ID788062

A SHORT-TITLE CATALOGUE
OF BOOKS PRINTED IN
ENGLAND, SCOTLAND, & IRELAND
AND OF ENGLISH BOOKS PRINTED ABROAD

1475–1640

VOLUME 2   I–Z

A SHORT-TITLE CATALOGUE
OF BOOKS PRINTED IN
ENGLAND, SCOTLAND, & IRELAND

AND OF ENGLISH BOOKS PRINTED ABROAD

1475—1640

FIRST COMPILED BY

A. W. POLLARD & G. R. REDGRAVE

SECOND EDITION, REVISED & ENLARGED

BEGUN BY

W. A. JACKSON & F. S. FERGUSON

COMPLETED BY

KATHARINE F. PANTZER

VOLUME 2

I—Z

LONDON
THE BIBLIOGRAPHICAL SOCIETY
1976

Oxford University Press, Ely House, London W. 1

OXFORD LONDON GLASGOW NEW YORK
TORONTO MELBOURNE WELLINGTON CAPE TOWN
IBADAN NAIROBI DAR ES SALAAM LUSAKA ADDIS ABABA
KUALA LUMPUR SINGAPORE JAKARTA HONG KONG TOKYO
DELHI BOMBAY CALCUTTA MADRAS KARACHI

ISBN 0 19 721790 7

BIBLIOGRAPHICAL SOCIETY PUBLICATION
FOR THE YEARS 1973, 1974, AND 1975
PUBLISHED 1976

*Printed in Great Britain
at the University Press, Oxford
by Vivian Ridler
Printer to the University*

PREFACE

THE Council of the Bibliographical Society has decided to issue the second volume of the revised Short-Title Catalogue before the first. This has been done in order to make the results of many years' work available to scholars as quickly as possible. The earlier completion of volume 2 is the result of Miss Pantzer's taking over the work of final revision on the death of William A. Jackson in 1964 at the letter R. The later letters of the alphabet represented a later stage in Jackson's own revision, and Miss Pantzer has felt that this, and the fact that she has personally overseen all these parts of the work, enable her and the Society to lay this volume before the public as having reached as definitive a stage as is possible in a work of this nature.

In order that this volume may be as easily consulted as possible, some preliminary matter has been attached, although this has been kept to a minimum. It is intended that the first volume shall contain, in the first place, a full account of the help the Society has received, both financial in the form of generous and whole-hearted support from foundations, trusts, firms, and institutions of learning, and intellectual in the form of help and advice from bibliographers, librarians, and others all over the world. There will be an account of the inception and progress of the work of revision which may be said indeed to have begun on the day that the original work was published in 1926, but which was officially inaugurated by the Society in 1946 and entrusted to W. A. Jackson and F. S. Ferguson.

Volume 1 will contain a detailed statement of the scope of the Short-Title Catalogue. The conventions of transcription and description which are summarily dealt with in the present volume will be presented at large. There will also be a list of reference books used and alluded to in the text.

At a later date the Society will publish a third volume containing an index of printers and booksellers. This volume will also contain further additions and corrections which, despite the thoroughness of the revision, inevitably occur. These should be sent to Miss Pantzer at the Houghton Library, Harvard University, Cambridge, Massachusetts 02138, U.S.A. and should furnish evidence for drawing up emendations comparable to those at the end of the present volume.

At the stage of revision which the work has now reached, the Council expects to publish the first volume containing letters A–H in 1980, and the final volume with the printers' index will follow in about two years' time.

CONVENTIONS OF TRANSCRIPTION

Titles   The first five words are almost always transcribed. An omission in these five words is denoted by '. . .' or [etc.].

Abbreviation   In titles after the first five words and in imprints, forenames have been abbreviated, and standard terms in imprints have been abbreviated or contracted.

Capitalization   Capitalization in the original has generally not been followed.

SYMBOLS, TERMS, AND ABBREVIATIONS

The revision of the text of STC has taken place over a period of 25 years, during which conventions of transcription and terminology have changed. Usage in STC (with some exceptions) has not been formalized, and the terms given below should be taken not as rules but as a guide to present practice.

[ ]   surrounds information at the beginning of an entry and words in the title, imprint, or date which are not present in the item itself. An exception is the formula: '[Init. T.L.]', which means that the author's initials, T.L., appear on the title-page or elsewhere. A hyphen within brackets has sometimes been used to indicate an unsigned preliminary quire, instead of the conventional π.

( )   surrounds words present in the item but not on the main or general title-page.

*   is placed after the location of a copy the particular variant, issue, or edition of which cannot be or has not been determined.

†   is placed after locations of 4° editions of the Book of Common Prayer which were not in Mr. Hetherington's original canvass; see the head-note preceding 16267.

+   placed after locations indicates that more copies exist than those in the libraries given.

⟨ ⟩   surrounds words conjecturally restored in the title of books known only by a copy or copies with defective title-page.

ą   = see Addenda and Corrigenda in this volume.

Issue   indicates the addition, deletion, and/or substitution of leaves or sheets constituting up to half of a book's original sheets. Where possible, further description in a heading or a note has been added, e.g. '[Anr. issue, w. cancel tp.]' or '[Anr. issue, w. quire A reprinted.]' When given simply as '[Anr. issue.]' it usually indicates a change in title or imprint which it was impossible to determine from available information whether it resulted from press alteration or cancellation.

Edition   indicates that more than half (usually all) of the sheets are from type that has been reset. In those cases where exactly half the sheets are reset and the other half remain in the original setting, the factor usually determining 'edition' or 'issue' has been whether the title-page is in the portion reset or not.

aed.	aedibus (house or shop)
app.	apparently
ass'd	assigned (transferred copyrights)
col.	colophon; *also* column
comp.	compartment
def.	defective
ed.	edition; *also* editor, edited by; *also* edibus (house or shop, in imprints)
ent.	entered (in the Stationers' Register)
exp.	expensis (at the cost of)
imp.	imperfect; *also* impensis (at the cost of, in imprints)
impr.	imprint
s.	see s.sh. below
SR	Stationers' Register
s.sh.	single sheet, a broadside

LOCATIONS

Below are listed all the locations in small caps and a selection of those in upper and lower case. Rare locations not found below are usually identified in the entries as C: College, NL: National Library, PL: Public Library, RL: Royal Library, U: University, UC: University College. Addresses, postal codes, and other information are generally available in reference books.

In the entries the Atlantic Ocean is represented by a semicolon. Up to five locations on each side have been listed with a view to geographical distribution. The prime British locations are: L, O, C, D, E; and the American: F, HN, HD, N, NY. In STC geography Australian and New Zealand libraries appear on the American side.

Imperfections other than missing blank leaves have been indicated where they were known. Where there are five or fewer locations, an attempt has been made to list multiple copies, and notations such as '2, 1 imp.' mean '2 copies, 1 of which is imperfect'. Where six or more locations are known, the extra copy or copies are indicated by a plus sign. In filling out the list of locations the STC revision has drawn on David Ramage's *A Finding-List of English Books to 1640 in Libraries in the British Isles*, Durham, 1958, and William W. Bishop's *A Checklist of American Copies of 'Short-Title Catalogue' Books*, second edition, Ann Arbor, 1950, and these two works can still be of use in finding extra copies of the more common items.

A	Aberdeen University Library
A²	St. Mary's College, Aberdeen Deposited at E
A³	Charter Room, Town House, Aberdeen
AAS	American Antiquarian Society, Worcester, Mass.
AMP	Ampleforth Abbey, York
ARP	Public Library, Armagh
AUG	Fort Augustus Abbey, Inverness-shire
B	Baptist College, Bristol Partly dispersed
BALT	George Peabody Department, Enoch Pratt Free Library, Baltimore, Md.
BALT²	Enoch Pratt Free Library, Baltimore, Md.
BALT³	Walters Art Gallery, Baltimore, Md.
BED	Central Library, Bedford (Old Bedford Library Collection)
BELVOIR	Belvoir Castle, Grantham, Leics. (Duke of Rutland)
BHP	Municipal Libraries, Bath
BIRM	University of Birmingham BIRM(Sh.Inst.): Shakespeare Institute
BIRM²	Reference Library, Birmingham BIRM²(K.N.): King's Norton, Hall Collection
Blickling Hall, Aylsham, Norf.	
BO	Boston Public Library, Boston, Mass.
BO²	Boston Athenaeum
BO³	Congregational Library, Boston, Mass.
BO⁴	not used
BO⁵	Massachusetts Historical Society, Boston, Mass.
BO⁶	Zion Research Library, Boston, Mass.
BODMER	Bibliotheca Bodmeriana, Cologny-Genève, Switzerland
BOWDOIN	Bowdoin College, Brunswick, Me.
BR	Brown University, Providence, R.I.
BRISTOL	Central Library, Bristol
BRISTOL²	University of Bristol
Britwell: sale at Sotheby's 30 March 1971, with lot numbers cited for a few rare items	
Broxbourne: Collection of the late Albert Ehrman Broxbourne(E): deposited with John Ehrman, London Broxbourne(O): deposited at O	

BRU	English Convent, Bruges
Bryn Mawr College, Bryn Mawr, Pa.	
BTL	Linen Hall, Belfast
BTU	Queen's University, Belfast
BURY	Bury St. Edmunds Cathedral Includes deposit of Assington Parish Library
BUTE	Marquess of Bute
C	University Library, Cambridge c(Bury deposit): Bury St. Edmunds Grammar School
C²	Trinity College
C³	Emmanuel College
C⁴	King's College
C⁵	St. John's College
C⁶	Pepysian Library, Magdalene College
C⁷	Corpus Christi College
C⁸	Jesus College
C⁹	Gonville and Caius
C¹⁰	Magdalene College
C¹¹	St. Catharine's College
C¹²	Christ's College
C¹³	Clare College
C¹⁴	Fitzwilliam Museum
C¹⁵	Pembroke College
C¹⁶	Queens' College
C¹⁷	Sidney Sussex College
C¹⁸	Selwyn College
C¹⁹	Peterhouse
C²⁰	Trinity Hall
C²¹	Downing College
C²²	Newnham College
C²³	Girton College
C²⁴	Cheshunt College
C²⁵	Westminster College
C²⁶	University Archives, University Library
CAL	University of California, Los Angeles
CAL²	University of California, Berkeley
CAL³	University of Southern California, Los Angeles
CAL⁴	Claremont Colleges, Claremont, Calif.
CAL⁵	County Law Library, Los Angeles, Calif.
CAL⁶	University of California, Davis

CAL⁷	University of California, Riverside
CAL⁸	University of California, Santa Barbara
CANT	Canterbury Cathedral
CANT²	Public Library, Canterbury Includes Canterbury Corporation Archives
CAR	Central Library, Cardiff
CARLISLE	Carlisle Cathedral
CARTMEL	Cartmel Priory Church, Lancs.
CASHEL	Cashel Cathedral, Co. Tipperary
CB	John Carter Brown Library, Providence, R.I.
CH	Chapin Library, Williams College, Williamstown, Mass.
CHATS	Chatsworth, Bakewell, Derbyshire (Duke of Devonshire)
CHEL	Sepulchrine Convent, New Hall, Chelmsford
CHEL²	Chelmsford Cathedral
CHES	Chester Cathedral
CHI	University of Chicago, Chicago, Ill.
CHI²	John Crerar Library, Chicago, Ill.
CHICH	Carmelite Convent, Chichester
CHICH²	Chichester Cathedral
COL	Public Library, Colchester
COLG	American Baptist Historical Society, Rochester, N.Y. (Samuel Colgate Collection)
COLG²	Rochester Center for Theological Studies, Rochester, N.Y.
COLWICH	St. Mary's Abbey, Colwich, Staffs.
CONN	Connecticut State Library, Hartford, Conn.
Copenhagen RL: Det Kongelige Bibliotek, Copenhagen	
COR	Cornell University, Ithaca, N.Y.
CREDITON	Crediton Parish Library Deposited at the University of Exeter
Crocker, C. Templeton, Estate of, San Francisco, Calif.	
CU	Columbia University, New York City
D	Trinity College, Dublin
D²	Marsh's Library, Dublin
D³	= CASHEL
D⁴	Public Record Office of Ireland, Dublin
D⁵	Honourable Society of King's Inn, Dublin
D⁶	National Library of Ireland, Dublin
D⁷	Representative Church Body, Dublin (Watson Collection)
D⁸	Royal Irish Academy, Dublin
D⁹	Public Library, Dublin
DAI	Douai Abbey, Woolhampton, Berks.
DALK	Duke of Buccleuch
DAR	Dartmouth College, Hanover, N.H.
DE	Downside Abbey, Bath
DEU	University of Dundee
DN	St. Clare's Abbey, Darlington
DNPK	Deene Park, Corby, Northants. (Edmund Brudenell) Collection partly dispersed in a sale at Bonham's, London, 26 Nov. 1975
Duke University, Durham, N.C.	
DUL	Dulwich College, London
DUR	Durham Cathedral
DUR(Bamb.)	Bamburgh Castle deposit at DUR⁵
DUR²	Squance Library Dispersed
DUR³	Cosin Library deposit at DUR⁵
DUR⁴	Cock Library Dispersed
DUR⁵	University of Durham
E	National Library of Scotland, Edinburgh
E²	Edinburgh University
E³	Signet Library, Edinburgh
E⁴	New College, Edinburgh University
E⁵	Royal College of Physicians of Edinburgh

E⁶	Scottish Record Office, General Register House, Edinburgh
E⁷	Society of Antiquaries of Scotland, Edinburgh
E⁸	Public Library, Edinburgh
E⁹	United Free Church Library Deposited at E⁴
E¹⁰	General Assembly of the Church of Scotland Library Deposited at E⁴
E¹¹	Speculative Society, Edinburgh University
E¹²	Edward Clark Library, Napier College of Science & Technology, Edinburgh
E¹³	Royal Observatory, Edinburgh
Edwards, Francis, Ltd., *Bookseller*, London	
ELY	= C
ETON	Eton College, Windsor, Berks.
EX	Exeter Cathedral
F	Folger Shakespeare Library, Washington, D.C.
FBL	Francis Bacon Library, Claremont, Calif.
Finedon: St. Mary's Church, Finedon, Northants.	
Finney, Theodore M., Pittsburgh, Pa.	
Fleming, John F., Inc., *Bookseller*, New York City	
FORDHAM	Fordham University, The Bronx, N.Y.
Freeman, Arthur. Items cited now = F	
G	= G²
G²	University of Glasgow
G³	= G²
G⁴	Public Library, Glasgow
GK	Sir Geoffrey Keynes
GLOUC	Gloucester Cathedral
Gordan, Mrs. John, New York City	
Goyder, George, Rotherfield Greys, Oxon.	
Graham, Howard Jay, Walla Walla, Wash.	
GRO	Buffalo and Erie County Public Library, Buffalo, N.Y.
Grolier Club, New York City	
HAGUE	Koninklijke Bibliotheek, The Hague
Hammond, W. F., *Bookseller*, Lymington, Hants.	
HART	Emory University, Atlanta, Ga. Collection formerly at Hartford Seminary Foundation
HART²	Trinity College, Hartford, Conn.
HAT	Hatfield House, Hatfield, Herts. (Marquess of Salisbury)
HD	Harvard University, Cambridge, Mass.
Hebrew Union College, Cincinnati, Ohio	
HER	Hereford Cathedral
HETH	John R. Hetherington Collection Bibles, Metrical Psalms, Books of Common Prayer deposited at BIRM; other items are partly dispersed
Hickmott, Allerton C., West Hartford, Conn.	
HN	Huntington Library, San Marino, Calif.
Hofmann & Freeman, Ltd., *Bookseller*, Sevenoaks, Kent	
HOLK	Holkham Hall, Wells, Norf. (Earl of Leicester)
Horblit, Harrison D., Ridgefield, Conn. Collection largely dispersed in sales at Sotheby's beginning 10 June 1974	
Houghton, Arthur A., Jr., New York City	
HP	Heythrop College, Cavendish Square, London
HUNT	Hunt Botanical Library, Carnegie-Mellon University, Pittsburgh, Pa.
Ickworth, Bury St. Edmunds, Suffolk (Marquess of Bristol)	
ILL	University of Illinois, Urbana, Ill.
IND	Indiana University, Bloomington, Ind.
INN	The Schoolhouse, Innerpeffray, by Crief, Perthshire

NLA	National Library of Australia, Canberra	O³⁶	Botany Department
NLM	National Library of Medicine, Bethesda, Md.		Partly deposited at O
		O³⁷	Campion Hall
NLW	National Library of Wales, Aberystwyth	O³⁸	Oxford University Press
	NLW(St. Asaph): St. Asaph Cathedral Library	O³⁹	English Faculty Library
		O⁴⁰	School of Geography
NMU	University of Nottingham	O⁴¹	Greyfriars Priory
NOR	Norwich Cathedral	O⁴²	Hope Collection, Ashmolean Museum
NOR²	Central Library, Norwich	O⁴³	Museum of the History of Science
NRO	Northamptonshire Record Office, Delapré Abbey, Northants.	O⁴⁴	Lady Margaret Hall
		O⁴⁵	not used
NW	Northwestern University, Evanston, Ill.	O⁴⁶	St. Anne's College
NWM	Northwestern University, Chicago, Ill. (Archibald Church Medical Library)	O⁴⁷	St. Hugh's College
		O⁴⁸	Philosophy Library
NY	New York Public Library, New York City	Oberlin College, Oberlin, Ohio	
NY²	New York Historical Society	OS	St. Mary's Seminary, New Oscott, Sutton Coldfield, Warwicks.
NY³	Engineering Societies Library, New York City		
		Otago University, Dunedin, New Zealand	
NY⁴	New York Academy of Medicine	OULT	St. Mary's Abbey, Oulton, Staffs.
NY⁵	Hispanic Society of America, New York City		
NY⁶	American Bible Society, New York City	P	Peterborough Cathedral
NY⁷	New York University		On long-term deposit at C
NY⁸	New York Society Library	PARIS	Bibliothèque Nationale
NY⁹	Jewish Theological Seminary, New York City		Includes Bliss Collection on Mary Queen of Scots
		PARIS²	Bibliothèque de l'Arsenal
NY¹⁰	New York Racket & Tennis Club	PARIS³	Bibliothèque Mazarine
NY¹¹	General Theological Seminary, New York City	Pearson, the late Norman H., New Haven, Conn.	
		PEN	University of Pennsylvania, Philadelphia, Pa.
NYS	New York State Library, Albany, N.Y.	PEN²	Pennsylvania State University, University Park, Pa.
		Penrose, Boies, Devon, Conn.	
O	Bodleian Library, Oxford		Collection partly dispersed in sales at Sotheby's in 1971, items from which cite lot numbers
	O(J): John Johnson Collection		
O²	Queen's College		
O³	Christ Church	PETWORTH	Petworth House, Petworth, Sussex (Lord Egremont)
	O³(E): Evelyn Library		
	O³(W): Wotton-under-Edge Parish Library	PETYT	Public Library, Skipton, Yorks. (The Petyt Library)
O⁴	Brasenose College		
O⁵	Corpus Christi College	PFOR	Carl H. Pforzheimer Library, New York City
O⁶	Worcester College	PH	Library Company of Philadelphia
	O⁶(D): Denchworth Parish Library	PH²	Free Library of Philadelphia
O⁷	Wadham College	PH³	= PH²
O⁸	St. John's College	PH⁴	Franklin Institute, Philadelphia, Pa.
O⁹	All Souls College	PH⁵	Presbyterian Historical Society, Philadelphia, Pa.
O¹⁰	Exeter College		
O¹¹	Merton College	PH⁶	Lutheran Theological Seminary, Philadelphia, Pa.
O¹²	Magdalen College		
O¹³	Lincoln College	PH⁷	Historical Society of Pennsylvania
O¹⁴	New College		Deposited at PH
O¹⁵	Oxford University Archives, Bodleian Library	Phillipps: sales at Sotheby's on 26–7 Nov. 1973 and 24–5 June and 25–6 Nov. 1974, items from which cite lot numbers	
O¹⁶	Trinity College		
O¹⁷	Balliol College		
O¹⁸	Jesus College	Pirie, Robert S., Hamilton, Mass.	
O¹⁹	Oriel College	PLUME	Plume Library, Maldon, Essex
O²⁰	Mansfield College	PML	Pierpont Morgan Library, New York City
O²¹	Manchester College	PN	Princeton University, Princeton, N.J.
O²²	Hertford College	PN²	Princeton Theological Seminary, Princeton, N.J.
O²³	not used		
O²⁴	Pembroke College	Private Owner: Requests for information should be addressed to the Hon. Secretary of the Bibliographical Society, for forwarding to the owner	
O²⁵	Pusey House		
O²⁶	St. Edmund Hall		
O²⁷	University College	PTS	Pittsburgh Theological Seminary, Pittsburgh, Pa.
O²⁸	Regents Park College		
	O²⁸(Bed.): Beddome Library		
	O²⁸(Bro.): Broughton Baptist Library	Quaritch, Bernard, Ltd., *Bookseller*, London	
O²⁹	Somerville College	Queen's University at Kingston, Ont.	
O³⁰	Taylor Institution		
O³¹	Keble College	R	Ripon Cathedral
O³²	St. Hilda's College	RD	Rothamsted Experimental Station, Harpenden, Herts.
O³³	Department of Agriculture		
O³⁴	Ashmolean Museum	RGU	University of Reading, Reading, Berks.
O³⁵	Blackfriars Priory	ROCH	University of Rochester, Rochester, N.Y.
		Rogers, David, The Old Mill, Blewbury, Berks.	

ROME	Ven. Collegio Inglese, Rome
ROS	Rosenbach Foundation, Philadelphia, Pa.
S	William Salt Library, County Record Office, Stafford
SAL	Salisbury Cathedral
SAU	University College, Swansea
SBK	St. Mary's Abbey, Stanbrook, Worcester
SC	University of South Carolina, Columbia, S.C.
Scheide: The Scheide Library	
	Housed at PN
SCL	Shropshire County Library, Shrewsbury
Seven Gables Bookshop, *Bookseller*, New York City	
Sexton, Eric H. L., Rockport, Me.	
SH	Shakespeare Centre, Stratford-upon-Avon
SHEF	University of Sheffield
SHR	Shrewsbury School
SMITH	Smith College, Northampton, Mass.
SMU	Southern Methodist University, Dallas, Tex.
SN	Syon Abbey, South Brent, Devon
SNU	University of Southampton
Sparrow, John, All Souls College, Oxford	
ST	Stonyhurst College, Whalley, Lancs.
STAN	Stanford University, Stanford, Calif.
STAPEHILL	Holy Cross Abbey, Stapehill, Dorset
STD	St. David's University College, Lampeter
Stevens Cox: James Stevens Cox, St. Peter Port, Guernsey, Channel Islands	
Stevens Cox, Gregory, St. Peter Port, Guernsey	
STL	St. Louis University, St. Louis, Mo.
STU	University of St. Andrews
SUNY(Buffalo)	State University of New York, Buffalo, N.Y.
Sydney, University of, Sydney, New South Wales	
Taylor, Henry C., Collection of. Now = Y	
Taylor, Robert H., Collection of	
	Housed at PN
TCU	Texas Christian University, Fort Worth, Tex.
TEX	University of Texas, Austin, Tex.
TMTH	St. Scholastica's Abbey, Teignmouth, Devon
TOKYO	Imperial University, Tokyo
TORONTO	Academy of Medicine, Toronto, Ont.

TORONTO²	University of Toronto
Traylen, Charles W., *Bookseller*, Guildford, Surrey	
U	Union Theological Seminary, New York City
USHAW	St. Cuthbert's College, Ushaw, Durham
V	University of Virginia, Charlottesville, Va.
VAL	Colegio-seminario de Ingleses, Valladolid, Spain
VER	Verulam Plays
	Deposited by the Earl of Verulam at O
W	St. Edmund's College, Ware, Herts.
WASH	= LC
WASH²	Catholic University of America, Washington, D.C.
WASH³	Georgetown University, Washington, D.C.
Washington Cathedral, Washington, D.C.	
Weissman, Stephen, Collection of	
	Dispersed
WEL	Wellesley College, Wellesley, Mass.
WES	Wesleyan University, Middletown, Conn.
Western Ontario, University of, London, Ont.	
	School of Library Science items are identified as (S.L.S.)
WI	Central Library, Wigan, Lancs.
WIN	Windsor Castle, Windsor, Berks.
WIN²	St. George's Chapter Library, Windsor Castle
WIS	University of Wisconsin, Madison, Wis.
WN	Winchester College
WN²	Winchester Cathedral
WOR	Worcester Cathedral
WOR²	= HP
WTL	Alexander Turnbull Library, Wellington, New Zealand
Y	Yale University, New Haven, Conn.
	Y(Pequot): Pequot deposit
Y²	Elizabethan Club, Yale University
Y³	= Y
YK	York Minster
YK²	Bar Convent, York
Z	Zentralbibliothek, Zürich

I. I pray you be not angry. 1624. *See* 3662.

14045.5 — I smell a rat. *Ballad.* 2 pts. s.sh.fol. [*W. Jones*] *f. H. Gosson*, [c. 1630.] c⁶.

14045.7 — I would you never had said so. *Ballad.* 2 pts. s.sh.fol. [*J. White*] *f. T. L[angley*, 1618.] Ent. 8 jy. 1618. c⁶.

Note: In the following, initials I. and J. are both transcribed as I.

14046   **I., A.** A godly ballad declaring by the scriptures the plagues that haue insued whoredome. *Ballad.* 1/2 sh. fol. *J. Allde*, 1566 (25 no.) Ent. 1566–67. L.
    On the verso is pr. 401.3.

  I., B. The comicall satyre of every man out of his humor. 1600. *See* 14767.
— Epicoene, or the silent woman. 1620. *See* 14763.
— The masque of augures. 1621. *See* 14777.
— *ed. See* 4932.5.

  I., C., *ed. See* 13478, 23345.

14047   **I., C.,** *Danus.* De prædestinatione. 1595. Now = 21555.1.

14048   **I., E.** Clavis theologiæ, quâ patet aditus ad SS. theologiæ adyta. fol. *T. Cotes*, 1632. Ent. to M. Sparke a. H. Robinson 17 my. o.
    A common-place book, w. tp, indexes, headings, and rules pr.; the rest left blank.

14049   **I., E.,** *Student in divinity.* A new-yeares gift for English catholikes, or a briefe explication of the new oath of allegiance. [Attrib. to R. Widdrington.] 8°. [*W. Stansby*,] 1620. L.O.C².E.W.+; NY¹¹.TEX.U.
    A&R 670. Answers 14910; tr. in 14050.5.

14050 — An adjoynder to the late catholike New-yeares gift. By E. I. the author of the New-yeares gift. [Attrib. to R. Widdrington.] 8°. [*Eliot's Court Press*,] 1620. L².O².C⁵.A².P.+; NY.
    A&R 660.

14050.5 — Strena catholica, seu explicatio breuis. [Attrib. to R. Widdrington.] 8°. *Augustæ, ap. B. Fabrum* [i.e. *London, J. Bill*,] 1620. L.L².O.O¹⁹.E.+
    A&R 675. A trans., w. additions, of 14049.

  I., G. A present consolacion for the sufferers of persecucion. 1544. *See* 14828.

  I., H. A briefe and cleare declaration of sundry pointes. 1611. *See* 13840.

14050a — An example for all those that make no conscience of swearing, and forswearing: shewing Gods judgement upon a maid-servant in London. *Ballad.* 2 pts. s.sh. fol. [*G. Purslowe*] *f. J. W[right*? c. 1625.] F.
— Institutiones piæ or directions to pray. 1630. *See* 599.

14051 — Jacob's ladder consisting of fifteene degrees to the knowledge of God. 1638. Now = 1839.5.

14052 — A position against vainglorious preaching. [Attrib. to H. Jacob.] 8°. [*Middelburg, R. Schilders*,] 1604. L. O⁵.; BO³.
— A treatise of the sufferings of Christ. 1598. *See* 14340.

  I., H., *Student in divinity, tr. See* 4056.

  I., I. *See* 1025.3.

14053   **I., L.,** *B. of Art.* The relection of a conference touching the reall presence. 1635. *See* 15351.3.

14054   **I., N.** A true relation of the ground, . . . of that murther committed by J. Bartram, upon sir J. Tyndall. 4°. *J. Beale*, 1616. L(destroyed).; HN.HD.LC.
    C4ᵛ init. 'N. J.'

14054.5 — [Anr. issue, w. inner forme of sheet A and C4ᵛ reset.] L⁸.O.; TEX.
    C4ᵛ init. 'N. T.'

14055 — A true relation of a most desperate murder, committed upon sir J. Tindall. 1617. = 24435.

14056   **I., R.** The history of Tom Thumbe, the little. [By Richard Johnson?] 8°. [*A. Mathewes*?] *f. T. Langley*, 1621. Ass'd by J. Trundle 13 de. 1620. PML.
— The inrichment of the weald of Kent. 1625. *See* 17363.
— Looke on me London. 1613. *See* 14676.
— The most pleasant history of Tom a Lincolne. 1631. *See* 14684.
— The new life of Virginea. 1612. *See* 14700.
— Nova Britannia. 1609. *See* 14699.
— Some just reflexions on a pasquill. 1606. *See* 14465.5.
— *tr. See* 3400.

  I., R., *Preacher.* Dives and Lazarus: or rather, divelish Dives. 1623, etc. *See* 14694.3 sqq.

  I., R., *Printer.* The treasurie of hidden secrets. 1596. *See* 19429.5.

14057   **I., S.** Bromleion. A discourse of the most substantial points of diuinitie. 4° in 8's. *T. Creede*, 1595. L.O. D.P.YK.; F.HN.HD.ILL.

14058 — Certaine godlie and learned sermons. Made upon sixe parables. 8°. *J. R[oberts*] *f. R. B[ankworth*,] 1601. L.; Otago U.

14058.3 — Two treatises, one of the latter day of judgement: the other of the joyes of heaven. 8°. *T. Creede*, 1600. o.

14058.7   **I., S.,** *M.A.* The soules centinell ringing an alarum against impietie and impenitencie. 4°. *Dublin, Soc. of Statrs.*, 1631. D.D².SAL.

14059   **I., S. A.** Carminum prouerbialium, . . . loci communes, . . . selecti. [Attrib. to H. Gembergius.] 8°. (*C. Barkar*,) 1577. Ent. 21 no. 1576. L.P.; HN.ILL.

14060 — [Anr. ed.] 8°. (*C. Barkerus*,) 1579. L.; F.

14060.5 — [Anr. ed.] 8°. (*C. Barkerus*,) 1583. E(imp.).G².LINC.P. SNU.+; AAS.ILL.

14061 — [Anr. ed.] 8°. (*T. Dawsonus, ex assig. C. Barkeri*,) 1588. L.O.D.E.E².+; F.N.

14062 — [Anr. ed.] 8°. (*T. Dawsonus, ex assig. C. Barkeri*,) 1595. L.LIV³.M.

14063 — [Anr. ed.] 8°. (*T. Dawsonus, ex assig. C. Barkeri*,) 1599. O.O⁵.C³.; HD.

14064 — [Anr. ed.] 8°. (*T. Dawsonus, ex assig. C.* [i.e. *R.?*] *Barkeri*,) 1603. L.D.D²(lacks tp).M.; HD.

14064.3 — [Anr. ed.] 8°. (*T. Dawsonus, ex assig. R. Barkeri*,) 1609. D.; F.HD(lacks tp, last 2 leaves).

14064.7 — [Anr. ed.] 8°. *in off. J. Haviland, imp. F. Constable, prost. ap. N. Butter*, 1637. Ent. to Constable 24 mr. C².; F.CU.Y.
    For order of court of Statrs. Co. to enter to Constable, *see Court-Book C*, p. 292.

14065 — [Anr. issue, w. imprint:] *Londini*, 1637. L.O.C.G². PLUME.+; HN.HD.ILL.

  I., S.R.N. Votivæ Angliæ. 1624. *See* 20946.1.
— Vox coeli. 1624. *See* 20946.4.

14066   **I., T.** A discourse, betweene Upright the shoomaker and master Pattent, the smith. 4°. *B. Alsop a. T. F[awcet*] *f. F. Groves*, 1640. Ent. 10 no. (E&R I.1). L⁸.o.

14067 — A joyful song of the royall receiuing of the Queenes maiestie into campe at Tilburie. *Ballad.* s.sh.fol. *J. Wolfe f. R. Jones*, 1588. Ent. to Wolfe 10 au. HN.
    Different text from 6565.

14068 — A miracle, of miracles. . . . Which lately happened at Dichet in Sommersetshire. Also a prophesie revealed by a poore countrey maide. Withall, Lincolneshire teares. For a great deluge. 4°. [*G. Eld*] *f. J. Trundle*, 1614. Ent. 15 no. 1613. L.
    (Formerly also 15652) Collates A–D⁴. **Contains** a revised version of 5681 and 21818.

14068.3 — [Anr. ed.] The miracle, [etc.] 4°. [*G. Eld*] *f. J. Trundle*, (1614). o(date on gen. tp cropt).
    (Formerly also 15652) Collates A–C⁴.

I., T.—*cont.*
— The soules solace. 1626, etc. *See* 14494 sqq.
14068.5 — A world of wonders. A masse of murthers. A couie of
cosonages. 4°. [*V. Simmes?*] *f. W. Barley,* 1595. C².;
HN. Arthur Freeman, Cambridge, Mass.
— *ed. See* 958.5.
— *tr. See* 4568.5, 20146.

14069 I., W. Dictionariolum quadruplex: or a foure-fold dictionarie [of similar Latin words that might be confused.] *Lat. a. Eng.* 4°. B. *A*[*lsop*] *f. H. Seile,* 1638.
Ent. 11 se. 1637. L(tp only, Harl.5919/313).C.
14070 — The excellencie of numbers. [n.d.] = 14089.
— *ed. See* 6980.
— *tr. See* 12462, 14534, 15517, 22992.7.
14071 — The whipping of the satyre. [In verse. By J. Weever?]
8°. [*S. Stafford*] *f. J. Flasket,* 1601. Ent. 14 au. O.;
F.HN.
(Formerly also 25352) Quires B, D, F have paper
with horizontal chainlines. For other items in this
controversy *see* 3672, 12504.5.

I., W., *of London, Printer.* A view of all the Lord Mayors.
1601. *See* 14343.

I., W., *Printer.* Somatographia. 1616. *See* 20782.

Iden, Henry, *tr. See* 11708.

If. If it plese ony man. [1477.] *See* 4890.
— If you know not me, you know no bodie. 1605, etc. *See*
13328 sqq.
— If you raile at the author I know what I know. [1629.]
See 1327.

Ignoramus. Ignoramus. Comœdia. 1630. *See* 21445.

Image. Image of idlenesse. [1555?] *See* 25196.
— Ymage of love. 1525. *See* 21471.5.

14072 Image of Pity. [To them that before this image of pity
say. . . . c. 1487.] Now = Indulgences 6.
14072a — To them that before this ymage. . . . [c. 1490.] Now =
Indulgences 8.
— *See also* Indulgences 7, 9–23.

Images. The images of a verye chrysten bysshop, and
of a counterfayte bysshop. [1536?] *See* 16983.5.

Imitation. The imytacyon and folowynge the blessed
lyfe of cryste. 1503, etc. For this and other editions
to whomsoever assigned, *see* Thomas, à Kempis.

Immerito, *pseud. See* 23089, 23095.

Imperiale. Imperiale, a tragedie. 1639. *See* 11369.

Ince, Hugh, *tr. See* 14959.5.

14073 Ince, William. Lot's little one. Or meditations on Gen.
19. vers. 20. 12°. *London, J. R*[*aworth,*] *sold by J.
Crook a. R. Sergier, in Dublin,* 1640. Ent. 26 au. L.
O.C.D.NEP.+; HD.ILL.PH².PML.PN².
Engr. tp dated 1641.

Inclination. Heir follows ane ballat Inclinatioun of our
king. 1567. *See* 22196.

14074 Increase. Encrease of blesse expected long. [In verse.]
s.sh.fol. [*Rheims, J. Foigny,* 1580?] L¹¹.
This poem also appears on verso of tp of 15507.

14075 Indagine, Joannes ab. Briefe introductions, . . . vnto
the art of chiromancy. *Tr.* F. Withers. 8°. *ap. J. Day
(f. R. Jugge,)* 1558. Ent. 1557–8. L⁸.P.; F.HN.NLM.
14075.5 — [Anr. ed.] Adding newely thereunto lovely pistares. . . .
8°. (*J. Daye f. R. Jugge,*) 1558. L(lacks col.).C(lacks
tp).
14076 — [Anr. ed.] 8°. *T. Purfoote,* 1575. O(imp.).; F.
14077 — [Anr. ed.] 8°. *T. Purfoot,* 1598. L.O.C⁵(lacks tp).P.;
HN.
14077a — The fourth edition. 8°. *T. Purfoot,* 1615. Ass'd from
Purfoot, sen., to jun. 6 no. F.ILL.
14077b — [Anr. ed.] 8°. *T. Purfoot,* 1633. HN.LC.

Index. Index poeticus. 1634. *See* 10702.

Indies. March 28. Numb. 1 Good and true tydings out
of the Indies. 1625. *See* Newsbooks 164.

INDULGENCES

It has been thought expedient to gather under this head all the
indulgences, letters of confraternity, certificates, and other ephe-
meral publications of that nature, nearly all printed in broadside
form, which must once have been very numerous but now survive
frequently only in fragments. The transfer of all those formerly
included has been recorded and cross-references have been inserted
for at least the latest Pope under whose authority they were granted,
the names of the commissaries, legates, cardinals, bishops, etc. who
issued them, and the foundations, orders, etc. who benefited from
their issue. They have been divided, somewhat arbitrarily, under
the following subheads:

CEDULAE AND CERTIFICATES OF CONFESSION

14077c.1 Vniuersis & singulis dñici gregis pastorib⁹. . . . Anno
M.d.xvii. [Lenten certificate of confession and absolution, issued by the Augustinians.] s.sh.*obl.*8°. [*R.
Pynson?,* 1517.] L(2 copies, C.18.e.2(10,11)). Lord
Kenyon.
(Formerly 956)
.2 — [Anr. ed.] UNiuersis et singulis dñici gregis pastorib⁹. . . .
Anno salutis M.D.xxiiii. s.sh.*obl.*8°. [*R. Pynson,*
1524.] O(Arch.A b.8(14)).
(Formerly 5626) 2 settings on 1 sheet; handle of
right-hand key touches inner border of one, covers
inner border of other.
.3 Per huius cedule et signi traditionē et concessionem cunctis
ecclesiarū rectoribus innotescat . . . M.D.xviii.
[Blank form, to be dated and signed.] s.sh.*obl.*4°.
[*London,* 1518.] L(C.121.g.10).
Line 4 begins 'ex'.
.4 — [Anr. ed.] s.sh.*obl.*4°. [*London,* 1518.] L(2 copies, C.121.
g.10 and Ames I.26).
Line 4 begins 'priuilegio'.
.5 UNiuersis ecclesiaȝ rectoribus ad quos presentes lře peruenerint Johēs [Young] Calipoleñ Ēpus magister
domus siue hospitalis sancti Thome martyris dicte
de Acoñ in Ciuitate Londoñ salutem. . . . [Blank
certificate that confession had been made.] s.sh.*obl.*8°.
[*R. Pynson,* c. 1517.] L⁵(Lemon Add. 3).

IMAGES OF PITY AND OTHER INDULGENCED PICTURES

The cuts below have letterpress or xylographic text, or show
evidence such text has been defaced or cut away. Merely pictorial
cuts, or cuts with text in MS. only, are not included.

The references to 'Dodgson' are to C. Dodgson, *English Woodcuts,* published in Paul Heitz, *Einblattdrucke des Fünfzehnten
Jahrhunderts,* 88. Band, Strasbourg, 1936.

Christ

.6 [To them that before this image of pity devoutly say .v. pater
noster, v. aves & a credo piteously.] [Xylographic,
w. 28 compartments, the text cut out.] s.sh.fol.
[*Westminster, W. Caxton,* c. 1487.] L(in 17720).
Dodgson 4.
(Formerly 14072)

Indulgences—IMAGES OF PITY, ETC.—*Christ—cont.*

.7 To þem þat before þis ymage off pyte. Deuoutly .v. tymes say. pr̄ nr̄ & aue. Pit⟨eous⟩ly beholding þies ar⟨ms.⟩ [Xylographic, w. 17 compartments.] s.sh.4°. [*Northern England*, c. 1490.] O(mutilated, Arch.G e.35). Dodgson 3.

.8 To them that before this ymage of pyte deuowtely say .v. Pr̄ nr̄. . . . [Xylographic, w. 18 compartments.] s.sh.4°. [*Westminster, W. Caxton*, c. 1490.] C(impression on blank last page of *Colloquium peccatoris*, Antwerp, M. van der Goes, c. 1487 = Oates 3948). Dodgson 10. (Formerly 14072a)

.8A [Image of pity. Xylographic, printed by frotton, the text defaced.] s.sh.8°. [*England*, c. 1480–90.] O(MS. Bodley 939). Dodgson 1.
　　The figure of Christ has diagonal shading. The text may have resembled that of nos. 10–11.

.9 Seynt gregor' with oþir' popes .&. bysshoppes yn seer'. Haue graūted of þdō .xxvj. dayes .&. xxvj. Mill' year' To þeym þat befor' þis fygur' on þeir knees. Deuoutly say .v. pater noster .&. v. Auees. [Xylographic, pr. by frotton.] s.sh.8°. [*Northern England?* c. 1490.] L(Dept. of P&D). Dodgson 2, a later version of the preceding.
　　The figure of Christ has no shading.

.10 The pdon for .v. pr̄ nr̄ .v. aues & a crede. is xxvj .m. yeres & xxvj. dayes: [Xylographic.] s.sh.16°. [*England*, c. 1490.] LINC. Dodgson 7.

.11 The pdou [*sic*] for .v. pr̄ nr̄ .v. aues & a crede. is xxvj .m. yeres. & xxvj. dayes. [flower; xylographic.] s.sh.16°. [*England*, c. 1490.] LC. Dodgson 8, a close copy of preceding.

.11A The pardon for .v. pater nr̄ .v. aues & a crede . . . is .xxxii. M.& lv. yeres. [Xylographic.] s.sh.4°. [*R. Copland?* c. 1525.] No copy traced. Known only through its use by Copland in 25421.2.
　　Christ's left arm is around a spear.

.11B [A similar cut, but reversed, w. the same xylographic text.] s.sh.4°. [*M. Fawkes?* 1534?] No copy traced. Known only through its use by Fawkes (Hodnett 2061) in 3275 sq.
　　Christ's right arm is around a spear; there is a cross on the top coin above Judas's head.

.11C [A similar cut, w. the same xylographic text.] s.sh.4°. [*H. Pepwell?* 1521?] No copy traced. Known only through its use by Pepwell (Hodnett 2279) in 20972.
　　Christ's right arm is around a spear; there is a small oval on the top coin above Judas's head.

.12 [Woodcut Image of Pity, within frame of 20 compartments, the indulgence cut out.] s.sh.8°. [*England*, c. 1490.] New York, Metropolitan Museum of Art. Dodgson 5.
　　The dice in this cut are at lower left corner.

.13 To them that before this ymage of pyte deuoutly say fyue Pater noster fyue Aueys & a Credo pytously beholdyng these armes of xp̄s passyon ar graunted xxxii M . vii . C . & lv. yeres of pardon. [Xylographic, w. 22 compartments.] s.sh.fol. [*England*, c. 1500.] O(MS.Rawl.D 403). Dodgson 9.

.14 To al thē yᵗ deuoutly say v. pr̄. nr̄. v. aues & a crede afor such a figᵣ ar graūted xxxii . m . vii . c . lv . yēs of pdō. [Xylographic, w. 20 compartments.] s.sh.8°. [*W. de Worde*, c. 1500.] L(Egerton MS.1821). Dodgson 6.
　　The dice in this are in lower right corner, and the borders of the cut are not joined at the corners.

.14A [A similar cut w. the same text.] s.sh.8°. [*W. de Worde*, c. 1505.] Y.
　　The dice in this are in lower right corner, and the borders of the cut are joined at the corners. In this example there are 3 lines of letterpress text below the cut.

.15 Ex domo Jhesu de Betheleem [the Carthusian Priory at Sheen]. Of your charyte in the worshyp of yᵉ .v. wondes of our lord & yᵉ .v. ioyes of our lady say. Pr̄ nr̄ &.Aue. [Xylographic, with arms of Christ. Only the first 5 words are in type.] s.sh.8°. [*W. de Worde?* c. 1505.] O(Arch.G f.14). Dodgson 18.

.16 Who sū euer deuoutely behoildeth thes armys of criste haith vjᵐ . viiᶜ . lv . ȳ peꝝ. [Xylographic, arms of Christ.] s.sh.8°. [*England*, c. 1500.] YK. Dodgson 20.

Indulgences—IMAGES OF PITY, ETC.—*Christ—cont.*

.17 [Image of pity, w. xylographic verses below, beginning:] The greatest comfort in all temptacyon. s.sh.4°. [*W. de Worde*, 1525?] No copy traced. Known only through its use by de Worde (Hodnett 456) in 14044 and later books.
　　The figure on the left, St. Francis, has a nimbus.

.17A [A similar cut, w. the same xylographic verses.] s.sh.4°. [*R. Copland?* c. 1525.] L(Egerton MS.1821). Dodgson 12.
　　The figure on the left, a Carthusian, has no nimbus. Used later by Copland in 25421.2.

.18 Surgite mortui. Venite ad judicium. Arma Beate Birgitte: De Syon. [Woodcut of Christ in Judgement, w. inscription in type.] s.sh.4°. [*R. Pynson*, c. 1510.] O(MS.Rawl.D 403). Dodgson 15.
　　Presumably issued for the Brigittine Convent of Syon, near Isleworth.

Our Lady

.19 Aue sc̄tissiā maria mr̄ dei regina celi . . . a sixto p̄p̄ q̄r̄to xj . m . ān cōced. [Xylographic, below virgin and child.] s.sh.8°. [*England?* c. 1490.] O(MS.Bodley 113). Dodgson 17.
　　This indulgence, which purports to be granted by Sixtus IV, has been declared a forgery; *see* W. L. Schreiber, *Manuel de l'Amateur*, No. 1053.

.19A [Virgin and child w. a kneeling suppliant, under an arch. Panel of text (xylographic?) cut away at foot.] s.sh.4°. [*England*, c. 1490.] L(Egerton MS.1821). Dodgson 16.

.20 Pro añ subscripta C. āni d' Johē p̄p̄ ij [Xylographic, below a close copy of the preceding.] 1/2 sh.fol. [*England*, c. 1490.] No copy traced. Known only through its later use by de Worde (Hodnett 463) in 14042 and 19213.

.21 [Woodcut of Pieta, within frame of 20 compartments, arranged as in no. 12, the indulgence cut out.] s.sh.8°. [*England*, c. 1490.] New York, Metropolitan Museum of Art. Dodgson 14.

.22 Who sum euer deuoutly beholdith. these armys off cristis passyon hat vi . m . vii c lv yeris of pardon: [Xylographic, Pieta w. 26 compartments of the instruments.] s.sh.4°. [*England*, c. 1500.] O(MS.Rawl.D. 403). Dodgson 13.

Saints

.23 Saynt Anne of Totnam. Pope Innocent hath graunted to all thē yᵗ deuoutly say .v. pr̄ nosters & .v. aues. . . . [Cuts of St. Anne w. virgin and child, St. George, a shield w. his cross, and instruments.] s.sh.fol. [*R. Pynson*, c. 1510.] L¹³.

.23A The hole īdulgēce of pdō graūted to blessed s. Cornelis. [Woodcut of St. Cornelius, Bp. of Rome.] s.sh.16°. [*London*, c. 1520.] L(frag., C.40.m.9(7) and Harl. 5968/72).L²(four settings, with four cuts, printed twice on folio sheet, Frag. No. 8).
　　Perhaps connected with Indulgences 83.

.23B [Henry VI with suppliants. Woodcut w. xylographic text.] s.sh.fol. [*England*, c. 1495.] O(MS.Bodley 277(f. 376)). Dodgson 22.
　　Cut mutil., text indecipherable.

INDULGENCES, LETTERS OF CONFRATERNITY, AND LISTS OF BENEFITS ISSUED ON BEHALF OF ENGLISH ESTABLISHMENTS AND ORDERS

General

Augustinian Order in England. *See* Indulgences 1 sq., 101 sqq., 102 sqq., 149, 150.

.23C Benedictines, English Congregation. Alphonsus Barrantes Doctour of Diuinitie Generall of the Holie Congregation of S. Bennet in Spaine, &c. Among other excellent graces. . . . [Letter of confraternity, w. spaces for name and date.] s.sh.fol. [*Douai, L. Kellam, jun.*, 1625?] C(imp., dated in MS. 26 Nov. 1625).W(Archive Cat.16.1(3), dated in MS. 28 Feb. 1626).
　　A&R 292.

Indulgences—INDULGENCES: ENGLISH ESTABLISHMENTS—
General—cont.

.24 Carmelite Order in England. FRater Robertus fratrū, ordinis beate Marie genitricis dei de monte Carmeli in puincia Anglie cōmorantiū Prior prouincialis. . . . [Letter of confraternity of Carmelite Friars in England, issued by the Prior-general.] s.sh.*obl.*fol. [*R. Pynson*, 1512.] NMU(Middleton MSS.).

.25 — Fratres will's breuie & Iohēs byrde . . . Baptiste mantuani cū plenitudine potestatis eiusdē in prouincia anglie. . . . [Letter of confraternity of Carmelite Friars in England.] s.sh.fol. [*R. Pynson*,] 1516. L(C.70.i.12). o(2 imp., MS.Rawl.D 366(ff.16,17)).O¹⁴(4 copies).
(Formerly 3717)

Local

.26 Beverley, Yorkshire, *Confraternity of St. John.* These folowynge be the priuyleges pardon and indulgence graunted to the bretherne and susters, & benefactours of the college church of seynt Johñ of Beuerley. [List of indulgences granted to members.] s.sh.fol. [*R. Pynson*, c. 1520.] o(2 imp., Arch.A b.8(2) and Gough York 57).
(Formerly 1984)

.27 Boston, Lincolnshire, *Church of St. Botolph, Guild or Confraternity of B. V. M.* VNiuersis xp̄ifidelib⁹ presentes litteras inspecturis. Nos aldermānus & camerarij gilde siue cōfraternitis ī honorē btē marie virgīs in ecclesia sctī Botulphi de Bostoñ. [Letter of confraternity, dated 7 Sept. 1504.] s.sh.*obl.*fol. [*R. Pynson*, 1504?] L(C.23.a.22).
(Formerly 17551)

.28 — [Anr. ed., dated 7 Sept. 1504.] VNiuersis xp̄ifidelib⁹ pñtes lr̄as inspecturis. Nos aldermānus. . . . s.sh.*obl.* fol. [*R. Pynson*, 1505?] L¹¹(Chancery Misc. (c. 47), Bundle 15, File 6, No. 31).

.29 — [Anr. ed., dated 16 May 1506.] VNiuersis xp̄ifidelib⁹ p̄sentes lr̄as īspecturis. Nos aldermann⁹. . . . s.sh.*obl.* fol. [*R. Pynson*, 1506.] L¹¹(Chancery Misc. (c. 47), Bundle 15, File 6).
In Indulgences 29–33 the 1st word is xylographic.

.30 — [Anr. ed., dated 11 Dec. 1511.] VNiuersis Xp̄ifidelibus pñtes lr̄as inspecturis. Nos aldermannus. . . . s.sh. *obl.*fol. p̄ *R. Pynson*, [1511.] L(Dept. of MSS., Wolley Charters 3.94).L¹³(Muniments 6655).

.31 — [Anr. ed., dated 1518.] VNiuersis et singulis cristifidelibus presentes litteras inspecturis Nos aldermānus. . . . s.sh.*obl.*fol. *per me R. Pynson*, [1518.] L¹³ (Muniments 6656).NMU(Middleton MSS.).

.32 — [Anr. ed., dated 1521.] Uniuersis et singulis xp̄ifidelibus presentes litteras inspecturis. Nos aldermānus & came/. . . . s.sh.*obl.* fol. *per me R. Pynsonū*, [1521.] PML.

.33 —[Anr. ed., dated 1522.] UNiuersis et singulis xp̄ifidelibus presentes litteras inspecturis. Nos aldermānus & came-/. . . .s.sh.*obl.*fol. *per me R. Pynsonū*, [1522.] L(C.37.f.31).
(Formerly 17550)

.34 — [Anr. ed., dated 1531.] UNiuersis et singulis xp̄ifidelibus . . . Nos aldermannus et camerarii. . . . s.sh.*obl.*fol. *per me R. Fakes*, [1531.] DE.

.35 Boston, Lincolnshire, *Guild of Our Lady of Scala Coeli.* [List in English of privileges of members of the Guild.] s.sh.fol. [*R. Pynson*, c. 1515.] c(imp.).
(Formerly 17549)

.36 Bosworth Field, *St. James' Chapel.* CHaryte hath caused our souereygne lorde the Kynge to consyder howe gracious howe meritorious & howe plesande a dede it is. . . . [Certificate for a contribution for chapel founded in memory of those slain at Bosworth Field.] s.sh.*obl.*4°. [*R. Pynson*?, c. 1511.] L(imp., C.39.h.5).O(Arch.A b.8(26a)). Lord Kenyon(2 imp.).; HD.
Line 11: 'Therfore'. This and following setting on same sheet in all copies but o.

.37 — [Anr. ed.] s.sh.*obl.*4°. [*R. Pynson*?, c. 1511.] L(imp., C.39.h.5).O(Arch.A b.8(26b)). Lord Kenyon.; HD.
Line 2: 'merytorious'; line 11: 'Therfor'.

.38 Burton Lazars, Leicestershire, *Hospital of St. Lazarus.* VNiuersis sctē mr̄is ecclesie filiis . . . Thomas Nortun miles ac mḡr hospitalis de Burton sctī Lazari Jerl'm in anglia . . . salutē. . . . [Letter of confraternity.] s.sh.*obl.*8°. [*R. Pynson*?, 1510.] L(C.18.e.2(7)).
(Formerly 4133)

Indulgences—INDULGENCES: ENGLISH ESTABLISHMENTS—
Local—cont.

.39 Colchester, Essex, *Monastery of the Holy Cross.* Frater Johēs Dryuer, prior monasterii ordīs fratrū sctē crucis in suburbiis Colcestrie. . . . [Indulgence.] s.sh.4°. p̄ *me R. Pynson*, [1523.] CHICH².M(deposit). Lord Kenyon.
(Formerly 5531) Woodcut lower left has cross on left shoulder. Line 4 begins 'cis'.

.40 — [Anr. ed.] s.sh.4°. p̄ *me R. Pynson*, [1523.] Lord Kenyon. Woodcut lower left has cross on right shoulder. Line 4 begins 'crucis'.

.41 Exeter, *Hospital of St. Roch.* The graces folowyng be graūted to al the bretherne and systers benefactours and good doers vnto the hospitall of yᵉ blessyd cōfessour saynt Rocke foūded & establyssyd wᵗin the of [*sic*] Cyte Excester. [Letter of confraternity.] s.sh.*obl.*8°. [*R. Faques*, 1522.] F.

.42 Hereford Cathedral, *Porch and Chantry Chapel.* Be it knowen to all cristen people. . . . [Indulgence issued by Cardinals Wolsey and Campeggio, papal legates.] s.sh.*obl.*4°. [*R. Faques*, 1518?] D².
(Formerly 13195)

Hounslow, Middlesex, *Trinitarians of.* See Indulgences 115A.

.43 Ipswich, Suffolk, *Franciscan Convent.* The holy & great indulgence & pardon of plenary remissiō a pena et culpa graūted by dyuerse popes, & newly confirmed with many amplycacions of . . . Leo the .x. that nowe is. . . . [Appointment by Abp. of Canterbury (really of York? as he is also called papal legate) as a house where the indulgences granted to the Hospital of the Holy Ghost, Rome, could be gained.] s.sh.*obl.*4°. [*W. de Worde*, 1518.] L(G.11899). M(deposit).
(Formerly 15475)

.44 Kirkby [i.e. Kirby] Bellars, Leicestershire. *Augustinian Priory.* Vniversis [xylographic] xp̄ifidelibus presentes litteras inspecturis, vel audituris Richard⁹ dei patiētia Prior prioratus de Kyrkeby super wrethik, alias vocatur Kyrkeby Beler. . . . [Letter of confraternity.] s.sh.*obl.*4°. [*W. Faques*, 1507.] L(C.18.e.1 (69)).L¹¹(Chancery Misc. (c. 47), Bundle 15, File 6).
(Formerly 15013)

.45 — ⟨B⟩E it knowen to all crysten pepull. . . . [Indulgence confirmed by Leo X to those visiting or giving alms to the conventual church of SS. Peter & Paul, 'Kyrkeby vpon wrethyke'.] s.sh.fol. [*J. Rastell*, 1520?] L¹³(2 imp. copies, H.2.19).

.46 Knaresborough, Yorkshire, *Trinitarian Priory of St. Robert.* Now = Indulgences 121B.

.47 — [Anr. ed.] Now = Indulgences 121C.

.48 Langley, Kent, *Monastery of the Virgin Mary and St. John the Evangelist.* UNiuersis. Sancte matris. Ecclesie filiis ad quos presentes. Littere puenerint. Nos. Iohānes. Braybornñ prior. Monasterij btē. Marie virginis & sanctti Iohānis euangeliste de. Langley Cantuariēsis dioc̄ & eiusdē loci conuentus. . . . [Letter of confraternity.] s.sh.*obl.*4°. [*York, U. Mylner*? 1519?] o(MS.Dodsworth 119(f.76)).
(Formerly 15201) This, like Indulgence 64, is a contemporary forgery; no such monastery existed.

.49 Lincoln, *Hospital of St. Katherine.* [Indulgence in favour of this hospital.] s.sh.*obl.*4°. [*R. Pynson*, c. 1510.] o (Douce frag. e.44).c(imp.).
(Formerly 21590)

Lincoln, *Hospital of St. Sepulchre.* See Indulgences 151 sq.

.50 London, *Bethlehem Hospital.* JOhēs Caualar custos siue magister & fratres domus sue [*sic*] hospitalis beate marie de Bethleem. . . . [Letter of confraternity.] s.sh.*obl.*4°. [*J. Rastell*, 1519.] L(6 copies, C.18.e.2 (12–14), Harl.5943/9, Ames I.27, and 804.k.15(3)). L⁵(2 copies, Lemon 2A, Add.4).O(2 copies, Arch.A b.8(8, 9)). M. Lord Kenyon.; F.
(Formerly 1975)

.51 London, *Monastery of the Holy Cross (Crutched Friars).* Be it knowen to alle true cristen peple . . . Thomas whete Prioure. [Letter of confraternity for benefactors, after destruction of the church by fire.] 1/2 sh.fol. [*R. Pynson*, 1491.] L(IA.55480). Broxbourne(O, left half).

Indulgences—INDULGENCES: ENGLISH ESTABLISHMENTS—*Local*
—London, *Monastery of the Holy Cross—cont.*

.52 — Vniuersis et singulis xp̄ifidelibus p̄ntes lr̄as inspecturis frater Will'ms Bowry. . . . [Letter of confraternity.] s.sh.*obl.*fol. [*R. Pynson?* 1515.] L(C.37.h.8).c⁷(2).

.53 — [Anr. ed.] FRater Wilhelmus Bowry, prior monasterii ordinis fratrum sancte crucis. . . . s.sh.*obl.*fol. [*W. de Worde*, 1519.] L(C.54.d.4(2)).
   (Formerly 13607) A dif. version from no. 52.

.54 — [Anr. ed.] s.sh.*obl.*4°. *R. Pynson*, [1528.] O(imp., Arch. A b.8(35b)).
   (Formerly 3433) Last word of text: 'Amen'.

.55 — [Anr. ed.] s.sh.*obl.*4°. *R. Pynson*, [1528.] O(imp., Arch. A b.8(35a)).
   (Formerly 3433) Last word of text: 'Amē'.

.55A London, *Hospital of St. Katherine's by the Tower, Guild of St. Barbara.* [Letter of confraternity specifying social as well as spiritual benefits, dated 1 Dec. 1518 and identifying 'Sir wyllyam Skeuīgton. knyght then beynge master.'] s.sh.*obl.*4°. [*J. Rastell*, 1518?] Seville, Biblioteca Colombina(imp. at beginning, bd. in J. Monaldus, *Summa . . . in utroque iure*, 1516).

.56 London, *Hospital of St. Thomas of Acres.* Johānes [Young] Calipoleñ episcop⁹ magister dom⁹ sctī Thome martyris Cātuariēs' dicte de Acoñ in ciuitate Londoñ. . . . [Letter of confraternity, dated 28 Feb. 1515.] s.sh. *obl.*4°. [*R. Pynson*, 1515?] L(C.18.e.2(122)).
   (Formerly 15471)

.57 — Be it know⟨n to all c⟩risten men and women, that thyse be the great indulgence. . . . [List of indulgences granted to confraternity.] s.sh.fol. [*R. Pynson*, 1515?] O (Arch.A b.8(3)).
   (Formerly 21592) In 95 mm. textura.

.57A — [Anr. ed.] Be it knowen [etc.] s.sh.4°. [*R. Redman*, c. 1532.] O(frags. of 2 copies, Vet.A 1 b.12).
   In 74 mm. textura.

.58 — Here after foloweth the newe pryuyleges and indulgēces graunted by our holy Father the Pope Leo .x. to the house of seynt Thomas of Acres in London. . . . [List of indulgences granted to the confraternity.] s.sh.fol. [*R. Pynson*, 1517?] L(imp., C.18.e.2(91)).C(bottom half, cropt).
   (Formerly 15474)

.59 London, *St. Lawrence in Jewry.* The confraternyte of seynt Ursula in seynt Laurence in the Iury. . . . [A picture issued to confraters.] s.sh.8°. [*W. de Worde*, c. 1520.] L(frag., C.18.e.2(33)).
   (Formerly 24541)

.60 London, *Savoy Hospital.* Julius Ep̄us seruus seruoɤ [xylographic] dei. . . . [Bull granting privileges on behalf of hospital at the request of the executors of King Henry VII, its founder.] s.sh.*obl.* fol. [*R. Pynson*, c. 1510.] O(imp., 3 frags. of single copy, Arch.A b.8 (16)).
   (Formerly 21803)

.60A London, *Unassigned.* [Fragment of the last 25 lines of a list, in English, of pardons granted to a confraternity in a parish church in the London diocese.] s.sh.fol. [*R. Pynson*, c. 1515.] O¹⁶(I.2.13).
   Pr. authentication in lower margin: 'Visa & examinata p̄ Me Johēm [Young] calipolensē [and] me Will'm Horsey'.

.61 Ludlow, Shropshire, *Palmers of St. Lawrence.* VNiuersis [xylographic] Et singulis . . . ego Richardus downe custos . . . fraternitatis gilde palmariorum . . . in ecclesia sancti Laurētij de Ludlow herfordeñ diocesis. . . . [Letter of confraternity.] s.sh.*obl.*fol. [*R. Pynson*, after 1511.] O(Arch.A b.8(6)).

.62 Newton, Isle of Ely, *Chapel of St. Mary in the Sea.* VNiuersis xp̄ifidelib⁹. . . . [Letter of confraternity.] s.sh.*obl.*4°. [*R. Pynson*, 1505.] L¹¹(Excheq. K. R. Eccles. Docs. 6/65).O(1.e.54).
   (Formerly 3280) Issued by W. Thornburgh.

.63 — [Anr. ed.] VNiuersis xp̄i fidelib⁹ presētes. . . . s.sh.*obl.*4°. [*York, H. Goes*, 1506.] O(2 copies, MS.Barlow 13 (ff.152,153)).

.64 Newton, Suffolk, *Hospital of Pity.* A deuoute inuocacyon of all the blessyd names of our lorde Jhesu Cryst . . . to euery mā woman & chyld gyuyng or sendyng ony parte of theyr goodys to the vpholdyng of the sayd

Indulgences—INDULGENCES: ENGLISH ESTABLISHMENTS—*Local*
—*cont.*

hospytall, they shall inioye the grete gyftes of grace. . . . [Indulgence.] s.sh.*obl.*4°. [*Southwark, P. Treveris*, c. 1530.] HD.
   This appears to be a contemporary forgery.

.65 North Newington, Oxfordshire, *Confraternity of Chapel of St. John the Baptist.* UNiuersis christifidelibus presentes literas inspecturis vel audituris, nos Joānes et Radulphus custodes. . . . [Letter of confraternity.] s.sh.*obl.*4°. [*R. Pynson*, 1521.] O(3 copies, Arch.A b.8(1*) and MS. Rawl.A 269(ff.50,51)).
   (Formerly 18661a) With Hodnett 1447; penultimate line: 'concedimus'.

.66 — [Anr. ed.] s.sh.*obl.*4°. [*R. Pynson*, 1521.] O(3 copies, Arch.A b.8(1*) and MS.Rawl.A 269(ff.50,51)).; HD. Pr. on same sheet as above. With Hodnett 1446; line 2: 'Joannes'; penultimate line: 'cōcedimus'.

.67 — OUr holy father the pope of Rome pope Boniface in his bull vnder leed doyth. . . . [List of indulgences.] s.sh.fol. [*R. Pynson*, 1521.] O(Arch.A b.8(1)). Lord Kenyon(frag.).

   Oxford, *Christ Church.* Vniuersis Christifidelibus, . . . [An inspeximus of a grant to Cardinal College (later Christ Church). 1529.] *See* 24323.5.

.67A Oxford, *Dominican Friary.* DEuot' in christo Iesu sibi dilect' [   ] Frater Henricus Osborñ sacre scientie humilis professor ac prior conuentus ordinis fratrum predicatorum Oxoñ. Salutem. . . . [Letter of confraternity.] s.sh.*obl.*4°. [*R. Pynson*, 1520.] L²²(2 copies, Hale MS.179(13)).

.68 Rickmansworth, Hertfordshire. Be it knowen to all crystē people which ioyeth in theyr hartes. . . . [Indulgences granted by Cardinal [Wolsey] and [John Longland] Bp. of Lincoln for restoration of church fired by heretics.] s.sh.4°. [*J. Skot*, c. 1525.] L(C.18.e.2(96)).
   (Formerly 21026)

.68A Ripon, Yorkshire, *Collegiate Church of St. Wilfrid.* UNiuersis christifidelibus de regno Anglie Walie he sunt indulgentie. . . . [List of indulgences granted to confraternity.] s.sh.*obl.*4°. [*R. Pynson*, c. 1520.] Muniments of the Earl of Aylesford, Packington Hall, Warwickshire.

.69 Salisbury, Wiltshire, *Hospital of the Trinity and St. Thomas.* Be it knowen vnto all trew crysten people that Laurence [Campeggio] by the grace of god bysshop of Salysbury . . . [List of indulgences granted to confraternity.] s.sh.4°. [*Southwark, P. Treveris*, 1530?] M(deposit).

.70 Southwark, *Guild of St. George.* UNto all manere & synguler crysten people beholdynge, or herynge these present letters. Knowe ye. . . . [Letter of confraternity.] s.sh.*obl.*4°. [*W. de Worde*,] 1514 (1 de.). L¹¹ (Chancery Misc. (c.47), Bundle 15, File 6).

.71 — [Anr. ed.] UNto all maner & synguler crysten people beholdynge or herynge these present lettres. Knowe ye. . . . s.sh.*obl.*4°. [*W. de Worde*,] 1514 (1 de.). L¹¹ (Chancery Misc. (c.47), Bundle 15, File 6).

.72 — [Anr. ed.] UNto all maner & singuler Cristen people beholdynge or herynge these present letters shall come gretynge, . . . s.sh.*obl.*4°. [*R. Pynson*, c. 1520.] M².
   Last line begins: 'seynt'.

.73 — [Anr. ed.] s.sh.*obl.*4°. [*R. Pynson*, c. 1520.] L⁵(imp., Lemon 2).
   Last line begins: 'George'.

.74 Stamford, Lincolnshire, *Benedictine Convent of Our Lady and St. Michael.* VNiversis [xylographic] Sanc⟨   ⟩. . . . [Letter of confraternity.] s.sh.*obl.*4°. [*Cambridge, J. Siberch*, c. 1523.] O(frag., Auct.7Q7.43).

.75 — [Anr. ed.] VNiuersis sctē matris ecclesie filiis ad quos presentes littere peruenerint nos Margareta Stanburne. Priorissa. . . . s.sh.*obl.*4°. [*W. de Worde*, 1524.] L(imp., Harl.5919/183).O(Arch.A b.8(15)).

.76 Strata Marcella, Montgomeryshire, *Monastery of B. Mary of.* UNiuersis sancte matris ecclesie filiis ad quos presentes littere peruenerint. Nos Iohannes dei paciencia abbas monasterij beate Marie de Stratamarcella Assaieñ dioc̄, & eisdē loci conuentus. . . . Cum reuerēdissimus pater dñs Thomas Cardinalis Eboɤ Anglie primas, . . . [Letter of confraternity.] s.sh.*obl.*4°. [*R. Pynson*, 1528.] L(imp., Egerton MS.2410 (f.3)).NLW(imp.).

Indulgences—INDULGENCES: ENGLISH ESTABLISHMENTS—*Local* —*cont.*

.77 Sudbury, Suffolk, *Hospital of St. Sepulchre.* Now = Indulgences 151.

.78 — [Anr. ed.] Now = Indulgences 152.

Thelsford, Warks., *Trinitarians of. See* Indulgences 122.

Thetford, Norfolk, *Hospital of St. Sepulchre. See* Indulgences 151 sq.

.79 Uxbridge, Middlesex, *Confraternity of Chapel of St. Margaret.* UNiuersis sancte matris ecclesie filiis ad quos presentes littere peruenerint Joħānes Herryes, wilelmus Myles, et, Ricardus Chapell gardiani capelle Sancte Margarete de woxbridge Londō diocesis. . . . [Letter of confraternity.] s.sh.*obl.*4°. *per me R. Fakes,* [1527.] L⁵(Lemon 3).

.80 Wakering, Essex, *Confraternity of St. John.* VEnerabilibus et in Christo carissime dilectis gardiano et magistris vna cum fratribus et sororibus gylde seu confraternitatis sancti Johannis in ecclesia perochiali sācti Nicholai de wakering Londoñ . . . Frater wilhelm⁹ Aiter. . . . [Letter of confraternity.] s.sh.*obl.*fol. [*R. Faques,* 1526.] L(C.18.e.2(16)).L⁵(Lemon 2B). (Formerly 15480)

.81 Walsoken, Norfolk, *Hospital of Holy Trinity.* UNiuersis sctē matris eccl'ie ad quos p̄sentes lr̄e puenerūt Thomas honyter Mgr̄ siue custos capelle et hospital' sctē Trinitatis de walsokyn norwic: diocesis. [Letter of confraternity.] s.sh.*obl.*4°. [*W. de Worde?* 1505.] NMU(Middleton MSS.).

.82 — [Anr. ed.] UNiuersis scē matris ecclesie filiis ad quos p̄ntes lr̄e puenerint Ioħēs wheth̄m, Mr̄ siue custos capelle & hospitalis scē t⟨rini⟩tatis de walsokon Norwyc dioc. . . . [Letter of confraternity.] s.sh.*obl.* 4°. [*R. Pynson,* c. 1515.] L(imp., C.18.e.2(9)). (Formerly 24521)

.83 Westminster, *Confraternity of St. Cornelius.* The pardon grauntyd to the fraternyte of Seynt Cornelys at Westmynster that vicet [*sic*] gyue or sende to it. . . . [Indulgence.] s.sh.4°. [*W. de Worde,* c. 1518.] O (Gough Gen. Top.364). (Formerly 25288) Perhaps connected w. Indulgences 23A.

.84 York, *Confraternity of St. Mary of Mt. Carmel.* UNiuersis et singulis Chris⟨tifidelibus⟩ Rafe Symson magister siue custos confrat⟨   ⟩ ciuitate Ebo♄ . . . et beate Marie de monte carmelo, in dicta ciuitate Ebo♄. . . . [Letter of confraternity.] s.sh.4°. [*R. Pynson,* 1520?] L(imp., Harl.5919/184).C(2 frags. in binding of 15822). 1 frag. at C includes the date 27 Oct. 'M.D. xx⟨   ⟩', i.e. 152⟨0?⟩.

.84A York, *Guild of SS. Christopher and George.* UNiuersis et sigulis xp̄ifidelib'. . . . Richard⁹ harbattyll. Magister siue custos ♄frat'nitat₃ siue gilde subĩuocatiõe Sccõ♄ Christofori & Georgii Martyrū In Ciuitate. Ebo♄. . . . [Letter of confraternity. 16 Oct. 1519.] s.sh.*obl.*fol. [*York, U. Mylner,* 1519.] Y.

INDULGENCES ISSUED ON BEHALF OF CONTINENTAL INSTITUTIONS

.85 Compostella, *Hospital of St. James.* In dei nomine Amen Nouerint vniuersi cristifideles. . . . [A certificate of contribution, w. woodcut signature of the commissary, Alfonsus de Losa.] s.sh.*obl.*4°. [*Westminster, W. de Worde,* 1497.] E². End of text dated 1497. Possibly issued in 2 settings like 86, 87.

.86 — [A variant, w. end of text dated 1498.] [*Westminster, W. de Worde,* 1498.] L(IC.55212).O(imp., Inc.d.E1. 1498.1).C(2).M. Hanover, Kestner-Museum(3).; PML (3). St. John's Seminary, Camarillo, California. Duff 213. (Formerly 14102) Line 1 ends: 're'. Pr. together on same sheet with 87. L, M, and Kestner have a sheet containing 2 impressions each, by halfsheet imposition, of this and 87.

.87 — [Anr. ed.] s.sh.*obl.*4°. [*Westminster, W. de Worde,* 1498.] L.O(imp.).C.E².M.+; LC.PML(2). Line 1 ends: 'felicis'.

Indulgences—INDULGENCES: CONTINENTAL INSTITUTIONS—*cont.*

.88 — Hereaft' foloweth the abreuiacõn of the graces, īdulgēces & staciõs which our moste holy fad' Pope Alexãder vi. graūteth to all true beleuīge people: . . . [List of indulgences.] s.sh.fol. [*W. de Worde,* c. 1505.] L(3 copies, imp., Harl.5919/131, C.18.e.2.(48), and Ames I.25).O(Arch.A b.8(25)).; F.HD(in binding of Ovid *Fasti,* Venice, 1520).MEL(Foxcroft 18). With cut of scallop-shell, top left corner. This is actually 2 folio sheets pasted together.

.89 — [Anr. ed.] s.sh.fol. [*W. de Worde,* c. 1505.] ETON.M (deposit, imp.). No cut of scallop-shell at top.

.90 Mount Sinai, *Abbey of St. Katherine.* Indulgences graunted to all and euery crysten man and whoman in what someuer party of the worlde they be entrynge in to the fraternyite [*sic*] of saynt Katheryn in the mounte of Synay. [List of indulgences.] s.sh.fol. [*J. Notary,* 1520?] O(Arch.A b.8(38)).LINC. Line 6 from bottom: 'Commaundement'. The collector is named as Dane Clement [Paleologus.]

.90A — [Anr. ed.] s.sh.fol. [*J. Notary,* 1520?] Virginia Theological Seminary, Alexandria, Va.(imp.). Line 6 from bottom: 'Cõmandement'. The collector is named as Brother Clement.

.91 Rome, *Hospital of the Holy Ghost.* FRater Philippus Mulart decretorum doctor sacri & apostolici hospitalis sancti Spirit⁹ in Saxia de vrbe Romana. . . . [Letter of confraternity, dated 1518.] s.sh.*obl.*fol. [*R. Pynson,* 1518.] O(Arch.A b.8(17)). Last full line of text ends: 'et'.

.92 — [Anr. ed., dated 1518.] s.sh.*obl.*fol. [*R. Faques,* 1518.] C(Add.MS.7519(f.27)). Line 2: 'Spirittus'; last full line ends: 'casi'.

.93 — [Anr. ed., dated 1519.] s.sh.*obl.*fol. *per me R. Fakes,* [1519.] L(C.39.k.14(5)).O(Arch.A b.8(18)). Broxbourne(O).; PML. Mellon. (Formerly 15477) Last full line of text ends: 'etiam'.

.94 — [Anr. ed., dated 1519.] s.sh.*obl.* fol. *per me R. Fakes,* [1519.] L(2 copies, C.39.k.14(6) and C.18.e.2(123)). O(Arch.A b.8(19*)). Last full line of text ends: 'casibus'.

.95 — [A variant, w. date altered to 1520.] s.sh.*obl.*fol. *per me R. Fakes,* [1520.] L(C.39.k.14(7)).; F.

.96 — [Anr. ed., dated 1520.] s.sh.*obl.*fol. *per me R. Pynson,* [1520.] L(C.18.e.2(15)).; St. John's Seminary, Camarillo, California. (Formerly 15478) Line 4 begins: 'nr̄ dñs Leo'.

.97 — [Anr. ed., dated 1520.] s.sh.*obl.*fol. *per me R. Pynson,* [1520.] L(C.122.e.8).O(Arch.A b.8(20)). Line 4 begins: 'noster dñs Leo'.

.98 — Our holy father pope Leo the .x. that now is (cõsiderynge the īfinite charite of our lorde Iesu christe, . . . [List of benefits.] fol(2). p̄ me R. Pynson, regiū Impressorē, [c. 1520.] O(top half, Vet.A 1 b.12).O¹⁹(bottom half of 2nd sheet). M(deposit).

.99 — [Anr. version.] fol(2). ⟨R. Pynson, regi⟩s Impressor, [1520.] L(2 frags. of 1 copy, C.18.e.1(48)). (Formerly 15479) In beginning of text: 'consyderynge that our Sauyour Lorde Ihesu criste'.

— *See also* Indulgences 43.

.100 Rome, *Jubilee.* [Bull ordaining 1500 as a Jubilee. 20 Dec. 1499.] s.sh.fol. [*R. Pynson,* 1500.] No copy traced. Offset of this in one HD copy of 3175. *See* Grolier Club *Gazette,* May 1922.

.101 Rome, *St. Peter's.* Universis [xylographic] Christifidelibus presentes litteras inspecturis, Frater Edmundus [Belland] Prior puincialis ordinis fratrū heremitarū sancti Augustini in Anglia. . . . [Letter, dated 12 Jan. 1517, admitting recipients to all the privileges granted by bull of Leo X of 6 May 1516 to contributors to St. Peter's and churches of the Austin Friars. Plural issue.] s.sh.*obl.*fol. [*R. Pynson,* 1517.] John Arundell, Wardour Castle. Next to last line: 'Dat' in cõuētu nr̄o Londoñ.'

.101A — [Anr. ed.] FRater wilhelmus [Wetherall] inter sacre theologie doctores minimus prior prouincialis. . . . s.sh.*obl.*4°. [*R. Pynson,* 1526.] C. Line 5 from bottom: 'Datū in conuentu nr̄o Londini.'

.101B — [Anr. ed.] F⟨rater⟩. . . . s.sh.*obl.*fol. [*R. Pynson,* 1526?] O(frag., Arch.A b.8(32)). Last line: 'Dat' in Cõuentu nostro Londoñ.'

Indulgences—INDULGENCES: CONTINENTAL INSTITUTIONS—
Rome, *St. Peter's*—*cont.*

.102 — Artycles of the great indulgence of plenary remissyon à pena et culpa graunted for the buyldynge of seynt Peters churche at Rome and the cõuentuall churchis of freres Angustyns [*sic*] of Oxford and other within the realme of Englond. [Indulgence.] s.sh.fol. [*R. Pynson*, 1516?] o⁸(imp., MS.253).PARIS³(imp., in *Fasciculus temporum*, 1524).

.103 — [Anr. ed.] The artycles of saynt Peters generall pardon graunted for the byldyng of saynt Peters church at Rome: and the cõuentuall churches of friers Augustines, within Englande, and Irelande. . . . [Indulgence.] s.sh.fol. [*R. Pynson?* c. 1518.] c¹⁹(imp., MS.O.1.26).

   Last paragraph begins: 'It' it hath pleased our souerayne lorde kyng Henry the .viii.'

.103A — [Anr. version.] s.sh.fol. *R. Pynson*, [c. 1518.] L(bottom half, recto of Harl.5919/132).

   Last paragraph begins: 'Also our soueraygne lorde kyng Henry the .viii.' L has Indulgences 150 pr. on the verso.

   — Uñiuersis [xylographic] Sancte matris ecclesie filijs. . . . [Inspeximus by Abp. Warham of bull of Julius II, dated 18 Mar. 1508, granting indulgences to contributors to the rebuilding of St. Peter's.] *See* 25071.5.

.103B — Willṁus [Warham] Permissione diuina Cãtuarieñ Archiepiscopus toci⁹ Anglie primas. . . . [Indulgence to choose a confessor, granted to contributors to building of St. Peter's.] 1/2 sh.fol. [*R. Pynson*, 1508.] L(C.11.b.11(1)).

   (Formerly 14841) Setting in second person singular throughout. Line 1 ends: 'Archiepis'. Cut of papal arms differs from both those in the following 104–5 groups; it has undamaged borders. Same xylographic 'Willṁus' as in 104–104B.

.104 — [Anr. ed., plural issue.] 1/2 sh.fol. [*R. Pynson*, 1508.] c(Syn.5.50.4).

   Top border of papal arms has damaged area 5 mm. long. Line 15: 'deuehy'.

   The 2 groups 104–104B and 105–105C represent twin settings, and the M copies of 104B and 105B still survive on the same sheet. In both groups line 1 ends: 'Archiepi', but each has its own xylographic 'Willṁus' and its papal arms. The 'impressions' of each are from standing type with a few press alterations, most noticeably in the use of 'tibi' or 'vobis' in line 5 to make singular or plural issues. That the orig. setting of each was for a plural issue is suggested by the readings in lines 8,9: 'confessione vestra . . . vestris pecca/tis', found in all impressions, even the singular issues.

   The 104 group can be recognized by the presence of dots inside the inner scallops of the init. 'W' and by the readings: 'confessorem idoneũ . . . regularẽ . . . pos-/' in line 7. The 105 group has no dots inside the inner scallops of the 'W' and has: 'confessorẽ idoneum . . . regularem . . . pos/' in line 7. Each group is arranged according to the progressive state of wear of the papal arms.

.104A — [Anr. impression, singular issue.] L⁵(Lemon Add. 2). o(J, imp.).

   Top border of papal arms has damaged area now 6 mm. long. Line 15: 'deuehy'.

.104B — [Anr. impression, singular issue.] M(R36318.2).

   As 104A, but left border of papal arms damaged near top. Line 15: 'deuehi'. Pr. simultaneously with 105B on 1 sheet.

.105 — [Anr. ed., singular issue.] 1/2 sh.fol. [*R. Pynson*, 1508.] o(J, imp.).

   2 sections of left border of this papal arms cut remain intact. For further distinctions *see* end of note to 104.

.105A — [Anr. impression, plural issue.] L(2 copies, C.18.e.1 (89) and Ames I.89).

   (Formerly 14840) Left border of papal arms gone; top border still intact.

.105B — [Anr. impression, singular issue.] M(R36318.1).

   As 105A. Pr. simultaneously w. 104B on 1 sheet.

.105C — [Anr. impression, plural issue.] o(Arch. A b.8(13).; PML(18221).

   (Formerly 25072) Top border of papal arms broken in 2 places.

Sinai. *See* Indulgences 90.

Indulgences—*cont.*

INDULGENCES ISSUED TO RAISE MONEY TO FIGHT THE TURKS OR TO RANSOM CAPTIVES

General

.106 [J]Ohannes [Sant] Abb⟨as⟩ Abendoñ sanctissimi in xp̄o prĩs et dm̄ nostri dm̄ Sixti diuina puidencia pape quarti. . . . [Indulgence, plural issue, to contributors for a fleet against the Turks.] s.sh.*obl*.fol. [*Westminster, W. Caxton*, 1476.] L¹¹(imp., dated in MS. 13 Dec. 1476).

.107 FRater Johannes kendale Turcipelerius Rhodi ac commissarius a sanctissimo in xpristo patre et domino nostro domino Sixto diuina prouidencia papa quarto . . . [Indulgence, singular issue, for contributors to the defence of Rhodes.] s.sh.*obl*.4º. [*Westminster, W. Caxton*, before 31 Mar. 1480.] L(IA.55024). Duff 204.
   (Formerly 22582)

.108 — [Anr. ed.] [F]Rater Johannes kendale turcipelerius Rhodi ac cõmissarius a sanctissimo in xp̄o patre et dño nostro dño Sixto. . . . s.sh.*obl*.4º. [*J. Lettou*, 1480.] c⁸.NRO(frags.). Duff 205.
   (Formerly 22582a)

.109 — [Anr. ed.] [F]Rater Johãnes Kendale turcipelerius rhodi ac cõmissarius a sanctissiõ in xp̄o patre et nr̄o Sixto. . . . s.sh.*obl*.4º. [*J. Lettou*, 1480.] c⁸. Duff 206.
   (Formerly 22583)

.110 [Frater Johannes Kendale . . . to line 7?] tis supplicationibʒ inclinati. vobis et vtrique vestrũ vt aliquẽ idoneum . . . [Indulgence, plural issue, for contributors to the defence of Rhodes.] s.sh.*obl*.4º. [*Westminster, W. Caxton*, 1480.] c²(frags.). Duff 207.
   (Formerly 22584)

.111 — [Anr. ed.] FRater Johannes kendale turcipelerius Rhodi ac cõmissarius a sanctissimo in xpristo patre et domino nostro domino Sixto. . . . [line 7] . . . supplicationibus inclinati. uobis et utrique uestrum ut aliquem idoneum. . . . s.sh.*obl*.4º. [*J. Lettou*, before 18 Apr. 1480.] L(IA.55403). Duff 208.
   (Formerly 22585)

.112 IOhannes de giglis iuris vtriusʠ doctor sanctissimi dñi nostri dñi Sixti diuina prouidencia pape quarti et sedis apostolice subdiaconus. . . . [Indulgence, singular issue, for contributors to the defence of Rhodes.] s.sh.*obl*.4º. [*Westminster, W. Caxton*, 1481.] L(IA.55052).c⁴(frag.).; PML.NCU(imp.). Duff 209.
   (Formerly 22586)

.113 IOhannes de giglis iuris vtriusʠ doctor sanctissimi dñi nr̄i dñi Sixti diuina puidencia pape quarti et sedis apostolice subdiaconus. . . . [Indulgence, plural issue, for contributors to the defence of Rhodes.] s.sh.*obl*. 4º. [*Westminster, W. Caxton*, 1481.] L(2 frags., IB.55051). o¹³(frags.).M(2 imp.). Duff 210.
   (Formerly 22587)

.114 IOhannes De Gigliis alias de liliis. . . . [Indulgence, w. blank terminations to suit either singular or plural grantee, to contributors to crusade.] s.sh.*obl*.4º. [*Westminster, W. Caxton*, before 24 Apr. 1489.] L(3 copies, IA.55126–8).c¹⁶.; PML. Duff 211.
   (Formerly 14100)

.115 — [Anr. ed.] IOhãnes de Gigliis. . . . s.sh.*obl*.4º. [*Westminster, W. Caxton*, 1489.] D. Duff 212.
   (Formerly 14101)

.115A Johẽs mĩster dom⁹ de Homideslowe [*sic* for Houndeslowe] Ordĩs scē Trinitatis & redẽpcioĩs captiuoɤ terre scē. . . . [Letter of confraternity for the Trinitarian Order for ransom of captives, dated 1503.] s.sh.*obl*.fol. [*J. Notary*, 1503.] HD.

.116 THe benygne grace, power, and vertue of our holy fader the pope July the seconde that now is as lyeutenaunt . . . [Indulgence to contributors to ransom of captives of Saracens.] s.sh.fol. [*R. Pynson*, c. 1510.] o(2 copies, Arch.A b.8(4,5)).

.117 — [Anr. ed.] s.sh.fol. [*R. Pynson*, c. 1510.] L(bottom, C.18.e.2(17)).o(top, Arch. A b.8(34)).
   (Formerly 19188) Line 2: 'lyeutenaũt'.

.117A BE it knowen vnto all Cristen people that by the cõmendacyon of our holy Fader the pope Julius the seconde . . . syr Mychaell of Paleolog. . . . [Indulgence to contributors to the appeal of M. de Paleologus for ransoming captives of Turks.] s.sh.fol. [*R. Pynson*, c. 1512.] YK(imp.).

Indulgences—INDULGENCES: TURKS OR CAPTIVES—*General—cont.*

.117B [Fragment begins:] ⟨afo⟩resayd hath sent in to this realme . . . [Licence (?) by W. Warham, Abp. of Canterbury, and E. Vaughan, Bp. of St. David's, as papal commissaries, to M. de Paleologus and his proctors to collect ransom money within the province of Canterbury, w. indulgences for benefactors. In English, with 5-line recommendation in Latin at foot.] s.sh.fol. [*R. Pynson*, c. 1512.] CASHEL(2 frags. of 1 copy, in binding of 9514).

.118 Michael de Palealogo frater consobrinus illustrissimi ducis Maior Cōstantinopolitañ. . . . [Indulgence to contributors to the appeal of M. de Paleologus for ransoming captives of Turks.] s.sh.fol. [*R. Pynson*, c. 1512.] L(C.110.e.10).

.119 — [Anr. issue.] s.sh.fol. [*R. Pynson*, c. 1512.] Sotheby 23 June 1958, Lot 133 (Ripon copy, bought by Green, untraced; photostats at L and O).
    In this issue there is no leading after lines 16 and 18.

.120 UNinersis [*sic*] christifidelib⁹ ad quos pñtes littere peruenerint in charitate et dilectiōe dñi nŕi Jesu xp̄i ex parte Michaelis de Palealogo. . . . [Indulgence to contributors to the appeal of M. de Paleologus for ransoming captives of Turks.] s.sh.fol. [*R. Pynson*, c. 1512.] O(frag., Arch.A b.8(33a)).O¹⁷(2 copies).
    Line 2 ends: 'Maioris'.

.121 — [Anr. ed.] Uniuersis christifidelibus. . . . s.sh.fol. [*R. Pynson*, c. 1512.] O(Arch.A b.8(33b)).
    Line 2 ends: 'Maioris Con-'.

.121A — [Anr. ed.] s.sh.fol. [*R. Pynson*, c. 1512.] L²²(Hale MS.77).
    Line 2 ends: 'Maioris Cō'.

.121B VNiuersis presentes litteras inspecturis Frater Oswaldus minister domus sctī Roberti iuxta Knaresburgh Eboŕ dioc̄ orddīs [*sic*] sctē Trinitatis & redēptionis captiuoᵤ terre sctē. . . . [Letter of confraternity for the Trinitarian Order for ransom of captives, dated 1526.] s.sh.fol. [*W. de Worde*, 1526.] O⁸(MS.253).

.121C — [Anr. ed., dated 1527.] UNiuersis presentes litteras inspecturis. Frater. Oswaldus. Minister domus sancti. Roberti. . . . s.sh.*obl*.fol. [*R. Pynson*, 1527.] Yorkshire Archaeological Society(DD 56 (1952) 26).

.122 Frater Johānes Brocden de Tellisforde wygorñieñ dioc. sancte Trinitatis et redemptionis captiuorum terre sancte. . . . [Letter of confraternity for the Trinitarian Order for ransom of captives.] s.sh.fol. [*R. Pynson*, 1529.] L²(4 copies, Frag. No. 4).

.123 For as moche ⟨ ⟩ men takē prysoners into the hādes of the Inf⟨id⟩eles, Turkes & Sarasy⟨ns⟩. . . . [Letter of confraternity issued by Mercedarians to those assisting in the ransom of captives of Turks, w. xylographic signature of the Master General, Benedictus Cafone.] s.sh.fol. [*Southwark, P. Treveris*, 1532.] O(2 copies, Arch.A b.8(20*,20**)).

Individual

.124 Busset, John and Richard. OUr holy father Pope Leo that now is cōsyderynge, that where .ii. certayne brotherñ Johñ busset and Richarde busset marchauntes of Auinien, . . . [Indulgences for contributors toward their ransom, w. letter of recommendation by Abp. Warham, dated Lambeth, 28 June 1515.] s.sh.fol. [*R. Pynson*, 1515.] O(2 copies, Arch.A b.8(31) and MS. Lat.misc.d.81).C.C².
    (Formerly 15472)

.125 — [Anr. ed., w. papal renewal for 3 years, dated 28 Aug. 1515.] Our holy ffader pope leo that noio [*sic*] is . . . s.sh.*obl*.4°. [*J. Notary*, 1515.] O(Arch.A b.8(10)).
    Text in 28 lines.

.125A — [Anr. ed.] s.sh.*obl*.4°. [*J. Notary*, c. 1515.] Broxbourne (O, right half).
    Text in 30 lines.

.126 — [Anr. ed.] Be it knowen to all trewe Cristen people we haue receyued a cōmaūdement. . . . [Recommendation by W. Warham, Archbishop of Canterbury, dated Lambeth, 31 May 1517.] s.sh.fol. [*R. Pynson*, 1517.] L²(Frag. No. 6).

Indulgences—INDULGENCES: TURKS OR CAPTIVES—*Individual—cont.*

.127 Cressy, Thomas. [Royal licence issued to Joan Cressy to collect alms for ransoming her husband, Thomas, 23 June 1515.] s.sh.fol. [*R. Pynson*, 1515.] MEL(2 frags., Foxcroft 24).
    The frags. represent 2 impressions on 1 sheet by halfsheet imposition.

.128 Homideslowe, John. Now = Indulgences 115A.

.129 Lascarina, Elizabeth. [Indulgences to contributors towards the redemption of the children of 'Lady Isabet lascarina', from the Turks. In English.] s.sh.fol. [*R. Pynson*, 1511.] O(top cropt, Arch.A b.8(12)). Lord Kenyon(2 frags., in binding of *Manipulus curatorum*).
    (Formerly 15473)

.130 — [Anr. version, w. 'Lady Elyzabeth Lasarina'.] s.sh.fol. [*R. Pynson*, 1511.] GLOUC(frags.).

Paleologus, Michael de. *See* Indulgences 117A sqq.

.131 Pyllet, *Sir* John. BE it knowen to all Cristē people that syr Johñ Pyllet . . . was taken by the Mauris & Infidels. [Indulgences for contributors to ransom.] s.sh.fol. [*R. Pynson*, 1517?] L(imp., C.18.e.2(49)).L⁵(imp., Lemon 1).
    (Formerly 7769) With King Henry's recommendation at the end.

.132 — [Anr. ed.] BE it knowen to all Cristen people that Johñ Pyllet. . . . s.sh.*obl*.4°. [*R. Pynson*, 1517?] O(Arch. A b.8(11)).
    Without King Henry's recommendation at the end.

.133 Sargy, John. These be the articles of the popes bulle under leade translated from latyn into englisshe. OOur [*sic*] holy father pope Leo the .x. of that name. . . . [Bull dated 21 May 1516 authorizing J. Sargy to collect ransom for captives of Turks, w. letter of protection of Henry VIII, dated 26 Oct. 1518.] s.sh.fol. [*R. Pynson*, 1518.] L(C.18.e.2(8)).M.
    (Formerly 15476)

LICENCES

.134 Robertus Castelleñ. . . . vt oēs & singulos. . . Parrochianos tuos. [Licence to clergy to absolve in cases usually reserved, 26 Feb. 1498. Singular issue.] s.sh.*obl*.4°. [*R. Pynson*, 1498.] O¹⁴(Auct.V.vi.15(f.33)). Duff 214.
    (Formerly 322) 13 lines.

.135 Robertus Castelleñ . . . vt cōfessorē idoneū. . . . [Licence granting choice of confessor to those who take no part in risings against the royal authority, 26 Feb. 1498. Singular issue.] s.sh.*obl*.4°. [*R. Pynson*, 1498.] L(IA. 55507). Duff 215.
    (Formerly 323) 13 lines.

.136 — [Anr. ed.] Robertus Castelleñ . . . vt ⁊fessorē idoneū. . . . s.sh.*obl*.4°. [*R. Pynson*, 1498.] M. Duff 215(variant).
    (Formerly 324) 12 lines.

.137 [R]Obertus Castelleñ . . . vt cōfessorē idoneū. . . . [Licence granting choice of confessors, 26 Feb. 1498. Plural issue.] s.sh.fol. [*R. Pynson*, 1498.] LC. Duff 216.
    (Formerly 325) 13 lines.

.138 Robertus Castelleñ cleric⁹ wulteranus . . . Vt oēs & singulos. . . . [Licence to clergy to absolve, 2 Feb. 1499. Singular issue.] s.sh.*obl*.4°. [*R. Pynson*, 1499.] O(Arch.A b.8(21)). Duff 217.
    (Formerly 326) 19 lines. Line 3 ends: 'prochianos'.
    In Indulgences 138–143 'Robertus' is xylographic.

.139 — [Anr. ed.] s.sh.*obl*.4°. [*R. Pynson*, 1499.] NY. Duff 217 (variant).
    (Formerly 327) 19 lines. Line 3 ends: 'parrochia-'.

.140 Robertus Castelleñ cleric⁹ wulteranus . . . Salutē. Dudū siquidē vobis vt ⁊fessorē idoneū seculare vel regularē. . . [Licence to choose confessors, 2 Feb. 1499. Plural issue.] s.sh.*obl*.4°. [*R. Pynson*, 1499.] c(frag.). c². Duff 218.
    (Formerly 328) 21 lines. Line 2 begins: 'mi dni nŕi'.

.140A — [Anr. ed.] s.sh.*obl*.4°. [*R. Pynson*, 1499.] O(frag. of 1st 11 lines, Vet.A 1b.12).
    Line 2 begins: 'dni nŕi'.

Indulgences—LICENCES—*cont.*

.141 Robertus Castelleñ cleric⁹ wulteran⁹ . . . Auctoritate apl'ica . . . vt ⁊fessorē idoneū. . . . [Licence to choose confessors. 2 Feb. 1499. Plural issue.] s.sh.*obl*.4°. [*R. Pynson*, 1499.] o(Douce frag.f.50). Duff 220.
(Formerly 329) 19 lines.

.142 — [Anr. ed.] s.sh.*obl*.4°. [*R. Pynson*, 1499.] c². Duff 219.
(Formerly 330) 18 lines. Line 2: 'simi dñi nr̄i pape cōmiarius [*sic*]. Vobis.'

.143 Robertus Castelleñ clericus wulteranus . . . Auctoritate apl'ica . . . vt ⁊fessorē idoneū. . . . [Licence to choose confessors, 2 Feb. 1499. Singular issue.] s.sh.*obl*.4°. [*R. Pynson*, 1499.] o².c⁵(Muniment Room, Drawer 56, No. 150).
18 lines. Line 2: 'dñi nr̄i pape cōmissarius. Tibi'.

.144 GAaspar Pow archidiaconus . . . ad hec [*sic*] cōmissari⁹ geñalis Tibi. . . . [Licence to choose confessor.] s.sh. *obl*. 4°. [*R. Pynson*, 1502.] o(Arch.A b.8(7)).
(Formerly 20139) Line 10 begins: 'Curia⁊, delationis . . .'.

.145 — [Anr. ed.] s.sh.*obl*.4°. [*R. Pynson*, 1502.] L¹¹(frags. of 2 copies, Chancery Misc. (c. 47), Bundle 15, File 6).
Line 10 begins: 'nam Curiam, delationis . . .'.

GENERAL INDULGENCES

.146 The most reuerende father in god, Thomas [Wolsey] cardynall of yorke, legate de latere of the see apostolyke. . . . [Indulgence in Latin and English granted to those who say a psalm, paternoster, and are for the prosperity of Henry VIII.] s.sh.fol. [*R. Pynson*, c. 1527.] Bryn Mawr C (in binding of Pliny, *Epistolarum*, [n.p., 1529]).

.147 Bulla plenarie indulgentiae per S.D.N. Julium diuina prouidentia papam, III. concessæ omnibus Christifidelibus, qui . . . pro vnione regni Angliæ sanctæ matri ecclesiæ . . . supplicauerint. [A plenary indulgence to the English people on the reconciliation w. Rome. 24 Dec. 1554.] s.sh.fol. *in æd*. I. Cawodi, [1554.] L⁵(Dyson Procs., no. 89).c⁷. Cr. 457.
(Formerly 14843) See also 26098.7.

.147A Bulla plenarie indulgentie per sanctissimum dominum nostrum Paulum diuina prouidentia papā .IIII. concesse Christifidelibus, pro pace concludanda inter principes Christianos, præcantibus. [A plenary indulgence upon the conclusion of war (apparently in reference to the Treaty of Vaucelles). 8 Mar. 1556.] s.sh.fol. *in æd*. I. Cauuodi, 1556. YK(imp.).

.148 WHo so euer beynge in the state of grace yᵗ deuoutly wyll say the sawter of our lady. . . . 16° in 8. [*Westminster, W. de Worde*, c. 1499.] L²(imp., Frag. No. 5). Duff 221.
(Formerly 19478)

STATIONS OF ROME

.149 Urbis Rome stationū exemplar cū indulgentiis vna & remissionibus earundē fundata⁊ & stabilita⁊ pro deuote porrigentibus manus . . . ordinis fratrum augustinensium in Anglia. . . . [Indulgences of the Stational churches in Rome, which could be gained in England by contributors to the rebuilding of St. Peter's.] s.sh.fol. [*R. Pynson*, c. 1520.] o(Arch.A b.8(37a)).

.150 The stations of Rome within the cite and without. s.sh.fol. [*R. Pynson*, c. 1520.] L(bottom half, verso of Harl. 5919/132).o(top half, Arch.A b.8(37b)).
L has Indulgences 103A pr. on the recto.

UNASSIGNED

.151 ⟨Be it known. . . .⟩ [List of indulgences.] s.sh.fol. [*Cambridge, J. Siberch*, 1522?] c(imp., Sayle 8279).
2nd paragraph begins: 'Fyrst our holy fader in Christe Alexander the thirde. . . .'
The tops of this and no. 152 are cropt, removing the city of the issuing Hospital of St. Sepulchre. Lincoln, Sudbury, and Thetford are all possibilities.

.152 — [Anr. ed.] s.sh.fol. [*Cambridge, J. Siberch*, c. 1522.] c (imp., Sayle 8280).
2nd paragraph begins: 'Fyrst our holy fader in christe Alexaader [*sic*] the theirde. . . .'

Indulgences—UNASSIGNED—*cont.*

.153 [Fragment of 15 lines from bottom right-hand corner of a list of indulgences in English, granted to contributors to the building of a hospital.] s.sh.fol. [*R. Pynson*, c. 1505.] L²(Frag. No. 43).

.154 [Fragment of 19 lines from lower portion of a letter of confraternity in Latin, specifying absolutions.] s.sh.fol. [*R. Pynson?* c. 1520.] Reading PL (in binding of MS. of Paschasius Radbertus from Reading Abbey).
See also Indulgences 60A.

———

Infancia. Infancia saluatoris. [c. 1477.] *See* 14551.

14078 **Informatio.** Libellulus, que Informatio puero⁊ appellatur, cum modico apparatu nouiter ⁊pilatus. *Eng. a. Lat.* 4° ⁶·⁴. (*Richard Pynson*,) [1499?] c⁶. Duff 223.
See the headnote to Stanbridge's Accidence (23139.5 sqq.)

14079 — [Anr. ed.] Libellus, qui Informatio puero⁊ appellatur. 4° ⁶·⁴. (*Here endeth the accidence made at the instaunce of G. Chastelayn* [*in Oxford*] *and J. Bars* [*in London*]: *emprynted by Rycharde Pynson*,) [1503.] L(G.7568). o(Mason H 35).; PML. Duff 224.
(Formerly also 14080)

14080 — = 14079.

14081 **Information.** Informacōn for pylgrymes vnto the holy londe. 4°. [*W. de Worde*, 1500?] E. Duff 225.

14082 — [Anr. ed.] The way to the holy lande. 4°. (*W. de worde*, 1515 (16 my.)) PML.

14083 — [Anr. ed.] 4°. (*W. de worde*, 1524 (26 jy.)) c⁵.
— Information from the Estaits of the kingdome of Scotland. 1640. *See* 21916.
— Information from the Scottish nation. [1640.] *See* 21917.
— An information to all good christians. 1639. *See* 21905.

14084 **Informations.** Informations, or a protestation, and a treatise from Scotland. 8°. [*W. Jones's secret press*,] 1608. L.O.C.E.STU.+; F.HD.U.Y.
Sheets A–D and F are from different settings in the 2 L copies, but in other copies these sheets appear to be mixed. *See also* 22236.

14085 **Ingelend, Thomas.** A pretie and mery new enterlude: called the Disobedient child. 4°. *T. Colwell*, [1570?] ? Ent. 1569–70. L.L⁶.O(2).; HN.HD.ILL.PFOR.Y². Greg 54.

14086 **Ingmethorp, Thomas.** A sermon vpon part of the second chapter of the first epistle of S. John. 8°. *Oxford, J. Barnes*, 1598. O.; F.
On 1 John ii.3–6.

14087 — A sermon vpon part of the second chapter of the first epistle of Saint John. 4°. *T. Creede*, 1609. L.O.C².PLUME.STU.+; F.HN.U.
On 1 John ii.21–3.

14088 — A sermon vpon the words of Saint Paul. 4°. *R. Field f. R. Flemming*, 1619. Ent. to R. Fleming a. R. Milbourne, 27 ja. L.O.YK.; HD.

14088.5 — [Anr. issue, w. imprint:] *R. Field f. R. Mylbourne*, 1619. O⁴.E⁴.; F(imp.).
— tr. See 16461.

14089 **Ingpen, William.** The secrets of numbers. (Numerorum secreta). 4°. *H. Lowns f. J. Parker*, 1624. L.L³⁸.O.C. C².+; F.HN.Y.
(Formerly also 14070)

Inimicus. Inimicus amicus. 1601. *See* 20053.

Injunctions. Injunctions set down by the L. Provest of Edinburgh. 1634. *See* 7484.
— For injunctions pertaining to the Church of England, see 10085 sqq.

14090 **Inman, Francis.** A light vnto the unlearned. 8°. *J. Legatt f. G. Lathum*, 1622. L.O.; Y.

14091 **Innes, William.** A bundle of myrrhe: or three meditations of teares. 12°. *f. R. Mylbourne*, 1620. Ent. 30 mr. L².O.E².

14092 **Innocent III,** *Pope*. The mirror of mans lyfe. Englished by H. K[erton from 'De contemptu mundi'. Anon. 8°. *H. Bynneman*, 1576. L.; F(last 2 leaves only).
For anr. trans. *see* 1st part of 11641.

Innocent III, *Pope—cont.*

14093 — [Anr. ed.] Englished by H. Kirton. 8º. *H. Bynneman,* 1576. F.CHI.

14094 — [Anr. ed.] 8º. *H. Bynneman,* 1577. O.C⁴.; F(lacks tp).

14094.5 — [Anr. ed.] 8º. *H. Bynneman,* 1580. L.

14095 — [Anr. ed.] 8º. *R. Robinson,* 1586. F(2, 1 imp.).
See Greg, *Register B,* p. 19.

14096 **Innocent VIII,** *Pope.* [Bull confirming the marriage of Henry VII and Elizabeth of York.] Our holy fadre the Pope Innocent . . . [27 mr. 1486.] *Eng.* s.sh.fol. [*W. de Machlinia,* 1486.] L.L⁵(cropt).M(cropt). Duff 227.

14097 — Alexander ep̄s . . . M.CCCC.lxxxxiiij. noñ Octobris. [A reissue by Pope Alexander VI of the Bull of 1486.] *Lat.* s.sh.fol. [*Westminster, W. de Worde,* 1494.] L²(Frag. No. 7).C⁵(2 copies of lower half only). ETON(2).M(deposit, bottom cropt).; HN. Duff 228.

14098 — Innocenti⁹ et Alexand' pontifices. . . . [An abridgement of the Bull of 1486 which occurs in 2 settings, here distinguished, both printed twice on the same sheet; all 4 being in each collection listed.] *Lat.* s.sh.*obl.*4º. [*Westminster, W. de Worde,* 1495.] L.O.O¹².C.ETON. Line 2: 'turam'. Duff 229.

14098.5 — [Anr. setting on same sheet.] s.sh.*obl.*4º. [*Westminster, W. de Worde,* 1495.] L.O.O¹².C.ETON. Line 2: 'turā'. Duff 229.

14099 — [Line 71:] . . . Oure moste holy faders, [etc.] [An exemplification of the Bull of 1486.] *Lat. a. Eng.* s.sh.fol. [*R. Pynson,* 1497.] CANT(imp.). Duff 230.

14100 — IOhannes de Gigliis. . . . [Indulgence to contributors to crusade against the Turks.] [1489.] Now = Indulgences 114.

14101 — [Anr. ed.] IOhānes de Gigliis. . . . [1489.] Now = Indulgences 115.

14102 — [Indulgence to contributors to the hospital of S. James, Compostella.] In dei nomine [etc.] [1498.] Now = Indulgences 86.

14103 — Regule ordinatiões et ꝗstitutiões cācellarie . . . Innocētii. . . . [*Louvain, J. Veldener,* 1485?] Duff 226.
As Veldener pr. this, not Machlinia, it does not belong in STC.

— *See also* Indulgences 23, 50, 85 sqq., 114 sq.

Inquisition. A discouery and playne declaration of practises of the Inquisition. 1568, etc. *See* 11996 sqq.

Institutio. Institutio compendiaria totius grammaticæ. 1540. *See* 15610.5.

— Institutio graecae grammatices compendiaria. 1595, etc. *See* 4511 sqq.

— Sacra institutio baptizandi. 1604. *See* 16157.5.

14104 **Institution.** The institucion of a gentleman. 8º. *T. Marshe,* 1555. L.O.P. A̶

14105 — [Anr. ed.] 8º. *T. Marshe,* 1568. Ent. to T. Orwin on death of T. Marsh ?23 jn. 1591. L.O(2).; F.HN.

Institutiones. Institutiones piæ, or directions to pray. 1630, etc. *See* 599 sqq.

Institutions. Institutions, or principall groundes of the lawes. 1543, etc. *See* 9292 sqq.

Instruction. A briefe and easye instrution [*sic*] . . . vnto the lute. 1568. *See* 15486.

— A breffe instruccyon . . . to teache a person wyllingly to dye. [1536?] *See* 11390.

14106 — A fruteful and a very christen instructiō for childrē. 8º. *W. Coplande [f.] (R. Kele,)* 1547. L.
Reprints parts of earlier primers; see 15986, etc.

— An instruction for all that intend to goe to the sacrament. 1634. *See* 16824.

14106.2 — [An instruction for children. Ends:] Here endeth thys lytle treatyse of the instruction of chyldren . . . [*Tr.*] 8º. (*London, J. Roux [Jean Le Roux],* 1543.) Finedon.

— A short and faythful instruction. [1556?] *See* 17864.

14106.5 — A short instruction veric [*sic*] profitable and necessarie for all those that delight in gardening. *Tr.* out of French. 4º. *J. Wolfe,* 1591. Ent. to Wolfe pt. 1, 29 de. 1590; pt. 2, 30 ap. 1591. Lownes.
Enlarged and reprinted in 18838.

14106.8 — [Anr. ed.] 4º. *J. Wolfe,* 1592. L.

Instructions. Brief instructions for church-wardens. [1637.] *See* 20454.3.

Instructions—*cont.*

14107 — Instructions, a holsome exercise, or meditations to be thought on. [1580–81.] Now = pt. 2 of 17278.4.

— Instructions for the curates. [1554?] *See* 26098.7.

— Instructions for musters and armes. 1623, etc. *See* 7683 sqq.

— Instructions for the increasing of mulberie trees. 1609. *See* 23139.

14107.5 — Instructions for your search into religion. 8º. [*Douai, L. Kellam,*] 1607. L².
A&R 409.

14107.7 — [Anr. ed., w. cancel tp:] Private instructions lately sent from a cath. gentleman beyond the sea's [*sic*], unto his protestant friend in Ireland. 8º. [*Douai, L. Kellam?*] 1634. D.
Cancel tp and 'Letter to the Reader' on A2 were printed by the Widow of C. Boscard. The date of the orig. printing of this ed. is not known.

— Instructions giuen by the princes of Nauarre, and Conde. [1570.] *See* 13104.

— Instructions sent be the committe [*sic*] of the Estates. 1640. *See* 21918.

14108 — Instructions when it ringeth to evensonge. [1580–81.] Now = pt. 5 of 17278.4.

Intentions. The intentions of the army of the kingdome of Scotland. 1640. *See* 21919.

Intercession. A deuout intercescion and praier. [1530?] *See* 14546.7.

Interest Table. [Table of interest at £8, etc. per centum. 1625?] *See* 19600.2 sqq.

14109 **Interlocution.** He [*sic*] begynneth an interlocucyon, with an argument, betwyxt man and woman. [*Tr.* from 'Le debat de l'ōme et de la fēme' by G. Alexis. In verse.] 4º in 6. [*W. de Worde,* 1525?] L.
Printer's name in device.

14109.2 **Interlude.** [Enterlude of detraction.] *See* Addenda.

14109.3 — [Enterlude of somebody and others.] 4º. [*W. Copland?* c. 1550.] L²(2 imp. leaves, Frag. No. 12). Greg 25.

14109.5 — [An enterlude of temperance.] 4º. [*W. de Worde,* c. 1528.] HN(1 leaf). Greg 7.

14109.7 — (The enterlude of the .iiii. cardynal vertues, & yᵉ vyces contrarye to them.) 4º. (*W. Myddylton,*) [c. 1545.] L(quire C only, imp.). Greg 21.5 (IV.1643–4).
Prob. a later ed. of 14109.5.

— [An interlude of the prodigal son. 1530?] *See* 20765.5.

14110 — An enterlude of welth, and helth. 4º. [*W. Copland f. J. Walley?* 1565?] Ent. to Walley 1557–58. L(2). Greg 27.

14111 — Thenterlude of youth. 4º. [*W. de Worde,* c. 1530.] L² (4 imp. leaves, Frag. No. 25). Greg 20.

14111a — [Anr. ed.] Thēterlude of youth. 4º. [*J. King f.?*] (*J. waley,*) [1557.] Ent. 1557–58. L.O(2).; HN.PFOR.Y².

14112 — [Anr. ed.] 4º. (*W. Copland,*) [1565?] L.; HN.

— A new and mery enterlude, called the Triall of treasure. 1567. *See* 24271.

— A new iuterlude [*sic*] and a mery of the nature of the .iiii. elements. [By J. Rastell. 1525?] *See* 20722.

— A newe enterlude . . . of godly queene Hester. 1561. *See* 13251.

14112.5 — A newe interlude of impacyente pouerte newlye imprynted. 1560. 4º. (*J. Kynge,*) [1560.] Ent. 10 jn. 1560. L. Greg 30.
(Formerly 14114)

14113 — [Anr. ed.] An new enterlude of impacient pouerte newly imprynted. 4º. [*W. Copland,* 1561?] HN (imp.).

14114 — Now = 14112.5.

— A new enterlude no lesse wittie. 1573. *See* 6150.

— A preaty interlude called, Nice wanton. [1560.] *See* 25016.

— A propre newe interlude of the worlde and the chylde. 1522. *See* 25982.

Interpretation. Here foloweth the interpretacoin [*sic*]. . . . [c. 1500.] *See* 17006.

14115 **Interpreter.** The interpreter wherin three principall termes of state are clearely vnfolded. [Attrib. to T. Scott, *B.D.* In verse.] 8º. [*Edinburgh?* 1622.] L.O.; HD.N.

Interrogatories. Interrogatories. For the doctrine and maners of mynisters. 1560. *See* 10133.5.

— Interrogatories vpon which . . . churchwardens shalbe charged. 1558. *See* 10117.

14116 **Intrationes.** Intrationū excellentissimus liber per Φ̅ necessarius oībus legȝ hominib⁹. fol. (*in off. R. Pynson,* 1510 (28 fb.)) L.O.C.D.M.+; F.HN.CU.HD. MIN.+

14117 — [A different text.] Intrationum liber omnibus legum Anglie studiosis apprime necessarius. fol. [*N. Hill f.*] *H. Smythe,* 1546 (1545 (1 no.)) L.O.C.D⁵.M².+; F.HN. CHI.CU.HD.+ Ⓐ

14118 **Introduction.** An introduction for to lerne to recken with the pen. 8⁰. (*N. Bourman,*) 1539. O.

14119 — [Anr. ed.] 8⁰. (*J. Herford,*) 1546. L(imp.).

14119.3 — [Anr. ed.] 8⁰. [*S. Mierdman f.*] (*J. Waley,*) 1552. HN.

14119.7 — [Anr. ed.] 8⁰. (*J. Awdely,*) 1566. HN.

14120 — [Anr. ed.] An introduction of algorisme. 8⁰. *J. Awdeley,* 1574. L.L¹⁶(imp.).; F.WIS.

14121 — [Anr. ed.] 8⁰. *J. Charlewood,* 1581. Ent. 15 ja. 1582. O(2).O⁶.

14121.5 — [Anr. ed.] 8⁰. *J. Roberts, solde* [*by R. Bankworth,*] 1595. Ent. to Roberts 31 my. 1594. L(tp only, Harl.5995/347).L⁴⁴.

14122 — [Anr. ed.] Arithmaticke: or, an itroduction [*sic*]. 8⁰. [*T. Cotes?*] 1629. L.

14123 — An introduction of the eyght partes of speche. 1542. = 15605.

14123.5 — An introduction to the catholick faith. 12⁰ in 6's. [*Rouen,*] *J. Cousturier,* 1633. USHAW. A&R 410.

14123.7 — An introduction to the knowledge and vnderstandyng to make . . . indentures. 8⁰. [*R. Grafton?* c. 1537.] L(tp only, Ames I.173).

14124 — [Anr. ed.] 8⁰. (*R. Toye,*) [c. 1545.] O. In title: 'knowledge', 'indētures'.

14125 — [Anr. ed.] 8⁰. [*R. Grafton f.*] (*J. Waylye,*) [c. 1550.] C. In title: 'knowlege', 'indentures'.

— A short introduction to grammar. 1632. *See* 25192.

14125.5 **Introductions.** Introductions in frensshe, for Henry yᵉ yonge Erle of Lyncoln. [Attrib. to P. Valence.] *Fr. a. Eng.* 4⁰. [*W. de Worde,* 1528?] L²(frag. 15). LONGLEAT. Text dated 1528 on B2ᵛ.

14126 **Invective.** An inuectyue agaynst dronkennes. 16⁰ in 8's. (*Ippiswiche, J. Oswen,*) [1548?] O(imp.).C. O copy is in sheets, unfolded.

14126.5 — An inuectiue ageinst glotony and dronkennes. 8⁰. (*R. Lant a. R. Bankes,* 1545.) F.

14127 **Invention.** A new invention of shooting fire-shafts in long-bowes. 4⁰. *H. L[ownes] f. J. Bartlet,* 1628. L. O.; BO⁵.NY⁴.

Inventions. Certaine new inventions to be known of all farmers. [1640.] *See* 19997.5.

Invocation. A deuout inuocacyon & prayer. [c. 1520.] *See* 14547.5.

Io., F. A treatise of the ministery. [1597.] *See* 14663.5.

Ipocras. *See* Hippocrates.

14128 **Ipomydon.** [The life of Ipomydon. c. 1522?] Now = 5732.5.

Ipswich, Suffolk, *Franciscan Convent. See* Indulgences 43.

Ireland.

CUSTOMS

14128.3 — [Book of rates.] The rates of marchandizes as they are set downe in the booke of rates. 4⁰. *Dublin, J. Franckton,* 1608. O²⁷(on deposit at O).

14128.5 — [Anr. ed.] The booke of rates. . . . 4⁰. *B. Norton a. J. Bill,* 1624. F(w. last quire from 14128.7).

14128.7 — [Anr. ed.] The booke of rates. . . . 1624. 4⁰. *R. Barker a. the assignes of J. Bill,* 1631 [1632.] O.D.; HD.LC.

LAWS AND STATUTES

14129 — In this volume are contained all the statutes [10 Hen. VI–14 Eliz.] made in Ireland. fol. (*R. Tottle,* 1572.) C.HOLK(2).; LC.

14129.5 — Statuta, ordinationes, acta, et prouisiones . . . [27–28 Eliz.] fol. *C. Barkerus,* [1585–86.] D(imp.).HOLK.; HD.

14130 — The statutes of Ireland, [3 Edw. II–13 Jas.] Newly perused [by Sir] (*R.* Bolton.) fol. *Dublin, Soc. of Statrs.,* 1621 (*Dublin, printed by the Co. of Statrs., of the citie of London,* 1620.) L.O.C.D.E².+; F.HN.CU. HD.WIS.+

Ireland—LAWS AND STATUTES—*cont.*

14131 — Lawes and orders of warre, established for the good conduct of the seruice in Ireland. 4⁰. [*Deputies of C. Barker?* 1599?] L.O.C.C².M².+; HN.

14131.5 — Lawes, and orders of warre, established for the good conduct of the service of Ireland. fol. *Dublin, Soc. of Statrs.,* 1625. L⁵(2). Cr. 258. (Formerly 14194)

14132 — Lawes and orders of warre; established for the good conduct of the service of Ireland. 4⁰. *Dublin, Soc. of Statrs.,* 1638. C.D.D⁶.; HD.ILL.Y. C1ʳ line 4 of heading ends: '*Army.*'

14132.5 — [Anr. ed.] 4⁰. *Dublin, Soc. of Statrs.,* 1638. D⁸. C1ʳ line 4 of heading ends: '*Armie*'.

14133 — An act for the graunt of one entier subsidie by the temporalitie. fol. *Dublin, J. Franckton,* 1615. L.

14134 — His maiesties directions for the . . . courts, of justice, within Ireland. 4⁰. *Dublin, Soc. of Statrs.,* 1622. L²¹. L²².C.

14134.3 — [Anr. ed.] 4⁰. *Dublin, Soc. of Statrs.,* 1632. Ellis Catalogue 263 (1929), item 9(untraced).

14134.7 — [Anr. ed.] 4⁰. *Dublin, Soc. of Statrs.,* 1638. O⁵.

14135 — An act for the granting of eight entire subsidies by the prelates and clergie of Ireland. fol. *Dublin, Soc. of Statrs.,* 1634. C.D.D².D⁵.G².

14135.3 — An act for the granting of four entire subsidies by the temporalitie. fol. *Dublin, Soc. of Statrs.,* 1634. D⁵. 8 leaves.

14135.7 — An act for the grant of foure entire subsidies by the temporalitie. fol. *Dublin, Soc. of Statrs.,* 1634. D². 28 pp.

14136 — An act for the Kings maiesties generall pardon. fol. *Dublin, Soc. of Statrs.,* 1635. C.D².D⁵.G².

14136.3 — Anno regni Caroli regis, . . . decimo & undecimo. At the Parliament 14. July, untill 28. [*sic*] Aprill. fol. *Dublin, Soc. of Statrs.,* 1635. O².C.D.D⁶.M².+ McK.&F. 274b.

14136.7 — [Anr. ed.] Anno . . . decimo & undecimo. . . . 14. July, . . . 18. Aprill. fol. *Dublin, Soc. of Statrs.,* 1635. C. D².D⁶.SHEF.YK.+; HD. McK.&F. 303.

14137 — [Anr. ed.] Anno . . . decimo et undecimo. . . . fourteenth July, . . . 18. Aprill. fol. *Dublin, Soc. of Statrs.* [i.e. *London, F. Kingston? a. R. Young,*] 1636. L.C.BTL. D.YK.+; F.HN.LC.WIS. McK.&F. 304.

PROCLAMATIONS

14138 — A proclamacyon set fourth by the Erle of Sussex . . . [Against Shane O'Neill. 8 June 1561.] fol(4). *Dublyn, H. Powell,* [1561.]L¹¹.O(sheet 1 only). Cr. 46.

14139 — A proclamacyon. Sett furthe by the Lorde Justice and Counsell. [Outlawry of rebels. 16 Aug. 1564.] fol(2). *Dublyn, H. Powell,* 1564 (16 au.) L¹¹. Cr. 54.

14140 — The offer and order giuen forth by Sir Thomas Smyth and his sonne vnto suche as be willing to accompanye the sayde sonne, in his voyage for the inhabiting some partes of the northe of Ireland. [1571.] Now = 22868.5.

14140.5 — (By the Lord Deputie.) A proclamation for the obseruation . . . of certayne statutes. And a summarie abridgement of the same statutes. 1576. 4⁰. *R. Jugge,* [1576.] D.

14141 — By the Queene. [Continuing the subsidy on wines. 18 Dec. 1578.] s.sh.fol. *C. Barker,* [1578.] L.O.O².; F.HD. Cr. 86.

14142 — By the Queene. [Against the Earl of Desmond. 26 April 1581.] fol(2). *C. Barker,* 1581. L.L⁵.O.O².; F.HD (sheet 1 only). Cr. 99.

14143 — By the Queene. [On the disposal of lands of rebels. 4 Nov. 1587.] s.sh.fol. [*Deputies of C. Barker,* 1587.] L.O.O².; F.HD. Cr. 126. 1st line of text ends: 'by'.

14144 — [Anr. ed.] s.sh.fol. [*Deputies of C. Barker,* 1587.] L⁵. Cr. 127. 1st line of text ends: 'some'.

14145 — The Queenes maiesties proclamation against the Earle of Tirone, [etc.] [12 June 1595.] fol(2). *Dublin, W. Kearney,* 1595. L¹¹. Cr. 145.

14145a — [The preceding in Irish.] fol(2).? *Dublin, W. Kearney,* 1595. No copy traced. The reference in Cr. 145 (*Cal.S.P. Ireland, 1592–1596,* p. 317, no. 82) is only to a report that the proclamation was pr. in Irish as well as English.

Ireland—PROCLAMATIONS—*cont.*

14146 — By the Queene. [On sending over the army into Ireland. 31 Mar. 1599.] fol(2). *Deputies of C. Barker,* 1599. L.L⁵.L²⁰.O.O².; F.HD. Cr. 153.

14147 — By the L. Deputie. [Offering a reward for Hugh O'Neill. 22 Nov. 1600.] s.sh.fol. *Dublin, J. Francke,* 1600. L¹¹. Cr. 159.

14147a — By the Queene. [As to a new coinage. 20 May 1601.] s.sh.fol. *Dublin, J. Francke,* 1601. L².L¹¹. Cr. 162.

14148 — By the L. Deputie. [Concerning frauds on the exchange. 9 June 1602.] s.sh.fol. *Dublin, J. Francke,* 1602. L¹¹. Cr. 166.

14149 — By the Queene. [Concerning the exchange. 24 Jan. 1603.] fol(2). *Dublin, J. Franckton,* 1602 [o.s.] L¹¹. Cr. 167.

14150 — By the Lord Deputie. [Against traffic with Spain. 10 Mar. 1603.] s.sh.fol. *Dublin, J. Franckton,* 1602 [o.s.] L². Cr. 168.

14151 — By the Lord Deputie. [Fixing a new standard of silver coin. 11 Oct. 1603.] s.sh.fol. *Dublin, J. Franckton,* 1603. L.L¹¹. Cr. 172.

14152 — By the Lord Deputie. [Revoking commissions of martial law. 20 Feb. 1605.] s.sh.fol. *Dublin, J. Franckton,* 1604 [o.s.] L¹¹. Cr. 178.

14153 — By the Lord Deputie. [Concerning the carrying of arms. 20 Feb. 1605.] s.sh.fol. *Dublin, J. Franckton,* 1604 [o.s.] L¹¹.HAT. Cr. 179.

14154 — By the Lord Deputie. [Pardon for offences before the King's accession. 11 Mar. 1605.] fol(4). *Dublin, J. Franckton,* 1604 [o.s.] L¹¹. Cr. 180.

14155 — By the King. [For uniformity in religion. 4 July 1605.] fol(2). *Dublin, J. Franckton,* 1605. L¹¹. Cr. 182.

14156 — By the Lord Deputie. [Against importation of arms, etc. 10 Mar. 1606.] fol(2). *Dublin, J. Franckton,* 1605 [o.s.] L¹¹. Cr. 185.

14157 — By the Lord Deputie. [For remedy of defective titles. 15 July 1606.] fol(2). *Dublin, J. Franckton,* 1606. L². Cr. 186.

14158 — By the Lord Deputie. [Abolishing the term 'sterling'. 11 Nov. 1606.] s.sh.fol. *Dublin, J. Franckton,* 1606. L¹¹. Cr. 187.

14159 — By the Lord Deputie. [Concerning the lands of Tyrone and Tyrconnell. 9 Nov. 1607.] s.sh.fol. *Dublin, J. Franckton,* 1607. L¹¹. Cr. 191.

14160 — By the Lord Deputie. [Against Lord Delvin. 23 Nov. 1607.] s.sh.fol. *Dublin, J. Franckton,* 1607. L¹¹. Cr. 193.

14161 — By the Lord Deputie. [Against Cahir O'Dogherty, etc. 23 Apr. 1608.] s.sh.fol. *Dublin, J. Franckton,* 1608. L¹¹. Cr. 194.

14162 — By the Lord Deputie. [Continuing the commission for surrendering lands in Tanistry, etc. 19 June 1609.] s.sh.fol. *Dublin, J. Franckton,* [1609.] L². Cr. 196.

14163 — By the Lord Deputy. [Republishing the proclamation of 4 July 1605. 13 July 1611.] fol(3). *Dublin, J. Franckton,* [1611.] L². Cr. 203.

14164 — A proclamation set forth by Sir James Carroll. [Enforcing certain laws. 31 Oct. 1612.] fol(2). *Dublin, J. Franckton,* 1612. L(Lansdowne MSS.). Cr. 206.

14165 — A proclamation set forth by Sir James Carroll. [Fixing wages. 3 Feb. 1614.] fol(2). *Dublin, J. Franckton,* 1613 [o.s.] L(Lansdowne MSS.). Cr. 213.

14166 — By the King. [Approving the Deputy of Ireland. 7 Feb. 1614.] fol(2). *R. Barker,* 1613 [o.s.] L²⁰.L²².O²(2).; HN.HD. Cr. 214.

14167 — ¶By the King. [For expulsion of priests and Jesuits. 31 May 1614.] fol(2). *R. Barker,* 1614. L⁵.L¹¹.L²⁰. L²².D⁶. Cr. 217.

14167a — [Anr. ed. Leaf orn.] fol(2). *R. Barker,* 1614. O². Cr. 218.

14168 — By the Lord Deputie. [For registering births, deaths, and marriages. 25 Apr. 1618.] fol(3). *Dublin, J. Franckton,* 1618. L⁵(sheets 1, 3 only). Cr. 223.

14169 — By the Lord Deputie. [Expelling Irish from Ulster plantations. 1 Oct. 1618.] s.sh.fol. *Dublin, F. Kingston,* 1618. L⁵. Cr. 224.

14170 — By the Lord Deputie. [Against usury. 3 Oct. 1618.] s.sh.fol. *Dublin, F. Kingston,* 1618. L⁵. Cr. 225.

14171 — By the Lord Deputie. [Appointing deputy postmaster. 9 Feb. 1619.] s.sh.fol. *B. Norton a. J. Bill,* 1618 [o.s.]; HN. Cr. 226.

14172 — By the Lord Deputie. [Against importation of arms, etc. 20 Mar. 1619.] fol(2). *Dublin, F. Kyngston,* 1619. L⁵. Cr. 227.

14173 — By the Lord Deputie. [Patent to F. Kingston and T. Downes. 15 July 1620.] s.sh.fol. *Dublin, Co. of Statrs.,* 1620. L⁵. Cr. 232.
See also 7154.5.

14174 — By the Lord Deputie. A proclamation concerning alehouses. [3 Mar. 1621.] fol(2). *Dublin, Co. of Statrs.,* 1620 [o.s.] L⁵. Cr. 233.

14175 — By the Lord Deputie. A proclamation concerning the customes, &c. for Dublin. [18 July 1621.] s.sh.fol. *Dublin, Co. of Statrs.,* 1621. L⁵. Cr. 234.

14175.5 — By the Lord Deputie. A proclamation for the suspending of sundry letters patents. [19 Jan. 1622.] s.sh.fol. *Dublin, Co. of Statrs.,* 1621 [o.s.] HD. Cr. 236.

14176 — By the Lords Justices. A proclamation concerning the commissioners proceedings. [27 July 1622.] s.sh.fol. *Dublin, Co. of Statrs.,* 1622. L⁵. Cr. 238.

14177 — By the Lords Justices. A proclamation concerning the late plantations, &c. [24 Aug. 1622.] s.sh.fol. *Dublin, Co. of Statrs.,* 1622. L⁵. Cr. 239.

14178 — By the Lords Justices. A proclamation concerning the payment of his Majest. revennue. [5 Sept. 1622.] s.sh.fol. *Dublin, Co. of Statrs.,* 1622. L⁵. Cr. 240.

14179 — By the Lord Deputie. A proclamation for the banishment of wandring Scottish-men. [21 Sept. 1622.] s.sh.fol. *Dublin, Co. of Statrs.,* 1622. L⁵. Cr. 241.

14180 — By the Lord Deputie. A proclamation for farthing tokens. [28 Sept. 1622.] fol(2). *Dublin, Co. of Statrs.,* 1622. L⁵. Cr. 242.

14181 — By the Lord Deputie. A proclamation against transportation of corne. [23 Nov. 1622.] s.sh.fol. *Dublin, Co. of Statrs.,* 1622. L⁵. Cr. 243.

14182 — By the Lord Deputie. A proclamation for prevention of dearth of corne. [18 Apr. 1623.] s.sh.fol. *Dublin, Soc. of Statrs.,* 1623. L⁵. Cr. 244.

14183 — By the Lord Deputie. A proclamation concerning iron ordnance, &c. [19 July 1623.] s.sh.fol. *Dublin, Co. of Statrs.,* 1623. L⁵. Cr. 245.

14184 — By the Lord Deputie. A proclamation prohibiting the use of logwood. [13 Jan. 1624.] s.sh.fol. *Dublin, Co. of Statrs.,* 1623 [o.s.] L⁵. Cr. 246.

14185 — By the Lord Deputie. A proclamation for the banishment of Jesuites and priests, &c. [21 Jan. 1624.] s.sh.fol. *Dublin, Soc. of Statrs.,* 1623 [o.s.] L.L².L⁵. E.; HN.HD(impr. cropt). Cr. 247.

14186 — By the Lord Deputie. A proclamation concerning the planters in Ulster. [21 Jan. 1624.] s.sh.fol. *Dublin, Co. of Statrs.,* 1623 [o.s.] L⁵. Cr. 248.

14187 — By the Lord Deputie. A proclamation prohibiting sale of cattell out of faires or markets. [26 Feb. 1624.] s.sh.fol. *Dublin, Soc. of Statrs.,* 1623 [o.s.] L⁵. Cr. 249.

14188 — By the Lord Deputie. A proclamation concerning the officers of the Custome-house. [27 Feb. 1624.] s.sh.fol. *Dublin, Co. of Statrs.,* 1623 [o.s.] L⁵. Cr. 250.

14189 — By the Lord Deputie. A proclamation touching weights and measures. [1 Mar. 1624.] s.sh.fol. *Dublin, Soc. of Statrs.,* 1623 [o.s.] L⁵. Cr. 251.

14190 — By the Lord Deputie. [Against unlicensed importation of arms. 5 Apr. 1624.] s.sh.fol. *Dublin, Soc. of Statrs.,* 1624. L⁵. Cr. 253.

14190.5 — [Anr. ed. 25 June 1625.] s.sh.fol. *Dublin, Co. of Statrs.,* 1625. L⁵. Cr. 259.
(Formerly 14195)

14191 — By the Lord Deputie. Tythes, offrings [etc.] to be taken by Ulster. [6 July 1624.] s.sh.fol. *Dublin, Soc. of Statrs.,* 1624. L⁵. Cr. 254.

14191a — By the Lord Deputy. [Accession of Charles I. 10 Apr. 1625.] s.sh.fol. *Dublin, Soc. of Statrs.,* 1625. L⁵. Cr. 255.

14192 — By the Lord Deputy. [The King's proclamation to his people. 10 Apr. 1625.] s.sh.fol. *Dublin, Soc. of Statrs.,* 1625. L⁵. Cr. 256.

14193 — By the Lord Deputy. A proclamation signifying that all men being in office shall continue. [10 Apr. 1625.] s.sh.fol. *Dublin, Soc. of Statrs.,* 1625. L⁵. Cr. 257.

14194 — Lawes and orders of warre. [11 June 1625.] Now = 14131.5.

14195 — By the Lord Deputie. [Against unlicensed importation of arms. 25 June 1625.] Now = 14190.5.

14196 — By the Lord Deputie. [For issue of warrants for gunpowder. 9 July 1625.] s.sh.fol. *Dublin, Co. of Statrs.,* 1625. L⁵. Cr. 260.

Ireland—Proclamations—*cont.*

14197 — By the Lord Deputie. [Against keeping markets on the sabbath. 23 July 1625.] s.sh.fol. *Dublin, Soc. of Statrs.*, 1625. L⁵.D⁴(2, destroyed). Cr. 261.

14198 — By the Lord Deputie. [Quarantine orders. 4 Aug. 1625.] fol(2). *Dublin, Co. of Statrs.*, 1625. L⁵.D⁴(2, destroyed). Cr. 262.

14199 — By the Lord Deputie. A proclamation for the banishing of idle persons. [22 Aug. 1625.] s.sh.fol. *Dublin, Co. of Statrs.*, 1625. L⁵.D⁴(3, destroyed). Cr. 263.

14200 — By the Lord Deputie. A proclamation forbidding drovers to drive cattle by night. [22 Aug. 1625.] s.sh.fol. *Dublin, Co. of Statrs.*, 1625. L⁵.D⁴(destroyed). Cr. 264.

14201 — By the Lord Deputie. An act of state touching beggers [etc. 24 Aug. 1625.] fol(2). *Dublin, Soc. of Statrs.*, 1625. L⁵.D⁴(3, destroyed). Cr. 265.

14202 — By the Lord Deputie. A proclamation for publike fasting. [13 Oct. 1625.] s.sh.fol. *Dublin, Soc. of Statrs.*, 1625. L⁵.D⁴(2, destroyed). Cr. 266.

14203 — By the King. A proclamation for the due administration of justice. [7 Nov. 1625.] s.sh.fol. *Dublin, Soc. of Statrs.*, 1625. L⁵. Cr. 267.

— By the King. A proclamation that ships carying victuals, or munition for Spaine, be lawfull prize. [31 Dec. 1625.] *See* 8813 sqq.

14204 — By the Lord Deputie. A proclamation to forbid trade within the dominions of the King of Spaine. [9 Jan. 1626.] s.sh.fol. *Dublin, Soc. of Statrs.*, 1625 [o.s.] L⁵.D⁴(3, destroyed). Cr. 269.

14205 — By the Lord Deputie. A proclamation concerning the payment of his maiesties revenues [etc. 20 July 1626.] s.sh.fol. *Dublin, Soc. of Statrs.*, 1626. D.D⁴(2, destroyed). Cr. 270.

14206 — By the Lord Deputie. A proclamation against the transportation of cattle. [23 Sept. 1626.] s.sh.fol. *Dublin, Soc. of Statrs.*, 1626. L¹¹.D⁴(3, destroyed). Cr. 271.

14207 — By the Lord Deputie. A proclamation concerning the obstinate returning of the transplanted Irish Septs. [30 Sept. 1626.] s.sh.fol. *Dublin, Soc. of Statrs.*, 1626. D⁴(4, destroyed). Cr. 272.

14208 — By the Lord Deputy. [Concerning heralds' fees at funerals. 4 Aug. 1627.] s.sh.fol. *Dublin, Soc. of Statrs.*, 1629. L⁵. Cr. 273.

14208a — [Anr. ed.] s.sh.fol. *Dublin, Soc. of Statrs.*, 1634. C. Cr. 274.

14208b — [Anr. ed.] s.sh.fol. *Dublin, Soc. of Statrs.*, 1636. D⁴ (destroyed). Cr. 275.

14209 — By the Lord Deputie. A stay of the transportation of cattle. [1 Sept. 1627.] s.sh.fol. *Dublin, Soc. of Statrs.*, 1627. D⁴(4, destroyed). Cr. 276.

14210 — By the Lord Deputie. [Renewing grants of Ulster undertakers. 13 Dec. 1627.] s.sh.fol. *Dublin, Soc. of Statrs.*, 1627. D⁴(4, destroyed). Cr. 277.

14211 — By the Lord Deputie. A proclamation for reformation of abuses in weights and measures. [5 Feb. 1628.] fol(2). *Dublin, Soc. of Statrs.*, 1627 [o.s.] O². Cr. 278.

14212 — By the Lord Deputie. A proclamation for bringing corne to serve the market. [27 June 1628.] s.sh.fol. *Dublin, Soc. of Statrs.*, 1628. D⁴(4, destroyed). Cr. 279.

14213 — By the Lord Deputie. A proclamation for restraint of rebellious persons. [23 Aug. 1628.] s.sh.fol. *Dublin, Soc. of Statrs.*, 1628. L⁵.D⁴(destroyed). Cr. 280.

14214 — By the Lord Deputie. A proclamation for deferring the assembly of Parliament. [20 Oct. 1628.] s.sh.fol. *Dublin, Soc. of Statrs.*, 1628. L⁵.D⁴(3, destroyed). Cr. 281.

14215 — By the Lord Deputy. [Against Roman ecclesiastical jurisdiction. 1 Apr. 1629.] s.sh.fol. *Dublin, Soc. of Statrs.*, 1629. L⁵.L¹¹. Cr. 282.

— By the King. Whereas there hath fallen out [etc. Announcing peace with France. 10 May 1629.] *See* 8924 sq.

14216 — By the Lords Justices. [Soldiers not to collect assignments. 23 Nov. 1629.] s.sh.fol. *Dublin, Soc. of Statrs.*, 1629. L⁵.D⁴(4, destroyed). Cr. 284.

14217 — By the Lords Justices. Instructions to be observed by the shiriffes [13 Jan. 1630.] s.sh.fol. *Dublin, Soc. of Statrs.*, 1629 [o.s.] L⁵.D⁴(2, destroyed). Cr. 285.

14218 — By the Lords Justices. A proclamation concerning dying woods. [20 May 1630.] s.sh.fol. *Dublin, Soc. of Statrs.*, 1630. L⁵. Cr. 286.

14219 — By the Lords Justices. [Revenue to be paid at fixed places. 30 June 1630.] s.sh.fol. *Dublin, Soc. of Statrs.*, 1630. L⁵. Cr. 287.

14220 — By the King. A proclamation to confirme defective titles. [14 Mar. 1631.] fol(2). *R. Barker*, 1630 [o.s.] L.M(deposit).; HN. Cr. 288.

14221 — By the Lords Justices. [Concerning export of grain, etc. 18 Mar. 1631.] s.sh.fol. [*Dublin, Soc. of Statrs.*, 1630 (o.s.)] L⁵(cropt). Cr. 289.

14222 — By the Lords Justices. [Concerning the monopoly of starch. 21 May 1631.] fol(2). *Dublin, Soc. of Statrs.*, 1631. D⁴(destroyed). Cr. 290.

14223 — By the Lords Justices. [Against unauthorized fasts and festivals. 21 July 1631.] s.sh.fol. *Dublin, Soc. of Statrs.*, 1631. D⁴(4, destroyed). Cr. 292.

14224 — By the Lords Justices. [Concerning licences of alehouses, etc. 4 Feb. 1632.] fol(2). *Dublin, Soc. of Statrs.*, 1631 [o.s.] D⁴(3, destroyed). Cr. 293.

14225 — By the Lords Justices. [Continuing impost on wine. 24 Feb. 1632.] s.sh.fol. *Dublin, Soc. of Statrs.*, 1631 [o.s.] D⁴(3, destroyed). Cr. 294.

14226 — By the Lords Justices. A proclamation upon the new Booke of rates. [20 Apr. 1632.] fol(2). *Dublin, Soc. of Statrs.*, 1632. D⁴(destroyed). Cr. 295.

14227 — By the Lords Justices. A proclamation to confirme defective titles. [21 July 1632.] s.sh.fol. *Dublin, Soc. of Statrs.*, 1632. D⁴(destroyed). Cr. 296.

14228 — By the Lords Justices. A proclamation to confirme defective titles. [22 Apr. 1633.] s.sh.fol. *Dublin, Soc. of Statrs.*, 1633. D⁴(4, destroyed). Cr. 298.

14229 — By the Lord Deputy. A proclamation prohibiting exportation of corne. [8 Oct. 1633.] s.sh.fol. [*Dublin, Soc. of Statrs.*, 1633.] D⁴(2, destroyed). Cr. 299.

14230 — By the Lord Deputy. An act for punishing rogues, [etc. 22 Oct. 1633.] fol(2). *Dublin, Soc. of Statrs.*, 1633. D⁴(destroyed). Cr. 300.

14231 — By the Lord Deputy. A proclamation concerning the payments of 12. pence in the pound, of all merchandizes [etc. 17 Dec. 1633.] s.sh.fol. *Dublin, Soc. of Statrs.*, 1633. D⁴(2, destroyed). Cr. 301.

14232 — By the Lord Deputy. A proclamation concerning the payment of his maiesties rents [etc. 27 Dec. 1633.] s.sh.fol. *Dublin, Soc. of Statrs.*, 1633. D⁴(destroyed). Cr. 302.

14233 — By the Lord Deputy. A proclamation concerning coales. [16 Jan. 1634.] s.sh.fol. *Dublin, Soc. of Statrs.*, 1633 [o.s.] D⁴(3, destroyed). Cr. 303.

14234 — By the Lord Generall. Instructions to be observed by officers of musters. [13 Mar. 1634.] fol(2). *Dublin, Soc. of Statrs.*, 1633 [o.s.] D⁴(3, destroyed). Cr. 304.

14235 — By the Lord Deputy. A proclamation concerning a Parliament, [etc. 23 May 1634.] s.sh.fol. *Dublin, Soc. of Statrs.*, 1634. D⁴(destroyed). Cr. 305.

14236 — By the Lord Deputy. A proclamation for the entertainment of souldiours. [6 June 1634.] s.sh.fol. *Dublin, Soc. of Statrs.*, 1634. D⁴(2, destroyed). Cr. 306.

14237 — By the Lord Deputy. A proclamation for farthing tokens. [16 Sept. 1634.] s.sh.fol. [*Dublin, Soc. of Statrs.*, 1634.] D⁴(4, destroyed). Cr. 308.

14238 — By the Lord Deputy. A proclamation concerning the reliefe of poore prisoners. [31 Mar. 1637.] s.sh.fol. *Dublin, Soc. of Statrs.*, 1637. D⁴(2, destroyed). Cr. 315.

14239 — By the Lord Deputy. A proclamation for avoyding of law suites, concerning lands. [31 Mar. 1637.] fol(2). *Dublin, Soc. of Statrs.*, 1637. D⁴(destroyed). Cr. 316.

14240 — By the Lord Deputy. A proclamation concerning the true making of cloath. [31 Mar. 1637.] fol(3). *Dublin, Soc. of Statrs.*, 1637. D⁴(2, destroyed). Cr. 317.

14241 — By the Lord Deputy. A proclamation concerning the abolishing of the title or name of Irish money. [6 Apr. 1637.] s.sh.fol. *Dublin, Soc. of Statrs.*, 1637. D⁴(2, destroyed). Cr. 319.

14242 — By the Lord Deputy. A proclamation for the preservation of phesants, &c. [3 Aug. 1637.] s.sh.fol. *Dublin, Soc. of Statrs.*, 1637. D⁴(4, destroyed). Cr. 321.

14243 — By the Lord Deputy. [For proving titles to lands. 31 Oct. 1637.] s.sh.fol. *Dublin, Soc. of Statrs.*, 1637. D⁴(4, destroyed). Cr. 322.

14244 — By the Lord Deputy. A proclamation concerning licences for selling wine. [31 Dec. 1637.] s.sh.fol. *Dublin, Soc. of Statrs.*, 1637. D⁴(3, destroyed). Cr. 323.

14245 — By the Lord Deputy. A proclamation concerning the importation of tobaccoe. [9 Jan. 1638.] s.sh.fol. *Dublin, Soc. of Statrs.*, 1637 [o.s.] D⁴(4, destroyed). Cr. 324.

Ireland—Proclamations—*cont.*

14246 — By the Lord Deputy. A proclamation concerning linnen yarne. [22 Feb. 1638.] s.sh.fol. *Dublin, Soc. of Statrs.*, 1637 [o.s.] D⁴(3, destroyed). Cr. 325.

14247 — By the Lord Deputy. A proclamation concerning the sealing of tobaccoe. [23 Feb. 1638.] s.sh.fol. *Dublin, Soc. of Statrs.*, 1637 [o.s.] D⁴(4, destroyed). Cr. 326.

14248 — By the Lord Deputy. A proclamation to prevent the defrauding of his majesties customes. [16 Oct. 1638.] fol(2). *Dublin, Soc. of Statrs.*, 1638. D⁴(4, destroyed). Cr. 327.

14249 — By the Lord Deputy. A proclamation prohibiting the importation of allome. [20 Dec. 1638.] fol(2). *Dublin, Soc. of Statrs.*, 1638. D⁴(3, destroyed). Cr. 328.

14250 — By the Lord Deputy. A proclamation touching times for passing of patents for defective titles. [20 Dec. 1638.] s.sh.fol. *Dublin, Soc. of Statrs.*, 1638. D⁴(4, destroyed). Cr. 329.

14251 — By the Lord Deputy. A proclamation touching glasses. [12 Feb. 1639.] s.sh.fol. *Dublin, Soc. of Statrs.*, 1638 [o.s.] D⁴(4, destroyed). Cr. 330.

14252 — By the Lord Lieutenant. [For officers to be at their posts. 28 Mar. 1640.] s.sh.fol. *Dublin, Soc. of Statrs.*, 1640. D⁴(4, destroyed). Cr. 334.

14253 — By the Lord Deputy. [Concerning pressed men. 5 May 1640.] s.sh.fol. *Dublin, Soc. of Statrs.*, 1640. D⁴(3, destroyed). Cr. 335.

— By the King. A proclamation for freedom of passage out of Ireland. [1640.] *See* 9174.

APPENDIX

14254 — A battell of birds most strangly fought in Ireland. [1621.] Now = 5764.7.

14255 — Brief discours de l'entreprise faicte sur Irlande [by Capt. Stuckley]. 4°. *Londres* [i.e. *Paris?*] 1579. L.O.; F.

14256 — A catalogue of the nobility of Ireland. 1628. = pt. of 7746.3.

14257 — Certaine aduertisements out of Ireland, concerning the losses to the Spanish nauie. 1588. = pt. 2 of 15412.

14257.5 — Een copye van eenen brief gesonden wt Irlant. 8°. [*J. Allde?*] 1581. An English version ent. to J. Perrin 20 de. 1580. L.

14258 — Cort verhael van den aenslach gheschiedt in Irlandt. 4°. (*Londen* [i.e. *Antwerp?*] 1579.) L.D

14258.5 — Victorie in Ir-landt, van de Coninghime van Engelandt, teghen de Spaignarden end Romanisten. 4°. *Londen* [i.e. *Netherlands*], 1581. L.

Ireland, Church of. A brefe declaration of certein principall articles of religion. [The 11 Articles of 1559.] 4°. *Dublin, H. Powel*, 1566 (20 ja.) D.

14260 — Articles of religion agreed upon in the convocation in 1615. 4°. *Dublin, J. Franckton*, 1615. L.O.C.D.D².+

14261 — [Anr. ed.] 4°. R. Y[oung] f. T. Downes, 1628. Ent. to Downes 26. ja. 1629, crossed out and 'ent. by order to the Irish stock.' L.O.C.DUR⁵.E.+; F.HN.NY.U.Y.+

14262 — [Anr. ed.] 4°. [R. Young] f. T. Downes, 1629. L.O.C.D. E.+; F.HN.HD.ILL.PML.+

14263 — [Anr. ed.] 4°. f. the Co. of Statrs. of the Irish Stocke, 1629. Ent. 29 jy. L.C.D⁹. Blickling.

14264 — Constitutions, and canons ecclesiastical, . . . 1634. 4°. *Dublin, A. Crook a. S. Helsham*, [1685–89.] L.O.O⁶. D².D⁸.; HD.Y(lacks tp).

14265 — [An earlier ed.] Constitutions, and canons ecclesiasticall, . . . 1634. 4°. *Dublin, Soc. of Statrs.*, 1635. L.O.C.CASHEL.E.+; F.NY(lacks tp).U.

14265.1 — [*Visitation articles.*] Articles to be inquired of by the churchwardens in the Lord Primates metropoliticall. 1629. s.sh.fol. *Dublin, Co. of Statrs.*, 1629. L⁵.

14265.3 — Armagh. [Archiepiscopal. Christopher Hampton.] Articles given in charge. . . . s.sh.fol. *Dublin, Soc. of Statrs.*, 1623. L⁵.

14265.5 —— [Archiepiscopal. James Ussher.] s.sh.fol. *Dublin, Soc. of Statrs.*, 1626. L⁵.

14265.7 — Cloyne. [George Synge.] 4°. *Dublin, Soc. of Statrs.*, 1639. O¹³.

14265.9 — Dublin. [Archiepiscopal. Lancelot Bulkeley.] 4°. *Dublin, Soc. of Statrs.*, 1638. O⁵.

14266 —— 4°. *Dublin, Soc. of Statrs.*, 1640. C³.

14267 **Ireland, Thomas.** The oath of allegeance, defended by a sermon. 4°. *N. Okes f. E. Aggas*, 1610. Ent. 7 mr. L.O.C.A.M⁴.+; CAL.U.

Irenicus Philodikaios, *pseud.* A treatise declaring, and confirming the title of James the sixt. [1599?] *See* 19881.5.

Irish prognostication. A new Irish prognostication. 1624. *See* 20993.

14268 **Ironside, Gilbert.** Seven questions of the sabbath briefly disputed. 4°. *Oxford, L. Lichfield, sold by E. Forrest*, 1637. L.O.C.D.E.; F.HN.HD.ILL.U.+

14269 **Isaacson, Henry.** Saturni ephemerides sive tabula historico-chronologica. fol. *B. A(lsop) & T. F(awcet) f. H. Seile a. H. Robinson*, 1633. Ent. 25 fb. 1632. L.O.C.D.E.+; F.HN.HD.N.Y.+

— ed. *See* 599, 600, 601.
— tr. *See* 1839.5.

Isabella Clara Eugenia, *Infanta of Spain.* A coppie of the proclamation. 1599. *See* 18470.

14270 **Isidore,** *Saint, Bp. of Seville.* Here be the gathered counsailes of saynct Isodorie to informe man, howe he shuld flee vices. [*Tr.* T. Lupset.] 8°. *T. Berthelet*, 1534. P.; F.
For a different trans. *see* 25420.

14270.5 — [Anr. ed.] 8°. *in æd. T. Bertheleti*, 1539. YK. Tobias Rodgers, London.; HD.

14271 — [Anr. ed.] 8°. *in æd. T. Bertheleti*, 1544. L.O.C⁴.; F.BO.

Isle. The ile of gulls. 1633. *See* 6414.

Isles. The fortunate isles. [1625.] *See* 14772.

14272 **Isocrates.** Ισοκρατους λογοι και επιστολαι. Isocratis orationes et epistolæ. Editio postrema. 8°. *ap. hæredes J. Norton & J. Bill* [i.e. *Geneva, P. Estienne?*] 1615. L(tp only, Harl.5990/132).O.O⁶.C.NEK.; F.BOWDOIN. CHI.CU.Y.+

14273 — [Heading A2ʳ:] Ισοκρατους προς Δημονικον λόγος παραινετικός. [With other works. c. 1585.] Now = 20054.3.

14274 — Isocratis orationes tres. . . . Item Plutarchi. . . . de liberis educandis libellus. *Gr.* 8°. *Cantabrigiæ, ap. T. Buck & R. Daniel*, 1638. C.C⁵.DUR³. Lord Kenyon.; F.
For other eds. of this combined text *see* 20054 sqq.

14275 — A perfite looking glasse for all estates: contained in three orations of morall instructions. *Tr.* into Lataine by Hieronimus Wolfius. Englished [by] (T. Forrest.) 4°. *T. Purfoote*, 1580. Ent. 4 ja. O.O³.E.; F.HN.HD.LC.

14276 — [*Ad Demonicum.*] The godly aduertisement or good counsell of Isocrates [*tr.*] (J. Bury), wherto is annexed Cato in meter [*tr.* B. Burgh.] 2 pts. 8°. (*W. Coplande,*) 1557 (1558 (1 ja.)) Pt. 1 ent. 1557–58. L.O.
Pt. 2 (formerly also 4856) reprints 4850.

14276.5 — Isocratis ad Demonicum oratio admonitoria. Item Plutarchi . . . de liberis educandis libellus. 12°. *Cantabrigiæ, ex acad. typographeo*, 1631. ETON.

14277 — = 14279.

14278 — [*Ad Nicoclem.*] The doctrinall of princis. *Tr.* syr Thomas Eliot. 8°. (*in the house of T. Berthelet,*) [1533?] L².L⁴.O(frag.).; F(2).

14279 — [Anr. ed.] The doctrinall of princes. 8°. (*in the house of T. Berthelet,*) [c. 1550.] L.L².BUTE.; HN.ILL.N. PML.
(Formerly also 14277) Tp border McK.&F. 30, dated 1534.

14280 — Archidamus, or, the councell of warre. *Tr.* T. Barnes. 4°. *W. Jones f. N. Bourne*, 1624. L.C.C⁷.M. PETWORTH.; F. HN.

Isselt, Michael ab. *See* 20862.

14280.5 **Isumbras,** *Sir.* The hystory of syr Isēbras. [In verse.] 4°. [*J. Skot*, c. 1530.] L¹³(2 leaves).; HD(frag.).
32 lines; B4ʳ line 5: 'quene a florence'.

14280.7 — [Anr. ed.] 4°. [*Southwark, P. Treveris*, c. 1530.] HD (frag.).
32 lines; B4ʳ line 5: 'quene of florence'.

14281 — [Anr. ed.] 4°. [*London*, c. 1560.] O(A2 only).
31 lines; A2ʳ line 15 ends: 'to see'.

14282 — [Anr. ed.] Here begynneth the history of the valyent knyght, Syr Isenbras. 4°. (*W. Copland,*) [1565?] L.
31 lines; A2ʳ line 15 ends: 'tose [*sic*]'.

Italian Convert. The Italian convert. 1635, etc. *See* 1235 sqq.

Italy. The affaires of Italy, with the crowning and inauguration of the new pope Barbarino a Florentine in Rome. 1623. *See* Newsbooks 133.

— Newes from Italy of a second Moses. 1608. *See* 1233.

14283 — Newes from Italy. Or, a prodigious accident concerning the citty of Pleurs [i.e. Piuro]. 4⁰. *N. O[kes] f. N. Newbery a. J. Pyper*, 1618. Ent. 6 oc. L.O.

14284 — [Anr. ed.] 4⁰ in 8. *Edinburgh, A. Hart*, 1619. L.

14285 — A true and perfect discourse of three great accidents in Italie. 8⁰. *J. Wolfe*, 1588. Ent. 19 fb. L.

14286 **Italy and France.** Grauissimae, . . . totius Italiæ, et Galliæ Academiarū censuræ. [On Henry VIII's marriage w. Catherine of Aragon. By E. Fox and others.] 4⁰. (*in off. T. Bertheleti*, 1530 (ap.)) L.O.C. D.E.+ ; F.BO.CH.HD.Y.

Italy and France—*cont.*

14287 — [A trans.] The determinations of the moste famous vniuersities of Italy and Fraunce. [*Tr.* T. Cranmer ?] 8⁰. (*in the house of T. Berthelet*, 1531 (7 no.)) L.O.C. LINC.YK.+ ; F.HN.HD.PML.

    Some copies (HD, 1 C) omit year date in colophon.

14288 **Item.** Here is an item for you. Or, the countrimans bill of charges. *Ballad.* 2 pts. s.sh.fol. *M. F[lesher, c.* 1630.] L.C⁶.

14289 **Ive, Paul.** The practise of fortification. 1589. = pt. 2 of 1708.5.

14290 — [Anr. ed.] Corrected and augmented. 4⁰. *F. Kingston . T. Cooke*, 1597. C⁸.HAT. Leeds PL.

    The author's name is spelled 'Ivie'.

— *tr. See* pt. 1 of 1708.5.

J

J. For initials I. or J. *see* I.

Jacchaeus, Thomas. *See* Jack, T.

Jack, *of Both Sides. See* 25612.

14291 **Jack,** *of Dover.* Jacke of Dover, his quest of inquirie. (. . . the penniles parliament of threed-bare poets.) 4°. [*W. White*] *f. W. Ferbrand*, 1604. Ent. 3 au. 1601. O.
    2nd pt. reprinted separately in 19307 sq.

14292 — [Anr. ed.] Jacke of Dovers merry tales. Whereunto is annexed The pennilesse parliament. . . . 4°. *J. B[eale,] sold by R. Higginbotham*, 1615. Ent. to J. Beale 12 no. 1614. O(lacks 2nd pt.).

Jack up Lande. *See* 5098.

14293 **Jack, Thomas.** Onomasticon poeticum siue, propriorum quibus in suis monumentis vsi sunt veteres poetae, breuis descriptio poetica. 4° in 8's. *Edinburgi, R. Walde-graue*, 1592. L.O.C².A.E.+; F.HN.HD.ILL.Y.+

14294 **Jackson, Abraham.** Gods call, for mans heart. A sermon. 8°. *T. S[nodham] f. R. Jackson*, 1618. Ent. 22 ja. O.

14295 — The pious prentice, or, the prentices piety. 12°. *E. G[riffin] f. M. Sparke a. J. Hardisty*, 1640. Ent. to Hardesty 9 no. 1639. O.

14296 — Sorrowes lenitive. Written upon occasion of the death of John, lord Harrington. [In verse.] 8°. *f. R. Jackson*, 1614. Ent. 15 mr. O.

14296.5 **Jackson, Bonaventure,** *O.F.M.* Manuductions to the pallace of trueth. By F. B. Observant. 8°. *Mackline, H. Jaye*, 1616. L⁹.O(imp.).A².AMP(imp.).USHAW.; F. A&R 411.

Jackson, Henry, *ed. See* 13706, 13707, 13708, 13711, 13722, 13723, 20612.5, 25592.

14297 **Jackson, John.** Ecclesiastes. The worthy church-man. 4°. [*M. Flesher*] *f. R. More*, 1628. Ent. 8 de. 1627. L.O.C².E².NLW.+; F(imp.).DAR.ILL.

14297a — The key of knowledge. . . . 12°. *F. Kingston f. R. Milbourne*, 1640. Ent. 28 no. 1639. O.C.P.; PN²(imp.).

14297a.3 — The soule is immortall: . . . 8°. *W. W(hite) f. R. Boulton (a. W. White,)* 1611. Ent. to Bolton a. White 24 no. 1610. O.C³.PARIS.; F. Lehigh U.
    (Formerly 13850) An anthology edited by Jackson.

14298 **Jackson, Thomas,** *Canon of Canterbury.* The converts happines. A comfortable sermon. 4°. *J. Windet f. C. Knight*, 1609. Ent. 24 ap. L.L¹⁵.C².D.PLUME.+; F.HN. CHI.HD.Y.+

14299 — Davids pastorall poeme: or sheepeheards song. Seven sermons, on the 23. psalme. 8°. *T. Purfoot, sold by E. Weaver*, 1603. Ent. to Purfoot 25 jn. L.D.LINC.; F.HN.BOWDOIN.HD.PN².

14300 — An helpe to the best bargaine. A sermon. 8°. *N. Okes f. M. Walbanke*, 1624. Ent. 23 no. 1623. L.CARLISLE.; F.U(imp.).

14301 — Judah must into captivitie. Six sermons. 4°. *J. Haviland f. G. Emondson a. N. Vavasour*, 1622. Ent. to Emonson, i.e. Emerson, 2 oc. L³.O.C.DUR⁵.E.+; F.L.C.U.Y.

14302 — [Anr. issue, w. imprint:] *J. Haviland f. J. Bulkley in Canterburie*, 1622. L.C⁵.M².

14303 — Londons new-yeeres gift. Or the uncouching of the foxe. A godly sermon. 4°. *J. W[indet] f. C. Knight*, 1609. Ent. 16 ja. L.O.C⁵.M.P.+; F.HN.HD.N.Y.+

14304 — Peters teares. A sermon. 4°. *W. W[hite] f. C. Knight*, 1612. Ent. 25 my. L.L¹⁵.O.O¹¹.; F.HN.TEX.Y.

14305 — The raging tempest stilled. The historie of Christ his passage, opened in weekly lectures. 4° in 8's. *J. Haviland f. G. Emondson a. N. Vavasour*, 1623. Ent. 12 my. L.O.C.A.D.+; F.HN.CHI.HD.N.

14305a — Sinnelesse sorrow for the dead. A sermon at the funerall of M. John Moyle. 8°. *T. S[nodham] f. R. Jackson*, 1614. Ent. 1 fb. C¹⁰.LINC.; F.

14306 **Jackson, Thomas,** *Dean of Peterborough.* Christs answer unto Johns question: . . . Delivered in certaine sermons. 4°. *G. P[urslow] f. J. Clarke*, 1625. Ent. 1 de. 1624. L.O.C.DUR.LINC.+; F.HN.HD.ILL.Y.+

— Commentaries upon the Apostles Creed. *See*
  1, 2. The eternall truth of scriptures. 14308.
  3. The blasphemous positions of Jesuites. 14315.
  4. Justifying faith. 14311.
  5. The originall of unbeliefe. 14316.
  6. The divine essence and attributes. 14318.
  7. The knowledg of Christ Jesus. 14313.
  8. The humiliation of the sonne of God. 14309.
  9. The consecration of the sonne of God. 14317.
  10, 11. Not published till 1654, 1657.
  12. A treatise of the holy catholike faith. 14319.

14307 — Diverse sermons, with a short treatise befitting these present times. 4°. *Oxford, L. Lichfield*, 1637. L.O.C⁵. D.E.+; F(imp.).HN.ILL.U.Y.+

14308 — The eternall truth of scriptures, . . . Delivered in two bookes of commentaries upon the Apostles Creede. 4°. *W. Stansby, sold by J. Budge*, 1613. Ent. to Stansby 23 jy. 1612. L.O.C.D.LEIC.+; F.HN.HD.NCU. Y.+
    Some copies (1 C, 1 HD) have errata list added on Zz4ᵛ.

14308.5 — [Anr. issue, w. imprint on cancel tp:] *W. Stansby f. E. Crossley*, 1613. F.

14309 — The humiliation of the sonne of God. 4° in 8's. *M. Flesher f. J. Clark*, 1635. Ent. 9 jn. L.O.C⁵.A.DUL.+; F.HN.ILL.U.Y.+

14310 — [A variant, w. date:] 1636. L.O.C¹⁵.D².NOR².+; F.HN. PTS.

14311 — Justifying faith, or the faith by which the just do live. 4° in 8's. *J. Beale*, 1615. Ent. 2 de. 1614, 'crost out to be entered to J. Clarke'. L.O.C.A.HER.+; F.HN. HD.NCU.PN.+

14312 — Second edition. 4° in 8's. *M. F[lesher] f. J. Clarke*, 1631. Ass'd to Clarke 1 mr. L.O.C.D.E.+; F.HN.ILL. U.Y.+
    See Court Book C, p. 225.

14313 — The knowledg of Christ Jesus. 4° in 8's. *M. F[lesher] f. J. Clarke*, 1634. Ent. 8 jy. 1633. L.O.C⁵.A.NOR².+; F.HN.HD.N.U.+

14314 — Nazareth and Bethlehem, . . . And, mankinds comfort. Two sermons. 4°. *Oxford, J. Lichfield a. w. Wrench*, 1617. L.O.C¹⁷.BIRM²(K.N.).P.+; F.HN.BO.HD.U.+

14315 — The third booke of commentaries upon the Apostles Creede, contayning the blasphemous positions of Jesuites concerning the authoritie of their church. 4° in 8's. *W. Stansby, sold by J. Budge*, 1614. L.L². O.C.HER.+; F.HN.HD.NCU.
    Sometimes found bd. w. 14308.

14316 — A treatise containing the originall of unbeliefe. 4° in 8's. *J. D[awson] f. J. Clarke*, 1625. Ent. 22 ja. L.O.C.D. E.+; F.HN.CHI.HD.U.+

14317 — A treatise of the consecration of the sonne of God to his everlasting priesthood. 4°. *Oxford, L. Lichfield*, 1638. L.O.C.D².E.+; F.HN.BR.ILL.U.+

14318 — A treatise of the divine essence and attributes. (The second part.) 2 pts. 4° (pt. 2 in 8's.) *M. F[lesher] f. J. Clarke*, 1628 (1629.) Ent. 4 oc. 1627 a. 20 au. 1628. L.O⁵.C⁵.D.E.+; F.HN.HD.N.Y.+
    Pt. 1, B1ʳ catchword: 'others'.

14318.5 — [Anr. ed. of pt. 1.] 4°. *M. F[lesher] f. J. Clarke*, 1628. L.O.C.A.YK.+; F.CHI.HD.TORONTO².
    B1ʳ catchword: 'My'.

14319 — A treatise of the holy catholike faith and church. Divided into three bookes. 4°. *M. F[lesher] f. J. Clarke*, 1627. Ent. 4 no. 1626. L.O.C⁵.G².LINC.+; F.HN.HD.N.U.+

— tr. *See* 20146.
— *See also* 17918, 24402.

14320 **Jackson, Timothy.** A brief and plaine, . . . exposition upon S. Pauls second epistle to the Thessalonians. 4°. *E. G[riffin] f. T. Pavier,* 1621. Ent. 26 ap. L (destroyed).O.CASHEL.; F.HN.HD.Y.

14321 **Jackson, William.** Aspice. יְהֹוָה Respice. The celestiall husbandrie. In a sermon at Pauls Crosse. 4°. *W. Jones, sold by E. Weaver,* 1616. Ent. to W. Jones 17 se. L.O.C.C⁵.WOR.+; F.HN.Y.

Jacob. Jacob's ladder. 1638. *See* 1839.5.

14322 **Jacob,** *ship.* A relation strange and true of a ship named the Jacob. 4°. [*Eliot's Court Press?*] *f. N. Butter,* 1622. Ent. 27 fb. C.
A different work from 20769.

14323 **Jacob,** *the Patriarch.* Thystory of Jacoby and his twelue sones. [In verse.] 4° ⁶·⁸. (*w. de worde,*) [1510?] L.O (frag.).
14323.3 — [Anr. ed.] [1510?] *See* Addenda.
14323.5 — [Anr. ed.] 4° ⁶·⁸. (*R. Pynson,*) [c. 1520.] HD(frags.).
14324 — [Anr. ed.] Thystory of Jacob & his. xii. sones. 4° ⁶·⁸. (*J. Skot,*) [1522–23.] L.
5-line init. on A1ʳ.
14324.5 — [Anr. ed.] 4° ⁶·⁴. [*J. Skot,* c. 1530.] L²(Frag. No. 28).; HN(3 leaves).MEL(1 leaf).
4-line init. on A1ʳ.
14325 — [A ghost.]
14326 — [Anr. ed.] The history of Jacob and his twelue sonnes. 4°. (*J. Allde f. J. Harison,*) [1570?] HN.
J. Walley was fined for pr. an ed. 1561–62; *see* Arber I.183.
14326.3 — [Anr. ed.] 4°. [*J. Awdley*](*f. Ant. Kytson,*) [1575?] DEU.
In the colophon 'for' is misprinted 'or'.
14326.5 — [An interlude upon the history of Jacob and Esau.] 4°. [*H. Sutton,* 1557.] Ent. to H. Sutton 1557–58. O¹⁴ (G⁴ only).
Headlines in B.L. This ed. not in Greg; *see* Bodleian Library Record, VII (1967), pp. 300–2, 304.
14327 — [Anr. ed.] A newe mery and wittie comedie or enterlude, newely imprinted, treating vpon the historie of Jacob and Esau. 4°. *H. Bynneman,* 1568. L.O.; F.HN. N.PFOR.Y². Greg 51.
Headlines in italic.

14328 **Jacob, Henry.** An attestation of many learned, . . . divines, that the church-governement ought to bee alwayes with the peoples free consent. 8°. [*Middelburg, R. Schilders,*] 1613. L.O.C.D².E.+; F.HN.CH.HD.U.+

14329 — A christian and modest offer of a conference, about the controversies betwixt the prelats, and deprived ministers. [Anon.] 4°. [*W. Jones's secret press,*] 1606. L.O.C.D².M.+; F.HN.HD(imp.).U.Y.+
— A collection of sundry matters. 1616. *See* 5556.

14330 — Anno domini 1616. A confession and protestation of the faith of certaine christians. [Anon.] 8°. [*Amsterdam, G. Thorp,*] 1616.] L.L³.O.C.PETYT.+; HD.
Often found bd. w. 5556.

14331 — = 14332.
14332 — A declaration and plainer opening of certain points, in the divine beginning of Christes true church. 8°. [*Middelburg, R. Schilders,*] 1612. O(imp.).C.C³.C⁵. E.; BO³.CH.HD.U.Y.

14333 — A defence of a treatise touching the sufferings and victorie of Christ. [Response to 3064.] 4°. [*Middelburg, R. Schilders,*] 1600. L.O.C.D.P.+; F.SMITH.U.Y.

14334 — = 14333.
14335 — A defence of the churches and ministery of Englande. (A short treatise [etc.]) 4°. *Middelburgh, R. Schilders,* 1599. L.O.C.E.M.+; F.HN.HD.U.Y.+
Reprinted in 14658.

14336 — The divine beginning and institution of Christs church. 8°. *Leyden, H. Hastings* [i.e. *van Haestens,*] 1610. L.O.C.D.E.+; BO³.CH.HD.Y. Detroit PL(imp.).

14337 — A plaine and cleere exposition of the second commandement. 8°. [*Leyden, H. van Haestens f. J. Marcus?*] 1610. L.O.C.C³.E.+; BO³.CH.HD.Y. Detroit PL.
— A position against vainglorious preaching. 1604. *See* 14052.

14338 — Reasons taken out of Gods word proving a necessitie of reforming our churches in England. 4°. [*Middelburg, R. Schilders,*] 1604. L.O.C.CASHEL.M.+; F.HN. HD.U.Y.+

14339 — To the right high and mightie prince, James, an humble supplication for toleration. [Anon.] 4°. [*Middelburg, R. Schilders,*] 1609. L.O.C¹⁰.D.E.+; F.HN.HD.N.U.+
Some copies (1 HD) have an erratum added on p. 48.

Jacob, Henry—*cont.*
14340 — A treatise of the sufferings and victory of Christ. [Init. H. I.] 8°. [*Middelburg, R. Schilders,*] 1598. L.O.C.D. WN.+; F.HN.BO.BO³.Y.

Jacobi, Joannes. *See* 4589 sqq.

Jacobus, *de Gruitroede. See* 6894.5.

Jacobus, *de Voragine. See* 24873.

14341 **Jaggard, William.** A catalogue of such English bookes, as lately have bene, or now are in printing for publication. 4°. *W. Jaggard,* 1618. O.
(Formerly also 10407)

14342 — Σωματογραφία ανθρωπίνη. Or a description of the body of man. 1616. = 20782.

14343 — A view of all the right honourable the Lord Mayors of London. By W. I. fol. [*E. Bollifant?*] *f. W. Jaggard a. T. Pavyer, sold* [*by T. Pavier,*] 1601. HN.

14344 **James I,** *King of England.* The workes of . . . James, . . . King of Great Britaine, . . . published by James [Mountague,] bishop of Winton. fol. *R. Barker a. J. Bill,* 1616. L.O.C.D.E.+; F.HN.HD.N.NY.+

14345 — [Anr. ed., w. supplement.] *R. Barker a. J. Bill,* 1616 (1620.) L.O.C².E².M.+; F.HN.HD.N.NY.+

14346 — [A trans.] Serenissimi . . . principis Jacobi, . . . opera, edita ab I. Montacuto, episcopo. [*Tr.* and revised by T. Reid and P. Young.] fol. *ap. B. Nortonium & J. Billium,* 1619. L.O.C(Bury deposit, lacks tp).D.E.+; BALT.HD.ILL.NY.Y.+
Text ends p. 609. The 4 unsigned prelim. leaves in this and the 2 following numbers vary in number present and arrangement; *see* Edinburgh Bibliographical Society Transactions, III (1948), pp. 17–30.
14346.3 — [Anr. issue, w. 'Hypotyposis' added on pp. 611–38.] L.O².D².E.P.+; F.HN.
Probably pub'd early in 1620. No colophon.
14346.5 — [Anr. issue, w. colophon on cancel of pp. 637–38:] (*ap. R. Barker & J. Billium,* 1620.) O.C(2).M.M².
— Apologia pro juramento fidelitatis. *See* 14400, 14403.

14347 — Βασιλικα δωρα, sive sylloge epistolarum, orationum, & carminum regalium. 8°. *Typis R. Badger,* 1640. L³. O(2).O⁸.C².C³.; HN.
(Formerly also 1186) Contains letters of Kings of England from Henry VIII to James I.

14348 — Βασιλικον δωρον. Deuided into three bookes. [Anon.] 4°. *Edinburgh, R. Walde-graue,* 1599. L.E.

14349 — [Anr. ed., revised.] Βασιλικον δωρον. Or his majesties instructions to his dearest sonne, Henry the prince. 8°. *Edinburgh, R. Waldegrave,* 1603. L.O.E.G².M⁴.+; F.HN.CAL.HD.ILL.+
From the method of leaf signatures this appears to have been only partly pr. by Waldegrave himself.

14350 — [Anr. ed.] 8°. *F. Kyngston f. J. Norton,* 1603. Ent. to a syndicate 28 mr. L.O.C.G².M.+; F.HN.HD.PML.Y.+
With royal arms on title. Apparently the demand for this book was such that Norton had it pr. by several printers, including those who appear on the various tpp of the Norton eds. and the Eliot's Court Press. Mixed sheets generally occur in 14350–53. For lists and charts of many of the differences, w. several reproductions, *see* Papers of the Bibliographical Society of America, LXIIII (1970), pp. 393–417.
14351 — [Anr. ed.] 8°. *F. Kyngston f. J. Norton,* 1603. L.O.C.E. M².+; F.HN.HD.N.Y.+
With McK. 273β on title.
14352 — = 14351.
14353 — [Anr. ed.] 8°. *R. Field f. J. Norton,* 1603. L.L³⁰.O.DUL. M⁴.+; F.HN.PN.Y.
At least sheet I was pr. by T. East; it has crowned rose orn. on I4ʳ.
14354 — [Anr. ed.] 8°. *E. Allde f. E. W[hite] a. others of the Co. of Statrs.,* 1603. L.O.C⁴.D.E.+; F.HN.HD.ILL.Y.+
See Court-Book C, pp. 2–3; Arber II.835.
14355 — [A trans.] Jacobi primi. . . . Βασιλικον δωρον, sive regia institutio. Lat. 8°. [*Eliot's Court Press? f.*] *J. Norton,* 1604. L.O.C.A.E.+; F.HN.HD.IND.U.+
14356 — [Anr. trans.] Βασιλικον δωρον: nev, Athrawiaeth i Fawredh yw anwylaf fab Henri'r Tywysog. *Tr.* R. Holland. Welsh. 4°. *S. Stafford f. T. Salisbury,* 1604. CAR(tp and prelims. only).NLW(imp.).
Epistle and half of tp in English. 12872 apparently intended to be issued w. this, and is linked to this on the tp. The plague may have prevented completion of this book.

James I, *King of England—cont.*

14357 — [An adaptation.] A princes looking glasse, or a princes direction, excerpted out of Βασιλικον δῶρον, and *tr.* into Latin and English verse by W. Willymat. 4°. *J. Legat, pr. to the Univ. of Cambridge,* sold [*in London*] *by S. Waterson,* 1603. L.C.C².E².; F.HN. HD.N(imp.).

14358 — [An anon. adaptation.] The fathers blessing: or second councell to his sonne. Appropriated to the generall, from that perticular example his majestie composed for the prince his son. 8°. [*B. Alsop*] *f. L. Becket,* 1616. Ent. 29 oc. 1615. L.

14358.5 — Third edition. 12°. *B. Alsop f. T. Jones,* 1619. Ass'd 27 my. BIRM(Sh. Inst.).
　　　　See Court-Book C, p. 105.

14359 — Fifth edition. 12°. *B. Alsop f. T. Jones,* 1624. L.

14360 — Sixt edition. 12°. *B. A*[*lsop*] *a. T. F*[*awcet*] *f. T. Jones,* 1630. L.; HD.

14360.5 — Seventh edition. 12°. *B. A*[*lsop*] *a. T. F*[*awcet*] *f. T. Jones,* 1632. F.

14361 — The copie of his majesties letter, sent 26. June 1604: to the Commons. 4°. [*F. Kingston f. C. Burby,*] 1604. Ent. 27 jn. L.O.C.C⁵.D.+; F.CHI.MCG.

14362 — The copie of the K. majesties letter to the L. Maior of London [28 Mar. 1603.] s.sh.fol. [*Edinburgh, R. Waldegrave,* 1603.] L.

14362.5 — [Anr. ed.] 4° in 2. [*R. Barker,* 1603.] M(deposit).; F.HN.
　　　　Dated at end. No tp; heading on A1ʳ.

14363 — A counter-blaste to tobacco. [Anon.] 4°. *R. B*[*arker*] 1604. O(1, plus a frag.).G².LIV³(imp.).; F.HN.BO⁵. HD.NY.+

14364 — Daemonologie, in forme of a dialogue [etc.] 4°. *Edinburgh, R. Walde-grave,* 1597. Ent. to R. Legat, 17 mr. 1598. L.L³⁰.O.E.G².+; F.HN.HD.ILL.PN.+
　　　　There are at least 3 states of the tp differing in the following points: headpiece: vase orn. or lace orn.; in line 2 of title the 1st letter is *G*[swash] or *G*.

14365 — [Anr. ed.] 4°. [*R. Bradock*] *f. W. Aspley a. W. Cotton,* 1603. Ent. to E. Edgar 3 ap. L.O.O².E.; F.HN.HD.LC. PN.

14365.5 — [Anr. issue, w. imprint:] *f. W. Cotton a. W. Aspley, sold at London bridge,* 1603. L³⁰.C¹⁷.; F.HD.N.

14366 — [Anr. ed.] 4°. *A. Hatfield f. R. Wald-grave,* 1603. L.O. C⁵.CASHEL.E.+; F.HN.HD.ILL.NY.+

14367 — Declaration du . . . Roy Jacques I. pour le droit des rois. (*Tr.* P. du Moulin.) 4°. *J. Bill,* 1615. L.
　　　　a2ʳ catchword: 'des'.

14367.5 — [Anr. issue, w. sheet a of preface expanded and reset.] O.C.CASHEL.D.LEEDS.+; F.HN.HD.ILL.NY.+
　　　　a2ʳ catchword: 'pour'.

14368 — [A trans.] Serenissimi Jacobi, . . . declaratio pro jure regio, adversus Cardinalis Perronii orationem. 4°. *ex off. Nortoniana, ap. J. Billium,* 1616. L.O.C.E². G².+; F.HN.HD.NY.

14369 — [Anr. trans.] A remonstrance of the most gratious King James I. for the right of kings. *Tr.* [by R. Betts] out of his majesties French copie. 4°. *C. Legge, pr. to the Univ. of Cambridge,* 1616. Ent. 10 jn. L.O.C. BRISTOL.G².+; F.HN.HD.ILL.TEX.+

14370 — [Anr. ed.] *Tr.* . . . by R. B[etts.] 4°. *C. Legge, pr. to the Univ. of Cambridge,* 1619. L.O.C.CASHEL.E.+; HN. CHI.ILL.MCG.WASH².+
　　　　Last p. numbered 288. May be a later ed. than 14371.

14371 — [Anr. ed.] 4°. *C. Legge, pr. to the Univ. of Cambridge,* 1619. L.O¹⁸.C.NEP.STU.+; F.N.WASH².
　　　　Last p. numbered 290. In some copies (C, F) tp is obviously a cancel. A

14372 — A declaratioun of the Kings maiesties intentioun toward the lait actis of Parliament. 1585. = 21948.
— Declaration du serenissime roy . . . touchant le faict de C. Vorstius. 1612. *See* 9229.

14373 — The essayes of a prentise, in the diuine art of poesie. 4°. *Edinbrugh* [sic], *T. Vautroullier,* 1584. L.C².E. M.G².+; F.HN.HD.PFOR. Arthur Houghton.
　　　　Author's name in an acrostic on A1ʳ.

14374 — [A variant, w. imprint:] *Edinburgh, T. Vautroullier,* 1585. L.O.C¹⁰.E.STU.+; HN.HD.PML.
　　　　The 2 E copies have different typesettings on P1ᵛ–2ʳ.

14375 — Flores regij. Or, proverbes and aphorismes, divine and morall. As spoken by his majestie. Collected by J. L. S. 8°. *B. A*[*lsop*] *a. T. F*[*awcet*] *f. B. Fisher,* 1627. L(2).C³.; F.HN.CAL.

James I, *King of England—cont.*

14376 — Ane fruitfull meditatioun [etc.] [On Rev. xx. 7–10.] 4°. *Edinburgh, H. Charteris,* 1588. L.L²(2).E.STD.

14376.5 — [Anr. ed.] 8°. *Newly reprinted by V. S*[*immes*] *f. J. Harrison the Yonger,* [1603.] Ent. 4 ap. 1589. C.
　　　　Collates A–B⁸ C⁶.

14377 — [Anr. ed.] 8°. *Newly reprinted* [*by V. Simmes*] *f. J. Harrison,* 1603. L.O.YK.; F.HD.ILL.
　　　　Collates A–B⁸.
— His majesties declaration, touching his proceedings in the late Parliament. 1621. *See* 9241.

14378 — His majesties gracious letter to the Earle of South-Hampton, and to the company of Virginia. Also a treatise of the art of making silke: by J. Bonoeil. 4°. *F. Kyngston,* 1622. L.G².; HN.HD.LC.N.NY.+
　　　　Bonoeil's treatise is a different work from 18761.

14379 — His Maiesties poeticall exercises at vacant houres. (The furies [*tr.* by King James from G. de Saluste du Bartas.]—The Lepanto of James the sixt.—La Lepanthe [*tr.* by Saluste] du Bartas.) 4°. *Edinburgh, R. Walde-graue,* (1591.) Ent. to R. Field 7 au. 1589. L.O.C².E.G².+; F.HN.HD.PML.Y.+
　　　　See Greg, *Register B,* p. 93; Arber II.38.

14379.3 — His majesties Lepanto, or, heroicall song, being part of his poeticall exercises at vacant houres. 4°. *S. Stafford a. H. Hooke,* 1603. Ent. 12 ap. O(frag.).O⁸.; HN.HD.
　　　　First pr. in 14379, w. a French trans.; for a Latin trans. *see* 14385.5.

14379.5 — [Heading A2ʳ:] The kings majesties letter to the Lords Grace of Canterbury, touching preaching, and preachers. (The Lord Archbishop of Canterburie [G. Abbot] his letters to the Bishop of Norwich.) 4°. [*London,* 1622.] C³.DUR⁵.
　　　　A different work from 33. Film of C³ copy is on Univ. Microfilms reel 649 ('33).

14379.7 — Lettre dy roy d'Angleterre. A madame la princesse de Condé. 8° in 4. [*London?*] 1617. HD.

14380 — Ane meditatioun vpon the . . . first buke of the chronicles of the Kingis [xv.25–9.] 4°. *Edinburgh, H. Charteris,* 1589. L.

14381 — [Anr. ed.] 8°. *reprinted* [*by J. Windet*] *f. F. Norton,* 1603. L.YK.; F(2).HD.ILL.

14381.5 — A meditation upon the 27, 28, 29. verses of the xxvii. chapter of Sᵗ. Matthew. Or a paterne for a kings inauguration. 8°. *R. Barker a. J. Bill,* 1620. C².
　　　　88 pp.

14382 — [Anr. ed.] 12°. *P. Barker,* 1620. L.O.C²(imp.).DUL. E².+; F.HN.HD.NY.PML.
　　　　127 pp.

14383 — [A trans.] Meditatio in cap. xxvii. evangelii S. Matth. 27, 28, 29. 8°. *ap. R. Barker et J. Billium,* 1620. L². L⁴³.DUR³.

14384 — A meditation upon the Lords prayer. 8°. *B. Norton a. J. Bill,* 1619. L.O.C.E².G².+; F.HN.CH.HD.PML.+

14385 — [A trans.] Serenissimi . . . Jacobi, . . . meditatio in orationem dominicam. [*Tr.* T. R.?] 8°. *ap. B. Nortonium & J. Billium,* 1619. L.C.E².M.YK.; F.U(lacks tp).

14385.5 — Naupactiados, sive Lepantiados Jacobi magni. Metaphrasis poetica authore T. Moravio. 4°. *R. Field, imp. J. Norton,* 1604. E.
　　　　A trans. of 14379.3.

14386 — [Anr. issue, w. cancel tp, w. imprint:] *J. Norton,* 1604. L².C.E²(2).; HN.HD.
　　　　(Formerly also 18298)

14387 — The peace-maker: or, Great Brittaines blessing. [Anon. By T. Middleton.] 4°. *T. Purfoot,* 1618. L.L². PETYT.PLUME.YK(C–E only).; BO.CB.TEX.Y.
　　　　C1ʳ catchword: 'Globe,'. *See* Greg, *Companion,* pp. 163–4.

14388 — [Anr. ed.] 4°. *T. Purfoot,* 1619. L.O.C.G⁴.YK.+; F.HN. HD.N.NY.+
　　　　C1ʳ catchword: 'canst'. Quires A–B reimposed from 14387. YK has 3 copies, 2 of which have quires C–E of 14387.

14388.3 — [Anr. ed.] 4°. *J. Beale,* 1619. WIN².; CAL.LC.U.Y(lacks tp).

14388.5 — [Anr. ed.] 4°. *J. Beale,* 1620. C⁹. Cecil Clarabut, London.

14388.7 — [Anr. ed.] 4°. *J. Beale,* 1621. L(tp only, Harl.5967/101). D.; F.

14389 — The psalmes *tr.* by King James. 1631. = 2732.
— Questions to be resoluit. 1597. *See* 21891.

14390 — [Speeches in chronological order.] The kings majesties speech, . . . in parliament, 19 March 1603. 4°. *R. Barker,* 1604. L².O².C.D.P.+; F.HN.HD.IND.PN.+
　　　　Text in italic type.

James I, *King of England—cont.*

14390.3 — [Anr. ed.] 4°. R. Barker, 1604. L³⁸.O.C⁵.G².M.+; F.HN.
HD.N.Y.+
Text in roman type.

14390.7 — [Anr. ed.] 4°. Edinburgh, T. Finlason, 1604. L.E.

14391 — [A trans.] Serenissimi regis oratio, . . . 19. Martij. 1603.
In Latinum sermonem versa: R. Marbeck, interprete.
8°. [R. Field,] imp. G. Bishop, 1604. L⁶.; F.CAL⁷.

14392 — His majesties speech in this last session of Parliament.
[Regarding Gunpowder Plot.] 4°. R. Barker, 1605.
L⁴³.O.C².P.SHEF.+; F.CAL²(imp.).HD.ILL.TEX.+
Ends M4ʳ; M1ʳ catchword: 'did'. The order of the
issues has not been established nor the amount of
resetting and possible mixture of sheets.

14392.5 — [Anr. issue, partially reset.] R. Barker, 1605. L.L³⁸.
O³.O⁵.; HD.MCG.PML. Pearson.
L4 cancelled; ends M4ᵛ; M1ʳ catchword: 'ple,'.

14393 — [Anr. issue, partially reset.] R. Barker, 1605. L.O.C.
CASHEL.E.+; F.HN.HD.ILL.NY.+
Ends M3ᵛ; M1ʳ catchword: 'of'. A page of text
about Sir Fulke Greville the elder (on L4 of 14392
and M1 of 14392.5) does not appear in this issue.

14394 — [A trans.] Regis oratio, habita in postremo regni
ordinum conuentu, Westmonasterii. 4°. R. Barker,
1606. L.O.C².D.YK.+; F.HN.NY.PML.Y.+

14395 — His majesties speech to . . . Parliament, the last day of
March 1607. 4°. R. Barker, [1607.] L.O.C.E.YK.+;
F.HN.HD.ILL.U.+
Copies vary; B2ᵛ line 4 ends 'when' or 'me'; both
at F.

14396 — The Kings majesties speach to the Lords and Commons the xxj. of March. 1609. 4°. R. Barker, [1609.]
L².O(lacks tp).C².D.E².+; HN.LC.N.NY.Y.+
A2ᵛ line 14 ends: 'impos-'; headpiece on tp: a
woodcut orn.

14396.3 — [Anr. ed.] 4°. R. Barker, [1609.] L⁴³.O.C.D.M.+; F.HD.
ILL.LC.Y.+
A2ᵛ line 14 ends: 'impossible'; headpiece on tp:
a woodcut orn.

14396.7 — [Anr. ed.] 4°. R. Barker, [1609.] L³⁰.O.C⁸.LAMPORT.P.;
F.
A2ᵛ line 14 ends: 'impossible'; headpiece on tp:
a block of type orns.

14397 — His majesties speech in the Starre-chamber, the xx. of
June. Anno 1616. 4°. R. Barker, [1616.] L.O².C.BED.
CASHEL.+; F.HN.HD.N.U.+
A3ʳ catchword: 'Dauid'; no asterisks at end of
text.

14397.3 — [Anr. ed.] 4°. R. Barker, [1616.] L.O¹³.C.E.YK.+; HN.
HD.MIN.PN.
A3ʳ catchword: 'Dauid'; 3 asterisks at end of text.

14397.7 — [Anr. ed.] 4°. R. Barker, [1616.] L.O².D.P.SHEF.+; F.
HD.ILL.PN².
A3ʳ catchword: 'Giue'; 3 asterisks at end of text.

14398 — [A ghost.]

14399 — His majesties speech in the upper house of parliament.
26. March, 1621. 4°. B. Norton a. J. Bill, 1621. L.
O.C.D.E.+; F(imp.).HN.HD.N.U.+

14399.5 — [Anr. ed.] 4°. Dublin, Soc. of Statrs., 1621. CASHEL.

— To the reverend fathers in God. [A royal letter for
further relief of Geneva. 1604.] See 9210.

14400 — Triplici nodo, triplex cuneus. Or an apologie for the
oath of allegiance, against the two breves of Pope
Paulus Quintus, and the late letter of Cardinal
Bellarmine to G. Blackwel the Arch-priest. [Anon.]
4°. R. Barker, 1607. L.O.C.CASHEL.E.+; F.HN.HD.U.
Y.+
Answered by 19408. See also 1702.

14401 — [Anr. ed., w. added 'Premonition' as pt. 1, w. gen. tp:]
An apologie for the oath of allegiance: first set forth
without a name, now acknowledged by James, King.
Together with a premonition to all most mightie
monarches. (Triplici nodo, triplex cuneus.) 2 pts.
4°. R. Barker, 1609. L.O.C.D.E.+; F.HN.ILL.U.Y.+
Imprint has no day and month date; no warning
against the unrevised copy on tp verso. HN has
warning inserted on an extra leaf at the end. Pt. 1
defended in 5474; answered in 15362.

14401.5 — [Anr. ed.] 2 pts. 4°. R. Barker, 1609 (8 ap.). C⁵.USHAW.;
F(2).HN.Y.
Imprint dated 'April. 8.'; no warning on tp verso.

14402 — [Anr. ed.] 2 pts. 4°. R. Barker, 1609 (8 ap.). L³⁰.O.C.
DUR⁵.E.+; F.HN.HD.N.U.+
With the warning against the unrevised copy dated
8 Apr. on the verso of the tp. There are at least

James I, *King of England—cont.*

2 settings of the majority of sheets in this and the
preceding ed., but a comparison of 4 copies (2 C,
HN, HD) shows that the sheets are found mixed.

14403 — [A trans. of 14400.] Triplici nodo triplex cuneus. Sive
apologia pro juramento fidelitatis. [Anon.] 4°. R.
Barkerus, 1607. L.O².C.D.E.+; F.HN.Y.

14404 — [Anr. ed.] 8°. [f.] J. Norton, 1608. L.D.; NYS.

14404a — [Anr. ed.] 1609. = pt. 2 of 14405.

14405 — [Anr. ed., w. a trans. of pt. 1 of 14401 added, w. gen.
tp:] Apologia pro juramento fidelitatis, primùm
quidem ανωνυμος: nunc verò ab ipso auctore, denuò
edita. Cui præmissa est præfatio monitoria. (Triplici
nodo, triplex cuneus.) 2 pts. 4°. [Eliot's Court Press f.]
J. Norton, 1609. L.O.C.D.E.+; F.HN.HD.ILL.U.+
(Pt. 2 formerly also 14404a) Defended in 24119.

14406 — [Anr. ed.] 2 pts. 12°. [f.] J. Norton, 1609. L.O.C.D.E.+;
F.HN.HD.ILL.PML.+

14407 — [Anr. ed.] Amsterdam, 1609.
Not an STC book. There is also a 12° ed. without
imprint, dated 1610, which was pr. abroad.

14408 — [Anr. trans. of 14401.] Apologie pour le serment de
fidelite. 2 pts. 8° in 4's. [Printed abroad] chez J.
Norton, 1609. L.O.C¹³.D².E.+; F.BO³.HD.WASH².Y.

14409 — The true lawe of free monarchies. [Signed C.
Φιλοπατρις.] 8°. Edinburgh, R. Walde-graue, 1598.
L.L².O.C.E.+

14410 — [Anr. ed.] 8°. T. C[reede] according to the copie printed
at Edenburgh, 1603. Ent. to E. Edgar 3 ap. L.O¹⁷.C².
BHP.E.; F.HN.HD.
On tp: 'Monarchies' in italic.

14410.5 — [Anr. ed.] 8°. T. C[reede] according . . ., 1603. L.O.C.E.
YK.+; F.HD.ILL.N.Y.+
On tp: 'Monarchies' in roman caps.

14411 — [Anr. ed.] 8°. R. Walde-grave [really T. Creede,] 1603.
DUR³.DUR⁵.USHAW(imp.).; HN.

14412 — Two meditations of the kings majestie; 1618, 1619. 8°.
R. Barker a. J. Bill, 1620. L².; F.
— See also 10731.

14413 — [Grant to Sir R. Stewart and R. Vaus of the roots and
stumps of trees in the royal parks.] 1610. = 8449.

14413.5 — [Heading A1ʳ:] A grant of the late kings majestie to
M. Burton of all Sir W. Ayloffs estate. 4°. [London,
1625.] O⁶.

APPENDIX

— [Tracts and verses on the accession of James.] See
5968, 5971, 6258, 7231, 7481, 10798, 12061, 12311,
13243, 14421, 14422, 14423, 14426.7, 14427, 14675,
14962, 15355, 17153, 18210, 19019, 19866, 20341,
20343, 21364, 24041, 25676.

14414 — Britannia triumphans sive icon quater maximi
monarchę, Jacobi Primi. 8°. [Eliot's Court Press f.]
J. Norton, 1607. L.L¹³.C.E.

14415 — Deus & Rex: sive dialogus, quo demonstratur Jacobum
regem immediatè sub Deo constitutum justissimè
sibi vendicare quicquid in juramento fidelitatis
requiritur. [By R. Mocket.] 4°. Londini, 1615. L².
L²².C.D.YK.+; HN.N.
Collates A–I⁴. See also notes to 14418.5, 14420.

14416 — [Anr. ed.] 8°. Londini, [Eliot's Court Press,] 1615. L.
O.C².CASHEL.E².+; F.HN.HD.PN².
Collates A–F⁸. One O copy has E–F⁸ reset, w.
F8ᵛ last line: 'ad iudicum.' instead of 'venite ad
iudicum.'

14417 — [Anr. ed.] 8°. Cantabrigiæ, [C. Legge,] 1615. O.C².C³.
C⁹.P.+; ILL.

14418 — [Anr. ed.] 8°. Londini, [E. Allde] pro regione Scotiæ,
1616. L.L³⁸.A.E².BRISTOL².; F.Y. Dickenson C.

14418.5 — [A trans.] God and the king: or, a dialogue shewing
that King James, being immediate under God doth
rightfully claime whatsoever is required by the oath
of allegeance. 4°. London, [J. Beale?] 1615. L².O.
BIRM.; HN.
Regarding patents and promulgation of this in
England see 8531 and Greg, Companion, pp. 157–
61; also 5870.3, 14484, 18228.5. For letters concerning petition for payment for printing costs by
J. Beale, W. Jaggard, T. Snodham, and E. Griffin
see Acts P.C., 1616–1617, pp. 145, 159.
Answered by 11110.7. See also 20337.5.

James I, *King of England*—APPENDIX—*cont.*

14419 — [Anr. ed.] 8°. *London,* [*J. Beale,*] 1615. L.C².D.E.YK.+; F.HN.HD.NY.U.
>Ends G7ʳ, p. 93.

14419.5 — [Anr. ed.] 8°. *London,* [*W. Jaggard, E. Allde, a. others?*] 1615. O⁴.; CHI.HD.ILL.N.NY.+
>Ends G6ᵛ, p. 92. Jaggard pr. at least sheet B, Allde at least sheet G.

14419.7 — [Anr. ed.] 8°. *London,* [*J. Beale,*] 1615. BTL.
>Ends F7ᵛ, p. 90. At least the 1st page of text is from the same typesetting as 14419.

14419a — [Anr. ed.] 8°. *Cambridge,* [*C. Legge,*] 1615. O(frag.). C⁵.USHAW.; PH(lacks tp)*.

14420 — [Anr. ed.] 8°. *London,* [*E. Allde,*] *to the onely use of J. Primrose, for the kingdome of Scotland,* 1616. L.E.E². DUR³.G².
>Regarding Primrose's privilege *see Register of the Privy Council of Scotland, 1613–1616,* pp. 534–8.

14420.3 — [Anr. ed.] 8°. *London,* [*T. Snodham?*] 1616. O.

14420.7 — [Anr. ed.] 8°. *Cambridge,* [*C. Legge,*] 1616. L.A.

— Dutifull and respective considerations upon foure heads of religion; proposed by James, King [etc.] 1609. *See* 15362.

14421 — Englands wedding garment. Or a preparation to King James his royall coronation. 4°. [*W. White?*] *f. T. Pavier,* 1603. HN.
>See *Court-Book C,* p. 4.

14422 — Englands welcome to James, . . . King of England. [In verse.] 4°. [*E. Allde?*] *f. E. W*[*hite*] *a. C. K*[*night,*] 1603. Ent. to E. White 8 ap. O.; HN.BO⁵.

14423 — An excellent new ballad, shewing the petigree of King James. s.sh.fol. [*f.*] *E. W*[*hite,* 1603.] ?Ent. to W. White 11 jn. 1603. L.

— Forth feasting. A panegyricke. 1617. *See* 7252.

14423.3 — A funeral elegie upon the lamentable losse of our late King. s.sh.fol. *f. J. Wright,* [1625.] ?Ent. 19 jn. 1625. L⁵(Lemon 258).

— God and the king: or, a dialogue shewing. . . . 1615, etc. *See* 14418.5 sqq.

— God and the king. Or a dialogue wherein. . . . [A reply to 14418.5.] 1620. *See* 11110.7.

14423.7 — Great Britaines sorrow for the death of her late deceased lord King James. [In verse.] s.sh.fol. [*London,* 1625.] S.; F.

14424 — [Grievances presented to his Majesty.] [1611.] = pt. of 7751.

14425 — An humble petition to the Kings most excellent majestie. 4°. [*Amsterdam, successors of G. Thorp,* 1625.] L.O³.C².E.G².+; HN.PN.
>Usually bd. w. 10404; both items are prob. by the same author as 19829; see *The Library,* V(1951), p. 239.

— In homines nefarios, qui scelere, parliamenti domum evertere. 1605. *See* 7737.

— Jacobi ara. 1617. *See* 19023.

14425.3 — The joyfull receiuing of James the sixt into Lyeth and Edenborough. 4°. [*J. Wolfe?*] *f. H. Carre,* 1590. Ent. 3 or 6 jn. L.; HN.

— King James his welcome to London. 1603. *See* 10798.

— The Kingis complaint. [1567.] *See* 22200.

14426 — Lucta Jacobi: or, a bonefire for his majesties double deliverie, [etc.] 4°. *T. C*[*reede*] *f. W. Welby,* 1607. Ent. 9 my. L.L³⁰.O.E(3).YK.; F.HN.HD.

14426.3 — Mirth in mourning: or, joyes conquest of sorrow, occasioned by the decease of King James. [In verse.] s.sh.fol. *f. J. T*[*rundle*] *a. H. G*[*osson,* 1625.] L⁵ (Lemon 259).

— A most humble supplication. 1620. *See* 563.5.

— The new man or, a supplication unto James, monarch. 1622. *See* 1705.

14426.7 — A new song to the great comfort and rejoycing of all true English harts. Ballad. 1/2 sh.fol. [*Edinburgh,*] *R. Walde-grave,* [1603.] HD.

14427 — Northerne poems congratulating the Kings majesties entrance to the crowne. *Lat. a. Eng.* 4°. *J. Windet f. E. Weaver,* 1604. Ent. 14 my. L.YK.

14428 — A petition to the Kings majestie, the Lords and Commons of the Parliament. [Arguments against their imprisonment by 'prisoners for debt, in the severall prisons of England.'] 4°. [*E. Allde,*] 1622. L.L³⁰.O. C.LINC.+; F.HN.HD.ILL.NY.+
>See also 14961.5, 14961.7.

14429 — Series patefacti nuper parricidii. 1605. = 1401.

— A short discourse of the good ends of the higher providence [etc.]. 1600. *See* 348 sq.

James I, *King of England*—APPENDIX—*cont.*

14429.5 — The supplication of certaine masse-priests [14432]. Published with a marginall glosse. 4°. [*G. Eld a. V. Simmes*] *f. W. Aspley,* 1604. Ent. 28 mr. L.O³.C⁸. LIV.M².+; ILL.N.Y.
>(Formerly 14431) Collates A–N⁴ O². Simmes pr. sheets F to end. Apparently attrib. to M. Sutcliffe on A2ʳ of 20144.

14430 — [Anr. ed.] Againe reuewed [*sic*] and augmented. 4°. [*G. Eld*] *f. W. Aspley,* 1604. L.O.C².NEK.PETYT.+; F.U.Y.
>Collates A–Q⁴; B3 missigned C3.

14430.5 — [Anr. ed.] 4°. [*G. Eld*] *f. W. Aspley,* 1604. L².O.C².D. DUL.+; HN.HD.NY¹¹.
>Collates A–Q⁴; B3 correctly signed; sheets P and Q from same setting as 14430.

14431 — Now = 14429.5.

14432 — A supplication to the kings most excellent majestie. [Anon. Attrib. to J. Colleton.] 4°. [*English secret press,*] 1604. L.O.C³.D².YK.+; F.HN.N.NY.U.
>A&R 247. Reprinted and answered in 14429.5, 20144. Some copies (L, 2 O, F) have errata added on G2ᵛ and alterations in sheet G.

— . . . To the kinges majestie. The humble petition of preachers. [1605?] *See* 16779.12.

— To the kings most excellent majestie: . . . The humble petition of . . . the prisoners for debt in the Kings Bench. [1621?] *See* 14961.5.

— To the right high and mightie prince, James, [etc.] 1609. *See* 14339.

— A treatise declaring, and confirming against all objections the title and right of prince, James the sixt. [1599.] *See* 19881.5.

— The triumphs of king James. 1610. *See* 17309.

— Triumphus Jacobi. [Engr. w. verses. c. 1624.] *See* 11511.5.

14433 — The true narration of the entertainment of his majestie, from his departure from Edenbrough. 1603. = 17153.

14434 — A true, modest, and just defence of the petition for reformation. 1618. = 6469.

James IV, *King of Scotland.* A ballade of the scottysshe kynge. [1513.] *See* 22593.

14435 **James V,** *King of Scotland.* Ad serenissimum . . . Jacobum Quintum . . . strena. [In verse.] 4°. (*Ediburgi* [*sic*], *ap. T. Dauidson,*) [1535–40?] L.

James, Dane, *tr.* See 4815.

14435.5 **James, Edward.** A retrayt sounded to certaine brethren. 4°. *S. Stafford,* 1607. Ent. 22 my. L.C¹⁷.; CAL⁶.

14436 **James, Leonard.** A true relation of the . . . murther, of Master James. Committed by one Lowe his curate. 4°. *f. R. Bonian a. H. Walley,* sold [*by R. Bonian,*] 1609. Ent. to R. Bonian 19 my. L.NOR².

14437 **James, Richard.** Anti-Possevinus, sive concio habita ad clerum in academiâ Oxoniensi. 4°. *Oxoniæ, J. Lichfield & G. Turner,* 1625. L(imp.).O.D.E.P.+; F.

14438 — An apologeticall essay for the righteousnes. 1632. = pt. of 14442.

14439 — Concio habita ad clerum Oxoniensem de ecclesia. 4°. *Oxoniæ, J. Lichfield & veneunt ap. T. Huggins,* 1633. L.O.C.A.P.+; F.HD.Y.

14440 — The muses dirge, consecrated to the remembrance of James, King of Great Brittaine. (Anagramata Anglica–Latina.) [In verse.] 4°. *A. M*[*athewes*] *a. J. N*[*orton*] *f. J. Browne,* 1625. L.; HN.

14441 — A sermon concerning the eucharist. Delivered in Oxford. [Anon.] 4°. [*T. Harper?*] *f. R. Allot,* 1629. L.O.E.NEP.P.+; HN.DAR.

14442 — A sermon concerning the times of receiving the sacrament. (An apologeticall essay. . . .) 4°. *J. B*[*eale*]. *f. N. Butter,* 1632. L.O.C.OS.P.+; F.HD(2nd pt. only). N.U.
>(14438 is pt. of this)

14443 — A sermon delivered in Oxford. Concerning the Apostles preaching and ours. (Concerning the observation of Lent-fast.) 4°. *W. Stansby f. N. Butter,* 1630. L.O.C. C².P.+; F(lacks 2nd pt.).HN.MCG(2nd pt. only).

— *ed. See* 18087.

— *tr. See* 17953.

14444 **James, Thomas,** *Captain.* The strange and dangerous voyage of captaine Thomas James. With an appendix concerning longitude, by H. Gellibrand. 4°. *J. Legatt f. J. Partridge,* 1633. Ent. 19 mr. L.O.C.D².M.+; F. HN.HD.N.NY.+
Copies vary; S4ᵛ signed 'X. Z.' or 'William Watts'; both at L, F.

14445 **James, Thomas,** *D.D.* An apologie for John Wickliffe. 4°. *Oxford, J. Barnes,* 1608. L.O.C.D.G².+; F.HN.HD.N.NY.+
Most (? all) copies issued w. 25589.

14446 — Bellum Gregorianum sive corruptionis Romanæ in operibus D. Gregorii editis, ex typographia Vaticana, loca insigniora. 4°. *Oxoniæ, J. Barnesius,* 1610. L.O.O³(A1,2 only).D.M².

14447 — Bellum papale, sive concordia discors circa Hieronymianam editionem. 4°. *G. Bishop, R. Newberie, & R. Barker,* 1600. Ent. 31 my. L.O.C.D.YK.+; HN.CHI.HD.LC.NY¹¹.
A2ʳ line 8 ends: 'Paulo'. Some copies (O, C, LC) have date altered in ink to '1606'.

14447.5 — [Anr. ed.] 4°. *G. Bishop, R. Nevvberie, & R. Barker* [*really printed abroad,*] 1600. L.O³.O⁶.C².WN.+; F.LC.U.WIS.
A2ʳ line 8 ends: 'sed'.

14448 — Catalogus interpretum S. Scripturæ. [*Ed.* J. Verneuil.] 4°. *Oxoniæ, J. Lichfield,* 1635. L.O.C.D.E.+; F.HN.CHI.HD.Y.+
Expanded version of pp. 163–79 of 14449.

14449 — Catalogus librorum bibliothecæ publicæ quam Thomas Bodleius in academia Oxoniensi nuper instituit. 4°. *Oxoniæ, ap. J. Barnesium,* 1605. L.O.C⁵.D.E².+; F.HN.LC.NY.Y.

14449.5 — [Anr. issue, w. headlines, borders, etc. removed and the text reimposed 9 pages to a sheet, pr. on 1 side only.] fol(at least 3). [*Oxford, J. Barnes,* 1605.] O(3 imp. sheets).
Intended for posting on the ends of Bodleian bookcases as a guide to the contents of the shelves.

14450 — [Anr. ed.] Catalogus universalis librorum in bibliotheca Bodleiana. 4° in 8's. *Oxoniæ, J. Lichfield a. J. Short, imp. Bodleianis,* 1620. L(2).O(6).C.D.E².+; F.HN.HD.N.NY.+
Most copies lack the 1620 Appendix, present in 1 L, 1 O, and have in its place 14451. R4 and Nn3 are usually cancels; the orig. leaves are present in 1 L, 1 O, O¹⁴(R4 only), O¹⁷, O¹⁹(R4 only), and Juel-Jensen.

14451 — Appendix ad catalogum librorum in bibliotheca Bodleiana. Editio secunda. [*Ed.* J. Rous.] 4°. *Oxoniae, J. Lichfield,* 1635. L.O.C.D.E².+; F.HN.CHI.HD.Y.+

14452 — Concordantiæ sanctorum patrum hoc est libri canticorum expositio. 4°. *Oxoniæ, J. Barnesius,* 1607. O.C.E².YK. Armagh PL.+
Ed. small, prob. less than 100 copies.

14453 — Ecloga Oxonio-Cantabrigiensis, tributa in libros duos. [A catalogue of manuscripts.] 2 pts. 4°. (*A. Hatfield,*) *imp. G. Bishop & J. Norton,* 1600. Ent. 25 jn. L.O.C.D.E².+; F.HN.HD.N.U.+

14454 — An explanation or enlarging of the ten articles in the supplication of doctor James [14455], lately exhibited to the clergy of England. 4°. *Oxford, J. Lichfield a. W. Turner,* 1625. L.O.C.D.DUR⁵.+; HN.BO.HART.NY.U.

14455 — [Heading A1ʳ:] The humble and earnest request of Thomas James, in the behalfe of bookes touching religion. 8°. [*Oxford?* 1625?] L(2).O.D².
Reprinted and explained in 14454.

14456 — The humble supplication of Thomas James, for reformation of the ancient fathers workes. s.sh.fol. *J. Windet,* [c. 1607.] O.

14457 — Index generalis librorum prohibitorum à pontificiis. 12°. *Oxoniæ, G. Turner,* 1627. L.O.C.D.E.+; HN.HD(imp.).N.NY.Y.+

14458 — Index generalis sanctorum patrum. . . . 8°. *ex off. J. Haviland, sumpt. P. Stephens,* 1624. Ent. 26 de. 1623. L³.O.C.D.YK.+
Really pr. at the expenses of Sir H. Lynde.

14459 — The Jesuits downefall, threatned against them by the secular priests. Together with the life of Father Parsons. 4°. *Oxford, Jos. Barnes, sold* [*in London*] *by John Barnes,* 1612. L.O.C.M².WOR.+; F.HN.HD.N.NY.+

14460 — A manuduction, or introduction unto divinitie. 4°. [*London, I. Jaggard,*] *f. H. Cripps a. H. Curteyne at Oxford,* 1625. L.O.C.D.E.+; F.HN.HD.N.U.+

James, Thomas, *D.D.—cont.*

14461 — Specimen corruptelarum pontificiarum in Cypriano. Inscriptum clero Anglicano. [Anon.] 4°. *G. Miller,* 1626. Ent. 25 mr. O.O².O⁹.O²⁴.

14462 — A treatise of the corruption of scripture, councels, and fathers, by the prelats, of the Church of Rome. Divided into V parts. 4°. *H. L[ownes] f. M. Lownes,* 1611. Ent. to H. Lownes 16 au. L.O.C⁴.D.E.+; F.HN.ILL.U.Y.+

14463 — [A variant, w. date:] 1612. L.O.C.D.E.+; F.HN.HD.N.Y.+
— *ed. See* 958.5, 25589, 25935.
— *tr. See* 3928, 7374.

14464 **James, William,** *Bp.* A sermon preached at Paules crosse the ix. of Nouember, 1589. 4°. *G. Bishop a. R. Newberie,* 1590. Ent. 25 jn. L.L².O.C.COL.+; HN.U.Y.

14465 — A sermon preached before the queenes maiestie the 19. of February laste paste. 8°. *H. Bynneman,* 1578 (24 ap.)Ent. 26 ap. L.L⁴.O.C.P.+; F.HN. Cincinnati U.
— *See also* 10192.6.

14465.5 **Jameson, R.** Some just reflexions on a nonsensical pasquill against the parson of Banchory. [Init. R. J.] 4°. *Edinburgh, A. Symson,* 1606 [i.e. 1706.] L.

14466 **Janua.** Janua linguarum, sive modus maxime accommodatus. [By W. Bathe.] Cum translatione Anglicana [by] (W. Welde.) *Lat. a. Eng.* 4°. *H. L[ownes] imp. M. Lownes,* 1615. Ent. 29 ja. 1614. L.L³⁰(imp.).O.; HN.N.
The Latin-Spanish text was first pub'd in Salamanca in 1611. Not to be confused with the *Janua linguarum reserata* of J. A. Komenský (15077.3 sqq.).

14466.5 — Editio secunda. 4°. *H. L[ownes] imp. M. Lownes,* 1616. O.O³(imp.). Aberystwyth UC.

14467 — [Anr. ed., revised and enlarged.] Janua linguarum, quadrilinguis. Or a messe of tongues: Latine, English, French, and Spanish. 4° in 8's. *R. F[ield] imp. M. Lownes,* 1617. L.O.C.BHP.G².+; F.HN.HD.N.TEX.+
French tr. by 'J. Barbier', probably a pseudonym for I. Habrecht; this version is expanded in 14472.3. Prelims. vary from 14466 and 14466.5.

14467.5 — [Anr. issue, w. A1,2 cancelled and replaced by 2 leaves, w. title:] Janua linguarum quadrilinguis: . . . Sive modus maximè accommodatus. *R. Field, imp. M. Lownes,* 1617. O.P.
The 2nd leaf has Welde's dedic. to C. Edmondes as in previous eds.

14467.7 — [Anr. ed. of 14466.] [1619?] *See* Addenda.

14468 — [Anr. ed. of 14466.] Janua linguarum, sive modus maxime accommodatus. Editio quarta. *Lat. a. Eng.* 4°. *H. L[ownes] imp. M. Lownes,* 1621. L.; ILL.

14468.5 — Editio quinta. 4°. *H. L[ownes] imp. M. Lowns,* 1623. D.; HD.ILL.Y.

14469 — [Anr. ed.] Janua linguarum, sive methodus et ratio compendiaria. Editio sexta. [*Ed.*] J. Harmar [the younger.] 4°. *in off. H. Lownes,* 1626. L.O.O¹². LEIC(lacks tp)*. St. Albans School, Hertfordshire.

14470 — [Anr. issue, w. date:] 1627. C.D.; ILL.

14471 — Editio septima. 4°. *in off. R. Young,* (sold by G. Lathum,) 1631. Ent. to R. Young 6 de. 1630. O(imp.).WN.; F(2).HD.
2nd tp in English: 'Janua linguarum, or, an easie and compendious method for attaining all tongues'.

14472 — Editio octava, opera T. Horne. Supplementum T. Poole. 8°. *in æd. R. Young,* (sold by G. Lathum,) 1634. O.C.DUL.M.NLW.+; HN.ILL.PN.

14472.3 — [A version in 6 languages.] Janua linguarum silinguis, Latina, Germanica, Gallica, Italica, Hispanica, Anglica. Cum introductione, et duplici indice. Auctore I. Habrechto. 8°. *Argentinæ* [*Strassburg,*] *sumpt. E. Zetzneri,* 1629. L.C.; F.HD.N.
Augmented from 14467.

14472.5 — [Anr. ed.] 8°. *Argentinæ* [*Strassburg,*] *sumpt. E. Zetzneri,* 1630. O.

14473 — Janua linguarum reserata. 1638. Now = 15077.5.

14474 — Fift edition. [*Ed.*] by J. Robotham. 1640. Now = 15077.7.

Japan. A briefe relation of the persecution . . . in Japonia. 1619. *See* 14527.

14475 — The theater of Japonia's constancy: in which martyrs suffered death in 1622. Also a briefe relation of the miracles, in Spayne. *Tr.* out of Spanish [by W. Lee.] 4°. [*St. Omer, English College Press,*] 1624. L.L⁴³.P. USHAW.YK.; HD.
A&R 812.

Japan—*cont.*
— *See* also 18482.

14476 **Jarret, John.** I tell you, John Jarret, you'l breake. *Ballad.* 2 pts. s.sh.fol. [*M. Flesher f. F. Grove,* 1630.] Ent. to F. Grove 20 de. 1630. c⁶.

Jasme, Jean. *See* 4589 sqq.

Jason. The veray trew history of the valiaūt knight Jasō. 1492. *See* 15384.

14477 **Jasper [Tudor],** *Duke of Bedford.* The epitaffe of the moste noble & valyaunt Iasper late duke of Beddeforde. [Signed 'Smerte maister de ses [Henry VII's] ouzeaus.' In verse.] 4⁰ ⁶·⁴. [*R. Pynson,* 1496.] c⁶. Duff 233.
(Formerly also 22605) Pynson's name in device McK 9a.

Jaurar Ben Abdella. The arrivall . . . of Alkaid Jaurar [etc.] 1637. *See* 18165.

14478 **Java.** A true report of the gainefull, voiage to Jaua the first of maie 1598. 4⁰. *P. S[hort] f. W. Aspley,* [1599?] L.L¹³.O⁵.G². Rotterdam, Prins Hendrik Maritime Museum.; F.LC.NY.

14479 **Jay, George.** A sermon preacht at the funerall of the Lady Mary Villiers [etc.] 8⁰. *f. T. Harper,* 1626. L³. L⁴⁶.C².

14479.3 — A sermon preached before his majestie at the court at Greenewich the 2. of July. 1632. 4⁰. *A. Mathewes,* 1632. Ent. 2 ja. 1633. P.PLUME.; F.HD.

Jay, Nicholas le. Le tocsin. 1611. *See* 1845.

14479.7 **Jeamie,** *of Woodicock Hill.* A proper new ballad, shewing a merrie jest of one Jeamie of Woodicock Hill, and his wife. 1/2 sh.fol. [*London,* c. 1610.] O.

14480 **Jeanes, Henry.** A treatise concerning a christians carefull abstinence from all appearance of evill. 12⁰. Oxford, *W. Turner f. H. Curteine,* 1640. L³.O³.C.BRISTOL. CARLISLE.+; U.

14481 **Jefferay, Richard.** The sonne of Gods entertainment by the sonnes of men. A sermon. 4⁰. *T. P[urfoot] f. H. Tomes,* 1605. Ent. 12 no. 1604. O.O¹⁶.; F.U.Y.

Jeffereys, Thomas. Almanacks. 1623, etc. *See* 464.5 sq.

14482 **Jeffray, William.** Ὁδὸς τεθλιμμένη. The narrow way to glory. Delivered in a sermon. 12⁰. *T. Cotes f. R. Hawkins,* 1634. Ent. 6 de. 1633. O.

14483 — The picture of patience. Or, a direction to perfection. 12⁰. *T. H[arper] f. R. Milbourne,* 1629. Ent. 18 ap. 1628. O.

14483.5 **Jeffreys, John.** [Newes from Virginia or Virginia stript naked.] 4⁰. [*R. Bird,* 1624.] Ent. to Bird 28 jy. 1624. No copy traced.
Frags. of the 1st 4 leaves, binder's waste, were examined by F. S. Ferguson.

14484 **Jegon, John,** *Bp.* [Direction to archdeacons enjoining the teaching of 14418.5.] s.sh.fol. Cambridge, *C. Legge,* 1616. O(2, 1 = J).
See also 5870.3, 18228.5.

14484.3 **Jehovah.** Jehovah. A free pardon. First written in Spanish. *Tr.* J. Danyel. 8⁰ in 4's. *T. East f. A. Maunsell,* [1576.] L².

14484.7 **Jemmatt, William.** Corona pietatis. The memoriall of the just. A sermon. 12⁰. *E. A[llde] f. S. Man,* 1627. Ent. 5 de. 1626. O²⁷.

14485 — A spirituall trumpet: exciting and preparing to the christian warfare. 12⁰. *J. H[aviland] f. J. Bartlet,* 1624. ?Ent. to J. Bartlet 29 mr. 1623. L.O.; Y.

14486 **Jeninges, Edward.** A briefe discouery of the damages that happen to this realme by disordered and unlawfull diet. 4⁰. *R. Ward,* 1590. Ent. 9 fb. L(2).; HN.HD.

14487 — [Anr. ed.] 4⁰. *R. Warde,* 1593. L.L².O⁸.C.HAT.+
— *ed. See* 23821, 23823, 23837, 23849.
— *tr. See* 3184.8, 14836.7.

14488 **Jenison, Robert.** The christians apparelling by Christ. 8⁰. *A. M[athewes] a. J. N[orton] f. J. Browne,* 1625. Ent. to R. Milbourne a. J. Browne 5 de. 1624 [i.e. 5 ja. 1625?] L.L²O.INN.; U.
John Browne 'at the signe of the crane in Pauls churchyard' is an apparently unrecorded, non-Catholic publisher.

Jenison, Robert—*cont.*
14489 — The cities safetie: or, a fruitfull treatise on psalm 127. 8⁰. *J. Haviland f. J. Bellamie,* 1630. Ent. 6 mr. L.O. C(3, 1 lacks tp).C³.INN.; F.HN.PN².

14490 — Directions for the worthy receiving of the Lords supper. 8⁰. [*G. Purslowe*] *f. J. Harrigat,* 1624. Ent. 27 mr. O.

14491 — The height of Israels heathenish idolatrie. 4⁰. (*G. Eld*) *f. R. Mylbourne,* 1621. Ent. 12 fb. L⁴.O.C.C⁵. Warwick County Record Office(imp.).; F.HN.HD.

14492 — Newcastles call, to her neighbour and sister townes and cities to take warning [etc.] 12⁰. *f. J. Coleby,* 1637. L.; HN.
— *See* also 11112, 11114.

Jenkinson, Anne, *tr. See* 2784.

14493 **Jenkinson, Daniel.** The triumph of faith. A . . . treatise. 8⁰. *E. Griffin f. S. Macham,* 1613. Ent. 1 no. O.; F.

14494 **Jenner, Thomas,** *Printseller, ed.* The soules solace, or thirtie and one spirituall emblems. [Init. T. I. In verse.] obl.8⁰. [*J. Dawson,*] sold by *T. Jenner,* 1626. L.
(Formerly also 22940)

14495 — [Anr. ed.] 8⁰. [*J. Dawson,*] sold by *T. Jenner,* 1631. L.O.; HN.
(Formerly also 22941)

14496 — [Anr. ed.] 8⁰. *E. P[urslowe] f. H. Overton,* 1639. HN.

14497 **Jenney, George.** A catholike conference, betweene a protestant and a papist. 4⁰. *J. D[awson] f. N. Bourne,* 1626. ?Ent. 24 mr. L.O.E.EX.LIV³.+; F.

Jennings, Miles, *tr. See* 17203.

Jennings, Ralph, *tr. See* 860.

14498 **Jenynges, Edward.** The notable hystory of two faithfull louers named Alfagus and Archelaus. *Tr.* by E. Jenynges. 1574. Now = 3184.8.

14498.5 **Jephtha.** ⟨ ⟩ When Jepha judge of Israel. *Ballad.* 1/2 sh.fol. *f. T. L[angley,* c. 1620.] Ent. to the ballad partners 14 de. 1624. M³(imp.).

Jeremiah [Katsaïtes], *Bp. of Mani. See* 3047.5.

14499 **Jeremiah,** *the prophet.* An epistle of the pphete Hieremie. [bef. 1540.] = 2792.
— The lamentations and holy mourninges of the prophet Jeremiah. [1587?] *See* 2779.5.

14500 **Jermin, Michael.** A commentary, upon the whole booke of Ecclesiastes. fol. *R. Hodgkinsonne f. J. Clark,* 1639. Ent. 7 de. 1638. L.O.C.D.E².+; F.HN.HD.ILL.U.+

14500.5 — [Anr. issue of 14500 and 14501, w. added gen. tp:] An exposition upon the two doctrinall bookes of King Solomon: the Proverbs, and Ecclesiastes. *R. H[odgkinson] f. P. Stephens a. C. Meredith,* 1639. GRO.

14501 — Paraphrasticall meditations, by way of commentarie, upon the proverbs of Solomon. fol. *R. Badger f. P. Stephens a. C. Meredith,* 1638. Ent. 12 de. 1637. L.O.C.D.E².+; F.HN.HD.ILL.U.+

Jerome, *of Brunswick. See* Hieronymus, *von Braunschweig.*

Jerome, *of Ferrara. See* Savonarola.

14502 **Jerome,** *Saint.* Certaine selected epistles of S. Hierome [etc.] *Tr.* [H. Hawkins.] 4⁰. [*St. Omer, English College Press,*] 1630. L.O.C.USHAW.W.+; F.HN.N.U. Y.+
A&R 412.
— Exposicio sancti Ieronimi in simbolum apostoloru3. 1468 [1478.] *See* 21443.

14503 — An exposicyon vpon the .li. psalme. 1538. = 21790.

14504 — [Anr. ed.] A pithie exposition upon the 51 psalme. 1578. = 21797.

14505 — [Four tokens of judgement.] As Iheronimus, sheweth in this begynnynge, so wyll I wryte of the. iiij. tokens, afore the dredefull daye of dome. (*Tr.* out of Duche by J. Dousbrugh [i.e. Doesborch.]) 8⁰ in 4's. (*R. Wyer,*) [1535?] L.
Reprinted from 793.3.

14505.5 — Here begynneth a lytell treatyse called the rewle of saynt Jherome. 4⁰ in 6's. [*R. Pynson,* c. 1510.] P(imp.).

14506 — The psalter of Sainct Hierome. 1576. = Pt. 2 of 14563.5.

Jerome, *Saint—cont.*

14507 — Vitas patrum. (Here foloweth the . . . lyff of the olde auncyent holy faders hermytes. *Tr.* out of Frensshe by W. Caxton.) fol. (*Westmynstre, W. de worde,* 1495.) L.O.C².G².M.+; F.HN.ILL.NY.Y.+ Duff 235.
One L copy has some leaves reprinted c. 1529 w. a woodcut of about that date; *see* Hodnett, p. 10 and no. 854.

14508 — [Vita.] The fyrst chapitre is the lyf of saint ierom as it is take of legenda aurea. [By S. Winter, of Syon Abbey.] 4° in 8's. [*Westminster, W. de Worde,* 1499?] L. Duff 236.
— *See* also 919.

14509 **Jerome, Stephen.** Englands jubilee, or Irelands joyes Io-pæn, for King Charles his welcome. 1625. Now = 14511.5.

14510 — The haughty heart humbled: or, the penitents practice. 4°. [*M. Flesher*] *f. R. More,* 1628. Ent. 15 no. 1627. O.O².DUL.EX.; HN.

14511 — Irelands jubilee, or joyes Io-pæn, for Prince Charles his welcome home. 4°. *Dublin, Soc. of Statrs.,* 1624. L.D.

14511.5 — [Anr. issue, w. title:] Englands jubilee, or Irelands joyes Io-pæn, for King Charles his welcome. 4°. *Dublin, Soc. of Statrs.,* 1625. O.C.D⁶.G².P.+
(Formerly 14509)

14512 — Moses his sight of Canaan. 8°. [*T. Snodham*] *f. R. Jackson,* 1614. Ent. 27 jn. 1613. L⁴.O(imp.).

14512.3 — [Anr. issue, w. dedic. and epistle added.] Seaven helpes to heaven. Second edition. 8°. [*T. Snodham*] *f. R. Jackson,* 1614. HD.
(Formerly 14514) Presumably a reissue of 14516 was also intended, but HD has only sheets of 14512, i.e. what becomes Helps 4–6 of 14512.7.

14512.7 — Third edition: corrected and enlarged. 8°. *J. W[hite] a. A. M[athewes] f. R. Jackson,* 1620 (1619.) L.O. C.; F.HD(imp.).LC.
(Formerly 14515)

14513 — Origens repentance: after he had sacrificed to the idols of the heathen. [In verse.] 4°. *J. Beale f. R. Jackson,* 1619. Ent. 20 jy. 1618. L.O(2).NLW.; F.HN.Y.
Regarding authorship of this *see* note to 13538.5.

14514 — Seaven helpes to heaven. 1614. Now = 14512.3.
14515 — Third edition. 1620. Now = 14512.7.
14516 — A serious fore-warning to avoide the vengeance to come. Wherto is added, a treatise; of joy in tribulation . . . with godly prayers. Together with S. Bernards meditations. Corrected and augmented, by S. Jerome. 2 pts. 8°. *G. Eld f. R. Jackson,* 1613. Ent. 9 no. 1612. L.O.
Prob. intended to be reissued in 14512.3; reprinted as Helps 1, 2, 7, 3 in 15412.7. In the preface Jerome disclaims authorship.

Jeronimo. The first part of Jeronimo. 1605. *See* 15085.

14516.5 **Jersey,** *Isle of.* The most wonderfull and strange finding of a chayre of gold, neare the Isle of Iarsie. 4°. [*T. Creede,* 1595.] Ent. to T. Creede 22 mr. 1595. Société Jersiaise, St. Hélier, Jersey(tp torn).

Jerusalem. The begynnynge and foundacyon of the knyghtes hospytallers of. 1524. *See* 15050.

14517 — The dystruccyon of Iherusalem by Vaspazyan and Tytus. 4°. (*R. Pynson,*) [1513?] C.

14518 — [Anr. ed.] 4° ⁴·⁸. (*w. de worde,*) [1510?] L.
This prob. precedes 14517.

14519 — [Anr. ed.] 4° ⁴·⁸. (*W. de Worde,* 1528 (23 ja.)) PML.
— The spiritual pilgrimage of Hierusalem. [1604–05.] *See* 12574.

14520 **Jessop, Edmund.** A discovery of the errors of the English anabaptists. 4°. *W. Jones f. R. Bird,* 1623. Ent. 6 jn. L.O.C.D⁵.E.+; F.HN.COLG(2).U.Y.
Authorship attrib. to J. Hetherington on G3ʳ of 6607.5. *See* also 15111.

Jest. Here begynneth a lytell geste how the plowman lerned his pater noster. [1510.] *See* 20034.
— Here begynneth a lytell propre ieste, called cryste crosse me spede. a.b.c. [c. 1530.] *See* 14546.5.
— A mery gest how a sergeāut woldel erne [*sic*] to be a frere. [1516?] *See* 18091.

14520.5 — [A merry jest of an old fool with a young wife. In verse.] 4°. (*Southwarke, by my P. Treueris,*) [1530?] L(2 leaves, B1 and its conjugate).
'Lenvoy of the prynter' begins: 'Go lytell boke vnto these olde foles/ That dooth them mary to lusty yonge [wives.]'

Jest—*cont.*

14521 — Here begynneth a merry ieste of a shrewde and curste wyfe. [In verse.] 4°. *H. Jackson,* [1580?] O(imp.). SH(frag.).; HN.

14522 — Here begynneth a mery geste of the frere and the boye. [In verse.] 4° in 8. (*W. de Worde,*) [1510–13.] C.

14522.5 — [Anr. ed.] 4°. (*W. Myddylton,*) [c. 1545.] Ent. to J. Waley, 1557–58. L(frag.).

14522.7 — [Anr. ed.] Heer beginneth a mery iest of of [*sic*] the frier and the boy. 4°. (*E. Alde,*) [1584–89.] Ent. to J. Allde 1568–69. O.
(Formerly 14524)

14523 — [Anr. ed.] The fryer, an⟨d⟩ the boy. 8°. *E. A[llde,]* 1617. O(tp cropt).

14524 — Now = 14522.7.
14524.3 — [Anr. ed.] Here beginneth a merry jest, of the fryer and the boy. 8°. *E. Allde,* 1626. F.

14524.5 — ⟨O⟩r, a pretty jest of a bride and a bridegroom, where the bridegroom was most neately deceived by a servingman. Ballad. 2 pts. s.sh.fol. [*G. Purslowe,* c. 1630.] C⁶(I.122–3ᵛ, cropt).
6366 is pr. on the verso.

14524.7 **Jesuits.** Aphorismi doctrinæ Jesuitarum & . . . pontificiorum doctorum. 12°. [*Eliot's Court Press,*] 1608. L.O.O³.O¹².D.; F.
There are 4° eds. of this date pr. abroad.

14525 — [A trans.] Aphorismes. Or, certaine selected points of the doctrine of the Jesuits. 4°. *London, printed by permission of the superiors,* [*W. Hall f. J. Bill,*] 1609. Ent. to J. Bill 9 my. L.O.C.E.CHATS.+; F.HN.CHI.HD. NY.+
— Articles made . . . touching the Jesuits. 1612. *See* 16829.5.

14526 — The articles which were propounded to the Jesuites the 14. of March, 1626. (Censure de la sacree faculte de theologie de Paris.) *Eng. a. Fr.* 2 pts. 4°. *Rouan, J. Besonge* [i.e. *London, B. Alsop a. T. Fawcet,*] 1626. L.O.C.
The French version may have been pr. by M. Flesher.

14526.5 — A bloody tragedie, or romish maske. Acted by five Jesuites, and sixteene young Germaine maides. Presented in Germanie in March 1607. *Tr.* out of High-Dutch. 4°. [*A. Islip?*] *f. E. E[dgar?]* 1607. Ent. to J. Trundle 7 no. F.

14527 — A briefe relation of the persecution lately made against the catholike christians, in Japonia. The first part. [Anon. By P. Morejon.] *Tr.* W. W[right.] 8°. [*St. Omer, English College Press,*] 1619. L.O.D.DUR⁵.HP. +; F.TEX.
A&R 550. Tr. from the Spanish orig. pr. in Mexico in 1616 (Medina II.72).
— Controversia illustris, hoc est, responsio ad libellum a patribus Soc. Jesu scriptum. 1625. *See* 5646.
— De studiis Jesuitarum abstrusioribus. 1609. *See* 4469.5.

14528 — A discoverie of the most secret and subtile practises of the Jesuites. *Tr.* out of French. 4°. [*G. Eld*] *f. R. Boulton,* 1610. Ent. 4 oc. L.O.DUR⁵.; F.HN.AAS.HD.PH.

14529 — An exact and sound discovery of the chiefe mysteries of Jesuiticall iniquity. Published in Italian, *tr.* I. B(argrave.) 12°. [*W. Jaggard*] *f. P. Paxton,* 1619. Ent. to W. Jaggard 8 mr. L(imp.).O(lacks tp).C² (imp.).C³(imp.).PLUME.
A trans. of 'Instruttione à prencipi . . . si governano li padri Giesuiti', Poschiavo, 1617, now attrib. to Fulgentio Micanzio. Prob. suppressed by order of Buckingham.
— Good newes from France. Containing the insolent demands of the Jesuites. 1624. *See* 11274.

14530 — Jesuita vapulans; or a whip for the fools back. [1681.] = Wing J 707.
— The Jesuites catechisme. 1602. *See* 19449.

14531 — The Jesuites comedie. Acted at Lyons. (Recit touchant la comedie jouee par les Jesuites, en la ville de Lyons.) 4°. *E. Allde, solde by A. Johnson,* 1607. Ent. to Allde a. Johnson 14 oc. O.; F.Y.
(2nd pt. formerly 14532) *See* also 21513.5.

14532 — Recit touchant la comedie jouee par les Jesuites. 1607. = 2nd pt. of 14531.

14533 — The Jesuites gospel. 1610. = 6016.
— The Jesuits miracles. 1607. *See* 20340.

14534 — The Jesuites pater noster given to Phillip III King of Spaine for his new yeares gift. Englished by W. I. [In verse.] 8°. *Oxford, Jos. Barnes* [really *London? T. Dawson?*] 1611. L(cropt).O(imp.).

Jesuits—*cont.*

14535 — The legend of the Jesuites. . . . Now done into English. 4°. *A. M[athewes] f. T. Dewe*, 1623. Ent. 31 de. 1622. L.O.C.LEIC.M(deposit).+; HN.

14536 — A peece of ordinance invented by a Jesuite. [1644?] = Wing P 2160.

14537 — A relation of the late journey of the Jesuites. 4°. [*G. Eld*,] 1620. L⁴.O².O⁵.O¹⁷.LEIC.; HN.BO.
 — The state-mysteries of the Jesuites. 1623. *See* 12092.
 — Troubles in Bohemia. Procured by Jesuites. 1619. *See* 3213.

14538 — Two spare keyes to the Jesuites cabinet. 1632. Now = 11346.3.

Jesus Christ. [Arms of, in woodcuts.] *See* Indulgences 15, 16.

14539 — A brife and faythfull declaration of the true fayth of Christ. Per me I. B. 1547. Now = 1034.7.

14540 — [Anr. ed.] A bryfe and faythfull declaration of yᵉ true fayth of Chryst. 1547. Now = 1035.5.

14540a — [Anr. issue of 14539, w. additional prelim. matter.] A bryefe and plaine declaracion of certayne sentēces in this litle boke. 1547. = 1035.
 — Certaine deuout petitions. 1575, etc. *See* 14563.3 sqq.
 — Christ in the clouds. 1635. *See* 25078.

14541 — Christ on his throne. Or, Christs church-government briefly laid downe. [Attrib. to H. Burton.] 4°. [*R. Hearne?*] 1640. L.O.C².D.P.+; F.HN.HD.N.U.+

14542 — Christs kingdome discovered. 1615. Now = 24175.3.

14543 — Christs teares over Ierusalem. Or, a caveat for England. *Ballad.* 2 pts. s.sh.fol. *f. H. Gosson*, [c. 1640.] Ent. to H. Gosson a. ballad ptnrs. 14 de. 1624. L.

14544 — A christian conference betweene Christ and a sinner. *Ballad.* 1/2 sh.fol. *assignes of T. Symcocke*, [1628–29.] Ent. to T. Nelson 7 no. 1586; to ballad ptnrs. 14 de. 1624. L.
 — Christus natus est. 1631. *See* 5209.5.
 — Christus redivivus. 1624. *See* 997.5.

14545 — A complaynt agaynst the wicked enemies of Christ. [In verse.] s.sh.fol. [*f. W. Pickering*, 1564.] Ent. to W. Pickering 4 se. 1564. HN.

14546 — Here begynneth a contemplacyon or medytacyon of the shedynge of the blood of our lorde Jhesu Cryste at seuen tymes. 4°. (*Westmynster, W. de worde*,) [1500?] R.; HN. Duff 107.

14546.3 — [Anr. ed.] The .vii. shedynges of the blode of Ihesu cryste. 4°. (*W. de Worde*, 1509.) C.DUR(Bamb.). (Formerly 14572)

14546.5 — Here begynneth a lytell propre ieste. Called cryste crosse me spede. a.b.c. How yᵗ good gosyps made a royall feest. [In verse.] 4°. (*W. de Worde*,) [1534?] Hofmann & Freeman Ltd.(imp.).
 — A demonstration of the trueth of that discipline which Christe hath prescribed. [1588.] *See* 24499.

14546.7 — A deuout intercescion and praier to our sauiour Jesu Christ. 4°. (*R. Fawkes*,) [1530?] C².

14547 — [Anr. ed.] 8°. (*R. wyer*,) [1550?] C².; F.

14547.5 — A deuout inuocacyon & prayer of all the blyssed names of Chryst. s.sh.fol. [*W. de Worde*, c. 1520.] L(Harl. 5919/143, imp.).

14548 — [D8ᵛ:] (Thus endeth the Dialogue or communicacion betwene our sauiour Jhesu Chryste and a sinner, lately *tr.* out of the Latin tonge.) 8°. (*south wark, J. Redman f. R. Redman*,) [1539?] F(lacks tp).
 — An exhortacion to the carienge of Chrystes crosse. [1555?] *See* 3480.5.

14549 — The generall signes and fore-runners of Christs comming. 8°. *M. F[lesher], sold by H. Gosson*, [c. 1625.] O.
 — Glad tydings from heaven: or Christs glorious invitation. [1633?] *See* 24065.

14550 — A gloryous medytacyon of Ihesus crystes passyon. 8°. (*R. Fakes*,) [c. 1523.] O.
 — The imytacyon and folowynge the blessed lyfe of cryste. 1503, etc. For this and other editions, to whomsoever assigned, *see* Thomas, à Kempis.

14551 — Hic incipit tractatus qui intitulatur Infancia saluatoris. 4°. [*Westminster, W. Caxton*, c. 1477.] MEL(1 leaf only).PML. Duff 222.
 — The hope of the faythful, declaryng the resurreccion of Jesys Chryst. [1555?] *See* 25249.

14552 — In the honor of yᵉ passion of our lorde. And the compassyon of our blyssed lady. 16° in 8's. (*R. Copland*, 1522.) A². (Formerly also 17535)
 — An inuocacyon gloryous. 1529. *See* 14563.

Jesus Christ—*cont.*

14552.3 — Itinerarium Iesu Christi: or, our blessed saviour his journall on earth. Digested into questions and answers. 12°. *J. Okes f. W. Lee*, 1639. Ent. to Okes 13 no. 1638; ass'd to Lee 11 ja. 1639. C.
 Engr. tp reads: 'Itinerarium Iesu Christi or the journeyes of our blessed saviour on earth.'
 — Jesus Psalter. *See* 14563.

14552.7 — [Life of Jesus Christ. In verse, w. woodcuts.] 16° in 8's. [*R. Copland*, 1533?] A²(imp.).
 — The manifold wisedome of God: in the grace of Jesus Christ. 1640. *See* 24959.5.

14553 — The myrrour or glasse of Christes passion. (*Tr.* J. Fewterer.) fol. (*R. Redman*, 1534 (12 de.)) L.O.C⁴ (lacks tp). Lord Kenyon.; F.HN.ILL.PML.Y³.+ For an extract *see* 20193.5.

14553.3 — A most godly and comfortable ballad of the glorious resurrection of our lord Jesus Christ. 2 pts. s.sh.fol. *f. F. Coules*, [1640?] Ent. to the ballad ptnrs. 14 de. 1624. L.
 — A new ditty, shewing the miracles of Jesus Christ. [c. 1625.] *See* 6922.7.

14553.7 — Here begȳneth yᵉ new notborune mayd vpō yᵉ passiō of cryste. [In verse.] 4°. (*J. Skot*,) [1535?] HN.
 A parody on 'The nutbrown maid', first published in 782.

14554 — [Begins:] O glorious Ihesu. [Death-bed prayers.] s.sh. fol. [*Westminster, W. Caxton*, c. 1484.] M. Duff 112. (Formerly also 6442)
 — O Ihesu endles swetnes. [1491.] *See* 20195.

14554.5 — O Lorde [etc. Poem in 8-line stanzas, each beginning with this phrase.] s.sh.fol. [*J. Day a. W. Seres?* 1549?] HN(2 frags.).
 The 2nd extant stanza begins: 'O Lorde thou dyddest thy fathers wrath pacify', and the poem also complains of slothful clergy.
 — Of the love of our only lord Jesus Christ. 1622. *See* 17658.

14555 — The opinion, judgement, and determination of two divines of the Church of England, concerning bowing at the name, Jesus. The one (H.B. Bachelour in Divinitie) of Cambridge, the other (I.H. Bachelour in Divinitie) of Oxford. [*Ed.*] (S.O[fwod?]) 8°. *Hambourgh, 1632. Reprinted [Amsterdam? successors of G. Thorp?]* 1634. L.O(2, 1 imp.).
 — Our lord his line of fathers. 1595. *See* 3874.5.

14556 — Our sauiour Iesus Christ hath not ouercharged his chirche with many ceremonies. [Attrib. to G. Joye.] 8°. (*Zijrik*) [i.e. Antwerp, the Widow of C. Ruremond?] 1543 (fb.). L.O.C.BUTE.; F.ILL.PML.

14557 — The passion of owr lord iesu christe wythe the contemplatiōs. (*Tr.*) 4° in 6's. [*Paris? f. A. Verard?* 1508?] L(frag., Harl.5919/37 and 44).L²(4 leaves, Frag. No. 38).O(imp.).C(frag.).G².+
 Regarding the Continental pr. and woodcuts *see* Hodnett, p. 41.

14558 — [Anr. ed., corrected and enlarged.] The passyon of our lorde. (*Tr.* out of frenche by A. Chertesey.) 4°. (*w. de worde*, 1521 (6 oc.)) O(lacks tp and last leaf).C(imp.).; BO.

14559 — [Anr. ed., w. colophon:] (Here endeth a goostly treatyse of the passyon of Christ.) 4°. (*W. de Worde*, 1532 (6 oc.)) L(lacks first 2 leaves).

14560 — The picture of Christ. 1611. = 12569.

14560.5 — A poeme declaring the real presence of Christ in the blessed sacrament of the aultar. s.sh.fol. *Doway, L. Kellam*, 1666. L.
 A&R 655.
 — The poor doubting christian drawne to Christ. 1635, etc. *See* 13726.5 sqq.

14561 — A proclamacyon of the hygh emperour Iesu Christ. 8°. (*R. Redman*,) [1534.] O.; CH.
 (Formerly also 14561b) No device; collates A⁸ B⁴.

14561a — [Anr. ed.] 8°. (*R. Redman*,) [1537.] F.
 McK. 3b on B8ᵛ; collates A–B⁸.

14561b — = 14561.

14562 — [Anr. ed.] 8°. [*J. Herford f.*] (*R. Kele*,) [1542–46.] L.

PSALTER OF JESUS

Note: The Psalter of Jesus was included in the text of some Salisbury Primers, e.g. 15978, and also printed as pt. 2 of 17263 sqq. and pt. 9 of 17278.4 sqq.

14563 — Ihesus. An inuocacyon gloryous named yᵉ psalter of Iesus. [Sometimes attrib. to R. Whitford.] 16° in 8's. (*R. Coplande*, 1529.) A².

Jesus Christ—PSALTER OF JESUS—*cont.*

14563.3 — [Anr. ed., revised.] Certaine deuout and godly petitions, commonly called, Iesus psalter. (Godly contemplations for the vnlearned.) 2 pts. 16° in 8's. *Antuerpiæ, ap. J. Foulerum,* 1575. O(lacks text of pt. 2).O⁵.

(Formerly 14565) A&R 413. Woodcut on verso of 1st tp. Sub tp pr. as D8ʳ of pt. 1.

The 'Godly contemplations' (= A&R 359) is a series of 61 woodcuts. It does not appear w. later eds. of the Psalter of Jesus but possibly was intended to be issued with 24626 sq., which have a short section w. the same heading but no woodcut series.

Attacked in 21685.

14563.5 — [Anr. ed.] (The psalter of Sainct Hierome.) 2 pts. 16° in 8's. *Antuerpiæ, ap. J. Foulerum,* 1575 (1576.) L.

(Formerly 14565 and 14506) A&R 414. No woodcut on verso of first tp.

14563.7 — [Anr. ed.] 16° in 8's. *Antuerpiæ, ap. J. Foulerum,* 1575 [i.e. *London, W. Carter?* 1579?] DE.M⁴.

A&R 415.

14564 — [Anr. ed.] 16° in 8's. *Rothomagi,* [*G. L'Oyselet*] *ap. H. Mareschalum,* 1580. L(imp.).; TEX(imp., bd. w. 24626.3).

A&R 416.

14565 — Now = 14563.3 and 14563.5.

14566 — [Anr. ed.] 1583. = pt. 2 of 17263.

14566.5 — [Anr. ed.] 8°. [*English secret press,* 1595–1600?] VAL.

A&R 417.

14567 — [Anr. ed.] 16° in 8's. [*J. Danter?*] 1596. L.

A&R 418. See Greg, *Register B,* p. 56.

14568 — [Anr. ed.] [1580–81.] Now = pt. 9 of 17278.4.

14568.3 — [Anr. ed., w. additions.] Six spiritual bookes, ful of marvelous pietie and devotion. [*Tr.* R. Gibbons? and J. Heigham; all *ed.* J. Heigham.] 2 pts. 12°. [*Douai, P. Auroi f. J. Heigham,*] (1604.) L²(books 1–3 only). COLWICH(imp.).

(Formerly 3369) A&R 766. Psalter of Jesus is book 4 and has an engr. tp, w. imprint: 'Doway, P. Ouroy, 1640 [*sic*]'; this tp w. the date erased is also found in the HN copy of 14569 and as the main tp in 14570.

Book 5 is correctly dated 1604.

14568.7 — The second edition. 2 pts. 12°. (*Douay,*) [*P. Auroi f.*] (*J. Heigham,*) 1611. L²⁶(lacks pt. 2).O(imp.).USHAW. Brailes Presbytery, near Shipston, Warks.(lacks tp).; F(lacks pt. 2).HD(lacks pt. 2).N(frag.).TEX(frag.).

A&R 767. Psalter of Jesus is pt. 2. N, TEX have only 'A tratise [*sic*] of the loue of God' by Luis, de Granada, tr. by J. Heigham, which appears only in this ed.

14569 — [Anr. ed.] 12°. *Douay,* [*P. Auroi f.*] *J. Heigham,* 1618. VAL(imp.).w. Claughton Presbytery, near Lancaster.; HN.

A&R 768. Psalter of Jesus is book 1; at least HN has the engr. sub tp mentioned in note to 14568.3.

14570 — [Anr. ed., without gen. tp, and w. engr. 1st tp:] The psalter of Jesus. Amplified, with figures. 12°. *Doway, P. Ouroy* (*f. J. Heigham—at s. Omers,* 1624.) L.C¹⁵. DE.HP.INN.+; HD(lacks Psalter of Jesus and engr. tp).

A&R 769. Psalter of Jesus is book 1; regarding its engr. tp *see* note to 14568.3.

14570.3 — [Anr. ed. of the Psalter of Jesus alone.] Certaine devout and godly petitions. 12°. [*St. Omer, English College Press,*] 1624. L.W.

A&R 419.

14571 — Here begynneth the rosary of our sauyour Iesu. [1526.] = pt. 2 of 3277.

14572 — The .vii. shedynges of the blode of Ihesu cryste. 1509. Now = 14546.3.

— The sinners redemption. Wherein is described the nativity of Jesus Christ. [1634?] *See* 22576.

14573 — A sparke of Christs beauty. [A sermon on Isai. ix. 6.] 4°. *Oxford, J. Lichfield a. J. Short,* 1622. L.L³⁰.; F.

14573.5 — A treatise of the principles of Christ his doctrine. Written Anno 1588. 16° in 8's. *T. Orwin f. T. Man,* [1588?] L².

14574 — A treatise, shewing the possibilitie, and conueniencie of the reall presence of our sauiour in the sacrament. 1596. Now = 26043.5.

14575 — A treatise wherin Christe and his techinges, are compared with the pope and his doinges. 8°. *in æd. T. Bertheleti,* 1534. F.

Jesus Christ—*cont.*

14576 — The true beliefe in Christ and his sacramentes. 1550. Now = 24223.5.

14577 — Two pleasant ditties, one of the birth, the other of the passion of Christ. *Ballad.* 2 pts. s.sh.fol. *assignes of T. Symcocke,* [1628–29.] Ent. to Mrs. Griffin 24 ap. 1640. L.

14577.5 — Whether the blode of Chryst suffyse to mānes redempcion. 8°. *J. Byddell,* [1536–37?] L(frag., Harl.5963/58).

— The wonderfull combate betweene Christ and Satan. 1592. *See* 629.

Jew. *See* Wandering Jew.

14578 **Jewel.** A jewel for gentlewomen. Containing divers godly prayers. 32° in 16's. *J. Beale,* 1624. L.

14579 **Jewel, John,** *Bp.* The works of the very learned J. Jewell, . . . And a briefe discourse of his life [by D. Featley]. 4 pts. fol. [*Eliot's Court Press f.*] *J. Norton,* 1609. L.O.C.D.E.+; F.HN.ILL.U.Y.+

14580 — [Anr. issue, w. date:] 1611. O.C.; N.

Sub tpp dated 1609.

14580.5 — [Anr. ed.] fol. *J. Norton,* 1611. L.O⁶.C.D².E.+; F.HN. HD.CHI.NY.+

Sub tpp dated 1611.

— Aduersus T. Hardingum, volumen. 1578. *See* 14607.5.

14581 — Apologia ecclesiæ anglicanæ. [Anon.] 8°. (*ap. R. wolfium,*) 1562. L.O.C.E².P.+; BO³.ILL.NY¹¹.PML.

Quire I, containing the 'Ecclesiæ anglicanæ administratio', was apparently an afterthought as the colophon containing Wolfe's name is on H4; it is lacking in many copies (L, C), but present in O.

14582 — [Anr. ed.] Authore J. Juello. 12°. *T. Vautrollerius,* 1581. L.O.C.A.M.+; F.HN.BO.N.U.+

14583 — [Anr. ed. Anon.] 8°. *Londini, ap. F. Bouuier,* 1584. L.O.C.C².C⁴.+; F.HN.

Prob. pr. abroad.

14584 — [Anr. ed.] Authore J. Juello. 12°. [*R. Robinson*] *imp. T. Chardi,* 1591. L.O.C.LEEDS.STD.+; F.HD.U.V.Y.+

Issued with 24750.

14585 — [Anr. ed.] 12°. *A. Hatfield,* 1599. Ent. to Bollifant a. Hatfield 13 jn. 1598. L.L¹⁵.O.C⁴.M.+; F.HD.ILL.MCG.

14586 — [Anr. ed.] 12°. [*Eliot's Court Press*] *imp. G. Bishop,* 1606. L.O.C.D.M.+; F.HN.COR.HD(imp.).N.+

14587 — [Anr. ed.] 12°. [*H. Lownes*] *imp. J. Boler,* 1626. Ass'd by A. Chard to J. Beale 10 oc. 1622. L.O.C.D.LYD.+; F.HN.N.TEX.U.+

14588 — [Anr. ed.] 12°. R. Y[oung] *imp. A. Boler,* 1637. L.O. C.D.M⁴.+; F.HN(frag.).HD.

14589 — [Anr. ed.] Cum versione Græca J. S(mith). 8°. *Oxonii, G. Turner imp. G. Webb,* 1639. L.O.C.D.E.+; F.HN. HD.ILL.Y.+

See also 14594, 17991.

14590 — [A trans.] An apologie, or aunswer in defence of the Church of England. [Anon.] *Tr.* 4°. (*R. Wolfe,*) 1562. Ent. 1561–2. L.O.C.DUR³.P.+; F.HN.HD.PML. Y.+

HN has 2 copies w. variations in sheet A. Trans. said to have been supervised by Abp. M. Parker. Answered by 12762, 20725, 21694.

14591 — [Anr. trans. Anon.] An apologie or answere in defence of the Churche of Englande. [*Tr.* Ann, Lady Bacon.] 8°. (*R. Wolfe,*) 1564. L.O.C.D.DUL.+; F.CH.PH.Y. Cleveland PL.

Dedic. to Lady Bacon init. M[atthew Parker]. C[antuariensis].

14592 — [Anr. ed. Signed.] The apologie of the Church of England. 12°. *J. R[oberts] f. T. Chard,* 1600. Ent. 8 oc. 1599. L(2).C⁴.BTL.CHATS. Hurd Episcopal Library, near Hartlebury, Worcs.; HN.ILL.

14593 — [Anr. ed.] 12°. *J. Beale,* 1635. Ass'd by A. Chard 10 oc. 1622. L⁴³.C. Goyder. Stevens Cox.; F(2).TORONTO². U.

1 F and Stevens Cox are variants with no date on tp.

14594 — [Anr. trans.] Απολογια της Αγγλων εκκλησιας. . . . Interprete J. S(mith.) 12°. *Oxoniæ, J. Barnesius,* 1614. L.O.O³⁸.C⁵.C¹⁵.+; F.HN.NY¹¹.

See also 14589.

14595 — [Anr. trans. Anon.] Deffynniad ffydd eglwys loegr. [*Tr.*] M. Kyffin. 8°. *R. Field,* 1595. NLW.; N.

— An apologie of priuate masse. 1562. *See* 14615.

Jewel, John, *Bp.—cont.*

14596 — Certaine sermons preached before the Queenes maiestie, and at Paules crosse. Whereunto is added a short treatise of the sacraments. [*Ed.*] (J. Garbrand.) 8⁰. *C. Barker,* 1583. Ent. to Barker a. Coldock 24 fb. L.O.C.G²·WI.+ ; F.HN.ILL(imp.).STAN.Y.
  (Formerly also 14598) In imprint: '*excellent Maiestie*' in italic type. A1ʳ heading: 'Certaine sermons . . .', in last line: 'guyded'.

14597 — [Anr. ed.] 8⁰. *C. Barker,* 1583. O.C¹⁵.P. ; F.HD.ILL.LC.Y. In imprint: 'excellent Maiestie' in roman type. A1ʳ heading: 'Sermons preached . . .', in last line: 'guided'.

14597.5 — [Anr. issue, w. 'excellent Maiestie' in roman; A1ʳ heading: 'Certaine sermons . . .', in last line: 'guided'.] L².O¹⁹. ; Weissman.

14598 — = 14596.

14599 — [Anr. ed.] 2 pts. 8⁰. [*R. Bradock?*] *f. W. Leake,* 1603. Ass'd 24 fb. L.O.C⁴.A.D.+ ; F.HN.HD.N.U.+ One HD copy, bd. in contemporary vellum, has a blank slip pasted over 'Wherunto . . . treatise of the sacraments . . .' and does not have pt. 2.

14599a — The copie of a sermon [on I Cor. xi. 23.] [1560.] = pt. 2 of 14612.

14600 — A defence of the Apologie of the Churche of Englande, an answeare to a certaine booke by M. Hardinge. fol. *H. Wykes,* 1567 (27 oc.) L³⁰.C².D.M.YK.+ ; F.CHI. ILL.NY¹¹(lacks Rrr4). Washington Cathedral. Ends Rrr⁴; line 4 of title: 'foorth'.

14600.5 — [Anr. ed.] fol. *H. Wykes,* 1567 (27 oc.) L.O.C.E.STD.+ ; F.HN.HD.ILL.U.+ Ends Rrr⁶; line 4 of title: 'foorthe'.

14601 — [Anr. ed.] Whereunto is also newly added an answeare vnto an other booke. fol. *H. Wykes,* 1570 (16 jn.) L.O.C.BHP.LINC.+ ; F.HN.HD.ILL.Y.+

14602 — [Anr. ed.] fol. *H. Wykes,* 1571 (16 se.) L.O.C².E².P.+ ; F.HN.BO.N.NY¹¹.+

14603 — An exposition vpon the two epistles to the Thessalonians. [*Ed.*] (J. Garbrand.) 8⁰. *R. Newberie a. H. Bynneman,* 1583. Ent. 24 fb. L.O¹⁷.C.E⁴.P.+ ; F.HN. HD.ILL.U.+

14604 — [Anr. ed.] 8⁰. *R. Newberie,* 1584. L(destroyed).O.C.EX. G².LINC.+ ; F.HN.BO.ILL.Y.

14605 — [Anr. ed.] 8⁰. [*V. Simmes*] *f. R. Newberie,* 1594. L (destroyed).O.O³.O⁵. Goyder.; F.HN.HD.

14606 — A replie vnto M. Hardinges answeare [12758]. fol. *H. Wykes,* 1565. L.O.C.D(lacks tp).E².+ ; F.HN.HD.N.U.+ Answered by 12760, 12761, 20729, 21694, 21696, 23234.

14606.5 — [Anr. ed.] fol. *H. Wykes,* 1565 (15 ja.) P.WN.; F.U.

14607 — [A variant, w. date:] 1566 (20 ja.) L.O².A.BHP.P.+ ; F.HN.HD.SMU.Y.+

14607.5 — [A trans.] Ioannis Iuelli, . . . aduersus Thomam Hardingum, volumen. Conuersum in Latinum, à Guilielmo Whitakero. 4⁰ in 8's. *T. Vautrollerius,* 1578. Ent. to T. Chard 3 no. NY¹¹. The order of printing the tpp—all conjugate— may have been 14609 (with '1588' a misprint), 14608, 14607.5.

14608 — [Anr. issue, w. tp reset, stating 'volumen alterum', and imprint:] *T. Vautrollerius, imp. T. Chardi,* 1578. L. O.C.A.D.+ ; F.HN.CAL.

14609 — [A variant, w. imprint:] *T. Vautrollerius, imp. T. Chardi,* 1588. O.; NY¹¹.

14609.5 — A sermon made in latine in Oxenforde. *Tr.* R. V[aux]. 8⁰. *T. Purfoote,* [1581?] L.O.C. Text in B.L.

14610 — [Anr. ed.] 8⁰. *T. Purfoote,* 1586. C⁵. Text in roman.

14611 — Seven godly and learned sermons. Never before imprinted. [*Ed.*] (I. K.) 8⁰. *imp. G. Bishop,* 1607. C⁴. STU.; F.

14612 — The true copies of the letters betwene John Bisshop of Sarum and D. Cole, vpon occasion of a sermon [on I Cor. xi. 23.] 2 pts. 8⁰. (*J. Day* (*J. daye*)), [1560.] Ent. 26 se. 1560. L.O.C.EX.P.+ ; F.HN.CHI.HD.U.+ Collates A–Q⁸ R⁴; A–H⁸. (Pt. 2 formerly 14599a) Sermon answered by 12758, 20726. *See also* 14615.

14613 — [Anr. ed.] 8⁰. [*J. Day,* 1560?] L.O(imp.).C.D.E.+ ; HN. ILL(imp.).NY¹¹.Y. Collates A–Z⁸ AA⁴.

14613.5 — A viewe of a seditious bul sent into Englande, 1569. [*Ed.*] (J. Garbrand.) 8⁰. *R. Newberie & H. Bynneman,* 1582. Ent. to H. Bynneman 12 fb. L.L¹⁵.O.O⁹.C.+ ; F.MIN.NY¹¹(imp.).U. Collates A⁴ B–M⁸.

Jewel, John, *Bp.—cont.*

14614 — [Anr. ed.] 8⁰. *R. Newberie & H. Bynneman,* 1582. L. L²(imp.).; HN.CAL. Collates A–O⁸ P⁴.

14615 — An apologie of priuate masse, spred a broade in writing, against the offer made in certayne sermons by the bisshop of Salsburie [in 14612]: with an answer for the defence of the trueth. Perused and allowed, . . . 8⁰. (*T. Powell,*) 1562 (no.) Ent. 1562–63. L.O.C. D.M².+ ; F.HD.U. Verso of tp blank. Prints the Apologie, followed by an anon. Answer by Bp. T. Cooper. Answered by 20728.

14615.5 — [Anr. issue, w. cancel tp:] A lewde apologie of pryuate masse, sedyciously spred abroade [etc.] L. (Formerly 14617) Title omits 'Perused . . .'; verso of tp blank.

14616 — [Anr. issue, w. cancel tp:] An apologie of priuate masse sediciously spredde abroade [etc.] L.O¹⁷.C.C⁷.; HN. Title omits 'Perused . . .'; 'To the reader' on verso of tp warns against copies of 14615 circulated without the Answer.

14617 — Now = 14615.5.
  — *ed. See* 13663.

14618 **Jewel, William.** The golden cabinet of true treasure: *tr.* out of French & enlarged, by W. Jewel. 8⁰. *H. L[ownes] f. J. Crosley,* 1612. Ent. to Lownes 20 au. 1611. L.O.G².; F.N.

14618.3 — [Anr. issue, w. imprint:] *H. L[ownes] f. J. Budge,* 1612. O¹⁰.C.LAMPORT.USHAW.; ILL.PN².

Jhonson, George. *See* Johnson, G.

Jig. A new northern jigge. [1628–29.] *See* 6191.

14618.5 **Joan.** Jone is as good as my lady. *Ballad.* 2 pts. s.sh.fol. *A. M[athewes,* c. 1620.] C⁶.

14619 — Joans ale is new. *Ballad.* [1680.] = Wing J 750. — Rocke the babie Joane. [1632?] *See* 21138.5.

Joanes, William. Almanacks. 1626, etc. *See* 464.9 sq.

Joannes, *Bp. of Callipolis. See* Indulgences 5, 56, 60A, 70.

14620 **Joannes,** *Campensis.* A paraphrasis vpon all the psalmes. 1539. Now = 2372.6.
  — *tr. See* 2995a.8.

14621 **Joannes,** *Canonicus.* [x5ʳ:] Expliciunt questioēs Johannis canonici super octo libros phisicorum aristotil. fol. (*ap. villam sancti Albani,* 1481.) L(frag.).O(3).C (frag.).C¹³(imp.).LIV³(frag.).+ ; ROS. Duff 237.

Joannes, *de Actona, ed. See* 17108.

Joannes, *de Mediolano.* For editions of the 'Regimen Sanitatis Salerni', *see* 21596, 21605, 21610.

14622 **Joannes,** *Metropolitanus Euchaitensis.* Joannis metropolitani Euchaitensis versus iambici. Editi cura Matthaei Busti. *Gr.* 4⁰. *Etonae,* [*M. Bradwood f.*] *J. Norton,* 1610. L.O.C.D².E².+ ; F.HN.HD.N.NY¹¹.+

14623 **Jobson, Richard.** The golden trade: or, a discovery of the river Gambra, and the golden trade of the Aethiopians. 4⁰. *N. Okes, sold by N. Bourne,* 1623. Ent. 18 jn. L.L⁴¹.O.C.D².+ ; F.HN.HD.ILL.NY.+

14624 **Joceline, Elizabeth.** The mothers legacie, to her vnborne childe. 12⁰. *J. Haviland f. W. Barret,* 1624. Ent. 12 ja. L.L³⁰.; F.

14624.5 — The second impression. 12⁰. *J. Haviland f. W. Barret,* 1624. O.; F.PN.

14625 — Third impression. 12⁰. *J. Haviland f. H. Barret,* 1625. L.; F.

14625.5 — The sixth impression. 12⁰. *E[liz.] A[llde] f. R. Allot,* 1632. Ass'd to M. Hodgets 19 de. 1625; to Allot 25 ja. 1626. O.E²(imp.).

14625.7 — The seventh impression. 12⁰. *F. K[ingston] f. R. Allot,* 1635. HN(imp.).

14626 **Jocelinus,** *Monk.* The life of the glorious bishop S. Patricke. . . . (*Tr.* B. B. [i.e. R. Rochford.]) 4⁰. *S. Omers,* [*G. Seutin?*] *f. J. Heigham,* 1625. L.O³.C. CAR.D.+ ; ILL. A&R 420. Reprinted in 24733, 24736.

27

14626.5 **Johann Justus**, *Landsberger*. An epistle or exhortation of Iesus Christ to the soule, that is deuoutly affected towarde him. [*Tr.* P. Howard.] 4°. [*London, Fr. Garnet's first press, 1592–93.*] LE.ST.
A&R 437.

14627 — [Anr. ed.] An epistle in the person of Christ to the faithfull soule. *Tr.* by one of no small fame. 8°. *Anwerpe,* [i.e. *English secret press,*] 1595. L.L².O (imp.).USHAW.YK².+; F.TEX.
A&R 438.

14628 — [Anr. ed.] An epistle or exhortation of Jesus Christ to the soule. 8°. [*St. Omers, English College Press,*] 1610. L.O.P.USHAW.W.+; HN.N.TEX. 𝔄
A&R 439.

14628.5 — [Anr. ed.] An epistle, or, exhortative letter sent from Jesus Christ, to every faithfull soule. *Tr.* (The manuell of St. Augustine.) 8°. *R.* H[odgkinson?] *f. W. Brookes,* 1637. Ent. 4 fb. D(imp.).

Johannides, Christophorus, *of Dalby.* De prædestinatione. 1595. *See* 21555.1.

John, *Bp. of Lincoln. See* Williams, J.

14629 **John**, *Chrysostom, Saint.* Τοῦ ἐν ἁγίοις πατρὸς ἡμῶν Ἰωάννου τοῦ Χρυσοστόμου τα εὑρισκόμενα. [*Ed.* Sir H. Savile.] 8 vols. fol. *Etonæ,* [*M. Bradwood f.*] *J. Norton,* 1610 (1611, 1612.) L.
Without prelims. except for the tpp. Tp dates vary: vols. 1, 2: 1610; vols. 3, 5, 6: 1611; vols. 4, 7, 8: 1612, all in arabic numerals except for vol. 8, which has: 'cIɔ. Iɔc. XII.' Colophons dated: vols. 1–3: 1610; vols. 5, 6: 1611; vols. 4, 7: 1612; vol. 8 dated 1613 on ¶¶¶4ᵛ. At the end of vol. 8 L has bd. in quires Iiii–Kkkk of vol. 4 and the over-all contents list from vol. 1 of 14629a.

14629.5 — [A variant.] L²(tpp dated: vols. 2, 3, 5, 6: 1611; vols. 1, 4, 7, 8: 1612).O¹⁰(tpp dated: vols. 1–3, 5, 6: 1611; vols. 4, 7, 8: 1612).
(Formerly 14629b) L² has at least the vol. 1 prelims. of 14629a. O¹⁰ has a complete set of the prelims. for 14629a bd. in vol. 8.

14629a — [Anr. issue, w. new prelims. for each vol., w. tpp dated 'cIɔ. Iɔc. XII [or XII]' and an added engr. tp in vol. 1, w. title:] S. Joannis Chrysostomi opera Græcé. *Etonæ, J. Norton,* 1613. L.O.C.D.E².+; F.HN.CU.HD.N.+
(Formerly also 14629c) Vol. 1 prelims. also include dedic., epistle, and over-all contents list; prelims. for the other vols. include only individual contents list.
The copy in St. Mark's Cathedral, Venice, has a pr. dedic. from Savile to Marcantonio Memmo, Doge, and to the Senate of Venice.

14629b — Now = 14629.5.
14629c — [Anr. issue, dated:] 1612. = 14629a.
— A cōpendious treatise. 1542. *See* 14640.

14630 — D. Ioannis Chrysostomi de prouidentia Dei, ac fato, orationes sex. J. Checo interprete. 8°. (*in off. R. Vuolfij,*) 1545 (ja.) L(2).CARLISLE.D².G².

14630.5 — An excellent treatise touching the restoring againe of him that is fallen. Put into English by R. W(olcomb.) 12°. *A. Hatfield f. J. Winnington,* 1588. Ent. 29 ja. HD.

14631 — [Anr. ed.] With an annexed epistle of comfort (T. C[ottesford.]) 12°. [*J. Windet*] *f. J. Helme,* (1609.) Ent. to J. Busby 30 oc. 1595. L.
'Epistle' pr. in 26140 and 5841.5.

14632 — An exposition vpon the epistle to the Ephesians. Truely and faithfully *tr.* out of Greeke. 4°. *H. Binneman a. R. Newberie,* 1581 (24 de.) Ent. 4 ja. 1582. L.O.C²(2).; F.HN.Y.
1581 in tp border.

14632a — [Anr. issue, w. outer forme of sheet A reset.] L². O(lacks tp).C.BTL. Athens, Gennadius Library.; F.
1581 in imprint; tp omits 'Truely and faithfully translated. . . .'

14633 — A godly exhortation made vnto the people of Antioch, touching patience by the examples of Job, [etc.] *Tr.* R. Rowse. 8°. *T. Creed,* 1597. L.M.

14634 — Τοῦ ἐν ἁγίοις Ἰωαννου τοῦ Χρυσοστόμου ὁμιλία δύο. [*Tr.*] J. Cheko. *Lat. a. Gr.* 2 pts. 4° w. perp. chainlines. (*ap. R. Vuolfium,*) 1543 (au.) L.O.C.D.R.+; F.HN.AAS.Y. 𝔄

14635 — D. Ioannis Chrysostomi . . . homiliæ sex, J. Harmari [the elder], opera. *Gr.* 8°. *Oxonii, ex off. J. Barnesii,* 1586. L.O.C.E².LIV³.+; F.PH.

John, *Chrysostom, Saint—cont.*

14636 — D. Ioannis Chrysostomi . . . homiliae ad populum Antiochenum, duæ & viginti. Opera J. Harmari [the elder.] *Gr.* 8°. *G. Bishop & R. Newberie,* 1590. Ent. 3 jy. 1591. L.O.C.M⁴.P.+; F.HN.CHI.HD.Y.+

14637 — An homilie of saint Johñ Chrysostome vpon that saying of Saint Paul, Brethren, I would not haue you ignorant, what is becom of those that slepe. With a discourse vpon Job, and Abraham, newly made out of Greke into latin by master Cheke, and englished by T. Chaloner [the elder.] 8°. (*in off.* T. Bertheleti,) 1544 (29 mr.) L.L⁴.O³.C.; F.MICH.

14637.5 — [Anr. ed.] 8°. (*in off.* T. Bertheleti,) 1553 (24 au.) O. C⁵.; HN.

14638 — A sermō . . . of pacience, of yᵉ end of yᵉ world. Wherunto is added an other homelie by J. Brentius. *Tr.* (into latin by J. Theophilus, and) into Englishe by T. Sãpson. 8°. (*N. Hyll f. J. Shefelde,*) 1550. L.C.; F.N.
For anr. trans. *see* 19893a.7.

14639 — A sermon . . . wherein besyde that it is furnysshed with heuenly wisedome & teachinge, he wonderfully proueth, that no man is hurted but of hym selfe: *tr.* T. Lupsette. 8°. (*in off.* T. Bertheleti, 1542.) L(2).O⁹.C.M.; F.HN.WIS.

14640 — [Anr. trans.] A cōpendious treatise of saynte Iohn Chrisostom prouing that no mã is hurte but of him selfe. [*Tr.*] (C. Chaualary.) 8°. (*J. Mayler f. J. Gough,* 1542.) O.; F.Y.

14641 — Theorremōn: or, the ancient . . . father, Sᵗ. Chrysostome treating on severall places of holy scripture: selected, and translated by J. Willoughbie. 8°. *Oxford, J. Barnes,* 1602. L.O(imp.).C.A.LONGLEAT. +; F.BOWDOIN.Y.

14642 — A treatise of S. John Chrisostome cōcerning the restitucion of a synner. Newly *tr.* 8°. (*R. Calye,*) 1553. L.L¹³.O².G².M.
— *See also* 12791, 20088, 25420.

John, *Don, of Austria.* The popes pittiful lamentation, for the death of don Joan. 1578. *See* 12355.

14643 **John**, *the Evangelist.* Here begynneth the enterlude of Johan the Euangelyst. 4°. [*W. Copland f.*] (*J. Waley,*) [c. 1550.] L(2). Greg 26.

14644 **John**, *King of England.* The troublesome raigne of John King of England, also the death of King John. (The second part.) 2 pts. 4°. [*T. Orwin*] *f. S. Clarke,* 1591. C².; F(lacks gen. tp).HN(lacks gen.tp). Greg 101.

14645 — The second part of the troublesome raigne of King John. 1591. = pt. 2 of 14644.

14646 — [Anr. ed.] The first and second part of the troublesome raigne of John King of England. Written by W. Sh. 4°. *V. Simmes f. J. Helme,* 1611. L(3, 1 imp.).O.O⁶. C².; F.HN.CAL.HD.Y.+

14647 — [Anr. ed.] Written by W. Shakespeare. 4°. *A. Mathewes f. T. Dewe,* 1622. L.L⁶.C.C².E².+; F.HN.CAL.HD.Y².+

14648 **John**, *of Arras.* [Melusine, a tale of the serpent fairy.] fol. [*W. de Worde,* 1510.] O(frags.).

14649 **John**, *of Capistrano, Saint.* [Capystranus; a metrical romance.] 4°. [*W. de Worde,* c. 1515.] L(10 leaves, A2–C3).
A3ʳ beneath Hodnett 1117: 'Now Machamyte that turke vntrue'; B1ʳ beneath Hodnett 1118: 'The emperour of Constantyne'.

14649.5 — [Anr. ed.] 4°. [*W. de Worde,* 1527?] L(2 leaves, C.40.m.9/18).
Beneath Hodnett 1117 (in a state earlier than 1528): 'Now Machamyte yᵗ turke vntrue'.

14650 — [Anr. ed.] 4°. [*W. de Worde,* 1530?] O(4 leaves).
Beneath Hodnett 1118 (in a state later than 1528): 'The Emperour of constantyne'.

14650.5 — The pope. De paus. O pope, o duke of Millyane, how foeminine is thy warre, [etc. With a contrasting account of John of Capistranus.] *Tr.* out of the old Dutch coppye, in print all most 50. yeares since. And now reprinted. s.sh.fol. [*London,*] 1621. C².

14651 **John**, *of the Cross.* The catholique judge: or a moderator of the catholique moderator. *Tr.* Sir A. A. 4°. *J. D[awson] f. R. Mylbourne,* 1623. Ent. 10 oc. L.O.C. G².M.+; F.HN.HD.ILL.U.+ 𝔄

14651.5 **John XXI,** *Pope.* The treasury of healthe conteynyng many profitable medycines gathered by Petrus Hyspanus & *tr.* by H. Lloyde. 8°. (*W. Coplande,*) [1550?] O.; N.NLM(prelims. only, in 14653).
Lord Stafford and Duchess of Northumberland mentioned on title and in prelims.

14651.7 — [Anr. issue, w. new prelims. omitting references to Stafford and the Duchess of Northumberland. After 22 Aug. 1553.] L.L[16](L[39] deposit).L[19].C(2, 1 imp.).G[2].; HN.NY[4](imp.).
(Formerly 14652a)

14652 — [Anr. ed.] The treasuri of helth. 8°. (*W. Coplande,*) [c. 1556.] L[8].L[16](3 imp.).O.CAR*.; HD.NLM.WIS.
No date in title.

14652a — Now = 14651.7.

14653 — [Anr. ed.] The treasuri of helth. . . . M.D.L VIII. The .vii. daye of October. 8°. (*W. Coplande,*) [1558.] L. O[8].M[2](imp.).; NLM(imp., w. prelims. of 14651.3).

14653.3 — [Anr. ed.] The treasurie of health. 8°. [*W. Copland,* c. 1560.] NLW(imp.).Dr. R. A. Hunter, London.; NLM(imp.).
Collates A[4] B–Y[8] a–g[8] h[4].

14653.7 — [Anr. ed.] 8°. *T. Hacket,* [c. 1570.] O.

14654 — [Anr. ed.] 8°. *T. East,* 1585. Ent. 12 ja. L.O.E[2].G[2].P.+

14655 **John Casimir,** *Count Palatine.* Certaine orations and answeres made vnto the French King in defence of peace. *Tr.* out of French. 8°. [*J. Day,*] 1579. C.

14656 **John George I,** *Elector of Saxony.* The Duke of Saxonie his jubilee: with a short chronologie. [Init. W. S.] 4°. *W. Jones,* 1618. Ent. 26 no. L.O.O[5].O[14].C[3].; F.

John Sigismund, *Elector of Brandenburg. See* 3541.

14656.5 **Johnson, Christopher.** Gulielmi Wiccammi Winton. Episcopi ortus atquè vita. 1564. December 14. [In verse.] s.sh.fol. [*London?* 1564.] O.
In italic.

14656.7 — [Anr. ed., w. 'Custodum nomina et series' added.] s.sh.fol. [*London?* 1564?] C(frag.).
In roman. Reprinted in 25671.

— *tr. See* 13625.

Johnson, D., *pseud.* Practicæ medicinæ liber. 1602. *See* 25954.

14657 **Johnson, Edward.** Hymnus comitialis, in honorem . . . Elisabethæ. s.sh.fol. [*London?* 1595?] L.

14657.5 **Johnson, Fabian.** True intelligence sent . . . Concerning the estate of the English forces now in Fraunce. 4°. [*J. Wolfe*] *f. T. Nelson,* 1591. Ent. to Wolfe 6 se. ILL.Y.

14658 **Johnson, Francis.** An answer to Maister H. Iacob his defence of the churches. 4°. [*Amsterdam?*] 1600. L.L[2].O.O[21].P.+; F.LC.Y.
Reprints and answers 14335.

14659 — A brief treatise . . . against two errours of the Anabaptists. 8°. [*Amsterdam? G. Thorp?*] 1609. C.LINC.

14660 — Certayne reasons and arguments proving that it is not lawfull to heare the present ministerie of the Church of England. 4°. [*Amsterdam, G. Thorp,*] 1608. L.O. C[5].D.P.+; F.LC.Y.
(Formerly also 10401) Answered in 3532.

14661 — A christian plea conteyning three treatises. 4°. [*Leyden, W. Brewster,*] 1617. L.O.C.A.DUR[3].+; F.HN.BO.U. Wisconsin Historical Society.+
Answered in 236.

14662 — An inquirie and answer of Thomas White his discoverie of Brownisme [25408]. 4°. [*Amsterdam, G. Thorp?*] 1606. O.DUR.

14663 — A short treatise concerning the exposition of those words of Christ, Tell the church, &c. 4°. [*Amsterdam?*] 1611. L.C[10].STU.; BO.BO[5].Y.

14663.5 — A treatise of the ministery of the Church of England. [Init. F. Io.] 4°. [*Low Countries?* 1595.] L.O.C.D[2].E[2].+; F.BO.HD.U.Y.+
(Formerly 13464) Prints and answers a letter by A. H., i.e. A. Hildersham. End of text on S1[r] dated 1595.

— *ed. See* 12340.

— *See also* 238, 18433.7.

14664 **Johnson, George.** A discourse of some trouble, . . . in the banished English church at Amsterdam. 4°. *Amsterdam,* 1603. L[2].L[4](imp.).C[2].LINC.; MCG(lacks tp).

14665 **Johnson, Jacobus.** Schediasmata poetica: sive, epigrammatum libellus. 8°. *ex off. J. Beale,* 1615. Ent. 29 no. 1614. CHATS.LINC.; F(2).NY.

14666 — [Anr. issue, w. cancel tp:] Epigrammatum libellus: sive, schediasmata poetica. *J. Beale, imp. R. Redmer,* 1115 [1615.] L.; CU.

14667 **Johnson, John,** *an humile professor, etc.* An confortable exhortation: of oure mooste holy christen faith. 8°. *Parishe, (Peter congeth,)* [*Malmö? J. Hoochstraten,*] 1535 (20 ja.) L(imp.).D(imp.).

14668 **Johnson, John,** *of Antwerp.* A true relation of Go⟨ds⟩ wonderfull mercies, in preserving one alive, which hanged five dayes, [i.e. J. Johnson.] 4°. *E. Allde,* [1605?] L(imprint cut).

Johnson, John, *of Colchester.* Almanacks. 1611, etc. *See* 465 sqq.

14668.5 — Johnsons arithmatick in 2. bookes. 8°. *A. Mathewes,* 1623. Ent. 21 fb. 1622. L[30].O.; HN.
(Formerly 14670)

14669 — [Anr. issue, w. imprint:] *A. Mathewes, sold by R. Moore,* (1623.) C(date cropt).

14670 — Now = 14668.5.

14670.3 — Johnsons arithmetick. . . . The second edition inlarged. 12°. *A. Mathewes, sold by J. Grismond,* 1633. L(date cropt).C[12].

14670.5 — [Anr. issue, w. imprint:] *A. Mathewes, sold by R. Milborne,* 1633. L[30].

Johnson, Laurence. *See* 1416.

14671 **Johnson, Richard.** Anglorum lacrimæ: in a sad passion complaynyng the death of Elizabeth. [In verse.] 4°. [*W. White*] *f. T. Pavier,* 1603. O.O[5].
Plagiarized from 21225.

14672 — A crowne-garland of goulden roses. [Songs.] 8°. *G. Eld f. J. Wright,* 1612. Ent. 18 fb. O.

14673 — [Anr. ed.] With new additions. 8°. [*Eliot's Court Press*] *f. J. Wright,* 1631. L.

14674 — The golden garland of princely pleasures. The third time imprinted. 8°. *A. M[athewes] f. T. Langley,* 1620. L.
See also 22919.5.

— The good shepheards sorrow. [1612.] *See* 13157.5.

— The history of Tom Thumbe. 1621. *See* 14056.

14675 — A lanterne-light for loyall subjects. 4°. *S. Stafford,* 1603. LAMPORT.; HN.

14676 — Looke on me London. . . . [Init. R. I.] 4°. *N. O[kes] f. T. Archer,* 1613. L.L[8].O[17].

14677 — The most famous history of the seauen champions of christendome. [The first part.] 4°. [*J. Danter*] *f. C. Burbie,* 1596. Ent. to J. Danter 20 ap.; to C. Burbie 6 se. HN(imp.).

14678 — The second part of the famous history of the seauen champions of Christendome. 4°. [*E. Allde?*] *f. C. Burbie,* 1597. Ent. 6 se. 1596. L.

14679 — [Anr. ed. of both pts.] The most famous history of the seuen champions of christendome. 2 pts. 4°. [*T. Dawson?*] *f. E. Burbie,* 1608 (22 no.) L.; F.NY(imp.).

14680 — [Anr. ed.] The famous historie [etc.] 2 pts. 4°. *T. Snodham,* (1616 (22 my.)) Ent. 25 jn. 1612. L.O[2](imp.).E.LINC.
Date at end of text of pt. 1.

14681 — Now = 4955.5.

14682 — [Anr. ed.] 2 pts. 4°. *W. Stansby,* [1626.] Ent. 23 fb. 1626. LINC(lacks tp to pt. 1).; HN.PFOR.

14682.5 — [Anr. ed.] 2 pts. 4°. *W. Stansby [a.] (R. Bishop,)* [1636?] Ass'd to Bishop 4 mr. 1639. L.; F.N.
Pt. 2 tp, line 5: 'christendome'.

14683 — [Anr. ed.] 2 pts. 4°. *R. Bishop,* [c. 1640.] L.BRISTOL[2].; F. Auckland PL. G. B. Evans, Harvard Univ.(imp.).
Pt. 2 tp, line 5: 'christendom'. Prob. post-1640.

14684 — The most pleasant history of Tom a Lincolne. The sixth impression. [Init. R. I.] 4°. *A. Mathewes, sold by R. Byrde a. F. Coules,* 1631. Ent. to W. White 24 de. 1599; pt. 2 to White 20 oc. 1607. F.

14685 — The seventh impression. [Init. R. I.] 4°. *A. M[athewes,] sold by F. Faulkner a. F. Coules,* 1635. O[6].; HN.BALT.

14685.5 — Musarum plangores: vpon the death of Sir Christopher Hatton. [In verse.] 4°. [*R. Jones?* 1591.] ?Ent. to Jones 24 no. 1591. F(sheet B only).

14685.7 — The nine worthies of London: explaining the honourable exercise of armes. [Verse and prose.] 4°. *T. Orwin f. H. Lownes,* 1592. O.
(Formerly 14687) A 2nd copy (Britwell) was sold at Sotheby's 8 Feb. 1922, lot 395, untraced.

Johnson, Richard—*cont.*

14686 — [Anr. issue, w. title:] The nine worthies of London. Explayning the honourable exercise of armes. *T. Orwin f. H. Lownes*, 1592. L.
In L copy is inserted the preface to 1485.

14687 — Now = 14685.7.

14688 — The pleasant conceites of old Hobson the merry Londoner. 4°. [*G. Eld*] *f. J. Wright*, 1607. L.O.

14689 — [Anr. ed., w. additions.] 8°. [*G. Eld*] *f. J. Wright*, 1610. O⁵.
27 lines a page.

14689.3 — [Anr. ed.] 8°. [*M. Flesher f. J. Wright*, 1634?] LIV(tp def. and lacks A1,8, B1, and all after D3).
28 lines a page. C has leaves D4–8, w. text continuous from D3ᵛ of LIV copy, which may belong to this ed. Hazlitt, *Handbook*, p. 303, mentions a tp, w. imprint: '*f. J. Wright*, 1634', among the Harl. frags. at L, but this particular item has not been traced.

14689.7 — [Anr. ed.] 8°. *f. W. Gilbertson*, 1640 [1649?] C(frag.). 30 lines a page.

14690 — The pleasant walkes of Moore-fields. [In verse and prose.] 4°. [*W. Jaggard?*] *f. H. Gosson*, 1607. Ent. 11 jn. O(3).; HN.

14691 — A remembrance of the honors due to Robert Earle of Salisbury. 4°. [*G. Eld*] *f. J. Wright*, 1612. Ent. 23 jy. L.O.O³(lacks tp).O⁵(imp.).CHATS.+; TEX. 𝔄
O⁵, TEX have an early state of A outer forme, w. tp dated 1512 [*sic*], and init. 'R. J.' on A3ʳ and A4ᵛ instead of signed 'Richard Jhonson'.
— *See also* 6769.5.

14691.1 **Johnson, Richard**, *Moralist*. The pilgrimage of man, wandering in a wilderness of woe. 4°. *J. Danter*, 1598. SAL.

14691.3 — [Anr. ed. Anon.] 4°. [*W. White*] *f. W. Barlie*, 1606. Ent. to White 5 de. 1605. L.
(Formerly 19919)

14691.5 — [Anr. ed.] 4°. *R. Blower*, 1612. O.
(Formerly 19920)

14691.7 — [Anr. ed.] 4°. *J. B[eale]* 1635. Ent. to Beale 12 no. 1614. C.

14691.9 — [A variant, w. imprint:] *J. B[eale], sold by J. Wright minor*, 1635. F.
(Formerly 19921)

14692 **Johnson, Robert**, *B.D.* The gospell and his maintenance. [A sermon.] 4°. *T. Cotes f. M. Sparke*, 1633. Ent. 4 se. L.O².C⁵.M.YK.+; HN.HD.Y.

14692.5 — [A variant, w. '*sold by J. Cartwright at Coventrie*' added to imprint.] C.D.; F.

14693 — The necessity of faith; or, nothing more necessarie for a christian. [A sermon.] 4°. *H. L[ownes] f. M. Lownes*, 1624. Ent. 27 ap. L.O.HER.
Reissued w. tp cancelled in 22240.5.

14693.5 — The way to glory: or, the preaching of the gospell. 4°. *N. Okes, sold by J. Pyper*, 1621. L².O.

14694 **Johnson, Robert**, *Chaplain to the Bp. of Lincoln.* Davids teacher, or the true teacher of the right-way to heaven. 4°. *T. Haveland f. M. Law*, 1609. L.O.C¹⁵.DUR³.NLW.+; F.Y.

14694.3 — Dives and Lazarus: or rather, divellish Dives: delivered in a sermon by R. I. Fourth edition. 8°. *W. J[ones] f. R. Bird*, 1623. Ent. 7 fb. NLW.

14694.5 — The eight edition. 8°. *W. J[ones] f. R. Bird*, 1628. P.; CU.

14694.7 — The eleventh edition. 8°. *J. N[orton] f. R. Bird*, 1633. HN.

14695 **Johnson, Robert**, *Gent.* Essaies, or rather imperfect offers. 8°. *J. Windet f. John Barnes*, 1601. Ent. 9 oc. L(imp.).L³⁰(imp.).O.O⁶.E².+; HN.PFOR.

14696 — [Anr. ed.] 8°. [*A. Islip*] *f. J. Bache*, 1607. Ent. to R. Walter 21 mr. L.L³⁰.O.G².; F.HN.HD.PFOR.PN.

14697 — [Anr. ed.] 16° in 8's. *G. Eld f. R. Wilson*, 1613. Ent. 19 no. 1610. L.; F.HN.CHI.HD.N.+

14698 — [Anr. ed.] Johnsons essayes: expressed in sundry exquisite fancies. 12°. *M. P[arsons] f. R. Wilson*, 1638. L.O.C⁵.PETYT.SHEF.+; F.HD.ILL.N.Y.+

14699 — Nova Britannia. Offring . . . fruites by planting in Virginia. [Init. R. I.] 4°. *J. Windet] f. S. Macham*, 1609. Ent. 18 fb. C(lacks tp)*.; NY.
Tp has headpiece of royal arms, 'offring' in line 2. Every sheet of this and the 2 following numbers is known in at least 2 different settings and they are found indiscriminately gathered. The ornamental inits. belonged to the King's Printing Office.

Johnson, Robert, *Gent.*—*cont.*

14699.3 — [A variant, w. no headpiece on tp, 'offring' in line 2.] L(2).; HN(2).CB(2).HD.PN. Penrose 128.

14699.5 — [A variant, w. no headpiece on tp, 'offring' in line 2.] O.G².; F.HN.BO.N.NY.+

14700 — The new life of Virginea: being the second part of Nova Britannia. [Init. R. I.] 4°. *F. Kyngston f. W. Welby*, 1612. Ent. 1 my. L.O.O⁵.CHATS.G².; F.HN.HD.N.NY.+
— *tr. See* 3398.

Johnson, Thomas, *tr. See* 10510.5.

Johnson, Thomas, *Astronomer.* Almanacks. 1598, etc. *See* 466 sqq.

14701 **Johnson, Thomas**, *Botanist.* Dainty conceits, with a number of rare and witty inventions. 1630. Now = 14708.1.

14702 — Descriptio itineris plantarum investigationis ergô suscepti in agrum Cantianum 1632. 12°. *T. Cotes*, 1632. L(2).O¹²(2).O³⁶.

14703 — Iter plantarum investigationis ergo susceptum a decem sociis, in agrum Cantianum, 1629. Julii. 13. 4°. [*A. Mathewes*, 1629.] L.O¹².A.ETON.

14704 — Mercurius botanicus. Sive plantarum gratiâ suscepti itineris, anno M.DC.XXXIV. descriptio. (Thermæ Bathonicæ, 1634.) 8°. *T. Cotes*, 1634. Ent. to T. a. R. Cotes 9 oc. 1634. L.O.C.E.NLW.+; HN.V.
Sheets I–M: 'Mercurii botanici pars altera. *T. a. R. Cotes*, 1641.' Some copies (C, NLW, HN, V) lack this.

14705 — A new booke of new conceits. 1630. Now = 14708.5.
— *ed. See* pt. 2 of 1592, 11751.
— *tr. See* 19189, 19192.

14706 **Johnson, Thomas**, *Minister.* Stand up to your beliefe, or, a combat betweene Satan and a Christian. [In verse.] s.sh.fol. London, *E. G[riffin,]* sold by *T. Hunt, Exeter*, [1640.] L.
Dated 1640 at bottom. Every 2nd line of this poem ends w. a consecutive portion of the Creed.

14707 **Johnson, Thomas**, *Miscellaneous writer.* Cornucopiæ, or diuers secrets: . . . newlie drawen out of diuers Latine authors. Eng. 4°. [*J. Danter*] *f. W. Barley*, 1595. Ent. to J. Danter 30 oc. 1594. L. London Museum(imp.).; HD.

14708 — [A variant, w. date:] 1596. O.G².; HN.BO⁵.

14708.1 — Dainty conceits, with a number of rare and witty inventions. 8°. *E[liz.] A[llde] f. H. Gosson a. F. Coules*, 1630. HN.
(Formerly 14701)

14708.3 — A lokinge glasse for eche estate, Wherin to weue the fickle fate. [In verse.] s.sh.fol. *A. Jeffs, soulde by W. Barley*, 1595. Ent. to Jeffes 18 my. O.

14708.5 — A new booke of new conceits. 8°. *E[liz.] A[llde] f. E. Wright a. C. Wright*, 1630. Ent. to J. Danter 8 mr. 1594; to Grismond, J. Wright, E. Wright, C. Wright, Coules, a. Gosson 7 de. 1629. L.O.
(Formerly 14705)

Johnson, William. An almanack. 1569. *See* 466.9.

Johnson, William, *Writer on Navigation. See* Blaeu, W. J.

Johnston, Sir Archibald, *Lord Wariston. See* 21904, 22036, 22039, 22047, 22060.

Johnston, Arthur. Canticum Salomonis, paraphraste A. Jonstono. 1633. *See* 2767.

14708.7 — Consilium collegii medici Parisiensis de mania G. Eglishemii. [Anon. In verse.] 8°. *Edinburgi, A. Hart*, 1619. L.E.

14708.8 — [Anr. ed.] 8°. *Parisiis* [i.e. London, *W. Stansby?*] 1619. L.

14708.9 — [Anr. ed.] 8°. *Edinburgi, J. Wreittoun*, 1631. E.

14709 — Elegiae duae: una ad episcopum Abredonensem, altera de pace rupta. [In verse.] 4°. *Aberdoniæ, E. Rabanus*, 1628. E².

14710 — Epigrammata. . . . [In verse.] 8°. *Abredoniæ, E. Rabanus*, 1632. L.O.E.G².M⁴.+; F.HN.HD.N.
Often found bd. w. 14714.

14711 — In obitum Jacobi pacifici, . . . elegia. [In verse.] 4°. [*M. Flesher,*] *imp. N. Butter*, 1625. L.

14712 — Musæ aulicæ, . . . interprete F. K[ynaston.] [In verse.] Lat. a. Eng. 8°. *ap. T. Harperum, imp. N. Butter*, 1635. L.; F.HN.

Johnston, Arthur—*cont.*

14713 — Musæ querulæ, de regis in Scotiam profectione. The muses complaint. [*Tr.*] (F. Kinaston.) [In verse.] *Lat. a. Eng.* 8°. *T. Harper f. N. Butter,* 1633. L.O.E. STU.; F.

14713.5 — Nicrina ad heroas Anglos. [Init. V. N. O. In verse.] 8°. *Heidelbergæ,* 1620 [really *London, W. Stansby,* 1622.] O.AE.

— Paraphrasis poetica psalmorum Davidis. 1637. *See* 2366.

14714 — Parerga Arturi Jonstoni Scoti, medici regii. [In verse.] 8°. *Aberdoniæ, E. Rabanus,* 1632. L.O.C².E.M⁴.+; F.HN.N.
Often found bd. w. 14710.

14714.5 — Querelæ Saravictonis & Biomeæ. [Anon. In verse.] 8°. [*W. Stansby,*] 1620. O.A.
Prob. pr. 1622, *cf.* 14713.5.

Johnston, John. *See* Jonston, J.

14715 **Johnston, Thomas.** Christs watch-word. Being the parable of the virgins. 4°. *W. J[ones] f. J. Bartlet,* 1630. Ent. 3 ap. L.O.A.D.M.+; HN.ILL.PN².Y.

14715.5 **Johnston, William.** Jobs creed explained in a sermon at the funerall of Francis Conyers. 8°. *Edinburgh, J. Wreittoun,* 1635. LINC.

Johnstoun, James. [Supplement to Sidney's Arcadia.] *See* 22550.

14716 **Jonah.** The historie of the prophet Jonas. *Ballad.* 2 pts. s.sh.fol. *E. A[llde,* c. 1620.] C⁶.

14717 **Jonas, Justus.** The true hystorie of the christen departynge of Martyne Luther. *Tr.* J. Bale. 8°. [*Wesel, D. van der Straten,* 1546.] L.O⁸.C.C³.D².+; HD(imp.).
Wrongly dated 1566 on C5ᵛ; correct date on C6ʳ.

— *See* also 5992.5.

Jonas, Richard, *tr. See* 21153.

Jones, Captain. The legend of captaine Jones. 1631. *See* 16614.

14717.5 **Jones, Anthony.** A spiritual chaine, and armour of choice, for Sion souldiers. 4°. *W. Jones f. R. Mylbourne,* 1622. Ent. 4 ap. L.O(imp.).; AAS.
(Formerly 4933)

Jones, Inigo. *See* 14776, 16768.22, 24156.

14718 **Jones, Inigo,** and **Davenant,** *Sir* **William.** Britannia triumphans: a masque, presented by the Kings majestie and his lords. 4°. *J. Haviland f. T. Walkley,* 1637. L.L⁶.O.O⁶.E.+; F.HN.HD.ILL.LC.+ Greg 526.

14719 — The temple of love. A masque. 4°. *f. T. Walkley,* 1634. L.L⁶.O.C.LONGLEAT.+; F.HN.HD.ILL.Y.+ Greg 497.
L and HN have 2 varying tpp; B4 intended to be cancelled.

14720 **Jones, John,** *B.D.* Our saviours journey to the Gadarens. [A sermon.] 8°. *N. Okes f. H. Bel,* 1615. Ent. 29 ja. L(imp.).O.A.LINC.; Y.

14721 **Jones, John,** *Eugenius.* Adrasta: or, the womans spleene, and loves conquest. A tragi-comedie. 4°. [*M. Flesher?*] *f. R. Royston,* 1635. L.O.E.ETON.SHEF.+; F.HN.HD.N.Y.+ Greg 501.

14721.5 **Jones, John,** *M.A.* The conquest of the saints. [A sermon.] 4°. *G. M[iller] f. W. Jones,* 1639. Ent. 8 mr. L.O.C¹⁷.G².NLW.+; F.MCG.Y.
(Formerly 14727)

14722 — Londons looking in backe to Jerusalem. [A sermon.] 4°. *W. Jones,* 1633. Ent. 15 de. 1632. L⁸.O.P.; F.Y.

14723 — [Anr. issue, w. imprint:] *W. J[ones] f. M. Sparkes,* 1635. O.A.; HN.

14724 **Jones, John,** *M.D.* The arte and science of preseruing bodie and soule in healthe. 4°. *H. Bynneman,* 1579. Ent. 9 jy. L.L².O.C.G².+; HD.ILL.LC.

14724a — [Anr. issue, w. imprint:] *R. Newberie* [*a.*] (*H. Bynneman,*) 1579. O⁵.USHAW.; F.HN.

14724a.3 — The bathes of Bathes ayde. 4°. (*T. East*) *f. w. Jones,* (1572 (13 my.)) L(lacks tp).O.C⁵.E.NLW.+; HN. Duke U.
Also issued as pt. 4 of 14725.

14724a.7 — The benefit of the auncient bathes of Buckstones, ... 1572. 4°. *T. East a. H. Myddleton f. W. Jones,* [1572] (18 ja.) L.O.C⁵.E.NLW.+; HN.NY⁴.
Also issued as pt. 3 of 14725.

Jones, John, *M.D.*—*cont.*

14724a.9 — A briefe, excellent, and profitable discourse, of the beginning of all liuing things. 4°. [*W. Williamson f.*] *w. Jones,* 1574 (8 my.) HN.

14725 — [Anr. issue, w. additions.] Hereunto is anexed Galens booke of elements, in the ende wherof is adioyned two other bookes. 4 pts. *w. Jones,* 1574. L.O.C.A. NLW.+; F(imp.).CAL.NLM(pts. 1, 2 only).Y.
Pt. 1 omits month date in col.; pts. 2–4 are re-issues of 11537.3, 14724a.7, 14724a.3, q.v. for imprints.

14726 — A dial for all agues. 8°. *W. Seres,* 1566. Ent. 1564–65. L(2 imp.).; HN.HD.

— Galens bookes of elementes. 1574. *See* 11537.3 and pt. 2 of 14725.

14727 **Jones, John,** *Minister.* The conquest of the saints. 1639. Now = 14721.5.

14728 **Jones, Philip.** Certaine sermons preached of late at Ciceter. 8°. *T. D(awson) f. T. Butter,* 1588. Ent. 3 my. C.D.YK. Gloucester PL.

— *tr. See* 17784.

14729 **Jones, Richard.** A briefe and necessarie catechisme. 8°. *T. East,* 1583. Ent. 12 ap. L.NLW.; F.

14730 — [Anr. ed.] 8°. *T. Snodham,* [1609.] Ass'd 17 jn. 1609. L.O.C³.E². Swansea PL.

14730.5 — [Anr. ed.] 8°. *W. Stansby,* [1626?] Ass'd 23 fb. 1626. L. In title: 'necessarie'.

14731 — [Anr. ed.] 8°. *W. Stansby,* [c. 1630.] L.M. In title: 'necessary'.

14732 **Jones, Robert.** The first booke of songes or ayres of foure parts with tableture for the lute. fol. *P. Short, with the assent of T. Morley,* 1600. L(lacks A1,2).; F(lacks all after F4).

14733 — The second booke of songs and ayres. fol. *P. S[hort] f. M. Selman, by the assent of T. Morley,* 1601. L.M³ (imp.).

14734 — A musicall dreame. [Xylographic.] Or the fourth booke of ayres. fol. [*J. Windet f.*] *the assignes of W. Barley, solde* [*by S. Waterson,*] 1609. L.G².

14735 — [Anr. issue, w. imprint:] *J. Windet, solde by S. Waterson,* 1609. HN.

14736 — The muses gardin for delights [xylographic], or the fift booke of ayres. fol. [*W. Stansby*] *by the assignes of W. Barley,* 1610. HN.

14737 — Cantus (Bassus) the first set of madrigals, of 3. 4. 5. 6. 7. 8. parts, for viols and voices. 2 ptbks. 4°. *J. Windet,* 1607. L.

14738 — Ultimum vale, with a triplicity of musicke. fol. *J. Windet, sold by S. Waterson,* 1605. L⁷(lacks tp). Fürst Dohna, Lörrach, Baden, Germany.

14739 **Jones, Thomas.** Mercy triumphing over judgement or, a warning for Sabbath-breakers. [In verse.] 8°. *E[liz.] P[urslowe] f. J. Wright the younger,* [1640?] O⁶(imprint cropt).; F(imprint cropt).
Prob. dated 1641.

Jones, William, *Almanack Maker. See* 464.9 sq.

14739.2 **Jones, William,** *of Dorset.* The mysterie of Christes nativitie. [A sermon.] 4°. [*W. Stansby*] *f. R. Hawkins,* 1614. Ent. 20 jy. L.O(imp.).O³.USHAW.; F.HN.HD.
(Formerly 14745)

14739.5 **Jones, William,** *of Suffolk.* A commentary upon the epistles to Philemon and to the Hebrewes. fol. *R. B[adger] f. R. Allot,* 1635. Ent. to Mrs. Allot 30 de. L³⁰.O.C.D².G⁴.; NY¹¹.U(imp.).*
(Formerly 14743) Imprint varies: w. Badger's inits. (most copies) or w. his name in full (L³⁰).

14739.8 — [Anr. issue, w. imprint:] *R. B[adger] f. R. Allot,* 1636. L(destroyed).L².L¹³.C⁴.C⁵.D.+; HD.PN².U.Y.
(Formerly 14744)

Jones, William, *of Usk.* Gods warning to his people of England. 1607. *See* 10011.

14740 = 14742.

14741 **Jones, William,** *of Wight.* A briefe exhortation to all men to set their houses in order. 4°. *W. Jones,* 1631. Ent. 30 mr. L.C.C².EX.NOR².+; CHI.

14742 — [Anr. ed.] 8°. *W. Jones,* 1637. L(date cropt).L³.
(Formerly also 14740)

Jones, William, *of Wight—cont.*

14743 — A commentary upon the epistles to Philemon and to the Hebrewes. 1635. Now = 14739.5.

14744 — [Anr. issue.] 1636. Now = 14739.8.

14744.5 — An exposition of the whole catechisme of the church of England. 8°. *W. Jones f. C. Greene,* 1633. Ent. to Jones a. Greene 9 jy. c⁴.; U.

14745 — The mysterie of Christes nativitie. 1614. Now = 14739.2.

14746 — A pithie and short treatise whereby a godly christian is directed how to make his last will. [Anon.] 1612. Now = 24229.5.

14747 — A treatise of patience in tribulation. [A sermon.] Hereunto are joyned the Teares of the Isle of Wight. [In verse.] 4°. *W. Jones,* 1625. Ent. 28 ap. L(2).O.O¹⁰. c.; F(1, plus 'Teares' only).HN.AAS.HD.

14748 — The true inquisition, or the sad soules search. [A visitation sermon.] 4°. *W. Jones,* 1633. Ent. 15 de. 1632. L³.O.

14749 — [Anr. ed.] Thought necessary to be republished, [etc.] 8°. *W. Jones,* 1636. L³.; HN.

Jones, *Sir* **William,** *tr. See* 12462, 15701, 18428.

Jones, Zachary, *tr. See* 15318, 15448.

14750 **Jonghe, Ellert de.** The true and perfect declaration of the mighty army by sea, made by the united Provinces. 4°. [*S. Stafford f.*] *J. Wolfe,* 1600. Ent. to C. Burby, 28 mr. L.O.

14751 **Jonson, Benjamin.** The workes of Benjamin Jonson. fol. *Imprinted at London by Will Stansby,* 1616. Unprinted court masques ent. 20 ja. 1615. L.O.C².A.D.+; F.HN.HD.N.NY.+

    The above imprint on the engr. tp by W. Hole is found mainly in large paper copies (L, HN). Other copies (O, HD, KAN, TEX) have a later state of the engr. tp, w. imprint: *London Printed by William Stansby.* Imprints on sub tpp for Every man out . . . and Poetaster vary, some mentioning J. Smethwick and M. Lownes, respectively. For these and other details *see* Greg III.1070–3.

14752 — [A variant, w. imprint on engr. tp:] *London printed by W: Stansby, and are to be sould by Rich: Meighen,* 1616. L.O⁷.C.DUR³.M.+; HN.O⁷.C.DUR³.M.ICH.Y².+

14753 — [Anr. ed.] fol. *R. Bishop, sold by A. Crooke,* 1640. Ent. to R. Bishop 4 mr. 1639. L.O.C.D.E.+; F.HN.HD.N.NY.+

    Poetaster sub tp has imprint: *by* [i.e. *for*] *R. Young.*

14753.5 — [The second volume of the works.] Bartholmew fayre. (The divell is an asse.—The staple of newes.) fol. *J. B[eale] f. R. Allot,* 1631. Bartholmew fayre ass'd to J. Legat a. A. Crooke 1 jy. 1637; The staple of news ent. 7 se. 1631. HN.CAL.HD.TEX(2).

    Apparently intended as a continuation of the 1616 vol. I and so sold. The unsold sheets were reissued in 14754 w. an added gen. tp. In the copies noted above the 1st leaf is a genuine blank. For a fuller analysis of this and the following *see* Greg III. 1075–81.

14754 — The workes of Benjamin Jonson. The second [and third] volume. Containing these playes, viz. 1 Bartholmew fayre. 2 The staple of newes. 3 The divell is an asse. [*Ed. vol. 2:* B. Jonson; *vol. 3:* Sir Kenelm Digby.] fol. *f. R. Meighen* [*a. T. Walkley*], 1640 (1631, 1641.) L.O.C.D².E².+; F.HN.HD.NY.TEX.+

    Includes the sheets of 14753.5 w. the original tpp, reissued by Meighen. The gen. tp was pr. by B. Alsop and T. Fawcet. Vol. 3 was pr. by J. Dawson for Walkley and contains The magnetick lady, A tale of a tub, and The sad shepherd (dated 1641) w. continuous signatures, as well as the masques and other works.

14754a — [Anr. issue, usually omitting Bartholmew fayre and The staple, and with The divell (= Wing J 1011) printed by T. Harper and dated 1641.] L³⁰.O.C².DUR³.E(lacks gen. tp).+; F(2).MCG.NW.Y.

14755 — The alchemist. 4°. *T. Snodham f. W. Burre, sold by J. Stepneth,* 1612. Ent. to W. Burre 3 oc. 1610. L.L⁶. O.C⁴.G².+; F.HN.HD.N.PML.+ Greg 303.

    — Bartholmew fayre. (The divell is an asse.—The staple of newes.) 1631. *See* 14753.5.

14756 — B. Jon: his part of King James his royall entertainement through his honorable cittie of London, 15. of March. 1603. (A particular entertainment of the

Jonson, Benjamin—*cont.*

    Queene and Prince to Althrope.) 2 pts. 4°. *V. S[immes a. G. Eld] f. E. Blount,* 1604. Ent. 19 mr. L.O.C²(pt. 1 only).B.M.+; F.HN.HD.ILL.NY.+ Greg 200.

    Simmes pr. 1st A–B; Eld the rest.

14757 — Ben: Jonson, his case is alterd. 4°. [*N. Okes*] *f. B. Sutton,* 1609. Ent. to H. Walley a. R. Bonion 26 ja.; to them a. B. Sutton 20 jy. L(2, 1 imp.).E.; F(imp.). TEX. Greg 281.

14758 — [Anr. issue.] A pleasant comedy, called: the case is alterd. *f. B. Sutton a. W. Barrenger,* 1609. L(imp.). L⁶(3).O.E.; HN.BO.HD.

    The HN copy has variant tp omitting 'Written by Ben. Jonson'.

14759 — Catiline his conspiracy. 4°. [*W. Stansby?*] *f. W. Burre,* 1611. L.O.C.E⁴.G².+; F.HN.BO.HD.N.+ Greg 296.

14760 — [Anr. ed.] 4°. *N. Okes f. J. S[pencer,]* 1635. Ass'd to W. Stansby 4 jy. by note of 10 jn. 1621. L.L⁶.; F.HN.BO. PFOR.WTL.

    B1ᵛ running title: 'CATILINE'.

14760.5 — [Anr. ed.] 4°. *N. Okes f. J. S[pencer,]* 1635. L.O.C³.; F.HD.PN.

    B1ᵛ running title: 'CATLINE [*sic*]'.

14761 — The characters of two royall masques. The one of blacknesse, the other of beautie. (The description of the masque.) 4°. [*G. Eld*] *f. T. Thorp, sold* [*by L. Lisle,*] 1608.] Ent. 21 ap. 1608. L(2).L⁶.O(imp.).C.; HN.BO.HD(imp.).PFOR(imp.). Greg 269.

    (14770 is pt. of this)

14762 — Chloridia. Rites to Chloris and her nymphs. A masque, 1630. [Anon.] 4°. *f. T. Walkley,* [1631.] L.L⁶.O.; F. HN.BO.HD.PFOR. Greg 452.

14763 — Epicoene, or the silent woman. [Title init. B. I.] 4°. *W. Stansby, sold by J. Browne,* 1620. Ent. to J. Browne a. J. Busby 20 se. 1610; ass'd to J. Browne a. ent. to W. Burre 28 se. 1612. O.; HD. Greg 304.

14764 — [Anr. issue, w. cancel tp:] The silent woman. . . . The author B. Jonson. *W. Stansby, sold by J. Browne,* 1620. L.L⁶(lacks tp)*.G⁴.; HN(2).MCG(lacks tp)*.N. WTL.Y(lacks tp)*.

14765 — Epigrams to severall noble personages in this kingdome. 1640. = pt. of 13798.

14766 — Every man in his humor. 4°. [*S. Stafford*] *f. W. Burre,* 1601. Ent. to C. Burby a. W. Burre 14 au. 1600. L(2).L⁶(2).O(2, 1 imp.).ETON.; F.HN.HD.PML.NY.+ Greg 176.

14767 — The comicall satyre of every man out of his humor. [Init. B. I.] 4° w. perp. chainlines. [*A. Islip*] *f. W. Holme,* 1600. Ent. 8 ap. L(imp.).L³⁰(imp.).; HN.BO. WTL. Greg 163.

    Collates A–R⁴. Quires P–R have horizontal chainlines.

14768 — [Anr. ed.] 4°. [*P. Short*] *f. W. Holme,* 1600. L⁶.O. Collates A–Q⁴.

14769 — [Anr. ed.] 4°. *f. N. Linge,* 1600. L(2).L⁶.O.ETON.; F. HN.HD.NY.Y.+

    Prob. pr. after 1600.

14770 — The description of the masque. With the nuptiall songs. Celebrating the marriage of Lord Ramsey. [1608.] = pt. of 14761.

14771 — Ben: Jonson's execration against Vulcan. With divers epigrams. [In verse.] 4°. *J. O[kes] f. J. Benson* [*a. A. Crooke,*] 1640. Ent. 16 de. 1639. L.L³⁸.O.O³.C².; F.HN. HD.N.NY.+

    Reprinted in 13798. There are 2 states of sheet A: w. the imprimatur dated 1640 or 1639; both at HN.

14772 — The fortunate isles and their union. A masque. 1624. [Anon.] 4°. [*London,* 1625.] L(3).L⁶.O(2).; HN.HD (lacks tp).PFOR. Greg 411.

14773 — The fountaine of selfe-love. Or Cynthias revells. 4°. [*R. Read*] *f. W. Burre,* 1601. Ent. 23 my. L(2).L⁶. O.C⁴.; HN.HD.LC.PML.Y².+ Greg 181.

    HN has added dedic. to W. Camden; CAL to Lucy, Countess of Bedford.

14774 — Hymenaei: or the solemnities of masque, and barriers. 4°. *V. Sims f. T. Thorp,* 1606. L.L⁶.O.G².M.; F.HN. CAL.HD.PFOR.+ Greg 237.

14775 — Lovers made men. A masque. [Anon.] 4°. [*London,*] 1617. O. Greg 350.

14776 — Loves triumph through Callipolis. A masque. The inventors. Ben. Jonson. Inigo Jones. 4°. *J. N[orton] f. T. Walkley,* 1630. L.O.STD.; F.HN.PFOR. Greg 437.

14777 — The masque of augures. . . . [Anon.] 4°. [*London,*] 1621. Ent. to Crooke a. Sergier 20 mr. 1640. L(2).O(2). Greg 381.

    One L copy has added note at end init. 'B.I.'

Jonson, Benjamin—*cont.*

14777a — The masque of the gypsies. 1640. = pt. of 13798.
14778 — The masque of queenes celebrated from the house of fame. 4°. *N. Okes f. R. Bonian a. H. Wally*, 1609. Ent. 22 fb. L(2).L⁶.O.; F.HN.HD.PFOR. Greg 280.
14779 — Neptunes triumph for the returne of Albion, a masque 1623. [Anon.] 4°. [*London*, 1624.] Ent. to Crooke a. Sergier 20 mr. 1640. L(imp.).O.; HN. Greg 407.
14780 — The new inne. Or, the light heart. 8°. *T. Harper f. T. Alchorne*, 1631. Ent. 17 ap. L.L⁶.L³⁰.O.O⁶.+; F.HN. HD.TEX.Y.+ Greg 442.
14781 — Poetaster or the arraignment. 4°. [*R. Bradock*] *f. M. L[ownes,]* 1602. Ent. to M. Lownes 21 de. 1601. L. L⁶.O.E.PETWORTH.; F.HN.HD.NY.Y.+ Greg 186.
— Q. Horatius Flaccus: his art of poetry. Englished by Ben: Jonson. With other workes of the author, never printed before. 1640. *See* 13798.
14782 — Sejanus his fall. 4°. *G. Elld f. T. Thorpe*, 1605. Ent. to E. Blount 2 no. 1604; ass'd to T. Thorpe 6 au. 1605. L.L⁶.O.O.C⁴.E.+; F.HN.HD.NY.Y.+ Greg 216.
Some copies read *Ellde*; both at L⁶.
— The silent woman. 1620. *See* 14763.
14782.5 — Time vindicated to himselfe, and to his honors. 1622. [Anon.] 4°. [*London*, 1623.] Ent. to A. Crooke a. R. Sergier 20 mr. 1640. PFOR. Greg 385.
14783 — Ben: Jonson his Volpone or the foxe. 4°. [*G. Eld*] *f. T. Thorppe*, 1607. Ent. to W. Burre 3 oc. 1610. L.O.C⁴ (2 imp.).D².E².+; F.HN.HD.IND.PML.+ Greg 259.
Two L copies have extra leaf of verses signed 'N. F.'
— *tr. See* 13798.
— *See also* 6769.5, 12018.

— A funerall elegie, in memory of B. Jonson. 1637. *See* 23759.
14784 — Jonsonus virbius: or, the memorie of Ben: Johnson revived. [In verse. *Ed.* B. Duppa.] 4°. *E. P[urslowe] f. H. Seile*, 1638. Ent. 3 fb. L.O.C².C⁴.LONGLEAT.+; F.HN.HD.N.NY.+
Some sheets are found in 2 states, bd. indiscriminately.

Jonston, Arthur. *See* Johnston, Arthur.

14785 **Jonston, John.** De cruenta morte Archibaldi Hunteri. [In verse.] s.sh.fol. *Edinburg, R. Walde-graue*, 1590. E.
14786 — Heroes ex omni historia Scotica lectissimi. [In verse.] 4°. *Lugduni Batavorum, C. Guyotius, sumt. A. Hartii, bibliopolæ Edinburgensis*, 1603. L.O.E.E².LINC.+; F(2). HN.HD.N.
One F copy has added dedic. to George Lauder.
14787 — Inscriptiones historicae regum Scotorum. . . . [In verse.] 4°. *Amsteldami, C. Claessonius A. Hartio, bibliopolæ Edemburgensi*, 1602. L.O.C.E.G⁴.+; F.HN. HD.IND.
Reissued in 1603 w. 2 added leaves of verses, 1 dated 1603, and 1 leaf of dedic. to James I, init. 'I. I.' Date on tp sometimes altered in ink to 1603. Examples of all at L.
At the end are 10 engr. portraits, w. Latin verse in letterpress below. There are 2 different plates each for James VI and Anne of Denmark; *see* Hind II.49–51 regarding their use in this and in 14787.2 sqq.
14787.2 — A trewe description of the nobill race of the Stewards. [Anon. The engr. portraits of 14787, w. letterpress English prose below.] fol. (*Amsterdam,*[*C. Claeszoon,*] *at the expensis of A. Hart*) [*in Edinburgh*, 1602?] O.E.
14787.4 — [Anr. issue, w. colophon:] (*Amsterdam, ad* [sic] *the expensis of A. Hart buikseller in Edinbrugh*, 1603.) L.O⁸.C.; HN.HD.NY.
(Formerly 12886) At least the texts under James VI and Anne of Denmark have been revised and reset.
14787.6 — Vera descriptio augustissimae Stewartorum familiae. [Anon. The engr. portraits of 14787, w. letterpress Latin verse below.] fol. (*Amsterodami,* [*C. Claeszoon,*] *sumpt. A. Hart bibliopolæ Edinburgensis,*) [1602?] O.
14787.8 — [Anr. issue, w. colophon:] (*Amsterdami, . . .,* 1603.) L.

Jordan, John, *ed. See* 21483.

14788 **Jordan, Thomas.** Poeticall varieties: or, varietie of fancies. 4°. *T. C[otes] f. H. Blunden*, 1637. L.O(2).O⁸. LIV³.; F.HN.DAR.HD.N.+
Reissued in 1646, w. prelims. cancelled and new tp, as Wing J 1045.
14789 **Jordanus.** Meditationes Jordani de vita et passione iesu christi. 16° in 8's. (*per R. Pynson,* 1513 (16 mr.)) C.
14790 **Jorden, Edward.** A briefe discourse of a disease called the suffocation of the mother. 4°. *J. Windet*, 1603. Ent. 14 mr. L.O.C.BRISTOL.ETON.+; F.BO⁵.HD.NLM.
14791 — A discourse of naturall bathes, and minerall waters. 4°. *T. Harper*, 1631. Ent. 1 jy. L.O.BRISTOL.E.EX.+; F. HN.BO⁵.CHI.HD.
14792 — Second edition, in many points enlarged. 4°. *T. Harper*, 1632. L.O.C³.D.M⁴.+; F(impr. cropt).HN.HD.NLM.Y.
Some copies have a cancel tp reading the same as the original but with the first 6 lines of the title condensed into 4. HD has copies with both tpp.
14793 — [Anr. issue.] Third edition, much enlarged. 4°. *T. Harper, sold by M. Sparke*, 1633. L¹⁶.C.BHP.E. Blickling.; F.HD.
14794 **Joriszoon, David.** David Gorge, borne in Holland, of his lyfe, and damnable heresi. [By J. Sphyractes.] *Tr.* out of Latyne. 4°. (*Basel, C. Mense,* 1560 (ja.)) L.C³.; HD(lacks tp).
Sheets A and B occur in 2 settings, but are found indiscriminately mixed.
14795 **Joseph,** *ben Gorion, pseud.* A compendious and most marueilous history of the latter tymes of the Jewes commune weale. *Tr.* P. Morwyng [from Abraham ben David's abstract in Bk. 3 of Sefer ha-Kabalah.] 8°. (*J. Daye f. R. Jugge,*) 1558. Ent. 1557–58. L³⁸. O¹².C¹⁵.; HN.CH(lacks tp; has 1567 tp added). Hebrew Union C.
14796 — [Anr. ed.] Newly corrected. 8°. (*R. Jugge,*) 1561. L. O(3).O¹⁴.C².M³.; F.HN.
14797 — [Anr. ed.] 8°. (*R. Jugge,*) 1567. L.L⁸.L³⁸.C.M³.; F.HN.LC.
14798 — [Anr. ed.] 8°. (*R. Jugge,*) 1575. L.L³⁸.E⁴.P.SHEF.+; F. HN.ILL.PML.NY⁹.
B1ʳ line 2: 'worshyp'.
14798.5 — [Anr. ed.] 8°. (*J. Jugge, wydowe,*) 1575 (1579.) O(2, 1 lacks colophon*).C(lacks colophon)*.; F(lacks colophon)*. Hebrew Union C(lacks colophon)*.
(Formerly 14800) B1ʳ line 2: 'worship . . . and striue'.
14799 — [Anr. issue, w. cancel colophon leaf:] (*W. Seres,*) 1575 (1579.) C.
14799a — [Anr. issue, w. cancel colophon leaf:] (*J. Wallie,*) 1575 (1579.) L.; N.Y.
14800 — Now = 14798.5.
14800.5 — [Anr. ed.] 8°. [*J. Charlewood f.*] *J. Wally,* [1585?] Hebrew Union C.
B1ʳ line 2: 'worship . . . & striue'.
14801 — [Anr. ed.] 8°. [*J. Roberts*] *f. T. Adames*, 1593. L.L³⁸.C.
14802 — [Anr. ed.] 8°. *V. Sims f. T. Adams*, 1596. L.; HD(imp.).
14803 — [Anr. ed.] 8°. [*R. Read?*] *f. T. Adams*, 1602. C.C⁵.; HN.HD.
14804 — [Anr. ed.] 8°. *f. T. Adams*, 1608. L³⁸.O(date trimmed).; NY⁹.Y.
14805 — [Anr. ed.] 8°. [*T. Creede*] *f. T. Adams*, 1615. L.L³⁸. O.C¹².M.+; NY. State College of Washington, Pullman, Wash.
14806 **Joseph,** *of Arimathea.* here after foloweth a treatyse takē out of a boke whiche Theodosius founde in Iherusalem in the pretorye of Pylate of Joseph of Armathy. 4°. (*W. de Worde,*) [1511?] L.C.
14807 — Here begynneth the lyfe of Joseph of Armathia. [In verse.] 4°. (*R. Pynson*, 1520.) L.
14808 **Joseph,** *the Patriarch.* A moste briefe and pleasant treatise of the interpretation of sundry dreames. 1626. Now = 13499.5.
— *See also* 19465.5.

Joseph, Anastasius. [Passport giving safe-conduct to A. Joseph. 2 July 1613.] *See* 13855.8.

14809 **Josephus, Flavius.** The famous and memorable workes of Josephus. *Tr.* by T. Lodge. fol. (*P. Short*) *at the charges of G. Bishop, S. Waterson, P. Short, a. T. Adams*, 1602. Ent. to R. Walley 7 mr. 1591; ass'd to P. Short 12 oc. 1591; ent. to S. Waterson, P. Short, a. T. Adams 26 jn. 1598. L.L³⁸.O⁶.C⁵.LEEDS.+; F.HN. HD(imp.).ILL.NY.+

Josephus, Flavius—*cont.*

14810 — [Anr. ed.] fol. *H. Lownes f. G. Bishop, S. Waterson, a. T. Adams,* 1609. L.O.C.LEIC².NEK.+; F.HN.ILL.NY. Y.+

14811 — [Anr. ed.] fol. (*H. Lownes*) [*a. J. Legat*] *f. T. Adams,* 1620. Ent. 14 mr. 1611. L³⁸.L⁴³.O³.C.NLW.+; HN. CAL⁸.HD(imp.).PN.Y.+
See Court-Book C, p. 134.

14811a — [Anr. issue, w. imprint:] *f. S. Waterson,* 1620. L.O. INN(imp.).; N.

14812 — [Anr. ed.] fol. *J. L[egat] f. A. Hebb,* 1632. Ent. 6 my. 1625. L.O.C.A.LIV³.+; F.HN.CHI.NY.Y.+

14812a — [Anr. issue, w. imprint:] *J. L[egat] f. S. Waterson,* 1632. L.BHP.NMU.; BO.IND.Y.

14813 — [Anr. ed.] fol. *J. L[egat] f. A. Hebb,* 1640. L³⁰.O.C². BIRM.M⁴.+; F.HN.HD.ILL.NY.+
See Court-Book C, pp. 310, 311, 312, 313, 315.

14813a — [Anr. issue, w. imprint:] *J. L[egat] f. J. Waterson* [*a.*] (*A. Hebb,*) 1640. Ent. 19 au. 1635. L.L¹⁶.C.CARTMEL. GLOUC.; F.Y.

14814 — Φλαβίου Ιωσηπου εις Μακκαβαίους λόγος ... cum latina interpretatione Joannis Luidi. 8°. *Oxoniæ, Jos. Barnesius,* 1590. L.O.C.A.P.+; HN.Y.

14815 **Josiah.** The reformation of religion by Josiah. a commendable example for all princes. 8°. [*f. T. Man,* 1590?] ?Ent. to T. Man 22 jn. 1590. L².O.C.E².P.+; F.

Josseline, John, *ed. See* 159, 11893, 19292.

14816 **Jourdan, Silvester.** A discovery of the Barmudas, otherwise called the Ile of Divels. 4°. *J. Windet, sold by R. Barnes,* 1610. L.; F.HN.

14817 — [Anr. ed.] A plaine description of the Barmudas, now called Sommer ilands. With an addition, [etc.] [Anon. Dedic. signed W. C., i.e. W. Crashaw.] 4°. *W. Stansby f. W. Welby,* 1613. L.O.C.CHATS.G².+; F.HN.CB.NY.Y.+

14818 Now = 11277.5.

Journal. A journall, or briefe report of the late seruice in Britaigne. 1591. *See* 13156.

Jovius, Paulus. *See* Giovio, P.

14819 **Joy.** The joy of tears or cordials of comfort. [In verse. By Sir W. Moore?] 8°. [*Edinburgh, J. Wreittoun?*] 1635 (30 jy.) L.

14820 **Joye, George.** An apologye made ... to satisfye w. Tindale: to the vnderstanding of hys new Testamēt printed in M.CCCCC.xxxiiij. in Nouember [2826]. 8°. [*J. Byddell,*] 1535. C.

14821 — A compendyouse somme of the very christen relygyon. *Tr.* [from Summa totius sacrae scripturae by] George Joye. 8° in 4's. (*J. Byddell,* 1535.) D².

14822 — A contrarye (to a certayne manis) consultacion: that adulterers ought to be punyshed wyth deathe. 8°. [*S. Mierdman f.*] (*G. Joye,*) [1549?] L.O.; F.
Answers 11235.

14823 — The exposicion of Daniel the prophete, gathered oute of P. Melanchton, [etc.] 8°. (*Geneue, G. I[oye].*) [i.e. *Antwerp, successor of A. Goinus,*] 1545 (au.) L.O.C. M.P.+; F.HN.LC.NY.Y.+

14824 — [Anr. ed.] The exposiciō [etc.] 8°. (*J. Daie a. W. Seres,* 1550 (9 ap.)) L.O.C.E⁸.M.+; F.HN.HD.NY(imp.).SMU.

14825 — [Anr. ed.] The exposycion [etc.] 8°. (*T. Raynalde,* 1550.) L.L².O.C.M.+; F.HN.HD.ILL.U.+
— A frutefull treatis of baptyme and the Lordis souper. 1541. *See* 24217.

14826 — George Joye confuteth, Winchesters false articles. 8°. (*Wesill in Cliefe lande* [i.e. *Antwerp, Widow of C. Ruremond,*] 1543 (jn.)) L.L⁴³.O.C.P.+

14827 — Now = 14828.5.

14828 — A present consolacion for the sufferers of persecucion. [Init. G. J.] 8°. [*Antwerp, S. Mierdman,*] (1544 (se.)) L.O.D.G².M.+

14828.5 — The refutation of the byshop of Winchesters derke declaratiō of his false articles. 8°. [*London, J. Herford,*] 1546. L.O.C.M.R.; F.HN.BO.BO³.U.
(Formerly 14827). Answers 11588.

14829 — The subuersiō of Moris false foundacion. 8°. (*Emdon, J. Aurik* [i.e. *Antwerp, G. van der Haghen,*] 1534.) L. O.DUR⁵.
Answers 18077.

14830 — The vnite and scisme of the olde chirche. 8°. [*Antwerp, Widow of C. Ruremond,*] 1543 (jn.) L⁴³(lacks tp). O.C.; HD.

Joye, George—*cont.*

— *ed. See* 2825, 2827, 20036.
— *tr. See* 2370, 2752, 2777, 2778, 13828.4, 17798, 18877, 26138.
— *See also* 845, 14556, 21804.

Joyeuse, Henri de, *Duke.* The life of the reverend Fa. Angel of Joyeuse. 1623. *See* 3902.

14830.3 **Joyner, Robert.** Itis, or three seuerall boxes of sporting familiars. 8°. *T. Judson f. J. Browne a. J. Harber,* 1598. Ent. 13 no. PFOR.

Joys. [The fifteen joys of marriage. c. 1507.] *See* 15257.5.

14830.7 **Juan,** *de Santa Maria.* Christian policie: or, the christian common-wealth. Written in Spanish, and *tr.* into English [by J. Mabbe.] 4° in 8's. *T. Harper f. E. Blount,* 1632. Ent. 4 jn. 1630. L.O³(E).C⁵.E.M².+

14831 — [Anr. issue, w. cancel tp, w. imprint:] *T. Harper f. R. Collins,* 1632. L.O.C.E².G².+; F.HN.CHI.U. Virginia Historical Society, Richmond, Va.+

14831a — [Anr. issue, w. cancel tp:] Policie vnveiled: wherein may be learned, the order of true policie. Written in Spanish and *tr.* into English, by I. M[abbe.] *T. Harper f. R. Collins,* 1632. L.L⁴.C.LK. Newport PL.; F.BO.HD.NY.Y.+

14832 — [Anr. issue, w. cancel tp, w. imprint:] *f. H. Mosley,* 1634. C.; Y.

14832a — [Anr. issue, w. cancel tp:] Policie vnveiled, or, maximes of state. Written by I. M[abbe.] *T. C[otes] f. H. Mosley,* 1637. L(tp only, Harl.5965/43).C.D.
In the C and D copies this letterpress tp is laid on an engraved tp. For these sheets reissued in 1650 see Wing J 1162.

Juda, Leo, *tr. See* 2760.3.

14833 **Judge.** The judge wherein is shewed, how Christ is to judge the world. 1621. = 741.

14834 **Judgement.** Hereafter foloweth the iudgemēt of all vrynes. Practysed by Doctor Smyth, and other at Mountpyller. 8° in 4's. (*R. Wyer,*) [1555?] L.G².; HD(imp.).
Contains most of text of 22153 sqq.
— The judgment of a catholicke English-man. 1608. *See* 19408.
— The iudgement of a most reuerend and learned man. [c. 1585.] *See* 2021.

14835 — The trew judgemēt and declaration of a faithful chrystyan, vppon the sacrament. 8°. *R. Stoughton,* [1548?] L(lost).O.D(2).; F.

14836 **Judicial.** The iudycyall of vrynes. fol. [*Southwark, P. Treveris,* 1527?] L.L¹⁶.C.G².; CAL.
A3ʳ line 1 begins: 'raysons'.

14836.3 — [Anr. issue, w. A2,3 reset.] L.L¹⁶(imp.).L¹⁹.O.G².; HN. HD.LC.NLM.TEX.
A3ʳ line 1 begins: 'te'.

14836.7 **Judith.** The famous history of the vertuous & godly woman Judyth. *Tr.* into Englysh meter by E. Jeninges. 8°. *T. Colwell,* 1565 (10 my.) L(tp only, Ames I.229).

14837 **Jugeler, Jack.** A new enterlued for chyldren to playe named Jacke Jugeler. Neuer before imprented. 4°. (*W. Copland,*) [1562?] Ent. 1562-63. ROS. Greg 35.

14837a — [Anr. ed.] Newly imprented. 4°. (*W. Copland,*) [1565?] HN.

14837a.5 — [Anr. ed.] 4°. *J. Allde,* [c. 1570.] F.HN(2 leaves). Greg 35c (IV.1644-5).

Jugge, Richard, *ed. See* 2867.
— *See also* Bookplates.

14838 **Juliers.** Newes from Gulick and Cleve. *Tr.* Charles Demetrius. 4°. [*E. Griffin*] *f. H. Holland a. G. Gibbs,* 1615. Ent. 16 oc. 1614. L.O.; HN.
See also 19512.

Julietta. Honour's Academie. 1610. *See* 18053.

Julius, *of Milan. See* Giulio, da Milano.

Julius II, *Pope.* The benygne grace, power, and vertue of our holy fader. [c. 1510.] *See* Indulgences 116 sq.
— Hereaft' foloweth the abreuiacōn of the graces. [c. 1505.] *See* Indulgences 88 sq.

34

Julius II, *Pope—cont.*

14839 — Vniuersis [xylographic] sancte matris ecclesie filijs. . . . [Inspeximus by Wolsey of a bull against Louis XII. 1512.] Now = 25947.7.

14840 — Willm̄us permissione diuina Catuariẽ Archiepiscopus toti⁹ Anglie. [1508.] Now = Indulgences 105A.

14841 — [Anr. ed.] [1508.] Now = Indulgences 103B.

14841.5 — The dialoge betwene Julius the seconde, genius, and saynt Peter. (*Tr.*) [Attrib. to D. Erasmus or F. Andrelinus.] 8°. (*R. Coplāde f. J. Byddell,*) [1534?] L(imp.).

14842 — [Anr. ed.] The dyaloge bytwene Jullius the seconde, genius, and saynt Peter. (*Tr.*) 4°. (*J. Byddell,* 1535.) L.C²(lacks tp).YK.
— *See also* Indulgences 44, 60, 81, 88 sq., 103B sqq., 116 sq., 129 sq.

14843 **Julius III,** *Pope.* Bulla plenarie indulgentiae. [1554.] Now = Indulgences 147.
— *See also* 26098.7.

14844 **Julius, Alexander.** Ad augustissimum Magnæ Britanniæ, regem [carmina]. 4°. [*J. Beale?* 1618?] L.C².D².; HN.

14845 — Ad ter maximum Magnæ Britanniae regem. Carmen εὐχαρίστικον. 4°. [*J. Beale?* 1614?] L.C².D².

14846 — Descriptio horrendi parricidii et nefariæ perduellionis. [Anon. In verse.] 4°. [*Edinburgh, R. Charteris,* 1606.] E(lacks tp).
Possibly issued separately but usually found as part of 14858.

14846.5 — Illustrissimae dominæ . . . Annabellæ Murraviæ vitæ & mortis speculum. [Anon. In verse.] 4°. *Edinburgi, R. Charteris,* 1603. L.
For a later ed. *see* 14850.

14847 — Illustrissimi domini Gordoniæ comitis . . . epithalamium. [Anon.] 4° in 8. *Edinburgi, R. Charteris,* 1607. L.O.C².D².E.+; HN.

14848 — In Henricum Fridericum primogenitum Jacobi, Walliae principem, lachrymæ. 4°. *Edinburgi, T. Finlason,* 1612. L.O.C².D².E.+; F.HN.

14849 — In illustrissimam dominam Annam Duglasiam, epicedium. [Anon.] 4°. *Edinburgi, R. Charteris,* 1607. L.O.C².D².E.+; F.

14850 — Mater compellat filium sibi superstitem. [Anon.] 4°. [*J. Beale,* c. 1615.] C².C¹⁷.D².E². Swansea PL.
For an earlier ed. *see* 14846.5.

14851 — Nobilissimi comitis Lothianae, . . . Roberti Cari, epithalamium. [Anon.] 4°. *Edinburgi, T. Finlason,* 1611. L.O.C².D².E².+; F.

14852 — Nobilissimi domini, domini Kethi, . . . epithalamium. [Anon.] 4°. *Edinburgi, R. Charteris,* 1609. L.O.C². D².E².+

14853 — Ob secundum et felicem eventum conjugii Frederici 5. et Elizabethæ filiæ regis Magnæ Britanniæ carmen εὐχαρίστικον. 4°. *Edinburgi, T. Finlason,* 1614 (16 fb.) L.O.C².D².E.+; HN.

14853.5 — Paraphrasis prophetiæ Maleaci poëtica. (Paraphrasis, 4. 5. & 11. capitum prophetiæ Jeschahiæ.) [Anon.] 4°. *Edinburgi, A. Hart,* 1611. L.
(Formerly 2791; 2nd pt. formerly 14856) Possibly issued separately but usually found as part of 14858; chap. 5 is a reissue of 14855.

14854 — Paraphrasis prophetiæ Chabakkuki poetica. [Anon.] 4°. *Edinburgi, R. Charteris,* 1610. E(2).
Possibly issued separately but usually found as part of 14858.

14855 — Paraphrasis quinti capitis Jeschahiæ. [Anon. In verse.] 4°. *Edinburgi, R. Charteris,* 1609. L.
Possibly issued separately but usually found as part of 14853.5 or 14858.

14856 — Paraphrasis, 4. 5. & 11. capitum prophetiæ Jeschahiæ. = pt. of 14853.5.

14857 — Pietas illustrissimi domini, . . . comitis Montis-rosarum in patrem è vita decedentem 9. Novemb. 1608. [Anon. In verse.] 4°. *Edinburgi, R. Charteris,* 1609. L.O.C².D².E.+

14858 — Alexandri Julii Edinburgeni Scoto-Britanni poemata sacra. 5 pts. 4°. *Edinburgi, T. Finlason,* 1614. L.O. C².D².E.+
Composed of sheets of 14854, 14853.5, 14855, and 14846 with added gen. tp, dedic., and Paraphrasis prophetiæ Hobadiæ.

14859 — Alexandri Julii Edinburgensis Scoto Britanni sylvarum liber. [In verse.] 4°. *Edinburgi, T. Finlason,* 1614. L.O.C².D².E².+; HN.
— *See also* 3989.

14860 **Junius, Adrian.** The nomenclator, or remembrancer. . . . Written in Latine, Greeke, French [etc.] now in English by J. Higins. 8°. *f. R. Newberie a. H. Denham,* 1585. Ent. to Newberie 12 oc. 1583. L.O.C.D.E.+; F.HN.CH.N.Y.+
Some copies have A. Fleming's name added to tp as compiler of index; both states at O, F. Both occur with and without Latin verses to Fleming on A1ᵛ.
Regarding foreign-printed eds. which include a little English *see* headnote preceding 6832.1.

14860.5 — Philippeis, siue, in nuptias . . . Philippi & Mariae carmen heroicum. 4°. (*in aed. T. Berthe[leti,*]) 1554. L. LINC.
(Formerly 14861a) No dedicatory letter.

14861 — [Anr. issue, w. cancel tp reading 'seu' for 'siue', w. dedicatory letter on verso.] L.L¹³.; F.HN.HD.

14861a — Now = 14860.5.
— *ed. See* 20762.5.
— *tr. See* 10566.

Junius, Andreas. *See* Young, A.

Junius, Franciscus. *See* Du Jon, F.

Junius, Patrick. *See* Young, P.

Junius, Richard. *See* Young, R.

14861a.5 **Jury.** The jury of inquisition de jure divino. Whether by divine right it is lawfull to inflict punishment upon lordly bishops. 4°. *Printed in the yeere, that Sea-Coale was exceeding deare* [*Eliot's Court Press,*] 1640. L.O.E. E².G².; F.Y.

Justice. The complete justice. 1636, etc. *See* 14887.3 sqq.

14862 **Justices (Justice) of Peace.** The boke of Iustices of peas the charge with all the processe of the cessions. 4°. (*R. pynson,*) [1505?] L.O(imp.).D⁵.ST.; HD.
Reprinted in 18394 sq.

14863 — [Anr. ed.] The boke of Iustyces of peas. 4°. (*W. de Worde,* 1506.) HN.

14864 — [Anr. ed.] The Iustyces of paes. The boke of iustyces of peas. 4°. (*w. de worde,* 1510.) L.O.; HN(lacks 14 leaves).

14864.5 — [Anr. ed.] The Iustices of peas. [etc.] 4°. (*w. de worde,* 1515.) O(colophon only, Vet.A1 b.12).; HN.

14865 — [A variant, w. colophon:] (*R. coplande,* 1515.) O.C.

14866 — [Anr. ed.] The boke of Iustyces of peas. 4°. (*J. Skot,* 1521 (3 oc.)) M.

14867 — [Anr. ed.] The boke of Iustices of peas. 4°. (*R. Pynson,* 1521.) C.

14868 — [Anr. ed.] 8°. (*R. Redman,* 1527.) O(colophon only, Douce Add.142/487).
Same ed. as 14869?

14869 — [Anr. ed.] The boke of iustices of peas. 8°. [*R. Redman,* 1527?] O(tp only, Douce Add.142/490).
In border McK.&F. 15. Same ed. as 14868?

14870 — [Anr. ed.] The boke of iustices of peace. 8°. (*R. Redman,*) [1530?] C(lacks first sheet).; HD.
In border of type orns. Prob. issued w. 15582, 7711, 7695.7, 20898, and 7728.

14871 — [Anr. ed.] The boke of the Iustyce of peas. 8°. [*J. Rastell,* 1526–30?] L.O. Broxbourne(E).; HD.
Issued with 15581.2, 7727, 20897, 7695.5, and 7712.

14871.5 — [Anr. ed.] Justice of peace. 8°. (*in ed. T. Bertheleti,*) [c. 1533.] HD.
In border McK.&F. 24. Prob. issued w. 7712.6, 15583.5, and 20898.3.

14872 — [Anr. ed.] The boke of Iustices of peas. 8°. (*R. Redman,*) [1533?] O.C¹⁸. London, Gray's Inn.; HD. MIN(imp.).
No border on tp; orn. at foot. Prob. issued w. 15583, 7712.4, 20899, and 7696.

14873 — [Anr. ed.] The boke for a Iustyce of peace neuer soo wel and diligently set forthe. 8°. *in æd. T. Berthel[eti],* [1535–37?] L.C(frag.).DNPK.P.; HD.MIN.
Prob. issued w. 7713, 20899.5, and 15583.7. HD also has 7696.5 bd. in same vol.

14874 — [A ghost.]

14875 — [Anr. ed.] The boke for a Iustyce of peace. 8°. *in ed. R. Redman,* [1538?] HD.MIN.PEN(imp.).
In border McK.&F. 22.

Justices (Justice) of Peace—*cont.*

14876 — [Anr. ed., w. additions.] The boke for a Iustice of peace, the boke that teacheth to kepe a courte baron. Returna breuium. Carta feodi. The boke of thordynance. A boke conteynynge those statutes. 6 pts. 8°. (*in æd. T. Bertheleti*, 1539.) L.C¹⁰.; F.HD(2).LC.
　　Although the pts. are called for on the gen. tp, vols. differ. Only copies of pt. 1 are listed above. Pt. 2 = 7713.3; pt. 3 = 20899.5 (HD) or 20900.5 (F); pt. 4 = 15584.5; pt. 5 = 7696.7 (HD) or 7697.5 (C¹⁰); pt. 6 = 9338.3 (HD) or 9338.5 (C¹⁰).

14877 — [Anr. ed.] The contentes of this boke. Fyrste the boke for a Iustice of peace. The boke that teacheth to kepe a court Baron. [etc.] 5 pts. 8°. (*in æd. T. Bertheleti*, 1544.) L.O.O⁸.C.; HN.CH.HD.MIN.Y.
　　Only copies of pt. 1 are listed above. Pt. 2 = 7713.5; pt. 3 = 20902.3; pt. 4 = 15584.9; pt. 5 = 7697.9.
　　This ed. does not contain the statutes (which are pt. 6 of 14876) but cf. 9339.

14878 — [Anr. ed. of 'Justices' only.] The boke for a Iustyce of Peace neuer so well set forthe. 8°. *in ed. Wilhelmum* [sic] *Middiltoñ*, [1543?] L.O⁶(lacks tp).

14878.3 — [Anr. ed.] 8°. *in ed. Wilhelmi Middiltoñ*, [1544?] L.O. Phillipps 2659.; HD.MIN.

14879 — [Anr. ed.] 8°. *in ed. N. Hyll*, 1546. O.; HD.LC.MIN(imp.).
　　This and the following variants issued w. 7717.4 sqq., 20903, 15586 sqq., 7699 sqq., and 7732 sqq. Herbert II.706 lists a variant w. H. Smith's name in the imprint, of which no copy is now known.

14879.5 — [A variant, w. imprint:] [*N. Hill*] *in ed. R. Kele*, 1546. HD.

14879a — [A variant, w. imprint:] [*N. Hill*] *in ed. R. Toye*, 1546. L.

14879b — [A variant, w. imprint:] [*N. Hill*] *in ed. J. Waley*, 1546. L.L⁸.; HD.

14880 — [Anr. ed., w. additions.] The contentes of this boke. Fyrst the booke for a Iustyce of peace [etc.] 6 pts. 8°. (*in ed. W. Powell*, 1550.) F(pt. 1).HD.
　　Pts. 2–6 in HD copy are 7721, 15585.5, 20904, 7734a, 7704, all also doubtless issued separately.

14881 — [Anr. ed. on continuous signatures, w. further additions.] Whereunto is added the boke called Articuli ad narratioñes nouas, & the diuersitie of courts. 8°. (*R. Tottle*, 1556 (13 my.)) L.G⁴.NLW.; HD.MIN.
　　Reprints of 812 and 10946 are included only in this ed.

14882 — [Anr. ed. Without the 'Articuli', etc.] The contentes of this boke. Fyrst [etc.] 8°. (*R. Tottil*, 1559 (13 my.)) L.P.; CAL⁵.CU.HD.MIN.NY.

14883 — [Anr. ed.] The contentes of this booke. Fyrste [etc.] 8°. (*R. Tottil*, 1559 (13 my.)) L.O.M⁴.; F.HN.HD.N.WIS.+

14884 — [Anr. ed.] 8°. (*R. Tottyl*, 1569.) L.O⁵.C⁷.BIRM²(K.N.). D⁵.+; HD.MIN.PH².Y.
　　Colophon varies: as above (HD) or 'Tottel' (L).

14885 — [Anr. ed.] 8°. (*R. Tottyl*, 1574.) L.L²².L³⁸.O.O⁴.+; F. HD.LC.MIN(imp.).NYS.

14886 — [Anr. ed. of 'Justices' only, w. a different addition.] The aucthoritie of al Iustices of peace, with diuers warrants. Whereunto is added a fourme for kepinge

Justices (Justice) of Peace—*cont.*

of Court leetes, [etc.] by John Kitchin. 8°. (*R. Tottell*,) 1580 (1579 (16 fb.)) L(destroyed).; HD.LC.
　　The 2nd pt., reprinted in 15017 sqq., was possibly planned as a separate publication as the text begins on 2nd B1ʳ, but in copies of this and the next the prelims. are on L4–8 of the 1st pt.

14887 — [A variant, w. colophon dated:] (1580 (10 ap.)) O.C⁵. C¹².DNPK.; F.CAL⁵.CU.HD.MIN.+

14887.3 — The complete justice. A compendium of the particulars incident to Justices of the Peace. 8°. *Cambridge, f. the assignes of J. More*, 1636. MIN.

14887.5 — [A variant, omitting imprint, w. date:] 1637. O.C⁵. BRISTOL².DUL.NEP.; HD.

14888 — [Anr. ed.] 8°. *London, by the assignes of J. More*, 1638. L(destroyed).L²².L³⁸.O.C.C².+; CHI.CU.HD.
　　— Loffice et auctoryte des iustyces de peas. 1538. *See* 10968.
　　— The new boke of Iustices of the peas by A. F. K. 1538, etc. *See* 10969 sqq.

Justinus, *the Historian. See* Trogus Pompeius.

14889 **Juvenalis, Decius Junius.** Junii Juvenalis et Auli Persii Flacci satyræ [*Ed.* T. Farnaby.] 8°. *R. Field, imp. G. Welby*, 1612. Ent. 29 ap. L.O.C.A.M⁴.+; F.HN.CU. HD.ILL.+

14890 — Secunda editio. 8°. *R. Field, imp. G. Welby*, 1615. L. O.C.M⁴.NEK.+; F.HN.HD.N.Y.+

14891 — Tertia editio. 8°. *T. Snodham, imp. J. Pyper*, 1620 (1621.) Ent. to T. Snodham 2 mr. 1618. L.O¹⁸.C¹⁵. G⁴.LEEDS.+; F.HN.HD.ILL.Y.+

14892 — Quarta editio. 8°. *J. Legat, imp. P. Stephani & C. Meredith*, 1633. L.O.C.M⁴.SNU.+; F.HN.HD(lacks tp). ILL.Y.+
　　See Court-Book C, p. 227.

14893 — That which seemes best is worst. Juvenals tenth satyre. With Virginias death. By W. B[arksted?] 8°. *F. Kyngston f. N. Newbery*, 1617. Ent. 14 oc. L.O. SHEF.; HN.CAL².
　　— *See also* 4979, 13784, 24821, 25225.

Juvenalis, Guido, *ed. See* 23885.3.

14893.5 **Juvencus, Caius Vettius Aquilinus.** Juuenci Hispani presbyteri historia euangelica, versu heroico descripta. . . . M.D.XXXIIII. 8°. [*Antwerp, J. Grapheus*,] (*væneunt Gypsuici, per R. Oliuerium*,) [1534.] C¹⁵.DUR.; HD(lacks tp).
　　Other copies (O) have the variant colophon: *Antuerpiae, typis J. Graphei*, 1534.

Juventus. An enterlude called lusty Juventus. [1550?] *See* 25148.

Juxon, William, *Bp.* London. Visitation Articles. *See* 10265, 10266.
　　— *See also* 16776.16.

K

K., A. F. *See* 10969.

14894   **K., F.** [Heading A2^r:] Of the crinitall starre, which appeareth this October and Nouember 1580. 8°. [*R. Watkins*, 1580.] Ent. to R. Watkins 1 no. 1580. L(lacks tp).

K., H., *tr. See* 14092.

K., I. or J. An exposition vppon the syxt psalme of Dauid. [1556?] *See* 15074.6.
— *ed. See* 14611.
— *tr. See* 21311, 24664.

K., M., *tr. See* 16899.3.

14894.3   **K., R.** ⟨L⟩illies light ⟨for⟩ the helpe of young schollers. [By] R. K. 8°. *T. Dawson*, 1599. L(tp only, Harl.5919/59).

K., W. The education of children. 1588. *See* 14926.
— The metamorphosis of Pigmalions image. 1598. *See* 17482.

14894.5   **Kalenberg.** [The parson of Kalenborowe. *Tr.* from P. Frankfurter's 'Die geschichdes pfarrers vom Kalenberg.'] 4°. [*Antwerp, J. van Doesborch*, c. 1520.] O (lacks first 2 leaves).

Kalendar. The Kalendar of shepherds. 1503, etc. *See* 22407 sqq.

Kalendars. *See* Almanacks.

Kanuti, Benedictus, *Bp. See* 4589 sqq.

Kay, John, *tr. See* 4594.

Kay, Thomas. *See* pt. 2 of 4344.

Kaye, Richard. Almanacks. 1608, etc. *See* 467 sq.

Kayll, R. *See* 14894.7.

Ke., F., *tr. See* 15487.

14894.7   **Keale** or **Kayll, Robert.** The trades increase. [Init. I. R.] 4°. *N. Okes, sold by W. Burre*, 1615. Ent. 12 fb. L¹³.L³⁰(lacks tp).O.C.M.+; F.HN.BO.CHI.CU.+ (Formerly 20579) B3^r catchword: 'this'; G1^r line 12: 'conceipt'. At least M, BO have a 10-line errata slip pasted on the verso of the tp. Answered by 6845.

14894.8   — [Anr. ed.] 4°. *N. Okes, sold by W. Burre*, 1615. L(2). L⁸.C.NLW.SAL.; ILL. NY.
B3^r catchword: 'new'; G1^r line 12: 'conceit'.

14894.9   — [Anr. ed.] 4°. *N. Okes, sold by W. Burre*, 1615. L³⁰. O¹⁷.C²(VI.9.102²).D.; F.CB.HD(2).NY.
B3^r catchword: 'new', (w. comma); G1^r line 12: 'cōceipt'. In this ed. the inner formes of B, D, and F, and both formes of C are reimposed from 14894.8. One C² copy (VI.9.17²) and RGU have mixed sheets.

14895   **Keckermann, Bartholomæus.** Gymnasium logicum, id est, de usu & exercitatione logicæ artis absolutiori & pleniori, libri tres. 8°. *imp. J. Bill*, 1606. Ent. 30 no. 1605. LEIC.M⁴.SAL.; HN.

14896   — Ουρανογνωσία. Heavenly knowledg. A manuduction to theologie. Written in Latin done into English by T. V[icars]. 8°. *A. Math[ewes*, 1622.] Ent. 27 mr. 1622. L.O.D(lacks tp).
The 1st 3 words of the title and the imprint are xylographic, part of a woodcut border made especially for this work.

14897   — [Anr. ed., enlarged, w. letterpress tp:] Heavenly know-ledge. Done into English by T. Vickars. 12°. *A. M[athewes] a. J. N[orton] f. T. Jones*, 1626 (1625.) Ass'd to T. Jones 22 mr. 1625. L³.O(1, plus J, engr. tp only). BUTE.; F.HD(lacks letterpress tp).
The F letterpress tp is a variant, dated 1625. There is a 2nd tp, engr. by W. van de Passe: 'The second edition with addition. *f. T. Jones*, 1625.'

Keckermann, Bartholomæus—*cont.*
14898   — Systema ethicæ, tribus libris adornatum. 8°. *ex off. Nortoniana*, 1607. L.O.C.C²(2).; HN.U.

Keene, John. Almanacks. 1612, etc. *See* 468 sqq.

14898.5   **Keep.** Keepe within compasse: or, the worthy legacy of a wise father to his beloved sonne. [Init. John T., i.e. Trundle?] 8°. [*G. Eld] f. J. Trundle*, [1619.] Ent. 19 fb. 1619. O.
Line 1 of imprint ends: 'Barbican.'

14899   — [Anr. ed.?] 8°. *f. J. Trundle*, 1619. L(tp only, Harl. 5921/178).
Line 1 of imprint ends: 'in'; rest of tp from same setting as 14898.5.

14899.3   — Fift impression. 8°. [*f. J. Trundle*, c. 1620.] E²(impr. cropt).

14899.7   — Sixth impression. 8°. [*f. J. Trundle?* c. 1620.] L(tp only, Harl. 5993/120; impr. cropt).

14900   — Tenth impression. 16° in 8's. [*f. J. Wright*, c. 1630.] Ass'd by Trundle to J. Wright 24 ja. 1623. O(impr. cropt).
Prob. issued w. 20583.
— Keepe your text. 1619. *See* 23924.

14901   **Keilwey, Robert.** Relationes quorundam casuum selec-torum ex libris Roberti Keilwey. [*Ed.*] (J. Croke.) fol. [*A. Islip?*] *in æd. T. Wight*, 1602. L.O.BRISTOL². D.M².+; F.HN.CU.HD.LC.+

14902   — [Anr. ed.] Relationes. . . . Necnon, relationes . . . per G. Dalison, & per G. Bendloes. fol. [*M. Flesher*] *per assignationem J. Moore*, 1633. L.L³⁸.O.O⁸.D.+; F.HN. CHI.HD.NY.+

Keith, *Lord.* Nobilissimi domini, domini Kethi, . . . epithalamium. 1609. *See* 14852.

Keith, William. *See* Kethe, W.

14903   **Kellet, Edward.** Miscellanies of divinitie divided into three books. fol. [*R. Daniel a. T. Buck*] *printers to the Univ. of Cambridge*, 1633. L.O.C.D.STU.+; HN. CHI.PN².U.Y.

14904   — [Anr. issue, w. imprint:] *printers to the Univ. of Cam-bridge, sold* [*in London] by R. Allot*, 1635. L.O⁶.C². D.G².+; F.BO³.MICH.PN².Y.

14905   — A returne from Argier. [Two sermons by E. Kellet and H. Byam.] 4°. *T. H[arper] f. J. P[arker], sold by R. Thrale*, 1628. L.O.C¹⁷.A.BRISTOL.+; F.ILL(imp., lacks gen. tp).N.SMU.Y.+

14905.5   **Kellicke, Richard.** Soli Deo gloria. Know all men by these present [*sic*], . . . [Advertisements of medicines discovered and sold by . . .] s.sh.fol. [*N. Okes*, c. 1625.] L⁵(Lemon 236).

14906   **Kellie,** *Sir* **Thomas.** Pallas armata, or militarie instruc-tions. 4°. *Edinburgh, heires of A. Hart*, 1627. L.O.E. E².STU.+; F.HN.LC.
The L and F tpp appear to be from different settings; line 7 of L copy ends 'the', line 7 of F copy ends 'downe'.

14907   **Kellison, Matthew.** The gagge of the reformed gospell. 1263 [1623]. Now = 13033.4.

14908   — [Anr. ed.] The touch-stone of the reformed ghospell. 1634. Now = 13033.8.

14909   — A reply to Sotcliffes answer [23464] to the survey of the new religion [14913]. 8°. *Rhemes, S. Foigny*, 1608. L.O.C³.D.E².+; F.HN.N.NY¹¹.TEX.+ A&R 426.

14910   — The right and jurisdiction of the prelate, and the prince. Compyled by J. E. student in divinitie. 8°. [*Douai, P. Auroi,*] 1617. L.O.C².OS.W.+; HD.TEX.U. A&R 427. Answered by 14049.

14911   — [Anr. ed.] Newlie rewewed and augmented by the authoure. 8°. [*Douai, P. Auroi,*] 1621. L.O.C.D.G².+; HN.TEX. A&R 428.

Kellison, Matthew—*cont.*

14912 — A survey of the new religion. 8°. *Doway, L. Kellam* [*a. Rheims, S. Foigny,*] 1603. L.O.C⁵.A².E.+; F.HD.TEX. U.WASH³.
A&R 429. All but a1 and a8 pr. by Foigny; a1 and a8 found in 2 different settings, distinguished by a1ᵛ reading 'Astum' (L) or 'Actum' (HD).

14913 — [Anr. ed.] Newly augmented by the author. 4°. *Doway, L. Kellam,* 1605. L.O.C.E².W.+; F.HN.HD.N(lacks tp). U.+
A&R 430. Answered by 23448, 23464.

14914 — A treatise of the hierarchie and divers orders of the church against the anarchie of Calvin. 8°. *Doway, G. Pinchon,* 1629. L.O.C².D².E.+; F.HD.TEX.U.Y.+
A&R 431. Answered by 25779.
— *See also* 17128, 17129, 17130.

14915 **Kello, John.** The confessioun of maister John Kello Minister of Spot, the fourt [*sic*] day of October, 1570. 8°. *Edinburgh, R. Lekpreuik,* 15[70?] F.

14916 **Kellus, Samuel.** Carmen gratulatorium, ad . . . Jacobum, . . . sextum. 4°. *Edinburgi, A. Hart,* 1617. L.A².E.

14917 **Kellwaye, Simon.** A defensatiue against the plague. 4°. *J. Windet,* 1593. Ent. 21 mr. L.O.O⁵.G². Preston PL.+; F.HN.NLM.NY⁴.Y.+

14918 **Kelton, Arthur.** A chronycle with a genealogie. Newly compyled in meter. 8°. (*R. Grafton,* 1547.) L.O.

14919 — [Headline a3ᵛ/4ʳ:] A cōmendacion/Of welshmen. [Anon. In verse.] 8°. [*R. Grafton?*] (1546.) HN (lacks 1st 2 leaves).

14920 **Keltridge, John.** The exposition, and readynges of John Keltridge: vpon the wordes in the .xi. of Luke. 4°. *W. How f. A. Veale,* 1578. Ent. 1 jy. L.O.D.P.PLUME. +; F.HN.CHI.PN².U.

14921 — Two godlie and learned sermons, appointed, and preached, before the Jesuites in the Tower of London. 4°. [*J. Charlewood a.*] *R. Jhones,* [1581.] Ent. 23 my. 1581. L.O.D.E.P.+; F.U.

Kelway, Thomas, *tr. See* 10833.

14922 **Kem, Samuel.** The new fort of true honour, made impregnable. Presented in a sermon. 4°. *R. Oulton,* 1640. Ent. to R. Mabb 3 oc. L.O.C¹³.; U.Y.

Kemnitz. A true and particular relation of the battell fought neare Kemnitz. 1639. *See* Newsbooks 308.

14923 **Kemp, William.** Kemps nine daies wonder. Performed in a daunce from London to Norwich. 4°. *E. A[llde] f. N. Ling,* 1600. Ent. 22 ap. O.; CU.

14924 **Kempe, Margerie.** Here begynneth a shorte treatyse of contemplacyon taken out of the boke of Margerie kempe. 4°. (*W. de worde,*) [1501.] C.
— *See also* 20972.

14925 **Kempe, William.** A dutiful inuectiue, against the moste haynous treasons of Ballard and Babington. [In verse.] 4°. *R. Jones,* 1587. Ent. 23 de. 1586. L.O³.C. C⁵.PARIS.

14926 — The education of children in learning. [Init. W.K.] 4°. *T. Orwin f. J. Porter a. T. Gubbin,* 1588. L.O.; F.HN. HD.
— *tr. See* 15241.3.

Kempis, Thomas à. *See* Thomas, à Kempis.

Kendale, Johannes. Frater Johannes Kendale, [etc.] [1480.] *See* Indulgences 107 sqq.

14927 **Kendall, Timothy.** Flowers of epigrammes, out of sundrie the moste singular authours. [In verse.] 8°. [*J. Kingston f.*] *J. Shepperd,* 1577. Ent. 25 fb. L.O. C².CASHEL.; F.HN.HD(lacks tp).

14928 **Kendrick, John.** The last will and testament of Mᵣ. John Kendricke draper of London. 4°. [*M. Flesher*] *f. N. Butter a. N. Bourne,* 1625. Ent. 13 fb. L.; Y.
Pagination in sheets D and E in top outer corner of page.

14928.5 — [Anr. ed.] 4°. [*M. Flesher*] *f. N. Butter a. N. Bourne,* 1625. L.L³⁰.O.D⁸.M⁴.+; F.HD.
Pagination in sheets D and E in centre of top of page; sheet A from same setting as 14928.

14929 **Kennedy, John.** The historie of Calanthrop and Lucilla. [In verse.] 8°. *Edinburgh, J. Wreittoun,* 1626. L.E (imp.).; F.HN.

Kennedy, John—*cont.*

14930 — [Anr. issue, w. cancel tp:] The ladies delight, or: the English gentlewomans history of Calanthrop and Lucilla. *T. Harper f. M. Sparke,* 1631. HN.

14931 — A theological epitome or divine compend. [In verse.] 8°. *Edinburgh, J. Wreittoun,* 1629. L.

14932 **Kennedy, Quintin.** Ane compendius tractiue conforme to the scripturis [etc.] 4°. [*Edinburgh, J. Scot,*] 1558. A²(2).BUTE.DUR³.E.
— Heir followeth the coppie of the ressoning which was betuix the Abbote of Crosraguell and J. Knox. 1563. *See* 15074.

Kennedy, Walter. *See* 7348.

14932.5 **Kenner, Mrs. John.** [Begins:] Thou shalte understande (chrysten reader) that the thyrde daye of August Anno .M.CCCCC.Lii, in Myddleton stonye . . . the good wyfe was deliuered of thys double chylde, begotten of her late husbande John Kenner. s.sh.fol. [*London,* 1553?] L(Dept. of P&D, mutilated).

Kenningham, William. An almanack. 1558. *See* 432.

14933 **Kenrick, Samuel.** The tell-troth's requitall, or, truth's recompence. [A sermon.] 4°. *M. Flesher f. R. Mylbourne,* 1627. Ent. 10 mr. L.O³.C⁵.LK.NEP.; F.HN. AAS.N.

Kent. The countie of Kent. [Wages and rates. 1563.] *See* 7957.9.
— A most true and lamentable report, of haile. 1590. *See* 20889.7.

14934 — Strange newes out of Kent, of a monstrous and mis-shapen child. 4°. *T. C[reede] f. W. Barley,* 1609. Ent. 26 au. L.

14935 **Kent Street.** A wonder woorth the reading, of a woman in Kent Street. 4°. *W. Jones,* 1617. L.

Kepler, Johann. *See* 24864.

14936 = 14937.

14937 **Ker, George.** A discouerie of the vnnaturall and trai-terous conspiracie of Scottish papists. 4°. *Edinburgh, R. Waldegraue,* [1593.] L.O.C².D.E.+; F(2).HD. W. Stirling Maxwell, Chicago, Illinois.
(Formerly also 14396) Pr. in B.L.; cf. 14940.

14938 — [Anr. ed.] 4°. *R. F[ield] f. J. Norton,* 1593. Ent. 26 jn. L.O.D.E. Bradford PL.+; F.HN.HD.

14939 — [Anr. ed.] 4°. *T. Snodham, sould at the house of T. Este,* 1603. Ent. to T. Snodham ?ap. 1603 (Arber III.35). L.O(imp.).O².DUR⁵(2).E(2).; U.

14939.5 — [Anr. issue, w. cancel tp, w. imprint:] *f. W. Barley,* 1603. O.

14940 — [Anr. ed.] 4°. *Edinburgh, R. Walde-grave* [really *J. Wreittoun?* c. 1625.] L.L³⁰.E(3).E².
Pr. in roman type.

Ker, William. *See* 21929.

Kerr, James. Theses aliquot logicae. Præside J. Caro. 1617. *See* 21555.30.

Kerr, Robert, *Earl of Lothian.* Nobilissimi comitis Lothianae, epithalamium. 1611. *See* 14851.

Kerton, H., *tr. See* 14092.

14941 **Kethe, William.** Of misrules contending, with gods worde by name. [In verse.] s.sh.fol. [*S. Mierdman? f.*] *H. Syngelton,* [1553?] L⁵(Lemon 16).

14942 — A ballet declaringe the fal of the whore of babylone intytuled Tye thy mare tom boye. [In verse.] 8°. [*W. Hill,* 1548?] O.; F.

14943 — A sermon made at Blanford Forū, in the countie of Dorset. 8°. *J. Daye,* [1571?] L.L².O.C.E².+; F.

14944 — [William Keth his seeing glasse.] [Heading A4ʳ:] Vnto the ryghte honorable the nobilitie and ientlemen of Englande. 16° in 8's. [*Printed abroad,* c. 1555.] F(lacks A1–3 and all after C1).
Title from Maunsell (17669), pt. 1, p. 64.
— *See also* 16563.

14944.5 **Kett, Francis.** An epistle sent to diuers papistes in Eng-land prouing the pope to bee the beast in the 13. of the Reuelations. 8° in 4's. *H. Marsh,* 1585. L².P.

14945 — The glorious and beautifull garland of mans glorifica-tion. 4°. *R. Ward,* 1585. L.L²(2).O(imp.).R.; F.U.

14945.5 Key. The key of paradise opening the gate, unto eternall salvation. Collected . . . by I. W[ilson] P[riest.] The third edition. 18° in 6's. [*St. Omer, Eng. Coll. press,*] 1623. BUTE.HP(imp.).
A&R 432.

14946 — The key to vnknowne knowledge. Or, a shop of fiue windowes. 4°. *A. Islip f. E. White,* 1599. L.O.C.G⁴. P.+; F.HN.HD.ILL.NY⁴.+

Key, Thomas, *tr. See* 2854.

14947 Keymis, Lawrence. A relation of the second voyage to Guiana. 4°. *T. Dawson,* 1596. Ent. 15 oc. L.O. CHATS.G².LINC.+; F.HN.CB.MICH.NY.+
There are variant spellings in title: 'Keymis' or 'Kemys'; both at HN.

Keynes, George, *tr. See* 17533.

14948 Kichener, Nathaniel. The worlds assises. A sermon. 8°. *L. Snowdon f. J. Harison,* 1616. Ent. to J. Harison the elder, 9 de. 1615. LINC(imp.).; Y.

14949 No entry.

Kidman, Thomas. Almanacks. 1631, etc. *See* 469 sqq.

14950 Kilby, Richard, *of Derby.* The burthen of a loaden conscience. [Anon.] 8°. *Cambridge, C. Legge,* 1608. L.
14950.5 — [Anr. ed., signed.] 8°. *Cambridge, C. Legge, sold [in London] by M. Law,* 1613. U(imp.).
14951 — Fift impression. 8°. *Cambridge, C. Legge, sold [in London] by M. Law,* 1614. O¹³.C.
14952 — The sixt impression. 8°. *Cambridge, C. Legge, sold [in London] by M. Law,* 1616. O.
14953 — Seauenth impression. 8°. *Cambridge, C. Legge, sold [in London] by M. Law,* 1618. L.
Prob. issued w. 14955.
14954 — Tenth edition. 12°. *H. L[ownes] f. J. Boler,* 1630. Ass'd by widow Legge to Boler 1 jn. 1629. L.C¹⁰.
Prob. issued w. 14956.
14954.3 — The twelfth edition. 12°. *R. Y[oung] f. J. Boler,* 1635. L(tp only, Ames II.1297).; F.
Prob. issued w. 14956.7.
14954.7 — Hallelu-iah: praise yee the Lord, for the unburthening of a leaden conscience. 8°. *Cambridge, C. Legge, sold [in London] by M. Law,* 1617. L(tp only, Ames II. 439).
14955 — [Anr. ed.] 8°. *Cambridge, C. Legge, sold [in London] by M. Law,* 1618. L.
Prob. issued w. 14953.
14956 — [Anr. ed.] 12°. *H. L[ownes] f. J. Boler,* 1630. Ass'd by widow Legge to Boler 1 jn. 1629. L.C¹⁰.
Prob. issued w. 14954.
14956.3 — [Anr. ed.] 12°. *f. J. Boler,* 1632. ILL.
14956.7 — [Anr. ed.] 12°. *[R. Young] f. J. Boler,* 1635. F.
Prob. issued w. 14954.3.

14957 Kilby, Richard, *of Oxford.* A sermon preached . . . in Oxford at the funerall of Thomas Holland. 4°. *Oxford, Jos. Barnes, sold [in London,] by John Barnes,* 1613. L.O.C.E.M.+; F.HN.Y.

14958 Killigrew, Henry. The conspiracy a tragedy. 4°. *J. Norton f. A. Crooke,* 1638. Ent. 13 mr. L.O.C².E. LEEDS.+; F.HN.HD.N.NY.+ Greg 537.

14959 Killigrew, Thomas. The prisoners and Claracilla. Two tragæ-comedies. 12°. *T. Cotes f. A. Crooke,* 1641 (1640). 'The prisoners' ent. 2 ap. 1640; 'Claracilla' ent. 4 au. 1640. L(2, 1 imp.).L⁶.O.O⁶.C³('The prisoners' only).; F.HN.HD.PEN.PML.+ Greg 619, 620.
Gen. tp and 'Claracilla' dated 1641; 'The prisoners' tp dated 1640. = Wing K 452.

14959.5 Kimedoncius, Jacobus. Of the redemption of mankind. Tr. H. Ince. 4° in 8's. *F. Kingston,* 1598. Ent. to E. Allde 2 no. L.BUTE.G⁴.P.; F.HN.HD.ILL.PN².
14960 — [A variant, w. imprint:] *F. Kingston f. H. Lownes,* 1598. L⁴⁶.O.E².ETON.SAL.+; HN.U(imp.).

14960.5 Kind. A mad kinde of wooing, or, a dialogue betweene Will the simple, and Nan the subtill. *Ballad.* 2 pts. s.sh.fol. *f. H. G[osson,* c. 1628.] C⁶.
14961 — [Anr. ed.] s.sh.fol. *assignes of T. Symcockc* [sic], [1628–29.] L.

Kinde, John. An almanack. 1625. *See* 469.9.

Kinder, Henry, *tr. See* 15454.5.

Kinder, Philip. Almanacks. 1619, etc. *See* 437 sq.

Kinesman, Edward. The lives of saints. 1623. *See* 24732.

King. The Kingis complaint. [1567.] *See* 22200.
— The Kings psalms [etc.] 1544, etc. *See* 3001.7 sqq.

14961.5 King's Bench, *Prisoners of.* To the kings most excellent majestie: the Lords . . . Commons. The humble petition of the prisoners for debt in the Kings Bench. [Against usury and imprisonment for debt.] s.sh.fol. [*London,* 1621?] L⁵(Lemon 213).
14961.7 — To the most honourable assembly of the Commons. The humble petition of the prisoners in the Kings Bench, and Fleete. [Urging an act for the release of prisoners of debt.] s.sh.fol. [*London,* 1624.] L(Harl. MS.7614/125).L⁸(GL 5777).
A bill was read 18 Mar. 1624; *see JHC* I.739, 836.
— *See also* 14428, 22639.

King, Mr., *tr. See* 1895.

14962 King, Adam. In Jacobum sextum Scotorum regem, Adami Regii panegyris. 4°. *Edenburgi, R. Charteris,* 1603. L.E².STU.; HN.
— *tr. See* 4568.

14963 King, Benjamin. The marriage of the lambe. [A sermon.] 12°. *T. Cotes f. R. H[arper?]* 1640. L.O.C¹⁰.

14964 King, Edward. Justa Edouardo King naufrago, ab amicis mœrentibus, amoris. (Obsequies. Lycidas, J. M[ilton].) 4°. *Cantabrigiæ, ap. T. Buck & R. Daniel,* 1638. L.O⁹.C.LINC.M.+; HN.HD.ILL.NY.Y².+

14965 King, Henry, *Bp.* An exposition upon the Lords prayer. 4°. *J. Haviland, sold by J. Partridge,* 1628. L.O.C. BIRM.NLW.+; F.HN.HD.ILL.U.+
14966 — [Anr. ed.] 4°. *A. Griffin,* 1634. L.O.C⁸.DUR.E⁴.+; HD. PH.SMU.
14967 — [A variant, w. 'Second impression' added to tp.] L.O. C.A.D.+; F.ILL.NY¹¹.PH.PN.
14968 — A sermon of deliverance. Preached on Easter Monday, 1626. 4°. *J. Haviland f. J. Marriot,* 1626. Ent. 21 ap. L.O.C.BHP.ETON.+; F.HN.HD.U. Wisconsin Historical Society.+
14969 — A sermon preached at Pauls Crosse, touching the supposed apostasie of J. King, late bishop of London. 4°. *F. Kyngston f. W. Barret,* 1621. Ent. 14 de. L³⁸. DUR⁵.GK.M.; F.SMU.
Takes exception to statement on p. 19 of 3895.5; *see also* 18305. All copies but L³⁸, GK have quire M from 14969.5 added.
14969.5 — [Anr. issue, w. quire M added and tp partly reset:] Whereunto is annexed the examination, and answere of T. Preston, P[riest, *alias* R. Widdrington] touching this scandall. L.O.C.D.DUR(Bamb.).+; HN.HD (lacks quire M).IND.PN².U.+
Some copies (2 O, C², HN, IND) have errata on M3ᵛ.
14970 — A sermon preached at St. Pauls March 27. 1640. 4°. *E. Griffin,* 1640. Ent. 29 ap. L.O.C.D.PETYT.+; F.HN.HD. U.Y.
14971 — Two sermons preached at White-Hall in lent. 4°. *J. Haviland,* 1627. Ent. to Mrs. Griffin a. Haviland 16 mr. L.O.C².C⁸.DUR⁵.+; F.HN.HD.U.Y.+
14972 — Two sermons. Upon the Act Sunday. (David's enlargement. By H. King.—Davids strait. By J. King.) 2 pts. 4°. *Oxford, J. L[ichfield] a. W. T[urner] f. W. Turner,* 1625. L.O.C.DUR⁵.YK.+; F.HN.HD.N.Y.+

14973 King, Humphrey. An halfe-penny-worth of wit, in a penny-worth of paper. Or, the hermites tale. The third impression. [In verse.] 4°. *f. T. Thorp, by assignement of E. Blount,* 1613. L.PLUME.; F.HN.NY.

14974 King, John, *Bp.* The fourth sermon preached at Hampton Court on Tuesday the last of Sept. 4°. *Oxford, Jos. Barnes,* 1606. L.O.C.G⁴.M².+; F.HN.HD.U.Y.+
14975 — [Anr. ed.] 4°. *Oxford, Jos. Barnes,* 1607. Ent. to John Barnes a. ass'd to T. Langley 28 ap. 1619. L¹³.O.C. D.E.+; F.HN.HD.U.Y.+
14976 — Lectures vpon Jonas, deliuered at Yorke in the yeare of our Lorde 1594. (A sermon preached at the funeralles of John [Piers, abp. of York.]—A sermon preached in Yorke.) 4° in 8's. *Oxford, Jos. Barnes, solde [in London by Joan Brome,]* 1597. L.O. C.D.E.+; F.HN.CHI.HD.Y.+
14977 — [Anr. ed.] Newlie corrected. 4° in 8's. *Oxford, Jos. Barnes, solde [in London by Joan Brome,]* 1599. L.O. C².CASHEL.M.+; F.HN.HD.MIN.U.+

King, John, *Bp.*—*cont.*
14978 — [Anr. ed.] Newly corrected. 4⁰ in 8's. *Oxford, Jos. Barnes, solde* [*in London by Joan Brome,*] 1600. Ent. to P. Short a. T. Hayes 31 ja. 1602. L.O.C.E⁸.M.+; F.HN.HD.U.Y.+

14979 — [Anr. ed.] Newly corrected. 4⁰ in 8's. *H. L(ownes,) sould by A. Johnson,* 1611. Ent. to H. Lownes 6 fb. 1604. L.O.C¹⁵.D.G².+; F.HN.ILL.LC.U.+
(Formerly also 14980; 14988 is pt. of this)

14980 — = 14979.

14981 — [Anr. ed.] 4⁰ in 8's. *H. Lownes,* 1618. L.O.C.E².G².+; F.HN.HD.N.PEN.+
(14989 is pt. of this)

14982 — A sermon at Paules Crosse, on behalfe of Paules church. 4⁰. *E. Griffin f. E. Adams,* 1620. Ent. 12 my. L.O.C.D.P.+; F.HN.ILL.U.Y.+

14983 — A sermon of publicke thanks-giving for the happie recoverie of his majestie. 4⁰. [*Eliot's Court Press*] *f. T. Adams,* 1619. Ent. 7 my. L.L¹³.C². Bradford PL.+; F.HD(tp mutil.).LC.NY¹¹.
Collates A–G⁴ H². This may be the 3rd ed., not the 1st.

14984 — [Anr. ed.] A sermon of publicke thanks-giving for the happy recovery of his majesty. 4⁰. [*Eliot's Court Press*] *f. T. Adams,* 1619. L.O.C⁵.D.E.+; F.HN.CHI.HD.ILL.+
Collates tp+B–H⁴; B1ᵛ line 1: 'dittie'.

14984.5 — [Anr. ed.] 4⁰. [*Eliot's Court Press*] *f. T. Adams,* 1619. L.L².O.C.DUR⁵.+; F.BO⁵.CAL².U.Y.
Sheets B–E reset, F–H same setting as 14984; B1ᵛ line 1: 'ditty'.

14985 — A sermon preached in Oxon: the 5. of November. 1607. 4⁰. *Oxford, Jos. Barnes,* 1607. L.O.C³.P. PLUME.+; F.HN.HD.NY¹¹.U.+
One L copy has 'in Oxford:' in the title.

14986 — A sermon preached at Whitehall the 5. of November. 1608. 4⁰. *Oxford, Jos. Barnes,* 1608. Ent. to John Barnes a. ass'd to T. Langley 28 ap. 1619. L.O.C.D². G².+; F.HN.CHI.HD.U.+
Sheets A–E occur in 2 settings, found mixed; F copies differ in A–E3, O copies in A–D only.

14987 — A sermon preached in Sᵗ. Maries at Oxford the 24. of March. 4⁰. *Oxford, Jos. Barnes,* 1608. Ent. to John Barnes a. ass'd to T. Langley 28 ap. 1619. L.O.C.D. M.+; F.HD.U.Y.

14988 — A sermon preached at the funerals of John [Piers], Arch bishop of Yorke, 1594. 1611. = pt. of 14979.

14989 — A sermon preached in York, 1595. 1618. = pt. of 14981.

14989.5 — Vitis Palatina. A sermon appointed to be preached after the mariage of the Ladie Elizabeth. 4⁰. [*Eliot's Court Press*] *f. J. Bill,* 1614. Ent. 22 ja. L.O.C.G². LINC.+; F.HN.HD.NY.Y.+
(Formerly 14991) Collates ¶⁴ A–F⁴.

14990 — [Anr. ed.] 4⁰. [*Eliot's Court Press*] *f. J. Bill,* 1614. L.O. C.E.YK.+; F.HD.ILL.PN².Y.
Collates ¶⁴ A–E⁴.

14991 — Now = 14989.5.
— The bishop of London his legacy. 1623. *See* 18305.
— *See also* 10258 sqq.

14992 **King, John,** *Public Orator of Oxford.* Cenotaphium Jacobi. Sive laudatio funebris. 4⁰. *Oxoniæ, J. Lichfield & G. Turner,* 1624. L.O.C².P.YK.+; F.HN.HD.Y.
— *See also* 14972, 19027.

14992.5 **King, Robert.** A funerall sermon that was prepared to have bene preached, by Robert King. 8⁰. (*R. Grafton,* 1552 (my.)) O¹⁰.

14993 **King, William,** *of Edinburgh.* Theses philosophicæ præs. G. Regio. 1612. Now = 7487.9.
14994 — — 1616. Now = 7487.13.
14995 — — 1620. Now = 7487.17.
14996 — — 1624. Now = 7487.21.
14997 — — 1628. Now = 7487.25.

14997.3 **King, William,** *Preacher.* The straight gate to heaven. A sermon. 8⁰. *G. Eld, sould by E. Wright,* 1616. HD.
14997.7 — [Anr. ed.] 8⁰. *G. Eld, sould by T. Langley,* 1617. F.
14998 — [Anr. ed.] 8⁰. *G. Eld,* 1622. L.
14998.3 — [Anr. ed.] 8⁰. *M. Flesher, sold by F. Coules,* 1630. F.
14998.7 — [Anr. ed.] 8⁰. *M. Flesher,* [c. 1633.] O.O³.
14999 — [Anr. ed.] 16⁰ in 8's. *M. Flesher,* 1636. O.

14999.5 **Kingdoms.** [Second line of title:] Alteraciõs of kingdoms, for despisĩg of god. [In verse.] s.sh.fol. [*R. Grafton,* c. 1550.] O(Vet.A1a.3(34*), imp.).

14999a **Kings.** This present boke called the Gouernaunce of kynges. 1511. = 17017.

15000 **Kingsmill, Andrew.** A most excellent and comfortable treatise, for all such as are troubled in minde. And also a conference betwixt a Christian & an afflicted consciēce. (A forme of thanksgiuing and praier to be vsed of all godlie Christians in their families.) [*Ed.*] (*F. Mylles.*) 3 pts. 8⁰. *C. Barkar,* 1577. L(pt. 1: 4400.i.35, pt. 2: 4411. de. 46, lacks pt. 3).O.C.; F.
(Pts. 2 and 3 formerly 21770)

15001 — [Anr. ed.] 8⁰. *C. Barker,* 1578. L⁴(imp.).O.; F.
Does not reprint pt. 3 of 15000, but substitutes another prayer 'conteining the duetie of euerie true Christian.'

15002 — [Anr. ed.] 8⁰. [*T. Dawson*] *by assignement of C. Barker, solde* [*by H. Carre,*] 1585. L.O.; F.HN.

15003 — A viewe of mans estate. [*Ed.* F. Mills.] 8⁰. *H. Bynneman f. L. Harison a. G. Bishop,* 1574. Ent. 1570–71. O.; HN.

15004 — [Anr. ed.] 8⁰. *H. Bynneman f. L. Harison a. G. Bishop,* 1576. L.O.LAMPORT. Stevens Cox.; F(lacks tp).

15005 — [Anr. ed.] 8⁰. [*J. Kingston*] *f. G. Bishop a. T. Woodcocke,* 1580. Ass'd to Woodcocke 15 jy. 1578. L.O.; F.

15006 **Kingsmill, Thomas.** Classicum poenitentiale, [etc.] (Tractatus de scandalo.) 4⁰. *Oxoniæ, Jos. Barnesius, prostant Londini, ap. S. Waterson,* 1605. L.O.O¹⁸.C. C⁵.+

15007 — A complaint against securitie in these perillous times. 8⁰. *imp. G. Bishop,* 1602. Ent. 2 au. O.

15008 — The drunkards warning. A sermon. 8⁰. *N. Okes f. R. Collins,* 1631. Ent. 29 ja. O.O¹².

15009 **Kingsmill, William,** *ed.* Encomion Rodolphi Warcoppi ornatissimi, qui extinctus est. 1605. Now = 19049.5.

Kingston, Felix. *See* 7154.7, 14173.

Kinsayder, W., *pseud. See* 17482, 17485.

Kinsman, Edward, *tr. See* 24730, 24732, 24738.

Kinsman, William, *tr. See* 24730.

Kinwelmarsh, Francis, *tr. See* 15487.

15010 **Kirbye, George.** Cantus. Prim⁹. (Cantus. Secund⁹.—Altus.—Tenor.—Bassus.—Sextus.) The first set of English madrigalls, to 4. 5. & 6. voyces. 6 ptbks. 4⁰. *T. Este,* 1597. Ent. 24 no. 1596. L(2, 1 imp.).O(altus only).; F(1, plus 2 tenor only).HN(lacks altus).LC.

15011 **Kirchmeyer, Thomas.** The popish kingdome, or reigne of Antichrist. By T. Naogeorgus, englyshed by B. Googe. (The spirituall husbandrie.) [In verse.] 4⁰. *H. Denham f. R. Watkins,* 1570. Ent. 1569–70. L. O(2 imp.).C.D².P.; F.HN.BO⁵.CH.Y.

15012 — [A ghost.]

15013 **Kirkby Bellars, Leicestershire,** *Augustinian Priory.* Vniuersis xp̃ifidelibus presentes litteras inspecturis, [etc.] [1507.] Now = Indulgences 44.
— *See also* Indulgences 45.

15014 **Kirke, John.** The seven champions of christendome. 4⁰. *J. Okes, sold by J. Becket,* 1638. Ent. to J. Okes 13 jy. L.O.C.ETON.M.+; F.HN.HD.N.NY.+ Greg 545.

15015 **Kirkham, W.** Ioyfull newes for true subiectes, to God and the crowne. [Signed W. Kyrkh.] *Ballad.* s.sh.fol. *W. How f. R. Johnes,* [1570.] Ent. 1569–70. L.

Kirton, H., *tr. See* 14092.

15015.3 **Kis, Stephanus.** Tabulæ analyticæ, . . . de fide, charitate, et patientia. Authore Stephano Szegedino. 4⁰ in 8's. *in æd. R. Fieldi, imp. T. Adams,* 1593. Ent. to Adams a. Oxenbridge 30 my. 1592. C⁵.
See Greg, *Register B,* p. 43.

15015.7 — [A variant, w. imprint:] *in æd. R. Fieldi, imp. J. Oxenbridge,* 1593. L(2 tpp. Ames I.539; Harl.5936/270).

15016 — [A variant, w. imprint:] *in æd. R. Fieldi, imp. G. Nortoni,* 1593. L.L².C.C¹⁷.D.

Kit, *of Kingston.* Westward for smelts. By kinde Kit of Kingstone. 1620. *See* 25252.

15017 **Kitchen, John.** Le court leete, et court baron. 8⁰. *in æd. R. Tottelli,* 1580 (4 oc.) Ent. 18 fb. 1583. D.G².; F(2).HN.HD.
First pr. as pt. of 14886. *See also* 7726.

Kitchen, John—*cont.*

15018 — [Anr. issue, dated 1581, w. 'Returna Breuium' added.] 2 pts. 8⁰. *in æd. R. Tottelli*, 1581 (4 oc.) L.O.O⁵.R. Rouen PL.; HD.LC(lacks pt. 2).MIN.NYS.
　　Pt. 2 reprints 20894.4, and the text is included in all the following eds.

15019 — [Anr. ed., enlarged.] 2 pts. 8⁰. *in æd. R. Tottelli*, 1585 (6 my.) L³⁸.O.C.D.NLW.+; HN.CAL⁵.CU.HD.MIN.

15020 — [Anr. ed., w. continuous signatures.] 8⁰. *in æd. R. Totelli*, 1587 (1 mr.) L.L².O.O⁶.C.+; HN.CU.HD.N.Y.+

15021 — [Anr. ed.] 8⁰. *in æd. R. Totelli*, 1592 (1 jy.) L.C³.DNPK.; F.HN.HD.LC.MIN.+

15022 — [Anr. ed.] 8⁰. [*A. Islip?*] *in æd. T. Wight & B. Norton*, 1598. L.L¹³(imp.).O.NMU.P.+; F.CAL.HD.MICH.PN.+

15023 — [Anr. ed.] 8⁰. [*A. Islip*] *f. the Co. of Statrs.*, 1607. O³. O²⁹.; HN.HD.MICH.N.
　　See Court-Book C, p. 23.

15024 — [Anr. ed.] 8⁰. [*A. Islip*] *f. the Co. of Statrs.*, 1613. L.C². E.P.WOR.+; F(imp.).HN.HD(imp.).LC.Y.

15025 — [Anr. ed.] 8⁰. [*A. Islip*] *f. the Co. of Statrs.*, 1623. Ent. to the English Stock 5 mr. 1620. L.O.O⁹.O¹⁹. Leeds PL.; F.HN.HD.WASH³.

15026 **Kittowe, Robert.** Loves load-starre. Lively deciphered in a historie. 4⁰. *T. Creede*, 1600. O.

15027 **Knack.** A most pleasant and merie new comedie, intituled, a knacke to knowe a knaue. 4⁰. [*f.*] *R. Jones*, 1594. Ent. 7 ja. L(imp.).L⁶.O.; HN. Greg 115.

15028 — A pleasant conceited comedie, called, a knacke to know an honest man. 4⁰. [*T. Scarlet*] *f. C. Burby*, 1596. Ent. 26 no. 1595. L⁶.O.; HN.HD. Greg 139.

Knaresborough, Yorkshire, *Trinitarian Priory of St. Robert. See* Indulgences 121B sq.

Knave. The knave of harts. 1612, etc. *See* 21390 sqq.

Knaves. Here begynneth the .xxiiii. orders of knaues. [c. 1561.] *See* 995.5.
— The xxv. orders of knaues. 1565, etc. *See* 993 sqq.

15029 **Knell, Thomas.** An A B C to the christen congregacion. [Signed T. Knell. In verse.] s.sh.fol. *R. Kele*, [1550?] HN.
　　Pr. on verso of 9512.8.

15030 — An answer to a papisticall byll, cast in the streetes of Northampton. [Anon. In verse.] s.sh.fol. *J. Awdely*, 1570. Ent. 1570–71. HN.

15030.5 — An answer at large, to a most hereticall, . . . byll, in English verse, which was cast abrode in the streetes of Northamton, 1570. [Signed T. Knell jun.] 4⁰. *J. Awdelye*, [1570.] C⁵.
　　The answers in this are longer than the ones in the preceding number. The text of the 'byll' is the same.

15031 — Certain true marks wherby to knowe a papist. [Signed T. Knell.] 8⁰. *J. Allde*, [1581.] Ent. 29 ap. 1581. L².

15032 — A declaration of such tempestious, and outragious fluddes, as hath been in England. 1570. [Signed T. Knell jun.] 8⁰ in 4's. (*W. How f. J. Allde a. W. Pickering*, 1571.) Ent. 1570–71. C.

15033 — An epitaph, or rather a short discourse made vpon the life & death of D. Boner, Bisshop of London. [Signed T. Knell jun. In verse.] 8⁰. *J. Allde*, 1569 (14 se.) L.O²⁴.C⁵.

15033.3 — A godlie and necesserie treatise, touching the vse and abuse of praier. Compiled and made by Thomas Knell the elder. 8⁰. *H. Denham*, 1581. L¹⁵(imp.).

15033.7 — An historicall discourse of yᵉ life and death of doctor Story. [Signed T. Knell jun. In verse.] 8⁰ in 4's. (*J. Allde*,) [1571.] D².
　　(Formerly 23298)

15034 — A piththy [*sic*] note to papists all and some that ioy in Feltons martirdome . . . viii. August. 1570. [Signed T. Knell jun. In verse.] 8⁰ in 4's. *J. Allde*, [1570.] L².

15035 **Knevet, Ralph.** Funerall elegies; consecrated to the immortall memory, of Lady Katherine Paston. 4⁰. *T. Cotes f. A. Crooke*, 1637. Ent. 22 ap. L.

15036 — Rhodon and Iris. A pastorall. 4⁰. [*J. Beale*] *f. M. Sparke*, 1631. Ent. 12 no. L.O.C².E.ETON.+; F.HN.HD. N.Y.+ Greg 449.

15036a — [A variant, w. imprint:] *f. M. Sparke, sold by E. Causon at Norwich*, 1631. L.; F.

15037 — Στρατιωτικόν. Or a discourse of militarie discipline. [In verse.] 4⁰. [*M. Flesher*,] 1628. HN.

15037.5 **Knewstub, John.** An aunsweare vnto certaine assertions, tending to maintaine the Churche of Rome. 4⁰. *T. Dawson f. R. Sergier*, 1579. Ent. 15 jn. L4.O¹⁷.C. C⁵(2).YK.; F.HN.U.
　　(Formerly 15039) Collates ☞⁴ A–G⁸ H⁴ I².

15038 — [Anr. ed.] 8⁰. *T. Dawson f. R. Sergier*, 1579. L.O. C(imp.).A.; F(2, 1 lacks tp).HN.HD.
　　(Formerly also 15041) Collates *⁴ A–N⁸ O⁴.

15039 — Now = 15037.5.

15040 — A confutation of monstrous and horrible heresies, taught by H. N[iclas in 18556 and 18557.] 4⁰ in 8's. *T. Dawson f. R. Sergier*, 1579. Ent. 11 my. L.O.C.D. E⁴.+; F.HN.HD.N.U.+
　　2nd section reprinted separately in 15046.

15041 — = 15038.

15042 — Lectures of . . ., vpon the twentith [*sic*] chapter of Exodus. 4⁰ in 8's. *L. Harrison*, 1577. Ent. 3 my. L. O.O².C.BTL.+; Washington Cathedral.

15043 — [Anr. ed.] 4⁰ in 8's. *L. Harrison*, 1578. L.O.C⁴.A.WI.+; F.HN.NY.U.Y.

15044 — [Anr. ed.] 4⁰ in 8's. *f. T. Woodcocke*, 1579. Ass'd 15 jy. 1578. O.BIRM.E².P.SCL(2).; F.

15045 — [Anr. ed.] 4⁰ in 8's. [*T. Dawson*] *f. T. Woodcocke*, 1584. L(tp only, Ames I.419).L².P.; F.BO.HD.NY¹¹.

15046 — A sermon preached at Paules Crosse the Fryday before Easter, 1579 [really 1576.] 8⁰. *T. Dawson f. R. Sergier*, 1579. L.O.C.DEU.ETON.+; F.HD(imp., lacks tp). TORONTO².
　　First pr. as part of 15040.

Knight. The knight of the burning pestle. 1613. *See* 1674.
— The knyght of the swanne. 1512, etc. *See* 7571 sqq.
— A poore knight his pallace of priuate pleasures. 1579. *See* 4283.

15047 **Knight, Edward.** The triall of truth, wherein are discouered three greate enemies vnto mankinde. 8⁰. *T. Dawson a. T. Butter*, 1580. Ent. 13 no. 1579. O.

15048 **Knight, Francis.** A relation of seauen yeares slaverie under the Turkes of Argeire. 4⁰. *T. Cotes f. M. Sparke, jun.*, 1640. Ent. 16 mr. O².O¹³.C.C⁶.D².; HN. N.NY.Y(2).

15048a — [Anr. issue, w. imprint:] *T. Cotes f. M. S[parke] jun., sold by T. Nicholes*, 1640. L(2).E.WIN²(imp.)*.; F.NY. WTL.

Knight, Richard. An almanack. 1638. *See* 469.11.

15049 **Knight, William.** A concordance axiomaticall: containing a survey of theologicall propositions. fol. [*W. Hall a. T. Haviland?*] *f. J. Bill*, 1610. Ent. to J. Norton a. Bill 18 de. 1609. L.O.C.E².SAL.+; F.HN.U. Y. Wisconsin Historical Society.+

15050 **Knights of Saint John.** [Heading A3ʳ:] The begynnynge and foundacyon of the . . . knyghtes hospytallers of saynt Iohan baptyst of Ierusalem. [A4ᵛ:] Here foloweth the syege, . . . of Rodes [of 1522. *Tr.* by R. Copland from Jacques de Bourbon.] fol. (*R. Coplande*, 1524 (23 jy.)) L(imp.).
　　Reprinted in 12626, vol. 2, pp. 72–95. The earliest known ed. of the French text is dated 1525.

15051 **Knolles, Richard.** The generall historie of the Turkes. fol. *A. Islip*, 1603. Ent. 5 de. 1602. L.O.C.DEU(lacks tp).M⁴.+; F.HN.HD.N.PML.+
　　One half of the copyright belonged to G. Bishop and J. Norton, *see* Arber III.223.

15052 — Second edition. [Enlarged.] fol. *A. Islip*, 1610. G. Bishop's part ent. to T. Adams 14 mr. 1611. L.O. C².LIV³.M.+; F.HN.HD.ILL.Y.+

15053 — Third edition. [Enlarged] by E. Grimston. fol. *A. Islip*, 1621 (1620.) Continuations from 1604 ent. 10 jn. 1629. L.O.C.E.NLW.+; F.HN.CU.HD.ILL.+

15054 — Fourth edition. With a new continuation. fol. *A. Islip*, 1631. Continuation ent. 20 de. 1630. L.O⁴.C.D.E⁸.+; F.HN.CU.HD.ILL.+
　　See Court-Book C, p. 195.

15055 — Fift edition. With a new continuation [by] (T. Nabbes.) fol. *A. Islip*, 1638. L.O.C.D.G².+; F.HN.HD.N.Y.+
　　See Court-Book C, pp. 299, 308, and Greg, *Companion*, pp. 105–6, 351–3.
— *tr. See* 3193.

15056 **Knots.** [Heading A1ʳ:] Certaine excellent and new invented knots and mazes, for plots for gardens. [Sometimes attrib. to G. Markham.] 4⁰. (*f. J. Marriott*, 1623.) L.O.; HN.

Knott, Edward, *pseud. See* 25774, 25777.

Knowles, Thomas. A second courante of newes from the East India. 1622. *See* 7458.

15057 **Knox, James.** Theses philosophicæ. 1601. Now = 7487.4.
15058 ——1605. Now = 7487.6.

15059 **Knox, John.** An admonition or warning that the faithful Christiãs in London, Newcastel Barwycke & others, may auoide Gods vengeãuce. 8°. (*Wittonburge, N. Dorcastor,*) [i.e. *London? J. Day?*] (1554 (8 my.)) O.O¹⁷.E(imp.).; F.
15059.5 — [Anr. ed., w. title:] A godly letter sent too the fayethfull in London, Newcastell, Barwyke, and to all other within the realme of Englande, that loue the cõminge of oure Lorde Iesus. (A confession & declaratiõ of praiers added therunto.) 2 pts. 8°. *Rome, before the castel of s. Aungel at the signe of sainct Peter,* [i.e. *Wesel? J. Lambrecht? f. H. Singleton,*] 1554 (jy.) Pt. 2 ent. to R. Waldegrave 10 ja. 1581. L.O⁸(imp.).C. D.E.+; F.HN.CH.ILL(pt. 2 only).
(Formerly 15073) With Singleton's device, McK. 127.
15060 — An answer to a great number of blasphemous cauillations. 8°. [*Geneva*] *J. Crespin,* 1560. L.O.C.E.G².+; F.HN.HD(tp mutilated).N.U.+
15061 — [Anr. ed.] 8°. [*R. Field*] *f. T. Charde,* 1591. Ent. to T. Cooke 11 ja. 1581. L².O.C².D.E.+; F.HN.HD.ILL.NY.+
15062 — An answer to a letter of a Iesuit named Tyrie, be Iohne Knox. 8°. *Sanctandrois, R. Lekpreuik,* 1572. L.O.A. E(2).E³.; F.
Reprinted and answered in 24476.
15063 — The appellation of John Knoxe from the cruell sentence pronounced against him by the false bishoppes and clergie of Scotland. (An admonition by A. Gilby.) 8°. *Geneva,* [*J. Poullain a. A. Rebul?*] 1558. L.O.C¹⁰. E.M.+; F.CH.PN².Y. New Brunswick U, Fredericton, N.B.
— A confession & declaratiõ of praiers vpon the death of king Edward the VI. 1554. *See* pt. 2 of 15059.5.
15064 — The copie of an epistle sent vnto the inhabitants of Newcastle, & Barwike. In the end wherof is added a briefe exhortation to England. 2 pts. 16° in 8's. *Geneva,* 1559. L.O.C.
(Formerly also 15065)
15065 — = 15064.
15066 — The copie of a letter, sent to the ladye Mary dowagire, regent of Scotland, in 1556. Here is also a sermon. 16° in 8's. [*Wesel? H. Singleton?* 1556.] L.C.E.E². M.+; F.
In same types as 9981.
15067 — [Anr. ed.] Nowe augmented by the author. 8°. *Geneva, J. Poullain a. A. Rebul,* 1558. L.O.C¹⁰.E.G².+; F. CH(2).N.
Omits the sermon added in 15066.
— An exposition vppon the syxt psalme of Dauid. [1556?] *See* 15074.6.
15068 — A notable and comfortable exposition of M. John Knoxes, vpon the fourth of Mathew. [*Ed.* J. Field.] 8°. *R. Walde-graue f. T. Man,* [1583.] Ent. 24 fb. 1583. L².D.E.ETON.G².+; TORONTO².
Man fined for printing this; see Arber II.854.
15069 — A faythfull admonition made by Iohñ Knox, vnto the professours of Gods truthe in England. 8°. (*Kalykow,*) [i.e. *Emden, E. van der Erve,*] (1554 (20 jy.)) L.O.C. C⁸.D².+; F.HN.CH.N.PML.
15070 — The first blast of the trumpet against the monstruous regiment of women. [Anon.] 8°. [*Geneva, J. Poullain a. A. Rebul,*] 1558. L.O.C.E.STU.+; F.HN.CH.
Answered in 1005.
15071 — [The first (second—thirde) book of the history of the reformation of religion within the realme of Scotland.] [Anon.] 8°. [*T. Vautrollier,* 1587.] L.O.C.D.E.+; F. HN.HD.PML.
Pp. 17–560 only; said to have been seized before completion of printing by Abp. Whitgift's order.
15072 — A fort for the afflicted. 1580. Now = 15074.8.
15073 — A godly letter sent too the fayethfull in London, Newcastell, [etc.] (A confession and declaratiõ of praiers.) 1554. Now = 15059.5.
15074 — Heir followeth the coppie of the ressoning which was betuix the Abbote of Crosraguell [Q. Kennedy] and John Knox. 4°. *Edinburgh, R. Lekpreuik,* 1563. E(2).; F.
See also 12968.

Knox, John—*cont.*
— A notable and comfortable exposition. *See* 15068.
15074.2 — The ordoure of excommunicatioun and of publict [*sic*] repentance, vsed in the church of Scotland. [Anon.] 8°. *Edinburgh, R. Lekpreuik,* 1569. L².E(2).
15074.4 — [Verso/recto headline:] A percel of the .vi./Psalme expounded. 8°. [*London? J. Day?,* 1554.] O(imp.).
15074.6 — [Anr. ed.] An exposition vppon the syxt psalme of Dauid, wherein is declared hys crosse, complayntes and prayers. (A comfortable epistell sent to the afflicted church of Chryste.) [Init. I.K.] 16° in 8's. [*Wesel? H. Singleton?* 1556?] E(2, 1 imp.).G². End of text dated 7 July 1556. In same types as 9981; 1 E and G² are bd. w. 15066.
15074.8 — [Anr. ed., revised.] A fort for the afflicted. [*Ed.* A. Fleming.] 8°. *T. Dawson,* 1580. Ent. 5 no. 1580; ?ent. to R. Field 29 oc. 1589 and crossed out 2 mr. 1590. L.O. Goyder.; HN.HD(lacks tp).
(Formerly 15072) Does not exactly duplicate text of 15074.4.
15075 — A sermon preached by Iohn Knox in the publique audience of the church of Edenbrough, the .19. of August .1565. For the which the said I. Knoxe was inhibite preaching for a season. To this is adioyned an exhortation for the reliefe of [ministers.] 8°. [*H. Denham?*] 1566. Ent. to Master Wood, prob. not a stationer, 1565–66. L.O.C.E.M.+; F.HN.CH.HD.PML.+
15076 — To his louing brethren whome God ones gathered in the church of Edinburgh. 8° in 4. *Striuiling, R. Lekpreuik,* 1571. E.
— ed. *See* 1340, 24357.
— *See also* 22041.

Knutsson, Bengt, *Bp. See* 4589 sqq.

Knyvet, *Sir* **Thomas.** [Certificate that the silver in the Irish shilling is worth 3ᵈ. 1604.] *See* 9209.5.

15077 **Komenský, Jan Amos.** Conatuum Comenianorum præludia ex bibliotheca S. H[artlib.] (Porta sapientiae reserata.) 4°. *Oxoniæ, G. Turnerus,* 1637. L.L¹⁵. O.O².C.+; HD(imp.).U(imp.).
15077.3 — Janua linguarum reserata: or a seed-plot of all languages. The third edition. *Tr.* T. Horne. *Lat. a. Eng.* 8°. *R. Young, sold by T. Slater,* 1636. Ent. to Young 10 jn. 1634. L.L⁴⁴.E.; F.
The same text as 15078 sqq. but in 2 languages only. Not to be confused w. the anon. Janua Linguarum (14466 sqq.).
15077.5 — The fourth edition. Corrected and enlarged. 8°. *R. Young, sold by T. Slater,* 1638. C.DUR³.G².LIV³.; Oberlin C.
(Formerly 14473)
15077.7 — The fift edition. Now reviewed by J. Robotham. 8°. *R. Young,* 1640. Ent. to Young a. T. Slater 21 no. (E&R I.2). L⁴⁴.C.DUL.G².
(Formerly 14474)
15078 — Porta linguarum trilinguis reserata. (The gate of tongues vnlocked. [*Ed.*] J. Anchoran.) *Lat., Eng., a. Fr.* 8°. *G. Millerus, sumpt. M. Sparkes & T. Slater* (*G. Miller f. T. Slater,*) 1631. Ent. to Sparkes a. Slater 28 jy. L.DUL.
Same text as 15077.3 sqq., but in 3 languages.
15078.5 — [Anr. issue, w. imprint on Eng. tp:] *G. Miller f. M. Sparke,* 1631. C.
15078a — [Anr. issue, w. imprints:] *G. Millerus, sumpt. authoris,* (*G. Miller f. the authour,*) 1631. L².O.C(imp.).C⁵.; F.HN.CU.HD.
HD copy has dedic. signed 'Ioh. Anchor., I. A. Comenius, Sam. Hartlib' on A2ᵛ.
15079 — Secunda editio. 8°. *T. Cotes, sumpt. M. Sparkes* (*T. Cotes f. M. Sparkes,*) 1633. L.O.C.DUL.M.+; F.HN (Lat. tp only).ILL. Vermont U.
21641 is an appendix to this and is sometimes found bd. with it.
15079.5 — [Anr. issue, w. imprint:] *T. Cotes, sumpt. T. Slater* (*T. Cotes f. T. Slater,*) 1633. G².MARL.; HD(lacks Lat. tp).TORONTO². St. Mark's Church Rectory, Niagara-on-the-lake, Ontario(Eng. tp only).
15080 — Tertia editio. (Clavis ad portam.) 8°. *A. Griffin, sumpt. M. Sparke* (*A. Griffin f. M. Sparke,*) 1637. L.L³.L³⁸. M⁴.NLW.+; F.HN.HD.N.Y.
15081 — Quarta editio. 8°. *E. Griffin, sumpt. M. Sparke* (*E. Griffin f. M. Sparke,*) 1639. L.C².CARTMEL.E(lacks Lat. tp)*.NEP.+; LC(lacks Lat. tp)*.Y(lacks Lat. tp)*.
(2nd pt. formerly also 21641a)

Komenský, Jan Amos—*cont.*

15081.5 — [A variant, w. date 1640 on Lat. tp, 1639 on Eng. tp.] o. Brno U, Czechoslovakia.; F.N.PN.

15081.7 — [A variant, w. both tpp dated 1640.] CU.

15082 — Reverendi et clarissimi viri Johannis Amos Comenii pansophiæ prodromus. 12°. *M. F[lesher,] sumpt. L. Fawne & S. Gellibrand,* 1639. Ent. to Gellibrand 17 oc. 1638. L.O[7].C.D.E.+; F.HN.HD.

Koran. *See* 15084.

15082.5 **Koresios, Georgios.** [Heading A1[r]:] Κυριου Γεωργιου Κορεσσιου . . . διάλεξις μετά τινος τῶν Φράρων. 4°. [*Eliot's Court Press,* c. 1625.] L.O.C.WIN[2]. Athens NL.+; HD.
Issued w. 19553.5, q.v.

15083 **Korydaleus, Theophilos,** *Abp.* Του σοφωτατου κυριου Θεοφιλου του Κορυδαλεως. Περι επιστολικων τύπων. ("Εκθεσις περὶ ῥητορηκῆς [*sic*].) 8°. *ex off. G. S[tansby,]* 1625. L.O.C.D.E[2].+; HN.HD.
The Library of the Greek Patriarch, Alexandria, has a copy w. dedic. to Pachomios Doxaras instead of the usual one to Bp. John Williams. *See also The Library,* XXII(1967), pp. 13–43 and *Harvard Library Bulletin,* XV(1967), pp. 140–68.

15083.5 **Kraus, Daniel.** Panegyricus in laudem . . . Gustavi Adolphi. . . . Authore Elia Denukrois [i.e. Daniel Kraus.] 4°. *Augustæ Trinobantum* [i.e. *London,* but really *printed abroad,*] 1629. L.PARIS.; F.
There is a reply to this (copy at C), w. title: 'Censura ad Panegyricum, . . . Augustæ Trinobantum evulgatum M.DC.XXVIII.[*sic*]' but without an imprint of its own. It was pr. abroad and does not belong in STC.

Kroeselius, Johannes, *ed. See* 1777.

15084 **Kur'ān.** Here begynneth a lytell treatyse of the turkes lawe called Alcaron. 4°. (*W. de worde,*) [1519?] L.

15085 **Kyd, Thomas.** The first part of Jeronimo. With the warres of Portugall, and the life and death of Don Andræa. [Anon. Attribution doubtful.] 4°. [*W. Jaggard*] *f. T. Pavyer,* 1605. L.L[6].O.; F.HN. Greg 221.

15086 — The Spanish tragedie, containing the lamentable end of Don Horatio, and Bel-imperia. Newly corrected and amended of such grosse faults as passed in the first impression. [Anon.] 4° w. perp. chainlines. *E. Allde f. E. White,* [1592.] Ent. to A. Jeffes 6 oc. 1592. L. Greg 110.
See Greg, *Register B,* p. 44.

15087 — [Anr. ed.] 4° w. perp. chainlines. *A. Jeffes, sold by E. White,* 1594. Göttingen U.

15088 — [Anr. ed.] 4°. *W. White,* 1599. Ass'd 13 au. HN.

15089 — [Anr. ed.] With new additions. 4°. *W. W[hite] f. T. Pavier,* 1602. Ent. 14 au. 1600. L.O(imp.).ETON (imp.).; HN(tp only, added to 15089a).
Tp has device McK. 165, w. no motto.

15089a — [Anr. ed.] 4°. *W. W[hite] f. T. Pavier,* 1603. E[2].; HN (lacks tp, has tp of 15089 instead).
Tp has device McK. 345, w. motto: 'Thou shalt . . .'

Kyd, Thomas—*cont.*

15090 — [Anr. ed.] 4°. *W. White (f. T. Pavier,)* 1610 (1611.) L.O.; F.HN.HD(tp mutil.).
Some copies (HD) have misprints in colophon uncorrected.

15091 — [Anr. ed.] 4°. *W. White, sold by J. White a. T. Langley,* 1615. C[2].

15091a — [A variant, w. imprint:] *W. White f. J. White a. T. Langley,* 1615. L.; F.HN.

15092 — [Anr. ed.] 4°. *J. White f. T. Langley,* 1618. L[6].O.; HN. HD.

15093 — [Anr. ed.] 4°. *A. Mathewes, sold by J. Grismand,* 1623. L.O.G[2].; F.HN.HD.N.Y.+

15093a — [A variant, w. imprint:] *A. Mathewes, sold by T. Langley,* 1623. C[4].; CH.

15094 — [Anr. ed.] 4°. *A. Mathewes f. F. Grove,* 1633. Ent. to E. Brewster a. R. Bird 4 au. 1626. L.O.C[3].E.ETON.+; F.HN.BO.HD.TEX.+

— The tragedye of Solyman and Perseda. [1592?] *See* 22894.

15095 — The trueth of the most wicked and secret murthering of John Brewen. [Anon. Not by Kyd.] 4°. [*T. Orwin?*] *f. J. Kid, sold by E. White,* 1592. Ent. 28 jn. L[2].

— *tr. See* 11622, 23702.5.

— *See also* 7605.

Kyffin, Edward. Car-wr y Cymru. 1631. *See* 24007a.

— *tr. See* 2743.

15096 **Kyffin, Maurice.** The blessednes of Brytaine, or a celebration of the Queenes holyday. [In verse.] 4°. *J. Windet,* 1587. Ent. 10 no. L[2].COL(mutil.).; HN.

15097 — [Anr. ed.] Newly set foorth . . . this yeere 88. 4°. [*J. Windet f.*] *J. Wolfe,* 1588. Ent. to Windet 17 oc. L. L[2].; HN.

15098 — A defence of the honorable sentence and execution of the Queene of Scots. [1587.] Now = 17566.3.

— *tr. See* 14595, 23895.

15099 **Kynaston,** *Sir* **Francis.** The constitutions of the musæum Minervæ. [Anon.] 4°. *T. P[urfoot] f. T. Spencer,* 1636. Ent. 15 ap. L.O.D.DUR[3].SHEF.+; F. HN.HD.N.Y.+
(Formerly also 16780)

15100 — Corona Minervæ. Or a masque. [Anon.] 4°. *f. W. Sheares,* 1635. L.L[6](2).O.E.; F.HN(2).Y. Greg 503.
(Formerly also 16781) Some copies have extra leaf of dedic. added between tp and A1 (1 L[6], F, 1 HN).

— *tr. See* 5097, 14712, 14713.

Kynder, Philip. Almanacks. 1619, etc. *See* 437 sq.

Kyninghame, Euphemia. In pious memorie. 1616. *See* 7252.3.

Kynnestar, John. A true report of a murder doen by J. Kynnestar. 1573. *See* 21485.

Kyrkh., W. *See* Kirkham, W.

15101 **Kyttes, G.** [Headline on versos:] The vnluckie Firmentie. [In verse.] 4°. [*T. Colwell,* 1572?] O(imp.).
With Wyer's old device, McK. 67δ, in a state a little later than in 5532.

L

L., *Eliensis*. Responsio ad apologiam Cardinalis Bellarmini. 1610. *See* 604.

L., *Lady C. of. See* 16610.

15102   L., A. Antimartinus, siue monitio cuiusdam Londinensis ad adolescentes vtriúsque academiæ. 4⁰. *G. Bishop & R. Newbery*, 1589. Ent. 3 jy. L.O.C.D.P.+; F.HN. HD.U.Y.+
(Formerly also 681)
— Newes of the complement of the art of navigation. 1609. *See* 15692.
— Speculum belli sacri. 1624. *See* 15432.

15103   — Spirituall almes: a treatise wherein is set forth the necessity of exhortation. 12⁰. *T. S[nodham] f. S. Man*, 1625. Ent. 18 de. 1624. L⁴.
— *ed. See* 5898.
— *tr. See* 4450.

15104   L., B. The soules lamentations, and love to God. Preces & lachrymae. Dumps and teares of repentence. 12⁰. *T. Purfoot*, 1614. Ent. 5 ja. O.

L., C., *Minister, tr. See* 21276.

L., C. F. *See* 12173.3.

L., D. Solitarinesse improved. [c. 1640.] *See* 16945.5.
— *tr. See* 7239.

L., E., *tr.* Romes monarchie. 1596. *See* 21296.

L., E. D., *I. C. See* 15137.

L., F., *tr. See* 18974.

L., G. A paumflet compyled by G. L. [really by G. C.] [1540.] *See* 4268.5.
— *tr. See* 15311, 20113.

L., H. Sundry christian passions. 1593. *See* 16697.
— *See also* 16857.

15105   L., H., *Oxon*. Gratiæ ludentes. Jests, from the universitie. 12⁰. *T. Cotes f. H. Mosley*, 1638. Ent. 19 de. 1637. L.O.; ROS.
O is correctly dated; L and ROS are misdated '1628' and corrected in ink to '1638'.

15106   L., I. or J. The birth, purpose, and mortall wound of the Romish holie league. [Verse and prose.] 4⁰. [*T. Orwin*] *f. T. Cadman*, 1589. L.L².O.; F.
Attrib. to James Lea.
— A book of grammar questions. [c. 1590?] *See* 15374.8.
— An elegie upon the death of Elizabeth. 1603. *See* 15189.
— The lawes resolutions of womens rights. 1632. *See* 7437.

15107   — A true and perfecte description of a straunge monstar borne in Rome in 1585. [Verse and prose.] 4⁰. *J. Wolfe f. W. Dight, sold by W. Wright*, 1590. ?Ent. to Wright 5 oc. O.
— *ed. See* 21583.
— *tr. See* 13996, 13996a, 13997, 13997a, 13997b, 13998.

15107.3   L., I., *Pastor*. A christian consolatory letter; written . . . to one of his loving parishoners and friends: upon the pestilence. [1 Aug. 1625.] s.sh.fol. [*London*, 1625.] L⁵(Lemon 262).
See also 12561.2.

L., I., *Turvallius*. Summus dux. [1623?] *See* 16695.5.

L., J. P. C. A perfect table . . . of bread. [1640.] *See* 19600.

L., Ja. V. The ages of sin. [c. 1635.] *See* 15193.5.

L., L. Certaine Englishe verses. 1586. *See* 16617.
— *tr. See* 778.

15108   L., M. A merry jest of John Tomson, and Jakaman his wife. *Ballad*. 2 pts. s.sh.fol. [*A. Mathewes*] *f. E. Wright*, [c. 1637.] Ent. to Y. James 1 au. 1586. L.

L., N. *See* Lesse, N.

L., P. The constant lover. [1638?] *See* 16868.

15109   L., R. Apologia innocentiae et integritatis . . . aduersus E. Osb[erne] calumnias. [Attrib. to R. Latewar.] 8⁰. *Oxoniæ, Jos. Barnesius*, 1594. O.O³.C⁵.

15109.3   — A copye of a letter contayning certayne newes, & the articles or requestes of the Devonshyre & Cornyshe rebelles. [Anon.] 8⁰. [*J. Day a. W. Seres*,] 1549. L².O(lacks articles).LINC.

15109.7   — [Anr. issue, w. B6–8 reset. Init. R. L. on B5ᵛ.] 8⁰. [*J. Day a. W. Seres*,] 1549. O⁵.
— A letter: whearin, . . . the entertainment vntoo the Queenz maiesty, iz signified. [1575.] *See* 15190.5.

L., R., *Gentleman*. Diella. 1596. *See* 17091.

L., R. S. The French tutour. 1625. *See* 22429.5.

15110   L., S. P. One and forty divine odes Englished, set to King Davids princely harpe. (An assay, or Buchanan his paraphrase on the first twentie psalmes.) 8⁰. *M. F[lesher a.] (R. Y[oung] f. R. Moore,)* 1627. Ent. to Flesher 16 mr. L.E.; HN.
Sometimes attrib. to Sir J. Sempill.

15111   L., T. Babylon is fallen. [Anon.] 8⁰. *E. Allde*, 1597. Ent. 3 ja. O.; F(imp.).
This, 15113, and the items cross-referenced below are reprinted in a Wing collection; *see* main entries for Wing references. Babylon is reprinted in Wing L 68 and there attrib. to T. L., who may be the Thomas Legate described on K3ʳ of 14520 as one of the orig. leaders of an Arian separatist group. *See also* Champlin Burrage, *Early English Dissenters*, I.214–20.

15111.3   — [Anr. ed., w. different prelims. and title:] A prophesie that hath lyen hid, above these 2000. yeares. 4⁰. [*E. Allde*] *f. N. Fosbrooke*, 1610. L.O(2).C.C³.; F.PH².
(Formerly 20441) A2ᵛ line 2 ends: 'lock'.

15111.5   — [Anr. ed.] 4⁰. [*E. Allde*] *f. N. Fosbrooke*, 1610. L(impr. defaced).O(imp.).SAL.SHEF(imp.).
A2ᵛ line 2 ends: 'locke'.

15111.7   — [Anr. ed.] 4⁰. [*E. Allde*] *f. N. Fosbrooke*, 1614. L.C.
(Formerly 20442)

15112   — [Anr. ed. of 15111.] Babilon is fallen. . . . Published according to the first copie, printed, Anno Dom. 1595. 8⁰. *E. All-de*, 1620. L.C¹⁰.
— De fide. 1592. *See* 12563.

15113   — An exposition of the XI. XII. and XIII. chapters of the Revellation. By a late writer, only these two letters T. L. are in his advertisement to queene Elizabeth. 8⁰. [*W. Jones?*] 1623. C.; PN².
Neither copy has the Advertisement, which is, however, reprinted in Wing L 83, where its 1st publication date is given as 1589. The Exposition is reprinted in Wing B 4593.
— The key of David. 1610. *See* 21520.5.
— To the church of Rome. 1599. *See* 21309.

L., T. *See also* Lodge, T.
— *tr. See* 18310.

L., T., *Doctor of Physic, tr. See* 16901.

L., T., G. *See* Lodge, T.

L., T., *of Lincoln's Inn, Gent. See* Lodge, T.

15113.5   L., V. The pleasaunt playne and pythye pathewaye leadynge to a vertues and honest lyfe. [In verse.] 4⁰. *N. Hyll f. J. Case*, [1552?] O².O¹³.LIV³(lacks tp.); F.HN.
(Formerly 15421) Attrib. to Urban Lynyng.

L., W. The conflict in conscience of Bessie Clarksone. 1632. *See* 16611.

15114 — An helpe for yong people, preparing them for the worthy receiving of the Lords Supper. 8°. *T. H[arper] f. N. Butter,* 1640. Ent. 19 my. E².; HN.

15115 — The incomparable jewell. Shewed in a sermon. 4°. *R. Young, sold by G. Lathum,* 1632. L(imp.).O.; F.HN. U.Y.

— Nothing for a new-yeares gift. 1603. *See* 15706.

La., Jo., *Gent. See* 15190.

15115.5 **La., R.** The true copie, of a letter written to a gentleman of worship in England. Lamentably discoursing the crueltie of Bashaw Mahomet. 4°. *J. D[anter] f. T. Gosson,* 1595. ?Ent. 5 ap. O.

Labé, Louise. The debate betweene follie and loue. 1584. *See* 12262.

Labyrinthus. Labyrinthus: comœdia. . . . 1636. *See* 12596.

15116 **Lace.** [A book of engraved lace patterns. c. 1605.] Now = 24765.7.

15117 **Lacey, William,** *pseud.* [i.e. William Wolfe, *S.J.*] The judgment of an university-man concerning M. William Chillingworth his late pamphlet [5138], in answere to Charity maintayned. (Heautomachia.) 4°. [*St. Omer, English College Press,*] 1639. L.O.C. C¹⁰.SAL.+; HN.HD.U(lacks 2nd pt.).
(2nd pt. formerly 5140) A.&R. 896.

15117.3 **La Croix, François de.** The little garden of our B. lady. *Tr.* (J. W[ilson].) 24° in 6's. [*St. Omer, English College Press,*] 1626. DE(imp.).M(imp.). A.&R. 433.

15117.7 — [Anr. ed.] 24° in 6's. [*St. Omer, English College Press,*] 1631. L⁰.COLWICH.CHEL(2 imp.).LE.; F. A.&R. 434.

15118 **Lactantius, Lucius Coelius.** L. Lactantii Firmiani carmen. . . . Gul. Lilii in laudem virginis deiparę carmen eruditum. Ab Erasmo Institutum christiani hominis feliciter ęditum. 4°. [*R. Pynson,* 1522?] L(lacks after b4).
The Lily and Erasmus are lacking; for separate eds. of the Erasmus *see* 10450.2 sqq.

15118.5 **Lacy, John.** wyl bucke his testament. [In verse.] 4°. *W. Copland,* [c. 1560.] O.; PML.
(Formerly 4001)

15119 **Ladies.** The ladies cabinet opened: wherein is found experiments in preserving, cookery and huswifery. 4°. *M. P[arsons] f. R. Meighen,* 1639. Ent. 25 ja. L.C.; NY.

15120 **Lady.** The lamenting lady, who for the wrongs done to her by a poore woman, was most strangely punished. *Ballad.* 2 pts. s.sh.fol. *f. H. Gosson,* [c. 1620?] C⁶.
— The lost lady. 1638. *See* 1901.5.

Lady, Our. *See* Mary, *the Blessed Virgin.*

Laet, Alphonse. An almanack. 1548. *See* 470.

15121 **Laet, Gaspar.** The pronosticaciõ of maister Jasper. [1516.] Now = 470.2.

15122 — [Prognostication. 1517.] Now = 470.3.

15123 — Prenostica effectuum celestium influentiarum corpora inferiora regulantium. [1518.] Now = 470.4.

15124 — Prenosticatio mg̃ri. Iasp. la⟨et.⟩ [1520.] Now = 470.5.

15125 — [Anr. ed.] The pnostication of maister Iasp Laet. [1520.] Now = 470.6.

15126 — A pronosticacyon of Master: Iasper Laet. [1524.] Now = 470.8.

15127 — Pronosticum . . . p̄ anno M.CCCCC.xxix. [1529.] Now = 470.9.

15128 — Pronosticum . . . pro anno domini M.CCCCC.xxx. [1530.] Now = 470.10.
— *See also* 385.7.

15129 **Laet, Gaspar,** *the Younger.* The pronosticacion. [1533.] Now = 471.5.

15130 — [A prognostication. 1534.] Now = 471.7.
15131 — Pronosticaciõ. [1541.] Now = 474.5.
15132 — Pronosticatiõ. [1544.] Now = 475.5.

La Faye, Antoine de. La main chrestienne. 1587. *See* 5160.5.
— *See also* 2053.

La Fontaine, Robert de. *See* Le Maçon, R.

15133 **La Framboisière, Nicolas Abraham de.** [Heading A1ʳ:] An easy method to know the causes of the humour in the body. [*Tr.* from Latin.] 4°. [*London?* 1640?] L.

15134 **Lake, Arthur,** *Bp.* Sermons with some religious and divine meditations. 2 pts. fol. *W. Stansby* (*R. Young, T. C[otes] a. R. C[otes]*) *f. N. Butter,* 1629 (1628.) Ent. 11 mr. 1628. L.O.C.D.E.+; F.HN.HD.ILL.U.+

15135 — Ten sermons upon severall occasions. 4°. *T. Badger f. H. Mosley,* 1640. Ent. 18 ap. L.O⁶.C.A.LINC.+; F.HN.HD.

15136 **Lake, Osmund.** A probe theologicall: or, the first part of the christian pastors proofe of his learned parishioners faith. 4° in 8's. [*F. Kingston*] *f. W. Leake,* 1612. Ent. 18 de. 1609. L.O.C.D.E.+; F.HN.PN².

Lakes, Thomas. An almanack. 1627. *See* 478.

15137 **L'Allouette, Edmond de.** A catholicke apologie against the libels, . . . made, by the League. [Init. E.D.L.I.C. By P. de Belloy? *Tr.* E. Aggas.] 8°. [*G. Robinson*] *f. E. Aggas,* [1585–86.] L.O.C.D.E.+; F.HN.HD.N.U.+ (Formerly also 1856)

15138 **Lalor, Robert.** The case of præmunire; or the attainder of R. Lalor, priest. = pt. of 6361.

15139 **La Marche, Olivier de.** The resolued gentleman. [Anon.] *Tr.* out of Spanishe by L. Lewkenor [from H. de Acuña's trans. of the French original.] 4°. *R. Watkins,* 1594. Ent. 2 de. L.O.O³.C(2, 1 imp.).P.; F(2, 1 imp.).HN(imp.).HD.
For another trans. *see* 1585.

15140 **La Martelière, Pierre de.** The argument of Mʳ. Peter de la Marteliere for the universitie of Paris, against the Jesuits. *Tr.* (G. B[rowne].) 4°. [*W. Hall,*] *sold* [*by N. Butter,*] 1612. L.L³⁸.O.C².A.+; F.HN.HD.U.
Epistle in L copy signed 'George Browne', in HD copy init. 'G. B.'

15141 — [Anr. issue, w. epistle cancelled and cancel tp:] The Jesuite stript & whipt. *f. W. Arundel,* 1616. O. CASHEL.; F.

Lambard, Thomas, *ed. See* 15144.

15142 **Lambard, William.** Αρχαιονομια, siue de priscis anglorum legibus libri. Gulielmo Lambardo interprete. Anglo-Sax. a. Lat. 4°. *ex off. J. Daij,* 1568. L.O.C.D. E.+; F.HN.HD.N.NY.+

15143 — Archion, or, a comentary upon the high courts of justice in England. 8°. *f. D. Frere,* 1635. Ent. 27 mr. L.O.C.D.E.+; F.HN.CU.HD.N.+

15144 — [Anr. ed.] Newly corrected [by T. Lambard.] 8°. *E. P[urslowe] f. H. Seile,* 1635. Ent. to Seile a. Frere 1 jy. L.O.C³.D².G².+; F.HN.CHI.HD.U.+

15145 — The duties of constables, borsholders, tithing-men, [etc.] 1582. 8°. *R. Newberie a. H. Middleton,* 1583. Ent. to Barker a. Newbery, ass'd to Middleton a. Newbery 26 mr. L(destroyed).O.D.; HN.HD.
Eds. of this are generally bd. w. eds. of the Eirenarcha that are roughly contemporary, but not necessarily of the same year.

15146 — [Anr. ed.] 1582. 8°. *R. Warde,* [1583?] C².; F.CAL².HD.

15146.5 — [Anr. ed.] 1583. 8°. *R. Ward,* [1583.] L.

15147 — [Anr. ed.] 8°. *R. Newberie a. H. Middleton,* 1584. L. HETH. Stevens Cox.; HN.HD.IND.LC.MIN.

15148 — [Anr. ed.] Enlarged . . . 1587. 8°. *R. Newberie a. H. Midleton,* 1587. L.O.O⁹.C².C⁹.; HD.

15149 — [Anr. ed.] 8°. *R. Newberie,* 1591. F.HN.BALT.CAL⁵.CU.

15150 — [Anr. ed.] Enlarged 1594. 8°. *f. R. Newberie,* 1594. Ass'd to J. Newbery 30 se. L.L².; HD.MIN.

15151 — [Anr. ed.] 8°. *C. Yetsweirt,* 1594. L.O.LK.; HD.MIN.
A paginary reprint of 15149 and possibly a piracy. *See also* Greg, *Register B,* p. 48, for limited patent.

15152 — [Anr. ed.] Now enlarged in 1599. 8°. *T. Wight a. B. Norton,* 1599. L.L³⁸.O.C²⁰.P.+; F.CU.HD(imp.).LC. N.+
See Greg, *Register B,* p. 70, for limited patent.

15153 — [Anr. ed.] 8°. *T. Wight,* 1601. O.

15154 — [Anr. ed.] Enlarged in 1602. 8°. *T. Wight,* 1602. L. L³⁰.O.C.NLW.+; F.CU.HD(2).LC.Y.

15155 — [Anr. ed.] Enlarged in 1604. 8°. *T. Wight,* 1604. L⁴⁸. O.; HN.HD(2).ILL.NYS.

15156 — [Anr. ed.] 8°. [*A. Islip?*] *f. the Co. of Statrs.,* 1605. F. HN.HD.
See Court-Book C, p. 16.

Lambard, William—*cont.*

15157 — [Anr. ed.] Enlarged in 1606. 8°. [*A. Islip*] *f. the Co. of Statrs.*, 1606. L.O.D.G².NRO.+; F.CU.HD.ILL.LC.

15158 — [Anr. ed.] Enlarged in 1610. 8°. [*A. Islip*] *f. the Co. of Statrs.*, 1610. L.O⁴⁷.C.M².SCL.+; F.HN.HD.N.NY.+

15158.5 — [Anr. ed.] Enlarged in 1610. 8°. [*A. Islip?*] *f. the Co. of Statrs.*, 1612. P.

15159 — [Anr. ed.] Enlarged in 1610. 8°. [*A. Islip*] *f. the Co. of Statrs.*, 1614. L.O.C².D².M.+; F.HN.HD.ILL.U.+

15160 — [Anr. ed.] Enlarged in 1610. 8°. [*A. Islip*] *f. the Co. of Statrs.*, 1619. Ent. to the English Stock 5 mr. 1620. L.O.C.D.M².+; HN.HD.ILL.LC.NY.+

15161 — [Anr. ed.] 8°. [*A. Islip*] *f. the Co. of Statrs.*, 1624. C³. P.; Vermont U.

15161.5 — [Anr. ed.] 8°. [*A. Islip*] *f. the Co. of Statrs.*, 1626. L. O³(2, 1 imp.).

15162 — [Anr. ed.] Now carefully corrected and augmented to 1631. 8°. *assignes of J. More*, [1631.] L.O.C²⁰.; HD.

15162.3 — [Anr. ed.] And now corrected to this present yeare 1633. 8°. *M. Flesher, J. Haviland, a. R. Young, the assignes of J. More*, [1633.] O.NLW.; F.HD.

15162.7 — [Anr. ed.] 8°. *M. Flesher, and R. Young, the assignes of J. More*, 1640. L(tp only, Ames II.1595).C²¹.; HD.

15163 — Eirenarcha: or of the office of the justices of peace, in two bookes. 8°. *R. Newbery a. H. Bynneman, by the ass. of R. Tot[tell] & C. Bar[ker,]* 1581. Ent. 3 ja. 1582. L(lacks last leaf).O.C.E².M².+; F.HN.CU.HD. ILL.+

    See Greg, *Register B*, p. 12. In some copies the errata is pr. on Ll 7ᵛ, in others on a separate slip from the same setting.

15164 — [Anr. ed.] 8°. *R. Newbery a. H. Binneman, by the assig. of R. Tottell a. C. Barker*, 1582. L(imp.).C⁴.COL.; F.HN.CAL⁵.HD.MIN.+

    Some copies (L) have 15164a.5 bd. in.

15164a — [Anr. ed.] 8°. *R. Newbery a. H. Bynneman by the ass. of R. Tot[tell] a. C. Bar[ker,]* 1582. L.O.O¹⁶.COL. LIV³.; HN(lacks tp).CU.HD.LC.N.+

    Partially from the same setting as 15164. Some copies (L, HN, 1 HD) have 15164a.5 bd. in.

15164a.5 —— [Heading A1ʳ:] A table of all the principall matters. . . . By C. Powell. 8°. (*f. R. Newberie*, 1583.) L(2).; HN.HD.

    Collates A⁸ and is found in copies of 15164 and 15164a.

15165 — [Anr. ed. of 15164a.] Now reuised, corrected, and enlarged. Whereunto is added an appendix of sundry precedents. 8°. *R. Newbery*, 1588. L.C².D.E².NEP.+; F.HN.HD.ILL.NYS.+

15166 — [Anr. issue, w. tp replaced by a halfsheet, and D–E⁸ revised and reprinted.] Whereunto is added the newly reformed commission of the peace. *R. Newbery*, 1591. L.O.O⁹.C¹⁵.M⁴.; F.HD.MIN.

    Colophon still dated 1588.

15167 — [Anr. ed.] Now secondly reuised. 8°. *R. Newbery*, 1592. L.O.C²¹.D.M⁴.+; F.HN.CU.HD.MIN.+

15168 — [Anr. ed.] Enlarged agreeably to the reformed commission. 8°. *R. Newbery*, 1594. Ass'd to J. Newbery 30 se. L.L⁴³.O.C².M.+; F.HN.CU.HD.ILL.+

15169 — [Anr. ed.] Now fourthly reuised. 8°. *T. Wight a. B. Norton*, 1599. L.O.C²⁰.P.STU.+; F.CAL⁵.CU.HD.N.+

15170 — [Anr. ed.] 8°. *T. Wight*, 1602. L.O.O².C.BHP.+; F.HN. CU.HD.ILL.+

15171 — [Anr. ed.] 8°. [*A. Islip*] *f. the Co. of Statrs.*, 1607. L.O D.G².NLW.+; F.CU.HD.ILL.MIN.+

    See Court-Book C, pp. 16, 22; p. 16, note 1, mentions an ed. of 1605, but its existence cannot be verified, and it may be a confusion w. 15156.

15172 — [Anr. ed.] Revised, in the eighth yeere of King James. 8°. [*A. Islip*] *f. the Co. of Statrs.*, 1610. L.O⁴⁷.C.M². NLW.+; F.HN.HD.ILL.NY.+

15173 — [Anr. ed.] 8°. [*A. Islip*] *f. the Co. of Statrs.*, 1614. L.O. C².D².NLW.+; F.HN.CU.HD.ILL.+

15174 — [Anr. ed.] 8°. *f. the Co. of Statrs.*, 1619. Ent. to the English Stock 5 mr. 1620. L.O.C.D.G².+; F.HN.HD. ILL.NY.+

15175 — A perambulation of Kent: conteining the description, . . . of that shyre. 4°. (*H. Middleton f. R. Newbery*) *f. R. Newberie*, 1576. L.O.D⁵.G².P.+; F.HN.HD.N. NY.+

    Only 600 copies pr. according to the errata list. Newbery's rights yielded to the Stat. Co. 8 Jan. 1584; *see* Arber II.789.

15175.5 — [A variant, omitting Middleton's name from the colophon.] C(2).A.BIRM.

Lambard, William—*cont.*

15176 — [Anr. ed.] Now increased and altered. 4° in 8's. *E. Bollifant*, 1596. Ent. to Mrs. Griffin a. J. Haviland 7 jn. 1621; to Haviland a. J. Wright 4 se. 1638. L.O.C.D.G².+; F.HN.CU.HD.ILL.+

15176.5 — The third edition. 8°. *R. Hodgkinsonne f. D. Pakeman*, [1640?] L(2).C.

    Reissued in 1656 w. cancel tp as Wing L 216.

15177 **Lambe, John.** A briefe description of the notorious life of J. Lambe. 4°. *Amsterdam*, [really *London, G. Miller?*] 1628. L.L³⁰.O.C(frag.).G².+

15178 **Lambert, François.** The minde and judgement of maister Fraūces Lambert of the wyll of man. *Tr.* N. L(esse.) M. D. xlviii. 8°. (*J. Day a. W. Seres*,) [1548.] L.O.C⁴.E².M.+; F.HN.COR.U(tp in facs.).

15179 — The summe of christianitie gatheryd out almoste of al placis of scripture. *Tr.* T. Reuel, 1536. 8°. [*R. Redman*, 1536.] L.GLOUC.P.; F(imp.).HN.

15180 **Lambert, John**, *the Martyr.* A treatyse made by Johan Lambert vnto Kynge Henry the .viij. concernynge hys opynyon in the sacramēt of the aultre. 1538. [*Ed.* J. Bale.] 8°. [*Wesel, D. van der Straten*, 1548?] L. O.C.D.; F.

15181 **Lambert, John**, *Minister of Elham.* Of predestinacion & election . . . M.D.L. 8° in 4's. (*Cātorbury, J. Mychell*,) [1550?] C.C³.

15182 **Lambert, Peter.** The successe of swaggering, swearing, . . . Described in the life of Peter Lambert. 4°. [*E. Allde*] *f. J. Busbie the elder*, [1610.] Ent. 29 mr. 1610. L(destroyed). Sotheby's, 20 June 1933, lot 480 (untraced).

15183 **Lambeth Articles.** Articuli Lambethani. 1631. An error for one of two editions of 1651; cf. Wing A 3890.

15184 **Lambi, Giovanni Battista.** A revelation of the secret spirit. Declaring the secret of alchymie. *Tr.* R.N.E. gent. 8°. *J. Haviland f. H. Skelton*, 1623. Ent. 16 ja. L.C¹⁰.A.G².; BO⁵.HD.PH.WIS.

Lambinus, Dionysius, *ed. See* 5266.4, 5297, 5303, 5309, 5309.2, 5309.3.

15185 **Lamentation.** A lamentation in whiche is shewed what ruyne cometh of seditious rebellyon. 1536. Now = 18113.3.
    — The lamētacyon of a christen. 1545. *See* 3765.
    — The lamentation of a male-content. [1597.] *See* 19338.

15186   — The lamentation of a new married man. *A Ballad.* 2 pts. s.sh.fol. *assignes of T. Symcock*, [1628–29.] L.

15186.5   — [Anr. ed.] 2 pts. s.sh.fol. *A. M[athewes*, c. 1630.] C⁶.
    — The lamētation of Edward Bruton, and James Riley. [1633.] *See* 3945.7.
    — The lamentacion of England. 1557. *See* 10014.

Lammie, William. Positiones aliquot logicæ. Praeside G. Lammio. 1613. *See* 21555.20.

Lamp. The burning lampe. 1635. *See* 12144.5.

15187 **Lamwell, Sir.** The treaty (se of Sir Lamwell.) [In verse.] 4°. [*J. Mychell*, 1548.] O(frag.).
    3rd line of recto of 2nd leaf: 'Ete nor drynke wolde he 〈 〉'.

15187.5   — [Anr. ed.] 4°. [*J. King*, 1560.] Ent. to King 1557–58. O(frag.).
    B3ʳ line 14: 'Eate nor drinke would he neuer,'.

Lancaster, County of. The seuerall rates . . . for the countie of. [30 Aug. 1595.] *See* 8245.

Lancaster, Duchy of. *See* 7705.4.

15188 **Lancaster, Thomas.** The ryght and trew vnderstādynge of the supper of the Lord. 8°. [*E. Whitchurch? f.*] (*J. Turke*,) [1550?] L.O.O⁶.BUTE.; F.HN.BO⁵.

15188.3 **Lancicius, Michael.** The glory of the B. father S. Ignatius of Loyola, founder of the Society of Jesus. [Anon.] 24° in 6's. *Gant, Joos Dooms*, 1628. L.MSM. A.&R. 435.

15188.7   — [Anr. ed.] 32° in 8's. *Rouen, J. Cousturier*, 1633. ST (lacks letterpress tp).YK².; F.
    Engraved tp dated 1632. A.&R. 436.

Land. How to order any land. [1637?] *See* 22391.5.

Landi, Ortensio. *See* 5059.

15189 **Lane, John.** An elegie upon the death of Elizabeth. [Init. I. L. In verse.] 4°. [*W. White*] *f. J. Deane*, 1603. Ent. 15 ap. (Arber III.36). O.

15190 — Tom Tel-Troths message, and his pens complaint. [Init. Jo. La. *Gent.* In verse.] 4°. [*F. Kingston*] *f. R. Howell*, 1600. Ent. to T. Orwin 23 jn. 1591; to Howell 26 ap. 1600. L.; F(lacks F4).HN.

15190.5 **Laneham, Robert.** A letter: whearin, part of the entertainment vntoo the Queenz maiesty, at Killingwoorth Castl, iz signified. [Init. R. L.] 8° in 4's. [*London*, 1575.] O.C³.; HD.
Collates A–L⁴.

15191 — [Anr. ed.] 8°. [*London*, 1575.] L.O(3).C⁵.SH.; F.HN.CH. HD.N.+
Collates A–E⁸ F⁴.

15192 **Lanfrancus,** *Mediolanensis.* A most excellent and learned woorke of chirurgerie, called Chirurgia parua Lanfranci, published in the Englyshe prynte by John Halle. A compendious worke of anatomie. An historiall [*sic*] expostulation [both by J. Hall.] 4°. *T. Marshe*, 1565. Ent. bef. 7 mr. 1565. L.O.C.A. G².+; HN.HD.NLM.WIS. Duke U.+ 𝔄
One O copy has no date on general tp.

Langbaine, Gerard, *ed. See* 16788.
— *tr. See* 20667.

15192.5 **Langdon, Thomas.** A lytell treatyse confoundyng the great eresyes yᵗ reygne now a dayes. [In verse.] 4°. (*Cantorbury, J. Mychell,*) [1549?] H. R. Creswick, Gifford, East Lothian, Scotland(frags.).

15193 **Langenes, Bernardt.** The description of a voyage made by certaine ships of Holland [under the command of C. Houtman] into the East Indies. *Tr.* out of Dutch by W. P(hillip.) 4°. [*J. Windet? f.*] *J. Wolfe*, 1598. Ent. 12 no. 1597 a. 17 fb. 1598. L.L².O(imp.).O⁵.C⁶.; HN.CHI.NY. Penrose 115(imp.).
Langenes was publisher of the Dutch ed.

15193.5 **Langeren, Jacob van.** The ages of sin, or sinnes birth and growth. [9 engravings w. verses, the last init. Ja. V. L.] 4°. [*London*, c. 1635.] L.; HN.
— *See also* 22634.5.

15193a **Langford, George.** Manassehs miraculous metamorphosis: . . . A sermon. 4°. *G. Eld. f. J. Clarke*, 1621. Ent. 30 my. L.O.C.C⁵.DUL.+; F.U.

15194 — Search the scriptures. Or, an enquirie after veritie. 4°. *G. P[urslowe] f. J. Clarke*, 1623. Ent. 30 ap. O.C.C². D.WIN².+; F.HN.BO.MIN.

15195 **Langham, William.** The garden of health. . . . 4° in 8's. [*Deputies of C. Barker*,] 1579 [i.e. 1597.] Ent. to Bishop, Newbury a. R. Barker 6 jn. 1597. L.O. C(imp.).D⁶.E².+; HN.CH.HD.WIS.Y.+
In some copies (O) the date is changed in MS. to 1597; in others (P, HN) to 1598.

15196 — Second edition corrected. 4° in 8's. *T. Harper, w. permission of the Co. of Statrs.*, 1633. Ent. 5 jy. L.O.C⁵. E⁵.M⁴.+; F.HN.HD.NLM.NY.+
See Court-Book C, p. 244.

15197 **Langhorne, Launcelot.** Mary sitting at Christs feet. A sermon preached at the funerall of Mʳⁱˢ Mary Swaine. 8°. [*N. Okes*] *f. A. Johnson*, 1611. Ent. 28 jn. L.O.

15198 — [Anr. ed.] Mary sitting at Christs feet. With the christian life, of Mʳⁱˢ Mary Swaine. 8°. *M. F[lesher] f. E. Wright*, [1624?] Ass'd 24 jn. 1624. L.; F.

15198.5 — [Anr. ed.] Mary sitting at Christs feet. With the christian life, . . . 8°. *M. F[lesher] f. E. Wright*, 1624. LINC.

15199 — [Anr. ed.] Mary sitting at Christs feet. A sermon. 8°. *M. F[lesher] f. E. Wright*, 1630. L⁴⁶.C.

15200 — [Anr. ed.] Mary sitting at Christs feet. With the christian life, . . . 8°. *M. F[lesher] f. E. Wright*, 1633. C.

Langland, William. The vision of Pierce Plowman. 1550. *See* 19906.

15201 **Langley, Kent,** *Monastery of the Virgin Mary and St. John the Evangelist.* UNiuersis. . . . [1519?] Now = Indulgences 48.

15202 **Langley, Henry.** The chariot and horsemen of Israel. 8°. *F. Kyngston f. E. Weaver*, 1616. Ent. 23 my. O.

Langley, Thomas. Almanacks. 1635, etc. *See* 479 sqq.

15203 **Langley, Thomas,** *ed. See* 24654.
— *tr. See* 11903.

15203 **Langlois de Fancan, François.** The favourites chronicle. [Anon. *Tr.* from the 'Chronique des favoris'.] 4°. [*London*,] 1621. L.O.C.D.M.+; F.HN.HD. N.NY.+ 𝔄

15204 **Langton, Christopher.** An introduction into phisycke, with an vniuersal dyet. 8°. *E. W(hytchurche,)* [1545?] L.O.C.G²(lacks tp).; HN.BO⁵.NLM.

15205 — A very brefe treatise, ordrely declaring the prīcipal partes of phisick. Gathered, M.D.XLVII. 8°. (*E. Whitchurche,*) [1547] (10 ap.) L.

15206 **Langton, Robert.** The pylgrimage of M. Robert Langton clerke to saynt Iames in Compostell. 4°. (*R. Coplande*, 1522 (18 no.)) LINC.

15206.5 **Languedoc,** *Reformed Churches.* Articles conteining the request presented to the French kyng by the deputies of the reformed churches of Languedoc. *Tr.* 8°. *H. Middleton f. T. Cadman*, 1574. L.R.

15207 **Languet, Hubert.** A short apologie for christian souldiours. [Stephanus Junius Brutus, *pseud.*] *Tr.* H. P. 8°. *J. Wolfe f. H. Carre*, 1588. Ent. to Wolfe 26 ap. L.; F.

15207.5 — The apologie or defence, of the most noble prince William. [Anon. *Tr.*] 4°. *Delft*, 1581. L².O.C².; F. HN(lacks last leaf).HD.IND.
Ornamental inits. on B2ʳ, P2ʳ, P3ʳ, R3ʳ. Attrib. to P. Loyseleur, revised by Languet. Copies of this or 15209 are also at C¹⁷, LINC, TEX.

15208 — [Anr. issue, w. cancel tp:] A treatise against the proclamation published by the king of Spayne, by which he proscribed the late prince of Orange. *Delft*, [1581.] L.
Tp pr. in London, 1584.

15209 — [Anr. ed.] The apologie [etc.] 4°. *Delft*, 1581 [i.e. *London*, 1584.] Ent. to T. Marshe 8 fb. 1582, 'neuer printed by him.' L.L².O.O¹⁸.D.+; HN.HD.ILL.N.Y.
No ornamental inits.

15210 — = 15209.

15211 — Vindiciae, contra tyrannos: siue, de principis in populum, populíque in principem, legitima potestate. [Stephanus Junius Brutus, *pseud.*] 8°. *Edimburgi* [i.e. *Basle, T. Guarinus?*] 1579. L.O.C³.E.NLW.+; F.HN. HD.N.NY.+
Also attrib. to P. de Mornay.

15212 — [Anr. ed.] [*Printed abroad*,] 1580. Not an STC book.

Lanier, Nicholas. Ayres made by severall authors [N. Lanier, etc.] 1614. *See* 4539.

15212.5 **La Noue, François de.** Declaration de Monsieur de la Noue, sur sa prise des armes. 8° in 4's. *Verdun, M. Marchant* [i.e. *London, J. Wolfe,*] 1588. Ent. 12 de. L(2).
1st line only of title in caps; the genuine French ed. w. this imprint has 1st 2 lines of title in caps.

15213 — [A trans.] The declaration of the lord de la Noue, vpon his taking armes. *Tr.* A. M[unday.] 4°. *J. Woolfe*, 1589. L.O.C.; F.HN.TEX.

15213.5 — — [An anon. response.] Discours sur la declaration faicte par le Sieur de la Noue. 8° in 4's. *Paris* [i.e. *London, J. Wolfe,*] 1589.] L.

15214 — — [A trans.] A discourse vpon the declaration, published by the Lord de la Noue. *Eng. a. Fr.* 4°. *J. Woolfe*, 1589. Ent. 25 ja. L².L¹³.O.; F.HN.Y.
Pr. in parallel columns. At least O, HN have the end of Wolfe's name in the imprint masked by the frisket.

15215 — The politicke and militarie discourses of the Lord de la Nouue. *Tr.* by E. A[ggas.] 4° in 8's. *f. T. C(adman) a. E. A(ggas) by T. Orwin*, 1587 (1588.) Ent. to Aggas 11 no. 1587. L.O.C.M.P.+; F.HN.HD.N.Y.+

15216 **La Noue, Odet de.** The profit of imprisonment. A paradox. *Tr.* J. Syluester. [In verse.] 4°. *P. Short f. E. Blunt*, 1594. Ent. 25 my. O¹³.; HN.

15217 **Lanquet, Thomas.** An epitome of cronicles . . . continued to the reigne of Edwarde the sixt by T. Cooper. 4°. (*in the house of T. Berthelet,*) 1569 (1549.) L.O.C.D.E².+; F(lacks col.).HN.HD.N.Y.+ 𝔄

Lanquet, Thomas—*cont.*

15217.5 — [Anr. ed.] To the reigne of Quene Elizabeth, by Robert Crowley. 4°. (*W. Seres*,) *in æd. T. Marshe*, (1559 (5 ap.)) L(2, imp.).O.C.D.E.+; F.HN.HD.ILL.MICH.+
(Formerly 15221) A pirated ed. repudiated by Cooper; *see* verso of tp in 15218 sqq.

15218 — [Anr. ed.] Coopers chronicle, . . . vnto the late death of Queene Marie by T. Cooper. 4°. [*T. Powell*,] (*in the house late T. Berthelettes*,) 1560. L.O.C.D.G².+; F.HN. CU.HD.N.+
Crowley's continuation replaced by one by Cooper. At least 1 F, 1 HD have the last halfsheet, C², cancelled and C–D⁴ of 15220 added.

15219 — [Anr. ed.] 4° in 8's. [*London*,] 1565 (20 ap.) L³⁰.C.C⁵. A.ST.; F.BO.PN.TEX.Y.+

15220 — [Anr. issue, partially reset.] 4° in 8's. [*London*,] 1565 (1 au.) L.O.C.D².E².+; F.HN.BO.NY.+

15221 — [Anr. ed.] An epitome of cronicles. . . . To the reigne of Quene Elizabeth, by R. Crowley. 1559. Now = 15217.5.

Lansbergen, Philippus van. *See* 21323, 24864.

Lanspergius, Johann Justus. *See* Johann Justus, *Landsberger.*

15222 **Lant, Thomas.** [Verso/recto headline:] The dailie exercise/of a Christian. 12°. [*H. Denham*, 1590.] Ent. to H. Denham 7 de. 1584. L(lacks tp and after M10). Maunsell (17669), pt. 1, p. 84, lists a Denham ed. of 1590.

15222.5 — [Anr. ed.] The daily exercise of a Christian. 12°. [*N. Okes*] *f. the Co. of Statrs.*, 1615. HD.

15223 — [Anr. ed.] 12°. *f. the Co. of Statrs.*, 1623. Ent. to the English Stock 5 mr. 1620. L.

15224 — Sequitur celebritas & pompa funeris [of Sir P. Sidney.] Here followeth the manner of the whole proceeding of his ffunerall. *Lat. a. Eng.* [Engravings w. text.] obl.fol. *Graven in copper by D. T. de Brij, London*, 1587 (1588.) L.O³.C⁶. London, College of Arms. Viscount De L'Isle.; F(imp.). Mrs. J. Nicholas Brown, Providence, R.I.
Mrs. Brown's copy (formerly BUTE) has early states of plates throughout. *See* also Hind I.132–7.

15225 **Lantern.** Here begynnethe the lanterne of lyght. [By J. Grime?] 8°. (*R. Redman*,) [1535?] L.O.P.; F(imp.). HN.

15225.5 — A lanthorne for landlords. *Ballad.* 2 pts. s.sh.fol. *f. J. Wright*, [c. 1630.] c⁶.
Line 1: 'will'.

15226 — [Anr. ed.] 2 pts. s.sh.fol. *f. John Wright*, [c. 1640.] L.
Line 1: 'wil'.

Lanton, *Usurer. See* 24167.5.

15227 **Lanyer, Æmilia**, *Mrs.* Salve deus rex Judæorum. Containing, the passion of Christ. . . . [In verse.] 4°. *V. Simmes f. R. Bonian*, 1611. Ent. 2 oc. 1610. HN. Imprint in 4 lines.

15227.5 — [Anr. issue, w. imprint in 5 lines.] L.L⁶*.O.BHP.; F(imp.).HN.CH.

15228 **La Perrière, Guillaume de.** The mirrour of policie. A worke no lesse profitable than necessary, for princes, magistrates, [etc.] [Anon. *Tr.* from 'Le miroir politique'.] 4°. *A. Islip*, 1598. Ent. 5 fb. 1597. G².; F.ILL.Y.
Prelims. in 4 leaves.

15228.5 — [Anr. issue, w. prelims. in 2 leaves:] The mirrour of policie. A worke nolesse [*sic*] profitable than necessarie, for all magistrates. *A. Islip*, 1598. L.O.C.P. STU.+; F.HN.HD.PFOR.WIS.+

15229 — [A variant, w. date:] 1599. L.O.C.DUR³.E.+; F.HN.HD. N.Y.+

15230 — The theater of fine devices, containing an hundred morall emblemes. *Tr.* T. Combe. 8°. *R. Field*, 1614. Ent. 9 my. 1593. G²(imp.).; HN.

La Place, Pierre de. The fyrst parte of commentaries, concerning the state of Fraunce. 1573. *See* 22241.

15230.5 — Politique discourses, treating of the differences and inequalities of vocations. [Anon.] *Tr.* Æ. Aggas, 1578. Ent. 25 no. 1577. L.O.C.C².P.+; F.HN.HD.N.NY.+
(Formerly 20745)

La Place, Pierre de—*cont.*

15231 — A treatise of the excellencie of a christian man. *Tr.* L. Tomson. 8°. *C. Barkar*, 1576. L(2).O(2).O¹².C.P.

15232 — [Anr. ed.] 8°. *C. Barkar*, 1577. L(2).C.

15232.5 — [Anr. ed.] 8°. *T. Dawson f. C. Barker*, 1589. L⁴.E².; F.HN.

La Placette, Jean. Of the incurable scepticism of the Church of Rome. 1588 [i.e. 1688.] *See* Wing L 429.

15233 **La Primaudaye, Pierre de.** The French academie, . . . newly *tr.* by T. B[owes.] 4° in 8's. *E. Bollifant f. G. Bishop a. R. Newbery*, 1586. Ent. 6 jy. L.C².D.P.YK.+; F.HN.HD.N.Y.+

15234 — Second edition. 4° in 8's. [*Eliot's Court Press*,] *imp. G. Bishop*, 1589. L.O.C.A.D⁵.+; F.HN.ILL.TEX.Y.+

15235 — Third edition. 4° in 8's. [*Eliot's Court Press*,] *imp. G. Bishop*, 1594. L.O.C².BIRM.BRISTOL².; F.HN.HD.ILL. Y.+

15236 — Fourth edition. 4° in 8's. [*Eliot's Court Press*,] *imp. G. Bishop*, 1602. L.O².C³.D².E.+; F.HN.HD.PML.Y.+

15237 — Fift edition. 4° in 8's. [*R. Field*] *f. T. Adams*, 1614. Ent. 14 mr. 1611. L.O.C.BRISTOL².NEP.+; F.CAL.CHI. CU.MICH.+

15238 — The second part of the French academie. *Tr.* out of the second edition. [Dedic. init. T. B., i.e. T. Bowes.] 4° in 8's. *G. B[ishop,] R. N[ewbery,] R. B[arker]*, 1594. Ent. to Bishop a. Newbery 4 jn. 1589. L.O. C².D⁵.STU.+; F.HN.HD.ILL.NY.+

15239 — [Anr. ed.] 4° in 8's. [*T. East*,] *imp. G. Bishop*, 1605. L.L³⁸.O.C.BTU.; F.HN.CAL.CHI.LC.

15240 — The third volume of the French academie. Englished by R. Dolman. 4° in 8's. [*Eliot's Court Press*,] *imp. G. Bishop*, 1601. Ent. 6 jn. 1594. L.O.C³.BIRM.BTU.+; F.HN.HD.ILL.NY.+

15241 — The French academie. Fully discoursed and finished in foure bookes. [Pt. 4 *tr.* by W. P., i.e. W. Philip?] fol. [*J. Legat*] *f. T. Adams*, 1618. Pt. 4 ent. 3 mr. L.O.C.E².WOR.+; F.HN.HD.N.PN.+

La Puente, Luis de. *See* Puente, L. de la.

15241.3 **La Ramée, Pierre de.** [*Arithmetica.*] The art of arithmeticke in whole numbers and fractions. *Tr.* W. Kempe. 8°. *R. Field f. R. Dextar*, 1592. Ent. 17 ja. L.

15241.7 — [*Dialectica.*] P. Rami regii professoris dialecticæ libri duo. Exemplis . . . illustrati. Per Rolandum Makilmenæum. 8°. *T. Vautrollerius*, 1574. L.C⁶.P. PARIS³.; F.

15242 — [Anr. ed.] 8°. *T. Vautrollerius*, 1576. O.BRISTOL².DUL. PLUME.R.

15243 — [Anr. ed.] Scholiis G. Tempelli illustrati. 8°. *Cantabrigiae, ex off. T. Thomasij*, 1584. L.O².C.P.WOR.+; HN.

15244 — [Anr. ed.] Authore Frederico Beurhusio. 8°. [*Eliot's Court Press*,] *imp. G. Bishop*, 1589. Ent. 9 de. 1588. O.C.LYD.M⁴.YK.+

15244.3 — [Anr. ed.] 24° in 12's. *Cantabrigiæ, ex off. J. Legat*, 1592. ILL.
Issued w. 23659.3. This and the following eds. list no editor's name.

15244.7 — [Anr. ed.] 12°. *Edinburgi, hæredes A. Hart*, 1637. O⁴⁸. E.

15245 — [Anr. ed.] 24° in 12's. *Cantabrigiæ, ex off. R. Danielis, et veneunt per Petrum Scarlet*, 1640. O.C.C².C¹⁵.M⁴.+; F.CHI.ILL.X.

15246 — [A trans.] The logike of . . . P. Ramus. *Tr.* per M. Roll. Makylmenæum Scotum. 8°. *T. Vautrollier*, 1574. L.; F.

15247 — [Anr. ed.] 8°. *T. Vautrollier*, 1581. O.C.STU.; HN.

15248 — [Anr. trans.] The art of logick. Gathered out of Aristotle, by P. Ramus. Published by A. Wotton. [*Tr.* S. Wotton.] 8°. *J. D[awson] f. N. Bourne*, 1626. L.O.C.D.E².+; CAL².LC.

15249 — [Anr. trans.] P. Ramus . . . his dialectica in two bookes. Not onely *tr.* but also digested by R. F(age) Gent. 8°. *W. J[ones]*, 1632. L.M⁴.

15249.3 — [Anr. issue, w. cancel tp:] *W. Jones f. A. Kembe in South-Worke* [sic], 1635. L³⁸.

15249.7 — [Anr. issue, w. imprint:] *f. N. Vavasour*, 1636. O.
— *See* also 1596.7, 1982, 11343.

15250 — [*Geometria.*] The elementes of geometrie. *Tr.* T. Hood. 8°. *J. Windet f. T. Hood, to be sold in the Staplers Chappel or at the house of F. Cook*, 1590. L.O(imp.).

La Ramée, Pierre de—*cont.*

15251 — Via regia ad geometriam. The way to geometry. *Tr.* and enlarged by W. Bedwell. [*Ed.*] (J. Clerke.) 4° in 8's. *T. Cotes, sold by M. Sparke,* 1636. Ent. to T. and R. Cotes 12 mr. 1635. L.O.C.D².G².+; F.HN.HD. ILL.Y.+

15251.3 — [*Grammatica Latina.*] P. Rami professoris regii grammatica, ab eo demùm recognita: et ex varijs ipsius scholis & prælectionibus breuiter explicata. 8°. *T. Vautrollerius,* 1585. G².LK(imp.).*

15251.7 — [Anr. ed.] Editio postrema. 8°. *ex æd. T. Orwinii, imp. T. Man & T. Gubbin,* 1589. L³⁸.

15252 — [A trans.] The latine grammar of P. Ramus. (The rudimentes of P. Ramus his Latine grammar.) *Tr.* into English. 2 pts. 8°. *R. Walde-graue,* 1585. L(tpp only, Ames I.445–6; Harl.5974/63).C.E².; F.
Pt. 1 is a pirated ed. of 15253; *see also* 25364b.

15253 — [Anr. ed.] Whereunto is joyned an epistle of Tullie. 8°. *Cambridge, T. Thomas,* 1585. L⁴⁴.C.D.

— [*Rhetorica.*] Ramæ rhetoricæ libri duo. 1597, etc. *See* 4196.5 sqq.
— *See also* 10765.5, 23659.3 sqq.

15254 — Rudimenta Græca e P. Rami grammaticis præcipue collecta: a B. Salignaco. 8°. *ap. H. Binneman,* 1581. L.O.D.; BO⁵.STL.

— The fyrst parte of commentaries. 1573. *See* 22241.
— Ode natalitia. In memoriam P. Rami. 1575. *See* 12902.5.

Larke, John, *tr. See* 3325, 3357.

15254.5 **Larke, Nicholas.** The practice of thankefulnesse; or Davids choyse directions how to prayse God. 8°. *G. P[urslowe] f. R. Jackson,* 1622. Ent. 14 mr. O.

15255 **La Roche de Chandieu, Antoine.** Antonii Sadeelis viri clarissimi vereque theologi de rebus grauissimis controuersis disputationes. 4° in 8's. *ex off. T. Thomasij . . . Academiæ Cantabrigiensis typographi,* 1584. O.C.DUR(Bamb.).P.STU.+; F.NY².PN.
1st 2 leaves in 2 settings; tp line 5 has 'controuersis' or 'controversis'; both at C.

15256 — Moste excellent meditations vppon the xxxii. Psalme, . . . *tr.* W. W(atkinson.) 8°. (*T. Dawson f.*) *T. Cooke a. T. Man,* 1579. Ent. to Cook 2 ap. L.C¹⁵.G².; F.

15257 — A treatise touching the word of God. Made by A. Sadeele. And *tr.* J. Coxe. 8°. [*T. East?*] *f. J. Harison,* 1583. O(imp.).O⁶.P.

La Rochefoucauld, François de, *Cardinal.* Articles concluded. 1619. *See* 16836.

La Rochelle. *See* Rochelle.

15257.5 **La Sale, Antoine de.** [The fifteen joys of marriage. Anon. *Tr.* In verse.] 4°. [*W. de Worde,* c. 1507.] O (2 leaves).
C4ʳ has small orn. at bottom. This trans. possibly by R. Copland; for anr. trans. *see* 6476.

15258 — [Anr. ed.] The fyftene joyes of maryage. 4°. (*W. de Worde,* 1509.) F(imp.).PML.
C4ʳ has catch title at bottom: 'xv. Ioyes.'

Lascarina, *Lady* **Elizabeth.** *See* Indulgences 129 sq.

15259 **Lasco, Joannes à,** *Bp.* Breuis et dilucida de sacramentis ecclesiæ Christi tractatio. 8°. *per S. Myerdmannum,* 1552. L.O.C.E.M.+; F.BO.NY. ⌘

15260 — De catechismus, oft kinder leere, diemen te Londen, is ghebruyckende. [*Tr.*] (J. Vtenhoue.) 8°. *S. Myerdman,* 1551. L.

15260.5 — [Anr. ed.] 8°. *Ghedruct tot Londen, by N. van den Berghe,* 1553. Emden, Grosse Kirche. Mainz, Stadtbibliothek.

15260.7 — De cleyne catechismus, oft kinderleere. Ghemaeckt doer M. Microen. [i.e. abridged from the larger one of J. à Lasco.] 8°. *Londen, N. vanden Berghe,* 1552 (8 oc.) Amsterdam U.

15261 — [Anr. ed.] 8°. *J. Daye,* 1561 (24 jn.) L.; PML. Union C, Schenectedy, N.Y.

15262 — [Anr. ed.] 8°. *J. Daye,* 1566 (12 se.) O.
Text in B.L.; for anr. ed. w. text in roman *see* pt. 2 of 2740.

15262a — [Anr. ed.] Den kleynen cathecismus. 8°. *G. Duwes,* 1566. C.

Lasco, Joannes à—*cont.*

15263 — Compendium doctrinæ de vera vnicaque Dei et Christi ecclesia. 8°. *in off. S. Mirdmanni,* 1551. L.O³.D. Warsaw U.
— *See also* 16571, 16573, 16574, 16575.

La Serre, Jean Puget de. *See* Puget de la Serre, J.

La Sierra, Pedro de. *See* 18866.

Lass. The countrey lasse. [1628–29.] *See* 19224.5.

15264 — The lovely northerne lasse. *Ballad.* 2 pts. s.sh.fol. *f. F. Coules,* [1632.] Ent. 2 ja. 1632. L.

15264.5 — [Anr. ed.] s.sh.fol. *f. F. Coles,* [c. 1635.] G².
In title: 'northern'.

Lassels, John. *See* 25591.

15265 **Lasso, Orlando di.** Nouæ aliquot et ante hac non ita vsitatæ ad duas voces cantiones suauissimæ. 2 ptbks. 4°. *T. Este,* 1598. Ent. 7 au. L(imp.).; F.HN.

15266 — Recueil du mellange d'Orlande de Lassus, contenant plusieurs chansons a quatre, & cinq parties. 5 ptbks.? obl.4°. *T. Vautrouller,* 1570. ?Ent. to Vautrollier 1570–71. O(quinta pars).; F(superius).

Late, Gaspar. *See* 470.2 sqq.

15266.5 **Latewar, Richard.** Rerum gestarum ab illustriss°: viro Th: White [founder of St. John's College, Oxford] . . . ἀπομνημόνευμα. [Anon. In verse.] s.sh.fol. [*Oxford, J. Barnes,* 1608?] L¹³(Muniments 32444).
See Anglia, LXXXIX (1971), pp. 424, 432.
— *See also* 15109.

15267 **Latham, Simon.** Lathams falconry or the faulcons lure, and cure. 4°. [*J. Beale*] *f. R. Jackson,* 1614. Ent. 5 se. O.; HN.KAN(imp.).Y.

15267.3 — [Anr. issue, w. imprint:] *J. B[eale] f. R. Jackson,* 1615. L.O.C².C³.DUL.; F.HN.KAN. Miss Clara S. Peck, New York City.
Usually bd. w. 15268.3. Has 2 sheets of new prelims. added.

15267.7 — [Anr. ed.] 4°. *T. Harper f. J. Harison,* 1633. Ass'd to F. Williams 16 ja. 1626. L.O.O¹¹(imp.).LONGLEAT. WI.+; F.HN.HD.N.Y.+
Usually bd. w. 15268.7.

15268 — Now = 15267.3 and 15268.3.

15268.3 — Lathams new and second booke of falconrie. 4°. *J. B[eale] f. R. Jackson,* 1618. Ent. 6 jy. L.O(2).C².C³. DUL.; F.HN.KAN.LC. Miss Clara S. Peck, New York City.
Usually bd. w. 15267.3.

15268.7 — [Anr. ed.] 4°. *T. Harper f. J. Harison,* 1633. L.O. O³(E).LONGLEAT.WI.+; F.HN.HD.N.Y.+
Usually bd. w. 15267.7.

15269 — Now = 15267.7 and 15268.7.

Lathbury, John. *See* Latteburius, J.

15270 **Lathum, William.** Phyala lachrymarum. Or a few friendly teares, shed over the dead body of Mʳ N. Weld. (Meditationes.) [In verse.] 12°. *R. Y[oung] f. G. Lathum,* 1634. L.; HN(imp.).
— *tr. See* 24820.

15270.5 **Latimer, Hugh,** *Bp.* The fyrste sermon of Mayster Hughe Latimer, whiche he preached before the kynges grace . . . M.D.XLIX. the viii. of Marche. [*Ed.*] (T. Some.) 8°. (*J. Daye a. W. Seres,*) [1549.] L. 0.0⁷(lacks tp).C²(w. tp to 15270.7 inserted).A(lacks tp).+; F.HD.V(imp.).Y.
B5ᵛ catchword: 'not'. This and the following eds. usually found bd. with eds. of 15274–15274.7. This ed. generally occurs w. 15274.

15270.7 — [Anr. ed.] 8°. (*J. Day a. W. Seres,*) [1549.] L.O(imp.). O³.C.ETON.+; F.HN.N.PFOR.SMU.+
(Formerly 15273) In title: 'kynges maiest.'; B5ᵛ catchword: 'lesse'.

15271 — Now = 15272.5.

15272 — [Anr. ed.] 8°. (*J. Daye a. W. Seres,*) [1549.] L.O.; F.HN. CH.CU.
In title: 'kynges maiest.'; B5ᵛ catchword: 'gilti-'.

15272.5 — [Anr. ed.] 8°. (*J. Day a. W. Seres,*) [1549.] L.C(lacks tp).C⁷.P.; F.HN(2).HD.
(Formerly 15271) In title: 'kinges maiestie'; B5ᵛ catchword: 'les'; 'to be sold at the new shop by the lytle conduyte in Chepesyde' omitted from colophon.

Latimer, Hugh, *Bp.*—*cont.*

15273 — Now = 15270.7.

15274 — The seconde [to seventh] sermon of Master Hughe Latemer, . . . preached . . . yᵉ .xv. day of Marche. M.cccc.xlix. 8º. [S. Mierdman f.] (J. Daye a. W. Seres,) [1549.] L.O.O⁷.C.A.+; F.HD(lacks tp and sheet A).Y.

> Side-notes in sheet A only; Ee1ʳ line 5 ends: 'attain'.
> This and the following eds. usually found bd. with eds. of 15270.5–15272.5. This ed. generally occurs w. 15270.5.

15274.3 — [Anr. ed.] 8º. (J. Daye a. W. Seres,) [1549.] L(2).O³.C².DUR³.; F.HN.CH.CU.

> Sheets A–E, T–Aa from the same setting as 15274. Sheets F–R, Bb–Cc reset w. side-notes: F1ᵛ note 1 ends: 'sed.'; O3ʳ note 1 ends: 'prai'; Cc2ᵛ note begins: 'Chryst'. Outer formes of sheets Dd and Ee reset without side-notes: Ee1ʳ line 5 of text ends: 'attayne'.
> Sheets N–S, Bb–Ee in this and the next present problems in the amount of resetting and mixture of sheets.

15274.7 — [Anr. ed.] 8º. (J. Day a. W. Seres,) [1549.] L.O.C(2).C⁷.P.; F.HN.HD.ILL.PFOR.+

> In title: 'Maister Hughe Latimer'; side-notes throughout. Sheets F–R, Cc–Ee reset from 15274.3: F1ᵛ note 1 ends: 'sed worthely.'; O3ʳ note 1 ends: 'praye.'; Cc2ᵛ note begins: 'Chryste'; Ee2ʳ note begins: 'Chryste' (L) or 'christ' (HD). L, HD also differ in sheet A; both have 'Latimer' but HD has 'Cum gratia . . .' below the tp border while L does not.

15275 — = pt. of 15276.

15276 — 27 sermons preached by the ryght reuerende . . . maister Hugh Latimer, as well such as in tymes past haue bene printed, as certayne other. (The seuen sermons preached at Westminster.—Certayn godly sermons vppon the lords prayer. Gathered, by A. Bernher.) 2 pts. 4º in 8's. J. Day, 1562. L.O⁴.C⁵.LEIC².M⁴.+; F.HN.BO.ILL.U.+

> Often found incorrectly bd. w. 'Certayn godly sermons' (pt. 2) first.

15277 — [Anr. ed., w. additions to pt. 2, also ed. A. Bernher.] Frutefull sermons . . . newly imprinted: 1571. 2 pts. 4º in 8's. J. Daye, (1572, 1571.) L.O.C.BTU.M².+; F.HN.HD(imp.).ILL(imp.).PH.+

> Pt. 2 (formerly also 15284) has sub tp 'Seuen sermons, vpon the Lordes prayer' dated 1572 and colophon dated 1571.

15278 — [Anr. ed.] 1575. 4º in 8's. J. Day, (1571) [really 1575.] L.O.O¹².C.NOR².+; F.HN.N.PH.PML.+

15279 — [Anr. ed.] 4º in 8's. J. Daye, (1578.) L.O.C².E.M.+; F.HN.ILL.LC.U.+

15280 — [Anr. ed.] 4º in 8's. J. Daye, 1584. L.O.C¹².BIRM.D.+; F.HN.CH.N.NY¹¹.+

> Table is blind reprint of 15279 and useless.

15281 — [Anr. ed.] 4º in 8's. reprinted by V. Sims, 1596. Ent. 6 de. 1594. L.O¹¹.C.LEIC². Southampton PL.+; F.HN.HD.ILL.Y.+

> See Greg, Register B, p. 82.

15282 — [Anr. ed.] 4º in 8's. [W. Jaggard,] f. the Co. of Statrs., 1607. L.O.C⁴.D.M.+; F.HN.HD.N.U.+

15283 — [Anr. ed.] 4º in 8's. T. Cotes f. the Co. of Statrs., 1635. L.O.C.E.NEK.+; F.HN.HD.ILL.NY.+

> See Court-Book C, pp. 254, 285.

15283.5 — [Anr. issue, w. cancel tp, w. imprint:] T. Cotes f. the Co. of Statrs., 1636. L².; F(tp mutil.).

15284 — Seuen sermons, made vpon the Lordes Prayer, preached before the Duches of Suffolke. 1572. = pt. 2 of 15277.

15285 — Concio quam habuit reuerediss. in Christo pater Hugo Latimer⁹, in coũetu spiritualiũ. Anno. 1537. 8º. (southwarke, p J. Nicolai pro J. Gough,) [1537.] L.L².C.C³.D(lacks tp).; F.HN.

> For a later ed. see 15288.

15286 — [A trans.] The sermon that . . . Hugh Latimer, made to the clergie, in the coũocatiõ, the 9. day of June, nowe tr. out of latyne. 8º. (T. Berthelet, 1537 (23 no.)) O.; F.CU.MICH.

15287 — [Anr. ed.] 8º. (T. Berthelet, 1537 (24 mr.)) C.C³.

> In title: 'in conuocation'.

15288 — Hugonis Latimeri . . . oratio, apud totum ecclesiasticorũ conuentũ. 8º. [T. Dawson?] imp. T. Chardi, 1592. O.D².DUR⁵.

> For an earlier ed. see 15285.

Latimer, Hugh, *Bp.*—*cont.*

15289 — A moste faithfull sermõ preached before the kynges most excellent maiestye, and hys most honorable Councell. M.D.L. 8º. (J. Day,) [1550.] L(2, 1 imp.). L².O.C⁷.CAR.; F(imp.).NY¹¹.

15290 — [Anr. ed.] M.D.L. 8º. (J. Day,) [1553?] L.P.; F.HN.CU.

> In title: 'excellēte', 'Councel'.

15291 — A notable sermõ [on the plough] of maister Hughe Latemer, whiche he preached in yᵉ shrouds at paules churche. 1548. 8º. (J. Day a. W. Seres,) [1548.] L.O.C⁷.A.P.+; F.HN.CU.HD.IND.

> With arms of the Duchess of Suffolk on verso of tp.

15292 — = 15291 or 15292a.

15292a — [Anr. ed.] M.DXLviii. 8º. (J. Daye a. W. Seres,) [1548.] L.O.C(lacks tp).DNPK. Lord Kenyon.; F.N.PFOR.

> Without arms of Duchess of Suffolk on verso of tp. This ed. prob. precedes 15291.

15293 — A sermon of Master Latimer, preached at Stamford the .ix. day of October. Anno .M.cccc. and fyftie. 8º. (J. Daye,) [1550.] L(2).O.C⁵.C⁷.P.; F.HN.CU.HD (lacks colophon).PFOR.

— See also 21047.3.

Latin Grammar. [b2ʳ begins:] case As I muste goo to the mayster. . . . [1482?] Now = 23163.13.

15295 — Latinæ grammaticæ pars prior. 1595. See 7351.

— [d3ʳ begins:] noĩatif case suponēt to the verbe. . . . [1497?] Now = 23163.8.

— Nova et expedita via comparandae linguae Latinæ. [c. 1590.] See 24695a.5.

— Rudimenta grammatices. 1618. See 21438.

— A short introduction to grammar. 1632. See 25192.

— [A1ʳ begins:] What nownys maketh comparison. [c. 1505.] See 23155.4.

Latomus, Bartholomew, *ed. See* 5266.5.

15296 **La Tour Landry, Geoffroy de.** [a1ʳ begins:] Here begynneth the book whiche the knyght of the toure made. [Anon.] (Tr. W. Caxton.) fol. (Westmynstre,) [W. Caxton, 1484] (31 ja.) L(2).O.C.M. Lord Kenyon(7 leaves).; NY. Duff 241.

15297 **Latteburius, Joannes.** [c1ʳ begins:] Incipit liber moraliũ sup trenis iheremie ꝑphete. fol. [Oxford, T. Rood,] (1482 (31 jy.)) L.O.C.LINC.M.+; F.PML(2). Mellon. Duff 238.

> Some copies (o¹⁴) have a border on a2ʳ.

15298 **Laud, William,** *Abp.* A relation of the conference betweene William Lawd, and Mʳ. Fisher the Jesuite. fol. R. Badger, 1639. Ent. 24 de. 1638. L.O.C.A.D.+; F.HN.HD.N.NY.+

> Ends Ddd2. Large paper copies, and some ordinary ones (o⁴⁶) read 'Lawd' instead of 'Lavvd' on tp and sometimes have A2–3, B2–3, K2–3, and Oo3, reset. This is actually the 2nd ed., greatly expanded, of this text (see A4ᵛ) as it was first printed as pt. 2 of 25382.

15299 — [Anr. issue, w. tp and A4 reset.] Second edition revised, with a table annexed. R. Badger, 1639. L¹³. O.C.DUR⁵.LYD.+; F.HN.HD.ILL.JH.+

> Ends Fff4.

— A replie to a relation, of the conference. 1640. See 4154.

15300 — A sermon preached at White-hall, on the 24. of March, 1621. 4º. B. Norton a. J. Bill, 1622. L.O.C.LINC.YK.+; F.N.NY¹¹.Y.

15301 — A sermon preached before his majesty, at Wansted. 4º. F. K[ingston] f. M. Lownes, 1621. L.O.C⁸.D⁸.G⁴.+; F.CAL⁶.HD.PEN².Y.

> Reissued w. tp cancelled in 22240.5.

15302 — A sermon preached before his majestie, on Sunday at White-hall [on Ps. lxxv.2,3.] 4º. B. Norton a. J. Bill, 1625. L.O.D⁸.P.PETYT.+; HN.HART².Y.

15303 — A sermon preached before his majestie, on the fift of July, at the solemne fast. 4º. [B. Norton a. J. Bill,] f. R. Badger, 1626. Ent. 18 jy. L.O.C².D⁸.NLW.+; HART².U.

15304 — A sermon preached on Munday, the sixt of February, at Westminster: at the opening of the parliament. 4º. B. Norton a. J. Bill, 1625. L.O.C.D⁸.NLW.+; HN.CAL⁶.CHI.HD.U.

15305 — A sermon preached on Munday, the seaventeenth of March, at Westminster. 4º. [B. Norton a. J. Bill] f. R. Badger, 1628. L.O³.O⁵.C²(lacks tp)*.

Laud, William, *Abp.—cont.*

15305.5 — [A variant, w. imprint:] *f. R. Badger, sold by H. Perrie,* 1628. O(2).C³.D⁸.WOR.YK.; BO.Y.

15305.7 — [A variant, w. imprint:] *f. R. Badger, sold by R. Allot,* 1628. O.

15306 — A speech delivered in the starr-chamber, at the censure of J. Bastwick. 4°. *R. Badger,* 1637. Ent. 1 jy. O³(E). O⁹.C¹⁵.STD.WIN².+; F.HN.SMU(2).

    Type orn. on tp. It is prob. that only 25 copies of this ed. were pr. There is also an 18th century reprint, w. tp orn. w. flowers and long leafy extensions.

15307 — [Anr. ed.] 4°. *R. Badger,* 1637. L.O(7).C(6).D.E(2).+; F(6).HN(2).HD(2).N.NY(2).+

    Orn. w. crown, rose, and thistle on tp. The sheets, formes, and even pages of this ed. were set from 1 to 4 times and occur in all possible combinations.

15308 — [Anr. ed.] 4°. *Dublin, Soc. of Statrs.,* 1637. CASHEL.; N.NY.

15309 — Divine and politike observations newly *tr.* out of the Dutch language, upon some lines in the speech of the Arch. B. of Canterbury, in the Starre-Chamber. [Dedic. signed Theophilus.] 4°. [*Amsterdam, Richt Right Press,*] 1638. L.O.C.D.E.+; F.HN.HD.N.NY.+ 𝔄

15310 — Articles exhibited in parliament against William Archbishop of Canterbury. 4°. [*London,*] 1640. O.O²⁵. M(deposit).; HN.CAL(2).

    Collates A²B⁴; dated 25 Feb. on tp. 1640 is an old style date as the articles were actually presented in Feb. 1641.

15310.1 — [A variant, w. 'Published by a true and perfect copy' added on tp.] O.O³.C².ETON.

    The added words appear only on this tp.

15310.3 — [Anr. ed.] 4°. [*London,*] 1640. L.O.O⁵(2).O⁶.E.; HD.U.

    Collates A⁴; A2 missigned B2; p. 1 has 7-line heading; p. 5, line 1 ends 'people'; tp not dated 25 Feb.

15310.4 — [A variant, w. p. 5, line 1 ending 'peolpe [*sic*].'] L. O²⁵.M(deposit).; F.HD.ILL.NY.

15310.6 — [Anr. ed.] 4°. [*London,*] 1640. O¹⁴.C.DUR⁵.STU.; F.HD. IND.NY.Y.+

    Collates A⁴; A2 missigned B2; p. 1 has 7-line heading; p. 5, line 1 ends 'and'; tp not dated 25 Feb.

15310.8 — [Anr. ed.] 4°. [*London,*] 1640. L⁸.O.C².D⁸.M(deposit).+; HN.HD.N.NY.PH.+

    Collates A⁴; A2 correctly signed; p. 1 has 10-line heading; p. 5, line 1 ends 'betweene'; tp not dated 25 Feb.; text rewritten and abridged from preceding eds.

— *ed. See* 602, 606, 16606.

— *See also* 10137.5 sq., 10147.7 sqq., 10147.10, 10245, 10263 sq., 10265.5, 10297, 10325, 10370, 16549, 19004, 20136.

15311 **Lauder, George.** The anatomie of the Romane clergie. *Tr.* into English verse by G. L. 4°. *R. Field f. R. Mylbourne,* 1623. Ent. 21 my. L.; IND.

15312 — The Scottish souldier. [In verse.] 4°. *Edinburgh, J. Wreittoun,* 1629. HN.PN.

15313 — Tears on the death of Evander. Occasioned by the losse of sir. John Svinton [*sic*]. [In verse.] 4°. *Hagh,* 1630. HN.

15313.5 — [Heading ¶1ʳ:] Tweeds tears of joy, to Charles great Brittains king. [Anon. In verse.] 4°. [*Edinburgh?* 1639.] E.

— *tr. See* 20113.

15314 **Lauder, William.** Ane compendious and breue tractate, concernyng ye office and dewtie of kyngis. [In verse.] 4°. [*Edinburgh, J. Scot,*] (1556.) L.; HN.

15315 — Ane godlie tractate or mirrour. Quhairintill may be easilie perceauit quho thay be that ar ingraftit in to Christ. Compyld in meter. 4°. [*Edinburgh, R. Lekpreuik,* 1569?] F.

15315.5 — Ane prettie mirrour or conference, betuix the faithfull protestant ād the dissemblit false hypocreit. [In verse.] 4°. [*Edinburgh, R. Lekpreuik,* 1570?] HN.

Laudivius, *da Vezzano.* The Turkes secretorie. 1607. *See* 17996.

15316 **Laudonnière, René de.** A notable historie containing foure voyages made by certayne French captaynes vnto Florida. *Tr.* R. H[akluyt.] 4°. *T. Dawson,* 1587. L.; HN.NY(imp.).

15316.5 **Laurence, John.** Politica, decorum, commentationes, quae J. Laurentius conscripsit. 8°. (*T. Orwinnus,*) *imp. J. Higini,* 1590. L².O³.

Laurence, Thomas. *See* Lawrence, T.

Laurent, *Dominican. See* 21429.

Laurentis, Bartholomaeus, *ed. See* 22980.

Laurentius, Andreas. *See* Du Laurens, A.

15317 **Lauzière, Pons,** *Marquis de Thémines.* The coppy of a letter written by the lord of Themines. Also, a decree of the court of parliament sitting at Chaalons. Done into English by E. A[ggas.] 4°. *J. Wolf,* 1593. Ent. 11 ja. O⁸.P.; Y.

15318 **La Vardin, Jacques de.** The historie of George Castriot, surnamed Scanderbeg, King of Albania. [*Tr.*] By J. de Lavardin, [from the Latin of M. Barlezio.] Newly *tr.* out of French by Z. J[ones] Gentleman. fol. [*R. Field*] *f. W. Ponsonby,* 1596. Ent. 12 oc. 1593. L.O.C.D.E.+; F.HN.HD.N.NY.+

15319 **Lavater, Ludwig.** The book of Ruth expounded in twenty eight sermons, published in Latine, and *tr.* by Ephraim Pagitt, a childe of eleuen yeares. 8°. *R. Walde-graue,* 1586. L(tp only, Harl.5990/77).O.O⁴.; F.HN.HD.Y.

15320 — Of ghostes and spirites walking by nyght. *Tr.* R. H[arrison.] 4°. *H. Benneyman f. R. Watkyns,* 1572. L.L³⁰.O.G². Dr. R. A. Hunter, London.+; F.HN.HD (lacks 3rd pt.).PML.WIS.+

    1st 2 leaves printed with R. Jugge's types; the rest by Bynneman.

15321 — [Anr. ed.] 4°. *T. Creede,* 1596. L.O.C.E.M².+; F.HN.HD.

15322 — Three christian sermons, of famine and dearth of victuals. *Tr.* W. Barlow. 8°. *T. Creede,* 1596. L.O. D.P(lacks tp).; F.HN.HD.

Lavender, Theophilus, *ed. See* 3051.

Law. The lawes resolutions of womens rights. 1632. *See* 7437.

— The true lawe of free monarchies. 1598. *See* 14409.

Lawe, Robert. *See* Loeus, R.

Lawes, Henry. *See* 17937, 21725.

Lawfulness. The lawfulness of our expedition into England manifested. 1640. *See* 21923.

15323 **Lawne, Christopher.** Brownisme turned the in-side out-ward. 4°. [*N. Okes*] *f. W. Burre,* 1613. Ent. 15 my. L.O.C¹⁰.D².; HN.BO³.Y.

15324 — The prophane schisme of the Brownists. Discovered by C. Lawne, J. Fowler, [etc.] 4°. [*W. Stansby f. W. Burre,*] 1612. Ent. to Burre 6 jy. L.O.C¹⁰.D².M.+; F.HN.HD.U.Y.+

    Answered by 5449.

15325 **Lawrence, John.** A golden trumpet, to rowse up a drowsie magistrate. [A sermon.] 4°. *J. Haviland,* 1624. Ent. to Mrs. Griffin a. Haviland 13 jy. L.O³. C.C³.E.+; F.HD.

Lawrence, John, *Fellow of CCC. See* Laurence, J.

Lawrence, Leonard, *tr. See* 778.

15326 **Lawrence, Thomas.** A sermon preached before the kings maiesty. 4°. *R. Badger,* 1637. Ent. 7 mr. O.O³. O⁹.C³.D.+; F.HN.GRO.HART².U.

15326.5 — [A variant, w. imprint:] *R. Badger, sold in Saint Dunstans church-yard in Fleet-street, at the little shop turning up to Cliffards-Inne,* 1637. L¹³.O.C.E².LINC.+; F.HD.N.Y.

15326.7 — [Anr. ed., w. 'maiestie' in title.] *See* Addenda.

Lawrence, Thomas—*cont.*

15327 — Second edition. 4º. *R. Badger, sold in S. Dunstans . . .,* 1637. L.L⁴⁷.O.C⁵.P.

15328 — Two sermons. The first preached . . . in Oxford the second, in . . . Sarum. 4º. *Oxford, J. Lichfield,* 1635. L.O.C¹⁰.DUR³.EX.+; F.GRO.HD.U.

Laws. The lawes of the markette. 1562, etc. *See* 16704.6, 16717, 16727.9.

15329 **Lawson, William.** A new orchard and garden. With the country houswifes garden. 4º. *B. Alsop f. R. Jackson,* 1618 (1617.) Ent. 7 jy. 1617. L.RD.; F.HD(1st pt. only).

15330 — [Anr. ed.] Now the second time corrected. Whereunto is newly added the Art of propagating plants (by S. Harwood.) 4º. *J. H[aviland a. G. Purslowe] f. R. Jackson,* 1623. L(lacks 1st pt.). O.C.C⁸.NLW.+; F. HN.HD(imp.). Washington, D.C., Dept. of Agriculture.
(Harwood section formerly also 12921) Also issued as pt. 4 of 17395.3 sqq. Purslowe pr. sheet H to the end.

15331 — [Anr. ed.] Now the third time corrected. 4º. *J. H[aviland] f. F. Williams,* 1626. Ass'd 16 ja. L.L³⁸.O³(E, imprint cropt).; F.HN.HUNT.

15331.3 — [Anr. ed.] Now the second [*sic*] time corrected. 4º in 8's. *N. Okes f. J. Harison,* 1631. Ass'd 29 jn. 1630. O(imp.).O³.RD.; ILL.
Also issued as pt. 6 of 17396 sq.

15331.7 — [Anr. ed.] Now the third time corrected. 4º in 8's. *E. [a.] (A.) Griffin f. J. Harison,* 1638 (1637.) NY. PML.
Also issued as pt. 6 of 17397.
— *ed. See* 6611.5.

Lawson, William, *Scotsman.* Abstene fra sin. *Tr.* W. Lawsoune. [1579?] *See* 17328.7.

15332 **Lawyer.** The just lawyer his conscionable complaint against private informing and soliciting of judges. 4º. *G. Purslowe,* 1631. Ent. 17 ap. L.L²².O.D.; F.HN. HD.

15333 **Layfielde, Edmund.** The mappe of mans mortality and vanity. A sermon, at the funerall of A. Jacob. 4º. [*M. Flesher*] *f. N. Bourne,* 1630. L.L².O.C⁸.EX.+; F.HN. HD(lacks prelims.).

15334 — The soules solace. A sermon at the funerall of W. Fawcit. 4º. *M. F[lesher] f. G. Gibbs,* 1632. Ent. 31 mr. L.L².O.O¹⁰.C.+; F.CU.HD. 𝔄
L, L³, I O, F, CU, and HD have the date altered in ink to 1633.

15335 — = 15334.

15336 **Lazarillo,** *de Tormes.* The pleasaunt historie of Lazarillo de Tormes. *Tr.* D. Rouland. [Sometimes attributed to D. Hurtado de Mendoza.] 8º. *A. Jeffes,* 1586. Ent. to T. Colwell 1568–69; sold to H. Bynneman 19 jn. 1573. L.O.; HN.ILL.
The title of a lost ed. pr. by H. Bynneman in 1576 is transcribed in Harl.MS.5910, vol. 3, f. 183.

15337 — [Anr. ed.] 4º. *A. Jeffes,* 1596. L.O.C².; HN.

15338 — [Anr. ed.] 8º. *J. H[aviland],* 1624. Ent. to Mrs. Griffin a. Haviland 7 jn. 1621. L.C.C³.; F.HN.ILL.
Usually found bd. w. copies of 16928. Dedic. signed by T. Walkley.

15339 — [Anr. ed., w. additions.] The third edition, corrected. (The pursuit of the historie.) 8º. *E. G[riffin] f. W. Leake,* 1639. Ent. to J. Haviland a. J. Wright 4 se. 1638. L.INN.; F.HN.HD.N.
2nd pt. reprinted from 16927.

15340 — The most pleasant and delectable historie of Lazarillo de Tormes. The second part. *Tr.* W. P[histon?] 4º. *T. C[reede] f. J. Oxenbridge,* 1596. Ent. 12 mr. O (imp.).; HN.HD.PEN.
— The pursuit of the historie. [A different text from 15340.] 1622, etc. *See* 16927 sq.

Lea, James. The birth, purpose, and mortall wound of the Romish holie league. 1589. *See* 15106.

League. An answere to the last tempest and villanie of the league. 1593. *See* 662.
— An aunswere to the league. [1586?] *See* 11373.

15341 — The necessarie league [against the house of Austria.] *Eng. a. Fr.* 8º. [*London?*] 1625 (30 se.) L.O.

15342 **Leake, Richard.** Foure sermons, preached and publikely taught within the countie of Westmerland. 8º. *F. Kingston f. T. Man,* 1599. Ent. to T. Man a. H. Lownes 10 oc. O.P.

15342.5 — [A variant, w. imprint:] *F. Kingston f. T. Man a. H. Lownes,* 1599. F.

15343 **Lear,** *King.* The true chronicle history of King Leir, and his three daughters. 4º. *S. Stafford f. J. Wright,* 1605. Ent. to E. White 14 my. 1594; to Stafford a. ass'd to J. Wright 8 my. 1605. L(2).; F.HN.N. Cincinnati PL. Greg 213.

Learning. The olde learnyng and the new, compared. 1548. *See* 20842.

15344 **Leather.** Leather: a discourse, tendered to the high court of Parliament. And a petition to the high court of Parliament, [to] redresse abuses. 4º. *T. C[otes] f. M. Sparke,* 1629. Ent. 22 de. 1628. L.L³⁰.O.C².D.; F.HN. HD.NY.Y.+
The petition is on a folding leaf (lacking in L, NY; present in F, HD) which begins: 'The generall greeuance of all England, man, woman, and child'; it may also have been issued separately.

15345 **Leaves.** The .iiii. leues of the trueloue. [In verse.] 4º. (*w. de worde,*) [1510?] L.; HN.

15346 **Lebenhain.** This horryble monster is cast of a sowe in a vyllage which is called lebēhayn. M.CCCCC. & xxxi. [With woodcuts.] s.sh.fol. [*Germany,* 1531.] L.
Orig. German title cut off and the English one added by P. Treveris; orig. state in L(Dept. of P&D).

Lecey, John, *ed. See* 4835.

15347 **Le Challeux, Nicolas.** A true and perfect description, of the last voyage attempted by Capitaine John Rybaut, into Terra Florida. 1565. 8º. *H. Denham f. T. Hacket,* [1566.] Ent. 1566–67. L.O⁵.G².

15347.5 **Lechmere, Edmund.** The conference (betwixt M. D. [Richard] Smith, now bishop of Chalcedon, and M. Featlie minister, about the reall presence) mentioned by Doctour Featly in the end of his Sacrilege [10733]. [Init. S. E.] 12º. *Doway, widdow of M. Wyon,* 1632. L.O.C.E.USHAW.+; F.U.WASH³.Y.
(Formerly 7436) A.&R. 442. Reprinted in 15351.3; answered by 24930.

15348 — A disputation of the church, wherein the old religion is maintained. [Dedic. init. F. E.] 8º. *Doway, M. Wyon,* 1629. L³⁵.O.C.A².D.+
A.&R. 443.

15349 — [Anr. ed.] 8º. *Doway, widdow of M. Wyon,* 1632. L.O. C.D²(lacks tp).M.+; F.HN.HD.ILL.U.+
A.&R. 444.

15350 — [Anr. ed., enlarged.] By E. S. F. 8º. *Doway, widdow of M. Wyon,* 1640. L.O.C.D.M.+; F.HN.N.U.Y.+
A.&R. 445.

15351 — A relection of certaine authors that are pretended to disavow the churches infallibilitie. [Init. F. E.] 8º. *Doway, widdow of M. Wyon,* 1635. L.O⁵.AUG.USHAW. W.+; U.
A.&R. 446.
— *See also* 6929.

15351.3 **Lechmere, John.** The relection of a conference touching the reall presence. Or a bachelours censure of a masters Apologie [24930]. By L. I. B. of Art. 8º. *Doway, L. Kellam,* 1635. L.O.AUG.ST.USHAW.+; F. HN.N.WASH³(imp.).Y.
(Formerly 14053 and 22814) A.&R. 447. Includes reprint of 15347.5.

Le Choyselat, Prudent. *See* 20452.

L'Écluse, Charles de, *tr. See* 6984.

15351.7 **Lecluse, Jean de.** An advertisement . . . of Mʳ. Thomas Brightman his book namely, A revelation of the Apocalyps [3754]. 4º. [*Amsterdam, G. Thorp,*] 1612. L³¹.O¹³.; BO⁵.
— *See also* 11212, 18789.

Lectures. Lectures or readings vpon the 6. verse of the 22. chapter of the Prouerbs. 1596. *See* 22400.5.

15352 **Ledenberch, Geilis van.** A true discovery of those treasons of which, G. van Ledenberch was a practiser. 4°. *E. Griffin f. N. Butter,* 1619. Ent. 26 my. L(tp only, Harl.5927/473).O.PETWORTH.STD.

15353 **Ledesma, Diego de.** The christian doctrine in manner of a dialogue betweene the master and the disciple. *Tr.* 8°. [*London, Fr. Garnet's second press?*] 1597. L².O.
A.&R. 448.

15353.3 **Ledoyen de la Pichonnaye, G.** A playne treatise to learne in a short space the Frenche tongue. 8°. *H. Denham f. certayne of the Companie,* 1576. HN.

15353.7 **Lee, George.** A true discourse of such straunge and woonderfull accidents, as hapned in the house of M. George Lee of North-Aston. 4°. [*E. Allde?*] *f. E. White,* 1592. Ent. to J. Kyd 21 jy. L.

15354 **Lee, Richard.** The spirituall spring. A sermon. 4°. *T. S[nodham] f. S. Man,* 1625. Ent. 24 oc. 1624. L². O.C.DUL.M².+; F.HN.HD.U.Y.

Lee, William, *tr. See* 14475.

15355 **Leech, Andrew.** Jovis arbitrium: sive jus hæreditarium, Jacobo D. G. primo. 4°. *V. S[immes] pro C. Knight,* 1603. Ent. by title in English and w. Knight's consent to E. Venge 31 my. (Arber III.36). O.E².

15356 **Leech, David.** Philosophia illachrymans. 1637. Now = 71.23.

15357 — Positiones nonnullæ philosophicae. 1633. Now = 71.18.

15358 — — 1634. Now = 71.19.
15359 — — 1635. Now = 71.20.
15360 — — 1636. Now = 71.21.
— — [1637?] *See* 71.24.
15361 — — [1638.] Now = 71.25.

15362 **Leech, Humfrey.** Dutifull and respective considerations upon foure severall heads of proofe and triall in matters of religion. Proposed in [pt. 1 of 14401]. [Anon. Continued by R. Parsons.] 4°. [*St. Omer, English College Press,*] 1609. L.O(lacks tp).C.D.YK.+; F.N.U.
(Formerly also 19404) A.&R. 449. Errata on Hh2ᵛ.

15362.5 — [Anr. ed.] 4°. [*St. Omer, English College Press,*] 1609. C.D.USHAW.
(Formerly 19405) Errata corrected in text; no list on Hh2ᵛ.

15363 — A triumph of truth. . . . 8°. [*Douai, L. Kellam,*] 1609. L.O.C².M.YK.+; F.HN.TEX.
A.&R. 450. Answered by 1867, 20292.

15363.3 **Leech, James.** A plaine and profitable catechisme. 8°. *J. Legat, printer to the Univ. of Cambridge,* 1605. C.; HD.
(Formerly 15365)

15363.7 **Leech, Jeremy.** A sermon, preached before the lords of the councel. At the funerall of the princess, the Lady Marie's grace. 8°. *H. L[ownes] f. S. Macham,* 1607. Ent. 12 oc. L.O⁴.LINC.; F.HN.
(Formerly 15374)

15364 — The trayne souldier. A sermon preached before the societie of captaynes and gentle men. 8°. *J. B[eale] f. N. Newbery,* 1619. Ent. 7 my. L.O.LINC.M.P.+

15365 Now = 15363.3.

15365.7 **Leech, John,** *Poet.* Joannis Leochaei Scoti, musæ priores, sive poematum pars prior. (Eroticon—Idyllia—Epigrammata.) 8°. [*J. Beale,*] 1620. L³⁸.O.C⁵.A.E⁸.; HN. HD.
Epigrammata, B2ʳ catchword: 'De'.

15366 — [Anr. issue, w. the Epigrammata enlarged and reset.] [*J. Beale,*] 1620 [1621.] L.O.C.E.M².+; F.HN.CU.HD. N.+
Epigrammata, B2ʳ catchword: 'Stipite'. Some of the epigrams are dated 1621, and the next-to-last one is 'De 2. editione epigrammatum'.

15367 — Joannis Leochaei. Epigrammatum libri quatuor. Editio tertia. 4°. *B. Alsopus,* 1623. Ent. 29 au. L.C³. A(imp.).; HN.

Leech, John, *Poet—cont.*

15368 — Jani maliferi strena calendis januarii 1617. 4°. *Edinburgi, T. Finlason,* 1617. L.E(2).E².; HN.

15369 — Jani sperantis strena calendis januarii 1617. 4°. *Edinburgi, T. Finlason,* 1617. L(2).E(2).E².; F.HN.

15370 — Jano bifronti strena, sive cornua. Calendis januarii 1622. 4° in 8. *Andreapoli, E. Rabanus,* 1622. E².; HN.

15370.5 — Joannis Leochæi, strenae: calendis Januarii. Anno Dom. M.DC.XXVI. 4°. *Augustæ Trinobantum* [i.e. London,] *B. Alsopus & T. Facetus,* 1626. E².

15371 — Lachrymæ in . . . Jacobi .I. . . . recessu de Scotiae in Anglorum fines. 4°. *Edinburgi, T. Finlason,* 1617. L.A.

15372 — Johan. Leochæi nemesis poetica. 4° in 8. *Edinburgi, A. Hart,* 1617. E².

15373 — Nemo calendis Maii. 1617. 4°. *Edinburgi, T. Finlason,* 1617. L.C¹⁷.E².

15374 Now = 15363.7.

15374.2 **Leech, John,** *Schoolmaster.* Certaine grammar questions for the exercise of young schollers in the learning of the accidence. [Anon.] 4°. [*London, c. 1590?*] L. (Formerly 12173)

15374.3 — [Anr. ed.] A book of grammar questions. [Init. I. L.] 4°. [*London, c. 1590?*] P.

15374.5 — Certaine grammar questions, for the better furthering of young scholars to understand the accidence. 8°. *J. Norton,* 1605. L.
This is a similar text to the above but not identical. In the preface Leech says 'I did many yeares since cause to be printed for mine own scholars a booke of Grammar questions'.

15374.7 — [Anr. ed.] A booke of grammar questions. Now the second time imprinted, corrected, and enlarged. (Foure little dialogues or colloquies.) 2 pts. 8°. *T. Dawson,* 1618. Mrs. Donald F. Hyde, Somerville, N.J.
A5ʳ catchword: 'full,'.

15374.9 — [Anr. ed.] A booke of grammar questions. Now the third time imprinted. 8°. *T. Harper f. G. W[inder?]* 1628. L(tp only, Harl.5927/427).O(imp.).
L also has the sub tp to the 2nd part, Foure little dialogues, w. the same imprint (Harl.5927/428). Although the O copy lacks both tpp, it was pr. by Harper and almost certainly belongs to this ed. It has A5ʳ catchword: 'or'.

15375 **Le Fèvre, Raoul.** hEre begynneth the volume intituled and named the recuyell of the historyes of Troye. *Tr.* W. Caxton. fol. [*Bruges, W. Caxton a. C. Mansion,* 1475?] L.L⁴.O(imp.).C.M.+; HN.NY(frag.). PML.PFOR. Robert Taylor(frag.). Duff 242.

15376 — [Anr. ed.] The recuyles or gaderige to gyder of yᵉ hystoryes of Troye. fol. (*W. de Worde,* 1502.) L (imp.).*.C⁴(date altered in MS. to 1503).C⁶(lacks 4 leaves.)

15377 — [A variant, w. date:] (*W. de Worde,* 1503.) LC.PML.
15378 — [Anr. ed.] The recuile of the histories of Troie. 3 pts. fol. w. *Coplād,* 1553. L.C.; F.HN.HD(imp.).Y.

15379 — [Anr. ed.] The auncient historie of the destruction of Troy. [Anon.] *Tr.* out of French by W. Caxton. Newly corrected, and the English much amended, by W. Fiston. 4° in 8's. *T. Creede* [a.] (*V. Simmes,*) 1596 (1597.) Ent. to T. Orwin 23 jn. 1591; to V. Simmes 6 ap. 1601. O(imp.).; F(imp.).

15380 — [Anr. ed.] 4° in 8's. *T. Creede,* 1607. L.O. Aberystwyth UC.; F(2, 1 imp.).HN.Y. Robert Taylor.

15381 — Newly corrected. The fifth edition. 4° in 8's. *B. Alsop,* 1617. L.O.C(imp.).C².; HN.N(imp.).TEX(imp.).

15382 — The sixth edition, now newly corrected. 4° in 8's. *B. Alsop a. T. Fawcet,* 1636. L⁴¹.O.C(imp.).M.SHEF.+; F.HN.CHI.HD.Y.+

15383 — fOr asmoche as late . . . I translated aboke named Recuyel of the histories of Troye . . . I entende to translate the boke of thistories of Jason. [Anon. *Tr.* W. Caxton.] fol. [*Westminster, W. Caxton,* 1477.] L.O.C.M. Vienna NL.; NY.PML. Duff 245.

15384 — [Anr. ed.] The veray trew history of the valiaũt knight Iasõ. fol. (*Andewarpe, G. Leeu,* 1492 (2 jn.)) L.C.D. Duff 246.

15385 **Legate, Robert.** A briefe catechisme and dialogue betwene the husbande and his wyfe. 1545. Now = 4797.3.

15386 **Legatum.** Legatum distribuendum in nuptiis mulierum pauperum, distribui debet in nuptiis virginum, non viduarum. 1586. Now = 4474.64.

15387 **Legatus.** De legato et absoluto principe perduellionis reo. 8°. *Oxoniæ, typis J. Barnesii,* 1587. L.L¹³.O.C.

Legenda Aurea. The golden legend. [1483, etc.] *See* 24873 sqq.

15388 **Legh, Gerard.** The accedens of armory. 4° in 8's. (*R. Tottill,* 1562 (31 de.)) Ent. 1562–63. L.O.C.E.M.+; F.HD.N.WIS. Cincinnati U.+

15389 — [Anr. ed.] 4° in 8's. (*R. Tottel,* 1568.) L.O.C².D².M.+; F.HN.ILL.

15390 — [Anr. ed.] 4° in 8's. (*R. Tottel,* 1576.) L.O⁸.C.D.E.+; F.HN.CH.HD.WIS.+

15391 — [Anr. ed.] 4° in 8's. (*R. Tottell,* 1591.) Ent. 18 fb. 1583. L.O.C³.G².M⁴.+; F.HN.ILL.NY.WIS.+

15392 — [Anr. ed.] 4° in 8's. (*H. Ballard,* 1597.) L.O.E.M.P.+; F.HN.N.PH.WIS.+

15393 — [Anr. ed.] 4° in 8's. [*W. Jaggard*] (*f. J. Jaggard,*) 1612. L.O.C².E.M.+; F.HN.N.NY.WIS.+
The PETWORTH copy has added at both beginning and end 2 leaves with a colophon reading: 'W. Stansby, sold by R. Meighen, 1621', possibly cut up and mounted from copies of 22634.

15394 **Legrand, Jacques.** [a1ᵛ:] Here begynneth the table of a book intytuled the book of good maners. (*Tr. W. Caxton.*) fol. [*Westminster, W. Caxton,*] (1487 (11 my.)) L(imp.).L²(imp.).C. Copenhagen RL. Duff 248.

15395 — [Anr. ed.] fol. (*R. Pynson,* 1494 (30 se.)) L(lacks a1,2). Duff 249.

15396 — [Anr. ed.] 4° in 6's. (*R. Pynson,*) [1500.] C⁴(imp.).; N(imp.). Duff 250.
Prob. later than 15397.

15397 — [Anr. ed.] Here begynneth a lytell boke called good maners. 4° in 6's. (*Westmynster, W. de worde,*) [1498.] L.C. Duff 251.

15398 — [Anr. ed.] The boke of good maners. 4° 8·4. (*W. de Worde,* 1507 (10 de.)) L(lacks tp).C(2 imp.).; F(imp.). HN.PML(imp.).

15399 — [Anr. ed.] 4° 8·4. (*w. de worde,*) [1526?] O.

15399.5 — [An extract.] Here begynneth a lytell necessarye treatyse the whiche speketh of the estate of the comonalte, and of good maners. [Anon.] 8° in 4's. (*R. wyer,*) [1531–34.] M.USHAW.

Le Grys, *Sir* **Robert,** *tr. See* 1393, 24633.

15400 **Le Hucher,** *M.* M. le Hucher minister of Amyens . . . compelled to fly. [1616.] Now = 24675.5.

Leicester, *Earl of. See* Dudley, R.

15401 **Leicestershire Lovers.** The two Lestershire lovers. Ballad. 2 pts. s.sh.fol. [*W. Jones?*] *f. J. Trundle,* [c. 1620.] L.
5612 is pr. on the verso.

Leiden. *See* Leyden.

15402 **Leigh, Dorothy.** The mothers blessing. Or the godly counsaile of a gentle-woman. 12°. *f. J. Budge,* 1616. Ent. 26 fb. O.

15402.5 — The third edition. 12°. [*G. Purslowe*] *f. J. Budge,* 16017 [*sic*]. Goyder.

15403 — The fourth edition. 12°. [*S. Stafford*] *f. J. Budge,* 1618. C.

15403a — The fift edition. 12°. *f. J. Budge,* 1618. HN.

15404 — The seventh edition. 12°. *f. J. Budge,* 1621. L.

15405 — The tenth edition. 12°. *f. R. Allot,* 1627. Ent. 4 se. 1626. L.; N.

15405.5 — The fourteenth edition. 12°. *f. R. Allot,* 1629. L(imp.).

15406 — The fifteenth edition. 12°. *f. R. Allot,* 1630. L.

15407 — [Anr. ed.] 12°. *f. R. Allot,* 1633. O.INN.; F.HD. Toronto PL.

15407.3 — [Anr. ed.] 12°. *f. R. Allot,* 1634. F.

15407.5 — [Anr. ed.] 12°. *f. T. Lambert,* 1636. N.

15408 — [Anr. ed.] 12°. *T. Cotes f. A. Crooke,* 1640. Ent. 2 se. 1639. C.; F.

15409 **Leigh, Edward.** Critica sacra: or, philologicall and theological observations, upon all the Greek words of the New Testament. 4° in 8's. *R. Young, sold by G. Latham a. P. Nevill,* 1639. Ent. to Young 5 oc. 1638. L.O.C.BIRM.LEIC.+; F.HN.HD.ILL.U.+

Leigh, Edward—*cont.*

15410 — Selected and choice observations concerning the twelve first Cæsars. 12°. *Oxford, L. Lichfield f. W. Webb,* 1635. L.O.C³.C⁵.; F.HN.HD(imp.).ILL.

15411 — A treatise of the divine promises. In five bookes. 4°. *G. Miller,* 1633. Ent. 8 jy. L.O.C.E.G².+; F.HN.HD. ILL.U.+

— *ed. See* 25317.

Leigh, Nicholas, *tr. See* 10499.

15412 **Leigh, Richard.** The copie of a letter sent out of England to don Bernardin Mendoza. Found in the chamber of R. Leigh a seminarie priest. Whereunto are adioyned certaine late Aduertisements, concerning the losses to the Spanish nauie. [By W. Cecil.] 2 pts. 4°. *J. Vautrollier f. R. Field,* 1588. L.O.C.D².P.+; F. HN.HD.ILL.NY.+
(Pt. 2 formerly also 14257) All the following distinctions are found in HD copies except for pt. 2, setting 3, which is at O(Wood 511). Examination of more copies would undoubtedly reveal further variations (at C there have been reported 2 settings of both formes of sheets A–C and of D outer forme). In pt. 1 the second of each copy pair of readings given below is that followed in 15413, except for quire C, q.v. Pt. 2 is lacking in some copies (2 c), found separately in at least setting 4 at O(4° C 16 (19)Art.BS.), or found with various combinations of pt. 1 sheets.
Pt. 1 collates A–E⁴ F² and is found at HD with the following differences. A2ᵣ last line ends 'countrey' or 'and'. C outer forme reset: C1ᵣ line 2 has 'infamie.' or 'infamy.' (the latter setting reimposed in 15413). C inner forme as follows: C3ᵛ line 12 from the bottom begins 'niards, and'; altered in press to 'niards, &'; completely reset with 'liques' (15413 reset with 'as it is'). E3,4 reimposed: without or with marginal notes; F2ᵣ altered in press: 'The [space] of Octob. 1588.' or 'The 9 of Octob. 1588.'
Pt. 2 occurs in four distinct settings, the first three collating A–B⁴ [–]², with [–]1ᵣ dated 26 Sept. 1588. A4ᵣ line 6 from the bottom ends 1) 'Bys-keyne'; 2) 'Byskeine'; 3) 'Biskeine' (this is partly reimposed in 15413); 4) Collates A–B⁴ and is probably by a different printer (T. Orwin?).
The French trans., 15414.3, was probably printed before the English text.

15413 — [Anr. ed.] 4°. *J. Vautrollier f. R. Field,* 1588. L².L³⁰. L³⁸.O.O⁵.; F.HN.HD.
Collates A–G⁴ H²; B2ᵣ line 1: 'Armie'; G2ᵣ line 2: 'soul-'.

15413.5 — [Anr. ed.] 4°. *J. Vautrollier f. R. Field,* 1588. C.G².OS*.; PH. W. Stirling Maxwell, Chicago.
Collates A–G⁴ H²; B2ᵣ line 1: 'Army'; G2ᵣ line 2: 'souldi-'.

15414 — [Anr. ed.] *G. Miller,* 1641. = Wing B 5729. One L copy, G.6068(2), has the date sophisticated to read 1601.

15414.2 — [A trans.] La copie d'vne lettre envoyee d'Angleterre a dom Bernardin de Mendoze. 8°. [*London, J. Vautrollier f. R. Field,*] 1588. O.
Collates A–D⁸ E⁴. No mention of 'Advertisemens' on tp, and they are not present. E4ᵣ has no orn., and the printer's address to the reader is dated 20 Sept. 1588.

15414.3 — [Anr. issue, w. F–H⁴ I² added and F1ᵣ beginning:] (Depuis l'impression de ceste derniere fueille. . . .) L.O.; HD.
H4ᵛ dated 27 Sept. 1588.

15414.4 — [Anr. ed.] 8°. [*London, J. Vautrollier f. R. Field,*] 1588. O.
Collates A–D⁸ E–H⁴ I², with F–I in the same setting as 15414.3. 'Advertissemens' mentioned on tp; E4ᵣ has an orn.
There are at least 2 other eds. in French dated 1588 and without imprint: (1) collates A–D⁸ E–H⁴(H4 blank) and is attrib. to Delft (copy at O); (2) collates A–G⁸ and is attrib. to La Rochelle (copy at PARIS). Neither mentions the 'Advertisse-mens' on the tp though they are present.

15414.6 — [Anr. trans.] Essempio d'vna lettera mandata d'Inghil-terra a don Bernardino di Mendozza. *Tr. di francese* [really from English.] 8°. *Leida, Arrigo del Bosco* [i.e. *London, J. Wolfe,*] 1588. Ent. to J. Wolfe 23 oc. L(2).O.; F.HD(2).
Collates A² B–G⁸ H⁶. F7ᵣ is dated 20 Sept. 1588, and H4ᵛ is dated 27 Sept. 1588.

15415 **Leigh, Valentine.** Deathes generall proclamation. Also fiue preceptes of vertuous and honest lyfe. 8°. (*H. Sutton*,) 1561 (8 ja.) L².

15416 — The moste profitable and commendable science, of surueying. 4°. [*J. Kingston*] f. A. Maunsell, 1577. Ent. 11 fb. O.C.C¹⁷(imp.).CAR.RD.+; F.TEX.WIS.

15416a — [A variant, w. imprint:] f. M. Jennings, 1577. L.O. C².RD.; LC. Horblit.

15417 — [Anr. ed.] Newly imprinted. 4°. [*J. Kingston*] f. A. Maunsell, 1578. L.L²⁸.O⁵.R.RD.+; HN.PEN.PH².Y.

15418 — [Anr. ed.] 4°. J. Windet f. A. Maunsell, 1588. L.L²⁸. O.C⁵.RD.; MICH.

15419 — [Anr. ed.] 4°. J. Windet f. R. Dexter, 1592. Ent. 2 no. 1590. L.L³⁸.C¹².D.RD.+; F.HN.N. Horblit.

15420 — [Anr. ed.] 4°. R. Robinson f. R. Dexter, 1596. L.O.O³. C⁷. Warrington PL.+; American U, Washington, D.C.

15421 — The pleasaunt playne and pythye pathewaye leadynge to a vertues and honest lyfe. [1552?] Now = 15113.5.

15422 **Leigh, William.** The christians watch: or, an heavenly instruction. Preached at the funerals of Thomas Leigh of Adlington . . . 1601. 8°. [*E. Allde*] f. E. White, 1605. Ent. 22 ja. O¹⁰.LINC.; F.HN.

15423 — The dampe of death: beaten backe. . . . In a sermon. 8°. T. Creede f. A. Johnson, 1613. O.C¹⁰.LINC.; F.U.

15423.3 — Davids palme and cedar, shewing the reward of the righteous. In a sermon. 8°. T. Creede f. A. Johnson, 1615. Ent. 12 jy. LINC.M.; F(imp.).

15423.5 — The dreadfull day, dolorous to the wicked. In two sermons. 8°. [T. Creede] f. A. Johnson, 1610. LINC.; F(2, 1 lacks tp).

15423.7 — The drumme of devotion, striking out an allarum. Together with the perfume of prayer. In two sermons. 8°. T. Creede f. A. Johnson, 1613. Ent. 31 my. L(tp only, Ames II.315).O.; F.

15424 — The first step, towards heaven, or, Anna, the prophetesse. With the second edition of Great Brittaines deliverance. [Two sermons.] 8°. N. Okes f. A. Johnson, 1609. Ent. 24 oc. 1608. L(imp.).INN.

15425 — Great Britaines, great deliverance, from the great danger of popish powder. 4°. [T. Creede] f. A. Johnson, 1606. Ent. 1 jy. 1602; crossed out and re-ent. 20 ja. 1606. L³⁰.O.C².M².YK.+; F.CAL.HD. Reprinted in 15424.

15426 — Queene Elizabeth, paraleld in her princely vertues. In three sermons. 8°. T. C[reede] f. A. Johnson, 1612. Ent. 13 de. 1611. L.L¹³(imp.).O.O⁴.; F.HN.

15427 — The soules solace. 1617. = pt. of 12869.

15428 — Strange newes of a prodigious monster, borne in Adlington in Lancaster, 1613. Testified by W. Leigh. 4°. J. P[indley] f. S. M[an,] 1613. Ent. to Man 12 jn. O.; F.
    Leigh is only cited as a witness by an anonymous narrator.

— *See* also 12866.

15428.5 **Leighton, Alexander.** An appeal to the parliament; or Sions plea against the prelacie. [Anon.] 4°. *Printed the year & moneth wherein Rochell was lost* [i.e. Amsterdam, successors of G. Thorp, 1629]. L.O.C².E. G².+; F.HN.CH.N.U.+
    (Formerly 15430) Leaf 5 signed A3; G3ʳ has 'J.C.' in swash italic. Though La Rochelle fell in Oct. 1628, the book was not pr. till early the following year. See also 8967.

15429 — [Anr. ed.] 4°. *Printed the year & moneth wherein Rochell was lost* [i.e. Amsterdam, J. F. Stam, 1629?] L.O.C.E.NLW.+; F.HN.HD.KAN.Y.+
    Leaf 5 signed A; G3ʳ has 'I.C.' in plain italic.

15430 — Now = 15428.5.
— The second edition. By Dr. Layton. [*Printed abroad*, 1644?] *See* Wing L 1022.

15431 — A friendly tryall of some passages contained in the Treatise of faith [6114], written by Mr. E. Culverwel. 8°. [Amsterdam, successors of G. Thorp,] 1624. C¹⁰. D.DUR³.

15431.5 — A shorte treatise against stage-playes. [Anon.] 4°. [Amsterdam, successors of G. Thorp,] 1625. L.L³.C². E. Leeds PL.; HN.BO.HD.PML.
    (Formerly 24232)

15432 — Speculum belli sacri: or the looking-glasse of the holy war. [Init. A. L.] 4°. [Amsterdam, successors of G. Thorp,] 1624. L.O.C².E.G².+; F.HN.HD.N.U.+

15433 **Leighton,** *Sir* **William.** The teares or lamentations of a sorrowfull soule. [In verse.] 4°. R. Blower, 1613. Ent. 25 ja. L.O.C.Britwell 236(imp.).; HN.CH(imp.). NY.
    HN copy has an added leaf w. pr. presentation epistle to T. Egerton, Lord Chancellor of England, by John Milton, father of the poet. The O copy differs from L in not having ∗∗1,2,4, though O does have ∗∗3, the dedic. to Prince Charles. Heading Bb3ᵛ: 'THE/Table of all [etc.]' (O) or 'The Table.' (L).

15434 — The teares . . . composed with musicall ayres. fol. W. Stansby, 1614. L.L⁷.C(frag.). St. Michael's C, Tenbury.; F.NY.
    Only the first 8 pieces are by Leighton.

15435 — Vertue triumphant, or a lively description of the foure vertues cardinall. [In verse.] 4°. M. Bradwood f. M. Lownes, 1603. Ent. 4 jy. L.L⁸.; F.HN.HD.SUNY (Buffalo).Y.+

15436 **Leith.** ane premonitioun to the barnis of Leith. 1572. Now = 22204.5.

15437 **Leius, Matthias.** Certamen elegiacum novem musarum, Apolline duce, contra Barbariem susceptum. [In verse.] 4°. per S. Staffordum, 1600. C².

15438 — Matthiæ Leij, . . . liber de triumphata Barbarie. (Liber epigrammatum.) [In verse.] 4°. [W. Stansby,] 1621. L.O.C.C².D.+; F.Y.

15439 — Mathiæ Lej Germani reginæ pecuniæ liber I. (Joannis Secundi et M. Lei reginæ pecuniæ regia.) [In verse.] 8°. [Eliot's Court Press,] 1623. Ent. to Mrs. Griffin a. J. Haviland 10 mr. L.O.C².D.LINC.+; ILL.

15440 **Leland, John.** Assertio inclytissimi Arturij regis Britanniae. 4°. [R. Wolfe] (ap. J. Herford,) 1544. L.O.C.D. E.+; F.HN.HD.N.NY.+

15441 — [A trans.] A learned and true assertion of the life of prince Arthure. Newly tr. by R. Robinson. 4°. J. Wolfe, 1582. Ent. 7 jn. L.L².O⁴.C.NLW(imp.).; F.HN. HD.N.Y.+

15441.7 — Bononia Gallo mastix. In laudem felicissimi victoris Henrici octaui. 4°. J. Mayler, 1545. C².G².

15442 — Ἐγκώμιον τῆς εἰρήνης. Laudatio pacis. [In verse.] 4°. (ap. R. Wolfium) 1546 (au.) L.O.C.E.M.+; F.HN. HD.N.NY.+
    The 'W' in Wolfe's name in the colophon is composed of an inverted italic 'I' and a 'V'.

15442.5 — Fatum Bononiæ Morinorum. [In verse.] s.sh.fol. [R. Wolfe,] 1544. G²(cropt to 4° size).

15443 — Genethliacon illustrissimi Eäduerdi principis Cambriae. [In verse.] 4°. (ap. R. Vuolfium,) 1543. L.O. C.D².G².+; F.HN.HD.N.NY.+

15444 — Κύκνειον ασμα. Cygnea cantio. (Commentarii.) Lat. 2 pts. 4°. [R. Wolfe, 1545.] L.O.O³.C.ETON.+; CAL². N.PN.Y.

15444.5 — [Anr. issue, w. imprint:] Londini, 1545. L.O.C⁹.E.G².+; F.HN.HD.IND.PML.

15445 — The laboryouse journey & serche . . . for Englandes antiquitees, geuen of hym as a newe yeares gyfte to Kynge Henry the viij . . . with declaracyons enlarged: by J. Bale. 8°. [S. Mierdman f.] (J. Bale,) to be sold [by R. Foster,] (1549.) L.O.C.BRISTOL². G².+; F.HN.N.PML.Y.+

15445.5 — Naenia in mortem splendidissimi equitis Henrici Duddelegi. [In verse.] 4°. J. Mayler, 1545. G².

15446 — Naeniae in mortem Thomæ Viati equitis incomparabilis [Sir T. Wyatt]. [In verse.] 4°. [R. Wolfe,] (ad signum ænei serpentis,) 1542. L.O.C.D².G².+; F.HN. HD.N.PML.+

15446a — [A ghost.]

15447 — Principum, ac illustrium aliquot & eruditorum in Anglia virorum, encomia. Quibus adiuncta sunt, aliquot herôum, hodiè viuentium, encomia à T. Newtono, exarata. [In verse.] 4°. ap. T. Orwinum, 1589. L.O.C.C².D.+; F.HN.HD.LC.N.+

— *See* also 3834.

15448 **Le Loyer, Pierre,** *Sieur de la Brosse.* A treatise of specters or straunge sights. [Tr.] (Z. Jones.) 4°. V. S[immes] f. M. Lownes, 1605. Ent. 11 ja. L.O.C.D.E.+; F.HN. HD.N.NY.+
    Copies vary: with or without Jones's name on A3ʳ; both at F, N, PEN.

15449 **Le Maçon, Robert,** *called De La Fontaine.* Catechisme et instruction familiere pour les enfans qui se præparent à communiquer à la saincte Cene selon la forme de l'eglise françois à Londres. 8°. *R. Field,* 1602. L.

15450 — [A trans. of an unknown earlier and shorter ed. of 15449.] A catechisme and playne instruction for children, which prepare thēselues to communicate according to the order of the Frenche church at London. *Tr.* T. W[ilcox.] 8°. *H. Middleton f. T. Man,* [1580.] Ent. 9 fb. 1580. L(2).; F.

15451 — Les funerailles de Sodome et de ses filles. 8°. *R. Field,* 1600. L.C³.C¹⁷.D².P.+; HD.

15452 — [Anr. ed.] Reveu & corrigé de nouveau. 8°. *R. Field* [really *France,*] 1610. L.O.C²⁵.D².G².+; F.HN.

15453 **Le Maire de Belges, Jean.** The abbreuyacyon of all generall councellys. *Tr.* J. gowgh [from Le traicte des schismes.] 8°. [*R. Wyer f.*] *J. gowgh,* (1539.) O. DUR⁵.

15453.3 **Leman, James.** To the high court of Parliament. . . . [A petition to restore the school at Ipswich to its original location.] s.sh.fol. [*London,* 1624.] L⁵(Lemon 228).

15453.7 **Le Mayre, Marten.** The Dutch schoole master. Wherein is shewed the way to learne the Dutch tongue. 8°. *G. Elde f. S. Waterson,* 1606. Ent. 15 au. 1603. O.

15454 **Lemnius, Levinus.** An herbal for the Bible. Drawen into English by T. Newton. 8°. *E. Bollifant,* 1587. Ent. to Bollifant a. A. Hatfield 4 my. L.O.C.E.P.+; F.HN.HD(imp.).MICH.Y.+

15454.5 — The sanctuarie of salvation, helmet of health, and mirrour of modestie. [*Tr.*] H. K(inder.) 8°. *H. Singleton,* [1592.] Ent. 31 mr. 1592. L.; HD.

15455 — [A ghost.]

15456 — The touchstone of complexions . . . englished by T. Newton. 8°. *T. Marsh,* 1576. L(2).L³⁹.O(lacks tp). O².P.; F(imp.).CHI².WIS.Y.

15457 — [Anr. ed.] 8°. *T. Marsh,* 1581. Ent. to T. Orwin 23 jn. 1591. L.O(2).O⁴³(imp.). Chester PL. Dr. R. A. Hunter, London.; F.HN.HD.N.Y.+

15458 — [Anr. ed.] Englished by T. N. 4°. *E[liz.] A[llde] f. M. Sparke,* 1633. L.L¹⁶.O.C.G².+; F.HN.CHI.HD.NLM.+

15459 **Le Moyne de Morgues, Jacques.** La clef des champs, pour trouuer plusieurs animaux. 1586. obl.8°. [*T. Vautrollier*] *imprimé aux Blackefreirs, pour J. le Moyne,* [1586.] Ent. 31 jy. 1587. L(2 imp.). With woodcuts of beasts, birds, and flowers pr. only on the recto.

15460 **Lennard, Sampson.** An exhortatory instruction to a speedy repentance. 12°. *M. B[radwood] f. E. Blount a. W. Barret,* 1609. Ent. to Blount 5 de. 1608. L. DUL.PLUME.; HN.
— *tr. See* 4103, 5051, 18147, 19768.5.

15461 **Lent, Jacke.** The recantaciō of Jacke lent late vicare generall to the mooste cruell Antichriste of Rome. 8°. (*J. Day a. W. Seres,*) 1548. F.

15462 **Lenthall, William.** Mᵣ. Speaker his speech to his majestie, in parliament, the fifth of November. 1640. 4°. [*T. Paine*] *f. W. Sheares,* 1640. O⁵. BRISTOL. ETON.P.PETYT.; F.HN.HD.N.Y. A2ʳ line 10 of text: 'Session'.

15462.3 — [Anr. ed.] 4°. *f. W. Sheares,* 1640. F.LC. A2ʳ line 10 of text: 'Sessions'.

15462.7 — [Anr. ed.] 4°. *Reprinted at Dublin,* 1640. D⁶.

15463 **Lenton, Francis.** Characterismi: or, Lentons leasures. Expressed in essayes and characters. 12°. *J. B[eale] f. R. Michell,* 1631. Ent. 29 ap. L.O.; HN.ILL.

15463.5 — [Anr. issue, w. cancel tp:] Spare time. Expressed in essayes and characters, never before written on. *f. J. Boler,* 1632. NY.

15464 — [Anr. issue, w. new tp and prelims:] Lentons leisures described, in divers moderne characters. *London,* 1636. HN.

15464.5 — [Anr. issue, w. new tp and prelims:] A piece of the world, painted in proper colours. *J. Raworth,* 1640. F.N. Sheets D and E apparently reset.

Lenton, Francis—*cont.*

15465 — Great Britains beauties, or, the female glory; epitomized, in encomiastick anagramms. 4°. *M. Parsons f. J. Becket,* 1638. Ent. 3 fb. O(2).O²¹.; HN.

15466 — The Innes of Court anagrammatist: or, the masquers masqued. [In verse.] 4°. [*T. Harper*] *f. W. Lashe,* 1634. Ent. 7 jy. L.L⁸.L³⁸.O⁶.O¹³.+; F.HN.CAL⁵.

15467 — The young gallants whirligigg: or youths reakes. [In verse.] 4°. *M. F[lesher] f. R. Bostocke,* 1629. Ent. 21 no. 1628. L.L⁴.O³⁸(frags. of 2 leaves).C(frag.).; F.HN.HD.

15467.5 — [Anr. issue, w. cancel tp and dedic.] The puisne gallants progresse. *London,* 1635. Robert Taylor. With verse dedic. to Henry Rich, Earl of Holland.

15468 [A ghost.]

15469 **Lentulo, Scipio.** An Italian grammer written in Latin and turned in Englishe: by H. G(ranthan.) 8°. *T. Vautroullier,* 1575. L(2).O(3).O⁵.C.M.; F(2).HN.BO.N.

15470 — [Anr. ed.] La grammatica di M. Scipio Lentulo . . . *tr.* H. G. An Italian grammer. . . . 8°. *T. Vautrollier,* 1587. Ent. to R. Field 11 ap. 1614. L.O.C³.EX*.RGU.; F.HN.Y.

15470.5 — [A variant, w. imprint:] *T. Vautrollier f. W. Norton,* 1587. Y.

15470a — [A variant, w. imprint:] *T. Vautrollier f. J. Harison,* 1587. HN.

15470a.5 **Lentulus, Publius.** Publius Lentulus, his newes to the Senate of Rome, concerning Jesus Christ. s.sh.fol. [*M. Flesher*] *f. H. Gosson,* [c. 1625.] L⁵(Lemon 81).

Leo I, *Pope and Saint. See* 20088.

Leo IX, *Pope. See* Indulgences 84.

15471 **Leo X,** *Pope.* JOhānes Calipoleñ episcop⁹ magister dom⁹ sctī Thome martyris Cātuariēꝑ dicte de Acoñ in ciuitate Londoñ. . . . [1515?] Now = Indulgences 56.

15472 — OUr holy father . . . that now is cōsyderynge, that where .ii. certayne brotherñ John busset and Richarde busset. . . . [1515.] Now = Indulgences 124.

15473 — [Indulgence in English for the redemption of the children of. . . . 1511.] Now = Indulgences 129.

15474 — Here after foloweth the newe pryuyleges and indulgēces graunted to the house of seynt Thomas of Acres in London. . . . [1517?] Now = Indulgences 58.

15475 — THe holy & great indulgence & pardon of plenary remissiō a pena et culpa graūted by dyuerse popes, . . . [1518.] Now = Indulgences 43.

15476 — These be the articles of the popes bulle under leade . . . OOur [*sic*] holy father. . . . [1518.] Now = Indulgences 133.

15477 — FRater Philippus Mulart . . . hospitalis sancti spiritus in Saxia de vrbe Romana. [1519.] Now = Indulgences 93.

15478 — [Anr. ed., dated 1520.] Now = Indulgences 96.

15479 — [Indulgence in English in favour of the 'Hospitall of the holy Ghoste', Rome. 1520.] Now = Indulgences 99.

15480 — VEnerabilibus et in Christo carissime dilectis gardiano et magistris vna cum fratribus et sororibus gylde seu confraternitatis sancti Johannis in ecclesia perochiali sācti Nicholai de wakering Londoñ. . . . [1526.] Now = Indulgences 80.
— *See also* Indulgences 45, 53 sqq., 57 sq., 91 sqq., 101 sqq., 123, 125 sqq., 131 sq., 144 sq.

15481 **Leo, John,** *Africanus.* A geographical historie of Africa, written in Arabicke and Italian. *Tr.* and [with additions] collected by J. Pory. fol. [*Eliot's Court Press,*] *imp.* G. Bishop, 1600. Ent. 1 se. L.O.C.D.M.+; F.HN. HD.N.NY.+

15481.5 — [Anr. issue, w. imprint:] *J. L[egat] f. A. H[ebb,] part of the impression, made over to be vented for the benefit of the children of J. Minsheu deceased,* [c. 1626.] Ass'd to Hebb 6 May 1625. Mrs. Charles W. Engelhard, Far Hills, New Jersey.

Leochæus. *See* Leech.

15482 **Leodius, Huburtus.** Epistola ad R. Ascham. [1590.] = pt. of 829.

Leone, Giovanni. *See* 15481.

Leoni, Tommaso. *See* 3357.

Leonicenus, Nicolaus, *tr. See* 11531.5, 11532.

15483 **Leowitz, Cyprianus von.** Breuis et perspicua ratio iudicandi genituras, ex physicis causis extructa. Praefixa est admonitio de vero astrologiæ vsu: per H. Wolfium. Adiectus est libellus de præstantioribus quibusdam naturæ virtutibus: J. Dee authore. 2 pts. 4°. [Colophon to pt. 1:] (*H. Suttonus,*) 1558 (jy.) L. O(2 imp.).C.C³(2).D². ; HD.Y(lacks col.).*
As copies of both pts. of this and the next occur separately or w. mixed colophons, only copies of pt. 1 are given here and all copies of pt. 2 are listed at 6463 sq.

15483.5 — [A variant, w. colophon:] (*H. Suttonus, imp. N. Englande,*) 1558 (jy.) L¹³.O.C¹⁰. ; F.

15484 — De coniunctionibus magnis insignioribus superiorum planetarum. 1573. Now = 479.8.

15485 **Le Petit, Jean François.** The Low-Country commonwealth contayninge an exact discription of the eight united provinces. *Tr.* E. Grimeston. 4° in 8's. *G. Eld,* 1609. L.O.C.D.E². ; F.HN.HD.N.Y. 𝔄
(Formerly also 19800)
— *See also* 17450.

Lermæus, Gabrielis, *tr. See* 21656.

15486 **Le Roy, Adrien.** A briefe and easye instruction [*sic* to learne the tableture to conducte and dispose thy hande vnto the lute englished by J. Alford. [Anon.] obl.4°. *J. Kyngston f. J. Roubothum,* 1568. L(imp.).
Reprinted in 15487.

15487 — A briefe and plaine instruction to set all musicke of eight diuers tunes in tableture for the lute. *Tr.* F. Ke. [i.e. Kinwelmarsh.] obl.4°. (*J. Kyngston f.*) *J. Rowbothome,* 1574. L(imp.).O.PARIS.
Includes reprint of 15486.

Le Roy, Guillaume. *See* 24796.

15488 **Le Roy, Louis.** Of the interchangeable course, or variety of things in the whole world. *Tr.* R. A(shley.) fol. *C. Yetsweirt, Esq.,* 1594. L.O.C.D².E². ; F.HN.HD. N.Y.
— *tr. See* 760.

15489 **Le Roy, Pierre.** A pleasant satyre or poesie: wherein is discouered the Catholicon of Spayne, and the chiefe leaders of the [French] League. [Anon. In prose. *Tr.* by T. W., i.e. T. Wilcox?, from Satire Menippée.] 4°. *Widdow Orwin f. T. Man,* 1595. Ent. to J. Hardie 28 se. 1594. L.O.C³.BIRM.WN. ; F.HN.CH. HD.Y.
The translator's inits. are on Aa1ᵛ. At least O, HD copies have an inserted halfsheet, ¶², w. epistle by T. M[an] Stationer to J. B., Merchant.

15490 — [Anr. issue, w. cancel tp:] Englandes bright honour. *J. Deane,* 1602. L. ; ILL.

15490.5 **Le Saulx, Marin,** *called du Saussé.* Théanthropogamie en forme de dialogue par sonnets chrestiens. [In verse.] 8°. *T. Vautrolier,* 1577. PARIS.

15491 **Lescarbot, Marc.** Nova Francia: or the description of that part of New France, which is one continent with Virginia. [Anon.] *Tr.* P. E(rondelle.) 4°. [*Eliot's Court Press,*] imp. G. Bishop, 1609. Ent. 12 jn. L.O. O³.D². ; F.HN.HD.N.NY.

15492 — [Anr. issue, w. dedic. and To reader cancelled, and w. cancel tp w. imprint:] *f. A. Hebb,* [after 1625.] L.C².CHATS. ; HN.HD.LC.N.NY.

Lesdiguières, François de Bonne, *Duc de. See* 6877.5.

Le Shalleux, Nicolas. *See* 15347.

15493 **Lesk, William.** A sermon preached aboard of the Globe. By the Cape of Good Hope. 4°. *G. Purslowe,* 1617. Ent. 24 oc. L.C.C³.PLUME. ; F.HN. Penrose 140.

Leslie, Alexander, *First Earl of Leven.* Articles and ordinances of warre; for the armie of Scotland. 1640. *See* 21914.

15494 **Leslie, Henry,** *Bp.* A sermon preached before his majesty at Windsore. 4°. *Oxford, J. L[ichfield] a. W. T[urner] f. W. Turner,* 1625. L.O.C.P.WOR. ; HN.HD.

Leslie, Henry, *Bp.—cont.*

15495 — A sermon preached before his majesty at Wokin. 4°. *H. L[ownes] f. J. Boler,* 1627. Ent. 22 se. L.O.C.E².P. ; F.HN.NY.

15496 — A speech, delivered at the visitation of Downe and Conner, held the 26ᵗʰ of September, 1638. [Anon.] 4°. *J. Raworth f. G. Thomason a. O. Pullen,* 1639. Ent. 23 mr. L.O.C.D⁸.E. ; F.HN.HD.N.U.

15497 — [Anr. issue, w. cancel tp:] A full confutation of the covenant, in a speech, 26ᵗʰ of September, 1638. *J. Raworth f. G. Thomason a. O. Pullen,* 1639. L.O.C². CASHEL.E. ; F.CHI.HD.PN².Y.

15498 — [A trans., w. author's name:] Examen conjurationis Scoticæ: sive, oratio habita Lisnegarvæ, in visitatione diœceseos Dunensis & Connorensis 26 Septemb. 1638. Latinitate donavit J. Portusius. 4°. *Dublinii, ex off. soc. bibliop.,* 1639. L.O.C.D.E.

15499 — A treatise of the authority of the church. [A sermon.] 4°. *Dublin, Soc. of Statrs.,* 1637. L.O.C.D.WOR. ; HD.

15500 — [Anr. issue, w. cancel tp, w. imprint:] *Dublin, Soc. of Statrs.,* 1639. L(2).C¹⁰.E.LIV³. ; HN.U.

15501 — A treatise tending to unitie: in a sermon. 4°. *Dublin, Soc. of Statrs.,* 1623. L.C⁵.D.D².

15502 — A warning for Israel, in a sermon. 4°. *Dublin, Soc. of Statrs.,* 1625. L.O.D⁶.D⁹.P.

15503 **Leslie, John,** *Bp. of Ross.* [Heading A1ʳ:] The copie of a letter writen out of Scotland, by an English gentlemā vnto a frind that desired to be informed of the truth of the slaunderous reportes of the quene of Scotland. [Anon.] 12°. [*Louvain, J. Fowler,* 1572.] C.
(Formerly 17566) A.&R. 451. Answers 17565.

15504 — A defence of the honor of the right high, right mighty, and noble princesse, Marie queene of Scotlande. [Anon.] 4°. [*Paris?*] 1569. L(frag., Add.MSS.48027, ff. 284–91).
A.&R. 452.

15505 — [Anr. ed.] A defence of the honour of the right highe, mightye and noble princesse Marie quene of Scotlande. 8°. *London, E. Dicæophile* [i.e. *Rheims, J. Foigny,*] (*solde in Paules church yearde, in the shoppes of P. a. N. Lycosthenes,*) 1569. L.BUTE.E.G².PARIS. ; F.HN.
A.&R. 452.

15506 — [Anr. ed., enlarged.] A treatise concerning the defence of the honour of Marie of Scotland. (A treatise touching the right.—A treatise that the regiment of women is conformable.) [M. Philippes, *pseud.*] 3 pts. 8°. *Leodii, ap. G. Morberium* [*a. Louvain, J. Fowler,*] 1571. L.O.C(pts. 2, 3 only).D².E. ; F.IND(pts. 1, 3 only).
A.&R. 453. The 3 tpp are cancels and are the only portions pr. by Morberius.

15507 — [Anr. version of pt. 2.] A treatise towching the right, of Marie, of Scotland, and of king James. By J. Lesley. 8°. [*Rouen, G. L'Oyselet,*] 1584. L.O³.C.D². E. ; F.HN.CU.TEX.Y.
A.&R. 455. This is a retranslation into English from the Latin trans. of 15506: De titulo et jure Mariae, Rhemis, 1580. *See also* 14074.
— A treatise of treasons. 1572. *See* 7601.

15508 **Leslie, William.** Propositiones. 1625. Now = 71.9.

15509 — Vindiciæ theologicae pro perseverantia sanctorum. 1627. Now = 71.15.

15510 **Lesly, John.** An epithrene: or voice of weeping: a meditation. 8°. *A. M[athewes] f. H. Robinson,* 1631. L. L².O.C.BUTE. ; F.HN.AAS.HD.

Lesly, Robert. Nouerint vniuersi. . . . 163[ ]. *See* 9253.5.

15510.5 **L'Espine, Jean de.** Comfort for an afflicted conscience. *Tr.* P. Allibond. 8°. *R. Field f. T. Man,* 1591. Ent. 29 oc. L(tp only, Harl.5936/267).O(imp.).C⁴. ; SMITH (imp.).
For other trans. of this text *see* 15514.5, 15515, 17238.

15511 — A confutation of the popish transubstantiation. [Anon.] *Tr.* P. Allibond. 8°. *T. Scarlet f. T. Man,* 1592. L.C.
(Formerly also 376) Only the 'Briefe summe' is by de l'Espine.

15511a — An excellent and learned treatise of apostasie. *Tr.* 8°. *T. Vautrollier,* 1587. Ent. to J. Morris 26 ap. L.O. D.YK.

L'Espine, Jean de—*cont.*

15512 — An excellent treatise of christian righteousnes. *Tr.* J. Feilde. 8°. *T. Vautrollier,* 1577. Ent. 10 de. O.

15512.5 — [Anr. issue, w. sheet A reset, w. imprint:] *T. Vautrollier,* 1578. L.SCL.
E5ʳ line 1: '9'.

15513 — [Anr. ed.] 8°. *T. Vautrollier,* 1578. L.; F.HN.U(imp.).
E5ʳ line 1: 'nynth'.

15513.5 — [Anr. ed.] 8°. *T. Vautrollier,* 1578. F.
E5ʳ line 1: 'ninth'.

15514 — [Anr. ed.] 8°. *T. Vautrollier,* 1580. L(2).

15514.3 — [Anr. ed.] 8°. *T. Vautrollier,* 1584. E².

— The foundation of christian religion. 1612. *See* 5188.

15514.5 — Three godly treatises. 1. To comfort the sicke. 2. Against the feare of death. 3. Of the resurrection. *Tr.* S. Veghelman. 8°. *W. Stansby f. R. Banckworth,* 1611. L.C¹⁰.
For other trans. *see* 15510.5.

15515 — A treatise tending to take away the feare of death. Newly *tr.* [Init. M.D.S.A., i.e. M. de Spina.] 12°. *W. J[ones,]* 1619. Ent. to W. Jones 21 au. O.
For other trans. *see* 15510.5.

15516 — A very excellent and learned discourse, touching the tranquilitie of the minde. *Tr.* E. Smyth. 4° in 8's. *J. Legate, Printer to the Univ. of Cambridge, solde [by A. Kitson] in London,* 1592. Ent. to G. Bishop 9 de. 1588. L.O.C.D.M⁴.+; F.CHI.HD.PN².U.+
— *See also* 21354, 24726.5.

Lesse, Nicholas. An apologie or defence of the worde of God. 1548. *See* 17792.
— *tr. See* 84, 166.5, 920, 10450, 15178, 17792.

15517 **Lessius, Leonardus.** A consultation what faith and religion is best to be imbraced. *Tr.* W. I. [i.e. W. Wright.] 8°. [*St. Omer, English College Press,*] 1618. L.AUG.DE.HP.W.+; F.HD.
A.&R. 456.

15518 — The second edition. Whereunto is annexed a little treatise whether the church of Rome hath fallen. 8°. [*St. Omer, English College Press,*] 1621. L.C.DAI.ST.W.+
(1701 is pt. of this) A.&R. 457.

15518.5 — [Anr. trans.] A consultatione which faith is to be beleued which religione is to be imbraced. Wryttin [i.e. *tr.*] be P. Andersone. 8°. *Flesh, J. Cock* [imprint false,] 1619. AMP.
A.&R. 458.

15519 — A controversy, in which is examined, whether every man may be saved in his owne faith. 8°. [*St. Omer, English College Press,*] 1614. E.ST.
A.&R. 459.

15520 — Hygiasticon: or, the right course of preserving life and health unto extream old age: done into English [by N. Ferrar.] (A treatise of temperance. By L. Cornarus, *tr.* G. Herbert.) 24° in 12's. *Cambridge, R. Daniel,* 1634. L.O.C.G².LEEDS.+; F.HD.NLM.TEX.Y.
Preface init. 'T. S.'

15521 — The second edition. 24° in 12's. [*R. Daniel a. T. Buck,*] *printers to the Univ. of Cambridge,* 1634. L.O³⁹.C.; HN.HD(2).ILL.

15522 — The third edition. 24° in 12's. [*R. Daniel a. T. Buck,*] *printers to the Univ. of Cambridge,* 1636. L.L¹⁶.O.C.A.+; CH.FBL.HD(imp.).NY.WTL.+

15523 — Rawleigh his ghost. Or, a feigned apparition of syr Walter Rawleigh, to a friend of his, for the translating into English, the booke of L. Lessius . . . entituled, De providentia numinis. *Tr.* A. B. [i.e. M. Wilson?] 8°. [*St. Omer, G. Seutin?*] 1631. L(2).O.C.D.USHAW.; F.TEX.Y.
A.&R. 460.

15524 — The treasure of vowed chastity in secular persons. Also the widdowes glasse [by F. Androzzi.] *Tr.* I. W[ilson] P[riest.] 18° in 6's. [*St. Omer, English College Press,*] 1621. L.ST.; F.HN.
A.&R. 827.

15525 **Lesson.** ⟨Here beginneth a⟩ good lesson for yonge men. [In verse.] 4°. [*London, c.* 1540.] C(A1,2).

Le Tellier, Jean Baptiste. *See* 23138.

Letter. A lettre frō the holy ghost. [*c.* 1540.] *See* 13608.4.
— A letter from the king. 1589. *See* 13098.
— A letter of a baker of Boulougne. 1607. *See* 3218.7.

Letter—*cont.*

— The letter of the French king . . . concerning the death of the marshall D'Ancre. 1617. *See* 16835.

15525.3 — A letter sent by a gentleman of England, to his frende, contayning a confutacion of a French mans errors, in the report of the myraculous starre nowe shyninge. 8°. (*T. Marshe,*) 1573. L².

— A letter sent by the French king. 1590. *See* 13113.5.
— A letter sent from a banished minister. 1554. *See* 10016.
— A letter written by a catholike gentleman. 1590. *See* 5400.3.
— A letter written by a French catholike gentleman. Concerning the late victories obtained by the king of Nauarre. 1588. *See* 18144.
— A letter, written by a french catholicke gentleman. Conteyning a briefe aunswer to slaunders. 1589. *See* 18145.
— A letter written by a French gent: concerning the emperour Ferdinand. 1620. *See* 10812.

15526 — A letter written by a true christian catholike. 1586. *See* 12752.5.
— A letter written by the king of Nauarre vnto the French king. 1585. *See* 13108.
— A letter written by the king of Nauarr, to the three estates of Fraunce. 1589. *See* 13112.
— A letter written out of England. 1599. *See* 10017.
— A letter written to the governours of the East Indian marchants. 1603. *See* 7448.
— A profitable, and comfortable letter. [1584?] *See* 25624.5.

Letters. Certaine letters declaring in part, the affaires in the Pallatinate. 1621. *See* 1037.

15527 — Certein letters wherin is set forth a discourse of the peace attempted by Holland and Zelande 1574. [*Tr.* from J. Perrenot and others.] 8°. *T. Marshe,* 1576. L.L².L¹³(frag.).O.HAGUE.
— Certain most godly, fruitfull, and comfortable letters. 1564. *See* 5886.
— Conceyted letters, newly layde open. 1618, etc. *See* 3637 sqq.

15528 — Foure letters: one from the Duke of Bouillon to the French king [etc.] 4°. *R. Field f. R. Mylbourne,* 1619. Ent. 22 mr. O(2).O³.O⁸.; F.N.
— Letters patents made by the French king. 1621. *See* 16840.
— Letters patents of the declaration of the king of France. 1626. *See* 16845.5.
— The letters pattents of the kings declaration. [1590.] *See* 13113.
— Severall letters betwixt the French king and the Q. mother. 1631. *See* 16847.5.
— Three letters written by the king of Nauarre. 1586. *See* 13111.

15529 — Two letters: one written by a protestant to his brother. . . . The other by master Ramon. *Tr.* 4°. *T. Este f. M. Law,* 1603. Ent. to T. Snodham 31 my. L.C.
— Two letters or embassies. 1620. *See* 3215.

Lettres. Lettres patentes de declaration du roy. 1634. *See* 16848.

15530 **Leurechon, Jean.** Mathematicall recreations. 1633. Now = 10558.5.

15531 **Leuwis, Dionysius de.** The lyfe of prestes. = 6894.

Le Vager, Jean. The voluntarie conversion, of foure fryers. [J. Le Vager and others.] 1604. *See* 5650.

15532 **Levens, Peter.** Manipulus vocabulorum. A dictionarie of English and Latin wordes. Gathered 1570. 4°. *H. Bynneman f. J. Waley,* [1570.] Ent. to R. Newbury 1569–70. L.O(imp.).; ILL.

15532.5 — A right profitable booke for all disseases. Called the pathway to health. 4°. [*H. Bynneman*] *f. E. White,* 1582. Ent. 7 my. L.L³⁹.; HD(2, 1 lacks tp).Y.

15533 — [Anr. ed.] 4°. *E. Allde f. E. White,* 1587. L.O⁸.C.BRISTOL².; CAL.NY⁴(imp.).

15533.3 — [Anr. ed.] Newly corrected and augmented. 4°. *J. Roberts f. E. White,* 1596 (1597.) O.CAR(2 imp.).; NLM.

15533.7 — [Anr. ed.] 4°. *J. Windet f. E. White,* 1608. L³⁸.; BO².

15534 — [Anr. ed.] 4°. *J. Beale f. R. Bird,* 1632. Ass'd to E. Brewster a. Bird 4 au. 1626. L.L¹⁶.O.C.G².+; F.HN.HD.NLM.Y.+

15535 **Lever, Christopher.** A crucifixe: or, a meditation upon repentance, and, the holie passion. [In verse.] 4°. V. S[immes] f. J. Budge, 1607. Ent. 17 de. 1606. L.L².BUTE.; CH.HD.LC.

15536 — Heaven and earth, religion and policy. 8°. H. B[allard] f. J. Chorlton, 1608. Ent. 24 my. L.L².O.C.YK.; F.HN. U.

15537 — The historie of the defendors of the catholique faith. 4° in 8's. G. M[iller] f. N. Fussell a. H. Moseley, 1627. Ent. to Fussell 8 mr. L.O.C.D.E.+; F.HN.HD. N.U.+
> Engr. tp omits printer's inits.

15537.5 — The holy pilgrime, leading the way to new Jerusalem. 8°. N. O[kes] f. B. Sutton a. W. Barrenger, 1609 (1610.) Ent. 13 no. 1609. G².; HN.

15538 — [Anr. ed.] The holy pilgrime, leading the way to heaven. 8°. B. Alsop f. W. Barringer, 1618 (1617.) L.DUL.YK.; F.N.

15539 — [Anr. issue, w. cancel gen. tp, w. imprint:] f. L. Faune, 1631. C.; HD(lacks A3–5).

15540 — Queene Elizabeths teares: or, her resolute bearing the Christian crosse, in the bloodie time of Queene Marie. [In verse.] 4°. V. S[immes] f. M. Lownes, 1607. Ent. 2 my. L(2).E². Bradford PL.; F.HN.CH.N.
> N copy has imprint in 2 lines, instead of 3, omitting 'at the signe of the Bishops head'.

15541 **Lever, Ralph.** The arte of reason, rightly termed, witcraft. 8°. H. Bynneman, 1573. L(lacks tp).O.C². E².LINC.+; F.HN.CH.HD.N.+

15542 — The most ancient and learned playe, called the philosophers game. [Anon.] Set forth by W. F[ulwood.] 8°. R. Hall f. J. Roubotham, 1563 (21 my.) Ent. 1562–63. F.
> Disclaimed by Lever on **3ʳ of 15541. Fulwood's name is in an acrostic on a8ʳ.

15542a — [Anr. issue, w. cancel tp:] The most noble auncient and learned playe, . . . Set forth by R. Leuer and augmented by W. F[ulwood.] J. Rowbothum, [1563?] L.DUR(Bamb.).; HD(lacks tp)*.

15542a.5 **Lever, Richard.** Tables of interest. [Tr. out of Dutch.] 2 pts. 4°. G. Miller, 1631. L(tp only, Ames II.951). O²⁶.
> The O²⁶ copy collates A–B⁴; a–q⁴ B¹ C⁴. Miller pr. the 1st 2 sheets; the rest (tables) is a reissue of an unidentified Dutch work pr. in Holland.

15543 **Lever, Thomas.** A fruitfull sermon made in Poules churche at London in the shroudes the seconde daye of February. 8°. (J. Daie a. W. Seres, 1550 (9 ap.)) L.O.C⁵.M. Bradford PL.+; F.
> A3ᵛ catchword: 'crysye'.

15543.5 — [Anr. ed.] 8°. (J. Daie a. W. Seres, 1550 (9 ap.)) L¹⁵. C⁴.
> In title: 'Februari'; A3ᵛ catchword: 'crysy'.

15543a — [Anr. ed.] 8°. (J. Daie a. W. Seres, 1550.) HN.HD.
> In title: 'Februari'; A3ᵛ catchword: 'crisie'.

15544 — A meditacion vpon the Lordes prayer, made M.D.Li. 8°. (J. Daye,) [1551] L.O.M.

15545 — [Anr. ed.] A meditacion vpõ the the [sic] lordes praier. 8°. [R. Grafton f.] (J. Kyngston, sold by A. Kyngston,) [1551.] O.; F.
> F has the title corrected in press.

15546 — A sermon preached at Pauls crosse, the .xiiii. day of December, . . . M.D.L. 8°. (J. Day,) [1551.] L¹⁵. C³(imp.).M².; HD.
> Collates A⁸ A–D⁸ dd⁸ E⁸(–E1) F⁸ G².

15546.3 — [Anr. ed.] 8°. (J. Day,) [1551.] L.O.C.C².M.+; F.HN. N.Y.
> Collates A–G⁸ H⁴; in title: 'Pauls'.

15546.7 — [Anr. ed.] 8°. [Worcester, J. Oswen, 1551?] O.BTU.
> Collates A–G⁸ H⁴; in title: 'Poules'.

15547 — A sermon preached the thyrd Sunday in Lent before the kynges maiestie. 8°. (J. Daie a. W. Seres, 1550 (9 ap.)) L.L¹⁵.O.O¹⁷.C¹⁰.+; F(imp.).HD.
> D1ʳ catchword: 'discharge:'; E2ʳ last line ends: 'with all.' Quire F is in the same setting as 15549.+

15548 — [Anr. ed.] A sermon preached the thyrd Sondaye in Lente [etc.] 8°. (J. Day,) [1550.] L.
> D1ʳ catchword: 'may'; E2ʳ last line ends: 'wythal.'

15548.5 — [Anr. issue, w. quire A reset and title corrected:] A sermon preached yᵉ fourth Sũdaye in Lente [etc.] (J. Day,) [1550.] L.O.O⁵. Bradford PL.; F.HN.
> (Formerly 15550) D1 and E2 are like 15548.

Lever, Thomas—cont.

15549 — [Anr. issue, w. quires D–E reset.] (J. Daie a. W. Seres, 1550 (9 ap.)) F.
> D1ʳ catchword: 'maye'; E2ʳ last line ends: 'wyth al.' Quires A–C are in the same setting as 15548.5; quire F is in the same setting as 15547.

15550 — Now = 15548.5.

15551 — Three fruitfull sermõs, made by T. Leuer. 1550. Now newlie perused by the aucthour. 8°. J. Kyngston f. H. Kirckham, (solde) [by H. Kirkham,] 1572. L.L². O.C⁵.G².+; F.HN.
> Reprints 15543, 15547, 15546.

15551.5 — A treatise of the right way frõ danger of synne . . . nowe newly augmented. 8°. H. Bynneman f. G. Byshop, 1571. L(tp only, Ames I.258).L².P.

15552 — [Anr. ed.] 8°. (H. Bynneman f. G. Byshop, 1575.) L. O.LAMPORT.LEEDS.

15553 **Levett, Christopher.** An abstract of timber-measures. 4°. W. Jones, 1618. Ent. 21 no. L(2).O.; HN.

15553.5 — A voyage into New England begun in 1623. 4°. W. Jones, 1624 (21 au.) L.

15554 — [Anr. issue, w. cancel tp, w. imprint:] W. Jones, sold by E. Brewster, 1628. L.A.; HN.CB.NY⁵.PH².

15555 **Levett, John.** The ordering of bees: or, the true history of managing them. 4°. T. Harper f. J. Harison, 1634. Ent. 10 no. 1631. L.O.C.E.LIV³.+; F.HN.CU.WIS.Y.+

15556 **Lewes, Richard.** A sermon preached at Paules Crosse, concerning Isaac his testament. 8°. Oxford, J. Barnes, 1594. L.O.LINC.; F.

Lewicke, Edward, tr. See 3184.6.

Lewis, Hugh, tr. See 25260.

15557 **Lewis, Jeremiah.** The doctrine of thankfulnesse: or, Israels triumph, a sermon. 4°. T. S[nodham] f. E. Brewster, 1619. Ent. 14 ja. L.O.C⁵.; N.

15557.5 — The right use of promises. Whereunto is added Gods free-schoole. [Ed.] (T. Shelton.) 12°. J. B[eale] f. H. Overton, (sold by H. Overton,) 1631. Ent. to J. Boler a. Overton 10 fb. M.; HD.PN².U.

15558 **Lewis, John.** Ignis cœlestis: or an interchange of divine love. 8°. T. S[nodham] f. N. N[ewbery], 1620. Ent. 17 jn. L.O.LINC.; F.

15559 — Melchizedech's anti-type: or the eternall priest-hood, with the scrutiny of the masse. 4°. N. Okes f. R. Whitakers, 1624. L.O(2).C³.HER.LIV³.; F.HN.HD.

15560 — [Anr. issue, w. cancel tp:] The unmasking of the masse-priest. By C. A. f. R. Whittaker, 1624. L.L².
> Retains Lewis's dedic., etc. The tp was pr. by Eliot's Court Press.

15561 **Lewkenor, Sir Edward.** Threnodia in obitum D. Edouardi Lewkenor equitis. Funerall verses. 4°. A. Hatfield f. S. Macham a. M. Cooke, solde [by M. Cooke,] 1606. Ent. 29 mr. L.L².O.C(imp.).A.+; F.HN.Y.

15562 **Lewkenor, Sir Lewis.** A discourse of the vsage of the English fugitiues, by the Spaniard. [Anon. Sometimes wrongly attrib. to J. Wadsworth.] 4°. London, T. Scarlet f. J. Drawater, 1595. Ent. 23 ja. L².O.O⁵. A.E.; F.HD.ILL.NY.
> Pr. without the author's permission.

15563 — [Anr. ed., unauthorized.] 4°. Lodon [sic], T. Scarlet f. J. Drawater, 1595. L.; HN.

15564 — [Anr. ed., enlarged and authorized, but still anon.] The estate of English fugitiues. 4°. [T. Scarlet] f. J. Drawater, 1595. L.O.C.D.G².+; F.HN.HD.N.NY.+

15565 — [Anr. ed.] Newly corrected and amended. 4°. [T. Scarlet] f. J. Drawater, 1596. Ent. to W. Ponsonby 26 au. 1595 a. 26 se. 1597. L.O.C.E.YK.+; F.HN.HD (imp.).NY. Lehigh U.+

— tr. See 5642, 15139, 24135.

15566 **Lewkenor, Samuel.** A discourse . . . for such as are desirous to know of forraine cities. Containing a discourse of citties wherein flourish universities. 4°. J. W[indet] f. H. Hooper, 1600. Ent. 11 de. 1599. L.O. C.D.E².+; F.HN.HD.N.NY.+

Lewyngton, Thomas, *tr. See* 791.

15567 **Ley, John.** A patterne of pietie. Or the religious life and death of M^rs. J. Ratcliffe. 8°. *F. Kingston f. R. Bostocke,* 1640. Ent. 14 se. 1639. L.O.C.M².NLW.+; F.HN.CAL.PN².

15568 **Ley, Roger.** The bruising of the serpents head. A sermon. 4°. *J. Dawson f. N. Bourne,* 1622. Ent. 20 ja. L.O.C.; HD.Y.

15569 — Two sermons, one preached at Paules Crosse by R. Lea. Another by J. Squire . . . [the first] (The scepter of righteousnes.) 4°. *W. J[ones] f. N. Bourne,* 1619. Ent. 4 ja. L.O.C.DUR³.E².+; F(imp.).HD.NY¹¹(imp.). PN².Y.

Leycester, John, *tr. See* 7681.3, 20610.

15569.5 **Leyden.** We the maiestrates and rulers of the towne of Layden send our frindelie gretinge. [Prohibitions concerning cloth manufacturing industry in Leyden.] s.sh.fol. [*Leyden,* 1587.] Leyden, Gemeente-archief (Secr. arch. 9241,607).

15570 **Leyden University.** A catalogue of all the cheifest rarities in the Publick Theater. *Leyden, J. Voorn,* 1591 [1691.] = Wing S 905.

15571 **L'Hermite, Jacques.** A true relation of the fleete which went under the admirall Jaquis Le Hermite through the straights of Magellane. [*Tr.* from Waerachtigh verhael, van het succes van de Vlote, 1625.] 4°. *f. Mercurius Britannicus,* 1625. L(2).; HN.CB.NY.PH².

Lhuyd. *See* Lloyd and Llwyd.

15572 **Libellulus.** Libellulus secundarū intentionū logicalium nouiter compilatus. pro scholaribus. 4°. [*R. Pynson,* 1498?] L. Duff 252.
        Collates a⁶ b⁴.

15573 — [Anr. ed.] 4°. [*R. Pynson,* 1502?] L(lacks tp).
        Collates A⁶ B⁴.

15574 — [Anr. ed.] Tractatus secundarum intentionum. 4°. [*Southwark, P. Treveris,*] *Venūdantur ap. J. Thorne,* [*Oxford,*] 1527. C.

15574.5 **Libellus.** Libellus sophistarum. [Colophon:] (ad vsum Cantibrigiē.) 4° in 6's and 8's. (*per R. pynson,* 1497.) C⁵.
        Collates A⁶ B⁸ C–D⁶ E–G⁸ H–I⁶ K–N⁸. This and 15576.6 are sometimes attrib. to R. Alington.

15575 — Now = 15576.6.

15575.5 — [Anr. ed.] Libellus sophistar⟨um⟩ [ad vsum Cantibrigiē.?] 4° in 6's. [*R. Pynson,* 1501?] C(tp def.).
        Collates a⁸ b–m⁶ n⁸; w. Pynson's device, McK. 9, w. his name. The text most closely resembles the Cambridge versions.

15576 — [Anr. ed.] Ad vsum Cantibrigiē. 4° ⁸·⁴. *per w. de worde,* (1510 (7 se.)) C.C⁵(lacks col.).

15576.4 — [Anr. ed.] Ad vsum Cātibrigiē. 4° ⁸·⁴. (*w. de worde,* 1524 (4 jn.)) L².O.
        (Formerly 15579)

15576.6 — Libellus sophistarum ad vsum Oxoniē. 4° in 6's. [*R. Pynson,* 1499–1500.] O.C⁵.; LC.
        (Formerly 15575) Collates A–M⁶ N⁸; w. Pynson's device, McK. 9, w. his name. This is essentially the same text as the preceding, but w. a different arrangement and details.

15576.8 — [Anr. ed.] Ad vsū Oxoniē. 4° ⁸·⁴. *W. de worde,* (1510 (15 ap.)) O.

15577 — [Anr. ed.] Ad vsū Oxoniē. 4° ⁸·⁴. *w. de worde,* (1512 (12 au.)) O.

15578 — [Anr. ed.] Ad vsum Oxoniē. 4° ⁸·⁴. *per w. de worde,* [1518?] L(imp.).

15578.3 — [Anr. ed.] [Ad vsum Oxoniē.] 4° ⁸·⁴. [*W. de Worde,* 1525?] C(imp.).

15578.5 — [Anr. ed.] Ad vsum Oxoniensium. Anno M.D. XXV. 4°. [*Cologne, P. Quentell,* 1525.] O.

15578.7 — [Anr. ed.] Ad vsum Oxoniē. 4° ⁸·⁴. *per W. de Worde,* (1530 (16 jy.)) L².C⁷.

5579 — Now = 15576.4.

— Libellus supplex imperatoriae maiestati. 1571. *See* 18440.

Libellus—*cont.*

Parvus Libellus or *Carta Feodi.*

15579.3 — Crata [*sic*] feodi simplicis cū littera atturnatoria. 4°. (*per R. Pynson,*) [1505?] D⁵.ST.; HD.
        Reprinted in 18394 sq.

15579.4 — [Anr. ed.] Carta feodi simplicis cum littera atturnatoria. 4°. (*per Winandum de Worde,*) [1505?] L.O.; HD.
        (Formerly 4688) Collates a–d⁸·⁴ e⁶.

15579.5 — [Anr. ed.] 4°. (*per Winandum de worde,*) [1507?] L(2). L²².M.
        (Formerly 4689) Collates a–e⁶ f⁴.

15579.6 — [Anr. ed.] 4°. (*per wynandum de worde,*) [c. 1510.] C.; HN(frag.).
        Collates AA⁸ BB⁴ CC–EE⁶·⁴. Possibly intended as part of a collection.

15579.8 — [Anr. ed.] 4°. (*per wynandum de worde,*) [c. 1515.] O.; HN.
        Collates A⁸ B⁴ C–E⁶·⁴.

15580 — [Anr. ed.] Paruus libellus continens formā multa⁊ rerū. 4°. (*per R. Pynson,*) [1521?] C.

15580.5 — [Anr. ed.] Carta feodi. 4°. (*per J. Skot,*) [1521.] M.

15581 — [Anr. ed.] Paruus libellus. 4°. [*W. de Worde,* 1523?] L.; HD.
        Collates A–H⁴; w. cut of royal arms on the tp.

15581.2 — [Anr. ed.] 8°. [*J. Rastell,* 1526–30?] O. Broxbourne(E).; HD.
        Issued w. 14871.

15581.5 — [Anr. ed.] 8°. (*per R. Redman,* 1527 (15 mr.)) L(col. only, Harl.5963/85).

15582 — [Anr. ed.] 8°. (*per R. Redman,* 1530.) L.C.; HD.
        Prob. issued w. 14870.

15583 — [Anr. ed.] 8°. (*per me R. Redmam [sic],* 1533.) O.C¹⁸.
        London, Gray's Inn.; HN.HD.LC.
        Prob. issued w. 14872.

15583.5 — [Anr. ed.] Carta feodi. 8°. (*in ed. T. Bertheleti,*) [c. 1533.] HD.MIN.
        In border McK.&F. 24; imprint only in colophon. Prob. issued w. 14871.5.

15583.7 — [Anr. ed.] 8°. *in æd. T. Bertheleti,* [1535?] L.P.; HD. MIN.
        (Formerly 4690) In border McK.&F. 34; imprint only on tp. Prob. issued w. 14873.

15584 — [Anr. ed.] Paruus libellus. 8°. (*per me R. Redman,* 1538.) L(destroyed).; F.HD.LC.
        1st line of colophon ends: 'Impressum'.

15584.3 — [Anr. ed.] 8°. (*per me R. Redman,* 1538.) O.; HD(lacks tp).
        1st line of colophon ends: 'Car'.

15584.5 — [Anr. ed.] Carta feodi. 8°. (*in æd. T. Bertheleti,*) 1539. L.C¹⁰.; F.HD.LC.MIN.
        Issued as pt. 4 of 14876.

15584.7 — [Anr. ed.] Paruus libellus. 8°. (*per me R. Redman,* 1541.) L.L²².; HD(2).MIN.

15584.9 — [Anr. ed.] Carta feodi. 8°. *in æd. T. Berth[eleti,]* 1543. L.O.O⁸.C.; HN.CH.HD.MIN.Y.
        Issued as pt. 4 of 14877.

15585 — [Anr. ed.] Paruus libellus. 8°. (*per me W. Myddylton,* 1543.) L(2).

15585.5 — [Anr. ed.] 8°. (*per me W. Myddylton,* 1545.) L.; HD. MIN.
        HD copy issued as pt. 3 of 14880.

15586 — [Anr. ed.] 8°. (*per R. Kele,*) 1546. O.; HART.HD.
        This and the following variants were all pr. by N. Hill and issued w. 14879 sqq.

15586.5 — [A variant, w. colophon:] (*per N. Hyll,*) 1546. MIN.

15586a — [A variant, w. colophon:] (*per H. Smyth,*) 1546. O(2).

15586b — [A variant, w. colophon:] (*per R. Toye,*) 1546. O.

15587 — [A variant, w. colophon:] (*per J. Waley,*) 1546. L.; HD.

15587.5 — [A trans.] The chartuary in English, necessary for al maner of persons that wyll serue for to wryte ye forme of makynge of indētures. 8°. (*N. Hyl f. J. Walley,*) [1545?] O(tp and col. only, Douce Add. 142/233).

———

Liber. Liber assisarum. [1514?] *See* 9599.
— Liber festiualis. 1483, etc. *See* 17957 sqq.
— Liber quorundam canonum disciplinæ ecclesiæ Anglicanæ. 1571. *See* 10036 sqq.

Liberality. Liberalitie and prodigalitie. 1602. *See* 5593.

Lichfield, *Diocese of. See* 21053.7.

Lichfield, Nicholas, *tr. See* 12538, 16806.

Lichfield, Richard, *pseud. See* 12906.

Lichfield, William. *See* 20881.3.

15588 **Lichfild, Henry.** The first set of madrigals of 5. parts. 5 ptbks. 4°. *f. M. L[ownes,] J. B[rowne,] a. T. S[nodham,] the assignes of W. Barley,* 1613. L(1 complete, plus 2 altus).L⁷.O(altus, tenor, quintus). M³(cantus, quintus).; F(cantus, altus, 2 bassus).HN (1 complete, plus bassus).CAL(imp.).
Bassus tp varies: dated 1613 or 1614; both at HN.

Licia. Licia, or poemes of loue. [1593?] *See* 11055.

Lidd. Lidd. The declaration . . . what wages seruantes, shall haue. 1565. *See* 7986.5.

Lidgate, John. *See* Lydgate, J.

Lidley, John. [Lidley's prayers. 1563? etc.] *See* 10617, 4028, 4029.5 sq., 4032 sq.

Liebault, Jean. *See* 10547.

15589 **Life.** Cyuile and vncyuile life. A discourse where, is disputed, what order of lyfe best beseemeth a gentleman. 4°. [*W. How f.*] *R. Jones,* 1579. Ent. 4 se. L.
Collates [–]² B–N⁴.

15589.5 — [Anr. issue, w. additional prefatory matter.] *R. Jones,* 1579. L.O.; F.ROS.
Collates A–N⁴.

15590 — [Anr. issue, w. cancel tp:] The English courtier, and the cūtrey-gentleman. *R. Jones,* 1586. HD.
— The noble lyfe & natures of man, [etc.] [1527?] *See* 13837.5.

15591 **Light.** A light for the ignorant or a treatise [of] the civill state, the true ecclesiasticall-state, and the false ecclesiasticall state. 4°. [*Amsterdam, Richt Right Press,*] 1638. L.C(3).C¹⁷.E(2).; F.CAL².HD.U.
Reprinted in 7435.5.

15591.5 **Lightbody, George.** Against the apple of the left eye of antichrist, or the masse book. [Anon.] 8°. [*Holland,*] 1638. E(3, 1 lacks Answers to the censures.).; HD.
Has same tp orn. w. motto: 'Het huys opeen steen rot ghegront . . .' as 664.7, which may be by the same author. The imperfect E copy, which prob. represents the pamphlet as originally issued, has a contemporary MS. ascription to Lightbody.

15592 — Quaestiones grammaticae in compendium digestæ. 8°. *Edinburgi, J. Wreittoun,* 1628. E².

Lighterfoote, Richard. An Almanack. 1607. *See* 480.

15593 **Lightfoot, John.** Erubhin or miscellanies christian and judaicall. 8°. *G. Miller f. R. Swayne a. W. Adderton, sold* [*by R. Michell,*] 1629. Ent. 29 my. L.O.C.D².E. +; F.HN.HD.N.NY¹¹. +

15594 — The temple service as it stood in the dayes of our saviour. [1649.] = Wing L 2072.

15595 **Lightfoot, William.** The complaint of England. Wherein it is prooued that the practices of papists against the realme are vnlawfull. 4°. *J. Wolfe,* 1587. Ent. 4 mr. L.L².O.C².E. +; F.HN.HD.ILL.NY. +

15596 **Lilburne, John.** Come out of her my people. 4°. [*Amsterdam, Richt Right Press,*] *printed in the yeare of hope,* 1639. L.L⁸.L³⁸.C².M(deposit).; F.WEL(imp.).

15597 — [Heading A1ʳ:] A coppy of a letter written by J. Lilburne, close prisoner in the wards of the Fleet to J. Ingram and H. Hopkins, wardens of the said Fleet. 4°. [*London?* 1640.] L.L⁶.L¹⁸.O.E.; HD.

15598 — The poore mans cry. Wherein is shewed the miserable estate of J. Lilburne. Published by a backe friend of the English popish prelates. 4°. [*Amsterdam, Richt Right Press,*] 1639. L.C².E.M⁴.NEK. +; WEL(imp.).

15599 — A worke of the beast or a relation of a most vnchristian censure, executed upon J. Lilburne. 4°. [*Amsterdam, Richt Right Press,*] *printed in the yeare the beast was wounded,* 1638. L.O(imp.).C.C².E². +; F.HD.U.WEL.

Lilly, John. *See* Lyly.

Lily, Dorothy, *ed. See* 15600.

Lily, George. [Map of the British Isles.] 1555. *See* 11713.5.

15600 **Lily, Peter.** Two sermons: [on Mark xvi.16, and Luke xxiv.5. *Ed.*] (D. Lilie.) 4°. *T. Snodham,* 1619. Ent. 27 my. O.C.C².C⁴. Finedon.; HN.U.Y.

15601 — Conciones duæ [on Acts xv.39 and John xix.9–10.] 4°. *T. Snodham,* 1619. Ent. 27 my. L².L³.O.C².C⁴. +; HN.Y.

15601.3 **Lily, William.** Libellus de constructione octo partium orationis. [Anon. *Ed.* D. Erasmus.] 4° in 6's. (*per R. pynson,* 1513.) O.
(Formerly 5544 and 10497) Also attrib. to Colet or Erasmus.

15601.5 — [Anr. ed.] 4°. [*Cambridge, J. Siberch,* 1521?] L¹³(frag. of sheet D).

15601.7 — [Anr. ed.] Absolutissimus de octo orationis partium constructione libellus, emendatus per Erasmum. [Anon.] 8°. *W. de Worde,* 1531 (fb.) M.

15602 — [Anr. ed.] 8°. *W. de Worde,* 1533 (mr.) L.

15603 — [Anr. ed.] Libellus de constructione octo partium orationis. 8°. *diligentia H. Pepwell,* 1539. C⁶.

15603.5 — [Anr. ed.] 8°. *T. Petyt,* 1539. Lord Kenyon(frags.).

15604 — [Anr. ed., enlarged and revised.] De octo orationis partium constructione libellus, aeditus a G. Lilio emendatus ab Eras. Roter. & scholijs H. Primæi, L. Coxi illustratus. 4°. (*ex off. T. Bertheleti,*) 1540. O.C.ETON.G².

15605 — Now = 15610.6.

15605a — Now = 15623.5.

15606 — Antibossicon. [In verse.] 4°. (*in aed. Pynsonianis,* 1521.) L(imp.).L².O.C⁵.C⁷. +; HN(2).ILL.
Prob. issued w. 13807. *See* also 25443.2.

15606.5 — Epigrammata Guil. Lilii Angli. [In verse.] 4°. [*W. de Worde,* 1521.] L².D.

15606.7 — [A trans. of the verses in honour of Charles V.] Of the tryūphe, and the v'ses that Charles themperour, & the kyng of England, Henry the .viii. were saluted with, passyng through London. *Lat. a. Eng.* 4°. (*R. Pynson,*) [1522.] HN.
(Formerly 5017)

15607 — Guilielmi Lilii . . . de generibus nominum, ac verborum præteritis & supinis regulæ. [*Ed.* J. Rightwise. In verse.] 4°. [*Southwark, P. Treveris,* 1528?] L.

15608 — [Anr. ed.] 8°. *ap. W. de Worde,* 1533 (mr.) L.

15609 — [Anr. ed.] 8°. (*per me H. Pepwell,* 1539.) C⁶.

15609.3 — Guilelmi Lilii Angli rudimenta. Paruulorū Lilii nuper impressa & correcta. *Eng.* 4°. [*York, U. Mylner,* 1516?] O(frag.).
Tp has a schoolmaster cut, Hodnett 918. For other eds. pr. as part of Colet's Aeditio, *see* 5542 sqq.

15609.5 — [Anr. ed.] 4°. [*Southwark, P. Treveris?* 1525?] CU (imp.).
Without tp; A1ʳ begins: '¶Guillelmi Lilij Angli Rudimenta./ ¶To make latyn'.

15610 — [Anr. ed.] 8°. [*J. Byddell,* 1538?] C(frag.).
Tp in border McK.&F. 29; in title: 'Paruulorum'; omits '& correcta.'
— *See* also 15118, 19598.6.

'LILY'S GRAMMAR'

This book, the authorized school text from 1540 onwards, is a composite work revised at various times, the main components of which are set out below. There are two parts, the first in English for the youngest pupils and the second in Latin for more advanced students. Each part has what is technically called an Accidence, analysing the eight parts of speech with special emphasis on the declension of nouns and conjugation of verbs; and a Grammar or Syntax, showing how sentences are constructed out of the parts of speech. In the course of time the term 'Accidence' apparently became appropriated to the whole of the English portion while 'Grammar' was reserved for the Latin part. For examples of this usage and of various conflicts over printing and publishing rights to this profitable book *see* the index to Greg's *Companion* under 'Accidence' and 'Grammars'. For fuller discussions of the sources of 'Lily's Grammar' and further references *see* T. W. Baldwin, *William Shakspere's Small Latin & Lesse Greeke*, Urbana, 1944, I.94–9, II.690–701, *Papers of the Bibliographical Society of America*, XXXVII (1943), pp. 85–113, and *The Library*, IX (1954), pp. 85–100.

Lily, William—'*Lily's Grammar*'—*cont.*

1. 'The Accidence', first entitled 'An introduction of the eight parts of speech' (15610.6) and later 'A short introduction of grammar' (15610.10). This incorporates, in a version revised and expanded by David Talley, the three main sections of the book called 'Colet's Aeditio' (5542 sqq.):

   a. Colet's Aeditio *per se*, the Accidence in English.

   b. Lily's Rudimenta, the Grammar in English, also apparently published separately (15609.3 sqq.)

   c. Lily's Carmen de moribus, beginning 'Qui mihi . . .'

2. 'The Grammar', first entitled 'Institutio compendiaria totius grammaticae' (15610.5) and later 'Brevissima institutio' (15611). Its main sections, selected and revised by anonymous editors, are:

   a. Orthographia, on spelling, pronunciation, and punctuation, the sources as yet unidentified.

   b. Etymologia, the Accidence in Latin, largely derived from Lily's De generibus nominum ac verborum praeteritis (15607) as revised and augmented by Thomas Robertson and published at Basle in 1532. This includes the following sections of mnemonic verse: Lily's rules on the gender of nouns beginning 'Propria quae maribus . . .'; Robertson's rules on heteroclite nouns beginning: 'Quae genus . . .'; Lily's rules on the preterites of verbs and the supine beginning 'As in praesenti . . .' Other portions draw on Linacre (15634) and Melanchthon.

   c. Syntaxis, the Grammar in Latin, derived in part from the Lily-Erasmus Libellus de constructione (15601.3) but with other portions allied to Linacre and Despauter, from whom the section on figures of speech is largely taken.

   d. Prosodia, on accents, quantities, and verse, based on Robertson's supplements (*see* 2b above), usually with a dictionary of the words used in the grammar: 'Omnium nominum . . . interpretatio' expanded from John Rightwise's list in Lily's De generibus (15607).

Warning: While an attempt has been made to give collations of editions where such information was readily available at the time copy was prepared for the printer, these collations derive from various sources and differ in their completeness and exactitude. Furthermore, as is evident from the note to 15623, in one format and probably more, type was kept standing. As a result, it is not clear to what extent a difference in date actually signifies 'Anr. ed.', that is, the bulk of the type reset.

15610.5 — Institutio compendiaria totius grammaticae. 4°. (*ex off.* T. Bertheleti, 1540.) L.L².
    Possibly issued as pt. 2 w. 15610.6.

15610.6 — ⟨An intro⟩duction of the eyght partes of speche. [*Ed.* D. Talley.] 4°. (*in off.* T. Bertheleti, 1542.) L.
    (Formerly 15605) Collates A–I⁴. Possibly issued as pt. 1 w. 15610.5, but o has a single leaf frag. w. proof corrections (Vet. A1a.3(1)) pr. [T. Berthelet, c. 1540]: the paragraph on Interjections at the end of the section on Concords has only 4 lines (15610.6 has 6 lines, H4ʳ) and 'Godly Lessons for Chylderne' follows on the same page.

15610.7 — [Anr. ed. of 15610.5 and 15610.6, which were issued together from this time.] 2 pts. 4°. (*in off.* T. Bertheleti, 1543.) ILL.
    Collates A–H⁴ I⁶; A–X⁴.

15610.8 — [Anr. ed.] 2 pts. 8°. (*in off.* T. Bertheleti,) 1544 (1543.) HN.
    Collates A–F⁸ G⁴; A–N⁸ O⁴.

15610.9 — [Anr. ed.] 2 pts. 4°. (*in æd.* T. Bertheleti, 1546.) G².
    Collates A–I⁴; A–V⁴.

15610.10 — [Anr. ed., w. title for pt. 1:] A shorte introduction of grammar. 2 pts. 4°. [R. Wolfe,] 1548. L²(a⁴ of pt. 1 only, Frag. No. 70).

15611 — [Anr. ed., w. title for pt. 2:] (Brevissima institutio.) 2 pts. 4° in 8's. (*ap.* R. Wolfium,) 1549. O(pt. 1 lacks A5,6; pt. 2 lacks I8, K1–4).
    Collates A–D⁸ E⁴; A–K⁸.

15611.3 — [Anr. ed.] 2 pts. 4° in 8's? [R. Wolfe,] (1553.) L(tp to pt. 2 only, Harl.5974/14).

15611.7 — [Anr. ed.] 2 pts. 8°. [Geneva, C. Badius,] 1557 (cal. mr.). L.C.
    Collates a–c⁸ d⁴; A–H⁸; L has at the end extra quires e–f⁸ w. Nominum interpretatio, not present in c. In title: 'vf [*sic*]', 'inowlege [*sic*]'. This and the 2 following eds. have Badius's 'Prelum Ascensianum' device.

Lily, William—'*Lily's Grammar*'—*cont.*

15612 — [Anr. ed.] 2 pts. 8°. [Geneva, C. Badius,] 1557 (cal. mr.) O.C.; F.ILL.
    Collates like 15611.7. At least O, C, F do not have e–f⁸. In title: 'vp', 'knowlege'; at end of d4ʳ, 2 lines in roman begin: 'Pulcherrimæ . . .'

15613 — [Anr. ed.] 2 pts. 8°. [Geneva, C. Badius,] 1557. R(pt. 2 only, imp.)*.; F.HN.
    Collates like 15611.7. At least F does not have e–f⁸. At end of d4ʳ, 5 lines in italic begin: 'Liberi . . .'

15613.3 — [Anr. ed.] 2 pts. 4° in 8's. (*ap.* R. Wolfium,) 1558. C¹⁵.

15613.5 — [Anr. ed.] 2 pts. 4° in 8's. (*ap.* R. Vuolfium,) 1560. C¹³ (w. 15621.3 bd. at the end).
    Colophon to pt. 1 on D6ᵛ.

15613.7 — [Anr. ed.] 2 pts. 4° in 8's. (*ap.* R. Wolfium, 1564.) F(pt. 1 lacks tp; pt. 2 lacks I7,8).
    Collates A–C⁸ D⁶; A–I⁸.

15614 — [Anr. ed.] 2 pts. 4° in 8's. (*ap.* R. Vuolfium, [col. to pt. 1:] 1566, [tp to pt. 2:] 1567.) O(pt. 1 lacks tp and A8; pt. 2 lacks F1–3, H1, 2 and all after H6).
    Pt. 1 collates A–D⁸ (colophon on D8ᵛ); pt. 2 may collate like 15614.2.

15614.2 — [Anr. ed.] 2 pts. 4° in 8's. (*ap.* R. Vuolfium, 1567.) F.
    Collates A–D⁸; A–H⁸ I⁶.

15614.4 — [Anr. ed.] 2 pts. 8°. (*ap.* R. Vuolfium, 1567.) NLW (imp.).
    Collates A–C⁸ d⁴; A–G⁸+ ?

15614.6 — [Anr. ed.] 2 pts. 4° in 8's. (*ap.* R. Vuolfium,) 1568. F.
    Collates like 15614.2. ILL has leaves G4,5 of pt. 2 from an ed. very similar to this, but sig. G.v. is under 'at' of 'seruat' while F has it under 'Ton' of 'Tonum'.

15614.8 — [Anr. ed.] 2 pts. 8°. [R. Wolfe,] (1569.) NMU(pt. 2 only).

15614.9 — [Anr. ed.] 2 pts. 4° in 8's. (*ap.* R. Vuolfium, 1570.) L(tp to pt. 2 only, Harl.5974/13).

15615 — [Anr. ed.] 2 pts. 4° in 8's. [Holland? c. 1570.] C.
    Collates A–C⁸ D⁴; A–H⁸ I⁴ A–B⁴ (Nominum interpretatio). A pirated ed., prob. pr. in Holland.

15616 — [Anr. ed.] 2 pts. 4° in 8's. (*ap.* R. Vuolfium,) 1572 ([tp to pt. 2:] 1573.) O.
    Collates like 15614.2.

15617 — [Anr. ed.] 8°. *assignes of* F. Flowar, 1574. O.
    Collates A–R⁸; sub tp on E7ʳ; also dated on R7ᵛ.

15618 — [Anr. ed.] 2 pts. 4° in 8's. (*per assig.* F. Floræ, 1575.) C(pt. 1 lacks all but C⁸).
    Pt. 2 collates A–G⁸ H⁴ I⁸; pt. 1 may collate like 15622.

15619 — No entry.

15620 — [Anr. ed.] 4° in 8's. *assignes of* F. Flowar, 1577. L(lacks D7 [colophon?], D8 [sub tp?]).
    Collates A–L⁸. May have had a final quire M⁸, w. Nominum interpretatio, as suggested in the note to 15622. There is a frag. of an unidentified 4° ed. at O¹⁴ w. this imprint, but the date is cropt.

— [Anr. ed.] 4°. 1578. See 15622.

15621 — [Anr. ed.] 8°. *assignes of* F. Flowar, 1584. HN.
    Collates like 15617.

15621.3 — [Anr. ed.] 8°. [*assignes of* F. Flowar,] ([R7ᵛ:] 1585.) C¹³(Q–R⁸ only, bd. w. 15613.7).
    Collates like 15617.

15621.5 — [Anr. ed.] 8°. (*per assig.* F. Floræ, 1585 ([R7ᵛ:] 1586.)) L(sub tp only, Ames I.451).; F(2nd pt. only, w. 15622.3).
    Collates like 15617. See Greg, Register B, pp. 20, 21.

15621.7 — [Anr. ed.] 8°. [T. Dawson f.] *assignes of* F. Flowar, 1585 ([P8ᵛ:] 1586.) London, St. Paul's School.
    Collates A–P⁸; sub tp on E4ʳ; also dated on P8ᵛ.

15622 — [Anr. ed.] 2 pts. 4° in 8's. *assignes of* F. Flowar, 1588 ([pt. 1, D7ᵛ:] 1589 [pt. 2 tp:] 1587 [pt. 2, 'I'8ᵛ:] 1578.) O.
    Collates A–D⁸; A–G⁸ H⁴ 'I'⁸. The last quire has Nominum interpretatio, w. the 1st 2 leaves signed 'M' and the 3rd 'I'. The outer sheet of this quire, including the 1578 colophon, prob. belongs to an ed. following the pattern of 15620. See Greg, Register B, p. 25.

15622.3 — [Anr. ed.] 8°. *assignes of* F. Flowar, 1590. F(A1–E6 only, w. 15621.5).
    Collates like 15617. See Greg, Register B, pp. 34, 36.

15622.7 — [Anr. ed.] 8°. (*per assig.* F. Floræ, 1592 (1594.)) O³ (lacks tp and R7,8).
    Collates A–R⁸. See Greg, Register B, p. 52.

15622.8 — [Anr. ed.] 8°. 1593. *See Addenda.*

Lily, William—*'Lily's Grammar'*—*cont.*

15623 — [Anr. ed.] 2 pts. 8°. [*T. Dawson f.*] *assignes of J. Battersbie*, 1597 (*per assig. F. Floræ*, 1596.) L.O⁵. O⁸(imp.).C⁴.; F(2).
    Collates A–E⁸; A–K⁸ L⁴ M⁸ N⁴. 15624, 15624.5, 15625 sq. are all largely in the same typesetting as this, so it is clear the type for this (and perhaps other formats) was left standing for considerable time. *See* Greg, *Register B*, pp. 58, 60.

15623.5 — [Anr. ed.] 8°. [*T. Dawson f.*] *assignes of J. Battersbie*, 1599. C(frags.).; ILL.
    (Formerly 15605a) Collates A–R⁸; sub tp on E7ʳ; colophon on R7ʳ.

15624 — [Anr. ed.] 2 pts. 8°. [*T. Dawson f.*] *assignes of J. Battersbie*, 1599. L(pt. 1 only, w. 15624.5).
    Collates like 15623.

15624.5 — [Anr. ed.] 2 pts. 8°. [*T. Dawson f.*] *assignes of J. Battersbie*, 1602. L(pt. 2 only, w. 15624).O.C(pt. 2 only, w. 15625).CHATS.
    Collates like 15623.

15625 — [Anr. ed.] 2 pts. 8°. [*T. Dawson f.*] *J. Norton*, 1606. O.C(pt. 1 only, w. 15624.5).; F.
    Collates like 15623.

15626 — [A variant, w. imprint to pt. 1:] *J. Norton*, 1607. L.C. E².ETON.; HN.
    Collates like 15623.

15626.1 — [Anr. ed.] 8°. *J. Norton*, 1608. L.
    Collates like 15626.2.

15626.2 — [Anr. ed.] 8°. *J. Norton*, 1610. HN.
    Collates A–Q⁸; sub tp on E8ʳ; colophon on Q7ᵛ; also dated on Q8ʳ.

15626.3 — [Anr. ed.] 8°. *J. Norton*, 1611. Y.
    Collates like 15626.2.

15626.4 — [Anr. ed.] 8°. *B. Norton*, 1613. L.O³.
    Collates A–Q⁸.

15626.5 — [Anr. ed.] 8°. *assignes of J. Battersbie*, 1613. LEEDS.; BO.
    BO collates A–Q⁸ (lacks Q7,8); sub tp on E8ʳ; also dated Q6ᵛ.

15626.7 — [Anr. ed.] 8°. (*per assig. J. Battersbij*, 1617.) L(E8–Q6 only).
    Prob. collates like 15626.5.

15626.8 — [Anr. ed.] 8°. (*Excudebat J. Battersbie*, 1619.) L(col. only, Ames II.509).

15627 — [Anr. ed.] 8°. *assignes of B. Norton*, 1621. L.

15627.2 — [Anr. ed.] 8°. *C. Legge, pr. to the Univ. of Cambridge*, 1621. C.; F.
    Collates A–O⁸; sub tp on E2ʳ; also dated on O8ʳ. Tp in border McK.&F. 204β, w. royal arms at top. *See* Greg, *Companion*, pp. 178–207.

15627.3 — [Anr. ed.] 8°. *C. Legg, pr. to the Univ. of Cambridge*, 1621. C(Bury deposit).
    Collates like 15627.2. Tp in border McK.&F. 206β, w. female figures at top.

15627.5 — [Anr. ed.] 8°. *assignes of B. Norton*, 1627. O⁶(lacks tp).
    Collates A–Q⁸.

15627.6 — [Anr. ed.] 8°. *B. Norton*, 1628. C.
    Collates like 15628.

15627.7 — [Anr. ed.] 8°. *prs. to the Univ. of Cambridge*, 1629 ([sub tp:] 1630.) C⁴.
    Collates A–O⁸.

15627.9 — [Anr. ed.] 4°. *B. Norton*, 1630. Maggs, *Mercurius Britannicus*, No. 10 (Jan. 1934), item 1179 (cannot now be traced).
    This may be the copy examined at some time by F. S. Ferguson and recorded as collating A–F⁴ G², like 15628.5.

15628 — [Anr. ed.] 8°. *B. Norton*, 1630 ([col:] 1631.) L(tp only, Harl.5974/28).O(2nd pt. only, imp.).; F.
    Collates A–Q⁸; sub tp on E8ʳ; colophon on Q8ʳ.

15628.3 — [Anr. ed.] 8°. *B. Norton*, 1631 ([sub tp:] 1632.) NLW.
    Collates like 15628.

15628.5 — [Anr. ed.] 4°. *B. Norton*, 1632. London, St. Paul's School.
    Collates A–F⁴ G² and consists only of pt. 1; there is no Brevissima institutio; cf. 15627.9.

15628.7 — [Anr. ed.] 8°. *assignes of B. Norton*, 1633 ([col.:] 1632.) F.
    Collates A–O⁸; sub tp on E5ʳ; colophon on O8ʳ.

15629 — [Anr. ed.] 8°. (*B. Norton*, 1634.) L(2nd pt. only).
    Collates like 15628.7.

15630 — [Anr. ed.] 8°. *prs. to the Univ. of Cambridge*, 1634. C.; ILL.
    Collates A–O⁸; sub tp on E5ʳ; no colophon.

15631 — [Anr. ed.] 8°. *assignes of R. Norton*, 1636 (*R. Nortonus*, 1637.) L(1st pt. only).O²⁸(Bed., frag.).; F.
    Collates like 15630.

Lily, William—*'Lily's Grammar'*—*cont.*

15632 — [Anr. ed.] 8°. *Oxford, W. Turner*, 1636. O.; HN.
    Collates A–P⁸; sub tp on E5ʳ; P8 blank.

15632.3 — [Anr. ed.] 8°. *Cambridge, T. Buck & R. Daniel*, 1638 ([sub tp:] 1637.) CU.
    Collates like 15630.

15632.7 — [Anr. ed.] 8°. *assignes of R. Norton*, 1639 (*R. Nortonus*, 1637.) L(A1–5 only, Harl.5974/74).NLW.
    Collates like 15630.

15633 — [Anr. ed.] 8°. *R. Daniel, pr. to the Univ. of Cambridge*, 1640. L(A1–B3, B6–E4 only).
    Prob. collates like 15630.

15633.2 — [Anr. ed.] 8°. *assignes of R. Norton* (*typis R. Nortoni*,) 1640. L(sub tp only, Harl.5974/3).LEEDS.PARIS.

15633.4 — [Extracts.] Lilies rules construed. The ninth edition corrected and amended. Whereunto are added T. Robertsons Hetroclites [*sic*], the Latine syntaxis, Qui mihi. [*Ed.*] (W. Heane [i.e. Hayne].) 8°. *T. Dawson*, 1603. Ent. to Dawson, Master [E.] White, W. Leake, a. C. Burby 29 no. 1603. NMU.

15633.6 — [Anr. ed.] 8°. *B. Norton*, 16(33?) F(date defaced).
    In this and the next, the editor's name is spelled 'Haine'.

15633.8 — [Anr. ed.] 8°. *R. Norton*, 1638. L.

— Animadversions upon Lillies grammar. 1625. *See* 25867.

— *See also* 14894.3, 21061, 23280, 23283, 23284.5.

Limbo-Mastix. Limbo-mastix, that is a canvise of Limbus patrum. 1604. *See* 25692.

15634 **Linacre, Thomas.** Thomae Linacri Britanni de emendata structura Latini sermonis libri sex. 4°. (*ap. R. Pynsonum*,) 1524 (de.) L.O.C.G².M.+; F.HN.ILL.
    See also 2b, 2c in headnote preceding 15610.5.

15635 — Linacri progymnasmata grammatices vulgaria. 4°. (*J. Rastell*,) [1512.] L.

15636 — Rudimenta grammatices Thomæ Linacri diligenter castigata denuo. *Eng.* 4°. (*in æd. Pynsonianis*,) [1525?] L.M.
    Collates A–M⁴; a different work from 21438 and 22564.

15637 — [Anr. ed.] 4°. (*in æd. Pynsonianis*,) [c. 1525.] L(lacks a⁴).
    Collates a–e⁴ A–E⁴; prob. earlier than 15636.

— *tr. See* 11531.5, 20398.3.

— *See also* 3382.5, 25737.

15638 **Linaker, Robert.** [A comfortable treatise for such as are afflicted in conscience. Perused the second time and enlarged.] 8°. [*V. Simmes f. R. Boyle*, 1595.] C(lacks tp and E8).
    With dedic. to the Earl of Essex, omitted in the following eds. The title and imprint are supplied from Herbert (II.1279), who had a copy.

15639 — [Anr. ed.] Perused the second time and enlarged. 8°. *J. R[oberts] f. W. Leake*, 1601. Ass'd from Boyle 9 jy. 1597. L(tp only, Ames II.26).C.

15640 — [Anr. ed.] Revised the third time. 8°. *H. L[ownes] f. W. Leake*, 1607. L.

15640.5 — [Anr. issue, w. imprint:] *H. L[ownes] f. W. Leake*, 1610. O.C.; LC.

15641 — [Anr. ed.] Revised the fourth time. 12°. *W. Stansby f. J. Parker*, 1620. Ass'd by W. Barrett 8 mr. L.; F.

15642 — [Anr. ed.] Revised the fifth time. 12°. *T. Snodham f. J. Parker*, 1625. C.C³.C¹⁰.

15643 — The sixth edition. 12°. *J. Haviland f. J. Bolar*, 1634. Ass'd to Haviland a. J. Wright 4 se. 1638. L.DUL.

15643.5 — A short catechisme: or a cordiall preservative for little children. 8°. [*T. Creede*] *f. W. Leake*, 1610. Ent. 11 jy. L(2).; HD(imp.).

15644 — A short and plaine instruction, for such as are carefull to know the way to euerlasting life. 8°. *T. Orwin f. T. Woodcock*, 1591. NY.

15645 **Lincoln.** A mournfull dittie on the death of certaine iudges and iustices, who died after the assises, holden at Lincolne. *Ballad.* s.sh.fol. *J. Wolfe f. W. Wright*, 1590. Ent. 21 my. L.

— The seuerall rates . . . made by the iustices of peace of Lincolne. [1563.] *See* 7957.3.

Lincoln, *Cathedral*—*Prebendary of. See* 24259.

Lincoln, *Countess of. See* 5432.

15646 Lincoln, *Diocese of.* An abridgment of that booke which the ministers of Lincoln diocess delivered to his maiestie. Being the first part of an apologye for themselves and their brethren that refuse the subscription, and conformitie which is required. 4°. [*W. Jones's secret press,*] 1605. L.O.C.D².M.+; BO.BO³.HD (imp.).IND.U.

15647 — [Anr. ed.] 8°. [*Leiden, W. Brewster,*] *Reprinted,* 1617. L.O⁵.O⁸.C.E.; HD(imp.).U.Y. Pilgrim Hall, Plymouth, Massachusetts.

15648 — [Anr. ed.] 8°. [*Holland?*] *Reprinted,* 1638. L³.DEU.E(3). G².LINC.; N.U.

15649 — Nouerint vniuersi per praesentes [etc. Form of receipt.] [1538.] = 16794.

Lincoln, *Hospital of St. Katherine. See* Indulgences 49.

Lincoln, *Hospital of St. Sepulchre. See* Indulgences 151 sq.

15650 Lincolnshire. Answere to the petitions of the traytours and rebelles in Lyncolneshyre. 1536. Now = 13077.5.

15651 — A briefe relation by the commoners of Lincolnshire. [1651?] Not an STC book.

15652 — Lamentable newes out of Lincolne-shire of the overflowing of waters. 1614. = pt. of 14068 sq.

15653 Lindanus, Willelmus, *Bp.* Certaine tables sett furth . . . wherein is detected the dangerous doctrine of the heretikes. *Tr.* L. Euans. 8°. *Antwerpe, Ægidius Diest,* 1565. L².O.P(imp.).; F. A.&R. 461.

Linde, *Sir Humphrey. See* Lynde, *Sir* H.

15654 Lindesay, David. An heavenly chariot. 1622. Now = 15683.5.

15655 Lindsay, David, *Bp.* De potestate principis. Aphorismi. 1617. Now = 21555.28.

15656 — The reasons of a pastors resolution, touching the communion. 8°. *G. Purslowe f. R. Rounthwaite,* 1619. Ent. 22 my. L.O.A.E.G².+; F.

15657 — A true narration of all the passages of the proceedings in the generall assembly of the church of Scotland, holden at Perth the 25. of August, 1618. Against a seditious pamphlet [4360]. 4° in 8's. *W. Stansby f. R. Rounthwait,* 1621. Ent. 16 de. 1620. L.O.C.D.E.+; F.HN.HD.ILL.NY.+

15657.5 — [Anr. issue, w. cancel tp:] A treatise of the ceremonies of the church. *f. R. Rounthwaite,* 1625. E⁹(tp only). PETYT.; HD.NY¹¹. Washington Cathedral. The tp is anon.; the preface retains the identification: 'David [Lindsay, Bp. of] Brechen'.

15658 Lindsay, *Sir* David. The warkis of the famous and vorthie knicht Schir Dauid Lyndesay. Newly correctit, and augmentit. [In verse.] 2 pts. 4° in 8's. (*Edinburgh,*) *J. Scot, at the expensis of H. Charteris,* 1568. WN.; F.HN.

15658.5 — [Anr. issue, w. date on R1ᵛ:] (1569.) C⁵(imp.).

15659 — [Anr. issue w. new prelims.:] *Edinburgh, J. Scot at the expensis of H. Charteris,* 1571. O(imp.).

15660 — [Anr. ed.] 4° in 8's. *Edinburgh, T. Bassandyne,* 1574. BUTE.E.

15661 — [Anr. ed.] 4° in 8's. *Edinburgh,* [*J. Ross,* 1580?] O(tp mutilated).

15662 — [Anr. issue, w. prelims. reset, w. imprint:] *Edinburgh, H. Charteris,* 1582. E.P(lacks tp). In this and the following 3 eds., The historie of Squyer Meldrum is called for in the contents but is not included.

15663 — [Anr. ed.] 4° in 8's. *Edinburgh, H. Charteris,* 1592. L.E.

15664 — [Anr. ed.] 4° in 8's. *Edinburgh, H. Charteris,* 1597. DUR(imp.).; Y. Heading B1ʳ: 'Ane Prologue'.

15664.3 — [Anr. ed.] 4° in 8's. *Edinburgh, H. Charteris,* 1597. E (imp.).; F. Heading B1ʳ: 'The Prologue'.

Lindsay, *Sir* David—*cont.*

15664.7 — [Anr. ed.] 4° in 8's. [*Edinburgh,*] *R. Charteris,* 1605. BUTE(imp.).

15665 — [Anr. ed.] 4° in 8's. *Edinburgh, T. Finlason,* 1610. HN.

15666 — [Anr. ed.] 8°. *Edinburgh, A. Hart,* 1614. L(imp.).; HN.

15667 — [Anr. ed.] 8°. *Edinbugh* [sic], *A. Hart,* 1617. E.

15667.5 — [Anr. ed.] 8°. *Edinburgh, A. Hart,* 1619. L.; F(imp.).

15668 — [Anr. ed.] 8°. *Aberdene, E. Raban f. D. Melvill,* 1628. E.; F.HN.

15669 — [Anr. ed.] 8°. *Edinburgh, heires of A. Hart,* 1630. E.

15670 — [Anr. ed.] 8°. *Edinburgh,* [*heirs of*] *A. Hart,* 1634. L. E.; HN.BO².

15671 — The complaynte and testament of a popiniay. [In verse.] 4°. (*J. Byddell,* 1538.) L.; HN.

15672 — Ane dialog betuix experience and ane courteour, off the miserabyll estait of the warld. And is deuidit in foure partis. [In verse.] 4° in 8's. [*Edinburgh, J. Scot,*] *at the expensis off Doctor, Machabeus, in Copmahouin,* [1554.] L.L²(imp.).O(2, 1 imp.).C(imp.).E².; F.HN. As originally issued, this contained only Ane dialog, commonly known as The monarche. The L, 1 O, and E² copies also have the extra texts from 15675 and prob. represent a later issue.

15673 — [Anr. ed., w. additions.] 4 pts. 4° partly in 8's. [*Rouen? J. Petit?*] *at the expenses of S. Jascuy, in Paris,* 1558. L.C².BTU(Testament only).E(2, 1 imp.).; F.HN(Tragedie only).TEX(lacks Dialog, imp.). Contains Ane dialog, The dreme of Shir Dauid Lindsay, The tragedie of maister reuerende fader Dauid, The testament and complaynt of our souueraine lordis papyngo. Parts may have been issued separately. For an earlier version in English of Tragedie *see* 15683, of Testament *see* 15671.

15674 — [Anr. ed.] 4 pts. 8°. [*Rouen? J. Petit?*] *at the expenses of S. Jascuy, in Paris,* 1558. HN.

15674.5 — [Anr. issue, w. d⁸ of pt. 1 cancelled and replaced by 12 leaves: d⁸ dd⁴.] E(1, plus a frag.*).P.

15675 — [Anr. ed.] 2 pts. 4° in 8's. [*Edinburgh, J. Scot,*] *at the expensis of Doctor Nachabeus* [sic] *in Copmanhouin,* [1559.] L(Tragedie, etc.).L².O(1, plus Tragedie, etc.). E²(Tragedie, etc.).; F.PFOR. The L, O, E² copies of Tragedie (S⁸) and the other texts (2nd A–G⁸) are bd. w. 15672.

15676 — [Anr. ed.] A dialogue betweene Experience and a Courtier, nowe newly corrected. 4° in 8's. (*T. Purfoote a.* [i.e. *for*] *W. Pickering,*) 1566. Ent. to R. Serle 1563–64; to W. Pickering 1565–66. L.O⁸.C.E(imp.). G²(imp.).+; F(imp.).HN.HD(imp.).TEX(6 leaves). Copies vary; tp line 17 has: 'pithy pieces' (C) or 'pithy posys' (L).

15677 — [Anr. ed.] Now the seconde time corrected. 4° in 8's. *T. Purfoote,* 1575. L.E(imp.).R.; F.HN.N.Y.

15678 — [Anr. ed.] Now the seconde time corrected. 4° in 8's. *T. Purfoote,* 1581. L.O.C².E.M.+; F.HN.N.NY.TEX.+

15679 — The historie of ane nobil and wailzeand squyer, William Meldrum. [In verse.] 4° in 8's. *Edinburgh, H. Charteris,* 1594. L.E. Aberdeen PL.; HN.

15680 — [Anr. ed.] 4°. *Edinburgh,* [*T. Finlason*] *f. R. Lawson,* 1610. HN. This and the next ed. may have been issued w. 15665 and 15670 respectively.

15680.5 — [Anr. ed.] 8°. *Edinburgh, heires of A. Hart,* 1634 (27 de.) E⁸(imp.).

15681 — Ane satyre of the thrie estaits. 4°. *Edinburgh, R. Charteris,* 1602. O.; HN. Greg 193.

15681.5 — [A variant, w. imprint:] *Edinburgh, R. Charteris, cum privilegio regis,* 1602. O.E.LINC.; F.

15682 — [Anr. issue, for sale in London, w. cancel tp:] The workes. Newly corrected. *Edinburgh, R. Charteris, sold in London by N. Butter,* 1604. L. The cancel tp has perpendicular chain lines. The 1602 colophon is retained.

15683 — The tragical death of Dauid Beatō bishoppe of sainct Andrews [in verse] wherunto is ioyned the martyrdom of maister George Wyseharte [by R. Burrant.] 8°. (*J. Day a. W. Seres,*) [1548?] L(2).O(lacks tp). O⁵(frag.).

15683.5 Lindsay, David, *Minister at Leith.* An heavenly chariot, layde open for transporting the new-borne babes of God. 4°. *Sainct-Andrewes, E. Raban,* 1622. O¹⁴.E. INN.; F. (Formerly 15654) Reprinted in 15684.

Lindsay, David, *Minister at Leith—cont.*
15684 — The godly mans journey to heaven. 8°. *R. F[ield] f. R. Bird,* 1625. Ent. 18 oc. 1624. L(imp.).O.DUL.E².STU. +; F.
    Includes reprint of 15683.5. Prob. pr. by G. Miller as Field died in the fall of 1624.

Lindsell, Augustine, *Bp.* Visitation Articles. *See* 10216, 10317.
— *ed. See* 23948.

Lindt, Willem van der, *Bp.* Certaine tables wherein is detected the doting dangerous doctrine of heretikes. *See* 15653.

Ling, N., *tr.* A sum or a brief collection of holy signes. 1563. *See* 23433.

15685 **Ling, Nicholas.** Politeuphuia wits common wealth. 8°. (*Lonlon* [sic],) *J. R(oberts) f. N. Ling,* 1597. Ent. 14 oc. L.
    Colophon also dated 1597. First in the 'Wits Series', which includes 381, 17834, 26014.
15685.5 — [A variant, w. tp and colophon dated:] 1598. Juel-Jensen(A1, Mm2–4 only, bd. w. 15686.3).
15686 — [Anr. ed., w. 'Second edition' on A3ʳ.] Newly corrected and augmented. 8°. *J. R[oberts] f. N. Ling,* 1598. L(imp.).L³⁰.E.M²(imp.). Juel-Jensen.; F.HN.HD.ILL.PFOR.+
15686.3 — [Anr. ed., w. 'Third edition' on A3ʳ.] 8°. *J. R[oberts] f. N. Ling,* 1598. Juel-Jensen(2, 1 imp. and completed by 15685.5).; F(imp.).PEN.
15686.7 — [Anr. ed., w. 'Fourth edition' on A3ʳ.] 8°. *H. B[allard?] f. J. Smithweck,* 1608. Ent. 19 no. 1607. BRISTOL (imp.). Juel-Jensen(imp.).
15687 — [Anr. ed., w. 'Fourth edition' on A3ʳ.] 8°. *W. S[tansby] f. J. Smethwicke,* [1608?] L.; HD(imp.).
    'Diall' in imprint.
15687.3 — [Anr. ed., w. 'Fourth edition' on A3ʳ.] 8°. *W. S[tansby] f. J. Smethwicke,* [after 1612.] BIRM(imp.). Juel-Jensen.; HD.
    'Dyall' in imprint.
15687.7 — [Anr. ed., w. 'Ninth edition' on A3ʳ.] 12°. *W. S[tansby] f. J. Smethwicke,* [c. 1615.] F(imp.).ILL.NY.Y.
15688 — [Anr. ed., w. 'Tenth edition' on A3ʳ.] 12°. *W. S[tansby] f. J. Smethwicke,* [1620?] L.L³⁰.CHATS. Juel-Jensen.; HN.HD.ILL.TEX.
15689 — [Anr. ed., w. 'Eleventh edition' on A3ʳ.] 12°. *W. S[tansby] f. J. Smithwicke,* [1626?] O.; HD.
    Collates A–Y¹²; 'Dyal' in imprint.
15689.5 — [Anr. ed., w. 'Eleventh edition' on A3ʳ.] 12°. *W. S[tansby] f. J. Smethwicke,* [1628?] O³.C⁴.NLW. Juel-Jensen.; F.HN.COR.
    Collates A–S¹² T⁶; 'Diall' in imprint.
15690 — [Anr. ed., w. 'Twelfth edition' on A3ʳ.] 12°. *R. Young f. J. Smethwicke,* [1630?] L.; HN.CHI.LC(imp.). TORONTO². Amherst C.
    Pp. 391.
15690.3 — [Anr. ed., w. 'New edition' on A4ʳ.] 12°. *R. Young f. J. Smethwicke,* [c. 1640.] HD.
    Pp. 321.
— *ed. See* 3191.

15690.7 **Lingham, J.** A true relation of all suche Englishe capetaines and lieuetenants, as haue been slaine in the Low Countries, together with those now liuing; as also of such as are fled to the enemy. 8°. *R. Ward,* 1584. L².

Lingua. Lingua: or the combat of the tongue. 1607, etc. *See* 24104 sqq.

15691 **Linschoten, Jan Huygen van.** John Huighen Van Linschoten. his discours of voyages into yᵉ Easte & West Indies. (*Tr.* out of Dutch by W. P[hilip].) fol. [*J. Windet f.*] *J. Wolfe,* (1598.) Ent. 21 jn. 1597. L.O.C.D.E.+; F.HN.HD.N.NY.+

15692 **Linton, Anthony.** Newes of the complement of the art of navigation. And of the mightie empire of Cataia. 4°. *F. Kyngston,* 1609. L.O⁵.O²².C⁶. London, Royal Institution of Naval Architects.+; F.HN.LC.MIN.NY.+

15693 **Lippomano, Luigi,** *Bp.* A copye of a very fyne and wyttye letter. *Tr.* M. Throckmerton. 8°. *Curtigiane of Rome,* [i.e. Emden, E. van der Erve,] 1556. O(2).

Lippomano, Luigi, *Bp.—cont.*
15693.5 — [Anr. ed.] A copye of a verye fyne and wytty letter. 8°. *Curtigiane of Rome,* [i.e. *London, J. Kingston a. H. Sutton? f. J. Wayland?*] 1556. L.O(frag.).; F.

15694 **Lipsius, Justus.** Iusti Lipsi de constantia libri duo. Iterata editio. 8°. *imp. G. Bishop,* 1586. Ent. 31 ja. L¹⁵.C.BRISTOL².HOLK.USHAW.+
15694.3 — [Anr. ed.] Quinta editio. 8°. *imp. G. Bishop,* 1592. C¹⁵. ETON.; ILL.
15694.7 — [A trans.] Two bookes of constancie. Englished by J. Stradling. 4°. [*P. Short f.*] *R. Johnes,* 1594 (1595.) Ent. 7 oc. 1594. CAR.; COR(imp.).PN².
15695 — [A variant, w. tp date:] 1595. L.O⁴.C.CARTMEL.E.; F.HD.N.
15696 — A direction for trauailers. Taken [by Sir J. Stradling] out of J. Lipsius [his Epistola de peregrinatione italica], and enlarged for the behoofe of the young Earle of Bedford. 4°. *R. B[ourne] f. C. Burbie,* 1592. Ent. 12 my. L.L¹⁶.; N.
15697 — Iusti Lipsi epistolarum selectarum centuria prima. 8°. *G. Bishop,* 1586. L¹⁵.O.C³.P.USHAW.+; F.
15698 — Iusti Lipsi epistolarum centuria secunda. 8°. [*Eliot's Court Press,*] *imp. G. Bishop,* 1590. Ent. 29 my. L. L¹³.L¹⁵.O.USHAW.+; F.ILL.Y.
    Sometimes bd. w. 15697; reissued as pt. 2 of 15699.
15699 — [Anr. ed. of 15697 and a reissue of 15698.] Iusti Lipsi epistolarum centuriæ duæ. 2 pts. 8°. *G. Bishop,* 1593 (1590.) C.C⁵.C¹⁹. Heidelberg U. Newport PL.; F.HN.HD(pt. 1 only).ILL.
15700 — Iusti Lipsi V. Cl. oratio in calumniam. 4°. *F. Kyngston,* 1615. O.C.C².E².PLUME.+; F.
    For a trans. *see* 23127.
15700.3 — [Anr. ed.] 4°. *F. Kyngston,* 1618. E.
15700.7 — Iusti Lipsi politicorum siue ciuilis doctrinæ libri sex. Editio altera. 2 pts. 8°. *G. Bishop,* 1590. Ent. to J. Wolfe 13 ja. 1590. L¹⁵.O(tp to pt. 2 only, Douce Add.142/50).C⁵(2).USHAW. Swaffham Parish Church, Norfolk.; CU.N.
    See also 24031.
15701 — [A trans.] Six bookes of politickes or ciuil doctrine. Done into English by [Sir] W. Jones. 4°. *R. Field f. W. Ponsonby,* 1594. Ent. to J. Wolfe 15 no. 1589 a. 13 ja. 1590; to E. Aggas 10 jy. 1590. L.O.C.D⁵.E.+; F.HN.HD.N.Y.+
15702 — Iusti Lipsi tractatus ad historiam Romanam cognoscendam. 8°. *Cantabrigiae, ex off. J. Legate,* 1592. L.O. O¹⁷.C.C³.+; F.HART.NY¹¹.
15703 — [Anr. issue, w. cancel tp, w. imprint:] *Lugduni Batauorum, ex off. Plantiniana ap. F. Raphelengium,* 1592. L.C.; Y.
15703.5 — [Anr. ed.] 8°. *Cantabrigiæ, ex off. J. Legate,* 1607. L(tp only, Ames II.127).O⁶.C.; F.
— *See also* 22213, 26064.

Lisander. *See* Lysandre.

Lisbon. The triumphant arch erected in Lisbone. 1619. *See* 19843.
15704 — Two most srange [sic] and notable examples, shewed at Lyshborne. 4°. [*A. Jeffes] f. W. Barley,* 1591. Ent. to A. Jeffes 29 ap. O.LINC.

L'Isle, François de, *pseud. See* 20855.

15705 **Lisle, William.** Divers ancient monuments in the Saxon tongue. 1638. Now = 160.5.
— The faire Æthiopian. [*Tr.*] *W. L'isle.* 1631. *See* 13047.
— The famous historie of Heliodorus. [*Tr.*] *W. Lisle.* 1638. *See* 13048.
15706 — Nothing for a new-yeares gift. [Init. W. L. In verse.] 4°. *T. C[reede] f. W. Lugger,* 1603. O.E.
— *ed. See* 160.
— *tr. See* 21662, 21663, 21670.

15706.5 **List.** A lamentable list, of certaine hidious, frightfull, and prodigious signes, which have bin seene, for these 18. yeares last past, to this present: that is to say, Anno. 1638. *Ballad.* 2 pts. s.sh.fol. [*J. Okes?] f. T. Lambert,* [1638.] Ent. to J. Okes 20 au. 1638. O.

15707 **Litany.** The golden letany in englysshe. 16° in 8's. (*R. Coplãd,* 1531 (19 jn.),) A².
15707.5 — [Anr. ed.] 16°. (*J. Skot,*) [1536?] M.
— For separate litanies used in the Church of England see 16453 sqq.

15708 Lithgow, William. A briefe and summarie discourse upon that lamentable disaster at Dunglasse. Anno 1640. the penult of August. [In verse.] 4°. *Edinburgh, R. Bryson,* [1640.] L.E.G².; HN.

15709 — The gushing teares of godly sorrow. [In verse.] 4°. *Edinburgh, R. Bryson, at the expences of the authour,* 1640. L.E(2).E²(imp.).E⁸.; F.HN.HD.

15710 — A most delectable, and true discourse, of an admired and painefull peregrination in Europe, Asia and Affricke. 4°. *N. Okes, sold by T. Archer,* 1614. Ent. to N. Okes 13 fb. L.O.O⁸.; F.HN.HD.Y.
>   *See Court-Book C, p. 355.* In some copies (F, L) the dedics. to the Earl and Countess of Somerset are cancelled and the address to the reader is reprinted w. heading: 'To all noble-minded gentlemen, and heroicke spirits'.

15711 — [Anr. ed.] Second impression. 4°. *N. Okes, sold by T. Archer,* 1616. L.E.; F.HN.

15712 — [Anr. ed.] Newly imprinted, and inlarged. 4°. *N. Okes,* 1623. L.O.O⁹.C³.LINC.; HN.NY.Y.

15712.5 — [Anr. ed., revised and enlarged.] The totall discourse, of the rare adventures, of long nineteene yeares travayles. 4°. *N. Okes,* 1632. C¹².A.E.G².LEEDS.; ILL. NY(2, 1 lacks tp*).WIS.
>   This and the following ed. contain a new dedic., 'To the high and mighty monarch, Charles'. They also contain a prologue to the reader, beginning 'Judicious lector', differing from that in the 1623 ed. The LEEDS copy has the date altered in ink to 1633.

15713 — [Anr. issue, w. imprint:] *N. Okes, sold by N. Fussell a. H. Mosley,* 1632. L.O.C¹⁷.D.E².+; F.HN.HD.N.Y.+

15714 — [Anr. ed.] 4° in 8's. *J. Okes,* 1640. L.O.C.DUR⁵.E.+; F. HN.HD.N.NY.+

15715 — The pilgrimes farewell, to his native countrey of Scotland: wherein is contained, in way of dialogue, the joyes and miseries of peregrination. [In verse.] 4°. *Edinburgh, A. Hart, at the expences of the author,* 1618. L.O.E(2).; HN.BO.

15716 — Scotlands welcome to her native sonne, King Charles. [In verse.] 4°. *Edinburgh, J. Wreittoun,* [1633.] L(2). O.E(2).M⁴.; F.HN.HD.

15717 — A true and experimentall discourse, upon the last siege of Breda [etc.] 4°. *J. Okes f. J. Rothwel,* 1637. Ent. 14 de. L.O.C.D.E.+; F.HN.HD.N.Y.+

15717.5 Littleton, Edmund. A briefe catechisme, containing the summe of the gospell. 8°. *G. Purslowe f. S. Stafford,* 1616. Ent. 1 se. 1602. HD.

15718 — [Anr. ed.] 8°. *J. Haviland f. H. Bell,* 1631. Ass'd to H. a. M. Bell 4 se. 1632. L.

Littleton, *Sir* Thomas.

TENURES—*Law French*

15719 — [Tenores novelli. Begins a2ʳ:] [T]enant en fee simple [etc. Ends i6ᵛ:] (Explicīūt tenores nouelli.) fol. (*p J. lettou & W. de machlinia,*) [1482.] L.O⁹.C.CHATS. M.+; LC.PML. Duff 273.
>   Reprinted in 18394 sq.

15720 — [Anr. ed.] fol. (*per w. de machlinia,*) [1483?] L.BIRM² (Cobham).M.; LC. Duff 274.

15721 — [Anr. ed.] fol. (*in ciuitate rothomagensi, per w. le tailleur ad instantiam R. pynson,*) [1490.] L(lacks A1).L²¹. O.C.M.+; HD.PML. Duff 275.

15722 — [Anr. ed.] fol. [*R. Pynson,* 1496.] L⁵.O(A1 only).; HN. HD(imp.).PML. Duff 276.

15722.5 — [Anr. ed.] fol. [*R. Pynson,* 1502?] L.D.; HN.HD.LC. (Formerly 15725)

15723 — [Anr. ed.] Leteltun teners newe correcte. fol. [*R. Pynson,* 1510?] L.L²².C.D.

15724 — [Anr. ed.] fol. (*per R. Pynson,* 1516.) L.O.M.; HD(lacks tp).

15725 — Now = 15722.5.

15725.5 — [Anr. ed.] Leteltun tenuris new correcte. fol. (*per R. Pynson,* 1522.) C(lacks tp).C⁴(2 imp.).

15726 — [Anr. ed.] Lytylton tenures newly and moost truly correctyd & amendyd. 16° in 8's. (*in ęd. R. Pynsoni,* 1525 (4 id. oc.)) L²².O.; HD(imp.).

15727 — [Anr. ed.] 16° in 8's. (*in ed. R. Redman,* 1528 (6 ap.)) L(destroyed).; HD.MIN(imp.).

15728 — [Anr. ed.] 16° in 8's. (*in ed. R. Pynsonis,* 1528 (18 jn.)) L(imp.).M.; HD. (Formerly also 15729)

15729 — = 15728.

Littleton, *Sir* Thomas—TENURES—*Law French—cont.*

15730 — [Anr. ed.] Lyttylton tenures newly imprinted. 8°. (*R. Redman,*) [c. 1530.] L.O¹⁰.C.; LC.

15731 — [Anr. ed.] 8°. (*in ed. T. Bertheleti,* 1530.) L.O.C.D.; HD. LC.

15731.5 — [Anr. ed.] 8°. (*R. Redman,*) 1539. P.; HD.

15732 — [Anr. ed.] Les tenures de Lyttelton nouelment imprimes. fol. (*R. Redman,*) [c. 1540.] L.L²².L³⁸.M.; HD.LC.NYS.

15732.5 — [Anr. ed.] Lytylton tenures newly imprynted. 8°. (*in ęd. T. Bertheleti,*) 1541. HD.LC.

15732.7 — [Anr. ed.] 8°. (*H. Smyth,*) 1545. HD.MIN. (Formerly 15734)

15732.9 — [Anr. issue, w. colophon:] (*P. Bounel f. J. Walley,*) 1545. S.
>   (Formerly 15764) This is the only book known in which Bounel's name occurs, and he is unknown to Arber.

15733 — [Anr. ed.] Newly reuised, with a table. [Ed.] (W. S[tanford?]) 8°. (*W. Myddylton,*) 1545 (26 mr.) L(lacks tp).; HD.LC.MIN.

15734 — Now = 15732.7.

15735 — Now = 15764.5.

15736 — [Anr. ed.] 8°. (*W. Powel,* 1553.) L.; HD.

15737 — [Anr. ed.] 8°. *R. Tottel,* 1554. L.

15738 — [Anr. ed.] Litletons tenures. Conferred with diuers true wrytten copies, and purged of sondry cases. 8°. *ap. R. Tottel,* 1557 (*R. Tottill,* 1557 (28 oc.)) L. M⁴.; HD.
>   In colophon: 'Flete-/strete'. 'Table' omitted in this and the following eds.

15738.3 — [Anr. ed.] Litletons tenures. 8°. *ap. R. Tottel,* 1557 (*R. Tottil,* 1557 (28 oc.)) L³⁸.O.O¹⁸.M.STU.; HN.CAL⁵.HD. MIN.NYS.
>   In colophon: 'Fletestrete'.

15738.7 — [Anr. ed.] 8°. *ap. R. Tottele,* 1557 (*R. Tottil,* 1557 (28 oc.)) L.ST.; CU.HD.LC.
>   In colophon: 'Flete stret'.

15739 — [Anr. ed.] Les tenures du monsieur Littleton, ouesque certein cases addes p auters de puisne temps, troueres signes. 8°. (*R. Tottil,*) 1567 (17 my.) L.M. M².; HD.

15740 — [Anr. ed.] 8°. (*R. Tottill,*) 1569. O.C⁷.LEEDS.NLW.P.; HN.HD.MIN.

15741 — [Anr. ed.] 8°. (*R. Tottill,*) 1572. L.O⁵.C².D.ST.+; F.HD.V.

15742 — [Anr. ed.] 8°. (*R. Tottyl,*) 1572 (1574.) O.ST(lacks tp).; F.HN.CU.HD.MIN.+

15743 — [Anr. ed.] 8°. (*R. Tottyl,*) 1577. L.L²².O.M.P.+; HD(2). BO².MIN.

15744 — [Anr. ed.] 8°. (*R. Tottyl,*) 1579. L.O.C.E.P.; HN.HD(3, 1 imp.).LC.MIN.

15745 — [Anr. ed.] [Ed.] (W. West.) 8°. (*R. Tottel,*) 1581. L. HAT. Cambridge, Squire Law Library.; HN.HD.MIN. PML.Y.+

15746 — [Anr. ed.] 8°. (*R. Tottill,*) 1583. Ent. 18 fb. L.O.O⁷. NLW.S.+; F.HN.HD.MIN.Y.+
>   Some copies (O, O⁷) are pr. on 4° paper.

15747 — [Anr. ed.] 8°. (*R. Tottill,*) 1585. L.O.C²⁰.D.G²(imp.).+; HN.CU.HD.LC.MIN.+

15748 — [Anr. ed.] 8°. (*R. Tottell,*) 1588. L.L³⁰.O.COL.D⁵.+; F. HN.HD.MIN.Y.+
>   Some copies (L, 1 L²², 1 HD) are pr. on 4° paper.

15749 — [Anr. ed.] 8°. (*R. Tottell,*) 1591. L.L²².C.D².LEEDS.+; F.HN.HD.MIN.Y.+
>   Some copies (L²², L³⁰, 1 F) are pr. on 4° paper.

15750 — [Anr. ed.] 12°. (*R. Tottell,*) 1591. L(tp only, Ames I.513).O.C.BRISTOL².BTU.+; F.HN.HD.LC.MIN.

15751 — [Anr. ed.] Reuieu & change. 12°. *in æd. C. Yetswerti armigeri,* 1594. L.; HD.LC.Y(2).

15752 — [Anr. ed.] Reuieu & corrige. 12°. *in æd. J. Yetsweirt relictæ C. Yetsweirt aⁿ nuper defuncti,* [1595?] L³⁸. C⁵.; F.HN.HD.MIN.N.+

15753 — [Anr. ed.] 12°. [*A. Islip*] *in æd. T. Wight & B. Norton,* 1599. L.O.D².; HD.LC.MIN.NYS.

15754 — [Anr. ed.] 8°. [*A. Islip*] *in æd. T. Wight,* 1604. L.L³⁸(2). O.C¹⁹.STU.; F.HN.CAL⁵.CU.HD(3).
>   Some copies (L) are pr. on 4° paper.

15755 — [Anr. ed.] 8°. [*A. Islip?*] *f. the Co. of Statrs.,* 1608. L²². ETON.; CU.HD.
>   Some copies (L²²) are pr. on 4° paper. *See Court-Book C, p. 16.*

15755.3 — [Anr. ed.] 12°. [*A. Islip*] *f. the Co. of Statrs.,* 1608. L. O.O⁶.HOLK.STU.; F.HN.HD.LC.

15755.7 — [Anr. ed.] 8°. [*A. Islip?*] *f. the Co. of Statrs.,* 1612. L(2).L²².S.; HN.CU.LC.N.
>   Some copies (2 L, L²²) are pr. on 4° paper.

Littleton, *Sir* **Thomas**—Tenures—*Law French*—*cont.*

15756 — [Anr. ed.] 12°. [*A. Islip*?] *f. the Co. of Statrs.*, 1612. L.L⁸.O.C.C².+; CAL⁵.HD.LC.NYS.
15756.5 — [Anr. ed.] 8°. [*A. Islip*?] *f. the Co. of Statrs.*, 1617. LC.
15757 — [Anr. ed.] 12°. [*A. Islip*?] *f. the Co. of Statrs.*, 1617. L.O.C².D.NEP.+; F.HN.HD.PN.Y.+
15758 — [Anr. ed.] 16° in 8's. [*A. Islip*?] *f. the Co. of Statrs.*, 1621. Ent. to the English Stock 5 mr. 1620. L.O. O¹³.C².E².+; HN.HD.LC.MIN.Y.+
Prob. issued w. 19644.5.
15759 — [Anr. ed.] 16° in 8's. *assignes of J. More Esq.*, 1639. L. O.C.D².NLW.+; F.HN.HD.LC.Y.+
Probably issued w. 19645.

Tenures—*English*

15759.5 — Lyttelton tenures in Englysshe, [*sic*]. fol. [*J. Rastell*, 1523–25.] Raphael King catalogue 46 (1947), item 185(untraced).; Nash(6 leaves).
Collates A–I⁶ K–L⁴; fol. xxx, line 1: '& dye'. With Rastell's device, McK. 37, on L4ᵛ.
15760 — [Anr. ed.] fol. [*J. Rastell*, 1528–30.] L.
Collates A–I⁶ K⁸; fol. xxx, line 1: 'and dye'. With Rastell's device, McK. 37, on K8ᵛ.
15761 — [Anr. ed.] Lyttilton tenures truely translated. M.D.XXXVIII. 8°. *in aed. T. Berthelet*, [1538.] L. O¹⁴.; HN.HD.
15761.2 — [Anr. ed.] Lytelton tenures in Englysshe. 8°. (*Robert Redman*,) [1538?] F.N.
15761.4 — [Anr. ed.] Lyttelton tenures in Englysshe. 8°. (*Robert Redman*,) [1539?] ST.
15761.6 — [Anr. ed.] Littelton tenures neuly imprinted. 8°. [*T. Berthelet*?] 1539. Sotheby's, 9 Dec. 1935, lot 46 (bought by B. F. Stevens & Brown, Ltd.; cannot be traced).
15761.8 — [Anr. ed.] Lyttelton tenures in Englysshe. 8°. (*Roberte Redman*,) [1540?] C⁵.; HD.
15762 — [Anr. ed.] 8°. (*T. Petyt*,) [1541?] L.O.C².OS.ST(imp.).; COR.CU.HD.LC.MIN.+
15763 — [Anr. ed.] 8°. (*W. Myddylton*, 1544 (4 my.)) O.P.; F. HD.LC.
15764 — Now = 15732.9.
15764.5 — [Anr. ed.] 8°. [*T. Berthelet*,] 1545. C⁵.ST.; HD(2). (Formerly 15735)
15765 — [Anr. ed.] 8°. (*W. Powell*,) 1548 (6 jy.) L.C.; HD.
15765.5 — [Anr. ed.] 8°. (*w. Powell*,) 1551 (6 se.) L(tp only, Harl. 5919/127).; HD.MIN.
15766 — [Anr. ed.] 8°. (*R. Tottle*, 1556 (16 ap.)) HD.MIN. Collates A–S⁸ T²; in colophon 'day'.
15766.5 — [Anr. issue, w. T² reset.] (*R. Tottle*, 1556 (16 ap.)) HD. In colophon 'daye'.
15767 — [Anr. ed.] 8°. (*R. Tottell*, 1556 (16 ap.)) L(2, 1 imp.). P.; HN.HD.LC.MICH.MIN.
(Formerly also 15769) Collates A–S⁸.
15767.5 — [Anr. ed.] Truly translated. 8°. [*London*,] 1556. HD.LC. MIN.
This and the next 2 eds. collate A–Y⁸ Z⁶ like 15765 sq. and prob. should precede 15766.
15768 — [Anr. ed.] Trulye translated. 8°. (*T. Marshe*,) 1556. L.O.C(imp.).
15768.5 — [Anr. ed.] Truelye translated. 8°. (*T. Marshe*,) 1556. S.; HD.
15769 — = 15767.
15769.3 — [Anr. ed.] 8°. (*R. Tottill*, 1568.) USHAW.; HD.MIN.
15769.7 — [Anr. ed.] 8°. (*R. Tottyl*, 1572.) HD(imp.).
15770 — [Anr. ed.] 8°. (*R. Tottyl*, 1574.) L.O.C.; HN.HD.ILL.LC. Y.+
15770.5 — [Anr. ed.] 8°. (*R. Tottyl*, 1576.) L.ST(lacks tp).; HD. LC.NYS.
15771 — [Anr. ed.] 8°. (*R. Tottel*, 1581.) L.C².C¹⁰.C²⁰.CAR.+; CU.HD.MICH.PML.Y.+
15772 — [Anr. ed.] 8°. (*R. Tottill*, 1583.) C³.BIRM(imp.).HETH. London, Royal Institution of Chartered Surveyors.; CAL⁵.CU.HD.LC.MIN.+
15773 — [Anr. ed.] 8°. (*R. Tottill*, 1586.) L.R.; F.HN.HD.LC. MIN.
15773.5 — [Anr. ed.] 8°. (*by the assignes for* [sic] *R. Tottle*, 1586.) O.C⁹.; CAL⁵.HD.
15774 — [Anr. ed.] 8°. *R. Tottell*, 1592 (1593.) O¹⁸.HETH(imp.). OS(imp.).; HD.LC.MIN.NYS.Y.+
15775 — [Anr. ed.] Lately . . . amended. 8°. *C. Yetsweirt Esq.*, 1594. L.M².; F.HD.MIN.NYS.Y.+
15776 — [Anr. ed.] 8°. *J. Yetsweirt*, 1597. L.; HD.MIN.
15777 — [Anr. ed.] 8°. *T. Wight*, 1600. L.C.C¹⁹.HOLK.RD.+; F.HD. ILL.MIN.NY.+
15778 — [Anr. ed.] 8°. *T. Wight*, 1604. L.L²².O.E.S.+; F.HD. MICH.

Littleton, *Sir* **Thomas**—Tenures—*English*—*cont.*

15779 — [Anr. ed.] 8°. [*A. Islip*?] *f. the Co. of Statrs.*, 1608. L.O.C⁵.CHATS.E.+; F.HN.CU.HD.MICH.+
See Court-Book C, p. 16.
15780 — [Anr. ed.] 8°. [*A. Islip*?] *f. the Co. of Statrs.*, 1612. L⁴⁸.O.O⁷.C⁵.P.; HN.CU.HD.ILL.LC.+
15781 — [Anr. ed.] 8°. [*A. Islip*?] *f. the Co. of Statrs.*, 1616. O⁷. NLW. Town End, Troutbeck, near Ambleside, Westmorland.; HN.BO.CU.HD.LC.
15782 — [Anr. ed.] 8°. [*A. Islip*?] *f. the Co. of Statrs.*, 1621. Ent. to the English Stock 5 mr. 1620. L.C.E².LEEDS. RGU.+; HN.CU.HD.LC.Y(2).
15783 — [Anr. ed.] 8°. [*A. Islip*?] *f. the Co. of Statrs.*, 1627. L. O.C.DUL.YK.+; F.HN.CU.HD.WIS.+

———

15784 — The first part of the institutes of the lawes of England. Or, a commentarie upon Littleton [i.e. on his 'Tenores novelli'], authore E. Coke. fol. [*A. Islip*] *f. the Soc. of Statrs.*, 1628. L.O.C.D.NLW.+; F.HN.CU. HD.MIN.+
Contains text of Littleton's Tenures in Law French and English, w. Coke's commentary. *See also* 15789.
15785 — The second edition, corrected: with an alphabeticall table. 2 pts. fol. [*M. Flesher, J. Haviland, a. R. Young*] *assignes of J. More Esq., sold by R. More*, 1629. L.O.C.A.NLW.+; HN.CU.HD.LC.N.+
(Pt. 2 formerly 15788) The tp of pt. 2 is pr. on Ggggg4 of pt. 1; the text of pt. 2 collates a⁴ B–D⁴ e⁴ F–G⁴ H⁶.
15786 — The third edition, corrected. fol. *M. F[lesher] J. H[aviland] a. R. Y[oung] assignes of J. More Esq.*, 1633. L.O.C⁹.D.ETON.+; F.HN.CU.HD.ILL.+
15787 — The fourth edition. fol. *M. F[lesher] J. H[aviland] a. R. Y[oung] assignes of J. More Esq.*, 1639. L.O.C.E². M(deposit).+; F.HN.CU.HD.MICH.+
15788 — A table. 1629. = pt. 2 of 15785.
15789 — [Anr. ed.] A table to the first part of the Institutes. fol. [*M. Flesher, J. Haviland, a. R. Young, assignes of J. More*,] 1630. L.O.LINC.; HD.CAL⁵.
Collates [–]² B–Q² and prob. was intended to supplement copies of 15784.

LITURGIES

Most bibliographers are hesitant to deal with liturgies from the period before, during, and after the Reformation. For the Latin-Rite liturgies the variety of texts is the main source of confusion; for Anglican liturgies it is primarily the multiplicity of editions. For both the problem is compounded by the sad state of the majority of copies, some surviving only as fragments rescued from bindings and others having undergone contemporary, near-contemporary, or modern mutilation and/or sophistication: 'made-up' copies in every possible sense.

STC, with its limitations, cannot provide satisfactory discriminations for binding fragments or for severely imperfect copies or even many mildly imperfect or sophisticated ones. What it can do is to help indicate the large heaps into which the various texts can be sorted. I have attempted in this section, by means of various headnotes, to point out a few important things to look for, adapted to the different texts. Considerable work still needs to be done, but in the meantime I hope all bibliographers as apprehensive as I was when first coming to grips with this section will receive a modicum of encouragement from the headnotes. KFP

Following is a list of the headings, subheadings, and cross-references.

Liturgies—*Headings*—**Latin Rite**—*cont.*
Directorium: *see* 17720 sqq.

Diurnals	15861.7
Graduals	15862

Hortulus: *see* 13828.2 sqq.

Hours and Primers
   Salisbury and Reformed   15866
   York   16101.8

Hymns
   Salisbury—Hymns and Sequences with Glosses   16110
   Salisbury—Hymns with Music   16129
   York—Hymns with Music   16135

Legenda   16136

Litany: *see* 15707 sq.

Manuals
   Salisbury   16138
   York   16160
   England, Scotland, and Ireland   16161.5

Martyrology: *see* 17532 sq.

Missals
   Hereford   16163
   Salisbury   16164
   York   16220
   Special Offices   16224.5
   England   16225
   England, Scotland, and Ireland   16227

Ordinals
   Salisbury   16228
   York   16232.4
   Reformed Roman   16232.5

Primers: *see* Hours above

Processionals
   Salisbury   16232.6
   York   16250.5

Psalters   16253
   Appendix   after 16266

Rituals: *see* Manuals above

Sequences: *see* Hymns above

CHURCH OF ENGLAND

Book of Common Prayer
   English   16267
   Translations   16423
   Selections   16441
   Appendix   16448.7

Litany   16453

Order of Communion   16456.5

Epistles and Gospels: *see* 2964.5 sqq.

Catechism   16461

The Form and Manner of making Archbishops, Bishops, etc. (The Ordinal)   16462

State Services
   Accession Days   16479
   Gowrie Conspiracy   16489
   Gunpowder Plot   16493
   Special Forms of Prayer on various Occasions   16503

OTHER PROTESTANT CHURCHES

Geneva   16560

The Netherlands   16560.5

Common Prayer used by English Calvinistic Congregations abroad   16561

Common Prayer used by Foreign Congregations in London   16571

The Scottish Book of Common Order   16577

Episcopal Church of Scotland—Book of Common Prayer, 1637   16606

Liturgies—*cont.*

Latin Rite

Latin-Rite liturgies, as they survive in separate printed STC texts, can be roughly sorted into five categories: choir books, closet books, altar books, and two varieties of 'walking' books, and listed analytically thus:

Breviary: a compendium of all the services said in the choir of the church, with the following supplemental and extracted publications:
   Antiphoner: the music for all the services
   Diurnal: the daytime services
   Legenda: the 'lectiones' or readings for all the services
   Psalter: the Psalms of King David
   Hymns: the set songs, with and without music
   Ordinal: the directions (rubrics) for ordering the services

Hours or Primer: a collection of devotions primarily for use in a lay person's room or closet

Missal: a compendium of all the services said at the altar of the church, with the following supplemental and extracted publications:
   Gradual: the music for all the services
   Sequences: the set songs, without music

Manual: a walking book (the earlier ones with music) for use on small occasions

Processional: a walking book with music for use on large festival occasions

Further descriptions will be found in the headnotes to the alphabetical listings below. These descriptions are intended primarily for beginners who have just stepped into the maze and are limited to those sections that give the basic structure of a text or striking features that distinguish one text from another. For example, if you have at hand a Salisbury Breviary of the 2-vol. pattern, you will be able to go through its sections and understand why it may be in two volumes or in one, and you can also pursue varieties of Psalters: you will begin to see, in a very practical and limited sense, how these two texts work.

Because editions of texts according to Salisbury use are in the overwhelming majority, the headnotes are geared to Salisbury contents and patterns, which will differ in some details from other uses. For further information and for analyses of the parts of the Breviary and of its related texts *see* Henry Bradshaw, Appendix II, in volume III of *Breviarium ad Usum Insignis Ecclesiae Sarum*, ed. F. Procter and C. Wordsworth, Cambridge, 1886; also Appendix I in the same volume and the Introduction to volume II. For a general discussion of the whole group of Latin-Rite liturgies *see* Christopher Wordsworth and Henry Littlehales, *The Old Service-Books of the English Church*, London, 1904. I have relied heavily on both works in drawing up the headnotes, but I have also modified or amplified explanations where I felt my own particularly thorny experiences gave warrant. KFP

In the entries below '[Anr. ed.]' has generally been restricted to those editions occurring consecutively in which the first five words of the title are the same or the title-page is lacking. For a different use of the term in the Hours and Primers section *see* the headnote preceding 15866.

ANTIPHONERS

These provide the music and directions (rubrics) for the services said in the choir, e.g. antiphons, responses, hymns, canticles, etc., and follow the 2-vol. pattern of the Breviary.

15790   Antiphonale ad vsū ecclesie Sa⁊. [Pars hiemalis.] fol. (*in alma Parisiorū acad., per w. hopyliū, imp*. **F**. byrckman [*in* London,] 1519.) L(imp.).O³.C.C²(frags.).DNPK (imp.).
   The C copy has the Psalter in the 'Hymn⁹' setting noted in 15790a.

15790a   Antiphōarij ad vsū Sa⁊ volumē secūdū: vulgo pars estiualis nūcupata. fol. (*in alma Parisiorū acad., per w. hopyliū, imp. F. byrckman* [*in* London,] 1520.) L.O (frags.).C.LIV.M.+
   L has on BB6ᵛ a repetition of the tp cut beneath which is: *Venales habetur Londonij a F. Byrckman*, not present in the C copies. The Psalter is in 2 settings; both at C: a3ʳ last word: 'Hymn⁹' (Syn. 2. 51.5) or 'agitur' (Rel.bb.51.2, Sel.2.25). C also has 2 leaves (a1,8) used as proof for the Psalter.

Liturgies—Latin Rite—*cont.*

BREVIARIES

These contain the daily services said in the choir, throughout the year. There are the following major sections:

Kal.   Kalendar of fixed festivals, with instructions for finding when the movable feasts occur, sometimes with information keyed to 'this present year. . . .'

Temp.   Temporale or Proprium de Tempore: services largely reserved for seasonal festivals, e.g. Advent (4th Sunday before Christmas), Easter, Trinity (8th Sunday after Easter), etc.

Pstr.   Psalter, with the Psalms of King David arranged for complete reading in the course of each week (*see* further details in the headnote for Psalters at 16253), followed by the Litany and the Vigiliae Mortuorum.

Com.SS.   Commune Sanctorum: services which are common to a number of occasions or frequently repeated, e.g. for an apostle, for several martyrs, for the dedication of a church; also selections of the mass from the Missal. This section was the latest to reach a regularized form, and early editions display considerable variety.

Prop.SS.   Proprium Sanctorum or Sanctorale: services for fixed festivals, e.g. St. Andrew's Eve, 29 November.

Totum   The folio Great Breviaries, e.g. 15812, and the earliest editions in the smaller sizes have the sections ordered in the above pattern, called *Totum*, with the Temporale and Proprium Sanctorum each having the services for the whole year. Some folio editions, e.g. 15805.5, 15812, 15830, have at the end the Accentuarium on the pronunciation of vowels, which more often is found with Missals.

2 vols.   In order to publish a volume of more manageable weight for carrying around (Portiforium), the Temporale and Proprium Sanctorum were each divided into a winter part (P.H., pars hiemalis) and a summer part (P.E., pars estivalis), and they were combined with the Kalendar, Psalter, and the Commune Sanctorum to form the following pattern in the Salisbury Breviaries:

P.H.   Temporale from Advent (4th Sunday before Christmas) to the week following Pentecost (Whitsun, 7th Sunday after Easter; latest possible date, 13 June).
Kalendar, Psalter, and Commune Sanctorum complete.
Proprium Sanctorum from St. Andrew's Eve (29 November) to the festival of Marcus and Marcellus (18 June).

P.E.   Temporale from the Eve of Trinity Sunday (8th Sunday after Easter; earliest possible date, 17 May).
Kalendar, Psalter, and Commune Sanctorum complete.
Proprium Sanctorum from St. Dunstan's day (18 May) to the festival of Saturninus and Sisinnius (29 November).

Note that the Kalendar, Psalter, and Commune Sanctorum were usually printed in double quantities so that these sections are in the same setting in all but a few Breviaries following the 2-vol. pattern. Regarding the early Psalters which are specifically P.H. or P.E. *see* the headnote at 16253. The Kalendar is sometimes printed in the same quire as the title-page, in which case it is bound first in each volume and distinguished as being P.H. or P.E. As copies survive today, occasionally one duplicate set of the Kalendar, Psalter, and Commune Sanctorum has been removed and the remainder bound as one volume, with a resulting pattern like the following: Temp.-P.H., Prop.SS.-P.H. | Kal., Pstr., Com.SS. | Temp.-P.E., Prop.SS.-P.E.

Aberdeen

15791   Breuiarij Aberdonēsis ad per celebris eccl'ie Scotoꝛ vsum pars hyemalis (estiualis). 2 vols. 8⁰. *ī Edībȳrgēsi oppido, īp. w. chepmā,* [P.H.:] 1509 (id. fb.) [P.E.:] (1510 (4 jn.)) L(P.E., imp.).A(imp.). E(imp.).E²(imp.). Lord Strathmore (imp.). +

15791.5   *Officium Novum.* [Begins A1ʳ:] Compassio beate Marie In festo dolorose compassionis beate Marie. quod celebratur ānuatim feria quarta post dominicam in ramis palmarñ [*sic*]. 8⁰. (*Edinburgi, ꝑ J. Story, mandato K. Stule,*) [c. 1520.] Lord Strathmore.

Abingdon, Benedictine Abbey

15792   Portiforium. 2 vols. 4⁰. (*ī monasterio Abēdonensi, per J. Scholarem,* 1528 (12 se.)) O¹⁰(imp.).C³(P.E., imp.).

Hereford

15793   Breuiariū secundū vsum herford'. [Pars estivalis.] 8⁰. [Pp3ʳ:] (*in Rothomageñ emporio [P. Olivier a. J. Mauditier,] imp. I. haghe [in London, at the expenses of Margaret, Countess of Richmond,]* 1505 (2 non. au.)) O.

St. Albans, Benedictine Abbey

15793.5   [Begins a1ʳ:] De aduentu. Primo sciendum ē qd' de oībus festis. . . . 2 vols. 8⁰. [*St. Albans, J. Herford,* c. 1535.] L(C.110.a.27).

Salisbury

15794   [Breviarium ad usum Sarum.] *Totum?* 4⁰. [*Southern Netherlands,* c. 1475 ?] O(frags.).O⁴(frags., missing). c(frags.). Lincoln, Grammar School Library (frags.). Duff 60.

15795   [Begins a2ʳ:] In nomine. . . . Incipit ordo breuiarij: secundum morem ecclesie Sarum: Anglicane. *Totum.* 8⁰. (*Venetijs, per R. de nouimagio,* 1483 (10 kal. oc.)) PARIS. Duff 61.

15795.5   [Begins a2ʳ:] In nomine. . . . Incipit ordo breuiarii scd'm morē ecclīe Saꝛ anglicane: in parte hyemali. 8⁰. (*Rothomagi, per M[artin] morin,* [1492 ?] (4 non. jn.)) O(lacks 2 leaves). Duff 69.
    (Formerly 15803)

15796   — Now = 15801.5.

15797   Breuiariū scd'm morem ecclesie Sarum. *Totum.* 8⁰. [*Venice, J. Hertzog de Landoia f. F. Egmont a. G. Barrevelt in London,* 1494.] L²(4 leaves of Temp.: Frag. No. 44; and ff. 204–9 of Prop.SS.).O(Temp., Pstr., Com.SS., imp.).O⁵(tp and 7 leaves of Temp.). Duff 63, 64.
    (Formerly also 15798)

15798   — = 15797.

15799   Breuiariū scd'm vsum Sarum. *Totum.* 8⁰. (*in paris'. suburbiis, per P. Leuet,* 1494 (3 id. fb.)) O⁴(2 leaves). c(lacks 2 leaves).D(imp.). Duff 65.

15800   — [Anr. ed.] *Totum.* fol. [*Venice, J. Hertzog de Landoia,* 1494.] c(10 leaves). Duff 66.

15801   Breuiarij secūdum morem Sarū pars estiualis. 16⁰ in 8's. (*Venetijs, per J. Hertzog de Landoia [f. F. Egmont a. G. Barrevelt in London,]* 1495 (cal. mr.)) O.O⁴(frags., missing). Duff 67.

15801.5   [f. 329ʳ begins:] Incipit propriū de sanctis tpe estiuali. 8⁰. [*Venice, J. Hertzog de Landoia f. F. Egmont a. G. Barrevelt in London,* 1495 ?] c⁵(ff. 329–36 only). Duff 62.
    (Formerly 15796)

15802   [B]Reuiarium ad vsum Saꝛ. *Totum.* fol. (*Rothomagensis, ere & īpensa J. richardi, industriaꝗ Martini Morin,* 1496 (3 no.)) L¹⁸(30 imp. leaves).DUR⁵(frags.).E² (imp.). Duff 68.
    a1ʳ heading at top of 1st column: 'In nomine . . . Incipit ordo breuiarii scd'm/ morē et ꞇsuetudinē eccl'e Saꝛ āglicane . . .'; cf. 15805.4.

15803   — Now = 15795.5.

15804   — [Anr. ed.] 2 vols. 8⁰. (*parisius,* [*J. Dupré,*] 1499.) L (P.E., imp.).c⁵(P.H., imp.).c⁸(imp.).PARIS(imp.). Duff 70.

15805   Breuiarium secūdū vsum ecclesie Sarum. 2 vols. 8⁰. (*imp. T. martini, in Louaniensiū acad.,* 1499 (4 cal. jn.)) Antwerp, Musée Plantin. Duff 71.

15805.1   — [Anr. ed.] 2 vols. 8⁰. (*Parisii, industria J. Philippi, exp. J. huuyn [in Rouen,]* 1501 (16 au.)) OS(P.E., lacks tp)

15805.2   — [Anr. ed.] 2 vols. 8⁰. [*London?* c. 1505.] USHAW(XVII. G.4.3, frag. of Pstr., AA(lombardic)⁸, w. only P.E. antiphons).

15805.4   [a1ʳ heading at top of 1st column:] In nomine . . . Incipit ordo breuiarii scd'm/ morē & ꞇsuetudinē eccl'e Saꝛ āglicane. *Totum.* fol. [*Paris, W. Hopyl,* c. 1505.] Rogers(imp.).
    Cf. 15802, 15812.

15805.5   — [Anr. ed.] *Totum.* fol. (*Parisius, per T. keruer, ere et imp. W. de worde & Michaelis Morin mercatoruꝛ Londoniis,* 1506 (17 ja.)) F(29 leaves, frags. of Kal., Pstr., Prop.SS., Accentuarium).

15805.7   Portiforium seu breuiarium ad vsum īsignis ecclīe sarū. 2 vols. 8⁰. (*Rothomagi, cura P. Violette, imp. J. biēayse [in Paris,]* 1506 (3 de.)) O⁵(P.H.).

15805.9   [Heading A2ʳ:] Breuiarii vna cū ordinali scd'm vsum Sarum pars estiualis. 8⁰. [*Paris,* c. 1506.] AMP(imp.).

15806 Portiforii ad vsuȝ Sarum . . . pars hyemalis (estiualis.) 2 vols. 8°. (*Parhysiis, exp. W. de worde bibliopole Lōdoniis*, 1507 (11 cal. jy.)) o(imp.).

15806a [Ends q8ᵛ:] Breuiariū secundū vsum Sarum. [Pars estiualis.] 4° in 8's. (*arte R. Pynson, imp. Margarete comitisse Richemondie et derbie*, 1507 (25 au.)) o(Masses only).M(imp.).; PML(imp.).
　　Collation of the P.E. is: aa–gg⁸ (Temp.), A⁸ (Kal.), A–F⁸ G⁶ H⁴ (Pstr., w. P.E. antiphons only), A–C⁸ (Masses), ā⁸ ē⁸ ī⁴ (Com.SS.), kk⁴ (Etheldrede, St. Thomas, BVM from Purification to Advent), ƥ⁸ (Dedic. church, St. Chad); a–q⁸ (Prop.SS.).

15807 [Breviarium secundum usum Sarum. Pars hiemalis.] 4° in 8's. [*R. Pynson*, 1507?] o(4 leaves of Prop.SS.).c (ū2,7 of Com.SS.). Private owner(imp.).; HD(h4,5 of Temp.).
　　The collation of the P.H. private copy is: a–t⁸ (Temp., all before d2 lacking), A⁸ (Kal., in same setting as 15806a), A–H⁸ I⁴ (Pstr., w. P.H. antiphons only), ā⁸ ē⁸ ī⁸ ō⁸ ū⁸ aa–gg⁸ (Com.SS., including St. Thomas, BVM from Advent to Purification, Dedic. church, St. Chad and ending aa3ʳ, where Prop.SS. begins).

15808 Portiforium seu breuiarium, ad legitimum Sarisburiēsis ecclesie ritū. Pars estiualis. 4° in 8's. [*Paris,*] *Venūdant̄ Lōdoniis ap. w. de worde*, (1509 (11 kl'. ja.)) o(2 imp.).c⁵.

15809 Portiforium seu breuiarium ad vsum īsignis ecclesie Sarum. 2 vols. 8°. (*Parisius*, [*J. Ferrebouc a. J. Bienayse,*] 1510 [P.H.:] (10 ja.) [P.E.:] (2 cal. fb.)) L(P.E., imp.).o(tp only).BUTE(P.H.).

15810 Portiforiū seu breuiariū ad vsū īsignis eccl'e Sarū. 2 vols. 8°. (*Parisiⁱ, per T. keruer, imp. F. Byrckman* [*in London,*] 1514 (25 ja.)) o.

15811 — [Anr. ed. ✠2ʳ begins:] KL. Prima dies mensis [etc.] 2 vols. 8°. [*Paris, T. Kerver*, 1515?] L(Kal. and Pstr. only).

15811.5 — [Anr. ed.] 2 vols. 8°. (*Parisius*, [*J. Ferrebouc a. J. Bienayse,*] 1515 (10 kal. my.)) c⁹(P.E., imp.).os (P.E.).
　　The c⁹ copy has added to the colophon: īp. R. mace [*in Caen or Rouen.*]

15812 Breuiariū seu horariū domesticū: . . . ad vsum Saƥ. Totum. fol. (*in Parisiorū acad.,* [*W. Hopyl,*] *imp. F. byrckman* [*in London,*]) 1516. o.c(frag.).A.D.DNPK.
　　Foliated; a1ʳ heading at top of 1st column: 'In nomine . . . Incipit ordo breuiarij secūdū more et consuetudinē/ eccl'ie Saƥ anglicane'; cf. 15813, 15805.4.

15813 — [Anr. ed.] Totum. fol. [*Paris, W. Hopyl f. F. Byrckman in London*, 1516?] o(top half of 4 leaves only, of Prop.SS. for 4–17 July).
　　No foliation; possibly earlier than 15812.

15814 Portiforium seu breuiarium ad vsum insignis ecclesie Sarū. 2 vols. 8°. [P.H. tp:] 1518; [P.H. col.:] (1518 (non. fb.)) [P.E. col.:] (*Parisiis*, 1518 (12 fb.)) c(leaf f3 of Pstr. only, imp.).ST(P.E.). Private owner (P.H.).

15815 Portiforium seu breuiarium ad vsum īsignis ecclesie Sarum. 2 vols. 8°. [*Paris*, 1518?] c(P.H., imp.).

15816 Portiforiū seu breuiariū ad īsignis Sarisburiēsis ecclesie vsum. 2 vols. 4° in 8's. [P.E.:] (*in alma vniuersitate Parisiēñ, per N. hygman, imp. F. regnault* [*in Paris*] *& F. Byrckmā* [*in London,*] 1519 [P.H.:] (7 fb.)) L(P.E.).o(P.H.).o²⁴.c(imp.).WOR.

15817 [Begins aa2ʳ:] In dei nōīe amen Breuiarij vna cum ordinali secundum vsum Sarum pars estiualis. 4°. [*Paris?* 1520?] o(aa2,3 only).

15818 — [Anr. ed.] 2 vols. 8°. (*parisijs*, [*Y. Bonhomme, the widow of*] *T. Keruer, imp. F. Byrckmā* [*in London,*] 1524 [P.H.:] (12 jn.) [P.E.:] (24 oc.)) c(Kal. only, bd. w. 15860).os(P.E.).YK.

15818.5 — [Anr. ed.] 2 vols. 16° in 8's. [*Antwerp, C. Ruremond f.*] *P. Kaetȝ* [*in London,*] 1524. o(P.H., imp.).

15819 — [Anr. ed.] 2 vols. 16° in 8's. [P.H.:] ([*Paris,*] *in off.* [*Y. Bonhomme,*] *vidue T. Keruer, imp. F. byrckman* [*in London,*] 1525 (3 kal. se.)) c(P.E., imp., Syn.8.52.27). Lord Kenyon(P.H., imp.).
　　Psalter, b2ʳ, 2nd column, last line: 'terio & cithara.'; cf. 15821a.

15820 — [Anr. ed.] 2 vols. 16° in 8's. (*Rothomagi,* [*P. Olivier,*] *imp. F. Regnault, Parisius*, 1525 (10 mr.)) c(P.E., imp., Rit.e.252.1).
　　P.E. Temporale, A3ʳ last line ends: 'sctā ma-'.

15821 — [Anr. ed.] 2 vols. 16° in 8's. (*Rothomagi,* [*P. Olivier,*] *imp. F. Regnault, Parisius*, 1525 (10 mr.)) L(P.E., imp.). Edinburgh, Theological College(P.E.).
　　P.E. Temporale, A3ʳ last line ends: 'scā ma'.

15821a — [Anr. ed.] 2 vols. 16° in 8's. [*Paris, Y. Bonhomme, the widow of T. Kerver*, after 1525.] c(P.E., imp., Rit. e.252.2).
　　Psalter, b2ʳ, 2nd column, last line: 'rio et cythara.'; cf. 15819, 15828.

15822 Portiforium seu breuiarium ad insignis Sarisburiēsis ecclesie vsum. Pars estiualis (hiemalis.) 2 vols. 4° in 8's. [P.H.:] (*Antwerpie, labore C. Ruremundensis, imp. F. Bryckman* [*in London,*]) 1525 (1526 (22 mr.)) L(P.H., imp.).c(imp.).WOR(P.H., imp.).SCL(P.E., imp.). Copenhagen RL(P.E., imp.).
　　The P.E. colophon has '*per C. Endouiēsem* [i.e. *Ruremond,*] . . . 1525.'

15822a — [Anr. ed.] 2 vols. 16° in 8's. [*Paris, J. Kerbriant or Huguelin*, before 1528.] c(P.H., imp.).
　　35 lines to a column.

15823 Portiforiū seu breuiariū ad vsum insignis eccl'ie Sarū. 2 vols. 16° in 8's. (*Parisijs, opera J. Kaerbriand: siue huguelin, imp. J. parui,*) 1528 (23 ap.) c.
　　34 lines to a column.

15824 Portiforiū seu breuiarium ad vsum ecclesie Sarisburiēsis. 2 vols. 4° in 8's. (*Parisijs, per F. Regnault*, 1528.) L (tp, Kal., Pstr. only).o(P.E., 3 imp. copies).
　　(Formerly also 15825)

15825 — = 15824.

15826 — [Anr. ed.] 2 vols. 8°. (*Parisijs, in ed. F. Regnault*, 1528 (18 my.)) L(P.E.).c.(P.E., imp.).; STL (P.H., imp.).
　　𝔄

15827 — = 15829.

15828 [Ends UU8ʳ:] Finis partis estiualis breuiarij insignis ecclesie Saƥ. 16° in 8's. (*Parisijs, arte* [*Y. Bonhomme*] *vidue T. Keruer*, 1530 (3 cal. no.)) o(imp.).
　　Psalter, b2ʳ, 2nd column, last line: 'rio et cithara.'; cf. 15821a.

15829 Portiforiū seu breuiariū ad vsum ecclesie Sarisburiēsis. 2 vols. 8°. [*Paris, J. Petit,*] (*imp.* [*Y. Bonhomme*] *vidue T. Keruer,*) 1530. o(imp.).c(P.H., imp.).
　　(Formerly also 15827.)

15830 Breuiariū seu horariū domesticū. Totum. fol. (*ere et īp. C. cheuallon & F. regnault in Parisiorū acad.,*) 1531. L.L².o¹⁰.C.C².+

15831 Portiforium seu breuiariū ad vsuȝ ecclesie Sarisbur'. 2 vols. 16° in 8's. (*Parisijs, per F. Regnault*) *Venūdatur Parisijs ap. F. Regnault*, 1532 (1531.) c(P.E. only: 2 imp.).os(P.E.).

15832 Portiforium seu breuiarium ad vsum ecclesie Sarisburiensis. 2 vols. 8°. (*Parisijs, p̄ F. Regnault*) *Venundat̄ Parisijs, ap. F. Regnault*, 1533. o(P.H.).o²⁷(P.E., tp and Kal. only).c(P.H.).USHAW(P.E., imp., XVIII.D. 7.14).

15833 Portiforiū seu breuiarium ad vsum ecclesie Sarisburiēsis. 2 vols. 4° in 8's. [P.H. col.:] (*Parisijs, per F. Regnault*, 1535); [P.E. col.:] (*in alma uniuersitate Parisiēñ., p̄ F. regnault*, 1535.) L(P.H. only: 2 copies).L²(P.E.). o(2, 1 imp.; plus P.H., imp.).c(P.E.).; F(P.E.).CH (P.E.).
　　The tp has separate border pieces w. Regnault's inits. The P.E. colophon on oo8ʳ is erroneously reprinted in 15840. The Psalter is in 2 settings, bd. indiscriminately w. P.H. or P.E.; both at o.

———

15833.5 Portiforium, seu breuiariū, ad vsum insignis ecclīe Sarisburiensis nouiter impressum. 2 vols. 16° in 8's. [P.E. col.:] (*per E. whytchurche*, 1541.) L⁴(P.E.).
　　The tp has border McK. & F. 46. This is the 1st ed. to be expurgated of all references to the authority of Rome over the English church.

15834 — [Anr. issue, w. cancel tpp:] Portiforiū secundū vsum Sarū, nouiter impressum & a plurimis purgatū mēdis. In quo nomen Romano pontifici falso ascriptum omittit̄, vna cum aliis que christianissimo nostri regis statuto repugnant. *per E. Whytchurch*, 1541 [P.H. col.:] (*ap. E. Whitchurche*, 1541 (fb.)) L.O (P.E.).o¹⁴.c.ST(P.E.).
　　The P.H. tp has McK. & F. 41; the P.E. tp has McK. & F. 33; for the P.E. colophon see 15833.5.

15835 — [Anr. ed.] 2 vols. 8°. [P.H.:] *per R. Grafton et E. whitchurch*, 1544, (*in ed. E. Whitchurche, veneunt in off. G. Telotson*, 1543 (de.)); [P.E.:] *per R. Grafton et*

Liturgies—**Latin Rite**—Breviaries—*Salisbury—cont.*
    E. Whitchurch, 1544, (*per R. Grafton, to bee solde by*
    W. Telotsō, 1544.) L.O.O³¹(P.H.).M²(P.E.).

15836 Portiforium seu breuiariū ad vsum insignis ecclesie Saris-
    buriensis. 2 vols. 8°. *Parisiis, ap.* (*M. Boursette*)
    viduam F. Regnault, 1554 (1555.) L.O.O³(imp.).c
    (lacks P.H. tp)*.os(P.H.).+; F(1 imp.*, plus P.E.).
    HN.ILL(lacks P.H. tp)*.STL(P.E., imp.).Y. 𝔄
15837 — [A variant, w. P.H. tp dated:] 1555. L.O.BURY.DUR
    (Bamb.).LINC.+; PML.
15838 — = 15839.
15839 Portiforium seu breuiarium, ad insignis Sarisburiensis,
    ecclesie vsum. 2 vols. 4° in 8's. *Londini,* 1555 [P.H.
    col.:] (*per J. Kyngston et H. Sutton,* 1555 (7 mr.))
    L(P.E., C.35.g.20).O.C⁶(P.H., imp.).CASHEL.ST.+; N.
    PML.
       (Formerly also 15838) The P.E. colophon (Ii6ᵛ)
      has no imprint or date.
15840 Portiforiū seu breuiarium ad vsum ecclesie Sarisburiensis.
    2 vols. 4° in 8's. [*R. Caly,*] 1555 [P.E. col.:] (*in alma*
    vniuersitate Parisieñ. p F. regnault, 1535.) L.O.C.C³.
    M.+; HN(P.H.).PML.
       (Formerly also 15841) The tp has border McK. &
      F. 48β w. Caly's inits. This is a reprint of 15833,
      including the P.E. colophon, which is on qq7ᵛ in
      the present ed. The P.H. has a 2-line explicit on
      G8ᵛ (o) or omits it (Rogers). The Psalter is in
      2 settings bd. indiscriminately; a1ᵛ column 1 ends:
      'saluum' (P, P.H.; c, P.E.) or 'meus' (c, P.H.).
15841 — = 15840.
15842 Portiforium seu breuiarium, ad insignis Sarisburiensis,
    ecclesie vsum. 2 vols. 4° in 8's. *per J. Kyngston & H.*
    Sutton, 1556 [P.H. col.:] (7 mr.) L(P.H.: C.35.g.19
    and C.35.g.22(1), imp.; P.E.: C.35.g.22(2), lacking
    tp).O.C.DE.ST.+; HN(P.E., w. tp and Kal. of 15840).
    HD.NY(P.H.).
       (Formerly also 15843) The P.E. colophon (Oo6ᵛ)
      has no imprint or date.
15843 — = 15842.
15844 Portiforium seu breuiarium ad īsignis Sarisbu̅rie̅sis eccle-
    sie vsum. 2 vols. 4° in 8's. [Tpp:] *Parisijs, ap. G.*
    Merlin, 1556; or *Parisijs, ap. M. Boursette viduam*
    F. regnault, 1556; [P.E. colophon:] (*industria J.*
    Amazeur pro G. Merlin.) L(P.H.).O(P.H.).C.D²(lacks
    tp of P.E.).WN.+; F(P.H.).
       (Formerly also 15845) The P.H. tp and colophon
      have Merlin's name and device (L, O, C, D², WN, F)
      or Boursette's (Rogers). The P.E. tp has Merlin's
      name and device (O³¹, C, WN) or Boursette's, seen
      by F. S. Ferguson in the copy sold at Sotheby's
      19 March 1936, lot 486 (W. Herbert–Faulkner–
      Methuen), not traced; it had Merlin's name in the
      P.E. colophon.
15845 — = 15844.
15846 — [Anr. ed.] 2 vols. 16° in 8's. *Rothomagi, ap. R. valen-*
    tinum & Florentium filium eius, 1556. L.L²(imp.).O
    (P.E.).C(P.E., imp.).D(imp.).+
15847 — [Anr. ed.] 2 vols. 8°. *Parisiis, ap. G. Merlin,* [P.H.:]
    1556, [P.E.:] 1557; [P.H. col.:] (*ex typog. J. le Blanc*
    pro G. Merlin, 1556) [P.E. col.:] (*typis J. le Blanc*
    pro G. Merlin, 1557.) L.L¹³.O.C.USHAW.+; F.BO.

15847.3 *Officia Nova.* [Begins a1ʳ:] Cōmemoracō lamētacōis sine
    [*sic*] cōpassiōis btē Marie ī morte filij . . . q̄ celebrari
    debet feria sexta īmediate p̄cedēte domīcā ī passione.
    4° in 8's. [*Westminster, W. Caxton,* 1490.] c³(b1,
    8 only). Ghent U. Duff 105.
       (Formerly 17534)

15848 [Festum visitationis beatae Mariae virginis. Celebrated
    2 July. Ends:] . . . cum gaudio tandem/ et exultatiōe
    ppetua renascamur. Per xp̄m̄/ dominū nostrū/ 4°.
    [*Westminster, W. Caxton,* 1480?] L(last 7 leaves).
    Duff 148.
       26 lines.
15849 — [Anr. ed.] 4°. [*W. de Machlinia,* c. 1488.] o(2 leaves).
    Duff 149.
       24 lines.
15850 — [Anr. ed. Begins a2ʳ:] de diuina iusticia seruos hūiles
    exultans mīa. ps. Magnificat [etc.] 4° in 8's. [*R.*
    Pynson, 1495?] L(imp.). Not in Duff.

Liturgies—**Latin Rite**—Breviaries—*Salisbury—cont.*

15851 Festum dulcissimi nominis iesu fiat septimo idus Augusti.
    4° in 8's. (*per me R. Pinson,*) [1493?] L. Duff 143.
15852 — [Anr. ed.] Festū dulcissimi nominis Ihesu. 4° in 8's.
    (*per R. Pynson,*) [1497.] L. Duff 144.
15853 [Festum transfigurationis Jesu Christi. Begins a1ʳ:]
    Octauo Idus Augusti fiat offm̄ [etc.] 4° in 8's. [*W. de*
    Machlinia, c. 1488.] LONGLEAT. Duff 145.
15854 — [Anr. ed. Begins a1ʳ:] Octauo Id⁹ Augusti fiat seruit'
    [etc.] 4° ⁶·⁴. [*Westminster,*] (*Caxton me fieri fecit,*)
    [1491?] L. Duff 146.
15855 — [Anr. ed. Begins A2ʳ:] Octauo idus Augusti fiat
    seruiciū [etc.] 4° ⁶·⁴. (*per me R. Pynson,*) [1496.] L
    (lacks 1st leaf). Duff 147.

York

15856 Breuiariū scd'm vsum ecclesie Eboracensis. *Totum.* 8°.
    (*venetijs, p J. hāman de Landoia dictuȝ hertzog, imp.*
    F. egmundt [*in London,*] 1493 (kal. my.)) L(leaves
    49–56, 129–35 only).o(lacks last 2 leaves).c(frags.).
    USHAW(frags.). St. Helen's Church, Ashby-de-la-
    Zouch, Leics.(imp.). Duff 59.
15857 [Begins a2ʳ:] In nomine . . . Incipit ordo Breuarii [*sic*]
    secundū morē & cōsuetudinē ecclesie Eboraceñ.
    2 vols. 8°. [*Rouen, P. Violette,* c. 1507.] c(imp.).
15858 Breuiarium ad vsum insigis [*sic*] metropolitane ecclesie
    Eboracēsis. 2 vols. 8°. *in Parrhisiensi acad., ī ed. F.*
    Regnault, exp. J. Gascheti in Eboracēsi ciuitate;
    1526 (15 oc.) L(P.H., imp.).o(P.H., imp., plus 8
    leaves of P.E. bd. w. 16251).c(P.E. Temp. only,
    bd. w. 15860).BUTE(P.H.).YK.
15859 Breuiarium insignis ac metropolitane ecclesie Eboracēsis.
    2 vols. 16° in 8's. *in Parisiorū acad., exp. F. Regnault*
    et J. Gascheti in Eboracensi ciuitate, 1533 (22 au.)
    L(imp.).
15860 — [Anr. ed.] 2 vols. 8°. [*Rouen,* 1555?] c(imp.).
       The c P.E. vol. has the Temporale replaced by
      that of 15858 and the Kalendar by that of 15818.
15861 *Officium Novum.* [Supplement to the Sanctorale. Text
    begins:] PAstor cesus ī gregis medio pacem emet
    cruoris precio. 8°. (*Eboȝ, per me U. Mylner,*) [1513?]
    c³(imp.).

Appendix

The general rubriques of the breviarie, put into English.
  1617. See 16232.5.

DIRECTORIUM

See 17720 sqq.

DIURNALS

These consist of the day services (Lauds–Vespers) from the various
sections of the Breviary, except for the Psalter, which is complete.
They follow the *Totum* pattern of the Breviary.

15861.7 Diurnale Sarum. [Ed.] (Gulielmus cowper.) 16° in 8's.
    (*in alma Parisiorum acad.,* [*W. Hopyl,*] imp. H.
    Jacobi, Londonii [*a. F. Byrckman,*] 1512.) L².
       The verso of the colophon leaf has Byrckman's
      device and Hopyl's motto: 'Fortuna opes . . .'

15861.8 Sarisburiensis jornalis siue diurnalis. 16° in 8's. (*Parrhysiis,*
    exp. F. Regnault, 1528 (3 se.)) Private owner.

GRADUALS

These provide the music and directions (rubrics) for the altar
services, including the Gregorian (e.g. introits and offertories),
Scriptural, and other texts such as Sequences. They follow the
pattern of the Missal: Temporale, Proprium Sanctorum, Commune Sanctorum.

15862 Graduale ad consuetudinē Sarum. fol. *in alma Parisiorū*
    acad., (*opera W. hopylii,*) imp. W. Bretton ciuis Lon-
    doneñ, Venundētur Londoñ., ap. [H. *Jacobi a. J.*
    Pelgrim,] 1508 (1507 (4 id. ap.)) HN.
15863 Graduale secundū morem & cōsuetudinem preclare eccle-
    sie Sarum. fol. *in alma Parisiorū acad.,* (*in off. N.*
    Preuost, imp. w. de worde, J. Renis [i.e. *Reynes,*] &
    L. suethon [i.e. *Sutton,* all in London,]) 1527 (17 cal.
    ja.) O.O³.O⁵(frag.).
15864 Graduale ad verā et integrā preclare ecclesie Sarū con-
    suetudinē. fol. *Parisijs,* (*in off. N. Preuost,*) *Venun-*
    datur Londonij a F. Byrckman, 1528 (6 cal. jy.) L.
    O(1 leaf).O⁹(frag.).C.LIV.+

Liturgies—Latin Rite—GRADUALS—*cont.*

15865 Graduale ad vsū ecclesie Sarisburiensis. fol. (*Parisijs, in off. N. Preuost, imp. F. Regnault,*) *Venundatur Londonij ap. R. Redman, et Parisijs ap. F. Regnault,* 1532 (6 cal. jy.) L.L¹³(tp only).O. Dundee, Town Council (12 leaves). Lord Kenyon.

HORTULUS

See 13828.2 sqq.

HOURS (OR OFFICE) OF THE BLESSED VIRGIN AND PRIMERS

These are primarily books of private devotion, although some of their contents could be used in services said in the choir. The main components, found in all Salisbury Hours up to 1534 and most of them thereafter, are:

Hours of the B.V.M. from Purification to Advent (Matins–Compline)
Seven Penitential Psalms
Fifteen Gradual Psalms
Litany
Vigiliae Mortuorum (Dirige)
Commendations of Souls

All editions have a Kalendar of fixed festivals at the beginning, frequently preceded or followed by an Almanack giving the date of Easter for a range of years. When editions listed below lack or omit any date on the title-page or in the colophon, the first year from the Almanack, if present, has usually been supplied. Supplementary sets of Hours, prayers, and other material differ from edition to edition, and for abstracts of the contents *see* Edgar Hoskins, *Horae Beatae Mariae Virginis or Sarum and York Primers and Primers of the Reformed Roman Use*, London, 1901, the item numbers from which are cited in the entries below. A few Hoskins items are to be found in STC under the headings 'Hortulus' (13828.2) and 'Primer' (20373 sqq.). A few more have been omitted as their present location could not be traced or they were too fragmentary.

The Hours and Primers are listed in purely chronological order. All editions up to 1534 and many later ones have the main components mentioned above in Latin, though some of the headings and an increasing number of the supplemental prayers and other material are in English. These editions, in spite of other variations, have been called '[Anr. ed.]' below when they immediately follow another Latin edition. In contrast, Primers with the main components in English or in English and Latin (the latter either in parallel columns or on facing pages) are represented by several distinct versions, reflecting varying shades of religious opinion and with increasing omissions of, or alterations to, the main components themselves. Only those that are known to be the same version as that immediately preceding are referred to as '[Anr. ed.]'. While some indication of the versions followed is given below, for a detailed treatment of the different sources *see* Charles Butterworth, *The English Primers (1529–1545)*, Philadelphia, 1953.

Salisbury and Reformed

15866 Now = 15926.5.
15867 [Horae ad usum Sarum.] 8°. [*Westminster, W. Caxton,* 1477–78.] O(4 leaves).; PML(62 leaves). Duff 174. Hoskins 1.
    12 lines.
15868 — [Anr. ed.] 4°. [*Westminster, W. Caxton,* 1480.] L(4 leaves). Duff 175. Hoskins 2.
    20 lines.
15869 — [Anr. ed.] 8°. [*W. de Machlinia,* 1485.] L(7 leaves).O (lacks 8 leaves).O¹⁴(16 leaves).C(2 leaves).LINC(4 leaves).+ Duff 176. Hoskins 3.
    17 lines.
15870 — [Anr. ed.] 16°. [*Paris, J. Dupré?* 1488?] C(4 leaves, plus duplicates of 2). Duff 177.
    15 lines.
15871 — [Anr. ed.] 8°. [*Westminster, W. Caxton,* 1490.] L(m⁸ only). Duff 178. Hoskins 4.
    16 lines in Caxton's type 5, pr. all in black.
15872 — [Anr. ed.] 8°. [*Westminster, W. Caxton,* 1490.] L(d1–4). C(4 leaves). Duff 179. Hoskins 5.
    16 lines in Caxton's type 5, pr. in red and black. Offset portions of 2 otherwise unknown eds. in Caxton's type 8 [1491–93], an 8° w. 16 lines and a 4° w. 22 lines, are in the L(imp.) copy of 20195; *see British Museum Quarterly*, XXVI (1962), pp. 52–3.
15873 — [Anr. ed.] 16° in 8's. [*Antwerp, G. Leeu,* 1491–92.] O⁴ (K⁸ only, missing). Duff 180. Hoskins 6.

Liturgies—Latin Rite—HOURS AND PRIMERS—*Salisbury and Reformed—cont.*

15873.5 — [Anr. ed.] 8°. [*R. Pynson,* 1493?] O(1 leaf, Vet. A 1 b.12(7)).
    17 lines in Pynson's type 4. The recto and verso have different settings of the same text, including Stella Celi; line 1 has 'sacrosanctum' or 'sacro sāctū'.
15874 — [Anr. ed.] Officia secūdum morem ecclesie Sarum. 16° in 8's. (*venetiis, per J. hertzog, imp. G. barreuelt & F. de egmont* [*in London,*] 1494.) L(frags.).O(frags.). DUR⁵(frag.).ETON(frags.).M(tp and Kal.).+ Duff 181. Hoskins 9*.
    All frags. are unfolded sheets coming from bindings; *see Essays in Honour of V. Scholderer*, pp. 363–6.
15875 — [Anr. ed.] 4° in 8's. [*Westminster, W. de Worde,* 1494.] L(A⁶ only).L².O(lacks 11 leaves).C(2 imp.). Duff 182. Hoskins 7.
    22 lines; l 7ʳ line 4: 'dieb₃'. This and many of the following eds. include the Fifteen Oes, reprinted from 20195.
15876 — [Anr. ed.] 4° in 8's. [*Westminster, W. de Worde,* 1494.] L(87 leaves). Duff 183. Hoskins 8.
    22 lines; l 7ʳ line 4: 'diebus'.
15877 — [Anr. ed.] 8°. [*Rouen, Martin Morin?* 1494?] L²³(2 sheets from a binding). Duff 184.
    17 lines; w. spaces left blank for inits.
15878 — [Anr. ed.] 8°. [*Westminster, W. de Worde,* 1494.] O⁵ (Y1–4, 6, 7). Duff 185. Hoskins 9.
    17 lines; w. the inits. pr. in red.
15879 — [Anr. ed.] 8°. [*Paris, P. Pigouchet?*] (*pro j. ricardo, rothomagi,* 1494.) L(imp.).
15880 — [Anr. ed.] Hore intemerate beatissime virginis scd'm vsum Sarum. 4° in 8's. [*Paris, P. Pigouchet?*] (1495.) L(imp.).O. Duff 186. Hoskins 10.
15881 — [Anr. ed. Begins a1ʳ:] Ianuarius habet dies .xxxi. 8°. [*Paris, E. Jehannot,* 1495?] L. Duff 187. Hoskins 11.
    23 lines, in 83 mm. bastard. This and the next ed. are more probably c. 1497–99.
15881.3 — [Anr. ed. Begins A1ʳ:] Mensis ianuarii h₃ dies .xxxi. 8°. [*Paris, E. Jehannot,* 1495?] O(Arch. B f.42, imp.).
    23 lines, in 83 mm. rotunda.
15881.5 — [Anr. ed.] 8°. [*Paris, E. Jehannot f. J. Poitevin?* c. 1495.] L(imp.).PARIS. Hoskins 11*.
    25 lines. PARIS app. has part of an extra leaf at the beginning w. Poitevin's device.
15882 — [Anr. ed.] 8°. [*R. Pynson,* 1495.] O(2 leaves).C⁹(4 leaves).M(6 leaves). Duff 188. Hoskins 12, 29.
    17 lines.
15883 — [Anr. ed.] 8°. [*Paris, P. Pigouchet,* 1495.] O(G1,4,5,8). Duff 189. Hoskins 13.
    27 lines.
15884 — [Anr. ed. Ends:] Hore beate marie scd'm vsu₃ Sa₃ [etc.] 8°. [*J. Notary, J. Barbier, a. J. H., i.e. J. Huvin?*] (*pro w. de worde* [*in Westminster,*] 1497 (3 ap.)) O(leaves 1,3,4,6 of last quire). Duff 190. Hoskins 14.
    With the device, McK. 8α, above the colophon.
15885 — [Anr. ed.] Hore beate Marie v'gîs secundū vsum Sarum. 8°. [*Paris, J. Philippe f. T. Kerver a.*] (*pro j. ricardo, rothomagi,* 1497.) L.O.C.M.; F.PML. Duff 191. Hoskins 15.
    Kerver's device is on the tp; Philippe's is below the colophon on r4ᵛ; the latter is omitted in the F copy.
15886 — [Anr. ed.] Hore intemerate beatissime virginis Marie. 8°. (*per R. Pynson,*) [1497.] O. Duff 192. Hoskins 16.
15887 — [Anr. ed.] Hore presentes ad vsum Sarum. 8°. *Parisius, per P. pigouchet, pro S. vostre,* 1498 (16 my.) L.L². O.C.C².+; PML. St. John's Seminary, Camarillo, California. Duff 193. Hoskins 17.
15888 — [Anr. ed.] Hore beate marie virginis secundum vsum Sarum. 8°. (*i vniv'sitat' parisieñ.,*) *J. Jehannot* (*pro n. coîtis* [i.e. *N. Lecomte*] *nunc in anglia mercatore,* 1498.) C(imp.).C²(lacks A1, B8).M(imp.).; HN(imp.). Duff 194. Hoskins 18.
15889 — [Anr. ed.] Incipiunt hore [etc.] 8°. *parisii,* [*P. Pigouchet*] *pro s. le vostre,* [1498.] M(lacks 1 leaf).ST.; F.PML. Duff 195. Hoskins 19.
15890 — [Anr. ed.] Hore ad vsū Sarrum. 8°. *parisius,* [*J. Jehannot*] *pro J. Poiteuin,* [1498.] D. Duff 196. Hoskins 20.
15891 — [Anr. ed.] 16°. [*R. Pynson,* 1498.] C(bb1–4). Duff 197. Hoskins 35.
    (Formerly also 15907) 21 lines.

Liturgies—Latin Rite—Hours and Primers—*Salisbury and Reformed—cont.*

15892 — [Anr. ed.] 64°. [*Paris*, 1499.] C(frag. of 1 leaf).
Duff 198 and Hoskins 20* note a 64° copy w. colophon: Paris, 1499, which was destroyed by fire in 1865 and may or may not have been the ed. to which the C leaf belongs.

15893 — [Anr. ed.] 8°. [*R. Pynson*, 1500.] DUR⁵(E–F⁸ only). Duff 199.
18 lines.

15894 — [Anr. ed.] 8°. [*R. Pynson*, 1500.] C⁷(2 leaves). Duff 200. Hoskins 22.
20 lines.

15895 — [Anr. ed.] 64° in 8's. (*westmynster, by me J. Noary* [sic], 1500 (2 ap.)) MEL(i–k⁸ only). Duff 201. Hoskins 21.

15895.5 — [Anr. ed.] Hore beate virginis marie ad vsum Sarum. 8°. [*Paris, J. Jehannot*, 1500?] CAL²(imp.). Arthur Vershbow, Newton Center, Massachusetts(imp.).
32 lines; calendar for 1500–21; types and cut of anatomical man as in 15888. Both copies have at the end A⁸ w. the Creed in Latin verse in the same setting as illustrated for E. Jehannot in A. Claudin, *Histoire de l'imprimerie en France*, II. 259.

15896 — [Anr. ed.] Hore p̄sentes ad vsū Sarū. 4° in 8's. *Parisius, p̄ P. pigouchet pro S. vostre*, 1501 (20 oc.) L.O(2).O³ (imp.).C². Hoskins 23.

15897 — [Anr. ed.] 8°. *Parisius, per P. pigouchet pro S. vostre*, 1502 (8 mr.) O.; F.PML. Hoskins 24.

15898 — [Anr. ed.] 8°. (*per me w. de worde*, 1502.) O(imp.).O⁵ (frag.). Nantwich Parish Church, Cheshire. Hoskins 25.

15899 — [Anr. ed.] Hore beate Marie virginis secundum vsum insignis ecclesie Sarum totaliter ad longum & sine require. 4° in 8's. (*p̄ me w. de worde*, 1503 (31 jy.)) L(lacks B8, O3). Hoskins 26.
See also 23443.5.

15900 — [Anr. ed.] 4° mostly in 8's. (*be me J. Notary,*) [1503?] L. Hoskins 28.

15901 — [Anr. ed.] 4° in 8's. [*Paris, W. Hopyl?*] (*pro a. verard,*) [c. 1503.] L(lacks a1–4).C(imp.). Copenhagen RL.; HD(imp.).PML. Hoskins 30.

15901.5 — [Anr. ed.] 8°. [*W. de Worde, c.* 1503.] LINC(imp.). Hoskins 27.
26 lines; the text of the Hours begins on A7ʳ.

15902 — [Anr. ed.] long 12°. [*Rouen, P. Guerin*, 1505?] L(imp.). Hoskins 47.
36 lines.

15903 — [Anr. ed.] Hore beatissime v'ginis marie [etc.] 8°. (*in alma Parrhisiorū acad., per w. hopylium,*) *imp. w. brettō ciuis Lōd'.,* (*venales habent̄ Londoñ. ap.* [*W. Bretton,*] 1506 (9 kal. ap.)) O(lacks 31 leaves).; NLA (imp.). Hoskins 31.

15904 — [Anr. ed.] [H]ore diue virginis Marie. 8°. (*Parisius, p̄ A. verard*, 1506 (24 ap.)) L(lacks b4).O(20 leaves, Vet. A 1 b.12(3)). Hoskins 32.

15904.5 — [Anr. ed.] Hore beate marie virginis ad vsū Sar̄. long 12°. (*Rothomagi, ī off. R. goupil p̄ G. candos,*) [1506?] PML.

15905 — [Anr. ed.] Hore presentes ad vsum Sarum. 8°. *Parisius,* [*P. Pigouchet*] *pro S. vostre,* [1507?] L.O⁷(imp.).C (imp.). Hoskins 33.

15906 — = 15913.
15907 — = 15891.
15908 — [Anr. ed.] 8°. [*W. de Worde*, 1508?] C(8 leaves). Hoskins 36.
19 lines.

15908.5 — [Anr. ed.] Hore beatissime virginis marie. 4° in 8's. (*w. de worde*, 1510.) L.
The inner sheet of quire D is in MS., w. woodcuts stamped in by hand.

15909 — [Anr. ed.] Hore beatissime v'ginis Marie ad vsum Sarisburiēsis ecclesie. 8°. (*parisius, per T. Keruer, imp. w. bretton* [*in London,*] 1510 (5 se.)) L(imp.). L¹⁵.O(imp.).C³(imp.).USHAW(imp.).+; F(lacks tp). Hoskins 37.
(Formerly also 15910)

15910 — = 15909.
15910.5 — [Anr. ed. C2ᵛ:] Sequn̄t hore intemerate virginis marie scd'm vsum Sarum. 8°. [*R. Pynson*, 1510?] DNPK (C–G⁸ only).
20 lines, in 116 mm. textura. O(Vet. A 1 b.12(2)) has a frag. of 10 leaves from quires C, K of a different 20-line Pynson ed., w. the Credo beginning on C4ʳ while in DNPK it begins on C1ʳ.

15911 — [Anr. ed.] Hore beate marie virginis. long 12°. [*Rouen,*] *pour P. guerī,* [1510?] L(lacks 4 leaves). Hoskins 49.

Liturgies—Latin Rite—Hours and Primers—*Salisbury and Reformed—cont.*

15912 — [Anr. ed.] Hore beatissime virginis Marie. 4° in 8's. (*in alma Parhisiorum acad.,* [*T. Kerver,*] *imp. F. byrckman* [*in London,*]) *Vendūtur Londoñ. ap. bibliopolas in cimiterio sancti Pauli,* (1511 (12 se.)) C(imp.). Hoskins 39.

15913 — [Anr. ed.] Officium beate Marie v'ginis [etc.] 8°. *Parisius, exp. S. vostre,* [1512.] O.C²(imp.).ST(imp.).; F. Hoskins 34, 40.
(Formerly also 15906) Ends q8; the O copy is bd. w. a non-STC item, which is included on University Microfilms reel 89.

15913.5 — [Anr. ed.] Hore Marie virginis scd'm vsum Sarū. 4° in 8's. *Parisiis, opa N. higmā, imp. S. vostre,* [1512.] C¹⁴(imp.).ST(lacks tp).; PML. James R. Tanis, Bryn Mawr College, Bryn Mawr, Pennsylvania(imp.). Arthur Vershbow, Newton Center, Massachusetts. Hoskins 57.
(Formerly 15927)

15914 — [Anr. ed.] 4° in 8's. (*by me w. de worde*, 1513.) L(imp.). Hoskins 41.

15915 — [Anr. ed.] 4° in 8's. [*R. Pynson*, 1513?] O³(frags.).YK (imp). Hoskins 42.

15916 — [Anr. ed.] Hore bt̄e marie viginis [sic] ad vsū Sarū pro pueris. 8°. *i alma Parisiorū acad., imp. F. byrckmā* [*in London,*] 1514 (1 ja.) C⁵(imp.). Hoskins 43.

15917 — [Anr. ed.] Hore beate marie virginis [etc.] long 12°. (*per R. Pynson*, 1514 (12 my.)) C¹³.; BO. Hoskins 44.

15918 — [Anr. ed.] 4° in 8's. (*in alma Parhisiorum acad.,* [*W. Hopyl?*] *imp. F. byrckman* [*in London,*] 1514 (12 jy.)) C(imp.).C⁹(imp.). Hoskins 45.

15919 — [Anr. ed.] Hore beate marie virginis [etc.] long 12°. (*per w. de worde*, 1514 (24 jy.)) C. Hoskins 46.

15920 — [Anr. ed.] Hore beatissime virginis Marie ad legitimum Sarisburiensis ecclesie ritum. 4° in 8's. (*in alma Parhisiorum acad.,* [*W. Hopyl?*] *imp. F. Byrckman* [*in London,*]) *Venduntur Londoñ. ap. bibliopolas in cimiterio sancti Pauli,* 1515 (1514 (12 oc.)) O. Hoskins 48.

15921 — [Anr. ed.] 4° in 8's. (*in alma Parhisiorum acad.,* [*W. Hopyl?*] *imp. F. byrckmā,*) *Venduntur Londoñ. a F. byrckman,* (1516 (19 no.)) O(2). Hoskins 50.

15922 — [Anr. ed.] 4° in 8's. (*W. de Worde*, 1519.) L(lacks A1,8). C(imp.).; HD(frag. of 1 leaf, f. xciiii, bd. w. 16259.7). Hoskins 73.
(Formerly also 15947)

15923 — [Anr. ed.] Hore beatissime virginis Marie ad legitimū Sarisburiēsis ecclesie ritū. 4° in 8's. (*in alma Parrhisiox̄ acad.,* [*P. Pigouchet?*] *imp. F. byrckman,*) *Venūdant̄ Londoñ. a F. byrckmā,* (1519 (14 ap.)) O(2). Hoskins 53.

15924 — [Anr. ed.] 4° in 8's. [ā4ʳ:] (*Parisius, per N. hicḡmā, imp. F. Birckmā* [*in London,*]) [ʒ 8ᵛ:] (*i alma Parrhisiox̄ acad., imp. F. regnault,* [both cols.:] 1519 (24 oc.)) O.C³(imp.).D². ; Y. Hoskins 54.
F. S. Ferguson noted that the copy sold at Sotheby's 24 Jan. 1950, lot 398, had 'regnault' instead of 'Birckmā' in the colophon on ā4ʳ.

15925 — [Anr. ed.] 4° in 8's. (*in alma Parhisiorū acad., imp. F. byrckman* [*in London,*]) *Venales habēt̄ Londoñ. ap. bibliopolas in cimiterio scti Pauli,* 1520 (14 jn.) O. Hoskins 55.

15926 — [Anr. ed.] Hore beate virginis Marie [etc.] 4° in 8's. *Parisiis, opa N. Hygmā, imp. S. vostre,* [1520?] L. O(2, 1 imp.).ST.; F.HN.PML(2). Hoskins 56.

15926.5 — [Anr. ed.] 4° in 8's. [*Paris?* 1520?] L(14 leaves). Hoskins 94.
(Formerly 15866 and 15967) The text of the Hours should begin on A1, lacking. This contains extra prayers to St. Thomas à Becket and other saints connected with Canterbury.

15927 — Now = 15913.5.
15928 — [Anr. ed.] long 12°. [*Rouen*, 1520?] L(lacks A1,2, N5,6). Hoskins 87.
(Formerly also 15960) Collates A–M¹² N⁶.

15929 — [Anr. ed.] 64° in 8's. [*Paris*, 1520?] L(28 leaves from quires e–h).
16 lines.

15930 — [Anr. ed.] Hore beate Marie ad ritū ecclesie Sarisburiensis. 4° in 8's. (*in alma Parrhisiox̄ acad., imp. F. byrckman,*) *Venūdant̄ Londoñ. a F. byrckmā,* (1521 (ja.)) O. Hoskins 58.

15931 — [Anr. ed.] 4° in 8's. (*in alma Parrhisiorum acad.,* [*T. Kerver,*] *imp. F. byrckman,*) *Venūdant̄ Londoñ. a F. byrckmā,* (1521 (9 ap.)) O.O².C. Hoskins 59.

Liturgies—Latin Rite—Hours and Primers—*Salisbury and Reformed—cont.*

15932 — [Anr. ed.] Hore beate marie virginis ad vsum Sarū. long 12°. (*Parisius, p J. bignon pro R. fakes Lōdoii* [sic] *librario,*) [1521?] O(imp.). Hoskins 60.
  With Fakes's device, McK. 56, on the tp, w. his name in type.

15932.5 — [Anr. ed.] 8°. [*W. de Worde,* after 1521.] London, College of Arms(frags. of 16 and of 40 leaves).
  20 lines; w. de Worde's device, McK. 46β.

15933 — [Anr. ed.] Hore beatissime virginis Marie ad legitimum Sarisburiensis eccl'ie ritum. 8°. (*per R. Pynson,* 1522 (18 ja.)) O. Hoskins 61.

15934 — [Anr. ed.] Hore beatissime virginis Marie ad cōsuetudinem insignis ecclesie Saꝛ. 4° in 8's. *per w. de worde,* (1523 (20 no.)) L(imp.).SAL(imp.). Hoskins 62.

15935 — [Anr. ed.] Hore beate marie virginis secundum vsum Sarum. 4° in 8's. [*Antwerp, C. Ruremond f. P. Kaetz in London,* 1523?] ST(imp.). Hoskins 63.
  With Kaetz's device, McK. 63.

15936 — [Anr. ed.] long 12°. (*p me w.* ⟨*de*⟩ *worde,* ⟨1523?⟩) C³(imp.). Hoskins 64.
  'D' of sig. D1 is under 'eu' of 'euangelistā'; cf. 15941.

15937 — [Anr. ed.] 4° in 8's. [*Antwerp, C. Ruremond,*] (1524 (19 au.)) L¹⁵(imp.).LIV(lacks tp). Hoskins 65.

15938 — [Anr. ed.] long 12°? (*Antuerpie, oper*⟨*a*⟩ *C. endouiensis* [i.e. *Ruremond,*] *imp. P. kaetz* [*in London,*] 1524 (22 no.)) L(frag. of last leaf, Harl.5918/21). Hoskins 66.

15938.5 — [Anr. ed.] Hore beate marie virginis [etc.] 4° in 8's. [*Antwerp, C. Ruremond,*] *Venundantur Londonij ap. P. kaetz,* (1524 (27 no.)) PML.

Hortulus anime ad vsum insignis ecclesie Sarum. 1524. *See* 13828.2.

15939 Hore btē marie virginis ad vsum Sarū. 4° in 8's. (*Antwerpie, per C. Endouiēn.* [i.e. *Ruremond,*] *imp. F. byrckman,*) *Venūdantur per F. byrckmā* [*in London,*] (1525 (my.)) C.; HN(lacks A1). Hoskins 67.

15940 — [Anr. ed.] long 12°. *Rothomagi, imp. J. cousin,* (1525 (28 jy.)) C. Hoskins 68.

15941 — [Anr. ed.] long 12°. [*W. de Worde?* 1525?] C(imp.). Hoskins 69.
  'D' of sig. D1 is under 'ne' of 'Johannem'; cf. 15936.

15942 — = 15944.

15943 — [Anr. ed.] narrow 8°. (*Parisius, in ed. F. regnault,* 1526 (11 ja.)) ST(lacks tp). Hoskins 70.

15944 — [Anr. ed.] Hore beatissime virginis Marie ad legitimū Sarisburiensis ecclesie ritum. 4° in 8's. (*Parisius, per F. Regnault,*) *Venūdaī Parisius a F. Regnault,* (1526 (1 mr.)) L(2, 1 lacks 1st A10, 1 imp., plus 2nd A⁸ only, imp.).O(imp.).C³.D².LIV.+; BO.ILL. Hoskins 71. (L frag. formerly 15942.)

15945 — [Anr. ed.] 4° in 8's. (*Parrhisiis, in ed. F. Regnault,*) *Venundatur Parisius a F. regnault,* 1526 (17 mr.) L. Hoskins 72.
  Reissued in 15949. C(Sayle 8068) is a 2-leaf frag., B(lombardic)1,2, which may belong to this or an earlier Regnault ed.

15946 — [Anr. ed.] 4° in 8's. (*Rothomagi, in ed. J. Cousin,* 1526 (1 au.)) Edinburgh, Theological College(lacks tp). Hoskins 72*.

15946.5 — [Anr. ed.] 64° in 8's. (*parrhisijs, arte J. preuel, sumpt. R. banckys, londoñ.,* 1526 (14 oc.)) C³(frags. of 4 quires).

15947 — = 15922.

15948 — [Anr. ed.] Hore beatissime virginis Marie ad consuetudinē eccl'ie Saꝛ. 4° in 8's. *per me w. de worde,* (1526 (4 non. au.)) L²(imp.).O(imp.). Hoskins 74.

15949 — [Anr. issue of 15945.] 4° in 8's. (*Parrhisijs, in ed. F. Regnault,* 1527 (17 mr.)) L(imp.).C(imp.). Hoskins 76.

15950 — [Anr. ed.] Hore beatissime virginis Marie ad legitimū Sarisburiēsis ecclesie ritum. 4° in 8's. (*Parisius per F. Regnault,*) *Venūdaī Parisiis a F. Regnault,* 1527 (27 jn.) L(3 imp.).C(imp.)*. Hoskins 77.
  In colophon: 'indulgētiis'.

15951 — [Anr. issue, w. the 1st quire reprinted.] Hore beatissime virginis Marie ad legitimum Sarisburiēsis ecclesie ritum. (*Parisius, per F. Regnault,*) *Venūdaī Parisius a F. Regnault,* 1527 (27 jn.) L(frags.).; LC(2, 1 imp.). Hoskins 78.
  In colophon: 'indulgentiis'.

Liturgies—Latin Rite—Hours and Primers—*Salisbury and Reformed—cont.*

15952 — [A mixed? copy, w. tp as in 15951 and colophon as in 15950.] L². Hoskins 78.

15953 — [Anr. ed.] Hore beatissime v'ginis Marie ad verū Sarisburiēsis ecclesie ritū. 4° in 8's. (*Parisiis, in off. N. Preuost, imp. F. Byrkman. Et ap. eundē venundātur Londonii,* 1527 (18 jy.)) L(imp.).L²(imp.).O(3, 1 imp.).C(imp.).C⁴.; CH. Hoskins 79.

15953.5 — [Anr. ed.] Hore beatissime virginis Marie ad verū Sarisburiensis ecclesie ritum. 4° in 8's. (*Parisiis, in off. N. Preuost, imp. F. Byrkman et ap. eundem venundātur Londinij,* 1527 (26 jy.)) C³.

15954 — [Anr. ed.] Hore beatissime virginis Marie ad legitimū Sarisburiēsis ecclesie ritum. 4° in 8's. (*Parisij p F. Regnault, imp. eiusdem,*) *Venūdāī Parisiis a F. Regnault,* 1527 (10 oc.) L(imp.).O(imp.).C(lacks last leaf).M².+; HN.LC.PML. Hoskins 80.

15955 — [Anr. ed.] This prymer of Salysbury vse is set out a lōg [etc.] (Expliciunt hore beatissime virginis Marie.) *Latin.* narrow 8°. Paris, (*in ed. F. regnault,*) 1527 (13 de.) O(imp.). Hoskins 81.

15956 — [Anr. ed.] 32° in 8's. (*Parisijs, in off.* [*Y. Bonhomme*] *vidue T. keruer, imp. F. Byrckmā, venūdatur Londinij a F. byrckmā,* 1527.) ST(imp.). Hoskins 82.

15957 — [Anr. ed.] Enchiridion, p̄clare ecclesie Sarum. 16° in 8's. *Parisiis, ex off.* [*Y. Bonhomme*] *vidue T. Keruer,* (*exp. A. plomier,*) 1528 (2 se.) L.L¹⁴.O.C³.LIV.+; HN. Hoskins 83.

15958 — [Anr. ed.] Hore beate marie virginis ad vsum Saꝛ. long 12°. *Rothomagi,* [*N. le Roux,*] *imp. J. cousin,* [1528.] O. Hoskins 84.

15959 — [Anr. ed.] 8°. *parisius, per G. Hardouyn,* [1528?] L(2, 1 imp.).O.O³¹.C².; JH.PML. Hoskins 85.

15960 — = 15928.

15961 — [Anr. ed.] 4° in 8's. [*Paris, F. Regnault,* 1528?] L (8 leaves).

15961.3 — [Anr. ed.] This prymer of Salysbury vse is set out a long w'tout ony serchyng. *Latin.* 8°. Parys, [*F. Regnault,*] 1529. PML(imp.).
  36 lines.

15961.5 — [Anr. ed., w. same title.] *Latin.* 16° in 8's. Parys, (*per F. Regnault,*) 1529 (30 ap.) F(imp.).
  27 lines.

15962 — [Anr. ed.] Hore beate marie virginis ad vsū ecclesie Saꝛ. 4° in 8's. (*Antwerpie, per C. Endouiensem* [i.e. *Ruremond,*]) *Venūdātur p C. Ruremūdeñ.,* (1530 (ja.)) C⁸(imp.).; ILL(imp.). Hoskins 88.

15963 — [Anr. ed.] Hore beate Marie ad vsum ecclesie Sarisburiensis. 4° in 8's. (*Parisiis, in ed. F. Regnault,*) *Venundātur Parisiis ap. F. Regnault,* 1530 (30 ap.) L⁴.O(lacks last leaf).O²(imp.). Hoskins 75, 89.

15964 — [Anr. ed.] 16° in 8's. (*Parisiis, per F. Regnault,* 1530 (30 ap.)) ST(lacks all before E1, f. xxxiii). Hoskins 90.
  The ST copy filmed on Univ. Microfilms reel 136 is actually 15981a.

15965 — [Anr. ed.] Enchiridion preclare ecclesie Sarum. 8°. (*Parisiis, in ed. G. Harduoyn* [sic], 1530 (11 my.)) L.O.C(imp.).DUR(Bamb.).ETON.+; F. Hoskins 91.
  Some copies (DUR(Bamb.), ETON) have the misprint in the colophon corrected to 'Hardouyn'.

15966 — [Anr. ed.] Hore beate marie virginis ad vsū ecclesie Saꝛ. 4° in 8's. (*Antwerpie, per C. Endouiensem* [i.e. *Ruremond,*]) *Venundantur in cimiterio sancti pauli sub intersignio sancti Augustini* [*in London,*] 1531 (1530 (oc.)) L(imp.).O. Hoskins 92.

15967 — Now = 15926.5.

15968 — [Anr. ed.] Hore beatissime virginis marie ad legitimum Sarisburiensis ecclesie ritum. 4° in 8's. (*Parisiis, per F. Regnault,*) *Venundantur Parisijs a F. Regnault,* 1530. L(imp.).O.O³(imp.).C(imp.).DUR³.+; F. Hoskins 93.

Ortulus anime. The garden of the soule: or the englisshe primers. 1530. *See* 13828.4.

15969 Hore btē marie virginis ad vsū ecclesie Saꝛ. 4° in 8's. [*Antwerp,*] (*ex off. C. Ruremundeñ.,*) *Venundantur in cimiterio sancti pauli sub intersignio sancti Augustini* [*in London,*] 1531 (14 my.) L.O.O³¹. Hoskins 95.
  This and many of the following eds. (e.g. 15973, 16002.5, 16008.5) contain a short treatise, The manner to live well, written by J. Quentin and tr. by R. Copland.

15970 — [Anr. ed.] This prymer of Salysbury vse is set out a long. *Latin.* 16° in 8's. Parys, (*per F. Regnault,*) 1531 (10 jn.) O(2, 1 imp.).ST. Hoskins 96.

Liturgies—Latin Rite—Hours and Primers—*Salisbury and Reformed—cont.*

15971 — [Anr. ed.] 8°. *Parys, (in ed. F. regnault,) venūdātur ap. F. Regnault,* (1531 (30 jn.)) C.YK.; F. Hoskins 97.

15972 Hortulus anime . . . scd'm vsum Saꝶ. 1531. Now = 13828.6.

15973 This prymer of Salysbury vse [etc.] *Latin.* 8°. *Parys, (per F. Regnault,)* 1531. L(imp.).O.C.ST.; NY¹¹(imp.)*. Hoskins 98.
 X8ᵛ last word: 'trinitatem'.

15974 — [Anr. ed.] This prayer [*sic*] of Salisbury vse [etc.] *Latin.* 8°. *Parys, (per F. Regnault,)* [1531.] L(2, 1 imp.).O(2, 1 imp.). Hoskins 99.
 X8ᵛ last word: 'trinitatem'.

15975 — [Anr. ed.] 8°. [*Paris, F. Regnault,* 1531?] O(imp.). Hoskins 100.
 X8ᵛ last word: 'actio'.

15976 — [Anr. ed.] 8°. (*w. Rastell,* 1532 (30 ap.)) C(imp.).; Nash(frags. of a⁸ and q⁴). Hoskins 101.
 The Nash frags. are of portions lacking in C and may belong to an earlier Rastell ed.

15977 — [Anr. ed.] This prymer of Salisbury vse [etc.] *Latin.* 16° in 8's. *Parys, (per F. Regnault,)* 1532 (7 au.) F. Hoskins 102.

15978 — [Anr. ed.] This prymer of Salysbury vse [etc.] *Latin.* 16° in 8's. *Parys, (opera y. Bonhomme vidue T. Keruer, imp. J. Growte [in London,])* 1532 (au.) L.O(3, 2 imp.).C(16 leaves)*.C⁶.; HN.PML. Hoskins 103.
 This has the Psalter of Jesus (cf. 14563) at the end on ✠–✠✠⁸.

15979 — [Anr. issue, w. quire a reprinted.] Thys prymer off salysburye vse [etc.] *Paris, wythyn the howse off T. keruer, att the expenses off J. growte boke seller yn london,* 1533 (1532 (au.)) L(2 imp.).; BO. Hoskins 104.

15980 — [Anr. ed.] This prymer of salysbury vse. *Latin.* 8°. *Parys, (in ed. F. regnault,) Venūdātur ap. F. Regnault,* (1532 (31 oc.)) O(2, 1 imp.). Hoskins 105.

15981 — [Anr. ed.] This prymer of Salysbury vse [etc.] *Latin.* 16° in 8's. *Parys, (ꝑ F. Regnault,)* 1533 (4 no.) C.DUR (Bamb.).; NY¹¹(imp., w. at least BB⁸ of 15986.7). Hoskins 109.
 N2ʳ line 18 begins: 'secula'.

15981a — [Anr. ed.] 16° in 8's. [*Paris, F. Regnault,* 1533?] L² (imp.).C(2 leaves).DE(imp.).ST(lacks all before B8, and also GG8). Hoskins 106.
 N2ʳ line 18 begins: 'la seculorum.' The ST copy is on Univ. Microfilms reel 136 ('15964').

15982 — [Anr. ed.] Enchiridiō preclare eccl'ie Sarisbāriēsis. 8°. (*Parisijs, in ed. G. Hardouyn,*) [1533?] L(lacks 1st leaf).O.C¹⁴(lacks 1st leaf).DE(imp.).ST.+; F(lacks 1st quire).ILL(imp.).Y. Hoskins 110.

15982.5 — [Anr. ed.] Horae ad vsum Sarum. 16° in 8's. (*T. Berthelet, printer to the kinges highnes,*) [1533?] ST.

15983 — [Anr. ed.] 8°. (*R. wyer,*) L¹⁵(lacks tp).O(last leaf only, Douce Add. 142/616). Hoskins 111.

15984 — [Anr. ed.] Hore beatissime virginis marie [etc.] 4° in 8's. (*Parisii, per F. Regnault,*) *Venundantur Parisiis a F. Regnault,* 1534. L(2 imp.).L².O(3, 1 lacks tp).C.ST.; F.HD.PML. Hoskins 113.

15985 — [Anr. ed.] Thys prymer of salysbury vse. *Latin.* 16° in 8's. *Paris, (ꝑ y. bōhōme, viduā T. keruer,) wythin the howse of T. keruer, at the expenses off J. growte boke-seller in London,* 1534. L.L⁸(imp.).O. Lord Kenyon. Hoskins 114.
 This has the Psalter of Jesus (cf. 14563) at the end on *–**⁸.

15985a — [Anr. ed.] 8°. (*Rothomagi, per me N. le roux, imp. J. cousin,*) [1534?] L(imp.).

15985a.5 — [Anr. ed.] 16° in 8's. *Parys, (imp. F. Reynault,)* 1534 (1535.) L(lacks 2 leaves).

15986 A prymer in Englyshe, with certeyn prayers & godly meditations, very necessary for all people that vnderstonde not the Latyne tongue. [*Ed.* W. Marshall.] 8°. (*J. Byddell f. w. Marshall,*) [1534.] O.; BO(imp.). Hoskins 115.
 The 1st Primer in English; partially based on Joye's Ortulus anime, 13828.4. Issued w. 21789.3? Extracts reprinted in 14106.

Liturgies—Latin Rite—Hours and Primers—*Salisbury and Reformed—cont.*

15986.3 This prymer of Salysbery vse bothe in Englyshe & in Laten, is set out a longe [etc.] 8°. (*R. Redman,*) [1535.] PARIS.

15986.7 This prymer of Salysbury vse. *Latin.* 16° in 8's. *Parys, [f. F. Regnault,]* 1535. L(imp.).C(imp.). Hoskins 107.

15987 — [Anr. ed.] Hore beatissime virginis Marie ad legitimū Sarisburiensis ecclesie ritum. 4° in 8's. (*Parrhisijs, per F. Regnault,*) *Venūdanꞇ Parisius a F. Regnault,* 1535 (1536 (25 my.)) L².O.C.DUR(Bamb.).M.+; HN. BO.PML. Hoskins 116.

15988 A goodly prymer in englyshe, newly corrected. 4°. (*J. Byddell f. w. Marshall,* 1535 (16 jn.)) L.O(imp.).C³ (imp.).C⁶(lacks tp).M.+; F(imp.).CAL(imp.). Hoskins 117, 119.
 (Formerly also 15989) A revision of 15986. Includes Savonarola on Psalm li, beginning on 1st M3ʳ; issued w. 21798.5?

15988a A primer in Englysshe, with dyuers prayers [etc.] 8°. (*T. Godfray,*) [1535?] C. Hoskins 118.
 Based largely on Joye's Ortulus anime, 13828.4, but differs from 15986 and 15988. Intended to be issued w. 21789.4?

15989 — = 15988.
15990 — Now = 15997.5.

15991 [The primer in Latin.] 16° in 8's. (*by me J. Byddell,* 1536.) L¹⁵(imp.). Hoskins 121.

15992 This prymer of Salysbery vse, bothe in Englyshe and in Laten [etc.] 8°. [*Antwerp, widow of C. Ruremond f.*] *J. Gowghe (in London,* 1536.) O(2).C(imp.). Hoskins 122.
 A composite of the texts of 15986.3, 15988, and 15988a. Issued w. 21789.5 and 21799; *see also* 23443.5. 2nd A1ʳ has John Colet's Seven petitions of the Pater Noster in 78 mm. Lettersnijder; a single leaf at C (Sayle 6096, Nijhof and Kronenberg 2691) has it in 79 mm. rotunda, possibly from a lost ed. pr. at Antwerp. The only other known eds. in which the Colet trans. appears are 15978 sq., 15983, and 15986.3.

15992.5 — [Anr. ed.] *Eng. a. Latin.* 8°. [*Rouen, N. le Roux f. F. Regnault in Paris,* c. 1536.] Sotheby's, 17 Oct. 1918, lot 131(imp., misdescribed, cannot be traced). Hoskins 117*, p. 93.

15993 Thys prymer in Englyshe and in Laten is newly trāslatyd after the Laten texte. 8°. (*Rowen, [N. le Roux?]* 1536.) O.O²(frag.).C(imp.). Hoskins 124.
 A revision of 15986.3. Issued w. 21789.6.

15994 Thys prymer of Salisbury vse. *Latin.* 8°. *Rowen, (per me N. le roux, imp. J. cousin,) [a. J. Marchant,]* 1537. O (imp.). Lord Kenyon(imp.). Hoskins 125.
 With Marchant's device on the tp.

15995 — [Anr. ed.] This prymer of Salysbury vse. *Latin.* 16° in 8's. *Rouen, [N. le Roux?] (pro F. Regnault [in Paris,])* 1537. O(3, 2 imp.).A².M.; CH. Hoskins 126.

15996 — [Anr. ed.] Hore beate Marie virginis, ad vsum insignis ecclesie Saꝶ. long 12°. [*R. Faques?*] (1537.) O. Hoskins 127.

15997 This prymer in Englyshe and in Laten [etc.] 4°. [*R. Redman,* 1537?] L²(imp.).C⁵(imp.).LEEDS. Lord Kenyon(imp.).; F(2,1 imp., plus a frag.).CAL(imp.). Hoskins 128.
 Based on 15993. Issued w. 2964.5 and 21789.7.

15997.5 The prymer with the pystles and gospels in Englysshe. *Eng. a. Latin.* 2 pts. 8°. (*J. Byddell,*) [1537?] O¹⁷(2, 1 imp.).C³(A–M⁸ only). Hoskins 120, 130.
 (Formerly 15990 and 15999) Based on 15988 and 15991.

15998 A goodly prymer in Englysshe, newly corrected. 4°. [*T. Gibson f. W. Marshall,* 1538?] L(2).O.C.C⁶.LINC (imp.).; F.HN.CU.N. Hoskins 129.
 Based on 15988. Includes Savonarola on Psalms li and xxxi on continuous signatures.

15999 — Now = 15997.5.
16000 — Now = 16075.5.

Liturgies—Latin Rite—HOURS AND PRIMERS—*Salisbury and Reformed—cont.*

16001   This prymer of Salysbury vse. *Latin.* 8°. *Rowen, (per N. le Roux, imp. F. Regnault, Parisiis,)* 1538. L.D². Hoskins 132.

16002   — [Anr. issue, w. colophon:] (*Parisijs, per F. Regnault,*) 1538. L.ST(imp.). Hoskins 134, 141.

16002.5 — [Anr. ed.] *Latin.* 8°. (*Rothomagi, per N. le roux,* 1538.) O³¹(imp.).
        Collates A–U⁸.

16002a — [Anr. ed.] This prymer of Salysbury vse. *Latin.* 8°. *Rowen,* 1538. Dr. C. Inglis. Hoskins 137. 𝔄

16003   Here after foloweth the prymer in Englysshe and in latin after the vse of Sarum. 8°. (*Paris, be me F. regnault,*) 1538. L¹⁵(imp.).A. Hoskins 133.
        Based on 15993.

16004   Hereafter foloweth the prymer in Englysshe after the vse of Sarum. 8°. (*Rowen, N. le Roux f. F. Regnault [in Paris,]*) 1538. L(imp.).C(imp.).; F(imp.).BO(lacks tp). PML.PN. Hoskins 135.
        Based on 15997. The PML copy is bd. w. 2966.3.

16005   — Now = 16008.3 sq.

16006   Thys prymer in Englyshe and in Laten. 8°. (*Rowen, [N. le Roux f. J. Marchant,]* 1538.) O.; F. St. Mary's Seminary, Perryville, Missouri. Hoskins 138.
        Based on 15997. With Marchant's device on the tp. Issued w. 2965.2. Possibly later than 16007.

16007   — [Anr. ed.] *Eng. a. Latin.* 8°. [*Rouen, N. le Roux,*] 1538. L²(imp.).O. Lord Kenyon(imp.).; F.CH.HD.ILL. Hoskins 139.
        Based on 15997. The 'Contentes' are on the tp. Issued w. 2965.4 and 21790.5. Possibly earlier than 16006.

16008   This prymer in Englyshe and in Latyn. 4° in 8's. [*R. Redman,*] 1538. L(lacks tp).O(imp.).O¹⁷.C.; CH(frag.). Hoskins 140.
        Based on 15997. Issued w. 2966.5 and 21792.

16008.3 Thys prymer in Englyshe and in Laten. 8°. [*Rouen, N. le Roux f. F. Regnault? in*] (*Parys,* 1538.) L.
        (This and the next formerly 16005) Based on 15993 w. same preface; St. Thomas à Becket in Kalendar for 29 Dec. Issued w. 2965 and 21791.

16008.5 — [Anr. issue, w. cancel quire B.] L.O.O⁵.C.C²(imp.).+; F.HN.NY¹¹. Hoskins 136.
        Has The preface and maner to lyue well (cf. 15969) beginning B6ᵛ; St. Thomas à Becket dropped from Kalendar in accordance w. 10086.

16009   The manual of prayers, or the prymer in Englysh & Laten. . . . Set forth by Jhon [Hilsey] by Goddes grace, at the Kynges callyng, bysshoppe of Rochester at the cōmaundemente of Thomas Crumwell. 4°. (*by me J. Wayland,* 1539 (15 jy.)) O(lacks 4 leaves).; F(imp.).CAL(imp.).N(frag.).*
        D1ᵣ does not mention Psalm li at the top.

16009.5 — [Anr. issue, w. quire D reset.] O³¹(imp.).C(imp.).C⁶.; HN. Hoskins 142.
        D1ᵣ mentions Psalm li at the top. C⁶, HN also have the title corrected to: '& the Kynges callyng,'.

16010   The manuall of prayers, or the prymer in Englyshe, . . . Set forth by Jhon [Hilsey] late bysshope of Rochester. 8° in 4's. (*by me J. Mayler f. J. Waylande, and be to sell by A. Hester a. M. Lobley,* 1539.) L.O(imp.).D².; BO(tp facs.). Hoskins 143.
        Issued w. 2966.7?

16011   — [An abridged ed.] The primer in Englishe moste necessary for the educacyon of chyldren abstracted oute of the Manuall of prayers or primer in Englishe and latē, set forth by Jhō, laet byshop of Rochester. 8°. (*J. Maylart f.*) *J. waylande, & be to sell by A. Hester a. M. Lobley,* [1539?] L. Hoskins 144.

16012   [Ends:] Expliciunt hore beate Marie virginis secundum vsum ecclesie Sarum. 8°. (*Rothomagi, venundātur ap. H. Marescalum,*) [1539?] YK(imp.). Hoskins 145.

16013   — [Anr. ed. Ends:] Expliciunt hore beate Marie virginis scd'm vsum ecclesie Sarum. 8°. [*Antwerp?* 1539?] L(C1–5,7,8, D–K⁸). Hoskins 147.

Liturgies—Latin Rite—HOURS AND PRIMERS—*Salisbury and Reformed—cont.*

16014   The primer in Englishe wyth the A. B. C. for children after the vse of Salisburye. Newlye imprinted. 8°. [*R. Grafton a. E. Whitchurch?* 1540?] L(tp only, C.35.b.15(2)). Hoskins 148.

16015   The prymer both in Englyshe and Latin. 8°. *R. grafton a. E. whytchurche,* 1540. L(tp mutilated).C.; F. Hoskins 151.
        A composite version. Issued w. 2971.5? The imprint is in the upper half of the tp.

16016   A primer or boke of prayers. Here vnton [*sic*] is added the pistles & gospels. *English.* 2 pts. long 12°. (*N. Bourman,*)1540. L²(imp.).LIV³(imp.). Goyder(imp.). Hoskins 152.
        Based on 16010.

16016.5 [The primer in English and Latin, with the Epistles and Gospels.] 2 pts. 8°. [*N. Bourman?* 1540?] F(imp.). Hoskins 153.

16017   The manuall of prayers or primer in englysh set forth by Jhon late bysshop of Rochester. 16° in 8's. (*T. Petyt,*) [1540.] L(π⁸ B⁸ only).O(π⁸ B⁸ only, Vet. A 1 b.12(4)). C¹⁴(frags.). Hoskins 154.
        Based on 16010.

16017.5 [The primer in English.] 16° in 8's. [*R. Copland?* c. 1540.] L¹⁵(imp.). Hoskins 150.
        A composite version based on 15988, 15993, and 20195.

16018   The primer in Englisshe and Laten . . . with the exposicion [of Savonarola] of Miserere and In te domine speraui and with the epistles and gospels. 3 pts. 8°. *J. mayler,* [1540?] O(8° C 70 Th.Seld.). Hoskins 158.
        A composite version. Matins begins on C8ᵣ; quires H–I are present.

16018.5 — [Anr. issue, w. quires D–I cancelled and replaced by D–G.] O(Douce BB 102).
        Matins begins on D1ᵣ (also on C8ᵣ, which should have been cancelled); quires H–I are omitted from the collation.

16019   Hore btē marie virginis. 32° in 8's. *per T. Petit,* 1561 (1541.) OS(imp.). Hoskins 159.
        The colophon date is the correct one.

16020   The prymer in Englysshe and Laten, after the vse of Sarum, . . . with the exposicion [of Savonarola] . . . with the epystles and gospels. 3 pts. 8°. (*T. Petyt,*) 1541. O(imp.).ST(imp.). Addington Church, Bucks.; F(lacks tp).ILL(imp.). Hoskins 160.

16021   A prymar of Salisbery vse, in Englyshe and Latyn. The exposytion [of Savonarola.] The gospels and pystels. 2 pts. 8°. [*N. Bourman? f.*] (*R. Toye,*) [1542?] C² (frag.).; F.NY¹¹(frags. of collects). Hoskins 155, 162.
        Based on 16008.

16021.5 [The primer in English and Latin.] 8°. [*London,* c. 1541.] C(imp.).
        A composite version.

16022   Hore beate marie virginis secundum vsū insignis ecclesie Sariburisburium [*sic*] de nouo īpresse. 16° in 8's. (*J. May⟨ler,⟩*) [1541] L(col. def.). Hoskins 161.

16023   — [Anr. ed.] Hore beate Marie virginis secundū verum vsum insignis ecclesie Sarisburiensis. 8°. [*Antwerp,*] 1542. L. Hoskins 163.

16024   — [Anr. ed. Ends:] Expliciūt hore beatissime virginis Marie secundum vsum Sarum. 8°. (*Rothomagi,* 1542.) L(lacks tp). Phillipps 3386. Hoskins 164.
        The Phillipps copy has the tp, beginning: 'This prymer of Sarysbury vse . . .'

16025   — = 16026.

16026   The prymer in Englyshe, and Latyn wyth the epystles and gospelles: . . . and also the exposycion [of Savonarola.] 2 pts. 4° in 8's. [*R. Grafton f.*] *W. Bonham,* 1542. L¹⁵(imp.).C(lacks tp).C⁵.LINC(frag., bd. w. 16048)*. M(lacks pt. 2).; F(lacks tp and last leaf).WIS(frag.). Hoskins 165, 166.
        (Formerly also 16025) Based on 15993.

Liturgies—Latin Rite—Hours and Primers—*Salisbury and Reformed*—*cont.*

16027 — [A variant, w. imprint:] *R. Toye,* 1542. C.; HN.BO. NY[11]. Hoskins 168.

16027.5 The prymer in Latin, and Englysh. 8°. *R. Grafton,* 1542. O[17](imp.).USHAW(imp.). Hoskins 157.

16028 The prymer in Englysshe and Laten, after the vse of Sarū ... with the epystles and gospels. 2 pts. 8°. (*T. Petyt*), 1542. O(imp.).; F. Hoskins 167.
　　Based on 15997.

16028.5 The prymer in Englysh and latyn, after the vse of Sarum, ... with the exposicyon [of Savonarola] ... with the epystels and gospels. 3 pts. 4° in 8's. (*T. Petyt,* 1543.) EX.
　　A reprint of 16028, with the addition of Savonarola; 3 hands below title. The date occurs only at the end of the Primer.

16029 — [A variant, w. 'Cum priuilegio ...' below title.] L.O. O[8].C.C[4].+; F.N. Hoskins 169.

16030 This is the prymer in Englysh. 16° in 8's. (*R. Kele,*) [1543?] C(bd. w. 2971). Hoskins 170*.
　　A composite version based on 15988 and 15993.

16031 — Now = 16033.5.

16032 This prymer of Salysbury vse. *Latin.* 16° in 8's. (*per T. Petit,*) 1544 (12 se.) L. Hoskins 171.

16033 [The primer in English and Latin.] 8°. (*T. petyt,* 1544.) L(imp.).O[2](imp.). Hoskins 172.
　　Based on 16028.

16033.5 [The primer in English.] 32° in 8's. (*R. Grafton,*) [1544–45.] L(8 leaves from quires t–u).C(frags.). Hoskins 170.
　　(Formerly 16031) Based on 16015.

—————

16034 The primer, set foorth by the kynges maiestie and his clergie, to be taught lerned, & read: and none other to be vsed throughout all his dominions. *English.* 4°. (*Within the precinct of the late dissolued house of the gray Friers, by R. Grafton,*) 1545 (29 my.) L.L[4].O. O[31]. Sir Richard Proby.; N(imp.).PML. Hoskins 174.
　　The 1st Primer in English authorized by the king and prepared under his supervision.

16035 — [Anr. ed.] 8°. (*R. Grafton,* 1545 (29 my.)) C[3](lacks tp). Hoskins 173.
　　In colophon: 'graye Friers'.

16036 — [Anr. ed.] 8°. (*R. Grafton,* 1545 (29 my.)) O(imp., bd. w. 2973.3). Hoskins 175.
　　In colophon: 'gray Friers'.

16037 — [Anr. ed.] 4°. (*E. Whitchurche,*) 1545 (19 jn.) L(2, 1 lacks 1st 8 leaves).O.C(imp.).C[2].DUR[5](imp.).+ Hoskins 176.

16038 — [Anr. ed.] 8°. (*E. Whitchurche,* 1545 (20 jn.)) L. Hoskins 177.
　　In colophon: '*AT London*'.

16039 — [Anr. ed.] 8°. (*E. Whitchurche,* 1545 (20 jn.)) LINC (lacks tp). Hoskins 178.
　　In colophon: '*AT LONDON*'.

16040 The primer, in Englishe and Latyn, set foorth by the kynges maiestie [etc.]. 4° in 8's. *R. Grafton,* 1545 (6 se.) L.O[2].C.M[3].YK.+; F.HN.BO.ILL.PML.+ Hoskins 179.

16041 This prymer of Saylbury [*sic*] vse [etc.]. *Latin.* 16° in 8's. (*per T. Petyt,*) 1545 (25 no.) L. Hoskins 180.

16042 Orarium seu libellus precationum per regiam maiestatem & clerū latinè æditus. 8°. (*ex off. R. Graftoni,*) 1546 (1545 (6 se.)) L(lacks last leaf).O(imp.).C(imp.). LINC.M.+; HN(imp.). Hoskins 186.
　　The authorized Latin ed. *See* also 16089 and 20378.

16042.5 — [Anr. ed.] *Latin.* 16° in 8's. [*R. Grafton,* 1546?] O[31] (lacks tp and last leaf).
　　Collates A–R[8]. The contents are the same as 16042, but the present item has 1546 as the 1st year in the Almanack while 16042 has 1545.

Liturgies—Latin Rite—Hours and Primers—*Salisbury and Reformed*—*cont.*

16043 [The primer in English.] 16° in 8's. (*E. Whitchurche,* 1546 (1 ap.)) ILL(lacks tp, bd. w. 2973.5). Hoskins 183.

16043.5 The primer in English and Latyne, sette furthe by the kynges maiestie [etc.]. 16° in 8's. (*R. Grafton,* 1546 (10 au.)) Private owner.

16044 The primer, set furth by the kinges maiestie [etc.] *English.* 4°. *R. Grafton,* 1546 (17 au.) L.O.NOR.YK. Blackburn PL.; F.HN.PN. Hoskins 184.
　　25 lines. For a reprint w. 32 lines, [c. 1710], w. the above imprint but at bottom of tp: 'Reprinted without any alteration' *see* Hoskins 262.

16045 — [Anr. ed.] The primer in Englysshe, set furth [etc.]. 8°. (*E. Whitchurche,*) 1546 (20 au.) L. Hoskins 185.
　　ILL has a frag. pr. only on one side: I1[r], I4[v]–5[r], I8[v], w. I1[r] line 3: 'wayle' and using w[5b] while 16045 has 'waile' and uses w[5a].

16046 The primer, in Englishe & Latin, set forth [etc.]. 8°. (*E. Whitchurche,*) 1546 (9 ja.) L(2 imp.).; PML. Hoskins 181.

16047 [The primer in English.] 32° in 8's. (*R. Graftō,* 1546 (16 mr.)) C(imp.). Hoskins 182.

16048 The primer set furth [etc.]. *English.* 4°. *R. Graftō,* (1547 (30 no.)) L.O(imp.).LINC(w. frag. of 16026). Hoskins 187.
　　In title: 'his dominions'.

16048a — [Anr. ed.] 4°. (*R. Grafton,* 1547 (30 no.)) O.O[3](imp.). SHR(imp.). Hoskins 188.
　　In title: 'his highnes dominions'.

16049 The primer in Englishe & Latin: set forth [etc.]. 8°. (*E. Whitchurche,* 1548 (9 ja.)) L(lacks A2).; Y. Hoskins 189.

16049.3 [The primer in English.] 16°. [*R. Kele*? c. 1548.] C(duplicates of N2,3,6,7). Hoskins 190.
　　15 lines.

16049.5 [The primer in English.] 8°. (*R. Grafton,*) [1548?] LONGLEAT(lacks tp, bd. w. 2975). Hoskins 191.

16049.7 [The primer in English.] 8°. (*E. Whitchurche,* 1549 (20 jn.)) M(duplicates of 4 leaves, one of them signed Ii (I1? or Ii1?), w. Litany and col.).

16050 The prymer set furth [etc.]. *English.* 8°. [*N. Hill*? *f.*] (*R. Grafton,* 1549.) O.C[3](imp., bd. w. 2975). Hoskins 193.
　　Heading ❡I1[r]: 'An iniūccion'.

16050.3 — [Anr. ed.] *English.* 8°. [*S. Mierdman,* c. 1549.] C(imp.). Hoskins 192.
　　Heading ❡I1[r]: 'An iniūccyon'.

16050.5 The primer and catechisme set furthe [etc.]. *English.* 8°. [*J. Day*?] 1549. O(leaves 1,4,5,8 of 1st quire only).

16051 [The primer in English.] 32° in 8's. (*T. Gaultier, at the costes of R. Toye,*) [c. 1550.] C(lacks all before C2). Hoskins 194.
　　O[3] has a frag. (H[8], ff. 42–9) which apparently represents an earlier printing of the text on N[8], ff. 85–92, in the C ed., where N4 is missigned H4.

16051.5 [The primer in English.] 16° in 8's. [*E. Whitchurch,* c. 1550.] Lord Kenyon(frags. of 3 quires, Sext–7 Psalms).
　　14 lines.

16052 [The primer in English and Latin. With the epistles and gospels.] 2 pts. 8°. (*Cantorbury, J. Mychell,*) [1550?] HN(lacks all before B1 of pt. 1).

—————

16053 The primer set furth . . . corrected accordynge to the statute. *English.* 4°. (*in æd. R. Graftoni,* 1551.) L(2, 1 imp.).O[10](imp.).DUR[5](imp.).; V(imp.).Y. Hoskins 195.
　　The 1st Edwardian revision.

16054 The primer, and catechisme, set furthe . . . corrected accordyng to the statute. *English.* 8°. (*R. Grafton,*) 1551. L(imp.).O(imp.).C[10]. Hoskins 196.

Liturgies—Latin Rite—Hours and Primers—*Salisbury and Reformed—cont.*

[The primer in English.] 8⁰. (*E. Whytchurche*, 1551.) L²(5 leaves of last quire, w. Litany, Graces, and col.; Frag. No. 3). *See* 20.3.
18 lines.

16055　This prymer of Salisbury vse is se tout [*sic*] along with houtonyser chyng [*sic*]. *Latin.* 8⁰. *Rouen*, (*per N. le Roux pro R. Valentinum* [*sic*],) 1551. L(2).O(2).O³. Lord Kenyon(imp.).; HN. Hoskins 197.

16056　— [Anr. ed.] Hore beate Marie virginis secūdū vsū Saʒ. 16⁰ in 8's. (*Rothomagi, ap. R. Valētinū,* 1551. O(imp.). Hoskins 198.

16057　The primer, and cathechisme, sette furthe [etc.] *English.* 8⁰. (*R. Grafton,*) 1552. CANT.D²(imp.).; ILL. Hoskins 199, 199*.

16058　This prymer of Salisbury vse. *Latin.* 8⁰. *Rouen*, (*per J. le prest pro R. Valentinum* [*sic*],) 1554. L(imp.).O(2, 1 imp.).CANT.M.; St. Mary's Seminary, Perryville, Missouri. Hoskins 203.

16059　— [Anr. ed.] Hore beate Marie, virginis secundum vsum ısignis ecclesie Sarisburiensis. 8⁰. (*T. Petit,*) 1554. O(imp.). Hoskins 204.

16060　An vniforme and catholyke prymer in Latin and Englishe, . . . to be only vsed of al the kyng and quenes maiesties louinge subiectes. 4⁰. *J. Waylande,* 1555 (4 jn.) L.L².C².D².LIV.+; HN. Hoskins 207.
The 1st Marian ed. Many of the prayers are reprinted in 21446.7.

16061　Hore beate Marie virginis secundum vsum insignie ecclesie Sarum. 8⁰. *in ed. R. Toy,* 1555 (10 au.) C. Hoskins 208.
Collates A–I⁸ K⁴; the canticle: 'Ego dixi . . .' begins I4ʳ line 18; cf. 16067.5.

16062　The primer in English and Latin, after Salisburie vse. 8⁰. *in æd. R. Caly,* 1555 (1 oc.) C⁷.; F(imp.).ILL. Hoskins 209.

16063　The primer in Englishe (after the vse of Sarum). Whereunto is added a treatise concerning the masse. 8⁰. *J. Wailande,* 1555. O³.C(imp.).C³(imp.).P(imp.). Hoskins 211.
For separate printings of the Treatise *see* 17629 sq.

16064　The primer in Latin and Englishe (after the vse of Sarum). [With] a treatise concerning the masse. 4⁰. *J. Waylande,* 1555. L(imp.).L¹⁵.O(imp.).O¹⁷(imp.). BUTE.; ILL(imp.).N. Hoskins 212, 213.
Quire P has 4 leaves. In some copies of this and the next the 1st word of the title is 'This'.

16065　— [Anr. issue.] *J. Waylande,* 1555. L.O.C.DUR⁵(imp.). M.+; PML(2, 1 imp.).WASH³.
Quire P has 11 leaves, orig. P1 being cancelled and replaced by two 4-leaf gatherings, the 1st leaves signed P.i. and P.v. respectively. The tp is a cancel (both L; 1st word: 'The'); extra quire R⁴ is added immediately following Q4; and c⁴ is a cancel quire in smaller type to allow inclusion of the 15 Psalms.

16066　Hore beate Marie virginis secundum vsum insignie ecclesie Sarisburieñ. 8⁰. *J. Waylande,* 1555. L. Hoskins 211*.
Collates A–I⁸ K⁴; the canticle: 'Ego dixi . . .' begins I1ᵛ line 2.

16067　— [Anr. ed.] Hore beate Marie virginis secundum vsum insignis ecclesie Sasburiensis [*sic*]. 8⁰. *J. Kyng f. J. waley,* 1555. L²³. Hoskins 214.
Collates A–I⁸ K⁴; the canticle: 'Ego dixi . . .' begins I3ᵛ line 18.

16067.5　— [Anr. ed.] *Latin.* 8⁰. [*London*, c. 1555.] C(imp.). Hoskins 228.
Collates A–I⁸ K⁴; the canticle: 'Ego dixi . . .' begins I1ᵛ line 13; cf. the 2 preceding items and 16061.

16068　— [Anr. ed.] This prymer of Salisbury vse is se tout [*sic*] a long [etc.] *Latin.* 8⁰. *Rouen*, (*per J. le prest, imp. R. valentini,*) 1555. L(imp.).O.O².C.C².+; HN.ILL(lacks tp). Hoskins 215.

Liturgies—Latin Rite—Hours and Primers—*Salisbury and Reformed—cont.*

16069　— [Anr. ed.] Hore beate marie virginis secūdum vsum insignis ecclesie Sarum. 16⁰ in 8's. [*Rouen,*] *per R. Valentinum, venales habentur Rothomagi in porticu bibliopolarum,* 1555. L. Hoskins 216.

16070　Here after foloweth the prymer in Englysshe and in latin. 8⁰. (*rothomagi*, [*J. le Prest?*] *imp. R. valentini,*) 1555. L.O(2).O³¹.C(imp.). Hoskins 219.

16071　Hereafter foloweth the prymer in Englysshe and in latin. 16⁰ in 8's. (*Rothomagi,*) *in ed. R. Valentini,* 1555. L. O(imp.).M.; F(imp.).HN(frag.). Hoskins 217.
K1ʳ last line of Latin: 'vum [*sic*] me festina.'; D(lombardic)3ʳ last line of Latin: 'lo: vt meditarer'.

16071.5　— [Anr. ed.] Here after foloweth [etc.] 16⁰ in 8's. (*Rothomagi,*) *in ed. R. Valentini,* 1555. PML.
K1ʳ last line of Latin: 'uandū me festina'; D(lombardic)3ʳ last line of Latin: 'culo vt meditarer'.

16072　This prymer of Sarysbury vse is set out a long [etc.] *Latin.* 8⁰. *Rouen,* [*J. le Prest,*] *venundantur ap. R. Valentinū,* 1555. L².M.; F.ILL.NY¹¹(2). Hoskins 218.
Issued w. 2978.5.

16073　The primer in English and Latin, after Salisburie vse. 8⁰. *in æd. R. Caly,* 1556 (1 oc.) L.C(imp.).DUR³. Hoskins 220.
C2ᵛ line 1 of English begins: 'heade'.

16073.5　— [Anr. ed.] *Eng. a. Latin.* 8⁰. [*R. Caly,* 1556?] LINC (imp., bd. w. 2975.5). Hoskins 227.
C2ᵛ line 1 of English begins: 'head'.

16074　The primer in English after Salysburye vse. 8⁰. (*J. Kynge,*) 1556. C. Hoskins 222.

16075　The prymer in Englyshe for children, after the vse of Salisburye. 8⁰. [*J. Day?*] (1556.) PML. Hoskins 222*.

16075.5　— [Anr. ed.] The primer in English for children, after the vse of Saʒ. 8⁰. [*J. Kingston?* 1556?] O. Hoskins 131. (Formerly 16000)

16076　This prymer of Salisbury vse is se tout [*sic*] along [etc.] *Latin.* 8⁰. *Rouen*, (*imp. R. valentini,*) 1556. L².O.O¹⁷. ST(imp.). Douai PL.; N.WES. Hoskins 223.

16077　Here after foloweth the prymer in Englysshe and in latin. 8⁰. (*Rothomagi,*) *R. Valentin,* 1556. ETON.ST. Hoskins 224.

16078　Hereafter foloweth the prymer in Englysshe, and in Latin. 16⁰ in 8's. (*Rothomagi,*) *in ed. Florenti Valentini,* 1556. O. Hoskins 225.

16079　The prymer in Latine. 8⁰. [*J. Day f.*] *thassignes of J. Wayland,* 1557. L(imp.).O(2).C(imp.).M. Goyder.; N.PML. Hoskins 231.

16080　The prymer in Englishe and Latine. 8⁰. *the assynes of J. Wayland,* 1557. L(imp.).C.BUTE.STD.USHAW(imp.).; F.HN.CH.ILL.PML.+ Hoskins 232.

16081　The primer in Englishe and Latine. 4⁰ in 8's. *J. Kyngston a. H. Sutton,* 1557. L(imp.).O.O³.O⁸.C.+; F.BO.PML. Hoskins 233.

16081.5　Hore beate Marie virginis secundum vsum insignis ecclesie Sarisburiēsis. 16⁰ in 8's. *Rothomagi, ap. Florentium Valentinum,* [1557?] PML.

16082　The primer in English and Latin. 16⁰ in 8's. *the assignes of J. Wayland,* 1558 (22 au.) C(2, 1 imp.). Hoskins 234.

16083　— [Anr. ed.] The prymer in English and Latin. 16⁰ in 8's. *the assignes of J. Wayland,* 1558 (22 au.) L.O³.LINC. Hoskins 235.

16084　Hore beate Marie virginis secundum vsum insignie ecclesie Sarum. 16⁰ in 8's. *At London by the assynes of J. Wayland,* 1558. O(imp.).P. Hoskins 236.

16084.5　— [Anr. ed.] Hore beate Marie virginis secūdum vsum insignis ecclesie Sarum. 16⁰ in 8's. *Londini,* (*by the assynes of J. Wayland,*) [1558?] Julian I. Edison, St. Louis, Missouri.

Liturgies—Latin Rite—HOURS AND PRIMERS—*Salisbury and Reformed—cont.*

16085 The prymer in English and Latine. 8°. *the assygnes of J. Wayland,* 1558. L.O.DE(imp.).M.YK.+; HN(imp.). ILL.PML. Hoskins 237.

16086 The primer in Englysh after Salysburie vse. 8°. *(the assygnes of J. Wayland,)* 1558. O.MARL.; F(imp.). ILL. Hoskins 238.

16087 The primer set furth at large, with many godly and deuoute prayers. *English.* 4°. (*W. Seres*) [*f.*] *the assignes of J. Wayland,* 1559. L(2 imp.).O³.C⁸. Hoskins 239, 239*.
    Based on 16053. For Seres's patent to print Primers *see* Arber II.60–1. For Primers printed by Seres based more closely on the Book of Common Prayer and omitting hymns *see* 20373 sqq.; *see also The Library,* XVIII (1937), pp. 192–4.

16088 — [A ghost.]

16089 Orarium seu libellus precationum per regiam maiestatem, latinè æditus. 8°. (*ex off. W. Seres,*) 1560. L.O.C.LIV. YK.+; F. Hoskins 244.
    Based on 16042. For Primers based more closely on the Book of Common Prayer in Latin *see* 20378 sqq.

16090 The primer and cathechisme set forth at large, with many godly prayers. *English.* 8°. [*W. Seres?* c. 1560?] Sotheby's, 22 Mar. 1937, lot 300 (Aldenham copy, untraced). Hoskins 245.
    Based on 16053.

16091 — [Anr. ed.] *English.* 16° in 8's. [*W. Seres,* c. 1565.] O(A–B⁸ only, imp.).
    The catechism begins on A1ʳ; the hymn 'Iam lucis orto sidere' begins on B5ᵛ. The L copy formerly included here is now at 20377.5.

16092 — [Anr. ed.] The primer, and cathechisme, set forth at large. *English.* 8°. W. Seres, 1566 (1575.) O(2 imp.). O¹⁷. Hoskins 252.
    The catechism begins on A1ʳ; the hymn 'Iam lucis orto sidere' begins on B1ᵛ.

16093 — Now = 20377.3.

16094 The primer, or office of the blessed virgin Marie, in Latin and English: according to the reformed Latin. [*Ed.*] (R. V[erstegan, i.e. R. Rowlands.]) 12°. Antwerp, A. Conings, 1599. L².O⁴.O¹³(imp.).C(imp.).E.+; HD(lacks tp). Hoskins 267.
    A&R 680. There are 2 issues: w. engravings (L², O⁴, C) or w. woodcuts (L², HD).

16095 — [Anr. ed.] *Eng. a. Latin.* 12°. Antwerp, A. Conings, 1604. L.O.C.W.YK.+; F.HART. Hoskins 268.
    A&R 681. There are 2 issues: w. engravings (L, O, O¹⁷, CANT, YK) or w. woodcuts (L², O, F).

16095.5 The office of the blessed Virg. Marie, with the rubriques in English. *Latin.* 32° in 8's. Douay, [*P. Auroi f.*] *J. Heigham,* 1614. W(imp.). Hoskins 269*.
    A&R 685.

16096 The primer, or office of the blessed virgin Marie, in English. 18°. *Mackline, H. Jaey,* 1615. L(destroyed). L²⁶(imp.). Rogers. Hoskins 270.
    A&R 688.

16096.5 The primer, or office of the blessed virgin Marie, in Latin and English. 12°. *S. Omers,* [*C. Boscard f.*] *J. Heigham,* 1616. L²³(imp.).L²⁶(imp.).WOR²(imp.).; F(imp.). Hoskins 271.
    A&R 682.

16097 The primer according to the last edition of the Roman Breviarie. *English.* 12°. [*English secret press,*] 1617. L²³.C.C².W.; TEX. Hoskins 272.
    A&R 689.

16098 The primer, or office of the blessed virgin Marie, in Latin and English. 12°. *S. Omers,* [*C. Boscard f.*] *J. Heigham,* 1621. L²⁶(lacks tp).O.C¹⁵.MAPL(lacks tp).; F(imp.).HN. Hoskins 272*, 273.
    A&R 683.

Liturgies—Latin Rite—HOURS AND PRIMERS—*Salisbury and Reformed—cont.*

16098.3 The office . . . with the rubriques in English. *Latin.* 16° in 8's. Douay, [*P. Auroi*] *f. J. Heigham,* 1623. L⁹. ST(imp.).USHAW.
    A&R 686.

A collection of private devotions: called the hours of prayer. 1627. See 5815.5.

16098.7 The primer, or office . . . in English. 12°. Rouen, J. le Boullenger, 1630. DE. Hoskins 273**.
    A&R 690.

16099 — [Anr. ed.] *English.* 18°. S. Omers, [*widow of C. Boscard f.*] *J. Heigham,* 1631. C.SBK(imp.). Hoskins 274.
    A&R 691. With engravings.

16100 — [Anr. issue.] S. Omers, *J. Heigham,* 1631. C.C².DE.W. Hoskins 274*.
    A&R 692. Quires D–F, Ee–Gg, Oo–Qq are reprinted w. woodcuts, possibly after 1640. The W copy has engravings pasted over the woodcuts. The other quires have the letterpress identical to 16099 but have blank spaces for the engravings.

16101 — [Anr. ed.] *English.* 12°. [*Antwerp*], 1632. L(destroyed).; F. Hoskins 275.
    A&R 693. The F tp is a cancel; the Almanack is for 1631–49.

16101.2 — [Anr. ed.] *English.* 12°. Roan [i.e. *St. Omer?*] 1632. O⁵. Hoskins 276.
    A&R 694.

16101.4 The primer . . . in Latin and English. 12°. [*Rouen,*] J. le Cousturier, 1633. L.O⁸.ST(lacks tp).W(imp.). Rogers (imp.). Hoskins 278.
    A&R 684.

16101.6 The office . . . with the rubriques in English. *Latin.* 24° in 8's. [*Rouen,*] J. le Cousturier, 1633. L.BUTE.HP.LIV (imp.).YK(lacks last leaf). Cuddesdon College, Cuddesdon, Oxon.(imp.). Hoskins 277.
    A&R 687.

York

At least 2 editions (16104, 16104.5) are called Horae 'secundum usum Anglicanum' in the colophon, though York is mentioned in the title and in the heading for Matins.

16101.8 [Horae ad usum Eborum.] 8°. [*Rouen?* c. 1510.] DUR³ (frag. of 1 sheet, in a binding).

16102 — [Anr. ed.] 32° in 8's. [*R. Pynson,* 1510?] L(6 leaves of quire P, 463.h.8, f.22). Hoskins 38.
    14 lines.

16102.5 — [Anr. ed.] 8°. [*W. de Worde,* c. 1515.] London, College of Arms(frag. of 24 leaves).

16103 — [Anr. ed. d8ᵛ:] Sequuntur hore beate marie virginis secundū vsū Eboraceñ. 4° in 8's. [*Rouen, f. G. Bernard a. J. Cousin,* 1516?] YK(imp.). Hoskins 51.

16104 — [Anr. ed.] Hore beatissime virginis Marie ad legitimū Eboracensis ecclesie ritum. 4° mostly in 8's. [*Rouen,*] (*sumpt. G. bernard et J. cousin,*) *Venūdātur Rothomagi, in off. J. cousin,* (1517 (26 ja.)) L.C⁵.USHAW (imp.). Hoskins 52.
    C(lombardic)6ᵛ: 'Seqūtur [*sic*] hore . . .'

16104.5 — [Anr. ed.] 4° mostly in 8's. (imp. *J. Caillard, Rothomageñ,* 1520 (29 ja.)) YK(imp.).
    C(lombardic)6ᵛ: 'Sequūtur hore . . .'

16105 — [Anr. ed. D1ᵛ:] Sequuntur horæ . . . secundum vsuȝ Eboȝ. 16° in 8's. [*France?* 1532?] YK(imp.). Hoskins 108.

16106 — [Anr. ed.] Hore bte Marie virginis scd'm vsum Eboȝ. 16° in 8's. (*Rothomagi, per N. le roux pro J. groyat* [i.e. *Growte, in London*] *et*) *J. Marchant, Rothomageñ.,* (1536.) LINC(imp.). Hoskins 123.

16107 — [Anr. ed.] Hore beate Marie virginis secundum vsum insignis ecclesie Eboracensis. 8°. *in ed. R. Toy,* 1555. YK. Hoskins 210.

16108 — [Anr. ed.] Hore beate Marie, virginis secundum vsum insignis ecclesie Eboracensis. 8°. J. Kingstone a. H. Sutton (*f. J. wyght,*) 1556. C³. Hoskins 221.

16109 — [Anr. ed.] Hore beate Marie virginis, secundum vsum insignis ecclesie Eboriensis. 8°. [*J. Kingston a. H. Sutton*] *f. J. Wight,* [1557?] C⁶.YK(frag.). Hoskins 226.

16109.5 — [Anr. ed.] 8°. [*J. Kingston a. H. Sutton?* 1557?] YK(C⁸ only). Hoskins 230.
    C1ᵛ line 5: '& dies'; both 16108 and 16109 have 'et dies' here.

Liturgies—Latin Rite—*cont.*

HYMNS

These are the set songs from the Breviary.

Salisbury

In addition to the two forms of Hymns listed below, there is a third, without gloss or music, printed as part of most editions of the separate Psalter, e.g. 16255. For detailed listings of the contents and arrangement of each form and their relation to the Breviary *see* Bradshaw, Appendix (fully cited in the headnote preceding 15790), pp. c–cxviii.

Hymns and Sequences with Glosses

The Hymns are collected from the Breviary and the Sequences from the Missal. Those deriving from the Officia Nova (e.g. 15847.3 sqq. for the Hymns) were first printed as an appendix (16111) and remain in later editions as separate units at the end of the Hymns and the Sequences respectively. These are school texts, each accompanied by a gloss or 'expositio'. They were presumably published in paired editions, though in a few cases only one or the other survives. The Sequences as a collection were printed only in this form.

16110   Expositio hymnorū scd'm vsum Sarum. (Expositio sequentiaȝ.) 2 pts. 4° in 6's. [*Cologne, H. Quentell,* 1496.] L.O.C.LINC.P(pt. 2 only).+; HN. Duff 138.
    Collates a–i⁶; A⁸ B–I⁶ K⁸.

16111   [*Supplements.*] Sequūtur hymni q̄plures in precedenti libro deficientes. (Incipiunt expositiones prosaȝ seu sequentiarū in presedentibus [*sic*] deficientium.) 2 pts. 4° in 8's. [*R. Pynson,* 1496.] O.LINC. Duff 139.
    Collates a–b⁸; L⁶. Pynson's device, McK. 9, is on b8ᵛ and L6ᵛ. Reprinted at the end of the respective pts. of all the following eds.

16112   Expositio hymnorum secūdum vsum Sarū. (Expositio sequentiarum secundum vsum Sarum.) 2 pts. 4° in 6's. [Pt. 1 col.:] (*p r. pynson,*) [pt. 2 col.:] (1497.) L(lacks tp to pt. 1).O(imp.).O⁸.LICH.NOR².+ Duff 140.

16113   — [Anr. ed.] 2 pts. 4° in 6's. [*R. Pynson;* pt. 2 col.:] (1498.) O⁹(lacks tp to pt. 2). Copenhagen RL.; St. Mary's Seminary, Perryville, Missouri(imp.). Duff 141.
    Pynson's device, McK. 9, is on L6ᵛ, k8ᵛ. Pt. 1 has no colophon.

16114   — [Anr. ed.] 2 pts. 4° in 6's. (*in westmonasterio, per w. de worde,* 1499; [pt. 1 col.:] (6 fb.) [pt. 2 col.:] (17 mr.)) O¹⁰(imp.).C¹⁰(imp., missing). Duff 142.
    The pt. 2 colophon gives the year as '.M. cccc. lxix. ix. [*sic*]'; from the state of the device it was actually pr. in 1500.

16115   — [A ghost.]
16116   Expositio hymnorum totius anni secundum vsnm [*sic*] Sarum: multis elucidationibus aucta. (Expositio sequentiarum.) [*Ed. by J. Badius Ascensius, w. his prefaces.*] 2 pts. 4° 8·4; pt. 2 in 6's. (*in inclyta Parrhisiorū Lutecia, ab. A. Bocardo: ere et impendio J. balduini seu boudins [in London,]* 1502; [pt. 1 col.:] (nonis mr.) [pt. 2 col.:] (15 cal. mr.)) L.O(1, plus pt. 2 only).C⁷.C¹⁶(pt. 1 only).; ILL.
    Badius's glosses are reprinted in most of the following eds., but the prefaces are sometimes omitted.

16116a   — [Anr. ed.] 2 pts. 4° 8·4; pt. 2 in 6's. (*per w. de worde,* 1502; [pt. 1 col.:] (7 oc.) [pt. 2 col.:] (29 de.)) L(tp to pt. 2 only, Harl.5974/58). Nantwich Parish Church, Cheshire(pt. 1 only).; PML(lacks I1,8 of pt. 1).

16116a.5   Expositio hymnoȝ scd'm vsum Saȝ. (Expositio sequentiarum.) 2 pts. 4° in 6's. [*R. Pynson;* pt. 2 col.:] (1502.) G².
    Pynson's device, McK. 9, is on L6ᵛ and K8ᵛ. Pt. 1 has no colophon.

16117   Expositio hymnorum totius anni secundum vsum Sarum. (Expositio sequentiarum.) 2 pts. 4° 8·4. (*J. Notary,* [pt. 2 col.:] 1505 (2 my.)) L.L².
    Pt. 1 has an undated colophon.

16117.5   Expositio hymnoȝ secūdū vsū Saȝ. (Expositio sequentiarum.) 2 pts. 4° in 6's. [Pt. 2 col.:] (*per me R. pynson,* 1506 (6 ja.)) C⁵.
    Pt. 1 has no colophon.

16118   Expositio sequentiarum. 4° in 6's. [*Rouen, P. Violette f. A. Myllar in Edinburgh,*] (1506 (10 jn.)) L.
    Myllar's device, McK. 22, is on k6ᵛ.

16119   Expositio hymnorum totius anni diligentissime recognitorum, multis elucidationibus aucta. (Expositio sequentiarum.) 2 pts. 4° 8·6·4; pt. 2 in 6's. (*Rothomagi, per P. violete, imp. G. wansfort in ciuitate Eboȝ,* 1507 (15 jn.)) O(imp.).M.
    Both titles omit 'ad usum Sarum' as perhaps not necessary for sale in York; cf. 16128.2.

16119.5   — [A variant of pt. 2, w. col.:] (*Rothomagi, per P. violete, imp. P. regnault, Cadom* [i.e. *Caen,*] 1507 (15 jn.)) Seville, Biblioteca Colombina(pt. 2 only).

16120   — [Anr. ed.] 2 pts. 4° 8·4; pt. 2 in 6's. [Pt. 1 col.:] (*p w. de worde,* 1508 (30 jn.)) L(lacks tp to pt. 1 and last 2 leaves of pt. 2).

16121   Expositio hymnoȝ. (Expositio sequentiaȝ.) 2 pts. 4° 8·4. *per w. de worde,* (1509; [pt. 1 col.:] (6 jy.) [pt. 2 col.:] (26 au.)) O(pt. 1 only).; F(2 pts., bd. separately).HN (pt. 1 only).

16121a   Expositio sequentiarum. 4° in 6's. (*per me R. pynson,* 1509 (17 oc.)) O(bd. w. 16123).

16122   Expositio hymnoru3 totius anni secūdum vsū Sarum. (Expositio sequentiarum.) 2 pts. 4° 8·4. [Pt. 1 tp:] *Venduntur in ed. J. notarii;* [pt. 2 col.:] (*per J. Notarii* [sic], 1510 (2 oc.)) L²(pt. 1 only).L¹⁵.C(lacks hh4 of pt. 2).
    Pt. 1 has an undated colophon.

16123   Expositio hymnorū secūdum vsum Sarum. 4° 8·4. (*per me R. pynson,* 1511 (2 oc.)) O(bd. w. 16121a).

16123a   Expositio sequentiaȝ toti⁹ anni. 4° 8·4. *p w. de worde,* (1512 (10 ja.)) O⁵(frag.).; F(bd. w. 16124).HN.

16124   Expositio hymnoȝ toti⁹ anni secūdū vsum Saȝ. 4° 8·4. *p w. de worde,* (1512 (8 my.)) F(bd. w. 16123a).

16125   Expositio hymnoȝ totius anni. (Expositio sequētiarū.) 2 pts. 4° 8·4. *p w. de worde,* (1514; [pt. 1 col.:] (12 jn.) [pt. 2 col.:] (8 jy.)) L.C²(pt. 2 only, lacking tp and last leaf).D².; Y.

16126   — [Anr. ed.] 2 pts. 4° 8·4. *per w. de worde,* 1515; [pt. 1 col.:] (14 jn.) [pt. 2 col.:] (8 jn.)) L.O(2, 1 imp.).O⁸. D². Lord Kenyon.; F(pt. 2 only, lacking last leaf).HN (pt. 2 only).

16127   — [Anr. ed.] 2 pts. 4° 8·4; pt. 2 in 6's. (*per me R. Pynson,* 1515; [pt. 1 col.:] (15 se.) [pt. 2 col.:] (3 jy.)) O¹⁶ (lacks tp to pt. 1).C.NLW.

16128   — [Anr. ed.] 2 pts. 4° 8·4. *p W. de Worde,* (1517.) L(lacks last leaf of pt. 2).; Y(pt. 2 only, bd. w. 16128.5).

16128.2   Expositio sequentiarum recentissime impressa. 8°. *Cadomi* [i.e. *Caen,*] imp. M. Angier, (1519 (12 mr.)) L².
    While the title does not mention Sarum and the colophon specifies: 'secundum vsum modernum in ecclesia Christi', these are the Sarum Sequences with the usual supplement at the end of the text. It was perhaps intended for sale in York; cf. 16119 sq.

16128.3   Expositio hymnorum totius anni secundū vsum Sarum. (Expositio sequentiarū.) 2 pts. 4° 8·4. *Antuerpie, per me M. Hillenium Hoochstratanum;* [pt. 2 tp:] (*Venundantur Londoñ in cemiterio sancti Pauli,*) [c. 1520.] L(tp to pt. 2 only, Harl.5927/4).L².O.C³. ETON.+

16128.5   Expositio hymnorū totius anni secundu [*sic*] vsum Saȝ. 4° 8·4. *p W. de Worde,* (1527.) Lord Kenyon(frag.).; Y(bd. w. pt. 2 of 16128).

16128.7   Expositio hymnorū totius anni secundū vsum Saȝ. (Expositio sequentiarum.) 2 pts. 4° 8·4; pt. 2 in 6's. *p W. de Worde,* [pt. 1 col.:] (1530 (8 oc.)) C(2 leaves, Sayle 8908).; LC.

Hymns with Music

The Hymns generally follow the arrangement of the Totum pattern of the Breviary: Temporale, Commune Sanctorum, Proprium Sanctorum. Except for very brief directions (rubrics) when the Hymns are to be sung, this gives only hymn texts, with the music from the Antiphoner repeated for each verse of a hymn and not just accompanying the first verse.

16129   Hymnoȝ cū notis opusculū diurno seruitio per totius anni circulū . . . secūdū vsū insignis ecclesie Sarisburiēsis. 4° in 8's. *in alma Parisiorū acad.,* [*T. Kerver,*] imp. F. byrchmā [*in London,*] (*Venale habetur Londonie in cimiterio sācti pauli ap. scolas nouas,* 1518 (10 ja.)) O²(imp.).C.

16129.3   Hymnorum cum notis opusculum . . . secundū exemplar Parisiis impressum. 4° in 8's. *Rothomagi, venale habetur in ed. J. cousin,* (1518 (5 no.)) O¹⁴.LIV.

Liturgies—Latin Rite—HYMNS—*Salisbury*—*Hymns with Music*
—*cont.*

16130 Hymnorum cum notis opusculū, secundū vsum insignis ecclesie Sarisburiensis. 4° in 8's. *Antwerpie, (arte C. endouiñ. [i.e. Ruremond,] sumpt. P. kaetz,) Venundantur Londonij ap. p. kaetz,* (1524 (5 ap.)) O(3). C(frag.).

16131 Hymnorum cum notis opusculū. 4° in 8's. *Antwerpie, (per C. Endouiensem [i.e. Ruremond,]) imp. F. brykman [in London,]* (1525 (31 my.)) L.L[15].O[10].C(imp.).DE.

16131.5 Hynorum [*sic*] cum notis opusculum ad vsum Sa₂. 4° in 8's. (*Antwerpie, per C. Endouiensem [i.e. Ruremond,] imp. G. de hagis [i.e. van der Haghen,]*) 1528. L.O[5].

16132 Hymnorum cum notis opusculū vsui insignis ecclesie Sarū subseruiens. 4° in 8's. (*Antwerpie, in off. vidue C. Ruremundeñ.,*) 1532 (1533 (oc.)) L(imp.).

16133 Hymnorū cum notis opusculū. 4° in 8's. (*Antwerpie, in off. vidue C. Ruremundeñ., imp. J. Coccij [in London,]*) 1541 (jy.) L.O.O[3](imp.).BUTE.W.; PML.

16134 Hymnorū cū notis opusculū. 4° in 8's. *per J. Kyngston & H. Sutton,* 1555. L(imp.).L[2].O(2).O[12]. Coughton Court, Alcester, Warks.

York

Hymns of York use which are not also of Sarum use are included, without music, at the end of most editions of the separate Psalter, e.g. 16255.

Hymns with Music

16135 Hymni canori cum iubilo secundum morem ecclesie Eboracēsis. 4° in 8's. (*Rothomagi, i off. P. Oliuier,*) imp. *J. gachet [in York,]* (1517 (5 fb.)) L(imp.).C[5].

LEGENDA

These contain the readings from the Old Testament, Gospels, and church fathers, and lives of saints belonging to the services said in the choir. They follow the *Totum* pattern of the Breviary: Temporale, Commune Sanctorum, Proprium Sanctorum.

16136 [Z4[v]:] Legēde festiuitatū tā temporaliū φ sancto₂ p totū annū scd'm ordinationē ecclesie Sa₂. fol. (*Parisius, per G. Maynyal [f. W. Caxton in Westminster,]* 1488 (14 au.)) L(lacks 21 leaves).C(2 frags., of 27 and of 2 leaves).C[7](2 leaves).C[13](1 leaf).PARIS(7 leaves). Duff 247.
    Caxton's device, McK. 1, is on z5[v]. For a detailed description of the L copy *see The Library,* XII (1957), pp. 225–39.

16137 Legende totius anni tam de tēpore φ de sanctis secūdum ordinem Sa₂. fol. (*Parisius, per w. hopylium, imp. F. byrckman [in London,]* 1518.) O(2).C(tp in facs.). LIV(lacks 7 leaves).

LITANY

The golden letany. 1531, etc. *See* 15707 sq.

MANUALS

Early editions of these provide the music, spoken texts, and directions for the priest's use when his position was not fixed either at the altar or in the choir, and so constitute a priest's walking book. There are services taken from the Missal, e.g. the night before Christmas, the Thursday of the Last Supper, the marriage ceremony; others from the Breviary, e.g. the Vigiliae Mortuorum; and others specially developed, e.g. baptism, visitation of the sick, burial of the dead. After Queen Mary's reign only those services were retained which occurred at no specified time, e.g. baptism, marriage (the 'occasional' offices), and the music was omitted.

Salisbury

16138 Manuale ad vsum insignis ecclesie Sarū. fol. [*Paris, B. Rembolt,* 1498.] C[9]. Duff 287.
    Rembolt's device is on the tp.

16139 — [Anr. ed.] 4° in 8's. *Rothomagi, (opera p. oliuier et J. de lorraine socio₂,) imp. J. richardi,* (1500 (primo in pascha.)) O(lacks 9 leaves). Duff 288.

16139.5 — [Anr. ed.] 4° in 8's. *Parisius, imp. A. verard,* [c. 1505.] MARL(imp.).

16140 — [Anr. ed.] fol. (*R. Pynson,* 1506.) L(lacks 7 leaves). C[7](lacks 14 leaves).ST(lacks 2 leaves).

16140.3 — [Anr. ed.] 4° in 8's. *Rothomagi, (opera P. Oliuier,) imp. J. richardi,* (1509 (27 ap.)) ST(imp.).

16140.5 — [Anr. ed.] 4° in 8's. [*Rouen, P. Violette,* c. 1509.] HN (n1,2,7,8).

Liturgies—Latin Rite—MANUALS—*Salisbury*—*cont.*

16140.7 — [Anr. ed.] 4° in 8's. (*Rothomagi,* [*P. Olivier,*] 1510 (22 ⟨ ?⟩)) O(imp.).
    O also has 4 leaves of an ed. pr. about this time, prob. at Rouen by Martin Morin.

16141 — [Anr. ed.] 4° in 8's. *Rothomagi, in off. M[artin] Morin, imp. J. Caillart,* (1515 (31 my.)) C[8]. Rogers.

16141.5 — [Anr. ed.] fol. (*in alma Parisiorū acad., [W. Hopyl,] imp. F. byrckman [in London,]* 1515.) LIV(lacks 2 leaves).; PML.

16142 — [Anr. ed.] 4° in 8's. *Rothomagi, in off. P. Oliuier, imp. J. cousin,* 1516 (10 de.) L(lacks 6 leaves).

16143 — [Anr. ed.] 4° in 8's. *Rothomagi, in off. P. oliuier, on les vent a Rouen en la maison P. coste,* [1520?] L(lacks 4 leaves).

16144 — [Anr. ed.] 4° in 8's. *pro J. caillart, Rothomageñ.,* (1522 (24 de.)) O.C.USHAW(imp.).

16145 — [Anr. ed.] fol. *Antwerpie, (arte C. Endouiēsis [i.e. Ruremond,]) Venūdantur Londini ap. P. kaetz,* (1523 (11 jy.)) L.L[8].O(imp.).O[16](imp.).

16146 — [Anr. issue, w. tp imprint:] *Venūdantur Londini ap. F. byrckman.* F.

16147 Manuale ad vsum percelebris ecclesie Sarisberieñ. fol. *Parrisijs, per D. maheu,* 1526 (5 id. oc.) L.

16148 Manuale ad vsum ecclesie Sarisburiensis. 4° in 8's. *Parisijs, per F. Regnault,* 1529 (17 de.) C(imp.). Lord Kenyon(imp.).

16148.2 — [A variant, w. tp date:] 1530. O(2, 1 imp.).LINC. F. J. Norton, Cambridge Univ. Library.
    The colophon is still dated 17 Dec. 1529.

16148.4 — [Anr. ed.] 4° in 8's. (*Parisijs,) pro J. Cousin, Rothomageñ.,* 1537 (14 jy.) C[5](imp.).; ILL(lacks last leaf).

16148.6 — [Anr. ed.] 4° in 8's. *Parisijs, p̄ F. Regnault,* 1537 (17 oc.) O.C[5](imp.).

16149 Manuale ad vsum insignis ecclesie Sarum. 4° in 8's. *Antuerpie, (in off. vidue C. Ruremundensis,)* 1542 (1543 (ja.)) O.C.C[9].ST.USHAW.+; F.

16150 Manuale ad vsum percelebris ecclesie Sarisburiensis. 4° in 8's. *Rothomagi, typis N. Rufi* [i.e. le Roux,] 1543. L.O(2).O[24].DUR(Bamb.).M(imp.).; F.

16151 — [Anr. ed.] Nouiter impressum. 4° in 8's. [*R. Caly,*] 1554. L(2, 1 lacks tp).L[3].L[15](imp.).O[31].
    The tp has border McK. & F. 48β w. Caly's inits. at the bottom.

16152 — [Anr. ed.] Recēter impressum. 4° in 8's. (*ex off. J. Kingston & H. Sutton,*) 1554. L.O.O[3].STU.YK.+; HN. HD(2).PML.

16153 — [Anr. ed.] Nouiter impressum. 4° in 8's. [*J. Kingston a. H. Sutton,*] 1554. L.L[27].O.O[5].C[5].+; F.N.
    The tp of this, 16152, and 16154 has border McK. & F. 38 w. winged cherub at the bottom.

16154 — [A variant, w. title reading:] Recenter impressū. L.L[2]. L[15].O.C.+; F.BO.

16155 Manuale ad vsum insignis ecclesie Sarisburiensis. 4° in 8's. *Rothomagi,* [*R. Hamillon,*] *venale habetur ap. R. valētinū,* 1554. L.O.C[2].DUR[3].M.+; HN.
    The O copies are in 2 different typesettings; a2[r] line 4 ends 'pulsētur' (Gough Missals 170, 181) or 'pulsentur' (Douce BB 167).

16155a — [Anr. ed.] 4° in 8's. *Rothomagi,* [*R. Hamillon,*] *venale habetur ap. R. valētinū,* 1555. L.L[2].O.O[31].D[2].+; F. PML.Y.

16156 Manuale ad vsum per celebris ecclesie Sarisburiensis. Recenter impressum. 4° in 8's. [*R. Caly,*] 1555. L[13].O.O[10].C(2).; BO.CH.
    The tp has border McK. & F. 51 w. sea horses at the bottom.

16157 — [A ghost.]

16157.5 Sacra institutio baptizandi: matrimonium celebrandi: . . . juxta usum insignis ecclesiæ Sarisburienfis [*sic*]. [*Ed.* E. Maihew.] 4°. *Duaci, L. Kellam,* 1604. L.O.C.DE. W.+; HD(lacks ā[2]).PML.TEX.Y.
    A&R 717. Copies should have ā[2], w. ā1 having an index on the recto and approbation dated 5 July 1604 on the verso; ā2 is blank.

16158 — [Anr. issue w. 8 additional leaves.] (Annotationes.) L.O.C.M.W.+; HN.NY[11].PML.TEX.
    A&R 718. The index/approbation leaf is retained but in some copies (1 C) is mispaginated '6'.

16159 Manuale sacerdotum hoc est. Ritus administrandi sacramenta baptismi, matrimonii, [etc.] 8°. *Duaci, L. Kellam,* 1610. L.O.C.CASHEL.W.+; HD.NY[11].TEX. WASH[3].
    A&R 719. Approbation dated 9 Feb. 1611 is on

Liturgies—Latin Rite—MANUALS—*Salisbury—cont.*

T5ᵛ; T6–8 are blank or have proofs. The 3 C copies have T6 blank and on T7 an earlier state of K8 w. the black portions of the recto imperfectly pr. One C copy retains T8, having the text of K1 w. the black portions of the verso imperfectly pr. This and a 2nd C copy have bd. in an earlier state of K1,8 w. only the red portions of the rectos pr., the versos being blank. HD has T6,7 cut out and T8 blank. DE has on T6 different proof of K1.

York

16160   Ad laudem dei et honorē tuāꝗ non immerito flos virgo maria ecce manuale quoddam secundu3 vsū matris eccl'ie Eboraceñ. 4° in 8's. (*per w. de Worde* [really *Paris?*] *pro J. Gaschet* [*in York*] *et J. ferrebouc* [*in Paris*] *sociis,* 1509 (4 ydus fb.)) L(imp.).O.C⁶.USHAW (imp.). Earl Fitzwilliam.; HN.N.

16161   — [Anr. ed.] 4° in 8's. [*Rouen, N. le Roux?*] *imp. J. Gachet, Eboraceñ.,* [1530?] AMP.D²(lacks 2 leaves).

England, Scotland, and Ireland

16161.5 Ordo baptizandi aliáque sacramenta administrandi, & officia quædam ecclesiastica ritè peragendi: ex rituali Romano, jussu Pauli quinti edito, extractus. Pro Anglia, Hibernia, & Scotia. 12° in 6's. [*St. Omer, English College Press,*] 1632. OS.
A&R 721. For earlier eds. *see* pt. 2 of 16226 sq.

16162   — [Anr. ed.] 24° in 8's. *Parisiis,* [*widow of J. Blagaert,*] 1636. L(destroyed).O.W. Rogers.
A&R 722.

16162.3 — [Anr. ed.] 12°. [*St. Omer, English College Press,*] 1639. L⁹.O.DAI(lacks tp).ST.W.; TEX.
A&R 723.

16162.7 — [Anr. ed.] 32°. [*Rouen,*] *per J. Cousturier,* 1639. DE.
A&R 724.

MARTYROLOGY

See 17532 sq.

MISSALS

These contain the services said at the altar throughout the year. There are the following sections:

Kal.   Kalendar of fixed feasts, with the blessings for salt, water, and bread (Salisbury) or with rules and prayers (York).

Temp.   Temporale or Proprium de Tempore: services for the seasonal festivals, running from the first Sunday in Advent through the last Saturday in Trinity term, followed by those for the dedication of a church.

Prop.SS.   Proprium Sanctorum or Sanctorale: services for fixed festivals, beginning with St. Andrew's Eve (29 November).

Com.SS.   Commune Sanctorum: services common to a number of occasions or frequently repeated, e.g. for an apostle, for several martyrs, the marriage ceremony.

Note that the main unit of the mass, including the ordinary and the canon of the mass, is associated with the Temporale. In this unit the canon of the mass is frequently given special treatment by being printed on vellum and/or in larger types than the rest of the Missal. In the earliest editions of Salisbury use this unit precedes the service for Easter Sunday; in most later editions this unit follows the Temporale. In editions of York use this unit precedes Trinity Sunday. Many editions, e.g. 16182, 16190, have at the end the Accentuarium on the pronunciation of vowels, also found in some folio Breviaries.

Hereford

16163   Anno incarnationis dominice . . . hoc nouum opus sacri missalis ad vsu famose ac percelebris eccl'ie Helfordeñ. nuper correctum et emendatum [etc.] fol. *Rothomagi, opera P. oliuerii et J. mauditier, imp. J. richardi,* 1502 (1 se.) L.O(2 imp.).O⁸(imp.).GLOUC (imp.).

Salisbury

16164   [a4ʳ:] Missale ad vsum Saꝝ incipit fe-/liciter. fol. (*Parisi⁹, arte G. Maynyal, imp. G. Caxton* [*in Westminster,*] 1487 (4 de.)) DUR³(3 leaves). Lyme Park, Disley, Cheshire(imp.). Duff 322.

Liturgies—Latin Rite—MISSALS—*Salisbury—cont.*

16165   [a4ʳ:] Missale ad vsum Saꝝ. inci/pit feliciter. fol. [*Basle, M. Wenssler,* 1489.] L.O. Le Havre PL(imp.). Duff 323.

16166   Missale secundum vsum ecclesie sarisburieñ. fol. [*Rouen,*] (*imp. et arte Martini morin,* 1492 (12 oc.)) L(lacks 1 leaf).O(lacks 27 leaves). Duff 323.

16167   Missale secundum vsum ecclesie Sarum Anglicane. fol. (*venetijs, p J. hertzog de landoia, imp. f. de egmont ac G. barreuelt* [*in London,*] 1494 (kal'. se.)) L(frags.). O(frags.).C(lacks 3 leaves). Bologna U(imp.). Il Castello di Monselice, nr. Padua, Italy.+ Duff 324.

16168   — [Anr. ed.] 8°. (*venetijs, per J. hertzog de landoia,* [*f.*] *F. egmont,* 1494 (kal'. de.)) L.O.C(imp.).A(imp.). Lord Kenyon.+ Duff 325.

16169   — [Anr. ed.] fol. (*Parisius, per U. Gerig & B. Renbolt, imp. w. de worde & Michael morin* [*both in London*] *necnō P. leueti* [*in Paris,*] 1497 (2 ja.)) L(lacks 7 leaves).; HN(last leaves defective).

16170   — [Anr. ed.] fol. [*Rouen, Martin Morin,* 1497?] L.; HD. Duff 326.
With Morin's device at the end, w. his name in type enclosed within a border. This may have been pr. [c. 1500.]

16171   — [Anr. ed.] fol. (*Rothomagi, opera Martini Morin, imp. J. richardi,* 1497 (4 de.)) L.C¹¹(lacks last leaf).A.W. WIN.; BO. Duff 327.

16172   — [Anr. ed.] fol. (*Londoñ., ap. westmonasteriū, per J. notaire et J. barbier, imp. w. de worde,* 1498 (20 de.)) L(imp.).C.E(imp.).M(imp.). Ossory Diocesan Library, Kilkenny, Co. Kilkenny.+ Duff 328.
2 cols., 37 lines.

16172.5 — [Anr. ed.] fol. [*London?* c. 1500?] O(1 leaf, Vet. A 1 b.12(11)), w. pt. of the marriage service).
2 cols., 38 lines. The types have some resemblance to Notary's 110 mm. textura and W. Fakes's 112 mm. textura, but they are rather mixed and worn.

16173   — [Anr. ed.] fol. (*p R. Pynson, mandato & imp. J. Morton Cantuarieñ Archiepi,* 1500 (10 ja.)) O.O²⁵(imp.).C² (imp.).C³(imp.).M. Duff 329.
Duff erroneously attrib. a copy to O⁸.

16174   — [Anr. ed.] fol. (*in Parhisioꝝ acad., per J. higmanū & W. hopyliū* [*f.*] *J B* [*a.*] *G H,* 1500 (10 kal. jy.)) O.O¹⁸ (frag.).WN². Duff 330.

16175   Ad vsum insignis ecclesie sarū missale. fol. *ab J. de prato alme parisiensis vniuersitatis librario jurato, Venales ap. bibliopolas in cimiterio sācti pauli Londoñ. inuenientur,* 1500 (2 kl'. oc.) L²³(imp.).O⁴(frag.).C¹² (imp.).ELY.NOR². Duff 331.
The date should prob. be interpreted as 1502 (kl'. oc.).

16176   Missale scd'm vsum insignis ecclesie Saꝝ. fol. [*Rouen, Martin Morin,*] (*imp. J. Huuyn,* 1501 (4 se.)) O.
— [Anr. ed.] 1502 (kl'. oc.)) See 16175.

16177   Missale ad vsum insignis ac famose ecclesie Sarū. 8°. (*parisiis, p T. Keruer,* 1503 (prid. non. ap.)) O(2, 1 imp.).ST(imp.).USHAW(2.; F.TEX(imp.).

16178   Ad vsū insignis ecclesie Sarū missale. fol. *ab artis successoribus J. de Prato Parisiēsis, Venales ap. bibliopolas in cimyterio sancti Pauli Londoñ inuenientur,* 1504 (9 kl' ja.) L(lacks pt. of Kal.). Rogers(lacks tp and f2).

16179   Missale ad vsum insignis eccclesie [*sic*] Sarum. fol. (*per R. Pynson, mandato & imp. regis Henrici septimi,* 1504 (10 kal. ja.)) L(imp.). O³¹(imp.).C³.M(imp.).WN² (2 leaves).; HN.

16180   — [Anr. ed.] fol. (*imp. A. verard Parisieñ,* 1504 (29 jn.)) L(imp.).C(lacks 3 leaves).

16181   Missale ad cōsuetudinē insignis ecclesie Sarū. fol. *in alma Parhisiorum acad.,* (*diligētia w. hopylij, imp. G. cluen et F. byrckmā sociorū* [*in London,*]) 1504 (13 kl'. se.) L.O(frag.).D.
In the colophon the month date is 'Kalēdas Septēbris', i.e. 1 Sept.

16182   Missale ad vsū insignis ecclesie Saꝝ. 4° in 8's. [1st col.:] (*Rothomagi, per Martinū Morin,* 1506 (12 my.)) [2nd col.:] (. . . *imp. J. richardi ac J. huuyn necnō P. coste et G. besnard,* 1506.) L².O².C(imp.).USHAW(imp.).; F.

16182a Missale scd'm vsum insignis ecclesie Saꝝ. fol. [*Paris, A. Verard,*] (*imp. J. huuyn et G. bernard* [*in Rouen,*] 1508 (27 ap.)) O(imp.).DUR⁵(frag.).
Verard's name occurs only in the 'M' of the xylographic 'Missale'.

16182a.5 — [Anr. issue, w. colophon:] (*imp. ⟨w.⟩ de worde, Londoñ.,* 1508(2⟨7⟩ ap.)) O⁵(frags. of 4 leaves).

Liturgies—Latin Rite—Missals—*Salisbury—cont.*

16183 — [Anr. ed.] fol. (*Rothomagi, arte Martini morin, imp. J. richardi,* 1508 (27 my.)) O(lacks tp).C(lacks 3 leaves).; NY[11].

16184 Missale ad vsū insignis ecclesie Saᵣ. 4° in 8's. [1st col.:] (*Rothomagi, p Martinū Mori,* 1508 (7 au.)) [2nd col.:] (. . . *imp. J. Richardi,* 1508 (6 au.)) L(imp.). BUTE.USHAW(imp.). Lord Kenyon.

16185 — [Anr. ed.] 4° in 8's. (*Rothomagi, in off. J. loys, imp. J. huuin,* 1508 (27 se.)) L.O.

16186 — [Anr. ed.] 4° in 8's. (*Rothomagi, in off. P. violette, imp. G. candos,* 1509 (2 au.)) L.L[8](imp.).YK.; PML.

16187 — [Anr. ed.] fol. (*Rothomagi, arte martini morin, imp. J. Richardi,* 1510 (26 no.)) O(16 leaves, bd. w. 16166).

16188 Missale ad cōsuetudinē insignis ecclesie Sarum. fol. *in alma Parisiorum acad.,* 1510 (10 kal. ap.) [col.:] (. . . *opera w. Hopylij, imp. F. byrchmā* [*in London,*] 1511 (7 fb.)) O.C.C[3].D.YK.+; HD(imp.).LC(1 leaf). PML.

16188.5 Missale ad vsū insignis eccl'ie Saᵣ. 4° in 8's. [1st col.:] (*Rothomagi, per Martinū Mori,* 1510 (27 fb.)) [2nd col.:] (. . . *imp. J. Richardi,* 1511 (21 jn.)) BUTE.

16189 Missale ad consuetudinem insignis ecclesie Sarū. fol. (*in alma Parhisioᵣ acad., diligentia R. sutoris* [i.e. Cousturier,] *imp. w. de worde, R. faques* [both in London,] *J. bienayse & J. ferrebouc* [both in Paris,] *Venundantur in ed. w. de worde, aut R. Facques, in cymiterio sancti pauli Londoñ.,* (1511 (6 kl'. my.)) L (lacks 1 leaf).O[24](frag.).C[8].

16190 Missale ad vsū insignis ac preclare ecclesie Saᵣ. fol. *per R. pynson,* (1512 (8 kal. mr.)) L(lacks tp and CC4).O. C(imp.).DUR(Bamb.).SCL.+

16191 Missale ad cōsuetudinem ecclesie Sarum. fol. (*Parrhisij, per B. Remboldt,* 1513 (21 ja.)) L.O[25].C(imp.).C[5]. Sir Richard Proby.

16192 — = 16194.

16193 Missale ad vsū ac cōsuetudinē Sarū. fol. (*in alma Parisiorum acad., opera w. Hopylij, imp. F. byrchman* [*in London,*] 1514 (28 no.)) L(imp.).O.C.DUR[3].LIV.+; PML.

16194 Missale ad vsū ac consuetudine ac preclare ecclesie Saᵣ. 4° in 8's. (*Rothomagi,*) *Martinus Morin,* (*ere et expensis G. bernard,* 1514 (15 fb.)) L(imp.).O(lacks 2 leaves).ST. (Formerly also 16192.)

16195 Missale ad vsum atᵩ consuetudinē insignis ecclesie Saᵣ. 8°. *in alma Parisiorū acad.,* (*a w. Hopylio,*) *imp. F. Byrkmā* [*in London,*] 1515. L.O.DE(imp.).HAT.YK (imp.).+; F.HN.HD.Y.

16195.5 Missale ad vsum insignis ac preclare ecclesie Saᵣ. 4° in 8's. (*Rothomagi,*) *Martinus Morin,* (*imp. J. huum* [i.e. Huvin] *et J. cousu* [i.e. Cousin,] 1515 (9 au.)) ST(imp.).

16196 — [Anr. ed.] 4° in 8's. (*Rothomagi, opera P. oliuier, imp. G. bernard,* 1516 (31 ja.)) L[2].

16197 — [Anr. ed.] 8°. *in alma Parisiorū acad.,* (*per J. kerbriant alias huguelin & J. Adam, socios, imp. eorūdē necnon J. Petit atᵩ J. Bienayse,*) 1516 (22 au.) L(lacks 4 leaves).O.C.E[2](lacks 2 leaves).USHAW(imp.).+; BO[6] (imp.).PML.

16198 — [Anr. ed.] 4° in 8's. (*Rothomagi, opera E. hardy, imp. J. caillard,* [15]18 (5 jn.)) L(imp.).C(imp.).

16199 — [Anr. ed.] fol. [*Rouen, M. Morin,*] (*imp. F. Regnault, Parisieñ,* 1519 (20 mr.)) L[23](imp.).O.C[16].D. Morin's name occurs in the init. 'M' on the tp.

16200 — [Anr. ed.] 4° in 8's. *in alma Parisiorum acad.,* (*per N. higman, imp. F. regnault et F. Byrckman* [*in London,*]) 1519 (29 oc.) O.O[31].C.C[16].ST.+; CH.PML.

16201 Missale ad vsum ac consuetudinem insignis ecclesie Sarum. fol. [*Rouen,*] (*opera P. oliuier, exp. J. cousin,* 1519 (24 de.)) L.C.C[5].SAL. The Proprium Sanctorum collates A–F[8] G[10].

16201.3 — [Anr. issue, w. Proprium Sanctorum reprinted, collating A–H[8] I[10].] C[2].LEIC.

16201.7 Missale ad vsum insignis ac preclare ecclīe Saᵣ. 4° in 8's. [*Rouen, f. J. Cousin,*] (1519.) O(imp.). Cousin's device is on the tp, and the date is on the tp verso.

16202 — [Anr. ed.] fol. (*per R. Pynson,* 1520 (9 kal. ja.)) L.O.C. C[3].G[2].+; HD.PML.

16202.5 — [Anr. ed.] 4° in 8's. [*Rouen, f. R. Macé a. N. Mullot?* c. 1520.] Lord Kenyon(imp.). Approx. 15 mm. below the signature line on k1,3, l1,3, p1,3, r3, A1, and E(lombardic)1 are pr. 'Mace' or 'Mace', and at the same position on A3 is 'Mulot', presumably to designate sheets allotted to each publisher.

Liturgies—Latin Rite—Missals—*Salisbury—cont.*

16203 — [Anr. ed.] fol. (*Parisius, imp. J. petit, J. bienayse & J. adā,* 1521 (30 jy.)) L(lacks 2 leaves).O[12](imp.). Copenhagen RL(imp.).

16204 — [Anr. ed.] 4° in 8's. (*Rothomagi, opera P. oliuier, imp. J. cousin,* [15]21 (5 se.)) L[2](imp.).O.

16204.5 — [A variant, w. colophon:] (*Rothomagi, opera P. oliuier, imp. J. caillard,* [15]21 (5 se.)) O(imp.).

16205 Missale ad vsum īsignis ecclesie Saᵣ. fol. *in alma Parrhisiorum acad.,* (*imp. F. Regnault,*) 1526 (30 oc.) O.C.A[2].MAYNOOTH.YK.+

16205.5 — [Anr. ed.] fol. (*Parisius, imp. J. petit,* 1527 (6 fb.)) C(imp.).

16206 Missale ad vsū ac cōsuetudinē Sarū. fol. (*in alma Parisiorum acad., opera N. Preuost, imp. F. Byrckman* [*in London,*] 1527 (3 kal. mr.)) L(imp.).O.C(imp.).DUR[5]. SAL.+; F.PML.

16207 Missale ad vsum insignis ecclesie Sarum. fol. (*Antwerpie, asscribēdū est C. Ruremūdñ,*) *Venundantur ap. F. byrckman* [*in London,*] 1527 (28 mr.) L(imp.).O.O[3]. C(imp.).USHAW(imp.).+; HN.

16208 Missale ad vsum insignis ac preclare ecclesie Saᵣ. 4° in 8's. *in alma Parisiorum acad.,* (*per F. regnault,*) 1527 (27 jy.) L.L[2].O(imp.).ST.YK.+; N.PML.

16209 Missale ad vsum insignis ecclesie Saᵣ. fol. [*Antwerp,*] (*opere, atᵩ imp. C. Ruremūdensis,* 1528 (14 ap.)) L.O (imp.).C(imp.).BUTE.

16210 Missale ad vsum ecclesie Sarisburiēsis. 4° in 8's. *Parisijs, per F. Regnault,* 1529. L.O.O[19].C[12].ST(imp.).+; ILL. In the 2 O copies the Canon of the Mass is in different settings. ETON has a frag. of a paginary reprint w. woodcuts as in 16210 but some of the types differing.

16211 — [Anr. ed.] fol. (*Parisius, imp. F. Regnault,* 1531 (31 my.)) L(lacks tp).O(lacks 3 leaves).D[2](lacks tp).PARIS.

16212 — [Anr. issue, w. date on tp and in colophon:] 1532. C. HER.

16212.5 — [Anr. ed.] fol. (*Parisijs, in ed. F. Regnault,*) [c. 1532.] C[5](lacks tp).

16213 Missale ad vsum insignis ac preclare ecclesie Saᵣ. 4° in 8's. *in alma Parisiorum acad.,* (*imp. F. regnault,*) 1533 (27 my.) L(lacks tp). O.C.LINC.P.+; PML.

16214 Missale ad vsum ecclesie Sarisburiensis. fol. (*Parisijs, in ed. F. Regnault,*) 1534. L(imp.).O.C.CHICH[2].W.+; F.

16215 — [Anr. ed.] 4° in 8's. (*Rothomagi, ex off. R. hamillonis, venale habetur in ed. R. valētini,*) 1554. L.O(2).O[3]. O[25].; F.HN. 2 cols., 40 lines.

16216 — [Anr. ed.] 4° in 8's. (*Rothomagi, ex off. R. hamillonis, venale habetur in ed. R. valentini,*) 1555 (1554.) L.O. C(imp.).D[2].DE.+ 2 cols., 47 lines.

16217 — [Anr. ed.] fol. *Parisijs,* (*typis J. Amazeur,*) *ap. G. Merlin,* 1555. L(imp.).O.C.D.ST.+; F.HN.HD.NY[11]. PML.

16218 — [Anr. ed.] 4° in 8's. (*per J. Kyngstō et H. Sutton,*) 1555. L.O.C.C[6].ELY.+; F.HN.CH.HD.PML.

16219 — [Anr. ed.] fol. [*J. Kingston a. H. Sutton,*] 1557. L.O.C. M.ST.+; ILL.PML. St. John's Seminary, Camarillo, California. The tp has McK. 115β, a modified form of J. Day's device.

York

16220 Missale secundū vsum insignis ecclesie Eboraceñ. fol. (*Rothomagi, imp. P. violette,*) [1509?] O(lacks 1 leaf). C.

16221 Missale ad vsum celeberrime ecclesie Eboracensis. fol. *Rothomagi,* (*opera P. oliuier,*) *sumpt. J. gachet* [*in York,*] 1516 (5 fb.) L(frags.).O.C(imp.).C[15](imp.). ST(lacks last leaf).+

16222 — [Anr. ed.] 4° in 8's. *Rothomagi,* (*opera P. oliuier,*) *ere et imp. G. bernard & J. cousin,* 1517 (26 oc.) L.O.DE. LINC.ST(lacks last 2 leaves).+; HN.

16223 Missale ad vsū celeberrime eccl'ie Eboracēsis. 4° in 8's. [*Rouen, N. le Roux?*] *sumpt. J. Gachet* [*in York,*] 1530 (2 jy.) O(2, 1 imp.).O[2](imp.).D[2](lacks 4 leaves). Printed w. some of P. Olivier's old material including the init. 'M' on the tp w. his name.

16224 Missale ad vsum ecclesie Eboraceñ. 4° in 8's. *parisijs, sumpt. F. Regnault,* 1533. L.O.C.BUTE.LIV(imp.).+; ILL.

Liturgies—Latin Rite—Missals—*cont.*

Special Offices

16224.5 Missa preciosissimi sanguinis domini nostri iesu xp̄i. 4°.
(*R. Pynson*,) [c. 1520.] Lord Kenyon(frag., bd. w.
16168).
Possibly written for Hayles Abbey; *see also*
12973.5.

16224.7 [Heading:] Orationes dicende in missis pro agendis deo
gratijs de recōciliatione regni cum ecclesia catholica.
[Three prayers set forth during Queen Mary's reign
to be said at mass.] 1/2 sh.fol. [*London*, 1555?] Truro
Cathedral(bd. w. 16205).

England

16225 Missæ aliquot pro sacerdotibus itinerantibus in Anglia.
Ex missali Romano reformato. 4°. [*St. Omer, English
College Press*,] 1615. L.O.C.USHAW.W.+; N.STL.TEX.
A&R 542. The outer forme of sheet T is in 2 set-
tings; T2ᵛ, 1st col., line 1 ends: 'Amen.' or 'Amē.';
both at C.

16226 Missale parvum pro sacerdotibus in Anglia itinerantibus.
Ordo baptizandi, aliaq; sacramenta ministrandi.
2 pts. 4°. [*St. Omer, English College Press*,] 1623.
L(tp mutilated).O.; ILL.
A&R 543. Pt. 2 (A&R 720) is reprinted in 16161.5
sqq. and 16227.

England, Scotland, and Ireland

16227 Missale parvum pro sacerdotibus in Anglia, Scotia, &
Ibernia itinerantibus. Ordo etiam baptizandi, [etc.]
2 pts. 4°. [*St. Omer, C. Boscard*,] 1626. L.O.C.D.E.+;
F.HN.HD.TEX.Y.+
A&R 544. E has 2 copies w. line 4 of tp in different
settings.

ORDINALS

In these are collected the rubrics (directions printed in red) dispersed throughout the Breviary giving rules for finding the proper
office for every day in the year and assigning priority when movable
and fixed festivals concur, i.e. happen on the same day.

Salisbury

For editions of Clement Maydeston's Directorium sacerdotum,
based on the Sarum Ordinal, with his 'Defensorium', some of
which were formerly listed below, *see* 17720 sqq.

16228 [Ordinale seu pica secundum usum Sarum. Begins:] ad
capud [*sic*] ieiunij et a capite ieiunij [etc.] 4°. [*Westminster, W. Caxton*, 1477.] L(8 leaves, 4 of them
defective).
For Caxton's advertisement for this *see* 4890.

16229 — No entry.
16230 — = 17728.
16231 — Now = 17728.3.
16232 — Now = 17728.5.

York

16232.4 [A1ʳ:] Incipit pica siue directorium sacerdotum ad vsum
Eboracum. 4° in 6's. ⟨*Eboraci, per me H. Goes*, 1509
(18 fb.)⟩ Cᶦ⁷(lacks V6).YK(imp.).
The colophon supplied above was once present in
the Cᶦ⁷ copy; *see* Herbert III.1437.

Reformed Roman

16232.5 The generall rubriques of the breviarie, put into English.
16° in 8's. *S. Omers*, [*C. Boscard f.*] *J. Heigham*, 1617.
DN.TMTH.W.
A&R 140.

PRIMERS
See above: Hours (15867 sqq.)

PROCESSIONALS

These provide the music, spoken texts, and directions (rubrics) for
festival processions, whether at the altar, in the choir, or elsewhere
inside and outside the church. Some editions have a few woodcuts
emblematically representing the positions of the officiators. While
the processions are ordered after the arrangement of the Missal
(Temporale, Proprium Sanctorum, Commune Sanctorum), they
are specially developed services, in particular those for Rogation
Days (following the 5th Sunday after Easter).

Liturgies—Latin Rite—Processionals—*cont.*

Salisbury

16232.6 [Ends:] Processionale cū diligenti cura & industria correct: ad vsū insignis p̄clareq̄ ecclesie Sar̄. [*Ed. R.
Fox, Bp. of Winchester.*] 4° in 8's. (*per R. Pynson*,
1501 (ydus no.)) BUTE.

16232.8 [Ends:] Processionalibᵍ [*sic*] . . . correct: ad vsū insignis
p̄clareq̄ ecclesie Sar̄ imp̄ssisq̄ . . . 4° in 8's. (*per R.
Pynson*, 1502 (prid. ydus no.)) o⁸(lacks tp).c(C2,7
only)*. Rogers(2 leaves).

16233 Processionale ad vsum insignis ac preclare eccl'ie Sar̄. 8°.
(*Rothomagi, per Martinum Morin, imp. J. Richardi*,
1508 (14 jy.)) o⁵.DUR(Bamb., imp.).
Unfoliated; 37 lines to the full page; cf. 16236.5.

16234 Processionale ad vsū eccl'ie Sar̄. 4° in 8's. (*Rothomagi, per
Martinum Morin, imp. J. caillard*, 1517 (14 au.)) o².
The tp has Morin's device w. his name in type
below.

16235 Processionale ad vsum insignis ac preclare ecclesie Sar̄.
4° in 8's. *Parisiꝰ, per w. hopylium, imp. F. byrckman,
Venundātur Londonij ap. F. byrckman in cimiterio
sancti Pauli*, 1519 (28 oc.) o(lacks last leaf).

16236 — [Anr. ed.] 4° in 8's. *Antwerpie, per C. endouieñ. [i.e.
Ruremond*,] *imp. F. byrckman, Venundantur Londonij
ap. F. byrckman, in cimiterio sancti Pauli (vel a suis
seruitoribus,)* 1523 (16 mr.) L(imp.).

16236.3 — [Anr. ed.] 4° in 8's. *Antwerpie, per C. endouieñ. [i.e.
Ruremond*,] *imp. P. kaetz, Venundantur Londini ap.
P. kaetz*, 1523; [tp:] (6 au.) [col.:] (15 oc.) o(lacks
c1).

16236.5 — [Anr. ed.] 8°. [*Rouen?* c. 1525.] o³(lacks tp).
Ff. cxcvi; 28 lines to the full page; cf. 16233.

16236.6 — [Anr. ed.] 4° in 8's. [*Rouen?* c. 1525.] o(G3–8, H–Q⁸
only).
32 lines to the full page.

16236.7 — [Anr. ed.] 4° in 8's. *Antwerpie, per C. endouieñ. [i.e.
Ruremond*,] *imp. P. kaetz, Venundantur Londonij ap.
P. kaetz*, 1525 (6 fb.) L(imp.).o(lacks c1).o²(lacks tp).
g2ʳ varies; the text under the next-to-last staff of
music begins: 'omnis et talis' (o) or is corrected
to 'omnis et mortalis' (D²).

16237 Processionale ad vsum Sar̄. 4° in 8's. [*Antwerp, C.
Ruremond*,] 1528. L.Lᶦ⁵.O².; F.
The tp has Ruremond's device enclosing his name
in type.

16238 — [Anr. ed.] 4° in 8's. [*Antwerp, C. Ruremond*, 1530?]
L(lacks tp and last quire).

16239 Processionale ad vsum ecclesie Sarisburiēsis. 4° in 8's.
Parisiis, in ed. F. Regnault, 1530. o(imp.).c(imp.).;
PML.

16240 Ad oīpotētis dei gloriā . . . hoc processionale ad vsum
insignis ecclesie Sarum [etc.] 4° in 8's. (*Parisijs, ex
off. N. Preuost, imp. F. byrckman [jun., in London*,])
1530 (3 cal. ja.) c.c⁵.

16240.5 Processionale ad vsum Sarum. 4° in 8's. (*Parisijs, ex off.
N. Preuost, imp. iunioris F. byrckman,*) *Venundatur
Londonij in ed. iunioris F. byrckman*, 1530. o(imp.).

16241 Processionale ad vsus insignis eccl'ie Sar̄ obseruandos
accōmodū. 4° in 8's. [*Antwerp, widow of C.
Ruremond*,] 1532. L(lacks last quire).

16241.5 — [Anr. ed.] 4° in 8's. [*Antwerp*,] (*in off. vidue C.
Ruremundensis*,) 1542. o²⁴.

16242 — [Anr. ed.] 4° in 8's. [*Antwerp*,] (*in off. vidue C.
Ruremundensis, imp. J. Raynes [in London*,]) 1544.
L.O.C(imp.).DE(imp.).YK.+; PML.

16243 — [Anr. ed.] 4° in 8's. [*Antwerp*,] (*in off. vidue C.
Ruremundensis*,) 1545. L.L².O.O².ST.+

16244 Processionale ad vsum insignis eccl'ie Sar̄. 4° in 8's. [*J.
Kingston a. H. Sutton*,] 1554. L.O⁵.C⁶.DUR³.LIV.+;
F.HN(imp.).HD.PML.
Collates a–z⁸ A⁸ B⁴.

16245 — [Anr. ed.] 4° in 8's. [*J. Kingston a. H. Sutton*,] 1555.
L.O.C⁵.D.BUTE.+; HN(imp.).Y.
Collates a–z⁸ A⁸ B⁴.

16246 — [Anr. ed.] 4° in 8's. [*T. Marsh?*] 1555. L.O.C.M(lacks
tp).ST.+; F(1, plus a1, 2 only, bd. w. 16247).
Collates a–t⁸; the tp has border McK. & F. 37β w.
inits. 'T R' at the bottom. At least F has an extra
leaf signed 'b.vij.' inserted after b6 and containing
the service for St. Thomas à Becket; it is not
present in L.

16247 — [Anr. ed.] 4° in 8's. [*J. Wayland?*] 1555. L.O(3). Sir
Richard Proby.; F(imp., w. a1,2 of 16246).
Collates a–t⁸; the tp has border McK. & F. 51,
w. sea horses at the bottom.

Liturgies—Latin Rite—Processionals—*Salisbury—cont.*

16248 Processionale ad vsum insignis ac preclare ecclesie Saȝ. 4° in 8's. *Rothomagi, (in off. R. hamilionis,) imp. R. valentini, Venale habetur ap. R. valentinū,* 1555 (18 oc.). L.O(3, 1 imp.).O³¹.COL(imp.).D.; HN.BO.PML.

16249 — [Anr. ed.] 4° in 8's. *Rothomagi, (in off. R. hamilionis,) imp. R. valentini, Venale habetur ap. R. valentinū,* 1557 (15 oc.). L.O.C.C⁵.

16249.5 — [Anr. ed.] 4° in 8's. *Antuerpie, (per M. Endouianum, typis C. Ruremundeñ.,) ap. M. Endouianū,* 1158 [1558.] L.O.C(imp.).*.D.

The date on the tp and in the colophon is misprinted: 'M C lviij' with the 'C' corrected in ink to 'D'.

16250 — [A variant, w. tp imprint:] *Antuerpie, ap. G. Simonem,* 1158 [1558.] O⁸.O¹⁴.

York

16250.5 Processionale completum per totum anni circulum ad vsum celebris ecclesie Eboracensis. 4° in 8's. *Rothomagi, opera p. oliuier, ere et imp. J. gachet, alias de france, Eboraci,* [1516?] L(tp def.).

16251 — [Anr. ed.] 8°. [*Rouen, N. le Roux?*] *imp. J. Gachet, Eboraci,* 1530. L.O.LINC.USHAW(lacks M8).

L has F⁸ K–L⁸ in a different setting from O and a 5-line colophon on M8ᵛ while O has a 7-line colophon.

16252 — [Anr. ed.] 4° in 8's. *per J. Kyngston et H. Suttō,* 1555. O(2).C⁵.; PML.

PSALTERS

These contain the Psalms of King David. There are three main varieties in Latin:

1. The psalms in numerical order, without directions when they are to be said and usually with editorial commentary. Editions of this variety are not liturgical and are listed at 2354 sqq.
2. The psalms in numerical order, sometimes with brief directions when they are to be said, including antiphons for some psalms, e.g. following Psalm 18 (Caeli ennarant). Editions of this variety are listed below. In them the psalms are followed by the twelve Canticles (including the Athanasian Creed, Quiqunque vult), the Litany, usually the Vigiliae Mortuorum, and frequently by the Hymns (*see* headnotes preceding 16110 and 16129) with a supplement of York hymns.
3. The psalms arranged according to the days and hours at which they are said, with canticles and hymns interspersed; e.g. in Salisbury Psalters, following the antiphon and responses after Psalm 20 (Domine in virtute tua, the last psalm for Matins on Sundays) is the canticle of Ambrosius and Augustinus (Te Deum laudamus), then antiphons and rubrics for Lauds, then Psalm 92 (Dominus regnavit, the first psalm for Lauds on Sundays). Editions of this variety form part of a Breviary and are included in the listings at 15971 sqq. A few Salisbury Psalters of this variety have only the (c) or summer antiphon noted below, e.g. 15805.2, 15806a, 15808. 15807 has, and the missing P.H. vols. of the other items probably had, a Psalter with (a) and Sarum (b) antiphons.

Note that the antiphons are of some help in distinguishing imperfect Psalters of different uses. Following Psalm 18 in Sarum and Aberdeen Psalters of variety 3 and in many Sarum Psalters of variety 2, there are three antiphons, to be employed beginning:

(*a*) the first Sunday in Advent: 'Nox praecessit dies . . .'
(*b*) the first Sunday after the octave of Epiphany (after 13 January): 'Praeceptum Domini . . .'
(*c*) the octave of Trinity (on the 9th Sunday after Easter) and sometimes simply labelled 'per estatem' or summer antiphon: 'Sponsus ut e thalamo . . .'

York and Hereford Psalters have (*a*) and (*c*) the same but have for (*b*): 'Non sunt loquelae . . .' The Hereford Psalter, in the only printed edition (part of 15793), describes (*b*) as being employed before Quadragesima (before Lent) and has an extra antiphon to be used in Quadragesima (during Lent): 'Legis tuae, Domine, . . .'

16253 [Begins a2ʳ:] Iheronimus de laude dei super psalterium. 4° in 8's. [*Westminster, W. Caxton,* 1480?] L(lacks a1, blank?). Duff 354.

16253.5 — [Anr. ed.] 8°. [*R. Pynson,* c. 1496.] M(k⁸ only, w. most of Psalms 68–75).

19 lines of 114 mm. textura, Pynson's type 6.

Liturgies—Latin Rite—Psalters—*cont.*

16254 [1st A1ʳ:] KL mēsis ianuarii. [2nd A1ʳ:] Beatus vir qui nō abiit [etc.]. 8°. (*ap. westmonasteriuȝ, per me w. de worde,* 1499 (20 my.)) C⁷(frags.).M(imp.). Duff 355.

16255 [Ends:] Psalteriū cū antiphonis dñicalib⁹ & ferialibus vna cū hymnis ecclesie Saȝ & Eboraceñ. deseruiētibus. 4° in 8's. (*per me W. de worde,* 1503 (12 ap.)) L(lacks 1st 9 leaves).D².

16256 Liber soliloquiorum. (Hoc presens psalteriū cū hymnis scd'm vsū Saȝ et Eboraceñ.) 16° in 8's. (*per w. de worde,* 1504.) C(imp.).

16257 [Title on [a]1ʳ:] Psalterium [xylographic] ex mādato victoriosissimi Anglie regis Henrici septimi cum psalmorū virtute feliciter incipit. 8°. (*per G. Faȝȝ,* 1504 (7 fb.)) L.O(imp.).C.C³.; HN.

16258 Psalterium cum hymnis scd'm vsum et cōsuetudinem Sarum et Eboraceñ. 4° in 8's. (*Parisius,* [*W. Hopyl,*] *exp. G. Brettoñ.,* [*H. Jacobi, a. J. Pelgrim,*] 1506 (22 [*sic*] kal. ap.)) O(2).; HN.

Jacobi and Pelgrim's device, McK. 17, is at the end of the Hymns.

16258.7 Psalteriū cū hymnis ad verū vsū Saȝ [col.:] (et Eboraceñ.) 8°. *Parisius, exp. F. byrckman* [*in London,*] 1516 (7 fb.) O. Rogers.

16259 Psalterium cum hymnis scd'm vsum et cōsuetudinem Saȝ et Eboraceñ. 4° in 8's. (*Parisij, exp. F. Byrkmam* [*sic*, *in London,*] 1516 (22 fb.)) L.O(2).O¹⁹(imp.).C⁵(imp.).; TEX.

16259.3 [B1ʳ:] Psalterium cum hymnis. ps. i. [y4ᵛ:] Sequuntur hymni . . . ad vsum Saȝ et Eboraceñ. 8°. [*W. de Worde?* c. 1517.] YK(lacks before B1 and after y4). 21 lines of 112 mm. textura.

16259.5 [Ends:] Psalterium cum antiphonis . . . vna cum hymnis eccl'e Saȝ et Eboraceñ. deseruientibus. 8°. (*per me winā⟨dum de Worde,⟩* [c. 1520?] O¹⁷(4 imp. leaves of last quire).

Possibly of the same ed. as 16259.3 or 16259.7.

16259.7 [2nd A1ʳ:] Psalterium cum Hymnis./ Psalmus. Primus. 8°. [*W. de Worde,* c. 1520.] HD(imp., partly completed by 16266). 𝕬 20 lines of 116 mm. textura. 1st A⁸ is the Kalendar; the last leaf, S7, concludes the Psalms and has the 1st Canticle. Pasted inside the front cover is a frag. of 15922.

16260 Psalterium cum hymnis secundū vsum & cōsuetudinē Sarum et Eboraceñ. 4° in 8's. (*Parisius, exp. F. Byrckman* [*in London,*] 1522 (7 jn.)) L².O.C(imp.). M.YK.+; TEX.Y.

16260.5 Psalteriū cū hymnis ad verū vsū Saȝ [col.:] (et Eboraceñ.) 8°. *in alma Parisioȝ acad., imp. F. byrchman* [*in London,*] 1522 (8 mr.) O(2 imp.).O²⁷(imp.).C¹⁰.

16261 Psalterium cum hymnis ad vsum insignis ecclesie Sarū et Eboraceñ. 8°. (*Antwerpie, opere C. Ruremundeñ.,*) *Venundantur Londonij ap. P. kaetz,* 1524 (13 no.)) L.O(imp.).

16262 Psalterium cum hymnis. 8°. (*per R. Pynson,* 1524.) O (imp.).D²(imp.).

16263 — [Anr. ed.] 16° in 8's. [*Paris?* 1529?] L(imp.).C(frag.).

16263a Psalterium ad decantāda in choro officia ecclesiastica accommodatissimum: cū hymnis . . . ad simpliciū sacerdotū clericorūȹ instructionem impressū. 16° in 8's. [*Antwerp, C. Ruremond,*] *Venundantur Londonij ap. J. renis* [i.e. *Reynes,*] 1530. O(2, plus tp only, Douce Add. 142/205).

16264 Psalterium Dauidicum, ad vsum ecclesie Sarisburiensis. 8°. [*T. Marsh f.*] *A. Kitson,* [1555.] O.C(2, 1 imp.).; ILL.

16265 — [A variant, w. imprint:] *T. Marshe,* [1555.] O.YK.

16266 — [Anr. ed.] 8°. *per J. Kyngston & H. Sutton,* 1555. O³¹. C⁶.LINC.LIV.; HD(tp, P4–Q7, R5–8 only, w. 16259.7). ILL.

Prob. earlier than 16264 sq.

Appendix

Psalteriū btē marie virginis cū articulis īcarnatiōis. [1510?] *See* 17543.

RITUALS

See above: Manuals (16138 sqq.).

SEQUENCES

These are the set songs from the Missal. They developed from mnemonic phrases devised to accompany the prolonged notes of 'Alleluia' sung while the priest moved from the right side to the

Liturgies—Latin Rite—Sequences—*cont.*
left side of the altar between readings from the Epistle and the Gospel for each day. They were printed as a collected text only in the form of schoolbooks paired with Hymns; *see* 16110 sqq.

Church of England

Note: For a list of the subheadings in this section *see* the headnote following 15789.

Book of Common Prayer

The section below, especially in regard to 4° editions, draws heavily upon the research and examination of copies pursued by John R. Hetherington in preparation for his bibliography of 4° editions of the Book of Common Prayer and of the Sternhold and Hopkins metrical Psalms before 1662, to be published as *Prayers and Psalms in Quarto: 1549–1661*. Through his generosity some of the essential findings are extracted below, but they are intended only as an earnest of the much fuller and more specific information in his bibliography, where pressmarks and imperfections of copies will be detailed, several signature positions for each edition recorded, and further distinguishing features noted. Among the latter the State Prayers, which Mr. Hetherington first organized systematically, will be listed with fuller variations in the formulae beginning in 1621.

For 4° editions I have cited from Mr. Hetherington's records the pressmark or some other fuller indication for one copy which is complete or most nearly so, to serve as a standard copy for that edition. For editions originally undated, or where there are two editions of the same date and series, or where no copy with an imprint survives, I have given a further minimal distinction, though by itself it is weak evidence for a perfect copy and of practically no use for an imperfect copy. Copies not originally included in Mr. Hetherington's canvass have been marked with '†' as they have not been checked against his complete findings and may not agree in all details.

Liturgies—Church of England—Book of Common Prayer— *Headnote—cont.*
For the other formats I have attempted to gather comparable information though on a more restricted scale. I have limited myself to identifying at least one copy of each STC entry by number of columns, typeface, and a series number referring to its collation. There undoubtedly exist other editions, not recorded below, which a canvass of all copies and a systematic comparison of signature positions and xeroxes would have turned up. Such an effort was impossible at this time; indeed I am deeply indebted to several librarians and collectors for their generous co-operation in the relatively modest compilation below of non-4° formats. Much work remains to be done, especially on the Edwardian folios and the Caroline octavos, but I hope that the overall scheme represented below will make the next bibliographer's task somewhat easier. KFP

Following is a chart of collations and a few kindred points. The 4° collations have been extracted from Mr. Hetherington's records. The others derive from a variety of sources and may occasionally suffer a lapse in accuracy. Not included are early 4°, 2-column, Black Letter editions printed on continuous signatures with Bibles, e.g. 2089 and 2144. It is to be noted that from 1552 in the smaller formats and from 1564 in folio, the prose Psalter after the translation of the Great Bible is a normal accompaniment to the Book of Common Prayer, whether on continuous signatures or separate. These Psalters are all printed, like the Book of Common Prayer itself, by the patentees of the office of the King's (or Queen's) Printer.

For other Psalters after the translation of the Great Bible published, as part of an adaptation of the Book of Common Prayer, by William Seres, his assigns, or for the Company of Stationers *see* the headnote preceding 2370. A few other early adaptations of the Book of Common Prayer together with prose Psalter are listed at 2376.5–2377, and 2380a.5. For another adaptation published by Seres but without a Psalter *see* the group of Primers at 20373 sqq.

Chart of Editions

fol. 1 col. B.L.	Series	Date	STC	Collation				State Prayer
	2/1	1549	16267	❧² πA⁸ A⁸ B–I⁶ K⁸ L–X⁶ Y⁸ ¶⁴ ¶a–¶e⁶ ¶f⁸				¶1ᵛ
	2/2	1549	16268	❧² πA⁸ A–I⁶ K⁸ L–T⁶ U⁸ (U8 blank) X⁶ Y⁸ AA–EE⁶ f⁸ ✠⁴				✠2ᵛ
	2/3	1549	16269 16269.5	❧² πA⁸ [or πA² ππA⁸] A–I⁶ K⁸ L–T⁶ U⁸ (U8 blank) X⁶ Y⁸ Aa–Ee⁶ f⁸ ✠⁴				✠2ᵛ
	2/4	1549	16270 16273	πA¹⁰ A–P⁸ Q⁴ R–T⁸ U¹⁰				Q2ᵛ
	2/5	1549	16274 16275	❧¹⁰ A–R⁸ S–T⁶				P5ʳ
	2/6	1549 (Worcester)	16276	✠¹⁰ A–N⁶ O⁴ P–U⁶ X⁴				Q5ᵛ
	2/7	1551 (Dublin)	16277	πA¹⁰ A–R⁸ S⁴				O6ʳ

	Series	Date	STC	Collation*	State Prayer	Communion Rubrics	Ordinal	Last Leaf
	2/11	1552	16279 16280.5	¶⁶ ¶¶⁸ A–Q⁸ R⁶	¶¶4ᵛ	O1	S/AA⁶ BB⁶ CC⁸	CC8ʳ: cut of Madonna, verso blank
	2/12	1552	16284.5	¶⁶ ¶¶⁸ A–Q⁸ R⁶	¶¶4ᵛ	O1	S/AA⁶ BB⁶ Cc⁸	Cc8ʳ: end of text and colophon, verso blank
	2/13	1552	16281 16281.5 (Worcester 16287)	A⁶ B–R⁸ S⁶	B5ʳ	P3ᵛ	AA⁸ BB¹²	BB12ʳ: errata and prices, verso blank
	2/14	1552	16282.3 16282.7	A–K⁸ L¹⁰ M–N⁸ O–P¹⁰	B2ᵛ	N3ʳ	AA⁸ BB¹⁰	BB10ʳ: prices (or prices and note about Ordinal), verso blank

* Beginning with Morning Prayer; for collation of Prelims., Act, and for extra leaves and cancels *see* headnote preceding 16279.

Liturgies—Church of England—BOOK OF COMMON PRAYER—*Chart of Editions—cont.*

	Series	Date	STC	Collation*	State Prayer	Communion Rubrics	Ordinal	Last Leaf
fol. 1 col. B.L. cont.	2/15	1552	16285 16286.3	A–U^6 X^8, ff. 128	B4^v	R6	Aa–Cc^6, ff. 17	Cc6 lacking or cancelled in early eds.; later eds. have 'truely . . . imprynted' and prices on recto, verso blank
	2/16	1552	16286.5	A–Y^6 z^6 &^{4}	B4^v	T6	Aa–Bb^6 Cc^{10}	Cc10 lacking, prob. had errata and prices

* See note on previous page.

	Series	Date Range	STC	Collation	State Prayer[s]	Psalter	Godly Prayers
	2/20	1559	16291	πA^{12} b^6 A–U^6 X^8, ff. 128	B6^r	none	none
	2/21	1559	16292	πA^{12} π^6 A–K^8 L^{10} M–N^8 O–P^{10}	B2^v	(Ordinal: AA^8 BB^{10})	none
	2/22	1559 [1561?]	16292a	[for prelims. *see* 16292a]+A–K^8 L^{10} M–N^8 O–P^{10}	B4^v	none	none
	2/23	1564 1577	16296 16306.3	*[or (. ⁕ .)]^8 ¶^{10} A–P^8 Q^6	B4^v	A–I^8 K^6	none
	2/24	1580 1592	16307 16316	(. ⁕ .)^8 ¶^{10} A–P^8 Q^6	B4^v	A–K^8	K5^r
	2/25	1594 1603	16318 16325	a^{10} b[or πB]^8 A–P^8 Q^6	B4^v	A–K^8	K5^r
	2/26	1603/4 1625	16326 16364	a^{10+2} [later a^{12}] πB^8 A^8 B^{10} C–N^8 O^{10} P^8 Q^6	B4^v–5^r	A–K^8	K5^r
	2/27	1627 1639	16368 16416	πA^{12} πB^8 A–Cc^8 Dd^4 (Dd4 blank)	B5^v–6^r	R4^r (sub tp)	Cc8^r
fol. 2 cols. B.L.	2/29	1616	16347	A^4 B–E^6 F^4	B3^r	D2^r	none
fol. 2 cols. rom.	2/30	1598	16322.3	A–C^6 D^4	A5^r	none	D3^r
	2/31	1607 1616	16332 16347a	A^4 B–G^6	B4^v	D6^r	none
	2/32	1629 (Cambridge)	16375	A^4 B–G^6	B3^v–4^r	D6^r	none
	2/33	1629	16374	A^4 B–H^6 I^4	C1^r	E5^v	none
	2/34	1633/2	16390	A^4 b^4 B–H^6 I^4	B4$^{r–v}$	E4^r	none
	2/35	1638 (Cambridge)	16410	A^6 (B)–(H)^6 (I)^4	(B)4^v	(E)4^r	none
	2/36	1638/9	16415	A^8 B–I^6 K^4	B3^v	E5^v	none
4° 1 col. B.L.	Heth. 1	1549 (Worcester)	16271	πA–πC^4 A–U^4 W^4 X^4 a–u^4 w^4 x–z^4 Aa–Ii^4	w4^r	Issued sep. as 2378	none
	Heth. 2	[1552] [1553]	16288 16288a	a^8 ¶^{8} A–P^8	B2^r	A–I^8 K^4 Aa^8	Aa2^r
	Heth. 3	1559	16293	a–b^8 c^6 A–T^8 U^{10}	B6^r	A–M^8	M2^r
	Heth. 4	1560 1562	16294 16295	πA–πB^8 πC^6 A–T^8 U^{10}	B6^r	A–N^8	M8^v
	Heth. 5	1565	16296.5	¶^{8} *^{6} A–T^8 U^{10}	B6^r	A–N^8	M8^v
	Heth. 6–7	1566 1568	16297.5 16298.5	¶^{8} ¶^{6} A–T^8 U^{10}	B6^r	A–N^8	M8^v
	Heth. 8	1570	16299	¶^{8} ¶^{6} A–T^8 U^{10} (U10 blank)	B6^r	A–M^8 N^4	M6^v
	Heth. 9–10	1571 1577	16301.3 16306.5	¶^{8} ¶^{6} A–U^8 (device U7^r; U7^v–8^v blank)	B6^r	A–M^8 N^4	M6^v
	Heth. 11	[1578]	16306.7	¶^{8} ¶^{6} A–X^8 Z^8 Aa–Ii^8 Kk^4	B6^r	T8^r (sub tp)	Ii5^r
	Heth. 12–14	[1579?] [1589?]	16306.9 16314.5?	¶^{8} ¶^{6} A–Y^8 Aa–Ii^8 Kk^4	B6^r	T8^r (sub tp)	Ii5^r
	Heth. 16	[1589?] [1598?]	16314.5? 16322.6	¶^{8} ¶^{8} A–Y^8 Aa–Ii^8 Kk^4	B6^r	T8^r (sub tp)	Ii5^r
	Heth. 20	1601	16324.5	A–Hh^8	D5^r	U5^r (sub tp)	Hh2^v

Liturgies—Church of England—BOOK OF COMMON PRAYER—*Chart of Editions—cont.*

	Series	Date Range	STC	Collation	State Prayer[s]	Psalter	Godly Prayers
4° 1 col. B.L. cont.	Heth. 21–3	1604 1626	16328 16365.5	A–C⁸ D¹⁰ E–R⁸ S¹⁰ T–Hh⁸	D5ʳ–ᵛ	U5ʳ (sub tp)	Hh2ᵛ
	Heth. 25	1627 1634	16369.3 16397	A–Ii⁸	D8ᵛ–E1ʳ	X3ʳ (sub tp)	Hh8ᵛ
	Heth. 26	[1636?] 1639	16403.5 16417	πA–πB⁸ πC⁴ A–Dd⁸ Ee⁶	B4ʳ	R3ʳ (sub tp)	Dd7ʳ
	Heth. 28	1621 (Dublin)	16358	πA–πB⁸ A–Bb⁸	B3ᵛ	Q6ʳ (sub tp)	Bb5ʳ
	Heth. 29	1637 (Dublin)	16407	A–B⁸ πC² C–Kk⁸ Ll² (Includes Ordinal, at Ii5)	D5ᵛ–6ʳ	U8ʳ (sub tp)	Hh5ᵛ
4° 2 cols. B.L.	Heth. 41	[1586?] 1603	16311.5 16325.3	πA⁴ A–E⁸	A3ᵛ	C1ᵛ	E6ᵛ
	Heth. 42–4	1603/4 1630	16326.5 16380.9	πA⁴ A⁸ B¹⁰ C–E⁸	A4ʳ	C1ᵛ	E6ᵛ
	Heth. 51–3	1632 1634	16386 16397.7	πA⁴ A–E⁸ F⁶	A4ʳ	C5ᵛ	F4ᵛ
	Heth. 54	1636 1639	16404 16417.3	πA⁴ A–E⁸ F⁴	A4ʳ	C4ᵛ	F2ᵛ
	Heth. 55	1637	16405	A⁴ B–G⁸ H⁶	B3ᵛ–4ʳ	F2ᵛ	none
	Heth. 57–9	1630 1640 (Cambridge)	16380 16420	πA⁴ A–E⁸	A4ʳ	C4ʳ	none
4° 2 cols. rom.	Heth. 61	1615	16344	πA⁴ A–E⁸ F²	A4ʳ	C4ʳ	F1ʳ
	Heth. 63	1619 1623	16351 16361	πA⁴ A–G⁸	A5ʳ	D2ʳ	G7ᵛ
	Heth. 65	1627 1633/2	16369.7 16391	A–H⁸	B5ʳ	E2ʳ	H7ᵛ
	Heth. 66	1636	16404.3	A⁴ B–G⁸ H⁶	B5ʳ	E2ʳ	none
	Heth. 67	1639	16417.5	A–R⁴ S²	C2ʳ	K1ʳ	I2ʳ
	Heth. 71–2	1630 1638 (Cambridge)	16380.3 16412	A⁴ B–H⁸ (H8 blank)	B5ʳ	E2ʳ	none
8° 1 col. B.L.	8/1	1552/3	16290	a–c⁸ A–Cc⁸ D[d]⁴	B7ʳ	| A–R⁸ S⁴	Q8ᵛ
	8/2	1553	16290.5	πAA–πBB⁸ A–Y⁸ Aa–Dd⁸ Ee⁴	C4ʳ	| AA–QQ⁸ aa⁸ bb⁴	aa1ʳ
	8/3	1559	16293.5	πA⁸ †⁴ w/⁸ A–Cc⁸ D[d]⁴ (D[d]4 blank)	C2ʳ	| A–Q⁸ R⁴ (R4 blank)	Q8ᵛ
	8/4	1560	16294a.3	πA–πB⁸ A–Dd⁸ (Dd8 blank?)	C3ʳ–ᵛ	| A–Q⁸ R⁴	R1ʳ
	8/5	1564	16296.3	*–**⁸ A–Dd⁸	—	| A–R⁸	—
	8/6	1572 1574	16302 16304.6	[π⁸] ‡⁸ A–Dd⁸	C2ᵛ	| A–R⁸ S⁴	S1ʳ
	8/7	1576	16306	¶⁸ ℂ⁸ A–Cc⁸	C2ʳ	| A–Q⁸	Q5ᵛ
	8/8	[1581?] [1583?]	16309.3 16309.7	[π–ππ⁸] A–Rr⁸	C1ʳ	Bb5ʳ (sub tp)	[Rr3ᵛ?]
	8/9	[1585?] 1600	16310.5 16324.3	π⁸ ℂℂ⁸ (*)⁴ A–Pp⁸ Qq⁴	C1ʳ–ᵛ	Aa7ʳ (sub tp)	Qq2ʳ
	8/10	1604 1613	16328a 16337a.5	π⁸ B–Z⁸ &⁴ Aa–Nn⁸	E2ʳ–ᵛ	Aa1ʳ	&3ʳ
	8/11	1612 1633	16337a.3 16393.7	π⁸ B–Z⁸ (Z8 blank)	D4ᵛ	P7ʳ	Z6ʳ
	8/12	1639	16417.7	π⁸ B–Y⁸	D4ʳ–ᵛ	P2ʳ	Y7ʳ
8° 2 cols. rom.	8/13	1615 1626	16345 16367	A–F⁸	B1ʳ	D1ʳ	F7ʳ
				also 1633 (16394) and 1634 (16399) at Edinburgh, and 1639 (16418c.5) printed after 1640			
	8/14	1627 1640	16370 16421	A–F⁸ G⁴	B5ʳ	D5ʳ	G3ʳ
	8/15	1639	16418	A–F⁸ G⁴	B5ʳ	D4ᵛ	G3ʳ
12° 1 col. B.L.	12/2	1616	16348a	A–P¹² Q⁶	B10ʳ	K10ʳ	none

Liturgies—Church of England—BOOK OF COMMON PRAYER—*Chart of Editions—cont.*

	Series	Date Range	STC	Collation	State Prayer[s]	Psalter	Godly Prayers
12° 2 cols. rom.	12/5	1633 [Amsterdam]	16394.7	A–F¹² (F12 blank)	B9ʳ	D5ʳ	F9ʳ
	12/6	1634 1640	16399.5 16421.3	A–E¹²	B1ᵛ	C8ʳ	E10ᵛ
	12/7	1634 (Edinburgh)	16399.7	A–E¹²	A9ʳ	C6ʳ	E11ʳ
	12/9	1639	16419	π⁴ A–B¹² C⁴ [or C1–4+?; *see* note at entry for 16419]	A5ᵛ	[C5ʳ?]	C2ᵛ
16° 1 col. B.L.	16/1	1570	16300	π⁸ C–Z⁸	E7ʳ⁻ᵛ	| A–O⁸	[O1ᵛ?]
	16/2	1571 1572	16301.5 16302.5	π⁸ C–Y⁸ Aa–Hh⁸	F4ᵛ	| A–S⁸	S2ʳ
	16/3	1575	16305a	A–Y⁸	D5ʳ	| A–O⁸	O1ᵛ
	16/4	[1577?]	16306.6	π⁸ B–X⁸ Aa–Yy⁸ Aaa–Ddd⁸	E3ʳ⁻ᵛ	Ii1ʳ	Ddd2ʳ
	16/5	1581	16309.4	[π⁸?] B–Ss⁸ Tt⁶	E2ʳ⁻ᵛ	Cc6ᵛ	Tt1ʳ
	16/6	1585	16311	[π⁸?] A–Xx⁸	—	—	—
	16/7 𝔄	[1590?]	16315	A–Ss⁸	E1ʳ⁻ᵛ	Cc4ʳ	Ss5ʳ
	16/8	1592	16317	*⁸ B–Z⁸ [χ⁴] Aa–Ss⁸	E1ʳ⁻ᵛ	Cc4ʳ	Ss5ʳ
	16/9	1624	16363.5	[A–B⁸?] C–Z⁸ &⁸ Aa–Ss⁸	D7ᵛ⁻⁸ʳ	Cc4ʳ	Ss5ʳ
	16/10	1636 1640	16404.7 16421.5	A–Yy⁸	F5ʳ	Gg2ʳ	Yy5ʳ
16° 1 col. rom.	16/11	1586	16311.6	π⁸ B–V⁸	C6ʳ	N2ʳ	V4ᵛ
	16/12	1587	16312	*⁸ A–Y⁸	B7ʳ	O2ᵛ	Y7ʳ
	16/13	1591? 1596	16315.5? 16321a	*⁸ A–Y⁸	C6ᵛ⁻7ʳ	O3ᵛ	Y4ᵛ
24° 1 col. rom.	24/1	1603	16324.9	A–P¹²	B10ᵛ	K5ʳ	none
	24/2	1604	16328a.5	A–P¹²	B8ʳ	K5ʳ	none
	24/3 𝔄	1606	16331	A–P¹²	B9ᵛ	K5ʳ	none
	24/4	1614? 1623	16342.7? 16362.3	A–P¹² Q⁶	B10ᵛ	K9ʳ	none
	24/5	1627 1640	16371 16422	A–R¹²	C10ᵛ	M2ᵛ	none

State Prayer for King Edward

[Accession to the throne 28 Jan. 1547]

The supplication for the Sovereign follows the first of the responses headed: 'We beseech . . .' in the Litany.

Note: Entries for the 1549 folios are largely based on the B.M. Catalogue and on copies in the University Microfilms series. While signature positions were compared when trouble arose with 16268–16269.5, the other entries have not received the same scrutiny.

16267   The booke of the common prayer and administracion of the sacramentes, and other rites and ceremonies of the Churche: after the vse of the Churche of England. fol. *in off.* E. *Whitchurche*, 1549 (7 mr.) L.O(imp.). c⁴.DUR³.M².+; HN.BO.PML.Y(tp only). Arthur Houghton.+
     1 col., B.L., ending ¶f8; series 2/1 (HN, BO). O1ʳ catchword: 'was'. For a list of the compilers *see* 16448.7.

16268   — [Anr. ed.] fol. *in off.* R. *Graftoni*, 1549 (8 mr.) L (C.25.l.12, imp.).O³(imp.).O⁴(imp.).DUR.; Crocker (Y⁸ only, w. 16269.5).
     1 col., B.L., ending ✠4; series 2/2 (L, O³, O⁴). O1ʳ catchword: 'surreccion:'; colophon w. month date on Y8ʳ. The O⁴ copy has following Y8 2 leaves signed ✠² w. Canticles and colophon: R. *Grafton*, 16 Mar., 3 Edw. VI [1549], and the prices, followed by the final quires of 16267.

16269   — [Anr. ed.] fol. *in off.* R. *Graftoni*, 1549 (mr.) L(C.21.d. 19, imp.).; HN.
     1 col., B.L., ending ✠4; series 2/3. O1ʳ catchword: 'surrec-'; no colophon on Y8ʳ. Other copies of this and the next may be at D², ETON, TEX. The c⁶ copy on Univ. Microfilms reel 95 is actually 16275.

16269.5   — [Anr. ed.] fol. *in off.* R. *Graftoni*, 1549 (mr.) L(C.25. l.2).O³¹.C(*see* note).c²(imp.).; PML. Crocker (w.Y⁸ of 16268).
     1 col., B.L., ending ✠4; series 2/3. O1ʳ catchword: 'raised'; no colophon on Y8ʳ. The preface is in 2 settings, signed '🖐.ii.' (O³¹, PML, Crocker) or 'A.ii.' (L). The c copy has quires B–D, E2–5, G–L, N–S, X of 16267; F, T–U, Y, and app. A1,6 of 16269.5; preface and M2–6 of 16269; and A2–5, E1,6, M1, Aa1 to the end in a setting different from any ed. at L, e.g. A2ʳ has headline: 'Mattins.' on a cancel slip pasted over erroneous: 'Communion.'

16270   — [Anr. ed.] fol. *in off.* E. *Whitchurche*, 1549 (4 my.) L(2, 1 imp.).O³(2).C.DUR⁵.E.; HN.NY¹¹.TEX.Y.
     1 col., B.L., ending U10; series 2/4 (L). C1 misnumbered 'xviii'.

16270a   — [Anr. issue, w. quires G, I, N, and A1,2,7,8; C4,5; R1,2,7,8 and S1–3,6–8 reprinted by N. Hill.] *in off.* E. *Whitchurche*, 1549 (4 my.) L.O(3, 2 imp.).c5.c8. LIV(lacks tp).+; HN.CB(frag.).
     1 col., B.L., ending U10; series 2/4 (L). C1 correctly numbered 'xvii'.

Liturgies—Church of England—BOOK OF COMMON PRAYER—
State Prayer for Edw.—cont.

16271 — [Anr. ed.] 4°. *Wigorniæ, in off. J. Oswæni,* (*they be also to sell at Shrewesburye,*) 1549 (24 my.) L.O⁵ (imp.).C(Syn.6.54.6).CANT(imp.).M(imp.).; HD(imp.). PML.SMU(Dd3 only).
    1 col., B.L., ending Ii4; Heth. 1.1. Some copies (L, HD) are bd. w. Oswen's Psalter, 2378.

16272 — [Anr. ed.] fol. *in off. E. Whitchurche,* 1549 (16 jn.) L.O.O⁵.C.BRISTOL.+; HN(tp only).CB.CH. John L. Cooley, Pigeon Cove, Massachusetts(lacks tp).
    1 col., B.L., ending U10; series 2/4 (C). A1ʳ (Matins) line 2 of text: 'Thy kingdome come'. At least certain sheets are in 2 settings; A1ʳ has the further distinction in line 6 of text: 'against' (L) or 'agaynst' (O, C).

16273 — [Anr. ed.] fol. *in off. E. Whitchurche,* 1549 (16 jn.) L.O.C².D.M.+; HN (lacks tp).IND.NY¹¹.PN.Y(lacks tp).+
    1 col., B.L., ending U10; series 2/4 (HN). A1ʳ (Matins), line 2 of text: 'Thy kingdom come'. At least HN has some sheets pr. by N. Hill, possibly mixed from 16270a.

16274 — [Anr. ed.] fol. *in off. R. Graftoni,* 1549 (mr. (jn.)) L. L³⁰.D²(imp.).; F.ILL. Peter W. Adams, New York City.
    1 col., B.L., ending T6; series 2/5 (L). A1ʳ (Matins), last line ends: 'handes prepared'.

16275 — [Anr. ed.] fol. *in off. R. Graftoni,* 1549 (mr. (jn.)) L.O(imp.).C.D⁷.M.+; BO.N.PML.
    1 col., B.L., ending T6; series 2/5 (BO, c⁶). A1ʳ (Matins), last line ends: 'the drie lande'. The c⁶ copy is on Univ. Microfilms reel 95 ('16269').

16276 — [Anr. ed.] fol. *Wigorniæ, in off. J. Oswæni,* 1549 (30 jy.) L(C.36.l.13, lacks 2 leaves).O(imp.).c.
    1 col., B.L., ending X4; series 2/6 (L). The shelf-mark of L is erroneously given as C.36.l.17 in the printed B.M. Catalogue.

16277 — [Anr. ed.] fol. *Dubliniae, in off. H. Poweli,* 1551. C³.D. D⁸(frag.).
    1 col., B.L., ending S4; series 2/7 (D).

16278 — Now = 2380a.5.

1552 Headnote

Early editions of the 1552 folio BCP received contemporary amendment; near-contemporary alteration was practised upon some copies of one late edition (16282.7); and succeeding owners of all editions, in their desire to have 'complete' copies or to repair the defects of time, have added not a little to the difficulty of this version of BCP. The analyses and entries below are based on a limited comparison of copies by me at L, O, BO, BO⁶, HD, NY¹¹, and PML, together with comparison of a few signature positions and xeroxes by long-suffering colleagues at those libraries and at L², C, HN, and CB. This considerable selectivity in points compared means the findings can only be provisional. In particular, gathering information on last leaves was a belated decision imperfectly carried out, especially for L copies, the first I examined after HD copies. A full-scale analysis of all sheets in all known copies must ultimately be done, but it lies beyond the scope of STC.

The results recorded below only attempt to impart a rudimentary order. The basic segregation of editions follows old STC and is by imprint: Whitchurch, Grafton, and Oswen. To identify a copy not included in my original canvass it is best to establish the series of the text according to the chart of collations at the beginning of the BCP section and then to compare the fuller details at the respective STC entries, coded to the analysis immediately below. It is, I fear, an unavoidably complex process, and there will surely be editions and issues not recorded below or not detectable by the limited discriminations. I hope, however, I have sketched in the large outlines and detailed the major points of danger. KFP

In the distinctions for the Prelims. and Act, '11-line "T"' means that 11 lines are indented to the right of the initial.

Preliminaries

1 a⁸ b⁶; a2ʳ has 11-line 'T', line 1 of text ends: 'thing by'
2 a⁸ B⁶; a2ʳ has 9-line 'T'
3 a⁸ B⁶; a2ʳ has 4-line 'T'
4A a⁸ b⁶; a2ʳ has 11-line 'T', line 1 of text ends: 'by the', line 2 has 'deuised'
4B a⁸ b⁶; a2ʳ has 11-line 'T', line 1 of text ends: 'by the', line 2 has 'deuysed'
5A a⁸ b⁶; a2ʳ has 13-line 'T', a2 is missigned 'a.i.'
5B a⁸ b⁶; a2ʳ has 13-line 'T', a2 is signed 'a.ii.', Preface has no border of rules

Liturgies—Church of England—BOOK OF COMMON PRAYER—
1552 Headnote—cont.

6 a⁸ b⁶; a2ʳ has 13-line 'T', a2 is signed 'a.ii.', Preface has **a** border of rules

Act of Uniformity

1 a²; a1ʳ has 7-line 'W', last line has 'theyr'
2 a²; a1ʳ has 10-line 'W'
3 a²; a1ʳ has 5-line 'W'
4 a²; a1ʳ has 7-line 'W', last line has 'their'
5 A²; A1ʳ has 11-line 'W'
6 A²; A1ʳ has 19-line 'W'

Text

For collations of the text, beginning with Morning Prayer and continuing through the Ordinal *see* the chart of collations at the beginning of the BCP section: series 2/11–16. Further distinctions for editions within a series are given in the STC entries below, where necessary.

Communion Rubrics

On 27 Oct. 1552 the Privy Council ordered the Lord Chancellor to require the inclusion, among the rubrics at the end of the section on Communion, of the 'Black Rubric' concerning kneeling, beginning: 'Although no order can be so perfectly devised, . . .'; *see Acts P.C., 1552–1554,* p. 154. The following variations occur:

1 Black Rubric omitted from text. The other rubrics, to a total of six, are found on:

   a O1 of series 2/11, 12; lines 1–2 of recto: 'to haue compassion . . . thinges which . . .' (16280.5: CB).
   b T6 of series 2/16; lines 1–2 of recto: 'to haue compassion . . . those/ thynges whiche . . .' (16286.5: O³).
   c P3ᵛ of series 2/13; all six rubrics on the verso (16281: O).
   d R6, foliated 'Fol.97.', of early eds. of series 2/15; line 1 of recto: 'And there . . . Sup-/' (16285: O⁴).

2 Inserts. The Black Rubric by itself on the recto of a leaf, the verso being blank. Usually found at the end or beginning of the section on Communion; sometimes bound in at the beginning or end of the volume.

   a **Last full line of text ends: 'bodye,/'.** Found in series 2/11 (16279: NY¹¹) and 2/13 (16281.5: HN).
   b **Last full line of text ends: 'bo-/'.** Found in series 2/12 (16284.5: L²) and 2/13 (16281: L; 16281.5: C).

3 Cancels. The Black Rubric along with others, the text on the first line of the recto continuing from the preceding verso.

   a Without foliation; 1st line of recto: 'to haue compassion . . . those thyn-/'. Found with series 2/11 (16280: L) and 2/16 (16286.5: O).
   b Foliated: 'Fol.97.'; 1st line of recto: 'And there . . . Supper,/'. Found with early eds. of series 2/15 (16285: HD).
   c Foliated: 'Fo.97.' (omits 'l'); otherwise same setting and distinction as Cancel 3b (16285.7: CB). Note: since the information I originally sent out was not very clear on this point, some copies listed below as having 3b may actually have 3c.

4 Black Rubric included in the text but not a cancel.

   a N3ʳ of series 2/14; line 1 of recto: 'hath, or mighte . . . suffyse/' (16282.3: O³¹; 16282.7: HD).
   b R6, foliated: 'Fo.97.', of later eds. of series 2/15; 1st line of recto ends: 'there/', 2nd line ends: 'his/' (16285a: L; 16286: L).
   c R6, foliated: 'Fo.102.', of later eds. of series 2/15; 1st line of recto ends: 'there/', 2nd line ends: 'hys/' (16286.2: L; 16286.3: L).

Errata

On 27 Sept. 1552 the Privy Council ordered R. Grafton to delay sale of the BCP until certain faults had been corrected; *see Acts P.C., 1552–1554,* p. 131. Four different errata lists are so far known, and there should probably be at least one more. In the examples below the correction indicated is from the error: 'called the field of blood' to 'called Acheldema, that is the field of blood', found two-thirds through the Gospel for the Sunday before Easter. The error is indicated as occurring on:

1 C8ᵛ line 31. One of 13 errata by Whitchurch to accompany series 2/11 as a cancel for CC8 (16280: O), or series 2/12 as an extra leaf (16284.5: L²). The prices are on the recto below the errata, and the verso is blank.

Liturgies—Church of England—BOOK OF COMMON PRAYER—
1552 Headnote—cont.

2 E8ʳ last line. One of 7 errata by Whitchurch to accompany
series 2/13; printed on BB12ʳ with the prices below and the verso
blank (16281.5: HN). The 7th erratum is N5ʳ line 22, for 'offences,
reade offence.' Note that these 7 errata are exactly those uncorrected in the text of 16281 (PML) and may more properly belong
with that edition of this series.

3 E8ʳ last line. One of 5 errata by Whitchurch, also to accompany
series 2/13; printed on BB12ʳ with the prices below and the verso
blank (16281.5: C). This list omits the last two errata of Errata 2,
which are corrected in the text of the C copy, and is in a different
typesetting.

4 Fol. 35ᵛ line 22. One of 30 errata by Grafton to accompany early
eds. of series 2/15 as a cancel for Cc6 (16285: HD) or perhaps not
a cancel (16285.5: O). The prices are on the verso.

[5 G3ᵛ lines 33–4, uncorrected in series 2/16 (16286.5: BO⁶). No
copy of this series so far examined has Cc10 present.]

Last Leaves

See the chart of collations at the beginning of the BCP section and
also additional information in the STC entries.

Note: In the listing of copies below it is to be assumed that copies
lack the final leaf and/or errata unless otherwise specified; rubric
inserts or cancels are noted where present; e.g. in 16279 L(C.21.d.
14) has no insert and lacks CC8 and errata.

16279   The boke of common prayer, and administracion of the
         sacramentes, and other rites and ceremonies in the
         Churche of Englande. (The fourme and maner of
         makynge . . . bisshoppes, [etc.]) fol. *in off. Edovardi
         Whytcherche,* 1552. L(C.21.d.14; C.36.l.18, imp.,
         has rubric insert 2a).O³(Gibbs 4, lacks tp).O⁸(b.1.3,
         imp., has rubric insert 2a).; NY¹¹(has rubric insert 2a
         and CC8).
              1 col., B.L., ending R6, CC8; series 2/11. Has
         Prelims. 1, Act 1, Rubric 1a. The bulk of the text
         sheets are also reissued in 16284.5 as well as in the
         following.
              Further copies of one or another of the Whit-
         church eds. may be at L¹³, C⁴, C⁵, C⁸, CANT, D, D⁷,
         DUR³, EX, LIV; CH, N, TEX, Y.

16280   — [Anr. issue, w. different Prelims.] *in off. Edwardi
         Whytcherche,* 1552. L(G.12099, has rubric insert
         3a; in place of CC8 is app. substituted BB10 as in
         16282.7).O(C.P. 1552 d.1, has errata 1).
              1 col., B.L., ending R6, CC8; series 2/11. Has
         Prelims. 5B, Act 1, Rubric 1a. (L copy formerly
         16282).

16280.5 — [Anr. issue, w. different Prelims.] *in off. Edwardi
         Whytcherche,* 1552. O³¹(A 22, lacks tp, has Act 1
         and rubric insert 2a).; BO(Benton 1.4, has Act 2,
         rubric cancel 3a, and CC8).CB(04695, lacks Act, has
         CC8).
              1 col., B.L., ending R6, CC8; series 2/11. Has
         Prelims. 2, Act as indicated, Rubric 1a.

16281   — [Anr. ed.] fol. *in off. Edovardi Whytcherche,* 1552.
         L(C.36.l.16, has Act 2 and rubric insert 2b; in place
         of BB12 is substituted Cc6 as in 16286).O(C.P. 1552
         d.2, imp., lacks Act).; PML(17309, has Act 1 and
         rubric insert 2b; in place of BB12 is substituted
         errata 1, not relevant to this series).
              1 col., B.L., ending S6, BB12; series 2/13, w. B1ʳ
         having in last line: 'magnified'. Has Prelims. 2,
         Act as indicated, Rubric 1c. The bulk of the text
         sheets are reissued in 16287.

16281.5 — [Anr. ed.] fol. *in off. Edovardi Whytcherche,* 1552. C
         (Sel.3.220, has rubric insert 2b, has BB12 = errata
         3).; HN(62282, has rubric insert 2a, has BB12 =
         errata 2).
              1 col., B.L., ending S6, BB12; series 2/13, w. B1ʳ
         having in last line: 'magnifyed'. Has Prelims. 1,
         Act 2, Rubric 1c.

16282   — = L copy of 16280.

16282.3 — [Anr. ed.] fol. *in off. Edovardi whitcherche,* 1552. L²
         (lacks Act).O³¹(Brooke 216, has Act 2, prob. added
         later).C(Sel.3.139, has BB10).; HN(350000, has
         BB10).
              1 col., B.L., ending P10, BB10; series 2/14, w.
         D1ʳ having in last line: 'bothe'. Has Prelims. 4A,
         Act 4, Rubric 4a. BB10ʳ has prices only, and the
         verso is blank.

Liturgies—Church of England—BOOK OF COMMON PRAYER—
State Prayer for Edw.—cont.

16282.7 — [Anr. ed.] fol. *in off. Edovard Wihitchurche* [sic], 1552.
         L²(imp., for Prelims. *see* note; lacks Act, has BB10).
         O(C.P. 1552 d.3, has Act 5).O⁵(Δ.11.8, lacks tp).
         O²¹.; HD(imp., for Prelims. *see* note; lacks Act).
              1 col., B.L., ending P10, BB10; series 2/14, w. D1ʳ
         having in last line: 'both'. Has Prelims. 4B, Act 4,
         Rubric 4a. BB10ʳ has prices and a statement that
         the Ordinal is to be omitted in the next ed.; the
         verso is blank.
              Both L² and HD have in the Prelims. quire ππA¹⁰
         as in 16292a (copy 2), w. Almanack beginning 1561
         on ππA3ᵛ. This quire replaces b⁶ in L² and a6–8 b⁶
         in HD.

16283   — Now = 16286.3.

16284   — Now = 16286.2.

16284.5 — [Anr. issue of 16279, w. last quire reset.] fol. *in off. R.
         Graftoni,* 1552 (au.). L²(has rubric insert 2b, has
         Cc8 and errata 1).
              1 col., B.L., ending R6, Cc8; series 2/12. Has
         Prelims. 5A, Act 5, Rubric 1a.

16285   — [Anr. ed.] fol. *in off. R. Graftoni,* 1552 (au.) L(C.25.l.3,
         has rubric cancel 3b).O⁴(lacks Act).; HD(Typ.505.
         52.280F, lacks Act, has rubric cancel 3b, and errata 4
         as a cancel for Cc6).
              1 col., B.L., ending X8, Cc6; series 2/15, w. N1ʳ
         numbered 'Fol.. 73' (2 stops only, in the middle);
         F4 misnumbered '31' instead of 34; B5 numbered
         11 w. recto headline: '*The Letanie.*' Has Prelims.
         5A, Act 5, Rubric 1d (present only in O⁴).
              Further copies of one or another of the foliated
         Grafton eds. may be at C⁴, C⁹, C¹⁵, BTU, BUTE, D⁷,
         E, M², WN²; TCU.

16285.5 — [Anr. issue, w. A–B⁶ of the text reset.] *in off. R. Graf-
         toni,* 1552 (au.) O(C.P. 1552 d.5, has Prelims. 5B,
         rubric cancel 3b, has errata 4, poss. pr. as Cc6).O³
         (Gibbs 5, imp., has Prelims. 5A, rubric cancel 3b,
         has errata 4 at beginning of vol.).
              1 col., B.L., ending X8, Cc6; series 2/15, w. N1
         and F4 like 16285; B5 numbered 11 w. recto
         headline: '*The Letany.*' Has Prelims. as indicated,
         Act 5, Rubric 1d?

16285.7 — [Anr. ed.] fol. *in off. R. Graftoni,* 1552 (au.) O⁸(a.3.24,
         very imp., w. mounted Whitchurch tp as in 16280;
         lacks Act, has rubric cancel 3b).; CB(16456, has
         rubric cancel 3c).
              1 col., B.L., ending X8, Cc6; series 2/15, w. N1
         numbered 'Fol..73.' (3 stops); G4 misnumbered
         '39' instead of 40; 'C' of sig. C2 is under 't' of
         'the'. Has Prelims. 5B, Act 5, Rubric 1d?

16285a — [Anr. issue, w. at least C2 and R1,6 of the text reset.]
         in off. R. Graftoni, 1552 (au.) L(C.25.l.7, lacks Act).
         C(Sel.3.222, imp., lacks Act).
              1 col., B.L., ending X8, Cc6; series 2/15, w.
         N1 and G4 like 16285.7; 'C' of sig. C2 is under
         'de' of 'shoulde'. Has Prelims. 5B, Act 5?,
         Rubric 4b.

16286   — [Anr. ed.] fol. *in off. R. Grafton* [sic, no 'i'], 1552 (au.)
         L(C.36.l.15, imp., has Prelims. 6 instead of 5B, lacks
         Act).O(C.P. 1552 d.4; Douce C.P. 1552 d.1).O³(W.M.
         4.22).O⁴(Wombridge 137, has Cc6).
              1 col., B.L., ending X8, Cc6; series 2/15, w. N1
         numbered 'Fol.73.' (2 stops, correctly placed); B4
         misnumbered '13' instead of 10. Has Prelims. 5B,
         Act 5, Rubric 4b. Cc6ʳ has: 'This booke is truely
         and diligently imprynted.' followed by the prices
         w. 5-line 'T'.

16286.2 — [Anr. ed.] fol. *in off. R. Graftoni,* 1552 (au.) L(C.25.l.8,
         has Cc6).; PML(5544, has Cc6).
              1 col., B.L., ending X8, Cc6; series 2/15, w. N1
         numbered 'Fol.lxxiij'; C2ʳ has init. 'A' larger than
         init. 'O'. Has Prelims. 6, Act 6, Rubric 4c. Cc6 was
         not specifically rechecked, but it is prob. like
         16286.3 rather than 16286. (Formerly 16284.)

16286.3 — [Anr. issue.] *in off. R. Graftoni,* 1552 (au.) L(C.36.l.17,
         has Cc6).; HN(62285, imp., has Cc6; Page 387, has
         Prelims. and Act from an ed. c. 1565).
              1 col., B.L., ending X8, Cc6; series 2/15, w. N1
         like 16286.2; C2ʳ has init. 'A' smaller than init.
         'O'. Has Prelims. 6, Act 6, Rubric 4c. Cc6ʳ (HN)
         has: 'This booke . . . imprynted.' like 16286, but
         followed by the prices w. 4-line init. 'T'. In the
         L copies of this and 16286.2 the only portions in
         a different setting are C2–5, F2–5, and quires E,
         H, K, X, Aa. (Formerly 16283)

Liturgies—Church of England—Book of Common Prayer—
State Prayer for Edw.—cont.

16286.5 — [Anr. ed.] fol. *in off.* R. Graftoni, 1552 (au.) o(Douce
C.P. d.1552.2, has Prelims. 5B, cancel rubric 3a; in
place of Cc10 is substituted errata 4, not relevant to
this series). o³(Gibbs 6, imp., has Prelims. 5A, lacks
Act, lacks Ordinal).; bo⁶(imp., Prelims. defective,
has cancel rubric 3a).
    1 col., B.L., ending &4, Cc10; series 2/16. Has
    Prelims. as indicated, Act 5, Rubric 1b (present
    only in o³). Cc10 should have errata 5.

16287 — [Anr. issue of 16281.] fol. *Wigorniæ, in off.* J. Oswen,
1552. o(C.P. 1552 d.6, imp., has rubric insert 2a at
beginning of vol., lacks Ordinal).
    1 col., B.L., ending S6, BB12?; series 2/13, w. B1ʳ
    having in last line: 'magnified'. Has Prelims. 3,
    Act 3, Rubric 1c. Oswen pr. only the Prelims., Act,
    and A⁶ and O1,2 of the text. Another copy of this
    ed. may be at WOR.

16288 — [Anr. ed., w. Psalter added:] (The psalter or psalmes
of Dauid, poynted as it shalbe sayde or songe in
churches.) 2 pts. 4° in 8's. *in off.* E. whitchurche,
[1552?] L(C.25.h.5).o³.c³.d⁷(imp., lacks Psalter).
HETH(imp.).; HN(imp., lacks Psalter).bo(imp.).N.NY
(Psalter only)†.
    1 col., B.L., ending P8, Aa8; Heth. 2.1. In pt. 1
    'C' of sig. C1 is under 'li' of 'life' (L, orig. C1).
    Some copies have a cancel (Heth.2.2, o³(Gibbs
    208)) w. 'C' under 'f' of 'of'. This and the next
    both have the Black Rubric in the text on M8ʳ.
    (Psalter formerly also 2381)

16288a — [Anr. ed.] 2 pts. 4° in 8's. *in off.* E. whitchurche, [1553?]
L(imp.).L¹⁵(imp.).c(imp.).d².m(328).; HN.
    1 col., B.L., ending P8, Aa8; Heth. 2.3. In pt. 1
    'C' of sig. C1 is under 'e' of 'worde'. (Psalter for-
    merly also 2382)

16289 — Now = 16290.5.

16290 — [Anr. ed.] 2 pts. 8°. (*in æd.* R. Graftoni,) 1552 (1553
(mr.)) L(lacks Psalter).; NY(Psalter only).NY¹¹(imp.).
    1 col., B.L., ending D[d]4, S4; series 8/1. The
    Black Rubric is in the text on Y1ᵛ–2ʳ.

16290.5 — [Anr. ed.] 2 pts. 8°. [E. Whitchurch,] 1553. L(imp.).
    1 col., B.L., ending Ee4, bb4; series 8/2. The
    Black Rubric is in the text on Y2ᵛ–3ʳ. (Formerly
    16289; Psalter formerly also 2383)

State Prayer for Queen Elizabeth

[Accession to the throne 17 Nov. 1558]

In addition to the supplication for the Sovereign earlier in the
Litany, a formal State Prayer for the Sovereign is now added near
the end of the Litany, beginning: 'O Lord our heavenly father. . . .'
This is the one noted in all the editions below.

16291 The boke of common praier, and administration of the
sacramentes, and other rites and ceremonies in the
Churche of Englande. fol. *in off.* R. Graftoni, 1559.
L.o.o⁵.c.c⁵(imp.).+ 𝔄
    1 col., B.L., ending X8; series 2/20 (L). The leaves
    are numbered; i.e. this is patterned after series
    2/15 (16285 sqq.) but without the Ordinal. As no
    other book with Grafton's imprint after 1553 is
    known, this ed. possibly represents an unsuccess-
    ful attempt by him to gain a share in the Queen's
    Printing Office. Mr. Hetherington suggests that
    this ed. was pr. by Grafton as agent for Jugge and
    Cawood and that he improperly put his name in
    the imprint, since his licence as Queen's Printer
    was revoked by Queen Mary in 1553 and never
    restored. The c copy has a cancel slip, originally
    pasted over the imprint but now on a flyleaf, w.
    imprint: *in off.* R. Jugge & J. Cawode. The tp
    verso is in the same typesetting as 16292, and sheet
    A4,9 in at least the L, o copies is from 16292, w. A4
    headlines in B.L.

16292 — [Anr. ed.] fol. *in off.* R. Jugge & J. Cawode, 1559. L.
L².LINC(imp.). Sir Richard Proby.; HN.BO(has no
Ordinal).
    1 col., B.L., ending P10, BB10; series 2/21 (L, BO).
    The leaves are not numbered, and this is patterned
    after series 2/14 (16282.3 sq.). This omits the
    expanded latter part of the Litany, including the
    new State Prayer (the old one appears on B2ᵛ).
    Mr. Hetherington suggests that the official printers
    were temporarily denied access to this part of the

Liturgies—Church of England—Book of Common Prayer—
State Prayer for Eliz.—cont.

new revisions. The Ordinal (formerly 16465)
appears for the last time on a double register,
though later eds. of it on separate signatures (*see*
16466 sqq.) are usually bd. w. folio, 1 col., B.L.
eds. of BCP.

16292a — [Anr. ed.] fol. *in off.* R. Jugge & J. Cawode, 1559
[1561?] L(2).o³¹(2).
    1 col., B.L., ending P10; series 2/22. The copies
    differ in the prelims., and at least 1 and 4 have
    been sophisticated.

    1. L(6.d.9, formerly 16292b) has prelims. collating
    πA¹²πB⁶. The tp (πA1) is undated and has been
    supplied from an ed. c. 1566. The Almanack
    on πA12ᵛ begins 1559. Quire D and L3,8,
    P4,7 are the same setting as 16292.

    2. L(C.25.l.6) has prelims. collating πA¹² ππA¹⁰.
    The tp is dated 1559, but the state of the border
    (McK. & F. 68) is probably later than 1559.
    πA9-12, with Almanack beginning 1559 on
    πA12ᵛ, were intended to be cancelled. ππA¹⁰
    includes an Almanack beginning 1561 on ππA3ᵛ
    and a revised Kalendar. L², HD have a copy of
    this quire ππA¹⁰ inserted in 16282.7. The text
    is the same setting as 1, except that P1,10 are
    reset.

    3. o³¹(Brooke 217) has prelims. collating πA¹²πB⁶.
    The tp is like 2 above. The Almanack on πA12ᵛ
    begins 1561.

    4. o³¹(A 66) has prelims. collating πA¹²(−πA12)
    ππA²πB⁸. πA1 is a faked tp dated 1561. The
    Almanack on πB1ᵛ begins 1561.

16292b — = copy 1 of 16292a.

16293 — [Anr. ed., w. Psalter added.] 2 pts. 4° in 8's. *in off.* R.
Jugge & J. Cawood, 1559. L(C.53.c.61, imp., lacks
Psalter).; Bernard Kottler, Purdue Univ., Lafayette,
Indiana(Psalter only).
    1 col., B.L., ending U10, M8; Heth. 3.1. R1ʳ of
    pt. 1 correctly omits the Black Rubric. The Kottler
    Psalter has M⁸ w. colophon: W. Seres, [n.d.],
    which may or may not belong; this copy is the one
    noted in McK. & F. 37β.

16293.3 — [Anr. ed.] 2 pts. 4° in 8's. *in off.* R. Jugge & J. Cawood,
1559. L(C.112.c.10, imp., w. M⁸ lacking in Psalter).
    1 col., B.L., ending U10, M8; Heth. 3.2. R1ʳ of
    pt. 1 has the Black Rubric (*see* headnote preceding
    16279), apparently erroneously added in this ed.
    as the page is 2 lines longer than the others. The
    prelims. of pt. 1 and all extant of the Psalter are
    in the same typesetting as 16293.

16293.5 — [Anr. ed.] 2 pts. 8°. [J. Kingston] *in off.* R. Jugge & J.
Cawoode, (1559.) PML.
    1 col., B.L., ending D[d]4, R4; series 8/3. NEK has
    a frag. of an unrecorded 8° ed., w. heading on A8ʳ:
    'A briefe declaration . . .'; this appears on w/ 8ᵛ
    of the present ed.

16294 — [Anr. ed.] 2 pts. 4° in 8's. *in off.* R. Jugge & J. Cawood,
1560. L(C.25.h.12).L⁵(imp.).o.LEIC²(imp., lacks
Psalter).; BO⁶(Psalter only, imp.).
    1 col., B.L., ending U10, N8; Heth. 4.1. The
    border of the Psalter tp varies: McK. & F. 113*(L)
    or McK. & F. 83 (o).

16294a — [A ghost.]

16294a.3 — [Anr. ed.] 2 pts. 8°. (R. Jugge a. J. Cawoode, 1560.)
o³(imp.).
    1 col., B.L., ending Dd8, R4; series 8/4.

— [Anr. ed.] fol. [1561?] *See* 16292a.

16295 — [Anr. ed.] 2 pts. 4° in 8's. *in off.* R. Jugge & J. Cawood,
1562. M(imp.).; BO(Benton 2.1).NY¹¹(imp.).
    1 col., B.L., ending U10, N8; Heth. 4.2.

16296 — [Anr. ed.] 2 pts. fol. *in off.* R. Jugge & J. Cawode,
(1564.) L.o(Psalter tp only).
    1 col., B.L., ending Q6, K6; series 2/23. Signa-
    tures have numbers in round brackets, e.g. A(iii).

16296.3 — [Anr. ed.] 2 pts. 8°. *in off.* R. Jugge & J. Cawood,
(1564.) Sotheby's, 28 Jan. 1946, lot 2151 (tp reproduced; Harmsworth copy, bought by Maggs; cannot
be traced).
    1 col., B.L., ending Dd8, R8; series 8/5.

16296.5 — [Anr. ed.] 2 pts. 4° in 8's. *in off.* R. Jugge & J. Cawood,
(1565.) NLW(St. Asaph, imp.). Goyder(complete).;
NY(Psalter only)†.
    1 col., B.L., ending U10, N8; Heth. 5.3. Signa-
    tures have numbers in round brackets, e.g. A(iii).

Liturgies—Church of England—Book of Common Prayer—
State Prayer for Eliz.—cont.

16297 — [Anr. ed.] 2 pts. fol. (*R. Jugge a. J. Cawood,* 1566.)
L(imp.).o(imp.).; HN.
    1 col., B.L., ending Q6, K6; series 2/23 (L). Signa-
tures have numbers in round brackets, e.g. A(iii).
(Formerly also 16301; Psalter formerly also
2385)

16297.5 — [Anr. ed.] 2 pts. 4° in 8's. (*R. Jugge a. J. Cawood,* 1566.)
HN(pt. 1 imp.: Page 731; Psalter: 13083).
    1 col., B.L., ending U10, N8; Heth. 6.2. Signa-
tures have numbers in round brackets, e.g. A(iii).

16298 — [Anr. ed.] 2 pts. 4° in 8's. (*R. Jugge a. J. Cawood,*
1567.) L(3407.c.14, imp.).
    1 col., B.L., ending U10, N8; Heth. 7.2.

16298.5 — [Anr. ed.] 2 pts. 4° in 8's. *in off.* R. Jugge & J. Cawood,
(1568.) c²(imp., lacks Psalter).; HN(Page 597).
    1 col., B.L., ending U10, N8; Heth. 7.3.

16299 — [Anr. ed.] 2 pts. 4° in 8's. *in off.* R. Jugge & J. Cawood,
(1570.) L(pt. 1 imp., Psalter bd. separately).; HN(2
copies: 62313 and Page 3). Washington Cathedral
(2 imp., both lack Psalter).
    1 col., B.L., ending U10, N4; Heth. 8.2. (Psalter
formerly also 2387)

16300 — [Anr. ed.] 2 pts. 16° in 8's. R. Jugge a. J. Cawood,
(1570.) L(destroyed).o.
    1 col., B.L., ending Z8, O8; series 16/1.

16301 — = 16297.

16301.3 — [Anr. ed.] 2 pts. 4° in 8's. *in off.* R. Jugge & J. Cawood,
(1571.) o³(Psalter only, imp., w. 16301.7).D(W.f.51,
lacks end of Psalter).HETH(imp.).M(imp.).
    1 col., B.L., ending U8, N4; Heth. 9.1.

16301.5 — [Anr. ed.] 2 pts. 16° in 8's. (*R. Jugge a. J. Cawood,*
1571.) o(Psalter only).D(pt. 1 only, imp.).
    1 col., B.L., ending Hh8, S8; series 16/2. (Psalter
formerly 2388) The D copy of pt. 1 has the colophon undated and may belong to an earlier ed.

16301.7 — [Anr. ed.] 2 pts. 4° in 8's. (*R. Jugge,* 1572.) L(3434.d.2,
Psalter only).o³(Gibbs 209, pt. 1 only, imp., w.
16301.3).
    1 col., B.L., ending U8, N4; Heth. 9.2. (Psalter
formerly 2390)

16302 — [Anr. ed.] 2 pts. 8°. (*R. Jugge,* 1572.) L(imp., lacks
Psalter).o(S⁴ only, of Psalter).; NY(Psalter only,
imp.).
    1 col., B.L., ending Dd8, S4; series 8/6. (o frag.
formerly 20197)

16302.5 — [Anr. ed.] 2 pts. 16° in 8's. (*R. Jugge,* 1572.) Goyder
(imp.).
    1 col., B.L., ending Hh8, S8; series 16/2.

16303 — [Anr. ed.] 2 pts. fol. (*R. Jugge,* 1573.) L(imp.).
    1 col., B.L., ending Q6, K6; series 2/23. Signa-
tures have numbers in round brackets, e.g.
A(iii).

16303.5 — [Anr. ed.] 2 pts. 4° in 8's. (*R. Jugge,* 1573.) Sotheby's,
28 Jan. 1946, lot 2155(imp., Harmsworth copy, with-
drawn from sale, cannot be traced).
    1 col., B.L., ending U8, N4; Heth. 10.3.

16304 — = pt. of 2109.

16304.5 — [Anr. ed.] 2 pts. 4° in 8's. (*R. Jugge,* 1574.) WN²
(49.B.11, imp.).
    1 col., B.L., ending U8, N4; Heth. 10.4.

16304.6 — [Anr. ed.] 2 pts. 8°. (*R. Jugge,* 1574.) L(Psalter only).
    1 col., B.L., ending Dd8? S4; series 8/6. (Psalter
formerly 2391)

16304.7 — [Anr. ed.] 2 pts. fol. *in off.* R. Jugge, (1575.) o³.; HD
(imp.).NY¹¹.
    1 col., B.L., ending Q6, K6; series 2/23 (HD, NY¹¹).

16305 — [Anr. ed.] 2 pts. 4° in 8's. *in off.* R. Jugge, (1575.) L
(Psalter only, destroyed).o(F3,6 of pt. 1 only)†.; F
(Psalter only).PML(17258, lacks Psalter).
    1 col., B.L., ending U8, N4; Heth. 10.5.

16305a — [Anr. ed.] 2 pts. 16° in 8's. (*R. Jugge,* 1575.) HN.
    1 col., B.L., ending Y8, O8; series 16/3. (Psalter
formerly also 2392)

16306 — [Anr. ed.] 2 pts. 8°. *R. Jugge,* (1576.) o.
    1 col., B.L., ending Cc8, Q8; series 8/7. (Psalter
formerly also 2393)

16306.2 — [Anr. ed.] 2 pts. fol. *in off.* R. Jugge, (1577.) Seven
Gables(Phillipps 2692).
    1 col., B.L., ending Q6, K6; series 2/23. Psalter
tp, dated 1577, has line 5 ending: 'poynted/'.

16306.3 — [Anr. ed.] 2 pts. fol. (*R. Jugge,* 1577.) BO⁶(imp.).HD
(imp.).
    1 col., B.L., ending Q6, K6; series 2/23. Psalter
tp, dated 1577, has line 5 ending: 'poyn-/'.

Liturgies—Church of England—Book of Common Prayer—
State Prayer for Eliz.—cont.

16306.5 — [Anr. ed.] 2 pts. 4° in 8's. (*R. Jugge,* 1577.) L(Psalter
only).; N(C.8726.577).NY¹¹(imp., lacks Psalter).
    1 col., B.L., ending U8, N4; Heth. 10.7. (Psalter
formerly 2395)

16306.6 — [Anr. ed.] 16° in 8's. (*C. Barkar,*) [1577?] NY¹¹(lacks
tp).
    1 col., B.L., ending Ddd8; series 16/4.

16306.7 — [Anr. ed.] 4° in 8's. *C. Barker,* [1578?] L(3408.c.42,
w. B5,6 inserted from an earlier ed.).o(imp.).
    1 col., B.L., ending Kk4; Heth. 11.1. 'C' of sig. C1
is under 'l' of 'shal'.

16306.9 — [Anr. ed.] 4° in 8's. *C. Barker,* [1579?] c(SSS.23.4).
    1 col., B.L., ending Kk4; Heth. 12.1. 'C' of sig. C1
is under 's' of 'shall'.

16307 — [Anr. ed.] 2 pts. fol. *C. Barker,* 1580. L.M(lacks
Psalter).
    1 col., B.L., ending Q6, K8; series 2/24 (L).

16308 — Now = 16309.1.

16309 — [Anr. ed.] 4° in 8's. (*C. Barker,* 1580.) HETH(frag.).;
ILL(imp.).
    1 col., B.L., ending Kk4; Heth. 12.2.

16309.1 — [Anr. ed.] 2 pts. fol. *C. Barker,* 1581. L(2 imp.).D⁷.; BO.
    1 col., B.L., ending Q6, K8; series 2/24 (L, BO).
Parts of the Psalter are in 2 settings; L(3406.e.11),
BO have 'F' of sig. F1 under final 'h' of 'hath';
L(C.25.l.10) has it under and to left of 'h' of
'he'. (Formerly 16308)

16309.2 — [Anr. ed.] 4° in 8's. *C. Barker,* [1581?] G²(G.x.27).
    1 col., B.L., ending Kk4; Heth. 12.3. 'C' of sig. C1
is under 'h' of 'shall'; 'B' of sig. B1 is under 'si' of
'confession'.

16309.3 — [Anr. ed.] 8°. (*C. Barker,*) [1581?] E(imp., bd. w.
2459).
    1 col., B.L., ending Rr8; series 8/8. 'c' of sig. Cc1
is under space before 't' of 'the'. The E copy has
the date 1581 stamped in at a later time.

16309.4 — [Anr. ed.] 16° in 8's. (*C. Barker,* 1581.) MICH(Clements,
imp.).
    1 col., B.L., ending Tt6; series 16/5.

16309.5 — [Anr. ed.] 4° in 8's. *C. Barker,* [1582?] HETH.; HN
(62260).
    1 col., B.L., ending Kk4; Heth. 13.1. 'C' of sig. C1
is under and to left of 's' of 'shall'.

16309.6 — [Anr. ed.] 4° in 8's. *C. Barker,* [1583?] o³(MS.336).;
BO⁶(imp.).
    1 col., B.L., ending Kk4; Heth. 12.5. 'C' of sig. C1
is under 'h' of 'shall'; 'B' of sig. B1 is under 2nd
'o' of 'confession'.

16309.7 — [Anr. ed.] 8°. (*C. Barker,*) [1583?] HETH(imp., bd.
w. 2466.3).
    1 col., B.L., ending Rr8; series 8/8. 'c' of sig. Cc1
is under 'f' of 'of'.

16309.8 — [Anr. ed.] 4° in 8's. (*C. Barker,*) [1584?] GLOUC(imp.,
w. faked tp w. imprint of J. Day).; ILL(C1 to the end,
w. 16310).PEN(imp.).
    1 col., B.L., ending Kk4; Heth. 12.6. 'C' of sig. C1
is under 'o' of 'roare'.

16310 — [Anr. ed.] 4° in 8's. *C. Barker,* [1585?] L(C.27.f.8).
HETH(frag.).; ILL(before C1 only, w. 16309.8).
    1 col., B.L., ending Kk4; Heth. 12.7. 'C' of sig. C1
is under and to left of 1st 'r' of 'roare'.

16310.5 — [Anr. ed.] 8°. [*C. Barker,* c. 1585?] o(imp., bd. w.
2466.3).
    1 col., B.L., ending Qq4; series 8/9. Qq4ᵛ line 2:
'kill al', line 18: 'folowe'; cf. 16320.5, 16323.3,
16324.3.

16311 — [Anr. ed.] 16° in 8's. (*C. Barker,* 1585.) L(destroyed).
    1 col., B.L., ending Xx8; series 16/6.

16311.3 — [Anr. ed.] 2 pts. fol. *C. Barker,* 1586. LIV.; HN.NY¹¹.
    1 col., B.L., ending Q6, K8; series 2/24 (NY¹¹).

16311.4 — [Anr. ed.] 4° in 8's. *C. Barker,* [1586?] o²⁴(imp.).;
TEX(complete).
    1 col., B.L., ending Kk4; Heth. 14.1. 'C' of sig. C1
is under 'e' of 'water'.

16311.5 — [Anr. ed.] 4° in 8's. *C. Barker,* [1586?] o³²(RBR).
DUR⁵.G⁴(imp.).SH(imp.).
    2 cols., B.L., ending E8; Heth. 41.1. 'E' of sig. E2
is under 'wa' of 'wayes'. Previous eds. of this
description were pr. as pt. of 4° Bibles, e.g.
2144.

16311.6 — [Anr. ed.] 16° in 8's. (*C. Barker,* 1586.) HD(imp.).
    1 col., rom., ending V8; series 16/11.

16311.7 — [Anr. ed.] 2 pts. fol. *C. Barker,* 1587. DUR.
    1 col., B.L., ending Q6, K8; series 2/24.

Liturgies—**Church of England**—Book of Common Prayer—
State Prayer for Eliz.—cont.

16311.9 — [Anr. ed.] 4° in 8's. [*C. Barker,* 1587?] c(Syn.6.58.
        20, imp.).
        2 cols., B.L., ending E8; Heth. 41.2. 'E' of sig. E2
        is under space between 'my' and 'wayes'.
16312   — [Anr. ed.] 16° in 8's. *Deputies of C. Barker,* 1587. O.
        1 col., rom., ending Y8; series 16/12.
16313   — [Anr. ed.] 4° in 8's. *Deputies of C. Barker,* 1588. L(C.
        36.f.12).O²⁰(imp.)*.LEIC²(imp.)*. Exeter U(frag.)*.;
        BO(imp.)*.BO⁶(imp.)*.
        2 cols., B.L., ending E8; Heth. 41.3.
16314   — [Anr. issue, w. imprint:] *Deputies of C. Barker,* 1589.
        c(Syn.6.58.18, plus 1 imp.*).BIRM².
        2 cols., B.L., ending E8; Heth. 41.4.
16314.5 — [Anr. ed.] 4° in 8's. (*Deputies of C. Barker,*) [1589?]
        Sotheby's, 28 Jan. 1946, lot 2160(imp., Harmsworth
        copy, bought by Orion, untraced; bd. w. 2475.7).
        1 col., B.L., ending Kk4; may belong to series
        Heth. 14 or 16.
16314a — [Anr. ed.] 2 pts. fol. *Deputies of C. Barker,* 1590. O.
        C³.DUR.; HN.
        1 col., B.L., ending Q6, K8; series 2/24 (HN).
16314a.5 — [Anr. ed.] 4° in 8's. [*Deputies of C. Barker,* 1590?]
        COL(imp.).HETH(C.V.44, imp.).
        2 cols., B.L., ending E8; Heth. 41.5. 'E' of sig. E2
        is under 'm' of 'my'.
16315   — [Anr. ed.] 16° in 8's. [*Deputies of C. Barker,* c. 1590.]
        L(destroyed).C²(imp.).
        1 col., B.L., ending Ss8; series 16/7. Cf. 16321a.5.
16315.5 — [Anr. ed.] 16° in 8's. (*Deputies of C. Barker,* 1591.)
        Douglas A. Jeffery, Sevenoaks, Kent(imp.).
        1 col., rom., ending Y8; prob. belongs to series
        16/13.
16316   — [Anr. ed.] 2 pts. fol. *Deputies of C. Barker,* 1592. L.
        C²(lacks tp).D.
        1 col., B.L., ending Q6, K8; series 2/24 (L).
16316.5 — [Anr. ed.] 4° in 8's. [*Deputies of C. Barker,* 1592?] L¹⁴
        (imp.).E(imp.).E⁴(M.H.4/5, imp.).HETH(2 imp.).; ILL
        (imp.).
        2 cols., B.L., ending E8; Heth. 41.7. 'E' of sig. E2
        is under 'w' of 'wayes'.
16317   — [Anr. ed.] 16° in 8's. *Deputies of C. Barker,* (1592.) O
        (lacks 4 leaves between Z8 and Aa1).
        1 col., B.L., ending Ss8; series 16/8.
16318   — [Anr. ed.] 2 pts. fol. *Deputies of C. Barker,* 1594. L
        (imp.).O(imp.).O³(imp.).C².; F.HN.MICH.
        1 col., B.L., ending Q6, K8; series 2/25 (F).
        (Psalter formerly also 2401)
16318.5 — [Anr. ed.] 4° in 8's. [*Deputies of C. Barker,* 1594?] L
        (1411.e.1, w. tp from 1614 ed.).L¹⁴(imp.).O³⁸(imp.)†.
        SH(imp.).STD(imp.).; Y(imp.).
        2 cols., B.L., ending E8; Heth. 41.9. 'E' of sig. E2
        is under 'y' of 'my'. (L copy formerly 16342)
16319   — = 16322.
16320   — [Anr. ed.] 4° in 8's. *Deputies of C. Barker,* 1595.
        L(imp.).C²(frag.).D⁷.HETH(X.2).SH(imp.).+;   MICH
        (frag.).
        2 cols., B.L., ending E8; Heth. 41.10.
16320.3 — [Anr. ed.] 4° in 8's. *Deputies of C. Barker,* [1595?]
        BO(Benton 2.3).
        1 col., B.L., ending Kk4; Heth. 16.2. 'C' of sig. C1
        is under space between 'shall' and 'roare'.
16320.5 — [Anr. ed.] 8°. *Deputies of C. Barker,* 1595. O³(imp.,
        Psalter tp dated 1595).; HN(Page 41, Psalter tp dated
        1597).
        1 col., B.L., ending Qq4; series 8/9. Qq4ᵛ line 2:
        'kill al', line 18: 'followe' (O³) or 'kill all' and
        'followe' (HN); cf. 16310.5.
16321   — [Anr. ed.] 4° in 8's. *Deputies of C. Barker,* 1596. L
        (C.25.h.7).CASHEL.E²(imp.).
        1 col., B.L., ending Kk4; Heth. 16.4.
16321.5 — [Anr. ed.] 4° in 8's. *Deputies of C. Barker,* 1596.
        L†.L¹⁴(HC.184).HETH(imp.).LEIC²(2   imp.).NLW(St.
        Asaph, w. quire A of 16341.5).; F(imp.)†.NY. Finney
        (w. quire A of 16344.5).
        2 cols., B.L., ending E8; Heth. 41.11.
16321a — [Anr. ed.] 16° in 8's. *Deputies of C. Barker,* 1596.
        LINC.; HN.
        1 col., rom., ending Y8; series 16/13 (HN).
16321a.5— [Anr. ed.] 16° in 8's. 1596; B.L. *See* Addenda.
16322   — [Anr. ed.] 2 pts. fol. *Deputies of C. Barker,* 1596 (1597.)
        L(3 imp.).O³(imp.).M.NOR(imp.).; F(imp.).ILL.
        1 col., B.L., ending Q6, K8; series 2/25 (L). (One
        L copy, C.25.m.5(2), formerly 16319)
16322.1 — [Anr. ed.] 4° in 8's. [*Deputies of C. Barker,* 1597?]

Liturgies—**Church of England**—Book of Common Prayer—
State Prayer for Eliz.—cont.

        HETH(C.V.113, imp.). Truro Cathedral(imp.).; NY⁶
        (lacks tp).
        2 cols., B.L., ending E8; Heth. 41.12. 'E' of sig. E2
        is under 'y' of 'wayes'.
16322.2 — [Anr. ed.] 4° in 8's. *Deputies of C. Barker,* [1597?] L¹³
        (lacks   Psalter).C⁵(Psalter   only).M(R28452).;   ILL
        (imp.).
        1 col., B.L., ending Kk4; Heth. 16.6. 'C' of sig. C1
        is under 'sh' of 'shall'; 'F' of sig. F1 is under 'il'
        of 'euill'. At least E outer sheet is the same type-
        setting as 16321. The ILL copy has C outer sheet
        in a different typesetting, w. 'C' of sig. C1 under
        and to left of 1st 'r' of 'roare'.
        — [Anr. ed.] 8°. 1597. *See* 16320.5.
16322.3 — [Anr. ed.] fol. *Deputies of C. Barker,* 1598. L².O³(lacks
        tp).; HN. Lehigh U.
        2 cols., rom., ending D4; series 2/30 (L², HN). This
        ed. has no Psalter.
16322.5 — [Anr. ed.] 4° in 8's. [*Deputies of C. Barker,* 1598?] LC
        (S84.1599 case, D5–E8 only).
        2 cols., B.L., ending E8; Heth. 41.13. 'E' of sig. E2
        is under 'a' of 'wayes' and '2' is under the 'e'.
16322.6 — [Anr. ed.] 4° in 8's. [*Deputies of C. Barker,* 1598?] L⁴
        (ARC.A35.1b/1621, imp., w. 1st 2 leaves of 16357.5
        and Psalter of 16358).
        1 col., B.L., ending Kk4; Heth. 16.8. 'C' of sig. C1
        is like 16322.2; 'F' of sig. F1 is under 1st 'h' of
        'hath'.
16322.7 — [Anr. ed.] 2 pts. fol. *Deputies of C. Barker,* 1599 (1598.)
        L.O(imp.).C¹⁷(part of Psalter only, w. 16339).CANT.;
        BO.NY¹¹(imp.).
        1 col., B.L., ending Q6, K8; series 2/25 (BO).
        (Psalter formerly 2402)
16323   — [Anr. ed.] 4° in 8's. *Deputies of C. Barker,* 1599. L.O
        (Bib.Eng. 1598 e.3, plus 1 imp.).LEIC²(2 imp.).; HN.
        Syracuse U†.
        2 cols., B.L., ending E8; Heth. 41.14. The L copy
        (3051.cc.6) has the date defective, sometimes mis-
        read as 1598.
16323.3 — [Anr. ed.] 8°. (*Deputies of C. Barker,* 1599.) The Rev.
        C. G. F. Dare, South Harrow, Middlesex(imp.).
        1 col., B.L., ending Qq4; series 8/9. Qq4ᵛ line 2:
        'kil all'; cf. 16310.5.
16323.5 — [Anr. ed.] 2 pts. fol. *R. Barker,* 1600. O.O²²(Psalter
        only).D⁷.DUR(imp.).E⁹.+; NY(Psalter only).PH.PML.Y.
        1 col., B.L., ending Q6, K8; series 2/25 (PML).
16324   — [Anr. ed.] 4° in 8's. *R. Barker,* 1600. L¹³(imp.).L³⁰
        (imp.).O²⁸(imp.).C(Syn.6.60.7, imp.).HETH(imp.).; HD
        (imp.).ILL(imp.).PH²(imp.).PTS(imp.).
        2 cols., B.L., ending E8; Heth. 41.15.
16324.3 — [Anr. ed.] 8°. (*R. Barker,* 1600.) NCU(imp.).
        1 col., B.L., ending Qq4; series 8/9. Qq4ᵛ line 2:
        'kill all', line 18: 'follow'; cf. 16310.5.
16324.5 — [Anr. ed.] 4° in 8's. *R. Barker,* 1601. M²(7.C.4.114(1)).;
        BO⁶(lacks Hh8).
        1 col., B.L., ending Hh8; Heth. 20.1.
16324.7 — [Anr. ed.] 4° in 8's. *R. Barker,* 1601. L(w. tp from
        1609 ed.).O(quires C–D, and E outer sheet only, w.
        16326.5).HETH(C.V.78, plus 1 imp.).; Finney(w. tp
        from 1599 ed.).
        2 cols., B.L., ending E8; Heth. 41.16.
16324.9 — [Anr. ed.] 24° in 12's. *R. Barker,* 1603. ILL.
        1 col., rom., ending P12; series 24/1.

                State Prayer for King James
        [Accession to the throne 24 Mar. 1603]

16325   — [Anr. ed.] 2 pts. fol. *R. Barker,* 1603. L(imp.).
        1 col., B.L., ending Q6, K8; series 2/25.
16325.3 — [Anr. ed.] 4° in 8's. [*R. Barker,* 1603.] L(3035.p.10,
        imp.).
        2 cols., B.L., ending E8; Heth. 41.18. 'E' of sig. E2
        is under 'a' of 'wayes' and '2' is under the 's'.
        Partly reissued in 16326.5.

State Prayers for King James / Queen Anne and Prince Henry
Following the revisions adopted at the Hampton Court conference
in early 1604 there appears, following the State Prayer for the
Sovereign near the end of the Litany, a second prayer for members
of his family. The variations noted here and below refer to names
in the text of the prayer and not to its heading.

16326   The booke of common prayer, and administration of the
        sacraments, and other rites and ceremonies of the

Liturgies—Church of England—BOOK OF COMMON PRAYER—
State Prayers for J / A, H—cont.

Church of England. 2 pts. fol. *R. Barker*, 1603 [o.s.] L(2 imp.).L²(2).L⁴⁶.C². Sir Richard Proby.; BO(lacks bifolium).

1 col., B.L., ending Q6, K8; series 2/26 (L, BO). The L copy on Univ. Microfilms reel 995 (C.25.m.11) lacks the added bifolium w. the proclamation, a reprint of 8344, the 1st leaf of which is signed a5. This copy also has 7748.3 bd. in before Morning Prayer.

16326.5 — [Anr. ed.] 4° in 8's. *R. Barker*, 1603 [o.s.] L¹⁴(HC. 208).O(quire B, and E inner sheet only, w. 16324.7). E⁴(imp.).; N(imp.).NY¹¹(imp.).

2 cols., B.L., ending E8; Heth. 42.1. Quires C–E are the same typesetting as 16325.3.

16327 — [Anr. ed.] 2 pts. fol. *R. Barker*, 1604. L(destroyed).O. HETH(imp.).INN.M.; CH.NY.NY¹¹(Psalter only, w. 16353).PML.Y.

1 col., B.L., ending Q6, K8; series 2/26 (O, NY¹¹, PML). The Psalter is in 2 settings; line 3 of title ends: 'transla-/' (formerly 2404; O, CH, NY, PML) or 'the/' (NY¹¹, Y).

16328 — [Anr. ed.] 4° in 8's. *R. Barker*, 1604. L(C.70.c.4). L². HETH(2 leaves).; HN.

1 col., B.L., ending Hh8; Heth. 21.4.

16328.5 — [Anr. ed.] 4° in 8's. *R. Barker*, 1604. O(Bib.Eng. 1630 e.1, plus 2 imp., w. 1630 tp).A(imp.).HETH(2, 1 imp.). LEIC²(2, 1 imp.). Southwell Minster.; MICH.NY¹¹.

2 cols., B.L., ending E8; Heth. 42.2.

16328a — [Anr. ed.] 8°. *R. Barker*, 1604. O.LINC.; PH⁷.

1 col., B.L., ending Nn8; series 8/10 (O). (Psalter formerly also 2405)

16328a.5 — [Anr. ed.] 24° in 12's. *R. Barker*, 1604. Halle U, East Germany.

1 col., rom., ending P12; series 24/2.

16329 — [Anr. ed.] 2 pts. fol. *R. Barker*, 1605. L(imp.).LINC.

1 col., B.L., ending Q6, K8; series 2/26 (L). Pt. 1, A1ʳ last line: 'afflictions'.

16329a — [Anr. issue, partly reset.] *R. Barker*, 1605. L.M.; HN. HD.LC.NY¹¹.Y.+

1 col., B.L., ending Q6, K8; series 2/26 (L, BO, HD). Pt. 1, A1ʳ last line: 'your afflictions.'

16329a.5 — [Anr. ed.] 4° in 8's. *R. Barker*, 1605. HETH(imp.).; HN(Page 402).

1 col., B.L., ending Hh8; Heth. 21.5.

16330 — [Anr. ed.] 4° in 8's. *R. Barker*, 1606. O(Douce C.P. e. 1606).A.

1 col., B.L., ending Hh8; Heth. 21.6.

16330.3 — [Anr. ed.] 4° in 8's. *R. Barker*, 1606. L(1411.e.2).L¹⁴. O.DUR⁵(imp.).HETH(imp.).+; CHI.HD.ILL(imp.).NY. PH².

2 cols., B.L., ending E8; Heth. 42.4.

16331 — [Anr. ed.] 24° in 12's. *R. Barker*, 1606. O.; N(lacks tp). TEX.

1 col., rom., ending P12; series 24/3 (O).

16332 — [Anr. ed.] fol. *R. Barker*, 1607. L.O¹⁹.C.C³.ELY.+; F. HN.HD.

2 cols., rom., ending G6; series 2/31 (HD).

16332.2 — [Anr. ed.] 2 pts. fol. *R. Barker*, 1607. O.O³.; HN.

1 col., B.L., ending Q6, K8; series 2/26 (O, O³). The Psalter is in 2 settings, w. tp dated 1606 (O) or 1607 (O³); both have Psalter colophon dated 1607.

16332.4 — [Anr. ed.] 4° in 8's. *R. Barker*, 1607. O¹⁴(imp.).O¹⁷ (imp.).O²⁰(imp.).G²(imp.).HETH(C.V.73, imp.).; MICH (imp.).

2 cols., B.L., ending E8; Heth. 42.5. A complete copy w. tp was in the stock of E. T. Webster, Stonham Parva, Stowmarket, Suffolk, in 1974.

16332.5 — [Anr. ed.] 4° in 8's. *R. Barker*, 1607 (1608.) D(W.f.54). LEIC².

1 col., B.L., ending Hh8; Heth. 22.7.

16332.6 — [Anr. ed.] 4° in 8's. [*R. Barker*, 1608.] L¹⁴(imp.).O⁶ (imp.).CANT(C.12.13, lacks tp).LIV³(imp.).OS(w. tp from 1630 ed.).+; HN(imp.). Washington Cathedral (imp.).

2 cols., B.L., ending E8; Heth. 42.6. 'E' of sig. E2 in under 'd' of 'changed'.

16332.8 — [Anr. ed.] 4° in 8's. *R. Barker*, 1608. L(lacks tp). B(imp.).HETH(imp.).M(imp.).NEK(imp.).; ILL(complete).

2 cols., B.L., ending E8; Heth. 42.7.

16333 — [Anr. ed.] 16° in 8's. (*R. Barker*, 1608.) L(destroyed). 1 col., B.L. Possibly resembled series 16/8 or 16/9.

Liturgies—Church of England—BOOK OF COMMON PRAYER—
State Prayers for J / A, H—cont.

16333.5 — [Anr. ed.] 4° in 8's. *R. Barker*, 1609. BO(Benton 3.3).

1 col., B.L., ending Hh8; Heth. 22.9.

16334 — [Anr. ed.] 4° in 8's. *R. Barker*, 1609. E(Ry.IV.c.24(1)). HETH(frag.).; F.HD(imp.).ILL.PML(2, 1 imp.).V(imp.).

2 cols., B.L., ending E8; Heth. 42.8.

16335 — = 16337.

16335.5 — [Anr. ed.] 4° in 8's. *R. Barker*, 1611 (1610.) O(C.P. 1611 e.1).; HN.

1 col., B.L., ending Hh8; Heth. 22.11.

16336 — [Anr. ed.] fol. *R. Barker*, 1611. L⁴³.O.C.BTU.M.+; CHI. HD(frag.).ILL.Y.

2 cols., rom., ending G6; series 2/31 (C, HD).

16337 — [Anr. ed.] 4° in 8's. *R. Barker*, 1611. L(imp.).O³⁸.C (Syn.6.61.33).B.M(lacks tp).+; F(imp.).ILL(2 imp.). MICH.TEX.

2 cols., B.L., ending E8; Heth. 42.9. (The L copy, 464.b.1, formerly 16335)

16337a — [A ghost.]

— [Anr. ed.] 4°. [1612?] *See* note on L² copy of 16337a.7.

16337a.3 — [Anr. ed.] 8°. *R. Barker*, 1612. O(lacks tp).; NY¹¹.

1 col., B.L., ending Z8; series 8/11. The NY¹¹ copy has a cancel slip, not present in O, substituting Prince Charles for Prince Henry in the State Prayers.

State Prayers for King James / Queen Anne and Prince Charles

[Death of Prince Henry 6 Nov. 1612]

16337a.5 — [Anr. ed.] 8°. *R. Barker*, 1613. TEX.

1 col., B.L., ending Nn8; series 8/10.

— *See* also 16348a.

State Prayers for King James / Queen Anne, Prince Charles, Prince Frederick, and the Lady Elizabeth

[Marriage of James's daughter Elizabeth and Prince Frederick, the Elector Palatine, 12 Feb. 1613]

16337a.7 — [Anr. ed.] 4° in 8's. *R. Barker*, 1613. L(lacks Psalter). L²(**H5145.A4.1613).L¹⁵(imp.).D†.HETH(imp.).; V.

1 col., B.L., ending Hh8; Heth. 22.13. The L² copy has State Prayers for J / A, H and so may represent the orig. setting of halfsheet D5,6; the other copies have the current State Prayers.

16338 — [Anr. ed.] 4° in 8's. *R. Barker*, 1613. L(lacks tp).O(Bib. Eng. 1613 e.3).C(imp.).G².M(imp.).+; HN†.ILL.TEX†.

2 cols., B.L., ending E8; Heth. 42.10. 'E' of sig. E2 is under 'my' of 'my wayes'.

16338.3 — [Anr. ed.] 4° in 8's. *R. Barker*, 1613. O⁹(q.12.8).O²⁶. C².D. Hull U.+; NY(imp.).V. Washington Cathedral (frag.).

2 cols., B.L., ending E8; Heth. 42.11. 'E' of sig. E2 is under and to right of 'y' of 'my waies' and '2' is under 'ai'. *See* also 16341.

16339 — [Anr. ed.] 2 pts. fol. *R. Barker*, 1613 (1614.) L(lacks tp).O¹⁹(Psalter only, w. 16343).C²(imp.).C¹⁷(imp., w 1st part of Psalter from 16322.7).; NY¹¹(Psalter only, w. 16343).

1 col., B.L., ending Q6, K8; series 2/26 (L, C²). The date 1614 appears only in the Psalter colophon.

16340 — [A ghost.]

16341 — [Anr. ed.] 4° in 8's. *R. Barker*, 1614. L(1008.cc.2). O¹⁰.C³(w. quire B of 16338.3).G². Essex U(lacks tp).+; HD(imp., w. B outer sheet of 16338.3).NY⁶(imp.). TEX†.

2 cols., B.L., ending E8; Heth. 42.12. 'E' of sig. E2 is under 'my' of 'my waies' and '2' is under 'w'. A outer and C outer sheets are from the same typesetting as 16338.3; copies of that, this, and the next have mixed sheets more frequently than usual.

16341.5 — [Anr. ed.] 4° in 8's. *R. Barker*, 1614. L¹⁴.O³(Gibbs 216). D⁷.E⁴.LEIC².+; HN†.HD(w. E outer sheet of 16341). ILL.

2 cols., B.L., ending E8; Heth. 42.13. 'E' of sig. E2 is under and to left of 'w' in 'wayes'. Quire B, and A inner, C inner, D outer sheets are from the same typesetting as 16341.

16342 — = 16318.5.

16342.3 — [Anr. ed.] 4° in 8's. *R. Barker*, 1614. L(lacks tp).O(w. quire A of 16349.7).O³(imp.).O¹²(lacks tp).NOR²(imp., but w. tp).+; ILL(w. tp from 1615 ed.).

1 col., B.L., ending Hh8; Heth. 22.14.

Liturgies—**Church of England**—BOOK OF COMMON PRAYER—
State Prayers for J | A, C, F, E—cont.

16342.5 — [Anr. ed.] 8°. *R. Barker*, 1614. O³.
    1 col., B.L., ending Z8; series 8/11.

16342.7 — [Anr. ed.] 24° in 12's. *R. Barker*, 1614. Sotheby's,
    21 June 1967, in lot 2049(Schiff-Abbey copy, format
    misdescribed, untraced).
    1 col., rom. Prob. belongs to series 24/4.

16343 — [Anr. ed.] 2 pts. fol. *R. Barker*, 1615. L.O.C(imp.).E.
    M.+; NY¹¹(w. Psalter of 16339).
    1 col., B.L., ending Q6, K8; series 2/26 (L).

16343.5 — [Anr. ed.] 4° in 8's. *R. Barker*, 1615. o(lacks Hh8).
    O³⁸.C⁵(T.9.48).D⁷.; HN.ILL.PML.
    1 col., B.L., ending Hh8; Heth. 22.15.

16344 — [Anr. ed.] 4° in 8's. *R. Barker*, 1615. L(1008.cc.1).O.
    C².D².G².+; F.HN.PML(imp.).
    2 cols., rom., ending F2; Heth. 61.1.

16344.5 — [Anr. ed.] 4° in 8's. *R. Barker*, 1615. L¹⁴(HC.283).
    O³¹†.D.G²(imp.).SNU(imp.).+; HN.NY¹¹(imp.). Finney
    (quire A only, w. 16321.5).
    2 cols., B.L., ending E8; Heth. 42.15.

16345 — [Anr. ed.] 8°. *R. Barker*, 1615. L.O.C.HETH.
    2 cols., rom., ending F8; series 8/13. A6ʳ has head-
    piece of type orns. Other copies of this or the next
    may be at L⁸, NOR², F, HN, ILL, NY.

16345.5 — [Anr. ed.] 8°. *R. Barker*, 1615. O.O².C(2, 1 imp.).; HD
    (imp.).
    2 cols., rom., ending F8; series 8/13. A6ʳ has
    woodcut headpiece.

16346 — [Anr. ed.] 24° in 12's. *R. Barker*, 1615. L.
    1 col., rom., ending Q6; series 24/4.

16347 — [Anr. ed.] fol. *R. Barker*, 1616. L.O³⁸.A.D⁷.M.+; HN.
    PML.
    2 cols., B.L., ending F4; series 2/29 (L).

16347a — [Anr. ed.] fol. *R. Barker*, 1616. L.O.C.D².E².+; F.HN.
    HD.ILL.PML.+
    2 cols., rom., ending G6; series 2/31 (HD).

16348 — [A ghost.]

16348a — [Anr. ed.] 12°. *R. Barker*, 1616. L.O.C(Psalter only).
    1 col., B.L., ending Q6; series 12/2. The State
    Prayers are for J | A, C; cf. 16337a.5. This is the
    only ed. of BCP observed that has pagination.

16349 — [Anr. ed.] 2 pts. fol. *R. Barker*, 1617. L.O¹⁷.O¹⁹.O²²
    (imp.).E.+; F(Psalter only, lacking tp).HD(frag.).ILL
    (Psalter tp only).
    1 col., B.L., ending Q6, K8; series 2/26 (L).
    (Psalter formerly also 2410)

16349.3 — [Anr. ed.] 4° in 8's. [*B. Norton a. J. Bill, assignes of R.
    Barker?* 1618?] L(frag.).L²(imp.).O¹³(frag.).c²(imp.).
    HETH(C.V.54, imp.).+
    2 cols., B.L., ending E8; Heth. 42.18. 'E' of sig. E2
    is under space between 'changed' and 'my'.

16349.7 — [Anr. ed.] 4° in 8's. *B. Norton a. J. Bill a. assignees of
    R. Barker*, 1618. L¹⁸(Clements bequest).O(quire A
    only, w. 16342.5).C²(imp.).HETH(imp.).; Finney.
    1 col., B.L., ending Hh8; Heth. 22.18.

16350 — [Anr. ed.] 8°. *B. Norton a. J. Bill, deputies a. assignes
    of R. Barker*, 1618. L.O.C⁹.D.; HN.NY. St. John's C,
    Auckland, N.Z.
    2 cols., rom., ending F8; series 8/13 (L).

*State Prayers for King James | Prince Charles, Prince Frederick,
    and the Lady Elizabeth*

[Death of Queen Anne 2 Mar. 1619]

16351 — [Anr. ed.] 4° in 8's. *B. Norton a. J. Bill*, 1619. L¹⁴.O
    (Bib.Eng. 1619 e.1).C.HETH.M.+; ILL.
    2 cols., rom., ending G8; Heth. 63.19.

16352 — [Anr. ed.] 8°. *B. Norton & J. Bill*, 1619. L(C.108.a.7).
    1 col., B.L., ending Z8; series 8/11. Other copies
    of this or the next may be at O¹⁰, JH, LC, NY.

16352.5 — [Anr. ed.] 8°. *B. Norton a. J. Bill*, 1619. L(3051.b.
    20, imp.).O²⁸(imp.).; F(lacks tp).PML. Washington
    Cathedral.
    2 cols., rom., ending F8; series 8/13.

16353 — [Anr. ed.] 2 pts. fol. *R. Barker a. J. Bill*, 1619 (1620.)
    L.O.DUR³.E.STU.+; HN.HD.ILL.NY¹¹(imp., w. Psalter of
    16327).
    1 col., B.L., ending Q6, K8; series 2/26 (HD).
    (Psalter formerly also 2413)

16354 — [Anr. ed.] 4° in 8's. *R. Barker a. J. Bill*, 1620. L(w. tp
    from 1630 ed.).C(SSS.23.6).EX.G²(w. date on tp
    altered in ink to 1612).HETH(imp.).; HN†.PML(lacks
    Psalter).
    1 col., B.L., ending Hh8; Heth. 22.20a. 1st tp
    dated in arabic numerals like all other eds. of this

Liturgies—**Church of England**—BOOK OF COMMON PRAYER—
State Prayers for J | C, F, E—cont.

    series; cf. 16359. The C, HETH copies (Heth. 22.20b)
    have an earlier setting of quire C, omitting 2 lines
    on C7ʳ and having the unique ending of C1ʳ line 1:
    'Morning and Eve-/' while the other copies have
    a corrected setting w. C1ʳ line 1 ending: 'Morning/'
    like the other eds. of this series.

16354.5 — [Anr. ed.] 4° in 8's. [*R. Barker a. J. Bill?* 1620?] HETH
    (9602, lacks before A1).
    2 cols., B.L., ending E8; Heth. 42.20. 'E' of sig. E2
    is under 'y' of 'my waies' and '2' is under the 'w'.
    B outer sheet is the same typesetting as 16349.3;
    quire A, and C outer, D inner sheets are the same
    typesetting as 16357.

16355 — [Anr. ed.] 8°. *R. Barker a. J. Bill*, 1620. C.; FORDHAM.Y.
    2 cols., rom., ending F8; series 8/13 (Y).

16356 — [Anr. ed.] 24° in 12's. *B. Norton a. J. Bill*, 1620. L.
    BIRM.
    1 col., rom., ending Q6; series 24/4 (L).

16357 — [Anr. ed.] 4° in 8's. *B. Norton a. J. Bill*, 1621. L†.C⁵
    (T.5.28).D.G².M(imp.).+; HN. Finney(lacks tp).
    2 cols., B.L., ending E8; Heth. 42.21. For anr. ed.
    of the same description w. later State Prayers see
    16357.7.

16357.3 — [Anr. ed.] 8°. *B. Norton a. J. Bill*, 1621. Y.
    1 col., B.L., ending Z8; series 8/11.

*State Prayers for King James | Prince Charles, Prince Frederick,
    the Lady Elizabeth, and issue*

[Birth of various children to Frederick and Elizabeth 1617–19]

16357.5 — [Anr. ed.] 4° in 8's. *B. Norton a. J. Bill*, 1621. L⁴
    (ARC.A35.1b/1621, 1st 2 leaves only, w. 16322.6).
    1 col., B.L., ending Hh8; Heth. 22.21. As the
    State Prayers are lacking, it is impossible to know
    if they mentioned 'issue' or not.

16357.7 — [Anr. ed.] 4° in 8's. *B. Norton a. J. Bill*, 1621. L
    (3054.d.14).CANT(imp.).E⁴(imp.).HETH(w. A outer,
    B outer sheets of 16357).M(2 imp.).; HN†.HART².
    2 cols., B.L., ending E8; Heth 43.1. For anr. ed.
    of the same description w. earlier State Prayers see
    16357. The present ed. is usually bd. w. items dated
    1623 and 1625.

16358 — [Anr. ed.] 4° in 8's. *Dublin, Soc. of Statrs.*, 1621. L
    (C.66.e.17).L⁴(Psalter only, w. 16322.6).c(imp.).D
    (imp.).; HN†.
    1 col., B.L., ending Bb8; Heth. 28.1.

16358.5 — [Anr. ed.] 2 pts. fol. *B. Norton a. J. Bill*, 1622. O³.O¹⁹.
    C.; BO.CAL²(lacks tp).
    1 col., B.L., ending Q6, K8; series 2/26 (BO).

16359 — [Anr. ed.] 4° in 8's. *R. Barker a. J. Bill*, MDCXX [*sic;*
    Psalter:] (*B. Norton a. J. Bill*, 1622.) L(Psalter only).
    L¹⁴(imp.).c(Syn.7.62.35, lacks A7).G⁴(lacks A8).;
    NY¹¹.
    1 col., B.L., ending Hh8; Heth. 23.1. Cf. 16354,
    which has a similar imprint on the 1st tp but is a
    different setting throughout. State Prayers omit
    mention of 'issue'.

16360 — [Anr. ed.] 8°. *B. Norton a. J. Bill*, 1622. O.O³.C².BTL.
    LINC.+; HD(imp.).
    2 cols., rom., ending F8; series 8/13 (O, HD).

16361 — [Anr. ed.] 4° in 8's. *B. Norton a. J. Bill*, 1623. L(3408.
    g.4).O(2, 1 lacks tp, 1 imp.).O²⁴.D(imp.).HETH(imp.).;
    NY(2).WTL†. Washington Cathedral†.
    2 cols., rom., ending G8; Heth. 63.23.

16362 — [Anr. ed.] 8°. *B. Norton a. J. Bill*, 1623. L.L⁴⁶.O³.D.;
    HD.WASH³.
    2 cols., rom., ending F8; series 8/13 (L, HD).

16362.3 — [Anr. ed.] 24° in 12's. *B. Norton a. J. Bill*, 1623. NLW
    (2, 1 imp.). Juel-Jensen(lacks tp).
    1 col., rom., ending Q6; series 24/4.

16363 — [Anr. ed.] 8°. *B. Norton a. J. Bill*, 1624. O.O¹⁹(imp.).
    HETH(lacks tp).STD. Broxbourne (O).
    2 cols., rom., ending F8; series 8/13 (O, HETH,
    Broxbourne).

16363.5 — [Anr. ed.] 16° in 8's. (*B. Norton a. J. Bill*, 1624.)
    HETH(imp.), bd. w. 2593.5).STD(imp., bd. w. 2587.3).
    1 col., B.L., ending Ss8; series 16/9.

*State Prayers for King Charles | Queen Mary, Prince Frederick,
    and the Lady Elizabeth*

[Accession to the throne 27 Mar. 1625; marriage to Queen
    Henrietta Maria 1 May 1625]

Although the 'issue' of Frederick and Elizabeth continue to be

Liturgies—Church of England—Book of Common Prayer—
State Prayers for C | M, F, E—cont.

mentioned, they no longer serve as a significant chronological distinction.

16364 — [Anr. ed.] 2 pts. fol. *B. Norton a. J. Bill,* 1625. L.L⁸.
O.O³.LINC.; ILL. NCU.
1 col., B.L., ending Q6, K8; series 2/26 (ILL).

16365 — [Anr. ed.] 8°. *B. Norton a. J. Bill,* 1625. L(destroyed).
C⁵.D.NLW(2, 1 = St. Asaph).; HD(lacks tp).ILL.NCU.
PML.SMITH(lacks tp).
2 cols., rom., ending F8; series 8/13 (HD, PML).
For an ed. of this series falsely dated 1639 and w.
the present State Prayers *see* 16418c.5.

16365.5 — [Anr. ed.] 4° in 8's. *B. Norton a. J. Bill,* 1626. L(imp.).
O(C.P. 1626 e.1).
1 col., B.L., ending Hh8; Heth. 22.26.

16366 — [Anr. ed.] 4° in 8's. *B. Norton a. J. Bill,* 1626. L(1411.
e.5).O²⁵(imp.).E⁴.LEEDS.LIV(imp.).+; NY. St. Olaf C,
Northfield, Minnesota.
2 cols., B.L., ending E8; Heth. 43.6.

16367 — [Anr. ed.] 8°. *B. Norton a. J. Bill,* 1626. L.O(J, tp
only).; HN(2).BALT.ILL.
2 cols., rom., ending F8; series 8/13 (L).

16368 — [Anr. ed.] fol. *B. Norton a. J. Bill,* 1627. L³⁰.O.C⁵.
CHICH.LEEDS.+; CH.ILL.NY¹¹.Y.
1 col., B.L., ending Dd4; series 2/27 (NY¹¹).

16369 — [A ghost.]

16369.3 — [Anr. ed.] 4° in 8's. *B. Norton a. J. Bill,* 1627. O⁸(imp.).
O²²(TTT 2.8).C².C²⁰.P(imp.)†.+; HD(imp.).PML.Y†.
1 col., B.L., ending Ii8; Heth. 25.1. Most (all?)
copies have the 1st tp dated 1626 in red, w. 1627
overprinted in black; Psalter tp dated 1627.

16369.7 — [Anr. ed.] 4° in 8's. *B. Norton a. J. Bill,* 1627. O²
(UU.e.355).O⁶(lacks tp).O³⁸†.CANT(lacks tp).STD†.;
ILL. MICH.NY¹¹.Y†.
2 cols., rom., ending H8; Heth. 65.4.

16370 — [Anr. ed.] 8°. *B. Norton a. J. Bill,* 1627. L(3406.b.28,
lacks tp).C.HETH.; NY(imp.).
2 cols., rom., ending G4; series 8/14. G3ʳ has orn.
w. 7 pairs of crossed sceptres (L, C, HETH). NY has
G4 in a different setting w. zigzag orn. on G3ʳ and
'G' of sig. G3 under 'h' of 'that'. Other copies of
this or the next may be at E, M, F, CAL, CAL², ILL, PN.

16370.5 — [Anr. ed.] 8°. *B. Norton a. J. Bill,* 1627. L(3407.a.14
(1), imp.).ELY.
2 cols., rom., ending G4; series 8/14. G3ʳ has orn.
w. crown between a rose and a thistle. (L copy
formerly 16373c)

16371 — [Anr. ed.] 24° in 12's. *B. Norton a. J. Bill,* 1627. L.;
St. John's Seminary, Camarillo, California.
1 col., rom., ending R12; series 24/5 (L).

16372 — [Anr. ed.] 4° in 8's. [*B. Norton a. J. Bill,* 1628?] O
(Bib.Eng. 1628 d.1, imp.).HETH(imp.).
2 cols., B.L., ending E8; Heth. 42.28. 'E' of sig. E2
is under 'w' of 'waies'.

16373 — [Anr. ed.] 8°. *B. Norton a. J. Bill,* 1628. L(3406.a.23).
1 col., B.L., ending Z8; series 8/11.

16373a — [Anr. ed.] 8°. *B. Norton a. J. Bill,* 1628. L(3050.a.43).
O⁹.; HD.NY.
2 cols., rom., ending G4; series 8/14 (L, HD). G3ʳ
has orn. w. salamanders in flames.

16373b — [Anr. ed.] 8°. *B. Norton a. J. Bill,* 1628. L(3434.ccc.58
(2)).O².; HN.AAS.CAL⁸.PML.
2 cols., rom., ending G4; series 8/14 (L, PML). G3ʳ
has zigzag orn.; 'G' of sig. G3 is under 'os' of
'those'.

16373c — Now = 16370.5.

16374 — [Anr. ed.] fol. *B. Norton a. J. Bill,* 1629. L.O.C².D.
ETON.+; HD(2).NY.
2 cols., rom., ending I4; series 2/33 (HD).

16375 — [Anr. ed.] fol. *T. a. J. Buck, prs. to the Univ. of
Cambridge,* 1629. L.O.C.D.E².+; F.HN.HD(imp.).PML.
TEX.+
2 cols., rom., ending G6; series 2/32 (HD).

16376 — [Anr. ed.] 4° in 8's. *B. Norton a. J. Bill,* 1629. L(imp.).
L¹⁴(2 imp.).HETH(imp.).; HN(Page 222).NY¹¹†.
2 cols., B.L., ending E8; Heth. 44.29.

16376.5 — [Anr. ed.] 4° in 8's. *B. Norton a. J. Bill,* 1629. L¹⁴
(lacks A8).O²⁹(220/8).G²(lacks tp).; NY.
2 cols., rom., ending H8; Heth. 65.6.

16376.7 — [Anr. ed.] 8°. *B. Norton a. J. Bill,* (1629.) C⁴.
1 col., B.L., ending Z8; series 8/11.

16377 — [Anr. ed.] 8°. *B. Norton a. J. Bill,* 1629. O.C.STD(lacks
tp). Broxbourne(O).
2 cols., rom., ending G4; series 8/14 (O, C). There

Liturgies—Church of England—Book of Common Prayer—
State Prayers for C | M, F, E—cont.

may be 2 settings, at least in part; G3ʳ has orn. w.
salamanders in flames (o) or w. knot between
birds (c). Other copies of this or 16376.7 may be
at Exeter U, PEN, ROS.

16377.5 — [Anr. ed.] 24° in 12's. *B. Norton a. J. Bill,* 1629.
O³⁸.M².; BO.HD. St. John's Seminary, Camarillo,
California.
1 col., rom., ending R12; series 24/5 (BO, HD).

16378 — [Anr. ed.] fol. *R. Barker a. J. Bill* [Psalter tp:] (*B.
Norton a. J. Bill,*) 1630. L.O¹⁷.C.DUR(2).ELY.; HN(2).
1 col., B.L., ending Dd4; series 2/27 (C, ELY).

16378.5 — [Anr. ed.] 4° in 8's. *R. Barker (& J. Bill,)* 1630. L
(imp.).O(C.P. 1630 e.3).O³.C¹⁷.
1 col., B.L., ending Ii8; Heth. 25.4.

16379 — [Anr. ed.] 4° in 8's. *R. Barker a. assignes of J. Bill,* 1630.
Now = 16380.9.

16380 — [Anr. ed.] 4° in 8's. *T. a. J. Buck, prs. to the Univ. of
Cambridge,* 1630. L¹⁴(HC.365(1)).C(imp.).ELY.HETH.
M.+
2 cols., B.L., ending E8; Heth. 57.1.

16380.3 — [Anr. ed.] 4° in 8's. *T. a. J. Buck, prs. to the Univ. of
Cambridge,* 1630. C(Rel.c.63.7¹).C¹⁵.D(imp.).HETH.;
HN.HD.
2 cols., rom., ending H8; Heth. 71.1.

16380.5 — [Anr. ed.] 8°. *B. Norton a. J. Bill,* 1630. Dr. J. McL.
Emmerson, New College, Oxford.
2 cols., rom., ending G4; series 8/14.

16380.7 — [Anr. ed.] 8°. *R. Barker a. J. Bill,* 1630. L(1480.a.31).;
LC.U.
2 cols., rom., ending G4; series 8/14 (L).

*State Prayers for King Charles | Queen Mary, Prince Charles,
Prince Frederick, and the Lady Elizabeth*

[Birth of Charles II 29 May 1630]

16380.9 — [Anr. ed.] 4° in 8's. *R. Barker a. assignes of J. Bill,*
1630. L(1474.c.17).L¹⁴(frag.).O.C².HETH(imp.).+; HD.
MICH(frag.). Washington Cathedral(frag.).
2 cols., B.L., ending E8; Heth. 44.30. (Formerly
16379)

16381 — [Anr. ed.] 8°. *R. Barker a. assignes of J. Bill,* 1630. L
(3408.c.30).O(2, 1 imp.).; HN.
2 cols., rom., ending G4; series 8/14 (L, O).

16381.5 — [Anr. ed.] 8°. (*R. Barker a. assignes of J. Bill,* 1630.)
O(imp.).
1 col., B.L., ending Z8; series 8/11.

16382 — [Anr. ed.] 24° in 12's. *R. Barker a. assignes of J. Bill,*
1630. L.PLUME.; IND.
1 col., rom., ending R12; series 24/5 (L). Largely
reissued in 16389.

16383 — [Anr. ed.] fol. *R. Barker a. assignes of J. Bill,* 1631. L.
O.C(imp.).C¹⁵.G².+; HN(2).NY¹¹.
1 col., B.L., ending Dd4; series 2/27 (L).

16384 — [Anr. ed.] 4° in 8's. *R. Barker a. assignes of J. Bill,*
1631. L(3049.d.12).O.O³.C.C³.+; NY¹¹.
2 cols., rom., ending H8; Heth. 65.8.

16384.7 — [Anr. ed.] 8°. *R. Barker a. assignes of J. Bill,* 1631.
L(1005.b.3, frags.).; HN.BO.NY.
2 cols., rom., ending G4; series 8/14. G3ʳ has
orn. w. a face in a sunburst.

16385 — [Anr. ed.] 8°. *R. Barker a. assignes of J. Bill,* 1631.
L(3408.c.29).
2 cols., rom., ending G4; series 8/14. G3ʳ has orn.
w. a face between 2 black and white flowers. Other
copies of this or 16384.7 may be at M, NLW, CAL²,
ILL, Rutgers U. Largely reissued in 16387.

*State Prayers for King Charles | Queen Mary, Prince Charles,
the Lady Mary, Prince Frederick, and the Lady Elizabeth*

[Birth of daughter Mary 4 Nov. 1631]

16385.7 — [Anr. ed.] 4° in 8's. *R. Barker a. assignes of J. Bill,*
1632. L².O(Bib.Eng. 1632 e.1).O³.LEIC²(w. tp from
1634 ed.).HETH(imp.).+; F(2, 1 imp.).Y†.
1 col., B.L., ending Ii8; Heth. 25.6.

16386 — [Anr. ed.] 4° in 8's. *R. Barker a. assignes of J. Bill,*
1632. L(3406.c.19).A(lacks tp).BRISTOL.D(imp.).;
HN(lacks tp)†.NY.PML. ending F6; Heth 51.1. For anr. ed.
2 cols., B.L., ending F6; Heth 51.1. For anr. ed.
of the same description w. later State Prayers *see*
16388a.5.

Liturgies—Church of England—Book of Common Prayer—
State Prayers for C | M, C, M, F, E—cont.

16386.7 — [Anr. ed.] 8°. (*R. Barker a. assignes of J. Bill*, 1632.)
O³(imp.).
1 col., B.L., ending Z8; series 8/11.

16387 — [Anr. issue of 16385, w. quire B reset w. current State
Prayers.] 8°. *R. Barker a. assignes of J. Bill*, 1632.
L(3407.c.15).O.O²⁵.C(lacks tp).C².; HN(2).HD.N.PML.
2 cols., rom., ending G4; series 8/14. B2ʳ, col. 1,
line 1 ends: 'sinner doth re-/'. Other copies of this
and the next 2 may be at O³, C⁵, OS, STD(imp.), ILL,
NY, NY¹¹, Y.

*State Prayers for King Charles | Queen Mary, Prince Charles,
the Lady Mary, and the Lady Elizabeth*

[Death of Prince Frederick 29 Nov. 1632]

Note: Other editions with these State Prayers besides the two
immediately below are 16391, 16392, 16393.7, 16394, 16394.7,
16395, 16399.7, 16400.

16388 — [Anr. ed.] 8°. *R. Barker a. assignes of J. Bill*, 1632.
L(3408.b.30).C.; NY.
2 cols., rom., ending G4; series 8/14. B2ʳ, col. 1,
line 1 ends: 'sinner doth/'; B3ʳ, col. 2, line 19 from
bottom has erroneous: 'altar'; cf. 16387 as well
as the next.

16388a — [Anr. issue, partly reset and reimposed.] 8°. [*R. Barker
a. assignes of J. Bill*, 1632.] L(3052.b.22, imp.).
2 cols., rom., ending G4; series 8/14. B2ʳ, col. 1,
line 1 ends: 'sinner doth/'; B3ʳ, col. 2, line 19 from
bottom has corrected: 'alter', the 3rd word in the
line. G3ʳ has orn. w. cherub in the centre.

State Prayers in 1632–33

Note: As so few copies of non-4° editions were checked for State
Prayers and the imprint dates and Prayers revealed no simple
correspondence, anomalous editions dated 1632 and all editions
dated 1633/32 or 1633 are listed below.

16388a.5 — [Anr. ed.] 4° in 8's. *R. Barker a. assignes of J. Bill*,
1632. L†.O(imp.).G²(Dp.f.16).HETH(imp.). Exeter
U.; HD.
2 cols., B.L., ending F6; Heth. 52.3. State Prayers
as in 16396. For anr. ed. of the same description
but with earlier State Prayers *see* 16386. The tp
of the present ed. is largely in the same typesetting
as 16397.7.

16389 — [Anr. issue of 16382.] 24° in 12's. *R. Barker a. assignes
of J. Bill*, 1632. L.WN.
1 col., rom., ending R12; series 24/5 (L). The State
Prayers are in the same setting and have the same
names as 16382 (L).

16390 — [Anr. ed.] fol. *R. Barker a. assignes of J. Bill*, 1633
(1632.) L.O³.C.A.BIRM.+; HN(2).ILL.PEN.
2 cols., rom., ending I4; series 2/34 (L). State
Prayers as in 16388 (1 HN) or 16396 (L, 1 HN). In
the 2nd HN copy B3,4 including the later State
Prayers are a cancel bifolium.

16391 — [Anr. ed.] 4° in 8's. *R. Barker a. assignes of J. Bill*,
1633 (1632.) L(destroyed).L¹⁴(HC.375).O.C³.D.E.+;
BO⁶.ILL(imp.).NY†.PML.TEX†.
2 cols., rom., ending H8; Heth. 65.10. State
Prayers as in 16388.

16392 — [Anr. ed.] fol. *R. Barker a. assignes of J. Bill*, 1633. L
(destroyed).O.C⁵.D7(lacks tp).DUR³.M.+; HN.HART.NY.
PML.WTL.
1 col., B.L., ending Dd4; series 2/27 (NY). State
Prayers as in 16388 (NY, early issue?) or 16396 (O,
HETH, late issue?).

16392.5 — [Anr. ed.] 4° in 8's. *R. Barker a. assignes of J. Bill*,
1633. Thomas Thorp catalogue 374 (1966), item 81
(Kenney 1943).
1 col., B.L., ending Ii8; Heth. 25.7. Tp all in
black; reissued in 16397. State Prayers as 16396.

16393 — [Anr. ed.] 8°. *R. Barker a. assignes of J. Bill*, 1633.
L(C.128.b.12).O.HETH.
2 cols., rom., ending G4; series 8/14. G3ʳ has orn.
w. lion's head in centre. State Prayers as in 16396
(HETH). Another copy of this or the next two may
be at TEX.

16393.5 — [Anr. ed.] 8°. *R. Barker a. assignes of J. Bill*, 1633.
L(C.108.d.14).C²(C.12.52¹, imp.).HETH(imp.).; HN.
2 cols., rom., ending G4; series 8/14. G3ʳ has orn.
w. knot between scrolls and leaves. State Prayers
as in 16388 (L) or 16396 (HN).

Liturgies—Church of England—Book of Common Prayer—
State Prayers in 1632–33—cont.

16393.7 — [Anr. ed.] 8°. (*R. Barker a. assignes of J. Bill*, 1633.)
HETH(imp.).
1 col., B.L., ending Z8; series 8/11. State Prayers
as in 16388.

16394 — [Anr. ed.] 8°. *Edinburgh*, [*R. Young*,] *prs. to the Kings
Majestie*, 1633. O.C.; HN.HD. Washington Cathedral.
2 cols., rom., ending F8; series 8/13. B1ʳ catch-
word: 'pride'; State Prayers as in 16388 (HD).
Other copies of this or the next may be at L, E, E²,
M, ILL, N, NY.

16394.3 — [Anr. ed.] 8°. *Edinburgh*, [*R. Young*,] *prs. to the Kings
Majestie* [*a. London, R. Barker a. assignes of J. Bill*,]
1633. C.; HD(imp.).
2 cols., rom., ending F8; series 8/13. B1ʳ catchword: 'abate'. Quire A is the same setting as
16394; quires B–F, including State Prayers as in
16396 (HD), were pr. in London. Sheets reissued
in 16399.

16394.7 — [Anr. ed.] 12°. [*Amsterdam?*] *Imprinted anno* 1633.
L.O².
2 cols., rom., ending F12; series 12/5. State
Prayers as in 16388. The tp is in a forged border
similar to McK. & F. Appendix no. 8.

16395 — [Anr. ed.] 24° in 12's. *R. Barker a. assignes of J. Bill*,
1633. L.O.
1 col., rom., ending R12; series 24/5 (L). State
Prayers as in 16388 (L).

*State Prayers for King Charles | Queen Mary and Prince
Charles*

[Birth of James II 14 Oct. 1633]

James, Mary, and later children are usually included as 'the rest of
the royal progeny'. Other editions above with these State Prayers
are 16388a.5, 16390, 16392, 16392.5, 16393, 16393.5, 16394.3.

16396 — [Anr. ed.] fol. *R. Barker a. assignes of J. Bill*, 1633
(1634.) L.C⁵.
1 col., B.L., ending Dd4; series 2/27 (L). Sheets
reissued in 16397.3.

16397 — [Anr. issue of 16392.5, w. tp in red and black.] 4° in
8's. *R. Barker a. assignes of J. Bill*, 1634 (1633.)
L(lacks Ii8).O7.C².D.LEIC².+; F.HN.ILL(imp.).N.
1 col., B.L., ending Ii8; Heth. 25.8.

16397.3 — [Anr. issue of 16396.] fol. *R. Barker a. assignes of J.
Bill*, 1634. O.O³.C².GLOUC.WOR.+; HN.LC(imp., w.
facs. tp dated 1632).PML.
1 col., B.L., ending Dd4; series 2/27 (PML).

16397.7 — [Anr. ed.] 4° in 8's. *R. Barker a. assignes of J. Bill*,
1634. L(3408.g.5).L¹⁴.O¹⁰(w. πA4 of 16380).C(lacks
tp)†.M.+; HN(lacks tp)†.ILL.NY¹¹.PML.
2 cols., B.L., ending F6; Heth. 53.4.

16398 — [Anr. ed.] 8°. *R. Barker a. assignes of J. Bill*, 1634. C.
D².LEIC².NMU.OS.; HN.HD(imp.).ILL.Y.
2 cols., rom., ending G4; series 8/14 (C, HD). G3ʳ
has orn. w. rose between lion and unicorn.

16399 — [Anr. issue of 16394.3, w. variant date.] 8°. *Edinburgh*,
[*R. Young*,] *prs. to the Kings Majestie* [*a. London, R.
Barker a. assignes of J. Bill*,] 1634. L.O.O³.D7.E.+;
F(lacks A5).HN.NY¹¹.PML.Y.+
2 cols., rom., ending F8; series 8/13 (L, PML).

16399.5 — [Anr. ed.] 12°. *R. Barker a. assignes of J. Bill*, 1634.
L(destroyed).D².
2 cols., rom., ending E12; series 12/6.

16399.7 — [Anr. ed.] 12°. *Edinburgh*, [*R. Young*,] *prs. to the Kings
Majestie*, 1634. O.C(lacks tp).A.E.; NY¹¹.
2 cols., rom., ending E12; series 12/7 (O, E, NY¹¹).
State Prayers as in 16388. Almanack on verso of
tp.

16400 — [Anr. issue, w. A1–3 replaced by A1–4, w. imprint:]
Edinburgh, R. Y[*oung,*] *pr. to the Kings Majestie*,
1634. L(imp.).E(2, 1 lacks before A5).HETH.
2 cols., rom., ending E12; series 12/7. State
Prayers as in 16388. Orig. A1–3 were possibly
damaged. The replacements, pr. in London at the
Barker-Bill press, have the tp verso blank, Almanack on A2ʳ, etc., so that the text on A4ᵛ (end
of Proper Lessons) duplicates that on A4ʳ retained
from 16399.7 though they are in different settings.

16401 — [Anr. ed.] 4° in 8's. *prs. to the Univ. of Cambridge*, 1635.
L(3407.d.11).L¹⁴.C.E.HETH(lacks tp).+; HN(imp.)†.
CAL†.LC†.NY⁶. Washington Cathedral(imp.).
2 cols., rom., ending H8; Heth. 72.5.

Liturgies—**Church of England**—Book of Common Prayer—
State Prayers for C | M, C—cont.

16402 — [Anr. ed.] 8°. *R. Barker a. assignes of J. Bill*, 1635.
L(2).O³(imp.).M.; HN.COR.ILL. New Brunswick U,
Fredericton, N.B.
2 cols., rom., ending G4; series 8/14 (L).

16402.5 — [Anr. ed.] 12°. *R. Barker a. assignes of J. Bill*, 1635.
L(03440.p.38(1)).HETH.; HN.PN(imp.).
2 cols., rom., ending E12; series 12/6 (L).

16402.7 — [Anr. ed.] 24° in 12's. *R. Barker a. assignes of J. Bill*,
1635. L(C.124.cc.10(3)).
1 col., rom., ending R12; series 24/5.

16403 — [Anr. ed.] fol. *R. Barker a. assignes of J. Bill*, 1636.
L.O.C.A.P.+; HN.HD.ILL.PML.WASH².+
1 col., B.L., ending Dd4; series 2/27 (HD). Copies
differ; C1ʳ line 4: 'thorowout' or 'throughout';
both at HD.

16403.5 — [Anr. ed.] 4° in 8's. [*R. Barker a. assignes of J. Bill*,
1636?] BO(Benton 3.6.5, imp., w. prelims. and end
of 16407).
1 col., B.L., ending Ee6; Heth. 26.2. 'B' of sig. B1
is under 'll' of 'shall'.

16404 — [Anr. ed.] 4° in 8's. *R. Barker a. assignes of J. Bill*,
1636. C(Syn.6.63.31).BRISTOL.D.E.LEIC².+; ILL.
2 cols., B.L., ending F4; Heth. 54.6. Sheets
reissued in 16417.3.

16404.3 — [Anr. ed.] 4° in 8's. *R. Barker a. assignes of J. Bill*,
1636. L(2).O(C.P. 1636 d.1).C.M².; HD.PML.
2 cols., rom., ending H6; Heth. 66.3. B1ʳ line 5
of heading: 'read'.

16404.4 — [Anr. issue, partly reset.] *R. Barker a. assignes of J. Bill*,
1636. O⁵.C(Syn.5.63.2).LEIC².M.WOR.+; NY⁶.NY¹¹
(imp.)†. Finney.
2 cols., rom., ending H6; Heth. 66.4. B1ʳ line 5
of heading: 'reade'.

16404.5 — [Anr. ed.] 8°. *R. Barker a. assignes of J. Bill*, 1636.
C²(2).; BO⁶(missing).DAR.
2 cols., rom., ending G4; series 8/14 (C²).

16404.7 — [Anr. ed.] 16° in 8's. (*R. Barker a. assignes of J. Bill*,
1636.) C(imp.).
1 col., B.L., ending Yy8; series 16/10.

16404.9 — [Anr. ed.] 4° in 8's. *R. Barker a. assignes of J. Bill*,
1637. O²⁸(lacks tp).; ILL(complete).
1 col., B.L., ending Ee6; Heth. 26.3.

16405 — [Anr. ed.] 4° in 8's. *R. Barker a. assignes of J. Bill*,
1637. L(3053.e.1).O.C⁷†.E⁴(imp.).HETH.+; HD(frag.).
LC(imp.)†.
2 cols., B.L., ending H6; Heth. 55.7.

16406 — [Anr. ed.] 4° in 8's. *prs. to the Univ. of Cambridge*, 1637.
L³⁸(SR.B 1637.B4).O³†.BIRM².BRISTOL(imp.).NMU.+;
Finney.
2 cols., B.L., ending E8; Heth. 58.7.

— [Anr. ed.] 4° in 8's. *T. Buck a. R. Daniel, prs. to the
Univ. of Cambridge*, 1637.
2 cols., rom., ending F1; = pt. of 2327.

16407 — [Anr. ed.] 4° in 8's. *Dublin, Soc. of Statrs.*, 1637. L
(3407.b.10).O(1, plus Ordinal only)†.O³¹(lacks Psalter
and Ordinal)†.C(imp.).D⁷.; HN.BO(frags., w. 16403.5).
NY¹¹.
1 col., B.L., ending Ll 2; Heth. 29.1. The Ordinal
(formerly also 16476) is on continuous signatures
only in this ed.

16408 — [Anr. ed.] 8°. *R. Barker a. assignes of J. Bill*, 1637. L.
L⁴⁶.O.EX.LICH.+; F.HN.ILL.LC.
2 cols., rom., ending G4; series 8/14 (F). The HN
copy has illustrations 'sold by R. Peake'; *see*
19518.5.

16408.5 — [Anr. ed.] 24° in 12's. *R. Barker a. assignes of J. Bill*,
1637. HD.
1 col., rom., ending R12; series 24/5.

16409 — [Anr. ed.] fol. *R. Barker a. assignes of J. Bill*, 1638.
L.O.C.C³.D(imp.).+; HN.PML.U.
1 col., B.L., ending Dd4; series 2/27 (HN).

16410 — [Anr. ed.] fol. *T. Buck a. R. Daniel, prs. to the
Univ. of Cambridge*, 1638. L.O.C.D.M.+; F.HN.ILL.
PML.Y.+
2 cols., rom., ending (I)4; series 2/35
(PML).

16411 — [Anr. ed.] 4° in 8's. *R. Barker a. assignes of J. Bill*,
1638. L†.C(G.3.51).C²(lacks tp).D.LEIC²(imp., lacks
Psalter).+; BO⁶.PML.
1 col., B.L., ending Ee6; Heth. 26.4.

16412 — [Anr. ed.] 4° in 8's. *prs. to the Univ. of Cambridge*, 1638.
L(imp.).L¹⁴.O(Bib.Eng. 1638 d.1).C.C².+; HN.ILL.NY.
Finney.
2 cols., rom., ending H8; Heth. 72.8.

Liturgies—**Church of England**—Book of Common Prayer—
State Prayers for C | M, C—cont.

16413 — [Anr. ed.] 8°. *R. Barker a. assignes of J. Bill*, 1638.
L(3050.b.36).O(3).O⁴⁶.C.; HD(imp.).
2 cols., rom., ending G4; series 8/14. B2ʳ has orn.
w. crossed stems at centre. Other copies of this or
the next 2 may be at C²⁵, D, E, YK(2), BALT, BO⁶, N,
STAN.

16413.3 — [Anr. ed.] 8°. *R. Barker a. assignes of J. Bill*, 1638.
L(C.123.e.19).O³.O³⁸.
2 cols., rom., ending G4; series 8/14. B2ʳ has orn.
w. bearded face at centre.

16413.5 — [Anr. ed.] 8°. *R. Barker a. assignes of J. Bill*, 1638.
C(Rel.d.63.7).
2 cols., rom., ending G4; series 8/14. B2ʳ has orn.
w. fleur-de-lis at centre.

16414 — [Anr. ed.] 12°. *R. Barker a. assignes of J. Bill*, 1638.
O⁶.; HD.
2 cols., rom., ending E12; series 12/6. 'C' of
sig. C3 is under 'ng' of 'blessing'.

16414.3 — [Anr. ed.] 12°. *R. Barker a. assignes of J. Bill*, 1638.
O¹⁷.C.; HN(imp.).
2 cols., rom., ending E12; series 12/6. 'C' of
sig. C3 is under 2nd 'e' of 'even'. The C copy has
tp border McK. & F. 272 like 16414. The O¹⁷ copy
has A1,12 pr. and inserted later; though the
imprint is the same, the tp border is McK. & F.
Appendix no. 8, prob. pr.: *Amsterdam, J. F. Stam?*
post-1640.

16414.5 — [Anr. ed.] 24° in 12's. *R. Barker a. assignes of J. Bill*,
1638. L(Davis).G⁴.
1 col., rom., ending R12; series 24/5 (L).

16415 — [Anr. ed.] fol. *R. Barker a. assignes of J. Bill*, 1638
(1639.) L.O(imp.).C.BIRM².M.+; HN.HD.ILL.NY.
Washington Cathedral.+
2 cols., rom., ending K4; series 2/36 (HD).

16416 — [Anr. ed.] fol. *R. Barker a. assignes of J. Bill*, 1639.
L.L².O(imp.).D.+; F.HN.CAL.NY.PML.+
1 col., B.L., ending Dd4; series 2/27 (NY).

16417 — [Anr. ed.] 4° in 8's. *R. Barker a. assignes of J. Bill*,
1639. L(472.a.10).O.BIRM.HETH.P(imp.)†.+; HN.BO.
ILL.
1 col., B.L., ending Ee6; Heth. 26.5. A1ʳ line 3:
'thorowout'.

16417.2 — [Anr. issue, partly reset.] *R. Barker a. assignes of J.
Bill*, 1639. L(473.a.10).O³.C.D.DUR.+; HN.PML.
1 col., B.L., ending Ee6; Heth. 26.6. A1ʳ line 3:
'throughout'.

16417.3 — [Anr. issue of 16404, w. cancel tp.] 4° in 8's. *R. Barker
a. assignes of J. Bill*, 1639. L¹⁵.O(imp.).*.C(Adams
5.63.2).BIRM²(imp.).*.; F(lacks tp)*.MICH.
2 cols., B.L., ending F4; Heth. 54.9.

16417.5 — [Anr. ed.] 4° (not in 8's). *R. Barker a. assignes of J. Bill*,
1639. E⁴(imp.).; Washington Cathedral(complete).
2 cols., rom., ending S2; Heth. 67.1.

16417.7 — [Anr. ed.] 8°. *R. Barker a. assignes of J. Bill*, 1639.
HETH.; NY¹¹.
1 col., B.L., ending Y8; series 8/12. HETH also has
an imp. copy of anr. ed. of this series w. 'T' of
sig. T1 under and to left of 't' of 'them' instead of
under 'n' of 'among' as in the present ed.

16418 — [Anr. ed.] 8°. *R. Barker a. assignes of J. Bill*, 1639.
L(2 copies, 3406.c.22; 219.g.13).L⁴⁴.O.; BO.ILL.TEX.
2 cols., rom., ending G4; series 8/15. Psalter
begins D4ᵛ.

16418a — [Anr. ed.] 8°. *R. Barker a. assignes of J. Bill*, 1639.
L(3006.aa.14).O.C.E.M.+; HN.NY.Y.
2 cols., rom., ending G4; series 8/14. Psalter
begins D5ʳ; B5ᵛ, last prayer in the Litany has:
'O most mercifull Father'.

16418b — [Anr. ed.] 8°. *R. Barker a. assignes of J. Bill*, 1639.
L(C.66.b.20).L⁴¹.C(imp.).C².; CAL.
2 cols., rom., ending G4; series 8/14. Psalter
begins D5ʳ; B5ᵛ, last prayer in the Litany has:
'O most most [*sic*] mercifull Father'.

16418c — [Anr. ed.] 8°. *R. Barker a. assignes of J. Bill*, 1639 [i.e.
printed abroad? c. 1647.] L(3050.b.38).NEP.; WEL.
2 cols., rom., ending G4; series 8/14. Psalter
begins D5ʳ; only ed. w. proclamation of James I
on A3ᵛ–4ʳ in roman type.

16418c.5 — [Anr. ed.] 8°. *R. Barker a. assignes of J. Bill*, 1639
[i.e. *London?* after 1640.] C².
2 cols., rom., ending F8; series 8/13. This has
State Prayers as in 16365. While it collates like
16365, it actually is a paginary reprint, w. omissions and rearrangement in the prelims. and

Liturgies—Church of England—BOOK OF COMMON PRAYER—
State Prayers for C / M, C—cont.

alteration of the State Prayers, of an ed. of series
8/14 of 1637 or later.

16419　— [Anr. ed.] 12°. *R. Barker a. assignes of J. Bill,* 1639.
E(imp.).; ILL(missing).
2 cols., rom.; State Prayers on A5ᵛ; series 12/9.
The E copy ends on C4 and has no Psalter; the ILL
copy was originally reported to be in 12's, except
for quire D, which has 14 leaves.

16419.5　— [Anr. ed.] 12°. *R. Barker a. assignes of J. Bill,* 1639.
HN.
2 cols., rom.; State Prayers on B1ᵛ; series 12/6.

16420　— [Anr. ed.] 4° in 8's. *T. Buck a. R. Daniel, prs. to the
Univ. of Cambridge,* 1640. L².L¹⁴(HC.418).O(imp.).
C.G².+ ; NY(lacks tp).
2 cols., B.L., ending E8; Heth. 59.1.

16421　— [Anr. ed.] 8°. *R. Barker a. assignes of J. Bill,* 1640.
L.O.O¹⁶.M.NLW(St. Asaph).+
2 cols., rom., ending G4; series 8/14 (L).

16421.3　— [Anr. ed.] 12°. *R. Barker a. assignes of J. Bill,* 1640.
O¹⁴.
2 cols., rom., ending E12; series 12/6.

16421.5　— [Anr. ed.] 16° in 8's. *R. Barker a. assignes of J. Bill,*
1640. C.
1 col., B.L., ending Yy8; series 16/10.

16422　— [Anr. ed.] 24° in 12's. *R. Barker a. assignes of J. Bill,*
1640. O.; Museum of Fine Arts, Boston, Massa-
chusetts(Textile Dept.).
1 col., rom., ending R12; series 24/5 (O).

Translations

16423　[*Latin.*] Ordinatio ecclesiæ, seu ministerii ecclesiastici, in
florentissimo regno Angliæ, conscripta sermone
patrio, & in Latinam linguam conuersa, ab Alexandro Alesio Scoto. 4°. *Lipsiæ, in off. W. Gunteri,* 1551.
L.O.O³.C.E.+ ; BO.CH.NY¹¹.
A trans. of the 1st prayer book of Edward VI.

16424　— Liber precum publicarum, seu ministerii ecclesiasticę
administrationis Sacramentorum, aliorūꝗ rituū &
ceremoniarum in Ecclesia Anglicana. [Revised *tr.* of
16423 by W. Haddon.] 4°. (*ap. R. Volfium,*) [1560.]
L.O³.C.D.E.+ ; HN(2).BO.PML.
Ends Qq4.

16424a　— [Anr. issue, w. the Occasional Offices added and Qq
reset.] L.L².O(2).O¹⁷.M.; HN.TEX.
Ends Tt4.

16425　— Now = 16429.5.

16426　— [Anr. ed., revised, w. Psalter added.] 2 pts. 16° in 8's.
(*ap. R. Wolfium,* 1571, 1572.) L.O.C².LINC.M.+ ; HN.
CAL.HD.N.NY¹¹.+
Only the Psalter (formerly also 2355) is dated,
1571 on the tp and 1572 in the colophon.

16427　— [Anr. ed.] 8°. (*T. Vautrollerius*) *per assig. F. Floræ,*
(1574.) L.O.C.D⁷.E².+ ; F.HN.HD.NY¹¹.Y.+

16428　— [Anr. ed.] 8°. (*J. Jacksonus*) *per assig. F. Floræ,* 1594.
L.O.C⁷.CASHEL.WN².+ ; HN.ILL.NY¹¹.PML.U.

16428.5　— [Anr. issue, w. imprint on tp:] *typis J. Norton,* 1594.
O³.

16429　— [Anr. issue, w. 1st sheet reset, w. imprint:] *typis J.
Norton,* 1604. L(destroyed).LINC.
Retains original colophon: *J. Jacksonus,* 1594.
— See also 17991.

16429.5　[*Latin and Greek.*] Liber precum publicarum ecclesiæ
Anglicanæ, in iuuentutis Græcarum literarum
studiosæ gratiam, latinè Græceꝗ editus. [*Tr.*] (W.
Whitaker.) 8°. (*ap. R. Wolfium,*) 1569. L.O.C.C².
LINC.+ ; TEX.
(Formerly 16425)

16430　[*French.*] Le liure des prieres communes, de l'administra-
tion des sacremens & autres ceremonies en l'église
d'Angleterre. *Tr.* F. Philippe. 4°. [*N. Hill f.*] *T.
Gaultier,* 1553. L².O.O³¹(imp.).C(imp.).LIV.+ ; HN.
BO.CB.
Pr. for use in the Channel Islands.

16431　— La liturgie angloise. Ou le livre des prieres publiques.
Nouuellement traduit en françois [by P. de Laune.]
(Le livre des Pseaumes de David.) 2 pts. 4°. *J. Bill,*
1616. L.O.C.M.STU.+ ; F.HN.HD(lacks sub tp).PML.
Y.+

16432　[*Greek.*] Λειτουργια Βρεττανικη. . . . Liber precum publicarum. Operâ & studio E. Petili. (Ψαλτηριον του

Liturgies—Church of England—BOOK OF COMMON PRAYER—
Translations—cont.

Δαβιδ.) 2 pts. 8°. *typis T. Cotesi pro R. Whitakero,*
1638. L.O.C.D.M.+ ; F.HN.HD.ILL.NY.+
(Psalter formerly also 2353)

16433　[*Irish.*] Leabhar na nurnaightheadh. [*Tr.*] (W. Daniel,
Abp. of Tuam.) fol. *Cljath* [i.e. *Dublin*,] *a dtigh
Shéon Francke alias Franckton,* 1608. L.O.C.A.D.+ ;
HN.CH.HD.N.PML.+

16434　[*Spanish.*] Liturgia Inglesa. [*Tr.* F. de Texeda.] 4°.
Augustæ Trinobantum [i.e. *London, B. Norton a. J.
Bill,*] CIƆ.IƆI.IXIIV [1623.] L.O.C.E.ETON.+ ; F.
HN.HD.PML.Y.+

16435　[*Welsh.*] Lliver gweddi gyffredin. [*Tr.* W. Salesbury, *ed.*
R. Davies.] fol. *H. Denham, at the costes a. charges
of H. Toy,* 1567. Ent. 1566–67. CAR(imp.).M.NLW
(imp.). Swansea PL(lacks tp).

16436　— [Anr. ed.] 4°. *J. Windet, at the costes a. charges of T.
Chard,* 1586. L².O(imp.).O⁵.O³⁸.NLW.

16437　— [Anr. ed.] 4°. *gan ddeputiaid C. Barker,* 1599. L.L².
O(imp.).C⁵.NLW(2, 1 imp., 1 = St. Asaph).

16438　— [Anr. ed.] 2 pts. 4° in 8's. *B. Norton a* [sic] *J. Bill,*
1621. L.O.NLW.; F.BO.HD.N.
See also 20952.

16439　— [Anr. ed.] 8°. *R. Barker a* [sic] *chan assignes J. Bill,*
1630. L(lacks tp).O(imp.).O³⁸.DUL.LIV³.; HN.HD.
Prob. issued w. 2746.

16440　— [Anr. ed.] 4° in 8's. *Assignes J. Bill ag i'w gwerthu gida.
R. Milborne,* 1634. L(lacks B8).O³.C³.D.NLW(imp.).
+ ; HN.PML.
Prob. issued w. 2747.

Selections

Note: For selections from the Book of Common Prayer published
with the Psalter 'after the translation of the Great Bible' *see* no. 2 in
the headnote preceding 2370. For different selections without a
psalter *see* 20373 sqq.

16441　The booke of common praier noted. [By] (J. Merbecke.)
[A2ʳ:] (In this booke is conteyned so muche of the
order of commõ prayer as is to be song in churches.)
4°. (*R. Grafton,*) 1550. L.O.C.D.M.+ ; HN.BO.ILL.
PML.Y.+

16442　[Heading A1ʳ:] The order of commen prayer, for mattins
and euensonge thorowe oute the whole yere. [1552.]
= pt. of 2089.

16443　Mornyng and euenyng prayer and communion. 1565.
= 6419.

16444　[The psalter or psalms of David, with the ordinary service
out of the Book of Common Prayer.] (*W. Seres,* 1567.)
Now = 2386.4.

16445　— [Anr. ed.] *W. Seres,* 1571. Now = 2387.7.

16446　— [Anr. ed.] *P. Short,* (1600.) = 2403.

16447　[*Latin.*] Liber precum publicarum in usum ecclesiæ
chathedralis [*sic*] Christi Oxon. (Liber psalmorum.)
8°. *Oxoniæ, J. Barnesius,* 1615. L.O.C³.C⁵.LINC.; Y.
Excerpts from 16426.

16448　— [Anr. ed., revised.] Liber psalmorum et precum in
usum ecclesiæ Cath. Christi Oxon. 12°. *Oxoniæ, L.
Lichfield,* 1639. O.O⁴.
Contents vary from 16447.

16448.3　[Heading A1ʳ:] Ad Mat. & Vesp. [Matins and Evensong
in Latin, probably for use at Peterhouse, Cambridge.]
fol. [*Cambridge,* 1634?] O³.C¹⁹.
The O³ copy is bd. w. 16397.3 and 16474 in a
binding w. Peterhouse stamp.

Appendix

16448.7　The compilers of the English common prayer book (as now
it is) . . . mense Maio 1549. s.sh.4°. [*London, c.*1640.]
DUR³.; Washington Cathedral.

16449　Reasons for refusal of subscription to the booke of common praier. 1605. = 14035.

16449a　The second and last part of Reasons for refusall of subscription. 1606. = 14036.

16450　A survey of the booke of common prayer, by way of 197.
queres grounded upon 58. places, ministring just
matter of question, with a view of London ministers
exceptions. 8°. [*Middelburg, R. Schilders,*] 1606. L.
O.C.D².LINC.+ ; F.ILL.LC.Y.
Includes reprint of 16779.12.

Liturgies—Church of England—BOOK OF COMMON PRAYER—
Appendix—cont.

16451 — [Anr. ed.] Reviewed, corected, and augmented. 8°.
    [*Middelburg, R. Schilders,*] 1610. L.O³.C.C¹⁰.G².+;
    F.U.Y.
        See 18541.

16452 The triall of the English liturgie. 4°. [*Leyden, W.
    Christiaens,*] 1637. L⁴.O².C.D.E(imp.).+; F.HN.HART.

16452.5 — [Anr. ed.] 4°. [*Leyden, W. Christiaens,*] 1638. L.O³⁸.
    C².E.M.+; MCG.U.

LITANY

Note: For other editions of 'A Letanie with suffrages', 1543, etc.
see 1744 sqq., 10619 sqq.

16453 [Begins:] O God the Father of heauē. [The litany and
    suffrages.] 8°. [*London?* 1554.] L.
        With prayer for King Philip and Queen Mary.

16453.5 — [Anr. ed. Begins:] Suffrages. O God, the father of
    heauen. 8°. [*London,* 1558.] L.
        With prayer for Queen Elizabeth; prayer against
        sedition mentions Bp. of Rome.

16453.7 — [Anr. ed.] 8°. [*London,* 1558.] C.
        With prayer for Queen Elizabeth; prayer against
        sedition omits Bp. of Rome.

16454 The letanye, vsed in the quenes maiesties chappel. 8°. (*R.
    Jugge,*) 1559. C³.COL.; Y.

16454.5 The letany. 16° in 8. [*W. Seres?* 1559.] O(bd. w. 3007).

16455 The letany, wyth certayne other deuoute and godlye
    meditations. 16° in 8's. *London,* 1562. O(imp.).

ORDER OF COMMUNION

16456 Now = 16458.3.

16456.5 The order of the communion. 4°. (*Rychard Grafton,* 1548
    (the .viii. daye of Marche.)) L.DUR⁵.; PML.
        (Formerly 16458)

16457 — [Anr. ed.] 4°. (*Rychard Grafton,* 1548 (the eyght daie of
    Marche.)) L.L¹⁵.O³¹.C.DUR³.+; F.HN(lacks tp).Y.

16458 — Now = 16456.5.

16458.3 — [Anr. ed.] 4°. (*Richard Grafton,* 1548 (the eyght daye
    of Marche.)) L.L¹⁵.
        (Formerly 16456)

16458.5 — [Anr. ed.] 8°. [*T. Raynalde a. W. Hill,* 1549?] O.

16459 [A trans.] Ordo distributionis sacramenti altaris sub
    utraque specie, et formula confessionis. [*Tr.*] (A. A.
    S. D. Th. [A. Alesius, Scotus, Dr. Theology.]) 8°.
    Londini, [i.e. *Leipzig, V. Bapst,*] 1548 (8 mr.) L.O.
    E.; F.HD.Y.

16460 Certaine notes . . . to be song at the morning communion.
    1560. = 6418.

EPISTLES AND GOSPELS

Note: For editions of the Liturgical Epistles and Gospels *see* the
headnote and entries at 2964.5 sqq.

CATECHISM

Note: For editions of the Catechism with commentaries *see* under
the names of the authors.

16461 A short catechisme, by law authorised in the Church of
    England. *Tr.* into Hebrew by T. Ingmethorpe. *Eng.
    a. Heb.* 8°. M. Flesher f. R. Milbourne, 1633. Ent.
    8 de. 1632. L.O.O⁴.C⁵.YK.+

THE FORM AND MANNER OF MAKING ARCHBISHOPS, BISHOPS, ETC. (THE ORDINAL)

16462 The forme and maner of makyng and consecratyng of
    archebishoppes bishoppes, priestes and deacons. 4°.
    (*R. Grafton,*) 1549 (mr.) L.O³(imp.).C³.C¹⁰.M.
        B1ʳ line 4 ends: 'pla-'.

16462.5 — [Anr. issue, w. sheet B reset.] L.O¹⁷.C.D².LINC.+; HN.
    PML.Y.
        B1ʳ line 4 ends: 'from'.

16463 — [Anr. ed.] 1552 (au.) = pt. of 16285 sqq.
16464 — [Anr. ed.] 1552. = pt. of 16279 sqq.
16465 — [Anr. ed.] 1559. = pt. of 16292.
16466 — [Anr. ed.] The fourme and maner of makyng and con-
    secratyng bishoppes, priestes, and deacons. 1559.
    fol. *R. Jugge,* [1575?] L.M.
        This and the following eds. are usually found bd.
        after folio 1-col., B.L. Books of Common Prayer
        of approximately the same date.

16466.5 — [Anr. ed.] fol. *Deputies of C. Barker,* 1596. L.

Liturgies—Church of England—THE FORM AND MANNER OF
MAKING ARCHBISHOPS, BISHOPS, ETC.—*cont.*

16467 — [Anr. ed.] fol. *R. Barker,* 1607. L.O³.C.C⁵.E.+; F.HN.
    NY¹¹.SMU.

16468 — [Anr. ed.] fol. *B. Norton a. J. Bill, deputies a. assignes
    of R. Barker,* 1618. L⁴.L⁵(Lemon 160).LINC.; ILL.
    NY¹¹.Y. Washington Cathedral.

16469 — [Anr. ed.] fol. *B. Norton a. J. Bill,* 1627. O(2).O³¹.G⁴.;
    ILL.

16470 — [Anr. ed.] fol. *B. Norton a. J. Bill,* 1629. L.C.ELY.; HN.
    Reprinted in 4° w. this imprint in 1661 and later
    as pt. of Wing S 4823 sqq.

16471 — [Anr. ed.] 4°. *R. Barker a. J. Bill,* [1660?] = Wing
    C 4105?

16472 — [Anr. ed.] fol. *R. Barker a. assignes of J. Bill,* 1631. L.
    O(2).C.; HN.ILL.

16473 — [Anr. ed.] fol. *R. Barker a. assignes of J. Bill,* 1633.
    L(destroyed).O.O¹⁶.C¹⁷.; HN.NY.PML.WTL.

16474 — [Anr. ed.] fol. *R. Barker a. assignes of J. Bill,* 1634.
    L.O.O³.C(lacks tp). Hull U.+; HN.LC.PML.

16475 — [Anr. ed.] fol. *R. Barker a. assignes of J. Bill,* 1636.
    L.O.O³.O⁵.C.+; HN.HD.ILL.JH.PML.+

16476 — [Anr. ed.] 4°. 1637. = pt. of 16407.

16477 — [Anr. ed.] fol. *R. Barker a. assignes of J. Bill,* 1638.
    L.O.C.D(imp.).M⁴.+; HN.PML.

16478 — [Anr. ed.] fol. *R. Barker a. assignes of J. Bill,*
    1639. L.O.O¹⁰.C.LIV.+; F.HN.ILL.PML. Washington
    Cathedral.
        Reprinted in 1660 w. date 1639 but w. 'assigns' in
        imprint (copy at L: 3407.e.8(2), w. BCP of 1660).

STATE SERVICES

Accession Days

16479 [*Elizabeth I.*] A fourme of prayer, with thankes geuyng,
    to be vsed euery yeere, the .17. of Nouember, beyng
    the day of the queenes maiesties entrie to her raigne.
    4° in 8. (*R. Jugge,*) [1576.] L.C².DUR³.LIV.

16479.5 — [Anr. ed.] 4° in 8's. (*C. Barkar* [sic],) [1578?] L².
16480 — [Anr. ed.] 4° in 8's. *C. Barker,* (1578.) L.C⁵.
    Expanded from 10 to 22 leaves.

16481 — [Anr. ed.] 4° in 8's. *C. Barker,* [1580?] L².C³.LINC.; HN.
16482 — [Anr. ed.] 4° in 8's. *Deputies of C. Barker,* [1590?] L.
    COL.

16483 [*James I.*] A fourme of prayer with thanksgiving, to be
    used the 24. of March: being the day of his highnesse
    entry to this kingdome. 4°. *R. Barker,* [1604.] L.O.
    C.CASHEL.M⁴.+; HN.

16484 — [Anr. ed.] 4°. *B. Norton a. J. Bill,* [1620.] L².O.C¹⁵.
    LINC.; BO.HD.

16485 [*Charles I.*] A forme of prayer, with thanksgiving, to bee
    used the 27. of March. Being the day of his highnesse
    entry to this kingdome. 4°. *B. Norton a. J. Bill,* 1626.
    L.L².O.C.LINC.+; Y.
        Colophon dated 1625 or 1626; copies of both at
        O³.

16485.3 — [Anr. ed.] 4°. *B. Norton a. J. Bill,* 1629. F.N.
16485.7 — [Anr. ed.] 4°. *R. Barker a. assignes of J. Bill,* 1631. L².
16486 — [Anr. ed.] 4°. *R. Barker a. assignes of J. Bill,* 1634.
    DUR³.

16486.3 — [Anr. ed.] 4°. *R. Barker a. assignes of J. Bill,* 1635.
    C¹⁵(2).PLUME.

16486.7 — [Anr. ed.] 4°. *R. Barker a. assignes of J. Bill,* 1637
    (1636.) O¹³.
        The colophon leaf, dated 1636, is a cancel.

16487 — [Anr. ed.] 4°. *R. Barker a. assignes of J. Bill,* 1638. L².
    O.C³.C⁵(2).C¹⁰.; BO.HD.ILL.HN.

16488 — [Anr. ed.] 4°. *R. Barker a. assignes of J. Bill,* 1640.
    L(2).O.C.C³.; HN.

Gowrie Conspiracy

16489 A fourme of prayer with thanksgiving, to be used every
    yeere the fift of August: being the day of his high-
    nesse happy deliverance from the bloody attempt of
    the earle of Gowry. 4°. *R. Barker,* 1603. L.O.C³.E.
    WN².+; F.HD. Sexton.

16490 — [Anr. ed.] 4°. *R. Barker,* 1606. L.L².O.O³.DUR³.+; HN.
16491 — [Anr. ed.] 4°. *B. Norton a. J. Bill,* 1618. L.O(2).C².E.
16492 — [Anr. ed.] 4°. *B. Norton a. J. Bill,* 1623. L.L².O¹³.LINC.

Gunpowder Plot

16493 A prayer to be used on Wednesday November 13. [1678?]
    Not an STC item.

Liturgies—Church of England—STATE SERVICES—*Gunpowder Plot*—cont.

16494 Prayers and thanksgiving to be used for the happy deliverance from the intended massacre the 5 of November 1605. 4°. *R. Barker*, [1606?] L.O.C³.D². E.+; F.HN.HD.ILL.PML.+

Tp line 13: 'Set foorth'; some copies have slight press alterations on A2, E2, F2, F4; A2ʳ line 1 of text ends 'prayers,' or 'sup-'; F4ʳ has orn. w. ram's head or orn. w. dolphins; both at HN, PML.

16495 — [Anr. ed.] Prayers and thanksgiving to bee used . . . the fift of November 1605. 4°. *R. Barker*, [1610?] L(destroyed).O¹³.C⁵.DUR.E.; HN.

Tp line 12: 'Set forth'.

16496 — [Anr. ed.] 4°. *R. Barker a. J. Bill*, 1620. L.L².C².C⁸.

16496.5 — [Anr. ed.] 4°. *B. Norton a. J. Bill*, 1623. LINC.; F.

16497 — [Anr. ed.] 4°. *B. Norton a. J. Bill*, 1625. L.L².O.

16497.1 — [Anr. ed.] 4°. *B. Norton a. J. Bill*, [before 1629.] O³.C³.

A3 signed correctly.

16497.3 — [Anr. ed.] 4°. *B. Norton a. J. Bill*, [before 1629.] F.

A3 signed '3 A'.

16497.5 — [Anr. ed.] 4°. *R. Barker a. assignes of J. Bill*, 1630. C.

16497.7 — [Anr. ed.] 4°. *R. Barker a. assignes of J. Bill*, 1631. L². C¹³.; HN.

16498 — [Anr. ed.] 4°. *R. Barker a. assignes of J. Bill*, 1634. L.; Y.

16499 — [Anr. ed.] 4°. *R. Barker a. assignes of J. Bill*, 1635. L². O(J).O¹³.C⁸.; HD.

16500 — [Anr. ed.] 4°. *R. Barker a. assignes of J. Bill*, 1636. L(2, 1 mutilated).O(2).C²(imp.).C¹⁹.; Y.

16501 — [Anr. ed.] 4°. *R. Barker a. assignes of J. Bill*, 1638. L. O.C³.E³.P.+; F.BO.

16502 — [Anr. ed.] 4°. *R. Barker a. assignes of J. Bill*, 1640. O. O⁴.C⁵.R.SHEF.+; HD(2).

Prayers for the Parliament. [1606?] *See* 7748.5.

SPECIAL FORMS OF PRAYER ON VARIOUS OCCASIONS

16503 A prayer for victorie and peace. 8°. (*in aed. R. Graftoni*, 1548.) C⁶.

16503.5 — [Anr. ed.] 8°. (*in ed. R. Jugge*, 1548.) L(imp.).

16504 A thankes geuing to God vsed in Christes churche on the Monday Wednisday and Friday. 1551. 8°. *R. Grafton*, [1551] (jy.) C⁶.

A prayer made by the deane of Westminster [H. Weston] and delyuered to the chyldren of yᵉ queenes maiesties gramer scole there. [1555.] *See* 25291.5.

16504.5 A forme of meditation, very meete to be daylye vsed of house holders in this daungerous, and contagious tyme. 8°. *A. Lacy*, [1563?] Ent. 1563–64. COL.

16505 A fourme to be vsed in common prayer twise a weeke, during this tyme of mortalitie. Set foorth by the queenes maiesties speciall commaundement, xxx. Iulij. 1563. 4°. (*R. Jugge a. J. Cawood*,) [1563.] L(692.d.33).L².YK.

'Homyly' divided into 2 parts; prob. later than the eds. listed below. For later adaptations *see* 16524, 16532, 16540, 16553.

16506 — [Anr. ed.] A fourme . . . twyse aweke. 4°. (*R. Jugge a. J. Cawood*,) [1563.] L.O(J).C.D².DUR³.+; F.BO(imp.). PML.Y.

'Homyly' not divided; A4ʳ catchword: 'thy'.

16506.3 — [Anr. ed.] 4°. (*R. Jugge a. J. Cawood*,) [1563.] L¹⁵.O. O¹³.C³.C⁴.+

'Homyly' not divided; A4ʳ catchword: 'We'.

16506.7 — [Anr. issue, w. E2–3, F2–4 reset.] C².C³.

'Homyly' divided into 2 parts.

16507 A short fourme of thanksgeuyng to God for ceassing the plague. Set forth by the Byshop of London [E. Grindal.] 4°. (*R. Jugge a. J. Cawood*, 1563 (22 ja.)) L.L².C².

16507.5 — [Anr. issue, undated, w. cancel tp and last leaf.] C³.C⁵.

In title: 'ceassyng'.

16508 A fourme to be vsed in common prayer euery Wednesdaye and Frydaye, within the cittie and dioces of London: for the deliuery of those christians, that are now inuaded by the Turke. 4°. *W. Seres*, [1565.] L.HAT.; PML.

16508.3 — [Anr. ed., for Norwich.] 4°. *J. Waley*, [1565.] L².

General Priory of the British Realm of the Order of the Hospital of St. John of Jerusalem, St. John's Gate, Clerkenwell, London.

16508.7 — [Anr. ed., for Salisbury.] 4°. *J. Waley*, [1565.] SAL.

Liturgies—Church of England—SPECIAL FORMS OF PRAYER—cont.

16509 A short forme of thankesgeuing for the delyuerie of the isle of Malta from the Turkes. Set forthe by Matthew [Parker] Archebyshop of Canturburye. 4°. (*W. Seres*, 1565.) L.SAL.

16510 A fourme to be vsed in common prayer, euery Sunday, Wednesday, and Fryday, through the whole realm: for the preseuration of those christians and their countreys, that are nowe inuaded by the Turke. Set foorth by Mathewe [Parker] Archbyshop of Canterbury. 4°. (*R. Jugge a. J. Cawood*,) [1566.] L.O.C². LINC.SAL.+; HD.PML.Y.

16510.5 A prayer to be sayd . . . (through the dioeces of Norwich) during the tyme of this hard and sharp wether. s.sh.4°. [*Norwich, A. de Solempne?* 1571?] C⁸.

16511 A fourme of common prayer to be vsed, by aucthoritie of the queenes maiestie, and necessarie for the present tyme and state. 1572. 27 Octob. [After the massacre of St. Bartholomew.] 4°. (*R. Jugge*,) [1572.] L.O.C³. COL.SAL.+; HN.ILL.

16512 The order of prayer, . . . to auert Gods wrath from vs, threatned by the late terrible earthquake. 4°. *C. Barker*, (1580.) Ent. 22 jn. L.C.DUR³(w. A3–6 from 16513).; HN.

Collates A⁴ B–D⁴; 'Psalm. xxx.' on A3(signed in B.L.). Tp in 2 settings found w. either 16512 or 16513. C, HN have added description of earthquake on E–F⁴; HN has orig. sub tp on E1ʳ: C has stub only.

16513 — [Anr. ed.] 4°. *C. Barker*, (1580.) L(lacks tp).O(lacks tp, bd. w. 16525.3).O¹³.C³.YK.+; F.HD.Y.

Collates A⁸ B–D⁴; A3(signed in roman type)–A6 contain 'A prayer for the estate of Christes church' inserted after tp (A2), sometimes misbound; 'Psalm. xxx.' on A7(unsigned). Quires B and D apparently from same setting as 16512. C³ has added description of earthquake on E–F⁴, w. E1 a cancel w. the recto blank.

16513a An order for publike prayers on Wednesdayes and Frydayes. [1586.] = 4587.

16514 A prayer for the estate of Christes church. [1580.] = pt. of 16513.

A prayer for all kings, princes, countreyes and people. *See* 19342 sqq.

16515 A necessarie and godly prayer appoynted by John [Aylmer], Bishop of London to be vsed throughout his dioces vpon Sondayes and Frydayes, for the turning away of Gods wrath. Aswell, conserning this vntemperate wether and raine. 4°. [*London*,] 1585. L.C⁵.

16516 An order of praier and thankes-giuing, for the preseuration of the queenes maiesties life and salfetie [*sic*]: to be vsed of the preachers of the dioces of Winchester. With a short extract of W. Parries voluntarie confession. 4°. [*H. Denham f.*] *R. Newberie*, [1585.] Ent. 25 fb. 1585. L.O(J). C⁵.E.SAL.+; F.HN. CB.HD(2).

16517 An order of prayer and thanksgiuing, for the preseuration of her maiestie and the realme, from the Lloodie practises of the pope. 4°. *C. Barker*, 1586. Ent. 25 au. L.C³.C⁵.SAL.; HN.NY¹¹.

An order for publike prayers to be vsed on Wednesdayes and Frydayes. [1586.] *See* 4587 sq.

16518 A prayer and thanksgiuing fit for this present and to be vsed in the time of common prayer. 4°. *C. Barker*, 1587. L².C³.COL(2).DUR³.; F(frag.). Sexton.

16519 A fourme of prayer, necessary for the present time and state. 4°. *Deputies of C. Barker*, 1588. L.O.C.DUR³. LINC.+; HN.BO.Y.

A godly prayer for the preseuration of the queenes maiestie. 1588. *See* 17489.5.

16520 A psalme and collect of thanksgiuing, not vnmeet for this present time: to be said or sung in churches. 4°. *Deputies of C. Barker*, 1588. L.C³.C⁵.; HN.

16520.5 [A form of prayer for the protection of Elizabeth of England and Henry [III] of France; against the Catholic Leagues. Begins:] O Lord our God, most gracious & most glorious, . . . 1/2 sh.fol. [*J. Charlewood*, 1589.] O.

(Formerly 21292)

16521 A forme of prayer, thought fitte to be dayly vsed in the English armie in France. 4°. *Deputies of C. Barker*, 1589. L.C³.COL.

16522 A fourme of prayer, necessarie for the present time and state. 4°. *Deputies of C. Barker*, 1590. L.L²(2).C³.COL.; Sexton.

Liturgies—Church of England—Special Forms of Prayer—
cont.

16523   Certaine praiers to be vsed at this present time for the good success of the French king, against the enemies of Gods true religion and his state. 4°. *Deputies of C. Barker,* 1590. L.C⁵.; HN.
> Last prayer ends: 'worlde without end, Amen.'

16523.3   — [Anr. ed.] 4°. *Deputies of C. Barker,* 1590. L².COL.; Sexton.
> Last prayer ends: 'now and foreuer. Amen.'; order of last 2 prayers reversed from 16523 w. some textual changes.

16523.5   A prayer to be vsed in euery parish church at morning and euening prayer, during the time of these present troubles in France. s.sh.fol. *Deputies of C. Barker,* [1590?] COL(2).
> Reprinted from 16523.3.

16523.7   A prayer vsed in the queenes maiesties house and chappell, for the prosperitie of the French king assayled by rebels 21 Aug. An. 1590. s.sh.fol. *Deputies of C. Barker,* [1590.] COL.

16524   Certaine praiers collected out of a fourme of godly meditations, set foorth . . . and commended vnto the ministers and people of London by John [Aylmer], bishop of London, &c. July. 1593. 4°. *Deputies of C. Barker,* [1593.] L.O.C.COL.YK.+; HN. 𝔄
> Adapted from 16505.

16525   An order for prayer and thankes-giuing (necessary to be vsed in these dangerous times) for the safetie and preseruation of her maiesty and this realme. 4°. *Deputies of C. Barker,* 1594. L.L².O.C.DUR³.+; F.HN. ILL.
> Collates A–D⁴; *see also* 16529.

16525.3   — [A variant, omitting date from tp.] O(tp only, bd. w. 16513).

16525.7   — [Anr. ed.] 4°. *Deputies of C. Barker,* 1594. L².C³.
> Collates A–C⁴.

16526   A prayer set forth by authoritie for the success of hir maiesties forces and nauie. s.sh.fol. *Deputies of C. Barker,* 1596. L⁵.O.COL.

16527   A prayer of thankesgiuing, and for continuance of good success to her maiesties forces. s.sh.fol. *Deputies of C. Barker,* 1596. L⁵.O.O².
> Line 2 of text ends: 'vnto'.

16527.5   — [Anr. ed.] s.sh.fol. *Deputies of C. Barker,* 1596. L.L⁵. O.COL(2).; F.
> Line 2 of text ends: 'vn-'.

16528   Certaine prayers set foorth by authoritie, to be vsed for the prosperous success of her maiesties forces and nauy. 4°. *Deputies of C. Barker,* 1597. L.O.DUR³.SHEF.; HN. HD.
> Collates A–C⁴; A3 has leaf signature in B.L. type, has headpiece of type orns., begins 'Most mighty God'.

16528.5   — [Anr. issue, w. quire A reset.] L².C².
> A3 unsigned, has headpiece of winged woman w. cornucopias, begins 'Most mighty God'.

16528a   — [Anr. ed.] 4°. *Deputies of C. Barker,* 1597. HN.
> Collates A–C⁴; A3 has leaf signature in roman type, has no headpiece, begins 'O God all-maker'; C3 unsigned.

16528a.5   — [Anr. ed.] 4°. *Deputies of C. Barker,* 1597. L.C⁵.COL.; BO.
> Collates A² B–C⁴; A2 missigned A3 and from the same setting as in 16528a; C3 signed.

16529   An order for prayer and thanksgiuing . . . for the safetie and preseruation of her maiestie and this realme. Set foorth 1594. And reuewed with some alterations vpon the present occasion. 4°. *Deputies of C. Barker,* 1598. L.; BO.
> A revised ed. of 16525 w. 2 prayers added.

16530   A prayer for the good successe of her maiesties forces in Ireland. s.sh.fol. *Deputies of C. Barker,* 1599. L(2). L²².O.O².; F.

16531   Certaine prayers fit for the time. 4°. *R. Barker,* 1600. L. L²(2).C⁵.HAT.YK.

16532   Certaine prayers collected out of a forme of godly meditations, to be used in the present visitation. 4°. *R. Barker,* 1603. L.O.C.D².DUR³.+; F.HN.HD.MIN.PML.+
> Adapted from 16505.

16533   A short forme of thanksgiuing to God, for staying the plague. 4°. *R. Barker,* 1604. L²(2).L¹⁶.C³.DUR³.SAL.
> Prayers for the Parliament. [1604?] *See* 7748.3.

16534   Prayers appointed to be used in the church at morning and evening prayer, for the queenes safe deliverance. 4°. *R. Barker,* 1605. L.L²(2).C³.DUR³.; HN.ILL. Sexton.

Liturgies—Church of England—Special Forms of Prayer—
cont.

16535   Thanksgiving for the queenes maiesties safe deliverance .9. April 1605. 4°. *R. Barker,* [1605.] L².C³.DUR³.M.; HN.
> Prayers for the Parliament. [1606?] *See* 7748.5.

16536   A prayer for the speaker of the commons house of Parliament. 4°. [*R. Barker,* 1606?] L.

16537   Prayers appointed to be used in the church for the queenes safe deliverance. 4°. *R. Barker,* 1606. L.L².

16538   A forme of praier to be used in London, and elsewhere in this time of drought. 4°. *R. Barker,* 1611. L.L².O.C³. DUR³.+; F.HD.

16539   A forme of prayer to be publikely used in churches, during this unseasonable weather, and aboundance of raine. 4°. *R. Barker,* 1613. L.; HN.HD.
> The gospel written [etc. against King's evil. Before 1620.] *See* 16551.

16539.5   A prayer for the king and queene of Bohemia and their affaires in this warre, to be used by the English companies. s.sh.fol. [*London,* c. 1620.] O³¹.

16540   A forme of common prayer, together with an order of fasting: for the averting of Gods heavy visitation upon many places of this kingdome, and for the drawing downe of his blessings upon us, and our armies. 4°. *B. Norton a. J. Bill,* 1625. L.O.C.D.LEIC². +; F.HN.HD.PML.Y.+
> B3ʳ line 1 of heading ends: 'one'. C has 5 copies, all w. some sheets or parts of sheets in different settings, apparently indiscriminately bd. Adapted from 16505.

16541   — [Anr. ed.] 4°. *B. Norton a. J. Bill,* 1625. L.O.C².D².E.+; HN.ILL.
> B3ʳ line 1 of heading ends: 'verse'.

16542   A short forme of thanksgiving to God for staying the contagious sickenesse of the plague. 4°. *B. Norton a. J. Bill,* 1625. L.O.C.E.M⁴.+; F.HN.HD.N.NY⁴.+

16543   A forme of prayer, necessary to bee used in these dangerous times, of warre and pestilence, for the safety and preservation of his maiesty. 4°. *B. Norton a. J. Bill,* 1626. L.O.C.D².LINC.+; F.CAL.HD.PML.U.+

16544   — [A variant, omitting 'of warre and pestilence' from the tp.] L(1st sheet only).L².O.O³.YK.; HN.CAL.HD.N.PML.

16545   A prayer, to be used . . . so long as his maiesties navie and forces are abroade. 1/2 sh.fol. [*B. Norton a. J. Bill,* 1628?] L⁵(Lemon 287).
> Line 6 ends: 'in'.

16545.5   — [Anr. ed.] 1/2 sh.fol. [*B. Norton a. J. Bill,* 1628?] L (Harl.5936/57).L⁵(Lemon 288).O³¹.; HN(2).
> Line 6 ends: 'Ar-'; HN copies pr. on same sheet.

16546   A prayer to bee publiquely used at the going foorth of the fleete this present yeere, 1628. 1/2 sh.fol. [*B. Norton a. J. Bill,* 1628.] L⁵(Lemon 286).LINC.; ILL.
> Line 1 of text ends: 'Father,'.

16546.5   — [Anr. ed.] 1/2 sh.fol. [*B. Norton a. J. Bill,* 1628.] O³¹. C³.
> Line 1 of text ends: 'Fa-'.

16547   A forme of prayer, necessary to bee used in these dangerous times of warre. 4°. *B. Norton a. J. Bill,* 1628. L.O.C.D.E.+; F.HN.ILL.NY¹¹.U.+
> Line 2 of title: 'Forme of'.

16547.5   — [Anr. ed.] 4°. *B. Norton a. J. Bill,* 1628. L².O.C.D². LINC.+; HN.BO.HD.N.Y.+
> Line 2 of title: 'of prayer'.

16548   A thanksgiving and prayer for the safe child-bearing of the queenes maiestie. 1/2 sh.fol. *B. Norton a. J. Bill,* 1628. L.L⁵(Lemon 289).O³¹.

16548.3   A thanksgiving and prayer for the safe child-bearing of the queenes maiestie. 1/2 sh.fol. *R. Barker a. J. Bill,* 1629. L⁵(Lemon 297).
> Line 3 of text ends: 'the'.

16548.7   — [Anr. ed.] 1/2 sh.fol. *R. Barker a. J. Bill,* 1629. O³¹.; HD.
> Line 3 of text ends: 'Kingdomes,'.

16549   A thanksgiving for the safe delivery of the queene, and happy birth of the yong prince. [By W. Laud.] 1/2 sh.fol. *R. Barker,* 1630. L.L⁵(Lemon 299).O³¹.; HD.

16549.5   A thanksgiving, and prayer for the safe child-bearing of the queenes maiestie. 1/2 sh. fol. *R. Barker a. assignes of J. Bill,* 1631. L⁵(Lemon 306).O³¹.

16550   A thanksgiving for the safe delivery of the queene, and happy birth of the yong princesse. 1/2 sh.fol. *R. Barker a. assignes of J. Bill,* 1631. L.O³¹.; HD(imp.).

16550.3   A thanksgiving for the happy recovery of his maiesties health [King Charles.] 1/2 sh.fol. *R. Barker a. assignes of J. Bill,* [1632.] O³¹.; HD.

Liturgies—Church of England—Special Forms of Prayer—cont.

16550.5 A thankesgiving, and prayer for the safe child-bearing of the queenes maiestie. 1/2 sh.fol. *R. Barker a. assignes of J. Bill,* 1633. O[31].

16550.7 A thankesgiving for the safe deliverie of the queenes maiestie, and happy birth of the duke of Yorke. 1/2 sh.fol. *R. Barker a. assignes of J. Bill,* 1633. O[31].; HD.

16551 [Begins:] The gospel written in the xvj. of Marke. [Form to be used at touching for the King's evil.] fol(2). [*R. Barker,* before 1620.] L.L[5](Lemon 161).

16552 A thankesgiving, and prayer for the safe child-bearing of the queenes maiestie. 1/2 sh.fol. *R. Barker a. assignes of J. Bill,* 1635. L.L[5](Lemon 308).O[31].D.

16553 A forme of common prayer, together with an order of fasting: for the averting of Gods heavie visitation. 4°. *R. Barker a. assignes of J. Bill,* 1636. L.L[2].O[3].C. CASHEL.+; F.HN.HD(2).NY[11].

B3[r] last line ends: 'full of compassion'. Adapted from 16505.

16553a — [Anr. issue, partly reset.] *R. Barker a. assignes of J. Bill,* 1636. L.O.C.D.M.+; HN.BO.HD.PML.Y.

(Formerly also 16554) B3[r] last line ends: 'against us'. Most of the text is reimposed from the standing type of 16553.

16554 — = 16553a.

16555 A thankesgiving, and prayer for the safe child-bearing of the queenes maiestie. 1/2 sh.fol. *R. Barker a. assignes of J. Bill,* 1636. L.O[31].

16555.5 A thankesgiving for the safe delivery of the queenes maiestie, and happy birth of the new-borne princesse. 1/2 sh.fol. *R. Barker a. assignes of J. Bill,* 1636. O[31].

16556 A prayer for the kings majestie, in his northern expedition: to be said in all churches. 1/2 sh. fol. *R. Barker a. assignes of J. Bill,* 1639. L.O.C[2].D.M.+; HD.WIS.

16557 A forme of common prayer; to be used upon the eighth of July: on which day a fast is appointed for the averting of the plague. 4°. *R. Barker a. assignes of J. Bill,* 1640. L.O.C.LINC.P.+; F.HN.HD.N.PML.+
See also 9159.

16558 A prayer for the kings majestie in his expedition against the rebels of Scotland; to be said in all churches. 1/2 sh.fol. *R. Barker a. assignes of J. Bill,* 1640. L.L[5](Lemon 311).O[16].; F.
Line 1 of text ends: 'Fa-'.

16558.5 — [Anr. ed.] 1/2 sh.fol. *R. Barker a. assignes of J. Bill,* 1640. L[8].O.O[31].C[2].; HD.
Line 1 of text ends: 'by'.

16559 A forme of common prayer: to be used upon the 17th of November, and the 8th of December: on which dayes a fast is appointed for the removing of the plague. 4°. *R. Barker a. assignes of J. Bill,* 1640. L.O.C.LINC. SAL.+; F.HN.BO.HD.PML.

Other Protestant Churches

Geneva

16560 Geneua. The forme of common praiers vsed in the churches of Geneua: made by J. Caluyne. In the ende are prayers translated by W. Huycke. 8°. (*E. Whitchurche,* 1550 (7 jn.)) L.O[17](lacks tp).C.D.DUL.; HN.

Netherlands

16560.5 A part of the lyturgy of the reformed churches in the Netherlands. *Tr.* out of Dutch. 4°. *Leyden,* [c. 1640.] U.

Common Prayer used by English Calvinistic Congregations Abroad

16561 The forme of prayers and ministration of the sacraments, &c. vsed in the Englishe congregation at Geneua: and approued, by J. Caluyn. (One and fiftie psalmes of Dauid in Englishe metre, 37 by T. Sternholde.— The catechisme.) 3 pts. 8°. *Geneua, J. Crespin,* 1556 (10 fb.) O(imp.).C.E.M.Z.+; F.HN.ILL(pt. 2 only).NY. PML.+ Cowan 1.
(Formerly also 11723) For an early issue of pt. 3 see 4380. Pt. 1 revised in 16567. For a Latin version of pt. 1 see 16565. Regarding the references to Cowan *see* headnote preceding 16577.

Liturgies—Other Protestant Churches—Common Prayer used by English Congregations Abroad—*cont.*

— [An extract? consisting of psalms and catechism only.] [1556?] *See* 2426.8.

16561.5 — [Anr. extract? consisting of Form of prayers only.] 16° in 8's. [*Geneva, M. Blanchier?*] (1557.) P(imp., bd. w. 2383.6).
On d8[v]: 'The end. M.D.LVII.' This has only a prose psalter with it and was possibly intended for private use.

16561a — [Anr. ed. of 16561, w. added psalms (to a total of 62) and prayers.] The forme of prayers and ministration of the sacraments, &c. . . . 2 pts. 16° in 8's. *Geneua, J. Poullain & A. Rebul,* 1558. L.E(imp.).; HN. Cowan 3.
Pt. 2 includes psalms and catechism.

16562 — [Anr. ed.] 2 pts. 8°. [*Printed abroad?*] 1561. C(imp.). C[2].E.PARIS(A 6234, has pt. 2, imp.).; BO(imp.). Cowan 4.
The psalms (pt. 2) are called for in the Table of Contents but are present only in the PARIS copy. This pt. collates A–S[8] T[2] (E–G[8] lacking) and contains the same psalms (80) as 2429; i.e. it conforms to the English rather than to the Geneva branch. The tp to pt. 2 is undated and has a close copy of Z. Durand's device, Silvestre 1075.

16563 — [Anr. ed.] 3 pts. 16° in 8's. *Geneua, Z. Durand,* 1561. L[15]. Cowan 5.
The psalms (pt. 2) are as in 16561a, w. added ones (to a total of 87) attrib. to W. Kethe. Sheets reissued in 16578.
— [Anr. ed. of psalms alone.] 16° in 8's. [*London,*] 1561. Cowan 6. *See* 2428.

16564 The forme of prayers and ministration of the sacraments &c. vsed in the English church at Geneua, also the praiers which they vse there in the Frēche churche. 8°. *Edinburgh, R. Lekprewik,* 1562. E. Cowan 7.
A transitional form from the Genevan service to the Scottish Book of Common Order (16577 sqq.).

16565 Ratio et forma publice orandi Deum, atque administrandi sacramenta, et cæt. In Anglorum ecclesiam, quæ Geneuæ colligitur, recepta: cum comprobatione D. I. Caluini. 8°. *Geneuæ, ap. J. Crispinum,* 1556. L.O[5]. C.E.LINC.+; BO.HD.U. Cowan 2.
For an English version *see* pt. 1 of 16561.

16566 Liturgia sacra, seu ritus ministerii in ecclesia peregrinorum profugorum propter euangelium Christi Argentinæ. [*Ed.*] Per V. Pollanum. 8°. (*per S. Mierdmannū,*) 1551 (23 fb.) L.O.O[5].C.D.+; HD.PML. Sexton.

16567 A booke of the forme of common prayer, administration of the sacraments: &c. agreeable to Gods worde, and the vse of the reformed churches. 8°. *R. Walde-graue,* [1585?] L.L[2].C[5](imp.).
A revised version of pt. 1 of 16561.

16568 — [Anr. ed.] 8°. (*Middelburgh, R. Schilders,*) 1586. L.O[5]. C.LINC.M.+; PML.

16569 — [Anr. ed.] 8°. *Middelburgh, R. Schilders,* 1587. L.L[2].; F.HN.AAS.

16570 — [Anr. ed.] Fourth editiō. 8°. *Middelburgh, R. Schilders,* 1602. L.L[2].O.C.E.+

Common Prayers used by Foreign Congregations in London

16571 Forma ac ratio tota ecclesiastici ministerii, in peregrinorum, potissimum vero Germanorum ecclesia: instituta Londini, per pientissimum regem Eduardum sextū: 1550. Autore J. a Lasco. 8°. [*Frankfurt, C. Egenolff a. Emden, E. van der Erve,* 1554?] L(2, 1 imp.).O.C.E.; F.HN.
Van der Erve pr. quires C–HH.

16571a — [A trans.] De christlicke ordinanciē . . . doer M. Microen. 8°. *buyten Londen, C. Volckwinner* [i.e. Emden, N. Hill a. E. van der Erve,] 1554. O(2).C. London, Dutch Church.

16572 — [Anr. ed.] 8°. [*Emden, E. van der Erve,*] 1563. L(imp.).

16572.3 La forme des prieres ecclesiastiques. Auec la maniere d'administrer les sacramens. 8°. [*London,*] 1552. O.

16572.7 Doctrine et forme d'icelle ainsi comme elle se practique en l'eglise des estrangiers à Londres. 8°. [*London,* 1552.] O.

Liturgies—Other Protestant Churches—COMMON PRAYERS
USED BY FOREIGN CONGREGATIONS IN LONDON—*cont.*

16573 L'ordre des prieres et ministere ecclesiastique de
l'eglise de Londres, et la confession de foy de
l'eglise de Glastonbury en Somerset. [By J. à
Lasco; *ed.* V. Poullain.] 16° in 8's. [*S. Mierdman?*]
1552. O⁵.C. Frankfurt am Main, Stadt- und
Universitätsbibliothek.

16574 Toute la forme & maniere du ministere ecclesiastique, en
l'eglise des esträgers, dressée a Londres. Par J. a
Lasco. *Tr.* de Latin. 8°. [*Emden*,] G. Ctematius [i.e.
E. van der Erve,] 1556. L(2).O.C.CANT.D(imp.).; NY.

16575 Kirchenordnung, wie die in der statt Londen geordnet
worden. Durch J. von Lasco beschrieben, aber durch
M. Micronium in eine kurze sum̃ verfasset, und
jetzund verdeutschet. 8°. *Heidelberg, J. Mayer*, 1565.
L.

16576 La forma delle publiche orationi, . . . la qual si vsa nella
chiesa de forestieri in Londra. [*Tr.* by P. P. Vergerio.]
8°. [*Zürich, A. Gesner*, 1551?] L.C⁵.

THE SCOTTISH BOOK OF COMMON ORDER

Note: Listed below are editions, frequently entitled 'The CL.
psalmes of David', which include the order of Baptism, Communion, etc. For editions of the psalms for the 'use of the Kirk of
Scotland' which do not include Baptism, etc. *see* 2701 sqq. The
references to Cowan in the entries there and below are to William
Cowan, 'A Bibliography of the Book of Common Order and Psalm
Book of the Church of Scotland: 1556–1644' in *Papers of the Edinburgh Bibliographical Society*, X (1913), pp. 71–98. The earliest
Cowan items are at 16561 sqq.

16577 The forme of prayers and ministration of the sacraments
&c. vsed in the English church at Geneua, approued
and receiued by the churche of Scotland, whereunto
are also added sondrie other prayers, with the whole
psalmes of Dauid in English meter. (The catechisme.)
2 pts. 8°. *Edinburgh, R. Lekpreuik*, 1564. O⁵. Cowan
8.
(Pt. 2 formerly also 4382)

16577a — [A variant, w. date on 1st tp altered:] 1565. L(2,
1 imp.).C⁵.E(imp.).*.LIV(imp.).*.; F.
(Pt. 2 formerly also 4382)

16578 — [Anr. issue of 16563, w. additions.] 3 pts. 16° in 8's.
[*Geneva, Z. Durand*,] pour H. le Mareschal, [*Rouen*,]
1566. P(imp.). Cowan 9.
The orig. tpp are cancelled and quires X–Nn are
largely new made, completing the psalms following
the English ed., 2430.

16578.5 — [Anr. ed. of the psalms.] The haill hundreth and
fyftie psalmes of Dauid, in Inglis meter, be T.
Sternholde. 8°. *Edinburgh, J. Scot*, 1567. Dundee
PL(tp only, bd. w. 2996.5).
Although psalms alone are called for on the tp, no
separate Scottish ed. of the psalms is known this
early; *see* 2701 for the first independent ed.

16579 — [Anr. ed. of the whole Book of Common Order.] The
forme of prayers and ministration of the sacraments
&c. 16° in 8's. [*Geneva, Z. Durand?*] 1571 [Cate-
chism sub tp:] (*Edinbrough, R. Lekpriuik*, 1570.) F.

16579.3 — [A variant, w. imprint on Catechism sub tp:] (*Imprinted*
1571.) E(imp.). Cowan 11.

16579.5 — [Anr. ed.] The forme of prayers [etc.] 8°. *Edinburgh,
J. Ros f. H. Charteris*, 1575. L¹⁵(1st quire only).
E(imp.). Cowan 13.

16580 — [Anr. ed., w. title:] The CL. psalmes of Dauid in Eng-
lish metre. With the forme of prayers, and ministra-
tion of the sacraments &c. vsed in the churche of
Scotland. (The catechisme.) 2 pts. 8°. *Edinburgh, T.
Bassandine*, 1575. O(3, 1 imp.).E. Cowan 12.
(Pt. 2 formerly also 4384)

16580.3 — [Anr. ed.] 2 pts. 8°. (*Edinburgh, [widow of] T.
Bassandyne*, 1578.) E(frags.). Cowan 14.

16580.7 — [Anr. ed.] 8°. [*Edinburgh, J. Ros?* 1578?] E⁷(imp., has
no catechism). Cowan 15.

16581 — [Anr. ed.] The forme of prayers and administration of
the sacramentes, . . . (The catechisme.) 16° in 8's.
[*Geneva?*] 1584. L.L².O.C.E.+; F.HN.CH. Cowan 16.
Omits psalms; except for this omission it follows
the arrangement in 16579.

16582 — [Anr. ed.] The CL. psalmes of Dauid in meter. For
the vse of the kirk of Scotland. 8°. *T. Vautrollier*,
1587. L²(imp.).O(catechism only).E.E²(imp.).G²
(psalms only).; F.ILL.NY(imp.). Cowan 17.
Psalms sub tp is on T1ʳ.

Liturgies—Other Protestant Churches—THE SCOTTISH BOOK
OF COMMON ORDER—*cont.*

16583 — [Anr. ed. D1ʳ begins:] Psalmes of Dauid. 8°. [K6ʳ:]
(*T. Vautrollier*, 1587.) L(imp.). Cowan 18.
L copy made up of at least 2 unidentified eds.;
partly pr. in Scotland and of later date; *see* also
16584.5.

16584 — [Anr. ed.] The CL. psalmes of Dauid in meter, for the
vse of the kirk of Scotland. 8°. *Middelburgh, R.
Schilders*, 1594. L(lacks A1,2).O.A.D(imp.).E.+; HN
(imp.). Cowan 19.

16584.5 — [Anr. ed.] 8°. *Edinburgh, H. Charteris*, 1594. E(tp only).
E⁴(imp.). Cowan 20.
16583 may be in part from this ed.

16585 — [Anr. ed.] 3 pts. 8°. *Edinburgh, H. Charteris*, 1596 [tp
to pt. 2:] (1595.) L(imp.).A(pt. 2 only).D(frags.).E.
LINC. Cowan 21.
Rearranged so that pt. 2 has psalms and catechism
and pt. 3 has orders of fasting and excommunication.

16585.5 — [A variant, dated 1596 throughout.] C(lacks 1st tp).;
F.CB(pts. 1,2 only, imp.).

16586 — [Anr. ed.] The CL. psalmes of dauid in meitir: with
the forme of prayeris vsit in the kirk of Scotland.
(The catechisme.) 2 pts. 8°. *Edinburgh, R. Smyth*,
1599 (1602.) L. Cowan 23.

16587 — [Anr. ed.] 3 pts. 16° in 8's. (*Middleburgh, R. Schilders*,
1599.) A(imp.). Dundee PL(lacks tp). Cowan 24.
The psalms (pt. 2), which for the first time appear
in prose as well as metre, are largely reimposed
in 2499.5.

16588 — [Anr. ed.] The CL. psalmes of David in prose and
meter. 2 pts. 16° in 8's. *Dort, A. Canin, at exp. of the
aires of H. Charteris, a. A. Hart*, [*Edinburgh*,] 1601.
E.; NY. Cowan 25.

16589 — [Anr. ed.] The CL. psalmes of David in meter, with
the prose. For the use of the kirk of Scotland. 3 pts.
8°. *Middelburgh, R. Schilders*, 1602. L.O.E.E⁴.M.+;
F.CU.NY(imp.).PN². Cowan 27.
(Pt. 3 formerly also 4388) The psalms (pt. 2) are
largely reimposed from 2507.5.

16589.5 — [Anr. ed.] The CL. psalmes of David in prose and
meter. Whereunto is newlie added: an notable
treatise of Athanasius. 16° in 8's. *Edinburgh, A.
H[art] f. James Cathkin a. R. Lauson*, 1607. E(imp.).

16590 — [Anr. ed.] The CL. psalmes of David in prose and
meeter. Where-unto is added, prayers commonly
used in the kirkes, and privat houses. 16° in 8's.
Edinburgh, A. Hart, 1611. E.E⁸(imp.). Cowan 30.

16591 — [Anr. ed.] The psalmes of David in meeter, with the
prose. 3 pts. 8°. *Edinburgh, A. Hart*, 1611. L(imp.).
O.A.CASHEL.E.+; F.HN.BO.ILL.NY.+ Cowan 31.
(Pt. 3 formerly also 4389)

16592 — [Anr. ed.] The CL. psalmes of David, in prose and
meeter. Hereunto is added the whole church discipline, [etc.] 3 pts. 8°. *Edinburgh, A. Hart*, 1615. L
(imp.).C.E.G².M⁴.+; F.HN.N.NY(imp.).PML. Cowan 33.
Pt. 3, which is the Heidelberg catechism instead
of Calvin's and is 'for the use of the kirke of
Edinburgh', was possibly also issued separately
as 13031.3.

— [Anr. ed.] 12°. 1615. *See* 2708.

16593 — [Anr. ed.] The whole booke of psalmes in prose and
meeter. Heereunto is adjoyned an exact kalendar,
with the forme of baptisme, the Lords Supper, [etc.]
16° in 8's. *Edinburgh, A. Hart*, 1617. E. Cowan
36.
This and the following eds. have no catechism.

16593.5 — [Anr. ed.] The CL. psalmes of David in prose and
meeter . . . whereunto is annexed the whole church
discipline. 8°. *Edinburgh, A. Hart*, 1618. E(1st quire
only, bd. w. 16599).

16594 — [Anr. ed.] The CL. psalmes of David in prose and
meeter. Newly corrected. Heereunto is adjoyned an
exact kalendar, [etc.] 8°. *Edinburgh, A. Hart*, 1622
(1621.) O³(imp.).A.E.G².G⁴.; BO⁶(imp.).HD(imp.).
Cowan 37.

16594.5 — [Anr. ed.] The psalmes of David, in prose and metre:
together with the order of baptisme, [etc.] 16° in 8's.
Aberdene, E. Raban f. D. Melvill, 1625. O(imp.).E.
G²(imp.). Cowan 38.
(Formerly 2709) Melvill's name is omitted from
the colophon.

16595 — [Anr. ed.] The CL. psalmes of . . . David, in English
metre, according as they are sung in the church of
Scotland. With manie godlie prayers, . . . and the

Liturgies—Other Protestant Churches—THE SCOTTISH BOOK OF COMMON ORDER—*cont.*

holie communion; [etc.] 4°. *Aberdene, E. Raban f. D. Melvill,* 1629. A(imp.).E.E².; F. Cowan 43.

In spite of the title, this contains no order of communion and perhaps belongs after 2714.

16595.5 — [Anr. ed.] (The CL. psalmes of David in prose and meeter [etc. With baptism, etc.]) 16° in 8's. (*Edinburgh, heires of A. Hart,* 1629.) E(psalms only, imp.).

An earlier issue of Cowan 47 (16596.5).

16596 — [Anr. ed.] The psalms of David in prose and metre, according to the church of Scotland. 16° in 8's. *Aberdene, E. Raban f. D. Melvill,* 1629 (1630.) NY. Cowan 45.

16596.5 — [Anr. issue of 16595.5.] (The CL. psalmes of David in prose and meeter [etc. With baptism, etc.]) 16° in 8's. (*Edinburgh, heires of A. Hart,* 1630.) NY(lacks 1st tp). Cowan 47.

(Formerly 2716)

16597 — [Anr. ed.] The psalms of David, in prose and metre: with the whole forme of discipline, and prayers, according to the church of Scotland. 8°. *Aberdene, E. Raban f. D. Melvill,* 1633. L.O.C⁴.E.M.+; F.HN. NY.PH⁵.PN².+ Cowan 53.

Cowan also notes a copy omitting Melvill's name from the psalms sub tp.

16598 — [Anr. ed.] The whole booke of psalmes, in prose & meeter. 2 pts. 16° in 8's. *Edinburgh, heires of A. Hart,* 1634. L(imp.).O.E(2, 1 imp.).; NY(imp.). Cowan 56.

16599 — [Anr. ed.] The psalmes of David in prose and meeter. With their whole tunes in foure or mo parts. Whereunto is added many godly prayers, [etc.] 2 pts. 8°. *Edinburgh, heires of A. Hart,* 1635. L.O.C²(lacks ∗⁸; w. 1st quire of Wing B 2384 substituted). D².E.+; F. HN.HD.NY.PN².+ Cowan 57.

(Formerly also 2418)

16600 — [Anr. ed.] The psalmes of David in meeter. With baptisme, the Lords Supper, [etc.] 12°. *Edinburgh, J. Wreittoun,* 1635. L².O.E.INN. Cowan 58.

16601 — [Anr. ed.] The whole book of psalmes in prose and meeter. With an exact kalendar, [etc.] 2 pts. 16° in 8's. *Edinburgh, J. Bryson,* 1640. L.C(lacks tp).E.; NY. Cowan 61.

16602 — [Anr. ed.] 12°. 1640. = 2724.

16603 — [Anr. ed.] 4°. 1640. = 2723.

16604 [A trans.] Foirm na nurrnuidheadh agas freasdal na sacramuinteadh. [*Tr.* J. Carswell.] 8°. *indún Edin, R. Lekpreuik,* 1567 (24 ap.) L(imp.).E²(imp.).; PML. Cowan 10.

The catechism is not that of Calvin.

The forme and maner of examination befoir the admission to ye table of ye Lord. 1581. *See* 11183.

16605 The forme and maner of ordaining ministers . . . used in the church of Scotland. 4°. *Edinburgh, T. Finlason,* 1620. E. Salton Kirk Library, The Manse, East Saltoun, East Lothian.

EPISCOPAL CHURCH OF SCOTLAND, BOOK OF COMMON PRAYER, 1637

16606 The booke of common prayer, and administration of the sacraments . . . for the use of the church of Scotland. (The psalter, . . . According to the last translation in king James his time.) [*Ed.* Abp. W. Laud.] 2 pts. fol. *Edinburgh, R. Young,* 1637 (1636.) L.O.C.D.E.+; F. HN.HD.N.PML.+

Quires A, C–E of the BCP are known in 2 partial or complete published settings, w. sample distinctions given below:

A3ʳ–5ᵛ; A4ᵛ line 1 ends: 'Dominus' or 'Do-'
C1ʳ–4ʳ, 5ᵛ–8ᵛ; C1ʳ last line: 'yee may' or 'ye may'
D1ʳ–8ᵛ; D1ʳ line 2 ends: 'Jeru-' or 'Jerusalem'
E3ᵛ, 6ʳ; E3ᵛ line 5 ends: 'exam-' or 'ex-'
The first are found at o²(80.b.15), the second at o⁴(Lath.R.3.18). For further details and identification of suppressed settings and proof sheets found as binding fragments, *see The Bibliotheck,* V (1967), pp. 1–23.

The Psalter is found in 2 complete settings (for the second *see* 16607). In the first, w. title as above, the title varies: line 9 has 'Pointed' (most copies) or omits this word (D, E, HD). Quire kk was intended to be in 8 leaves; kk6ᵛ has the catchword: 'Cer-

Liturgies—Other Protestant Churches—EPISCOPAL CHURCH OF SCOTLAND, BOOK OF COMMON PRAYER, 1637—*cont.*

taine'; kk7,8 are cancelled in most copies but are present in at least o(Douce C.P. d.1637) and PML.

In this and 16607, hh3 is found in 4 settings, all at o; hh3ᵛ line 1 ends: 'blot-' (orig. 16606, C.P. 1637 d.3); 'blotted' (orig. 16607, MS. Auct. V 3.17); 'he' (cancel, Douce C.P. d.1637); or 'may' (cancel, C.P. 1637 d.2).

16606a — = 16606.

16607 — [Anr. ed. of pt. 2, w. title:] The psalter, . . . After the translation set forth by authority in king James his time of blessed memory. fol. *Edinburgh, R. Young,* 1636. L.O.D.DUR.E.+; HN.CH.ILL.N.PML.+

Quire kk intended to have only 6 leaves; no catchword on kk6ᵛ. For orig. leaf hh3 *see* end of note to 16606.

16608 **Lively, Edward.** Eduardi Liuelei, . . . annotationes in quinq; priores ex minoribus prophetis. 8°. *G. Bishop,* 1587. Ent. 4 de. L.O.C.A.D.+; F.HN. Hebrew Union C.

16609 — A true chronologie of the times of the Persian monarchie. 8°. *F. Kingston f. T. Man, J. Porter, a. R. Jacson,* 1597. Ent. 17 de. L.O.C.D.E.+; F.HN.HD.N. NY.+

Lives. The lives, apprehensions . . . of the 19. late pyrates. [1609.] *See* 12805.

16610 **Livingston, Helen,** *Countess of Linlithgow.* The confession and conversion of . . . my lady C[ountess] of L[inlithgow.] 8°. *Edinburgh, J. Wreittoun,* 1629. HN.

16611 **Livingstone, William.** The conflict in conscience of Bessie Clarksone. Newly corrected. [Init. W. L.] 12°. *Edinburgh, J. Wreittoun,* 1632. L.

16611.5 **Livius, Titus.** Titi Liuij Patauini Romanae historiæ principis, libri omnes. 8°. *per E. Bollifantum,* 1589. O.C.DUR(Bamb.).M.STU.+; F.CHI(2).Y.

No colophon.

16612 — [A variant, w. colophon:] (*imp.* G. Bishop.) L.O⁸.O¹¹. C.P.; F.HN.HD. Indiana State U.

16612a — [A variant, w. colophon:] (*imp.* R. Watkins.) C.BIRM. WOR.; ILL.Y.

16612a.3 — [A variant, w. colophon:] (*imp.* J. Harison.) O(frag.). O⁵.; F.

16612a.7 — An argument, wherin the apparaile of women is both reproued and defended. (*Tr.* W. Thomas.) 8°. (*in the house of T. Berthelet,*) 1551. HD.

In tp border McK.&F. 30, dated 1534 at the bottom. A trans. of the fourth decade of Livy.

— The historie . . . of Anniball and Scipio. 1544, etc. *See* 5718 sqq.

16613 — The Romane historie. . . . Also, the breviaries of L. Florus. *Tr.* P. Holland. fol. *A. Islip,* 1600. Ent. 11 no. 1598. L.O.C.E².NEK.+; F.HN.HD.N.NY.+

Llandaff, *Bp. of. See* Field, Theophilus.

16614 **Lloyd, David.** The legend of captaine Jones. [Anon. In verse.] 4°. [*R. Young*] f. J. M[arriott,] 1631. Ent. to Marriott 26 my. L.L⁴.; HD.

16615 — [Anr. ed.] 4°. [*M. Flesher*] f. J. M[arriott,] 1636. L. NLW.; F.Y.

L copy has engr. tp from a later ed. added.

Lloyd, Evans. Almanacks. 1582, etc. *See* 480.3 sq.

Lloyd, George, *Bp. See* 10176.

Lloyd, Humphrey. *See* Llwyd, H.

Lloyd, John, *Vicar of Writtle, ed. See* 22552.
— *tr. See* 1430, 14814.

16616 **Lloyd, Lodowick.** A briefe conference of divers lawes 4°. *T. Creede,* 1602. L.O.C.E².NLW.+; F.HN.HD.LC (imp.).MCG.

16617 — Certaine Englishe verses, presented vnto the Queenes maiestie. (The triumphs of trophes.) [Init. L. L.] 4°. [*R. Ward f.*] H. Haslop, 1586. L.

Lloyd, Lodowick—*cont.*

16618   — The choyce of jewels. 4⁰. *T. Purfoot*, 1607. Ent. 22 se.
      1606. L.O.M.NLW.; F(2).HN.HD.N.ROCH.

16619   — The consent of time, disciphering the errors of the
      Grecians [etc.] 4⁰ in 8's. *G. Bishop a. R. Newberie*,
      1590. Ent. to T. Adams 14 mr. 1611. L.O.C.D².NLW.
      +; F.HN.N.NY.Y.+

16620   — An epitaph vpon the death of syr Edward Saunders
      the .19. of Nouember. 1576. [In verse.] s.sh.fol.
      H. S[ingleton] f. H. Disle, [1576] (3 de.) Ent. 3 de.
      HN.

16621   — The first part of the diall of daies, containing 320.
      Romane triumphes. 4⁰. *f. R. Ward*, 1590. L.O.C.
      NLW.P.+; F(2).HN.CHI.Y. Lehigh U.

16622   — Hilaria: or the triumphant feast for the fift of August.
      [In verse.] 4⁰. *S. Stafford*, 1607. Ent. 28 jy. O(2).;
      HN.

16623   — The iubile of Britane. 4⁰. *T. Purfoot*, 1607. Ent. 22 se.
      1606. L.O.HAT.HOLK.NLW.+; F.HN.ILL.Y.

16623a — Linceus spectacles. 4⁰. *N. Okes*, 1607. L.O.C(2).C³.
      Dedic. begins on A3ʳ, in 2 leaves.

16623a.5 — [Anr. issue, w. dedic. expanded.] L.L¹³.O.SHEF.; F.HN.
      Dedic. begins on A2ʳ, in 3 leaves.

16624   — The pilgrimage of princes. 4⁰. [*J. Charlewood a. J.
      Kingston? f.*] *W. Jones*, [1573?] L(2).O.C².CAR.NLW.;
      F.HN.HD.N.WIS.+
        Copies occur w. minor variations in quires ** and
        A.

16625   — [Anr. ed.] Newly published. 4⁰. *J. Wolfe*, 1586. L.O.C.
      NLW.PETYT.+; F.HN.N.PML.TEX.+

16626   — [Anr. ed.] 4⁰. *W. White*, 1607. L.O.E.LEEDS.NLW.+; F.
      HN.ILL.N.Y.+

16627   — The practice of policy. 4⁰. *S. Stafford*, 1604. L(imp.).
      O(2).C³(imp.).C⁵.; HN.HD.

16628   — Regum gemma e sacris bibliis desumpta. 12⁰. *ap. J.
      Windet*, [1600?] L².O.YK.; F.

16629   — [Anr. ed.] 12⁰. *ap. T. Creede*, 1602. LICH.P.; HN.

16630   — The stratagems of Jerusalem: with the martiall lawes.
      4⁰. *T. Creede*, 1602. Ent. 12 au. L.O.C.A.NLW.+; F.
      HN.CHI.HD.NY.+
        Some copies (L, F) have Latin quotation above
        device on tp.

16631   — The tragicocomedie of serpents. 4⁰. *T. Purfoot, sold by
      A. Johnson*, 1607. Ent. to T. Purfoot jun. 22 se. 1606.
      L.O.D.E².; HN.N.

16631.5 — [Anr. issue, w. imprint on cancel tp:] *T. Purfoot*, 1607.
      O.

16632   — The triplicitie of triumphes. Containing, the order,
      solempnitie and pompe, of the feastes, [etc.] 4⁰. *R.
      Jhones*, 1591 (ja.) Ent. 16 de. 159c. L(lacks dedic.)*.
      O.NLW(lacks dedic.)*.; HN.
        Dedic. signed 'Lod. Lloyd'.

16632.5 — [Anr. issue, w. prelim. leaf reset.] O.; N.Y.
        Dedic. signed 'Lodowike Lloyd'.

16633   — [Anr. issue, w. prelims. cancelled and new tp:] The
      order, solemnitie, and pompe, .. upon the nativities
      of emperours. [Anon.] *London*, 1610. L.; F.HN.HD.
        The cancel tp was prob. pr. by W. White; *see*
        16675.

16634 **Lloyd, Richard.** A briefe discourse of the . . . actes and
      conquests of the nine worthies. [In verse.] 4⁰. *R.
      Warde*, 1584. O.

      Lloyd, Robert, *tr. See* 6639, 6671.

      Lluhsnym, Yarffeg. *See* Mynshul, G.

16635 **Llwyd, Humphrey.** Angliæ regni florentissimi noua
      descriptio. [*Printed abroad,*] 1573.
        Not an STC item.

16636   — The breuiary of Britayne. Englished by T. Twyne,
      1573. 8⁰. (*R. Johnes*,) [1573.] L.O.C.G².NLW.+; F.
      HN.HD.LC.N.+

16637   — Cambriæ typus. [*Printed abroad*, n.d.]
        Not an STC item.
      — *tr. See* 4606, 14651.5, 24595.
      — *See* also 20309.

16638 **Llyfr Plygain.** Llyfer plygain sef Christianu ddiaeth.
      16⁰ in 8's. [*E. Alldc*] *dros E. White*, 1612. Ent. to T.
      Chard 8 oc. 1599; ass'd to E. White, sen., 19 oc.
      1607. HN.

16639   — [Anr. ed.] 16⁰ in 8's. *dros E. White*, 1618. NLW
      (21 leaves only).

Llyfr Plygain—*cont.*

16640   — [Anr. ed.] 16⁰. *J. Beale*, 1633. Ass'd by widow Chard
      to Beale 10 oc. 1622; by widow White to Ed. Allde
      29 jn. 1624; by Eliz. Allde to J. Beale 1 ap. 1629. C³.
      Collates B–G¹⁶; B5ʳ catchword: 'Ebrill'.

16640.5 — [Anr. ed.] 16⁰. *J. Beale*, 1633. NLW(photostat only).
      Weimar U(missing).
      Collates B–G¹⁶; B5ʳ catchword: 'Ebril'.

16641   — [Anr. ed.] 16⁰ in 8's. [*J. Beale*, c. 1635.] NLW(lacks
      tp).
      Collates A–K⁸.

16641.3 — [Anr. ed.] 16⁰ in 8's. [*J. Beale?* c. 1640.] NLW(imp.).
      Collates A–B⁸ C⁴; A–H⁸.

16641.5 **Loarte, Gaspare.** The exercise of a christian life. Written
      in Italian. *Tr.* J. S(ancer [*pseud.*, i.e. S. Brinkley.])
      8⁰. [*W. Carter*, 1579.] L.L².DE.YK².; F(lacks tp).
      A.&R. 462.

16641.7 — [Anr. ed.] Newly perused and corected. With certaine
      deuout exercises and prayers added. 12⁰ ⁸·⁴. [*Rouen,
      R. Parsons' Press*,] 1584. L.O.C.W.YK.+; F.ILL.Y.
      (Formerly 16643) A.&R. 463.

16642   — [Anr. ed.] 8⁰. [*Fr. Garnet's second press?* 1596–97.] L.
      O.AMP.OS.ST.+; F.
      A.&R. 464.

16643   — Now = 16641.7.

16644   — [Anr. ed.] *Tr.* by S. B. 8⁰. [*S. Omer, English College
      Press*,] 1610. L.C².A².AUG.ST.
      A.&R. 465.

16644.5 — [A protestant adaptation.] The exercise of a christian
      life, written by G. L(oarte.) Being the first ground
      whence the two treatises [19355, 19380] were made
      by R. P(ersons.) [*Ed.* and *tr.* by Mr. Banister, son of
      J. Banister.] 8⁰. (*P. Short*) *f. W. Leake*, 1594. Ent.
      14 se. L.; HN.HD.
        Based on same original as preceding, but very
        differently interpreted.

16645   — The exercise of a christian life. Written by Lewis de
      Granada. 1634. Now = 16922a.7.

16645.3 — The godlie garden of Gethsemani, furnished with
      holsome fruites of meditacion & prayer. [Anon. *Tr.*]
      16⁰ in 8's. [*W. Carter*, c. 1576.] L(imp.).OS(imp.).
      A.&R. 466. Collates **⁴ A–S⁸+?

16645.5 — [Anr. ed.] 16⁰ in 8's. [*W. Carter*, c. 1580.] M⁴(imp.).;
      F.
      (Formerly 11803a) A.&R. 467. Collates A–S⁸. In
      title: 'godly'.

16645.7 — [Anr. ed.] Meditations, of the life and passion of our
      lord Jesus Christ. By G. Loart. 16⁰ in 8's. [*Fr.
      Garnet's second press*, 1596–98.] O.
      (Formerly 16648) A.&R. 468.

16646   — Instructions and aduertisements, how to meditate the
      misteries of the rosarie. *Tr.* [J. Fen.] 8⁰. [*W. Carter*,
      1579.] L.O.C⁹.OS.SN.+; F.HN.Y.
      A.&R. 469.

16647   — [Anr. ed.] Wher unto is annexed meditations for the
      evenings, and mornings, of the weeke. 12⁰. *Rouen,
      C. Hamillon*, 1613. L.L⁴².O⁵.DE(imp.).OS.
      A.&R. 470.

16648   — Meditations. Now = 16645.7.

16649 **L'Obel, Matthias de.** Balsami, opobalsami, carpobal-
      sami, & xylobalsami, cum suo cortice explanatio. 4⁰.
      A. Hatfield, imp. J. Norton, 1598. L(2).O.C.C⁹.; HD.
      NLM.

16650   — Matthiae de L'Obel . . . in G. Rondelletii . . . Pharma-
      ceuticam officinam animaduersiones. 1605. Now =
      19595.5.

16650.5 — Perfuming of tabacco, and the great abuse committed
      in it. *Tr.* I. N[asmith] G. 4⁰. *W. Stansby*, 1611. NY.
      — Stirpium aduersaria noua. 1570. *See* 19595.

      Lochinvar. *See* 12069.

      Locke, Henry. *See* Lok, H.

16651 **Lockyer, Nicholas.** Christs communion with his church
      militant. 8⁰. *E. G[riffin] f. J. Rothwell*, 1640. C. D.

16652   — A divine discovery of sincerity. 8⁰. *E. G[riffin] f. J.
      Rothwell*, 1640. Ent. 29 ap. L.O²⁸(Bed.).C.C¹⁰.A.; F.
      HN.HD.PN².U.

16653 **Lodge, Thomas.** An alarum against vsurers. Containing
      tryed experiences against worldly abuses. 4⁰. *T. Este
      f. S. Clarke*, 1584. Ent. 4 no. 1583. L(imp.).O.; F
      (lacks tp).HN.HD(imp.).

Lodge, Thomas—*cont.*

16654 — Catharos. Diogenes in his singularitie. By T. L. of Lincolns Inne, Gent. 1591. 4°. *W. Hoskins & J. Danter f. J. Busbie*, [1591.] Ent. to H. Chettle 17 se. 1591. L.O.; F.HN.HD.

16655 — The diuel conjured. [Init. T. L.] 4°. *A. Islip f. W. Mats*, 1596. L.O.C². ; F.HN.HD.PFOR.Y.

16656 — Euphues shadow, the battaile of the sences. Hereunto is annexed the deafe mans dialogue. By T. L. Gent. 4°. *A. Jeffes f. J. Busbie*, 1592. Ent. to Busbie a. N. Ling 17 fb. L.C².CAR.; F.HN(imp.).Y.

16657 — The famous, true and historicall life of Robert second duke of Normandy, surnamed Robin the diuell. By T. L. G. 4°. [*T. Orwin*] *f. N. L*[*ing*] *a. J. Busbie*, 1591. HN.
 Based on 21070.

16658 — A fig for Momus: containing pleasant varietie. [In verse.] 4°. [*J. Orwin*] *f. C. Knight*, 1595. Ent. 2 ap. L.O.; F.HN.HD.PFOR.

16659 — The life and death of william Long beard. By T. L. of Lincolns Inne, Gent. 4°. *R. Yardley a. P. Short*, 1593. L⁸(imp.).O(lacks dedic.).; HD.
 Title found in 2 states: with (HD) or without (L⁸, O) a Latin motto.

16660 — A margarite of America. 4°. [*A. Jeffes*] *f. J. Busbie*, 1596. L(2).O.
 — A most pleasant historie of Glaucus and Scilla. 1610. *See* 16675.

16661 — Paradoxes against common opinion. 1602. Now = 6467.5.

16662 — Phillis: honoured with pastorall sonnets. Where-vnto is annexed, the tragicall complaynt of Elstred. 4°. [*J. Roberts*] *f. J. Busbie*, 1593. L.C²(imp.).E².; F(imp.).HN.
 B1, cancelled in most copies, is present in HN. Sheets H–L prob. by a second pr.

16662a — Prosopopeia: containing the teares of the holy, Marie. [Dedic. init. T. L.] 8°. [*T. Scarlet*] *f. E. White*, 1596. L².

16662b — [Anr. issue, w. dedic. init. L. T., omitting 'containing' from title.] O.E².

16663 — [Begins A1ʳ:] Protogenes can know Apelles by his line [etc. A defence of poetry, music, and stage plays in answer to 12097. Anon.] 8°. [*H. Singleton?* 1579.] O.; HN.

16664 — Rosalynde. Euphues golden legacie. 4°. *T. Orwin f. T. G*[*ubbin*] *a. J. Busbie*, 1590. Ent. to Busbie a. N. Ling 6 oc. F(imp.).PFOR.

16665 — [Anr. ed.] 4°. *A. Jeffes f. T. G*[*ubbin*] *a. J. Busbie*, 1592. L.O(2).

16666 — [Anr. ed.] 4°. [*A. Jeffes*] *f. N. Lyng a. T. Gubbins*, 1596. L(imp.).; HN.

16667 — [Anr. ed.] 4°. [*V. Simmes*] *f. N. Lyng a. T. Gubbins*, 1598. F.HN.

16668 — [Anr. ed.] 4°. *J. R*[*oberts*] *f. N. Lyng*, 1604. Wroclaw U.; HN. Pirie(lacks tp).

16668a — [A ghost.]

16669 — [Anr. ed.] 4°. [*J. Windet*] *f. J. Smethwick*, 1609. Ent. 19 no. 1607. L.O.C².; F.

16670 — [Anr. ed.] Euphues golden legacie. [*W. Stansby*] *f. J. Smethwick*, 1612. L.C².E².; F.PML.

16671 — = 16673.

16672 — [Anr. ed.] 4°. *f. J. Smethwick*, 1623. L⁶.O.C².E².; F.HN. Hickmott.

16673 — [Anr. ed.] 4°. *f. J. Smethwicke*, 1634. L(2). Lord Latymer.; F.HN.BO.
 One L copy (formerly 16671) has the date altered in ink to 1614.

16673.5 — [A variant, w. imprint:] *f. Francis Smethwicke*, 1634. PFOR.
 A genuine imprint although not transferred to F. Smethwick until 24 Aug. 1642 (E.&R. I.50).

16674 — Scillaes metamorphosis: enterlaced with the vnfortunate loue of Glaucus. [In verse.] 4°. [*T. Orwin f.*] *R. Jhones*, 1589. Ent. to Jones a. T. Lodge 22 se. L⁶.O(imp.).; F.HN.
 Tp varies: 1st 2 words of title in 1 line (F, HN) or 2 lines (L⁶, O, 16674.5).

16674.5 — [A variant, w. date:] 1590. L.; PFOR.

16675 — [Anr. issue, w. cancel tp:] A most pleasant historie of Glaucus and Scilla. *London*, 1610. HD.
 For two other Jones remainders reissued this year, prob. by W. White, *see* 7200, 16633.

16676 — A treatise of the plague. 4°. [*T. Creede a. V. Simmes*] *f. E. White a. N. L*[*ing*], 1603. L.O.C.E².LINC.+; F.HN. HD(tp mutilated).NLM.PFOR.

Lodge, Thomas—*cont.*

16677 — Wits miserie, and the worlds madnesse. 4°. *A. Islip, sold by C. Burby*, 1596. L(2, 1 imp.).O(3).O³(imp.). C².; F.HN.HD.NY.PFOR.+
 One O copy has tp reading 'Wils'.

16678 — The wounds of ciuill war. Liuely set forth in the true tragedies of Marius and Scilla. 4°. *J. Danter, sold* [*by A. Kitson or R. Bankworth*,] 1594. Ent. to Danter 24 my. L.L⁶.O.SHEF.VER.+; F.HN.HD.ILL (imp.).PFOR.+ Greg 122.
 — *ed. See* 5432, 21002.
 — *tr. See* 14809, 16901, 16916.3, 21666, 22213.

16679 **Lodge, Thomas**, and **Greene, Robert**. A looking glasse for London and England. 4°. *T. Creede, sold by W. Barley*, 1594. Ent. to Creed 5 mr. HN. Robert Taylor. Greg 118.

16680 — [Anr. ed.] 4°. *T. Creede, solde by W. Barley*, 1598. L. O(2).; HN.

16681 — [Anr. ed.] 4°. *T. Creede f. T. Pavier*, 1602. Ent. to Pavier 14 au. 1600. L.

16681.5 — [Anr. ed.] 4°. [*R. Blower*, 1605?] CHI(lacks tp).

16682 — [Anr. ed.] 4°. *B. Alsop*, 1617. L(2).L⁶.O.C⁶.PETWORTH.; F.HN.HD.PFOR.SUNY(Buffalo).+

16683 **Loe, William**, *the Elder*. Come and see. The blisse of brightest beautie: shining out of Sion. 4°. *R. Field f. M. Law*, 1614. L.G².GLOUC.WI.; F.U.

16684 — = 16690.

16685 — The joy of Jerusalem: and woe of the worldlings. A sermon. 8°. *T. Haveland f. C. Knight a. J. Harrison*, [*sold by C. Knight*,] 1609. Ent. 25 se. L.L¹⁵.YK.; F(2, 1 imp.).

16686 — The kings shoe. Made, and ordained to trample on, Edomites. A sermon. October the ninth, 1622. 4°. *J. L*[*egat*] *f. W. Sheffard*, 1623. Ent. 16 no. 1622. L.L³.O.C.PLUME.+; F.N.U.

16687 — Now = 16691.5.

16688 — The merchant reall. [A sermon.] 4°. *Hamboroughe, P. Lang*, 1620. O.C.C⁸. Hamburg, Staats- und Universitätsbibliothek.

16689 — The mysterie of mankind, made into a manual. 12°. *B. Alsop f. G. Fayerbeard*, 1619. Ent. 18 ja. O.PLUME. Hamburg, Staats- und Universitätsbibliothek.; F.

16690 — [Headline †4ʳ:] Songs of Sion. [In verse.] 12°. [*Hamburg*, 1620.] L(imp.).O(imp.).DUL(imp.).; HN(imp.).
 (Formerly also 16684) Apparently issued without a tp. Dated Hamburg, 24 Jan. 1620 on B1ʳ.

16691 — Vox clamantis. Mark. 1. 3. A stil voice, to the three thrice-honourable estates of parliament. 4°. *T. S*[*nodham*] *f. J. Teage*, 1621. Ent. 12 mr. L.O.C.C³.; HN.BO.HD.N.U.+

16691.5 **Loe, William**, *the Younger*. The merchants manuell, being a step to stedfastnesse. 12°. *A. M*[*athewes*] *f. T. Walkley*, 1628. Ent. 30 oc. 1627. L.
 (Formerly 16687)

Loeaecheus, Andreas. *See* 17894.

16692 **Loeus, Robertus**. Effigiatio veri sabbathismi. 4°. [*Eliot's Court Press f.*] *J. Norton*, 1605. Ent. 5 jn. L.O.C.D. E².+; HD.LC.

Logarithms. Logarithmorum chilias prima. [1617.] *See* 3741.

Logica. Logicæ artis compendium. 1615. *See* 21701.

16693 **Logici.** [Begins A2ʳ:] [Q]Voniā ex t'mis [etc.] 4° in 6's. [*Oxford, T. Rood*, 1483?] L(3 leaves).O¹¹(lacks B3,4). O¹⁴.C²(27 leaves).R(frag.).+; HD(1 leaf).Y(1 leaf). Duff 277.

16694 **Logie, Andrew.** Cum bono deo. Raine from the clouds. 4°. *Aberdene, E. Raban*, 1624. L.O.C.D.E.+; F.HN.

16695 **Lohetus, Daniel.** Sorex primus oras chartarum primi libri de republica ecclesiastica corrodens. 8°. *ap. J. Billium*, 1618. L².O.C.D.E².+; HD.

16695.5 **Loiseau de Tourval, Jean.** [Heading A1ʳ:] Summus dux, cum duce redux. [On Prince Charles and the Duke of Buckingham's visit to Paris, Feb. 1623. Init. I. L. Turvallius. In verse.] 4°. [*W. Stansby*, 1623?] L(1040.m.40(4*)).
 — *tr. See* 4752.

Lok, Anne, *tr. See* 4450.

16696 **Lok, Henry.** Ecclesiastes, otherwise called the preacher. Abridged, and dilated in English poesie. Whereunto are annexed sundrie sonets. 4° in 8's. *R. Field,* 1597. Ent. 11 no. 1596. L.L².O.C.P.; F.HN.HD(imp.).NY.Y. (Formerly also 2765) Includes a reprint of 16697. The L² copy has the complimentary sonnets at the end cancelled and the one addressed to Abp. J. Whitgift pr. on a special leaf, facing the tp.

16697 — Sundry christian passions contained in two hundred sonnets. [Init. H. L.] 16° in 8's. *R. Field,* 1593. Ent. 2 my. HN.NY.Y.
Reprinted in 16696.

Lok, Michael, *tr. See* 650, 810.5.

16698 **Lomazzo, Giovanni Paolo.** A tracte containing the artes of curious paintinge [etc.] Englished by R. H(aydocke.) fol. (*Oxford, Jos. Barnes f. R. H[aydock,]* 1598.) Ent. to John Barnes a. ass'd to Roger Jackson 16 oc. 1619. L.O.C.G².M.+; F.HN.HD.N.NY.+

Lon, Henry. Almanacks. 1554, etc. *See* 481 sqq.

16699 **Loncq, Hendrik Cornelius.** A true relation of the vanquishing of the towne Olinda. Also a map. [*Tr.*] 4°. *Amstelredam, J. F. Stam,* 1630. L.; CB. 𝕬

Londius, Thomas. Utrum episcopus Romanus. 1602. *See* 21555.8.

London.

ORDERS AND REGULATIONS

16700 — The decree for tythes to be payed in London. fol. *T. Berthelet,* 1546. L.

16701 — [Anr. ed.] 8°. (*J. Cawood,*) 1546 [1554.] L.

16702 — [Anr. ed.] M.D.LXXX. 8°. (*T. East*) *f. G. Cawood,* [1580.] L.L²(2).BRISTOL.; F.

16703 — [Anr. ed.] 8°. [*J. Windet f.*] *J. Wolfe,* 1596. L⁸.L²².L³⁰.

16703.5 — [Anr. ed.] 4°. *J. Wolfe,* 1596 [*Oxford, H. Hall,* c. 1662.] C⁵.D².DUR³. Finedon.
Perhaps = pt. of Wing W 654.

16704 — [Anr. ed.] 8°. [*J. Roberts?*] *f. G. Cawood,* 1597. O(tp only, Douce Add.142/218.).D.; HN.

16704.1 — By the mayre. [of London; against forestalling and regrating.] s.sh.fol. [*E. Whitchurch?* c. 1550.] L² (complete, Frag. No. 13).

16704.3 — Orders taken, and enacted, for orphans and their porcions. 8°. (*J. Cawood,*) 1551. L².L⁸.; HN.
(Formerly 18843a) *See also* 16706.7, 16708.

— The order of the hospitalls of K. Henry . . . and K. Edward. 1557 [c. 1690.] *See* Wing O 389.

16704.6 — The lawes of the markette, anno 1.5.62. 8°. (*J. Cawoode,*) [1562.] HN.
See also 16717, 16727.9.

16704.7 — An admonition to be redde in the churches of the citie and subburbes of London, by the pastours and ministers of the same. [From the Bp. of London, E. Grindal, by order of the Privy Council regarding provisions against the plague. 4 Mar. 1563 (o.s.)] s.sh.fol. *W. Seres,* [1564.] M(deposit).

16704.9 — Wyllyam Cecill knight, high Stewarde [etc. Regulations for Westminster regarding the plague. 12 Mar. 1563 (o.s.)] s.sh.fol. *R. Jugge,* [1564.] L⁵. Cr. 591.
(Formerly 7971) *See also* 16723.

16705 — By the maior. [Orders for cleansing the streets.] s.sh.fol. *J. Daye,* [1564.] O².

16705.3 — By the maior of London. [Proclamation regarding the lottery of 1567.] s.sh.fol. *H. Bynneman,* 1567 (13 se.) HD.
See also 8000, 8000.7, etc.

16705.7 — The ordre of my lorde mayor, the aldermen & the shiriffes, for their metings throughout the yeare. 8°. *J. Daye,* 1568. HN.
See also 16718.7, 16728, 16729.4, 16730 sq.

16706 — By the maior. [It is ordered that all poulters observe these prices.] s.sh.fol. *J. Daye,* 1572 (5 ap.) O.

16706.3 — For the alderman of the warde. Meanes deuised for better execution of the statute for reliefe of the poore in London. 1/2 sh.fol. *J. Daye,* [1572.] L⁵ (Lemon 64).
Possibly issued w. 9187.6.

16706.7 — O⟨rders⟩ taken, ⟨and enac⟩ted, for ⟨orphans.⟩ 8°. *J. Daye,* 1575. L(imp.).
See also 16704.3, 16708.

16707 — By the mayor. [Order directing all commodities to be sold only in the public market.] fol(2). *J. Day,* [1576.] O.

16707.1 — Articles to be enquired of, [etc. Orders regarding the plague. Oct. 1577.] 1/2 sh.fol. [*J. Day,* 1577.] L⁵. Cr. 723.
(Formerly 8097) *See also* 16723.

16707.3 — Articles concerning the deliuery of the Bibles mentioned in the peticion of C. Barker. [6 Oct. 1578.] 1/2 sh.fol. [*C. Barker,* 1578.] L⁵(Lemon 70).
For the petition *see* 1417.5.

16708 — Orders taken & enacted, for orphans. 8°. (*T. East*) *f. G. Cawood,* [1580.] L.O(2, 1 lacks tp).
See also 16704.3.

16708.5 — Commune consilium [etc. Act regarding the freeing of apprentices before their terms expire. 1 June 1526.] s.sh.fol. *J. Daye,* [c. 1580.] L⁸(Records Office).
See also 16727.3.

16709 — Orders appointed to bee executed in the citie of London, for setting roges and idle persons to work. 4°. *J. Daye,* [1582.] L⁸.D².; F.TEX.
See also 16712, 16718.6.

16710 — By the maior. When I and my brethren the aldermen, . . . [Order regulating the price of firewood.] s.sh.fol. *J. Daye,* [1584] (20 jy.) L.

16711 — Wolstan Dixey maior. The abridgement of an acte of Common Counsel, 2 July, 1586, for the better seruice of hir maiestie in her cariage for better gouernement of cartes, carters, carres and carre men. 8°. [*London, R. Waldegrave?* 1586.] L⁸(imp.).

16712 — Orders appointed to be executed in the cittie of London, for setting roges and idle persons to worke. 4°. [*J. Charlewood?* f.] *H. Singleton,* [1587?] L.O(2).; HN.HD.
There is a c. 1750 type facsimile, copies at L, L⁴⁷, CU. *See also* 16709.

16713 — An acte of Common Councell [regarding 'hallage' dues by cloth-buyers, etc. 10 Nov. 1587.] s.sh.fol. *H. Singleton,* [1587.] L.
See also 16716, 16719, 16728.7, 16732.

16713.5 — An order to be published by the Lord Maior, for auoyding of beggars. [17 Apr. 1593.] s.sh.fol. *H. Singleton,* [1593.] O². Cr. 859.
(Formerly 8228) Line 4 of title: 'statutes'; *see* 16727.5.

16714 — Now = 16727.5.

16715 — Retailing brokers. Commune concilium [etc. Act for reforming abuses by them.] fol(3). [*J. Windet f.*] *J. Wolfe,* 1595. O.

16716 — By the mayor. Orders for Blackwellhall. fol(3). [*J. Windet f. J. Wolfe?* 1595.] L(impr. cropt).
See also 16713.

16717 — The lawes of the market. 8°. [*J. Windet f.*] *J. Wolfe,* 1595. O.
See also 16704.6.

16718 — Now = 16727.9.

16718.3 — By the Mayor. Forasmuch as all transgressors. . . . [Ordinance regarding the keeping of watch and ward, payment of taxes, etc. by non-citizens.] fol(2). [*J. Windet,* c. 1595.] L(Harl.5943/61–2).

16718.5 — [Heading:] Generall matters to be remembred of the lord maior, throughout the whole yeare. 8°. [*J. Windet,* c. 1600.] L⁸.

16718.6 — By the maior. To all constables. . . . [Order for the execution of the statute against rogues and vagabonds. 30 Sept. 1603.] s.sh.fol. *J. Windet,* [1603.] L⁸.
See also 16709.

16718.7 — The order of my lord mayor, the aldermen, and the sheriffs, for their meetings. 8°. *J. Windet,* 1604. L⁸.
See also 16705.7.

16719 — By the maior. Orders set downe for Blackewelhall. [29 Nov. 1604.] fol(3). *J. Windet,* [1604.] L.L⁸.
See also 16713.

16720 — [A collection of acts and reports of Common Council dated 1606–40. *Printed, post-1640.*]
Not an STC book.

16721 — By the maior. Orders . . . concerning the rates of cariages. [25 Nov. 1606.] fol(3). *J. Windet,* [1606.] L.

16722 — By the mayor. An act of Common Councell, prohibiting all strangers to use any trades, within this citty. [15 Apr. 1606.] fol(3). *J. Windet,* 1606. L.

London—Orders and Regulations—*cont.*

16723 — Orders conceived and thought fit, as well by the Lord Maior . . . to be observed in the time of the infection of the plague. fol(2). *J. Windet,* 1608. HN.
    See also 16704.9, 16707.1, 16723.5, 16729.1, 16729.3, 16731.

16723.5 — Orders conceived and agreed to be published, . . . by the lord mayor and aldermen [regarding the plague.] fol(4?). *J. Windet,* [1608?] HD(3 sheets only, lacking at least 1 before the 2nd sheet).
    See also 16723.

16724 — M. T[homas] C[ambell] 1610. [Proclamation specifying the true measure of colliers' sacks.] s.sh.fol. [*W. Jaggard,* 1609.] L.
    As Cambell was Lord Mayor in 1608–9, the proclamation is post-dated.

16724.5 — Commune conciliū [etc.] An acte for the reformation of apparell to be worne by prentices. [21 Jan. 1611.] s.sh.fol. *W. Jaggard,* [1611.] L⁸(Records Office).

16725 — Commune consilium [etc.] Whereas the company of painter-stainers . . . [Act requiring membership in the company. 11 July 1612.] s.sh.fol. [*W. Jaggard,* 1612.] L⁸.

16725.3 — M. T[homas] M[iddleton] Where, in all well-governed kingdomes, . . . care have ever beene had . . . that breade, meats, . . . should bee good. fol(3). *W. Jaggard,* [1613.] HN.

16725.7 — I[ohn] I[olles] By the major. Whereas divers good acts and ordinances [etc. Proclamation regarding prices of ale, etc.] fol(2). *W. Jaggard,* [1615.] O¹⁵.

16726 — Now = 16728.7.

16727 — An acte for the reformation of divers abuses in the wardmote inquest. 12°. *W. Jaggard,* 1617. L(2).L⁸.
    See also 16729.5, 16731.7, 16736.5, 16737.

16727.1 — By the maior. A proclamation for reformation of abuses, in the gaole of New-gate. [23 Sept. 1617.] fol(2). *W. Jaggard,* 1617. L⁸(Records Office).
    See also 16733.3.

16727.3 — Commune concilium. [etc. Act regarding the freeing of apprentices before their terms expire. 1 June 1526.] s.sh.fol. *W. Jaggard,* 1617. L⁸(Records Office).
    See also 16708.5.

16727.5 — An order to be published by the lord maior, for auoyding of beggers. [17 Apr. 1593.] s.sh.fol. *H. Singleton* [*B. Norton a. J. Bill,* 1618?] L.O.; F.HD. Cr. 858.
    (Formerly 8227 and 16714) Line 4 of title: 'statues [*sic*]'; *see* 16713.5.

16727.7 — By the major. A proclamation for the prices of tallow and candles. [14 Sept. 1620.] s.sh.fol. *W. Jaggard,* 1620. O¹⁵.; HN.

16727.9 — The lawes of the market. 8°. *W. Jaggard,* 1620. L⁸.; CH.HD.
    (Formerly 16718) *See also* 16704.6.

16728 — The order of my lord maior, the aldermen, and the sheriffs, for their meetings. 8°. *W. Jaggard,* 1621. O.
    See also 16705.7.

16728.3 — Commune consilium [etc.] An act for reformation of the negligences of constables. [7 Apr. 1621.] fol(2). *W. Jaggard,* [1621.] HN.
    See also 16729.9.

16728.5 — Commune consilium [etc.] Whereas by a common councell holden the ninth day of Aprill, . . . an act was made, for prevention of theft, [etc. 19 June 1622.] s.sh.fol. *W. Jaggard,* 1622. HN.

16728.7 — E[dward] B[arkham] M[ayor] Commune concilium [etc. Orders regarding Blackwell-hall. 3 Oct. 1622.] fol(2). *W. Jaggard,* [1622.] L.
    (Formerly 16726) *See also* 16713.

16728.9 — An acte of common councell, concerning the preservation and clensing of the river of Thames. s.sh.fol. *I. Jaggard,* [1623?] L⁸(Records Office).

16729 — Orders conceived and published concerning the infection of plague. [1665.] = Wing O 397.

16729.1 — Orders to be used in the time of the infection of the plague within the citie of London, till further charitable provision may be had. fol(2). *I. Jaggard,* 1625. L.
    See also 16723.

16729.2 — I[ohn] G[oare] M[ayor] By the maior. Whereas the infection of the plague is daily dispersed more & more in divers parts of this city [etc. 5 Apr. 1625.] s.sh.fol. *I. Jaggard,* 1625. L.

London—Orders and Regulations—*cont.*

16729.3 — Orders [regarding the plague] heeretofore conceived and agreed to bee published, . . . now revived. fol(4?). [*I. Jaggard,* 1625.] L(1st 3 sheets only, dated in MS. 30 Apr. 1625).
    See also 16723.

16729.4 — [The order of my lord mayor, the alderman, and the sheriffs for their meetings.] 8°. [*I. Jaggard?* c. 1625.] O(quire B only).
    No marginal note on B5ᵛ; *see* 16730 sq. *See also* 16705.7.

16729.5 — Commune concilium [etc. Order for the reformation of abuses in electing the foreman of the wardmote inquests. 8 Oct. 1617.] s.sh.fol. *R. Young,* 1628. L⁸(Records Office).
    See also 16727, 16737.

16729.7 — Commune concilium [etc. When St. Thomas's day falls on Sunday, wardmotes are to be conducted on the following Monday. 16 Dec. 1617.] s.sh.fol. *R. Young,* 1628. L⁸(Records Office).

16729.9 — Commune concilium [etc.] An act for the reformation of the negligences of constables. [7 Apr. 1621.] fol(2). *R. Young,* 1628. L⁸(Records Office).
    See also 16728.3.

16730 — The order of my lord mayor, the aldermen, and the sheriffes, for their meetings. 8°. *R. Young,* 1629. L.L⁸.
    B5ᵛ marginal note: 'Cappe'; *see* 16729.4. *See also* 16705.7.

16730.5 — [Anr. issue, w. quire B partly reset.] c³. Phillipps 2702.; HD.
    B5ᵛ marginal note: 'Capp'.

16731 — By the mayor. [Orders regarding the plague. 22 Apr. 1630.] s.sh.fol. *R. Young,* 1630. L⁵.
    See also 16723.

16731.3 — Commune concilium [etc. Order regarding the election of constables. 31 Aug. 1621.] fol(2). *R. Young,* 1630. L⁸(Records Office).
    See also 16729.9, 16737.7.

16731.5 — Anno primo Iacobi regis. An act for the charitable reliefe and ordering of persons infected with the plague. fol(2). *R. Young,* 1630. HD.

16731.7 — By the mayor. [Charge for wardmotes.] fol(3). *R. Young,* [c. 1630.] L⁸(Records Office).
    See also 16727.

16732 — Commune concilium [etc.] An act . . . touching bringing of commodities to Blackwell-hall and Leaden-hall. [20 July 1631.] fol(3). *R. Young,* 1631. L.
    See also 16713.

16733 — Commune concilium [etc.] An act . . . for the reformation of sundry abuses practised upon the common markets. [20 July 1631.] fol(2). *R. Young,* 1631. L.L⁵.

16733.3 — Orders devised and agreed upon 7 March 1632 [o.s.], for and concerning the good government of the gaole of Newgate. fol(2?). [*R. Young,* 1633?] L⁸ (Records Office, 1st sheet only).
    See also 16727.1.

16733.7 — By the mayor. Whereas [etc. Order for observing established rates for poultry (16734.) 7 Jan. 1633 (o.s.)] s.sh.fol. *R. Young,* [1634.] L.L⁸.O².
    (Formerly 16736)

16734 — By the mayor. [Table of] Rates and prices of all sorts of poultry. [7 Jan. 1633 (o.s.)] fol(2). *R. Young,* [1634.] L.L⁸.RD.

16735 — By the mayor. A proclamation concerning the prices of butter and candles. [21 Feb. 1633 (o.s.)] fol(2). [*R. Young?* 1634.] O²(1st sheet only).O¹⁵.

16736 — Now = 16733.7.

16736.5 — The articles of the charge of the wardmote inquest. fol(3). *R. Young,* [c. 1635.] L⁸(Records Office).
    See also 16727.

16737 — Commune concilium [etc. Order for the reformation of abuses in electing the foreman of the wardmote inquests. 8 Oct. 1617.] s.sh.fol. *R. Young,* 1637. O.
    See also 16727, 16729.5.

16737.3 — Commune concilium [etc. Order regarding the election of aldermen and sheriffs. 19 Dec. 1639.] s.sh.fol. [*R. Young?* 1639?] L⁸(Records Office).

16737.7 — Commune concilium [etc. Order regarding the election of constables. 31 Aug. 1621.] fol(2). *R. Young,* 1640. L⁸(Records Office).
    See also 16731.3.

16738 — The articles of the charge of the wardmote enquest. [1649.] = Wing A 3870.

London—*cont.*

BILLS OF MORTALITY

Yearly

16738.5 — [Heading E1ʳ:] The number of all those that hath dyed in the citie of London, & the liberties from the 28, of December 1581. vnto the 27, of December 1582. 8°. [*J. Charlewood, after 1582.*] L⁸(quire E only, GL 3948).
        This is not an official bill, and the work of which it is a section has not been identified. It is prob. based on information gathered by John Stow.

16739 — The true copie of all the burials and christenings [13–20 Oct. 1603, etc.] Now = 16743.9, nos. 14, 16.

16739.5 — 1602. 1603. A true report of all the burials and christnings within London from the 23. of December, 1602. to the 22. of December, 1603. s.sh.fol. *J. Windet*, [1603.] Ent. 1 au. 1603. HN.HD.
        Royal arms without 'I R'.

16739.7 — [Anr. ed.] s.sh.fol. *J. Windet*, [1603.] L.
        Royal arms with 'I R'.

16740 — 1602. 1603. A true report. . . . (1624. 1625. A true report . . . 22 December, 1624. to 23. December, 1625.) 2 pts. s.sh.fol. *W. Stansby*, [1625.] Ass'd to Stansby 11 se. 1611. o(impr. mutilated).
        Royal arms alone at top.

16740.5 — [Anr. ed. of pt. 1:] 1602. 1603. A true report. . . . s.sh.fol. *W. Stansby*, [1625.] L⁸.
        Has both royal arms and arms of London at top.

16741 — 1624. 1625. A generall or great bill for this yeere, . . . 16. December, 1624. to 15. December 1625. s.sh.fol. *W. Stansby*, 1625. L⁸.L¹¹(S.P.D., Chas. I, vol. 11, doc. 70).

16741.3 — A generall or great bill 20. December 1624 to 22 December 1625. s.sh.fol. [*London, 1625.*] L⁸.
        Possibly a piracy.

16741.7 — A generall or great bill for . . . Westminster, Lambeth, Newington, Stepney, Hackney, and Islington: 30. December, 1624. to 22. December, 1625. s.sh.fol. *W. Stansby*, 1625. L⁵(Lemon 267).L⁸.L¹¹(S.P.D., Chas. I, vol. 12, doc. 39).o.C²⁶(CUR 54(9), imp.).
        (Formerly 25287)

16742 — A generall bill for this present yeere, ending the 17 of December 1629. s.sh.fol. *R. Hodgkinson*, [1629.] L⁸. L¹⁸(Forster).

Note: The following annual bills are all s.sh.fol. and all printed at the Parish Clerks' Press, by R. Hodgkinson in 1630–33 and T. Cotes in 1636. *See* James Christie, *Some Account of Parish Clerks*, 1893, pp. 187–8.

16743 — A generall bill for this present yeere, ending the 16 of December 1630. s.sh.fol. [*Parish Clerks' Press, 1630.*] L(MS. Egerton 2645, f. 234).L⁸.L¹⁸(Forster).
    — — 15 Dec. 1631. L⁸.L¹⁸(Forster).
    — — 20 Dec. 1632. L⁸.L¹⁸(Forster).
    — — 19 Dec. 1633. L⁸.
    — — 18 Dec. 1634. L⁸.
    — — 17 Dec. 1635. L⁸.
    — — 15 Dec. 1636. L⁸.

Part of the Year

16743.1 — A generall bill for 8. weeks . . . from the 14. of July, 1603. to the 8. day of September 1603. s.sh.fol. *J. Windet*, [1603.] HD.

16743.2 — A true bill of the whole number that hath died since this last sicknes began to October the sixt day, 1603. [Signed:] H. Chettle. s.sh.fol. *J. R[oberts] f. J. Trundle*, [1603.] HD.

16743.3 — [Anr. ed.] . . . to . . . October the 20. day, 1603. [Anon.] s.sh.fol. *J. R[oberts] f. J. Trundle*, [1603.] o.
    — A true relation of al that have bin buried from 14 of July last past, 1603, to the 17. of November following. 1603. *See* 18248.

Blank Bills (Briefs)

16743.4 — 1608. From the [ ] to the [ ] s.sh.4°. [*London, 1609.*] Ent. to J. Windet 1 au. 1603. D(filled out in MS. for 16 Feb.–23 Feb.).

16743.5 — 1609. From the [ ] to the [ ] s.sh.4°. [*London, 1609.*] F(frag., filled out in MS. for 24 Aug.–31 Aug.).

16743.6 — From the [ ] to the [ ] 1610. s.sh.4°. [*London, 1610.*] L¹¹(S.P.D., Jas. I, vol. 58, doc. 102, 4 blank weekly bills printed on 1 sheet).

London—BILLS OF MORTALITY—*cont.*

16743.7 — From the [ ] to the [ ] 1621. s.sh.4°. [*London, 1621.*] Ass'd to Stansby 11 se. 1611. HN(in binding of 23344, altered in MS. to yearly bill for 23 Dec. 1619 to 25 Dec. 1620).

16743.8 — From the [ ] to the [ ] 1625. s.sh.4°. [*W. Stansby, 1625.*] o(Vet. A 1 b.10(55), filled out in MS. for 8 Dec.–15 Dec.).

Weekly

Note: Unless otherwise indicated, each bill has the same heading, format, and imprint as the preceding bill. Bills covering the period 1 January–24 March retain the old-style date of the previous year.

16743.9 — [Series 1. No. 1.] 1603. Buried in London from 14 July, to the 21. of the same. s.sh.fol. *J. Windet*, [1603.] Ent. 1 au. 1603. L.; HD.
    — — [No. 2.] 21 July–28 July. L.; HD.
    — — [No. 3.] 28 July–4 Aug. L.; HD.
    — — [No. 4.] 4 Aug.–11 Aug. L.; HD.
    — — No. 5. 11 Aug.–18 Aug. L.; HD.
        There are 2 settings; in heading: 'neere' (L) or 'nere' (HD).
    — — No. 6. 18 Aug.–25 Aug. L.; HD.
    — — No. 7. 25 Aug.–1 Sept. L.; HD.
        There are 2 settings: royal arms with (HD) or without (L) 'I R'.
    — — No. 8. The true copie of all the burials and christnings from the first of September 1603. to the 8. of September. s.sh.fol. *F. Kyngston*, [1603.] L.; HD.
        There are 2 settings; line 3 of heading ends 'to the' (L) or 'the Kings' (HD). *See Court-Book C*, p. 8.
    — — No. 9. 8 Sept.–15 Sept. L.; HD.
    — — No. 10. 15 Sept.–22 Sept. HD.
    — — No. 11. 22 Sept.–29 Sept. s.sh.fol. *J. Windet*, [1603.] L.; HD.
        With only weekly totals, like the previous bills.
    — — [Anr. ed., with weekly and cumulative totals.] L (frag., Harl.5919/71).
    — — No. 12. 29 Sept.–6 Oct. HD.
        With only weekly totals.
    — — [Anr. ed., with weekly and cumulative totals.] No. 12. . . . Wherunto is added the number of all that have dyed. . . . L.
        All the following bills include both weekly and cumulative totals.
    — — No. 13. 6 Oct.–13 Oct. L.M(deposit).; HD.
        Royal arms with 'I R'.
    — — No. 14. 13 Oct.–20 Oct. L.L⁸(imp.).; HD.
        (Formerly 16739) Royal arms without 'I R'.
    — — No. 15. 20 Oct.–27 Oct. HD.
        Royal arms with 'I R'.
    — — No. 16. 27 Oct.–3 Nov. L.L⁸.; HD.
        (Formerly 16739) There are 2 settings: royal arms with (L, HD) or without (L⁸) 'I R'.
    — — No. 17. 3 Nov.–10 Nov. L.; HD.
        Royal arms with 'I R'.
    — — No. 18. 10 Nov.–17 Nov. L.; HD.
        There are 2 settings: royal arms with (L) or without (HD) 'I R'.
    — — No. 19. 17 Nov.–24 Nov. L.; HD.
        There are 2 settings: royal arms with (HD) or without (L) 'I R'.
    — — No. 20. 24 Nov.–1 Dec. L.; HD(top cropt).
        Royal arms with 'I R'.
    — — No. 21. 1 Dec.–8 Dec. L.; HD.
        Royal arms with 'I R'.
    — — No. 22. 8 Dec.–15 Dec. L.; HD(top cropt).
        Royal arms with 'I R'.
    — — No. 23. 15 Dec.–22 Dec. L.; HD.
        There are 2 settings: royal arms with (L) or without (HD) 'I R'.

16743.10 — [Series 2.] No. 1. 1603. The true copie. . . . 29 Dec. 1603–5 Jan. [1604.] s.sh.fol. *J. Windet*, [1604.] L.; HD.
    — — No. 2. 5 Jan.–12 Jan. L.; HD.
    — — No. 3. 12 Jan.–19 Jan. L.
    — — No. 4. 19 Jan.–26 Jan. HD.
    — — No. 5. 26 Jan.–2 Feb. HD.
    — — No. 6. 2 Feb.–9 Feb. L.; HD.
    — — No. 7. 9 Feb.–16 Feb. L.; HD.
    — — No. 8. 16 Feb.–23 Feb. HD.
    — — No. 9. 23 Feb.–1 Mar. M²(mutilated).; HD.
    — — No. 10. 1 Mar.–8 Mar. HD.

London—Bills of Mortality—*Weekly* (1604)—*cont.*
— — No. 11. 8 Mar.–15 Mar. HD.
— — No. 12. 15 Mar.–22 Mar. HD.
— — No. 13. 22 Mar.–29 Mar. HD.
  This and No. 14 are dated 1604 at the top of the bill, but 1603 is retained in the text of the heading.
— — No. 14. 29 Mar.–5 Apr. HD.
— — No. 15. 5 Apr.–12 Apr. HD.
  Both the top of the bill and the text of the heading are dated 1604.

16743.11 — [Series 3.] No. 1. The true copie. . . . 24 May–31 May 1604. s.sh.fol. *J. Windet*, [1604.] HD.
— — No. 2. 31 May–7 June. HD.
— — No. 3. 7 June–14 June. HD.
— — No. 4. 14 June–21 June. HD.

16744 — [Series 4.] The generall bill for this whole weeke, . . . 14 July–21 July 1625. s.sh.4°. *W. Stansby*, 1625. Ass'd 11 se. 1611. O.
— — 4 Aug.–11 Aug. L.
— — No. 15. 20 Oct.–27 Oct. O.

Note: All the following series of bills are printed on both sides.

16744.5 — [Series 5. Heading on verso: 'The diseases and casualties this weeke.'] No. 50. 26 Nov.–3 Dec. 1635. s.sh.4°. [*Parish Clerks' Press*, 1635.] HN.

16745 — [Series 6. Heading on verso: 'The diseases. . . .'] No. 20. 28 Apr.–5 May 1636. s.sh.4°. [*T. Cotes at the Parish Clerks' Press*, 1636.] O.
— — No. 21. 5 May–12 May. O.
— — No. 22. 12 May–19 May. O.
— — No. 23. 19 May–26 May. O.
— — No. 24. 26 May–2 June. O.
— — No. 27. 16 June–23 June. O.
— — No. 29. 30 June–7 July. O.
— — No. 30. 7 July–14 July. O.
— — No. 33. 28 July–4 Aug. O.
— — No. 34. 4 Aug.–11 Aug. O.
— — No. 35. 11 Aug.–18 Aug. O.
— — No. 37. 25 Aug.–1 Sept. O.
— — No. 38. 1 Sept.–8 Sept. O.
— — No. 39. 8 Sept.–15 Sept. O.
— — No. 40. 15 Sept.–22 Sept. O.
— — No. 41. 22 Sept.–29 Sept. O.
— — No. 42. 29 Sept.–6 Oct. O.
— — No. 43. 6 Oct.–13 Oct. O.
— — No. 44. 13 Oct.–20 Oct. O.
— — No. 45. 20 Oct.–27 Oct. O.

16745.3 — [Series 7. Heading on verso: 'The diseases. . . .'] No. 25. 31 May–7 June 1638. s.sh.4°. [*Parish Clerks' Press*, 1638.] O.
— — No. 27. 14 June–21 June. O.
— — No. 28. 21 June–28 June. O.
— — No. 29. 28 June–5 July. O.
— — No. 30. 5 July–12 July. O.
— — No. 31. 12 July–19 July. O.
— — No. 32. 19 July–26 July. O.
— — No. 33. 26 July–2 Aug. O.
— — No. 34. 2 Aug.–9 Aug. O.
— — No. 36. 16 Aug.–23 Aug. O.
— — No. 37. 23 Aug.–30 Aug. O.
— — No. 38. 30 Aug.–6 Sept. O.
— — No. 39. 6 Sept.–13 Sept. O.
— — No. 40. 13 Sept.–20 Sept. O.
— — No. 41. 20 Sept.–27 Sept. O.
— — No. 42. 27 Sept.–4 Oct. O.
— — No. 43. 4 Oct.–11 Oct. O.
— — No. 44. 11 Oct.–18 Oct. O.
— — No. 45. 18 Oct.–25 Oct. O.
— — No. 48. 8 Nov.–15 Nov. O.
— — No. 49. 15 Nov.–22 Nov. O.
— — No. 50. 22 Nov.–29 Nov. O.

16745.5 — [Series 8. Heading on verso: 'The diseases. . . .'] No. 3. 27 Dec. 1638–3 Jan. [1639.] s.sh.4°. [*Parish Clerks' Press*, 1639.] O.
— — No. 4. 3 Jan.–10 Jan. O.
— — No. 5. 10 Jan.–17 Jan. O.
— — No. 6. 17 Jan.–24 Jan. O.
— — No. 7. 24 Jan.–31 Jan. O.
— — No. 8. 31 Jan.–7 Feb. O.
— — No. 10. 14 Feb.–21 Feb. O.

London—Bills of Mortality—*Weekly* (1639)—*cont.*
— — No. 11. 21 Feb.–28 Feb. O.
— — No. 12. 28 Feb.–7 Mar. O.
— — No. 13. 7 Mar.–14 Mar. O.
— — No. 14. 14 Mar.–21 Mar. O.
— — No. 15. 21 Mar.–28 Mar. O.
  The heading is dated 1639 beginning with this bill.
— — No. 16. 28 Mar.–4 Apr. O.
— — No. 17. 4 Apr.–11 Apr. O.
— — No. 18. 11 Apr.–18 Apr. O.
— — No. 19. 18 Apr.–25 Apr. O.
— — No. 20. 25 Apr.–2 May. O.
— — No. 21. 2 May–9 May. O.
— — No. 22. 9 May–16 May. O.
— — No. 23. 16 May–23 May. O.
— — No. 24. 23 May–30 May. O.
— — No. 25. 30 May–6 June. O.
— — No. 26. 6 June–13 June. O.
— — No. 27. 13 June–20 June. O.
— — No. 28. 20 June–27 June. O.
— — No. 29. 27 June–4 July. O.
— — No. 30. 4 July–11 July. O.
— — No. 31. 11 July–18 July. O.
— — No. 32. 18 July–25 July. O.
— — No. 34. 1 Aug.–8 Aug. O.
— — No. 35. 8 Aug.–15 Aug. O.
— — No. 36. 15 Aug.–22 Aug. O.
— — No. 37. 22 Aug.–29 Aug. O.
— — No. 38. 29 Aug.–5 Sept. O.
— — No. 39. 5 Sept.–12 Sept. O.
— — No. 40. 12 Sept.–19 Sept. O.
— — No. 41. 19 Sept.–26 Sept. O.
— — No. 42. 26 Sept.–3 Oct. O.
— — No. 43. 3 Oct.–10 Oct. O.
— — No. 44. 10 Oct.–17 Oct. O.
— — No. 45. 17 Oct.–24 Oct. O.
— — No. 46. 24 Oct.–31 Oct. O.
— — No. 47. 31 Oct.–7 Nov. O.
— — No. 48. 7 Nov.–14 Nov. O.
— — No. 49. 14 Nov.–21 Nov. O.
— — No. 50. 21 Nov.–28 Nov. O.
— — No. 51. 28 Nov.–5 Dec. O.
— — No. 52. 5 Dec.–12 Dec. O.

16745.7 — [Series 9. Heading on verso: 'The diseases. . . .'] No. 4. 7 Jan.–14 Jan. 1640 [1641.] s.sh.4°. [*Parish Clerks' Press*, 1641.] O.
— — No. 5. 14 Jan.–21 Jan. O.

— For other broadsides which contain statistics on plague deaths *see* 4273, 4472.3, 4472.5, 19251.3, 20206, 20823, 20824, 20875. *See also* 18248.

APPENDIX

16746 — The ancient customes and approved usages. = pt. of Wing C 4353.
— The belman of London. 1608, etc. *See* 6480 sqq.
16747 — A breefe discourse, declaring and approuing the necessarie maintenance of the laudable customes of London. 8°. *H. Midleton f. R. Newberie*, 1584. Ent. 4 my. L.L².O.C(imp.).P.+; F.HN.HD.Y.
16748 — The briefe of the ministers bill for London tithe. [1621.] Now = 16779.10.
16749 — The cities advocate. 1629. = 3219.
16750 — The cities comfort: or, Patridophilus his preservatives against the plague. [1625?] Now = 19598.2.
— Civitatis amor. 1616. *See* 17878.
— A commyssion sent to the byshop of London. [1557?] *See* 3286.
16751 — A courtly new ballad of the wooing of the faire maid of London. (The faire maid of Londons answer.) *Ballads*. 1/2 sh.fol. *f. H. Gosson*, [1640?] Ent. to W. White 1 mr. 1600; to ballad ptnrs. 14 de. 1624. L. 1st stanza begins: 'Faaire [*sic*] Angell of England,'.
16751.5 — [The cries of London. 12 woodcuts w. letterpress verses.] s.sh.fol. [*London*, c. 1630.] ?Ent. to J. Wolfe 16 my. 1599. L(Dept. of P&D, 1.7.–65*).
  c⁶ has an impression [c. 1610] of these cuts and 12 others, without verses. *See also* 16761.
16752 — [Deed of admission to a London company. 1636?] Now = 16786.18.
— The disclosing of . . . the deuyl in two maydens within the citie of London. [1574.] *See* 3738.
— The discovery of a London monster. 1612. *See* 14030.

London—APPENDIX—*cont.*

— The great frost. Cold doings in London. 1608. *See* 11403.

— In this booke is conteyned the names of yᵉ baylifs. . . . [1503?] *See* 782.

16753 — Lachrymæ Londinenses. Or, Londons teares and lamentations, for the plague. 4°. [*B. Alsop a. T. Fawcet*] *f. H. Holland a. G. Gibbs,* 1626. L⁸.O³ (imp.).; F. 𝕬
F has half-title: Lachrymæ Londinenses: or, Londons lamentations and teares.

16754 — A larum for London, or the siedge of Antwerpe. 4°. [*E. Allde*] *f. W. Ferbrand,* 1602. Ent. to J. Roberts 29 my. 1600. L(imp.).L⁶(2).O.PETWORTH.; F(2).HN. HD.LC. Greg 192.

16754.5 — A letter sent by the maydens of London, . . . in the defense of their lawfull libertie. 8°. *H. Binneman f. T. Hacket,* 1567. Ent. 1567–68. L².

16755 — London looke backe, at that yeare of yeares 1625. 4°. *A. M[athewes], sold by E. Blackmoore,* 1630. L⁸.L¹⁵.
Attrib. to T. Dekker. *See Court-Book C,* p. 224. A different work w. the same title is included in 6175.

16755.5 — [Londons affright.] ⟨ ⟩ pitty, to all people that shall heare of it in ⟨ ⟩ull fire that happned on London bridge. *Ballad.* 2 pts. s.sh.fol. [*f. E. Blackmore,* 1633.] Ent. to E. Blackmore 13 fb. 1633. M³(imp.).

16756 — [Headline:] Londons complaint. [In verse.] 4°. [*London,* c. 1585.] C(1 leaf).

— Londons jus honorarium. 1631. *See* 13351.

16756.5 — Londons lotterie: with an incouragement to the furtherance thereof, for the good of Virginia. *Ballad.* 2 pts. s.sh.fol. *W. W[hite] f. H. Robards,* 1612. Ent. 30 jy. C⁶.
See also 24833.4.

— Londons love, to the royal prince Henrie. 1610. *See* 13159.

16757 — Londons mourning garment. 1603. = 18248.

16758 — Londons ordinarie, or every man in his humour. *Ballad.* 2 pts. s.sh.fol. *assignes of T. Symcocke,* [1628–29.] L.

16758.3 — [Anr. ed.] s.sh.fol. [*Eliz. Allde*] *f. J. Wright,* [c. 1630.] C⁶.

16758.7 — London soundes a trumpet, that the countrey may heare it. [Woodcut w. letterpress text.] s.sh.fol. *f. H. Gosson,* 1630. L⁵(Lemon 304).

16759 — London tryacle, being the enemie to all infectious diseases. [*Ed.*] (R. Band). 4°. *E. Allde,* 1612. L.

16760 — [Anr. ed.] 4°. *E. Allde,* 1615. L.; HN.
Dedic. signed R. Browne.

16761 — [The manner of crying things in London. 32 engr. plates.] 4°. [*London,* c. 1640.] HN.
See Hind III.368. *See also* 16751.5.

16761.3 — A merry progresse to London to see fashions, by a young country gallant. *Ballad.* 2 pts. s.sh.fol. [*W. White*] *f. J. White,* [c. 1615.] C⁶.

— The names of all the high sheriffes. 1628. *See* 10018.5.

16761.5 — The othe of eurye free man. s.sh.4°. [*R. Jugge,* c. 1575.] F.
Foliated init. 'Y'.

16762 — [Anr. ed.] The othe of euery free man. s.sh.4°. [*C. Barker,* c. 1580.] L.
Init. 'Y' has bearded old man w. cane.

16762.5 — [Anr. ed.] The othe of euery free man, of the citie of London. s.sh.4°. [*J. Day?* c. 1580.] L⁸.
Init. 'Y' has human-headed, 2-tailed fish.

16763 — [Anr. ed.] The othe of euerie free man, of the city of London. s.sh.4°. *H. Singleton,* [1590?] L(Huth 50/47).

16763.3 — [Anr. ed.] *J. Wolfe,* [c. 1595.] *See* Addenda.

16763.5 — [Anr. ed.] The oath of every free man, of the citie of London. s.sh.4°. *J. Windet,* [c. 1605.] O.

16764 — [Anr. ed.] The oath of every free-oath of the citty of London. s.sh.4°. *W. Jaggard,* [c. 1610.] L.
Foliated init. 'Y'.

16764.3 — [Anr. ed.] s.sh.4°. *W. Jaggard,* [c. 1610.] O.M.
Historiated init. 'Y'.

16764.5 — [Anr. ed.] The oath of every free-man of the citie of London. s.sh.4°. *R. Young,* [1628?] HD.

16764.7 — [Anr. ed.] The oath of every free-man of this [*sic*] citie of London. s.sh.4°. *R. Young,* [1634?] L⁸.

16765 — A pleasant new ballad, both merry and witty, that sheweth the humours, of the wives in the city. *Ballad.* 2 pts. s.sh.fol. *f. H. G[osson,* c. 1630.] C⁶.

16766 — = 16767.

London—APPENDIX—*cont.*

16767 — A profitable and necessarie discourse, for the meeting with the bad garbelling of spices, composed by diuers grocers of London. 4°. *R. B[ourne] f. T. Man,* [1592.] L.L⁸.O.C.CHATS.+; HN.CU.HD(imp.).NY. (Formerly also 16766)

16768 — [A ghost.]

⸻

16768.2 **London,** *Apprentices.* [Indenture for an unidentified company, stipulating: 'And the sayd master his sayd Apprentize . . . shall teach and instruct' and 'he shall not waste the goods of his said master'.] s.sh.*obl.*fol. [*London,* c. 1605.] Ent. to H. Lownes 14 no. 1604. S. Pottesman, London(imp., in binding of a copy of 10982).
Printed in civilité. *See also* 16777.10, 16778.8, 16787.9.

London, *Archdeaconry of.* Visitation articles. *See* 10268 sqq.

16768.4 **London,** *Barber Surgeons.* To the honourable house of Commons, . . . The humble petition of the masters or governors of the mysterie of barbers and chirurgions of London. [Against the patent obtained by the Physicians to supervise the Barber Surgeons as well as the Physicians.] s.sh.fol. [*London,* 1624?] L⁸ (GL 225).M(deposit).

London, *Bethlehem Hospital.* See Indulgences 50.

16768.6 **London,** *Bookbinders.* A generall note of the prises for binding of all sorts of bookes. s.sh.fol. *London,* 1619. L⁵(Lemon 171).

16768.8 — To the most honorable assembly of the Commons house. . . . The binders of bookes in London doe shew. . . . [against the monopoly of the Company of Goldbeaters for the importation and sale of gold foliat.] s.sh.fol. [*W. Stansby,* 1621.] L⁵(Lemon 186). L⁸(GL 5776).
See also 16776.6, 16777.14.

16768.10 — To the most honorable assembly of the Commons. . . . The binders of bookes in London, doe shew, that whereas G. Withers hath lately composed a book, which he calleth, The songs or hymnes of the church [25908], . . . [Objections against Wither's patent, 8704.5.] s.sh.fol. [*London,* 1624.] L⁵(Lemon 225).O.

16768.12 **London,** *Brewers.* To the honourable house of Commons. . . . The humble petition of the company of brewers in London. [Requesting relief from the burden of 4ᵈ a quarter on malt.] s.sh.*obl.*fol. [*London,* 1621.] L⁸(GL 454, cropt).
Petition presented 25 May 1621; *see* Notestein VI.476–7.

16768.14 **London,** *Bridewell Hospital.* [Proclamation of the governors.] Worshipfull, the cause of your repaire hither is to give you knowledge, that you are elected . . . s.sh.fol. [*A. Islip,* c. 1630.] HD.
— *See also* 23228.5.

16768.16 **London,** *Brokers.* To the most honorable assemblie the Commons house. . . . The humble petition of the English brokers. [Requesting the suppression of foreign brokers.] s.sh.fol. [*London,* 1621.] L(Harl. MS.7608/214).L⁸(GL 5779).
A bill was first read 14 May 1621; *see* Notestein VI.153.

16768.18 **London,** *Butchers.* Reasons tendred by the free butchers of London, against the bill in Parliament, to restraine butchers from grazing of cattle. s.sh.fol. [*London,* 1624.] L⁵(Lemon 217).
The bill was first read 19 Apr. 1624; *see* JHC I.770.

16768.20 **London,** *Carpenters.* Abuses vsed concerning the heawing, sawing, and measuring of timber, . . . [Against the sale by wharfingers and merchants of wood not cut to lawful size.] s.sh.fol. [*London,* 1593.] L(Lansdowne MS.161, no. 22).
Endorsed in MS.; 'preferred to the consideration of the parliament howse 35 Eliz.' Printed in civilité.

London, *Carpenters—cont.*
16768.22 — To the most hon^ble assemblie of the high court of Parliament. The humble petition of many thousands of poore carpenters, bricklayers, . . . and other handycrafts men. [Complaining of the restrictions of the Building Commissioners on repairing houses.] s.sh.fol. [*London,* 1621?] L⁵(Lemon 137).
Mentions that Inigo Jones had failed to attend a hearing in Parliament. Regarding this and the following *see* Notestein VII.273–7, 332–8.

16768.24 — To the most honourable assembly of the house of Commons. The humble petition of thousands of carpenters, bricklayers, . . . and other handicrafts men. [Requesting another hearing in Parliament.] s.sh.fol. [*London,* 1621?] L(Harl.MS.7614/118).

16768.26 — Arguments and reasons mentioned in the petition unto the right honourable assembly of the Commons house, . . . [Showing why houses should be repaired and why forefronts ought to be made of timber rather than stone or brick.] s.sh.fol. [*London,* 1621?] L(Harl.MS.7614/119).

16768.28 **London,** *Cloth-workers.* To the most honorable assembly of the Commons house. . . . The humble petition of the artizan cloth-workers of London. [Requesting confirmation of the order of the Common Council of London, 24 Sept. 1618, concerning the excessive number of apprentices.] s.sh.fol. [*London,* 1624?] L⁵(Lemon 216).

16768.30 — To the right honourable, . . . the knights and burgesses of Parliament: the humble petition of the artizan cloth-workers of London. [Requesting restrictions on the exportation of white cloth, i.e. undyed and undressed.] s.sh.fol. [*London,* 1621?] L⁸(GL 5784).

16768.32 **London,** *College of Heralds.* To the high-constables of the towne of [ ] or to any of them, greeting. These are to require you, . . . [Form of visitation summons to gentry to present evidence of claims to gentility to R. Treswell and A. Vincent.] Office of Armes in London, fift day of August 1623. s.sh.fol. [*W. Jaggard,* 1623.] L(Harl.MS.4204/11).

16769 **London,** *College of Physicians.* Certain necessary directions, aswell for the cure of the plague, as for preventing the infection. 4°. *R. Barker a. assignes of J. Bill,* 1636. L⁸.O.C².D².G².+; F.HN.CHI.HD.NLM.+
C1ʳ catchword: 'demeanour'.

16769.5 — [Anr. ed.] 4°. *R. Barker a. assignes of J. Bill,* 1636. L.L⁸.O.C².P.+; F.HD.MICH.NLM(2).NWM*.
C1ʳ catchword: 'demenour'; at least sheets P–S are from the same setting as 16769.

16770 — The kings medicines for the plague. Prescribed for the yeare 1604. by the whole colledge of physitians. 12° 8.4. *f. H. Gosson, sold by F. Coules,* 1630. L.

16771 — [Anr. ed.] 12° 8.4. *f. H. Gosson, sold by F. Coules,* 1636. L.L¹⁶.

16772 — Pharmacopœa Londinensis, in qua medicamenta antiqua et nova describuntur. fol. *E. Griffin, sumpt. J. Marriot,* 1618. Ent. 16 ja. L.L¹⁶.O.C⁹.STU.+; HD.Y.
See 8565 and Greg, *Companion,* pp. 162–3.

16773 — [Anr. ed.] Diligenter revisa. fol. [*E. Griffin*] *f. J. Marriott,* 1618. L(2).O.O⁶.O¹⁴.C.; TEX.

16774 — Tertia editio. fol. [*Eliot's Court Press*] *f. J. Marriott,* 1627. L.L¹⁶.O.C.E⁵.+; WIS.

16775 — Quarta editio. fol. *f. J. Marriott,* 1632. L(tp only).L¹⁶.L³⁹.O(2).C⁹.; HN.HD.LC.
The date on the engr. tp is apparently altered in MS. from 1627; the printer's note at the end is dated 8 Apr. 1632.

16776 — Quinta editio. fol. *f. J. Marriott,* 1639. L.L³⁹.O⁸.C⁴.E².+; F.NLM.TEX.
The date on the engr. tp is apparently altered in MS. from 1627; the printer's note at the end is dated 18 Mar. 1638 [o.s.]

— *See also* 16768.4.

16776.2 **London,** *Cooks.* [Oath.] You shalbe true to our soveraigne lord James. . . . s.sh.4°. [*London,* c. 1620.] HD.
A contemporary inscription attributes this to the Cooks' Company.

London, *Convent of the Crutched Friars. See* London, *Monastery of the Holy Cross.*

London, *Customs House.* Officers fees for Englishmen. 1615. *See* 8519.

16776.4 **London,** *Customs House—Clerks.* An abstract of the grievances of the poore clerkes of his majesties Custome-house London, by reason of letters pattents lately obtained for the erecting of a new office called the Office of clerke of the bils. s.sh.fol. [*W. Jones,* 1621.] L⁸(GL 11).
Petition presented to Parliament 6 Apr. 1621; *see* Notestein VII.347–8.

16776.6 **London,** *Cutlers.* An abstract of the grievances of the cutlers, paynter-stainers, and book-binders concerning the pattent of gold and silver foliat conteyned likewise in a petition [to] the Commons house. s.sh. fol. [*W. Jones,* 1621.] L⁸(GL 10).
Answered by 16777.14; *see also* 16768.8. The patent was declared a grievance 2 May 1621; *see* Notestein VII.371–2.

London, *Diocese of.* Articles and Injunctions. *See* 10247 sqq.

16776.8 — Instructions for the ministers, and churchwardens, of the citie of London. [Regulating lecturers in the parishes. Signed T. Paske.] s.sh.fol. [*London,* 1630.] L⁵(Lemon 298, dated in MS. Jan. 1629 [o.s.]).

16776.10 — John by the prouidence of God bishop of London. . . . [Brief of Bp. John Aylmer for collections for the relief of T. Butler of Colchester, gunpowder maker. 15 Sept. 1586.] s.sh.fol. [*G. Robinson,* 1586.] L⁵ (Lemon 82).

16776.12 — To all and every the ministers, . . . of London. . . . [Regarding deportment during church services. Signed 'Geo: London', prob. G. Abbot rather than G. Montaigne.] s.sh.fol. [*London,* 1611?] L⁵(Lemon 121).; HN.

16776.14 — To my very loving brethren the ministers, . . . of London. . . . [Requiring attendance at prayers Wednesdays and Fridays. Signed T. Paske. 10 Dec. 1627.] s.sh.fol. [*London,* 1627.] L⁵(Lemon 279).

16776.16 — [Fragments of Latin marriage licences, in different typesettings, apparently all issued by W. Juxon, Bp. of London, 1633–60.] s.sh.obl.fol. [*London,* 1633–60.] o³.c(Sayle 7061, 8375, 8376).; HD.
Printed in civilité.

16777 **London,** *Distillers.* The distiller of London. Compiled for the sole use of the company of distillers of London. And by them to bee duly observed. fol. *R. Bishop,* 1639. Ent. 30 ja. 1640. L.L⁸.; HN.HD. NLM.NY⁴.

16777.2 **London,** *Dyers.* The briefe contents of the bill exhibited against logwood, and abuses in dying. 1620. s.sh.fol. [*London,* 1621.] L⁵(Lemon 181).
The bill was first read 12 Mar. 1621; *see* Notestein VII.410.

— Directions given by the patentees, . . . in dying. [c. 1610.] *See* 6903.5.

16777.4 — To the most honourable assembly of the Commons house. . . . The petition of the wardens . . . of the art or mysterie of dyers. [Requesting the prohibition of logwood in dyeing.] s.sh.fol. [*London,* 1621.] L⁵ (Lemon 187).L⁸(GL 1835).L¹¹(S.P. 15/42: 49).

16777.6 **London,** *Felt Makers.* To the most honorable assembly of the Commons house. . . . The petition of the felt-makers. [Requesting prohibition of the importation of felts and hats made abroad.] s.sh.fol. [*W. Stansby,* 1621?] L⁵(Lemon 185).L⁸(GL 1997).

16777.8 **London,** *Fustian Makers and Merchants.* To the honourable . . . the Commons house of Parliament: the humble petition, of divers merchants and . . . makers of fustians. [Requesting that fustians not be subject to export taxes as the raw materials employed in their manufacture are taxed on importation.] s.sh.fol. [*London,* 1621?] L⁸(GL 5756).

16777.10 **London,** *Girdlers.* This indenture witnesseth. . . . [Apprenticeship indenture.] s.sh.4°. [*London,* c. 1630.] Ent. to H. Lownes 14 no. 1604. o¹⁶(imp.).
Line 6 from bottom ends: 'taught and'.

16777.12 — [Anr. ed.] s.sh.4°. [*London,* c. 1630.] o¹⁶(imp.).
Line 6 from bottom ends: 'taught'.

16777.14 **London,** *Goldbeaters.* The answer of the gold-beaters of London, to the grievances exhibited by the cutlers [16776.6]. s.sh.fol. [*London,* 1621.] L(Harl.MS. 7608/421). L⁸(GL 107).
See also 16768.8.

London, *Goldbeaters—cont.*
— A briefe of the charter to the company. [1619.] *See* 8613.

London, *Goldsmiths.* A declaration of an order for making cases for ballaunces. [1588, etc.] *See* 8170 sq.
— To the right honourable . . . privie counsell. The petition of T. Crosse on behalfe, of goldsmiths. [c. 1620.] *See* 6071.5.

16777.16 London, *Grocers.* [Apprentice's oath.] s.sh.4º. [*London*, 1611.] M(Clowes deposit).
— *See also* 16767.

16778 London, *Hanse Merchants.* Den wirdigen . . . heren Burgemeysteren der Stat Coelln. . . . Ex Londen den derden dach in Martio. xvc.xxvi. [A letter relating an attempt to suppress importation of Lutheran books.] s.sh.fol. [*Cologne, M. von Neuss*, 1526.] L. Cologne, Stadt Archiv.; PML.
Not properly an STC item.

London, *Hospital of St. Katherine's by the Tower. See* Indulgences 55A.

London, *Hospital of St. Thomas of Acres. See* Indulgences 5, 56 sqq.

16778.2 London, *Hot Pressers.* To the most honorable assembly the Commons house. . . . The humble petition of divers hott-pressers. . . . Shewing that whereas sir G. Douglas hath obteyned a pattent. . . . s.sh.fol. [*W. Stansby*, 1621.] L(Harl.MS.7614/114).L⁸(GL 5778).
This and the following prob. presented in Apr. 1621; *see* Notestein VII.378.
16778.4 — To the right honourable assembly of the Commons house. The reasons moving the hot-pressers to draw themselves into an orderly forme of governement. . . . s.sh.fol. [*London*, 1621.] L(Harl.MS.7608/213).L⁸ (GL 5786).

16778.6 London, *Leathersellers.* The oath of every freeman of the company. s.sh.4º. [*London*, c. 1610.] O.

London, *London Company for the colonization of South Virginia. See* Virginia Company.

London, *Merchant Adventurers.* A briefe demonstration of the benefit [of] freedome of trade for cloth. [1640?] *See* 16779.2.
— The course of the tare of cloth in Holland. 1627. *See* 5875.
— *See also* 16779.8.

16778.8 London, *Merchant Tailors.* This indenture witnesseth. . . . [Apprenticeship indenture.] 1/2 sh.fol. [*London*, 1616.] Ent. to H. Lownes 14 no. 1604. O¹⁷(2).
In last line 'JAMES' has swash italic '*A*'.
16778.10 — [Anr. ed.] 1/2 sh.fol. [*London*, 1616.] O¹⁷(2).
In last line 'JAMES' has roman 'A'.
16778.12 — [A prayer to be said by the poor of the company.] Oh almightie God. . . . s.sh.fol. [*F. Kingston?* 1603?] L⁵(Lemon 110).

16779 London, *Merchants.* The case of the company of merchants trading into France. [1667?]
Not an STC item.

16779.2 London, *Merchants of the Staple.* A briefe demonstration of the great benefit arising through the freedome of trade for cloth and other woolen manufactures. [Against restraints the Merchant Adventurers are attempting to impose.] fol(2?). [*London*, 1640?] L (1st sheet only, 816.m.14(81)).
Last date in the text is 1639.
16779.4 — A briefe of the act for the reliefe of the marchants of the estaple. [Requesting permission to sell wool and woolfells in England whenever they are prohibited from trading abroad.] s.sh.fol. [*London*, 1624?] L (Harl.MS.7614/116).
Prob. in response to 8687.
16779.8 — Wooll being the cheife comoditie of this kingdome, it is thus thought good for this common weale, to advance it to the highest rate that conveniently it may be. [Requesting an act for free trade to remedy

encroachments of the Merchant Adventurers.] s.sh. fol. [*London*, 1621.] L(Harl.MS.7617/87).
The bill had its 2nd reading 7 May 1621 and was passed 24 Nov. 1621; *see* Notestein III.188–90, 442–4, and *passim*.

16779.10 London, *Ministers.* The briefe of the ministers bill for London tithe. [Requesting more equitable assessments.] s.sh.fol. [*London*, 1621.] L(2, 1 = Harl.MS. 7610/93).L⁸(GL 480). O.
(Formerly 16748) The bill was read and rejected 21 Mar. 1621; *see* Notestein II.249.
16779.12 — The printer to the reader. . . . To the kinges majestie. The humble petition of two and twentie preachers, . . . [Requesting relief from conformity with 'certayne Ceremonies', 10069.] s.sh.fol. [*W. Jones's secret press?* 1605?] L⁵(Lemon 114). Broxbourne(O). Reprinted in 16450.
— For anonymous tracts relating to the 'Popish Apparell' *see* 10387 sqq.

London, *Monastery of the Holy Cross (Crutched Friars). See* Indulgences 51 sqq.

16780 London, *Museum Minervæ.* The constitutions. 1636. = 15099.
16781 — Corona Minervæ. 1635. = 15100.

London, *Painter-Stainers. See* 16725, 16776.6.

16782 London, *Pewterers.* Anno .IIII. Henrici octaui. These be the statutes established in diuerse Parliamentes for the mistery of yᵉ pewterers. 4º. (*G. How*,) [bef. 1590.] C.
16783 — [Anr. ed.] 4º. (*London*, 1593.) L³.O.

16783.5 London, *Pin Makers.* To all haberdashers. . . . [Giving the new address of the hall. May 1619.] s.sh.fol. [*J. Bill*, 1619.] L⁵(Lemon 166).; HN.

16784 London, *Royal Exchange.* The merchants new-royal-exchaunge. 8º. *T. C*[reede] f. *C. Burbey*, 1604. Ent. 25 ja. O.D.; HN.Y.

London, *St. Lawrence in Jewry. See* Indulgences 59.

London, *Savoy Hospital. See* Indulgences 60.

16785 London, *Shipwrights.* [Charter of the company.] 4º. [*T. Dawson*, 1612?] C.
Collates A–I⁴. The charter is dated 10 Sept. 1612.
16785.3 — [Anr. ed.] 4º. [*J. Bill f.*] (*T. Beadle*, 1618.) Y.
Collates A–Z⁴. The cut of the ship was apparently borrowed from E. Allde.
16785.7 — By the master, wardens and assistants of the companie . . . [Orders for the government of the company.] s.sh.fol. [*London*, 1621.] L⁵(2, Lemon 178 and Procs. Jas. I, no. 234).

16786 London, *Society of Arms.* Orders established, condiscended, and agreed unto by the societie. 8º. [*A. Islip*,] 1616. Ent. to Islip 5 oc. O.

16786.2 London, *Stationers.* A briefe of the bill concerning printers, booksellers and bookbinders. [Proposing restrictions on the importation of books pr. and/or bd. on the Continent.] s.sh.fol. [*London*, 1614?] L (Ames I.169).
Apparently refers to the act read 2 May 1614; *see* JHC I.470. Pr. in civilité.
— Ordinaunces decreed for reformation in pryntyng. [1566.] *See* 7757.5.
16786.4 — These shall be to warne and require you. . . . [Summons to freemen to attend a meeting at Stationers' Hall Monday, 30 Mar. 1640.] s.sh.fol. [*London*, 1640.] O¹²(2, in p.15.16).
16786.6 — To the right honourable the house of Commons. . . . The humble petition of T. Man, [and others. Against the patent of R. Wood and T. Symcock, 8815.] s.sh.fol. [*London*, 1621.] L⁸(Broadsides 23:115).
Petition presented 23 Mar. 1621; *see* Notestein VII.426 and Greg, *Companion*, pp. 168–9. Answered by 3217.5.

London, *Stationers—cont.*

16786.8 — To the right reverend and right honourable, the Lords spirituall and temporall. . . . An abstract of the generall grievances of the poore free-men and journeymen printers oppressed. [Against the 'unlawfull', i.e. monopolistic, ordinances of the company.] s.sh.fol. [*London,* 1621.] L(Harl.5910/137, imp.). L⁵(Lemon 214, a proof copy).
  This and the next presented before 29 May 1621; *see* Notestein III.336, n. 65 and Greg, *Companion,* pp. 152–3.

16786.10 — [Anr. issue, w. heading altered:] To the honourable house of Commons. . . . [*London,* 1621.] L(Harl.MS. 7614/115).L⁸(GL 5752).

16786.12 — Vicesimo octavo Januarij, 1611. . . . Present, the master, wardens, and assistants of the company. . . . [Order that 1 perfect copy of every book pr. shall be supplied to the Bodleian.] s.sh.fol. [*R. Barker,* 1612.] L⁵(Lemon 126).

16786.14 **London,** *Tilers and Bricklayers.* 1570. The book of ordinances belonging to the company. 4º. *London,* [c. 1640.] L⁸.

16786.16 — That the statute of 17. Edwardi 4. . . . [Petition of the tilers and bricklayers proposing fines on bricks, etc. unlawfully made and impositions to pay for the expense of searching and examining.] s.sh.fol. [*T. Snodham,* 1621.] L⁵(Lemon 138).L⁸(GL 5994).
  A bill was rejected in Parliament 17 Feb. 1621; *see* Notestein VII.449.

London, *Tobacco-Pipe Makers.* An abstract of his majesties charter to the tobacco-pipe makers of Westminster. [1619.] See 8611.

16786.18 **London,** *Tradesmen and Artificers within three miles of.* [ ] admissus fuit in libertatem communitatis officinatorum et artificium . . . [ ] die 163[ ]. s.sh.*obl.*slip. [*London,* 1636?] c(frags., Sayle 8546).
  (Formerly 16752) Pr. in civilité with 3 or more settings to a sheet. For the grant of incorporation on 8 Apr. 1636 *see Cal. S.P.D., 1635–1636,* pp. 359–60. E. Purslowe entered an abstract of the charter in the SR on 8 Mar. 1637.

16787 **London,** *Watermen.* The contents of the water-mans bill. [Reasons for forming a company.] fol. [*London,* 1621.] L⁸(GL 6138).
  A bill was first read 5 May 1621; *see* Notestein VI.138. See also 23813.3.

16787.2 — The prices of fares and passages to be paide from London to Grauesende, . . . and also betwene London Bridge and Windesoure, . . . fol(4). (*J. Cawood,*) [c. 1555.] L⁵(2, Lemon 49 and 50).
  The 1st sheet is in 2 settings; heading as above (no. 49) or 'payde', 'also betwene London Brydge and Wyndesoure' (no. 50).

16787.4 — The rates and pryces . . . for fare or passage from London Brydge to Wyndesoure, . . . s.sh.fol. [*J. Cawood?* c. 1555.] L⁵(2, Lemon 51 and 52).

16787.6 — The prices and rates . . . for fayre or passage, from Londō to Grauesende, . . . s.sh.fol. [*J. Cawood,* c. 1555.] L⁵(2, w. 16787.4).
  — The watermens suit. [1614?] *See* 23813.3.

16787.8 **London,** *Water-Tankard-Bearers.* To the honourable assembly of the Commons house. . . . The humble petition of the companie of water-tankerd-bearers . . . Robert Tardy in the name of the rest. [Requesting suppression of private branches and cocks, which withdraw water from public conduits.] s.sh.fol. [*London,* 1621?] L⁸(GL 6135).

16787.9 **London,** *Weavers.* This indenture witnesseth . . . [Apprenticeship indenture.] s.sh.4º? [*London,* c. 1615.] HD(frag.).

16787.10 **London,** *Wharfingers.* To the honorable assembly of the Commons house . . . and to the committees, for grievances of the same house. The humble petition of Edward Hopkins, . . . and other wharfingers. [Against abuses by the Woodmongers in regulating use of carts.] s.sh.fol. [*London,* 1621.] L(Harl.MS. 7614/126).L⁸(GL 2456).
  A bill on their behalf was first read 2 Mar. 1621; *see* Notestein VII.482. Answered by 16787.12.

16787.12 **London,** *Woodmongers.* To the honorable assembly of the Commons house . . . the answere of the woodmongers, to the complaint of some few wharfingers [16787.10]. s.sh.fol. [*London,* 1621.] L⁸(GL 6452).

16787.14 — To the honorable assembly of the Commons house . . . the reasons why the wood-mongers should continue their government of carres. s.sh.fol. [*London,* 1621.] L⁸(GL 6453).

Londoners. Londoners their entertainment in the countrie. 1604. See 19807.7.

Long, Kingesmill, *tr.* See 1392.

16788 **Longinus, Dionysius Cassius.** Διοννσιου Λογγινου ρητοπος περι υψους λογου βιβλιον Dionysii Longini liber de grandi loquentia. [Ed.] G. L(angbaine.) *Gr. a. Lat.* 8º. *Oxonii,* G. T[urner,] *imp.* G. Webb, 1636. L.O.C.E.ETON.+; F.HN.HD.ILL.Y.+
  Some copies (o³, o⁴, o³⁸, 1 c) have errata added on Y4ᵛ; many copies lack the index (Z⁸), which is present in 1 o, o⁶, o¹⁶. Some copies of this and the next have a folding leaf (o⁹, 5 C, 2 HD).

16789 — [Anr. issue.] Editio postrema. 8º. *Oxonii,* [*W. Turner,*] *imp.* G. Webb, 1638. L.O.C.D².E.+; F.HN.HD.ILL.Y.+
  Some copies (L, C, HD) have errata added on Y4ᵛ.

16790 **Longland, John,** *Bp.* Joannis Longlondi, dei gratia Lincolnien episcopi, tres conciones. (Quinque sermones.) [*Tr.* T. Caius?] fol. (*per* R. Pynson,) [1527?] L.L².O.C(imp.).D.+
  Frequently bd. w. 1 or more of the Sermones, cf. 16797.

16791 — Psalmus trisesimus [*sic*] septi. Conciones expositiuæ . . . in tertium psalmum pœnitentialem. Anno. do. 1520. fol. [*R. Pynson,* 1527?] O.C⁵.D.LINC.YK.+
  Collates X–MM⁶. This and the 4 following items were intended to be issued together, but they were printed by 2 different printers using the same types at different times; *see also* 16797.

16791.5 — Psalmus quinquagesimus. Conciones expositiuae. . . . Anno do. 1521. et 1522. fol. (R. Redman, 1532 (28 my.)) O¹⁰.C⁵.D.LINC.YK.+; HD.
  Collates NN–OOO⁶ PPP⁴.

16792 — Psalmus centesi. pri. Expositio concionalis. . . . Annis do. 1523. 1524. 1525. 1526. 1527. 1528. 1529. fol. [*R. Redman?* 1532?] L.C.
  Collates QQQ–ZZZ⁶ a–zz⁶ A–GG⁶ HH⁸.

16793 — Psalmus tricesi. pri. Expositio concionalis. . . . An. do. 1519. fol. [*R. Pynson?* 1527?] L².O.C.D.YK.+
  Collates L–S⁶ T–V⁴.

16793.5 — Psalmus sextus. fol. (*per me* R. Pynsoñ,) [1527?] L².O. C.D.YK.+
  Collates B–I⁶ K⁴.

16794 — Nouerint vniuersi per præsentes, [etc. Form of receipt, as collector of the king's tenths.] s.sh.*obl.*8º. [*R. Redman?* 1538.] O.
  (Formerly also 15649)

16794.5 — Johannes pmissione diuina Lincolñ Episcopus. . . . Ye shall vnderstande. . . . [Mandate to the clergy against the pope, recognizing the supremacy of the king as head of the English church. 19 June 1535.] s.sh.fol. [*T. Berthelet,* 1535.] Mrs. Donald W. Henry, Middlebury, Connecticut.

16795 — A sermõd spoken be fore the kynge at Grenwiche, vppon good fryday: M.CCCCC xxxvj. 4º. [*London,* 1536.] L.; F.
  In types used by J. Mayler beginning in 1539.

16795.5 — A sermõd made be for the kynge at Rychemunte, vppon good fryday, M.CCCCC.xxxvj. [really 1535.] 4º. [*London,* 1535.] O³.C²(imp.).P.
  The king was at Richmond on Good Friday of 1535.

16796 — A sermonde made before the kynge, at grenewiche, vpon good Frydaye. M.D.xxxviij. 4º. (*T. Petyt,*) [1538.] L.L².O(imp.).DNPK.; F.

16797 — Sermones . . . habiti corã illustrissimi regis Henrici octaui, . . . summa maiestate, . . . M.D.XVII. [really 1527?] fol. [*R. Pynson?* 1527?] L².O¹⁷.C.D.YK.+; HD.
  Tp and prelims. only, w. border McK.&F. 8 in a state after 1525; intended to preface the collection of which 16791, 16791.5, 16792, 16793, and 16793.5 were to form the parts. Most copies have 1517 on the tp altered in ink to 1518; O¹², O¹⁷, LINC, YK apparently have M.D.XVIII. pr. on the tp.

— See also Indulgences 68.

Longolius, Gilbertus, *ed. See* 5323.5.

16798 Longueval, Charles Bonaventure de, *Comte de Bucquot.* The lamentable death of the earle of Bucquoy. 4º. *Paris, P. Rocolet* [i.e. *London, E. Allde,*] 1621. L.P.; HN.N.
At least P, HN have the misprint 'LAMENTA/TLE' in the title, with the second 'T' altered in ink to 'B'.

Longus. Daphnis and Chloe. 1587. *See* 6400.

Longwater, Nicholas, *tr. See* 470.2.

16799 Look. A pleasant commodie, called Looke about you. 4º. [*E. Allde*] *f. W. Ferbrand,* 1600. L.L⁶.O(2, imp.).E.; F.HN.HD. Greg 174.

16800 — Looke about you. 4º. [*London,*] *Printed at the Cat and Fidle, for a dauncing mouse,* 1630. L.D(lacks tp).; HN.NY.
— Looke up and see wonders. 1628. *See* 1904.

16801 Lookes, John. The rag-man: or, a company that fell at oddes one day. *Ballad.* 2 pts. s.sh.fol. *f. F. Grove,* [post-1640.] = Wing R 132.

16801.3 — A famous sea-fight: or, a ⟨blood⟩y battell, which was fought between the Spaniard ⟨and th⟩e Hollander. *Ballad.* 2 pts. s.sh.fol. [*M. Parsons*] *f. F. Grove,* [1639.] Ent. 23 se. 1639. M³.

Looking-glass. A looking-glasse for all lordly prelates. 1636. *See* 20466.

16801.7 — A looking-glasse for city and countrey. [Woodcut w. letterpress text.] s.sh.fol. *f. H. Gosson, sold by E. Wright,* [1630.] L⁵(Lemon 303).
— A looking-glass for corne hoorders. [1631?] *See* 21457.

16802 — A looking-glasse for drunkards. 12º ⁸·⁴. [*M. Flesher*] *f. F. C[oules?]* 1627. L.

16802.3 — A looking-glasse, for murtherers and blasphemers; wherein they ⟨see⟩ Gods judgement showne upon a keeper neere Enfield C⟨hase.⟩ *Ballad.* 2 pts. s.sh. fol. [*M. Flesher*] *f. J. T[rundle,* 1626.] ?Ent. to J. Wright 16 jy. 1634. C⁶(I.232–3ᵛ).
1105.5 is pr. on verso.

16802.7 — A lokinge ⟨glass⟩ . . . or a worthy table to be had in euery good christian⟨ ⟩ s.sh.fol. [*London?* c. 1590.] H. W. Davies Catalogue 1 (1937), item 357(top left portion only, untraced).
Text begins: 'Why make you suche hast my frende or ye passe on?'
— The poore mans looking-glasse. 1640. *See* 12582.1.

16803 = 16804.

16804 Loper, Christian. Laniena Paswalcensis: that is, a tragicall relation of the plundring, of the towne of Pasewalke in Pomerland. First *tr.* into Nether dutch and now into English. 4º. [*Holland?*] 1631. L.O(2). C.

16805 Lopes, Duarte. A report of the kingdome of Congo. [Gathered] by P. Pigafetta. *Tr.* A. Hartwell. 4º. [*J. Windet f.*] *J. Wolfe,* 1597. Ent. 26 au. 1595. L.O.C. D.E.+; F.HN.ILL.NY.Y.+
Apparently intended to be issued w. 2 tpp, the first w. the device McK. 269, the second w. McK. 258 and the reading 'reporte'. Copies sometimes lack one or the other of the tpp or are misbound.

16806 Lopes de Castanheda, Fernam. The first booke of the discouerie and conquest of the East Indias. *Tr.* N. L(ichefield.) 4º. *T. East,* 1582. Ent. 19 de. 1581. L.O. C.E.P.+; F.HN.HD.N.NY.+

16807 Lopez de Gómara, Francisco. The pleasant historie of the conquest of the Weast India, atchieued by H. Cortes. *Tr.* T. N(icholas.) 1578. [Anon.] 4º. *H. Bynneman,* [1578.] Ent. 7 fb. 1578. L.O.C¹⁵.E. CHATS.+; F.HN.HD.N.NY.+

16808 — [Anr. ed.] 4º. *T. Creede,* 1596. Ent. 28 ja. L(3).O.D DUL.E².; F.HN.HD(imp.).N.NY.+

16809 Lopez de Mendoza, Iñigo, *Marqués de Santillana.* The prouerbes of . . . sir James Lopez de Mendoza with the paraphrase of P. Diaz. *Tr.* B. Googe. 8º. *R. Watkins,* 1579. Ent. 3 jy. L.O.C⁵.; HN.N.

16810 Loque, Bertrand de. Discourses of warre and single combat, *tr.* J. Eliot. 4º. *J. Wolfe,* 1591. Ent. 11 ap. 1589. L.L³⁰.O.C²(imp.).PETYT(imp.).+; F(2).HN.HD. ILL.NY.

16811 — [Anr. issue, w. cancel tp, w. imprint:] *London,* 1631. C.C².M.

16812 — A treatie of the churche. *Tr.* T. W[ilcox.] 8º. [*T. Dawson*] *f. R. Langton,* 1581. Ent. to T. Man 15 de. 1580. L.O⁹.C.D.P.+; F.HN(imp.).BO.CHI.U.+

16813 — [Anr. ed.] An excellent and plaine discourse of the church. 8º. (*T. Dawson*) *f. T. Man,* 1582. L.O.; BO³.U.

Lord. Lord have mercy upon us. [1636.] *See* 20206, 20875.
— O Lorde [etc. Poem w. stanzas beginning w. this phrase. 1549?] *See* 14554.5.
— Our Lord his line of fathers from Adam. 1595. *See* 3874.5.

Lord Bishops. Lord Bishops, none of the Lord's bishops. 1640. *See* 20467.

Lord's Day. The Lords day, the Sabbath day. 1636. *See* 4137.9.

Lord's Prayer. A deuout treatise vpon the paternoster. [1526?] *See* 10477.

16814 — A familiar and christian instruction vpon the Lordes prayer. *Tr.* out of french by G. C[hapelin.] 12º. *T. Vautrollier f. A. Maunsell,* 1582. Ent. to A. Mansfield [*sic*] 17 oc. 1581. C.C⁰.
Dedic. init. E. R.

16814.5 — A godly and short treatise vpon the Lordes prayer, the xii. articles of the christian faith, and the ten commaundementes. 8º. *T. Dawson f. G. Bishop,* 1580. Ent. 30 jn. 1579. L².LEEDS.; PN²(imp.).Y.
(Formerly 4465)

16815 — In the name of the Father. . . . The pater noster in Englyshe. [1535?] Now = pt. 2 of 20200.3.

16816 — A metricall declaration of the .vij. petitions of the pater noster. 4º in 6. [*R. Wyer?* c. 1530.] HN.

16817 — Oratio Dominica: symbolum apostolorum: mandata catalogi: sacramenta ecclesiæ, cum nonnullis aliis, carmine reddita: per Mameranum poetam laureatum. 4º. *T. Marshęus,* 1557. L.HAT.

16818 — The pater noster spoken of yᵉ sinner: God answerynge him at euery peticyon. 8º. (*T. Godfray,*) [c. 1535.] F. Reprinted in 21789.5.

16819 — Now = 16821.7.

16820 — The pater noster. yᵉ crede. & the cōmaundementes in englysh. 8º in 4's. (*J. Byddell,* 1537.) O.
C2ʳ line 6: 'al'.

16820.3 — [Anr. ed.] 8º in 4's. (*J. Byddell,* 1537.) Y(lacks 1st 2 leaves, completed by 16820.5).
C2ʳ line 6: 'all'. At least K4ᵛ, including the colophon, is from the same setting as 16820.

16820.5 — [Anr. ed.] The pater noster, the crede, and the commaūdementes in Englyshe. 8º. [*London,* 1537?] Y (1st 2 leaves only, w. 16820.3).
2nd leaf missigned B2; w. the same init. 'I' and from the same press as 16821.

16821 — [Anr. ed.] The pater noster, the crede, and the commaundementes in Englysh. 8º. [*London,* 1537?] C.
Prob. from the same press as 24455.5.

16821.3 — [Anr. ed.] The pater noster: the crede: and the commaundementes in Englysh. 8º. [*R. Redman?* c. 1538.] C³.

16821.5 — [Anr. ed.] The pater noster, the crede, & the commaundementes in Englyshe. 8º. (*T. Petyt,*) 1538. BUTE.

16821.7 — [Anr. ed.] The pater noster, the aue, crede, and .x. cōmaūdemētes in Englishe with other godly lessyōs. 8º. (*R. Redman,* 1539.) L.
(Formerly 16819)

16822 — Preparatio ad orandū. A preparation vnto the lordes prayer. 8º. (*J. Day a. W. Seres,*) [1548?] L(destroyed). C.
— The proude wyues pater noster. 1560. *See* 25938.

16823 — A short interpretation of the Lords praier. The third impression. s.sh.fol. *J. Okes, sold by A. Driver,* 1627. O.

16823.5 Lord's Supper. [Heading A1ʳ:] Certaine rules, to bee observed in the administration of the Lords supper. 4º in 2. [*London,* c. 1640.] O¹³.

Lord's Supper—*cont.*

16824 — An instruction for all those that intend to goe to the sacrament. s.sh.fol. *W. Jones*, 1634. O.
— The mysterie of the Lords supper. 1614. *See* 3922.
— The souper of the Lorde. 1533. *See* 24468.
— A treatise of the Lords supper. 1591. *See* pt. 2 of 22685.

16825 **Lord, Henry.** A display of two forraigne sects in the East Indies viz[t]: the sect of the Banians and the sect of the Persees. 4°. (*T. a. R. Cotes*) *f. F. Constable*, 1630. Ent. 22 fb. L.O.C.D².E.+; F.HN.BO.N(lacks engr. tp). PML.+
Letterpress sub tpp read: 'A discoverie of the sect of the Banians'; 'The religion of the Persees'.

16826 **Loreto.** The miraculous origin and translation of the church of our B. lady of Loreto. 1635. Now = 23884a.6.

16826.5 **Loris, Daniel.** Le thresor des parterres de l'universe, contenant les figures et pourtraits. . . . Descripts en Latin, François, Allemand & Anglois. 4°. *Geneve, E. Gamonet*, 1629. L.; BO.HD.HUNT.

16827 **Lorkyn, Thomas.** Recta regula & victus ratio pro studiosis & literatis. 8°. *Londini*, [*J. Cawood?*] 1562. C(2, 1 imp.).

Lorraine, *Cardinal of. See* 5010.5 sq.

Losa, Alphonsus de. *See* Indulgences 85 sqq.

16828 **Losa, Francisco de.** The life of Gregorie Lopes. [*Ed.*] A. Remon. [*Tr.*] (N.N.) 24° in 8's. *Paris*, [*widow of J. Blagaert,*] 1638. L.O.M².; F. A&R 471.

Loudun. A relation of the devill Balams departure out of . . . the nuns of Loudun. 1636. *See* 1232.

16828.5 **Lougher, Robert.** A sermon preached at Cern, in Dorset, the 18. day of September 1623. 4°. *J. Legatt f. F. Constable*, 1624. O.O³(2).O²⁸.RGU.YK.; F.HN.HD.NY¹¹.

Loughfoyle. Newes from Lough-foyle. 1608. *See* 18784.

16829 **Louis IX,** *King of France.* St. Lewis; the king: or a lamp of grace. 1615. = pt. 2 of 23582.

Louis XII, *King of France. See* 25947.7.

Louis XIII, *King of France.*

Arrangement chronological

— The apologies of the most christian kinges. 1611. *See* 13124.
— Epicedium Ludoici [*sic*] regis Galliae. 1611. *See* 23625.5.

16829.5 — Articles made . . . by the king of France, touching the re-establishment of the Jesuits. 4°. [*J. Beale?*] *f. T. Archer*, 1612. Ent. to Archer a. R. Redmer 24 ja. L. O².O³.C².HAT.+

16830 — The kings declarations upon his edicts for combats. *Tr.* E. A[ggas?] 4°. *T. Creed f. W. Wright*, 1613. Ent. 29 ap. L.O.; F.HN.KAN.Y. Lewis.
This includes a reissue of A4–B4 from 1976.

16831 — The kinges declaration and confirmation of the proclamation of Nantes. *Tr.* J. B. 8°. *f. J. Barnes*, 1613. Ent. 13 ap. O.

16831.5 — [Anr. issue, w. title:] The French kinges declaration [etc.] *f. J. Barnes*, 1613. L.; HN.

16832 — = pt. of 16833.

16833 — A true relation of the conferences betweene the king of France, and prince of Conde. (The publication of the peace according to the pleasure of the king.) 4°. *E. Griffin f. N. Butter*, 1616. Ent. 3 jn. L.O(2nd pt. only). LEIC.P.; F.
(2nd pt. formerly also 16832)

16834 — The French kings declaration against the dukes of Vendosme and Mayenne, [etc.] 4°. [*W. Stansby*] *f. W. Barret*, 1617. Ent. 18 fb. L(imp.).O(2).O⁸.C.D.; F.HN.MCG.PN.

16835 — The letter of the French king, to the parliament of Roan, concerning the death of the marshall D'Ancre. 4°. *H. L[ownes] f. N. Newbery*, 1617. Ent. 23 ap. L.O.O¹⁸.P.; F(2).HN.HD.Y.

Louis XIII, *King of France—cont.*

16835.5 — The French kings declaration made in favour of the princes . . . who had withdrawne themselves from his majesty. 4°. *F. Kyngston f. W. Arondell*, 1617. Ent. 3 jn. F.

16836 — Articles concluded and agreed upon by the lords, the cardinalls, de la Roche-Foucaud, and de Bethune, in the name of the king. *Tr.* 4°. *G. E[ld] f. G. Fairebeard*, 1619. Ent. 17 jn. L.; F.LC.

16837 — A letter written by the king of France. 1619. = pt. of 11284.
— An edict made the ninth of November [1619.] 1620. *See* 21673.5.

16838 — A declaration, made and published by the king of France, 6. of August 1620. *Tr.* 4°. [*J. Beale?*] 1620. Ent. to J. Beale a. T. Jones 12 au. L.; HN.

16839 — Certaine articles or ordinances made by the French kinge and the duke d'Espernon. 4°. *Amsterdam, G. Veseler*, 1621. O.; HN.

16840 — Letters patents made by the French king, touching those of the reformed religion. 4°. [*J. Beale?*] 1621. L.C¹³.D.M.; HN.

16841 — The 4. of November. The peace of France. Or the edict, granted by the French king. *Eng. a. Fr.* 4°. *J. D[awson a. T. Snodham] f. N. Newbery*, 1622. Ent. 1 no. L.O.; HN.HD.Y.
13 articles. For a piracy *see* Newsbooks 87.

16842 — [Anr. ed.] 4°. *Edinburgh, T. Finlason*, 1622. E(2).

16843 — November the 29. The true originall edict of Nants. 4°. *R. F[ield] f. W. Garrat*, 1622. Ent. 21 no. L.L⁴³.; Y.
92 articles. *See also* 13120.

16844 — [Anr. issue, omitting 'November the 29.' from tp, w. imprint:] *R. F[ield] f. W. Garrat*, 1623. L.L³⁸.O.C (impr. cropt).C².; HN (date cropt).

16845 — The French kings edict upon the peace. 4°. [*B. Alsop a. T. Fawcet?*] *f. Mercurius Britannicus*, 1626. Ent. to N. Butter 4 jy. L.O.O¹⁷.; F.HN.

16845.5 — Letters patents of the declaration of the king of France, for the demolishing of the strong places, townes or castles. 4°. *f. Mercurius Britannicus*, 1626. LONGLEAT.

16846 — [Page:] (1) Articles of agreement made betweene the French king and those of Rochell. Also a relation of a sea-fight made by sir K. Digby. *Eng. a. Fr.* 4°. *f. N. Butter*, 1628. L.O⁶.C². London, Foreign Office.; HN.
There are 2 states of the tp, dated 24. of October (HN) or 30. of October (L).

16847 — Newes of certaine commands. 1629. *See* Newsbooks 200.

16847.5 — Severall letters betwixt the French king and the Q. mother, concerning the present troubles. *Tr.* 4°. [*B. Alsop a. T. Fawcet*] *f. N. Butter a. N. Bourne*, 1631. E(lacks tp).; HN.

16848 — Lettres patentes de declaration du roy, pour la reformation du luxe des habits. *Fr. a. Eng.* 4°. *E. P[urslowe] f. H. Seile*, 1634. Ent. 28 jn. L.O¹³.C⁵.; F.HD.
English and French pr. on facing pages; imprint on English tp only.

16849 **Louis I,** *Prince de Condé.* A declaration made by the prynce of Conde. 8°. *R. Hall f. E. Sutton*, 1562. Ent. 1561–62. L.L².

16849.3 — [Anr. ed.] 8°. *R. Hall f. E. Sutton*, 1562. O.C(imp.).
In title: 'by my lord prince'; sheet B from same setting as 16849.

16849.7 — [Anr. ed.] 8°. *R. Hall f. E. Sutton*, 1562. M.P.
In title: 'by the prince'.

16850 — A seconde declaration of the prince of Conde. 8°. *H. Sutton f. E. Sutton*, [1562.] Ent. 1561–62. L.L².L³⁰ (sheet A only).O.M.

16851 — A declaration of the prince of Conde and his associates to the queene. 8°. *L. Harryson*, [1562.] Ent. 1562–63. L².; HD.

16852 — The treaty of thassociation made by the prince of Condee. 8°. [*W. Seres,*] 1562. L².O.M.P.; HD.
Init. 'W.S.' at end of text.

16853 — The copy of a letter sent by one of the camp, of the prince of Conde to a freend of his. 8°. (*J. Allde*, 1569 (24 ja.)) Ent. 1568–69. O.

16854 **Loukaris, Cyril,** *Patriarch.* The confession of faith, of Cyrill, patriarch of Constantinople. Confessio fidei . . . *Eng. a. Lat.* 4°. *f. N. Bourne*, 1629. Ent. 1 jy. L.O.O⁷.C³.YK.+; F.Y.

Loukaris, Cyril, *Patriarch—cont.*
16854.3 — [Heading A1ʳ:] Τοῦ μακαριωτάτου . . . Κυρίλλου
σύντομος πραγματεία κατὰ Ἰουδαίων. 4°. [*London, N.
Metaxas in J. Haviland's shop,* 1626?] Athens NL
(2 imp.). Loverdos Library, Kifissia, Athens.; HD.
The prelims. and a 2nd pt., Bp. Maximos's
'Ὁμιλίαι, were pr. in Constantinople; *see Harvard
Library Bulletin,* XV (1967), pp. 159–61.

16854.5 **Louvain,** *English College of the Society of Jesus.* Rules of
the Englishe sodalitie, of the immaculate conception
of the virgin Mary . . . in the Englishe Colledge of
the Society of Jesus in Lovaine. 12°. *Mackline, H.
Jaey,* 1618. O.ST.USHAW.
A&R 744.

16855 **Love.** Fond love why dost thou dally: or, the passionate
lovers ditty. *Ballad.* 2 pts. s.sh.fol. [*A. Mathewes*] f.
F. Coules, [c. 1630.] L.

16856 — Loves garland or, posies for rings, hand-kerchers, and
gloves. 8°. *N. O*[*kes*] f. *J. Spencer,* 1624. Ent. 28 se.
O(sheet A only).

16856.3 — Loves up to the elbowes. *Ballad.* 2 pts. s.sh.fol. [*M.
Flesher*] f. *H. G*[*osson,* c. 1629.] Ent. to F. Coules a.
ballad ptnrs. 20 jn. 1629. C⁶(imp.).
Signed at end: 'William ⟨ ⟩', possibly W. Meash.

16856.7 — Love without lucke, or the maidens misfortune. *Ballad.*
2 pts. s.sh.fol. f. *J. G*[*rismond,* c. 1631.] Ent. to F.
Coules a. ballad ptnrs. 5 se. 1631. C⁶.

16857 — ⟨ ⟩ o⟨r⟩ loues complai⟨nts;⟩ with the legend of Orpheus
and Euridice. [In verse.] 8°. *J. R*[*oberts*] f. *H.
Lownes,* 1597. L(imp.).; HN(imp.).
Dedic. init. 'H. L.' i.e. H. Lownes.

16857.3 — The true loves knot untied. Being the right path,
whereby to advise princely virgins . . . lady Arabella,
and the second son to the lord Seymore. *Ballad.*
2 pts. s.sh.fol. f. *F. G*[*rove,* c. 1630.] G².

Love, George. An almanack. 1625. *See* 480.7.

Love, Nicholas, *tr. See* 3259.

16857.7 **Lovell, Robert.** The high way to honor: as it was
delivered in two sermons. 4°. *E. A*[*llde*] f. *N.
Bourne,* 1627. L.; F.
16857.9 — Index postillanum [*sic*]. *See* Addenda.
16858 — The publican becomming a penitent. Two sermons.
4°. *T. S*[*nodham*] f. *N. Newbery,* 1625. Ent. 28 ap.
L.O.M².; F.
16859 — Two soveraigne salves for the soules sicknesse. 4°. *T.
S*[*nodham*] f. *N. Newbery,* 1621. O.E².; HD.

16860 **Lovell, Thomas.** A dialogue between custom and veritie
concerning dauncing and minstrelsie. [In verse.] 8°.
J. Allde, [1581.] Ent. 23 my. 1581. HN.

16861 **Lover.** The despairing lover, whose mind was much tormented. (A constant and a kinde maid.) *Ballad.*
2 pts. s.sh.fol. f. *F. Coules,* [1633?] Ent. to J. Wright
a. ballad ptnrs. 8 jy. 1633. L.
(Pt. 2 formerly 17186) Pr. on the verso of 11154.
16862 — The discontented lover. [Post-1640.]
Not an STC item.
16862.1 — The deceased maiden-lover. *Ballad.* 2 pts. s.sh.fol.
assignes of T. Symcocke, [1628–29.] L.
16862.3 — [Anr. ed.] The diseased [*sic*] maiden lover. 2 pts.
s.sh.fol. f. *J. Wright,* [c. 1635.] C⁶.
Pr. on the verso of 19224.7.
16862.5 — The faythfull lovers resolution, being forsaken. *Ballad.*
2 pts. s.sh.fol. [*J. White?*] f. *P. Birch,* [1618?] C⁶.
— The faithlesse lover. *See* pt. 2 of 16862.1.
16862.7 — A lover forsaken of his love. *Ballad.* 1/2 sh.fol. *G.
P*[*urslowe,* c. 1630.] G².
16862.9 — [Anr. ed.] A lover forsaken of his best beloved. *Ballad.*
1/2 sh.fol. *assignes of T. Symcocke,* [1628–29.] L.
— A lovers complaint being forsaken of his love. [c. 1620.]
See 5608.6.
16863 — The lovers complaint for the losse of his love. *Ballad.*
1/2 sh.fol. *assignes of T. Symcocke,* [1628–29.] L.M³.
Both copies are pr. on same sheet w. 16864a.11.
16864 — The lovers delight: or, a pleasant pastorall sonnet.
Ballad. 2 pts. s.sh.fol. f. *F. Coules,* [1640?] L.
16864.5 — A lovers desire for his best beloved: or, come away,
come away. *Ballad.* 2 pts. s.sh.fol. *assignes of T.
Symcocke,* [1628–29.] L.
16864a — The lovers dreame: . . . *Ballad.* 2 pts. s.sh.fol. f. *J.
W*[*right,* 1633?] Ent. to ballad ptnrs. 8 jy. 1633. L.

Lover—*cont.*
16864a.1 — The lovers guift, or a fairing for maides: being a dialogue betweene Edmund and Prisilly. *Ballad.* 2 pts.
s.sh.fol. [*E. Allde*] f. *J. Trundle,* [c. 1615.] C⁶.
16864a.3 — A lovers lamentation to his faire Phillida. *Ballad.*
1/2 sh.fol. *G. P*[*urslowe,* c. 1627.] C⁶.
16864a.5 — The lovers lamentation to his love Nanny. (The
flattering lovers farewell.—The comfortable answere
of Nanny.) *Ballads.* s.sh.fol. [*G. Eld*] f. *E. W*[*right,*
c. 1617.] C⁶.
— A lovers newest curranto, or the lamentation of a young
mans folly. [c. 1625.] *See* 1487.5.
— A most excellent ditty of the lovers promises. [1628–
29.] *See* 6922.4.
16864a.7 — The passionate lover. *Ballad.* 2 pts. s.sh.fol. [*A.
Mathewes*] f. ⟨ ⟩ [c. 1625.] C⁶(impr. cropt).
In the imprint only the top half of the 1st init. of
the publisher's name remains and may be 'E' or
'F'.
16864a.9 — The revolted lover. Or a young maiden is apt to be
wonne. *Ballad.* 2 pts. s.sh.fol. *assignes of T. Symcock,*
[1628–29.] Ent. to J. Wright a. ballad ptnrs. 1 jn.
1629. L.

Lovers. Lovers made men. 1617. *See* 14775.
16864a.11 — A pleasant new ballad of two lovers. 1/2 sh.fol.
[*assignes of T. Symcock,* 1628–29.] L.M³.
Both copies are pr. on same sheet as 16863.
16864a.12 — [Anr. ed.] 1/2 sh.fol. [*E. Allde*] f. *H. G*[*osson,*
c. 1628.] C⁶.
16865 — The two kinde lovers: [etc.] *Ballad.* 2 pts. s.sh.fol.
assignes of T. Symcocke, [1628–29.] L.
16865.3 — [Anr. ed.] 2 pts. s.sh.fol. f. *F. Coules,* [c. 1633.] C⁶.
16865.7 — The two scornfull lovers or I care not whether I have
her or no. *Ballad.* 2 pts. s.sh.fol. [*G. Eld*] f. *J.
T*[*rundle,* c. 1623.] M³.
16866 — Two unfortunate lovers, or, a true relation of the
lamentable end of John True, and Susan Mease.
Ballad. 2 pts. s.sh.fol. f. *H. Gosson,* [c. 1640.] Ent.
to F. Coules 13 jn. 1631. L.
— *See also* Amantes.

Low, Henry. Almanacks. 1554, etc. *See* 481 sqq.
16867 — A prognostication. [1564.] = 482.7.

16868 **Lowberry, Peter.** The constant lover. Who his affection
will not move. [Init. P. L.] *Ballad.* 2 pts. s.sh.fol.
f. *H. Gosson,* [1638?] Ent. 8 ja. 1638. L.
16869 — A new ditty: of a lover tost hither and th⟨i⟩ther. *Ballad.*
2 pts. s.sh.fol. [*E. Purslowe?*] f. *E. Wright,* [c. 1640.]
Ent. to H. Gosson 8 ja. 1638. L.

Low Countries. *See* Flanders, Holland, Netherlands,
Newsbooks, etc.

16869.5 **Lowe, Peter.** The whole course of chirurgerie. Whereunto is annexed the Presages of Hippocrates. 2 pts.
4°. *T. Purfoot,* 1597. Ent. 16 fb. O(imp.).C¹⁷.E⁵.P.;
HN.HD.NY⁴.Y(imp.).
16870 — [Anr. ed.] A discourse of the whole art of chyrurgerie.
Second ed. 2 pts. 4° in 8's. *T. Purfoot,* 1612 (1611.)
L.O³.C⁹.D.E.+; NLM.NY⁴.WTL.
16871 — Third edition. 2 pts. 4° in 8's. *T. Purfoot* [2], 1634. Ent.
6 no. 1615. L.O.C¹³.E.SAL.+; F.HN.HD.ILL.NY.+
16872 — An easie, certaine, and perfect method, to cure
Spanish sicknes. 4°. *J. Roberts,* 1596. L.

16873 **Lower,** *Sir* **William.** The phaenix in her flames. A
tragedy. 4°. *T. Harper* f. *M. Young,* 1639. L.O(lacks
tp).C.E.SHEF.+; F.HN.HD.N.Y.+ Greg 569.

16874 **Lowin, John.** Conclusions upon dances, both of this age,
and of the olde. [J. L. Roscio, *pseud.*] 4°. [*N. Okes
a. W. White*] f. *J. Orphinstrange,* 1607. Ent. 20
no. 1606. L. Stevens Cox (imp.).; HN.
White pr. quires C–D.
16875 — [Anr. issue, w. tp:] Brief conclusions of dancers and
dancing. f. *J. Orphinstrange,* 1609. L.
Tp pr. by W. Hall on A1, originally blank; the tp
and dedic. (A2,3) of 16874 are cancelled in the L
copy.

16876 **Lownes, Lawrence.** An abstract of the case of L. Lownes esquire, concerning the mannors of Hutton, Wandisley, and Angram. [Grievances against a decree in Chancery.] s.sh.fol. [*London*, 1628?] o.
> An act to reverse the decree was 1st read in Commons 18 Apr. 1628; *see JHC* I.885; but *see* also 13179.5.

Lowth, William, *tr. See* 1591.

Loyalty. Loyalty's speech to England. 1639. *See* 10018.

16876.5 **Loyola, Ignatius de,** *Saint.* Annotations to the exercise. [Anon.] 8°. [*Rouen, J. Cousturier*, c. 1630.] L⁹.L³⁵. ST.W.YK².+
> A&R 30. Title within border of type orns. F has a single leaf in a different typesetting.
— Conclave Ignati. [1611.] *See* 7026 sqq.
— The glory of the B. father S. Ignatius of Loyola. 1628, etc. *See* 15188.3 sq.
— Ignatius his conclave. 1611, etc. *See* 7027 sqq.

16877 — A manuall of devout meditations and exercises, instructing how to pray mentally. Drawne out of the spirituall exercises of B. F. Ignatius by T. de Villa-castin. *Tr.* [H. More.] 12°. [*St. Omer, English College Press,*] 1618. L.O.C.CHEL.ST.+; F.
> A&R 848. Dedic. init. 'J. W.' i.e. J. Wilson.

16877.5 — [Anr. ed.] *Tr.* H. M[ore.] 12°. [*St. Omer, English College Press,*] 1623. O.COLWICH.YK².
> A&R 849.

16878 — [Anr. ed.] 12°. [*St. Omer, English College Press,*] 1624. L.O.BUTE.ST.W.+; F(imp.).TEX.
> A&R 850.

Loyseleur, Pierre. *See* 15207.5.

16879 **Lubin, Eilhard.** Clavis Græcæ linguæ cum sententiis Græcis. Opusculum... hac alterâ editione adauctum. 8°. [*G. Purslowe,*] *ex off. Soc. Stationariorum*, 1620. Ent. to Leake a. ptnrs. in the Latin Stock 22 oc. 1618; ent. to R. Field a. ptnrs. in the Latin Stock 6 au. 1619. L.O.C².D.; BO.

16880 — Editio tertia. Duabus partibus distincta. 8°. *in off. J. Haviland, sumpt. J. Partridge*, 1629. O.; ILL.

16881 — Editio nouissima. Operâ & cura J. H[armar, the Younger?] 8°. *in off. E. Griffini, sumpt. J. Partridge*, 1640. C.D.PLUME.; F.TORONTO².

16882 **Lucanus, Marcus Annaeus.** M. Annæi Lucani, de bello ciuili, libri decem. [*Ed.* J. Sulpitius.] 16° in 8's. *imp. G. Bishop*, 1589. Ent. 3 jy. L(tp only, Ames I.494).O.C.C⁵(2).; F.HN.HD.ILL. Queen's U.

16883 — M. Annæi Lucani Pharsalia, sive, de bello civili . . . adjectis notis T. Farnabii. 8°. *R. Field*, 1618. Ent. 28 jn. L.O.C.E.YK.+; F.HN.HD.N.TEX.+

16883.5 — Lucans first booke translated line for line, by Chr. Marlow. [In verse.] 4°. w. perp. chainlines. *P. Short, sold by W. Burre*, 1600. Ent. to J. Wolfe 28 se. 1593; ass'd from P. Linley to J. Flasket 26 jn. 1600. L.; F.
> Also issued as pt. 2 of 17415.

16884 — Lucans Pharsalia: containing the civill warres betweene Cæsar and Pompey. *Tr.* into English verse by Sir A. Gorges. fol. [*N. Okes*] *f. E. Blount*, 1614. Ent. to W. Burre 27 my. L.O⁷(imp.).C.A.WN.+; F. BO.CHI.ILL.TEX.+

16885 — [Anr. issue, w. imprint:] *f. W. Burre*, 1614. L³⁰.C². LIV³.; HN.CH.HD.ILL.PN.

16885a — [Anr. issue, w. imprint:] *f. T. Thorp*, 1614. O.C⁵.LICH. WN.; HN.HD.ILL.N.Y.+

16886 — Lucan's Pharsalia: or the civill warres of Rome, betweene Pompey the great, and Julius Cæsar. The three first bookes. *Tr.* T. M[ay.] 8°. *J. N[orton] & A. M[athewes,] sold by M. Law*, 1626. Ent. to Norton a. Mathewes 18 ap. L.L⁴⁴.

16887 — [Anr. ed., w. additions.] Lucan's Pharsalia. . . . The whole ten bookes. Englished, by T. May. 8°. [*A. Mathewes*] *f. T. Jones a. J. Marriott*, 1627. Ent. 12 mr. L.O.C.E.NEK.+; F.HN.HD.N.Y.+
> Number of leaves of dedic. sonnets varies (HD has 8, L and Y have 6, etc.).

16888 — Second edition. 8°. *A. Mathewes f. T. Jones*, 1631. Ass'd to Jones 11 de. 1630. L.O.C.A.D⁹.+; F.HN.HD. N.Y.+
> Engr. tp has imprint: *f. T. Jones*, 1631.

16889 — Third edition. 8°. *A. M[athewes], sold by W. Sheares*, 1635. Ass'd to Mathewes 24 oc. 1633. L.O.C.LIV³. NEK.+; F.HN.HD.ILL.Y.+
> Engr. tp has imprint: *A. M. f. T. Jones*, 1635.

Lucar, Cyprian. Three bookes of colloquies. *Tr.* by C. Lucar. Also Lucar appendix. 1588. *See* 23689.

16890 — A treatise named Lucarsolace . . . in part deuised by C. Lucar. 4°. *R. Field f. J. Harrison*, 1590. Ent. 26 mr. a. 4 my. L.L³⁰.O.C.P.+; HN.LC.WIS. Horblit.

16891 **Lucian,** *of Samosata.* Complures Luciani dialogi à D. Erasmo . . . in Latinum côuersi. 8°. (*W. de Worde*, 1528 (27 jn.)) L.

16892 — Luciani dialogi aliquot per D. Erasmum versi. 8°. (*R. Redman*, 1531.) C.

16892.3 — Luciani Samosatensis dialogorum selectorum liber primus (secundus). Græcolatinus 12°. *ap. T. Harperum*, 1634 (1636.) L(1st date shaved).L³⁰.

16892.7 — [Anr. issue, w. cancel 1st tp:] Libri duo, Graeco-Latiné. *ap. T. H., imp. G. Emerson*, 1636. L(1st tp only, Harl.5967/168).O³.C⁵.YK. Athens, Gennadius Library.; F.PH(lacks 1st tp)*.

16893 — Certaine select dialogues of Lucian. *Tr.* F. Hickes [*Ed.*] T. H(ickes). 4°. *Oxford, W. Turner*, 1634. L O.C.D(lacks B1).E².+; F.HN.HD.N.Y.+

16894 — A dialogue. betwene Lucian and Diogenes of . . . life. [*Tr.* Sir T. Elyot.] 8°. (*in aed. T. Bertheleti,*) [1532?] O.; HN(lacks last leaf).

16895 — Necromantia. A dialog of the poete Lucyan. *Eng. a. Lat.* fol. [*Southwark, P. Treveris? f.*] (*J. Rastell,*) [1530?] O(frags.). Earl of Macclesfield.
> The Latin trans. is by Sir T. More.

16896 — Lepidissimum Luciani opusculū περὶ διψάδων, H. Bulloco interprete. 4°. *ex acad. Cantabrigiensi,* (*per J. Siberch,*) 1521. L(2).L²(1st sheet only).C⁵.
> Includes a reprint, w. additions, of 4082.
— *See* also 20054.

16897 **Lucinge, René de.** The beginning, continuance, and decay of estates. *Tr.* J. F(inet.) 4°. [*Eliot's Court Press*] *f. J. Bill*, 1606. Ent. 9 jy. L.O.C.D.E².+; F.HN. HD.N.NY.+

16898 **Lucretia,** *of Siena.* [Lucretia and Euryalus. 1515? etc.] *See* 19969.8 sqq.

Lucydarye. *See* 13685.5.

Ludham, John, *tr. See* 11755, 11758, 11760, 25012.

Ludlow, Hertfordshire, *Palmers of St. Lawrence. See* Indulgences 61.

Ludlow, *Mr.* [Ludlow's prayers. 1563?] *See* 10617.

Ludovico, Joannes Baptista Guardano, *puncto. See* 18229.

Ludus. Ludus Scacchiæ. 1597. *See* 6216.

16899 **Lugo, Peregrinus de.** Principia seu introductiones . . . in via doctoris subtillis. 4° in 6's. *Venūdanī in alma vniuersitate Oxoniēse,* (*p R. pynsō, cuჳ cura H. Meslier, exp. g. castellani, oxonii morantis,*) [1508?] L.O(imp.).C.LINC.M.+; F.

Luidus, Johannes. *See* Lloyd, J.

16899.3 **Luis,** *de Granada.* [Heading A1ʳ:] A breefe treatise . . . commonly called, the conuersion of a sinner. [Anon. *Tr.* M. K.] 8°. [*f. G. Cawood*, 1580?] L.; F.N.
> (Formerly 5648) All known copies lack tp and prelims.; for anr. trans. *see* 16901.

16899.5 — [Anr. ed.] The conuersion of a sinner: faithfully *tr.* out of Italian by M. K. 8°. *T. Creed f. J. P[arnell,* 1598.] Ent. 18 mr. 1598. L².O⁹.
> (Formerly 5649) Attrib. to Luis de Granada in the prelims.

16899.7 — [Anr. ed. Signed.] 12°. *Edinburgh, R. Waldegraue*, 1599. HD.

16900 — An excellent treatise. 1601. = pt. of 16910.5.
— The exercise of a christian life. 1634. *See* 16922a.7.

16901 — The flowers of Lodowicke of Granado. The first part. *Tr.* T. L[odge] doctor of phisicke. 12°. *J. R[oberts] f. T. Heyes*, 1601. Ent. 23 ap. L.; F(imp.).N.
> For anr. trans. *see* 16899.3.

16902 — Granados deuotion. Exactly teaching how a man may dedicate himselfe vnto God. Englished, by F. Meres. 12°. *E. Alldt f. C. Burby*, 1598. Ent. 28 mr. L(imp.). L³⁰.O.BTU.P +; F.HN.HD.U.Y.

Luis, *de Granada—cont.*

16903 — A memoriall of a christian life. Wherein are treated all such thinges, as apperteyne vnto a christian to doe. (*Tr.* R. Hopkins.) 8°. *Rouen, G. L'oyselet,* 1586. L. O.C.BTU. DUR³.+; F.HD.TEX.WASH³. St. Mary's Seminary, Perryville, Missouri.+
A&R 472. In this and the following eds. only the first 4 treatises were pub'd.

16904 — [Anr. ed.] 8°. *Rouen, G. Loyselet* [i.e. *London, V. Simmes?*] 1599. L.O.C.USHAW.W.+; F.HN.N. TEX.U.+
A&R 473.

16905 — [Anr. ed.] 8°. *Douay,* [*P. Auroi f.*] *J. Heigham,* 1612. O.HP.W.; F.LC.STL.TEX.Y.
A&R 474.

16906 — [Anr. ed.] 8°. *S. Omers,* [*G. Seutin?*] *f. J. Heigham,* 1625. L.O.C.DE.W.+; F.N.STL.TEX.Y.
A&R 475.

16906.5 — A most fragrant flower or deuout exposition of the Lords praier, *tr.* J. G(olburne.) 12°. *R. Bradocke f. J. Browne,* 1598. Ent. 22 jy. D.

16907 — Of prayer, and meditation. Wherein are conteined fowertien deuoute meditations. (*Tr.* R. Hopkins.) 8°. *Paris, T. Brumeau,* 1582. L.O.C.DE.YK².+; F. HART².HD.N(imp.).
A&R 476.

16908 — [Anr. ed.] 12° ⁸·⁴. *Rouen, G. L'oiselet,* 1584. L.O.C². W.YK.+; F(imp.).ILL.TEX.
A&R 477.

16908.5 — [Anr. ed.] 8°. *Douay,* [*P. Auroi f.*] *J. Heigham,* 1612. L.O⁵.C.M.W.+; F(imp.).HN.N.TEX.Y.+
(Formerly 13769 and 16912) A&R 478.

16909 — [An altered version.] Of prayer and meditation. Contayning foure-teene meditations. (An excellent treatise of consideration and prayer.) [*Ed.* Mr. Banister, son of J. Banister.] 2 pts. 12°. [*J. Charlewood?*] *f. T. Gosson a. J. Perin, solde* [*by J. Perrin,*] 1592. Ent. 7 jy. F.
First of a series of Protestant eds. which use basically the same trans. but rearrange the parts.

16909.5 — [Anr. ed.] 12°. (*J. Roberts*) *f. T. Gosson a. R. Smith,* 1596. TMTH.; HD.

16910 — [Anr. ed.] 12°. *P. Short f. W. Wood,* 1599. Ent. 6 no. 1598. L.E.; F.

16910.5 — [Anr. ed.] 12°. *J. Harison f. W. Wood,* 1601. L²⁶.O (Treatise only).STD.
(16900 is pt. of this)

16911 — [Anr. ed.] 12°. *J. R[oberts]* f. *E. White,* 1602. Ent. 2 au. C.
See Greg, *Register B,* p. 90.

16911.5 — [Anr. ed.] 12°. *W. J[aggard]* f. *E. White,* 1611. L(sub tp only, Harl.5963/251).L²⁶.C¹⁹.SBK.WOR.
See Court-Book C, p. 49.

16912 — Now = 16908.5.

16913 — [Anr. ed.] Granada's meditations. . . . Sixt impression. 12°. *E. Allde, solde by J. Grismond* [*a.*] (*J. Browne,*) 1623. L³.O(2 imp.).DUL(imp.).

16914 — [Anr. issue, w. cancel tp:] F. L. Granada's meditations. . . . Sixth edition. *f. J. Browne,* 1623. C³.

16915 — [Anr. ed.] 12°. *E(liz.) All-de, sold by R. Allot,* 1633 (1634.) Ent. to R. Allot 25 ja. 1626. L.O.C¹⁵.BIRM. STU.+; HN.Y.
Engr. tp: 'Granada's meditations. The 7ᵗʰ impression. 1634.'

16916 — [A ghost.]

16916.3 — A paradise of praiers, containing the puritie of devotion, and meditation. [*Tr.* T. Lodge?] 12°. *T. Haveland f. M. Law,* 1609. Ent. as tr. by T. L. to A. Wise 22 my. 1601. CHATS.

16916.7 — [Anr. ed.] 12°. *R. Field f. M. Law,* 1614. ILL.

16917 — The fourth edition. [*Ed.*] (H. P.) 12°. *J. Norton, sold by W. Sheares,* 1633. O.C¹⁵.; HD.
— Prayer and meditation. 1630. *See* 16922a.

16918 — The sinners guyde. . . . Wherein sinners are reclaimed from the by-path of vice. Digested into English, by F. Meres. 4° in 8's. *J. Roberts f. P. Linley & J. Flasket,* 1598. Ent. to P. Linley 2 au. 1597. L.O.C. M.P.+; F.HN.CAL.ILL.

16919 — [Anr. ed.] 4° in 8's. *R. Field f. E. Blount,* 1614. Ent. to J. Flasket 26 jn. 1600. L.O.C.D².E².+; F.PN.TORONTO². U.

16920 — Granados spirituall and heauenlie exercises. Englished by F. Meres. 12°. *J. Robarts f. I. B[ing,]* 1598. Ent. to Bing a. Gosson 6 no. O.; HD(imp.).

16921 — [Anr. ed.] 12°. *Edinburgh, R. Walde-grave,* 1600. L.

Luis, *de Granada—cont.*

16922 — A spiritual doctrine, conteining a rule to liue wel, with diuers praiers and meditations. *Tr.* (R. Gibbons.) 8°. *Louan, L. Kellam,* 1599. L.O.C.E.YK.+; HN.HD.TEX.Y.
A&R 479.

16922a — [Anr. issue, omitting prelims., w. tp:] Prayer and meditation. *S. Omers,* [*English College Press,*] 1630. L.O.BUTE.DN.
A&R 480.

16922a.3 — [Anr. issue, w. tp:] A spiritual doctrine. [*St. Omer, widow of C. Boscard,*] 1632. L².
A&R 481. Retains prelims. of 16922.

16922a.7 — [Anr. issue, w. tp:] The exercise of a christian life. Contayning many godly, and devout prayers & meditations . . . by the reverend father, Lewis of Granada . . . *tr.* into English by S. B. The second edition. [*St. Omer, English College Press,*] 1634. L². C².AUG.W.
(Formerly 16645) A&R 482. Beginning of title and translator erroneously taken from 16644. Substitutes new prelims. for those of 16922.

— *See also* 14568.7.

Lull, Ramón. Le libre del orde de cauayleria. *Tr.* W. Caxton. [1484.] *See* 3356.7.

16923 **Luminalia.** Luminalia, or the festivall of light. Personated in a masque at court, by the queenes majestie, and her ladies. [Attrib. to Sir W. Davenant.] 4°. *J. Haviland f. T. Walkley,* 1637. L.L⁶.O.BHP.LINC.+; F.HN.HD.N.Y.+ Greg 527.

16924 **Lumesden, Alexander.** A heavenly portion. Set downe in a sermon preached at the funerall of mistris Frances Sentleger. 8°. *T. C[reede] f. A. Johnson,* 1614. Ent. 17 my. O.

Lumsden, Charles, *tr. See* 21276.

16925 **Luna, Juan de.** Arte breve, y conpendiossa para aprender a leer, la lengua Española. (A short art [etc.]) *Span. a. Eng.* 8°. *Juan Guillermo* (*W. Jones,*) 1623. Ent. 10 mr. L.C.C³.D². Madrid NL.; F.HD.
Spanish and English on facing pages, including tpp.

16926 — [A ghost.]
— Familiar dialogues in Spanish. [1622.] *See* 18897.

16927 — The pursuit of the historie of Lazarillo de Tormez. *Tr.* T. W[alkley.] 8°. *B. Alsop f. T. Walkley,* 1622. Ent. 26 oc. O(2).; F.
Reprinted in 15339.

16928 — [Anr. ed.] 8°. *G. P[urslowe] f. R. Hawkins,* 1631. Ass'd 20 no. 1628. L.C.C³.; HN.ILL.

Luna, Miguel de. *See* 354

16929 **Lunan, Alexander.** Theses philosophicae, . . . Praeside Alexandro Lunano. 1622. Now = 71.6.

16930 **Lundie, John.** Oratio eucharistica & encomiastica, in benevolos universitatis Aberdonensis benefactores. 4°. *Aberdoniis, E. Rabanus,* 1631. L.A.G².
— Propositiones aliquot logicae. 1627. *See* 71.13.
— Theses logicæ & philosophicae. 1626. *See* 71.10.

16931 **Lundie, Thomas.** Utrum episcopus Romanus sit Antichristus necne? 1602. Now = 21555.8.

16932 **Lupset, Thomas.** Tho. Lupsets workes. 8°. (*in æd. T. Bertheleti,*) 1546. L.O(imp.).C.M.P.+; F.HN.PN.U.Y.
Includes a reprint without attribution of Sir T. Elyot's trans. of Pico's Twelve Rules from 6157; see also 19898a.3.

16933 — [Anr. ed.] 8°. (*J. kynge,*) 1560. Ent. 20 se. L.O.C.E.P.+; F.HN.HART.HD.N.+

16934 — A compendious and a very fruteful treatyse, teachynge the waye of dyenge well. 8°. (*T. Berthelet,* 1534.) L(2, 1 imp.).D⁸.; HN.

16935 — [Anr. ed.] 8°. (*ex ęd. T. Bertheleti,* 1541.) L.O.C.D.M. +; F.HN.HD.ILL.Y.+

16936 — An exhortation to yonge men. 8°. (*in aed. T. Berthlet,* 1535.) L.C(frag.).; F.

16937 — [Anr. ed.] 8°. (*in aed. T. Bertheleti,* 1538.) L.C.BUTE. YK.; F.NY¹¹.

16938 — [Anr. ed.] 8°. (*in æd. T. Bertheleti,* 1544.) L.O⁹. Rogers.

16939 — A treatise of charitie. [Anon.] 8°. (*in aed. T. Bertheleti,* 1533.) L.L¹⁷(imp.).; HN.

Lupset, Thomas—*cont.*

16940 — [Anr. ed.] 8º. (*in aed. T. Berthelet*, 1535.) L(imp.).
16941 — [Anr. ed.] 8º. (*in æd. T. Bertheleti*, 1539.) L.O.Oº.C².
Rogers(lacks tp).; F(lacks tp).
— *tr. See* 5550, 14270, 14639.

16942 **Lupton, Donald.** Emblems of rarities: or choyce observations out of worthy histories. 12º. *N. Okes*, 1636.
L.O.C.E.M.+; F.HN.BO⁵.MICH.N(imp.).+
16943 — Gather [etc.] The glory of their times. Or the lives of
yᵉ primitive fathers. [Anon.] 4º. *J. Okes, sold [by P.
Nevill,]* 1640. ?Ent. 6 fb. 1637. L.O.C.D.E.+; F.HN.
HD.N.NY.+
— The history of the moderne protestant divines. *Tr.* D.
L(upton.) 1637. *See* 24660.
16944 — London and the countrey carbonadoed and quartred
into severall characters. 8º. *N. Okes*, 1632. L.L⁸.
L¹⁵.O.O⁶.+; F.HN.HD.
16945 — Objectorum reductio: or, daily imployment for the
soule. 8º. *J. Norton f. J. Rothwell*, 1634. Ent. 17 my.
L.O.C³.; F.BO. Fleming.
16945.5 — [Anr. issue, w. prelims. cancelled and cancel tp:]
Solitarinesse improved, in occasionall meditations.
[Init. D. L.] *f. J. Rothwell*, [c. 1640.] F.

16946 **Lupton, Thomas.** The christian against the Jesuite.
Wherein a booke, intituled A discouerie [19402] is
reproued. 4º. (*T. Dawson*) *f. T. Woodcocke*, 1582.
Ent. 19 mr. L.L².O.O⁴.YK.; F.U.
In support of 18533.
16947 — A dream of the deuill, and Diues. 8º. *J. Charlewood f.
H. Car*, 1584. Ent. 6 my. 1583. L².
16947.5 — [Anr. ed.] 8º. *T. Dawson f. H. Carre*, 1589. HN.
16948 — [Anr. ed.] 8º. *E. Allde f. S. White*, 1615. Ass'd to E.
White 17 fb. 1603. L.
16949 — A moral and pitieful comedie, intituled, All for money.
4º. *R. Warde a. R. Mundee*, 1578. Ent. to R. Ward
25 no. 1577. L.O(lacks tp). Greg 72.
16950 — A persuasion from papistrie: . . . 4º. *H. Bynneman*,
1581. Ent. 22 fb. L.O.D.E.E².+; F.HN.
16951 — Siuqila. Too good, to be true: . . . Herein is shewed by
waye of dialoge, the wonderfull maners of the people
of Mauqsun. 4º. *H. Bynneman*, 1580. Ent. 31 mr.
L.M².; HD.N.
No privilege.
16951.5 — [Anr. ed.] 4º. *H. Bynneman*, 1580. O.; F.HN.
In title: 'way of dialogue'; privilege on tp and in
colophon.
16952 — [Anr. ed.] 4º. [*Deputies of*] *H. Bynneman*, 1584. O.C².;
F(lacks tp).
16953 — [Anr. ed.] 4º. *A. Jeffs*, 1587. L.L⁴.O.O³⁹.C.; F.HN.
16954 — The second part and knitting vp of the boke entituled
Too good to be true. 4º. *H. Binneman*, 1581 (6 se.)
Ent. 11 au. L.O.O³⁹(imp.).; F.HN.
Ends Dd1.
16954.5 — [Anr. ed.] 4º. *H. Binneman*, 1581 (6 se.) L⁴.C.C².P.; F(2).
Ends Cc4; sheet A from same setting as 16954.
16955 — A thousand notable things, of sundry sortes. 4º. *J.
Charlewood f. H. Spooner*, [1579.] Ent. 25 se. 1578.
L.O.C(imp.).C¹²(imp.).SH(imp.).; F.
16956 — [Anr. ed.] 4º. [*G. Robinson*] *f. E. White*, 1586. Ent.
8 au. Town End, Troutbeck, near Ambleside,
Westmorland.; HD.
16957 — [A ghost.]
16957.5 — [Anr. ed.] 4º. [*J. Charlewood?*] *f. E. White*, [c. 1590.]
C⁵.; F.CH.N.
(Formerly 16958a)
16958 — [Anr. ed.] 4º. *J. Roberts f. E. White*, 1595. O.; F.
16958.5 — [A variant, undated.] G².
16958a — Now = 16957.5.
16959 — [Anr. ed.] 4º. *J. Roberts f. E. White*, 1601. L.C(imp.).
P.; F.
16959.5 — [Anr. ed.] 4º. *E. Allde f. E. White*, 1612. L.G².; WIS.
16960 — [Anr. ed.] 4º. *E. All-de f. N. Fosbrooke, by the assignes
of J. Wright a. R. Bird*, 1627. Ass'd to T. Pavier a.
Wright 13 de. 1620; to E. Brewster a. Bird 4 au.
1626. L.L¹⁶.O¹⁹.CHATS.G².; F.HN.N.PH.Y.+
16961 — [Anr. ed.] 8º. *J. Haviland f. R. Bird*, 1631. L.L¹⁰.
C².G².; F.HN.CAL.LC.NLM.+

Lusing, René de. *See* 16897.

16962 **Luther, Martin.** A boke made by a certayne great clerke,
agaynst the newe idole, and olde deuyll. [Anon.] 8º.
(*R. Wyer,*) [1534.] F.COR(lacks tp).
16963 — The boke of the discrypcyon of the images of a verye
chrysten bysshop. [1536?] Now = 16983.5.

Luther, Martin—*cont.*

16964 — The chiefe and pryncypall articles of the christen
faythe, with thre bokes. [*Tr.* W. Lynne?] 8º. [*S.
Mierdman*] (*f. G. Lynne*, 1548.) L.O³(frag.).C.M.
Göttingen U.+; F.HN.N(imp.).U.Y.
16965 — A commentarie . . . vpon the epistle to the Galathians.
Tr. 4º in 8's. *T. Vautroullier*, 1575. L.O.C.E².EX.+;
F.HN.HD.ILL.Y.+
Some copies (1 F, HD) have Vautrollier's device
on the verso of the tp, others lack it (O⁹, 1 F,
HN).
16966 — [Anr. ed.] Diligently reuised. 4º in 8's. *T. Vautroullier*,
1577. L.O.C².A.M².+; F.HN.HD(tp def.).ILL.NY.+
16967 — [Anr. ed.] 4º in 8's. *T. Vautroullier*, 1580. L.O.C²⁵.D².
E⁴.+; F.HN.HD.ILL.U.+
16968 — [Anr. ed.] 4º in 8's. *T.* [*a. J.*] *Vautroullier*, 1588. L.C.
LIV.+; F.HN.CAL(imp.).ILL(imp.).PN(2).
See Greg *Register B*, p. 27.
16969 — [A variant, w. imprint:] *T. Vautroullier f. W. Norton*,
1588. L.O.C¹².; HD.
16970 — [Anr. ed.] 4º in 8's. *R. Field*, 1602. Ent. 5 mr. 1599,
crossed out. L(destroyed).C¹².BIRM.D.SHEF(imp.).;
F.HN(w. some sheets from 16973).ILL.PN.Y.
In some copies (F, HN) the date is altered in MS.
to 1603.
16971 — No entry.
16972 — = 16973.
16973 — [Anr. ed.] 4º in 8's. *R. Field*, 1616. Ent. 22 jn. 1615.
L.O.C⁴.E⁴.M.+; F.HN.CU.HD.N.+
(Formerly also 16972)
16974 — [Anr. ed.] 4º in 8's. *G. Miller*, 1635. Ass'd 3 ap. 1626.
L.O.C.E.M.+; F.HN.ILL.U.Y.+
16975 — A commentarie vpon the fiftene psalmes, called psalmi
graduum. *Tr.* H. Bull. [*Ed.*] (J. Fox.) 4º in 8's. *T.
Vautroullier*, 1577. Ent. 10 de. L.O.C.EX.P.+; CAL.
ILL.LC.N.NY.+
Address to reader signed 'John Fox'.
16975.5 — [Anr. ed.] 4º in 8's. *T. Vautroullier*, 1577. L³⁰.O²⁸
(Bed.).R.; F.HN.CHI.HD.
Address to reader signed 'John Foxe'.
16976 — [Anr. ed.] 4º in 8's. *R. Field*, 1615. Ent. 22 jn. L.O.C⁴.
D.G².+; F.HN.HD.ILL.NY¹¹.+
16977 — [Anr. ed.] 4º in 8's. *G. Miller*, 1637. Ass'd 3 ap. 1626.
L(lacks tp).O.C.D.M.+; F.ILL.U.V.Y.+
16978 — A commentarie or exposition vppon the twoo epistles
generall of Sainct Peter, and that of Sainct Jude. *Tr.*
T. Newton. 4º. [*J. Kingston*] *f. A. Veale*, 1581. Ent.
25 jn. L.O.CAR.SHEF.STU.+; F.HN.HD.IND.U (lacks tp).+
— Every dayes sacrifice. . . . Written by D. M. Luther.
1607. *See* 6396.5.
16979 — An exposition of Salomons booke, called Ecclesiastes.
[Anon. *Tr.*] 8º. *J. Daye*, 1573. L.O.C⁴.C¹⁵.P.+; F(3,
1 imp.).BO.LC.Y.
(Formerly also 2763)
16979.3 — An exposition vpon the Cxxx. psalme. *Tr.* T. Potter.
8º. *H. Singleton*, 1577. O.
(Formerly 20137)
16979.7 — An exposicion vpon the songe of the blessed virgine
Mary, called Magnificat. *Tr.* J. Hollybush [*pseud.*,
i.e. M. Coverdale]. 8º. (*Southwarke, J. Nicolson,*)
1538. L.O(imp.).O³.
(Formerly 17536)
16980 — A faythfull admonycion of a certen trewe pastor.
[Anon.] *Tr.* (Eusebius Pamphilus.) [*Ed.*] P.
Melancthon. 8º. (*Grenewych, C. Freeman* [i.e.
Strassburg, W. Rihel,] 1554 (my.)) L.L⁵(2 leaves,
Lemon 36A).O.C.M.+; F(lacks tp).
16981 — [Anr. ed.] A faithful admonition [etc.] 8º. (*Grenewych,
C. Freeman* [i.e. *London, J. Day?*] 1554 (my.)) L.
— [Fourteen consolations. 1535? etc.] *See* pt. 4 of 20200.3,
and 20193, 16988.5, 16989.
16982 — A frutefull and godly exposition of the kyngdom of
Christ, vpō Jeremye in the xxiij. chapter, . . . where-
unto is annexed a sermon, of U. Regius, vpon the
ix. chapter of Mathewe . . . *tr.* (G. Lynne.) 8º. [*S.
Mierdman*] *f. G. Lynne*, 1548. L(2).O.C.; F.Y.
— A fruteful sermon of Mart[er] concernynge
matrimony. [1548?] *See* 21826.6.
16983 — A frutfull sermon of the moost euangelicall wryter
M. Luther, made of the angelles. *Tr.* (J. Fox.) 8º.
H. Syngleton, [1548?] L.O.O⁴.; HN.
16983.5 — The images of a verye chrysten bysshop, and of a
counterfayte bysshop. [Anon.] 8º. [*R. Wyer f.*] (*W.
Marshall,*) [1536?] L(2 imp.).CHATS. Lord Kenyon.; F.
(Formerly 16963) This does not appear to be a
trans. of any known work by Luther.

Luther, Martin—*cont.*

16984 — The last wil and last confession of martyn luthers faith. *Tr.* 8°. [*Wesel, D. van der Straten?* 1543.] L.O. D(imp.). Blickling.

16985 — A methodicall preface prefixed before the epistle to the Romanes. *Tr.* W. W[ilkinson.] 8°. [*T. Dawson*] *f. T. Woodcocke,* [bef. 1594?] L.O(1 imp., plus a frag.). O¹⁰.; F.

16986 — [Anr. ed.] 12°. [*London,*] 1632. L(destroyed).; F(impr. cropt).

16987 — A prophesie out of the nienth chapter of Esaie. 8°. *H. Bynneman f. G. Seton,* 1578. Ent. 10 mr. L.L⁴.O. C(imp.).C⁴.; F.HD.

16988 — Here after ensueth a propre treatyse of good workes. [Anon.] 8°. (*R. wyer,*) [1535?] O³.O⁸(imp.).; HN.

16988.5 — A treatice cõteining certain meditatiõs of trew & perfect consolatiõ. [Anon.] Wrytten in Frenche and *tr.* by R. Filles. 8°. (*J. Alde,*) [1564.] Ent. 1563–64. L.C.
     (Formerly 10868) For another trans. *see* also 20200.3.

16989 — [Anr. trans.] A right comfortable treatise containing fourteene pointes of consolation for them that labor. Englished by W. Gace. 8°. *T. Vautrollier,* 1578. Ent. 1 jy. F.

16990 — [Anr. ed.] 8°. *T. Vautrollier,* 1579. Ent. 6 ap. WI.; F.

16991 — [Anr. ed.] 8°. *T. Vautrollier,* 1580. L.O.C¹²(imp.).M.

16992 — A ryght notable sermon, made vppon the twenteth [*sic*] chapter of Johan. [*Tr.*] (*R. Argentyne*) 8°. *Ippeswich, A. Scoloker,* 1548. Ent. to R. Waldegrave 10 ja. 1581. L.O.C.; F.HN.HD.

16993 — Special and chosen sermons. Englished by W. G(ace.) 4° in 8's. *T. Vautroullier,* 1578. Ent. 6 ap. 1579. L. O.C.G⁴.M².+; F.HN.HD.N.Y.+
     See Arber II.848. Admonition to reader signed either 'Foxe' (HD) or 'Fox' (HN).

16994 — [Anr. ed.] 4° in 8's. *T. Vautroullier,* 1581. L.O.C.D. M.+; F.HN(imp.).HD.ILL.NY.+
 — A treatice cõteining certain meditatiõs. [1564.] *See* 16988.5.

16995 — A treatise, touching the libertie of a christian. *Tr.* J. Bell. 8°. *R. Newbery a. H. Bynneman,* 1579. Ent. to Newbery 24 ja. O.C(imp.). Goyder.; F.BO.PN².
     Collates A–B⁸ C² D–I⁸ K². Herbert, I.489, owned a copy of an earlier trans. pr. by J. Byddell, [c. 1537.]

16996 — [Anr. ed.] 8°. *R. Newbery a. H. Bynneman,* 1579. L.O. BUTE.M.P.; F.HN.HD.PN.Y.
     Collates A–H⁸.

16997 — [Anr. ed.] 4°. [*T. Harper*] *f. W. Sheares,* 1636. L.O.O³. LEEDS.M².; F.HN.HD(2).ILL.U(2, 1 imp.).

16997.5 — A very comfortable, and necessary sermon, concerning the comming of Christ. *Tr.* (T. B[econ].) 8°. (*J. Daye,* 2570 [i.e. 1570.] Ent. 1569–70. L.C⁵.; F.ILL.

16998 — [Anr. ed.] 8°. *J. Daye,* (1578.) L.L².YK(imp.). Stevens Cox.; F.

16999 — A very excellent and swete exposition vpon the two & twentye [23rd] psalme. [Anon.] *Tr.* M. Coverdale. 8°. (*Southwark, J. Nycolson f. J. Gough,*) [1537.] O. C.; CH.PML.
     Dated 1537 in tp border McK.&F. 33.

17000 — [Anr. ed., w. additions.] MDXXXVIII. (How. . . . A sermon out of the .xci. psalme, by A. Osiander.) 8°. (*Southwarke, J. Nicolson,*) [1538.] L.
     2nd pt. reprinted from 18878.

17000a — [A variant, w. date misprinted:] M D CCCCC. C¹⁵.; F.
 — *See* also 10493, 11394, 17119, 17626.

—Luthers predecessours. 1624. *See* 1787.
— *See* also 14008.5, 17797.

Lutssolof. An example of Gods judgement. [c. 1582.] *See* 10608.5.

Lutzen. The great and famous battel of Lutzen. 1633. *See* 12534.

17001 **Luzvic, Stephanus.** The devout hart or royal throne of the pacifical Salomon. *Tr.* (H. A. [i.e. H. Hawkins?]) Enlarged by F. St. Binet. 12°. [*Rouen,*] *J. Cousturier,* 1634. L.ETON.HP.USHAW.
     A&R 483. ETON and HP (A&R 484) have slips reading '1638' pasted over the date.

17002 **Lycophron.** Λυκοφρονος του Χαλκιδεως Αλεξάνδρα. Lyco-phronis Chalcidensis Alexandra. In vsum Academiæ Oxoniensis. [In verse.] *Gr.* 4°. [*Oxford,*] *J. Barnesius,* 1592. L.O(2).C.; F.HN.Y.

17003 — [Anr. ed.] 8°. [*Cambridge,*] *J. Legatus,* 1595. O.C.

17003.3 **Lycosthenes, Conrad.** Apophthegmatum ex optimis vtriusque linguae scriptoribus. . . . Loci communes. 8°. *sumpt. H. François,* 1579. Ent. to J. Harrison 1, G. Bishop, a. W. Norton 5 ja. L.C²⁰.

17003.7 — [Anr. ed.] Apophthegmata, ex probatis Graecae linguae scriptoribus collecta. Postremâ hac editione aucta. Editio altera. 8°. *J. Jacksonus,* 1596. L.O.C¹⁰. Rogers. St. Albans School, Hertfordshire.; HN.BO.BO².

17004 — [Anr. ed.] Postremâ hac editione expurgatâ, locupletata. 8°. *ap. T. Harperum pro Soc. Stat.,* 1635. Ent. to the Latin Stock 22 oc. 1618; to the English Stock 22 jn. 1631. L.O.C.G⁴.M².+; F.HN.HD.N.PN.+
     See Court-Book C, p. 303.
 — The doome warning all men. 1581. *See* STC 1582.
 — *See* also 19196.

17005 **Lydgate, John.** [The assembly of the gods.] Hrre [*sic*] folowyth the interpretacõn of the names of goddis and goddesses. [In verse.] fol. [*Westminster, W. de Worde,* 1498.] L.; HN(imp.).PML. Duff 253.
     The attrib. to Lydgate at the end of the text is erroneous, and it is omitted from the following eds.

17006 — [Anr. ed.] Here foloweth the interpretacoin [*sic*]. [Anon.] 4° in 6's. [*Westminster? W. de Worde,* c. 1500.] C. Duff 254.
     This is the latest of the first 3 eds.

17007 — [Anr. ed.] Here foloweth the interpretacyon. 4° in 8's. [*Westminster? W. de Worde,* 1500?] L.; HN(imp.). Duff 255.

17007.5 — [Anr. ed.] Here foloweth the interpretacyon. 4° ⁸·⁶. (*R. Pynson,*) [c. 1505.] O(2 leaves).; HN(imp.).
     (0 frag. formerly 24844a)

17007a — [Anr. ed.] Here folowith the interpretaciõ. 4° ⁴·⁶. [*J. Skot f.*] (*R. Redman,*) [after 1529.] HN.

17008 — [Ends:] .Explicit the chorle and the birde. [Anon. In verse.] 4° in 10. [*Westminster, W. Caxton,* 1477?] L(2 leaves). C. Duff 256.
     1st page, line 6: 'writyng'.

17009 — [Anr. ed.] Explicit the chorle and the birde. 4°. [*Westminster, W. Caxton,* 1478?] PML. Duff 257.
     1st page, line 6: 'wrytyng'.

17010 — [Anr. ed.] Here endeth the tale of the chorle & the byrd. 4°. (*R. Pinson,*) [1493.] L. Duff 258.

17011 — [Anr. ed.] Here begynneth the chorle & the byrde. 4° in 8. (*Westmynstre, W. de worde, in Caxtons house,*) [1497?] L. Duff 259.

17012 — [Anr. ed.] Here begynneth the chorle and the byrde. 4° in 8. (*W. de Worde,*) [1510?] C.

17013 — [Anr. ed.] Here foloweth the churle and the byrde. 4°. (*Cantorbury, J. Mychel,*) [1550?] O.; HN.

17014 — [Anr. ed.] The churle and the byrde. 4°. (*W. Copland,*) [c. 1565.] F.HN.
 — The cronycle of all the kynges. [c. 1552, etc.] *See* 9983, 9983.3.

17014.3 — [The complaint of the black knight.] Here begynnys the mayng or disport of chaucer. [Anon. In verse.] 4° ⁸·⁶. (*Edinburgh, W. chepman a. A. myllar,* 1508 (4 ap.)) E.
     (Formerly 5099)

17014.7 — [Anr. ed.] The cõplaynte of a louers lyfe. 4° in 6's. (*W. de worde,*) [1531?] L.

17015 — [The court of sapience. b7ʳ:] Explicit liber primus de curia sapiencie. [Anon. Not by Lydgate. In verse.] *Eng.* fol. [*Westminster, W. Caxton,* 1480.] L.O(frag.). O⁸.M. Duff 260.

17016 — [Anr. ed.] The courte of sapyence. 4° ⁸·⁴. (*W. de Worde,* 1510.) L.
 — Here begynnethe the boke calledde the falle of princis. 1494, etc. *See* 3175 sqq.

17017 — This present boke called the Gouernaunce of kynges. [*Tr.* from Aristotle's Secreta secretorum by J. Lydgate and completed by B. Burgh? In verse.] 4°. (*R. Prynson* [*sic*], 1511 (17 ap.)) L(lacks tp). O(2 leaves).; HN.
     (Formerly also 12140 and 14999a) *See* also 770.
 — The hystorye, sege and dystruccyon of Troye. 1513, etc. *See* 5579 sqq.

Lydgate, John—*cont.*

17018 — [Fol. 14ᵛ:] Thus endeth the horse the ghoos & the sheep. [Anon. In verse.] 4º ⁸·¹⁰. [*Westminster, W. Caxton,* 1477?] L(4 leaves).C(lacks 2 leaves). Duff 261.

17019 — [Anr. ed.] The hors. the shepe & the ghoos. 4º ⁸·¹⁰. [*Westminster, W. Caxton,* 1477–78.] C(imp.).; PML. Duff 262.

17020 — [Anr. ed.] Here begynneth a lytell treatyse of the horse, the sheep, and the ghoos. 4º in 6's. [*Westminster, W. de Worde,* c. 1495.] C. Duff 263.

17021 — [Anr. ed.] Here begynneth a lytyll treatyse of the horse, the sheep, and the goos. 4º in 6's. [*Westminster, W. de Worde,* 1499?] L. Duff 264.

17022 — [Anr. ed.] Here begynneth a lytell treatyse of the horse, the shepe, & the goos. 4º in 6's. [*Westminster? W. de Worde,* 1500.] PML(lacks last leaf). Duff 265.

— Hrre [*sic*] folowyth the interpretacōn of the names of goddis and goddesses. *See* 17005 sqq.

— The lamentacyon of our Lady. [1509–10.] *See* 17537.

— The life and death of Hector. 1614. *See* 5581.5.

17023 — [Fol. 94ᵛ:] Here endeth the book of the lyf of our lady. [In verse.] fol. [*Westminster,*] (*W. Caxton,*) [1484.] L.O.C(imp.).G²·M. + ; PML(2, 1 imp.).Y(quire E only). Duff 266.

a6ᵛ line 1 of heading ends: 'yeftes'.

17024 — [Anr. ed.?] fol. [*Westminster, W. Caxton,* 1484.] L(a2, 3,6,7).L⁴¹(a3,6).O(a3,6).C(a3,6).M(2 sets of a3,6).; N(1 leaf).PML(a3,6). Gordan(a3,6). Duff 266a.

a6ᵛ line 1 of heading ends: 'yeftes of'. The frags. prob. represent cancelled leaves rather than a new ed.

17025 — [Anr. ed. Hh5ᵛ:] Here endeth the lyfe of our lady. 4º. (*R. Redman,* 1531 (1 no.)) L.; HN.MEL(2 leaves).

— Here begynneth the lyfe of seint Albon. 1534. *See* 256.

— Here begynnys the mayng or disport of chaucer. 1508. *See* 17014.3.

— The payne and sorowe of euyll maryage. [c. 1530.] *See* 19119.

— This book is intytled the pylgremage of the sowle. 1483. *See* 6473.

17026 — The puerbes of Lydgate. [In verse.] 4º ⁶·⁸. (*W. de Worde,*) [1510?] C.; PML.

14 leaves. Consists largely of extracts from 3175.

17027 — [Anr. ed.] 4º. (*W. de Worde,*) [1520?] L.C(frag.).; HN. (Formerly also 17978) 12 leaves.

17027.5 — This lytell treatyse compendiously declareth the damage . . . caused by the serpente of diuision. [Anon.] 8º. (*R. Redman,*) [c. 1535.] O¹⁰.

17028 — [Anr. ed.] The serpent of diuision . . . . Set forth after the auctours old copy, by I. S[tow.] Anno. M.D.L.IX. the .iiii. of May. 8º. (*O. Rogers,*) [1559.] C.; HN.

17029 — [Anr. ed.] Whereunto is annexed the tragedye of Gorboduc. 2 pts. 4º. *E. Allde f. J. Perrin,* 1590. L.O.C⁶. DUL.PETWORTH.; F(pt. 2 only).HN.HD(pt. 2 only, imp.). PML(pt. 2 only).Y. + Greg 39.

Pt. 2 may also have been issued separately; for earlier eds. *see* 18684 sq.

17030 — Stans puer ad mensam. [In verse.] *Eng.* 4º. [*Westminster, W. Caxton,* 1477?] C.; HN. Duff 269.

Lydgate is named in the envoy on fol. 3ʳ. The 1st line of verse is: My dear child first thyself enable. For other texts resembling this *see* 3303, 20953, 23428, 24866.

17030.5 — [Anr. ed., w. additions.] Stans puer ad mēsā [xylographic.] (Here begynneth Lytell Johan.) 4º. (*W. de Worde,*) [1510?] C.

(Formerly 23430) Little John is reprinted from 3303. A3ʳ line 1 begins: 'Who spareth the rodde . . .'

17030.7 — [Anr. ed.] 4º. [*W. de Worde,* c. 1520.] O(a3 only).

a3ʳ line 1 begins: 'Be meke in measure . . .'

17030.9 — [Anr. ed.] Stans puer ad mensa. otherwyse called the boke of norture, newly imprinted. 4º. (*Southwarke, by me J. Redman,*) [bef. 1540.] L.

A3ʳ line 1 begins: 'who spareth the rodde . . .'

17031 — [Fol. 2ʳ:] Prologus/ Here begynneth the prologue of the storye of Thebes. [In verse. Anon.] 4º in 8's. [*Westminster, W. de Worde,* 1497?] L(lacks 4 leaves). Duff 268.

17032 — The temple of glas. [Anon. In verse.] 4º in 8's. [*Westminster, W. Caxton,* 1477?] C. Duff 270.

17032a — [Anr. ed.] Here begynneth the temple of glas. 4º in 8's. [*Westminster, W. de Worde,* 1495?] L.C(imp.).; HN. Duff 271.

(Formerly also 12955)

Lydgate, John—*cont.*

17033 — [Anr. ed.] Here begynnyth yᵉ temple of glas. 4º in 8's. [*Westminster? W. de Worde,* 1500?] E. Duff 272.

17033.3 — [Anr. ed.] (The temple of glas.) 4º. (*R. Pynson,*) [1503.] O(frag.).

(Formerly 12954)

17033.7 — [Anr. ed.] Here begynneth the temple of glas. 4º. (*W. de Worde,*) [1506?] L.

17034 — [Anr. ed.] This boke called the tēple of glasse, is in many places amended. 4º ⁴·⁶. (*in the house of T. Berthelet,*) [1529?] O.; HN.

(Formerly also 12955a)

17035 — Here begynneth the testamēt of Johñ Lydgate. [In verse.] 4º. (*R. Pynson,*) [1520?] L.C.; HN.

— Here begynneth a treatyse of a galaūt. [1510? etc.] *See* 24240 sqq.

17036 — Here begynneth a treatyse of the smyth whych that forged hym a new dame. [Anon. Not by Lydgate. 1565?] Now = 22653.9.

17037 — [Verses on the seven virtues. Xylographic. Doubtfully attrib. to Lydgate.] s.sh.fol. [*London?* 1500?] L (imp.).

17037.5 — [The virtue of the mass. Anon. In verse.] 4º. [*W. de Worde,* 1500.] L²(1 leaf, Frag. No. 10).

29–30 lines a page.

17038 — [Anr. ed.] The vertue of yᵉ masse. 4º. (*W. de worde,*) [1520?] C.

32 lines a page.

— *See also* 4476.5.

Lydiat, Thomas. Ad clarissimum virum, D. H. Savilium, epistola astronomica. 8º. *typis H. Lowns,* 1621 (29 mr.) L.O.C.D.DUR(Bamb.). + ; HN.HD.

17040 — Defensio tractatus de variis annorum formis contra J. Scaligeri obtrectationem. 8º. *F. Kyngston,* 1607. Ent. 26 fb. L.O.C.D.E². + ; F.HN.CU.HD(imp.).ILL. +

17041 — Emendatio temporum compendio facta ab initio mundi. 8º. *F. Kyngston,* 1609. Ent. 17 fb. L.O.C.D. ETON. + ; F.HN.BALT.

17042 — Numerus aureus melioribus lapillis insignitus factusque Gemmeus; è thesauro anni magni, restauratore T. Lydyat. s.sh.fol. *G. Jones,* 1621 [o.s.](fb.) L⁵(Lemon 193).O.

17043 — Prælectio astronomica de natura cœli. 8º. [*Eliot's Court Press*] excudi curavit *J. Bill,* 1605. Ent. 25 ja. L.O.C. D.E¹³. + ; F.HN.CHI.CU.Y. +

17044 — [A ghost.]

17045 — Recensio et explicatio argumentorum productorum libello emendationis temporum compendio factæ. 12º. [*Geneva, E. Le Preux,*] sumpt. *G. Harper, Londini,* 1613. L².O².O¹³.C.SCL.; F.HD.

These sheets were also issued w. Le Preux's imprint and omitting Harper's (copies at L, O, C, ETON, LC).

17046 — Solis et lunæ periodus [etc.] 8º in 4's. *typis G. S[tansby,]* 1620. L.O(2).O⁵.D.D². ; HD.TEX.

See Court-Book C, p. 465.

17047 — Tractatus de variis annorum formis. 8º. [*Eliot's Court Press,*] ex off. Nortoniana, 1605. Ent. to J. Bill 12 au. L.O.C.D.E. + ; F.HN.CU.HD.ILL. +

Lyford, William, *ed. See* 19941, 19942.

17047.5 **Lyly, John.** A moste excellent comedie of Alexander, Campaspe, and Diogenes. [Anon.] 4º. [*T. Dawson*] f. *T. Cadman,* 1584. DUL.; HN.HD(lacks last leaf). IND.PFOR. Greg 84.

(Formerly 17048b)

17048 — [Anr. ed.] Campaspe, played beefore the queenes maiestie by her maiesties childrē. [Anon.] 4º. [*T. Dawson*] f. *T. Cadman,* 1584. L.O.; F(lacks prelims.).

17048a — [Anr. ed.] Campaspe, played beefore the queenes maiestie by her maiesties children. [Anon.] 4º. [*T. Dawson*] f. *T. Cadman,* 1584. L⁶(imp.).

17048b — Now = 17047.5.

17049 — [Anr. ed.] 4º. *T. Orwin f. W. Broome,* 1591. Ass'd by T. Cadman to J. Broome 12 ap. 1597. L.L⁶.O.C².E. + ; HN(imp.).Y.

17050 — Endimion, the man in the moone. [Anon.] 4º. *J. Charlewood f. the widdowe Broome,* 1591. Ent. 4 oc. L.; HN.Y². Greg 99.

17051 — Euphues. The anatomy of wyt. 4º. [*T. East*] f. *G. Cawood,* [1578.] Ent. 2 de. 1578. L.C².

17052 — [Anr. ed.] Euphues. . . . Corrected and augmented. 4º. f. *G. Cawood,* [1579.] C²(imp.).

With a leaf orn. before the imprint.

Lyly, John—*cont.*

17053 — [Anr. ed.] 4°. (*T. East*) *f. G. Cawood,* (1579.) L²⁴(imp.).
O.; F(imp.).Y.
With '¶' before the imprint.

17053.5 — [Anr. ed.] 4°. (*T. East*) *f. G. Cawood,* (1580.) Robert
Taylor.
Line 2 of imprint ends: 'dwelling'.

17054 — [Anr. ed.] 4°. (*T. East*) *f. G. Cawood,* (1580.) L.O(2
imp.).C.C³.; F.PN(imp.).
Line 2 of imprint ends: 'dwel-'.

17055 — [Anr. ed.] 4°. (*T. East*) *f. G. Cawood,* (1581.) L.O³⁸
(imp.).; IND.N.
Tp line 4 ends: 'all'.

17055.5 — [Anr. ed.] 4°. (*T. East*) *f. G. Cawood,* (1581.) STU.; HD.
Tp line 4 ends: 'Gen-'.

17056 — [Anr. ed.] 4°. (*T. East*) *f. G. Cawood,* (1585.) HN.CH.

17057 — [Anr. ed.] 4°. (*T. East*) *f. G. Cawood,* (1587.) L.
BODMER.SH(lacks tp).; F.Y.

17058 — [Anr. ed.] 4°. [*W. Howe*] *f. G. Cawood,* [1590?] Britwell 244.; F.CU.N(imp.).Y(imp.).

17059 — [Anr. ed.] 4°. *J. Roberts f. G. Cawood,* [1593?] L³⁰.O.;
F.HN.PML.Y.
Tp line 7: 'contained'.

17060 — [Anr. ed.] 4°. *J. Roberts f. G. Cawood,* [1597?] L.
Lord Latymer.; F.HD.NY. Hickmott.
Tp line 7: 'contayned'.

17061 — [Anr. ed.] 4°. [*H. Lownes*] *f. W. Leake,* 1606. Ent. 2 jy.
1602. L⁴(lacks tp).DUR⁵.G². Wroclaw U.; F(2).ILL.
LC(imp.). Pirie.

17062 — [Anr. ed.] 4°. [*H. Lownes*] *f. W. Leake,* 1607. L.; F.HN.
IND.Y.

17063 — [Anr. ed.] 4°. [*H. Lownes*] *f. W. Leake,* 1613. L.O.C⁴.;
F.HN.HD.IND.

17064 — [Anr. ed., w. additions.] Euphues the anatomy of wit.
(Euphues and his England.) 4° in 8's. *G. Eld f. W.
B[arrett,] sold by A. Johnson,* 1617. Ass'd to Barrett
16 fb. L.O.C(imp.).ETON.NOR.+; F.HN.CU.HD.IND.+
2nd pt. reprinted from 17068.

17065 — [Anr. ed.] 4° in 8's. *J. Beale f. J. Parker,* (1623.) Ent.
8 mr. 1620. L.O.C.E.NEK.+; F.HN.HD.N.Y.+

17066 — [Anr. ed.] 4° in 8's. *J. H[aviland,] sold by J. Boler,*
1631. L.O.BIRM.E.P.+; F.HN.CH.PN. De Paul U,
Chicago, Illinois.+
Some copies (O, P, F) are dated 1630 in pt. 2.

17067 — [Anr. ed.] 4° in 8's. *J. Haviland,* 1636. Ent. to J.
Haviland a. J. Wright 4 se. 1638. L.O.C(lacks tp).
A.M.+; F.HN.N.NY.Y.+
Quires A and Q–Aa have perpendicular chainlines.

17068 — Euphues and his England. Containing his voyage and
aduentures. 4°. (*T. East*) *f. G. Cawood,* 1580. Ent.
24 jy. 1579. L²⁴(imp.).; F(imp.).PFOR.
Collates A⁴ ¶⁴ B–Nn⁴ Oo².

17069 — [Anr. ed.] 4°. (*T. East*) *f. G. Cawood,* 1580. O(2,
1 imp.).; Y(imp.).
Collates A⁴ ¶⁴ B–Ll⁴; ¶1ʳ line 2: 'Gentlewoemen'.

17070 — [Anr. ed.] 4°. (*T. East*) *f. G. Cawood,* 1580. L.O.C.C³.;
Robert Taylor.
Collates A⁴ ¶⁴ B–Ll⁴; ¶1ʳ line 2: 'Gentlewomen'.

17071 — [Anr. ed.] 4°. (*T. East*) *f. G. Cawood,* 1581. HN.

17072 — [Anr. ed.] 4°. (*T. East*) *f. G. Cawood,* 1582. O³⁸(imp.).;
HD.N.Y.

17072.5 — [Anr. ed.] 4°. (*T. Este*) *f. G. Cawood,* 1584. Y.

17073 — [Anr. ed.] 4°. (*T. East*) *f. G. Cawood,* 1586. HN.CH.KAN.
MCG.

17074 — [Anr. ed.] 4°. (*T. East*) *f. G. Cawood,* 1588. L.BODMER.
LIV³.SH.; F.HD.Y. Dr. Kenneth Rapoport, Middle-
town, N.Y.

17074.5 — [Anr. ed.] 4°. (*A. Jeffes*) *f. G. Cawood,* 1592. F.CU.N.

17075 — [Anr. ed.] 4°. *J. R[oberts] (imp.) f. G. Cawood,* 1597. L.L³⁰.
O.; F.HN.LC(imp.).NY(imp.).PML.

17076 — [Anr. ed.] 4°. *J. R[oberts] f. G. Cawood,* 1601. F.HD.Y.
Hickmott.

17077 — [Anr. ed.] 4°. [*E. Allde?*] *f. W. Leake,* 1605. Ent. 2 jy.
1602. Lord Latymer.; F.HN.WTL.Y.

17078 — [Anr. ed.] 4°. [*E. Allde?*] *f. W. Leake,* 1606. L.L⁴.O.
Wroclaw U.; F.IND.

17079 — [Anr. ed.] 4°. [*W. Hall?*] *f. W. Leake,* 1609. L.O.C²
(imp.).DUR⁵.; F(2).HN(lacks tp).ILL.IND. Pirie.
For later eds. *see* 17064 sqq.

17080 — Gallathea. [Anon.] 4°. *J. Charlwoode f. the widdow
Broome,* 1592. Ent. to G. Cawood 1 ap. 1585, to J.
Broome 4 oc. 1591. L.E.; HN. Greg 105.

17081 — = pt. of 17088.

17082 — Loves metamorphosis. A wittie and courtly pastorall.
4°. [*S. Stafford*] *f. W. Wood,* 1601. Ent. 25 no. 1600.
L.L⁶.O.O⁶.C⁶.+; F.HN.HD.IND.PFOR. Greg 178.

Lyly, John—*cont.*

— Mar-Martine, I know not why [etc.] [1589.] *See* 17461.

17083 — Midas. Plaied before the queenes maiestie. [Anon.] 4°.
T. Scarlet f. J. B[roome,] 1592. Ent. to J. Broome
4 oc. 1591. L.L⁶.O.O⁵(lacks tp).E.; F.HN.CH.HD(lacks
tp).N. Greg 106.

17084 — Mother Bombie. As it was sundrie times plaied. [Anon.]
4°. *T. Scarlet f. C. Burby,* 1594. Ent. 18 jn. L.O.
Greg 125.

17085 — [Anr. ed.] 4°. *T. Creede f. C. Burby,* 1598. L(2).L⁶.
O(2).C⁶.E.; F.HN.BO.HD.PFOR.

— Pappe with an hatchet. [1589.] *See* 17463.

17086 — Sapho and Phao. Played beefore the queenes maiestie.
[Anon.] 4°. (*T. Dawson*) *f. T. Cadman,* 1584. Ent.
6 ap. L. Greg 82.
A3ʳ catchword: 'his'.

17086.5 — [Anr. ed.] 4°. (*T. Dawson*) *f. T. Cadman,* 1584. O⁶.E.;
HN.
A3ʳ catchword: 'forge. What'.

17087 — [Anr. ed.] 4°. *T. Orwin f. W. Broome,* 1591. Ent. to J.
Broome 12 ap. 1597. L(2).L⁶.O(lacks last leaf).E
(lacks tp).; F.HN.HD.Y².

17088 — Sixe court comedies. . . . 12°. *W. Stansby f. E. Blount,*
1632. Ent. 9 ja. 1628. L.O.C².E.M.+; F.HN.HD.ILL.Y.+
In title: 'Witie'. Includes reprints of 17048, 17050,
17080, 17083, 17084, and 17086.

17089 — [A variant, w. 'wittie' in title.] L¹⁵.L³⁰.O².C.G⁴.+; HN.
BO.N.NY.TEX.+

— A whip for an ape. [1589.] *See* 17464.

17090 — The woman in the moone. 4°. [*J. Roberts*] *f. W. Jones,*
1597. Ent. to R. Fynche 22 se. 1595. L(2).L⁶.O.O⁶.;
HN.HD.IND.PFOR. Greg 144.

Lynch, John. Pascha Christianum; the Christian passe-
over. 1637. *See* 23120.

17091 **Lynche, Richard.** Diella, certaine sonnets, adioyned to
the amorous poeme of Dom Diego and Gineura.
[Init. R. L., Gentleman.] 8°. [*J. Roberts*] *f. H.
Olney,* 1596. L.O.; F.HN.

17092 — An historical treatise of the travels of Noah into
Europe: done into English by R. Lynche [from G.
Nanni.] 4°. *A. Islip,* 1601. L.O.O⁸.C.E.; F.HN.HD.N.
Y.+

17092.5 — [Anr. issue, w. cancel tp, w. imprint:] *A. Islip f. M.
Law,* 1602. CHI.

— *tr. See* 4691.

Lynde, *Sir* Humphrey. A case for the spectacles. 1638.
See 17101.

17093 — A letter of Sʳ. Humfrey Linde, to a lady of great worth,
much afflicted for syr Humphreys sake. [A satire on
Lynde, written by J. Floyd?] 8°. [*St. Omer, English
College Press,*] 1634. O.C¹⁰.E.

17094 — [A ghost.]

17095 — Via devia: the by-way: mis-leading the weake by
colourable shewes of apocryphall scriptures. 12°. *A.
M[athewes] f. R. Milbourne,* 1630. Ent. 17 oc. 1629.
L.O.C.DUR⁵.M².+; F.HN.HD.N.NY.+

17096 — Second edition. 12°. *A. Mathewes f. R. Milbourne,*
1632. L.O.C.E².YK.+; F.HN.HD.ILL.NY¹¹.+
Most, if not all, copies have a cancel tp.

17097 — Via tuta: the safe way. Leading all christians to the
true, ancient, and catholique faith, now professed
in the church of England. 12°. *G. M[iller] f. R.
Milbourne,* 1628. Ent. 18 ap. L.O.O¹³.C.; F(2).HN.U.
Y.
Answered by 11112, 23630.

17098 — Second edition. 12°. *T. H[arper] f. R. Milbourne,* 1629.
L.O.C.DEU.USHAW.+; F.BO².HD(imp.).

17099 — Third edition. 12°. *F. K[ingston] f. R. Milbourne,* 1629.
L².O.C.M.P.+; F.HN.HD.ILL.U.+
Copies vary: errata on Q9ʳ or Q12ʳ; both at F.

17100 — Fourth edition. 12°. *A. M[athewes] f. R. Milbourne,*
1630. L.O.C.DUR⁵.SHEF.+; F.HN.HD.N.U.

17100a — Fifth edition. 12°. *A. Math[ewes] f. R. Milbourne,* 1632.
L.O.C⁹.E².PETYT.+; F.HN.BO³.HD.

17101 — A case for the spectacles, or, a defence of Via tuta,
together with Stricturæ in Lyndomastygem, and a
sermon preached at his [i.e. Lynde's] funerall by D.
Featley. 2 pts. 4°. *M. P[arsons] f. R. Milbourne,* 1638.
Ent. 23 de. 1636. L.O.C.D.E².+; F.HN.BO³.N.U.+
Answers 11112.

— *ed. See* 20752.

— *See also* 23528.

17102 **Lyndewode, William,** *Bp.* [Constitutiones provinciales. S9ᵛ:] Explicit opus . . . super constitucõnes prouinciales. fol. [*Oxford, T. Rood,* 1483.] L.O.C(imp.). E(imp.).M.+; HD.N. Scheide. Duff 278.
  Most of a1–k2 is in 2 settings (e.g. c2ʳ, col. 1, last line has 'aggregationis' or 'aggrauationis'; leaf signature f1 is under 'ꝙuis' or under 'glosa'), but copies are often found mixed. This and the continental fol. eds. (17107, 17109, 17111) include Lyndewode's text and commentary; English-printed 8º eds. have only the text.

17103 — [Anr. ed.] Constitutiones prouinciales ecclesie anglicæ. 8º. (*ap. westmonasteriũ. in domo caxston* [sic], *per w. de worde,* 1496 (31 my.)) L.L².O.C.M.+; HN.HD.PML. Gordan. Duff 279.

17103.5 — [Anr. issue, w. 4 quires reset.] L.; HN. Duff 279. In title: 'Constituciones'.

17104 — [Anr. ed.] 8º. (*ap. westmonasteriũu* [sic], *ꝑ w. de worde,* 1499 (15 ap.)) L².O.O⁵.M.OS(imp.).; F. Grolier Club. Duff 280.

17105 — [Anr. ed. A7ʳ:] Explicit opus . . . super constituciones ꝓuinciales. 8º. (*R. Pynson,*) [1499.] L.O.DNPK.M.; HD.LC.N.PML. Gordan. Duff 281.

17106 — [Anr. ed. a1ʳ:] De sũma trinitate [etc.] 8º. (*per R. Pynson,*) [1499.] L.M(imp.). Duff 282.

17107 — [Anr. ed.] Prouinciale seu constitutiones Anglie cum summariis. [*Ed.*] (J. Badius Ascensius.) fol. (*in parisiana acad., A. Bocard,* 1501 (28 my.)) L.O.C. DUR.STU.+; F.HN.HD.MICH.NY.+
  The Badius ed. is reprinted in 17109, 17111. Though no English bookseller is mentioned in the imprint of 17107 and 17108, both items were clearly intended for sale in England.

17108 — [A different text, not by Lyndewode.] Constitutiones legitime seu legatine regionis anglicane: cũ interpretatione Johannis de Athon. [*Ed.*] (J. Badius Ascensius.) fol. *Parisijs, co impresse* (*arte w. hopilij, imp. eiusdem et J. cõfluẽtini,* 1504 (id. se.)) L.O.C.E. M.+; F.CAL⁵.HD.Y(2).
  Often bd. w. 17111. Reprinted in 17109 w. the commentary and in 17109.3 sqq. without the commentary, as Constitutiones Othonis.

17109 — [Anr. ed. of 17107 and 17108 together. a1ʳ:] Prouinciale, seu cõstitutiones Anglie . . . reuise. [✠1ʳ:] (Constitutiones legitime seu legatine.) 2 pts. fol. (*in Parisorũ acad., diligentia w. Hopylij, imp. mercatoris Londoñ. w. Brettoñ,*) *venales habentur Londoñ. ap.* [*H. Jacobi a. J. Pelgrim,*] (1505 (23 mr.)) L.O.C.D². E².+; HN.HD.LC.N.PML.+

17109.3 — [Anr. ed. H6ʳ:] Explicit opus super constitutiones prouinciales. (Constitutiones Othonis.) 2 pts. 8º. (*per me R. Pynson,*) [c. 1505.] L.O.

17109.7 — [Anr. ed.] Incipiunt opera super cõstitutines [sic] prouinciales et Othonis. 8º. (*per me w. de worde,* 1508.) L.
  (Formerly 10081)

17110 — [Anr. ed.] Incipiunt opera super cõstitutiones prouinciales & Othonis. 8º. (*per me w. de worde,* 1517.) C. LIV³. Chester PL.; HN.

17111 — [Anr. ed. of 17107, i.e. of Lyndewode's text alone, w. commentary.] Prouinciale seu cõstitutiones Anglie. fol. (*Antwerpie, diligentia C. Endouieñ,* i.e. *Ruremond,*]) *venales habẽtur Londoñ. ap. F. bryckman,* (1525 (20 de.)) L.O.C.DUR⁵.M.+; HN.CU.HD.N.PML.+
  Often bd. w. 17108.

17111.5 — [Anr. ed. of both texts, without commentary.] Incipiunt opera sup cõstitutiones ꝓuinciales et Othonis. 8º. (*ap. w. de worde,* 1526 (16 ka. au.)) HD.
  (Formerly 10082)

17112 — [Anr. ed.] 8º. (*ap. w. de worde,* 1529 (28 no.)) L.; F. HD.Y.

17112.5 — [Anr. ed.] Constitutiones Angliæ prouinciales. 8º. *T. Marshe,* 1557. Ent. to T. Orwin 23 jn. 1591. L.O.C. A.D.+; F.HN.HD.MIN.NYⁱⁱ.+
  (Formerly 17114) Most copies misdated 2557; copies of both at O.

Lyndewode, William, *Bp.*—*cont.*

17113 — [A trans.] Constitutions ꝓuincialles, and of Otho, and Octhobone, *tr.* in to Englyshe. 8º. (*R. Redman,* 1534.) L.L².O(2).C.BTL.; F.HN.HD.
  (Formerly also 10083)

17114 — Now = 17112.5.

Lyne, Richard, *Engraver. See* 4349.

17115 **Lynne, Walter.** The beginning and endynge of all popery. (*Tr.* G. Lynne.) 4º. (*J. Herforde, at the costes of G. Lynne,*) [1548?] L.L².O(3).C.E(lacks tp).; HN.SMU(E4 only).
  Based on a German trans. of the Vaticinia sive prophetiae by Joachimus, Abbot of Fiore.

17116 — [Anr. ed., revised.] A most necessarie treatise, declaring the beginning and ending of all poperie. 4º. *J. Charlewoode,* 1588. Ent. 22 jy. L.L².O¹⁷.D.HETH (imp.).; F.HD(imp.).

17117 — A briefe and compendiouse table, in a maner of a concordaunce, of the whole Bible. Gathered by H. Bullynger [etc.] 8º. [*S. Mierdman*] (*f.* G. Lynne,) 1550. L.L¹⁵.O(3).C(imp.).C⁵(imp.).; F.HN.CAL.HD.NY. (Formerly also 3015)

17118 — [Anr. ed.] 8º. (*J. Tysdale,*) 1563. L.L⁻⁵.O.P.; F. (Formerly also 3016)

17119 — A briefe collection of all such textes of the scripture as do declare yᵉ happie estate of thẽ that be vyseted wyth syckenes. Wherunto are added two sermons by M. Luther. 8º. [*S. Mierdman*] (*f.* G. Lynne, 1549.) O. Sheffield PL.; PML.
  — *tr. See* 4079, 4626, 16964, 16982, 20843, 21826.6.

17120 **Lyon, John.** Teares for the never sufficientlie bewailed death of Alexander earle of Dumfermeling. 4º. *Edinburgh, heires of A. Hart,* 1622. HN.

17120.5 **Lyons.** A note of such things as were stollen in Lyons, on Munday night the eleventh of June 1630. [List of pearls and other jewelry.] If any such thing shall be heard of, let them repaire to Mʳ. de la Barre in Crutchet-Fryers. s.sh.fol. [*W. Jones?* 1630.] L⁵ (Lemon 300).
  See also 23952.7.

Lysandre. A tragi-comicall history . . . of Lisander, and Calista. 1627, etc. *See* 906 sq.

Lyshborne. *See* 15704.

17121 **Lysias.** Eratosthenes, hoc est, breuis et luculenta defensio Lysiæ, prælectionibus illustrata A. Dunæi. *Gr. a. Lat.* 8º. *J. Legatus, Acad. Cantab. typographus,* 1593. L.O.C.D.E.+; F.HN.CAL.HD.ILL.+

17122 **Lyster, John.** A rule how to bring vp children. 8º. (*T. East,* 1588.) D².; F.ILL(lacks colophon).

17122.5 **Lyte, Henry,** *the Elder.* The light of Britayne. A recorde of the honorable originall & antiquitie of Britaine. 8º. [*J. Charlewood?*] 1588. O³(E).; F.
  — *tr. See* 6984.

17123 **Lyte, Henry,** *the Younger.* The art of tens, or decimall arithmeticke. 8º. *E. Griffin,* 1619. Ent. 21 au. L.O. C³.E.WOR.+; HN.

17123.5 — To be taught in [ ] The foure principles of arithmetic in six houres, to any that hath but a reasonable capacity. s.sh.4º. [*E. Griffin,* 1619.] Rogers(2 cropt).
  Poster advertising lectures, mentioning 'my little booke' (17123).

M

M., A. A deuoute mans purposes. 1597. *See* 17231.
— Himatia-Poleos. 1614. *See* 18274.
— Metropolis coronata. 1615. *See* 18275.

17124 — The true reporte of the prosperous successe which God gaue vnto our English souldiours in Ireland, 1580. More at large set foorth then in the former printed copie. 4°. [*J. Charlewood*] *f. E. White*, [1581.] Ent. 20 de. 1580. C.
Epistle on A2. Possibly by A. Munday.

17124a — [Anr. issue, anon., w. verses on A2^r.] C.

17125 — A relation of the passages of our English companies from time to time, [etc.] 4°. [*E. Allde*] *f. H. Gosson*, 1621. F.HD.
— Sidero-Thriambos. 1618. *See* 18278.
— The strangest adventure [etc.] 1601. *See* 23864.
— A watch-woord to Englande. 1584. *See* 18282.
— *ed. See* 3189, 23344.
— *tr. See* 7, 190, 543, 544, 11513, 12498, 19159, 19161, 19447, 20367, 23864.

17126 **M., A.,** *Minister in Henley.* An amulet. 1617. Now = 17238.5.

M., B. R. Adagia in Latine and English. 1621. *See* 10441.5.

17126.5 **M., C.** The first part of the nature of a woman. Fitly described in a Florentine historie. 4°. *V. Simmes f. C. Knight*, 1596. Ent. 30 de. 1595. O.
Attrib. to C. Middleton.

17127 — The second part of the historie, called the nature of a woman. 4°. *the widow Orwin f. C. Knight*, 1596. O.
Attrib. to C. Middleton.
— *tr. See* 18931.

17128 **M., Ch.** Meditations, and devout discourses upon the B. sacrament. [By M. Kellison.] 8° in 4's. *Doway, L. Kellam* [*the younger*,] 1639. O.C.OS.USHAW.
A&R 485.

17129 — A myrrhine posie of the bitter dolours of Christ his passion. [By M. Kellison.] 8°. *Doway, L. Kellam* [*the younger*,] 1639. L.L^{35}.TMTH.YK^2.; F.TEX.U.
A&R 486.

17130 — Paraphrasticall and devout discourses upon the psalme Miserere. [By M. Kellison.] 8°. [*Douai, G. Pinchon*,] 1635. L.O.C.A^2.USHAW.+; F.TEX.
A&R 487.

M., D. *See* 18294.5.

17131 **M., D. F. R. de.** Respuesta y desengano contra las false-dades enbituperio de la Armada Inglesa. 4°. *en casa de A. Hatfildo, por T. Cadmano*, 1589. L.O(tp only, Douce Add. 142/230).HAT.; HD.

17132 — [A trans.] An answer to the vntruthes, published in Spaine, in glorie of their supposed victorie against our English nauie. *Tr. J. L*(ea.) 4°. *J. Jackson f. T. Cadman*, 1589. Ent. 1 fb. L.O.C^2.DUR^3.P.+; F.HN.COR.HD.NY.

M., E. A deuoute mans purposes. 1597. *See* 17231.

17133 — Humors antique faces. 1605. Now = 21385.5.
— The man in the moone. 1638. *See* 11943.

M., E., *of Christ Church, Oxford, tr. See* 7371.5 sq.

M., F., *tr. See* 19935.

M., G. Cheap and good husbandry. 1631. *See* 17339.
— A compendious treatise in metre. 1554. *See* 17469.
— The English husbandman. 1613. *See* 17355.
— Hobsons horse-load of letters. 1613. *See* 17360.
— Honour in his perfection. 1624. *See* 17361.
— The loue of the soule. 1578. *See* 17504.

17134 — [Anr. ed.] 1619. = 17506.
— The second and last part of the first booke of the English Arcadia. 1613. *See* 17352.

M., G.—*cont.*
— The second part of the soldiers grammar. 1627. *See* 17392.
— A second part to the mothers blessing. 1622. *See* 17387.3.
— The souldiers accidence. 1625. *See* 17388.
— Vox militis. 1625. *See* 20980.
— *ed. See* 3314.
— *tr. See* 741.

M., G., *Gent.* The souldiers grammar. 1626, etc. *See* 17391, 17393.

M., H. To the catholickes of England. [1636.] *See* 21505.

17135 **M., H.,** *of the Middle Temple.* The strange fortune of Alerane: or, my ladies toy. [In verse.] 4°. *V. S*[*immes*] *f. M. L*[*ownes*,] 1605. Ent. 8 fb. L(tp only, Harl. 5927/239).L^4(frag.).O^{13}.; HN.

M., I. or J. The abridgement or summarie of the Scots chronicles. 1633. *See* 18015.
— Adams tragedie. Declaring Satans malice. 1608. *See* 17156.3.
— The anatomie of pope Joane. 1624. *See* 17754.
— Antonios revenge. 1602. *See* 17474.
— A briefe abstract of all the English statutes [etc.] 1625. *See* 17836.7.

17136 — A breefe directory, and playne way howe to say the rosary of our blessed lady: whereunto be adioyned the prayers of S. Bryget, w. others. 16° in 8's. *Bruges, H. Holost* [*i.e. London, W. Carter a. J. Lion*,] 1576. L.
A&R 488.

17137 — A briefe recantacion of maystres missa. 1.54.8. 8°. [*R. Wyer?* 1548.] F.
— A christian almanacke. 1612. *See* 18019.
— Conceyted letters. 1618. *See* 3637.

17138 — Ane fruitful and comfortable exhortatioun anent death. 1597. Now = 17815.5.

17139 — The generall practise of medecine. By Φιλιατρεύς. 8°. *Edinburgh, J. Wreittoun*, 1634. L.A.
Possibly by J. Makluire.

17140 — A health to the gentlemanly profession of seruingmen. 4°. *W. W*[*hite*,] 1598. Ent. 15 my. L.O(2).; F.
Attrib. to G. Markham.
— The history of Antonio and Mellida. 1602. *See* 17473.
— A most exact, ready and plaine discourse, how to trayne horses to amble. 1605. *See* 17384.5.
— A new booke of cookerie. 1615. *See* 18299.
— The poem of poems. [1596.] *See* 17386.
— A sixe-fold politician. 1609. *See* 17805.
— The teares of the beloved. 1600. *See* 17395.
— *tr. See* 535.5, 1074.5.
— *tr. See* also Mabbe, James.

M., I., *Counselor.* A terrible sea-fight. 1640. *See* 21479.5.

M., J., *Gent.* The most famous historie, of Mervine. 1612. *See* 17844.

17141 **M., J.,** *Master of Arts.* The soules pilgrimage to celestial glorie. 4°. *A. Mathewes, sold by W. Sheares*, 1634. L.C.D.EX.; F.HD.ILL.Y.
Possibly by J. Maxwell.

17141a — Spiritual food, and physick. 1623. = 17861.

17142 **M., J.,** *Mr.* A funerall sermon, preached at the buriall of the lady Jane Maitlane. Together with diverse epitaphs. 4°. *Edinburgh,* [*R. Young*,] *printers to the kings majestie*, 1633. L.E.E^2.; F.HN.
Presumably by a J. Maitland.

17143 **M., Jo.** Phillippes Venus. Wherin is pleasantly discoursed sundrye arguments. 4°. [*E. Allde*] *f. J. Perrin*, 1591. O.; F(lacks tp).

M., L. A booke of fishing with hooke & line. 1590. *See* 17572.
— An excellent ditty. [1634.] *See* 18104.5.
— *tr. See* 17590, 20180.7.

M., L., *Gent., ed. See* 652.

17144 **M., M.** An ease for a diseased man. 8°. *W. Jones, sold by J. Wright,* [*Senior,*] 1625. L.
— Ane godlie dreame. 1603. *See* 17811.
— Vienna [etc.] [1628.] *See* 17201.

M., M. T. The life of sir T. Moore. [1631.] *See* 18066.

M., P. The christians combat. 1591. *See* 17842.7.
— A commentarie vpon the booke of the Prouerbes of Salomon. 1592. *See* 18245.
— The excellencie of the mysterie of Christ Jesus. 1590. *See* 18247.
— The fatall dowry. 1632. *See* 17646.
— Newes from Malta. 1603. *See* 17215.
— The powerfull favorite. 1628. *See* 17664.
17144.5 — Religions complaint to the honourable ladyes of Scotland. [In verse.] s.sh.fol. [*Edinburgh, J. Wreittoun,* 1639?] L(Harl.5938/95–96).
By P. MacKenzie?

17145 **M., P.,** *Gentleman.* King Charles his birthright. [In verse.] 4°. *Edinburgh, J. Wreittoun,* 1633. L.O.; HN.
Attrib. to P. Maitland.

M., P. D. The image of bothe churches. 1623. *See* 19480.

17145.3 **M., R.** An epytaphe vpon the death of M. Rycharde Goodricke esquier. 1/2 sh.fol. [*London,* 1562.] E.
17145.7 — An exercise for a christian familie; . . . By R. M. 12°. *R. Waldegraue,* 1585. CAR.
17146 — Micrologia. Characters, or essayes. 8°. *T. C[otes] f. M. Sparke,* 1629. Ent. 22 de. 1628 as 'a booke called Rodes Charecters'. O(2).
17147 — A newe ballade, O dere lady Elysabeth [etc.] *Ballad.* s.sh.fol. [*London,* 1560?] L.L⁵(Lemon 48).
17148 — Newes of Sᵣ. Walter Rauleigh. With the true description of Guiana. 4°. [*G. Eld*] *f. H. G[osson,] sold by J. Wright,* 1618. Ent. to J. Trundle a. H. Gosson 17 mr. L.O.; F.HN.CB.NY.
List of ships on G3ᵛ.
17148.3 — [Anr. issue, w. sheets B–D reset.] L.L³⁰.O(2).; HN.HD (lacks tp).MICH.NCU.NY.
G3ᵛ blank.
— The translation of certaine latine verses vppon her majesties death. 1603. *See* 18252.
— *ed. See* 6103.

17148.7 **M., R.,** *Minister of Gods Word.* Three treatises religiously handled. 8°. *J. Windet,* 1603. L(tp only, Harl. 5993/105).

17149 **M., R.,** *Student in Divinity.* A profitable dialogue for a perverted papist. 4°. *S. Stafford,* 1609. Ent. 18 mr. F.HD.
17149.5 — A true touchstone for a counterfeite catholike. 8°. *W. White,* 1609. Ent. 16 no. YK.

17150 **M., S.** A sermon concerning internall and externall workes. 4°. *J. Legatt,* 1632. Ent. 8 jn. L.O.O³.G². Finedon.; F.
Dedic. indicates S. M. is not the author.

M., S. T., *tr. See* 911.

M., T. The ant, and the nightingale. 1604. *See* 17874.3.
— The blacke booke. 1604. *See* 17875.
17151 — The copie of a letter written from Master T. M. neere Salisbury to Master H. A. at London. 4°. *R. B[arker,]* 1603. L.O.C².DUR⁵.P.+; F.HN.HD.
There are 2 states of A outer forme: A3ᵣ catchword 'the' (HD) or 'warrant' (L). HD copy has A outer forme perfected w. inner forme of 17151a.
17151a — [Anr. issue, w. title:] The copie of a letter written from Master C. S. neere Salisbury [etc.] L.O.O⁵.C.SHEF.+; HN.HD.
In some copies (O, HD) A outer forme is perfected w. inner forme of 17151.
17152 — Digesta scholastica, in gratiam puerorum edita. 8°. *Oxoniæ, J. Lichfield et G. Wrench,* 1617. O.
Attrib. to T. Morrice.
— A discourse of trade, unto the East-Indies. 1621. *See* 18255.
— An exact discoverie of Romish doctrine. 1605. *See* 18184.

M., T.—*cont.*
— Father Hubburds tales. 1604. *See* 17874.7.
— A mad world, my masters. 1608. *See* 17888.
— The manner of his Lordships entertainment. 1613. *See* 17904, pt. 2.
— The tragedy of Julia Agrippina. 1639. *See* 17718a.
— A trick to catch the old-one. 1608. *See* 17896a.
— The tryumphs of honor and industry. 1617. *See* 17899.
17153 — The true narration of the entertainment of his royall majestie, from Edenbrough; till London. 4°. *T. Creede f. T. Millington,* 1603. Ent. to C. Burby a. T. Millington 9 my. L.O.O³(imp.).E.M.+; F.HN.HD. PFOR.Y.+
(Formerly also 14433) The inits. may merely be those of the publisher.
— The two gates of salvation. 1609. *See* 17904.3.
— *tr. See* 743.

M., T., *A Countrie Farmer.* The silkewormes. 1599. *See* 17994.

M., T., *Esq.* The tragedy of Julia Agrippina. 1639. *See* 17718.

M., T., *Gent.* The ghost of Lucrece. 1600. *See* 17885.5.
— A mad world, my masters. 1640. *See* 17889.
17154 — Micro-cynicon. Six snarling satyres. 8°. *T. Creede f. T. Bushell,* 1599. O.; HN. 𝔄
Sometimes attrib. to T. Middleton.

M., T., *Physition, tr. See* 12411.5.

17154.5 **M., W.** [Heading on recto of first leaf:] A description of the creation . . . set downe in manner of alphabet by W. M. Edinburgs alphabet. [In verse.] 8°. [*Edinburgh, J. Wreittoun,* 1632.] E.
Commonly attrib. to W. Mercer.
17155 — The man in the moone, telling strange fortunes, or the English fortune-teller. 4°. *J. W[indet] f. N. Butter,* 1609. Ent. 13 no. L.O.; F.
17155.5 — The lamentation of Englande: for the late treasons conspired against the queenes maiestie . . . by F. Throgmorton. 1584. *Ballad.* s.sh.fol. *R. Jhones,* [1584.] Private owner.
— *tr. See* 11550.

M., W., *S.J., tr. See* 20967, 23948.5.

17156 **M., W.,** *Servitor.* A true discourse of the late battaile fought betweene our Englishmen, and the prince of Parma. 4°. *R. Ward,* 1585. HN.

M. I. G. Prognostication. 1639. *See* 446.3.

17156.3 **Mabb, John.** Adams tragedie. Declaring Satans malice. [Init. I. M.] 8°. *W. W[hite] f. T. Downe a. E. Dawson,* 1608. Ent. to White 26 mr. HD.
17156.7 — The afflicted mans vow: with his meditations and prayers. 8°. *T. Snodham, sould by J. Helme,* 1609. Ent. to Helme 19 oc. P.; F.HD.

Mabbe, James, *tr. See* 288 sqq., 4911, 4914, 11126, 14830.7 sqq.

Macalpine, John. *See* Machabæus, J.

17157 **MacCaghwell, Hugh.** Scᴀᴛhᴀn ꝛhᴀcꝼᴀmuinᴛe nᴀ hᴀiᴛꝼiꝛohe. 12° in 6's. [*Louvain, press of the Irish Franciscans,*] 1618. L.O.C.D.E².+; HD(imp.).N(imp.). A&R 489.

17158 **Macchiavelli, Niccolò.** Lasino doro di Nicolo Macchiauelli, con tutte laltre sue operette. 8°. *Roma* [*London, J. Wolfe,*] 1588. Ent. to J. Wolfe 17 se. L.O.C.E.M.+; F.HN.HD.NY.Y.+
17159 — I discorsi di Nicolo Machiauelli, sopra la prima deca di T. Liuio. Nouellamente emmendati. 8°. *Palermo, heredi d'Antoniello degli Antonielli* [*London, J. Wolfe,*] 1584 (28 ja.) L.O.C.M⁴.RGU.+; F.HD.ILL.N.Y.+
In title: 'con somma cura'.
17159.5 — [Anr. issue, w. first quire reset.] E.; F.HN.NY.PN.
In title: 'con somma diligenza'.
17160 — Machiavels discourses. upon [*sic*] the first decade of T. Livius. Tr. E. D(acres.) 12°. *T. Paine f. W. Hills a. D. Pakeman,* 1636. Ent. 15 mr. L.O.C.E.M.+; F.HN.HD.N.NY.+
Some copies (L, O) have both cancel and cancellandum for B1. Tp lines 6–7 vary: 'animadversions' in italic (L, HD) or roman (F).

Macchiavelli, Niccolò—*cont.*

17161 — [Florentine history.] Historie. . . . Nuouamente ammendate. 12°. *Piacenza, heredi di G. Giolito [London, J. Wolfe,]* 1587. Ent. to J. Wolfe 18 se. L.O.C(2).YK.; F.BALT.HD.IND.Y.+

17162 — The Florentine historie. *Tr.* T. B(edingfeld,) esquire. fol. *T. C(reede) f. W. P(onsonby,)* 1595. Ent. 2 oc. 1594. L.O.C.D.E.+; F.HN.HD.N.NY.+

17163 — Libro dell'arte della guerra. Nouamente corretti [*sic*]. 8°. *Palermo, Antonello degli Antonelli [London, J. Wolfe,* 1587.] L(both tpp).O.M⁴(both tpp).; HN.

At least HN has A8ʳ line 3 from bottom: 'non vēga'.

17163.5 — [Anr. issue, w. cancel bifolium A1, 8 with title:] I setti libri dell'arte della guerra. [*London, J. Wolfe,*] 1587. O.E.RGU.; F.HD.

At least HD has A8ʳ line 3 from bottom: 'nō venga'.

17164 — [A trans.] The arte of warre. (Certain waies for the orderyng of souldiers.) *Tr.* P. Whitehorne. 2 pts. 4°. (*J. Kingston f. N. Englande,*) 1560 (jy.) (1562 (ap.)) Ent. 1562–63. L.O.C².A.M.+; F.HN.CH.HD.Y.+

17165 — [Anr. ed.] Newly imprinted with other additions. 2 pts. 4°. (*W. Williamson f. J. Wight,*) 1573 (se.) L.L¹⁰.O (pt. 2 only).E².G².+; F(pt. 2 only).HN.LC.MICH(pt. 2 only).N.

Issued w. 4790 as pt. 3.

17166 — [Anr. ed.] 2 pts. 4°. (*T. East f. J. Wight,*) 1588. L.O.C⁴.DUL.P.+; F.HN.BO⁵.COR.LC.+

Issued w. 4791 as pt. 3.

17167 — Il prencipe di Nicolo Machiauelli. Con alcune altre operette. 8°. *Palermo, heredi d'Antoniello degli Antonielli [London, J. Wolfe,]* 1584 (28 ja.) L.O.C.E. YK.+; F.HN.HD.N.NY.+

Some copies (L, C) read 'dagli' in imprint.

17168 — [A trans.] Nicholas Machiavel's Prince. Also, the life of Castruccio Castracani of Lucca. *Tr.* E. D(acres.) 12°. *R. Bishop f. W. Hils, sold by D. Pakeman,* 1640. Ent. 16 jn. 1639. L.O.C.D.E.+; F.HN.CU.HD.N.+

1 PN copy at least has uncorrected state of tp line 11 reading 'Paul, the and'.

— A discourse upon the meanes of wel governing. Against N. Machiavell. 1602. *See* 11743.
— Grandsire Graybeard. Or Machiavell displayed. 1635. *See* 3704.9.

17169 — Machivells dogge. 1617. Now = 3664.5.
17170 — The uncasing of Machivils instructions to his sonne. 1613. Now = 3704.3.
17171 — [Anr. ed.] 1615. Now = 3704.7.

Macdowell, William. Theses aliquot logicæ. Præside G. Makdowello. 1613. *See* 21555.21.

17172 **Macer, Æmilius.** Macers herbal. Practysyd by Doctor Lynacro. [1542?] Now = 13175.9.
17173 — A newe herball of Macer. [1535?] Now = 13175.3.

17173.5 **Macey, George.** A sermon preached at Charde in the countie of Somerset. 8°. [*R. Bradock?*]*f. R. D[exter,] soulde by M. Hart, Exceter,* 1601. Ent. to Dexter 3 au. F.

17174 **Machabæus, Joannes.** Enarratio in Deuteronomium [etc.] 8°. *typis R. Hall,* 1563. Ent. 1562–63. L².L¹³. O.C(2).C¹⁰.

Machin, Lewis. The dumbe knight. 1608. *See* 17398.
— *See also* 1429.

Machin, Lewis, and **Bacster, William.** The insatiate countesse. 1613. *See* 17476.5.

MacKenzie, Patrick. Religions complaint to the honourable ladyes of Scotland. [1639?] *See* 17144.5.

MacIlwain or **Macilmane, Roland.** *See* Makilmenæus, R.

17175 **Macollo, Joannes.** Iatria chymica, exemplo therapeiæ luis venereæ illustrata. 8° in 4's. *ap. J. Billium,* 1622. L.O.C.E².G².+; F.

17175.3 **Macguire, Patrick.** Teares for the death of the most gracious prince Lodovicke, duke of Richmond. [In verse.] s.sh.fol. *f. J. Wright,* [1624.] L⁵(Lemon 219).

17175.7 **Macropedius, Georgius.** (Methodus) de conscribendis epistolis. Accessit C. Hegendorphini epistolas conscribendi methodus. 8°. *T. Vautrollerius,* 1576. L(tp only, Harl.5990/23, cropt at top).

17176 — [Anr. ed.] 8°. *T. Vautrollerius,* 1580. Ent. to J. Harrison the elder 5 se. L(tp only, Harl.5990/32).O(imp.).; F.

Macropedius, Georgius—*cont.*

17176.1 — [Anr. ed.] 8°. *T. Vautrollerius,* 1581. C¹⁷.
17176.2 — [Anr. ed.] 8°. *ex off. R. Field,* 1592. O⁶.SHEF.; CHI.ILL.
17176.3 — [Anr. ed.] 8°. *ex off. R. Field,* 1595. Ass'd 7 my. 1594. HD.
17176.4 — [Anr. ed.] 8°. *ex off. R. Field, sunt venales ap. R. Dexter,* 1600. L.P.
17176.5 — [Anr. ed.] 8°. *ex off. R. Field,* 1604. O.
17176.6 — [Anr. ed.] 8°. *ex off. R. Field,* 1609. O.YK.; HN.
17176.7 — [Anr. ed.] 8°. *ex off. R. Field,* 1614. L(tp only, Ames II.341).
17176.8 — [Anr. ed.] 8°. *ex off. R. Field,* 1621. L(tp only, Ames II.600).DUR⁵.; ILL.
17176.9 — [Anr. ed.] 8°. *ex off. G. Miller,* 1637. Ass'd 3 ap. 1626. L(2 tpp, Ames II.1378, Harl.5936/391).O⁶.A.ETON.; F.

Madd., I. *See* 24903.

Maddie. The bird in the cage. 1570. *See* 22187a.5.
— Maddeis lamentatioun. 1570. *See* 22201.
17177 — Maddeis proclamatioun. [1570.] Now = 22201.5.

17178 **Maddison, Sir Ralph.** Englands looking in and out. Presented to the high court of parliament now assembled. 4°. *T. Badger f. H. Mosley,* 1640. Ent. 17 fb. 1641. L.O.C.DUR⁵.LINC.+; F.HN.CU.HD.Y.+

17179 **Maden, Richard.** Christs love and affection towards Jerusalem. Delivered in sermons. 4°. *M. F[lesher] f. J. Clark,* 1637. Ent. 9 mr. L.O.C.A.M².+; F.HN.HD. ILL.PN².+

17180 **Madoxe, Richard.** A learned and a godly sermon, especially for all marryners . . . 1581. 8°. *J. Charlwood,* [1581.] L(1, also tp Harl.5927/290).L².C.SCL. Tp incorrectly calls author 'John Madoxe'.

Madrid. Articles of peace. In a treaty at Madrit. 1630. *See* 9251.

Maestricht. A journall of . . . that famous siege of Mastricht. 1632. *See* Newsbooks 276.

17181 **Maffei, Giovanni Pietro.** Fuga sæculi. Or the holy hatred of the world. Conteyning the lives of 17. holy confessours of Christ. *Tr.* H. H[awkins.] 4°. *Paris* [*St. Omer, English College Press,*]1632. L.O.C.M.W.+; F.HN.TEX.Y.

A&R 490. *See also* 24735.

17181.5 **Maffeus, Celsus.** [A1ʳ:] Celsi Veronensis dissuasoria. 4° in 6's. (*R. Pinson,* 1505.) O³.

17182 **Magini, Giovanni Antonio.** The Italian prophecier. That is, a prognostication made for 1622. *Tr.* out of Italian into Dutch and now into English. 4°. [*E. Allde?*] 1622. L.L³⁰.E.

17183 — A strange and wonderfull prognostication. *Tr.* 4°. *f. N. Butter,* 1624. Ent. 3 my. L.
— *See also* 3160.

17183.5 **Magirus, John.** Joannis Magiri physiologiae peripateticæ libri sex. Accessit C. Bartholini enchiridion metaphysicum. 8°. [*B. Norton a. J. Bill*] *ap. J. Billium,* 1619 (1618.) Ent. 20 jn. 1618. O¹⁰.CARTMEL.D. DNPK. Lord Kenyon.; F.HD(imp.).

17184 **Magnet.** The magnes. 1585. = frag. of 18648.

Magna Carta. *See* 9266 sqq.

Magnificat. An exposicion vpon the songe of the blessed virgine Mary, called Magnificat. 1538. *See* 16979.7.

17185 **Magnus, Valerianus.** A censure about the rule of beleefe practised by the protestants. *Tr.* R. Q. gentleman. 4°. *Doway, L. Kellam, [the younger,]* 1634. L(tp only, Harl.5961/75, impr. cropt).O.

A&R 491.

Magor. A true relation . . . of the great Magor. 1622. *See* 20864.

Mahomet. *See* Mohammed.

17186 **Maid.** A constant and a kinde maid. [1633?] = pt. 2 of 16861.
— The fayre mayde of the Exchange. 1607. *See* 13317.
17186.5 — A love-sick maids song, lately beguild, by a run-away lover that left her with childe. *Ballad.* 1/2 sh.fol. *f. J. W[right?* c. 1625?] c⁶.
— The maydes answere. [c. 1625.] *See* 546.5.
17187 — The maids comfort: or, the kinde young man. *Ballad.* 2 pts. s.sh.fol. *assignes of T. Symcocke,* [1628–29.] L.

Maid—*cont.*

17188 — The maydes metamorphosis. 4°. *T. Creede f. R. Olive,* 1600. Ent. 24 jy. L.L⁶.O.E.ETON.+; HN.HD. Greg 164.
— The maides tragedy. 1619. *See* 1676.

17189 — This maide would give tenne shillings for a kisse. *Ballad.* 2 pts. s.sh.fol. *J. White,* [c. 1620.] c⁶.

17189.3 — The true mayde of the south: or, a rare example of a mayde dwelling at Rie. *Ballad.* 2 pts. s.sh.fol. *f. F. Coules,* [c. 1630.] c⁶.

17189.7 — [Anr. ed.] 2 pts. s.sh.fol. *f. F. Coules,* [c. 1635.] L. Title line 3: 'a maide'.

Maiden. The deceased maiden-lover. [1628–29.] *See* 16862.1 sq.

17190 —The maidens complaint of her loves inconstancie. *Ballad.* 2 pts. s.sh.fol. *f. H. G[osson,* 1620?] L.

17191 — [Anr. ed.] 2 pts. s.sh.fol. *f. E. W[right,* 1625?] L.

17192 — Here is a necessarye treatyse . . . and hath to name, the maydens crosse rewe. [In verse.] 4°. (*R. wyer,*) [1540?] HN.

17192.3 — A maydens lamentation for a bedfellow. Or, I can, nor will no longer lye alone. *Ballad.* 2 pts. s.sh.fol. [*W. White*] *f. J. White,* [c. 1615.] c⁶. Title line 2 ends: 'beene'.

17192.7 — [Anr. ed.] 2 pts. s.sh.fol. [*W. White*] *f. J. White,* [c. 1617.] c⁶. Title line 2 ends: 'alone'.

17193 — The maidens nay, or, I love not you. [1685?] = Wing M 271. *See also* 12573.5.

17194 **Maidstone.** The forme and shape of a monstrous child, borne at Maydstone . . . 1568. s.sh.fol. *J. Awdeley,* [1568] (23 de.) Ent. to J. Sampson [i.e. Awdley] 1568–69. L.

Maidstone, Clement. *See* Maydeston.

17195 **Maie, Edward.** A sermon of the communion of saints. 4°. *J. Dawson f. G. Lathum,* 1621. Ent. 13 jn. L.C. PLUME(imp.)*.; F.Y.
Answered in 22394.

17196 — [Anr. ed.] 4°. *J. Legatt f. G. Lathum,* 1621. O(2).C⁵. NLW.; F.HN.HD.U.Y.
Called 2nd impression in 'To the reader'.

17196.3 **Maierus, Michael.** Arcana arcanissima. Hoc est hieroglyphica Ægyptio-Græca. 4°. [*T. Creede,*] 1614. Ent. to T. Creede 28 my. 1613. L.O(lacks tp).DUR³.LEEDS.

17196.5 — [Anr. issue, w. engr. tp, undated.] L(2).L³.C.; HD.LC.
In some copies 2nd engr. leaf has special dedic. stamped (in L³ to L. Andrewes).

17196.7 — [Anr. issue, w. cancel letterpress tp:] De hieroglyphicis Ægyptiorum libri sex. *prostat ap. Soc. Londinensem,* 1625. Y.

17197 **Maihew, Edward.** A paradise of praiers and meditations. The first part. 16° in 8's. *Doway, widdow of L. Kellam,* 1613. O.
A&R 492.

17197.5 — A treatise of the groundes of the old and newe religion. Devided into two parts, whereunto is added a briefe confutation of [6014]. [Anon.] 4°. [*English secret press,*] 1608. L.O.C.E.W.+; F.HD.NY¹¹.TEX.U.
(Formerly 24247) A&R 493. Printer's preface signed 'Thom. R.'
— *ed. See* 16157.5 sq.

17198 **Mailliet, Marc de.** A la louange du serenissime roy. Ode. 4°. *G. Purslowe,* 1617 (27 se.) L(imp.).

17199 — Balet de la revanche du mespris d'amour. 4°. [*Eliot's Court Press,*] 1617 (28 ja.) L.

Maimonides. *See* Moses ben Maimon.

17200 **Mainardi, A.** An anatomi, that is to say a parting in peeces of the mass. [Anthoni de Adamo, *pseud.*] 8°. [*Strassburg, heirs of W. Köpfel,*] 1556. L.O.C.D.E.+; F.BO³.COR.HD.Y.

17201 **Mainwaringe, Matthew.** Vienna. Noe art [etc.] Wherein is storied, yᵉ valorous atchievements, of Sʳ Paris of Viennæ and the faire Vienna. [Init. M. M.] 4°. [*A. Mathewes*] *f. G. Percivall,* [1628.] Ent. 25 my. 1628. L.O.USHAW(imp.). Chester PL.; F.

17202 — [Anr. ed.] 4°. [*B. Alsop a. T. Fawcet*] *f. R. Hawkins,* [1632?] Ass'd by Hawkins to Mead a. Meredith 29 my. 1638. L.O.C.M.; HN.HD(imp.).N.
(Formerly also 24717)
— *See also* 19206.

17203 **Maisonneuve, Étienne de.** The gallant, delectable and pleasaunt hystorie of Gerileon of Englande. *Tr.* (M. Jennynges.) 4°. [*J. Kingston*] *f. M. Jennynges,* 1578. Ent. to J. Jugge 20 my. 1577; ass'd to M. Jennynges 6 ap. 1579. O(2, 1 date torn, 1 imp.).; HN.
(Formerly also 17204, 17205)

17204 — = 17203.
17205 — = 17203.

17206 — Gerileon of England. The second part. *Tr.* A. M(undy). 4°. [*T. Scarlet?*] *f. C. Burbie,* 1592. Ent. to T. Scarlet 8 au. L.

Maitland, Patrick. *See* 17145.

17206.5 **Makcouldy, Allan.** A true perpetuall prognostication for . . . 1632. 8°. *Dubline* [*Edinburgh, J. Wreittoun,*] *printed for my comerauds,* 1632. E.

Make-peace, Mary. Divers crabtree lectures. 1639. *See* 23747.

Makilmenæus, Roland, *ed. See* 15241.7, 15246.

17207 **Makluire, John.** The buckler of bodilie health. 8°. *Edinburgh, J. Wreittoun,* 1630. L.

17208 — Sanitatis semita. . . . Cum tractatu de febre pestilente. 8°. *Edinburgi, J. Wreittoun,* 1630. C.
— *See also* 17139.

17209 **Malbie, *Sir* Nicholas.** A plaine and easie way to remedie a horse that is foundered in his feete: [etc.] 4°. *T. Purfoote,* 1576. L.
Copies of 17209 sqq. often found bd. w. corresponding eds. of 20870 sqq.

17210 — [Anr. ed.] 4°. *T. Purfoote,* 1583. L.O⁵.; HN.ILL.Y.
17210.3 — [Anr. ed.] 4°. *T. Purfoote,* 1586. L.
17210.7 — [Anr. ed.] 4°. *T. Purfoote,* 1588. D.; Clark Art Institute, Williamstown, Mass.

17211 — [Anr. ed.] 4°. *T. Purfoot,* 1594. L.STU.
— Remedies for diseases of horses. [Sometimes attrib. to Sir N. Malbie.] 1576. *See* 20870.
— *tr. See* 11621.

Malet, Francis, *tr. See* 2854.

Malim, William, *ed. See* 4938.
— *tr. See* 17520.

17212 **Malmerophus.** [A ballad of Malmerophus and Sillera.] *Ballad.* s.sh.fol. *J. Wolfe f. E. White,* 1582. O(lower half only).

17213 **Malone, William.** A reply to Mʳ. James Ussher his answere. 4°. [*Douai?*] 1627. L.O.C.D².E.+; F. HD.N. NY¹¹.TEX.+
A&R 494. Answer to 24542; answered in 20520, 23604.

Malory, *Sir* Thomas. Thus endeth thys book entytled le morte darthur. [*Tr.* and *ed.* Sir T. Malory.] 1485. *See* 801.

17213.5 **Malta.** ⟨C⟩ertayn and tru good nues, frō the syege of the isle Malta. Translat owt of Frenche yn to Englysh. 8° in 4's. *Gaunt,* [*G. Manilius,*] 1565 (27 au.) L².
A&R 226.

17214 — A copie of the last aduertisement that came frō Malta, of the miraculous deliuerie of the isle from the Turke. *Tr.* out of Italian. 8°. *T. Marshe,* 1565 (21 no.) Ent. 1565–66. L(frags., Harl.5919/242, 5963/56, 346–7, 5995/26).C(frags.).

17215 — Newes from Malta, written by a gentleman of that Iland. *Tr.* according to the Italian copie. [Init. P. M.] 4°. *T. Creede f. J. Hippon,* 1603. O.

17216 **Maltbey, John.** A grand-fathers legacy; or, Maltbey's morsels for mourners. 8°. *N. Okes* [*a. J. Okes,*] *sold* [*by S. Waterson,*] 1633. L.O.; F.

17217 **Malthus, Francis.** A treatise of artificial fire-works. Written in French, and Englished by the authour Tho: [*sic*] Malthus. 8°. [*W. Jones*] *f. R. Hawkins,* 1629. Ent. 29 my. L.O⁵.C¹⁰.E².G².+; F.HN.HD(lacks engr. tp).PH.PH².
Engr. tp correctly signed 'by F. Malthus'. Advertised in 10558.5.

17218 **Malvezzi, Virgilio.** Il Davide perseguitato David persecuted: done into English by R. Ashley. 12°. *J. Haviland f. T. Knight, sold by T. Alchorn,* 1637. Ent. 9 mr. L⁴.O.LINC.; F.HD(imp.).PN.

Malvezzi, Virgilio—*cont.*

17219 — Romulus and Tarquin. First written in Italian and now taught English, by [H. Carey.] 12°. *J. H[aviland] f. J. Benson,* 1637. Ent. 20 fb. L.O.C(lacks engr. tp). CARLISLE.G². + ; F.HD.N.PN.Y. +
    The translator's name is given in HCL monogram.

17220 — Second edition. [*Tr.*] H. Cary. 12°. *J. H[aviland] f. J. Benson,* 1638. L.L¹³.O.D.; F.HN.HD.N.Y. +

17221 **Malynes, Gerard de.** The center of the circle of commerce. 4°. *W. Jones, sold by N. Bourne,* 1623. Ent. to Jones 20 no. L.O⁸.C².RGU.YK. + ; F.HN.CU.LC(imp.).
    In answer to 17985.

17222 — Consuetudo, vel lex mercatoria, or the ancient law-merchant. fol. *A. Islip,* 1622. Ent. 1 au. L(destroyed). L³⁰.O.C.G².LIV³. + ; F.HN.HD.ILL.Y. +

17223 — [Anr. issue, w. cancel tp:] *A. Islip, sould by N. Bourne,* 1629. L.C⁵.D.LIV³.NLW. + ; CAL.HD(2).LC.N.Y.

17224 — [Anr. ed.] Whereunto is annexed the Merchants mirrour, by R. Dafforne. 2 pts. fol. [Gen. tp, impr. for pt. 1:] *A. Islip, sould by N. Bourne;* [gen. tp, impr. for pt. 2:] *R. Young f. N. Bourne,* 1636 (1635). Pt. 2 ent. 21 mr. 1635.
    Gen. tp divided into 2 sections with 2 imprints; pt. 2 tp has same imprint as bottom of gen. tp, but dated 1635.
    Copies survive in the following combinations:
      1. with gen. tp only in pt. 1, and
      a. with pt. 2 dated 1635. L³⁰.O²².DUR⁵.; BO².NYS.
      b. lacking pt. 2. HD.
      2. with two tpp in pt. 1, the gen. tp preceded by the 'cancel' tp 17224.5, and
      a. with pt. 2 dated 1635. O³.LEEDS.SHEF.; BO⁵. ILL.
      b. with pt. 2 reset and dated 1651 (= Wing D 102). L.L³⁸.; V.
    O has a separate copy of pt. 2 dated 1635.

17224.5 — [Anr. issue, w. cancel tp in border McK&F 232, omitting all mention of Dafforne.] *A. Islip, sould by N. Bourne,* 1636.
    Copies with the cancel tp only in pt. 1 survive in the following combinations:
      a. lacking pt. 2. L¹³.L³⁰.D.; HN.CU.HD.LC.MICH. +
      b. with pt. 2 dated 1635. Y.
      c. with pt. 2 dated 1651. Y.

17225 — Englands view, in the unmasking of two paradoxes. 8°. *R. Field,* 1603. Ent. 23 de. 1602. L.L³⁰.C.M². ; CU.HD (2, 1 imp.).IND(imp.).Y.

17226 — The maintenance of free trade. 8°. *J. L[egatt] f. W. Sheffard,* 1622. Ent. 22 oc. L.L³⁰.O.E.RGU. + ; F.HD. IND.NY.Y. +
    In answer to 17986.

17226a — Saint George for England, allegorically described. 8°. *R. Field f. W. Tymme,* 1601. Ent. 13 my. L.L³⁰.O.E. M². ; HN.HD.Y.

17227 — A treatise of the canker of Englands common wealth. 8°. *R. Field f. W. Johnes,* 1601. Ent. 3 mr. L(imp.). L³⁰.O.M².RGU. + ; F.HN.CU.HD.Y.

17228 **Mameranus, Nicolaus.** Beso las manos et point dictionis gallicæ vsus. Cum carmine de leone et asino. 4°. *T. Marshus,* 1157 [1557?] C⁴. Leiden U.
    Partially reprinted in 17228.5.

17228.5 — Beso las manos, clausula quid significet apud Hispanos. [In verse.] s.sh.fol. [*Cambridge?* c. 1600.] C.
    A partial reprint of 17228.
— See also 16817.

Mammon. Newes from Millaine. The copie of a letter . . . concerning prince Mammon. 1630. *See* 17916.3.

17229 **Mamora.** Newes from Mamora, or, a summary relation of the taking of Mamora. *Tr.* (W. Squire.) 4°. [*N. Okes*] *f. T. Archer,* 1614. L⁴³.O.

17229.5 **Man.** The deadmans song, whose dwelling was neere unto Basing Hall in London. *Ballad.* 1/2 sh.fol. *f. E. Wright,* [1625?] Ent. to Wright a. others 14 de. 1624. C⁶.

17230 — [Anr. ed.] 2 pts. s.sh.fol. *f. F. Coules,* [c. 1640.] L.

17231 — A deuoute mans purposes. Being zealous and comfortable meditations. 12°. *J. W[indet] f. E. Mats,* 1597. Ent. to W. Mattes 24 se.; to E. Mattes 7 no. L.O.
    Dedic. signed 'A. M.' in L, 'E. M.' in O.

17232 — The discontented married man. Or, a merry new song. *Ballad.* 2 pts. s.sh.fol. *f. R. Harper,* [c. 1640.] L.
— The man in the moone. 1638. *See* 11943.

Man—*cont.*

17232.5 — Mans arraignement, and Gods mercy in delivering him. [Sermons.] 4°. *F. Kyngston f. J. Flasket,* 1607. Ent. 21 ap. O³(imp.).; F.

17233 — The marryed mans lesson. [1634.] = 19254.
— The new man. 1622. *See* 1705.

17234 — O yes. If any man or woman, any thing desire. *Ballad.* 2 pts. s.sh.fol. [*M. Flesher*] *f. F. Coules,* [c. 1630.] L.C⁶.

17235 — The poore man payes for all. This is but a dreame. *Ballad.* 2 pts. s.sh.fol. *f. H. G[osson,* 1625 ?] Ent. to F. Grove 12 mr. 1630. L.
— A poore mans mite. 1639. *See* 1589.5.
— The poore-mans plaster-box. 1634. *See* 12942.

17236 — Remember man both night and day, thou must nedes die there is no nay. *Ballad.* 1/2 sh.fol. *J. Tysdale a. J. Charlewood,* [1554–58.] L⁵(Lemon 43).

17237 — [Anr. ed.] 1/2 sh.fol. *W. Powell f. W. Pickering,* 1566 (21 au.) Ent. 4 se. 1564. HN.

17238 — The sicke-mans comfort, against death. *Tr.* out of [J. de L'Espine's] Frenche by J. E[liot?] 8°. *J. Wolfe,* 1590. Ent. 11 ap. 1589. L.O(imp.).
    For other trans. *see* 15510.5.
— A yong-mans most earnest affection. [c. 1620.] *See* 26118.

17238.5 **Man, Abraham,** *Minister in Henley.* An amulet or preservative against sicknes and death. [Init. A. M.] 12°. *R. F[ield] f. T. Man,* 1617. Ent. to master a. J. Man 29 mr. L⁴.
    (Formerly 17126)

Man, Judith, *tr.* An epitome of the history of Argenis and Polyarchus. *Tr.* (J. Man.) 1640. *See* 1396.

17239 **Man, Stephen.** A relation of certaine things in Spaine, worthy of observation. 8°. [*T. Snodham*] *f. J. Browne,* 1619. Ent. 1 jy. L(imp.).

Manchester. The description of a moste dreadfull and mervelous monster borne in Manchester. [1579.] *See* 6772.5.
— Manchester al mondo. 1633. *See* 18026.

Mancinellus, Antonius. *See* 23427.3.

17239.3 **Mancinus, Dominicus.** Mancinus de quatuor virtutibus. [In verse.] 8°. *T. Marsh,* 1584. ILL.

17239.5 — [Anr. ed.] 8°. *ap. R. Dexter,* 1601. Robert O. Dougan, Huntington Library (imp.).

17239.7 — [Anr. ed.] 8°. [*R. Field*] *ex typ. Soc. Stationariorum,* 1613. L.O.WOR.

17240 — [Anr. ed.] 8°. *ex typ. E. P[urslowe,] imp. Soc. Stationariorum,* 1638. Ent. to the English Stock 5 mr. 1620. L.

17241 — [A trans.] The englysshe of Mancyne apon the foure cardynale vertues. (Mancinus de quattuor virtutibus.) 2 pts. 4° in 8's. [*R. Pynson,* 1520?] L(pt. 1 only).O(2, 1 of pt. 2 only).
    Errata given Eng. before Latin.

17242 — [Anr. trans.] Here begynneth a ryght frutefull treatyse, intituled the myrrour of good maners, côteynyng the .iiii. vertues. *Tr.* A. Bercley. [In verse.] *Lat. a. Eng.* fol. (*R. Pynson, at the instance of Rychard yerle of kent,*) [1518?] L.C⁷.

17242.5 — [Anr. ed.] Here begynnyth a treatyse intitulyd the myrrour of good maners. fol. (*R. Pynson, at the instâce of Richard yerle of Kêt,*) [1520?] LINC.; HN.

17243 — = pt. of 3546.

17244 — [Anr. trans.] A plaine path to perfect vertue: *tr.* G. Turberuile. [In verse.] 8°. *H. Bynneman f. L. Maylard,* 1568. Ent. 1567–68. L.WN.

17245 **Mandevill, Robert.** Timothies taske: or a christian sea-card. [*Ed.*] (T. Vicars.) 4°. *Oxford, J. Lichfield a. J. Short,* 1619. L.O.O³⁸.D.M. + ; F.AAS.U.

17246 **Mandeville,** *Sir* **John.** [k4ʳ:] Here endeth the boke of Iohn Maunduyle. knyght of wayes to Ierusalem & of marueylys of ynde [etc.] 4° in 8's. (*R. Pynson,*) [1496.] L(imp.).O(frag.). Duff 285.

17247 — [Anr. ed. fol. 5ʳ:] here begynneth a lytell treatyse or booke named Iohan Maûdeuyll [etc.] 4° in 6's. (*Westmynster, W. de worde,* 1499) [bef. de.] C(imp.). ST(imp.). Duff 286.

17248 — Now = 17249.5.

17249 — [Anr. ed.] 4° in 6's. (*W. de worde,* 1503.) O(2, 1 imp., 1 frag.).

Mandeville, *Sir* **John**—*cont.*

17249.5 — [Anr. ed.] 4°. [*W. de Worde*, 1510?] L(1 leaf, Harl. 5919/16). O(2 leaves).
(Formerly 17248) 33 lines a full page.

17250 — [Anr. ed.] The voiage and trauayle, of syr J. Maunde-uile. 4° in 8's. (*T. East*, 1568 (6 oc.)) L.

17251 — [Anr. ed.] 4°. *T. Este*, [1582?] Ent. 12 mr. 1582. O.; F.

17251.5 — [Anr. ed.] 4°. *T. Snodham*, 1612. Ass'd 17 jn. 1609. LC.

17252 — [Anr. ed.] 4°. *T. S⟨nodham,⟩* 1618. L(imprint mutilated).

17253 — [Anr. ed.] 4°. *T. Snodham*, 1625. CHATS.; F(date cropt). HN.

17253.5 — [Anr. ed.] 4°. *W. Stansby*, 1632. Ass'd 23 fb. 1626. Y.

17254 — [Anr. ed.] 4°. *R. Bishop*, [1639?] Ass'd 4 mr. 1639. F.HN.

Mandozze, John, *Lord.* See 17820.

Manelli, Giovanni Maria, *tr.* See 23649.

Manfield, Henry, *tr.* See 4603.

Manifest. The manifest, or declaration of his maiesty. 1620. *See* 10809.

Manifestation. A manifestation of the great folly of certayne . . . secular priestes. 1602. *See* 19411.

Manner. The maner, and forme of examination befoir the admission to ye tabill of ye Lord. 1581. *See* 11183.5.

17255 — The maner of the world now a dayes. *Ballad.* 1/2 sh.fol. [*G. Simson*? c. 1590.] HN.

— The perfect manner of handling the sword. [1626.] *See* 17467, pt. 2.

17256 **Mannheim.** A letter sent from Maynhem concerning the late defeate. 1622. Now = Newsbooks 54.

17257 **Manning, James.** A new booke, intituled, I am for you all, complexions castle. 4°. *J. Legat, printer to the Univ. of Cambridge, sold* [*in London*] *by S. Waterson*, 1604. L.O.CA. Preston PL.+; F.HN.HD.

17257.5 **Manning, Peter.** An acte to avoyde a decree in Chancery betweene one F. Verzelline, plaintiffe; and P. Manning, M. Palmer, and others, defendants. [Brief of a bill in Parliament favouring the defendants.] s.sh.fol. [*London,* 1621.] L(Harl.MS.7617/17).
The bill was read 24 Apr. 1621 and committed 17 May 1621; see *JHC* I. 588, 623. For Verslyn's response *see* 24690.

17258 **Manojo, Fernando.** Newes from Spaine. A relation of the death of don Rodrigo Calderon. Faithfully *tr.* 4°. [*London,*] 1622. L.CASHEL.; F.

17259 **Mansel,** *Sir* **Robert.** A true report of the service done upon certaine gallies. 4°. *F. Kyngston, sold by J. Newbery,* 1602. L.O.O⁶.; F.
See also 6910.4.

Mansfeld, Ernst von, *Count.* The appollogie of the earle of Mansfield. 1622. *See* 24915.

17260 — Count Mansfields directions of warre. [*Ed.*] W. G. 4°. *E. Allde f. R. Whittaker,* 1624. L.O.O³(W).

17261 — The ninth of September. 1622. Count Mansfields proceedings since the last battaile. 1622. Now = Newsbooks 76.
— See also Newsbooks 71, 73, 74.

17261.5 **Mansfield,** *Miller of.* [A ballad of King Henry II and the miller of Mansfield.] 2 pts. s.sh.fol. [*E. Allde?* 1588?] HN(pt. 1 only, on verso of 7557, imp.).

17262 — [Anr. ed.] A pleasant new ballad of the miller of Mansfield, in Sherwood and of King Henry the second. 2 pts. s.sh.fol. *f. E. Wright,* [1640?] Ent. to Pavier, the Wrights, a. ballad ptnrs. 14 de. 1624. L.

17262.5 **Mantua, Council of.** The causes why the Germanes wyll not go, nor consente vnto that counsel, called at Mantua. [*Tr.* M. Coverdale.] 8°. (*southwarke, J. Nicolson,*) 1537. C⁹.SCL.

Mantuanus, Baptista. See Spagnuoli, B.

17263 **Manual.** A manual of prayers newly gathered out of many and diuers famous authours. [Compiled and *tr.*] (G. F[linton].) 2 pts. 16° in 8's. [*Rouen, Fr. Parsons' Press,*] 1583. O(imp.).C⁹.DUL.
A&R 495. (Pt. 2 formerly 14566) For earlier separate eds. of the Jesus Psalter *see* 14563 sqq.

Manual—*cont.*

17264 — [Anr. ed.] Whereunto is addid a sommarie of the christian belefe. 2 pts. 16° in 8's. [*Rouen, G. L'Oyselet,*] 1589. C.
A&R 496.

17264.5 — [Anr. ed.] 2 pts. 16° in 8's. [*London, Fr. Garnet's first Press,* c. 1593.] O.
A&R 497.

17265 — [Anr. ed.] Whereunto is added a newe callender. 2 pts. 8° in 4's. [*English secret press,* c. 1595.] L.L².
A&R 498.

17265.5 — [Anr. ed.] 2 pts. 16° in 8's. [*English secret press,* 1596.] USHAW(imp.).W.
A&R 499.

17266 — [Anr. ed.] Distributed according to the daies of the weeke. 12°. *Calice,* [*English secret press,*] 1599. L.L².
A&R 500.

17267 — [Anr. ed.] 12°. [*English secret press,* 1604.] L²(2, 1 imp.).
(Formerly also 17272) A&R 501.

17267.5 — [Anr. ed.] Gathered out of manie famous authors. 12°. [*English secret press,* 1602–5.] HAT.
A&R 502.

17268 — [Anr. ed.] Now newly corrected. 8°. *Doway, L. Kellam,* 1604. L².L¹³.O(2).MAPL.
A&R 503.

17269 — [Anr. ed.] 12°. [*V. Simmes,*] 1604. O.
A&R 504.

17270 — [Anr. ed.] Augmented with pointes collected out of the Princes manual. 12°. [*Douai, C. Boscard,*] 1605. L². PARIS(imp.).
A&R 505.

17271 — [Anr. ed.] 12°. [*Douai, C. Boscard,*] 1609. L².
A&R 506.

17272 — = 17267.

17273 — [Anr. ed.] 12°. (*Doway,* [*P. Auroi f.*] *J. Heigham,*) 1613. L.; F.
A&R 507.

17274 — [Anr. ed.] A manual of godly praiers, and litanies newly annexed. . . . 12°. *Rouen, C. Hamillon,* 1613. O.YK.
A&R 508.

17275 — [Anr. ed.] Newly augmented. 12°. *Rouen, C. Hamillon,* 1614. L.
A&R 509.

17275.3 — [Anr. ed.] 12°. *Douway, f. J. Heigham,* 1615. E.

17275.5 — [Anr. ed.] 2 pts. 12°. [*English secret press,*] 1616. F.
A&R 510.

17275.7 — [Anr. ed.] 2 pts. 16° in 8's. [*Rouen?*] 1617 (1618). W.
A&R 511.

17276 — [Anr. ed.] Taken out of many famous authors and distributed [etc.] [*Ed.* and enlarged] (by J. Heigham.) 12°. *S. Omers,* [*C. Boscard f.*] *J. Heigham,* 1620. L². PLUME.
A&R 512.

17276.2 — [Anr. ed.] All lately reviewed and corrected. 2 pts. 12°. [*Lancs., Birchley Hall Press?*] 1620. O¹³(imp.). DE(lacks O1).
A&R 513.

17276.3 — [Anr. ed.] Taken out of many famous authors and distributed [etc.] 2 pts. 12°. *S. Omers,* [*C. Boscard*] *f. J. Heigham,* 1623. L.

17276.4 — [Anr. ed.] Newly annexed. 12°. *S. Omers,* [*C. Boscard*] *f. J. Heigham,* 1625. C(imp.).DE.MAPL.
A&R 514.

17276.6 — [Anr. ed.] Distributed. . . . With a forme of confession. 24° in 6's. *S. Omers, f. J. Heigham,* 1625. F(imp.).
A&R [514a].

17276.8 — [Anr. ed.] 2 pts. 24°. [*St. Omers, English College Press,*] (1625). MAPL(imp.).
A&R 515.

17277 — [Anr. ed.] Augmented with divers points of the princesse manuall. 8°. *Paris,* [*English secret press,*] 1630. O(imp.).O¹³(imp.).
A&R 516.

17277.3 — [Anr. ed.] Newly annexed. [Init. W. H.] 12°. *Rouen, f. J. Cousturier,* 1630. C².
A&R 517.

17277.7 — [Anr. ed.] 12°. [*Rouen,*] *J. Cousturier,* 1637. W(imp.). YK.
A&R 518.

17278 — [Anr. ed.] Newly perused. [Init.] (B. T. A[nderton?]) 16° in 8's. *Paris,* 1640. L².COLWICH.
A&R 519.

17278.1 — [A protestant version.] 12°. *B. A[lsop] f. C. Knight,* 1620. ?Ent. 17 mr. 1607. O.

17278.4 Manual or Meditation. [A manual or meditation.] 9 pts. 16º in 8's. (*Doway, I. R.*) [really *Greenstreet House Press, England,* 1580–81.] c(lacks general tp, imp. at end).
    (Formerly 17776a, 14107, 25131, 20194, 14108, 5183, 11182, 20199, and 14568) A&R 520. Pt. 7 includes a rearranged version of 18843. Pt. 1 reprints 17775.

17278.5 — [Anr. ed.] A manual o [*sic*] meditation, and most necessary prayers: . . . [*Ed.*] (I. R.) 9 pts. 16º in 8's. [*Greenstreet House Press, England,* 1580–81.] o(lacks pt. 4).
    A&R 521. Partially from same setting as 17278.4.

17278.6 — [Anr. ed.] 16º in 8's. [*English secret press,* c. 1596.] O.
    Continuous signatures; A&R 522; *see* Greg, *Register B,* p. 57.

Manuale. [Manuale ad vsum Sarum. 1498, etc.] *See* 16138 sqq.

Manudiction. A manudiction for Mʳ. Robinson. 1614. *See* pt. 2 of 3532.
— A second manudiction. 1615. *See* 556.

Manuel, *King of Kilang.* An ambassage. 1621. *See* 17670.5.

Manutius, Paulus. *See* Manuzio, P.

17278.8 Manuzio, Aldo. Phrases linguae Latinae . . . nunc primùm in ordinem abecedarium adductae, & in Anglicum sermonem conuersae. 8º. *ex off. T. Vautrollerij,* 1573. HD(imp.).
    Vautrollier granted 10-year patent for this 22 Apr. 1573; *see* Arber II.886.

17278.9 — [Anr. ed.] 8º. *ex off. T. Vautrollerij,* 1579. L.M.SHR.

17279 — [Anr. ed.] 8º. *ex off. T. Vautrollerij,* 1581. L.DUL.; HN.HD(imp.).SMITH.

17279.5 — [Anr. ed.] 8º. *ex off. T. Vautrollerij,* 1585. I. A. Shapiro, Birmingham.; ILL.

17280 — [Anr. ed.] 8º. *R. F*[*ield,*] *imp. J. Harisoni,* 1595. Ent. to Harrison, sen., a. Field 29 oc. 1594. L(tp only, Ames I.156).O.

17281 — [Anr. ed.] 8º. *R. F*[*ield,*] *imp. J. Harisoni,* 1599. L.C. DUL.PLUME.

17281.3 — [Anr. ed.] 8º. *R. Field pro J. Harisono,* 1608. LIV².

17281.5 — [Anr. ed.] 8º. [*R. Field*] *ex typ. Soc. Stat.,* 1613. Ass'd to the English Stock 21 se. 1612. L⁴⁴.; BO.

17282 — [Anr. ed.] 8º. [*R. Field*] *ex typ. Soc. Stat.,* 1618. Ent. 5 mr. 1620. L.DUR⁵.; Y.

17283 — [Anr. ed.] 8º. [*G. Miller*] *ex typ. Soc. Stat.,* 1625. Ass'd to Miller 3 ap. 1626. L(tp only, Harl.5937/241).L⁸.LK.; ILL.

17283.3 — [Anr. ed.] 8º. [*G. Miller*] *ex typ. Soc. Stat.,* 1628. ILL.

17283.5 — [Anr. ed.] 8º. [*A. Islip*] *ex typ. Soc. Stat.,* 1630. L(tp only, Ames II.924).CHATS.ELY.; HART.ILL. Library Co., Burlington, N.J.

17284 — [Anr. ed.] 8º. [*B. Alsop*] *pro Soc. Stat.,* 1636. L.O.D². LIV³.LK.; BOWDOIN.CAL(imp.).HD. Edwin Wolf II, Philadelphia.

17285 — [Anr. ed.] 8º. *Cantabrigiæ, ex acad. typ.* [*T. Buck a. R. Daniel,*] 1636. L.L³.L⁴⁴.C.C².; F.

17286 Manuzio, Paolo. Epistolarum . . . libri x. Quinque nuper additis. Eiusdem quæ præfationes appellantur. 8º. *ap. J. Kyngstonum, G. Nortoni sumpt.,* 1573. L(tp only, Harl.5927/88).L³.O²².C⁵.CAR.; F.

17286.5 — [Anr. issue, w. cancel tp:] *imp. G. Nortoni,* 1573. G⁴. USHAW.; HD.ILL(imp.).

17287 — [Anr. ed.] 16º in 8's. *T. Vautrollerius* [*f. W. Norton,*] 1581. L.C⁴.E.; HN.PH(impr. cropt).
    Norton's device on Kk8.

17287.3 — [Anr. issue, w. imprint:] *T. Vautrollerius pro G. Nortono,* 1581. O.O⁷.C⁸.

17287.7 — [Anr. issue, w. imprint:] *T. Vautrollerius pro I. Harrisono,* 1581. C¹⁵.WOR.; F.

17288 — [Anr. ed.] Libri xii. 16º in 8's. *R. Robinsonus,* 1591. L.O.C.C².DUL.+; F.HD.ILL.

17289 — [Anr. ed.] 16º in 8's. [*R. Bradock?*] *ap. R. Dexter,* 1603. L.L².C.CHES.DUR⁵.+.
— *ed. See* 5266, 5297, 24788.

Manwaring, Roger. *See* 17751.

17290 Manwood, John. A brefe collection of the lawes of the forest. 4º. [*London,* 1592?] L.C²⁰.NEP.; HD(2).Y.
    This ed. pr. for private circulation.

17291 — A treatise and discourse of the lawes of the forrest. 4º in 8's. [*A. Islip f.?*] *T. Wight a. B. Norton,* 1598. L.O.C.D.E.+; F.HN.HD.N.NY.+.

Manwood, John—*cont.*

17292 — [Anr. ed., enlarged.] 4º in 8's. [*A. Islip?*] *f. Soc. of Statrs.,* 1615. Ent. to the English Stock 5 mr. 1620. L.O.C.D.E².+; F.HN.HD.N.NY.+.
    Includes much material from 17290 not found in 17291.

17293 Manzini, Giovanni Battista. Politicall observations upon the fall of Sejanus. *Tr.* Sʳ. T. H[awkins.] 4º. *A. Griffin f. G. Emondson* [i.e. Emerson,] 1634. C⁵ (imp.).; F.MICH.Y.

17293.5 — [Anr. issue, w. cancel tp:] *A. Griffin f. G. Emerson,* 1634. L.O.D.NEP. Lord Kenyon.; HN.CHI.HD.MCG.
    Reissued as pt. 2 of 17668; reprinted in 17667.

Manzolli, Pietro Angelo. *See* 19138.5.

17294 Map. The map of mortalitie. [In verse.] s.sh.fol. *R. B*[*lower?*] *f. W. Lugger,* [1604.] Ent. 4 my. 1604. HN.

Map, Walter. *See* 6915, 19880.

17295 Maplet, John. The diall of destiny. 8º. *T. Marshe,* 1581. Ass'd to T. Orwin by E. Marshe 23 jn. 1591. L(imp.).o. Lord Kenyon.
    In place of table at end L has 2 leaves: 'A description of such dayes as are most happie and vnhappie', possibly also pr. by Marsh.

17296 — A greene forest, or a naturall historie, . . . 1567. 8º. *H. Denham,* (1567(3 jn.)) Ent. 1566–67. L.L¹⁶.O.C(imp.). P.+; F(imp.).HN.CHI.

17297 Mappamundi. Mappa mundi. Otherwyse called the compasse, and cyrcuet of the worlde. 8º in 4's. (*R. wyer,*) [c. 1550.] L.; F(imp.).
    This is taken from 782. The copies are from different typesettings; A3ʳ last line ends 'and mesu-' (F) or 'and wonders' (L).

Mar., G. *See* 17505.

17298 Marandé, Léonard de. The judgment of humane actions. Englished by J. Reynolds. 8º. *A. Mathewes f. N. Bourne,* 1629. Ent. 24 no. 1628. L.O.C.DUL.E². +; F.HN.N.PH.Y.

Marbecke, John. The booke of common praier noted. 1550. *See* 16441.

17299 — A booke of notes and common places. 4º in 8's. *T. East,* 1581. Ent. 17 oc. 1580. L.O.C.D².E².+; F.HN.HD.N. NY¹¹.+

17300 — A concordāce, that is to saie, a worke wherein ye maie finde any worde conteigned in the whole Bible. fol. (*R. Grafton,*) 1550 (jy.) L(lacks Ttt6).O.C.D.G².+; F.HN.HD.N.NY.+

17300.5 — [Headline A4ʳ:] A dialogue betweene youth and olde age. 8º. [*T. East?* 1584?] L⁴³(imp.).
    Maunsell (17669), pt. 1, p. 69, lists an ed., possibly this, pr. for R. Yardley, 1584, which is 6 years earlier than Yardley's name appears on any extant book.

17301 — Examples drawen out of holy scripture. 8º. *T. East,* 1582. Ent. 9 mr. 1582. O.E.; F.

17302 — The holie historie of king Dauid, . . . Drawne into English meetre. 4º. *H. Middleton f. J. Harison,* 1579. L.LONGLEAT.

17303 — The lyues of holy sainctes, contayned in holye scripture. 4º in 8's. (*H. Denham a. R. Watkins,*) 1574. L.O.C. D.M.+; F.HN.BR.N.PML.+

17304 — [Anr. ed.] fol. (*H. Denham a. R. Watkins,*) 1574. L.O. C⁷.E.M.+; F.HN.NY(imp.).

Marbecke, Roger. A defence of tabacco. 1602. *See* 6468.

17305 Marbury, Francis. A fruitful sermon necessary for the time, preached at the Spittle. 8º. *P. Short,* 1602. Ent. 17 ap. L.O.C.E².YK.+; F.HN.

17306 — Notes of the doctrine of repentance. 8º. *P. Short,* 1602. Ent. 17 no. L.LK.

17307 — A sermon preached at Paules crosse. 8º. *P. Short, sold* [*by C. Burby,*] 1602. Ent. 18 jn. L.L¹⁵.C.C¹⁵.YK.; F.

17308 Marcelline, George. Epithalamium Gallo-Britannicum. 4º. [*Eliot's Court Press*] *f. T. Archer,* 1625. Ent. 4 de. 1624. L.O³⁴.C⁵.E.P.+; F.HN.HD.ILL.N.
    For a large engr. of Charles and Henrietta Maria, with verses and imprint: *sold by T. Archer,* intended to accompany this *see* Hind II.64–5.

17308.5 — A funerall elegie upon the death of Lodovick duke of Lenox, and Richmond. s.sh.fol. *f. J. Trundle,* 1624. L⁵(Lemon 210).

Marcelline, George—*cont.*

17309 — The triumphs of king James. [Anon.] 4⁰. [*W. Jaggard*] *f. J. Budge*, 1610. Ent. to W. Jaggard 11 jn. L.O.C. DUR⁵.E.+; F.HN.

17310 — Les trophees du roi Jacques I. [*Printed abroad*,] 1609. Not an STC book.
— Vox militis. 1625. *See* 20980.
— *See also* 11374.

17311 **Marcellinus, Ammianus.** The Roman historie, [etc.] *Tr.* P. Holland. fol. *A. Islip*, 1609. L.O.C.D.E.+; F. HN.CU.HD.N.+.

17311.5 **Marckant, John.** [A notable instruction.] *See* Addenda.

17312 — The purgacion of the ryght honourable lord Wentworth, concerning the crime layde to his charge. [In verse.] s.sh.fol. *O. Rogers*, 1559 (28 ap.) HN.
Rogers fined for printing without entering; *see* Arber I.101.

Marcoduranus, Franciscus Fabricus, *ed. See* 23886.5.

17313 **Marconville, Jean de.** A treatise of the good and euell tounge. 8⁰. [*J. Wolfe*] *f. J. Perin*, [c. 1592.] L(1, also tp only: Harl.5927/177).C².
— *See also* 20182a.5.

17313.3 **Marcort, Antoine.** The boke of marchauntes, . . . Newly made by the lorde Pantapole, [etc.] *Tr.* [Anon.] 8⁰. (*T. Godfraye*,) [1534.] HN.
(Formerly 3321)

17313.7 — [Anr. ed.] Newly perused and augmented. 8⁰. [*J. Day?*] (*sold by R. Jugge*,) 1547. O.O¹⁷(imp.).C³.CHATS.
(Formerly 3322)

17314 — A declaration of the masse, . . . Trāslated newly out of French. 8⁰. (*Wittenberge, H. Lufte*) [i.e. London, *J. Day*,] 1547. L.O.C.BUTE.CHATS.+; F.

17314a — [Anr. ed.] 8⁰. (*Wyttenberge, H. Luft*) [i.e. London, *J. Day*,] 1547. O(2).C.C⁶.Broxbourne(E.); BO.Y.

17315 — [Anr. ed.] 8⁰. [*Ipswich, J. Oswen*,] 1548. L.O.; HD.

17316 — [A variant, w. colophon:] (*Ippyswyche, J. Oswen.*) O. O¹³.

Marcos, *da Lisboa. See* Silva, M. da.

Marcus Aurelius. The golden boke of Marcus Aurelius. 1535. *See* 12436.

17317 **Mardeley, John.** A declaration of thee [*sic*] power of Gods worde, . . . M.D.XLVIII. 8⁰. (*T. Raynald*,) [1548.] O.C(2).BUTE.D(2).LINC.; F.BO³.

17318 — Here is a shorte resytal of certayne holy doctours whych proueth that the naturall body of christ is not in the sacramēt . . . collected in myter. 8⁰. (*T. Raynalde*,) [1548?] L².O.C(2).BUTE.

17319 — Here beginneth a necessarie instruction for all couetous ryche men. 8⁰. (*T. Raynalde*,) [1548?] L².C(2).D.

Margaret, *Countess of Richmond and Derby, tr.* The mirroure of golde. [1506?] *See* 6894.5.
— *See also* 23954.7.

Margaret, *Duchess of Parma.* A briefe request presented vnto the duchesse of Parme. 1566. *See* 11028.

17320 **Margaret,** *of Angoulême.* A godly medytacyon of the christen sowle, . . . *tr.* by Elyzabeth doughter to our late souerayne kynge Henri the .viij. [*Ed.*] (J. Bale.) 8⁰. [*Wesel, D. van der Straten*,] (1548 (ap.)) L(2). O.C.C⁴(lacks tp).LINC.; F.HN.BO.

17320.5 — [Anr. ed., w. additions.] (Godly meditations.) [By J. Cancellar.] 8⁰. [*H. Denham*, 1568?] Ent. to H. Denham 1567–68. L(lacks tp).
Bale's epistle omitted in this and following ed.

17321 — [Anr. ed.] 16⁰ in 8's. [*J. Charlewood? f.*] (*H. Denham*,) [1580?] L².O.O³(E).M.
Dedic. signed: 'J. Canceller'. Text reprinted in 1892, Lamp 2.

17322 — = 17321.

17322.5 — [Anr. ed.] 8⁰. *R. Ward*, 1590. HD.
Has Bale's epistle; omits Cancellar's meditations.

17323 — The queene of Nauarres tales. Now newly *tr.* 4⁰. *V. S[immes] f. J. Oxenbridge*, 1597. Ent. to F. Norton 1 se. 1600. O.
Preface signed: 'A. B.'

17323.5 **Margaret,** *of Austria.* A briefe discourse of the voyage and entrance of the queene of Spaine into Italy. *Tr.* H. W. 4⁰. [*J. Windet f.*] *J. Wolfe*, [1599.] Ent. 30 ja. 1599. L.

Margaret, *of Austria*—*cont.*

17324 — The happy entraunce of the high borne queene of Spaine, in the citty of Ferrara. *Tr.* 4⁰. [*J. Windet f.*] *J. Woolfe*, 1599. Ent. 11 ja. L.O.
Reprinted in 19834.

17324.5 **Margaret,** *of Scotland, Saint.* [Life of St. Margaret. b3ʳ line 1:] Of god & man but with out p⟨enite⟩nce. [In verse.] 4⁰. [*J. Rastell?* c. 1530.] O(2 leaves).

Margaret, *of Uxbridge, Saint. See* Indulgences 79.

17325 **Margaret,** *Saint, Virgin, and Martyr.* Here begynneth of seint margarete. The blissid lif that is so swete. [In verse.] 4⁰. [*R. Pynson,* 1493.] O(4 leaves, 1 blank). Duff 289.

17326 — [Anr. ed.] Here begynneth the lyfe of saynte. Margarete. 4⁰. (*R. Redman*,) [1530?] HN.

17327 — [Anr. ed.] 4⁰. (*J. Mychell*,) [1548?] C(frag.).

17328 **Margariton.** Margariton. A rich treasure discovered of problemes and their resolves. *Tr.* out of French. [By] (T. S.) 12⁰. *B. Alsop a. T. F[awcett] f. D. Frere*, 1640. L.L⁴³.O.; F.HN.MICH.
Reprinted, w. preface altered, from 5059.

17328.7 **Marienburg.** Abstene fra sin [etc. An account of a miracle at Marginburgh, i.e. Marienburg.] *Tr.* furth of Duche in Scottis be W. Lawsoune. s.sh.fol. [*Edinburgh, A. Arbuthnet,* 1579?] A(2).

17329 **Mariscal Academy.** Lachrymae Academiæ Marischallanæ. 1623. Now = 71.30.

17330 **Market.** The market or fayre of vsurers. A newe pasquillus or dialogue. Newely *tr.* by W. Harrys. 8⁰. (*S. Mierdman*,) 1550. L.O¹⁰(imp.).E.; HN.
Epistle signed 'E. aellen'.

17330.5 **Market Harborough.** To all christian people, to whom these presents shall come, . . . & especially . . . of the parish church of S. Marie in Arden in the Field. [Letters from W. Barlow, Bp. of Lincoln, and James I regarding joining of 2 parishes, 25 Mar. and 27 Apr. 1613.] fol(4). [*R. Barker,* 1613.] O³.

17331 **Markham, Francis.** The booke of honour. Or, five decads of epistles of honour. fol. *A. Matthewes a. J. Norton*, 1625. Ent. 23 my. L.O.C.E².M².+; F.HN.CU. HD.N.+

17332 — Five decades of epistles of warre. fol. *A. Matthewes*, 1622. Ent. 21 no. 1621. L.O.C.E².GLOUC.+; F.HN. CU.HD.N.+

17333 **Markham, Gervase.** The art of archerie. 8⁰. *B. A[lsop] a. T. F[awcett] f. B. Fisher*, 1634. L.O.O³.O¹⁸.NEK.+; F.HN.LC.N(imp.).Y(imp.).+

17334 — Cavelarice, or the English horseman. 3 pts. 4⁰. [*E. Allde a. W. Jaggard*] (*f. E. White,* 1607.) Ent. 3 mr. L.O.C(imp.).STD. Royal Veterinary College, London. +; F.CAL.HD.ILL.NY.+
Prob. issued w. 17387.5 sq. An issue? dated 1609 in Maggs cat. 792 (1950), n. 277, now untraced.

17335 — [Anr. ed.] 16 Cavalarice, 17. Newly imprinted. 4⁰ in 8's. (*E. Allde f. E. White,* 1617, 1616, 1617.) L. O(J, imp.).C.M.STU.+; F(2).HN.PN.WIS. Miss Clara S. Peck, New York City.
— Certaine excellent and new invented knots. [Sometimes attrib. to G. Markham.] 1623. *See* 15056.

17336 — Cheape and good husbandry [etc.] 4⁰. *T. S[nodham] f. R. Jackson*, 1614. Ent. 13 de. 1613. L.L¹⁶.O.D.P.+; HN.
Abridged in 17380.

17337 — [Anr. ed., enlarged.] 4⁰. *T. S[nodham] f. R. Jackson*, 1616. L.RD.; F.NY.
Includes abridged version of 17350.

17338 — Third edition. 4⁰. *T. S[nodham] f. R. Jackson*, 1623. L.O(2).RD(2).SNU.NEK(lacks tp).+; HN.PEN.PN.Y. Dept. of Agriculture, Washington, D.C.+
Also issued as pt. 2 of 17395.3 sqq.

17339 — Fift edition. [Init. G. M.] 4⁰ in 8's. *N. Okes f. J. Harison*, 1631. Ass'd 29 jn. 1630. L.L¹⁶.O.NLW.RD.+; F.CAL.HD(imp.).ILL.Y.+
Also issued as pt. 1 of 17396 sq.

17340 — Sixt edition. 4⁰ in 8's. *A. Griffin f. J. Harison*, 1631 [1637?] L¹⁶(imp.).O.O².A.M².; CAL.GRO.MICH.PML. Missouri U.+
Also issued as pt. 1 of 17397.

Markham, Gervase—*cont.*

17341 — The complete farriar, or the kings high-way to horsmanship. 8°. *J. D[awson] f. R. Young, sold by P. Nevill*, 1639. Ent. to B. Fisher 29 au. 1631; to R. Young 27 mr. 1637. L.C.C⁹.; F.L.C.
An abridgement of 17350.
— Conceyted letters, newly layde open. 1618. *See* 3637.

17342 — Countrey contentments, in two bookes: the first, of riding great horses. Likewise of hunting, hawking, [etc.] The second, The English huswife. 4°. *J. B[eale] f. R. Jackson*, 1615. Ent. 5 se. 1614. L(2, 1 imp.).L¹⁶.O(2, 1 imp.).; F.HN.IND(pt. 1 only). NY(pt. 2 only).
1st bk. includes abridged version of 17350. *See* also 17344.

17343 — [Anr. ed., enlarged, of 2nd bk. only.] Country contentments, or the English huswife. 4°. *J. B[eale] f. R. Jackson*, 1623. L.L⁴⁰.L⁴³.O. Women's Service Library, London.; F.HN.MICH.NY. Dept. of Agriculture, Washington, D.C.
Also issued as pt. 3 of 17395.3 sqq. For later eds. *see* 17353 sq.

17344 — [Anr. ed. of 1st bk. of 17342.] Country contentments: or, the husbandmans recreations. The fourth edition. 4° in 8's. *N. Okes f. J. Harison*, 1631. Ass'd 29 jn. 1630. L.O(2).O³.; F.ILL.PN.
Also issued as pt. 2 of 17396 sq. Text of pt. 2 of 17356 replaces abridged version of 17350.

17345 — Fift edition. 4° in 8's. *T. Harper f. J. Harison*, 1633. L.L⁴⁰.M².W.; CAL⁸.HD(imp.).ILL.MICH. Missouri U.+
Also issued as pt. 2 of 17396.5 sq.

17346 — A discource of horsmanshippe. 4°. *J. C[harlewood] f. R. Smith*, 1593. Ent. to J. Charlewood 29 ja. O. Duke of Gloucester.

17347 — [Anr. ed., enlarged.] How to chuse, ride, traine, and diet, horses. Also, a discourse of horsmanship. Together w. a newe addition for the cure of horses diseases. 4°. *J. R[oberts] f. R. Smith*, 1595. DALK.; HD. Miss Clara S. Peck, New York City.

17347.5 — [Anr. ed.] 4°. *J. R[oberts] f. R. Smith*, 1596. HN. Clark Art Institute, Williamstown, Mass.
Sheets A-G reissued from preceding.

17348 — [Anr. ed.] 4°. *J. W[indet] f. R. Smith*, 1597. O³(imp., with K–L⁴ of 17349).; HN (P3 mutil.).

17349 — [Anr. ed.] 4°. *J. Roberts*, 1599. Ent. to W. Wood 6 no. 1598. L.; Mellon.
See Greg, *Register B*, p. 68.

17350 — [Anr. ed., enlarged.] 4°. *E. A[llde] f. E. White*, 1606. Ent. 2 au. 1602. L.O.INN. Wrocław U.
See Greg, *Register B*, p. 90. For later abridgements of the text *see* 17337 sqq., 17341, 17342.

17350.5 — The English Arcadia, alluding his beginning from Sir P. Sydneys ending. 4°. *E. Allde, solde by H. Rocket*, 1607. Ent. to E. Allde 16 ja. 1606. HN.

17351 — [Anr. issue, w. tp reset: 'Sydnes'.] *E. Allde, solde by H. Rocket*, 1607. O.

17352 — The second and last part of the first booke of the English Arcadia. [Init. G. M.] 4°. *N. Okes f. T. Saunders*, 1613. Ent. 22 my. L.O.; F.HN.CH.

17353 — The English house-wife. The fourth time augmented. 4° in 8's. *N. Okes f. J. Harison*, 1631. Ass'd 29 jn. 1630. L¹⁶.O.O³.G².LEEDS.; F.LC.PH.
Anr. ed. of 17343. Also issued as pt. 3 of 17396 sq.

17354 — [Anr. ed.] Now the fifth time augmented. 4° in 8's. *A. Griffin f. J. Harrison*, 1637. L¹⁶.M².; COR.GRO.HD. PML. Missouri U.+
Also issued as pt. 3 of 17397.

17355 — The English husbandman. The first part. 4°. *T. S[nodham] f. J. Browne*, 1613. Ent. 25 jn. 1612. L.O.D.RD.WI.+; F.HN.CU.ILL(imp.).Y.+
Tp signed 'G. Markham' or 'G. M.'; both at F.

17356 — The second booke of the English husbandman. (The pleasures of princes.) [Init. G. M.] 2 pts. 4°. *T. S[nodham] f. J. Browne*, 1614. Ent. 7 ap. L.L¹⁶(imp.). D.RD.; F.HN.BO⁵(pt. 2 only). CAL²(pt. 2 only).Y.+
Pt. 2 is a prose paraphrase of 6611 w. additions.

17356a — [A variant, w. date:] 1615. L(2 imp.).O³⁰(imp.).SNU(pt. 1 only). Norman Comben, London(pt. 1 only).; F. HN(pt. 2 only).HD(pt. 2 only).ILL(pt. 1 only).Y.+
Text of pt. 2 reprinted in 17344.

17357 — [Anr. ed. of all 3 parts.] The English husbandman, drawne into two bookes. Newlie reviewed. (The pleasures of princes.) 3 pts. 4°. [*A. Mathewes a.*] (*J. Norton*) *f. W. Sheares*, 1635. Ass'd to J. Marriott 17 fb. 1623. L.O.O³⁰(imp.).C(imp.).RD.+; F(pts. 1, 2 only).HN(pt.3 only).HD.WIS.Y.+

Markham, Gervase—*cont.*

Mathewes pr. pt. 1 only. O also has a separate leaf which appears to be a sub tp to pt. 1: '⟨The⟩ / En⟨glish⟩ / Hus⟨ban⟩d-/man. / Containing the / [etc.] *f. W. Sheares*, 1635.'

17358 — [A variant, w. imprint:] (*J. Norton*) *f. H. Taunton*, 1635. L.C².LEIC².M.RD.+; F(pts. 1, 2 only).HN.CU. PN.Y.+

17359 — The famous whore, or noble curtizan: conteining the lamentable complaint of Paulina. 4°. *N. O[kes] f. J. Budge*, 1609. L. Duke of Gloucester.; HN.HD.
— A health to the gentlemanly profession of seruingmen. 1598. *See* 17140.

17360 — Hobsons horse-load of letters: or a president for epistles. The first booke. [Init. G. M.] 4°. [*T. Snodham*] *f. R. Hawkins*, 1613. Ent. 23 se. O.

17360a — [Anr. ed., enlarged.] (The second part.) 4°. *G. P[urslow] f. R. Hawkins*, 1617. 2nd pt. ent. 23 de. 1614. HN.

17361 — Honour in his perfection: or, a treatise in commendations of the vertues of Henry Earle of Oxenford. Henry Earle of Southampton. [etc.] [Init. G. M.] 4°. *B. Alsop f. B. Fisher*, 1624. L(4).O(2).C.BTU.; F.HN.HD.Y.
— How to chuse, ride, traine, and diet horses. 1595. *See* 17347.

17362 — Hungers prevention: or, the whole arte of fowling. 8°. *A. Math[ewes] f. A. Helme a. T. Langley*, 1621. Ent. to Langley, P. Birch, a. Helme 15 my. 1620. L.L¹⁶(imp.).O.C.C⁴.+; F.HN.HD(date cropt).N(imp.). Y.+

17363 — The inrichment of the weald of Kent. [Anon.] 4°. *G. P[urslowe] f. R. Jackson*, 1625. Ent. 28 ap. L.L³⁰.O. A.WN².+; F.HN.HD.LC.PH.
Dedic. init.: 'R. J[ackson].'

17364 — [Anr. ed.] Inlarged, and corrected. By G. Markham. 4° in 8's. *N. Okes f. J. Harison*, 1631. Ass'd 29 jn. 1630. L.O.C².BRISTOL².WI.+; F.CAL⁸.HART².KAN.Y.+
Also issued as pt. 4 of 17396 sq.

17365 — [Anr. ed.] 4° in 8's. *A. Griffin f. J. Harison*, 1636. L.L². M².W. Royal Institution of Chartered Surveyors, London.; CAL².ILL. PML. Missouri U. Rutgers U.
Also issued as pt. 4 of 17397.

17366 — Markhams faithful farrier. 8°. *T. a. R. Cotes f. M. Sparke*, 1629. Ent. 13 se. 1628. O⁵.
Derived from 17376.

17367 — [Anr. ed.] 8°. *T. C[otes] f. M. Sparke, sold by R. Royston*, 1630. Royal Veterinary College, London.; HN.

17368 — [Anr. ed.] 8°. *Oxford, W. Turner f. M. Sparke,* [*London,*] 1631. HN.Y.

17369 — [Anr. ed.] 8°. *T. C[otes] f. M. Sparke*, 1635. O.

17369.5 — [Anr. ed.] 8°. *T. C[otes] f. M. Sparke Junior*, 1636. WIS.

17370 — [Anr. ed.] 8°. *T. Cotes f. M. Sparke Junior*, 1638. L.O.; F.

17371 — [Anr. ed.] 8°. *T. Cotes f. M. Sparke Junior*, 1640. C.

17372 — Markhams farwell to husbandry. 4°. *J. B[eale a. A. Mathewes] f. R. Jackson*, 1620. Ent. 19 au. 1617. L(2).O.O⁸.RD.; F.HN.BO⁵.NY.Y.+
See Court-Book C, p. 95. For Markham's promise to write no more books on animal diseases *see* Arber III.679. Also issued w. tp cancelled as pt. 1 of 17395.3. Mathewes pr. quires H to the end.

17373 — [Anr. ed.] Newly reviewed. 4°. *M. F[lesher] f. R. Jackson*, 1625. L.O.C.M.RD.+; F.HN.BR.HD. Dept. of Agriculture, Washington, D.C.
Also issued as pt. 1 of 17395.5 sq.

17374 — Now the third time, revised. 4° in 8's. *N. Okes f. J. Harison*, 1631. Ass'd 29 jn. 1630. L³⁰.O.C².BRISTOL². RD.+; F.HD.ILL.WIS.
Also issued as pt. 5 of 17396 sq. Variant imprint: 'Hrison [*sic*]'; both at HD.

17375 — Fourth time, revised. 4° in 8's. *E. Griffin f. J. Harison*, 1638. W. L(2).A.M².PETYT. Aberystwyth UC.; GRO. MICH.NYS. Rutgers U. Dept. of Agriculture, Washington, D.C.+
Also issued as pt. 5 of 17397.

17376 — Markhams maister-peece. Or, what doth a horse-man lacke. Devided into two bookes. 4°. *N. Okes, sold by W. Welby*, 1610. Ent. to N. Okes 24 no. 1609. O.; F(imp.).HN.
Contains copies of cuts from 17387.5.

17376.5 — [A variant, w. imprint:] *N. Okes, sold by A. Johnson*, 1610. L(imp.).L¹⁶.

Markham, Gervase—*cont.*

17377 — [Anr. ed.] Now newly imprinted. 4° in 8's. *N. Okes,* 1615. L.C²(imp.).SHR. Stevens Cox.; CAL².N. Dept. of Agriculture, Washington, D.C.
   Engr. tp: 'The second impression.'

17377a — [Anr. ed.] 4° in 8's. *N. Okes, sold by R. Whitakers,* 1623. L.O.RD.SNU(imp.). Royal College of Veterinary Surgeons, London.+; HD.
   Engr. tp: 'The third impression.'

17378 — Now the fourth time imprinted. 4° in 8's. *N. Okes, sold by N. Fussell a. H. Mosley,* 1631 (1630.) L¹⁶(imp.). C⁴.A.RD.RGU.+; F.HN.HD.NY(2).Y.

17379 — Now the fifth time imprinted. 4° in 8's. *N. a. J. Okes,* 1636. L.L¹⁶.O.O⁹.C².+; F.HN.NLM.Y.

17379.5 — [Anr. issue, w. cancel tp, w. imprint:] *N. a. J. Okes f. J. Smithwicke,* 1636. Royal College of Veterinary Surgeons, London.
   Tp pr. as Qq8 of 17379, where it appears in copies at L¹⁶, O⁹. NLM has it separate. *See* also 17366.

17380 — Now = 17381.5.

17381 — Markhams methode or epitome. 8°. *G. E[ld] f. T. Langley,* [1616?] O(impr. cropt).
   An abridgement of 17336.

17381.5 — [Anr. ed.] 8°. *T. S[nodham] f. R. Jackson,* 1616. Ass'd by T. Langley to Jackson 10 jn. L.
   (Formerly 17380) *See Court-Book C,* p. 86.

17382 — Third edition. 8°. *J. H[aviland] f. R. Jackson,* 1623. L.

17383 — Fourth edition. 8°. *f. M. Sparke,* 1628. Ass'd to F. Williams 16 ja. 1626. L²(missing).
   A piracy.

17383.5 — Fifth edition. 8°. [*Oxford, W. Turner] f. M. Sparke, sold by R. Royston, London,* 1630. Hodgson's 23 Feb. 1928, lot 495 (bought by Maggs, untraced).
   Regarding this pirated ed. *see* Greg, *Companion,* pp. 268–73 and Madan II.520–4.

17384 — The sixth edition. 8°. *T. Harper f. J. Harison, sold by R. Royston,* 1633. Ass'd 29 jn. 1630. HN.NY⁴.
   — Marie Magdalens lamentations. 1601. *See* 17569.

17384.5 — A most exact, ready and plaine discourse, how to trayne and teach horses to amble. [Init. J. M.] 4°. *G. E[ld] f. E. Blount,* 1605. Ent. 10 ja. Duke of Gloucester.; Clark Art Institute, Williamstown, Mass.
   — The most famous historie of Mervine. 1612. *See* 17844.

17385 — The most honorable tragedie of Sir R. Grinule, knight. [In verse.] 8°. *J. Roberts f. R. Smith,* 1595. Ent. to J. Roberts 20 se. L.O.; F(imp.).HN.N.
   — The pleasures of princes. 1614. *See* 17356.

17386 — The poem of poems. Or, Sions muse, contayning the diuine Song of king Salomon, deuided into eight eclogues. [Init. J. M.] 8°. *J. Roberts f. M. Lownes,* [1596.] O(impr. cropt).

17386.5 — A schoole for young souldiers. [Anon.] s.sh.fol. *f. J. Trundle,* [1615.] Ent. 26 se. 1615. L⁵(Lemon 239). Illustrations copied from 11810.

17387 — [Anr. ed.] s.sh.fol. *f. R. Higginbotham,* 1616. Ass'd 26 fb. L(date altered in MS. to 1618).; HD.

17387.3 — A second part to the mothers blessing, or a cure against misfortunes. [Init. G. M.] 12°. *G. P[urslowe] f. T. Dewe,* 1622. Ent. 7 my. PFOR.
   Beginning of title prob. refers to 3670 or 15404.

17387.5 — The shape and porportion [*sic*] of a perfit horse, together w. three anotomies [*sic*] of horses bodies. [Anon.] s.sh.fol. *f. E. White,* 1607. Ent. 5 jy. O.
   Prob. issued w. 17334. Cuts copied in 17376.

17387.7 — [Anr. issue, omitting imprint and date.] O.

17388 — The souldiers accidence. Or an introduction into military discipline. Also, the cavallarie [etc.] [Init. G. M.] 4°. *J. D[awson] f. J. Bellamie,* 1625. Ent. 3 ja. L.L¹⁰.O.LAMPORT.

17389 — The second edition corrected by G. Markham. 4°. *W. J[ones] a. T. P[aine] f. J. Bellamie,* 1635. O³.; MICH. Unsold sheets reissued as pt. 1 of 17390.

17390 — The souldiers exercise: in three bookes. 3 pts. 4°. *J. Norton f. J. Bellamy, H. Perry, a. H. Overton,* 1639. L(tp only, Harl.5961/141).O.O¹¹.PARIS. London, Royal Artillery Institution.; HN.
   A reissue of 17389 and 17393 w. gen. tp printed as A1 of pt. 2 of 17393.

17391 — The souldiers grammar. [Init. G. M. *Gent.*] 4°. [*A. Mathewes*] *f. W. Shefford,* 1626. Ent. 24 jy. L.O (impr. cropt).
   (Formerly also 17394).

Markham, Gervase—*cont.*

17391.5 — [Anr. issue.] Unto which, is added the booke of postures, [etc.] *f. W. Shefford,* 1626. C³.LAMPORT.; HD.
   Contents = 17391; prob. intended to be issued w. plates like those bd. w. HN copy of 7684; *see* also 794.5.

17392 — The second part of the soldiers grammar. [Init. G. M.] 4°. [*A. Mathewes*] *f. H. Perry,* 1627. L.O.; HD(imp.).

17393 — [Anr. ed. of both pts.] 2 pts. 4°. (*J. N[orton]*) *f. H. Overton* [*a.*] (*H. Perry,*) 1639. L(tp to pt. 2 only, Harl.5961/139).O¹¹.; HD.
   Also issued as pts. 2, 3 of 17390.

17394 — = 17391.

17395 — The teares of the beloved: or, the lamentation of saint John. [Init. J. M. In verse.] 4°. *S. Stafford, sold by J. Browne,* 1600. L.C.D².; F.HN.Y.
   — Verus Pater, or, a bundell of truths. 1622. *See* 24693.

17395.3 — A way to get wealth. The first three bookes gathered by G. M(arkham.) The last by W. Lawson. 4 pts. 4°. *f. R. Jackson,* 1623. O³(E).
   A reissue under a gen. tp of 17372 (w. tp cancelled), 17338, 17343, and 15330.

17395.5 — [Anr. issue, w. imprint on gen. tp:] *f. R. Jackson,* 1625. ILL.
   Tp line 4 ends: 'good'; 17373 replaces 17372.

17395.7 — [Anr. issue, w. gen. tp line 4 ending: 'Huswiferie'.] *f. R. Jackson,* 1625. L.L¹⁶(imp.).; F(pt.1 only).N.WIS.

17396 — [Anr. ed., enlarged.] The first five bookes gathered by G. M. The last by W. L. All the fift time corre&ed [*sic*]. 6 pts. 4° in 8's. *N.Oakes f. J. Harrison,* 1631. Ass'd 29 jn. 1630. L.O(imp.).C.E².RD.+; F.HN.CHI. HD.Y.+
   A reissue of 17339, 17344, 17353, 17364, 17374, 15331.3 with gen. tp. Gen. tp varies; as above (HD) or 'corrected' and 'Okes' (HN).

17396.5 — [Anr. issue, w. imprint on cancel gen. tp:] *f. J. Harrison,* [1633?] HD(date cropt).Y(date cropt).
   Contents as in 17396, except Y has 17345 (1633) substituted for 17344.

17397 — [Anr. ed.] The sixt time corrected. 6 pts. 4° in 8's. *E. G(riffin) f. J. Harison,* 1638. L.O.C.E.RD.+; F.HN. HD.PH.Y.+
   A reissue of 17340, 17345, 17354, 17365, 17375, 15331.7 with gen. tp.
   — ed. *See* 3314, 10549, 13202.
   — tr. *See* 744, 6785, 19793.

17398 **Markham, Gervase,** and **Machin, Lewis.** The dumbe knight. A historicall comedy. [Preface signed 'L. Machin'.] 4°. *N. Okes f. J. Bache,* 1608. Ent. 6 oc. O.; HN. Greg 277.
   Tp line 4: 'Reuels.'

17398a — [A variant, w. tp line 4: 'Reuelles.'] O(4° T39 Art.).

17399 — [Anr. issue, w. cancel tp:] The dumbe knight. A pleasant comedy. Written by Jarvis Markham. *N. Okes f. J. Bache,* 1608. L.; F.HN.HD(imp.).

17400 — [Anr. ed.] 4°. *A M[athewes] f. W. Sheares,* 1633. Ent. to R. Wilson 19 no. 1610. L.O.C.E.SHEF.+; F.HN.CU. HD.N.+

17401 **Markham, Gervase,** and **Sampson, William.** The true tragedy of Herod and Antipater. 4°. *G. Eld f. M. Rhodes,* 1622. Ent. 22 fb. L.L⁶.O.ETON. Stockholm RL.+; F.HN.HD.N.Y.+ Greg 382.
   Printer's Epistle signed by Rhodes.

17402 — [Anr. issue, w. new prelims.] O.SHEF.; BO.
   Dedic. signed by Sampson.

Markham, Jervis. *See* Markham, Gervase.

17403 **Markham, Robert.** The description, of that ever to be famed knight, Sⁱʳ John Burgh. [In verse.] 4°. [*A. Mathewes,*] 1628. L.O.NEK.; F.HN.HD.

Marl., C. *See* 17429.

17404 **Marlorat, Augustine.** A catholike and ecclesiasticall exposition of ... S. Mathewe. *Tr.* T. Tymme. fol. *T. Marshe,* 1570. Ent. 1569–70. L.O.C.M.P.+; F.HN. ILL. U.Y.+

17405 — A catholike and ecclesiasticall exposition of ... S. Marke and Luke. *Tr.* T. Timme. 4°. *T. Marsh,* 1583. Ent. 1570–71. L.C.D².P.SCL.+; F.

17406 — A catholike and ecclesiasticall exposition of ... S. John. *Tr.* T. Timme. fol. *T. Marshe,* 1575. Ent. 1570–71. L.O.A.HER.P.+; F.HN.HD.ILL.NY¹¹.+
   ILL copy has slip reading 'J. Harrison, 1575' pasted over imprint, apparently lost from some other copies.

Mariorat, Augustine—*cont.*

17406.5 — A catholike and ecclesiasticall exposition vppon the epistle of S. Jude. *Tr.* I. D. 8°. *G. Dewes a. H. Marshe,* 1584. U.

17407 — A catholike . . . exposition vppon the two last epistles of Jhon. 4°. [1580.] = pt. 2 of 4433.

17408 — A catholike exposition vpon the reuelation of Sainct John. [*Tr.*] (A. Golding.) 4° in 8's. *H. Binneman f. L. Harison a. G. Bishop,* (1574.) Ass'd to T. Woodcock 15 jy. 1578. L.O.C.CAR.M.+; F.HN.HD.ILL.U.+

17409 — Propheticæ, et apostolicæ, id est, totius diuinæ ac canonicæ scripturæ, thesaurus. fol. *T. Vautrollerius,* 1574. L.O.C.D.G².+; F.HN.PH.WASH³.

17410 — A treatise of the sin against the holy ghost. . . . Translated. 8°. (*J. Allde f.*) *L. Harison,* [1570?] L.C.; F.

17411 — [Anr. ed.] 8°. *R. Walde-graue f. T. Woodcocke,* 1585. L(tp only, Harl.5990/84).L².

— *See also* 2957.7.

Marlowe, Christopher. Epigrammes and elegies. By J. D[avies] and C. M(arlow). [c. 1599?] *See* 6350; for later eds. *see* 18931.

17412 — The famous tragedy of the rich Jew of Malta. [*Ed.*] (T. Heywood.) 4°. *J. B[eale] f. N. Vavasour,* 1633. Ent. to N. Ling a. T. Millington 17 my. 1594; to Vavasour 20 no. 1632. L.L⁶.O.C².E.+; F.HN.HD.N. NY.+ Greg 475.
Earliest surviving ed., not the first.

17413 — Hero and Leander. [In verse.] 4°. *A. Islip f. E. Blunt,* 1598. Ent. to J. Wolfe 28 se. 1593. F.

17414 — [Anr. ed.] Begun by C. Marloe; and finished by G. Chapman. 4°. *F. Kingston f. P. Linley,* 1598. Ass'd from Blount 2 mr. L.; HN.

17415 — [Anr. ed.] Whereunto is added the first booke of Lucan *tr.* by the same author. 2 pts. 4° w. perp. chainlines. [*F. Kingston*] *f. J. Flasket* (*P. Short,* sold by *W. Burre,*) 1600. Both pts. ass'd from Linley to Flasket 26 jn. 1600. O.; HN.
Pt. 2 is a reissue of 16883.5.

17416 — [Anr. ed. of pt. 1:] 4° w. perp. chainlines. [*F. Kingston*] *f. J. Flasket,* 1606. L.O.; PML.WEL.

17417 — [Anr. ed.] 4° w. perp. chainlines. *f. E. Blunt a. W. Barret,* 1609. L⁶.; F(imp.). Hickmott.

17418 — [Anr. ed.] 4°. *W. Stansby f. E. Blunt a. W. Barret,* 1613. Ass'd to J. Pindley from Wolfe 27 ap. 1612. L.; HN.

17419 — [Anr. ed.] 4°. *G. P[urslowe] f. E. Blount,* 1617. Ass'd to Purslowe from Pindley 2 no. 1613. O⁶.BODMER. M.; HN.

17420 — [Anr. ed.] 4°. *G. P[urslowe] f. E. Blount,* 1622. F.HN. Y². Hickmott. Pirie.

17421 — [Anr. ed.] 4°. *A. M[athewes] f. R. Hawkins,* 1629. Ass'd by Blount a. Thorpe to S. Vicars 3 no. 1624; to Hawkins 27 de. 1625? L.L⁶.O.C².; F.HN.CH.LC. TCU.

17422 — [Anr. ed.] 4°. *N. Okes f. W. Leake,* 1637. Ass'd from Hawkins 6 jn. L.L⁶.C².BTU.E.+; F.HN.HD.ILL.PML.+

17423 — The massacre at Paris: with the death of the Duke of Guise. 8°. *E. A[llde] f. E. White,* [1594?] L.L⁶.O.C⁶.; F.HN.CH.LC(lacks tp).N.+ Greg 133.

— A most excellent ditty of the lovers promises. [1628–9.] *See* 6922.4.

— Ouids elegies. [after 1602.] *See* 18931.

17424 — [A ghost.]

17425 — Tamburlaine the great. Who, from a Scythian shephearde, . . . Now first, and newlie published. (The second part.) [Anon.] 8°. *R. Jhones,* 1590. Ent. 14 au. O(imp.).; HN.COR(tp only). Greg 94.
Collates A–K⁸ L².

17426 — [Anr. ed.] Now newly published. 8°. [*R. Robinson f.*] *R. Jones,* 1593. L.; COR(lacks tp).
Collates A–I⁸; L tp date tampered with and has been read as both 1592 and 1593.

17427 — [Anr. ed.] 8°. *R. Johnes,* 1597. HN.
Collates A–L⁸.

17428 — [Anr. ed. of pt. 1:] Tamburlaine the greate. Who, from the state of a shepheard [etc.] 4° w. perp. chainlines. [*E. Allde*] *f. E. White,* 1605. L.L⁶.O.C⁶.; F(imp.). HN(3).BO.N. Pearson.

17428a — [Anr. ed. of pt. 2:] Tamburlaine the greate. With his impassionate furie, for the death of his lady. 4° w. perp. chainlines. *E. A[llde] f. E. White,* 1606. L.L⁶. O.O⁶(imp.).C⁶.; F.HN.N.PEN². Pearson(imp.).

17429 — The tragicall history of D. Faustus. Written by Ch. Marl. 4°. *V. S[immes] f. T. Bushell,* 1604. Ent. 7 ja. 1601. O. Greg 205.

Marlowe, Christopher—*cont.*

17430 — [Anr. ed.] 4°. *G. E[ld] f. J. Wright,* 1609. Ass'd 13 se. 1610. PETWORTH. Hamburg PL.; HN.

17431 — [Anr. ed.] 4° w. perp. chainlines. *G. E[ld] f. J. Wright,* 1611. HN.

17432 — [Anr. ed., revised and enlarged.] Written by Ch. Mar. 4°. *f. J. Wright,* 1616. L.

17433 — [Anr. ed.] With new additions. 4°. *f. J. Wright,* 1619. PN.
A reprint of the text of 17432 w. no further additions.

17434 — [Anr. ed.] 4°. *f. J. Wright,* 1620. L.O⁶.; NY. Robert Taylor.

17435 — [Anr. ed.] 4°. *f. J. Wright,* 1624. L.

17435.5 — [Anr. ed.] 4°. *f. J. Wright,* 1628. O¹³. Stockholm RL.

17436 — [Anr. ed.] 4°. *f. J. Wright,* 1631. L.O(2).E(2).; F.HN.HD. N.Y.+

17437 — The troublesome raigne and lamentable death of Edward the second. 4° w. perp. chainlines. [*R. Robinson*] *f. W. Jones,* 1594. Ent. 6 jy. 1593. z(dates altered in ink to '1694'). Kassel, Landesbibliothek (destroyed?). Greg 129.

17438 — [Anr. ed.] 4°. *R. Bradocke f. W. Jones,* 1598. L(2). L⁶(imp., w. MS. tp dated 1593).O.E.; F(impr. cropt). HN(2).

17439 — [Anr. ed.] 4°. [*W. Jaggard*] *f. R. Barnes,* 1612. Ass'd 16 de. 1611. L⁶.L³⁰.; F.HN.HD. Pearson.
K2ʳ duplicates text of I4ᵛ; text ends K2ᵛ.

17439.5 — [Anr. issue, w. no duplication.] L.E.; HN.HD.
Text ends K2ʳ.

17440 — [Anr. ed.] As it was publikely acted by the Earle of Pembrooke his servants. 4°. [*Eliot's Court Press*] *f. H. Bell,* 1622. Ass'd 17 ap. 1617. L.O.O⁶(imp.)*.; F(imp.).BO.HD.NY.TCU.+

17440a — [A variant.] As it was publikely acted by the late queenes maiesties servants. L.L⁶.C⁴. Vienna NL.; F.HN.LC.N.Y.+

— *See also* 20406.

17441 **Marlowe, Christopher,** and **Nash, Thomas.** The tragedie of Dido queene of Carthage. 4°. *the widdowe Orwin f. T. Woodcocke,* 1594. O.; F.HN. Greg 128.

17442 **Marmion, Shakerley.** A fine companion. [A comedy.] 4°. *A. Mathewes f. R. Meighen,* 1633. Ent. 15 jn. L. O.E.ETON.LEEDS.+; F.HN.HD.N.Y.+ Greg 481.

17443 — Hollands leaguer. An excellent comedy. 4°. *J. B[eale] f. J. Grove,* 1632. Ent. 26 ja. HN. Greg 461.
In imprint: 'Swan-Alley'; inner forme of sheet A wrongly imposed.

17443.5 — [Anr. issue.] L.O.C.E.LEEDS.+; F.HN.HD.N.NY.+
In imprint: 'Swan-Yard'; inner forme of sheet A correctly imposed.

17444 — A morall poem, intituled the legend of Cupid and Psyche. 4°. *N. a. J. Okes,* sold by *H. Sheppard,* 1637. Ent. to J. Okes 24 jn. L.L⁶.O(imp.).O⁶(lacks engr. tp)*.WN.; CH.N(imp.)*.
Engr. tp: Cupid and Psiche. *J. Okes f. H. Sheppard,* 1637. There are press alterations in sheet A in this and the following.

17444a — [A variant, w. engr. tp date altered to 1638.] L.O(lacks letterpress tp).P.; F.HN.HD.Y.

17445 **Marnix van Sant Aldegonde, Philips van.** The bee hiue of the Romishe church. *Tr.* G. Gylpen. [By Isaac Rabbotenu, *pseud.*] 8°. *T. Dawson f. J. Stell,* 1579. Licensed 21 ja. 1577; copy received 15 ap. 1579. L.C.C³.
See Greg, *Register B*, p. 8, concerning R. Schilders' part in printing this.

17445.5 — [Anr. issue, w. cancel tp:] *Tr.* G. Gilpin. 8°. (*T. Dawson f. J. Stell,*) soulde [by *A. Maunsell,*] 1579. C.P. Broxbourne(E).; F. HN. 𝕬

17446 — [Anr. ed.] Newly imprinted w. a table (by A. Fleming). 8°. (*T. Dawson f. J. Stell,*) solde [by *A. Maunsell,*] 1580. L.O.C.D.M.+; F.HN.HD.N.U.+

17447 — [Anr. ed.] 8°. *T. Dawson,* 1598. Ent. 7 fb. 1597. L (imp.).L³⁸.O⁶.NOR².STU.+; F(2).HN.HD.LC(imp.).NY¹¹.

17448 — [Anr. ed.] 8°. *J. Dawson,* 1623. Ent. 20 mr. 1621. L.O.C.BIRM.LINC.+; F.HN.HD.ILL.U.+

17448.5 — [Anr. ed.] 8°. *M. Dawson,* 1636. L⁸.O.D.E.M⁴.+; F.HD. ILL.Y.

17449 — [Anr. issue, w. cancel tp:] *M. Dawson,* sold by *M. Simmons,* 1636. L(both tpp).O.C².G²(both tpp).M.+; HN.ILL.N(lacks tp)*.SMU. Iowa U.

Marnix van Sant Aldegonde, Philips van—*cont.*
17450 — Chronyc. Historie der Nederlandtscher oorlogen. Beschreuen durch A. Henricipetri. Wt den Hooch-duytschen ouèrgesedt (Theophilus translator.) [i.e. C. Ryckewaert.] 8°. *Noortwitz, [A. de Solempne,]* 1579. L.O.C.M.NOR². + ; F.HN.HD.NY.Y. +
　　Partially based on 'General historien der aller namhafftigsten [etc.]' of A. Henricpetri; attrib. to Marnix doubtful; may actually be by Ryckewaert; tp information intentionally misleading. The French ed. 'Histoire des troubles', 1582, is doubtfully attrib. to J. F. Le Petit in *Bibliotheca Belgica*, 1st series, XIV, L 54.
17450.3 — [A trans.] A tragicall historie of the troubles and ciuile warres of the lowe countries. *Tr.* out of French by T. S(tocker.) [By] (Theophile, *D.L.*) 4° in 8's. *J. Kyngston [a. T. Dawson] f. T. Smith,* [1583.] Ent. 5 oc. 1582. L.O.C.G².M². + ; F.HN.HD.LC.N. +
　　(Formerly 23945). Dawson pr. quires A–S. Dedic. dated 15 Mar. 1583.
17450.7 — A pithie, and most earnest exhortation, concerning the estate of Christiandome. [Anon.] 8°. *Antwerpe [London, R. Waldegrave,]* 1583. L.O.C.D².P. + ; F.HN. (Formerly 5147)

17451 **Marolois, Samuel.** The art of fortification, or architecture militaire. Augmented A. Girard. *Tr.* H. Hexham. fol. *Amsterdam, f. M. J. Johnson,* 1638. L.; F.BO².
　　Eng. title and imprint pasted over Dutch engr. tp. The plates are from the 1627 Amsterdam Dutch ed.

Marot, Clément. *See* 18688.

17452 **Marphoreus,** *pseud.* Martins months minde, that is, a certaine report, of the death, and funeralls, of olde Martin Marreprelate, the great makebate of England. [Dedic. signed Mar-phoreus. Attrib. to T. Nash.] 4°. *[T. Orwin,]* 1589. L.L².O.C².M. + ; F.HN.HD.KAN.NY. +

17453 **Marprelate, Martin,** *pseud.* [Tracts in chronological order.] Oh read ouer D. John Bridges [3734], for it is a worthy worke: or an epitome of the fyrste booke, of that right worshipfull volume, written against the Puritanes. 4°. *Printed ouersea, in Europe, within two furlongs of a bounsing priest, at the cost and charges of M. Marprelate, gent. [East Molesey, R. Waldegrave,* 1588 (oc.)] L.O.C.M.YK. + ; F.HN.HD.NY.Y. +
　　Prelim. 'Epistle' only; 54 pp. collating [–]⁴ B–G⁴. *See* 19605.5.
17454 — Oh read ouer D. John Bridges, for it is worthy worke: [etc.] 4°. *Printed on the other hand of some of the priests [Fawsley, R. Waldegrave,* 1588 (no.)] L.L². O.C.DUR³. + ; F.HN.CH.NY.Y. +
　　'Epitome' only; collates [–]² B–F⁴ G². *See* 19605.5.
17455 — Certaine minerall, and metaphisicall schoolpoints to be defended by the reuerende bishops [etc.] s.sh.fol. *[Coventry, R. Waldegrave,* 1589 (20 fb.)] L².O(imp.).
17456 — Hay any worke for Cooper [5682]: or a briefe pistle directed to the reuerende byshopps. 4°. *Printed in Europe, not farre from some of the bounsing priestes [Coventry, R. Waldegrave,* 1589 (mr.)] L.O.C.D. NLW. + ; F.HN.HD.NY.Y. +
　　There is a post-1640 reprint of this in roman type.
17457 — Theses Martinianae: that is, certaine demonstratiue conclusions. Published by Martin junior. 8° in 4's. *[Wolston, J. Hodgkins,] by the assignes of Martin junior, without any priuiledge of the Catercaps,* [1589 (22 jy.)] L.L².O.C².DUR(Bamb.). + ; F.HN.PML.U.Y. +
17458 — The iust censure and reproofe of Martin iunior. By Martin senior. 8° in 4's. *[Wolston? J. Hodgkins,* 1589 (29 jy.)] L(2).L²(2).O.C².C³.; F.HN.PML.U.Y. +
17459 — The protestatyon of Martin Marprelat. 8° in 4's. *Published by the worthie gentleman D. martin mar prelat D. in all the faculties primat and metropolitan [Hasely? R. Waldegrave?* 1589 (se.)] L.L²(2).O.C.; HN.PFOR.U.Y. Pirie.

[Anonymous anti-martinist tracts in the controversy.]
— An almond for a parrat, or Cutbert Curry-knaues almes. Fit for the knaue Martin. [Attrib. to T. Nash. 1589?] *See* 534.
— Antimartinus, siue monitio cuiusdam Londinensis ad adolescentes vtriúsque academiæ contra Martin Marprelate. 1589. *See* 15102.
— A countercuffe giuen to Martin iunior by the venturous hardie and renowned Pasquil of England. [Sometimes attrib. to T. Nash.] 1589. *See* 19456.
— The first parte of Pasquils apologie. 1590. *See* 19450.

Marprelate, Martin, *pseud.*—*Anonymous anti-martinist tracts*—*cont.*
17460 — A dialogue. Wherin is plainly layd open the tyrannicall dealing of Lord Bishops. 1640. Now = 6805.3.
17461 — [Begin:] Mar-Martine, I know not why a trueth in rime set out [etc. Attrib. to T. Nash and J. Lyly?] 4°. *[London?* 1589.] L(2, 1 imp.).L²(2).O.M.NLW.; HN.NY.U.
17461.5 — [Begin:] Mar-Martin. I knowe not why a frutelesse lye in print; ... [In verse.] 4°. *[London?* 1589?] HN.
　　No tp; 2 leaves.
17462 — [Anr. ed.] Marre Mar-Martin: or Marre-Martins medling, in a manner misliked. [In verse.] 4°. *Printed with authoritie [T. Orwin?* 1589?] L.L²(2). L³.O(2, 1 imp.).M.; F.HN.U.
　　4 leaves; text corrected.
— Martins months minde, that is, a certaine report, of the death, and funeralls, of olde Martin Marreprelate. 1589. *See* 17452.
17463 — Pappe with an hatchet. Alias, a figge for my God sonne. [Attrib. to J. Lyly. Preface signed Double V.] 4°. *J. Anoke a. J. Astile f. the Bayliue of Withernam [T. Orwin,* 1589.] L(2).O⁸(imp.).O²⁸.C⁴.LIV³(lacks tp).; F.HN.HD.NY.PML. +
　　B2ᵛ line 26: 'abusde.'; D4ᵛ lines 11–12: 'next/ booke, shall be . . .'
17463.3 — [Anr. issue, w. textual corrections.] L³.O.M.; IND.Y.
　　B2ᵛ line 26: 'abusde:'; D4ᵛ lines 11–12: 'next/ book, shall be . . .'
17463.7 — [Anr. ed.] 4°. *J. Anoke a. J. Astile f. the Bayliue of Withernam [T. Orwin,* 1589.] L²(2).O.C².DUR⁵.; HN. PFOR.TEX.
　　B2ᵛ line 26: 'abusde,'; D4ᵛ line 11: 'next booke, shall bee/'.
— The returne of the renowned caualiero Pasquill of England, and his meeting with Marforius at London vpon the Royal Exchange. 1589. *See* 19457.
17464 — A whip for an ape: or Martin displaied. [By J. Lyly?] 4°. *[London? T. Orwin?* 1589?] L.L².M.; HN.
17465 — [Anr. ed., w. no imprint and w. title:] Rythmes against Martin Marre-prelate. 4°. *[T. Orwin,* 1589.] L.L².O.C⁹.; HN.U.
— *See* also Penry, John; Throckmorton, Job; 1346, 1521, 12342, 12903, 12914, 12915, 22912, 23450, 23451, 23628, 26030.

Marquino, F., *tr. See* 13101.

17466 **Marriage.** A new and pleasaunt enterlude intituled the mariage of witte and science. 4°. *T. Marshe,* [1570.] Ent. 1569–70. O. Greg 55.

17467 **Mars.** Mars his feild or the exercise of armes. (The perfect manner of handling the sword and target.) 2 pts. 8°. *sold by R. Daniell,* [1625?] L.O.
　　Plates copied from 11810 and 794; pt. 1 based on 11810. The copies differ in number of plates.

17468 **Marseilles.** A true report of the taking of Marseilles. *Tr.* out of French [by E. Aggas?] 8°. *J. Windet f. E. Aggas,* [1585.] L.L².

17469 **Marshall, George.** A compendious treatise in metre declaring the firste originall of sacrifice. By G. M. 4°. *(in ed. J. Cawodi,)* 1554 (18 de.) L².L⁴.; HN.
　　Author's name occurs in acrostic in prologue.

Marshall, Hamlett. *See* 23096.

17469.2 **Marshall, Thomas.** [Keepsake. 30 Sept. 1640.] s.sh.8°. *[Oxford, L. Lichfield,* 1640.] O.

Marshall, William, *ed. See* 15986, 25127.
— *tr. See* 5641, 10498, 10503.5, 17817, 21789.3, 24238, 26119.

17469.6 **Marshall, William,** *Engraver.* [The four elements. 4 engraved plates.] Earth. (Aire. Fire. Water.) 4°. *(sould by T. Jenner,)* [c. 1640.] L(Print Dept.).
　　See Hind III.190–1.

17469.8 **Marshalsea Prison.** A zealous prayer to God, used and said every day by the poore prisoners of the Marshalsey, for all their good benefactors. s.sh.fol. *[W. Jones,* c. 1620.] L⁵(Lemon 235).

17470 **Marshe, Richard.** A sermon preached at the consecration of R. Senhouse, Bp. of Carlile. 4°. *H. Lownes f. M. Lownes,* 1625. O.C¹⁵.DUR³.ETON.G². +
　　Reissued w. tp cancelled in 22240.5.

Marsilius, *of Padua. See* 17817

Marsixtus, Martin. *See* 24913.

17471 **Marston, John.** The workes of M[r]. J. Marston, being tragedies and comedies, collected into one volume. 8°. [*A. Mathewes*] *f. W. Sheares,* 1633. L.L[38].O.A. M.+; F.HN(both tpp).HD.ILL.PML.+
All sub tpp signed.

17472 — [Anr. issue, w. cancel tp:] Tragedies and comedies collected into one volume. [Anon.] *A. M[athewes] f. W. Sheares,* 1633. L.O[2].C.ETON.M.+; F(gen. tp only).HN. CHI.HD.NY.+
Omits Sheares' dedic.; all sub tpp replaced by anon. cancels. O[3] has a binding frag. w. cancels R6, R7, and E7 pr. in a row.

17473 — [Antonio and Mellida.] The history of Antonio and Mellida. The first part. [Init. I. M.] 4°. [*R. Bradock*] *f. M. Lownes a. T. Fisher,* 1602. Ent. 24 oc. 1601. L(3).L[6].O.; F.HN.BO.HD.PFOR.+ Greg 184.
Reissued in 1652 with gen. tp 'Comedies, Tragicomedies & Tragedies' (copy HN) containing also 17474, 17475, 17478, 17479, 17483, 17487, 17488. *See* also 4963 and 11156.

17474 — Antonios revenge. The second part. [Init. I. M.] 4°. [*R. Bradock*] *f. T. Fisher, soulde [by M. Lownes,]* 1602. Ent. 24 oc. 1601. L.L[6].O.; F.HN.HD.ILL.PFOR.+ Greg 185.
Sheets G, H, I have perp. chainlines.

17475 — The Dutch courtezan. 4°. *T. P[urfoote] f. J. Hodgets,* 1605. Ent. 26 jn. L(2).L[6](2).O.; F.HN.CH.HD.PFOR.+ Greg 214.

— Histrio-mastix. Or, the player whipt. 1610. *See* 13529.

17476 — The insatiate countesse. A tragedie. Written by J. Marston. 4°. *T. S[nodham] f. T. Archer,* 1613. L (imp.).L[6].O.E.; HN.MCG.PFOR. Greg 315.
Attrib. to Marston doubtful; in some copies (O, HN, PFOR) tp mutilated to cut out his name.

17476.5 — [Anr. issue, w. cancel tp:] Written by L. Machin, and W. Bacster. 4°. *f. T. Archer,* 1613. F.

17477 — [Anr. ed. Anon.] 4°. *N. O[kes] f. T. Archer,* 1616. L. O.; F.HN.

17478 — [Anr. ed. Signed.] 4°. *I. N[orton] f. H. Perrie,* 1631. Ent. 10 fb. L.O.C[2].E.M.+; F.HN.HD.N.PN.+

17478a — [Anr. issue, w. cancel tp.] Written, by W. Barksteed. *f. H. Perrie,* 1631. HN(imp.).
Tp pr. by R. Badger.

— Jacke Drums entertainment. [Mainly by J. Marston.] 1601. *See* 7243.

17479 — The [xylographic] malcontent … 1604. 4°. *V. S[immes] f. W. Aspley,* [1604.] Ent. to Aspley a. T. Thorpe 5 jy. L.L[4].L[6].O.; F.HN.HD(tp def.).NY.Y.+ Greg 203.
Collates A–H[4]. Quires B–E in this and 17480 are by another printer.

17480 — [Anr. ed.] 1604. 4°. *V. S[immes] f. W. Aspley,* [1604.] L(2).SHEF.; HN.BO(imp.).LC(imp.).PFOR.
Collates A–H[4] I[2]; partly from same setting as 17479 w. prologue and epilogue added and corrections.

17481 — [Anr. ed.] Augmented. With the additions written by J. Webster. 1604. 4°. *V.S[immes] f. W. Aspley,* [1604.] L.L[6].O.CHATS.ETON.+; F.HN.HD.ILL.NY.+
Collates A–I[4].

17482 — The metamorphosis of Pigmalions image. And certaine satyres. [In verse. Dedic. init.] (W. K[insayder.]) 8°. (*J. Roberts*) *f. E. Matts,* 1598. Ent. 27 my. L.L[13].O.; F(2).HN.PFOR.PML.
See also 4275 sqq. for reprints of first part. *See* Arber III.677–8.

17483 — Parasitaster, or the fawne. 4°. *T. P[urfoote] f. W. C[otton],* 1606. Ent. 12 mr. L.L[6].C[4](imp.).E[2].VER.; F.HN.BO.PFOR.Y. Greg 230.

17484 — [Anr. ed.] Now corrected of many faults. 4°. *T. P[urfoote] f. W. C[otton,]* 1606. L.L[6].O.E[2].ETON.+; F.HN.HD.N.NY.+
Partly from the same setting as 17483.

17485 — The scourge of villanie. Three bookes of satyres. (W. Kinsayder, *pseud.*) 8°. *J. R[oberts,] sold by J. Buzbie,* 1598. Ent. to Roberts 8 se. L.O.; F.HN.PFOR. H. Bradley Martin, New York City. Robert Taylor.
See Arber III.677–8.

17486 — [Anr. ed.] Corrected. 8°. *J. R[oberts,]* 1599. L[13].O.; F.HD.
G8[r], 2nd heading: 'Maister'.

17486.5 — [Anr. ed.] 8°. *J. R[oberts,]* 1599. L. Lord Harlech.; F.N.Y.
G8[r], 2nd heading: 'Master'.

Marston, John—*cont.*

17487 — What you will. 4°. *G. Eld f. T. Thorppe,* 1607. Ent. 6 au. L.O.O[6].C[2].ETON.+; F.HN.HD.N.NY.+ Greg 252.

17488 — The wonder of women or the tragedie of Sophonisba. 4°. *J. Windet,* 1606. Ent. to E. Edgar 17 mr. L.L[6]. O.C[2].E.+; F.HN.HD.PFOR.Y.+ Greg 231.

17488.3 — [Anr. issue, w. cancel tp:] The tragedie of Sophonisba. *J. Windet,* 1606. E.
— *See* also 4275.

17488.7 **Marstrand.** A breefe coniecturall discourse, vpon the caracters found vpon fower fishes, taken neere Marstrand the 28. of Nouember 1587. 4°. *E. Allde,* 1589. Ent. 12 my. O(2, 1 lacks tp).
(Formerly 17650)

17489 **Marten, Anthony.** An exhortation, to stirre vp the mindes of all her maiesties faithfull subiects, to defend their countrey. 4°. *J. Windet, sold [by A. Maunsell,]* 1588. Ent. to Windet 2 se. L.O(imp.).O[5].C.DUL.+; F(3). HN.CH.HD.NY.
Contains reprint of 17489.5.

17489.5 — A godly prayer for the preseruation of the queenes maiestie, and for her armies both by sea and land. [Anon.] s.sh.fol. *J. Wolfe f. T. Woodcocke,* 1588. Ent. 31 jy. COL.
Reprinted in 17489.

17490 — A reconciliation of all the pastors and cleargy of this church of England. 4°. *J. Windet,* 1590. Ent. 14 jy. L(imp.).L[3].O.C.SAL.+; F.HN.CAL.U(tp mutil.).Y.

17491 — A second sound, or warning of the trumpet vnto iudgement. 4°. *T. Orwin f. A. Maunsell,* 1589. Ent. to Orwin 26 ap. L.O.C.P.YK.+
— *tr. See* 1925, 24669.

17492 **Martialis, Marcus Valerius.** M. Val. Martialis epigrammatων libri. [*Ed.*] (T. Farnaby.) 8°. *F. Kingstonius, imp. G. Welby,* 1615. Ent. 25 mr. 1613. L.O.C.DUR[3].M[4].+; F.HN.HD.ILL.Y.+ 𝔞

17493 — [Anr. ed.] 8°. *R. Junius, imp. P. Stephani & C. Meredith,* 1633. Ass'd to T. Snodham 2 mr. 1618; to Stansby 23 fb. 1626. L.O.C.DUL.M.+; F.HN.HD. ILL.Y.+
See Court-Book C, p. 227, and Greg, *Companion,* pp. 84, 275–6.

17494 — Selected epigrams of Martial. Englished [in verse] by T. May. 16° in 8's. [*H. Lownes*] *f. T. Walkley,* 1629. Ent. 31 mr. 1628. L.L[6].O(2).O[7].HETH(imp.).; F.HN. HD.N.Y.+

17495 — Martial to himselfe, treating of worldly blessednes, in Latin, English and Walsch. [In verse. *Tr.*] S. Vachan. s.sh.fol. *J. Awdely,* [1571.] M[2].

17496 **Martiall, John.** A treatyse of the crosse gathred out of the scriptures. 8°. *Antwerp, J. Latius,* 1564. L.O.C.E. W.+; F.HN.CHI.WASH[3].Y.
A&R 524.

17497 — A replie to M. Calfhills blasphemous answer [4368] made against the treatise of the crosse. 4°. *Louaine, I. Bogard,* 1566. L.O.E.P.YK.+; F(imp.).
A&R 523; answered in 11456.
— *ed. See* 12759.

Martin, jun. *See* 17457.

17498 **Martin, St., Abp. of Braga.** Seneca moralissmus [*sic*] philosophus [or rather St. Martin] de quattuor virtutibus cardinalibus. 4° in 8's. (*per w. de worde,* 1516.) L.O.

17499 — [Anr. ed.] 4° in 8's. (*w. de worde,* 1523.) O.
17499.5 — [Anr. ed.] 4° in 8's. (*W. de Worde,* 1529.) Copenhagen RL.

17500 — [A trans.] The rule of an honest lyfe. *Tr.* Here vnto is added the Encheridyon of a spyrytuall lyfe. 8°. [*R. Redman?* 1538?] F(imp.).

17501 — [Anr. trans.] A frutefull worke of Lucius Anneus Seneca [or rather St. Martin] named the forme and rule of honest lyuynge. *Tr.* R. Whyttynton and now newlye imprynted. *Lat. a. Eng.* 8°. (*W. Myddylton,* 1546 (21 jy.)) L(3).O.; HN.

17502 — A frutefull worke of Lucius Anneus Senecæ [or rather St. Martin.] Called the myrrour or glasse of maners. *Tr.* R. whyttynton. Nowe newely imprynted. *Lat. a. Eng.* 8°. (*W. Myddylton,* 1547.) L.O.; F.HN.CU(1st quire only, bd. w. 22216).
A different work from 17501.

Martin, sen. *See* 17458.

Martin, A. *See* Marten.

17503 **Martin, Gregory.** A discouerie of the manifold corruptions of the holy scriptures by the heretikes. 8⁰. *Rhemes, J. Fogny*, 1582. L.O.C.E⁴.M.+; F.HN.HD.N. NY.+
A&R 525; answered by 11430.

17504 — The loue of the soule made by G. M. 16⁰ in 8's. *Roane, [London, Fr. Garnet's second press,]* 1578 [c. 1597.] L.LK.
A&R 526; first pr. in 17507.

17505 — [Anr. ed.] Made by G. Mar. Where-unto are annexed certain Catholike questions. [Anon., not by Martin. In verse.] 16⁰ in 8's. *Roan, [English secret press, 1602?]* O.
A&R 527. Verses answered by 13388, 20959, 21307a.3.

17505.5 — [Anr. ed.] Made by G. M. 12⁰. *[English secret press, 1614?]* L⁹.CAR.
A&R 528 and 529; collates A–D¹².

17506 — [Anr. ed.] With a catalogue of the popes and professors of the catholike faith; and a challenge to Protestants. 12⁰. *[Lancs., Birchley Hall Press,]* 1619. O(2, 1 imp.). USHAW ('Catalogue' only).W.; F.
(Formerly also 17134) A&R 530. *See also* 10912, 10914.

17506.3 — [Anr. ed.] Wherinto is annexed, a rule, for the interpretation of holy scripture. Taken out of the Apology of F. Staphilius [23230]. 8⁰. *S. Omers, [widow of C. Boscard] f. J. Heigham*, 1630. A².VAL(imp.).
A&R 531.

17506.5 — [Anr. ed.] 24⁰ in 6's. *[St. Omer, G. Seutin?]* 1633. OS (imp.).
A&R 532.

17506.7 — [Anr. ed.] 12⁰. *[English secret press, 1640?]* A².
A&R 533. Collates A–C¹² D⁶. Omits Staphylus excerpt.

17507 — A treatyse of christian peregrination. Whereunto is adioined certen epistles. 8⁰. *[Paris, f. R. Verstegan,]* 1583 [c. 1597.] L.O.C.OS.W.+; HD.Y.
A&R 534. 'Epistles' reprinted as 17504.

17508 — A treatise of schisme. 8⁰. *Duaci, ap. J. Foulerum* [really *London, W. Carter,*] 1578. L.L².O.OS.W.+; F.
A&R 535. *See* Greg, *Companion*, p. 20.
— *tr. See* 2207, 2884.

Martin, *Sir* Henry. *See* 11904.

17509 **Martin, James,** *M.A.* Via regia. The kings way to heaven. With a letter of I. Casaubon. 8⁰. *N. Okes f. G. Norton*, 1615. Ent. 3 mr. L.O(2).A.LINC.; F.HD. ('Letter' formerly 4746)

17509.5 — [A variant, w. imprint:] *f. G. Norton*, 1615. C³.; HN. FBL.
— *ed. See* 19020, 23580, 25369.
— *tr. See* 21752.
— *See also* 736.

Martin, James, *of Dunkeld. See* 17524.

17510 **Martin, Richard.** A speach delivered, to the kings majestie in the name of the sheriffes. 4⁰. *[R. Read] f. T. Thorppe, sould by W. Aspley*, 1603. Ent. to Aspley 12 my. (Arber III. 36). L.L².O.O⁵.C³.+; F.HN.BO.HD.

17511 — [Anr. ed.] 4⁰. *Edinburgh, R. Walde-grave*, 1603. L⁸.; F.
The tpp of L⁸ and F are variant in setting.

17511.5 **Martin, Robert,** *bibliopola.* Catalogue des diverses livres francoises: recueilées dans la France . . . ils se vendent a [R. Martin.] 4⁰. *chez T. Harper*, 1640. O.A². D.STU.; ILL.

17512 — Catalogus librorum quos (in ornamentum reipublicæ literariæ) ex Italia selegit R. Martine, apud quem prostant venales. 4⁰. *typis A. Mathewes*, 1633. L.O (2).C.D.DUR⁵.

17513 — Catalogus librorum tam impressorum quam manuscriptorum, quos ex Roma, Venetiis, aliisque Italiæ locis, selegit R. Martine apud quem væneunt. 4⁰. *typis J. Haviland*, 1635. L.O(4, 2 imp.).O³(frags.).C. McK. 306 on tp, which is conjugate w. table of contents.

17513.5 — [Anr. issue, w. McK. 227 on cancel tp.] O.
Tp a single leaf pr. by T. Harper.

17514 — Catalogus librorum, ex præcipuis Italiæ emporiis selectorum per R. Martinum. Apud quem venales habentur. 4⁰. *typis T. Harper*, 1639. L.O.O¹⁸.C.D.+

Martin, Robert, *bibliopola—cont.*

17515 — Catalogus librorum, plurimis linguis scriptorum: ac è diversis Europæ regionibus congestorum: prostant venales apud R. Martinum. 4⁰. *typis T. Harper*, 1640. O.O¹¹.C.D.P.; CAL.

17516 **Martin, Thomas.** Historica descriptio complectens vitam, Guilielmi Wicami. [Anon.] 4⁰. *P. S[hort,]* 1597. L.O.O¹⁴.C¹⁸.WN.+

17517 — A traictise declaryng and plainly prouyng, that the pretensed marriage of priestes, is no mariage. . . . Herewith is comprised a full confutation of [20176]. 4⁰. *in æd. R. Caly*, 1554. (my.) L.O.C.D².E.+; F.HN.HD. N.PML.+
Answered by 20175; attrib. to S. Gardiner. *See also* 21804, 24514.

17518 — A defence of priestes mariages, . . . agaynst T. Martin. [By Sir R. Morison? *Ed.* Abp. M. Parker.] 4⁰. (*J. Kingston f. R. Jugge,*) [1567?] Ent. 1566–67. L.O.C³.D.WI.+; F.HN.HD(2).Y.
Ends Pp⁴; some copies (L, O) have variant sp. in colophon: 'Kinston'.

17519 — [Anr. issue, w. sheets Oo and Pp reprinted, and Qq–Zz⁴ &&⁴ ??⁶ added.] 4⁰. (*R. Jugge,*) [1567?] L. O.C.D².M.+; F.HN.HD.MIN.U.+
Additions by Abp. M. Parker.
— *See also* Bookplates.

Martin, William. *See* Martyn, W.

Martine, William. Positiones aliquot philosophicæ. Præside G. Martino. 1618. *See* 21555.31.

17520 **Martinengo, Nestore,** *Count.* The true report of all the successe of Famagosta. Englished by W. Malim. 4⁰. *J. Daye*, 1572. L.O(imp.).C³(imp.).; F(imp.).HN.HD. LC(imp.).
Collates A–F⁴ G².

17521 — [Anr. ed.] 4⁰. *J. Daye*, 1572. General Priory of the British Realm of the Order of the Hospital of St. John of Jerusalem, St. John's Gate, Clerkenwell, London. Gennadius Library, Athens.; Y.
Collates A–F⁴.

Martínez, Marco. *See* 18868 sqq.

17522 **Martini, Matthias.** Græcæ linguæ fundamenta: . . . limatiora & pleniora ex quarta editione. 8⁰. *typis J. Haviland, imp. J. Partridge*, 1629. Ent. to W. Garrett 6 fb. 1626; to J. Partridge 18 se. 1627. L.O.C(imp.). C⁵.D.+; F.HN.HD.PH.WASH³.+
Martini is only the editor; dedic. is signed 'Schola Bremensis'.

17523 **Martinius, Petrus.** מַפְתֵּחַ לְשׁוֹן הַקֹּדֶשׁ that is the key of the holy tongue: wherein is conteineid, first the Hebrue grammar out of P. Martinius. Secondly, a practize vpon the psalmes. Thirdly, a short dictionary. All Englished by J. Udall. 8⁰. *Leyden, F. Raphelengius*, 1593. L.O.C.G².M.+; F.HN.HD.N.NY.+

17524 **Martinus, Jacobus.** Jacobi Martini . . . de prima simplicium, & concretorum corporum generatione disputatio. 8⁰. *Cantabrigiae, ex off. T. Thomæ*, 1584. L.O.C.E².P.+; LC.Y.

Martius, Laurentius. *See* 21806.

17525 **Martyn, Joseph.** New epigrams, and a satyre. [In verse.] 4⁰. *G. Eld*, 1621. Ent. to Eld a. M. Flesher 8 my. L.O.; F.HN.NY.

17526 **Martyn, William.** The historie, and lives, of twentie kings of England. With the successions of the dukes [etc.] fol. *W. Stansby f. H. Fetherstone*, 1615. Ent. 20 au. 1614. L².O.C.LINC.M.+; F.HN.HD.WIS.Y.+
See Acts of the Privy Council, 1615–16, p. 100. Martin forced to apologize for offensive passages.

17527 — [Anr. issue, w. tp:] The historie, and lives, of the kings of England. (The successions of the dukes [etc.]) fol. [*W. Stansby*] *f. J. Bill, W. Barret a. H. Fetherstone*, 1615. L.O.C.GLOUC.SHEF.+; F.HN.ILL.IND.WASH².+

17528 — [Anr. ed.] fol. [*H. Lownes*] *f. J. Boler* [*a.*] (*f. G. Tompson,*) 1628. Ass'd to Boler, R. Young, a. G. Thomason 1 no. 1627. L.O.C.D².DUR(Bamb.).+; F.HN.MICH.N.Y.+
Plates from 13581 in this and 17529. Text apparently not changed from 17526.

17529 — [Anr. ed.] Whereunto is now added the historie of king Ed. VI. [etc.] by B. R. Mʳ. of arts. fol. *R. Young, f. himselfe & others*, 1638. Addition ent. to Boler a. Young 26 no. 1633. L.O.C.D.E.+; F.HN.HD.N.U.+

Martyn, William—*cont.*

17530 — Youths instruction. Composed and written by W. Martyn esquire. 4°. *J. Beale*, 1612. Ent. to W. Hall 9 ap. L(2).O(3).C²(2).; F.

17531 — Second edition. 4°. *J. Beale f. R. Redmer*, 1613. Ent. to J. Beale 7 ap. 1614. L(1, also tp Harl.5927/191).L³⁰. BHP.BRISTOL².; F.HN.Y.

Martyne, Bp. of Dumience. *See* Martin, St., Abp. of Braga.

Martyr, Petrus, *Anglerius. See* Anglerius.

Martyr, Petrus, *Vermilius. See* Vermigli.

17532 **Martyrology.** The martiloge in englysshe after the vse of salisbury. [*Tr.*] (R. Whytford.) 4°. (*W. de worde*, 1526 (15 fb.)) L.O.C¹⁹.D².LINC.+; HN.

17533 — The roman martyrologe, according to the reformed calendar. *Tr.* G. K[eynes.] 8°. [*St. Omer, English College Press*,] 1627. L.O.C.A².D².+; F.HN.MICH.Y. A&R 536. Dedic. init. J. W., i.e. J. Wilson.

17534 **Mary, the Blessed Virgin.** Cōmemoracō lamētacōis sine [*sic*] cōpassiōis btē Marie. [1490.] Now = 15847.3.

— Compassio beate Marie. [c. 1520.] *See* 15847.5.

17535 — The compassyon of our lady. 1522. = 14552.

17536 — An exposicion vpon the songe of the blessed virgine Mary, called Magnificat. 1538. Now = 16979.7.

17537 — The lamentacyon of our lady. 4° in 6. (*W. de Worde*,) [1509–10?] C. Sometimes attrib. to J. Lydgate.

17538 — A methode, to meditate on the psalter, or great rosarie of our blessed ladie. 16° in 8's. *Antwerp* [*English secret press*,] 1598. L(imp.).O. A&R 541. 15 engrs. pasted in.

— Miracles lately wrought [etc.] 1606. *See* 18746.

17539 — The myracles of oure blessyd lady. 4° in 6's. (*Westmynster in Caxtons house, W. de Worde*,) [1496.] G². Duff 297.

17540 — [Anr. ed.] 4° ⁸·⁴. (*W. de Worde*, 1514.) L.

17541 — [Anr. ed.] 4°. (*W. de Worde*, 1530.) F.

17542 — Here after folowith the boke callyd the Myrroure of oure lady. 2 pts. fol. (*R. Fawkes*, 1530 (4 no.)) L.O.C(lacks tp). M.P.+; F(2).HN.ILL.PML. Sometimes attrib. to T. Gascoigne.

17542.3 — The mistical crowne of the most glorious virgin Marie, *tr.* R. H. 8°. *Douay, D. Hudsebaut*, 1638. L(imp.). DAI. A&R 557. Tr. R. Howard? or R. Hungate?

17542.5 — Our ladyes chambre, or parler. 8°. [*R. Wyer*, 1533?] O(tp only, Douce Add. 142/612).

17542.7 — The psalter of the B. virgin Mary. Conteyning many deuout prayers & petitions. Composed in the French tongue by a father of the Society of Jesus [i.e. adapted by A. Sucquet? from the 'Psalterium parvum'.] *Tr.* into English by R. F. 12°. [*St. Omer, English College Press*,] 1624. L.OS(imp.).W. A&R 129.

17543 — Psalteriū btē marie virginis cū articulis īcarnatiōis dñi nr̄i iesu xp̄i nup editū. 4°. [*Paris, W. Hopyl f.*] (*London, S. Voter*,) [c. 1515] (21 oc.) O(2 leaves).

17544 — Here begynneth the Rosarye of our lady in englysshe with many goodly petyciōs dyrect to her. 16° in 8's. [*Antwerp, W. Vorsterman*, c. 1525.] C.

17545 — [Anr. ed.] 16° in 8's. (*R. Coplande*, 1531.) A².

17545.5 — [Anr. ed.] The rosary with the articles of the lyfe & deth of Jesu Chryst and peticiōs directe to our lady. 16° in 8's. (*J. Skot*, 1537.) M. A revision of the text of 17544.

17546 — The rosarie of our ladie. Otherwise called our ladies psalter. 12°. *Antuerpiæ, ap. J. Keerbergium*, 1600. L.L².O.O⁸.DE.+; F.Y. A&R 918. Preface init. T. W. P., i.e. T. Worthington, Priest.

17547 — The song of Mary the mother of Christ. [In verse.] 4°. *E. Allde f. W. Ferbrand*, 1601. Ent. 23 jy. L.E.; F.HN.NY. L, NY have quire F not in most other copies.

17548 **Mary, the Blessed Virgin.**—*Archconfraternity of the Rosary.* The arch-confraternity of the holy rosary of our blessed lady. . . . [A description with indulgences, prayers, etc.] 24° in 12's. [*English secret press*,] 1636. L. A&R 36.

17549 **Mary, the Blessed Virgin.**—*Guild of Our Lady of Scala Coeli, at Boston.* [Notification of privileges of members. c. 1515.] Now = Indulgences 35.

17550 **Mary, the Blessed Virgin.**—*Confraternity of, at St. Botulph's, Boston.* UNiuersis et singulis xp̄ifidelibus [etc. 1522.] Now = Indulgences 33.

17551 — [Anr. ed.] VNiversis xp̄ifidelibus [etc. 1504?] Now = Indulgences 27.

— *See also* Indulgences 28, 29, 30, 31, 32, 34, 50, 123.

17552 **Mary, the Blessed Virgin.**—*Monastery at Brussels.* Statutes compyled for the better observation of the holy rule of S. Benedict. 3 pts. 8°. *Gant, J. Dooms*, (1632.) L.O²⁵.DE.OULT.W.+; F.Y. A&R 800. Sometimes bd. as pts. 2–4 of 1860.

Mary, the Blessed Virgin.—*Church of Our Lady of Loreto.* *See* 23884a.4 sqq.

17553 **Mary, de' Medici.** Declaration de la reyne mere du roy tres-crestien, contenant les raisons de sa sortie des pais-bas. 4°. *G. Thomason*, 1638. Ent. to Thomason a. O. Pulleyn 23 ja. 1639. L.O.C.D.P.+; F.Y.

17554 — [A trans.] A declaration of the queene, mother of the most christian king. Containing the reasons of her departure out of the Low-Countreys; [etc.] 4°. *J. Raworth f. J. Kirton a. T. Warren*, 1639. Ent. 29 ap. L.O.C.DUR.SAL.+; HN.CHI.LC.Y.

— Newes out of France: . . . Contayned in the letters of the queene mother. 1619. *See* 11284.

17555 — The remonstrance made by the queene-mother of France, to the king. *Tr.* 4°. *T. S[nodham] f. N. Newbery*, 1619. Ent. 15 ap. L(2, 1 lacks tp).O(3).M.; HN.

17556 — A true discourse of the whole occurrences in the queenes voyage from Florence, until Marseilles. Hereunto is annexed, the first Savoyan. [By A. Arnauld.] *Tr.* E. A[ggas.] 4°. *S. Stafford f. C. Burby*, 1601. Ent. 16 ja. L.L¹³.O.M.YK(2nd pt. only).; F.HD (2nd pt. only).LC.

17557 **Mary, of Nimeguen.** Here begynneth a lyttell story . . . of a mayde that was named Mary of Nēmegen. 4°. (*Anwarpe, J. Duisbrowghe*,) [1518?] HN.

17558 **Mary, Queen Consort of Louis XII.** The solempnities. & triumphes doon at the spousells of the kyngs doughter to the archeduke of Austrige. 4°. (*R. Pynson*,) [1509.] L(imp.). A trans. of 4659.

17559 **Mary I, Queen of England.** The epitaphe upon the death of quene Marie, augmented by the first author. [In verse. By L. Stopes?] s.sh.fol. *R. Lant*, [1559.] L⁵ (Lemon 46). Prob. the 'ballad' for which Lant was 'sent to warde' (Arber I.101), with verses in praise of Elizabeth added.

17560 — [A genealogical table of Philip and Mary.] 1554, = pt. of 5207.

17561 — Now singe, nowe springe, oure care is exild, Oure vertuous quene, is quickned with child. *Ballad.* 1/2 sh.fol. *W. Ryddaell*, [1554.] C⁷.

17562 — A supplicacyō to the quenes maiestie. 8°. *J. Cawoode*, (1550) [really *Strassburg, W. Rihel*, 1555.] L.L². L⁸(imp. at end)*.BUTE.; F.

17562a — [A variant, w. date 1555 on last leaf.] L.O.C²(lacks tp). C⁵.; SMU.

17563 — [Anr. issue, w. tp reset, without imprint.] A suplicacyon [etc.] (1555.) F.HD. — *tr. See* 2854.

17564 **Mary, Queen of Scotland.** Allegations against the surmisid title of the quine [*sic*] of Scotts and the fauorers of the same. 4°. (*Excusum S A 7 decembris*, 1565.) L.E. Wherever 'S A' may have been, the marginal notes were pr. by a second impression and the printing is primitive.

17565 — The copie of a letter written by one in London concernyng the credit of [G. Buchanan's] late published detection of the doynges of the ladie Marie of Scotland. 8° in 4's. [*J. Day*, 1572.] L.O¹⁰.C.E.P.+; F(2). HN.HD. Supporting 3981; answered by 15503.

17566 — The copie of a letter writen out of Scotland [against] the slaunderous reportes of the quene of Scotland. [1572.] Now = 15503. — A defence of the honor of Marie queene of Scotlande. 1569. *See* 15504.

Mary, *Queen of Scotland—cont.*

17566.3 — A defence of the honorable sentence and execution of the queene of Scots: [etc.] (Anthony Babingtons letter.) 4⁰. *J. Windet,* [1587.] Ent. 11 fb. 1587. L.L². O¹⁷.E.G².+; F.HN.HD.N.

(Formerly 15098) Halfsheet L in 2 states: L1ʳ lace orn.; L1ʳ orn. w. putti playing music (L, HD). In some copies (HN) 1st F1 reset, beginning 'hath &'.

— De Maria Scotorum regina. [1571.] *See* 3978.

17566.5 — [A description of Mary's wedding to the dauphin. Scottish *tr.* with additions of 'Discours du grand et magnifique triumphe'.] 4⁰. [*Edinburgh, J. Scot?* 1558.] L²(4 leaves)

— Epitaphs, the first, upon the death of Marie, late queene of Scots. 1604. *See* 10432.7.

17566.7 — 1589. Est natura hominum [etc.] The Scottish queens buriall at Peterborough, 1587. 8⁰ in 4. *A* [sic] *J[effes],* [sic] *f. E. Venge,* [1589.] E.; F.

— Histoire de Marie royne d'Escosse. 1572. *See* 3979.

— Martyre de la royne d'Escosse. 1587. *See* 3107.

— The Scottish queens buriall. [1589.] *See* 17566.7.

— *See also* 13869.

17567 **Mary,** *Saint of Egypt.* A sacred poeme describing the miraculous life and death of S. Marie of Ægipt. 4⁰. (*Doway, widowe of M. Wyon,* 1640.) L.O.M.ST. USHAW.; F.HN.Y.

A&R 406. By R. Howard, O.F.M. All copies but O, ST, USHAW lack last leaf w. colophon.

17568 **Mary Magdalen,** *Saint.* [B6ᵛ:] Here endeth the complaynte of the louer of cryst Saynt mary Magdaleyn. [In verse.] 4⁰ in 8's. (*w. de worde,*) [1520?] F(imp.).

17569 — Marie Magdalens lamentations for the losse of her master Jesus. [In verse.] 4⁰. *A. Islip f. E. White,* 1601. L.O¹³.D².; F.HN.HD.

Attrib. to G. Markham.

17570 — [Anr. ed.] 4⁰. *J. R[oberts] f. T. Clarke,* 1604. Ent. 24 ap. L.BUTE.

'Ad autorem' init. W. F. *See* Court-Book C, p. 8.

— Marie Magdalens loue. 1595. *See* 3665.

17571 **Maryland.** A relation of Maryland: together, with a map of the countrey, his majesties charter. 4⁰. *to bee had, at W. Peasley esq; his house or at J. Morgans house,* 1635 (8 se.) L(3).O(2).M.; HN.HD.LC.N.NY.+

— *See also* 4371.

17572 **Mascall, Leonard.** A booke of fishing with hooke & line. Another of sundrie engines and trappes. [Init. L. M.] 4⁰. *J. Wolfe, solde by E. White,* 1590. Ent. to J. Wolf 23 my. 1587. L.LINDLEY.; F.HD.PN.ROS.Y(2).

Taken partly from 3309.

17573 — [Anr. ed.] 4⁰. [*A. Islip? f.*] *J. Wolfe, sold by E. White,* 1600. M(2, 1 imp.).; PN.ROS.Y(2, 1 imp.).

17573.5 — A booke of the art and maner, howe to plante and graffe all sortes of trees . . . with diuerse other newe practises, by [D. Brossard.] *Tr.* L. Mascal. 4⁰. *H. Bynneman f. J. Wight,* [1569.] Ent. 1568–69. L(imp.).C¹⁴.G².M.RD.; F.WIS(imp.).

Some copies (M, F) misdated '1589' on C3ᵛ; some (L) undated.

17574 — [Anr. ed.] 4⁰. *H. Denham f. J. Wight,* [1572.] L.O.O²⁴. G².RD.+; HN.HD.HUNT.

17575 — [Anr. ed.] 4⁰. [*H. Denham a. J. Charlewood?] f. J. Wight,* 1575. L(1, also tp only Harl.5995/27).L⁴⁰. RD.; F.HN(imp.).CHI.HD.WIS.+

17576 — [Anr. ed.] 4⁰. [*J. Kingston] f. J. Wight,* 1582. L.RD. Warrington PL.; HN.Y.

— [Anr. ed.] 1589. *See* note to 17573.5.

17577 — [Anr. ed.] 4⁰. *T. Este f. T. Wight,* 1590. C.A.D⁶.G²(2).; ROCH.WIS.

17578 — [Anr. ed.] 4⁰. *T. East f. T. Wight,* 1592. L.STU.; COR. HUNT.LC.N(imp.).

17579 — [Anr. ed.] 4⁰. [*V. Simmes,*] 1596. L.O⁵.; HN.HD(imp.).

A pirated ed. w. woodcuts copied.

17579.5 — [Anr. ed.] 4⁰. *T. Este f. T. Wight,* 1599 (1592.) C²⁰.G².

For a later ed. *see* 5874.

17580 — The first booke of cattell. (The second booke.—The third booke.) 4⁰ in 8's. *J. Wolfe,* 1587. Ent. 23 my. L.; F(imp.).HN.

Quires A–N, V, and Gg in 4's.

17581 — [Anr. ed.] 4⁰ in 8's. *J. Wolfe, solde by J. Harrison the elder,* 1591. L.O³³.D.G².RD.+; HN.CU.Y.

17582 — [Anr. ed.] 4⁰ in 8's. [*J. Windet f.*] *J. Wolfe, sold by J. Harrison the elder,* 1596. L.O.D.RD(1st bk. only).

17583 — [Anr. ed.] 4⁰ in 8's. *J. Harison,* 1600. Ent. 29 oc. 1599. L(lacks tp).O.RD(lacks 1st bk.).

Mascall, Leonard—cont.

17584 — [Anr. ed.] 4⁰ in 8's. *J. Harison,* 1605. L.C¹⁹.RD(lacks 1st bk.). Norman Comben, London.

17585 — [Anr. ed.] 4⁰ in 8's. *N. Okes f. J. Harison,* 1610 (1609.) G².; HN.WIS.Y.

17586 — [Anr. ed.] The government of cattell. 4⁰ in 8's. *T. S[nodham] f. R. Jackson,* 1620 (1619.) Ent. 1 mr. 1614. L.RD.SNU.; F.HD.

17587 — [Anr. ed.] 4⁰ in 8's. *T. Purfoot f. F. Falkner* [a.] (*F. Williams,*) 1627. Ent. to F. Williams 16 ja. 1626. L. C.E.RD. Royal Institution of Chartered Surveyors, London.; HN.BO⁵.HD.

17588 — [Anr. ed.] 4⁰ in 8's. *T. Harper f. J. Harison,* 1633. Ent. 29 jn. 1630. L.O.NLW(St. Asaph).RD. School of Agriculture Library, Cambridge.+; F.HD.LC.

17589 — The husbandlye ordring and gouernment of poultrie. 8⁰. *T. Purfoote f. G. Dewse,* 1581. L.C⁵(lacks tp).G².

17590 — A profitable boke declaring dyuers approoued remedies, to take out spottes and staines. Englished by L. M[ascall.] 4⁰. *T. Purfoote a. W. Ponsonbie,* 1583. Ent. 1 fb. L.O.G².

This and following eds. sometimes bd. w. corresponding eds. of 24254 sqq.

17591 — [Anr. ed.] 4⁰. *T. Purfoote,* 1588. L¹⁶(tp mutilated).O. G².; F(lacks tp). HD.Y.

17592 — [Anr. ed.] 4⁰. *T. Purfoot,* 1596. C.G².; HN.HD(impr. mutilated).LC.

17593 — [Anr. ed.] (A proper treatise, wherein is briefly set forth the art of limming.) 4⁰. *T. Purfoot,* 1605. L.O⁵.; HN (1st pt. only).LC(2nd pt. only).PH²(1st pt. only). (2nd pt. formerly 24257) Pr. w. continuous signatures.

— *tr. See* 20180.3 sq.

17594 **Mason, Edmund.** A sermon preached before his majestie at Oatelands. 4⁰. *J. Bill,* 1622. L.O.C.D².YK.+; F. HN.HD(lacks tp).

17595 **Mason, Francis.** The authoritie of the church in making canons and constitutions. Delivered in a sermon. And now enlarged. 4⁰. [*Eliot's Court Press] f. J. Norton,* 1607. Ent. 9 ap. L.O.C.E.M.+; F.HN.HD.N.U.+ Answered in 13395.

17596 — Second edition revised. 4⁰. *Oxford, J. Lichfield,* 1634. Ent. to Joyce Norton a. R. Whitaker 26 au. 1632. L.O.C.A.D.+; F.HN.HD.KAN.U.+ Quire A partially reset: tp 'reuised' or 'revised'; both at HD.

17597 — Of the consecration of the bishops in the church of England: five bookes. fol. *R. Barker,* 1613. L.O.C.D. E⁴.+; F.HN.HD.N.PML.+ Answered by 4960.

17598 — [A trans., enlarged.] Vindiciæ ecclesiæ Anglicanæ; sive de legitimo eiusdem ministerio, id est, de episco-porum successione, consecratione, [etc.] Editio secunda. Opus traductum ab ipso authore. [*Ed.*] (N. Brent.) fol. *per F. Kyngstonum,* 1625. Ent. 19 jn. 1624. L.O.C.D.E.+; F.HN.HD.ILL.PML.+

17599 — [Anr. issue, w. cancel tp:] imp. E. Blackmore, 1638. L.O.C².D.E².+; F.HN.PEN.Y. Tp pr. by T. Harper.

17600 — Two sermons, preached at the kings court. 8⁰. *H. L[ownes] f. N. Newbery,* 1621. Ent. 19 fb. L.O.BURY. LINC.; HN.

17600.3 **Mason, George,** *Merchant.* Grammaire Angloise. Con-tenant reigles bien exactes. Fr. a. Eng. 12⁰. [*W. Stansby*] *chez N. Butter,* 1622. Gdańsk, Biblioteka Gdańska PAN. Vienna NL.

17600.7 — [Anr. ed.] 12⁰. *chez N. Butter,* 1633. C².PARIS. Mons PL. Munich, Bayerische Staatsbibliothek.

17601 **Mason, George,** and **Earsden, John.** The ayres that were sung and played, at Brougham Castle. fol. *T. Snodham,* 1618. L.; HN.

17602 **Mason, Henry.** Christian humiliation, or, a treatise of fasting. 4⁰. *G. P[urslowe] f. J. Clarke,* 1625. Ent. 15 oc. 1624. L.O.C.E².M(deposit).+; F.HN.HD.ILL. U.+

17603 — [Anr. ed.] Christian humiliation, or, the christians fast. Second edition, enlarged. 4⁰. *M. F[lesher] f. J. Clarke,* 1627. L.O.C³.A.CASHEL.+; F.ILL.NY¹¹.Y.

17603.5 — [Anr. issue, w. variant tp:] Whereunto is added The epicures fast. 2 pts. 4⁰. *M. F[lesher] f. J. Clarke,* 1627. O⁶.C.C³.C⁵.D.; HD.NY¹¹. Pt. 2 a reissue of 17608.

Mason, Henry—*cont.*

17604 — Contentment in Gods gifts. 12°. [*M. Flesher*] *f. J. Clarke*, 1630. Ent. 30 oc. 1629. O.O⁵.PLUME.
Reprinted in 17606 sq.

17605 — The cure of cares. 4°. *M. F*[*lesher*] *f. J. Clarke*, 1627. Ent. 25 au. L.O.C.LINC.PLUME.+; PN.U.

17605a — [A variant, w. date:] 1628. L.O⁵.C.D.NEP.+; F.HN.

17606 — Second edition, enlarged with Contentment in Gods gifts. (The tribunall of the conscience. Third edition.) 12°. [*M. Flesher*] *f. J. Clarke*, 1630. L. Dr. R. A. Hunter, London.; F.HN.Y.
Includes reprints of 17604, 17614.

17607 — Third edition enlarged [etc.] 1634. = 17612 lacking general tp; appears bd. w. unsold sheets of 17611 in 1653 w. cancel gen. tp: 'Four treatises. *f. R. Clark*' (Juel-Jensen) and in 1656 as Wing M 914.

17608 — The epicures fast: or: a short discourse, discovering the licenciousnesse of the Romane church. 4°. *G. P*[*urslow*] *f. J. Clarke*, 1626. Ent. 14 ap. L.O.D. M⁴.P.+; F.HN.CHI.U.Y.+
Also issued as pt. 2 of 17603.5.

17609 — Hearing and doing the ready way to blessednesse. 12°. *M. F*[*lesher*] *f. J. Clark*, 1635. Ent. 14 ja. L.O.C.D. WI.+; PN².U.Y.

17610 — The new art of lying, covered by Jesuits under the vaile of equivocation. 4°. *G. Purslowe f. J. Clarke*, 1624. Ent. 18 ja. L.O.C.D.E.+; F.HN.HD.ILL.NY¹¹.+

17611 — [Anr. ed.] 12°. [*M. Flesher*] *f. J. Clark*, 1634. L.O.C.A. D.+; F.CAL.HD.N.U.+
For post-1640 reissues *see* 17607.

17612 — Three treatises. 1. The cure of cares. 2. Contentment in Gods gifts. 3. The tribunall of the conscience. 12°. [*M. Flesher?*] *f. J. Clark*, 1634. L³.O.C⁵.E.YK.+; F.HN(lacks gen. tp).PN².
For post-1640 reissues *see* 17607.

17613 — The tribunall of the conscience. 4°. *G. P*[*urslowe*] *f. J. Clarke*, 1626. Ent. 14 ja. L.O.C.E².LINC.+; F.HN.HD. PN².U.+

17614 — Second edition, enlarged. 4°. *G. P*[*urslowe*] *f. J. Clarke*, 1627. L.O.C.D.NEP.+; F(2).HD.MIN.NY¹¹.Y.
Later eds. pub'd as pt. of 17606 sq.

— *See also* Bookplates.

17615 **Mason, James.** The anatomie of sorcerie. 4°. *J. Legatte, sold by S. Waterson*, 1612. L.O.C.E.LIV².+; F.HN.HD. N.NY.+
Some copies (one O, NY) read 'anotomie' in title.

17616 **Mason, John,** *Governor of Newfoundland.* A briefe discourse of the New-found-land. 4°. *Edinburgh, A. Hart*, 1620. L.O³.E.; HN.CB.PH².ROS.

17617 **Mason, John,** *of Cambridge.* The Turke. A worthie tragedie. 4°. *E. A*[*llde*] *f. J. Busbie* [*jun.,*] 1610. Ent. 10 mr. 1609. L.L⁶(2).O(2).O⁵.E(imp.).; F.HN.HD.ILL. Y².+ Greg 286.

17618 — [Anr. ed.] An excellent tragedy of Mulleasses the Turke, and Borgias governour of Florence. 4°. *T. P*[*urfoot*] *f. F. Falkner in Southwarke*, 1632. Ass'd 22 jn. 1631. L.O.C.E.M.+; F.HN.CU.HD.N.+

Mason, Sir John. *See* 5605a.

17618.5 **Mason, Richard,** *Fr. Angelus à S. Francisco.* A manuell of the arch-confraternitie of the cord of the passion. By Br. Angelus Francis. 2 pts. 12°. *Doway, M. Bogart*, 1636. MSB. Capuchin Friary, Olton, Birmingham(imp.).
A&R 537.

— *tr. See* 11314.4.

17619 **Mason, Robert.** Reasons academie. 8°. *T. Creede f. J. Browne*, 1605. Ent. 19 oc. 1604. D.; HN.
A4: To reader; B1ʳ line 1 of text ends: 'to dis-'.

17620 — [Anr. issue.] A mirrour for merchants. With an equal table to discover the excessive taking of usurie. [*T. Creede*] *f. J. Browne*, 1609. L.C².; CAL(imp.).
A3–4: different To reader; B1ʳ as in 17619.

17620.3 — [Anr. issue.] A new post: with soveraigne salve to cure the worlds madnes. By sir I. D. knight. *f. J. Mariot*, [1620.] C.; HN.
(Formerly 6354) Copies differ; C has tp as above +B–H⁸ of 17619; HN has 4 new leaves, pr. by G. Eld: tp as above; A2–3 new preface; A4 = cancel B1 w. recto line 1 of text ending: 'consist'.

17620.5 — [Anr. ed.] *f. J. Barnes*, 1620. O.C.
(Formerly 6353) Prelims., pr. by E. Allde, as in 17620.3 (HN) but 4th leaf is unsigned and recto line 1 of text ends: 'consist of'.

Mason, Robert—*cont.*

17621 — Reasons monarchie. 8°. *V. Sims*, 1602. L.O(imp.).O⁴² C(2, 1 imp.). M².; F.CAL.

17622 **Mason, Thomas.** Christs victorie over Sathans tyrannie. fol. *G. Eld a. R. Blower*, 1615. Ent. to Blower 1 au. 1614. L.O.C.E².P.+; F. HN.HD.N.U.+
An abridgment of 11222 w. additions. *See* also 24892, Arber V.lviii.

17623 — A revelation of the Revelation. . . . Whereby the pope is declared to bee Antichrist. 8°. *G. Eld*, 1619. Ent. to Eld a. M. Flesher 9 ja. L.O.C.

17624 **Mason, William.** A handful of essaies. Or imperfect offers. 12°. *A. Mathewes f. J. Grismand*, 1621. L.O.P.; HN.

Masque. The masque of augures. 1621. *See* 14777.

17625 — The maske of flowers. Presented by the gentlemen of Graies-Inne. [Dedic. init. I. G., W. D., T. B.] 4°. *N. O*[*kes*] *f. R. Wilson*, 1614. Ent. 21 ja. L(3).L⁸. O(2).CHATS.; HN.HD.PFOR.Y². Greg 320.
One L copy has earlier state of tp, altered in press.

— The masque of the Inner Temple and Grayes Inne. [1613.] *See* 1664.

— The masque of the League and the Spanyard discouered. 1592. *See* 7.

17625.5 **Mass.** Against the detestable masse, and more then abhominable popishe heresie. *Tr.* out of French. Articles moste certain and true. 1566. 8°. *I. Kingston*, [1566.] D.; F(imp.).

— An apologie of priuate masse. 1562. *See* 14615.

— A briefe recantacion of maystres missa. [1548.] *See* 17137.

17626 — The dysclosyng of the canon of yᵉ popysh masse, with a sermon annexed of Marten Luther. 8°. (*Hans hitprycke*) [*W. Copland?* 1548?] L.O.O⁹.C³.NLW.+; F.

17627 — [Anr. ed.] The dysclosīg of the canon of the popysh masse, wyth a sermon [etc.] 8°. (*Hans hitpricke,*) [*London?* 1547?] C.NLW. Phillipps 7722. 𝕬

17628 — Doctissimi cuiusdam viri tractatus contra missæ sacrificium. 1578. = pt. 2 of 1492.

17629 — [Heading:] A plaine and godlye treatise, concernynge the masse [etc.] 8°. [*J. Wayland?* 1555?] L(2).L². O.BUTE.DUR(Bamb.).; F.HN.
Line 3 of heading: 'sacrament'; no tp; also sometimes pr. as part of English *Primers* (see 16063 sqq.); see Arber I. 394, no. 31; possibly later than 17629.5.

17629.5 — [Anr. ed.] 8°. [*J. Wayland?* 1555?] O³.DUR⁵.
Line 3 of heading: 'sacra-'; possibly earlier than 17629.

17630 — The vpcheringe of the messe. [In verse. By Luke Shepherd] 8°. *J. Daye a. W. Seres*, [1548?] O(2). C.NLW.; HN.

— [The virtue of the mass. c. 1500.] *See* 17037.5.

Mass Priests. The supplication of certaine masse-priests. 1604. *See* 14429.5.

Massan, William, *tr. See* 19741.

17631 **Massie, William.** A sermon preached at Trafford at the mariage of a daughter of Sir E. Trafforde. 8°. *Oxford, J. Barnes, sold* [*in London by T. Cooke,*] 1586. O.C.; F.

Massinger, John, *tr. See* 20491.

17632 **Massinger, Philip.** The bond-man: an antient storie. 4°. *E. Allde f. J. Harison a. E. Blackmore*, 1624. Ent. 12 mr. L(4).L⁶.O.E(lacks A4).PETWORTH.; F.HN.HD. N.PML.+ Greg 408.

17633 — [Anr. ed.] 4°. *J. Raworth f. J. Harrison*, 1638. L.O.C⁶. E.NEK.+; F.HN.HD.N.Y.+

17633a — [A variant, w. imprint:] *J. Raworth f. E. Blackmore*, 1638. L.L⁴.L³⁸.C.C².; F.HN.HD.PFOR.TEX.+

17634 — The duke of Millaine. A tragædie. 4°. *B. A*[*lsop*] *f. E. Blackmore*, 1623. Ent. to Blackmore a. G. Norton 20 ja.; to Blackmore 5 my. L.L⁶.O.C¹⁰.E.+; F.HN. BO.N.PN.+ Greg 386.
First gathering consists of 2 separate halfsheets; the one containing tp and dedic. shows press corrections.

17635 — [Anr. ed.] 4°. *J. Raworth f. E. Blackmore*, 1638. L.O.C. G².M.+; F.HN.HD.N.Y.+

17636 — The emperour of the east. A tragæ-comœdie. 4°. *T. Harper f. J. Waterson*, 1632. Ent. 19 no. 1631. L.O. C.E.M.+; F.HN.HD.N.NY.+ Greg 459.
HD copy has sheet E wrongly perfected.

Massinger, Philip—*cont.*

17637 — The great duke of Florence. A comicall historie. 4⁰. [*M. Flesher*] *f. J. Marriot*, 1636. Ent. 7 de. 1635. L.O.C.E.M².+; F.HN.HD.N.NY.+ Greg 505.

17638 — The maid of honour. 4⁰. *J. B*[*eale*] *f. R. Allot*, 1632. Ent. to [J.] Waterson 16 ja. O(2).O³(lacks K4).C⁴.; F.CH.PML. Greg 470.
  Quire K wrongly perfected; 4th leaf of quire signed K2.

17638.5 — [Anr. issue, w. quire K reset.] L.O.C.E.LIV³.+; F.HN. HD.N.Y².+

17639 — A new way to pay old debts a comoedie. 4⁰. *E. P*[*urslowe*] *f. H. Seyle*, 1633. Ent. 10 no. 1632. L.O.C.G².M.+; F.HN.HD.N.NY.+ Greg 474.

17640 — The picture a tragæcomædie. 4⁰. *J. N*[*orton*] *f. T. Walkley*, 1630. Ent. to J. Waterson 8 au. 1634. O.; F.HN.CH.CHI.TEX. Greg 436.

17640.5 — [A variant, w. tp reset.] The picture. A tragecomedie. L.O.E.LEEDS.M.+; F.HN.HD.N.PML.+
  In some copies of this issue (2F, PML) sheet I is reset.

17641 — The renegado, a tragæcomedie. 4⁰. *A. M*[*athewes*] *f. J. Waterson*, 1630. Ent. 22 mr. L.O.C.E.M⁴.+; F.HN. HD.N.PML.+ Greg 430.

17642 — The Roman actor. A tragædie. 4⁰. *B. A*[*lsop*] *a. T. F*[*awcet*] *f. R. Allot*, 1629. Ass'd by Allot's widow to Legat a. A. Crooke 1 jy. 1637. L.O.C⁴.DUR(Bamb.). E.+; F.HN.HD.N.PML.+ Greg 424.
  H3ᵛ and H4ʳ occur in 2 states, reversed and in proper order.

17643 — The unnaturall combat. A tragedie. 4⁰. *E. G*[*riffin*] *f. J. Waterson*, 1639. Ent. 14 fb. L.O.C.E.M.+; F.HN.HD. N.PML.+ Greg 559.

17644 **Massinger, Philip,** and **Dekker, Thomas.** The virgin martir, a tragedie. 4⁰. *B. A*[*lsop*] *f. T. Jones*, 1622. Ent. 7 de. 1621. L(3).L⁶(2).; HN. Greg 380.
  Prob. the later state.

17644a — [A variant, w. 'Alsop' in full in imprint.] O(2).; HN.
  Prob. the earlier state.

17645 — [Anr. ed.] 4⁰. *B. A*[*lsop*] *a. T. F*[*awcet*] *f. T. Jones*, 1631. L.O.C¹⁰.E.LIV³.+; F.HN.HD.PML.TEX.+

17646 **Massinger, Philip,** and **Field, Nathan.** The fatall dowry: a tragedy. [Init. P. M. and N. F.] 4⁰. *J. Norton f. F. Constable*, 1632. Ent. 30 mr. L.O.C.G². LEEDS.+; F.HN.HD.N.PML.+ Greg 464.

17647 **Masson, Jean.** De libero arbitrio theses theologicæ. 1597. Now = 21555.2.

Massonius, Robert, *ed. See* 24664, 24667, 24668.

17648 **Masterson, Thomas.** T. Masterson his first booke of arithmeticke. (His second booke.) 4⁰. *R. Field*, 1592. L.L³⁰(imp.).O.C(2).D.; F(2).HN.CU.HD(2).

17648.3 — T. Masterson his addition to his first booke. 4⁰. *R. Field*, 1594. L.L³⁰.O.C(2).D.; F(2).HN.CU.HD(2).

17648.7 — T. Masterson his third booke. 4⁰. *R. Field*, 1595. L.O.C.D.P.+; F(2).HN.CU.HD(2).

17649 — [Anr. ed. of first book, w. new second and third books added.] Mastersons arithmetick newly set forth by H. Waynman. 8⁰. *G. Miller*, 1634. L.O³(2).C.NOR².; HN.

17650 **Mastrand.** A breefe coniecturall discourse. 1589. Now = 17488.7.

17651 **Matelief, Cornelius.** An historicall and true discourse, of a voyage made by C. Matelife. *Tr.* out of Dutch. 4⁰. [*G. Eld*] *f. W. Barret*, 1608. Ent. 21 my. L(2). O⁹.O¹³. Rotterdam, Prins Hendrik Maritime Museum.; Penrose 159.

Mater. Mater compellat filium sibi superstitem. [1606?] *See* 14850.

Mathew, Peter. *See* 22246.

Mathew, William. Almanacks. 1602, etc. *See* 483 sqq.

Matter. Here begynneth a ryght frutefull mater: [etc.] 1523. *See* 11005.

Matters. Certaine matters composed together. [1594?] *See* 18016.

17652 **Matthæus,** *Westmonasteriensis.* Elegans, illustris, et facilis rerum, præsertim britannicarum, ad annum domini 1307. narratio. [*Ed.* Abp. M. Parker.] fol. [*R. Jugge*,] 1567 (20 oc.). L.O⁷.C.D⁵.M.+; F.HN.HD.N.NY.+

Matthaeus, *Westmonasteriensis—cont.*

17653 — [Anr. ed.] Matthæus Westmonasteriensis . . . de rebus britannicis [etc.] fol. *ex off. T. Marshij*, 1570 (2 jn.) Ent. to T. Orwin on Marsh's death 23 jn. 1591. O⁹. C.C⁹.D⁵.NEK.+

17653a — [Anr. issue, w. title:] Flores historiarum [etc.] *ex off. T. Marshij*, 1570 (2 jn.) L.O.C².D.E.+; F.CU.HD.PML. Y.+ A
  A3ʳ catchword: 'Tem-'; K3 signed 'I iij.'; sig. O2 under 'vt vnns [*sic*]'; in index, **3ʳ catchword: 'Ventus'. Quires A–X and index sometimes found mixed w. 17653a.3.

17653a.3 — [Anr. issue, w. quires A–X and part of index-errata reset.] L.O³¹.C³.E.M.+; F.HN.IND.LC.N(imp.).
  A3ʳ catchword: 'Temporibus'; K3 signed 'R.iij.'; sig. O2 under 'q; lõ'; in index, **3ʳ catchword: 'Tractatus'. Quires A–X and index sometimes found mixed w. 17653a.

17653a.7 — [Anr. issue, w. tp dated:] 1573. M²(quires A–X of 17653a).USHAW(quires A–X mixed sheets of 17653a and 17653a.3).

17654 **Matthew, Roger.** The flight of time. [A sermon.] 4⁰. *G. Miller f. G. Edwards*, 1634. Ent. 5 ap. L¹³.O.C.DUR⁵. EX.+; F.HD. Sydney U.

17654a — [A variant, w. imprint:] *G. Miller f. E. Langham at Banbery.* L.C.M⁴.; HN.

17654a.5 — Peters net let downe. [A sermon.] 4⁰. *G. Miller f. G. Edwards*, 1634. Ent. 5 ap. L.O¹⁹.; F(2).HD.ILL.U.

17655 — [A variant, w. imprint:] *G. Miller, sold by E. Langham at Banbury.* L.O(2, 1 imp.).D.; HN.MIN.

17656 **Matthew, Simon.** A sermon made in the cathedrall churche of saynt Paule. 8⁰. (*in the house of T. Berthelet*, 1535 (30 jy.)) L.

Matthew, Thomas, *tr. See* 2066, 2077, 2083 sqq., 2841, 2857.

17657 **Matthew, Tobias,** *Abp.* Piissimi et eminentissimi viri, D. Tobiæ Matthæi archiepiscopi olim Eboracensis concio apologetica adversus Campianum [4536.5]. 12⁰. Oxoniæ, L. Lichfield, imp. E. Forrest, 1638. L⁴. O.C².A.D².+; F.
  — York. Visitation articles. *See* 10377.5 sqq.

17658 **Matthew,** *Sir Tobie.* Of the love of our only lord Jesus Christ. [Anon.] 8⁰. [*St. Omer, English College Press*,] 1622. L²⁶.DE.ST.W.WOR.+; HN.N.
  A&R 538.
  — The widdowes mite. 1619. *See* 11490.
  — *tr. See* 741, 742.7, 743, 910, 983, 1153, 3134, 20483, 21145, 21148, 21150.5.
  — *See also* 25774.

17658.5 **Matthiae, Johannes.** Libellus puerilis, in quo continentur, quinque primaria capita doctrinae christianae, cum precationibus aliquot sacris, quinque linguis comprehensa, Latina, Suetica, Gallica, Germanica, Anglica. obl. 8⁰ in 4's. Holmiæ, Ignatus Meurerus, 1626. L. Stockholm RL.

17659 **Matthias,** *Emperor of Germany.* Articles of the peace agreed upon, between the Archduke Mathias, and the Lord Botzkay. 4⁰. [*Eliot's Court Press?*] *f. N. Butter*, 1607. O.O².PETWORTH.; F.HN.Y.

17660 — Newes from Francfort, concerning the election of the Emperor Matthias. *Tr.* out of Dutch. 4⁰. [*G. Eld*] *f. H. Holland*, 1612. Ent. 27 jy. L.O(3).D².; HN.HD.

17661 **Matthieu, Pierre.** The heroyk life and deplorable death of Henry the fourth. *Tr.* E. Grimeston. (A panegyre.—The tropheis. *Tr.* J. Syl[vester].) 4⁰. *G. Eld*, 1612. Ent. to J. Bill a. A. Islip 10 oc. 1611. L.O.C. D.M.+; F.HN.HD.N.NY.+

17662 — The history of Lewis the eleventh. *Tr.* E. Grimeston. (Maximes, . . . of P. de Commines.) fol. *G. Eld* [*a. N. Okes*], 1614. Ent. 23 se. 1611. L.O.C.D.NEK.+; F. HN.HD.N.Y.+
  Okes pr. quires Aaa–Ffff.

17663 — The historie of S. Elizabeth daughter of the king of Hungarie. *Tr.* Sʳ. T. H[awkins]. 8⁰. Bruxelles, widdow of H. Antony called Velpius, 1633. L.
  A&R 540.

17664 — The powerfull favorite, or, the life of Ælius Sejanus. [*Tr.* as a satire on the Duke of Buckingham. Init. P. M.] 4⁰. Paris [London?] 1628. L.L².O.C.LIV³.+; F. HN.HD.N.Y.+
  154 pp.

Matthieu, Pierre—*cont.*

17665 — [Anr. trans.] The powerfull favorite, or the life of Ælius Sejanus. [Init. P. M.] 4°. *Paris* [*London?*] 1628. L.O.C.LINC.PETYT.+ ; F.HN.HD.N.U.+
  62 pp.

  — Remarkeable considerations. *See* 17668.

17666 — Unhappy prosperitie expressed in the histories of Ælius Seianus and Philippa. *Tr.* S[r]. T. Hawkins. 4°. *J. Haviland f. G. Emondson,* 1632. Ent. 9 fb. L.O.C. DUL.E.+ ; F.HN.HD.N.Y.+
  Most copies lack letterpress tp; present in 1F copy.

17667 — Second edition. *Tr.* S[r]. T. H. 12°. *T. Harper, sold by N. Vavasour,* 1639. Ass'd to Harper 22 se. 1638. L.O.C.D.STU.+ ; F.HN.HD.N.NY.+
  Includes reprints of both pts. of 17668.

17668 — Remarkeable considerations upon the life of M. Villeroy. *Tr.* Sir T. H[awkins]. 2 pts. 4°. *E. G[riffin] f. G. Emerson,* 1638. Ent. 26 jy. 1637. O(imp.).C.M. Lord Kenyon.; F.HN.CAL(imp.).N(imp.).Y.+
  Pt. 2 is a reissue, w. tp cancelled, of 17293.
  — *See* also 11275, 22244, 22246, 23582.

Maulette, Genevuefue. *See* 19793.

17669 **Maunsell, Andrew.** The first part of the catalogue of English printed bookes: which concerneth diuinitie. (The seconde parte . . . which concerneth the sciences.) 2 pts. fol. *J. Windet* (*J. Roberts*) *f. A. Maunsell,* 1595. Ent. to Windet 8 my. L.O.C.E.M.+ ; F.HN.HD.N.ROS.+
  The C, COL, HN, HD, and other copies have useful annotations.

Maunsell, John, *ed. See* 26077.

Maunsell, Richard. *See* 23235.

17670 **Maupas, Charles.** A French grammar and syntaxe. *Tr.* w. additions by W. A(ufeild.) 8°. *B. A[lsop] a. T. F[awcet] f. R. Mynne,* 1634. Ent. 8 my. L.O.C². G⁴.M.+ ; F(imp.).HN.HD.ILL.NY⁵.+

17670.5 **Maurice,** *Prince of Orange.* An ambassage of two Indian kings sent unto Prince Maurice. [*Tr.* from the Dutch *Missive van twee. . . .*] 4°. *s'Graven-Haghe* [i.e. *London?*] 1621. O.; F.

  — The articles of the giuing ouer of the large, cittie of Groning. [1594.] *See* 12392.5.

17671 — The battaile fought betweene Count Maurice of Nassaw, and Albertus Arch-duke of Austria, the xxij. of June 1600. 4°. *P. S[hort,]* 1600. L.CAR.DALK.; HD.

17671a — [A variant, w. imprint:] *f. A. Wise.* L.

  — A briefe discourse of the cruell dealings of the Spanyards. 1599. *See* 23008.

  — A discourse of the ouerthrowe giuen by Morris of Nassawe. 1597. *See* 22993.

17672 — The faithfull and wise preventer: or, considerations to be thought upon by Prince Maurice. 4°. *Graven-hage, Aert Meuris* [i.e. *London, E. Allde?*] 1621. O.C.SAL.

17673 — The honorable victorie obteined by Graue Maurice against the cittie of Rhyne-berg, the 20. of August. 1597. *Tr.* A. Hendrickson. 4°. *E. Allde f. T. Stirrop,* [1597.] Ent. 22 au. 1597. L.

17674 — The 13. of August. The post of the prince. 1622. *See* Newsbooks 70.

17674a — February 19. Numb. 19. A relation of the treason. 1623. *See* Newsbooks 98.

17675 — A short report of the honourable journey into Brabant, by Graue Mauris. *Tr.* out of Dutch. 4°. *T. C[reede] f. T. Pavier,* 1602. Ent. to Creede 29 jy. L.E⁴.

17676 — The triumphs of Nassau. [By J. J. Orlers a. H. de Haestens.] *Tr.* W. Shute. fol. *A. Islip,* 1613. Ent. 23 ap. 1612. L.O.C.D.M.+ ; F.HN.HD.N.NY⁵.+

17677 — [Anr. issue, w. cancel tp:] *A. Islip, sold by R. Moore,* 1620. L.EX.G².; HD. McMaster U.

17678 — A true discourse of the ouerthrowe giuen to the common enemy at Turnhaut, the 14. of January by count Moris of Nassaw. Sent from a gentleman to a friend in England. 4°. *P. Short, sold* [by *J. Flasket a. P. Linley,*] 1597. Ent to Linley 29 ja. L.O.HAGUE.
  For a different account *see* 22993.

17679 — A true relation of the famous & renowmed [*sic*] victorie latelie atchieued by the Counte Maurice neere to Newport in Flaunders against the arch-duke Albertus. *Tr.* out of Duch. 4°. *R. Blower f. C. B[urby,* 1600.] Ent. to Burby 30 jn. 1600. L.; ILL.

Maurice, *Prince of Orange*—*cont.*

17680 — A true report of all the proceedinges of Grave Mauris before the towne of Bercke. *Tr.* out of Dutch. 4°. [*R. Read?*] *f. W. Jones,* 1601. Ent. 3 au. L.C.DALK. HAGUE.
  — *See* also Newsbooks for items not specifically listed above.

Mausoleum. Mausoleum or, epitaphs, on Prince Henrie. 1613. *See* 13160.

17681 **Mavericke, Radford.** The grieving of Gods spirit. Contayning the summe of a sermon. 4°. *W. Stansby,* 1620. L².O.; F.HD.

17682 — The practice of repentance. Or a sermon. 4°. *W. Stansby,* 1617. L.O(lacks tp).; F.

17683 — Saint Peters chaine: consisting of eight golden linckes. [A sermon.] 8°. *J. Windet,* 1596. Ent. 9 jn. L.O.; F(imp.).

17683a — Saint Peters watch word. 8°. *J. W[indet,]* 1603. Ent. 12 my. LINC.; HD.

17683a.5 — Three treatises religiously handled. . . . The mourning weede. The mornings joy. The kings rejoycing. 4°. *J. Windet,* 1603. Ent. 12 my. L(tp only, Harl.5993/105).; F.

17684 **Maxey, Anthony.** The sermon preached before the king, at White-Hall, the eight of Januarie. 1604 [o.s.] 4°. *H. Lownes f. C. Knight,* 1605. Ent. 8 fb. L¹³.O.C⁸. ETON.; HD.

17684.5 — [A variant, w. title:] The copie of the sermon, preached [etc.] L².

17685 — [Anr. ed.] The goulden chain of mans salvation, . . . set downe in two severall sermons. (The second sermon.) 8°. *T. Este f. C. Knight,* 1606. L.O.C².C⁵.
  (2nd sermon formerly also 17689)

17685.5 — [Anr. ed.] 8°. *G. Eld f. C. Knight,* 1606. COL.NLW.

17686 — [Anr. ed.] Third edicion [*sic*]. Preached in three severall sermons. 8°. *T. E[ast] f. C. Knight,* 1607. L.O.C.CHATS.
  Contains a reprint of 17690.

17687 — [Anr. ed.] Together with the Agony of Christ. Fourth edition. 2 pts. 8°. *F. K[ingston] f. C. Knight,* 1610. L.O.C⁴.NLW.P.+ ; F.HN.ILL.Y. ℥
  The 2nd pt. was apparently issued separately as 17691, but is linked on title. For later eds. of 17687 *see* 17692 sqq.

17688 — An other sermon preached before the king at Greenewich 26. of March 1605. 4°. *G. a. L. Snowdon f. C. Knight,* 1605. Ent. 6 my. O.PETYT.; F.HD.

17689 — [Anr. ed.] 1606. = pt. of 17685.

17690 — The churches sleepe, expressed in a sermon preached at the court. 8°. *T. Este f. C. Knight,* 1606. Ent. 5 ap. L.O.C².LINC.NLW.+
  Usually found bd. w. 17685; reprinted in 17686.

17691 — The copie of a sermon preached at Whitehall. 2 of March, 1610. 8°. *F. K[ingston] f. C. Knight,* 1610. Ent. 18 jn. O.C(imp.).P.YK.; F.ILL.
  Also issued as pt. 2 of 17687.

17692 — [Anr. ed. of 17687.] Five sermons preached before the king. The fift edition. (The copie of a sermon.) 2 pts. 4°. [*T. Snodham*] *f. C. Knight,* 1614. Fifth sermon ent. 2 no. 1613. L.O.O⁶.C.C².+ ; F.HN. Sydney U.

17693 — [Anr. ed.] Certaine sermons preached before the kings maiestie. The sixt edition. (A sermon preached at Bagshot, September 1, 1616.) 2 pts. 8°. *H. L[ownes] f. C. Knight,* 1619. 6th a. 7th sermons ent. 8 oc. 1616; 9th sermon ent. 2 de. 1618. L.O.; U(lacks tp). Y.
  Contains 9 sermons.

17694 — [Anr. ed.] Seventh edition. 2 pts. 8°. *T. Harper f. T. Knight,* 1634. Ass'd 12 oc. 1629. L.C.C³.BIRM².NOR². + ; F(lacks gen. tp).HN.PN².U.

17694.5 — [Anr. issue, w. imprint on gen. tp:] *f. T. Alchorn,* 1636. Ass'd 8 mr. E².; HD(imp.).

17695 **Maxey, Edward.** A new instuction [*sic*] of plowing and setting of corne. 4°. *F. Kyngston,* 1601. Ent. 7 au. L.

17696 **Maximilian II,** *Emperor of Germany.* A brief rehersal & discription, of the coronatiō of the hye and myghtī prince Maximilian kyng of Romans, at Francford yn 1562. 8°. *Newli prented yn Gaunte,* [*G. Manilius,*] 1565 (27 au.) L.L².
  A&R 144.
  — Libellus supplex imperatoriæ maiestati. 1571. *See* 18440.

17697 **Maximinus, James.** Whereas the professor hereof, Jacobus Maximinus, . . . Foure most strange and rare artificiall stones. [A quack medicine handbill. 24 Oct. 1622.] s.sh.fol. [*London*, 1622.] o.

17697.3 **Maximos,** *Bp. of Cythera.* [Michael Margounios.] Μαξίμου τοῦ Μαργουνίου . . . Διάλογος. 4°. [*W. Jones*, 1625–26.] L. L².L¹⁵.O.WIN². + ; HD.
Issued w. 11728.4 and 12343.5, for which it has errata. The errata may have been pr. by the Eliot's Court Press. *See also The Library*, XXII(1967), pp.13–43 and *Harvard Library Bulletin*, XV(1967), pp. 140–68.

17697.7 **Maxwell, James.** Admirable and notable prophesies, uttered in former times by 24. famous Romain-catholickes, concerning the church of Rome's defection. [*Tr.* from Latin.] 4°. E: *A*[*llde*] *f. W. a. T. Harper*, 1614. Ent. to C. Knight a. T. Harper 2 jy. 1614. HD(tp only).

17698 — [Anr. ed.] 4°. *E. Allde f. C. Knight*, 1615. L.O.C.D.E.+ ; F.HN.CHI.HD(tp mutil.).U.+

17699 — Carolanna, that is to say, a poeme in honour of our king. By J. Anne-son [i.e. J. Maxwell.] 4°. E. *All-de*, [1619.] L.O.DUL.E.E².+ ; F.HN.CH.HD.

17699.5 — An English-royall pedigree: common to the two most noble princes lately married. Friderick, . . . and Elizabeth. s.sh.fol. [*E. Allde*] *f. H. Gosson*, [1613.] L⁵(Lemon 133).

17700 — The golden art, or the right way of enriching. Comprised in ten rules. 4°. [*F. Kingston*] *f. W. Leake*, 1611. L.; F(imp.).

17700.5 — The imperiall and princely pedigree of . . . Friderick . . . and Elizabeth. s.sh.fol. [*E. Allde f. H. Gosson?* 1613.] L⁵(Lemon 134).

17701 — The laudable life, and deplorable death, of prince Henry. Together, with some other poemes. 4°. *E. Allde f. T. Pavier*, 1612. Ent. 28 no. L.O.A.E.LONGLEAT.+ ; F.HN.HD.N.Y.+

17702 —The mirrour of religious men, and of godly matrones. 8°. [*E. Allde*] *f. E. White*, 1611. Ent. 1 ap. o.

17703 — A monument of remembrance, erected in Albion, in honor of the departure from Britannie, and honorable receiving in Germany, of Fredericke, & Elizabeth. [In verse.] 4°. *N. Okes f. H. Bell*, 1613. Ent. 30 mr. L.L¹³.O(2).E(2, 1 imp.).; F.HN.HD.N.U.+

17704 — A new eight-fold probation of the church of Englands divine constitution. (A demonstrative defence or tenfold probation.) 4°. *J. Legatt*, 1617. ?Ent. 22 oc. L.O.C.D.E.+ ; F.U.

17705 — Queene Elizabeths looking-glasse of grace and glory. 8°. (*E. Alde f. E. White*, 1612.) L.O.O⁶.; HN.

17706 — The speedy passage to heaven. [Anon. Not by Maxwell.] 1612. Now = 19458.5.
— *tr. See* 7359, 13222, 24209.
— *See also* 17141.

17707 **May.** The fetching home of May: or, a pretty new ditty. *Ballad.* 2 pts. s.sh.fol. *f. J. Wright, jun.*, [1635?] ?Ent. to T. Lambert 18 jn. 1636 for 1635–6. L.

May, Edward, *tr. See* 4426.8.

May, Edward, *Chaplain. See* Maie.

17708 **May, Edward,** *Gent.* Epigrams divine and morall. 8°. *J. B*[*eale*] *f. J. Grove*, 1633. Ent. 17 ja. L.L⁴.O.; HN.

17709 **May, Edward,** *Physician.* A most certaine and true relation of a strange serpent found in the heart of John Pennant. 4°. *G. Miller*, 1639. Ent. 14 oc. L.O.C.E⁵. M.+ ; F.HN.HD.NLM.NY⁴.+

17710 **May, John.** A declaration of the estate of clothing now used within this realme of England. 4°. *A. Islip*, 1613. Ent. 30 no. 1612. L.L³⁰.O.O².C¹⁰.+ ; CU.HD.

17711 **May, Thomas.** A continuation of Lucan's historicall poem till the death of Julius Cæsar. 8°. [*J. Haviland*] *f. J. Boler*, 1630. Ent. 3 mr. L.O.C.LINC.PETYT.+ ; F.HN.HD.WIS.Y.+

17712 — The 2ᵈ edition. 8°. [*T. Cotes*] *f. J. Boler*, 1633. L.O.C.E. M⁴.+ ; F.HN.HD.N.Y.+
The 1st quire may be by a different printer.

17713 — The heire an excellent comedie. 4°. B. *A*[*lsop*] *f. T. Jones*, 1622. O.O³(imp.).O⁸.PETWORTH.; F.HN.BO.HD. N. Greg 384.

17714 — [Anr. ed.] 4°. *A. Mathewes f. T. Jones*, 1633. Ass'd by Jones to Mathewes 24 oc. L.O(both tpp).C(both tpp). E.M.+ ; F.HN.CHI.HD.PML.+

May, Thomas—*cont.*

17714a — [Anr. issue, w. cancel tp pr. as I4, w. 'second impression' added.] O(2).C(tp only).M.; F.HN.HD.ILL.PEN.+

17715 — The reigne of King Henry the second. [In verse.] 8°. *A. M*[*athewes a. J. Beale*] *f. B. Fisher*, 1633. Ent. 30 no. 1632. L.O.C.DUL.E.+ ; F.HN.HD(imp.).N.PFOR.+

17716 — The tragedy of Antigone. 8°. *T. Harper f. B. Fisher*, 1631. L(2).L⁶.O.C³.E.; F.HN.CU.HD.Y.+ Greg 450.

17717 — The tragedie of Cleopatra. 12°. *T. Harper f. T. Walkly*, 1639. Ent. 26 oc. 1638. L.L⁶.O.E.LEEDS.+ ; F.HN.CHI. HD.Y.+ Greg 553.
Intended to be issued w. 17718, for they were entered together, have one dedic. and are commonly bd. together; reissued in 1654 with cancel tp and added nonce tp as part of 'Two tragedies', Wing M 1416.

17718 — The tragedy of Julia Agrippina. By T. M., Esq. 12°. *R. Hodgkinsonne f. T. Walkly*, 1639. Ent. 26 oc. 1638. L.L⁶.O.O⁶.C(frag.).+ ; HN.HD.LC.TEX.Y.+ Greg 554.
Intended to be issued w. 17717; reissued in 1654 w. cancel tp as part of 'Two tragedies', Wing M 1416.

17718a — [A variant, omitting 'Esq.' from tp.] E.; HN.PN.

17719 — The victorious reigne of King Edward the third. [In verse.] 8°. [*J. Beale?*] *f. T. Walkley a. B. Fisher*, 1635. Ent. 15 ja. L.O.C.D.WI.+ ; F.HN.HD.N.NY.+
— *tr. See* 1392, 1393, 1399, 16886, 16887, 17494, 24823.

17720 **Maydeston, Clement.** [Directorium sacerdotum. Begin.:] KL Prima dies mensis. [etc. Fol. 139ʳ:] Explicit directoriũ sacerdotũ et incipit defensoriũ eiusd'. [Based on Sarum Ordinal.] fol. (*p w. Caxton ap. westmonasteriũ prope London,*) [1487.] L(lacks leaf 1).LINC(2 leaves, lost).; HD(1 leaf). Duff 290.

17721 — [Anr. ed.] 4° in 8's. (*Antwerpie, p G. Leeu*, 1488.) L(2, 1 lacks 6 leaves).O.C(imp.).C⁵. Duff 291.

17722 — [Anr. ed.] fol. (*per W. Caxton ap. westmonasteriũ prope London,*) [1489.] L(1 leaf, Harl.5919/2). O.O³(frag.). O¹¹(frag.). Duff 292.

17723 — [Anr. ed. Begin.:] KL Ianuarius [etc.] 4° in 8's. (*in westmonasterio, per w. de worde*, 1495.) L.C(1 imp., plus 2 leaves). Duff 293.

17724 — [Anr. ed. Begin.:] Animaduertendũ . . . magister clerke correctõis. 4° in 8's. *R. pynson ad imprimendũ dedit*, 1497. L.C⁷(1 leaf). Duff 294.

17725 — [Anr. ed. Begin.:] Animaduertendum . . . magister Clerke correctõis. 4° in 8's. *R. pynson ad imprimendũ dedit*, 1498. O¹³.M(lacks last leaf). Duff 295.

17726 — [Anr. ed. Begin.:] KL Ianuarius [etc.] 4° in 8's. [*Westminster, W. de Worde*, 1499.] C(lacks last leaf). Duff 296.

17727 — [Anr. ed. Begin.:] Animaduertendum . . . magister clerke [etc.] 4° in 8's. *R. pynsõ ad imprimendum dedit*, 1501. L(lacks last 4 leaves).CASHEL(imp.).Lord Kenyon.

17728 — [Anr. ed.] Ordinale sarum. 4° in 6's. (*per me R. pynson*, 1503 (31 au.)) O.C(leaves i3 and i6).C⁶.
(Formerly also 16230)

17728.3 — [Anr. ed.] 4° ⁸·⁴. (*W. de worde*, 1504 (23 fb.)) O.O⁵.
(Formerly 16231)

17728.5 — [Anr. ed.] 4° in 6's. (*R. pynson*, 1508 (10 kal. de.)) O(2, 1 lacks tp).
(Formerly 16232) O¹⁴ has a frag. of leaves P3, 4 in a different setting; P3ʳ column 1, line 1 begins: 'de resurre.' (O) or 'de resur.' (O¹⁴).

17728.7 **Mayenne, Henri de Lorraine.** The Duke de Mayennes ghost speaking to the princes, of France. *Tr.* [Anon.] 4°. *Hage, H. Jacobson* [*London? B. Alsop?*] 1622. F.

17729 **Mayer, John.** An antidote against popery. 4°. *M. F*[*lesher*] *f. J. Grismand*, 1625. Ent. 18 oc. 1624. L.O.C.D.E².+ ; F. NYS.PN²(imp.).U.Y.+

17730 — A commentarie upon the new testament. The first (second) volumne. 2 pts. fol. *T. Cotes f. J. Bellamie* (*J. Haviland f. J. Grismond,*) 1631. Pt. 2 ent. 16 jn. L(lacks gen. tp).O.C.E.M.+ ; F.HN.NY¹¹.U(pt. 1 only).Y. For 'The third volumne' *see* 17731.7; pt. 1 = anr. ed. of 17744.

17730.5 — [Anr. issue of pt. 2, w. cancel tp:] A commentarie upon all the epistles of Saint Paul. fol. *J. Haviland f. J. Grismond*, 1631. L.

17731 — Ecclesiastica interpretatio: or the expositions upon the seven epistles called Catholike, and the Revelation. 4° in 8's. *J. Haviland f. J. Grismand*, 1627. Ent. mr. L.O.C.D.E.+ ; F.HN.HD.U.Y.+

Mayer, John—*cont.*

17731.3 — [Anr. issue, w. cancel tp:] A commentarie upon the seven smaller epistles, and the booke of the revelation. 4° in 8's. *J. Haviland f. J. Grismond,* 1631. E².; HD.

17731.7 — [Anr. issue, w. cancel tp:] A commentarie upon the new testament. The third volumne. 4° in 8's. *J. Haviland f. J. Grismond,* 1631. HN.U.
Intended as pt. 3 of 17730.

17732 — The English catechisme. Or a commentarie on the short catechisme. 4° in 8's. [*Eliot's Court Press*] *f. J. Marriot,* 1621. Ent. 8 jy. 1620. L.O.O¹³.BTL.; F.HN.HD.NY¹¹.
Engr. tp reads 'Marriott'.

17733 — Second edition. 4° in 8's. *A. Mathewes f. J. Marriot,* 1622. C³.SCL.YK.; F.ILL.SMU.U. Notre Dame U.+

17734 — Third edition. 4° in 8's. *A. Mathewes f. J. Marriot, sold by J. Grismand,* 1623. L.O.C.NLW(imp.).; F.HN.HD.ILL.U.+

17735 — Fourth edition. 4° in 8's. *A. Mathewes f. J. Grismand,* 1630. Ass'd 22 jn. 1626. L.C.E².M.SAL.+; F.HN.CONN.WASH².Y.+

17736 — = 17740.

17737 — Fifth edition, corrected. 4° in 8's. *M. Flesher f. J. Marriot,* 1634. Ass'd 6 de. 1631. O.

17738 — [A variant, w. date:] 1635. L.O.C².LICH.NLW.+; F.HN.HD.N.Y(imp.).+

17739 — Mayers catechisme abridged. Or, the A.B.C. inlarged. The second edition made more compleat. 8°. *A. M[athewes] f. J. M[arriot], sold by J. Grismand,* 1623. F.HD(imp.).
Collates A–E⁸.

17739.5 — [Anr. ed.] 8°. *A. M[athewes] f. J. M[arriot], sold by J. Grismand,* 1623. C.
Collates A–D⁸; sheet A is same setting as 17739.

17740 — The fift edition. 8°. [*M. Flesher*] *f. J. Marriot,* 1632. L(2).C¹⁰.DUR(Bamb.).
(Formerly also 17736)

17740.5 — The seventh edition. 8°. *f. J. Marriot,* 1639. O(2).; Y.

17741 — A fourefold resolution, digested into two bookes; very necessary to salvation. 12°. [*T. Dawson*] *f. E. Burby,* 1609. Ent. to Dawson 2 oc. O.; F.HN(imp.).PN².

17742 — A patterne for women: setting forth the life of Mrs. Lucy Thornton. [A sermon.] 12°. *E. Griffin f. J. Marriot,* 1619. Ent. 20 au. L.O.

17743 — Praxis theologica: or, the epistle of the apostle Sᵗ James resolved. 4° in 8's. *J. B[eale] f. R. Bostocke,* 1629. Ent. 13 no. 1628. L.O.C.D.G².+; F.HN.HD.ILL.U.+

17744 — A treasury of ecclesiasticall expositions. [On the Gospels and Acts.] 4° in 8's. *J. D[awson] f. J. Bellamie,* 1622. Ent. 27 au. L.O.C.E(tp def.).NOR².+; F.HN.HD.ILL.U.+
Reprinted as pt. 1 of 17730.

17745 **Mayeres, Randulph.** Mayeres his travels: containing a true recapitulation of . . . the authors peregrination. [In verse.] 8°. *T. H[arper] f. R. Harper,* [1638.] L(impr. cropt).

17746 **Mayerne, Patrick.** The patterne of all pious prayer. Also, a short panigyre on Mary-Land in America. [In verse.] 8°. *Doway,* 1636. O(lacks panegyric).
A&R 598. Author's name in anagram.

17747 **Mayerne Turquet, Louis de.** The generall historie of Spaine. Tr. E. Grimeston. fol. *A. Islip a. G. Eld,* 1612. Ent. to Islip 19 no. 1608. L.O.C.CASHEL.E².+; F.HN.HD.N.NY.+

Mayerne Turquet, Théodore de, *ed. See* 17993.

17748 **Mayfield.** A most horrible & detestable murther committed at Mayfield in Sussex. 4°. *J. Danter, sold by W. Barley,* 1595. O.

Mayhew, Edward. *See* Maihew, E.

17748.5 **Mayle, John.** An act for the selling of the lands, . . . of J. Mayle of London, scrivener, for payment of his debts. [Brief of a bill in Parliament.] s.sh.fol. [*London,* 1621.] L⁸(GL 5493).
Text ends: 'That it may be enacted, . . .' The first reading was 16 May 1621; *see JHC* I.621.

Mayler, John. A joyfull new tidynges of the goodly victory. (*Tr.* J. Mayler.) *See* 977.5.

17749 **Maynard, John.** The XII. wonders of the world. Set and composed for the violl de gambo, [etc.] fol. *T. Snodham f. J. Browne,* 1611. L.O.

Mayne, Duke de. Remonstrances. 1593. *See* 5012.

17750 **Mayne, Jasper.** The citye match. A comoedye. [Anon.] fol. *Oxford, L. Lichfield,* 1639. L.O.C.DUL.LEEDS.+; F.HN.HD.N.Y.+ Greg 568.

17751 **Maynwaring, Roger.** Religion and alegiance: in two sermons. 4°. *J. H[aviland] f. R. Badger,* 1627. Ent. 7 no. O.C².DUL.DUR⁵.G².+; CAL.U.
1st B4ᵛ catchword: 'preames'. For the proclamation calling in these sermons *see* 8896.

17751.5 — [Anr. ed.] 4°. *J. H[aviland] f. R. Badger,* 1627. L.O³.C.DUR⁵.STU.+; F.HN.HD.N.Y.+
1st B4ᵛ catchword: 'supreames;'. In the DUR⁵ copies quires 1st D–F and 2nd F–H are apparently reimposed from 17751.

17752 **Mayo, John.** The popes parliament, . . . Whereunto is annexed an Anatomie of pope Ioane. 4°. *R. Field,* 1591. L.L²D.; F.AAS.Y.

17753 — [A ghost.]

17754 — The anatomie of pope Joane. [Init. J. M.] 8°. *R. Field,* 1624. L.O.; HD.

17755 — A sermon of fasting, and of Lent preached at Shaftesbury. 8°. *W. Hall f. J. Helme,* 1609. Ent. 23 no. 1608. L.G².PLUME.; F.HD.

17756 — The universall principle; the common justice of the world, delivered in a sermon. 4°. [*F. Kingston*] *f. J. Smithwike,* 1630. Ent. 15 fb. L.LINC.

Mayr, George, *ed. See* 1843.

17757 **Mean.** The golden meane. Lately written, to a great lord. 12°. [*H. Lownes*] *f. J. Chorlton,* 1613. Ent. 14 jn. L.O(imp.).
Attrib. to J. Ford and to A. Stafford.

17758 — [Anr. ed.] The golden meane. Enlarged by the first authour. Second edition. 12°. [*H. Lownes*] *f. J. Chorlton,* 1614. L.O.LINC.OS.; HN.CAL.

17759 — Third edition. 12°. *J. H[aviland] f. J. Benson,* 1638. L.L³⁰(lacks letterpress tp)*.o(lacks letterpress tp)*. o⁶.; F(2, 1 imp.; both lack letterpress tp)*. Syracuse U.
See Court-Book C, pp. 285, 487.

17759.5 — [A variant, w. 'Third edition' omitted from tp.] L.L². C(2).; PEN.

17760 — The meane in spending. 1598. = pt. of 24477.

17760.5 — [Headline B1ʳ:] A meane to dye wel. 8°. (*W. Myddleton,*) [c. 1545.] C²(frag.).
See also 786.

17761 **Meara, Dermitius de.** Ormonius; sive, illustrissimi herois ac domini, Thomæ Butleri, commemoratio. [In verse.] 8°. *T. Snodhamus,* 1615. Ent. 7 no. 1614. L.O.C.BTU.D.+; F.

17762 — Pathologia hæreditaria generalis, sive de morbis hæreditarijs tractatus spagyrico-dogmaticus. 12°. *Dubliniae,* [*F. Kingston a. T. Downes*] *typis deputatorum J. Franctoni,* 1619. L.O.C.D.E².+

17763 **Meash, William.** Leanders love to loyall Hero. *Ballad.* 2 pts. s.sh.fol. [*W. White*] *f. J. W[hite,* 1614.] Ent. to White 2 jy. 1614. C⁶.
— *See also* 16856.3.

Measure. The measure of expence. 1626. *See* 12805.5.

17764 **Mecare.** True newes from ⟨Mecare:⟩ and also out of Worcestershire. 4°. *f. W. Barley,* [1598.] C(cropt). A

17764.5 **Mechlin.** ⟨   ⟩ of a meruylous and a terrible destruction now lately done in the yere M.CCCC.xlvi. the .vii. day of August. . . . *Tr.* by R. Olyuer. s.sh.fol. *R. Lant f. Thomas* ⟨*Purfoot?*⟩ [1546.] O(2 cropt).

Meddus, James, *tr. See* 22125.

17765 **Mede, Joseph.** Churches, that is, appropriate places for christian worship. 4°. *M. F[lesher] f. J. Clark,* 1638. Ent. 4 jn. L.O.C.D.E.+; F.HN.HD.ILL.U.+
Unsold sheets reissued in some copies of Wing M 1596; reprinted w. tp dated 1638 as pt. of Wing M 1597.

17766 — Clavis apocalyptica ex innatis et insitis visionum characteribus demonstrata. [Anon.] 4°. *Cantabrigiæ,* [*T. a. J. Buck,*] *imp. authoris, in gratiam amicorum,* 1627. L².O.C.C¹².WOR.+; HN.

Mede, Joseph—*cont.*

17767 — Editio secunda. (In sancti Joannis Apocalypsin commentarius.) 2 pts. 4°. *Cantabrigiæ, ap. T. Buck,* 1632. L.O.C.D.G².+; F.HN.HD.ILL.NY¹¹.+

17768 — The name altar, or θυσιαστήριον, anciently given to the holy table. 4°. M. F[lesher] f. J. Clark, 1637. Ent. 11 jn. L.O.C.D.E⁸.+; F.CAL.N.U.Y.+
  In imprint: 'Sᵗ Peters'.

17768.5 — [Anr. ed.] 4°. M. F[lesher] f. J. Clark, 1637. L³⁸. O.C².E.G².+; F.HN.HD.ILL.Y(2).
  In imprint: 'S. Peters'.

17769 — The reverence of Gods house. 4°. M. F[lesher] f. J. Clark, 1638. Ent. 23 oc. L.O.C.D.E.+; F.HN.HD.N.U.+
  Unsold sheets reissued in some copies of Wing M 1596 sq.

17770 **Medeley, Thomas.** Misericors, μικροκοσμος, or, Medeleyes offices. 12°. J. B[eale,] 1619. Ent. 9 ap. O.

17770.3 **Medicine.** A marvellous medicine to cure a great paine. *Ballad.* 1/2 sh.fol. [W. Jones] f. H. G[osson, 1624.] Ent. 14 de. 1624. c⁶.

17770.5 — [Heading A1ʳ:] A medicine for the soule, as well for them that are whole of body as for them that be sick. 16° in 8's. [R. Tottell, c. 1550.] F(imp.).

Medicines. Mediciues [sic] for horses. [1565?] *See* 20439.7.

17770.7 — The seven soveraigne medicines and salves, to be diligently applied to the seven deadly wounds and sores. [In verse.] 1/2 sh.fol. S. Stafford, 1603. L(MS Harley 514, 2 copies, fol. 1 and 119). 𝕬

17771 **Medina, Pedro de.** The arte of nauigation. *Tr.* J. Frampton. 1581. fol. T. Dawson, (1581) [after 4 au.] Ent. 28 fb. L.L³⁰.C⁶.; F. Henry Taylor.

17772 — [Anr. ed.] 4° in 8's. T. Dawson, 1595. E(lacks tp). London, Royal Institution of Naval Architects.; HN. BO².NCU.

Medina Sidonia, Alonso, *Duke de. See* 19625.

17773 **Meditation.** An excellent and a right learned meditacion, compiled in two prayers, to be vsed in these daungerous daies of affliction. 8°. *Roane, M. Wodde,* [J. Day?] 1554 (3 ja.) c³.; HN.
  (Formerly also 1293)
  — A gloryous medytacyon of Ihesus crystes passyon. [c. 1523.] *See* 14550.

17773.5 — A godly meditation day and night to be exercised. [Engr. W. Rogers.] s.sh.fol. [London, c. 1600.] L (Print Dept.).
  See Hind, I.279.

Meditationes. Meditationes Jordani de vita et passione iesu christi. 1513. *See* 14789.

17774 — Variæ meditationes et preces piæ. 8°. C. Barkerus, 1582. Ent. 12 ap. c³.

17775 **Meditations.** Certayne deuout meditations very necessary for christian men to meditate vpon euery day in the weeke: concerning Christ his lyfe and passion. 16° in 8's. (Duaci, ap. J. Bogardi [i.e. London, W. Carter,] 1576.) L.O.
  A&R 227. By P. Canisius; reprinted as pt. 1 of 17278.4.
  — Deuout meditacions, psalmes and praiers. 1548. *See* 2998.5.

17775.5 — Divine meditations. contayning remedies against . . . death. *Tr.* out of French, by E. Grimston. 12°. G. Eld, sold by E. Blount a. F. Burton, 1606. L(tp only, Ames II.119).

17776 — Godly meditacions verye necessarie to bee sayde of all christen men. 16° in 8's. [E. Whitchurch? 1546?] L.

17776a — Meditations. [1580–81.] Now = pt. 1 of 17278.4.
  — Meditations miscellaneous, holy and humane. 1637. *See* 13171.

17777 — Meditations of consolation. 1621. Now = pt. 2 of 6427.5.

Medley. An excellent medley, which you may admire. [c. 1630.] *See* 19231.5.

17777.5 — An excellent new medley. To the tune of the Spanish Pavin. *Ballad.* 1/2 sh.fol. [London, c. 1620?] c⁶.
  What are sometimes interpreted as author's inits. 'F.D.' at the end, are only the tops of 'FIN' in FINIS.

17777.7 — [Anr. ed.] 1/2 sh.fol. *assignes of T. Symcocke,* [1628–29.] L.

17778 **Medwall, Henry.** Here is cõteyned a godely interlude of Fulgens cenatoure of Rome. 4° in 6's. (J. rastell,) [1512–16.] L(2 leaves).; HN. Greg 1.
  Based on B. da Montemagno's De vera nobilitate; *see also* 5293.

17779 — Nature. A goodly interlude of Nature. fol. [W. Rastell, 1530–34.] L(2, 1 cropt, 1 frag.). O(frag.).C.; HN (frag.).MEL(frag.). Greg 17.

17780 **Meene, Joshua.** A liberall maintenance is manifestly due to the ministers of the gospell. 4°. T. Harper f. L. Chapman a. W. Certain, 1638. Ent. 30 mr. L.O.C. NOR².P.+; F.HN.N.NY.Y.+

17780.5 — [Anr. issue, w. cancel tp:] The vickers challenge. Claiming a maintainance as due by proofes out of the gospell. 4°. Printed a. sold by N. Vavasour, 1640. O⁸.; HD.

17781 **Meeting.** The meeting of gallants at an ordinarie: or the walkes in Powles. 4°. T. C[reede,] solde by M. Lawe, 1604. Ent. to R. Serger a. J. Trundle 8 ja. 1608. L.O(2).; PML.
  Attrib. to T. Dekker.

Meetkerke, Edward, *tr. See* 7371.5.

Meg, *of Herefordshire. See* 12032.

17782 **Meg,** *of Westminster.* The life and pranks of long Meg of Westminster. 1582. L.
  Tp and colophon forged from 6749; rest of text c. 1650.

17782.5 — The life of long Meg of Westminster, containing the mad merry pranks shee played. 4°. E. All-de f. E. White, 1620. Ass'd to T. Pavier a. J. Wright by E. White 13 de. Robert Taylor.
  See Court-Book C, pp. 112–13.

17783 — [Anr. ed.] 4°. [J. Beale] f. R. Bird, 1635. Ent. to E. Brewster a. R. Bird 4 au. 1626. F.HN.

17783.3 — [Anr. ed.] 4°. f. R. Bird, 1636. L⁴⁷.

Meggs, William. *See* 3432.5, 18102a.2.

Megiser, Hieronymus. Thesaurus polyglottus. 1603. *See* headnote preceding 6832.1.

17784 **Meierus, Albertus.** Certaine briefe, and speciall instructions for gentlemen, merchants, &c. employed in seruices abrode. [Tr.] (P. Jones.) 4°. J. Woolfe, 1589. Ent. 20 ja. L(2).L².C⁶.WN.; F.HN. Penrose 162(imp.).

Meigret, Louis, *tr. See* 20098.

17785 **Mela, Pomponius.** The worke of P. Mela. The cosmographer, concerninge the situation of the world. *Tr.* A. Golding. 4°. [J. Charlewood] f. T. Hacket, 1585. L.O.C².; F.HN.BO.LC.WIS.+

17786 — [Anr. ed., enlarged.] The rare and singuler worke of P. Mela. Whereunto is added, that of J. Solinus Polyhistor. 2 pts. 4°. (J. Charlewoode) f. T. Hacket, 1590 (1587.) L.O.C.CHATS.G².+; F.HN.CU.HD.LC(pt. 1 only).
  Pt. 2 a reissue of unsold sheets of 22896 sq., q.v.

17787 **Melampus.** The contemplation of mankinde. 1571. = 13482.

Melanchthon, Philipp. Augsburg confession. *See* 908.

17788 — A ciuile nosgay wherin is contayned the offyce and dewty of all magestrates and subiectes. *Tr.* J. G[oodale.] [Anon.] 8°. (R. wyer f. J. goodale,) [1550?] Ent. to J. King 1557–58. L.L².O.
  (Formerly also 12005)
  — The confessyon of the fayth of the Germaynes. 1536. *See* 908.

17789 — The epistle of the famous and great clerke Philip Melancton made vnto kynge Henry the eight, for the reuokinge of the six articles. Trãslated out of laten by J. C. 8°. (Weesell [Antwerp, S. Mierdman,] 1547 (18 my.)) L(2).O².O¹⁷.M.; F.HD.Y.
  Tp line 2 ends: 'Philip Me-'. An earlier ed. of this was issued under R. Bankes's imprint for R. Grafton; *see P. C. Proceedings,* VII.107; *L. & P. Henry VIII,* XVI.166, 212, 214, etc.

17789.5 — [Anr. ed.] 8° in 4's. (Weesell [London, R. Wyer,] 1547 (18 my.)) c.
  Tp line 2 ends: 'Philip'.
  — A famous and godly history, contaynyng the lyues of three reformers. 1561. *See* 1881.

17790 — A godly and learned assertion in defence of the true church. *Tr.* R. R(obinson.) 8°. T. Dawson, 1580. O(imp.).; F.HD.

Melanchthon, Philipp—*cont.*

17790.5 — Godly prayers, meete to be vsed in these later times: collected out of Philip Melancthon and others. *Tr.* [R. Robinson.] 8°. *assigne of W. Seres (H. Denham,)* 1579. Ent. to Denham 24 mr. BUTE.; F.
  Dedic. init. 'Ric. R.'

17791 — A godlye treatyse of prayer, *tr.* by J. Bradforde. 8°. [*S. Mierdman f.*] (*J. Wight,*) [1553.] L.O(2).O¹⁷.C.BUTE.; F(2).HN.

17792 — The iustification of man by faith only. *Tr.* N. Lesse. An apologie or defence of the worde of God, by N. Lesse. 8°. (*W. Powell,* 1548 (11 oc.)) L.O.O⁹.; ILL.

17793 — A newe work cōcerning both partes of the sacrament to be receyued of the lay peple. *Tr.* out off [*sic*] latyn. 8°. [*Zurich, C. Froschouer?*] 1543. L.L².O.C.G².+; F.Y.

17794 — = 17795.

17795 — [Anr. ed.] A newe work concernyng [etc.] 8°. [*S. Mierdman f.*] (*R. Jugge,*) [1548?] L.O.O³.C⁹.M.+; F.HN.HD.

17796 — [Anr. ed.] A newe worck [etc.] 8°. [*S. Mierdman f.*] (*R. Jugge,*) [1548?] L⁴.O²¹.C.D.M.+; N.

17797 — Of two woonderful popish monsters, to wyt, of a popish asse and of a moonkish calfe. Witnessed, the one by Melanchthon, the other by M. Luther. *Tr.* out of French by J. Brooke. 4°. (*T. East,*) sould [*by A. Maunsell,*] (1579.) Ent. to East 24 mr. L.O.C².; F.

17798 — A very godly defense, full of lerning, defending the mariage of preistes. *Tr.* lewis beuchame [i.e. G. Joye]: M.CCCCC.XLI. in Auguste. 8°. (*Lipse, U. Hoff*) [i.e. *Antwerp, widow of C. Ruremond,* 1541.] L.O.C.LINC.P.+

17799 — A waying and considering of the Interim. *Tr.* J. Rogers [*Martyr.*] 8°. (*E. Whitchurche,*) 1548 (6 au.) L.O (imp.).C(lacks colophon).D.; F.

— *ed. See* 5266.5, 5290, 16980, 23944.

— *See also* 5947, 10391.5, 11394, 14823, 20906, 24728, and 2b in the head-note preceding 15610.5.

17800 **Melanthe.** Melanthe fabula pastoralis acta cum Jacobus rex, Cantabrigiam inviseret. 4°. [*Cambridge,*] C. *Legge,* 1615 (27 mr.) L.O.C.ETON.WOR.+; BO.HD (date cropt).PN.Y. Greg L 7.
  Attrib. to S. Brooke.

17800.5 **Melbancke, Brian.** Philotimus. The warre betwixt nature and fortune. 4°. *R. Warde,* 1582 (1583.) C².

17801 — [A variant, w. tp dated:] 1583. L.L⁴.O.C⁵.P(imp.).; F.HN.HD.

Meletios, *Patriarch of Alexandria. See* 19553.5.

17802 **Mell, George.** A proper new balad of the bryber Gehesie. s.sh.fol. *T. Colwell,* [1566.] Ent. 1566–67. L.

Mellis, John, *ed. See* 18794, 20802.

17803 **Mellys, John.** The true description of two monsterous children. 1566. Ballad. s.sh.fol. *A. Lacy f. W. Lewes,* [1566.] Ent. 1565–66. L.

Melody. The mindes melodie. 1605. *See* 18051.

17804 **Melton,** *Sir* **John.** Astrologaster, or, the figure-caster. 4°. *B. Alsop f. E. Blackmore,* 1620. Ent. to J. Harrison a. Blackmore 8 ap. L.O.C.A.PLUME.+; F.HN.HD.N.Y.+

17805 — A six-folde politician. Together with a six-folde precept of policy. [Init. J. M.] 8°. *E. A[llde] f. J. Busby,* 1609. Ent. 15 de. 1608. L.O.C².DUR³.M.+; F.HN.HD.N.NY.+

17806 **Melton, William de.** Sermo exhortatori⁹ cancellarij Eboꝝ. hijs qui ad sacros ordines petunt promoueri. [Anon.] 4° in 8. [*W. de Worde,* 1510?] L.P.
  Printer's name in device.

Melusine. [Melusine, a tale of the serpent fairy. 1510.] *See* 14648.

17807 **Melville, Andrew.** Principis Scoti-Britannorum natalia. [In verse.] 4°. *Edinburgi, R. Walde-graue,* 1594. L.E².

17808 — Scholastica diatriba, A. Meluino moderante. 1599. Now = 21555.3.

17809 — Στεφανισκιον. Ad Scotiae regem, habitum in coronatione reginae. [In verse.] 4°. *Edinburgi, R. Walde graue* [sic, 2 words], 1590. L.L².DUL.E.E².+; F.HN.

17810 — Viri clarissimi A. Melvini musae et P. Adamsoni vita et palindoia [sic]. 4°. [*Edinburgh?*] *E. Raban?*] 1620. L.O.C.E.M⁴.+; F.HN.HD.NY.Y. 𝕬

— *See also* 148.5.

17811 **Melville, Elizabeth.** Ane godlie dreame, compylit in Scottish meter. [Init. M. M., i.e. Mistress Melville.] 4°. *Edinburgh, R. Charteris,* 1603. O(imp.).E.

17812 — [An Eng. version.] A godlie dreame. 4°. *Edinburgh, R. Charteris,* [1604?] E.

17813 — [Anr. ed.] A godlie dreame. 4°. *Edinburgh, R. Charteris,* 1606. HN.

17814 — [Anr. ed.] 8°. *Edinburgh, A. Hart,* 1620. L.LINC.

17815 **Melville, James.** The black bastel, or, a lamentation in name of the kirk of Sscotland [sic]. Abridged by N. [i.e. D. Calderwood? In verse.] 8° in 4's. [*Edinburgh, J. Wreittoun,*] 1634. L.O.E.; F(date cropt).

17815.5 — Ane fruitful and comfortable exhortatioun anent death. [Init. J. M.] 8°. *Edinburgh, R. Walde-graue,* 1597. O.C³.E.P.
  (Formerly 17138)

17816 — A spirituall propine of a pastour to his people. 4°. *Edinburgh, R. Walde-graue,* 1589 [i.e. 1598.] L.E(lacks tp).

Melvin, Andrew. *See* 17810.

Melvin, William, *tr. See* 11550.

17816.5 **Memento mori.** Memento mori remember to die [xylographic] s.sh.4°. [*London,* c. 1640.] F.
  Woodcut compartment w. letterpress quatrain beginning: 'It is appointed'; *see also* 26038.2.

Memorials. General and rare memorials. 1577. *See* 6459.

Men. Two wise men [etc.] 1619. *See* 4991.

17817 **Menandrinus, Marsilius.** The defence of peace: lately translated out of laten in to englysshè, (by W. Marshall.) fol. (*R. wyer f. w. marshall,* 1535 (jy.)) L.O.C(lacks folio 139).M.P.+; F.HN.HD.NY.WIS.+
  Regarding financing of this ed. *see L. & P. Henry VIII,* VII.422–3; XI.1335.

17818 **Menantel, François de.** A congratulation to France, upon the happy alliance with Spaine. 4°. [*G. Eld*] f. *T. Thorp, sold by W. Burre,* 1612. Ent. to Thorpe 27 ap. O.

Mendoza, Andres de. *See* 533.

Mendoza, Bernardino de. The copie of a letter sent to Don B. Mendoza. 1588. *See* 15412.

17819 — Theorique and practise of warre. *Tr.* out of the Castilian tonge by Sʳ. E. Hoby. 4°. [*Middelburg, R. Schilders,*] 1597. L.O.CHATS.; F.HN.CH.N.Y.+

Mendoza, *Don* **Diego Ilustado de.** A proclamation made in the name of his majesty of Spaine. 1630. *See* 17916.5 sq.

17820 **Mendoza, Juan.** [Heading B1ʳ:] The historie of John lorde Mandozze. [*Tr.,* w. additions, from Boaistuau's version of Bandello's *Novelle,* by] (T. Delapeend.) 8°. [*T. Colwell,* 1565.] Ent. to Colwell 1565–66. L(imp.).

17821 **Menewe, Gracious.** A confutacion of that popishe and antichristian doctryne, whiche mainteineth yᵉ ministracyon of the sacrament vnder one kind, [etc.] 16° in 8's. [*Wesel? H. Singleton?* 1555?] L.O(2).C(2).E.M.; F.HN.CH.
  In same type as 9981. Attrib. to T. Becon. Prob. issued w. 17822.

17822 — A plaine subuersyon . . . of all the argumentes, for the maintenaunce of auricular confession, [etc.] 16° in 8's. [*Wesel? H. Singleton?* 1555?] L.O(2).C(2).E.M.; F.HN.CH.
  In same type as 9981. Attrib. to T. Becon. Prob. issued w. 17821.

Menippean Satire. A pleasant satyre or poesie. 1595. *See* 15489.

Mennher, Valentin. *See* 23677.

Menyman, William, *ed. See* 18846.

Merbecke, John. *See* Marbecke, J.

17823 **Merbury, Charles.** A briefe discourse of royall monarchie. Wherunto is added a collection of Italian prouerbes, [etc.] Eng. a. Ital. 4°. *T. Vautrollier,* 1581. Ent. to Marsh, w. note: 'vantrollier [sic] this' 23 no. HD(2, 1 imp.). 𝕬
  Address to favourers and friends on *2.

17823.5 — [Anr. issue, w. new prelims.] L.O.C.E².G².+; F.HN.CHI.
  Dedic. to Queen Elizabeth on *2.

17824 **Mercator, Gerard.** Historia mundi: or Mercator's atlas. Lately rectified by J. Hondy. Englished by W. S(altonstall.) fol. *T. Cotes f. M. Sparke a. S. Cartwright,* 1635. Ent. 8 no. a. 19 de. 1632 a. 3 mr. 1635. L.O.C. D.E.+; F.HD(imp.).N.NY.Y.+
    Verses on verso of 1st leaf occur in 2 settings: one signed 'F. Q[uarles]', the other 'M. S[parkes]' or unsigned. *See* also Greg, *Companion,* pp. 310–18.

17824.5 — [A variant, w. impr. on letterpress tp:] *T. Cotes f. M. Sparke,* 1635. L.; F.HN.

17825 — [Anr. issue, w. engr. tp:] Second edytion. *f. M. Sparke,* 1637. L.O.D².NLW. Southwell Minster.+; F.HN.HD. N.NY.+

17826 — [Anr. issue, w. engr. tp dated:] 1639. ILL.NY.

17827 **Mercator, Gerard,** and **Hondius, Jodocus.** Atlas or a geographicke description of the world. *Tr.* H. Hexham. 2 vols. fol. *Amsterdam, H. Hondius a. J. Johnson,* 1636. L.O⁸.O¹⁰.C³.M²(vol. 1 only).+; HN.HD.ILL.NY(lacks sub tp).V.+
    English title and imprint slips pasted over engr. Fr. title and imprint: vol. 1: '*chez H. Hondius, 1633*' or '*1636*'; vol. 2: '*sumptibus & typis H. Hondij, 1633*' or '*1636*'. In some copies (O²¹, HD,N) one or both of the imprint slips are missing. In the Latin 'Editio decima' of 1630 and 1631 is a map by T. Pont: 'A new description of the shyres Lothian and Linlitquo. *J. Hondius cœlavit sumptibus A. Hart,* [1630.]' In later eds. including 17827 the imprint is altered to: '*H. Hondius excudit*'.

17828 — [Anr. issue, w. imprint:] *Amsterdam, chez H. Hondius (sumptibus & typis H. Hondij,)* 1638. O.DUR⁵(frag.). M²(vol. 2 only).PETYT(vol. 2 only).; PEN(vol. 2 only).
    Apparently issued without English imprint slips.

Mercedarians, *Order of Our Lady of Mercy. See* Indulgences 123.

Mercer, James. Theses aliquot logicae. Praeside J. Mercero. 1630. *See* 21555.39.
— — 1632. *See* 21555.43.

17828.5 **Mercer, William.** Bon-acords decorement. Or, newes from the north. Wherein is expressed the forme of new Aberdeene. 4°. [*Edinburgh, J. Wreittoun,*] 1633. E. W. F. Taylor, Aberdeen.
— *See* also 17154.5.

Merchants. The merchants new-royall-exchaunge. 1604. *See* 16784.
— The marchants auizo. 1589. *See* 3908.4.

Mercurius. Mercurius Botanicus. 1634. *See* 14704.
— Mercurius Britannicus. Mundus alter et idem. [1607?] *See* 12685.
— *tr. See* 11541.

17829 — Mercurius Carolinus. No. 1. 1649.
    Not an STC item.

17829a — Mercurius Davidicus; or a patterne of loyall devotion. 8°. *Oxford, L. Leichfield,* 1634 [i.e. 1643.] L.STD.; HN. = Wing M 1761.
— Mercurius Gallo-Belgicus. A relation of all matters passed. 1614. *See* 20862.

17830 **Meredeth, John.** The judge of heresies, one God, one faith, one church. 4°. *A. M[athewes] f. J. Grismand,* 1624. Ent. 12 ja. L.L³.O.C.D.+; F.HN.

17831 — The sinne of blasphemie against the holy ghost. 4°. [*E. Allde*] *f. J. Marriot,* 1622. Ent. 28 jy. 1621. L.O.O¹⁸. C.; F.HN.AAS.BO.Y.

17832 **Meredeth, Richard.** Two sermons preached before his majestie. 4°. *G. Eld. f. S. Waterson,* 1606. Ent. 3 mr. L.O.C⁵.D.YK.+; U.Y(deposit).
— *See* also Bookplates.

17833 **Meres, Francis.** Gods arithmeticke. Written by Francis Meres. 8°. *R. Johnes,* 1597. L.O.E.; F.HD.

17834 — Palladis tamia. Wits treasury being the second part of Wits Common wealth. [*Ed.* N. Ling.] 8°. *P. Short f. C. Burbie,* 1598. Ent. 7 se. L.L³⁸.O.C².P.+; F.HN (imp.).ILL.N.PFOR.+
    All copies but PFOR, ROS lack A2–A4. L,O,HN have cancel and cancellandum of B1. Second in the 'Wits Series' which includes 381, 15685, 26014.

17835 — [Anr. ed.] Wits Common wealth. The second part. A treasurie of similies, [etc.] 12°. *W. Stansby, sold by R. Royston,* 1634. Ass'd to Stansby 23 fb. 1626. L.O.C⁴.BIRM.SH.+; F.HN.HD.ILL.Y.+

Meres, Francis—*cont.*

17836 — [Anr. issue, w. engr. tp:] Witts academy a treasurie of goulden sentences. *f. R. Royston,* 1636. L.C⁴.; F. HN(engr. tp only).BO.PEN.Y.+
    Date on engr. tp altered from 1635.
— *tr. See* 16902, 16918 sq., 16920 sq.

17836.3 **Mericke, John.** A compendious collection and breefe abstract of all the auncient English-statutes now in force within Ireland. 8°. *Dublin, J. Franckton,* (1617). L(frag., Ames II.230, 440). BTL.D(imp.).D⁵.D⁶.

17836.7 — [Anr. issue, omitting prelims. w. title:] A briefe abstract of all the English statutes [etc. Init. J. M.] 8°. *Dublin, Societie of Stationers,* 1625. D⁹. St. Fin Barre's Library, Cork.

Merideth, John. *See* Meredeth, J.

17837 **Meriton, George.** The christian mans assuring house. And a sinners conversion. Two sermons. 4°. *E. Griffin f. R. Mab,* 1614. L.O.P.YK.; HN.CHI.

17838 — A sermon of nobilitie. 4°. [*G. Eld*] *f. T. Clarke,* 1607. Ent. 16 my. L.O.C.P.YK.+; HN.HD.U.

17839 — A sermon of repentance. 4°. [*G. Eld*] *f. T. Clarke,* 1607. Ent. 27 my. L.O.C.COL.YK.+; F.HN.

17840 — A sermon preached before the generall assembly at Glascoe. 4°. *W. Stansby f. H. Featherstone,* 1611. Ent. 6 jn. L.O.C².E.YK.+; F.HN.HD.Y.

17841 **Merlin.** Here begynneth a lytel treatyse of yᵉ byrth & pphecye of Marlyn. [In verse.] 4° ⁸·⁴. (*W. de Worde,* 1510.) O⁵(frag.).; LC(frag.).PML.

17841.3 — [Anr. ed.] 4°. (*W. de Worde,* 1529.) L(last leaf only, Harl.5919/30).

17841.7 — The whole prophesie of Scotland, England, & some-part of France, and Denmark. [In verse.] 8°. *R. Walde-grave,* 1603. HN.HD.
    Not pr. by Waldegrave; possibly a London piracy. Quire C partly reset; C1ʳ line 1 'gowrie' (HD) or 'Gowrie' (HN).

17841.9 — [Anr. ed.] 8°. *Edinburgh, A. Hart,* 1615. Abbotsford, Melrose, Roxburghshire.

17842 — [Anr. ed.] 8°. *Edinburgh, A. Hart,* 1617. L.; F.

17842.3 — [Anr. ed.] 8°. [*Edinburgh?*] 1639. BUTE(imp.).

17842.7 **Merlin, Pierre.** The christians combat: wherein is set downe that daungerous fight wherunto all the elect are called. [Init. P. M.] *Tr.* G. C[hapelin.] 8°. *R. Field f. R. Dexter,* 1591. Ent. 29 se. L.; NY⁸.

17843 — A most plaine and profitable exposition of the booke of Ester. *Tr.* 8°. *T. Creede,* 1599. L.O.DUL.E².LINC.+; F.WASH³.

17844 **Mervin.** The most famous and renowned historie, of that woorthie knight Mervine. [*Tr.*] by I. M[arkham?], Gent. 2 pts. 4° in 8's. *R. Blower a. V. Sims,* 1612. Ent. to R. Jones 3 fb. 1596; ass'd by Simmes to E. Griffin 20 de. 1619. L.O.; F.HN.HD.N.Y.+

Meslier. The true history of the tragicke loves. 1628. *See* 13516.

Message. A message, termed Marke the truth of the worde of God. 1570. *See* 19974.2.

Messia, Pedro. *See* Mexia, P.

17845 **Mestrezat, Jean.** The divine pourtrait; or representation of the Lords supper. Englished by J. Reynolds. 12°. *A. M[athewes] f. G. Baker,* 1631. Ent. 4 ap. L³. PLUME.

Metamorphosis. The metamorphosis of tabacco. 1602. *See* 1695.
— A strange metamorphosis of man. 1634. *See* 3587.

Metcalfe, Nicholas, *tr. See* 7318.

17845.3 **Meteren, Emanuel van.** Commentarien ofte memorien van den Nederlandtschen staet. fol. *Schotlandt buyten Danswijck, H. van Loven (Londen, voor E. van Meteren,* 1609.) Dutch Church, London.

17845.7 — [Anr. ed.] fol. *Schotland buyten Danswijck, H. van Loven (Londen, voor E. van Meteren,* 1610.) L.
    Possibly some sheets from same setting as 17845.3.

17846 — A true discourse historicall, of the succeeding governours in the Netherlands. *Tr.* T. C(hurchyard) and R. Ro(binson.) 4°. [*F. Kingston*] *f. M. Lownes,* 1602. Ent. 16 de. 1601. L.O.C.E.M.+; F.HN.HD.N.NY.+
    Dedic. signed 'T. C.' or 'T. Churchyard'; both at F. Juel-Jensen and CH have a rare variant w. tp signed: 'T. Churchyard'.

Method. A short method for the declining of French verbes. 1623. *See* 21504.5.

17847 **Meung, Jean de.** The dodechedron of fortune. Englished by S[r]. W. B. knight. [In verse.] 4°. *J. Pindley f. H. H[ooper] a. S. M[an,]* 1613. Ent. 20 my. L.O[5].; F. HN.N.

17847.2 — [Anr. issue, w. imprint:] *J. Pindley f. S. Man,* 1613. O.

17847.4 **Meurier, Gabriel.** Communications familieres non moins propre que tresutiles.... Familiare communications no leasse proppre then verrie proffytable. *Fr. a. Eng.* 8°. *Anuers, chez P. de Keerberghe,* 1563. L.; ILL.

17847.6 — Coniugaisons Francois-Angloises mises en lumiere. *Fr. a. Eng.* 8°. *Anuers, chez J. waesberge,* 1563. ILL.

17847.8 — The coniugations in Englishe and Netherdutch, according as G. Meurier hath ordayned the same in Netherdutche, and Frenche. De coniugatien in Engelsch ende Nederduytsche. [*Tr.* T. Basson.] 8°. *Leyden, T. Basson,* 1586. Bamberg, Staatsbibliothek.

— The nosegay of morall philosophie. 1580. *See* 6039.

Mexia, Pedro. Αρχαιο-πλουτος. 1619. *See* 17936.5.

17848 — A pleasaunt dialogue, concerning phisicke and phisitions. (*Tr.* out of the Castlin tongue by T. N[ewton?]) 8°. *J. Charlewood,* 1580. Ent. 11 jn. L.L[17].BRISTOL[2].
2nd tp on A2: 'A delectable dialogue [etc.]'

17849 — The foreste or collection of histories, dooen out of Frenche [from the trans. of C. Gruget] by T. Fortescue. 4°. [*H. Wykes a.*] *J. Kyngston f. W. Jones,* 1571. Ent. 1570–71. L.O.C[2].G[2].M.+; F.HN.CB.HD.N.+
Wykes pr. quires A–N. *See also* 24330.

17850 — [Anr. ed.] 4°. [*J. Kingston f.*] *J. Day,* 1576. L.O.C[2].DUL.P.+; F.HN(imp.).CHI.HD.PML.+
See Arber II.788. Some copies (L) misdated '1476'.

17851 — The historie of all the Romane emperors. Englished by W. T(raheron.) fol. [*F. Kingston*] *f. M. Lownes,* 1604. Ent. 10 de. 1601. L.O.C.E.M.+; F.HN.HD.N. NY.+

17852 — [Anr. ed.] The imperiall historie: continued by E. Grimeston. fol. *H. L[ownes] f. M. Lownes,* 1623. L.O.C.E.M.+; F.HN.HD.N.Y.+
— A pleasaunt dialogue. 1580. *See* 17848.
— The treasurie of auncient and moderne times. 1613. *See* 17936.

17853 **Michael,** *de Ungaria.* Euagatorium modus p̄dicandi sermones. xiii. [etc.] 8°. (*R. Pynson,*) [1510?] L.
(Formerly also 10580) Continental eds. are known containing some English sentences but without imprints indicating English sale.

17854 **Michaelis, Sebastien.** The admirable history of the possession and conversion of a penitent woman. (A discourse of spirits.) *Tr.* W. B. 4° in 8's. [*F. Kingston*] *f. W. Aspley,* [1613.] Ent. 17 jn. 1613. L[13].L[30].O(2). DE.; F.PEN.PN.
(2nd part formerly also 17855)

17854a — [Anr. issue, w. new prelims., dated:] 1613. L.O.C.G[2].P. +; F.HN.HD.ILL.NY.+
Quire ¶[4] substituted for A1 of 17854.

17855 — = 2nd part of 17854.

Michaelmas Term. Michaelmas terme. 1607. *See* 17890.

17856 **Michaelson, John.** The lawfulnes of kneeling, in the sacrament. 8°. *E. Raban, printer to the universitie of Sainct-Andrewes,* 1620. L.A.E.M[4].STU.+; F.U.
Answers 4364; answered by 4354.

17857 **Michel, William.** Epitaphs upon the untymelie death of W. Michel. 4°. *Aberdoniæ, E. Rabanus,* 1634. L.A(imp.).; F.

17857.5 **Micheli, Raphel.** The premier liure des poemes. 8° in 4's. [*J. Charlewood,*] 1569. L.

17857.7 **Michell,** *Sir* **John.** *See* Addenda.

Michelsone, Niels, *ed. See* 18572.

17858 **Mico, John.** A pill to purge out poperie. [Anon.] 8°. *f. B. Fisher,* 1623. LEEDS.; HN.
Reprinted in 17861.

17859 — [Anr. ed.] 8°. [*G. Purslowe*] *f. B. Fisher,* 1624. O. Stevens Cox.; U.

17860 — [Anr. ed.] 8°. *B. A[lsop] f. B. Fisher,* 1624. L.O.ETON.; F.

17861 — Spirituall food, and physick: [etc.] Second edition [of 17858.] [Init. J. M.] 8°. *H. L[ownes] f. B. Fisher,* 1623. Ent. 25 au. C.
(Formerly also 17141a)

Mico, John—*cont.*

17862 — The third edition, corrected by the author J. Mico. 8°. *B. A[lsop] a. T. F[awcett] f. B. Fisher,* 1628. C(2, 1 imp.).

17863 — The fourth edition. 8°. *f. J. Boler, sold by T. Hunt in Exeter,* 1631. Ass'd to Boler 22 fb. O.

Microcosmography. Micro-cosmographie. 1628. *See* 7439.

Micron, Marten. De christlicke ordinancie der Nederlätscher ghemeynten Christi. 1554. *See* 16571a.
— De kleyne catechismus. 1552. *See* 15260.7.

17863.3 — Een claer bewijs, van het recht ghebruyck des nachtmaels Christi. 8°. (*Lonnen, S. Mierdmā,*) 1552 (9 ap.) Amsterdam U.

17863.5 — [Anr. ed.] 8°. (*buyten Londen, C. Volckwinner* [i.e. *Emden, E. van der Erve a. N. Hill,*] 1554.) L.O.

17864 — [A trans.] A short and faythful instruction, for symple christianes, whych intende worthely to receyue the holy supper. (*Tr.* T. C[ranmer?]) 8°. [*Emden, E. van der Erve,* 1556?] L.L[2].C[3].; F.

17864.5 — [Anr. ed. Anon.] 8°. (*H. Sutton,*) [1560?] O.
(Formerly 3035)
— *See also* 18812.

Microphilus, *pseud.* The new-yeeres gift. 1636. *See* 22631.

Midas. Midas. 1592. *See* 17083.

17865 **Middelburg.** Middleborow. A briefe rehersall of the accorde and agreement, that the captaynes, and armie of Middleborow and Armew: haue made. *Tr.* out of the ducthe [*sic*] 1574. 8°. *R. Jhones,* [1574.] L[2](2).O.C.
— A true relation written from Midelbourg. 1622. *See* Newsbooks 39.

17866 **Middleton, Christopher.** The famous historie of Chinon of England. 4°. *J. Danter f. C. Burbie,* 1597. Ent. to T. Gosson a. Danter 20 ja. 1596. L.C(imp.).; HN.

17867 — The historie of heauen. [In verse.] 4°. [*J. Orwin*] *f. C. Knight,* 1596. L.O.; HN(cropt).

17868 — The legend of Humphrey duke of Glocester. [In verse.] 4°. *E. A[llde] f. N. Ling,* 1600. Ent. 15 ap. L(2).O.; F.Y.
— *See also* 17126.5 sq.
— *tr. See* 6840.

17869 **Middleton,** *Sir* **Henry.** The last East-Indian voyage. 1606. = 7456.

17869.5 **Middleton,** *Sir* **Hugh.** This indenture made [   ] in the fourteenth yeare of James betweene Hugh Middellton and [   ]. [Form for a lease of supply of water by pipe.] s.sh.fol. [*London,* 1616.] L(MS. Dept., Add.Ch.56224).O(J).
Pr. in civilité; dated in MS. 17 July 1616 (O) or 17 Mar. 1617 (L).

Middleton, Marmaduke, *Bp. of St. David's.* Injunctions. *See* 10324.5.

17870 **Middleton, Richard.** The carde and compasse of life. Directing all men to arrive at the harbour of heaven. 8°. *W. S[tansby] f. W. Burre,* 1613. Ent. 15 my. L. O.DUR.; F(2).Y.

17871 — Goodnes; the blessed mans badge: in two sermons. 12°. *N. Okes,* 1619. Ent. 7 ja. L[4].Broxbourne(O).; F.PN[2].
Prob. issued w. 17873.

17872 — The heavenly pro:gresse. By Rich. Middleton. 12°. *N. Okes, (sold by T. Adams,)* 1617. Ent. 5 ap. O.

17872a — [Anr. issue, w. imprint:] *N. Okes, (sold by W. Burre,)* 1617. L(tp only, Print Dept.)PLUME.; HN.PN[2].

17872a.5 — [Anr. issue, w. colophon:] (*N. Okes, sold by S. Waterson,* 1617.) L[4](lacks tp).

17873 — The key of David. By Rich. Middleton. 12°. *N. Okes,* 1619. Ent. 7 ja. L[4].O. Broxbourne(O).; F.HN(engr. tp only).
Prob. issued w. 17871.

17874 **Middleton, Richard,** *of York.* Epigrams and satyres. (Times metamorphosis.) 4°. *N. Okes f. Joseph Harison,* 1608. Ent. 4 my. E[2].; NY.

17874.3 Middleton, Thomas. The ant, and the nightingale: or father Hubburds tales. [Init. T. M.] 8° in 4's. T. C[reede] f. T. Bushell, solde by J. Chorlton, 1604. Ent. to Bushell 3 ja. O.; F(imp.).HN.
    (Formerly 17881)

17874.7 — [Anr. ed., w. title:] Father Hubburds tales: or the ant, and the nightingale. [Init. T. M.] 8° in 4's. T. C[reede] f. W. Cotton, 1604. L.HAT.
    (Formerly 17880)

17875 — The blacke booke. [A satire. Init. T. M.] 4°. T. C[reede] f. J. Chorlton, 1604. Ent. 22 mr. L.O(2).O⁸.; F.HN.HD.NY.
    Title xylographic.

17876 — Blurt master-constable. Or the Spaniards night-walke. As it hath bin acted. [Anon.] 4°. [E. Allde] f. H. Rockytt, 1602. Ent. to E. Allde 7 jn. L(2).L⁶.O.E.; F(imp.).HN.BO. Greg 188.

17877 — A chast mayd in Cheape-side. A pleasant conceited comedy. 4°. f. F. Constable, 1630. Ent. 8 ap. L.L⁶.O. O⁶.E.+; F.HN.CH.HD(imp.).PML.+ Greg 433.

17878 — Civitatis amor. The cities love. An entertainment by water. 4°. N. Okes f. T. Archer, 1616. L.L⁸.A.; HN. PFOR.Y. Greg 338.

17879 — The famelie of love. Acted by the children of his maiesties revels. [Anon.] 4°. [R. Bradock] f. J. Helmes, 1608. Ent. to Helme a. J. Browne 12 oc. 1607. L(imp.).L³⁰.O.O⁶(imp.)*.; HN.ILL.PFOR.PML. Greg 263.

17879a — [A variant, w. title:] The familie of love. L(2).L⁶.C⁶.; F.HN.HD.TEX.Y.

17880 — Father Hubburds tales: or the ant, and the nightingale. 1604. Now = 17874.7.

17881 — Now = 17874.3.

17881a — [A ghost.]

17882 — A gamᵉ at chæss as it was acted. [Anon.] 4°. [London, 1625]. L.L⁶.O.O⁶.C³.; F.HN.HD.PH.Y.+ Greg 412.
    B1ʳ line 4: 'me Disciples'.

17883 — [Anr. ed.] 4°. [London, 1625?] L(2, 1 imp.).L⁶.O(lacks A1).DUL(imp.).E.; F.HD.N(imp.).NY.Y.+
    B1ʳ line 4: 'my Disciples'. Reissued w. new prelims. in 17885.

17884 — [Anr. ed.] A game at chesse as it hath bine acted. 4°. Lydden, J. Masse, [1625?] L.O.O⁶.E².ETON(lacks tp). +; F(2, 1 imp.).HN.HD.

17885 — [Anr. issue of 17883, w. new prelim. halfsheet.] A game at chesse. As it was acted. 4°. [London?] 1625. C.; HN.Y².

17885.5 — The ghost of Lucrece. [Init. T. M. Gent.] [In verse.] 8°. V. Simmes, 1600. F.

17886 — Honorable entertainments, compos'de for the service of this noble cittie. 8°. G. E[ld,] 1621. HN.

17887 — The Inner-Temple masque. Or masque of heroes. 4°. [W. Stansby] f. J. Browne, 1619. Ent. 10 jy. L(2). L⁶.O.E(3).; F.HN.HD.N.Y.+ Greg 358.

17888 — A mad world, my masters. As it hath bin lately in action. [Init. T. M.] 4°. H. B[allard] f. W. Burre, 1608. Ent. to Burre a. E. Edgar 4 oc. L(2).L⁶.L¹⁵. O.VER.; F.HN.HD.N.NY.+ Greg 276.

17889 — [Anr. ed. Init. T. M., Gent.] 4°. [J. Okes] f. J. S[pencer,] sold by J. Becket, 1640. Ass'd to J. Spencer 3 jy. 1630. L.O.C³.E.M.+; F.HN.HD.N.PML.+

— The mariage of the old and new testament. See 17904.5.

17890 — Michaelmas terme. As it hath been acted. [Anon.] 4°. [T. Purfoot a. E. Allde] f. A. J[ohnson,] 1607. Ent. to A. Johnson 15 my. L(2).L⁶.L¹⁵.O.PETWORTH.; F. HN.CH.HD.Y².+ Greg 244.

17891 — [Anr. ed.] Newly corrected. 4°. T. H[arper] f. R. Meighen, 1630. Ass'd 29 ja. L.O.C².E.M².+; F.HN. HD.N.Y².+

— The peace-maker. 1618. See 14387.

17892 — The phoenix, as it hath beene acted. [Anon.] 4°. E. A[llde] f. A, [sic] J[ohnson,] 1607. Ent. to Johnson 9 my. L(2).L⁶.O.C⁶.; F.HN.HD.NY.Y.+ Greg 243.
    HN has inserted leaf w. prologue from 17617.

17893 — [Anr. ed.] 4°. T. H[arper] f. R. Meighen, 1630. Ass'd 29 ja. L.O.C⁴.E.ETON.+; F.HN.HD.N.PML.+

— The puritane or the widdow of Watling-streete. 1607. See 21531.

17894 — Sir Robert Sherley, sent ambassadour in the name of the king of Persia, to Sigismond the third, king of Poland. His royal entertainment into Cracovia, [etc. Anon. A prose trans., w. additions, of Encomia nominis et negocii D. R. Sherlaii by A. Loeaecheus.] 4°. J. Windet f. J. Budge, 1609. Ent. 30 my. O.CHATS.; F.Y.
    Dedic. not signed. See Court-Book C, p. 443.

Middleton, Thomas—*cont.*

17894.5 — [Anr. issue, w. new cancel dedic. signed: 'T. Middleton'.] L.

17895 — The sunne in Aries. A noble solemnity at the establishment of E. Barkham, lord maior. 4°. E. All-de f. H. G[osson,] 1621. L.E.; HN. Greg 367.

17896 — A trick to catch the old-one. As it hath beene lately acted. [Anon.] 4°. G. Eld, 1608. Ent. 7 oc. 1607. L (tp only).O. Greg 262.

17896a — [Anr. issue, w. tp init.: 'T. M.'] 4°. G: [sic] E[ld,] sold by H. Rockytt, 1608. L(2).L⁶(2).O.E(lacks H4).ETON.; HN.HD(impr. torn).PFOR.TEX.Y.

17897 — [Anr. ed., w. tp signed: 'T. Midleton'.] 4°. G. Eld f. T. Langley, 1616. L.L⁶.O.O⁶.E.+; F.HN.BO.HD.Y.

17898 — The triumphs of health and prosperity. A noble solemnity at the inauguration of C. Hacket, lord maior. 4°. N. Okes, 1626. L⁸.; HN. Greg 413.

17899 — The tryumphs of honor and industry. A solemnity at establishment of G. Bowles, lord maior. [Init. T. M.] 4°. N. Okes, 1617. L.L⁸.E.; HN. Greg 351.

17900 — The triumphs of honor and vertue. A noble solemnitie, at the establishment of P. Proby, lord maior. 4°. N. Okes, 1622. L(imp.).E.; F.HN(date cropt). Greg 383.

17901 — The triumphs of integrity. A noble solemnity, at the establishment of M. Lumley, lord maior. 4°. N. Okes, 1623. HN.PML. Greg 387.

17902 — The triumphs of love and antiquity. An honourable solemnitie at the establishment of Sir W. Cockayn, lord maior. 4°. N. Okes, 1619. L.O.O¹⁴.E.LONGLEAT.; HD(lacks D1). Greg 359.

17903 — The triumphs of truth. A solemnity at the establishment of Sir T. Middleton, lord maior. 4°. N. Okes, 1613. Ent. 3 no. L.L⁸.LONGLEAT. Greg 311.

17904 — [Anr. issue, enlarged, w. title:] The triumphs [etc.] Shewing also his lordships entertainment upon Michaelmas day last. 2 pts. N. Okes, 1613. L.L⁸(pt. 2 only).O.E(2).; F.PFOR. Robert Taylor. Greg 311–2.

17904.3 — The two gates of salvation, or the mariage of the old and new testament. [Init. T. M.] 4°. N. Okes, 1609. C³.
    (Formerly 11682)

17904.5 — [Anr. issue, w. title:] The mariage of the old and new testament. 4°. [N. Okes,] 1620. L.
    (Formerly 3001) Dedic. signed: 'T. Middleton'. First halfsheet apparently pr. by G. Purslowe: McK. 311 on tp.

17904.7 — [Anr. issue, w. cancel title:] Gods parliament-house: or the marriage of the old and new testament. 4°. J. Okes, 1627. L(w. dedic. signed 'S. Collins' inserted from 5561).L⁴.O.; BALT.
    (Formerly 5560)

17905 — = 17906.

17906 — The wisdome of Solomon paraphrased. [In verse.] 4°. V. Sems [sic], 1597. L(imp.).O.O⁵(frags.).; HN.Y.

17907 — Your five gallants. As it hath beene often in action. 4°. [G. Eld] f. R. Bonian, [1608.] Ent. 22 mr. 1608. L(2).L⁶(2).O.E(2, 1 lacks tp).ETON.; HN.HD.LC(imp.). PFOR.Y². Greg 266.

— See also 6501, 17154.

17908 Middleton, Thomas, and Dekker, Thomas. The roaring girle. Or Moll Cut-purse. 4°. [N. Okes] f. T. Archer, 1611. L.L⁶.O.O⁵.E.+; F(imp.).HN.BO.PFOR. Robert Taylor.+ Greg 298.

17909 Middleton, Thomas, and Rowley, William. A courtly masque: the device called The world tost at tennis. 4°. G. Purslowe, sold by E. Wright, 1620. Ent. to Purslowe a. J. Trundle 4 jy. L. Greg 365.
    Orn. w. leaves and flowers on tp.

17910 — [Anr. issue, w. woodcut illustration on tp, w. imprint:] G. Purslowe, sold by [E. Wright,] 1620. L(2, 1 imp.). L⁶.O.O⁶.; F.HN(2).HD.LC.
    In all copies the imprint is considerably or totally cropt.

17911 — A faire quarrell. As it was acted before the king. 4°. [G. Eld] f. J. T[rundle,] sold [by E. Wright,] 1617. L.O.E.; F(impr. cropt).HN.CHI.HD.NY.+ Greg 352.

17911a — [Anr. issue, w. cancel tp:] With new additions. L⁶. ETON(imp.).; HD.
    3 leaves inserted in quire H.

17912 — [Anr. ed.] 4°. A. M[athewes] f. T. Dewe, 1622. Ass'd by J. Trundle to T. Dewe 2 se. 1621. L.L⁶.O.E.SHEF. +; F.HN.BO.HD.Y.+

17913 **Middleton, William,** *B. D.* Papisto-Mastix, or the protestants religion defended. 4°. *T. P[urfoot] f. A. Johnson,* 1606. Ent. 17 fb. L.O.C.D.M.+; F.HN.HD.

17914 **Middleton, William,** *Captain.* Bardhoniaeth, neu brydydhiaeth, y llyfr kyntaf. 4°. *T. Orwin,* 1593. O. NLW.; HN.

17915 — Psalmae y brenhinol brophwyd Dafydh. 1603. = 2744.
— *tr. See* 2742.5.

17915.5 **Midhurst.** An excellent ballad of the mercers sonne of Midhurst. (A new ballad intituled, The old mans complaint.) *Ballad.* 2 pts. s.sh.fol. *f. H. G[osson,* c. 1630.] Pt. 1 ent. to ballad ptnrs. 24 de. 1624; pt. 2 ass'd by M. Trundle to ballad ptnrs. 1 jn. 1629. C⁶(Pepys I.334, 137).

17915.7 **Midwife.** The wicked midwife, the cruell mother, and the harmelesse daughter. Or, a cruell murther committed upon a new-borne childe. *Ballad.* 2 pts. s.sh.fol. [*London,* c. 1640.] M³(imp.).

Mierbeck, Tobias. Theses physicae de generatione et corruptione. [1600.] *See* 21555.5.

17916 **Mihil Mumchance.** Mihil Mumchance, his discouerie of the art of cheating in false dyce play. 4°. *J. Danter, sold by W. Jones,* 1597. Ent. to Danter 22 au. O(date cropt).; F.HN.
Largely reprinted from 24961.

17916.3 **Milan.** Newes from Millaine. The copie of a letter written from Millaine to Venice, by Signior Padre, concerning prince Mammon. *Tr.* out of the Italian copie. Also, the abridgment of the articles of pacification of Italie. 4°. [*Eliz. Alldle*] *f. N. Butter,* 1630. L.
1st pt. reprinted in 17916.5.

17916.5 — Newes from Millaine and Spaine. The copy of a letter . . . by Signior Padre. A proclamation made . . . for the apprehending of all sent out of Millaine, [etc.] *Tr.* out of the Spanish copy. 4°. [*N. Okes*] *f. N. Butter a. N. Bourne,* 1630. HD.
1st pt. reprinted from 17916.3; 2nd pt. reprinted from 17916.7.

17916.7 — A proclamation made in the name of his majesty of Spaine, for the apprehending of all sent out of Millane by prince Mammon. A letter written from S. Lucas. *Tr.* out of the Spanish. 4°. [*W. Jones*] *f. N. Butter a. N. Bourne,* 1630. HD.
Reprinted in 17916.5.

17916.9 — [Anr. issue, w. a 2nd pt. (Newsbooks 207) linked on tp:] A proclamation [etc.] Novem. 18 Num. 17 Allso the continuation of our newes [etc.] [*W. Jones*] *f. N. Butter a. N. Bourne,* 1630. F.

17917 **Milborne, Richard.** Concerning imposition of hands. A sermon. 8°. (*J. W[indet]*) *f. M. Law,* (1607.) O. C¹⁰.LINC.WOR.; F.U.
Tp line 5: 'Motropolital [*sic*]'; a corrected tp pr. as D4 w. 'Metropolitical'.

17918 **Milbourne, William.** Sapientia clamitans, wisdome crying out to sinners. 8°. *J. Haviland f. R. Milbourne,* 1638. Ent. 12 de. 1637. O.O⁸.C.C².WI.+; F(imp.).HN.
Contains 2 sermons by T. Jackson, Dean of Peterborough, and 1 by J. Donne, edited by W. Milbourne. Keynes 28.

17918.5 — [Anr. issue, w. imprint:] *J. Haviland, sold by J. Colby,* 1638. DUL.; PN².

17919 — [Anr. issue, w. cancel tp:] Wisdome crying out to sinners. [Anon.] *M. P[arsons] f. J. Stafford,* 1639. L³.C.C².CARLISLE.; U.
Keynes 28a.

17920 — [Anr. issue, w. date:] 1640. L².C³.C⁹.

Mildapettus, Franciscus, *pseud. See* 23872.

Mildmay, Humphrey, *tr. See* 7263.

Miles. Miles christianus. 1590. *See* 21238.

17920.5 **Miles, James.** Brevis cathechismus pro hereticis Anglicis, Scotis, & alijs ad fidem captolicam [*sic*], & apostolicam reductis. Ex romano cathechismo Latino in Anglicum idioma confectus. *Lat. a. Eng.* 8°. *Neapoli, ap. O. Beltranum,* 1635. L(imp.).

Military Art. The military art of trayning. 1622. *See* 794.

17921 **Mill, Humphrey.** A nights search. Discovering the nature of all sorts of night-walkers. Digested into a poeme. 8°. *R. Bishop f. L. Blaicklock,* 1640. Ent. 24 fb. L.O(2).O⁶.; F.HN.HD.N.PML.+
A 2nd pt. appeared in 1646 as Wing M 2058.

17922 — Poems occasioned by a melancholy vision. 8°. *J. D(awson) f. L. Blaikelocke,* 1639. Ent. 27 no. 1638. L(3).L⁴.O.C(imp.).; F.HN.HD.N.PML.+

17923 **Mill, Tom.** O yes, O yes; I do cry. [A political satire in verse.] s.sh.fol. *Printed new at Pomadie,* [1639.] L. L¹¹(S.P.D., Chas. I Add., vol. 538, doc. 140).

17923.5 **Miller, William.** A sermon preached at the funerall of G. Davies esquire. 4°. *F. Kyngston,* 1621. Ent. to M. Sparke 20 no. 1620. L.O.BIRM²(K.N.).; F.

17924 **Milles, Robert.** Abrahams suite for Sodome. A sermon. 8°. *W. Stansby f. M. Lawe,* 1612. L.C.C².

17924.5 — [Anr. ed., w. title:] Abrahams sute [etc.] 8°. *W. Hall f. M. Lawe,* 1612. L⁴.O.; HD.

17925 **Milles, Thomas.** [Heading:] An abridgement of the customers apologie [17928], to be read more at large in Thesaurario Bodleyano. [Anon.] fol. [*W. Jaggard?* 1613?] L(lacks tp).
Expanded in 17930; part of that text from same setting.

17925.5 — [Heading:] Acroamata. Or serious observations, . . . upon sections, of [17927]. Concerning bullion, money, and exchange at free-staples. fol. [*W. Jaggard,* 1609?] O.

17926 — The catalogue of honor or tresury of true nobility peculiar to Great Britaine. fol. *W. Jaggard,* 1610. L.O. C.D².E.+; F.HN.HD.N.NY.+
Includes a trans. of 11922. 22008 intended to be issued w. some copies of this. *See also* 22824.7.

17927 — The custumers alphabet and primer. Conteining, their creede. Their ten commandmentes, [etc.] fol. [*W. Jaggard?*] 1608. L.L².O.O⁵.; HN.CU.

17928 — The custumers apology. That is to say, a generall answere to informers of all sortes. [Anon.] fol. [*J. Roberts,* 1599.] L¹¹.O.HAT.; HN.HD(imp.).
Only 50 copies were printed. All copies have author's signature; most copies dated by hand '1599.' Abridged in 17925, 17931.

17929 — = 17928.

17930 — The custumers apologie. To be read more at large [etc.] fol. [*W. Jaggard?* 1613?] L.; CU.
An expansion of 17925; part of text from same typesetting.

17931 — An abstract, almost verbatim (with some necessarie additions) of the customers apologie [17928], written 18. yeares ago. fol. [*W. Jaggard?* 1617?] L.; CU.

17932 — The customers replie. Or second apologie. fol. *J. Roberts,* 1604. Ent. 12 fb. L.L³⁰(imp.).O.; HN.HD.Y.
Answer to 25330.

17933 — The mistery of iniquity. Discovered in these acroamaticall lessons, shewing the ascension or descention of summum bonum, and summa miseria. fol. [*W. Jaggard?* 1609?] L.O.C².; HN.
L tp dated 1609 in MS.

17934 — The misterie of iniquitie. Plainely layd open by a lay-christian. fol. [*W. Jaggard,*] 1610. L.L².O¹⁴.D.; F.HN. CU(2).HD.Y.
Date altered in MS. to 1611.

— Nobilitas politica vel civilis. 1608. *See* 11922.

17935 — An out-port-customers accompt, of all his receipts. fol. [*W. Jaggard,* 1612?] L.L².O.; HN.CU.

17936 — The treasurie of auncient and moderne times. *Tr.* out of P. Mexio and F. Sansovino, [etc.] [Anon.] fol. *W. Jaggard,* 1613. L.O.C.D.E.+; F.HN.HD.N.NY.+
Vol. 2 now = 17936.5.

17936.5 — [A 2nd vol.] Αρχαιο-πλουτος. Containing, ten following bookes to the former. *Tr.* out of P. Mexia [etc. Anon.] fol. *W. Jaggard,* 1619. L.O.C.D.E².+; F.HN.HD.N.NY.+
(Formerly pt. of 17936) Engr. tp: 'Times storehouse'. Includes a trans. of 11922.

— *ed. See* 11922.

Mills, Francis, *ed. See* 15000, 15003.

17937 **Milton, John.** A maske [Comus] presented at Ludlow castle, 1634. [Anon.] 4°. [*A. Mathewes*] *f. H. Robinson,* 1637. L.L⁶.O.C².M.+; HN.HD.ILL.NY.Y².+ Greg 524.
Dedic. signed 'H. Lawes.' 23 copies can now be located.

Milton, John—*cont.*
— Epitaphium Damonis. [1639?] *See* 6218.
— Lycidas. 1638. *See* 14964.

17938 **Milton, Richard.** Londoners their entertainment in the countrie. 1604. Now = 19807.7.

17939 — Londons miserie, the countryes crueltie: with Gods mercie. [In verse.] 4°. *N. Okes*, 1625. L.

17940 **Milton, Thomas.** A note of the headlands of England. [1605.] = 10019.

17941 **Milward, Matthias.** The sword-bearer, or, magistrates charge. A sermon. 1641. = Wing M 2187.

17942 **Milwarde, John.** Jacobs great day of trouble, and deliverance. A sermon. 4°. [*W. Stansby*] *f. E. Edgar*, 1610. Ent. 26 oc. 1609. L.L¹⁵.O.C.DUR³.+; F.HN. CAL².HD.LC.

Mimi Publiani. *See* 4841.5, 10437, 20482.5.

17943 **Minadoi, Giovanni Tommaso.** The history of the warres betweene the Turkes and the Persians. *Tr.* A. Hartwell. 4°. [*J. Windet f.*] *J. Wolfe*, 1595. Ent. 28 my. 1589. L.O.C.D.P.+; F.HN.BO.N.Y.+

Mind. The mindes melodie. 1605. *See* 18051.

Minerva. Corona Minervæ. 1635. *See* 15100.
— A revelation of the true Minerva. 1582. *See* 3132.

Ministers. Reasons why the surplice, . . . should not be pressed upon ministers. [c. 1610.] *See* 20792.7.

17944 **Minsheu, John.** Ἡγεμὼν εἰς τὰς γλώσσας. id est, ductor in linguas, the guide into tongues. In undecim linguis. (Vocabularium hispanicolatinum. . . . A most copious Spanish dictionarie.) 2 pts. fol. [*W. Stansby a. M. Bradwood*] *at the charges of J. Minsheu published and printed, sold at J. Brownes shop*, 1617. L.O.C.D.E.+; F.HN.HD.N.NY.+
(Pt. 2 formerly 17949) Imprint on sub tp 'ap. J. Browne' (o²,o⁶,o¹⁸), sometimes left blank, and sometimes filled in by pen (last two both at HD). In some copies individual dedics. are inserted: to E. of Southampton, Sir H. Montagu, T. Wilbraham (all L³⁸), G. Carew (HD). *See* 17947.5.

17944a — [A leaf inserted in 17944, entitled:] A catalogue and true note of the names of such persons which . . . have receaved the Etymologicall dictionary. 1/2 sh. fol. *at Mr.* [*J.*] *Brownes a Booke-binder in Little-Brittaine without Aldersgate,* [1617–20.]
The variants given below are distinguished by the name ending the list. For nos. 3, 7, 9, the type was completely reset; at least nos. 3–6 were printed by E. Allde. *See Joseph Quincy Adams Memorial Studies,* pp. 755–73.
  1 Sir J. Deckham. L³⁸.
  2 Mr. C. Chibborne. L³⁸.
  3 Sir J. Franckline. O.; N. Sexton.
  4 Mr. P. Grevill. L³⁸.
  5 Mr. E. Smith. o⁹.c.
  5A Sir H. Carey. o²,o³,o¹²,o¹³,o¹⁴.
  6 Sir T. Metham. o.o⁵,o⁸,o¹¹,E².+; HD.
  7 The Lo: Mountjoy. L.L⁸.L³⁸.O(J).o⁶.+; COR. ROS.V. Sexton.
  7A Sir R. Hare. o³.
  8 Edw. L. Fitzwarren. F.ROS.
  9 Mr. Welles. L.L³⁸.o¹⁰.c(Bury deposit).STD.+; F.HN.BOWDOIN.HD.NY.+
  10 Sir R. Tichborne. L.L³⁸. Stevens Cox.; F(2). ILL.

17945 — [Anr. ed. of pt. 1 of 17944.] Minshaei emendatio, vel à mendis expurgatio, sui Ductoris in linguas. In nine languages. By the industrie, and at the charges of J. Minsheu published and printed. 22°. July, anno 1625. The second edition. fol. *J. Haviland,* 1625. L.L³⁰.O.C¹⁷.NEK.+; HN.HD(3).ILL.
A leaf of advts. without impr., entitled: 'A few words and matters of a multitude [etc.]' appears in 1 F copy. *See Court-Book C,* p. 165.

17945.5 — [Anr. issue, w. imprint:] *sold at J. Brownes shop,* 1625 (22 jy.) E.M².NLW(St. Asaph).; F.BALT.HD.

17946 — [Anr. issue, w. imprint:] *J. Haviland,* 1626. L.L⁴⁴.O. O¹⁹.C.+; CAL.ILL.NY⁵.PH.PN.+

17947 — [Anr. issue, w. imprint:] *J. Haviland,* 1627. Ent. to B. Fisher 27 ap. 1635. L.O.C.D.E.+; F.HN.HD.N.Y.+

Minsheu, John—*cont.*

17947.5 — Glosson-etymologicon. (Id est) the etymologie of tongues, or a most ample dictionary etymologicall. [2-leaf prospectus for 17944.] fol. [*London,* 1611?] O(J).
Minsheu's patent for printing 17944 was granted under the title as given above; *see* Greg, *Companion,* p. 157.

17948 — Pleasant and delightfull dialogues in Spanish and English. 1623. = pt. of 19621.

17949 — = pt. 2 of 17944.
— *See also* 19620, 19622.

17950 **Minucius Felix, Marcus.** M. Minucii Felicis Octavius. 12°. *Oxoniæ,* [*W. Turner,*] *imp. T. Huggins, & H. Curteyn,* 1627. L.O.D².EX.PLUME.+; F.HN.HD.ILL.Y.

17951 — [Anr. ed.] 12°. *Oxoniæ, G. Turner, imp. T. Huggins,* 1631. L.O.O³⁸.C¹⁵.M².; F.HD.Y.

17952 — [Anr. ed.] 12°. *Oxonii, G. Turner,* 1636. L.O.C.CASHEL. DUR⁵.+; F.PH.Y.

17953 — [A trans.] Minucius Felix his dialogne [*sic*] called Octavius. *Tr.* R. James. 12°. *Oxford, L. Lichfield f. T. Huggins,* 1636. L.O.C.DUR⁵.M².+; F.HN.HD.N.Y.+

Miracles. [   ] dyuerse my⟨racles⟩ in Hay⟨les.⟩ [c. 1515.] *See* 12973.5.
— Miracles lately wrought . . . at Mont-aigu. 1606. *See* 18746.

17954 **Mirandula, Octavian.** Illustrium poetarum flores: per O. Mirandulam collecti. 16° in 8's. *ex typ. T. Creed,* 1598. Ent. 13 fb. L.L⁴⁴.; F(lacks tp).HD(imp.).

17955 — [Anr. ed.] Poetarum illustrium flores. . . . Nunc repurgati, a T. Pulmanno Craneburgio. 16° in 8's. [*T. Creede,*] *imp. A. Johnson,* 1611. O.C.D.; HN.ILL.

17956 **Mirandula, Scipio.** Cynthia coronata seu serenissima Maria Austriaca Carolo cincta. [*Printed abroad,* 1623?]
Not an STC book.

17957 **Mirk, John.** [Liber festivalis and Quatuor sermones.] [a2ʳ:] tHis day is callyd [etc. Anon.] 2 pts. fol. (*west-mynster, w. Caxton,* 1483 (30 jn.)) L.L².O(imp.). M(imp.).STU.+; HN. Duff 298–99.
The Quatuor sermones are found in two typesettings: a1ʳ heading: 'book'; d5ʳ line 3 ends 'cum cete' (L²,O⁸,M) or 'booc' and 'cum ce' (L,O,STU,HN). For further distinctions *see Essays in Honour of Victor Scholderer,* pp. 407–25.

17958 — [Anr. ed. from anr. MS. of pt. 1 only. [-]1ᵛ:] The helpe & the g̅ce [etc. z3ʳ:] (Here endith the boke that is callid festiuall.) fol. [*Oxford, T. Rood a. T. Hunte,*] (1486 (the day aftir seint Edward the kyng [14 oc.])) L(1 leaf, Harl. 5919/139). L².O(2 imp.).c(frag.). M(lacks 1st 2 leaves).+ Duff 300.

17959 — [Anr. ed. of both pts. a2ʳ:] The helpe and grace [etc.] 2 pts. fol. [*Westminster, W.*] (Caxton,) [1491.] L(imp.).O(pt. 1 only, imp.).c(imp.).M(imp.).; HN. PFOR(pt. 1 only, imp.).PML(pt. 2 only). Gordan (imp.). Duff 301–02.
Reprints text of 17957.

17960 — [Anr. ed.] 2 pts. fol. (*R. Pynson,*) [1493.] C(pt. 2 only). c6(lacks 3 leaves). Duff 303–04.
Pt. 1 ends on n4.

17961 — [Anr. ed., w. 10 leaves added to pt. 1.] 2 pts. fol. (*R. Pynson,*) [1493.] C(pt. 1, imp.).D. Duff 305–06.
Pt. 1 ends on p4.

17962 — [Anr. ed.] 2 pts. 4° in 8's. (*in westmonesterio,* [*W. de Worde,*] 1493 (1494.)) L.O.C².C⁴.; PML. Duff 307–08.
All copies imp.

17963 — [Anr. ed.] Incipit liber qui vocatur festialis. 2 pts. 4° in 8's. [Col. to pt. 1:] *Rothomagi,* 1495 (4 fb.) [Col. to pt. 2:] *J. rauynell.* L.O(fol. 201 only).C⁴(imp.). Duff 309–10.

17963.5 — [A variant, w. col. to pt. 1:] *J. rauynell.* L(imp.).

17964 — [Anr. ed.] De nouo correctus et impressus. 4° in 8's. (*in celeb. vrbe Parisiensi, per w. hopyl,* [*i*]*mp. N. Comitis,* 1495 (26 fb.)) L(2, 1 imp.).O(2, 1 imp.). Duff 311.

17965 — [Anr. ed.] Incipit liber (qui Festialis appellatur) [*sic*]. 2 pts. 4° in 8's. (*in Westmonasterio,* [*W. de Worde,*] 1496.) L(pt. 1 only, lacks tp). O(imp.).C².M(imp.).; MEL(col. only). Duff 312–13.

17966 — [Anr. ed.] Incipit liber qui vocatur festiualis. 4° in 8's. *rothom̄* [*Rouen,*] (*per M. Morin, imp. J. Richardi,* 1499 (22 jn.)) L(imp.).O.C(imp.).SAU.; Y. Duff 314.

Mirk, John—*cont.*

17966.5 — [Anr. ed.] 2 pts. 4° in 8's. (*R. Pynson*, 1499 (6 jy.)) L(imp.).O(imp.). Broxbourne(E, imp.). Duff 315–16.

17967 — [Anr. ed.] Incipit liber qui Festialis appellatur. 2 pts. 4° in 8's. (*in Westmonasterio*, [*W. de Worde*,] 1499.) L(imp.).O(pt. 1, imp.).M(pt. 1, imp.).; N(imp.). Duff 317–18.

17968 — [Anr. ed.] 2 pts. 4° in 8's. (*ap. westmonasterium, p̄ J. notarii*, 1499 (2 ja.)) L(imp.).C(imp.).; LC. Duff 319–20.

17969 — [Anr. ed.] Incipit liber qui vocatur ffestiualis. 2 pts. 4° in 8's. (*per R. Pinsone*, 1502 (10 jy.)) L(imp.). O(2, imp.).; MEL(col. only).

17970 — [Anr. ed.] Incipit liber qui vocatur festiualis. 2 pts. 4° in 8's. (*J. Notary*,) [1506?] L(imp.).O(pt. 1 only). P(imp.).PLUME.

17970.5 — [Anr. ed.] 4° 6.4. [*R. Pynson*, 1507?] O(q1–5 only, bd. in 17972).OS(imp.). Lord Kenyon(1 leaf).
2 cols., 31 lines a page. The cuts are in the same state as 21430 sq.

17971 — [Anr. ed.] The festyuall. 4° 8.4. (*W. de worde*, 1508 (11 my.)) C(imp.).C³(lacks Ll 4).; LC.

17971.5 — [Anr. ed.] 4° 8.4 (*w. de worde*, 1511 (1 au.)) O⁴(imp.).M.

17972 — [Anr. ed.] 4° 8.4. (*w. de worde*, 1515 (5 my.)) O(2 imp.). O³(imp.).YK(imp.).

17973 — [Anr. ed.] Here begynneth the festyuall. 4° 8.4. (*R. Faques*,) [c. 1512.] L².O(imp.).

17973.5 — [Anr. ed.] 4° 8.4 (*w. de worde*, 1519 (5 my.)) HN.

17974 — [Anr. ed.] The festyuall. 4° 8.4. (*W. de worde*, 1528 (5 no.)) L.L²³.O.

17975 — [Anr. ed.] 4° 8.4. (*W. de Worde*, 1532 (23 oc.)) O.C².; HART²(imp.).

17976 **Miroir.** Le myrouer de verite. 1532. Now = 11919.5.

17977 **Miropsius, Nicolaus,** called **Prepositus.** Prepositas [*sic*] his practise, a worke very necessary. 1588. Now = 20180.7.

17978 = frag. of 17027.

Mirror. A myrrour for English souldiers. 1595. See 10418.
— A myrroure for magistrates. [1559.] See 1247.
— The first parte of the Mirour for magistrates. 1574. See 13443.
— The seconde part of the Mirrour for magistrates. 1578. See 3131.
— A mirrour for murtherers. [1633.] See 10581.5.

17978.5 — [Heading B1ʳ:] The mirrour of complements. 8°. [*T. Harper*, 1634.] Ent. to Harper 2 ap. 1634. HN(imp.).

17979 — [Anr. ed., enlarged.] The mirrour of complements. Or: a pleasant academy. 12°. *T. Harper, sold by L. Chapman*, 1635. L.

17979.3 — [Anr. ed.] The mirrour of complements. Or: a manuell of choice . . . ceremonies. The third edition. 12°. *T. Harper, sold by L. Chapman*, 1637. Y(imp.).

17979.5 — Here foloweth the maner of good & salutary lyuynge for euery mā & womā called the muroure [*sic*] of conscyence. 8°. [*York, U. Mylner*, 1517?] L(1st leaf only, C.18.e.2/113*).

17979.7 — The mirrour of friendship: both how to knowe a perfect friend, and how to choose him. *Tr.* out of Italian by T. Breme. (An excellent aduertisement . . . not to trust fortune. Collected by. I. B.) 8°. *A. Jeffes (a. W. Dickenson,)* 1584. Ent. 28 au. HN.
— The mirroure of golde for the synfull soule. [1506?] See 6894.5.

17980 — The mirrour of madnes, or a paradoxe maintayning madnes to be most excellent. *Tr.* J. San[ford,] gent. 8°. *T. Marshe*, 1576. Ass'd by Marsh to T. Orwin 23 jn. 1591. L².O.
— Mirror of mans lyfe. 1576. See 14092.

17981 — Mirror of new reformation. 1634. Now = 3605.7.
— The myrroure of oure lady. 1530. See 17542.
— The mirrour of policie. 1598. See 15228.

17981.5 — A mirrour of presence, or a miscellany. Whereby the popish transubstantiation, and the Lutheran [*sic*] consubstantiation are touched. Lastly, extraordinary astronomicall observations of some stars and comets. 8°. [*The Netherlands?* 1638?] E.
— The mirrour of princely deedes. [1578.] See 18859.
— The myrrour of the worlde. [1481.] See 24762.

17982 — A myrrour or glasse for them that be syke. [1536?] Now = 11470.5.
— A mirour or glasse to know thy selfe. [1536?] See 11390.
— A mirrour to all that loue to follow the warres. 1589. See 1041.7.

Mirror—*cont.*
— A mirrour to confesse well. [1604.] = 1st bk. of 14568.3.
— This is the myrour or glasse of helthe. [bef. 1531.] See 18214a.
— A trewe mirrour or glase. 1556. See 21777.
— A worthy myrrour, wherin ye may marke, an excellent discourse of a breeding larke. 1589. See 3411.

Mirth. Mirth in mourning. [1625.] See 14426.3.

Misacmos, *pseud.* See 12779.

Mis-Amaxius, *pseud.* See 19501.

17983 **Miserere.** Miserere mei domine. A thought upon the latter day. Whereunto are annexed, Of the time before Christs comming . . . five hymnes. [In verse.] 12°. R. Y[oung] f. P. Nevill, 1638. Ent. to Young 18 ap. L.C².

17983.5 — [Anr. issue, w. imprint on gen. tp:] *R. Young*, 1638. O.

Misodiaboles, *pseud.* See 12782.

17984 **Misophonus,** *pseud.* De caede et interitu Gallorum regis, Henrici tertii, epigrammata. 1589. = 13099.

Missa, *Maystres.* See 17137.

17985 **Misselden, Edward.** The circle of commerce. Or the ballance of trade, in defence of free trade. 4°. *J. Dawson f. N. Bourne*, 1623. Ent. 20 my. L.O.C.D.E.+; F.CU.HD.MICH.Y.+
Answered in 17221.

17986 — Free trade. Or, the meanes to make trade florish. 8°. *J. Legatt f. S. Waterson*, 1622. Ent. 15 jn. L².O³.C. D².M².+; HD(lacks K4).
Answered in 17226.

17987 — Second edition with some addition. 8°. *J. Legatt f. S. Waterson*, 1622. L.O.C.D².DUR⁵.+; F.CHI.CU.HD.Y.+

Mitchell, S., *ed.* See 3921.5, 3925.

17988 **Mitchil, Jonathan.** A discourse of the glory to which God hath called believers. 1677. = Wing M 2289.

Mo., Tho. The boke of the fayre gentylwoman. [c. 1540.] See 18078.5.

Mocenigo, Giovanni, *Doge of Venice.* See 22588.

17989 **Mock-beggar Hall.** The map of Mock-beggar hall, with his scituation in the spacious countrey, called, Anywhere. *Ballad.* 2 pts. s.sh.fol. f. *R. Harper*, [1635?] L.
Line 1 of text begins: 'I reade in ancient times . . .' = line 25 of 17990.

17990 — [Anr. version, w. title:] Mock-beggers hall, [etc.] 2 pts. s.sh.fol. f. *R. Harper*, [1640?] L.
Line 1 of text begins: 'In ancient times when as . . .'; on verso of L is printed Wing C 7280.

Mocket, Richard. Deus & Rex. 1615. See 14415.

17991 —Doctrina et politia ecclesiæ anglicanæ. [Anon.] 4° in 8's. *ap. J. Billium*, 1616. Ent. 17 jn. L.L¹³.C⁸.D.D². *See Court-Book C*, p. 86. Includes Mocket's Latin trans. of the Prayer Book (cf. 16423) and reprints of 14581, 18712.

17992 — [Anr. issue, w. quires A, V–Z reset, dated:] 1617. L.O. C.D.E².+; F.HN.NY¹¹.U.Y.+

Modus. Modus tenendi curiam baronum. [c. 1500.] See 7705.7.
— Modus tenendi unum hundredum. [1520?] See 7726.

17993 **Moffett, Thomas.** Insectorum sive minimorum animalium theatrum: olim ab E. Wottono. [etc.] inchoatum. [*Ed.*] (T. de Mayerne.) fol. *ex off. T. Cotes et venales ap. B. Allen*, 1634. Ent. to T. a. R. Cotes 12 de. 1633. L.O³(E).G².M².P.+; CAL².HD.MICH.NY⁴. WASH².+
Regarding a tp engraved by W. Rogers c. 1604, when publication was originally planned, *see* Hind I.276–7.

17993a — [A variant, w. imprint:] *ex off. T. Cotes et venales ap. G. Hope*, 1634. L.O.C².D.E².+; F.HN.HD.KAN.NY.+

17993b — [A variant, w. imprint:] *ex off. T. Cotes*, 1634. L¹⁶. L³⁸.O.D.E.+; F.CAL².ILL.MIN.NY.+

17994 — The silkewormes, and their flies. [Init. T. M. a countrie farmar. In verse.] 4°. V. S[immes] f. N. Ling, 1599. L.L⁶.O.C³.E².+; F.HN.BO.CHI.Y.+

17994.5 **Mohammed**, *the prophet*. Here after foloweth a lytell treatyse agaynst Mahumet and his cursed secte. 8°. (*Southwarke, P. Treuerys,*) [c. 1530.] USHAW.; HD.

17995 — Mohammedis imposturæ: that is, a discovery of the manifold forgeries, of the blasphemous seducer Mohammed. Written in Arabicke, *tr.* W. Bedwell. Whereunto is annexed the Arabian Trudgman. 4°. *R. Field,* 1615. Ent. 16 ja. L.O.C.D.E.+; F(2).HN. HD(2).PH.Y.
(2nd pt. formerly 1072)

17995.5 — [Anr. issue, w. cancel tp:] Mahomet unmasked. Or a discoverie [etc.] *f. T. Dewe,* 1624. L³⁸.O³.C⁵.; IND. U(imp.).

17996 **Mohammed II**, *Sultan*. The Turkes secretorie, conteining his sundrie letters to divers emperours. *Tr.* out of the Latine copie [of Laudivius, *da Vezzano.*] 4°. *M. B[radwood,] solde [by C. Burby,]* 1607. Ent. to E. Edgar 16 ja. L.L³⁸.C(lacks tp).D².DUR⁵.+; F.HN. HD(imp.).
Dedic. signed 'M. Hermann.'

17997 **Mohammedan History**. The Mahumetane or Turkish historie. *Tr.* R. Carr. 4°. *T. Este,* 1600. Ent. 29 my. L.L³⁸.O.C.P.+; F.HN.ILL.TEX.Y.

17998 **Molina, Antonio de.** Spiritual exercises, very profitable for active persons desirous of their salvation. *Tr.* by (E. A.) of the house of Shene. 12°. *Mechlin, H. Jaey,* 1621. L⁹.
A&R 545.

17999 — [Anr. issue, w. date:] 1623. L.
A&R 546.

18000 — A treatise of mental prayer. [*Tr.* J. Sweetnam.] Whereunto is adjoined a treatise of exhortation to spirituall profit. Written by F. Francis Arias. [*Tr.* T. Everard.] 12°. [*St. Omer, English College Press,*] 1617. L.O. USHAW. Manresa College, Roehampton.; F.HN.HD.Y.
A&R 829.

18001 — A treatise of the holy sacrifice of the masse. *Tr.* I. R. [i.e. J. Floyd.] 16° in 8's. [*St. Omer, English College Press,*] 1623. L.AUG.DE.HP. Rogers(imp.).
A&R 547.

Molineus, Petrus. *See* Du Moulin, P.

18002 **Molinier, Etienne.** Essayes: or, morall and politicall discourses. 1636. Now = 18003.1.

18003 — A mirrour for christian states. *Tr.* W. Tyrwhit. 4°. *T. Harper,* 1635. Ent. to Parker [Harper?] 18 jy. 1634. L.O.C.D.E.+; F.HN.HD.N.NY.+

18003.1 — [Anr. issue, w. 1st sheet reprinted, w. title:] Essayes: or, morall and politicall discourses. [*T. Harper*]*f. W. Sheares,* 1636. L.O.C⁵.D.E².+; F.HD.LC.N.Y.+
(Formerly 18002)

Molle, Emer. *See* 18003.7.

Molle, John, *tr. See* 4528, 18162.

18003.3 **Molyneux, Emery.** [The gores for the celestial globe, designed by Molyneux and engr. by J. Hondius.] *sumptibus G. Sanderson,* 1592. L²⁵. Kassel, Hessisches Landesmuseum. Nürnberg, Nationalmuseum.
This and the following are discussed in 3146, 13698, 13906. *See also* Hind I.168–73.

18003.4 — [The gores for the terrestrial globe, designed by Molyneux and engr. by J. Hondius.] *sumptibus G. Sanders,* 1592. PETWORTH.

18003.5 — [Anr. issue, w. date:] 1603. L²⁵. Nürnberg, Nationalmuseum.

18003.7 — The mariners compasse: By which hee sayleth to all yᵉ parts of the world this being set upon a needle touch'd with a loadstone. s.sh.fol. *T. Jenner,* 1623. L⁵(Lemon 207).
Signed: 'Emer. Molle.' Engraving intended for mounting on a needle; *see* Hind I.169n.

18003.9 **Mompesson, Sir Giles.** The description of Giles Mompesson late knight censured by parliament the 17th of March A° 1620. s.sh.fol. [*London,* 1620.] L(Print Dept.).L⁵(Lemon 182).; F.
See 8659, 8661. Engraving of figures in 3 panels w. verses; *see* Hind II.396.

18004 **Monacius, Janus Julius.** Tres excellente, & nouelle description contre la peste. Premierement, vn poeme nouueau, fait sur l'origine de la roine, auec quelques autres euures poetiques. *Lat. a. Fr.* 8°. *T. Purfoot,* [1570?] L.L¹⁶.

18005 **Monardes, Nicolas.** The three bookes written in the Spanishe tonge. *Tr.* J. Frampton. 4°. [*J. Kingston f.*] *W. Norton,* 1577. L.A.; F(lacks Ee2).NY(lacks Ee2). F copy includes tp to 18005a, and Ee2–Zz2 of 18006.5.

18005a — [Anr. issue, w. cancel tp, entitled:] Ioyfull newes out of the newe founde worlde. L.O(2).C.C¹⁵.M.; F.HN. BO.NY.WIS.+

18006 — [Anr. ed.] Newly corrected. Whereunto are added three other bookes of the bezaar stone, [etc.] 4°. (*T. Dawson f.*) *W. Norton,* 1580. L.L¹⁹.C².M.ST.; F.HN. BO.N.NY.+
Ss3ᵛ catchword: 'the'.

18006.5 — [Anr. issue, corrected, w. Ss3ᵛ ending: 'The end of the Dialogue of Yron.'] L.O.O⁵.C.DUL(imp.).+; F(imp.). CB(imp.).HD(imp.).HUNT.NY.+

18007 — [Anr. ed.] 4°. *E. Allde, by the assigne of B. Norton,* 1596. L.O.C.D.E.+; F.HN.HD.ILL.NY.+

18008 **Monday.** Mondayes worke. Or, the two honest neigbours [*sic*] both birds of a feather. *Ballad.* 2 pts. s.sh.fol. *f. F. Grove,* [1632.] Ent. 16 jy. 1632. L.
Possibly by the author of 13843.

18009 **Money.** Money is my master: yet once it was a servant unto mee. *Ballad.* 2 pts. s.sh.fol. *f. F. Coules,* [1635?] L.

18010 **Moneymonger.** The money monger. Or, the usurers almanacke. 1626. Now = 24209.5.

Monfart, Henri de. *See* 10840.

18011 **Monginot, François.** A resolution of doubts. Or a summarie decision of controversies betwixt the reformed church and the romaine. (*Tr.* R. C[oxe.]) 4°. *B. Alsop f. G. Norton,* 1618. Ent. 9 jy. L(imp.).O.C.E². P.+; F.U.
Ent. as tr. by 'Coxe'; may be Roger Cocks, scholar of Trinity College, Cambridge, 1611.

18012 — [Anr. trans.] A resolution of doubts: or, a summary, deciding of controversies betweene the reformed and the romish churches. *Tr.* S. Williams. 8°. *E. Griffin,* 1620. L³⁰.O.C.; F.

18013 **Monings, Edward.** The landgraue of Hessen his princelie receiuing of her maiesties embassador. [H. Clinton, 2nd earl of Lincoln.] 4°. *R. Robinson,* 1596. Ent. 26 oc. L.O¹¹(frag.).; HN.

18014 **Monipennie, John.** The abridgement or summarie of the Scots chronicles. (A short description of the westerne iles of Scotland.) 2 pts. 4°. [*W. Stansby f.*] *J. Budge,* 1612. [Col. to pt. 2:] (*S. Stafford.*) Ent. to Stafford 14 au. L.O.E.M².PARIS.+; F(pt. 1 only).HN (pt. 1 only).HD.ILL.PML.
On tp: 'Monipennie'; title ends: 'generall, with a memoriall of . . . things in Scotland.' In some copies (L,M²,HD) date altered in ink to 1614.

18014.5 — [Anr. issue of pt. 1 only, w. cancel tp w. 'Monnipennie' and title ending: 'generall.'] *J. Budge,* 1612. O⁷.D.E.M.

18014a — [Anr. ed.] 8°. *S. Stafford,* 1612. O.E(2).G².LINC.STU.; F.ILL.
This and 18015 sq. include the 'Description'.

18015 — [Anr. ed.] Latelie corrected. [Init. J. M.] 8°. *Edinburgh, J. W[reittoun] f. J. Wood,* 1633. L.O.C.E.SHEF.+; F. HN.HD.N.NY.+

18015.5 — [Anr. issue, w. imprint:] *Edinburgh, J. Wreittoun,* 1633. O.E(2).G².M⁴.

18016 — Certaine matters composed together. [Anon.] 4°. *Edinburgh, R. Walde-graue,* [1594?] L.L¹⁶(lacks tp). O.C(lacks tp).E.+; HN.
The last date in the text (on E1ᵛ) is 1593.

18017 — [Anr. ed.] Certayne matters concerning the realme of Scotland, composed together. 1597. 4°. [*S. Stafford*] *f. J. Flasket,* 1603. Ent. 2 ap. L.O.C.D².E.+; F.HN. HD.N.PML.+

18018 — [Anr. ed.] 4°. *A. Hatfield f. J. Flasket,* 1603. L.O.C. DUR⁵.E.+; F(2).HN.CAL.CHI.LC.

18019 — A christian almanacke. Needefull and true. Written by J. M[onipennie.] 8°. [*W. Stansby*] *f. J. Budge,* 1612. Ent. 2 jy. 1611. L.O.

18020 **Monlas, John.** Quadrivium Sionis or the foure wayes to Sion. 4°. *A. Mathewes,* 1633. Ent. 14 au. 1632. L. L⁴.O.O²²(lacks tp).P.; PN².

18021 **Monmouthshire.** 1607 Lamentable newes out of Monmouthshire. 4°. [*E. Allde*] *f. W. W*[*elby*, 1607.] Ent. to W. Welby 12 fb. 1607. L.O(impr. cropt).O⁶. DALK.; HN.

Monomachie. A monomachie of motiues. 1582. *See* 11048.

Monro, Alexander. Theses aliquot philosophicae. Præside A. Monroo. 1628. *See* 21555.35.
—— 1632. *See* 21555.42.

Monro, David. ⟨Theses aliquot logicæ.⟩ Præside D. Monroo. 1615. *See* 21555.24.

18022 **Monro, Robert,** *Major General.* Monro his expedition with the worthy Scots regiment. fol. *W. Jones,* 1637. Ent. 23 de. 1636. L.O.C.E.M².+; F.HN.CU.HD.N.+
The Royal Artillery Institution copy has the MS. note: 'This book [was] printed at the sole expense of Lord Rhees, and most of the copies (which were but few) given to his friends.'

18023 **Monson,** *Sir John.* Since the recommitment of sir J. Monsons bill [etc.]. s.sh.fol. [*London,* c. 1662.] Not an STC item.

Monster. This horryble monster is cast of a sowe. [1531.] *See* 15346.

Mont. Prisacchi Retta, Bengalasso del. A new yeeres gift. The courte of ciuill courtesie. 1577. *See* 21134.5.

Montacutius, Richard, *Bp. See* Montagu, R.

18023.5 **Montagu, Henry,** *Earl of Manchester.* Contemplatio mortis, et immortalitatis. [Anon.] *Eng.* 12°. *R. Barker a. assignes of J. Bill,* 1631. L.O.; F.HN.HD.
(Formerly 18025) 129 pp.; errata on p. 129.

18024 — [Anr. ed.] 12°. *R. Barker a. assignes of J. Bill,* 1631. L.O³(imp.).; F.Y.
147 pp.; errata of 18023.5 corrected. Verses on A2ᵛ signed 'R. B.'

18025 — Now = 18023.5.
18026 — [Anr. ed.] Manchester al mondo. Contemplatio mortis, & immortalitatis. The former papers not intended to the presse, have pressed the publishing of these. 12°. *R. Barker a. assignes of J. Bill,* 1633. L.O.C.BIRM.NLW.+; F.HN.HD.MICH.NY.

18026.5 — [Anr. ed.] 12°. *J. Haviland f. F. Constable,* 1635. Ent. 29 au. O.C.LINC.; HN.HD.

18027 — [Anr. issue, w. cancel tp:] Third impression much inlarged. *J. Haviland f. F. Constable,* 1635. L.O.O³⁹. DUL.; ILL.

18027a — [Anr. ed.] Third [*sic*] impression much inlarged. 12°. *J. Haviland f. F. Constable,* 1636. L.O.O¹².M.; F.HD. ILL.
O copy has engr. tp dated 1639; see 18028.5.

18028 —Fourth impression much inlarged. 12°. *J. Haviland f. F. Constable,* 1638. O.BURY. Stevens Cox.; F.NY¹¹.

18028.5 — [Anr. issue, w. added engr. tp:] *f. F. Constable,* 1639. L(imp.).O(engr. tp only).E².P.SHEF.+; HN.HD.N.PN².

Montagu, James, *Bp. See* Mountague.

18029 **Montagu, Richard,** *Bp.* Analecta ecclesiasticarum exercitationum: collectore R. Montacutio. 1622. fol. [*J. Haviland a. A. Islip*] *pro Soc. Bibliop.,* [1622.] L.O.C.D.E².+; F.HN.HD.ILL.U.+
See Court-Book C, p. 140. Haviland pr. prelims. and quires B–K, Mm–Ddd; Islip pr. the rest.

18030 — Appello Caesarem. A just appeale from two vnjust informers [J. Yates and S. Ward.]. 4°. [*H. Lownes*] *f. M. Lownes,* 1625. Ent. 18 fb. L.O.C.D.E.+; F.HN. HD.N.NY¹¹.+
Suppressed in 1629 by proclamation; see 8912. Answered by 4633, 18032, 26003, 26083.

18030.5 — [Anr. ed.] 4°. *H. L*[*ownes*] *f. M. Lownes,* 1625. L⁴³.O. C².DUR⁵.NEP.+; F(2).HN.ILL.PH².Y(2).
In imprint: 'Matthew'. Quires a and A in same typesetting as 18030.

18031 — [Anr. ed.] 4°. *H. L*[*ownes*] *f. M. Lownes,* 1625. L.O.C. E.M².+; F.CAL.HD.U. Iowa U.+
In imprint: 'Mathew'; the O³ copy has 'Mathow [*sic*]'.

18032 —— [Headline:] A briefe Censure upon/An appeale to Caesar. 4°. [*Oxford,* 1625?] O.O².C⁵(2).LINC.; CAL. All copies imp. O² contains B–F⁴.

18033 — Apparatus ad origines ecclesiasticas. fol. *Oxoniæ, L. Lichfield,* 1635. L.O.C.D.G².+; F.HN.HD.ILL.U.+

Montagu, Richard, *Bp.—cont.*

18034 — R. Montacutii, episcopi Cissacestriensis, de originibus ecclesiasticis commentationum tomus primus. fol. *per M. Flesher & R. Young,* 1636. Ent. to M. Flesher 14 no. 1635. L.O.C.D.E.+; F.HART.HD(w. tp of 18035a inserted).ILL.U.

18035 — [Anr. issue, w. title:] Θεανθρωπικον: seu, de vita Jesu Christi. Libri duo. fol. *typis M. Flesher & R. Young,* 1640. L.O¹⁰.C⁴.D.DUR⁵.+; F.
This and following issued w. 18036 sq. as pt. 2.

18035a — [A variant, w. imprint:] *typis M. Flesher & R. Young, venales ap. J. Kirton & T. Warren,* 1640. L.O¹³.C. DUR³.E.+; F.HN.CHI.HD(tp only).

18036 — Θεανθρωπικον . . . pars posterior. fol. *typis R. Olton & E. Purslow, venales ap. J. Kirton & T. Warren,* 1640. Ent. to H. Seile 5 my. 1638. L.O².C.D².DUR⁵.+; HN. HD.U.
This and following issued as pt. 2 of 18035 sq.

18036.5 — [A variant, w. imprint:] *typis M. Flesher & R. Young, venales ap. J. Kirton & T. Warren,* 1640. O.C⁴.C¹⁹. DUR³.ETON.; F.ILL.

18037 — Diatribæ upon the first part of the late history of tithes [22172.] 4° in 8's. *F. Kyngston f. M. Lownes,* 1621. Ent. 24 no. 1620. L.O.C.D.E.+; F.HN.CU.HD.N.+

18038 — A gagg for the new gospell? No: a new gagg for an old goose. Or an answere to a late abridger of controversies. 4°. *T. Snodham f. M. Lownes a. W. Barret,* 1624. L.O.C.D.G².+; F.HN.HD.N.U.+
Answers 13033.2; answered by 26003.

18039 — Immediate addresse unto God alone. 4°. *W. Stansby f. M. Lownes a. W. Barret,* 1624. L.O.C.D.E².+; F.HN. HD.N.Y.+
— ed. *See* 4745, 12346.
— *See also* 10182 sqq., 10299, 10734, 10737.

18040 — Anti-Montacutum. An appeale or remonstrance . . . against R. Mountagu. 4°. *Edenburgi* [i.e. *London, B. Alsop a. T. Fawcet,*] 1629. L.O.O⁶.E.; F.
Unsold sheets reissued in 1641 w. cancel tp as Wing A 3566.
— A dangerous plot discovered. That, R. Mountague, [etc.] 1626. *See* 26003.

18040.5 **Montagu, Walter.** The shepheard's paradise. A comedy. 8°. *f. T. Dring,* 1629 [1659.] Ent. 27 se. 1658. L(2). L⁶.O.O⁶.; F.HN.CH.HD.Y. Greg 797. = Wing M 2475.

Montague, *Viscount. See* Browne, A., *Viscount Montague.*

Montaigne, George, *Bp.* Visitation Articles. *See* 10239, 10261 sqq.
— *See also* 16776.12, 25375a.4, 25375a.7.

18041 **Montaigne, Michel de.** The essayes or morall, politike and millitarie discourses. Done into English by (J. Florio.) fol. (*V. Sims f. E. Blount,* 1603.) Ent. to E. Aggas 20 oc. 1595; to E. Blount 4 jn. 1600. L.O.C². E.M.+; F.HN.HD.N.NY.+

18042 — [Anr. ed.] Essayes written in French. fol. *M. Bradwood f. E. Blount a. W. Barret,* 1613. L.O.C.D⁶.E.+; F.HN. HD.N.NY.+

18043 — [Anr. ed.] The essayes or, morall, [etc.] Third edition. Whereunto is now newly added an index. fol. *M. Flesher f. R. Royston,* 1632 (1631.) L.O.C.D².E.+; F.HN.HD.N.NY⁸.+
— *See also* 21551.7.

Montanus, Jacobus, *Spirensis. See* 24766.

Montanus, Philippus, *tr. See* 23948.

Montemagno, Buonaccorso da, *the Younger. See* 5293, 17778.

18044 **Montemayor, Jorge de.** Diana of George of Montemayor: tr. by B. Yong. fol. *E. Bollifant, imp. G. B*[*ishop*,] 1598. Ent. 9 se. L.O.C.E².M.+; F.HN.HD.N. NY.+ 𝔄
— *See also* 153.3.

18045 **Montenay, Georgette de.** Monumenta emblematum christianorum virtutum. Interpretatione metrica, Latina, Hispanica, Italica, Germanica, Anglica & Belgica, donata. 8°. *Francofurt. ad Mœnum, curâ & imp. J.-C. Unckelii,* 1619. L(lacks A3).C.G².Göttingen U.; HD.
Same plates as in Lyon, J. Marcorelle ed. of 1571, engr. by P. Woeriot.

Montenay, Georgette de—*cont.*

18046 — [Anr. issue, w. title:] A booke of armes, or remembrance, wherein ar one hundred godly emblemata. *Franckfurtt an Mayn, by charges of J.-C. Unckels,* 1619. L.C.; BR(lacks tp)*.

18046.5 — [Anr. issue, w. title:] Cien emblemos christianos tracados y declarados de diversas doctrinas provechosas y pias. *Francoforte, a cuestas de J. C. Unckel,* 1619. G².

> A copy with the Italian title, 'Cento emblemi' is listed in A. G. C. de Vries, *De Nederlandsche Emblematen,* 1899, no. 112, untraced.

18046.7 — [Anr. issue, w. title:] Livre d'armoiries en signe de fraternite. *Francfort au Mayn, es frays de J. C. Unckel,* 1619. PARIS.; F.HD. Arthur Vershbow, Newton Center, Mass.

18047 — [Anr. issue, w. title:] Stamm Buch, darinnen Christlicher Tugenden Beyspiel, Einhundert ausserlesener Emblemata. *Franckfurt am Mayn, in Verlag J.-C. Unckels,* 1619. O.; HD.

18048 **Montfort, Elizabeth.** [Two sermons preached at the funerals of Mrs. E. Montfort (text: Rev. 14.13), and of Dr. T. Montfort (text: Rom. 2.16).] 8°. [*J. Norton,* 1632.] L(imp.).

18049 **Montgomery, Alexander.** The cherrie and the slaye. Composed into Scottis meeter. 4°. *Edinburgh, R. Walde-graue,* 1597. HN.

18049.5 — [Anr. ed.] The cherrie and the slae. . . . Prented according to a copie corrected be the author himselfe. 4°. *Edinburgh, R. Walde-graue,* 1597. E.

18050 — [Anr. ed.] The cherrie and the slae. Compyled into meeter. 8°. *Edinburgh, J. Wreittoun,* 1636. L.
— The flyting betwixt Montgomery and Polwart. 1621. *See* 13954.3.

18051 — The mindes melodie. Contayning certayne psalmes of David, applyed to a new pleasant tune. [Anon. In verse.] 8°. *Edinburgh, R. Charteris,* 1605. HN.

18051.3 — [Anr. ed.] 8°. *Edinburgh, R. Charteris,* 1606. G².

18051.5 **Months.** The months. [Set of 12 engr. roundels w. verses around circumference.] 4°. *sold by T. Johnson,* [c. 1630.] L(Print Dept., 166.c.1, interleaved w. 12561.8).

> Not mentioned in Hind; an earlier half-erased imprint is discernible: 'sould by R. Daniell'.
— [The months. 12 engr. plates c. 1621.] *See* 12561.4.

18051.7 **Montmorency, Henri I,** *Duke de.* [Heading A1ʳ:] A declaration of the protestation of monseigneur the mareschal d'Anville. 8°. [*London,* 1575.] L.
> End of text dated '1575.'

18052 **Montpellier.** The practyse of cyrurgyons of Mountpyller: and of other that neuer came there. 4°. [*R. Wyer f.*] (*R. Banckes,*) [1540?] L.

18053 **Montreux, Nicolas de.** Honours academie. Or the famous pastorall, of Julietta. With divers histories. [Anon.] Englished by R. T(ofte.) fol. *T. Creede,* 1610. Ent. to M. Lownes 2 ap. 1607; ass'd to T. Creede 11 no. 1609. L.O.C².G².LEEDS.+; F.HN.CU.HD.N.+

Montulmo, Antonius de. An almanack. 1555. *See* 483.14.

18054 — A ryghte excellente treatise of astronomie for this present yeare . . . 1554, & 1555, next folowing. *Tr.* F. van Brunswike. 8°. [*J. Kingston f.*] *T. Marshe,* [1554.] L³⁸.O.O⁵. Bos.clxv.

Monument. A monument of mortality. 1630. *See* 6427.5.

18055 **Moone, Peter.** A short treatyse of certayne thinges abused in the popysh church, longe vsed. [In verse.] 4°. (*Ippyswyche, J. Oswen,*) [1548.] L.C¹³(frag.).; HD.
> In 8-line stanzas.

18056 — [Anr. ed.] 4°. (*W. Copland,*) [1548?] C(2 leaves only).; HN.HD(frag.).

18056.5 — [Verse sermon in 7-line stanzas against papists. Last stanza beg.: 'Prayse we the heauenly lorde,'. Anon.] 4°. (*Ippiswiche, J. Oswen,*) [1548.] O(Douce frag.e. 30. 2 leaves only).

Moore, Mr. A shorte catechisme for housholders. With prayers. First made by maister Moore, and augmented by M. Dearing. 1603. *See* 6717.

18057 **Moore, John.** A mappe of mans mortalitie. . . . Whereunto are annexed two consolatory sermons. 2 pts. 4°. *T. S[nodham] f. G. Edwards, sold [by R. Mabb,]* 1617. Ent. 3 ja. L.O(imp.).C.E(imp.).STU.+; F(lacks tp).HN.NY¹¹.U.

18057a — [Anr. issue, w. a dedication to Sir F. Greville inserted, ¶².] C.E.; PN².

18058 — A target for tillage. 8°. [*R. Field*] *f. W. Jones,* 1612. Ent. 18 se. O.LINC.

18059 — [Anr. ed.] 8°. [*R. Field*] *f. W. Jones,* 1613. O.C.
— A two-fold cord of consolation. 1617. = pt. 2 of 18057 sq.

Moore, Philip. Almanacks. 1567, etc. *See* 484 sqq.

18059.5 — The hope of health wherin is conteined a goodlie regimente of life. 8°. *J. Kyngston,* 1564 (my.) HN.HD.

18060 — [Anr. ed.] The hope of health, wherein [etc.] 8°. *J. Kingston,* 1565 (no.) L.L¹⁶(imp.).C.P.

Moore, Richard, *ed. See* More, R.

Moore, Robert. An almanack. 1570. *See* 486.5.

18061 — Diarium historicopoeticum, in quo . . . declarantur cuiusque mensis dies fere singuli, regum, imperatorum, natalibus, nuptiis, [etc. In verse.] 4°. *Oxonii, J. Barnesius,* 1595. L.L².O.C.M.+; F.HN.Y.

18062 **Moore,** *Sir* **William.** A counter-buff to Lysimachus Nicanor [i.e. J. Corbet.] By Philopatris, *pseud.* [In verse.] 4°. [*Edinburgh, R. Bryson,*] 1640. O.E(2).; HN.
> Answers 5751.
— Doomes-day. 1628. *See* 3445.

18063 — The true crucifixe for true catholickes. [In verse.] 8°. *Edinburgh, J. Wreittoun,* 1629. L.O.E.E².G⁴.+; F.HD.ILL.
— *tr. See* 3445.
— *See also* 14819.

18064 **Moraes, Francisco de.** The honorable, pleasant and rare conceited historie of Palmendos. [Anon.] *Tr.* A. M(onday.) 4°. *J. C[harlewood] f. S. Watersonne,* 1589. Ent. to J. Charlewood 9 ja. L.O(imp.).; HN.
> For anr. trans. *see* 4910.
— Palmerin of England. 1596. *See* 19161.

18065 **Moraius, Kentegernus.** Theses aliquot philosophicae. Præside K. Moraio. 1628. Now = 21555.36.
— — 1634. *See* 21555.44.

Moravius, Thomas. *See* Murray, T.

Moray, John. A farewell to the renowmed captaine, A. Gray. 1605. *See* 12200.5.

More, Agnes, *tr. See* 11316.

18066 **More, Cresacre.** D. O. M. S. The life and death of Sir Thomas Moore. Written by M. T. M[ore, or rather C. More.] 4°. [*Douai, B. Bellère,* 1631?] L.O.C².D² (lacks tp).M.+; F.HN.HD.N.U.+
> A&R 548. The dedic. to Marie Henriette refers to 'the hope-full yssue': Prince Charles, born 29 May 1630. Dedic. begins ✱2ʳ; a post-1640? reissue has it beginning ¶3ʳ (San Francisco U); 1642 reissues (cf. Wing M 2630) omit dedic.

18067 **More, Edward.** A lytle and bryefe treatyse, called the defence of women, made agaynst [12105.] [In verse.] 4°. (*J. Kynge,*) 1560. Ent. 1557–58. L.O(2, imp.).; HN.PFOR.
> HN has variant colophon: 'John h Kynge'.

18068 **More, George,** *Esquire.* Principles for yong princes: collected out of sundry authors. 12°. *N. Okes,* 1611. L(imp.).C.WI.; F.HN.N.
> The author may be identical with Sir George More, q.v.

18068.5 — [Anr. ed.] 4°. [*G. Purslowe*] *f. J. Day,* 1629. L⁴³.O.O⁶.PETYT.; HN.NY.PN².

18069 — [Anr. issue, w. cancel tp, w. imprint:] *Printed at London,* 1629. L.L⁴.C²(lacks tp)*.PLUME(lacks tp)*.; HD.

18070 **More, George,** *Preacher.* A true discourse concerning the certaine possession and dispossessiō of 7 persons in one familie in Lancashire. 8°. [*Middelburg, R. Schilders,*] 1600. L.L².O.O⁸.LINC.; F.HN.
> Supports 6280.5 sqq.; answers 12883.

18070.5 — [Anr. ed.] 8°. [*Middelburg, R. Schilders,*] 1600. O.; HD.
> In title: 'dispossession'.

18071   **More,** *Sir* **George.** A demonstration of God in his workes. 4°. *J. R[oberts] f. T. Charde,* 1597. Ent. 28 se. L.O².C.C³.; F.HN.TEX.U.
    Tp signed: 'George More'. *See* also 18068.

18071.5 — [Anr. issue, w. cancel tp signed: 'George More, Esquire'.] *J. R[oberts] f. T. Charde,* 1597. O.O⁶. P(lacks tp)*.; HN.

18072 — [Anr. issue, w. cancel tp, w. imprint:] *J. Ro[berts] f. T. Charde,* 1598. L.O⁹.C(2).C².; F.HD.

  More, Henry, *tr. See* 16877, 20001.

  More, John, *tr. See* 11966, 18414.

18073   **More, John,** *Preacher.* A liuely anatomie of death. 8°. *G. S[imson] f. W. Jones,* 1596. Ent. 25 oc. 1595. L.; F.

18074 — A table from the beginning of the world to this day. [*Ed.*] (N. Bownd.) 8°. *J. Legate, pr. to the Univ. of Camb., sold in London* [by A. Kitson,] 1593. Ent. 12 ap. L.O.C.D.E⁴.+; F.HN.HD.N.Y.+

18074.5 — Three godly and fruitfull sermons, . . . now first published by N. Bownd: whereunto he hath adioyned of his owne, a sermon of comfort and, a short treatise of a contented mind. 4°. *J. Legatt, pr. to the Univ. of Camb., solde in London* [by A. Kitson,] 1594. L.P.; PN².

  More, Philip. *See* Moore.

18075   **More, Richard,** *Carpenter.* The carpenters rule, or, a booke shewing many plaine waies, truly to measure ordinarie timber. 4°. *F. Kyngston,* 1602. Ent. 10 ap. L.O.C.C⁵(imp.).A.+

18075.5 — [Anr. issue, w. cancel tp, w. imprint:] *f. W. Welby,* 1616. L³⁸.

  More, Richard, *Publisher, ed. See* 3192.

18076   **More,** *Sir* **Thomas.** The workes of Sir T. More . . . wrytten by him in the Englysh tonge. [*Ed.*] (W. Rastell.—A table by T. Paynell.) fol. *at the costes of J. Cawod, J. Waly, a. R. Tottell,* 1557 (ap.) L. O(imp.).C.D.E.+; F.HN.HD.N.NY.+
    1st quire pr. by J. Cawood, the rest by R. Tottell. Imprint varies: first line: 'Printed at' or 'IN LONDON'; both at L.

18077 — The answere to the fyrst parte of the poysened booke, whych a namelesse heretyke [W. Tyndale] hath named the souper of the lorde [24468]. 8°. (w. Rastell, 1534.) L.O.D.LINC(lacks tp).M.+; F(lacks col.).HN.
    Answered by 14829.

18078 — The apologye of syr T. More knyght. 8° in 4's. (w. Rastell, 1533.) L.O(lacks tp).C.M.P.+; F.HN.HD(imp.). N(imp.).Y.+
    Answers 21586; answered by 21584.

18078.5 — The boke of the fayre gentylwoman, . . . lady Fortune. [Init. Tho. Mo. In verse.] 8° in 4's. (R. Wyer,) [c. 1540.] L².

18079 — The cōfutacyon of Tyndales answere [24437]. fol. w. Rastell, 1532. L.O.C.D.E.+; F.HN.N.Y³. San Francisco U.+

18080 — The second parte of the cōfutacion of Tyndals answere. fol. w. Rastell, 1533. L.O.C.D.E.+; F.CHI.Y³(lacks tp). San Francisco U. Scheide.
    Answers 24437, 1470.

18081 — The debellacyon of Salem and Bizance. 8°. (w. Rastell, 1533.) L(imp.).L².O.C.M.+; F.HN.N.PN.Y³.+
    Answers 21584.

18082 — A dialoge of comfort against tribulacion. 4° in 8's. *in aed. R. Totteli,* (1553 (18 no.)) L.O.C².NOR².USHAW. +; F.HN.ILL.N.Y.+

18083 — [Anr. ed.] Now newly set foorth, with many places restored and corrected. [*Ed.* J. Fowler.] 8°. *Antuerpiae, ap. J. Foulerum,* 1573. L.O.C.D.G².+; F.HN.HD. TEX.Y.+
    A&R 549. *See* Arber I.492.

18084 — A dyaloge of syr Thomas More . . . wherin be treatyd dyuers maters, as of the veneration & worshyp of ymagys. fol. [*J. Rastell,*] (1529 (jn.)) L.L⁸.O(tp defective).O²(imp.).; F.HART².LC.
    Answered by 24437. This may have been in part pr. by P. Treveris.

18085 — [Anr. ed.] Newly ouersene. fol. [*W. Rastell,*] 1530. L.O.C.D.E.+; F.HN.HD(lacks tp).N.PML.+
    Privilege dated May 1531 at end; in O,HD copies it is altered to 1530 by erasure of the 'i'.

  More, *Sir* **Thomas**—*cont.*

18086 — Epigrammata Thomæ Mori Angli. 16° in 8's. *typis J. H[aviland,] prostant ap. H. Mosley,* 1638. Ent. 18 my. L.O.C.A.LYD.+; F.HN.HD.N.Y.+

18087 — Epistola Thomæ Mori ad Academiam Oxon. [etc. *Ed.* R. James.] 4°. *Oxoniæ, J. Lichfield, imp. T. Huggins,* 1633. L.O.C.A.D.+; F.HN.HD.PN.Y.+

18088 — Thomae Mori epistola ad Germanū Brixiū. 4°. (*in æd. Pynsonis,*) 1520. L.C(2).C²(2).C⁴.C⁹.; F.

18088.5 — Eruditissimi viri Ferdināadi Barauelli [i.e. *Sir* T. More] opus elegās, quo refellit Lutheri calumnias: quibus Anglie, regem Henricum octauum insectatur. 4°. [*R. Pynson,*] 1523. DUR⁵.

18089 — [Anr. issue, w. new prelims. and quire H enlarged.] Eruditissimi viri Guilielmi Rossei opus elegans, [etc.] L.O.C.DUR³.SAL.+; F.HN.CH.Y.

18090 — A letter of syr Tho. More knyght impugnynge the erronyouse wrytyng of J. Fryth. 8° in 4's. (w. Rastell, 1533.) O.OS. Goyder(lacks tp).; F.
    Answered by 11381, 24468.
  — A fruteful, and pleasaunt worke. *See* 18094.

18091 — A mery gest how a sergeaūt woldel erne [sic] to be a frere. [Anon. In verse.] 4°. (J. Notary,) [1516?] HN.
    Reprinted in 79.

18092 — The supplycacyon of soulys: . . . Against the supplycacyon of beggars [10883]. fol. [*W. Rastell,* bef. 25 Oct. 1529.] L⁸.O².C(2 leaves).DNPK.LIV.; U. New Rochelle College, N.Y.
    Collates a² b–l⁴ m². Answered by 11386.5.

18093 — [Anr. ed.] fol. [*W. Rastell,* 1529.] L.O.C².D.M.+; F.HN. BO.N.Y.+
    Collates A–L⁴.

18094 — [*Utopia.*] A fruteful, and pleasaunt worke of the beste state of a publyque weale, and of the newe yle called Vtopia. *Tr.* R. Robynson. 8°. [*S. Mierdman f.*] *A. Vele,* 1551. L.L⁸.O.C².M.+; F.HN.HD.N.NY.+
    The first (1516) and other early Latin eds. were pr. abroad.

18095 — [Anr. ed.] A frutefull pleasaunt, & wittie worke. Seconde edition newlie corrected. 8°. [*R. Tottell f.*] *A. Vele,* [1556.] L(2).O(2).C(lacks last leaf)*.c⁵. DUL.; HN.CB.CU.PFOR.Y.

18095.5 — [A variant, w. colophon dated:] 1556. L.L⁸.O⁵.C⁵.E.+; F.HN.HD.ILL.PN.+

18096 — [Anr. ed.] A most pleasant, fruitfull, and wittie worke. Third edition. 4°. *T. Creede,* 1597. L.O.A.G².; F.HN. HD.PN.Y.+

18097 — [Anr. ed.] Sir Thomas Moore's Utopia: . . . Now after many impressions, newly corrected. 4°. *B. Alsop,* 1624. L.O.C.D.E.+; F.HN.HD.N.NY.+

18098 — [Anr. ed.] The common-wealth of Utopia. 12°. *B. Alsop & T. Fawcet, sold by W. Sheares,* 1639. L.O. C.D⁶.M.+; F.HN.HD.N.Y.+
  — *tr. See* 16895, 19897.7.
  — *See* also 11181.

  Morejon, Pedro. *See* 14527.

18099   **Morel, Jean.** De ecclesia ab Antichristo per eius excidium liberanda. 4°. [*Eliot's Court Press,*] *imp. G. Bishop,* 1589. Ent. 10 ja. L.O.C³.DUR.M.+; F.HD.Y.
    (Formerly also 671)

18100 — [Anr. issue.] 8°. *ap. G. Bischop* [sic], 1594. L.O.O⁹.C.; U.
    A reissue of the sheets of Tractatus de Ecclesia, *Hanouiæ, G. Antonius,* 1594.

18100.5 — Le vray agnus dei pour descharmer le peuple francois. Escrit pour Henry III. roy de France sur le poinct de son massacre. Dedié au Henri IIII. roy de France. 8°. *R. Field,* 1589. Ent. 7 au. Vatican Library (Palatine Collection).
    Dedic. signed 'Jean de Morely Sieur de Choisy'.

18101   **Morelius, Gulielmus.** Verborum Latinorum cum Graecis Anglicisque coniunctorum, commentarij. fol. *in æd. H. Bynnemani, per assig. R. Huttoni,* 1583. Ent. to Newberie a. Denham 30 de. 1584. L.O.C.E².M².+; F.HN.HD.ILL.N.+
    HN has a leaf of this w. MS. corrections used as copy for 24008.

  Morély, Jean. *See* 18100.5.

18102   **Moresinus, Thomas.** Papatus, seu deprauatae religionis origo et incrementum. 8°. *Edinburgi, R. Walde-graue,* 1594. L.O.C.E².P.+; F.HN.CHI.HD.
    '1582' in orn. at top of tp.

18102a — [A variant, w. 2 reclining figures in headpiece on tp.] C.E.

Morg., Ll. *See* 18104.

18102a.2 Morgan, George. George Morgan plaintife, William Megges, Richard Bowdler, [and others] defendants. [Abstract of events in the bankrupt Alum Company, for which Morgan was factor in Middelburg.] (. . . The most humble petition of Morgan is, that the said decree [in Chancery, of 26 June 1620] may be established, by act of Parliament.) fol(2). [*London,* 1621.] L(Harl.MS.7607/395, 397).L⁸(1st sheet only, GL 3701).

Morgan's bill was entered 23 Mar. 1621; *see* Notestein, V.318. For Bowdler's answer *see* 3432.7.

18102a.3 — The particulars of . . . 22600. l. sterling, owing the 20 of May 1612. for the allom account. [With 97 items, numbered in the left column.] s.sh.fol. [*London,* 1621.] L(Harl.MS.7607/403).

This was app. printed in Aug. 1621, as at the end of the text is stated: 'The Defendants had 14 moneths . . . since the said . . . Decree [of 26 June 1620]'. Most of the text is reprinted in sheet 3 of the following.

18102a.5 — A briefe of Morgans bill in Parliament. (Inter Georgium Morgan quer.—The particulars . . . owing in Middleborough, the 20. of May 1612. [With the items unnumbered and totalled '97' in MS.]) fol(3). [*London,* 1624?] L(Harl.MS.7607/393, 399, 401).O²(1st sheet only).

The last date on sheet 1 is 14 July 1623, but the next Parliament did not meet until 12 Feb. 1624.

The 3 sheets are apparently linked by the reference at the end of sheet 1: 'The Certificate of the Knights and Aldermen [i.e. sheet 2], which is Decreed, ariseth by 97. ['7' in MS.] particulars, sent into the Court annexed to their said Certificate.'

Item 404 in the Harl. collection is a partly printed sheet with many gaps filled in by hand. It begins: 'A Breefe of [Morgans Bill in Parliamt]' with the bracketed words in MS. Presumably it also is [1624?]

18103 Morgan, John. A short analysis of a part of the second chapter of S. James, from the 14. verse to the end. 8°. *T. Orwin f. E. Aggas,* 1588. Ent. 20 no. L.

18104 Morgan, Llewellyn. Every mans condition. Or every man has his severall opinion. [Signed 'Ll. Morg.'] *Ballad.* 2 pts. s.sh.fol. [*M. Flesher*] *f. F. Coules,* [c. 1630.] C⁶.

18104.5 — An excellent ditty, both merry and witty, expressing the love of the youthes of the city. [Init. L. M.] *Ballad.* 2 pts. s.sh.fol. *f. J. Grismund,* [c. 1627.] Ent. to J. Wright a. ballad ptnrs. 16 jy. 1634. C⁶.

18105 Morgan, Nicholas. Up and be doing, [etc.] The perfection of horse-manship. 4° in 8's. [*E. Allde*] *f. E. White* [*sen.,*] 1609. Ent. 6 oc. L.O.E.; F.HN.HD(imp.). PN.Y.+

18105.3 — [Anr. issue, w. cancel prelims. A–D⁴, w. title:] The horse-mans honour: or, the beautie of horse-manship. [Anon.] *f. J. Marriott,* 1620. L(imp.). BHP.D(imp.).; Y. Mellon.

New quires pr. by A. Mathewes.

18105.7 — [Anr. issue, w. cancel tp, w. imprint:] *f. the widdow Helme a. J. Marriott,* 1620. PEN.

Morgan, Thomas. *See* 5742.9.

18106 Morice, James. A briefe treatise of oathes exacted by ordinaries and ecclesiasticall iudges. [Anon.] 4°. [*Middelburg, R. Schilders,* 1590?] L.O.C.D.DUR³.+; F.HN.HD.MICH.U.+

18107 — = 18106.

Morillon, Claude. *See* 13136.

18108 Morindos. The famous & renowned history of Morindos. 4°. [*E. Allde*] *f. H. R*[*ockett,*] 1609. Ent. 4 jy. 1608. O(2).

18109 Morison, *Sir* **Richard.** Apomaxis calumniarum, convitiorumque, quibus Ioannes Coclęus, . . . Henrici octaui, famam impetere, . . . studuit. 4°. (*in aed. T. Bertheleti,* 1537.) L.O.C.D.YK.+; F.N.

Dedic. app. misdated: '1538. 12. calendas Iulii.'

18109.5 — A comfortable consolation wherin the people may se, howe far greatter cause, they haue to be glad for the ioyful byrth of prince Edwarde, than sory for the dethe of quene Iane. 8°. (*in aed. T. Bertheleti,* 1537.) M.

Morison, *Sir* **Richard**—*cont.*

18110 — An exhortation to styrre all Englyshe men to the defence of theyr countreye. 8°. (*in æd. T. Bertheleti,* 1539.) L.

A2ʳ line 5 ends: 'gy-'.

18110.5 — [Anr. ed.] 8°. (*in æd. T. Bertheleti,* 1539.) O.C⁵.; F(2, 1 lacks tp).

A2ʳ line 5 ends: 'gi-'.

18110.7 — [Anr. ed.] 8°. (*in æd. T. Bertheleti,* 1539.) C⁷.

A2ʳ line 5 ends: 'hauynge'.

18111 — An inuectiue ayenste the great and detestable vice, treason. 8°. (*in æd. T. Bertheleti,* 1539.) L.C.; HD.

A4ᵛ catchword: 'brink'.

18112 — [Anr. ed.] 8°. (*in æd. T. Bertheleti,* 1539.) L².; F. HN(mixed sheets, w. quires a,C,F of 18111 and B of 18113).

A4ᵛ catchword: 'brinke'.

18113 — [Anr. ed.] 8°. (*in æd. T. Bertheleti,* 1539.) L.O.C⁵.; STAN.

A4ᵛ catchword: 'brynke'.

18113.3 — A lamentation in whiche is shewed what ruyne cometh of seditious rebellyon. [Anon.] 4°. (*in aed. T. Bertheleti,*) 1536. L.L².C⁵.; HN(lacks last leaf).NW.

(Formerly 15185)

18113.5 — A remedy for sedition. [Anon.] 4°. (*in aed. T. Bertheleti,*) 1536. L.L².O.C.E⁴.+; F(lacks tp).ILL.Y.

(Formerly 20877) A2ʳ line 1 ends: 'consyde-'.

18113.7 — [Anr. ed.] 4°. (*in aed. T. Bertheleti,*) 1536. C.C².E.; HN.

A2ʳ line 1 ends: 'conside-'.

— *tr. See* 11402, 23407, 24846.5.

— *See also* 17518.

Morisot, Claude. *See* 1397.

18114 Morletus, Petrus. Ianitrix siue institutio ad perfectam linguæ Gallicæ cognitionem acquirendam. *Lat. a. Fr.* 8°. *Oxoniæ, J. Barnesius,* 1596. O.LIV³.

18114.5 Morley, Caleb. To the most honorable assembly of the commons [etc. A brief concerning rights of Morley or Alan Bishop to the parsonage of Stalbridge.] s.sh. fol. [*London,* 1621.] L⁵(Lemon 191).

The petition was rejected on 2 Mar. 1621; *see* Notestein, VI.278.

18114.6 — [Anr. version, addressed:] To the lords spirituall and temporall . . . of Parliament. s.sh.fol. [*London,* 1621.] L⁸(GL 3704).

18115 Morley, Henry. The cleansing of the leper. 8°. H. L[*ownes*] *f. C. Knight,* 1609. L.L².O.C⁹.; F.HN.

18115.5 Morley, Thomas. The first booke of ayres. Or little short songs, to sing and play to the lute, with the base viole. fol. [*H. Ballard f.*] *W. Barley, the assigne of T. Morley,* 1600. F(imp.).

18116 — Of Thomas Morley the first booke of balletts to five voyces. 5 ptbks. 4°. *T. Este,* 1595. Ent. 6 de. 1596. L.L⁷.O(cantus, altus, tenor, quintus).O³.E².+; F.HN. HD(cantus, altus, bassus, quintus).LC.N.+

18117 — [Anr. ed.] 5 ptbks. 4°. *T. Este, the assigne of T. Morley,* 1600. L(cantus, bassus).O.Juel-Jensen(altus).; F(cantus, bassus, quintus).

18118 — [A trans.] Di Tomaso Morlei il primo libro delle ballette a cinque voci. 5 ptbks. 4°. *T. Este,* 1595. Ent. 6 de. L(alto).O¹⁸(canto).; F(canto).HN.

18119 — Of Thomas Morley the first booke of Canzonets to two voyces. 2 ptbks. 4°. *T. Este,* 1595. Ent. 6 de. 1596. L.L⁷.D².; F(cantus).HN(tenor).LC.

18120 — [Anr. ed.] 2 ptbks. 4°. *T. Snodham f. M. Lownes a. J. Browne,* 1619. Ent. to J. Browne 22 de. 1610; to M. Lownes, J. Browne, a. T. Snodham 11 se. 1611. L(1, plus cantus only).; HN.

18121 — Canzonets. Or little short songs to three voyces. 3 ptbks. 4°. *T. Est, the assigne of W. Byrd,* 1593. Ent. 6 de. 1596. L(2).L⁷.O(altus, bassus).D²(cantus, altus). St. Michael's College, Tenbury; F(1 w. cantus imp.). HN(altus, bassus).LC(cantus imp. and 2 bassus, 1 imp.).

18122 — [Anr. ed.] Now newly imprinted with some songs added by the author. 3 ptbks. 4°. *T. Este, the assigne of T. Morley,* 1602. C(bassus).

18123 — [Anr. ed.] 3 ptbks. 4°. *T. Este, the assigne of W. Barley,* 1606. L.L⁷.O(bassus imp.).C.E².+; F.HN.CAL.HD.N.+

See Court-Book C, pp. 19–20.

18124 — [Anr. ed.] 3 ptbks. 4°. *W. Stansby, R. Hawkings* [sic], *G. Latham,* 1631. Ass'd to W. Stansby 23 fb. 1626. L.

Morley, Thomas—*cont.*

18125 — Canzonets. Or little short songs to foure voyces. 4 ptbks. 4°. *P. Short,* 1597. Ent. 10 oc. L.L⁷.O.C.A.+; F.HN.Y².

18126 — Canzonets or litle short aers to fiue and six voices. 5 ptbks. 4°. *P. Short,* 1597. Ent. 31 oc. L(2).O. E(altus).; F(cantus, altus, bassus, quintus).HN.
The sextus part is pr. in the tenor ptbk.

18127 — Madrigalls to foure voyces. The first booke. 4 ptbks. 4°. *T. Est,* 1594. Ent. 6 de. 1596. C².E². YK.+; F(tenor). HN.LC(1, plus bassus only).

18128 — [Anr. ed.] Now newly imprinted with some [2] songs added. 4 ptbks. 4°. *T. Este, the assigne of T. Morley,* 1600. L(tenor, bassus).O.D²(cantus, altus).E².M³(cantus).+; F(cantus).HN.

18129 — Madrigals to fiue voyces. 5 ptbks. 4°. *T. Este,* 1598. Ent. 7 au. L.O.; F(cantus, tenor, quintus). HN.CAL.LC.

18130 — Madrigales the triumphes of Oriana, to 5. and 6. voices. 6 ptbks. 4°. *T. Este, the assigne of T. Morley,* 1601. Ent. 15 oc. 1603. L.O³.C(bassus).; F.HD.
Tp line 6 ends: 'Morley,'.

18130.5 — [Anr. ed.] 6 ptbks. 4°. *T. Este, the assigne of T. Morley,* 1601. L⁷(2).O(2, plus altus only).C(altus, tenor, quintus, sextus).E².P(quintus imp.)*.; F(altus, sextus).HN.ILL(tenor, bassus, quintus).
Tp line 6 ends: 'Morley'.

18131 — The first booke of consort lessons, made by diuers authors, for six instruments. 6 ptbks. 4°. [H. Ballard f.] *W. Barley, the assigne of T. Morley,* [1599.] L (bass-violl).O(cithern).O³(pandora, flute).
Tp dated '1599' in compartment.

18132 — [Anr. ed.] Now newly corrected and inlarged. 6 ptbks. 4°. *T. Snodham f. J. Browne, the assigne of W. Barley,* 1611. L(flute).L⁷(treble-violl).; HN(pandora). NY.
See Court-Book C, pp. 19–20.

18133 — A plaine and easie introduction to practicall musicke. fol. *P. Short,* 1597. Ent. to P. Short a. W. Hoskins 9 oc. 1596. L.O.C².E⁴.M³.+; F.HN(tp torn).HD.N.NY.+

18134 — [Anr. ed.] fol. *H. Lownes,* 1608. L.O.C.D.M³.+; F.HN. HD.N.NY.+

18134.3 **Mornay, Philippe de.** A briefe refutation of a certaine calumnious relation of the conference passed betwixt the lord Plessis Marli, and J. Peron, calling himself bishop of Eureux, the fourth of May last. 4°. *A. Hatfield,* 1600. ROME.
Answers 1st ed. of 19413, no copy of which is known. See also 6381, 6385.5.

18134.7 — Christian meditations, vpon the sixt, twentie fiue, thirtie, and two and thirtie psalmes. . . . And moreouer, a meditation vpon the 137. psalme by P. Pilesson [i.e. Pellison.]. *Tr.* J. Feilde. 16° in 8's. *J. Wolfe f. J. Harrison the yonger,* [1587?] Broxbourne(E).
See entry to R. Field 29 oc. 1589; Greg, *Register B,* p. 34.

18135 — [Headline A3ᵛ:] A christian view of life and death. (*Tr.* A. W.) 8°. [*R. Field,* 1593.] C(lacks tp).
Maunsell (17669) pt. 1, p. 74, has entry: 'Christian and godly view of death, & life, as also of humane actions. *Tr.* by A. W. Printed by R. F[ield] for R. B[allard.] 1593. in 8.'

18136 — The defence of death. Contayning a most excellent discourse written in Frenche. And doone into English by E. A[ggas]. (Certain collections gathered out of Seneca.) 8°. *J. Allde f. E. Aggas,* 1576. Ent. 1 jy. 1577. O.; F.

18137 — [A variant, w. date:] 1577. L.L².

18138 — [Anr. trans.] A discourse of life and death. . . . Antonius, a tragoedie by R. Garnier. Both done in English by the countesse of Pembroke. 4°. [*J. Windet*] *f. W. Ponsonby,* 1592. Ent. 3 my. L.O(2 imp.).C³.; F.HN.Y. Greg 108.
The trans. of Mornay appears to be edited from 18136. 'Antonius' reprinted in 11623.

18139 — [Anr. ed. of the Discourse only.] 8°. [*R. Field*] *f. W. Ponsonby,* 1600. L(2, 1 w. tp defective). O.D.; F.N.Y. Arthur Houghton.

18140 — [Anr. ed.] 12°. *H. L[ownes] f. M. Lownes,* 1606. Ent. 5 no. 1604. L.; HD.N.
All copies bd. w. 18155.

18141 — [A variant, w. date:] 1607. L. Juel-Jensen.; ILL.

18141.5 — [Anr. ed.] 12°. *H. L[ownes] f. M. Lownes,* 1608. O.E. E bd. w. 18155.

Mornay, Philippe de—*cont.*

18142 — Fowre bookes, of the institution, vse and doctrine of the sacrament. [*Tr.* by R. S. from] The second [French] edition. fol. *J. Windet f. I. B[ing,] T. M[an] a. W. P[onsonby,]* 1600. Ent. to Man 31 mr. 1598; to Bing a. Ponsonby 17 oc. 1598. L.O.C.D.E.+; F.HN. HD(imp.).ILL.U.+
See Greg, *Register B,* p. 67. First ed. in English. Some copies (L, HN) have extra leaf signed A2 w. translator's inits.

18143 — An homily upon these words of saint Matthew, Chap. 16. v. 18. Tu es Petrus. *Tr.* I. V[erneuil?] 12°. Oxford, *J. Barnes,* 1615. O.C.

18144 — A letter written by a French catholike gentleman, to the maisters at Sorbonne. Concerning the late victories obtained by the king of Nauarre. [Anon.] 8°. *J. Wolfe f. E. Aggas,* 1588. Ent. 3 fb. O.O⁵.

18145 — A letter, written by a french catholicke gentleman. Conteyning a briefe aunswere to the slaunders of a certaine pretended Englishman [Louis d'Orléans]. [Anon.] 4°. *J. Woolfe,* 1589. L(2).O.C².C¹⁷.; F.HN.

18146 — Meditations vpon psal. 101. Written first in French. *Tr.* T. W(ilcocks). 8°. *A. Islip f. T. Man,* 1599. Ent. 5 mr. L³⁰.D.P.; F.NW.

18147 — The mysterie of iniquitie: that is to say, the historie of the papacie. Englished by S. Lennard. fol. *A. Islip,* 1612. Ent. 28 se. 1611. L.O.C.D.E.+; F.HN.HD.N.NY.+
— A notable treatise of the church. *See* 18159.

18148 — [A ghost.]

18149 — A woorke concerning the trewnesse of the christian religion. Begunne to be *tr.* by Sir P. Sidney and finished by A. Golding. 4° in 8's. [*J. Charlewood a.*] (*G. Robinson*) *f. T. Cadman,* 1587. Ent. to T. Smith 13 oc. 1581; to T. Cadman 7 no. 1586. L.O.C. A.D.+; F.HN.HD.N.NY.+

18150 — [Anr. ed.] 4° in 8's. *R. Robinson f. J. B[rome,]* 1592. Ent. to J. Brome 12 ap. 1597. L.O.E².M².P.+; F.HN. CHI.HD.NY¹¹.+

18151 — [Anr. ed.] Reviewed, and now the third time published, and purged from faults. [*Ed.*] (T. Wilcocks.) 4° in 8's. [*G. Eld*] *f. G. Potter,* 1604. Ent. 23 au. 1601. L.O.C².BIRM.M².+; F. HN.HD.ILL.NY.+
See Arber II.840.

18152 — The fourth time published. 4° in 8's. *G. Purslowe,* 1617. Ass'd 2 de. 1616. L.O.C.D.M.+; F.HN.ILL.HD.NY.+

18153 — Philip Mornay, lord of Plessis his teares. For the death of his sonne. Englished by J. Healey. 8°. *G. Eld,* 1609. L.O.LK.; F.HN.HD. Pirie.

18154 — The shielde and rewarde of the faithfull. Or a meditation vpon Genesis 15. chap. vers. 1. *Tr.* (J. Bulteel.) 12°. *T. D[awson] f. N. Newbery,* 1620. Ent. 12 ap. O.; F.

18155 — Six excellent treatises of life and death, collected by P. Mornay and now *tr.* 12°. *H. L[ownes] f. M. Lownes,* 1607. Ent. 15 ja. L.E.; F.HD.N.
Contains selections from Plato (Axiochus), Cicero, Seneca, St. Ambrose, St. Cyprian, and the Bible. Translator's note on A2ᵛ mentions, and extant copies are bd. w., 18140 sqq.

18156 — Three homilies upon these three sentences following. [Psalms 55.22, John 14.27, Luke 10.42.] *Tr.* A. R[atcliffe.] 12°. *J. D[awson] f. N. Newbery,* 1626. Ent. 15 de. 1625. O.C.

18156a — Three meditations upon these three places of Scripture: 1 Cor.2.2. Psal. 6.1. Prov. 3.11,12. *Tr.* J. Bulteel. 12°. *J. H[aviland] f. N. Newbery,* 1627. O.
The last leaf is a 2nd tp which, instead of Bulteel's name as translator, gives that of Philip of Mornay Lord of Plessis Marly.

18156a.5 — Traicte. De l'eglise, auquel sont disputees les principalles questions, en nostre temps. 8°. *T. Vautrollier,* 1578. O.; F.HD.

18157 — [A variant, w. date:] 1579. O¹⁴.D.; HD. Iowa U.

18158 — [A trans.] A treatise of the church. *Tr.* J. F(eilde.) 8°. *C. Barker,* 1579. Ent. 20 ja. L.C².A.; F(imp.).Y.
See Greg, *Register B,* p.34.

18159 — [Anr. ed., w. title:] A notable treatise of the church. 8°. *C. Barker,* 1579. L.O.M².P.; F.ILL.U.

18160 — [Anr. ed.] 8°. *C. Barker,* 1580. L.O.C.D.M.+; F(2).HN. HD.N.U.

18161 — [Anr. ed., w. title:] A treatise of the church. 8°. *C. Barker,* 1581. L.L².L⁴⁸.G².; F.HN.CHI.
A2ʳ line 2: 'Lorde, . . . Lorde'.

18161.5 — [Anr. ed.] 8°. *C. Barker,* 1581. O³.C(2).E.NEK.P.; F.HD(lacks tp).
A2ʳ line 2: 'Lorde, . . . Lord'.

Mornay, Philippe de—*cont.*

18162 — [Anr. trans.] Reviewed and enlarged by the author. *Tr.* (J. Molle.) 4°. L. S[*nowden*] *f. G. Potter,* 1606. Ent. to the Company a. to G. Potter 18 jn. 1604. L.C.D.E.LINC.+; F.HN.HD(imp.).N.U.+
    Verso of tp blank or w. royal arms; both at F. Ddd²: 'Conclusions' and errata (F); cancel Ddd²: table and errata (L).

18163 — The true knowledge of a mans owne selfe. *Tr.* A. M(undy.) 12°. *J.* R[*oberts*] *f. W. Leake,* 1602. Ent. 27 oc. 1601. L(2).O¹⁸.; F.

18164 — Two homilies concerning the meanes how to resolve the controversies of this time. *Tr.* out of French. 12°. *Oxford, J. Barnes,* 1612. L.O.C³.; HN.

18164.5 — [A variant, omitting author's name from tp.] O.D².
  — Vindiciae. 1579. *See* 15211.
  — A woorke concerning the trewnesse of the christian religion. *See* 18149.
  — *See also* 5010, 12508, 13106, 13109.

18165 **Morocco.** The arrivall and intertainements of the embassador, Alkaid Jaurar ben Abdella. From the emperor of Morocco. 4°. *J. Okes,* 1637. Ent. 28 no. L.L².O.E.LINC.+; F.HN.NY.TEX.

18166 **Morray, William.** Nyne songs collected out of the holy scriptures. 8°. *Edinburgh, J. Wreittoun,* [1631?] E²(date cropt).

18167 — A short treatise of death in sixe chapters. 8°. *Edinburgh, J. Wreittoun,* 1631. L.E.; F.

18168 — [Anr. ed.] 8°. *Edinburgh, J. Wreittoun,* 1633. E².

18169 **Morrell, William.** New-England. Or a briefe enarration of the ayre, earth, water, fish and fowles of that country. In Latin and English verse. 4°. *J. D[awson,]* 1625. L.; HN.BO⁵(lacks tp).

18170 **Morrice, Thomas.** An apology for schoole-masters. 8°. *B. Alsop f. R. Flemming,* 1619. Ent. 12 ja. L.O(2).
  — *See also* 17152.

Morrice Dance. The passoinate [*sic*] morrice. [1593.] *See* STC 1.

Mors, Roderigo, *pseud. See* 3759.5, 3764.

Morse, Henry. *See* 21505.

18171 **Morton, Andrew.** Theses theologicæ de sacramentis. 1602. Now = 21555.9.

18171.5 **Morton, David.** Sacris ordinibus non rite initiati tenentur ad eos ritus ineundos. [In verse.] s.sh.fol. [*Cambridge,*] 1633 [i.e. 1663]. L.
    (Formerly 18195)

Morton, John, *Cardinal. See* Indulgences 51 sqq.

18172 **Morton, Thomas,** *Bp.* Antidotum adversus ecclesiæ Romanæ de merito propriè dicto ex condigno venenum. 4°. *Cantabrigiæ, ex acad. typog.* [*T. Buck a. R. Daniel,*] 1637. L.O.C.D.E.+; F.CAL.HD.N.U.+

18173 — [Anr. issue, w. cancel tp, w. imprint:] *Cantabrigiæ, ex acad. typog., væneunt à J. Sweeting* [*London,*] 1639. O¹².; HN.HD.

18173.5 — Apologiæ catholicæ, in qua paradoxa, haereses, blasphemiae, scelera, quae Jesuitæ, impingunt, diluuntur. Tomus primus. (Liber secundus.) 4°. [*Eliot's Court Press,*] *imp. G. Bishop & J. Norton,* 1605. R.; HD.
    For pt. 2 see 18175.5.

18174 — [Anr. issue, w. cancel tp:] Apologia catholica ex meris Jesuitarum contradictionibus conflata, in qua paradoxa [etc.] Libri duo. *imp. G. Bishop,* 1605. L.O.C. D.M.+; HN.
    Pt. 2 = 18175.5.

18174a — [Anr. issue, w. cancel tp, w. imprint:] *J. Norton,* 1605. L(tp defective).O¹⁰.C.DUR³.M².+; F.HD(tp only).ILL. U.Y.

18175 — [Anr. ed.] Apologiae catholicæ, in qua paradoxa, [etc.] Libri duo. Editio castigatior. 8°. [*Printed abroad f.*] *J. Norton,* 1606. L.O.D.E².P.+; HD.NY¹¹(imp.).U.

18175.5 — Apologiæ catholicæ pars secunda, judicem ecclesiæ demonstrans . . . in libros quinque digesta. 4°. [*R. Field*] *imp. G. Bishop & J. Norton,* 1606. L.O.C.D.DUR³.+; F.Y.
    (Formerly pt. of 18174)

18176 — A catholike appeale for protestants. fol. [*R. Field*] *imp. G. Bishop & J. Norton,* 1609. L².O.C⁴.CASHEL.DEU.+; F.HN.BOWDOIN.HD.U.
    Answers 3604.5.

Morton, Thomas, *Bp.*—*cont.*

18177 — [A variant, w. date:] 1610. L.O.C.D.E.+; F.HN.HD. ILL.U.+

18178 — Causa regia, sive, de authoritate, et dignitate principum christianorum, dissertatio; adversus R. Bellarmini tractatum. 4°. *ap. J. Billium,* 1620. L.O.C².D.E.+; HN.CAL.U.
  — De pace inter evangelicos procuranda sententiæ quatuor. 1638. *See* 20447.

18179 — A defence of the innocencie of the three ceremonies of the church of England. 4°. [*R. Field*] *f. W. Barret,* 1618. Ent. 10 se. L.O.C.E.YK.+; F.HN.HD(date altered in MS. to 1616). N.U.+
    Answered by 559, 560; defended by 4113.

18180 — Second impression. 4°. [*W. Stansby*] *f. W. Barret,* 1619. L.O.C.D.E.+; F.HN.FORDHAM.HD.ILL.+ **A**
    D² copy has extra halfsheet S containing: 'An answere to a popular objection.'

18181 — A direct answer unto the scandalous exceptions, which T. Higgons hath lately objected against D. Morton. 4°. [*R. Field*] *f. E. Weaver,* 1609. Ent. 2 my. L.O.C. D.E².+; F.HD.SMU.U.
    Answers 13454.

18182 — A discharge of five imputations of mis-allegations, falsly charged upon the bishop of Duresme, by an English baron [T. Arundell of Wardour?] 8°. *M. F*[*lesher*] *f. R. Milbourne,* 1633. Ent. 6 fb. L.O.C. D.G².+; F.HN.HD.ILL.NY¹¹.+
    In defence of 18189.

18183 — The encounter against M. Parsons, by a review of his last sober reckoning, [etc.] 4°. [*W. Stansby a. Eliot's Court Press*] *f. J. Bill,* 1610. Ent. 27 ap. L.O.C². D.E.+; HN.BO³.Y.
    In some copies (L, I O) the date is omitted. Answers 19412.

18184 — An exact discoverie of Romish doctrine in the case of conspiracie and rebellion. [Init. T. M.] 4°. F. *Kyngston f. C. B*[*urby*] *a. E. W*[*eaver,*] 1605. Ent. 5 de. to C. Burby a. E. Weaver. O.C.E.M.YK.+; MIN. N.NY¹¹.U.Y.+
    Erratum on H3ᵛ. B1ʳ last line: 'prooued'; D4ʳ line 1 begins: 'cession'. o(4°.P.39.Th.) has these readings. Sheets are sometimes mixed w. 18184.5. Answered by 18188, 19417.

18184.5 — [Anr. ed.] 4°. F. *Kyngston f. C. B*[*urby*]⁵ *a. E. W*[*eaver,*] 1605. L.O.C.D.DUR⁵.+; F(2).HN.BO³.HD.
    No erratum on H3ᵛ. Quires B and D are in two settings: B1ʳ last line: 'proued'; B2ʳ line 1: 'prooued' or 'proued'; D4ʳ line 1 begins: 'inveterate' or 'late'. o(4°S.10.Jur.) has the former readings and o(Pamph.C.3) the latter.

18185 — A full satisfaction concerning a double Romish iniquitie; hainous rebellion, and more then heathenish æquivocation. 4°. *R. Field f. E. Weaver,* 1606. L.O.C.D.M².+; F.HN.HD.N.U.+
    Answers 18188; answered by 18185a, 19417.

18185a — A plaine patterne of a perfect protestant professor: which is to be a false corrupter, of authorities, &c. Taken forth of (A ful satisfaction) written by T. Morton. [By R. Broughton.] 4°. [*English secret press,* 1608–10.] L².L²⁵.
    A&R 167.

18186 — The grand imposture of the (now) church of Rome. 4° in 8's. *G. Miller f. R. Mylbourne,* [1626?] Ent. 11 jy. 1626. L.O.C.D².E².+; F.HN(imp.).NY¹¹. PML.Y.+
    Answered by 20308.

18187 — The second edition, revised w. additions. 4° in 8's. *G. Miller f. R. Milbourne,* 1628. L.O.C.D.E.+; F.HN. CHI.HD.U.+

18188 — A just and moderate answer to a most injurious, and slaunderous pamphlet, [18184]. [By R. Broughton.] 4° in 2's. [*English secret press,* 1606.] L.O.C².BED. YK.+; F.HN.HD.Y.
    A&R 164. Answered by 18185.

18189 — Of the institution of the sacrament of the blessed bodie and blood of Christ. fol. *W. Stansby f. R. Mylbourne,* 1631. Ent. 10 fb. L.O.C.D.E.+; F.HN. HD.ILL.U.+
    Defended in 18182.

18190 — Second edition, much enlarged w. particular answers to objections raysed against this worke. fol. [*A. Mathewes*] *f. R. Milbourne,* 1635. L.O.C.D.G².+; F.HN.ILL. Allegheny C.
  — A plaine patterne of a perfect protestant professor. *See* 18185a.

Morton, Thomas, *Bp.*—cont.

18191 — A preamble unto an incounter with P. R. [i.e. R. Parsons.] Concerning the romish doctrine of rebellion and of aequivocation. 4°. *M. Bradwood f. J. Bill a. E. Weaver,* 1608. L.O.C.D.E.+; F.U.Y.
Answers 19417; answered by 19412.

18192 — Prioris Corinthiacæ epistolæ expositio quædam. 1598. Now = 18197.3.

18193 — Replica. Seu, adversus nuperrimam confutationem aliquotæ particulæ partis prioris Apologiæ T. Mortoni, (authore C. R. theologo [i.e. R. Smith, *Bp. of Chalcedon*]) brevis velitatio. 4°. *R. B[adger,] imp. R. Whitaker & R. Badger,* 1638. Ent. 13 jn.; half Badger's share ass'd to N. Bourne 15 jn. L.O.C.D. DUR⁵.+; F.U.WASH².

— A reply to Dr. Mortons Defence. 1622, 1623. See 559, 560.

18194 — Salomon or a treatise declaring the state of the kingdome of Israel. 1596. Now = 18197.7.

18195 — Sacris ordinibus non rite initiati tenentur. 1633. Now = 18171.5.

18196 — A sermon preached before the kings majestie, in the cathedrall church of Durham. 4°. *London, R. Barker a. assignes of J. Bill,* 1639. L.L¹³.O.C².D.+; F.HN. HD(A2 defective).N.

18196a — [Anr. issue, w. A1 and A2 partially reset, w. imprint:] *Newcastle upon Tyne, R. Barker a. assignes of J. Bill,* 1639. L.O⁶.C².DUR.NEK.+; F.HN.HD.U(imp.).Y.+
Lion mask orn. on tp.

18196a.5 — [Anr. ed.] 4°. *Newcastle upon Tyne, R. Barker a. assignes of J. Bill,* 1639. C.DUR⁵(imp.).E².; F.
Dolphin orn. on tp. Pr. by J. Legatt; *see The Library,* II(1901), pp. 368–9.

18197 — Totius doctrinalis controversiæ De eucharistia decisio. 4° in 8's. *Cantabrigiæ, ex off. R. Danielis,* 1640. L.O.C.D.E².+; F.BO².CAL.CHI.

— *See also* 10176.5, 10192.8, 10193, 10227, 10227.2, and Bookplates.

18197.3 **Morton, Thomas,** *of Berwick.* Prioris Corinthiacæ epistolæ expositio quædam. 8°. *[R. Robinson] ap. R. Dexter,* 1596. L².O.C³.D.G⁴.+; HN.PN².
(Formerly 18192)

18197.7 — Salomon or a treatise declaring the state of the kingdome of Israel. Whereunto is annexed another treatise, . . . of the right constitution of a church. 4°. *R. Robinson f. R. Dexter,* 1596. L.O.C³.D.G².+; F.HN.BO³.U.Y.
(Formerly 18194)

18198 — A treatise of the nature of God. [Anon.] 8°. *T. Creede f. R. Dexter,* 1599. Ent. to Ralph Jackson a. R. Dexter 18 ja. L.O.C.E⁴.M.+; F.HD.

18198.5 — [A variant, w. imprint:] *T. Creede f. Raphe Jackson,* 1599. F.HN.U.Y.

18199 — A treatise of the threefolde state of man. 8°. *[R. Robinson] f. R. Dexter a. Ralph Jackeson,* 1596. Ent. 12 mr. L.O.C².C³.PLUME.+; F(2).ILL.U.

18200 — [Anr. ed.] 12°. *B. A[lsop] a. T. F[awcett] f. R. Dawlman,* 1629. Ent. to G. Latham 31 ja. 1620. L.O. DUL.ELY.YK.+; F(2).HN.HD.ILL.U.

18200.5 — Two treatises concerning regeneration, [etc. Anon.] 8°. *T. Creede f. R. Dexter a. Raph Jackson,* 1597. Ent. 7 fb. L.P.; F.

18201 — [Anr. ed.] 8°. *E. Griffin f. E. Bishop,* 1613. L³.O.D.E⁴.; F.

18202 **Morton, Thomas,** *of Clifford's Inn.* New English Canaan or New Canaan. Containing an abstract of New England, [etc.] 4°. *Amsterdam, J. F. Stam,* 1637. Ent. to C. Greene 18 no. 1633. L.O.C¹³.D.G².+; F.HN.HD.N.NY.+
Tp is a cancel.

18203 — [Anr. issue, w. cancel tp, w. imprint:] *f. C. Greene,* [1637?] L.CHATS.

18203.5 **Morus, Horatius.** Tabulae universam chirurgiam miro ordine complectentes. fol. *H. Denham,* 1584. L¹⁶. L¹⁹.O¹⁴.NEK(tp def.).

18204 — [A trans.] Tables of surgerie, brieflie comprehending the whole art and practise thereof. *Tr.* R. Caldwall. fol. *H. Denham,* 1585. Ent. to R. Newbery 13 au. L.L¹⁶.O.

Morwen, John. See 19931.

Morwyng, Peter, *tr.* See 11800, 14795.

Morysine, Richard. See Morison, *Sir* R.

18205 **Moryson, Fynes.** An itinerary written by Fynes Moryson Gent. (Containing his ten yeeres travell through the twelve dominions of Germany, Bohmerland, . . . France, England, Scotland, and Ireland.) fol. *J. Beale,* 1617. Ent. 5 ap. L.O.C.D.E.+; F.HN.HD.N.NY.+
2nd page of title varies: description of pts. in roman or italic (a cancel); both at O,M,HD. Regarding Moryson's patent to publish this *see* Arber V.lviii.

Mosan, Jacob, *tr.* See 25862.

Moscorovius, Hieronymus. See 20083.3.

Moscow. The reporte of a bloudie massacre in Mosco. 1607. *See* 21461.

Mosellanus, Petrus. See 21810.

18206 **Moses** *ben Maimon.* חלכות תשובה. Canones poenitentiæ Hebraicè. *Tr.* G. N. [i.e. W. Norwich?] 4°. *Cantabrigiæ, ex acad. typog.* [*T. a. J. Buck,*] 1631. L.O.C.D.DUR⁵.+; F(2).HD.ILL.

Moskorzewski, Hieronim. Catechesis ecclesiarum. 1609. *See* 20083.3.

18207 **Mosse, Miles.** The arraignment and conuiction of vsurie. In six sermons. 4°. *widdow Orwin f. T. Man,* 1595. Ent. to T. Man a. J. Porter 18 fb. L.O.O³.C. Bangor UC.+; F.HN.HD.ILL.N.

18208 — [A variant, w. imprint:] *widdow Orwin f. J. Porter,* 1595. L³⁰.O.C⁸.C⁹.; F.CU.HART².LC.PEN.

18209 — Justifying and saving faith. . . . In a sermon. 4°. *C. Legge, Pr. to the Univ. of Cambridge, sold by M. Law [London,]* 1614. L.O.C.E².P.+; F.HN.HD.U. Sydney U.+

18210 — Scotlands welcome. A sermon preached at Needham. 8°. *M. Bradwood f. T. Man,* 1603. Ent. to T. Man a. J. Porter 21 my. L.O.C.D.P.+; F.HN.BO⁵.HART.

— *See also* 21204.5, 21238.

18211 **Mote, Humphrey.** The primrose of London, with her valiant aduenture on the Spanish coast. 4°. *[R. Ward?] f. T. Nelson,* 1585. L.; HN. Penrose 176.

Mother. Mother Bombie. 1594. *See* 17084.

18212 — A mothers teares over hir seduced sonne: or a dissuasive from idolatry. 1627. Now = 24903.5.

Motives. Humble motives [etc.] 1601. *See* 3518.
— Motives to induce the protestant princes [etc.] 1639. *See* 7367.5.

18213 — Motives to godly knowledge: with a briefe instruction. 8°. *f. W. Bladon,* 1613. Ent. 29 ap. O.

Motulind, Antonius de. An almanack. 1555. *See* 483.14.

Motus. Motus Medi-terraneus. 1626. *See* 13585.5.

Moufet, Thomas. See Moffett, T.

Moulin, Pierre du. See Du Moulin, P.

18214 Now = 18223.7.

18214a **Moulton, Thomas.** [*Series I. Author named in 1st chap.: on pestilence. Title reads:*] This is the myrour or glasse of helthe, necessary and nedefull [etc.] 8° in 4's. *(R. wyre,)* [bef. 1531.] O(2).
In colophon: 'Norwytche rents.' 120 chapters in text.

18214a.3 — [Anr. ed.] 8° in 4's. *(R. wyre,)* [bef. 1536.] G².
In colophon: 'Norwytche rentys.' 121 chapters in text.

18214a.5 — [Anr. ed. 121 chapters.] *See* Addenda.

18214a.7 — [Anr. ed.] 8° in 4's. *(R. wyer,)* [bef. 1536.] F(imp.).
In colophon: 'Norwytche rentes.' 134 chapters in text.

18215 — = 18220.

18215a — Now = 18223.7.

18216 — [Anr. ed.] 8°. *(R. Redman,)* [1540?] L.G²(lacks G1).; HN.
This and following eds. have 133 chapters in text.

18217 — Now = 18225.8.

18218 — Now = 18225.2.

18219 — [Anr. ed.] 8°. *(Elysabeth [Pickering] late wyfe vnto R. Redman,)* [1541?] L.C(lacks col.).; HN.

18220 — [Anr. ed. w. title:] The myrrour or glasse [etc.] 8°. *(W. Myddelton,)* [1545?] L.L¹⁶.L¹⁹.C(lacks tp).G².; HN.NLM.PML.
(Formerly also 18215)

18221 — [Anr. ed., w. title:] This is the myrrour [etc.] 8°. *[N. Hill f.] (R. Toye,)* [bef. 1546.] L¹⁶.C.

Moulton, Thomas—*cont.*

18221.3 — [A variant, w. colophon:] (*f. R. Jugge,*) [bef. 1546.] L[16].

18221.5 — [A variant, w. colophon:] (*f. T. Petyt,*) [bef. 1546.] HD.
  Collates A–G[8] H[4]; cf. 18225.4.

18221.7 — [A variant, w. colophon:] (*f. J. Wally,*) [bef. 1546.] L[17].

18221a — [A variant, w. colophon:] (*R. Kele,*) [bef. 1546.] L.C.

18222 — Now = 18225.4.

18222.5 — [Anr. ed.] 8°. [*R. or W. Copland f.*] (*J. waley,*) [1548?] O.; HD.
  Collates A–G[8] H[6].

18223 — [Anr. ed.] 8°. [*W. Copland f.*] (*J. Waley,*) [1560?] L.; HN.
  Collates A–G[8] H[4].

18223.3 — [A variant, w. colophon:] (*A. Vele,*) [1560?] Philadelphia, College of Physicians.

18223.7 — [Anr. ed.] 8°. [*T. Colwell,* 1561?] L(2, 1 imp.).L[16].O[8].C.G[2](2).; NLM.WIS(lacks B1).
  (Formerly 18214 and 18215a) Only known ed. without colophon; one L copy (C.31.c.16) has R. Wyer colophon inserted. Leaf orn. precedes title; in title: 'glasse', 'helth'.

18224 — [Anr. ed.] 8°. (*T. Colwel,*) [1566.] L.O.P.; HN.NLM.
  Leaf orn. precedes title; in title: 'glass', 'healthe'.

18225 — [Anr. ed., w. title:] The mirrour or glasse [etc.] 8°. *H. Jackson,* [1580.] O.C.

18225.2 — [*Series II. Anon. 1st chap. on planets. Title reads:*] This is the glasse of helth, a great treasure. 8° in 4's. (*R. wyer,*) [1540?] L.; NY[4].
  (Formerly 18218) This and the next ed. have 132 chapters in the text. In colophon: 'paryssh besyde'.

18225.4 — [Anr. ed.] 8°. [*T. Petyt,*] [1545?] O.
  (Formerly 18222) Collates a–d[8] e[4]; cf. 18221.5.

18225.6 — [Anr. ed.] 8° in 4's. (*R. wyer,*) [1547?] G[2].; WIS. ℨ
  This and the next ed. have 133 chapters in the text. In colophon: 'seynt . . . parysshe, at'.

18225.8 — [Anr. ed.] 8° in 4's. (*R. wyer,*) [1555?] L.G[2].; PML.
  (Formerly 18217) In colophon: 'saynt . . . parysshe, at'.

Moundeford, Abigail. [Bookplate.] *See* Bookplates.

18226 **Moundeford, Thomas,** *Minister.* A sermon preached at S. Martins in the Fields. At the funerall of the lady Blount. [Anon.] 8°. *B. Alsop f. J. Hodgets,* 1620. Ent. as by T. Mountford 6 mr. O.O[10](tp mutilated).C.
  (Formerly also 3135)

18227 **Moundeford, Thomas,** *Physician.* Vir bonus. Q. Vir bonus est quis? 8°. *per F. Kingstonum,* 1622. Ent. 7 ja. 1623. L.O.C.A.D.+
— *tr. See* 7303.

Mounslowe, Alexander. Almanacks. 1561, etc. *See* 488 sqq.

18228 — A prognosticatitiŏ [*sic*]. [1579.] = pt. of 488.5.

Mount Sinai, St. Katherine's Abbey. *See* Indulgences 90.

18228.3 **Mount Taragh.** Mount Taraghs triumph. 5. July. 1626. *Ballad.* s.sh.fol. *Dublin,* [1626.] L[5](Lemon 271).

Mountague, A. *See* Browne, A., *Viscount Montague.*

18228.5 **Mountague, James,** *Bp.* [Direction to archdeacons, etc. enjoining the teaching of 14418.5.] s.sh.fol. *London,* 1616. L[5].
  For a variant *see* 5870.3; for anr. ed. *see* 14484.
— *ed. See* 14344, 14346.

Mountain, Didymus, *pseud. See* Hill, T.

Mountain, George, *Bp. See* Montaigne, G.

Mountaine, James, *tr. See* 7334.

18229 **Mountebank.** The skilfull mountebanke. Or, come, and I'le cure you. By Joannes Baptista Guardano Ludovico puncto. 8°. *J. O[kes] f. T. Lambert,* 1638. HN.

Mountford, Thomas. *See* Moundeford, T., *Minister.*

Mourt, George. A relation or journall. 1622. *See* 20074.

Mousgrove. The lamentable ditty of little Mousgrove. [1630.] *See* 18316.3.

18230 **Mucedorus.** A most pleasant comedie of Mucedorus. Newly set foorth. 4°. *f. W. Jones,* 1598. L.; HN. Greg 151.

Mucedorus—*cont.*

18231 — [Anr. ed.] 4°. [*W. White*] *f. W. Jones,* 1606. L[6].

18232 — [Anr. ed.] Amplified with new additions. 4°. [*W. White*] *f. W. Jones,* 1610. L.C[2].; HN.

18233 — [Anr. ed.] With new additions. 4°. [*W. White*] *f. W. Jones,* 1611. O.; HN.

18234 — [Anr. ed.] 4° w. perp. chainlines. [*G. Eld?*] *f. W. Jones,* 1613. L.; F.BO.

18235 — [Anr. ed.] 4°. *N. O[kes] f. W. Jones,* 1615. L.; HN.

18236 — [Anr. ed.] 4°. [*G. Eld?*] *f. J. Wright,* 1618. Ass'd by widow S. Jones 17 se. HN.

18237 — [Anr. ed.] 4°. [*G. Eld?*] *f. J. Wright,* 1619. L.O.; HN.BO.HD.

18237.5 — [Anr. ed.] 4°. [*G. Eld?*] *f. J. Wright,* 1621. Gdańsk, Wojewódzka i Miejska Biblioteka Publiczna.

18238 — [Anr. ed.] 4°. [*G. Purslowe*] *f. J. Wright,* 1626. L[6].; F.HN.

18238.5 — [Anr. ed.] 4°. [*G. Purslowe f. J. Wright,* 1629?] C[2](lacks tp).

18239 — [Anr. ed.] 4°. [*G. Purslowe*] *f. J. Wright,* 1631. L.O[14].

18240 — [Anr. ed.] 4°. [*E. Purslowe*] *f. J. Wright,* 1634. L.

18241 — [Anr. ed.] 4°. [*R. Young*] *f. J. Wright,* 1639. C[2].; BO.PML.Y.

Much Horksley. *See* 12207.

18242 **Muenster, Sebastian.** A briefe collection and compendious extract of straūge and memorable thinges, gathered oute of the Cosmographye of S. Munster. 8°. *T. Marshe,* 1572. L(imp.).HAT.
  For anr. trans. *see* 18662.

18243 — [Anr. ed.] 8°. *T. Marshe,* 1574. L.E.; BO.

18243.5 — [Anr. ed.] 8°. *T. Marshe,* 1576. Ent. to T. Orwin, on Marshe's death, 23 jn. 1591. Vermont U.

18244 — A treatyse of the newe India, . . . after the descripcion of S. Munster. Tr. R. Eden. 8°. [*S. Mierdman f.*] (*E. Sutton,* 1553.) L.; CB.MICH.NY.PH[2].PH[7].

18245 **Muffet, Peter.** A commentarie vpon the booke of the Prouerbes of Salomon. [Init. P. M.] 8°. *R. Field f. R. Dexter,* 1592. Ent. 20 jn. L.O.C.C[10].P.; F.HN. CAL.HD.

18246 — The second time perused, much enlarged. Whereunto is newly added an exposition of a fewe prouerbs set downe here and there in the scriptures. 8°. *R. Robinson f. R. Dexter,* 1596. L.C.E.P.YK.+; F.HN.ILL.

18247 — The excellencie of the mysterie of Christ Jesus. [Init. P. M.] 8°. *T. Orwin f. R. Jackson a. W. Young,* 1590. Ent. to R. Jackson 4 no. L.O.LK.; HD.

18248 **Muggins, William.** Londons mourning garment, or funerall teares. [In verse.] (A true relation of al that have bin buried of all diseases, in every severall parish, from 14 of July last past, 1603, to the 17. of November following.) 4°. *R. Blower,* 1603. L.O.; HN.
  (Formerly also 16757)

Mulart, Philippus. Frater Philippus Mulart [etc.] *See* Indulgences 91 sqq.

18249 **Mulcaster, Richard.** Catechismus Paulinus. In vsum scholae Paulinae conscriptus. 8°. *J. Windet, imp. M. Law,* 1601. O.C[5].C[10].G[2]. London, St. Paul's School (imp.). ℨ
  See Greg, *Register B*, p. 77.

18249.5 — Cato Christianus. In quem conijciuntur ea omnia, quae in sacris literis ad parentum, puerorumq́; pietatem videntur maximè pertinere. [In verse.] 8° in 4's. *V. Simsius,* [1600.] C[10].
  Preface dated 6 May 1600.

18250 — The first part of the Elementarie which entreateth of right writing of our English tung. 4°. *T. Vautroullier,* 1582. L.O.C[10].P.SHR.+; F(lacks tp).HN.CU.HD.N.+

18251 — In mortem serenissimæ reginæ Elizabethæ. [In verse.] 4°. *pro E. Aggas,* 1603. L.L[2].L[13].; F.HN.
  Issued w. 18252.

18252 — The translation of certaine latine verses written vppon her majesties death, called a comforting complaint. [Init. R. M. In verse.] 4°. *f. E. Aggas,* 1603. L[2].L[13].; F.HN.
  Issued w. 18251.

18253 — Positions wherin those primitiue circumstances be examined, necessarie for the training vp of children. 4°. *T. Vautrollier f. T. Chare* [sic], 1581. Ent. to T. Chard 6 mr. L[30].O[7].C.DUL.LIV[3].+; F.HN.BO.CU. ILL.+

Mulcaster, Richard—*cont.*

18253a — [A variant, w. imprint:] *T. Vautrollier,* 1581. L.O.C¹⁰.
E.P.+; F.HD.N.WTL.Y(2).
— *See also* 7589.5.

Mulcaster, Robert, *tr. See* 11194.

18254 **Mulheim.** The lamentable destruction of Mulheim. . . .
Printed according to the Dutch originall. 4°. *G. Eld*
f. R. Lea, sold by E. Marchant, 1615. L.

Multibibus, Blasius, *pseud. See* 3585.

18255 **Mun, Thomas.** A discourse of trade, from England unto
the East-Indies. [Init. T. M.] 4°. *N. Okes f. J. Pyper,*
1621. Ent. 12 ap. L.L².O.C.LINC.+; F.CU.HD.LC.Y.+

18256 — Second impression corrected. 4°. *N. Okes f. J. Pyper,*
1621. L.O⁸.C².LINC.M.+; HN.CAL².MIN.N.Y.

18257 **Munda, Constantia,** *pseud.* The worming of a mad
dogge: or, a soppe for Cerberus. 4°. [*G. Purslowe*]
f. L. Hayes, 1617. Ent. 29 ap. L.O(2).; F.HN.BO.
HD.N.
Answers 23533.

18258 **Munday, Anthony.** The admirable deliverance of 266.
christians by J. Reynard [i.e. J. Fox] Englishman
from the Turkes. [Anon.] 4°. *T. Dawson, sold* [*by*
T. Archer,] 1608. Ent. to T. Dawson a. S. Peele
23 jy. 1579. L.C³.; F.HN.

18259 — An aduertisement and defence for trueth against her
backbiters, and specially against fauourers, of
Campions. 1581. Now = 153.7.

18259.3 — The araignement, and execution of a wilfull and
obstinate traitour, named E. Ducket, alias Hauns.
[Init. M. S.] 8°. *J. Charlewood a. E. White,* [1581.]
C⁵.E.
Answered by 12934.

18259.7 — [Ballad in praise of the navy in 12-line stanzas. Last
stanza begins: 'God saue our gratious Queen, / that
dooth a royall fleet maintain:'.] 1/2 sh.fol. *J. Allde f.*
R. Ballard, [c. 1584.] O⁵(bottom half only).

18260 — A banquet of daintie conceits. Furnished with verie
delicate and choyse inuentions, either to the lute,
bandora, virginalles, or anie other instrument. [In
verse.] 4°. *J. C*[*harlewood*] *f. E. White,* 1588. Ent. to
T. Hacket 6 jy. 1584. L.

18261 — A breefe and true reporte, of the execution of certaine
traytours at Tiborne. 4°. [*J. Charlewood*] *f. W.*
Wright, 1582. Ent. 31 my. L(2).L²(2).E.LK(imp.).;
F.HN.

18262 — A breefe aunswer made vnto two seditious pamphlets.
8°. *J. Charlewood,* 1582. Ent. to E. White 12 mr.
L.E.; F.HN.
Answers 4537.

18262a — [A variant, w. imprint:] *f. E. White,* 1582. L².O.; PFOR.

18263 — A briefe chronicle, of the successe of times, from the
creation. 8°. *W. Jaggard,* 1611. L.O.C.G².M.+; F.HN.
HD.ILL.NY.+
Halfsheet B (dedic. to Goldsmiths) often lacking;
present in HN,HD.

18264 — A breefe discourse of the taking of Edmund Campion.
8°. [*J. Charlewood*] *f. W. Wright,* 1581. Ent. 24 jy.
L².
Answered by 7629.
— A breefe treatise of the vertue of the crosse. *Tr.* out of
French. 1599. *See* 24216.

18265 — [Headline:] Camp-bell, or the ironmongers faire field.
[A pageant at the installation of Sir T. Cambell as
Lord Mayor.] 4°. [*E. Allde,* 1609.] L(sheet B only).
Greg 282.

18266 — Chrysanaleia: the golden fishing: or, honour of fish-
mongers. Applauding the advancement of J. Leman,
to lord maior. 4°. *G. Purslowe,* 1616. Ent. 29 oc.
L.L⁸.O.O⁵.LONGLEAT.; F.HN. Greg 335.

18267 — Chruso-thriambos. The triumphes of golde. At the
inauguration of Sir J. Pemberton, in the dignity of
lord maior. 4°. *W. Jaggard,* 1611. HN. Greg 295. ꝺ
Tp line 10 ends: 'Golde-'.

18267.5 — [Anr. ed.] 4°. *W. Jaggard,* 1611. C².
Tp line 10 ends: 'Gold-'.

18268 — A courtly controuersie, betweene looue and learning.
8°. *J. Charlewood f. H. Carre,* 1581. L.

18269 — The death of Robert, earle of Huntington. [A play. By
A. Munday and H. Chettle. Anon.] 4°. [*R. Bradock*]
f. W. Leake, 1601. Ent. 1 de. 1600. L.O.C⁶.E.NEK
(imp.).+; F.HN.HD.NY.Y.+ Greg 180.
Prob. issued w. 18271.

Munday, Anthony—*cont.*

18270 — A discouerie of Edmund Campion, and his con-
federates. 8°. [*J. Charlewood*] *f. E. White,* 1582
(29 ja.) Ent. 12 mr. L.O.C.C³.C⁵(imp.).; F.HN.HD.Y.
B1ʳ catchword: 'Seas,'.

18270.5 — [Anr. ed.] 8°. [*J. Charlewood*] *f. E. White,* 1582 (29 ja.)
C³.M.; F.NY.
B1ʳ catchword: 'Countrie'.

18271 — The downfall of Robert, earle of Huntington. [A
tragedy. By A. Munday and H. Chettle. Anon.] 4°.
[*R. Bradock*] *f. W. Leake,* 1601. Ent. 1 de. 1600.
L.L⁶.O.C⁶.E.+; F.HN.CH.HD. Cleveland PL.+ Greg
179.
Prob. issued w. 18269.

18272 — The English Romayne lyfe. 4°. *J. Charlewoode f. N.*
Ling, 1582. Ent. to J. Charlewood a. N. Ling 21 jn.
L.O.C⁶.DUR⁵.G².+; F(2).HN.HD.ILL.

18273 — [Anr. ed.] 4°. *J. Charlewoode f. N. Ling,* 1590. L.O(2).
DUR⁵.; F.CAL.
— Fedele and Fortunio. *Tr.* [by A. Munday.] 1585. *See*
19447.

18274 — Himatia-Poleos. The triumphs of olde draperie. At the
enstalment of Sʳ. T. Hayes in the high office of
lord maior. [Init. A. M.] 4°. *E. Allde,* 1614. L.
Greg 322.
— The first part of the historie, of Sir J. Oldcastle. [By
A. Munday and others.] 1600. *See* 18795.

18275 — Metropolis coronata, the triumphes of ancient drapery.
In honour of the advancement of Sir J. Jolles, to the
high office of lord maior. [Init. A. M.] 4°. *G. Purs-*
lowe, 1615. L(2).L⁸.O.LONGLEAT.; F.HN.HD. Greg
332.

18276 — The mirrour of mutabilitie, or principall part of the
mirrour for magistrates. [In verse.] 4°. *J. Allde, solde*
by R. Ballard, 1579. Ent. to J. Allde 10 oc. L.SH
(lacks tp).; F.HN.PFOR.

18277 — The paine of pleasure. [In verse.] 4°. [*J. Charlewood*]
f. H. Car, 1580 (17 oc.) Ent. to R. Jones 9 se. 1578.
C⁶.
B1ʳ catchword: 'ⅭIn'. SR entry states: 'compiled
by N. Britten.' First poem is 'Authors Dreame';
see Arber II.847.

18277.5 — [Anr. ed.] 4°. [*H. Bynneman?* 1583?] L(imp.).
B1ʳ catchword: 'What'.

18278 — Sidero-Thriambos. Or steele and iron triumphing.
Applauding the advancement of Sir S. Harvey, to
the dignitie of lord maior. [Init. A. M.] 4°. *N. Okes,*
1618. L. Greg 355.

18279 — The triumphes of re-united Britania. Performed in
honor of Sir L. Holliday lorde mayor. 1605. 4°.
W. Jaggard, [1605.] L(lacks C4).O.; HN. Greg
218.

18280 — The triumphs of the golden fleece. For the enstaulment
of M. Lumley in the maioraltie. 4°. *T. S*[*nodham,*]
1623. L.

18281 — A view of sundry examples. Reporting many straunge
murthers. 4°. [*J. Charlewood*] *f. W. Wright, sold* [*by*
J. Allde, 1580.] Ent. 27 ap. 1580. L².; F.
See also 1325.

18282 — A watch-woord to Englande to beware of traytours.
[Init. A. M.] 4°. [*J. Charlewood*] *f. T. Hacket,* 1584.
L.O(2).; HN.PFOR.
B1ʳ line 2: 'England.'

18282a — [Anr. ed.] 4°. [*J. Charlewood*] *f. T. Hacket,* 1584.
L.O.C.DUL.M.+; F.HN.HD.N.U(imp.).+
B1ʳ line 2: 'Englande.' Sheets B–N only reset.

18283 — Zelauto. The fountaine of fame. 4°. *J. Charlewood,*
1580. O.
— *ed. See* 3189, 4461, 12430, 21801, 23344 sq.
— *tr. See* 7, 190, 541, 543, 544, 684, 5326, 5541, 6467,
11262, 15213, 17206, 18064, 18163, 19157 sq.,
19161, 19165, 19447, 20366 sqq., 23864, 23867,
24216.
— *See also* 13159, 17124, 19974.6, 21677.

Mundus. Mundus & Infans. 1522. *See* 25982.
— Mundus alter et idem. [1607?] *See* 12685.

18284 **Mundy, John.** Songs and psalmes composed into 3. 4.
and 5. parts. 5 ptbks. 4°. *T. Est, the assigne of W.*
Byrd, 1594. Ent. 6 de. 1596. L(2).O(1, plus contratenor). O³.C(tenor).YK.

Munich. A strange report of six witches, executed in
Manchen. 1601. *See* 20890.

18285 **Munster.** A most true relation of a very dreadfull earthquake, in Munster. *Tr.* out of Dutch by C. Demetrius. 4⁰. *Rotterdame* [*London, T. Snodham,* 1612?] L.O.
— A treuue nyeuu tydinges of the rebaptisers of Mūster. [1535?] *See* 564.

Munster, Sebastian. *See* Muenster, S.

Murad IV, *Sultan.* The great Turks terrible challenge. [1640.] *See* 23424.7.
— A true and fearfull pronouncing of warre. 1640. *See* 23424.5.

18286 — A vaunting, daring, and a menacing letter, sent from sultan Morat [etc.] 4⁰. *J. Okes, sold by J. Cowper,* 1638. Ent. to Okes 4 jn. L.C.C¹⁰.LONGLEAT. Athens, Gennadius Library.; HD.LC.

Murder. A horrible, creuel and bloudy murther. 1614. *See* 12630.
— The horrible murther of a young boy. 1606. *See* 6552.
— A most straunge, rare, and horrible murther committed by a Frenchman. [1586.] *See* 11377.

18286.5 **Murders.** Sundrye strange and inhumaine murthers, lately committed. 4⁰. *T. Scarlet,* 1591. L².

18287 — Three bloodie murders: the first, committed by F. Cartwright upon W. Storre, [etc.] 4⁰. [*G. Eld?*] *f. J. Trundle,* 1613. L(destroyed.)O(2).; HD(tp cropt). TEX.
Includes reprint of 23295.

18288 — Two most unnatural and bloodie murthers: the one by Maister Caverly, a Yorkshire gentleman. The other, by Mistris Browne. 4⁰. *V. S[immes] f. N. Butter,* 1605. Ent. 12 jn. O.LONGLEAT.
For plays on this subject, *see* 22340, 25635.

18289 — Two notorious murders. One committed by a tanner (J. Wright), [etc.] 4⁰. [*Eliot's Court Press*] *f. W. Blackwall & G. Shaw,* ⟨1595.⟩ Ent. 17 jy. 1595. L(destroyed).; HD(photostat of L).

18290 **Mure, Andrew.** Πιδαξ Πετρεια or, the discoverie of S. Peters well, at Peter-head. 8⁰. *Edinburgh, heirs of A. Hart,* 1636. L.O.E².

Mure, *Sir* **William.** *See* Moore, W.

Muretus, Marcus Antonius, *ed. See* 23886.

18291 **Murford, Nicholas.** At the court at Oatelands. [1640?] Now = pt. of 21636.5.

18292 **Muriell, Christopher.** An answer unto the catholicks supplication, [etc.] 4⁰. *R. R[ead] f. F. Burton,* 1603. Ent. 25 jn. L.O.O².C⁸.YK.+; F. Bp. Medley Library, Church Hall, Fredericton, N.B.
For another answer *see* 20141.

18292.3 — [Anr. ed.] Newlie corrected and augmented. 4⁰. *R. R[ead] f. F. Burton,* 1603. L¹³.O.O⁵.E.WI.+; HN.HD.

18292.7 **Murmellius, Joannes.** Composita verborum et verba cōmunia ac deponētalia. 4⁰. [*W. de Worde,* c. 1521.] P(imp.).; PML(imp.).

18293 — [Anr. ed.] 4⁰ ⁸·⁴. (*W. de Worde,* 1529.) O.
— *ed. See* 22980.

Murmurer. A murmurer. 1607. *See* 3671.

Murray, Annabella. *See* 14846.5.

18294 **Murray,** *Sir* **David.** A paraphrase of the CIV. psalme. 4⁰. *Edinburgh, A. Hart,* 1615. E².E⁸.

18294.5 — The complaint of the shepheard Harpalus. [Init. D. M.] *Ballad.* 1/2 sh.fol. [*M. Flesher*] *f. H. G[osson,* c. 1625.] C⁶.G².
Issued w. 15.3. Reprinted in 18296.

18295 — [Anr. ed.] 1/2 sh.fol. *assignes of T. Symcocke,* [1628–29.] L.
Issued w. 15.5.
— A paraphrase of the CIV. psalme. *See* 18294.

18296 — The tragicall death of Sophonisba. (Cælia. [etc.]) [In verse.] 8⁰. [*G. Eld*] *f. J. Smethwick,* 1611. Ent. 18 fb. L(lacks tp).E.E².; F.HN.HD. Robert Taylor.
Includes reprint of 18294.5.

Murray, James, *Earl of.* The deploratioun of the murther. 1570. *See* 22192a.3 sq.

18297 **Murray, John,** *Earl of Annandale.* A letter writt⟨en to⟩ the L. viscount Anan decl⟨aring the nature of the⟩ late clemency to the lay-recusants in England.⟩ 4⁰. [*London?* 1622.] L(tp mutilated).

Murray, John, *Minister. See* 22236.

Murray, Mungo. *See* 21555.36, 21555.44.

18298 **Murray, Thomas.** Naupactiados. 1604. = 14386.

Murray, William, *Bp.* Llandaff. Visitation Articles. *See* 10246.

18299 **Murrell, John.** A new booke of cookerie. Wherein is set forth the fashion for dressing or sowcing, eyther flesh, fish, or fowle. [etc. Init. J. M.] 8⁰. [*T. Snodham*] *f. J. Browne,* 1615. Ent. 14 oc. 1614. O.

18300 — [Anr. ed., signed in full.] 8⁰. [*T. Snodham*] *f. J. Browne,* 1617. Ent. 4 ja. 1618. L.O.
Reprinted in 18302.5.

18301 — A daily exercise for ladies and gentlewomen. Whereby they may learne the whole art of making pastes, preserves, [etc.] 12⁰. [*T. Snodham*] *f. the widow Helme,* 1617. Ent. to J. Browne 29 ap. L.LEEDS.; HD(imp.).LC.

18302 — A delightful daily exercise for ladies and gentlewomen. Whereto is added a booke of cookery. 2 pts. 12⁰. [*A. Mathewes*] *f. T. Dewe,* 1621. Ent. to A. Helme 28 mr. L.; HN.
The recipes differ from those in Murrell's other books.

18302.5 — Murrels two bookes of cookerie and carving. The fourth time printed. 8⁰. *M. F[lesher] f. J. Marriot,* 1631. Ent. 17 fb. 1623. O(sub tp only).; NY.
Reprints 18299; carving reprinted from 3289.

18303 — The fifth time printed. 8⁰. *M. F[lesher] f. J. Marriot,* 1638. L.L⁴¹.LEEDS.; F.LC.

Murton, John. A discription of what God hath predestinated. 1620. *See* 6773.
— Objections. Answered by way of dialogue. 1615. *See* 13054.
— *See also* 563.5, 21107a.

Musæ. Musarum deliciae. 1635. *See* 20522.
— Musarum plangores. [1591.] *See* 14685.5.

18304 **Musaeus.** The divine poem of Musaeus. *Tr.* by G. Chapman. 32⁰ in 8's. *I. Jaggard,* 1616. Ent. to W. Jaggard 27 jy. O.

18305 **Muschet, George,** *Priest.* The bishop of London his legacy. Or certaine motives of D. King, late bishop of London, for his change of religion. [Init. A. B.] 4⁰. [*St. Omer, English College Press,*] 1623. L⁴.O.C. A.D².+; F(2).HD.TEX.
A&R 555. *See also* 14969.

18306 — [A variant, w. date:] 1624. L.C².M.USHAW.W.+; TEX.U. A&R 556.

18307 **Muschet, George,** *Poet.* The complaint of a christian soule. Newlie written in meter. 4⁰. *Edinburgh, R. Charters* [sic], 1610. L.E.E².

18307.5 **Musculus, Wolfgang.** The comentarye or exposition of W. Musculus vppon the li. psalme. Newlye *tr.* [by J. Cox?] out of Latine into Englishe the xii. of December. 1565. 16⁰ in 8's. *R. Serle f. W. Lobley,* [1566?] Ent. 1565–66. L¹⁵(imp.).

18308 — Common places of christian religion. Hereunto are added two other treatises, one of othes, and an other of vsurye. *Tr.* (J. Man.) fol. [colophon on 587ᵛ:] (*R. Wolfe,*) 1563. L.O.C.BIRM.YK.+; F.HN.HD(lacks errata).U.Y.+
Another colophon on 570ᵛ: 'Reynolde Woulfe' (HN,HD) or 'Reginalde Wolfe' (L). Copies vary: HN has col. on 587ᵛ dated 1563 and on 570ᵛ dated 1562; HD is vice versa; L has both cols. dated 1563. Includes anr. trans. of 18310.

18309 — [Anr. ed.] 4⁰ in 8's. *H. Bynneman,* 1578. L.O.C.A.P.+; F.HN.N.PN.Y.+
See Arber II.788.

18309.5 — Den eersten psalm Davids, seer fijn ende christelick wtgheleit. 12⁰. (*bwten Lonnen, Theophilū Brugensem* [i.e. *Emden? E. van der Erve?*] 1554.) Frederik Muller & Co., Amsterdam, *Troubles Religieux* (Catalogue Oct. 1904) no. 296, as cited in E. J. Worman, *Alien Members of the Book-Trade during the Tudor Period,* 1906, p. 19.

18310 — Of the lawful and vnlawful vsurie amōgest christians. *Tr.* (T. L.) 16⁰ in 8's. [*Wesel? H. Singleton?* 1556?] L.O.C(2).; F.
This is pr. in the types of 9981. For anr. trans. *see* 18308.

Musculus, Wolfgang—*cont.*

18311 — Le Temporiseur. . . . Auec plusieurs bons conseilz. [E. Myonius, *pseud.*] (*Tr.* V. Poullain.) 8°. (*E. Mierdman*,) 1550. L.O(imp.).P.PARIS.; HD.

18312 — [A trans.] The temporysour (that is to saye: the obseruer of tyme, or he that chaungeth with the tyme.) Compyled in Latyn by W. Musculus, and *tr.* into Frenche by M. V. Pullain. And out of Frenche by R. P[ownoll.] (A excellent admonicion of Cœlius Secundus Curio.) 8°. [*Wesel? H. Singleton?*] 1555 (jy.) L.
Pr. in same types as 9981.

18313 — [A variant, w. title:] The temporisour [etc.] O.O[17] (imp.).BUTE.; F.

18314 — [Anr. ed.] 16° in 8's. *Edinburgh, T. Vautroullier*, 1584. L(tp only, Ames I.432).YK.; F.
— *See also* 13210.

18314.5 **Muse.** A muse and maze of a sicke-mans minde, through the feare of death and hell. [In verse.] 8°. *G. Eld*, 1616. P.

Muser, Peter, *Engraver. See* 12734.7.

18315 **Muses.** The muses fire-works upon the fifth of November. s.sh.fol. *f. W. Miller*, [c. 1680.] = Wing M 3142.

Museum. The constitutions of the musæum Minervæ. 1636. *See* 15099.

18316 **Musgrave, Christopher.** Musgraves motives, and reasons, for his secession from the church of Rome. 4°. *F. K[ingston] f. R. Moore*, 1621. Ent. 6 mr. L.O.C.DUR(Bamb.).YK.+; F.HN.N.Y. Sexton.

18316.3 **Musgrove.** The lamentable ditty of little Mousgrove, and the lady Barnet. *Ballad.* 2 pts. s.sh.fol. *f. H. Gosson*, [1630.] Ent. to F. Coles 24 jn. 1630. C[6].

18316.7 **Mush, John.** An abstracte of the life and martirdome of Mistres M. Clitherowe. [Anon. Abridged from the MS. life by J. Mush.] 8°. *Mackline, H. Jaey*, 1619. St. Augustine's Priory, Newton Abbot, Devon. A&R 551.
— Declaratio motuum. 1601. *See* 3102.
— *See also* 25124.

Musket, George. *See* Muschet, G., *Priest.*

Musophil., Anonym., *ed. See* 24397.

Musophilus, *pseud. See* 3568.5, 3574, 3575.

18317 **Mussemius, Joannes.** Prognosticon D. Ioannis Mussemij Germa. 1544. Now = 488.9.

Mustapha. The tragedy of Mustapha. 1609. *See* 12362.
— November 11. Number 3. The wonderfull resignation of Mustapha. 1623. *See* Newsbooks 132.

Muzio, Girolamo. *See* 21788.

Myddelmore, Henry. The translation of a letter. 1564. *See* 24565.

Myddelton. *See* Middleton.

18318 **Mynshul, Geffray.** Certaine characters and essayes of prison and prisoners. Compiled by Novus Homo a prisoner in the Kings Bench. [Signed: 'Yarffeg Lluhsnym'.] 8°. *W. Jones*, 1618. Ent. 11 fb. L.

18319 — [Anr. ed., signed: 'G. Mynshul'.] Essayes and characters of a prison and prisoners. 4°. [*G. Eld*] *f. M. Walbancke*, 1618. L.O(2).DUL(imp.).NLW. Chester PL.; F.HN.ILL.NY. Arthur Houghton.

18320 — [Anr. ed.] With some new additions. 4°. *J. O[kes] f. M. Walbancke*, 1638. L.O.O[6].BHP.; F(2).BO.HART[2]. HD.N.

Myonius, Eutichius, *pseud. See* 18311.

Myriel, Henry, *ed. See* 5549.7.

18321 **Myriell, Thomas.** The christians comfort. In a sermon. 4°. *G. P[urslowe] f. J. White*, 1623. Ent. 19 fb. L[8].O. C[2].P.YK.+; F.BO[6].

18322 — Christs suite to his church. A sermon. 8°. [*T. Snodham*] *f. N. Butter*, 1613. Ent. 6 de. O.LINC.

18323 — The devout soules search. In a sermon. 8°. *T. C[reede] f. J. Budge*, 1610. Ent. to J. Budge a. R. Bonian 12 fb. L.O.C[3].LINC.; Weissman.

18323a — [Anr. issue, w. imprint:] *T. C[reede] f. R. Bonian a. H. Walley*, 1610. C.
— *See also* 25663.

Mystery. The mysterie of Megiddo. 1589. *See* 12579.5.
— The mysterie of the Lords supper. 1614. *See* 3922.

N

18324　**N.** To the maior, aldermen, and inhabitants of N. A dialogue against playing at cardes. [1600?] Now = 1335.7.
— *ed. See* 17815.

18324.5　**N.,** *Christian.* Cuiusdā fidelis christiani epistola, ad christianos oēs. Subsequitur & diui Augustini de miseria, mortalis uitæ, sermo. 4°. *ap. præclaram Cantabrigiam,* (*J. Siberch,* 15)21. O.

N., A. The Bible-bearer. 1607. *See* 18495.
— Catechismus. 1570. *See* 18701.
— Elizaes memoriall. 1603. *See* 18586.
— Great Brittaines generall joyes. 1613. *See* 18587.
18325　— A true relation of the travels of M. Bush, a gentlemen: . . . from Lamborne, a place in Bark. shire, to London. [By A. Nixon.] 4°. *T. P[urfoot] f. N. Butter,* 1608. L.; Pearson.
18325.3　— [A variant, w. title:] A true relation of the admirable voiage and travell of William Bush gentleman. F (impr. cropt).
— Two faces under a hood. 1607. *See* 18495.5.
18325.7　— A warning to all trayterous papistes. Who by continual practise, and especialie by this late & horrible treason, [etc. In verse.] 4°. *R. Waldegraue f. T. Man a. W. Brome,* 1586. C⁵.LONGLEAT.

N., B.; N., B., *Gent.;* **N., Ber.,** *Gent. See* Breton, N.

18326　**N., C.** Our Ladie hath a new sonne. 8°. *Dowaie* [i.e. *English secret press,*] 1595. L.O.LINC(imp.).; HN. A&R 558.
— The unfortunate politique. 1638. *See* 4876.

18327　**N., D.** Londons looking-glasse. Or the copy of a letter, written by an English travayler, to the apprentices of London. 8°. [*St. Omer, English College Press,*] 1621. O. A&R 559.
18327.5　— A toung-combat, lately happening, between two English soldiers; in the tilt-boat of Gravesend. 8°. [*Malines, H. Jaye,*] 1623. L⁹.C³.M.; HN.HD. (Formerly 22091) A&R 560. Answered by 13264.8.
— *See also* 13576.
— *tr. See* 18443.

N., E. Cæsars dialogue. 1601. *See* 18432.

18328　**N.,** *Sir F.* The true copies of two especiall letters. 1622. Now = Newsbooks 55.

N., H. *See* Niclas, H.

18328.5　**N., I.** or **J.** A path-way to penitence. With sundry deuout prayers. 16° in 8's. *J. Wolfe,* 1591. Ent. 20 no. 1590 a. 25 fb. 1591. L. Possibly by J. Norden.
— The pensive mans practise. The second part. 1609. *See* 18626a.5.

N., I., *G., tr. See* 16650.5.

N., L., *ed. See* 3191.

N., M. Remaines . . . concerning Britaine. 1605. *See* 4521.

N., M., *B.D. P.P.* A catechisme, composed according to the order of the catechisme in the Common Prayer Booke. The second edition. *See* 18531.

18329　**N., N.** De conventu Cæsaris Ferdinandi cum quibusdam imperii electoribus Ratisbonæ celebrato, anno M.DC.XXX. epistola. 4°. *B. A[lsop] & T. F[awcett] pro N. Butter & N. Bourne,* 1631. L.O.O¹¹.C. PLUME.+; HN.CHI.COR.

N., N.—*cont.*
18330　— An epistle of a catholicke young gentleman, (being for his religion imprisoned.) To his father a protestant. 8°. *Doway* [i.e. *English secret press,*] 1623. O.; Robert Taylor. (Formerly also 10431) A&R 561. End of text on C6ᵛ dated 15 Aug. 1614.
18331　— Maria triumphans. Being a discourse, wherin the B. Virgin Mary is defended. 12°. [*St. Omer, English College Press,*] 1635. L.AUG(imp.).USHAW.W(imp.). St. Joseph's College, Upholland, near Wigan, Lancs. A&R 562.
— The progenie of catholicks and protestants. 1633. *See* 579.
— The triple cord. 1634. *See* 580.
— *tr. See* 7266, 16828.

N., N., *Catholic Gentleman, tr. See* 22889.

N., N., *P. See* 576.

18332　**N., Nicolaus.** Epistola cuiusdam angli, qua asseritur consensus veræ religionis doctrinæ & ceremoniarum in Anglia. [*Paris,*] 1061 [i.e. 1561.] Not an STC book.

18333　**N., O.** An apology of English Arminianisme or a dialogue. 8°. [*St. Omer, English College Press,*] 1634. L.O(2).O⁹.O¹⁷.D.; ILL. A&R 563.

18334　**N., R.** The christians manna. Or a treatise of the eucharist. Written by a catholike devine. 4°. [*St. Omer, English College Press,*] 1613. L.O.C².A².W.+; F.HD.TEX.U.Y.+ A&R 564.
— The furies. 1614. *See* 18521.
— A table of boorde and timber measure. [1615?] *See* 18676.5.

N., R., *Oxon.* Sir Thomas Overburies vision. 1616. *See* 18524.

N., R.P.N. Clavis Homerica. 1638. *See* 21072a.

N., S. An antidote. 1615. *See* 18657.
— An appendix to the Antidote. 1621. *See* 18658.5.
18334.5　— The copie of a letter written to a very worshipful catholike gentleman in England. 8°. [*Antwerp, A. Conincx?*] 1601. USHAW. A&R 565.
— The guide of faith. 1621. *See* 18659.

18335　**N., T.** The disposition or garnishmente of the soule. 1596. Now = 26038.8.
18335.5　— A pleasant dialogue. betweene a lady called Listra, and a pilgrim. Concerning the gouernment of Crangalor. 1579. (The second part of the painefull iorney of the poore pylgrime.) 2 pts. 8°. *J. Charlewood,* [1579.] Ent. 5 my. 1579. HN.
— *ed. See* 1356.5.
— *tr. See* Newton, Thomas, and Nicholas, Thomas.

N., T., *Student in Cambridge, tr. See* 22229.

18336　**N., W.,** *gent.* Barley-breake, or, a warning for wantons. [In verse.] 4°. *S. Stafford,* 1607. Ent. 16 my. O.O³.; HN.HD(imp.). Robert Taylor.

18337　**Nabbes, Thomas.** Playes, maskes, epigrams, elegies, and epithalamiums. Collected into one volumne. 4°. *J. Dawson, sold* [*by N. Fussell,*] 1639. L.E.M²(imp.).; BO.PFOR.
This gen. tp app. was intended to be issued w. plays having cancel tpp: 18340.5 or 18340, 18345a or 18345, and 18343a (E,M²,PFOR). Copies of this title at L,BO are bd. w. 18339, 18345 or 18344, and 18343 or 18343a. All known copies now have bd. in also 2 or more other Nabbes plays.

Nabbes, Thomas—*cont.*

18338 — The bride, a comedie. 4°. *R. H[odgkinson] f. L. Blaikelocke*, 1640. Ent. 8 jy. 1639. L.O.D.E.M².+; F.HN.HD.N.NY(lacks I4).+ Greg 576.

18339 — Covent garden: a pleasant comedie. 4°. *R. Oulton f. C. Greene*, sold [*by N. Fussell*,] 1638. Ent. 28 my. L.L⁶.O.D.M.+; F.HN.CU.HD.ILL.+ Greg 542.
Also issued as pt. of 18337.

18340 — [Anr. issue, w. cancel tp, w. imprint:] *R. Oulton, sold* [*by N. Fussell*,] 1639. L(3).L⁶.O.E.(lacks tp)*.; F.HN. HD.LC.
Cancel tp pr. by J. Dawson; also issued as pt. of 18337.

18340.5 — [A variant, w. imprint:] *R. O[ulton]*, sold [*by N. Fussell*,] 1639. E(pt. of 18337).ETON.

18341 — Hannibal and Scipio. An historicall tragedy. 4°. *R. Oulton f. C. Greene*, 1637. Ent. 6 au. 1636. L.O.C⁴.D.E.+; F.HN.HD.N.NY.+ Greg 513.

18342 — Microcosmus. A morall maske. 4°. *R. Oulton f. C. Greene*, 1637. Ent. 6 au. 1636. L.O.C⁴.D.E.+; F.HN. HD.N.PML.+ Greg 514.

18343 — The springs glorie. Vindicating love. . . . Moralized in a maske. With other poems, epigrams, elegies, and epithalamiums of the authors. 4°. *J. D[awson] f. C. Greene*, sold by *N. Fussell*, 1638. Ent. to C. Greene 23 jn. L(2).L⁶.O(2).O⁶.E.; F.HN.CH.HD.Y.+ Greg 543.
Variant dedics. to B. Roberts or W. Ball; both at O,F,HN. Also issued as pt. of 18337.

18343a — [Anr. issue, w. cancel tp:] The springs glory, a maske. *J. Dawson*, sold [*by N. Fussell*,] 1639. L.L⁶.O.ETON (frag.).; F(2).HN(2).HD.N.Y.
Variant dedics. as in 18343; both at HN. Also issued as pt. of 18337.

18344 — Totenham Court. A pleasant comedie: acted in the yeare MDCXXXIII. At the private house in Salisbury-Court. The author T. Nabbes. 4°. *R. Oulton f. C. Greene*, 1638. Ent. 5 ap. L.O.C⁴.D.E.+; F.HN.HD.N.NY.+ Greg 540.
Also issued as pt. of 18337.

18345 — [Anr. issue, w. cancel tp:] Totenham-Court, a pleasant comedy. Acted at the private house in Salisbury-Court. By T. Nabbs. *R. Oulton, sold* [*by N. Fussell*,] 1639. L(3).E.; HN.ILL.Y.
Also issued as pt. of 18337. Cancel tp pr. by J. Dawson.

18345a — [A variant, w. 'Salisburie-Court'.] L⁶.L³⁰.O.SHEF.; F.CU.ILL.Y.
Also issued as pt. of 18337.

18346 — The unfortunate mother: a tragedie. Never acted. 4°. *J. O[kes] f. D. Frere*, 1640. Ent. 4 no. 1639. L.O.D. E.M.+; F.HN.HD.N.NY.+ Greg 581.
— See also 15055.

18347 **Naile, Robert.** A relation of the royall, magnificent, and sumptuous entertainment, given to Queene Anne, at Bristoll. [In verse.] 4°. [*Eliot's Court Press*] *f. J. Budge*, 1613. Ent. 8 oc. L.O.; HN.

Namen. See 18347.5.

Names. The names of all the high sheriffes. 1628. *See* 10018.5.

18347.5 **Namur.** A true relation of the birth of three monsters in the city of Namen in Flanders: as also Gods judgement upon an unnaturall sister. . . . (*Tr.*, according to the Dutch copy.) 4°. (*S. Stafford f. R. Bunnian*, 1609.) Ent. 25 ap. L(col. only, Harl.5927/159).; F.

Nanni, Giovanni. See 17092.

18348 **Nannini, Remigio.** Civill considerations upon many and sundrie histories. Done into French by G. Chappuys, and into English by W. T[raheron?] fol. *F. K[ingston] f. M. Lownes*, 1601. Ent. 30 mr. L.O.C.D.E².+; F.HN.HD.N.NY.+

Nannius, Petrus, *ed.* See 23885.7.
— *tr.* See 886.

Nantes. The kinges declaration . . . of Nantes. 1613. *See* 16831.
— November the 29. The true originall edict of Nants. 1622. *See* 16843.

Naogeorgus, Thomas. See 15011.

18349 **Napier, John.** Mirifici logarithmorum canonis descriptio. 4°. *Edinburgi, ex off. A. Hart*, 1614. Ent. to E. Aggas 16 ja. 1615. L³⁸.O. CASHEL.E(imp.). Cambridge, Philosophical Lib.+; HN.BO.IND.MICH.Y.+

Napier, John—*cont.*

18349a — [Anr. issue, w. 'Admonitio' on m1ᵛ.] L.O.C.D.E².+; CH.CHI.LC.NY⁸.TEX.+

18350 — [Anr. issue, w. cancel tp to pt. 1, and pt. 2 added.] (Mirifici logarithmorum canonis constructio; . . . Unà cum annotationibus H. Briggii.) 2 pts. *Edinburgi, A. Hart*, 1619. L³⁸.O.C.D.E.+; F(imp.).HN. BO.NY. Horblit.
Most copies do *not* have the reissue of pt. 1, which is present in 2 E,F,HN. BO has both pts., without the cancel tp to pt. 1.

18351 — [A trans.] A description of the admirable table of logarithmes. *Tr.* E. Wright. With an addition of an instrumental table invented by the translator, and described by H. Brigs. 12°. *N. Okes*, 1616. Ent. 3 jy. L.O.C¹⁶.E.M⁴.+; CAL².CH.CHI.PH. Horblit.

18352 — [Anr. issue, w. tp cancelled and replaced by πA¹², w. Appendix to the Logarithmes and new tp:] Whereunto is added new rules. [*N. Okes*] *f. S. Waterson*, 1618. L³⁰.O.C.E².LIV³.+; F(imp.).BO.MICH.NY.Y.+
— Logarithmicall arithmetike. First invented by J. Neper. 1631. *See* 3740.

18353 — No entry.

18354 — A plaine discouery of the whole Reuelation of Saint John. 4° in 8's. *Edinburgh, R. Walde-graue*, 1593. L.O.C.E.YK.+; F.HN.HD.NY.Y.+
Outer sheet of quire B in two settings: B1ʳ line 4: 'euidentlie' (HD) or 'euidently' (HN).

18355 — [Anr. ed.] Newlie imprinted. 4° in 8's. [*Edinburgh, R. Waldegrave*] *f. J. Norton*, [*London*,] 1594. L.L³⁸.O. CASHEL.E.+; F. HN(imp.).MIN.N.U.+

18356 — [Anr. ed.] Now revised, and inlarged. 4° in 8's. *Edinburgh, A. Hart*, 1611. C.C³.E(2).E⁴.; F.HN.MICH.NY.

18356a — [A variant, w. imprint:] *f. J. Norton*, 1611. L.O.C.D.E.+; F.HN.CAL.HD.NY.+

18357 — Rabdologiæ, seu, numerationis per virgulas libri duo. 12°. *Edinburgi, A. Hart*, 1617. Ent. to N. Okes 22 my. L.O.C.D.E.+; F.HN.CHI.HD.NY.+
Tp line 5 varies: 'expeditissi-' (HN,HD) or 'expeditis-' (F). On leaf C8 of 420.11 is an advt. that Napier's Rods are 'made by Nathaniel Gosse in Hosier-lane.'
— See also 12518, 23063.

18358 **Naples.** The great wonders that are chaunced in the realme of Naples. *Tr.* out of Frenche by J. A. 1566. [With a poem: 'An admonition or warning to England' by J. Partridge.] 8°. (*H. Denham f. T. Hacket*,) [1566.] Ent. 1565–66. O.

18359 **Narne, William.** Christs starre: or, a christian treatise. 4°. *J. L[egat] f. P. Stephens a. C. Meredith*, 1625. Ent. to R. Rounthwaite 29 se. 1624. L.C(imp.). D(imp.).E⁸.LINC.+; F.BO⁶.HD.PN².

18359.5 — [A variant, w. imprint:] *J. L[egat] f. R. Rounthwaite*, 1625. O.

18360 — The pearle of prayer most pretious, and powerfull. 8°. *Edinburgh, J. Wreittoun*, 1630. C.E².; F.HD.U.

Narration. A narration, briefely contayning the history of the French massacre. 1618. *See* 3950.
— Cent. 3. . . . A true narration of a late sea-fight. 1640. *See* Newsbooks 328.

Narrationes. Articuli ad narrationes nouas. [1525?] *See* 812.

18361 — [Novae Narrationes. 1st a1ʳ (index):] De recto patens defens replicacio [etc. 2nd a2ʳ:] noue narrationes [etc.] Law Fr. 4° in 6's. [*London?* bef. 1501?] L(imp.). c(lacks e4).; HN.HD. Duff 334.
On folio-sized paper w. horizontal chainlines. The types, 83 mm. bastard, resemble J. Rastell's except for 'w' and abbreviations; if Rastell was involved in the printing, the date is more likely c. 1512.

18362 — [Anr. ed.] fol. [*R. Pynson*, 1504?] L(lacks F6).O(lacks F6).C⁴(imp.).
A1ʳ line 1 of text ends: 'ē'.

18362.5 — [Anr. ed.] fol. [*R. Pynson*, 1519?] L(2, 1 lacks F6).C⁴ (lacks F6).
A1ʳ line 1 of text ends: 'illōques'.

18363 — [Anr. ed.] Herein is contained the booke called Nouae narrationes, Articuli ad nouas narrationes [812], and the booke of diuersitees of courtes [10946]. Newly imprinted. 8°. *in aed. R. Tottell*, 1561 (1 ap.) Ent. 18 fb. 1583. L.O.C.D.G².+; F.HN.HD.N.PML.+

Nash, Thomas. An almond for a parrat. [Attributed to T. Nash.] [1589?] *See* 534.

Nash, Thomas—*cont.*

18364 — The anatomie of absurditie: contayning a breefe confutation of the slender imputed prayses to feminine perfection. 4°. *J. Charlewood f. T. Hacket,* 1589. Ent. 19 se. 1588. L³⁰(lacks tp)*.o.; F.HN.

18365 — [A variant, w. date:] 1590. L.
— The apologie of Pierce Pennilesse. *See* 18378.

18366 — Christs teares ouer Ierusalem. 4°. *J. Roberts, solde by A. Wise,* 1593. Ent. to A. Charlewood 8 se. L.O.O³.; HN(imp.).PFOR.

18367 — [Anr. issue, w. new prelims., w. imprint:] *f. A. Wise,* 1594. L(imp.).O.O³(lacks X2).; HN.HD(imp.)*.
Prelims. pr. by R. Field. O has both orig. and cancel of X3.

18368 — [Anr. ed.] 4°. [*G. Eld*] *f. T. Thorp,* 1613. L.O.C.C⁹.NOR². P.; F(2).HN.HD.N.Y.
— A countercuffe [etc. Doubtfully attributed to T. Nash.] 1589. *See* 19456.
— The first part of Pasquils apologie. [Doubtfully attributed to T. Nash.] 1590. *See* 19450.

18369 — Haue with you to Saffron-walden. 4°. *J. Danter,* 1596. L(3).L⁶.O(3, 2 imp.).C⁶.C⁹(lacks tp).; F.HN.HD. NY.TEX.+

18370 — Nashes Lenten stuffe, containing the description of Great Yarmouth. With a new play of the praise of the red herring. 4°. [*T. Judson a. V. Simmes*] *f. N. L[ing] a. C. B[urby]* 1599. Ent. to C. Burby 11 ja. L.O.O³(imp.).C².C⁶.+; F.HN.HD.ILL.NY.+
Sheets B–F pr. by Judson; sheet A and prob. the rest pr. by Simmes. *See also* 19933.5.

18371 — Pierce Penilesse his supplication to the diuell. 4°. [*J. Charlewood f.*] *R. Jhones,* 1592. Ent. 8 au. L. L¹³(imp.).; F.HD.NY.
See also 20905.

18372 — [Anr. ed.] 4°. *A. Jeffes f. J. Busbie,* 1592. L(tp only, Harl.5921/135).O.O⁸.C²(lacks tp).; F.CH.N. Robert Taylor.

18373 — [Anr. ed.] 4°. *A. Jeffes f. J. B[usby,]* 1592. L(tp facs.).; HN.

18374 — [Anr. ed.] 4°. *A. Jeffes f. J. B[usby,]* 1593. L.O⁵(imp.).

18375 — [Anr. ed.] 4°. (*T. C[reede]*) *f. N. Ling,* 1595. L(2).L⁶. O(3).C.C⁹(lacks tp).; F.HN.Y. Hickmott.

18376 — A pleasant comedie, called Summers last will and testament. 4°. *S. Stafford f. W. Burre,* 1600. Ent. to C. Burby a. W. Burre 28 oc. L.L⁶.O.C⁶.E.+; F. HN. HD.ILL.Y.+ Greg 173.
Imprint varies: 'Water' or 'Walter'; both at L.
— The returne of Pasquill. [Doubtfully attributed to T. Nash.] 1589. *See* 19457.

18377 — Strange newes, of the intercepting certaine letters. 4°ª w. perp. chainlines. [*J. Danter,*] 1592. Ent. to J. Danter 12 ja. 1593. L(2).O(2, 1 lacks C4).
L(Ashley 1257) has horizontal chainlines.

18377a — [Anr. issue, w. A1,2 reset, w. imprint:] *J. Danter,* 1592. HN.

18377b — [A variant, w. date:] 1593. CH.

18377b.5 — [Anr. issue, omitting 'To . . . carminist' and w. 'To . . . readers' on verso of tp.] *J. Danter,* 1593. F.

18378 — [Anr. issue, w. prelims. of 18377 reprinted on 2 leaves.] The apologie of Pierce Pennilesse. *J. Danter,* 1593. O.; HD.

18378a — [A variant, w. imprint:] *J. Danter, sold by W. Barley,* 1593. O.; HN.

18379 — The terrors of the night or, a discourse of apparitions. 4°. *J. Danter f. W. Jones,* 1594. Ent. to J. Danter 30 jn. 1593 a. 25 oc. 1594. L(2).; F.HN.
— The tragedie of Dido. 1594. *See* 17441.

18380 — The vnfortunate traueller. Or, the life of Iacke Wilton. 4°. *T. Scarlet f. C. Burby,* 1594. Ent. to J. Wolfe 17 se. 1593. L.; F(imp.).HN.HD(imp.).

18381 — [Anr. ed.] Newly corrected and augmented. 4°. *T. Scarlet f. C. Burby,* 1594. L(lacks tp).O.O³.O⁵.
— *See also* 12272, 17452, 17461.

18382 **Nash, Thomas,** *Philopolites.* Quaternio or a fourefold way to a happie life. 4°. *J. Dawson,* 1633. Ent. 5 jy. 1632. L.O.C.DUL.LEEDS.+; F.HN.HD.N.NY.+
O,F copies have a pr. leaf before tp: 'Ex dono authoris; pignus amoris.'

18383 — [Anr. issue, w. cancel tp, w. imprint:] *N. Okes, sold by J. Benson,* 1636. L.O⁶.C.C².D(lacks tp)*.; F.CU.HD. ILL.Y.+
Tp only pr. by N. Okes.

18384 — [Anr. issue, w. cancel tp, w. title:] Miscelanea or a fourefold way [etc.] *J. Dawson, sold by T. Slater,* 1639. L.C⁵.LK.; HN.N.

Nash, Thomas, *Philopolites*—*cont.*
— *See also* Bookplates.

Nasmith, John, *tr. See* 16650.5.

18385 **Natura Brevium.** [*Editions in Law French.*] [a2ʳ:] Dicitur q̄ [etc.] [i3ʳ:] Here endith the boke of Natura breuium. fol. (*R. Pynson,*) [1494.] O(frag.).C⁴.; HN.HD.LC.PML. Duff 332.
Linked to 23877.7 in the latter's colophon.

18386 — [Anr. ed. a1ʳ:] Dicitur que [etc.] [i6ʳ:] Here endeth [etc.] fol. (*R. Pynson,*) [1500.] O.C.D. Duff 333.

18387 — [Anr. ed. Headline A1ʳ:] Natura breuiū. fol. (*R.Pynson,*) [1506?] L.; HN.HD.

18388 — [Anr. ed.] Newly corrected, with diuers addiciōs. fol. (*p̄ R. Pynson,*) [1518?] L.C(lacks M6).C⁴.LEEDS.; HD.

18389 — [Anr. ed.] Newly and moost trewly corrected. [*Ed.* R. Chidley.] 16° in 8's. (*in ęd. R. Pynsoni,* 1525 (4 id. oc.)) L.L²².O.; HD.

18390 — [Anr. ed.] 16° in 8's. (*in ęd. R. Pynsoni,* 1528.) L.O¹⁰.C.; HN.HD.

18391 — [Anr. ed.] 16° in 8's. (*in ed. R. Redman,*) 1529 [1530] (23 mr.) L.M.; HD.LC.MEL(frag.).MIN.Y.

18392 — Now = 18395.5.

18393 — [Anr. ed.] 8°. (*in æd. T. Bertheleti,* 1531 (kal. oc.)) L(2, 1 lacks z8).O.; HD.MIN.
(Formerly also 18395)

18394 — [Anr. ed.] Natura Breuium. The olde tenures. [etc. *Ed.*] (W. Rastell.) 4° w. perp. chainlines. (*w. Rastell,* 1534.) L.O.C(imp.).E.RGU.+; HN.HD(imp.).LC.NYS. WIS.+
(816 is pt. of this) Double column. Includes texts of 23877.7, 15719, 18361, 812, 10946, 14862, 15579.3, 7714, 7726, 20894.4, and 7695.5.

18394.5 — [Anr. issue, reimposed for 12°.] 12°. (*w. Rastell,* 1534.) O(imp.).O⁵(imp.).NEK(imp.).; HD(imp.).MICH. TEX(imp.).
Single column.

18395 — = 18393.

18395.5 — [Anr. ed. of Natura Brevium only.] fol. (*R. Redman,*) [1534?] L(2).O(col. only).C⁴(imp.).; HD(lacks tp).Y.
(Formerly 18392)

18396 — [Anr. ed.] 8°. (*W. Myddylton,*) [1545?] L(imp.).; HD(2).LC.

18397 — [Anr. ed.] (The olde tenures.) 2 pts. 8°. [*N. Hill f.*] (*H. Smyth,*) 1545. L.; F.HD.MIN.
Old Tenures reprinted from 23877.7.

18397.5 — [Anr. ed. of Natura Brevium only.] 8°. (*W. Powel,* 1551.) P.

18398 — [Anr. ed.] Natura breuium in frenche. 8°. *in æd. R. Tottell,* 1557. O³.O¹⁸.; HD(2).

18398.5 — [Anr. ed.] Natura breuium in french. 8°. *in æd. R. Tottell,* 1557. L.D.; HD.LC.

18399 — [Anr. ed.] 8°. *in æd. R. Tottell,* 1566 (1567 (21 ja.)) L.C⁷.M².NLW.ST.+; HN.HD.LC.MIN.NYS.

18400 — [Anr. ed.] La vieux natura breuium, dernierment corrigee. 8°. *in æd. R. Tottill,* 1572. L.O⁶.G². NLW.P.+; F.HD.MICH.MIN.NYS.+

18401 — [Anr. ed.] 8°. *in æd. R. Tottelli,* 1580 (1 jn.) L.L³⁰. BRISTOL².HAT.HOLK.; F.CAL⁵.HD.MICH.Y.+

18402 — [Anr. ed.] 8°. *in æd. R. Tottelli,* 1584 (1 ap.) Ent. 18 fb. 1583. L.O.C.D.E.+; HN.HD.LC.MIN.NY.+

18402.5 — [*English*]. Natura breuium newly corrected in Engglysshe, with dyuers addicōs. [*Tr.* T. Phaer.] fol. (*R. Redman,*) [1530?] C⁴.; Y.

18403 — [Anr. ed.] 8°. (*R. Redman,* 1532.) HD(2, 1 imp.).MIN.

18404 — [Anr. ed.] 8°. (*R. Redman,* 1535.) L.O.; HD.

18405 — [Anr. ed.] 8°. (*R. Redman,* 1540.) L.O(imp.).C⁵.; HN.HD.

18406 — [Anr. ed.] 8°. (*T. petit,* 1544.) L.O.C¹⁵.C¹⁹.; COR.

18407 — [Anr. ed.] 8°. (*W. Myddylton,* 1544.) L(lacks R5).; HD.LC.

18408 — [Anr. ed.] 8°. [*R. Tottell? f.*] (*T. petit,*) [1550?] L.L⁸.O.C.E.+; HD(2, 1 imp.). MICH.
Tp orn. varies: Beale cut 11 or 32; both at HD.

18408.5 — [Anr. ed.] 8°. (*W. Powell,* 1553 (6 my.)) O.O⁴⁷.P.; HD.

18408.7 — [Anr. ed.] Natura breuium newly corrected, in Englishe. 8°. (*R. Tottell,* 1557 (27 fb.)) E.NLW.; HD. MIN.NYS.

18409 — [Anr. ed.] Natura breuium in Englishe newelye corrected. 8°. (*R. Tottil,* 1557 (27 fb.)) L. London U, Institute of Advanced Legal Studies.; F.HD.LC.MIN.

18410 — Now = 18411.5.

18411 — [Anr. ed.] 8°. (*R. Tottill,* 1576 (22 fb.)) C.; CU.HD.MIN.

18411.5 — [Anr. ed.] 8°. (*R. Tottill,*) [1580?] HN(imp.).CU.HD.LC.
(Formerly 18410)
— La nouel natura breuium. 1534. *See* 10958.

Nature. Natures cruell step-dames. 1637. *See* 12012.

18412 **Naumburg.** The actes of the ambassage, passed at Naumburg concerning the matters there moued by pope Pius the .iiii. in 1561. *Tr.* out of Dutche by R. W. 8°. *J. Day,* [1561.] L.; F.

18412.5 — [Anr. ed. No 'R. W.' on tp.] 8°. *J. Day,* [1561.] C.

18413 **Nausea, Fridericus,** *Bp.* Of all blasing starrs in generall. *Tr.* A. Fleming. 8°. [*H. Middleton?*] f. T. Woodcocke, 1577. Ent. 1 jy. 1578. L.; HN.

18413.3 — [Anr. ed.] A treatise of blazing starres in generall. [Anon.] 4°. B. Alsop, solde by H. Bell, 1618. L.O(2). C. Cambridge, Whipple Museum.; MCG.PH.Y. (Formerly 11051)

18413.5 — [Anr. ed.] 4°. B. Alsop, sold by H. Bell, 1618. F.

18413.7 — [Anr. issue, w. imprint:] B. Alsop, sold by E. Wright, 1618. L[16].O.P.; HN. (Formerly 11051a)

18414 — A sermon of the sacramēt of the aulter. *Tr.* J. More. 8° in 4's. (*w.* Rastell, 1533.) F.
— *See also* 11037.

Naugerius, Andrea, *ed. See* 18927, 18928, 18951.5, 18976.8.

18415 **Nautonier, Guillaume de.** The mecographie of ye loadstone. [Pt. 2 of the French ed. of 1604.] *Scots, Fr. a. Lat.* fol. *Tolose & Venez, R. Colomies & A. de Courteneufue, aux frais de l'autheur,* 1603. L.PARIS. London, Royal Institution of Naval Architects.; F.

Navarre, *Prince de. See* Henry IV, *King of France.*

18416 **Neade, William.** The double-armed man, by the new invention. 4°. [*Eliot's Court Press*] f. J. Grismand, 1625. Ent. 4 fb. L.O(imp.).C[3].D[6].SHEF.+; F.HN(2).HD. Mellon. New York, Metropolitan Museum of Art. *See also* 9002.

18416.3 — Objections against the use of the bow with the pike: and the answers thereunto. [Anon.] s.sh.fol. [*W. Jones, c.* 1630.] L(bd. w. G.2292).; HD. Mellon.

18416.7 **Neale, Thomas.** A wench for a weaver. *Ballad.* 2 pts. s.sh.fol. [*M. Flesher*] f. F. Coules, [c. 1630.] C[6].

Nebrissa, Aelius Antonius of. *See* 688.

18417 **Neck, Jacob Corneliszen van.** The journall, or dayly register, contayning a true manifestation, and historicall declaration of the voyage. (*Tr.* W. Walker.) 4°. [*S. Stafford a. F. Kingston*] f. C. Burby & J. Flasket, 1601. Ent. 16 ja. L.L[30](imp.).O.C.C[6].; HN. NY(imp.).WTL. Quires A–G pr. by Stafford; ¶2 and quires H–Q pr. by Kingston. *See* Greg, *Register B,* p. 80.

18418 **Needleworks.** A booke of curious and strange inuentions, called the first part of needleworkes. 1596. Now = 5323a.8.

18419 **Negri de Bassano, Francesco.** A certayne tragedie wrytten fyrst in Italian, by F. N. B. entituled, Freewyl. *Tr.* H. Cheeke. 4°. [*R. Jugge,* 1573?] L(imp.).O(2 imp.).; F.HN(imp.).HD.ILL.PFOR. Greg 63.

Negus, Jonathan, *ed. See* 18420.

18420 **Negus, William.** Mans active obedience, or the power of godlines. [*Ed.*] (J. Negus.) 4° in 8's. F. Kyngston f. N. Newbery, 1619. Ent. 23 jy. 1618. L[4].O.C.D.DUL.; F.HD.U.

18421 **Neile, Richard,** *Bp.* M. Ant. de Dn̄is arch-bishop of Spalato, his shiftings in religion. 4°. [*A. Mathewes f.*] J. Bill, 1624. L.O.C.D.E.+; F.HN.HD(imp.).N.NY.+ ꝧ A2[r]: 'collected by the ... Bishop of Duresme ...'

18421.5 — Richardus, providentia divina, Lincol. episcopus: Dilectis nobis in Christo, [etc. Form of precept for collecting arrears of tenths of clergy. 8 Jan. 1615 o.s.] obl.fol. slip. [*London?* 1616.] L[5](Lemon 149).
— *ed. See* 7006.
— *See also* 10192.7, 10226, 10238, 10361, 10362.5, 10380 sqq.

18422 **Nelson, Henry.** Speculum christianum or, a christian survey for the conscience. Englished. By H. N. 1614. Now = 26121a.7.

18422.5 **Nelson, Thomas.** The blessed state of England. Declaring the sundrie dangers which by Gods assistance, the queenes maiestie hath escaped in the whole course of her life. 4°. [*R. Robinson?*] f. W. Wright, 1591. Ent. 5 ja. F.

Nelson, Thomas—*cont.*

18423 — The deuice of the pageant: set forth by the companie of the fishmongers, for J. Allot: established lord maior. 4°. *London,* 1590. L. Greg 96.

18424 — A memorable epitaph, made vpon the lamentable complaint of the people for the death of Sir F. Walsingham ... 7. April. 1590. [In verse.] s.sh.fol. [*J. Charlewood*] f. W. Wright, [1590.] Ent. 27 ap. 1590. HN.

18425 — A short discourse: expressing the substaunce of all the late pretended treasons against the queenes maiestie. 1586. [In verse.] 4°. G. Robinson f. T. Nelson, [1586.] Ent. to G. Robinson 6 oc. 1586. L.C[5].; HN.

18425.5 — [A variant, w. imprint:] G. Robinson f. E. White. O[3].; F.

18426 — [A reprint of A3[r]–A4[v].] The substance of all the late entended treasons [etc.] *Ballad.* s.sh.fol. G. Robinson f. E. White, [1586.] L[2].

18426.5 — [Anr. ed. Anon.] A proper newe ballad, declaring the substaunce [etc.] s.sh.fol. T. Purfoote f. E. White, [1586.] L[5](Lemon 84).

Nemausum. Academiæ Nemausensis responsio. 1584. *See* 18581.

18427 **Nemesius,** *Bp.* The nature of man. A learned and usefull tract. *Tr.* G. Wither. 12°. M. F[lesher] f. H. Taunton, 1636. Ent. to M. Flesher a. H. Taunton 23 fb. L.O.C[4].D.E.+; F.HN.HD.N.NY.+ Unsold sheets reissued in 1657 without prelims. and w. cancel tp as Wing N 418.

18428 **Nenna, Giovanni Battista.** Nennio, or a treatise of nobility. *Tr.* [Sir] W. Jones. 4°. P. S[hort] f. P. Linley a. J. Flasket, 1595. Ent. to P. Linley 27 se. L.O.C.M.P.+; F.HN.HD.N.Y.+ The comma at end of line 1 of tp of L copy has dropped out.

18429 — [Anr. issue, w. cancel tp.] A discourse whether a noble man by birth or a gentleman by desert is greater in nobilitie. P. Short, solde [by J. Flasket,] 1600. L.; F.CHI.LC.

Neperus, Joannes. *See* Napier, J.

Neptune. Neptunes triumph. [1624.] *See* 14779.

Nero, *Emperor of Rome.* Nero Cæsar, or monarchie depraved. 1624. *See* 3221.

18430 — The tragedy of Nero, newly written. 4°. A. Mathewes a. J. Norton f. T. Jones, 1624. L.O.A.ETON.Bradford PL.+; F.HN.HD.PN.Y.+ Greg 410.

18431 — [Anr. ed.] 4°. A. Mathewes f. T. Jones, 1633. Ass'd to A. Mathewes 24 oc. L.O.DUR(Bamb.).E.G[2].+; F.HN. CU.HD.ILL.+

Nero, Claudius Tiberius. *See* Tiberius.

18432 **Nesbit, E.** Cæsars dialogue or a familiar communication containing the first institution of a subject, in allegiance to his soveraigne. [Init. E. N.] 8°. T. Purfoot, [jun.,] 1601. Ent. 22 de. 1593 a. 26 jn. 1601. L.L[2].O.C.STU.+; F.HD(lacks A8).N. Tp line 3 ends: 'Com-'.

18432.5 — [Anr. ed.] 8°. T. Purfoot, 1601. HN. Tp line 3 ends: 'Commu-'.

Netherlands. A brief and necessary discourse. *See* 18439.

18433 — A briefe cronicle, and perfect rehearsall of all the memorable actions hapned not onelie in the low-Countries, but also in Germanie, Italy, Fraunce, and other countries since the yeare 1500. 16° in 8's. [*J. Windet f.*] J. Wolfe, 1598. Ent. 23 de. 1597. L.
— Certein letters of the peace attempted by Holland and Zelande in 1574. 1576. *See* 15527.

18433.7 — A true confession of the faith, which wee falsely called Brownists, doo hould. [Attrib. to H. Ainsworth and F. Johnson.] 4°. [*Amsterdam?*] 1596. L.L[2].O.O[21].C[2].+; HN.BO[3].Y. (Formerly 237) Reprinted in 238, 7298.

18434 — [Anr. ed.] The confession of fayth of certayne English people, living in exile in the Low Countreyes. 1602. = pt. of 7298.

18435 — [Anr. ed.] 8°. [*Amsterdam, G. Thorp,*] 1607. L.L[2]. O(2).E.

18436 — [Anr. ed.] 8°. [*Amsterdam?*] 1640. C[3].
— A declaration of faith of English people remaining at Amsterdam in Holland. 1611. *See* 13053.5.
— A defence and true declaration. 1571. *See* 18441.

Netherlands—*cont.*

18437 — A description of the prosperitie, strength, and wise government of the United Provinces. 4°. *F. Kyngston f. E. Marchant,* 1615. O.C⁵.C¹⁷.HAGUE.; F.HN.Y.

18437.5 — [Anr. issue, w. cancel tp.] Newes of the Netherlands. Relating the whole state of those countries at the present. *F. Kyngston f. E. Marchant,* 1615. L.O.; HN.
(Formerly 18444) L,O copies bd. w. 18445.7.

18438 — 24. of August. 1578. A discourse of the present state of the wars in the lowe Countryes. Wherein is contayned the pittifull spoyle of Askot. 8° in 4's. [*J. Charlewood f.*] (*W. B[artlett,*]) [1578.] O.

18439 — A briefe and necessarie discourse concerning the meanes to preserue both the religion and estate of the lowe Countries. 8°. *f. T. Charde,* 1584. Ent. 29 my. L².

18440 — Libellus supplex imperatoriæ maiestati . . . nomine Belgarum ex inferiori Germania, euangelicæ religionis causa per Albani ducis tyrannidem eiectorum. (Apologeticon.) 2 pts. 8°. *ap. J. Daium,* 1571. Ent. 1570–71. L.O.C.D.LINC.+

18441 — [A trans.] A defence and true declaration of the thinges lately done in the lowe countrey. (*Tr.* E. Newcomen.) 8°. *J. Daye,* (1571.) L(lacks 2nd tp).O².HAGUE.; HD(lacks 2nd tp).

18442 — Newes from the Low Countries. 1621 (29 jy.) Now = Newsbooks 26.
— Newes from the Low Countries. 1621 (9 au.) *See* Newsbooks 13.

18443 — Newes from the Low-Countreyes. Or the anatomy of Calvinisticall calumnyes. *Tr.* D. N. 8°. [*St. Omer, English College Press,*] 1622. L²⁵.C³.
A&R 566.

18444 — Newes of the Netherlands. 1615. Now = 18437.5.

18445 — A request presented to the king of Spayn. . . . By the inhabitantes of the lowe countreyes, protesting that they will liue according to the reformation of the Gospell: the xxij. of Iune. 1578. 4°. *Edinburgh, Leighe Mannenby,* [i.e. *London, H. Bynneman,*] 1578. Ent. to H. Bynneman 22 jn. O⁸.C⁵.LINC.M.
(Formerly also 19837)
— Treves endt. The funerall of the Netherlands peace. [1621.] *See* 24268.3.

18445.5 — A ⁺rue and perfect relation of the newes sent from Amsterdam, the 21. of February, 1603. Concerning the fight of five Dutche shippes in the E. Indies, against the Portugall fleete. 4°. *T. C[reede] f. T. Archer,* 1603. Ent. 19 mr. L. Rotterdam, Prins Hendrik Maritime Museum.

18445.7 — A vision or dreame contayning the whole state of the Netherland warres. (A short . . . narration from . . . Goch.) *Eng. a. Dutch.* 4°. [*G. Purslowe a. N. Okes*] *f. E. Marchant,* 1615. L.O.; F.Y.
(Formerly 18447; 2nd pt. formerly 11925) L,O copies bd. w. 18437.5. Quires A–D pr. by Purslowe; the rest by Okes.

18446 — [Anr. issue, w. cancel gen. tp:] A true relation of the treasons attempted against foure townes in the Low Countries. *f. W. Welbie,* 1615. O.

18446a — [Anr. issue, w. a variant cancel gen. tp:] A true relation . . . townes in the Netherlands. *f. E. Marchant,* 1615. O(tp only, bd. w. 18445.7).; HN.

18447 — Now = 18445.7.

OFFICIAL DOCUMENTS

BEFORE 1577

18447.5 — These ben the ordynaũces, that the emperour hath caused to be red to thestates . . . aswell to the auoydynge of the Lutherayn secte, as for the pourueyaũce of the dysordre of his coyne, & ordres to be sette in the sayde countrees. [7 Oct. 1531.] 8° in 4's. (*R. wyer,*) [1532?] O.
(Formerly 5016)

STATES GENERAL

— The aduise and answer of yᵉ prince of Orenge, made by the estates generall. [1577?] *See* 25709.

18448 — A treatise of the peace made between the states and the prince of Orenge. 1576. *Tr.* out of dutch. 8° in 4's. [*J. Allde f.*] *W. Broome,* [1577.] Ent. 1 jy. 1577. L.; F.

18449 — The ordinance and edict, vppon the fact of the execution of both the religions, statuted by the bailiefes, of Ghaunt. 1579. = 11808.

Netherlands—STATES GENERAL—*cont.*

18450 — The answere of the states generall of the vnited Prouinces of the low countries vnto the ambassadors of Germanie, their proposition. 4°. *J. Wolfe,* 1591. C⁵.LINC.

18451 — [A trans.] Copie de la responce de messieurs les estats generaux sur la proposition a eux faite, par les ambassadeurs des circles d'Alemagne. [*Tr.* from German by] (P. Verheile.) 4°. *J. Wolfe,* 1591. Ent. 17 de. 1590. L.HAT.

18451.5 — The aunswere of the lords the estates generall of the vnited prouinces of the Lowe-Countries, to the letter of the archduke of Austria. Also, the extract of certaine letters, written out of the campe before Groning. Printed first at Middleburgh by R. Schilders . . . 1594. 2 pts. 4°. [*J. Windet f.*] *J. Wolfe,* (1594.) Pt. 1 ent. 8 au.; pt. 2 ent. 2 au. HAGUE.; ILL(pt. 1 only).Y.

18452 — The answere made by the noble lords the states, unto the ambassadour of Polonia. 4°. *J. Windet,* 1597. Ent. 26 au. L².

18453 — A proclamation made by the states of the vnited Netherlands, touching the defence of the safegard of the enemy. *Tr.* out of Dutch. Also a copie of a letter, 21 of March 1599. 4°. [*J. Windet f.*] *J. Wolfe,* 1599. L.L².

18454 — A proclamation of the lords the generall states, of the vnited Prouinces, whereby the Spaniards are declared to be lawfull prize. *Tr.* out of the Dutch coppy. 4°. [*E. Allde f.*] *J. Wolfe,* 1599. Ent. 17 ap. L.L².C.; F.HD.
— A true report of a voyage made this last summer by a fleete of the states generall of the vnited prouinces to the coast of Spaine and the Canary-Isles. 1599. *See* 4555.5.

18454.5 — An admonition published by the generall states of the Netherlandish united Prouinces: touching his now intended proceedings, against the Spaniards. *Tr.* out of the Dutch printed coppy. 4°. [*E. Allde*] *f. W. Dight, solde by T. Pavier,* 1602. Ent. 12 jn. C⁵.
— Newes from Flanders and Ostend. A true declaration how the United Provinces have set forth a navie. [1604.] *See* 11029.5.

18454.7 — A proclamation [*sic*], by the which is prohibited in the research of the passengers ships betweene France and England, not to use any disorder in wordes nor deedes. *Tr.* out of Dutch. 4°. *T. Purfoot f. W. Fearbrand,* [1605.] Ent. to T. Purfoot 12 au. 1605. HD.
End of text dated 19 July 1605.

18455 — Articles of agreement, concerning the cessation of warre, betweene the arch-duke and the states. *Tr.* (W. B B.) 4°. [*S. Stafford*] *f. T. Archer,* 1607. L.; HN.Y.
See also 3471.

18455.3 — A briefe declaration of the proceedings of the peace that is now intreating of betweene the king of Spaine, the archduke, and the generall states. *Tr.* out of Dutch. 4°. [*Eliot's Court Press*] *f. P. Harison,* 1608. Ent. 5 mr. L.L³⁰.; F.HN.Y.
— Propositions made by monsieur vander Hurst at the assembly of the generall states. 1609. *See* 25934.

18455.7 — Articles, of a treatie of truce. Made in Antwerp, the 9. of April, 1609. 4°. [*J. Windet*] *f. G. Potter a. N. Browne* [*sic*], 1609. L.L².O.; F.HN.

18456 — [A variant, w. corrected imprint:] *f. G. Potter a. N. Bourne,* 1609. L.M⁴.; F.HN.HD.Y.

18457 — An edict or proclamation; published by the states generall how all Jesuits, priests and monkes shall behave themselves. 4°. *E. A[llde] f. T. Archer,* 1612. Ent. to E. Allde 13 ap. L.O.C⁵.C⁹.
— [Proclamation concerning herring fishing. 1615.] *See* 21486.

18458 — A proclamation made by the generall states . . . prohibiting secret assemblies. 4°. *T. D[awson] f. N. Newbery,* 1619. Ent. 23 jy. O.C⁵.

18459 — The declaration of the decree made by the generall states . . . against certaine Arminians. *Tr.* out of the Dutch copy. 4°. *F. Kyngston f. N. Newbery,* 1619. L.C².C⁵.
See also 11707.

18459.5 — Letters patents graunted by the states of the united Netherland Provinces, to the West Indian company of merchants, at this present resident in those countries. [9 June 1621.] s.sh.fol. [*The Hague?* 1621.] L.

Netherlands—STATES GENERAL—*cont.*

18460 — Orders and articles granted by the states general concerning the erecting of a West India companie. 4°. [*London*,] 1621. L.O.C⁵.; F.HN.NY.Y.

18460.3 — A message or ambassage made by Sir P. Pecquius . . . upon the 23. day of March, 1621. unto the generall states. Together with the answer. 4°. *Middleburgh, H. vander Hellen*, [i.e. *London*,] 1621. O.

18460.7 — [Anr. trans.] Proposition of the ambassadour Peckius. In the congregation of the general states. With the answer the xxv. of March, 1621. *Tr.* out of Dutch, according to the copy, pr. by A. Meurs, the Hague. 4°. [*Printed abroad*, 1621.] C⁵.; HD.

18461 — A copie of the agreement made betweene Hurian Bassa, governour of Tunis. And the states of the Netherlands. 4°. [*B. Alsop*,] 1622. O.

18462 — A proclamation made and proclaimed in Holland, &c. by the lords the generall states of the united Netherland Provinces, prohibiting all Jesuites, priests, monkes, friers to come into the Provinces. 4°. *The Hage, H. Jacobson* [i.e. *London, B. Alsop*,] 1622. L.O⁹.

— A compendious card or map of the two armies . . . the one of the states of Holland. [1624?] *See* 4606.5.

— Three severall treatises concerning the truce at this present propounded. 1630. *See* 24258.

18463 — Lawes and ordinances touching military discipline. *Tr.* I. D. 4°. *The Haghe, widowe & heires of H. Jacobs van Wouw*, 1631. L.

18464 — Advice given unto the states of of [*sic*] the Low-Countries. 1632. Now = Newsbooks 262.

SOUTHERN PROVINCES

18464.5 — A proclamation set out by the K. of Spaine. Wherein order is taken for the vse and trafficke of merchandise, with those of Holland Zealand and others. *Tr.* out of the Dutch copy. 4°. *J. Wolfe, sold by W. Wright*, 1592. Ent. to J. Wolfe 23 mr. HD.

18465 — A true coppy of the admonitions sent by the subdued prouinces to the states of Holland: [etc.] First *tr.* out of French into Dutch, and now into English by H. W. 4°. [*J. Windet f.*] *J. Wolfe*, 1598. Ent. 12 jy. L.L².O.C¹³.HAT.+; F.HN.HD(tp cropt).NY⁵.Y.

18466 — [Anr. ed.] 4°. *Edinburgh, R. Walde-graue*, 1598. L.

18467 — The second admonition, sent by the subdued prouinces to Holland. *Tr.* out of Dutch by H. W. 4°. [*J. Windet f.*] *J. Wolfe*, 1598. Ent. 28 oc. L.C.C⁵.; HD.

18468 — A true coppie of the transportation of the Lowe Countries, . . . Doone by the king of Spayne, for the dowrie of his daughter. *Tr.* out of Dutch by H. W. Nouember, 1598. 4°. *J. R[oberts] f. P. Linley*, [1598.] Ent. 7 no. L.L².L¹³.O.; F.HN.HD.ILL.Y.

18468.5 — Aplacarde [*sic*] or statute concerning the musters. Reniewed and decreed the 4ᵗʰ· of Febr. 1599. 4°. *Leyden, T. Basson*, 1599. Leiden U.

18469 — [Anr. ed.] 4°. *the Hage, widowe & heires of H. Jacobs van Wouw*, [1630?] Leiden U.

18470 — A coppie of the proclamation made by the illustrous [*sic*] infanta Isabella. Touching the defence, of all communication, with Holland. *Tr.* out of the copie, printed at Antwerpe. 4°. [*E. Allde f.*] *J. Wolfe*, 1599. L.L².C.; F.HN.ILL.

18471 — A proclamation or proscription, set foorth & published by the arch-duke Albertus, against his mutinous soldiers. *Tr.* out of the Dutch coppy printed at Middleborough. 4°. [*E. Allde a. R. Read*] *f. T. Pavier*, 1602. Ent. 20 se. L.C.; F.
Quire B pr. by Read; the rest by Allde.

18472 — A proclamation or edict. Touching the opening of the traffique, of Spain, with these countries. *Tr.* out of the Nether-landish tongue. 4°. [*E. Allde*] *f. T. Archer*, 1603. Ent. 8 my. L.L³⁰.

18472a — [Anr. ed.] 4°. *W. W[hite] f. T. Archer*, 1603. O.O².O³. C.C².; LC.
(Formerly also 22998)

18472a.5 — A proclamation of the truce betweene his majesty of Spayne, and the States generall. *Tr.* out of Dutch. [14 Apr. 1609.] s.sh.fol. [*S. Stafford*] *f. J. Budge*, 1609. Ent. 14 ap. L.O.O².M(deposit).; Y.
(Formerly 19841)

— *See* also Brabant, Flanders, Holland, etc.

Netherlands East India Company. *See* 7450.

18473 **Nethersole,** *Sir* **Francis.** Memoriæ sacra illustriss. potentiss. principis Henrici Walliæ principis, laudatio funebris. 4°. *Cantebrigiæ, ex off. C. Legge*, 1612. L.O.C.D.E.+; F.HN.HD.ILL.Y.+
— *See* also Newsbooks 55.

18474 **Nettles, Stephen.** An answer to the Jewish part of Mʳ Selden's History of Tithes. 4°. *Oxford, J. Lichfield & W. Turner*, 1625. L.O.C.D.STU.+; F.HN. HD.ILL.U.+

Neutrales. De neutralibus et mediis. 1562. *See* 25612.

Neve, Jeffery. Almanacks. 1604, etc. *See* 489 sqq.

Neve, John. Almanacks. 1626, etc. *See* 490 sqq.

Nevile, Thomas. [Bookplate.] *See* Bookplates.

18475 **Nevill, William.** The castell of pleasure. [*Ed.?*] (R. Coplande.) [In verse.] 4° in 6's. (*W. de worde*,) [1530?] HN.
On a1ᵛ Copland calls himself: 'Coplande the prynter'. This is later than 18476.

18476 — [Anr. ed.] 4° in 6's. (*H. Pepwell*, 1518.) L.

Neville, Alexander. Academiae cantabrigiensis lacrymæ tumulo P. Sidneij sacratæ. 1587. *See* 4473.

18477 — Alexandri Neuylli ad Walliæ proceres apologia. 4°. *ex off. H. Binnimani*, 1576 (12 my.) L.L¹³.O⁸.O¹⁷. HOLK.; F.

18478 — Alexandri Neuylli Angli, de furoribus Norfolciensium Ketto duce, liber vnus. Eiusdem Noruicus. [In verse.] 4°. *ex off. H. Binnemani*, 1575. L.O.C.D.E.+; F.HN.CU.HD.N.+
R2ʳ catchword: 'portaeq̃;'.

18478a — [Anr. issue, w. R2,3 cancels.] O⁵.C³.C⁵.C⁶.; F.HN.
R2ʳ catchword: 'alteram)'.

18478a.5 — [Anr. issue, w. R2,3 new cancels.] L.NLW.
R2ʳ catchword: 'extra'.

18479 — [Anr. ed. of 'Kettus' only.] 1582. = pt. 3 of 18773 sqq.

18480 — [A trans.] Norfolkes furies, or a view of Ketts campe: necessary for the malecontents, with a table of the maiors and sheriffes of this worshipfull city of Norwich. *Tr.* R. W[oods.] 4°. *W. Stansby f. H. Fetherstone*, 1615. Ent. 4 au. L.O.O¹³.C²(imp.)*.; F. NOR².; HN.

18480.5 — [Anr. issue, w. imprint:] *f. E. Casson* [*Norwich*,] 1615. NOR².; HN.

18481 — [Anr. ed., enlarged.] Norfolke furies, and their foyle. Under Kett, their accursed captaine. With a description of Norwich, and a catalogue of the governours. *Tr.* R. Woods. 4°. [*London, A. Mathewes*,] *f. E. Casson in Norwich*, 1623. L.O.O⁶.C¹⁷.NOR².+; F.HN. HD(imp.).
— *tr. See* 22225.

18482 **Neville, Edmund.** The palme of christian fortitude. Or the glorious combats of christians in Japonia. [*Anon.*] 8°. [*St. Omer, widow of C. Boscard*,] 1630. L.L⁹.O³.C. USHAW.+; F.HN.HD.STL.
A&R 741. A trans. by Neville from J. Rodriguez Girão.

18482.5 **Neville, George,** *Abp.* The great feast at the intronization of the reuerende father in God George Neuell, archbishop of Yorke. fol(5). [*J. Cawood?* 1570?] O(on verso of 25073).

New Custom. A new enterlude . . . entituled new custome. 1573. *See* 6150.

18483 **New England.** A briefe relation of the discovery and plantation of New England. 4°. *J. Haviland, sold by W. Bladen*, 1622. Ent. to A. Griffin a. J. Haviland 15 jy. L(2).O².O⁵.CHATS.; F.HN.CH.N.NY.+
This book is advertised in 25855.

18484 — [Anr. issue, w. cancel tp:] An historicall discoverie and relation of the English plantations, in New England. *f. J. Bellamie*, 1627. L.
Includes quire B of 20074 and quires B–E of 18483.

18485 — The humble request of his majesties loyall subjects, the governour and the company late gone for New-England. [By G. Phillips, *Colonist?*] 4°. [*M. Flesher*] *f. J. Bellamie*, 1630. Ent. 21 my. O.O⁹.C.LINC.; HN.BO.CB.MICH(2).
(Formerly also 25858)

— New-Englands plantation. 1630. *See* 13449.

New England—*cont.*

18486 — A proposition of provisions needfull for such as intend to plant themselves in New England, [etc.] s.sh.fol. *f. F. Clifton,* 1630. L.LINC(bd.w.18485).

— A true relation of the late battell fought in New England. 1637. *See* 24758.

New Man. The new man or a supplication unto James. 1622. *See* 1705.

18487 **New Mexico.** New Mexico. Otherwise, the voiage of Anthony of Espeio. [By J. Gonzales de Mendoza.] *Tr.* [by A. F.] out of the Spanish copie printed first at Madreel, 1586, and afterward at Paris in the same yeare. 8°. [*T. East?*] *f. T. Cadman,* [1587.] Ent. to E. Aggas 2 my. 1587. HN.

Trans. from an extract of the Spanish original of 12003.

New Sarum. The seuerall rates . . . for New Sarum. [30 Aug. 1595.] *See* 8247.

New Windsor. The seueral rates . . . made by the Justices of peace of new Winsour. [1563?] *See* 7957.7.

New Year's Gift. A bloudy new-yeares gift. 1609. *See* 13018.3.

18488 — A heavenly new years gift. 1620. = pt. of 3580.

18489 — A new yeres gift, or an heauenly acte of parliament. 1569. Now = 97.5.

— The sixt new-yeres gift. 1579. *See note to* 22185.

18490 — The third newyeeres gift and the second protest . . . against all the learned papists. 4°. (*J. Allde,* 1576.) Ent. 31 de. 1576. O.WN².

18491 — Newbery, Thomas. A booke in Englysh metre, of the great marchaunt man called Diues Pragmaticus. 4°. *A. Lacy,* 1563 (25 ap.) Ent. 1562–63. M. Leeds PL.

Newcomen, Elias, *tr. See* 18441.

Newell, William. *See* 8400.5.

Newfoundland. A commission for the well governing of our people, in New-found-land. 1633. *See* 9255.

— A short discourse of the New-found-land. 1623. *See* 4311.

Newgate. The discovery of a London monster called, the black dog of Newgate. 1612. *See* 14030.

18492 — Of the endes and deathes of two prisoners, lately pressed to death in Newgate. 1569. [In verse.] s.sh.fol. *J. Awdely,* [1569.] Ent. to J. Sampson [Awdely] 1568–69. HN.

18493 **Newhouse, Thomas.** Certaine sermons, preached by . . . T. Newhouse. And now set foorth by R. Gallard. 8°. *F. Kyngston f. E. Weaver a. W. Welby,* 1614. Ent. 15 my. L.O.NOR².P.YK.+ ; F.

18494 — A learned and fruitfull sermon, preached in Christs Church in Norwich. [*Ed.*] (R. Hill.) 8°. [*T. Snodham*] *f. Jonas Man,* 1612. Ent. 19 no. 1611. O.C.LINC.YK.

18495 **Newman, Arthur.** The Bible-bearer. By A. N[ewman.] 4°. *W. J[aggard] f. J. C[horlton,]* 1607. Ent. to J. Trundell 22 ap. L.L⁴³.O.C².; F.HN.NY¹¹.

18495.5 — [Anr. issue, w. cancel tp:] Two faces under a hood, or, the cloake of hypocrisie, worne thred bare. Now newly turned. [Init. A. N.] 4°. *f. J. Trundle,* 1607. O⁶.

18496 — Pleasures vision: with deserts complaint. [In verse.] 8°. *G. E[ld] f. T. Bayly,* 1619. Ent. 24 no. 1618. L.O.; HN.COR.HD.PFOR(imp.).

Newman, George. *See* 4587.7.

18497 **Newman, John.** A looking-glasse for petitioners. . . . In a sermon preached at Framlingham Castle in high Suffolke. 8°. *E. Griffin f. J. Barnes,* 1619. Ent. 4 my. L.O.C. Sparrow.; F.HN.

Newman, Thomas, *tr. See* 23897.

18498 **Newnham, John.** Newnams nightcrowe. A bird that breedeth brawles in many families and housholdes. Wherein is remembred that kindely regard which fathers ought to haue towards their sonnes. 4°. *J. Wolfe,* 1590. Ent. 10 se. L.O.; F.HN.CH.

O copy has a cancel D4ʳ pasted over the original page w. 7 lines omitted from the original setting. L,F,HN have D4 corrected and app. conjugate, w. ¶ at the bottom of the verso.

18499 **Newport, Frances.** An epytaphe, of the godlye constaūt, & counfortable cōfessor mystres (Darothye [*sic*] Wynnes) whiche slepte in Christ the yere of Grace. M.D.LX. [In verse.] 8°. (*O. Rogers,*) [1560.] L(tp only, Harl. 5919/161).O(1, plus frag.).

18500 — = 18499.

(Formerly also 10386, 18500)

News. *See also* Newsbooks.

— ⟨C⟩ertayn and tru good nues, frō the isle of Malta. 1565. *See* 17213.5.

— Certayne newes of the whole discription, [etc. 1574?] *See* 5182.

— The certaine newes of this present weeke. 1622. *See* Newsbooks 68, 72, etc.

18501 — The fourth of September. Newes from sundry places. 1622. Now = Newsbooks 75.

— The last newes. [etc.] 1623. *See* Newsbooks 111, 113, etc.

18501.5 — Late newes from the north: being, a relation of the skirmish betwixt the English and Scots, neere the river of Tine. 8°. [*T. Harper*] *f. R. Harper,* 1640. Ent. 15 se. O⁶.

Two poems on A7ᵛ are reimposed from 22007.5.

18502 — July 22. Numb. 41. More newes of the Duke of Brunswicke. 1623. Now = Newsbooks 120.

18503 — July 29. Numb. 42. More newes of the good successe of the Duke of Brunswicke. 1623. Now = Newsbooks 121.

— Most true and more admirable newes, of a maiden of Glabbich. 1597. *See* 12531.5.

— Newe newes contayning a shorte rehersall [etc.] 1579. *See* 23406.

18504 — Newes come from hell of loue, vnto vserers. [Init. J. E.] 8°. *W. Copland,* 1565. Ent. 1565–66. L².

— Newes come latle frō Pera. [1561.] *See* 4102.3.

18504.5 — Newes from diuers countries. As, from Spaine, Antwerpe, Collin, [etc.] 4°. *V. Sims, sold* [*by W. Barley,*] 1597. L(2).; LC.

— Newes from Francfort. 1612. *See* 17660.

— Newes from Gulick. 1615. *See* 14838.

— 1624. Newes from Holland. 1624. *See* 13574.

— Newes from Ireland. 1608. *See* 18785.

— Newes from Lough-foyle. 1608. *See* 18784.

— Newes from Malta. 1603. *See* 17215.

— Newes from Mamora. 1614. *See* 17229.

— Newes from Millaine. 1630. *See* 17916.3.

— Newes from Rome concerning the papisticall masse. [1550?] *See* 14006.

— Newes from Rome. Of two mightie armies. [1606.] *See* 4102.5.

— Newes from Spayne and Holland. 1593. *See* 22994.

— Newes from Spaine. The king of Spaines edict. 1611. *See* 22992.7.

— Newes from the Low Countries. 1621. *See* Newsbooks 13, 26.

— Newes from Vienna. 1566. *See* 24716.

18505 — Newes good and new. (Too good to be true.) *Ballad.* 2 pts. s.sh.fol. [*W. Jones?*] *f. J. Trundle,* [c. 1623.] C⁶.

— May 5. Numb. 32. Newes of certaine commands lately given by the French king. 1629. *See* Newsbooks 200.

— February 28, Numb. 20. The newes of forraine parts. 1623. *See* Newsbooks 99.

— Newes sent to the ladie princesse of Orenge. 1589. *See* 18834.

18506 — The 20th. of September. The newes which now arrive. 1622. Now = Newsbooks 78.

18507 — [The strange newes. Headline:] The history of strange wonders. 8°. (*R. Hall,* 1561.) Ent. betw. 24 jn. a. 8 jy. HN(lacks tp).

Title supplied from the SR entry.

— Strange newes out of Kent. 1609. *See* 14934.

— True and most certaine newes, sent from Vienna. 1595. *See* 24716.5.

— True newes, concerning the winning of Corbeyll. 1590. *See* 13146.

— True newes from one of sir F. Veres companie. 1591. *See* 24652.

— Wofull newes from the west-parts of Englane. 1612. *See* 10025.

NEWSBOOKS, 1620–1640

The entries below are in the order set forth by Folke Dahl in
*A bibliography of English corantos and periodical newsbooks 1620–
1642*, London, The Bibliographical Society, 1952. Many news
pamphlets of a non-periodical nature remain under various other
headings in the STC. For items in the section below cross references have been provided from all the STC entries where they
were previously entered. The main headings and sub-headings are:

CORANTOS

Amsterdam, P. Keerius	.1
Amsterdam, B. Jansz	.18
'Altmore'	.26
The Hague	.28
London, N. Butter	.29

NEWSBOOKS

Unnumbered, Oct. 1621–4 Oct. 1622	.35A
Numbered, Butter et al., 15 Oct. 1622–2 Feb. 1640 [o.s.]	.82
T. Archer, 1624–1628	.346
Amsterdam, 1633	.359

CORANTOS

Amsterdam, P. Keerius

18507.1 [Begins:] The new tydings out of Italie are not yet com.
s.sh.fol. *Amsterdam, G. Veseler, soulde by P. Keerius*,
1620 (2 de.) L. Dahl 1.
(Formerly 5745)

2 Corrant out of Italy, Germany, &c. s.sh.fol. *Amsterdam,
G. Veseler, soulde by P. Keerius*, 1620 (23 de.) L.O.
Dahl 2.
(Formerly 5745)

3 Corrant out of Italy, Germany, &c. s.sh.fol. *Amsterdam,
G. Veseler, soulde by P. Keerius*, 1621 (4 Nanuari
[*sic*]). L. Dahl 3.
(Formerly 5745)

4 Corrant out of Italy, Germany, &c. s.sh.fol. *Amsterdam,
G. Veseler, soulde by P. Keerius*, 1621 (21 ja.). L.
Dahl 4.
(Formerly 5745)

5 Courant out of Italy, Germany, &c. s.sh.fol. *Amsterdam,
G. Veseler, soulde by P. Keerius*, 1621 (31 mr.) L.
Dahl 5.
(Formerly 5745)

6 Courant out of Italy, Germany, &c. s.sh.fol. *Amsterdam,
G. Veseler, soulde by P. Keerius*, 1621 (9 ap.)
L(Harl.MS.389/56). Dahl 6.
(Formerly 5745)
Courant newes out of Italy, Germany, Bohemia,
Poland, &c. s.sh.fol. *Amsterdam, G. Vesel⟨er, sold
by P. Keerius*, 1621⟩ (25 my.) L(Harl.MS.389/79,
mutil.). Dahl 7.
(Formerly 5745)

8 Corante, or, newes from Italy and Germanie. s.sh.fol.
Amsterdam, J. Veselde, 1621 (13 jn.). CANT.
Imprint prob. false, prob. pr. in England.

9 Corante, or, newes from Italy and Germanie. s.sh.fol.
Amsterdam, J. Veselde, 1621 (20 jn.) L(Harl.MS.
389/106). Dahl 8.
(Formerly 5745) Prob. pr. in England.

10 Courant newes out of Italy, Germany, Bohemia,
Poland, &c. s.sh.fol. *Amsterdam, G. Veseler, [sold by
P. Keerius*, 1621] (5 jy.) L. Dahl 9.
(Formerly 5745)

11 Courant newes out of Italy, Germany, Bohemia, Poland,
&c. s.sh.fol. *Amsterdam, G. Veseler, [sold by P.
Keerius*, 1621] (9 jy.) L. Dahl 10.
(Formerly 5745)

12 Courant newes out of Italy, Germany, Bohemia,
Poland, &c. s.sh.fol. *Amsterdam, G. Veseler, [sold
by P. Keerius*, 1621] (15 jy.) L. Dahl 11.
(Formerly 5745)

13 Newes from the Low Countries. s.sh.fol. *Amsterdam,
J. Veseler*, 1621 (9 au.) L. Dahl 12.
(Formerly 5745) Prob. pr. in England.

14 The courant out of Italy and Germany, &c. s.sh.fol.
Amsterdam, G. Veseler, [sold by P. Keerius], 1621
(6 se.) L. Dahl 13.
(Formerly 5745)

15 The courant out of Italy and Germany, &c. s.sh.fol.
Amsterdam, G. Veseler, [sold by P. Keerius,] 1621
(12 se.) L. Dahl 14.
(Formerly 5745)

18507.16 The courant out of Italy and Germany &c. s.sh.fol.
Amsterdam, G. Veseler, [sold by P. Keerius,] 1621
(12 se.) L. Dahl 15.
(Formerly 5745) Contains some of same news as
the preceding, but tr. from a different original.

17 The courant out of Italy and Germany, &c. s.sh.fol.
Amsterdam, G. Veseler, [sold by P. Keerius,] 1621
(18 se.) L. Dahl 16.
(Formerly 5745)

Amsterdam, B. Jansz

Note: This entire series may have been printed in London, possibly for T. Archer.

18 Courante, or, newes from Italy and Germany. s.sh.fol.
Amsterdam, [B. Jansz?] 1621 (9 ap.) L. Dahl 17.
(Formerly 5747)

19 Courante, or, newes from Italy and Germany, &c.
s.sh.fol. *Amsterdam, [B. Jansz?]* 1621 (22 ap.)
L(Harl.MS.389/68). Dahl 18.
(Formerly 5747)

20 Corante, or, newes from Italy and Germanie. s.sh.fol.
Amstelredam, B. Janson, 1621 (6 jn.) L(Harl.MS.
389/82, mutil.). Dahl 19.
(Formerly 5747)

21 Corante, or, newes from Italy, Germanie, Hungarie and
Spaine. 1621. s.sh.fol. *Amstelredam, B. Jonson*, 1621
(25 jn.) L(Harl.MS.389/83). Dahl 20.
(Formerly 5747)

22 Corante, or, newes from Italy, Germanie, Hungarie,
Spaine and France. 1621. s.sh.fol. *Amstelredam,
B. Jonson*, 1621 (3 jy.) L(Harl.MS.389/84, mutil.).
Dahl 21.
(Formerly 5747)

23 Corante, or, newes from Italy, Germanie, Hungarie,
Spaine and France. 1621. s.sh.fol. *Amstelredam,
B. Jonson*, 1621 (9 jy.) L(2, 1 = Harl.MS.389/87).
Dahl 22.
(Formerly 5747)

24 Corante, or, newes from Italy, Germanie, Hungarie,
Poland, Bohemia and France. 1621. s.sh.fol. *Am-
stelredam, B. Jonson*, [1621] (20 jy.) L(2, 1 = Harl.
MS. 389/104). Dahl 23.
(Formerly 5747)

25 Corante, or, newes from Italy, Germany, Hungaria,
Bohemia, Spaine and Dutchland. 1621. s.sh.fol.
[Amsterdam,] B. Johnson, 1621 (2 au.) L. Dahl 24.
(Formerly 5747)

'Altmore'

26 Newes from the Low Countries. s.sh.fol. *Altmore, M H
[London,]* 1621 (29 jy.) L.O. Dahl 25.
(Formerly 18442)

27 Corrant or newes from Italie, Germanie, [etc.] s.sh.fol.
From Altmore by M H [London,] 1621 (6 au.) LC.
Dahl 26.

The Hague

28 Corante, or, newes from Italy, Germany, Hungaria,
Polonia, France, and Dutchland. 1621. s.sh.fol. *the
Hage, A. Clarke [London,]* 1621 (10 au.) L. Dahl 27.
(Formerly 5746)

London, N. Butter

29 Corante, or, newes from Italy, Germany, [etc.] s.sh.fol.
f. N. B[utter,] 1621 (24 se.) L. Dahl 28.
(Formerly 5748)

30 Corante, or weekely newes from Italy, Germany, [etc.]
s.sh.fol. *f. N. B[utter,]* 1621 (30 se.) L. Dahl 29.
(Formerly 5748)

31 Corant or weekly newes, from Italy, Germany, [etc.]
s.sh.fol. *f. N. B[utter,]* 1621 (2 oc.) L. Dahl 30.
(Formerly 5748)

32 Corante, or weekely newes from Italy, Germany, [etc.]
s.sh.fol. *f. N. B[utter,]* 1621 (6 oc.) L. Dahl 31.
(Formerly 5748)

33 Corant or weekly newes, from Italy, Germany, [etc.]
s.sh.fol. *f. N. B[utter,]* 1621 (9 oc.) Edison Dick,
Chicago. Dahl 32.

34 Corant or weekly newes, from Italy, Germany, [etc.]
s.sh.fol. *f. N. B[utter,]* 1621 (11 oc.) L.; LC. Dahl 33.
(Formerly 5748)

35 Corant or weekly newes, from Italy, Germany, [etc.]
s.sh.fol. *f. N. B[utter,]* 1621 (22 oc.) L. Dahl 34.
(Formerly 5748)

NEWSBOOKS

Unnumbered Newsbooks

18507.35A Newes from Poland. Wherein is inlarged the Turks formidable threatning of Europe. With many repulses even to this present moneth of October. 4°. F. K[ingston] f. B. D[ownes] a. W. Lee, 1621. Ent. to W. Lee 23 oc. L.O(1, plus frag.).
(Formerly 20083)

35B — [A variant, w. date:] 1622. L.

35C The certaine and true newes, from Germany and Poland, to this present 29. of October, 1621. 4°. F. K[ingston] f. B. D[ownes,] 1621. Ent. to B. Downes a. W. Lee 6 no. O.
(Formerly 11788)

36 Newes from Turkie and Poland. 4°. *The Hage* [London, E. Allde,] 1622. L.O(imp.).C². London, Foreign Office.; F.HN.HD. Dahl 35.
(Formerly 24332)

37 Newes from the Palatinate. 4°. *The Hage* [London, E. Allde,] 1622. L(2).O.C². Dahl 36.
(Formerly 19132)

37A A true relation of such battailes as have beene fought of late, . . . since the 12. of March. 1622. All which came in letters by Mr Balam. 4°. [London,] 1622. G⁴.

38 More newes from the Palatinate; and more comfort to every true Christian. 4°. [London?] 1622. L.C².C¹⁰.G⁴. Mrs. Folke Dahl, Lund, Sweden. Dahl 37.

39 A true relation written from Midelbourg the seaventh of Aprill, 1622. 4°. [Holland?] 1622. O⁹.G⁴

40 Good newes for the King of Bohemia? 4°. [B. Alsop,] 1622 (17 ap.) O(2).C².BELVOIR.YK.; HN. Dahl 38.
(Formerly 11354)

41 Propositions made by Captaine Ferentes to the King of Bohemia. April 19. 1622. 4°. [n.p. 1622.] LIV³(imp.).

42 The King of Bohemia's welcome to Count Mansfield. 4°. [E. Allde,] 1622. L.O.PETWORTH.; F. Dahl 39.
(Formerly 11355)

43 The safe returne of the King of Bohemia. 4°. [n.p.] 1612 [i.e. 1622] (1 my.) O.

44 Three great overthrowes one in the Palatinate, [etc.] 4°. [B. Alsop,] 1622 (4 my.) L.L⁴.O(2).PETWORTH.; TEX(tp def.). Dahl 40.
(Formerly 18923)

45 [Begins:] It is certified from Palermo in Sicilia, [etc.] 4° in 8. [N. Bourne a. T. Archer? 1622 (14 my.)] ? Ent. to Bourne a. Archer 18 my. 1622. L(lacks tp). Dahl 40A.

46 The 23. of May. Weekely newes from Italy, [etc.] 4°. J. D[awson] f. N. Bourne a. T. Archer, 1622. Ent. 22 my. L. Dahl 41.

47 A true relation of all such battailes in the Palatinate, untill this present the 24. of May. 4°. E. A[llde] f. N. Bourne a. T. Archer, 1622. Ent. 27 my. L(2).O. PETWORTH.YK. Leiden U. Dahl 42.
(Formerly 19135)

48 The 30. of May. Weekly newes from Italy, [etc.] 4°. E. A[llde] f. N. Bourne a. T. Archer, 1622. Ent. 29 my. L. Dahl 43.

49 More newes from the Palatinate the 3. of June. 4°. W. Jones f. N. Butter a. W. Sheffard, 1622. Ent. to Butter 29 my. L(tp mutil.). Mrs. Folke Dahl, Lund, Sweden. Dahl 44.

50 — [Anr. issue, w. sheet A reset:] More newes from the Palatinate, the second time imprinted June the 5. 4°. W. Jones f. N. Butter a. W. Sheffard, 1622. L.C³. Dahl 45.
(Formerly 19133)

51 Good newes from Alsasia and the Palatinate, the fift of June. 4°. B. A[lsop] f. N. Bourne a. T. Archer, 1622. ?Ent. 3 jn. L(tp def.).; HN. Dahl 46.
(Formerly 538)

51A A continuation of more newes from the Palatinate, the 13. of June. 4°. J. H[aviland] f. N. Butter, 1622. Ent. 10 jn. HD. Dahl 48.
A true relation . . . Palatinate. 1622. *See* 25233.

52 The true copie of a letter sent from Franckfort. 4°. J. D[awson] f. N. Bourne a. T. Archer, 1622. Ent. 14 jn. BELVOIR.D. Dahl 49.

53 The 18. of June. Weekely newes from Italy, [etc.] 4°. J. D[awson] f. N. Newbery a. W. Sheffard, 1622. Ent. 17 jn. L. Dahl 50.

54 A letter sent from Maynhem concerning the late defeate. 4°. B. Alsop f. N. Butter, 1622. BELVOIR.; HN. Dahl 51.
(Formerly 17256)

18507.55 The true copies of two especiall letters verbatim sent from the Palatinate by Sir, F. N[ethersole]. 4°. W. Jones [a. E. Allde] f. N. Bourne a. T. Archer, 1622 (21 jn.) Ent. 20 jn. HN. Dahl 52.
(Formerly 18328)

56 — [A variant, omitting 21 jn. from tp.] L.O.D.LAMPORT.

56A Coppies of letters sent from personages of accompt; truely relating occurences in the Palatinate. 4°. J. D[awson] f. J. Bartlet, 1622 (21 jn.) Ent. 20 jn. L.YK.; F.
(Formerly 19128) The F copy has variant date: 22 jn.

57 The late proceedings in all troubled parts of Christendome. 4°. W. Jones f. N. Bourne a. T. Archer, 1622 (25 jn.) Ent. 24 jn. L.O(lacks tp).; HN. Dahl 53.

57A The true relation of that worthy sea fight, in the Persian gulph. With the lamentable death of captaine A. Shilling. Printed this 2. of July. 4°. J. D[awson] f. N. Newbery a. W. Sheffard, 1622. Ent. to Sheffard, 28 jn. L.O.C.G².; F. Penrose 227.
(Formerly 22433)

58 The third of July. A continuation of the warres. 4°. E. A[llde] f. N. Bourne a. T. Archer, 1622. O. Dahl 54.

59 The safe arrivall of Christian Duke of Brunswick. 4°. J. D[awson] f. N. Bourne a. T. Archer, 1622 (3 jy.) Ent. 2 jy. L.O(2). Dahl 55.

60 A true relation of the murther of Osman the great Turke. 4°. B. A[lsop] f. N. Butter, 1622. Ent. 3 jy. L. Dahl 56.

61 A true relation of the proceedings of the Bavarian forces. 4°. f. N. Bourne a. T. Archer, 1622 (11 jy.) Ent. 11 jy. O(tp mutil.). Sheffield PL. Dahl 57.
(Formerly 1595)

62 The strangling and death of the great Turke. 4°. J. D[awson] f. N. Bourne a. T. Archer, 1622 (15 jy.) Ent. 17 jy. L⁴.O(2).PETWORTH.; F. Dahl 58.
(Formerly 18883)

63 The relation of all the last passages of the warres in the Palatinate. 4°. J. D[awson] f. N. Newbery a. W. Sheffard, 1622 (18 jy.) Ent. to Sheffard 17 jy. O. Ghent U. Dahl 59.
(Formerly 19134)

64 The 19. of July. In this weekly newes [etc.] 4°. J. D[awson] f. N. Bourne a. T. Archer, 1622. O. Dahl 60.

65 The surprisall of two imperial townes by Count Mansfield. 4°. J. D[awson a. E. Allde] f. N. Bourne a. T. Archer, 1622 (19 jy.) Ent. 18 jy. L.O. Dahl 61.

66 A continuation of more newes from the Palatinate. 4°. B. A[lsop] f. N. Bourne a. T. Archer, 1622 (26 jy.) O. Dahl 62.

67 The 26. of July. 1622. A true, plaine, and compendious discourse. 4°. E. A[llde] f. N. Bourne a. T. Archer, 1622. Ent. 25 jy. O(2).HAGUE(imp.).; F.HD. Henry Taylor. Dahl 63.
(Formerly 1899)

68 The certaine newes of this present weeke. 4°. J. H[aviland] f. N. Butter, 1622. Ent. 1 au. BELVOIR. Dahl 64.

69 August II. 1622. A remonstration of the French subjects. 4°. J. D[awson] f. N. Bourne a. T. Archer, 1622. Ent. 1 au. L.O(2).O⁸. Blickling.; HN. Dahl 65.
(Formerly 11307)

70 The 13. of August 1622. The post of the prince. 4°. J. D[awson] f. N. Bourne a. T. Archer, 1622. Ent. 10 au. L.O(2).O⁸. Mrs. Folke Dahl, Lund, Sweden.; F. Dahl 66.
(Formerly 17674)

71 The 19. of August. The entertainment of Count Mansfield. 4°. E. A[llde] f. N. Bourne a. T. Archer, 1622. Ent. 19 au. O. Dahl 68.

71A A true and faithfull relation, . . . concerning the death of sultan Osman. 4°. [F. Kingston] f. B. Downes, sold [by B. Downes] a. W. Sheffard, 1622. Ent. to B. Downes 19 au. L.O.C.C².C³.+; F.HD.
(Formerly 18882) Written by Sir T. Roe.

72 The 23. of August. The certaine newes of this present weeke. 4°. G. E[ld] f. N. Butter, 1622. Ent. 21 au. O.BELVOIR. Dahl 70.

73 The 27. of August. Mansfields arrivall in the Dukedome of Brabant. 4°. J. D[awson] f. N. Bourne a. T. Archer, 1622. Ent. 24 au. O. Mrs. Folke Dahl, Lund, Sweden.; ILL. Dahl 71.

Newsbooks—NEWSBOOKS—*Unnumbered Newsbooks—cont.*

18507.74 The 2. of September. Two great battailes very lately
fought. 4°. *J. D[awson] f. N. Bourne a. T. Archer,*
1622. Ent. 30 au. L.O.O⁸. Dahl 72.

75 The fourth of September. Newes from sundry places.
4°. *f. N. Butter,* 1622. Ent. 2 se. L.O⁸.YK. Dahl 73.
(Formerly 18501)

76 The ninth of September. 1622. Count Mansfields pro-
ceedings since the last battaile. 4°. *E. A[llde] f. N.
Bourne a. T. Archer,* 1622. Ent. 7 se. L.O.BELVOIR.
Dahl 74.
(Formerly 17261)

77 The 14. of September. A relation of many memorable
passages from Rome, [etc.] 4°. *f. N. Butter, B.
Downes, a. W. Shefford,* 1622. O(imp.).M(frag.).
Dahl 75.
(Formerly 21295)

78 The 2oth. of September. The newes which now arrive
from divers parts. 4°. *f. N. Butter a. W. Sheffard,*
1622. O².O⁸.Z. Dahl 76.
(Formerly 18506)

79 The 25. of September. Newes from most parts of
Christendome. Continued from the twentieth. 4°.
[G. Eld?] f. N. Butter a. W. Sheffard, 1622. L.Z.;
HD. Dahl 77.

80 The 27. of September. A relation of letters, and other
advertisements of newes. 4°. *[Eliot's Court Press?]
f. N. Butter a. T. Archer,* 1622. L.BELVOIR.YK.Z.
Dahl 78.

81 The 4. of Octob: 1622. A true relation of the affaires of
Europe. 4°. *[B. Alsop?] f. N. Butter a. N. Bourne,*
1622. L.O.O⁸.BELVOIR.Z.; F.HN. Dahl 79.
(Formerly 10571) There are variant tpp.
November 12. A relation of a sea-fight between the
Duke of Guise and the Rochellers. 1622. *See* 5011.5.
Too late for an unnumbered Newsbook.

*Numbered and dated
Newsbooks*

82 [First Series.] October 15. 1622. Novo. 1. A relation of
the late occurrents. 4°. *B. A[lsop] f. N. Butter a. N.
Bourne,* 1622. L.O.YK. Dahl 80.
(Formerly 5148)

83 — October 15. 1622. No. 2. A continuation of the
affaires of the Low-Countries. 4°. *[Eliot's Court
Press?] f. N. Butter a. B. Downes,* 1622. Ent. 14 oc.
L.BELVOIR. Dahl 81.

84 — Octob. 22. Nou. 3. A relation of the weekely oc-
curences of newes. 4°. *f. N. Butter, B. Downes, a.
W. Shefford,* 1622. L(tp only, Harl.5967/7). BEL-
VOIR.YK(2). Dahl 82.

85 — October 30. 1622. No. 4. A continuation of the
weekly newes. 4°. *[Eliot's Court Press?] f. N. Butter,
N. Bourne, a. T. Archer,* 1622. ?Ent. to Butter 26 oc.
O⁹.BELVOIR. Dahl 83.

86 — [A variant w. imprint:] *f. N. Butter a. B. Downes,*
1622. L. Dahl 84.

87 — November 5. 1622. Numb. 5. A continuation of the
newes. 4°. *[Eliot's Court Press?] f. B. Downes a.
T. Archer,* 1622. Ent. to Bourne a. Downes 3 no.
L.C²¹.Z. Dahl 85.
See Court-Book C, pp. 154, 469; *see also* 16841.

88 — Novem. 7. 1622. Numb. 6. A coranto. 4°. *[T.
Snodham?] f. N. Butter, N. Bourne, a. W. Shefford,*
1622. L.O.Z. Dahl 86.
(Formerly 5749)

89 — Novemb. 16. 1622. Numb. 7. A continuation of the
newes. 4°. *[G. Eld?] f. N. Butter, N. Bourne, a. W.
Shefford,* 1622. L.YK. Dahl 87.

90 — Novemb. 21. 1622. Numb. 8. The continuation of
the former newes. 4°. *[Eliot's Court Press?] f. N.
Butter, B. Downes, a. T. Archer,* 1622. L.BELVOIR.
Dahl 88.

91 — Novemb. 28. Numb. 9. Briefe abstracts out of
diverse letters. 4°. *B. A[lsop] f. N. Butter, N. Bourne,
a. W. Shefford,* 1622. L.O. Dahl 89.
(Formerly 83)

92 — January the 20. Numb 14. Weekely newes, containing the imprisonment of the Cardinall Clossell. 4°.
[G. Eld?] f. N. Butter, N. Bourne, a. B. Downes,
1623. L.Z. Dahl 93.

93 — January the 28. Numb. 15. Weekely newes, containing the late proceedings in the Grisons country.
4°. *[Eliot's Court Press?] f. N. Butter, N. Bourne,
a. B. Downes,* 1623. L.C²¹.Z. Dahl 94.

Newsbooks—NEWSBOOKS—*Numbered and dated—cont.*

18507.94 — January the 30. Numb. 16. Weekly newes, con-
taining the propositions of the ambassador of the
Emperor. 4°. *[G. Eld?] f. N. Butter, N. Bourne, a.
W. Sheffard,* 1623. Ent. to Butter a. Bourne 27 ja.
D⁷. Dahl 95(location given is erroneous).

95 — [Anr. issue, dated 'January the 31.', w. 'To the
reader' added to verso of tp.] L. Dahl 96.

96 — A new survey of the affaires of Europe. 4°. *[G. Eld?]
f. N. Butter, B. Downes, a. T. Archer,* 1623. Ent. to
Butter a. Bourne 5 fb. C. Dahl 97.
(Formerly 10569)

97 — February the 11. Numb. 18. Weekly newes, containing these particulars: [etc.] 4°. *[G. Eld, E. Allde,
a. others] f. N. Butter, N. Bourne, a. W. Sheffard,*
1623. Ent. to Butter a. Bourne 8 fb. L.YK. Dahl 98.

98 — February 19. Numb. 19. A relation of the late
horrible treason. 4°. *[J. Dawson, E. Allde, a. G. Eld]
f. N. Butter, B. Downes, a. T. Archer,* 1623. Ent. to
Butter a. Downes 17 fb. L.L⁴. Dahl 99.
(Formerly 17674a)

99 — February 28, Numb. 20. The newes of forraine
partes. 4°. *[J. Dawson, E. Allde, W. Jones, a. another]
f. N. Butter, N. Bourne, a. W. Sheffard,* 1623. L.
Dahl 100.

100 — March 7, 1623. Numb. 21. A proclamation by the
states of Utrecht. 4°. *[J. Dawson a. G. Eld] f. N.
Butter, N. Bourne, a. T. Archer,* 1623. O.BELVOIR.
Dahl 101.
(Formerly 24561)

101 — March 7. 1623. Numb. 22. The sentence and execution [etc.] 4°. *[Eliot's Court Press?] f. N. Butter a.
W. Sheffard,* 1623. L.BELVOIR.; MIN. Dahl 102.

102 — March 14, 1623. Numb. 23. Weekly newes, con-
taining the great treason. 4°. *[J. Dawson?] f. N.
Butter, N. Bourne, a. T. Archer,* 1623. L.SHEF.
Dahl 103.

103 — March 31, 1623. Numb. 24. Weekly newes, from
forraine parts. 4°. *[J. Dawson?] f. N. Butter, N.
Bourne, a. W. Sheffard,* 1623. Ent. to Butter 26 mr.
L. Dahl 104.

104 — Aprill 8, 1623. Numb. 25. A relation of the last
newes from severall parts of the world. 4°. *[J. Dawson?] f. N. Butter, N. Bourne, a. T. Archer,* 1623.
L. Dahl 105.

105 — April 17. Numb. 26. The continuation of our former
newes. 4°. *[Eliot's Court Press?] f. N. Butter, N.
Bourne, a. T. Archer,* 1623. Ent. to Butter 17 ap.
L. Dahl 106.

106 — April 21. Numb. 27. The continuation of our weekly
newes. 4°. *[G. Eld?] f. N. Butter a. N. Bourne,* 1623.
Ent. to Butter 17 ap. L. Dahl 107.

107 — April 24. Numb. 28. The continuation of our
former newes. 4°. *[Eliot's Court Press?] f. N. Butter,
N. Bourne, a. T. Archer,* 1623. Ent. to Butter 24 ap.
L.D⁸ (apparently erroneously dated 1625). Dahl 108.

108 — May 2. Numb. 29. The continuation of our weekly
newes. 4°. *[Eliot's Court Press?] f. N. Butter a. W.
Sheffard,* 1623. Ent. 30 ap. L. Dahl 109.

109 — May 7. 1623. Numb. 30. A relation of the Duke of
Brunswicks march. 4°. *[E. Allde a. J. Dawson?] f.
N. Butter, N. Bourne, a. T. Archer,* 1623. Ent. to
Butter a. Bourne 5 my. L. London, Press Club.
Dahl 110.

110 — May 12. Numb. 31. The newes of this present weeke.
4°. *[G. Eld?] f. N. Butter, N. Bourne, a. W. Sheffard,*
1623. Ent. to Butter a. Bourne 12 my L. Dahl 111.

111 — May 17. Numb. 32. The last newes. 4°. *[Eliot's Court
Press?] f. N. Butter a. W. Sheffard,* 1623. L. Dahl
112.

112 — May 26, 1623. Numb. 33. A relation of Count
Mansfeilds last proceedings. 4°. *[J. Dawson?] f.
N. Butter, N. Bourne, a. W. Sheffard,* 1623. L.
Dahl 113.

113 — May 30. Number 34. The last newes. 4°. *[Eliot's
Court Press?] f. N. Butter a. T. Archer,* 1623. Ent.
to Butter a. Bourne 29 my. L. Dahl 114.

114 — June 10. Numb. 35. More newes of the affaires of
the world. 4°. *[G. Eld?] f. N. Butter a. T. Archer,*
1623. L. Dahl 115.

115 — June 16. Numb. 36. The affaires of the world. 4°.
[G. Eld?] f. N. Butter a. N. Bourne, 1623. Ent. to
Butter 13 jn. L. Dahl 116.

116 — June 26. Numb. 37. More newes. 4°. *f. N. Butter a.
T. Archer,* 1623. O. Dahl 117.
(Formerly 11793)

Newsbooks—NEWSBOOKS—*Numbered and dated—cont.*

18507.117 — July 4. Numb. 38. The relation of our last newes. 4⁰. [*Eliot's Court Press?*] *f. N. Butter a. T. Archer*, 1623. Ent. to Butter a. Sheffard 3 jy. L. Dahl 118.

118 — July 10, 1623. Numb. 39 The last newes continued. 4⁰. [*J. Dawson?*] *f. N. Butter a. W. Sheffard*, 1623. Ent. 17 jy. L. Dahl 119.

119 — July 18. Numb. 40. The weekely newes continued. 4⁰. [*Eliot's Court Press*] *f. N. Butter a. N. Bourne*, 1623. Ent. to Butter a. Sheffard 17 jy. L. Dahl 120.

120 — July 22. Numb. 41. More newes of the Duke of Brunswicke. 4⁰. [*Eliot's Court Press*] *f. N. Butter a. W. Sheffard*, 1623. L.O. Dahl 121.
(Formerly 18502)

121 — July 29. Numb. 42. More newes of the good successe of the Duke of Brunswicke. 4⁰. [*Eliot's Court Press?*] *f. N. Butter a. N. Bourne*, 1623. L.O.O⁹. Dahl 122.
(Formerly 18503)

122 — August 21. Numb. 44. Our last weekly newes. 4⁰. [*Eliot's Court Press?*] *f. N. Butter a. N. Bourne*, 1623. L. Dahl 123.

123 — Aug. 27. Numb. 45. More newes for this present weeke. 4⁰. *E. Allde f. N. Butter a. W. Sheffard*, 1623. Ent. 17 jy. L.O⁹. Dahl 124.

124 — August 29. Numb. 46. Ital: Gazet. Nū. prī⁰. More newes from Europe. 4⁰. [*J. Dawson?*] *f. N. Butter a. T. Archer*, 1623. Ent. to Butter a. Bourne 26 au. L.C¹⁷(imp.). Dahl 125.
An extraordinary issue.

125 — September. 5. Numb. 46. Our last weekely newes. 4⁰. *E. Allde f. N. Butter a. W. Sheffard*, 1623. Ent. to Butter 4 se. L. Dahl 126.

126 — September 12. Numb. 47. Our last weekly newes. 4⁰. [*Eliot's Court Press?*] *f. N. Butter a. N. Bourne*, 1623. Ent. to Butter 10 se. L.O⁹. Dahl 127.

127 — September. 17. Numb. 48. Weekely newes. 4⁰. *E. Allde f. N. Butter a. W. Sheffard*, 1623. L. Dahl 128.

128 — September 24. Number 49 More newes for this present weeke. 4⁰. *E. Allde f. N. Butter a. W. Sheffard*, 1623. Ent. to Butter 23 se. L.O⁹.P. Dahl 129.

129 — October 2. Number 50 Our last newes containing, a relation of the last proceedings. 4⁰. *E. Allde f. N. Butter a. T. Archer*, 1623. Ent. to Butter 1 oc. L.O⁹. Dahl 130.

130 [Second Series.] October 11. Number 1. Our last weekely newes. 4⁰. *E. Allde f. N. Butter a. T. Archer*, 1623. Ent. to Butter 10 oc. L. Dahl 131.

131 — October 28. Number 2. A most true relation. 4⁰. *E. Allde f. N. Butter a. W. Sheffard*, 1623. L.O⁹. Dahl 132.

132 — November 11. Number 3. The wonderfull resignation of Mustapha. 4⁰. *E. Allde, sold by N. Butter a. N. Bourne*, 1623. Ent. to Butter 11 no. L.O⁹. Dahl 133.

133 — Novemb. 20. Numb. 4. The affaires of Italy. 4⁰. [*G. Eld?*] *f. N. Butter*, 1623. L.; ILL('Numb. 4.' deleted). Dahl 134.

134 — [Nov. 26? No. 5.] The proceedings of Bethelem Gabor in Hungary. 4⁰. *f. N. Butter*, 1623. L(cropt).

135 — Decem: 11. Number 6. First from Constantinople. 4⁰. *E. Allde f. N. Butter a. N. Bourne*, 1623. L. Dahl 135.

136 — Decemb. 13. Number 7. Weekely newes from Germanie. 4⁰. *E. Allde f. N. Butter a. N. Bourne*, 1623. L.O⁹. Dahl 136.

137 — The newes of Europe. 4⁰. *E. Allde f. N. Butter a. N. Bourne*, 1623. O⁹(numbered '8' in MS.).

138 — January 7. Number 9. The newes and affaires of Europe. 4⁰. *E. Allde f. N. Butter a. N. Bourne*, 1624. L.O⁹. Dahl 137.

139 — January 15. Number 10. The newes and affaires of Europe. 4⁰. *E. Allde f. N. Butter a. W. Sheffard*, 1624. L.O⁹. Dahl 138.

140 — January 29. Number 12. The affaires and occurances of Europe. 4⁰. *E. Allde f. N. Butter a. W. Sheffard*, 1624. O⁹.

141 — February 24. Number 14. The affaires and generall businesse of Europe. 4⁰. [*G. Eld?*] *f. N. Butter*, 1624. Ent. to Butter w. 12 previous numbers 23 fb. L.O⁹. Dahl 139.

142 — February 27. Numero 15. Newes from Europe. 4⁰. *E. Allde f. N. Butter a. T. Archer*, 1624. O⁹.

143 — March 6. Numero 16. The newes and affaires of Europe. 4⁰. *E. Allde f. N. Butter a. N. Bourne*, 1624. Ent. to Butter 5 mr. L.O⁹. Dahl 140.

Newsbooks—NEWSBOOKS—*Numbered and dated—cont.*

18507.144 — March 12. Numero 17 Newes of Europe. 4⁰. *A. Mathewes f. N. Butter, a. W. Sheffard*, 1624. O⁹.YK. Dahl 141.

145 — March 19. Numero 18. Newes from Europe. 4⁰. [*G. Eld?*] *f. N. Butter*, 1624. L.O⁹. Dahl 142.

146 — April 7. Numb. 20 Extraordinary newes containing many . . . passages. 4⁰. [*E. Allde?*] *f. N. Butter*, 1624. L.O⁹. Dahl 143.

147 — Aprill 20. Numero 21. The newes of Europe. 4⁰. *E. Allde f. N. Butter a. N. Bourne*, 1624. L. Dahl 144.

147A — Aprill 28. Numero 22. The generall newes of Europe. 4⁰. *E. Allde f. N. Bu tt* [sic] *a. N. Bourne*, 1624. G⁴.

148 — May 12. Num. 24. A true relation of the newes of this present weeke. 4⁰. [*G. Eld?*] *f. N. Butter a. N. Bourne*, 1624. L. Dahl 145.

149 — July. 3. Numb. 30. Late newes or true relations. 4⁰. [*G. Eld?*] *f. N. Butter a. N. Bourne*, 1624. L. Dahl 146.

150 — September 1. Numb. 31. A true & particuler relation. 4⁰. *f. N. Butter*, 1624. Ellis Cat. 204, no. 361 (untraced). Dahl 147.

151 — Septemb. 11. Numb. 32. The continuation of the weekely newes from the first of September to the 11. of the same 1624. 4⁰. [*E. Allde?*] *f. N. Butter, N. Bourne, N. Nuberry, a. W. Sheffard*, 1624. Ent. to Butter a. Bourne 10 se. L. Dahl 148.
From no. 32 on in the second series all numbers have the same title reading at the beginning of the tp, unless otherwise indicated, and almost all indicate the date of the preceding number.

152 — September 16. Number 33. 4⁰. *f. N. Butter a. N. Bourne*, 1624. Ent. 16 se. L. Dahl 149.
Contains advertisement for 4606.5.

153 — [P. 1 begins:] Septemb. 22. Numb. 34. A continuation of the weekly newes. 4⁰. [*f. N. Butter, etc.*, 1624.] Philadelphia, College of Physicians (1 leaf only). Dahl 149A.

154 — October. 5. Numb. 36. The continuation of of [sic] the weekly newes. 4⁰. *f. N. Butter & N. Bourne*, 1624. L. Dahl 150.

155 — October 20. Numb. 38. The newes of this present weeke continued. 4⁰. [*E. Allde?*] *f. N. Butter a. N. Bourne*, 1624. YK. Dahl 150A.

156 — Novem. 15. Numb. 41. The continuation of our weekly newes. 4⁰. *E. All-de f. N. Butter a. N. Bourne*, 1624. L. Dahl 152.

157 — Novem. 22. Numb. 42. 4⁰. *E. A*[*llde*] *f. N. Butter a. N. Bourn*, 1624. O. Dahl 153.
(Formerly 25201)

158 — Decemb. 4. Numb. 43. 4⁰. *f. N. Butter a. N. Bourne*, 1624. L.LAMPORT. Dahl 154.

159 [Third Series.] Januar. 5. Numb. 2. The continuation of our weekly newes. 4⁰. *f. Mercurius Britannicus*, 1625. L. Dahl 160.
Unless otherwise indicated all titles in this and the following (fourth) series begin as above and include the date of the preceding number. 'Mercurius Britannicus' undoubtedly is a pseud. for N. Butter and N. Bourne, who may be assumed to have published these two series.

160 — Januar. 21. Numb. 4. 4⁰. *f. Mercurius Britannicus*, 1625. YK. Dahl 160B.

161 — Februar. 1. Numb. 6. 4⁰. *f. Mercurius Britannicus*, 1625. L. Dahl 162.

162 — Febru. 8. Numb. 7. 4⁰. *E. A*[*llde a. another*] *f. Mercurius Britannicus*, 1625. Ent. to Butter 8 fb. L. Dahl 163.

162A — Februar. 18. Numb. 9. 4⁰. *f. Mercurius Britannicus*, 1625. L⁸.

163 — March 2. Numb. 11. 4⁰. *f. Mercurius Britannicus*, 1625. Ent. to Butter 7 mr. London, Press Club. Dahl 165.

164 — [March 29. No. 15. Sub tp reads:] March 28. Numb. 1 Good and true tydings out of the Indies. 4⁰. [*f. Mercurius Britannicus*,] (1625). BELVOIR (sheet C only). Dahl 166.

165 — April 7. Numb. 16. The continuation of our weekly newes. 4⁰. *f. Mercurius Britannicus*, 1625. L. BELVOIR. Dahl 167.

166 — Aprill 14. Numb. 17. 4⁰. [*E. Allde?*] *f. Mercurius Britannicus*, 1625. L(2).C²¹. Dahl 168.

167 — April 21. Numb. 18. 4⁰. *f. Mercurius Britannicus*, 1625. L.L³⁸. Dahl 169.

Newsbooks—NEWSBOOKS—*Numbered and dated*—cont.

18507.168 — April 27. Numb. 19. 4°. f. *Mercurius Britannicus*, 1625. L.L³⁸. Dahl 170.

169 — May 5. Numb. 20. 4°. f. *Mercurius Britannicus*, 1625. L.O. Dahl 171.
(Formerly 25201a)

170 — May 19. Numb. 22. 4°. [E. *Allde*?] f. *Mercurius Brittanicus*, 1625. L(2). Dahl 173.

171 — May 24. Numb. 23. 4°. f. *Mercurius Britannicus*, 1625. L. Dahl 174.

172 — May. 30. Numb. 24. 4°. f. *Mercurius Britannicus*, 1625. Ent. to Butter w. other newsbooks 19 jn. L.D(lacks tp). Dahl 175.

173 — June 28. Numb. 28. 4°. f. *Mercurius Britannicus*, 1625. YK. Dahl 175B.

174 — Julie 22, Numb. 31. 4°. f. *Mercurius Brittanicus*, 1625. L.

175 — August 4. Numb. 32. 4°. f. *Mercurius Britannicus*, 1625. L.

176 — Number 40. [Undated; news reports for 4–26 Oct.] The continuation of our newes. 4°. [E. *Allde*? f.] *Mercurius Britanicus*, 1625. D(imp.). Dahl 176.

177 — January 18. Numb. 49. The continuation of our weekly newes. 4°. f. *Mercurius Britanicus*, 1626. YK. Dahl 176B.

178 [Fourth Series.] [After 12 March.] 4°. [f. *Mercurius Britannicus*? 1626.] L(2 leaves, pp. 19–22, Harl.MS. 390). Dahl 177.

179 — May 23. Numb. 13. The continuation of our weekely newes. 4°. f. *Mercurius Britannicus*, 1626. BELVOIR. Dahl 179.

180 — June 14. Numb. 16. 4°. f. *Mercurius Britannicus*, 1626. London, Press Club (imp.). Dahl 181.

181 — August 24. Numb. 26. 4°. f. *Mercurius Britannicus*, 1626. BELVOIR. Dahl 184.

182 — August 29. Numb. 27. 4°. f. *Mercurius Britannicus*, [1626.] L.

183 — November 8. Num. 37. 4°. [J. *Norton*?] f. *Mercurius Brittanicus*, 1626. HD(tp only).

184 — December 8. Num. 42. The third newes continued for this moneth of December. 4°. f. *Mercurius Brittanicus*, 1626. BELVOIR. Dahl 189.

185 [Fifth Series.] June 8. The con⟨tinuation of⟩ our weekly n⟨ewes which have⟩ beene sent fr⟨om several parts of⟩ Christen⟨dome⟩. 4°. f. ⟨*Mercurius Britannicus*.⟩ O(imp., mutil.). Dahl 194.
In this series the beginning of the title remains as above unless otherwise indicated.

186 — Aug. 1. Num. 25. 4°. [G. *Purslowe*?] f. *Mercurius Britanicus*, 1627. BELVOIR. LAMPORT. Dahl 197.
This and most of the following include accounts of the Duke of Buckingham's siege on the Isle of Ré; *see* especially Newsbooks 193; *see* also 20779.5, 24739.5 sqq.

186A — Aug. 8. Numb. 27. Certaine avisoes of private letters. 4°. f. *N. Butter*, 1627. Ent. 7 au. LAMPORT. Dahl 198.

187 — Aug. 17. Numb. 29. The continuation of our weekly newes. 4°. f. *N. Butter*, 1627. Ent. to Butter a. Bourne 16 au. L. Dahl 199.

188 — Septemb. 12. Numb. 32. 4°. f. *N. Butter*, 1627. BELVOIR. Dahl 202.

189 — October 4. [No. 36]. 4°. f. *N. Butter*, 1627. Ent. 4 oc. L. Dahl 204.

190 — October. 9. Numb. 37. 4°. f. *N. Butter*, 1627. ILL.

191 — October 17. Numb. 38. 4°. f. *N. Butter*, 1627. L.

192 — October. 24. Numb. 39. 4°. f. *N. Butter*, 1627. Ent. 23 oc. L. Dahl 205.

193 — A true report of all the speciall passages of note lately happened in the Ile of Ree. . . . Novemb. 1. Numb. 40. The continuation of our weekly newes. 4°. [W. *Stansby*] f. *N. Butter*, 1627. Ent. 30 oc. F. Dahl 206.
Film of F copy on Univ. Microfilms reel 944 ('25201aa'). *See* note to Newsbooks 186.

194 — Novemb. 7. Numb. 41. The continuation of our weekly newes. 4°. f. *N. Butter*, 1627. L.

195 — January 25. Numb. 47. The further continuation of our weekly newes. 4°. f. *N. Butter*, 1628. BELVOIR. Dahl 210.

196 — [Heading:] June 10, Num. 49. The continuation of our weekly newes. 4°. (f. *N. Butter*, 1628.) L(sheet A, no tp).
The reason for the gap in date is not known.

197 — [Heading:] June 19. Num. 50. 4°. (f. *N. Butter*, 1628.) L(sheet A, no tp).

Newsbooks—NEWSBOOKS—*Numbered and dated*—cont.

18507.197A [Unidentified Series.] April 21. Numb. 55. The continuation of our late extraordinarie private avisoes since the 3. of Aprill. 4°. f. *N. Butter*, 1628. L.
Contents fit this date but no known series is numbered beyond 50 until 1639.

198 [Sixth Series.] October 28. Num. 19. The continuation of our weekly newes. 4°. f. *N. Butter*, 1628. Z(imp.). Dahl 211.

199 — November 19. Num. 22. The continuation of our weekly newes. 4°. f. *N. Butter*, 1628. O. Dahl 212.

200 — May 5. Numb. 32. Newes of certaine commands lately given by the French king. 4°. f. *N. Bourne*, 1629. Ent. 2 my. C. Dahl 214.
(Formerly 16847) First two words of the title are pr. on the same line as, and between, the date and no.

201 — June 4. Num. 34. The continuation of the weekely newes. . . . 1629. 4°. f. *N. Bourne*, [1629.] PARIS. Dahl 216.

202 — August [18.] Num. 40. The continuation of the weekly newes. 4°. f. *N. Bourne*, 1629. L.LAMPORT. Dahl 217.

203 — August 25. Num. 41. The continuation of the weekly newes. 4°. f. *N. Bourne*, 1629. LAMPORT.Z. Dahl 218.

203A — September 28. Numb. 43. The continuation of the weekly newes. 4°. [G. *Purslowe*] f. *N. Bourne*, 1629. Mrs. Folke Dahl, Lund, Sweden.
Quire D has another setting of 11363.

204 [Seventh Series.] April 21. Numb. [blank] The continuation of the weekely newes, from the 31 of March. 4°. f. *N. Bourne*, 1630. L.
See ent. 24 jn. for 28 'currentes'.

205 — July. 16. Numb. 9. The continuation of the most remarkable occurrences of newes. 4°. [G. *Purslowe*?] f. *N. Bourne*, 1630. L. Dahl 220.
(Formerly 18762) Date tampered with in ink and could read July. 19. instead.

206 — October. 12. Numb. 15. The continuation of our weekly newes. 4°. f. *N. Butter a. N. Bourne*, 1630. O(imp.). Dahl 222.

207 — November 18. Numb. 17. The continuation of our newes. 4°. [W. *Jones*] f. *N. Butter a. N. Bourne*, 1630. F.
Issued as pt. 2 of 17916.7.

208 — A relation of the King of Sweden. . . . Febr. the 18. Unto which is added our weekly avisoes. 4°. f. *N. Butter a. N. Bourne*, 1631. PARIS.; HN. Dahl 223.
(Formerly 12536)

209 — March 14. Numb. 23. The continuation of our weekly newes, from the 18. of February. 4°. [G. *Purslowe*?] f. *N. Butter a. N. Bourne*, 1631. C. Dahl 224.
(Formerly 25201b)

210 — Aprill 7. Numb. 24. The copie of a letter written from Hambrough. 4°. [G. *Purslowe*?] f. *N. Butter a. N. Bourne*, 1631. Z. Dahl 225.

211 — Aprill 18. Numb. 25. The continuation of our weekly avisoes from forraine parts. 4°. [G. *Purslowe*?] f. *N. Butter a. N. Bourne*, 1631. L.Z. Dahl 226.

212 — May 3. Numb. 26. The solemnity of the marriage of the Emperours sonne. 4°. [G. *Purslowe*?] f. *N. Butter a. N. Bourne*, 1631. Z. Dahl 227.

213 — May 9. Numb. 27. The continuation of our forreigne newes. The first part. 4°. [W. *Jones*?] f. *N. Butter a. N. Bourne*, 1631. Z. Dahl 228.

214 — May 16. Numb. 28. The continuation of our forreigne newes. The second part, being promised in our former aviso. 4°. [W. *Jones*?] f. *N. Butter a. N. Bourne*, 1631. Z. Dahl 229.

215 — [June 4. No. 29.] The continuation of our weekly avisoes, since the 16. of May to the 4. of June. 4°. f. *N. Butter a. N. Bourne*, 1631. E(tp cropt).

216 — A relation of that which hath passed in France. 1631. Dahl 230.
See 11288.5. As this is unnumbered and undated, it is not properly part of this series.

217 — June, 10. Numb. 30. The continuation of our forreigne newes, since the 4. [of June.] 4°. f. *N. Butter a. N. Bourne*, 1631. L.

218 — June, 25. Numb. 31. The continuation of our weekly newes from forraine parts. 4°. f. *N. Butter a. N. Bourne*, 1631. C. Dahl 231.
(Formerly 25201b) *See* ent. 15 jy. to Butter for 'currentes' from 16 se. 1630.

Newsbooks—NEWSBOOKS—*Numbered and dated—cont.*
18507.219 —August, 4. Numb. 34. The continuation of our
weekly newes. 4º. *f. N. Butter a. N. Bourne,* 1631.
BELVOIR. Dahl 233.

220 —August, 20. Numb. 35. The continuation of our
forraine occurrences. Devided into two parts. The
first part. 4º. *f. N. Butter a. N. Bourne,* 1631. O.
Dahl 234.
    The second part, apparently numbered 36, no
longer exists in any known copy.

221 —Septemb. 2. Numb. 37. The continuation of our
forraine avisoes. 4º. *f. N. Butter a. N. Bourne,* 1631.
L.O. Dahl 236.
    (Formerly 11177)

222 —Septemb. 9. Numb. 38 The continuation of our
forraine occurrences. 4º. *f. N. Butter a. N. Bourne,*
1631. L. Dahl 237.

223 —Septemb. 19. Numb. 39. The continuation of our
forreine newes. 4º. *f. N. Butter a. N. Bourne,* 1631.
O.BELVOIR.Z. Dahl 238.

224 —October. 3. Numb. 41. The continuation of our
weekely newes. 4º. *f. N. Butter a. N. Bourne,* 1631.
O.Z. Dahl 240.

225 —October. 6. Numb. 43 [i.e. 42]. The continuation of
our weekely newes. 4º. *f. N. Butter a. N. Bourne,*
1631. Z. Dahl 241.

226 —October. 13. Numb. 43. The continuation of
our newes from forraigne parts. 4º. *f. N. Butter
a. N. Bourne,* [1631.] BELVOIR(date cropt). Dahl
242.

227 —October. 20. Numb. 44. The continuation of our
late avisoes from forreine parts. 4º. *f. N. Butter a.
N. Bourne,* 1631. O.BELVOIR. Dahl 243.

228 —Novemb. 9. Numb. 46. The continuation of our
weekely newes. The first part. 4º. *f. N. Butter a.
N. Bourne,* 1631. NEK. Dahl 245.

229 —November 10. Numb. 47. The continuation of our
weekely newes. The second part. 4º. [*J. Dawson?*]
f. N. Butter a. N. Bourne, 1631. NEK. Dahl 246.

230 —November 19. Numb. 48. The continuation of our
weekely newes. 4º. *f. N. Butter a. N. Bourne,* 1631.
O(lacks all after A4). Dahl 247.

231 —November 22. Numb. 49. The continuation of our
weekely avisoes. 4º. *f. N. Butter a. N. Bourne,* 1631.
O. Dahl 248.

232 —November 29. Numb. 50. The continuation of our
forraine intelligence. The first part. 4º. [*J. Dawson?*]
f. N. Butter a. N. Bourne, 1631. O.BELVOIR.E.
Dahl 249.

233 [Eighth Series.] November 29. Numb. 1. The continuation of our weekely intelligence. The second
part. 4º. [*J. Dawson?*] *f. N. Butter a. N. Bourne,*
1631. O.BELVOIR.E. Dahl 250.

234 —December 8. Numb. 2. The continuation of our
forraine newes. 4º. *f. N. Butter a. N. Bourne,* 1631.
O.BELVOIR. Dahl 251.

235 —December 17. Numb. 3. The continuation of our
weekely newes. 4º. *f. N. Butter a. N. Bourne,* 1631.
BELVOIR(2). Dahl 252.

236 —January 2. Numb. 5. The continuation of our
weekely avisoes. 4º. *f. N. Butter a. N. Bourne,* 1632.
O.BELVOIR(lacks tp). Dahl 253.

237 —January 12. Numb. 6. The continuation of our
weekely avisoes. 4º. [*J. Dawson?*] *f. N. Butter a.
N. Bourne,* 1632. L.BELVOIR. Dahl 254.

238 —January 24. Numb. 8. The continuation of our
forraine avisoes. 4º. [*J. Dawson?*] *f. N. Butter a.
N. Bourne,* 1632. BELVOIR. Dahl 256.

239 —January 30. Numb. 9. The continuation of our
forraine newes. 4º. [*J. Dawson?*] *f. N. Butter a.
N. Bourne,* 1632. BELVOIR(2). Dahl 257.

240 —February 8. Numb. 10. The continuation of our
forraine intelligence. 4º. [*J. Dawson?*] *f. N. Butter a.
N. Bourne,* 1632. L. Dahl 258.
    (Formerly 11179)

241 —February 27. Numb. 13. The continuation of our
forraine avisoes, . . . the second part. 4º. [*J. Dawson?*] *f. N. Butter a. N. Bourne,* 1632. BELVOIR.
Dahl 261.
    No copy of the first part is known. From no. 13
on all numbers in this series have the same title
beginning, unless otherwise indicated.

242 —March 6. Numb. 14. 4º. [*J. Dawson?*] *f. N. Butter
a. N. Bourne,* 1632. BELVOIR.E. Dahl 262.

243 —March 15. Numb. 15. 4º. [*J. Dawson?*] *f. N. Butter
a. N. Bourne,* 1632. BELVOIR. Dahl 263.

Newsbooks—NEWSBOOKS—*Numbered and dated—cont.*
18507.244 —March 24. Numb. 16. 4º. [*J. Dawson?*] *f. N. Butter
a. N. Bourne,* 1632. BELVOIR. Dahl 264.

245 —Aprill 9. Numb. 17. 4º. [*J. Dawson?*] *f. N. Butter a.
N. Bourne,* 1632. BELVOIR(2). Dahl 265.

246 —Aprill 14. Numb. 18. The continuation of our
forraine avisoes, . . . the 2. part of the 9. 4º. [*J. Dawson?*] *f. N. Butter a. N. Bourne,* 1632. C.BELVOIR(2).
E. Dahl 266.
    (Formerly 11178)

247 —Aprill 24. Numb. 19. 4º. [*J. Dawson?*] *f. N. Butter
a. N. Bourne,* 1632. C.BELVOIR(2). Dahl 267.
    (Formerly 11178)

248 —Aprill 28. Numb. 20. 4º. [*J. Dawson?*] *f. N. Butter
a. N. Bourne,* 1632. L.O.C.BELVOIR(2). Dahl 268.
    (Formerly 11178)

249 —May 4. Numb 21. . . . The first part. 4º. [*J. Dawson?*] *f. N. Butter a. N. Bourne,* 1632. BELVOIR.P.
Dahl 269.

250 —May 4. Numb. 22. . . . The second part. 4º. [*J. Dawson?*] *f. N. Butter a. N. Bourne,* 1632. BELVOIR.
Dahl 270.

251 —May 21. Numb. 23. 4º. [*J. Dawson?*] *f. N. Butter a.
N. Bourne,* 1632. LINC(imp.). Dahl 271.
    (Formerly 11178)

252 —May 16. Numb. 24. 4º. [*J. Dawson?*] *f. N. Butter a.
N. Bourne,* 1632. BELVOIR. Dahl 272.

253 —May 28. Numb. 26 [i.e. 25]. 4º. [*J. Dawson?*] *f. N.
Butter a. N. Bourne,* 1632. BELVOIR. Dahl 273.

254 —June 6. Numb. 26. 4º. [*J. Dawson?*] *f. N. Butter a.
N. Bourne,* 1632. L.C(imp.).BELVOIR. Dahl 274.
    (Formerly 11178 and 25201c)

255 —June 9. Numb. 27. 4º. [*J. Dawson?*] *f. N. Butter a.
N. Bourne,* 1632. BELVOIR. Dahl 275.
    See also 23520, advertised at end.

256 —June 23. Numb. 29. 4º. [*J. Dawson?*] *f. N. Butter a.
N. Bourne,* 1632. L.BELVOIR. Dahl 277.
    (Formerly 11178)

257 —July 6. Numb. 32. The continuation of our weekely
avisoes. 4º. *J. D[awson] f. N. Butter a. N. Bourne,*
1632. Ent. 2 jy. C.BELVOIR. London, Press Club.
Dahl 280.
    (Formerly 25198)

258 —July 19. Numb. 34. 4º. *J. D[awson] f. N. Butter a.
N. Bourne,* 1632. Ent. 27 jy. BELVOIR. Dahl 282.
    See also 23520, advertised at end. *See* ent. 16 jy.
for 'currentes' from 19 ja. to 14 jy.

259 —July 25. Numb. 35. 4º. *J. D[awson] f. N. Butter a.
N. Bourne,* 1632. Ent. 27 jy. C.BELVOIR(2). Dahl 283.
    (Formerly 25198)

260 —July 30. Numb. 36. 4º. *J. D[awson] f. N. Butter a.
N. Bourne,* 1632. Ent. 27 jy. BELVOIR.D. Dahl 284.

261 —August 3. Numb. 37. 4º. *J. D[awson] f. N. Butter a.
N. Bourne,* 1632. O.BELVOIR(2). Dahl 285.

262 —August. 3. Numb. 38. Advice given unto the States
of of [*sic*] the Low-Countries. 4º. B. A[lsop] a.
T. F[awcet] f. N. Butter a. N. Bourne, 1632. BEL-
VOIR.; F. Dahl 286.
    (Formerly 18464) Last 6 lines in F and BELVOIR
copies from different settings.

263 —August 13. Numb. 39. The continuation of our
weekely avisoes. 4º. *J. D[awson] f. N. Butter a.
N. Bourne,* [1632.] BELVOIR(date cropt). Dahl 287.

264 —August 23. Numb. 40. 4º. *J. D[awson] f. N. Butter
a. N. Bourne,* 1632. O⁵.BELVOIR. Dahl 288.

265 —August 30 Numb. 41. 4º. *J. D[awson] f. N. Butter
a. N. Bourne,* 1632. BELVOIR. Dahl 289.

266 —September 1. Numb. 42. The continuation of our
Swedish intelligence. 4º. *J. D[awson] f. N. Butter a.
N. Bourne,* 1632. C.C⁵. Dahl 291.

267 — [A variant, w. title corrected:] The continuation of
our weekely avisoes. L.BELVOIR. Dahl 290.

268 —September 4. Numb. 43. The continuation of our
Swedish and French, with some Low-Country
newes. 4º. *J. D[awson] f. N. Butter a. N. Bourne,*
1632. O¹⁰.BELVOIR. Dahl 292.

269 —September 12. Numb. 44. The continuation of our
forraine avisoes. 4º. *J. D[awson] f. N. Butter a.
N. Bourne,* 1632. BELVOIR(2). Dahl 293.

270 —September 19. Numb. 45. . . . The first part. 4º.
J. D[awson] f. N. Butter a. N. Bourne, 1632.
BELVOIR. Dahl 294.

271 —September 22. Numb. 46. . . . Being the second part.
4º. *J. D[awson] f. N. Butter a. N. Bourne,* 1632.
C.BELVOIR. Dahl 295.
    (Formerly 11178)

Newsbooks—NEWSBOOKS—*Numbered and dated—cont.*

18507.272 — September 26. Numb. 47. 4°. *J.* D[*awson*] *f. N. Butter a. N. Bourne*, 1632. BELVOIR. Dahl 296.

273 — October 3. Numb. 48. 4°. *J.* D[*awson*] *f. N. Butter a. N. Bourne*, 1632. L.BELVOIR. Dahl 297.

274 — October 10. Numb. 49. The continuation of our weekely newes. The first part. 4°. *J.* D[*awson*] *f. N. Butter a. N. Bourne*, 1632. BELVOIR. Dahl 298.

275 — October 12. Numb. 50. The continuation of our forraine avisoes. The second part. 4°. *J.* D[*awson*] *f. N. Butter a. N. Bourne*, 1632. D. Dahl 299.

276 [Ninth Series.] October 16. Numb. 1. A journall of all the principall passages of that late famous siege of Mastricht. 4°. *J.* D[*awson*] *f. N. Butter a. N. Bourne*, 1632. L(2).O.C.E. Leiden U.; HD.NY. Dahl 300.

(Formerly 11365) On 17 Oct. 1632 a Star Chamber decree prohibited the further publication of newsbooks. *See also* Greg, *Companion,* pp. 291–2. The first word of the title is pr. on the same line as, and between, the date and no.

277 [Tenth Series.] Numb. 1. An abstract of some speciall forreigne occurrences, . . . of the 20 of December. 4°. [*T. Harper?*] *f. N. Butter a. N. Bourne*, 1638. Ent. 19 de. L.O. Rolf Wistrand, Stockholm.; F.MIN. Dahl 301.

(Formerly 82) Patent for printing newsbooks awarded to Butter and Bourne 20 Dec. 1638. Continuous pagination and signatures throughout the entire series of 100 numbers, beginning at least w. no. 6 and possibly w. no. 2.

278 — Num. 6, From Norimberg. 4°. [*R. Oulton?*] (*f. N. Butter a. N. Bourne*, 1639 (1 ja.)) MIN. Dahl 302.

279 — Numb. 7. 25 Ordinary weekly currantoes from Frankford. 4°. (*f. N. Butter a. N. Bourne*, [1639] (1 ja.)) MIN. Dahl 303.

280 — [No. 8.] Ordinary weekly currantoes from Holland. 4°. [*R. Oulton?*] (*f. N. Butter a. N. Bourn*, [1639] (1 ja.)) MIN(top shaved). Dahl 304.

281 — Num. 9. 29 The articles and other circumstances and particulars of the taking of Brisack. 4°. (*f. N. Butter a. N. Bourne*, 1639 (1 ja.)) MIN. Dahl 305.

282 — Num. 10. 41 The weekly curranto from Norimberg. 4°. (*f. N. Butter a. N. Bourn*, 1639 (9 ja.)) MIN. Dahl 306.

283 — Numb. 11. 45 The continuation of the Frankford curranto. 4°. [*R. Hodgkinson?*] (*f. N. Butter a. N. Bourne*, 1638 [o.s.] (9 ja.)) MIN. Dahl 307.

Includes 'The weekely curranto of Holland'.

284 — Nnmb. [*sic*] 16. 65 The weekly curranto from Norimberg. 4°. [*T. Harper?*] *f. N. Butter a. N. Bourne*, 1639 (18 ja.)) Z. Dahl 308.

285 — Num. 17. 69 The weekly curranto from Frankford. 4°. [*R. Hodgkinson?*](*f. N. Butter a. N. Bourne*, 1638 [o.s.] (18 ja.)) Z. Dahl 309.

286 — Num. 21. Ordinarie weekely currantos from Norimberg. 4°. [*R. Oulton? f.*] (*N. Butter a. N. Bourne*, [1639] (1 fb.)) MIN. Dahl 310.

287 — Num. 22. 89 Ordinary weekely curranto from Franckford, [*sic*] 4°. (*f. N. Butter a. N. Bourn*, 1639 (1 fb.)) MIN. Dahl 311.

288 — Num. 23. 93 The ordinary weekly curranto from Holland. 4°. [*R. Hodgkinson?*] (*f. N. Butter a. N. Bourne*, 1639 (1 fb.)) MIN. Dahl 312.

289 — Num. 29. 117 Ordinary weekely curranto from Norimberg. 4°. (*f. N. Butter a. N. Bourne*, 1639 (17 fb.)) MIN. Dahl 313.

290 — Numb. 30. Ordinary weekly curranto from Frankford. 4°. (*f. N. Butter a. N. Bourne,*) [1639 (17 or 18 fb.)] MIN (margins trimmed, esp. last leaf). Dahl 314.

291 — Num. 31. 125 The ordinary weekly curranto from Holland. 4°. [*R. Hodgkinson?*] (*f. N. Butter a. N. Bourne*, 1639 (18 fb.)) MIN. Dahl 315.

292 — Numb. 35. 141 The ordinary weekly curranto from Norimberg. 4°. [*T. Harper?*] (*f. N. Butter a. N. Bourne*, 1639 (1 mr.)) MIN. Dahl 316.

293 — [No. 36. 145.] The ordinary weekly currantoes from Franckford. 1638. 4°. [*R. Hodgkinson?*] (*f. N. Butter a. N. Bourne*, 1639 (1 mr.)) MIN(first leaf trimmed). Dahl 317.

294 — Num. 37. 149 The ordinary weekly curranto from Holland. 4°. [*R. Hodgkinson?*] (*f. N. Butter a. N. Bourne*, 1639 (1 mr.)) MIN. Dahl 318.

Newsbooks—NEWSBOOKS—*Numbered and dated—cont.*

18507.295 — Num. 38. pag. 153. The ordinary curranto from Norimberg. 4°. (*f. N. Butter a. N. Bourne*, 1639). MIN. Dahl 319.

296 — Num. 39. 157 The ordinary weekly curranto from Frankford. 4°. [*R. Hodgkinson?*] (*f. N. Butter a. N. Bourne*, 1639 (12 mr.)) MIN. Dahl 320.

297 — Numb. 40. 161 The ordinary weekly curranto from Holland. 4°. [*B. Alsop?*] (*f. N. Butter a. N. Bourne*, 1639 (12 mr.)) MIN. Dahl 321.

298 — [No. 47. 189.] The ordinar(y) weekly curranto from Norimberg. 4°. (*f. N. Butter a. N. Bourne*, 1639 (3 ap.)) MIN(trimmed). Dahl 322.

299 — Num. 48. 193 The ordinary weekly curranto from Frankford. 4°. [*R. Hodgkinson?*] (*f. N. Butter a. N. Bourne*, 1639 (3 ap.)) MIN. Dahl 323.

300 — [No. 49. 197.] The ordinary weekly curranto from Holland. 4°. (*f. N. Butter a. N. Bourne*, 1639 (3 ap.)) MIN(trimmed). Dahl 324.

301 — [No. 64. 257.] Extractes of private letters from Germany, [etc.] 4°. (*f. N. Butter a. N. Bourne*, 1639 (13 my.)) MIN(trimmed). Dahl 325.

302 — Num. 65. [261.] The ordinary weekly curranto from Norimberg. 4°. [*R. Hodgkinson?*] (*f. N. Butter a. N. Bourne*, 1639 (13 my.)) MIN(trimmed). Dahl 326.

303 — Numb. 66: [265.] The ordinary weekely curranto from Franckford. 4°. [*R. Oulton?*] (*f. N. Butter a. N. Bourne*, 1639 (13 my.)) MIN(trimmed). Dahl 327.

304 — [No. 67. 269.] The ordinary weekely currantoes from Holland. 4°. [*B. Alsop a. T. Fawcet?*] (*f. N. Butter a. N. Bourne*, 1639 (13 my.)) MIN(trimmed). Dahl 328.

305 — [No. 68. 273.] The ordinary weekly curranto from Norimberg. 4°. [*T. Harper?*] (*f. N. Butter a. N. Bourne*, 1639 (22 my.)) MIN(trimmed). Dahl 329.

306 — 277 Numb. 69. The ordinary weekely curranto from Franckford. 4°. [*R. Oulton?*] (*f. N. Butter a. N. Bourne*, 1639 (21 my.)) MIN(trimmed). Dahl 330.

307 — [No. 70. 281.] The ordinary weekly curranto from Holland. 4°. [*R. Hodgkinson?*] (*f. N. Butter a. N. Bourne*, 1639 (22 my.)) MIN(trimmed). Dahl 331.

308 — [No. 71. 285.] A true and particular relation of the battell fought neare Kemnitz. 4°. [*f. N. Butter a. N. Bourne*, 1639 (my.)] MIN(trimmed). Dahl 332.

An extraordinary issue.

309 — Numb. 72. [289.] The ordinary weekely curranto from Holland. 4°. [*R. Oulton?*] (*f. N. Butter a. N. Bourne*, 1639 (27 my.)) MIN(trimmed). Dahl 333.

310 — [No. 73.] 293. The ordinary weekly curranto from Frankford. 4°. [*R. Hodgkinson?*] (*f. N. Butter a. N. Bourne* [*sic*], 1639 (27 my.)) MIN(trimmed). Dahl 334.

311 — [No. 74. 297.] The ordinary weekly curranto from Norimberg. 4°. (*f. N. Butter a. N. Bourne*, 1639 (27 my.)) MIN(trimmed). Dahl 335.

312 — Num. 84. 337 The Norimberg curranto of this week. 4°. (*f. N. Butter a. N. Bourn*, 1639 (21 jn.)) C. Dahl 336.

(Formerly 18751)

313 — Numb. 86. 345 The curranto this weeke from Holland. 4°. [*T. Harper?*](*f. N. Butter a. N. Bourne*, 1639 (21 jn.)) C. Dahl 337.

(Formerly 13571)

314 [Eleventh Series.] Century 2. Num. 40. 161 The curranto of this week from Holland. 4°. (*f. N. Butter a. N. Bourn*, 1639 (18 oc.)) Rolf Wistrand, Stockholm. Dahl 338.

This series, like the preceding one, has continuous pagination and signatures throughout the entire series of 100 numbers.

315 — Century 2. Num. 41. 165 An extraordinary curranto: wherein is related, the late sea-fight betwixt the Spaniards and the Hollanders. 4°. [*R. Hodgkinson?*] (*f. N. Butter a. N. Bourn*, 1639 (18 oc.)) C. Rolf Wistrand, Stockholm. Dahl 339.

(Formerly 5750)

315A — Cent. 2. Numb. 165 [corrected in MS. to 67]. 165 The curranto for this weeke from Franckford. 4°. [*M. Flesher?*] (*f. N. Butter,* ⟨1639⟩ (de.)) Mrs. Folke Dahl, Lund, Sweden (colophon def.)

316 — Cent. 2. Num. 86. 241 The curranto this weeke from Norimberg. 4°. [*T. Harper?*] (*f. N. Butter,* 1640 (12 fb.)) BELVOIR. Dahl 340.

317 — Cent. 2. Numb. 87. 245 The curranto for this weeke from Franckford. 4°. [*B. Alsop a. T. Fawcet?*] (*f. N. Butter,* 1639 [o.s.] (11 fb.)) BELVOIR. Dahl 341

Newsbooks—NEWSBOOKS—*Numbered and dated—cont.*

18507.318 — Century 2. Numb. 88. 249 The curranto for this weeke, from Holland. 4°. [*R. Oulton?*] (*f. N. Butter,* 1640 (11 fb.)) BELVOIR. Dahl 342.

319 — Cent. 2. Numb. 90. 275 The curranto for this weeke from Franckford. 4°. [*T. Harper?*] (*f. N. Butter,* 1639 [o.s.] (22 fb.)) BELVOIR. Dahl 343.

320 — Century 2. Numb. 91 279 The curranto for this weeke, from Franckford. 4°. [*R. Oulton?*] (*f. N. Butter,* 1640 (22 fb.)) BELVOIR. Dahl 344.

321 — 293 [i.e. 283.] Numb. 92. The curranto for this weeke from Holland. 4°. (*f. N. Butter,* 1640 (22 fb.)) BELVOIR. Dahl 345.

322 — Century 2. Num. 93. 297 The curranto for this weeke from Norimberg. 4°. (*f. N. Butter,* 1640 (24 fb.)) BELVOIR. Dahl 346.

323 — Century 2. Numb. 94 301 The curranto for this week from Frankeford. 4°. (*f. N. Butter,* [1640] 24 fb.)) BELVOIR. Dahl 347.

324 — Cent. 2. Numb. 95. 305 The curranto this weeke from Holland. 4°. (*f. N. Butter,* 1640 (24 fb.)) BELVOIR. Dahl 348.

325 [Twelfth Series.] Cent. 3. Num. 8. 29 The curranto for this weeke from Norimberg. 4°. [*B. Alsop a. T. Fawcet?*] (*f. N. Butter,* 1640 (25 mr.)) BELVOIR. Dahl 349.
This series also has continuous signatures and pagination, but the format changed with 337, reverting to the format of earlier series.

326 — Century 3. Numb. 9. 33 The curranto for this weeke from Franckford. 4°. [*T. Harper?*] (*f. N. Butter a. N. Bourne,* 1639 [o.s.] (24 mr.)) BELVOIR. Dahl 350.

327 — Century 3. Numb. 10 37 Th ecurranto [*sic*] for this weeke, from Holland. 4°. (*f. N. Butter,* 1640 (25 mr.)) BELVOIR. Dahl 351.

328 — Cent. 3. Num. 11. 41 A true narration of a late sea-fight betwixt 15. men of warre. 4°. [*B. Alsop a. T. Fawcet?*] (*f. N. Butter,* 1640 (27 mr.)) BELVOIR. Dahl 352.

329 — Cent. 3. Num. 12. The curranto for this weeke from Norimberg. 4°. [*B. Alsop a. T. Fawcet?*] (*f. N. Butter,* 1640 (31 mr.)) BELVOIR. Dahl 353.

330 — Century 3. Numb. 13 49 The curranto for this weeke, from Franckford. 4°. (*f. N. Butter,* 1640 (31 mr.)) BELVOIR. Dahl 354.

331 — Century 3. Numb. 14. [5]5 The curranto for this weeke from Holland. 4°. [*T. Harper?*] (*f. N. Butter,* 1640 (31 mr.)) BELVOIR. Dahl 355.

332 — Cent. 3. Num. 15. 57 The curranto for this weeke from Norimberg. 4°. [*B. Alsop a. T. Fawcet?*] (*f. N. Butter,* 1640 (10 ap.)) BELVOIR. Dahl 356.

333 — Century 3. Numb. 16. 61 A true and fearefull pronouncing of warre . . . by Soloma Hometh. 4°. [*T. Harper?*] (*f. N. Butter,* 1640 (10 ap.)) BELVOIR. Dahl 357.
Includes 'The curranto for this weeke from Franckford.' *See also* 23424.5 sq.

334 — Century 3. Numb. 17. 65 The curranto for this weeke from Holland. 4°. [*T. Harper?*] (*f. N. Butter,* 1640 (10 ap.)) BELVOIR. Dahl 358.

335 — Cent. 3. Num. 18. 69 The curranto for this weeke from Franckford. 4°. [*B. Alsop a. T. Fawcet?*] (*f. N. Butter,* 1640 (20 ap.)) BELVOIR. Dahl 359.

336 — Century 3. Numb. 19 73 The curranto for this weeke, from Holland. 4°. [*R. Oulton?*] (*f. N. Butter,* 1640 (20 ap.)) BELVOIR. Dahl 360.

337 — Century 3. Numb. 20. The newes for this week from Norimberg, Frankford and Holland. 4°. [*T. Harper?*] *f. N. Butter,* 1640 (23 ap.) o. Dahl 361.
(Formerly 18750) With this number the earlier practice of printing all the week's news in one number instead of several is re-established, and the series returns to 50 numbers instead of 100.

338 — Century 3. Numb. 27. Newes of this present weeke from Germany, Italy, and Spaine. 4°. [*T. Harper?*] *f. N. Butter,* 1640 (6 jn.) BELVOIR.; N(trimmed). Dahl 362.

339 — A true relation of a late very famous sea-fight, . . . in Brasil. 4°. [*T. Harper?*] *f. N. Butter,* 1640 (12 jn.) L.L⁸.o.; COR. Dahl 363.

340 — Century 3. Numb. 31. Newes of this present weeke from severall places. 4°. [*T. Harper?*] *f. N. Butter,* 1640 (27 jn.) BELVOIR. Dahl 364.

341 — Cent. 3. Num. 46. The continuation of our two last weeks printed newes from forraigne parts. 4°. [*T. Harper?*] *f. N. Butter,* 1640 (4 de.) o³. Dahl 365.

Newsbooks—NEWSBOOKS—*Numbered and dated—cont.*

18507.342 — Cent. 3. Num. 47. The continuation of the forraine avisoes. 4°. *f. N. Butter,* 1640 (10 de.) o³. Dahl 366.

343 — Cent. 3. Numb. 48. The continuation of the forraine occurrents for 5. weekes. 4°. *f. N. Butter,* 1640 [o.s.] (11 ja.) Dahl 367.

344 — ⟨Cent. 3.⟩ Numb. 49. The ⟨co⟩ntinuation ⟨of⟩ the forraine avisoes for two weekes last past. 4°. ⟨*f. N. Butter,*⟩ 1640 [o.s.] (23 ja.) N(tp mutil.). Dahl 368.

345 [Thirteenth Series.] Cent. 4. Numb. I. The forraine aviso's [*sic*] continued. 4°. *f. N. Butter,* 1640 [o.s.] (2 fb.) BELVOIR. Dahl 369.
This is the last known issue of this series to bear the date '1640'.

T. Archer, 1624–1628

346 Septemb. 9. Numb. 23. (Numb. 32.) A continuation of the former newes. 4°. *f. T. Archer a. B. Fisher,* [1624.] Ent. to Archer 7 se. 1624. o. Dahl 390.
(Formerly 25200)

347 — [Anr. issue, w. tp:] Septemb. 10. Numb. 23. (Numb. 32.) Extraordinary newes. [etc.] L. Dahl 391.

348 October 11. Number 2. Two wonderful and lamentable accidents. 4°. [*Eliot's Court Press?*] *f. T. Archer,* 1624. L.; HD(quire C only). Dahl 392.

349 October 21. Number 3. A relation of the chiefest and last proceedings of the campe of the Prince of Orange. 4°. [*J. Dawson?*] *f. T. Archer,* 1624. YK. Dahl 393.

350 [End of October. No. 4.] 4°. [*f. T. Archer,* 1624.] o(imp.). Dahl 394.

351 November the 10. Number the 5. In this weekes newes is related the occasions and successes of Count Mansfield. 4°. *B. A[lsop] f. T. Archer,* 1625 [i.e. 1624]. ? Ent. 15 no. 1624. L. Dahl 395.

352 Novem. 24. Num. 7. The weekely newes, containing these particulars. 4°. *W. J[ones] f. T. Archer,* 1624. Ent. 22 no. o. Dahl 396.
(Formerly 25199)

353 A certaine and perfect relation of the encounter and bloody slaughter. 4°. *B. A[lsop] f. T. Archer,* 1625. M. Dahl 397.

354 A continuation of all the principall occurrences which hath happened to the leaguers. 4°. *B. A[lsop] f. T. Archer,* 1625. L.BELVOIR. Dahl 398.
(Formerly 3594) Both known copies trimmed at top of tp.

355 A true and very memorable relation, of certaine speciall matters. 4°. *f. T. Archer,* 1628. C².BELVOIR. Dahl 399.

356 July 2 Num. 2. The continuation of our weekly newes. 4°. *f. T. Archer,* 1628. L.

357 (1) August 7. Num. 6. The continuation of our weekly newes. 4°. *f. T. Archer,* 1628. L¹¹. Dahl 400.

358 (1) August 15. Num. 7. The continuation of our weekly newes. 4°. *f. T. Archer,* 1628. L¹¹. Dahl 401.

Amsterdam, 1633

359 Briefe relations from marchans letters. 4°. *Amsterdam,* [*f. J. van Hilten,*] 1633. Rolf Wistrand, Stockholm. Dahl 402.

360 (1) The continuation of newes from diverse parts, . . . *tr. at Amsterdam* 1633. 4°. [*Amsterdam, J. F. Stam? f. J. van Hilten,* 1633.] Rolf Wistrand, Stockholm. Dahl 403.

361 (1) The last weekes letters printed at Amsteldam by I. H. the 26. off [*sic*] Feb. 1633. 4°. [*Amsterdam, J. F. Stam f. J. van Hilten,* 1633 (26 fb.)] Rolf Wistrand, Stockholm. Dahl 404.

See also English Mercury, Swedish Intelligencer, and 24739.5 sqq.

———

18508 **Newstead, Christopher.** An apology for women: or, womens defense. 8°. *E. G[riffin] f. R. Whittakers,* 1620. Ent. 27 de. 1619. O.O³.; F.HN.
Answers 23533.

Newton, *Cambridge, Chapel of St. Mary in the Sea. See* Indulgences 62, 63.

Newton, *Suffolk, Hospital of Pity. See* Indulgences 64.

Newton, *Sir* **Adam,** *tr. See* 9232, 21764.

18509 **Newton, Robert.** The countesse of Mountgomeries
Eusebeia: expressing briefly, the soules praying
robes. 12°. *G. Purslow f. A. G[ilman,]* 1620. Ent.
to A. Gilman 9 no. L.; F.

18510 **Newton, Thomas.** Approoued medicines and cordiall
receipes, with the natures, of simples. 8°. *T. Marshe,*
1580. Ent. to T. Orwin on decease of T. Marsh,
23 jn. 1591. L.L¹⁹.L³⁹.O.E².

18511 — Atropoïon Delion. 1603. Now = 18513.5.
18512 — An epitaphe vpon the worthy and honorable lady, the
lady Knowles. s.sh.fol. *W. How f. R. Johnes,* [1568.]
Ent. 1568–69. HN.
— A notable historie of the saracens. 1575. *See* 6129.

18513 — The olde mans dietarie. Englished out of Latine by
T. Newton. 8°. [*G. Robinson*] *f. E. White,* 1586. Ent.
11 ja. O(frag.). Chester PL.; HN.HD.
— The true tryall and examination of a mans owne selfe.
1586. *See* 11761.3.
— A view of valyaunce. 1580. *See* 21469.
— *ed. See* 1356.5, 3944, 6129, 22221, 23188.
— *tr. See* 5274, 5294, 5314, 6230, 12193a, 15454, 15456,
16978, 17848, 19293a, 22221.
— *See also* 15447.

18513.5 **Newton, Thomas,** *gent.* Atropoïon Delion, or, the death
of Delia. [In verse.] 4°. [*W. White*] *f. W. Johnes,*
1603. L⁶.O(2).; HN.N.
(Formerly 18511)

Neyle, Richard, *Bp. See* Neile, R.

Nicanor, Lysimachus, *pseud. See* 5751.

18514 **Niccholes, Alexander.** A discourse, of marriage and
wiving. 4°. *N. O[kes] f. L. Becket,* 1615. O(2).;
F.HN.HD.N.

18515 — [Anr. ed.] 4°. *G. Eld f. L. Becket,* 1620. L.O.; F.HN.
Iowa U.

18516 **Niccols, Richard.** The beggers ape. [In verse. Anon.]
4°. *B. A[lsop] a. T. Fawcet f. L. Chapman,* 1627.
Ent. 25 no. 1626. L(date cropt).O(2).; F.HN.HD(impr.
cropt).Y.

18517 — The cuckow. [In verse.] 4°. *F. K[ingston,]* sold by
W. C[otton,] 1607. L.L⁶(lacks tp).O(2, 1 lacks tp).;
F.HN.CH.

18518 — A day-starre for darke-wandring soules. 1613. Now =
18526.5.
18519 — = 18520.
18520 — Expicedium. A funeral oration, vpon the late deceased
princesse Elizabeth queen of England. By Infelice
Academico Ignoto. Wherunto is added, the true
order of her highnes funerall. [Anon.] 4°. [*E. Allde*]
f. E. White, 1603. L(2).O.E.; HN.CH.HD(2, 1 misbound w. 19804).

18521 — The furies. With vertues encomium. Or, the image of
honour. In two bookes of epigrammes. [Init. R. N.]
8°. *W. Stansby,* 1614. HN.

18522 — Londons artillery, briefly containing the noble practise
of that wothie [*sic*] Societie. [In verse.] 4°. *T. Creede
a. B. Allsopp f. W. Welby,* 1616. Ent. 3 ja. L.L⁸.
O(2).A.; HN.CH.IND.

18523 — Monodia or Walthams complaint, upon the death of
the lady Honor Hay. [In verse.] 8°. *W. S[tansby] f.
R. Meighen a. T. Jones,* 1615. Ent. to W. Stansby 7
no. 1614. O.; HN.

18524 — Sir Thomas Overburies vision. With the ghoasts of
Weston, Mᵗⁱˢ. Turner, [etc.] By R. N[iccols] Oxon.
[In verse.] 4°. *f. R. M[eighen] & T. J[ones,]* 1616.
L.C.C³.DUL.; F.HN.CH.HD.

18525 — The three sisters teares. Shed at the funerals of Henry,
prince of Wales. [In verse.] 4°. *T. S[nodham] f. R.
Redmer,* 1613. Ent. 17 de. 1612. L(imp.).O.;
F.HN.BO.HD.

18526 — A winter nights vision. 1610. = pt. of 13446.
— *ed. See* 13446.
— *tr. See* 13142.

18526.5 **Niccols, Richard,** *of the Inner Temple.* A day-starre for
darke-wandring soules. Published by I. C. 8°.
[*T. Snodham*] *f. J. Budge,* 1613. O.; F.U.
(Formerly 18518)

18527 **Nicetas,** *Bp.* Catena Græcorum patrum in beatum Job
collectore Niceta. [*Ed.* and *tr.* P. Young.] fol. *ex
typ. regio,* 1637. L.O.C.D.E.+; F.CHI.HD.NYⁱⁱ.U.+
(Formerly also 10581)

18528 **Nicholas,** *Saint.* Saynt Nycholas of tollētyne. 4° in 8.
(*W. de worde,*) [1525?] L.
Orns. at end of paragraphs.
18528.5 — [Anr. ed.] 4°. [*W. de Worde,* 1525?] L(frag.).
No orns. at end of paragraphs.

Nicholas, Henry. *See* Niclas, Hendrik.

Nicholas, Thomas, *tr. See* 5141, 16807, 26123.

18529 **Nicholas y Sacharles, Juan.** Hispanus reformatus. 12°.
Gualterus Burre, 1621. Ent. 20 mr. L.L².O.C.D².+
18530 — [A trans.] The reformed Spaniard: to all reformed
churches. *Tr.* 4°. *W. Burre,* 1621. Ent. 29 mr.
L.O.D².DUR(Bamb.).E².+; HD(impr. torn).N.U.
C2ʳ catchword: 'Here-'. Cancel tp pr. as E4; orig.
tp line 7: 'And especially to'; cancel tp: 'In
speciall, To'; both at O,HD.
18530.5 — [Anr. ed.] 4°. *W. Burre,* 1621. C³.; F.HN.NYⁱⁱ.
C2ʳ catchword: 'Heere-'.

18531 **Nicholes, Martin.** A catechisme, composed according
to the order of the catechisme in the Common Prayer
Booke. The second edition. [Init. M.N. B.D. P.P.]
8°. *R. Y[oung] f. J. Boler, sold by W. Russell in
Plimmouth,* 1631. Ent. to Boler 24 ap. 1630. O.; HD.
According to ent. 7 se. 1638 this is 'by Master
Nicholls'.
18531.3 — [Anr. ed.] By M. Nicholes, B.D. P.P. The third
edition, corrected. 8°. *f. J. Boler,* 1632. C¹⁰.
18531.7 — The fifth edition. 8°. *R. Y[oung] f. A. Boler,* 1636. M.
— *See also* 1313.3.

18532 **Nicholl, John.** An houre glasse of Indian newes. . . .
Shewing the miseries, indured by 67 Englishmen,
sent to the planting in Guiana. 1605. 4°. [*E. Allde*] *f.
N. Butter,* 1607. Ent. 25 jn. L(2, 1 imp.).G².;
HN.CB.CH.NY.PH².
Dedic. signed: 'John Cooke' (NY) or 'I. C.' (L,HN).
There is a half-title on A1ʳ: 'An hower-glasse
[etc.]'

Nicholls, Edward. The dolphins danger. 1617. *See*
23748.5.

18533 **Nichols, John.** A declaration of the recantation of J.
Nichols (for the space almost of two yeeres the
popes scholer in the English seminarie at Rome).
8°. *C. Barker,* 1581 (14 fb.) L.O.C.D.G².+; F.HN.HD.
ILL.U.+
Tp in two settings; above the imprint the spacing
of the colon in 'God: Honour' is 'd: H' (HN) or
'd : H' (G²,YK,HD). Quartersheet N² set in duplicate; N1ʳ line 3 from bottom ends: 'from' (G²,
HN,HD) or 'frõ' (YK). First 8 lines of L1ʳ in 3
settings: line 1 begins: 'tichrist' (O,C); 'ry' (O,
HN,HD); or 'gory' (O⁵,G²). The last is the only one
that properly fits the text on K8ᵛ.
18533.5 — [Anr. ed.] 8°. *H. Binneman f. C. Barker,* 1581 (14 fb.)
O(imp.).O⁴.C².D(imp.).
— A discouerie of J. Nicols. [1581.] *See* 19402.
18534 — John Niccols pilgrimage, whrein [*sic*] is displaied the
liues of the proude popes. 8°. *T. Dawson f. T. Butter
a. G. Isaac,* 1581. Ent. to T. Butter 4 se. L.O.C.D.
YK.+; F(2).HN.LC.Y.
See Arber II.853.
18535 — The oration and sermon made at Rome, . . . the xxvij.
daie of Maie. 1578. 8°. *J. Charlewood, seruant to the
earle of Arundell,* [1581.] Ent. 22 ap. 1581. L²(imp.).
O⁴.D(imp.).; F.
Answered in 19402.
18536 — [A variant, w. imprint:] *J. Charlewood, sold by E.
White,* 1581. L.O.C.D.YK.+; F.CAL².HD.U.
Author's postscript dated: 'Anno 1581. Aprill. 25'.
18536a — [A variant, without the date to the postscript.] C.DUR⁵.
18537 — A true report of the late apprehension of John Nicols
minister, at Roan. [By W. Allen.] 8°. *Rhemes, J.
Fogny,* 1583. L.L².O.C.P.+
A&R 12.

18538 **Nichols, Josias.** Abrahams faith: that is, the olde religion.
4°. *T. Wight,* 1602. O.D.YK.; F.HN.BO³.U.Y.+
Copies vary: with (HN) and without errata (O,F).
18539 — [Anr. issue, w. cancel tp, w. imprint:] *T. Wight, sold by
E. Weaver,* 1603. Ent. to E. Weaver 6 my. 1605.
L.D.E(lacks tp)*.P(lacks tp)*.; PEN².
18539.5 — An order of household instruction. 8°. *the widowe
Orwin f. T. Man,* 1595. Ent. 17 mr. 1596. C⁵.
18540 — [Anr. ed.] 8°. *the Widowe Orwin f. T. Man,* 1596.
L.; F.

Nichols, Josias—*cont.*

18541 — The plea of the innocent: Wherein is averred; that the ministers & people falslie termed puritanes, are iniuriouslie slaundered. 8°. [*J. Windet?*] 1602. L.O.C².E.YK.+; F.BO⁵.NY¹¹.
> 229 pp. In 'Publisher to the reader' of 1645¹ it is stated that the present work was pr. by permission of James I 'not longe before he came out of Scotland'. Answered by 5882.

18542 — [Anr. ed.] 8°. [*Middelburg, R. Schilders,*] 1602. L.O. C².P.PETYT.+; HN.BO³.HD.Y.
> 251 pp.; on tp 1st line of Micah quotation ends: 'fall I'.

18542.5 — [Anr. ed.] 8°. [*Middelburg, R. Schilders,*] 1602. L.C¹⁰.E.; F.BALT.U(imp.).
> 251 pp.; on tp 1st line of Micah quotation ends: 'shal'.

18543 **Nichols, Nicholas.** A spirituall poseaye contayning most godly consolations and prayers. 8°. *W. Williamson f. J. Harrison,* 1573. L.O⁹.

18544 **Nichols, Philip.** Sir Francis Drake revived: calling upon this dull age, by this memorable relation, of a third voyage, when Nombre de Dios was surprised. 4°. *E. A[llde] f. N. Bourne,* 1626. Ent. 32 oc. L.ETON.; F.HN.HD(lacks N4).NY.Y.+
> PH² copy has unique dedic. to Elizabeth of Bohemia.

18545 — [Anr. ed.] 4°. [*W. Stansby*] *f. N. Bourne,* 1628. L.L². O.C⁴(2).STD.; F.HN.HD.NY.Y.+
> Possibly some copies intended to be issued w. 7161.3.

18546 **Nicholson, Samuel.** Acolastus his after-witte. [In verse.] 4°. [*F. Kingston*] *f. J. Baylie,* 1600. Ent. 8 se. L.O.C.; F.HN.

18547 — A sermon, called Gods new-yeeres-guift, sent unto England. [Anon.] 8°. *W. White, sold by Y. James,* 1602. Ent. to W. White 22 mr. O.

18548 — [Anr. ed., signed.] Gods new-yeeres gift sent unto England. 8°. *S. Stafford,* 1602. Ent. 27 ap. L(2).

18548.5 **Niclas, Hendrik.** All the letters of the A. B. C. in ryme. *Tr.* out of Base-almaine. [Init. H. N.] s.sh.fol. [*Cologne, N. Bohmberg,*] 1575. G².

18549 — Cantica. Certen of the songes of HN. *Tr.* out of Base-almayne. 8°. [*Cologne, N. Bohmberg,* 1575.] F.HN.

18550 — Comoedia. A worke in ryme, contayning an enterlude of myndes, witnessing the mans fall from God. Set forth by HN, and by him newly amended. *Tr.* out of Base-almayne. 8°. [*Cologne, N. Bohmberg,* 1574?] L.L⁶.O.C⁵.P.+; F.HN.CH.HD.Y². Greg 64.
> In at least HD copy the virgule after 'ryme' has dropped out.

18551 — Dicta HN. Documentall sentences: eauen-as those-same were spoken-fourth by HN. *Tr.* out of Base-almayne [by C. Vitell.] 8°. [*Cologne, N. Bohmberg,* 1574?] L.L².O.C.D.+; F(2).BO.U.Y.

18552 — Epistolæ HN. The principall epistles of HN. *Tr.* out of Base-almaine. 8°. [*Cologne, N. Bohmberg,* 1575?] L.L²(imp.).C(imp.).; F.U(frag.).Y.

18553 — An epistle sent unto two daughters of Warwick from H. N. The oldest father of the Familie of Love. With a refutation of the errors that are therin; by H. A(insworth.) 4°. *Amsterdam, G. Thorp,* 1608. L.O(3).C.G².; HN.CAL.U.Y.

18554 — Epistola XI. HN. Correctiō and exhortation out of heartie loue. *Tr.* out of Base-almayne [by C. Vitell.] 8°. [*Cologne, N. Bohmberg,* 1574?] L.L².C.D.P.+; F.HD.

18555 — The first epistle of H. N. A crying-voyce of the holye spirit of loue. *Tr.* out of Base-almayne. 8°. [*Cologne, N. Bohmberg,* 1574?] L².C.E⁴.LINC.; F.

18556 — Euangelium regni. A ioyfull message of the kingdom. Set-fourth by HN. *Tr.* out of Base-almayne [by C. Vitell.] 8°. [*Cologne, N. Bohmberg,* 1575?] L.O.C.D.E².+; F.HN.HD.Y.
> HD copy has stamped on tp and as colophon: 'Imprinted at Harlem, M. CCCCXLVIII.' Partially reprinted and answered in 15040.

18557 — Exhortatio. I. The first exhortation of H. N. to his children, and to the famelye of loue. by him newlye perused. *Tr.* out of Base-almayne. 8°. [*Cologne, N. Bohmberg,* 1574?] F.
> Answered in 15040. Ends w. chap. 22.

18557.5 — [Anr. issue, w. chaps. 23, 24 added.] L.L².C.LINC.; F.

Niclas, Hendrik—*cont.*

18558 — Introductio. An introduction to the holy vnderstanding of the glasse of righteousnes. Sett-forth by HN. 8°. [*Cologne, N. Bohmberg,* 1575?] L.L².O³.; U.Y.

18559 — A new balade or songe, of the Lambes feaste. 1574. = 21529.

18560 — The prophetie of the spirit of loue. Set-fourth by HN. *Tr.* out of Base-almayne [by C. Vitell.] 8°. [*Cologne, N. Bohmberg,*] 1574. L.L².C.C⁸.D.; F(2).HN.Y.

18561 — Prouerbia HN. The prouerbes of HN. *Tr.* out of Base-almayne [by C. Vitell.] 8°. [*Cologne, N. Bohmberg,* 1575?] L.L².C.C⁵.BUTE.; F.HN.Y.

18562 — A publishing of the peace vpon earth . . . published by HN. *Tr.* out of Base-almayne [by C. Vitell.] 8°. [*Cologne, N. Bohmberg,*] 1574. L.L².C.D.P.; F.PML.

18563 — Reuelatio Dei. The reuelation of God, and his great propheatie. Set-fourth by HN. *Tr.* out of Base-almayne. 8°. [*Cologne, N. Bohmberg,* 1575?] L.L²(2). C.D.; F.HN.HD.Y.

18564 — Terra pacis. A true testification of the spirituall lande of peace. Set-foorth by HN. *Tr.* out of Base-almayne. 8°. [*Cologne, N. Bohmberg,* 1575?] L.O.C³.D.M.+; F.HN.Y.

18564.5 — Thre groūdlie refreines, which HN hath set-fourth against his enemies. obl. 16° in 8's. [*Cologne, N. Bohmberg,* 1574.] L².

— *See also* 77, 1858, 7573, 10681.5, 10843, 21180, 22378, 24095, 25665. For a proclamation ordering the burning of these books, *see* 8125.

18565 **Nicodemus.** Here begynneth the treatys of Nycodemus gospell. 4°. (*J. Notary,* 1507.) D².

18566 — [Anr. ed.] Nychodemus gospell. [Xylographic.] 4° 8.4. (*w. de worde,* 1509 (23 mr.)) O.C.

18567 — [Anr. ed.] 4° 8.4. (*w. de worde,* 1511.) L.; PML.

18567a — [Anr. ed.] 4°. (*W. de Worde,* 1512 (20 fb.)) O(2 leaves only).

18568 — [Anr. ed.] Nychod'mus gospell. [Xylographic.] 4° 8.4. (*w. de worde,* 1518 (10 mr.)) L.

18569 — [Anr. ed.] 4°. (*J. Skot,* 1529 (6 ap.)) O(imp.).

18570 — [Anr. ed.] Nychodemus gospell. 4°. (*W. de worde,* 1532 (12 ap.)) C.

18570a — [Anr. ed.] 4°. (*J. Skot,*) [1537?] C.

18571 — Nichodemus his gospel. [*Ed.*] (J. Warrin, *priest*). 8°. [*Rouen,*] *J. Cousturier,* [c. 1635.] L.O.C.DUR(Bamb.). NLW.+; F.HD.N.Y.
> A&R 572. Reissued in 1646 with prelims. revised and reset (copy at O).

18571.5 **Nicolai, Gilbertus.** Tractatus de tribus ordinibus beatissime virginis dei genitricis Marie. 8°. (*per R. Pynson,*) [c. 1515.] Seville, Biblioteca Colombina.

18572 **Nicolai, Philipp.** Chronologia sacra, by the high illuminate doctor Phil. Nicolai. [*Ed.*] N. Michelsone. *Tr.* out of the German and Dence tongue by D. Forbes. 16° in 8's. *Edinburgi, J. Wreittoun,* 1630. E.

18573 — [Anr. issue, w. cancel tp:] A prophesie of Doomes-day. The second edition. *Edinburgh, J. Wreittoun,* 1631. L.

Nicolaus, *de Clemangiis. See* 5397.

Nicolaus, *Leonicenus, tr. See* 11531.5, 11532.

18574 **Nicolay, Nicolas de.** The nauigations, peregrinations and voyages, made into Turkie. *Tr.* T. Washington. 4° in 8's. *T. Dawson,* 1585. Ent. 28 fb. 1581. L.O.C. BIRM.E.+; F.HN.HD.ILL.NY.+
> On ¶3ᵛ: 'printed in English at [J. Stell's] costes & charges'. Cuts copied from Dutch ed. *Antwerp, W. Silvius,* 1576.

18575 **Nicolls, Philip.** The copie of a letter sente to one maister Chrispyne chanon of Exceter for that he denied yᵉ scripture to be the touche stone of al other doctrines. 8°. (*J. Day a. W. Seres,*) [1548?] L.L².; F.
> End of text dated 7 Nov. 1547.

18576 — Here begynneth a godly newe story of .xii. men that moyses sent to spye owt the land of canaan. 8°. (*w. hill,* 1148 [i.e. 1548] (10 my.)) L(2, 1 imp.).O.C.G².; F.PN².U.

18577 — [Anr. ed.] The history of the xii. men that were sent to spye [etc.] 8°. *J. Allde f. J. Harisō,* [1575?] L.L².G².

Nicolls, Thomas, *tr. See* 24056.

Nicols, John. *See* Nichols, J.

Nicols, Thomas. A pleasant description of . . . the ilands of Canaria. 1583. *See* 4557.

18578 **Nicolson, James.** A prognosticacion. [1563.] Now = 490.20.

Nicolson, Thomas. [Bookplate.] *See* Bookplates.

18579 **Nid, Gervase.** Certaine sermons upon divers texts of scripture. 8°. *N. Okes f. W. Burre,* 1616. L.O.LINC.; HN.HD(imp.).

Nieuport. A true and briefe relation of the bloody battel of Nieuport . . . 1600. [1641.] *See* 13264.9.

Niger, Franciscus. *See* 25509.3.

18580 **Nightingale.** The nightingale: whose curious notes are here explain'd. *Ballad.* 2 pts. s.sh.fol. *f. F. Coules,* [1633.] Ent. to the ballad ptnrs. 8 jy. 1633. L.

Nilus, *Metropolitan of Thessalonica.* *See* Cabasilas, N., *Abp.*

18581 **Nîmes University.** Academiæ Nemausensis breuis et modesta responsio. Ad professorum Turnoniorum societatis, vt aiunt, Iesu assertiones. 8°. *T. Vautrollerius,* 1584. L.C.D.P.WOR.; F.

Nisbet, E. *See* Nesbit, E.

18582 **Nixon, Anthony.** The blacke yeare. Seria jocis. 4°. *E. Allde f. W. Timme,* 1606. Ent. 9 my. L.O.; F.TEX.
  In O,F copies the first 'l' in Allde has dropped out. D4v–E3r are mainly extracted from 22666.

18583 — The christian navy. Wherein is playnely described the perfit course to sayle to the haven of eternall happinesse. [In verse.] 4°. *S. Stafford,* 1602. Ent. 27 se. L.; F.HN.

18584 — The dignitie of man, both in the perfections of his soule and bodie. 4°. *E. Allde,* 1612. L.L43.O.O3.C.; F.CHI.U.

18585 — [Anr. issue, init. N. A., w. imprint:] *Oxford, Jos. Barnes f. John Barnes, [London,]* 1616. L.G2.; F. Cancel sheet A including imprint pr. by E. Allde.

18586 — Elizaes memoriall. King James his arrivall. And Romes downefall. [Init. A. N. In verse.] 4°. *T. C[reede] f. J. Baylie,* 1603. Ent. 12 ap. L.O.; HN.

18587 — Great Brittaines generall joyes. Londons glorious triumphes. Dedicated to the memorie of the mariage of Fredericke and Elizabeth. [Init. A. N. In verse.] 4°. *[W. White] f. H. Robertes, sold by T. P[avier,]* 1613. Ent. to H. Roberts 14 fb. L13.O.CHATS.; F.HN.

18588 — Londons dove: or a memoriall of maister Robert Dove. 4°. *T. Creede f. J. Hunt,* 1612. Ent. 12 my. L8.O.; HN.

18588.5 — [Anr. issue, w. imprint:] *T. Creede f. J. Hunt, sold by E. Marchant,* 1612. L.O.; PFOR.

18589 — Oxfords triumph: in the royall entertainement of his majestie, [etc.] 4°. *E. Allde, solde by J. Hodgets,* 1605. Ent. to E. Allde, J. Trundle a. J. Hunt 19 se. L(tp defective).C.

18590 — The scourge of corruption. Or a crafty knave needs no broker. 4°. *[J. Beale] f. H. Gosson a. W. Houlmes,* 1615. Ent. 2 de. 1614. L(lacks A2).O.O17(lacks tp).; HN.HD.
  In imprint of O copy: 'Goston'.

18591 — A straunge foot-post, with a packet full of strange petitions. 4°. *E. A[llde]* 1613. L.; F.HN(2, 1 frag.).

18591a — [Anr. issue.] The foot-post of Dover. *E. Allde, solde by J. Deane,* 1616. HN.
  HN bd. w. 1st 2 leaves of 18591.

18592 — The three English brothers. Sir Thomas Sherley his travels. Sir Anthony Sherley his embassage to the christian princes. Master Robert Sherley his wars against the Turkes. 4°. *[A. Islip?] sold by J. Hodgets,* 1607. Ent. to E. Edgar 8 jn. L.O5(imp.).*.BUTE.; F.HN.Y. Penrose 225.

18593 — [Anr. issue, w. cancel tp:] The travels of three English brothers. F(impr. cropt).

18594 — The warres of Swethland. . . . As also the state and condition of that kingdome. 4°. *[J. Windet] f. N. Butter,* 1609. Ent. 16 jn. L.O.O2.E.

18595 — [Anr. issue, w. cancel tp:] The warres of Swethland. . . . With a certificate of the service of three Englishmen. *f. N. Butter,* 1609. O.C(2, 1 imp.).; F.

18596 — Swethland and Poland warres. A souldiers returne out of Sweden, and his newes from the warres. 4°. *[R. Blower] f. N. Butter,* 1610. O2.; F.
— *See also* 18325.

Nobilitas. Nobilitas politica vel civilis. 1608. *See* 11922.

18597 **Nobody.** No-body, and some-body. With the true chronicle historie of Elydure. 8° in 4's. *[J. Roberts] f. J. Trundle,* [1606.] Ent. 12 mr. 1606. L.L6(2 imp.). O(imp.).O6(imp.).; F.HN.HD(impr. cropt).ILL.PFOR (imp.).+ Greg 229. 𝔄

18598 — Nobody his counsaile to chuse a wife. *Ballad.* 2 pts. s.sh.fol. *A. M[athewes, c.* 1622.] C6.

18598.5 — No body loves mee. *Ballad.* 2 pts. s.sh.fol. *[G. Eld] f. E. W[right, c.* 1615.] C6.

18599 — The welspoken nobody. God that is all good [etc. In verse.] s.sh.fol. *[S. Mierdman? c.* 1550.] F(imp.).HN.
  A trans. of a poem by Georg Schans, Strassburg, 1533. In riband of cut: '.Nobody.is.my..name. that.beyreth.euery.bodyes.blame.' This work not related to 6437.

18599.5 **Noel, William, and others.** [Heading A1r:] Factum, or rehearsall of the whole cause, with proofes to defend it. [Petition to reverse a decree of the French Privy Council of 27 Jan. 1622, concerning piracy committed by Andrew de Launay off the coast of Brittany.] 4°. *[J. Dawson,* 1622?] HD.

Nogaret de la Valette, Jean Louis de, *Duc d'Épernon.* *See* 24096.

18600 **Noot, Jan van der,** *Physician.* The gouvernance and preseruation of them that feare the plage. Now newly set forth. 1569. 8°. *W. How f. A. Veale,* [1569.] O5.C3.

18600.5 **Noot, Jan van der,** *Poet.* Het Bosken van H. I. Vander Noot. Inhoudende verscheyden poëtixe wercken. 8°. *[H. Bynneman,* 1570?] Ghent U(imp.). Haarlem PL.; F.

18601 — Het theatre oft Toon-neel, waer in ter eender de ongelucken die den werelts gesinden ende boosen menschen toecomen. 8°. *[J. Day,* 1568.] HAGUE. Antwerp PL. Brussels RL. Haarlem PL.; F(frag.).
  Etchings by Marcus Gheeraerts the elder; also used in 18603.

18602 — A theatre wherein be represented as wel the miseries & calamities that follow the voluputous worldlings. (*Tr.* out of French by T. Roest) [and E. Spenser.] 8°. (*H. Bynneman,* 1569.) Ent. 1569–70. L(2).O.; F.HN.COR.HD.ILL(imp.).+
  Cuts copied from 18601.

18603 — Le theatre auquel sont exposés . . . les miseres qui suiuent les mondains. 8°. (*chez J. Day,* 1568.) L.O.C.CHATS.; F.
  Same plates as in 18601. The L copy has the title in a border of type orns. while O,C,F have it in the engr. compartment of 18601.

18604 **Norden, John.** A christian familiar comfort and incouragement not to dismaie at the Spanish threats. 4°. *[T. Scarlet a. J. Orwin] f. J. B[rome,]* 1596. Ent. to mistris Brome 5 ap. L.O(imp.).O2.; F.HD.N.
  First 3 quires pr. by Scarlet; the rest by J. Orwin.

18604.5 — Civitas Londini. [A map.] fol(4). [*London,* 1600.] Stockholm RL.
  L has an imperfect copy of a later state; *see* Hind I.199–202.

18605 — England an intended guyde, for English travailers. 4°. *E. All-de,* 1625. L.L5(frags., Lemon 254, 256). O.C(imp.).WN.; F(imp.).HN.HD(imp.).
  Tables copied in 10420.

18606 — An eye to heaven in earth. 12°. *W. Stansby f. R. Meighen,* 1619. Ent. 20 mr. O.

18607 — The fathers legacie. With precepts morall, and prayers divine. [Anon.] 12°. *[M. Flesher] f. J. Marriot,* 1625. Ent. as by J. Norden 1 de. 1623. O.

18608 — A godlie mans guide to happinesse. 12°. *A. M[athewes] f. J. Marriott,* 1624. Ent. 19 jn. 1623. L.C(imp.).

18609 — A good companion for a christian. 12°. *G. P[urslowe] f. R. Collins,* 1632. L(without engr. tp).O.; HART.
  O, HART have engr. tp dated: '1634'.

18610 — The imitation of David his godly and constant resolution. 12°. *J. Haviland f. R. Whittakers a. G. Latham,* 1624. L4.C.; HN.

18611 — The labyrinth of mans life. Or vertues delight and envies opposite. [In verse.] 4°. *[G. Eld] f. J. Budge,* 1614. Ent. 17 ja. L.O.; F.HN. Arthur Houghton.

18612 — A load-starre to spirituall life. 12°. *W. Stansby,* 1614. C.

18613 — A mirror for the multitude, or glasse, wherein maie be seene, the violence, of the multitude. 8°. *J. Windet,* 1586. Ent. 5 de. O.C.; N.

188

Norden, John—*cont.*

18614 — The mirror of honor: wherein euerie professor of armes, may see the necessitie of the feare of God. 4°. *the widowe Orwin f. T. Man,* 1597. Ent. 17 ja. L.L².O(2).D.; F(2).HN.N.

— Nordens Preparative to his Speculum Britanniæ. *See* 18638.

18615 — A pathway to patience, in all manner of crosses. 12°. *E. A[llde] f. T. Harper,* 1626. Ent. 9 jy. 1625. L⁴.; HD.

18616 — [Pt. 1.] A pensiue mans practise very profitable for all personnes. 8°. *H. Singleton,* 1584. Ent. 6 au. C.
See Greg, *Register B,* p. 33. The publishing rights to pt. 1 were kept strictly separate from pts. 2 and 3. Though now frequently bd. together, they were never issued together except for the piracy 18618.3. For pts. 2 and 3 *see* 18626a.1 sqq.

18617 — [Anr. ed.] 12°. [*R. Robinson*] *f. H. Singleton,* 1589. F(lacks M6,7).

18617.3 — [Anr. ed.] 12°. *R. Robinson, by the assigne of H. Singleton,* 1592. Ent. 25 jn. 1593. F.
D3ʳ last line: 'diuerse'.

18617.5 — [Anr. ed.] 12°. [*R. Robinson,* 1592.] Florida State U(lacks tp). A
D3ʳ last line: 'diuers'; some sheets from same setting as 18617.3.

18617.7 — [Anr. ed.] 12°. *R. Bradocke,* 1598. O(lacks 1st 2 leaves).C(lacks tp, w. tp to 18626a.4 inserted).; F(lacks M12).
See Greg, *Register B,* pp. 64, 66.

18618 — Now = 18626a.4.

18618.3 — [Anr. ed., w. pt. 2 added.] 2 pts. 12°. (*Edinburgh,*) *R. Waldegrave,* 1600. C¹⁹.

18618.7 — [Anr. ed. of pt. 1 only.] 12°. *T. Haveland f. R. Bradocke,* 1609. L.

18619 — Now = 18626a.5.

18620 — [Anr. ed.] 12°. *W. Hall f. R. Bradocke,* 1610. L.L³.; F.

18620.5 — [Anr. ed.] 12°. *W. Hall f. R. Bradocke,* 1612. HN.

18621 — [Anr. ed.] 12°. *J. Beale f. T. Pavier,* 1615. Ent. 3 mr. L⁴.C.
See Court-Book C, pp. 73, 109.

18622 — Now = 18626a.6.

18623 — [Anr. ed.] Newly corrected after above forty impressions. 12°. *J. Beale f. T. Pavier,* 1620. O.O²².E.

18624 — Now = 18626a.7.

18624.5 — [Anr. ed.] 12°. *J. Beale f. T. Pavier,* 1624. L(lacks tp, w. tp to 18626a.7 inserted).; F.CHI.

18625 — [Anr. ed.] 12°. *f. E. Brewster a. R. Bird,* 1627. Ass'd 4 au. 1626. L.; HN.

18625.5 — [Anr. ed.] 12°. *f. E. Brewster & R. Bird,* 1629. O⁶.

18626 — [Anr. ed.] Above 41. impressions. 12°. *J. Beale f. R. Bird,* 1635. L.INN.

18626.5 — [Anr. ed.] Newlycorrected [*sic*] . . . above 42. impressions. 12°. *J. Beale f. R. Bird,* 1636. L.M².; F.

18626a — [Anr. ed.] 12°. *J. Beale f. R. Bird,* 1640. L(lacks tp). O.; BALT.

18626a.1 — [Pt. 2.] The pensiue mans practise. The second part. Or the pensiue mans complaint and comfort. 12°. *J. Windet f. J. Oxenbridge,* 1594. Ent. 2 ap. 1595. L(lacks G11).LAMPORT.

18626a.2 — [Anr. ed.] 12°. *J. W[indet] f. J. Oxenbridge,* 1599. O(imp.).

18626a.3 — [Pt. 3.] A progresse of pietie, being the third part of the Pensiue mans practise. 12°. *V. S[immes] f. J. Oxenbridge,* 1598. O(lacks I12).
Reprinted from 18633, q.v.

18626a.4 — [Pts. 2 and 3.] The pensiue mans practise. The second (third) part. Third time corrected and augmented. 2 pts. 12°. *A. Hatfield f. F. Norton,* 1600. Ent. 1 se. C.C¹⁹(pt. 3 only).; F(pt. 2 only, imp.).
(Formerly 18618) *See* Greg, *Register B,* p. 76.

— [Anr. ed.] *Edinburgh, R. Waldegrave,* 1600. *See* 18618.3.

18626a.5 — [Anr. ed. Init. J. N.] 12°. *M. Bradwood f. W. Aspley,* 1609. Ent. 28 ja. 1605. L.; F.
(Formerly 18619)

18626a.6 — [Anr. ed.] 12°. *E. G[riffin] f. W. Aspley,* 1616. L³.L⁴.O.C.
(Formerly 18622)

18626a.7 — [Anr. ed.] 12°. *J. H[aviland] f. W. Aspley,* 1623. L.E.; F.
(Formerly 18624)

18626a.8 — [Anr. ed.] 12°. *J. B[eale] f. W. Aspley,* 1633. L.O.M².

18627 — A pensive soules delight. [In verse.] 4°. *T. C[reede] f. W. Lugger,* 1603. O.; F(2 leaves only).HN.

18628 — [Anr. ed.] 12°. *W. Stansby f. J. Busby,* 1615. Ent. 8 de. 1614. O.C².INN.

Norden, John—*cont.*

18629 — A poore mans rest: . . . . Now the eight time augmented. 12°. [*T. Snodham*] *f. J. Budge,* 1620. Ent. 25 au. 1619. L.

18630 — Now the ninth time augmented. 12°. *T. S[nodham] f. J. Budge,* 1624. L.

18630.3 — Now the tenth time augmented. 12°. *G. W[ood] f. R. Allot,* 1627. Ass'd 4 se. 1626. L(tp only, Ames II.794).

18630.7 — Now the eleventh time augmented. 12°. *J. L[egat] f. R. Allott,* 1629. SNU.; HN(imp.).

18631 — Now the twelfth time augmented. 12°. *Eliz. A[llde] f. R. Allot,* 1631. L.; F(imp.).

18631.5 — Now the thirteenth time augmented. 12°. *J. L[egat] f. R. Allot,* 1633. O(imp.).

18632 — A prayer for the prosperous proceedings of the earle of Essex in Ireland. 4°. *E. Allde,* 1599. L.

18633 — A progresse of pietie. Or the harbour of heauenly harts ease. 12°. *J. Windet f. J. Oxenbridge,* 1596. Ent. 30 au. 1591. F.
Reprinted in 18626a.3. F has a separate proof leaf of a presentation epistle from 'R. M. to his most louing wife' dated 2 Jan. 1597 intended for insertion in a copy of this or 18626a.3. An imp. ed. of 1590–1 belonging to George Stokes was reprinted by the Parker Society, 1847.

18634 — A sinfull mans solace: most sweete and comfortable, for the sicke soule. 8°. *R. Jones,* 1585. Ent. 7 de. 1584. L(imp.).C(imp.).; HN.

18635 — Speculum Britanniae. The first parte an historicall discription of Middlesex. 4°. [*Eliot's Court Press,*] 1593. L.O.C.D.E².+; F.HN.HD.N.NY.+
See Arber II.16 for patent to print this. The engr. tp occurs with and without the engraver's name; both at O. One O copy (Douce N 253) has quire A in a different, prob. earlier, setting without the Anglo-Saxon alphabet on A4ᵛ.

18636 — = 18635.

18637 — 1598 Speculi Britanniæ pars the desc^ription of Hartfordshire. 4°. [*T. Dawson,* 1598.] L.L³⁸.O.C.D.+; F.HN. Sexton.

18638 — Nordens preparatiue to his Speculum Britanniæ. 8°. [*J. Windet,*] 1596. L.; HN.

18638.5 — Surrey. Jo: Nordenus delineauit 1594 C. Whitwell sculpsit. s.sh.fol. *imp. R. Nicolsoni gener,* [1594.] L(maps C.2.cc.7). London, Royal Geographical Society.
There is a later state c. 1610 also at L w. James's unicorn instead of dragon in royal arms at upper left; *see* Hind I.223.

18639 — The surveyors dialogue. Divided into five bookes. 4° in 8's. [*S. Stafford*] *f. H. Astley,* 1607. Ent. 30 oc. 1606. L.O.BRISTOL².DUL.E.+; HN.HD.MICH.NY.Y.+

18640 — [Anr. ed.] Now newly imprinted. And a sixt booke added. 4°. *W. S[tansby] f. J. Busby,* 1610. Ent. to T. Man, jun., a. J. Busby, jun., 16 jn. 1609. O¹⁶. C.D⁶.RD.; F.LC.
In C copy the date has been tampered with. Quires M and N are unsold sheets of 18639.

18640a — [A variant without the printer's initials.] L(2).A.SHEF. London, Royal Institution of Chartered Surveyors.; HN.LC.Y.

18640b — [A variant, w. imprint:] *J. W[indet] f. J. Busby,* 1610. L³⁸.O.
This is probably the earliest variant.

18641 — Now the third time imprinted. 4° in 8's. *T. Snodham,* 1618. L.O.C.BIRM.D.+; F.HN.CU.HD.N.+
In some copies dedic. to R. Cecil cancelled and new dedic. to Sir R. Smith inserted; both at L.

18641.2 — Sussex. Johēs Norden deliniauit anno 1595, Christof. Shwytzer scul. s.sh.fol. [*London,* 1595.] London, Royal Geographical Society. A

— A table shewing the distances betweene all the cities, . . . in England. = pt. of 18605.
Line 1 ends: 'Cities,'.

18641.4 — [Anr. ed., including Wales.] s.sh.fol. [*E. Allde?* 1625?] L⁵(Lemon 255).
Line 1 ends: 'Townes'. This has not been found in any copy of 18605.

— A table shewing the distances of the moste of the chiefe townes in Wales. = pt. of 18605.

18642 — Vicissitudo rerum. An elegiacall poeme, of the interchangeable courses and varietie of things. The first part. 4°. *S. Stafford,* 1600. L.O(lacks tp).; F.HN. Arthur Houghton.

Norden, John—*cont.*

18643 — [Anr. issue, w. cancel title:] A store-house of varieties, briefly discoursing the change and alteration of things in this world. *London*, 1601. O.; HN.

18643.3 — The view of London bridge from east to west. 1597. s.sh.fol. [*London*, 1597.] F(2).
Engr. dedic. to Sir R. Saltonstall, Lord Mayor 1597–98.

18643.5 — [Anr. state, w. letterpress dedic. to J. Gore, Lord Mayor 1624–5.] s.sh.fol. [*London*, 1624.] O³⁴(Sutherland 73–298).
Regarding this and a later copy of this *see* Hind I.197–9.
— *See also* 18328.5.

18643.7 **Norfolk.** ⟨T⟩he bew⟨ailing⟩ of a true subiect, for the late conspired rebellion in Northfolke . . . 1570. 8⁰ in 4's. *J. Awdely*, 1570. Ent. 1570–71. O²⁴(imp.).
— The cooper of Norfolke. [1625?] *See* 19223.5.

18644 **Norfolk gentleman.** The Norfolke gentleman his last will and testament. *Ballad.* 2 pts. s.sh.fol. *f. J. W[right*, c. 1635.] Ent. to T. Millington 15 oc. 1595; to J. Wright a. ballad ptnrs. 14 de. 1624. M³(imp.).
First line beg.: 'Now ponder well'. Line 1 of heading ends: 'Testament:'; line 2 of heading ends: 'Brother,'.

18644.3 — [Anr. ed.] 2 pts. s.sh.fol. *f. J. W[right*, c. 1635.] L.
Line 1 of heading ends: 'Testament:'; line 2 of heading ends: 'brother,'.

18644.5 — [Anr. ed.] 2 pts. s.sh.fol. [*f. J. Wright*, c. 1635.] o(impr. torn).
Line 1 of heading ends: 'And'.

18645 **Norice, Edward.** The new gospel, not the true gospel. Or a discovery of the life and death, doctrin, and doings of Mr. J. Traske. 4⁰. *R. Bishop f. H. Hood*, 1638. Ent. 21 ap. L.O.C³.BRISTOL.D².+; F(tp defective).HN.HD.U.
Answers 24178.5.

18646 — A treatise maintaining that temporall blessings are to bee sought with submission to the will of God. Wherein is confuted [3450]. 12⁰. [*R. Badger*] *f. R. Milbourne*, 1636. Ent. 9 ap. L.O.

18647 **Norman, Robert.** The newe attractiue, containing a short discourse of the magnes or lodestone. (A discours of the variation of the cumpas. By W. Borough.) 2 pts. 4⁰. *J. Kyngston f. R. Ballard*, 1581. Ent. 3 au. L.O.C³.D.G².; F(pt. 2 only). David P. Wheatland, Topsfield, Mass.
(Pt. 2 formerly also 3389; 'Table of the sunnes declination' formerly also 23121)

18648 — [Anr. ed.] Newly corrected by M. W. B(orough.) 2 pts. 4⁰. *T. East f. R. Ballard*, 1585. L.L³⁸.O.C³.A.+; HN.HART².HD.Y.
(Pt. 2 formerly also 3390; 17184 a frag. of this)

18649 — [Anr. ed.] 2 pts. 4⁰. *E. Allde f. H. Astley*, 1592. L⁴⁴. London, Royal Institution of Naval Architects. Stevens Cox.; NY.NY³.WIS.
Subtp misdated: '1562'.

18650 — [Anr. ed.] 2 pts. 4⁰ in 8's. *E. Allde f. H. Astley*, 1596. Ent. 1 mr. 1596 a. 3 no. 1600. L(2).O⁵.C⁶.C¹⁵.; Horblit.
(Pt. 2 formerly also 3391)

18651 — [A ghost.]

18652 — [Anr. ed., revised.] 4⁰ in 8's. *T. C[reede] f. J. Tappe*, 1614. Ass'd to T. Man, jun., 16 jn. 1609. L.L³⁰. C.A.E.+; CAL⁴.
— The safegard of sailers. *Tr.* R. Norman. 1584. *See* 21545.
— *ed. See* 4700.

18653 **Norris,** *Sir* **John.** Ephemeris expeditionis Norreysij & Draki in Lusitaniam. [*Ed.*] (O.H.) 4⁰. [*T. Orwin,*] *imp. T. Woodcocke*, 1589. Ent. 28 oc. L.L².O.C¹³.D.+; F.HN.HD.MICH.NY.+

18654 — Newes from Brest. A diurnal of al that Sir J. Norreis hath doone. 4⁰. *P. Short f. T. Millington*, 1594. Ent. 21 no. L.DALK(imp.).; F.Y.

18654.3 — Newes sent out of Britayn [i.e. Brittany], and other places. . . . Concerning the seuerall exploits of Sir J. Norris. 4⁰. *J. Wolfe*, 1591. Ent. 5 jn. 1591. L.; HN.
App. continued in 13156.

18654.7 — Norrice the mariner, shewing what the world is; and the world that was. *Ballad.* s.sh.fol.? *Edinburgh, J. Wreittoun*, 1625. Andrew Jervise Sale, Dowell's, Edinburgh, 5 Dec. 1878, lot 1206.

Norris, *Sir* **John**—*cont.*

18655 — The true reporte of the seruice in Britanie. Performed by Sir J. Norreys before Guingand. 4⁰. *J. Wolfe*, 1591. L(2).O.BIRM.E².P.; HN.

18656 **Norris, Ralph.** A warning to London by the fall of Antwerp. *Ballad.* s.sh.fol. *J. Allde*, [1577?] HN.

18657 **Norris, Silvester.** An antidote or soueraigne remedie against the pestiferous writings of all English sectaries. The first part. [Init. S. N.] 4⁰. [*St. Omer, English College Press,*] 1615. L.O.C.E.YK.+; F.BO³. HD.NY¹¹.U.
(Pt. 2 now = 18657.5) A&R 572a.

18657.5 — An antidote. . . . The second part. [Init. S. N.] 4⁰. [*St. Omer, English College Press,*] 1619. L.C.DAI. DE.E.+; N.NY¹¹.STL.
(Formerly pt. of 18657) A&R 572b.

18658 — [Anr. ed. of both pts.] An antidote or treatise of thirty controuersies. [Init. S. N.] 2 pts. 4⁰. [*St. Omer, English College Press,*] 1622. L.O.C.D.M.+; F.HN.HD.N.U.+ 𝔄
A&R 573.

18658.5 — An appendix to the antidote. [Init. S. N.] 4⁰. [*St. Omer, English College Press,*] 1621. O.C.HP.OS.W.+; TEX.
A&R 575. Defended in 23528.

18659 — The guide of faith. Or, a third part of the Antidote. [Init. S. N.] 4⁰. [*St. Omer, English College Press,*] 1621. L.O.C.E.W.+; F.HN.NY¹¹.TEX.Y.+
A&R 574.

18660 — The pseudo-scripturist. Or a treatise . . . that the wrytten word of God is not the sole iudge of controuersies. [Init. N. S., *priest.*] 4⁰. [*St. Omer, English College Press,*] 1623. L.O.AMP.DE.HP.+; F.
A&R 576.

18661 — A true report of the private colloquy betweene M. Smith, alias Norrice, and M. Walker. . . . With a briefe confutation of [24960]. 4⁰. [*St. Omer, English College Press,*] 1624. L.AUG.D².LEIC.; F.
A&R 577.

18661a **North Newington.** UNiuersis christifidelibus presentes literas [etc. 1521.] Now = Indulgences 65 sq.
— OUr holy father the pope of Rome pope Boniface [etc. 1521.] *See* Indulgences 67.

18662 **North, George.** The description of Swedland, Gotland, and Finland. Collected out of sundry laten aucthors, but chieflye S. Mounster. 4⁰. *J. Awdely*, 1561 (28 oc.) L.C(imp.).D². Stockholm RL.; F.HN.
Stockholm copy has cancel dedic. to Nils Gyllenstierna. Almost entirely a trans. of Muenster's Cosmographia; cf. 18242.
— *ed. See* 10552.
— *tr. See* 19832.

North, *Sir* **Thomas,** *tr. See* 3053, 12427, 20065, 20071.

Northampton. The seuerall rates . . . made by the Justices of peace, of Northampton. [June 1566.] *See* 7995.5.

18662.5 **Northamptonshire.** The Northampton-shire lover, or a pleasant dialogue. *Ballad.* 2 pts. s.sh.fol. [*M. Flesher*] *f. H. Gosson*, [c. 1625.] C⁶.
— The witches of Northamptonshire. 1612. *See* 3907.

18663 **Northbrooke, John.** Spiritus est. . . . A breefe and pithie summe of the christian faith. 4⁰. *J. Kingston f. W. Williamson*, 1571. L.O.A.D.P.+; F.U.

18663.5 — [Anr. ed.] 8⁰. *J. Charlewood*, [1582?] Ent. 15 ja. 1582. C.M²(imp.).; F(lacks Oo8).

18664 — [Anr. ed.] Newlie corrected. 8⁰. *J. Charlewood*, 1582. L.O.BIRM²(K.N.).BRISTOL².P.; F.HN.HART.N(imp.).U.+

18664.5 — Spiritus est. . . . The poore mans garden. 4⁰. *J. Kingston f. W. Williamson*, 1571. L(tpp only, Ames I.252; Harl.5936/112).L².L³⁸.ETON.G².; F.

18665 — [Anr. ed.] Newly corrected. 8⁰. *W. Williamson*, 1573. L.O¹⁷.C(imp., Sayle 7301).; TEX.
F1ʳ headline: 'The poore mans Garden.'

18666 — [Anr. ed.] 8⁰. (*W. Williamson,*) [1575?] C(Sayle 1795). G²(imp.).HETH.
Device in colophon dated 1573. F1ʳ headline: 'after his fall.'

18667 — [Anr. ed.] 8⁰. *J. Charlewood*, [1582?] Ent. 15 ja. 1582. L.O.C⁴.M.WI.+; ILL.NY¹¹.WIS.
Tp line 4 in italic.

18667a — [Anr. ed.] 8⁰. *J. Charlewood*, [1582?] L.L³⁸.O³.C¹².G².; F. Columbia Theological Seminary, Decatur, Georgia (lacks tp).
Tp line 4 in roman.

Northbrooke, John—*cont.*

18667b — [Anr. ed.] 8°. (*J. Charlewood*,) [1582?] L.C[15].
18668 — [Anr. ed.] 8°. *J. Roberts*, 1600. Ent. 31 my. 1594. L[3].P.; F.HN.
18669 — [Anr. ed.] 8°. *J. Roberts*, 1606. L.O.C[2].D.LIV[2].; F.
18670 — Spiritus est. . . . A treatise wherein dicing, dauncing, vaine playes or enterluds are reproued. 4°. *H. Bynneman f. G. Byshop*, [1577?] Ent. 2 de. 1577. L(imp.).C.; F.HN.HD.PH.
18671 — [Anr. ed.] 4°. *T. Dawson f. G. Bishoppe*, 1579. L(2).O. O[8].C.D.; F.HN.CH.N(imp.).PML.+

Northern Beggar. The cunning northerne begger. [1634.] *See* 1799.

18671.3 **Northern Turtle.** The northerne turtle: wayling his unhappy fate. *Ballad.* 1/2 sh.fol. *f. J. H[ammond?* c. 1628.] C[6].
  In line 4 of title: 'Northerne'.
18671.7 — [Anr. ed.] 1/2 sh.fol. *f. J. H[ammond?* c. 1630.] C[6].
  In line 4 of title: 'Northern'.
18672 — [Anr. ed., with a first part added, w. title:] The paire of northerne turtles. 2 pts. s.sh.fol. *f. F. Coules*, [c. 1640.] L.
  (Formerly also 24370)

Norton, Humfrey. Almanacks. 1579, etc. *See* 491 sq.

18673 **Norton, Robert.** The gunner shewing the whole practise of artillerie. fol. *A. M[atthewes] f. H. Robinson*, 1628. Ent. 27 de. 1627. L.O.C.A.DUL.+; F.HN.HD.N.NY.+
  Title in engr. compartment (L, HD) or in wdct. comp., w. sp.: 'Artillery' (O). Engr. comp. and plates from Fr. and Ger. translations of D. Ufano's *Artilleria*, Frankfurt, 1614 and 1621. Unsold sheets reissued in 1664 w. cancel tp (copy at L).
18674 — The gunners dialogue. With the art of great artillery. 4°. [*Eliot's Court Press*] *f. J. Tap*, 1628. O.DUL.; F.BO[5].ILL(date cropt).
18675 — A mathematicall apendix [*sic*], containing many propositions for mariners at sea. 8° in 4's. *R. B[radock?] f. R. Jackson*, 1604. L.L[10]. Kenney 3176.; Horblit.
18676 — Of the art of great artillery, viz. the explanation of [6848 and 6858] by T. Digges. 4°. *E. Allde f. J. Tap*, 1624. L(2).BTU.DUL.; F.BO[5].CHI.
18676.5 — A table of boorde and timber measure, ... Calculated by R. N[orton.] s.sh.fol. [*London*, 1615?] L[5](Lemon 100).
  Prob. intended to be issued w. 20806.5.
— *tr. See* 4500, 23264.
— *See also* 13697, 20806.5.

Norton, Robert, *Minister, tr. See* 25010.

Norton, *Sir* **Thomas.** VNiuersis sctē mr̄is ecclesie filiis . . . T. Norton [etc. 1510.] *See* Indulgences 38.

18677 **Norton, Thomas.** All such treatises as haue been lately published by T. Norton. 6 pts. 8°. *J. Daye*, [1570.] O(lacks pt. 6).PARIS(lacks pt. 4).; HN.
  A reissue w. gen. tp of one or another ed. of 18679.5, 18685.3, 18678, 18679, 18678a, 18685.
18677.5 — A bull [Noveritis quod anno] graunted by the pope to doctor Harding and other. [14 Aug. 1567. Anon.] fol(2). *J. Day*, [1570.] O[5].D[2](2nd sheet only).
18678 — [Anr. ed.] 8° in 4's. *J. Daye*, [1570.] L.O.C[2].D.YK.+; F.HN.HD.N.NY[11].+
  (Formerly also 12764)
18678a — An addition declaratorie to the bulles. Scene [*sic*] and allowed. [Anon.] 8° in 4's. *J. Daye*, [1570.] L.O.C[2]. D.P.+; F.HN.CHI.NY[11].Y.+
  The second bull is Regnans in excelsis; *see also* 19974.2.
18678a.5 — [Anr. ed.] Seen and allowed. 8° in 4's. *J. Daye*, [1570.] L.L[2].O.C[2].E.+; BO[3].HD(w. quire B from 18678a).N.
— A catechisme, or first instruction. 1570. *See* 18708.
18679 — A disclosing of the great bull. [Anon.] 8° in 4's. *J. Daye*, [1570.] L.O.C[2].D.YK.+; F.HN.HD.N.NY.+
  (Formerly also 12765) 'An answer to the Bull' ent. 1569–70.
— A message, termed Marke the truth. 1570. *See* 19974.2.
18679.5 — To the queenes maiesties poore deceiued subiectes of the northe contreye. [Anon.] 8° in 4's. (*H. Bynneman f. L. Harrison*, 1569.) Ent. 1569–70. L(2).M.; F.
18680 — [Anr. ed.] To the quenes maiesties poore deceyued subiectes of the north countrey. 8° in 4's. (*H. Bynneman f. L. Harrison*, 1569.) L.O.C.D[2].E.+; HN.CHI.HART.HD.PML.

Norton, Thomas—*cont.*

18681 — [Anr. ed.] To the . . . poore deceiued subiects of the northe contrey. 8° in 4's. (*H. Bynneman f. L. Harrison*, 1569.) L.C.BUTE.D.
18682 — [Anr. ed.] To the . . . poore deceiued subiectes. Newly perused and encreased. 8°. (*H. Bynneman f. L. Harrison*, 1569.) L.O.C.E.YK.+; F.HN.CHI.N.
18683 — The seueral confessions of T. Norton and C. Norton. [1570.] Now = 18687.5.
18684 — The tragedie of Gorboduc, whereof three actes were wrytten by T. Nortone, and the two laste by T. Sackuyle. Sett forthe as the same was shewed before the quenes most excellent maiestie. 1561. 8°. *W. Griffith*, 1565 (22 se.). Ent. 1565–66. O(tp only, Douce Add. 142/217).; HN. Greg 39.
18685 — [Anr. ed., w. title:] The tragidie of Ferrex and Porrex, set forth without addition or alteration, but altogether as the same was shewed on stage before the queenes maiestie, about nine yeares past. 8° in 4's. *J. Daye*, [1570.] L.L[6].O.PARIS.; F.HN.HD(imp.).IND. NY.+
— [Anr. ed.] The tragedy of Gorboduc. 1590. *See* 17029, pt. 2.
18685.3 — A warning agaynst the dangerous practises of papistes. [Anon.] 8° in 4's. [*J. Day*, 1569?] Ent. to J. Day 1569–70. L.
18685.7 — [Anr. issue.] Sene and allowed. (*J. Daye, solde*) [*by L. Harrison*, 1569.] L.O.C.D[2].E.+; F.HN.CHI.NY[11].Y.+
  (Formerly 18687)
18686 — [Anr. ed., signed 'T. Norton.'] Newly perused and encreasced [*sic*]. 8° in 4's. (*J. Daye*,) [1570?] L.O.C[7]. D.P.+; F.HN.HD.N.U.+
  Partly from same setting as 18685.7. Tp in two settings: 'agaynst' or 'against'; both at L.
18687 — Now = 18685.7.
— *tr. See* 785, 4415, 18708, 18730, 24666.
— *See also* 2866, 13869, and 17823 (Addenda).

18687.5 **Norton, Thomas,** and **Christopher,** *of the Northern Rising.* The seuerall confessions of T. Norton and C. Norton. 8°. *W. How f. R. Johnes*, [1570.] Ent. 1569–70. C[5].
  (Formerly 18683)

18688 **Norvell, Robert.** The meroure of an chrstiane [*sic*]. [In verse.] 4° in 8's. *Edinburgh, R. Lekprewik*, 1561. C(frag.).E[2](frag.).; F.HD(frag.).MEL(frag.).
  Largely a trans. from C. Marot.

18688.5 **Norwich,** *City of.* [Heading A2r:] At an assembly of the maior, sheriffs, aldermen, and common councell of the city of Norwich, [etc. Ordinances for regulating trades and occupations within the city. 19 Aug. 1622.] 4°. [*F. Kingston*, 1622.] O(lacks tp).

18689 **Norwich,** *Diocese of.* Orders for the redresse of abuse in diet. [By W. Redman, *Bp.*] s.sh.fol. [*London*, 1595.] O.
  Cf. 9202.

Norwich, William, *tr. See* 18206.

18690 **Norwood, Richard.** Fortification or architecture military. 4°. *T. Cotes f. A. Crooke*, 1639. Ent. 12 au. 1637. L.O.C[2].E.YK.+; LC.
18691 — The sea-mans practice, contayning a fundamentall probleme in navigation, experimentally verified. 4°. [*B. Alsop a. T. Fawcet*] *f. G. Hurlock*, 1637. Ent. 24 jn. L.L[30].L[33].; F.Y.
18692 — Trigonometrie. Or, the doctrine of triangles. 2 pts. 4°. *W. Jones*, 1631. Ent. 15 se. L.O.C.D.ETON.+; HN. CAL[2].NY[8]. Horblit.
  Errata on &4v. In some copies (HN) sheets R–&[4] reset; errata on [*]1v.
18693 — [Anr. issue, w. cancel tp:] Second edition. *W. Jones*, 1634. L.

Nostradamus, Michael. Almanacks. 1559, etc. *See* 492 sqq.

18694 — An excellent tretise, shewing suche infirmities, as shall insue. 1559. and 1560. *Tr.* into Englysh at the desire of L. Philotus, Tyl. 8°. *J. Day*, (1559 (mr.)) O.
  See Arber I.101 for Day's fine for printing this without licence.
18695 — The prognostication. [1559.] Now = 492.3.
18696 — [B8v:] Here endeth the prognostication. [1567.] Now = 493.3.

Notaras, Gerasimos, *Saint. See* 3047.5.

18697 **Notari, Angelo.** Prime musiche nuoue . . . à una, due, et tre voci. fol. *Londra, intagliate da G. Hole,* [1613.] L.
　　Entirely engr.; *see* Hind II.338.

18698 **Notarius Rusticus.** Vox ruris reverberating Vox civitatis [23075], complaining this yeare 1636. 4°. *T. C[otes] f. J. W[illiams,]* 1637. L.O⁸(frag.).C.; F.

Note. A briefe note of the benefits that growe to this realme, by fish-daies. [1595.] *See* 9976.5.
— A note of the head-lands of England. [1605.] *See* 10019.
— A note of the severall sorts of bookes. [c. 1623.] *See* 7705.5.

Notes. Certaine briefe notes upon a briefe apologie. [1602.] *See* 7628.

18699 **Nothing.** There's nothing to be had without money. *Ballad.* 2 pts. s.sh.fol. [*A. Mathewes*] *f. H. G[osson,* 1633?] Ent. to ballad ptnrs. 8 jy. 1633. L.
　　Possibly by Martin Parker.

18699.3 **Nottingham.** Villa Nottingham ss. Whereas at the general sessions [etc. Blank form for granting licence to ale- and victualling-house keepers.] s.sh.fol. [*London,* 1631?] HN.

Nottingham, *Earl of. See* Howard, C.

18699.7 **Nottinghamshire Lovers.** The two Nottinghamshire lovers. *Ballad.* 2 pts. s.sh.fol. *f. H. Gossen,* [c. 1630.] C⁶.

18700 — [Anr. ed.] 2 pts. s.sh.fol. *f. H. G[osson,* 1635?] L.

Nova Francia. Nova Francia: or the description of New France. 1609. *See* 15491.

Novations. Answeres to certaine novations. [c. 1638.] *See* 664.7.

18700.5 **November.** November. Thou sun that shed'st the dayes, looke downe and see a month more shining by events, than thee. *Ballad.* s.sh.fol. [*London?* 1640?] Private owner.
　　Contains allusion to the Parliament of 3 Nov. 1640.

Novimola, Sebastianus, *ed. See* 6781, 6783.

Novus Homo, *pseud.* Certaine characters and essayes of prison. 1618. *See* 18318.
— Supplicatio ad imperatorem, reges. 1513 [i.e. 1613.] *See* 1703.

Nowell, Alexander.
THE LARGER CATECHISM
18701 — Catechismus, siue prima institutio, disciplináque pieta- tis christianæ. [Init. A. N.] 4°. *in off. R. Wolfij,* 1570 (16 cal. jul.) L.L⁴.O.O³.C.+; F.CH.ILL.U.
　　B1ʳ line 6 of text: 'rationem'. *See Cal. S.P.D., 1547–1580,* p. 382. *See also* 7627.7.

18701a — [Anr. ed.] 4°. *in off. R. Wolfij,* 1570 (16 cal. jul.) O(imp.).O⁵.O¹⁰.C.M.+; F.
　　B1ʳ line 6 of text: 'ratiõe'. Sheet A is from the same setting as 18701.

18702 — [Anr. ed.] 4°. *in off. R. Wolfij,* 1571 (3 cal. jun.) O.O⁴. C.HAT.; F.

18702.5 — [Anr. ed.] 4°. *in off. R. Wolfij,* 1571. L.O.O⁴.C¹⁵.D.+; ILL.U.

18703 — [Anr. ed.] 4°. *in off. R. Wolfij,* 1572. L.O.C.DUR⁵. LINC.+; HD(lacks tp).U.

18704 — [Anr. ed.] 4°. *ap. J. Dayum,* 1574. L.O.C⁵.D.YK.+; V.

18705 — [Anr. ed.] 4°. *ap. J. Dayum,* 1576. L.L².O⁴.C⁵.; F.HN. BO.HD.

18706 — [Anr. ed.] 4°. *ap. J. Dayum,* 1580. L.O.O¹².C⁵.P.+

18706a — [Anr. ed.] 8°. *pro assign. R. Daij,* 1595. C⁸.

18707 — [*Latin a. Greek.*] Κατηχισμος, ἡ πρώτη παίδευσις. . . . Catechismus, siue prima institutio, [etc. Anon. *Tr.* W. Whitaker.] 8°. (*ap. R. Wolfium,*) 1573. L.O.C. D.E.+; F.HN.BO.CHI.U(imp.).+

18708 — [*English.*] A catechisme, or first instruction of christian religion. *Tr.* (T. Norton.) [Anon.] 4°. *J. Daye,* 1570. This or 18730 ent. 1569–70. L.O.O⁴.C(imp.).C⁸.; F(3).PML.U.
　　See Greg, *Register B,* p. 7. *See also* 7627.7.

18709 — [Anr. ed., signed 'A. Nowell.'] 4°. *J. Daye,* 1571. L.L¹⁵.O.O⁴.E.+; F.HN.HD.ILL.WASH².

18710 — [Anr. ed.] 4°. *J. Daye,* 1573. L.O(lacks tp).; CU.ILL.

18710a — [Anr. ed.] 4°. *J. Daye,* 1575 (1576.) L.O.O⁴.C⁹.; BO. IND.PML.

Nowell, Alexander—*cont.*
18710a.5 — [Anr. ed.] 4°. *J. Daye,* 1577 (1576.) O.O⁴(lacks col.).; F.HD(imp.).PH.
　　Some sheets reset in F copy.

THE SHORTER CATECHISM
18711 — Catechismus paruus pueris primùm Latinè qui edi- scatur, proponendus in scholis. [The Church of England Catechism, *tr.* by A. N., w. prayers, etc.] 8°. *ap. J. Dayum,* 1573. F.
　　See 7627.7.

18711.5 — [Anr. ed.] 8°. *ap. J. Dayum,* 1583. ILL.

18711a — [*Latin a. Greek.*] Catechismus paruus [etc. *Tr.* W. Whitaker. Init. A. N.] 8° in 4's. *ap. J. Dayum,* 1574. L.O.O¹⁷.C.P.+

18711b — [Anr. ed.] 8°. *ap. J. Dayum,* 1584. L.O.O¹⁴.D.ETON.

18711b.5 — [Anr. ed.] 8°. *sumptibus bibliopolarum,* 1619. O⁴.

18711c — [Anr. ed.] 8°. *A. Matth[ewes] pro soc. bibliop. Lond.,* 1633. Ent. 5 mr. 1620. O.O⁵.; F.

THE MIDDLE CATECHISM
18712 — Christianæ pietatis prima institutio ad vsum scholarum Latinè scripta. 8°. *in æd. J. Daij,* 1574. O³.O²¹. PLUME.; HN.
　　Following imprint: 'Cum gratia & priuilegio Regiæ Maiestatis, alijs omnibus interdicente huius Catechismi impressione [*sic*].' Reprinted in 17991. *See* 7627.7.

18713 — [Anr. ed.] 8°. *in æd. J. Daij,* 1576. F.

18713.5 — [Anr. ed.] 8°. *ap. J. Daium,* 1577 (18 de.) P.

18714 — [Anr. ed.] 8°. *ap. J. Daium,* 1581. L.

18714.5 — [Anr. ed.] 8°. *ap. J. Dayum,* 1584 (6 au.) C¹⁹(imp.).
　　C4ʳ line 1 ends: 'Euangelii'.

18714.7 — [Anr. ed.] 8°. *ap. J. Dayum* [i.e. *R. Waldegrave a. R. Day?*] 1584 (6 au.) O.
　　C4ʳ line 1 ends: 'fi-'. Partly signed in Waldegrave's manner.

18715 — [Anr. ed.] 8°. *ap. J. Wolfium, pro assign. R. Daij,* 1586. O⁴.

18715.5 — [Anr. ed.] 8°. *ex off. J. Wolphij pro assign. R. Daij,* 1590. L¹⁵.

18716 — [Anr. ed.] 8°. *ex off. J. Windet, pro assign. R. Daij,* 1593. D².

18717 — [Anr. ed.] 8°. *ex off. J. Windet, pro assign. R. Daij,* 1595. O.

18718 — [Anr. ed.] 8°. *ex off. J. Windet, pro assign. R. Daii,* 1598. O⁴.

18718.5 — [Anr. ed.] 8°. *imp. bibliopolarum,* 1608. D.

18719 — [Anr. ed.] 8°. *imp. bibliopolarum,* 1610. O.; F.

18720 — [Anr. ed.] 8°. [*E. Allde,*] *imp. bibliopolarum,* 1615. O.

18720.5 — [Anr. ed.] 8°. [*H. Lownes,*] *imp. bibliopolarum,* 1621. Ent. 5 mr. 1620. DUL.

18721 — [Anr. ed.] 8°. [*H. Lownes,*] *imp. bibliopolarum,* 1625. L.C³.DUR(Bamb.).

18722 — [Anr. ed.] 8°. *Cantabrigiæ, ex typ. Acad. typographorum,* 1626. L⁴.M².NOR.; F.

18723 — [Anr. ed.] 8°. [*W. Stansby,*] *imp. bibliopolarum,* 1630. L. C(Sayle 7608) has an imp. copy of an ed. pr. by A. Mathewes of about this date.

18724 — [Anr. ed.] 8°. *Cantabrigiæ, ex Acad. typog.,* 1633. L.O⁴.O¹⁷(imp.).C(2, 1 imp.).C¹⁹(imp.).; F. 𝕬

18725 — [Anr. ed.] 8°. *Cantabrigiæ, ex Acad. typog.,* 1636. L.L². c.c². Lord Kenyon.

18725.5 — [Anr. ed.] 8°. *J. Nortonus pro soc. bibliopolarum,* 1639. CARLISLE.

18726 — [*Latin a. Greek.*] Χριστιανισμου στοιχειωσις. . . . Chri- stianæ pietatis prima institutio . . . Graecè & Latinè scripta. [*Tr.* W. Whitaker.] 8° in 4's. *ap. J. Dayum,* 1575. L.O.C⁹.COL.M².+; F.

18727 — [Anr. ed.] 8°. *ap. J. Dayum,* 1577. L.O.C.BIRM²(K.N.). M.+; F.CU.U.

18728 — [Anr. ed.] 8°. *ap. J. Dayum,* 1578. L.L³⁸.O.O⁴.C.+; F.HN.BO.ILL.N.+

18729 — [Anr. ed.] 12°. *M. Parsons pro soc. stat.,* 1638. Ent. 5 mr. 1620. L.O.C⁵.D.E².+; HN.BO.HD.NY¹¹.U.

18730 — [*English.*] A catechisme, or institution of christian religion, to bee learned of all youth next after the little catechisme: appointed in the booke of common Prayer. [Init. A. N. *Tr.* and abridged from 18701 by T. Norton.] 8°. *J. Daye,* 1572. This or 18708 ent. 1569–70. L².O(imp.).NLW.
　　Collates A–G⁸ H¹⁰. *See* 7627.7.

18730.3 — [Anr. ed.] 8°. [*J. Day,* 1575?] O(lacks tp).
　　Collates A–H⁸; B1ʳ line 1 of text ends: 'Com- maun-'.

18730.7 — [Anr. ed.] 8°. *J. Daye,* 1576. U.
　　Collates A–H⁸; B1ʳ line 1 of text ends: 'Cõmaun-'.

Nowell, Alexander—*cont.*

18731 — [Anr. ed.] 8°. *J. Daye*, 1577. L.O(lacks tp).
　　　　　Collates A–G⁸.

18732 — [Anr. ed.] 8°. *J. Daye*, 1579. O⁴.

18733 — [Anr. ed.] 8°. [*J. Kingston f.*] *J. Daye*, 1583. L.O.; HD.

18733.3 — [Anr. ed.] 8°. *R. Warde f. the assignes of R. Day*, 1584. YK.

18733.5 — [Anr. ed.] 8°. *J. Windet f. the assignes of R. Day*, 1593. F.

18733.7 — [Anr. ed.] 8°. *J. Windet f. the assignes of R. Day*, 1597. L(tp only, Harl.5936/326).

18734 — [Anr. ed.] 8°. *f. the co. of statrs.*, 1609. O.

18735 — [Anr. ed.] 8°. *f. the co. of statrs.*, 1614. L.O⁴.; F.HN.

18736 — [Anr. ed.] 8°. *f. the co. of statrs.*, 1625. Ent. 5 mr. 1620. L(imp.).DUR(Bamb.).

18737 — [Anr. ed.] 8°. *A. M[athewes] f. the co. of statrs.*, 1633. L.

18737.5 — [Anr. ed.] 8°. *f. the co. of statrs.*, [c. 1635.] O⁴.

18738 — [Anr. ed.] 8°. *J. N[orton] f. the co. of statrs.*, 1638. L.O.C³.E².; HART.

18739 — A confutation, as wel of M. Dormans last boke [7061] as also of D. Sander [21694]. 4°. *H. Bynneman*, 1567 (24 no.). Ent. 1566–67. L².O.C.D.DUR⁵.+; F.ILL.PML. U(frag.).

18740 — A reproufe, . . . of a booke entituled, A proufe of certayne articles [7062]. 4°. *H. Wykes*, 1565 (30 my.). Ent. to H. Denham 1564–65. L.O.C.D.DUR⁵.+; F(2).PML.U.
　　　　　Includes reprint of 7062. Answered by 7061, 21694.

18741 — [Anr. ed.] 4°. *H. Wykes*, 1565 (13 jy.) L.L².O⁴.C. PETYT.+; HN.CHI.Y.

18742 — [Anr. ed., enlarged.] The reproufe of M. Dorman his proufe of certaine articles . . . continued. 4°. *H. Wykes*, 1566. L.O.C².D.P.+; F.HN(imp.).CHI(imp.). PML.U.+

18743 — A sword against swearers and blasphemers. 1611. Now = 3050.5.

18743a — [Anr. ed.] 1618. Now = 3050.7.

18744 **Nowell, Alexander**, and **Day, William**, *Bp.* A true report of the disputation with E. Campion. Whereunto is ioyned a true report of the other three dayes conferences (by J. Feilde.) 4°. *C. Barker*, 1583 (1 ja.) Ent. 27 de. 1582. L.O.C.D.E.+; F.HN.ILL. NYᴵᴵ.U.+
　　　　　Errata on verso of tp.

18744.5 — [Anr. ed.] 4°. *C. Barker*, 1583 (1 ja.) L.O.C².DUR⁵.M.+; F.HD.N.TEX.U.+
　　　　　Verso of tp blank.

Nuce, Thomas, *tr. See* 22229.

18745 **Nugent, Richard.** Rich: Nugents Cynthia. Containing direfull sonnets, madrigalls, and passionate intercourses. [In verse.] 4°. *T. P[urfoot] f. H. Tomes*, 1604. Ent. 4 jn. L.; HN.

Nukrois, Elias de, *pseud. See* 15083.5.

18746 **Numan, Philips.** Miracles lately wrought by the intercession of the glorious virgin Marie, at Mont-aigu. *Tr.* R. Chambers. [Anon.] 8°. *Antwarp, A. Conings*, 1606. L.O.C.A².W.+; F.HN.HD.N.Y.+
　　　　　A&R 578. Attacked in 24472.

18747 **Nun.** A nunnes prophesie, or. The fall of friers. 4°. *W. White, sold by E. Marchant*, 1615. Ent. to J. Trundle 13 fb. L.L³O.O.; U.

18748 **Nun, Thomas.** A comfort against the Spaniard. 4°. *J. Windet f. J. O[xenbridge,]* 1596. L.D.; F.

Nuncius. Nuncius inanimatus. 1629. *See* 11944.

18749 **Nuptial.** The fatall nuptiall. 1636. Now = 3567.5.

18750 **Nuremberg.** Century 3. Numb. 20. The news for this week from Norimberg. 1640 (23 ap.) Now = Newsbooks 337.

18751 — Num. 84. 337 The Norimberg curranto of this week. (1639 (21 ap.)) Now = Newsbooks 312. For other weekly corantos from Nuremberg *see* Newsbooks [Tenth Series], etc.

Nutbrown Maid. Here begȳneth yᵉ new notborune mayd vpō yᵉ passiō of cryste. [c. 1535.] *See* 14553.7.

Nycolson, James. Almanacs. 1563. *See* 490.18 sq.

Nye, Philip, *ed. See* 22486, 22488, 22492, 22513, 22515, 22521.

18752 **Nyndge, Edward.** A booke declaringe the fearfull vexasion, of one Alexander Nyndge. Beynge moste horriblye tormented wyth an euyll spirit. In the yere 1573. [Init. I. W.] 8° in 4's. *T. Colwell*, [1573?] L.

18753 — [Anr. version.] A true and fearefull vexation of one Alexander Nyndge. Written by his owne brother E. Nyndge. 4°. [*W. Stansby*] *f. W. B[arrett?] sold by E. Wright*, 1615. L.G².
　　　　　Text has minor changes from 18752. In L copy date altered in ink to 1616.

O

O. O per se O. 1612. *See* 6487.

O., C. The valiant actes of the English nation. 1585. *See* 18777.

O., Christoph. The fountaine of all variance. 1589. *See* 18778.

18754 **O., E.** A detection, of divers notable untruthes. Gathered out of Mʳ Sutcliffes Newe Challenge [in 23453], and Mʳ Willets Synopsis [25697 sq.] and Tetrastilon [25702 sq.] According to the platforme of that conference, betwixt the R. bishoppe of Evreux, and the lorde of Plessis. [By P. Woodward.] 8°. [*V. Simmes?*] 1602. L.O.C.USHAW.YK.+; F.HD.N.TEX.Y.
    A&R 906. Answered in 1822, 23454, 25694.

O., H., *tr. See* 10865.

18755 **O., I.** The lamentation of Troy, for the death of Hector. Whereunto is annexed an old womans tale in hir solitarie cell. [In verse.] 4°. *P. Short f. W. Mattes,* 1594. Ent. 22 fb. L.L⁴.LAMPORT.; F.HN. Arthur Houghton.
    Prob. by Sir J. Ogle.
— A plea for the reall-presence. 1624. *See* 11113.
— ed. *See* 21047.3.
— tr. *See* 23554.

O., L. Enchiridion controversiarum. 1633. *See* 18881.
— Speculum Jesuiticum. 1629. *See* 18997.

O., N. Rede me and be nott wrothe. [1528?] *See* 1462.7.

18756 **O., S.** A relation of sundry particular wicked plots of the Spaniards. [By S. Ofwod.] 4°. [*London?*] 1624. L.C⁵.G⁴.
    Reprinted from 2nd pt. of 18837.
18757 — An adioynder of sundry other plots. 1624. = pt. of 18837; *see also* 22078.5.
— ed. *See* Ofwod, S.

O., V. N. Nicrina ad heroas Anglos. 1620 [1622.] *See* 14713.5.

O., W. The description and use of the double horizontall dyall. 1636. *See* 18900.

18758 **Oat-meale, Oliver,** *pseud.* A quest of enquirie, by women to know, whether the tripe-wife were trimmed by Doll yea or no. 4°. *T. G.,* 1595. HN.
    Printer purposely unidentifiable. *See also* 19855.

18759 **Oberndoerffer, Johann.** The anatomyes of the true physition, and counterfeit mounte-banke. *Tr.* F. H[erring.] (A discovery of certaine stratagems [by F. Herring.]) 4°. [*T. Creede*] *f. A. Johnson,* 1602. Ent. 14 ap. L.L⁸.L¹⁹.; F.NLM.
18759.5 — [Anr. issue, w. cancel tp:] Beware of pick-purses. Or, a caveat for sick folkes to take heede of unlearned phisitions. By F. H., Doctor in Physick. *London,* 1605. HN.NLM.

Objections. Objections against the use of the bow w. the pike. [c. 1630.] *See* 18416.3.
— Objections. Answered by way of dialogue. 1615. *See* 13054.

Observations. Divine and politike observations. 1638. *See* 15309.
18760 — Especiall observations, and approved physicall rules; which have beene well tryed in the last time of pestilence. 4°. *B. Alsop a. T. Fawcet by the assignes of R. B[arker,]* 1625. L.L¹⁶.O.C³.NEK.+; F.HD.
— Observations concerning the present affaires of Holland. 1621. *See* 13576.

Observations—cont.
18761 — Observations to be followed, for the making of fit roomes, to keepe silkewormes in. [By J. Bonoeil.] 4°. *F. Kyngston,* 1620. L¹¹(frag., C.O.I., item 24). O.CHATS.; HN.CB.HD.Y.
    HD copy has date altered in ink to 1629. *See The Library,* XV (1960), pp. 130–1; *see also* 14378.

Occam, William of. *See* Gulielmus, *de Occam.*

Occurrences. The chiefe occurrences of both armies. 1592. *See* 11260.
18762 — July. 16. Numb. 9. The continuation of our remarkable occurrences of news. 1630. Now = Newsbooks 205.

18763 **Oceander,** *Prince.* The heroicall adventures of the knight of the sea . . . prince Oceander. 4°. [*R. Bradock*] *f. W. Leake,* 1600. Ent. 26 ap. L.; HN.HD(lacks Hh4).

18764 **Ochino, Bernardino.** Sermons [five] of Barnardine Ochine of Sena . . . *tr.* [*Lady* A. Bacon.] 8°. (*R. C[ar] f. W. Reddell,*) 1548 (jy.) L³.O.O¹⁰.D(frag.).DUR⁵.; F.HD.
    Reprinted in 18766, 18768.
18765 — Sermons [six] of the ryght famous ād excellent clerke master B. Ochine. [*Tr.*] (R. Argentyne.) 8°. *Ippeswych, A. Scoloker,* 1548. L.O.C.D.E².+; F.
    All sermons different from those in 18764; reprinted in 18766, 18768.
18766 — Certayne sermons of the ryghte famous and excellente clerk [etc.] 8°. *J. Day,* [1551?] L(2, 1 imp.).O(2, 1 imp.).C.DNPK.P.; F.HD.ILL(imp.).NY¹¹.Y.+
    Sermons 1–6 reprinted from 18765; 7–11 from 18764; 12–25 from 18767.
18767 — Fouretene sermons . . . concernyng the predestinacion and eleccion of god. *Tr.* out of Italian in to oure natyue tounge by A. C[ooke, *Lady* Bacon.] [*Ed.*] (G. B.) 8°. (*J. Day & W. Seres,*) [1551?] L.O.C².C⁵. STU.; N.
    Reprinted in 18766, 18768.
18768 — Sermons of Barnardine Ochyne, (to the number of .25.) concernyng the predestination and election of God. *Tr.* A. C[ooke, *Lady* Bacon and R. Argentine.] 8°. *J. Day,* [1570?] L.C⁴.DUR⁵.LINC.P.+; F.HN(imp.).
    Sermons 1–14 reprinted from 18767; 15–20 from 18765; 21–5 from 18764.
18769 — Certaine godly and very profitable sermons, of faith, hope and charitie. *Tr.* W. Phiston. 4°. *T. East,* 1580. Ent. 10 or 20 ap. L.O.C.E⁴.P.+; F.HD.STAN.U.
18770 — A tragoedie or dialoge of the uniuste primacie of the bishop of Rome. *Tr.* J. Ponet. 4°. [*N. Hill*] (*f. G. Lynne,*) 1549. Ent. to R. Waldegrave 11 se. 1587. L.O.C.A.D.+; HN.CHI.HD.Y.
    [-]2ᵛ ends: 'the lorde Protector'.
18771 — [Anr. issue, amended.] L.O.C¹⁰.E.E².+; F.HN.
    [-]2ᵛ ends: 'the Counseill'.

18772 **Ockland, Christopher.** Anglorum prælia, ab anno domini 1327. vsque ad annum 1558. [In verse.] 4°. [*H. Bynneman f.*] *R. Neuberie, ex assign. H. Binnemani,* 1580. Ent. to H. Bynneman 18 au. L.O.C. E².P.+; F.HN.HART.ILL.
18772.5 — [Anr. issue, w. cancelled tp replaced by halfsheet.] Anglorum prælia: . . . . Item: de pacatissimo Angliæ statu. 2 pts. *ap. R. Nuberie, ex assign. H. Bynneman,* 1582. L.O³.C⁴.LINC. Witwatersrand U.; F.
    (Formerly 18775) Pt. 2 a reissue of 18775a.
18773 — [Anr. ed.] Anglorum prælia. . . . Item, de pacatissimo Angliæ statu. . . . . Hijs A. Neuilli Kettum: . . . adiunximus. 8°. [*H. Bynneman*] *ap. R. Nuberie, ex assign. H. Bynneman,* 1582. L.L³⁸.O.C.NEK.+; F(3, 1 imp.).HD.NY⁷.
    (3rd pt. formerly also 18479) N1ᵛ last line begins: 'Londini:'. Copies of this and the following eds. sometimes have mixed sheets.

Ockland, Christopher—*cont.*

18773.3 — [Anr. ed.] 8°. [*H. Bynneman*] *ap. R. Nuberie, ex assign. H. Bynneman,* 1582. L.O⁹.C.D².G².+; F.CU.ILL.MICH.NY.+
N1ᵛ last line begins: 'bus meis'.

18773.7 — [Anr. ed.] 8°. [*H. Bynneman*] *ap. R. Nuberie, ex assign. H. Bynneman,* 1582. L³⁸.O.C.DUR(Bamb.).G².+; F.HN(imp.).BO(imp.).CU.ILL(imp.).+
N1ᵛ last line begins: 'ni ex'.

18774 — [Anr. ed.] 8°. [*H. Bynneman*] *ap. R. Nubery, ex assign. H. Bynneman,* 1582. L.O.C.D.E².+; F.HN(imp.).CHI.HD(imp.).LC.+
N1ᵛ last line begins: 'meis'.

18775 — Now = 18772.5.

18775a — Ειρηναρχια *siue* Elizabetha. De pacatissimo Angliæ statu. [In verse.] 4°. *C. Barkerus,* 1582. Ent. to T. Woodcock a. C. Barker 21 mr. L.O.C⁴.D⁵.NLW.+; F.HN.BO.PN.Y.
Also issued as pt. 2 of 18772.5.

18776 —Elizabetheis. Siue de pacatissimo et florentissimo Angliæ statu, liber secundus. [In verse.] 4°. *ex off. T. Orwini,* 1589. Ent. 6 ja. L.O²⁷.BIRM²(K.N.).D.M.+; F.

18777 — [A trans. of 18772 and 18775a, init. C. O.] The valiant actes and victorious battailes of the English nation. (Elizabeth queene. Or a short declaration of the peaceable state of England.) *Tr.* J. S(harrock.) [In verse.] 2 pts. 4°. *R. Walde-graue,* (1585.) L(2, 1 of pt. 2 only).; F.HN.HD(imp.).
Only partly signed in Waldegrave's manner; the orns. app. belonged to J. Day.

18778 — The fountaine and welspring of all variance, sedition, and deadlie hate. [Init. Christoph. O.] 4°. *R. Ward,* 1589. L.L².D.; HN.

18779 **Octavian,** *Emperor of Rome.* Here begynneth Octauyan the Emperoure of Rome. 4° ⁸·⁴ [*W. de Worde,* 1505?] HN(imp.).

Octavianus, Sixtus, *ed.* See 4866.

18780 **Odell, Thomas.** A brief and short treatise, called the christians pilgrimage to his fatherland. [In verse.] 4°. *Amsterdam, J. F. Stam,* 1635. L.

18781 —Isaacks pilgrimage a brief and short treatise of the strife that Isaack had with his heard-men. [In verse.] 4°. *Amsterdam, J. F. Stam,* 1635. L.

18782 **Odingsells, Charles.** The pearle of perfection sought after. 4°. *M. D[awson] f. J. Williams,* 1637. Ent. 27 mr. L.C⁵.P.; HN.MIN(lacks tp).

18782.5 — Prophecying, casting out of devils, and miracles: briefly discoursed in two sermons. 8°. *W. Stansby,* 1619. L.

18783 — [Anr. issue, w. cancel tp.] Two sermons, lately preached at Langar in Belvoir. *W. Stansby, sold by J. Parker,* 1620 (1619.) L.O(2).C³.LINC.; PN².

18784 **O'Dogherty,** *Sir Cahir.* Newes from Lough-foyle in Ireland. 4°. [*E. Allde*] *f. N. Butter,* 1608. Ent. 19 my. L.O.O⁵.C.D⁶.+

18785 — [Anr. ed., w. title:] Newes from Ireland. . . . Newly imprinted and inlarged. 4°. [*E. Allde*] *f. N. Butter,* 1608. L.D.; F.

18785.5 — [Anr. issue, w. cancel tp:] Later newes from Ireland. *f. N. Butter,* 1608. HN.

18786 — The over-throw of an Irish rebell, in a late battaile: or the death of sir C. Adoughertie. 4°. (*Dublin, J. Franckton*) [i.e. *London, G. Eld] f. J. Wright,* 1608. Ent. to H. Gosson a. J. Wright 12 au. L.L¹³.C².D.

18787 **Œcolampadius, Joannes.** A sarmon, of Ihon Oecolampadius, to yong men, and maydens. (*Tr.* J. Foxe.) 8°. (*H. Powell, sould by H. Syngleton,*) [1548?] L.O.O¹⁰.C.D.+; F.N.

Offer. A christian and modest offer of a conference. 1606. See 14329.

18787.5 — A most excellent offer of a certaine invention for a new kind of fire. . . . First found out by Mr. H. Platte, in [19991] and now disclosed by Mr. Gosling. s.sh.fol. *T. C[otes] f. M. S[parke],* 1628. Ent. to M. Sparke 5 de. 1627. L⁵(Lemon 291).
See also 19995.

Office. Loffice et auctoryte des iustyces de peas. 1538. See 10968.

Office—*cont.*

18788 — The office of generall remembrance. Of matters of record, created by his maiesties letters pattents. Is kept in Cursitors Court. 4°. *G. Eld for the remembrancers generall the patentees, to bee had of R. Wilson,* 1617. L.L³⁰.O.C.RGU.+; F.HN.HD.MICH.Y.+
E has variant title: 'remembrance [*sic*]'; 'To the reader' in two settings: signed ¶ or ℂ; both at E.

Offices. In this booke is contayned yᵉ offices of sheryffes. [1538?] See 10984.

18789 **Ofwod, Stephen.** An advertisement to Jhon Delecluse and Henry May the elder. 4°. [*Amsterdam?* 1633?] D².
— *ed.* See 555, 4748, 11129, 14555.
— *tr.* See 18837, 22078.5.
— See also 18756.

Ogilvie, John. A true relation, of the proceedings against J. Ogilvie. 1615. See 23104.

Ogle, *Sir John.* See 18755.

18790 **Ogston, William.** Oratio funebris, in obitum maximi virorum Georgii, Marischalli Comitis, D. Keith. 2 pts. 4°. *Abredoniæ, E. Rabanus,* 1623. L.L³.A.E².

18790.5 **Oh.** Oh faine would I marry yet divers occasions a while make me tarry. *Ballad.* 2 pts. s.sh.fol. [*M. Flesher,* c. 1635.] M³(pt. 1 only, imp.).
First line begins: 'Oh faine would I wive,'; it is possible a first portion of the title is missing.

18791 **O'Hussey, Giollabrighde,** *otherwise* **Bonaventura.** Ⱦⱥn ⷄⱥ ⱃⱙⱀⱀⰵ ⱘⱀ ⰳⱃⰰⱅⱀⱖ ⰳⱁⱃ ⷄⱁⱃⱃⱁ S. Ꝑⱃⰹⱁⱞⱃⱖⱕ ⷄⱁⱀⰰⰷⰵⱀⱅⱖⱃⰰ ⱁ ꝱⰵⱁⷄⰰⱃⱖ ⰳⰰⱑⰷⱖⰰⱀ [etc.] 16° in 8's. [*Louvain, press of the Irish Franciscans,* c. 1614.] L.C.
A&R 581. A metrical version of pt. of St. Bernard's De Contemptu Mundi.

18791.5 — Ⱥn ⱅⰵⰰⰳⰰⱃⰳ ⱍⱃⰹⱁⱃⷄⰰⱃⱀⰵ. [The christian catechism.] 16° in 8's. *Antuerpiae, ap. J. Mesium,* 1611. L.L⁴⁴.O.C.D⁶.+; N.
A&R 583. Marginal notes in roman type.

18792 — [Anr. ed.] 16° in 8's. [*Louvain, press of the Irish Franciscans,* c. 1614.] L.O.C.
A&R 582. Marginal notes in Irish type.

18793 **O'Kearney, John.** Ⱥⰹⰷⱃⱁⰹⱀ ⰳⰰⱁⰹⷄⰵⰹⱀⰳⰵ, ⱀ ⱌⰰⰹⱅⰹⱌⰹⱁⱃⱞⰰ. 1571. Now = 22.3.

18793.5 **Old Christmas.** [An interlude with the characters Old Christmas, Good Order, Riot, Gluttony, and Prayer.] fol. (*w. Rastell,* 1533.) Nash(2 leaves). Greg 14.5.
Not by J. Skelton.

18794 **Oldcastle, Hugh.** A briefe instruction and maner how to keepe bookes of accompts. Newely augmented by J. Mellis. 8°. *J. Windet (f. H. Singleton,)* 1588. Ent. to Windet a. Singleton 4 de. 1587. L.L³⁰.L⁴⁵.E².; HN.CAL².
Based on L. Pacciolo's *Summa de Arithmetica,* Venice, 1494.

18795 **Oldcastle, John,** *Baron Cobham.* The first part of the true and honorable historie, of the life of Sir J. Oldcastle. [By A. Munday and others.] 4°. *V. S[immes] f. T. Pavier,* 1600. Ent. 11 au. L(lacks tp).O(2, 1 imp.).BODMER.; F.HN.CAL. Greg 166.

18796 — [Anr. ed., with 'Written by William Shakespeare' added to the title.] 4°. [*W. Jaggard*] *f. T. P[avier,]* 1600 [1619.] L.O.C².E.LEEDS.+; F.HN.HD.N.NY.+
— See also 24045.

18797 **Olde, John.** The acquital or purgation of the moost catholyke prince Edwarde the .VI. and of the churche of Englande refourmed. 8°. (*Waterford* [i.e. *Emden, E. van der Erve,*] 1555 (7 no.)) L.O³.C.D.DUR⁵.+; F.HD.

18798 — A confession of the most auncient and true christē catholike olde belefe. 8°. *Sothewarke, C. Truthal* [i.e. *Emden, E. van der Erve,*] 1556 (ap.) L.O.C.ETON.M.+; F.
— A short description of Antichrist. [Attrib. to J. Olde. c. 1555.] See 673.
— *ed.* See 21047.3.
— *tr.* See 2854.6, 23554, 25009.

18799 **Oldenbarneveld, Jan van.** The arraignment of John van Olden Barnevelt. 4°. *E. Griffin f. R. Rounthwait,* 1619. Ent. 17 my. L.O.C.D².STU.+; F.HN.COR.N.Y.+

18800 — Barnevels apology: or Holland mysterie. With marginall castigations. [*Tr.*] 4°. [*W. Jones*] *f. T. Thorp,* 1618. Ent. 27 oc. L.O.C.E.M.+; F.HN.HD.N.PN².+
Dedic. signed: 'Francfurt this 27. of June. 1618. . . . Robert [i.e. Petrus] Holderus.'

18801 — Barnevelt displayed; or the golden legend of new St John. *Tr.* out of Dutch. 4°. *G. Eld f. N. Butter,* 1619. Ent. 13 ja. L.O(2).O¹⁸.M. Blickling.; F(2).HN. Rutgers U.

18802 — Murther unmasked, or Barneviles base conspiracie discovered. *Ballad.* 2 pts. s.sh.fol. *W. J[ones? 1619.]* C⁶.

18803 — Newes out of Holland: concerning Barnevelt and his fellow-prisoners . . . the oration made unto the generall states by the ambassadors of the French king. With their answere. 4°. *T. S[nodham] f. N. Newbery,* 1619. Ent. 6 ap. L.L³⁸.O.M.HN.N.

18804 — [Anr. issue, w. cancel tp and new prelims.] The true description of the execution of justice, done upon Sir J. van Olden Barnavelt. *Tr.* according to the Dutch copie. *F. Kyngston f. N. Newbery,* 1619. Ent. 17 my. O.O².C.M.; F.HN.

18805 **Oldmayne, Timothy.** Gods rebuke in taking from us Sir E. Lewkenor. 8°. *E. Griffin f. J. Parker,* 1619. Ent. 20 ap. L³.O.; F.HN.

18806 — Lifes brevitie and deaths debility. Evidently declared in a sermon preached at the funerall of E. Lewkenor. 4°. *N. a. J. Okes,* 1636. L.L³.O.C.P.+; F.CHI.MIN. Imprimatur misdated 1625.

Oldwanton, Oliver, *tr. See* 25196.

18807 **Olevian, Caspar.** An exposition of the symbole of the apostles. *Tr.* J. Fielde. 8°. *H. Middleton f. T. Man a. T. Smith,* 1581. Ent. to T. Smith 9 jn. 1580. L.O³.C³.; F.HN.ILL.U.

18807.3 — [Anr. ed.] 8°. *H. Middleton f. T. Man a. T. Smith,* 1582. L(tp only, Ames I.388).L⁴³.C².
— *See also* 13023.

Olinda. A true relation of the vanquishing of Olinda. 1630. *See* 16699.

18807.7 **Oliphant, Robert.** In obitum C. V. et eximii theologi D. T. Bezæ Vezelii ad civeis Reip. Genevensis elegia. s.sh.fol. [*London?* 1606?] M(deposit).

18808 **Oliver,** *of Castile.* [End:] Here endeth yᵉ hystorye of Olyuer of Castylle, and of the fayre Helayne. [*Tr.* H. Watson.] 4° ⁸·⁴. (*w. de worde,* 1518.) Ent. to T. East 12 mr. 1582. PML(lacks tp).

Oliver, Reynold, *tr. See* 17764.5.

18809 **Oliver, Thomas.** Thomæ Oliverij Buriensis philiatri. De sophismatum præstigijs cavendis admonitio. . . . De rectarum linearum parallelismo. . . . De missione sanguinis. . . . De circuli quadratura. 4 pts. 4°. *Cantabrigiæ, ex off. J. Legat,* 1604. L.O.C.D.E².+; F(imp.).NY.

18810 — A new handling of the planisphere. 4°. *F. Kyngston f. S. Waterson a. Rafe Jacson,* 1601. Ent. 22 ap. L.O.C.DUR⁵.E.+; F.HN. Horblit. Henry Taylor.

18811 **Olmstead, Richard.** Sions teares leading to joy. 12°. *Dublin, Society of Stationers,* 1630. O.D⁶.

18811.5 — A treatise of the union betwixt Christ and the church, or mans felicitie and happinesse. Preached in severall sermons. 12°. *Dublin, Soc. of Statrs.,* 1627. O.

Olney, Henry, *ed. See* 5780.7.

18812 **Onderzoeking.** Een korte onsoeckinghe des gheloofs. [By M. Micron.] 8°. *J. Daye,* 1561 (3 jy.) L.

18813 **O'Neill, Con Bacach,** *1st Earl of Tyrone.* The copye of the submissyon of Oneyll, which he made the .xxiiii. daye of September, in the .xxxiiii. yere of his maiesties raygne. s.sh.fol. *R. Lant f. J. Gough,* [1542.] L.

18814 **O'Neill, Hugh,** *Earl of Tyrone.* Declaratio de Tyronensis et Tirconelii comitum, sociorumque fuga. 4°. *R. Barkerus,* 1607. C.

18815 **Onosander.** Onosandro Platonico, of the Generall Captaine, and of his office, *tr.* out of Greke into Italyan, by F. Cotta, and out of Italian into Englysh by P. Whytehorne. 8°. *W. Seres,* 1563. Ent. 1563–64. L.O.C⁸.

18816 **Openshaw, Robert.** [*Short version, anon., collating* A–B⁸C⁴.] Short questions and answeares, conteyning the summe of christian religion. 8°. *T. Dawson,* 1579. O. 𝕬

18817 — [Anr. ed.] 8°. *T. Dawson,* 1580. L.
Running title on recto: 'of Christian Religion'.

18817.5 — [Anr. ed.] 8°. *T. Dawson,* 1580. L.
Running title on recto: 'Christian Religion'.

18818 — [Anr. ed.] 8°. *T. Dawson,* 1581. C³.

18819 — [Anr. ed.] 8°. *T. Dawson,* 1582. F.HD.

18820 — [Anr. ed.] 8°. *T. Dawson,* 1583. O.

18821 — [Anr. ed.] 8°. *T. Dawson,* 1584. L.O.

18822 — Now = 18830.3.

18822.2 — [Anr. ed.] 8°. *T. Dawson,* 1598. Ent. 1 au. 1586. HD.

18822.6 — [Anr. ed.] 8°. *T. Dawson,* 1603. C¹⁹.

18822.8 — [Anr. ed.] 8°. *T. Dawson,* 1609. D.

18823 — [Anr. ed.] 8°. *T. Dawson,* 1614. C.

18824 — Now = 18830.7.

18825 — [Anr. ed.] 8°. *T. Dawson,* 1618. L.

18826 — [Anr. ed.] 8°. *J. Dawson,* 1622. C³.

18826a — [Anr. ed.] 8°. *J. Dawson,* 1623. O(2 leaves).

18827 — Now = 18830.8.

18828 — [Anr. ed.] 8°. *J. Dawson,* 1629. L.

18828.5 — [Anr. ed.] 8°. *J. Dawson,* 1633. DUR(Bamb.).

18829 — [Anr. ed.] 8°. *J. Dawson,* 1634. O.; F.HD(2 leaves).

18830 — [A variant, w. imprint:] *M. Dawson,* 1635. O.; Y. Both copies have horizontal chainlines.

18830.1 — [Anr. ed.] 8°. *M. Dawson,* 1637. L(tp only, Harl.5921/ 376).

18830.2 — [Anr. ed.] 8°. *J. Dawson,* 1639. M.

18830.2A — [*Enlarged version, signed in full at end, collating* A–E⁸.] [Short questions and answers. Newly enlarged.] 8°. [*T. Dawson,* 1586?] Ent. to Dawson 1 au. 1586. NY¹¹(lacks tp).
This differs from all known eds. in having C1ʳ catchword: 'S. paule'; in the heading on A2ʳ this has 'R. O.' while other eds. have 'Robert O.'

18830.3 — [Anr. ed.] Short questions and answeares, ... Newly enlarged with the testimonies of scripture. 8°. *T. Dawson,* 1586. O.
(Formerly 18822)

18830.4 — [Anr. ed.] 8°. *T. Dawson,* 1589. O.

18830.4A — [Anr. ed.] 8°. *T. Dawson,* 1599. TEX.

18830.5 — [Anr. ed.] 8°. *T. Dawson,* 1600. BO².

18830.6 — [Anr. ed.] 8°. *T. Dawson,* 1602. U.

18830.7 — [Anr. ed.] 8°. *T. Dawson,* 1617. L.; F.
(Formerly 18824)

18830.8 — [Anr. ed.] 8°. *J. Dawson,* 1627. O.DUR(Bamb.).; F.
(Formerly 18827)

18830.9 — [Anr. ed.] 8°. *J. Dawson,* 1633. E².; HD.

18831 **Opitz von Boberfeld, Martin.** An oration to the most illustrious prince Frederick king of Bohemia. *Tr.* out of Latin. 4°. [*London,*] 1620. L.L⁴.O².O¹¹.E.; HN.HD.

18832 **Optatus,** *Saint.* Optati Afri Milevitani episcopi de schismate Donatistarum. In eosdem notæ & emenda-tiones M. Casauboni. 8°. *typis J. Legat,* 1631. Ent. 17 oc. L.O.C.D.E.+; F.HN.ILL.
Copies vary: with or without errata on verso of tp; both at O.

Opus. Opus eximium, de vera differentia regiae potestatis et ecclesiasticae. 1534. *See* 11218.

Opusculum. Opusculum affabre recognitium [etc. 1511?] *See* 25479.

18833 — Compilatū est hoc opusculum insolubilium secundū vsum īsignis schole paruisi ī alma vniuersitati. 4°. [*Oxford, J. Scolar,* 1517?] L(lacks A4).

18833a — [Anr. ed.] 4°. [*Southwark, P. Treveris,*] *venundantur ap. I. T[horne or Dorne, Oxford,* c. 1526.] O⁵.C.

Orandus, Eiræneus, *tr. See* 11027.

Orange, *Prince of. See* Frederick Henry, *Prince of Orange* (1625–47).
— *See also* Maurice, *Prince of Orange* (1618–25).
— *See also* William I, *Prince of Orange* (1544–84).

18834 **Orange,** *Princess of.* Newes sent to the ladie princesse of Orenge [i.e. Louise de Coligny, widow of William I.] *Tr.* out of French by J. E[liot?] 4°. *J. Wolfe,* 1589. Ent. 9 jn. L.D.P.YK.

18835 **Oratio.** Oratio hominis Belgae de virtute ac laudibus Britannorum in defendenda aliorum contra potentiores dynastas salute. Habita in celeberrimâ Oxoniensi academiâ xxix. April. A. CIƆ IƆ CII. 4°. *R. Field*, 1602. Ent. 28 jn. L³.O.D.HAT.; F.
— Oratio perstringens historiolam lanienæ Gallicæ. 1619. *See* 3949.

18836 — Supplex ad diuinam maiestatem oratio, pro defensione nostri. s.sh.fol. [*London*, 1585.] C³.
Bd. before, app. dated from, and perhaps related to 4089.

Oration. The oration and declaration. 1590. *See* 13114.
— The oration made unto the French King. 1617. *See* 11305.

18836.5 — An oration militarie to all naturall Englishmen, whether protestants, or otherwise in religion affected, to moue resolution in these dangerous times. 8°. *T. Orwin a. T. Cadman*, 1588. HN.

18837 — An oration or speech appropriated unto the princes of christendom. Wherein the right of the Netherlandish warre, against Phillip of Spain is approved. Englished by T. Wood. According to the printed copie at Amsterdam, 1608. (An adjoynder of other plots. Gathered and *tr.* by S. O[fwod.]) 4°. [*Amsterdam, successors of G. Thorp,*] 1624. L.O.C.E.LIV².+; F. HN.HD.
(2nd pt. formerly also 18757) The oration is a trans. of W. Verheiden's *De jure belli Belgici*, first pub'd 1596. Partly reprinted in 22078.5; 2nd pt. only reprinted in 18756.

18838 **Orchard.** The orchard, and the garden. Gathered from the Dutch and French. Also to know the time when it is good to sow. 4°. *A. Islip*, 1594. L.O⁵.; HUNT (imp.).
An enlarged reprint of 14106.5; reprinted in 11562.

18839 — [Anr. ed.] 4°. *A. Islip*, 1596. O⁵.STU.; WIS.
18839.5 — [Anr. ed.] 4°. *A. Islip*, 1597. LINDLEY.RD(frag.).
18839a — [Anr. ed.] 4°. *A. Islip*, 1602. C.LINDLEY.

Orchestra. Orchestra or a poeme. 1596. *See* 6360.

18840 **Order.** An easie and profitable order in tilling of ground. = pt. of Wing S 3021.
— An order made to a select committee. 1640. *See* 7747.
18841 — The order of matrimony. 8°. *A. Scoloker*, [1549.] L.O. C(frag.).; HN.
18841.3 — [Anr. ed.] 8° in 4's. *R. Waldegraue*, 1580. D.
Dedic. init. 'R. W[aldegrave].'
— The order of orthographie. 1622. *See* 20186.7.
— The order of the hospitalls of K. Henry. 1557 [c. 1690.] *See* Wing O 389.
18841.7 — Heere foloweth the ordre or trayne of warre, that a prynce, or a heed captayne, ought to take, that wyll conquere, or assege a place. 8° in 4's. (*R. Wyer f. J. Gowgh,*) [c. 1540.] Sotheby's 27 June 1898, lot 1293 (bought by Thorold, untraced).
For a fuller description *see* M. J. D. Cockle, *A Bibliography of Military Books up to 1642*, pp. 2–3.
— The order, solemnitie, and pompe. 1610. *See* 16633.
18842 — An order, whych a prince in battayll must obserue. 8°. (*T. Raynold a. W. Hyll,*) [1548?] L.M.
Based on F. Vegetius Renatus, De re militari.
18843 — A short and an absolute order of confession. 16° in 8's. [*W. Carter*, c. 1577.] L.L³⁰.
A rearranged version of this pr. in pt. 7 of 17278.4 sqq.
— ⟨A table⟩ shewing the most profitable order and m⟨ethod for r⟩eading of history. [c. 1620.] *See* 13528.5.

18843a **Orders.** Orders taken, and enacted, for orphans. 1551. Now = 16704.3.

18844 **Ordinal.** The ordynal or statutȝ concernynge artyfycers. [1542?] Now = 9343.8.

Ordinance. This is a true copy of thordināuce to be obseruyd in the kynges Eschequier. [1526–30?] *See* 7695.5.

Ordinances. Ordinaunces decreed for reformation in pryntyng. [1566?] *See* 7757.5.
— Ordinances set foorth by the King. 1591. *See* 13116.

Ordinary. The ordenarye for all faythfull chrystiās. 1548. *See* 5199.7.

Ordo. Ordo baptizandi. 1632. *See* 16161.5.

18845 **Origan, David.** Annorum quinque sequentium ephemerides. Curâ J. Evans. 8°. *J. Haviland*, 1633. O.
A later version ent. to R. Hodgkinson and D. Frere 27 au. 1638.
18845a — [A trans.] An ephemerides for five yeares to come. Revised by J. Evans. 8°. *J. Haviland*, 1633. L(lacks V8).; F(imp.).AAS.HD(lacks A4).
Dedic. on A2ʳ varies: *see* Addenda.

18846 **Origen.** [Heading A1ʳ:] Omelia origeīs de beata maria magdalena. [*Ed.* W. Menyman.] 8° in 10. *In alma ciuitate londoñ ad rogatū w. Menymā* [*W. Faques,* 1505?] L.M.
1st 2 words of title xylographic.

18847 — [A trans.] An homilie of Marye Magdalene, declaring her feruēt loue and zele towards Christ. Newly translated. (An homilye of Abraham.) 16° in 8's. (*R. Wolfe,*) 1565. L.

18848 — [Anr. trans.] 8°. (*f. H. Sutton,*) [1555?] O(frag.).

18849 **Original.** The original & sprynge of all sectes & orders by whome, whā or were [*sic*] they beganne. *Tr.* out of hye Dutch [by M. Coverdale?]. 8°. (*Southwarke, J. Nicolson f. J. Gough,*) 1537. L(2).O.C.C⁹.SCL.; F.
Copies vary only in numbering of fol. 23; misnumbered '2' in I L; corrected to '23' in I L,O,C,C⁹,F.
— The originall of idolatries. 1624. *See* 4747.

Orlando. The historie of Orlando Furioso. 1594. *See* 12265.

Orlers, Jean Janszoon. *See* 17676.

18850 **Ormerod, Oliver.** The picture of a papist: or, a relation of the damnable heresies. Together with a discourse of the late treason. Whereunto is annexed Pagano-Papismus. 4°. [*R. Bradock*] f. *N. Fosbrooke*, 1606. Ent. 9 de. 1605. L.O.C.D.YK.+; F.HN.LC.U.Y.
18851 — The picture of a puritane: or, a relation of the opinions, and practises of the Anabaptists in Germanie, and of the puritanes in England. Wherunto is annexed Puritano-papismus. 4°. *E. A[llde]* f. *N. Fosbroke*, 1605. Ent. 1 oc. L.O.C².D.E.+; F.BO³.LC.NY(imp.).U.+
18852 — [Anr. ed.] Newly corrected and enlarged. 4°. *E. A[llde]* f. *N. Fosbroke*, 1605. L.O².C².C⁵.M.+; HN.HD.N.Y(2).

18853 **Ornithoparchus, Andreas.** Andreas Ornithoparcus his Micrologus, or introduction: containing the art of singing. *Tr.* J. Douland. fol. [*T. Snodham*] f. *T. Adams*, 1609. Ent. 20 ja. L.O³.O⁵.C.E².+; F.HN.CAL. CH.NY.+

Orpheus. Heire begynnis the traitie of Orpheus. [1508?] *See* 13166.

Orpheus Junior, *pseud. See* 24609.

18854 **Orphinstraunge, John.** The blessed publicane. Briefly shewing foorth the happy estate of humble repentant sinners. [In verse.] 4°. *T. C[otes]* f. *J. Orphinstraunge*, [1625–30?] F.

18855 **Ortelius, Abraham.** Theatrum orbis terrarum. The theatre of the whole world. *Tr.* by W. B[edwell?] fol. [*Eliot's Court Press* f.] *J. Norton* (*a. J. Bill,*) 1606 [1608?] L.O.C.E.LIV³.+; F.HN.CB.MICH.N.+
Maps pr. in Antwerp by the Officina Plantiniana.
18856 — Abraham Ortelius his epitome of the Theater of the worlde nowe latlye, renewed and augmented by M. Coignet. (An addition to the Epitomies.) obl.8°. [*Antwerp,*] f. *J. Shawe, London*, 1603. Ent. 16 ap. 1602. L.C(imp.).C⁵.D.E².+; F.HN.CB.HD.N.+
Letterpress tp, usually cancelled, present in a copy sold Sotheby's 20 Jan. 1948, lot 357. Tr. from Coignet's French abridgement, Antwerp, 1602.
18857 — [Anr. trans.] An epitome of Ortelius his Theatre of the world. Amplyfied with new mappes wanting in the Latin editions. obl.8°. [*Antwerp,*] (*typis H. Swingenij*) [f.] *J. Norton, London*, [1601?] L.O³.C.; F.CB.HD (lacks col.).N.NY.+
Tr. from Latin abridgement, Antwerp, 1595.

Orthius, Wygandus. *See* 11758.

Orthographical Declaration. The orthographiall [*sic*] declaration: containing, a briefe advertisement. 1616. *See* 6455.5.

18858 **Ortiz, Antonio.** A relation of the solemnetie wherewith the catholike princes were receyued in the Inglish colledge of Valladolid. *Tr.* F. Rivers. 8°. *Printed at N.* [*Antwerp, A. Conincx,*] 1601. L.L².BUTE.; F.Y. A&R 584.

18859 **Ortuñez de Calahorra, Diego.** The mirrour of princely deedes and knighthood. *Tr.* M. T(yler.) [Anon.] 4° in 8's. *T. East,* [1578.] Ent. 4 au. 1578. L.; HN.

18860 — [Anr. ed.] The first part of the mirrour of princely deedes. 4° in 8's. *T. East,* [1580?] L(lacks tp). C(imp.).; F.HN.

18861 — [Anr. ed.] 4° in 8's. *T. Este,* [1599?] L.O.C(imp.).; HN.HD.

18862 — The second part of the first booke of the myrrour of knighthood. [Anon.] *Tr.* R. P[arry.] 4° in 8's. *T. Este,* 1585. Ent. 24 au. 1582. F.HN.

18862.5 — [A variant, w. imprint:] *T. Est,* 1585. P.

18863 — [Anr. ed.] 4° in 8's. *T. Este,* 1599. L.O.; HN. Cleveland PL.

18864 — The third part of the first booke, of the mirrour of knighthood. [Anon.] *Tr.* R. P[arry.] 4° in 8's. *T. East,* [1586?] F.HN.

18865 — [Anr. ed.] 4° in 8's. *T. Este,* [1598–99?] L(lacks Ll4). O.; F.HN.

18866 — The second part of the myrror of knighthood. [i.e. Bks. 4, 5; by P. de la Sierra.] Now newly *tr.* by R. P[arry.] 4° in 8's. *T. Este,* 1583. L.; F.HN.

18867 — [Anr. ed.] 4° in 8's. *T. Este,* 1598. O.DUL.; F(lacks tp). HN(lacks tp).

18868 — The sixth booke of the myrrour of knighthood. [By M. Martínez.] *Tr.* R. P[arry.] 4°. *E. Allde f. C. Burby,* 1598. Ent. 12 ap. 1597. O.C.; F(2).HN.

18869 — The seuenth booke of the myrrour of knighthood. [By M. Martínez.] Englished [by] (L. A.) 4°. *T. Purfoot f. C. Burby,* 1598. Ent. 12 ap. 1597. L.O.C.; F.HN.

18870 — The eighth booke of the myrror of knighthood. [By M. Martínez.] Englished [by] (L. A.) 4°. *T. Creede f. C. Burbey,* 1599. Ent. 12 ap. 1597. L.O.C.; F.HN.

18871 — The ninth part of the mirrour of knight-hood. [By M. Martínez. *Tr.* R. Parry?] 4°. [*S. Stafford*] *f. C. Burbie,* 1601. Ent. 12 ap. 1597. L(imp.).O.C.; F.HN.

Ortus. *See* Hortus.

18872 **Os.** Os facies mentū. *Lat. a. Eng.* 4°. (*Rothomagi, in off. L. hostingue et J. loys f. M. coeffin dwelyng at exeter,*) [1505.] F.

18873 — Now = 23196a.2.

18873.3 — [Anr. ed.] 4°. (*W. de worde,* 1508 (11 mr.)) L. (Formerly 23194)

18873.5 — [Anr. ed.] 4°. (*Antwerpie, per me J. de Doesborch,*) [c. 1510.] L(imp.).; HN. (Formerly 23195) Title xylographic. Third line of English text begins: 'an eyelyde anye [*sic*]'.

18873.7 — [Anr. ed.] 4°. [*Antwerp, G. Back,* c. 1510.] L²(frag. 17). Same line of English text as 18873.5 begins: 'an eyelyde an eye'.

18874 — [Anr. ed.] 4°. (*W. de worde,* 1512.) F.

18874.5 — [Anr. ed.] 4°. (*per R. Pynson,* 1516.) c(Syn.6.51.22, two leaves). (Formerly 1380 and pt. of 23180)

18875 — [Anr. ed.] 4°. (*W. de worde,* 1518.) L(imp.).

Osb., M. *See* 18876.

Osborne, George. Almanacks. 1622, etc. *See* 494 sqq.

Osborne, Henry. *See* Indulgences 67A.

18876 **Osborne, M.** A newe ballade of a louer extollinge his ladye. [Signed M. Osb.] *Ballad.* s.sh.fol. *W. Gryffith,* 1568. ?Ent. to T. Colwell 1562–63. L.

18877 **Osiander, Andreas.** The coniectures of the ende of the worlde, *tr.* by G. Joye. 8°. [*Antwerp, S. Mierdman,*] 1548 (my.) L.O.C.M.; F.

18878 — How and whither a christen man ought to flye the horrible plage of the pestilence. [On Psalm 91.] *Tr.* (M. C[overdale.]) 8°. (*Southwarke, J. Nicolson f. J. Gough,*) 1537. L.; F. Reprinted in 17000; enlarged in 4303.

18879 — [Anr. ed. Anon.] 8°. L. *Askell* (*f. T. Purfoote,*) [1564.] Ent. 1563–64. L(destroyed).O.O¹⁴.C⁵.C¹⁰.; F.HN. — *See also* 5992.5.

18880 **Osiander, Lucas.** A manuell or briefe volume of controuersies of religion. Written in Latine and now Englished with some additions and corrections. 8°. *H. Lownes,* 1606. Ent. 7 oc. 1605. L.C.YK.; F.HART. HD(2, 1 imp.).U.

18881 — [Anr. issue, w. cancel tp, init. L. O.] Enchiridion controuersiarum: or, a briefe manuell of controuersies. 8°. *J. B[eale] f. J. Boler,* 1633. C.D.

18882 **Osman II,** *Sultan of Turkey.* A true and faithfull relation, . . . concerning the death of Sultan Osman. 1622. Now = Newsbooks 71A.

— A true relation of the murther of Osman. 1622. *See* Newsbooks 60.

18883 — The strangling and death of the great Turke. 1622. Now = Newsbooks 62.

18884 **Osorio da Fonseca, Jeronimo,** *Bp.* Hieronymi Osorii . . . de gloria, libri V. . . . Eiusdem de nobilitate, libri V. Omnia nunc castigatiora edita. 16° in 8's. *H. Middletonus, imp. W. N[orton],* 1580. Ent. to J. Harrison the elder 3 se. L.L².C.EX.

18884.3 — [A variant, w. imprint:] *H. Middletonus, imp. J. H[arrison,]* 1580. C².Cecil Clarabut, London.; F.ILL. Williams C.

18884.7 — [A variant, w. imprint:] *H. Middletonus, imp. F. C[oldock,]* 1580. O.C¹⁷.A.E².STU.

18885 — [Anr. ed.] 16° in 8's. *R. Field, imp. J. Harrisoni,* 1589. L(tp only, Harl.5990/62). C.WIN².

18886 — [A trans.] The fiue bookes of the famous, . . . man, H. Osorius, contayninge a discourse of ciuill, and christian nobilitie. *Tr.* W. Blandie. 4°. *T. Marsh,* 1576. Ent. to T. Orwin 23 jn. 1591. L.O.C.G².P.+; F.HN.CHI.Y.

18887 — An epistle of the reuerend father to Elizabeth quene of England. *Tr.* R. Shacklock. 8°. *Antwerp, Æ. Diest,* 1565. L.O.C².C⁴.YK(lacks tp).+; F.STL.Y. A&R 586. Running title: 'A pearle for a prynce'; answered by 7679, 12598. Probably later ed. than 18888.

18888 — [Anr. ed.] 8°. *Antwerp, J. Latius,* 1565. L.L².O(2).DE.; F.HN.N. A&R 585.

18889 — A learned and very eloquent treatie [*sic*], writen in Latin by H. Osorius, wherein he confuteth a certayne aunswere made by M. W. Haddon. *Tr.* J. Fen. 8°. *Louanii, ap. J. Foulerum,* 1568. L.L².O.P.W.+; F.CH.CU.TEX. A&R 587. Answers 12598; answered by 12593.

18890 **Ossoliński, Jerzy,** *Count.* A true copy of the Latine oration of the excellent lord George Ossolinski. With the translation. 4°. [*G. Purslowe*] *f. W. Lee,* 1621. Ent. 5 ap. L.O.C.D.E.+; F.HN.HD.N.Y.+ Italic text A3ʳ–A4ᵛ in two settings: A3ʳ 3rd line from bottom: 'Ottomanarum' (HN) or 'Otto-manorum' (HD). Knuttel I.3159 lists a Dutch tr. w. tp stating: 'Na de copy, ghedruct te Londen by B. Norton ende J. Bill.'

18891 **Ostend.** A breefe declaration of that which is happened as-well within as without Oastend. 4°. *Middle-borrow printed by R. Schilders. At London printed for M. Law,* 1602. Ent. 2 fb. L.O.; F.HN.

18892 — A dialogue and complaint made vpon the siedge of Oastend, made by the king of Spaine, the archduke, . . . to the prince Morrice, *tr.* 4°. [*R. Read*] *f. M. Law,* 1602. Ent. 25 fb. O.O⁵.DUL.HAGUE.; HN.

18892.3 — The oppugnation, and fierce siege of Ostend, by the archduke Albertus his forces, the fift day of June (after their writing). *Tr.* out of Dutch. 4°. *V. S[immes] f. T. Pavier,* 1601. Ent. 5 au. HN. Text begins A3ʳ. This and following 2 issues are, except for added paragraphs at end, from the same setting reimposed.

18892.7 — [Anr. issue, w. text beginning A2ʳ.] HD(lacks tp).

18893 — [Anr. issue, w. title:] Newes from Ostend, of, the oppugnation, . . . the fift day of Julie [*sic*] (after their writing). Now newly imprinted; whereunto are added other newes. L. Text begins A1ᵛ.

18894 — Further newes of Ostend. Wherein is declared such accidents as haue happened since the former edition. 4°. *V. S[immes] f. T. Pavier,* 1601. Ent. 9 se. L.

18895 — A true historie of the memorable siege of Ostend. *Tr.* E. Grimeston. 4°. [*V. Simmes*] *f. E. Blount,* 1604. Ent. 20 se. L.O.C².D⁶.E².+; F.HN.HD(imp.).N.NY.

18895.5 **Oteringham.** A most certaine report of a monster borne at Oteringham in Holdernesse, the 9. of Aprill. 1595. 4°. *P. S[hort,] sold by T. Millington*, [1595.] Ent. to P. Short a. T. Millington 26 my. 1595. L.G².

18896 **Otes, Samuel.** An explanation of the generall epistle of saint Jude. Delivered in one and forty sermons. fol. *E. Purslow f. N. Bourne*, 1633. Ent. 12 my. 1630. L.O.C⁵.D.G².+ ; F.HN.HD.NY¹¹.Y.+

Other. Other thus it is: [etc. 1570?] *See* 7550.

18897 **Oudin, César.** A grammar Spanish and English. *Tr.* J. W[odroephe?] Who hath also *tr.* the five dialogues of J. de Luna, annexed. 8°. *J. Haviland f. E. Blount*, 1622. L.O.C³.G².M².+ ; F.HN.HD.NY⁵.PH.+

18898 **Oughtred, William.** Arithmeticæ in numeris et specie-bus institutio. 8°. *ap. T. Harperum*, 1631. L.O.D.E². ETON.+ ; HN.CU.ILL.MICH. Lownes.

18899 — The circle of proportion, and the horizontall instrument. *Tr.* W. Forster. 4°. *A. Mathewes*, 1632. Ent. 18 my. 0.0³.C(w. engr. tp of 18899b.5 inserted).PLUME. Regarding cancels and the contents of individual copies of the various issues (some including 18899c and 18901a) *see Transactions of the Cambridge Bib. Soc.*, IV (1968), pp. 372–7, 382.

18899a — [Anr. issue, w. engr. tp:] The circles. *f. E. Allen maker of these and all other mathematical instruments*, 1632. L.L³⁰.O⁸.C.YK.+ ; F.HN.ILL.PH. Horblit.

18899b — [Anr. issue, w. cancel letterpress tp:] With an Additament [18899c]. *A. Mathewes, sold by N. Bourne*, 1633. L.L³⁸.O.C⁴.ETON.+ ; HD.WIS(lacks tp)*. Horblit.

18899b.5 — [Anr. issue, w. engr. tp, w. imprint:] *f. E. Allen . . .*, 1639. L.C(engr. tp only, bd. w. 18899).; Horblit.

18899c — An addition unto the use of the circles of proportion. And is to follow after the 111 page of the first part. [Anon.] 4°. *A. Mathewes*, 1633. L.L³⁰.O.C.ETON.+ ; CU.HD.WIS. Horblit.
This is linked on the tp of 18899b, but also found bd. w. the other issues.

18899c.5 — The description and use of the double horizontall dyall. [Anon.] 8°. *M. Flesher*, 1632. L¹⁹.C¹⁵.PLUME.; HD.

18900 — [Anr. ed. Init. W. O.] 8°. *M. Flesher*, 1636. L.O.; LC.

18901 — The new artificial gauging line or rod. 8°. *A. Mathewes*, 1633. Ent. 19 oc. 0.0³.; HN. Horblit.

18901a — To the English gentrie, . . . against R. Delamain, in a pamphlet called Grammelogia [6542]. 4°. [*A. Mathewes*, 1634?] L.L³⁰.O.C.E.+ ; HD. Horblit(2). Bd. w. various issues of 18899 sqq.
— *tr. See* 10558.5.

Outis, Benthelmai, *pseud. See* 24174.

18901a.5 **Outlawry.** An act to stay the reversing of utlaries after judgement, and to put in baile upon writtes of error, [etc. Brief of a bill in Parliament.] s.sh. 4°. [*London*, 1624.] L(Harl.MS.7617/16).
The MS. endorsement notes a committee meeting on 20 Apr. 1624.

Outred, Marcelline, *tr. See* 5723, 5723.5.

18902 **Outreman, Philippe d'.** The true christian catholique or the maner how to live christianly. *Tr.* J. Heigham. 8°. *S. Omers*, [*C. Boscard,*] 1622. L.L².O.USHAW. YK.+ ; F.HN.CAL².KAN.TEX. A&R 588.

Overall, John, *Bp.* Norwich. Visitation Articles. *See* 10292.
— *See also* 8578.5.

18903 **Overbury, Sir Thomas.** Sir Thomas Overbury his observations in his travailes 1609. 4°. [*B. Alsop f. J. Parker,*] 1626. Ent. to W. Barrett a. L. Lisle 28 ja. 1616; to J. Parker 13 ap. 1626. L.O.C.D.E.+ ; F.HN. HD.N.Y.+

18903.5 — A wife, now a widowe. [In verse. Anon.] 8°. [*T. Creede*] *f. L. L'isle*, 1614. Ent. 13 de. 1613. O.C².

18904 — [Anr. ed., enlarged.] A wife now the widdow of Sir T. Overburye. Whereunto are added many witty characters. 4°. [*E. Griffin*] *f. L. Lisle*, 1614. L.O(2).; F.

18905 — Third impression; with addition of other characters. 4°. *E. Griffin f. L. Lisle*, 1614. L.L³⁰.WN.; HN.HD.Y². Pirie.
HD, HN have an added halfsheet, w. 1st leaf signed C4 and containing 4 characters, not present in L.

18906 — Fourth impression, enlarged with more characters. 4°. *G. Eld f. L. Lisle*, 1614. L.O.C².; F.

Overbury, Sir Thomas—*cont.*

18907 — Fift impression. 4°. *T. C[reede] f. L. Lisle*, 1614. L.O⁵.; F.HD.

18908 — [Anr. ed.] New and choise characters, of seueral authors: together with The wife, written by Syr T. Overburie. With other things added to this sixt impression. 8°. *T. Creede f. L. L'isle*, 1615. L.O (imp.).; F.
32 of the additional characters have been attrib. to J. Webster.

18909 — [Anr. ed.] Sir Thomas Overburie his wife, with new elegies, [etc.] Editio septima. 8°. *E. Griffin f. L. L'isle*, 1616. L.O³⁸.E.; F.BO⁵.HD. Pirie.

18910 — Eight impression. 8°. *E. Griffin f. L. L'isle*, 1616. O(imp.).; F.BO(imp.).ILL.JH².Y.+

18911 — Ninth impression augmented. 8°. *E. Griffin f. L. L'isle*, 1616. L.C².BTL.; F.HN.ILL.NY. Pirie.+

18912 — Tenth impression. 8°. *E. Griffin f. L. L'isle*, 1618. L.L³⁸.O(lacks ¶8).C¹⁵.DUL.+ ; F(imp.).HN.HD. Pirie.

18913 — Eleventh impression. 8°. [*A. Griffin*] *f. L. Lisle, sold by H. Seile*, 1622. L.L³.O(2, 1 imp.).C.M⁴.; F.HN.HD.PN. Pirie.+

18914 — Twelfth impression. 8°. *Dublin*, [*A. Johnson f.*] *Co. of Statrs.*, 1626. L.C(2).D⁶(2).; F. Pirie.
Unsold sheets reissued in 1655 w. cancel tp as Wing O 610.

18915 — Twelfth [*sic*] impression. 8°. *I. J[aggard] f. R. Swayne*, 1627. Ent. 28 jy. 1626. L.L⁶.O.C⁴.USHAW.+ ; F.HN. CHI.HD.Y.+

18916 — Thirteenth impression. 8°. [*J. Legat*] *f. R. Allot*, 1628. Ent. 8 ap. L.O.CHATS.LIV³.SHEF.+ ; F.HN.CHI.HD.Y.+

18917 — Foureteenth impression. 8°. [*B. Alsop a. T. Fawcett*] *f. R. Allot*, 1630. L.O.C.CARTMEL.E.+ ; F.HN.COR. Pirie.

18918 — Fifteenth impression. 8°. *R B[adger] f. R. Allot*, 1632. L.O.C.D⁹.M.+ ; F.HN.HD.N.Y.+

18919 — Sixteenth impression. 8°. *J. Haviland f. A. Crooke*, 1638. Ent. to Legat a. Crooke 1 jy. 1637. L.O.C. C².E².+ ; F.HN.HD.ILL. Hunter C.+
— *tr. See* 18975.

18919.3 — The bloody downfall of adultery. Murder, ambition, at the end of which are added Westons, and Mistris Turners last teares, who suffered execution the 14. of Nouember last. 1615. 4°. [*G. Eld*] *f. R. H[iggen-botham*, 1615.] C.; F(lacks tp).HN.HD.
(Formerly 18921) This app. reprints the poem 'Mistris Turnores teares' ent. to J. Trundle 29 no. 1615.

18919.7 — [Anr. issue reimposed w. altered headlines and title:] The just downefall of ambition, adultery. Murder. *f. R. H[iggenbotham*, 1615.] O.; F(lacks tp).
(Formerly 18920a)

18920 — [Anr. ed.] The just down ⟨fall of⟩ ambition, adultery, and murder. Where-unto are added 3. notorious sinners. Weston. M. Turner and Fran⟨klin.⟩ To these ⟨is⟩ joyned an elegy, [by I. T.] 4°. [*G. Eld*, 1616?] L(tp defective). 𝕬

18920a — Now = 18919.7.
18921 — Now = 18919.3.
18921.3 — The portracture of Sir Thomas Overbury knight. [Engr. with verses by W. B.] s.sh.fol. *C. Holland*, [1616?] Ent. to L. Lisle 20 ja. 1616. L⁵(Lemon 141). C⁶.; National Gallery of Art, Washington, D.C.
See Hind II.186–8.

18921.5 — [Anr. state, w. imprint:] *sould by J. Hind*, [1620?] L(Print Dept.).

18921.7 — A sorrowfull song. Made upon the murther and untimely death of Sir Thomas Overbury knight. *Ballad.* 2 pts. s.sh.fol. [*G. Eld*] *f. J. W.* [i.e. *White or Wright*, 1615.] C⁶(I.216–17ᵛ).
13541.3 pr. on verso.
— For other works dealing with Overbury's murder, see 3720, 6342, 7626, 7627.5, 11332, 11332.5, 18524, 21406.

18922 **Overs, John.** The true history of the life and death of old J. Overs. 8°. *N. a. J. Okes*, 1637. Ent. to J. Okes 25 ja. HN.

18923 **Overthrows.** Three great overthrowes one in the Palatinate, [etc.] 1622 (4 my.) Now = Newsbooks 44.

18924 **Overton, John.** Jacobs troublesome iourney to Bethel. [A treatise on Gen. 33. 1–4.] 8°. *Oxford, J. Barnes*, 1586. L.O.C.P.; F.

18925 Overton, William, *Bp.* A godlye, and pithie exhortation, made to the iudges of Sussex. 8°. *R. Newbery a. H. Bynneman,* [1579?] Ent. to H. Bynneman 12 fb. 1579. L.L².O.P.YK.; F(lacks D7).

18926 — Oratio doctissima et grauissima, . . . ad præbendarios, in visitatione ecclesiæ. 4°. *Oxoniæ, J. Barnesius,* 1601. O.O¹³.C.PLUME.YK.+

— *See also* 10224.

18926.1 Ovidius Naso, Publius. [*Collections.*] P. Ouidii Nasonis opera, veterum exemplarum auxilio emendata. H. Glareani annotationes in Metamorphosin. Item, fragmenta epigramaton, & carmen ad Pisonem. 8°. *J. Kingstonus,* 1570. ETON.M.OS.; F.
Text apparently includes only the Metamorphoses and a Vita.

18926.3 — [Anr. ed.] 8°. *in aed. H. Binneman,* 1572. L(tp only, Harl.5927/126).

18926.5 — [Anr. ed.] 8°. *T. Vautrollerius,* 1576. O.
Vautrollier granted 10-year patent to pr. Ovid's works in Latin 19 June 1574; *see* Arber II.746, 886. *See also* Greg, *Companion,* pp. 266–8.

18926.7 — [Anr. ed.] 8°. *H. Mideltonus, imp. J. Harison,* 1585. C².

18926.9 — [Anr. ed.] 8°. *J. H*[*arrison 3,*] *imp. J. Harisoni* [*1,*] 1602. L(tp only, Harl.5919/55).

18927 — P. Ouidii Nasonis. Fastorum lib. vi. Tristium lib. v. De Ponto lib. iiii. In Ibim. Ad Liuiam. [*Ed.* A. Naugerius and others.] 16° in 8's. *T. Vautrollerius,* 1583. O.C(imp.).EX.
For Vautrollier's patent *see* 18926.5.

18927.5 — [Anr. ed.] Pub. Ouidii Nasonis, [etc.] Ex A. Naugerij, castigationibus. 16° in 8's. *ex typ. Soc. Stat.,* 1614. Ass'd by J. Harrison to the English Stock 21 se. 1612; 5 mr. 1620. L(tp only, Harl.5937/290).O. Swaffham Parish Church, Norfolk.

18928 — Publii Ouidii Nasonis Heroidum epistolae. Amorum libri iii. De arte amandi libri iii. De remedio amoris lib. ii. Omnia ex acuratiss. A. Naugerij castigatione. 16° in 8's. *T. Vautrollerius,* 1583. L(tp only, Ames I.412).C.DUR⁵.
For Vautrollier's patent *see* 18926.5. Includes A. Sabinus' Epistolae tres.

18928a — [Anr. ed.] 16° in 8's. *T. Vautrollerius,* 1583. Eustace F. Bosanquet (lacks tp, untraced).

18929 — [Anr. ed.] 8°. *R. F*[*ield,*] *imp. J. Harisoni,* 1594. L(tp only, Harl.5936/271, date cropt).O⁶.; HN.

18929.3 — [Anr. ed.] 8°. *J. H*[*arrison 3,*] *imp. J. Harisoni* [*1,*] 1602. L(tp only, Harl.5993/88).

18929.5 — [Anr. ed.] 8°. [*W. Stansby*] *ex typ. Soc. Stat.,* 1631. Ass'd by J. Harrison to the English Stock 21 se. 1612; 5 mr. 1620. C.; HD.

18929.7 — [Anr. ed.] 8°. [*F. Kingston*] *ex typ. Soc. Stat.,* 1635. L(tp only, Ames II.1224).Quaritch.

18930 — [Anr. ed., w. title:] Pub. Ouidii Nasonis Heroidum epistolæ, unà cum A. Sabini epistolis tribus. Amorum, libri III. [etc.] Accesserunt annotatiunculæ quædam. 8°. [*Cambridge,*] *ex Acad. typog.,* 1635. O.C.C².ETON.; F.ILL. Western Ontario U(S.L.S.).

— [*Amores.*] Certaine of Ouids elegies. By C. Marlow. [c. 1599?] *See* 6350.

18931 — Ouids elegies: three bookes. By C. M[arlowe.] Epigrames by J. D. [*Sir J. Davies.*] 8°. *Middlebourgh* [i.e. *London,* after 1602.] O(Douce O 31).
Collates A–F⁸G⁴; oblong woodcut orn. on tp. This ed. is later than 18931a, q.v.

18931a — [Anr. ed., w. title:] All Ouids elegies: 3. bookes. By C. M. Epigrams by J. D. 8°. *Middlebourgh* [i.e. *London,* after 1602.] L⁶.O(Mason AA 207).; HN.
Collates A–F⁸G⁴; orn. of asterisks on tp. This is earlier than 18931. Regarding the order of eds. *see Studies in Bibliography,* XXV(1972), pp. 149–72, especially p. 172 for evidence bearing on the date.

18932 — [Anr. ed.] 8°. *Middlebourgh* [i.e. *London,* c. 1630.] L.L⁶.O(Mal. 368/3).Juel-Jensen.; F.HN.HD.PML.Y.+
Collates A–F⁸; orn. of 3 leaves and 2 hands on tp.

18933 — [Anr. ed.] 8°. *Middlebourgh* [i.e. *London, T. Cotes?* c. 1640.] L(2).O(Mal. 133/12).O⁷.C³.SHEF.; F.HN.HD. N.NY.+
Collates A–F⁸; square of 4 type orns. on tp. L,HD copies bd. w. other Ovid works printed by Cotes 1639–40; probably M. Sparke was the publisher.

18934 — [*Ars Amatoria.*] The flores of Ovide de arte amandi with theyr englysshe afore them. 4°. (*in ed. wynandi de worde,* 1513.) L.YK(lacks tp).

Ovidius Naso, Publius—*cont.*
Note: in 18935–7 former STC numbering is disregarded.

18935 — [Heading A1ʳ:] Publii. [*sic*] Ouidii Nasonis de arte amandi: or, the art of loue. [*Tr.* T. Heywood.] 8°. [*London?* c. 1625.] L³⁰.O.C³.; F(3).HD(2).ILL(2).Y.
C1ʳ line 11 of text: 'to thee by my new art,'; C1ʳ line 9 of text: 'barke'. In some copies p. 10 misnumbered '01'; both at F,ILL. At L is a copy of this ed. w. added tp dated 1650.

18935.3 — [Anr. ed., w. heading A1ʳ:] Publii Ouidii [etc.] 8°. [*London?* c. 1625.] O.
C1ʳ line 11 of text: 'to thee by my new art,'; C1ʳ line 9 of text: 'Barke'.

18935.5 — [Anr. ed.] 8°. [*London?* c. 1625.] L.
C1ʳ line 11 of text: 'to thee by my new Art,'.

18935.7 — [Anr. ed.] 8°. [*London?* c. 1625.] F.N.
C1ʳ line 11 of text: 'to thee by new art,' (omits 'my').

18935a — [Anr. ed.] 8°. [*London?* c. 1625.] O.HETH.; HN.
C1ʳ line 11 of text: 'for thee by my new art,'.

18936 — [Engr. tp only:] Loues schoole. Publii Ouidii Nasonis de arte amandi. Or the art of loue. 8°. *Amsterdam, N. J. Visscher,* [c. 1625.] L.L³⁰.O.C³.G⁴.+; F(2).HN. HD.ILL.Y.
Since the engr. tp is found bound w. copies of most of the preceding eds. it is impossible to determine which, if any, it properly belongs to.

18937 — [Anr. ed., w. letterpress tp:] Publii [etc.] 8°. [*T. Cotes,* c. 1640.] L.L¹³.O⁷(lacks tp).SHEF.; F.HN.HD.Y. Pearson.
C1ʳ line 11 of text: 'for thee by my new Art,'.

18938 — [*Epistolæ ex Ponto.*] Ovid de Ponto. Containing foure books of elegies. *Tr.* [into verse] by W. S(altonstall.) 8°. *T. Cotes f. M. Sparke junior,* 1639. Ent. 13 fb. 1638. L.O.C³.G⁴.SHEF.+; F.HN.HD.ILL.Y.+

18939 — [A variant, w. 'Veniam . . .' on tp of 18938 replaced by:] Second edition. *T. Cotes f. M. Sparke junior,* 1640. L.O.C.C¹².LINC.+; F.HN.CAL⁷.HD.NCU.+

18939.5 — [*Epistolæ Heroidum.*] The heroycall epistles of . . . Publius Ouidius Naso, in Englishe verse: *tr.* G. Turberuile with A. Sabinus aunsweres. 8°. *H. Denham,* 1567. Ent. 1566–67. L(imp.).; F(imp.). ILL(imp.).
The colophon is undated; 'D' of sig. D1 is beneath the space following 'fall.' in the line above. This ed. has errata on X3ᵛ. The tp, present but not conjugate in F, ILL copies, is the same setting as 18940.

18940 — [Anr. ed.] 8°. *H. Denham,* 1567 (19 mr.) L(lacks col.). C²(lacks col.).; HN(quires L,U,X only, w. 18940.5). N(imp.).PFOR.
The colophon is dated '19. Mar. 1567.'; 'D' of sig. D1 is beneath 's' in 'drops'.

18940.5 — [Anr. ed.] 8°. *H. Denham,* 1567. O(lacks col.).; HN(imp.).HD.
The colophon is dated '1567.'; 'D' of sig. D1 is beneath 'to'. The HN copy on University Microfilms reel 347 has the 2nd quire from 18941, quires L,U,X from 18940, and the rest from the present ed.

18941 — [Anr. ed.] 8°. *H. Denham,* 1569. O(lacks col.).; F.HN.

18942 — [Anr. ed.] 8°. *H. Denham,* [1570?] L.O.; F.

18943 — [Anr. ed.] 8°. *J. Charlewoode,* [c. 1584.] L(2, 1 imp.). O.LIV.M.; F.HN.ILL.WIS.
Denham's rights yielded to Statrs. Co. 8 Jan. 1584; *see* Arber II.789.

18944 — [Anr. ed.] 8°. *S. Stafford,* 1600. Ent. 3 mr. L(lacks X8). O.C¹².M²(imp.)*.Juel-Jensen.; F(2).N.

18945 — Ovid's heroicall epistles. Englished by W. S(altonstall.) 8°. *R. B*[*adger*] *f. M. Sparke,* 1636. Ent. 7 de. 1635. BTU(imp.).; F.

18945.5 — [Anr. issue, w. engr. tp:] Second edytion. *R. B*[*adger*] *f. M. Sparke,* 1637. O(impr. cropt).; HD.

18946 — [Anr. ed.] 8°. *J. D*[*awson*] *sold by M. Sparke junior,* 1639. L.O(lacks plates).C.G⁴.LINC.+; F.HN.CAL.HD (lacks some plates).Y.+
At least L, C, HN have engr. tp as in 18945.5. Copperplates pasted in.

18947 — Ovids heroical epistles, Englished by J. Sherburne. 12°. *E. G*[*riffin*] *f. W. Cooke,* 1639. Ent. 16 oc. 1638. L(2).O.C³.; F.HN.HD.ILL.

18947.5 — [*Fasti.*] P. Ouidii Nasonis Fastorum ad Caesarem Germanicum, libri sex. 8°. *T. Vautrollerius,* 1574. L(tp only, Harl.5990/18, date cropt).R.
For Vautrollier's patent *see* 18926.5.

Ovidius Naso, Publius—*cont.*

18948 — Ovids festivalls, or Romane calendar, *tr.* into English verse equinumerally, by J. Gower, master of arts. 8°. *R. Daniel, pr. to the Univ. of Cambridge, sold by M. S[parke] junior, London,* 1640. Ent. to A. Griffin 12 oc. 1639. L.O.C².E.P.+; F.HN.HD. N.NY.+

Copies vary in the red printing on tp.

18948.5 — [A variant, w. imprint:] *R. Daniel, pr. to the Univ. of Cambridge,* 1640. O⁷.; BO.NY.

18949 — [*Ibis.*] Ovid his inuectiue against Ibis. *Tr.* into English meeter (T. Underdown.) 8°. *T. East & H. Middleton,* 1569. Ent. to T. East 1568–69. L.O(3).M.; HN.CAL. ILL(imp.).

18950 — [Anr. ed.] 8°. *H. Bynneman,* 1577. Ent. 1 jy. L.O(2). c(lacks M4).C².; F.HN.HD.N(imp.).

18951 — [*Metamorphoses.*] Fabularum Ouidii interpretatio, ethica, physica, et historica, tradita in academia Regiomontana à G. Sabino, & edita industria T. T[homas.] Accessit ex N. Comitis mythologijs de fabularum vtilitate, tractatio. 8°. *Cantabrigiæ, ex off. T. Thomæ,* 1584. L.O.C.A.D.+; F.HN. CHI.HD.

See also 18926.1.

18951.5 — P. Ouidii Nasonis Metamorphoseon libri xv. Ab A. Naugerio castigati, & V. Giselini scholijs illustrati. 16° in 8's. *T. Vautrollerius,* 1582. L.; F.ILL.

For Vautrollier's patent *see* 18926.5.

18952 — [Anr. ed.] 16° in 8's. *R. Field, imp. J. Harrisoni,* 1589. L(tp only, Harl.5990/63).O.

18952.1 — [Anr. ed.] 16° in 8's. *ex typ. J. H[arrison 3,] imp. J. Harisoni senioris,* 1601. Berthold Wolpe, London.

18952.3 — [Anr. ed.] P. Ovdii [*sic*] Nasonis. Metamorphosis. Ex accuratissimis castigationibus emendata. 8°. *N. Okes pro J. Harrison,* 1612. Ass'd by J. Harrison to the English Stock 21 se. C.DNPK.

18952.4 — [Anr. ed.] 8°. [*R. Field*] *ex typ. Soc. Stat.,* 1617. F.

18952.5 — [Anr. ed.] 8°. [*R. Field*] *ex typ. Soc. Stat.,* 1620. Ent. 5 mr. O.

18952.6 — [Anr. ed.] 8°. *ex typ. Soc. Stat.,* 1628. Y.

18952.7 — [Anr. ed.] 8°. *ex typ. Soc. Stat.,* 1630. L(tp only, Ames II.925).

18952.8 — [Anr. ed.] P. Ovidii Nasonis Metamorphosis. Ex accuratissimis castigationibus emendata. 8°. *ex typ. Soc. Stat.,* 1633. L(tp only, Ames II.1022).C.

18952.9 — [Anr. ed.] 8°. [*F. Kingston,*] *ex typ. Soc. Stat.,* 1636. O(J, tp only).

18953 — P. Ovidii Nasonis Metamorphoseωn libri xv. Editio prioribus castigatior. (G. Bersmanni annotationes.) 8°. *Abredoniae, E. Rabanus, imp. D. Melvill,* 1630. A.M.

18954 — [Anr. ed.] 12°. *Cantabrigiæ, ex acad. typog.,* 1631. C.C².C⁴.BIRM²(K.N.).

18954.5 — Metamorphoseωn libri xv. Ad fidem editionum optimarum & codicum manuscriptorum examinati. Operâ & studio T. Farnabii. 8°. *typis A. Griffin, sumpt. Jocosæ Norton & R. Whitakeri,* 1636. O¹⁴.; J. E. Anderson, Cambridge, Mass.

18955 — The fyrst fower bookes of P. Ouidius Nasos worke, intitled Metamorphosis. *tr.* into Englishe meter by A. Golding. 4°. *W. Seres,* 1565. Ent. 1564–65. L.O.; F.HN.PFOR.

18956 — The .xv. bookes of P. Ouidius Naso, entytuled Metamorphosis, *tr.* into English meeter, by A. Golding. 4° in 8's. *W. Seres,* 1567. L.O.C.D⁵.G².+; F.HN.HD. ILL.Y.+

18957 — [Anr. ed.] 4° in 8's. *W. Seres,* 1575. L.O.C¹².E.SH.+; F.HN.HD.Y.

18958 — [Anr. ed.] 4° in 8's. *J. Windet a. T. Judson,* 1584. L.C⁵(imp.).; F.ILL.

H. Denham yielded his rights in this bk. to Statrs. Co. 8 Jan. 1584; *see* Arber II.789.

18959 — [Anr. ed.] 4° in 8's. *R. Walde-graue,* 1587. L.O.C¹²(tp defective).D.NEK(lacks tp).+; F(2).HN.HD.ILL.TEX.

Not signed in Waldegrave's usual manner. Lace orn. on tp belonged to J. Day.

18960 — [Anr. ed.] 4° in 8's. *J. Danter,* 1593. L³⁸.O⁶ (2, 1 imp.). C¹².; F.HN.N.WEL.Y.+

See Greg, *Register B,* p. 42.

18961 — [Anr. ed.] 4° in 8's. *W. W[hite,]* 1603. L.L⁶.C².SHEF. Warrington PL.+; F(2).HN.CHI.HD.ILL.

18962 — [Anr. ed.] 4° in 8's. *T. Purfoot,* 1612. L.O.C⁸.A.WN.+; F.HN.HD.N.NY.+

See also Court-Book C, p. 129.

Ovidius Naso, Publius—*cont.*

18963 — Ovids Metamorphosis translated grammatically, and also according to the propriety of our English tongue, so farre as grammar and the verse will well beare. To be used according to the directions in [3768]. *Tr.* (J. B[rinsley, *the elder.*]) 4°. *H. Lownes f. T. Man,* 1618. Ent. 23 fb. L.L³⁰.C⁵.; F.CU.

Contains only pt. of the 1st bk.

18963.3 — The first five bookes of Ovids Metamorphosis: edit: 2ᵈ. [*Tr.* G. Sandys.] 12°. *f. W: B[arrett,]* 1621. Ent. to M. Lownes a. W. Barrett 27 ap. 1621; 'crost out' 8 ap. 1628. F(imp.).HD.

18963.7 — Edit: 3ᵈ. 12°. *f. W: B[arrett,]* 1623. WN.

18964 — Ovid's Metamorphosis Englished by G. S(andys.) fol. (*W. Stansby,*) 1626. L.O.C.DUR(Bamb.).E.+; F.HN. HD.N.NY.+

A royal patent granted Sandys to print this 24 ap. 1626; *see Court-Book C,* p. 201, n. 4.

18965 — [Anr. ed.] 12°. *R. Young, sold by J. Grismond,* 1628. Ass'd to T. Lownes 10 ap. 1627. L.L³⁸.O.; F.HN. CHI.HD.NY.+

An unauthorized ed.; *see Court-Book C,* p. 201.

18966 — [Anr. ed.] Ovid's Metamorphosis Englished, mythologiz'd, and represented in figures. An essay to the translation of Virgil's Æneis [a *tr.* of Bk. 1.] fol. *Oxford, J. Lichfield,* 1632. L.O.C.D.E.+; F.HN.HD. N.NY.+

The prelims. and one setting of Vvv² (w. 3-line initials on Vvv2ᵛ) were printed in London by W. Stansby; *see The Library,* III(1948), pp.193–212. According to O3ʳ of 18967, this fol. ed. was sold in London by A. Hebb. Regarding an attempted piracy *see Court-Book C,* p. 235. The plates for this ed. reprinted w. Latin text edited by T. Farnaby, *Paris, A. Morelli,* 1637; also in 18968.

18967 — The 3ᵈ. edition. 12°. *R. B[adger] f. A. Hebb,* 1638. L.O.C.BIRM.M⁴.+; F.HN.HD.IND.NY.+

Reprints trans. of Metamorphoses only.

18968 — [Anr. ed. of 18966.] fol. *J. L[egat] f. A. Hebb,* 1640. L.O.C.DUR⁵.E².+; F.HN.HD.ILL.NY.+

18969 — — [*Extracts.—Cinyras.*] The picture of incest. Lively portraicted in the historie of Cinyras and Myrrha. [*Tr.*] By J. Gresham. [In verse.] 12°. *f. R. A[llot,]* 1626. L.; Y.

— — [Anr. trans.] The scourge of Venus: or, the wanton lady. With the rare birth of Adonis. Written by H. A[ustin.] 1613. *See* 968.

18969.5 — — [*Judgement of Midas.*] Of such as on fantesye decree & discuss: on other mēs works, lo Ouids tale thus. [*Tr.*] T. Hedley. [In verse.] s.sh.fol. (*H. Sutton,*) [1552?] L⁵(Lemon 33).

Reprinted in 5225.

18970 — — [*Narcissus.*] The fable of Ouid treting of Narcissus, *tr.* into Englysh mytre [by T. H., i.e. T. Howell]. 1560. 4°. [*J. Tisdale f.*] *T. Hackette,* [1560.] L.O(2).; HN.

— — *See also* 20939.

18971 — — [*Salmacis and Hermaphroditus.*] The pleasant fable of Hermaphroditus and Salmacis [*tr.*] by T. Peend. [In verse.] 8°. (*T. Colwell,*) 1565 (de.) Ent. 1565–66. O.M.

18972 — — [Anr. trans.] Salmacis and Hermaphroditus. [*Tr.* by F. Beaumont? In verse.] 8°. [*S. Stafford*] *f. J. Hodgets,* 1602. O.; F(2).

(Formerly also 1666) Reprinted in 1665.

18973 — [*Nux.*] Ovid's Walnut-tree transplanted. [*Tr.*] (R. Hatton.) [In verse.] 12°. [*W. Stansby*] *f. R. Milbourne,* 1627. Ent. 20 ap. L.

18974 — [*Remedia Amoris.*] Ovidius Naso his remedie of love. *Tr.* (F. L.) [In verse.] 4°. *T. C[reede] f. J. Browne,* 1600. Ent. to J. Browne a. J. Jaggard 25 de. 1599. O.O⁵.C².

18975 — The first and second part of the Remedy of love. [*Tr.*] Sir T. Overbury. [In verse.] 8°. *N. Okes, sold by J. Wels,* 1620. L.L³⁰.O.; HN.HD.

18976 — Ovid's Remedy of love. [*Tr.* J. Carpenter. In verse.] 8°. [*N. a. J. Okes*] *f. F. Smith,* 1636. Ent. 31 my. L.L³⁰.SHEF.

A2ʳ line 2 of text: 'Warres'.

18976.2 — [Anr. ed.] 8°. [*N. a. J. Okes*] *f. F. Smith,* 1636. HN.HD.

A2ʳ line 2 of text: 'Wars'.

18976.4 — [*Tristia.*] P. Ouidii Nasonis de tristibus libri quinque: cum annotationibus minime reiiciendis. 8°. *T. Vautrollerius,* 1574. HD.

For Vautrollier's patent *see* 18926.5.

Ovidius Naso, Publius—*cont.*
18976.6 — [Anr. ed.] 8°. *T. Vautrollerius,* 1581. L(tp only, Harl.5990/37).
18976.8 — [Anr. ed.] Publii Ovidij Nasonis Tristium libri V. Ex accuratissima A. Naugerii castigatione. 8°. *Edinburgi, A. Hart,* 1612. Ass'd by J. Harrison to the English Stock 21 se. E(imp.).
18977 — [Anr. ed.] Pub. Ovidii Nasonis de tristibus libri V. 8°. *Cantabrigiæ, ap. T. Buck & R. Daniel,* 1638. L.
18977a — The thre first bookes of Ouids de tristibus. *Tr.* T. Churchyard. 4° in 8's. *T. Marshe,* [1572.] Ass'd on Marsh's death to T. Orwin 23 jn. 1591. L.
18977b — [Anr. ed.] 4° in 8's. *T. Marshe,* 1578. M.
18978 — [Anr. ed.] 4° in 8's. *T. Marsh,* 1580. O.; HN(imp.).
18979 — Ovids tristia containinge five bookes of mournfull elegies. *Tr.* W. S(altonstall.) 8°. *[T. a. R. Cotes] f. F. Grove,* 1633. Ent. 20 oc. 1632; ass'd to R. Cotes 9 no. 1633. L.L³⁰.; HN.
18980 — [Anr. ed.] 8°. *[T. a. R. Cotes] f. F. Grove,* 1637. L.O. C⁴.G⁴.LINC.+; F.HN.CHI.HD.Y.+
18981 — Publ [*sic*] Ovid. De tristibus: or mournefull elegies. *Tr.* Z. Catlin. 8°. *T. Cotes f. J. Bellamie,* 1639. Ent. 18 my. L.L³⁰.O.O²⁶.C.; F.HN.BO.N.Y.+
　　　1 HN copy has special dedic. to Sir W. Spring, *bt.*
— *See also* 13366.

— Ouids banquet of sence. By G. Chapman. 1595. *See* 4985.

18981.5 **Ovum Zephyrium.** Ovum Zephyrium: a winde-egg; fil'd with more imagination then judgement: yet it can make a golden bed for a sicke foole. [A satire in verse.] 4°. *[T. Snodham] f. C. Knight,* 1613. BTU.

Owein, Guillame, *ed. See* 9516.

18982 **Owen, David.** Anti-paræus: sive determinatio de jure regio . . . contra D. Paræum, paulò auctior. 8°. *ex off. C. Legge acad. Cantab. typographi,* 1622. L.O.C. A.NLW.+; F.CU.
18983 — Herod and Pilate reconciled: or, the concord of papist and puritan. 4°. *C. Legge, pr. to the Univ. of Camb., sold in Pauls churchyard [by M. Lownes,]* 1610. L.O⁴.C.LINC.NLW.+; F.BO³.HD. Iowa U.
18983.5 — [Anr. ed.] 4°. *C. Legge, pr. to the Univ. of Camb.,* 1610. L².O.C².D.E.+; F.HN.U. Ronald Mansbridge, New York.

18984 **Owen, Jane.** An antidote against purgatory. 12°. *[St. Omer, English College Press,]* 1634. O.AUG.ROME. A&R 589.

18984.5 **Owen, John.** Epigrammatum libri tres. Autore Joanne Owen Britanno. 8°. *ap. J. Windet, sumpt. S. Watersonii,* 1606. Ent. 29 jn. WN.; HD.
18984.7 — Secunda editio. 8°. *ap. J. Windet, sumpt. S. Watersonii,* 1606. O.C¹⁰.D.; F.
18985 — = 18986.
18986 — [Anr. ed., enlarged.] Epigrammatum Joannis Owen Cambro-Britanni libri tres. Ad Mariam Neville. Editio tertia. (Epigrammatum . . . ad Arbellam Stuart, liber singularis. Editio prima.) 2 pts. 12°. *ex off. H. Lownes, sumt. S. Waterson,* 1607. L³⁰.O.C⁵. D².M².+; F.HN.ILL.NY.Y.
　　　(Formerly also 18985)
18987 — Editio quarta. (Editio secunda.) 12°. *ex off. J. Legati, sumt. S. Waterson,* 1612. L.O.C.NLW.WN.+; F.HN. HD.N.Y.+
　　　Also issued as pt. 1 of 18988.5.
18988 — Epigrammatum . . . libri tres. Ad Henricum principem [etc.] Editio prima. (Epigrammatum. . . . Ad tres Mecaenates, libri tres. Editio prima.) 2 pts. 12°. *ex off. N. de Quercubus [i.e. Okes], sumt. S. Waterson,* 1612. Pt. 1 ent. 11 se. L.O(pt. 1 only).C⁴.E².M.+; F.HN.HD.N.Y.+
　　　Also issued as pts. 2 and 3 of 18988.5.
18988.5 — [Anr. issue of 18987 and 18988 w. gen. tp:] Epigrammatum libri decem. Editio quarta. 3 pts. 12°. *ex off. N. de Quercubus, sumt. S. Waterson,* 1612. O.C³. CHATS.; F.
　　　The gen. tp was pr. as C12 of pt. 2 of 18988, where it is found in many copies (1 F, HN, HD).
18989 — [Anr. ed. of both pts. of 18988.] Editio secunda. 12°. *ex off. N. de Quercubus, sumt. S. Waterson,* 1618. L.O.C.NLW.YK.+; F(2nd pt. only).FBL.HD.HN.ILL.

Owen, John—*cont.*
18990 — [Anr. ed. of all 10 bks., w. no gen. tp.] Epigrammatum . . . libri tres. Editio quinta. (Editio tertia.) 12°. *ex off. N. de Quercubus, sumpt. S. Waterson,* 1622. L.O.C.E².NLW.+; F.HN.ILL. Lehigh U. 𝔄
18991 — [Anr. ed., w. gen. tp:] Epigrammatum. . . . Libri decem. Editio sexta. (Editio quarta.—Monostica [by M. Verino.]) 12°. *ex off. A. Math[ewes,] sumpt. S. Waterson,* 1633. L.O.C.E.NLW.+; F.HN.NY. SMITH.Y.+ 𝔄
18992 — [Anr. issue, w. engr. tp dated:] 1634. O.C.NLW.; BO².CHI.ILL.HD.PH.+
　　　Regarding John Waterson's objections in 1637 to an ed. imported from abroad *see* Greg, *Companion,* p. 317.
18993 — Epigrams of that most wittie and worthie epigrammatist Mr. J. Owen. *Tr.* J. Vicars. 8°. *W. S[tansby] f. J. Smethwicke,* 1619. Ent. 17 se. 1618. O.; HN.HD.
18994 — Certaine epigrams out of the first foure bookes. *Tr.* R. H[ayman.] 1628. = pt. 2 of 12974.

Owen, John, *Bp.* Saint Asaph. Visitation articles. *See* 10324.

18995 **Owen, Lewis.** The key of the Spanish tongue. Eng. a. Span. 12°. *T. C[reede] f. W. Welby,* 1605. L.; F.HD.
18995.5 — [Anr. issue, w. cancel tp, w. imprint:] *T. C[reede] f. W. Welby,* 1606. L⁴⁴.O(lacks tp)*.C³(lacks tp)*. E²(lacks tp)*.
18996 — The running register: recording a true relation of the state of the English colledges, in all forraine parts. 4°. *[F. Kingston] f. R. Milbourne,* 1626. Ent. 12 jn. L.O.C.D.E.+; F.HN.CHI.HD.NY.+
18997 — Speculum Jesuiticum. Or, the Jesuites looking-glasse. [Init. L. O.] 4°. *T. C[otes] f. M. Sparke,* 1629. Ent. 29 ap. L.O.C.D².E.+; F.HN.HD.N.U.+
　　　Also issued as pt. 2 of 21720. There is a rare issue at C²,C¹³ signed: 'Lewis Owen' on A2ᵛ and A4ᵛ.
18998 — The unmasking of all popish monks, friers, and Jesuits. 4°. *J. H[aviland] f. G. Gibs,* 1628. Ent. 19 oc. 1627. L.O.C.E.NLW.+; F.HN.HD.N.U.+
　　　Unsold sheets reissued w. cancel tp in 1646 as Wing O 828.
— *tr. See* 10561.

18999 **Owen, Thomas.** The copie of a letter sent from Paris. Contayning an answere to [5861]. [Init. F. G.] 4°. *[St. Omer, English College Press,]* 1611. L.O¹⁸.C². ST.YK.+
　　　A&R 590.
19000 — A letter of a catholike man beyond the seas, including another of Peter Coton priest, to the queene regent of France. Touching the death of Henry the IIII. *Tr.* [Init. T. A., i.e. Audoenus or Owen.] 8°. *[St. Omer, English College Press,]* 1610. L.O(imp.). AUG.ST.WOR.; F.
　　　A&R 591.
— *tr. See* 6383.

Owl. The owles almanacke. 1618. *See* 6515.

19001 **Owsolde, Walter.** The varietie of memorable and worthy matters. 4°. *J. R[oberts] f. J. Charlton,* 1605. Ent. 10 ap. L.; F.HN.N.NY.
19002 — [Anr. issue, without printer's initials.] C.

OXFORD UNIVERSITY
OFFICIAL DOCUMENTS

19002.3 — [*Orders for the market.*] Robert [Dudley] earle of Leicester [etc.] fol(2). [*London,* 1575.] O¹⁵.
　　　Dated in MS. '17° Eliz'.
19002.5 — — Thomas [Sackville] baron of Buckurst [etc.] fol(2). [*Oxford, J. Barnes,* 1601?] O⁴(imp.).
19002.7 — — Thomas [Sackville] earle of Dorset [etc.] s.sh.fol. [*Oxford, J. Barnes,* 1606.] O¹⁵(2). Cr. 1036.
　　　(Formerly 21539) Dated in MS. 2 July 1606.
19003 — — Orders made and set downe by the justices of peace, [etc. 11 Jan. 1614.] fol(2). [*Oxford, J. Barnes,* 1614.] F. Cr. 1141.
19004 — — A proclamation, for the well ordering of the market [etc. By Abp. W. Laud.] fol(3). *Oxford, J. Lichfield,* 1634. L.O.C.BRISTOL².M.+; HN.HD.LC.MICH.Y.+
　　　L⁸ and O¹⁵ copies dated in MS. 17 Dec. 1634.

Oxford University—OFFICIAL DOCUMENTS—*cont.*

19005 — [*Statutes.*] Corpus statutorum universitatis Oxon. [*Ed.* B. Twyne and R. Zouch.] fol. *Oxoniæ, J. Lichfield & G. Turner,* 1634. L.O.O².O³.O⁴.+; Sexton.
Prelims. and A–Kk² pr. by Lichfield; a–ee² pr. by Turner.

19006 —— Synopsis seu epitome statutorum. [*Ed.* T. Crossfield?] s.sh.fol. *Oxonii, G. Turner, imp. G. Webb,* 1635. O.O³(2 frags.).O¹⁵.C(2).NLW(2).

19007 —— Statuta selecta è corpore statutorum universitatis Oxon, [etc. Compiled by T. Crossfield.] 8°. [*Oxford,*] *typis G. Turner pro G. Webb,* 1638. L.O.C.D².E².+; F.HN.HD.ILL.Y.+
An engr. chart of the lectures: 'Encyclopædia seu orbis literarum' often bound w. this; an earlier state sometimes found w. 19006.

19008 —— Statuta. 1 Schedula sive repertorium seriei & circuitus praedicti, manu propria Cancelarij, [etc.] s.sh.fol. *Oxoniæ, J. Lichfield, imp. G. Davis,* 1629. O.O¹⁵.; HD.
Issued w. 19009.

19009 —— Carolus. R. Ordo sive series electionis procuratorum. [By P. Turner, *the younger.*] Engr.] s.sh.fol. [*Oxford, J. Lichfield,* 1629.] O.O¹⁵.; HD.
Issued w. 19008.

19010 — The answere of the vicechancelour, the doctors, both the proctors, and other the heads of houses in the universitie of Oxford. To the humble petition of the ministers of the Church of England, desiring reformation of certaine ceremonies and abuses. 4°. *Oxford, J. Barnes,* 1603. L.O³.; CAL.Y.
¶¶3ᵛ–4ᵛ blank. Answered by 238, 6469.

19010.5 — [Anr. issue, w. letter from Camb. Univ. on ¶¶3ᵛ–4ᵛ.] *Oxford, J. Barnes,* 1603. L².L³.L¹³.C.C².; F.N.

19011 — [Anr. ed.] 4°. *Oxford, J. Barnes, sold by S. Waterson* [*London,*] 1603. L.O.C.DEU.M.+; F.HN.HD.NY¹¹.Y.+

19012 — [Anr. ed., w. new prelims. On tp:] Confirmed by the . . . universitie of Cambridge. 4°. *Oxford, J. Barnes, sold by S. Waterson* [*London,*] 1603. L.O.C³.M.YK.+; F.ILL.U.Y.
A–D⁴ from same setting as 19011.

19012a — [Anr. ed.] 4°. *Oxford, J. Barnes,* [1603.] O.O⁵.C⁹.C¹⁰. LINC.; V.

19013 — [Anr. ed.] 4°. *Oxford, J. Barnes, sold by S. Waterson* [*London,*] 1604. L.O.C.DUR(Bamb.).E.+; F.HN.HD. N.U.+

19014 — Decretum universitatis Oxoniensis damnans propositiones [based on D. Pareus] . . . sive Jesuitarum, sive puritanorum. 4°. *Oxoniæ, J. Lichfield & J. Short,* 1622. L⁴.O(3).O⁸.O¹³.LINC.; U.
For an ed. in Dutch and Latin, pr. in the Netherlands, which repeats the Oxford imprint *see* Madan II, no. 500. In the Latin text the Dutch ed. has B1ʳ catchword: 'tuma-' (E, frag.) while the Oxford ed. has: 'di,'.

— The foundation of the universitie of Oxford. *See* 19052.2 sqq.

19014.5 — To all christian people [etc. Blank form of licence to ale-house keepers issued by C. Potter.] s.sh.fol. [*Oxford,* 1640?] O.

QUÆSTIONES

— De philosophia, panathenaica duae: in comitiis Oxonii habitæ. [1586.] *See* 19887.
— Quæstiones sex. Anno. 1597. 1598. *See* 36.
— Theses Mʳⁱ Bret respondentis in comitiis. 1597. *See* 3716.5.

19015 — Quæstiones (Christo propitio) in vesperiis discutiendæ. [10 July 1602.] = pt. of 13886.

19016 — Quæstiones, Deo propitio, discutiendæ. . . . Oxon. 1605. s.sh.fol. [*Oxford, J. Barnes,* 1605.] O.

19016.1 — Quæstiones favente deo in sacra theologiâ, . . . 1608. 4°. *Oxoniæ, J. Barnesius,* 1608. O⁵.; F.

19016.2 — Quaestiones in sacra theologia. [9 July 1614.] s.sh.fol. [*Oxford, J. Barnes,* 1614.] O.

19016.3 — Quaestiones. [12 July 1617.] s.sh.fol. [*Oxford,* 1617.] c⁵(right half). A

19016.4 — Quaestiones. [11 July 1618.] s.sh.fol. [*Oxford,* 1618.] O.

19016.5 — Quaestiones. [10 July 1619.] s.sh.fol. [*Oxford,* 1619.] O.

19016.6 — Quaestiones. [7 July 1621.] s.sh.fol. [*Oxford,* 1621.] L⁵(Lemon 188).

19016.7 — Quaestiones. [6 July 1622.] s.sh.fol. [*Oxford,* 1622.] O.

Oxford University—QUÆSTIONES—*cont.*

19016.8 — Quæstiones. [10 July 1624.] s.sh.fol. [*Oxford,* 1624.] HD.

19016.9 — Quaestiones. [7 July 1627.] s.sh.fol. [*Oxford, J. Lichfield a. W. Turner,* 1627.] L⁵(Lemon 278).O.

19016.10 — Quaestiones. [12 July 1628.] s.sh.fol. [*Oxford,* 1628.] O.O¹⁴.

19016.11 — Quaestiones. [11 July 1629.] s.sh.fol. [*Oxford,* 1629.] O(Douce frag. d.12/15).

19016.12 — Quaestiones. [10 July 1630.] s.sh.fol. [*Oxford, W. Turner,* 1630.] L⁵(Lemon 301).

19016.13 — Quaestiones. [7 July 1632.] s.sh.fol. [*Oxford,* 1632.] O.

19016.14 — Quaestiones. [6 July 1633.] s.sh.fol. [*Oxford,* 1633.] O⁵.

19016.15 — Quæstiones. [12 July 1634.] s.sh.fol. [*Oxford, W. Turner,* 1634.] O.O⁵.; HD.
Three orns. at top of left-hand col.

19016.16 — [Anr. ed.] s.sh.fol. [*Oxford, W. Turner,* 1634.] O.
One orn. at top of left-hand col.

19016.17 — Quaestiones. [11 July 1635.] s.sh.fol. [*Oxford,*] L. *Lichfield,* [1635.] O.

19016.18 — Quaestiones. [6 July 1639.] s.sh.fol. [*Oxford,* 1639.] L¹¹(S.P.D. Chas. I., vol. 425, doc. 29).O¹⁵.

19016.19 — Quaestiones. [11 July 1640.] s.sh.fol. [*Oxford,* 1640.] O.

19017 — Quaestiones. [1605–40.] Now entered separately at 19016 sqq.

VERSES, ADDRESSES, ETC.

Arranged chronologically and by college.

— [*The University.*] In illustrissimi comitis Leicestrensis, adventum. 1585. *See* 7287.
— Exequiæ illustrissimi equitis, D. Philippi Sidnaei. 1587. *See* 22551.

19017.5 — Oxoniensium στεναγμὸς siuè, carmina ab Oxoniensibus conscripta in obitum illustrissimi C. Hattoni. 4°. *Oxonii, ex off. J. Barnesii,* 1592. L².
— Funebria nobilissimi equitis, D. H. Untoni. 1596. *See* 24520.
— Ecloga Oxonio-Cantabrigiensis, tributa. 1600. *See* 14453.

19018 — Oxoniensis Academiæ funebre officium in memoriam Elisabethæ, reginæ. 4°. *Oxoniæ, J. Barnesius,* 1603. L.O.C⁷.DUR⁵.E².+; F(2).CH.CHI.TEX.Y.

19019 — Academiæ Oxoniensis pietas erga serenissimum et potentissimum Jacobum regem. 4° in 8's. *Oxoniæ, J. Barnesius,* 1603. L.O.C².E.M.+; F.HN.HD.N.Y.+
Copies vary: N8ᵛ blank, or w. 'Votum typographi'; both at L,O.

19020 — Eidyllia in obitum fulgentissimi Henrici Walliæ principis. [*Ed.* J. Martin.] 4°. *Oxoniæ, J. Barnesius,* 1612. L.O.C.ETON.WN.+; F.HN.HD.N.Y.+

19021 — Justa Oxoniensium. (Lachrymæ Oxonienses stillantes in tumulum principis Henrici.) [*Ed.* S. Fell?] 4°. [*E. Griffin?*] *imp. J. Bill,* 1612. L.O.C.E².YK.+; F.HN. HD.N.Y.+
E3ʳ last line: 'Colleg. Nov. Socius.'

19021.5 — [Anr. issue, w. at least quires C–E, I–L, N reset.] L.O.C.E².LEEDS.+; F.HN.N.Y.
E3ʳ last line: 'Nov. Coll. Socius.'

19022 — Epithalamia. Sive lusus Palatini in nuptias Friderici comitis Palatini ad Rhenum. Et Elisabethæ, Jacobi regis filiæ. 4°. *Oxoniæ, Jos. Barnesius, & Londini væneunt ap. Joh. Barnesium,* 1613. L.O.C.DUR⁵.M.+; F.HN.HD.N.Y.+
Regarding cancellation of F3 and P1 *see Cal. S.P.D., 1611–1618,* p. 176; both cancels and cancellanda at L,F.

— Justa funebria Ptolemæi Oxoniensis T. Bodleii. 1613. *See* 3194.

19023 — Jacobi ara ceu, in Jacobi, regis reditum e Scotia in Angliam, gratulatoria. 4°. *Oxoniæ, J. Lichfield & G. Wrench,* 1617. L.O.C².BIRM²(K.N.).E².+; F.HN. HD.N.Y.+

19024 — Academiæ Oxoniensis funebria sacra. Æternæ memoriæ reginæ Annæ dicata. 4°. *Oxoniæ, J. Lichfield & J. Short,* 1619. L.O.C².D.E².+; F.HN.N.TEX.

19025 — Ultima linea Savilii sive in obitum H. Savilii. Justa academica. (Oratio funebris. A T. Goffe.) 4°. *Oxonii, J. Lichfield & J. Short,* 1622. L.O.C.A.D.+; F.HN. HD.N.Y.+

19026 — Votiva, sive ad . . . Jacobum, regem. De Caroli, Walliæ principis, in regiam Hispanicam adventu. 4°. *F. Kyngstonus,* 1623. L.O.C².D².YK.+

Oxford University—Verses, Addresses, etc.—*cont.*

19027 — Carolus redux. (Πανακαδημικος. Sive, gratulatio pro Carolo reduce, Oxoniensium nomine recitata, à J. King, *public orator*.) 4°. *Oxoniæ, J. Lichfield & J. Short*, 1623. L.O.C.A.D.+; F.HN.HD.ILL.Y.+

19028 — Camdeni insignia. [In honour of W. Camden.] (Parentatio historica: sive commemoratio G. Camdeni per D. Whear.) 4°. *Oxoniæ, J. Lichfield & J. Short*, 1624. L.O.C.D.E.+; F.HN.DAR.Y.

19029 — Schola moralis philosophiae Oxon. In funere Whiti [i.e. T. White, *founder of Sion College*] pullata. (Oratio funebris . . . per G. Price.) 4°. *Oxoniæ, J. Lichfield & J. Short*, 1624. O.O².O¹³.O³⁸.; HD.

19030 — Oxoniensis academiae parentalia. Sacratissimæ memoriæ Jacobi, regis, dicata. 4°. *Oxoniæ, J. Lichfield & G. Turner*, 1625. L.O.C.D.M.+; F.HN.HD.N.NY¹¹.+ Sheet Ee, lacking in many copies, present in L,O¹⁷,F.

19031 — Epithalamia Oxoniensia. In . . . Caroli, regis, &c. cum Henretta [*sic*] Maria, connubium. 4°. *Oxoniæ, J. Lichfield & G. Turner*, 1625. L.O.C³.D.E.+; F.HN. HD.N.Y.+

19032 — Britanniae natalis. [Acad. verses on the birth of Charles II.] 4°. *Oxoniæ, J. Lichfield*, 1630. L.O.C. D.E.+; F.HN.HD.KAN.Y.+

19032.5 — Ad magnificum . . . virum dominum Johannem Cirenbergium. Ob acceptum synodalium epistolarum concilii Basileensis Αὐτόγραφον, quod T. Roe Oxoniensi bibliothecæ transmisit. Carmen honorarium. [*Ed.*] (J. Rous.) 4°. *Oxoniæ, J. Lichfield*, 1631. L(2).O.O¹⁷.C⁷.; F.Y. (Formerly 21351)

19033 — Solis Britannici perigæum. Sive itinerantis Caroli periodus. 4°. *Oxoniæ, J. Lichfield & G. Turner*, 1633. L.O.C².DUR⁵.M.+; F.HN.HD.N.Y.+ In some copies (O¹⁷,HD) quire ii⁴ added and K⁴ reset.

19034 — Musarum Oxoniensium pro rege suo soteria. 4°. *Oxoniæ, J. L[ichfield a.] W. T[urner,]* 1633. L.O.C². M.YK.+; F.HN.LC.N.Y.+

19034a — [Anr. copy, for the king, with a special title-page partly pr. in gold, w. imprint:] *Oxoniæ, J. L[ichfield] et G. T[urner,]* 1633. L(C.122.e.2/1).

19035 — Vitis Carolinæ gemma altera sive ducis Eboracencis genethliaca. 4°. *Oxoniæ, J. Lichfield & G. Turner*, 1633. L.O.C⁵.E².M.+; F.HN.CAL⁴.HART.Y. Text ends on L3ᵛ.

19035a — [Anr. issue, w. cancels L3,4.] O¹².C².ETON.LIV³.M.+; HN.ILL.N.TEX.Y. L4ʳ catchword: 'When'.

19035a.5 — [Anr. issue, enlarged, w. new cancels L3,4.] O.O³⁸. C².C⁵.E².+; F.HD.ILL.N.Y.+ L4ʳ catchword: 'And'.

19036 — Coronae Carolinæ quadratura. Sive perpetuandi imperii Carolini augurium. 4°. *Oxoniæ, L. Lichfield*, 1636. L(imp.).O.C².M.WN.+; F(2).HN.N.TEX.Y(imp.). (Formerly also 5021)

19037 — Flos Britannicus veris novissimi filiola Carolo & Mariæ nata. [On the birth of Princess Anne, 17 Mar. 1637.] 4°. *Oxoniæ, typis L. Lichfield*, [1637?] L.O.C².DUR⁵. WN.+; F.HN.HD.N.Y.+ The sheets of this book vary in number and arrangement; *see* Madan I.193, II.135. Five varieties at O; two others at O⁶,O¹⁷.

19038 — Musarum Oxoniensium Charisteria pro serenissima regina Maria, recens e nixus laboriosi discrimine receptâ. 4°. *Oxoniæ, typis L. Lichfield*, 1638. L.O.C. G².YK.+; F.HN.HD.N.Y.+

19039 — Horti Carolini rosa altera. 4°. *Oxoniæ, L. Lichfield*, 1640. L.O.C.D.DUR⁵.+; F.HN.CHI.HD.Y.+

19039.5 — [Anr. issue, w. cancel title:] Horti . . . altera. Claroque surculo sese feliciter exerenti, musarum Oxoniensium acclamatio. *Oxoniæ, L. Lichfield*, 1640. F.N. Halfsheets F and cc cancelled because of derogatory references to Scots.

19040 — [*Bodleian Library*.] [Heading:] Munificentissimis atque optimis cuiusvis ordinis, dignitatis, sexus, qui bibliothecam hanc libris ampliarunt [etc. The official Register of Benefactors.] fol. [*London, R. Barker*, 1604.] O. Intended to be handwritten throughout; for lack of a satisfactory scribe the entries for 1600–mid 1604 were privately pr. at Sir Thomas Bodley's expense.
— *See also* 14449, 14451, 16786.12, 19032.5.

19041 — [*Colleges. — Christ Church*.] Carmina funebria, in obitum G. de Sancto Paulo. Now = 19043.5.

Oxford University—Verses, Addresses, etc.—*cont.*

19042 — Death repeal'd by a thankfull memoriall sent from Christ-Church in Oxford, celebrating the deserts of Vis-count Bayning. [In verse.] 4°. *Oxford, L. Lichfield f. F. Bowman*, 1638. L(imp.).O.O³.C².PLUME.+; F(3).HN.HD.Y. (Formerly also 1652)

— Liber precum publicarum in usum ecclesiæ chathedralis [*sic*] Christi Oxon. 1615. See 16447.

19043 — Musa hospitalis ecclesiæ Christi Oxon. In adventum Jacobi regis, ad eandem ecclesiam. 4°. *Oxoniæ, ap. J. Barnesium*, 1605. L.O.C⁷.D.HAT.+; F.HN.TEX.Y.

— Vniuersis Christifidelibus, [etc. An inspeximus regarding privileges. 1529.] See 24323.5.

19043.5 — [*Corpus*.] Carmina funebria, in obitum clarissimi viri Georgii de Sancto Paulo C.C.C. 4°. *Oxoniæ, J. Barnesius*, 1614. O⁵.WN.; HN. (Formerly 19041)

19044 — [*Exeter*.] Threni Exoniensium in obitum . . . Johannis Petrei, Baronis de Writtle. (Oratio funebris [by M. Styles.]) 4°. *Oxoniæ, J. Barnesius*, 1613. L.O.O⁵. C.C².+; Y.

19045 — [*Lincoln*.] In aduentum illustrissimi Lecestrensis comitis ad collegium Lincolniense. 1585. = 7286.

19046 — [*Magdalen*.] Beatæ Mariae Magdalenae lachrymæ, in obitum Gulielmi Grey. [*Ed.*] (Rob. Barnes, *of Greys*.) 4°. *Oxoniæ, J. Barnesius*, 1606. L.O.O¹².HAT.WN.+; F.HN.HD.PN.Y.

19047 — Luctus posthumus sive erga defunctum Henricum Walliæ principem, Magdalenensium officiosa pietas. (Oratio funebris [by A. Frewen.]) 4°. *Oxoniæ, J. Barnesius*, 1612. L.O.C.D.M.+; F.HN.HD.N.Y.+

19048 — [*Merton*.] Bodleiomnema. (Memoriæ sacrum. Viro clarissimo, T. Bodleio, . . . collegium Mertonense, . . . dicat.—Oratio funebris, à J. Halesio.) 4°. *Oxoniæ, J. Barnesius*, 1613. L.O.C⁷.LIV³.WN.+; F.HN.HD.N. NY.+ 𝔄

19049 — Merton colledge case. [Arguments directed to Parliament concerning a dispute over the lease of the manor of Malden in Surrey.] fol. [*London?* 1625.] L.O.O⁵. In the archives at O¹¹, the Bursar's accounts for 25 July–21 Nov. 1625 record the payment of 13ˢ 4ᵈ for the printing of this brief. A bill on the College's behalf was read in Parliament 11 and 16 Feb. 1626; *see JHC* I.818,820.

19049.5 — [*New College*.] Encomion Rodolphi Warcoppi ornatissimi, quem habuit Anglia, qui extinctus est 1605. [By men of New College; ed. W. Kingsmill.] 4°. *Oxoniæ, ap. J. Barnesium*, 1605. O.O³.WN.; HN. (Formerly 15009 and 25021)

19050 — Musæ hospitales Wicchamicæ in adventum principis Friderici-Ulrici. Exhibitæ Oxoniæ in Collegio Novo. 1610. 4°. [*R. Barker*, 1610.] L.O.

— Peplus. Illustrissimi viri D. P. Sidnaei supremis honoribus dicatus. 1587. See 22552.

19051 — [*Trinity*.] Decretum de gratiis collegio rependendis. [12 Dec. 1602.] 47 lines. Post 1640.

19052 — [Anr. ed.] 52 lines. Post 1700.

APPENDIX

— Compilatum est hoc opusculum insolubilium. [1517?] *See* 18833.

19052.2 — The foundation of the universitie of Oxford. With a catalogue of the principall founders. fol(2). [*Cambridge*,] C. Legg f. J. Scot, sold [by G. Humble, London,] 1622. Ent. to W. Stansby 11 se. L⁵(Lemon 196). Compiled by John Scot, *Antiquarian*.

19052.4 — [Anr. ed.] fol(2). *Prs. to the univ. of Camb., f. J. Scot the elder, sold by G. Humble* [*London*,] 1634. L².O.; Y. (Formerly 21868)

19052.6 — [A trans.] Fundatio academiae Oxoniensis. Cum catalogo [etc.] fol(2). [*Cambridge*,] C. Legg pro J. Scot, veneunt [by G. Humble, London,] 1622. L⁵(Lemon 197).

19052.8 **Oxley, Robert.** A sermon preached at Gouldsbrough in Yorke-shire. 4°. *J. Haviland f. R. Moore*, 1622. HD. Sydney U.

19053 **Oxley, Thomas.** The shepheard, or a sermon, preached in Durisme minster. 4°. [*W. Jaggard*] *f. E. Edgar*, 1609. L.O.O¹⁰.C².YK.+; F(2, 1 imp.).HD. Sydney U. Halfsheet A set in duplicate; orn. on A2ʳ: urn between volutes or crowned rose between amoretti; both at C².

P

P. The double PP. 1606. *See* 6498.

19054 **P., A.** The compasse of a christian, directing them that be tossed in the waues of this worlde vnto Christ Jesus. 8°. *J. Wolfe f. J. Harison the yonger,* [1582.] O.; F.HN(lacks tp).
Dedic. dated 26 May 1582.

19054.5 — Natural and morall questions and answeres. Intermingled with many riddles, and darke sentences, written by A. P. With a manner of ordering the body for health through euery month. In Latin verse by J. Camerarius. 8°. *A. Islip,* 1598. Ent. to J. Wolfe 21 jy. 1592. HD(imp.).

19055 — [Heading A1ʳ:] A payre of two mornings meditations. [1644?] = Wing P 4.

19056 — A reply [by R. Charnock] to a notorious libell intituled A briefe apologie [19391.5]. Whereunto is also adjoyned an answere [by J. Bennett] to the Appendix [19392.5]. 4°. [*R. Barker,*] 1603. L.O.D.W.YK.+; F.TEX.
A&R 236.
— tr. *See* 13246, 14002, 24748.

19057 **P., B.** The prentises practise in godlinesse, and his true freedome. Divided into ten chapters. Written by B. P. 8°. *N. Okes f. J. Bach,* 1608. Ent. 22 jy. L.L⁸.; F.U.

19057.3 — [Anr. ed.] Written by W. P. 8°. *G. Eld f. R. Wilson,* 1613. Ass'd 19 no. 1610. P.
Author's epistle init. B. P.

19057.7 — [Anr. issue, w. cancel tp:] The young-mans guide to godlinesse. Devided into tenne chapters by W. P. *f. R. Wilson,* 1619. O.
(Formerly 19081)

P., C. The history of the quarrels of Paul .V. 1626. *See* 21766.

19058 — Judicium theologicum. 8°. [*Printed abroad,*] 1622.
Not an STC book.

19059 — Two briefe treatises. The one . . . concerning catechisme. The other, touching peace. 8°. *W. Stansby f. W. Butler,* 1616. Ent. 26 se. O.
— ed. *See* 244.

19060 **P., D.** Certaine brief and necessarie rules of geographie, seruing for the vnderstanding of chartes and mappes. 8°. *H. Binneman,* 1573. L.O.

19061 **P., D. B.** A reformation of a catholike. 1604. = 3096.
19062 — The second part. 1607. = 3097.

P., E. A godly and fruitefull sermon. [1584?] *See* 19104.
— A helpe to discourse. 1619. *See* 1547.

19062.5 — A table, expressing the words of art in the exercise of the science militarie. fol(2). [*London?* c. 1620–25.] O(Ashm. H 24(135)).
Possibly connected w. H. Petowe and the Artillery Garden; cf. 19802.5.
— tr. *See* 2962, 5996.

P., F., *an Italian, ed. See* 6760.

P., G. The old wiues tale. 1595. *See* 19545.
19063 — The true report of the lamentable death, of William of Nassawe. 8°. *Middleborough, D. van Respeawe,* 1584. L.O²⁴.
— A true reporte, of the late discoueries, of the Newfound Landes. 1583. *See* 19523.
— ed. *See* 21072a.
— tr. *See* 4876.

P., G., Br., *tr. See* 4469.

19064 **P., G.,** *Cantabrigiensis.* Antidicsonus cuiusdam Cantabrigiensis G. P. Accessit Libellus, in quo explicatur impia Dicsoni Artificiosa memoria. 8°. *H. Midletonus, pro J. Harisono,* 1584. L.C.
Answers 6823; answered by 21809. Possibly by W. Perkins.

19065 — Libellus de memoria, verissimaque bene recordandi scientia. 8°. *R. Walde-graue,* 1584. Ent. to W. Welby 2 my. 1608. L.O(3).O⁵.C²(2).DUR(Bamb.).; HN.
Possibly by W. Perkins.

P., Guil., G. A moorning diti. [1580.] *See* 19120.7.

P., H. Cures for the itch. 1626. *See* 19328.
19066 — Digitus Dei. 1631. Now = 19798.3.
— The duty of all true subjects. 1639. *See* 19505.
— Elizabetha quasi vivens. 1603. *See* 19803.5.
— Epigrams by H. P. 1608. *See* 19330.
— The mastive. 1615. *See* 19333.
— A merry discourse of meum, and tuum. 1639. *See* 19510.
— Milk for babes. 1630. *See* 19798.5.
— The mous-trap. 1606. *See* 19334.
— ed. *See* 16917.
— tr. *See* 15207.

P., H., *Esq.* Sundrie new remedies against famine. 1596. *See* 19996.

19067 **P., H.,** *Gent.* The more the merrier. 1608. Now = 19511.5.

P., H., *Miles.* Certaine philosophical preparations. [c. 1607.] *See* 19977.3.

19068 **P., I. or J.** Anabaptismes mysterie of iniquity unmasked. [By J. Paget?] Also, wisedomes bountie unmasking the man of sinne. 8°. *A. M[athewes] f. G. Winder,* 1623 (1622). Ent. 24 se. 1622. L(imp.).O²⁷.BIRM²(K.N.).
19072.5 intended to be reissued as pt. 2 of this.

19069 — Christs confession and complaint, concerning his kingdom and servants. 4°. [*Printed abroad,*] 1629. L⁴.O.O³.C.; F.HD.
O,C copies bd. w. 19072.

19070 — The coat armour of a christian. [1584.] Now = 19863.3.
— A commemoration of the life and death of Dame Helen Branch. [1594.] *See* 19863.7.
— An elegant description of spirituall life. 1632. *See* 20221.5.

19070.3 — The English schoole, teaching to read English distinctly, and to write it both faire and true. 12°. *T. C[otes] f. J. Bellamy,* 1635. Ent. 23 mr. 1635; 'crost out' 13 no. 1637. L⁴⁴.
See Court-Book C, p.301.

19070.5 — A godlie and zealous prayer, . . . for the preseruation of Elizabeth, queene. s.sh.fol. *H. Singleton,* [1586?] L⁵(Lemon 85).
Heading line 2: 'Subiecte,'.

19070.7 — [Anr. issue, partly reset, w. heading line 2: 'subiecte,'.] HD.

19071 — A meruaylous straunge deformed swyne. [By John Phillips? or John Partridge?] *Ballad.* s.sh.fol. *W. How f. R. Johnes,* [1570?] Ent. 1570–71. L.

19072 — Romes ruin. Or a treatise of the certaine destruction of Rome. 4°. [*Printed abroad,*] 1629. L.O.C.SAL.; F.
O,C copies bd. w. 19069.
— Three godly and learned treatises. 1632. *See* 20221.7.

19072.3 — A treatise shewing how the sarifice [*sic*] of the holy masse . . . halpe christians to salvation. 8°. *Rouen, in the prent hous of M. Michel,* 1614. PARIS. Prinknash Abbey, Cranham, Gloucestershire.
A&R 592.
— The weakenes of nature. [c. 1630.] *See* 20370.5.

P., I. or J.—*cont.*
19072.5 — Wisedomes bountie to heavenly pilgrims . . . unmasking the man of sinne. 8°. *G. Eld, sold by J. Budge,* 1622. Ent. as by 'Master Pecke' to G. Eld a. M. Flesher 10 jy. 1622. O²⁷.
    Linked on tp of 19068.

19072.7 **P., I.,** *D. D.* Foode from heaven, or nourishment for the soule being prayers and meditations. 3ᵈ. Ed. 24° in 12's. *T. Harper f. R. Harper,* 1639. Lord Rothschild.

P., J., *Knight.* An invitation unto prayer. 1624. *See* 19774.

P., J., *Master of Arts.* The heart of the king. 1626. *See* 20521.6.

19073 **P., J.,** *Priest.* The safegarde from ship-wracke, or heavens haven. [By J. Pickford.] 8°. *Douay, P. Telu,* 1618. L.O.C.STU.W.+; F.N.(frag.).TEX.U.
    A&R 647.

P., J., *Scr. Pub.* [Table of interest.] 1625. *See* 19600.4.

P., I. B. The reformed protestant. 1621. *See* 3607.5.

19074 **P., I. B. S. P.** Tractatus de persecutione toleranda. 8°. [*Printed abroad,*] 1622.
    Not an STC book.

P., J. R. A word of comfort. 1623. *See* 11118.

P., J. W. *See* Wilson, J., *Priest.*

P., Jaco., *Ep. D.* Aggeus and Abdias. 1562. *See* 19927.

P., L., *Ballad Writer. See* Price, L.

P., M. Grandsire Graybeard. 1635. *See* 3704.9.
19075 — Lord have mercy upon us. This is the humble petition of England. [1636.] Now = 19251.3.

P., M., *Ballad Writer and Versifier. See* Parker, Martin.

P., M. C. A briefe admonition to all English catholikes. 1610. *See* 24992.

19076 **P., N.** Come worldling see what paines I here do take. [By M. Parker?] *Ballad.* 2 pts. s.sh.fol. *f. H. Gosson,* [1638.] Ent. under title, app. cropt in L copy, 'Gathergood the father Scattergood the son' 9 ap. 1638. L.
    Wrongly entered as Wing C 5503.

19076.5 **P., N.,** *Master of Arts.* The vertue and operation of this balsame. s.sh.fol. [*Eliot's Court Press,* c. 1615.] L⁵(Lemon 247).

P., N. N. Miscellania. 1640. *See* 576.

19077 No entry.

P., O. Sermons, vpon the 101. psalme. 1591. *See* 19916.7.

P., P., *Gent., tr. See* 10713.5.

P., P. S., *tr. See* 4551.

19078 **P., R.** [Heading:] An admonition to the towne of Callays. [By R. Pownoll?] 8°. [*Wesel? P. A. de Zuttere?* 1557.] L.
    End of text dated 12 Apr. 1557.
— A booke of christian exercise. 1582, etc. *See* 19353, 19355.
— A christian directorie. 1585, etc. *See* 19354.1 sqq.
— The Jesuits miracles. 1607. *See* 20340.
— Parvus catechismus. 1573. *See* 20105.
— *tr. See* 18312, 18862, 18864, 18866, 18868.
— *See also* 16644.5.

P., R., *B. D.* The historie of tithes. 1640. *See* 19770.5.

P., R., *Minister, ed. See* 6099.7.

P., R. B. A manual of praiers. 1618. *See* 3899.
— Seaven sparkes. [1604–05?] *See* 4008.

19078.4 **P., S.** An epitaph of the vertuous life and death of Dame Helen Branch. [In verse.] 4°. *T. Creede,* 1594. HN.
— The pope in his fury. [1571.] *See* 19550.

19078.6 **P., S. C.** A letter written by a French gentleman to his friend at Rome on the treaty between the queen mother of France and the king of Navarre. 8°. [*T. Orwin? f. E. Aggas,*] 1587. L². 𝔄

19078.8 **P., T.** A fruitfull conference, or communication, touching the receiving of the holy communion, set downe in forme of a dialogue. 8°. *H. Lownes f. R. Bonian,* 1608. Ent. to H. Lownes 21 se. YK.

P., T.—*cont.*
— A gorgious gallery, of gallant inuentions. 1578. *See* 20402.
— Of the knowledge of warres. 1578. *See* 20403.
— The poore mans appeale. 1620. *See* 19791.
19079 — A short catechisme for householders. 8°. *F. K[ingston] f. G. Winder,* 1624. O.
    A different work from 6710.5.
— *ed. See* 19751.5, 22877.4.
— *tr. See* 19625, 24140.5.

P., T. L. D. M., *tr. See* 21666.

P., T. W. The rosarie of our ladie. 1600. *See* 17546.
— Whyte dyed black. 1615. *See* 26001.

P., Tho. *See* 12354.

19080 **P., W.** Foure great lyers. Also, a resolution to the countri-man. [1585?] Now = 19721.7.
19080.5 — The gossips greeting. [In verse.] 4°. *B. A[lsop] f. H. Bell,* 1620. Ent. 11 jy. HN.
    (Formerly 19331) Ent. as by 'H. Parratt' but not by him.
— A new dialoge called the endightment agaynste mother Messe. 1548. *See* 20499.
— The prentises practise. 1613. *See* 19057.3.
19081 — The young-mans guide to godlinesse. 1619. Now = 19057.7.

P., W., *tr.* A booke of secrets. 1596. *See* 3355.
— The honorable ouerthrow of the duke of Sauoyes troopes. [1597.] *See* 5043.5.
— The necessarie, . . . education of a gentlewoman. 1598. *See* 3947.
— *See also* 450.7, 929, 4115.5, 11727, 15241, 15691, 19799, 21828, 22992.3.

P., W., *G.* Luctus consolatorius. 1591. *See* 19120.3.

P., W., *Master of Arts in Cambridge, ed. See* 1919.

P., W. B. The second question, of traditions. [1612–23.] *See* 3098.5.

P., W. J., *tr. See* 1699.

Pacciolo, Luca. *See* 18794.

19081a **Pace, Richard.** Oratio Richardi Pacei in pace nuperime composita. 4° ⁶·⁴. (*per R. Pynson,* 1518 (nonis de.)) L.O.C².LIV³. Seville, Biblioteca Colombina.; HN.
19082 — Praefatio. D. Richardi Pacei in Ecclesiasten recognitum ad Hebraicam ueritatem. 4°. [*R. Pynson,* 1526?] O.LK(imp.).
— *tr. See* 10898.
— *See also* 24943.

Pacius, Julius. Iul. Pacii a Beriga institutiones logicae.
19083   12°. *Cantabrigiæ, ex off. J. Legat,* 1597. C.DUL.P.; F.
19083a — Logicae. Rudimenta. Secunda editio. 12°. *ap. G. Stansby,* 1612. O.
    A different work from 19083.

Pack. A packe of Spanish lyes. 1588. *See* 23011.

19084 **Packer, Thomas.** The sinners sanctuary. 12°. *J. Haviland f. E. Blackmore,* 1638. Ent. 6 no. 1637. L⁴.O.
19085 — The true catholike: collected out of the oracles, and psalteries of the holy Ghost. [Preface *tr.* by T. Packer out of F. de Ribera.] 12°. [*G. Miller*] *f. E. Blackmore,* 1628. O.C.DUL.
    (Formerly also 4831)
19086 — Third edition enlarged. 12°. *G. Miller f. E. Blackmore,* 1632. L⁴.O.C.; F.HD(imp.).

19087 **Packman.** The pack-mans pater noster, or a dialogue betwixt a chapman and a priest. 1624. Now = 22185.5.

19087.5 **Padilla y Manrique, Martin de,** *Adelantado Mayor of Castile.* [Begins:] Consideringe the obligation, which his catholike magestye my lord and master [etc. An address to English catholics.] s.sh.fol. [*Lisbon, S. Lopes?* 1597?] L¹¹(S.P.D., Eliz., vol. 270, doc. 88.1.)
    (Formerly 19842) A&R 593.

Padre, *Signior.* Newes from Millaine. 1630. *See* 17916.3 sq.

Paeschen, Jan van. The spiritual pilgrimage of Hierusalem. [1604–05.] *See* 12574.

19087.7 **Page, Phillip.** To the right reverend . . . the Lords spirituall and temporall, in Parliament. An abstract of the greevances of P. Page against Foxwell, Hutton, Sherbon, Day, and Cason. [In a dispute over land.] s.sh.fol. [*W. Jaggard*, 1621.] L⁸(GL 3927). Sherburn and Day, servants of Lord Chancellor Bacon, are accused of accepting bribes. The appeal ends: 'For to leaue him [Page] to the Law, is to leaue a mastlesse sinking shippe in a raging sea . . .'

19088 **Page, Samuel.** The allegeance of the cleargie. A sermon. [Contains 9 sermons.] 4°. *N. Okes f. S. Waterson*, 1616. Ent. 6 ja. L.O.C².EX.M.+; F.HN.ILL.U. Sydney U.

19088.3 — [Anr. issue, w. added gen. tp:] Nine sermons upon sundrie texts. *N. Okes f. S. ⟨Wate⟩rson*, 1616. HD(tp def.).

19088.7 — [Anr. issue, w. gen. tp:] Nine sermons: preached uppon speciall occasion. *f. S. Waterson*, 1630. C. (Formerly 19093)

19089 — The broken heart: or, Davids penance. Published by N. Snape. 4°. *T. Harper*, 1637. Ent. 8 ap. 1636. L.O. C⁵.D.PETYT.+; F.HN.HD.ILL.PN².+

19090 — Divine sea-service. 1616. = pt. of 19091.

19091 — God be thanked. A sermon [on Ps.126.2.] Hereunto are added sundry formes of prayer for such as travell by sea. 4°. *N. Okes f. S. Waterson*, 1616. L.O.C.EX.G².+; F.HN.HD.ILL. (2nd pt. formerly 19090)

19092 — A godly learned exposition, together w. apt notes on the Lords prayer. Published by N. Snape. 4°. *T. Harper*, 1631. Ent. 19 jy. L.O.C.G².M.+; F.HN.NY¹¹. PN².U.

19093 — Nine sermons. 1630. Now = 19088.7.

19094 — A sermon, preached at the funerall of S[ir]. Richard Leueson. 16° in 8's. *W. White*, 1605. L.

— *See also* 4275.

19095 **Page, Ulalia,** *Mrs.* The lamentation of Master Pages wife of Plimmouth. [1640?] Now = 6557.4.

19096 **Page, William.** A treatise or justification of bowing at the name of Jesus. By way of answere to an Appendix [in 20458]. Together with an examination of reasons made by Mr Prinne to Mr Widdowes [in 20465]. 4°. *Oxford, J. Lichfield*, 1631. L.O.C.D².BIRM.+; F.CAL. HD.U.Y.+ Supports 25593. Extra errata for this are bd. in c⁴ copy of 24884.

19096a — [Anr. issue, w. cancel tp, w. 'Published by command' added.] L⁴.O.C.DUR⁵.NEP.+; F.HN(lacks tp)*.HD.U. 𝕬

— *ed. See* 23993.

Page, William, *tr. See* 6130.

Pageant. A pageant of Spanish humours. 1599. *See* 23010.

19097 **Paget, John.** An answer to the unjust complaints of W. Best. Also an answer to Mr. J. Davenport [6311]. 4°. *Amsterdam, J. F. Stam*, 1635. L(tp only, Harl. 5930/458).L³.O(2).O¹¹.C. Answered by 1973.5 and 6310.

19098 — An arrow against the separation of the Brownists. 4°. *Amsterdam, G. Veseler*, 1618. L.O.C³.D².NOR².+; HN.HD.LC(lacks tp).NY.Y.+

19099 — Meditations of death. 12°. (*Dort, H. Ash*, 1639.) L.O. C.PLUME. Chester PL.; F.HN.Y.

19100 — A primer of christian religion. 8°. *J. Harison f. T. Man*, 1601. O⁶(imp.).C.CHES.; U.

— *See also* 19068.

19101 **Pagit, Eusebius.** Eusebii Pagetti catechismus Latine æditus, authore N. Baxtero. 8°. *T. Vautrollerius*, 1585. C¹⁰.; F. 𝕬

19102 — A godlie and fruitefull sermon [on Gen.xiv.20,21]. 8°. *J. Wolfe f. T. Man*, 1583. Ent. 24 fb. L.C.; F. *See* Arber II.854.

19103 — [Anr. ed. Anon.] 8°. [*R. Waldegrave*, 1584?] L.O.P. A piracy; signed in Waldegrave's manner.

19104 — [Anr. issue, w. cancel tp. Init. E. P.] L.; F.

19105 — A godly sermon: preached at Detford. [Anon.] 8°. *f. T. Man*, 1586. L(2).C(2).C⁵.

Pagit, Eusebius—*cont.*

19105.5 — The history of the Bible briefly collected by way of question and answere. Read and corrected by the author. 12°. *J. Legat, pr. to the Univ. of Camb., sold by S. Waterson*, [*London,*] 1602. Ent. to Waterson a. Burby ? 3 fb. 1603. F(imp.).

19106 — [Anr. ed.] The historie [etc.] 12°. *J. Legate, pr. to the Univ. of Camb., sold by S. Waterson*, [*London, c.* 1605.] O.C.

19106.5 — [Anr. ed.] 12°. *J. Legat, sold by S. Waterson*, 1611. Y.

19107 — [Anr. ed.] 12°. *J. Legat, sold by S. Waterson*, 1613. L.; HD.

19107.5 — [Anr. ed.] 12°. *J. Legat*, 1623. Ass'd to Legat 31 my. 1615. E⁴. Burby's share ass'd to W. Welby 16 oc. 1609. In the assignment to Legat 31 my. 1615, 75 copies of each impression reserved to Waterson and Welby. Welby's rights ass'd to T. Snodham 2 mr. 1618; to W. Stansby 23 fb. 1626.

19108 — [Anr. ed.] 8°. *J. L[egat,] sold by S. Waterson*, 1627. L.L³.O(2).C.HETH.; F.HN.NY. Tp lines 9–10: 'bind/them'.

19108.5 — [Anr. ed.] 8°. *J. L[egat,] sold by S. Waterson*, 1627. ILL. Tp lines 9–10: 'and/bind'.

19108.7 — [Anr. ed.] 8°. *J. L[egat,] sold by S. Waterson*, 1627. C.HETH.; HD.ILL.NY.Y. Tp lines 9–10: 'and/binde'.

19109 — [Anr. ed.] 12°. *J. L[egat,] sold by S. Waterson*, 1628. L.O.C².DUL.; HN. F1ʳ line 10: 'Aialon'; line 15: 'kings'.

19109.2 — [Anr. ed.] 12°. *J. L[egat] and are [sold by S. Waterson*, *c.* 1630.] o(imprint cropt). F1ʳ line 10: 'Aialon'; line 15: 'Kings'; tp lines 3–4: 'BIBLE,/BRIEFLY'.

19109.3 — [Anr. ed.] 12°. *J. L[egat,] sold by S. Waterson*, 1632. L². F1ʳ line 10: 'Aijalon'.

19109.4 — [Anr. ed.] 12°. *J. L[egat,] sold by S. Waterson*, [1634?] BR(imp.). The imprint was clearly never dated; tp lines 3–4: 'BRIEFELY/collected'.

19109.5 — A verie fruitful sermon, necessary to be read . . . concerning predestination. [Anon.] 8°. *R. Warde f. T. Man*, 1583. Ent. 24 fb. O.E². (Formerly 22240) *See* Arber II.854.

19109.7 — [Anr. ed.] 8°. *R. Walde-graue f. T. Man*, [1583?] O(frag., Douce Add.142/663).

— *tr. See* 2962, pt. 1.

19110 **Pagitt, Ephraim.** Christianographie, or the description of the multitude and sundry sorts of christians not subject to the pope. 4°. *T. P[aine] a. W. J[ones] f. M. Costerden*, 1635. Text ent. to Costerden 3 no. 1634; map ent. to Jones 6 jn. 1635. L.O.C⁹.M.STU.+; F.HN.HD.IND.U(imp.).+

19110.5 — — [A prospectus for 19110.] 1635. *See* Addenda.

19111 — Second edition inlarged. 4°. *W. J[ones] a. N. O[kes] f. M. Costerden*, 1636. Ent. 4 mr. L.O.C.D².E.+; F.HN. HD.N.NY.+

19111.5 — — [A publisher's prospectus for 19111, w. engr. map.] fol(2?). *W. Jones*, 1636. Broxbourne (O). The letterpress, apparently pr. on a single sheet, is cut up in 3 strips and pasted around the map.

19112 — Third edition inlarged. fol. *J. Okes f. M. Costerden*, 1640. L.O.C.D.E.+; F.HN.HD.N.U.+

19113 — A relation of the christians in the world. 4°. *J. Okes*, 1639. Ent. 26 au. L.O(imp.).LAMPORT.M.WIN².; NY.U.

— *tr. See* 15319.

19114 **Paglia, Antonio dalla.** The benefite that christians receiue by Jesus Christ crucified. [Anon.] *Tr.* out of French by A. G[olding?] 8°. (*T. East*) *f. L. Harison a. G. Bishop*, 1573. L.; HD. Improperly attrib. to Palerio [i.e. dalla Paglia.] Actually by Benedetto da Mantova and revised by M. A. Flaminio.

19115 — [Anr. ed.] 8°. *H. Bynneman f. L. Harison a. G. Bishop*, [1575?] L.L⁴.L¹⁵.O.; F.

19115.5 — [Anr. ed.] 8°. [*T. Dawson?*] *f. L. Harison a. G. Byshop*, [1577?] LAMPORT.

19116 — [Anr. ed.] 8°. *T. D(awson) f. G. Bishop a. T. Woodcocke*, 1580. Ass'd to Woodcock 15 jy. 1578. L.C¹²(lacks tp).; NY¹¹(imp.).

Paglia, Antonio dalla—*cont.*
19116.5 — [Anr. ed.] The benefit of Christs death, or the glorious riches of Gods free grace. 8º. *J. L[egat] f. A. Hebb*, 1631. Ent. 26 se. STD.

19117 — Third edition. 8º. *J. L[egat] f. A. Hebb*, 1633. o⁶(imp.). C.P.; F.

19118 — Fourth edition. 8º. *E. G[riffin] f. A. Hebb*, 1638. L.

19119 **Pain.** The payne and sorowe of euyll maryage. [*Tr.* by J. Lydgate from De coniuge non ducenda.] 4º. (*W. de Worde,*) [c. 1530.] HN.

19120 **Painter, Anthony,** Anthony Paint⟨er⟩ the blaspheming caryar. Who sunke into the ground vp to the neck, not to bee drawne out by the strength of hor⟨ses,⟩ and there dyed the 3. of November. 1613. 4º. [*G. Eld*] *f. J. Trundle*, 1614. Ent. 21 ja. o(tp cropt).

19120.3 **Painter, William.** Luctus consolatorius. Super morte nuper D. cancellarij Angliæ [C. Hatton], Nouembr. 1591. [In verse. Init. W. P. G. i.e. W. Painter, *Gent.*] 4º. *ap. T. Orwinum*, 1591. F.

19120.7 — A moorning diti vpon the deceas of Henry Earl of Arundel. [Init. Guil. P. G. i.e. W. Painter, *Gent.*] s.sh.fol. *J. Allde*, [1580.] Ent. 28 mr. 1580. L⁵ (Lemon 73).; HN.
(Formerly 10932)

19121 — The palace of pleasure. [Vol. I.] 4º. [*J. Kingston a.*] *H. Denham f. R. Tottell a. W. Jones*, 1566 (26 ja.) Ent. to W. Jones 1565–66. L.L⁴(imp.).; F(imp.). HN(lacks tp). ILL(imp.).PFOR.TCU.+
Kingston pr. quires A–Oo.

19122 — [Anr. ed.] 4º in 8's. *T. Marshe*, 1569. o(2, 1 imp.). c²(imp.).M. Charlecote Park, Warwickshire.; F(3, 2 imp.).HN.ILL(imp.).LC(imp.). Hickmott.

19123 — [Anr. ed.] Corrected and augmented. 4º in 8's. *T. Marshe*, 1575. Ass'd on T. Marsh's death to T. Orwin 23 jn. 1591. L.L³⁰.o(lacks tp).c.; F(imp.).ILL. PML.TEX.Y.+

19124 — The second tome of the palace of pleasure. 1567. 4º. *H. Bynneman f. N. England*, (1567 (8 no.)) Ent. 1566–67. L.o.M.M².STU(lacks tp).; F.HN.CH.ILL.PFOR.+
Outer forme of 1st quire in 2 settings: tp line 11: 'Clarke' (F,CH) or 'Clerke' (L,O,HN).

19125 — [Anr. ed.] Agayn corrected and encreased. 4º in 8's. *T. Marshe*, [1580?] Ass'd on T. Marsh's death to T. Orwin 23 jn. 1591. L.L³⁰.C(imp.).c²(imp.). Charlecote Park, Warwickshire.+; F.ILL.PML.TEX.Y.+
— *tr. See* 5059, 6130, 11420.

19125.5 **Painter, William,** *Aphorist.* [Heading B1ʳ:] Chaucer new painted. [In verse.] 8º. [*G. Eld a. M. Flesher*, 1623.] Ent. to G. Eld a. M. Flesher 14 my. 1623. HN(imp.).

Pair. A paire of turtle doves. 1606. *See* 11094.

Paiva, Hieronymus de. *See* 13431.

Palamas, Gregorios. *See* 12343.5.

19126 **Palatinate.** A briefe information of the affaires of the Palatinate. [By T. Scott, *B.D.?*] 4º. [*London?*] 1624. L.O.C.D.E.+; F.HN.HD(2, 1 imp.).N.
Also issued as pt. of 22064.
— Catechesis religionis christianæ: quæ in ecclesiis Palatinatus traditur. 1591, etc. *See* 13023 sqq.

19127 — Certaine letters declaring . . . affaires in the Pallatinate. 1621. = 1037.
— The copy of a letter . . . concerning the present business of the Palatinate. 1622. *See* 5742.7.

19128 — Coppies of letters . . . relating occurrences in the Palatinate. 1622. Now = Newsbooks 56A.

19129 — A faithfull admonition of the Paltsgraves churches. Englished by J. Rolte. 4º. *E. Griffin f. G. Gibbes*, 1614. Ent. 20 de. 1613. L³⁸.O.DUR⁵.E².M².+; F.U.Y.

19130 — A full declaration of the faith and ceremonies professed in the dominions of Fredericke, Elector Palatine. *Tr.* J. Rolte. 4º. [*F. Kingston*] *f. W. Welby*, 1614. Ent. 30 jy. L.O.C.LINC.NEP.+; F.BO.

19131 — [Anr. ed., abridged.] A declaration of the Pfaltzgraves: concerning the faith professed in his churches. *Tr.* J. R[olte.] 4º. [*B. Alsop a. T. Fawcet*] *f. T. Jones*, 1637. L.O.C.D.E.+; F.HN.HD.U.Y.+

19132 — Newes from the Palatinate. 1622. Now = Newsbooks 37.

19133 — More news from the Palatinate. 1622. Now = Newsbooks 50. *See also* Newsbooks 38, 49.

Palatinate—*cont.*
19134 — The relation of all the last passages. 1622. Now = Newsbooks 63.
— The true copies of two letters from the Palatinate by Sir, F. N. 1622. *See* Newsbooks 55.

19135 — A true relation of all such battailes. 1622. Now = Newsbooks 47.
— *See also* Newsbooks 44, 51, etc.

Palatinus, Musaeus, *pseud.* The two Lancashire lovers. 1640. *See* 3590.

Paleario, Aonio, *pseud. See* 19114.

Paleologus, Clement. *See* Indulgences 90 sq.

Paleologus, Michael de. *See* Indulgences 117A, 117B, 118 sq., 120 sqq.

Palermo. [Begins:] It is certified from Palermo. [1622.] *See* Newsbooks 45.

19136 **Palfreyman, Thomas.** [Headline:] Diuine meditations. 8º. (*H. Bynneman f. W. Norton*, 1572.) o(lacks tp).

19137 — A myrrour or cleare glasse, for all estates, to looke in, conteinyng the true knowlege and loue of god. 8º. (*H. Sutton, at the costes of M. Lobley a. J. Waley,*) 1560 (7 my.) Ent. to Lobley 1559–60. C.

19137.5 — A paraphrase vppon the epistle of the holie apostle S. Paule to the Romanes. [*Ed.*] (T. Palfreyman.) 4º. *H. Bynneman f. W. Norton*, [1572?] L(lacks tp).L⁴⁶.
Includes a letter by Zwingli, several tracts by M. Cellarius, and a reprint of 22268.

19138 — The treatise of heauenly philosophie. 4º in 8's. [*H. Middleton*] *f. W. Norton*, 1578. L.O.M.WI.; F(2).HN. LC.NY¹¹.
— *ed. See* 1255.5, 1257, 1259, 1260a.

19138.5 **Palingenius, Marcellus** [i.e. P. A. Manzolli]. Marcelli Palingenii Stellati poetæ doctissimi Zodiacus vitæ. [In verse.] 8º. *ex off. T. Marshi*, 1569. R.; ILL.

19139 — [Anr. ed.] 8º. *in æd. H. Bynneman*, 1572. C¹⁰.; HN.

19140 — [Anr. ed.] 16º in 8's. *ap. T. Marsh*, 1574. L(2).O²².E².P. Stevens Cox.; F.HN.ILL.

19141 — [Anr. ed.] 8º. *ap. T. Marsh*, 1575. L.; F.HN.CU.

19142 — [Anr. ed.] 16º in 8's. *ap. T. Marsh*, 1579. L.L¹⁶.; CHI.

19143 — [Anr. ed.] 8º. *R. Robinsonus*, 1592. L.L¹⁶.o⁶.C³.P.+; F.HD.ILL.

19143.5 — [Anr. ed.] 8º. *ap. R. Dexter*, 1599. C.; F. Halifax, King's College U.

19144 — [Anr. ed.] 8º. [*R. Bradock,*] *ap. R. Dexter*, 1602. L.O.C.DUR(Bamb.).NLW.+; F.ILL.

19145 — = 19146.
19146 — [Anr. ed.] 8º. [*J. Legat,*] *ex off. Soc. Stat.*, 1616. L.O. C.BIRM. Edinburgh, Royal High School.+; F.HN. CAL.HD.ILL.

19147 — [Anr. ed.] 8º. *ex off. Soc. Stat.*, 1639. Ent. to the English Stock 5 mr. 1620. L.O¹⁰.C.A.DUL.; F.HN.ILL(2). STAN.Y.

19148 — [A trans.] The firste thre bokes of the most christiã poet M. Palingenius, called the zodyake of lyfe: newly *tr.* by B. Googe. [In verse.] 8º. *J. Tisdale f. R. Newberye*, 1560. Ent. bef. 4 my. L(imp.).C(frag.).; HN.HD.ILL.IND(imp.).

19149 — The firste syxe bokes. *Tr.* B. Googe. 8º. *J. Tisdale f. R. Newbery*, 1561. L(2).O.P.; F.HN.ILL.N.Y.+

19150 — The zodiake of life wherein are twelue bokes *tr.* B. Googe. 8º. *H. Denham f. R. Newberye*, 1565 (18 ap.) L.L⁶.O.C².WN.+; F.HN.HD.N.WIS.+

19151 — [Anr. ed.] Newly recognished. 4º in 8's. [*H. Middleton f.*] *R. Newberie*, 1576. L.L³⁰.C.E.SHEF.; F.HN.

19152 — [Anr. ed.] 4º in 8's. *R. Robinson*, 1588. Ass'd 11 de. 1587. L.O.C²(lacks tp).P.STU.+; F.HN.CU.HD(lacks T1).Y.+

Palladine. The famous, pleasant, and variable historie, of Palladine. 1588. *See* 5541.

19152.5 **Palladius, Peter.** Isagoge ad libros propheticos & apostolicos. 8º. *imp. G. Bishop*, 1592. C⁹.C¹⁰.; HART.

19153 — [A trans.] An introduction into the bookes of the prophets and apostles. *Tr.* E. Vaughan. 8º. *G. S[haw] f. W. Holme*, 1598. L(tp only, Ames I.620).O.C. PETYT. Juel-Jensen.; F.HN.HD(cropt).

Pallas. Palladis palatium. 1604. *See* 26014.

19154 **Pallavicino, Sir Horatio.** Album, seu nigrum amicorum. Author in libri nomen. [Verses on the death of Sir H. Pallavicino. *Ed.*] (T. Field.) 4º. *per T. Creed pro A. Wise*, 1600. L².O.

Pallavicino, *Sir* **Horatio**—*cont.*

19154.3 — An Italians dead bodie, stucke with English flowers. Elegies, on the death of Sir Oratio Pallavicino. [Verses by Jos. Hall and others. *Ed.*] (T. Field.) 4°. *T. Creede f. A. Wise,* 1600. L².

Palmendos. The honorable, . . . historie of Palmendos. 1589. *See* 18064.

Palmer, Anthony, *ed. See* 22801.

19154.5 **Palmer, Herbert.** An endeavour of making the principles of christian religion plain and easie. [Anon.] 8°. *Cambridge, R. Daniel,* 1640. L.C⁵.
(Formerly 5187)

19154.7 **Palmer, Robert.** A godly and fruitfull sermon vpon the 2. and 3. verses of the first chapter of the prophet Malachie. 8°. *J. Wolfe,* 1591. Ent. 17 de. 1590. D.

19155 **Palmer, Thomas.** Bristolls military garden. A sermon. 4°. *F. Kyngston,* 1635. Ent. 6 mr. 1636. L.L³.O.C⁶.; HD.Y.

19156 **Palmer,** *Sir* **Thomas.** An essay of the meanes how to make our travailes, more profitable. 4°. *H. L[ownes] f. M. Lownes,* 1606. Ent. 3 jn. L.O.C.D.M.+; F.HN.HD.N.NY.+
Imitated from T. Zwinger's Methodus Apodemica, 1577.

19157 **Palmerin,** *de Oliva.* Palmerin d'Oliua. [Pt. 1] The mirrour of nobilitie. Turned into English by A. M(unday.) 4°. *J. Charlewoode f. W. Wright,* 1588. L.; F.

19158 — The [first] second part of the historie of Palmerin d'Oliua. *Tr.* A. M(unday.) 2 pts. 4° in 8's. *T. Creede,* 1597. Ass'd from Wright 9 au. 1596. L(imp.).; HN(pt. 2 only, imp.).

19159 — [Anr. ed. of pt. 1:] Palmerin d'Oliva. The mirrour of nobilitie. [*Tr.*] A. M[unday.] 4° in 8's. *T. Creede,* 1615. L⁴.

19159a — [Anr. issue of pt. 1, w. cancel tp, w. pt. 2 added.] Palmerin d'Oliva the first (second) part. 2 pts. 4° in 8's. *T. C[reede] a. B. A[lsop] f. R. Higgenbotham,* 1616. Ass'd 4 de. 1615. L(imp.).L⁴(pt. 2 only).HETH(pt. 1 only, lacking tp)*.; HN(pt. 2 only).

19160 — [Anr. ed.] 2 pts. 4° in 8's. *f. [by] B. Alsop a. T. Fawcet,* 1637. L.O.C(imp.).G⁴.M.+; F.HN.HD(imp.).N.Y.+
M copy has variant imprint to pt. 1 reading: '*by B. Alsop a. T. Fawcet,* 1637.'

19161 **Palmerin,** *of England.* The [first] seconde part, of the no lesse rare, historie of Palmerin of England. [By F. de Moraes.] *Tr.* A. M[unday.] 2 pts. 4° in 8's. *T. Creede,* 1596. Ent. to J. Charlewood 13 fb. 1581; to T. Creede 9 au. 1596. L(imp.).

19162 — [Anr. ed. of pt. 1.] The [xylographic] first part [etc.] 4° in 8's. *T. Creede,* 1609. L(tp only).; F(lacks A8). HD(imp.).
Dedic. signed 'A. Munday'. HD also has leaves G1,8 and H4,5 from an ed. of pt. 2 prob. intended to accompany this. They are in the binding of 24622.5 and have chapter arguments in italic whereas the other eds. have them in roman.

19163 — [Anr. ed.] The first (second) part, [etc.] 2 pts. 4° in 8's. *T. Creede a. B. Alsop,* 1616. L(pt. 2 only).O.LIV³ (pt. 1 only).HETH(imp.).; F.HD.MCG.

19164 — [Anr. ed.] 2 pts. 4° in 8's. *B. Alsop a. T. Fawcet,* 1639. L.L⁴.O.C.E.+; F.HN.CH.CU.N.+

19165 — The third and last part of Palmerin of England. *Tr.* A. M(undy.) 4°. *J. R[oberts] f. W. Leake,* 1602. Ent. 10 mr. 1595. L.L⁵(imp.).O.E.; F.HN. Cleveland PL.

19165.5 **Palmus.** A most excellent song of the love of young Palmus, and faire Sheldra. To the tune of Shackleyhay. *Ballad.* 2 pts. s.sh.fol. *f. J. W[right,* c. 1630.] Ent. to widow of E. White sen. 16 mr. 1613; to J. Wright a. ballad ptnrs. 14 de. 1624. C⁶.

Palsgrave, John. Joannis Palsgraui ecphrasis Anglica. 1540. *See* 11470.

19166 — Lesclarcissement de la langue francoyse, [etc.] fol. [*R. Pynson,* c. 1524;] (*fynysshed by J. Haukyns,*) 1530 (18 jy.). L.O.C.M.SHR.+; F.ILL.LC.TEX.Y.
Pynson pr. 2nd A–D⁶ F–K⁶. *See L.&P. Henry VIII,* III², pp.1522–23; IV¹, p.16.

19167 **Paludanus, Franciscus.** A short relation, of the life, of S. Elizabeth. Queen of Portugall. *Tr.* out of Dutch, by Sister Catherine Francis [i.e. C. Greenbury.] 8°. *Bruxelles, J. Pepermans,* 1628. L.
A&R 595.

Pammelia. *See* 20759.

Pamphilus, Eusebius, *tr. See* 16980.

19168 **Panacea.** Panacea: or, select aphorismes, divine and morall. (A characterisme of the foure cardinall vertues [by *Sir* R. G., *Knight.*]) 8°. *A. Mathewes,* 1630. Ent. 12 mr. L.P.; F(lacks 1st A3).HD.

Panarete. *See* 3553 sqq.

Panedonius, Philogenes, *pseud.* Ar't asleepe husband? 1640. *See* 3555.

19169 **Panke, John.** Collectanea. Out of St Gregory and St Bernard against the papists. 8°. *Oxford, J. Lichfield a. J. Short,* 1618. L.O.STD.

19170 — Eclogarius, or briefe summe of the truth of that title of Supreame Governour, given to his majestie in causes spirituall, and ecclesiasticall. 8°. *Oxford, J. Barnes,* 1612. L(2, 1 imp.).WOR.; F(imp.).

19171 — The fal of Babel. By the confusion of tongues, proving against the papists that it cannot be discerned what they would say, in the question of the sacrifice of the masse. 4°. *Oxford, J. Barnes,* 1608. L.O.C.D.; HD.

19171a — [Anr. issue, w. cancel tp, w. imprint:] *Oxford, Jos. Barnes, sold by John Barnes, [London,]* 1613. L.C⁵.
Tp pr. by W. White.

19172 — A short admonition by way of dialogue, to all those who have with held themselves from the Lordes table. 8°. *Oxford, J. Barnes, sold by S. Waterson, [London,]* 1604. L.O.; HD.

19172.3 **Panke, William.** A most breefe, easie and plaine receite for faire writing. Both for the Roman and secretary handes. 8°. *E. A[llde] f. J. Perin,* [1591.] HN.
To the Reader dated 30 Sept. 1591. Examples added in MS.

19172.7 **Panter, Patrick.** Academiae Sancti Andreae, serenissimo suo principi, Carolo advenienti gratulatio. [In verse.] 8° in 4. *Edinburgi, hæredes A. Hart,* 1633. E.; F.
(Formerly 21552) Prob. issued w. 19173.

19173 — Valliados libri tres, opus inchoatum. [In verse.] 8°. *Edinburgi, hæredes A. Hart,* 1633. A.E.STU.; F.
Prob. issued w. 19172.7.

Paolo, *Servita. See* Sarpi, P.

Papa. Papa confutatus. 1580. *See* 11240.

19174 **Papal Exchequer.** Fiscus Papalis. Sive, catalogus indulgentiarum. A part of the popes exchequer. *Tr.* [W. Crashaw.] *Lat. a. Eng.* 4°. *N. Okes f. G. Norton,* 1617. L.O⁵.C.DUR.M².+; F.HN.CHI.HD.NY.+

19174a — [Anr. ed.] 4°. *B. Alsop,* 1621. L.O.C.D².E.+; F.HN.CHI.HD.NY¹¹.+
Orig. tp signed: 'W. Crashaw' (D²,C³,F, 1 HD); cancel tp not signed (C, 1 HD).

Papatus Romanus. Papatus romanus: liber de origine. 1617. *See* 7002.

Papist. A spectacle for a blind papist. [1582.] *See* 23030.

19175 **Papists.** Dialogus contra papistarum tyrannidem. 8°. *W. S[eres],* 1562 (10 au.) Ent. 1562–63. L.L².; HD.
Possibly by W. Haddon; includes his poem 'Contra evangelicorum hostes, precatio.'

19176 — [A trans.] A dialogue agaynst the tyrannye of the papistes. *Tr.* E. C. 8°. *W. S[eres,]* 1562 (17 se.) Ent. 1562–63. L(imp.).L².O.; F.HD(lacks D1).
Tp varies: with (O) or without (HD) the translator's inits.

19177 — A litel treatise ageynste the mutterynge of some papistis in corners. [By T. Swinnerton.] 1534. Now = 23551.5.

19178 — Mercyful father we humbly thee pray, Frō the tirāny of papists defēd vs alway. s.sh.12°. *J. Awdely,* [1570?] L.
Prob. a colophon leaf of an unidentified work.

19179 — A reply with the occasion thereof, to a rayling, libel, of the papists, set vpon postes, and also in Paules church. 4°. [*H. Singleton,* 1579?] Ent. to H. Singleton 6 ap. 1579. L².O¹⁷.; F.HN.HD.

— A warning agaynst the dangerous practises of papists. [1569?] *See* 18685.3.

19179.5 **Paracelsus.** A hundred and fourtene experiments and cures. Collected by J. H[ester.] 8°. [*H. Middleton*, 1583?] O.
(Formerly 19181) An abridged trans. of the Latin text, *Lyons*, 1582.

19180 — [Anr. ed.] Collected by J. Hester. 4°. *V. Sims*, 1596. H. Bynneman's copy ent. to Simmes 1 mr. L.L¹⁶.O. O¹⁷.G²(3).; F(imp.).CH.NLM.Y.

19181 — Now = 19179.5.

19181.3 — The true and perfect order to distill oyles out of al maner of spices . . . gathered out of sundry aucthors. As Gualterius, [etc. *Tr.*] J. H(ester.) [Not by Paracelsus but reprinted in the following eds.] 8°. [*J. Charlewood*,] (1575.) G².

19181.5 — [Anr. ed., enlarged, w. title:] The first part of the key of philosophie. Wherein is contained secretes of physicke and philosophie, deuided into twoo bookes. In the firste is the order to distill, oiles. In the seconde is the order to prepare, mineralles. First written by T. Paraselsus [*sic*], and now published by J. Hester. 8°. *R. Day*, 1580. E⁵(imp.).G².; Y.

19181.7 — [Anr. ed.] 8°. *V. Simmes*, 1596. L.BRISTOL².G²(2).M² (imp.).; F.
(Formerly 13252)

19182 — [Anr. ed.] The secrets of physick and philosophy. 12°. *A. M[athewes] f. W. Lugger*, 1633. L(destroyed). L¹⁶.G²(2).; HN.CAL.HD.NLM.WIS.

19182.5 — [Anr. ed., anon., substituting printer's preface for Hester's.] A storehouse of physicall and philosophicall secrets. The first (second) part. 4° in 8's. *T. Harper*, 1633. L(2, 1 imp.).L⁴.O(2).M⁴.; F. WIS.Y.
(Formerly 23293) Also issued as pt. 3 of 1357.

19183 **Paradin, Claude.** The heroicall deuises of M. Claudius Paradin. *Tr.* P. S. 16° in 8's. *W. Kearney*, 1591. Ent. to T. Scarlet 17 au. 1590. L.O(2).O⁶(imp.).D⁶.; F. ILL.

19184 — The true and lyuely historyke purtreatures of the woll bible. 1553. = 3043.

19185 **Paradoxes.** Foure paradoxes. 1 A byshop and a minister is all one. [etc.] 8°. [*London?* c. 1570.] O.
— Paradoxes against common opinion. 1602. *See* 6467.5.

19186 **Paragon.** A peerelesse paragon. *Ballad.* 2 pts. s.sh.fol. *f. T. Lambert*, [1633.] Ent. 18 no. 1633. L.

Parallel. A parallel.—Parallelismus.—A second parallel. 1626. *See* 10735, 10734, 10737.

Parasynagma. Parasynagma Perthense. 1620. *See* 4361.

19187 **Pardon.** A generall free pardon or charter of heuyn blys, very necessary for all true christē people. Not gyuen by any popysh collusyon, but by Jesu Christ. Compyled in our old Englyssh tong, in the yere M.iiii.C. 8° in 4's. (*R. Lant f. J. Gough*,) [1542?] F.
— The general pardon, [etc. 1570?] *See* 13012.
— *See also* Indulgences 10 sqq.

19188 **Pardons.** [Ends:] The somme is fyue yeres [etc. c. 1510.] Now = Indulgences 117.

19189 **Paré, Ambroise.** The workes of that famous chirurgion A. Parey. *Tr.* T. Johnson. [Bk. 29 *tr.* G. Baker.] fol. *T. Cotes a. R. Young*, 1634. Ent. to Young a. R. Cotes 28 se. 1629. L.O.C.E².M².+; F.HN.CU.HD.MICH.+
Variant settings of dedic. to Sir Edward Herbert or Edward Lord Herbert of Cherbury; both at Y. Bk. 22 reprinted from 19192. Young pr. quires Aaa–Yyyy.
— An explanation of the fashion of instruments of chirurgery. 1631. *See* 6063.

19190 — [Anr. ed.] 1634. = pt. of 20783.

19191 — The method of curing wounds made by gun-shot. Done into English by W. Hamond. 4°. *I. Jaggard*, 1617. Ent. to W. Jaggard 2 de. 1616. O.; Y(imp.).

19192 — A treatise of the plague. Collected out of the workes of A. Parey. [*Tr.* T. Johnson.] 4°. *R. Y[oung] a. R. C[otes], sold by M. Sparke*, 1630. Works ent. to R. Young a. R. Cotes 28 se. 1629. L¹⁷.O.C³.A.P.+
A,P misdated: '1930'. Reprinted as bk. 22 of 19189.

Pareus, Daniel, *ed. See* 13220, 20567.3.

19193 **Pareus, David.** Pareus. [A Latin poem.] 1585. Now = 19340.5.

Pareus, David—*cont.*

19194 — Davidis Parei theologi Archipalatini. In S. Matthæi evangelium commentarius. Cui subjungitur in duas S. Petri Epistolas: [etc.] commentarius. 4° in 8's. *Oxoniæ, J. Lichfield, imp. T. Huggins*, 1631. O.O¹⁹. A.LEIC.SCL.+; HD.ILL.
Last 120 pp. pr. in London by Eliz. Allde. Pareus's works ordered burned; *see Acts P.C., 1621–1623*, p.237. *See also* 18982, 19014.

19194.5 — [A variant, w. imprint:] *Oxoniæ, J. Lichfield, imp. H. Curteyne*, 1631. L².O⁵.C⁵.BIRM.D.+; LC.

19194.7 — [A variant, w. imprint:] *Oxoniæ, J. Lichfield, imp. H. Crypps*, 1631. L(destroyed).O²⁶.O³⁸.; F.V.
— *ed. See* 24527, 24536.

19195 **Parfeius, Gulielmus.** Speculum iuuenum uxores impetuose affectantiū. 8°. (*ex off. J. Herfordie*, 1547.) O.P.

Pargiter, William. *See* 25759.5.

19196 **Parinchef, John.** An extracte of examples, apothegmes, and histories. Collected out of Lycosthenes, Brusonius and others. *Tr.* J. P(arincheffe.) 8°. *H. Bynneman f. H. Toie*, [1572.] O(imp.).O⁵(imp.).; HN.
Epistle dated 1572. HN has variant tp w. inits. 'A. P.'

19197 **Paris.** The miserable estate of the citie of Paris at this present. With a true report of sundrie straunge visions, lately seene in the ayre vpon the coast of Britanie. 4°. [*J. Wolfe*] *f. T. Nelson*, 1590. Ent. 24 au. L.P.

19198 — A rare example of a vertuous maid in Paris. *Ballad.* s.sh.fol. *by a. for A. M[ilbourne,] sold by the booksellers of London*, [after 1692.]
Not an STC item.

19199 — A treatise concerning the famine of Paris. 1590. = pt. of 10004.

19200 — [*Parlement.*] A newe order for banqueroupts. (A notable decree of the parliament of Paris against W. Buhique.) 8°. *T. Dawson f. T. Charde*, 1582. Ent. 24 au. O.
— An extract of the registers of the Court of Parliament of Paris. 1611. *See* 1845.

19201 — An act or decree of the court of Parliament of Paris. Against a booke, intituled F. Suares Defensio fidei catholicæ. *Tr.* J. B[arnes?] 4°. [*T. Snodham*] *f. John Barnes*, 1614. L.O.O³.DUR³.E.; F.

19202 — A decree of the court of Parliament at Paris, the second day of Januarie, 1615. Touching the soueraigntie of the king. 4°. [*W. Jaggard*] *f. N. Bourne*, 1615. Ent. 9 ja. O.

19203 — A copie of the first arrest or decree of the Parlament [*sic*] of Paris, against the booke of Santarellus the Jesuite. [13 Mar. 1626, etc.] 4°. *R. Badger, sold [by R. Allott,*] 1634. O.WOR.; TEX.

19203.3 — Arrest of the court of Parliament, whereby the pretended marriage of Monsieur, with the princesse Margaret of Lorraine, is declared not valuably contracted. [5 Sept. 1634.] (Arrest de la cour.) *Eng. a. Fr.* 2 pts. 4°. *R. Raworth f. N. Butter a. N. Bourne*, 1634. Ent. 15 se. F.
Pt. 2 pr. by T. Harper, although sub tp has imprint: 'Paris, A. Estiene, P. Mettayer & C. Prevost, 1634.'

Paris, *Physicians of. See* 3841.

19203.7 **Paris University.** The censure of the sacred facultie of divinitie of Paris against the four bookes concerning the ecclesiastical cōmonwealth, composed by M. A. de Dominis [6994]. *Tr.* by a student in divinitie. 8°. *Doway, widdowe of L. Kellam a. Thomas his sonne*, 1618. L.O¹⁷.
— Censurs of certaine propositions. 1631. *See* 4911.5.

19204 — The copie of a late decree of the Sorbone condemning the murthering of princes. Together, with the arrest of the parliament. [8 June 1610.] *Tr.* into English. [*Ed.*] (J. B.) *Eng., Lat. a. Fr.* 4°. *R. B[arker,]* 1610. L.O.C.D.DUR⁵.+; F.HN.HD.U.
Answered in 24992.

19205 — Summa actorum facultatis theologiæ Parisiensis contra librum inscriptum, Controversia Anglicana. Now = pt. 2 of 1703.
— A true coppie of a letter sent vnto Sixtus by those of the Sorbonne. [1590.] *See* 5744.
— *See also* 14526.

19206   **Paris,** *le chevalier.* Here begynneth thystorye of the noble knyght Parys, and of the fayr Vyēne. (*Tr.* w. Caxton.) fol. (*at westmestre, p Caxton,* 1485 (19 de.)) L. Duff 337.

19207   — [Anr. ed.] Thystorye [etc.] fol. (*andewarpe, G. Leeu,* 1492 (23 jn.)) D(a3 torn). Duff 338.

19207a — [Anr. ed.] 4°. [*W. de Worde, c.* 1505.] O(frags., D1,4; F1,4).
        From similarity of type and makeup, this and the following may be the same ed.

19208   — [Anr. ed. C1ʳ begins:] all the thre baners [etc.] 4°. [*W. de Worde, c.* 1505.] Ent. to T. Purfoot 8 au. 1586. L(frag., C4).
  — *See also* 17201.

19208.5 **Paris, John de.** A true recitall of the confession of the two murderers J. de Paris, and J. de la Vigne: touching the murder of J. de Wely, of Amsterdam. 4°. [*T. Snodham*] *f. N. Bourne,* 1616. Ent. 5 jn. F(imp.). HN(cropt).

19209   **Paris, Matthæus.** Matthæi Paris, monachi Albanensis, Angli, historia maior. [*Ed.* Abp. M. Parker.] fol. (*ap. R. Wolfium,*) 1571 (1570.) L.O.C.D.G4.+; F.HN. HD.N.NY11.+
        Wolfe's device in colophon.

19209a — [A variant, w. device in colophon replaced by Latin motto.] L.O.C.DUR5.G2.+; F.ILL.PML. Auckland PL. 𝔄

19210   — [Anr. ed.] Accesserunt, duorum Offarum . . . vitæ. Editore W. Wats. 2 pts. fol. *R. Hodgkinson* (*M. Flesher*), *sumpt. C. Bee & L. Sadler,* 1640 (1639.) 1st pt. ent. to R. Hodgkinson 21 mr. 1638; 2nd pt. ent. to Flesher 14 de. 1638. L.O.C.D.E8.+; F.HN.HD. N.NY.+

Parisians. The proces . . . committed by the Parisians leaguers. 1590. *See* 11287.5.

Parke, Robert, *tr. See* 12003.

19211   **Parker, Henry,** *Baron Morley.* The exposition and declaration of the psalme, Deus ultionum dominus. 8°. (*in æd. T. Bertheleti,* 1539.) L.L2.O.
  — *tr. See* 19811.

19212   **Parker, Henry,** *D.D.* [Begins:] RIche and pore [etc. Ends:] Here endith a . . . dyalogue. of Diues & paup. [Anon. Prob. not by Parker.] fol. (*R. Pynson,* 1493 (5 jy.)) L.O.C.G2.M.+; F(imp.).HN.CH.ILL.NY.+ Duff 339.

19213   — [Anr. ed.] Diues & pauper [xylographic]. fol. (*Westmonstre, W. de worde,* 1496 (3 de.)) L.O.C.D(imp.). M.+; MCG.NY.PML(imp.). Mellon. Philip Hofer, Cambridge, Mass.+ Duff 340.

19214   — [Anr. ed.] Diues and pauper. 8°. *in æd. T. Bertheleti,* (1536 (16 oc.)) L.L15.O.C4.M.+; F(lacks tp).HN.CHI. HD.

19215   **Parker, Henry,** *of Lincoln's Inn.* The case of shipmony briefly discoursed, according to the grounds of law, policy, and conscience. [Anon.] 4°. [*T. Harper,*] 1640. L.O.C.D.E11.+; F.HN.HD.N.NY.+

19216   — [Anr. ed.] 4°. [*E. Purslowe,*] 1640. L.O.C.D8.E.+; HN. CU.HD.LC.WIS.+
        In title: 'policie'; 49 pp.

19216.5 — [Anr. ed.] 4°. [*E. Purslowe?*] 1640. L30.DEU.E.; CU.
        In title: 'policie'; 30 pp.

19217   **Parker, John.** A true patterne of pietie, meete for all christian house-holders to looke vpon. 8°. [*J. Danter?* f.] *J. Wolfe,* 1599. Ent. 1 mr. 1592. F.

19217.5 **Parker, Martin.** An abstract of the historie of the renouned maiden queene Elizabeth. Briefly relating the principall matters throughout her raigne. In English meeter. [Init. M. P.] 32° in 8's. *T. Cotes,* 1631. Ent. to T. a. R. Cotes 16 no. 1630. Arthur Houghton.

19218   — A bill of fare: for, a Saturday nights supper. [Init. M. P.] *Ballad.* 2 pts. s.sh.fol. *M. P*[*arsons*] *f. F. Grove,* [1637.] Ent. 4 oc. 1637. L.

19219   — A banquet for soveraigne husbands. Or, the rosting of the ramme whole the twenty foure of June, 1629. [Init. M. P.] *Ballad.* 2 pts. s.sh.fol. [*M. Flesher*] *f. F. Coules,* [1629?] c6(torn).
        (Formerly also 1366)

19220   — The bonny bryer, or a Lancashire lasse, her sore lamentation. [Init. M. P.] *Ballad.* 2 pts. s.sh.fol. *f. F. G*[*rove,* 1630?] L.

Parker, Martin—*cont.*

19221   — A briefe description of the triumphant show made by Aulgernon Percie, earle of Northumberland, at his installation . . . into the garter, upon the 13. of May, 1635. [Init. M. P.] *Ballad.* 2 pts. s.sh.fol. *f. F. Coules,* [1635.] L.

19222   — A briefe dissection of Germaines affliction. [In verse.] 8°. *T. Cotes f. F. Grove,* 1638. Ent. 9 fb. L.; HD.

19223   — Britaines honour. In the two valiant Welchmen, who fought against fifteene thousand Scots. [Init. M. P.] *Ballad.* 2 pts. s.sh.fol. *E. G*[*riffin,*] *sold* [*by T. Lambert,* 1640.] O. 𝔄

19223.5 — The cooper of Norfolke: or, a pretty jest of a brewer, and the coopers wife. [Anon.] *Ballad.* 2 pts. s.sh.fol. [*M. Flesher, c.* 1627.] c6(impr. cropt?).
        Stanza 1, line 5: 'cride'.

19224   — [Anr. ed. Init. M. P.] 2 pts. s.sh.fol. *f. F. Grove,* [1630?] L.
        Stanza 1, line 5: 'cry'd'.

19224.3 — The countrey lasse. To a dainty new note. [Init. M. P.] *Ballad.* 2 pts. s.sh.fol. [*G. Purslowe, c.* 1628.] c6.

19224.5 — [Anr. ed. Anon.] 2 pts. s.sh.fol. *assignes of T. Symcocke,* [1628–29.] L.

19224.7 — [A cruel Cornish murder.] [Init. M. P.] *Ballad.* 2 pts. s.sh.fol. *f. F. Coules,* [1624.] c6(imp., I.360–1ᵛ).
        16862.3 pr. on verso.

19225   — ⟨   ⟩ Or, Cupids wrongs vindicated. [Init. M. P.] *Ballad.* 2 pts. s.sh.fol. *f. F. G*[*rove,* 1633.] Ent. as 'The faire maides appology or Cupids . . .' to F. Grove 29 my. 1633. L(cropt).

19226   — A description of a strange and miraculous fish, cast upon the sands in Worwell. [Init. M. P.] *Ballad.* 2 pts. s.sh.fol. *f. T. Lambert,* [1635?] O. 𝔄

19227   — The desperate damsells tragedy. Or the faithlesse young man. [Init. M. P.] *Ballad.* 2 pts. s.sh.fol. *f. H. G*[*osson,* 1630?] L.

19228   — The distressed virgin: or, the false young-man and the constant maid. [Init. M. P.] *Ballad.* 2 pts. s.sh.fol. *f. F. Coules,* [1633.] Ent. to the ballad ptnrs. 1 jn. 1629. L.

19229   — Dreadfull newes: or a true relation of the earthquake. Hapned at Callabria. 1638. Now = 4349.5.
        Not by Parker; for his poem *see* 19273.

19229.5 — Englands honour revived. By the valiant exploytes of captaine Kirke. [Init. M. P.] *Ballad.* 2 pts. s.sh.fol. [*A. Mathewes*] *f. M. Trundle widdow,* [1628.] Stevens Cox.

19230   — An exact description of the manner how his majestie went to the Parliament, the thirteenth day of April, 1640. [Init. M. P.] *Ballad.* s.sh.fol. *sold* [*by T. Lambert,* 1640.] Ent. to T. Walkley 9 ap. 1640. O.
        (Formerly also 5024)

19231   — An excellent new medley, which you may admire. [Init. M. P.] *Ballad.* 2 pts. s.sh.fol. *f. H. G*[*osson,* c. 1625.] L(Rox.I.112 and I.13).

19231.5 — [Anr. ed., w. 3 added stanzas. Anon.] An excellent medley, [etc.] 2 pts. s.sh.fol. *f. F. Grove,* [c. 1630.] ? Ent. to F. Grove 26 no. 1629; to J. Wright, jun., 24 my. 1639. G2.

19232   — The father hath beguild the sonne. [Init. M. P.] *Ballad.* 2 pts. s.sh.fol. [*A. Mathewes*] *f. F. Coules,* [1629.] Ent. 20 jn. 1629. c6.

19233   — A fayre portion for a fayre mayd. [Init. M. P.] *Ballad.* 2 pts. s.sh.fol. *f. F. G*[*rove,* 1633.] Ent. to F. Grove 1 my. 1633. L.

19234   — Fayre warning, or, happy is he whom other mens harms can make to beware. [Init. M. P.] *Ballad.* 2 pts. s.sh.fol. *f. R. Harper,* [c. 1635.] L.

19235   — Four pence halfe penny farthing: or, a woman will have the oddes. [Init. M. P.] *Ballad.* 2 pts. s.sh.fol. [*M. Flesher*] *f. C. W*[*right,* 1629?] Ent. to F. Grove 22 jn. 1629. c6.

19236   — Good counsell for young wooers. [Init. M. P.] *Ballad.* 2 pts. s.sh.fol. [*A. Mathewes*] *f. F. G*[*rove, c.* 1635.] Ent. to F. Grove 15 mr. 1633. L.
        Line 3 of title: 'Woman'.

19236.5 — [Anr. ed. Anon.] 2 pts. s.sh.fol. [*A. Mathewes*] *f. F. G*[*rove, c.* 1635.] M3(imp.).
        Line 3 of title: 'Mayden'.

19237   — The good fellowes best beloved. [Init. M. P.] *Ballad.* 2 pts. s.sh.fol. *f. J. Wright, junior,* [1634.] Ent. 13 de. 1634. L.

19238   — Good newes from the north, truly relating how about a hundred of the Scottish rebels, [etc. 18 Sept. 1640. Init. M. P.] *Ballad.* 2 pts. s.sh.fol. *E. G*[*riffin,*] *sold* [*by T. Lambert,*] 1640. Ent. to E. Griffin 29 se. O.

Parker, Martin—*cont.*

19239 — A good throw for three maiden-heads. [Init. M. P.] *Ballad.* 2 pts. s.sh.fol. *f. J. Grissmond,* [1629.] Ent. as 'Three maids coosened. by &c.' 1 jn. 1629. c⁶.

19240 — A good workeman needes never want worke. [Init. M. P.] *Ballad.* 2 pts. s.sh.fol. [*A. Mathewes*] *f. F. Grove,* [c. 1635.] L.

19241 — Grandsire Graybeard. Or Machiavell displayed. 1635. Now = 3704.9.

19242 — Harry White his humour. [Init. M. P.] 16° in 8's. [*T. Cotes?*] *f. T. Lambert,* [1637.] Ent. 16 my. 1637. O.

19242.5 — Have among you good women or, a high-way discourse betweene old William Starket and Robin Hobs. [Init. M. P.] *Ballad.* 2 pts. s.sh.fol. *f. T. Lambert,* [1634.] Ent. 17 ap. 1634. L.

19243 — A hee-divell: or, if this womans husband use her well, [etc. Init. M. P.] *Ballad.* 2 pts. s.sh.fol. *f. F. Grove,* [1630.] Ent. 12 mr. 1630. c⁶.

19244 — Hold your hands honest men. [Init. M. P.] *Ballad.* 2 pts. s.sh.fol. [*M. Flesher*] *f. T. Lambert,* [1634.] Ent. 11 au. 1634. L.

19245 — The honest plaine dealing porter. [Init. M. P.] *Ballad.* 2 pts. s.sh.fol. *f. F. Coules,* [c. 1630.] c⁶.

19245.5 — The honor of the Inns of Court gentlemen; or, a briefe recitall of the magnificent show, that past from Hatton to White-hall on the third of February. [Init. M. P.] *Ballad.* 2 pts. s.sh.fol. *f. T. Lambert,* [1634.] Private owner.
A description of Shirley's masque: 22459.

19246 — Houshold talke, or; good councell for a married man. [Init. M. P.] *Ballad.* 2 pts. s.sh.fol. *assignes of T. Simcocks, sold by F. Grove,* [1628–29.] L.

19246.5 — John and Joan: or, a mad couple well met. [Init. M. P.] *Ballad.* 2 pts. s.sh.fol. *f. T. Lambert,* [1634.] Ent. 15 se. 1634. L.

19247 — Keep a good tongue in your head. [Init. M. P.] *Ballad.* 2 pts. s.sh.fol. [*M. Flesher*] *f. T. Lambert,* [1634.] Ent. 7 jy. 1634. L.

19248 — The king and a poore northerne man. [Init. M. P. In verse.] 8°. *T. Cotes f. F. Grove,* 1633. Ent. to R. Cotes 9 no. O.

19249 — [Anr. ed. Init. M. P.] 8°. *T. Cotes, sold by F. Grove,* 1640. L.

19249.5 — [An abridgement. Init. M. P.] s.sh.fol. *f. F. Grove,* [c. 1635.] O.

19250 — Knavery in all trades, or, here's an age would make a man mad. [Init. M. P.] *Ballad.* 2 pts. s.sh.fol. *f. F. Grove,* [1632.] Ent. 16 jy. 1632. c⁶.

19250.5 — Labour in vaine. Or an imperfect description of love. [Init. M. P.] *Ballad.* 2 pts. s.sh.fol. *f. T. Lambert,* [1636.] Ent. 18 jn. 1636. L.

19250.7 — A lamentable relation of a fearfull fight at sea, between the Spaniard and the Hollander, on Friday being the eleventh of October. [Signed 'Martin Parkin'.] *Ballad.* s.sh.fol. *M. F[lesher] f. T. Lambert,* [1639.] Ent. 15 oc. 1639. E.

19251 — The legend of Sir Leonard Lack-wit. 8°. *E. P[urslowe,] sold by S. Pemmell,* 1633. Ent. 8 ja. L.

19251.3 — Lord have mercy upon us. This is the humble petition of England [etc. In verse. Init. M. P. With plague statistics for 1593, 1603, 1625, 1636.] s.sh.fol. *f. T. Lambert,* [1636.] L⁸.O(imprint mutil.).
(Formerly 19075) *See also* 16739 sqq.

19251.5 — The lovers joy and griefe: or a young mans relation. [Init. M. P.] *Ballad.* 2 pts. s.sh.fol. *f. T. Lambert,* [1635?] Ent. 12 mr. 1635; 18 jn. 1636. L.

19251.7 — A lovers teares: or, the constancy of a yong mans mind. [Init. M. P.] *Ballad.* 2 pts. s.sh.fol. *f. T. Lambert,* [1634.] Ent. 19 au. 1634. L.

19252 — Loves solace: or the true lovers part. [Init. M. P.] *Ballad.* 2 pts. s.sh.fol. *f. F. Grove,* [1632.] Ent. to F. Grove 3 se. 1632; to J. Wright a. ballad ptnrs. 8 jy. 1633. L.

19252.5 — A man cannot lose his money, but he shall be mockt too. [Init. M. P.] *Ballad.* 2 pts. s.sh.fol. [*G. Purslowe*] *f. F. Grove,* [c. 1625.] c⁶(I.466–7ᵛ).
25333.5 is pr. on the verso.

19253 — Mans felicity and misery: which is a good wife and a bad. [Init. M. P.] *Ballad.* 2 pts. s.sh.fol. *f. F. Grove,* [1632.] Ent. 16 jy. 1632; ?20 mr. 1638. c⁶.
Stanza 1, line 1: 'Cozen'.

19253.5 — [Anr. ed.] 2 pts. s.sh.fol. *f. F. Grove,* [c. 1635.] L.
Stanza 1, line 1: 'Couzen'.

Parker, Martin—*cont.*

19254 — The marryed mans lesson: or, a disswasion from jealousie. [Init. M. P.] *Ballad.* 2 pts. s.sh.fol. [*Eliz. Allde*] *f. J. Wright the younger,* [1634.] Ent. 13 de. 1634. L.
(Formerly also 17233)

19254.5 — The married-womans case: or good counsell to mayds. [Init. M. P.] *Ballad.* 2 pts. s.sh.fol. [*E. Allde*] *f. H. G[osson,* c. 1625.] c⁶(torn).

19255 — The maunding souldier: or, the fruits of warre is beggary. [Init. M. P.] *Ballad.* 2 pts. s.sh.fol. *f. F. Grove,* [1629?] L.

19256 — A messe of good fellows. [Init. M. P.] *Ballad.* 2 pts. s.sh.fol. *f. T. Lambert,* [1634.] Ent. 15 se. 1634. L.

19257 — The milke-maids life: or, a pretty new ditty. [Init. M. P.] *Ballad.* 2 pts. s.sh.fol. *f. T. Lambert,* [1634.] Ent. 22 mr. 1634. L.

19258 — A new medley or, a messe of all-together. [Init. M. P.] *Ballad.* 2 pts. s.sh.fol. *f. H. Gosson,* [1640?] ? Ent. to J. Wright, jun., 24 my. 1639. L.

19258.5 — Newes from New-castle with an advertisement. [Init. M. P.] *Ballad.* 2 pts. s.sh.fol. *E. G[riffin,] sold [by T. Lambert,* 1640.] M³(torn).

19259 — Newes from the Tower-hill: or, a gentle warning to Peg and Kate. [Init. M. P.] *Ballad.* 2 pts. s.sh.fol. *f. E. B[lackmore,* 1631?] Ent. to E. Blackmore 4 no. 1631. c⁶.

19260 — The nightingale warbling forth her owne disaster. [In verse.] 8°. *G. P[urslowe] f. W. Cooke,* 1632. L(imp.).; HN.

19261 — No naturall mother, but a monster. [Init. M. P.] *Ballad.* 2 pts. s.sh.fol. [*E. Purslowe?*] *f. F. Coule⟨s,* [1634.] Ent. 16 jy. 1634. M³(torn).

19262 — A paire of turtle-doves. *Ballad.* 2 pts. s.sh.fol. *f. T. Lambert,* [1640?] L.

19263 — A penny-worth of good counsell. [Init. M. P.] *Ballad.* 2 pts. s.sh.fol. [*f. H. Gosson?* 1638.] Ent. to H. Gosson 9 ap. 1638. L.

19264 — A proverbe old, yet nere forgot, Tis good to strike while the irons hott. *Ballad.* 2 pts. s.sh.fol. [*A. Mathewes*] *f. F. Grove,* [c. 1625.] c⁶.

19265 — Robin and Kate: or, a bad husband converted by a good wife. [Init. M. P.] *Ballad.* 2 pts. s.sh.fol. *f. T. Lambert,* [1634.] Ent. 9 my. 1634. L.

19266 — Robin Conscience, or, conscionable Robin. [In verse. Init. M. P.] 8°. *f. F. Coles,* 1635. Ent. to M. Sparke 20 ap. 1630; ass'd to F. Coules 13 jn. 1631. O.
29 lines a page.

19266.5 — [Anr. ed. Anon.] 8°. [*f. F. Coules,* c. 1640.] F(imp.).
38 lines a page.

19267 — Rochell her yeelding to the obedience of the French king. [28 Oct. 1628.] [Init. M. P.] *Ballad.* 2 pts. s.sh.fol. [*M. Flesher*] *f. J. Wright,* [1628.] c⁶.

19267.5 — Saylors for my money. A new ditty. [Init. M. P.] *Ballad.* 2 pts. s.sh.fol. [*W. Jones*] *f. C. Wright,* [c. 1630?] c⁶.

19268 — A scourge for the pope. *Ballad.* 2 pts. s.sh.fol. [*G. Purslowe*] *f. J. Trun⟨dle,⟩* [1624.] c⁶(torn).

19269 — Take time while 'tis offerd. [Init. M. P.] *Ballad.* 2 pts. s.sh.fol. *f. R. Harper,* [1634.] Ent. 29 ap. 1634. L.

19270 — The three merry coblers. Who tell how . . . they are still on the mending hand. [Init. M. P.] *Ballad.* 2 pts. s.sh.fol. *f. F. Grove,* [1634.] Ent. 5 fb. 1634. L.

19271 — Times alteration: or, the old mans rehearsall, what brave dayes he knew. [Init. M. P.] *Ballad.* 2 pts. s.sh.fol. *assignes of T. Symcocke,* [1628–29.] L.

19271.5 — [Anr. ed. Anon.] 2 pts. s.sh.fol. [*A. Mathewes,* c. 1630.] c⁶.

19272 — The tragedy of doctor Lambe, the great suposed conjurer. [14 June 1628.] [Init. M. P.] *Ballad.* 2 pts. s.sh.fol. [*Eliz. Allde*] *f. H. G[osson,* 1628.] c⁶.

19273 — A true and terrible narration of a horrible earthquake, in Calabria. From pregnant atestation, written in English verse. 8°. *T. Cotes f. R. Mabb a. F. Grove,* 1638. Ent. to R. Mabb 26 my. L(3).; HN.

19274 — A true subjects wish. For the happy successe of our royall army. [Init. M. P.] *Ballad.* 2 pts. s.sh.fol. *E. G[riffin,] sold [by T. Lambert,* 1640.] Ent. to A. Griffin 24 ap. 1640. O.

19274.5 — A true tale of Robbin Hood. [In verse.] 8°. [*T. Cotes f. F. Grove,* 1632?] Ent. to F. Grove 29 fb. 1632. O(impr. cropt).
Tp line 3: 'Touch'.

Parker, Martin—*cont.*

19275 — [Anr. ed.] 8⁰. *f.* [*by*] *T. Cotes, sold by F. Grove,* [1632?] Ass'd to R. Cotes 9 no. 1633. L(imp.).
Tp line 3: 'touch'.

19276 — Tryall brings truth to light. [Init. M. P.] *Ballad.* 2 pts. s.sh.fol. [*M. Flesher*] *f. T. Lambert,* [1634.] Ent. 31 my. 1634. L.

19277 — The two inseparable brothers. *Ballad.* 2 pts. s.sh.fol. [*M. Flesher*] *f. T. Lambert,* [1637.] L(torn).M³.
For an engr. w. Latin verses on the same subject *see* 11728.6.

19278 — The two Welsh lovers, or the British nymph. *Ballad.* 2 tabs. s.sh.fol. [*G. Purslowe*] *f. J.* ⟨*Trundle,*⟩ [c. 1625.] C⁶(impr. torn).

19279 — The wandring Jews chronicle. *Ballad.* s.sh.fol. *f. F. Grove,* [1660?]
Not an STC item.
— A warning for all lewd livers. 1633. *See* 20324.

19280 — A warning for wives, by the example of one Katherine Francis, alias Stoke. [21 Apr. 1629.] [Init. M. P.] *Ballad.* 2 pts. s.sh.fol. *f. F. G*[*rove,* 1629.] C⁶.

19281 — Well met neighbour: or, a dainty discourse betwixt Nell and Sisse. [Init. M. P.] *Ballad.* 2 pts. s.sh.fol. *f. T. Lambert,* [1640?] L.G².

19282 — The whoremongers conversion, and his exhortation. [Init. M. P.] *Ballad.* 2 pts. s.sh.fol. *f. F. Cowles,* [1629.] Ent. 20 jn. 1629. L.

19283 — The wiving age. Or a great complaint of the maidens of London. [Init. M. P.] *Ballad.* 2 pts. s.sh.fol. [*M. Flesher*] *f. F. Coules,* [c. 1627.] C⁶.

19283.5 — The woman to the plow and the man to the hen-roost, or a fine way to cure a cotquean. [Init. M. P.] *Ballad.* 2 pts. s.sh.fol. *f. F. Grove,* [1629.] Ent. 22 jn. 1629. G².

19284 — The wooing lasse, and the way-ward lad. [Init. M. P.] *Ballad.* 2 pts. s.sh.fol. *f. J. Wright, junior,* [1635?] L.

19285 — The wooing maid, on a faire maid neglected. [Init. M. P.] *Ballad.* 2 pts. s.sh.fol. *f. T. Lambert,* [1635?] Ent. 18 jn. 1636. L.
— *See also* 6809, 18699, 19076, 25869.

19285.2 **Parker, Matthew,** *Abp.* An admonition—for the necessitie of the presente tyme tyll a furder consultation—to all suche as shall intende hereafter to enter the state of matrimonye godly and agreablye to lawes. s.sh.fol. *R. Wolfe,* 1560. C⁷(MS.113.44/3).
With Parker's MS. corrections.

19285.4 — [Anr. ed.] An admonition to all suche . . . godlie and agreably to laws. s.sh.fol. [*R. Wolfe?* c. 1560.] C⁷(MS.113.44/1).

19285.6 — [Anr. ed.] s.sh.fol. *J. Walley,* [c. 1560.] PML.

19285.8 — [Anr. ed.] s.sh.fol. *R. Wolfe,* 1563. O¹⁰.
At C⁷(MS.113.44/2) is an undated post-1640 ed. w. text ending: 'Set forth . . . 1563.' It has the tables of affinity cols. 2 and 3 in roman whereas other STC eds. have cols. 2 and 3 in B.L.

19286 — [Anr. ed.] s.sh.fol. *R. Wolfe,* 1571. O.
O is mounted in a roll with 25073.

19287 — [Anr. ed.] s.sh.fol. *P. Short f. J. Harrison,* 1594. Ent. to J. Harrison, sen., 2 jy. 1578. O.

19287.3 — [Anr. ed.] s.sh.fol. *f. T. Adams,* [c. 1600.] C².C¹⁰.

19287.7 — [Anr. ed.] s.sh.fol. [*London,* c. 1600.] L⁵(Lemon 54).
Heading line 2 ends: 'godlily and agreeably to lawes'.

19288 — [Anr. ed.] s.sh.fol. *f. E. White,* [1605?] L.C⁸.

19289 — [Anr. ed.] s.sh.fol. *N. Okes f. J. Harison,* 1620. L.O(2, 1 = J).C.

19289.5 — [Anr. ed.] s.sh.fol. [*Oxford, W. Turner,* c. 1630.] L.O.
Heading line 2 ends: 'of ma-'. (Formerly 19291)

19290 — [Anr. ed.] s.sh.fol. *J. Okes f. J. Harrison,* 1639. O⁹.

19291 — Now = 19289.5.
— A briefe examination . . . of a certaine declaration. [1566?] *See* 10387.

19292 — De antiquitate Britannicæ ecclesiæ & priuilegiis ecclesiæ Cantuariensis, cum archiepiscopis eiusdem 70. (Catalogus cancellariorū, [etc.]) [By Abp. Parker assisted by G. Acworth and J. Josseline.] fol. *Londini, in æd. J. Daij,* 1572 [–1574.] L.L²(.).O.C.M.+; F.
Copies vary considerably. Tp in 3 states: imprint as above (1L,1C,ETON); a variant, omitting imprint, dated: 'An. Dom. 1572.' (1L,O³,1C); anr. setting, omitting imprint, dated: 'Anno Domini. 1572.' Parker added to and rearranged contents. Early and late issues at L,C. Latter usually includes

Parker, Matthew, *Abp.*—*cont.*
errata, lives of Augustine and Parker, list of bks. given to C by Parker in 1574. For the description of a copy with all 3 tpp and 2 settings of some other leaves *see Bibliotheca Lindesiana,* III, cols. 6859–61.

19292a — — The life off the 70. archbishopp off Canterbury . . . Englished [from the anonymous Latin attack 'Historiola'], and to be added to the 69. [*Tr.* J. Stubbs?] 8⁰. [*Zürich, C. Froschauer?*] 1574. L.O.C.D.M.+; F.HD(imp.).N.TEX.Y.+
In at least 1L,4 O,1HD,TEX copies is a folding leaf: 'A table Englished out off that legend off Canterbury tales entituled in Latin. De antiquitate Britannicæ ecclesiæ [etc.]'

19293 — Howe we ought to take the death of the godly. a sermon made in Cambrydge at the buriall of the noble clerck. D. M. Bucer. 8⁰. *R. Jugge,* [1551?] C⁷(2).LINC (imp.).LK.P.

19293a — [Anr. version.] A funerall sermon, both godlye, learned and comfortable, preached 1551. at the buriall of M. Bucer. (*Tr.* T. Newton [from an abridged Latin version pr. abroad.]) 8⁰. *T. Purfoote,* [1587.] F.
Dedic. dated 24 Feb. 1587.
— The whole psalter translated into English metre. [1567?] *See* 2729.
— *ed. See* 159, 863, 17652, 19209, 25004, 25005.
— *tr. See* 24265.
— *See also* 10151 sqq., 10287 sq., 10352.5, 16509, 16510, 17518.

19294 **Parker, Robert.** A scholasticall discourse against symbolizing with Antichrist in ceremonies. [Anon.] fol. [*Middelburg, R. Schilders,*] 1607. L.O.C.D.E².+; F. HN.BO.N.U.+

19295 **Parkes, Richard.** An apologie: of three testimonies of holy Scripture. (The second booke containing, A rejoynder to a reply [25692.]) 4⁰ in 8's. *G. Eld* [*a. W. Jaggard?*] 1607. Ent. 11 jn. L.O.C².D.G².+; F.HN.U.
Apparently Eld pr. only ¶1–E8. First bk. a revision of 19296. Answered by 25693.

19296 — A briefe answere unto certaine objections and reasons against the descension of Christ into hell. [Anon.] 4⁰. *Oxford, J. Barnes, sold by S. Waterson,* [*London,*] 1604. L.O.C.G².M⁴.+; F.HN.HD.U.Y.
Revised version pr. as 1st bk. of 19295. Answered by 25692.

19297 — [Anr. issue, w. cancel tp.] *Oxford, f. John Barnes,* [*London,*] 1613. O.O³.C².C³.D.+
Tp pr. in London by W. White.

19298 **Parkes, William.** The curtaine-drawer of the world. [Partly in verse.] 4⁰. [*N. Okes*] *f. L. Becket,* 1612. Ent. 22 ja. L.O(2).; F.HN.CH. Arthur Houghton.

19299 **Parkhurst, John,** *Bp.* Iohannis Parkhursti ludicra siue epigrammata iuuenilia. 4⁰. *ap. J. Dayum,* 1573. L. O.C.M².P.+; F.HN.CU.HD.N.+
— *See also* 10286, 10289.

Parkin, Martin. A lamentable relation of a fight at sea. [1639.] *See* 19250.7.

Parkins, John. *See* Perkins, J.

19300 **Parkinson, John.** Paradisi in sole paradisus terrestris. Or a garden of flowers with a kitchen garden and an orchard [xylographic]. fol. (*H. Lownes a. R. Young,*) 1629. Ent. to Young 10 ap. L.O.C.DUR (Bamb.).E.+; F.HN.HD.NY. Notre Dame U.+
RD and 1HD copies have quire A reset w. A1ʳ line 4 ending 'amend the' instead of 'amend'. The reset quire pr. by T. Cotes and possibly intended for issue w. 19301, though the NY copy of the latter has orig. quire A.

19301 — [Anr. issue, w. added letterpress tp, w. imprint:] *T. Cotes, sold by R. Royston,* 1635. NY.

19302 — Theatrum botanicum: the theater of plants. Or, an herball of a large extent. fol. *T. Cotes,* 1640. Ent. to R. Cotes 3 mr. 1635. L.O.C.D.E.+; F.HN.HD.N. PML.+
See Court-Book C, p. 265.

19303 **Parks, William.** The rose, and lily. Delivered at the lecture, in Ashby de-la-zouch. [Four sermons.] 4 pts. 4⁰. *J. Norton f. G. Wilne,* 1639 (1638). Ent. 10 au. 1638. L.O(pt. 4 only).C(pt. 2 only).; F.

Parks, William—*cont.*

19303.3 — [Anr. issue, w. cancel gen. tp, w. imprint:] *J. N[orton] f. G. Wilne, sold by S. Man,* 1640. D.; HD.
Sub tpp cancelled.

19303.7 **Parliament.** [A2^r catch title:] Parlyament of byrdes. [In verse.] 4° in 6. [*W. de Worde,* c. 1520.] L(imp.).
32 lines a page.

19304 — [Anr. ed.] The parlament of byrdes. 4°. [*J. Awdley,*] (*f. A. Kytson,*) [c. 1565.] O.
30 lines a page.

19305 — The plyament of deuylles. [In verse.] 4°. (*W. de worde,* 1509.) C.; HN.

19305.5 — [Anr. ed. Heading 1^r:] The parlyament of deuylles. 4°. (*R. Fakes,*) [1522?] Y.

— The parlament of vertues royal. [1614.] *See* 23581.

19306 — The parlament of women. With the merry lawes by them newly enacted. 8°. *J. O[kes], sould by J. Wright the younger,* 1640. Ent. 18 jn. HN.

19307 — The penniles parliament of threed-bare poets. 4°. *f. W. Barley,* 1608. Ent. to J. Beale by consent of widow M. Barley 12 no. 1614. F.HN.
For other eds., *see* 14291 sq.

19307.5 — [Anr. ed.] The . . . poets, or the merry fortune-teller. By Doctor Merry-man. 8°. *J. B[eale,]* 1637. HD.

Parma, *Duchess of. See* 11028.

Parma, *Prince of. See* 331 sqq.

19308 **Parmenius, Stephen.** De nauigatione illustris et magnanimi equitis aurati Humfredi Gilberti, carmen. 4°. *ap. T. Purfutium,* 1582. L.; HN.
(Formerly also 4015)

19308.5 — Pæan Stephani Parmenii Budeii ad psalmum Dauidis CIV. conformatus. fol. *T. Vautroullerius,* 1582. L. ETON.
(Formerly 4016)

Parnassus. Newes from Pernassus. 1622. *See* 22080.

19309 — The returne from Pernassus: or the scourge of Simony. [A comedy.] 4°. *G. Eld f. J. Wright,* 1606. Ent. 16 oc. 1605. L.O(2).O^6.C^2(imp.).; F.HN.HD.N.NY.+
Greg 225.
Collates A–H^4 I^2.

19310 — [Anr. ed.] 4°. *G. Eld f. J. Wright,* 1606. L.L^6.O.C. ETON.+; F.HN.HD.NY.Y^2.+
Collates A–H^4. Tp from same setting as 19309.

19311 **Parr, Elnathan.** The workes of that faithfull preacher, M^r. E. Parr. The third edition [of 19319, 19320]: corrected and enlarged. fol. *G. P[urslowe a.] (J. Norton) f. S. Man,* 1632. L.O.C.BIRM^2(K.N.).E^2.+; F.HN.CHI.HD.NY^{11}.+
Includes 5th ed. of 19314 and 4th ed. of 19312.

19311.5 — [A variant, w. gen. tp dated:] 1633. O^{10}.O^{28}.C^5.D.; F.HN.HD.ILL.Y.+

19312 — Abba Father: or, a plaine and short direction concerning private prayer. 12°. *F. K[ingston] f. S. Man,* 1618. Ent. 1 de. 1617. O.
— Fourth edition. 1632. = pt. of 19311.

19313 — Fifth edition. 12°. *N. Okes f. S. Man,* 1636. L(2).L^3. D.; F.

19314 — The grounds of divinitie, . . . propounded familiarly in divers questions and answeres. 8°. *N. O[kes] f. S. Man,* 1614. Ent. 13 fb. O.C.

19315 — [Anr. ed.] Newly corrected, and enlarged. Second edition. 8°. *T. Snodham f. S. Man,* 1615. L.O^{26}.; F.HN.U(imp.).

19316 — Third edition. 8°. *E. Griffin f. S. Man,* 1619. L.L^3.O. C(imp.).DUL.; HD.U.

19316.3 — Fourth edition. 8°. *N. O[kes] f. S. Man,* [c. 1625.] F. TEX.Y.
All copies have the date cropt.
— Fift edition. 1632. = pt. of 19311.

19317 — Seaventh edition. 12°. *J. Norton f. S. Man,* 1633. L.; F.PH.

19318 — Eight edition. 12°. *f. S. Man,* 1636. L.O.C^2.INN.; F.

19319 — A plaine exposition upon the whole 8. 9. 10. 11. chapters of the Epistle of Saint Paul to the Romans. 4° in 8's. *G. Purslowe f. S. Man,* 1618. Ent. 11 ap. L.L^{43}. L^{46}.INN.M^4.; F.HN.NY^{11}.Y.

19320 — Second edition corrected, with the twelfth chapter not before printed. 4° in 8's. *G. Purslowe [a. J. Beale?] f. S. Man,* 1620. Ent. 9 oc. 1619. L.O.C^3(frag.).; F.HN. U.V.

Parr, Elnathan—*cont.*

19321 — A plaine exposition upon the whole thirteenth, fourteenth, fifteenth, and sixteenth chapters of the Epistle of saint Paul to the Romanes. 4° in 8's. *G. Eld f. S. Man,* 1622. Ent. 20 se. 1621. L(destroyed). O.DUL.LEIC.; F.HN(2).BO^5.NY^{11}.U.

19322 **Parr, Richard,** *Bp.* Concio ad clerum habita Oxoniæ Jul. 12. 1625. 8°. *Oxon., G. Turner,* 1628. O.O^4.C.

19323 — The end of the perfect man. A sermon preached at the buriall of Sir R. Spencer. 4°. *Oxford, W. Turner,* 1628. L.L^3.O.M.NOR^2.+; F.HN.CHI.HD.U.+
— *See* also Bookplates.

Parr, Thomas. The wonder of this age. [Engraving.] 1635. *See* 13372.5.

19324 **Parret,** *Sir* **James.** An invitation unto prayer. 1624. = 19774.

19325 **Parron, William.** Ad serenissimū . . . dñm Henricū . . . anni presentis. M.d. pronosticon libellus. 1499. Now = 494.8.

19326 — Ad serenissimū . . . dñm henricū . . . anni p̄sentis millesimi quingētesimi [se]cūdi pronosticon libellus. [1501.] Now = 494.9.

19327 — [A prognostication for 1498.] Now = 385.3.

19328 **Parrot, Henry.** Cures for the itch. Characters. Epigrams. Epitaphs. [Init. H. P.] 8°. [*J. Haviland a. M. Flesher*] *f. T. Jones,* 1626. Ent. 21 ap. O.
Apparently Flesher pr. the Characters only, and this section may be a reissue.

19329 — = 19330.
19330 — Epigrams by H. P[arrot.] Mortui non mordent. 4°. *R. B[radock,] soulde by J. Helme,* 1608. Ent. to J. Busby a. J. Helme 11 ap. L.; HN.HD.

19331 — The gossips greeting. [Formerly attrib. to H. Parrot.] 1620. Now = 19080.5.

19332 — Laquei ridiculosi: or springes for woodcocks. Caveat emptor. [In verse.] 16° in 8's. [*T. Snodham*] *f. J. Busby,* 1613. Ent. 9 my. 1612. L.O.DUL.E^2.; F.PFOR.
8 leaves in quire A; no inits. on tp.

19332.5 — [Anr. issue, w. quire A compressed to 4 leaves and tp init. H. P.] O(2, 1 lacks tp).O^6(imp.).*.C^{16}.; F.HN.HD. N.TEX.

19333 — The [xylographic] mastive, or young-whelpe of the olde-dogge. Epigrams and satyrs. [Init. H. P. In verse.] 4°. *T. Creede f. R. Meighen a. T. Jones,* 1615. Ent. to R. Meighen 4 jy. L.O(2).; F.HN.HD.ILL.NY.+
In most copies the date is cropt or restored; orig. date at ILL.

19334 — The mous-trap. [Epigrams. Init. H. P. In verse.] 4°. [*W. Jaggard*] *f. F. B[urton,]* 1606. Ent. to F. Burton 17 oc. L.O^5.; HN.

Parry. *See* also Pareus.

Parry, Daniel, *ed. See* 13220.

19335 **Parry, Henry,** *Bp.* De regno Dei, et victoria christiana, conciones duæ. 4°. *ex typog. Kyngstoniano, imp. C. Burbæi & E. Weaver,* 1606. L.O^{10}.C.DUR^3.E.+; F(2, 1 imp.).HN.U.
Copies vary: with or without erroneous 'FELIX' before 'KYNGSTONIANO' in the imprint; with or without errata on H4^v (all at C^2).

19336 — Victoria christiana. Concio ad clerum: habita Oxoniæ anno Domini. 1591. 8°. *Oxoniæ, J. Barnesius,* 1594. L.O.; F.
Reprinted in 19335.
— *tr. See* 20630, 24532.

19337 **Parry, Robert.** [Heading 2nd A1^r:] Moderatus, the most delectable & famous historie of the blacke knight. 4°. (*R. Jhones,* 1595.) Ent. 21 mr. 1594. O(lacks tp).; F(imp.).

19338 — Sinetes passions vppon his fortunes. (The lamentation of a male-content vpon this enigma. Maister thy desiers or liue in despaire.) [In verse.] 2 pts. 8°. *T. P[urfoot] f. W. Holme,* 1597. Ent. 5 oc. 1596. HN.
Pt. 2, though bd. w. pt. 1 in the HN copy, may be a separate, anon. work.
— *tr. See* 18862, 18864, 18866, 18868, 18871.

19339 **Parry, William,** *Doctor of Laws.* The last words of W. Parry. [Post-1640.]
Not an STC book.

19340 — In Guil. Parry proditorem odæ & epigrammata. [By W. Gager?] 8° in 6. *Oxoniae, ex off. J. Barnesij,* 1585. O(tp only).WN.; HN.

Parry, William, *Doctor of Laws—cont.*

19340.5 — Pareus. [A Latin poem. By G. Peele?] 8°. *Oxoniæ, typis J. Barnesii,* 1585. WN.; HN.
(Formerly 19193)

19341 — = 19342.

19342 — A true and plaine declaration of the horrible treasons, practised by W. Parry. (A prayer for all kings, princes, countreyes and people.) 4°. *C. B[arker,* 1585.] Ent. to R. Newbery 27 fb. 1585. L.O.C.E. LEEDS.+; F.HN.HD.ILL.PML.+
(Prayer formerly 20192) Tp line 7 ends: 'of his/'; letter on D2ʳ begins: 'Monsignor, the Holines'.

19342a — [Anr. issue, w. D2ʳ⁻ᵛ partially reset; letter begins: 'Monsignor, his Holinesse'.] C¹⁷.LINC.; F.HN.HD.

19342a.5 — [Anr. issue, partially reset and reimposed.] L.O.O⁸.C². D.+; F.CHI.ILL.
Tp line 7 ends: 'of his and/'.

— See also 13960.5, 16516.

19343 **Parry, William,** *Traveller.* A new and large discourse of the travels of sir A. Sherley [etc.] 4°. *V. Simmes f. F. Norton,* 1601. Ent. to W. Aspley a. F. Norton 11 no. L.O.O³.CHATS.HAT.; F(2).N.Y.

Parson. [The parson of Kalenborowe. c. 1520.] *See* 14894.5.

19344 **Parsons, Bartholomew.** The barren trees doome: a sermon. 4°. *N. Okes f. M. Law,* 1616. Ent. 12 ap. O. O³(imp.).G².; F.HN.

19345 — Boaz and Ruth blessed: or a sacred contract. 4°. *Oxford, J. Lichfield f. W. Webbe,* 1633. L.O.C.C².P.+; BO. HD.Y.

19346 — Dorcas: or, a perfect patterne of a true disciple. A sermon. 4°. *Oxford, W. Turner,* 1631. L.O.P.;*HD(tp defective).
See also 21636.

19347 — The first fruites of the Gentiles. In three sermons. 4°. *N. Okes f. J. H[arrison] a. E. Blackmore,* 1618. Ent. to Harrison a. Blackmore 5 my. L.L³.O(2, 1 imp.). O²¹(imp.).C².; HN.HD.Y.

19347.5 — The historie of tithes: or, tithes vindicated. 4°. *Oxford, W. Turner f. W. Webb,* 1637. O³.C².C⁵.PLUME.STU.; BO.HD.Y.

19348 — [Anr. issue, w. cancel tp:] Honos & onus Levitarum, or, tithes vindicated. *Oxford, W. Turner f. W. Webb,* 1637. L.O.O².STU.

19349 — The magistrats charter examined, or his duty and dignity opened. In a sermon. 4°. *N. Okes f. M. Law,* 1616. Ent. 12 ap. L.O.O³.G².PLUME.+; F.HN.BO.HD.Y.

19350 — A Romane centurion becomming a good souldier of Jesus Christ. In foure sermons. 4°. *M. D[awson] f. T. Slater,* 1635. Ent. to W. Hammond 16 se. 1634. L.O.BTL.E.P.+; F.HN.HD(imp.).NY¹¹.

19350.5 — [A variant, w. imprint:] *M. D[awson,] sosd* [sic] *by H. Hammond, in Salsbury,* 1635. L(imp.).

19351 — A sermon preached at the funerall of Sʳ Francis Pile. 4°. *Oxford, L. Lichfield f. W. Webb,* 1636. L.O.C⁴. D².M.+; F.HD.U.

19352 **Parsons, Robert.** An answere to the fifth part of Reportes [5504] lately set forth by syr E. Cooke. [Anon.] 4°. *[St. Omer, F. Bellet,]* 1606. L.O.C.D.DUR⁵.+; F.HN. HD.N.U.+
A&R 611. Both sides of tp in 2 settings: orig. title line 7 ends: 'Kinges'; cancel title line 7: 'Kings'; both at HD.

— An appendix to the Apologie. [1602.] *See* 19392.5.

19353 — [A Book of Christian Exercise.] The first booke of the christian exercise, appertayning to resolution. [Init. R. P.] 12°. *[Rouen, Fr. Parsons' press,]* 1582. L.O.C DE.P.+; F.HN.HD.Y.
A&R 619. For eds. w. E. Bunny's alterations, *see* 19355 sqq.

19354 — [Anr. ed. Anon.] Corrected and newlye imprinted. 1584. 12°. *(Rone, [G. L'Oyselet,]* 1584.) L.; F. Holy Cross College, Worcester, Mass.
A&R 620. An unauthorized reprint, not corrected.

19354.1 — [Anr. ed., enlarged, w. title:] A christian directorie.... Deuided into three bookes. The first wherof . . . is only conteined in this volume, with reprofe of the falsified edition by E. Buny. [Init. R. P.] 12° ⁸·⁴. *[Rouen, Fr. Parsons' press,]* 1585 (30 au.) L.O.C.OS. YK.+; F.HN.TEX.U.Y.
(Formerly 19362) A&R 621. No more published. Answered by 4088. Some revised and new material in this ed. adapted for Protestant use in 19380 sqq.

Parsons, Robert—*cont.*

19354.3 — [Anr. ed., enlarged.] 8°. *Louan, L. Kellam,* 1598. L.O.C.A.D².+; F.HN.TEX.TORONTO².U(lacks tp).+
(Formerly 19368) A&R 622.

19354.5 — [Anr. ed., enlarged. Anon.] The christian directory.... Lately reviewed, corrected, and not a little altered by the author himselfe. 12°. *[St. Omer, F. Bellet,]* 1607. L.O³.C.USHAW.W.+; F.HN.HD.ILL.Y.+
(Formerly 19371) A&R 623.

19354.6 — [Anr. issue, w. tp cancelled and replaced by a bifolium with contents and title:] A christian directory.... By R. Persons. *[St. Omer, English College Press,]* 1620. HP.

19354.7 — [Anr. ed., enlarged.] A christian directory,.... Written by R. Persons. The sixt, and last edition. 12° in 6's. *[St. Omer, English College Press,]* 1622. L.O.C.DUR³. W.+; HN.U.
(Formerly 19376) A&R 624. The LINC copy has 'sixth,' in the title.

19354.9 — [Anr. ed.] The seaventh, and last edition. 8°. *[St. Omer, English College Press,]* 1633. L.L⁹(lacks tp).O.C (imp.).
(Formerly 19378) A&R 625.

19355 — [A Protestant adaptation.] A booke of christian exercise, appertaining to resolution, by R. P. Perused [i.e. edited and altered], and accompanied now with a Treatise tending to pacification: by E. Bunny. 8°. *N. Newton a. A. Hatfield f. J. Wight,* 1584. Ent. 28 au. L.O.C²(imp.).C¹⁵(imp.).P.; F.U.
See also 16644.5.

19356 — [Anr. ed.] 12°. *(Middleborough, R. P[ainter, i.e. Schilders,])* 1584. C³.C⁵.

19356.5 — [Anr. ed.] 8°. *N. Newton a. A. Hatfield f. J. Wight,* 1585. Bangor UC.

19357 — [Anr. ed.] 8°. *N. Newton f. J. Wight,* 1585. O.C.; F.HN. PN².

19357.5 — [Anr. ed.] 8°. *[N. Newton?] f. J. Wight,* 1585. L(imp.). ST.; F.HN(lacks tp).

19358 — [Anr. ed.] 8°. *[T. Dawson,]* 1585. O(lacks tp).C.LK.P.; HD.U.
In title: 'Resolution'.

19358.5 — [Anr. ed.] 8°. *[T. Dawson,]* 1585. O¹⁷.O²⁷.DUR⁵.; F.
In title: 'Resolulution [sic]'.

19359 — [Anr. ed.] 12°. *London, [J. Windet,]* 1585. L.L².C².C⁵. OS.+; F.
For other Windet piracies *see* 19363, 23022.

19359.1 — [Anr. ed.] 8°. *Oxford, J. Barnes,* 1585. O.O³(imp.). C¹⁵(imp.).; F(2).
Tp line 7: 'in deed: by'. See Arber II.793–4; *see* also 3072. Presumably most of the 'Oxford' eds. are London forgeries.

19359.3 — [Anr. ed.] 8°. *Oxford, J. Barnes,* 1585. O¹⁰.; ILL.
Tp line 7: 'indeede: by'.

19359.5 — [Anr. ed.] 12°. *Oxford, J. Barnes,* 1585. O.C⁹.NLW (imp.).; F.TEX.Y.
(Formerly 19361) Tp line 7: 'resolue our/'; line 13: 'EDM.'

19359.7 — [Anr. ed.] 12°. *Oxford, J. Barnes,* 1585. L.ETON.; F.
Tp line 7: 'resolue our/'; line 13: 'EDMVND'.

19359.9 — [Anr. ed.] 12°. *Oxford, J. Barnes,* 1585. O.
Tp line 7: 'shoulde/'.

19360 — [Anr. ed.] 12°. *Oxford, J. Barnes,* 1585. O.C.; HD.
Tp line 7: 'should re-/'; *2ʳ line 4: 'provi-/'.

19360.3 — [Anr. ed.] 12°. *Oxford, J. Barnes,* 1585. O.; F.
Tp line 7: 'should re-/'; *2ʳ line 4: 'proui-/'.

19360.5 — [Anr. ed.] 12°. *Oxford, J. Barnes,* 1585. O.E⁴.OS.
Tp line 7: 'should re/' (no hyphen); *2ʳ line 7 begins: 'lande,'. 'ij' of sig. Aij is beneath the space before 'to' in the line above. E⁴ and OS copies have this signature position but *2ʳ reading like 19360.7.

19360.7 — [Anr. ed.] 12°. *Oxford, J. Barnes,* 1585. L(imp.).O. HER.; NY¹¹.
Tp line 7: 'should re/' (no hyphen); *2ʳ line 7 begins: 'land,'. 'ij' of sig. Aij is directly beneath 'to' in the line above.

19361 — Now = 19359.5.

19362 — Now = 19354.1.

19363 — [Anr. ed.] 12°. *London, [J. Windet,]* 1586. L.C³(lacks tp).BUTE.D.P.; HD(2 imp.).U.
(2nd pt. formerly 4095) *See* note to 19359.

19364 — [Anr. ed.] 8°. *J. Charlewood f. J. Wight,* 1589. L.C⁵.

19365 — [Anr. ed.] 12°. *E. Bollifant f. T. Wight,* 1594. L.O.C.
In this and following eds. Bunny's Treatise is not included.

Parsons, Robert—*cont.*

19365.5 — [Anr. ed.] 12°. *J. Jackson f. T. Wight,* 1596. L²⁶.
USHAW.; HD(imp.).

19366 — [Anr. ed.] 12°. *A. Hatfield f. T. Wight,* 1597. L.M².

19367 — [Anr. ed.] 12°. *London,* [*P. Short?*] 1598. Ent to F.
Kingston 25 ja. L(tp only, Harl.5993/82).O¹⁷(imp.).
O²⁸.C(2, 1 imp.).; F.
See Greg, Register B, p. 62.

19368 — Now = 19354.3.

19368.5 — [Anr. ed.] 8°. [*f.*] *T. Wight,* 1599. L.L⁴⁶.

19369 — [Anr. ed.] 12°. [*f.*] *T. Wight,* 1602. O⁶.C(imp.).; HN.
DAR.TORONTO².

19370 — [Anr. ed.] 12°. *F. Kyngston f. E. Weaver,* 1607. Ent.
6 my. 1605 a. 2 mr. 1607. L⁴⁶.O²⁸.; F.

19371 — Now = 19354.5.

19372 — [Anr. ed.] 12°. *F. Kyngston f. E. Weaver,* 1609. L.O.O³.
C.C¹².+; F.

19373 — [Anr. ed.] 12°. *F. Kyngston f. E. Weaver,* 1612. O.SH.;
HN.

19374 — [Anr. ed.] 12°. *F. Kyngston f. E. Weaver,* 1615. L.O.
C.M.; F.N.

19375 — [Anr. ed.] 12°. *J. Dawson f. E. Weaver,* 1621. L.L⁴⁶.
O.E.PLUME.+; HD.Y.

19376 — Now = 19354.7.

19376.5 — [Anr. ed.] 12°. *G. Purslowe f. T. Weaver,* 1630. L.O¹².
BIRM².INN.ST.; F.

19377 — = 19388a.

19378 — Now = 19354.9.

19379 — [Anr. ed.] Both parts joyned together. 12°. *T. Harper,*
sold by J. Waterson, 1640. Ass'd to T. Weaver 19 de.
1638; to G. Miller 28 jn. 1639. L.O¹⁷.C⁹.BIRM.DUL.
+; HN.ILL.
L,C⁹,DUL bd. w. 19389; HN,ILL bd. w. 19388a.

19380 — The seconde parte of the booke of christian exercise.
Or a christian directorie. Written by the former
author R. P(arsons.) 8°. *J. Charlwoode a.* [i.e. *for*]
S. Waterson, 1590. Ent. 30 ja. L.L³.O.C⁵.BUTE.;
F.HN.
Anonymously adapted for the use of Protestants
largely from the new material in 19354.1. *See also*
16644.5.

19381 — [Anr. ed.] 12°. *J. Charlewood f. S. Waterson,* 1591.
L(2).C⁵.HER.; F.HN.

19382 — [Anr. ed.] 12°. *J. Charlewood f. S. Waterson,* 1592. L
(tp only, Ames I.523).O.C.E.; F.NY¹¹.U.

19383 — [Anr. ed.] 12°. *J. Roberts f. S. Waterson,* 1594. Ent.
31 my. L(2).L²⁶.O.C¹⁰.P.; F(imp.).

19384 — [Anr. ed.] 12°. *J. Roberts f. S. Waterson,* 1598. L.O.C.;
ILL.NY¹¹.

19384.5 — [Anr. ed.] 12°. *J. Roberts f. S. Waterson,* 1599. O⁶.;
F.HD(imp.).

19385 — [Anr. ed.] 12°. *J. Roberts f. S. Waterson,* 1601. L.
BIRM.; HN.TORONTO².U.Y.

19385.5 — [Anr. ed.] 12°. *W. Jaggard f. S. Waterson,* 1608. L⁴⁶.
O²⁸.

19386 — [Anr. ed.] 12°. *W. Jaggard f. S. Waterson,* 1610. L.O.C.P.

19387 — [Anr. ed.] 12°. *W. Jaggard f. S. Waterson,* 1615. O.C.;
F.HN.

19388 — [Anr. ed.] 12°. *W. Jaggard f. S. Waterson,* 1619. L.
L⁴⁶.O.O⁶(imp.).C.; HD.U.

19388a — [Anr. ed.] 12°. *A. M*[*athewes*] *f. S. Waterson,* 1631.
L.O¹².C³.G².NLW.+; F.HN.ILL.
(Formerly also 19377) This and following ed.
found bd. as pt. 2 of 19379.

19389 — [Anr. ed.] 12°. *T. Cotes f. S. Waterson,* 1633. Ent. to
T. a. R. Cotes 19 jn. 1627. L.O¹⁹.O²⁸.C⁹.DUL.

19390 — [A trans.] Llyfr y Resolusion, . . . Wedi ei gyfieithu yn
Gymraeg y gan J. D[*avies, of Mallwyd.*] 12°. *J.*
Beale tros yr un J. D[*avies,*] 1632. L.NLW.

19391 — A brief, and cleere confutation, of a chalenge, made by
O. E. 1603. Now = 24994.5.

19391.5 — A briefe apologie, or defence of the catholike ecclesiastical hierarchie. [Anon.] 8°. [*Antwerp, A. Conincx,*
1601.] L³⁰.O.D².DUR⁵.P.+; F.HN.HD.TEX.Y.
A&R 613. Collates †–††⁸ A–Ee⁸ Ff². Answered
by 19056, 7628. A passage on p.201 is obliterated
in the HD copy and prob. others, according to
instructions on E2ʳ of 19392.5.

19392 — [Anr. ed.] 8°. [*R. Barker,* 1601.] L.L².C.YK.
(Formerly also 4832) A. & R. 614. Collates ¶⁸
A–Ee⁸. Reprinted by order of Bp. Bancroft.

19392.5 — An appendix to the Apologie, lately set forth. Wherin
two other bookes [1884, 3106] are examined.
[Anon.] 8°. [*Antwerp, A. Conincx,* 1602.] L²⁶.L³⁰.
O⁴.HP.MSB.; F.HN.Y.
A&R 612. Answered in 19056. *See* 19391.5.

Parsons, Robert—*cont.*

19393 — A brief censure vppon two bookes [12745 and 5005]
written in answere to E. Campions offer of disputation. [Anon.] 8°. *Doway, J. Lyon* [i.e. *house of F.*
Browne, Greenstreet House Press,] 1581. L.O.E.OS.
P.+; F.HD.
(Formerly also 4534) A&R 615. Answered by
12746, 5007; supported by 19401.

19394 — A brief discours contayning certayne reasons why
catholiques refuse to goe to church. Dedicated by
J. H(owlet, *pseud.*) to the queenes maiestie. 8°.
Doway, J. Lyon [i.e. *East Ham, Greenstreet House,*]
1580. L.O.C².D².DUR⁵.+; F.CAL.
A&R 616. Answered by 10844, 11421, 25586. In
at least L,O,D² copies the tp is a cancel.

19395 — [Anr. ed.] 16° in 8's. *Doway* [i.e. *English secret press,*]
1599. L.LK.
A&R 617.

19396 — [Anr. ed.] 12°. *Doway* [i.e. *English secret press,*] 1601.
L.O.D.E.OS.+; F.HN.
A&R 618.

19397 — [A ghost.]
— A christian directory. *See* 19354.1 sqq.

19398 — A conference about the next succession to the crowne
of Ingland. Where vnto is added a genealogie. Pub-
lished by R. Doleman, *pseud.* [By R. Parsons, R.
Rowlands, and others.] 8°. *Imprinted at N.* [*Antwerp,*
A. Conincx,] 1594 [1595.] L.O.C.D².E.+; F.HN.HD.
N.U.+
A&R 271. Answered by 5638.5, 25245.

19399 — The copie of a leter, wryten by a master of arte of
Cambrige. [Not by Parsons.] 1584. Now = 5742.9.
— The copies of certaine discourses. 1601. *See* 5724.

19400 — A declaration of the true causes of the great troubles.
1592. = 10005.

19401 — A defence of the censure [19393], gyuen vpon two
bookes of w. Charke and M. Hanmer against E.
Campian. [Anon.] 8°. [*Rouen, Fr. Parsons' Press,*]
1582. L.O.C.E.OS.+; F.HN.HD.U.Y.+
A&R 626. Partially reprinted in 19409.5. Answers
5007; answered by 5008, 5009.

19401a — — An answeare for the time, vnto that Defence of the
censure. 1583. = 5008.

19402 — A discouerie of J. Nicols minister, misreported a
jesuite. Wherin is contayned a ful answere to his
recantation [18533]. There is added a reproofe of an
oration [18535]. [Anon.] 8°. [*Stonor Park, Green-*
street House Press, 1581.] O.C⁵.OS.W.YK.+; F.
A&R 627. Answered by 16946, 10764.
— A discussion of the answere of M. W. Barlow. *See*
19409.

19403 — The dolefull knell, of Thomas Bell. 1607. Now =
25972.4.

19404 — Dutifull and respective considerations. 1609. = 15362.

19405 — [Anr. ed.] 1609. Now = 15362.5.

19406 — An epistle of the persecution of catholickes in Englande.
Tr. owt of frenche and conferred with the Latyne
copie. by. G. T. To whiche is added an epistle by
the translator to the preeuie councell. [Anon.] 8°.
Douay in Artois [i.e. *Rouen, Fr. Parsons' Press,* 1582.]
L.O.C².DUR⁵.W.+; HD.STL.U.WASH³.Y.
(Formerly also 3724 and 4834) A&R 629. A.
Briant wrote 'The copie of a letter' (L6–M2) only.
Translator's epistle answered by 24181.

19407 — The fore-runner of Bels downefall. 1605. Now =
25972.5.

19407a — The second time set forth. [1605?] Now = 25972.6.

19408 — The judgment of a catholicke English-man. Concerninge Triplici nodo, triplex cuneus [14400]. [Anon.]
4°. [*St. Omer, English College Press,*] 1608. L.O.C.D.
DUR.+; F.HD.U. Gonzaga U, Spokane, Wash.
A&R 630. Answered by 1446, 24472.

19409 — A discussion of the answere of M. William Barlow
[1446], to the booke intituled: The judgment of a
catholike Englishman. Written by R. Persons.
Wherunto since the said fathers death, is annexed
a generall preface, [by E. Coffin.] 4°. [*St. Omer,*
English College Press,] 1612. L.O.C.D².DUR⁵.+; F.HN.
HD.N.U.+ 𝔄
A&R 628. *See also* 11021, 11022.

19409.5 — A little treatise concerning triall of spirits. Written
first by R. Parsons, . . . against Master Charke.
Newly set forth, with an Appendix taken out of a
later writer. 8°. [*Lancs., Birchley Hall Press?*] 1620.
L(tp only, Harl.5961/62).C⁵(imp.).P(lacks tp).ST.; STL.
A&R 631. Reprinted from 19401.

Parsons, Robert—*cont.*

19410 — [Anr. issue, enlarged, w. cancel tp:] Whereunto is added a comparison of a true Roman catholike with a protestant. 2 pts. 8°. [*Lancs., Birchley Hall Press?*] 1620. L(cancel tp and pt. 2 only).O¹³(both tpp).YK.
A&R 632.

19411 — A manifestation of the great folly of certayne in England calling themselves secular priestes. [Anon.] 4°. [*Antwerp, A. Conincx,*] 1602. L.O.USHAW.W.YK.+
A&R 633. Answered by 4321.
— Newes from Spayne and Holland. 1593. *See* 22994.

19412 — A quiet and sober reckoning with M. Thomas Morton . . . concerning . . . a Treatise of P. R. [i.e. R. Parsons, 19417.] 4°. [*St. Omer, English College Press,*] 1609. L.O.C.D.YK.+; F.HN.HD.N.U.+
A&R 635. Answers 18191; answered by 18183.

19412.5 — A relation of the king of Spaines receiuing in Valliodolid [*sic*]. Wryten by an Inglish priest. [Anon.] 8°. [*Antwerp, A. Conincx,*] 1592. L².O.C.
(Formerly 19836a) A&R 636.

19413 — A relation of the triall . . . betweene the bishop of Evreux, and L. Plessis Mornay. Newly reveued, and sett forth againe, with a defence therof. [Init. N. D., i.e. R. Parsons.] 8°. [*St. Omer, F. Bellet,*] 1604. L.O.C².DUR⁵.M².+; F.HN.N.TEX.U.+
A&R 637. Also issued as pt. 3 of 19416. 1st ed., of which no copy is known, answered by 18134.3, 23453 sq. which this work in turn attacks.

19414 — A review of ten publike disputations . . . under K. Edward & Qu. Mary, concerning some principall points in religion. [Init. N. D.] 8°. [*St. Omer, F. Bellet,*] 1604. L.O.C².D.YK.+; F.HD.N.STL.U.
A&R 638. Also issued as pt. 5 of 19416.

19415 — A temperate ward-word, to the turbulent and seditious Wach-word of Sir F. Hastinges [12927]. [Init. N. D.] 4°. [*Antwerp, A. Conincx,*] 1599. L.O.C².D.E.+; F.HN.HD.N.U.+
A&R 639. Answered by 12928, 23453.
— The third part of a treatise. *See* 19416, vols. II and III.

19416 — A treatise of three conversions of England. Divided into three partes. The former two whereof are handled in this booke [i.e. Vol. I.] [Vol. II:] (The third part of a treatise. An examen of the calendar of protestant saints, martyrs and confessors, divised by J. Fox, and prefixed before [11222 sqq.] The first six monethes. Wherunto is annexed [19413].) [Vol. III:] (The third part of a treatise. The last six monethes. Wherunto is annexed [19414].) [All init. N. D.] 5 pts. 8°. [*St. Omer, F. Bellet,*] 1603 (1604.) L.O.C.D.M.+; F.HN.HD.N.U.+
A&R 640. Answered by 23469, 23470.

19417 — A treatise tending to mitigation towardes catholicke-subjectes in England. Against the seditious wrytings of T. Morton [18184, 18185]. [Init. P. R.] 8° in 4's. [*St. Omer, F. Bellet,*] 1607. L.O.C.D.E.+; F.HN.HD.N.U.+
A&R 641. Supports 19412; answered by 18191. Yyy4 intended to be cancelled and Conclusion, etc. (Zzz–Aaaa⁴) inserted before Table (Zzz⁴Aaaa²). Quires Vvv to end have horizontal chainlines.

19418 — The warn-word to sir Francis Hastinges Wast-word [12928]: conteyning the issue of three former treateses. Wherunto is adjoyned a breif rejection of [23453]. [Init. N. D.] 8°. [*Antwerp, A. Conincx,*] 1602. L.O.C.D.E².+; F.HN.HD.TEX.U.+
A&R 642. Answered by 23465.
— *See also* 19885.

Part. A parte of a register, contayninge sundrie memorable matters, for the reformation of our church. [1593?] *See* 10400.

Parthenia. Parthenia or the maydenhead of the first musicke. [1613.] *See* 4251.5.

19419 **Partridge, James.** Ayme for Finsburie archers. Or an alphabeticall table of the names of every marke within the same fields. 16° in 8's. G. M[iller] f. *John Partridge,* 1628. L.

19420 — The letters patents of the presbyterie. By J. Peregrin. 1632. Now = 19622b.5.

19421 **Partridge, John.** The ende and confession of J. Felton, . . . the viii daie of August 1570. 8°. R. Jones a. T. Colwell, [1570.] Ent. to R. Jones 1570–71. C⁵.

19422 — = 19421.

19423 — = 19421.

Partridge, John—*cont.*

19424 — The most famouse and worthie historie, of the worthy lady Pandauola. [*Tr.* In verse.] 8°. T. Purfoote, 1566. Ent. 1566–67. C⁶.

19425 — The notable hystorie of two famous princes, Astianax and Polixena. 1566. [In verse.] 8°. H. Denham f. T. Hacket, [1566] (7 my.) Ent. 1565–66. O.C⁶.

19425.5 — The treasurie of commodious conceits, & hidden secrets. and may be called, the huswiues closet, of healthfull prouision. 8°. R. Jones, 1573. HN.
Herbert, II.1043, owned a 2nd ed. 1580.

19426 — The fourth tyme corrected. 8°. R. Jhones, 1584. L.; HD.

19427 — [Anr. ed.] Now amplified and inlarged. 8°. [*Eliot's Court Press*] f. H. Car, 1584. O⁵.; HN.
Same contents as 19426.

19428 — [Anr. ed.] 8°. f. H. Car, 1586. L.

19429 — [Anr. ed.] 8°. [*J. Charlewood? f.*] R. Jones, 1591. O.; WIS.
See also 3298.

19429.5 — [Anr. ed., anon., w. title:] The treasurie of hidden secrets. Commonlie called, the good huswives closet . . . newly enlarged. 4°. [*J. Danter? f.*] R. Johnes, 1596. G².; NLM.
Preface init. R. J., *Printer.*

19430 — [Anr. ed.] 4°. J. R[oberts] f. E. White, 1600. Ent. 3 jy. 1601. L.O⁸.BRISTOL².; F(tp def.).NY(date torn).WIS.

19430.5 — [Anr. ed.] 4°. J. W[indet] f. E. White, 1608. G². Hatchards Booksellers, London(imp.).
Preface init. I. W., *Printer.*

19431 — [Anr. ed.] 4°. [*Eliot's Court Press*] f. E. B[rewster] a. R. B[ird,] 1627. Ent. to E. Allde 29 jn. 1624. O.; F. HD.NLM.

19431.5 — [A variant, w. imprint:] f. J. Wright, 1627. L¹⁶(imp.).; Duke U.
See 19436.5.

19432 — [Anr. ed.] 4°. Eliz. All-de, 1633. O(frag.).O¹⁸.C.C².C⁹.; HN.

19433 — [Anr. ed.] 4°. R. Oulton, 1637. Ent. 22 ap. 1640. L.C.; Duke U.

19433.2 — The widowes treasure. 1582. *See* Addenda.

19433.3 — The widowes treasure, plentifully furnished with secretes in phisicke. Hereunto are adioyned, sundry pretie practises of cookerie. [Anon.] 8°. R. Waldegraue f. E. White, 1585. Ent. to T. Rider 6 ap. 1584; ass'd to E. White 11 ap. 1584. LEEDS.

19433.5 — [Anr. ed.] 8°. [*G. Robinson f. E. White,* 1586?] L(imp.). (Formerly 19436) Collates A–G⁸; not signed in Waldegrave's manner; A2ʳ line 1 of text ends 'writ-'.

19433.7 — [Anr. ed.] 8°. E. Alde f. E. White, 1588. O⁵.; HD.
A2ʳ line 1 of text ends 'written'.

19434 — [Anr. ed.] 8°. J. Roberts f. E. White, 1595. L.
This and following eds. collate A–F⁸.

19435 — [Anr. ed.] 8°. J. Roberts f. E. White, 1599. L.

19436 — Now = 19433.5.

19436.3 — [Anr. ed.] 8°. [*J. Windet,* c. 1610.] BRISTOL²(lacks tp).
A2ʳ has init. 'T' with satyrs.

19436.5 — [Anr. ed.] 8°. J. Haviland f. J. Wright, 1627. Ass'd to T. Pavier a. J. Wright 13 de. 1620; Pavier's share ass'd to E. Brewster a. R. Bird 4 au. 1626. C².
See Court-Book C, p.113.

19437 — [Anr. ed.] 8°. E. Allde, sold by R. Bird, 1631. O.

19437a — [Anr. ed.] 8°. R. B[adger] f. R. Bird, 1639. L.

19438 — The worthie hystorie of the most noble and valiaunt knight Plasidas. 1566. [In verse.] 8°. H. Denham f. T. Hacket, [1566.] Ent. 1565–66. O.C⁶.; F(frag.).HN.
— *See also* 18358, 19071.

19439 **Parvula.** Here begynneth a treatyse called. Peruula. [1497?] Now = 23163.7.

19440 — [Anr. ed.] Peruula. [1496?] Now = 23163.6.

19441 — [Anr. ed.] [1501?] Now = 23163.11.

19442 — [Anr. ed.] [1500.] Now = 23163.9.
— Long Parvula. *See* 23163.13.

Pascalius, Carolus. *See* Pasquale, C.

Paske, Thomas. Instructions for the ministers, and churchwardens. [1630.] *See* 16776.8.
— To my very loving brethren the ministers, . . . of London. [1627.] *See* 16776.14.

Paskewet. *See* 20127.

19443 **Pasor, George.** Lexico-Græco-Latinum. 8°. W. Jaggard, 1620. Ent. to Field, Swinhowe, Jaggard and ptnrs. in the Latin Stock 11 my. J(untraced).

Pasor, George—*cont.*

19444 — [Anr. ed.] Lexicon Græco-Latinum. In Novum Domini nostri Jesu Christi Testamentum. 8°. *ap. J. Billium,* 1621. L.O.C.G⁴.LIV³.+; F.ILL.Y.

19445 **Pasor, Matthias.** Oratio pro linguæ Arabicæ professione. 8°. *Oxoniæ, J. Lichfield & G. Turner,* 1627. L.O. C².D.P.+; PN².

19446 **Pasquale, Carlo.** False complaints. Or the censure of an unthankful mind. *Tr.* W. C. 4°. *H. Lownes,* 1605. Ent. as tr. by W. Covell 2 fb. L.O⁵.C.; F. Iowa U.

19447 **Pasqualigo, Luigi.** Fedele and Fortunio. The deceites in loue. *Tr.* out of Italian [by A. Munday. Anon.] 4°. [*J. Charlewood?*] *f. T. Hacket,* 1585. Ent. 12 no. 1584. F(2, 1 imp.).HN(imp.). Greg 86.
  Dedic. varies: to Maister M. R. by M. A. (1F); or to J. Heardson, Esquier by A. M. (HN).

19448 **Pasquier, Étienne.** The jesuite displayed. Containing the original and proceedings of the jesuites. *Tr.* E. A[ggas.] 4°. [*E. Allde*] *f. E. Aggas,* 1594. Ent. 10 oc. O.O⁸.C.D.; BO³.

19449 — The jesuites catechisme. Or examination of their doctrine. *Tr.* [by W. Watson. Anon.] 4°. [*J. Roberts,*] 1602. L.O.C.D.E.+; F.HN.HD.N.U.+
  A&R 596.
  — See also 5066, 10797.

19450 **Pasquil.** The first parte of Pasquils apologie. Wherin he gallops the fielde with the Treatise of reformation [19612]. [Doubtfully attrib. to T. Nash.] 4°. *Printed where I was, and where I will bee . . .* [*J. Charlewood,*] 1590. L.L².O.C²·M.+; F.HN.HD(imp.).NY.TEX.+

19451 — Pasquils jests, mixed with Mother Bunches merriments. [By W. Fennor?] 4°. [*S. Stafford?*] *f. J. Browne,* 1604. L.

19451.5 — [Anr. ed.] Newly corrected with new additions. 4° w. perp. chainlines. [*J. Windet*] *f. J. Browne,* 1609. Ass'd by Browne's widow to J. Marriot 17 fb. 1623. F(lacks G2).

19452 — [Anr. ed.] 4°. *M. F[lesher,] sold by F. Grove,* 1629. O.; HN.

19453 — [Anr. ed.] 4°. *M. F[lesher,] sold by F. Coles,* [1632?] F.

19453.3 — [Anr. ed.] 4°. *M. F[lesher,] sold by A. Kembe, Southwarke,* 1635. C².
  — Pasquils mad-cap. 1600. See 3675.

19453.7 — Pasquils Palinodia, and his progresse to the taverne. [By W. Fennor? In verse.] 4°. *T. Snodham,* 1619. Ent. as by 'William F.' 6 ap. HN.

19454 — [Anr. issue, w. cancel tp, w. imprint:] *T. Snodham, sold by F. Parke,* 1619. L.L¹³.O.C(impr. faked).; F.N.

19455 — [Anr. ed.] 4°. *T. H[arper] f. L. Chapman,* 1634. Ass'd to W. Stansby 23 fb. 1626. L.L⁶.L⁴⁰.O.; F.HN.DAR (date cropt).HD(date cropt). Pearson.
  — Pasquil the playne. 1533. See 7672.

19456 **Pasquill,** *of England.* A countercuffe giuen to Martin junior. [Formerly attrib. to T. Nash.] 4°. *Printed between the skye and the grounde,* [*J. Charlewood,*] 1589. L.L²(2).; F.CH.HD.NY.U.+
  Both L²,U copies dated 'sixt' of August on A4ᵛ; all other copies dated 'eyght'.

19456.5 — [Anr. ed.] 4°. *Printed, betweene the skye and the grounde,* [*J. Charlewood*] 1589 [October?] L.O.O⁸.M.; F.HN.

19457 — The returne of the renowned caualiero Pasquill of England. [Formerly attrib. to T. Nash.] 4°. *If my breath be so hote that I burne my mouth, suppose I was printed by Pepper Allie* [*J. Charlewood*] 1589. L(2). L².L³.L⁴.; HN.HD.ILL.TEX.Y.+
  B4ʳ line 31: 'hee should'.

19457.3 — [Anr. issue, partially reset, w. B4ʳ line 31: 'she should'.] L.L².O⁸.C².M.+; F.NY.PFOR.

19457.7 — [Anr. issue, further reset, w. B4ʳ line 31: 'he should'.] L².O.C.; CH. Pirie.
  Only A1ʳ,B3ᵛ,C1ᵛ–C4ᵛ,D3ᵛ,D4ʳ from same setting as 19457.

19458 **Pasquilla.** Pasquillorum versus aliquot ex diuersis auctoribus collecti. 4°. *Edimburgi, R. Lekpreuik,* 1565. C².

Pasquin, Petrus, *of Rome.* See 24913a.5.

Passage. The passage of our most drad soueraigne lady. 1558. See 7590.
  — The quenes maiesties passage through the citie. 1558. See 7589.5.
  — The royall passage of her maiesty. 1604. See 7592.

Passage—*cont.*

19458.5 — The speedy passage to heaven. 8°. [*T. Creede?*] *f. T. Bushell,* 1612. Ent. 6 jy. L.O.
  (Formerly 17706)

19458.7 — [A variant, with imprint:] [*T. Creede?*] *f. T. B[ushell,]* 1612. L.

19459 **Passe, Crispin van de,** *the Younger.* A garden of flowers, wherein very lively is contained a true discription of al the flowers in these foure followinge bookes. *Tr.* out of Netherlandish [by E. W. or T. Wood?] 2 pts. obl.fol. *Utrecht, S. de Roy f. C. de Passe,* 1615. L.O. O¹².C.; F.HN(imp.).WIS.

19460 **Passing Bell.** A passing bell towling to call us to mind, Our time evill spending, a plague now we find. *Ballad.* 2 pts. s.sh.fol. [*London,* 1625?] Ent. to J. Allde 30 oc. 1582; to ballad ptnrs. 14 de. 1624. O(imp.).
  1st line: 'Hark man what I thy God shal speak,'.

Passion. The passion of a discontented minde. 1601. See 3679.5.
  — The passion of owr lord iesu christe. [1508?] See 14557.

Passions. The passions of the spirit. 1599. See 3682.5.

Pastime. The pastyme of people. [1530?] See 20724.

Pastor. The pastor and the prelate. 1628. See 4359.

Pater. Erra Pater. [1540? etc.] See 439.3 sqq.
  — [Pater, Filius, et Uxor. An interlude. 1530?] See 20765.5.
  — Verus Pater. 1622. See 24693.

Pater Noster. See Lord's Prayer.

19461 **Paterson, William.** The protestants theologie, containing, the true solutions, and groundes of religion. The 1. part. 4°. [*Malines, H. Jaye,*] 1620. L.O.E.W.YK.+; WASH².
  A&R 597. No more published?

19462 **Pathomachia.** Pathomachia: or, the battell of affections. Now first published by a friend of the deceassed author. 4°. *T. a. R. Coats f. F. Constable,* 1630. Ent. 16 ap. L.O.C.E.SHEF.+; F.HN.HD.N.Y².+ Greg 434.

19463 **Pathos.** Pathose, or an inward passion of the pope for the losse of hys daughter the masse. [In verse. By L. Shepherd?] 8°. (*J. Daye a. W. Seres,*) [1548?] C (imp.).

Pathway. A path way ĩto the holy scripture. [1536?] See 24462.
  — The pathway to knowledge. 1596. See 19799.

19464 — The pathway to musicke, contayning sundrie familiar rules. [*Ed.* W. Barley?] obl.4°. [*J. Danter*] *f. W. Barley,* 1596. L.
  Intended to be issued with 1433.
  — The path-way to please god. 1617. See 24991.5.

19465 — No entry.
  — A plaine pathway to the French tongue. 1575. See 11376.
  — The pleasant playne and pythye pathwaye. [1552?] See 15113.5.

19465.3 **Patriarchs.** [Headline:] The testament of Gad. (The testament of Aser.) [*Tr.* from the Latin version of R. Grosseteste.] 8° in 4's. (*R. Lant,*) [1542?] F(imp.).
  Not same trans. as in 19465.7 sqq. Film of F copy on Univ. Microfilms reel 718 ('23918a').

19465.5 — The testament of Joseph whych was *tr.* oute of Greke into Latyne by Grosthede [R. Grosseteste], and into Englishe by, w. Freloue [i.e. A. Gilby.] 8°. *R. grafton a. E. whytchurch,* 1539. L(frag.).O(frag.).P.; F(frag.). HD(1 imp., plus frag.).
  This trans. reprinted in 19465.7 sqq.

19465.7 — The testaments of the twelue patriarches, the sonnes of Iacob: *tr.* out of G⟨reek⟩e into Latine by R. Grosthed, and Englyshed by A. G[ilby.] With the testament of Iacob their father: prefixed. [*Ed.*] (R. D[ay.]) 8°. *J. Daye,* 1574. F.

19466 — [Anr. ed., w. pref. signed R. Day.] 8°. *J. Day,* 1575. L(imp.).

19467 — [Anr. ed.] To the credit whereof an auncient Greeke copye written in parchment, is kept in the uniuersitie librarye of Cambridge. 8°. *J. Day* [*a. J. Kingston,*] 1576. c(tp defective).
  Kingston pr. quires C–K.

19467.5 — [Anr. ed.] 8°. [*J. Kingston f.*] *J. Day,* 1577. L.O⁹.

Patriarchs—*cont.*

19468 — [Anr. ed.] 8°. *J. Daye [a. J. Kingston,] 1581.* L.O.C.
LIV³. Rogers.
Kingston pr. quires C–K.

19468.5 — [Anr. ed.] 8°. *P. Short f. the assignes of R. Day, 1595.*
C.D(lacks tp).

19469 — [Anr. ed.] 8°. *P. Short f. the assignes of R. Daye, 1601.*
O.C.; F.PN.
Translator's inits. omitted from tp.

19469.5 — [Anr. ed.] 8°. *f. the Co. of Statrs., 1606.* L(imp.).O.;
LC(imp.).Y.
Translator's inits. appear on tp of this ed., but
not hereafter.

19470 — [Anr. ed.] 8°. *[H. Lownes] f. the Co. of Statrs., 1610.*
C.; HN.

19470.5 — [Anr. ed.] 8°. *f. the Co. of Statrs., 1614.* BTL.

19471 — [Anr. ed.] 8°. *[H. Lownes] f. the Co. of Statrs., 1619.*
O⁶.; F.PEN.

19471.5 — [Anr. ed.] 8°. *f. the Co. of Statrs., 1628.* PH.

19472 — [Anr. ed.] 8°. *[R. Young] f. the Co. of Statrs., 1633.*
C.LK.; HD.

19472.5 — [Anr. ed.] 8°. *Edinburgh, J. Wreittoun, 1634.* C.

19473 — [Anr. ed.] 8°. *R. Y[oung] f. the Co. of Statrs., 1638.*
L.L⁴³.O.M.; St. Mary's Seminary, Perryville, Missouri.

Patrick. [Patrick's places. 1531, etc.] *See* 12731.4 sqq.

Patrick, *Saint.* The life of the glorious bishop S. Patricke.
1625, etc. *See* 14626, 24733, 24736.

19474 — [Saint Patricks purgatory. A description of the cave so
called.] 4°. *[Dublin, W. Bladen, 1632?]*
Sheets reissued w. new prelims. in 1647 as by H.
Jones = Wing J 946. No copy is known of the
orig. issue. Authorship sometimes erroneously
attrib. to J. Spottiswood.

Patrick, *Simon, tr. See* 6036, 11743.

Patridophilus, *Pseud. See* 19598.2, 19598.4.

19475 **Patrizi, Francesco,** *Bp.* A moral methode of ciuile
policie. Abridged oute of the Cōmentaries of F.
Patricius. *Tr.* R. Robinson. 4°. *T. Marsh, 1576.*
Ass'd by E. Marsh to T. Orwin 23 jn. 1591. L.C.
NLW.; F.HN.CU.HD.ILL.+

Patrizi, Francesco, *Philosophical Writer. See* 3161.

19476 **Patten, William.** The calender of scripture. 1575.
[Anon.] 4°. *[R. Jugge, 1575.]* L.O.C.BTU.G².+; F.
HN(imp.).HD.ILL.U.+
HD copy has author's signature on tp.

19476.5 — The expedicion into Scotlāde of Edward, duke of
Soomerset. 8°. *(R. Grafton, 1548 (30 jn.))* L.O.C.E.
M.+; F.HN.HD.N.PML.
(Formerly 19479) Quartersheet d in 2 settings:
d1ʳ catchword: 'nauntes' (O) or 'tes' (L,HN).

19477 — In mortem W. Wynter equitis aurati. Monumentum
diutinæ mutuæᵭ; amicitiæ ergò. [In verse.] 4°. *ap.
T. Orwinum, 1589.* HN.

19478 **Patten, William,** *Bp.* Who so euer beynge in the state
of grace [etc. c. 1499.] Now = Indulgences 148.

19479 Now = 19476.5.

19480 **Pattenson, Matthew.** The image of bothe churches,
Hierusalem and Babel. By, P[attenson] D. M. 8°.
Tornay, A. Quinqué, 1623. L.C.C².DE.VAL.; F.BO².Y.
A&R 599. P. 81, line 2: 'mere'.

19481 — [Anr. ed.] 8°. *Tornay, A. Quinqué, 1623.* L.O.C.E.M.+;
F.HN.HD.N.NY.+
A&R 600. P. 81, line 2: 'more'.

Pattern. A patterne of catechisticall doctrine. 1630. *See*
603.

Patterns. Here foloweth certaine patterns. [1624.] *See*
21826.

— New and singular patternes & workes of linnen. 1591.
See 24765.3.

Paul IV., *Pope. See* Indulgences 147A.

19482 **Paul V.,** *Pope.* A declaration of the variance betweene the
pope, and the segniory of Venice. 4°. *[R. Barker,]*
1606. L.O.C.C².D⁸.+; F.HN.HART².HD.N.+

— The history of the quarrels of Paul .V. 1626. *See* 21766.

19483 — The popes complaint to his minion cardinals, against
the good successe of the Bohemians. [A satire, in
verse.] 4°. *[London, 1620?]* L.L⁴.O.O².SHEF.+; F.HN.
CH.HD.

Paul V., *Pope*—*cont.*

— Prosopopoeia. Or, a conference held at Angelo castle
between the pope, the emperor and the king of
Spain. [1619?] *See* 20443.

— *See also* 16161.5, 24719.

Paul, *of the order of Servites. See* 21757, 21759, 24719.

19484 **Paule, Sir George.** The life of the most reverend prelate
J. Whitgift. 4°. *T. Snodham, 1612.* Ent. to T. Pavier
14 oc. 1611. L.O.C.CASHEL.E.+; F.HN.HD.N.NY.+

19485 **Paulet, William,** *Marquis of Winchester.* The lord
marques idlenes: conteining manifold matters of
acceptable deuise; as sage sentences, [etc.] 4°. *A.
Hatfield, 1586.* Ent. to E. Bollifant, A. Hatfield, J.
Jackson, a. N. Newton 8 no. L.L³⁸.O.; F(2).HN.WIS.
Lewis.

19486 — [Anr. ed.] 4°. *E. Bollifant, 1587.* L.LIV³(imp.).; F.HN.
HD.N.Y.+
Prelims. from same setting as 19485 except for a
few alterations such as imprint and date.

Paulett, Alice. [Bookplate.] *See* Bookplates.

Paulfreyman, Thomas, *ed. See* Palfreyman, T.

Paulilli, Anello. *See* 19530.

Pauncefote or **Paunchfoot, John,** *tr. See* 4868.

19487 **Pavonius, Franciscus.** Summa ethicae: sive, introductio
in Aristotelis, et theologorum doctrinam moralem.
12°. *Oxonii, sumpt. G. Turner, 1633.* L.O³.C³.
CARLISLE.E².+; HD.ILL.

19488 **Paybody, Thomas.** A just apologie for the gesture of
kneeling in the act of receiving the lords supper.
4° in 8's. *W. Jones, 1629.* Ent. 22 se. 1628. L².O.C.D.
E².+; F.HN.FORDHAM.U.Y.+

19489 **Payne, John.** Royall exchange: to suche worshipfull
citezins, marchants, gentlemen and other occupiers
of the contrey as resorte therunto. Try to retaine, or
send back agayne. 4°. *Harlem, G. Romaen, 1597.*
L³.L⁸.O.; F.Y.

19489.5 **Payne, John,** *Engraver.* The true portraicture of his
maᵗⁱᵉˢ royall ship the Soveraigne of the Seas built
in 1637. [With Latin verses by H. Jacob and
Eng. verses by T. Cary.] s.sh.fol. *[London, 1638.]*
L(Print Dept).L⁵.L³³(3). London, Science Museum.
Plate subscribed: 'Archinaupego Petro Pett jun:
scultore J. Payne. Cum privilegio ad imprimendum
solum.' This engr. mentioned in 13368, p. 50.
See also Hind III.28–30.

19490 **Payne, Robert.** A briefe description of Ireland: made in
this yeare, 1589. Truely published, by N. Gorsan.
8°. *T. Dawson, 1589.* O(2).

19491 — [Anr. ed.] With diuers notes sithenes the first impression. 8°. *T. Dawson, 1590.* L.

19491.5 — The vale mans table. Herein is taught . . . howe to
draine moores, [etc.] s.sh.fol. *[London, 1583.]* L⁵
(Lemon 78).; HD.
Text dated 16 Nov. 1583.

Paynell, Thomas. The assaute and cōquest of heuen.
Tr. T. Paynel. 1529. *See* 862.

— The ciuilitie of childehode. *Tr.* T. Paynell. 1560. *See*
10470.3.

— The conspiracie of Lucius Catiline. *Tr.* T. Paynell.
1541. *See* 10751.

19492 — A frutefull booke of the comon places of all S. Pauls
epistles. 8°. *(J. Tisdale,) 1562.* Ent. 1561–62. L
(destroyed).O(2).C⁵(imp.).BUTE.P.; F.HN.HD(imp.).N.

— A moche profitable treatise against the pestilence, *tr.*
T. Paynel. [1534?] *See* 24226.

19493 — The pādectes of the euangelycall lawe. 8°. *(N. Hyll f.
W. Seres a. A. Vele,)* 1553. BUTE.; F.HN.NY.

19494 — The piththy [*sic*] and moost notable sayinges of al
Scripture. 8°. *(T. Gaultier, at the costes of R. Toye,)*
1550. L.O.BUTE.LIV.NEK.; F.

19494.3 — [A variant, w. colophon:] *(T. Gaultier, at the costes of
R. Kele,)* 1550. O.

19494.7 — [A variant, w. colophon:] *(T. Gaultier, at the costes of
W. Bonham,)* 1550. C⁸(imp.).

19495 — [Anr. ed.] Newly augmēted & corrected. 8°. *(W.
Copland f. R. Jugge,)* [1552?] L(lacks tp).; HD.

Paynell, Thomas—*cont.*

19495.3 — [A variant, w. colophon:] (*W. Copland f. J. Waley,*) [1552?] NY.

19495.7 — [A variant, w. colophon:] (*W. Copland f. J. Whight* [i.e. *Wight,*]) [1552?] N.

19496 — [Anr. ed.] 8°. (*W. Copland,*) 1560. L.O.C⁵.; F.LC.
— Regimen sanitatis Salerni. This boke is *tr.* by T. Paynell. 1528. *See* 21596.
— *ed. See* 1873, 23187.
— *tr. See also* 193, 545, 548.7, 923, 1908, 6156, 6274.5, 10465.5, 10466, 10470.8, 12742, 14024, 24318, 24848.5, 24855.
— *See also* 18076.

19496.5 **Paynter, Henry.** Saint Pauls rule for religious performances. A sermon. By H. Paynter preacher in Exeter. 4°. *J. B[eale] f. N. Butter,* 1632. E².G².; F.U.

Peacemaker. The peace-maker: or, Great Brittaines blessing. 1618, etc. *See* 14387 sqq.

19497 **Peacham, Henry,** *the Elder.* The garden of eloquence conteyning the figures of grammer and rhetorick. 4°. *H. Jackson,* 1577. L.O(2).; F.HN.ILL.LC.Y.

19498 — [Anr. ed.] Corrected and augmented. 4°. *R. F[ield] f. H. Jackson,* 1593. L.L⁴.O.CHATS.E².+; F.HN.HD. N.Y.+

19498.5 — A sermon vpon the three last verses of the first chapter of Job. 8°. *R. Jones & E. Aggas,* 1591. Ent. to R. Jones 4 ja. O⁹.LK.

19499 **Peacham, Henry,** *the Younger.* An Aprill shower; shed in abundance of teares, for the death of R. Sacvile, earle of Dorset. [In verse.] 4°. *E. Allde,* 1624. O.

19500 — The art of drawing with the pen, and limming in water colours. 4°. *R. Braddock f. W. Jones,* 1606. Ent. 23 oc. L.; F.
An expanded version reprinted as 1st bk. of 19507 sqq.

19500.5 — [Anr. issue, w. cancel tp, w. imprint:] *R. Bradock f. W. Jones,* 1607. D.M².; HN.LC.

19501 — Coach and Sedan, pleasantly disputing for place and precedence. [Mis-Amaxius, *pseud.*] 4°. *R. Raworth f. J. Crowch, sold by E. Paxton,* 1636. Ent. 9 fb. L. O(2).C².; F.HN.BOWDOIN.NY.TEX.

19501.5 — [A variant, w. imprint:] *R. Raworth f. J. Crowch,* 1636. HD.

19502 — The compleat gentleman. 4°. [*J. Legat] f. F. Constable,* 1622. Ent. 3 jy. L.O.C.D.G²(lacks tp).+; F.HN.CU.HD. N.+
1 L(G.16576) and O copies have cancellandum X4.

19503 — [Anr. ed.] Whereunto is annexed the order of a maine battaile. 4°. [*G. Wood] f. F. Constable,* 1627. O(lacks engr. tp).C².BRISTOL².DUL.M².+; F.HN.HD(lacks engr. tp).N.Y.+
Engr. tp: 'Second impression much enlarged'. F has earlier state w. Constable's address: 'yᵉ Greene man in Leaden hall street right over Billeter lane' and at foot of right pedestal: 'Sculp. Anno 1625'. This latter date is altered to 1626 in the 1627 and 1634 states of the engr. tp.

19504 — [Anr. ed.] With the art of limming newly enlarged. 2 pts. 4°. [*J. Legat] f. F. Constable,* 1634. L.O.C³.M³. NEK.+; F.HN.HD.N.NY.+
Pt. 2 also issued sep. as 19509, q.v. for imprint. Copies vary; 1st quire X has 4 leaves (O³²,HN,HD) or 7 (L,HN).

19505 — The duty of all true subjects to their king. [Init. H. P.] 4°. *E. P[urslowe] f. H. Seyle,* 1639. Ent. 13 ap. L.O. C.C².D.+; HD.N.U.

19506 — No entry.

19507 — Graphice or the most auncient and excellent art of drawing and limming. 4°. *W. S[tansby] f. J. Browne,* 1612. Ent. 16 de. 1611. L(2).D.D⁶.; F.HD.LC.NY.
1st book an expanded version of 19500.

19508 — [Anr. issue, w. cancel tp:] The gentlemans exercise. Or an exquisite practise, as well for drawing as also the making of all kinds of colours. *f. J. Browne,* 1612. L.L⁴.L¹⁸.O. London, Courtauld Institute.; F.HN.LC.

19509 — [Anr. ed.] 4°. [*J. Legat] f. J. Marriott, sold by F. Constable,* 1634. Ass'd 17 fb. 1623. L⁸.O³².C².; F.HD. ILL(imp.).
Also issued as pt. 2 of 19504. Some copies have var. impr.: *f. J. M., sold by F. Constable,* 1634; both at HD.

Peacham, Henry, *the Younger*—*cont.*

19510 — A merry discourse of meum, and tuum. By H. P[eacham.] 4°. *assignes of T. P[urfoot,] f. J. Clark,* 1639. Ent. 27 se. 1638. L.O.; F.HN.HD.Y. Pirie.

19511 — Minerva Britanna, or a garden of heroical devises. [In verse.] 4°. *W. Dight,* [1612.] Ent. 9 au. 1611. L.L³⁰. O.G².WN.+; F.HN.HD.N.PML.+
Copies vary: text ends Ff1ᵛ or has added 'Authors Conclusion', dated 1612 on Ff4ʳ; both at F.

19511.5 — The more the merrier. Containing: threescore and odde head-lesse epigrams. [Init. H. P., *Gent.*] 4°. *J. W[indet] f. G. Chorleton, a. T. Man,* 1608. Ent. 2 ap. F.HN.
(Formerly 19067)

19512 — A most true relation of the affaires of Cleve and Gulick. With the articles of the peace, propounded at Santen. 4°. *W. Stansby f. J. Helme,* 1615. Ent. 18 ja. L.O.O².G².YK.+; F.HD.N.Y.
Claims to correct the account in 14838.

19513 — The period of mourning. Disposed into six visions. Together with nuptiall hymnes. [In verse.] 4°. *T. S[nodham] f. J. Helme,* 1613. Ent. 8 fb. L¹³.O(both tpp).O⁹.C⁴.CHATS.; ILL(both tpp).Y.

19513.5 — [Anr. issue, w. cancel tp printed as H4, continuing:] Also the manner of the solemnization of the marriage at White-Hall. *T. S[nodham] f. J. Helme,* 1613. L. O. Juel-Jensen.; F.HN.HD.

19514 — Prince Henrie revived. Or a poeme. 4°. *W. Stansby f. J. Helme,* 1615. Ent. 18 ja. L.O.O⁹.C²(imp.).; HN.

19515 — Thalias banquet: furnished with an hundred and odde dishes of newly devised epigrammes. 8°. *N. Okes f. F. Constable,* 1620. O.; F.HN.

19516 — Thestylis atrata: or a funeral elegie upon Frances, late countesse of Warwick. 4°. *J. H[aviland] f. F. Constable,* 1634. HN.HD.

19517 — The truth of our times: revealed out of one mans experience, by way of essay. 12°. *N. O[kes] f. J. Becket,* 1638. Ent. 26 jy. 1637. L.O(2).C⁵.INN.; F(2). HN.HD.N.Y.

19518 — The valley of varietie: or, discourse fitting for the times, containing passages out of antiquity, philosophy, and history. 12°. *M. P[arsons] f. J. Becket,* 1638. Ent. 10 mr. L.O.C.E.LEEDS.+; F.HN.HD.N.NY.+

Peake, Robert, *Painter, tr. See* 22235.

19518.5 **Peake,** *Sir Robert, Printseller.* [Bible illustrations.] 8°. *sold by R. Peake,* [1637?] L(in C.123.e.19).C.; HN.
Sometimes found in Bibles, BCP's of 1637 and later; e.g. C copies of 2327, 2328; HN copy of 16408. Regarding controversy about the prints, *see* DMH no. 476 headnote.
— Effigies regum Anglorum à Wilhelmo Conquestore. [c. 1640?] *See* 10007.5.

19518.7 **Pearce, Edward.** Edward Pearce inventor [Engr. designs for friezes.] obl.fol. *sould by T. Hinde,* 1640. CU(Avery Lib.).

19519 **Pearl,** *Ship.* To the most honourable assembly of knights, citizens, . . . of Parliament. The humble petition of the adventurers in the ship called the Pearle. s.sh.fol. [*London,* 1621?] L⁸.
A complaint that they have been deprived of their goods or the value thereof since Apr. 1615.

19520 **Pearston, Thomas.** A short instruction vnto christian religion. 8°. *J. Wolfe,* 1590. Ent. to Wolfe a. E. Aggas 23 jy. 1590. O.; Y.

19521 **Pecke, Edward.** A godly exhortation, whereby Englande may knowe: what sinfull abhomination there nowe dooth flowe. 8°. *E. Allde, solde by H. Astley,* 1588. Ent. to Allde 8 au. 1586. L(imp.).

Pecke, J. *See* 19072.5.

19522 **Pecke, Richard.** Christs watch-word. Occasioned on the funerall of L. Bodley. 4°. *A. Griffin, sold by J. Moungwell a. E. Dight in Exeter,* 1635. Ent. 18 fb. L⁴⁶.C.DUR⁵.

19522.5 — Two sermons delivered at Sᵗ. Peters in Exeter. (The great day dawning.—The spirituall plowman.) 2 pts. 4°. *T. Harper f. A. Ritherdon,* 1632. Ent. 16 jn. C².C¹⁰.YK.; F.HD(lacks gen. tp).

19523 Peckham, *Sir* **George.** A true reporte, of the late dis-coueries, of the Newfound Landes. [Init. G. P.] 4°. *J. C[harlewood] f. J. Hinde,* 1583. L.O⁵.C.G²(2). LONGLEAT.; F.HN.N.NY.Y.+
Copies vary in the prelims. and final quires: (*a*) *4, B–G⁴ H¹ (IL); (*b*) *4 §² B–G⁴ H¹ (F); (*c*) *4 §⁴ B–G⁴ H¹ I² [–]² (IL,C,HN). H¹ set in duplicate, signed: 'H.' or 'H.I.' I² partially reset, I1ʳ line 1 of text: 'adventured with' or 'adventured in money . . . with' (both at L). [–]2 is the table, usually bd. after the prelims.

Peckham, John, *Abp.* Exornatorium curatorum. [1515?] *See* 10627.5.

Peckius, Pieter. A message or ambassage made by Sir P. Pecquius. 1621. *See* 18460.3.
— Proposition of the ambassadour. [1621.] *See* 18460.7.

19524 Pedantius. Pedantius. Comœdia, olim Cantabrig. acta in Coll. Trin. [Attrib. to E. Forset.] 12°. *W. S[tansby,] imp. R. Mylbourn,* 1631. Ent. 9 fb. L.O.C.D².SHEF.+; F.HN.HD.N.NY.+ Greg L 9.

19525 Pedersen, Christiern. The richt vay to the kingdome of heuine is techit heir. [*Tr.* J. Gau. Anon.] 8°. (*Malmw, J. Hochstraten,* 1533 (16 oc.)) F.
(Formerly also 11686)

19526 Pedlar. The joviall pedler: or, a merry new ditty. *Ballad.* 2 pts. s.sh.fol. [*f. R. Harper?* 1640?] L(imp.).

19527 — The pedler opening of his packe, to know of maydes what tis they lacke. *Ballad.* 2 pts. s.sh.fol. *E. A[llde,* c. 1620.] C⁶.
W. Pickering ent. a ballad 'pedler and his packe' 1568–69.
— The pedlers prophecie. 1595. *See* 25782.

19528 Peebles. The thrie tailes of the thrie priests of Peblis. [In verse.] Supplyit with sundrie merie tailes. 4°. *Edinburgh, R. Charteris,* 1603. O(imp.).E.; F.

19529 Peeke, Richard. Three to one: being, an English-Spanish combat, performed by a westerne gentle-man, of Tavystoke. 4°. [*A. Mathewes*] *f. J. T[rundle,]* 1626. Ent. to J. Trundle 18 jy. L(lacks tp).O(lacks tp).C².C³(imp.).; HN(impr. cropt).
Collates A–E⁴.

19529.5 — [Anr. ed.] 4°. [*A. Mathewes f. J. Trundle,* 1626.] O(impr. cropt).
Collates A–E⁴.

19530 Peele, George. The araygnement of Paris a pastorall. [Anon.] 4°. *H. Marsh,* 1584. L.C².; HN. Greg 83.
Based on Paulilli's Giuditio di Paride, 1566.

19531 — The battell of Alcazar. [Anon.] 4°. *E. Allde f. R. Bankworth,* 1594. L(2).L⁶.O.O⁶(2 imp.).ETON.; F.HN. HD.ILL.PML.+ Greg 127.

19532 — Descensus Astrææ. The device of a pageant, borne before W. Web, lord maior of London, 1591. 4°. [*T. Scarlet*] *f. W. Wright,* [1591.] L⁸. Greg 100.

19533 — The device of the pageant borne before W. Dixi lord maior of London. 4°. *E. Allde,* 1585. O. Greg 87.

19534 — An eglogue. Gratulatorie. Entituled: to the honorable shepheard of Albions arcadia: Robert earle of Essex. 4°. [*J. Windet f.*] *R. Jones,* 1589. Ent. 1 au. O.

19535 — The famous chronicle of king Edward the first. 4°. *A. Jeffes, solde by W. Barley,* 1593. Ent. to Jeffes 8 oc. L.O.E(lacks tp).; F(imp.).HN(imp.). Greg 112.

19536 — [Anr. ed.] 4°. *W. White,* 1599. Ass'd 13 au. L(2).L⁶. O.; F(2, 1 imp.).HN.HD.TEX.

19537 — A farewell. Entituled to the famous and fortunate generalls of our English forces: sir J. Norris & syr F. Drake. Whereunto is annexed: a tale of Troy. [In verse.] 4°. *J. C[harlewood,] solde by W. Wright,* 1589. Ent. 23 fb. L.; HN.
2nd pt. revised in 19546.5.

19538 — The historie of . . . syr Clyomon and Clamydes. [Anon. Not by Peele.] 1599. = 5450a.

19539 — The honour of the garter. Displaied in a poeme gratu-latorie: entitled to the earle of Northumberland. Created knight of that order, and installd anno regni Elizabethæ .35. die Iunij 26. 4°. *widdowe Charlewood f. J. Busbie,* [1593.] L.L⁶.O(1, plus a frag.).HN.

19540 — The loue of king Dauid and fair Bethsabe. 4°. *A. Islip,* 1599. Ent. to A. Islip cancelled a. E. White's name substituted 14 my. 1594. L.L⁶.O.C⁶.E.+; F.HN.HD. ILL.Y².+ Greg 160.
Based in part on Saluste du Bartas.

Peele, George—*cont.*

19541 — Merrie conceited jests of George Peele. 4°. *N. Okes f. F. Faulkner a. H. Bell,* 1607. Ent. to F. Faulkner 14 de. 1605. HN.

19542 — Now = 19544.5.

19543 — [Anr. ed.] 4°. *G. P[urslowe] f. F. Faulkner,* 1627. L.L⁶.

19544 — [Anr. ed.] 4°. *f. H. Bell,* 1627. Robert Taylor.

19544.5 — [Anr. ed.] 4°. [*Eliot's Court Press*] *f. H. Bell,* [c. 1630.] L⁴.O.; F.HN.PML.Y.
(Formerly 19542)

19545 — The old wiues tale. A pleasant conceited comedie. Written by G. P[eele.] 4°. *J. Danter, sold by R. Hancocke a. J. Hardie,* 1595. Ent. to R. Hancock 16 ap. L.L⁶(imp.).; HN.PFOR. Greg 137.

19546 — Polyhymnia describing, the honourable triumph at Tylt. [In verse.] 4°. *R. Jhones,* 1590. E²(imp.).; HN.

19546.5 — The tale of Troy: by G. Peele. 128°? in 8's. *A. H(atfield, sold by N. Ling,)* 1604. Arthur Houghton.
— *See also* 19340.5, 21528.

19547 Peele, James. The maner and fourme how to kepe a perfecte reconyng. 1553. fol. *R. Grafton,* [*J. Kingston a. H. Sutton,* 1554?] L(imp.).L⁴⁵.
Grafton pr. title and verso only.

19548 — [Anr. ed., enlarged, w. title:] Fame dothe. . . . 1569. The pathe waye to perfectnes, in th' accomptes of debitour, and creditour. Verie muche enlarged. fol. *T. Purfoote,* [1569] (16 au.). L.L⁴⁴.O⁶.; HN.HD(frag.). LC(imp.).PEN.

19549 Peele, Steven. A letter to Rome, to declare to yᵉ pope, J. Felton his freend is hangd in a rope. *Ballad.* s.sh.fol. *A. Lacie f. H. Kyrkham,* [1571.] Ent. 1570–71. HN.

19550 — The pope in his fury doth answer returne, To a letter yᵉ which to Rome is late come. [Init. S. P.] *Ballad.* s.sh.fol. *A. Lacie f. H. Kyrkham,* [1571.] Ent. 1570–71. L.

19551 — A proper new balade expressyng the fames, concerning a warning to al London dames. *Ballad.* s.sh.fol. *A. Lacie f. H. Kyrkham,* [1571.] Ent. 1570–71. HN.

Peend, Thomas de la. The pleasant fable of Her-maphroditus and Salmacis [*tr.*] by T. Peend. 1565. *See* 18971.
— *tr. See* 17820.

19552 Peerson, Martin. Mottects or grave chamber musique. [Lyrics by F. Greville.] 6 ptbks. 4°. *W. Stansby,* 1630. L(2).O³.E.G².; HN.Y.

19553 — Private musicke, or the first booke of ayres and dialogues. 4°. *T. Snodham,* 1620. L(imp.).O.

Peeter, Stubbe. *See* Stubbe Peeter.

19553.5 Pegas, Meletios, *Patriarch of Alexandria.* Του μακαριωτα-του πατρος ημων Μελετιου περι της αρχης του παπα ὡς ἐν εἴδει ἐπιστολῶν. 4°. [*Eliot's Court Press,* c. 1625.] L.O.C.WIN². Athens NL.+; HD(lacks tp).
Issued w. 15082.5, 4325.5, 11511.7. *See also The Library,* XXII (1967), pp. 13–43 and *Harvard Library Bulletin,* XV(1967), pp.140–68.

19554 Peggy. A new ballad of the souldier and Peggy. *Ballad.* 2 pts. s.sh.fol. [*J. Okes*] *f. F. Coules,* [1640?] L.
(Formerly also 22892) This has been attrib. to R. Climsell.

Pelagius. Pelagius redivivus. 1626. *See* 10736.

19555 Pelegromius, Simon. A description of S'hertogenbosh: written in the yeere 1540. *Tr.* out of Dutch. 4°. [*G. Purslowe*] *f. N. Bourne,* 1629. Ent. 18 my. L.O.BED.; F.HN.MICH.PH²(imp.).

19556 — Synonymorum sylua olim a Simone Pelegromio col-lecta, nunc è Belgarum sermone in Anglicanum transfusa, & redacta per H. F. Accesserunt huic editioni synonyma quædam poetica. *Lat. a. Eng.* 8°. *T. Vautrollerius,* 1580. O.P.; ILL(imp.).WASH³.
For Vautrollier's patent *see* Arber II.746, 886.

19557 — [Anr. ed.] 8°. *T. Vautrollier,* 1585. O³.C³. Stevens-Cox.; HN.ILL.

19557.3 — [Anr. ed.] 8°. *Londini, sumpt. trium virorum* [i.e. *Frankfurt?*] 1594. DUL(2).

19557.7 — [Anr. ed.] 8°. *R. Field, imp. J. H[arrison,]* 1598. L(tp only, Ames I.617).

19558 — [Anr. ed.] 8°. *J. Harison* [3,] *imp. J. H[arrison 1,] J. N[orton,] H. F[rancis,]* 1603. Ent. to Harrison, sen., a. B. Norton 3 no. 1602. L(tp only, Harl.5927/170). O.C.C¹³(imp.). SHR(lacks tp).

Pelegromius, Simon—*cont.*

19558.3 — [Anr. ed.] 8°. [*G. Snowdon*,] *ex off. Nortoniana*, 1606. E²(imp.).

19558.7 — [A variant, w. imprint:] *G. S*[*nowdon*,] *imp. J. Harisoni*, 1606. O²⁴(1st sheet only).

19559 — [Anr. ed.] 8°. [*N. Okes*,] *imp. J. Harisoni*, 1609. L. NLW.

19559.5 — [A variant, w. imprint:] *imp. J. Norton*, 1609. O.

19560 — [Anr. ed.] 8°. [*W. Hall*,] *imp. J. Norton & J. Bill*, 1612. Ent. to J. Norton 9 mr. L(lacks tp).O.; F.

19561 — [Anr. ed.] 8°. [*Eliot's Court Press*,] *imp. J. Bill*, 1615. C.; F.HD.ILL.MCG.MICH.

19562 — [Anr. ed.] 8°. *ap. J. Billium*, 1619. L.C.

19562.5 — [Anr. ed.] 8°. [*Eliot's Court Press*] *ap. J. Billium*, 1627. DUL.NLW.; F.ILL.PH.

19563 — [Anr. ed.] 8°. *ap. Joyce Norton & R. Whittaker*, 1632. Ass'd 26 au. L.O.C.E.LYU.+

19564 — [Anr. ed.] 8°. *typis E. Griffini, sumpt. R. Whitakeri*, 1639. L.O.C.GLOUC.WI.+; F.HN.CHI.HD.Y.+

19564.5 **Pell, John.** [An idea of mathematics. Begins:] Sir: The summe of what I have heretofore written or spoken to you concerning the advancement of mathematickes, [etc. Anon.] s.sh.fol. [*London*, 1638?] L (528.n.20(5*), printed on both sides).

19565 **Pelletier, Pierre.** A lamentable discourse, upon the paricide and assasination: committed on Henry the fourth king of France. *Tr.* 4°. [*J. Windet*] *f. E. Blunt a. W. Barret*, 1610. Ent. to W. Barret 14 my. L.O. C.C³.M.+; F(2).HN.HD.PN.Y.

19566 **Pellham, Edward.** Gods power and providence: shewed, in the miraculous preservation of eight Englishmen, left by mischance in Green-land. With a description of that countrey. 4°. *R. Y*[*oung*] *f. J. Partridge*, 1631. Ent. 30 se. L.L⁸.O.C(date cropt).PLUME.; F.HN.HD. N.NY.+
Map from same plate as 20509, pt. 3, pp.472–3. Dedic. to Muscovy Co. varies: begins w. or omits Sir J. Merick; both at F.

19566.5 **Pellham,** *Sir* **William.** Meditations upon the gospell by saint John. 12°. *G. P*[*urslowe*] *f. J. Budge*, 1625. YK.; F.

19567 **Pelling, John.** A sermon of the providence of God. 4°. *N. Okes f. N. Butter*, 1607. Ent. 18 no. L(destroyed). L⁸.O.O³.C.C⁵.+; F.HN.HD.U.Y.+

Pellison, Pierre. See 18134.7.

19568 **Pemberton, William.** The charge of God and the king, to judges and magistrates. In a sermon preached at the assises at Hartford. 8°. *E. Griffin f. S. Man*, 1619. Ent. 16 de. 1618. L.O¹⁸.C³.G².M.+; F.HD.U.

19569 — The godly merchant, or the great gaine. A sermon preached at Paules-crosse. Octob. 17. 8°. *E. Griffin f. S. Macham*, 1613. Ent. 10 no. L.L¹⁵.O.O³(imp.).; F.BO.

19569a — Second impression. 8°. *H. L*[*ownes*] *f. W. Butler*, 1616. L².LINC. Finedon.; F.

19569a.5 **Pemble, William.** The workes of that late learned man W. Pemble. 4°. *f. J. Bartlet*, 1629. O⁴.; BALT.
A reissue w. gen. tp pr. by J. Beale calling for 19592, 19584, 19586, 19578, 19579 (O⁴) or 19580 (BALT) and 19573 (12°, not included). Also bd. w. this are 19590, and 19576a (O⁴) or 19577 (BALT). All Pemble's works were pub'd posthumously; *ed.* by R. Capel unless otherwise noted.

19570 — [Anr. ed., enlarged.] Third edition. 4 pts. fol. *T. Cotes f. J. Bartlet*, 1635. L.O.C.D.E.+; F.HN.CHI.HD.Y.+
(Pts. 2, 4 formerly 19571a; pt. 3 formerly 19573a) This reprints all the works except 19588, of which a trans. is included, and 19575. Cotes printed all but pts. 2, 4 which are by *M. Flesher*. The main publisher is Bartlet, but reprints of 19589, 19576, 19571, 19574, 19587 are *f. E. Forrest*, [Oxford,] *sold by R. Royston*; reprint of 19579 is *f. J. Boler*.
Gen. tp varies: 'That late learned minister . . . sometimes Fellow of' (HD,U) or 'That learned minister . . . late of' (C²).

19570.5 — [Anr. issue, w. gen. tp w. imprint:] *T. Cotes f. E. F*[*orrest, Oxford*,] *sold by R. Royston*, 1635. L³⁸.O¹⁶. O²⁸(Bed.).C³.EX.; HD.U.

19571 — A briefe introduction to geography. 4°. *Oxford, J. Lichfield f. E. Forrest*, 1630. L.L³⁰.O.C¹⁰.G⁴.; F.HN. AAS.NY.Y.+

Pemble, William—*cont.*

19571a — [Anr. ed.] A brief introduction. (A summe of moral philosophy.) = pts. 2, 4 of 19570 sq.

19572 — De formarum origine. Editio posthuma. *Cantabrigiæ, ex off. R. Daniel, pro J. B*[*artlet, c.* 1650.] = Wing P 1115.

19573 — [Anr. ed.] De formarum origine. Guilielmi Pembeli, tractatus. Editio posthuma. 12°. *R. Young, sumpt. J. Bartlet*, 1629. Ent. 27 ja. L.L³.O¹².C³.CARLISLE.+; HN.HD.Y.

19573a — [Anr. ed.] 1635. = pt. 3 of 19570 sq.

19574 — De sensibus internis. Tractatus Gulielmi Pembeli. Editio posthuma. 12°. *Oxoniæ, J. Lichfield, imp. E. Forrest*, 1629. L.O¹².C.C³.CARLISLE.+; HN.Y.

19575 — Enchiridion oratorium. A Guilielmo Pembelo. 4°. *Oxoniæ, ap. J. Lichfield, pro E. Forrest*, 1633. L.O. C².D.NLW.+; AAS.HD.

19576 — = 19576a.

19576a — Five godly, and profitable sermons. [*Ed.*] (J. Tombes). 4°. *Oxford, J. Lichfield, sold by E. Forrest*, 1628. L.O.O³.C.C⁵.+; F.HN.N.PEN².Y.+

19577 — Second edition. 4°. *Oxford, J. Lichfield f. E. Forrest*, 1629. L.L³⁰.CARLISLE.D.P.+; F.HN.AAS.U.

19578 — A fruitfull sermon, on 1 Cor. 15. 18, 19. 4°. *R. Y*[*oung*] *f. J. Bartlet*, 1629. Ent. 27 ja. L.O.C.A.LYU.+; F.HN. HD.U.Y.+

19579 — An introduction to the worthy receiving the sacrament. 4°. *H. L*[*ownes*] *f. J. Boler*, 1628. Ent. 11 mr. L.O. ETON. G².LEEDS.+; F.HN.HD.PEN².Y.+

19580 — [Anr. ed.] 4°. *H. L*[*ownes*] *f. J. Boler*, 1629. L.O.C.D.E. +; F.HN.AAS.NY¹¹.U.+

19580.5 — [Anr. ed.] 4°. *J. B*[*eale*] *f. J. Boler*, 1633. SAU.; F.HD. U.

19580.7 — Third edition. 12°. *R. Y*[*oung*] *f. J. Boler*, 1635. O.

19581 — [Anr. ed.] Third edition. 12°. *E. Griffin f. F. Eaglesfield*, 1639. Ent. 'in trust f. sons of J. Boler', 7 se. 1638. O⁵.O¹².PETYT.

19582 — The period of the Persian monarchie. Extracted, and englished, much of it out of doctor Raynolds [i.e. J. Rainolds], by W. Pemble. Published and enlarged by R. Capel. 4°. *R. Y*[*oung*] *f. J. Bartlet*, 1631. Ent. 15 jy. L.O.C¹⁰.D.STU.+; F.HN.AAS.U.Y.+
Tp varies: line 13 ends: 'by his friend,' or 'by'; both at U.

19583 — Salomons recantation and repentance: or, the booke of Ecclesiastes explained. 4°. *J. H*[*aviland*] *f. J. Bartlet*, 1627. Ent. 30 my. L.O.C².E.LYU.+; F.AAS. CHI.

19584 — [A variant, w. date:] 1628. L.O.C.D.G⁴.+; F.Y. Otago U.

19585 — [Anr. ed.] 4°. *R. B*[*adger*] *f. J. Bartlet*, 1632. O³.O⁵. O⁶.O¹².G².; F.AAS.U.Y.

19586 — A short and sweete exposition upon the first nine chapters of Zachary. 4°. *R. Young f. J. Bartlet*, 1629. Ent. 11 mr. 1628. L.L³⁰.O.C.D.+; F.HN.CHI.HART.U.+

19587 — A summe of morall philosophy. 4°. *Oxford, J. Lichfield f. E. Forrest*, 1632. L.O.C.D.G⁴.; F.HN. AAS.N.PH.+

19588 — Tractatus de providentia Dei. Editio posthuma. 12°. *J. B*[*eale*], *sumpt. J. Bartlet*, 1631. Ent. 15 jy. L.O. C³.D.P.+; F.HN.HD.Y(imp.).
Trans. in 19570 sq. The undated Latin ed. *imp. J. B*[*artlet*] at F is c. 1650; cf. 19572.

19589 — Vindiciae fidei, or a treatise of justification by faith. Delivered in certaine lectures at Magdalen Hall in Oxford. 4°. *Oxford, J. Lichfield a. W. Turner f. E. Forrest*, 1625. L.O.C¹⁷.D.G².+; F(2).HN.NY¹¹.Y.

19590 — Second edition. 4°. *Oxford, J. Lichfield f. E. Forrest*, 1629. L.O.C.D.G².+; F.HN.AAS.U.Y.+

19591 — Vindiciæ gratiæ: a plea for grace. 4°. *R. Young f. J. Bartlet*, 1627. Ent. 26 se. 1626. L.O.C².D.G⁴.+; F. CHI.HART.Y. Otago U.

19592 — Second edition. 4°. *H. L*[*ownes*] *f. J. Bartlet*, 1629. L. L².O.C.LYU.+; F.HN.ILL.U.Y.+

19593 **Pembroke, Simon.** A most strange and rare example of the iust iudgement of God executed vpon a coniurer (S. Pembroke). 8°. *H. Bennyman* [sic], [1577.] Ent. 25 ja. 1577. L.

Pen, George, *tr.* See 11720.

19594 **Peña, Juan Antonio de la.** A relation of the royall festivities, made by the king of Spaine. *Tr.* out of Spanish. 4°. [*G. Purslowe*] *f. H. Seyle*, 1623. Ent. 15 se. L.PETWORTH.YK.; F.

19595 **Peña, Petrus,** and **L'Obel, Matthias de.** Stirpium aduersaria noua, perfacilis vestigatio. fol. (*exc. prelum T. Purfœtij,*) 1570 (1571 (cal. ja.)) Ent. 1569–70. L.O.C³.D.E.+; F.HD.ILL.NY.STAN.+

19595.3 — [Anr. issue, enlarged, w. cancel tp:] Nova stirpium aduersaria. *Antuerpiæ, ap. C. Plantinum,* 1576. L. O.C.E.PARIS.+; HD.HUNT. Lownes.
  Issued as pt. 2 of L'Obel's Plantarum seu stirpium historia, 1576. Plantin bought 800 sets of sheets; in 1580 he also acquired the woodblocks. New index covers both pts. The orig. Purfoot colophon sometimes uncancelled.

19595.5 — [Anr. issue, w. different additions, as pt. 2 of:] Matthiae de L'Obel medici insulani, in G. Rondelletii Pharmaceuticam officinam animaduersiones. Accesserunt Auctaria, Adversariorumque volumen. 2 pts. fol. *exc. præelum T. Purfootij,* 1605 (id. ap.) L. O.C.D.E.+; F.HN.HD.KAN.NY.+
  (Formerly 16650) Cancel tp to pt. 2: 'Dilucidae simplicium medicamenorum [*sic*] explicationes, & Stirpium adversaria. Quibus accessit altera pars.'

19595.7 — [Anr. issue, w. cancel gen. tp:] Pharmacopoeia Rondeletii: cum Matthiæ Lobelii & Lyd. Myrei animaduersionibus. Item Stirpium aduersaria, auctioria. *Lugduni Batavorum, ap. J. Maire,* 1618. Lownes.

Pendryck, William. The application of the lawes. 1623. *See* 7435.

19596 **Penitents, Order of.** In the name of god here begynneth the rule of the lyuynge of the bretherne and systers of the order of penytentes. 4°. (*W. de Worde,* 1510.) DUR(Bamb.). 𝕬

19596.5 **Penkethman, John.** Accompts of merchandise ready computed. As also tables for the speedy measuring of timber boord, glasse and land. Supplyed at this new impression with other tables. 24° in 12's. E. G[riffin] f. R. Whitaker, 1639. L. 𝕬

19597 — Additions to Hoptons Concordancy. 1635. = pt. 2 of 13781.

19598 — Artachthos or a new booke declaring the assise of bread. 4°. E. G[riffin] a. R. B[ishop,] 1638. Ent. to Mrs. Griffin a. R. Bishop 17 jy. L.L³⁰.O.C.E.+; F(lacks letterpress tp).HN.CU.HD.ILL.+
  See 9125 and Greg, *Companion,* pp. 350–1. Engr. tp: R. Bishop & E. Griffine, sold at ye Stationers shops, or at ye chamber of J. Penkethman in Simonds Inn in Chancerie lane, 1638.

19598.2 — The cities comfort: or, Patridophilus his preservatives against the plague. [Anon.] s.sh.fol. G. P[urslowe,] *sold at the scriveners shop in Cliffords Inn Lane,* [1625?] L⁸.
  (Formerly 16750) Based on 5478.

19598.4 — [An expanded version in verse.] A preservative poem or Patridophilus his precepts De arte praeservandi. 8°. A. Griffin f. W. Leake, 1636. Ent. to Mrs. Griffin 7 no. HD.

19598.6 — The fairest fairing for a schoole-bred sonne; . . . or Lillies lesson to his schollers. [In verse.] 8° in 4. [*London,* c. 1630.] L(bd. w. 19599).
  A trans. of the Carmen de moribus, concerning which *see* 1c in the headnote preceding 15610.5.
— [Interest tables.] *See* 19600.2 sqq.
— The measure of expence. 1626. *See* 12805.5.

19599 — Onomatophylacium: or, the christian names of men and women. 8°. G. P[urslowe,] 1626. Ent. to G. Purslowe 29 mr. L.O⁵.
— Penkethman his president. *See* 19600.8.

19600 — A perfect table declaring the assise or weight of bread by troy and avoirdupois weights. [Init. J. P. C. L.] s.sh.fol. R. Bishop, [1640.] Ent. to Mrs. Griffin a. R. Bishop 11 ja. 1640. L(2 imp.).

19600.2 — A plaine and perfect two-fold table: readily shewing the [simple] interest of monyes, after the rate of 10. or 8.l. for the use of 100.l. for a yeere: which table you may divide in three parts, and insert in your almanack, this first title being cut away. [Anon.] s.sh.fol. G. P[urslowe,] *sold at the scriveners shop in Cliffords Inne Lane,* [1624.] Ent. as by Penkethman to Purslowe 11 jn. 1624. L⁵(Lemon 257).

19600.4 — [A revised ed., without title, 'at 8, 7, and 6 li. per cent.' Init. I. P., Scr[ivener] Pub.] fol(2). G. Purslow sold at the scriveners shop in Cliffords Inne-Lane, 1625. O⁵(cut up and bd. w. 19599).

Penkethman, John—*cont.*

19600.6 — [A preparative to purchase or a table of compound interest at £8 per centum. Anon.] fol(4). [G. Purslowe, 1625?] Ent. to Purslowe 20 fb. 1625. O⁵(cut up and bd. w. 19599).
  Title from SR entry.

19600.8 — The purchasers pinnace, or, the bargainees brigantine. Also, Penkethman his president, or, the new art of accompt. obl.4°. J. Haviland, sold at the authors shop against the Rolles in Chancerie Lane, (1629.) Ent. 14 ja. 1630. L(imp., Harl.5949/168, 170–71).; F.
— tr. See 4861, 24825.

19601 **Pennington, Robert.** A catechisme common place booke. 8°. F. K[ingston] f. N. Newbery, 1619. Ent. 6 my. 1618. L².O.; PH.

Penny-wise. Penny-wise pound foolish. 1631. *See* 6516.

19602 **Penry, John.** Th' appellation of John Penri, vnto the highe court of Parliament. 8° in 4's. [*La Rochelle, R. Waldegrave,*] 1589. L.O.C.DUR³.M.+; F.NY.Y. Pirie.

19603 — A briefe discouery of the vntruthes and slanders contained in a sermon, preached the 8. of Februarie 1588. by D. Bancroft [1346]. [Anon.] 4°. [*Edinburgh, R. Waldegrave,*] 1590.] L.O.C².D.E.+; F.HN.HD.U.Y.+
  (Formerly also 1351)

19604 — [Heading B1ʳ:] A defence of that which hath bin written in the questions of the ignorant ministerie, and the communicating with them. 8° in 4's. [*East Molesey, R. Waldegrave,* 1588.] L.L².O.C¹⁰(imp.).M.+; F.U.Y.
  Answers 22908; supported by 12342; reprinted and answered in 22909.

19605 — An exhortation vnto the gouernours and people of Wales. 8° in 4's. [*London, R. Waldegrave,* 1588.] L².O.C.; HN.
  (Formerly also 19606a) 66 pp.

19605.5 — [Anr. ed.] There is in the ende something not in the former impression. 8° in 4's. [*Aldermanbury? R. Waldegrave,*] 1588. NLW.
  110 pp., of which 41 sqq. is new material. Section cancelled in next issue forms basis of 19613 and 17453, 17454. Answered by 22908.

19606 — [Anr. issue, w. pp. 65–110 cancelled and replaced by a single leaf, p. 65.] L.O.D.E.NLW.+; F.HN.HD.Y.

19606a — = 19605.

19607 — The historie of Corah, Dathan, and Abiram, &c. Applied to the prelacy ministerie and church-assemblies of England. 4°. [*Middelburg, R. Schilders?*] 1609. L.O.O⁸.C¹³.D.+; U.Y.
— An humble motion with submission. 1590. *See* 7754.

19608 — [Heading:] I John Penry doo heare . . . set downe the whole truth which I hold in regard of my faith towards my God and dread soueraigne queene Elizabeth. 4° in 2's. [*Printed abroad?* 1593?] L.C².E.; F.BO. Philadelphia, American Philosophical Society.
  Prob. 19610 issued w. this.

19608.5 — Mr John Penry, his apologie, or clearing, against the evil collections & hard dealings of his adversaries. 4°. [*Amsterdam, G. Thorp,*] 1611. LYU.

19609 — The state of the church of England. [1588.] = 24505.

19610 — [Heading:] To my beloved wife Helener Penry. 4° in 2. [*Printed abroad?* 1593.] L.C².E.; F.BO. Philadelphia, American Philosophical Society.
  Prob. issued w. 19608.

19611 — A treatise containing the aequity of an humble supplication. [Anon.] 8°. Oxford, J. Barnes, sold [by T. Cooke, London,] 1587. L.L².O.C.; F.HN.Y.

19612 — A treatise wherein is manifestlie proued, that reformation and those that fauor the same, are vniustly charged to be enemies, vnto hir maiestie. 4°. [*Edinburgh, R. Waldegrave,*] 1590. L.O.C².D.E.+; F.HN.HD.U.Y.+
  Answered by 19450. See also Greg, *Register B,* p. 34.

19613 — A viewe of some part of such publike wants & disorders as are in the seruice of God, within Wales. 8°. [*Coventry, R. Waldegrave,* 1589.] L.O⁸.C²(imp.). NLW.P.+; F.HN.TORONTO².Y. Pirie(2, 1 lacks tp).
  See also 19605.5.
— tr. See 2053.
— See also Marprelate, M., *pseud.*

19614 **Penryn.** Newes from Perin in Cornwall: of a most bloody murther. 4°. E. A[llde,] 1618. L.O.

19615 **Penuen, Sands.** Ambitions scourge, described in the morall fiction of Ixyon. [In verse.] 8°. *f. J. Helme*, 1611. Ent. 8 no. 1610. O(imp.).

Pera. Newes come latle frō Pera. [1561.] *See* 4102.3.

Percevall, *Plaine.* Plaine Perceuall the peace-maker of England. [1590.] *See* 12914.

Percy, Algernon, *Earl of Northumberland.* Lawes and ordinances of warre. 1640. *See* 9336.
19615.5 — ⟨A⟩ list of his majesties ships, with others . . . under the command of A. Percy, . . . gone to sally against the Turkish pirats. 1637. s.sh.fol. [*London*, 1637.] L⁵(Lemon 309).
    The engr. portrait has imprint: *sould by T. Jenner.* An earlier state of the portrait alone is at L(Print Dept.), O³⁴, etc. *See* Hind III.254.
19616 — A list of the colonels . . . as also of the names of the ships, captaines, and lieutenants under A. Percy . . . 1640. s.sh.fol. *T. Paine f. T. Walkley,* [1640.] Ent. 8 my. 1640. L.
    This has a later state of the engr. portrait in 19615.5.

19617 **Percy, Henry,** *Earl of Northumberland.* A true and summarie reporte of the earle of Northumberlands treasons, 1585. 4°. *in æd. C. Barker,* [1585.] L.O.C². D.E.+ ; F.HN.HD.N.TEX.+
    Tp line 12: 'Towre'.
19617.5 — [Anr. ed.] 4°. *in æd. C. Barker,* [1585.] L.O⁵.C².E.NEK. + ; CH.HD.ILL.Y.
    Tp line 12: 'Tower'.

Percy, John. *See* Fisher, J., *S.J.*

19618 **Percy, William.** Sonnets to the fairest Coelia. 4°. *A. Islip f. W. P[onsonby?]* 1594. L. Duke of Northumberland.; HN.

19619 **Percyvall, Richard.** Bibliotheca Hispanica. Containing a grammar, with a dictionarie in Spanish, English, and Latine. 2 pts. 4°. *J. Jackson f. R. Watkins,* 1591. Ent. 26 de. 1590. L.O.C.D².G².+ ; F.HN.HD.N.NY.+
19620 — A dictionarie in Spanish and English. Now enlarged. All done by J. Minsheu. Hereunto is annexed an English dictionarie. fol. *E. Bollifant,* 1599. Ent. to A. Hatfield a. E. Bollifant 28 jn. L.O.C.D.E.+ ; F.HN. HD.N.NY.+
    Issued w. 19622.
19620a — = 19620.
19621 — [Anr. ed., enlarged.] (A Spanish grammar.—Pleasant dialogues.) fol. *J. Haviland f. W. Aspley,* 1623. Ent. to Haviland 26 my. L³⁸.O.C.D.G².+ ; F.HN.MICH.NY⁵. Y.+
    (Pts. of this formerly also 17948, 19622b)
19621a — [A variant, w. imprint:] *J. Haviland f. E. Blount,* 1623. L³.O¹³.BED.ETON.USHAW.+ ; ILL.NY.NY⁵.
19621b — [A variant, w. imprint:] *J. Haviland f. G. Latham,* 1623. O².C⁵.C¹⁰.C¹².DUR³.+ ; F.CAL².HD(impr. torn). N.TEX.+
19621b.5 — [A variant, w. imprint:] *J. Haviland f. M. Lownes,* 1623. O¹⁹.C³.BIRM.E².NLW.+ ; F.CAL.HD.NY⁵.Y.+
19622 — A Spanish grammar, . . . Now augmented. Done by J. Minsheu. (Pleasant dialogues.) fol. *E. Bollifant,* 1599. L.O.C.D.E.+ ; F.HN.HD.N.NY.+
    Issued w. 19620.
19622a — = 19622.
19622b — [Anr. ed.] 1623. = pt. of 19621 sqq.
19622b.5 **Peregrin, James.** The letters patents of the presbyterie. By J. Peregrin. [Formerly attrib. to James Partridge.] 4°. [*Printed abroad?*] 1632. L.O.C.D².E.+ ; F.BALT.
    (Formerly 19420)

19623 **Peregrinatio.** [Heading of verso:] Peregrinatio humani generis. 1508. Now = 19917.5.

Peregrine, An. Almanacks. 1636, etc. *See* 494.12 sq.

Peregrino, Raphael, *pseud.* Pedaços de historia. [1593.] *See* 19624.5.

19624 **Peretto, Francesco.** Gli occhi. Oda. All'illust. contessa Lucia Bedford. Con altri vari componimenti heroici. regii. 4°. *presso G. Purslow,* 1616. L².LINC.

19624.5 **Pérez, Antonio.** Pedaços de historia, ô relaçiones. [By R. Peregrino, *pseud.*] 4°. *Impresso en Leon* [*London, R. Field,* 1594.] L.L³⁸.O.C.M⁴.+ ; F.HN.HD.N.NY⁵.+
    An expanded reprint of the ed. pr. at [Pau, 1593?] Dedic. to Earl of Essex.
— *See also* 19837.5 sqq.

19625 **Perez de Guzman, Alonso,** *Duke de Medina Sidonia.* Orders, set downe by the duke of Medina, to be obserued in the voyage toward England. *Tr.* T. P. 4°. *T. Orwin f. T. Gilbert,* 1588. L(2).L³³.O⁵.LINC.; HN.HD. Penrose 161.

19626 **Perez de Pineda, Juan.** An excelent comfort to all christians. *Tr.* J. Daniel, with diuers addicions by him. 8°. *T. East f. W. Norton,* 1576 (9 au.) O.O⁷(lacks tp)*.
19626.5 — [A variant, w. imprint:] *T. East f. A. Vele,* 1576 (9 au.) O⁷.P(2).

19627 **Perez de Valentia, Jacobus,** *Bp.* [Begins A2ʳ:] ⟨B⟩eatus qui custodit [etc. p10ʳ:] Expliciunt doctoris Valēcii sup psalteriū expōnes. fol. (*per me J. lettou ad exp. W. Wilcok,* 1481.) L(imp.).O.O²(imp.).C.C⁵. Duff 396.

19628 **Pericles,** *Prince of Tyre.* The painfull adventures of Pericles prince of Tyre. 1608. Now = 25638.5.

Periers, Bonaventure des. The mirrour of mirth. 1583, etc. *See* 6784.5 sq.

Perin. Newes from Perin. 1618. *See* 19614.

Perkins, George, *ed. See* 21072a.

19629 **Perkins, John.** Incipit perutilis tractat⁹ magistri Johĩs Parkins [*sic*] siue explanacio quorūdam capitulo₹ . . . nouiter edita. *Law Fr.* 8°. *in ed. R. Redman,* 1528 (24 oc.) C([A]4 def.).; HD.LC.
19630 — [Anr. ed.] 8°. *in ed. R. Redm̃,* 1532 (oc.) L²².O.; HN. HD(2).
19631 — [Anr. ed.] 8°. *in ed. W. Myddylton,* 1541 (au.) C.; HN.
19632 — [Anr. ed.] 8°. *in ed. H. Smyth,* 1545. LONGLEAT.; HN. CU.HD(2).
19633 — [Anr. ed.] Here beginneth a verie profitable booke treating of the lawes of this realme wherunto is added a newe table, and also is conferred w. the abridgementes and other booke cases, nowe newelye imprinted. 8°. *in aed. R. Totteli,* 1555. L.C¹³.; HD. LC.MIN.
19634 — [Anr. ed.] A profitable booke . . . treating of the lawes of Englande. 8°. *ap. R. Totell,* [1560?] O.; CAL⁵.HD.
19634.5 — [Anr. ed.] 8°. *ap. R. Tottell,* [1565?] L.L³⁸.O.USHAW.; F.CAL.CU.HD.MIN.+
19635 — [Anr. ed.] 8°. *ap. R. Tottell,* (1567.) M².NLW(lacks tp). SH.; F.HD.LC.MIN.Y.+
    Tp: '¶ A PROFITABLE/booke . . .'
19635.5 — [Anr. ed.] 8°. *ap. R. Tottell,* (1567.) L.O.O⁵.C².A.+ ; F. HN.CHI.HD.LC.+
    Tp: 'A profitable/Booke . . .'
19636 — [Anr. ed.] 8°. *ap. R. Tottell,* (1576 (14 de.)) L.C.C¹⁵. BIRM.SHEF.+ ; F.HD.ILL.MIN.Y.+
19637 — [Anr. ed.] 8°. *ap. R. Tottell,* (1581 (31 au.)) L.O.O¹⁹. House of Lords.; F.HN.HD.MIN.Y.+
19638 — [Anr. ed.] 8°. *ap. R. Tottell,* (1586.) Ent. 18 fb. 1583. L.O.C(imp.).D.M.+ ; F.HN.HD.MIN.Y.+
19639 — [Anr. ed.] 8°. *ap. R. Tottell,* (1593.) L.O.DNPK.E.; HN. CU.HD.LC.MIN.+
    Same setting reissued in 4° in 8's; both at HN.
19640 — [Anr. ed.] 12°. *in æd. Janæ Yetsweirt,* 1597. L.L³⁰.L³⁸. C⁵.D.; F.HN.CU.HD.MIN.+
19641 — [Anr. ed.] 12°. [*A. Islip*] *in æd. T. Wight,* 1601. L. L³⁸.O.C².LIV².+ ; F.HN.CU.HD.ILL.+
19642 — [Anr. ed.] 12°. [*A. Islip*] *f. the Co. of Statrs.,* 1609. L. L³.O.BIRM.LIV².+ ; F.HN.HD.ILL.Y.+
    See Court-Book C, p.16.
19643 — [Anr. ed.] 12°. [*A. Islip*] *f. the Co. of Statrs.,* 1614. L. O².C⁵.D.E.; F.HN.CU.HD.Y.+
19644 — [Anr. ed.] 12°. [*A. Islip*] *f. the Co. of Statrs.,* 1621. Ent. to the English Stock 5 mr. 1620. L.O.O¹⁴.C⁵.D².+ ; F.HN.CU.HD.NY¹¹.+
    Text mostly in B.L.
19644.5 — [Anr. ed.] 16° in 8's. [*A. Islip?*] *f. the Co. of Statrs.,* 1621. O.O⁷.O¹³.C².Cambridge, Squire Law Lib.; HN. CU.HD.LC.MIN.
    Text in roman. Prob. issued w. 15758.
19645 — [Anr. ed.] 16° in 8's. *M. Flesher a. R. Young, assignes of J. More,* 1639. L.O.C⁴.BRISTOL².NLW.+ ; F.HN. CHI.HD.LC.+
    Prob. issued w. 15759.

Perkins, Samuel. Almanacks. 1625, etc. *See* 495 sqq.

Perkins, William. [Works.] [Note: Possibly the earliest form of collected Works appeared in 1597, when 19663, 19712, 19743, and 19761, containing 11 treatises in all, were published in uniform format. Since they have no general tp and, except for 19712, have separate signatures, they have been left at their respective numbers.]

19646 — A golden chaine: or, the description of theologie. [With 12 other treatises, on continuous signatures.] 4° in 8's. *J. Legat, pr. to the Univ. of Camb.,* 1600. L.O.C.G⁴.LYU.+; F.HN.CHI.HD.MICH.+
  Other publishers mentioned on sub tpp are J. Porter, R. Jackson, and T. Man.

19647 — [Anr. ed., w. 5 treatises added.] The works of that famous and worthie minister of Christ, in the universitie of Cambridge, M. W. Perkins: gathered into one volume, and newly corrected according to his owne copies. fol. *J. Legat, pr. to the Univ. of Camb.,* 1603 (1602.) L.O.C.BRISTOL.LYD.+; F.BALT.CAL. MICH.NY¹¹.+
  Other publishers mentioned are J. Porter and R. Jackson; the latter died in 1601.

19648 — [Anr. ed.] fol. *J. Legat, pr. to the Univ. of Camb.,* sold [by *S. Waterson, London,*] 1605. L.O.C.A.DUR⁵.+; F.HN.HD(imp.).MIN.NY¹¹.+
  The following works, pub'd separately, are usually bd. w. this edition: 19707, 19724.3, 19732, 19733a, 19748; they are also reprinted in vol. 3 of 19649 sqq. *See also* 19724.9.

Note: 3-vol. 'sets' are frequently found composed of vols. from different editions.

19649 — [Anr. ed., enlarged.] 3 vols. fol. [Vols. 1, 2:] *J. Legate, pr. to the Univ. of Camb.,* sold by *S. Waterson,* [*London,*] 1608 (1609.) [Vol. 3:] (*C. Legge, pr. to the Univ. of Camb.,* 1609.) L.O.C.ETON.WN.+; F. CAL.CHI.HD(1,3).Y.+
  Other publishers mentioned on the sub tpp to vol. 3 are L. Greene in Cambridge and widow Burbie, E. Edgar, F. Kingston, T. Man, and W. Welbie in London; *see also* 19721.3, 19721.7.

19650 — [Anr. ed.] 3 vols. fol. [Vols. 1, 2:] *London, J. Legatt,* 1612 (1613.) [Vol. 3:] (*C. Legge, pr. to the Univ. of Camb.,* 1613.) L.O(1,3).C(1,2).A.BRISTOL².+; F.HN. HD(1,2).NY.Y(v.1).+
  Added to vol. 2 is a trans. of 19734. Other publishers in vol. 3 are as in 19649, except widow Burbie is omitted.

19651 — [Anr. ed.] 3 vols. fol. [Vols. 1,2:] *J. Legatt,* 1616 (1617.) [Vol. 3:] (*C. Legge, pr. to the Univ. of Camb.,* 1618.) L.O⁸.C.BRISTOL².WI.+; F.HN(1,3).HD(1,3).ILL(2,3).U.+
  Other publishers in vol. 3 are as in 19649, except widow Burbie is omitted; and W. B[urre] appears for the only time, on one variant of the sub tp to Clowd of witnesses; both at C.

19652 — [Anr. ed. of vol. 1] fol. *J. Legatt,* 1626 (1623, 1626.) Ass'd to J. Legat, jun., 2 ja. 1621. L.O.C.D.STU.+; F.CAL.HD(lacks tp)*.N.Y.+

19652.5 — [Anr. issue, w. cancel tp, w. imprint:] *J. Legatt,* sold by *J. Boler, G. Lathum, J. Grismond, R. Milbourne, a. J. Bellamie,* 1631. C²⁵.A.; PTS.

19653 — [Anr. ed. of vol. 2] fol. *J. Legatt,* 1631. Ass'd to J. Legat, jun., 2 ja. 1621. L.O.C¹².E².STD.+; F.HN.BO². N.Y.+

19653.5 — [Anr. issue, w. cancel tp, w. imprint:] *J. Legatt,* sold by *J. Boler, G. Lathum, J. Grismond, R. Milbourne, a. J. Bellamie,* 1631. O(J, tp only).C.C²⁵.A.; Y.

19653a — [Anr. ed. of vol. 3.] fol. *J. Haviland,* 1631. Portions of vol. 3 ass'd to J. Haviland 3 jy. 1630, 4 se. 1638; to J. Boler 1 jn. 1629, 13 de. 1629; to P. a. J. Man 3 my. 1624. L.O.C⁸.D.E².+; F.CAL.HD.N.Y.+
  Other publishers mentioned on sub tpp are J. Boler and assignes of T. Man. *See also Court-Book C,* p.109.

19653b — [A variant, w. imprint:] *J. Haviland f. J. Boler,* 1631. O¹⁹.C⁸.BIRM²(K.N.).D.PETYT.+; CH.PTS.TORONTO².Y.

19653b.5 — [Anr. issue, w. cancel tp, w. imprint:] *J. Haviland, sold by J. Boler, G. Lathum, J. Grismond, R. Milbourne, a. J. Bellamie,* 1631. C(w. tp to 19653b uncancelled). A(w. tp to 19653a uncancelled).; NY¹¹.Y.

19654 — [Anr. ed. of vol. 1.] fol. *J. Legatt,* 1635. L.O.C.D.DUR.+; F.CAL².MICH.U.Y(imp.).+

19655 — Armilla aurea, id est, miranda series causarum et salutis & damnationis iuxta verbum Dei. 8°. *Cantabrigiæ, ex off. J. Legatt,* 1590. L.O(lacks table). C(frag.).C³.C⁹.; F.NY⁸.

Perkins, William—*cont.*

19655a — [Anr. ed., enlarged.] Armilla aurea, id est, theologiæ descriptio. Editio secunda. Accessit practica T. Bezæ. 8°. *Cantabrigiæ, ex off. J. Legatt, extant Londini ap. A. Kitson,* [1591?] L.O.C.C².C¹⁰.+
  The L copy was bought on 10 May 1591.

19656 — Editio tertia. 8°. *Cantabrigiæ, ex off. J. Legatt, extant Londini ap. A. Kitson,* [1592.] Ent. to J. Legat 27 jy. 1592. O(lacks table).C(2).C².C⁵.C⁹.

19656.5 — [A variant, w. date:] 1592. C.; NY.

19657 — [A trans.] A golden chaine, or the description of theologie, containing the order of the causes of saluation and damnation according to Gods woord. Hereunto is adioyned the order which M. T. Beza used. *Tr.* [R. Hill.] 8°. *E. Alde, sold by E. White,* 1591. Ent. to T. Newman a. T. Gubbin 1 se. 1590. L.O.; U. *See* Greg, *Register B,* pp. 45–6.

19658 — [Anr. ed.] 8°. *J. Legate, pr. to the Univ. of Camb.,* sold [by *A. Kitson,*] *London,* [1591?] C.C².CARLISLE.P.

19659 — Now = 19661.5.

19660 — [Anr. ed.] 8°. *E. Alde, sold by E. White,* 1592. HETH.; F.HN.ILL.
  Except for the date, the tp is from the same setting as 19657.

19661 — [Anr. ed.] 12°. *Edinburgh, R. Walde-graue,* 1592. O(lacks last leaf). Vienna NL.

19661.5 — [Anr. ed.] *Tr.* R. H(ill.) Second edition, much enlarged. 8°. *J. Legate, pr. to the Univ. of Camb.,* 1592. Ent. 27 jy. C.C².M.; F.HD.
  (Formerly 19659)

19662 — [Anr. ed.] 4°. [*London, A. Islip f.*] *J. Legat, pr. to the Univ. of Camb.,* 1595. C.C¹².; F.HN(imp.).

19663 — [Anr. ed.] 4° in 8's. [*London, J. Orwin f.*] *J. Legate, pr. to the Univ. of Camb.,* 1597. L.L³⁸.O.C.BTL.+; F.HN. HD.TEX.U.+
  Possibly intended as part of a collected Works.

— [Anr. ed.] 4° in 8's. 1600. *See* 19646.

19664 — [A revision.] *Tr.* R. Hill, and by him now drawne into familiar questions and answers. 8°. *London, J. Legatte,* 1612. C.C¹².SHEF. Warrington PL.; ILL.
  The earlier version continues to be pr. in the Works.

19664.5 — [Anr. ed.] 8°. *J. Legatt,* 1621. Ass'd to J. Legat, jun., 2 ja. O.; F.HD.N.

— The arte of prophecying. *See* 19735.4.

19665 — A case of conscience, . . . Whereunto is added a discourse, taken out of H. Zanchius. 8°. *T. Orwin f. J. Porter a. T. Man,* 1592. Ent. to Man 27 ja. L.L⁴³ (imp.).O.D.G⁴.
  The imprint in the O copy is a variant, giving Man's name before Porter's.

19665.5 — [Anr. ed.] 8°. *R. Robinson f. T. Man a. J. Porter,* 1592. C².; F(imp.).ILL.

19666 — [Anr. ed.] 8°. *Edinburgh, R. Walde-graue,* 1592. L.

19667 — [Anr. ed.] 4°. *London,* [*A. Islip*] *f. J. Legat,* [*Cambridge,*] 1595. L.C.LICH.; F.HN.HD.LC.U.

19668 — The first part of the cases of conscience. [*Ed.*] (T. Pickering.) 8°. *J. Legat, pr. to the Univ. of Camb., sold by S. Waterson,* [*London,*] 1604. O⁶.C.P.; F.HN (imp.).

19669 — [Anr. ed., enlarged.] The whole treatise of the cases of conscience, distinguished into three bookes: the first whereof is revised and the other two annexed. 8°. *J. Legat, pr. to the Univ. of Camb., sold by S. Waterson,* [*London,*] 1606. Ent. to Legat a. Waterson 23 fb. 1607. O.C.C¹⁸(imp.).DUL(imp.).E.+; F.BO³.Y(2, 1 lacks tp).
  Continuous signatures.

19670 — [Anr. ed.] Newly corrected. 3 pts. 8°. *J. Legat, pr. to the Univ. of Camb., sold by S. Waterson,* [*London,*] 1608. L.C(lacks tp to bk. 2).C¹³(imp.).INN.; F(imp.). HN.MIN.Y.
  Each pt. has separate signatures. Bk. 2 has impr.: *f. J. Porter,* 1606.

19671 — [Anr. ed.] 4° in 8's. *London, J. Legat, sold by S. Waterson,* 1611. L.O.C.E(imp.).LIV².+; F.MIN.U(impr. cropt).Y(lacks tp).

19671.5 — [Anr. ed.] 4° in 8's. *J. Legatt, sold by S. Waterson,* 1614. L.O.BRISTOL.E.SHEF.+; F.CU.ILL.NY¹¹.

19672 — [Anr. ed.] 4° in 8's. *J. Legatt,* 1619. L.O²⁸(Bed.).C.E. NLW.+; HN.WIS(date cropt).

19673 — [Anr. ed.] 4° in 8's. *J. Legatt, sold by S. Waterson,* 1628. Ass'd to J. Legat, jun., 2 ja. 1621. O.LYD.; F.HN.HD. N.V.+

19674 — [Anr. ed.] 4° in 8's. *J. Legatt, sold by S. Waterson,* 1632. L.O.E.M⁴.; F.CAL.DAR.NY¹¹.

Perkins, William—*cont.*

19675 — [Anr. ed.] 4° in 8's. *J. Legatt, sold by J. Waterson*, 1635. Ass'd 19 au. O.C.BIRM.E(tp def.)*.; F.HN.FORDHAM.Y.

19676 — [A variant, w. date:] 1636. L.O.C³.CASHEL.LIV³.+; F.HN. ILL.U(tp def.).Y.+

19676.5 — Christian consolations for afflicted consciences. Comfortable for all repentant sinners. 8°. *W. J[ones] f. T. Pavier*, 1623. HN.
        Reprinted in large part from 19752.

19677 — Christian oeconomie: or, a short survey of the right manner of ordering a familie according to the Scriptures. Written in Latine and now set forth in the vulgar tongue by T. Pickering. 8°. *F. Kyngston, sold by E. Weaver*, 1609. Ent. to W. Cotton a. L. Green 2 jn. L.

19677.3 — [A variant, w. imprint:] *F. Kyngston*, 1609. F.ILL.N.
        — A christian and plaine treatise. 1606. *See* 19683.

19677.5 — A cloud of faithfull witnesses, leading to the heavenly Canaan: or a commentarie upon the 11. chapter to the Hebrewes. Published by W. Crashawe, and T. Pierson: who wrote it from his mouth. 4° in 8's. *H. Lownes f. L. Greene, [Cambridge,]* 1607. Ent. to W. Cotton 12 no. 1602; to L. Green 12 jn. 1607. L¹⁵. C¹⁵.NEP.; PTS.

19678 — [A variant, w. date:] 1608. O.C.OS(lacks tp)*.SHEF.; F(2).HD.U.WTL.

19679 — [Anr. ed.] 4° in 8's. *W. Stansby f. H. Fetherstone a. J. Parker*, 1622. Ass'd 2 no. 1618. L(destroyed).L⁴⁸. O.BIRM.; F.HN.BR.U.
        See Court-Book C, p.109.
        — The combat betweene Christ and the diuell displayed. Second edition. *See* 19748.

19680 — A commentarie or exposition, upon the five first chapters of the Epistle to the Galatians. With a supplement upon the sixt chapter, by R. Cudworth. 4°. *J. Legat, pr. to the Univ. of Camb.*, 1604. L.C.C². LIV². Kilmarnock PL.+; F.HN.HD(imp.).NY.PH.

19681 — [Anr. ed.] 4° in 8's. *London, J. Legatt*, 1617. Ent. to Legat a. S. Waterson 23 fb. 1607. L.O.C².D.E².+; F. HD.NY¹¹.PTS.Y.+

19682 — De praedestinationis modo et ordine. 8°. *Cantabrigiae, ex off. J. Legat*, 1598. L.O.C.P.SAL.+; HN.

19683 — [A trans.] A christian and plaine treatise of the manner and order of predestination. *Tr.* F. Cacot and T. Tuke. 8°. *[F. Kingston] f. W. Welby a. M. Clarke*, 1606. Ent. 12 au.; Clark's rights ass'd to C. Burby 10 no. 1606; all ass'd to J. Legat 29 ja. 1607. L.C². C³.C⁹.DUL.+; F.

19684 — Deaths knell: or, the sicke mans passing-bell. Ninth edition. 8°. *[G. Purslowe] f. M. Trundle*, 1628. F.

19684.1 — Tenth edition. 8°. *T. Cotes a. R. C[otes] f. M. Trundle*, 1629. Stevens Cox(frag.).

19684.2 — Eleventh edition. 8°. *[T. Cotes?] f. J. Wright*, 1629. Ass'd by M. Trundle to J. Wright a. others 1 jn. F.

19684.7 — Sixteenth edition. 8°. *f. J. Wright*, 1637. F.

19685 — A declaration of the true manner of knowing Christ crucified. 8°. *J. Legate, pr. to the Univ. of Camb.*, 1596. Ent. 19 ja. G².; HN.N.

19686 — [Anr. ed.] 4° in 8's. 1597. = pt. of 19743.

19686.5 — [Anr. ed.] 12°. *London, J. Legate, sold by S. Waterson*, 1611. F.

19687 — [Anr. ed.] 12°. *J. Legatt*, 1615. L.; F.

19687.5 — [Anr. ed.] 12°. *J. Legatt*, 1621. C.; F.

19687.7 — [Anr. ed.] 12°. *J. Legatt*, 1625. L.

19687a — [Anr. ed.] 12°. *J. Legatt*, [c. 1638.] L.C(2, 1 imp.). BURY.RGU.; F.

19688 — A direction for the gouernment of the tongue. 8°. *J. Legate, pr. to the Univ. of Camb., solde by A. Kitson in London*, 1593. Ent. to Legat 14 fb. C.; F.CAL.

19689 — [Anr. ed.] 8°. *Edinburgh, R. Waldegraue*, [1593?] E².
        — [Anr. ed.] 1595. *See* 19760.5.
        — [Anr. ed.] 1597. *See* 19761.

19689.5 — [Anr. ed.] 12°. 1600. *See* Addenda.

19690 — [Anr. ed.] 12°. *J. Legat, pr. to the Univ. of Camb., sold by S. Waterson, [London,]* 1603. C.; F.

19691 — [Anr. ed.] 12°. *London, J. Legate, sold by S. Waterson*, 1611. C.

19692 — [Anr. ed.] 12°. *J. Legatt*, 1615. L.; F.

19693 — [Anr. ed.] 12°. *J. Legatt*, 1621. Ent. to J. Legat, jun., 2 ja. L.C.; F.

19693.5 — [Anr. ed.] 12°. *J. Legatt*, 1625. L.

19694 — [Anr. ed.] 12°. *J. Legatt*, 1632. O⁶.; HN.

19694.5 — [Anr. ed.] 12°. *J. Legatt*, [c. 1638.] C(2, 1 imp.).BURY (lacks tp).; F.DAR.

19695 — [Anr. ed. Anon.] 8°. *Edinburgh, J. Wreittoun*, 1634. F.PEN.

Perkins, William—*cont.*

19696 — A discourse of conscience. 8°. *J. Legate, pr. to the Univ. of Camb.*, 1596. Ass'd to J. Legat, jun., 2 ja. 1621. L.L⁴.NEP.P.; F.HN.N.
        HN has 9 lines of errata pasted over orig. 7 lines.
        — Second edition. 1597. *See* 19743.

19697 — A discourse of the damned art of witchcraft. Published by T. Pickering. 8°. *C. Legge, pr. to the Univ. of Camb.*, 1608. L.O.C.DUL.M.+; F.HN.CU.HD.ILL.+

19698 — [Anr. ed.] 8°. *C. Legge, pr. to the Univ. of Camb.*, 1610. Ent. to J. Boler by consent of widow Legge 1 jn. 1629. L.O.C.G².M.+; F.HN.HD.N.NY.+

19699 — 'Επιείκεια: or, a treatise of christian equitie and moderation. Published by (W. Crashawe.) 8°. *J. Legat, pr. to the Univ. of Camb., sold by S. Waterson, [London,]* 1604. Ent. to Legat a. Waterson 23 fb. 1607. C³. Brussels RL.; F.

19699.5 — Perkins vpon the Lords praier: by order of catechising. 8°. *R. B[ourne,] solde by E. White*, 1592. Ent. to R. Bourne 4 ja. L¹⁵.HETH.
        An unauthorized version; *see* Advt. to Reader in 19700.

19700 — [Anr. ed., corrected by author and enlarged.] An exposition of the Lords prayer, in the way of catechising. 8°. *[J. Wolfe f.] R. Bourne a. J. Porter*, 1592. Ent. 1 mr. L.O.C(imp.).C².

19700.5 — [Anr. ed., enlarged.] (A preface to praier.) 8°. *[J. Wolfe f.] R. Bourne a. J. Porter*, 1593. C⁹.; F.

19701 — [Anr. ed.] 12°. *Edinburgh, R. Walde-graue*, 1593. c(imp.).

19702 — = 19702a.

19702a — [Anr. ed.] 4°. *London, [A. Islip] f. J. Legat, [Cambridge,]* 1595. L(destroyed).L³⁸.C(2, 1 imp.).LICH.; F.HN.HD.

19702a.5 — [Anr. ed.] 8°. *Widow Orwin f. J. Porter a. R. Jackson*, 1596. LINC.
        — [Anr. ed.] 4° in 8's. 1597. *See* 19712.

19703 — An exposition of the symbole or creed of the apostles. 4° in 8's. *J. Legatt, pr. to the Univ. of Camb., solde [by R. Bankworth,] in London*, 1595. Ent. to Legat 24 ap. L.O.C.C².LICH.+; F.HN.HD.NY.PML.+

19704 — [Anr. ed.] Reuewed and corrected. 4° in 8's. *J. Legat, pr. to the Univ. of Camb.*, 1596. L³⁸.O.C.C².BTL.+; F.HN.PEN.TEX.U.+

19705 — [Anr. ed.] 8°. *J. Legate, pr. to the Univ. of Camb.*, 1597. L.O.C.C².INN.+; F.HART².

19705.4 — [Anr. ed.] 4°. *London, J. Legate, solde by S. Waterson*, 1611. L.O.C.E(imp.).LAMPORT.+; HD.

19705.7 — [Anr. ed.] 4° in 8's. *J. Legatt*, 1616. L.O.LEEDS.SHEF.; F.HN.CHI.Y.

19706 — [Anr. ed.] 4° in 8's. *J. Legatt, sold by S. Waterson*, 1631. Ass'd to J. Legat, jun., 2 ja. 1621. C.; F.NY.PML.U.Y.

19706.5 — M. Perkins, his exhortation to repentance, out of Zephaniah: preached in 2. sermons. Together with two treatises of the duties and dignitie of the ministrie. With a preface touching the publishing by (W. Crashaw.) 2 pts. 8°. *T. C[reede] f. W. Welby*, 1605. Ent. 7 de. 1604. C.C².DUL.M.
        Pt. 1 collates A⁸ *⁸ B–G⁸ H⁴. Pt. 2 reprinted from 19733.

19706.7 — [Anr. ed. of Zephaniah alone.] 8°. *[G. Snowdon f. W. Welby*, 1605.] c(lacks tp).
        Collates A–H⁸. c copy bd. w. 19733.

19707 — [Anr. ed., w. title:] A faithfull and plaine exposition upon the two first verses of the second chapter of Zephaniah. Third impression. fol. *T. Creede f. W. Welby*, 1606. L.O⁷.C.P.; HN.HD.NY¹¹.PTS.SMU.+
        Usually bd. w. 19648.

19707.5 — Fourth impression. 12°. *T. C[reede] f. W. Welby*, 1607. BURY.

19708 — Fift impression. 12°. *T. C[reede] f. W. Welby*, 1609. C.
        — The first part of the cases of conscience. 1604. *See* 19668.

19709 — The foundation of christian religion. 8°. *T. Orwin f. J. Porter*, 1590. ?Ent. to Porter a. T. Gubbin 21 au. 1588. NY.
        This is Perkins's Catechism. *See also* 21107.5.

19710 — [Anr. ed.] 8°. *T. Orwin f. J. Porter*, 1591. L.

19710.5 — [Anr. ed., enlarged.] 8°. *f. T. Gubbin & J. Porter*, 1592. C².
        'Proofs' of principles on 8 unsigned leaves at end; in all later eds., the proofs are distributed through the 1st section of the text.

19711 — [Anr. ed.] 4°. *[J. Orwin] f. J. Porter a. J. L[egat Cambridge,]* 1595. c(2, 1 frag.).; F.HN.LC(imp.).

Perkins, William—*cont.*

19712 — [Anr. ed., w. 4 other works.] 4° in 8's. *Widow Orwin* [*a.*] (*F. Kingston*) *f. J. Porter*, 1597. L³⁰.L³⁸.O(lacks tp).C(imp.).BTL.+; HN.HD(imp.).PEN.TEX.U.+
Collates Aa–Qq⁸ Rr⁴; possibly intended as part of a collected Works. Includes reprints of 19752, 19665, 19700, 19724.5. Other publishers mentioned on sub tpp are T. Man, R. Jackson, and H. Burwell, [Cambridge.]

19713 — [Anr. ed. of 19711.] 8°. [*Cambridge, J. Legat*] *f. J. Porter*, 1061 [i.e. 1601.] C.

19713.5 — [Anr. ed.] 8°. [*Cambridge, J. Legat*] *f. J. Porter*, 1604. YK.

19714 — [Anr. ed.] 8°. *f. J. Porter*, 1606. L.

19715 — [Anr. ed.] 8°. *J. Legate, pr. to the Univ. of Camb.*, 1608. Ent. to L. Greene 4 au. J(untraced).

19715a — [Anr. ed.] 8°. *London, J. Legatt*, 1615. O.

19715a.5 — [Anr. ed.] 8°. *J. Legatt*, 1616. D.

19716 — [Anr. ed.] 8°. *J. Legatt*, 1617. F.

19717 — [Anr. ed.] 8°. *J. Legatt*, 1618. C³.

19717.5 — [Anr. ed.] 8°. *J. Legæt* [sic], 1627. Ent. to J. Legat, jun., 2 ja. 1621. C¹⁰.

19718 — [Anr. ed.] 8°. *J. Legatt, sold by R. Allott*, 1629. L.

19718.5 — [Anr. ed.] 8°. *J. Legatt, sold by R. Allot*, 1632. L.

19719 — [Anr. ed.] 8°. *J. Legatt, sold by R. Allot*, 1633. L.O. DUR(Bamb.).

19720 — [Anr. ed.] 8°. *J. Legatt, sold by M. Allott*, 1636. O.

19721 — [Anr. ed.] 8°. *J. Legatt*, 1638. M.

— Regarding the trans. of this bk. into Welsh, *see Court-Book C*, p.145 (6 May 1622.) No edition earlier than 1649 is known.

19721.3 — Foure godly treatises; very necessary to be considered of all christians. The first is concerning the ende of the worlde. The second sheweth how farre a wicked man and a reprobate may goe in the profession of the gospell. The third is of the conflicts of Sathan with the christian. The fourth, of the right applying of Gods word to the conscience. 8°. *J. Wolfe f. R. Watkins*, 1587. Ent. to Watkins a. J. Porter 19 oc. 1587; to W. Welby 2 my. 1608. USHAW(imp.).
1st treatise reprinted as A Fruitful Dialogue in vol. 3 of 19649 sqq.

19721.7 — Foure great lyers, striuing who shall win the siluer whetstone. Also, a resolution to the countri-man, prouing it vnlawfull to buye prognostications. [Init. W. P.] 8°. *R. Walde-graue*, [1585?] L.O⁵.; HN.
(Formerly 19080) 'Resolution' reprinted in vol. 3 of 19649 sqq. Against almanack writers B (Buckminster, 422 sqq.), F (Frende, 444 sqq.), T (Twyne, 518.8 sq.), D (Dade? 434 sqq.).

19722 — A godly and learned exposition of Christs sermon in the mount. Published by T. Pierson. 4° in 8's. *T. Brooke a. C. Legge, prs. to the Univ. of Camb.*, 1608. Ent. to C. Burby 2 ap. 1604; to C. Legge 14 jn. 1608. L.O.C.D.ST.+; F.NY¹¹.PN.SMU. Case Western Reserve U.
See also 19735.6.

19723 — [Anr. ed.] 4° in 8's. *C. Legge, pr. to the Univ. of Camb.*, 1611. O.C(Cambridge Univ. Press).E.; F.HN. HD.Y.

— A godly and learned exposition upon Revelation. *See 19732.*

19724 — A godlie and learned exposition upon the whole Epistle of Jude, published by T. Taylor. 4°. *F. Kyngston f. T. Man*, 1606. L⁴⁶.C.BRISTOL.; F.

19724.3 — [Anr. ed.] fol. *F. Kyngston f. T. Man*, 1606. Ass'd by T. Man to P. a. J. Man 3 my. 1624. L.O.C.P.; HN. HD(2 imp.).PTS.
Usually bd. w. 19648.

— A golden chaine: or, the description of theologie. 1591, etc. *See* 19657 sqq. For the 1600 ed. with 12 other works *see* 19646.

19724.5 — A graine of musterd-seed. 8°. *T. Creed f. R. Jackson a. H. Burwell*, [Cambridge,] 1597. Ent. to R. Jackson 7 fb. O(lacks tp).; F.
— [Anr. ed.] 4° in 8's. 1597. *See* 19712.

19724.7 — [Anr. ed.] 12°. *J. Legat, pr. to the Univ. of Camb., sold by S. Waterson*, [London,] 1603. Ass'd to C. Burby 27 ap. 1602. Berthold Wolpe, London.
See Court-Book C, p.439.

19724.9 — [Anr. ed.] fol. [*A. Islip*] *f. C. Burbie*, 1607. O.USHAW.
Collates A⁶; a different typesetting from the text on Xxx2–Yyy1 of 19648.

19725 — [Anr. ed.] 12°. *London, J. Legate, sold by S. Waterson*, 1611. C.; F.

19726 — [Anr. ed.] 12°. *J Legatt*, 1615. L.; F.

19726.5 — [Anr. ed.] 12°. *J. Legatt*, 1621. Ass'd to J. Legat, jun., 2 ja. C.; F.

19726.7 — [Anr. ed.] 12°. *J. L[egat,]* 1625. L.

19727 — [Anr. ed.] 12°. *J. Legatt*, [c. 1638.] L(imp.).O.C(2). BURY.RGU.; F.

19728 — How to live, and that well. 12°. *J. Legat, pr. to the Univ. of Camb., sold by S. Waterson*, [London,] 1601. Ent. to J. Legate 7 de. L. Arbury Hall, Nuneaton, Warks.; DAR.

19728.5 — [Anr. ed.] 12°. *J. Legat, pr. to the Univ. of Camb., sold by S. Waterson*, [London,] 1603. BURY.

19729 — [Anr. ed.] 12°. *London, J. Legat, sold by S. Waterson*, 1611. C.; F(imp.).

19730 — [Anr. ed.] 12°. *J. Legatt*, 1615. L.; F.

19730.3 — [Anr. ed.] 12°. *J. Legatt*, 1621. Ass'd to J. Legat, jun., 2 ja. C.

19730.5 — [Anr. ed.] 12°. [*J. Legat,* 1625.] L(lacks tp).
Bd. w. 19687.7, 19693.5, 19726.7, 19746.6, 19762.5.

19730.7 — [Anr. ed.] 12°. *J. Legatt*, [c. 1638.] L.O.C(lacks tp). BURY.; F.DAR.

19731 — Lectures upon the three first chapters of the Revelation: published by R. Hill. To which is added an excellent sermon, in which is proved that Rome is Babylon, and that Babylon is fallen. 4°. *R. Field f. C. Burbie*, 1604. Ent. 21 mr. O.BTL. Bristol Cathedral. Vatican Library (Palatine Collection).; HN.N.U.
Sermon not reprinted in later eds.

19732 — [Anr. ed., enlarged.] A godly and learned exposition or commentarie upon the three first chapters of the Revelation. Second edition revised and enlarged by T. Pierson. fol. *A. Islip f. C. Burbie*, 1606. L.O⁷.P.; NY¹¹.PTS.SMU.
This or the following usually bd. w. 19648. The text reprinted in 19649 sqq. is called 'Second edition'.

19732a — Third edition. fol. *A. Islip f. C. Burbie*, 1607. L.O.C. USHAW.; HN.HD.

19733 — Of the calling of the ministerie two treatises, published, by (W. Crashawe.) With a preface prefixed touching the publishing of maister Perkins his works. 8°. *J. R[oberts] f. W. Welby*, 1605. Ent. 22 ja. L.O.C.C¹². LEEDS.+; F.HD.ILL.Y.
Reprinted in 19706.5.

19733a — Third impression. fol. *T. Creede f. W. Welby*, 1606. L.O⁷.C.P.; HN.HD.NY¹¹.PTS.SMU.+
Usually bd. w. 19648.

— M. Perkins, his exhortation to repentance. 1605. *See* 19706.5.

— Perkins vpon the Lords praier. 1592. *See* 19699.5.

19734 — Guilielmi Perkinsi problema de Romanæ fidei ementito catholicismo. Editum operâ S. Wardi. 4°. *Cantabrigiæ, ex off. J. Legat, extant Londini ap. S. Waterson*, 1604. L.O.C.D.E².+; F.HN.CHI.HD.U.+
A trans. of this is in vol. 2 of 19650 sqq.

19735 — Prophetica, siue de sacra et vnica ratione concionandi tractatus. 8°. *ex off. J. Legatt, Acad. Cantab. typog.*, 1592. L.C².G².GLOUC.YK(frag.).

19735.2 — Editio secunda auctior. 8°. *ex off. J. Legate, Acad. Cantab. typog.*, 1592. L(tp only, Ames I.525).O³.C. C⁹.PARIS.+; F.

19735.4 — [A trans.] The arte of prophecying: or a treatise of preaching. *Tr.* T. Tuke. 8°. *F. Kyngston f. E. E[dgar,] sold* [*by C. Burby,*] 1607. Ent. to C. Burby a. E. Edgar 10 de. 1606; ass'd to J. Legat 29 ja. 1607. C¹⁰.; HD.U(imp.).

19735.6 — The reformation of covetousnesse. Written upon the 6. chapter of Mathew, from the 19. verse to the ende. [*Ed.*] (H. Clapham.) 12°. [*T. Creede*] *f. N. Ling a. John Newbery*, 1603. Ent. to T. Bushell 23 no. 1602; ass'd from N. Ling to J. Smethwick 19 no. 1607. F.
An earlier version than the one pr. as pt. of 19722.

19735.8 — A reformed catholike: or, a declaration shewing how neere we may come to the present church of Rome. 8°. *J. Legat, pr. to the Univ. of Camb.*, 1597. Ent. 1 au. L(tp only, Ames I.599).C(tp def.).P.PETYT. Uppsala U.; F.HD.ILL(lacks tp).
Answered by 3096, 3097; defended by 48, 26004.

19736 — [Anr. ed.] 8°. *J. Legat, pr. to the Univ. of Camb.*, 1598. L.O.C.BIRM.E⁴.+; HN.TEX. 𝕬

19737 — [Anr. ed.] 8°. *Cambridge, J. Legat, sold by S. Waterson*, [London,] 1604. L⁴.L⁴³.O⁷.DUL.

19738 — [Anr. ed.] 8°. *London, J. Legatte, sold by S. Waterson*, 1611. L.O.C(tp def.).C⁵.D.

19739 — [Anr. ed.] 8°. *J. Legat*, 1619. C.C².; F.HN.HD.MIN.

Perkins, William—*cont.*

19740 — [Anr. ed.] 8°. *J. Legatt*, 1634. Ass'd to J. Legat, jun., 2 ja. 1621. L.O.C.C¹².NLW.+; F.HN.U.WIS.Y.+

19741 — [A trans.] Catholico reformado . . . trasladado por G. Massan. 8°. *R. del campo* [i.e. *R. Field*,] 1599. L. O(2).C⁶.HOLK.; F.PH.

— A reformation of a catholike deformed. 1604, etc. *See* 3096, 3097.

19742 — A salue for a sicke man, or, the right manner of dying well. 8°. *J. Legate, pr. to the Univ. of Camb.*, 1595. Ent. 6 oc. L.C.; F.HN.N. 𝔄
   (Formerly also 1766)

19742.5 — [Anr. ed.] 8°. *J. Legate, pr. to the Univ. of Camb.*, 1596. L(tp only, Harl.5929/377).

19743 — [Anr. ed., w. 2 other works.] 4° in 8's. *J. Legat, pr. to the Univ. of Camb.*, 1597. L.L¹³⁸.O.C.BTL.+; F.HN. HD.TEX.U.+
   (2nd pt. formerly 19686) 3rd pt. reprints 19696. Possibly intended as part of a collected Works.

19743.3 — [Anr. ed. of 19742.5.] 12°. 1600. *See* Addenda.

19743.5 — [Anr. ed.] 12°. *J. Legat, pr. to the Univ. of Camb., sold by S. Waterson*, [*London*,] 1603. BURY.

19744 — Now = 19747.3.

19745 — [Anr. ed.] 12°. *London, J. Legat, sold by S. Waterson*, 1611. C.; F.

19746 — [Anr. ed.] 12°. *J. Legatt*, 1615. L.; F.

19746.3 — [Anr. ed.] 12°. *J. Legatt*, 1621. Ass'd to J. Legat, jun., 2 ja. C.; F.

19746.7 — [Anr. ed.] 12°. *J. Legatt*, 1625. L.

19747 — [Anr. ed.] 12°. *J. Legatt*, 1632. O⁶.E⁴.; F.

19747.3 — [Anr. ed.] 12°. *J. Legatt*, [c. 1638.] L(imp.).O.C(2, 1 imp.).BURY.RGU.; F.DAR.
   (Formerly 19744)

19747.5 — Satans sophistrie answered by our saviour Christ, and in diuerse sermons further manifested. To which is added, a comfort for the feeble minded. [*Ed.*] (R. Hill.) 8°. *R. Field f. E. E*[*dgar*,] *sold* [*by C. Burby*,] 1604. Ent. to E. Edgar 15 au. 1603. O(imp.).

19747.7 — [Anr. ed.] 8°. *R. Field f. E. E*[*dgar*,] *sold* [*by C. Burby*,] 1604. L(tp only, Harl.5990/58, date cropt).O.C⁵(date cropt).; U.
   In title: 'diuers'.

19748 — [Anr. ed., w. title:] The combat betweene Christ and the divell displayed. The second edition much enlarged by a more perfect copie, by T. Pierson. fol. *M. Bradwood f. E. E*[*dgar*,] *solde* [*by C. Burby*,] 1606. L.O.C.; HN.HD(2).PTS.
   Usually bd. w. 19648.

19749 — Specimen digesti, siue, harmoniae bibliorum Veteris et Novi Testamenti. fol. (*Cantabrigiae, ex off. J. Legat*, 1598.) Ent. 17 mr. L.O(lacks last quire).C³. D²(imp.).LINC(imp.).+
   A trans. of this is in vol. 2 of 19649 sqq.

19750 — A treatise of Gods free grace, and mans free will. 8°. *J. Legat, pr. to the Univ. of Camb., sold by S. Waterson*, [*London*,] 1602. Ass'd to J. Legat, jun., 2 ja. 1621. C.LK.; F.Y.

19751 — A treatise of mans imaginations. [*Ed.*] (T. Piersonn.) 12°. *J. Legat, pr. to the Univ. of Camb., sold by S. Waterson*, [*London*,] 1607. Ent. to Legat a. Waterson 23 fb. O.C.; U.

19751.5 — A treatise of the vocations, or, callings of men. [*Ed.*] (T. P[ickering].) 8°. *J. Legat, pr. to the Univ. of Camb., sold by S. Waterson*, [*London*,] 1603. Ass'd to J. Legat, jun., 2 ja. 1621. C². Phillipps 2798.

19752 — A treatise tending vnto a declaration whether a man be in the estate of damnation or in the estate of grace. 8°. *R. Robinson f. T. Gubbin a. J. Porter*, [1590?] ?Ent. 21 au. 1588. HN.
   Dedic. dated 24 Nov. 1589. Tp line 4: 'damnation'; line 12: 'dilligence'. Item 7: Consolations for the troubled consciences, is reprinted in 19676.5 and 21204.5.

19752.3 — [Anr. ed.] 8°. *R. Robinson f. T. Gubbin a. J. Porter*, [1590?] C.; F.
   Tp line 4: 'damnation'; line 12: 'diligence'.

19752.5 — [Anr. issue, w. quire A reset.] *R. Robinson f. T. Gubbin a. J. Porter*, [1590?] P.
   Tp line 4: 'Damnation'.

19753 — [Anr. ed.] Newly corrected and augmented. 8°. *T. Orwin f. J. Porter a. T. Gubbin*, 1591. L.O²⁸(imp.). C.C².; F.
   1st ed. to include: 'A declaration of certen spirituall desertions.'

19753.5 — [Anr. ed.] Reuewed and corrected by the author. 8°. *T. Orwin f. J. Porter a. T. Gubbin*, 1592. O.C².M.

Perkins, William—*cont.*

19754 — [Anr. ed.] 4°. *Widdow Orwin f. J. Porter a. J. Legate*, [*Cambridge*,] 1595. L.O.C.C⁴.; F.HN.LC(imp.).
   Collates A–Aa⁴; 19754.3 collates A–T⁸.

19754.3 — [Anr. ed.] 8°. *Widdow Orwin f. J. Porter a. J. Legate*, [*Cambridge*,] 1595. F.

— [Anr. ed.] 4° in 8's. 1597. *See* 19712.

19754.7 — [Anr. ed.] 12°. [*London*,] *f. J. Porter a. J. Legat*, [*Cambridge*,] 1600. C¹².

19755 — [Anr. ed.] 12°. *f. L. Greene*, [*Cambridge*,] 1608. Ent. 4 au. L.; HD.

19756 — [Anr. ed.] 12°. *London, J. Legat, sold by A. Johnson*, 1619. Ass'd to J. Legat, jun., 2 ja. 1621. C.; F.

19757 — The true gaine: more in worth then all the goods in the world. 8°. *J. Legat, pr. to the Univ. of Camb.*, 1601. Ent. 7 de. L(2, 1 imp.).L².O²⁷(imp.).C.C².; U.
   Issued w. 19763.5.

19757.5 — [Anr. ed.] 8°. *J. Legat, pr. to the Univ. of Camb., sold by S. Waterson*, [*London*,] 1601. C.; F.
   Issued w. 19764.

19758 — Two treatises. I. Of . . . repentance. II. Of the combat of the flesh and spirit. 8°. *J. Legate, pr. to the Univ. of Camb., sold* [*by A. Kitson*,] *London*, 1593. Ent. to Legat 29 no. C.; F(2).LC.

19759 — Now = 19760.5.

19760 — Second edition corrected. 8°. *J. Legate, pr. to the Univ. of Camb., sold* [*by R. Bankworth*,] *London*, 1595. L. C(imp.).C². 𝔄

19760.5 — [Anr. ed.] (A direction for the gouernment of the tongue.) 4° in 8's. *J. Legate, pr. to the Univ. of Camb., sold* [*by R. Bankworth*,] *London*, 1595. L.C(2, 1 imp.). C⁹.; F.HN.
   (Formerly 19759)

19761 — [Anr. ed.] 4° in 8's. [*London, R. Field f.*] *J. Legate, pr. to the Univ. of Camb.*, 1597. L.L¹³⁸.O.C.BTL.+; F.HN. HD.TEX.U.+
   Possibly intended as part of a collected Works.

19761.1 — [Anr. ed.] 12°. *J. Legate, pr. to the Univ. of Camb.*, 1600. L(tp only, Ames II.14). NLW.
   This and other 12° eds. omit 'A direction'.

19761.3 — [Anr. ed.] 12°. *London, J. Legat, sold by S. Waterson*, 1611. O.; F.

19761.5 — [Anr. ed.] Fifth edition. 12°. *J. Legatt*, 1615. F.

19761.7 — [Anr. ed.] 12°. *J. Legatt*, 1619. L(tp only, Ames II.527).

19761.9 — [Anr. ed.] 12°. *J. Legatt*, 1621. Ass'd to J. Legat, jun., 2 ja. C.; F.

19762 — Now = 19763.3.

19762.5 — [Anr. ed.] 12°. *J. Legatt*, 1625. L.

19763 — [Anr. ed.] 12°. *J. Legatt*, 1632. F.

19763.3 — [Anr. ed.] 12°. *J. Legatt*, [c. 1638.] L.C(2, 1 imp.). BURY.RGU.; F.
   (Formerly 19762)

19763.5 — A warning against the idolatrie of the last times. 8°. *J. Legat, pr. to the Univ. of Camb.*, 1601. Ent. 7 de. L(2).L².O²⁷.C(2).C².; U.
   Issued w. 19757. In some copies ¶2, 3 are cancels; orig. dedic. begins: 'To . . . Henry Lord Gray of Ruthen,' the cancel begins: 'To . . . Lord Henry Earle of Kent,' both at L.

19764 — [Anr. ed.] 8°. *J. Legat, pr. to the Univ. of Camb., sold by S. Waterson*, [*London*,] 1601. C.M.; F(2).HN.
   Issued w. 19757.5.

— The whole treatise of the cases of conscience. *See* 19669 sqq.

— *See also* 19064, 19065, 21204.5.

19765 — No entry.

19766 **Pernau.** A true reporte of three straunge and wonderful accidents, lately hapened at Pernaw. *Tr.* out of Dutch. 4°. *R. B*[*lower*,] 1603. L.

19766.3 — [A variant, w. imprint:] *f. W. Barley*, 1603. F.

19766.5 **Perneby, William.** A direction to death: teaching man the way to die well. Made in the forme of a dialogue. 8°. [*F. Kingston*] *f. H. Lownes*, 1599. Ent. to H. Lownes a. John Harrison, jun., 15 ja. 1599. PN².

19766.7 — [A variant, w. imprint:] *f. T. Man*, 1599. P.; HD.

19767 **Pernius, Joannes.** Exemplar literarum, missarum, e Germania, ad G. Cecilium. [By J. Creswell; answers 8207.] 8°. [*Rome, V. Accolto*,] 1592.
   Not an STC book.

19767.3 **Perottus, Nicolaus.** Grammatica nicolai Perotti cum textu iodoci Badii Ascensii. 4° ⁴·⁸. (*per w. de worde*, 1512 (15 no.)) L⁴⁴.; HN.

Perottus, Nicolaus—*cont.*

19767.7 — [a1ᵛ:] Prefatio in regulas grāmaticales Nicolai perotti [etc. a2ʳ:] Nicolai perotti episcopi sypontini. . . . Ad Pyrrhum perottum nepotem. 4° in 8's. [*Louvain*,] (*E. de herstraten*,) [1486.] O.C.M.SHR. Utrecht U. Duff 346.

    Contains many passages in English.

— *See also* 695.

Perrenot, J. *See* 15527.

19768 **Perrenot de Granvelle, Antoine**, *Cardinal*. Letters conteyning sundry deuises, touching the state of Flaunders and Portingall. 8°. *T. Dawson f. T. Charde*, 1582. Ent. 23 jy. L.

19768.5 **Perrin, Jean Paul.** The bloudy rage of that great Antechrist [*sic*] of Rome . . . against the true church of Christ. . . . In the historie of the Waldenses and Albingenses, . . . *Tr.* S. Lennard. 4°. *f. N. Newbery*, 1624. Ent. 17 fb. 1623. L⁴.O².C.CASHEL.LICH.+; HN.BO⁶.CHI.LC.U.+

    The 4 sets of signatures were pr. by R. Field, J. Beale, Eliot's Court Press, and T. Snodham respectively. Unsold sheets reissued in 1655 w. prelims. cancelled as Wing P 1592.

19769 — [Anr. issue, w. cancel? tp:] Luthers fore-runners: or, a cloud of witnesses, . . . In the historie of the Waldenses: who for divers hundred yeares . . . *f. N. Newbery*, 1624. L.O.C.D.E.+; F.HD.N.U.Y.+

    Some copies (L⁴⁶,O,A,E,U) have the 'bloudy' tp cancelled; others (L,M,F,HD) retain it. Most copies have the 'Luthers' tp printed in red and black; L⁴⁶ and A have the same typesetting but printed all in black.

19769.3 — [Anr. issue, w. cancel tp:] Luthers fore-runners: . . . In the historie of the Waldenses. Whereunto is prefixed, a Treatise of the perpetuall visibilitie, . . . of the true church. . . . 2 pts. *f. N. Newbery*, 1624. L². Sparrow.

    Both copies have the 'bloudy' tp cancelled and have 39.7 as pt. 2. This 'Luthers' tp is printed all in black and has Field's 'Anchora spei' device, McK. 192; the F copy of 19769 has an offset of it on the verso of a flyleaf.

19769.7 **Perrot, François.** Auiso piaceuole dato alla bella Italia, sopra la mentita data dal re di Nauarra a papa Sisto V. [*Anon.*] 4°. *Monaco, G. Swartz* [*London, J. Wolfe*,] 1586. L.O(2).PARIS(2). Rogers.; HN.HD.

    Extensive quotations in Italian from Dante, Petrarch, and Boccaccio.

Perrot, George, *tr. See* 4469.

19770 **Perrot, Richard.** Jacobs vowe, or the true historie of tithes. 4°. *T. a. J. Bucke, prs. to the Univ. of Camb.*, 1627. L.O.C.D.G².+; F.HN.BO.HART².

    Tp varies: with comma or with colon after 'vowe'; both at C⁸.

19770.5 — [Anr. issue, w. prelims. cancelled, w. title:] The historie of tithes. By R. P., *B. D. Prs. to the Univ. of Camb.*, 1640. L³⁰.O³(2).O⁸.; F.

19771 **Perrott, Humphrey.** An assize sermon. [After 1738.]

19772 **Perrott,** *Sir* **James.** Certaine short prayers and meditations upon the Lords prayer and the ten commandements. 12°. *A. Mathewes f. R. Swayne*, 1630. Ent. to R. Swayne, sen., 20 de. 1629. L.; F.

19772.5 — A discouery of discontented mindes, wherein their seuerall sortes and purposes are described, especially such as goe beyond the seas. 4°. *Oxford, J. Barnes*, 1596. O.; CAL⁴.

19773 — The first part of the consideration of humane condition. 4°. *Oxford, Joseph Barnes, solde* [*by J. Broome, London,*] 1600. Ent. to John Barnes 7 jn. 1602. O(3). P.; HN.

    No more pub'd.

19774 — An invitation unto prayer, and the practise of piety, directing the way to true happinesse. [Init. J. P. Knight.] 12°. *Isaac Jaggard f. R. Bird*, 1624. Ent. 1 ap. O.NLW.

    (Formerly also 19324)

19775 **Perry, Henry.** Eglvryn Phraethineb. Sebh, dosparth ar retoreg. 4° in 2's. *J. Danter*, 1595. L(2, both lack folding leaf). NLW.; F.HD.

Perry, William. The boy of Bilson. 1622. *See* 1185.

19776 **Persians.** A briefe relation of the late martyrdome of five Persians. 8°. *Doway*, 1623. HN. **A** A&R 145.

Persiles. The travels of Persiles and Sigismunda. 1619. *See* 4918.

19777 **Persius Flaccus, Aulus.** Auli Persii Flacci satyræ sex. Cum posthumis commentariis, J. Bond. 8°. *F. Kingstonius, imp. G. Aspley & N. Butterij*, 1614. Ent. 8 jy. 1613. L.O.C.CASHEL.E.+; F.HN.CU.HD.N.+

    See also 13784, 14889.

19777.5 — [A trans.] Aulus Persius Flaccus his satires *tr.* into English [verse], by B. Holyday. 8°. *Oxford, Jos. Barnes*, 1616. F.HN.HD.Y.

    Type orns. on tp.

19778 — [Anr. ed.] 8°. *Oxford, Jos. Barnes*, 1616. Ent. to John Barnes 14 no. L.O.; HN.

    Oxford device (McK.336) on tp.

19778.5 — [A variant:] Second impression. *Oxford, Jos. Barnes*, 1616. O.O³⁸.; F.HD.

19779 — [Anr. ed.] Newly reviewed. 8°. *W. Stansby f. W. Arondell*, 1617. Ent. 29 mr. L(imp.).O¹¹.C⁵.E².SH.+; F.HN.CU(lacks tp).HD.ILL.

19780 — Third edition. 8°. *W. Stansby f. R. Higginbotham*, 1635. L.O.C².BTU.E.+; F.HN.HD.N.Y+

— *See also* 25225.

19781 **Person, David.** Varieties: or, a surveigh of rare and excellent matters. 4° in 8's. *R. Badger* [*a. T. Cotes*] *f. T. Alchorn*, 1635. Ent. 14 ja. L.O.C.BRISTOL².E.+; F.HN.HD.N.NY.+

    Cotes pr. (a)–(e)⁴, Aa–Nn⁴Oo²; Badger pr. the rest, using R. Barker's materials. In most copies Aa1 cancelled and replaced by (Aa)², including dedic. to Thomas [Hamilton], Lord Binning; both at O,C.

Personages. Eight learned personages. 1601. *See* 1073.

— Ten learned personages. 1601. *See* 1074.

Persons, Robert. *See* Parsons, R.

19781.5 **Persuasion.** An earnest perswasion vnto the pastours of Christes churche, especially vnto his churche of Englande: that as thei haue thruste the plough share into the grounde, so zelously to walke forth right. [In verse.] 8°. [*London, c.* 1580.] L².

Perth Assembly. Parasynagma Perthense. 1620. *See* 4361.

— Perth Assembly. Containing the proceedings. 1619. *See* 4360.

19782 — The questions to be resoluit at the conuention of the Estaits and Generall Assemblie, at Perth. 1597. = 21891.

— A re-examination of the five articles enacted at Perth. 1636. *See* 4363.

19783 **Perussellus, Franciscus.** Summa christianae religionis exarata primum Gallice a F. Perussello Gallico concionatore Londini: deinde Latine versa per P. Bellopoelium. 8°. [*S. Mierdman*] *per J. Gybkinum*, 1551 (ap.) C.; NY.

19784 **Peryn, William.** Spirituall exercyses and goostly meditacions, . . . Set foorthe by F. Wyllyam Peryn. [Trans. and adapted from 'Exercitia' of N. van Ess.] 8°. [*J. Kingston f.*] *J. Waley*, 1557. L.L².O.C³.G².+; F.HN.CHI.

19785 — [Anr. ed.] Neulye imprynted. 8°. *Caen, P. le Chandelier*, 1598. L³.L³⁵.O.W.; F.TEX. A&R 643.

19785.5 — Thre godlye and notable sermons, of the sacrament of the aulter. 8°. (*J. Herforde, at the costes of R. Toye,*) [1546?] L.O(imp.).O²¹.C.D.+; F.HN.Y. (Formerly 19787)

19786 — [Anr. ed.] 8°. (*N. Hyll, at the costes of R. Toye,*) [1546.] L⁴(lacks tp).O.O².C³.P(imp.).+

    Slot in sill of tp border of Mc K&F 33 dated 1546.

19787 — Now = 19785.5.

19788 **Pestell, Thomas.** Gods visitation: in a sermon preached at Leicester, at an ordinary visitation. 4°. *F. Kyngston f. R. Allott*, 1630. O.C³.C⁵.E. Leicester PL.+; HN.

19789 — The good conscience. Or, the soules banquet royall. In a sermon. 4°. *T. Creede f. A. Johnson*, 1615. Ent. 16 au. L.O.O³.C².C³.; F.HN.

19790 — Morbus epidemicus, or the churles sickenesse. In a sermon. 4°. *T. Creede f. A. Johnson*, 1615. Ent. 16 au. L.O.C¹⁷.; F.HN.HD.PN².

Pestell, Thomas—*cont.*

19791 — The poore mans appeale. In a sermon. [Init. T. P.]
4°. *E. Griffin f. A. Johnson*, 1620. Ent. 9 no. O.STU.;
HD.

Pet, Cornelius, *tr. See* 10608.5.

19792 **Pet, Edmond.** Lamentable newes, shewing the wonderfull deliverance of maister E. Pet. With other strange
things concerning these great windes. 4°. *T. C[reede]
f. W. Barley*, 1613. Ent. 5 ja. L.O.; TEX(impr. cropt).
See also 10511.7, 25840, 25949, 26092.

19793 **Pétau Maulette, Geneviève.** Deuoreux. Vertues teares
for the losse of the most christian king Henry, third
. . . and the vntimely death, of W. Deuoreaux. Paraphrastically *tr.* J. Markham. [In verse.] 4°. *J. Roberts
f. T. Millington*, 1597. L(tp only, Harl.5921/52).
O.; HN.

19794 **Peter,** *of Alcantara, Saint.* A golden treatise of mentall
praier. *Tr.* G. W(illoughby.) 16° in 8's. *Bruxelles,
widowe of H. Antone, called Velpius*, 1632. L.O.C
(imp.).OS.W.+; F.HN.CHI.HD(imp.).TEX.+
A&R 644.

Peter, *of Blois. See* 20412.

Peter, *of Lucca. See* 19815.

19795 **Peter,** *of Luxemburg, Saint.* The boke entytuled the next
way to heuen. 4° in 6's. (*W. de Worde,*) [1520?] L.;
HN.

19796 **Peter,** *Saint.* Peters fall. A godlie sermon: preached
before the queenes maiestie. [On Mark xiv.66–72.]
8°. [*J. Charlewood*] *f. J. Perin*, 1585. L.

19796.5 — [Anr. issue, w. title:] Peters fall. A godlie sermon,
preached [etc.] *f. J. Perrin*, 1585. P(2).SCL.; HN.
One P copy is bd. w. 22237, and both items may
be by the same author.

— Saint Peters complaint. 1595, etc. *See* 22955.7 sqq.

19797 — Saint Peters ten teares. [In verse.] 4°. *G. Simson f. W.
Jones*, 1597. ?Ent. to A. Jeffes 5 ap. 1595; to W.
Jones 15 oc. 1597. L.; HN.HART.

19798 — [Anr. ed.] Saint Peters teares. 4°. [*W. White*] *f. W.
Jones*, 1602. L.; F.HN.

Peter, *Stubbe. See* 23375.

19798.3 **Peters, Hugh.** Digitus Dei. Or good newes from Holland.
[Init. H. P.] 4°. *Rotterdam, A. Neringh*, 1631. L.O.
O[11].HAGUE. YK.; F.HD.Y.
(*Formerly* 19066)

19798.5 — Milk for babes, and meat for men. [Init. H. P.] 8°.
[*Amsterdam, successor of G. Thorp,*] 1630. HD.

19799 **Peters, Nicholaus.** The pathway to knowledge. Con-
teyning tables of English waights [*sic*], and measures.
[Anon.] Written in Dutch, and *tr.* by W. P[hilip.] 4°.
[*V. Simmes?*] *f. W. Barley*, 1596. Ent. to T. Nelson
31 my. 1592. L(lacks tp).L[16].C(imp.).P.ST.+; F.HN.
CAL[2].CU.

Peterson, Robert, *tr. See* 3405, 4738.

19800 **Petit, Jean François.** The Low-Country commonwealth.
1609. = 15485.

Petition. The humble petition of the communaltie.
[1588?] *See* 7584.
— The petition and remonstrance of the governor and
company. 1628. *See* 7449.
— A petition apologeticall. 1604. *See* 4835.

19801 **Petley, Elias.** The royall receipt: or, Hezekiahs physicke.
A sermon. 4°. *B. A[lsop] f. E. Blackmore*, 1623. Ent.
10 ja. L.L[15].O.O[27].C.+; F.HN.BO[5].HD.PN[2].+
— *tr. See* 16432.

Peto, William, *ed. See* 23966.

19802 **Petowb, Mariscal.** An honourable president. [1630.]
Now = 19807.3.

19802.5 **Petowe, Henry.** The artillery garden London, magnificent and tryumphant: or, the mother of armes
reviv'd. . . . 1635. [In verse.] s.sh.fol. [*London*, 1635.]
O(imp.).

19803 — The countrie ague. Or, London her welcome home to
her retired children. Together, with a true relation
of the warlike funerall of captaine R. Robyns. 4°.
[*B. Alsop a. T. Fawcet*] *f. R. Allot*, 1626. L.
In the L copy the orig. date '1625' has been overprinted '1626'.

Petowe, Henry—*cont.*

19803.5 — Elizabetha quasi vivens, Eliza's funerall. [Init. H. P.
In verse.] 4°. *E. Allde f. M. Lawe*, 1603. O(quire
B only).; HN. Mrs. Donald Hyde, Somerville, N.J.
(*Formerly* 19805) Tp line 8: 'Subject'. A2 (dedic.?)
cancelled. Law fined for pirating 5122 in this; *see*
Arber II.836.

19804 — [Anr. ed., partly reimposed.] 4°. *E. Allde f. M. Lawe*,
1603. L.O.C[6].; F.HN.HD(2, 1 misbound w. 18520).
Tp line 8: 'Subiect'. A2 dedic. signed in full.

19805 — Now = 19803.5.

19806 — Englands Cæsar. His majesties most royall coronation.
[In verse.] 4°. *J. Windet f. M. Law*, 1603. L.; F
(imp.).

19807 — The second part of Hero and Leander. [In verse.] 4°.
T. Purfoot f. A. Harris, 1598. Ent. 14 ap. O(2).

19807.3 — An honourable president for great men. To the memory
of J. Bancks, citizen and mercer of London, dyed
the 9.th day of September. 1630. [Signed Mariscalus
Petowb [*sic*]. In verse.] s.sh.fol. [*B. Alsop a. T.
Fawcet*, 1630.] L[5](Lemon 302).L[8].
(*Formerly* 19802)

19807.7 — Londoners their entertainment in the countrie. Or the
whipping of runnawayes. [Anon.] 4°. *H. L[ownes] f.
C. B[urby,]* 1604. Ent. as by Henry Petoe to C.
Burby 26 de. 1603. O(imp.).; HN.HD.
(*Formerly* 17938)

19808 — Philochasander and Elanira the faire lady of Britaine.
[In verse.] 4°. *T. Purfoot*, 1599. Ent. 19 au. 1598.
L.; HN.
— *See also* 19062.5.

19809 **Petrarca, Francesco.** Phisicke against fortune, aswell
prosperous, as aduerse. Englished by T. Twyne.
4° in 8's. [*T. Dawson f.*] *R. watkyns*, 1579. Ent.
22 fb. 1578; a 'copy' 13 ja. 1579. L.O.C.E[2].PETYT.+;
F.HN.HD.N.NY[4].+

19810 — Petrarchs seven penitentiall psalms, paraphrastically
translated: with other philosophicall poems. Written
by G. Chapman. 8°. [*R. Field*] *f. M. Selman*, 1612.
Ent. 13 ja. O.; HD(lacks tp).

19811 — The tryumphes of Fraunces [*sic*] Petrarcke, *tr.* H.
Parker, lorde Morley. (Vyrgyll in his epigrames of
Cupide and Dronkenesse.) 4°. (*J. Cawood,*) [1555?]
L(2).L[4].O.; HN.
— *See also* 19769.7, 19992.

Petre, John, *Baron of Writtle.* Threni Exoniensium.
1613. *See* 19044.

Petrie, John. Theses aliquot philosophicæ. Præs. J.
Petreio. 1603. *See* 21555.10.

19812 **Petronilla.** [Begins:] The parfite lyfe [etc. In verse.] 4°.
(*R. Pynson,*) [1495?] L.O.; PML. Duff 347.

19812.5 **Petrucci, Ludovico.** Apologia equitis Ludovici Petrucci
contra calumniatores suos. *Lat., Ital. a. Eng.* 4°. *Imprinted [in London, Eliot's Court Press, 1619?]*
Emblems ent. to R. Meighen a. W. Arundell 7 mr.
1617. O(2).
1 O copy (Wood 483(24)) has imprint cropt; the
other (4° Rawl.550) lacks tp but has variants, and
MS. and pr. additions, including cuts, some of
which occur in 11496; *see Bodleian Library Record,*
VIII(1967), pp.40–7.

19813 — [Anr. issue, w. new prelims. and C2–D1 cancelled and
replaced by ¶4.] *Excusum Londini*, 1619. L.O(Pamph.
C 16(17)).O[13](*4 ¶4 only).O[17].C.; F.
The C copy has 2 extra leaves with an address to
J. Prideaux.

19814 — Raccolta, d'alcune rime, del cavaliere L. Petrucci, con
la selva delle sue persecutioni. Farrago poematum.
Ital. a. Lat. 4°. *Oxoniæ, J. Barnesius*, 1613. L(imp.).
O.C[2].C[9].GLOUC.+; F(2).HD.Y.
2 extra leaves of cuts and errata (in both F copies)
may have been pr. in London.

Petrus, *Hispanus. See* 14651.5.

19815 **Petrus,** *Luccensis.* A dialogue of dying wel. First written
in the Italian tongue. . . . *Tr.* first into French, and
now into English [by] (R. V[erstegan, i.e. R. Rowlands.]) 8°. *Antwerp, A. C[onincx,]* 1603. L[2].O.C[3].E.
OS.+; F.HN.TEX.
(*Formerly also* 6802) A&R 645.

Petrus, *Ravennas. See* 24112.

19816 **Petrus, Galfredus.** Fratris Galfredi Petri Baioceñ. Galli, . . . De vita, ac moribus, atɕ panis miraculo sancti Nicholai de Tollentino, comedia. [*Ed.*] (E. Soppeth.) 8°. [*R. Pynson*, 1510?] L.L².

19816.5 — Fratris Galfredi Petri Baiocensis, . . . opus sane de deorū, dearumɕ gentilium genealogia. [In verse.] 4°. *in ed. T. Bertheleti*, 1524 (5 cal. oc.) O⁹.

19817 **Pett, John.** The great cicle of Easter containing a short rule. 1583. 8°. *J. C[harlewood] f. T. Butter*, [1584.] L.L¹³(imp.)*.WI(imp.)*.
D2ᵛ blank.

19817.5 — [A variant, w. colophon dated 1584 on D2ᵛ.] HN.

19818 **Pett, Peter.** Times iourney to seeke his daughter Truth. [In verse.] 4°. *F. K[ingston] f. H. Lownes*, 1599. HN.

19819 **Pettie, George.** A petite pallace of Pettie his pleasure; conteyning many pretie histories. [*Ed.*] (R. B.) 4°. (*R. W[atkins*, 1576.]) Ent. to R. Watkins 6 au. 1576. L.C(imp.).; N.PFOR.PML.
Collates A–Ff⁴.

19819.5 — [Anr. ed.] 4°. [*T. Dawson f.*] (*R. W[atkins*, 1578?]) Arthur Houghton.
Collates A² B–Y⁴ Aa–Bb⁴.

19820 — [Anr. ed.] 4°. [*T. Dawson f.*] (*R. W[atkins*, c. 1585.]) L.O(tp only).; HN.
Collates [–]² B–Y⁴ Z²; B1ʳ line 2: 'Sinorix cheefe'. Prelims. omitted in this and following eds.

19821 — [Anr. ed.] 4°. (*R. W[atkins*, c. 1590.]) L.O(imp.).; F.
Collates [–]² B–Y⁴ Z²; B1ʳ line 2: 'Sinorix chiefe'.

19822 — [Anr. ed.] 4°. *G. Eld*, 1608. Ent. to F. Burton 11 mr. 1605. L.O.; F.PEN(imp.).

19823 — [Anr. ed.] 4°. *G. Eld*, 1613. O.HETH(frag.).; BO. Iowa U(imp.).
— *tr. See* 12422.

19824 **Peyton, Thomas.** The glasse of time, in the two first ages. Divinely handled. [In verse.] 4°. *B. Alsop f. L. Chapman*, 1620. Ent. 27 jy. L(lacks 1st tp)*.L³ (imp.)*.O.O⁵(imp.)*.; F.HN.HD(2, 1 imp.*).
L and the imp. HD copies have a 'second age' sub tp (M1) in place of the missing 1st tp; L may have had a slip pasted over 'second'; HD has it erased and 'firste' substituted in ink.
F and both HD have a dedic. to James I lacking in O,HN and the next 2 issues.

19825 — [Anr. issue, w. cancel tp, w. imprint:] *B. Alsop*, 1623. O.

19825.5 — [Anr. issue, w. cancel tp, w. imprint:] *B. A[lsop] a. T. F[awcet*, after 1625.] HN.HD.

Pfalzgraf. *See* 19129, 19131.

19826 **Pflacher, Moses.** Analysis typica omnium cum veteris tum noui Testamenti librorum historicorum. Editio secunda. 4° in 8's. *E. Bollifantus, imp. G. B[ishop,]* 1587. Ent. to G. Bishop 11 jn. L.O.C.D².P.+; F.HN. PN².U.Y.+

Phaedrus. *See* 23410.

Phaer, Thomas. [The book of children. 1544, etc.] *See* 11967 sqq.
— A new booke entyteled the regiment of lyfe. [*Tr.* T. Phaer. 1543? etc.] *See* 11966.5 sqq.
— A newe boke of presidentes. [With a preface by Phaer and often ascribed to him. 1543, etc.] *See* 3327 sqq.
— *tr. See* 18402.5, 24799.

19827 **Phalaris.** [Begin a1ᵛ:] Carmeliani Brixiensis poete ad lectorem carmen. [a2ʳ:] Francisci Aretini . . . in Phalaridis epistolas. 4° in 8's. (*in vniuersitate Oxonie, T. rood atɕ t. hunte*, 1485.) O(6 leaves).O⁵.O⁷.O¹⁹(4 leaves).M.+ Duff 348.
The Latin trans. is that of F. Griffolini of Arezzo.

19828 — [A trans.] The epistles of Phalaris. *Tr.* W. D. 12°. *R. Badger.f. G. Latham*, 1634. L.O.C.E².LEEDS.+; F.HN. N.HD.U.+

19829 **Philadelphos, Theophilos.** Ad reverendissimos patres, . . . Ecclesiarum Anglicarum episcopos. [*Amsterdam, successor of G. Thorp,*] 1625.
Not an STC book.

Philadelphus, Eusebius. *See* 1463.

Philagathus, *tr. See* 6582.

19830 **Philalethes, Andreas,** *pseud.* An answere made by one of our brethren, a secular priest, now in prison, to a letter of G. Blackwels, written to Cardinall Caietane, 1596. Newly imprinted. [By R. Charnock.] 4°. [*A. Islip,*] 1602. L.O¹⁷.C.P.YK.+; F.HN.HD.ILL. TEX. 𝕬
A&R 235. Includes Blackwell's letter.

Philanactophil, *pseud. See* 3221, 11103.

Philarete. Faire-Virtue. 1622. *See* 25903.

Philaretes. Work for chimny-sweepers. 1602. *See* 12571.

Philaretus, Gilbertus. A brief discourse of the water of Spaw [partly from G. Philaretus. 1612?] *See* 22975.

Philargyrie. Philargyrie of greate Britayne. 1551. *See* 6089.5.

19831 **Philiatros.** Philiatros, or, the copie of an epistle, to a young student of physicke. 8°. *W. White*, 1615. Ent. 5 se. L.; PH.

19832 **Philibert,** *de Vienne.* The philosopher of the court. Englished by G. North. 8°. *H. Binnemā f. L. Harison a. G. Byshop*, 1575. Ass'd from L. Harrison to T. Woodcock 15 jy. 1578. L(2).L².L⁴.O.; F(lacks col.). HN.HD(imp.).

Philip I, *King of Spain. See* 22996.

19833 **Philip II,** *King of Spain.* The edict and decree of Phillip, king of Spaine, touching the exchanging of monyes. 1597. Now = 22992.3.

19833.5 — A briefe and true declaration of the sicknesse, last wordes and death of Philip the second. *Tr.* into English. 4°. *E. Bollifant f. W. Aspley*, 1599. Ent. 9 ja. L.C².

19834 — [Anr. ed., including:] (The happy entrance of Margaret of Austria). 4°. *Edinburgh, R. Walde-graue*, 1599. HD.
The 2nd pt. reprints 17324.
— [Begins:] Consideringe the obligation, [etc. An address to English catholics. 1597?] *See* 19087.5.
— A discourse more at large of the late ouerthrowe giuen to the king of Spaines armie. 1597. *See* 22993.

19835 — Een nieuu tiidinghe, hoe dat die prince van Spaengien triumphelick aengecomen is in Enghelandt. [*Printed abroad*, 1554.]
Not an STC book.

19836 — Oratio pia, & erudita pro statu Philippi & Mariæ. [By H. Weston?] 8°. (*in æd. J. Cawodi,*) [1554?] O.
— A proclamation set out by the K. of Spaine. For the vse and trafficke of merchandise, with those of Holland. 1592. *See* 18464.5.

19836a — A relation of the king of Spaines receiuing in Valliodolid [*sic*]. 1592. Now = 19412.5.

19837 — A request presented to the king of Spayn. 1578. = 18445.

19837.5 — Traicte paraenetique c'est à dire exhortatoire. *Tr.* J. D. Dralymont [i.e. J. de Montlyard.] Imprimé nouvellement. 8°. [*Eliot's Court Press?*] 1598. L.O.
Erroneously attrib. to A. Pérez and J. Teixeira.

19838 — [A trans.] A treatise parænetical, that is to say: an exhortation. Wherein is shewed the way to resist the Castilian king. By a Pilgrim Spaniard. Now Englished. 4°. [*R. Field*] *f. W. Ponsonby*, 1598. Ent. 17 mr. L.O.C.D.STU.+; F.HN.HD.IND.Y.+
Signed on S3ᵛ: 'P. Ol.'

19838.5 — [Anr. ed., w. title:] The Spanish pilgrime: or, an admirable discovery of a Romish catholicke. 4°. *B. A[lsop,] sold by T. Archer*, 1625. L.O.C.D².E.+; F.HN.HD.N.Y.+ 𝕬
(Formerly 23863) Dedic. to Earl of Pembroke on A2,3 lacking in most copies; present in IC,HD.
— A true discourse of the armie which the king of Spaine assembled. 1588. *See* 22999.

Philip III, *King of Spain.* A briefe declaration of the proceedings of the peace. 1608. *See* 18455.3.

19839 — The coppy of a letter and commission, of Phillip the third touching the trade of Holland and England. 4°. [*E. Allde*] *f. T. Pavier*, 1602. Ent. 8 no. L.
— Newes from Spaine. The king of Spaines edict. 1611. *See* 22992.7.

19840 — The severall proclamations lately published by the king of Spaine, and the French king. 2 pts. 4°. *T. C[reede] f. C. Burbie*, 1604. O⁷.DUR.
Pt. 2 also issued sep. as 13122.

Philip III, *King of Spain—cont.*

19841 — A proclamation of the truce betweene his majesty of Spayne, and the States generall. 1609. Now = 18472a.5.

19842 — [Begins:] Consideringe the obligation, [etc. An address to English catholics. 1597?] Now = 19087.5.

19843 — The triumphant and sumptuous arch erected by the company of English marchants in Lisbone, upon the Spanish kings entry. *Tr.* out of Spanish. 4°. *E. G[riffin] f. H. Seile,* 1619. Ent. 3 au. L.O.; HN.HD.
— The true copie of an edict, concerning christians in Portugall. [1602.] *See* 20128.

19843.5 **Philip IV,** *King of Spain.* The copy of two letters sent from Spaine: containing the kings censure for the rooting out of vices. 4°. *F. K[ingston] f. W. Lee,* 1621. Ent. to B. Downes a. W. Lee 6 no. L.

19844 — A proclamation for reformation, published . . . by Philip the fourth. [1623.] Now = 22992.9.
— A proclamation made in the name of his majesty of Spaine. 1630. *See* 17916.7.

19844.5 **Philip,** *son of Conn Crosach.* Duan Annso ó Pilip mac Cuinn Crosaig. [A poem on the day of doom.] s.sh.fol. [*Dublin, W. Kearney, at the expense of J. Usher,*] 1571. C⁷(2).
C⁷ copies on recto and verso of same sheet; possibly a proof sheet or type specimen.

19845 **Philip, John.** The examination and confession of certaine wytches. 1566. Now = 19869.5.

Philip, William, *tr.* Newes from Bohemia. 1619. *See* 3211.
— *See also* 450.7, 3355, 4115.5, 5043.5, 11727, 15193, 15241, 15691, 19799, 21828, 22992.3, 24628.

19846 **Philipot, John.** The catalogue of the chancellors of England, [etc.] 2 pts. 4°. *T. Cotes, sold by A. Crooke,* 1636. Ent. to R. Cotes 19 mr. L.O.C.D.G⁴.+; F.HN.CU.N(imp.).Y.+
— The cities advocate. [Formerly attrib. to J. Philipot.] 1629. *See* 3219.

19846.5 — To the [   ] of the hundred of [   ] These are to require you [etc. Form of summons for registering all gentry south of the Trent.] s.sh.4°. [*London,* 1634.] O.
Dated in MS. 8 July 1634.
— *ed. See* 4525.

Philippe, François, *tr. See* 6003.5, 16430.

Philippes, Morgan, *pseud. See* 15506.

19847 **Philippson, Joannes,** *Sleidanus.* Jo. Sleidani de quatuor summis imperijs. Libri tres. 8°. *R. Walde-graue, imp. T. Woodcock,* 1584. L.O.C.C³.LINC.+; F.HN.
Trans. in 19849, 19850.
— An epitome of Frossard. 1608. *See* 11399.

19848 — A famouse cronicle of oure time, called Sleidanes Commentaries, concerning the raigne of the emperour Charles the fift. *Tr.* J. Daus. fol. (*J. Daye f. A. Veale a. N. England,* 1560 (25 se.)) L.O.C².G².M.+; F.HN.HD(lacks tp).N.Y.+

19848a — [Anr. issue, w. cancel colophon:] (*J. Daie f. N. Englande,* 1560 (26 se.)) L.O.C.M.NEK.+; F.HN.MICH.PN.Y.+

19848b — [A ghost.]

19849 — A briefe chronicle of the foure principall empyres. Englished by S. Wythers. 4°. *R. Hall,* 1563. Ent. 1562–63. L.O.P.; F.HN.CH.LC.MICH.
Tp in 2 states; line 4 ends: 'Wherein, very' (HN,CH) or 'Wherein, is' (F,CH). A trans. of 19847.

19850 — The key of historie. Or, a most methodicall abridgement of the foure chiefe monarchies [19847]. *Tr.* from Latin (A. Darcie.) 12°. *M. Flesher f. W. Sheeres,* 1627. Ent. to R. Swain 17 ja. 1625; to W. Sheares 28 my. 1625. L.O.C⁹.E⁸.PETYT.+; F.HN.ILL.LC.MICH.+
Dedics. vary: w. Darcie's name (F,HN) or his inits. (LC). In some copies (1 L,L³,O) the dedics. are cancelled.

19851 — Second edition. 12°. *N. Okes] f. W. Sheeres,* 1631. L.O(lacks letterpress tp).C.G⁴.M².+; F.HN.CU.HD.N.+
Omits Darcie's dedics.

19852 — Third edition. 12°. *f. W. Sheares,* 1635. L.L³⁰.O.C.SHEF.; F.HN.HD.N.Y.+
Engr. tp dated 1636, lacking in L,O,C.

19853 **Philips, Edward.** Certaine godly and learned sermons. Taken by the pen of H. Yelverton. 4° in 8's. *R. Field f. C. Burbie,* 1605. Ent. 10 se. 1604. L.O.C.BTL.YK.+; F(2).HN.U.NY.

19854 — [Anr. ed.] 4° in 8's. *A. Hatfield f. Eliz. Burbie,* 1607. L.O.C.EX.SCL.; F.HN(imp.).PN².TORONTO².
— *See also* 1547.

19855 **Philips, Judith.** The brideling, sadling and ryding, of a rich churle in Hampshire, by one Judeth Philips. With a true discourse of her vnwomanly vsing of a trype wife. 4°. *T. C[reede,] solde by W. Barley,* 1595. HN.
See also 18758.

19855.5 **Philips,** *Sir* **Thomas.** Illustrissimus dominus, Tho. Philips. Eques auratus, [etc. Declaration of the style and titles of the ambassador to Sultan Murad IV.] 1626. s.sh.fol. [*London,* 1626.] L⁵(Lemon 274).

19856 **Phillida.** The obsequy of faire Phillida. *Ballad.* 1/2 sh.fol. [*London,* 1630?] L.

Phillip, Bartolome. *See* 10753.

Phillip, John. *See* Phillips, J.

Phillip, William, *tr. See* Philip, W.

19856.3 **Phillips, George.** The Aprill of the church. 8°. [*J. Danter] f. T. Gosson,* 1596. D.
Text begins A4ʳ.

19856.7 — [Anr. ed.] 8°. [*P. Short f. W. Leake?* 1598?] Ass'd from T. Gosson to W. Leake 16 mr. 1598. LINC(lacks tp). Text begins A2ʳ.

19857 — The embassage of Gods angell. 8°. [*P. Short] f. W. Leake,* 1597. Ent. 31 au. 1596. L.O.; F.

19858 — Fiue godly and learned sermons. 8°. *J. Roberts,* 1594. Ent. 14 de. 1593. LINC.

19859 — Gods generall summons to his last parliament. [A sermon.] 8°. [*P. Short] f. W. Leake,* 1595. Ent. 9 au. L.; F(imp.).

19859a — [Anr. ed.] 8°. [*P. Short] f. W. Leake,* 1597. O.

19860 — The good sheepeheardes dutie. Now = 19861.7.

19861 — The life and death of the rich man and Lazarus. 8°. [*E. Allde] f. E. White,* 1600. Ent. 22 ja. HN.

19861.3 — The paines of a faithful pastor. 8°. [*P. Short] f. W. Leake,* 1595. Ent. 21 my. L(tp only, Ames I.570). Phillipps 2802.

19861.5 — [Anr. ed.] 8°. [*P. Short] f. W. Leake,* 1596. L.; F.

19861.7 — [Anr. issue, w. cancel tp:] The good sheepeheardes dutie. [*P. Short] f. W. Leake,* 1597. L.C(lacks tp)*. (Formerly 19860)

Phillips, George, *Colonist. See* 18485.

19862 **Phillips, Jerome.** The fisherman. A sermon preached at a synode in Nottinghamshire. 4°. *for* [i.e. *by*] *W. J[ones] f. R. Bird, sold* [*by T. Pavier,*] 1623. Ent. 7 fb. L.O.C.D.YK.+; F.HN.PN².U.Y.

19863 **Phillips, John.** A balad intituled, a cold pye for the papistes. Wherin is contayned: the trust of true subiectes. *Ballad.* s.sh.fol. *W. How f. R. Johnes,* [1570?] Ent. 1570–71. HN.

19863.3 — The coat armour of a christian. 12°. [*R. Waldegrave*] *f. J. Harrison the yonger,* [1584.] Ent. 22 se. 1584. L².
(Formerly 19070) Dedic. signed 'J. Phillipus'.

19863.7 — A commemoration of the life and death of Dame Helen Branch. 1594. [In verse. Init. J. P.] 4°. [*J. Danter,* 1594.] HN.

19864 — A commemoration of the right noble and vertuous ladye, Margrit Duglasis good grace. 1578. [In verse.] 4°. (*J. Charlewood,*) [1578?] L.E.; HN.

19865 — The commodye of pacient and meeke Grissill. 4°. *T. Colwell,* [1566?] Ent. 1565–66; 1568–69. Y². Greg 52.

19866 — An epitaphe on the death of the right noble and most vertuous lady Margarit Duglasis. 1578. [In verse.] s.sh.fol. *f. E. White,* [1578.] HN.

19867 — An epitaph on the death of the right honorable lord H. Wrisley, earle of South hampton: . . . 1581. [In verse.] s.sh.fol. [*London,* 1581.] L.

19868 — An epitaph on the death of the vertuous ladie maioresse, late wyfe to (A. Auenet [i.e. Avenon]) lord maior. 1570. [In verse.] s.sh.fol. *R. Johnes,* [1570.] Ent. 1570–71. L(printed on verso of 11836).

Phillips, John—*cont.*

19869 — An epytaphe, or lamentable discourse: wherein is bewayled the death of sir W. Garrat. [In verse.] s.sh.fol. [*W. Williamson f.*] *R. Johnes*, 1571 (4 oc.) HN.

19869.5 — The examination and confession of certaine wytches at Chensforde [*sic*] the xxvi. daye of July 1566. (The second examination [27 July 1566].—The end and last confession of mother Waterhouse [29 July 1566].) 3 pts. 8°. (*W. Powell f. W. Pickeringe*, 1566 (13 au.)) Ent. 1566–67. L².
(Formerly 19845) Verses only by Phillips.

19870 — A frendly larum, or faythfull warnynge to the true harted subiectes of England. [In verse.] 8°. *W. How f. R. Johnes*, [1570.] Ent. 1569–70. L².; HN.

19870.5 — [Headline:] The history of Cleomines and Juliet. [In verse.] 8°. [*H. Jackson*, 1577?] Ent. to H. Jackson 14 oc. 1577. F(1 leaf only).

19871 — The life and death of sir Phillip Sidney. His funerals with the whole order of the mournfull shewe. [In verse.] 4°. *R. Walde-graue*, 1587. Ent. 22 fb. L.

19872 — The perfect path to paradice: contayning diuers most ghostly and wholsome prayers. 12°. *H. Jackson*, 1588. F.

19873 — [Anr. ed.] 12°. *H. Jackson*, 1590. F. Hickmott.

19873.5 — [Anr. ed.] Also a summons to repentance. 12°. *J. Beale f. R. Jackson*, 1617. H. Jackson's copies ass'd 22 jy. 1616. F(imp.).
2nd pt. is an abridged version of 19874.5.

19874 — [Anr. ed.] 12°. *T. Purfoot f. F. Williams*, 1626. Ass'd 16 ja. L.L⁴¹.; F.

19874.5 — [A summons to repentance.] 8°. [*H. Jackson*, 1584.] Ent. to H. Jackson 13 au. 1584. O(lacks tp).
Dedic. to Sir R. Constable, etc. Abridged in 19873.5.

19875 — [Anr. ed.] A sommon to repentance. 8°. *H. Jackson*, 1584. L.
Dedic. to Sir E. Osborne, etc.

19875.3 — [Anr. ed.] 8°. *H. Jackson*, 1590. C⁵.
Dedic. to George Devorax, Esq.

19875.5 — The tryumph of true subiectes. Wherein they are incouraged to continue their loue to hir maiestie. Wherunto is annexed hir going on the xxiiii. of Nouember, to Paules, and her receiuing into London, by the L. maior. 4°. *H. Jackson*, 1588. O⁸.HAT.; SMU.

19876 — Vt hora, sic fugit vita. A commemoration on the life and death of sir C. Hatton. [In verse.] 4°. [*E. Allde*] *f. E. White*, 1591. HN.

19877 — The wonderfull worke of God shewed vpon a chylde, W. Withers, who laye in a traunce tenne dayes. 8°. *R. Waldegraue*, 1581. Ent. 9 ja.; ass'd to E. White 13 ja. L.
— *See also* 19071.

19877.5 **Phillips, John**, *Minister of Feversham*. The christians A.B.C. Or, a christian alphabet, contayning grounds of knowledge vnto salvation. 12°. *T. Harper f. F. Clifton*, 1629. Ent. 5 jn. HD.

19878 — The way to heaven. 4°. *F. Kingston*, 1625. Ent. 2 my. L.O¹⁰.C².NOR².P.+; F.HN.U.Y.

19878.5 **Phillips, Thomas.** The booke of Lamentations; or, Γεεννηλογια a treatise of hell. As also. The booke of Genesis. 12°. *J. D[awson] f. P. Cole*, 1639. Ent. 7 au. 1638. L.O.C⁵.DUL.LINC*.; CAL.

19879 — [Anr. issue, w. cancel tp:] The booke of Lamentations. . . . Delivered in a sermon in Lincolne. (The booke of Genesis.) 12°. *J. D[awson] f. P. Cole*, 1639. L³.C. D(both tpp).; F.LC.

19880 **Phillis.** Phillis and Flora. The sweete and ciuill contention of two amorous ladyes. *Tr.* out of Latine [of W. Map] by R. S[tapleton?] Esquire. [In verse.] 4°. *W. W[hite] f. R. Johnes*, 1598. L.D².; F.ILL. Arthur Houghton.
Reprinted from 4985.
— The tragedie of Phillis. [1628–29.] *See* 15.5.

Philo, *Judaeus*. *See* 13964.

19881 **Philo-Balladus.** A womans birth. Or a perfect relation . . . to declare the descent of a woman. *Ballad.* 2 pts. s.sh.fol. *f. F. Grove*, [1638?] Ent. 20 fb. 1638. L.

Philo-Britannicos, *tr. See* 21757a.

19881.5 **Philodikaios, Irenicus**, *pseud.* A treatise declaring, and confirming against all obiections the just title of James the sixt, to the succession of the croun of England. 4°. [*Edinburgh, R. Waldegrave*, 1599?] Ent. to H. Hooper 6 ap. 1603. D.E.
Signed in Waldegrave's manner.

19882 **Philogamus.** Phylogamus. [In verse. By Luke Shepherd.] 8°. [*W. Hill*, 1548?] L(imp.).O⁰(lacks tp).

19882.5 **Philomusus.** The academy of complements. Wherein ladyes, . . . may accommodate their courtly practice. [Anon. By J. Gough?] 12°. by [*T. Badger*] *the assigne of T. P[urfoot] f. H. Mosley*, 1639. Ent. 7 no. 1638. F(imp.).ILL(imp.).

19883 — [Anr. ed.] Perused by the author with additions of witty amorous poems. 12°. *T. B[adger] f. H. Mosley*, 1640. L(imp.).O.; HD.
To the Reader signed Philomusus.

19883.5 — [Anr. ed.] 12°. *T. Badger f. H. Mosley*, 1640. F.

Philopatris, *pseud.* A counter-buff to Lysimachus Nicanor. 1640. *See* 18062.

19884 — An humble petition offered to this present parliament wherein the wandring ghost of the late pyramis [*sic*] demolished in Paris, discourseth his fortunes. 4° w. perp. chainlines. [*H. Lownes*] *f. M. Lownes*, 1606. Ent. 17 ja. L.O.C.C².D.+; F.HN.HD.N.NY.+
See also 20444.

Philopatris, C. The true lawe of free monarchies. 1598. *See* 14409.

19885 **Philopatris, John.** An aduertisement written to a secretarie of my L. treasurers of Ingland. Concerninge an other booke newly written in Latin . . . against her maiesties late proclamation [8207]. 8°. [*Antwerp*,] 1592. L(2, 1 imp.).O(imp.).LINC.YK.; F(imp.).NY.
A&R 264. An abridged trans. of R. Parsons's Elizabethae . . . saeuissimum in catholicos edictum, *Augustae*, 1592. The trans., formerly attrib. to J. Creswell, is more prob. by R. Rowlands.

Philophrastes, *pseud., tr. See* 22215a.

19886 **Philos.** A pleasant and delightfull poeme of two lovers, Philos and Licia. 4°. *W. S[tansby] f. J. Smethwick*, 1624. Ent. to W. Aspley 2 oc. 1606. O.

19887 **Philosophia.** De philosophia panathenaicae duae: in comitiis Oxonii habitæ. [5 id. Jul. 1585; 3 id. Jul. 1586.] 8°. [*Oxford, J. Barnes*, 1586.] O.O³⁸.; F. Detroit PL(imp.).

19888 **Philotus.** Ane verie excellent and delectabill treatise intitulit Philotus. Quhairin we may persaue the greit inconveniences that fallis out in the mariage betwene age and zouth [*sic*]. 4°. *Edinburgh, R. Charteris*, 1603. L.C¹⁶.E. Greg 199.

19889 — [Anr. ed.] 4°. *Edinburgh, A. Hart*, 1612. L(2).; HN.HD.

Philotus, Laurentius, *Tyl. See* 18694.

19890 **Philpot, John.** The trew report of the dysputacyon had & begōne in the conuocacyō hows at london the xviij. daye of October M.D.LIIII. [really 1553.] [Anon.] 8°. (*Basil, A. Edmonds* [i.e. *Emden, J. Gheylliaert a. S. Mierdman?*]) [1554.] L.L².O.C. DUR⁵.+; F.HN.PML.U.

19891 — [A trans.] Vera expositio disputationis, institutae in synodo ecclesiastica, Londini [etc.] 8°. (*Romae coram castro S. Angeli ad signum S. Petri*, [i.e. *Cologne*,] 1554.)
Not an STC book.

19892 — The examinacion of the constaunt martir of Christ, J. Philpot. (An apologie for spitting vpon an Arrian.) 2 pts. 8°. [*Emden, E. van der Erve*, 1556?] L.O.C.M. P.+; F.HD.PML.

19893 — [Anr. ed.] 2 pts. 8°. (*H. Sutton*, 1559.) L(2, 1 with 1st A⁸ of 19893a).; F.HN.HD(2 leaves).
In title: 'constante martir'; 1st B1ʳ line 1 of text ends 'vnto'. Sutton fined for printing this; *see* Arber I.101.

19893a — [Anr. ed.] 2 pts. 8°. (*H. Sutton*, 1559.) L(1st A⁸ only). O(lacks tp).STU.; F(lacks pt. 2).Y.
In title: 'constant martyr'; 1st B1ʳ line 1 of text ends 'mayster'.

Phinch, Richard. *See* 10877.5 sq.

Phioravanti, Leonardo. *See* 10879 sqq.

Phiston, William. *See* 10922 sqq.

Phoenix. The phoenix, as it hath beene acted. 1607. *See* 17892.

— The phoenix of these late times. 1637. *See* 25226.5.

Phoenix, Anne. The saints legacies. 1633. *See* 10635.3.

Phrases. Phrases elegantiores. 1625. *See* 10706.4.

19893a.3 — Phrases françoises: fort necessaires pour ceux qui apprennent a parler françois, en forme de question. 8°. *R. Field,* 1624. L.

— Phrases oratoriæ elegantiores. 1631. *See* 10707.

19893a.7 **Physic.** Phisicke for the soule, verye necessarie to be vsed in the agonie of death. *Tr.* out of Latine by H. Thorne. (A sermon of pacience, by saint John Chrisostome.) 8°. *H. Denham,* [1567?] Ent. 1566–67. F(imp.).

Text begins A1ʳ. The sermon is anr. trans. of 14638.

19894 — [Anr. ed.] 8°. *H. Denham,* (1568.) C⁵.; F(imp.).

Text begins B1ʳ.

19895 — [Anr. ed.] 16° in 8's. *H. Denham,* 1570. F.

19896 — [Anr. ed.] 16° in 8's. (*J. Charlewood*) f. *H. Denham,* (1578.) O.

19896.5 **Physiologus.** A familiar dialogue betwixt one Physiologus a gentleman student of Athens and his country friend Geoponus, wherein he doth make manifest many secrets in the soyling, plowing, and sowing of the earth. 4°. Oxford, *J. Barnes,* 1612. RD.

Piatti, Girolamo. *See* 20001.

Picardus, Odo, *ed. See* 23939.5.

Pichonnaye, G. Ledoyen de la. A playne treatise to learn the Frenche tongue. 1576. *See* 15353.3.

19897 **Pick, Samuel.** Festum voluptatis, or the banquet of pleasure. Containing divers choyce love-posies, songs, [etc.] 4°. *E. P[urslowe]* f. *B. Langford,* 1639. Ent. 17 oc. 1638. L(2).O.; F.HN.HD.

19897.3 **Pickering, Peter.** A myroure or glasse for all spiritual ministers. Gathered out of holy scripture and catholyke doctours, by P. Pykeryng for a newe yeres gyfte. M.D.L.I. 8°. (*R. Crowley,* 1550.) L.

Pickering, Thomas, *ed. See* 19668, 19669, 19697, 19751.5.

— *tr. See* 19677.

Pickford, John. *See* 19073.

19897.7 **Pico della Mirandola, Giovanni,** *Count.* Here is côteyned the lyfe of Johan Picus erle of Mirādula [written by his nephew, G. F. Pico.] (Here begin .xii. rulys. [In verse.]) [*Tr.* Sir] (t. more.) 4° in 6's. (*J. Rastell,*) [1510?] L.

(Formerly 19898a.)

19898 — [Anr. ed.] 4° in 6's. (*W. de worde,*) [c. 1525.] L(2).O.; HN.CH.LC(imp.).PML.

19898a — Now = 19897.7.

19898a.3 — Twelue rules, and weapons concerning the spirituall battel. Together w. a briefe exposition vpon the sixteene psalme: with two worthie epistles. *Tr.* (W. H.) 4°. *J. Windet* f. *J. Daldern,* 1589. Ent. to Windet 23 jn. HN.

For other trans., see 6157 (reprinted in 23968, 23988), 16932, 19897.7.

Pico della Mirandola, Giovanni Francesco, *Count. See* 19897.7.

Pictagoras. A brefe and pleasaunte worke. [1560?] *See* 20524.

19898a.7 **Picture.** The picture of a carnal man and a true christian: or a looking-glasse for christians. 12°. *F. Kyngston, sold by E. Weaver,* 1607. Ent. to Kingston 13 ap. Arbury Hall, Nuneaton, Warks.

19899 **Pie, Thomas.** Epistola ad ornatissimum virum D. Johannem Housonum qua dogma eius novum & admirabile de Judæorum divortijs refutatur [13886]. 4°. *A. Hatfieldus,* 1603. Ent. 22 jn. L.O.C.D.E.+; PH².

Answered by 13887.

19900 — An houreglasse contayning I a computation from the beginning of time to Christ by X. articles. II a confirmation of the same. 4°. [*R. Robinson* f.] *J. Wolfe,* 1597. Ent. 21 ap. L.O.C.D.P.+; F.HN.CAL.HD.Y.

Pie, Thomas—*cont.*

19901 — Usuries spright conjured: or a scholasticall determination of usury. With [an] answere to a treatise, written in defence of usurie. 4°. *M. Bradwood,* 1604. Ent. to G. Seton 2 ap. L.O.C.D.YK.+; CU.HART².HD.

— *ed. See* 2762.

Piementelli, Diego. *See* 19935.

Pierce, Matthew. Almanacks. 1634, etc. *See* 496 sqq.

Pierce, William, *Bp.* Visitation Articles. *See* 10137.9, 10316.

19902 **Pierius, Johannes,** *Valerianus.* A treatise writen by Johan Valerian a greatte clerke of Italie, which is intituled in latin Pro sacerdotum barbis. 8°. (*in aed. T. Bertheleti,* 1533.) L.O.O⁶(imp.).G².; HN.

19903 **Piers,** *Ploughman.* A godly dyalogue & dysputacion betwene Pyers plowman, and a popysh preest, concernyng the supper of the lorde. 8°. [*W. Copland,* c. 1550.] C³.M.

19903.5 — [Anr. ed.] A goodly dyalogue. . . . 8°. [*W. Copland,* c. 1550.] F.

19903a — I playne Piers which can not flatter [etc. A satire against Catholics, sometimes attrib. to W. Roy.] 8°. [*N. Hill?* 1550?] L².C³.E.; HN.

19903a.5 — [Anr. ed.] O read me, for I am of great antiquitie. I plaine Piers [etc.] I am the gransier of Martin mareprelitte. Newly corrected. 4° in 2's. *Printed either of this side, or of that side of some of the priestes,* [1589?] L(imp.).

Last 3 quires are proof sheets w. MS. corrections. This ed. is pr. as verse.

19904 — Pierce the Ploughmans crede. [In verse.] 4°. (*R. wolfe,* 1553.) L.C.; HN(2).WEL.

Reprinted in 19908.

19905 — Pyers plowmans exhortation, vnto the lordes, knightes and burgoysses of the parlyamenthouse. 8°. *A. Scoloker,* [1550?] L.O.

19906 — The vision of Pierce Plowman, now fyrste imprynted. [Attrib. to W. Langland. The B text. In verse.] 4°. [*R. Grafton* f.] (*R. Crowley,* 1550.) L.O.C.G².M.+; F.HN.BO(lacks tp).IND.NY.+

Tp misdated 1505, which is usually overprinted w. an orn. and the correct date stamped below.

19907 — Nowe the seconde tyme imprinted . . . whereunto are added notes in the mergyne. 4°. [*R. Grafton* f.] *R. Crowley,* 1550. L.O.C⁴.BTU.E.+; F.N.PML.WEL.Y.+

This may actually be the 3rd ed.

19907a — [Anr. ed.] Nowe the seconde time imprinted. 4°. [*R. Grafton* f.] *R. Crowley,* 1550. L.O.C².LEEDS.M.+; F.HN.HD.ILL.NY.+

19908 — [Anr. ed.] Newlye imprynted after the authours olde copy. Whereunto is also annexed the Crede of Pierce Plowman. 2 pts. 4°. *O. Rogers,* 1561 (21 fb.) Ent. 1560–61. L.O.C.D.E.+; F.HN.HD.N.PML.+

Pt. 2 reprints 19904.

Piers, John, *Bp.* Visitation Articles. *See* 10327, 10377.

Piers, Matthew. Almanacks. 1634, etc. *See* 496 sqq.

19909 **Pierse, Charles.** Vertues anatomie. Or a compendious description of lady Cheany. [In verse.] 8°. *W. Jones,* 1618. Ent. 9 my. O.

19910 **Pierson, Thomas.** The cure of hurtfull cares and feares. 12°. *R. B[adger]* f. *P. Stephens a. C. Meridith,* 1636. L².L⁴.D.P.; F.

App. issued w. 12897.5.

— *ed. See* 19677.5, 19722, 19732, 19748, 19751.

Pieta. *See* Indulgences 21, 22.

19910.5 **Pietro,** *Aretino.* A paraphrase upon the seaven penitentiall psalmes. . . . [Anon.] *Tr.* out of Italian by J. H(awkins.) 8°. [*Douai, G. Pinchon,*] 1635. L.L⁴. LAMPORT.USHAW.W.

A&R 758. Also erroneously attrib. to G. Savonarola. See also 2726.

19911 — Quattro comedie del divino Pietro Aretino. 8°. [*J. Wolfe,*] 1588. Ent. to J. Wolfe 20 se. L.O.C.D.M.+; F.HD.N.NY.Y.+

Pietro, *Aretino—cont.*

19911.5 — La prima (seconda) parte de Ragionamenti. (Commento di ser Agresto da Ficaruolo [i.e. A. Caro.]) 3 pts. 8°. (*Bengodi* [i.e. *London, J. Wolfe,*]) 1584 (21 oc.) Ent. to J. Wolfe 14 oc. 1588. L(2).O⁶. C¹³.DNPK.; Y.
　　Collates A–O⁸ P⁴; A–Z⁸; 𝔛⁸ A–H⁸.

19912 — [Anr. ed.] 2 pts. 8°. (*Bengodi* [i.e. *London, J. Windet f. J. Wolfe,*]) 1584 (21 oc.) [c. 1595.] L.O.O³.C.G².+; HD(2).
　　Collates A–P⁸; A–Mm⁸. There is also an [*Amsterdam,* c. 1620] ed. w. the *Bengodi,* 1584 (21 oc.) imprint at L,D,G²,F,ILL collating A–N⁸ Aa–Yy⁸ AA–GG⁸ HH⁴.

19913 — La terza, et ultima parte de Ragionamenti. 8°. *G. A. del Melagrano* [i.e. *London, J. Wolfe,*] 1589. Ent. to J. Wolfe 14 oc. 1588. L.O.C².DNPK.HOLK.+; F.HD. LC.N.Y.+

Pietro, *da Lucca.* See 19815.

19914 **Pigafetta, Marco Antonio.** Itinerario di Marc'antonio Pigafetta gentil'huomo Vicentino [from Vienna to Constantinople.] 4°. *G. Wolfio,* 1585. L.; NY.Y.

Pigafetta, Philippo, *ed.* See 16805.

19915 **Pigge, Oliver.** A comfortable treatise upon the latter part of the fourth chapiter of the first epistle of saint Peter. 8°. *R. Walde-graue f. J. Harison the yonger a. T. Man,* 1582. Ent. to T. Man 23 mr. L(destroyed).; F.

19916 — Meditations concerning praiers to almightie God, for the saftie [*sic*] of England, when the Spaniards were come into the narrow seas. 8°. *R. R[obinson] f. T. Man,* 1589. Ent. 3 mr. L.C(lacks tp).D.

19916.3 — [Anr. ed.] With a spirituall song of praises by P. Turner doctor of phisicke. 8°. *R. R[obinson] f. T. Man,* 1589. O.D.; F.

19916.7 — Sermons, vpon the 101. psalme, conteyning profitable instruction for all, especially for such as haue any gouernement ouer others. [Init. O. P.] 8°. *T. Orwin f. T. Man,* 1591. F(imp.).

Pigot, Francis. An almanack. 1630. *See* 497.

Pike, Richard. See 19529.

19917 **Pikeryng, John.** A newe enterlude of vice conteyninge, the historye of Horestes. 4°. *W. Gryffith,* 1567. L. Greg 48.

Pilesson, Pierre. See 18134.7.

Pilgrim. The pilgrime of Casteele. 1621. *See* 24629.
— [The Pilgrim's tale. 1538.] *See* 24650.

19917.5 **Pilgrimage.** [Book of the pilgrimage of mankind. In verse.] 4°. (*R. Pynson,* 1508 (5 de.)) O(last leaf only). (Formerly 19623)

19918 — [Anr. ed. Heading a1ᵛ:] The table. Here begynneth a boke in Frenche called le pelerynage de Lhomme, . . . & in oure tunge the pylgrymage of man kynd incompendiouce [*sic*] prose cōpoūded by william hendred prioure of Leomynstre, and now newly at the specyal commaundemente of the same compyled in metre. 4° in 6's. (*R. Faques,*) [1520?] O².
　　— Here begynneth . . . the pylgrimage of perfection. 1526. *See* 3277.

19919 — The pilgrimage of man. 1606. Now = 14691.3.
19920 — [Anr. ed.] 1612. Now = 14691.5.
19921 — [Anr. ed.] 1635. Now = 14691.9.
　　— This book is intytled the pylgremage [*sic*] of the sowle. 1483. *See* 6473.

19922 **Pilkington, Francis.** The first booke of songs or ayres of 4. parts: with tableture. fol. *T. Este,* 1605. Ent. 23 au. 1604. L.G².; F.HN.

19923 — The first set of madrigals and pastorals of 3. 4. and 5. parts. 5 ptbks. 4°. *f. M. L[ownes] J. B[rowne] a. T. S[nodham,]* the assignes of W. Barley, 1613. L. O¹³(altus only).M³(cantus, quintus only).; F(cantus, bassus only).HN.ILL(bassus only).
　　Cantus and tenor orig. dated 1614, altered in ink to 1613; other pts. dated 1613.

19924 — The second set of madrigals, and pastorals, of 3. 4. 5. and 6. parts. 6 ptbks. 4°. *T. Snodham f. M. L[ownes] a. A. B[rowne,]* 1624. L.O¹³(altus only).M³(imp.).; HN.
　　The altus pt. contains a pavanne for the orpharion by Wm. Stanley, Earl of Derby.

19925 **Pilkington, Gilbert.** The turnament of Tottenham. Published by W. Bedwell. [In verse.] (A briefe description of the towne of Tottenham. By W. Bedwell.) 4°. *J. Norton,* 1631. Ent. to W. Garrett 16 mr. L.L⁸.O.D².M.+; F.HN.HD.NY.Y.+
　　(2nd pt. formerly also 1795) The ascription to Pilkington is doubtful.

19926 **Pilkington, James,** *Bp.* Aggeus the prophete declared by a large commentarye. 8°. *W. Seres,* 1560 (2 se.) Ent. 2 se. L².O.; F.
　　Without 'J.P.L.C.' on tp.

19926.3 — [Anr. issue, w. tp reset.] L.L⁴.C.P.YK.+; F(imp.).ILL (lacks tp)*.
　　Tp init.: 'J.P.L.C.'; in title: 'commentarye.'

19926.7 — [Anr. issue, w. quires A,B,Ee,Ff reset.] C⁵.M.; F(imp.).
　　Tp init.: 'J.P.L.C.'; in title: 'commentary.'

19927 — Aggeus and Abdias prophetes, the one corrected, the other newly added, and both at large declared. [Signed Jaco. P., *Ep. D.*] 8°. *W. Seres,* 1562. L.O.C. C⁵.D².+; F.NY.Y.
　　(2nd pt. formerly also 19928)

19928 — An exposition vpon Abdyas. [1562.] = 2nd pt. of 19927.

19929 — A godlie exposition vpon certeine chapiters [i–v] of Nehemiah. Newlie published. In the latter end, because the author could not finish that treatise of oppression . . . is added that by R. Some. [*Ed.*] (J. Fox.) 4° in 8's. *T. Thomas, pr. to the Univ. of Camb.,* 1585. L.O.C.G².YK.+; F.HD. Allegheny C.
　　Some's treatise is reprinted from 22910.

19929.5 — [An extract, reprinting I8ʳ–L1ᵛ of 19929.] Two godlie and fruitful treatises of oppression. The one taken out of the Exposition vppon the fift chapter of Nehemiah, by J. Pilkington. The other by R. Some. 8°. *T. Thomas, pr. to the Univ. fo* [*sic*] *Camb.,* 1585. L².C².D.; Y(imp.).

19930 — The true report of the burnyng of the steple and churche of Poules. [Anon.] 8°. *W. Seres,* 1561 (10 jn.) Ent. 11 jn. L.C⁷. 𝔄

19930.5 — [A trans.] Exemplum literarum amici cuiusdam ad amicum quendam suum, de vera origine conflagrationis pyramidis, & templi Paulini Londinensis. [Anon.] 4°. *in off. J. Day,* 1561. L¹¹(S.P.D., Eliz., vol. 17, doc. 28).

19931 — The burnynge of Paules church in London in 1561. 8°. *W. Seres,* (1563 (10 mr.)) Ent. 1562–63. L.O.C.D.G². +; F.HN.HD.PML.Y.+
　　Reprints and confutes some Catholic propaganda entitled 'An addicion', ascribed to John Morwen, former Bp. Bonner's chaplain.

19932 — [A ghost.]
　　— Two godlie and fruitful treatises of oppression. 1585. *See* 19929.5.

19933 **Pilkington, Richard.** Parallela: or the grounds of the new romane catholike, and of the ancient christian religion, compared together, in answere to [4958]. 4°. *J. Bill,* 1618. L².O.C.P.YK.+; HN.
　　Answered by 4959.

19933.5 **Pill.** A pil to purge melancholie: or, a preprative [*sic*] to a purgation: or, topping, copping, and capping. 4°. [*W. White,* 1599.] PFOR.
　　Apparently connected w. the Harvey-Nash controversy, esp. 18370.
　　— A pill to purge out poperie. 1623. *See* 17858.

Pillet, *Sir* **John.** *See* Indulgences 131 sq.

19934 **Pilovius, Conradus.** Epicedium: in obitum . . . Ludovici Linoxiæ & Richmondiæ ducis. 4°. [*B. Alsop,*] 1624. L.C².

19935 **Pimentel, Diego.** The deposition of don D. Piementelli [concerning the Armada]. *Tr.* out of Dutch by F. M. 4°. [*J. Charlewood f.*] *J. Woolfe,* 1588. Ent. 29 oc. L.O.O⁸.C.G².+; F.HN.CH.HD.Y.

19936 **Pimlico.** Pimlyco. Or, runne red-cap. Tis a mad world at Hogsdon. (Skeltons tunning of Elynor Rumming.) [In verse.] 4°. [*T. Purfoot*] *f. J. Busbie a. G. Loftis,* 1609. O.; HN.N.
　　(2nd pt. formerly also 22612)

Pimm, Timothy, *tr. See* 953.5.

Pindar, Elizabeth. [Bookplate.] *See* Bookplates.

Pine, John. *See* 20521.2 sqq.

19937 **Pinelli, Luca.** Breife [*sic*] meditations of the most holy sacrament. [*Ed.* H. Garnet.] 12⁰. [*V. Simmes,* c. 1600.] L.L².L⁹.L³⁵.HP.+; F.
A&R 648.

19937.5 — [Anr. trans.] Meditations of the most B. sacrament of the altar. *Tr.* [T. Everard.] 8⁰. [*St. Omer, English College Press,*] 1622. PARIS.SBK(imp.).USHAW.W. Prinknash Abbey, Cranham, Gloucs.; TEX.
A&R 649.

19938 — The mirrour of religious perfection devided into foure bookes. *Tr.* [T. Everard.] 8⁰. [*St. Omer, English College Press,*] 1618. L.L⁹.CAR.SN.USHAW.+; F.N.TEX.
A&R 650.

19939 — The societie of the rosarie. 1624. Now = 11617.6.
19939a — [Anr. ed.] [1596–97.] Now = 11617.5.
19940 — The virgin Maries life, faithfully gathered out of auncient and holie fathers. *Tr.* R. G[ibbons.] 8⁰. *Doway, L. Kel*[*lam,*] 1604. L².L¹³.O.HP.W.+; F.TEX. Loyola U, Chicago, Illinois.
A&R 651. Reprinted in 11617.6.

19940.5 — [Anr. ed.] 12⁰. *Roan,* [*English secret press,*] 1604. DE. Société des Bollandistes, Brussels.
A&R 652.

19941 **Pinke, William.** The tryall of our sincere love to Christ. [Sermons on Ephes.vi.24. *Ed.* W. Lyford.] 2 pts. 4⁰. *Oxford, W. Turner f. E. Forrest,* 1630. L⁴.O.O³.O¹². PLUME.
Reissued w. tp cancelled as pts. 2,3 of 19942.

19942 — The tryall of a christians syncere love unto Christ. [*Ed.*] (W. Lyford.) 4 pts. 4⁰. *Oxford, J. Lichfield f. E. Forrest,* 1631. L³.O.O³.C³.BTU.+; F(pts. 1,4 only). HN(pt. 1 only).HD(imp.).N.NY.+
Pts. 2,3 a reissue of 19941; pt. 1 on 1 Cor.xvi.22; pt. 4 on Luke xiv.26.

19943 — Second edition. 12⁰. *Oxford, J. Lichfield f. E. Forrest,* 1634. L.O.C.PLUME.; F.Y.

19944 — Third edition. 12⁰. *Oxford, L. Lichfield f. E. Forrest,* 1636. O.C.BURY.ELY.
— *tr. See* 4531.

Pinkney, Miles. *See* Car, M., *pseud.*

19945 **Pinner, Charles.** A sermon, vpon the wordes of Paul the apostle [1 Tim.iv.8]. Preached at Litlecot. 8⁰. *Oxford, J. Barnes, sold* [*by J. Broome, London,*] 1597. O.

19945a — [A sermon at Marlborough on 1 Tim.iv.16.] 8⁰. [*Oxford, J. Barnes,* 1596?] O(lacks tp).
Epistle dated 20 Oct. 1596.

19946 — Two sermons, on these wordes of Peter the apostle [1 Peter ii.17]. Preached at Marlebrough. 8⁰. *T. Creede,* 1597. O.LINC.; F.

Piot, Lazarus, *tr. See* 4182.

19947 **Pirckheimer, Bilibaldus.** The praise of the gout, or, the gouts apologie. *Tr.* W. Est. 4⁰. *G. P*[*urslowe*] *f. J. Budge,* 1617. Ent. 10 no. L(2).L⁸.O(2).O¹³.E⁵.; HN. HD.N.

Pisan, Christine de. *See* 7269 sqq.

19948 **Piscator, Johann.** Analysis logica euangelii secundum Matthæum. 8⁰. *R. F*[*ield,*] *imp. B. Nortoni,* 1594. Ent. to J. Norton 1 oc. L(destroyed).O.C.D.LEIC. NEP.+; F.HN.U.
See Greg, *Register B,* p.54.

19949 — Analysis logica euangelii secundum Marcum. 8⁰. *ex off. R. Field,* 1595. Ent. to J. Norton 10 my. O.C⁵. D.LEIC.NEP.+; F.ILL.
See Greg, *Register B,* p.54.

19950 — [A ghost.]
19951 — [Anr. ed.] 8⁰. *A. Hatfield,* 1598. L(destroyed).O.DUL.; HN.U.

19952 —Analysis logica euangelii secundum Lucam. 8⁰. *R. Field,* 1596. Ent. to B. Norton 13 ap. L(destroyed). L⁴⁶.O.C.LEIC.NEP.+; F.HN.HD.ILL.U.
See Greg, *Register B,* p.54.

19953 — Analysis logica euangelii secundum Johannem. 8⁰. [*Eliot's Court Press,*] *imp. G. Bishop,* 1591. Ent. to E. Bollifant a. ptnrs. 27 my. L³.C⁹.LEIC.LINC.; HN. BO(imp.).

19954 — [Anr. ed.] 8⁰. [*Eliot's Court Press,*] *imp. G. Bishop,* 1595. L(destroyed).O.C.C⁵.NEP.WOR.+; F.HN.HD.

19955 — Analysis logica libri S. Lucæ qui inscribitur Acta Apostolorum. 8⁰. *F. Kingstonus,* 1597. Ent. to B. Norton 23 se. L(destroyed).L⁴⁶.O.C.LEIC.NEP.+; F. HN.HD.U.

Piscator, Johann—*cont.*

19955.5 — Analysis logica Epistolarum Pauli ad Romanos. [etc., to] Thessalonicenses. 8⁰. [*Eliot's Court Press,*] *imp.* G. Bishop, 1590 (1589.) Ent. 19 ja. L.C.; William and Mary C, Williamsburg, Virginia.

19956 — [Anr. ed.] 8⁰. [*Eliot's Court Press,*] *imp.* G. Bishop, 1591. L³.L⁴⁶.C.A.YK.+; HN.BO.Y.

19957 — [Anr. ed., enlarged.] Analysis logica omnium Epistolarum Pauli. Editio secunda. 4 pts. 8⁰. [*Eliot's Court Press,*] *imp.* G. Bishop, 1594. L(destroyed).L⁴³.C. LINC.WI.WOR.+; HN.HD.
Includes reprint of 19957.7.

19957.3 — Editio tertia. 8⁰. [*R. Field,*] *imp.* G. Bishop, 1608. L(1, plus N2 sub tp only, Harl.5936/273).NLW(St. Asaph).USHAW.; F.HD(imp.).ILL.NLA.

19957.7 — Analysis logica quinque postremarum Epistolarum Pauli. 8⁰. [*Eliot's Court Press,*] *imp.* J. Wolfe, 1592. Ent. 18 ap. L⁴⁶.A.E².LEIC.LK.
Reprinted in 19957.

19958 — Analysis logica septem Epistolarum apostolicarum, quæ catholicæ appellari solent. 8⁰. [*Eliot's Court Press,*] *imp.* J. Wolfe, 1593. Ent. 10 my. L(destroyed). O.C⁹.A.LINC.WOR.+; F.HN.HD.

19959 — Editio secunda. 8⁰. G. Bishop, 1597. L.O.C.C².USHAW.+; F.
— Animaduersiones in dialecticam. 1583. *See* 19962.
— Aphorismi doctrinæ christianæ. 1595, etc. *See* 4372.5 sq.

19960 — Expositio capitum catecheseos religionis christianæ. 8⁰. *ap.* R. Field, 1603. Ent. 18 my. L.C³.DUL.P.WOR.; AAS.

19961 — In P. Rami Dialecticam [15241.7] animaduersiones. 8⁰. *ex off. typog.* H. Bynneman, 1581. Ent. to J. Harrison a. G. Bishop 12 de. 1580. L.O⁷.

19962 — [Anr. ed.] Animaduersiones Joan. Piscatoris Arg. in dialecticam P. Rami. Editio Secunda. 8⁰. H. Middletonus, pro J. Harrisono & G. Bishop, 1583. L.O.CARLISLE.D².LINC.+; HN.ILL.
Usually bd. w. 23873 sq.

19963 — A learned and profitable treatise of mans justification. 8⁰. T. Creede f. R. Jackson, 1599. Ent. to T. Creede 18 ja. O.YK.

19964 — [Anr. issue, w. imprint:] T. Creede f. R. Dexter, 1599. LK.; F.HD.WASH².
— *See also* 23873.

Pit, J., *Minister. See* 19969.2.

19965 **Pitcher, John.** A fearefull example. Shewed vpon a periured person. (John Pitcher.) 4⁰. [*E. Allde*] f. T. Nelson, [1591.] O.
Text dated 14 May 1591.

19966 **Pitiscus, Bartholomew.** A canon of triangles: or, the tables, of sines, [etc. Anon.] 4⁰. [*B. Alsop a.* T. Fawcett] f. J. Tap, 1630. L.O³.C.E¹³.LIV³.+; F.HN. BO.MICH.Y.+
Reprints pt. 2 of 19967; prob. issued w. 19968.

19967 — Trigonometrie: or the doctrine of triangles. *Tr.* R. Handson. (A canon of triangles.) 2 pts. 4⁰ in 8's. (*E. Allde*) f. J. Tappe, (1614.) Ent. 17 ja. L.O.C².A.NEP.+; HN.BR(pt. 2 only). Horblit.
Pt. 2 is without imprint or date and is reprinted in 19966.

19968 — [Anr. ed. of pt. 1] 4⁰ in 8's. B. A(lsop) a. T. Fawcet f. J. Tap, (1630.) L.L³⁸.O³.C⁴.LIV³.+; HN.BO.WASH².Y. U.S. Naval Observatory, Annapolis, Maryland.
Prob. issued w. 19966.

19968a — [Anr. ed.] 4⁰ in 8's. T. F[awcet] f. G. Hurlock, [1642?] Ass'd to Joseph Hurlock 1 au. 1631; to George Hurlock 16 ja. 1634. L⁴⁴.C.E¹³. Royal Observatory, Greenwich.; F.ILL.MICH.SMITH.WEL.+
Now considered post–1640.

19969 **Pits, John.** A poore mannes beneuolence to the afflicted church. 8⁰. A. Lacy, 1566 (29 ja.) Ent. 1565–66. L².O.C.M.; HN.

19969.2 — A prayer, and also a thankesgiuing vnto God, for preseruing our queene . . . 1577. [Signed J. Pit, *Minister.* In verse.] s.sh.fol. C. Barkar, [1577.] L⁵(Lemon 68).

19969.4 — A prayer or supplication made vnto God by a yonge man, that he woulde be mercifull to vs. [Signed J. Pyttes. In verse.] s.sh.fol. W. Herforde, 1559 (23 mr.) L⁵(Lemon 53).

19969.6 **Pity.** Pitties lamentation for the cruelty of this age. *Ballad.* 2 pts. s.sh.fol. [M. Flesher] f. J. W[right, c. 1625.] C⁶.

Pius II, *Pope* [Enea Silvio Piccolomini]. [De miseria curialium.] *See* 1383.5, 1384, 3546.

19969.8 — [Euryalus and Lucretia. Anon.] 4°. [*Antwerp, J. van Doesborch,* 1515?] L(4 leaves of quire e).E³(frag., missing).

19970 — [Anr. ed.] The goodli history of the moste noble and beautyfull ladye Lucres of Scene in Tuskane. 4°. [*J. Day,* 1553?] L(lacks last leaf).

19971 — [Anr. ed.] The goodly history [etc.] 8°. (*J. Kynge*) 1560. Ent. 10 jn. L.

19972 — [Anr. ed.] The goodli history of . . . Lucres . . . and Eurialus. 8°. (*W. Copland,*) 1567. c⁶.

19972.5 — [Anr. trans. Headline:] A pleasaunt Historie. [In verse.] 8°. [*London,* c. 1570.] ?Ent. to W. Norton 1569–70. DNPK(2 imp. copies of sheet E).
  28 lines a page. The other trans. are prose.

19973 — [Anr. trans.] The historie of Eurialus and Lucretia. Tr. C. Allen. 8°. *T. Cotes f. W. Cooke,* 1639. Ent. 3 oc. 1638. L.O.C.; HN.Y.
  Wing P 2322 is wrong; the imprint date above is genuine.

19974 — [Anr. trans.] The m⟨ost⟩ excell⟨ent⟩ historie, of Euryalus and Lucresia. [*Tr.*] (W. Braunche) 4°. *T. Creede, solde by W. Barley,* 1596. Ent. to T. Creede 19 oc. L.

Pius IV, *Pope. See* 18412.

19974.1 **Pius V,** *Pope.* The braineles blessing of the bull [of 27 Apr. 1570, Regnans in excelsis.] *Ballad.* s.sh.fol. *A. Lacie,* [1570.] Ent. 1570–71. L.

19974.2 — A message, termed Marke the truth of the worde of God, in these .xiii. bloes, at the popes bull [of 27 Apr. 1570, Regnans in excelsis.] 8°. (*W. How f. J. Arenolde,*) [1570.] Ent. 1569–70. c⁵.c⁹.YK.
  Attrib. to T. Norton; *see also* 18678a.
  — [Regarding the bull of 14 Aug. 1567, *see* 18677.5, 18678a, 18679.]

Pius, Thomas. Epistola ad Johannem Housonum. 1603. *See* 19899.

19974.4 **Places.** The severall places where you may hear news. [In verse.] s.sh.fol. [*London,* c. 1640.] c⁶.

Plague. Good councell against the plague. 1592. *See* 5871.3.
  — Present remedies against the plague. 1594, etc. *See* 5871.5 sq.
  — *See also* London, *Bills of Mortality* (16739 sqq.)

19974.5 **Plain Clerk, Thomas,** *Pseud.* A proclamation against the home-loyterers, recusants to the common cause, within the Colledge of Justice. [In verse.] s.sh.fol. [*London,* 1640.] E.

Plain Dealing. Plaine-dealing, or, a precedent of honestie. 1616. *See* pt. 2 of 125.

Planter. The planters plea. 1630. *See* 25399.

Planudes, Maximus. *See* 170.7, 175.

Platin, Claude, *tr. See* 3055.

19974.6 **Plato.** Axiochus. A most excellent dialogue, written in Greeke by Plato [*pseud.*] Tr. by Edw. [Edmund?] Spenser. Heereto is annexed a speech spoken at the tryumphe at White-hall by the page to the earle of Oxenforde. 4°. [*J. Charlewood a. J. Danter*] *f. C. Burbie,* 1592. Ent. 1 my. PFOR.
  Based on the Latin text of R. Welsdalius's ed., 1568. For anr. trans. *see* 18155. Both the trans. and the speech have been attrib. to A. Munday. The triumph was held 22 Jan. 1581; *see also* 13868.5.

19974.8 — Platonis Menexenus, siue, funebris oratio. (Exhortatio ad patriam amandam atᵹ defendendam.) *Lat. a. Greek.* 4°. *Cantebrigiæ, ex off. T. Thomasii,* 1587. L.

19975 — Platoes cap. Cast at this yeare 1604, being leape-yeere. 4°. [*T. Purfoot*] *f. J. Chorlton,* 1604. Ent. to T. Bushell a. J. Charlton 21 mr. L(imp.).O.; HN.JH.
  Dedic. signed 'Adam Eavesdropper.'

19976 **Platt,** *Sir* **Hugh.** The accomplisht ladys delight in preserving, physick and cookery. [Anon. Not by Platt.] = Wing W 3268.

19977 — [Heading:] A briefe apologie of certaine new inuentions. fol. (*R. Field,* 1593.) Ent. 5 mr. L⁵(Lemon 91).
  L⁵ copy pasted in columns; *see also* 19991.

Platt, *Sir* **Hugh—**cont.

19977.3 — [Heading:] Certaine philosophical preparations of foode and beverage for sea-men, in their long voyages. [Init. H. P., *Miles.*] 1/2 sh.fol. [*H. Lownes,* c. 1607.] L¹⁶.; CAL.

19977.7 — Delightes for ladies, to adorne their persons, tables, closets, and distillatories. 12°. *P. Short,* [1600?] Ent. 5 oc. 1599. L. Juel-Jensen.
  (Formerly 19979) Without heading to Table which is in all later eds.

19978 — [Anr. ed.] 12°. *P. Short,* 1602. L.

19978.5 — [Anr. ed.] 12°. *P. Short,* 1603. G².; HN.

19979 — Now = 19977.7.

19979.5 — [Anr. ed.] 12°. *H. L*[*ownes,*] 1605. LEEDS.

19980 — [Anr. ed.] 12°. *H. L*[*ownes,*] 1608. L.; F. Horblit.
  This and following eds. often found bd. w. 5434 sqq.

19981 — [Anr. ed.] 12°. *H. Lownes,* 1609. L.C.LEEDS. Juel-Jensen.; HN.NY.WIS.

19982 — [Anr. ed.] 12°. *H. Lownes,* 1611. L¹⁶.O.LEEDS. Juel-Jensen(imp.).

19983 — [Anr. ed.] 12°. *H. L*[*ownes,*] *sould by A. Johnson,* 1615. L. Bradford PL. Juel-Jensen(imp.).; HN.

19983.3 — [Anr. ed.] 12°. *H. L*[*ownes,*] *sould by A. Johnson,* 1617. Juel-Jensen.; HD.WIS. Kraus.

19983.5 — [Anr. ed.] 12°. *H. Lownes,* 1624. L.; Horblit.

19983.7 — [Anr. ed.] 12°. *H. L*[*ownes*] *a. R. Y*[*oung,*] *sold by J. Boler,* 1628. Ent. to H. Lownes a. R. Young 30 my. 1627. L.LINC.; F.

19984 — [Anr. ed.] 12°. *H. L*[*ownes*] *a. R. Y*[*oung,*] *sold by J. Boler,* 1630. Ass'd to G. Cole a. G. Lathum 6 no. 1628. L(destroyed).O(imp.). Juel-Jensen(imp.).; CHI².

19985 — [Anr. ed.] 12°. *R. Y*[*oung,*] *sold by J. Boler,* 1632. Ass'd to R. Young 6 de. 1630. L.M. Juel-Jensen.; HN.LC(2).PML.

19986 — [Anr. ed.] 12°. *R. Y*[*oung,*] *sold by J. Boler,* 1635. O.; HN.

19987 — [Anr. ed.] 12°. *R. Young,* 1636. L(imp.). Juel-Jensen.

19987.5 — [Anr. ed.] 12°. *R. Young,* 1640. L(tp only, Ames II.1600). G².; HD.

19988 — A discouerie of certaine English wants. 4°. *P. S*[*hort*] *f. W. Ponsonby,* 1595. L.L¹⁰.O. London, Royal Institution of Naval Architects.; F.HN.HD.Y.
  — Diuers chimicall conclusions. 1594. *See* pt. 3 of 19991.

19989 — Diuerse new sorts of soyle. 1594. = pt. 2 of 19991.

19990 — Floraes paradise, beautified and adorned with sundry sorts of delicate fruites and flowers. With an offer of an English antidote. 8°. *H. L*[*ownes*] *f. W. Leake,* 1608. Ent. 18 jn. L.O¹².C³.RGU. Juel-Jensen.; F.HD. WIS.
  Unsold sheets reissued in 1653 w. cancel tp as Wing P 2384.

19990.5 — The floures of philosophie, with the pleasures of poetrie annexed to them. 8°. *H. Bynneman a. F. Coldocke,* 1572. Woburn Abbey, Bedfordshire (imp.).

19990.7 — [Anr. ed.] 8°. *F. Coldocke a. H. Bynneman,* 1581. L.

19991 — The jewell house of art and nature. (Diuerse new sorts of soyle.—Diuers chimicall conclusions.) 3 pts. 4°. *P. Short,* 1594. Ent. 8 au. L.O.C.G²(imp.).M².+; F(imp.).HN.HD.WIS.Y.+
  (Pt. 2 formerly also 19989) *See also* 18787.5, 19977, 19995 for other treatments of Platt's inventions. Some copies (1 O,G²,RD) have a folding leaf repeating the cuts in the text.

19991.5 — [Anr. issue, w. imprint:] *P. Short, sold by W. Ponsonby,* 1594. c.

19992 — Hugonis Platti armig: manuale, sententias aliquot diuinas & morales complectens: partim è sacris Patribus. Partim è Petrarcha decerptas. 16° in 8's. *P. Short,* 1594. Ent. 18 no. L.O.C.C⁵.RD.+; F.HN.HD.

19993 — The new and admirable arte of setting of corne. 4°. *P. Short,* 1600. Ent. 25 no. L.LINC.RD.; BO⁵*.
  A2ʳ line 1 of text ends: 'probably'; C1ʳ line 7 of text ends: 'the'. This is a different setting in all quires from the following items, except 19994.5, q.v. Title varies: ending 'page the following' (L) or 'the page following' (RD).

19993.5 — [Anr. ed.] 4°. *P. Short,* 1600. L(C.54.b.28).O. Cambridge, School of Agriculture.
  A2ʳ line 1 of text ends: 'probable', line 3 has 'new'; C1ʳ line 7 of text ends: 'cause', line 11 has 'wormes'.

Platt, *Sir Hugh—cont.*

19993.7 — [Anr. issue, w. quires C and D reset.] [*P. Short,* 1600?]
L(966.b.15, lacks tp).
Cı[r] line 7 of text ends: 'cause', line 11 has 'wourmes'.

19994 — [Anr. issue, w. quires A and C reset.] *P. Short,* 1601.
L(7077.bbb.34).L[30](lacks tp).RD.; HN.HUNT.WIS.
A2[r] line 1 of text ends: 'problable', line 3 has 'newe'; Cı[r] line 7 of text ends: 'cause', line 11 has 'woormes'.

19994.5 — [A variant of 19993, w. imprint:] *P. Short,* 1601.
London, Royal Agricultural Society.
In the same typesetting, with the same readings as 19993; only the last digit of the date is altered.

19995 — A new, cheape and delicate fire of cole-balles. 4°. *P. Short,* 1603. Ent. 31 de. 1602. L.L[10].G². Juel-Jensen.; F.HN.
See also 19991.

19996 — Sundrie new and artificiall remedies against famine. Written by H. P[latt] Esq. 4°. *P. S[hort,]* 1596. Ent. to P. Short 23 au. L.L[30].O[8].RD. London, Royal Institution of Naval Architects.+; F.HN.CU.HD.NY.+

19997 **Platte, T.** Anne Wallens lamentation, for the murthering of her husband the 22 of June. 1616. *Ballad.* 2 pts. s.sh.fol. *f. H. Gosson,* [1616.] C[6].

19997.5 **Plattes, Gabriel.** Certaine new inventions and profitable experiments necessary to be known of all farmers, and others. [Advertisement where a device can be seen for setting corn and other seeds deep. 6 Apr. 1640. Anon.] s.sh.fol. [*R. Bishop? f. A. Hebb,* 1640.] Ent. as by Plattes to A. Hebb 11 ap. 1640. BO[5].

19998 — A discovery of infinite treasure hidden since the worlds beginning. [On husbandry.] 4°. *J.* L[egat,] *sold by G. Hutton,* 1639. Ent. to J. Legat 10 de. 1638. L.O.BRISTOL².E.RD.+; F.HN.CU.HD.ILL.+
Some copies have cancel tp w. same imprint and added leaf of errata; both at L.

19999 — [A ghost.]

20000 — A discovery of subterraneall treasure, viz. of all manner of mines and mineralls. 4°. *J. Okes f. J. Emery,* 1639. Ent. 22 fb. L.O.C³.D.E.+; F.HN.HD.ILL.NY.+
Unsold sheets reissued in 1653 w. cancel tp as Wing P 2410.

20001 **Platus** or **Piatti, Hieronymus.** The happines of a religious state divided into three bookes. *Tr.* [H. More.] 4°. [*Rouen, J. Cousturier,*] 1632. L.O.C.USHAW.W.+; F.HN.HD.N.Y.+
A&R 653.

20001.5 — [Anr. issue, w. imprint:] [*Rouen,*] *ap. J. Cousturier,* 1632. Holy Cross Abbey, Stapehill, Dorset.
A&R 654.

20002 **Plautus, Titus Maccius.** Menaecmi. A pleasant and fine conceited comædie, taken out of Plautus. Written in English, by W. W[arner.] 4°. *T. Creede, sold by W. Barley,* 1595. Ent. to T. Creede 10 jn. 1594. L.; F(3).HN. Greg 135.
— *See also* 11787.

Play. A mery play betwene Iohan Iohan [etc.] 1533. *See* 13298.
— A mery play betwene the pardoner [etc.] 1533. *See* 13299.
— The most ancient and learned playe, called the philosophers game. 1563. *See* 15542.
— The pleasaunt and wittie playe of the cheasts renewed. 1562. *See* 6214.

20003 **Playfere, Thomas.** The whole sermons of that eloquent divine, of famous memory; T. Playfere. 3 pts. 8°. *T. S(nodham) f. M. Law,* 1623 (1617, 1621.) L.O.C. BRISTOL².ELY.+; CHI.COR.
Pt. 1 in the O copy is a reissue of 20019; in the L copy it is reset, w. sub tp on 16[r] also dated 1623. Pts. 2 and 3 are reissues of 20012, 20006.

20003.5 — Fift edition. 3 pts. 8°. *J. Norton,* (*J.* L[egate a.] *J.* B[eale,]) *sold by J. Bowler,* 1633. Nine Sermons ass'd from C. Legge to J. Boler 1 jn. 1629. DUR[5].; F.
(Pt. 2 formerly also 20013; pt. 3 formerly also 20007)

Playfere, Thomas—cont.

20004 — [A variant, w. gen. tp:] Sixt edition. *J. Norton, sold by J. Bowler,* 1633. L.O.C.D.YK.+; F.HD.ILL.U.WIS.+

20005 — Ten sermons preached by that eloquent divine of famous memorie, T. Playfere. [*Ed.*] (D. C.) 8°. *C. Legge, pr. to the Univ. of Cambridge,* 1610. L.O.C.C⁵.; F.NY[11].Y.
9 sermons only, of which 6, 7, 8, 5 are reprinted from 20026.

20005a — [Anr. ed., w. title:] Nine sermons [etc.] 8°. *C. Legge, pr. to the Univ. of Cambridge,* 1612. L.C.C³.G². LAMPORT.; F(3).HN.

20006 — [Anr. ed.] 8°. *C. Legge, pr. to the Univ. of Camb.,* 1621. O.O².C.C².D.; F.HN.
Also issued as pt. 3 of 20003.

20007 — [Anr. ed.] 1633. = pt. 3 of 20003.5 sq.

20008 — Caesaris superscriptio. Sive conciuncula, coram duobus potentissimis regibus, in superiori atrio splendidae illius domûs, quae vocatur Theobaldus. 4°. [*Eliot's Court Press,*] *imp. J. Bill,* 1606 (30 jy.) Ent. 29 jy. L(1213.l.7(3)).O.C.C³.P.+; HN.Y.

20009 — A funerall sermon, preached 10. May. 1605. = pt. of 20026.

20010 — Hearts delight. A sermon preached at Pauls crosse in Easter terme. 1593. 8°. *J. Legat, pr. to the Univ. of Camb., sold by S. Waterson,* [*London,*] 1603. L⁴.L[15].O.

20011 — [Anr. ed., including:] (The power of praier.—The sick-mans couch.) 8°. *J. Legat, sold by S. Waterson,* 1611. L.C.C³.D.NOR².+; F.PN².Y.
(2nd pt. formerly also 20025a; 3rd pt. formerly also 20027a)

20012 — [Anr. ed.] 8°. *J. Legatt, sold by M. Lawe,* 1617. Ass'd from J. Legat, sen., to jun. 2 ja. 1621. L.O.C.C². G².+; F.HN.CAL(pt. 3 only).CHI.
(3rd pt. formerly also 20027b) Also issued as pt. 2 of 20003.

20013 — [Anr. ed.] 1633. = pt. 2 of 20003.5 sq.

20014 — A most excellent and heauenly sermon: vpon the 23. chapter of the gospell by saint Luke. [Anon.] 8°. [*J. Orwin*] *f. A. Wise,* 1595. O.; HN.
Collates A–G⁸. Wise fined for pr. 2 eds.; see Greg, *Register B,* pp. 51, 57; Arber II.823, 827.

20014.3 — [Anr. ed., w. alterations.] 8°. [*J. Danter*] *f. A. Wise,* 1595. L.; F(tp def.).
Collates A–G⁸ H⁴; A3[r] line 3: 'betraied'.

20014.5 — [Anr. ed.] 8°. [*J. Danter*] *f. A. Wise,* 1595. F.
Collates A–G⁸ H⁴; A3[r] line 3: 'betrayed'.

20015 — [Anr. ed., revised by the author, w. title:] The meane in mourninge. By T. Playfere. 8°. *Widow Orwin f. A. Wise,* 1596. Ent. 30 ap. L².LK.; N.
Issued w. 20020.

20016 — [Anr. ed.] 8°. *J. Roberts f. A. Wise,* 1597. L.C⁴.LK.; HD.

20017 — [Anr. ed., including:] (The pathway to perfection.) 8°. *F. Kyngston f. M. Law,* 1607. Ass'd 25 jn. 1603. L. O.C(imp.).
(2nd pt. formerly also 20022)

20018 — [Anr. ed.] 8°. *T. Haveland f. M. Law,* 1611. L.C.C³.C⁵.; F.LC.SMU.Y.
(2nd pt. formerly also 20023)

20019 — [Anr. ed.] 8°. *N. Okes f. M. Law,* 1616. L.O.C.C².G².+; F.HN.CHI.NY[11].
(2nd pt. formerly also 20024) Also issued as pt. 1 of 20003.

20020 — The pathway to perfection. A sermon. 8°. *Widow Orwin f. A. Wise,* 1596. Ent. 30 ap. L².O.LK.; N.
Issued w. 20015.

20021 — [Anr. ed.] 8°. *J. Roberts f. A. Wise,* 1597. L.O(tp only, Douce Add.142/532).C⁴.LK.; HD.

20022 — [Anr. ed.] 1607. = pt. of 20017.

20023 — [Anr. ed.] 1611. = pt. of 20018.

20024 — [Anr. ed.] 1616. = pt. of 20019.

20025 — The power of praier. A sermon. 8°. *J. Legat, pr. to the Univ. of Camb., sold by S. Waterson,* [*London,*] 1603. L⁴.O.C⁴.; NY[11].

20025a — [Anr. ed.] 1611. = pt. of 20011.

20026 — A sermon preached before the kings majestie at Drayton the sixt day of August. 1605. (A sermon preached the 27. of August. 1605.—A funerall sermon preached 10. May. 1605.—A sermon preached [on Matt.v.19.]) 4°. *C. Legge, pr. to the Univ. of Camb., sold by S. Macham,* [*London,*] 1609. L².O.C.DUL.E².+; F.HN.U.
(3rd pt. formerly also 20009) 1st sermon apparently also issued separately (L,IC,D,YK). Reprinted in 20005.

Playfere, Thomas—*cont.*
20027 — The sick-mans couch. A sermon. 4°. *J. Legat, pr. to the Univ. of Camb., sold by S. Waterson,* [*London,*] 1605. O.O¹⁷.C.C².
20027a — [Anr. ed.] 1611. = pt. of 20011.
20027b — [Anr. ed.] 1617. = pt. of 20012.
20028 — Sufficit. Sive, de misericordia dei. 4°. [*F. Kingston,*] *imp. T. Chard, & venundantur in off. N. Fosbrooke,* 1607 (3 ap.) L.O.C³.D.STU.+; HN.

20028.5 **Playstowe,** *Mr.* Mr. Playstowe's epithalamium; or, the marriage of Pandarus and Flora. *Ballad.* 2 pts. s.sh.fol. *G. E[ld, c.* 1615.] L(on verso of 5612).
See Court-Book C, pp.53–4.

Pleasures. The pleasures of princes. 1614. *See* 17356.

Pleurs. Newes from Italy. Concerning the citty of Pleurs. 1618. *See* 14283.

20029 **Plinius Secundus, Caius.** The [xylographic] historie of the world. *Tr.* P. Holland. The first (second) tome. 2 pts. fol. *A. Islip,* 1601. Ent. 20 my. 1600. L.O.C. D².E².+; F.HN.CU.HD.N.+
20029.5 — [Anr. issue, w. cancel tp, w. imprint:] *imp. G. B[ishop,]* 1601. Bishop's pt. ass'd to T. Adams 14 mr. 1611. O.O²¹.C¹².INN.SH.+; F.HD.NLM.NY.Y.+
20030 — [Anr. ed.] 2 pts. fol. *A. Islip,* 1634. L.O.C.DUR³.E.+; F.HN.CH.CHI.CU.+
20030a — [Anr. issue, w. imprint:] *A. Islip, sold by J. Grismond,* 1635. L.O.C.D.E.+; F.HD.KAN.N.NY.+
20031 — A summarie of the antiquities, and wonders of the worlde, out of the sixtene first bookes of Plinie, *tr.* oute of [the French abridgement by P. de Changy] by I. A. 8°. *H. Denham f. T. Hacket,* [1566.] Ent. 1565–66. L.; HN.
20032 — [Anr. ed.] The secrets and wonders of the world. 4°. [*H. Denham*] *f. T. Hacket,* 1585. L.; HN.
Omits translator's inits. and Changy's dedic.
20033 — [Anr. ed.] 4°. [*J. Wolfe*] *f. T. Hacket,* 1587. L.G².; F(imp.).LC.

20034 **Ploughman.** Here begynneth a lytell geste how the plowman lerned his pater noster. [In verse.] 4°. [*W. de Worde,* 1510.] Ent. to J. Sampson, i.e. Awdley, 14 au. 1560; ass'd to J. Charlewood 15 ja. 1582. C.
20035 — The plough-mans tale. 1606. = 5101.
20036 — The praierand [*sic*] complaynte of the ploweman vnto Christe. [*Ed.* W. Tyndale? or G. Joye?] 8°. [*Antwerp, M. de Keyser,* 1531?] L.; HN.PML.
Preface dated 28 Feb. 1531.
20036.5 — [Anr. ed.] The prayer and . . . vnto Christ. 8°. [*T. Godfrey, c.* 1532.] O.
Preface init. 'w. T.'

20037 **Plowden, Edmund.** Abridgment des touts les cases reportez alarge per monsieur Plowden, composee & digest p T. A[she.] 8°. *in æd. J. Yetsweirt,* [1598?] L.O.C⁵.E.P.+; HN.HD(2).LC.MIN.
1 HD copy has preface, cancelled in most copies.
20038 — [Anr. ed.] 8°. [*A. Islip,*] *f. the Co. of Statrs.,* 1607. Ent. to the English Stock 5 mr. 1620. L.O.C.D.RGU.+; F.HN.HD.MIN.Y.+
20039 — No entry.
20040 — [*Commentaries, Pt.* 1.] 1571. Les comentaries, ou les reportes . . . de dyuers cases [Edw. VI—Eliz.] fol. *in æd. R. Tottelli,* (1571 (24 oc.)) O.C⁷.A.CASHEL. NLW.+; F.HN.CU.HD.MIN.+
1 HD copy has tp w. variant date: 22 oc.
20041 — [Anr. ed.] 1578. . . . Ouesque vn table per W. Fleetewoode. fol. *in æd. R. Tottelli,* (1578 (20 oc.)) L.O⁵.C.D².NLW.+; F.HN.CU.HD.MIN.+
See also 20046.3.
20042 — Now = 20046.3.
20043 — Now = 20046.7.
20044 — [Anr. ed.] fol. *in aed. R. Tottelli,* 1588. Ent. 18 fb. 1583. L.O³.C.C¹².CHATS.+; F.HN.CU.HD.MIN.+
20045 — [Anr. ed.] fol. [*A. Islip*] *in aed. T. Wight & B. Norton,* 1599. L.O.C.D.M.+; HN.HD.LC.MIN.Y.+
20046 — [Anr. ed.] fol. [*A. Islip*] *f. the Co. of Statrs.,* 1613. Ent. to the English Stock 5 mr. 1620. L.O¹⁹.C.D.M².+; F(2).HN.CU.DAR.HD.
(Pt. 2 now = 20047.5)

Plowden, Edmund—*cont.*
20046.3 — [*Commentaries, Pt. 2.* Though paged continuously w. pt. 1, edits. of pt. 2 were pub'd separately and are found bd. w. pt. 1 in various combinations.] Cy ensuont certeyne cases reportes [etc.] (The table by W. Fleetewoode.—Vn report fait per vn vncerteine author.) fol. (*in æd. R. Tottelli,*) 1579 (15 jn.) L. O⁶.C.D².M.+; F.HN.CU.HD.MIN.+
(Formerly 20042) 'Vn report' is in 2 settings: A2ʳ 2nd line below init. begins: 'Henry Bridg3' or 'Henry Bridges'; both at HD.
20046.7 — [Anr. ed.] fol. (*in æd. R. Tottelli,*) 1584 (15 fb.) Ent. 18 fb. 1583. L(destroyed).C(imp.).P. Cambridge, Squire Law Lib.; F.HN.HD(3, 2 imp.).MIN.
(Formerly 20043; 'Vn report' formerly 20049)
20047 — [Anr. ed., w. tp:] 1594 La second part de les reports. fol. [*T. Dawson*] *in æd. C. Yetsweirti,* (1594.) L.O². C.C².D.+; HN.HD.LC(2). Auckland PL.
20047.5 — [Anr. ed.] fol. [*A. Islip*] *f. the Co. of Statrs.,* 1610. Ent. to the English Stock 5 mr. 1620. L.O¹⁹.C.D.M².+; F.HN.CU.DAR.HD.+
(Formerly pt. 2 of 20046)
20048 — Les quæres del mounsieur Plowden. 8°. [*A. Mathewes?*] *f. W. Lee a. D. Pakeman,* [1635?] L.O(2).C.C⁵. Lord Kenyon.; CAL⁵.HD.LC.MIN.Y.+
20049 — Vn report fait per vn vncerteine authour. 1584. = pt. of 20046.7.

Plowman. *See* Ploughman.

20050 **Plummer, Timothy.** The favorite: or, a plaine demonstration of Gods especiall love to the righteous, in a sermon. 8°. *f. S. Man,* 1622. Ent. 2 ja. 1622. L.O. LINC.NOR².; HD.

20051 **Plumptre, Huntingdon.** Epigrammatων opusculum duobus libellis distinctum. Quibus lepôris gratiâ, Homeri Batrachomyomachia Latino carmine reddita, subiungitur. 8°. *typis T. Harper, imp. R. Allot,* 1629. Ent. 17 jn. 1628. L.O.C².ETON.M.+; F.HN.HD. N.NY.+

20052 **Plutarch.** [*De capienda ex inimicis utilitate.*] Howe one may take profite of his enmyes [*sic*], *tr.* [*Sir* T. Elyot?] 8°. (*T. Berthelet,*) [1531?] L.O⁶.C⁷.; HN.HD. Prob. issued w. 4890.5; reprinted in 4891 sq.
20053 — [Anr. trans.] Inimicus amicus: an excellent treatise, shewing, how a man may reape profit by his enemy. [Anon.] 8°. *V. S[immes] f. T. Bushel,* 1601. Ent. 26 ja. HN.
For anr. trans. *see* pt. 2 of 20063.5 sq.
— *See also* 20612.7.
20054 — [*De educatione puerorum.*] Plutarchi Chæronei opusculum de liberorum institutione. Item Isocratis orationes tres. i. Ad Demonicum. ii. Ad Nicoclem. iii. Nicoclis. (Luciani Cupido.) *Greek.* 8°. *ex off. H. Bynneman,* 1581. L.O.D.; ILL.
20054.3 — [Anr. ed.] 8°. [*Eliot's Court Press? c.* 1585.] O(lacks tp).
(Formerly 14273)
20054.5 — [Anr. ed.] 8°. *typis G. Bishop,* 1589. O.
20054.7 — [Anr. ed.] 8°. *R. Field, imp. J. Harrisoni,* 1592. Isocrates ent. to J. Harrison the elder 1 de. 1589; ? to G. Bishop 3 jy. 1591. O.
20055 — [Anr. ed.] 8°. [*Eliot's Court Press?*] *typis G. Bishop,* 1599. L.
20055.5 — [Anr. ed.] 8°. *ex typ. Soc. Stat.,* 1614. ILL.
20055.7 — [Anr. ed.] 8°. [*F. Kingston,*] *ex typ. Soc. Stat.,* 1620. Ent. to the English Stock 5 mr. Athens, Gennadius Lib.
20056 — [Anr. ed.] 8°. [*F. Kingston,*] *ex typ. Soc. Stat.,* 1627. L.C².C⁵.OS.; PH⁶.
20056.5 — [Anr. ed.] 8°. [*F. Kingston,*] *ex typ. Soc. Stat.,* 1635. L(tp only, Ames II.1243). Stevens Cox.
— For other eds. *see* 14274, 14276.5.
20056.7 — [A trans.] The educacion or bringinge vp of children, *tr.* by T. Eliot esɋer, one of yᵉ kingis most honorable counsayle. 4°. (*in the house of T. Berthelet,*) [bef. June, 1530.] N.
20057 — [Anr. ed.] The education . . . *tr.* by syr T. Eliot. 4°. (*in the house of T. Berthelet,*) [1532?] L.O.; HN.
20057.5 — [Anr. trans.] A president for parentes, teaching the vertuous training vp of children and holesome information of yongmen. *Tr.* and partly augmented by E. Grant. 1571. 8°. *H. Bynneman,* (1571.) Ent. 1570–1571. P.; HN.

Plutarch—*cont.*

20058 — [*De recta audiendi ratione*.] Πλουταρχου. . . . Περὶ του ἀκούειν. 8°. *J. Legatus, Acad. Cantab. typog.*, 1595. C.

20058.5 — [*De tranquillitate animi*.] Tho. wyatis translatyon of Plutarckes boke, of the quyete of mynde. 8°. (*R. Pynson*,) [1528.] HN.
Dedic. dated 31 Dec. 1527.

20059 — [Anr. trans.] A philosophicall treatise concerning the quietnes of the mind. *Tr.* out of Greeke into French by J. Amyat. Now turned into English by J. Clapham. 8°. *R. Robinson f. T. Newman*, 1589. O.
For anr. trans. *see* pt. 3 of 20063.5 sq.

20060 — [*De tuenda sanitate praecepta*.] Plutarchi Chaeronensis de tuenda bona valetudine precepta Erasmo Rotero- damo interprete. 4° 8.4. (*in ed. R. Pynson*, 1513 (5 cal. au.)) L. Fribourg U, Switzerland.

20060.5 — [A trans.] The gouernaūce of good helthe, Erasmus beynge interpretoure. 8° in 4's. (*R. Wyer*,) [1549?] O.G². ; Y.
C1r line 1 of text begins: 'thus ordereth'.

20061 — [Anr. ed.] 8° in 4's. (*R. Wyer*,) [c. 1555.] L.L19.C.; HN.
C1r line 1 of text begins: 'Socrates'.

20061.7 —— [*Extracts*.] Practica Plutarche the excellent phylo- sopher. 8° in 6. (*R. Wyer*,) [c. 1545.] L.
(Formerly 20073) Contains most of chap. 2 and the final prescriptions in 20060.5 sq.

20062 —— [Anr. trans.] The preceptes of the excellent clerke & graue philosopher Plutarche for the preseruacion of good healthe. [*Tr.*] (J. Hales.) 8°. *in off. R. Graftoni*, 1543. L.; F.HD(imp.).

20063 — [*Moralia*.] The philosophie, commonlie called, the morals. *Tr.* out of Greeke by P. Holland. fol. *A. Hatfield*, 1603. Ent. to W. Ponsonby 18 ap. 1600; to G. Bishop et al. 5 jy. 1602. L38.O.C.D.E2.+; F.HN.CU. HD.N.+

20063.5 — [Anr. trans.] Three ⟨moral⟩ treatises, no lesse pleasa⟨nt⟩ than necessary, wherof the one is called the learned prince, the other the fruites of foes, the thyrde the porte of rest. [*Tr.*] (T. Blondeuille.) [Pts. 1, 2 in verse.] 3 pts. 4°. *W. Seres*, (1561 (7 jn.)) Fruits of Foes ent. to R. Tottell 1558–59; Learned Prince to W. Seres 11 my. 1561. HN.
For other trans. of pt. 2 *see* 20052 sq.; of pt. 3 *see* 20058.5 sq.

20064 — [Anr. ed.] 8°. *H. Denham*, 1580. L.C.

20065 — [*Vitae parallelae*.] The liues of the noble Grecians and Romanes. *Tr.* out of Greeke into French by J. Amyot, out of French by T. North. fol. *T. Vautroullier*, 1579. Ent. to Vautrollier a. J. Wight 6 ap. O.C2.BIRM2. D.NLW.+; F.HN.ILL.NY.Y.+

20066 — [A variant, w. imprint:] *T. Vautroullier a. [for] J. Wight*, 1579. L.O.C2.BTU.M4.+; F.CAL.HD.N.NY.+

20067 — [Anr. ed.] fol. *R. Field f. B. Norton*, 1595. L.O.C2.M.; F.CU.HD.ILL.Y.+

20067.5 — [A variant, w. imprint:] *R. Field f. T. Wight*, 1595. L.O4.C12.BIRM2.NEK.+; F.HN.PN.WEL.

20068 — [Anr. ed.] Hereunto are also added the lives of Epami- nondas, [etc.] 2 pts. fol. *R. Field f. T. Wight*, 1603. L.O.BED.LEEDS.NOR2.+; F.HD(lacks o7).ILL.LC.Y.+
Pt. 2 is a reissue of 20071, w. var. tp dated 1603 and a table added.

20068a — [A variant, w. imprint:] *R. Field f. G. Bishop*, 1603. L.DUL.; HN.LC.NY.PN.Y.+

20068b — [A variant, w. imprint:] *R. Field f. J. Norton*, 1603. O.O7.C.BIRM.BRISTOL2.+; F.DAR.HART2.ILL.V.

20069 — [Anr. ed.] fol. *R. Field*, 1612 (1610.) Ent. 2 mr. 1607. L.O.C.D.E2.+; F.HN.HD.PN.Y.+

20070 — [Anr. ed.] fol. *G. Miller, sold by R. Allot*, 1631. Ass'd to G. Miller 3 ap. 1626. L.O.C.BIRM.E.+; F.HN.BO2. CHI.NY.+

20071 — The lives of Epaminondas, of Philip of Macedon, [etc.] *Tr.* Sir T. North. fol. *R. Field*, 1602. C2.HAT.; HN.CAL2.
Reissued as pt. 2 of 20068 sqq., q.v.

20072 — The amorous and tragicall tales. *Tr.* J. Sanford. 8°. *H. Bynneman f. L. Maylard*, 1567. L(lacks tp).; F.
Includes a portion trans. from Heliodorus.

20073 — [Appendix.] Practica Plutarche. [c. 1545.] Now = 20061.7.
— *See also* 20612.7.

20074 **Plymouth,** *New England*. A relation or journall of the beginning of the English plantation at Plimoth. [*Ed.*] (G. Mourt.) 4°. [*J. Dawson*] *f. J. Bellamie*, 1622. Ent. 29 jn. L.O.BHP.CHATS.G2.; F.HN.BO.N.NY.+
Copies vary: orig. C1r heading begins 'New-

Plymouth, *New England*—*cont.*
England'; the cancel begins: 'A relation or'; both at NY,Y. This book is advertised in 25855. Quire B reissued in 18484.
— A sermon preached at Plimmoth. 1622. *See* 6149.

20075 **Pocklington, John.** Altare christianum: or, the dead vicars plea. Wherein the vicar of Gr[antham]. being dead, yet speaketh [etc.] 4°. *R. Badger*, 1637. Ent. 7 mr. L(lacks Y2).O.C.A.D.+; F.HN.CHI.HD.U.+
See 13270. The F copy has hand-stamp in red ink below impr.: 'sould by N. Vavasour'. Answered in 20474. Ordered burned 12 Feb. 1641; *see JHL* IV.161,180. Regarding publication of the sermon (Wing B 4316) by W. Bray, the licenser, disavow- ing Pocklington's ideas *see* Greg, *Companion*, p.108.

20076 — Second edition. 4°. *R. Badger*, 1637. L.O.C2.D.G2.+; F.HN.N.PN2.Y.+

20077 — Sunday no Sabbath. A sermon. 4°. *R. Young*, 1636. Ent. 24 fb. L.O.C.D.E.+; F.HN.CHI.PN2.Y.+
Ordered burned w. 20075.

20078 — Second edition. 4°. *R. Young, sold by T. Brisco a. J. Williams*, 1636. L.O.C2.D.E.+; F.HN.HD.N.U.+

Poem. A pleasant poeme of two lovers. 1624. *See* 19886.
— A poeme declaring the real presence of Christ. 1606. *See* 14560.5.

Poemata. Poemata miscellanea. 1612. *See* 13248.2.

20079 **Poeniteas.** Peniteas cito libellus. 4° 8.6. (*per wynadundum* [sic] *de worde*,) [1514?] L.D.; Ravenstree Co., Pasadena, California(Huth copy).

20080 — [Anr. ed.] 4° 8.6. (*per wynandū de worde*,) [1515?] F.
20081 — [Anr. ed.] 4° 8.6. (*per winandū de worde*,) [1516?] L.

Poeton, Edward, *ed. See* 3279.

Poggio, *Fiorentino. See* 170.7, 175, 179.5.

Points. Certaine easie and profitable points in husbandrie. 1637. *See* 22391.3.

20082 **Pointz, Robert.** Testimonies for the real presence of Christes body and blood . . . *tr.*, out of six auncient fathers with certain notes. 8°. *Louanii, ap. J. Foulerum*, 1566. L.O.M.P.W.+; F.HN.TEX. A&R 656.

20083 **Poland.** Newes from Poland. 1621. Now = Newsbooks 35A.

20083.3 — [*Socinian Churches*.] Catechesis ecclesiarum quæ in regno Poloniæ . . . affirmant, patrem domini nostri Jesu Christi, esse illum unum Deum Israëlis: [etc.] [By H. Moscorovius, i.e. Moskorzewski.] 12°. *Racoviæ*, 1609 [i.e. *London, H. Lownes*, 1614?] L.O. O3.O17.O21.; HD. 𝕬
279 pp. There are 2 eds. w. this imprint pr. abroad, both w. 317 pp.

Polano, Pietro Soave. *See* 21760, 21761.

20083.5 **Polanus, Amandus.** Amandi Polani a Polansdorf par- titiones theologicæ iuxta naturalis methodi leges conformatæ duobus libris. Editio secunda, auctior. 8°. *per E. Bollifantum*, 1591. Ent. 10 ap. L(tp only, Ames I.510).C.C7.P.; HD.

20083.7 — [A trans.] The substance of christian religion, soundly set forth in two bookes, by definitions and partitions, framed according to the rules of a naturall method. *Tr.* E. W(ilcocks.) 8°. *R. F[ield] f. J. Oxenbridge*, 1595. Ent. 25 oc. 1594. O.; U.

20083.9 — Second edition corrected and augmented. 8°. *R. F[ield] f. J. Oxenbridge*, 1597. L.

20084 — [Anr. ed., enlarged, w. new prelims.] [*Ed.*] (T. Wilcocks.) 8°. *A. Hatfield f. F. Norton*, 1600. Ass'd 1 se. L.NLW.; F.HN.BO(lacks tp).HART.ILL.
See Greg, *Register B*, p.76.

20085 — [Anr. ed.] According to the last edition, lately cor- rected. 8°. *A. Hatfield f. W. Aspley*, 1608. Ass'd 28 ja. 1605. L2.O.; HD.

20086 — A treatise of Amandus Polanus, concerning Gods eternal predestination. [*Tr.*] (R. Gostwyke.) 8°. *J. Legat, pr. to the Univ. of Camb.*, 1599. L.L4.O.O28 (Bed.).E.+; HD.N.SMU.

20087 **Pole, Reginald,** *Cardinal.* The seditious and blasphemous oration of cardinal Pole intytuled the defence of the eclesiastical vnitye. *Tr.* F. Wythers. 8°. (*O. Rogers,*) [1560.] Ent. 2 se. 1560. L.L².C.C⁵.M.+; F.HN.

20088 — A treatie [*sic*] of iustification. Founde emong the writings of cardinal Pole. Item, certaine translations touching the said matter of iustification. [By SS. Augustine, Basil, Cyprian, John Chrysostom, Pope Leo I. *Tr.* Sir T. Copley?] 4°. *Louanii, ap. J. Foulerum,* 1569. L(imp.).O.C.D².YK.+; TEX.
(Formerly also 24245) A&R 657.

20088.5 — The trew copy of the transumpt [*sic*], or wrytinge of late sente to the byshoppe of London, by the lorde cardinal Pole concerning the due vse of confessionals. Anno (1557) 6 idus Ian. s.sh.fol. *in aed. J. Cawodi,* [1557.] C⁷(MS.III.159).
— *See also* 10149.

20089 **Polemon, John.** All the famous battels that haue bene fought in our age. 4°. *H. Bynneman & F. Coldock,* [1578.] Ent. to Bynneman 1 jy. 1577. L.O.C.D(impr. def.).P.+; F.HN.CAL(imp.).

20090 — The second part of the booke of battailes, fought in our age. [Anon.] 4°. [*T. East*] *f. G. Cawood,* 1587. Ent. 10 ja. L.O.C.E².P.; F.HN.BO.N.Y.+

Politianus, Angelus, *tr. See* 761.

Politique. La politique reforme. 1589. *See* 11371.5.

20091 **Pollard, Leonard.** Fyue homilies of late, made by a ryght good and vertuous clerke, called master L. Pollarde. 4°. (*W. Gryffyth,*) 1556. L.L²(imp.).C³.BUTE.; F.
Contains same inits. as 3375 and may have been pr. by W. Powell.

Polo, Gaspar Gil. *See* Gil Polo, G.

20092 **Polo, Marco.** The most noble and famous trauels of Marcus Paulus, into the east partes of the world. *Tr.* (J. Frampton.) 4°. [*H. Bynneman f.*] *R. Newbery,* 1579. Ent. 3 de. 1578. L(2, 1 imp.).L².C¹³.; HD.MIN.WIS.

20092.5 **Polotzk.** A true reporte of the taking of the great towne and castell of Polotzko, by the king of Polonia. With the manner of the assaults from the 11. of August to the 30. of the same month. 1579. 8°. [*London,* 1579.] L.

20093 **Polter, Richard.** The pathway to perfect sayling. Being the six principall pointes, concerning navigation. 4°. *E. Allde f. J. Tappe,* 1605. Ent. 12 fb. L(2).; NY.
1 L copy has MS. attribution to W. Borough.

20094 **Poltrot, Jean de.** An answere to the examination. 1563. = 5553.

20095 **Polyander, John.** A disputation against the adoration of the reliques of saints departed. *Tr.* H. Hexham. 8°. *Dordrecht, G. Walters,* 1611. C.C³.; HD.

20096 — The refutation of an epistle, written by a doctor of the Augustins order. *Tr.* H. Hexham. 4°. *F. K[ingston] f. T. Man,* 1610. Ent. 19 ja. O.C².D.DUR(Bamb.).M.+; F(imp.).HD.

20097 **Polybius.** The hystories of the most famous and worthy cronographer Polybius: discoursing of the warres betwixt the Romanes & Carthaginenses. Englished by C. W(atson.) Annexed an abstract of the worthy acts perpetrate by king Henry the fift. 8°. *H. Bynneman f. T. Hacket,* (1568.) Ent. 1565–66. L(2).O.; F.HN.HD(imp.).

20098 — The history of Polybius. *Tr.* [from the *Fr.* of L. Meigret] by E. Grimeston. fol. *N. Okes f. S. Waterson,* 1633. Ent. to Waterson a. Okes 30 ap. O.; HN.BOWDOIN.LC. Missouri U.

20099 — [A variant, w. imprint:] *N. Okes f. S. Waterson,* 1634. L.O⁷.C⁵.BIRM.E.+; F.HN.CHI.HD.Y.+

20099a — [A variant, w. imprint:] *N. Okes f. C. Bee,* 1634. L.O.C.E².NEK.+; F.HN.N.NY. Amherst C.+

20099a.5 — [Anr. issue, w. cancel tp:] The antient and noble historian Polybius. *T. Cotes f. J. Waterson,* 1635. O.

Pomander. The pomāder of prayer. [By T. Becon.] 1558, etc. *See* 1744 sqq.
— The pomander of prayer. [*Ed.* R. Whitford.] 1528, etc. *See* 25421.2 sqq.

Pomerane, John. A compēdious letter. [1536.] *See* 4021.

Pond, Edward. Almanacks. 1601, etc. *See* 501 sqq.
— *See also* 1547.

Ponet, John, *Bp. See* Poynet, J.

20100 **Pont, Robert.** Against sacrilege, three sermons preached by R. Pont. 8°. *Edinburgh, R. Waldegraue,* 1599. D.E.E².G².LINC.+; F.

20101 — De sabbaticorum annorum periodis chronologica digestio. 4°. *per G. Jones,* 1619. Ent. 2 fb. L.O.C.D.E.+; MICH.U.

20102 — [Anr. issue, w. cancel tp, w. imprint:] *per G. Jones pro M. Sparke,* 1626. L.O⁴.O¹¹.A.STU.

20103 — De unione Britanniæ, seu de regnorum Angliæ et Scotię consolidatione, dialogus. 8°. *Edinburgi, R. Charterus* [sic], 1604. L.O.D.E.M⁴.+; F.HN.HART.NY⁸. Dickinson C.

20104 — A newe treatise of the right reckoning of yeares, and ages of the world. 4°. *Edinburgh, R. Walde-graue,* 1599. L.O.C.D.E.+; F.HN.ILL.NY⁴.

20105 — Paruus catechismus quo examinari possunt iuniores qui ad sacram cœnam admittuntur. [Init. R. P.] 8°. *Andreapoli, R. Lekpreuik,* 1573. E.
— *ed. See* 2765.5.

Pont, Timothy. *See* 17827.

20106 **Pontanus, Lodovicus.** Meditations. 1610. = 20485.

Pontanus, Robert. *See* Pont, R.

20106.5 **Pont-aymery, Alexandre de.** A state discourse vpon the late hurt of the French king. *Tr.* out of French, by E. A[ggas.] 4°. [*E. Allde*] *f. E. Aggas,* 1595. Ent. 21 ja. O.; F.

20107 **Ponthus.** [The noble history of king Ponthus. *Tr.* H. Watson?] 4° ⁸·⁴. [*W. de Worde,* 1509?] O(d⁴ only). Signatures in lower case.

20107.5 — [Anr. ed.] 4° ⁸·⁴. [*R. Pynson?* c. 1510.] O(I2,6 only, Douce frag. f. 53).
(Formerly 23435a) Signatures in upper case; I2ʳ last line ends: 'that he wold ha⟨ve⟩'.

20108 — [Anr. ed.] [Q8ᵛ:] (Here endeth the noble hystory of . . . kynge Ponthus of Galyce & of lytell Brytayne.) 4° ⁸·⁴. (*W. de Worde,* 1511.) O(lacks tp).
Signatures in upper case; I2ʳ last line ends: 'come play you'.

20109 **Ponticus, Ludovicus Virunius.** Pontici Virunnii viri doctissimi Britannicæ historiæ libri sex, quibus præfixius est catalogus regum Britanniæ: per Dauidem Pouelum. (Itinerarium Cambriæ: . . . auctore Giraldo Cambrense.—Cambriæ descriptio.) 8°. *ap. E. Bollifantum, imp. H. Denhami & R. Nuberij,* 1585. L.O.C.D.G².+; F.HN.HD.N.NY.+
The main text is actually an abridgement by Ponticus of Geoffrey of Monmouth.

Poole, Timothy, *ed. See* 14472.

Poor. The poores lamentation for the death of Elizabeth. 1603. *See* 7594.

Poor Man. The poore-mans plaster-box. 1634. *See* 12942.

20110 **Pope.** A blowe for the pope, touching the popes prerogatives. Extracted out of the Booke of Martyres [11222 sqq.] 4°. *Edinburgh, J. Wreittoune,* 1631. L. E(2).E².E⁸.
— A commission sent to the pope. 1586. *See* 21769.

20111 — A gagge for the pope, and the jesuits. 4°. *J. D[awson] f. E. Blackmore,* 1624. Ent. as by 'H.G.' to N. Bourne a. E. Blackmore 25 ja. L.O.D.G².P.+; F.HN. AAS.HD.U.+

20112 — A new-yeeres-gift forthe [*sic*] pope. *Ballad.* 2 pts. s.sh.fol. [*London,* c. 1625.] C⁶(pt. 1 only).
— The popes complaint to his minion cardinals. [1620?] *See* 19483.
— The pope confuted. 1580. *See* 11241.

20112.5 — The popes eschucheon, or coate of armes. *Ballad.* s.sh.fol. [*S. Stafford,* 1606.] Ent. to S. Stafford 17 fb. 1606. L.

20113 — The popes new-years gifts, anno 1622. *Tr.* G. L[auder?] 4°. *Sainct-Andrewes, E. Raban,* 1622. E(2).

20113.5 — The popes pyramides. The fruites of Rome, thou here protractur'd [*sic*] seest, [etc. Woodcut w. verses.] s.sh.fol. [*R. Shorleyker,* 1624?] L⁵(Lemon 248).
— The popes wound is deadly. 1624. *See* 24912.5.
— Prosopopoeia. Or, a conference between the pope, [etc. 1619?] *See* 20443.
— Den sack met die stucken voor den Paus van Roomen. 1578. *See* 6581.

Popery. The beginning and ending of all poperie. [1548?] *See* 17115.
— A pill to purge out poperie. 1623. *See* 17858.

20114 **Popes.** A solemne contestation of diuerse popes, out of their own canon law. 8º. *J. Daye,* [1560.] Ent. 26 se. 1560. L.O.DUR⁵.ETON.P.+; F.HN.LC.ILL.
ETON copy dated in MS. 26 Sept. 1560; MS. note in DUR⁵ copy attributes this to J. Foxe.

20115 **Popham, Edward.** A looking-glasse for the soule. 12º. *T. S[nodham] f. N. Newbery,* 1619. Ent. 22 mr. O.

Popish Idolatry. The originall of popish idolatrie. 1630. *See* 4748.

20116 **Porcia, Jacopo di,** *Count.* The preceptes of warre, set-forth [*sic*] by James the erle of Purlilia, and trāslated into englysh by P. Betham. 1544. 8º. (*E. Whytchurche, solde by W. Telotson,*) [1544.] O.C.; HN.

20117 **Porder, Richard.** A sermon of gods fearefull threatnings for idolatrye. 8º. *H. Denham,* (1570.) Ent. 1569–70. L.L³⁰.; F(2).
— *tr. See* 886.

20118 **Porta, Giovanni Battista della.** De furtiuis literarum notis. 4º. *ap. J. Wolphium,* 1591. Ent. 2 no. 1590. L.O.C.D.E.+; F.COR.FBL.HD.ILL.+
Dedic. to Earl of Northumberland by J. Castel-vetro.

20118a — [Anr. issue, w. imprint:] *Neapoli, ap. Io. Mar. Scotum,* 1563 [*London, J. Wolf,* 1591.] L.O.; F.HN.
Imprint and dedic. to Joannes Sotus copied from the Naples, 1563 ed. Wolf's reprint has a mask orn. on tp while the orig. tp has arms of the king-dom of Naples.
— *See also* 21445, 24100.

20119 **Portau, Thomas.** A declaration . . . of the conversion of M. du Tertre. 1616. Now = 7371.5.

20120 **Porteous.** Here endis the Porteous of noblenes. 1508. Now = 5060.5.

20121 Now = 20124.5.

20121.5 **Porter, Henry.** The pleasant historie of the two angrie women of Abington. 4º. [*E. Allde*] *f. J. Hunt a. W. Ferbrand,* 1599. L(2, 1 imp.).L⁶(imp.).; F.HN.HD. Greg 161.
(Formerly 20123)

20122 — [Anr. ed.] 4º. [*E. Allde*] *f. W. Ferbrand,* 1599. L.O.C⁶. ETON.LEEDS.+; F.HN.CH.N(imp.).PFOR.

20123 — Now = 20121.5.

20124 **Porter, Jerome.** The flowers of the lives of the most renowned saincts of England Scotland, and Ireland. The first tome. 4º. *Doway,* 1632. L.O.C.E².M.+; F. HN.HD.N.NY¹¹.+
A&R 658. No more printed.

Porter, Thomas. An almanack. 1585. *See* 501.32.

20124.5 **Porter, Walter.** Madrigales and ayres. Of two, three, foure and five voyces, with the continued base, with toccatos, sinfonias and rittornellos to them. 6 ptbks. 4º. *W. Stansby,* 1632. L.; F(tenor only).
(Formerly 20121)

20125 **Portius, Placentius.** Pugna porcorum per Placentium Portium poetam. [In verse.] 8º. (*imp. T. Woodcock,*) 1586. C.

20126 **Portrait.** Le vray purtraict d'un ver monstrueux qui a esté trouué dans le cœur d'un cheual qui est mort en Londres le 17. de Mars. 1586. s.sh.fol. *chez J. Wolfe,* [1586.] HN.

20126.3 **Portraiture.** A true purtraiture of sundrie coynes found the 8 of April 1611. in the Harkirke [Sefton, Lancs.] [Engr.] s.sh.fol. [*London,* 1611.] M(deposit).

20126.7 — The true portraiture of the valiant English soldiers in their proceedings to the wars for the seruice of their prince; and honour of their countrey. [Woodcuts w. verses.] s.sh.fol. [*London,* 1588?] ? Ent. to J. Wolfe 9 jy. 1588. C⁶(2973/396–97).
— A very lively portrayture, of the arch-bishops, [etc.] 1640. *See* 10406.

Portraitures. The pourtraitures at large of nine moderne worthies. 1622. *See* 24602.

20127 **Portskewett.** A right strange and woonderful example of the handie worke of God, by the birth of three chil-dren, borne in Paskewet, in Monmouth. 4º. *R. Jones,* 1585. L(tp only).

Portsmouth. The exemplification of the letters, pattents, for Portesmouth. [1580.] *See* 8121.

Portugal. The historie of the uniting of Portugal to the crowne of Castill. 1600. *See* 5624.
— Of the new lādes. [1520?] *See* 7677.

20128 — The true copie of an edict, made by the king of Spaine, concerning the new christians dwelling in Portugall. *Tr.* out of the Portugall language. 1602. 4º. *R. B[lower] f. T. Pavier,* [1602.] Ent. to R. Blower 18 jn. 1602. L.O.

Pory, John, *tr. See* 15481.

Positions. Daungerous positions and proceedings. 1593. *See* 1344.

20128.3 **Posselius, Johannes.** Οἰκέων διαλογων βιβλιον ἑλληνιστι και Ῥωμαιστι. Familiarium colloquiorum libellus Graecè et Latinè auctus. 8º. *in off. Soc. Bibliop.,* 1622. Ent. 14 jn. C⁵.

20128.5 — [Anr. ed.] 8º. *in off. Soc. Bibliop.,* 1630. BIRM²(K.N.).; BO.

20128.7 — [Anr. ed.] 8º. *in off. Soc. Bibliop.,* 1635. L(tp only, Ames II.1292).C².; F.

20129 — [A trans.] Dialogues containing all the most usefull words of the Latine tongue. Construed into English. [By] (E. Rive.) 4º. *E. Allde, sold by Christ-Church greater South doore* [i.e. *by E. Rive,*] 1623. Ent. 14 jn. L.L⁴.O.C.; Y.

20130 — Johannis Posselii Σύνταξις Graeca, . . . unà cum Varennii tractatu. 8º. *Cantabrigiæ, ex off. R. Danielis, prostant ap. F. Eaglesfield,* [*London,*] 1640. L.O⁵.C.A.DUR³.+; HN.HD.ILL.PH.Y.+

20130.5 **Possevino, Antonio.** A treatise of the holy sacrifice of the altar, called the masse. *Tr.* T. Butler. 12º. *Louanii, ap. J. Foulerum,* 1570. O²¹.OS.ST.; F(imp.).
A&R 659.

20131 **Postil.** A postill or collection of moste godly doctrine. 1550. = 5806.
— A new postil. 1566. *See* 1736.

20131.5 **Posy.** A posie of rare flowers, gathered by a young-man for his mistrisse. *Ballad.* 2 pts. s.sh.fol. *f. H. Gosson,* [c. 1630.] Ent. to J. Wright 12 ap. 1627. C⁶.

20132 — [Anr. ed.] 2 pts. s.sh.fol. *f. H. G[osson, c. 1630.]* L.

20132.5 **Potion.** A potion for the heart-plague, as a soueraigne remedie for the other: set downe in a letter sent vnto the humble in spirit. 8º. *A. Hatfield f. S. Waterson,* 1603. Ent. 9 au. O.O⁹(pt. of sheet A only, in i.10.7). Ent. under heading of text: 'To all that loue [etc.]'. Author's name on B5ᵛ: T. Darling.

Pots, Richard. *See* 22791.

20133 **Potter, Barnaby,** *Bp.* The baronets buriall, or a funerall sermon at Sʳ Edward Seymours buriall. 4º. *Oxford, J. Barnes,* 1613. L.L³.O.O¹⁰.P.+; F.HN.NY¹¹.Y.
— *See also* 10173, 10174.

20134 **Potter, Christopher.** A sermon preached at the con-secration of B. Potter bishop of Carlisle. Hereunto is added an advertisement touching [21766]. 8º. [*M. Flesher*] *f. J. Clarke,* 1629. L.O.C².D.E.+; F.HN.NY¹¹. Y.
Tp may be a cancel.

20135 — Want of charitie justly charged, on all such Romanists, as dare affirme, that protestancie destroyeth salva-tion. In answer to a late popish pamphlet Charity mistaken [25774]. 8º. *Oxford, prs. to the Univ. f. W. Webb,* 1633. Ent. to J. Clarke 1 au. L².O⁴.C.D.DUR.+; F.HD.NY¹¹.U.Y.
Answered by 25778.

20135.3 — [A variant, w. imprint:] *Oxford, prs. to the Univ.,* 1633. O.DUR⁵.YK.; F.HD.

20135.7 — [Anr. issue, w. imprint:] *Oxford, prs. to the Univ., sold by J. Clarke,* [*London,*] 1633. L.O.C².D.E.+; F. HN.ILL. 𝔄

20136 — Second edition, revised [at the suggestion of Bp. Laud.] 8º. *M. F[lesher] f. J. Clarke, sould by W. Webb,* [*Oxford,*] 1634. L.O².C.D².E².+; F.HN.

20136.3 — [A variant, w. imprint:] *M. F[lesher] f. J. Clarke,* 1634. L.O.C².D.G⁴.+; F.CU.HD.U.Y.+

Potter, Christopher—*cont.*

20136.7 — [A variant, w. imprint:] *M. Flesher f. W. Webb,* [*Oxford,*] 1634. O³.D.; HN.
— *ed. See* 244, 245.
— *tr. See* 21766.
— *See also* 19014.5.

20137 **Potter, Thomas.** An exposition vpon the Cxxx. psalme. *Tr. T. Potter.* 1577. Now = 16979.3.
— *tr. See* 4070.

20138 **Potts, Thomas.** The wonderfull discoverie of witches in the countie of Lancaster. 4°. *W. Stansby f. J. Barnes,* 1613 (1612.) Ent. 7 no. 1612. L.L³⁸.O(3).E.G².; F(lacks tp).HN.HD.N.Y.+
Most copies (2 O,HD) have the title signed 'Thomas Potts' and errata on A4ʳ. The 3rd O copy (4°.W. 9(2)Art.) is an earlier variant with 'T. P. Esquier' on the tp and A4ʳ blank.

Poullain, Valérand, *ed. See* 16566, 16573.
— *tr. See* 18311, 18312.

Poverty. A newe interlude of impacyente pouerte. [1560.] *See* 14112.5.

20139 **Pow, Gaspar.** Gaaspar Pow . . . ad hec cõmissariꝰ [etc.] [1502.] Now = *Indulgences* 144.

Powel, Daniel. *See* Powell, D.

Powel, David, *ed. See* 4606, 20109.

20140 **Powel, Edward.** Propugnaculum summi sacerdotij euangelici, . . . aduersus M. Lutherum. 4°. (*in ed. Pynsonianis,* 1523 (3 no[nas] de.) L.O.C.G².R.+; F.N.

20141 **Powel, Gabriel.** The catholikes supplication vnto the kings majestie; for toleration of catholike religion in England: with short notes. Whereunto is annexed parallel-wise, a Supplicatorie counterpoyse of the protestants. 4°. *F. Kyngston f. E. Weaver,* 1603. Ent. 1 jn. L.O².C.E.M².+; F.HART.N.U. 𝔄
Supplication begins: 'Such are the rare perfections . . .'; cf. 20144. *See also* 18292.
20141.3 — [Anr. issue.] *F. Kyngston f. E. Weaver,* 1603. L².O.C. D².E.+; F.HN.HD.LC.Y. 𝔄
20141.5 — [Anr. issue, w. the same imprint.] *See* Addenda.
20142 — A consideration of the deprived and silenced ministers arguments, for their restitution . . . exhibited in their late supplication, unto parliament [7736]. 4°. *G. Eld f. T. Adams,* 1606. Ent. 4 ap. L.O.C.A.D.+; F.HN. BO.MCG.U.
Answered in 3522.
— A myld defence of certeyne arguments, . . . against an intemperat consideration by G. Powell. 1606. *See* 3522.
20143 — A rejoynder unto the mild defence. [1607.] = pt. of 20146.
20144 — A consideration of the papists reasons for toleration of poperie in England, intimated in their Supplication vnto the kings majestie [14432]. 4°. *Oxford, J. Barnes, sold by S. Waterson,* [*London,*] 1604. L.O.C.G².M².+; F.TEX.U.
Supplication begins: 'So many causes concurre . . .'; cf. 20141.
20145 — Gabrielis Poueli Ordovicis Britanni, de adiaphoris theses theologicæ ac scholasticæ. 8°. *R. Barkerus,* 1606. L².O¹⁰.C.D.YK.+; HN.
20146 — [A trans.] De adiaphoris. Theological and scholastical positions, concerning things indifferent. *Tr. T. J[ackson, Dean of Peterborough?]* (A rejoynder unto the mild defence [3522.]) 4°. *F. Kyngston f. E. White,* 1607. Ent. 3 mr. L.O.C².D.YK.+; F. Detroit PL.
(2nd pt. formerly also 20143) Has half-title: 'Two profitable and necessarie treatises'.
20146.5 — G. Poueli Ordovicis Britanni, de extremo humiliationis Christi actu . . . theses theologicae ac scholasticae. 8°. *Hanoviae, ap. J. Radaeum* [*Oxford, J. Barnes,*] 1602. O.O¹¹(6).O¹⁴(2).
All copies are of sheet A only.
20147 — Gabrielis Poueli . . . disputationum theologicarum & scholasticarum de Antichristo & eius ecclesia, libri II. 8°. *ex typog. J. Windeti, imp. T. Man,* 1605. L. O.C.D.E.+; U.Y.
20147.5 — The mysterie of redemption. . . . With divers sweet and comfortable prayers. 12°. *F. Kyngston f. W. Cotton,* 1607. Ent. 24 no. 1606. F.

Powel, Gabriel—*cont.*

20148 — Prodromus. A logicall resolution of the I. chap. of the epistle unto the Romanes. 8°. *Oxford, Jos. Barnes, soulde by John Barnes,* [*London,*] 1602. L(destroyed). L².L³.O.C.WOR.+; HN.PN².
20149 — A refutation of an epistle apologeticall [10431.5]. 4°. *A. Hatfield f. T. Man, Junior,* 1605. L².O.C².D.E.+; F.HN.HART.HD.U.+
Includes text of the Epistle.
20150 — The resolved christian, exhorting to resolution. 8°. *V. S[immes] f. T. Bushel,* 1600. Ent. 26 ap. O.M.; F.HN.
20151 — [Anr. ed.] Corrected and enlarged. The third edition. 8°. *V. S[immes] f. T. Bushel,* 1602. L(tp only, Harl. 5993/107). L².BIRM²(K.N.).NLW.YK.; F.
20151.5 — Fourth edition. 8°. *f. T. Bushell,* 1603. U(imp.).
20152 — Fift edition. 12°. [*M. Bradwood*] *f. W. Cotton,* 1607. Ent. 25 se. 1605. L².C.BRISTOL².
20153 — [Anr. ed.] 8°. *T. S[nodham] f. R. Moore,* 1616. L.L⁴⁶. C².; U.
20154 — [Anr. ed.] 8°. *T. S[nodham] f. R. Moore,* 1623. Ent. to W. Barrett 16 fb. 1617. L.C.C⁴.NLW.; F.HN.MICH.NY.
20155 — Theologicall and scholasticall positions concerning usurie. 8°. *Oxford, Jos. Barnes, solde by John Barnes,* [*London,*] 1602. L.
20155.5 — [Anr. ed.] 8°. *Oxford, Jos. Barnes* [*London, V. Simmes,*] *sold by John Barnes,* 1602. L².O.C.C¹⁰.; HD.
20156 — Theologicall positions concerning the lawfulnesse of borrowing upon usurie. 8°. *F. Kingston f. E. Weaver,* 1605. Ent. 27 my. L.L².L³⁰.L⁴³.C.; HN.LC.
A different work from 20155.
— Two profitable and necessarie treatises. *See* 20146.

20157 **Powel, Griffinus.** Analysis analyticorum posteriorum sive librorum Aristotelis de demonstratione. 8°. *Oxoniæ, J. Barnesius,* 1594. O.O¹⁸.C.C².LEIC.
(Formerly also 756)
20157.5 — Editio secunda. 8°. *Oxoniæ, J. L[ichfield,] imp. H. Cripps,* 1631. O.O⁴.O¹⁸.C.M².+; ILL.STL.
(Formerly 757)
20158 — Analysis lib. Aristotelis de sophisticis elenchis. 8°. *Oxoniæ, ex off. J. Barnesii,* 1598. L.L²(2).O.O²⁴.; HN.

20158.5 **Powel, Joan.** The ⟨t⟩rue reporte, ⟨an⟩d tragicall discourse of ⟨Jo⟩an Powel mayden, late dwelling in the olde Baylie in London. 8°. *J. Wolfe f. H. Kirkham,* [1582?] Ent. 14 de. 1581. L(tp only, Harl.5927/27).

Powell, C. *See* 15164a.5.

20159 **Powell, Daniel.** The love of Wales to their soveraigne prince, expressed in a true relation of the solemnity held at Ludlow. 4°. *N. Okes,* 1616. O.; HN.
— The redemption of lost time. [*Tr.*] (D. Powel.) 1608. *See* 20825.

Powell, John. The assize of bread. Newly corrected. 1592, etc. *See* 870 sqq.

20160 **Powell, Robert.** Depopulation arraigned, convicted and condemned, by the lawes of God and man. 8°. *R. B[adger,]* 1636. Ent. to T. Badger 16 my. L.L³⁰.O. C.C³.+; F.HN.CHI².CU.HD(imp.).+
20161 — The life of Alfred, or Alvred. Together w. a parallell of K. Charles. 12°. *R. Badger f. T. Alchorn,* 1634. Ent. 21 jn. L.O.C.D².E.+; F.HN.HD.N.NY.+

20162 **Powell, Thomas,** *Londino-Cambrensis.* The art of thriving. Or, the plaine path-way to preferment. Together with the mysterie and misery of lending and borrowing. 8°. *T. H(arper) f. B. Fisher,* 1635 (1636.) F.HN.CU.PN².
Reprinted from 20168, 20171.
20163 — The attourneys academy: or, the manner and forme of proceeding, upon any suite. 4°. [*G. Purslow*] *f. B. Fisher,* 1623. L.O.BRISTOL².NLW(lacks errata).WOR. +; F.HN.CU. 𝔄
With extra leaf of errata; B2ʳ last line: 'Proces'. *See* Greg, *Companion,* pp.218–19.
20163.5 — [Anr. ed.] 4°. [*N. Okes a. B. Alsop*] *f. B. Fisher,* 1623. L¹³.O.D.M.NLW(St. Asaph).+; F.COR.FBL.HD.ILL.+
No errata; B2ʳ last line: 'Processe'. Okes pr. through quire Z.
20164 — Third impression corrected w. additions of the Verge Court. 4°. [*B. Alsop a. T. Fawcet*] *f. B. Fisher,* 1630. L.L³⁰.O.C.; BO.HART²(imp.)*.HD.NYS.
A1ᵛ orn. at bottom w. cherub's head in foliage.

Powell, Thomas, *Londino-Cambrensis—cont.*

20164a — [Anr. ed.] Third impression. 4°. [*B. Alsop a. T. Fawcet*] *f. B. Fisher,* 1630. L.O.C⁵.D².M².+; F.ILL.Y.
A1ᵛ orn. at bottom w. bird upside down and foliage.

20164a.5 — [Anr. ed.] Third impression. 4°. [*B. Alsop a. T. Fawcet*] *f. B. Fisher,* 1630. L⁸.O⁶(imp.).C.C².E.; HN. LC.
A1ᵛ orn. at bottom w. interlocking circles and flowers at ends.

20165 — The attornies almanacke. Provided & desired for the use of all such as shall remove any cause from an inferiour court to any higher. 4°. *B. A*[*lsop*] *a. T. F*[*awcet*]*f. B. Fisher,* 1627. Ent. 30 ap. L.O.C.D.E.+; F.HN.HD.N.Y.+

20166 — Direction for search of records. 4°. *B. A*[*lsop*] *f. P. Man,* 1622. Ent. to Alsop a. P. Man 18 jy. L.O.C.D². E.+; F.HN.BR.HD.N.+
See Greg, Companion, pp. 218–19.

20166.5 — Loues leprosie. [Etc. In verse.] 4°. *W. White,* 1598. N.

20167 — The passionate poet. With a description of the Thracian Ismarus. [In verse.] 4°. *V. Simmes,* 1601. HN.
— The repertorie of records. [*Ed.* T. Powell.] 1631. *See* 194.

20168 — Tom of all trades. Or the plaine path-way to preferment. 4°. *B. Alsop a. T. Fawcet f. B. Fisher,* 1631. L.O.C².D.E².+; F.HN.CHI.HD.Y.
Reprinted in 20162.

20169 — Vertues due: or, a true modell of the life of Katharine Howard. [In verse.] 8°. *S. Stafford,* 1603. HN.

20170 — A Welch bayte to spare prouender. Or, a looking backe upon the times past. 4°. *V. Simmes,* 1603. Simmes fined for printing without license 5 de. 1603. L.O. E.P.; HN.
See also Arber II.837.

20171 — Wheresoever you see mee, trust unto your selfe. Or, the mysterie of lending and borrowing. 4°. [*Eliot's Court Press*] *f. B. Fisher,* 1623. Ent. 12 my. L.O(2). O⁵.NLW.PETYT(imp.).; HN(imp.).NY.
Reprinted in 20162.

20172 **Powell, Thomas,** *of Brasenose Coll., Oxford.* A sermon preached in saint Maries. 4°. *Oxford, J. Barnes,* 1613. O.O³⁸.CARTMEL.EX.LK.; F.HN.CAL.HD.

20173 **Powlter, Richard.** The fountain of flowing felicity. With the waters of life. 16°. *T. East,* 1583. L²(missing).

20174 **Pownoll, Nathaniel.** The young divines apologie for his continuance in the universitie. [*Ed.*] (G. Fletcher, *the younger.*) 12°. *C. Legge, pr. to the Univ. of Camb., sold by M. Lownes,* [*London,*] 1612. L.O.C².C³.DUR⁵. +; F.ILL.

Pownoll, Robert. A moste pythye and excellent epistell. *Tr.* R. Pownoll. 1556. *See* 10432.
— *tr. See* 7376.5, 18312.
— *See also* 19078.

20175 **Poynet, John,** *Bp.* An apologie fully aunsweringe by scriptures and aunceāt doctors, a blasphemose book gatherid by D. Steph. Gardiner, and other papists [1517?]. 8°. [*Strasburg, heirs of W. Köpfel?*] (1555 (ap.)) L⁴.O.O⁵.O¹⁷.P.; F.
Text in italic.

20175a — [Anr. ed.] Newly correctid. 8°. [*Strasburg, heirs of W. Köpfel?*] (1556.) L.O.C.DUR⁵.M².+; F.HN.HD.NY¹¹.Y.
Text in B.L.
— Catechismus breuis.—A short catechisme. 1553. *See* 4807, 4812.

20176 — A defence for mariage of priestes, by Scripture and aunciente wryters. 8°. *R. Wolff,* (1549.) L.O.O⁵.C. P.+; F.N.U.
Answered by 17517.
— A defence of priestes mariages. [Sometimes attrib. to J. Poynet.] [1567?] *See* 17518.
— Diallacticon. [*Strasburg, W. Rihel,*] 1557.
Not an STC book.
— The humble and vnfained confessiō. 1554. *See* 5630.

20177 — A notable sermon concerninge the ryght vse of the lordes supper. 8°. [*S. Mierdman*] (*f. G. Lynne,* 1550.) L.O.O¹⁷.C.P.+; F.HN.ILL.

20178 — A shorte treatise of politike power, and of the true obedience with an Exhortacion compyled by. D. J. P[oynet,] B[p. of] R[ochester and] W[inchester.] 8°. [*Strasburg, heirs of W. Köpfel,*] 1556. L.O.C.D.E.+; F.HN.HD.N.U.+

Poynet, John, *Bp.—cont.*

20179 — [Anr. ed.] 4°. [*Paris?*] 1639. L.O.C.D.E.+; F.HN.HD (date torn).N.U.+
Omits the Exhortation.
— *tr. See* 18770.

20180 **Poyntz, Adrian.** New and singular patterns & workes of linnen. 1591. Now = 24765.3.
— The treasure of the soule. *Tr.* A. P[oyntz.] 1596. *See* 24208.

Poyntz, *Sir* **Francis,** *tr. See* 4890.5.

PP. The double PP. 1606. *See* 6498.

Practice. The practise how to finde ease. 1618. *See* 7072.5.
— The practise of the faithfull. 1613. *See* 24314.

Practices. Practises touching the state of France. 1575. *See* 11287.
— The vnlawful practises of prelates. [1584?] *See* 20201.

20180.3 **Præpositi, Nicolaus.** A compendious treatise, of Nicholas Prepositas, of medicines gathered and collected, both out of the old and new writers of phisicke. [*Tr.* L. Mascall?] 4°. *J. Wolfe f. E. White,* 1588. Ent. to Wolfe 14 oc. 1587. O⁸.
Various prescriptions extracted from the 'Dispensarium ad Aromatorios'.

20180.7 — [Anr. issue, w. new prelims.] Prepositas his practise, a worke very necessary. Wherein are approued medicines. *Tr.* L. M[ascall?] *J. Wolfe f. E. White,* 1588. L.L¹⁶.O.C.; F(5).HN.HD.NLM.NY⁴.
(Formerly 17977)

20181 **Prague.** A true relation of the bloudy execution, lately performed by the commaundment of the emperours maiestie, of some states-men, and others; in Prague. Faithfully *tr.* out of the Dutch copye. 4°. [*London,*] 1621 (21 jy.) L.O(3).C.; F.

20182 **Praise.** The prayse and commendacion of suche as sought comenwelthes. 8°. (*A. Scoloker,*) [1549?] L².O(2). C.M.; HN.
(Formerly also 20182a)

20182a — = 20182.

20182a.5 — The praise and dispraise of women: gathered out of sundrye authors. Written in the French tongue, and brought into our vulgar, by J. Allday. 8°. (*T. East*) *f. W. Ponsonby,* 1579. Ent. 17 jn. 1577; copy received 3 jy. 1579. F.
Largely based on J. de Marconville's De la bonte et mauvaistie des femmes.

20183 — The praise of a pretty lasse: or, the young mans dissimulation. *Ballad.* 2 pts. s.sh.fol. *M. P*[*arsons*] *f. F. Grove,* [1638?] L.

20184 — The praise of musicke. 8°. *Oxenford, J. Barnes,* 1586. L.L².O.BUTE.WN.+; HN.BALT².CH.LC.NY.+
Attrib. to J. Case in 4246.

20185 — The praise of nothing. *Ballad.* 2 pts. s.sh.fol. *f. H. Gosson,* [1635?] L.G².

20186 — The praise of our country barly-brake. *Ballad.* 2 pts. s.sh.fol. *f. H. Gosson,* [1634.] Ent. to J. Wright a. ballad ptnrs. 16 jy. 1634. L.

20186.3 — The praise of sailors, heere set forth. *Ballad.* 2 pts. s.sh.fol. [*M. Flesher*] *f. J. Wright,* [c. 1630.] ?Ent. to J. Wright a. ballad ptnrs. 1 jn. 1629. C⁶.
1st line: 'As I lay musing in my bed,'.

20186.7 **Prat, Joseph.** The order of orthographie. [Anon.] 8° in 4's. *A. Mathews f. W. Lee,* 1622. BO⁵.

Prat, William, *tr. See* 3196.5.

20187 **Pratt, William.** The arithmeticall jewell: or the use of a small table: whereby is speedily wrought, as well all arithmeticall workes in whole numbers, as all fractionall operations. Published by his majesties priviledge, granted to the inventor. 12°. *J. Beale, sold by N. Bourne,* 1617. Ent. to Beale 21 jn. C(bd. w. instrument).
Advertised on C8 of 420.11.

20187a — [A variant, w. imprint:] *J. Beale,* 1617. O.O³.; F.HN.

20188 **Pratte,** *Poore, pseud.* The copie of a pistel or letter sent to Gilbard Potter in the tyme when he was in prison, for speakeing on our most true quenes part the lady Mary. 8°. [*R. Jugge f.*] (*H. Singelton,*) 1553 (1 au.) L.

Prayer. A booke of private prayer. [1566.] *See* 20376.

Prayer—*cont.*

20188.3 — A compendious forme of prayer, for the whole estate of Christes church necessarye to be vsed of all estates at tyme conuenient. Newely collected and set forth, in 1565. 8°. *R. Serll f. H. Sanderson,* [1565.] Ent. 1564–65. ETON(2 leaves only, in FG 8.8).

20188.7 — [Heading *1ʳ:] A fourme of prayer to be vsed in priuate houses euery mornyng and euenyng. 4°. [*R. Jugge,* c. 1570.] HN(*4 only).

    The prayers are those usually found at the end of Sternhold and Hopkins (cf. 2442, etc.) but this frag. does not belong to any of the known eds.

— A forme of thankesgiuing and praier. 1577. *See* pt. 3 of 15000.

— A godly prayer for the preseruation of the queenes maiestie. 1588. *See* 17489.5.

20189 — A good and godly prayer to be said at all tymes, with a prayer vpon the Pater noster. 8°. *J. Alde f. M. Lobley,* 1563. L.

20190 — In the name of almightie God. [Text begins:] Gratious Lord God [etc.] s.sh.fol. [*T. Scarlet?* c. 1595.] L.

    Possibly pr. f. R. Boyle, publisher of 1335.7 and 2751 with which this is bound.

20191 — Lorde omnipotent and moste mercyfull father, [etc. New Year's prayer for Ed. VI and sisters.] s.sh. 4°. [*N. Hill? f.*] *R. Jugge,* [c. 1552.] L.

— O Lord our God, most gracious & most glorious, [etc. For the protection of Queen Elizabeth. 1589.] *See* 16520.5.

— The patterne of all pious prayer. 1636. *See* 17746.

— The praierand [*sic*] complaynte of the ploweman vnto Christe. [1531?] *See* 20036.

20192 — A prayer for all kings, princes, countreyes and people. [1585.] = pt. of 19342.

— A prayer meete to be sayd of all true subiectes. [1586?] *See* 7594.5.

— A prayer sayd in the kinges chappell. [1553.] *See* 7508.

20192.5 — A praier very comfortable and necessary to be used of all christians every morning and evening, amongst their families. [Against the plague.] s.sh.fol. *f. T. Pavyer,* [c. 1603.] L⁵(Lemon 109).

Prayers. [For prayers ordered for liturgical use:] *See* Liturgies, *esp.* 16479 sqq., 16503 sqq.

— A booke of christian prayers. [*Ed.* R. Day.] 1578. *See* 6429.

20192.7 — [A book of prayers?] 16° in 8's. (*Ippyswyche, J. Oswen,*) [1548.] C(H1, 2, 7, 8 only).

    H1ᵛ has a prayer: 'For a woman conceyued with childe.' and H2ʳ: 'For those that gouerne vs.'

20193 — Certeine prayers and godly meditacyons very nedefull for euery Christen. 16° in 8's. (*Malborow, per J. Philoponon* [Antwerp, H. Peetersen van Middelburch?] 1538.) L.

    On F6 begins 'Consolacyon for troubled consciences', a trans. of Luther's Fourteen Consolations reprinted from pt. 4 of 20200.3. This also includes Savonarola on Psalm 51.

    The printing was formerly attrib. to J. Hoochstraten.

20193.5 — Deuoute prayers in englysshe of thactes of our redemption. 8°. (*R. Redman,*) [1535?] M.

    Text is extracted from 14553.

20194 — Devout prayers to be sayde: before, at, and after masse. [1580–81.] = pt. 4 of 17278.4.

20195 — [Fifteen Oes.] O Jhesu endles swetnes of louyng soules, [etc. By St. Bridget.] *Eng. a. Lat.* 4° in 8's. [*Westminster,*] (*W. Caxton,*) [1491.] L(1, plus frag. of a3–6). Duff 150.

    Outer forme of frag. from a different setting. Reprinted in 15875, 16017.5, and various other Sarum Primers.

20196 — [Anr. ed.] The .XV. oos. [C4ᵛ:] (Here endeth the .xv. oos ī Englysshe wᵗ diuers other prayers.) 16° in 8's. (*R. Coplāde,* 1529.) A².

20196.5 — [Anr. ed.] 16°. (*R. wyer,*) [c. 1545.] L(2 leaves only, Harl.5919/104,132).

20197 — Godlye prayers. [1572.] = pt. of 16302.

— Godly prayers, meete to be vsed in these later times. 1579. *See* 17790.5.

— Godlye priuate praiers for householders. 1574, etc. *See* 6684.5 sqq.

Prayers—*cont.*

20197.3 — Here after foloweth twoo fruitfull and godly praiers, the one in laude of the trinitie, and the other desiryng grace to with stande the feare of death. [In verse.] 8° in 4. *R. Lante a. R. Bankes,* 1545. F.

    Film of F copy on Univ. Microfilms reel 714 ('13194a').

— Here folowe certayne prayers of holy men & women, taken oute of the Bible. [1550?] *See* 2379.

20197.7 — In the time of Gods visitation by sickenesse, . . . may be vsed by gouernours of families. s.sh.fol. *V. Simmes,* [1607?] L⁵(Lemon 119).

20198 — Praiers. 1601. = 5181.

20199 — Prayers, before and after confession. [1580–81.] = pt. 8 of 17278.4.

— Prayers for the Parliament. [1606?] *See* 7748.7.

20200 — [Heading A1ʳ:] Praiers of holi fathers, patryarches, prophetes, [etc.] 16° in 8's. (*R. Grafton, solde by W. Tylotson,*) [1544?] HN.

    An expanded version of pt. 1 of 20200.3.

20200.3 — Prayers of the Bible takē out of the olde testament and the newe, as olde holy fathers bothe men and women were wont to pray in tyme of tribulation deuyded in vi. partes. 6 pts. 32° in 8's. (*R. Redman,*) [1535?] L(pt. 2 only).L²(lacks pt. 5).; CH(lacks pts. 4, 5).PML.

    Pt. 1 based on O. Brunfels's 'Precationes Biblicae,' Antwerp, M. de Keyser, 1531; different versions given in 2379 sq., 2748, 2996, 20200. Pt. 2 (formerly 16815): Pater noster in Englyshe. Pt. 3: The crede. Pt. 4: A consolation for troubled consciences (a tr. of Luther's Fourteen consolations; reprinted in 20193). Pts. 5, 6: Savonarola on Psalms 51, 31.

— Prayers or meditacions. [The 'Queen's Prayers' of Catharine Parr.] 1545, etc. *See* 4818 and 3009.

20200.7 — [Heading:] Three and thirty most godly & deuout prayers or salutations. 12°. [*St. Omer, English College Press,* 1640?] L.O³.AUG.OS.W.+ A&R 823.

— Three prayers. 1591. *See* 22703.

Precationes. Precationes priuatę. Regiæ E. R. 1563. *See* 7576.7.

Precedent. A president to the nobilitie. 1612. *See* 1234.

Precepts. Certaine precepts, or directions. 1617, etc. *See* 4897 sqq.

Preces. I. Preces. II. Grammaticalia. 1616. *See* 21106.

— Preces in usum scholae Paulinae. 1600. *See* 21591.5.

— Preces privatæ. 1564, etc. *See* 20378 sqq.

Pregethau. Pregethau a osodwyd. 1606. *See* 13678.

20201 **Prelates.** The vnlawfull practises of prelates against godly ministers. 8°. [*R. Waldegrave,* 1584?] L.O.C.D. E.+; F.U.Y.

20202 **Prempart, Jacques.** A historicall relation of the famous siege of the citie called the Busse. Hereunto is added a generall mappe. fol. *Amsterdam,* (*J. F. Stam*) *f. H. Hondio,* 1630. L.O.C.CASHEL.E.+; F.HN.BO².HD(lacks maps).WASH².

    O copy has date altered by hand to 1631.

Preparatio. Preparatio ad orandū. [1550?] *See* 16822.

Preparation. Of the preparation to the crosse. 1540. *See* 11393.

— [Anr. ed.] 1627. *See* pt. 2 of 11395.

20203 — A preparation to the due consideration and reuerent comming to the holy communion. [*Ed.*] (C. Barker.) 16° in 8's. *C. Barker,* 1580. Ent. 1 ap. F.

Prepositas, Nicholas. A compendious treatise. 1588. *See* 20180.3.

— Prepositas his practise. 1588. *See* 20180.7.

20203.5 **Preservative.** A godlye and holesome preseruatyue against desperatiō. [By L. Shepherd?] 8°. [*J. Herford f.*] (*J. Burrel,*) [1548?] L(lacks tp).C¹⁵.NOR².; HD. (Formerly 20205)

20204 — [Anr. ed.] 8°. (*W. Copland f. R. Kele,*) 1551. O.USHAW.; F.

20205 — Now = 20203.5.

20205.5 — A spirituall preservative against the plague. In two parts. Whereunto is annexed a sermon of mortalitie, by S. Cyprian. 8°. *f. B. Fisher,* 1625. F(tp only).

20206 **Preservatives.** Lord have mercy upon us. Preservatives and medicines [for the plague, w. weekly death totals for 1603, 1625, and 1636.] s.sh.fol. [*R. Young a. M. Flesher*] *f. T. S*[*later?* 1636.] L⁸(2).
 1 L⁸ copy has printed totals through 23 June 1636; the other through 14 July. *See also* 16739 sqq.

20207 **Presse, Symon.** A sermon preached at Eggington. 8°. *Oxford, J. Barnes, solde* [*by J. Broome, London,*] 1597. O.
 B7, 8 are app. cancels.

20208 **Preston, John.** The breast-plate of faith and love. Delivered in 18. sermons. [*Ed.*] (R. Sibs, J. Davenport.) 4° in 8's. *W. J*[*ones a. G. Purslowe*] *f. N. Bourne,* 1630. 1st pt. ass'd by R. Dawlman to Bourne 13 oc. 1629; 2nd and 3rd pts. ent. to Bourne 9 jy. and 22 oc. 1629. L.L³.O.O⁶.O¹¹.+; F.CAL².HD.N.NY¹¹.+
 Prelims. and quires Aa to end pr. by Jones; the rest by Purslowe.

20209 — Second edition, corrected. 4° in 8's. *W. J*[*ones a. G. Purslowe*] *f. N. Bourne,* 1630 (1631.) L².C.D².E².M.+; F.HN.HD.ILL.U.+
 Prelims., quires [B]–[C], and Aa to end pr. by Jones; the rest by Purslowe.

20210 — [Anr. ed.] Second edition, corrected. 4° in 8's. *W. J*[*ones a. G. Purslowe*] *f. N. Bourne,* 1631. HER.
 Jones pr. the prelims. only; the rest by Purslowe.

20211 — [Anr. issue, w. cancel tp:] Third edition. *W. J*[*ones a. G. Purslowe*] *f. N. Bourne,* 1632. L²².O²¹.C³.E.WI.+; F.CAL.HD(lacks tp)*.ILL.Y.+

20212 — Fourth edition. 4° in 8's. *R. Y*[*oung*] *f. N. Bourne,* 1634. L.O.C.D².E.+; F.HN.HD.N.NY¹¹.+

20213 — Fifth edition. 4° in 8's. *R. Y*[*oung*] *f. N. Bourne,* 1634 (1637.) L.O.C.D.E².+; F.HN.HD.ILL.U.+

20214 — The cuppe of blessing: in three sermons. 1633. = pt. 3 of 20262.

20215 — The deformed forme of a formall profession. Or, the description of a true and false christian. 4°. *Edinburgh, J. Wreittoun,* 1632. L.O.C.E.M⁴.SHEF.+; F.HN.HD.U.

20216 — [Anr. issue, w. cancel tp, w. imprint:] *Edinburgh, J. Wreittoun,* 1634. L.O.C.E.; CHI.ILL.

20217 — The doctrine of selfe-deniall. = pt. of 20221.7.
20218 — Now = 20221.3.
20219 — The doctrine of the saints infirmities. [*Ed.*] (T. Goodwin, T. Ball.) 12°. *N. a. J. Okes f. H. Taunton,* 1636. Ent. 8 ap. L.C(engr. tp only).DUL.LINC.WI.; F.HN.Y.

20220 — [Anr. ed.] 12°. *N. a. J. Okes f. H. Taunton,* 1637. L⁴. O.C.D.NLW.+; F.HN(engr. tp only).DAR.HD(engr. tp only).U.

20221 — [Anr. ed.] 4°. *J. Okes f. H. Taunton,* 1638. L.O.C.E².M. +; F.HN.HD.ILL.U.+

20221.1 — [Anr. ed.] 12°. *J. Okes f. S. Taunton,* 1638. M⁴.; F.
 Engr. tp as in 20220.

20221.3 — [Anr. ed.] 8°. *Amsterdam,* [*Richt Right Press,*] *f. T. L., sold at his chamber in Flowingburrow neare unto the English church,* [c. 1638.] L.O.
 (Formerly 20218) o bd. w. 12035 and 13726.4.

20221.5 — An elegant and lively description of spirituall life and death. [On John v.25. Init. J. P.] 4°. *T. Cotes f. M. Sparke,* 1632. Ent. 12 no. 1631. L.GLOUC.; HN. 𝔄
 (Formerly 20279)

20221.7 — [Anr. issue, w. additions.] Three godly and learned treatises. Intituled, I. A remedy against covetousnesse. II. An elegant description. III. The doctrine of selfe-deniall. [Init. J. P.] 4°. *B. A*[*lsop*] *a. T. F*[*awcett*] *f. M. Sparke,* 1632. Ent. 12 no. 1631. L². L²².O.O.C².M.+; F(lacks gen. tp).HN.HD.ILL.Y.+
 (Formerly 20280) 'Remedy' collates Aa–Ff⁴; reprinted in 20275. 'Doctrine' (formerly 20217) collates Gg–Ll⁸; for anr. version *see* 20228. Mm² has errata for all 3 treatises.

20222 — [Anr. ed.] Foure godly and learned treatises. . . . IV. Upon the sacrament of the Lords supper. By J. Preston. Third edition. 4° in 8's. *T. C*[*otes*] *f. M. Sparke,* 1633 (1632.) L.O.C.BIRM²(K.N.).CASHEL.+; F.HN.HD.ILL.U.+
 4th pt. reprinted from 20280.3. In some copies (1F,HN,HD) 'Remedy' and 'Doctrine' are sheets of 20221.7.

20223 — Fourth edition. 4° in 8's. *A. G*[*riffin*] *f. M. Sparke,* 1636. L.O.C.E.WN².+; F.HN.HD.N.U.+

20224 — The fulnesse of Christ for us. 12°. *M. P*[*arsons*] *f. J. Stafford,* 1639. Ent. 6 oc. 1638. O.C³.C⁵.

Preston, John—*cont.*

20225 — [Anr. ed.] 4°. *J. Okes f. J. Stafford,* 1640. L.O.C.E.M⁴.+; F.HN.HD.ILL.U.+
 F copy has engr. portrait of James I dated 1641.

20226 — The golden scepter held forth to the humble. With the churches dignitie by her marriage. And the churches dutie in her carriage. In three treatises. [*Ed.*] (T. Goodwin, T. Ball.) 4° in 8's. *R. Badger* [*a.*] (*E. Purslow*) *f. N. Bourne, A. Boler a. R. Harford,* 1638. Ent. to Bourne a. Harford 6 my. 1637; pt. ass'd to T. Boler 7 se. 1638. L.O.O².C.E.+; F.HN.HD.Y.
 Engr. tp has imprint as above. In some copies the letterpress tp has 'R. B.' instead of 'R. Badger'; both at C,F.

20227 — [Anr. ed.] 4° in 8's. *R. Badger f. N. Bourne, R. Harford, a. F. Eglesfield,* 1638. L.O.O⁸.C.M⁴.+; F. HD.N.NY.U.+
 Engr. tp dated 1639, w. impr. unchanged from 20226.

20228 — Grace to the humble. As preparations to receive the sacrament. 12°. *T. Cotes f. M. Sparke junior,* 1639. Ent. 8 oc. 1638. O(2).; F.V.
 For a different version of this text *see* Doctrine of Self-Denial in 20221.7.

— A heavenly treatise, of the divine love of Christ. 1640. *See* 20240.3.

— Judas's repentance. 1634. *See* 20249.

20229 — The Law out lawed. Or, the charter of the Gospell. 4°. *Edinburgh, J. Wreittoun,* 1631. L.L³.O. Finedon.; F.HN.NY¹¹.U.

20230 — [Anr. issue, w. cancel tp, w. imprint:] *Edinburgh, J. Wreittoun,* 1633. L.O.C.E(3).SHEF.; F.CHI.ILL.

20231 — Life eternall or, a treatise of the divine essence and attributes. [*Ed.*] (T. Goodwin, T. Ball.) 4° in 8's. *R. B*[*adger a. W. Jones,*] *sold by N. Bourne a. R. Harford,* 1631. Ent. to Bourne a. Harford 13 oc. 1629. L.O.C.D.E.+; F.HN.HD.N.NY¹¹.+
 Jones pr. quires Aa–Qq.

20232 — Second edition, corrected. 4° in 8's. *R. B*[*adger,*] *sold by N. Bourne a. R. Harford,* 1631. L.O.C².D².E².+; F.HN.DAR.ILL.Y.+

20233 — Third edition. 4° in 8's. *R. B*[*adger,*] *sold by N. Bourne a. R. Harford,* 1632. L.O.C.LINC.STU.+; F.HN.CU.U. McMaster U.

20233a — [A variant, w. date:] 1633. L.O²¹.C.CASHEL.E.+; F.HD. WASH².Y.

20234 — Fourth edition. 4° in 8's. *E. P*[*urslowe,*] *sold by N. Bourne a. R. Harford,* 1634. L.O.C.D².E.+; F.HN.HD. ILL.U.+

20235 — A liveles life: or, mans spirituall death in sinne. Sermons upon Ephes. 2.1,2,3. Whereunto is annexed a sermon at Lincolnes Inne, on Gen. xxii.xiv. 4°. *J. Beale f. A. Crooke,* 1633. Ent. 19 fb. and 8 ap. 1630. L.O¹².C.A.M⁴.+; HD.ILL.PN².Y. Haverford C.

20236 — The last edition. 4°. [*E. Purslowe*] *f. M. Sparke,* 1633. C.BTL.CASHEL.E.; F.HN.LC.NY.

20237 — Third edition. 4°. [*J. Beale*] *f. A. Crooke, sold by D. Frere,* 1635. L.O.C.D.G².+; F.HN.HD.N.NY¹¹.+
 (2nd pt. formerly 20269) Reissued as pt. 2 of 20282.

20238 — Mount Ebal, or a heavenly treatise of divine love. 4°. *M. P*[*arsons*] *f. J. Stafford,* 1638. Ent. to R. Milborne a. Stafford 29 no. 1637; to Stafford 26 ap. 1638. L.O.C.E.M.+; F.HN.HD.ILL.U.+
 Some copies (STD,HN,U) have the misprint 'Safford' in the imprint.

20239 — Now = 20240.3.
20239.5 — [A different version of 20238.] The onely love of the chiefest of ten thousand: or an heavenly treatise of the divine love of Christ. In five sermons. 12°. *f. J. Stafford,* 1639. Ent. 16 jy. L(tp only, Ames II.1488).

20240 — [Anr. issue?] 12°. *f. J. Stafford,* 1640. C.C³.; HD.Y.
 Tp from same setting as 20239.5, w. date altered in press.

20240.3 — [Anr. ed.] A heavenly treatise of the divine love. 4°. *T. Paine f. J. Stafford,* 1640. L.O.C.LYU.STU.+; F.HN. CHI.HD.ILL.+
 (Formerly 20239) Unsold sheets reissued in a collection under gen. tp: 'Sun-beams of Gospel-light, *f. J. Stafford,* 1644.' (HD)

20241 — The new covenant, or the saints portion. A treatise delivered in fourteene sermons upon Gen. 17.1.2. Whereunto are adjoyned foure sermons upon Eccles. 9.1.2.11.12. [*Ed.*] (R. Sibs, J. Davenport.) 4° in 8's. *J. D*[*awson*] *f. N. Bourne,* 1629. Ent. 12 ja. L.L³.O. C.M⁴.+; DAR(4 Serm. only).TORONTO².U.

Preston, John—*cont.*

20241.3 — Second edition, corrected. 4° in 8's. *J. D[awson, G. Purslowe a. W. Jones] f. N. Bourne*, 1629. O².C¹³. DUL.STU.; DAR(very imp.).HD.ILL.PN.

Quires A–T pr. by Dawson, V–1st Ll by Purslowe, 2nd Aa–Mm by Jones in 20241.3–20244.

20241.7 — Third edition. 4° in 8's. *J. D[awson, G. Purslowe, a. W. Jones] f. N. Bourne*, 1629. O.BHP.; F.CHI.HD. MICH.N.+

20242 — Fourth edition. 4° in 8's. *J. D[awson, G. Purslowe, a. W. Jones] f. N. Bourne*, 1630. O.C.LYU.NLW.SHEF.+; F.CHI.ILL.PN².Y.+

20243 — Fifth edition. 4° in 8's. *J. D[awson, G. Purslowe, a. W. Jones] f. N. Bourne*, 1630. L.L².O.O³.G⁴.+; F.HN.CU. PH².Y.+

20244 — Sixth edition. 4° in 8's. *J. D[awson, G. Purslowe, a. W. Jones] f. N. Bourne*, 1631. L.O.C².E⁸.LINC.+; F.HN. HD(lacks tp).NW.PN².+

20245 — Seventh edition. 4° in 8's. *J. D[awson] f. N. Bourne*, 1633. L.O. CASHEL.E.M.+; F.NY¹¹.Y.

20246 — Eighth edition. 4° in 8's. *J. D[awson] f. N. Bourne*, 1634. L.O.C.E.G².+; F.HN.HD.N.NY¹¹.+

20247 — Ninth edition. 4° in 8's. *J. D[awson] f. N. Bourne*, 1639. L.O.C².E.LYU.+; F.HN.HD(imp.).ILL.U.+

— The new creature. 1633. *See* pt. 2 of 20262.

— The onely love. 1639. *See* 20239.5.

20248 — The patriarchs portion. 1619. Now = 20282.3.

— A preparation to the Lords supper. 1635, etc. *See* 20281a.3 sq.

20249 — Remaines of . . . John Preston. Containing three excellent treatises, namely, Judas's repentance. The saints spirituall strength. Pauls conversion. 4°. [*J. Beale*] *f. A. Crooke*, 1634. Ent. 28 au. 1633, 23 fb. 1634. L.O. C.D.E.+; F.HN.HD.ILL.U.+

20250 — Second edition. 4°. *R. B[adger a.] (J. L[egate]) f. A. Crooke*, 1637. L.O.C.E.LYU.+; F.HN.HD.ILL.U.+

Legate pr. quires R to end.

— A remedy against covetousnes. 1632. *See* 20221.7.

20251 — The saints daily exercise. A treatise concerning prayer. In five sermons upon 1 Thess. 5.17. [Ed. R. Sibbes and J. Davenport.] 4°. *W. J[ones,] sold by N. Bourne*, 1629. Ent. 8 jy. L³⁰.O².O⁶.C.C².; F.CAL.CAL². CHI.U.

20252 — Second edition, corrected. 4°. *W. J[ones] f. N. Bourne*, 1629. L⁴.O.O¹²(2).C²⁵.BHP.; F.CHI.

20253 — Third edition. 4° in 8's. *W. J[ones] f. N. Bourne*, 1629. L.O.C(imp.).BTU.WOR.+; F.HN.HD(imp.).U. Syracuse U.+

20254 — Fourth edition. 4° in 8's. *W. J[ones] f. N. Bourne*, 1630. L⁴⁸.O.C.E.SHEF.+; F.BO.PN².U.Y.+

20255 — Fifth edition. 4° in 8's. *R. B[adger] f. N. Bourne*, 1631. L.O.C.BIRM.G⁴.+; F.HN.ILL.MICH.PN².+

20256 — Sixth edition. 4° in 8's. *W. J[ones] f. N. Bourne*, 1631. L²².C².D².DUL.NOR².+; HN.HART.SMU.

20257 — Seventh edition. 4° in 8's. *E. P[urslowe] f. N. Bourne*, 1632. L.O²⁸.C³.E⁸.EX.; F.HN.HD.LC.NY¹¹.+

20258 — Eighth edition. 4° in 8's. *E. Purslow f. N. Bourne*, 1633. L².O.C.CASHEL.E.+; LC.U.

20258.5 — [Anr. issue, w. cancel tp, w. imprint:] *E. P[urslowe] f. N. Bourne, sold by W. Hope*, 1634. L(2, 1 lacks tp). C.; F.BO².HD(2, 1 lacks tp).ILL.NY¹¹.

(Formerly 20260)

20259 — Ninth edition. 4° in 8's. *E. Purslow f. N. Bourne*, 1634. O.E².LYU.NLW.PETYT.+; F.BO.HD.NY.NY¹¹.+

20260 — = 20258.5.

20260a — [Anr. issue, w. imprint:] *E. Purslow f. N. Bourne*, 1635. L.O.C.E.SAU.+; F.HN.BO⁵.ILL.U.+

20261 — = 20260a.

20262 — The saints qualification: or a treatise I. Of humiliation, in tenne sermons. II. Of sanctification, in nine sermons: whereunto is added a treatise of communion w. Christ in three sermons. [Ed.] (R. Sibs, J. Davenport.) 3 pts. 4° in 8's. *R. B[adger] f. N. Bourne*, 1633. Ent. 22 oc. 1629; 22 de. 1632; 26 jn. 1633. L.O.C.D. M⁴.+; F.HN.HD.U(tp def.).Y.+

(Pt. 3 formerly also 20214)

20263 — Second edition, corrected. 4° in 8's. *R. B[adger] f. N. Bourne*, 1634 (1633.) L.O.C.DUR⁵.G².+; F.HN.HD. ILL.U.+

20264 — [A variant:] Third edition. *R. B[adger] f. N. Bourne*, 1634. L.C⁵.C¹⁵.

In the title 'third' is a misprint, corrected in press in 20263.

20265 — Third edition. 4° in 8's. *R. B[adger] f. N. Bourne, sold by T. Nicholes*, 1637. L.O.C⁵.E².M⁴.+; HN.CHI. HD.N.PN².+

Preston, John—*cont.*

20265.5 — [Anr. issue, w. imprint:] *R. B[adger] f. N. Bourne, sold by W. Hope*, 1637. L³.O.E.EX.STU.+; F.HN.BO. PN².U.+

— The saints spirituall strength. 1634. *See* 2nd pt. of 20249.

20266 — The saints submission, and Sathans overthrow. Or, sermons on James 4.7. 12°. *J. D[awson,] sold by P. Cole*, 1638. Ent. 18 my. L.O².

— A sermon of spiritual life. *See* 20278.

20267 — A sermon preached at the funerall of J. Reynel. 1615. Now = 20282.5.

20268 — A sermon preached at the funeral of A. Upton. 1619. Now = 20282.7.

20269 — A sermon preached at Lincolnes Inne. 1635. = pt. of 20237.

20270 — Sermons preached before his majestie; and upon other occasions. [Ed.] (T. G[oodwin,] T. B[all.]) 4°. [*Eliot's Court Press a. R. Young] f. L. Greene of Cambridge, sold by J. Boler*, [*London*], 1630. Ent. to Boler a. Greene 14 a. 22 ja. L.O.O³.C.SHEF.+; F. MICH.PN².U.Y.

Tp on A2. Eliot's Court Press pr. A⁴, L–S⁴; Young the rest.

20270.5 — [Anr. ed.] 4°. [*Eliot's Court Press a. R. Young] f. L. Greene of Cambridge, sold by J. Boler*, [*London,*] 1630. L⁴⁸.C.C².E.G⁴.; F(imp.).HN.HD(imp.). ILL.U.+

Tp on A1. Eliot's Court Press pr. A⁴, O–X⁴; Young the rest.

20271 — [Anr. ed.] 4° in 8's. *J. Beale f. J. Boler a. Joane Greene*, 1631. L.O.O²⁸.C².E⁸.+; F.HART.HD.LC.NY¹¹.+

20271a — [Anr. issue, w. imprint:] *f. J. Boler a. Joane Greene*, 1631. HN.

20272 — [Anr. ed.] 4°. *f. M. Sparke*, 1631. O.C.C³.BIRM.CASHEL. +; F.HN.PN².PTS.

W. Turner of Oxford, M. Sparke and others were charged w. pirating an ed. of 'five sermons', probably this; *see* Greg, *Companion*, p. 271 and Madan II, p.521.

20273 — Fourth impression, corrected. 4°. [*J. Beale*] *f. J. Boler a. Joane Greene*, 1634. L.O.C.BIRM.E².+; F.HN.HD. ILL.U.+

20274 — Fift impression. 4° in 8's. *J. Norton f. A. Boler*, 1637. Ent. 15 se. L.O.C⁵.E.NLW.+; F.HN.HD.N. NY.+

20275 — Sins overthrow: or, a godly and learned treatise of mortification. Upon Colos. iii.v. 4°. *J. Beale [a. A. Mathewes] f. A. Crooke*, 1633. Ent. 8 ap. 1630. O. DUL.SHEF.; F(2).HN.HD.

Last section reprinted from Remedy of Covetousness in 20221.7.

20276 — Second edition, corrected and enlarged. 4°. *J. Beale f. A. Crooke*, 1633. L.O.C³.CASHEL.M⁴.+; F.HN.CHI.HD. U.+

20277 — Third edition. 4°. *F. Kingston f. A. Crooke, sold by D. Frere*, 1635. L.O.C.D.E.+; F.HN.HD.N.Y.+

Reissued in 20282.

20278 — A sermon of spirituall life and death. [On 1 John v.12.] 4°. *T. C[otes] f. M. Sparke*, 1630. L(tp only, Harl. 5973/84).O.

Title in compartment.

20278.5 — [Anr. issue, w. title in border of rules.] L.M⁴.P.

20279 — An elegant and lively description of spirituall life and death. [On John v.25.] Now = 20221.5.

20280 — Three godly and learned treatises. 1632. Now = 20221.7.

20280.3 — Three sermons upon the sacrament of the Lords supper. 4°. *Oxford, f. W. Turner a. H. Curteyn, sold by M. Sparkes*, [*London,*] 1631. Ent. to Sparke, Turner, a. Curteyn 17 no. 1630. L.C.BRISTOL.; MICH.

(Formerly 20281a) Reprinted in 20222 sq.

20280.5 — [A variant, w. imprint:] [*Oxford,*] *f. W. Turner a. H. Curteyn, sold by M. Sparkes*, [*London,*] 1631. M.; F.

20280.7 — [A variant, w. imprint:] [*Oxford,*] *f. W. Turner a. H. Curteyn, sold [by M. Sparke, London,*] 1631. O¹².; HN.HD.NY¹¹.

20281 — [Anr. ed.] 4°. *T. Cotes f. M. Sparke*, 1631. L²².O.C.D². E².+; F.HN.HD.SMU.U.+

20281a — Now = 20280.3.

20281a.3 — [Anr. ed., w. title:] A preparation to the Lords supper. Fourth edition. 8°. *T. C[otes] f. M. Sparke*, 1635. L(tp only, Ames II.1228).

20281a.7 — Fift edition. 12°. *J. Dawson f. M. Sparke*, 1638. O.; F.HN.

Preston, John—*cont.*

20282 — Two godly and learned treatises upon mortification and humiliation. 2 pts. 4°. *f. A. Crooke, sold by D. Frere,* 1635. L.O⁵.DUR⁵.; F(pt. 1 only).HD(2).N.U.Y.
A reissue, w. added gen. tp pr. by J. Beale, of 20277, 20237.

20282.3 **Preston, John,** *of East Ogwell.* The patriarchs portion. Or, the saints best day. Delivered in a sermon at the funerall of sir Thomas Reynell. 8°. *A. M[athewes] f. R. Jackeson,* 1619. Ent. 22 ap. O.C².WOR.
(Formerly 20248)

20282.5 — A sermon preached at the funerall of Mʳ. Josiah Reynel. 4°. *N. Okes f. Richard Boulton,* 1615. Ent. 12 fb. L.L³.O.O¹⁰.; HN.
(Formerly 20267)

20282.7 — A sermon preached at the funeral of Mʳ. Arthur Upton. 4°. *W. Jones,* 1619. Ent. 19 jy. L³.L¹³.L⁴⁶.O(2).O¹⁰.; F.HN.
(Formerly 20268)

20283 **Preston, Richard.** The doctrine of the sacrament of the lords supper. 8°. *N. O[kes] f. J. Bellamie,* 1621. Ent. 6 ja. L⁴.O.C².; HN.

20284 — The duties of communicants. 8°. *J. D[awson] f. J. Bellamie,* 1621. Ent. 6 mr. L⁴.O.C².

20285 — The godly mans inquisition, lately delivered in two sermons. 4°. *J. Dawson f. J. Bellamie,* 1622. Ent. 13 ja. O.BED.EX.SHEF.YK.+; F.BO⁶.HD.LC.

20286 — Short questions and answers, plainely explaining the nature and use of the sacraments. 8°. *N. O[kes] f. J. Bellamine* [sic], 1621. L⁴.C².; HN.HD.

Preston, Thomas, *Benedictine Monk. See* Widdrington, R., *pseud.*

20286.3 **Preston, Thomas,** and **Green, Thomas.** Appellatio qua reverendi patres, Thomas Prestonus, & Thomas Greenæus Angli Benedictini, ad pontificem provocarunt. 4°. *Augustae, ap. B. Fabrum* [*London, E. Griffin,*] 1620. Ent. to E. Griffin 14 de. L.L².O.C³.D.+; N.
A&R 677.

20286.7 — Reverendorum patrum D. Thomæ Prestoni . . . & Fr. T. Greenæi ad Gregorium decimum quintum, supplicatio. 4°. *Augustae, ap. B. Fabrum* [*London, E. Griffin,*] 1621. L².O.O³.C².HP.; N.
A&R 678.

20287 **Preston, Thomas,** *Dramatist.* A lamentable tragedy mixed ful of pleasant mirth, conteyning the life of Cambises king of Percia. 4°. (*J. Allde,*) [1570?] Ent. 1569–70. L.; HN. Greg 56.

20287.5 — [Anr. ed.] 4°. (*E. Allde,*) [c. 1585.] O(F2,3 only).
In colophon: 'Imprinted at London at the Long Shop . . . by'.

20288 — [Anr. ed.] 4°. (*E. Allde,*) [c. 1595.] L(3).L⁶.O. PETWORTH.; F.HN.HD.N.NY.+
In colophon: 'Imprinted at London by'.

20289 — A lamentation from Rome, how the pope doth bewayle. *Ballad.* s.sh.fol. *W. Gryffith,* 1570. Ent. 1569–70. HN.

Preventer. The faithfull and wise preventer. 1621. *See* 17672.

20290 **Price, Daniel.** The creation of the prince. A sermon. 4°. *G. Eld f. R. Jackson,* 1610. Ent. 14 jn. L.O.C.DUR³. WOR.+; F.HN.HD.

20291 — David his oath of allegeance to Jerusalem. The sermon. 4°. *Oxford, J. Barnes,* 1613. L.O.O³⁸.CASHEL.LINC.+; F(2).HN.U.Y.

20292 — The defence of truth against a booke falsely called The triumph of truth sent over from Arras 1609. By H. Leech [15363]. 4°. *Oxford, J. Barnes,* 1610. L.O.A. BIRM²(K.N.).YK.+; F.HN.Y.

20293 — A heartie prayer, in a needful time of trouble. The sermon preached at Theobalds, before his majestie, an houre before the death of king James. 4°. *M. Flesher f. J. Grismand,* 1625. Ent. 27 jn. L.O.O¹⁹.; F.HN.

20294 — Lamentations for the death of prince Henry. Two sermons. 4°. *T. Snodham f. R. Jackson,* 1613. Ent. 5 de. 1612. L.O.O⁵.E².LINC.+; F.HN.HD.ILL.NY.
43 pp.

20295 — [Anr. ed.] 4°. *T. Snodham f. R. Jackson,* 1613. L.O. C².P.STU.+; F.HN.HD.N.NY¹¹.+
38 pp.

Price, Daniel—*cont.*

20296 — The marchant. A sermon preached at Paules Crosse. 4°. *Oxford, J. Barnes,* 1608. L.O.C.LINC.M.; F(2). HN.N.Y.

20297 — Maries memoriall. A sermon preached at Sᵗ. Maries Spittle. 4°. *E. Griffin,* 1617. Ent. 23 oc. L⁴.O.C.EX. LINC.+; NY¹¹.

20298 — Prælium & præmium. The christians warre and rewarde. A sermon. 4°. *Oxford, J. Barnes,* 1608. L. L¹³.O.C.LINC.+; F.NY¹¹.

20299 — Prince Henry his first anniversary. 4°. *Oxford, J. Barnes,* 1613. L.L³.O.C³.E².+; F.HN.Y.

20300 — Prince Henry his second anniversary. 4°. *Oxford, Jos. Barnes, sold by John Barnes,* [*London,*] 1614. L.O. O¹⁰.E².PLUME.; F.HN.LC.Y.

20301 — Recusants conversion: a sermon preached at Sᵗ. James. 4°. *Oxford, J. Barnes,* 1608. L.O.C.EX.M.+; F.HN.

20302 — Sauls prohibition staide. Or the apprehension, and examination of Saule. With a reproofe of those that traduce the honourable plantation of Virginia. Preached in a sermon. 4°. [*J. Windet*] *f. M. Law,* 1609. L.O.C.LINC.YK.+; F.HN.HD.N.PN.+

20303 — Sorrow for the sinnes of the time. = pt. of 20304 sq.

20304 — Spirituall odours to the memory of prince Henry, in foure of the last sermons. (Sorrow for the sinnes of the time.—Teares shed over Abner.) 4°. *Oxford, Jos. Barnes, sold by John Barnes,* [*London,*] 1613. L³.O. C³.CASHEL.E.+; F(2 imp.).HN.HD.N.Y.+
All tpp have McK. 336: w. break in upper left scroll.

20304.5 — [Anr. ed.] 4°. *Oxford, Jos. Barnes* [i.e. *London, G. Eld,*] *sold by John Barnes,* [*London,*] 1613. L.L¹³(lacks gen. tp).o('Sorrow' and 'Teares' only).O¹⁰.E².+
All tpp have McK. 338: without break in upper left scroll.

20305 — The spring. A sermon preached before the prince. 4°. [*J. Windet*] *f. R. Jackson,* 1609. Ent. 12 jn. L.O.C². LINC.NLW.+; F.HN.

20306 **Price, Gabriel.** The laver of the heart. Preached at Pauls Crosse. 8°. *F. Kyngston f. T. Man,* 1616. Ent. 20 de. 1615. L.L¹⁵.O.LINC.M.; F.PN².V.

20307 **Price, Henry.** The eagles flight or six principall notes, or sure markes for euery true christian. As it was deliuered in a sermon. 8°. *R. Bradocke f. J. Busbie,* 1599. Ent. 14 ap. L.L².O.; F.U.Y.
— *See also* 11500.

Price, James, *ed. See* 1018.

20308 **Price, John.** Anti-Mortonus or an apology in defence of the church of Rome. Against the grand imposture of doctor T. Morton [18186]. [Init. J. S.] 4°. [*St. Omer, English College Press,*] 1640. C⁵.A².HP.OS.W.+; TEX. WASH³.
A&R 679.

20309 **Price,** *Sir* **John.** Historiae Brytannicae defensio, Joanne Priseo authore. (De Mona Druidum insula, epistola H. Lhuyd.) 4°. *in æd. H. Binneman, imp. H. Toy,* 1573. L.O.C.D.E.+; F.HN.HD.N.PML.+

20310 — Yny lhyvyr hwnn ỹ traethir. [Anon.] 8°. [*E. Whitchurch,*] 1546. NLW.

20311 **Price, Lawrence.** The batchelors feast, or, the difference betwixt, a single life and a double. [Init. L. P.] *Ballad.* 2 pts. s.sh.fol. *f. J. W[right,] the younger,* [1636.] Ent. to J. Wright, jun., 28 jn. 1636. L(Rox. I.12,17).

20312 — Bee patient in trouble. [Init. L. P.] *Ballad.* 2 pts. s.sh. fol. *f. J. Wright, junior,* [1636.] Ent. 28 jn. 1636. L.

20313 — A compleate gentle-woman. [Init. L. P.] *Ballad.* 2 pts. s.sh.fol. [*f. J. Wright,* 1633.] Ent. to J. Wright a. ballad ptnrs. 8 jy. 1633. L.

20314 — Cupids wanton wiles. [Init. L. P.] *Ballad.* 2 pts. s.sh. fol. *f. J. Wright, the younger,* [1640?] L.

20315 — The honest age, or there is honesty in all trades. [Init. L. P.] *Ballad.* 2 pts. s.sh.fol. *f. H. G[osson,* 1632.] Ent. to H. Gosson a. F. Coles 24 my. 1632. C⁶.

20316 — The merry conceited lasse, whose hearts desire was set on fire, a husband for to have. [Init. L. P.] *Ballad.* 2 pts. s.sh.fol. *f. T. Lambert,* [1640?] L.

20317 — A monstrous shape. Or a shapelesse monster. [On the swine-faced woman. Init. L. P.] *Ballad.* 2 pts. s.sh. fol. *M. F[lesher] f. T. Lambert,* [1639.] ?Ent. 11 de. 1639. O.

Price, Lawrence—*cont.*

20318 — A new Spanish tragedy. Or, more strange newes from the narrow seas. [Init. L. P.] *Ballad.* 2 pts. s.sh.fol. *f. S. Rand,* [1639.] Ent. to J. Stafford 15 oc. 1639. O.

20319 — Newes from Hollands Leager: or Hollands Leager is lately up broken. [Init. L. P.] *Ballad.* 2 pts. s.sh.fol. *f. J. W[right,* 1632.] Ent. to H. Gosson a. F. Coles 24 my. 1632. C⁶.

20319.5 — Oh grammercy penny: being a Lancashire ditty. [Init. L. P.] *Ballad.* 2 pts. s.sh.fol. [*G. Purslowe*] *f. M. Trundle, viddow,* [c. 1628.] C⁶.

20320 — Rocke the cradle John: or, children after the rate of twenty foure in a yeere. [Init. L. P.] *Ballad.* 2 pts. s.sh.fol. *f. E. B[lackmore,* 1631.] Ent. to E. Blackmore 4 no. 1631. L.

20320.5 — [Anr. ed., signed 'Lau. Price'.] 2 pts. s.sh.fol. *f. E. B[lackmore,* c. 1635.] C⁶(title cropt).

20321 — Round boyes indeed. Or the shoomakers holy-day. [Init. L. P.] *Ballad.* 2 pts. s.sh.fol. [*M. Flesher*] *f. J. Wright,* [c. 1632.] ?Ent. to J. Wright, jun., as 'A merry round' 24 jn. 1637. C⁶.

20322 — Seldome cleanely: or, a merry new ditty. [Init. L. P.] *Ballad.* 2 pts. s.sh.fol. *f. J. Wright, junior,* [1635?] L.G².

20322.3 — Strange and wonderfull news of a woman which lived neer unto the famous city of London. [Init. L. P.] *Ballad.* 2 pts. s.sh.fol. *f. F. Grove,* [c. 1630.] L.

20322.7 — Tis a wise child that knows his own father. [Init. L. P.] *Ballad.* 2 pts. s.sh.fol. *R. Oulton f. J. Wright the younger,* [c. 1640.] M³.

20323 — The two fervent lovers. [Init. L. P.] *Ballad.* 2 pts. s.sh.fol. *f. F. Coules,* [1632.] Ent. to H. Gosson a. F. Coles 24 my. 1632. L.

20324 — A warning for all lewd livers. [Init. L. P.] *Ballad.* 2 pts. s.sh.fol. *f. T. Lambert,* [1633.] Ent. 14 jy. 1633. L(Rox. I.442).
　　　A post-1640 ed. at L is init. M. P., and this ballad is sometimes attrib. to M. Parker.

20325 — A wonderfull wonder, being . . . the life and death of T. Miles, who did forsweare himselfe, and died the 8 of August 1635. [Init. L. P.] *Ballad.* 2 pts. s.sh.fol. *f. J. Wright, junior,* [1635.] L.

20326 — The young-mans wish. [Init. L. P.] *Ballad.* 2 pts. s.sh. fol. *f. J. Wright, the younger,* [1635?] Ent. to F. Grove 25 ja. 1638. L.SAL.

Price, Richard. The cryes of the dead. Or the late murther in South-warke, committed by one R. Price. *Ballad.* 2 pts. s.sh.fol. [*W. Jones*] *f. T. L[angley,* c. 1620.] C⁶.

20328 **Price, Sampson.** The beauty of holines: or the consecration of a house of prayer. A sermon. 4°. B: A[lsop]: *f. R. Meighen,* 1618. Ent. 30 mr. L.O.C.D.G⁴.+; F.HN.

20329 — The clearing of the saints sight. A sermon. 4°. [*G. Purslowe*] *f. John Barnes,* 1617. L.O.C.SHR.WOR.+; HN.AAS.CAL.CHI.

20330 — Ephesus warning before her woe. A sermon preached at Pauls Crosse. 4°. *G. Eld f. John Barnes,* 1616. Ent. 4 ap. L.O.C.BIRM²(K.N.).D.+; F.HN.CAL.HART.Y.
　　　Copies vary: in title: 'Bachelour . . . Oxford:' (L,C²,F) or 'Bachelour . . . Oxford: and Lecturer at S. Olavs.' (O,C²,HN).

20331 — A heavenly proclamation to fly Romish Babylon. A sermon. 4°. *Oxford, J. Barnes,* 1614. O.O¹³.C².C⁵.; F.HN.
　　　O¹³ has frags. in bindings to make more than 2 complete copies.

20332 — Londons remembrancer: for the staying of the plague. In a sermon. 4°. E. *All-de f. T. Harper,* 1626. L.L⁸.O.G⁴.WOR.+; F.NY.

20333 — Londons warning by Laodicea's luke-warmnesse. Or a sermon. 4°. [*T. Snodham*] *f. John Barnes,* 1613. Ent. 14 oc. L.L¹⁵.O.P.PETYT.+; F.BO⁶.HD.

20334 — The two twins of birth and death. A sermon. Upon the funeralls of sir W. Byrde. 4°. E. *All-de f. J. Hodgets,* 1624. L.O.C².M.NOR².+; F.HN.HD.N.Y.+

Price, Thomas, *tr. See* 24140.5.

Price, William, *of Oxford. See* 19029.

20335 **Price, William,** *Vicar of Brigstock.* Janitor animæ: the soules porter. A treatise of the feare of God. 12°. J. *D[awson] f. J. Cowper,* 1638. Ent. 5 jn. 1637. O.C.

Prick. [The prick of conscience.] *See* 3360, 24228.

20336 **Pricke, Robert.** The doctrine of subjection. 1616. Now = 20337.5.

20337 — The doctrine of superioritie, and of subjection, contained in the fift commandement. [*Ed.*] (R. Allen.) 8°. [*T. Creede*] *f. E. Dawson a. T. Downe,* 1609. Ent. to W. Young 21 jn. 1608. L.O(imp.).

20337.3 — [A variant, w. imprint:] *f. T. Downe a. E. Dawson,* 1609. DUR⁵.

20337.5 — [Anr. issue, w. cancel tp replacing A2,3:] The doctrine of subjection to God and the king. *f. T. Downes a. E. Dawson,* 1616. O.
　　　(Formerly 20336) Change in title is an attempt to capitalize on 14418.5.

20338 — A verie godlie and learned sermon, treating of mans mortalitie. [*Ed.*] (R. Allen.) 4°. *T. Creede,* 1608. L. O.O¹⁰.COL.D.+; HD.

20339 **Pricket, Robert.** Honors fame in triumph riding. Or, the life and death of the earle of Essex. [Init. R. P. In verse.] 8° in 4's. *R. B[lower] f. R. Jackson,* 1604. O.; HN.
　　　Apparently suppressed; *see H.M.C.,* Tenth Report, Appendix 2, p. 92.

20340 — The Jesuits miracles, or new popish wonders. [Init. R. P. In verse.] 4°. [*N. Okes*] *f. C. P[urset] a. R. J[ackson,*] 1607. Ent. to Jackson a. Purset 21 mr. L.L³.O(3).; F.HN.HD.WTL.
　　　In some copies (L³,2 O) the inits. following the dedic. are omitted.

20341 — A souldiers wish unto his soveraigne lord king James. [In verse.] 4°. *J. Harison,* 1603. Ent. 3 ap. L.O.; HN. HD.IND.

20342 — Times anatomie [*sic*]. Containing: the poore man's plaint, Brittons trouble, and her triumph. [In verse.] 8° in 4's. *G. Eld, sold by J. Hodgets,* 1606. L.O.HAT. YK.; F.HN.

20343 — Unto the most high and mightie prince, king James. A poore subject sendeth, a souldiors resolution. [Prose.] 4°. *J. Windet f. W. Burre,* 1603. L.O.D(lacks tp).P(imp.).; F.HN.PFOR.U.
　　　Collates A–F⁴; A3ʳ catchword: 'by'. F. S. Ferguson examined a copy, presently untraced, which collated A–E⁴ F²; A3ʳ catchword: 'banner'.

— *ed. See* 5491.

Prid, W., *tr. See* 929 sqq.

20343.7 **Prideaux, John,** *Bp.* [Heading A1ʳ:] Alloquium serenissimo regi Jacobo Woodstochiæ habitum 24. Augusti. Anno 1624. [Init. J. P. V[ice-chancellor] Ox.] 4°. [*Oxford,* 1624.] O.
　　　Reprinted in 20358.5.

20344 — Castigatio cuiusdam circulatoris, qui R. P. Andream Eudaemon-Johannem Cydonium seipsum nuncupat. Opposita ipsius calumnijs in epistolam I. Casauboni ad Frontonem Ducæum. 8°. *Oxoniæ, J. Barnesius,* 1614. L.O.C.D.E.+; HN.HD.
　　　Defends 4742.

20345 — Certaine sermons preached by John Prideaux. 4° in 8's. *Oxford, L. Lichfield,* 1637. (1636.) L.O.C(16 serm.).D(9 serm.).M(deposit).+; F(lacks gen. tp).HN (5 serm.).HD(11 serm., lacking gen. tp).ILL(9 serm.). U(16 serm., lacking gen. tp).+
　　　(Pts. of this formerly 20353, 20354, 20355, 20360, 20365) Contains 20 sermons, all dated 1636, w. continuous signatures and separate pagination; *see* Madan I.199. First 9 sermons reissued in 1641 w. cancel gen. tp as Wing P 3432.

20346 — Christs counsell for ending law cases. In two sermons. 4°. *Oxford, Jos. Barnes,* 1615. Ent. to John Barnes a. ass'd to J. Budge 1 oc. 1619. L³.O.O³.C⁵.G².
— [Anr. ed.] 1621. *See* 20351.
— [Anr. ed.] 1636. *See* 20345.

20347 — Concio habita Oxoniæ ad artium baccalaureos. 4°. *Oxoniæ, J. Lichfield & G. Turner,* 1626. L⁴.O.C.D². E.+; F.HN.HART.HD.Y.+

20348 — The doctrine of the sabbath. Delivered in the Act at Oxon. 1622. *Tr.* into English. 4°. E. *P[urslowe] f. H. Seile,* 1634. L.O.C.D.E².+; F.HN.HD.ILL.U.+

20349 — Second edition. 4°. E. *P[urslowe] f. H. Seile,* 1634. L. O.C.D.E.+; F.HN.HD.N.Y.+

20350 — Third edition. 4°. E. *P[urslowe] f. H. Seile,* 1635. L.O. C.E.LINC.+; F.HN.HD.ILL.U.+

20351 — Eight sermons. 4° in 8's. *F. Kyngston f. J. Budge,* 1621. Ent. 25 jn. L.O(imp.).C³.WOR. Rochester Cathedral. +; F.HART.NY¹¹.

Prideaux, John, *Bp.—cont.*

20352 — Ephesus backsliding considered and applyed in a sermon. 4°. *Oxford, Jos. Barnes,* 1614. Ent. to John Barnes a. ass'd to J. Budge 17 oc. 1619. L.O.D.LK.; U.

20353 — The first fruits of the resurrection. 1636. = pt. of 20345.

20354 — Heresies progresse. 1636. = pt. of 20345.

20355 — Hezekiahs sicknesse and recovery. 1636. = pt. of 20345.

20356 — Lectiones novem de totidem religionis capitibus præcipuè hoc tempore controversis prout publicè habebantur Oxoniæ. 4°. *Oxoniæ, J. Lichfield & G. Turner pro H. Crypps,* 1625. L².L³.O.C³.YK.+; HART.N.NY¹¹.U.

20357 — [Anr. ed.] Lectiones decem. . . . Editio secunda, auctior. 4°. *Oxoniæ, J. Lichfield & G. Turner,* 1626. L⁴⁶.O.C.D².E.+; F.HART².NY¹¹.Y.

20358 — Orationes novem inaugurales, de totidem theologiæ apicibus. Accedit de Mosis institutione concio. 4°. *Oxoniæ, J. Lichfield & G. Turner, imp. G. Turner,* 1626. L.O.C.D².LINC.+; F.CHI.HART.NY.NY¹¹.

20358.5 — Perez-Uzzah: or the breach of Uzzah. 4°. *Oxford, J. Lichfield a. W. Turner,* 1624. NY¹¹. Includes reprint of 20343.7.

20359 — [Anr. issue, w. imprint:] *Oxford, J. Lichfield a. W. Turner,* 1625. L.O.C.DUL.WOR.+; F.U. Sydney U. Pocumtek Valley Historical Association, Old Deerfield, Massachusetts.

20360 — A plot for preferment. 1636. = pt. of 20345.

20361 — A sermon preached on the fifth of October 1624: at the consecration of St James chappel in Exceter Colledge. 4°. *Oxford, J. Lichfield a. W. Turner,* 1625. L.O.C. DUR⁵.WOR.+; F.HD.NY¹¹.Y. Sydney U.

20362 — Tabulæ ad grammatica Græca introductoriæ. (Tyrocinium [etc.]) 2 pts. 4°. *Oxford, J. Barnesius,* 1607. L(pt. 1 only).O(pt. 1 only).S(pt. 2 only).; ILL.

20363 — [Anr. ed.] 2 pts. 4°. *Oxoniæ, J. Lichfield, væn. ap. E. Pearse,* 1629. L.O.C³.D.DUR⁵.+; Y.

20364 — Editio tertia. (Heptades logicae.) 4°. *Oxoniæ, L. Lichfield, imp. E. Pearse a. T. Allam,* 1639. L.L³. O.C³.CREDITON.+; HN.CHI.

20365 — Wisedomes justification. 1636. = pt. of 20345.

Primaeus, Henricus, *ed. See* 15604.

20366 **Primaleon,** *of Greece.* The first booke of Primaleon of Greece. [*Tr.* A. Munday.] 4°. [*J. Danter*] *f. C. Burby,* 1595. Ent. to J. Charlewood 9 ja. 1589; to C. Burby 10 au. 1594. L.

20366a — The second booke of Primaleon of Greece. *Tr.* A. M(undy.) 4°. *J. Danter f. C. Burby,* 1596. Ent. 10 au. 1594. L(frag.).

20367 — The famous and renowned historie of Primaleon of Greece. The first (second–third) booke. *Tr.* A. M[unday.] 3 pts. 4° in 8's. *T. Snodham,* 1619. Ent. 2 mr. 1618, 20 ap. 1619. L.O(2).C(imp.).NLW. Juel-Jensen(pt. 2 only).; F.HN.HD(imp.).N.Y.

20368 **Prime, John.** The consolations of Dauid, breefly applied to queene Elizabeth: in a sermon. 8°. *Oxford, J. Barnes, sold* [*by T. Cooke, London,*] 1588. L.O(3).

20368.5 — An exposition, and obseruations vpon saint Paul to the Galathians. 8°. *Oxford, J. Barnes, sold* [*by T. Cooke, London,*] 1586. D.

20369 — [A variant, w. imprint:] *Oxford, J. Barnes, sold* [*by T. Cooke, London,*] 1587. L(destroyed).O.C.P.YK.+; PN².

20370 — A fruitefull and briefe discourse in two partes: the one of nature, the other of grace. 8°. *T. Vautrollier f. G. Bishop,* 1583. Ent. 20 ap. O.P.; F.

20370.5 — [Anr. issue, w. prelims. cancelled, w. title:] The weakenes of nature, and the strength of grace; or, an antidote against Arminianisme. [Init. J. P.] *f. J. Boler,* [c. 1630.] F.

20371 — A sermon briefly comparing the estate of king Salomon and his subiectes with queene Elizabeth and her people. Preached in sainct Maries in Oxford. 8°. *Oxford, J. Barnes,* 1585. L.O(2).; F.HN.

20371.5 — [Anr. ed.] 8°. *Oxford, J. Barnes,* 1585. P.; F(2). In title: 'subiects'.

20372 — A short treatise of the sacraments. 8°. *C. Barker,* 1582. Ent. 5 fb. L⁴.c(lacks tp).LK.; CAL⁶.

Primer. For liturgical primers *see* Liturgies, especially 15867 and 15986.

20373 — A prymmer or boke of private prayer. 8°. *ex off. W. Seres,* 1553. O.; PML(imp.). Hoskins 200.
a1^r line 1: 'A Catechis-'. Based on the Book of Common Prayer; *see The Library,* XVIII(1937), pp.192–4. For another Seres imitation of BCP *see* headnote preceding 2370. For liturgical primers

Primer—*cont.*

pub'd by Seres *see* 16087 sqq. *See also* Greg, *Companion,* p.4.

20373.5 — [Anr. ed.] 8°. [*W. Seres,* 1553?] O(imp.).Hoskins 202. With prayer for King Edward. ¶1^r line 1: 'The catechisme, that'.

20374 — [Anr. ed.] A primmer [etc.] 16° in 8's. *ex off. W. Seres,* [1553.] L. Hoskins 201. With prayer for Queen Mary.

20375 — [Anr. ed.] 8°. *ex off. W. Seres,* 1560. L.; CAL(imp.).*. Hoskins 243.

20376 — [Anr. ed.] A booke of private prayer. 16° in 8's. *W. Seres,* [1566?] M. Hoskins 249.

20377 — [Anr. ed.] A primer, or booke [etc.] 8°. *ex off. G. Seresii,* 1568. C. Hoskins 251.

20377.3 — [An abridged ed., w. title:] A primer and a cathechisme, and also the notable fayres. 16° in 8's. *T. Purfoote, assigned by W. Seres,* [c. 1570.] L(tp only, Harl. 5937/117).; F(imp.). Hoskins 253.
(Formerly 16093) Catechism begins B3^r; F8^v line 1 begins: 'godlye'; there are no hymns, cf. 16091. The tp is in the types of 9981.

20377.5 — [Anr. ed.] 16° in 8's. [*T. Purfoot? assigned by W. Seres,* c. 1570.] L(imp.). Hoskins 248.
The L copy (formerly 16091) has quire B from the same setting as 20377.3; F8^v line 1 begins: 'godly'.

20377.7 — [Anr. ed.] 16°. [*assigns of W. Seres,* c. 1580?] C(imp.). Hoskins 254.
Gathered in 16's; catechism begins B1^r. *See* Greg, *Register B,* pp.10, 14, 38, 56, and Arber II.350.

20378 — Preces priuatæ, in studiosorum gratiam collectæ & regia authoritate approbatæ. 16° in 8's. *G. Seres,* 1564. L.O.C³.D.ETON.+; HN.BO.HD.ILL.NY¹¹. Hoskins 247.
Text related to 16042, 16089; a different work from 7576.7.

20379 — [Anr. ed.] 16° in 8's. *G. Seresius,* 1568. L(imp.).L¹⁵. C²(imp.).DUR⁵.; F.NY¹¹.
Date in colophon misprinted 1668.

20380 — [Anr. ed.] Nouiter impressæ & auctæ. 16° in 8's. *G. Seres,* 1573. L.O.C.E.M.+; F.HN(lacks col.).BO.N.Y.+

20381 — [A variant, w. imprint:] *G. Seres,* 1574 (1573.) BUTE.

20382 **Primerosius, Jacobus.** Academia Monspeliensis a Jacobo Primirosio descripta. 4°. *Oxoniæ, ap. J. Lichfield, pro G. Webbe,* 1631. L.O.C.E².SAL.+
Cancel tp pr. as F4, w. Oxford device replacing dedic. to T. Clayton; both at L,O¹³,YK.

20383 — The antimoniall cup twice cast. *Tr.* R. Wittie. 8° in 4's. *B. A[lsop] a. T. Fawcet,* 1640. Ass'd by Fawcet to N. Bourne 11 ja. 1641. L.

20384 — Jacobi Primirosii, doctoris medici, de vulgi in medicinâ erroribus libri quatuor. 12°. *B. A[lsop] & T. F[awcet] pro H. Robinsonio,* 1638. Ent. 8 se. L.O.C.D².LEEDS.+; F.HN.NLM.TEX. Dickinson C.
ELY lacks the last digit in the date.

20385 — Jacobi Primirosii . . . exercitationes, et animadversationes in librum, de motu cordis. Adversus G. Harveum. 4°. *G. Jones pro N. Bourne,* 1630. Ent. 23 mr. L.O.C.D.E.+; F.HD.NLM.NY⁴.Y.+

20385.5 **Primrose, David,** *Advocate.* An apologie for advocates. Declaring the dignitie, merites, and necessitie of their calling. Against P. Hay [12971]. 4°. *Edinburgh, J. Wreittoun,* 1628. O(imp.). Earl of Rosebery.

20386 — Scotlands complaint. Upon the death of king James. [In verse.] 4°. *Edinburgh, J. Wreittoun,* 1625. E(2).; HN.
— Scotlands welcome to king Charles. [1633.] *See* pt. 2 of 7486.
— *See also* 24523.

20387 **Primrose, David,** *Minister.* A treatise of the sabbath and the Lords-day. Englished out of French by G. P[rimrose.] 4° in 8's. *R. Badger f. W. Hope,* 1636. Ent. to N. Bourne 26 ja.; ass'd to W. Hope 14 ap. L.O.C.D².E.+; F.HN.HD.ILL.U.+
Tp is a cancel.

20388 **Primrose, Diana.** A chaine of pearle. Or a memoriall of queene Elizabeth. [In verse.] 4°. [*J. Dawson*] *f. T. Paine, sold by P. Waterhouse,* 1630. Ent. 15 ja. L.E. SNU(imp.).; HN. PML.

20389 **Primrose, Gilbert.** The christian mans teares. 12°. *f. J. Bartlet,* 1625. Ent. 6 no. 1624. O.

20390 — Jacobs vow, opposed to the vowes of monkes and friers. Written in French. And *tr.* J. Bulteel. 4°. *F. Kyngston f. N. Newbery,* 1617. Ent. 10 fb. L.O.C.D.E².; F.CAL².

Primrose, Gilbert—*cont.*

20390.5 — Panegyrique a tres-grand et tres-puissant prince, Charles prince de Galles, &c. 8° in 4's. *Londres* [i.e. *Paris,*] 1624. E.
   (Formerly 5027) L has a variant, w. imprint on tp: *Paris, chez P. Auvray,* 1624.

20391 — The righteous mans evils. 4°. *H. L[ownes] f. N. Newberry,* 1625. Ent. 10 se. 1624. L.L⁴.O.C³.BUTE.; F.PN².

20392 — The table of the Lord. [Two sermons.] 12°. *J. D[awson] f. N. Bourne,* 1626. C.; F.ILL.

20392.5 — [Anr. issue, w. cancel tp and added 3rd sermon.] Three sermons of the table of the Lord, shewing against the papists. (A sermon of the table.) 2 pts. 12°. *W. S[tansby] f. N. Bourne,* 1627. Ent. 3 ja. L(tp to pt. 2 only, Ames II.795).PLUME.
   — *tr. See* 20387.
   — *See also* 12641.

20393 **Primrose, W.** [Heading ¶1ʳ:] A funerall poeme upon the death of Mʳ. Hugh Broughton, who deceased in anno 1612. August the 4. Interred the 7. 4° in 2. [*W. Jaggard?* 1612.] L(now lost).O³.CHATS.; HN.NY⁹.
   CHATS and NY⁹ bd. w. 3887.5; O³ w. 3870.

20393a **Prince.** The princes prayers. 1610. Now = 12582.24.
20393b — Now = 12582.24.

20394 **Principia.** Principia siue maxima legū Anglie a Gallico illo (ut fertur) sermone collecta, et sic in Latinum translata. 8°. *R. Lant,* (38 Henry VIII [1546] (24 de.)) O.; PEN.

20395 — Principia quædam, et axiomata ex iure ciuili sparsim collecta. 16° in 8's. *ex off. H. Binneman,* 1581. HN.

Principle. The principle of all principles. 1624. *See* 1021.5.

20396 **Principles.** The principles of astronomy. Shewing the motions of the planets, and stars. 8°. *E. P[urslowe] f. H. Gosson,* 1640. Ent. 24 no. 1640. L.

Prior, Thomas. *See* 22808.

Priscianus. En Priscianus verberans et vapulans. 1632. *See* 12967.

Priseus, Joannes. *See* 20309.

20397 **Pritchard, Thomas.** The schoole of honest and vertuous lyfe. Also, a laudable discourse, of honorable wedlocke. By. I. R. 4°. [*J. Charlewood f.*] *R. Johnes,* [1579.] O(imp.).; F.HN.

Problema. Problema theologicum. 1607. *See* 23624.3.

Proby, Peter. [Licence to Peter Proby. 1578.] *See* 11108.

Proceedings. The proceedings of the Grisons. 1619. *See* 12390.

Proces. The proces or vnpardonable crimes committed by the Parisians Leaguers. 1590. *See* 11287.5.

Proclamation. A proclamation against the homeloyterers. [1640.] *See* 19974.5.
   — A proclamation by the lords and states. 1618. *See* 11707.
   — A proclimation [*sic*], by the which is prohibited in the research of the passengers ships [etc. 1605.] *See* 18454.7.
   — A proclamacyon of the hygh emperour Iesu Christ. [1534.] *See* 14561.

Proclamations. *See* England (7758 sqq.).

20398 **Proclus, Diadochus.** Προκλου σφαιρα. . . . Procli sphæra. Ptolemæi de hypothesibus planetarum liber singularis. Cui accessit Ptolemæi canon regnorum. Latinè reddidit J. Bainbridge. *Gr. a. Lat.* 4°. *G. Jones,* 1620. L.O.C.D.STU.+; F.HN.BO.NY. Loyola U, Chicago, Illinois.+

20398.3 — Procli diadochi sphæra Thoma Linacro Anglo interprete. 8° in 4's. (*p̄ me R. Pynson,*) [1522?] L.

20398.7 — [A trans.] The descripcion of the sphere or the frame of the worlde, . . . Englysshed by w. Salysbury. 8° in 4's. (*R. Wyer,* 1550 (11 fb.)) G².
   With errata on F2ʳ.

20399 — [Anr. ed., w. additions.] 8° in 4's. (*R. Wyer,*) [1550?] L.L².C⁶.; NLM. 𝔄
   Without errata.

20400 **Procter, Thomas,** *Esq.* A worthy worke profitable to this whole kingdome. Concerning the mending of all high-waies. 4°. *E. Allde,* 1607. L.C².ETON.; HN.BO⁵.

20401 — [Anr. issue, w. cancel tp:] A profitable worke to this whole kingdome. *London,* [*E. Allde,*] 1610. L. O(lacks tp)*.; WIS.

20402 **Procter, Thomas,** *Poet.* A gorgious gallery, of gallant inuentions. [In verse.] 4°. [*W. How f.*] *R. Jones,* 1578. Ent. 5 jn. 1577. L.O. Duke of Northumberland.
   Signed 'T. Proctor' on K4ʳ.

20403 — Of the knowledge and conducte of warres, two bookes. [Init. T. P.] 4°. *in æd. R. Tottelli,* 1578 (7 jn.) Ent. 2 jn. L.O.C(lacks ¶2).DUR(Bamb.).E².+; F.HN.CHI². HD.Y.+
   This is probably by a different Procter.

20404 — The triumph of trueth. [In verse.] 8°. [*London,* 1585?] Ent. to Y. James 28 jn. 1582. O(frag.).

20405 **Procter, William.** The watchman warning. A sermon. 4°. *A. Mathewes, sold at the New Exchange,* 1625. Ent. 25 no. 1624. L.L⁴.C.P.YK.+; F.HN.HD.U.Y.

20406 **Proctor, John.** The fal of the late Arrian. 8°. (*W. Powell,* 1549 (9 de.)) L.O.C.WIN².; F.CHI.
   L,O misdated 1049. This contains the list of reasons for doubting the divinity of Christ w. refutations, found among Marlowe's papers in Kyd's possession.

20407 — The historie of wyates rebellion. 8°. (*R. Caly,*) 1554 (22 de.). L.O⁵.O¹⁷.C.P.+; F.CAL(imp.).HD.MICH.PML.

20408 — [Anr. ed.] 8°. (*R. Caly,*) 1555 (10 ja.) L(2, 1 imp.). L².O.M.STU.+; F.HN.CAL.HD.Y.
   — *tr. See* 24754.

20408.5 **Proctor, Thomas.** Englands purginge fire. Conteyninge two petitions . . . shewinge how the church in England might be ordered, yet more consormably [*sic*] to the will of God. 4°. [*Amsterdam, G. Veseler,*] 1621. L³⁸.C².

20409 — Religions crowne. Wherein are conteyned very proffitable directions, tendinge to meditation, upon the guifts [*sic*] and promises of God in Christe. 4°. *Amsterdam, G. Veseler,* 1621. LINC.

20410 — The right of kings, conteyning a defence of their supremacy. 4°. [*Amsterdam, G. Thorp,*] 1621. L.C⁵. LINC.

20411 — The righteous mans way. Wherein . . . men may meditate upon the commandments of God. 4°. [*Amsterdam, G. Thorp,*] 1621. L.L⁴.SAL.; F.

Proctor, Thomas, *Poet. See* 20402 sqq.

Proditor. Proditoris proditor. 1606. *See* 11924.

Professions. The professions of the true church. 1579. *See* 13066.5.

20412 **Profits.** Here begynnethe a lytyll treatyse whiche is called the .xii. profytes of trybulacyon. [*Tr.* from Peter, *of Blois,* w. other items on the same theme prefixed.] 4° in 6's. (*Westmyster, Wynkyn the worde,*) [1499.] DUR(Bamb.).M. Duff 400.
   For the Caxton ed. [1491] *see* pt. 2 of 3305.

20413 — [Anr. ed.] The .xii. profytes of tribulacyon. 4°⁶·⁴. (*W. de Worde,* 1530 (28 my.)) L.O.O¹⁰.; F.HN.CAL.

Prognostications. *Anonymous*

20414 — [A prognostication for 1498.] Now = 385.3.
20415 — [A prognostication. 1498?] Now = 385.7.
20416 — [A prognostication for 1517.] Now = 470.3.
20417 — [A prognostication for 1523.] Now = 389.3.
20418 — [A prognostication for 1523.] Now = 470.7.
20418.5 — A faythfull and true pronosticacion vp̄ō the yeare .M.CCCCC.xxxvi. gathered out of the prophecies and scriptures of God . . . *tr.* out of hye Almayne by M. Couerdale. (A spirituall almanacke.) 8°. [*Southwark, J. Nicholson f. J. Gough, London,* 1535?] c⁰(lacks col.).
   For later eds. *see* 20423 sq.
20419 — [A prognostication. 1539?] Now = 392.5.
20420 — [A prognostication. 1539?] Now = 392.7.
20421 — [A prognostication for 1541?] Now = 392.9.
20422 — A mery pnosticacion. [1544.] Now = 394.5.
20423 — A faythfull and true pronosticatiō vp̄ō the yere .M.CCCCC.xlviii. (A spirituall almanacke.) *Tr.* M. Couerdale. 8°. [*J. Herford f.*] (*R. Kele,*) [1547?] O(2, 1 imp.).; F.
   For an earlier ed. *see* 20418.5.

Prognostications—*cont.*

20424 — [Anr. ed.] A fayfhful & true pronosticatiō vpō the yeare .M.CCCCC.xlix. 8⁰. [*J. Herford f.*] (*R. Kele,*) [1548?] c(2nd pt. only).LEEDS.; F(1st pt. only). (397 is pt. of this)

20425 — Prognostycacion, and almanacke of two shepherdes. [1556.] Now = 399.7.

20426 — [A prognostication for 1551.] Now = 398.7.

20427 — [A prognostication for 1575?] Now = 401.7.

20428 — [A prognostication for 1594?] Now = 401.8 and 403.7.

20429 — A generall prognostication for ever. 1626. Now = 435.63.

20430 — Prognostication for 1626, for Scotland. Now = 405.5.

— *See* also other anonymous and fragmentary prognostications at the beginning of the Almanack section.

20431 — No entry.

Progress. A merry progresse to London to see fashions. [c. 1620.] *See* 16761.3.

Progymnasma. Progymnasma scholasticum. 1597. *See* 23281.

Promise. The promisse of matrimonie. [1485?] *See* 9176.

Prompter. The prompter, or a cleare explication. 1625. *See* 12792.5.

20432 — The prompters packet of private and familiar letters. 8⁰. *M. Bradwood f. S. Macham,* 1612. Ent. 7 se. 1610. O.

20433 — [Anr. ed.] 4⁰. [*J. Beale?*] *f. S. Macham,* 1633. Ent. 11 ja. 1632. L.

20434 **Promptorium.** Incipit prologus in libellū qui dicitur promptorius puerorum. [t3ʳ:] Finit op⁹ qđ nūcupatur Medulla grāmatice. [By Galfridus, *Anglicus.*] *Eng. a. Lat.* fol. (*per R. pynson in exp. F. egmōdt & P. post pascha,* 1499 (15 my.)) L.O.C.G²(lacks t3).M.+; HN. ILL.MEL (t3 only).PML. Duff 352.

20435 — [Anr. ed.] Promptoriū paruulorum clericorum quod apud nos Medulla grāmatice appellatur [etc.] 4⁰. (*per J. notarium, venundatur ap. bibliopolas in cimetario sancti pauli,* 1508 (12 au.)) L.L²(frag.). c⁷(imp.). Blickling.; Y. According to Ad Lectorem, this and following eds. intended to be issued w. Hortus vocabulorum; *see* 13828.8 sqq.

20436 — [Anr. ed.] Promptuariū paruulorum. 4⁰ ⁸·⁴. *per w. de worde,* (1510 [1511] (17 ja.)) L.

20437 — [Anr. ed.] 4⁰ ⁸·⁴. *per w. de worde,* (1512 (26 my.)) c(imp.).; F.HN.

20438 — [Anr. ed.] 4⁰ ⁸·⁴. *per w. de worde,* 1516 (5 se.) L.O.C.M. WN.+; HN.HD.

20439 — [Anr. ed.] 4⁰ ⁸·⁴. (*per w. de worde,* 1528 (13 my.)) L.

Pronouncing. Century 3. . . . A true and fearefull pronouncing of warre. 1640. *See* Newsbooks 333.

20439.3 **Properties.** Here begynneth the proprytees and medycynes for hors. 4⁰ in 6's. [*W. de Worde,* 1502?] HN(imp.). Duff 353.

20439.5 — [Anr. ed.] Proprytees & medycynes of horses. 4⁰. (*W. de Worde,*) [c. 1525.] Earl Fitzwilliam.

20439.7 — [Anr. ed., w. title:] Mediciues [*sic*] for horses. 4⁰. [*W. Copland,* 1565?] Ent. to J. Rowbotham 1564–65. c²(imp.).LINC.; Mellon.

— The properties of an honest heart. 1638. *See* pt. 2 of 23240.

Prophecies. XII Sibyllarum icones the prophecies of the twelve sybills. [c. 1625.] *See* 22527a.5.

20440 **Prophecy.** A prophesie of the judgment day. Being lately found in saint Denis church in France. *Ballad.* 2 pts. s.sh.fol. [*A. Mathewes*] *f. J. W[hite,* 1620?] c⁶(imp.). With prophecies for 1620–30.

20441 — A prophesie that hath lyen hid, above these 2000. yeares. 1610. Now = 15111.3.

20442 — [Anr. ed.] 1614. Now = 15111.7.

20442a — [A ghost.]

Proposition. A proposition. Concerning kneeling. 1605. *See* 3524.

— A proposition of the princes. 1593. *See* 11288.

Propositiones. Propositiones catholicæ. 1633. *See* 12704.

20443 **Prosopopoeia.** [Heading A1ʳ:] Prosopopoeia. Or, a conference held at Angelo castle, between the pope, the emperor, and the king of Spaine. [A satire in verse.] 4⁰. [*London,* 1619?] L.O.O².; HN.

Prosopopoeia—*cont.*

20444 — Prosopopeia. Or the complaint of the Pyramis, erected by the French king now pulled downe. *Tr.* out of French. 4⁰. *G. Eld,* 1606. Ent. to F. Kingston 27 jy. 1605. L.O.O².C.D.+; F.HN.ILL. *See* also 19884.

20444.5 **Prosper.** Prosper his meditation with his wife. *Lat. a. Eng.* 4⁰. *R. Watkins,* [c. 1570.] c⁷(MS.448²).

20445 **Protestant.** The second part of the protestants plea. 1625. Now = 3895.7.

— Sixe demaunds (from an unlearned protestant.) 1609. *See* 6574.

— Two letters: one written by a protestant. 1603. *See* 15529.

Protestant Divines. History of the modern protestant divines. 1632. *See* 24660.

20446 **Protestant History.** An ecclesiastical protestant historie. 1624. = 3895.

Protestant Princes. Motives to induce the protestant princes. 1639. *See* 7367.5.

Protestants. Catalogus protestantium: or, the protestants kalender. 1624. *See* 25160.7.

20447 — De pace inter evangelicos procuranda sententiæ quatuor: Tho. (Mortoni.) Jo. (Davenantii.) Jos. (Halli.) Ultima ab quibusdam in Gallia theologis. Traditæ J. Duræo. Ab autoribus revisæ. 12⁰. *G. M[iller] pro G. Hammond, prostant ven. per B. Langford,* 1638. Ent. to W. Hammond 4 ja. L.O³.C. E⁴.D.+; F.CAL.CHI.HD.U.+ This book is frequently catalogued under John Durie, the translator.

20447.5 — [A variant, w. imprint:] *G. M[iller] pro G. Hammond,* 1638. O.C³.E.; F.ILL.

— A declaration of the afflictions of the protestants in Saluce. 1620. *See* 21673.5.

— The displaying of the protestantes. 1556. *See* 13557.

20448 — The first part of protestants proofes, for catholikes religion and recusancy. [By R. Broughton?] 4⁰. [*English secret press,*] 1607. L.O.C³.CASHEL.W.+; F. A&R 160. On E3ᵛ is the imprint copied from the orig. French ed.: *Paris, chez F. Gueffier,* 1607.

20449 — The protestants and jesuites up in armes in Gulickeland. Also, a true and wonderfull relation of a Dutch maiden (called Eve Fliegen of Meurs). *Tr.* according to the Dutch coppy. 4⁰. [*N. Okes*] *f. N. Bourne,* 1611. O. *See* also 11088.3.

20449.5 — [A variant, w. title:] The protestants and jesuites together by the eares in Gulicke-land. [Etc.] *f. N. Bourne,* 1611. F.

20450 — Protestants demonstrations, for catholiks recusance. [By R. Broughton?] 8⁰. *Douay,* [*P. Auroi f.*] *J. Heigham,* 1615. L⁴.O.DE.OS.ST. A&R 168.

20450.5 — [Anr. issue, w. tp reset:] Protestants demonstration; for catholicks recusancie. [*Douai,* 1615?] c.; TEX.

20451 — A shorte declaration of the lives and doctrinde [*sic*] of the protestants and puritans. 8⁰ in 4's. *Rouen, in the prnt* [*sic*] *hous of M. Michel,* 1615. L.E².; F. A&R 763.

Protestatio. Protestatio christianissimi regis Gallorum. 1560. *See* 11309.5.

Protestation. A protestation of the kings supremacie. 1605. *See* 3525.

— The protestation of the noblemen. 1638. *See* 21903, 21904.

Proude, Richard. A rutter of the northe. [1555?] *See* 11551.

Prouninck, G. *See* 23228.7.

Provence. A true discourse of an ouerthrow of the Leaguers in Prouince. [1591.] *See* 11290.

Prowse, Anne, *tr. See* 23652.

20452 **Prudent le Choyselat.** A discourse of housebandrie, no lesse profitable then delectable. *Tr.* R. E. 4⁰. *J. Kyngston f. M. Jenynges,* 1577. Ent. to A. Maunsell 11 fb. F.CH.

20453 — [Anr. ed.] 4⁰. *J. Kyngston f. M. Jennynges,* 1580. Ass'd 6 ap. 1579. L.RD(lacks tp).; HD(imp.).

20453.5 Prudentius, Aurelius Clemens. Cathemerinon liber. [Devotional verse. *Ed.*] (Martinus Hegiensis.) 4° [6.4?] [*W. de Worde,* 1523?] o(frags. of 1st 2 quires).

Prynne, William. Anti-Arminianisme. 1630. *See* 20458.
20454 — A breviate of the prelates intollerable usurpations. Edition 3. much enlarged. [W. Huntley, *pseud.*] 4°. [*Amsterdam, J. F. Stam,*] 1637. L.O.C.D.E.+; F.HN.HD.N.NY.+
Often bd. w. 20454.5.
— A brief answer to a late treatise of the Sabbath day. [*Anon.*] [1635?] *See* 4137.7.
20454.3 — [Heading A1ʳ:] Brief instructions for church-wardens and others to observe in all episcopal or archdiaconal visitations and spititual [*sic*] courts. [*Anon.*] 4° in 2. [*G. Dexter a. W. Taylor?* 1637.] E.
See Cal. S.P.D., 1637, pp. 174–5.
20454.5 — [Anr. ed., w. heading ¶1ʳ:] Briefe instructions [etc.] 4° in 2. [*London?* 1637.] L.L³⁸.O.O².C.+; F.HN. HD.
App. not pr. by Stam, though usually bd. w. 20454.
20455 — A briefe survay and censure of Mr. Cozens his couzen-ing devotions [5815.5]. 4°. [*T. Cotes,*] 1628. L⁴.O. C.D.DUR⁵.+; HN.LC.N.NY¹¹.
¶2ʳ catchword: 'Deuotions.'; C3ʳ catchword: 'But'. Some copies (1 o) have prelims. of 20455a.
20455a — [Anr. ed.] 4°. [*T. Cotes,*] 1628. L.O.C.E.M.+; F.CAL². HD.ILL.NY.+
¶2ʳ catchword: 'and'; C3ʳ catchword: 'Spirit'. ¶–¶¶⁴, A–B⁴, N–O⁴ are reimposed from 20455.
— A catalogue of such testimonies. 1637. *See* 4788.
20456 — Certaine quæres propounded to the bowers at the name of Jesus. Fourth edition. [*Anon.*] 4°. [*Amsterdam, J. F. Stam,*] 1636. L.O.C.C².E.+; F.BO³. HD.
20457 — The Church of Englands old antithesis to new Armi-nianisme. 4°. [*A. Mathewes a. Eliz. Allde f. M. Sparke,*] 1629. L.O.C.D.E.+; F.HN.HD.N.U.+
Prob. issued w. 20460 as a 2nd pt. This is one of the bks. Sparke and others printed without licence; *see* Greg, *Companion,* pp. 243–50. Mathewes ad-mitted pr. 10 sheets, prob. A⁴ a–c⁴ B–G⁴.
20458 — [Anr. ed.] Anti-Arminianisme. Or the Church of Englands antithesis. The second edition much en-larged. (An appendix concerning bowing.) 4°. [*Eliz. Allde f. M. Sparke,*] 1630. L.O.C.D.E.+; F.HN.HD.N. U(lacks tp).+ 𝕬
A⁴ a–c⁴ same sheets as 20457, w. A1 a cancel. Linked by errata and table to 20461. 1 HD copy has slip w. 3 extra margin errata pasted on last page. Appendix answered by 19096, 25593.
20459 — A divine tragedie lately acted. [*Anon.* By H. Burton.] 1636. Now = 4140.7.
20459.3 — [Heading *1ʳ:] God no impostor nor deluder. [*Anon.*] 4° in 8. [*London?* 1629?] D.D².; HD.
Pp. 16.
20459.7 — [Anr. ed., revised, w. heading a1ʳ:] God; no impostor, nor deluder. (A coppie of a recantation.—The nine assertations of Lambheth [*sic*].) 4° in 8's. [*A. Mathewes,* 1629?] L.O⁸.C.D.M.+; HN.HD.KAN. U(imp.).
Pp. 37. This is the only ed. w. A coppie and Nine assertions (pp. 29–37), which are reprinted in 20458.
20460 — [Anr. ed., revised, w. title:] God, no impostor nor deluder: or, an answer to a popish and Arminian cavill. 4°. [*Eliz. Allde,*] 1629. L.O.C.M.YK.+; F.HN. HD.ILL.U.+
Pp. 34. Prob. issued w. 20457.
20461 — [Anr. ed., revised.] God, no impostor, nor deluder. Or, [etc.] 4°. [*Eliz. Allde,*] 1630. L.O.C.D.E.+; HN.HD. LC.N.U.+
Pp. 36. Linked w. 20458, which has some errata for this. a*1 cancelled and replaced by 2 leaves: tp as above and dedic. to J. Tolson signed by Prynne.
20462 — Healthes: sicknesse. Or a compendious discourse; proving, the drinking of healthes, to be sinfull. 4°. *Printed at London,* [*A. Mathewes,*] 1628. L.O.C.A.M +; F.HN.HD.N.NY.+
Pp. 86. One o copy, in a contemporary binding, has prelims. of 20463 bd. w. this ed.
20463 — [Anr. ed., corrected.] 4° in 8's. *Printed in London,* [*A. Mathewes,*] 1628. L.O.DUR.G².P.+; F.HN.HD.ILL.U.+
Pp. 95.

Prynne, William—*cont.*
20464 — Histrio-mastix. The players scourge. 4°. E. A[llde, A. Mathewes, T. Cotes] a. W. J[ones] f. M. Sparke, 1633. Ent. 16 oc. 1630; cancelled 1 de. 1634. L³⁰. O⁶.DUR⁵.E.M.+; HN.BO.CHI.JH.NY.+
⁎⁎4ᵛ blank. *See Court Book C,* pp.256–7, 262 and Greg, *Companion,* pp.277–90. Mathewes pr. quires B–M; Cotes N–Z; Allde Aa–Zzz, Aaa*–Kkk*, and Vvvvv to the end; Jones the tp, prelims. and Aaaa–Ttttt, including a cancel for Xxxx2,3.
20464a — [Anr. issue, w. 'Errataes' on **⁎**⁎4ᵛ.] L.O.C².D.E.+; F. HN.HD.N.NY.+
20465 — Lame Giles his haultings. Or, a briefe survey of Giles Widdowes his confutation [25593.] (A short relation of bowing.) 2 pts. 4°. f. G. Widdowes [or rather f. M. Sparke,] 1630. L.O.C.D⁸.DUR⁵.+; F.HN.HD.ILL.U.+
Answered by 19096. M. Sparke and others charged w. printing this without licence; *see* Greg, *Com-panion,* 268–73.
20466 — A looking-glasse for all lordly prelates. [*Anon.*] 4°. [*London?*] 1636. L.O.C.D.E.+; F.HN.HD.N.U.+
20467 — Lord Bishops, none of the Lords bishops. (Good councel for the present state of England.) [*Anon.*] 4°. [*Amsterdam, Cloppenburg Press,*] 1640 (no.) L.O.C. D.E.+; F.HN.HD.N.U.+
20468 — The Lords day, the Sabbath day. The 2. edition. [*Anon.* By H. Burton, revised by W. Prynne.] 1636. Now = 4137.9.
20469 — Newes from Ipswich: discovering certaine late de-testable practises of domineering lordly prelates. [M. White, *pseud.*] 4°. *Ipswich,* [*Edinburgh, G. Anderson,* 1636?] L.O.CASHEL.E.G².+; F.HN(imp.). COR(lacks A3).HD.NY¹¹.
Collates A⁴ B². Copies vary; last page dated 20 Oct. (L,HN) or 12 Nov. (O,F,HD).
20469.3 — [Anr. ed.] 4°. *Ipswich,* [i.e. *London?*] 1636. C.; F.U.
Collates *⁎**⁎4; tp line 4: 'extripate [*sic*]'.
20469.7 — [Anr. ed.] 4°. *Ipswich,* [i.e. *London?*] 1636. HD.NY.
Collates ¶4; tp line 4: 'extirpate'.
20470 — Edition 3. 4°. *Ipswich,* [i.e. *London?*] 1636. L.O.; NY. PH.
Collates ¶4.
20471 — The perpetuitie of a regenerate mans estate. 4°. W. Jones, 1626. Ent. 7 ap. L.O.C.BRISTOL.E⁴.+; F.HN. HD(lacks Fff2).MICH.U.+
20472 — Second edition perused and inlarged. 4° in 8's. W. Jones, 1627. L.O.C.D.YK.+; F.HN.HD.U(w. added sheets of 20473).Y.+
In HD copy ¶8 is cancelled and replaced by §4§§1 answering a speech by B. Duppa at Oxford 10 July 1627.
20473 — [Anr. issue, enlarged, w. cancel tp:] Third edition. [W. Jones] f. M. Sparke, 1627. L.O².C.A.M.+; HN. CU.HD.LC.N.+
Ll8–Mm2 cancelled and replaced by Mm–Rr⁸ Ss⁴.
20474 — A quench-coale. Or a briefe disquisition and inquirie, in what place of the church the Lords-table ought to be situated. All the pretences, of Mr. R. Shelford [22400], E. Reeve [20830], Dr. J. Pocklington [20075], and A late coale from the altar [13270], are here fully answered. By a well-wisher to the truth of God. [*Anon.*] 4°. [*Amsterdam, Richt Right Press,*] 1637. L.O.C.D.E(date cropt).+; F.HN.HD.N.U.+ 𝕬
20475 — XVI. new quæres proposed to our lord prælates. [*Init.* M. E.] 4°. [*Amsterdam, J. F. Stam,*] 1637. L.O⁹.C. D.E.+; HD.NY¹¹.PH.U.Y.+
20476 — The unbishoping of Timothy and Titus. Or a dis-course, prooving Timothy to be no bishop. [*Init.* A. B. C.] 4°. [*Amsterdam, J. F. Stam,*] 1636. BO³. U.WTL.
Collates A–X⁴.
20476.5 — [Anr. issue, w. V3–X4 cancelled and replaced by X–Y⁴ Z² plus an extra leaf of errata.] 1636. L.O.C.D.E. +; F.HN.HD.ILL.U.+
The new quires were possibly pr. in London.
20477 — The unlovelinesse, of love-lockes. Or, a summarie dis-course. 4°. *London,* 1628. L.O.C.D.G⁴.+; F.HN.HD. N.Y.+
D2ʳ line 2: 'needes'.
20477.5 — [Anr. ed.] 4°. *London,* 1628. L.O¹⁷.C⁴.E.YK.+; CH.NY. D2ʳ line 2: 'needs'. Prelims. and quires H–I from same setting as 20477.
— *See also* 1569.

Prys, Edmund, *tr.* *See* 2745.

Psalm. Psalme of prayer and praise. [1614.] *See* 5208.

20478 **Psalms.** Deuout psalmes and colletes. 1567 (1547.) = 2999.

20479 — [Anr. ed.] [1550?] Now = 2999.5.

Psalter. The psalter of the B. virgin Mary. 1624. *See* 17542.7.

Psalterium. Psalteriū btē marie virginis cū articulis īcarnatiōis. [c. 1515.] *See* 17543.
— For liturgical psalters *see* 16253 sqq.

Pseudo-martyr. Pseudo-martyr. 1610. *See* 7048.

20480 **Ptolemy, Claudius.** Here begynneth the Compost of Ptholomeus, *tr.* oute of Frenche. 8° in 4's. (*R. Wyer,*) [1530?] L.; F(imp.).HN.
Consists of extracts from 22407.

20480a — [Anr. ed.] The Compost, of Ptholomeus. 8° in 4's. (*R. Wyer,*) [1540?] HN.
Tp line 1 ends: 'COM'.

20481 — [Anr. ed.] 8° in 4's. (*R. Wyer,*) [1550?] L.
Tp line 1 ends: 'Compost'; B1ʳ line 4 of text: 'almyghty'.

20481.3 — [Anr. ed.] 8° in 4's. (*R. Wyer,*) [1552?] HN.
Tp line 1 ends: 'Compost'; B1ʳ line 4 of text: 'almyghtye'.

20481.7 — [Anr. ed.] 8°. (*T. Colwell,*) [1562?] Ent. 1561–62. HD. NY.

20482 — [Anr. ed., corrected.] 8°. *M. P[arsons] f. H. Gosson, sold by E. Wright,* [1638?] Ent. to H. Gosson 22 de. 1632. L.
— *See* also 20398.

Publication. The publication of the peace. 1616. *See* 16833.

20482.5 **Publilius Syrus,** *Mimus.* [Heading A4ʳ:] Mimus sentences. [In verse.] 16° in 8's. [*London?* c. 1630.] O(frag. of quire A).
A trans. of the so-called *Mimi Publiani* into English couplets. For another version *see* 4841.5, 10437.

20483 **Puccini, Vicenzo.** The life of the holy and venerable mother suor Maria Maddalena de Patsi. *Tr.* (G. B. [or rather *Sir* T. Matthew].) 8°. [*St. Omer, English College Press,*] 1619. L(imp.).L²⁶.O.W.YK²(imp.).+; STL.TEX.
A&R 695.

Puck. The merry Puck, or; Robin Good-fello[w]. [1633?] *See* 12015.5.

20484 **Puckell, Stephen.** A true table of all such fees as are due to the bishop of London. 4°. [*Amsterdam, successors of G. Thorp,*] 1631. L.O.C¹⁰.WIN².; F.HD.

Puede-Ser, Diego, *tr. See* 288, 4911, 4914.

20485 **Puente, Luis de la.** Meditations upon the mysteries of our holy faith. *Tr.* R. Gibbons. The first (second) part. 2 pts. 8°. [*Douai, C. Boscard*; Pt. 2: *P. Auroi,*] 1610. L.O.C.DE.SN.+; F(pt. 1 only).HD.Y.
(Formerly also 20106) A&R 696–7.

20486 — [Anr. ed., enlarged, w. pts. 3–6:] Translated out of Spanish by J. Heigham. The first (second) tome. 2 pts. 4°. *S. Omers,* [*C. Boscard,*] 1619. L.O.C.DE. USHAW.+; F.HN(imp.).HD.N.TEX.+
A&R 698.

20487 — [An abridgement.] Meditations upon the mysteries of our faith. Abbridged [by N. Arnaya], and *tr.* [by T. Everard.] 12° in 6's. [*St. Omer, English College Press,*] 1624. L.L⁹.M².USHAW.W(imp.).+; N.TEX.
A&R 699.

Puer. Stans puer ad mensam. [By J. Lydgate. 1477.] *See* 17030.
— Stans puer ad mensam. [By H. Rhodes. 1545?] *See* 20953.
— Stās puer ad mensā. [By J. Sulpitius.] 1515. *See* 23428.

20487.5 **Puget de la Serre, Jean.** An alarum for ladyes. By the sieur de la Serre. Newly turn'd out of Franch [*sic*] by F. Hawkins, drawing on to the tenth yeare of his age. 8° in 4's. *Paris, chez N. & J. de la Coste,* 1638. L.L¹⁶(imp.).PARIS.
A&R 440.

Puget, de la Serre, Jean—cont.

20488 — Histoire de l'entree de la reyne mere dans la Grande-Bretaigne. Enrichie de planches. fol. *J. Raworth pour G. Thomason & O. Pullen,* 1639. L.O.C⁶.D. HAT.+; F.HD.NY.PML.PN.+

20489 — Histoire de l'entree de la reyne mere dans les provinces unies des Pays-Bas. Enrichie de planches. fol. *J. Raworth pour G. Thomason & O. Pullen,* 1639. L. L⁸.O(2).C.C⁶.; F.HD.NY.NY⁵.PML.+

20490 — The mirrour which flatters not. Transcrib'd English by T. C(ary.) 8°. *E. P[urslowe] f. R. Thrale,* 1639. Ent. 22 oc. 1638. L.O.C.G².LEEDS.+; F.HN.CU.HD.N.+
Copies vary; with and without imprimatur on R8ʳ; both at F.

20491 — The secretary in fashion: or, a compendious and refined way of expression in letters. *Tr.* J. Massinger. 4°. *J. B[eale] a. S. B[ulkley] f. G. Emerson,* 1640. Ent. 19 jn. L.O⁶.; F.HN.HD.N.NY.+

20492 — The sweete thoughts of death, and eternity. [*Tr.*] (H. H[awkins].) 8°. *Paris,* [i.e. *St. Omer, English College Press,*] 1632. L.O.LINC.USHAW.W.+; F.HN.TEX.
A&R 441.

20493 **Pullein, Thomas.** Jeremiahs teares, or a sermon preached in York-minster 1604. 4°. *W. Jaggard f. C. Knight,* 1608. Ent. 21 de. 1607. O.C.M².YK. Bradford PL.; F.HD.

20494 **Pulley, William.** The christians taske: shewing the matter measure reward manner of his salvation. 12°. *G. Eld a. M. Flesher,* 1619. Ent. 17 oc. 1618. L².O.; F.CHI.HD.PN².

Pulmannus, Theodore, *ed. See* 17955, 23886.5.

Pulton, Ferdinand. An abstract of all the penall statutes. 1577, etc. *See* 9527 sqq.
— A collection of sundrie statutes. 1618, etc. *See* 9328 sqq.

20495 — De pace regis et regni. viz. a treatise declaring the great and generall offences of the realme. Collected out of the reports of the common lawes. fol. [*A. Islip*] *f. the Co. of Statrs.,* 1609. L.O.C².BTU.DUR⁵.+; F.HN.CU.HD.ILL.+

20496 — [Anr. ed.] fol. [*A. Islip*] *f. the Co. of Statrs.,* 1610. L.O.C.DUR⁵.NEK.+; F.CHI.HD.LC.Y.+

20497 — [Anr. ed.] fol. [*A. Islip*] *f. the Co. of Statrs.,* 1615. L.O.C⁵.D.SHR.+; F.HN.CHI.HD.U.+

20498 — [Anr. ed.] fol. [*A. Islip*] *f. the Co. of Statrs.,* 1623. L²². O.C.D.E.+; F.HN.CU.HD.N.+
— A kalender, or table, comprehending the effect of all the statutes. 1606, etc. *See* 9547 sqq.

20499 **Punt, William.** A new dialogue called the endightment agaynste mother Messe. [Init. W. P.] 8°. (*W. Hyll a. W. Seres,* 1548 (17 de.)) L².O.C(imp.).NLW.; F.

20500 — [Anr. ed.] 8°. (*W. Hyll a. W. Seres,* 1549 (2 ja.)) O(2). NLW.
Init. W. P. on C6ʳ.

20500.5 — [Anr. ed.] 8°. (*W. Hyll a. W. Seres,* 1549 (2 ja.)) C³.; F.HN.
Punt's name in full on C6ʳ. Most of quire A and part of the outer forme of quire B are corrected and reimposed from 20500.

Purcas, William. The wofull lamentation. [1624?] *See* 20509.7.

20501 **Purchas, Ambrose.** Purchas, his paradise. A sermon. 8°. *R. Raworth,* 1635. L.

20502 **Purchas, Samuel.** The kings towre, and triumphant arch of London. A sermon. 8°. *W. Stansby, sold by H. Fetherstone,* 1623. Ent. to Stansby 5 my. L¹⁵.O.

20503 — Purchas his pilgrim. Microcosmus, or the historie of man. 8°. *W. S[tansby] f. H. Fetherstone,* 1619. Ent. 12 jn. L.O.C.D.E².+; F.HN.CHI.HD.NY.+
App. D1 is a cancel in all copies.

20504 — [Anr. issue, w. cancel tp, w. imprint:] *f. T. Alchorn,* 1627. L.C.C².C⁴.; F.HN.CB.ILL.Y.+
Tp pr. by B. Alsop a. T. Fawcet.

20505 — Purchas his pilgrimage. Or relations of the world and the religions observed in all ages. fol. *W. Stansby f. H. Fetherstone,* 1613. Ent. 7 au. 1612. L.O.C.M.STU. +; F.HN.HD.N.NY.+

20506 — Second edition, much enlarged. fol. *W. Stansby f. H. Fetherstone,* 1614. L.O.C.LIV.WN.+; F.HN.BO.N.NY.+
A

20507 — Third edition, much enlarged. fol. *W. Stansby f. H. Fetherstone,* 1617. L.O.C.A.D².+; F.HN.HD.N.NY.+

Purchas, Samuel—*cont.*

20508 — Fourth edition. fol. *W. Stansby f. H. Fetherstone*, 1626.
CH.MICH.
Title begins: 'Purchase'.

20508.5 — [Anr. issue, w. first quire reset.] E.+; F.HN.HD.N.NY.+
tp).E.+; F.HN.HD.N.NY.+
Title begins: 'Purchas'; w. added dedic. to King
Charles.

20509 — Hakluytus Posthumus or Purchas his pilgrimes. 4 vols.
fol. *W. Stansby f. H. Fetherstone*, 1625. Ent. 11 de.
1621. L.O.C.D.E.+; F.HN.HD.N.NY.+
Engr. tp dated 1624 or 1625; both at HN,HD.

20509.3 **Purchas, Thomas.** The communicants duty, set forth
in eight sermons, preached at Kings-Lynne. 12°. *J.
Norton f. W. Edmonds*, 1639. Ent. 4 mr. L(tp only,
Ames II.1487).; PN².

20509.7 **Purchas, William.** The wofull lamentation of William
Purcas, who for murtherin [*sic*] his mother at
Thaxted in Essex was executed at Chelmsford.
Ballad. 2 pts. s.sh.fol. *f. F. Coules*, [1624?] Ent. to
ballad ptnrs. 14 de. 1624. L.

20510 **Purgation.** A spirituall purgation. [1548?] = 4312.

Purlilia, James, *Earl of. See* 20116.

20511 **Purmerend.** A strange and miraculous accident happened
in the cittie of Purmerent. 4°. [*E. Allde? f.*] *J. Wolfe*,
1599. Ent. 19 fb. L.

20512 **Purser,** *Pirate.* A true relation, of the lives and deaths of
the two English pyrats, Purser, and Clinton. [By
T. Heywood.] 8°. *J. Okes*, 1639. O.

20513 **Purser, William.** Compound interest and annuities.
The grounds and proportions thereof, containing
the art of decimall arithmetick. 8°. [*A. Mathewes*]
f. R. M[ilbourne,] sold by R. Roydon of Bristoll, 1634.
Ent. to Milbourne 5 ap. O.O³.O¹⁰.; HD.Y(imp.).

20514 **Purset, Christopher.** The crib of joy. [Anon. Not by
Purset.] 1611. Now = 6039.5.

Purvey, John. A compendious olde treatyse. 1530. *See*
3021.

20515 **Puteanus, Erycius.** Eryci Puteani amoenitatum huma-
narum diatribæ duæ. 12°. *Oxoniæ, G. Turner, imp.
J. Westall*, 1640. L.O.C.D.E.+; COR.ILL.

20516 — Eryci Puteani Comus, sive phagesiposia Cimmeria.
Somnium. 12°. *Oxonii, G. Turner, imp. H. Curteyne*,
1634. L.O.C.A.CASHEL.+; F.HN.CHI.CU.HD.+

20517 — Eryci Puteani historiæ Insubricæ libri VI. 12°. *Oxonii,
G. Turner*, 1634. L.O.C.A.CASHEL.+; F.HN.CHI.COR.
HD.+

20518 — Eryci Puteani suada attica, sive orationum selectarum
syntagma. Item palæstra bonæ mentis, prorsus
innovata. 8°. *Oxoniæ, G. Turner, imp. T. Robinson*,
1640. L.O⁷.D².ETON.GLOUC.+; F.HN.

20519 **Puttenham, George.** The arte of English poesie. [Anon.]
4°. *R. Field*, 1589. Ent. to T. Orwin 9 no. 1588;
ass'd to Field 7 ap. 1589. L.L³⁰.O.C.E.+; F.HN.CH.NY.
WIS.+

Puttenham, George—*cont.*

20519.5 — [Anr. issue, w. 4 leaves inserted following quire N.]
L(2). L³⁰.; HN.Y.

20520 **Puttock, Roger.** A rejoynder unto W. Malone's Reply
[17213] to the first article. 4° in 8's. *Dublin,* [*W.
Bladen f.*] *Co. of Statrs.*, 1632. L.O.C.D.DUR³.+; F.
HD.
In at least 2C,HD copies this is bd. w. the prelims.
of 23604 and vice versa.

Pye, Thomas. *See* Pie, T.

Pygott, Thomas, *ed. See* 22877.4.

Pyke, Richard. Three to one. [1626?] *See* 19529.

Pykering, Peter. *See* 19897.3.

20521 **Pylbarough, John.** A commemoration of the inestimable
graces and benefites of God . . . composed uppon
the psalme of Benedictus Dominus Deus Israel. &c.
4°. (*in æd. T. Bertheleti,*) 1540. L².O.C⁵.; F.

Pyllet, *Sir* **John.** *See* Indulgences 131 sq.

Pyne, Arthur, *ed. See* 20522.

20521.2 **Pyne, John.** Anagrammata regia. In honorem maximi
regis Caroli conscripta. Opusculum nunc auctoris
operà auctum. [Anon.] 4°. [*W. Stansby*, 1626.] Ent.
to Stansby 20 fb. 1627. L.O(2).O⁴.SHEF.; F.HN.NY.
(Formerly 5020) Prob. issued w. 20521.4. 20521.2–
20521.8 attrib. to Pyne in the stationers' entries.

20521.4 — Epigrammata religiosa, officiosa, jocosa. Anglo-latina,
Latina, Anglica. [Anon.] 4°. [*W. Stansby*, 1626.]
Ent. to Stansby 20 fb. 1627. L.O(2).; HN.NY.
(Formerly 10428) Prob. issued w. 20521.2. Ana-
gram on author's name on L3ᵛ.

20521.6 — Καρδία τοῦ βασιλέως. . . . The heart of the king; and the
king of the heart. [Init. J. P., *Master of Arts.*] 4°.
W. Stansby, 1626. Ent. 20 fb. 1627. O.

20521.8 — [Anr. issue, w. cancel tp, w. imprint:] *W. Stansby*,
1628. HD.

20522 — Musarum deliciae. Contayning more then a select
century of royall Latine anagrams, besides diverse
written in English. Perused anew, and now published
(with the authors assent) by Arthur Pyne. [Anon.]
4°. *A. Griffin*, 1635. Ent. 26 my. L.CHATS.; HN.

Pynner, Charles. *See* 19945 sqq.

Pyott, Lazarus, *tr. See* 542, 4182.

Pyramus. Pyramus and Thisbe. 1617, etc. *See* 11527 sq.

20523 **Pyrrye, C.** The praise and dispraise of women, very
fruitfull to the well disposed minde. And a dialogue
vppon the sentence, know before thou knitte. [In
verse.] 8°. *W. How*, [1569]. Ent. 1568–69. HN.
An earlier version was ent. to R. Serle 1563–64.

20524 **Pythagoras.** A brefe and plesaunte worke, and sience
[*sic*], of Pictagoras. 8°. *W. Copland*, [1560?] L.

Pyttes, John. *See* 19969.4.

Q

Q., G. Elogium serenissimi regis. [1620?] *See* 20564.5.

Q., R., *Gentleman, tr. See* 17185.

Quæstio. Quæstio quodlibetica. 1630. *See* 21768.

20525 **Quæstiones.** Quæstiones (Christo propitio) in vesperiis discutiendae. [1602.] Now = pt. of 13886.
— For other Oxford quæstiones *see* 19016 sqq.

20526 **Quarles, Francis.** Argalus and Parthenia. [In verse.] 4°. *f. J. Marriott*, 1629. Ent. 27 mr. L.O.C³.C¹⁰.E².+; F.HD.
Pp. 160.

20526.5 — [Anr. ed.] 4°. *f. J. Marriott*, 1630. DUL.
Pp. 154; Bk. II line 2 ends: 'neere.'

20527 — [Anr. ed.] Newly perused perfected and written. 4°. *f. J. Marriott*, 1632. O⁹.C.C².E².; F.
Pp. 154; Bk. II line 2 ends: 'neer.'; Bk. III line 1 ends: 'ouerblowne'.

20527.5 — [Anr. ed.] 4°. *f. J. Marriott*, 1632. L.O²⁸(imp.).C¹⁷. CARLISLE.SH(lacks tp).; F.PML.PN². Pirie.
Pp. 154; Bk. II line 2 ends: 'neer.' Bk. III line 1 ends: 'overblowne'. L,C¹⁷, CARLISLE,F,PML have this text, but w. date erased from engr. tp.

20528 — [Anr. ed.] 4°.*f. J. Marriott*, [c. 1635.] O. Juel-Jensen.; F.
Pp. 152; Bk. II line 1 ends: 'cleare,'; Bk. III line 2: 'showrs'.

20528.5 — [Anr. ed.] 4°. *f. J. Marriott*, [c. 1635.] HN.BO.
Pp. 152; Bk. II line 1 ends: 'cleare,'; Bk. III line 2: 'show'rs'.

20528a — [Anr. ed.] 4°. *f. J. Marriott*, [c. 1635.] L³⁰.O.C.C².C¹². ; F.HD.ILL(imp.).SUNY(Buffalo).WEL.
Pp. 152; Bk. II line 1 ends: 'clear,'.

20528a.5— [Anr. ed.] 4°.*f. J. Marriott*, [c. 1635.] L⁶.O⁶.WI.; HN. CAL.HD.N.
Pp. 152; Bk. II line 1 ends: 'clar,'.

20529 — Divine fancies: digested into epigrammes, meditations, and observations. [In verse.] 4°. *M. F[lesher] f. J. Marriot*, 1632. Ent. 7 fb. L.O.O⁹.E.WI.+; F.HN.HD. NY.TEX.+

20530 — [Anr. ed.] 4°. *M. F[lesher] f. J. Marriot*, 1633. L.O. Nottingham PL.; F.HN.HD.ILL.N.+

20531 — [Anr. ed.] 4°. *M. F[lesher] f. J. Marriot*, 1636. L.C.C¹². INN. Juel-Jensen.+; F.HN.HD.ILL.Y.+

20532 — [Anr. ed.] 4°. *M. F[lesher] f. J. Marriot*, 1638. L.L⁶.O⁹. C.LEIC².+; F.HN.CHI.HD.Y.+

20533 — Divine poems: containing the history of Jonah. Ester. Job. Sions sonets. Elegies. 8°. (*M. Flesher*) *f. J. Marriott*, 1630. Pt. ass'd to M. Flesher 21 my. 1628; the rest to J. Marriot 29 ap. 1630. L.O.O⁶(2).C¹². DUL.; F.HN.HD.N.Y.+
(2nd pt. formerly also 20547) Reprints 20544, 20546, 20550, 2782, 2776.

20534 — [Anr. ed.] Newly augmented. 8°. *M. F(lesher) f. J. Marriot*, 1633 (1632.) L.O.C.M.NLW.+; F.HN.HD (lacks A1).PML. Missouri U.+
Engr. tp in this and following eds. dated 1632.

20535 — [Anr. ed.] 8°. *M. F(lesher) f. J. Marriot*, 1634. L.O.C. COL.NLW.+; F.HN.HD.N.U(lacks engr. tp).+

20536 — [Anr. ed.] 8°. *M. F(lesher) f. J. Marriot*, 1638. L⁶.O³⁹. C(lacks A1).BIRM².E.+; F.HN.CAL.ILL.PML.+

20536.5 — [Anr. issue, w. cancel letterpress tp w. imprint:] *M. F[lesher] f. J. M[arriot] sold by L. Blaikelocke*, 1638. L.O¹¹(lacks letterpress tp)*.O⁴⁴.G².; HD.ILL.Y. Lehigh U.

20537 — An elegie upon my deare brother, the Jonathan of my heart, Mʳ. J. Wheeler. 8°. *T. C[otes] f. N. Alsop a. T. Nicholes*, 1637. Ent. 27 ja. L.; F.HN.

20538 — An elegie upon the truely lamented death of sir Julius Cæsar. 8°. [*M. Flesher*] *f. J. Marriott*, 1636. HN.

20539 — An elegie. Upon the death of sir J. Wolstenholme. 1640. = pt. of 20552.

Quarles, Francis—*cont.*
20540 — Emblemes by Fra: Quarles. (Quarleis. [By E. Benlowes.]) 8°. *G. M[iller], sold at J. Marriots shope*, 1635. Ent. 2 my. 1634. L.O.C¹⁹.G²(lacks Quarleis).; F.HN.HD.N.NY.+
A2ʳ line 9: 'playd'; N4ʳ: quotation from St. Augustine. Quarleis (X1–Y2) is from the same typesetting in this and 20540.5. In some copies (L,HD) there is inserted bef. X1 a letterpress tp (formerly 1878): 'Lusus Poëticus Poëtis. *G. M[iller],* 1634.'

20540.5 — [Anr. ed.] 8°. *G. M[iller], sold at J. Marriots shope*, 1635. L(lacks Quarleis).L⁵.W.; F.HN.BO.HD(quires I–V only).PFOR(lacks Quarleis).+
A2ʳ line 9: 'played'; N4ʳ: no quotation from St. Augustine.

20541 — [Anr. ed.] = Wing Q 80.

20542 — [Anr. ed., enlarged.] Emblemes. (Hieroglyphikes.) 8°. *J. D(awson) f. F. Eglesfeild* [sic], 1639. Ass'd to J. Williams a. Eaglesfield 13 oc. 1640. L.L⁶.L¹⁶.O.D.; F.HN.HD.WTL.
This does not reprint Quarleis. Regarding lawsuit between Quarles and Eaglesfield *see The Library* XV(1934), pp.97–109.

20543 — Enchyridion containing institutions. Divine. Morall. [etc.] 24° in 12's. *T. Cotes*, 1640. Ent. to N. Alsop 21 no. 1639. L.

20544 — A feast for wormes. Set forth in a poeme of the history of Jonah. (A hymne to God.—Eleven meditations.— Pentelogia.) 4°. *F. Kyngston f. R. Moore*, 1620. Ent. 11 ap. L.L².O.C.C⁸.+; HN.HD.LC(lacks tp).N.NY.+

20545 — [Anr. ed.] 4°. *F. Kyngston f. R. Moore*, 1626. L.O.C¹⁰. LEEDS.M.+; F.HN.HD.ILL.PML.+

20546 — Hadassa: or the history of queene Ester: with meditations. [In verse.] 4°. [*F. Kingston*] *f. R. Moore*, 1621. Ent. 10 ja. L.O.C⁸.E.M.+; F.HN.HD.N.NY.+

20547 — [Anr. ed.] 1630. = pt. of 20533.

20548 — Hieroglyphikes of the life of man. [In verse.] 8°. *M. Flesher f. J. Marriott*, 1638. Ent. 10 ja. L.L⁵.O.C.G². +; F.HN.HD.NY.PML.+

20549 — The historie of Samson. [In verse.] 4°. *M. F[lesher] f. J. Marriott*, 1631. Ent. 8 no. 1630. L.O.O¹¹.E².G².; F.HN.HD(imp.).ILL.PML.+

20550 — Job militant: with meditations divine and morall. [In verse.] 4°. *F. Kyngston f. G. Winder*, 1624. Ent. 13 oc. 1623. L.O.C.E.M.+; F.HN.HD.N.NY.+

20551 — Memorials upon the death of sir R. Quarles. 8°. *T. Cotes f. N. Alsop*, 1639. Ent. 25 jn. L.; HN.HD.
Set as a monumental inscription.

20552 — Sighes at the contemporary deaths of the countesse of Cleaveland and mistrisse C. Killegrue. (An elegie. Upon sir J. Wolstenholme.) [In verse.] 8°. *T. Cotes f. N. Alsop*, 1640. Ent. 10 fb. L(1st pt. only).; HN. HD.NY.
(2nd pt. formerly 20539)

20553 — Sions elegies. 1624. = 2782.
20554 — Sions sonets. 1625. = 2776.

Quarles, Francis, *Minister, ed. See* 25292.3.

Queen. The Queenes Arcadia. 1606. *See* 6262.
— The queenes praiers. 1545, etc. *See* 3009 sqq., 4818 sqq.

20555 **Quelch, William.** Church-customes vindicated: in two sermons. 4°. *M. F[lesher] f. N. Butter*, 1636. L.O.C. P.WOR.+; F.HN.HD.U.Y.+

Quench-coal. A quench-coale. 1637. *See* 20474.

Quentin, John. *See* 15969.

Quercitanus, Josephus. *See* Du Chesne, J.

Querelæ. Querelæ Saravictonis & Biomeæ. 1620. *See* 14714.5.

Queries. Certaine quæres propounded. 1636. *See* 20456.
— XVI. new quæres. 1637. *See* 20475.

20556 **Querimonia.** Querimonia ecclesiæ. [etc.] 4°. *ex typ. J. Windet pro R. Watkins,* 1592. L².O.C.D.E.+; F.ILL. TEX.
  (Formerly also 10399)
— Querimonia Europæ. 1625. *See* 10570.

Questionary. The questyonary of cyrurgyens. [1543.] *See* 12468.

20557 **Questions.** Certaine questions by way of conference betwixt a chauncelor and a kinswoman of his concerning churching of women. 8°. [*Middelburg, R. Schilders,*] 1601. L.C².WIN².
— Certayne questions demaunded by the realme of Englande. [1555.] *See* 9981.
20557.5 — [Heading A1ʳ:] Certaine questions propounded to archbishops, bishops, archdeacons, . . . and other audacious usurpers upon his majesties royall prerogative, lawes, and his loyall subjects lawfull liberties. [Regarding the canons of May 1640.] 4°. [*London,* 1640?] O.WIN².; PN.
20558 — Certayne short questions and answeres. Very profitable for yong children, to be instructed in the principles of the christian faith. 8°. *H. Middleton f. T. Man,* 1580. Ent. 27 jn. C².D(imp.).; F.
20559 — [Anr. ed.] 8°. *R. Waldegraue f. T. Man,* 1582. O.E.
20560 — [Anr. ed.] 8°. *J. K[ingston] f. T. Man,* 1584. L.
20560.3 — Questions propounded to the professors of the chuch[*sic*]-assemblies of England. 1/2 sh.fol. [*Amsterdam?* c. 1608?] HD.
20560.7 — Questions worthy to be consulted on for the weale publyque. s.sh.fol. [*J. Kingston,* c. 1555.] L⁵(Lemon 15).
— Short questions and answers. 1579, etc. *See* 18816 sqq.

20561 **Quevedo, Francesco de.** Visions, or, hels kingdome, and the worlds follies and abuses, strangely displaied by [i.e. *tr.*] R. C(roshawe,) of the Inner Temple. [Anon.] 12°. *E. G[riffin] f. S. Burton,* 1640. Ent. 12 fb. 1639. L.O.; F.PN².

20562 **Quilibet.** Let Quilibet beware of Quodlibet. 8°. [*London?* 1602.] L.O².O⁵.O¹⁷.C.; F.COR.
  Answers 25123.

20563 **Quin, Walter.** Corona virtutum principe dignarum, . . . in usum D. Caroli principis. 12°. [*W. Stansby*] *ap. J. Billium,* 1613. L.O.O⁵.C.DUR⁵.+; F.HN.CAL.N.
20563.5 — [Anr. ed.] 12°. *ap. J. Billium,* 1615. E.
20564 — [Anr. ed.] 12°. *ap. J. Billium,* 1617. L.O.O³.BIRM. Warrington PL.+; F.HN.ILL.WTL.
20564.5 — Elogium serenissimi regis, carmina acrostica [etc. Init. G. Q.] s.sh.fol. [*G. Purslowe?* 1620?] E.
20565 — In nuptiis principum incomparabilium Caroli, et Henriettæ Mariæ, gratulatio quadrilinguis. 4°. *G. Purslow,* 1625. L. A
20566 — The memorie of the most worthie Bernard Stuart, lord D'Aubigni renewed. [In verse.] 4°. *G. Purslow,* 1619. Ent. 7 fb. L.O(2).BUTE.E.; F.HN.
20567 — Sertum poeticum, in honorem Jacobi sexti. [In verse.] 4°. *Edinburgi, R. Walde-grave,* 1600. L.E².D.; HN.
  E bd. w. 20566.

20567.3 **Quintilianus, Marcus Fabius.** M. Fabii Quintiliani institutionum oratoriarum libri duodecim. Novæ huic editioni adiecit Fabianarum notarum spicilegium Daniel Pareus. Accesserunt Declamationes. 8°. *Francofurti, sumpt. H. Robynson,* [*London,*] *& G. Fitzeri,* 1629. C.
  Pref. by H. Fetherstone.

20567.7 **Quip.** A quip for a scornfull lasse. Or, three slips for a tester. *Ballad.* 2 pts. s.sh.fol. [*M. Flesher*] *f. F. Grove,* [c. 1627.] Ent. 5 mr. 1627. C⁶.

Quips. Pleasant quippes for vpstart newfangled gentlewomen. 1595. *See* 12096.
— Quips upon questions. 1600. *See* 775.5.

R

20568   **R.** Death's loud allarum. [1635?] = 5420.

R., A. Clavis Homerica. 1638. *See* 21072a.
— Κουρεὺς ἀπόξυρος. 1627. *See* 21327.

20569   — True and wonderfull. A discourse relating a strange serpent in Sussex . . . August. 1614. 4°. [*E. Allde f.*] *J. Trundle,* [1614.] Ent. 24 au. 1614. O.O⁵.

R., B. Spirituall encrease. 1620, etc. *See* 21098.5 sq.

R., B., *Master of Arts. See* 17529.

R., C. Friendly counsaile. [1633?] *See* 20821.
— A mostpleasant [*sic*] dialogue. [1632.] *See* 20822.5.

20570   — The true discripcion of this marueilous straunge fishe, whiche was taken in the yeare .M.DLX.ix. s.sh.fol. (*T. Colwell,*) [1569.] Ent. 1568–69. L.

R., D., *B. in Divin.* A practicall catechisme. 1632, etc. *See* 21166 sqq.
— A treatise of the two sacraments. 1633, etc. *See* 21169 sqq.

R., E. A familiar and christian instruction. 1582. *See* 16814.

20571   — Two fruitfull exercises, the one: a christian discourse vpon the 16. and 17. verses of the 16. chapter of Judges, the other: a godly meditation. Also a buckler against a Spanish brag. 8°. [*Eliot's Court Press,*] *imp. G. Bishop,* 1588. Ent. 19 se. L.; F.PN².Y.
— *See also* 25232.

R., F. Meditations of instruction. 1616. *See* 21342.
— Thule. 1598. *See* 21348.

R., G. Theses philosophicæ. 1596. *See* 7487.1.
— Y drych cristianogawl. 1587. *See* 21077.
— *tr. See* 13112.

R., H. A defiance to fortune. 1590. *See* 21078.
— Honours conquest. 1598. *See* 21082.
— Lancaster his allarums. [1595.] *See* 21083.
— Mythomystes. [1632.] *See* 20939.

20572   — Newes from the Leuan[t]e seas. Discribing the many perrilous euents of Edward Glenham. [By Henry Roberts?] 4°. [*J. Roberts*] *f. W. Wright,* 1594. Ent. 19 au. L.
— Our Ladys retorne to England. 1592. *See* 21087.3.

R., H., *Esq.* Γαμηλια on the happy marriage. 1640. *See* 21179.

R., I. or **J.** An answere to a romish rime. 1602. *See* 20959.
— The countrie mans comfort. 1637. *See* 20961.
— Daphnes trophees. 1619. *See* 20664.
— The displaying of an horrible secte. [1578.] *See* 21181.

20573   — An elegie upon the death of the most illustrious Gustavus Adolphus. [In verse. By J. Russell, *of Magd. Coll., Cambridge.*] s.sh.fol. [*Cambridge, T. a. J. Buck,* 1633?] L.
     Reprinted in 21460. Incorrectly entered as Wing R 22.

20574   — An epitaph, on the death of the late most reuerend father in God, John [Whitgift]: arch-byshop of Canterburie. [In verse. By J. Rhodes?] 8°. *W. White,* 1604. L.; HN.

20575   — A most straunge, and true discourse, of the wonderfull judgement of God. Of a monstrous, deformed infant. 4°. [*E. Allde*] *f. R. Jones,* 1600. Ent. 28 ap. O.

20575.5   — Organon reipublicæ. [A treatment in outline form of such topics as studies, government, war.] obl. 4°. *ex off. R. Bradoci,* 1605. Ent. 24 ja. D.

20575.7   — [A trans.] Organon reipublicæ, or the north starre of pollicie. [Anon. *Tr.*] (E. Sadler.) obl.4°. *T. C[reede] f. W. Welby,* 1605. Ent. 12 au. BO⁵.
— A paire of spectacles for Sir H. Linde. 1631. *See* 11112.

R., I. or **J.**—*cont.*

20576   — A poeme, on the kings most excellent majesties progresse into Scotland. May. 1633. 8°. *London,* [*f. F. Grove,*] 1633. Ent. to F. Grove 10 my. L.
— Purgatories triumph. 1613. *See* 11114.

20577   — The spy discovering the danger of Arminian heresie and Spanish trecherie. [In verse. By John Russell, *of Magd. Coll., Cambridge.*] 4°. *Strasburgh* [i.e. *Amsterdam, successors of G. Thorp,*] 1628. L.O.C.STU.YK.+; F.HN.HD.N.U.+

20578   — The taming of a shrew: or, the onely way to make a bad wife good. [Verses signed J. R.] [after 1665.]
     Not an STC item; perhaps = Wing R 19.

20579   — The trades increase. 1615. Now = 14894.7.
— *ed. See* 17278.5.
— *tr. See* 1845, 3398, 18001, 19131.
— *See also* 20397.

R., I., *Cantabrigiensis.* De hypocritis vitandis. 1595. *See* 20599.

R., I., *D.D.* The dove-like soule. [1625.] *See* 1st sermon of 20774.

R., I., *D. of Divinity.* The discovery of the man of sinne. 1614. *See* 20609.

R., I., *P.* A word of comfort. 1623. *See* 11118.

R., I., *Student in Divinity.* The overthrow of the protestants pulpit-babels. 1612. *See* 11111.

R., I. H. The most excellent historie of Lysimachus. 1604. *See* 13510.

20579.5   **R., James.** [The perfect pathway to salvation.] 16° in 8's. [*T. Orwin,* 1590?] Ent. to J. Judson 29 oc. 1580 a. 4 oc. 1585; to T. Orwin 1 jn. 1590. c(lacks tp).
     Prayers at end for Queen Elizabeth. James R. is prob. James Rowbotham, who had the orig. copyright; *see* Arber II.380.

20580   — [Anr. ed.] The perfect path-way to salvation. 16° in 8's. [*E. Allde*] *f. H. Astley,* 1603. Ass'd to T. Gosson 26 jn. 1590; ent. to T. Dawson 1 mr. 1596; to H. Astley 3 no. 1600. L.O.
     Prayers at end for King James.

20581   — [Anr. ed., enlarged.] 16° in 8's. *T. Snodham,* 1618. Ass'd to T. Man, jun., 16 jn. 1609. F(imp.).

R., L. An antidot for lazinesse. 1624. *See* 21138.

20582   — The boke Reade me frynde. 1546. Now = 1462.9.

20582.5   — A subtill practise, wrought in Paris by fryer Frauncis, who to deceiue fryer Donnet of a sweet skind nun which he secretly kept, procured him to go to Rome. 4°. [*A Islip*] *f. T. Nelson,* 1590. Ent. 26 jn. HN.

R., L., *Presbyter.* The genealogie of protestants. 1621. *See* 21138.3.

20583   **R., M.** The mothers counsell, or, live within compasse. 16° in 8's. *f. J. Wright,* 163[0?] Ent. 24 ja. 1623. L(tp mutil.).O(2, w. tpp. mutil.).
     Prob. issued w. 14900.

20584   — A president for young pen-men. Or the letter-writer. 4°. *G. Eld f. R. Wilson,* 1615. L.O(2).

20584.5   — Third impression, corrected and amended. 4°. *N. Okes f. M. Walbancke,* 1620. Sotheby's 11 June 1902, lot 711. Bought by W. Carew Hazlitt (*see* his *Bibliographical Collections* IV.322), but, according to notes by W. A. Jackson, the item was returned as imperfect since it lacked quire D and had a duplicate of quire G.

20585   — Fourth impression, newly corrected. 4°. *J. Okes f. M. Walbanke,* 1638. Ass'd from N. Okes to Walbank 3 mr. 1626. L.; HD.

R., N. A copie of a lettre. 1587. *See* 370.5.

R., N., *Gent.* Poems. Divine, morall. 1632. *See* 21010.7.

20585.3 **R., O.** An easie entraunce into the chiefe poynts of christian religion: gathered, by a minister. 8°. *R. Walde-graue,* [c. 1585.] L².
   Not same text as 11833, 13826.

20585.5 **R., P.** The art to dye well. Or a briefe and easy methode, how to direct ones life, to a secure & happy end. 12°. [*St. Omer, English College Press,*] 1626. AUG.
   A&R 700. A different work from 1838.5.
— The lamentatiõ of lady Scotland. 1572. *See* 22011.

20585.7 — A pensiue mans praiers. 12°. *T. Scarlet,* 1596. HN.
— A quiet and sober reckoning with M. T. Morton. 1609. *See* 19412.
— A treatise tending to mitigation. 1607. *See* 19417.

20586 **R., R.** The house-holders helpe, for domesticall discipline. [Init. R. R., *Minister,* i.e. R. Rogers?] 8°. *G. Purslowe f. J. Budge,* 1615. Ent. 30 oc. O.; F.HD(frag.).

20587 — Post nubila sudum. (In obitum Elisabethae [etc.]) [In verse.] 4°. *Oxoniæ, ap. J. Barnesium,* 1603. L.C⁵.

20587.5 — Questions, concernyng conie-hood, and the nature of the conie. . . . As they were studiously acted in Germanie. 4°. [*R. Jones,* 1595.] Ent. to R. Jones 5 jn. 1595. F(imp.).
   Dedic. dated 4 June 1595.
— *ed. See* 21289.
— *tr. See* 3902, 20885.

R., R., *Minister. See* 20586.

20588 **R., R.,** *of Lincoln's Inn.* A consort of the creatures, with the creator, and with themselues. [By R. Rawlyns.] 8°. *T. Orwin f. W. Young a. R. Jac-son,* 1591. Ent. to T. Orwin 11 ja. F.

R., Ric. Godly prayers. 1579. *See* 17790.5.

R., S. [For items initialled 'S. R.' *not* listed below, *see* Rowlands, S.]
— An answer to T. Bels challeng. 1605, etc. *See* 22809 sq.
— Greenes ghost haunting conie-catchers. 1602, etc. *See* 12243 sq.
— Martin Mark-all. 1610. *See* 21028.5.
— The noble souldier. 1634. *See* 21416.

20588.5 — Ruth reuiued. [A verse paraphrase of the Book of Ruth.] 8°. *Oxford, L. Lichfield f. T. Allam,* 1639. O⁵.
— *tr. See* 712.

R., S., *Gent.* The choise of change. 1585, etc. *See* 21132 sqq.
— *tr. See* 21134.5.

R., T. The catechisme in meter. 1583. *See* 4800.3.

20589 — A confutation of the tenne great plagues, prognosticated by J. Doleta [in 6992] . . . 1587. 8°. *R. Walde-graue,* [1587.] Ent. 5 de. 1586. O.
   Collates A–B⁸.

20589.5 — [Anr. ed.] 8°. *R. Walde-graue,* [1587.] St. Paul's School, London (frag., in binding of 15621.7).; HN.
   Collates [–]⁸.
— Cornelianum dolium. 1638. *See* 20691.
— Deuteromelia. 1609. *See* 20757.
— Melismata. 1611. *See* 20758.
— The muses looking-glasse. 1638. *See* 20694.

20590 — Robin Hood and the beggar. [after 1660.]
   Not an STC item.

20591 — Robin Hood and the butcher. [after 1660.]
   Not an STC item.

20592 — [Anr. ed.] [after 1660.] Perhaps = Wing R 1629.
— *tr. See* 14385.

R., T., *Minister, ed. See* 26037a.

R., V., *tr. See* 1838.

R., W. An advice how to plant tobacco. 1615. *See* 23612.
— A brief, and cleere confutation. 1603. *See* 24994.5.
— The English ape. 1588. *See* 20698.
— A match at mid-night. 1633. *See* 21421.

20593 — The most horrible and tragicall murther of John lord Bourgh. Togeather with the sorrowfull sighes of a sadde soule, vppon his funerall: written by W. R. a seruaunt of lord Bourgh. 4°. *R. R[obinson,]* 1591. Ent. to Robinson 26 ja. L².O.; HN.
   W. R. wrote only the verses. *See also* 5813, 5814.

20594 — A treatise of the sacrament of confirmation. [By R. Smith, *Bp. of Chalcedon.*] 8°. *Doway, G. Pinchon,* 1629. L⁹.O(imp.).C.A².W.+; F.Y.
   A&R 778.

20595 **R., W.,** *Esquire.* Mount Tabor. 1639. = 25752.

R., W., *Gent.* A merrie and pleasant comedy. 1638. *See* 21422.

20595.5 **R., W. S.,** *tr.* True newes of a notable victorie obtayned against the Turkes. By the lorde, Adolph baron of Swartzburg, anno 1598. Before Raab. *Tr.* out of the high Dutch coppy. 4°. *J. R[oberts]f. R. Olive,* [1598.] Ent. 13 my. 1598. L.
— *See also* 6396.5.

R. de M., D. F. *See* 17131.

20596 **Raban, Edward.** The glorie of man consisting in the excellencie of woman. Gathered out of holie scriptures, [etc.] Whereunto is annexed The duetie of husbands (drawne out of [4698]). [Anon.] 8°. *Aberdene, printed by the author* [E. Raban,] 1638 (6 jn.) E(w. Raban's signature on tp).

20597 — [Heading B1ʳ:] Rabans resolution against drunkennes and whoredome: [etc.] 8°. [*St. Andrews, E. Raban,* 1622.] C(quire B only).

Rabbards, Ralph, *ed. See* 21057.

Rabbotenu, Isaac, *pseud. See* 17445.

20598 **Raben, Gottfried.** The confession and publike recantation of thirteene personages. 1602. Now = 1074.5.

Rablet, Richard, *ed. See* 5452.

Racan, Honorat de Bueil, *Marquis de. See* 4016.5.

20599 **Racster, John.** De hypocritis vitandis. Auctore I. R[acster]. Cantabrigiensi. 4°. *Cantabrigiæ, ex off. J. Legatt,* 1595. L².C.C².C⁵.; F.

20600 — The true art of living well. The right use of things indifferent. The plaine foot-path to God. Three sermons. 8°. [*R. Field*] f. *T. Clarke,* 1605. Ent. 9 oc. 1604. O(imp.).LINC(tp torn).; HN.

20601 — A booke of the seuen planets, or, seuen wandring motiues, of W. Alablasters [i.e. Alabasters] wit, retrograded or remoued. 4°. *P. Short f. A. Wise,* 1598. Ent. 7 oc. L².O.C.C³.D.+; F(2).HN.NY.U.
   Tp varies: with or without '(Aut mentiuntur papistæ.)'; both at F. *See also* 10799.

20601.5 — [Anr. issue, w. cancel tp pr. as M4.] William Alablasters seuen motuies [*sic*]. Remoued and confuted. *P. Short f. A. Wise,* 1598. L.O.C.; HD.Y.
   In many copies (L, O, HD, Y) the orig. tp is uncancelled.

Radegunde, *Saint.* Here begynneth the lyfe of saynt Radegunde. [c. 1525.] *See* 3507.

20602 **Radford, John.** A directorie teaching the way to the truth in a discourse against the heresies of this time. Whereunto is added, a short treatise against adiaphorists. 8°. [*English secret press,*] 1605. L.C.D.M. USHAW.+ ; F.HN.HD.N.U.+
   A&R 701.

20602.5 **Ragged.** Ragged, and torne, and true. Or, the poore mans resolution. *Ballad.* 2 pts. s.sh.fol. *assignes of T. Symcocke,* [1628–29.] Ent. to F. Grove 20 de. 1630. L.

20603 **Rainbow, Edward,** *Bp.* Labour forbidden, and commanded. A sermon. 4°. [*J. Beale*] f. *N. Vavasour,* 1635. Ent. 15 ja. L.O.C.D.YK.+ ; F.HN.HD.N.U.+

Rainold, Thomas. A compendious declaration. 1551. *See* 20779.

20604 **Rainolde, Richard.** A booke called the foundacion of rhetorike. 1563. Now = 20925a.5.

20605 **Rainolds, John.** An answere to a sermon preached the 17 of April 1608, by G. Downame [7125]. [Anon. Not by Rainolds.] 2 pts. 4°. [Pt. 1: *Amsterdam, J. Hondius*; Pt. 2: *Amsterdam, G. Thorp,*] 1609. L.O.C. D.E.+ ; F.HN.HD.N.U.+

20606 — Johannis Rainoldi, de romanæ ecclesiæ idololatria [*sic*], in cultu sanctorum, reliquiarum, . . . libri duo. 4° in 8's. *Oxoniæ, ap. Jos. Barnesium,* 1596. Ent. to John Barnes 7 jn. 1602. L.O.C.D.E.+ ; F.HN.CHI.HD.NY.+

20607 — A defence of the judgment of the reformed churches [touching adultery and remarriage]. Wherin both R. Bellarmin and an English pamphlet are cõfuted. [Ed.] 4°. [*Dort, G. Waters,*] 1609. L.O.C.D.E.+ ; F. HN.HD.N.NYᴵᴵ.+

Rainolds, John—*cont.*

20608 — [Anr. ed.] 4°. [*Dort,*] *G. Walters* [*sic*], 1610. L.O.C.D. DUR(Bamb.).+; F(2).CHI.HD.U.Y.+

20609 — The discovery of the man of sinne: wherein is set forth the changes of Gods church. First preached in divers sermons by J R[ainolds] D. of Divinity and now published by W. H(inde.) 4°. *Oxford, J. Barnes,* 1614. L.O.C⁵.CASHEL.E.+; F.U.

20609.5 — [Anr. issue, w. prelims. cancelled and new tp, signed in full.] *Oxford, Jos. Barnes, sould by John Barnes,* [*London,*] 1616. CAL(lacks G1).

20610 — An excellent oration of that late famously learned J. Rainolds. Very usefull for all such as affect the studies of logick and philosophie. *Tr.* J. L(eycester.) 12°. *T. Harper f. T. Slater a. W. Aderton,* 1638. Ent. 25 ap. O.O⁴.; HN.LC.PN².

20611 — A letter of Dʳ Reinolds to his friend, concerning his advice for the studie of divinitie. 12°. *J. Beale f. J. Man,* 1613. Ent. 31 au. O.O¹⁷.C.LINC.

— Liber Collegii [etc. Gift-plate.] *See* Bookplates.

20612 — Johannis Rainoldi orationes duæ: ex ijs quas habuit in collegio Corporis Christi, anno 1576. 8°. *Oxoniæ, ex off. J. Barnesij,* 1587. O.O³.P.YK.; Queen's U.

20612.2 — [Anr. ed.] 8°. *Oxoniæ, ex off. J. Barnesij,* 1597. BTU.

20612.3 — [Anr. ed.] 12°. *Oxoniæ, ex off. J. Barnesij,* 1608. O⁶.C². BRISTOL.

20612.5 — Johannis Rainoldi olim Græcæ linguæ prælectoris orationes quinq[ue]. [*Ed.*] (H. Jackson.) 12°. *Oxoniæ, J. Barnesius,* 1613. O.O²⁵.CHICH².
    Collates ¶⁸ A–L⁸; 1st oration begins: 'Si quis'.

20612.7 — [A different work.] D. Johannis Rainoldi . . . orationes 5. cum aliis quibusdam opusculis. Omnia nunc primum edita. (Plutarchi Chæronensis lib. II. 1 De utilitate ex hostibus capienda. 2 De morbis animi & corporis.—Maximi Tyrii philosophi Platonici disputationes tres [all *tr.* by J. Rainolds].) 12°. *Oxoniæ, J. Barnesius,* 1613 (1614.) O.C.
    Collates A–N¹² w. tp pr. as N12; 1st oration begins: 'Pythagorā'.

20613 — V. Cl. D. Joannis Rainoldi, . . . orationes duodecim; cum alijs quibusdam opusculis. Adjecta est oratio funebris, in obitu eiusdem habita à I. Wake. 3 pts. 12°. *Oxoniæ, J. Barnesius,* 1614 (1613.) L¹⁶(lacks pt. 2).O(lacks pt. 2).O³.O³⁸(lacks sub tp to pt. 3).
    (Wake's oration formerly 24937) Reprints 20612 (A–D¹²) and reissues 20612.5, 20612.7.

20614 — [Anr. ed.] 12°. *imp. G. Stansbeius pro H. Fetherstone,* 1619. L.O.C.D.E.+; F.HN.CU.ILL.Y.+

20615 — [Anr. ed.] 12°. *G. Stansbeius,* 1628. L¹⁵(impr. def.).O⁶.; HN.

20615.5 — [Anr. issue, w. cancel tp, w. imprint:] *G. Stansbeius, & vænum dantur à R. Allot,* 1628. L.O⁵.C.A.YK.+; CHI.COR.ILL.U.
    Tp in 2 settings: line 12 has 'à' under 'br' in line 11 or under 'eb'; both at PLUME.

20616 — Th' ouerthrow of stage-playes, by the way of controuersie betwixt D. Gager and D. Rainoldes. Whereunto are added certeine latine letters betwixt maister Rainoldes, and D. Gentiles. 4°. [*Middelburg, R. Schilders,*] 1599. L.O.C.CASHEL.E².+; F.HN.HD.N. PML.+

20617 — [Anr. issue, w. quires A–E reset.] *Middelburgh, R. Schilders,* 1600. L.O¹¹(imp.).SH.; F(2).HN.HD.+

20618 — Second edition. 4°. *Oxford, J. Lichfield f. E. Forrest a. W. Webbe,* 1629. L.O.C.D.E².+; F.HN.HD.N.NY.+

20619 — The prophecie of Obadiah opened and applyed in sundry sermons preached by J. Rainolds. Published by W. H(inde.) (A sermon upon . . . the eighteenth psalme.) 4°. *Oxford, Jos. Barnes,* 1613. Ent. to John Barnes, ass'd to Master [Roger] Jackson 29 jy. 1619. L.O.C³.E².M.+; F.HN.CHI.HD.U.+
    (2nd pt. formerly 20622) An issue or ed. w. imprint: *Oxford, J. L[ichfield] a. J. S[hort,]* 1620, noted in Madan's *Oxford Books,* II, no. 490, as being at PLUME, can no longer be found; the only copy at PLUME lacks the tp.

20620 — A replye answering a Defence [7115] of the sermon, preached at the consecration of the bishop of Bathe and Welles [17 April 1608], by G. Downame. [Anon. Not by Rainolds.] 2 pts. 4°. [*Amsterdam, G. Thorp,*] 1613 (1614.) L.O.C.D.YK.+; F(pt. 1 only).HD(pt. 2 only).U(pt. 2 only).TORONTO².Y.

20621 — A sermon vpon part of the eighteenth psalm: preached in the vniuersitie of Oxford. 8°. *Oxford, J. Barnes,* 1586. L².O(2).O⁵(2).C³.DUR⁵.; F.
    Tp line 11: 'thankes'.

Rainolds, John—*cont.*

20621.5 — [Anr. ed.] 8°. *Oxford, J. Barnes,* 1586. L.LINC.P.; F.HD. Y(imp.).
    Tp line 11: 'thanks'.

20622 — [Anr. ed.] 1613. = pt. of 20619.

20623 — A sermon vpon part of the prophesie of Obadiah: preached on the 28. of October last. 1584. 8°. (*T. Dawson,*) 1584. L.C³.LK.; F.HD.

20623.5 — [Anr. ed.] Preached . . . October 1584. 8°. (*T. Dawson,* 1586.) P.; F.

20624 — Sex theses de sacra scriptura, et ecclesia. Publicis in academia Oxoniensi disputationibus, explicatae. 8°. *H. Middletonus, imp. G. Bishopi,* 1580. Ent. 9 fb. L.O.C.P.YK.+; F.HN.NY¹¹.
    An Eng. trans. in 20626.

20625 — [Anr. ed., revised and enlarged.] Johannis Rainoldi Angli sex theses . . . nunc autem recognitæ, & apologia contra pontificios . . . auctæ. 8°. [*Eliot's Court Press,*] *imp. G. Bishop,* 1602. L.O.C.D.E.+; HN.HART. HD.ILL.U.+

20626 — The summe of the conference betwene J. Rainoldes and J. Hart [*Jesuit*]: touching the head and the faith of the church. Perused by J. Hart. Whereto is annexed Six conclusions [a *tr.* of 20624]. 4° in 8's. (*J. Wolfe,*) *imp. G. Bishop,* 1584. 1st pt. ent. 1 jn. 1584; 2nd pt. ent. 9 fb. 1580. L.O.C.CASHEL.E.+; F. HN.CAL.HD.NY¹¹.+

20627 — [Anr. ed.] 4° in 8's. *G. Bishop,* 1588. L.O.C⁵.D.DUR.+; F.CAL².NY¹¹. Hebrew Union C.

20628 — [Anr. ed.] 4° in 8's. [*Eliot's Court Press f.*] *G. Bishop,* 1598. L.O.C.G².M.+; F.HN.ILL.U.Y.+

20628a — [Anr. ed.] 4° in 8's. *W. Hall f. T. Adams,* 1598. L.WN. YK.

20629 — [Anr. ed.] 4° in 8's. *W. Hall f. T. Adames,* 1609. Ass'd 14 mr. 1611. L.O.C.D.E².+; F.HN.CHI.HD.U.+

20630 — [A trans.] Summa colloquii Johannis Rainoldi cum J. Harto. Jussu, curáq̉ R. Bancrofti in lucem emissa. H. Parraeo, interprete. fol. *Oxoniæ, J. Barnesius,* 1610. L.O.C.E.YK.+; F.NY¹¹.
    The trans. was made in 1586.

20631 — [Anr. issue, w. imprint:] *London, J. Norton,* 1611. L. C³.C⁸.DUR³.ETON.+; F.

— *See* also Bookplates and 19582.

Rainolds, William. A refutation of sundry reprehensions, cauils, and false sleightes, by which M. Whitaker [in 25357] laboureth to deface the late English translation, and catholike annotations of the new Testament [2884]. 8°. *Paris,* [*f. R. Verstegan?*] 1583. L.O.C³.D².E².+; F.HN.HD. ILL.U.+
    A&R 702. Answered by 25364. Pp² set in duplicate: Pp1ʳ line 11: 'See Heauen' (HD) or '107. See Heauen' (HN).

20633 — A treatise conteyning the true catholike and apostolike faith of the holy sacrifice ordeyned by Christ with an answere to [3924]. By W. Reynolde. 8°. *Antwerpe, J. Trognesius,* 1593. L.O.C³.D².E².+; F.HN. HD.N.U.+
    A&R 703.

Raleigh, Sir Walter. The discouerie of the large, rich, and bewtiful empire of Guiana. Performed in the yeare 1595. by sir W. Ralegh. 4°. *R. Robinson,* 1596. CHATS.M.; F.HN.NY.PH².
    P. 60 line 12 begins: 'vpon it, there'.

20635 — [Anr. ed.] 4°. *R. Robinson,* 1596. L.L³⁰.O⁵.C.; F.HN.HD. MICH.NY.+
    P. 60 line 12 begins: 'on it, there'; tp varies: in line 6: 'City' or 'Citie'; both at HD.

20636 — [Anr. ed.] 4°. *R. Robinson,* 1596. L.O.C¹⁷.D.G².+; F.HN. CB.N.NY.+
    P. 60 line 12 begins: 'it, there'; some copies (O, C⁴, IF, IHN) have on p. 1 line 22 the misprint: 'Gallie' for 'Gallego'.

— An excelent ditty, of the shepheards woing. [c. 1615.] *See* 6921.5.

20637 — The history of the world. [Anon.] fol. (*W. Stansby*) *f. W. Burre,* 1614. Ent. 15 ap. 1611. L.O.C.D².E⁸.+; F. HN.HD.N.NY.+
    See Court-Book C, pp. 77, 355, 357, and Greg, *Companion,* p. 52. In 20637–20641 the engr. tp is dated 1614.

20637a — [A ghost.]

20638 — [Anr. ed.] fol. (*W. Stansby f. W. Burre,* 1617.) L.L². O.C¹³.C¹⁸.+; F.CAL². MICH.NY.Y.+

Raleigh, *Sir* **Walter**—*cont.*

20638a — [Anr. ed.] By sir W. Ralegh. fol. (*W. Jaggard,* [*W. Stansby a. N. Okes*] *f. W. Burre,* 1617 [i.e. 1621.]) L.O.C.BIRM.LEIC.+; COR.NCU.PN.Y. Williams C.
Stansby pr. quires 2nd A–K; N. Okes pr. the preface, Jaggard the rest. *See Court-Book C,* p. 134.

20639 — [A variant, w. colophon:] (*W. Jaggard f. W. Burre,* 1621.) L.O.C.D.E².+; F.HN.CHI.HD.Y.+

20640 — [Anr. ed.] fol. [*H. Lownes*] (*f. H. Lownes, G. Latham a. R. Young,* 1628.) Ass'd by widow Burre to M. Lownes a. Latham 13 de. 1622; to T. Lownes 10 ap. 1627; to H. Lownes a. R. Young 30 my. 1627; to G. Cole a. Latham 6 no. 1628. L.O.C².DUR⁵.E.+; F.HN. HD.N.PN.+
☛ *See Court-Book C,* p. 152.

20641 — [Anr. ed.] fol. [*R. Young*] (*f. G. Latham a. R. Young,* 1634.) Ass'd to R. Young 6 de. 1630. L.O.C.E.M².+; F.HN.HD.N.NY.+
Copies vary: 'Minde of Front.' on sep. leaf or on verso of engr. tp; both at HD.

20641.5 — Sir Walter Raleighs Instructions to his sonne and to posterity. small 8°. [*J. Beale?*] *f. B. Fisher,* 1632. Ent. 13 ap. HN.NCU.PN(bd. w. 156).

20642 — [Anr. issue, w. tp partially reset:] Sir Walter Raleighs Instructions to his sonne, and to posterity. Whereunto is added Advice of a loving sonne to his aged father. [*J. Beale?*] *f. B. Fisher,* 1632. L.O.E.; F.
Issued w. 156 as pt. 2.

20642.5 — Second edition, corrected and enlarged according to the authors owne coppy. [*Ed.*] (B. F[isher].) small 8°. *f. B. Fisher,* 1632. DUL.; F.HD(frag.).
Tp of this and following eds. does not mention Advice; issued w. 156.3.

20643 — Third edition. small 8°. *f. B. Fisher,* 1633. L.C⁵.; N.
Issued w. 156.7.

20643.5 — [Anr. issue, w. tp reset:] Fourth edition. *f. B. Fisher,* 1633. F.LC(imp.).
B1ʳ line 4: 'bee'. Issued w. 156.7.

20644 — [Anr. ed.] Fourth edition. small 8°. *f. B. Fisher,* 1633. L.O.C³.; F.Y.
B1ʳ line 4: 'be'; quire A is same setting as 20643.5. Issued w. 156a.

20645 — [Anr. ed. of 20641.5 (unrevised text) with reprints of 156 and 24905 on continuous signatures.] 8°. *Edinburgh, J. Wreittoun,* 1634. L.RGU.; CU.NCU.

20646 — [Anr. ed. of revised Instructions.] Fifth edition. small 8°. *R. Raworth f. B. Fisher,* 1636. O⁵.O¹⁸.C(imp.).; F.NY.PN.
Issued w. 156a.5.
— The ladies prudent answer to her love. [1628–29.] *See* pt. 2 of 6922.4.

20647 — The life and death of Mahomet. 12°. *R. H[odgkinson] f. D. Frere,* 1637. Ent. 11 my. 1636. L.O.C.DUR⁵.M². +; F.HN.ILL.N.NY.+
— Newes of Sʳ. Walter Rauleigh. 1618. *See* 17148.

20648 — Now = 20649.7.
20648a — Now = 20649.1–20649.5.
20649 — The prerogative of parlaments [*sic*] in England. Written by sir W. R(alegh). Kᵗ. deceased. 4°. *Hamburgh* [*London, T. Cotes,*] 1628. L.O.C.C².BRISTOL.+; F.HN. HD.ILL.Y.+
D3ᵛ line 17 ends: 'is'.

20649.1 — [A variant, w. tp reset:] The prerogative of parliaments. . . . Written by sir Walter Raleigh knight, deceased. *Midelburge* [*London, T. Cotes,*] 1628. L⁵.O.C³.C⁴.; F.CAL⁵.HD.MCG.
D3ᵛ line 17 ends: 'is'.

20649.3 — [Anr. ed.] 4°. *Midelburge* [*London, T. Cotes,*] 1628. L.O. C².D.M.+; CAL².ILL.LC.NCU.NY.+
D3ᵛ line 17 ends: 'more'; D1ʳ line 6 from bottom: 'seized'. Quire A is reimposed from 20649.1.

20649.5 — [Anr. issue, w. quires C–G reset.] *Midelburge* [*London, T. Cotes,*] 1628. L.O.C.D.E.+; HN.BALT.CU.HD.N.+
D3ᵛ line 17 ends: 'more'; D1ʳ line 6 from bottom: 'seised'.
The AAS copy is an early state, omitting D3ᵛ line 12, the single word 'trust.' so that the reading 'more' is on line 16.

20649.7 — [Anr. ed.] 4°. *Midelburge* [*London, T. Cotes?*] 1628. L.O.C.D.E.+; F.CU.HD.IND.Y.+
(Formerly 20648) D3ᵛ line 17 ends: 'none' (roman).

20649.9 — [Anr. issue, w. cancel tp:] The prerogative. . . . [*London, T. Cotes?*] 1640. L.O²(lacks tp)*.O⁶.A.; F.HD.LC. NY.
D3ᵛ line 17 ends: 'none' (roman).

20650 — [Anr. ed.] The perogative [*sic*]. . . . 4°. [*London, T. Cotes,*] 1640. L.O.C.D.E.+; F.HN.HD.N.NY.+
D3ᵛ line 17 ends: 'none' (italic).

20651 — A report of the truth of the fight about the iles of Açores, this last sommer. Betwixt the Reuenge, and an armada. [Anon.] 4°. [*J. Windet*] *f. w. Ponsonbie,* 1591. Ent. 23 no. L.O.O⁵.O⁶.C⁶.+; HN.HD. Pearson.
A3ʳ–4ʳ is in 2 settings; A3ʳ line 1 ends: 'parciali-' or 'parciall-'; both at L.

20652 — Tubus historicus: an historicall perspective; discovering all the empires of the world. 4°. *T. Harper f. B. Fisher,* 1636. L.L³.O.O¹⁹.C.; F.ILL(lacks tp).NY.PN.V.+
— [Wine licences.] *See* 9187.8.
— *See also* 23077.

20652.5 — A declaration of the demeanor and cariage of sir W. Raleigh, aswell in his voyage, as in, his returne. 4°. *B. Norton a. J. Bill,* 1618. L.O.C².E.M.+; F.HN.HD.N. NY.+
(Formerly 20654) Collates A² A–H⁴. Colophon from same setting as 23401; *see also The Library,* III (1948), 124–34.

20653 — [Anr. issue, partially reset and reimposed.] *B. Norton a. J. Bill,* 1618. L.L³⁰.O.C.D.+; F.HN.HD.N.NY.+
Collates A² A–H⁴ I². Imprint varies, line 3: 'Printers to' (1L, F, most copies); 'Printers for' (C); or 'deputie Printers for' (L (292.e.18)).

20654 — Now = 20652.5.
20654a — [A ghost.]
20655 — Sir Walter Rauleigh his lamentation: who was beheaded the 29. of October. 1618. *Ballad.* 2 pts. s.sh.fol. [*R. Blower*] *f. P. Birch,* [1618.] C⁶.
— Sir Walter Rawleighs ghost. 1626. *See* 22085.
— *See also* 8569.

Ram, William, *ed.* Rams little Dodeon. 1606. *See* 6988.

Ramon, *Master. See* 15529.

20656 **Ramsay, Andrew.** Poemata sacra, Andreæ Ramsæi pastoris Edinburgeni. 8°. *Edinburgi, hæredes A. Hart,* 1633. L.O.C(imp.).E.YK.+; F.HN.CHI.ILL.Y.+

20657 — A warning to come out of Babylon, in a sermon preached at the receiving of Mʳ. T. Abernethie, sometime jesuite, into the church of Scotland. 4°. *Edinburgh, G. Anderson,* 1638. L.O.C.E.M(deposit). +; F.HN.HD.U(lacks F1).Y.+

20658 **Ramsay, David.** A sermon, or litle treatise, upon the three last verses of the seaventeenth chapter of Deuteronomie. 4°. *Aberdene, E. Raban,* 1629. L. E(imp.).

20659 — [Anr. issue, w. cancel tp and dedic. to King Charles. *Aberdene, E. Raban,* 1633. L.
In title 'seventeenth' is misprinted 'seventh'.

Ramsay, John, *of St. Andrews.* Decermina quaedam philosophica. 1629. *See* 21555.37.

Ramsay, John, *Visct. Haddington. See* 20664.

20660 **Ramsden, Henry.** A gleaning in Gods harvest. Foure choyce handfuls. [Sermons. *Ed.*] (J. Goodwine.) 4°. [*J. Dawson*] *f. J. D[awson] a. R. M[abb],* sold by T. Slater, 1639. Ent. to J. Dawson a. R. Mabb 1 mr. L.O.C³.D.YK.+; F.HN.HD.ILL.Y.+

20661 **Ramsey, John.** A corosyfe to be layed hard vnto the hartes of all fayhfull professours of Christes gospel. Gathered out of the scriptures. 8°. [*W. Hill,* 1548?] L.O.; F.

20662 — A plaister for a galled horse. [A protestant pamphlet in verse.] 4°. (*T. Raynalde,*) 1548. HN.

20663 — [Anr. ed.] 4°. (*Ippyswitche, J. Oswen,*) 1548. C¹³.

20664 **Ramsey, John,** *Visct. Haddington.* Daphnes trophees wherin is delyneated the power of beautie and the wonders of affection. [In verse. Init. J. R.] 8° in 4's. *Paris, R. Giffart,* 1619. BIRM².
Engr. title plate altered and used in 7224.

20665 **Ramsey, Laurence.** The practise of the diuell . . . in his papistes, against the true professors. [In verse.] 4°. [*J. Charlewood*] *f. T. Rider,* (*solde by H. Kyrkham,*) [1577?] ?Ent. to R. Jones 4 ap. 1577. O.E².

20666 — A short discourse of mans fatall end with an vnfaygned, commendation of syr Nicholas Bacon. [In verse.] s.sh.fol. *f. T. Ryder,* [1579?] ?Ent. to R. Jones 24 mr. 1579. HN.

Ramus, Petrus. *See* La Ramée, Pierre.

20667 **Ranchin, Guillaume.** A review of the Councell of Trent. *Tr.* G. L(angbaine.) fol. *Oxford, W. Turner f. W. T[urner,] E. Forrest a. W. Web,* 1638. L.O.C.D.E.+; F.HN.CHI.HD.Y.+
O³, O⁶ copies have as pastedowns a leaf signed ✱✱2 with Summary of the Contents covering pp. 112–241 of the text and set in roman type; possibly a trial setting. As published most of this material is on A3,4 and is set in italic. O¹⁶ has this leaf and ✱✱3 also.

20668 **Randall, John.** The workes of that famous divine, master J. Randall. All published since the authors death by master Holbrooke. (The great mysterie of godlinesse.) 2 pts. 4°. *H. L[ownes] f. N. Newbery,* 1629 (1630). O.CREDITON.LK.M(frag.).; N.
A reissue of 20680 and 20673 w. gen. tp.
20668.5 — [Anr. issue, w. imprint:] *H. L[ownes,] sold by J. Grismond,* 1629. F.
20669 — The description of fleshly lusts. Or a sermon. Now published by W. Holbrooke. 4°. *J. D[awson] f. N. Newbery a. W. Sheffard,* 1622. Ent. 16 jy. L.L³.O. C⁴.BIRM.+; HD.U.
20670 — [Anr. ed.] *f. H. L., R. Y., a. N. N.,* [1629.] = pt. of 20680.
20671 — [Anr. ed.] 1640. = pt. of 20681.
20672 — The great mystery of godlines. Now published. By W. Holbrooke. 4°. *J. Legatt f. R. Redmer a. W. Sheffard,* 1624. Ent. 20 ja. L.O.C².A.BIRM.+; F.HD.N.NY¹¹.U.+
In some copies (A,HD,NY¹¹) is the misprint 'Sheffeard' in the imprint.
20673 — Second edition. 4°. *H. L[ownes] a. R. Y[oung,]* 1630. Ent. to N. Newbery 26 mr. L(2).C(2). BIRM.NLW.; CHI.ILL.
Also issued as pt. 2 of 20668.
20674 — Third edition. 1640. = pt. of 20681.
20675 — The necessitie of righteousnes. Or a profitable and fruitfull sermon. Published, by W. Holbrooke. 4°. *J. D[awson] f. N. Newbery a. W. Sheffard,* 1622. Ent. 16 jy. L.L⁸.O.BIRM.E.+; F.HN.BALT.HD.U.+
20676 — [Anr. ed.] *f. H. L., R. Y., a. N. N.,* [1629.] = pt. of 20680.
20677 — [Anr. ed.] 1640. = pt. of 20681.
20678 — Saint Pauls triumph, or Cygnea illa & dulcissima cantio, of J. Randall, . . . uttered by him (in eleaven sermons). Now published by W. Holbrooke. 4°. *T. S[nodham] f. R. Redmer a. N. Newbery,* 1623. Ent. 9 oc. 1622. O.O²⁴.D.E.PLUME.; F.HART.U.
20679 — The second time published, revised, and enlarged. 4°. [*H. Lownes*] *f. R. Redmer a. N. Newbery,* 1626. L.O. C².A.NOR².; HD.U.Y.
20680 — Third edition. 4°. [*H. Lownes a. R. Young*] *f. H. L[ownes,] R. Y[oung] a. N. Newberry,* 1629. Ent. to R. Young 11 mr. 1628, 12 my. a. 29 jn. 1630. L.O.C. BIRM.NLW.; F.CHI.ILL.TORONTO².
(Pts. of this formerly also 20670, 20676) Also issued as pt. 1 of 20668.
20681 — Fourth edition. 4°. [*R. Young*] *f. R. Young a. S. Enderby,* 1640. L.O(imp.).O².BIRM.NLW.; F.HN.CU.HD.N.+
(Pts. of this formerly also 20671, 20674, 20677)
20682 — Three and twentie sermons, or, catechisticall lectures upon the sacrament of the Lords supper. Published by Josh. Randall. 4°. [*M. Flesher*] *f. J. Bellamie,* 1630. Ent. to Bellamie a. F. Clifton 17 mr. L.O.A. BIRM.D.; F.HART.PN².U.Y.+
20682a — [Anr. issue, w. imprint:] *f. F. Clifton,* 1630. O.O¹³.C.; HN.CHI.HD(imp.).ILL.U.
20683 — Twenty nine lectures of the church. Published by the late W. Holbrooke. 4° in 8's. *F. Kyngston f. N. Newbery,* 1631. Ent. 2 mr. L³.O.C.D.E⁴.+; F.HN.BO. N.U.+

Randall, Joshua, *ed. See* 20682.

20684 **Randol, John.** Noble Blastus: the honor of a lord chamberlaine. A sermon preacht the 27. of March, 1631. with speciall relation to the coronation-day, and the plague and dearth then among the people. 4°. [*B. Alsop a. T. Fawcett*] *f. T. Lambert,* 1633. Ent. 12 se. L.O.C.C⁴.P.+; HN.AAS.CAL.U(imp.).
20685 — A sermon preacht at St Maries in Oxford. Concerning the kingdomes peace. 4°. *Oxford, J. Lichfield a. W. Turner,* 1624. L.O.O³⁸.C².E.+

Randolph, Robert, *ed. See* 20694.

20686 **Randolph, Thomas.** Aristippus, or the joviall philosopher: . . . . To which is added, The conceited pedlar. [Anon.] 4°. *T. Harper f. J. Marriot, sold by R. Mynne,* 1630. Ent. 26 mr. L.L⁶.L⁴⁰✱.C.C⁴.; F.CH.LC.NY.PEN. Greg 431.
20686.5 — [Anr. ed.] 4°. *T. Harper f. J. Marriot, sold by R. Mynne,* 1630. O.O⁸.; F.HN.HD.N.NY.+
A2ʳ line 2 of speech: 'steept'.
20687 — [Anr. ed.] 4°. [*J. Beale?*] *f. R. Allot,* 1630. ?Ent. 8 ap. L(2).O.CREDITON.E.PETWORTH.; F.HN.
20688 — [Anr. ed.] 4°. [*Eliz. Allde*] *f. R. Allot,* 1631. L.O.DNPK.; F.HN.BO.ILL.Y.+
20689 — [Anr. ed.] 4°. [*E. Purslowe*] *f. R. Allot,* 1635. L.O.C.C². G².+; F.HN.CH.PEN.TEX.+
20690 — [Anr. ed.] 4°. *Dublin, Soc. of Statrs.,* [1635?] L(tp def.).
20691 — Cornelianum dolium. Comœdia lepidissima, ... Auctore, T. R[andolph and R. Brathwait.] 12°. *ap. T. Harperum, væneunt per T. Slaterum & L. Chapman,* 1638. Ent. to Harper a. Slater 30 mr. L.O.C².D².M².+; F.HN.HD.N.Y.+ Greg L 16.
20692 — The jealous lovers. A comedie presented to their majesties at Cambridge. 4°. [*T. a. J. Buck*] *prs. to the Univ. of Cambridge,* 1632. L.C².LEEDS.; HN.HD. Greg 469.
20692a — [A variant, w. imprint:] *prs. to the Univ. of Cambridge, sold by R. Ireland,* 1632. L.O.C.DUR(Bamb.).G².+; F.HN.HD.N.Y.+
20693 — [Anr. ed.] 4°. [*T. Buck a. R. Daniel*] *prs. to the Univ. of Cambridge, sold by R. Ireland,* 1634. L.O.C.E.M⁴. +; F.HN.HD.N.NY.+
Copies vary: orn. above imprint right-side-up or inverted; both at C².
20693a — [Anr. ed.] 8°. *R. Daniel, pr. to the Univ. of Cambridge, sold by R. Ireland,* 1640. L.O.C.E².ETON.+; F.HN.HD. ILL.Y.+
Unsold sheets reissued in 1643 as pt. of Wing R 241.
— The muses looking-glasse. [Init. T. R.] 1638. *See* pt. 2 of 20694.
20694 — Poems with the Muses looking-glasse: and Amyntas. [*Ed.*] (R. Randolph.) 2 pts. 4°. *Oxford, L. Lichfield f. F. Bowman,* 1638. L.O.C.G⁴.NEK.+; F.HN.HD.N.NY.+ Greg 548.
20695 — Second edition enlarged. 2 pts. 8°. *Oxford, L. Lichfield f. F. Bowman,* 1640. L.O.C(lacks engr. tp).D.E².+; F.HN.HD.N.PEN.+
Letterpress tp varies; in imprint: 'Leonard' or 'L.'; both at O.
20695.5 — [Anr. issue, w. imprint on cancel gen. tp:] *Oxford, f. F. B[owman,] sold by L. Chapman [in London,]* 1640. M.

Ranger, Philip. Almanacks. 1615, etc. *See* 502 sqq.

20696 **Rankine, Robert.** Theses philosophicæ. 1627. Now = 7487.24.
20697 — Theses philosophicæ. 1631. Now = 7487.28.

20698 **Rankins, William.** The English ape, the Italian imitation, the footesteppes of Fraunce [etc. Init. W. R.] 4°. *R. Robinson,* 1588. L.O(lacks tp).O¹⁷.
20698.5 — [Anr. ed.] 4°. *R. Robinson, sold by R. Jones,* 1588. CHATS.; F.HN.
20699 — A mirrour of monsters: wherein is plainely described the manifold vices, & spotted enormities, that are caused by the infectious sight of playes. 4°. *J. C[harlewood] f. T. H[acket,]* 1587. Ent. to T. Hacket 26 ap. L.O.C.; F.HN.
20700 — Seauen satyres applyed to the weeke. [In verse.] 8°. *E. Allde f. W. Ferbrand,* 1598. Ent. 3 my. HN.

Raphael, Solomon, *pseud. See* 20963.

Rastell, John, *Barrister and Printer.* [Abridgement of the statutes in English. 1519, etc.] *See* 9517.7 sqq.
20700.3 — [Away mourning.] [4-line stanzas with music, with repeated phrase 'a wey mornyng', with Rastell's device, McK. 40.] s.sh.fol. [*J. Rastell,* c. 1525.] L(K.8.k.8, imp.).
See The Library, XXVI (1971), pp. 197–214.
20701 — Exposiciões t̄mioꝛ legū angloꝛ. [With prologue signed by J. Rastell.] *Law Fr. a. Eng.* fol. [*J. Rastell,* c. 1523.] C.C⁴.
Both copies bd. w. 23879.7.

Rastell, John, *Barrister and Printer—cont.*

20702 — [Anr. ed.] Exposiciones t̄mino꜀ꝛ legū angloꝛ. fol. [*J. Rastell*, c. 1525.] L.; HD.
    (Formerly also 10010) Tp line 2: 'breuiū'. HD bd. w. 23880.3.

20703 — [Anr. ed. Anon.] Expositiones terminorū legum anglorū. *Law Fr.* 16° in 8's. [*J. Rastell,*] (1527 (15 jy.)) L.O.C(3, 1 imp.).E.; F.HN.HD.LC.PH².+

20703.3 — [Anr. ed., with Rastell's name in the prologue.] Exposiciones t̄minoꝛ legū angloꝛ. *Law Fr. a. Eng.* fol. [*J. Rastell*, c. 1530.] HD. Henry R. Stern, Jr., Old Westbury, Long Island, New York (lacks tp).
    Tp line 2: 'breuium'.

20703.5 — [Anr. ed.] The exposicions of the termes of the lawes of England, with diuers rules. Whereunto are added the olde tenures. 8°. *in æd. R. Tottell*, 1563 (29 ap.) L³⁰.L³⁸(imp.).; HD.MIN. Boston, Social Law Library.
    Old Tenures reprinted from 23877.7.

20704 — [Anr. ed.] 8°. *in æd. R. Tottell*, 1567 (17 fb.) L.L²².L²³. O⁵.C⁷.+; F.HD.MICH.MIN.

20705 — [Anr. ed.] 8°. *in æd. R. Tottel*, 1572. L.O⁹.C².NLW.; HN.HD.LC(imp.).V.

20706 — [Anr. ed.] 8°. *in æd. R. Tottel*, 1575. L²³.YK.; HN.HD. MIN. Oberlin C.

20706.5 — [Anr. ed. Anon.] An exposition of certaine difficult and obscure words, and termes of the lawes of this realme, newly set foorth and augmented. 8°. *in æd. R. Tottelli*, 1579. L².O⁵.E².P.; F.HN.HD. MIN.Y.+
    Ff. 224.

20707 — [Anr. ed.] 8°. *in æd. R. Tottelli*, (1579.) L.O(2).C.C⁵.; F.HD(imp.).MIN.PH².Y.+
    Ff. 211.

20708 — [Anr. ed.] 8°. *in æd. R. Tottelli*, 1592. Ent. 18 fb. 1583. O.O⁸.C.BIRM.BRISTOL².+; F.HN.HD.LC.MIN.+
    This and following eds. omit Old Tenures.

20709 — [Anr. ed.] 8°. *by th'assignee of C. Yetsweirt Esq. deceased*, 1595. O.NLW.YK.; F.HD.CU.MIN.PH².+

20710 — [Anr. ed.] Newly amended and augmented. 8°. *T. Wight a. B. Norton*, 1598. L⁴.O.C²⁰.; F.HD. MIN.Y(2).

20711 — [Anr. ed.] 8°. *T. Wight*, 1602. L.O.C.E.NLW.+; HN.HD. ILL(imp.).N.

20712 — [A ghost.]

20713 — [Anr. ed.] 8°. [*A. Islip*] *f. the Co. of Statrs.*, 1607. L.C. C⁵.M².; F.HN.ILL.LC.MIN.
    See Court-Book C, pp. 16, 23.

20714 — [Anr. ed.] 8°. [*A. Islip*] *f. the Co. of Statrs.*, 1609. L(tp only, Harl.5937/284).O.C(imp.).C⁵.LIV³.; F.CAL².HD. MICH.PN.+

20715 — [Anr. ed.] 8°. [*A. Islip*] *f. the Co. of Statrs.*, 1615. L. O³⁹.C.M.NLW.+; HN.CAL⁵.CU.HD.Y.+

20715a — [Anr. ed.] 8°. [*A. Islip*] *f. the Co. of Statrs.*, 1618. O¹⁴. C¹⁵.LINC.M. Town End, Troutbeck, near Ambleside, Westmoreland.; BO³.HD.

20716 — [Anr. ed.] Les termes de la ley: or, certaine difficult and obscure words. Now newly imprinted, and much inlarged. 8°. [*A. Islip*] *f. the Co. of Statrs.*, 1624. Ent. to the English Stock 5 mr. 1620. L.O.NLW. Sheffield PL.; F.CU.HART².HD.N.+
    L also has tp only, Harl.5937/305 w. the date altered in ink to 1634.

20717 — [Anr. ed.] 8°. [*A. Islip*] *f. the Co. of Statrs.*, 1629. L.O. C.D.M.+; F.HN.BALT.HD.NY.+

20718 — [Anr. ed.] With a new addition of above two hundred and fifty words. 8°. [*M. Flesher, J. Haviland, a. R. Young*] *the assignes of J. More*, 1636. L.O.C.BIRM. NLW.+; HN.CU.HD.LC.ILL.+

20719 — A new boke of purgatory whiche is a dyaloge betwene Comyngo & Gyngemyn. fol. (*J. Rastell*, 1530 (10 oc.)) L.O.DNPK*. GLOUC. Broxbourne(E).; CHI.HD.
    Line 1 of colophon on h4ᵛ: 'gedered'; heading a3ʳ: 'merueylous'. Answered in 11386.5.

20719.5 — [Anr. ed.] fol. (*J. Rastell*, 1530 (10 oc.)) Graham(imp.).
    Line 1 of colophon on h4ᵛ: 'gydered'; heading a3ʳ: 'marueylous'.

20720 — [A variant, omitting colophon on h4ᵛ. Anon.] [*J. Rastell*, 1530.] O¹⁷.; F.

20721 — [Heading A1ʳ:] A new cōmodye in englysh in maner of an enterlude wherein is dyscrybyd as well the bewte & good propertes of women as theyr vycys. [Adapted by Rastell from acts 1–4 of Celestina by F. de Rojas?] fol. (*J. rastell me imprimi fecit,*) [c. 1525.] L(frags., Harl.5995/188, 192, 195, 197, 199, 201). O. Greg 10.
    See also 4911.

Rastell, John, *Barrister and Printer—cont.*

20722 — [Heading A1ʳ:] A new iuterlude [*sic*] and a mery of the nature of the .iiij. elements. [Anon.] 8°. [*J. Rastell*, 1520?] L(imp.). Greg 6.
    Regarding the date *see The Library*, XXVI (1971), pp. 197–214.

20723 — [Heading A1ʳ:] Of gentylnes & nobylyte a dyaloge. [Anon.] fol. (*J. rastell me fieri fecit,*) [c. 1525.] L(imp.: A1,6; C2,3 in facs.).O(imp.).C.C⁶.; Nash (frags.). Greg 8.

20724 — The pastyme of people. The cronycles of dyuers realmys and most specyally of Englond cōpyled & empryntyd [by J. Rastell.] 2 pts. fol. [*J. Rastell*, 1530?] L.O(imp.).G².LONGLEAT.M.+; F.HN(2 imp.). LC(imp.).
    Title as above xylographic. There is a letterpress title: 'The cronycles of Englande and of dyuers other realmes: breuely compyled with the pyctures and armes of all the kynges of Englande syth the conquest', which may have been a trial tp before the xylog. was ready; both at LC.

— Table to 'La Graunde abridgement de le Ley'.—Magnum abbreuiamentum librorum legum Angliæ. 1517, etc. *See* 10955 sqq.

— *tr. See* 10455.

Rastell, John, *Jesuit.* A briefe shew of the false wares in the Apology of the churche of England [14590]. 8°. *Louanii, ap. J. Foulerum*, 1567. L.O.D.A².P.+
    A&R 704. Abridged from 12762.

20726 — A confutation of a sermon, pronoūced by M. Juell, at Paules Crosse, M.D.LX [14612, pt. 2]. 8°. *Antwerp, Æ. Diest*, 1564 (21 no.) L.O.C.D.DUR⁵.+; F.NY¹¹.U.
    A&R 705. Answered by 11433.

20727 — A copie of a challenge, taken owt of the confutation of M. Juells sermon. 8°. *Antwerp, Æ. Diest*, 1565 (20 ja.) O.WOR.
    A&R 706. Reprints ff. 160–76 of 20726.

20728 — A replie against an answer (falslie intitled) in defence of the truth [14615]. 8°. *Antwerp, Æ. Diest*, 1565 (10 mr.) L.O.C.D.W.+; F.HN.STL(imp.).WASH³.Y.
    A&R 707.

20728.5 — The third booke, declaring by examples out of auncient councels, Fathers and later writers, that it is time to beware of M. Jewel. 8°. *Antuerpiae, ex off. J. Fouleri*, 1566. L.DE.DUL.SAL.W.; F.HD.N(imp.).U.
    A&R 708. A continuation of 20729.

20729 — A treatise intitled, Beware of M. Jewel. 8°. *Antuerpiae, ex off. J. Fouleri*, 1566. L.O.C⁵.E.W.+; F.HN.U.Y.
    A&R 709. Answers 14606.

Rastell, William. A colleccion of all the statutes (vnto 1557.) *See* 9306 sqq.

20730 — A colleccion of entrees, of declaracions, barres, replicacions, reioinders, issues verdits, [etc.] fol. *in æd. R. Tottell*, 1566 (14 my.) L(destroyed).O.C⁷.DUR (Bamb.).NEK.P.+; F.HN.CU.HD.MIN.+

20731 — [Anr. ed.] fol. *in æd. R. Tottel*, 1574 (22 ja.) Ent. 18 fb. 1583. L.O.C.E.NLW.+; CU.HD.LC.MICH.Y.+

20732 — [Anr. ed.] 1596. . . . . Newly amended, and much enlarged. fol. [*A. Islip?*] *in æd. Janę Yetsweirt*, [1596.] L(destroyed).L³⁸.O.D.M².NLW.+; F.HN.CU.HD.N.+

20732.5 — A table collected of the yeres of our Lorde God, and of the yeres of the kynges of England. [Anon.] 8°. (*ex off. J. Waley,*) 1558 (22 de.) Ent. 1558–59. L(tp only, Harl.5928/51).HAT.; HN.Y.

20733 — [Anr. ed.] 8°. [*J. Kingston f.*] *J. Waley*, 1561 (3 no.) L.; F.HN(imp.).

20734 — [Anr. ed.] 8°. *J. waley*, 1562 (1561 (3 no.)) C².
    Quire L from same setting as 20733.

20735 — [Anr. issue, w. quire L reset.] *J. waley*, 1562 (1563 (mr.)) O.; F.Y.
    L1ʳ right col.: '24. of Henry. 8'.

20735.5 — [Anr. ed.] 8°. *J. waley*, 1563 (mr.) P.
    L1ʳ right col.: '24 of Hēry. 8.' Reset throughout from other known eds.

20736 — [Anr. ed.] 8°. *J. Kyngston f. J. Waley*, 1564 (1563 (mr.)) L.ST.
    Quire L from same setting as 20735: '24. of Henry. 8'.

20736a — [Anr. issue, w. quire L reset.] *J. Kyngston f. J. Waley*, 1564 (1565 (jy.)) L.O(2).C.C⁸.STU.; HD.
    L1ʳ right col.: '24. of Hē. 8.'

20737 — [Anr. ed.] 8°. *J. Waley*, 1567 (mr.) L.O.D.M.

20738 — [Anr. ed.] 8°. [*H. Middleton? f.*] *J. Waley*, 1571 (mr.) L.C.ST.; HN.PH.

Rastell, William—*cont.*

20739 — [Anr. ed.] 8°. [*J. Charlewood f.*] *J. Waley,* 1576. L.O (lacks tp).; F.
    Tp and colophon dated '1576'. There is a tp from a different setting at L (Harl.5963/384) w. line 2 ending 'our' instead of 'of'. The 'of' setting appears in the reissues below.

20739.3 — [Anr. issue, w. M² added, w. colophon:] (*ex off. J. Waley,* 1579.) C⁴.; HD.

20739.7 — [Anr. issue, w. 2 unsigned leaves at end, w. colophon:] (*ex off. J. Walley,* 1583.) Ent. to R. Walley 7 mr. 1591. L³⁸.

20740 — [Anr. ed.] Written by W. Rastal, and now newly corrected and augmented. 8°. *F. K[ingston] f. T. Adames,* 1598. Ent. 12 oc. 1591. L.O.P.; F(2).HN.

20741 — [Anr. ed.] Continued, untill the fift year of James. 8°. *W. J[aggard] f. T. Adams,* 1607 (1606.) L.O(3).D.; F.

20742 — [Anr. ed.] Continued, untill the twelfth yeare of James. 8°. [*W. Jaggard*] *f. T. Adams,* 1614. L.; F.BO².WTL.

20743 — [Anr. ed.] Continued untill the fifteenth yeare of Charles. Corrected and augmented, 1639. By J. Booker. 8°. *R. B[adger] f. A. Hebb,* 1639. Ent. 6 my. 1625. L.O.C.A.M.+; F.HN.
— Table to 'La nouuelle natura breuium'. 1553, etc. *See* 10959 sqq.
— *ed. See* 18076, 18394, 20836.

20744 **Ratcatcher.** The famous ratketcher, with his travels into France, and of his returne to London. (The ratketchers returne.) *Ballad.* 2 pts. s.sh.fol. [*W. White*] *f. J. Trundle,* [1616?] C⁶.

20745 **Ratcliffe, Ægremont.** Politique discourses. *Tr. Æ. Ratcliffe.* 1578. Now = 15230.5.

Ratcliffe, Anthony, *tr. See* 18156.

20746 **Ratcliffe, Thomas.** A short summe of the whole catechisme . . . for the greater ease of the common people of Saint Saveries in South-warke. First gathered by T. Ratliffe. 8°. *E. All-de f. H. Gosson,* 1619. O.
    Dedic. dated 22 Oct. 1592. Maunsell (17669) pt. 1, p. '33' (C4ʳ), lists an ed. 'f. W. Barley, 1594.'

20747 — [Anr. ed.] 8°. *E. All-de f. H. Gosson,* 1620. L.O⁴.; HD.

Rates. The rates of marchandizes. 1604, etc. *See* 7690.5 sqq.
— The rates of the custome house. 1545, etc. *See* 7687 sqq.

20748 **Rathborne, Aaron.** The surveyor in foure bookes. fol. *W: Stansby f. W: Burre,* 1616. L.O.C.D².E².+; F.HN. HD.ILL.NY.+
    Advertised on C8 of 420.11.

20748.5 **Ratramnus,** *Monachus.* The boke of Barthram priest intreatynge of the bodye and blode of chryst. [*Tr.* W. Hughe?] 8°. (*T. Raynalde a. A. Kyngstone,*) 1548. O.O¹⁷.C⁵.C⁹.BUTE.

20749 — [Anr. ed.] 8°. (*T. Raynalde a. A. Kyngstone,*) 1548. L. C.C⁷.CHATS.; HN.HD.NY.
    In title: 'intreating . . . bloude . . . Christ.' Quire C from same setting as 20748.5.

20750 — [Anr. ed.] 8°. *T. Raynalde,* 1549. L.O.BUTE.E.; F.HN. ILL.PML.

20751 — [Anr. trans.] A booke of Bertram the priest. Reviewed, and corrected [by] (T. W[ilcox.]) 8°. *T. D[awson] f. T. Woodcocke,* 1582. L.O.; CAL⁶.Y.

20752 — [Anr. ed., w. added preface.] Now the third time published. [*Ed.*] (H. Lynde.) 8°. *J. Dawson,* 1623. L.C. C⁵.C¹⁰.NLW.; HN.HD.

20752.5 — Now the fourth time published. 8°. *J. Dawson f. E. Jaggard,* 1623. L(tp only, Harl.5921/373).; F.
— *See* also 12492.

20753 **Ratsey, Gamaliel.** [Heading A2ʳ:] The life and death of Gamaliell Ratsey. 4°. [*V. Simmes,* 1605.] Ent. to J. Trundle 2 my. 1605. O(lacks tp).

20753a — Ratseis ghost. Or the second part of his madde prankes and robberies. 4°. *V. S[immes,] sold by J. Hodgets,* [1605.] M.

20754 **Ravaillac, François.** The copie of a letter written from Paris. Declaring the maner of the execution of F. Ravaillart. Together w. two edicts. 4°. [*R. Barker f.* J. Budge] *at Britaine Burse,* 1610. L.O.O²,O⁶.BED.+; F.HN.CHI.Y.

Ravaillac, François—*cont.*

20755 — The terrible and deserved death of F. Ravilliack, shewing the manner of his execution. Together w. an abstract out of divers proclamations, (turned into English by R. E.) 4°. [*R. Blower a. E. Allde*] *f. W. Barley a. J. Baylie,* 1610. ?Ent. to W. Barley 30 my. L.L⁴.O.C³.LINC(frag.).; F.HD.N.Y.
    Blower pr. the 1st quire, Allde the rest.

20755.5 — [Anr. ed.] 4°. *Edinburgh, R. Charteris,* 1610. HD.

Raven. The ravens almanacke. 1609. *See* 6519 sqq.

Ravennas, Petrus. *See* 24112.

20756 **Ravenscroft, Thomas.** A briefe discourse of the true (but neglected) use of charact'ring the degrees in measurable musicke. 2 pts. 4°. *E. Allde f. T. Adams,* 1614. L(2).L⁷.O.C. London, Gresham College.; F. HN.LC.NY.Y.+
    One HN copy has a comma after 'discourse'.

20757 — Deuteromelia: or the second part of musicks melodie. [Init. T. R.] 4°. [*T. Snodham*] *f. T. Adams,* 1609. Ent. 12 oc. L.L⁷.O.G².; F(2).CAL.HD.LC(2, 1 imp.). 𝔄

20758 — Melismata. Musicall phansies. Fitting the court, citie, and countrey humours. To 3, 4, and 5. voyces. [Init. T. R.] 4°. *W. Stansby f. T. Adams,* 1611. Ent. 19 mr. L.L⁷.O(3).G².; CAL.LC(2).

20759 — Pammelia. Musicks miscellanie. Or, mixed varietie of pleasant roundelayes. [Anon.] 4°. [*J. Windet*] *f. R. B[onian] a. H. W[alley,]* 1609. L.L⁷.O.; HN.HD (imp.).LC.Y.

20760 — [Anr. ed.] 4°. *T. Snodham f. M. Lownes a. J. Browne,* 1618. L(2).L⁷.O.; CAL.HD(lacks D2).LC.N.
— The whole booke of psalmes: with the hymnes. 1621, etc. *See* 2575, 2648.

Ravis, Thomas, *Bp.* London. Visitation Articles. *See* 10257.

20761 **Ravisius, Joannes.** Joan. Rauisii Textoris Niuernen: dialogi aliquot festiuissimi. Item eiusdem epigrammata. [*Ed.*] (L. Faber.) 16° in 8's. *ex off. H. Bynnemani,* 1581. Ent. 11 mr. L.O¹³.C.D.M⁴.+; F.N.

20761.2 — Joannis Ravisii Textoris epistolæ. 8°. *J. Kyngstonus,* 1574. LK.

20761.3 — [Anr. ed.] Epistolæ Joannis Ravisii Textoris, non vulgaris eruditionis. Nunc recèns emendatiores in lucem editæ. 8°. [*T. Snodham*] *ex typ. Soc. Stat.,* 1616. O⁶.; F.

20761.5 — [Anr. ed.] 8°. *ex typ. Soc. Stat.,* 1628. O.

20761.7 — [Anr. ed.] 8°. *Cantabrigiæ, ex acad. typog.,* 1631. L.O¹⁰. ETON.

20761.9 — [Anr. ed.] 8°. *ex typ. Soc. Stat.,* 1631. C².

20762 — [Anr. ed.] 8°. *ex acad. typog. Cantabrigiæ,* 1635. L.

20762.3 — [Anr. ed.] 8°. [*F. Kingston*] *ex typ. Soc. Stat.,* 1637. DUL.

20762.4 — [Anr. ed.] 8°. *Cantabrigiæ, ex acad. typog.* 1639. Rogers.

20762.5 — Epithetorum Joann. Rauisii Textoris epitome, ex Hadr. Junii medici recognitione. Accesserunt Synonyma poëtica, locupletiora. 16° in 8's. *ex off. H. Middletoni pro J. Harisono* [*1*,] 1579. L(tp only, Harl.5993/95). DUL.ETON.; F.ILL.

20762.7 — [Anr. ed.] 16° in 8's. *ex off. J. Jacksoni pro J. Harisono,* 1588. L.

20763 — [Anr. ed.] 16° in 8's. *ex off. J. Jacksoni pro J. Harisono,* 1595. O.C(imp.).DUL(imp.).; HD.Y.

20763.2 — [Anr. ed.] 16° in 8's. *N. Okes, imp. W. Welby,* 1608. O.

20763.3 — [A variant, w. imprint:] *N. Okes, imp. R. Banckworth,* 1608. L(tp only, Harl.5993/65).

20763.4 — [A variant, w. imprint:] *N. Okes, imp. J. Harison,* 1608. L(tp only, Ames II.166).

20763.5 — [A variant, w. imprint:] *N. Okes, imp. T. Man,* 1608. LK.

20763.7 — [Anr. ed.] 12°. [*R. Field*] *ex off. typ. Soc. Stat.,* 1617. Ass'd by J. Harrison, sen., to the English Stock 21 se. 1612. L(tpp only, Harl.5937/292, 294).; HD. Pilgrim Hall, Plymouth, Mass.

20764 — [Anr. ed.] 12°. [*J. Haviland?*] *ex off. typ. Soc. Stat.,* 1626. Ent. to the Latin Stock 22 oc. 1618; to the English Stock 5 mr. 1620. L.O.O²⁶.LIV³.

20765 — [Anr. ed.] 12°. [*T. Cotes?*] *ex off. typ. Soc. Stat.,* 1634 (1633.) L.O.; F(lacks last leaf).HN.

20765.5 — [Pater, Filius, et Uxor, or The prodigal son. An interlude related to Ravisius' *Iuvenis Pater et Uxor.*] fol. [*W. Rastell,* 1530?] C(1 leaf only). Greg 19.
— *See* also 23949.

20766 **Rawlidge, Richard.** A monster late found out and discovered. Or the scourging of tiplers. 4°. *Amsterdam* [i.e. *London,*] 1628. L(imp.).O.; HN.

20767 **Rawley, William.** A sermon of meekenesse, preached at the Spittle. 4°. *J. Haviland f. M. Lownes,* 1623. Ent. 16 my. L.L⁸.O.D.DUR³.; F.HD.Y.
Reissued w. tp cancelled in 22240.5.
— *ed. See* 1108, 1109, 1124, 1158, 1168, 1177.

20768 **Rawlin, Thomas.** Admonitio pseudo-chymicis. Seu alphabetarium philosophicum: . . . in quo D. D. Antonii aurum potabile obitèr refutatur. 4°. *per E. Allde,* [1610?] L.L¹³.O.C.C¹⁷.; NLM.Y.
Answers 668.

20769 **Rawlins, John.** The famous and wonderfull recoverie of a ship of Bristoll. 4°. [*Eliot's Court Press*] *f. N. Butter,* 1622. O.
A different work from 14322.

20770 **Rawlins, Thomas.** The rebellion: a tragedy. 4°. *J. Okes f. D. Frere,* 1640. Ent. 20 no. 1639. L.O.C².E.LEEDS.+; F.HN.CU.HD.N.+ Greg 582.
Unsold sheets reissued w. cancel tp in 1652 (LC).

20771 **Rawlinson, John.** The dove-like soule. = pt. of 20774.
20772 — Fishermen fishers of men. A sermon. 4°. *A. Hatfield f. E. Blount a. W. Barret,* 1609. Ent. to W. Barret 30 mr. L.O.C².D.G².+; F.HN.HD.N.U.+

20773 — The foure summons of the Shulamite. A sermon. 8°. *Oxford, J. Barnes, sold by S. Waterson,* [*London,*] 1606. L³.O.

20773a — Mercy to a beast. A sermon. 4°. *Oxford, J. Barnes,* 1612. L¹⁵.O.EX.G².WI.+; F.HN.HD.U.

20774 — Quadriga salutis. Foure quadragesimal, or Lent-sermons, preached at White-hall. 4°. *Oxford, J. Lichfield a. W. Turner f. E. Peerse,* 1625. L.L².O.C. G².+; F.HN.HD.U.Y.+
(1st sermon formerly also 20771)

20775 — The Romish Judas. A sermon. 4°. *W. Hall f. J. Hodgets,* 1611. Ent. 22 ja. L.O.C.D.G².+; F.HN.HD.U.Y.+

20776 — The unmasking of the hypocrite. A sermon. 4°. *E. Griffin f. R. Mabbe,* 1616. Ent. 12 my. L³.O.C.DUR⁵. G².+; F.HN.HD.U.

20777 — Vivat rex. A sermon preached on the day of his majesties inauguration, March 24°. 1614. 4°. *Oxford, J. Lichfield a. J. Short,* 1619. L.L⁸.O.C.G².+; F.HN.HD. NY¹¹.

Rawlyns, Roger, *tr. See* 24060.
— *See also* 20588.

Ray, John, *ed. See* 3990, 5301.6.

20778 **Raymond, Henry.** The maiden queene entituled the Britaine shepheardes teares for the death of Astrabomica, 1607. Augmented [by] the worldes vanitie. Both in verse. 4°. *J. W[indet] f. J. Browne,* [1607.] L.M⁴.; HN.

Raynalde, Thomas. The byrth of mankynde. Newly set furth. By T. Raynold phisition. 1545, etc. *See* 21154 sqq.

20779 — A compendious declaration of the excellent uertues of a certain lateli inuentid oile. [*Tr. from A. Vesalius' Radicis chynae usus.*] 8° in 4's. *Venetiis, J. Gryphius,* 1551. L.; HN.

Raynolds, John. *See* Rainolds and Reynolds.

20779.5 **Ré,** *Isle of.* A true and exact relation of the most remarkeable passages which have happened in the Ile of Ree, . . . since the 6. of August last past to the 24. of the same. *Tr. out of French.* 4°. [*W. Stansby*] *f. N. Butter,* 1627. Ent. to N. Butter a. N. Bourne 25 au. LAMPORT.; HD.
See also Newsbooks 186 sqq. and 24739.5 sqq.

Read. Rede me and be nott wrothe. [1528.] *See* 1462.6.

20780 **Read, Alexander,** *D.D.* A sermon preached April, 8. 1635 at a visitation at Brentwood in Essex. 4°. [*B. Alsop a. T. Fawcet*] *f. J. Clark,* 1636. Ent. 16 my. L.O.C.C¹⁵.

20781 **Read, Alexander,** *M.D.* The chirurgicall lectures of tumors and ulcers. Delivered in the Chirurgeans Hall. 4° in 8's. *J. H[aviland] f. F. Constable a. E. B[ush,]* 1635. Ent. to Constable a. E. Bush 22 au. 1634. L.O.C.E².M⁴.+; HN.HD.MIN.NLM. Duke U.

Read, Alexander, *M.D.—cont.*
20782 — Σωματογραφία ανθρωπίνη. Or a description of the body of man. By W. J[aggard] printer. 8°. *W. Jaggard,* 1616. L¹⁶.O.C.A.G².+; HN.HD.NLM.Y. Philip Hofer, Cambridge, Mass.
(Formerly also 14342) Preface signed by Read; reprints plates and identifications from 6062.

20783 — [Anr. ed., enlarged.] With the practise of chirurgery, and the use of three and fifty instruments. 8°. *T. Cotes, sold by M. Sparke,* 1634. L.C.BRISTOL².G².M⁴. +; F.HN.HD.NLM.NY⁴.+
(2nd pt. formerly also 19190) The 2nd pt. is a slightly abridged reprint of 6063.

20783.5 — A manuall of the anatomy of the body of man. 12°. *J. L[egate] f. F. Constable a. E. Bush,* 1634. Ent. 12 no. 1633. L(lacks tp).L¹⁷.L¹⁹.E⁵.G².; Philadelphia, College of Physicians.

20784 — [Anr. ed.] Enlarged and digested into 6. books. 12°. *J. H[aviland] f. F. Constable,* 1638. L(imp.).L¹⁶.L³⁰. O(lacks engr. tp).G²(w. prelims. to 20785 uncancelled).+; HN.HD.Y. Duke U.
Bk. 6 a reissue of 20785.

20785 — A treatise of all the muscules of the whole bodie. 12°. *R. Y[oung] f. F. Constable,* 1637. Ent. 19 de. 1636. L¹⁹.C.
Unsold sheets reissued w. prelims. cancelled as pt. of 20784.

20786 — A treatise of the first part of chirurgerie. Delivered in lectures. 4°. *J. Haviland f. F. Constable,* 1638. Ent. 26 jy. 1637. L¹⁹.O.C.BRISTOL².E².+; HN.HD.NLM.NY⁴. Amherst C.

Read, John, *Surgeon, tr. See* 723.

20787 **Reading, John.** Characters of true blessednesse. A sermon. 12°. *E. G[riffin] f. J. Norton a. R. Whitakers,* 1638. O.C¹⁰.

20788 — Davids soliloquie. Containing many comforts for afflicted mindes. As they were delivered in sundry sermons. 12°. [*J. Legat*] *f. R. Allot,* 1627. Ent. 7 my. 1626. L.L³.L³⁰.O.C.+; F.HN.

20789 — A faire warning. Declaring the comfortable use both of sicknesse and health. Delivered in severall sermons. 4°. *B. Alsop f. J. Hodgets,* 1621. Ent. 4 de. 1620. L.O(2).C.NOR².P.; F.HN.HD.

20790 — Jobs house: a sermon preached at the funerall of mistresse E. Trumball. 4°. *N. Okes f. J. Hodgets,* 1624. Ent. 12 au. L.O.O¹⁰.P.; F.HN.HD.

20791 — Moses and Jethro: or the good magistrate: admonitions delivered in a sermon. 8°. *J. Legatt f. R. Allott,* 1626. Ent. 7 my. L.O.C².A.P.+; F.HN.ILL.Y.

20792 — The old mans staffe, two sermons. 4°. *B. Alsop f. J. Hodgets,* 1621. L.O.C.D.P.+; F.HN.

Reasons. Certaine reasons and arguments of policie. 1624. *See* 22073.
— Reasons why the bill against the customary tenth of lead oare [etc. 1624.] *See* 6674.5.
— Reasons why the contribution of one pennie per tunne [etc. 1621.] *See* 25856.5.
— Reasons, why the county of Glocester, ought to joyne in repayring of a bridge. [1621.] *See* 23918.5.
20792.5 — Reasons, why the Lordes boorde shoulde rather be after the forme of a table, than of an aulter. 4° in 2. (*R. Grafton,*) 1550. C⁷.
20792.7 — Reasons why the surplice, crosse in baptisme, kneeling in receiving, &c. should not be pressed upon ministers, or people. [Grievances addressed to Parliament on behalf of nonconforming and deprived ministers.] s.sh.fol. [*London, c.* 1610.] E.

Rebuffus, Petrus. Tractatus de decimis. 1585. *See* 7262.

20793 **Recantation.** The voluntarie recantation of foure learned men. 1615. Now = 5650.5.

Receipt. A receyt to stay the plague. 1625, etc. *See* 26037 sqq.

Recital. A recitall of that which hath happened in the Kings armie. 1590. *See* 13139.
— A true recitall of the armie leuied by the princes of Germanie. 1591. *See* 11795.5.
— A true recitall of the confession of J. de Paris. 1616. *See* 19208.5.
— A true recital of those things done in the court of France. 1617. *See* 11292.

20794 **Reckoner.** [A ready reckoner.] 8°. (*R. Wolfe*,) [bef. 1573.] c(4 leaves).

20795 **Reckoning.** The iust reckenyng or accompt of the whole nomber of the yeares, from the beginnyng of the world. *Tr.* out of the Germaine tonge by A. Scoloker the .6. daye of July. 1547. 8°. [*London? 1547.*] c(imp.). Brighton Museum & Art Gallery.; Mellon. In the same types as 24514.

Record. A record of some worthy proceedings: in the howse of Commons. 1611. *See* 7751.

20795.3 **Record, Erasmus.** To the most honourable assemblie of the Commons house. . . . E. Recorde humbly beseecheth for the confirmation of a decree in Chancery. [For the recovery of money due him.] s.sh.fol. [*London,* 1624.] L⁸(GL 4947).
This is a somewhat different version of the text in 20795.5.

20795.5 **Record, Erasmus,** and **Vaughan, Millicent.** To the right honorable the Lords spirituall and temporall in Parliament. [A similar text to 20795.3, with the addition of another petitioner's name.] s.sh.fol. [*W. Stansby,* 1624.] L⁵(Lemon 227).L⁸(GL 4948).
Petition reported on 28 May 1624; *see JHL* III.416.

20796 **Record, Robert.** The castle of knowledge. fol. (*R. Wolfe,* 1556.) Ent. to W. Norton 6 ap. 1577. L.O.C.E².M.+; F.HN.HD.N.NY.+

20797 — [Anr. ed.] 4°. *V. Sims,* assigned by B. Norton, 1596. Ent. to J. Charlewood 15 ja. 1582; to J. Roberts 3 my. 1594. L(lacks folding leaf).L³⁰.O.LIV³.P.+; HN.CU.PN.SMITH.Y.+

20797.5 — The groũd of artes teachyng the worke and practise of arithmetike. With dyuers newe additions. 8°. (*R. Wolfe,* 1543 (oc.)) L.; Horblit.
(Formerly 20799)

20797.7 — [Anr. ed.] 8°. *R. Wolff,* 1549. c(imp.).PARIS.

20798 — [Anr. ed.] 8°. *R. Wolff,* [1551?] O.

20799 — Now = 20797.5.

20799.3 — [Anr. ed.] 8°. *R. Wolfe,* 1552 (8 oc.) L(imp.).
This ed. has Record's dedic. to King Edward, which is in all the following eds. except 20800 and 20800.2.

20799.5 — [Anr. ed.] 8°. (*R. Wolfe,* 1558.) Ent. 1558–59. CU.

20800 — [Anr. ed.] Now of late ouerseen & augmented. [By] J. D[ee]. 8°. (*R. Wolfe,* 1561.) L.L³⁰.; CU.LC.

20800.2 — [Anr. ed.] 8°. (*R. Wolfe,* 1566.) L⁴⁴.; F.

20800.4 — [Anr. ed., enlarged.] 8°. (*R. Wolfe,*) 1570 (30 no.) O¹².

20800.6 — [Anr. ed.] 8°. (*R. Wolfe,* 1571.) c⁴(lacks tp).

20800.8 — [Anr. ed.] 8°. (*R. Wolfe,*) 1573. L³⁰.C⁷.; HD.ILL.

20801 — [Anr. ed.] 8°. (*H. Binneman a. J. Harison,*) 1575. O(imp.).; F. Mount Holyoke C.

20801.3 — [Anr. ed.] 8°. *H. Binneman* (a. *J. Harison,*) 1579 (1577.) L³⁸(imp.)*.; CU.

20801.7 — [A variant, w. imprint:] *J. Harison,* 1579. L(tp only, Ames I.350).

20802 — [Anr. ed.] Afterwards augmented by J. Dee. And now corrected, with some newe rules and a thirde part. By J. Mellis. 8°. *J. Harison a. H. Bynneman,* 1582. L.C.BIRM²(K.N.).; F.

20802.5 — [Anr. ed.] 8°. *H. Midleton f. J. Harison,* 1586. L¹⁶(imp.).; MCG.WIS. Toronto PL.

20803 — [Anr. ed.] 8°. *R. Field f. J. Harison,* 1590. YK.; COR.

20803.5 — [Anr. ed.] 8°. *T. D(awson) f. J. Harison,* 1594. L³⁰.O.C⁵.; F.CU.ILL.

20804 — [Anr. ed.] 8°. *R. Field f. J. Harison,* 1596. L¹⁶(imp.).O.; HN.CU(lacks tp).ILL(lacks col.).

20804.3 — [Anr. ed.] 8°. *J. H[arrison 3,] f. J. Harison* [1,] 1600. L(tp only, Ames II.13).O.

20804.7 — [Anr. ed.] 8°. *J. Harison,* 1605. Bryn Mawr C.

20805 — [Anr. ed.] 8°. [*N. Okes] f. J. Harison,* 1607. L.; F.

20806 — [Anr. ed.] 8°. [*W. Hall] f. J. Harison,* 1610. C².NLW. Bangor UC.; HN.

20806.5 — [Anr. ed.] Records arithmeticke: contayning the ground of arts. Also the art of decimall arithmeticke: a table of board and timber measure [etc.] By R. N(orton). 8°. *T. S[nodham] f. R. Jackson,* 1615. Ent. 1 mr. 1614. O(imp.).O⁶(imp.).O³⁸(imp.).NLW(imp.). Keele U(tp def.).; HN.HD(imp.).Y.
(Formerly 20815) No known copy has the table of board and timber measure, but it was prob. the folding sheet 18676.5. The table is reprinted in 8° format in the following eds.

Record, Robert—*cont.*

20807 — [Anr. ed.] The ground of arts. . . . Now perused, and inlarged; with an appendix of figurate numbers, by R. Hartwell. 8°. *J. B[eale] f. R. Jackson,* 1618. L.O.C.; HN.

20808 — [Anr. ed.] Now the second time perused. New tables of interest, by R. C. 8°. *J. Beale f. R. Jackson,* 1623. L.L¹⁶(lacks tp).O.WOR. London, Sir John Soane's Museum.; HN.HD.NY³.V(imp.).Y.

20808.5 — [Anr. ed.] 8°. *T. Harper f. J. Harison, sold by R. More,* 1631. Ass'd to F. Williams 16 ja. 1626; to J. Harrison 29 jn. 1630. L³⁸(tp only, w. text from a Wing ed.). C⁵.CHATS.G².NLW.; F.BO.ILL. Toronto PL.
The G² copy has the date altered in ink to 1632.

20809 — [Anr. ed.] 8°. *T. Harper f. J. Harison,* 1632. L.O³.C.G². NLW.+; HN.CU(2).LC(lacks tp).Y.
The G² copy has the date erased.

20810 — [Anr. ed.] 8°. *T. Harper f. J. Harison,* 1636. L.L³⁸.O.O⁴³. PLUME.; HN.ILL.Y.

20811 — [Anr. ed.] 8°. *J. Raworth* [a.] (*J. Okes) f. J. Harison,* 1640. L¹⁶.O.C.M³.NLW.+; ILL.PEN.Y.

20812 — The pathway to knowledg, containing the first principles of geometrie. (The second booke.) 2 pts. 4°. (*R. wolfe,* 1551.) L.O.C.G².NLW.+; F.HN.LC.PH².WIS.

20813 — [Anr. ed.] 2 pts. 4°. [*J. Kingston f.*] (*J. Harrison,*) 1574. L(lacks m2).L³⁰.O.C⁵.WOR.+; CU.MICH.Y. Horblit.

20814 — [Anr. ed.] 2 pts. 4°. *J. Harison* [3,] *f. J. Harison* [1,] 1602. L(imp.).L³⁸.O⁵.E².PETYT.+

20815 — Records arithmeticke. 1615. Now = 20806.5.

20816 — The vrinal of physick. 8°. (*R. Wolfe,*) 1547. L¹⁷.O(imp.). c(lacks tp)*.G²(2).; F(lacks tp)*.

20817 — [A variant, w. date on tp:] 1548. L(lacks col.).L³⁰. G².M.NLW.+; HN.HD(imp.).

20818 — [Anr. ed.] 8°. (*R. Wolfe,*) 1567. L.P(2).; HN.

20818.5 — [Anr. ed.] 8°. *T. Dawson,* 1582. Ent. 23 jn. 1581. WIS.

20819 — [Anr. ed.] 8°. *T. Dawson,* 1599. L.C¹⁰.DUR(Bamb.). London, British Medical Association.; HD.Y.

20820 — The whetstone of witte, whiche is the seconde parte of arithmetike. 4°. (*Imprinted*) [a.] *solde, by J. Kyngstone,* (1557.) Ent. to T. Orwin 7 my. 1593. L.O.C.E².M.+; F.HN.CU.HD.ILL.+

20821 **Records, Charles.** Friendly counsaile. Or, here's an answer to all demanders. [Init. C. R.] *Ballad.* 2 pts. s.sh.fol. *f. R. Harper,* [1633?] Ent. 22 my. 1633. L(Rox I.16,113).

20822 — The good-fellowes advice. *Ballad.* 2 pts. s.sh.fol. *f. J. Wright, junior,* [1635?] L.

20822.5 — A mostpleasant [*sic*] dialogue: or a merry greeting betweene two lovers. [Init. C. R.] *Ballad.* 2 pts. s.sh.fol. *f. H. G[osson,* 1632.] Ent. to Gosson a. F. Coles 24 my. 1632. c⁶.
— *See also* 21025.

20823 **Red Cross.** The red-crosse: or, Englands lord have mercy upon us. A lamentable relation of many visitations by the plague. [With plague statistics.] s.sh.fol. *f. J. Trundle,* 1625. L(2).L⁸.; NY.
L copies pr. on both sides of same sheet. *See also* 16739 sqq.

20824 — [Anr. ed.] s.sh.fol. *f. H. Gosson,* 1636. L⁸.

Red, William. Almanach ephemerides. [1507.] *See* 504.

20825 **Redemption.** The redemption of lost time. [*Tr.*] (Daniel Powel.) 12°. *N. O[kes] f. R. Sergier,* 1608. Ent. 23 mr. F. 𝔄

20826 **Redman, John.** A compendious treatise called the cõplaint of grace. Set furth by T. Smyth. 8°. *in æd. R. Caly,* [1556?] L(imp.).c(2).D.

20826.5 — [Anr. ed., revised.] The complaint of grace. Printed in popish times, falsly and corruptly, many places being left out. Restored now, and those places put in out of a manuscript coppy. Out of the library of W. Crashawe. 8°. *N. O[kes] f. R. Boyle a. W. Welby,* 1609. O¹⁷.C².D.

20827 — A reporte of maister doctor Redmans answeres, to questions concernynge certaine poyntes of religion. 8°. (*T. Raynalde f. W. Seres,*) 1551. C.D.
Adapted in 11222, p. 867 sqq.

Redman, William, *Bp. See* 18689.

20828 **Reeks, Richard.** Faith and good workes united: in a sermon. 4°. *T. Harper f. J. Harrigat,* 1630. Ent. 6 my. L.O.G².; HD.NY¹¹.

20829 Reeve, Edmund. The christian divinitie, contained in the divine service of the church of England. 4° in 8's. [*T. Harper*] *f. N. Fussell a. H. Mosley*, 1631. Ent. 29 my. 1630. L.O.C.D.E².+; F.HN.ILL.U.Y.+

20830 — The communion booke catechisme expounded. 4°. *M. Flesher*, 1635. Ent. 23 ap. L.C⁵.; Y.
Answered in 20474.

20831 — [A variant, w. imprint:] *M. F[lesher] f. H. Mosley*, 1636. O¹³.C.C¹⁰.P.WOR.+; HN.PH.U.

— For other works and translations by this author *see* Rive, E.

20832 Reeve, Thomas. The churches hazard delivered in a sermon. (Nabals arraignement.—Moses old square.) 4°. *A. Mathewes f. J. Grismond,* (sold by E. Martin of Norwich,) 1632. O.C³.C⁵(imp.).BIRM²(K.N.).NOR².; HD.
(Formerly also 20833, 20834.)

20832.3 — [A variant, w. impr. on 1st tp:] *A. Mathewes f. J. Grismond, solde in Norwich by E. Martin*, 1632. O³.

20832.5 — [Anr. issue, w. added gen. tp:] Three sermons. . . . Delivered upon severall occasions in Norwich. *A. Mathewes f. J. Grismond, sold by E. Martin* [*Norwich,*] 1632. E(imp.).

20832a — Mephibosheths hearts-joy upon his soveraignes safetie. Upon the happy returne of prince Charles. Delivered in a sermon. 8°. *A. Math[ewes] f. R. Milbourne,* 1624. CARLISLE.LINC.; F.HD.U.

20833 — Moses old square. = pt. of 20832.
20834 — Nabals arraignement. = pt. of 20832.

Re-examination. The re-examination of two of the articles abridged. 1636. See 4363.5.

Reformatio. Reformatio legum ecclesiasticarum. 1571. See 6006.

20834.3 Reformation. Of publique reformation of a church. s.sh.fol. [*Cambridge?* 1589?] L².
L² bd. w. 25365.5.
— The reformation of religion by Josiah. [1590?] *See* 14815.

Regensburg, *Diet of. See* 13612 sq.

Reges. Reges, reginæ, nobiles, & alij in ecclesia Petri Westmonasterij sepulti. 1600, etc. *See* 4518 sqq.

Regimen. [De regimine principium bonum consilium. 1508.] *See* 3307.

20834.7 Reginald, Bathsua. Ad Annam . . . reginam. [An engr. card measuring 3¼×4 in., w. specimens of script, including 'Radiography' or shorthand.] [*London,* 1616?] L³⁰.

20835 — Musa virginea Græco-Latino-Gallica, Bathsuæ R. (filiæ H. Reginaldi) anno ætatis suæ decimo sexto edita. 4°. *E. Griffin, imp. J. Hodgets,* 1616. L.O.C.; HN. Detroit PL(imp.).

20835.5 Reginald, Henry. Magæ Britanniae chronographa imperialia, seu trophaea trina. [In verse.] s.sh.fol. [*London,*] 1625. L⁵(Lemon 260).

Reginald, Henry, *tr. See* 13021, 13022.

Register. A briefe register in meter. 1599. *See* 3727.

20836 Registrum. Registrum omniū breuium tam originaliū ꝗ iudicialium. [*Ed.* W. Rastell.] 2 pts. fol. *ap. G. Rastell* [col. on P3ᵛ:] (*by W. Rastell and it is to sell at the house of the sayde Wyllyam, or of R. Redman,*) 1531. L.O.C.DUR.M.+; HN.CU.HD.MIN.Y.+

20836.5 — [A variant, omitting colophon on P3ᵛ and adding one on P4ʳ:] (*by w. Rastell,* 1531 (28 se.)) O(2 copies of P4 only, 1 = J).C.WOR.; LC(2).

20837 — [Anr. issue, w. new tp, and tables reprinted.] Registrum omnium breuium . . . nouiter impressum. *ap. R. Tottelum,* 1553. Ent. 15 fb. 1583. L.L³⁸.O¹⁹.C.NEP.+; F.HN.CU.HD.MIN.+

20838 — [Anr. ed.] 1595. Correctum ad vetus exemplar manuscriptum. fol. *in æd. Janæ Yetsweirt relictæ C. Yetsweirt,* [1595.] L.O.C.D.DUR³.+; HN.CU.HD.LC.MIN.+

20839 — [Anr. ed.] 1634. fol. [*J. Haviland a. R. Young*] *per assign. J. More,* [1634.] Ent. to the English Stock 5 mr. 1620. L³⁰.O¹⁰.C⁸.DUR.M².+; HD.LC.PN.Y(2).

Regius, A. In Jacobum sextum panegyris. 1603. *See* 14962.

Regius, G. Theses philosophicæ. 1612, etc. *See* 7487.9, etc.

20840 Regius, Urbanus. A cōparison betwene the olde learnynge & the newe, *tr.* out of latin by W. Turner. 8°. *Sowthwarke, J. Nicolsō,* 1537. L.; F.

20840.5 — [Anr. ed.] 8°. (*Sowthwarke, J. Nicolson f. J. Gough,*) 1537. O.M(imp.).

20841 — [Anr. ed.] 8°. (*Sowthwarke, J. Nicolson,*) 1538. L.C.C⁹.; F.

20842 — [Anr. ed. Anon.] The olde learnyng and the new, compared together. Newly augmented by W. Turner. 8°. (*R. Stoughton,* 1548.) L.O.C.OS.P.+; F.HN.HD.WIS.Y.

20843 — A declararation [*sic*] of the twelue articles of the christen faythe. And the righte foundation and comon places of scripture. [*Tr.*] (G. Lynne.) 8°. [*S. Mierdman*] (*f. G. Lynne, solde by R. Jugge,* 1548.) L.O(imp.).C.C⁸.STU.+; F.HN.ILL.U.Y.

20844 — An homelye or sermon of good and euill angels. *Tr.* R. Ro[binson.] 1583. 8°. *J. Charlewoode,* [1583?] Ent. 14 de. 1582. L².; F.

20845 — [Anr. ed.] 8°. *J. Charlwood,* 1590. L(2).; F.

20846 — [Anr. ed.] *Tr.* R. Robinson. 8°. *widdowe Charlwood,* 1593. L.O.P.; F.HN.U.

20847 — An instruccyon of christen fayth howe to be bolde vpon the promyse of God. *Tr.* (J. Fox[e.]) 8°. *H. Syngelton,* [1548?] L.O(2).C.D.

20848 — [Anr. ed.] A necessary instruction of christian faith and hope. Newly recognised by J. F(oxe.) 8°. *H. Singleton,* 1579. Ent. 6 ap. L(tp only, Harl.5936/412).O(1 leaf).C.D.

20849 — A lytle treatise after the maner of an epystle . . . wherin he declareth the dyuersyte betwene ryght worshyppyng and ceremonis inuented by mannis institucion. 8°. [*S. Mierdman f.*] (*G. Lynne,* 1548.) L(Print Dept.).L².O.D.; F(lacks col.).HN.TEX.

20850 — The sermon, which Christ made on the way to Emaus set downe in a dialogue. [*Tr.*] (W. Hilton.) 4° in 8's. *J. Daye,* 1578. Ent. 26 mr. 1579. L.L³⁰.O.C.P.+; F. HN.HD(imp.).ILL.U.+

20851 — [Anr. ed.] 4° in 8's. *W. White,* 1612. Ent. to J. Sheldrake 29 oc. 1594. L.O.C.D.E⁴.+; F.CAL.HD.ILL.Y.+

20851.5 — The shelde of saluacion. Newly sette forthe in Englysshe. [Anon. *Tr.* by T. B., i.e. T. Becon, from Dialogus inter Satanam et peccatorem.] 8°. *R. Wyer,* [1548?] C¹⁵.; PML.
Reprinted w. new preface as The Christian Knight in 1710, vol. 2.

20852 — The solace of Sion, and ioy of Ierusalem. Beeing a godly exposition of the Lxxxvij. psalme. *Tr.* into english by R. Robinson 1587. 8°. [*R. Jones,* 1587.] O(cropt).
Tp line 2 ends: 'SION, and' while the later eds. end: 'Ioy of'.

20853 — [Anr. ed.] 8°. [*J. Charlewood f.*] *R. Jones,* 1591. C.; HD.U.
Tp varies: line 5: 'latter age, redeemed: by' (U) or 'latter age: redeemed by' (HD).

20854 — [Anr. ed.] 8°. [*J. Roberts f.*] *R. Jones,* 1594. L.; F.
— *See* also 16982.

Reglas. Reglas gramaticales. 1586. *See* 5789.

20855 Regnier de la Planche, Louis. A legendarie, conteining an ample discourse of the life of Charles cardinal of Lorraine. [F. de L'Isle, *pseud.*] 8°. [*London?*] 1577. L.O.C.M².SHEF.+; F.HN.HD.PML.Y.

Rehearsal. A brief rehersal & discription, of the coronatiō. 1565. *See* 17696.
— A brief rehersall of the beleef of the good willing in Englande. [1575.] *See* 10681.5.
— A brief and true rehersall of the victory. 1573 (2 no.) *See* 13570.
— A rehearsall both straung and true. [1579.] *See* 23267.
— A true rehersall of the victory. 1573 (6 ap.) *See* 13578.

20856 Reid, James. Theses philosophicæ. 1610. Now = 7487.8.
20857 — — 1614. Now = 7487.11.
20858 — — 1618. Now = 7487.15.
20859 — — 1622. Now = 7487.19.
20860 — — 1626. Now = 7487.23.

Reid, Thomas, *tr. See* 14346.

Reiginalde, H. *See* Reginald, H., *tr.*

Reina, Casiodoro de, *tr. See* 2959.

Reinolds, John. *See* Reynolds.

20860.5 **Rejaule, V.** Newes from Spain. (A true relation of the lamentable accidents, caused by the inundation of rivers of Spaine. Written in Spanish and *tr*.) 4°. [*G. Eld*] *f. W. Blackwall*, 1618. Ent. 1 mr. L.O.

Relation. [For anonymous 'relations' not listed below *see* also, for 1622: Newsbooks 37A, 39, 47, 60, 61, 63, 71A, 82, 84; for 1623: Newsbooks 98, 104, 109, 112, 117, 131, 148, 150; for 1624: Newsbooks 349; for 1628: Newsbooks 355; for 1631: Newsbooks 208; for 1639: Newsbooks 308.]

— A briefe relation of the late martyrdome. 1623. *See* 19776.

— A briefe relation of the Scots entrance into England. 1640. *See* 22007.5.

20861 — A briefe relation, of what is hapned since the last of August 1598. by comming of the Spanish campe into the dukedome of Cleve. Also a letter of the emperour of Germany. *Tr.* out of the Dutch coppy. 2 pts. 4°. [*E. Allde f.*] *J. Wolfe*, 1599. Ent. 19 fb. L².L¹³(lacks map).C(2, 1 imp.).HAGUE.; F.HN.Y.

— A certaine and perfect relation of the bloody slaughter. 1625. *See* Newsbooks 353.

— The exact and true relation of that bloody battell. 1633. *See* 12532.5.

— A relation containing the manner of the coronation. 1620. *See* 10816.

— A relation of a new league. 1626. *See* 10817.

— A relation of a sea-fight. 1622. *See* 5011.5.

20862 — A relation of all matters passed, especially in France and the Low-countries. *Tr.* (R. Boothe) according to the originall of Mercurius Gallo-Belgicus [i.e. M. ab Issell]. 4°. [*F. Kingston*] *f. W. Welby*, 1614. Ent. 2 no. L.O.; N. Penrose. Henry Taylor.

— The 27. of September. A relation of letters. 1622. *See* Newsbooks 80.

— A relation of some speciall points concerning Holland. 1621. *See* 22083.

— A relation of that which hath passed. 1631. *See* 11288.5.

— A relation of the state of religion. 1605. *See* 21716.

— A relation strange and true. 1622. *See* 14322.

— A true and exact relation of the most remarkeable passages in the Ile of Ree. 1627. *See* 20779.5.

— A true and most exact relation of the taking of the Saint Esprit. 1627. *See* 24268.7.

— A true and perfect relation of the newes sent from Amsterdam. 1603. *See* 18445.5.

— A true and perfect relation of the proceedings. 1606. *See* 11618.

— A true and perfect relation of the whole proceedings. 1606. *See* 11619 sqq.

20863 — A true and strange relation of fire, which by an eruption made one of the islands of the Tercera's. 4°. [*T. Harper*] *f. N. Butter a. N. Bourne*, 1639. L.; HN.

— A true and very memorable relation, of certaine speciall matters. 1628. *See* Newsbooks 355.

— The true relation and description of 2. sea-fights against the Turkes. 1637. *See* 24335.5.

— A true relation brought by the lord of Buisson. [1622.] *See* 7268.5.

— A true relation of a late very famous sea-fight. 1640. *See* Newsbooks 339.

— A true relation of a wonderfull sea fight. 1621. *See* 22130.

— A true relation of Go⟨ds⟩ wonderfull mercies. [1605?] *See* 14668.

— The true relation of that worthy sea fight. 1622. *See* Newsbooks 57A.

— A true relation of the birth of three monsters. 1609. *See* 18347.5.

— A true relation of the conferences. 1616. *See* 16833.

— A true relation of the entertainment. 616. *See* 11292.5.

— A true relation of the famous victorie. [1600.] *See* 17679.

— A true relation of the French Kinge his good successe. 1592. *See* 13147.

— A true relation of the great Spanish fleet. 1623. *See* 23009.

— A true relation of the unjust proceedings at Amboyna. 1624. *See* 7451.

— A true relation of this present siege of Shertoken-Busse. 1629. *See* 13248.6.

Relation—*cont.*

20864 — A true relation without all exception, of strange accidents, in the kingdome of the great Magor, or Magull, greatest monarch of the East Indies. As also a report of the manners in the countrey. 4°. *J. D[awson] f. T. Archer*, 1622. Ent. to N. Bourne a. T. Archer 27 my. L(582.e.37).PETWORTH.; F.MIN.

Relations. Briefe relations from marchans letters. 1633. *See* Newsbooks 359.

— Relations, of the most famous kingdoms. 1608, etc. *See* 3401 sqq.

20865 — Two memorable relations. The former, of conflicts at Surat. The latter, the copie of a letter from Bergen-up-Zoom. 4°. [*B. Alsop, T. Fawcet a. R. Young*] *f. N. Butter a. N. Bourne*, 1631. L.LK.; F.HN.
  Alsop and Fawcet pr. quire A; Young the rest.

20866 — Two very lamentable relations: the one, the grievances for religion, of those under Ferdinand emperour. The other, the supplication, of certayne states. Done out of Dutch. 4°. [*Holland?*] 1620. O.O².; F.

Religion. The maine grounds of religion. 1630. *See* 12402a.6.

— True religion explained. 1632. *See* 12400.

20867 **Remedies.** Present remedies against the plague. 1594. Now = 5871.5.

20868 — [Anr. ed.] 1603. Now = 5871.7.

20869 — Remedies against discontentmēt, drawn into seuerall discourses, from the writinges of auncient philosophers. By Anonymus. 8°. [*T. Purfoot*] *f. R. Blower*, 1596. Ent. to Blower a. Purfoot 2 jn. L.; F.HN.CHI.

20870 — Remedies for diseases in horses. Approued and allowed by diuers very auncient learned mareschalles. [Often wrongly ascribed to Sir N. Malbie.] 4°. *T. Purfoote*, 1576. L.
  Usually bd. w. corresponding eds. of 17209 sqq.

20871 — [Anr. ed.] 4°. *T. Purfoote*, 1583. L(lacks tp).O⁵.; HN. ILL.Y. Mellon.

20872 — [Anr. ed.] 4°. *T. Purfoote*, 1586. L.

20873 — [Anr. ed.] 4°. *T. Purfoote*, 1588. L(imp.).D.; Clark Art Institute, Williamstown, Mass.

20874 — [Anr. ed.] 4°. *T. Purfoot*, 1594. STU.; HN.

20874.5 — Sundrie approued remedies against the plague. s.sh. fol. *E. Allde f. E. White*, [1603?] O.

20875 **Remedy.** Lord have mercy upon us. [xylographic] A speciall remedy for the plague. [With plague statistics for 1603, 1625, 1636.] s.sh.fol. [*R. Young a. M. Flesher*] *f. M. S[parke,] junior*, [1636.] Ent. to M. Sparke 28 my. 1625. L(imp.).L⁸.
  L has printed totals through 9 June 1636; L⁸ through 16 June. *See* also 16739 sqq.

20875.5 — [The remedy against the troubles of temptations.] 4° in 6's. (*w. de worde*, 1508 (4 fb.)) L(imp.).
  (Formerly 21262) B1ʳ last line ends: 'shall repent'. Except for a few quotations this is not by R. Rolle.

20876 — [Anr. ed.] The remedy ayenst the troubles of temptacyons. 4° in 6's. (*w. de worde*, 1519 (21 ja.)) L(2). C(imp.).
  (Formerly also 21263) B1ʳ last line ends: 'shal repent'.

20876.5 — [Anr. ed.] 4° in 6's. [*W. de Worde*, c. 1525.] F(imp.). In title: 'temtacyons'; B1ʳ last line ends: 'shal repēt'.

20877 — A remedy for sedition. 1536. Now = 18113.5.

Remembrance. A remembraunce for the maintenaunce of the liuynge of ministers. [1551.] *See* 21435.5.

Remigio, *of Florence.* Civill considerations. 1601. *See* 18348.

20878 **Remigius.** [A1ʳ:] Dominus que pars nomen quare quia significat substantiam [etc. Anon.] 4°. [*W. de Worde*, 1500.] O. Duff 356.

20878.5 — [Anr. ed.] 4°. (*W. de Worde,*) [1518?] O.

— *See* also 7016.

20879 **Remnant, Richard.** A discourse or historie of bees. Whereunto is added the causes, and cure of blasted wheat. 4°. *R. Young f. T. Slater*, 1637. Ent. 13 my. L.O¹³.E.; F.LC.WIS.

Remon, Alonzo, *ed. See* 16828.

Remonstrance. An humble remonstrance. 1640. *See* 12675.

Remonstrance—*cont.*

20880 — A remonstrance concerning the present troubles. 1640. = 21928.

— The remonstrance of the nobility. 1639. *See* 21907.

20881 — A remonstrance: or plaine detection of faults in a booke, entituled, A demonstration of discipline [24499]. 4°. *G. Bishop a. R. Newberie*, 1590. Ent. 3 jy. 1591. L.O.C.D².E.+; F.HN.HD.U.Y.+

— A true remonstrance of the state of the salt businesse. [1640?] *See* 21636.5.

Remonstrances. Remonstrances made by the Kings maiesties ambassadour. 1615. *See* 9237.

— Remonstrances, to the Duke de Mayne. 1593. *See* 5012.

20881.3 **Remorse.** The remors of conscyence. [In verse. The text is W. Lichfield's Complaint of God.] 4° in 6's. [*W. de Worde*, c. 1510.] C(imp.).
(Formerly 20883) Tp line 4 begins: 'remors'.

20881.7 — [Anr. ed.] 4° in 6's. [*W. de Worde*, c. 1515.] L⁴(frag.). Tp line 4 begins: 'mors'.

20882 — [Anr. ed.] 4°. (*W. de Worde*,) [1534?] L.LIV³(sheet B, and C1, 4).; HN(lacks tp).
(Formerly also 5605) Tp line 4 begins: 'stracyons'.

20883 — Now = 20881.3.

Remy, *Lord.* Civill considerations. 1601. *See* 18348.

20884 **Renaudot, Theophraste.** Numb. 1. A question. Whether there bee nothing new. *Tr.* 1640. (2. Which is most to be esteemed.—3. Whether truth beget hatred.— 4. Of the cock.—5. Why dead bodies bleed.) 5 pts. 4°. *R. B[adger a. R. Bishop?] f. J. Emery*, (1640.) Ent. 2 de. 1640. L.O⁶.O¹³(pts. 1, 2, 5).C(pts. 1–4). C²(pts. 1, 2, 4, 5).+; F(pt. 5).HN(pts. 1, 2, 5).CAL. ILL(pts. 1, 2).Y.+
R. Badger pr. pts. 1 and 3; R. Bishop prob. pr. pts. 2, 4, 5.

20885 **Renichon, Michel de.** The confession of Michael Renichon. Concerning, the bloudy enterprise, which should have bene committed vpon Maurice, prince of Orange. *Tr.* R. R[obinson.] 4°. [*J. Windet f.*] *J. Wolfe*, 1594. Ent. 26 jn. L.

20886 **Reniger, Michel.** De Pii quinti et Gregorii decimi tertii furoribus. Contra Elizabetham. 8°. *T. Dauso., pro R. Watkins*, 1582. L.O.C.D.E.+; HD.ILL.

20887 — Syntagma hortationum . . . ad Angliæ regem. 8°. *T. Dauson*, 1604. Ent. 2 jy. L².O.C.C²·YK.+; F.

20888 — A treatise conteining two parts. 1 An exhortation to true loue, to her maiestie. 2 A treatise against treasons. 8°. *T. Dawson*, 1587. Ent. 10 de. 1586. O(2).C.D(lacks tp).; F(imp.).HD.

20889 **Rennecherus, Herman.** The golden chayne of salvation. *Tr.* (P. Allibond.) 4° in 8's. *V. Simmes f. T. Man*, 1604. Ent. 4 jn. L.L³.O.C.; F.N.U.

20889.3 **Repairing.** A repayring of the breach. Wherein, is shewed the benefit that comes by a christian communion among the saints. 4°. [*Amsterdam, Richt Right Press*,] 1639. F.

Reply. An apologeticall reply. 1636. *See* 6310.

— A replie to a relation. 1640. *See* 4154.

— A reply to M. Nicholas Smith. 1630. *See* 6929.

— A reply with the occasion thereof, to a libel. [1579?] *See* 19179.

Réponse. Responce d'un surveillant de Bearn. 1615. *See* 11306.5.

20889.5 **Report.** A most rare & true report, of such great tempests, and accidents, which happened in Hereford shire, at a place called the Hay. 4°. *f. T. Lawe*, 1585. N.

— A most strange and true report of a monsterous fish. [1604.] *See* 11501.5.

20889.7 — A most true and lamentable report, of a great tempest of haile which fell vpon a village in Kent, called Stockbery. 4°. [*J. Wolfe*] *f. the widow of T. Butter*, 1590. Ent. 9 jy. F.
Film of F copy on Univ. Microfilms reel 717 ('23276a').

— A most wonderfull, and true report of diuerse vnknowne foules. [1586.] *See* 6074a.7.

— A reporte of a discourse. 1606. *See* 13001.

Report—*cont.*

— A report of the fight about the Açores. 1591. *See* 20651.

20890 — A strange report of six most notorious witches, who murdred above foure hundred small children: who were executed in Manchen in high Germanie. *Tr.* 4°. *W. W[hite] f. T. Pavier*, 1601. O(3).; HN.

20891 — A true and credible report, of a great fight at sea, betwene ships belonging to merchants of England, and the king of Spaines the 25. of May 1600. within the straightes of Gibraltare. 4°. *E. A[llde] f. W. Burre*, [1600.] Ent. 17 jy. 1600. L(C.71.bb.10).O.O⁶.

20892 — A true report and exact description of a mighty seamonster, or whale, cast upon the Langar-shore over against Harwich in Essex. 4°. *f. H. Holland, sold by C. H[olland,]* 1617. Ent. 15 fb. O.

— The true report of a great galley. 1592. *See* pt. 2 of 11285.

— A true report of a most famous victorie. 1600. *See* 7064.

— A true report of all the proceedinges before Bercke. 1601. *See* 17680.

— A true report of sundry horrible conspiracies. 1594. *See* 7603.

— The trew report of the dysputacyon. [1554.] *See* 19890.

— A true report of the gainefull, voiage to Iaua. [1599?] *See* 14478.

— A true report of the inditement. 1588. *See* 25229.

— A true reporte of the overthrowe. 1605. *See* 1900.

— A true reporte of the prosperous successe [of] English souldiours. [1581.] *See* 17124a.

— A true reporte of the skirmish. [1578?] *See* 4322.

Representation. A true representation of the proceedings of the kingdome of Scotland. 1640. *See* 21929.

Request. A briefe request or declaracion presented vnto the duchesse of Parme. 1566. *See* 11028.

Requests. The requests presented unto the French King, by the Generall Deputies. 1623. *See* 11306.

— The requestes presented vnto the Frenche Kinge by the three rulers. [1562?] *See* 5042.

Requests, *Court of.* The ancient state, of the Court of Requests. 1597. *See* 4341.

20893 **Res.** Eadem res duobus vendita, cui prius tradita, debetur. 1586. = 4474.32.

20894 **Ressold, William.** Foure sermons, I. Sinnes contagion. II. The description of a christian. III. The blindnesse of a sinner. IV. A race to heaven. 4°. *H. L[ownes] f. G. Lathum*, 1627. L.O.; U(imp.).

Restorer. The restorer of the French estate. 1589. *See* 11289.

Retofortis, Joannes. *See* 21463.

20894.4 **Retorna.** Returna bm̄. 4° ⁸·⁴. (*R. Pynson*, 1516.) O. Reprinted in 14880 sqq., 15018 sqq., 18394 sq.

20894.7 — [Anr. ed.] 4° ⁸·⁴. (*w. de worde*, 1519.) C(A4, 5 only, imp., Sayle 7697).M.; HN.

20895 — = 20897.

20896 — [Anr. ed.] Retourna breuium. 4° ⁶·⁴. (*R. Pynson*,) [1523–4?] C.

20897 — [Anr. ed.] Returna breuium. 8°. [*J. Rastell*, 1526–30?] L.O. Broxbourne(E).; HD.
(Formerly also 20895) Issued as pt. of 14871.

20898 — [Anr. ed.] 8°. (*R. Redman*, 1532 (18 fb.)) C.; HD. Prob. issued as pt. of 14870.

20898.5 — [Anr. ed.] 8°. (*in ed. T. Bertheleti*,) [c. 1533.] HD. In McK.&F. comp. 24 (architectural, with Christ at top). Prob. issued w. 14871.5.

20899 — [Anr. ed.] 8°. (*R. Redman*,) [1533?] O.C².C¹⁸. London, Gray's Inn.; HN.HD(2, 1 lacks col.). Includes Hundred Court. Prob. issued as pt. of 14872.

20899.5 — [Anr. ed.] 8°. *in æd. T. Bertheleti*, [1537–40?] L.P.; HD. In McK.&F. comp. 34 (architectural, w. vase at top). Foliated. Prob. issued as pt. of 14873. HD copy issued as pt. of 14876.

20900 — [Anr. ed.] 8°. (*R. Redman*, 1537 (31 au.)) [1538?] L(destroyed).L⁵.; F.HD.

20900.5 — [Anr. ed.] 8°. *in æd. T. Bertheleti*, [1538–40?] F.HD. MIN. In McK.&F. comp. 30 (architectural, w. angel at top). F copy issued as pt. of 14876.

Retorna—*cont.*

20901 — [Anr. ed.] 8°. (*R. Redman*, 1541 (6 my.)) L(2).O.; HD. MIN.
 Redman died in 1540 so this book is either misdated or pr. by his widow.

20902 — [Anr. ed.] 8°. (*per me W. Myddylton,*) 1543 (oc.) L.

20902.3 — [Anr. ed.] 8°. *in aed. T. Bertheleti,* [1543?] L.O.O⁸.C.; HN.CH.HD.MIN.Y.
 In McK.&F. comp. 34 (architectural, w. vase at top). Not foliated. Issued as pt. 3 of 14877.

20902.5 — [Anr. ed.] 8°. (*per me W. Myddylton,*) 1545 (se.) MIN.

20903 — [Anr. ed.] 8°. [*N. Hill,*] 1546. L(2).O.; HN.HD(3).MIN.U.
 Issued as pt. of 14879 sqq.

20904 — [Anr. ed.] 8°. *in ed. W. Powel,* [1552?] HD.MIN.
 HD copy issued as pt. 4 of 14880.

— [Anr. ed.] 1581. Issued as pt. 2 of 15018.

— [Anr. ed.] 1585. Issued as pt. 2 of 15019.

20905 **Return.** The returne of the knight of the poste from hell, with the divels aunswere to the Supplication of Pierce Penilesse [18371]. 4°. *J. Windet f. N. Butter,* 1606. Ent. 15 ja.; cancelled 17 fb. L(2).O.; HD (tp facs.).

20906 **Reuchlin, Johann.** De arte concionandi formulæ, ... Eiusdem Melancthonis discendæ theologiæ rationem, adiecimus. 8°. *per H. Bynneman pro J. Waley,* 1570. L.O.C.C²¹.P.; HD.

20907 **Reusner, Nicolaus.** Nicolai Reusneri . . . symbolorum imperatoriorum classis prima (secunda—tertia.) Quarta editio. 3 pts. 8°. *ap. J. Billium,* 1619. Ent. 19 oc. 1618. L.O.C.DUL.E.+; BO.

20908 — Quinta editio. 12°. *Oxonii, ap. G. Turner,* 1633. Ent. to Joyce Norton a. R. Whitaker 26 au. 1632. L.O.C².; HD.

20909 — Sexta editio. 12°. *Oxonii, ap. G. Turner,* 1638. L.O. C¹⁰.M².NEK.+; HN.HD(imp.).ILL.PH.TORONTO².+

20910 **Reuter, Adam.** Contra conspiratorum consilia orationes duæ. Habitæ, diebus regiæ liberationis à conspiratione Gowrie. 4°. *M. Bradwood,* 1612. Ent. to A. Hatfield 28 se. L.O⁵.C¹⁷.DUR⁵.M².+; F(2).

20911 — De consilio tractatus quem nobilissimo Suffolciæ comiti consecrat A. Reuter. 4°. *Oxoniæ, J. Lichfield & G. Turner,* 1626. L.O.O¹⁸.C.DUR⁵.+; Y.

20912 — Delineatio consilii brevissima: quam societati mercatorum Belgarum consecrat A. Reuter. 4°. [*W. Stansby,*] 1614. Ent. to W. Stansby 8 ap. O⁵.D².M².; HD.

20913 — Eadgarus in Jacobo redivivus seu pietatis Anglicanæ defensio. 4°. *Londini,* 1614. O.C².M².; HD.

20914 — Ex L. Ut Vim 3. D. Just: et jure. Quæstiones juris controversi 12. 4°. *Oxoniæ, J. Barnesius,* 1609. L.O.C². C¹⁷.P.+; F.

20914a — Henrici Fitzsimonis, Soc. Jes. contra ius, rationem, Deum, pugna: quam, demonstratam ex eiusdem Britannomachia, Henrico Wallopp consecrat A. Reuter. 4°. [*W. Stansby,*] 1616. O⁵.O¹⁷.; HD.

20915 — Libertatis Anglicanae defensio, seu demonstratio: regnum Angliæ non esse feudum pontificis. 4°. *J. Beale,* 1613. Ent. 8 de. L.O.C.DUR⁵.M².+; F.HN.HD.U.

20916 — Oratio: quam, papam esse bestiam . . . apud Johan: Apoc. 17. ver. 8. in fine probantem. 4°. *typis H. Lownes,* 1610. O(2).O⁵.C².E².M².; F.HD.

— *See also* 22890.5, 25858.3.

Revel, Tristram, *tr. See* 15179.

20917 **Revelation.** The prologe of this reuelacion. How a monke of Euishamme was rapte in spirite [etc. *Tr.* from the Latin Visio written down by Adam, *of Eynsham.*] 4°. [*W. de Machlinia,* 1483.] L.O. Duff 357.

— A revelation of the secret spirit. Declaring the secret of alchymie. 1623. *See* 15184.

20917.5 **Revels.** The revells of Christendome. [Engr. with verse.] s.sh.fol. *sould by Mary Oliver in Westminster Hall,* [1609.] L(Print Dept.).O³⁴(S.71–158). 𝕬

Revenger. The revengers tragædie. 1607. *See* 24149.

Rex. Vivat rex. 1633. *See* 25194.

20918 **Reyman, Matthæus.** Noctes musicæ. [*Leipzig,*] 1598. Not an STC book.

Reyna, Casiodoro de, *tr. See* 2959.

Reynard, John. The admirable deliverance of 266. christians. 1608. *See* 18258.

20919 **Reynard the Fox.** [a2ʳ:] This is the table of the historye of reynart the foxe. (*Tr. w.* Caxton.) fol. [*Westminster, W. Caxton,*] (1481 (6 jn.)) L(2).ETON.M.; PML. Kraus. Duff 358.
 29 lines a page.

20920 — [Anr. ed.] fol. [*Westminster, W. Caxton,* 1489.] C⁶ (lacks i5,6). Duff 359.
 31, 32 lines a page.

20921 — [Anr. ed.] Here begynneth the hystorye of reinard the foxe. fol. [*R. Pynson,* 1494.] O(imp.). Duff 360.
 38 lines a page.

20921.5 — [Anr. ed.] 4°. [*R. Pynson,* bef. 1506.] E(frag.).
 31 lines a page, pr. in 95 textura with w¹ and w⁶; *see* Isaac I, figs. 13, 14.

20921a — [Anr. ed.] 4°. [*W. de Worde,* c. 1525.] C(2 leaves).
 31 lines a page; printed in 95 textura with s³, w², w³; *see* Isaac I, fig. 8.

20922 — [Anr. ed.] Here beginneth the booke of Raynarde the Foxe. 8°. *T. Gaultier,* 1550. Ent. to W. Powell 30 no. 1560. L.O.; F.

20922.5 — [Anr. ed.] 4°. [*E. Allde,* c. 1600.] ? Ent. to J. Charlewood 15 ja. 1582; to E. Allde 4 oc. 1586. BIRM(imp.).
 In this ed. chap. 36 is 'How Reynard the Fox excused him selfe before the kyng.' This text appears as chap. 28 in 20922 and earlier eds. The revised text appears as chap. 19 in 20923 sqq.

20923 — [Anr. ed., revised.] The most delectable history of Reynard the fox. Newly corrected. As also augmented with sundry moralls and expositions. 4°. *Ed. All-de, solde by R. Aldred,* [1620.] O(date cropt).

20924 — [Anr. ed.] 4°. *Eliz. All-de,* 1629. L.O.; F.

20925 — [Anr. ed.] 4°. *R. Oulton f. J. Wright the younger,* 1640. Ent. to R. Oulton 22 ap. F.

20925a — [A variant, w. imprint:] ⟨*R. Oulto*⟩*n f. J. Salter,* 1640. O(tp def.).

Reyner, Clement. A treatise of indulgences. 1623. *See* 1023.5.

Reynolde, William. *See* Rainolds, W.

20925a.5 **Reynoldes, Richard.** A booke called the foundacion of rhetorike, made by R. Rainolde. 1563. mens. marcij. vj. [Based on the *Progymnasmata* of Aphthonius.] 4°. *J. Kingston,* [1563.] Ent. 1562–63. L³.O.C.BIRM² (K.N.).P.+; F.CH(imp.).
 (Formerly 20604) Issued w. 25802.

20926 — A chronicle of all the noble emperours of the Romaines. 4° in 8's. *T. Marshe,* 1571. Ent. 1566–67. L(imp.). O.C.A.P.+; F.HN.BO.CU.N.+

20927 **Reynolds, Edward,** *Bp.* An explication of the hundreth and tenth psalme. 4° in 8's. *F. Kyngston f. R. Bostocke,* 1632. Ent. 15 mr. L.O.C².D.E.+; F.HN.CHI. HD(imp.).U.+

20928 — Second edition. 4° in 8's. *F. Kyngston f. R. Bostocke,* 1635. L.O.C.DUR³.G².+; F.HN.N.U.Y.+

20929 — Meditations on the holy sacrament of the Lords last supper. 4°. *F. Kyngston f. J. Maynard,* 1638. Ent. 1 se. 1637; to Maynard a. Bostock 7 my. 1638. L¹³. O.C³.D.G².+; F.HN.U.Y.

20929a — [A variant, w. imprint:] *F. Kyngston f. R. Bostock,* 1638. L.L¹³.O⁶.O²⁰.LINC.; F(2).HN.NY¹¹.U.Y.

20930 — Second edition corrected and revised. 4°. *J. Norton f. J. Maynard,* 1639. O.DUR⁵.E².LYU.YK.+; F.HN.HD (imp.).

20930a — [A variant, w. imprint:] *J. Norton f. R. Bostock,* 1639. L.L⁴.O¹⁸.C.E².; F.BO.BO⁶.U.Y.

20931 — A sermon touching the peace & edification of the church. 4°. *F. Kyngston f. R. Bostock,* 1638. Ent. 29 mr. L.O.C.D.E⁴.+; F.HN.BO.PEN.U.+

20931.5 — [Anr. ed.] 4°. *f. R. Bostock,* 1638 [really c. 1650.] L³.O. C².BHP.NOR².+; ILL. Weissman.

20932 — The shieldes of the earth. A sermon. 4°. *F. Kyngston f. R. Bostock,* 1636. Ent. 2 my. L.O.C.M.PETYT.+; F. HN.BO.HD.U.+

20932.5 — [Anr. ed.] The shields [etc.] 4°. *f. R. Bostock,* 1636 [really c. 1650.] L³.O.C².G⁴.NOR².; F. Weissman.

20933 — The sinfulnesse of sinne. The fourth edition. 8°. *R. Bishop f. R. Bostocke,* 1639. N.WASH³(imp.).
 Eds. 1–3 are pt. 2 of 20934 sqq.

20934 — Three treatises of the vanity of the creature. The sinfulnesse of sinne. The life of Christ. 4° in 8's. *F. Kyngston f. R. Bostocke,* 1631. Ent. 8 fb. L.L¹².O. C(imp.).G².+; F.HN.BO.MICH.Y.+

20934.5 — [A variant, w. imprint on gen. tp:] *F. Kyngston, sold by H. Curteyne,* [*Oxford,*] 1631. O⁵.; STAN.

Reynolds, Edward, *Bp.—cont.*

20935 — Second edition, revised and corrected. 4° in 8's. *F. Kyngston f. R. Bostocke,* 1632 (1631.) L.O.C.A.NOR². +; F.HN.CHI.PN².U.+

20936 — Third edition. 4° in 8's. *R. Badger f. R. Bostocke,* 1634. L.O.C.DUR³.E².+; F.HN.HD.PEN². Bp. Medley Library, Church Hall, Fredericton, N.B.+

20936.5 — [Anr. ed. of pt 1.] The vanitie of the creature. By E. Reynolds. 12°. *F. Kyngston f. R. Bostocke,* 1637. O.G².; F.HN.HD.

The G² copy has the cancel tp 20937 at the end. All copies but G² have an inserted dedic. and verses dated 22 Jan. 1654.

20937 — [Anr. issue, w. cancel tp:] The vanitie of the creature, and vexation of the spirit. *F. Kyngston f. R. Bostocke,* 1637. L(2, 1 w. the inserted dedic.).

20938 — A treatise of the passions and faculties of the soule of man. 4°. *R. H[earne] f. R. Bostock,* 1640. Ent. 3 ja. L.O.C.D.E.+; F.HN.CHI.HD.U.+

20939 **Reynolds, Henry.** Mythomystes wherein a short survay is taken of true poesy. To which is annexed the Tale of Narcissus. [Init. H. R.] 4°. [*G. Purslowe*] *f. H. Seyle,* [1632.] Ent. as by Henry Reynolds to J. Waterson 10 au. 1632, 'crost out and resigned to the author'. L.O.C³.D.LIV³.; HN.HD.NY.ROS.

'Narcissus' paraphrased from G. Anguillara's version of Ovid.

— *tr. See* 23696.

20940 Now = 20941.7.

20941 **Reynolds, John,** *Epigrammatist.* Epigrammata, auctore Joanne Reinoldo . . . Novi Collegij socio. (Prima chilias complectens disticha anthrôpina.—Prima centuria reges Britannici.) 8°. *Oxoniæ, J. Barnesius,* 1611. L.O.O³.O⁵.; HD.

20941.3 — Prima chilias id est disticha classis epigrammatum sive carminum inscriptorum. Prima centuria continens ea quae pertinent ad Deum. (Secunda centuria . . . ad angelos.) 8°. *Oxoniæ, ap. J. Barnesium,* 1612. O. Duke of Portland(frag.).

20941.7 **Reynolds, John,** *Merchant.* Dolarnys primerose. Or the first part of the passionate hermit. [In verse.] 4°. *G. Eld, sold by R. Boulton,* 1606. Ent. 13 jn. F. Arthur Houghton.

(Formerly 20940)

20942 — The triumphs of Gods revenege [*sic*], against the crying, and execrable sinne of murther. The first booke. 4°. *F. Kyngston f. W. Lee,* 1621. Ent. 7 jn. L.O(2). C.M.YK.; F.HN.CH.

For separate eds. of Bks. 2 and 3 *see* 20943.3 sqq.

20943 — [Anr. ed.] 4°. *A. Mathewes f. W. Lee,* 1629. L.BTL.; F.

20943.3 — The triumphs. . . . Booke II. 4°. *F. Kyngston f. W. Lee,* 1622. L(2).O.C.C⁵.M.; F(2).HN.CH.

20943.5 — The triumphs. . . . Booke. III. 4°. *A. Mathewes f. W. Lee,* 1623. L.O.; F(2).

20943.7 — [A variant, w. imprint:] *A. Mathewes f. W. Lee,* 1624. M.; HN.CH.

20944 — The triumphs. . . . [Bks. 1–6.] fol. [Bks. 1,2,5:] (*A. Mathewes;*) [Bks. 3,4,6:] (*J. Haviland*) *f. W. Lee,* 1635 (1634.) Bks. 4–6 ent. to W. Lee, jun., 19 de. 1633; 14 jn. a. 20 au. 1634. L.O.C.M⁴.NEK(imp.).+; F.HN.N.NY¹¹.Y.+

Mathewes's name appears only on the sub tp to Bk. 2.

20945 — [Anr. ed.] fol. *E. Griffin f. W. Lee,* 1639. L(2, 1 imp.). O¹⁴.; U.

20946 — [Anr. issue, w. added gen. tp:] Second edition. *E. Griffin f. W. Lee,* 1640. L(destroyed).C.HETH.LIV³. PLUME.; F.HN.HD(w. 1639 tp cancelled).MICH.U.+

20946.1 — Votivæ Angliæ: or the desires and wishes of England. To perswade his majestie to drawe his sword, for the restoring of the Pallatynat, to prince Fredericke. [Init. S.R.N.I., i.e. IohN ReynoldS.] 4°. *Utrecht* [i.e. *London,*] 1624. L.O.C.C².D².+; F.HN.HD.ILL.U.+

(Formerly 22092) *2ʳ last line ends: 'seeing your'. *See* Greg, *Companion,* pp. 225–6.

20946.2 — [Anr. ed.] 4°. *Utrecht* [i.e. *London,*] 1624. O(2).C².C⁹.; HN.HD.N.NY.NY¹¹.

(Formerly 22093) *2ʳ last line ends: 'on her'; *3ʳ line 3 ends: 'and'. One O and HD copies are bd. w. 22064.

20946.3 — [Anr. ed.] 4°. *Utrecht* [i.e. *London,*] 1624. L.O.O².C.D. +; F.HD.ILL.U.Y.+

*2ʳ last line ends: 'on her'; *3ʳ line 3 ends: '&'.

Reynolds, John, *Merchant—cont.*

20946.4 — Vox cœli, or newes from heaven. Of a consultation there held by king Hen. 8. king Edw. 6. . . . wherein Spaines ambition and trecheries are unmasked. [Init. S.R.N.I., i.e. IohN ReynoldS.] 4°. *Elisium* [i.e. *London, W. Jones,*] 1624. C².C⁵.D².DUL.SHEF.+; F.HD.

(Formerly 22094) Pp. 92. *See* Greg, *Companion,* pp. 225–6.

20946.5 — [Anr. ed.] 4°. *Elisium* [i.e. *London,*] 1624. L.O.C².E. NOR².+; F.HN.ILL.MCG.NY(2).

Pp. 92; in title: 'treacheries'.

20946.6 — [Anr. ed.] 4°. *Elisium* [i.e. *London,*] 1624. L.L⁴.O¹³.YK. Blickling.; F.CAL.HD.N.U.+

(Formerly 22095) Pp. '70' (i.e. 60), B1ʳ last line: 'latinate.'; line 8 ends: 'ver-'. The HD copy is bd. w. 22064.

20946.7 — [Anr. ed.] 4°. *Elisium* [i.e. *London,*] 1624. L.O.C.DUR⁵. M(deposit).+; F.CAL.HD.ILL.Y.+

(Formerly 22096) Pp. 60; B1ʳ last line: 'Palatinate.' One C copy (H*.12.7(E)) and L¹³ have quire B in a different setting: B1ʳ last line: 'latinate.'; line 8 ends: 'verti-'.

20946.8 — [Anr. ed.] 4°. *Elesium* [*sic*], [i.e. *London,*] 1624. L³⁰.O. C⁴.C⁹.E.+; F.CH.HD.

(Formerly 22096a) Pp. 60; B1ʳ last line: 'his Palatinate.' One O copy is bd. w. 22064.

— *tr. See* 7367, 11293, 17298, 17845.

20946.9 **Reynolds, John,** *of the Mint.* An advice. Touching the currancie in payment of our English golde. As also, a table of the severall worths of all pieces, uncurrant through want of weight, at his majesties exchanges at London. [Anon.] 8°. *B. A[lsop] a. T. F[awcet] f. B. Fisher,* [1627.] Ent. 11 jy. 1627. RGU(date cropt).; HN(date cropt).

The copies vary on C7ᵛ; where HN has 'some small Profit' the RGU copy has the press alteration: 'a reasonable and sufficient Profit'.

20946.10 — [Anr. ed.] 8°. *f. F. Constable,* 1627. L³⁰.RGU.

20947 — [Anr. issue of 20946.9.] Corrected and amended. Disclaiming a booke, intituled The free exchanger [10614]. *f. B. Fisher,* 1627. L.

20947.3 — [Anr. issue of 20946.10.] Corrected [etc.] *f. B. Fisher,* 1628. L³⁰.

20947.7 — [Anr. ed.] An advice, or, directions as well for the paymaster as receiver of any English gold now currant. 8°. *f. B. Fisher,* 1629. BALT(tp def.).

20948 — [Anr. ed., revised.] Perfet [*sic*] directions for all English gold, now currant in this kingdome. 8°. *N. Okes f. B. Fisher,* 1631. L(2).O(date cropt).O³.O⁵.C⁵(lacks tp and C8).; ILL(date cropt).

Advt. for John East, goldsmith, at end of text. In both L copies B7 is cancelled; in O it is replaced by a bifolium, in C⁵ by a single leaf. On orig. C8 the tables for ounce and pennyweight troy are transposed; they are corrected on a cancel; both at L.

20949 — = 20950.

20950 — [Anr. ed., w. omissions and additions.] And two tables for valuing of gold and silver of any finesse; not heretofore published. 8°. *N. Okes f. B. Fisher,* 1632. L(impr. cropt).L³⁰.O.C¹⁰.

Advt. for John East at end of text.

20951 — [Anr. ed.] 8°. *N. O[kes] f. B. Fisher,* 1633. L.O(lacks tp).; F(date cropt). CU.HD(imp.).

No advt. for John East at end of text.

Rhaesus, J. D. *See* 20966.

Rhegius, Urbanus. *See* 20840 sqq.

20952 **Rheol.** Rheol o gyfarwyddyd iw harfer wrth ymweled ar clâf. [Order for the visitation of the sick; a different text from that in 16438.] 4°. (*gan T. Harper,* 1629.) NLW.

Rhodes, Island of. [The siege of Rhodes. c. 1482.] *See* 4594.

— [The siege of Rhodes. 1524.] *See* 15050.

— *See* also Indulgences 107 sqq.

Rhodes, Mr. Micrologia. 1629. *See* 17146.

20953 **Rhodes, Hugh.** [Heading A1ʳ:] The boke of nurture for men, seruantes and chyldren, with Stans puer ad mensam, newly corrected. 4°. (*T. Petyt,*) [1545?] O(lacks A2,3).

34 lines a page. Stans puer is in verse. Its 1st

Rhodes, Hugh—*cont.*
line, though lacking in the O copy, is: All ye that would learn, and would be called wise. For other texts resembling this *see* 3303, 17030, 23428 (in Latin), 24866 (French and English, etc.)

20954 — [Anr. ed.] 4°. (*A. Veale*,) [1560?] Ent. to J. King 1557–58. L.DE.
See also 20957; 35 lines a page; A2ʳ line 1: 'knowe your maisters'; B3ʳ line 2: 'selfe'.

20955 — [Anr. ed.] 4°. (*T. Colwell, dwellynge in the house of R. Wyer,*) [1560?] HN(lacks tp).
This is prob. earlier than 20954; 34 lines a page.

20956 — [Anr. ed. Anon.] obl. 4°. *T. East,* 1568. Ent. 12 mr. 1582. L.

20957 — [Anr. ed.] 4°. [*London, c.* 1570.] L(B3 only).; HD(A2, 3 only).
L,HD may belong to different eds. *See also* 20954; 35 lines a page; A2ʳ line 1: 'know your Masters'; B3ʳ line 2: 'self'.

20958 — [Anr. ed. Signed, revised, and enlarged.] 8°. *H. Jackson,* 1577. L.O.

20959 **Rhodes, John.** An answere to a romish rime lately printed [in 17505], and entituled, a proper new ballad, wherein are contayned catholike questions to the protestant. [In verse. Init. J. R.] 4°. *S. Stafford,* 1602. Ent. 22 my. L.C.
C1ʳ line 1: 'playnly'.

20959.5 — [Anr. ed., signed on A2ᵛ.] 4°. *S. Stafford,* 1602. L.O. O⁵(imp.).; HN.HD.
C1ʳ line 1: 'plainely'. Quires B, F from same setting as 20959.

20960 — A briefe summe of the treason intended against the king & state, November. 5. 1605. [In verse.] 4° w. perp. chainlines. *E. A[llde] f. E. White,* 1606. L.; F.HN.

20960.5 — [Anr. ed.] The second time printed, corrected, and amended. 4° w. perp. chainlines. *E. Allde f. E. White,* 1606. F.

20961 — The countrie mans comfort. Or religious recreations. Printed in 1588, and since corrected by the author J. R[hodes. In verse.] 8°. *M. D[awson,] sold by A. Boler,* 1637. Ent. to A. Hill 16 de. 1588. L.
— An epitaph, on the death of John, the archbyshop of Canterburie. [By J. Rhodes?] 1604. *See* 20574.

20961.5 **Rhodes, Mathew.** The dismall day, at the Black-fryers. Or, a deplorable elegie, on the death of almost an hundred persons, slaine by the fall of a house in the Black-fryers. [In verse.] s.sh.fol. *G. Eld,* 1623. L⁵ (Lemon 205).

20962 **Rhodomannus, Laurence.** Historia ecclesiæ siue populi Dei. 8°. *H. Bynneman p̄ F. Coldocko,* 1582. O.C³.

20963 **Rhumel, Johann Pharamund.** Avicula hermetis catholica. De mercurio sulphure & sale philosophorum in uno subjecto. [Solomon Raphael, *pseud.*] 12°. *ap. T. Harperum,* 1638. L.; NY⁴.

20964 — Canticum canticorum. Quod est Schelemonis de medicina universali. [Anon.] 12°. [*T. Harper,* 1638?] L.; NY⁴.

20965 — Compendium Hermeticum, de macrosmo [*sic*] et microcosmo, totius philosophiæ. 12°. [*T. Harper,* 1638?] L.; NY⁴.

Rhyme. *See* Rime.

Rhymer. *See* Rimer.

20966 **Rhys, John David.** Cambrobrytannicæ cymraecæue linguae institutiones. Ad intelligend. Biblia sacra nuper in Cambrobrytannicum sermonem versa [2347]. fol. *T. Orwinus,* 1592. Ent. 24 de. 1591. L.O. C.D².E.+; F.HN.CU.HD.N.+

20967 **Ribadeneira, Pedro de.** The life of B. father Ignatius of Loyola. *Tr.* out of Spanish by W. M. [*S. J.*, i.e. M. Walpole.] 8°. [*St. Omer, English College Press,*] 1616. L.L⁹(3).O.W. The Oratory, Birmingham.; F.
A&R 712.

20968 — [Anr. issue, w. cancel tp:] The life of the holy patriarch. [*St. Omer, English College Press,*] 1622. L.L²⁶.CHEL. HP.W.+; HN.
A&R 713.
— The lives of saints. 1621, etc. *See* 24731b sqq.

20969 No entry.

20970 **Ribaut, Jean.** The whole and true discouerye of Terra Florida. Nowe newly set forthe in Englishe the .xxx. of May. 1563. 8°. *R. Hall f. T. Hacket,* [1563.] Ent. 1562–63. L.L².
L² copy has inserted dedic. to Sir Martin Bowes.

20971 **Ribera, Francisco de.** The lyf of the mother Teresa of Jesus. [Not by Ribera.] 1611. Now = 23948.5.
— *See also* 19085.

Ricardus, *Dunelmensis. See* 958.5.

20972 **Ricardus,** *Prior.* Here foloweth a veray deuoute treatyse (named Benyamyn) of the myghtes and vertues of mannes soule, & of the way to true contemplacyon, compyled by Rycharde of saynt Vyctor. 4° ⁴·⁶. (*H. Pepwell,* 1521 (16 no.)) L.C². Louvain U.
Includes extracts from Saint Catharine of Siena, Margerie Kempe, and Walter Hylton.

20973 **Rice, Richard.** An inuective againste vices taken for vertue. 8° in 4's. *J. Kyngston f. H. Kirckham,* [c. 1575.] L².O(2).; F(imp.).

20974 — [Anr. ed.] Also certaine necessary instructions of the holy communion. Doen by D. w. *Arch[deacon].* 8°. *J. Kyngston f. H. Kirkham,* 1579. L.C(2).
2nd pt. reprinted in 24901.

20975 — [Anr. ed.] 8°. *R. Waldegaue* [*sic*] *f. H. Kirkham,* 1581. C².; F.
Though Necessary Instructions are called for on tp of this and following eds., they are omitted. This ed. has 'A fewe verses against, pastimes'.

20976 — [Anr. ed.] 8°. *T. O[rwin] f. H. Kirkham,* 1589. F.
This ed. has 'A forme of thanksgiuing, and prayer' following main text.
— *tr. See* 13210.

Rich. Riche and pore. 1493, etc. *See* 19212 sqq.

20977 **Rich, Barnaby.** The aduentures of Brusanus prince of Hungaria. 4°. [*T. Orwin*] *f. T. Adames,* 1592. Ent. to Adams a. J. Oxenbridge 23 oc. L(imp.).; F.

20977.5 — [A variant, w. imprint:] *f. J. Oxenbridge,* 1592. L³⁰. DUL.

20978 — Allarme to England, foreshewing what perilles are procured, where the people liue without regarde of martiall lawe. 4°. (*C. Barker,*) 1578. Ent. 26 ap. L.O. C⁵.D.P.+; F.Y. W. Stirling Maxwell, Chicago.

20979 — [Anr. ed.] 4°. (*H. Middleton f. C. B[arker,]*) 1578. L.; HN(tp facs.).
Probably the 1st ed.

20980 — [An adaption.] Vox militis: foreshewing what perils [etc. Init. G. M., i.e. G. Marcelline.] 4°. *B. A[lsop] f. T. Archer,* 1625. L(2).O.C.C⁵.C⁹.+; F.HN.BO².HD. TEX.
1st quire has 4 leaves; above imprint: 'Dedicated to Count Mansfield. . . .'

20980.5 — [Anr. issue, w. new prelims.] *B. A[lsop] f. T. Archer,* 1625. L.
1st quire has 2 leaves; above imprint is a rule. Dedic. to T. Style signed 'G. Marceline' is not conjugate w. tp.

20981 — A catholicke conference betweene Sʸʳ Tady Mac. Mareall and Patricke Plaine. 4°. [*T. Dawson*] *f. T. Adams,* 1612. Ent. 9 jn. L.O.C.D.SCL.+; F(2, 1 imp.). HN.HD(cropt).LC(lacks tp).Y.

20982 — The excellency of good women. 4°. *T. Dawson,* 1613. Ent. to J. Dawson 12 ja. L.O.; HN.Y.

20983 — Faultes [xylographic] faults, and nothing else but faultes. 4°. [*V. Simmes*] *f. J. Chorleton,* 1606. Ent. 25 ja. L.O.D.; F.HN.HD.N.NY.+

20984 — Now = 20991.7.

20985 — Roome for a gentleman, or the second part of Faultes ['Faultes' xylographic] collected for the true meridian of Dublin. 4°. *J. W[indet] f. J. Chorlton,* 1609. Ent. 3 oc. 1608. L.O.; F.HN.
— The fruites of long experience. 1604. *See* 21001.
— Greenes newes both from heauen and hell. 1593. *See* 12259.

20986 — The honestie of this age. 4°. [*T. Dawson*] *f. T. A[dams,]* 1614. Ent. to T. Adams 22 jn. L.C.D.; F(impr. cropt).HN.

20987 — [Anr. ed.] 4°. [*J. Legat*] *f. T. A[dams,]* 1615. O.O³.; F(imp.).HN.NY.
On tp: 'Barnabe Rych'.

20987.5 — [Anr. ed.] 4°. [*J. Legat*] *f. T. A[dams,]* 1615. L.O(2).C.
On tp: 'Barnabe Rich'.

20988 — [Anr. ed.] 4°. [*J. Legat*] *f. T. Adams,* 1616. L.C(lacks tp).D.; F(lacks tp).NCU.PH.TEX.WIS.

Rich, Barnaby—*cont.*

20988.5 — [Anr. ed.] 4°. *Edinburgh,* ⟨*A.*⟩ *Hart,* [1616?] HN(tp def.).

20989 — The Irish hubbub or, the English hue and crie. 4°. [*G. Purslowe*] *f. J. Marriot,* 1617. Ent. 14 my. L.O. C.; HN.HD.PH².TEX.
Tp line 8 in italic.

20989.3 — [Anr. ed., revised.] 4°. [*G. Purslowe*] *f. J. Marriot,* 1617. NY.
Tp line 8 in roman.

20989.7 — [Anr. ed., w. additions.] (Aphorismes.) 4°. [*G. Purslowe*] *f. J. Marriot,* 1618. C¹⁰.LONGLEAT. Blickling.; Robert Taylor.

20990 — [Anr. issue, w. imprint:] *f. J. Marriot,* 1619. L(lacks I2).O.C.; F.NY.

20991 — [Anr. ed.] 4°. *A. Mathewes f. J. Marriot,* 1622. L.L⁴³. O(2).D⁶.DUL(impr. cropt).; F.

20991.3 — A martial conference, pleasantly discoursed betweene two souldiers, the one captaine Skil, trained vp in the French and Low country seruices, the other captaine Pill, only practised in Finsburie fields. 4°. *f. J. Oxenbridge,* 1598. L(tpp only, Harl.5961/133 and Harl.5995/24).C⁸.
See also 21000.

20991.7 — My ladies looking glasse. Wherein may be discerned a wise man from a foole. 4°. [*J. Legat*] *f. T. Adams,* 1616. Ent. 6 jn. L.L².O.C.D⁶.+; HN.HD.ILL.NY.
(Formerly 20984) A different text from 20983.

20992 — A new description of Ireland: wherein is described the disposition of the Irish. 4°. [*W. Jaggard*] *f. T. Adams,* 1610. Ent. 30 ap. L.O.C.D.E.+; F.HN.HD.N.Y.+
Defended in 21003.

20993 — [Anr. issue, w. A3–B4 cancelled and new title:] A new Irish prognostication, or popish callender. [Anon.] *f. F. Constable,* 1624. L.L⁴³.O.C.D.+; HN.HD(2, 1 imp.).ILL.

20994 — Opinion diefied [*sic*]. Discovering the ingins, traps, and traynes, that are set to catch opinion. 4°. [*T. Dawson*] *f. T. Adams,* 1613. Ent. 5 jn. L(3).L³⁰.O(2).C.D.; F.HN. NY.Y. Robert Taylor.
Variant dedics.: to Prince Charles or Sir T. Rydgeway; both at L.

20995 — A path-way to military practise. 4°. *J. Charlewood f. R. Walley,* 1587. Ent. 22 mr. L.L².O.O⁶. London, Royal Artillery Institution.; HN.LC.

20996 — Riche his farewell to militarie profession. 4°. [*J. Kingston f.*] *R. Walley,* 1581. O.

20996.3 — [Anr. ed.] 4°. [*J. Kingston f.*] *R. Walley,* 1583. F(2 imp.).

20996.7 — [Anr. ed.] 4°. *V. S[immes] f. T. Adams,* 1594. Ass'd from R. Walley 12 oc. 1591. F(imp.).

20997 — [Anr. ed.] Newly augmented. 4°. *G. E[ld] f. T. Adams,* 1606. O.; F.TCU.

20998 — A right exelent and pleasaunt dialogue, betwene Mercury and an English souldier. Wrytten 1574. 8°. [*J. Day,*] sold [*by H. Disle,* 1574.] L.O.; F(imp.).
J. Day's rights yielded to the company 8 Jan. 1584; *see* Arber II.788.
— Roome for a gentleman. 1609. *See* 20985.

20999 — A short survey of Ireland. Truely discovering who hath armed that people with disobedience. 4°. *N. O[kes] f. B. Sutton a. W. Barenger,* 1069 [1609.] Ent. 3 mr. 1609. L.O.C.D.D⁶.; F.HN.LC.N(lacks tp).

21000 — A souldiers wishe to Britons welfare. [A dialogue betwen Captains Pill and Skill.] 4°. [*T. Creede*] *f. J. Chorlton,* 1604. Ent. 21 my. O(2).
See also 20991.3.

21001 — [Anr. issue, w. cancel tp:] The fruites of long experience. *T. Creede f. J. Chorlton,* 1604. L.O.DUL.; HN.

21002 — The straunge and wonderfull aduentures of Dō Simonides. [Corrected by] (T. Lodge.) 4°. [*J. Kingston f.*] *R. Walley,* 1581. Ent. 23 oc. L.O.; F(imp.).HN(lacks tp).HD.

21002a — The second tome of the trauailes and aduentures of Don Simonides, enterlaced with historie. 4°. [*J. Kingston*] *f. R. Walley,* 1584. Ass'd from Walley to T. Adams 12 oc. 1591. L.O(2).P.; F(imp.).HN.HD.

21003 — A true and a kinde excuse written in defence of that booke, intituled A newe description of Irelande [20992]. 4°. [*T. Dawson*] *f. T. Adams,* 1612. L.O.C.D. SCL.+; F(imp.).HN.HD.NY.WIS.+
In several copies (at least C, F, HD) the date has been cropt or defaced; it is intact in 1 O.

21004 — The true report of a late practise enterprised by a papist, with a yong maiden in Wales. 4°. [*J. Kingston f.*] *R. Walley,* 1582. Ent. 23 ap. L.L².O.D.

Rich, Edmund [i.e. *Saint* Edmund, *Abp. of Canterbury*]. *See* 965.

21005 **Rich, R.** Newes from Virginia. The lost flocke triumphant. [In verse.] 4°. *E. Allde, solde by J. Wright,* 1610. L.DUR³.; HN.PN.
Allde fined for printing without licence; *see Court-Book C,* p. 446.

Rich, William. [Binder's ticket. c. 1615.] *See* 3908.3.

21006 **Richard,** *Duke of York.* The true tragedie of Richard duke of Yorke, and the death of good king Henrie the sixt. [An abridged and mangled version of Shakespeare's *Henry VI,* pt. 3.] 8°. *P. S[hort] f. T. Millington,* 1595. O. Greg 138.

21006a — [Anr. ed.] 4°. *W. W[hite] f. T. Millington,* 1600. Ass'd from Millington to T. Pavier 19 ap. 1602. L.O. VER(lacks tp).; F(2, 1 imp.).HN(2).BO.HD.PFOR.
Reprinted in 26101.

21007 **Richard I,** *King.* Kynge Rycharde cuer du lyon. [In verse.] 4° 8·4. (*w. de worde,* 1509.) O.M.

21008 — [Anr. ed.] 4° 8·4. (*w. de worde,* 1528.) Ent. to T. Purfoot 1568–69. L(G8 in facs.).O.; PML.

Richard II, *King.* The tragedie of king Richard the second. 1597. *See* 22307.

Richard III, *King.* The ghost of Richard the third. 1614. *See* 3830.
— The tragedy of king Richard the third. 1597. *See* 22314.

21009 — The true tragedie of Richard the third. 4°. *T. Creede, sold by W. Barley,* 1594. Ent. to Creede 19 jn. F. HN(A2, 3 in facs.).PFOR. Greg 126.

Richard, *of Saint Victor. See* 20972.

21009.5 **Richards, John.** The crowne of a christian martyr, with the citie or church of Christ, and the fall of Babylon. 4°. [*Delft, J. P. Waelpots,*] 1634. O¹¹.

21010 **Richards, Nathaniel.** The celestiall publican. A sacred poem. 8°. *F. Kyngston f. R. Michell,* 1630. Ent. 6 mr. L.; F(2).HN.
L, 1 F copies have uncancelled dedic.: 'To the heavenly lover of divine poems'; the other F copy has 'Richarde' on tp instead of 'Richards'.

21010.3 — [Anr. issue, w. cancel tp:] Seven poems: divine, morall, and satyricall. *f. R. Michell,* 1631. HD(imp.). With dedic. uncancelled.

21010.7 — [Anr. issue, w. cancel tp:] Poems. Divine, [etc. Init. N. R., *Gent.*] *f. J. Boler,* 1632. ROS.

21011 — The tragedy of Messallina the Roman emperesse. 8°. *T. Cotes f. D. Frere,* 1640. Ent. 3 oc. 1639. L(2).L⁶. O(2).E.; F.HN.HD.N(imp.).NY.+ Greg 578.

21012 **Richardson, Alexander.** The logicians school-master: or, a comment vpon Ramus logicke. 4°. [*M. Flesher*] *f. J. Bellamie,* 1629. Ent. 7 de. 1622. L³.O.C.D.YK.+; HN.BO². Tufts U.
— *See also* 26085.

Richardson, Augustine, *tr. See* 24821.5.

21013 **Richardson, Charles.** The benefite of affliction. A sermon. 8°. *L. Snowdon f. W. Butlar* [1,] 1616. O.C¹⁰.; F.

21013.5 — [Anr. ed.] 8°. *E. G[riffin] f. T. Pavier,* 1621. O³.YK.

21014 — The doctrine of the Lords supper. 8°. *L. Snowdon f. W. Butlar* [1,] 1616. L.O.

21015 — The price of our redemption. A sermon preached at Paules Crosse. 8°. *W. Jaggard f. W. Butler,* 1617. Ent. to W. Butler, sen., 12 my. L.L⁴.LINC.; F.

21016 — The repentance of Peter and Judas. 4°. *W. Stansby f. E. Edgar,* 1612. Ent. to Edgar a. Jos. Browne 6 de. 1611. L.L³.C.E⁴.WI.+; HN.PN².

21016a — [A variant, w. imprint:] *W. Stansby f. Jos. Browne,* 1612. L.A.; HD(imp.).U.

21017 — A sermon against oppression and fraudulent dealing. 4°. *G. Purslowe f. Jos. Browne a. T. Harper,* 1615. Ent. to Browne 31 ja. L.L¹³.O.C².YK.+; F.HN.CAL.HD. Weissman.

21018 — A sermon concerning the punishing of malefactors. 4°. [*R. Blower?*] *f. W. Butlar* [1,] 1616. L.O.C².E.EX.+; F.HN.CAL.HD.

21019 — A workeman, that needeth not to be ashamed. A sermon describing the duety of a godly minister. 4°. *W. Stansby f. W. Barret,* 1616. Ent. 17 jy. L.O.C².E.P.; F.HN.HD.N.NY¹¹.+

21020 **Richardson, Gabriel.** Of the state of Europe. XIIII. bookes. Containing the historie, and relation of the many provinces hereof. fol. *Oxford,* [*J. Lichfield*] *f. H. Cripps,* 1627. L.O.C.E².M.+; F.HN.HD.N.NY¹¹.+

21020.5 **Richardson, John.** A sermon of the doctrine of justification. On Rom. 3.24.25.26. 4°. *Dublin, Soc. of Statrs.,* 1625. D(2).; PH².

21021 **Richardson, Robert.** A briefe and compendious exposition vpon the psalme called Deprofundis [*sic*]. 8°. (*T. Purfoote f. W. Norton,*) [1570.] Ent. 1569–70. F.

Richardus, *Dunelmensis. See* 958.5.

Richelieu, *Cardinal de. See* Du Plessis, A. J.

21022 **Richeome, Louis.** Holy pictures of the mysticall figures of the sacrament of the eucharist: set forth in French and *tr.* C. A. 4°. [*Lancs., Birchley Hall Press?*] 1619. L.O.CA.D.+; F.HN.N.U.Y.+
 A&R 714. Some copies (1 O, DAI, DE) have a leaf w. 31-line errata, sometimes pasted over original 20-line errata.

21023 — The pilgrime of Loreto. Performing his vow. Conteyning divers devout meditations. Tr. E. W[alpole.] 4°. *Paris,* [i.e. *St. Omer, English College Press,*] 1629. L.O.DE.HP.W.+; F.HN.N.PML.Y.+
 A&R 715.

21023a — [A variant, w. date:] 1630. L.O.C.ST.USHAW.+; F.
 A&R 716.

21024 **Richer, Edmond.** A treatise of ecclesiasticall and politike power. *Tr.* out of the Latin originall. [Init. *Δ.*] 4°. *W. S*[tansby,] *sold by J. Budge,* 1612. Ent. 23 mr. L.O.C(imp.).E.YK.+; COR.U.

Richworth, William. The dialogues. 1640. *See* 21454.

21025 **Rickets, Charles.** Charles Rickets his recantation. [By C. Records?] *Ballad.* 2 pts. s.sh.fol. *f. J. Wright,* [1633?] ?Ent. as 'Long runns that neere turnes' 8 jy. 1633. C⁶.

21026 **Rickmansworth.** Be it knowen to all crystē people. [c. 1525.] Now = Indulgences 68.

21027 **Rid, Samuel.** The art of jugling or legerdemaine. 4°. [*E. Allde*] *f. T. B*[ushell,] *solde by S. Rand,* 1612. Ent. to T. Bushell 16 ja. O(2).; HN.

21028 — [Anr. ed.] 4°. *G. Eld,* 1614. L.L³⁰.G².+; F.

21028.5 — Martin Mark-all, beadle of Bridewell; his defence and answere to the Belman of London [6480, 6485]. By S. R[id.] 4°. [*E. Allde*] *f. J. Budge a. R. Bonian,* 1610. Ent. 31 mr. L(2).L⁸.O(2). London, Bridewell School.; F.HN(lacks ¶2).CH.HD.Y.
 (Formerly 21400) Tp app. is a cancel.

Riddles. [Book of riddles.] *See* 3288.5, 3322.5.

Rider, Henry, *tr. See* 13804.

21029 **Rider, John,** *Bp.* Bibliotheca scholastica. 1589. Now = 21031.5.

21030 — The coppie of a letter sent from M. Rider, concerning the newes out of Ireland. 4°. [*F. Kingston*] *f. T. Man,* 1601. O.

21031 — A friendly caveat to Irelands catholickes. 4°. *Dublin, J. Franckton,* 1602. L(2).L²⁵.C².DUL.

21031.5 — Bibliotheca scholastica. A double dictionarie. *Eng.-Lat.* 4° in 8's. *Jos. Barnes, pr. to the Univ. of Oxford, sold* [*in London by T. Cooke,*] 1589. Ent. to John Barnes 7 jn. 1602 and 6 de. 1602 'vpon condicon that yt shalbe printed onely in London and not elsewhere'. L.L²⁶.O(imp.).NLW.; F.ILL(imp.).
 (Formerly 21029)

21032 — [Anr. ed.] Riders dictionarie corrected and augmented. *Eng.-Lat.* Wherein Riders index is transformed into a dictionarie etymologicall. Many words added. *Lat.-Eng.* By F. Holyoke. 4° in 8's. *A. Islip,* 1606. Ass'd to C. Burby 27 ja. 1603; to T. Man a. partners 26 no. 1604. O(imp.).C¹⁷.P. Copenhagen RL.; F(2).
 Partly based on the dictionary of Thomas Thomas; *see Court-Book C,* pp. 18, 175.

21033 — [Anr. ed.] Riders dictionarie corrected, and with the addition of above five hundred words enriched. Hereunto is annexed a dictionarie etymologicall by F. Holyoke. Third edition. 4° in 8's. *Oxford, Jos. Barnes,* 1612. L.O.O⁶(imp.).C. Birkenhead PL.+; HN.ILL.TORONTO². Indiana State U(imp.).

Rider, John, *Bp.—cont.*

21034 — [Anr. ed.] 4° in 8's. *A. Islip f. T. Man,* 1617. L. Copenhagen RL.; ILL.
 See Court-Book C, p. 104.

21034.3 — [A variant, w. imprint on gen. tp:] *A. Islip f. J. Bill,* 1617. NMU. Hull U. Versailles PL.; ILL(pt. 1 only).

21034.7 — [A variant, w. imprint on gen. tp:] *A. Islip f. W. Leake,* 1617. ILL.LC.

21034a — [A variant, w. imprint on gen. tp:] *A. Islip f. T. Adams,* 1617. O.

21035 — [Anr. ed.] To which are joyned . . . alterations by N. Gray. (Rideri dictionarium severiore trutina castigatum.) 4° in 8's. *A. Islip,* 1626. Pt. ent. to Islip 8 no. 1624. L.L³⁰.M.NLW. London, Birkbeck College.; HART².PEN.

21035.3 — [A variant, w. imprint on gen. tp:] *A. Islip f. W. Leake,* 1626. Oberlin C.

21035.5 — [A variant, w. imprints:] *A. Islip f. J. Bill* (*F. Kyngston*), 1626. Pt. 2 ent. to F. Kingston 26 my. 1623. O².; CAL.ILL.NWM.

21035.7 — [A variant, w. imprint on gen. tp:] *A. Islip f. J. Grismand,* 1626. Pt. ent. to Grismond 5 no. 1635. Y(imp.).
 See Court-Book C, p. 271.

21036 — [Anr. ed.] Riders dictionarie. 4° in 8's. *Oxford, J. Lichfield a. W. Turner,* 1627. L.O.O⁹.BIRM.NLW.+; CU.ILL.NY.Y. Indiana State U.
 Issued as pt. of 13619.5.

21036a — [Anr. ed.] Newly corrected. 4° in 8's. *A. Islip a. F. Kyngston,* 1633. L.O.C⁵.BIRM.NLW.+; HN.BO.ILL.NY⁷.Y.+
 Issued as pt. of 13620.

21036a.3 — [Anr. ed.] 4° in 8's. *F. Kingston,* 1640. Pt. ent. to Kingston 4 jy. 1635. C.C².C⁵.M².NEK.; HD(lacks tp)*. ILL.
 This ed. and following variants issued w. 13620.5 sqq. *See Court-Book C,* p. 330, and Greg, *Companion,* pp. 318–19.

21036a.7 — [A variant, w. imprint:] *F. Kingston f. J. Waterson,* 1640. Pt. ent. to Waterson 19 au. 1635. L¹⁶.LIV³.; F.N.

21036b — [A variant, w. imprint:] *F. Kingston f. R. Whitaker,* 1640. Pt. ent. to Joyce Norton a. R. Whitaker 26 au. 1632. L.O.C⁸.BRISTOL².SAU.; BO.HD.MICH.ROCH.SMITH.+

21036b.3 — [A variant, w. imprint:] *F. Kingston f. A. Crooke,* 1640. F.

21036b.7 — [A variant, w. imprint:] *F. Kingston f. P. Nevill,* 1640. Kent U.

21037 **Rider, T.** A merie newe ballad intituled the pinnyng of the basket. *Ballad.* s.sh.fol. *f. H. Kirkham,* [1590?] L.

Ridge, Oliver. *See* 26050.18.

Ridley, Lancelot. Annotations in the boke of Josue. [c. 1537.] *See* 2351.5.

21038 — A commentary in Englyshe vpon sayncte Paules epystle to the Ephesyans. 1540. 8°. (*R. Redman,*) [1540.] L.O.C.P.
 In title: 'vnlerned'.

21038.5 — [Anr. ed.] 8°. (*R. Redman,*) [1540.] L¹⁵.C.
 In title: 'vnlearned'.

21039 — An exposicion in Englishe vpon the epistle of .S. Paule, to the Colossians. 1548. 8°. (*in aed. R. Graftoni,* 1548.) L.O.C⁵.D.LINC.+; F.

21040 — An exposytion in Englyshe vpon the epistyll of saynt Paule to the Philippiās. 8°. (*Cantorbury, J. Mychell,*) [1550?] L.O.C.D.M.+; F.

21041 — [Anr. issue, w. quires G and H reprinted and A expanded.] Ouer seen by Thomas [Cranmer] archebysshop of Cantorbury. (*Cantorbury, J. Mychyll f. E. whitchurche,*) [1550?] L.NLW.

21042 — An exposition in the epistell of Jude. [Anon.] 8°. (*in the house of T. Gybson,*) [1538.] L.L¹⁵(lacks col.).C(lacks col.).
 Tp comp. dated 1538.

21042a — = 21042.

21043 — [Anr. ed., revised.] 8°. (*W. Copland f. R. Kele,*) [1549?] L⁴.L¹⁵.O.C(3).; F.NY.

— [Exposition on II and III John. 1537?] *See* 24443.5.

21044 **Ridley, Mark.** Magneticall animadversions. . . . Vpon certaine Magneticall advertisements, from W. Barlow [1442]. 4°. *N. Okes,* 1617. L.C.C⁶.C⁹.E².; PEN. Horblit. Henry Taylor.
 Answered by 1443. According to 420.11, apparently there was an Appendix to this pub'd; *see The Library,* X (1929), p. 378.

Ridley, Mark—*cont.*

21045 — A short treatise of magneticall bodies and motions. 4°. *N. Okes*, 1613. Ent. 15 my. L.O.C.A.LIV³.+; HD.NY. Y. Horblit. Cambridge, Massachusetts Institute of Technology (2).
No errata on X3ʳ.

21045.5 — [Anr. issue, w. errata on cancel X3ʳ.] L³⁸.C².C³.C²⁵.G².+; F.HN.LC.WIS. Horblit.+

21046 **Ridley, Nicholas,** *Bp.* A brief declaracion of the Lordes supper. 8°. [*Emden, E. van der Erve,*] 1555. L.O².O⁹. C⁸.C¹⁰.+; F.HN.PML.U.
Reprinted in 21048.

21047 — [Anr. ed.] 8°. [*T. Dawson?*] *f.* (*A. Veale*), 1586. L¹⁵.O. C. Goyder.; CAL.
Veale's name is in round brackets in the tp imprint.

21047.3 — Certein godly, learned, and comfortable conferences, betwene N. Rydley and H. Latimer. (A cōclusion to the reader [init. J. O., i.e. J. Olde]) 8°. [*Emden, E. van der Erve,*] 1556. L.O.O².C¹⁰.M.+; F.U.
(Formerly 21049)

21047.7 — [Anr. ed.] Certayne godly, [etc.] 8°. [*Emden, E. van der Erve?*] 1556. C.; F.

21048 — [Anr. ed.] Certē godly, . . . Wherunto is added. A treatise agaynst transubstantiation. M.D.LVI. 8°. [*Strasburg, heirs of W. Rihel,* 1556.] L.O³.C.BTU. DUR⁵.+; F.HN.CH.PML.Y.
Omits the Conclusion; 2nd pt. reprints 21046.

21049 — Now = 21047.3.

21050 — [Anr. ed.] Now newly againe imprinted. 8°. *J. Awdeley,* 1574 (14 oc.) Ass'd from Awdley to J. Charlewood 15 ja. 1582. L.O.C.C³.D.+; F.HN.HD(lacks A2).ILL. U(lacks tp).+

21051 — A frendly farewel, which master doctor Ridley, did write vnto all his true louers and frendes in God, a litle before that he suffred. Newly setforth [*sic*]. [Ed.] (J. Foxe.) 8°. *J. Day,* 1559 (10 no.) L.L².O.C³.; F.HN.PML.

21052 — A pituous lamentation of the miserable estate of the church of Christ in Englande, in the time of the late reuolt from the gospel. Neuer before imprynted. Whereunto are also annexed letters of J. Careles. 8°. (*W. Powell,* 1566.) Ent. 1565–66. L.L².D(imp.).YK.; HN.HD.N.
(2nd pt. formerly 4612) Dated on sub tp.

21052.5 — [Anr. ed.] 8°. (*W. Powell,* 1566.) O.C.; F.NY¹¹.
Tp lines 6–7: 'in the time of queene Mary.' Quires A, C are largely reimposed from 21052.

21053 — = 21052.
— A treatise agaynst the errour of transubstantiation. = pt. of 21048.
— *See also* 10247.

Ridley, R., *ed. See* 11892.

21053.7 **Ridley,** *Sir* **Thomas.** Forasmuch as I have lately seene [etc. Order to Wm. Bramsgrove of Lichfield to see that all parishes in the diocese provide themselves with folio Royal Bibles and Books of Common Prayer according to the order of the last metropolitical visitation, and to deliver copies of 8566. 5 June 1618.] s.sh.fol. [*London,* 1618.] L⁵(Lemon 158). 𝕬

21054 — A view of the civile and ecclesiastical law. 4°. [*A. Islip?*] *f. the Co. of Statrs.,* 1607. Ent. to the English Stock 5 mr. 1620. L.O.C.D.NOR².+; F.HN.HD.N.U.+

21055 — Second edition, by I. G[regory,] Mʳ. of arts. 4°. *Oxford, W. Turner,* 1634. O¹⁰.O¹⁷.; HN.
On tp: 'by Thomas Ridley.'

21055.5 — [Anr. issue, w. cancel tp, w. 'by Sʳ Thomas Ridley Knight'.] L.O.C.D².E.+; F.HN.HD.N.U.+
L³ copy has orig. tp uncancelled.

21056 — Third edition. 4°. *J. Dawson* [*a. Oxford, W. Turner,*] 1639. L.O.O².C⁵.C⁹.+; F.CHI.HD.MIN.V.+
Inits. I. G. omitted. Only the 1st quire pr. by Dawson; the rest by Turner.

21056.2 **Rig, William.** Guilielmus Rig, trecentas minas ad bibliothecam academiæ Edinburgenæ augendam testamento reliquit. [List of 26 books bought w. this legacy.] s.sh.fol. [*Edinburgh, A. Hart?*] 1619. L. E.E²(6).M(2, on deposit).; F.Y. Sexton.

Rikes, Richard, *tr. See* 21801.

21056.4 **Riley, Thomas.** Triall of conscience. In a quotidian exercise. 24° in 12's. *J. Okes f. J. Benson,* 1639. Ent. 8 oc. 1638. F.HD.

21056.6 **Rime.** [Headline:] A mery rime. [In verse. 2nd stanza begins: 'Agaynst good skoolemasters: / I speke not here one worde, / Nor agaynst good bochers:'.] 8°. [*London,* 1563?] Ent. to J. Tisdale 1562–63 'a mery Ryme Consernynge butchers [etc.]' HD(1 leaf only).

21056.8 **Rimer.** The rimers new trimming. *Ballad.* 1/2 sh.fol. [*W. White*] *f. T. Langley,* [1614?] C⁶.

Riolan, Jean, *the Elder. See* 1196, 24617.

21057 **Ripley, George.** The compound of alchymy. Or the ancient hidden art. Set foorth by R. Rabbards. [In verse.] 4°. *T. Orwin,* 1591. Ent. 12 my. L.O.C².C⁶. G².+; F.HN.HD.NY.WIS.+

21057.5 **Ripon.** The proceedings of the ecclesiasticall colledge of Rippon lately founded and erected by the authoritie of the queene. 1596. s.sh.fol. [*London?* 1596.] R.

Ripon, *Collegiate Church of St. Wilfrid. See* Indulgences 68A.

21058 **Rishton, Edward.** A notable discourse. 1575. = 274.
— An offer made by a catholike to a protestant. 1575. *See* pt. 2 of 274.

21059 **Rive, Edmund.** A briefe treatise concerning the necessity of the knowledge of the principall languages. 4°. *f. E. Wright,* 1621. LINC.

21060 — An heptaglottologie, that is, a treatise concerning seven languages. 8°. *W. Jones, sold by M. Lownes,* 1618. Ent. to Jones 25 no. O(2).C.
The 3 copies differ: one O(Opp.add.12° 138) and C have an extra quire, E⁸, with a Catalogue of Learnings. These 2 also agree in having 6 leaves in the 1st quire, w. verses on a5, while O(8° R 39 Art) has 4 leaves. However, O(8°) and C have in the title: 'languages, To wit,' while the O(Opp.) title, partly rephrased, has 'languages, Wherein,'.

21061 — Ten grammaticall chapters, with latine, construed . . . for to introduct into Lillies grammar [1561O.5 sqq.] 4°. [*E. Allde,*] 1620. Ent. to E. Allde 28 fb. 1621. O.STU.; ILL.

21062 — Twelve rules introducting to the art of Latine. 4°. *W. Jones,* 1620. Ent. 1 fb. O.; F.
— *tr. See* 2766, 20129.
— For other works by this author *see* Reeve, E.

Rivers, Francis, *tr. See* 18858.

21063 **Rivers, George.** The heroinæ: or the lives of Arria, Paulina, Lucrecia, Dido, [etc.] 12°. *R. Bishop f. J. Colby,* 1639. Ass'd from Coleby to R. Royston 5 se. 1640. L.O.C.PETYT(imp.).; F.HD.N.NY.Y.+

Rivers, Peregrine. Almanacks. 1625. etc. *See* 505 sqq.

Rivers, William. An almanack. 1628. *See* 505.17.

21063.3 **Rivet, André.** Six godly meditations or sermons upon certaine select texts of scripture. 12°. *J. Norton,* 1639. Ent. 31 au. 1638. PLUME.

21063.7 — [Anr. issue, w. cancel tp, w. imprint:] *J. Norton, sold by J. Kirton a. T. Warren,* 1639. A.
— *See also* 12092.

21064 **Rivius, Joannes.** A guide vnto godlinesse, moste worthy to bee followed. Englished by W. G(ace.) 8°. *G. Seton,* (1579.) Ent. 10 ap. L.O(imp.).

21064.5 — [Anr. tr.] A notable discourse of the happinesse of this our age, and of the ingratitude of men to God . . . newly Englished by W. W(atkinson.) 4°. (*T. Dawson*) *f. T. Cooke a. P. Eede,* 1578. Ent. to Cooke 11 se. O.; F.PH.Y(imp.).

21065 — [Anr. trans.] A treatise against the folishnesse of men in differringe the reformation of their liuing. *Tr.* J. Bankes. 8°. (*W. Powell,*) [1550?] L.

21066 — [Anr. trans.] Of the foolishnes of men in putting-off the amendement of their liues. Newlie *tr.* T. Rogers. 8°. (*J. Charlewood*) *f. A. Maunsel,* [1582.] Ass'd from G. Seton 26 ja. 1581. L.C⁵. Chester PL.; HD.

21067 — [Anr. ed.] 8°. (*T. Dawson*) *f. A. Maunsel,* 1583. C.

21067.3 — [Anr. ed.] Now againe reuised. 12°. *J. Windet f. A. Maunsell,* 1586. F.HN(imp.).
— *See also* 5600.5.

Rivius, Thomas. *See* Ryves, *Sir* T.

Ro., Ric., *tr. See* 20844.

21068 **Robartes, Foulke.** Gods holy house and service, according to the primitive forme thereof. 4°. *T. Cotes, sold [by J. Crooke a. R. Sergier,]* 1639. Ent. to R. Cotes 1 fb. L.O.C.D.E.+; F.HN.CHI.HD.U.+

21069 — The revenue of the gospel is tythes. 4°. *C. Legge, pr. to the Univ. of Camb.,* 1613. L.O.C.CASHEL.E².+; F.HN.CHI.HD.U.+

Robarts, Henry. *See* Roberts, H.

Robert, *Earl of Huntingdon.* The death. 1601. *See* 18269.
— The downfall. 1601. *See* 18271.

Robert I, *King of Scotland.* [The acts and life. 1571? etc.] *See* 1377.5 sqq.

Robert, *of Shrewsbury. See* 21102.

21070 **Robert,** *the Devil.* [Heading A2ʳ:] Here beginneth the lyf of the moste myscheuoust Robert the deuyll whiche was afterwarde called yᵉ seruaunt of god. 4° 8·4. (*W. de worde,*) [1500?] c(lacks tp).
31 lines a page. For a later adaptation *see* 16657.

21071 — [Anr. ed.] Robert the deuyll. [A1ᵛ:] Here begyñeth [etc.] 4° 8·4. (*W. de Worde,*) [1517?] L.
32 lines a page.

21071.5 — [Anr. version. In verse.] 4° 8·4. [*R. Pynson?* 1510?] O(frag. of 2 leaves of quire B and 6 leaves of quire C).
30 lines a page; C2ʳ line 1: 'That he had robbed syns the fyrst houre'.

21072 **Roberti, Antonius.** Clavis Homerica. 1638. = 21072a.
21072a — Clavis Homerica, reserans significationes, etymologias, derivationes. Huic adjicitur brevis appendix de dialectis. Authore R. P. N. N. Anglo, Oxoniensi [i.e. A. Roberti.] Editio secunda, priori correctior. Opera G[eorge] P[erkins.] 8°. *typis E. G[riffin,] sumpt. G. Emersoni,* 1638. Ent. 1 ja. L.O.C.C².A.+; F.HN.ILL.PH.Y.+
Preface init. A. R.

Roberts. An Almanack. 1639. *See* 505.19.

21073 **Roberts, Alexander.** An exposition upon the hundred and thirtie psalme. 4°. *J. Windet f. R. Banckworth,* 1610. L.O.C².NOR².PETYT.+; F.BO.HD.NYᴵᴵ.PN.
HD date altered in ink to 1616.

21074 — A sacred septenarie, or the seven last wordes of our saviour. 4° in 8's. *E. G[riffin] f. S. Man,* 1614. Ent. 11 mr. L.L².O.C.G².+; F.HN.HD.NY.+

21075 — A treatise of witchcraft. . . . With a true narration of the witchcrafts which Mary Smith, did practise. 4°. *N. O[kes] f. S. Man,* 1616. Ent. 3 jn. L.O.C².G².M⁴.+; F.HN.HD.N.NY.+

21076 **Roberts, Griffith.** Dosparth byrr ar y rhann gyntaf i ramadeg cymraeg. [Pt. 1 of a Welsh grammar. Anon.] 8° in 4's. [*Milan, V. Giradoni?*] 1567 (1 mr.) L(2).C².NLW(3, 1 imp.).SAU.; N(imp.).Y.
A&R 726.

21076.5 — Dosparth ar yr ail rann i ramadeg a eluir cyfiachydiaeth. [Anon.] 5 pts. 8° in 4's. [*Milan?* 1584–94.] L.NLW (imp.).
A&R 727. Pts. 2–6 of same grammar. There are no tpp, and pts. 2, 6 break off unfinished.

21077 — Y drych cristianogawl. [Init. G. R.] 8°. *Rhotomagi, ap. haeredes J. Favonis* [i.e. *Wales, Rhiwledyn Press,*] 1585 [1587.] L(imp.).CAR(imp.).NLW. G. J. Williams, Cardiff.
A&R 728.

21077.5 — Ynglynion ar y Pader, y Credo, ag ar deggor chymyn o waith D: G: R: yr athraw mawr odre Fulan. [In verse.] 8° in 4. [*Wales? Thackwell?* c. 1585?] NLW.
A&R 729.
— ed. *See* 5450.5.

21078 **Roberts, Henry.** A defiance to fortune. Proclaimed by Andrugio, noble duke of Saxony. [Init. H. R.] 4°. [*A. Jeffes*] *f. J. Proctor,* 1590. 2nd pt. ent. to A. Jeffes 7 au. 1592. L(lacks A4).O.CREDITON.
Copies vary: imprint has: 'Proctor.' (L), or continues: 'Proctor, and are to be sold at his shop. . . .' (O). HN has only a photostat of the L copy.

21079 — Englands farewell to Christian the fourth, famous king of Denmarke. 4°. [*S. Stafford*] *f. W. Welby,* 1606. Ent. 19 au. L.L³⁰.C.; F(2).HD.ILL.Y. 𝔄

21080 — Fames trumpet soundinge. Or commemorations of sir W. Mildmay, and sir M. Calthrop. [In verse.] 4°. *J. C[harlewood] f. T. Hacket,* 1589. Ent. 29 jy. L.

Roberts, Henry—*cont.*
21081 — Haigh for Devonshire. A pleasant discourse of six gallant marchants of Devonshire. 4°. *T. Creede,* 1600. HN.ROS.
An imitation of an early ed. of 6569 of which no copy is known.

21081a — [Anr. ed.] 4°. *T. Creede,* 1612. HN.
— The historie of Pheander. *See* 21087.

21082 — Honours conquest. Wherin is conteined the famous hystorie of Edward of Lancaster. [Init. H. R.] 4°. *T. Creede,* 1598. Ent. to J. Danter 5 mr. 1593. O(S4 def.).

21083 — Lancaster his allarums, honorable assaultes, and supprising of block-houses in Brasill. [Init. H. R.] 4°. *A. J[effes] f. W. Barley,* [1595.] Ent. to A. Jeffes 29 jy. 1595. HN(C3 in facs.).CB.
HN has added leaf in quire C in praise of Captain Cotton, not in CB.

21084 — A most friendly farewell, giuen by a welwiller to sir Frauncis Drake . . . 1585. 4°. [*T. East f.*] *W. Mantell a. T. Lawe,* [1585.] LINC.; HN(B4 def.).

21085 — The most royall and honourable entertainment, of Christiern the fourth. 4°. [*G. Eld*] *f. H. R[oberts,]* sold by W. Barley, 1606. Ent. to H. Roberts 30 jy. L.L⁸.L³⁰.O.E.+; F(2).HN.HD.Y.

21086 — Pheander, the mayden knight; describing his honourable trauailes. 4°. *T. Creede,* 1595. Ent. 10 mr. L(imp.).

21087 — [Anr. ed.] The [xylographic] historie of Pheander the mayden knight. Newly corrected, and augmented. The fourth edition. 4°. *B. Alsop,* 1617. F(lacks F3).

21087.3 — Our Ladys retorne to England, accompanied with saint Frances [*sic*] and the good Iesus of Viana in Portugall [captured ships], who comming from Brasell, ariued at Clauelly in Deuonshire. [Init. H. R.] 4°. *A. J[effes,] sold by W. Barlye,* 1592. HN(cropt).

21087.7 — A true relation of a most worthy and notable fight, performed the nineteenth of June now last past, by two small shippes of London against sixe great gallies of Tunes. 4°. [*G. Eld?*] *f. J. White, sold by T. Langley,* [1616.] L(impr. cropt).; HN.
Dedic. dated 2 Feb. 1616.

21088 — The trumpet o(f) fame: or sir Fraunces Drakes and sir John Hawkins f(are)well. [In verse.] 4°. *T. Creede, sold by W. Barley,* 1595. HN(cropt).
— See also 20572.

21089 **Roberts, Hugh.** The day of hearing: or, six lectures upon part of the thirde chapter of the Epistle to the Hebrewes. Hereunto is adjoyned a sermon against certaine mischievous May-games. 8°. *Oxford, J. Barnes, sold [by J. Broome, London,]* 1600. L.O.

21090 **Roberts, Humphrey.** An earnest complaint of diuers vain, wicked and abused exercises, practised on the Saboth day. 8°. *R. Johnes,* 1572. L(lacks tp).DUR³.

21091 **Roberts, John.** Compendium belli: or the touchstone of martiall discipline. 4°. *J. Norton a. A. Mathewes,* 1626. O.C⁸.

21091.5 — The compleat cannoniere: or, the gunners guide. 4°. *J. Okes,* 1637. Ent. 25 ja. O¹¹.

21092 — [Anr. ed.] 4°. *J. Okes, sold by G. Hurlock,* 1639. L.O³.C.C¹⁵.E.+; F.HN.
F has date altered in ink to 1640.

21093 — Great Yarmouths exercise. In a very compleat and martiall manner performed by their artillery men. 4°. *T. Harper, sold by Ellis Morgan,* 1638. L.

Roberts, John, *pseud.* A mustre of scismatyke bysshoppes of Rome. 1534. *See* 23552.

21094 **Roberts, Lewis.** The merchants mappe of commerce. fol. *R. O[ulton, Eliot's Court Press?, T. Harper, a. F. Kingston] f. R. Mabb,* 1638. Ent. 14 no. 1637. L.O.C.G².M².+; F.HN.CHI.HD.NY.+
The letterpress tp is a cancel. The printing appears to be divided as follows: Kingston, Aa–Kk*; Eliot's Court Press? Kk–Qq; Harper, Rr–Xx; Nnn–Qqq unidentified; the rest by Oulton, w. occasional Eliot's Court Press inits. and orns.

21095 — Warre-fare epitomized, in a century, of military observations. 4°. *R. Oulton f. R. Mabb,* 1640. L(tp only, Harl.5961/142).C.SHEF. Leiden U.; F.HN.HD.
Tp varies: w. (L, F) or without (C, HN, HD) hyphen in 'Warre-fare'.

Roberts, William, *Bp.* Bangor. Visitation Articles. *See* 10136.

Robertson, Bartholomew. Adagia. 1621. *See* 10441.5.

21096 — The anatomie of a distressed soule. 12⁰. *N. Okes f. D. Speed,* 1619 (1618.) Ent. 8 se. 1618. O.

21096.5 — A blow for the pope: or, a discourse had in S. Giles church in Elgen of Murray, at a conference with certaine papists. 8⁰. *G. Eld f. R. Jackson,* 1615. Ent. 5 ja. L.

21097 — The crowne of life. Containing the combate betwixt the flesh and the spirit. Also a comfortable dialogue betweene Christ and the soule. 2 pts. 12⁰. *E. G(riffin) f. J. Marriot,* 1618. Ent. 26 au. 1617. O.C.E(pt. 2 only).

21098 — The heavenly advocate: or a short direction for understanding the New Testament, together with a briefe catechisme. 8⁰. *J. B[eale] f. R. Jackson,* 1617. Ent. 12 fb. L.O.E².

21098.3 — Sapientia secundùm pietatem: seu, fundamenta religionis christianæ. 8⁰. *J. Beale,* 1618. Ent. 8 se. CHATS.

21098.5 — Spirituall encrease: or, conclusions for pacifying the perplexed conscience. [Init. B. R.] 12⁰. *N. Okes, sold by W. Lee,* 1620. Ent. to Lee 21 ja. O.

21098.7 — [Anr. issue, w. quire A reimposed.] *N. Okes f. W. Lee,* 1621. O.ELY.; HD.
(Formerly 21103)

Robertson, David. Thesium aliquot logicarum. Præs. D. Robertsono. 1610. *See* 21555.14.

21099 **Robertson, George.** Serenissimi et potentissimi monarchæ Caroli . . . comitia calata, Edini habita. [In verse.] 4⁰. *Abredoniae, E. Rabanus,* 1633. A.

21100 — Theses philosophicæ. 1596. Now = 7487.1.

21101 — Vitæ & mortis D. Roberti Rolloci Scoti narratio. 8⁰. *Edinburgi, ap. H. Charteris,* 1599. L.O.BUTE.E(2). E².; F.

Robertson, Thomas. *See* 15633.4, headnote to 15610.5.

Robertus, *Castellensis.* Robertus Castelleñ. [1498, etc.] *See* Indulgences 134 sqq.

21102 **Robertus,** *Prior of Shrewsbury.* The admirable life of saint Wenefride virgin, martyr, abbesse. *Tr.* into English. By J. F[alconer, *S.J.*] 8⁰. [*St. Omer, English College Press,*] 1635. L.O.C⁹.NEK.W.+; F.HN. TEX.WASH².Y.
A&R 725. For anr. trans. *see* 25853.

21103 **Robinson** or **Robertson, Bartholomew.** Spirituall encrease. 1621. Now = 21098.7.

21104 — [Anr. ed.] 1630. A ghost.

21104.5 **Robinson, Clement.** [A handful of pleasant delights. In verse.] 8⁰. [*W. How? f. R. Jones,* c. 1575.] Ent. to R. Jones 1565-66. HN(D2,3,6,7 only).
D3ᵛ last line: 'All slayest the hart whom thou maist helpe.' *See* Greg, *Register B,* p. 86.

21105 — [Anr. ed.] A handefull of pleasant delites, containing sundrie new sonets. With new additions. By C. Robinson. and diuers others. 8⁰. *R. Jhones,* 1584. L(lacks B6).
D3ᵛ last line: 'All slaiest the hart, whom thou maist help.'

21105.5 — [Anr. ed.] 8⁰. [*J. Danter? f. R. Jones,* 1595?] L(D2 only).
D2ʳ line 1: 'All flayest the heart, whom thou maist help.' *See* Court-Book C, p. 113.

21106 **Robinson, Hugh.** I. Preces. II. Grammaticalia quædam. III. Rhetorica brevis (ex Valerio et Talaeo constructa.) [Anon.] 4⁰. *Oxoniæ, J. Barnesius,* 1616. L. O.WN(2).
L copy has MS. dedic. by author.

Robinson, John, *Pastor of Leyden.* [An answer to a censorious epistle. 1610.]
Orig. not known. Reprinted with a reply in 12649.

21107 — An appeale on truths behalf. [1624.] = pt. of 227.

21107.5 — An appendix to Mʳ. Perkins his six principles of christian religion [19709]. 8⁰. [*Amsterdam, successors of G. Thorp,*] *Reprinted in the yeare,* 1635. D²; Y.

21107.7 — [Anr. ed.] 8⁰. [*Amsterdam, successors of G. Thorp,*] *Printed, Anno Domini,* 1636. W. F. Hammond.
The text is partly reimposed from 21107.5.

21107a — A defence of the doctrine propounded by the synode at Dort: against J. Murton and his associates, in A description [6773]. 4⁰. [*Amsterdam, successors of G. Thorp,*] 1624. L.O.C.A.G².; F.BO.BO⁵.U.Y.+

— Essayes; or observations. *See* 21114.

Robinson, John, *Pastor of Leyden—cont.*

21108 — A just and necessarie apologie of certain Christians, commonly called Brownists or Barrowists. By J. Robinson, first published in Latin . . . after *tr.* into English by himself. 4⁰. [*Amsterdam, successors of G. Thorp,*] 1625. L.O.O²⁰.; F.BO.CH.U.Y.+

21109 — A justification of separation from the church of England. Against R. Bernard his invective, The separatists schisme [1927]. 4⁰. [*Amsterdam, G. Thorp,*] 1610. L.O.C.D².YK.+; BO⁵.BO⁶.NY¹¹.U.Y.+

21110 — [Anr. ed.] 4⁰. [*Amsterdam, Richt Right Press,*] 1639. L.O.C.D.E².+; F.HN.BO.U.Y.+

21111 — A manumduction [pt. 2 of 3532]. 4⁰. [*Amsterdam, G. Thorp,*] 1615. L.O⁶.C².; BO³.LC.
Answered by 556.

21112 — Observations divine and morall. For the furthering of knowledg, and vertue. 4⁰. [*Amsterdam, successors of G. Thorp,*] 1625. L.O.C⁵.E².G².+; F.HN.HD.U.Y.+

21112a — [Anr. issue, w. A² reprinted in London.] New essayes or observations. [*M. Flesher,*] 1628. Ent. to J. Bellamy 18 oc. 1626. L.O.C.D².YK.+; F.HN.BO³.U.Y.+

21113 — [Anr. issue, w. cancel tp, w. date:] 1629. O(lacks Preface).DUL.; LC.Y.

21114 — [Anr. ed.] Essayes; or, observations. Second edition, with two tables. 12⁰. *J. D[awson] f. J. Bellamie,* 1638. L.O.C⁵.G².YK.+; F.CHI.HD.U.Y.+

21115 — Of religious communion private, & publique. With the silenceing of the clamours raysed by T. Helwisse [in 13055]. As also a survey of the confession of fayth published by Mʳ Smithes company [in 22877.4]. 4⁰. [*Amsterdam?*] 1614. L.L³.C.D². Blickling.; BO⁵. HD.Y.

21115a — The peoples plea for the exercise of prophesie. Against Mʳ. John Yates his monopolie. 8⁰. [*Leyden, W. Brewster,*] 1618. L³.; F.BO(2).NY.Y.

21116 — A treatise of the lawfulnes of hearing of the ministers in the church of England. 8⁰. [*Amsterdam?*] 1634. L.L³.C¹⁰.E(2).; BO.Y.

21117 **Robinson, John,** *Preacher.* Vox ducis: or, an alarme from the trumpet of God, to every souldier in Jesus Christ. In a sermon. 8⁰. *T. Harper,* 1631. Ent. 11 oc. C.C².C³.LIV³.M(2).

Robinson, Ralph, *tr. See* 18094.

21118 **Robinson, Richard.** Certain selected histories for christian recreations. Brought into English verse. 8⁰. [*J. Kingston?*] *f. H. Kirkham,* [1577?]. Ent. to T. East 5 de. 1576. L(imp.).
Dedic. dated 31 Dec. 1576.

21119 — A golden mirrour. 1589. Now = 21121.5.

21120 — The rewarde of wickednesse. [1574.] Now = 21121.7.

21121 — The vineyarde of vertue collected, composed, and digested into a tripartite order. 8⁰. *T. Dawson,* [1579?]. Ent. 26 au. 1579. F.
Dedic. to E. Uvedale.

21121.3 — [Anr. ed.] 8⁰. *T. Dawson,* 1591. Y.
Dedic. to H. Uvedale.

— *ed. See* 21288.

— *tr. See* 800, 5644, 13059.4, 15441, 17790, 17790.5, 17846, 19475, 20844, 20852, 20885, 23358, 23359, 23360, 23361, 23362, 23363.

21121.5 **Robinson, Richard,** *of Alton.* A golden mirrour. Conteining certaine pithie and figuratiue visions prognosticating good fortune to England. [In verse.] 4⁰. *R. Ward f. J. Proctor,* 1589. L.
(Formerly 21119)

21121.7 — The rewarde of wickednesse discoursing the sundrye monstrous abuses of wicked worldelinges. [In verse.] 4⁰. (*W. Williamson,*) [1574.] Ass'd from Williamson to J. Charlewood 15 ja. 1582. L.PARIS.; F(2, 1 lacks col.).HN(col. in facs.).HD(lacks col.).TEX.
(Formerly 21120) Device at end dated 1573; dedic. dated 19 May 1574.

21122 **Robinson, Robert.** The art of pronuntiation, digested into two parts. Vox audienda, & vox videnda. 12⁰. *N. Okes,* 1617. O.
Advertised on C8 of 420.11 as being sold by S. Waterson.

21123 **Robinson, Thomas.** The anatomy of the English nunnery at Lisbon. 4⁰. *G. Purslowe f. R. Mylbourne a. P. Stephens,* 1622. Ent. 11 my. L.O.C.C².DUR⁵.+; F(2). HN.N.

Robinson, Thomas—*cont.*
21124 — [Anr. ed.] 4°. [*G. Eld,*] *sould by R: Milbourne a.*
    P. Stephens, 1623. L(4).L².O.; F(lacks A1).HD.ILL.
    Sexton.
21125 — [Anr. ed.] 4°. [*G. Purslowe*] *f. P. Stephens & C.*
    Meredith, 1630. Ass'd 6 oc. 1629. L¹³.O.C².LINC.
    ST.; F(frag.).HN.HD.ILL.
21126 — [Anr. ed.] 4°. [*M. Parsons*] *f. P. Stephens & C.*
    Meredith, 1637. L².O.O³.M.WIN².+; F(imp.).HN.
    Unsold sheets reissued with cancel imprint slip:
    'f. Ed. Brewster, 1662' (copy at L).

21127 **Robinson, Thomas,** *Musician.* New citharen lessons,
    with perfect tunings of the same. 4°. [*J. Windet f.*]
    W. Barley, 1609. L.
21128 — The schoole of musicke: wherein is taught, true finger-
    ing of the lute, pandora, orpharion, and viol de
    gamba. fol. *T. Este f. S. Waterson,* 1603. L.L⁷(imp.).
    C.

Robotham, James, *ed. See* 20579.5.

21129 **Robotham, John.** Omen Romæ. Sive Cippus & θρηνῳδια
    in duos jesuitas & centum circiter gregarios ponti-
    ficios. [In verse.] 4°. *in off. H. L[ownes,] sumpt. R.*
    Moore, 1627. Ent. 10 ap. L.O.O⁹.; F.
    — *ed. See* 15077.7.

21129.5 **Robrough, Henry.** Balme from Gilead, to cure all
    diseases, especially the plague. Foure and twentie
    sermons on 2 Chron. 7.13,14. And two sermons of
    thankesgiving. 8°. *J. N[orton] a. A. M[athewes,] sold*
    by W. Shefford [sic], 1626. Ent. to J. Norton a. A.
    Mathewes 20 jn. BIRM².(K.N.).E.; F.HN.PN².

21130 **Robson, Charles.** Newes from Aleppo. A letter written.
    By C. Robson. 4°. [*J. Dawson*] *f. M. S[parke,]* 1628.
    Ent. 21 oc. L.O.D².; F.HN.HD.ILL.Y.+

21131 **Robson, Henry.** The examination, confession, and con-
    demnation of H. Robson fisherman of Rye, who
    poysoned his wife. [Init. L. B.] 4°. *F. Kingston f. R.*
    W[alker,] 1598. Ent. to R. Walker 17 mr. O.

21131.5 **Robson, Simon.** The choise of change: containing the
    triplicitie of diuinitie, philosophie, and poetrie.
    [Init. S. R., *gent.*] 4°. *R. Ward,* 1585. F.HD(imp.).
    Tp line 3 ends: 'Triplicitie . . . Diuini-/'.
21132 — [Anr. issue, w. outer forme of 1st quire reset.] *R.*
    Warde, 1585. F.TEX.
    Tp line 3 ends: 'Triplicitie . . . and/'; tp line 5 has:
    'necessarie'.
21132.1 — [Anr. ed.] 4°. *R. Warde,* 1585. M².
    Tp line 3 ends: 'Triplicitie . . . and/'; tp line 5
    has: 'necessary'.
21132.3 — [Anr. ed.] 4°. *R. Warde,* 1585. HN.HD.
    Tp line 3 ends: 'Triplicitie . . . Poetrie./'; B1ʳ
    no. 1: 'Three things do witnesse the / worde of
    God ['God' in B.L.]'
21132.5 — [Anr. ed.] 4°. *R. Warde,* 1585. L.O⁸.; HN.
    Tp line 3 ends: 'Triplicitie . . . Poetrie./'; B1ʳ
    no. 1: 'Three things doe witnesse the / worde of
    God ['God' in roman]'. 1st quire from same set-
    ting as 21132.3.
21132.7 — [Anr. ed.] 4°. *R. Warde,* 1585. F.HD.
    Tp line 3 ends: 'Triplicity . . . Poetrie/'; tp line 6
    has: 'ignorant'.
21132.9 — [Anr. ed.] 4°. *R. Warde,* 1585. O.C.
    Tp line 3 ends: 'Triplicity . . . Poetrie/'; tp line 6
    has 'Ignorant'.
21133 — [Anr. ed.] 4°. *T. Este,* 1598. Ent. 7 au. L.
    B1ʳ line 1: 'firt [sic]'.
21134 — [Anr. ed.] 4°. *T. Este,* 1598. L.O.C².
    B1ʳ line 1: 'first'.
21134.5 — A new yeeres gift. The courte of ciuill courtesie:
    assembled in the behalfe of all younge gentlemen,
    to frame their behauiour in all companies. Out of
    Italian, by S. R[obson] Gent. 4°. *R. Jhones,* 1577
    (1 ja.) Ent. 17 jy. 1576. L.C⁶.A.; HD(imp.). ¶
    Purports to be a trans. from B. del Mont. Prisacchi
    Retta but is actually by Robson.
21135 — [Anr. ed.] 4°. *R. Jhones,* 1582. HN.
21136 — [Anr. ed., w. title:] The court [etc.] 4°. *R. Jhones,* 1591.
    L.O.BRISTOL².; F.HD.

21137 **Roche, Robert.** Eustathia or the constancie of Susanna.
    [In verse.] 8°. *Oxford, J. Barnes, solde [by J. Broome,*
    London,] 1599. O.

Rochelle. A letter written by those of the Assembly in
    Rochell. 1621. *See* 11304.
— A true and most exact map of the siedge of Rochell.
    1628. *See* 23716.5.

Rochester, *Bp. of. See* Fisher, *St.* John, *Cardinal.*

Rochford, John, *Viscount.* [Bookplate.] *See* Bookplates.

Rochford, Robert, *tr. See* 14626.

Rochfort, Henry. An almanack. 1561. *See* 506.3.

21138 **Rochfort, Luke.** An antidot for lazinesse, or a sermon
    against sloth. [Init. L. R.] 4°. [*Dublin, Soc. of Statrs.,*]
    1624. C.; Y.
    A&R 730.
21138.3 — The genealogie of protestants, or a briefe discoverie of
    the first authours, founders & parents of their reli-
    gion. [Init. L. R., *Presbyter.*] 8°. *Paris,* 1621. AUG
    (imp.).E².
    A&R 731.
21138.5 **Rock.** Rocke the babie Joane: or, John his petition to his
    loving wife Joane. *Ballad.* 2 pts. s.sh.fol. *f. H.*
    G[osson, 1632?] Ent. to F. Coles 2 ja. 1632. C⁶.
    Printed on verso of 21551.3.
21138.7 **Rocquigny, Adrian de.** Muse chrestienne. Divisée en
    trois parties. Par A. de Rocquigny. [In verse.] 4°.
    [*G. Miller,*] 1627. Ent. to G. Miller 25 no. 1626.
    C⁵.
21139 — [Anr. ed.] Reveuë [sic], embellie & augmentee d'une
    seconde partie par l'autheur. 4°. [*G. Miller,*] 1634.
    L.PARIS.; NY.

Rod. The blacke rod. 1630. *See* 6492.5.

Rode, M. Micrologia. 1629. *See* 17146.

21140 **Rodes, Francis.** Life after death. Containing many reli-
    gious instructions. 12°. [*G. Purslowe*] *f. T. Dewe,*
    1622. Ent. 2 se. 1621. O.

21141 **Rodoginus, Irenæus,** *pseud.* Differences in matters of
    religion, betweene the Easterne and Westerne
    churches. 4°. *A. Mathewes f. J. Budge,* 1625. Ent.
    14 de. 1624. L.O.C.D.G².+; F.HN.HD(lacks tp).ILL.
    U.+

21142 **Rodriguez, Alonso.** The christian mans guide. Wherein
    are contayned two treatises. The one shewing us the
    perfection of our ordinary workes. The other the
    purity of intention we ought to have in all our actions.
    Tr. into English. 8°. [*St. Omer, G. Seutin,*] 1630.
    L.O⁶.C.OS.W.+; F.N(1st treatise only).TEX.U.
    A&R 732. Collates *⁴ A–E⁸ (text ends E8ᵛ)
    *⁴ F–L⁸ M⁴. The 2nd treatise is called the 'third'
    and is a reissue of pt. of 21149.5, q.v. For anr.
    trans. of the 1st treatise *see* pt. 2 of 21150.5.
21143 — The two first treatises. 1631. Now = 21150.5.
21144 — A short and sure way to heaven, and present happines.
    Taught in a treatise of our conformity with the will
    of God. *Tr.* out of Spanish (I. C.) 8°. [*St. Omer,*
    widow of C. Boscard,] 1630. L.O.C.USHAW.W.+; F.
    HN.N.TEX.Y.
    A&R 733.
21145 — A treatise of humilitie. . . . *Tr.* into English [*Sir* T.
    Matthew.] 12°. *Rouen,* [*J. Cousturier,*] 1631. L.L⁴.
    DE.USHAW.W.+; HN.Y.
    A&R 734.
21146 — [Anr. issue, w. cancel tp:] The stoope gallant. Or a
    treatise of humilitie. *Rouen,* [*J. Cousturier,*] 1631.
    L.O.AUG.; F.
    A&R 735.
21147 — [Anr. issue, w. cancel tp and added table:] A treatise
    of humility. [*St. Omer, widow of C. Boscard,*] 1632.
    L.O²⁵.C.ST.W.+; N.TEX.
    A&R 736.
21148 — A treatise of mentall prayer. With another of the
    presence of God. *Tr.* out of the Spanish [*Sir* T.
    Matthew.] 8°. [*St. Omer, English College Press,*]
    1627. L.O.C.E⁴.W.+; F.HN.
    A&R 737. Dedic. init. 'I. W[ilson.]'
21149 — [Anr. issue, w. new prelims.] Two treatises. Of mentall
    prayer, [etc.] [*St. Omer, English College Press,*] 1627.
    L(lacks tp).L⁹.SN.W.YK².+; F.TEX.
    A&R 738. Dedic. init. T. B., i.e. Sir T. Matthew,
    the translator.

Rodriguez, Alonso—*cont.*

21149.5 — [Heading A1ʳ:] A treatise of modesty and silence. [Heading E6ʳ:] (The third treatise of the right and pure intention.) [Anon.] 8°. [*St. Omer, G. Seutin,* 1630?] N.

Collates A–L⁸ M⁴. The 'third' treatise is reissued in 21142, w. E6–8 cancelled and replaced by *⁴.

21150 — [Anr. issue of A1–E5, w. added tp and table.] A treatise of modesty and silence. By A. Rodriguez. *Tr.* into English. [Additions printed: *St. Omer, widow of C. Boscard,*] 1632. C.SBK.; HD(lacks tp).TEX.

A&R 739. The tp and table are conjugate in C.

21150.5 — The two first treatises of the fisrt [*sic*] part of christian perfection. The one Of the estimation and affection to spirituall thinges. And the other, Of the perfection of our ordinary actions. *Tr.* out of Spanish [*Sir T. Matthew.*] 2 pts. 8°. [*St. Omer, G. Seutin,*] 1631. L.O.C.USHAW.W.+; F.HD(pt. 2 only).N(pt. 1 only, imp.).TEX.

(Formerly 21143) A&R 740. Collates ã⁸ A–N⁸; A–E⁸ (E8 is The table of chapters). For anr. trans. of pt. 2 *see* 21142.

— Two treatises. 1627. *See* 21149.

Rodriguez Girão, João. *See* 18482.

Roe, Alban, *tr. See* 10890.

21151 **Roe, Nathaniel.** Tabulæ logarithmicæ, or two tables of logarithmes: the first by N. Roe. The other, by E. Wingate. 8°. *M. Flesher f. P. Stephens a. C. Meridith,* 1633. Ent. 4 ap. L.O.C.D.E².+; F.HN.HD.ILL.MICH.+

Roe, Sir Thomas. The devotions used in the king of Swedens army. 1632. *See* 23519.5.

— The Swedish discipline. 1632. *See* 23520.

— *tr. See* 21757a.

— *See also* Newsbooks 71A.

21152 **Roe, William.** Epilogus ad quatuor colloquia dⁿⁱ· dʳⁱˢ· Wrighti. 4°. *T. Snodham, imp. M. Lownes,* 1615. Ent. 2 oc. O.C.D.LINC.M².+; HN.NY¹¹.

Defends Sir T. Roe against the account in Quatuor Colloquia, *Mechliniæ,* 1614, by T. Wright, *Priest.*

21153 **Roesslin, Eucharius.** The byrth of mankynde, newly *tr.* out of Laten. (R. Jonas.) 4°. (*T. R[aynald,]* 1540.) L(imp.).L¹⁶.O.C(imp.).G².+; HN.Y.

Copies vary: with and without 'Cum privilegio' on tp; both at L¹⁷. One L¹⁷ copy and Y have engr. plates.

21154 — [Anr. ed. Anon.] The byrth of mankynde, otherwyse named the womans booke. Newly set furth, corrected and augmented. By T. Raynold phisition. 8°. (*T. Ray[nald,]*) 1545. L.L³.L¹⁷.C.G².+; HN.LC.NLM.NY⁴.Y.+

21155 — [Anr. ed.] 4° in 8's. (*T. Ray[nald,]*) 1552. L¹⁶.O.C.E⁵.P.+; ROCH(imp.).

21156 — [Anr. ed.] 4° in 8's. [*R. Jugge?*] 1560. L.A.M⁴.P. Warrington PL.+; HN(w. quire B from 21157).NWM. Medical Society of the City and County, Denver, Colorado.

21157 — [Anr. ed.] Newly set forth. 4° in 8's. [*R. Jugge,*] (1565.) O(2).G².; LC.NLM.PEN.WIS.

21157.5 — [Anr. ed.] Newely set foorth. 4° in 8's. [*R. Jugge,*] (1565.) O.O⁸.E².M. Dr. Alistair Gunn, London.; HD. NLM.MICH.

21158 — [Anr. ed.] Newly set foorth. 4° in 8's. *R. J[ugge]* (1565) [1572?] L.L¹⁶.L¹⁷.BIRM.G².+; HN.LC.PH.WIS. Duke U. A2ᵛ catchword: 'harde'. L¹⁶ has copies w. this title and distinction in 2 different settings; one has the device McK. 123 at the end and B6ʳ catchword: 'forte'; the other has no device at the end and B6ʳ catchword: 'comfort'.

21159 — [Anr. ed.] Newly set foorth. 4° in 8's. [*J. Jugge?* 1585?] L.L¹⁶.G².; HN. A2ᵛ catchword: 'hard'.

21160 — [Anr. ed.] 4° in 8's. *R. Watkins,* (1598.) Ent. 7 oc. 1588. L.L¹⁶(imp.).O⁵.C.G².+; HN.HD.NLM.NY⁴.TEX.+

21161 — [Anr. ed.] 4° in 8's. [*G. Eld?*] *f. T. Adams,* (1604.) Ass'd 5 de. 1598. L.L¹⁶.C⁴.G².M.+; HN.CHI.LC.NLM. NY⁴.

21162 — [Anr. ed.] 4° in 8's. [*T. Dawson*] *f. T. Adams,* (1613.) L¹⁶.L¹⁷.L¹⁹.C.BRISTOL².+; HN.NLM.NWM.NY⁴.

21163 — [Anr. ed.] 4° in 8's. [*H. Lownes*] *f. A. H[ebb,]* sold by *J. Boler,* 1626. Ass'd to A. Hebb 6 my. 1625. L(2). L¹⁷.E².; F.NLM.NY⁴.Y.

Roesslin, Eucharius—*cont.*

21164 — [Anr. ed.] 4° in 8's. [*R. Barker, B. Alsop, a. T. Fawcet*] *f. A. H[ebb,]* sold by *J. Morret,* 1634. L.L¹⁷.O.M. NEK.+; HN.LC.NLM.NY⁴.Y.

Barker pr. quire A; Alsop and Fawcet the rest.

Roest, Theodore, *tr. See* 18602.

Roger, *of Hovenden. See* 21783.

Rogers, *Master, of Needham.* The glory . . . of a christian. 1618. *See* 21186.

Rogers, *Mr., of Oxford.* An answer to Mʳ. Fisher. 1623. *See* 21177.

21165 **Rogers, Daniel.** Davids cost. Wherein everyone, who is desirous to serve God aright, may see what it must cost him. Preached first, since enlarged. 12°. *F. K[ingston] f. S. Man,* 1619. Ent. 19 au. 1618. L. O(2).PLUME.; F.HN.NY¹¹.PN².U.+

21166 — A practicall catechisme: or, a view of principall truths. [Init. D. R., B. of Divin.] 4°. *J. N[orton] f. S. Man,* 1632. Ent. 26 mr. L⁴³.E.GLOUC.P(lacks tp).; F.HN.Y.

21167 — Second edition, corrected, enlarged. 4° in 8's. *T. Cotes f. J. Bellamie,* 1633. Ass'd 30 jy. L.O.C.D.G².+; F.HN. HD.N.U.+

21168 — [Anr. ed., signed in full.] Third edition, corrected and much enlarged. 4° in 8's. *J. D[awson] f. J. Bellamie a. R. Smith,* 1640. L.DUL.; HART.HD.NY⁸.

Also issued as pt. of 21173.

21169 — A treatise of the two sacraments of the gospell. [Init. D. R., B. of Divin.] 4° in 8's. *T. Cotes f. J. Bellamie,* 1633. Ent. 5 jn. L.O.C³.A.D.+; F.BO².ILL.NY¹¹.PN.+

21170 — Second edition. 4° in 8's. *T. Cotes f. J. Bellamie,* 1635. L³.O⁶.C.C³.C⁴.+; F.HN.HD.ILL.U.+

21171 — Third edition. 4° in 8's. *T. Cotes f. J. Bellamie,* 1635. L.L².A.BIRM²(K.N.).E².; HN.N.Y.

Also issued as pt. 2 of 21173.

21172 — [Anr. issue, w. date:] 1636. O.C⁵.; CHI.FORDHAM.

Also issued as pt. 2 of 21173.

21173 — Two treatises, first, the practicall catechisme. Secondly. A treatise of the two sacraments. 2 pts. 4° in 8's. *J. D[awson a.] (T. Cotes) f. J. Bellamie a. R. Smith,* 1640 (1635 *or* 1636.) L².O.C.STU.WOR.+; F.HN.HD. PN².TORONTO².+

Pt. 1 also issued sep. w. gen. tp cancelled as 21168; pt. 2 also issued as 21171 sq.

21174 **Rogers, Francis.** A sermon of love. Instructing all men to unite in love. 4°. *T. S[nodham] f. G. Norton,* 1613. Ent. 25 fb. O.; BO⁵.HD.LC.Y.

21175 — A sermon preached on September the 20. 1632. At the funerall of W. Proud. 4°. *J. Norton f. W. Adderton,* 1633. Ent. 19 de. 1632. L.L⁴.O.C⁴.NLW.+; F.HN.ILL. Y.

21176 — A visitation sermon, preached at the lord archbishops visitation, Aprill the fift, 1630. 4°. *J. Norton f. W. Adderton,* 1633. Ent. 19 de. 1632. L.L⁴.O.D.YK.+; F. HN.ILL.Y.

21176.5 **Rogers, Griswell.** To the right reverend and right honorable the Lords. . . . An abstract of the grievances done by Sir A. Ingram to G. Rogers widow [in a dispute over land.] s.sh.fol. [*London,* 1624.] L⁵(Lemon 226).

Petition reported on 28 May 1624; see *JHL* III. 415.

21177 **Rogers, Henry,** *of Herefordshire.* An answer to Mʳ. Fisher the jesuite, his five propositions concerning Luther. Hereunto is annexed Mr. W. C[rashaw] his dialogue of the said argument. 4°. [*London?*] 1623. L.O.C.D.WOR.+; F.HN.HD.NY¹¹.U.+

21178 — The protestant church existent, and their faith professed in all ages. 4°. *R. Badger,* 1638. Ent. 30 ja. L.O.O¹².C.STD.+; HN.

21178.3 — [Anr. issue, w. cancel tp and leaf of errata.] *M. Parsons, sold in St Dunstan's Church-yard, at the little shop turning up to Cliffords Inne,* 1638. O⁶.C².M².; HD.

21178.7 **Rogers, Henry,** *of Sussex.* Balme for the bruised: or, a treatise of comfort on the eighteenth and nineteenth verses of the fifth chapter of Job. [Anon. *Ed.*] (T. Rogers, *of Sussex.*) 12°. *F. Kyngston f. R. Allot,* 1631. PLUME.

Dedic. ends: 'From my fathers poore vicarage at Salmiston.' i.e. Selmeston, Sussex.

21179 **Rogers, Hugh.** Γαμηλια on the happy marriage of H[ugh] R[ogers] Esq. and A. B[aynton.] [In verse.] 4°. *Oxford, L. L[ichfield,]* 1640. L.; HN.

21180 **Rogers, John,** *Author of 'The Summe of Christianity'.* An answere vnto a wicked & infamous libel made by Christopher Vitel, one of the chiefe English elders of the pretended Family of loue. 8°. *J. Daye,* 1579. L.O.O³.D.P.; F.
See also 18548.5 sqq.

21181 — The displaying of an horrible secte of grosse and wicked heretiques, naming themselues the Familie of loue. Newely set foorth by I. R[ogers.] 1578. Whereunto is annexed a confession of articles, made the 28. of May 1561. 8°. [*H. Middleton*] *f. G. Bishop,* [1578.] Ent. 3 no. 1578. O.C.C².; F.
B1ʳ line 7 begins: 'land Christopher Vittel'.

21181.5 — [Anr. ed., partially reimposed.] 8°. [*H. Middleton*] *f. G. Bishop,* [1578.] L.O.C³.P.; HN.U.
B1ʳ line 7 begins: 'and Christopher vittel'.

21182 — [Anr. ed.] Whereunto is added certeine letters. 8°. (*H. Middleton*) *f. G. Bishop,* 1579. L.O.C.D.M.+; F.U.

21183 — The summe of christianitie, reduced vnto eight propositions. [Anon.] 8°. [*T. Dawson,* 1578?] L.
Tp comp. has inits. 'O R'.

21184 — [Anr. ed.] 8°. *T. Dawson,* 1679 [1579.] L(lacks tp).O.; F.BO⁶.
Tp comp. has inits. 'O R'.

21184.5 — [Anr. ed.] 8°. [*T. Dawson,* 1580?] L.
Tp has no comp.

Rogers, John, *Martyr, ed. See* 2841.
— *tr. See* 17799.

21185 **Rogers, John,** *of Chacombe.* A discourse of christian watchfulnesse. 8°. *W. Jones,* 1620. Ent. 24 se. 1619. L.O.C.PLUME.
See Court-Book C, p. 121.

21186 — The glory and happines of a true christian. A sermon preached by master Rogers at Needham. 8°. *W. J[ones] f. T. P[avier,]* 1618. Ent. to Pavier 23 ja. L⁴.O.C.CARLISLE.LINC.; U.

21186.5 **Rogers, John,** *of Dedham.* The doctrine of faith, wherein are handled ten principall points. 12°. [*H. Lownes*] *f. N. N[ewbery] a. W. Sheffard,* 1627. Ent. to Newbery a. Sheffard 19 fb. 1626. O²⁸.CHATS*.; F.HD.

21186.7 — [Anr. ed.] Wherein are handled twelve principall points. Second edition, newly corrected, and inlarged. 12°. [*Eliot's Court Press?*] *f. N. Newbery a. W. Sheffard,* 1627. L³.

21187 — Third edition. 12°. [*J. Dawson*] *f. N. Newbery a. H. Overton,* 1629. L.NLW.; F(imp.).BO.HD.

21187.5 — Fourth edition. 12°. *f. N. Newbery a. H. Overton,* 1632. Ass'd to H. Overton 13 my. 1630. L(tp only, Ames II.1047).O.G⁴.; HART².U.

21188 — Fifth edition. 12°. *J. D[awson] f. N. Newbery a. H. Overton,* 1633. L.O.C.; F.LC.PN².SMU.

21189 — Sixth edition. 12°. *G. M[iller] f. N. Newbery a. H. Overton,* 1634. L.L².C¹⁰.; F(imp.).U.

21190 — Seventh edition. 12°. *J. Dawson f. Jone Newbery a. H. Overton,* 1638. L.C³.; BO.

21190.5 — Eighth edition. 12°. *E. G[riffin] f. H. Overton a. S. Enderby,* 1640. L⁴⁶.O²⁸(Bed.).; F(2).U.

21191 — A treatise of love. 12°. *H. Lownes a. R. Young f. N. Newbery,* 1629. Ent. 5 de. 1628. L.O⁵.D.

21192 — Second edition. 12°. *J. Dawson f. N. Newbery,* 1632. L.O²⁸.C.; F.HD.SMU.U.

21193 — Third edition. 12°. *M. Dawson f. Jone Newbery,* 1637. L.O²⁶.C¹⁰.COL.; F(2, 1 imp.).BO.U.Y.

21194 **Rogers, Nehemiah.** Christian curtesie: or, Sᵗ. Pauls ultimum vale. Delivered in two sermons, on 2. Cor. 13.11. 4°. *H. L[ownes] f. E. Brewster,* 1621. Ent. 11 jy. L.O.C.BIRM²(K.N.). D.+; F.HN.HD.N.U.+
— The good houswife. 1632. *See* pt. 2 of 21202.

21195 — The good Samaritan. 1640. = pt. 2 of 21196.
⁓ The indulgent father. 1632. *See* pt. 3 of 21202.

21196 — A mirrour of mercy, and that on Gods part and mans. Set out in two parables, I. The penitent citizen. II. The good Samaritan. 2 pts. 4° in 8's. *G. M[iller] f. E. Brewster,* 1640. Pt. 2 ent. 17 se. 1639; pt. 1 ent. 24 ap. 1640. L⁴⁶(lacks gen. tp).O.C⁵.BIRM²(K.N.).G⁴ (lacks gen. tp).+; F.HN.HD(lacks gen. tp).ILL.NY¹¹.+
(Formerly also 21197, 21195) Errata on 1st A5ʳ covers both pts.

21197 — The penitent citizen. 1640. = pt. 1 of 21196.

Rogers, Nehemiah—cont.

21198 — A sermon preached at the second trienniall visitation of William [Laud] lord bishop of London. 4°. *G. Miller f. E. Brewster,* 1632. Ent. 31 de. 1631. L.L². O.A.RGU.+; F.HN.HD.ILL.U.+

21199 — A strange vineyard in Palæstina: in an exposition of Isaiahs parabolical song of the beloved, discovered. 4° in 8's. *J. Haviland f. E. Brewster,* 1623. Ent. 30 no. 1622. L.O.C.BIRM²(K.N.).STU.+; F.HN.HD. NY¹¹.Y.+

21200 — [Anr. issue, w. cancel tp:] The wild vine: or, an exposition. *f. E. Brewster,* 1632. L.O.O².C.INN.; F(2). HN.BO³.CHI.U.
Cancel tp pr. by G. Miller.

21201 — The true convert. Or an exposition upon the whole parable of the prodigall. Delivered in sundry sermons. 4° in 8's. *E. Griffin f. E. Brewster,* 1620. Ent. 30 no. 1619. O.O⁶.C(imp.).A.; HN.BO.HD.U.

21202 — The true convert: or, an exposition upon three parables. The lost sheepe. The lost groat. The lost sonne. 3 pts. 4° in 8's. *G. Miller f. E. Brewster,* 1632. Ent. 16 my. 1631. L.O.C.G².LINC.+; F.HN.HD.N.U.+
— The watchfull shepheard. 1632. *See* pt. 1 of 21202.
— The wild vine. 1632. *See* 21200.

21203 **Rogers, Richard.** Certaine sermons preached and penned. Whereunto are annexed sermons of S. Wright. 4° in 8's. *F. Kyngston f. T. Man,* 1612. Ent. to T. a. J. Man 16 ap. 1611. L.O.C.C⁵.; F.HN.HD. SMU.U(2, 1 imp.).

21204 — A commentary upon the whole booke of Judges. Preached in sundrie lectures. fol. *F. Kyngston f. T. Man,* 1615. Ent. to T. a. J. Man 29 oc. 1613. L.O. C¹².D.E².+; F.HN.HD.U.Y.+

21204.5 — A garden of spirituall flowers. Planted by Ri. Ro(gers.) Will. Per(kins.) Ri. Gree(nhame.) M. M[osse?] and Geo. Web(be.) 8°. *T. Snodham f. T. Pavier,* 1609. O.
The Perkins selection is reprinted from 19752.

21204.7 — The third time imprinted, with new additions. 8°. [*W. White*] *f. T. Pavier,* 1609. HN.

21205 — The fift time imprinted. 8°. [*W. White*] *f. T. Pavier,* 1609. L.

21206 — [Anr. ed.] 8°. [*W. White*] *f. T. Pavier,* 1610. F.

21207 — [Anr. ed.] 8°. *T. S[nodham] f. T. Pavier,* 1612. L.
For eds. of pt. 2 *see* 21213.1 and 21212 sqq.

21207.3 — [Anr. ed.] 1 Part. 8°. *T. S[nodham] f. T. Pavier,* 1613. L⁴(lacks H7).

21207.5 — [Anr. ed.] 8°. *W. White f. T. Pavier,* 1616. GK.; F.HD.

21207.7 — [Anr. ed.] 8°. *T. S[nodham] f. T. Pavier,* 1619. O.O¹⁸.; F(imp.).
O tp altered in ink to 'in 2 Parts.'

21208 — [Anr. ed.] 8°. *T. S[nodham] f. T. Pavier,* 1620. WOR.; HN.

21209 — [Anr. ed.] 8°. *T. S[nodham] f. T. Pavier,* 1622. L.O.

21210 — [Anr. ed.] Corrected and inlarged. 8°. *T. S[nodham] f. T. Pavier,* 1625. O⁶(H8 def.).C.; F.U.

21210.3 — [Anr. ed.] 8°. *J. D[awson] f. E. B[rewster] a. R. Bird,* 1628. Ass'd by widow Pavier to Brewster a. Bird 4 au. 1626. O.

21210.5 — [Anr. ed.] 8°. *T. B[rudenell] f. R. Bird,* 1630. Y.

21211 — [Anr. ed.] 8°. *J. B[eale] f. R. Bird,* 1631. O.

21212 — [Anr. ed., w. both pts. on continuous signatures.] 12°. *R. B[adger] f. R. Bird,* 1632. L.

21212.3 — [Anr. ed.] 12°. *Edinburgh, heirs of A. Hart,* 1634. INN.

21212.7 — [Anr. ed.] 12°. *R. B[adger] f. R. Bird,* 1635. F.

21213 — [Anr. ed.] 12°. *R. B[adger] f. R. Bird,* 1638. L.O.

21213.1 — A garden of spirituall flowers. 2. [i.e. second] part. 8°. *T. S[nodham] f. T. Pavier,* 1612. O.

21213.2 — [Anr. ed.] 8°. *T. S[nodham] f. T. Pavier,* 1613. F.

21213.3 — [Anr. ed.] 8°. *L. S[nowdon] f. T. Pavier,* 1615. GK.; F.

21213.4 — [Anr. ed.] 8°. *T. S[nodham] f. T. Pavier,* 1617. HD.

21213.5 — [Anr. ed.] 8°. *T. S[nodham] f. T. Pavier,* 1619. L(tp only, Harl.5910, Pt. IV, no. 35).O(lacks tp).O¹⁸.

21213.6 — [Anr. ed.] 8°. *T. S[nodham] f. T. Pavier,* 1620. HN.

21213.7 — [Anr. ed.] 8°. *T. S[nodham] f. T. Pavier,* 1622. L.O.; F.

21213.8 — [Anr. ed.] 8°. *T. S[nodham] f. T. Pavier,* 1625. O(imp.). C.; U(imp.).

21213.9 — [Anr. ed.] 8°. *T. C[otes] f. R. Bird,* 1629. Ass'd by widow Pavier to E. Brewster a. Bird 4 au. 1626. Y.

21213.10 — [Anr. ed.] 8°. *R. B[adger] f. R. Bird,* 1630. O.
For later eds. of pt. 2 *see* 21212 sqq.
— The practice of christianitie. *See* 21221 sq.

Rogers, Richard—*cont.*

21214 — Samuels encounter with Saul. Preached and penned, by R. Rogers. And published according to his owne coppy, finished before his death. 12°. *E. Griffin f. S. Man,* 1620. Ent. 18 mr. L.O.DUL.YK.; F.PN².U. Western Ontario U.

21215 — Seven treatises, containing such direction as is gathered out of the holie scriptures, leading and guiding to true happines. fol. *F. Kyngston f. T. Man a. R. Dexter,* 1603. Ent. 1 de. 1602. L.O.C¹².G⁴.YK.+; F.HN.BOWDOIN.MICH.U.+

21216 — [Anr. ed., enlarged.] Set foorth the second time, corrected. fol. *H. Lownes f. T. Man,* 1604. Dexter's pt. ent. to Stat. Co. 28 no. 1603. L(tp only, Ames II.64). C.A.G².; BO.PH. Amherst C.

21216a — [A variant, w. date:] 1605. L.O.C.D.M².+; F.N.NY¹¹.

21217 — [Anr. ed., enlarged.] Set forth the third time, corrected and enlarged. fol. *F. Kyngston f. T. Man,* 1610. L⁴. O.C.D⁶.E².+; F.CHI.HD(lacks O3).U.Y.+

21218 — [Anr. ed.] Set forth the fourth time. fol. *F. Kyngston f. T. Man,* 1616. L.O².O¹⁴.DUL.LYD.+; F.COR.ILL. TORONTO².

21219 — [Anr. ed.] Set forth the fourth [*sic*] time. 2 pts. 4° in 8's. *J. Dawson* [*a. A. Islip?*] *f. J. Bellamie by the assign. of P. a. J. Man,* 1627. Ass'd to P. a. J. Man 3 my. 1624. L.O³.; CAL.HART.

21219a — [Anr. issue, w. imprint:] *J. Dawson f. R. Meighen by the assign. of P. a. J. Man,* 1627. O.C³.C¹⁰.LYD.STD(lacks tp)*.; F.BR.U.

21220 — [Anr. ed.] Set forth the fifth time. 4° in 8's. [*J. Haviland f.*] *the assignes of T. Man f. R. Thrale,* 1630. Ass'd to B. Fisher 6 jy. 1629. L.C.DUL.LEIC. E⁸.+; F.HN.N.PTS.U.

21221 — [An abridgement.] The practice of christianitie. Or, an epitomie of Seven treatises. Contracted long since for private use, and now published [by] (S. E[gerton].) 12°. *F. K[ingston] f. T. Man,* 1618. Ent. to T. a. J. Man 10 jn. L.L⁴.O.C.LK.; F.

21221.5 — Second edition corrected. 12°. *R. Field f. T. Man,* 1619. L(tpp only, Ames II.511, 532).O.; Y.

21222 — Third edition. 12°. *B. Alsop f. T. Man, sold by B. Fisher,* 1623. L.C.SHEF.STU.; HN.HD.

21223 — Fourth edition. 12°. *assignes of T. Man, &c., sold by J. Wright,* 1629. Ent. to T. Man 1 mr. 1624; ass'd to P. a. J. Man 3 my. 1624; to B. Fisher 6 jy. 1629. L.L⁴.YK.; BO⁶.

21223.3 — Fifth edition. 12°. *assignes of T. Man, &c., sold by J. Boler,* 1635. O.

21223.7 — [Anr. issue, w. imprint:] *assignes of T. Man, &c., sold by D. Frere,* 1635. L(tp only, Ames II.1328). CARLISLE.; HN.

— *See also* 20586.

21224 **Rogers, Robert.** A living remembrance of master Robert Rogers, marchant adventurer & leather seller. Buried 1601. [In verse.] Leagacies bequeathed to charitable uses. s.sh.fol. *f. M. Allde,* [1601.] HN.

21225 **Rogers, Thomas,** *Esq., of Bryanston.* Celestiall elegies of the goddesses and the muses, dedeploring [*sic*] the death of ladie Fraunces countesse of Hertford. Whereunto are annexed verses touching the death of M. Ewens esquire. 8°. *R. Bradocke f. J. B[roome,]* 1598. Ent. to J. Broome 22 jn. HN. Plagiarized in 14671.

21226 **Rogers, Thomas,** *M.A.* The English creede, consenting with the true, auncient, catholique, and apostolique church. The first parte. fol. *J. Windet f. A. Maunsel,* 1585. Ent. 4 no. 1584. L.L².BIRM.D(date cropt).E² (date cropt).+; F.
   Tp line 6: 'euery'. Tp varies: with (L) or without (L tp only, Ames I.435) comma after 'true'.

21226.5 — [Anr. ed.] The English creede, ... true auncient catholique, [etc.]. fol. *J. Windet f. A. Maunsel,* 1585. L³⁸. O.C.C².YK.+; HN.BO³.HD.ILL.U.
   Tp line 6: 'euerie'.

21227 — The English creede, ... The second part. fol. *R. Walde-graue f. A. Maunsel,* 1587. Ent. 3 ap. L.O.C. DUR⁵.YK.+; F.HN.HD.ILL.NY¹¹.+
   The orns. are app. those of J. Day and T. East.

21228 — The faith, doctrine, and religion, professed, in England, expressed in 39 articles. 4°. *J. Legatt, pr. to the Univ. of Camb.,* 1607. L.O.C.E².YK.+; F.HN.HD.ILL. U.+
   See also 25972.2.

Rogers, Thomas, *M.A.*—*cont.*

21229 — [Anr. ed.] 4°. *J. Legatt,* 1621. Ent. 2 ja. L²(2).O.C.C²(2). BURY.; F(2).HN.N.U.

21230 — [Anr. ed.] 4°. *J. Legatt, sold by A. Hebb,* 1625. L.O.O³. E.G².+; F.HN.HD.ILL.U.+

21230a — [Anr. issue, w. cancel tp, w. imprint:] *J. Legatt, sold by W. Sheffard,* 1625. L.C².C⁵.LINC.PETYT.+; F.HD. MIN.NY¹¹.

21231 — [Anr. ed.] 4°. *J. Legatt, sold by M. Sparke,* 1629. L.O. C.DUR⁵.E.+; F.HN.CHI.CU.HD.+

21232 — [Anr. ed.] 4°. *J. Legatt,* 1633. L.O.O.C.D.M.+; F.HN.CHI. HD.U.+

21233 — [Anr. ed.] A treatise upon sundry matters contained in the thirty nine articles. 4°. *J. Legatt, sold by R. Thrale,* 1639. L.O.BIRM²(K.N.).D².E².+; F.HN.HD. N.U.+

21233.3 — The general session, conteining an apologie of the doctrine concerning the ende of this world. The first part. 8°. *H. Middleton f. A. Maunsell,* 1581. Ent. 6 no. C⁵.; F.CHI.
   B3ʳ catchword: 'nora-'; C1 cancelled. A different text from 11804.

21233.7 — [Anr. issue, w. quire B reset and C1 uncancelled.] F(lacks tp).
   B3ʳ catchword: 'norable'.

21234 — Gloucesters myte. 1612. Now = 21241.5.

— A godlie treatice concerning the lawfull vse of ritches. 1578. *See* 2nd pt. of 4342.

21235 — A golden chaine, [xylographic] taken out of the psalmes of king David: also, The pretious pearles of king Salomon. 12°. *H. Denham (the assigne of W. Seres,)* 1579. Ent. 18 se. O. Chester PL.; F(imp.).HD.

21236 — [Anr. ed.] 12°. *H. Middleton,* 1587. L.L⁴.D.E.ELY.+; F(lacks tp).NY.

21237 — An historical dialogue touching antichrist and poperie. 8°. *J. Windet f. A. Maunsell,* 1589. Ent. to Windet 29 au. L.L².O.O⁹.YK.

21238 — Miles christianus or a iust apologie of all necessarie writings and writers, specialie of them which in a diffamatorie epistle [by M. Mosse], are vniustly depraued. [Anon.] 4°. *J. Wolfe,* 1590. Ent. 2 no. L. L².O(imp.).C¹³.; Y.

— Of the ende of this worlde. [*Tr.* T. Rogers.] 1577, etc. *See* 11804 sqq.

21239 — A philosophicall discourse, entituled, The anatomie of the minde. 8°. *J. C[harlewood] f. A. Maunsell,* 1576. L(lacks O1).O.C.M³.P.+; F(3, 1 imp.).HN.
   For an abridgement *see* 24905.3.

21240 — A sermon vpon the 6. 7. and 8. verses of the 12. chapter of Romanes; made to the confutation of another sermon [4926]. 4°. *J. Windet,* 1590 (13 ap.) Ent. 22 mr. L.L².O.C².; F.BO³.HD(B1 def.).U.

— A treatise. 1639. *See* 21233.

21241 — Two dialogues, or conferences. .... Concerning kneeling in receiving the supper of the Lord. 4°. *H. Ballard,* 1608. L.O.C.D.YK.+; HN.BO³.HD.U.
   Answered in 13395.

— ed. *See* 10542.

— tr. *See* 938, 944, 950, 4342, 11804, 12582.2, 12582.20, 13059, 13066.5, 21066, 23973, 23995.

Rogers, Thomas, *of Sussex, ed.* Balme for the bruised. 1631. *See* 21178.7.

21241.5 **Rogers, Thomas,** *of Tewkesbury.* Gloucesters myte, delivered with the mournefull records of Great Britaine, into the worlds register. For the remembrance of prince Henrie. [In verse.] 4°. *W. Hall f. J. Man,* 1612. O.
   (Formerly 21234)

21241.7 **Rogers, Timothy.** Good newes from heaven: or, safe-conduct, discovering many treasons against every ones soule. 12°. *G. M[iller] f. E. Brewster,* 1627. Ent. 4 my. HD.PN².

21242 — Second edition. 12°. *G. M[iller] f. E. Brewster,* 1628. L.LAMPORT.

21243 — Third edition. 12°. *G. M[iller] f. E. Brewster,* 1631. L.; CHI.

21243.5 — Fourth edition. 12°. *R. Y[oung] f. E. Brewster,* 1635. TORONTO².

21244 — The righteous mans evidences for heaven. 12°. *J. B[eale] f. E. Bruster,* 1619. Ent. 19 de. 1618. O.

21244.5 — Fourth edition, corrected and inlarged. 12°. *E. G[riffin] f. E. Brewster,* 1621. L³.

21245 — Sixt edition. 12°. *J. Beale f. E. Brewster,* 1624. L.BTL.; HN.

Rogers, Timothy—*cont.*

21246 — Seaventh edition. 12°. *G. M[iller] f. E. Brewster,* 1627.
c.

21247 — Eighth edition. 12°. *G. M[iller] f. E. Brewster,* 1629.
L.; F.

21247.5 — Ninth edition. 12°. *G. M[iller] f. E. Brewster,* 1631.
Stevens Cox.; F.HN.HD(lacks M1).

21248 — Tenth edition. 12°. *G. M[iller] f. E. Brewster,* 1632. O.

21249 — Twelfth edition. 12°. *R. Young f. E. Brewster,* 1637. L.
PLUME.

21250 — The roman-catharist: or, the papist is a puritane. 4°.
[H. Lownes] f. E. Brewster, 1621. Ent. 30 my. L
(lacks tp).O.C.D.DUR³.+; F.N.SMU.U.Y.+

21251 **Rogers, William.** Youths warning-piece. In a true relation of the woefull death of W. Rogers. *Ballad.* 2 pts.
s.sh.fol. *f. A. K[embe, Southwark,]* 1636. Ent. to A.
Kembe 8 ap. L.
See also 60.3.

Rogers, William, *engraver. See* 775.7, 17773.5, 17993.

Rohan, Henri, *duc de.* The complete captain. 1640. *See*
4338.

21252 — A declaration of the duke of Rohan. Containing the
motives which have obliged him to implore the
assistance of the king of Great Britaine. *Tr.* according to the French copie. 4°. *[M. Flesher] f. N. Butter,*
1628. Ent. 28 mr. L.O.C.C². LINC.+; F(2).HN.HD.Y.

21253 — A treatise of the interest of the princes and states of
christendome. *Tr.* H. H(unt.) 4°. *Paris,* 1640. Ent.
to R. Bostock 29 jy. L⁴.O.C.LINC.PLUME.; HD.MCG.
PN.Y. Cincinnati U.
The dedic., ¶2, pr. in London; at least HD copy
has imprimatur on a sep. leaf.

Rojas, Fernando de. The Spanish bawd. 1631. *See* 4911
sq.
— *See also* 20721.

Rokyczanus, Johannes Sictor. *See* Sictor, J.

21254 **Rolland, John.** The seuin seages translatit out of prois in
Scottis meter. 4° in 8's. *Edinburgh, J. Ros f. H.
Charteris,* 1578. HN.
Loosely based on 21297.

21255 — [Anr. ed.] Heir beginnis the seuin seages. small 4° in
8's. *Edinburgh, R. Smyth,* 1592 (1595). L(imp.).

21256 — [Anr. ed.] The seven sages. 8°. *Edinburgh, A. Hart,*
1620. F. 🅰
All headlines have 'seuen'.

21257 — [Anr. ed.] 8°. *Edinburgh, heires of A. Hart,* 1631. F(B1
in facs.).
Quire B has 'seuen' in headlines; quire D headlines mixed 'seuen' and 'seven'.

21257.3 — [Anr. ed.] 8°. *[Edinburgh, heirs of A. Hart,* c. 1635.]
E(imp.).
Quire B has 'seven' in headlines; quire D has
'seuen'. Quires C and R are same setting as 21257.

21257.7 — [Anr. ed.] 8°. *[Edinburgh, heires of A. Hart,* c. 1635.]
G²(imp.).; HD(imp.).
All headlines have 'seven'. Quires B, E–I, Q,
S–Aa reimposed from 21257.3.

21258 — Ane treatise callit the court of Venus. [In verse.] 4° in
8's. *Edinburgh, J. Ros,* 1575. L.O(frag.).

21259 **Rolle, Richard,** *of Hampole.* Rycharde Rolle hermyte of
Hampull in his contemplacyons of the drede and
loue of God. [Not by Rolle.] 4° ⁸·⁴. *(w. de worde,*
1506.) L.DUR(Bamb.).M.; Mellon.

21260 — [Anr. ed.] 4° ⁸·⁴. *(W. de Worde,)* [1519?] O(lacks last
leaf).c(lacks last leaf).; F.HN.LC. Mellon.

21261 — [Heading a2ʳ:] Explanationes notabiles deuotissimi viri
Ricardi Hampole heremite sup lectioēs illas beati
Job. (Sermo beati Augustini de misericordia.) 4° in
6's. *[Oxford, T. Rood,* 1483.] L(frag.).c(2).c⁵(2
leaves).M.; PML. Duff 363.

21262 — [The remedy against the troubles of temptations. Not
by Rolle.] 1508. Now = 20875.5.

21263 — [Anr. ed.] 1519. = 20876.
— Speculum spiritualiū. 1510. *See* 23030.7.
— *See also* 3360.

21264 **Rollenson, Francis.** Sermons preached before his majestie. 4°. *T. Snodham f. R. Jackson,* 1611. Ent. 20 oc.
1610. L⁴.O.; HD.

Rollenson, Francis—*cont.*

21265 — Twelve prophetical legacies. Or twelve sermons
upon Jacobs last will. 4°. *T. C[reede] f. A. Johnson,*
1612. Ent. 30 oc. 1611. L.O.C.A.D.+; F.HN.HD.ILL.
U.+
Copies vary: with and without errata on Nn4ᵛ;
both at c.

21266 **Rollock, Hercules.** De augustissimo Iacobi 6. Scotorum
regis, & Annæ Frederici 2. Danorum regis filiæ
coniugio. Epithalamium. 4°. *Edinburgi, H. Charteris,*
1589. L.L².DUL.E.LINC.

21267 **Rollock, Robert.** Analysis dialectica Roberti Rolloci
Scoti, in epistolam ad Romanos. 8°. *Edinburgi, R.
Walde-graue,* 1593. L(destroyed; also tp only, Harl.
5990/88).INN.; F.

21268 — [A variant, w. imprint:] *Edinburgi, R. Walde-graue,*
1594. L.O⁴.C.E.P.+; F.PEN².

21269 — Analysis logica in epistolam Pauli apostoli ad Galatas.
8°. *F. Kyngstonus, imp. E. Weaver,* 1602. O.C.A.E.E².

21269.5 — [A variant, w. imprint:] *F. Kyngstonus,* 1602. L(destroyed).C¹³.A.; F.

21270 — Analysis logica in epistolam ad Hebræos. Accessit tractatus de justificatione eodem authore. 8°. *Edinburgi,
R. Charteris,* 1605. L.O.E.ELY.G².+; F.HN.
— Analysis logica, Roberti Rolloci in epistolam Pauli
apostoli ad Philemonem. *See* 21279.

21271 — Certaine sermons vpon severall places of the epistles
of Paul. 8°. *Edinburgh, H. Charteris,* 1599. L.E.E².;
F.HD(imp.). Cincinnati U.

21272 — [Anr. ed., enlarged.] Certaine sermons, upon severall
texts of scripture. Whereof the first eleven were
before published, and the remnant seven are newly
adjoyned. 8°. *Edinburgh, A. Hart,* 1616. O.E².; HN.
TORONTO².

21273 — [Anr. ed.] 8°. *Edinburgh, heires of A. Hart,* 1634.
L.E⁸.

21274 — Commentarius D. Roberti Rolloci, . . . in epistolam
Pauli ad Colossenses. 8°. *Edinburgi, R. Walde-grave,*
1600. O.A.CASHEL.E.P.+; F.HD.ILL.

21275 — De aeterna mentis diuinae approbatione et improba-
tione, doctrina explicata. s.sh.4°. *[Edinburgh,] R.
Walde-graue,* 1594. E.

21276 — An exposition upon some select psalmes of David. *Tr.*
out of Latine by C. L[umsden] minister of Dudings-
toun. 8°. *Edinburgh, R. Walde grave,* 1600. L.L³.L⁴³.
E.E².; F.NY.

21277 — Five and twentie lectures, upon the last sermon of our
Lord. 4° in 8's. *Edinburgh, A. Hart,* 1619. O.E.E².E⁸.
G⁴.; F.HN.

21278 — In epistolam Pauli apostoli ad Ephesios, commentarius.
4°. *Edinburgi, R. Walde-graue,* 1590. L.O.C³.D².E.+;
F.HN.Y.

21279 — In epistolam Pauli apostoli ad Thessalonicenses
priorem (posteriorem) commentarius. (Analysis
logica, in epistolam ad Philemonem.) 8°. *Edinburgi,
R. Walde-graue,* 1598. L.O.A.D.E.+; F.HN.

21280 — In librum Danielis prophetae, . . . commentarius. 4°
in 8's. *Edinburgi, R. Walde-graue,* 1591. L.O.C.A.E.+;
F.HN.BO.HD.

21281 — Lectures upon the first and second epistles of Paul to
the Thessalonians. [*Ed.*] (H. C[harteris a.] W. A.)
4° in 8's. *Edinburgh, R. Charteris,* 1606. L.C.BIRM²
(K.N.).E.M.+; F.HN.HD.ILL.U.+

21282 — Lectures upon the epistle of Paul to the Colossians.
[*Ed.*] (H. Holland.) 4° in 8's. *F. Kyngston,* 1603.
L.O.C.E.G⁴.+; F.HN.HD.ILL(imp.).U.+

21283 — Lectures, upon the history of the passion, of Jesus
Christ. [*Ed.*] (H. C[harteris and] W. A.) 4° in 8's.
Edinburgh, A. Hart, 1616. L.O.E.E².E⁸.; F.HN.HD
(imp.).U.

21284 — Quæstiones et responses aliquot de foedere Dei. 8°.
Edinburgi, H. Charteris, 1596. E.E².G².; F.

21285 — Tractatus de vocatione efficaci, quae inter locos theologiæ communissimos recensetur. 8°. *Edinburgi, R.
Walde-graue,* 1597. L.O.C.D.E.+; F.HN.HD.

21286 — [A trans.] A treatise of Gods effectual calling. *Tr.*
Henry Holland. 4°. *F. Kyngston,* 1603. L.O.D.E.WN.
+; F.HN.U.

Rolte, John, *tr. See* 19129, 19130.

Roman Histories. An abridgement. 1608. *See* 11413.

Roman Martyrology. *See* 17533.

21286.2 **Romans.** [Gesta Romanorum. 1502?] *See* Addenda.
21286.3 — [Anr. ed.] Gesta Romanorum. 4° 8.4. (*W. de Worde,*) [c. 1510.] c⁵.
  G1ʳ lines 1,2: 'Emperour / named Folemᵒ'. The 16th story begins D4ᵛ line 7 from bottom: 'Somtyme there dwelled . . . Pompey'.
21286.5 — [Anr. ed.] 4° 8.4. [*W. de Worde,* c. 1515.] L⁴¹(5 leaves with cuts).
  G1ʳ lines 1,2: 'Emperoure / named Folemus'.
21286.7 — [Anr. ed.] 4°. [*W. de Worde,* c. 1525.] HN(1 leaf, imp.).
  The 16th story begins on the verso 22 lines from the bottom: 'There dwelled somtyme . . . Pōpey'.
21287 — [Anr. ed.] Here after foloweth the hystorye of Gesta Romanorum. 4°. (⟨*J.*⟩ *Kynge,* 1557.) O.
21288 — [Anr. ed., revised.] A record of auncient histories, intituled in Latin: Gesta Romanorum. Now newly perused by R. Robinson. 8°. *T. Est,* 1595. O(imp.).
21288.3 — [Anr. ed.] 8°. *T. Este,* 1600 (1599.) BO.
  Dedic. to the Leathersellers dated 1 July 1600.
21288.5 — [Anr. ed.] With some addition. 8°. *T. Este,* 16⟨02.⟩ O(imp.).
  Dedic. to Bp. of Chichester dated 25 Mar. 1602. Collates A–X⁸.
21288.7 — [Anr. ed.] 8°. [*T. East,* c. 1605.] F(imp.).
  No dedic. Collates A–U⁸; 43rd History begins on U1ᵛ.
21289 — [Anr. ed.] With some thing added, by R. R[obinson.] 8°. *T. Snodham,* 1610. Ass'd from widow East to T. Snodham 17 jn. 1609. O.; HD(U8 def.).PN.
  Collates A–U⁸; 43rd History begins on U1ʳ.
21289.5 — [Anr. ed.] 8°. *T. Snodham,* [c. 1620.] F(lacks O1).
  Collates A–S⁸.
21290 — [Anr. ed.] 8°. *W. Stansby,* [c. 1630.] Ass'd 23 fb. 1626. F.
21290a — [Anr. ed., omitting Robinson's initials.] 8°. *R. Bishop,* [c. 1640.] Ass'd 4 mr. 1639. O(3, 1 imp.).C.ETON.; HN.
  Also listed as Wing R 632.

21291 **Rome.** The ceremonies, solemnities, and prayers, used at the opening of foure churches, within Rome, in the yere of jubile. Together with the bull of pope Clement [VIII.] 4°. [*S. Stafford*] *f. J. Wolfe,* 1600. L.O⁶.O⁷.EX.PETYT(2).; F.HN.HD.Y.
  See also 24578.5.
— Dialogo en quo se tratan las cosas acaecidas en Roma. 1586. *See* 24568.
21292 — [Form of prayer against the boars of Rome, beginning: 'O Lord our God, most gracious & most glorious,' etc. 1589.] Now = 16520.5.
21292a — A letter lately written from Rome, by an Italian gentleman, to a freende of his in Lyons. Wherein is declared the suddaine death of pope Gregory the thirteenth. The election of the newe pope, [etc.] *Tr.* J. F(lorio.) 8°. *J. Charlewoode,* 1585. L.O⁴.; HN.
  Supplies gap for April and May in MS. account in *Cal. S. P. Foreign, 1584–85.*
— Newes from Rome. Of two mightie armies. [1606.] *See* 4102.5.
21293 — Newes from Rome, Spaine, Palermo, [etc. Partly in verse.] 4°. [*J. Wolfe?*] *f. T. Nelson, sold by W. Wright,* 1590. Ent. to Nelson 11 ap. L².O.O².P.; F.
21294 — Newes from Rome, Venice, and Vienna, touching the present proceedinges of the Turkes against the christians. 4°. *J. Danter f. T. Gosson,* 1595. Ent. 10 mr. L(2).L².YK.
— O Lord our God, most gracious & most glorious, [etc. 1589.] *See* 16520.5.
21295 — The 14. of September. A relation of many memorable passages from Rome. 1622. Now = Newsbooks 77.
  For other 'Relations' from Rome *see* Newsbooks 80, 82, etc.
21296 — Romes monarchie, entituled The globe of renowmed glorie. *Tr.* out of the French and Italian histories by E. L. [In verse.] 4°. *widdow Orwin f. M. Lawe,* 1596. Ent. to widow Orwin 5 ja. HN.
— Romes wickednes. 1624. *See* 21302a.
— The sacke of Roome. 1590. *See* 24569.
— The seuin seages *tr.* be J. Rolland. 1578, etc. *See* 21254 sqq.
21297 — [Seven wise masters of Rome.] 4°. [*R. Pynson,* 1493.] c²(P4, 5 only). Duff 370.
  For an adapted version in verse *see* 21254.
21298 — [Anr. ed. Heading A2ʳ:] Here begynneth thystorye of yᵉ .vii. wyse maysters of rome. 4° in 6's. (*W. de worde,*) [1506?] L(imp.).
21299 — [Anr. ed. Heading A2ʳ:] Here beginneth thystory [etc.]

Rome—*cont.*
  8°. (*W. Copland,*) [c. 1555.] Ent. to T. Marsh 1558–59. F(imp.).
  Collates A–Q⁸ R⁴; B1ᵛ last line begins: 'perour were'.
21299.3 — [An earlier ed. of 21299.5.] 1576. *See* Addenda.
21299.5 — [Anr. ed.] The hystorie of the seven wise maisters of Rome, now newlye corrected with a pleasaunt stile, and purged from all old and rude words. 8°. *T. Purfoote,* 1602. Ent. 1565–66. HN.
  Collates A–Q⁸ R⁴; B1ᵛ last line begins: 'bey his'.
21299.7 — [Anr. ed.] 8°. [*T. Purfoot,* c. 1602.] c(imp.).
  Collates A–Q⁸ R⁴; B1ᵛ last line begins: 'his'.
21300 — [Anr. ed.] Enlarged with many pretty pictures. 8°. *T. Purfoot,* 1633. Ent. 6 no. 1615. F.
21301 — A terrible deluge or ouerflowing in Roome. 4°. [*E. Allde f.*] *J. Wolfe,* 1599. Ent. 1 fb. L.L².
— The triades or trinites of Rome. [c. 1535.] *See* 14027.5.

21302 **Rome,** *Church of.* The abuses of the romish church anatomised. [Signed 'Anonymus.'] 8°. *A. Mathewes, sold by J. Grismand,* 1623. Ent. to A. Mathewes 28 se. L.; F.
21302a — [Anr. ed., revised, w. title:] Romes wickednes: or, wicked Rome with her seven deadly sinnes. 8°. *A. Mathewes, sold by J. Grismand,* 1624. L.
21303 — [Anr. ed.] 8°. *A. M[athewes] f. J. Wright, the younger,* 1637. O.LK.
21304 — An answere or admonition to those of the church of Rome, touching the jubile. [1600.] Now = 24578.5.
— An apology of the Holy Sea. 1630. *See* 11109.
— [Articles.] In this boke is cōteyned the articles of oure fayth. [1509?] *See* 3359.
— Aviso a los de la iglesia Romana. 1600. *See* 24578.3.
— The braineles blessing of the bull. [1570.] *See* 19974.1.
— Cardinalium, . . . cæterorúmque . . . sententia. 1625. *See* 4609.
21305 — Here begynneth a boke, called the faull of the romyshe churche. 8°. [*N. Hill?* 1547?] L(3932.a.18).; F(2).
21305.3 — [Anr. ed.] Here begynneth a boke, called the faule [etc.] 8°. [*N. Hill?* 1548?] L(3932.a.3). O(2).; F. (Formerly 21307)
21305.7 — [Anr. ed.] Here begynneth a booke, called the faule of the romyshe churche. 8°. [*S. Mierdman?* c. 1550.] M.; PML.U.
21306 — [Anr. ed.] Here begynneth a booke called the fal of the romish church. 8°. [*W. Copland?* c. 1550.] L².O.C.
21307 — Now = 21305.3.
21307.3 — [A trans.] Den val der roomscher kercken, met alle haer afgoderie. 8°. (*London, S. Mierdmā,*) 1553. London, Dutch Church.
  Printer's name xylographic.
21307.5 — [Anr. ed.] Dē val der roomscher kercken, met alle haer afgoderije. 8°. [*Norwich, A. de Solempne?* c. 1570.] L.
21307.7 — Holy churches complaint, for her childrens disobedience. [In verse.] 4°. [*English secret press,* 1600?] L².
  A&R 402.
21307a — Indulgentiae sunt adulatorum Romanorum nequiciae. 1521. = pt. of 13083.
— Instructions for the curates. [1554?] *See* 26098.7.
21307a.1 — [The plucking down of the romish church.] *Ballad.* s.sh.fol. *J. Awdeley,* 1566 (17 au.) Ent. 1566–67. HD(bottom half only).
  Title from Stationers' Register; left column, 2nd stanza from bottom begins: 'Pul down her shop of wares'.
— Romes wickednes. *See* 21302a.
21307a.3 — Runne from Rome. Or a breif treatise, shewing the necessity to forsake that false church, and to cleave onely unto Christ. [In verse.] 8°. [*Printed abroad,*] 1640. O.; U.
  (Formerly 26007) Answers verse at end of 17505.
21307a.5 — The sum of the actes & decrees made by dyuers byshopes of Rome. (*Tr.* out of latyn.) 8° in 4's. (*in yᵉ house of T. gybson,*) [1538.] c⁴.
  Tp comp. dated 1538.
21307a.7 — [Anr. ed.] The sum of the actes and decrees made by dyuerse bysshops. 8° in 4's. [*R. Lant f.*] (*T. Gybson,*) [1539?] F.
21308 — [Anr. ed.] The sum . . . by diuerse bisshops. 8°. [*W. Copland f.*] (*T. gybson,*) [1552?] L.L².; PML.
  As nothing is known of Gibson after 1539, his name in the colophon is prob. a carry-over from previous eds.

Rome, *Church of—cont.*
21309 — To the church of Rome. 16° in 8's. [*E. Alldef.*] *J. Wolf*,
1599. Ent. 10 my. 1589. L².
L(Harl.5927/9) has the lower half of a tp, doubtfully identified in MS. as this text, w. imprint:
f H. Carre, 1589. Reprinted in Wing L 83 and
there attrib. to T. L., w. the 1st ed. stated to have
been dated 1588; *see also* 15111.
— A treatise prouynge that the byshops of Rome, [etc.]
1538. *See* 24248.
— The weather-cocke of Romes religion. 1625. *See* 5661.
21310 — [*Curia Romana.*] Diuino implorato praesidio. De
licentia ac concessione sanctissimi. D. N. et ad
instantiam regis Angliæ. [Minutes of the hearing of
Henry VIII's suit for divorce.] 8°. (*T. Berthelet,*)
[1532.] L.L².O.C.D(lacks tp).+
(Formerly also 5399)
— [*Papal Legate.*] Thomas [Wolsey] Miseratione diuina
[etc. Notification of Wolsey's visitation as papal
legate. 1525?] *See* 25947.3.

21310.5 **Rome,** *Hospital of the Holy Ghost.* The discripcion, and
foūdacion of the holy apostolyke hospitall, and con-
fraternite of the holy Goost in Rome, and by whome
it was fyrste founde and edified. 4° in 2. [*R. Pynson*,
c. 1520.] L⁵.
— *See also* Indulgences 91 sqq.

Rome, *Jubilee.* [1500.] *See* Indulgences 100.
— [1600.] *See* 21291, 24578.3 sq.

Rome, *St. Peter's Basilica. See* Indulgences 101 sqq.

Rome, *Stations of. See* Indulgences 149 sq.

21311 **Romei, Annibale,** *Count.* The courtiers academie: com-
prehending seuen seuerall dayes discourses. *Tr.*
J. K. 4°. *V. Sims*, [1598.] Ent. 11 se. 1598. L.O.
C.DUR⁵.LIV³.; F.HN.HD.ILL.N.+

Romeo. An excellent conceited tragedie of Romeo and
Juliet. 1597. *See* 22322.

21312 **Romney Marsh.** The charter of Romney Marsh. *Lat. a.*
Eng. 8°. [*J. Windet f.*] *J. Wolfe*, 1597. Ent. 22 mr.
L(2).L⁸.O.D. House of Lords.; F.HN.HD.MICH.Y.+
Reprints 21313 and adds a trans.
21313 — The grantes ordinances and lawes of Romeney marshe.
Lat. 8°. (*in aed. T. Berth[eleti]*, 1543.) L.M.

21314 Now = 21315.2.

Rondelet, Guillaume. *See* 19595.5 sq.

21315 **Ronsard, Pierre.** A discours of the present troobles in
Fraunce, *tr.* T. Jeney. (Elegia D. Rogerii.) [In
verse.] 4°. *Andwerpe*, [i.e. *Paris?*] 1568. PFOR.

Ronsovius, Henricus. *See* 21604, 21608.

Rookwood, Robert, *tr. See* 3902.

21315.2 **Room.** Roome, for a messe of knaves. 4°. [*E. Allde*] *f. N.*
F[osbrook,] 1610. HN.
(Formerly 21314)
21315.4 — Roome for companie, heere comes good fellowes.
Ballad. 2 pts. s.sh.fol. [*G. Eld*] *f. E. W[right*, c. 1617.]
Ent. to J. Trundle 22 oc. 1614. c⁶.

Roos, *Lord.* Relation of the late entertainment. 1617. *See*
4909.

21315.6 **Roos, Wilfride.** A combat betwixt the spirite and the
fleshe. A sermon, vpon the 6. and 7. verses of the
2. chap. to the Collossians. 8°. *R. Walde-graue*, 1587.
LC(date shaved, lacks B8).

21315.8 **Rope Dancing.** At the [   ] this present day shall bee
showne rare dancing on the ropes, acted by his
majesties servants. And the merry conceites of Jacke
Pudding. s.sh.4°. [*T. Cotes*, after 1630.] L(C.18.e.2.
(74)).
Filled out in MS. for the Rose in Wine Street.

Roper, Margaret, *tr. See* 10477.

21316 **Roper, William.** The mirrour of vertue in worldly great-
nes. Or the life of syr Thomas More. 12°. *Paris*,
[*St. Omer, English College Press,*] 1626. L.L⁸.L³⁰.O⁷
(lacks tp).O¹⁷(imp.).+; F(2).HN.HD(2, 1 lacks tp).Y.
A&R 742.

Ros. Ros cœli. Or, a miscellany of ejaculations. 1640. *See*
13219.

Rosa. Rosa Hispani-Anglica. [1623?] *See* 7376.

21317 **Rosa, Thomas.** Idæa, sive de Jacobi Magnæ Britanniæ,
regis, virtutibus enarratio. 8°. [*R. Field f.*] *J. Norton*,
1608. L.O.C.E.M.+; F.HN.HD.N.NY.+
21317.5 — [Anr. issue, w. cancel tp, w. imprint:] *ap. Soc. Biblio-*
polar., 1626. F.

21318 **Rosary.** The mystik sweet rosary of the faythful soule.
8°. *Anwerpe, M. Emprowers*, 1533. L.O.C(imp.).
— The rosary with the articles of the lyfe & deth of Jesu
Chryst and peticiōs directe to our lady. 1537. *See*
17545.5.
21319 — The societie of the rosary. [1593–94.] Now = 11617.4.

Roscio, J. L., *pseud. See* 16874.

21319.3 **Roscio, L.,** *Piemontois.* Double forteresse foy-sacramen-
tale. Ou telle deduction de foy et de sacrement,
qu'on ne luy peut contreuenir. 8°. *par T. Purfoot*,
1590. Ent. 28 ap. HOLK.
21319.7 — [A trans.] A double fortresse faith-sacramental; [etc.]
8°. *T. Purfoot*, 1590. Ent. 28 ap. D.

21320 **Rosdell, Christopher.** A godlie and short discourse,
shewing not onely what time the inhabitants of this
land first receyued the christian faith: but also what
maner of doctrine. 8°. *J. Wolfe*, 1589. Ent. 6 my.
L.C³.
— *tr. See* 4399.

Rose. The Spanish-English rose. [1623?] *See* 7376.

Roselli, Giovanni de. Epulario. 1598. *See* 10433.

Rosemary Flowers. The admirable vertue, of rosemary
flowers. [1615?] *See* 24844.7.

21321 **Rosenburg.** Strange signes seene in the aire, about the
citie of Rosenberge. *Tr.* out of the high Dutch. 4°.
J. Danter, solde by W. Barley, 1594. Ent. to J. Danter
22 au. O.

Roseo da Fabriano, Mambrino, *tr. See* 24330.

21322 **Rosier, James.** A true relation of the most prosperous
voyage made in the discovery of Virginia. 4°. [*Eliot's*
Court Press,] *imp. G. Bishop*, 1605. L.G².; F.HN.N.
NY.Y.+

Rosny, *Lord of. See* 1976.

Ross, *Bp. of. See* Leslie, J.

Ross, Abraham. *See* 21324.

21323 **Ross, Alexander.** Commentum de terræ motu circulari:
duobus libris refutatum. Quorum prior [P.]
Lansbergi, posterior [J.] Carpentari, argumenta
refellit. 4°. *ap. T. Harperum*, 1634. Ent. 16 de. 1633.
L.O.C.E².ETON.+; BO².HD.Y.
21324 — An exposition on the fourteene first chapters of Genesis, by way of question and answere. By Abraham
[*sic*] Rosse. 2 pts. 8°. *B. A[lsop]* a. *T. F[awcet] f. A.*
Upphill, 1626. L.L³.C(lacks N8).E(imp.).G².+; HN.
HD.𝕬
Pt. 2 is a reissue w. tp cancelled of 21325.5.
21325 — The first booke of questions and answers upon Genesis.
8°. *N. Okes f. F. Constable*, 1620. Ent. 6 my. O.C³.D.
21325.5 — The second booke of questions and answers upon
Genesis. 8°. *J. Legatt f. F. Constable*, 1622. Ent.
8 ja. L.C³.D.
Reissued in 21324, 21326.
21326 — [Anr. issue of 21325 and 21325.5 w. gen. tp:] The
first and second booke [etc.] *J. Legatt f. F. Constable*,
1622. L(destroyed).
21327 — Κουρευς αποξυρος, id est, tonsor ad cutem rasus; ex
Ingolstadiana tonstrina emissus; remissus. Operâ A.
R[oss] tonsoris Aberdonensis. 8°. *M. Flesher, imp.*
N. Butter, 1627. L.C.A.E.LINC.+; F.BO.

Ross, Alexander—*cont.*

21328 — Rerum Judaicarum memorabiliorum . . . liber primus. (Secundus.—Tertius.) [In verse.] 3 pts. 8°. *E. Griffin, imp. F. Constable*, 1617 (1619.) Ent. 22 no. 1617. O(2).DUR(bks. 2, 3 only).DUR(Bamb.).G²(bk. 1 only). Aberdeen PL(bk. 2 only).

21329 —— Liber quartus. [In verse.] 4°. *T. Harperus, sumpt. auctoris*, 1632. L.O⁵.C³. Blickling.

21330 — [Anr. issue?] 4°. *imp. G. Sheres*, 1635. O²(tp only). Probably intended as cancel tp.

21331 — Three decads of divine meditations. [In verse.] 4°. *A. M[athewes] f. F. Constable*, [1630.] L.C³.E.E².; F. HN.Y.
— Virgilius evangelisans. 1634. *See* 24826.

Ross, Thomas. *See* 21317.

Rossem, Maarten van, *Heer van Pouderoyen.* Of the great treason and syege of Andwerpe. [1542?] *See* 692.5.

21332 **Rosseter, Philip.** A booke of ayres, set foorth to be song to the lute, orpherian, and base violl. (. . . the rest of the songs.) fol. *P. Short, by the assent of T. Morley*, 1601. Ent. 8 my. L.; HN(lacks 2nd pt.).HD(imp.). Lyrics of 1st pt. by T. Campion.

21333 — Lessons for consort. Made by sundry excellent authors, and set to six seuerall instruments: namely, the treble lute, treble violl, base violl, bandora, citterne, and the flute. fol. *T. Este alias Snodham f. J. Browne*, 1609. Ent. 14 ap. L⁷(cittern only).O(frags. of treble lute only).; NY(flute only).

Rosseus, Guilielmus, *pseud. See* 18089.

21334 **Rote.** The rote or myrour of consolacyon & conforte. 4° in 8's. [*Westminster, W. de Worde*, 1496.] DUR(imp.). Duff 364.

21335 — [Anr. ed.] 4° in 8's. (*Westmyster, W. de Worde*,) [after jy. 1499.] C⁶.; Y. Duff 365.

21336 — [Anr. ed.] 4° 8·4. (*W. de Worde*, 1511.) L.O¹⁰(imp.).C.

21337 — [Anr. ed.] 4° 6·4. (*W. de Worde*, 1530 (23 mr.)) C. C²(colophon def.).; PML.

Roulanson, James. A sermon preached at Jesus chappell. 1627. *See* 21415.5.

21338 **Rous, Francis,** *the Elder.* The arte of happines. Consisting of three parts. 12°. *W. Stansby f. J. Parker*, 1619. Ass'd by H. Fetherstone to Parker 3 ap. 1626. L.O E².; HN.N.U.

21339 — [Anr. ed.] 12°. *J. Haviland*, 1631. Ass'd to Haviland a. J. Wright 4 se. 1638. L.O.C³.ETON.; F.HD.Y.

21340 — The diseases of the time, attended by their remedies. 12°. *W. Stansby f. J. Parker*, 1622. Ent. 21 no. 1621. O.; F.NY¹¹.PN².

21340a — [A variant, w. title beginning:] Diseases [etc.] C.C³. P.SCL.; F.HN.NY¹¹.Y.

21341 — The heavenly academie. Iam hic videte [etc.] 12°. *R. Young f. J. Bartlet*, 1638. Ent. 23 no. 1637. L.O.C². A.ETON.+; ILL.U.

21341.5 — [Anr. issue, w. title:] The heavenly academie: or the highest school. *R. Young f. J. Bartlet*, 1638. HN.

21342 — Meditations of instruction, of exhortation, of reprofe: indeavouring the edification of the house of God. [Init. F. R.] 12°. *J. L[egat] f. G. Gibbs a. F. Constable*, 1616. Ent. 2 de. 1615. L.O.C.E⁸.P.; F.ILL.U.

21342.5 — The mysticall marriage. Experimentall discoveries of the heavenly marriage betweene a soule and her saviour. 12°. *W. Jones*, 1631. Ent. 30 mr. ETON. Stevens Cox.; F. Haverford C.

21343 — [Anr. ed.] 12°. *W. J[ones] a. T. P[aine] f. J. Emery*, 1635. L.O.C.BTL.DUL.+; F.HN.HD.ILL.NY¹¹.+ F,HD have added engr. tp w. 'the 2ᵈ. Edition.'

21344 — Oile of scorpions. The miseries of these times turned into medicines. 12°. *W. Stansby f. J. Parker*, 1623. Ent. 27 my. L.O.C².A.P.+; F.HN.AAS.ILL.U.+

21345 — [A variant, w. imprint:] *W. Stansby f. J. Parker*, 1624. C.; F(2).

21346 — The onely remedy, that can cure a people. 12°. [*H. Lownes*] *f. J. Boler*, 1627. Ent. 24 my. L³.O.C.C³. ETON.; F.U.

21347 — Testis veritatis. The doctrine of king James. Of the church of England. Of the catholicke church. Shewed to bee one in the points of prædestination, free-will, certaintie of salvation. 4°. *W. J[ones,]* 1626. L.O.C.A. CASHEL.+; F.HN.CU.HD.U.+
      Pp. 107.

Rous, Francis, *the Elder*—*cont.*

21347.3 — [Anr. ed.] 4°. *W. J[ones,]* 1626. L³⁸.C².A.ETON.PETYT.; HD.U.
      Pp. 92. With added 'Advertisement concerning the Allegations' at the end.

21347.7 — [Anr. issue, anon., w. A1,2 cancelled and cancel tp:] The truth of three things; viz, the doctrine of predestination, free-will, and certainty of salvation. [*London*,] 1633. O.C(2).BURY.; F. (Formerly 21349 and 24300)

21348 — Thule, or vertues historie. . . . By F. R[ous. In verse.] 4°. *F. Kingston f. H. Lownes*, 1598. L.L⁴.O.E².ETON (lacks tp).; HN(1, plus a frag.).HD(1st bk. only).Y. 1st tp varies: w. Rous's name in full (E²) or his inits. (HN,HD); with 'The first Booke.' (E²,HD) or without (HN).

21349 — The truth of three things. 1633. Now = 21347.7.

21350 **Rous, Francis,** *the Younger.* Archæologiæ Atticæ libri tres. Three bookes of the Attick antiquities. 4°. *Oxford, L. Lichfield f. E. Forrest*, 1637. L.O.C.DUR⁵.E.+; F.HN.CU.HD.ILL.+

21351 **Rous, John.** Ad magnificum . . . J. Cirenbergium. 1631. Now = 19032.5.
— *ed. See* 14451.

21351.5 **Rouspeau, Yves.** A treatise of the preparation to the holy supper. Ttanslated [*sic*] by R. B. 8°. (*J. Allde f.*) *L. Harison*, [1570?] C⁵.; F.

21352 — [Anr. ed.] 8°. (*T. Dawson*) *f. T. Woodcocke*, 1578. Ass'd from L. Harrison to Woodcock 15 jy. O.

21353 — [Anr. ed.] 8°. (*T. Dawson*) *f. T. Woodcoke*, 1579. L.; F.

21354 — Two treatises of the Lord his holie supper. By Y. Rouspeau and J. de l'Espine. 8°. *T. Thomas, pr. to the Univ. of Camb.*, 1584. L.C(2).C².YK.; F. 1st treatise is anr. trans. of 21351.5.

21355 **Rovenzon, John.** A treatise of metallica. But not that which was published by S. Sturtevant [23411] upon his patent, now cancelled. Whereupon patent, is granted to J. Rovenzon. 4°. [*N. Okes*] *f. T. Thorp*, 1613. L.D.D².; HD.Horblit.

Rowbotham, James. The pleasant playe of the cheasts. 1562, etc. *See* 6214 sq.
— *See also* 20579.5.

Rowe, *Sir* **Thomas.** *See* Roe, *Sir* T.

Rowghton, Thomas, *tr. See* 7681.8.

21356 **Rowland, David.** A comfortable ayde for scholers, full of varietie of sentences, gathered out of an Italian authour. [*Tr.* from G. A. Grifoni's Specchio della lingua latina.] *Eng. a. Lat.* 8°. *H. Wykes*, 1568. Ent. 1567–68. O.

21357 — [Anr. ed.] 8°. *T. Marshe*, 1578. L.
— *tr. See* 15336.

Rowlands or **Verstegan, Richard.** A declaration of the true causes. 1592. *See* 10005.

21358 — Englands joy. [Init. R. V.] [1601?] Now = 24636.3.

21359 — Odes. In imitation of the seaven penitential psalmes, with sundry other poemes. [Init. R. V.] 8°. [*Antwerp, A. Conincx,*] 1601. L.O.; F.HN.HD(missing).ILL. A&R 845.

21360 — The post of the world. Wherein is contayned the antiquities and originall of the most famous cities in Europe. With their trade and traficke. (The post for diuers partes of the world.) [*Tr.* from German, w. additions.] 8° in 4's. *T. East*, 1576. L.L².L¹³.O.C(imp.). +; F.HN(imp.).BO⁵.HD.ROS.+ 𝕬

21361 — A restitution of decayed intelligence: in antiquities. Concerning the English nation. By the studie and trauaile of R. V(erstegan.) 4°. *Antwerp, R. Bruney, sold at London by J. Norton a. J. Bill*, 1605. Ent. to Bill 21 mr. a. 6 my. L.O.C.D.E.+; F.HN.HD.N.NY.+ A&R 846.

21362 — [Anr. ed.] 4°. *J. Bill [a. J. Norton]*, 1628. L.O.C.D.E.+; F.HN.HD.N.U.+ Quires O–L1 pr. by Norton. One Y copy made up w. sheets from 21361.

21363 — [Anr. ed.] 4°. *John Norton f. Joyce Norton a. R. Whitaker*, 1634. Ass'd 26 au. 1632. L.O.C.D.E.+; F. HN.HD.N.NY.+

Rowlands or **Verstegan, Richard**—*cont.*
— *ed. See* 16094.
— *tr. See* 19815, 19885, 24627a.8.
— *See also* 19398.

21364   **Rowlands, Samuel.** Ave Cæsar. God save the king. The
         joyfull ecchoes of loyall English hârtes, entertayning
         his majesties late arivall in England. [Init. S. R. In
         verse.] 4°. [*W. White*] *f. W. F[erbrand*] *a. G. L[oftus,*]
         1603. O.O⁵.LONGLEAT.; HN.
         Provisionally entered to Ferbrand 16 ap.; *see*
         Arber III.36.
21365   — The betraying of Christ. Judas in despaire. [Init. S. R.
         In verse.] 4°. *A. Islip*, 1598. L(2).O(2).G².; HN.TEX.
         One L copy has the imprint faked to read: 'A.
         Islip, sold by H. Toms, 1598.'
21365.5 — The bride. By S. R[owlands. In verse.] 4°. *W. J[ones]*
         f. T. P[avier,] 1617. Ent. to T. Pavier 22 my. HD.
         — A crew of kind gossips. 1613. *See* 21414.
21366   — Democritus, or doctor Merry-man his medicines,
         against melancholy humors. [Init. S. R. In verse.] 4°.
         [*W. Jaggard*] *f. J. Deane,* ⟨1607.⟩ Ent. 24 oc. 1607.
         L(date cropt).; HN(date cropt).
21367   — [Anr. ed., omitting preliminary verse, w. title:] Doctor
         Merrie-man: or, nothing but mirth. 4°. [*W. White*]
         f. J. Deane, 1609. HD.
         For later eds. *see* 21372.5 sqq. Quire A has perp.
         chainlines.
21368   — Diogines [*sic*] lanthorne. [In verse.] 4° w. perp. chain-
         lines. [*E. Allde*] *f. T. Archer*, 1607. Ent. 5 de. 1606.
         O.; F(imp.).ROS.
21368.5 — [Anr. ed.] 4°. [*E. Allde*] *f. T. Archer*, 1628 [i.e. 1608?]
         HN.
         Tp has the same woodcut as 21368.7 but in an
         earlier state.
21368.7 — [Anr. ed.] 4°. [*E. Allde*] *f. T. Pavier*, 1608. HN.
21369   — [Anr. ed.] 4°. [*R. Blower*] *f. T. P[avier*, c. 1615.] L
         (imp.).; F(imp.).HD.
21369.5 — [Anr. ed.] 4°. [*R. Blower*] *f. T. Archer*, [c. 1615.] CU.
         — [Anr. ed.] *f. T. Archer*, 1628. *See* 21368.5.
21370   — [Anr. ed.] 4°. *J. H[aviland*] *f. R. Bird*, 1628. Ass'd by
         widow Pavier to E. Brewster a. R. Bird 4 au. 1626.
         L.; F.HD.
21371   — [Anr. ed.] 4°. [*J. Beale*] *f. R. Bird*, 1631. F.HN.HD.Y.
21372   — [Anr. ed.] 4°. *J. N[orton*] *f. R. Bird*, 1634. L.O.
21372.5 — Doctor Merrie-man: or, nothing but mirth. [Init.
         S. R.] 4°. [*W. White*] *f. S. Rand*, 1614. L(tp only,
         Harl.5921/328).
         For earlier eds. *see* 21366 sq.
21373   — [Anr. ed.] 4°. [*W. White*] *f. S. Rand*, 1616. L.
21374   — [Anr. ed.] 4°. [*J. White*] *f. S. Rand*, 1618. L.
21375   — [Anr. ed.] 4°. *A. M[athewes*] *f. S. Rand*, 1619. HD.
21376   — [Anr. ed.] 4° w. perp. chainlines. *A. M[athewes*] *f. S.
         Rand*, 1623. L.
21377   — [Anr. ed.] 4°. *A. M[athewes*] *f. S. Rand*, 1627. Pt. 2
         ent. to F. Coules 4 jy. 1626. O(imp.).
21378   — The famous historie of Guy earle of Warwick. [In
         verse.] 4°. ⟨*E. A[llde*] *f. W. Ferbrand*, 1609.⟩ Ent. to
         Ferbrand 23 jn. 1608. F(impr. shaved).
         Based on 12540. C3ʳ line 4 of text ends: 'earth,'.
21378.3 — [Anr. ed.] 4°. [*E. Allde*, c. 1620.] HD(imp.).
         C3ʳ line 4 of text ends: 'Earth,'.
21378.7 — [Anr. ed.] 4°. *Edw. All-de*, [c. 1625.] HD(imp.).
         C3ʳ line 4 of text ends: 'Earth;'.
21379   — [Anr. ed.] 4°. *Eliz. All-de*, 1632. L(imp.).
21380   — [Anr. ed.] 4°. *Eliz. All-de*, 1635. Ass'd from Eliz.
         Allde to R. Oulton 22 ap. 1640. O(impr. shaved).
21381   — A fooles bolt is soone shott. [Init. S. R. In verse.] 4°.
         [*E. Allde?*] *f. G. Loftus, sold* [*by A. Johnson,*] 1614.
         Ent. to A. Maunsell 4 my. C².
21382   — Good newes and bad newes. [Init. S. R. In verse.] 4°.
         [*G. Purslowe*] *f. H. Bell*, 1622. O(2).; HN.
         — Greenes ghost haunting conie-catchers. 1602, etc. *See*
         12243 sq.
21383   — Heavens glory, seeke it. Earts [*sic*] vanitie, flye it. Hells
         horror, fere [*sic*] it. (Godly prayers.—The common
         cals, of the bell-man.) 12°. [*T. Cotes*] *f. M. Sparke*,
         1628. Ass'd by A. Islip to Sparke 10 ja. O.DUL.
         Includes reprint of 13048.5, which may be the
         only pt. by Rowlands, the rest prob. added by
         M. Sparke (*see* 23015.7, which has a few of the
         prayers and verses).
21384   — [Anr. ed., w. letterpress tp:] A most excellent treatise
         containing the way to seek heavens glory. Third
         edition. 12°. *G. M[iller*] *f. M. Sparke junior*, 1639. L.
         Engr. tp as in 21383 w. date altered to 1638.

Rowlands, Samuel—*cont.*
21385   — Hell's broke loose. [Init. S. R. In verse. On the Dutch
         rebel, John Leyden.] 4°. *W. W[hite,*] *sold by G.
         Loftus*, 1605. Ent. to W. White 29 ja. F.HN.PML.
         — Hels torments. 1601, etc. *See* 13048.5 sq.
21385.5 — Humors antique faces. Drawne in proportion to his
         severall antique jestures. [Init. E. M. In verse.] 4°
         w. perp. chainlines. [*E. Allde*] *f. H. Rockett*, 1605.
         Ent. 8 ja. M.; F.HN.
         (Formerly 17133)
21386   — Humors looking glasse. [In verse.] 4°. *E. Allde f. W.
         Ferebrand*, 1608. Ass'd by widow Ferbrand to T.
         Archer 12 oc. 1609. L.O.E².; HN. 𝔞
         — Humors ordinarie. *See* 21394 sq.
21387   — The knave of clubbes. [Init. S. R. In verse.] 4°. [*E.
         Allde*] *f. W. Ferebrand*, 1609. Ent. to C. Burby 2 se.
         1600; ass'd to W. Welby 16 oc. 1609. HD.
         The 1st ed., of which no copy is known, entitled
         A merry meeting or 'tis merry when knaves meet,
         1600, ordered burned; *see* Greg, *Register B*, p. 79.
21388   — [Anr. ed.] 4° w. perp. chainlines. *E. A[llde,*] 1611. O⁵.;
         HN.
21389   — [Anr. ed.] 4° w. perp. chainlines. *E. A[llde,*] 161[2?]
         L(date cropt).O(date shaved).
21390   — The knave of harts. Haile fellow. well met. [Anon. In
         verse.] 4°. *T. S[nodham,*] *solde by G. Loftus*, 1612.
         Ent. to T. Snodham 30 ap. O.; HN.
21390.5 — [Anr. ed.] 4°. [*T. Snodham*] *f. J. Bache*, 1612. Pirie.
         Pts. of quires A and E reimposed from 21390.
21391   — [Anr. ed.] 4°. [*T. Snodham*] *f. J. Bache*, 1613. L.
21392   — More knaves yet? The knaves of spades and diamonds.
         [Init. S. R. In verse.] 4° w. perp. chainlines. [*E.
         Allde*] *f. J. Tap*, [1613.] Ent. 27 oc. 1613. L(frag.,
         bd. w. 21392.3).O(date cropt, lacks C4).
21392.3 — [Anr. ed., signed in full.] With new additions. 4° w.
         perp. chainlines. [*E. Allde f. J. Tap*, 1613?] L(quires
         B–F only).; HN(impr. cropt).
         The L copy has a tp facs., and rest of quire A from
         21392.
21392.7 — The letting of humors blood in the head-vaine. [Init.
         S. R. In verse.] 8°. *W. White f. W. F[erbrand,*] 1600.
         Ent. to White 16 oc. O.
         O has inserted verse presentation epistle to Hugh
         Lee, Esq., signed 'Samuell Rowlands.' *See* Greg,
         Register B, pp. 79, 81; Arber II.832–3.
21393   — [Anr. ed.] 8°. *W. White f. W. F[erbrand,*] 1600. O(2,
         1 lacks A3).
         In title: 'humours'; B2ʳ line 4: 'feeelde [*sic*]'.
21393.5 — [Anr. ed.] 8°. *W. White f. W. F[erbrand,*] 1600. L.
         In title: 'humours'; B2ʳ line 4: 'fielde'.
21394   — [Anr. ed., signed in full, w. title:] Humors ordinarie,
         where a man may be verie merrie, and exceeding
         well used for his sixe-pence. 4°. *f. W. Firebrand*,
         [1605?] L.; HN.
21395   — [Anr. ed.] 4°. *E. Allde f. W. Firebrand*, 1607. L.; NY.
         With additional poems not in other eds., some of
         which are reprinted in 21386. Quires E–G have
         perp. chainlines.
21395.5 — [Anr. ed.] 4° w. perp. chainlines. [*E. Allde*] *f. T.
         Archer*, 1610. Stourhead, near Mere, Wilts.
         Without the added poems.
21396   — [Anr. ed., init. S. R., w. title:] The letting of humours
         blood. 8°. *W. White*, 1611. L.
21397   — [Anr. ed., init. R. S.] 8°. *W. W[hite,*] 1613. HN.
21398   — Looke to it: for, Ile stabbe ye. [Init. S. R. In verse.]
         4° w. perp. chainlines. *E. Allde f. W. Ferbrand a. G.
         Loftes*, 1604. Ent. to Ferbrand 19 no. 1603. O.;
         HN.
21399   — [Anr. ed.] 4° w. perp. chainlines. *W. W[hite*] *f. W.
         Ferbrand, sold by W. F[erbrand*] *a. G. L[oftus,*] 1604.
         NY.
21400   — Martin Mark-all. 1610. Now = 21028.5.
21401   — The melancholie knight. By S. R[owlands. In verse.]
         4°. *R. B[lower,*] *sold by G. Loftus*, 1615. Ent. to J.
         Beale 2 de. 1614. O.; IND.
21401.5 — [Anr. ed.?] The melancholy knight. 4°. *f. G. Loftus*,
         1615. L(tp only, Harl.5995/35).
         — [A merry meeting. 1600.] *See* 21387.
21402   — The night-raven. By S. R[owlands. In verse.] 4°. *G:
         Eld f. J. Deane a. T. Baily*, 1620. Ent. 18 se. 1619.
         O.; F.HN.NY.
21402a — = 21402.
21403   — [Anr. ed.] 4°. *W. J[ones*] *f. T. Baily*, 1634. L.; N.
21404   — [Headline:] A paire of spy-knaves. [Init. S. R. In
         verse.] 4°. [*G. Purslowe*, 1620?] Ent. to P. Birch 6 de.
         1619; ass'd to R. Bird 7 fb. 1623. L(imp.).

Rowlands, Samuel—*cont.*

— The penniles parliament of threed-bare poets. By Doctor Merry-man. 1637. *See* 19307.5.

21405 — A sacred memorie of the miracles wrought by Jesus Christ. [In verse.] 4º. *B. Alsop*, 1618. Ent. 16 ap. L. O. Gregory Stevens Cox.; HN.

21406 — Sir Thomas Overbury, or the poysoned knights complaint. [In verse.] s.sh.fol. [*G. Eld?*] *f. J. White*, [1614?] L⁵(Lemon 142).

21407 — A terrible battell betweene the two consumers of the whole world: time, and death. [In verse.] 4º. [*W. Jaggard*] *f. J. Deane*, [1606?] Ent. 16 se. 1606. O.

21408 — A theater of delightfull recreation. [In verse.] 4º. [*R. Field*] *f. A. Johnson*, 1605. Ent. 8 oc. BTU.; F(imp.).

21409 — Tis merrie when gossips meete. [Init. S. R. In verse.] 4º. *W. W[hite,]* sold by *G. Loftus*, 1602. Ent. to W. White 15 se. HN(imp.).

21410 — [Anr. ed.] 1609. = pt. of 21413.

21410.5 — [Anr. ed.] Newly enlarged. 4º. *W. W[hite f. J.] Deane*, [1613?] F(imp.).

21411 — [Anr. ed., anon., w. title:] Well met gossip: or, tis merrie when gossips meete. 4º. *J. W[hite] f. J. Deane*, 1619. L.O.

21412 — [Anr. ed.] 4º. *A. Mathewes*, sold by *M. Sparkes*, 1627. NY.

21413 — A whole crew of kind gossips, all met to be merry. [Init. S. R. In verse.] 4º. [*W. Jaggard*] *f. J. Deane*, 1609. O.
   (21410 is pt. of this) The only known ed. to include 'Tis merrie' on continuous signatures.

21414 — [Anr. ed.] A crew of kind gossips, all met to be merrie. Newly inlarged. 4º. *W. W[hite] f. J. Deane*, 1613. L.

21415 **Rowlandson, James.** Gods blessing in blasting, and his mercy in mildew. Two sermons. 4º. *J. Haviland f. W. Bladen*, 1623. L³.O.CARLISLE.DUR⁵.G².+; F.HN. CAL².

21415.5 — A sermon preached at Jesus chappell, neere Southampton. At the consecration thereof. Delivered by J. Roulanson. 4º. *G. M[iller] f. E. Blackmore*, 1627. L¹⁵.SNU.

21416 **Rowley, Samuel.** The noble souldier. Or, a contract broken, justly reveng'd. A tragedy. Written by S. R[owley.] 4º. [*J. Beale*] *f. N. Vavasour*, 1634. Ent. as by T. Dekker to J. Jackman 16 my. 1631; to N. Vavasour 9 de. 1633. L.O.C.E.LEEDS.+; F.HN.HD.N. PML.+ Greg 490.

21417 — When you see me, you know me. Or the famous chronicle historie of king Henrie the eight. 4º. [*H. Lownes a. others*] *f. N. Butter*, 1605. Ent. 12 fb. O.; BO. Greg 212.

21418 — [Anr. ed.] 4º. [*T. Purfoot*] *f. N. Butter*, 1613. L.O.O⁶.; HN.PFOR.Y.

21419 — [Anr. ed.] 4º. [*T. Purfoot*] *f. N. Butter*, 1621. L⁶(impr. cropt).O(2).ETON(impr. cropt).; HN.HD(impr. cropt). ILL.

21420 — [Anr. ed.] 4º. *B. A[lsop] a. T. F[awcet] f. N. Butter*, 1632. L(2).O.O⁶.; F(2, 1 w. date cropt).HN.CAL.ILL.N.

Rowley, William. All's lost by lust. *See* 21425.

21420.5 — For a funerall elegie on the death of Hugh Atwell, seruant to prince Charles, who died the 25. of Sept. 1621. [In verse.] s.sh.fol. [*London*, 1621.] L⁵(Lemon 190).

21421 — A match at mid-night. A pleasant comœdie. Written by W. R[owley.] 4º. *A. Mathewes f. W. Sheares*, 1633. Ent. 15 ja. L.O.C⁴.E.LEEDS.+; F.HN.HD.N. PML.+ Greg 476.

21422 — A merrie and pleasant comedy: called A shoo-maker a gentleman. Written by W. R[owley] gentleman. 4º. *J. Okes*, sold by *J. Cowper*, 1638. Ent. to J. Okes 28 no. 1637. L(2).L⁶.O(2).E.ETON.; F.HN.HD.N.Y.+ Greg 531.

21423 — A new wonder, a woman never vext. 4º. *G. P[urslowe] f. F. Constable*, 1632. Ent. 24 no. 1631. L.L⁶.O.C⁴. E.+; F.HN.HD.N.PML.+ Greg 460.

21424 — A search for money. Or the lamentable complaint for the losse of mounsieur l'Argent. 4º. [*G. Eld*] *f. J. Hunt*, 1609. Ent. to J. Wright a. J. Hunt 10 my. L.; HN.

— A shoo-maker a gentleman. *See* 21422.

21425 — A tragedy called All's lost by lust. 4º. *T. Harper*, 1633. Ent. 27 se. 1632. L.O.C⁴.E.LEEDS.+; F.HN.HD.N.NY.+ Greg 471.

Rowley, William—*cont.*

— The travailes of the three English brothers. 1607. *See* 6417.

— *See also* 17909, 17911, 23760.5.

Rowse, John. The unnaturall father. 1621. *See* 23808a.

Rowse, Robert, *tr. See* 14633.

21426 **Rowzee, Lodowick.** The queenes welles. That is, a treatise of the nature and vertues of Tunbridge water. 8º. *J. Dawson*, 1632. Ent. 5 jn. L(2).O.C¹⁰. G².; F(cropt).HN.HD.

Roxana. Roxana tragædia. 1632. *See* 249.

21427 **Roy, William.** Rede me and be nott wrothe. [1528.] Now = 1462.7.

21428 — [Anr. ed.] The boke Reade me frynde and be not wrothe. 1546. Now = 1462.9.

— *tr. See* 10493, 24223.3.

— *See also* 1462.3, 19903a.

21429 **Royal Book.** [a2ʳ:] When I remember [etc. a3ʳ:] Here foloweth the table of the rubriches of thys presente book entytled & named Ryal. (*Tr. w. Caxtou [sic] from the Somme du Roi of Laurent, Dominican.*]) fol. [*Westminster, W. Caxton*, 1488?] L(a2 in facs.). C(2, 1 lacks i1).M.; F(imp.).HN.CB(imp.).HD.PML. Duff 366.

21430 — [Anr. ed.] The boke named the royall. [xylographic] 4º in 6's. (*W. de worde,*) [1507.] L.O(imp.).OS(col. defaced)*.YK(imp.).; F.NY. Penrose(lacks tp).

21430a — [A variant, w. colophon:] [*W. de Worde f.*] (*R. Pynson,*) [1507.] L(imp.).C⁶.NEP. Lord Kenyon.; HN.

Roydon, Humphrey, *ed. See* 174.7.

21431 **Roye, Guy de.** [A1ʳ:] This that is writen . . . ought the prestres to lerne. [L10ʳ:] (Thus endeth the doctrinal of sapyence . . . *tr.* out of Frenshe in to englysshe by w. Caxton at westmestter [sic] fynysshed the .vij. day of may M,cccc lxxx ix.) fol. [*Westminster,*] (*Caxton me fieri fecii* [sic],) [1489.] L(imp.).O(2 imp.).C.M(1, plus a frag.).WIN.; F(imp.).HN.ILL.PML.Mellon(imp.). Duff 127.
   WIN copy has extra chapter: 'Of the necligences happyng in the masse.'

21432 **Rudd, Anthony,** *Bp.* A sermon preached at Richmond before queene Elizabeth upon the 28. of March, 1596. [*Ed.*] (R. S.) 8º. [*R. Field*] *f. T. Man*, 1603. L.O.C³.C¹⁰.YK.+; F.BO⁵.

21433 — A sermon preached at Greenwich before the kings majestie. 8º. *J. H[arrison] f. T. Man a. C. Knight*, 1603. Ent. 27 jn. O.C¹⁰.BURY.P.YK.; HD.

21433.5 — [Anr. ed.] 8º. *T. E[ast] f. T. Man a. C. Knight*, 1604. C¹⁰.

21434 — A sermon preached at the court at White Hall [on Ps. ci. 2. *Ed.*] (T. W.) 8º. [*R. Field*] *f. T. Man*, 1604. Ent. 18 jn. L.O.C.; F.Y.

21435 — A sermon preached before the kings majestie at White-Hall [on Ps. iii.8. *Ed.*] (T. S.) 4º. *H. Lownes f. C. Knight*, 1606. Ent. 18 fb. L.O.O¹⁷.C².C³.+; F.HN(tp only).WIS. Sydney U.

21435.5 **Ruddoke, Thomas.** A remembraunce for the maintenaunce of the liuynge of ministers. 1551. 8º. *W. Seres*, [1551.] L².C².

21435.7 **Rudierd, Sir Benjamin.** [Heading A1ʳ:] Sir Benjamin Ruddierd's speach in behalfe of the cleargy. 4º. [*Oxford, J. Lichfield*, 1628.] L.O(4).O².O¹³.P.; F.HD. ILL.Y.

21436 — [Anr. issue, w. added tp:] Sir Benjamin Rudierd his speech in behalfe of the clergie, and of parishes destitute of instruction, through want of maintenance. *Oxford*, [*J. Lichfield,*] sold by *P. Stephens a. C. Meredith*, [*London,*] 1628. L.O.C.D².E.+; F.HN. CHI.HD.U.+
   The tp may have been pr. in London.

21437 **Rudierd, Edmund.** The thunderbolt of Gods wrath or an abridgement of The theater of Gods fearefull judgements [1659.] 4º. *W. J[ones] by the assign. of A. Islip, f. T. Pavier*, 1618. L.O.O¹³.C.E.+

21438 **Rudimenta.** Rudimenta grammatices, in gratiam juventutis Scoticæ conscripta. Prioribus æditionibus longè emendatior. 8°. *Edinburgi, A. Hart,* 1618. L.
Collates A–D⁸; a different work from 15636 and 22564.

21439 — [Anr. ed.] 8°. *Edinburgi, haeredes A. Hart,* 1631. O.

21440 — [Anr. ed.] 8°. *Edinburgi, J. Wreittoun,* 1633. L(tp only).; F.

21440.5 — [Anr. ed.] 8°. *Edinburgi, G. Anderson,* 1638. CU.

21440.7 — [Anr. ed.] 8°. [*Edinburgh, R. Bryson?* c. 1640.] STU (lacks tp).
Headlines D2ᵛ–D3ʳ incorrectly read: '*ELEMENTA/GRAMMATICES*'.
— Rudimenta pietatis. 1595. *See* 7352.

21441 **Rudiments.** The rudiments of militarie discipline. Conteining short instructions for pike and musquet. 4°. *Edinburgh, f. J. Bryson,* 1638. E(2).

21441.3 — [Anr. ed.] 4°. *Glasgow, G. Anderson,* 1639. L(tp only, Harl.5961/143).

21441.7 **Rudolf II,** *Emperor.* A great and glorious victorie obtained by the emperour Rodolph the second against the Turke. Verbatim according to the Dutch copies printed at Augspurg. 4°. [*Eliot's Court Press*] *f. W. Holme,* 1595. W. Stirling Maxwell, Chicago.
— The letter of the emperour of Germanie. 1599. *See* pt. 2 of 20861.

Rudston, John. Almanacks. 1615, etc. *See* 506.7 sqq.

Rudston, Thomas. Almanacks. 1606, etc. *See* 507 sqq.

21442 **Rueff, Jacob.** The expert midwife, or an excellent and most necessary treatise of the generation and birth of man. Six bookes. *Tr.* into English. 4° in 8's. *E. G[riffin] f. S. B[urton,] sold by T. Alchorn,* 1637. Ent. to S. Burton 2 au. L.L¹⁶.E².G².M⁴.+; F.Y. Duke U. Philadelphia, College of Physicians.

21443 **Rufinus, Tyrannius.** Incipit exposicio sancti Ieronimi in simbolum apostoloruʒ. [Anon.] 4° in 8's. (*Oxonie,* [*T. Rood,*] 1468 [1478] (17 de.)) L.O.O¹⁹.C.M.+; HN.CH.LC.PML. Mellon. Duff 234.

21444 **Rugbie, Ralph.** A briefe treatise against detractors of dignities. 4°. *G. Eld,* 1622. Ent. to Eld a. M. Flesher 31 oc. L.L¹³.; F.

21445 **Ruggle, George.** Ignoramus. Comœdia coram regia majestate Jacobi regis Angliæ. &c. [Anon.] 12°. (*T. P[urfoot,]*) *imp. J. S[pencer,]* 1630. Ent. to W. Burr 18 ap. 1615; to J. Spencer 3 jy. 1630. L.O.C.D.E².+; F.HN.HD.N.NY.+ Greg L 8.
Partly based on G. B. della Porta's La Trappolaria. In some copies B6ᵛ–B7ʳ misimposed; both at O,C. *See also* 23251.

21446 — Secunda editio auctior. 12°. *typis T. H[arper,] sumpt. G. E[merson] & J. S[pencer,]* 1630. Ent. to G. Edmondson, i.e. Emerson, a. J. Spencer 20 jy. 1630; Spencer's share ass'd to Emerson 2 ap. 1631. L.O. C².E.LINC.+; F.HN.CHI.HD.Y.+

21446.3 **Ruin.** The ruine of Calvinisme. 12°. *Doway, L. Kellam,* 1623. L²⁵.W.
A&R 743.

Rule. In the name . . . the rule of the lyuynge of the order of penytentes. 1510. *See* 19596.

21446.7 — A right godly rule; how all faithfull christians ought to occupie and exercise themselves in their dayly prayers. 16° in 8's. *F. Kyngston,* 1602. Ent. to T. Marsh 1562–63; ass'd to T. Orwin ?23 jn. 1591. F(imp.).
Largely based on prayers in 16060. Film of F copy on Univ. Microfilms reel 717 ('21056b').
— A short rule of good life. [1597? etc.] *See* 22968.5 sqq.

21447 **Rules.** Certayne briefe rules of the regiment or construction of the eyght partes of speche, in englishe and latine. 8°. (*in aed. T. Bertheleti,*) 1537. O(2).

21447.5 — [Anr. ed.] 8°. [*T. Berthelet,*] 1538. London, St. Paul's School(imp.).
— Certaine godly rules concerning christian practice. 1634, etc. *See* 6168.5 sq.

21448 — [Heading A2ʳ:] Foure and twenty certaine godly rules [concerning prayer.] 8°. [*London?* c. 1640.] L.

Rules—*cont.*
21449 — The rules and righte ample documentes, touchinge almanackes. [1558?] Now = 10878.7.
— Rules of the Englishe sodalitie. 1618. *See* 16854.5.

21450 — No entry.

Runaway. The runawyaes [*sic*] answer. 1625. *See* 24562.

Ruscelli, Girolamo. *See* 293 sqq.

Rusdorf, Johan Joachim. *See* 11404.

21451 **Rush,** *Friar.* The historie of frier Rush. 4°. *E. All-de,* 1620. Ent. to J. Allde 1568–69. L.
C3ʳ line 2 from bottom begins: 'said he'; D4ᵛ line 2 from bottom: 'shoone, and I'.

21452 — [Anr. ed.] 4°. *E. All-de, solde by F. Grove,* 1626. HN.
C3ʳ line 2 from bottom begins: 'said, he'; D4ᵛ line 2 from bottom: 'shooes and, I'.

21452.5 — [Anr. ed.] 4°. *E. All-de,* 1629. F(tp only).
Bd. w. text of post-1640 ed., possibly Wing H 2121. F also has two single leaves, with cuts in slightly later state than 21452, which may belong to the 1629 ed. C3ʳ line 2 from bottom begins: 'thing'; D4ᵛ line 2 from bottom: 'shooes, and I'.

21453 **Rushe, Anthony.** A president for a prince. Wherein is to be seene by the testimonie of auncient writers, the duetie of kings. 4° in 2's. (*H. Denham,* 1566.) Ent. 1566–67. L.C.C³.; F(imp.).HN.

21454 **Rushworth, William.** The dialogues of William Richworth or the judgmend [*sic*] of common sense in the choise of religion. 12°. *Paris, J. Mestais,* 1640. L.O.C.USHAW.W.+; F.HN.CHI.U.Y.+ A&R 745.

21455 **Russel, Thomas.** Diacatholicon aureum: or a generall powder of gold, purging all offensive humours in mans bodie. 4°. [*S. Stafford*] *f. J. Flasket,* 1602. Ent. 8 de. 1601. L.

21456 **Russell,** *Lady* **Elizabeth.** A way of reconciliation of a good and learned man, touching the nature, of the sacrament. *Tr.* out of Latin by Lady E. Russell. 4°. *R. B[arker,]* 1605. O.YK.; F.CAL.

21456.5 **Russell, Francis,** *2nd Earl of Bedford.* ⟨The poor people's complaint, bewailing the death of their famous⟩ benefactor, the worthy earle of Bedford. *Ballad.* 1/2 sh.fol. [*London,* c. 1600?] Ent. to Y. James 1 au. 1586. M³(imp.).

21457 **Russell, John,** *Corn-hoarder.* A looking glasse for cornehoorders, by the example of J. Russell whose horses sunke into the ground the 4 of March 1631. *Ballad.* 2 pts. s.sh.fol. [*Eliz. Allde*] *f. H. Gosson,* [1631?] C⁶.

21458 **Russell, John,** *Diplomat and Bp.* [Heading 1ᵛ:] Propositio clarissimi oratoris. Magistri Johannis Russell [etc.] 4°. [*Bruges* or *Westminster? W. Caxton,* 1476?] L.M. Duff 367.

21459 **Russell, John,** *Edinburgh Advocate.* Verba Ioann. Russelli iureconsulti pro senatu populoque Edinburgensi habita, ad reginam Annam, dum Edinburgum ingreditur 19. Maij. 4°. *Edinburgi, R. Walde-graue,* 1590. DUL.E².; PEN.

21460 **Russell, John,** *of Magd. Coll., Cambridge.* The two famous pitcht battels of Lypsich, and Lutzen; wherein Gustavus the great died a conquerour: with an elegie. [In verse.] 4°. [*T. a. J. Buck,*] *prs. to the Univ. of Camb., sold by Philip Scarlet,* 1634. L.C.BHP.P.; F(imp.).HN.HD.TEX. Sexton.
Includes reprint of 20573.

21460.3 — [A variant, w. imprint:] *Prs. to the Univ. of Camb.,* 1634. O.; LC.
— *See also* 20577.

21460.7 **Russell, Thomas.** To the kings most excellent majestie, the lords . . . in parliament assembled. [Requesting a loan of £20,000 for the manufacture of saltpetre by a new method.] s.sh.fol. [*London,* 1626.] L⁵(Lemon 272).
Petition reported to Lords 24 March 1626; *see* *JHL* III.541. *See also* 8848.

21461 **Russell, William.** The [xylographic] reporte of a bloudie massacre in the citty of Mosco, with the fearefull end of Demetrius. [Anon.] 4°. *V. Sims f. S. Macham a. M. Cooke,* 1607. Ent. 13 de. 1606. L.O.C⁵.; F. NY.
　　For a description of earlier events *see* 22869.

21462 **Russia.** Newes of the present miseries of Rushia. 1614. = 3609.

21463 **Rutherford, John.** Commentariorum de arte disserendi libri quatuor. J. Retoforti authore. 4°. [*London, T. Vautrollier*] *ap. H. Charteris, Edinburgi,* 1577. C⁹.E. E².STU(2).

21464 **Rutherford, Samuel.** Christ and the doves heavenly salutations, or a sermon before the communion in Anwoth. Anno 1630. 4° in 2's. [*Scotland?* c. 1660.] L.O.E².G⁴(2).; F.HN.HD.MIN.U.

21465 — Christ's napkin: or, a sermon preached in Kirkcubright at the communion, May 12. 1633. Never before printed. 4° in 2's. [*Scotland?* c. 1660.] L.O.E².G⁴.; HN.HD(tp def.).U(missing).Y.

21465.5 **Ruthven, John,** *Third Earl Gowrie.* Gowreis conspiracie a discourse of the unnaturall and vyle conspiracie attempted against the kings majesties person at Sanct-Johnstown upon Twysday the 5. of August. 1600. 8°. *Edinburgh, R. Charteris,* 1600. E.

21466 — [Anr. ed., w. title:] The earle of Gowries conspiracie against the kings majestie of Scotland. 4°. *V. Simmes,* 1600. Ent. 11 se. L.E(2).; HD.
　　B1ʳ last line begins: 'by'.

21466.3 — [Anr. issue, partially reset and reimposed.] *V. Simmes,* 1600. L(imp.).L⁴.O.M.; F.HN.TEX.
　　B1ʳ last line begins: 'ring'.

21466.5 — [Anr. ed.] 4°. *V. Sims,* 1603. DUR⁵.
　　Tp line 7: 'sixteene hundred yeere of'; D1ʳ line 17 ends: 'about'.

21466.7 — [Anr. ed.] 4°. *V. Sims,* 1603. O⁹.LINC.; HN.
　　Tp line 7: 'sixteene hundred yeeres of'; D1ʳ line 17 ends: 'tenne'.

21467 — [Anr. ed.] 4°. *V. Simmes,* 1603. L.C³.; HD.PN.
　　Tp line 7: 'sixteene hundred yeares of'; D1ʳ line 17 ends: 'ten'.

21467.5 — [Anr. ed.] 4°. *V. Simmes,* 1603. O.D².E.; F(2, 1 lacks D4).Y.
　　Tp line 7: 'sixteenth hundred yeare of'; D1ʳ line 17 ends: 'houres'.

21468 — [A trans.] De execrabili et nefanda fratrum Ruvenorum, conjuratione, narratio. [With preface by P. Galloway?] 4° in 2's. *Edinburgi, R. Charteris,* 1601. L.O. C.D.E.+; F.HN.

21468.5 **Ruthven, Patrick,** *Earl of Forth.* Upon the miserable estate of generall Ruthven, now captaine of the castle of Edinburgh. [In verse.] s.sh.fol. [*London?* 1640.] E.

21469 **Rutilius Rufus, Publius.** A view of valyaunce. Describing the famous feates, of Romains and Carthaginians, for the possession of Spayne. *Tr.* [i.e. *ed.* or written by?] (T. Newton.) 8°. *T. East,* 1580. Ent. 13 my. L.O.

21469.5 [*blank*]

Rutland. The seuerall rates . . . made by the Justices of peace of Rutland. [1563.] *See* 7957.

Rutter. The rutter of yᵉ see. 1528, etc. *See* 11550.6 sqq.

21470 **Rutter, Joseph.** The shepheards holy-day. A pastorall tragi-comædie. 8°. *N. a. J. Okes f. J. Benson,* 1635. Ent. 19 ja. L(3).L⁶.O(2).O⁵.SHEF.; F.HN.HD.N.Y.+ Greg 499.
— *tr. See* 5770.

21471 **Ruytinck, Symeon.** Gulden legende vande Roomsche kercke: aenden toet-steen der waerheyd beproeft. 4°. *T. Snodham,* 1612. Ent. 24 de. 1611. L.; F.U.

Ry, Henry. An almanack. 1544. *See* 523.

21471.5 **Ryckes, John.** The ymage of loue. [Anon. *Tr.* J. Gowghe.] 4°. (*W. de worde,* 1525 (7 oc.)) C².ST. Lord Kenyon (lacks tp).; HN.
　　(Formerly 21473) For a revised text, which attributes original authorship to A. Savorine, *see* 21801. *See also* A. W. Reed, *Early Tudor Drama,* pp. 166–8.

21472 — [Anr. ed.] Cōpyled by J. Ryckes. 8°. (*W. de Worde f. J. Gough,*) [1532?] O.

21473 — Now = 21471.5.
— *tr. See* 421.17.

Ryckewaert, Carl, *tr. See* 17450.

Rye. The first anointed queene. . . . O happy Rye. [1573?] *See* 7582.5.

Rykmersworthe. Be it knowen to all crystē people. [c. 1525.] *See* Indulgences 68.

Ryther, Augustine, *Engraver. See* 12734.7, 13696.5, 24881a.

21474 **Ryves, Sir Thomas.** Historia navalis. Autore Tho. Rivio. (Liber primus.) 8°. *typis T. Harperi,* 1629. Ent. 22 ja. L.O⁴.C.M.P.+; F.HN.HD.N.NY.+

21475 — Historia navalis antiqua, libris quatuor. 8°. *ap. R. Barker et hæred. J. Billii,* 1633. L.O.C.D.E.+; F(lacks cuts).HN.HD.N.NY.+

21476 — Historiæ navalis mediæ libri tres. 8°. *ap. R. Hodgkinsonne, et væneunt in vico vulgariter dicto Little-Britaine* [by G. Emerson?] 1640. Ent. to Hodgkinson 3 mr. L.O.C.D.E.+; F.HN.HD.ILL.NY.+

21477 — Imperatoris Justiniani defensio adversus Alemannum. 12°. *G. Stansbeius,* 1626. L.O.C.D.DUR⁵.+; F.CHI.

21478 — The poore vicars plea. Declaring, that a competencie of meanes is due to them out of the tithes notwithstanding the impropriations. 4°. *J. Bill,* 1620. L.O. C.D.DUR⁵.+; F.HN.CU.HD.N.+
　　Copies vary: with or without 'Sit laus Deo.' on V4ᵛ; both at F.

21479 — Regiminis anglicani in Hibernia defensio, adversus Analecten. Libri tres. 3 pts. 4°. [*H. Lownes, J. Dawson a. J. Haviland*] *pro J. Bartlet,* 1624. Ent. 13 de. L.O.C.D.E.+; F.HN.N.Y.
　　1st A⁴ pr. by Lownes; bk. 3 by Haviland, the rest by Dawson.

S

S., *Mr., Master of Art.* A ryght pithy, comedie: intytuled Gammer gurtons nedle. 1575. *See* 23263.

21479.5 S., **A.** A terrible sea-fight: related in the copie of a letter sent to I. M. councellour, pensioner, and bailiffe to the citie of Batavia. Betweene nine East India ships of the Hollanders, and three great gallions; . . . about Goas bare September, 1639. 4º. *T. Harper f. N. Butter*, 1640. L.; F.WTL.
— *tr. See* 7333.

S., **A.**, *Gent.* The booke of bulls. 1638. *See* 4941.5.
— *tr. See* 7344, 24145.

21480 S., **A.**, *Preacher of the Word.* Πανολβιον, or, the blessednes of the saints. 4º. [*A. Mathewes?*] *f. W. Sheares*, 1634. L⁴.O⁴.C³.

S., **A. C.** A manual of controversies. 1614. *See* 4958.

S., **A. L.** and **D., F.** Anagrammata . . . T. Egertoni. 1603. *See* 6165.

21481 S., **A. P.** Ode natalitia. 1575. Now = 12902.5.

S., **B.**, *tr. See* 12641.

21482 S., **C.** A briefe resolution of a right religion. Touching the controuersies, that are nowe in England. [By C. Shutte?] 4º. *R. Ward f. J. Proctor*, 1590. L(2, 1 imp.).L².L³.O.YK.; U.Y.
Tp varies: with or without quotation from Proverbs above orn.; both at L.

S., **C.**, *Master.* The copie of a letter. 1603. *See* 17151a.

S., **C.**, *Preacher.* The testimonie of a true fayth. 1577. *See* 22467.

21483 S., **D.** A godly learned and fruitfull sermon. Made on the fourteenth of John. [*Ed.*] (J. Jordan.) 8º. *f. Y. James a. T. Lawe*, [1584.] L(2).O.
L² copy of 21483.5 has MS. attrib. to D. Squire.

21483.5 — [Anr. ed., init. R. C.] 8º. *f. T. Lawe & T. Nelson*, [1584?] L².P.

21484 — To all the clothiers of England. fol. [*T. Harper?* post-1640.]
Not an STC book.

21485 — A true reporte or description of an horrible, wofull, and moste lamentable murther, doen by J. Kynnestar. [Init. D. S., i.e. D. Sterrie?] (An admonishment [by Jude Smith.]) [In verse.] 8º. *H. Kirkham*, 1573 (25 ja.) L.

S., **D. D.**, *tr. See* 24072.

21486 S., **E.** Britaines busse. Or a computation aswell of the charge of a busse or herring-fishing ship. As also of the gaine and profit thereby. With the [Netherlands] states proclamation concerning herring-fishing [19 July 1615.] By E. S[harpe?] 4º. *W. Jaggard f. N. Bourne*, 1615. Ent. as by H. Sharpe 10 my. L.O. C.D⁹.NEK.+; F.HN.CU.HD(2).Y.
Copies vary: with or without errata after 'Finis'; both at HD.

21487 — [Anr. issue, w. cancel tp:] Englands royall fishing revived. *f. N. Bourne*, 1630. L⁴.L³⁰.O².D.D⁶.; F.HN(imp.).CU.HD.LC.+

21487.5 — A consideration upon death, conceived through the decease of Robert [Cecil] late earle of Salisburie. 4º. *Dublin, J. Franckton*, 1612. L²⁵.
— Cupids whirligig. 1607, etc. *See* 22380 sqq.

21488 — De rebus gestis Britanniæ commentarioli tres. 12º. *ex off. H. Binneman*, [1582?] L.O.O⁵.C.E.+; F.HN.HD.N. Weissman.
Has been attrib. to J. T. Clain and to E. Spenser. For a later ed. *see* 10013. F² in 3 settings: F1ᵛ line 4 of text begins 'sita est' (O⁵,O¹⁰); 'fictae' (O); or 'est' (O¹⁰,HD).

S., **E.**—*cont.*

21489 — The discouerie of the knights of the poste: or knightes of the post, or cōmon common [*sic*] baylers newly discried. [By E. Sharpham?] 4º. *G. S[imson,] solde [by R. Walker,]* 1597. Ent. to R. Walker 14 no. L.O.O³.C².; HN. A. Freeman, Cambridge, Mass.

S., **E.**, *B. of D.* Anthropophagus. 1623. *See* 23495.5.

21490 S., **E. C.** The government of Ireland under sir John Perrot. 4º. [*A. Mathewes*] *f. T. Walkley*, 1626. Ent. 5 se. L.O.C.D.NLW.+; F.HN.HD.N.Y.+
Sometimes attrib. to E. Cecil, Vct. Wimbledon.
— *tr. See* 5318.

21491 S., **E. F.** A disputation of the church. 1640. = 15350.

S., **F.** Pans pipe. 1595. *See* 21537.

21491.3 — The picture of a wanton: her leawdnesse discouered. 4º. *W. White f. T. P[avier,]* 1615. Ent. to T. Pavier 29, i.e. 19, jn. HN.
Based on Erasmus's Adolescentis . . . colloquium.
— The scoole of vertue. [c. 1550, etc.] *See* 22134.5 sqq.

21491.7 S., **F.**, *Minister of Gods Word.* Jerusalems fall, Englands warning . . . of Gods word. 4º. *T. S[nodham] f. T. Pavior [sic]*, 1617. Ent. 15 ja. 1616. L³.; F(lacks tp).

S., **F. W.** A treatise of penance. 1617. *See* 23212.

S., **G.** A paraphrase upon the psalmes. 1636. *See* 21724.

21492 — Sacræ heptades, or seaven problems concerning Antichrist. [Doubtfully attrib. to G. Sandys.] 4º. [*Amsterdam, successors of G. Thorp,*] 1625. L.O.C.C³.E.+; F.HN.HD.U.Y.+

21493 S., **G. W. P.** To the most irreuerend pope-holy fathers of the two seminaries at Rheimes and Rome. [In verse.] s.sh.fol. [*London?* 1600?] L(1865.c.10(44)).

21493.5 S., **H.** A divine dictionarie, or, the Bible abreviated. By T [*sic*]. S. 4º. *E. Allde f. F. Constable*, 1615. O.

21494 — [Anr. issue, w. cancel tp, w. author's inits. corrected to 'H. S.'] *E. Allde f. F. Constable*, 1615. C.PETYT.

21494.5 — [Anr. issue, w. cancel tp, w. imprint:] *E. Allde f. F. Constable*, 1616. HN.

21495 — [Anr. issue, w. cancel tp:] A christian and heavenly dictionary. The second impression, newly perused and amended by H. S. *E. Griffin f. F. Constable*, 1617. O.M².
— The examination of vsury. 1591. *See* 22660.

21496 — Jonah, the messenger of Ninevehs repentance. 1637. Now = 22677.5.

21496.3 — The mother and the child. In a little catechisme to teach little children the principles of religion. 8º. *B. A[lsop] a. T. F[awcet] f. B. Fisher*, 1628. ?Ass'd by T. a. J. Man to B. Fisher 6 jy. 1629. W. H. Robinson Catalogue 68 (1939), item 60 (untraced).
The tp is reproduced in Robinson Catalogue 63 (1937), item 44. The text may be related to 5961.5.

21496.5 — Elizaes losse, and king James his welcome. [Anon. In verse.] 4º. *T. C[reede] f. J. Smythicke*, 1603. O⁵.

21497 — [Anr. ed., init. H. S., w. additions and title:] Queene El'zabeths losse, and king James his welcome. 4º. *T. C[reede] f. J. Smythicke*, 1603. HN.
— Vita supplicium. 1590. *See* 22712.5.
— Your dedes in effecte, [etc. 1548?] *See* 11593.5.
— *ed. See* 22540.

S., **H.**, *of Gray's Inn, tr. See* 5061.

S., **I.** or **J.** Anti-Mortonus. 1640. *See* 20308.

21498 — Be wise and be warned. [An anti-Catholic exhortation.] 8º in 4's. *T. East f. F. Coldock*, 1573 (1 ja.) L².; HN(A3 def.).
— Certaine rare and new inventions. 1636. *See* 22391.6.

S., I. or J.—*cont.*

21499 — Certaine worthye manuscript poems of great antiquitie. Now first published by J. S[tow?] 1 The statly
tragedy of Guistard and Sismond [from Boccaccio's
Decameron, IV.1]. 2 The northren mothers blessing.
3 The way to thrifte. 8⁰. (*R. Robinson*) *f. R. D(exter,)*
1597. Ent. 31 mr. 1597. L.O.C.M.NOR².+; F.HN.HD.
N.NY.+
Sometimes regarded as pt. 3 of 12716 sqq.

21500 — A christian exhortation taken oute of the holy scriptures, for the great comfort of euery person being in
the agonie of deathe. Therewith is a briefe catechisme. [*Tr.* from French.] 8⁰. *H. Bynneman,* 1579.
C.
— Cinthia's revenge. 1613. *See* 23248.

21501 — Clidamas, or the Sicilian tale. 8⁰. *T. Payne, sold by J.
Cowper,* 1639. Ent. to Payne 25 fb. 1637. L(lacks
engr. tp).; F.HN.HD.N.
— A direction to finde all those names in genealogies
gathered by J. S. [1595?] *See* 3859.5.
— A discourse wherin is debated. 1554. *See* 23207.
— The duello or single combat. 1610. *See* 22171.

21502 — The errors of men. 1627. Now = 23250.5.
— The genealogies recorded in the sacred scriptures.
[1611?] *See* 23039.
— Ilium in Italiam. 1608. *See* 21743.
— Masquarade du ciel. 1640. *See* 21542.

21503 — Match me this wedding. *Ballad.* 2 pts. s.sh.fol. *f. T.
Lambert,* [1640?] L.
— A newe reuenge for an olde grudge. [1567.] *See* 23498.

21504 — The pitifull estate of the time present. A christian consideration of the miseries of this time. [By J. Stubbs?]
8⁰. *H. Denham,* (1564.) Ent. 1563–64. O.

21504.5 — A short method for the declining of French verbes,
nounes and pronounes, [etc. Anon.] 8⁰. *R. Field,*
1623. Ent. as by J. S. 30 jn. HD.
The author apparently is French.
— Soli gloria Deo. Certaine rare and new inventions.
1636. *See* 22391.6.
— The summarie of Englyshe chronicles abridged. [1566.]
See 23325.4.

21505 — To the catholickes of England. [Appeal for charity to
plague victims. 6 Oct. 1636. By J. Southworth and
H. Morse.] s.sh.fol. [*London?* 1636.] O.W.
A&R 792.

21506 — Truthe tryed, very comfortable to the faithfull . . .
Newly sette forth by I. S[tubbs?] 8⁰. (*H. Sutton f.
E. Sutton,* 1562 (21 de.)) Ent. 1562–63. L².
— *ed. See* 3227, 3234.5, 12363, 22608.
— *tr. See* 2004, 2017, 24778.
S., J., *of the Society of Jesus.* The paradise of delights.
1620. *See* 23531.
— S. Mary Magdalens pilgrimage. 1617. *See* 23532.
— The triall of the protestant private spirit. 1630. *See*
22370.

S., J. L., *ed. See* 14375.

21507 **S., J. V.** The sea fight in the road of Gibraltar the 25. of
Aprill last, betwixt the K. of Spaines carackts and
the Hollandish men of warre, *tr.* [from the Dutch of
J. van Spilbergen?] 4⁰. [*J. Windet*] *f. J. Hardie, sold
by Robert Jackson,* 1607. Ent. to C. Burbie, E. White,
jun., a. Robert Jackson 28 my. L.O.; HN.NY.

21507.5 **S., Joh.** A sweete consolation for all such as are afflicted
and oppressed with the weight and burden of their
sinnes. Whereunto is ioyned a treatise against the
feare of death. Gathered out of the Fathers. 8⁰. *C.
B[arker,]* 1580. Ent. to C. Barker 4 my. O⁰.
The Treatise is trans. from P. Viret by J. Shute?

21508 **S., L.** Resurgendum. A notable sermon concerning the
resurrection. 4⁰. [*R. Field f.*] *J. Wolfe,* 1593. Ent.
1 oc. L².O(imp.).C(2).C⁸.; BO.

S., M. [Almanack. bef. 1521.] *See* 388.
— The araignment, and execution of E. Ducket, alias
Hauns. [1581.] *See* 18259.3.
— The crums of comfort. 1628, etc. *See* 23016 sqq.
— The money monger. 1626. *See* 24209.5.

21509 — The poore orphans court, or orphans cry. 1636.
Now = 23017.7.
— A true relation of Englands happinesse. 1629. *See*
23467.
— *tr. See* 206.

S., M., *Doctor of Divinity.* The blessings on mount
Gerizzim. [1625?] *See* 23466.

S., M. A. Rudimenta grammatices. 1607. *See* 22564.

S., M. M., *tr. See* 4739.

21510 **S., N.** Merry jests, concerning popes, monkes and friers.
Written first in Italian by N. S. and thence *tr.* into
French by G. I. and now into English, by R.
W(illet.) 8⁰. *G. Eld,* 1617. Ent. to John Barnes a.
ass'd to J. Wright 26 fb. 1621. O⁶.; HN.
— N. S. arithmeticæ compendium. 1623. *See* 22562.

S., N., *Priest.* The pseudo-scripturist. 1623. *See* 18660.

21511 **S., P.** Fearefull newes. Of thunder and lightning, on a
place called Olveston, Glocester the 28. of November
last. 4⁰. *G. Eld f. F. Burton,* 1606. Ent. 13 ja. O(2).;
HD.
— *tr. See* 19183.

S., P., *Gent.* A christal glasse for christian women. 1591.
See 23381.

S., Sir P. Syr P. S. his Astrophel and Stella. *See* 22536.

S., R. Ad serenissimam Angliæ reginam Elizabetham oratio. [1573.] *See* 23101.5.

21512 — A briefe treatise, to prooue the necessitie and excellence
of the vse of archerie. Abstracted out of ancient and
moderne writers. 4⁰. *R. Johnes,* 1596. L(2).L².O.O⁸.;
F.HN.
— The counter-scuffle. 1623, etc. *See* 23051 sqq.

21512.5 — A description of the king and queene of fayries. [In
verse. By R. Herrick and others.] 12⁰. [*T. Harper?*]
f. R. Harper, 1634. Ent. 29 ap. ROS.

21513 — [Anr. ed.] 12⁰. [*T. Harper*] *f. R. Harper,* 1635. O.
— An epistle of a religious priest. [1597?] *See* pt. 2 of
22968.5.

21513.5 — The jesuites play at Lyons in France, as it was there
presented. 4⁰. [*W. Jaggard a. J. Windet*] *f. N.
Butter,* 1607. Ent. to J. Busby 26 oc. CASHEL.; F.HD.
Y(imp.).
Tp line 2 ends: 'Lyons'. First 2 quires pr. by
Jaggard, the last 2 by Windet. *See also* 14531.

21514 — [Anr. ed.] 4⁰. [*J. Windet*] *f. N. Butter,* 1607. L.O.C.C².
PLUME*.; HN(tp def.).HD.
Tp line 2 ends: 'Ly-'.
— Late newes out of Barbary. 1613. *See* 12857.2.
— The letting of humours blood. 1613. *See* 21397.
— Mœoniæ. Or, certaine excellent poems. 1595. *See* 22955.

21515 — The new prophetical king of Barbary. 1613. Now =
12857.4.

21516 — The phoenix nest. Built vp with the most rare and
refined workes of noble men. Set foorth by R. S. of
the Inner Temple. [In verse.] 4⁰. *J. Jackson,* 1593.
Ent. 8 oc. L.L⁴.O(2, plus a frag.).; F.HD.
— St Peters Complaint. 1620, etc. *See* 22965 sqq.
— A short summe of the principall things. 1624. *See*
22152.5.
— Straunge, lamentable, and tragicall hystories. *Tr.* R.
S[mythe.] 1577. *See* 1356.5.

21517 — The triumphs over death. 1595. *See* 22971.
— Vindiciæ Danielis. 1629. Now = 21631.5.
— *ed. See* 21432.
— *tr. See* 18142.

S., R., *D. D.* The churches visitation. 1634. *See* pt. 2 of
22507.
— Of the author of the protestant church. 1621. *See* 22812.

S., R., *Esquire.* Phillis and Flora. *Tr.* R. S. 1598. *See*
19880.

S., R., *Gentleman, tr. See* 7325, 22879.

S., R., *Londoner.* The French tutour. 1625, etc. *See*
22429.5 sq.

S., R., *of the Inner Temple, ed.* The phoenix nest. 1593.
See 21516.

S., R., *of the Society of Jesus.* An epistle of comfort. 1616.
See 22948.
— S. Peters Complaint. 1616. *See* 22963.

S., R., *Preacher of the word at Arley.* The countryman
with his houshold. 1620. *See* 22427.

S., R., *Priest.* Certain general reasons. 1611. *See* 22393.

S., R. V., *tr. See* 3472.

21518 **S., S.** A briefe instruction for all families. 8⁰. [*T. Dawson*]
f. W. Ponsonby, 1583. O.; Y.
Tp compartment init. T. D.

S., S.—*cont.*

21519 — The honest lawyer. Acted [etc.] 4º. *G. Purslowe f. R. Woodroffe, and are to be sold at his shop neere the great North-dore,* 1616. Ent. to R. Redmer a. ass'd to R. Woodroffe 14 au. 1615. L.L⁶.O⁵.E.ETON.+; HN.HD. LC.PEN.Y.+ Greg 337.
  Later than 21519a.

21519a — [A variant, w. imprint:] *G. Purslowe f. R. Woodruffe and are to be sold at the great North-dore,* 1616. L.O.; HN.
  Earlier than 21519.

S., S., *A. M.* Aditus ad logicam. 1613. *See* 22825.

S., S., *of the congregation of S. Elias. See* 7072.7.

S., S. G. *See* 21662, 21663, 21670, 24529.

S., T. Christus redivivus. 1624. *See* 997.5.
— The crums of comfort. 1627. *See* 23015.7.
— An exposition upon the cxii. psalme. 1621. *See* 23269.
— A divine dictionarie. 1615. *See* 21493.5.

21520 — A jewell for gentrie. Being an exact dictionary, to make any man understand all the art, belonging to hawking, hunting, fowling and fishing. Now newly published. [Based on 3308 sqq.] 4º. [*T. Snodham*] *f. J. Helme,* 1614. Ass'd by widow Olive to Helme 18 no. 1613. L.O(frag.).O⁵.STD.; F.HN.NY.Y. Miss Clara S. Peck, New York City.

21520.5 — The key of David, that openeth the gates to the citie of God: also, of faith and repentance. 8º. *T. Haueland f. N. Fosbrooke,* 1610. M².; U.
  A trans. by T. S. of 12563, q.v. The author of the Latin original was prob. T. L.; *see* 15111.
— Margariton. *Tr.* (T. S.) 1640. *See* 17328.
— A mirrhor mete for all mothers. [1579.] *See* 21634.

21521 — A psalme of thanksgiving. 1610. Now = 5208.5.
— Sermons, meditations, and prayers. 1637. *See* 23509.

21522 — A song or psalme of thanksgiving, in remembrance of our deliverance from the gun-powder treason. [In verse.] s.sh.fol. *W. Jones,* 1625. L⁵(Lemon 268).
— Vox regis. [1623.] *See* 22105.
— *ed. See* 997.5, 21435.
— *tr. See* 2029, 5010.5.

S., T., *D. D.* Vindiciae senectutis. 1639. *See* 22391.8.

S., T., *of U.* The second part of Vox populi. 1624. *See* 22103.

S., T. M. De Turco-papismo. 1604. *See* 23461.

21523 **S., Tho.** The touch-stone of prayer. Or a true and profitable exposition of the Lords prayer. 8º. *f. A. Johnson,* 1602. Ent. to R. Read 3 no. 1601. C.C³.

S., V. V., *tr. See* 3538.

S., W. An aunswere to the proclamation of the rebels in the north. 1569. *See* 22234.

21524 — Bought wit is best. Or, Tom Longs journey to London, to buy wit. 8º. *E. A[llde] f. F. Smith,* 1634. Ent. 2 ja. O.

21525 — The complaint of Time against the tumultuous and rebellious Scots. 1639. Now = 21643.5.

21525.5 — The country-mans commonwealth. Containing divers golden sentences. 8º. *T. H[arper] f. R. Harper,* 1634. O³.; HN(date cropt).
— Cupids schoole. 1632. *See* 6123.

21526 — A funerall elegye in memory of William Peter of Whipton neere Excester. 4º. *G. Eld,* 1612. O.O¹⁷.

21527 — An hundred heavenly thoughts. And resolutions, tending to draw the minde from evill to good. By W. S. preacher in S. Johns of Mathermarket in Norwich [i.e. W. Stinnet.] 12º. *G. Eld, sold by C. W[right,]* 1616. Ent. to Eld a. T. Bushell 6 my. O. PLUME.
— Instructions for the increasing of mulberie trees. 1609. *See* 23138 sq.

21528 — The lamentable tragedie of Locrine, the eldest sonne of king Brutus. Newly set foorth, ouerseene and corrected. 4º. *T. Creede,* 1595. Ent. 20 jy. 1594. L(3). O.C².BIRM²(imp.).; F.HN.CAL.ILL.PML. Greg 136.
  Has been attrib. to R. Greene and G. Peele.

21529 — A new balade or songe, of the Lambes feaste. (Another, out of goodwill.) [Init. W. S., *Veritatis Amator.*] *Ballad.* 2 pts. s.sh.fol. [*Cologne, N. Bohmberg,*] 1574. L.O.; HN.HD(2, 1 imp.).
  (Formerly also 18559) Copies vary: with (2 HD) or without (HN) notes in rt-hand margin of pt. 2.

21530 — No entry.

S., W.—*cont.*
— The proceedings of the English colonie in Virginia. 1612. *See* pt. 2 of 22791.

21531 — The puritaine or the widdow of Watling-streete. [By T. Middleton.] 4º. *G. Eld,* 1607. Ent. 6 au. L.O.C². E.SH(imp.).+; F.HN.HD.NY.Y².+ Greg 251.

21532 — The true chronicle historie of . . . Thomas lord Cromwell. 4º. [*R. Read*] *f. W. Jones,* 1602. Ent. to W. Cotton 11 au. L.O.; F(imp.).NY. Greg 189.

21533 — [Anr. ed.] 4º. *T. Snodham,* 1613. Ass'd by Jones to J. Browne 16 de. 1611. L.L⁶.O.C².E.+; F.HN.CAL.HD. Y².+
— *ed. See* 22761, 22766, 22775.5, 22781, 22791.
— *tr. See* 6999, 14656.

21533.3 **S., W.,** *Christ's unworthy minister.* [An exposition of the Ten Commandments, set forth in a table in the form of genealogical descent.] s.sh.fol. *W. White,* 1607. L⁵(Lemon 117).

S., W., *Doctor in divinity.* The black-smith. A sermon. 1606. *See* 22880.9.

S., W., *Gentleman.* A compendious examination. 1581. *See* 23133.5 sqq.

21533.7 — The true copie of such conference as passed (concerning the comming to the church, hearing of the diuine seruice,) betweene W. S. gent. and L. Euans, in the yeare. 1577. 8º. *T. Purfoote,* 1577. D.P.

S., W., *Preacher.* An hundred heavenly thoughts. 1616. *See* 21527.

S., W., *Veritatis Amator. See* 21529.

21534 **Sabie, Francis.** Adams complaint. The olde worldes tragedie. Dauid and Bathsheba. [In verse.] 4º. *R. Johnes,* 1596. L.; HN.HD.

21535 — The fissher-mans tale: of the famous actes, life and loue of Cassander a Grecian knight. [A verse paraphrase of 12285.] 4º. *R. Johnes,* 1595. Ent. 21 no. 1594. L.; HN.
  This and the following also intended to be issued w. 21537.

21536 — Flora's fortune. The second part of the Fishermans tale. [In verse.] 4º. *R. Jhones,* 1595. Ent. 21 no. 1594. L.; HN.

21537 — Pans pipe, three pastorall eglogues, in English hexameter. The printer hath annexed the Fisher-mans tale. [Init. F. S.] 3 pts.? 4º. *R. Jhones,* 1595. Ent. 3 ja. L(lacks Tale).; HN(w. tp only of Tale).
  HN tp to Tale is same setting as 21535.

Sabinus, Angelus. *See* 18928, 18939.5.

Sabinus, Georgius. *See* 18951.

Sabinus, Tarquinius Gallatius, *ed. See* 5476.

21537.3 **Sabunde, Raymundus de.** Theologia naturalis, sive liber creaturarum, specialiter: de homine, et de natura eius. Cum elencho & serie titulorum, nec non indice rerum & verborum. 8º. *Francofurti (ad Moenum, W. Hoffmannus,) imp. G. Thomasoni & O. Pulleni, bibliopol. Londinens.,* 1635. O.O³.C.E.NEP.+

21537.5 **Sachs, Hans.** A goodly dysputatyon betwene a christen shomaker and a popysshe parson. [Anon.] *Tr.* out of the Germayne tongue [by A. Scoloker.] 8º. *Ippeswich, A. Scoloker,* 1548. M(imp.).

21537.7 — [Anr. ed.] *Tr.* A. Scoloker. 8º. *A. Scoloker a. W. Seres,* 1548. L.O.
  (Formerly 5191)

21538 **Sack.** Muld sacke: or the apologie of Hic Mulier: to the late declamation against her [13374]. 4º. [*W. Stansby*] *f. R. Meighen,* 1620. Ent. 29 ap. L.O(imp.).; HN.HD.
  Cut on tp copied from the engr. of John Cottington by R. Elstrack; *see* Hind II.170.
— Den sack met die stucken voor den Paus van Roomen. 1568. *See* 6581.

Sackville, Thomas, *Earl of Dorset.* Thomas baron of Buckurst [etc. Orders for the market at Oxford. 1601?] *See* 19002.5.

21539 — Thomas earle of Dorset [etc. Orders for the market at Oxford. 1606.] Now = 19002.7.
— *See also* 1247, 18684.

21540 **Sacrifice.** Of the visible sacrifice of the church of God. 1637. Now = 7072.4.

Sadeel, Antonius. *See* 15257.

21541 **Sadleirus, Richardus.** Richardi Sadleiri de procreandis, eligendis, alendis, frænandis et tractandis equis, experientia. 4°. *H. Midletonus*, 1587. L.O⁸.

Sadler, Edmund. Organon reipublicæ, or the north starre of pollicie. 1605. *See* 20575.7.

21542 **Sadler, John.** Masquarade du ciel: presented to the great queene of the little world. A celestiall map. By J. S[adler.] 4°. *R. B[adger] f. S. C[artwright,]* 1640. Ent. to Cartwright 24 no. L.O.C.E¹³.LINC.+; F.HN. CU.HD.Y.+ Greg 595.
    F, I HN, Y copies omit the errata on F2ᵛ.

21543 — Praxis medicorum vel, formula remediorum, per alphabeticum ordinem digesta. 12°. *ap. R. Oulton, imp. P. Stephens & C. Meredith*, 1637. L.O.O².C.E⁵.+; HN. Dickinson C. Philadelphia, College of Physicians.
    At least one L copy lacks *⁴ (Index), which may represent a later addition to the contents.

21544 — The sicke womans private looking-glasse. 12°. *A. Griffin f. P. Stephens a. C. Meridith*, 1636. Ent. 25 ja. L.O.C².BRISTOL².G².; HN.NLM.

Sadler, John, *tr. See* 24631.

21545 **Safeguard.** The safegard of sailers, or great rutter, con⟨tain⟩ing the courses, distances, depthes, of sundrie harboroughs, both of England, Fraunce, Spaine, [etc.] *Tr.* out of Dutch by R. Norman [from C. Anthonisz, 'Het Leeskartboek van Wisbuy'.] 4°. *J. Windet a. T. Judso⟨n⟩ f. R. Ballard*, 1584. Ent. 17 jn. 1581. O(cropt).

21546 — [Anr. ed.] 4°. *E. Allde*, 1587. Ent. 2 oc. O¹⁸.; HN.Y.

21546.5 — [Anr. ed.] 4°. *E. Allde*, 1590. DUL.; WIS. Horblit 41.
    Collates A–X⁴Y².

21547 — [Anr. ed.] 4° in 8's. *E. Allde*, 1590. L.L³³.C⁶.
    Collates A–K⁸ L⁴ M².

21548 — [Anr. ed.] 4° in 8's. *A. Islip*, 1600. Ent. to T. Dawson to print for Astley 1 mr. 1596; crossed out 5 ap. 1596; ent. to H. Astley 3 no. 1600. L.O.O³.C¹⁵(imp.).

21549 — [Anr. ed.] Newly corrected and augmented by E. W[right.] 4° in 8's. *E. Allde f. H. Astley*, 1605. L.

21550 — [Anr. ed.] 4° in 8's. *E. A(llde) f. J. Tap*, 1612. L(2, 1 lacks tp).C(imp.).E².; BO²(imp.).PH².

21550.5 — [Anr. ed.] 4° in 8's. *B. A[lsop] a. T. F[awcet] f. J. Hurlocke*, 1632. Ass'd by widow Tapp 1 au. 1631. London, Trinity House.

21551 — [Anr. ed.] 4° in 8's. *B. A[lsop] a. T. F[awcet] f. G. Hurlock*, 1640 (1638.) Ass'd 16 ja. 1634. L.L³⁸.E⁸.

21551.3 **Sailor.** A sayler new come over: and in this ship with him those of such fame. *Ballad.* 2 pts. s.sh.fol. [*A. Mathewes] f. H. Gosson*, [1631?] Ent. to ballad ptnrs. 13 jn. 1631. C⁶(I.396–7ᵛ).
    21138.5 is pr. on the verso.

21551.7 **Sainct Sernin, Jonatan de.** Essais et observations sur les Essais du seigneur de Montagne. 8°. *E. Allde*, 1626. L(2, 1 w. tp def.).PARIS.

Sainctes, Claude de. *See* 24726.5.

21552 **Saint Andrews University.** Academiae Sancti Andreae, Carolo gratulatio. 1633. Now = 19172.7.

21553 — Antiquissimae celeberrimaeque academiæ Andreanæ Χαριστηρια. In adventum Jacobi primi. [In verse.] 4°. *Edinburgi, A. Hart*, 1617. L(2).E.E².; BO⁵.

21554 — Decermina quaedam philosophica. 1629. Now = 21555.37.

21555 — Gymnasma philosophicum. 1611. Now = 21555.16.

Theses
Arranged chronologically

21555.1 — De prædestinatione. Siue de causis salutis et damnationis disputatio, præside A. Meluino. C. Johannides [of Dalby] respondebit. 4°. *Edinburgi, R. Waldegraue*, 1595. A.E².G².STU.
    (Formerly 14047)

21555.2 — De libero arbitrio theses theologicæ. Præside A. Meluino. Respondente J. Massonio. 4°. *Edinburgi, R. Walde-graue*, 1597. A.
    (Formerly 17647)

21555.3 — Scholastica diatriba de rebus diuinis. A. Meluino moderante. 4°. *Edinburgi, R. Walde-graue*, 1599. A.E².D.G².
    (Formerly 17808)

21555.4 — De justificatione hominis coram Deo, theses theologicæ, quas A. Melvino, moderante, tueri conabitur P. Geddaeus. 4°. *Edinburgi, R. Walde-grave*, 1600. A.
    (Formerly 11696)

21555.5 — Theses physicae de generatione et corruptione quas defendere conabor sub præsidio J. Echlini. T. Mierbekius. 4°. *Edinburgi, R. Charteris*, [1600.] E².

21555.6 — Theses theologicæ de peccato quas A. Melvino moderante tueri conabor. J. Scharpius. 4°. *Edinburgi, R. Walde-grave*, 1600. A.
    (Formerly 22368)

21555.7 — Theses theologicae. De ecclesia catholica, quas sub praesidio A. Melvini sustinere conabor J. Wallasius. 4°. *Edinburgi, ap. R. Charteris*, 1601. D.

21555.8 — Utrum episcopus Romanus sit Antichristus necne? A. Melvino præside, T. Londius respondebit. 4°. [*Edinburgh,*] *R. Walde-grave*, 1602. A.E.P.
    (Formerly 16931)

21555.9 — Theses theologicæ de sacramentis, & missa idololatrica, quas A. Melvino moderante tueri conabitur A. Mortonus. 4°. *Edinburgi, R. Walde-grave*, 1602. A.E(imp.).
    (Formerly 18171)

Note: in the following, 'St. S.' denotes theses from St. Salvator's College; 'St. L.' those from St. Leonard's.

21555.10 — Theses aliquot philosophicae. . . . Præside J. Petreio. [St. S.] 4°. [*Edinburgh,*] *R. Walde-grane* [sic], 1603. O⁶.E. 𝔄

21555.11 — Theses philosophicæ quædam, . . . sub presidio D. Willikij. [St. L.] 4°. [*Edinburgh,*] *R. Walde-grave*, 1603. STU.

21555.12 — Theses aliquot logicae, . . . præside G. Wedderburno. [St. S.] 4°. *Edinburgi, R. Charters* [sic], 1608. O⁶.E².

21555.13 — [Theses logicæ. St. L.] 4°. [*Edinburgh,* 1608?] O⁶(imp.).

21555.14 — Thesium [sic] aliquot logicarum, . . . Præside D. Robertsono. [St. S.] 4°. [*Edinburgh,*] *A. Hart*, 1610. O⁶.

21555.15 — Theses aliquot logicæ, . . . Præside P. Brusio. [St. L.] 4°. *Edinburgi, A. Hart*, 1610. O⁶(imp.).

21555.16 — Gymnasma philosophicum de rebus logicis. A. Henrisono [Henderson] præside. [St. S.] 4°. *Edinburgi, A. Hart*, 1611. L.O⁶(frag.).
    (Formerly 21555)

21555.17 — Theses ex uberrimis logicæ, . . . Sub præsidio J. Strangii. AD. 1611. [St. L.] 4°. *Edinbur⟨gi,⟩ A. ⟨Hart, 1611.⟩* O⁶(imp.).E²(tp def.).

21555.18 — Exerc⟨itationes⟩ philosoph⟨icæ.⟩ Sub præsidio J. Blairij. [St. S.] 4°. *Edinburgi, T. Finlason*, 1612. O⁶(tp def.).

21555.19 — Theses philosophicae. . . . Sub præsidio J. Wemii. [St. L.] 4°. *Edinburgi, A. Hart*, 1612. O⁶.E(2).

21555.20 — Positiones aliquot logicæ, . . . Praeside G. Lammio. [St. S.] 4°. *Edinburgi, A. Hart*, 1613. O⁶.E².

21555.21 — Theses aliquot logicæ, . . . Præside G. Makdowello. [St. L.] 4°. [*Edinburgh,*] *A. Hart*, 1613. O⁶.

21555.22 — Theses logicæ, . . . Præside J. Schevezio. [St. S.] 4°. *Edinburgi, A. Hart*, 1614. O⁶.

21555.23 — Theses aliquot logicæ . . . 1614 . . . præside A. Brusio. [St. L.] 4°. *Edinburgi, T. Finlason*, [1614.] O⁶(imp.). E²(imp.).

21555.24 — ⟨Theses aliquot logicæ . . .⟩ Præside D. Monroo. [St. S.] 4°. *Edinburgi, A. Hart*, 1615. O⁶(frag.).

21555.25 — [Theses.] 4°. [*Edinburgh, c.* 1615.] O⁶(frag.).
    B1ʳ line 1 begins: '1. Anima humana'.

21555.26 — [Theses.] 4°. [*Edinburgh, c.* 1615.] O⁶(imp.).
    B1ʳ line 1 begins: '1 Hinc variæ'.

21555.27 — Theses philosophicae, . . . sub praesidio J. Vemii [Wemyss. St. L.] 4°. *Edinburgi, A. Hart*, 1616. O⁶. c².

21555.28 — [Heading 2ʳ:] De potestate principis. Aphorismi. [Theses, not for graduation, disputed by *Bp.* D. Lindsay at St. Mary's College before James I, with R. Howie presiding.] 4°. (*Edinburgi, T. Finlason*, 1617.) L.; HN.
    (Formerly 15655) Reprinted in 140, which also includes notes of R. Barron's disputation on the same occasion.

21555.29 — Positiones aliquot philosophicæ . . . Præside R. Barronio. [St. S.] 4°. *Edinburgi, A. Hart*, 1617. O⁶.

21555.30 — Theses aliquot logicae, . . . Præside J. Caro [Kerr. St. L.] 4°. *Edinburgi, T. Finlason*, 1617. O.O⁶.E².

21555.31 — Positiones aliquot philosophicæ . . . Præside G. Martino. [St. S.] 4°. *Edinburgi, A. Hart*, 1618. O⁶.

21555.32 — Theses aliquot logicæ . . . Præside A. Brusio. [St. L.] 4°. *Edinburgi, A. Hart*, 1618. O⁶(frag.).

21555.33 — Positiones, et disputationes aliquot philosophicæ, sub præsidio R. Baronii. [St. S.] 4°. *Andreapoli, E. Rabanus*, 1621. E.

Saint Andrews University—*Theses*—*cont.*

21555.34 — Theses aliquot philosophicae, . . . Præside J. Barronio. [St. S.] 4°. *Edinburgi, J. Wreittoun*, 1627. L.E²(imp.).

21555.35 — Theses aliquot philosophicae, . . . Præside A. Monroo. [St. S.] 4°. *Edinburgi, J. Wreittoun*, 1628. E²(imp.).

21555.36 — Theses aliquot philosophicae, . . . 1628. Præside K. Moraio [Mungo Murray. St. L.] 4°. *Edinburgi, J. Wreittoun*, 1⟨628.⟩ E²(imp.).
(Formerly 18065)

21555.37 — Decermina quaedam philosophica sive theses. Præside J. Ramisæo. [St. S.] 4°. *Edinburgi, J. Wreittoun*, 1629. C.E.
(Formerly 21554)

21555.38 — Theses philosophicae, . . . Præside J. Wedderburno. [St. L.] 4°. *Edinburgi, J. Wreittoun*, 1629. E.

21555.39 — Theses aliquot logicae, . . . Præside J. Mercero. [St. L.] 4°. *Edinburgi, J. Wreittoun*, 1630. E.E².

21555.40 — Theses philosophicæ . . . 1631. Praeside J. Barclaio. [St. S.] 4°. *Edinburgi, J. Scribonius*, [1631.] E.

21555.41 — Theses aliquot philosophicæ . . . 1631. Præside G. Wemio. [St. L.] 4°. *Edinburgi, J. Wreittoun*, [1631.] E.

21555.42 — Theses aliquot philosophicæ . . . Præside A. Monroo. [St. S.] 4°. *Edinburgi, J. Wreittoun*, 1632. E.

21555.43 — Theses aliquot logicae . . . Præside J. Mercero. [St. L.] 4°. *Edinburgi, hæredes A. Hart*, 1632. E.

21555.44 — Theses aliquot philosophicæ, . . . Præside K. Moraio [Mungo Murray. St. L.] 4°. *Edinburgi, hæredes A. Hart*, 1634. E.E².

21555.45 — Theses logicae, . . . Præside J. Armourio. [St. S.] 4° in 2's. *Edinburgi, J. Scribonius*, 1635. E.E².

21555.46 — Theses aliquot logicae, . . . Præside G. Wemio. [St. L.] 4°. *Edinburgi, hæredes A. Hart*, 1635. E.

Saint Anne of Totenham. *See* Indulgences 23.

21556 **Saintbarb, Richard.** [Heading B1ʳ:] Certaine points of christian religion. [In question and answer.] 8°. [*f. W. Young a. R. Jackson*, 1589.] Ent. to R. Jackson 1 oc. L(lacks tp).E(imp.).
Imprint is from Maunsell (pt. 1 of 17669), who lists 2 works w. this imprint: C4ʳ: 'Rich. Saintbarb. his Catechisme, wherein are chiefly handeled such things as are omitted in other Catechismes.' and H6ʳ: 'Rich. Saintbarb, his Exposition on the Creed, the Lords praier, Commandementes and Sacraments, in questions and Aunsweeres.' The present text is prob. the former.

21557 **Saint Bartholomew's Hospital.** The ordre of the hospital of .S. Bartholomewes in westsmythfielde in London. 8°. (*R. Grafton*,) 1552. L.L⁸.L⁴⁷.O.C⁶.+; F.

21558 **Saint Christophers.** Newes and strange newes from St. Christophers of a hurry-cano. 1638. Now = 23778.5.

Saint Denis. A briefe declaration of the yeelding vp of Saint Denis. 1590. *See* 13128.
— The coppie of a letter sent into England from Saint Denis. 1590. *See* 10004.

Saint Esprit. A true relation of the taking of the ship Saint Esprit. 1627. *See* 24268.7.

21558.5 **Saint German, Christopher.** An answere to a letter. [On the royal supremacy and various points of religion. Anon.] 8°. (*T. Godfray*,) [1535?] L(imp.).O².; F.HN.
(Formerly 659)

21559 — Dialogus de fundamentis legum Anglie et de conscientia. [Anon.] 8°. (*p J. Rastell*, 1528.) L.O.C.P.LINC.+; CH.HD(2, 1 imp.).MICH.MIN.PH².
Copies vary: with or without tp foliated; both at O, HD. In some copies the bifolium C1.8 is a cancel; orig. C8ʳ line 19: 'quia secūdum leges anglie'; the cancel has 'vnde ad/ puniendum'; both at L.

21560 — [Anr. ed., with the author's name.] 8°. [*A. Islip?*] in æd. T. Wight, 1604. L.O.C.D.G⁴.+; F.HN.CU.HD. MIN.+
With J. Bale's biography reprinted from 1295, p. 600.

21561 — [A modified trans.] Hereafter foloweth a dyaloge in Englysshe, bytwyxt a doctoure of dyuynyte, and a student in the lawes of Englande. [Anon.] 8° in 4's. (*R. wyer*,) [1530?] L.C.COL. Goyder.; F.HD.LC.
Reprinted in 21567.

Saint German, Christopher—*cont.*

21562 — [Anr. ed., revised.] The fyrste dyaloge in Englysshe, with newe addycyons. 8° in 4's. (*R. wyer*,) [1531.] L(2).O.O⁵.C.C⁴.; F.CH.HD.LC.MIN.+
(Formerly also 21569) There are additions within the text; *see* also 21563 sqq.

21563 — Here after foloweth a lytell treatise called the newe addicions. (To be added to yᵉ secōde dialoge in englysshe . . . the sayd additions treate of the power of the parlyament concernynge the spiritualtie.) [Anon.] 8°. (*T. Bertheletus*, 1531.) L.; HN.
Errata on D8ʳ. This and the following 2 eds. are, except as noted, found bd. w. 21562 and 21566. This text was not reprinted till 1751.

21563.5 — [Anr. ed.] 8°. (*T. Bertheletus*, 1531.) L.O.O⁵.C.C⁵.+; LC.
No errata on D8ʳ; with the abbr. 'Fo.' before folio numbers. C⁵, LC, and Goyder are not bd. w. 21562 or 21566.

21564 — [Anr. ed.] 8°. (*T. Bertheletus*, 1531.) O.D².M²(lacks tp).; CH.HD.MIN.
No errata on D8ʳ; without the abbr. 'Fo.' before folio numbers.

21565 — The secūde dyaloge in Englysshe bytwene a doctour of dyuynytye and a student. [Anon.] 8°. (*Southwarke, P. Treueys*, 1530 (24 no.)) L.C.C⁴.; F.HD(2).LC.MIN.

21566 — [Anr. ed., revised.] The secunde dyalogue i englysshe wyth new addycyons. Newly correctyd and emprentyd. 8°. (*Southwarke, P. Treueris*, 1531.) L.O.C.E.P. +; F.CH.HD.MIN. Peter W. Adams, New York City.
There are additions within the text; *see* also 21563 sqq.

21567 — [Anr. ed. of the unrevised texts 21561 and 21565.] Here after foloweth a dialoge in Englysshe. (The seconde dyaloge.) 2 pts. 8°. (*R. Redman*, 1531 (1 jn.)) O.

21568 –- [Anr. ed. of the revised texts.] The fyrst (seconde) dialogue in Englisshe, with newe additions. 2 pts. 8°. (*R. Redman*, 1532 (1 jy.)) L.O.; HN.HART².HD(imp.). N.PH²(pt. 1 only).+

21569 — = 21562.

21570 — [Anr. ed.] The dialogues in Englysshe. 8°. (*W. Myddylton*, 1543.) L(destroyed).; HN.CAL.HD.

21570.5 — [Anr. ed.] 8°. (*in aed. R. Toteli*, 1554.) D.; HD.MICH. MIN.PEN. Bp. Medley Library, Church Hall, Fredericton, N.B.
A2ʳ last line ends: 'wille dooe'.

21571 — [Anr. ed.] 8°. (*in aed. R. Totteli*, 1554 [i.e. 1556?]) L(2, 1 imp.).E.P.; DAR(imp.).HD.LC.PH².
A2ʳ last line ends: 'wyll dooe'.

21571.5 — [Anr. ed.] 8°. (*in æd. R. Totteli*, 1554 [i.e. 1565?]) L. O.C²(lacks col.).C⁴.BRISTOL².+; F.HN.CU.HD.MIN.+
A2ʳ last line ends: 'will doe'.

21572 — [Anr. ed.] 8°. (*in æd. R. Tottelli*, 1569.) L.O.C(w. quire A of 21571.5).DUL.P.+; F.HN.HD.LC.WIS.+

21573 — [Anr. ed.] 8°. (*in æd. R. Tottelli*, 1575.) L.DUR⁵.LEEDS. LEIC².NLW.+; HN.CU.HD.LC.MIN.+

21574 — [Anr. ed.] 8°. (*in æd. R. Tottelli*,) 1580. L(destroyed). L³⁸.C.BTL.M.M⁴.; F.HD.ILL.PEN.PH².+
In title: 'Englishe,'.

21574.5 — [Anr. ed.] 8°. (*in æd. R. Tottelli*,) 1580. O.C².C⁴.M. ST(lacks tp).+; F.HN.HD.IND.PH².+
In title: 'English,'.

21575 — [Anr. ed.] The dialogue in English. 8°. R. Tottill, 1593. Ent. 18 fb. 1583. O(imp., w. quires A, C of 21574.5 and col. of 21571.5). C.E².G².P(w. col. of 21571.5).; F.HN.CU.HD.MIN.+

21576 — [Anr. ed.] 8°. [*A. Islip f.*] T. Wight a. B. Norton, 1598. L.O¹⁷.C⁴.BTU.G².+; F.HN.CU.HD.MIN.+

21577 — [Anr. ed.] 8°. [*A. Islip f.*] T. Wight, 1604. L.O.C.LIV³. M⁴.+; F.HN.HD.ILL.U.+

21578 — [Anr. ed.] 8°. [*A. Islip*] f. the Co. of Statrs., 1607. L.O. C⁵.LINC.USHAW.+; F.HN.CU.HD.ILL.+
See Court-Book C, pp. 16, 27.

21579 — [A ghost.]

21580 — [Anr. ed.] 8°. [*A. Islip?*] f. the Co. of Statrs., 1613. L. C.D.G².M⁴.+; HN.HD.ILL.LC.Y.+

21581 — [Anr. ed.] 8°. f. the Co. of Statrs., 1623. Ent. to the English Stock 5 mr. 1620. L.O.C².BIRM.SHEF.+; F. HN.HD.ILL.NY¹¹.+

21582 — [Anr. ed.] 8°. assignes of J. More, 1638. O.O⁴⁶.A.; F. HD.ILL.NY¹¹.TEX.+
Tp line 4: 'Divinity,'.

21582.5 — [Anr. ed.] 8°. assignes of J. More, 1638. L.O³⁹.G²· P YK.+; F.HN.HD.LC.N.+
Tp line 4: 'Divinitie,'.

Saint German, Christopher—*cont.*

21583 — An exact abridgement of that excellent treatise called Doctor and student. [Anon. *Ed.*] (I. L.) 8°. [*J. Haviland f.*] *assignes of J. More f. M. Walbancke*, 1630. L(destroyed).O[11].C.D[6].DUL.G[2].+; F.HN.CU.HD. MIN.+
  Imprint varies: 'for' M. Walbancke (C,HD) or 'sold by' (F,O[11],O[17],O[19],O[27]).
— Here after foloweth a lytell treatise called the newe addicions. 1531. *See* 21563.

21584 — Salem and Bizance. (A dialogue betwixte two englyshe men.) [Anon.] 8°. (*in aed. T. Bertheleti*, 1533.) L. O(2).C.C[6].
  Answers 18078; answered by 18081.

21585 — The addicions of Salem and Byzance. [Anon.] 8°. *in aed. T. Bertheleti*, 1534. O.
— A treatise cōcernynge diuers of the constitucyons. [1535?] *See* 24236.

21586 — A treatise concernynge the diuision betwene the spiry-tualtie and temporaltie. [Anon.] 8°. (*R. Redman*,) [1532?] L.C.C[5].CHATS.
  Answered by 18078. Pr. after some of the Berthelet eds.; *see L.&P. Henry VIII*, VI.215.

21587 — [Anr. ed.] 8°. (*in aed. T. Bertheleti*,) [1532?] L[2](lacks tp).O.C[2](imp.).M.; F.LC.Y.
  A1[v] line 6: 'moost'; line 8: 'weyghtier'.

21587.3 — [Anr. ed.] 8°. (*in ed. T. Bertheleti*,) [1532?] C.
  A1[v] line 6: 'moost'; line 8: 'weyhtier'.

21587.5 — [Anr. ed.] 8°. (*in ed. T. Bertheleti*,) [1532?] C[6].; HN.
  A1[v] line 6: 'moste'; line 8: 'weightier'.

21587.7 — [Anr. ed.] 8°. (*in aed. T. Bertheleti*,) [1532?] L.O[17].
  A1[v] line 6: 'most'; line 8: 'weightier'.

21588 — A treatyse concernige the power of the clergye, and the lawes of the realme. [Anon.] 8°. (*T. Godfray*,) [1535?] L.O.O[2].C.; CU.HD.

21588.3 **Saint Giles without Cripplegate.** The register booke belonging to the parish church . . . according to the canon made in the 40. yere of her maiesties reigne. Written in the time of L. Andrewes, vicar. [For 1561–1606.] s.sh.fol. [*Deputies of C. Barker*, 1598?] L[8].
  Only the tp is pr.

21588.5 — The register booke, belonging to the parish church . . . beginning the first day of March 1606. Written in the time of J. Buckeridge vicar, lord bishop of Rochester. [For 1606–1634.] s.sh.fol. [*R. Barker*, 1612?] L[8].
  Only the tp is pr.

St. Ives. *See* 7686.6.

Saint James' Chapel. *See* Indulgences 36 sq.

21588.7 **Saint Jean-d'Angély.** A briefe declaration of all things that have past and beene done before the towne of Saint John Dangely from the 27. of May, untill this present time, by the duke de Guise. 4°. [*London*?] 1621. O.

21589 **Saint John, Oliver.** Mr S.-John's speech to the lords concerning ship-money. 4°. [*E. Purslowe*,] 1640 [o.s.] Ent. to H. Seile 11 fb. 1641. L[2].L[30].O.P.SHEF.+; HD.NY.PN.WTL.
  This and the following eds. are also listed as Wing S 331. Device (McK.281) on tp; E1[r] line 2 from bottom ends: 'Lord *Finches* soli-'. Ordered suppressed 6 Feb. 1641; *see JHC* II.80a.

21589.3 — [Anr. issue, w. quires C, E, F reset.] [*E. Purslowe*,] 1640 [o.s.] C[9].NEK.P. Stevens Cox.; F.HD.N.NY.Y.+
  Device on tp; E1[r] last 2 lines: 'L. *Finches* sollici-/ tation only, and'.

21589.5 — [Anr. issue, further reset.] 8°. [*E. Purslowe*,] 1640 [o.s.] L.O.C.D.E.+; F.HN.CU.HD.ILL.+
  Device on tp; E1[r] line 2 from bottom ends: 'Lord *Finches* solli-'. Quires A, E, and F outer forme reset; C inner forme reimposed. Copies vary: A2[r] heading has: 'SPEECH' or 'ARGUMENTS'; both at HD.

21589.7 — [Anr. ed.] 8°. [*T. Harper*,] 1640 [o.s.] L[2].O.C[2].D[8].YK.+; F(2).HD(2).LC.MCG.Y.
  Block of 8 type orns. on tp; E1[r] last 2 lines: 'L. *Finches* sollici-/tation only, &'.

Saint John Dangely. *See* 21588.7.

Saint Katherine's Abbey, *Mount Sinai. See* Indulgences 90.

21590 **Saint Katherine's Hospital,** *Lincoln.* Now = Indulgences 49.

Saint Katherine's Hospital by the Tower, *London. See* Indulgences 55A.

Saint Margaret's Chapel, *Uxbridge. See* Indulgences 79.

21590.5 **Saint Martin's Fort,** *Isle of Ré.* A true and perfect description of the cittadell or fort of St. Martins in the isle of Ree. [Engr. w. letterpress text.] s.sh.fol. *f. T. Walkley*, 1627. L[5](Lemon 277).
  See also 23716.5, 24742.

Saint Mary in Arden in the Field, *Leicestershire. See* 17330.5.

21591 **Saint Mary's Island.** A true report and description of the taking of the iland of S. Maries [Santa Maria in the Azores], by a shippe of Amsterdam, and foure English pinnasses. 1599. *Tr.* out of Dutch. 4°. [*J. Windet f.*] *J. Wolfe*, 1600. O.

Saint Michael's Convent without Stamford. *See* Indulgences 74 sq.

Saint Patrick's Purgatory. *See* 19474.

Saint Paul, *Sir George de.* Carmina funebria. 1614. *See* 19043.5.

Saint Paul's Cathedral. The burnynge of Paules church. 1563. *See* 19931.
— Exemplum literarum . . . de vera origine conflagrationis templi Paulini. 1561. *See* 19930.5.
— The meeting of gallants or the walkes in Powles. 1604. *See* 17781.

21591.3 — [Begins:] Received the [ ] day of [ ] . . . money . . . for repairing of the decayes and ruines of the cathedrall church of S[t] Paul in London. 1/2 sh.fol. [*London*, 1633?] L[11](S.P. 16/534: 2, dated in MS. 29 Jan. 1632 [o.s.]).
  See also 9254.
— The true report of the burnyng of the steple. 1561. *See* 19330.

21591.5 **Saint Paul's School.** Preces in usum scholae Paulinae, ideo impressae, ut accurate a singulis pueris ediscantur. 8°. *S. Staffordus, venduntur per M. Lawum*, 1600. Ent. to T. Stirrop 10 jn. 1597; to Stafford 12 jn. 1600. C[10].

Saint Robert's Priory, *Knaresborough. See* Indulgences 121B sq.

Saint Roch's Hospital, *Exeter. See* Indulgences 41.

Saint Savior's Parish, *Southwark.* A rate of duties. 1613. *See* 22945.5.

Saint Sepulchre's Hospital. *See* Indulgences 151 sq.

Saint Sernin, Jonatan de. *See* 21551.7.

21592 **Saint Thomas of Acres' Hospital,** *London.* Be it known [etc. 1515?] Now = Indulgences 57.
— *See also* Indulgences 5, 56, 58.

Saint Victor, Richard of. Here foloweth a veray deuoute treatyse. 1521. *See* 20972.

Saint Wilfrid's Collegiate Church. *See* Indulgences 68A.

Saints. The saints comforts. 1638. *See* 22502.
— The saints cordials. 1629. *See* 22503.
— The saints legacies, etc. 1633, etc. *See* 10635.5.

21593 **Saker, Austin.** Narbonus. The laberynth of libertie. 2 pts. 4°. (*W. How f.*) *R. Jhones*, 1580. Ent. 8 mr. L[4](imp.).O.; F(imp.).

Sal., W. Englands complaint. 1640. *See* 21644.

21594 **Sala, Angelo.** Opiologia. Or, a treatise concerning the nature, and safe use of opium. Done into English, and something inlarged by T. Bretnor. 8°. *N. Okes*, 1618. Ent. 26 au. 1617. L.L[16].O.O[17].C(2).; CHI.HD.
  Advertised on C8 of 420.11.

21595 **Salamanca University.** An extracte of the determinacion, and censure of the doctours of the universities of Salamanca and Valledolid touching the warres of Ireland, and declaracion of the poape his breve concerning the same warres. s.sh.fol. [*Salamanca, A. Tavernier*, 1603.] L.
  A&R 298.

Salem. The addicions of Salem and Byzance. 1534. *See* 21585.
— Salem and Bizance. 1533. *See* 21584.

21596 **Salerno.** [Schola Salernitana.] Regimen sanitatis Salerni. This boke techyng al people to gouerne them in helthe, is *tr.* by T. Paynell. *Lat. a. Eng.* 4°. (*T. Berthelet*, 1528 (au.)) L(imp.).M.
   With the orig. Latin verse of Joannes, *de Mediolano*, and a trans. of the Latin commentary of Arnaldus, *de Villa nova.*

21597 — [Anr. ed.] Amended, augmented, and diligently imprinted. 4°. (*T.Berthelet*, 1530 (fb.)) L.O.C.ST(imp.).; HN.

21598 — [Anr. ed.] 4°. (*in aed. T. Bertheleti*, 1535.) L.L³⁸.O⁶ (imp.).BIRM(Med.).; NLM.Y.

21599 — [Anr. ed.] 4°. (*in aed. T. Bertheleti*, 1541.) L.L¹⁶.O.C. M⁴.+; HN.HD.ILL.NLM.NY.+

21600 — [Anr. ed.] 8°. [*W. Copland f.*] (*A. Vele*, 1557.) L.O.C. BRISTOL².STU.+; HN.HART².HD.N.NLM.+

21601 — [Anr. ed.] 1575. 8°. *W. How f. A. Veale*, [1575.] L.O. C.D⁶.E.+; F(3).HN.NLM.NY⁴.

21602 — [Anr. ed.] 4°. *T. Creede*, 1597. Ent. 5 oc. 1596. L.L¹⁶. L³⁰.C.C⁵.+; MICH.NLM.NY.PN.Y.+

21603 — [Anr. ed.] Regimen sanitatis Salerni. The schoole of Salernes directorie. Perused, and corrected with the Latine verses reduced into English [by P. Holland.] 4°. *B. Alsop, sold by J. Barnes*, 1617. L.O.C.D.E⁵.+; F.HN.NLM.NY⁴.V.+
   Dedic. to Jos. Fenton signed 'Anonymus.' This and the following items omit Paynell's name as trans. of the commentary.

21603.3 — [Anr. issue, w. cancel tp, w. imprint:] *B. Alsop by the assignes of C. Knight, sold by J. Barnes*, [1617?] F.

21603.7 — [Anr. issue, w. new tp and dedic.:] *B. Alsop*, 1620. Duke U.
   Dedic. to Henry [Percy] Earl of Northumberland signed by John Barnes the publisher.

21604 — [Anr. ed.] Reviewed. Whereunto is annexed, a discourse of fish. 4°. *B. Alsop a. T. Fawcet*, 1634. L.O. C².D².G².+; F.HN.CHI².HD.NY⁴.+
   Preface init. R. H., i.e. H. Ronsovius? A copy seen by F. S. Ferguson w. the above imprint but w. the date altered in press to 1635 was offered for sale at Sotheby's 24 Oct. 1922, lot 525 (bought by Francis Edwards, untraced).

21605 — The Englishmans docter. Or, the Schoole of Salerne. [*Tr.* by Sir J. Harington from Joannes, *de Mediolano*'s Latin verse. In verse.] 8°. [*W. Jaggard*] *f. J. Helme a. J. Busby, junior*, 1607. Ent. 27 au. L.O.M⁴.; HN.MICH.
   Reprinted in 21610.

21606 — [Anr. ed.] 8°. [*R. Bradock*] *f. J. Helme a. J. Busby, junior*, 1608. L.; NLM.

21607 — [Anr. ed.] 8°. [*S. Stafford*] *f. J. Helme*, 1609. L.O⁶.; HD.WIS.

21608 — [Anr. ed.] Whereunto is adjoyned precepts for the preservation of health. Written by H. Ronsovius. (Now published. By S. H[obbs?]) 8°. *W. Stansby f. the widdow Helme*, 1617. L.; F.NLM.

21609 — [Anr. ed.] 8°. *A. M[athewes] f. T. Dewe*, 1624. L.L¹⁶.O. G².; HN.NLM.Y. Duke U.
   This is the 1st ed. to name Sir John Harington as the translator.

21610 — Conservandæ bonæ valetudinis præcepta. The Salerne schoole. [In verse.] *Eng. a. Lat.* 8°. *Edinburgh, A. Hart*, 1613. E(imp.).E².E⁵.ST.; HN.
   An anonymous reprint of Harington's trans. (21605), w. the addition of the Latin verses.

21611 **Salesbury, Henry.** Grammatica Britannica in vsum eius linguæ conscripta. 8° in 4's. [*Eliot's Court Press f.*] *T. Salesburius*, 1593. L².L¹³.C³.C¹⁰.NLW.; HD.

21612 **Salesbury, William.** Ban wedy i dynny air yngair allā o hen gyfreith Howel da. A certaine case extracte out of the auncient law of Hoel da, kyng of Wales whereby it maye gathered [*sic*] that priestes had lawfully maried wyues at that tyme. *Welsh a. Eng.* [Anon.] 4°. [*R. Grafton f.*] (*R. Crowley*, 1550.) L(C.40.b.58).C⁷(MS.454).NLW.

21613 — The baterie of the popes botereulx, commonlye called the high altare. 8°. [*R. Grafton f.*] (*R. Crowley*, 1550.) L.L².NLW.; F.

21614 — A briefe and a playne introduction, teachyng how to pronounce the letters in the British tong. 4°. [*R. Grafton f.*] *R. Crowley*, 1550. NLW.

21615 — [Anr. ed.] A playne and a familiar introductiō, teaching how to pronounce Welshe. Perused and augmēted. 4°. *H. Denham f. H. Toy*, 1567 (17 my.) Ent. 1566–67. L(2).NLW(2).; F.HN.HD(lacks tp).

Salesbury, William—*cont.*

21616 — A dictionary in Englyshe and Welshe. 4°. [*N. Hill f.*] (*J. Waley*, 1547.) L.O.D.E.NLW.+; F.HN.HD(tp def.). ILL.N.

21617 — Kynniver llith a ban. 1551. = 2983.
   — *ed.* See 12404 sq.
   — *tr.* See 2960, 16435, 20398.7.

21618 **Salignacus, Bernardus.** The principles of arithmeticke, . . . Englished by W. Bedwell. 8°. *R. Field*, 1616. Ent. 15 mr. L.O.
   — *ed.* See 15254.

Salisbury, Wiltshire, *Hospital of Trinity and St. Thomas.* See Indulgences 69.

21619 **Salisbury, John.** Siarles Arglwydd Howard. [Brief authorizing collections in behalf of Sion Salisburi. 1591.] = 13856.

21619.5 **Salisbury, Sir Thomas, Bart.** The life of Joseph. [In verse.] 4°. *T. Harper*, 1636. Ent. to R. Hodgkinson 21 no. 1635. Sparrow.

21620 — [Anr. issue, w. cancel tp, w. title:] The history of Joseph: a poem. *T. Harper f. R. Ball*, 1636. L.O.C. DUL.WI.+; F.HN.HD.NY.

Salisbury, Thomas, Printer, ed. See 2744.

21621 **Salkeld, John.** A treatise of angels. Of the nature, essence, and all other proprieties of angels. By J. Salkeld, lately fellow of the jesuites colledges in Conimbra, [etc.] 8°. *T. S[nodham] with authoritie of superiours, f. N. Butter*, 1613. Ent. 23 oc. 1612. L.O.C(imp.).E. LEEDS.+; F.HN.CHI.HD.NY.+

21622 — A treatise of paradise. And the principall contents thereof. 8°. *E. Griffin f. N. Butter*, 1617. Ent. 8 mr. L.O.C.LEEDS.M.+; F.HN.HD.N.NY.+

Salusbury, Sir Thomas. See 21619.5 sq.

21622.2 **Sallustius Crispus, Caius.** C. Crispi Sallustii de L. Sergii Catilinæ coniuratione, ac bellum [*sic*] Jugurthino historia. Cum alijs quibusdam. 8°. *ex off. T. Marshi*, 1569. F.
   The Latin eds. differ slightly in contents and arrangement.

21622.4 — C. Salustii Crispi coniuratio Catilinae, et bellum Jugurthinum. Eiusdem alia. 8°. *ap. H. Middletonum*, 1573. L.C.; F.ILL.
   Page 3, line 1 ends: 'Amiter-'.

21622.6 — [Anr. ed.] 8°. *ap. H. Middletonum*, 1573. O.C.DUL.; BO.
   Page 3, line 1 ends: 'Ami-'. Quires Q–Aa from same setting as 21622.4.

21622.8 — C. Sallusti Crispi opera omnia quae exstant: cum P. Ciacconii Toletani notis, denuo excusa. 8°. (*typis J. Harisoni* [3,]) *ap. R. Dexter*, 1601. Ent. to J. Harrison, sen., 21 my. 1595. L(tp only, Ames II.36).C².; F.

21623 — [Anr. ed.] 8°. [*H. Lownes*] *ex off. Stat.*, 1615. Ent. to the English Stock 5 mr. 1620. L(tp only, Harl. 5937/289).C.C⁵.; F.

21623.5 — C. Sallustius Crispus cum veterum historicorum fragmentis. 12°. *Oxoniae, G. Turner*, 1639. C⁵(2).D.DUL.

21624 — [A trans.] The workes of Caius Crispus Salustius. [*Tr.*] (W. Crosse.) 12°. [*Eliz. Allde,*] *sould by T. Walkley*, (1629.) L.O.C.BTU.DUR⁵.+; F.HN.HD.N.Y.+
   Engr. tp dated 1629 at bottom.

21625 — [Anr. trans.] The two most worthy and notable histories the Conspiracie of Cateline, and the Warre which Jugurth maintained. [*Tr.*] (T. Heywood.) fol. [*W. Jaggard*] *f. J. Jaggard*, 1608 (1609.) Ent. to W. Jaggard 15 fb. 1608. L.O.C.DUL.E.+; F.HN.HD.N. NY.+

21626 — [Anr. trans.] Here begynneth the famous cronycle of the warre, which the romayns had agaynst Iugurth. Tr. syr A. Barclay. *Lat. a. Eng.* fol. (*R. Pynson*,) [1520?] L.O.C(imp.).C⁷.M.+; CH.ILL.PFOR. Mellon. Colophon on Q5ʳ.

21627 — [Anr. ed.] fol. (*R. Pynson*,) [1525?] L(2 imp.).C(2, 1 imp.).M.; HN.CAL.PFOR.Y.
   Colophon on P4ᵛ.
   — [Anr. ed.] 1557. See pt. 2 of 10752.

21628 **Salo, Alessio Segala de.** An admirable method to love, serve and honour the B. virgin Mary. Englished by R. F. 12°. [*Rouen,*] *J. Cousturier*, 1639. C³.
   A&R 746.

Salo, Alessio Segala de—*cont.*

21628a — [A variant, without printer's name.] 1639. L(2, 1 imp.). c³.CHEL(lacks tp)*.HP(lacks tp)*.w.
A&R 747.

21629 **Salomon**, *the Jew and Physician*. A wounderfull prophecie or pronosticatiõ begynnynge from the yere M.D.XXXI. to the lawde of Charles the fyfthe. 8°. [*Antwerp, widow of C. Ruremond*, 1543.] c.
End of text dated May 1543.

21630 **Salter, Robert.** Wonderfull prophecies from the beginning of the monarchy of this land. Together with an essay touching the late prodigious comete. [On the Book of Daniel.] 4°. *W. Jones*, 1626. o.

21631 — [A variant, w. imprint:] *W. Jones*, 1627. L.O.C.LEIC. SHEF.+; HD.U.

21631.5 — [Anr. issue, w. first sheet reprinted.] Vindiciæ Danielis, strange prophecies from the monachie [*sic*] of this land. Or an essay of the comet. [Init. R. S.] [*Oxford, W. Turner*,] 1629. L.O.O³.CASHEL.E⁴.+; F.
(Formerly 21517)

21632 **Salter, Thomas.** A contention betweene three bretheren. 1581. Now = 1968.5.

21633 — [Anr. ed.] 1608. Now = 1968.7.

21634 — A mirrhor mete for all mothers, matrones, and maidens, intituled the mirrhor of modestie. 8°. [*J. Kingston*] *f. E. White*, [1579.] Ent. 7 ap. 1579. L.O.

21635 **Saltern, George.** Of the antient lawes of great Britaine. 4°. [*E. Allde*] *f. J. Jaggard*, 1605. Ent. to J. Jaggard a. J. Smethwick 20 my. L.O.C.D.E.+; F.HN.CU.HD. ILL.+

21636 **Saltern, Thomas.** Dorcas: a true patterne of a goodly life. 4°. *M. F[lesher] f. R. Jackson*, 1625. Ent. 4 de. 1623. O.O⁶.C².; Y.
o, y copies have date altered in ink to 1631; *see also* 19346.

21636.5 **Saltmakers**, *Society of*. A true remonstrance of the state of the salt businesse, undertaken by the societie of saltmakers. (At the court at Oatelands, 29 July 1638. A draught of the contract about salt, on the behalf of N. Murford, [etc.]) [An address to both houses of parliament, urging restrictions against imported salt.] fol(2). [*London*, 1640?] L(2nd sheet only). L⁵(Lemon 310, imp.).E.; HD(1st sheet only).
(2nd sheet formerly 18291)

21637 **Saltmarsh, John.** Holy discoveries and flames. 12°. *R. Y[oung] f. P. Nevill*, 1640. Ent. 6 my. L.O.C(letterpress tp def.).E.YK.+; F.HN.CH.N.U.+

21638 — Poemata sacra, Latinè & Anglicè scripta. (Poems upon some of the holy raptures of David.—The picture of God in man.) 8°. *Cantabrigiæ*, [*T. Buck a. R. Daniel*] *ex acad. typog.*, 1636. L.O²¹.C.C³.G².+; F.HN. CH.CU.ILL.+

21639 — The practice of policie in a christian life. 12°. *E. G[riffin] f. S. Endarby*, 1639. Ent. 26 jn. L.O.C³.C¹⁰. E.+; F.HN.CHI.PN².U.+

21640 **Saltonstall, Charles.** The navigator. Shewing and explaining all the chiefe principles of navigation. 4°. [*B. Alsop a. T. Fawcet*] *f. G. Herlock*, 1636. L(lacks engr. tp).C²².PARIS. London, Royal Institution of Naval Architects.; HN(lacks portrait).CB.LC(lacks engr. tp).Y(lacks letterpress tp).

21641 **Saltonstall, Wye.** Clavis ad portam, or a key fitted to open the gate of tongues. Wherein you may readily finde the Latine and French for any English word necessary for all young schollers. 8°. *Oxford, W. Turner*, 1634. Ass'd by Turner to M. Sparke 17 mr. 1635. L.O(2).C.; CU.ILL.
Issued as an appendix to 15079 and often found bd. together.

21641a — [Anr. ed.] [1639.] = pt. of 15081.

21642 — The country mouse, and the city mouse. Or a merry morrall fable. Enlarged out of Horace. Second edition. [Anon. In verse.] 8°. *T. Cotes f. M. Sparke junior*, 1637. Ent. 31 mr. 1636. O.

21643 — A description of time: applied to this present time. [Anon.] 8°. *J. O[kes] f. F. Grove*, 1638. Ent. as by W. Saltonstall 16 ja. L.

Saltonstall, Wye—*cont.*

21643.5 — The complaint of Time against the tumultuous and rebellious Scots. [Init. W. S. In verse.] 4°. B. A[lsop] a. T. F[awcet] f. R. Harper, 1639. Ent. 29 my. L.E.; F.
(Formerly 21525)

21644 — [Anr. ed., w. added prelims.] Englands complaint: against her adjoyning neighbours the Scots. By W. Sal. 8°. [*T. Harper*] *f. R. Harper*, 1640. Ent. 15 au. O⁶.; HN.

21645 — Picturæ loquentes. Or pictures drawne forth in characters. With a poeme of a maid. 12°. *T. Cotes, sold by T. Slater*, 1631. Ent. to T. a. R. Cotes 20 ap. L.O.; F.Y.

21646 — Second edition enlarged. 12°. *T. Cotes, sold by W. Hope*, 1635. L.O.C.; HN.

— *tr. See* 10576, 17824, 18938, 18945, 18979.

21647 **Saltwood, Robert.** A comparyson bytwene .iiij. byrdes, the larke, the nyghtyngale, yᵉ thrusshe & the cucko. [In verse.] 4°. [*London*,] (*J. Mychel*,) [1548?] HN.
Printed in the same types as 3186.

Saluce. A declaration of the afflictions. 1620. *See* 21673.5.

21648 **Salus.** Salutis cuique suae certa sunt inditia. 1586. Now = 4474.108.

21649 **Saluste du Bartas, Guillaume de.** [Letterpress tp:] Bartas his devine weekes and workes translated: . . . by J. Sylvester. [In verse.] 4° in 8's. *H. Lownes*, 1605. Ent. to Lownes 22 no. 1604; Quadrains ent. to E. Blount 22 ja. 1605. HN(B1 is a type facs. of 21650). ILL.
(7290 is pt. of this) Large paper copies of this and the following issues have B1ʳ w. royal arms within double rules (1 L, 1 ILL); regular paper copies have B1ʳ w. royal arms within single rules (O²) or without royal arms (C², HD).

21649a — [Anr. issue, w. cancel engr. tp, without imprint.] Bartas his devine weeks & workes. [T2ʳ:] (*H. Lownes*, 1605.) L.L³⁸(imp.)*.O.O².D(lacks tp)*.+; F. HD.ILL.N.U.+

21649a.5 — [Anr. issue, w. added quires Kk*–Ggg*:] (I Posthumus Bartas. The third day of his second weeke.) [*H. Lownes*,] (1606.) Added portion ent. to E. Blount 13 no. 1605. L.O.C.BIRM².E².+; F.HN.HD(imp.).PML. WIS.+
(Added portion formerly 21664)

21650 — [Anr. ed., including:] (The historie of Judith. Englished by T. Hudson.) 4° in 8's. *H. Lownes*, (1608.) Judith ent. 18 ja. L.O.O².C.SHEF.+; F.HN.CHI.CU. HD(imp.).+
See also 21665. This ed. omits some of the Fragments. Engr. tp usually w. printer's name as above and Anagrammata Regia on the verso. Some copies (1 C, F) have an earlier state without printer's name, w. the verso blank, and w. the anagram on A1ᵛ.

21651 — Now thirdly corrected & augm. 4°. *H. Lownes*, (*sould by A. Johnson*, 1611.) L.O.C.A.NEK.+; F.HN.CHI.HD. NY.+
With both Judith and the Fragments.

21652 — Now fourthly corr: & augm. 4°. *H. Lownes*, (1613.) Blount's rights ass'd to Lownes 11 ap. 1614. L.O. C.D.E².+; F.HN.HD.N.NY.+
(7291 is pt. of this)

21653 — [Anr. ed., enlarged.] With a compleate collectiõ of all the other workes *tr.* and written by J. Sylvester. fol. *H. Lownes*, (1620, 1621.) L.O.C.E.M.+; F.HN.CHI.HD. NY.+
Sylvester's works previously pub'd in 23575 sq. At least HN, HD have folding sheet near Mmmmm1 w. poem 'The Mysterie of Mysteries'; L has it separate: 1875.d.8(62); in this setting the middle column line 1 of verse has 'coeternal' while the leaf usually bd. after Hhh1 of 21654 has 'co-eternall'.

21654 — [Anr. ed., enlarged.] fol. *R. Young*, 1633 (1632.) Ent. to H. Lownes a. R. Young 30 my. 1627; to G. Cole a. G. Latham 6 no. 1628; to R. Young 6 de. 1630. L.O.C.E(lacks tp).SHEF.+; F.HN.HD.N.NY.+

21655 — Foure bookes of Du Bartas. 1637. Now = 21663a.5.

21656 — Guilielmi Salustii Bartassii Hebdomas a G. Lermæo latinitate donata. [In verse.] 12°. [*J. Windet?*] *ap. R. Dexter*, 1591. Ent. 6 fb. L.O.C².E.M.+; F.HN.HD.

Saluste du Bartas, Guillaume de—*cont.*

21657 — Hadriani Dammanis a Bysterveldt DN. de Fair-hill, Bartasias; qui de mundi creatione libri septem; liberius tralati et acuti [*sic*]. [In verse.] 8°. *Edinburgi, R. Walde-grave*, 1600. L.O.C³.E.YK.+; F.HN(tp def.). ILL.

21658 — The first day of the worldes creation. [*Tr.* In verse.] 4°. *J. Jackson f. G. Seaton*, 1595. Ent. 14 au. 1591. O.; HN.CAL.

21658.5 — [A variant, w. imprint:] *J. Jackson f. G. Seaton*, 1596. L.

21659 — The second day of the first weeke. Done out of French into English heroicall verse by T. Winter. 4°. [*R. Field*] *f. J. Shaw*, 1603. Ent. 18 no. 1602. HN.PH² (imp.).

21660 — The third dayes creation. Done verse for verse out of the French by T. Winter. 4°. [*R. Field*] *f. T. Clerke*, 1604. Ent. 13 se. L.

21661 — The second weeke or childhood of the world, *tr.* J. Syluester. [In verse.] 8°. *P. S[hort,]* 1598. Ent. 21 ap. HN.

21661.5 — [Anr. issue, w. inserted quires E–K:] (A sequele of the second weeke. (The furies.—The handy-crafts.—The arke.) *P. Short f. W. Wood*, 1598.) F. L (Harl.5927/179) has a variant sub tp to 'The handy-crafts' w. imprint: *P. Short f. W. Wood*, 1599.

21662 — Babilon, a part of the seconde weeke. With the commentarie, of S. G[oulart de] S[enlis]. Englished by W. L'isle. [In verse.] 4°. *E. Bollifant f. R. Watkins*, 1595. HN.

21662a — [A variant, w. imprint:] *E. Bollifant f. R. Watkins*, 1596. L.O.D.; F.HN.Y.

21663 — Part of Du Bartas, [la seconde semaine; jour 2] English and French, and in his owne kinde of verse, so neare as may teach an English-man French. With the commentary of S. G[oulart de] S[enlis.] By W. L'isle. 4°. *J. Haviland*, 1625. L.O.C.C².CANT.+; F.HN.ILL.Y. Wake Forest C, Wake Forest, N.C.+

21663a — = 21663.

21663a.5 — [Anr. issue, w. first quire reprinted.] Foure bookes of Du Bartas. *T. Paine f. F. Egelsfielde*, 1637. L(tp only, Harl.5967/159).O.C⁴.STD.; F(date cropt).HN. HD.V. (Formerly 21655)

21664 — I Posthumus Bartas. 1606. = pt. of 21649a.5.

21665 — II. Posthumus Bartas. The fore-noone of the fourth day of his second week. *Tr.* J. Sylvester. [In verse.] 4° in 8's. *H. Lownes*, 1607. Ent. to E. Blount 16 de. 1606. L.O.; F.HN.CH.WEL. A separate issue of quires Aaa–Eee of 21650, w. special added tpp and dedics. Sometimes bd. w. 21650 (WEL) or 21649a.5 (O, CH).

21666 — A learned summary [by S. Goulart] upon the famous poeme of W. of Saluste. *Tr.* out of French, by T. L[odge], D.M.P. fol. [*G. Purslowe,*] *f. J. Grismand*, [1621.] Ent. as tr. by Dr. Lodge 8 no. 1620. L.O.G². STU.WN.+; F.HN.HD.N.Y.+ Engr. tp dated 1621 at bottom.

21666.5 — [Anr. issue, w. cancel letterpress tp, w. imprint:] *f. R. M[ilborne?]* 1636. c(lacks tp)*.C⁵(lacks tp)*.; CAL².

21667 — [Anr. issue, w. cancel letterpress tp, w. imprint:] [*A. Mathewes*] *f. A. Crooke*, 1637. L²¹*.L⁴³.C.M⁴.; F.LC.Y.

21667.5 — [Anr. issue, w. cancel letterpress tp, w. imprint:] [*A. Mathewes*] *f. A. C[rooke] and part of the impression to be vented for the benefit of E. Minshew, the sonne of J. Minshew deceased*, 1637. L.; F.HD(imp.).ILL.

21668 — [Anr. issue, w. cancel letterpress tp, w. imprint:] [*R. Young*] *f. P. Nevill*, 1638. O².DUR(Bamb.).M².; HN.BALT.ILL.

21669 — A canticle of the victorie obtained by the French king, Henrie the fourth. *Tr.* J. Siluester. [In verse.] 4°. *R. Yardley*, 1590. Ent. to J. Wolfe 15 ap. and 19 my. L(lacks tp).O⁵(frag.).; F.HN.Y. Also issued as pt. 2 of 21672.

21670 — The colonies of Bartas. With the commentarie of S. G[oulart de] S[enlis,] enlarged by the translatour [W. Lisle. In verse.] 4°. *R. F[ield]* *f. T. Man*, 1598. Ent. 13 de. 1597. HN.

— The furies. 1591. *See* 14379.

21671 — The historie of Judith in forme of a poem. Englished by T. Hudson. 8°. *Edinburgh, T. Vautroullier*, 1584. Ent. to H. Lownes 18 ja. 1608. L.L¹³.O⁵(imp.). E(lacks tp).PARIS².+; HN.

— The miracle of the peace. Celebrated by the ghost of Du Bartas. 1599. *See* 7353.5.

Saluste du Bartas, Guillaume de—*cont.*

21672 — The triumph of faith. The sacrifice of Isaac. The shipwracke of Jonas. With a song of the victorie at Yury. *Tr.* J. Siluester. [In verse.] 2 pts. 4°. *R. Yardley a. P. Short*, 1592. L.O.O¹⁰(frag.).C¹⁰.; HN.N. All copies but o and c¹⁰ lack pt. 2, the reissue of 21669 called for.

21673 — L'Uranie ou muse celeste. Urania Roberti Ashelei de Gallica delibata. [In verse.] *Fr. a. Lat.* 4°. *J. Wolfius*, 1589. Ent. 10 my. L.L¹³.O.C².LK.; F(lacks D4).

— *tr. See* 14379.

— *See also* 19540, 23579, 23581, 23582.

21673.5 **Saluzzo.** A declaration of the afflictions and persecutions of the protestants in the marquisate of Saluce. Also other letters sent to the king, from the reformed churches in France. With an edict made by the French king, the ninth of November last past: wherein the prince of Conde is declared innocent. *Tr.* out of French. 4°. [*Eliot's Court Press*] *f. R. Rounthwaite*, 1620. Ent. 22 ja. L.

21674 **Salvianus.** Sancti Salviani . . . De gubernatione Dei, libri VIII. Eiusdem epistolarum lib. I. Timothei nomine ad ecclesiam catholic. lib. IV. (Annotationes . . . autore J. A. Brassicano.) 12°. *Oxoniæ, G. Turner, imp. H. Curteyn*, 1629. L.O.C.E.M².+; F.HN.BO⁵.HD(2). Y.

21675 — [Anr. ed.] 12°. *Oxoniæ, J. Lichfield, imp. H. Curteyn*, 1633. L.O.C.A.D.+; HN.U.

21676 — Quis dives salvus. How a rich man may be saved. *Tr.* into English by N. T. [i.e. J. Cresswell.] 8°. [*St. Omer, English College Press,*] 1618. L.O.C.ST.W.+; F.HN.U. A&R 748.

21677 — A second and third blast of retrait from plaies and theaters. Set forth by Anglo-phile Eutheo. 8°. (*H. Denham, the assigne of W. Seres,*) 1580. Ent. 18 oc. L.L²(lacks col.).O.C.P.+; F.HN. The 1st blast was 12097. The 2nd is trans. from bk. 6 of an ed. of 21674; the 3rd is by a former playwright, sometimes identified as A. Munday.

Sampson. A most excellent and famous ditty. [c. 1625, etc.] *See* 21688.5 sq.

Sampson, John. *See* Awdely, J.

21678 **Sampson, Richard,** *Bp.* Richardi Sampsonis . . . in D. Pauli epistolam ad Romanos, atq; in priorem ad Corinthios breuissima explanatio. 8°. (*in æd. J. Herfordiæ,*) 1546 (5 oc.) C(2).C⁵.D.; BO⁵.

21679 — Richardi Sampsonis episcopi Cicestr. in priores quinquaginta psalmos Dauiticos, familiaris explanatio, iam primū ædita. fol. *in æd. T. Bertheleti*, (1539.) L².L¹⁵.O.C.C⁵.+; ILL.

21680 — Richardi Sampsonis . . . explanationis psalmorum, secunda pars. fol. (*in æd. J. Herfordi*, 1548.) L(tp only, Harl.5963/388).L¹³.O(imp.).C(2).; HD(imp.).

21681 — Richardi Sampsonis, regii sacelli decani oratio, qua docet, anglos, regiæ dignitati ut obediant, [etc.] 4°. *in aed. T. Bertheleti*, [1535?] O(2).O⁸.; F.

21682 **Sampson, Thomas,** *Dean of Christ Church.* A briefe collection of the church, and of certayne ceremonies thereof. 8°. *H. Middleton f. G. Bishop*, 1581. Ent. 17 my. L².L³.O.D.P.

— A discourse touching the pretended match. [Sometimes attrib. to T. Sampson. 1569–70, etc.] *See* 13869 sqq.

21683 — A letter to the trew professors of Christes gospell, inhabiting in the parishe off Allhallowis, in Bredstrete in London. 8°. *Strasburgh in Elsas, at the signe of the goldē Bibell* [i.e. *Wesel? J. Lambrecht?*] 1554 (au.) L.L².O.C.; F(2).HN. At least c copy has the misprint 'Brebstrete' in the title.

21684 — Prayers and meditations apostolike. That is, prayers and meditations gathered and framed out of the epistles of the apostles. 16° in 8's. *Cambridge, J. Legate*, 1593. L¹⁵(frag.).O⁴³(pp. 161–92 only).C(pts. of quires X and Y).C⁵(pts. of 1st sheet and quires A, N, O, Aa, Bb, Cc). Southwell Minster (1st sheet, w. tp).+

21685 — A warning to take heede of Fowlers psalter [14563.3]. 8°. *T. Vautrollier f. G. Bishoppe*, 1578. Ent. 10 de. 1577. L.C(lacks tp).D.; F.

— *ed. See* 3499.5.

— *tr. See* 14638.

21686 **Sampson, Thomas**, *Poet*. Fortunes fashion, pourtrayed in the troubles of the ladie Elizabeth Gray, wife to Edward the fourth. [In verse.] 4°. [*R. Field*] *f. W. Jones*, 1613. Ent. 13 jy. L.O.O⁸.

21687 **Sampson, William.** Virtus post funera vivit or, honour tryumphing over death. Being true epitomes of honorable, personages. [In verse.] 4°. *J. Norton*, 1636. Ent. to G. Blackwall 26 ap. L.

21688 — The vow breaker. Or, the faire maide of Clifton. 4°. *J. Norton, sold by R. Ball*, 1636. L.L⁶.O.E.ETON(lacks A2).+; F.HN.HD.N.Y.+ Greg 510.
— *See also* 17401.

21688.5 **Samson.** A most excellent and famous ditty of Sampson judge of Israell. *Ballad.* 1/2 sh.fol. [*London*, c. 1625.] ? Ent. to T. Colwell 1563–64; to H. Carre 15 au. 1586. C⁶(impr. cropt?).
Line 2 of heading ends 'and'.

21689 — [Anr. ed.] 1/2 sh.fol. *assignes of T. Symcocke*, [1628–29.] L.
Line 2 of heading ends: 'propoun-'.

Samuel, John. The most strange discouerie of the three witches of Warboys. [J. Samuel, etc.] 1593. *See* 25018.5.

21690 **Samuel, William.** An abridgemēt of all the canonical books of the olde Testament, written in Sternholds meter. 8°. *W. Seres*, 1569. L.O(frag.).; HN.
(Formerly also 3044)

21690.2 — The abridgemente of goddes statutes [the Pentateuch] in myter. 8°. *R. Crowley* [really *R. Grafton*] *f. R. Soughton* [sic], 1551. HN.
Reprinted w. alterations in 21690.
— [Headline:] The arte of angling. 1577. *See* 793.7.

21690.4 — [Heading 1ʳ:] The loue of God. Here is declared, if you wyl rede that god doth loue this lād in dede by felynge his rod. [In verse.] 8° in 4. [*London*, 1559?] HN.
Alludes to the accession of Elizabeth.

21690.6 — [Heading A1ʳ:] The practice practiced by the pope and his prelates. which they haue vsed synce they came to their estates. [In verse.] 4°. (*H. Powell, solde by H. Syngleton,*) [1550?] L.

21690.8 — [Heading 1ʳ:] A warnyng for the cittie of London. That the dwellers, there in may repent their euyll lyues for feare of Goddes plages. [In verse.] 4°. (*H. Powell, soulde by H. syngelton,*) [1550?] L.; HD(frag.).

Sancer, James, *pseud, tr. See* 16641.5.

San., James, *tr.* The mirrour of madnes. 1576. *See* 17980.

Sandæus, Patricius. Memoriæ sacrum Jacobi sexti-primi. [1625.] *See* 21712.5.

Sanders, George. *See* Saunders, G.

Sanders, Nicholas. Antisanderus. 1593. *See* 5898.

21691 — A briefe treatise of vsurie. 8°. *Louanii, ap. J. Foulerum*, 1568. L(imp.).L².O.O³.C.+; CU.HD.
A&R 749.
— De visibili Rom'anarchia contra N. Sanderi Monarchiam. 1573. *See* 99.
— Fidelis serui, vnà cum errorum examine in septimo libro de visibili ecclesiæ monarchia a N. Sandero conscripta. 1573. *See* 5407.

21692 — The rocke of the churche wherein the primacy of S. Peter and of his successours is proued. 8°. *Louanii, ap. J. Foulerum*, 1567. L.O.E.OS.USHAW.+; F.TEX.
A&R 750. Answered by 11449.

21693 — [Anr. ed.] 8°. *S. Omers*, [*C. Boscard*,] *f. J. Heigham*, 1624. L.C.DE.OS.USHAW.+; N.TEX.
A&R 751.

21694 — The supper of our Lord set foorth in six bookes. (The seuenth booke.) 4°. *Louanii*, [*J. Fowler,*] 1565. L. C⁹(imp.).
A&R 752. Answers 14590, 14606, 18740; answered by 18739.

21695 — [Anr. issue, w. cancel tp and A4, and w. colophon and errata added.] *Louanii*, (*ap. J. Foulerum,*) 1566 (ja.) L.O.C.D.DUR⁵.+; F.HN.HD.N(imp.).NY.+
A&R 753.

Sanders, Nicholas—*cont.*

21696 — A treatise of the images of Christ, and of his saints: and that it is vnlaufull to breake them, and lauful to honour them. With a confutation of [14606]. 8°. *Louanii, ap. J. Foulerum*, 1567. L².O.C⁸.E.P.+; HD.
A&R 754. Answered by 11433. With 'The Preface conteining a Brief Declaration, which is the true Churche of Christ.'

21697 — [Anr. ed.] 8°. *S. Omers*, [*C. Boscard*] *f. J. Heigham*, 1624. L.L²⁶.L³⁵.OS.YK.
A&R 755. Omits preface.

21697.5 — [Anr. issue, w. tp cancelled and w. preface reprinted, w. imprint:] *S. Omers, f. J. Heigham*, 1625. L.A².
AUG(both tpp, imp.).DE.USHAW.
A&R 756.
— *See also* 25357.

21698 **Sanderson, John.** Institutionum dialecticarum libri quatuor. Editio tertia. 8°. *Oxoniæ, Jos. Barnesius*, 1602. Ent. to J. Jackson, A. Hatfield, a. E. Bollifant 2 jn. 1590; to John Barnes 7 jn. 1602. O.C(2).C⁵.LK.; TORONTO².

21699 — = 21698.
21700 — Editio quarta. 8°. *Oxoniæ, Jos. Barnesius*, 1609. O.

21701 **Sanderson, Robert**, *Bp.* Logicæ artis compendium. In quo universæ artis synopsis, breviter proponitur. [Anon.] 8°. *Oxoniæ, Jos. Barnesius*, 1615. O².

21702 — Secunda hac editione recognitum, duplici appendice auctum, à R. Sanderson. 8°. *Oxoniæ, J. Lichfield & J. Short*, 1618. L.O.C.BIRM²(K.N.).DUL.+; F.HN.HD. ILL.PH.+
11031 often bd. w. this.

21703 — Tertia hac editione recognitum. 8°. *Oxoniæ, J. Lichfield, imp. G. Davis*, 1631. L.O³.C².D.DUR⁵.+; HN.BO⁵.

21704 — Editio quarta. 8°. *Oxoniæ, L. Lichfield, imp. G. Davis*, 1640. L³.O.C³.CARLISLE.LINC.+; F.CHI.ILL.N.
— A soueraigne antidote against Sabbatarian errours. [Sometimes attrib. to R. Sanderson.] 1636. *See* 679.

21705 — Ten sermons preached I. Ad clerum .3. II. Ad magistratum .3. III. Ad populum .4. 4° in 8's. (*R. Y[oung]*) *f. R. Dawlman*, 1627. Ent. 5 mr. L.O⁴.C³.LINC.NLW. +; F.HN.COR.
See 21708.5.

21706 — [Anr. ed., enlarged.] Twelve sermons. 4°. *A. Math[ewes] f. R. Dawlman, sold by R. Allet*, 1632. L.O.C.DUR⁵.E².+; F.CAL². HD.N.U.+

21707 — [Anr. ed., enlarged.] Twelve sermons, . . . Whereunto are added two sermons more. The third edition. 4° in 8's. *R. B[adger] f. R. Dawlman* (*a. L. Fawne,*) 1637 (1636.) R. Allot's share ass'd to J. Legat a. A. Crooke 1 jy. 1637. L.O.C⁵.D.G².+; F.HN.CHI.HD.U.+
The extra sermons reprint 21710. The sub tp on I5ʳ has 'Faulne' and is dated 1636. Some copies (L, L¹⁵, HD) have the cancel tp to 21710.3 inserted before Pp1; DUR³ has a variant of this last tp dated 1637.

21708 — Two sermons: [on Rom. xiv.3 and Rom. iii.8.] 4°. *G. P[urslowe] f. J. Budge*, 1622. L.O.O⁵.C².; F.

21708.5 — Two sermons [on 1 Tim. iv.4 and Gen. xx.6] preached at Paules-Crosse London. Being the fifth and sixth ad populum. 4°. *B. A[lsop] a. T. F[awcet] f. R. Dolman* [sic], 1628. O.; Y.
Intended to supplement 21705, though the variant most often found w. 21705 is 21709. Both variants have B1 cancelled, w. the cancellans pr. on A4.

21709 — [A variant.] Two sermons preached . . . London. The one November 21. the other Aprill 15. 1627. *B. A[lsop] a. T. F[awcet] f. R. Dawlman*, 1628. L¹⁵.O. O⁴.C³.OS.+; F.COR.
The L¹⁵, F copies have imprint identical with the O 'Dawlman' setting, but the title is altered: '. . . London. The one Nonemb. [sic] 21. the other Aprill, 15. 1627. Being the Fifth and Sixth ad Populum.'

21710 — Two sermons: [on 1 Pet. ii.16 and Rom. xiv.23.] 4°. *M. F[lesher] f. R. Dawlman a. L. Fawne*, 1635. Ent. 9 my. L.O.C.D².E.+; F.HN.HD.U.Y.+
Tp varies; line 8: 'May 6.' or '6. May 1632.'; both at O.

21710.3 — [Anr. issue, w. cancel tp:] *R. B[adger] f. R. Dawlman a. L. Fawne*, 1636. C⁸.
The tp also issued w. some copies of 21707.
— *See also* Bookplates.

21710.7 **Sanderson, Thomas.** A briefe summe of christian religion. Collected for a preparation to the Lords supper.
4°. E. P[urslowe] f. F. Coules, 1640. U.

21711 — Of Romanizing recusants, and dissembling catholicks
... Or an answere to the posthume pamphlet of R.
Buckland [4007]. 4°. T. Purfoot, 1611. Ent. 27 au.
O.O²⁷.C.D(imp.).DUR³.

21712 **Sands, George.** The life and death of M. Geo: Sands,
who was executed the 6 of September, 1626. Ballad.
2 pts. s.sh.fol. f. F. Couls, [1626.] C⁶.

21712.5 **Sands, Patrick.** [Heading A1ʳ:] Memoriæ sacrum
sacratissimi monarchæ Jacobi sexti-primi. [In
verse.] 4°. [B. Norton a. J. Bill, 1625.] E².

21713 **Sandys, Edwin,** *Abp.* Sermons made by the most reue-
rende Edwin, archbishop of Yorke. 4° in 8's. H.
Midleton f. T. Charde, 1585. L.O.C.D(imp.).DUR⁵.
+; F.HN.BO⁵.ILL.U.+

21714 — [Anr. ed.] 4° in 8's. J. Beale f. T. Chard, 1616. L.O.C.D.
E⁴.+; F.HN.HD.ILL.U.+ 𝔄
— See also 10250, 10250.5, 10376.

21715 Now = 21717.5.

21716 **Sandys,** *Sir* **Edwin.** A relation of the state of religion:
and with what hopes and pollicies it hath beene
framed, and is maintained in the severall states of
these westerne parts of the world. [Anon.] 4°. [G. a.
L. Snowdon] f. S. Waterson, 1605. Ent. as by Sandys
21 jn. L.O.C⁴.D². Carlisle PL.+; F.MIN.
H3ʳ line 1 ends: 'factions &'; device on tp:
McK. 316. Publicly burned 2 Nov. 1605; see
Letters of John Chamberlain, ed. N. E. McClure,
I.214.

21717 — [Anr. ed.] 4°. V. Sims f. S. Waterson, 1605. L.O.C.
CASHEL.E².+; F.HN.COR.HD.Y.+
H3ʳ line 1 ends: 'practi-'.

21717.5 — [Anr. ed.] 4°. f. S. Waterson, 1605 [i.e. W. Stansby?
1622?] L.O.C.D.E.+; F.HN.HD.N.U.+
(Formerly 21715) H3ʳ line 1 ends: 'haue'. The tp
device (McK. 317) and the headpiece and factotum on A3ʳ are forgeries of those used in 21716;
the headpiece was used by Stansby in 1624 on
A4ʳ of 5396. The HD tp has MS. price and date:
'8ᵈ 1622'. The L, O, and BO² copies have differing
MS. corrections.

21718 — [Anr. ed., w. author named in preface.] Europæ speculum. Or, a view or survey of the state of religion in
the westerne parts of the world. Neuer before till
now published according to the authours originall
copie. 4°. Hagæ-Comitis [f. M. Sparke, London,]
1629. Ent. to M. Sparke 10 fb. 1630. L.O.C.D.E.+;
F.HN.HD.N.U.+
With note at end: 'From Paris. IX°. Aprill. 1599.
Copied out by the Authors originall, and finished,
2. Octob. An. M.DC.XVIII.' HD has a presentation copy inscribed by M. Sparke.

21719 — [Anr. ed.] Published according to the authours originall
copie, and acknowledged by him for a true copie. 4°.
T. Cotes f. M. Sparke, 1632. L.O.C.D.BRISTOL².+;
F.HN.HD.N.Y.+
With misprint at end: 'M.DC.XIII.'

21720 — [Anr. issue, w. variant tp and added pt. 2.] Whereunto
is added an Appendix of the Jesuits pilgrimage, by
L. O[wen.] 2 pts. T. Cotes f. M. Sparke, 1632. L.
O(imp.).C⁵.E.P.+; F.HN(lacks sub tp).NLA(lacks sub
tp).NY¹¹.WASH².
Pt. 2 is a reissue of 18997, q.v. for imprint; this
is the only ed. of Sandys w. which the Owen
text appears.

21721 — [Anr. ed.] 4°. T. Cotes f. M. Sparke, sold by G. Hutton,
1637. L.O.C.D.E.+; F.HN.HD.N.Y.+

21722 — [Anr. ed.] 12°. T. Cotes f. M. Sparke, 1638. L.O.C².D.
NOR.+; F.HN.BO.CHI.NY.+

21723 — Sacred hymns. Consisting of fifti select psalms of
David and others, paraphrastically turned into Eng-
lish verse. And by R. Tailour, set to be sung in five
parts. [Anon.] 4°. T. Snodham, by assign. of the Co.
of Statrs., 1615. Ent. to Snodham 29 (i.e. 19) jn. L.
O.CHICH.E.M³.+; F.HN.N.NY.Y.+
See Court Book C, p. 456.
— See also 13712, 13718.

21724 **Sandys, George.** A paraphrase upon the psalmes of
David. And upon the hymnes dispersed throughout
the Old and New Testaments. 8°. London, at the

Sandys, George—*cont.*
[shop of A. Hebb,] 1636. L.O.C.D.E.+; F.HN.CHI.HD.
NY.+
Tp varies: with (L, HD) or without (O, F) stop after
'David'. Regarding Sandys's patent to print this
for 14 years see Greg, Companion, pp. 321–2.

21725 — [Anr. ed., w. additions.] A paraphrase upon the divine
poems. (Job.—Psalmes. Set to new tunes. By
H. Lawes.—Ecclesiastes.—Lamentations.—A paraphrase upon the songs collected out of the Old and
New Testaments.) fol. (J. Legatt,) [sold] at the [shop
of A. Hebb,] 1638 (1637.) Ent. to A. Hebb 1 se.
1637. L.O.C.E.M².+; F.HN.HD.N.NY.+
Copies vary: with or without dedic. to King
Charles on verso of tp; both at F; one F copy of
the former has inserted dedic. to Queen Elizabeth
of Bohemia. Aaa1, half-title to Lamentations, is
cancelled in most copies; present in 1 O, 1 F, PML,
1 Y.

21726 — A relation of a journey begun An: Dom: 1610. Foure
bookes. Containing a description of the Turkish
empire, of Ægypt, [etc.] fol. [R. Field] f. W: Barrett,
1615. Ent. 3 jy. L.O.C.DUR(Bamb.).M⁴.+; F.HN.HD.
N.NY.+
Sheet C1,6 in 2 settings: C1ʳ catchword 'proclai-'
or 'pro-'; both at HD. Sheet D3,4 in 2 settings: w.
D3ᵛ line 1 beginning 'Turkish: built' or 'Turkish.
Built'; both at HD.

21727 — Second edition. fol. [R. Field] f. W. Barrett, 1621. L.
O.C.D.M.+; F.HN.HD.N.NY.+

21728 — Third edition. fol. [T. Cotes] f. R. Allot, 1627. Ass'd to
Mrs. Hodgets 19 de. 1625; to R. Allot 25 ja. 1626.
L.O.C.E².M.+; F.CAL.HD.ILL.NY.+

21729 — [Anr. ed.] Third edition. fol. [G. Miller] f. R. Allot,
1632. L.O.C.E.M.+; F.HN.CHI.HD.NY.+

21730 — Fourth edition. fol. [T. Cotes] f. A. Crooke, 1637. Ass'd
to J. Legat a. A. Crooke 1 jy. L³⁸.O.C.D⁶.E.+; F.HN.
HD.NW.PH.+
— tr. See 12397, 18963.3, 18964.
— See also 21492.

21731 **Sandys,** *Sir* **Miles.** Prima pars parvi opusculi, scripta
per M. Sandys, militem. The first part of a small
worke. 12°. [A. Mathewes] f. W. Sheares, 1634. Ent.
2 ja. 1635. L.C.LINC.USHAW.; F.LC.N.Y.
At least the L copy has F11–G6 cancelled and replaced by (G)–(I)¹²; and I10–K3 cancelled and
replaced by a single leaf; it also has an added leaf
of errata. C and F copies do not have the cancellations and additions.

21732 — [Anr. issue, w. cancel engr. tp.] Prudence the first of
the foure cardinall virtues. f. W: Sheares, (1634.) L.
O.C².DUR⁵(imp.). Carlisle PL.+; HN(both tpp).
FORDHAM.HD.ILL.PN².+
Copies checked (L, O, HN, HD) do not have the
cancellations and additions. The copy at Williams
College has both tpp.

Sanford, Hugh, *ed.* See 22540.

Sanford, James, *tr.* See 204, 3810, 10423, 12464, 17980,
20072.

21733 **Sanford, John.** Apollinis et musarum Εὐκτικὰ εἰδύλλια,
in Elizabethae auspicatissimum Oxoniam aduentum,
M.D.LXXXXII. [In verse.] 4°. Oxonii, J. Barnesius,
[1592.] L(2).; F.

21734 — Gods arrowe of the pestilence. [A sermon.] 8°. Oxford,
J. Barnes, sold by S. Waterson, [London,] 1604. L.
C.LK.; F(2, 1 lacks tp).

21735 — A grammer or introduction to the Italian tongue. 4°.
Oxford, J. Barnes, sold by S. Waterson, [London,]
1605. L(G2 in facs.).O(2, both lack folding Table).
O⁵.O¹².; F.HN.

21736 — Le guichet françois. Sive janicula et brevis introductio
ad linguam Gallicam. Lat. a. Fr. 4°. Oxoniæ, J.
Barnesius, 1604. L.L¹⁵.O.O⁵.MARL.+; F.ILL.

21737 — A briefe extract of the former Latin grammer [of the
French language written in Latin], done into Eng-
lish. 4°. Oxford, J. Barnes, sold by S. Waterson,
[London,] 1605. L(2).O.; HD.

21738 — Προπύλαιον, or an entrance to the Spanish tongue. 4°.
T. Haveland f. N. Butter, 1611. Ent. 25 ja. L.O.C.P.
STD.+; F.NY⁵.
Most copies have a dedic. to William Langton on
A2ʳ. One O(Wood 310(3)) has a dedic. to Lady
Beatrice Digbie on A2ʳ–4ʳ.

Sanford, John—*cont.*

21739 — [Anr. ed.] The Spanish grammar. Or, an entrance to the understanding of the Spanish tongue. 4°. *T. Harper f. N. Butter,* 1633. C³.; HN.
— *tr. See* 7322.

San Pedro, Diego de. [Arnalte y Lucenda.] For translations of this work *see* 546, 778, 6758.

21739.5 — The castell of loue, *tr.* out of Spanishe by J. Bowrchier, lorde Bernis. The whiche boke treateth of the loue betwene Leriano and Laureola. [Anon.] 8°. [*R. Wolfe f.*] (*J. Turke,*) [1548?] L.O(K6, 7 only). (Formerly 21741)

21740 — [Anr. ed. *Ed.*] (A. Spigurnell.) 8°. (*R. wyer f. R. Kele,*) [1552?] L.; HN.

21741 — Now = 21739.5.

21742 — [Anr. ed.] 8°. (*J. Kynge,*) [c. 1555.] Ent. to T. Purfoot 1564–65. HN.

21743 **Sansbury, John.** Ilium in Italiam. Oxonia ad protectionem regis sui omnium optimi filia, pedisequa. [Init. I. S. In verse, with a set of woodcut arms of Oxford Colleges.] 8°. *Oxoniæ, J. Barnesius,* 1608. L.O(4).O⁵.; HN.Y.

21744 **Sansovino, Francesco.** The quintesence of wit, being a corrant comfort of conceites. *Tr.* out of Italian. (R. Hichcock.) 4°. *E. Allde,* 1590 (28 oc.) L.O.C.D.E².+; F(imp.).HN.HD(imp.).*.N(imp.).PML.+

21744a — [A variant, without 'Octobris. 28.' in imprint.] HN. WTL.
— *See also* 17936.

Sant, John. *See* Indulgences 106.

Saona, Laurentius Gulielmus de. *See* Traversanus, L. G.

21745 **Saparton, John.** Sapartons alarum, to all such as do beare the name of true souldiers. *Ballad.* s.sh.fol. *W. How f. R. Johnes,* [1569.] Ent. 1568–69. L.
1st stanza begins: 'Al Mars his men drawe neere,'.

Sappho. Sapho and Phao. 1584, etc. *See* 17086 sqq.

Sarate, Augustine. The strange and delectable history of Peru. 1581. *See* 26123.

21746 **Saravia, Hadrianus.** De diuersis ministrorum euangelii gradibus, . . . liber unus: cui duo alij additi, alter de honore qui debetur pastoribus, alter de sacrilegijs. 4°. *G. Bishop & R. Newberie,* 1590. Ent. 25 jn. L.O.C.D.E.+; F.HN.HD.U.Y.+ ℋ
Translated in 21749 sq.; a different trans. of the 2nd pt. is in 21752.

21747 — De imperandi authoritate, et christiana obedientia, libri quatuor. 4°. *Reg. typog.* [*Deputies of C. Barker,*] 1593. Ent. to G. Bishop 1 fb. L.O.C.D.E.+; F.HN. HART.PN.U.

21748 — Defensio tractationis de diuersis ministrorum euangelij gradibus, contra Responsionem T. Bezæ. 4°. *Reg. typog.* [*Deputies of C. Barker a. Eliot's Court Press*] 1594. L.O.C.E.LINC.+; HN.U.
Eliot's Court Press pr. quires B–1st Ddd.

21749 — D. Saravia. 1. Of the diuerse degrees of the ministers of the gospell. 2. Of the honor due vnto priestes. 3. Of sacrilege. [*Tr.* from 21746.] 4°. *J. Wolfe, sold by J. Perin,* 1591. L².O.C¹³.D.; F.

21750 — [A variant, w. imprint:] *J. Wolfe, sold by J. Perin,* 1592. L.O.O³.DUR⁵.P.+; F.CAL.U.

21751 — Diversi tractatus theologici, ab Hadriano Saravia editi. fol. [*R. Field*] *ex typ. Soc. Stat.,* 1611 (1610.) L².O.C.D.E².+; F.HN.U.Y.
Reprints 21746, 21747, 21748, and includes: 'Responsio ad convitia quædam Gretseri jesuitæ' and 'Examen tractatus D. Bezae de triplici episcoporum genere.'

21752 — Vindiciæ sacræ. A treatise of the honor due to ecclesiasticall persons. Done out of the Latin [in 21746 by] (J. Martin.—An appendix . . . answering foure maine arguments which usurpers of the churches right usually alledge.) 8°. *T. a. R. Cotes f. J. Boler,* 1629. Ent. 26 no. 1628. L(2).L¹⁵.PETYT.; HART.

21752.5 **Sarcerius, Erasmus.** Cōmon places of scripture ordrely set forth. *Tr.* R. Tauerner. 8°. (*J. Byddell,* 1538.) L.LINC(lacks tp).; F.HN.
(Formerly 10465) Tp comp. of this and next ed. (McK. 29) has Byddell's name in the sill.

21753 — [Anr. ed.] 8°. (*J. Byddell,* 1538 (12 au.)) L¹⁵.O.C(imp.). BUTE.

Sarcerius, Erasmus—*cont.*

21754 — [Anr. ed.] 8°. (*N. Hyll,* 1553.) L(tp only, Harl.5993/32)*.O³(lacks colophon)*.C⁴.; NY.
Tp comp. of all issues of this ed. (McK. 33) has Hill's inits. in the sill.

21755 — [Anr. issue, w. colophon:] (*N. Hyll f. J. Walley,* 1553.) L.

21755a — [Anr. issue, w. colophon:] (*N. Hyll f. R. Toye,* 1553.) L.O(imp.).

21755a.5 — [Anr. issue, w. colophon:] (*N. Hyll f. A. Vele,* 1553.) Milton Reed, Raynham Center, Mass.

21756 — [Anr. ed.] 8°. *T. East,* 1577. L.L⁴.O.C¹⁹.G².+; F.BO⁶. U.Y.

Sargent, James. *See* 10834.

Sargy, John. *See* Indulgences 133.

21757 **Sarpi, Paolo.** An apology, or, apologiticall answere, made by father Paule of the order of Servi, unto the exceptions of cardinall Bellarmine, against certaine treatises and resolutions of J. Gerson, concerning excommunication. First published in Italian, and now *tr.* 4°. *N. O[kes] f. W. Welby,* 1607. Ent. 5 jn. L.O.C.D²(lacks tp).E²(lacks tp).+; F.HN.COR.
B1ʳ has a reference to the Italian ed.: *Venice, R. Meietti,* 1606.

21757a — A discourse upon the reasons of the resolution taken in the Valteline against the tyranny of the Grisons and heretiques. *Tr.* (Philo-Britannicos.) With the translators epistle to parliament. [Anon.] 4°. [*M. Flesher*] *f. W. Lee,* 1628. Ent. 28 jn. L.O.C.D.E.+; F.HN.HD.N.U.+
Unsold sheets reissued in 1650 as Wing S 695, w. cancel tp attributing the trans. to Sir T. Roe, who was not, however, of Lincoln's Inn, as the translator claims on D4ʳ.

21758 — The free schoole of warre, or, a treatise, whether it be lawfull to beare armes for the service of a prince that is of a divers religion. [Anon. *Tr.*] (W. B[edel].) 4°. *J. Bill,* 1625. Ass'd by B. Norton to Joyce Norton a. R. Whitaker 26 au. 1632. L.O.C.D.M.+; F.HN.CU. HD.N.+
For a Latin trans. *see* 21768.

21759 — A full and satisfactorie answer to the late unadvised bull, thundred by pope Paul the fift, against Venice. *Tr.* out of Italian. 4°. [*Eliot's Court Press*] *f. J. Bill,* 1606. Ent. to R. Barker 9 se. L.O.C.D⁸.E².+; F.HN. HD.NY¹¹.Y.+

21760 — Historia del concilio Tridentino . . . Di Pietro Soave Polano. [*Ed.*] (M. A. de Dominis.) fol. *appresso G. Billio,* 1619. L.O.C.D.E.+; F.HN.HD.NY¹¹.Y.+

21761 — [A trans.] The historie of the councel of Trent. *Tr.* N. Brent. [Pietro Soave, *pseud.*] fol. *R. Barker a. J. Bill,* 1620. L.O.C.E.M.+; F.HN(imp.).HD.N.U.+

21762 — [Anr. ed.] Unto this second edition are added divers observable passages, and epistles. fol. *B. Norton a. J. Bill,* 1629. L.O.C.D.E.+; F.HN.CHI.HD.U.+
Tp varies: 'second edition' in large caps., or in large and small caps.; both at HD.

21763 — [Anr. ed. etc.] Unto this third edition [etc.] fol. *R. Young a. J. Raworth f. R. Whittaker,* 1640. Ass'd by B. Norton to Joyce Norton a. R. Whitaker 26 au. 1632. L.O.C.D².E.+; F.HN.CHI.FBL.HD.U.
Raworth pr. quires Hh–Hhhh.

21764 — [Anr. trans.] Petri Suavis Polani historiae concilii Tridentini libri octo, Latini facti [by *Sir A. Newton.*] fol. *Augustæ Trinobantum* [i.e. *London, B. Norton a. J. Bill,*] 1620. L.O.C.A.ETON.+; F.HN.CU.HD.

21765 — The history of the Inquisition. *Tr.* out of Italian by R. Gentilis. 4°. *J. Okes f. H. Mosley,* 1639. Ent. 29 no. and 4 de. 1638. L.O.C.CASHEL.STU.+; F.HN.HD.N.U.+

21766 — The history of the quarrels of pope Paul .V. with the state of Venice. [Anon.] *Tr.* out of the Italian, and compared with the French copie. (C. P[otter].) 4°. [*Eliot's Court Press f.*] *J. Bill,* 1626. Ent. 19 mr. L. O.C.D.G⁴.+; F.HN.HD.N.U.+
See also 20134.

21767 — [Anr. trans.] Interdicti Veneti historia de motu Italiæ sub initia pontificatus Pauli V commentarius. Recèns ex Italico conversus. (G. Bedellus.) 4°. *Cantabrigiæ, ap. T. Bucke, J. Bucke et L. Greene,* 1626. L.O.C.D. E.+; F.HN.CHI.CU.NY¹¹.+

21767.5 — [Anr. issue, w. cancel tp, w. imprint:] *Cantabrigiæ, ap. T. & J. Buck,* 1630. Armagh PL.

Sarpi, Paolo—*cont.*

21768 — Quæstio quodlibetica. An liceat stipendia sub principe religione discrepante merere. [Anon.] [*Tr.* W. Bedel?] 4°. *Cantabrigiæ,* [*T. a. J. Buck,*] 1630. L.O. C.D.E².+; F.HN. Syracuse U.
For an English trans. *see* 21758.
— *See also* 24635, 24719.

21769 **Satan.** A commission sent to the pope, cardinals, [etc.] by king Satan the deuill of hell. 8° in 4's. *T. Purfoote,* 1586. Ent. 4 oc. 1586; crossed out 27 fb. 1587. L²(2).

21770 — A conference, containing a conflict had with Satan. (A forme of thankesgiuing.) 1577. = pts. 2 and 3 of 15000.

21771 **Satiræ.** Satyræ seriæ: or, the secrets of things; written in morall and politicke discourses. 12°. *J. Okes f. A. Roper,* 1640. Ent. to W. Adderton 16 se.; ass'd to A. Roper 4 oc. 1639. L.C.; Y.

21771.5 — [Anr. issue, w. cancel tp, w. 'observations' instead of 'discourses' in the title.] *J. Okes f. A. Roper,* 1640. L.O(imp.).C³.BTU.; F.HN.CHI.ILL.

Satire. A pleasant satyre or poesie. 1595. *See* 15489.

21772 **Saul, Arthur.** The famous game of chesse-play. 8°. [*T. Snodham*] *f. Roger Jackson,* 1614. Ent. 4 oc. 1613. L.O.; HN. H. Bradley Martin, New York City.

21773 — [Anr. ed.] Now augmented. By J. Barbier. 8°. *B. Alsop f. Roger Jackson,* 1618. L(destroyed).L⁸(imprint cropt).O(date cropt).C²(date cropt).C⁵(imprint cropt).; HN.HD(lacks folding table: 'A Briefe of the Lawes of Chesse-Play').

21774 — [Anr. ed.] 8°. [*T. Paine*] *f. J. Jackson,* 1640. Ass'd to F. Williams 16 ja. 1626. L.O.C. St. Michael's C, Tenbury.; F(date shaved).HN.HD(date cropt).Y.

21775 **Saulnier, Gilbert,** *Sieur du Verdier.* The love and armes of the greeke princes. Or, the romant of romants. *Tr.* for Philip, earle of Pembroke and Montgomery. 3 pts. fol. *T. Harper* (Tome III: *J. Dawson*) *f. T. Walkley,* 1640. Ent. 27 jn. L.O.C.D⁶.DUR³.+; F.HN. HD.N.NY.+

21776 **Saunders, Clement.** A shield of defence. 1612. = 11212.

21776.3 **Saunders, George,** *Gent.* Save a thiefe from the gallowes and he'll hang thee if he can. (The confession of G. Saunders gentleman, who killed his uncle. He writ this song the first of January, 1616.) *Ballad.* 2 pts. s.sh.fol. *W.* [*Jones*? c. 1618.] M³(impr. defective).

21776.7 — [Anr. ed.] s.sh.fol. [*W. Jones?*] *f. Edw.* [*Wright,* c. 1635.] Ent. to ballad ptnrs. 14 de. 1624. M³(imp.). Heading of pt. 2 omits the date.

Saunders, George, *Master.* A briefe discourse of the late murther of master G. Saunders. 1573, etc. *See* 11985 sq.
— A warning for faire women. Containing, the murther of master G. Sanders. 1599. *See* 25088.

21777 **Saunders, Laurence.** A trewe mirrour or glase wherin we maye beholde the wofull state of Englande. [Anon.] 8°. [*Wesel? H. Singleton?*] 1556. L(2).L².O. C³.BUTE.; F.LC(2).
Printed in the types of 9981. The attribution to Saunders is doubtful. 1 L, O copies have 2 extra leaves w. metrical paraphrase of the Lord's Prayer.

21778 **Saunders, Thomas.** A true discription and breefe discourse, of a most lamentable voiage, made to Tripolie in Barbarie. 4°. *R. Jones f. E. White,* 1587 (15 ap.) Ent. to Jones a. White 31 mr. L.O.

Saunderson, Robert. *See* Sanderson, R.

21779 **Sauter, Daniel.** The practise of the banckrupts of these times. Written in Latine and made to speake English. 8°. *J. Norton f. W. Garret,* 1640. Ent. 19 fb. L.L³⁰.O.

Sauvage, James. Almanacks. [1547, etc.] *See* 507.11 sqq.
21780 — A prognostication. [1550.] Now = 507.15.

21781 **Savage, Francis.** A conference betwixt a mother a devout recusant, and her sonne a zealous protestant. 8°. *J. Legat, pr. to the Univ. of Camb.,* 1600. L.O.; F.

Savage, William. Almanacks. 1610, etc. *See* 508 sq.

Savelli, Troilo. A relation of the death, of T. Savelli. 1620. *See* 3134.

21781.5 **Savile,** *Sir* **George,** *Baronet.* [Heading:] The state of the cause. [In a dispute over land between the baronet and his grandson, George, the latter represented by his mother's brother, Sir T. Wentworth.] s.sh.fol. [*London,* 1621?] L⁸(GL 5471).
This is very likely part of a petition to Parliament of which 1 or more sheets are missing.

Savile, Henry, *Esquire.* A libell of Spanish lies. With an answere by H. Sauile esquire. 1596. *See* 6551.

21782 **Savile,** *Sir* **Henry.** Praelectiones tresdecim in principium elementorum Euclidis. 4°. *Oxonii, J. Lichfield & J. Short,* 1621. L.O.C.D.E².+; F.HN.CU.HD.ILL.+ Tp varies: with (most copies) or without Oxford device (one O, presentation copy).

21783 — Rerum Anglicarum scriptores post Bedam praecipui, nunc primum editi. [Libri] Willielmi Malmesburiensis. Henrici Huntindoniensis. Rogeri Hovedeni. [etc.] (Fasti regum et episcoporum Angliae.) fol. *G. Bishop, R. Nuberie & R. Barker,* 1596. L.O.C.D. E².+; F.HN.HD.N.NY.+
— Ultima linea Savilli. 1622. *See* 19025.
— *ed. See* 3534, 14629, 26065.
— *tr. See* 23642.

21784 **Savile, John.** King James his entertainment at Theobalds: with his welcome to London, together with a salutatorie poeme. 4°. *T. Snodham, sould at the house of T. Este,* 1603. Ent. to Snodham 14 my. L. O.; F.HN.HD.

21785 **Savile, Thomas.** Adams garden. A meditation of thankfulnesse. 4°. *T. Haveland,* 1611. O.O³.

21786 — The prisoners conference. Handled by way of dialogue, between a knight and a gentleman. 8°. *W. Jaggard,* 1605. Ent. 26 ap. O.

21787 — The raising of them that are fallen. A discourse profitable to christians dialogue wise, betwixt a knight and a gentleman. 4°. [*R. Blower*] *f. W. Welby,* 1606. Ent. 14 ap. L.O.C³.YK.; F.HN.Y.

21788 **Saviolo, Vincentio.** Vincentio Saviolo his practise. In two bookes. The first intreating of the use of the rapier and dagger. The second, of honor and honorable quarrels. 4°. [*T. Scarlet f.*] *J. Wolfe,* 1595 (1594.) Ent. 19 no. 1594. L.L³⁰.O.C.G².+; F.HN.HD.N.PML.+ The 2nd bk. is largely a trans. of G. Muzio's Il Duello.

21789 — [Anr. issue, w. cancel tp, w. imprint:] [*J. Orwin*] *f. W. Mattes,* 1595. DUL.; HN.PEN. Syracuse U.

21789.1 **Savonarola, Girolamo.** Eruditoriū cōfessorum fratris Hieronymi Sauonarolae. 8°. [*Paris,*] (*in ed. Ascensianis,*) *venundātur a J. Paruo, H. Jacobi* [*London?*] *et Ascensio,* (1510 (14 cal. oc.)) L.L².O⁹.O¹⁷(imp.). PARIS.+
Though Jacobi was in Paris 1510–11 and the imprints of this and 21799.4 sqq. do not mention his London shop (and so may not qualify for STC), it is likely he brought back copies to sell in London.

21789.3 — [Heading A1ʳ:] An exposition after the maner of a cōtemplacyon vpon yᵉ .li. psalme, called Miserere mei Deus. [Anon. *Tr.* W. Marshall?] *Eng.* 8°. (*J. Byddell f. w. Marshall,*) [1534.] O.C(2).; BO(imp.). (Formerly 21795) Issued w. 15986?

21789.4 — [Anr. ed.] 32° in 8's. (*R. Redman,*) [1535.] *See* pt. 5 of 20200.3.

21789.4 — [Anr. ed.] An exposytion vpon [etc.] 8°. (*T. Godfray,*) [1535?] O.
Intended to be issued w. 15988a?

21789.5 — [Anr. ed.] An exposition after the maner of a contemplacyon vpon [etc.] 8°. [*Antwerp, widow of C. Ruremond,* 1536.] L(lacks A8).O.; NY.
(Formerly 21795a) Issued w. 15992, 21799. NY copy has tp 21790 inserted. This ed. has some extra prayers and 'The pater noster, spokē of the synner' not included in other eds. The pater noster is reprinted from 16818.

21789.6 — [Anr. ed., naming 'Hierom of Farrarye' in the heading and including the exposition on Psalm xxxi.] *Eng. a. Lat.* 8°. (*Rowen,* [*N. le Roux?*] 1536.) O.O².
Issued w. 15993.

21789.7 — [Anr. ed.] 4°. (*R. Redman*) [1537?] L(Ps. li only, w. tp 21790 inserted). L².O¹⁷.C⁵.M.+; F(2).
Issued w. 15997. Copies vary in the setting of the red text on A1ʳ; in the English heading F has virgules after 'Psalme' and 'Deus', and has 'Farrarye'; L has no virgules and has 'Ferrarye'.

Savonarola, Girolamo—*cont.*

21790 — [Anr. ed.?] An exposicyon vpon the .li. psalme. made by Hierom of Ferrarye. 4°. *Parys*, [*f. F. Regnault?*] 1538. L(tp only, bd. w. 21789.7).BUTE(tp only, bd. w. 21791).; NY(tp only, bd. w. 21789.5).
(Formerly also 14503) Tp w. architectural compartment, possibly intended to go with 21791, though only BUTE has this combination.

21790.5 — [Anr. ed. of Ps. li and xxxi.] An exposycyon after the maner [etc.] *Eng. a. Lat.* 8°. [*Rouen, N. le Roux,*) [1538.] L².O. Lord Kenyon.; F.CH.HD.ILL.
Issued w. 16007.

21791 — [Anr. ed.] 8°. [*Rouen, N. le Roux f. F. Regnault,*] (*Parys*, 1538.) L.L².O.C.ST.+; F(2).HN(2).
Issued w. 16008.3 sq. The BUTE copy has Ps. li only and has the tp 21790 bd. w. it.

21792 — [Anr. ed.] *Eng.* 4°. (*R. Redman*, 1539.) L.O.O¹⁷.
Issued w. 16008.

21793 — [Anr. ed. of Ps. li only.] A goodly exposycyon, [etc.] *Eng.* 8°. (*T. petyt,*) [c. 1540.] C.CHATS.
The CHATS copy is identical in setting to C except for the press variant: 'exposytyon,' in the title.

21794 — [Anr. ed. of Ps. li and xxxi.] An exposicyon [etc.] *Eng.* 4°.(*J. Herforde f. R. Toye,*) [1542?] L.O³.O¹⁷.C.M³.+; F(2).
— [For other early eds. of Ps. li on continuous signatures *see* 15988, 20193; for eds. of both Ps. li and xxxi on continuous signatures or linked on tp of Sarum primers, *see* 15998, 16018 sq., 16020, 16021, 16026 sq., 16028.5 sq.]

21795 — Now = 21789.3.
21795a — Now = 21789.5.
21796 — [Anr. ed.] 16° in 8's. (*T. Marshe f. M. Lobley,*) [1558.] Ent. 1557–58. L.

21797 — [Anr. ed.] A pithie exposition . . . Newly augmented and amended, by A. Fleming. 16° in 8's. *T. Dawson*, 1578. Ent. 17 se. L.
(Formerly also 14504)

21798 — Expositio vel meditatio fratris Hieronimi sauonarole . . . in psalmū In te domine speraui [Ps. xxxi.] 4° 8.⁶. (*per W. de worde,*) [1500?] O⁵.; F.
— [A trans.] A meditation of the same Ierom, vpon the psalm of In te domine speraui. 32° in 8's. (*R. Redman,*) [1535.] *See* pt. 6 of 20200.3. For other eds. printed on continuous signatures with Ps. li, *see* 21789.6 sqq.

21798.5 — [Anr. ed.] A goodly exposition [etc.] 4°. (*J. Byddell f. W. Marshall*, 1535?] c⁶(bd. w. 15988).M.

21799 — [Anr. ed.] A meditacyon [etc.] 8°. [*Antwerp, widow of C. Ruremond,*) 1536.] O.C.
Issued w. 15992, 21789.5.

21799.2 — [Anr. ed.] An other meditatiō [etc.] 8°. [*Emden, E. van der Erve*, 1555?] C.

21799.4 — Introductorium confessorum fratris Hieronymi Sauonarole. 8°. [*Paris,*] (*in ed. Ascensianis,*) *venundātur ab J. paruo, H. Jacobi* [*London?*] *& Ascensio,* (1510 (14 cal. mr.)) O⁹.C.PARIS.
See also 21789.1.

21799.6 — Libri fratris Hieronymi de ferraria . . . de simplicitate christiane vite. 8°. (*Parrhisiis, in calcog. Ascēsiana,*) *venundātur ab J. Paruo, H. jacobi* [*London?*] *& Ascensio,* (1510 (3 cal. mr.)) Avignon PL. Cambrai PL. Le Mans PL.
See also 21789.1.

21799.8 — [Anr. ed.] 8°. (*Parrhisiis, in chalcog. Ascensiana,*) *venundantur ab J. paruo, H. jacobi* [*London?*] *& Ascensio,* (1511(6 cal. jn.)) L.L².O.C.PARIS².+
— A paraphrase upon the seauen penitentiall psalmes. 1635. *See* 19910.5.

21800 — [Heading A1ʳ:] Sermo fratris Hieronymi de Ferraria in vigilia natiuitatis domini. (De lingua vernacula Italoᵫ in latinum conuersus per Bartholomeum, Mutilanensem.) 4°. [*R. Pynson*, 1509.] L(2). Florence NL.; HN.
End of text dated 8 Sept. 1509; the device has Pynson's name.

21801 **Savorine, Adrian.** The true image of christian love. Written in Latin by A. Savorine a Dominican frier, and *tr.* 50. yeeres ago by Richard Rikes, & now truely conferred with the auncient copies, and published by A. M(onday.) 8°. *J. Charlwood*, 1587. Ent. 28 no. 1586. L².
A revised reprint of 21471.5, q.v.

Savoy. The oracle of Savoy. 1600. *See* 5044.

Savoy—*cont.*

21802 — A true discourse of the occurrences in the warres of Savoy, and the winning of the forte of Mont-millan: by the king of France Henrie the fourth. Whereunto is annexed, the oration of sir P. Cauriana, knight. *Tr.* E. A[ggas.] 4°. [*R. Read*] *f. W. Burre*, 1601. Ent. 27 ja. L.O.C².

Savoy, *Duke of. See* Charles Emmanuel I.

21803 **Savoy Hospital**, *London*. Julius Eᵖus seruus [etc. Bull granting privileges. c. 1510.] Now = Indulgences 60.

Savoyan. The first Savoyan. 1601. *See* 17556.

21804 **Sawtry, James**, *pseud.* The defence of the mariage of preistes: agenst Steuen Gardiner. [By G. Joye.] 8°. (*Auryk, J. Troost*, [i.e. Antwerp, widow of C. Ruremond,] 1541 (au.)) L.O.NOR².
See also 17517.

21805 **Saxey, Samuel.** A straunge and wonderfull example of the iudgement of almighty God, shewed vpon two adulterous persons . . . this thirde of Februarie. 1583. 8°. [*H. Bynneman? f.*] *H. Jackson*, [1583?] D.; F.HD(tp def.).

Saxon, *of Antiquity. See* 24557.5.

Saxony, *Duke of. See* 14656.

21805.1 **Saxton, Christopher.** [Atlas of the counties of England and Wales. Sponsored by T. Seckford.] fol. [*London*, 1579.] L(Maps C.7.c.2, lacks port.).G²(w. index of 21805.5).M².; LC(lacks index).
Index: 1 col. roman, dated 1579 at bottom. The maps are dated 1574–79. LC,G²,M² have portrait of Elizabeth in 1st state (port. I) w. dress stretched square between the knees. For a fuller description of the plates *see* Hind I.88–95 and Skelton 1. At L¹¹(Patent Roll 19 Eliz., pt. 9 (no. 1159), m.21) is Saxton's 10-year patent to sell these maps, granted 22 July 1577. *See also* 23034.5.

21805.2 — [Anr. issue, w. index reset.] fol. [*London*, 1580?] L (118.e.1, w. port. II).C¹⁹(w. port. I).
Index: 1 col. roman, undated. In the 2nd state of the portrait the dress falls in folds between the knees.

21805.3 — [Anr. issue, w. index reset.] fol. [*London*, c. 1585.] LC(w. port. II, lacks map of Lancaster).
Index: 1 col. italic, which is bd. separately before the port. After the port. this copy also has the 3-col. index and double plate as in 21805.5.

21805.5 — [Anr. issue, w. index reset, and added double plate w. coats of arms on left-hand page and catalogue of cities on right-hand page.] fol. [*London*, 1590?] L. O.C.D.YK.+; F.HN.LC.N.PML.+
Index: 3 col. At least L³³ and one HN copy have the right-hand page of the double plate blank. 1 copy each at L and Royal Geographical Society is bd. w. 24481a.

21805.7 — Britannia insularum in oceano maximo . . . 1583. [Large map of England and Wales. Sponsored by T. Seckford.] fol(20). [*London*, 1583.] BIRM²(mounted together as one large map).
At L are later states, prob. post-1640; *see* Hind I.100–2.

Sc., An. Diaphantus. 1604. *See* 21853.

Scala Cœli. Scala coeli. Nineteene sermons. 1611. *See* 605.

21805.9 **Scapula, Joannes.** Lexicon Græcolatinum novum in quo ex primitivorum et simplicium fontibus derivata atque composita ordine non minùs naturali, quàm alphabetico, deducuntur. Editio ultima, cum auctario. Dialectorum omnium à J. Zuingero in tabulas redactarum. fol. *Londini, ap. Soc. Bibliopolarum*, 1619. Ent. to the Latin Stock 22 oc. 1618. L.C(2, 1 = Bury deposit).P. R. C. Alston, Leeds Univ.; HD.
This is a variant of the ed. pr. at Geneva, *ap.* P. Albertum, 1619 (copies at O, O²⁴).

21806 — [Anr. ed., enlarged.] Lexicon Græco-Latinum. Editio novissima. (Index Latinus. Operâ L. Martii.—Lexicon etymologicum. Autore J. Harmaro.) 3 pts. fol. *typis T. Harperi* ([pt. 2:] *T. Cotes,* [pt. 3:] *typis A. Griffin,*) *imp. Jocosæ Norton & R. Whitakeri*, 1637 (1636). Ent. 9 jn. 1635. L.O.C.D⁶.E.+; F.HN.HD.N. NY.+
The colophon to pt. 1 is dated 1636. Apparently Cotes and Griffin also pr. sections of pt. 1.

Scapula, Joannes—*cont.*
— *See also* 23408.2.

21806.5 **Scarbrough, Gervase.** The summe. 1623. *See* Addenda.

21807 **Scarperia.** Heuy newes of an horryble earthquake in Scharbaria in this present yeare of .xlij. Also how that a cytie in Turky is sonke. 8° in 4. (*N. Bourman,*) [1542.] L(1 imp.; also tpp only, Harl.5919/155, Harl.5936/283, both w. colophon pasted below title).

21808 — [Anr. ed.] 8° in 4. (*R. Lant,*) [1542.] L(tp and col. only, Harl.5919/169).LONGLEAT.; F.HD.
In title: 'erthquake, in Scarbaria.'

21809 **Scepsius, Heius,** *pseud.* Heii Scepsii defensio pro Alexandro Dicsono aduersus G. P. Cantabrigien [19064]. 8°. *T. Vautroullerius pro F. Coldoco,* 1584. O.C.
Written by A. Dickson; *see also* 6823.

21810 **Schade, Petrus,** *Mosellanus.* Paedologia Petri Mosellani protegensis, in puerorum vsum conscripta & aucta. Dialogi .37. Dialogi pueriles C. Hegendorphini XII. lepidi æque ac docti. 8°. (*ap. W. de Worde,*) 1532 (jn.) L.; HD(frags. of quire D).

21810.3 — P. Mosellani tabulæ de schematibus et tropis in Rhetorica. Item in Erasmi Roterodami libellum de duplica copia. 8°. *J. kyngstonus,* 1573. F.

21810.7 — [Anr. ed.] Tabulae . . . P. Mosellani [etc.] 8°. *ex typ. J. Kyngstoni,* 1577. C[10].

Scharbaria. *See* 21807.

Scharpius, Patricius. *See* 22369.

21811 **Scheibler, Christoph.** Christophori Scheibleri, . . . liber commentariorum topicorum. Additi sunt duo indices. Editio nova correctior. 8°. *Oxoniæ, G. Turner, imp. J. Adams, junioris,* 1637. L[3].O.C[3].D.G[2].+; Y.

21812 — Christophori Scheibleri, . . . metaphysica, duobus libris. Quibus accessit exercitationum auctarium. Per T. B(arlow.) Editio ultima. 4° in 8's. *Oxoniæ, G. Turner pro J. A[dams,]* 1637. O[3](impr. torn).O[7].C[3]. G[4](tp def.).
(2nd pt. formerly also 1441)

21812.2 — [A variant, w. imprint:] *Oxoniæ, G. Turner pro J. Adams,* 1637. C[9].

21812.3 — [A variant, w. imprint:] *Oxoniæ, G. Turner pro J. Adams, & væneunt ap. J. Godwin,* 1637. O.O[2].O[5].; Y.

21812.5 — [A variant, w. imprint:] *Oxoniæ, G. Turner pro J. Adams, & væneunt ap. T. Allam,* 1637. CHI.

21812.7 — [A variant, w. imprint:] *Oxoniæ, G. Turner pro J. Adams, & væneunt ap. J. Westall,* 1637. L(tp only, Ames II.1392).

21812.9 — [Anr. issue, w. cancel gen. tp, w. imprint:] *Oxoniæ, G. Turner pro J. Westall, T. Allam & J. Godwin,* 1637. LK.

21813 — [Anr. issue, w. cancel gen. tp, w. imprint:] *Oxoniæ, G. Turner pro J. Westall, T. Allam & J. Godwin,* 1638. L.O.C.D.E[2].+; F.HN.BO.CHI.CU.+

21814 — Philosophia compendiosa seu philosophia exhibens logicae, physicae [etc.] compendium. Addita est H. Buscheri Arithmetica. Editio quarta recognita. 8°. *Oxoniæ, G. Turner, imp. T. Huggins & H. Curteine,* 1628. O[10].C.C[2](impr.).D.

21814.5 — Editio quinta. 8°. *Oxoniæ, G. Turner, imp. H. Curteine,* 1631. L(tp only, Ames II.981).; Y.

21815 — Editio sexta prioribus correctior, & auctior. Huic editioni 1 præfigitur Technologia proœmialis. 2 Annectitur Arithmetica plenior quàm illa Buscheri. 8°. *Oxoniæ, G. Turner, imp. H. Curteine,* 1639. L[3].O. O[22].C.E[2].+; HN.HD(2).

Scheprevus, Joannes. *See* 22405.

Scheves, James. Theses logicæ. Præside J. Schevezio. 1614. *See* 21555.22.

21816 **Schickard, Wilhelmus.** Wilhelmi Schickardi horologium Hebræum, . . . hâc septimâ vice recusum. (Rota Hebræa.) [*Ed.* N. Homes.] 8°. *typis T. Paine, imp. P. Stephani & C. Meredith,* 1638 (1639.) Ent. 14 no. 1637. C.C[3].

21816.5 — [Anr. issue, w. tp cancelled and replaced by a[4].] Septies comprobatum. Emendatum, a N. H[omes] S. T. D. *typis T. Paine, venit ap. P. Stephanum & C. Meredith,* 1639. L(orig. tp uncancelled).O.C[2].A.G[2].+; F.HN.HD.ILL(orig. tp uncancelled).NY.+

21817 **Schilander, Cornelius.** Cornelius Shilander his chirurgerie. Containing a briefe methode for the curing of woundes and ulcers. *Tr.* out of Latin. By S. Hobbes. 4°. *R. Johnes f. C. Burbie,* 1596. Ent. 1 de. 1595. L.L[39].LEEDS.P.; HD.NLM.

21817.3 **Schindler, Valentin.** Schindleri lexicon pentaglotton, Hebraicum, Chaldaicum, Syriacum, Talmudicorabbinicum, et Arabicum, in epitomen redactum à G. A[labaster.] fol. *G. Jones, prostant ap. C. Bee et L. Sadler,* 1635. L.O.E.LEEDS.USHAW.+; F.HN.HD (lacks Rasche Theboth). Hebrew Union C. Queen's U.
(Formerly 247) A reissue, w. added tp and preface, of pt. 2 of 251, q.v.

21817.5 — [Anr. issue, without preface, w. title:] Epitome lexici Hebraici, . . . Una cum observationibus circa linguam Hebream et Grecam authore H. Thornidicke. *typis G. Jones,* 1635. Ent. under this title 22 jn. 1632. O[2].C.A.D.SAL.+; F.ILL. Hebrew Union C.
(Formerly 24040) Omits all mention of Schindler and Alabaster. There are no added observations, and Thorndike's part in this is conjectural. Tp varies: 'Thornidicke' (c) or 'Thornedike' (O[2], O[3], O[18], F).

21817.7 — [Anr. issue, reprinting preface of 21817.3 but omitting mention of Schindler in title:] Lexicon pentaglotton, . . . Authore G. Alabastro. *G. Jones, [sold by A. Hebb,]* 1637. L.D[2].LEEDS.M[2].
(Formerly 248)

21818 **Schlichtenberger, Eyriak.** A prophesie vttered by the daughter of an honest countrey man, called Adam Krause. This happened at a towne called Rostorff a mile from Melwing. 1580. (*Tr.* according to the highe Dutche.) 8°. (*J. Charlewood f. W. Wright,* 1580.) Ent. 18 au. F.
Reprinted w. the dates altered in 14068.

21819 **Schloer, Friedrich.** The death of the two renowned kings of Sweden and Bohemia. A sermon. *Tr.* out of the High-Dutch coppie [by T. H.] 4°. *J. D[awson] f. N. Bourne,* 1633. Ent. as tr. by T. H. 18 fb. L.O. C.D.E.+; F.AAS.PN[2].U.

Scholar. Alas poore scholler. [1641.] *See* 25632.

21820 **Schomberg, Henri de.** A relation sent to the French king by the marshall de Schomberg, of the fight neere to Castelnau d'Ary. *Tr.* out of French. 4°. *J. D[awson] f. N. Butter a. N. Bourne,* 1632. O.C.

21821 **Schonæus, Cornelius.** Terentius christianus, siue comoediæ duæ Terentiano stylo conscriptæ. Tobaeus. Juditha. His accessit Pseudostratiotes, fabula iocosa ac ludicra. 8°. *R. Robinsonus, imp. R. D[exter,]* 1595. L.

21821.2 — [Anr. ed.] 8°. *ap. R. Dexter,* 1601. O[3].P.

21821.4 — [Anr. ed.] 8°. [*J. Windet?*] *ex typ. Soc. Bibliopolarum,* 1607. O[6].; ILL(2).

21821.6 — [Anr. ed.] 8°. [*W. Hall,*] *ex typ. Soc. Stat.,* 1610. HD.

21821.8 — [Anr. ed.] 8°. [*E. Allde,*] *ex typ. Soc. Stat.,* 1615. L(tp only, Ames II.383).

21822 — [Anr. ed.] 8°. [*T. Snodham,*] *ex typ. Soc. Stat.,* 1620. Ent. to the English Stock 5 mr. L.O[10].; HN.

21822.5 — [Anr. ed.] 8°. *ex typ. Soc. Stat.,* 1625. C[10].; ILL.

21823 — [Anr. ed.] 8°. *Cantabrigiæ, ex Acad. Typog.* [*T. a. J. Buck,*] 1632. O.C.D.DUL.G[2].+; AAS.ILL.PH. St. Mark's Church Rectory, Niagara-on-the-lake, Ontario.

21824 — [Anr. ed.] 8°. *Cantabrigiæ, ex Acad. Typog.* [*T. Buck a. R. Daniel,*] 1635. L.L[15].C.C[5].; F.HN.Y.

21825 **Schonerus, Lazarus.** De numeris geometricis. Of the nature and proprieties [*sic*] of geometricall numbers. Englished, enlarged and illustrated with tables [by W. Bedwell] teaching the use of a rular, invented by T. Bedwell. 4°. *R. Field,* 1614. Ent. 17 ja. L.L[30].O. C.E[2].+; F.HN.
At least L, 4 O copies have a folding table signed 'N' at the foot: 'Trigonum architectonicum' and separately ent. 1 mr.; table reprinted in 1798.

School. The free schoole of warre. 1625. *See* 21758.
— A schoole for young souldiers. [1615, etc.] *See* 17386.5 sq.
— The schoole of good manners. 1609, etc. *See* 10923 sq.
— The schoole of slovenrie. 1605. *See* 6457.
— The schoole of vertue. [c. 1550, etc.] *See* 22134.5 sqq.

School—*cont.*

— The schoole of vertue, the second part. 1619. *See* 25265.

21826　**Schoolhouse.** A schole-house, for the needle. (Here foloweth certaine patterns of cut-workes: newly invented and never published before. Also sundry sortes of spots, as flowers, [etc.] But once published before.) obl.4°. *R. Shorleyker,* 1624. W. Dight's copies ass'd to Shorleyker 4 jn. 1627. O(2nd pt. only). Brussels, Musée des Arts Décoratifs.
　　Sub tp is undated.

21826.2　— [Anr. issue? w. imprint on 1st tp:] *R. Shorleyker, sould by J. Gresmond,* 1624. Brussels, Musée des Arts Décoratifs (tp only).

21826.4　— [Anr. ed.] obl. 4°. *[widow of] R. Shorleyker,* 1632. L(tp only, Harl.5919/265).L[18](imp.).

　　— Here begynneth . . . the schole house of women. 1541, etc. *See* 12105 sq.

21826.6　— The vertuous scholehous of vngracious women. A godly dialogue or communication of two systers. (A fruteful sermon of Mart. Luth[er] concernynge matrimony, [on Heb. xiii.4.]) [*Tr.*] (W. Lyn.) 8°. [*S. Mierdman f. W. Lynne,* 1548?] L.
　　(Formerly 12104) The 1st pt. is a trans. of 'Der bösen Weiber Zuchtschül.'

21826.8　— [Anr. ed., w. title:] A watchword for wilfull women. An excellent pithie dialogue betweene two sisters. [Init. R. B.] 8°. *T. Marshe,* 1581. Ass'd to T. Orwin by E. Marsh 23 jn. 1591. C.WI.
　　(Formerly 1063) Luther's sermon begins on E4[v].

　　Schoolmaster. The schoolemaster. 1583. *See* 24412.

　　Schoolpoints. Certaine minerall, and metaphisicall schoolpoints to be defended by the reuerende bishops. [1589.] *See* 17455.

　　Schoppe, Caspar. Is. Casauboni corona regia. 1615. *See* 4744.

21827　**Schottenius, Hermannus.** Instructio prima puerorum, à legendi peritia, tum in grammaticæ, tum morū præceptis. 8°. *ap. W. de Worde,* 1533. O.

21828　**Schouten, Willem Cornelis.** The relation of a wonderfull voiage. Shewing how south from the straights of Magelan, he found a newe passage and sayled round about the world. [*Tr.*] (W. P[hilip].) 4°. *T. D[awson] f. N. Newbery,* 1619. Ent. 13 ap. L.L[2]. L[33].O.O[2].+; HN.HD.MICH.NY.PH[2].+

　　Schwarzenberg, Adolph von, *Count.* True newes of a notable victorie. [1598.] *See* 20595.5.

21828.5　**Schwarzenberg, Georg Ludwig von,** *Count.* The oration or substance of that which was delivered before his majestie of Great Brittaine, by the emperours embassador. *Tr.* out of high Dutch. 4°. [*B. Alsop*] *f. T. Acrher* [sic], 1622 (18 ap.) L.O.; HD.NY.

21829　— [Anr. trans.] The oration . . . This is the true copie in English by Sir R. Anstruther. 4°. [*E. Allde*] *f. T. Archer,* 1622 (18 ap.) L[11].O.; F.HD.

21830　**Sclater, William,** *the Elder.* A briefe exposition with notes, upon the second epistle to the Thessalonians. 4° in 8's. *G. Miller f. G. Vincent,* 1627. Ent. 4 no. 1626. L.C.BIRM[2](K.N.).G[4].M.+; F.HN.HD.U.Y.+
　　This and following eds. usually bd. as pt. 2 of 21835 sqq.

21831　— Second edition corrected. 4° in 8's. *A. Mathewes f. R. Thrale,* 1629. Ass'd to J. Haviland 25 jn. O.O[18].C. BRISTOL.M[4].+; F.CHI.HD(lacks X2).ILL.PH[5].

21832　— Third edition. 4° in 8's. *J. Haviland, sold by R. Thrale,* 1632. L.O.C[2].G[2].M[4].+; F.HN.CHI.HD.Y.+

21833　— The christians strength. By William Sclater. [A sermon.] 4°. *Oxford, Jos. Barnes,* 1612. Ent. to John Barnes a. ass'd to J. Parker 10 jy. 1619. L[3].O.C. BRISTOL.STD.+; F.HD.ILL.NY[11].Y.

21834　— An exposition with notes upon the first epistle to the Thessalonians. 4° in 8's. *W. Stansby f. J. Parker,* 1619. Ent. to H. Fetherstone a. J. Parker 2 jy. 1618. L.O.C[4].+; F.HN.BALT.U(lacks tp)*.

21834a　— [A variant, w. imprint:] *W. Stansby f. H. Fetherstone,* 1619. O.O[6].C[3].G[4].SCL.; HD.

21835　— [Anr. ed., w. title:] An exposition with notes upon the first and second epistles to the Thessalonians. 2 pts.

Sclater, William, *the Elder—cont.*
　　4° in 8's. [*M. Flesher a. J. Haviland*] *f. J. Parker, sold by G. Vincent,* 1627. Ass'd to J. Parker 3 ap. 1626. L.O.C.BRISTOL.M.+; F.HN.HD.U.Y.+
　　Eds. of pt. 2, called for on the tp to this and the following eds., are bd. indiscriminately and are therefore sep. listed at 21830 sqq. Haviland pr. quires Aa–Oo of pt. 1.

21836　— [Anr. ed.] 4° in 8's. *J. Haviland, sold by R. Thrale,* 1630. L.O.C.G[4].M[4].+; F.HN.CHI.HD.Y.+

21837　— [Anr. ed.] 4° in 8's. *J. Haviland,* 1638. Ass'd to Haviland a. J. Wright 4 se. L.L[3].O[3].G[2].M.+; CHI.

21838　— A key to the key of scripture: or an exposition with notes, upon the epistle to the Romanes; the three first chapters. 4° in 8's. *T. S[nodham] f. G. Norton,* 1611. Ent. to R. Bonian a. G. Norton 19 fb. L(destroyed). O.BIRM[2](K.N.).M[2].PLUME.; F.HN.HD.ILL.Y.+

21839　— [A variant, w. imprint:] *T. S[nodham] f. R. Bonian,* 1611. C.C[3].E[2].G[2].NEP.+; HD.PN[2].U.

21840　— Second edition, corrected. 4° in 8's. *T. C[otes] f. N. Fussell a. H. Mosley,* 1629. Ass'd from G. Norton to R. Rounthwait 12 my. 1619; to N. Fussell 4 jy. 1626. L(destroyed).L[2].O.C[2].A.BRISTOL.+; F.BO.Y.

21841　— The ministers portion. By William Sclater. 4°. *Oxford, Jos. Barnes,* 1612. Ent. to John Barnes a. ass'd to J. Parker 10 jy. 1619. L.L[3].O.O[5].C.+; F.HN.ILL.Y.

21842　— The quæstion of tythes revised. Objections more fully, and distinctly answered. Mr Seldens Historie [22172], over-ly viewed. 4°. *J. Legatt,* 1623. Ent. 12 jn. L.O.C.E.M[4].+; F.HD.ILL(date cropt).WIS.U.+
　　Though this has the headline: 'The Ministers portion', it is a different work from 21841.

21843　— A sermon preached at the last generall assise holden at Taunton. 4°. *E. Griffin f. H. Fetherstone,* 1616. Ent. 31 au. L[3].O.C.BRISTOL.G[2].+; F.AAS.ILL.Y.
　　Reprinted in 21846.

21844　— Sermons experimentall: on psalmes CXVI. & CXVII. Published by his son W. Slater. 4°. *J. Raworth f. N. Butter,* 1638. L.O.C.A.BRISTOL.+; F.HN.HD.NY[11].U. ᴙ

21845　— The sick souls salve. By William Sclater. [A sermon.] 4°. *Oxford, Jos. Barnes,* 1612. Ent. to John Barnes a. ass'd to J. Parker 10 jy. 1619. L[3].O.C.BRISTOL.STD. +; F.HN.HD(lacks tp).ILL.Y.

21846　— Three sermons . . . Now published by his sonne (W. Sclater.) (A sermon preached at S[t]. Maries in Cambridge.—A sermon preached at Tanton.—A funerall sermon at the buriall of John Colles.) 4°. *T. Harper f. R. Allot,* 1629. Ass'd from R. Allot to J. Legat a. A. Crooke 1 jy. 1637. L.O.C.A.BRISTOL.+; F.BO.HD. ILL.Y.+

21847　— A threefold preservative against three dangerous diseases of these latter times. 1. Non proficiency in grace. 2. Fals-hearted hypocrisie. 3. Back-sliding in religion. Prescribed in a sermon at S. Pauls Crosse. 4°. *S. S[tafford] f. R. Bonian a. H. Walley,* 1610. L.L[3].L[15].O.C[4].+; F.HN.HD.

21848　— Utriusque epistolæ ad Corinthios explicatio analytica. Nunc à filio suo (G. Sclater) in lucem edita. 4°. *Oxoniæ, G. Turner,* 1633. Ent. to R. Allot 11 my. 1631. L(destroyed).L[3].O.C.D.E[2].+; F.HN.BO.ILL.Y.+
　　Tp as above on *1[r]; 2nd tp on A1[r] has 'analytica;' in title.

21849　**Sclater, William,** *the Younger.* Death's summons, and the saints duty. Laid forth first in a sermon on 2. King .20.1 at the funerall of a citizen [Peter Taylor.] Since somewhat enlarged. 4°. [*M. Parsons f.*] *R. Hodgkinson,* 1640. Ent. 3 mr. O.; F.HN.Y.

21850　— The worthy communicant rewarded. Laid forth in a sermon. 4°. *R. Y[oung] f. G. Lathum,* [1639.] L.L[3]. O.C.D.+; F.CAL[2].Y. Haverhill PL, Massachusetts. Sydney U.
　　Dedic. dated 11 May 1639.

　　— *ed. See* 21844, 21846, 21848.

21850.3　**Scoggin, John.** [Headline:] The iestes of Skogyn. 8°. [*T. Colwell,* c. 1570.] Ent. to T. Colwell 1565–66. L (frags. of quire K, Harl.5995/210, 328, 331–2).
　　23 lines a page.

21850.7　— [Anr. ed.] The first and best part of Scoggins jests: full of witty mirth and pleasant shifts, done by him in France. Gathered by A. Boord. 8°. [*M. Flesher*] *f. F. Williams,* 1626. Ass'd by H. Jackson to Roger Jackson 22 jy. 1616; to F. Williams 16 ja. 1625; to J. Harrison 4 on 29 jn. 1630. L.
　　(Formerly 21852) 30 lines a page.

Scoggin, John—*cont.*

21851 — Scoggins jestes. Wherein is declared his pleasant pastimes in France; and of his meriments among the fryers. 8°. *R. Blower*, 1613. Pt. of T. Pavier's rights ass'd by Blower to E. Wright 10 fb. 1615; anr. pt. of Pavier's rights ass'd to E. Brewster a. R. Bird 4 au. 1626. o(lacks F6).

A different text, continuing Scoggin's adventures.

21852 — Now = 21850.7.

21853 **Scoloker, Anthony**, *Poet*. Diaphantus, or the passions of love. [Init. An. Sc. In verse.] 4°. *T. C[reede] f. W. Cotton*, 1604. o.; Haverford C.

Scoloker, Anthony, *Printer*, tr. See 3017, 4626.3, 5199.7, 20795, 21537.5, 24781.

Scory, Edmund. See 22629.

21854 **Scory, John**, *Bp.* An epistle wrytten vnto all the faythfull that be in pryson in Englande. 1555. 8°. [*Emden, E. van der Erve*, 1555.] L.L².O³.C⁸.D.+; F.BO³.HD.

The F tp has the verso blank and is conjugate; the DUR⁵ tp w. verso blank is from the same typesetting but is pasted on a stub, the verso of which shows the remains of a woodcut.

— tr. See 921, 6152.

21855 **Scot, Gregory.** A briefe treatise agaynst certayne errors of the Romish church. [In verse.] 8°. *J. Awdeley*, 1574. L.; HN.

21856 **Scot, John**, *Adolescens*. In serenissimi et invictissimi regis Jacobi sexti, e Scotia sua decessum, Hodœporicon, per J. Scotum adolescentem. Adjecta insuper J. Scoti, à Scottistarvet, patruelis Schediasmata miscellanea. [In verse.] 4°. *Edinburgi, A. Hart*, 1619. L.C².E.E².

Edited by Sir John Scot of Scotstarvet, who also wrote the Schediasmata.

Scot, John, *Antiquarian*. See 4484.5, 4489.7, 19052.2.

Scot, Sir John. See 21856.

21857 **Scot, Patrick.** Calderwoods recantation: or, a tripartite discourse. Directed to such of the ministrie, in Scotland, that refuse conformitie to the ordinances of the church. [Anon.] 4°. *B. Alsop*, 1622. Ent. 4 no. L.O.C².D.E.+

21858 — Omnibus & singulis. Affording matter profitable for all men, alluding to a Fathers advice or last will to his sonne. 8°. *W. Stansby*, 1619. Ent. 12 jn. L(imp.).; HN.Y(imp.).

Collates A–G⁸.

21858.5 — [Anr. ed., revised and enlarged.] Omnibus & singulis. 8°. *W. Stansby*, 1619. L¹³.O.; F.

Collates A–G⁸ H⁴.

21859 — [Anr. issue, w. cancel tp:] A fathers advice or last will to his sonne. *W. Stansby, sold by J. Parker*, 1620. L.; F.

21860 — A table-booke for princes. 8°. *B. Alsop*, 1621. Ent. 31 mr. L.O.DUL.E.SHR.+; F.HN.HD.PN².

21861 — [Anr. issue, w. cancel tp, w. imprint:] *B. A[lsop,] sold by R. Swaine*, 1622. Ass'd 18 se. 1621. C.

21862 — The tillage of light. Or, a true discouerie of the philosophicall elixir, commonly called the philosophers stone. 8°. [*A. Mathewes] f. W. Lee*, 1623. L.E.G².; F.HN.

21863 — Vox vera: or, observations from Amsterdam. Examining the late insolencies of some pseudo-puritans. 4°. *B. Alsop*, 1625. L.O.C².D.E.+; F.HN.HD.U.Y.+

21864 **Scot, Reginald.** The discouerie of witchcraft, wherein the lewde dealing of witches is notablie detected, the knauerie of coniurors, [etc.] 4° in 8's. [*H. Denham f.*] (*W. Brome*,) 1584. L.O.C.D².E.+; F.HN.HD.N.Y.+

21865 — A perfite platforme of a hoppe garden. 4°. *H. Denham*, 1574. L.O.O¹⁷.C.M².+; NY(2).

21866 — [Anr. ed.] Newly corrected and augmented. 4°. *H. Denham*, 1576. L.L².O.G².RD.+; F.HN.ILL.PML.Y.+

21867 — [Anr. ed.] 4°. *H. Denham*, 1578. L.O.D⁶.RD.STU.+; F. HN.HD(imp.).HUNT.Y.+

Reprinted in 5874. Denham's rights yielded 8 Jan. 1584; see Arber II.789.

21868 **Scot, Robert.** The foundation of the universitie of Oxford. 1634. Now = 19052.4.

21869 **Scot, Thomas**, *Gent.* Philomythie or philomythologie. Wherin outlandish birds, beasts, and fishes, are taught to speake true English plainely. (Certaine pieces of this age paraboliz'd.) [In verse.] 8°. (*J. Legatt*) *f. F. Constable*, 1616 (1615.) Ent. 4 jy. 1615. L.L⁶.C².D.; F.HN.HD.N(lacks tp).NY.+ 𝔄

21870 — Second edition, much inlarged. 8°. (*E. Griffin*) *f. F. Constable*, 1616. L(2).O.D.E.SHEF.; F.HN.HD(lacks tp).N.NY.+

A8ᵛ line 1: 'sodaine'.

21871 — [Anr. ed.] Second edition, much inlarged. 8°. [*J. Legat*] *f. F. Constable*, 1622 (1616.) L(2, 1 imp.).L¹⁶.O(w. tp to 21870).; F.HN.CHI.

A8ᵛ line 1: 'sodain'd'. This was apparently pr. after 21871a, and is the ed. usually bd. w. 21872.

21871a — [Anr. ed.] Second edition, much inlarged. 8°. [*J. Legat*] *f. F. Constable*, 1622 (1616.) L.O⁶.; F.CU(imp.)*.Y.

A8ᵛ line 1: 'sodaind'.

21871a.3 — [Anr. issue, w. imprint on gen. tp:] *f. F. Constable*, 1640. HD.

21871a.7 — The second part of Philomythie, or Philomythologie. Containing certaine tales of true libertie. [In verse.] 8°. [*E. Griffin*] *f. F. Constable*, 1616. Ent. 12 ap. L. O.SHEF.; HN.HD.LC.PN.

21872 — [Anr. ed.] 8°. *J. Legatt f. F. Constable*, 1625. L(2).L¹⁶. O.; F.HN.CHI.ILL.Y.+

21873 **Scot, Thomas**, *of Ipswich*. God and the king, in a sermon preached at the assises holden at Bury S. Edmonds, June 13. 1631. 4°. *prs. to the Univ. of Camb.*, 1633. L.O.O²¹.C.C⁸.; F.HD.U.

21873.5 — Vox Dei: injustice cast and condemned. In a sermon preached the twentieth of March 1622. At the assises holden in St. Edmunds Bury. 8°. *J. L[egat] f. R. Rounthwait*, 1623. Ent. 6 my. L.O.C³.LINC.NOR².+; F.HN.U.

(Formerly 22097)

21874 **Scot, William.** The course of conformitie, as it hath proceeded, is concluded, should be refused. [Anon.] 4°. [*Amsterdam, G. Thorp*,] 1622. L.O.C².E.YK.+; F (imp.).HN.HD.ILL.U.+

Sometimes attrib. to D. Calderwood.

SCOTLAND

Statutes and other Public Documents

(Arranged by date of contents)

21875 — The actis and constitutiounis of the realme of Scotland maid be Iames the first, secund, [etc. 1424–1564. *Ed.*] (E. Henrison.) fol. (*Edinburgh, R. Lekpreuik*, 1566 (12 oc.)) L².O.E.E⁸. House of Lords.

Tp line 3 ends: 'the'. Ideally this should have fols. 113, 118, 132, 145, w. acts favouring Catholics, uncancelled as in O copy.

21876 — [Mixed copies, w. tp of 21875 and colophon of 21876a.] L.O.C.E.M.+; F.HN.HD.MIN.U.

21876a — [Anr. issue, w. cancel tp and colophon:] (*Edinburgh, R. Lekpreuik*, 1566 (28 no.)) L.O.A.E.G².+; F.CU.HD. MICH.

Tp line 3 ends: 'First'. This should also have cancels for fols. 113, 118, 132, and 145, the latter followed by an unnumbered leaf; 2 unnumbered leaves following 158 and 168; 181 replaced by 2 leaves, including the new colophon; and 133 cancelled and not replaced.

21877 — [Anr. ed., revised, including Parliaments 1–15 James VI.] The lawes and actes of parliament, maid be king Iames the first, and his successours. (Ane table of the principall maters.—A table of all the kinges of Scotland.—De verborum significatione the exposition of the termes . . . collected be J. Skene.) fol. *Edinburgh, R. Walde-graue*, 1597 (15 mr.) L.O.C².D².E.+; F.HN. CHI.HD.NY.+

(22014, 22622 are pt. of this) Copies usually have either the letterpress or the engr. tp; both at L, F.

21877.5 — [Anr. issue, w. quires 2nd H to the end, De verborum, reprinted, w. subtitle:] (Second edition. *Edinburgh, R. Walde-graue*, 1599.) L³⁸.O².C(imp.).E.LEEDS.+; F.HN.HD.N.Y.+

(22623 is pt. of this)

21878 — = 21892.

Scotland—STATUTES AND OTHER PUBLIC DOCUMENTS—*cont.*

21878.5 — The new actis and constitutionis of parliament maid be
Iames the fift kyng of Scottis. 1540. fol. [Col. on E5ʳ:]
(*Edinburgh, T. Dauidson,* 1541 (8 fb.)) E(2).HAT.

21879 — The actis and constitutionis of parliament maid be
Marie quene of Scottis. fol. (*Edinburgh, R. Lekpreuik,*
1565.) Private owner.

21880 — The actis of parliament of Iames the sext, king of
Scottis. [15 Dec. 1567.] fol. (*Edinburgh, R. Lekpreuik,*
1568 (6 ap.)) L.O.C²(lacks tp).E(lacks tp).M.+; F.HN.
CU.HD.MIN.+
Partially reprinted in 21946.5 sq.

21881 — [Anr. ed.] fol. *Edinburgh, J. Ros,* 1575. L.O.C.A.E.+;
F.HN.CH.HD.MICH.

21882 — In the parliament . . . be gunne at Striuiling. [28 Aug.
1571 and 26 Jan. 1572.] fol. *Sanctandrois, R.
Lekpreuik,* 1573. L.O.C.E.M.+; CU.HD.MIN.

21883 — [Anr. ed., enlarged, w. parliament of 30 Apr. 1573.]
fol. *Edinburgh, J. Ros,* 1575. L.O.C.A.E.+; F(3).HN.
CH.HD.MICH.

21884 — In the parliament haldin at Striuiling. [25 July 1578
and 20 Oct. 1579.] (Ane proclamatioun for publischeing of the actis of parliament. [23 Jan. 1579 o.s.])
fol. *Edinburgh, J. Ros,* 1579 [1580.] L.O.C.E.M.+;
F(2).HN.CH.HD(2).MIN.
(Proclamation formerly 21946)

21885 — In the parliament haldin and begun at Edinburgh.
[24 Oct. 1581.] fol. *Edinburgh, H. Charteris,* 1582.
L.O.C.E.M.+; F.HN.CH.HD(2, 1 imp.).

21886 — Ane declaratioun of the just and necessar causis,
mouing vs of the nobillitie [etc. By J. Colville.] 8°.
[*Edinburgh, R. Lekpreuik?*] 1582. L.L².E.A.

21887 — In the current parliament haldin at Edinburgh.
[22 May 1584.] fol. *Edinburgh, A. Arbuthnet,* [1584.]
L.O.BUTE(imp.).E(7).E².; F.HD.IND.

21887.5 — The act for furthering of iustice in criminall causes.
[9 Nov. 1588.] 4°. (*Edinburgh, H. Charteris,*) [1588.]
E².

21888 — Actis of parliament, past sen the coronatioun of the
kingis maiestie, in furtherance of the progres of
religioun, as alswa, concerning the puir. 4°. *Edinburgh, R. Walde-graue,* 1593. L.O.E.G².; F.

21889 — In the parliament haldin at Edinburgh, the aucht day
of Junii, 1594. fol. *Edinburgh, R. Waldegraue,* 1594.
E.E².; F.HN.

21890 — The decree . . . of parliament against J. Chastel. 1595.
= 5067.

21891 — The questions to be resoluit at the conuention of the
Estaits and Generall Assemblie, at Perth. [By King
James.] 4°. *Edinburgh, R. Walde-graue,* 1597. L.L¹¹
(S.P. Scot. Eliz., Vol. 60, doc. 31).E.E⁸.G².+; F.
(Formerly also 19782)

21892 — The lawes and acts of parliament made be James king
since his majesties XV. parliament the XIX day of
December 1597. [Parliaments 16–20. Ed.] (Sir J.
Skene.) fol. *Edinburgh, T. Finlason,* 1611. L.O.E.G².
LEEDS.+; F.HN.CU.HD.MIN.+
(Formerly also 21878) Collates tp+A⁴ B–G⁶ H²;
there is a 1647 reprint (pt. of Aldis 1258) some-
times lacking tp, collating A–H⁴ I¹.

21892.3 — Apud Falkland . . . Ane acte anent the registring of
saisings, reversions, and some vther writtes. [31
July 1599.] s.sh.fol. *Edinburgh, R. Walde-graue,*
1599. O.A³. Lord Rosebery(imp.). Cr.908.
(Formerly 21956) *See also* 21959.

21892.5 — Act of parliament anent registration of seasings.
[15 Nov. 1600.] s.sh.fol. [*Edinburgh,*] R. W⟨alde-⟩
grave, [1600.] E⁶(imp.).; F(impr. def.).

21892.7 — Certaine acts particularlie recommended by our
soveraine to the estates of parliament. [20 June 1609.]
fol. *Edinburgh, R. Charteris,* 1609. E.; HD(missing).

21893 — Some particulare actes made 24 of June 1609. fol.
Edinburgh, R. Charteris, 1609. E.E².

21894 — The rates of marchandizes as they are set down in the
booke of rates for payment of the kings majesties
customes, and impost of wynes within his kingdome
of Scotland. [29 Apr. 1611.] 4°. *Edinburgh, T. Finlason,* 1611. L.E(lacks tp).
See also 7693.

21894.5 — Articles concerning the authoritie of justices of peace
and constables, established within the kingdome of
Scotland. 4°. *Edinburgh, T. Finlason,* 1611. E.

21895 — [Anr. ed., w. additions.] Since enlarged . . . the xvj day
of Julie, 1612. 4°. *Edinburgh, T. Finlason,* 1612.
L(destroyed).E(imprint cropt).
Last item in text dated 27 Oct. 1612.

Scotland—STATUTES AND OTHER PUBLIC DOCUMENTS—*cont.*

21896 — The XXj parliament. [23 Oct. 1612.] fol. *Edinburgh,
T. Finlason,* 1612. L.O.C.E.G².+; F.HN.CU.HD.MIN.+
Collates tp+A–C² [–]².

21897 — The acts made in the XXII. parliament. [28 June 1617.]
fol. *Edinburgh, T. Finlason,* 1617. L.O.E⁸.G⁴.LEEDS.
+; HD.MIN. Cincinnati U.
Collates tp+A–F² F–I².

21898 — [Anr. ed. Heading A1ʳ:] God, and my right . . . The
XXII parliament. fol. [*Edinburgh, T. Finlason,* 1617.]
L.O.C(imp.).E.G⁴.+; F.HN.CU.HD.N.+
Collates A–K².

21899 — The act anent the setling of measures and weghts.
[19 Feb. 1618.] fol. [*Edinburgh, T. Finlason,* 1618.]
L⁴³.O.C.E.M⁴.; F.HN.CU.NY.
Collates L–M²; issued as a supplement to
21898.

21900 — The XXIII parliament. [4 Aug. 1621.] fol. *Edinburgh,
T. Finlason,* 1621. L.O.C.E².G⁴.+; F.HN.CU.HD.MIN.+
Tp line 3: 'by'; R2ᵛ ends: 'The end of the XXiij.
[etc.]'

21901 — [Anr. ed.] fol. *Edinburgh, T. Finlason,* 1621. L.E.G².
LEEDS.M⁴.+; F(imp.).HN.HD.LC.N.+
Tp line 3: 'bee'; R2ᵛ ends: 'Finis'.

21901.2 — [Heading A1ʳ:] God, and my right . . . Act anent the
taxation granted to his majestie of thirtie shillings
tearmelie upon the pound land, and the twentie
pennie of all anwelrentes. [27 Oct. 1625.] fol.
[*Edinburgh, T. Finlason,* 1625.] E.

21901.4 — [Heading A1ʳ:] God, and my right. . . . Act anent the
collecting of the taxation, and releife to prelates.
[27 Oct. 1625.] fol. [*Edinburgh, T. Finlason,* 1625.]
E.

21901.6 — [Heading A1ʳ:] God, and my right . . . Act anent
the taxation [etc. as 21901.2. 28 July 1630.] fol.
(*Edinburgh, heires of T. Finlason,* 1630.) O(2).;
MIN.N.
Enforced by the proclamations 21988 sq.

21901.8 — [Heading A1ʳ:] God, and my right . . . Act anent the
collecting of the taxation [etc. as 21901.4. 28 July
1630.] fol. [*Edinburgh, heirs of T. Finlason,* 1630.]
O.; MIN.N.

21902 — The acts made in the first parliament of our soveraigne
Charles, at Edinburgh. [28 June 1633.] fol. *Edin-
burgh, R. Young,* 1633. L.O.C⁹.E.M.+; F.HN.CU.HD.
MIN.+

21902.5 — [Anr. ed.] fol. *Edinburgh, E. Tyler,* 1633 [post-1640.]
C.A.BUTE.STU.; HN.CAL⁵.HD.LC.MIN.

— Generall demands, concerning the late covenant. 1638.
See 64.

— [Protestation of the noblemen 22 Feb. 1638.] *See*
22013.

21903 — The protestation of the noblemen, barrons, . . . and
commons, made the 4. of Julij immediatly after the
reading of the proclamation, dated 28. June 1638
[21996]. 4°. [*Edinburgh, G. Anderson,*] 1638.
CASHEL.E.G².M.YK.+
C1ʳ last line: 'to bee granted'.

21903.3 — [Anr. ed.] 4°. [*Edinburgh, G. Anderson,*] 1638. L.O.
E.E².M.+; F.HN.HD.ILL.NY.+
C1ʳ last line: 'to be granted'.

21903.5 — [Anr. ed.] 4°. [*Edinburgh, G. Anderson,*] 1638. DEU.
E(4).E².G².M².; F.HN.U. Brandeis U.
C1ʳ last line: 'to be graunted'.

21903.7 — [Anr. ed.] 4°. [*Edinburgh, J. Wreittoun,*] 1638. L.O.C.D.
E.+; F.HD.Y.
C1ʳ last line: 'Finis.'

21904 — The protestation of the noblemen, barrons, . . . and
commons; made the 22. of September, immediatly
after the reading of the proclamation, dated September 9. 1638 [21998]. [By A. Henderson and Sir A.
Johnston.] 4°. [*Edinburgh, G. Anderson,*] 1638. L³.
O.C.D.E.+; F.HD.ILL.NY.Y.+
A2ʳ line 4 from bottom begins: 'liklie'; C2ʳ line 1
begins: '(if'. Copies (e.g. L) may have mixed
sheets w. 21904.3.

21904.3 — [Anr. issue, w. quire A, and C inner forme reset.]
[*Edinburgh, G. Anderson,*] 1638. L¹⁵.D.DUR⁵.E.G².+;
F.HN.HD.
A2ʳ line 4 from bottom begins: 'likelie'; C2ʳ line 1
begins: 'adhere'.

Note: Items dated 1639 are arranged alphabetically.

21904.5 — Articles of militarie discipline. 4°. *Edinburgh, J. Bryson,*
1639. L.L¹⁵.O.E.G².+; F.HN.HD.Y.
(Formerly 811)

Scotland—Statutes and other Public Documents—*cont.*

21904.7 — Copye van eenen brief, ghesonden door seeckere hooghe graven ende heeren van Schotland, . . . aen den grave van Essex. 8°. *Edinburgh, J. Bryson* [i.e. *Amsterdam, Richt Right Press,*] 1639. HAGUE.
> App. a trans. of the letter sent 19 April 1639; no copies of the orig. Scottish ed. are known.

21905 — An information to all good christians within the king-dome of England, from the noblemen, and commons of the kingdome of Scotland. 4°. *Edinburgh, J. Bryson,* 1639. L.O¹⁸.E.LYU.M².+; F.HN.HD(2).NY¹¹.Y.
> Imprint in 3 lines; end of text dated: 'Edinb. 4 of Feb.' Sometimes erroneously attrib. to J. Durie.

21905a — [A variant.] *Edinburgh, J. Bryson,* 1639. L.O.C.E.M.+; F(2).ILL.N.PN².U.
> Imprint in 2 lines; end of text dated: 'Edinb. 4 of Feb.'

21905b — [A variant.] *Edinburgh, J. Bryson,* 1639. O.C.E.M⁴.
> Imprint in 2 lines; end of text dated: 'Edinburgh the 4 of February'.

21905b.5 — [A trans.] Informatie aen alle goede christenen in het coninckrijck van Enghelant. 4°. *Edinburg, J. Brysons,* [i.e. *Holland,*] 1639. D.

21906 — A large declaration concerning the late tumults in Scotland, from their first originalls: together with the seditious practices of the prime leaders of the Covenanters: collected out of their owne foule acts and writings. By the king. [Drawn up by W. Balcanquhall.] fol. *R. Young,* 1639. L.O.C.D².E.+; F.HN.HD.N.U.+
> Copies vary: tp with or without comma after 'Scotland' (both at C², HD); p. 41 with or without marginal note (both at L, C, F). Answered by 21929.

21906a — = 21906.

21907 — The remonstrance of the nobility, barrones, . . . and commons . . . vindicating them from the crymes, wherewith they are charged by the late proclamation in England, Feb. 27. 1639 [9135]. [22 Mar. 1639. Attrib. to A. Henderson.] 4°. *Edinburgh, J. Bryson,* 1639. L.O.C.D.E.+; F.HN.HD.N.U.+
> Pp. 32.

21908 — [Anr. ed.] 4°. *Edinburgh, J. Bryson,* [i.e. *Amsterdam, Richt Right Press,*] 1639. L.O.C.D.E¹¹.+; F.HD.
> Pp. 22.

21908.5 — [A trans.] Remonstrantie vande edelen, baronnen . . . van Schotlandt. 4°. *Edinburgh, J. Bryson,* [i.e. *Amsterdam, Richt Right Press,*] 1639. D.E(2, 1 imp.). HAGUE.; NY.

21909 — Some speciall arguments which warranted the Scotch subjects lawfully to take up armes. 4°. [*Amsterdam, Richt Right Press,* 1642.] L(8142.b.42).
> A variant of Wing S 4619 at L(E.239(3)).

Note: Official broadsides of 1640 with date of enactment are chronological; other items follow alphabetically.

21910 — Act anent masterles men, beggars, loytters at home, and others refusing to goe out beeing enrolled. [30 June 1640.] s.sh.fol. *Edinburgh, J. Bryson,* 1640. E².E³. Cr.1714.

21910.3 — Act anent the out comming of horses, as well conforme to their rents as voluntiers. [30 June 1640.] s.sh.fol. *Edinburgh, J. Bryson,* 1640. O.
> (Formerly 21913)

21910.5 — Act anent the inbringing of money. [15 July 1640.] s.sh.fol. *Edinburgh, J. Bryson,* 1640. O⁶.; HN.

21910.7 — Instructions anent the borrowing of money, and receiving of silver plate. [23 July 1640.] s.sh.fol. *Edinburgh, J. Bryson,* 1640. E.

21911 — Act against runawayes, masterlesse men, and those who travels [*sic*] without testimonials. [20 Aug. 1640.] s.sh.fol. *Edinburgh, J. Bryson,* 1640. E.E³ (impr. cropt). Cr.1716.

21912 — Act against run-awayes, and fugitives, and those who recepts, intertaines, conceals, and not apprehends, or delates them. [11 Nov. 1640.] s.sh.fol. *Edinburgh, J. Bryson,* 1640. O.E³. Cr.1719.

21912.3 — Instructions sent be the committe [*sic*] of the Estates to the committies of warre. [16 Nov. 1640.] s.sh.fol. *Edinburgh, J. Bryson,* 1640. O⁶.E³. Cr.1720.
> (Formerly 21918)

21912.7 — Act anent the pryces of shooes, bootes, hydes, and tanning of leather. [26 Nov. 1640.] s.sh.fol. *Edinburgh, J. Bryson,* 1640. L³⁰.

21913 — Now = 21910.3.

Scotland—Statutes and other Public Documents—*cont.*

21914 — Articles and ordinances of warre; for the present expedition of the armie of the kingdome of Scotland. [By A. Leslie, First Earl of Leven.] 4°. *Edinburgh, J. Bryson,* 1640. O.C⁸.E(2).; F.HD.Y.

— Declaratio consilii exercitûs Scoticani. 1640. *See* 21922.

21915 — The demands and behaviour of the rebels of Scotland. 4°. *R. Young,* 1640. Ent. 19 se. L.O.C.E.M.+; F.HN.HD.N.Y.
> Copies vary: with or without imprimatur on A4ᵛ; both at M.

— From the commissioners of Scotland, 24 February, 1640 [o.s.] *See* Wing S 976A, Cr.1836–7 (England).

21916 — Information from the Estaits of the kingdome of Scotland, to the kingdome of England. 4°. [*Edinburgh, J. Bryson,*] 1640. L.O.C.E.M⁴.+; F.HN.PN².Y.
> Ordered publicly burned; *see* 9154.

21916.5 — [Anr. ed.] An information from the States [etc.] 8°. [*Amsterdam, Cloppenburg Press,*] 1640. L(tp only, Harl.5938/65).O.O⁶.C¹⁵.LINC.; F.HD(def.).MCG.

21917 — Information from the Scottish nation, to all the true English, concerning the present expedition. s.sh.fol. [*Edinburgh, R. Bryson?* 1640.] L(190.g.13(245)).L³.O⁶.E.STU.

— Instructions anent the borrowing of money. 1640. *See* 21910.7.

21918 — Instructions sent be the committe [*sic*] of the Estates. 1640. Now = 21912.3.

21919 — The intentions of the army of the kingdome of Scotland. 4°. *Edinburgh, R. Bryson,* 1640. O.C.A.E.G².+; F.HD.U.
> Collates A–B⁴ C²; Bryson's device w. monogram (McK. 358β) on tp.

21919.5 — [Anr. ed.] 4°. *Edinburgh, R. Bryson* [i.e. *Leyden, W. Christiaens,*] 1640. L.O.C⁸.
> Collates A–B⁴ C²; orn. w. cupids and musical instruments on tp.

21920 — [Anr. ed.] 4°. [*Edinburgh, R. Bryson,*] 1640. L.L³.O.E.G².+; HN.HD.ILL. Iowa U.
> Collates A–D⁴ E². This is prob. the earliest ed.

21921 — [Anr. ed.] 4°. [*Amsterdam, Cloppenburg Press,*] 1640. L.O¹³.C².E.M.+; F.HD.N.NY.Y.+
> Collates A–B⁴; B1ʳ line 5: 'troubles,'.

21921.5 — [Anr. ed.] 4°. [*Amsterdam, Cloppenburg Press,*] 1640. O(2).O⁵.C.E(2).WIN².; HN.Y.
> Collates A–B⁴; B1ʳ line 5: 'troubles,'.

21922 — [A trans.] Declaratio consilii exercitûs Scoticani, ad fratres Anglos. 4°. *Edinburgi, R. Bryson,* 1640. L³.O⁶.E.G².G⁴.+

21923 — The lawfulnesse of our expedition into England manifested. 4°. *Edinburgh, R. Bryson,* 1640. L.O.C².E.E². +; F.HD.
> Bryson's device w. monogram on tp. Tp varies: line 3: 'of our' or 'of'; both at E.

21923.5 — [Anr. ed.] 4°. *Edinburgh, R. Bryson,* [i.e. *Leyden, W. Christiaens,*] 1640. L¹¹(S.P.D. Chas. I, Vol. 469, doc.87).O.
> Orn. w. woman's head above imprint. The L¹¹ copy has Laud's MS. notes.

21924 — [Anr. ed.] 4°. *Reprinted in England, by Margery Mar-Prelat* [i.e. *Amsterdam, Cloppenburg Press,*] 1640. L.O.C³.D.E¹¹.+; F.HN.HD.N.NY.+

21925 — [A trans.] Vertoog van het wettelyckheyt van onsen tocht in Engelant. Na de copye gedruckt by R. Brison. [*Holland,*] 1640.
> Not an STC book.

21926 — Our demands of the English lords manifested, being at Rippon Oct. 8. 1640. With answers to the complaints . . . said to be committed by our army. 4°. *Margery Mar-Prelat* [i.e. *Amsterdam, Cloppenburg Press,*] 1640. L.O.C².E.M.+; F.HN.N.Y. Pirie.

21927 — The proceedings of the commissioners. [1640.] = pt. 2 of 21929.

21927.5 — A remonstrance concerning the present troubles, from the meeting of the Estates. 4°. [*Edinburgh, R. Bryson,*] 1640. L³.O.C².E.G².+; F.HN.HD.MICH.U.+
> Pp. 39.

21927.7 — [Anr. ed.] 4°. [*Leyden, W. Christiaens,*] 1640. E.G².INN.
> Pp. 38.

21928 — [Anr. ed.] 4°. [*Amsterdam, Cloppenburg Press,*] 1640. L.O.C².D⁸.E.+; F.CAL.HD.N.NY.+
> (Formerly also 20880) Pp. 25; in title: 'estaees [*sic*]'.

Scotland—Statutes and other Public Documents—*cont.*

21929 — A true representation of the proceedings of the king-dome of Scotland; since the late pacification. (The proceedings of the commissioners sent from the parliament of Scotland.) [By W. Ker.] 2 pts. 4°. [*Edinburgh, R. Bryson,*] 1640. L.O.C.E.G⁴.+; F.HN. HD.U.Y.+

(Pt. 2 formerly also 21927) Answers 21906.

PROCLAMATIONS

21930 — Heir followis the proclamatioun that the nobilitie and lordis made . . . declaring the effect of thair assemblie in armour. [11 June 1567.] s.sh.fol. *Edinburgh, R. Lekpreuik,* [1567.] L¹¹(2, S.P. Scot. Eliz., Vol. 13, docs. 54, 55). Cr.172.

21931 — Heir followis ane act that the lordis of Secreit Counsall maid . . . declaring James erle Bothwell to be the murtherar of the kingis grace. [12 June 1567.] s.sh.fol. *Edinburgh, R. Lekpreuik,* 1567. L¹¹(2, S.P. Scot. Eliz., Vol. 13, docs. 56, 57). Cr.173.

21932 — Heir followis ane proclamation that the lordis of Secreit Counsall maid [etc. For apprehension of Earl Bothwell. 26 June 1567.] s.sh.fol. *Edinburgh, R. Lekpreuik,* 1567. E. Cr.174.

21933 — ane proclamatioun anent the tressonable conspiratouris [etc. 7 May 1568.] s.sh.fol. *Edinburgh, R. Lekpreuik,* [1568.] L(Cotton MSS. Cal. C.I. fol. 56).L⁵.L¹¹(3, S.P. Scot. Eliz., Vol. 15, docs. 12–14). Cr.195.

21934 — ane proclamatioun set furth be my lord regent, declaring the purpose of thame quha assistit with our souerane lordis mother. [14 May 1568.] fol(3). *Edinburgh, R. Lekpreuik,* 1568. L(Cotton MSS. Cal. C.I. fol. 60).L¹¹(1st sheet only, S.P. Scot. Eliz., Vol. 14, doc. 75). Losely House, Surrey. Cr.197.

21935 — [Begins:] Forsamekill as the contempt of the kingis authoritie [etc. Enforcement of letters of horning. 27 Dec. 1569.] fol(2). *Edinburgh, R. Lekpreuik,* 1570. E. Cr.225.

21936 — The kingis maiesteis proclamatioun . . . Confuting the pretensis of his hienis rebellis [etc. 8 May 1570.] fol(3). *Edinburgh, R. Lekpreuik,* 1570. L⁵.L¹¹(S.P. Scot. Eliz., Vol. 18, doc. 9). Cr.242.

21937 — The answer to the sclanderous misreport of thame that be seditious, craftie, and fals narratioun labouris to deface the kingis authoritie, and the establisching of his regent. [5 Aug. 1570.] s.sh.fol. *Edinburgh, R. Lekpreuik,* 1570. L¹¹(S.P. Scot. Eliz., Vol. 19, doc. 3). Cr.242.

21938 — The forme of the abstinance, grantit be my lord regentis grace, to the lordis within the castell and toun of Edinburgh. [30 July 1572.] s.sh.fol. *Edinburgh, T. Bassandyne,* [1572.] L¹¹(S.P. Scot. Eliz., Vol. 23, doc. 68). Cr.276.

(Formerly also 11184) Signed: 'John, Regent, [etc.]'

21939 — [Anr. ed., signed: 'James Hamilton'.] Cr.277. A ghost, occurring only in MS.

21940 — The copie of the proclamatioun . . . for ane conuentioun of the professouris of the trew religioun to consult vpon the conspiracies of the papistis. [3 Oct. 1572.] s.sh.fol. *Sanctandrois, R. Lekpreuik,* 1572. L.L⁵.L¹¹(S.P. Scot. Eliz., Vol. 23, doc. 95).O. Cr.280.

21941 — A breif declaration how materis hes procedit during the lait abstinence and how . . . the war is renewit. [1 Jan. 1572 o.s.] fol(2). *Edinburgh, T. Bassandyne,* 1572 [1573.] L¹¹(S.P. Scot. Eliz., Vol. 24, doc. 2). Cr.283.

21942 — The kingis maiesteis proclamatioun beiring the verie occasioun of the present incūming of the Inglis forces, with his hienes commandement for thair gude intreatment and freindly vsage. [13 Apr. 1573.] s.sh.fol. *Edinburgh, T. Bassandyne,* [1573.] L(Cotton MSS. Cal. C.IV. fol. 63).L¹¹(S.P. Scot. Eliz., Vol. 25, doc. 10). Cr.290. 'Imprentit'.

21943 — [Anr. ed.] s.sh.fol. *Edinburgh, T. Bassandyne,* [1573.] L⁵. Cr.291. 'Imprintit'.

21943a — [Anr. ed.] s.sh.fol. *Edinburgh, T. Bassandyne,* [1573.] L⁵. Cr.292. 'Imprinted'.

— By Sir William Drury knight. [Proclamation of the entry of the English forces into Scotland.] 1573. *See* 8055.

Scotland—Proclamations—*cont.*

21943a.5 — [Proclamation concerning provision for the poor. 1 Mar. 1574 o.s.] s.sh.fol. *Edinburgh, J. Ros,* [1575.] Lord Rosebery(imp.).

21944 — The proclamatioun of the crying doun of the new plakkis and hardheidis. [Concerning counterfeit coins. 3 Mar. 1574 o.s.] s.sh.fol. *Edinburgh, J. Ros,* [1575.] L(Cotton MSS. Cal. C.IV. fol. 263). Cr.324.

21944.5 — James be the grace of God . . . fforsamekle as oure richt traist [etc. Letter of the Privy Council charging each parish to advance to A. Arbuthnet £5 Scots for printing the Bible (2125). 8 Mar. 1575.] s.sh.fol. [*Edinburgh, T. Bassandyne,* 1575.] E(MS.3135.f.35).

21945 — The act and proclamatioun anent the vniuersall course of the new markit money. [31 May 1575.] s.sh.fol. *Edinburgh, J. Ros,* [1575.] L.L⁵.O.E.E².+; F. Cr.328.

21946 — Ane proclamatioun for publischeing of the actis of parliament. [23 Jan. 1579 o.s.] Cr.420. = leaf H1 of 21884.

21946.5 — [The kingis maiesteis proclamatioun, etc. as 21947.] fol(3). [*Edinburgh, J. Ros,* 1580.] E(2nd sheet only). In roman types; the second sheet has the text of cap. 5, 6, 9, and heading of cap. 3, in that order, from 21880. Barker's B.L. reprint, below, follows the Scottish spelling very closely and includes the text of cap. 3 and the whole of cap. 4.

21947 — [Anr. ed. Heading A2ʳ:] The kingis maiesteis proclamatioun togidder with certane actis of parliament maid anent the aduersaris of Christis euangell. [9 Apr. 1580.] 4°. (*Edinburgh, J. Ros* [i.e. *London, C. Barker,*] 1580.) Ent. to C. Barker 19 no. L².C². Cr.421.

21948 — A declaratioun of the kings maiesties intentioun and meaning toward the lait actis of parliament. [By P. Adamson.] 4°. *Edinburgh, T. Vautroullier,* 1585. E.; HD. Cr.543.

(Formerly also 14372) Tp device w. oval border but no outer frame (McK. 232). Reprinted w. this imprint but w. royal arms on tp on pp. 11–22 of Wing J 132.

21948.3 — [Anr. ed.] 4°. *Edinburgh, T. Vautroullier* [i.e. *London, R. Field?*] 1585 [1588?] L.L².C³.E.E².; F.HN.HD. Tp device w. oval border in scroll-work frame (McK. 192); line 5 of title: 'PARLIAMENT.'

21948.7 — [Anr. issue, w. quire A and C1ʳ mostly reset, and the rest reimposed.] *Edinburgh, T. Vautroullier* [i.e. *London, R. Field?*] 1585 [1588?] L.O.; HN. Tp device as 21948.3; line 5 of title: 'PARLIAMENT' (no stop).

21949 — [Anr. ed.] 4°. *Edinburgh, by the assignement of T. Vautroullier,* [i.e. *London, G. Robinson?*] 1585. O. C².G⁴.; HN.

21949.5 — [An Anglicized version.] Treason pretended against the king of Scots, by certaine lordes and gentlemen. With a declaration of the kinges maiesties intention. Out of Skottish into English. 8° in 4's. *f. T. Nelson,* 1585. L(Add.MS.48117).L²(2).; F.

(Formerly 23402) With a letter by C. Studley.

21949.7 — Ane act for cunzie. [13 Jan. 1591 (o.s.)] *See* Addenda.

21950 — James be the grace of God . . . Forsameikle as the ambitious [etc. Ordering a general muster on 2 February and calling for peace on the borders. 2 Jan. 1596.] s.sh.fol. [*Edinburgh,*] R. Walde-graue, 1596. L¹¹(S.P. Scot. Eliz., Vol. 60, doc. 1). Cr.813. Last line to the right of the init. begins: 'quhairin'.

21951 — [Anr. ed.] s.sh.fol. [*Edinburgh,*] R. Walde-graue, 1596. L(imp., Cotton MSS. Cal. D.II. fol.200).L⁵.DUL. Cr.814. Last line to the right of the init. begins: 'ses'.

21951a — [Anr. ed.] s.sh.fol. [*Edinburgh,*] R. Walde-graue, 1596. E. Cr.814a. Last line to the right of the init. begins: 'to'.

21952 — At Halirud-hous . . . The articles set downe be his maiestie to be performit be the erle of Huntlie afore he ressaue ony licence to returne or remane in Scotland. [22 Nov. 1596.] s.sh.fol. [*Edinburgh, R. Waldegrave,* 1596.] L¹¹(S.P. Scot. Eliz., Vol. 59, doc. 69). E(missing). Cr.836.

21953 — James be the grace of God. . . . Forsameikill as we are surely informit [etc. Concerning the return of the Earls of Huntly and Erroll. 22 Nov. 1596.] s.sh.fol. [*Edinburgh, R. Waldegrave,* 1596.] L¹¹(S.P. Scot. Eliz., Vol. 59, doc. 70). Cr.837.

21954 — Ane proclamation dischargeing the support of the rebellis of Ireland. [8 Aug. 1598.] s.sh.fol. *Edinburgh, R. Waldegraue,* 1598. L¹¹(S.P. Scot. Eliz., Vol. 62, doc. 61). Cr.887.

Scotland—PROCLAMATIONS—*cont.*

21955 — Ane acte of Counsell anent the cunzie. [Requiring yielding up of foreign coins at fixed rates. 18 Dec. 1598.] s.sh.fol. [*Edinburgh,*] *R. Walde-graue,* 1598. L[11](S.P. Scot. Eliz., Vol. 63, doc. 79). Cr.893.

21956 — Ane acte anent the registring of saisings, reversiones, and some vther writtes. [31 July 1599.] Now = 21892.3.

21957 — Ane act made be his hienes [etc. Forbidding purchase of goods from any foreign ship not duly entered at a free port. 30 June 1600.] s.sh.fol. *Edinburgh, R. Walde-grave,* 1600. L[11](S.P. Scot. Eliz., Vol. 66, doc. 38). Cr.940.

21958 — By the king Forasmuch as it hath pleased the almighty God [etc. Proclamation upon the accession of King James to the crown of England. 4 Apr. 1603.] s.sh.fol. *Edingburgh* [sic], *R. Walde-grave,* 1603. O. E[6]. Cr.1029.

21959 — Ane act of counsell anent the inserting of the clause of registration in seasings. [5 Jan. 1604.] s.sh.fol. [*Edinburgh,*] *widdowe Walde-grave,* 1604. O.E(2). Cr.1043a.
 See also 21892.3 sq.

21960 — Whereas Bevis Bulmer Englishman [etc. An order of Council for search for mines. 16 Feb. 1604.] *Edinburgh, widdowe Waldegrave,* 1604. Cr.1047.
 The L[11] copy cited in Cr. is wholly in MS.; E[6] does not have a pr. item either.

— By the king. [Proclamation against calumnies concerning the Scottish church. 26 Sept. 1605.] *See* 8377.

21960.3 — Ane act and ordinance set down be the lords of Privie Counsell and Session, anent the pryces to be taken heir-efrer [sic] be the clerks and writters, bering publick function and office. 4°. *Edinburgh, T. Finlason,* 1606. E[3].

21960.5 — A declaration of the just causes of his majesties proceeding against those ministers, attainted of high treason. Set forth by his majesties Counsell of Scotland. [7 Mar. 1606. By Sir T. Hamilton?] 4°. [*Edinburgh, R. Charteris,* 1606.] E.; F. Cr.1078.

21960.7 — [A variant, w. colophon:] (*Edinburgh, R. Charteris,* 1606.) E.

21961 — [Anr. ed.] 4°. *R. Barker,* 1606. L.O.C[2].E.G[2].+; F.HN. HD.N.NY.+ Cr.1079.

21962 — James be the grace of God . . . Forsameikill as the three estates of our kingdome of Scotland convenit [etc. Proclamation for better inbringing of the land tax. 9 July 1606.] s.sh.fol. [*Edinburgh, R. Charteris,* 1606.] E[6]. Cr.1088.
 Last line to the right of the init. begins: 'und'.

21963 — [Anr. ed. For the third instalment due 1 Feb. 1609.] s.sh.fol. [*Edinburgh, R. Charteris,* 1608.] A[3]. Cr. 1089.
 Last line to the right of the init. begins: 'ders'.

21964 — By the king. Whereas divers of the ministrie [etc. Prohibiting prayers for the imprisoned ministers. 26 Sept. 1606.] s.sh.fol. *Edinburgh, R. Charteris,* 1606. E. Cr.1094.

21965 — By the king. Whereas during our stay [etc. Enforcing laws against Jesuits, etc. 26 Sept. 1606.] s.sh.fol. *Edinburgh, R. Charteris,* 1606. E. Cr.1095.

21965.5 — God save the king A proclamation for reforming sundrie inconveniences touching the coynes of his M. realmes. [25 Nov. 1619.] s.sh.fol. *Edinbourgh, T. Finlason,* [1619.] E. Cr.1320(MS. only).
 Printed on a sheet and a half pasted together before printing.

21966 — A proclamation for keeiping the actes of the last generall Assemblies of the Kirk. [8 June 1620.] s.sh.fol. *Edinburgh, T. Finlason,* [1620.] E. Cr.1336.
 Pr. on 2 sheets pasted together before printing.

21967 — Ane act against all unlawfull alienations. [12 July 1620.] s.sh.fol. [*Edinburgh,*] *T.Finlason,* [1620.] M(deposit). Cr.1337.
 Printed on 2 sheets pasted together before printing. L[5], L[11], and O[2] do *not* have copies of this.

21968 — A proclamation anent tanning and barking of hydes. [29 June 1620.] fol(2). *Edinburgh, T. Finlason,* [1620.] A[3]. Cr.1340.
 Each sheet is made of 2 small sheets pasted together before printing.

21969 — A declaration of his M. pleasure anent the religion & present Kirk government. [26 July 1625.] s.sh.fol. *Edinburgh, T. Finlason,* [1625.] A[3]. Cr.1428.

Scotland—PROCLAMATIONS—*cont.*

21970 — By the king . . . Forsamekle as wee being willing [etc. Appointing a commission on church lands. 11 July 1626.] fol(2). *Edinburgh, T. Finlason,* 1626. A[3]. Cr.1447.

21971 — [Forsameekle as by ane act, etc. Concerning the holding of weaponshaws, i.e. musters. 25 Jan. 1627.] fol(2). *Edinburgh, T. Finlason,* [1627.] A[3](2nd sheet only). Cr.1458.

21972 — God save the king . . . Forsamekle, as wee being of late humbly petitioned [etc. Appointing a commission for settlement of teinds, i.e. tithes, etc. 3 Feb. 1627.] fol(4). *Edinburgh, T. Finlason,* [1627.] E[6]. Cr. 1459.

21973 — God save the king . . . Forsamekle as the commissioners [etc. Appointing sub-commissioners for settlement of teinds. 12 Apr. 1627.] s.sh.fol. *Edinburgh, T. Finlason,* [1627.] E[6]. Lord Rosebery. Cr.1462.

21974 — Charles by the grace of God . . . Forsamekle as in the warre [etc. Concerning the levies in aid of the king of Denmark. 16 May 1627.] s.sh.fol. *Edinburgh, T. Finlason,* [1627.] E. Cr.1466.

21975 — God save the kin⟨g⟩ . . . Forsameekle as wee with advise of the lordes of our privie counsell [etc. Teind sellers to meet commissioners. 28 Feb. 1628.] s. sh.fol. *Edinburgh, T. Finlason,* [1628.] E[6](5 imp.). Cr.1487.
 Last line to the right of the init. begins: 'who'.

21975.5 — [Anr. ed.] s.sh.fol. *Edinburgh, T. Finlason,* [1628.] E[6](imp.). Cr. 1488.
 Last line to the right of the init. begins: 'teresse'.

21976 — God save the ⟨king⟩ . . . Forsameekle as it is our gratious will and pleasure [etc. Teind buyers to meet commissioners. 28 Feb. 1628.] s.sh.fol. *Edinburgh, T. Finlason,* [1628.] A[3].E[6](2 imp.). Cr. 1490.

21977 — Charles by the grace of God . . . Forsamekle as information [etc. Concerning the yearly certification of papists. 10 July 1628.] s.sh.fol. *Edinburgh, T. Finlason,* [1628.] E. Cr.1496.

21978 — Charles by the grace of God . . . Forsamekle as wee beeing resolved to proceed in the maters [etc. Concerning teinds. 14 July 1628.] s.sh.fol. *Edinburgh, T. Finlason,* [1628.] E. Cr.1498.

21979 — Charles by the grace of God . . . . Forsamekle as wee beeing resolved to proceed in the matters [etc. Commissioners to appoint sub-commissioners, etc. 16 July 1628.] s.sh.fol. *Edinburgh, T. Finlason,* [1628.] A.E. Cr.1501.

21980 — Charles by the grace of God . . . Forsamekle as by an act [etc. Objections against sub-commissioners to be heard. 8 Aug. 1628.] s.sh.fol. *Edinburgh, T. Finlason,* [1628.] A[3]. Cr.1506.

21981 — Charles by the grace of God . . . Forsamekle as in the [etc. Lords of erections to produce their titles. 8 Aug. 1628.] s.sh.fol. *Edinburgh, T. Finlason,* [1628.] A[3]. Cr.1507.

21982 — Charles by the grace of god . . . Forsamekle as wee have by divers acts [etc. A proclamation by the commissioners of teinds that presbyteries are to appoint sub-commissioners. 27 Sept. 1628.] s.sh.fol. *Edinburgh, T. Finlason,* [1628.] A.E. Cr. 1510.
 Printed on 2 sheets pasted together before printing.

21983 — Charles by the grace of God . . . Forsamekle as wee having by diverse acts [etc. A proclamation by the commissioners of teinds concerning sellers and buyers. 3 Dec. 1628.] s.sh.fol. *Edinburgh, heirs of T. Finlason,* [1628.] E. Cr.1516.
 Printed on a sheet and a half pasted together before printing.

21984 — Apud Halyrudhouse . . . Forsomeekle as by expresse warrand [etc. Sub-commissioners to meet at once, 24 Mar. 1629. Concerning teinds, 5 June 1629. Concerning wages of valuers, 1 July 1629.] s.sh.fol. *Edinburgh, heirs of T. Finlason,* [1629.] E[3].; N. Cr.1524, 1529, 1533.
 (Formerly also 21985, 21986) The 3 proclamations are pr. on a single sheet w. the imprint at the bottom.

21985 — Anent the proposition [etc. 5 June 1629.] = pt. of 21984.

21986 — Forsameekle, as one of the causses [etc. 1 July 1629.] = pt. of 21984.

Scotland—PROCLAMATIONS—*cont.*

21987 — Charles by the grace of God, . . . for so meekle as wee having now after good advice [etc. Publication of decrees, some of which are dated 2 September, on the general submissions. 18 Sept. 1629.] fol. (*Edinburgh, heires of T. Finlason,*) [1629.] L.C.E.E⁸.G⁴.+; HN.ILL.MIN.N.U. Cr.1536.

21987.5 — His majesties approbation of the actes underwritten: at Holy-rude-House the 3. day of November, 1629. fol. (*Edinburgh, heirs of T. Finlasone* [sic], 1629.) E.

21988 — Charles by the grace of God . . . Forsamekle as the [etc. For the collection of the twentieth penny. 28 July 1630.] s.sh.fol. [*Edinburgh, heirs of T. Finlason,* 1630.] A³. Cr.1549.
　　See 21901.6.

21988.5 — Charles by the grace of God . . . forsomuch as our estates of our kingdome [etc. For the collection of the 30/- tax for four years. 28 July 1630.] s.sh.fol. [*Edinburgh, heirs of T. Finlason,* 1630.] Lord Rosebery.

21989 — Charles by the grace of God . . . Forsomekle as the trade [etc. For selling yarn by weight. 28 July 1631.] s.sh.fol. [*Edinburgh, heirs of T. Finlason,* 1631.] Cr.1568.
　　The A³ and E⁶ copies cited in Cr. are wholly in MS.

21990 — Charles by the grace of God . . . Forsomuch as in our Parliament [etc. For collecting the 30/- tax. 28 June 1633.] s.sh.fol. [*Edinburgh, R. Young,* 1633.] A³(2). Cr.1592.
　　Last full line ends: 'at'.

21991 — Charles by the grace of God . . . Forsomuch as in our Parliament [etc. For collecting the sixteenth penny. 28 June 1633.] s.sh.fol. [*Edinburgh, R. Young,* 1633.] A³(2).M(deposit). Cr.1593.
　　Last full line ends: 'and'.

21992 — Charles by the grace of God . . . Forsomuch as our lieges and subjects [etc. Savings from reduced rate of interest to be paid to the Crown for three years. 28 June 1633.] s.sh.fol. [*Edinburgh, R. Young,* 1633.] L. Cr.1594.

21993 — Charles by the grace of God . . . Forsomuch as we and the estates [etc. For collecting the tax for the College of Justice. 28 June 1633.] s.sh.fol. [*Edinburgh, R. Young,* 1633.] E.E⁶. Lord Rosebery. Cr.1595.
　　Last full line of text ends: 'and'.

21994 — [Anr. ed. 28 June 1633.] s.sh.fol. [*Edinburgh, R. Young,* 1633.] A³. Cr.1596.
　　Last full line of text ends: 'sig-'.

21995 — [Anr. ed. for the fourth instalment.] s.sh.fol. [*Edinburgh, R. Young,* 1633.] A³. Cr.1597.
　　Last full line of text ends: 'ninth'.

— Charles &c. For soe much as wee out of our princely care [etc. Against convocations or meetings against the Service book. 19 Feb. 1638.] *See* 22013.

21996 — Charles by the grace of God . . . Forsameikle as wee are not ignorant [etc. Concerning canons, Service book, etc. 28 June 1638.] s.sh.fol. [*Edinburgh, R. Young,* 1638.] L.O.CASHEL.E.M.+; F.HN.HD.ILL.NY.+ Cr.1679.
　　Last line to the right of the init. begins: 'so'. *See* 21903.

21997 — [Anr. ed.] s.sh.fol. [*Aberdeen, E. Raban,* 1638.] A³.E. Cr.1680.
　　Last line to the right of the init. begins: 'Greeting'.

21998 — [Heading A2ʳ:] Charles, by the grace of God, . . . Forsomuch as the cause and occasion of all the distractions [etc. For the settlement of religious affairs. 9 Sept. 1638.] 4° in 2's. *Edinburgh, R. Young,* 1638. L.O.C.D.E.+; F.HN.CAL.HD.Y(frag.).+ Cr.1684.
　　A2ᵛ line 2 ends: 'Lawes:'; E2ʳ line 2: 'read and'. Copies may have mixed sheets. This reprints the Confession and Bond from 22023, and includes several proclamations by the Privy Council dated 22 and 24 Sept. 1638. *See also* 21904.

21998.5 — [Anr. issue, partially reset and reimposed.] *Edinburgh, R. Young,* 1638. A.DEU.E(3).E²(2).M.; F.NY.
　　A2ᵛ line 2 ends: 'Laws:'; E2ʳ line 2: 'read &'.

21999 — Charles by the grace of God, . . . Forsameikle as out of the royall and fatherly care [etc. Dissolving the General Assembly. 29 Nov. 1638.] fol(2). *Edinburgh, R. Young,* 1638. O.CASHEL.E.E³(imp.).M.+; HN.Y. Cr.1692.
　　See also 22047.

21999.5 — [Anr. ed., including reprints of 12728 and 22000.] 4° in 2's. *Aberdene, E. Raban,* 1638. Aberdeen PL.; F.

Scotland—PROCLAMATIONS—*cont.*

— [Begins A2ʳ:] Whereas some have given out. 1638. *See* 12728.

22000 — [Heading a2ʳ:] Charles R. Charles by the grace of God . . . Whereas for the removing of the disorders [etc. Against acknowledging the Glasgow Assembly. 8 Dec. 1638.] 4°. *Edinburgh, R. Young,* 1638. L.O. CASHEL.E.M.+; F.HN.HD.ILL.PML.+ Cr.1693.
　　Reprinted in 21999.5; *see also* 22050.

22001 — [Anr. ed., enlarged.] His majesties proclamation in Scotland: with an explanation of the meaning of the Oath and Covenant. By the lord marquesse. 4°. *London, R. Young, sold at the Gun in Ivie-lane* [*by P. Nevill?*] 1639. O⁵.O¹³.C².E(2).; F.HD(w. a2–b4 of 22000). Cr.1694.
　　(2nd pt. formerly 12727, 22010.)

22001.5 — [A variant, w. imprint:] *London, R. Young, sold at the Starre on Bread-street hill* [*by R. Young,*] 1639. L. O.C.D.E.+; F.HN.HD.ILL.NY.+
　　Copies vary: with or without arms of the Marquess of Hamilton on c1ᵛ; both at O⁵.

22002 — Charles R. . . . Whairas we have by many fair and calme waies, [etc. Against rebels in arms in Scotland. 20 Apr. 1639.] fol(4). *London, R. Young,* 1639. O². Cr.1698.
　　Ordered suppressed by King Charles in favour of the following proclamation; *see Calendar of Clarendon State Papers in the Bodleian,* ed. O. Ogle and W. H. Bliss, I.175.

22003 — [A revision.] Charles R. . . . Whairas we have by many fair [etc. Against rebels in arms in Scotland. 25 Apr. 1639.] fol(3). *R. Young,* 1639. L.O.C⁸.D.E.+; F.PML. Cr.1699.
　　Royal arms 223, w. 9 lines of shading between 'HONI' and 'SOIT'.

22004 — [Anr. ed.] fol(3). *R. Young,* 1639. M(deposit). Cr.1700.
　　Royal arms 222, w. 5 lines of shading between 'HONI' and 'SOIT'. O² does *not* have this ed.

22005 — By the king . . . Whereas we are thus farre advanced [etc. Warning Scots against invading England. 14 May 1639.] s.sh.fol. *Newcastle, R. Barker & assignes of J. Bill,* 1639. L¹¹(2, S.P.D., Chas. I, Vol. 420, doc. 166; Coll. Procs., Chas. I, no. 225). O²(2). Cr.1701.

22006 — His majesties declaration, concerning his proceedings with his subjects of Scotland. 1640. = 9260.

APPENDIX

22007 — A briefe chronicle, of all the kinges of Scotland. 8°. *Aberdene, E. Raban f. D. Melvill,* 1623. L.; HN.

22007.5 — A briefe relation of the Scots hostile entrance into this kingdome of England, over the river of Tweed. 8°. [*T. Harper*] *f. R. Harper,* 1640. Ent. 3 se. O⁶.P.
　　2 poems on A8ʳ are reimposed in 18501.5.

22008 — A catalogue of the kings of Scotland. [By T. Milles.] fol. [*W. Jaggard,*] 1610. L.E.; F.Y.
　　Issued w. some copies of 17926.

— Certayne matters concerning the realme of Scotland. 1603. *See* 18017.

— The complaint of Scotland. [1567.] *See* 22189.

22009 — [Headline:] The complaynt of Scotland. 16° in 8's. [*Paris, c.* 1550.] L(2).E(2).
　　All copies lack tp; all but one L(G.5438) lack other leaves.

— A discription of Scotland. 1626. *See* 25228.5.

— Ane discourse tuiching the estait present in October 1571. 1572. *See* 6909.5.

22010 — An explanation of the meaning of the Oath and Covenant. 1639. = pt. of 22001 sq.

— [The first book of the history of the reformation of religion within the realm of Scotland. 1587.] *See* 15071.

— Informations, or a protestation, and a treatise from Scotland. 1608. *See* 14084.

22011 — The lamentatioũ of lady Scotland . . . speiking in maner of ane epistle. [In verse. Init. P.R.] 8°. *Sanctandrois, R. Lekpreuik,* 1572. E.

22012 — The lamentatiõ of the cõmounis of Scotland. 1572. Now = 22200.5.

— The late expedicion in Scotlande. 1544. *See* 22270.

22013 — [Heading A1ʳ:] Newes from Scotland being two copies, the one, a proclamation of the king [19 Feb. 1638]: the other, a protestation against it, by the noble men, of Scotland, both published the 22 day of Febr: 1638. 4° in 2. [*Amsterdam, Richt Right Press,* 1638.] L⁴.O⁶.; F.Y.

Scotland—APPENDIX—*cont.*

— Newes from Scotland. Declaring the life of Doctor
Fian. [1592?] *See* 10841.

22013.5 — Scotlands encouragement. Scotlands triumph in spight
of Rome and Spaine, who would curst Jerichos wals
heer build againe. [In verse.] s.sh.fol. [*London?*
1640.] E.

22013.7 — Scotlands triumph over Rome, the second part, in
which the scarlet whore [is] stabd to the heart. [In
verse.] s.sh.fol. [*London?* 1640–41.] E.

22014 — A table of all the kinges of Scotland. = pt. of 21877.

SCOTLAND, CHURCH OF

BOOK OF COMMON ORDER

See Liturgies (16577 sqq.)

BOOK OF DISCIPLINE

22015 — The first and second booke of discipline. Together
with some acts of the Generall Assemblies, and an
act of parliament. [*Ed.* D. Calderwood?] 4°. [*Amsterdam, G. Thorp,*] 1621. L.O.C.E.M.+; F.HN.HD.ILL.Y.+

CONFESSION OF FAITH

22016 — The confessioun of faith professit, and beleuit, be the
protestantes within the realme of Scotland. Pub-
lischved be thaim in parliament. [17 July, i.e. Aug.
1560.] 4°. [*Edinburgh,*] (*Jhone Scott,* 1561.) L.
Preamble begins: 'Long haue we thrustede [i.e.
thirsted]'; Chap. 1 begins: 'We confes and ack-
nawledge ane only God,'. Reprinted in 22022,
22027, 5155; tr. in 22028.

22017 — [Anr. ed.] The confession of the faythe and doctrine
[etc.] 8°. R. *Hall,* 1561. Ent. 1561–62. L.O.C.D.E.+;
F.HD.

22018 — [Anr. ed.] The confessione of the fayht [*sic*] and doctrin [etc.] 8°. *Edinburgh, R. Lekprewik,* 1561. L².C³.
E.G⁴.; PML.

22019 — Ane shorte and generall confession of the trewe christiane faith . . . subscriued be the kingis maiestie and
his housholde. [28 Jan. 1580 o.s.] s.sh.fol. *Edinburgh,
R. Lekprewike,* [1581.] E. Cr.436.
Text begins: 'We all and euerie one of vs . . .'
Reprinted in 22022, 22023, 22024 sqq., 5141.5,
5155; tr. in 5141.5 and 22030.7.

22019.5 — [Anr. ed.] s.sh.fol. *Edinburgh, R. Lekprewike,* [1581.]
HD.
In heading: 'fayth'.

22020 — [A variant, w. imprint:] *London, R. Waldegraue,*
[1581.] Ent. 15 mr. 1581. L⁵. Cr.437.

22021 — Now = 22024.7.

22022 — The confession of the true & christian fayth, according
to Gods word, and actes of parliament. [28 Jan.
1581.] 8° in 4's. R. *Waldegraue,* [1581.] Ent. 10 ja.
a. 15 mr. 1581. L(2).O.C.C⁹.E.; F.HD(lacks F4).PML.
Reprints 22019 and 22016.

22023 — The confession of faith, subscriued by the kingis
maiestie and his houshold: togither with the copie
of the bande, maid touching the maintenance of the
true religion. 4°. *Edinburgh, R. Walde-graue,* 1590.
L².C².E.STD.YK.+; F.
Reprints 22019, adding the Bond and the act of
the Privy Council 6 Mar. 1589. Confession and
Bond reprinted in 21998.

22024 — [Anr. ed. of 22019.] Ane shorte and generall confession.
s.sh.fol. *Edinburgh, H. Charteris,* 1596. E.

22024.3 — [Anr. ed.] s.sh.fol. [*T. East*] *f. T. Man,* 1603. PML.

22024.5 — [Anr. ed.] 4°. [*Edinburgh, R. Charteris* or *A. Hart,*
c. 1610.] O.
Collates a⁴.

22024.7 — [Anr. ed.] s.sh.fol. *f. J. Man,* [c. 1615.] L⁵(2, Lemon
74; Scot. Proc. 18).L¹¹(S.P. Scot. Eliz., Vol. 28,
doc. 36).; HD.
(Formerly 22021)

22025 — [Anr. ed., w. additions. Commonly called The Covenant.] The confession of faith, subscribed by the
kings majestie . . . 1580. And now subscribed in
1638. By us, noblemen, barrons, [etc.] fol(2). [*Edinburgh,* 1638.] Cr.1673.
The former Haigh Hall copy has not been traced.

22025.5 — [Anr. ed.] fol(2). [*Edinburgh,* 1638.] E(deposit, printed
on vellum).
This differs from the transcription for 22025 in
Cr.1673 in that where the latter has in line 3

Scotland, Church of—CONFESSION OF FAITH—*cont.*
'Household', in line 10 'maintanance', and in
line 17 'Parliament.', this vellum copy has
'HOUSHOLD', 'maintainance', and 'Parlament,'.

22026 — [Anr. ed.] The confession of faith of the kirk of Scotland, subscribed by the kings majestie . . . 1580. With
a designation of such acts of parlament, as are expedient, for justefying the union, after mentioned. And
subscribed by the nobles, 1638. 4°. [*Edinburgh, G.
Anderson,* 1638.] L¹⁵.C.D.E.M.+; F.HD.U.Y. Scheide.
B1ʳ line 9 begins: 'they were publickly'. This and
following eds. frequently bd. w. 22031.5 sqq.; *see*
also 22036. For a Latin trans. *see* 22030.

22026.2 — [Anr. ed.] 4°. [*Edinburgh, G. Anderson,* 1638.] A.D.E.
E².M.+; ILL.N.
B1ʳ line 9 begins: 'were publicklie'.

22026.4 — [Anr. ed.] 4°. [*Leyden? W. Christiaens?* 1638.] L.O.C.D.E.
+; F.HN.HD.ILL.PML.+
B1ʳ line 9 begins: 'were presentlie'.

22026.6 — [Anr. ed., enlarged.] 4°. [*Amsterdam, Richt Right Press,*]
1638. O¹⁸.C².G².LINC.YK.+; F.NY.U.
B1ʳ line 9 begins: 'no other'. This and the next
ed. include a reprint of 22037.

22026.8 — [Anr. ed.] 4°. [*Amsterdam, Richt Right Press,*] 1638. L.
B1ʳ line 9 begins: 'is no other'.

22027 — The confession of the faith, and doctrine believed and
professed by the protestants of Scotland, exhibited
to parliament holden the 25 day of December, 1568.
4°. *Edinburgh, G. Anderson,* 1638. L¹⁵.O.D.E.M.+;
F.HD.PML.U.Y.
Reprints 22016. Copies usually have 2 tpp; the
original, w. woodcut, gives the year of authoriza-
tion as 1568; the cancel, without cut, gives the
correct year 1567.

22028 — Confessio fidei et doctrinæ per ecclesiam reformatam
regni Scotiæ. [*Tr.* by P. Adamson?] 8°. *Andreapoli,
R. Lekpreuik,* 1572. O¹⁸.A.E.E².STU.
A trans. of 22016.

22029 — Confessio fidei ecclesiæ Scoticanæ. [A Latin trans. of
18435.] 8°. [*Amsterdam, G. Thorp,* 1607.]
Not an STC book.

22030 — Confessio fidei ecclesiæ Scoticanæ. 4°. [*Edinburgh, G.
Anderson,*] 1638. L.O⁶.C³.E.E².+; ILL.N.PML.
A trans. of 22026. B4ʳ line 1: 'iustissimis'.

22030.3 — [Anr. ed.] 4°. [*Edinburgh, G. Anderson,*] 1638. L¹⁵.O.
D.E.M².+; F.HN.HD.Y.
B4ʳ line 1: 'justissimis'.

— Examen confessionis fidei Calvinianæ, quam Scotis
proponunt. Auctore G. Cheisolmo. [With Eng. and
Lat. texts of 22019.] 1601. *See* 5141.5.

22030.7 — Confession generale de la vraye foy & religion chrestienne selon la parole de Dieu & les actes de nostre
parlement. 8° in 4's. *Imprimée nouuellement à Londres*
[really in *France,*] 1603 (1 jn.) L⁴³.E.
A trans. of 22019.

APPENDIX

22031 — Ane admonition to the antichristian ministers in the
deformit kirk of Scotland. [In verse. By N. Burne.]
8° in 4's. [*Paris, T. Brumen,*] 1581. O⁶.BUTE.E.;
F(2).WIS.
A&R 182. Sometimes bd. w. 4124.

— Answeres to the particulars proponed by his majesties
commissionar. [1638.] *See* 665 sq.

22031.5 — The beast is wounded. Or information from Scotland,
concerning their reformation. Hereto is added some
fruitfull observations. By John Bastwicks yonger
brother. The first part. 4°. [*Leyden? W. Christiaens?*]
*Printed in the year that the bishops had their downfall
in Scotland,* [1638.] O.
Tp has device w.: 'Sol justitiae Christus.' Though
the Confession of Faith should be inserted between
quires B and C of this and the following eds., it
is frequently missing or misbound, and eds. of
it have been listed separately at 22026 sqq.

22032 — [Anr. ed.] 4°. [*Amsterdam, Richt Right Press,*] *Printed
in the yeare that the bishops had their downfall in
Scotland,* [1638.] L¹⁵.O.C.CASHEL.E.+; F.HN.HD.N.
U.+
Tp has Richt Right device; tp line 14: 'JUDG.'

22032.5 — [Anr. ed.] 4°. [*Amsterdam, Richt Right Press,*] *Printed
in the yeare that the bishops had their downefall in
Scotland,* [1638.] L(2).O⁶.E(2).
Tp has Richt Right device; tp line 14: 'IVDG.'

22033 — Boanerges. 1624. = 3171.

Scotland, Church of—Appendix—*cont.*

— De disciplina ecclesiastica . . . dissertatio, ad ecclesiam Scoticam. 1622. *See* 24067.

— A dispute against the English-popish ceremonies, obtruded upon the church of Scotland. 1637. *See* 11896.

— The forme and maner of examination befoir the admission to ye tabill of ye Lord. 1581. *See* 11183.

22034 — The grievances given in by the ministers before the parliament holden in June 1633. [By John Spotiswood.] 8°. [*Printed abroad?*] 1635. L.E(2).; F(2).U.

(Formerly also 10405) Usually bd. w. 739.5.

22035 — Kirk patronage the peoples privilege. 1836 [*sic*].
Not an STC book.

— A large declaration concerning the late tumults in Scotland. 1639. *See* 21906.

— The maner, and forme of examination. 1581. *See* 11183.5.

— The ordoure of excommunication. 1569. *See* 15074.2.

— Quaeres concerning the state of the church of Scotland. 1621, etc. *See* 4361.5 sqq.

22036 — [Heading C1ʳ:] Reasons against the rendering of our sworne confession. [By Sir A. Johnston?] 4° in 2. [*Edinburgh, G. Anderson?* 1638.] O.E.G².G⁴.M.+; F.HN.HD(2).

C2ʳ line 1: 'prelats'. This and the following prob. intended to be issued as a supplement to 22026, but they are also found bd. after 22030, 22054, and other items.

22036.5 — [Anr. ed.] 4° in 2. [*Edinburgh, G. Anderson?* 1638.] L.C.D.E.M.+; F.HD.MCG.U.Y.

C2ʳ line 1: 'prelates'.

22037 — [Heading A1ʳ:] Reasons for which the service booke, ought to bee refused. [By G. Gillespie?] 4° in 2. [*Edinburgh, G. Anderson,*] (1638.) L.O.C.D.E.+; F.HN.PML.U.Y.+

A1ʳ catchword: 'by'. Reprinted in 22026.6.

22038 — [Anr. ed.] 4° in 2. [*Edinburgh, G. Anderson,*] (1638.) L.O.CASHEL.E.G⁴.+; F.HD.PML.U.Y.

A1ʳ catchword: 'English'.

— Refutatio libelli de regimine ecclesiae Scoticanae. 1620. *See* 23103.

22039 — A short relation of the state of the kirk of Scotland since the reformation. [By Sir A. Johnston?] 4°. [*Edinburgh, J. Wreittoun?*] 1638. L.O.C.D.E.+; F.HN.HD.U.Y.+

22040 — The speach of the kirk of Scotland. 1620. = 4365.

GENERAL ASSEMBLY

22041 — The ordour and doctrine of the generall faste, appointed be the Generall Assemblie. [By J. Knox and J. Craig.] 8°. *Edinburgh, R. Lekpreuik,* 1566. C³.E(2). LINC(imp.).

22042 — = 22044.

22043 — [Anr. ed., enlarged.] (Certaine chapters of the scriptures vsed be the ministers of Edinburgh in the tyme of the pest.) 8°. *Edinburgh, R. Lekpreuik,* 1574. L². O(2).C².D.; F.

22044 — [Anr. ed.] 16° in 8's. [*H. Middleton?* f. *J. Harrison a. T. Man,* 1580.] L.O.C³.; F.

(Formerly also 22042) All copies bd. w. 24251.5.

22045 — [Anr. ed.] 8°. [*W. White*] f. *T. P[avier,*] 1603. L.E(imp.).LK.; HD.

— The ordoure of excommunication. 1569. *See* 15074.2.

22046 — The determination of the Generall Assemblie. Anent the obedience to the kinges maiestie his authoritie. [7 July 1570.] 1/2 sh.fol. [*Edinburgh, R. Lekpreuik,* 1570.] L¹¹(S.P. Scot. Eliz., Vol. 18, doc. 77).

22047 — The protestation of the Generall Assemblie, made in the high kirk, and at the Mercate Crosse of Glasgow. [28–29 Nov. 1638. By Sir A. Johnston.] 4°. *Glasgow, G. Anderson,* 1638. L.O.CASHEL.E.M.+; F.HN.ILL.

A2ʳ catchword: 'intruded'; A2ᵛ line 1 begins: 'intruded'.

Some copies (L¹⁵, C, E², G², Y) have quire A erroneously perfected w. outer forme of 22047.5 and have: 'intruded/of'. *See also* 21999.

22047.5 — [Anr. issue, w. quire A partially reset.] *Glasgow, G. Anderson,* 1638. O.C.E².E⁴.G⁴.YK.+; F.HN.HD.N. Scheide.

A2ʳ catchword: 'of'; A2ᵛ line 1 begins: 'of'.

Scotland, Church of—General Assembly—*cont.*

22048 — An answer to the profession and declaration. Made by James marques of Hammilton [in pt. 1 of 64.5], imprinted at Edinburgh anno 1638, in December. 4°. *Edinburgh, J. Bryson,* 1639. L.O.C.E.M.+; F.HN.U. PML.Y.+

G² set in duplicate; G1ʳ line 13: 'cleare' (L, O) or 'clear' (YK).

22048a — [A variant, omitting imprint from tp.] L¹⁵.E.G⁴.M. YK.+; F.HN.HD(2).ILL.

22049 — The principall acts of the solemne Generall Assembly . . . at Glasgow the xxi. of November 1638. fol. *Edinburgh, heirs of A. Hart,* 1639. L.O.C.E.M.+; F. CAL⁵.HD.N.U.+

22050 — The protestation of the Generall Assembly of the kirke of Scotland, made at the Mercate Crosse of Edinburgh the 18. of December. 1638. 4°. *Edinburgh, J. Bryson,* 1639. L.O.E.E².G⁴.+; F.HN.PN².U.Y.+

No approbation on G2ᵛ. *See also* 22000.

22051 — [A variant, w. Latin approbation on G2ᵛ: 'Perlegi hunc tractatum . . .'] *Edinburgh, J. Bryson,* 1639. L.O. CASHEL.E.M.+; F(2).HN.ILL.N.Y(2).

The Y copies vary in the marginal notes.

22051.5 — [Anr. ed.] 4°. *Edinburgh, J. Bryson,* 1639. L.O.A.E.M (deposit).; HD.

In title: 'Kirk'; approbation in English on G2ᵛ: 'Revised according to the ordinance . . .'

22052 — Assembly at Glasgow. Dec. 6, 1638. s.sh.fol. [Printed in the 1800's.]
Not an STC item.

— A briefe and plaine narration of proceedings at an assemblie in Glasco. 1610. *See* 11915.

22053 — A faithfull report . . . anent the assemblie at Abirdeen 2. July 1605. 1606. = 63.

— The questions to be resoluit at the conuention of the Estaits and Generall Assemblie, at Perth. 1597. *See* 21891.

22054 — Reasons for a Generall Assemblie. 4°. [*Edinburgh, G. Anderson,*] 1638. L.O.C.D.E.+; HN.HD.LC.N.U.+

A2ʳ line 4 of text: 'nation'.

22054.5 — [Anr. ed.] 4°. [*Edinburgh, G. Anderson,*] 1638. L. CASHEL.E.M².YK.+; F.MCG.NY.Y.

A2ʳ line 4 of text: 'Nation'; quire B in same setting as 22054.

Scotland, Episcopal Church of. Canons and constitutions ecclesiasticall gathered and put in forme, for the government [*sic*] of the church of Scotland. [*Ed. R. Baron.*] 4°. *Aberdene, E. Raban,* 1636. L.O. C².E.M.+; F.HN.HD.ILL.U.

22056 — The catechisme, . . . set furth be Johne Aschibischop [*sic*] of sanct Androus. 1552. = 12731.

22057 — Een cort verhael van de misdaden die de Schotse bisschoppen te laste gheleyt werden; om't welcke sy verworpen sijn uyt de kercke van Schotland. [etc.] 8°. *Edinburgh, J. Bryson* [i.e. *Amsterdam, Richt Right Press,*] 1639. L(4175.de.20).HAGUE.

22058 — The declinator and protestation of the archbishops and bishops. 4°. *J. Raworth* f. *G. Thomason a. O. Pullen,* 1639. Ent. 23 ja. L(4175.a.86; 110.a.8).O.C.E.M.+; F.HN.HD.N.U.+ ⅀

Quire B in 2 settings: B3ᵛ line 14 has 'Deliberations' or 'deliberations'; both at O.

22059 — [Anr. ed.] 4°. *Aberdene, E. Raban,* 1639. O.; F.

22060 — The declinatour and protestation of the some sometimes [*sic*] pretended bishops. Refuted. [By Sir A. Johnston.] 4°. *Edinburgh, J. Bryson,* 1639. L(110.a. 9).O.C.E.M(deposit).+; F.HN.CHI.HD.U.+ ⅀

Scots. A briefe relation of the Scots hostile entrance. 1640. *See* 22007.5.

22061 **Scott, Edmund.** An exact discourse of the subtilties, fashishions [*sic*], pollicies, religion, and ceremonies of the East Indians, as well Chyneses as Javans [etc.] 4°. *W. W[hite]* f. *W. Burre,* 1606. L(2).L².O.; F.CU. MIN.NY.PH².+

22061.5 **Scott, Sir Michael.** The philosophers banquet: furnished with few dishes for health; but large discourse for pleasure, *tr.* [from the Mensa Philosophica, also attrib. to T. Anguilbertus] by W. B. Esquire. 12°. *N. O[kes]* f. *L. Becket,* 1609. Ent. 29 my. O⁹.G².; HN.N.

For a different adaptation of the Mensa *see* 24411.

Scott, *Sir* **Michael**—*cont.*

22062 — The second edition, newly corrected and inlarged. 8°. T. C[reede] f. L. Becket, 1614. L.O.O⁶.G².; F.HN. NY(2).TEX.

22063 — Third edition [w. additions and deletions.] 12°. [J. Beale] f. N. Vavasour, 1633. Ass'd 18 my. 1636. L(3).L¹⁰.G².; F.CAL.HD.N.Y.+

22064 **Scott, Thomas,** *B.D.* The workes of the most famous and reverend divine Mr. Thomas Scot. 4°. *Utrick,* 1624. O(25 items).A(9 items).; HD(24 items). 𝕬
    A reissue w. general tp. Following are the items in the O and HD copies, w. the nine A items marked '(A)': 3171.3, 5864.4(O only), 19126, 13264.8 (A), 20946.2, 20946.6 (HD) *or* 20946.8 (O), 22065, 22069a (A), 22072 (A), 22073.2, 22075, 22076, 22077, 22078.5, 22079 (A), 22080 (A), 22081 (A), 22084, 22086, 22088 (A), 22089, 22097a, 22100.6 (A; O and HD have quires A–B from 22100.4), 22103.3 (A and O; HD has quires B–H from 22103), 22105.5.
    The O copy was presented to the Bodleian by Michael Sparke in 1627.

22065 — Aphorismes of state: or certaine secret articles for the re-edifying of the romish church agreed upon, by the colledge of cardinalls. Whereunto is annexed a censure upon the chiefe points. *Tr.* according to the Latine, and Netherlandish Dutch. 4°. *Utrech* [i.e. *London,*] 1624. L.O.C³.D.M.+; F.HN.HD.NY.Y.+
    A3ʳ, Art. 9, line 8 begins: 'tion'. O and HD copies are in 22064.

22066 — [Anr. ed.] 4°. *Utrech* [i.e. *London,*] 1624. L.O(3).C².E. NOR².+; F(2).HN.HD.N.U.
    A3ʳ, Art. 9, line 8 begins: 'extirpation'. Quires C and D in same setting as 22065.

22067 — [Anr. ed.] 4°. *Utrech* [i.e. *London, J. Beale?*] 1624. L.C².LIV³.; F.CHI.ILL.
    A3ʳ, Art. 9, line 8 begins: 'reticks be'.

22068 — [Anr. ed.] 4°. *Utrech* [i.e. *London,*] 1624. L.; F.ILL. NY⁵.
    A3ʳ, Art. 9, line 8 begins: 'be againe'.

22069 — The Belgicke pismire: stinging the slothfull sleeper, and awaking the diligent to fast, watch, pray; [etc. Anon.] 4°. *London* [i.e. *Holland,*] 1622. L.O.C².NOR². G².+; F.HN.N.NY.U.+
    A3ʳ line 9: 'vvisedome'. One L copy (3670.aaa.13) has quire A of this, and the rest from 22069a.

22069a — [Anr. ed.] 4°. *London* [i.e. *Holland,*] 1622. L.O.C.A.M. +; F.HN.HD.ILL.NY.+
    A3ʳ line 9: 'wisdome'. O, A, and HD copies are in 22064.

22069a.5 — [Anr. issue, w. A⁴ aa² reset.] *London* [i.e. *Holland,*] 1622. C.
    A3ʳ line 9: 'wisedome'.

22070 — [Anr. ed., w. Scott's name on sub tp.] Whereunto is added the Projector. 8°. [*J. Dawson,*] 1623. L.O.C.D². NOR².+; F(2).HN.TEX.
    (2nd pt. formerly also 22082) Copies vary: with or without Scott's name on gen. tp; both at O.

22071 — The Belgick souldier: warre was a blessing. [Anon.] 4°. [*London,*] 1624. L.O.O⁴.C².SHEF.+; F.HN.HD.U.

22072 — [Anr. ed., revised and enlarged.] The Belgick souldier: dedicated to the parliament. Or, warre was a blessing. 4°. *Dort* [i.e. *London,*] 1624. L.O.C.A.D.+; F.HN.HD.N. NY.+
    D3–G2 reimposed from C3–F2 of 22071. O, A, and HD copies are in 22064.

— Boanerges. Or the humble supplication of the ministers of Scotland. [Attrib. to T. Scott.] 1624. *See* 3171.

— A briefe information of the affaires of the Palatinate. [Attrib. to T. Scott.] 1624. *See* 19126.

22073 — Certaine reasons and arguments of policie, why the king of England should enter into warre with the Spaniard. [Anon.] 4°. [*London,*] 1624. C(imp.). LAMPORT.; ILL.
    (Formerly also 9982) A3ʳ line 14 ends: '*Spani*-'; line 2: 'al me̅'.

22073.2 — [Anr. ed.] 4°. [*London,*] 1624. L(2).O.O².C².E(2).; F.HD. MIN.NY⁵.U.
    A3ʳ line 14 ends: '*Spani*-'; line 2: 'all men'. O and HD copies are in 22064. Both L, O², C², MIN copies have quire B of 22073.4.

22073.4 — [Anr. ed.] 4°. [*London,*] 1624. O.C⁵.D.M.SHEF.+; CAL. IND.LC.N.PML.+
    A3ʳ line 14 ends: '*Spani*-' (double hyphen). For copies of quire B *see* 22073.2.

Scott, Thomas, *B.D.*—*cont.*

22073.6 — [Anr. ed.] 4°. [*London,*] 1624. O.O¹⁸.C⁹.; F.HN.
    A3ʳ line 14 ends: '*Spaniard* is'; line 9 begins: '*Spaniards*' (no comma).

22073.8 — [Anr. ed.] 4°. [*London,*] 1624. O.; F.Y.
    A3ʳ line 14 ends: '*Spaniard* is'; line 9 begins: '*Spaniards*,'. Part of quire B is same setting as 22073.6.

22074 — Christs politician, and Salomons puritan. Delivered in two sermons preached before the kings majestie. 4°. *E. Griffin f. F. Constable,* 1616. Ent. 19 no. 1615. L.O.C.E.NOR².+; F.HD.TEX.U.Y.+ 𝕬
    Tp varies: verses arranged in 1 set of 4 lines or 2 sets of 2 lines; both at F.

22075 — Exod. 8. 19. Digitus Dei. [Etc. A sermon on Luke xiii.1–5. Anon.] 4°. [*Holland,* 1623.] L.O.C.DUR⁵.E.+; F.HD.N.NY.TEX.+

22076 — Englands joy, for suppressing the papists, and banishing the priests and jesuites. [Anon.] 4°. [*N. Okes?*] 1624. L.O.C⁴.E.M⁴.+; F.HN.HD.N.U.+ 𝕬

22077 — An experimentall discoverie of Spanish practises or the counsell of a well-wishing souldier. [Anon. By H. Hexham?] 4°. [*London,*] 1623. L.O.C⁵.SHEF.YK (imp.).+; F.CH.HD.NY.Y.+
    A2ʳ line 11 of text: 'faire opportunityes'. O and HD copies are in 22064. For pt. 2 *see* 22078.5.

22077.3 — [Anr. ed.] 4°. [*London,*] 1623. L.O.C.C².NOR².+; CB.N.V. Cleveland PL.
    A2ʳ line 11 of text: 'faire opportunities'; line 8 ends: 'attaine'. Quires B–D and E inner forme are same setting as 22077.

22077.5 — [Anr. ed.] 4°. [*London,*] 1623. L.O.O².D.YK.+; HN.CB. IND.U.
    A2ʳ line 11 of text: 'faire opportunities'; line 8 ends: 'attain'.

22077.7 — [Anr. ed.] 4°. [*London,*] 1623. L³⁸.O².C.C³.E.+; F.HN. ILL.PN.
    A2ʳ line 11 of text: 'fair opportunities'.

22078 — [Anr. ed. Heading A1ʳ:] A true souldiers councel. Anno 1624. 4°. [*N. Okes?* 1624.] O.O⁶.C.; NY⁵.

22078.5 — A second part of Spanish practises. Or, a relation of more plots. [Anon. Probably not by Scott.] Whereunto is adjoyned a worthy oration. (An adjoynder. [By S. Ofwod.]) 4°. [*N. Okes,*] 1624. L.O.C.E.M.+; F.HN.HD.N.NY.+
    The Oration and Adjoinder are partially reprinted from 18837.

22079 — The high-waies of God and the king. Wherein all men ought to walke in holinesse here, to happinesse hereafter. Two sermons. 4°. *London* [i.e. *Holland,*] 1623. L.O.C.D.E.+; F.HN.HD.N.NY.+

— The interpreter wherin three principall termes of state are unfolded. [Attrib. to T. Scott. 1622.] *See* 14115.

22080 — Newes from Pernassus. The politicall touchstone, whereon the governments of the world are touched. [Anon.] 4°. *Helicon* [i.e. *Holland,*] 1622. L.O.C.D². E².+; F.HN.HD.N.NY.+
    Adapted from T. Boccalini and partly reprinted in 3185.

22081 — The projector. Teaching a direct, sure, and ready way to restore the decayes of the church and state. In a sermon in Norwich, 1620. 4°. *London* [i.e. *Holland,*] 1623. L.O.C.D².E.+; F.HN.HD.N.NY.+

22082 — [Anr. ed.] 8°. 1623. = pt. of 22070.

22083 — A relation of some speciall points concerning the state of Holland. Shewing, why for the security of the united Provinces warre is better then peace. [Anon.] 4°. *The Hage, A. Muris* [i.e. *London, E. Allde,*] 1621. L.O.C⁵.; F.HN.HD. 𝕬

22084 — Robert earle of Essex his ghost, sent from Elizian: to the nobility, gentry, and communaltie of England. (A post-script, or, a second part.) [Anon.] 4°. *Paradise* [i.e. *London, J. Beale?*] 1624 [sub tp misdated:] (1642.) L.O.O².C².LIV³.+; F.CU.HD.NY (imp.).Y.+
    A2ʳ line 10 of text ends: 'parti-'. O and HD copies are in 22064.

22084a — [Anr. ed.] 4°. *Paradise* [i.e. *London, J. Beale?*] 1624. L.O.C.C².D⁸.+; F.HN.N.NY⁵.Y.+
    Sub tp correctly dated 1624; A2ʳ line 10 of text ends: 'partici-'.

— A second part of Spanish practises. 1624. *See* 22078.5.

— A short view of the long life and raigne of Henry the third king of England. 1627. *See* 5864.

Scott, Thomas, *B.D.—cont.*

22085 — Sir Walter Rawleighs ghost, or Englands forewarner. Discovering a secret consultation, newly holden in the court of Spaine. [Anon.] 4°. *Utricht, J. Schellem* [i.e. *London?*] 1626. L.O.C.D.G⁴.+; F.HN.HD.N.NY.+

22086 — The Spaniards perpetuall designes to an universall monarchie. *Tr.* according to the French. [Anon.] 4°. [*London,*] 1624. L.O.C.D.G².+; F.HN.HD.N.NY⁵.+
O and HD copies are in 22064.

22086.5 — [Heading A1ʳ:] A speech made in the lower house of parliament, anno 1621. By sir Edward Cicill colonell. [Anon.] 4°. [*Holland?* 1621.] E.; F.HN.COR.HD.
Possibly by C. Tourneur rather than Scott; *see TLS* 5 Aug. 1949, p. 505.

22087 — [Anr. ed., w. tp:] A speech made . . . By sir Edward Cicill, colonell. 4°. [*London,*] 1621. L.O.O².C.YK.+; F.HN.ILL.N.U.+

22088 — [Anr. ed.] By sir Edward Cicell, colonell. 4°. [*London,*] 1624. L.O.C.A.D².+; F.HN.CHI.HD.ILL.+
O, A, and HD copies are in 22064.

22089 — Symmachia: or, a true-loves knot. Tyed, betwixt Great Britaine and the United Provinces. [Anon.] 4°. [*Holland,* 1624.] L.O.C⁵.D².M.+; F.HN.HD.N.NY.+

22090 — A tongue-combat, lately happening betweene two English souldiers in the tilt-boat of Gravesend. [Preface signed 'H. Hexam'.] 1623. Now = 13264.8.

22091 — A toung-combat. [Init. D. N.] 1623. Now = 18327.5.

22092 — Votivæ Angliæ. [Init. S. R. N. I.] 1624. Now = 20946.1.

22093 — [Anr. ed.] 1624. Now = 20946.2.

22094 — Vox coeli. [Init. S. R. N. I.] 1624. Now = 20946.4.

22095 — [Anr. ed.] 1624. Now = 20946.6.

22096 — [Anr. ed.] 1624. Now = 20946.7.

22096a — [Anr. ed.] 1624. Now = 20946.8.

22097 — Vox dei: injustice cast and condemned. 1623. Now = 21873.5.

22097a — Vox Dei. [Anon.] 4°. [*Holland?* 1623?] O.C.BIRM.DUL. PLUME(imp.).; F.HN.HD.NY.NY⁵.+

22098 — Vox populi. Or newes from Spayne, *tr.* according to the Spanish coppie. Which may serve to forewarn both England and the United Provinces how farre to trust to Spanish pretences. [Anon.] 4°. [*London?*] 1620. L.O⁶.C.D.E.+; F.HD.MICH.N.NY⁵.+
In title: 'how farre/'; A2ʳ line 6 of text: 'Warre,'; D1ʳ line 22: 'Vigilant'. Quire D also found w. 22099. *See* Greg, *Companion,* pp. 176–8.

22098.5 — [Anr. ed.] 4°. [*London?*] 1620. L(lacks tp).O¹⁰.D².E. YK.+; F.HN.HD.ILL.NY.+
In title: 'how farre/'; A2ʳ line 6 of text: 'warre,'; D1ʳ line 22: 'vigilant'.

22099 — [Mixed sheets, with quires A–C of 22100.4 and quire D of 22098.] L.O(see note).O².O³(E, see note).DUL.+; TEX.
In title: 'how farre to/'; A3ʳ last line: 'cōmander'; D1ʳ line 22: 'Vigilant'. The O copy (Pamph.C.22 (13)) has *⁴ of 22101 inserted. The O³ copy lacks quire A, which is replaced w. an anomalous 1st quire signed 'B' imitated from 22101, q.v.
Copies at O¹³ and C⁵ have quire D from 22098.5 with 'vigilant'. O¹³ has quires A–C of 22100.4. The C⁵ copy has *⁴ of 22101, anomalous quire 'B' like the O³ copy, B–C of 22100.4.

22100 — [Anr. ed.] 4°. [*London?*] 1620. L(lacks tp, w. *⁴ of 22101 inserted, 1103.e.12(1)).O.O².D(imp.).M.+; F. CH.DAR.HD.TEX.
In title: 'how farre to/'; A3ʳ last line: 'Cōmāder'. This ed. has more typographical errors than usual.

22100.2 — [Anr. ed.] 4°. [*London,*] 1620. L.O.O⁵.C².DUL.+; F.HD.
In title: 'how farre to/'; A3ʳ last line: 'Cōmander'.

22100.4 — [Anr. ed.] 4°. [*London,*] 1620. L⁴³.O(see note).C.C³.DUL.; F.CHI.HD(see note).ILL.TEX.
In title: 'how farre to/'; A3ʳ last line: 'cōmander'. Quires A–C also found in 22099, q.v. The O(4° D59 Th.) and HD copies in 22064 have quires A–B of this, C–D of 22100.6.
This, 22100.6, and 22100.8 have quire B in the same setting; it is the same setting, w. signatures and headlines reimposed, as quire B of 22100.2.

22100.6 — [Anr. ed.] 4°. [*London,*] 1620. L².L¹³.O⁹.C⁴.A(in 22064). +; F.HN.HD(see note to 22100.4).ILL.NY.+
In title: 'how farre to/'; A3ʳ last line: 'commander'; line 1 begins: 'gouerne'. ILL has quire D in a different setting from any of the known eds., with 'D' of sig. D1 under first 'a' of 'a Catholique'.

Scott, Thomas, *B.D.—cont.*

22100.8 — [Anr. issue, w. quire A and C outer forme reset.] [*London,*] 1620. C⁴.D².LIV².NOR².YK.+; F.CB.U.
In title: 'how farre to/'; A3ʳ last line: 'commander'; line 1 begins: 'governe'.

22101 — [Anr. ed., w. preface signed: 'Thom: Scott'.] 4°. [*Holland,*] 1620 [1624.] L.O(*⁴ only, in 22099). C⁵(*⁴ only, see note at 22099).; F.NY.
This ed. collates *⁴ B–E⁴ and is reissued w. tp usually cancelled in 22102.
Quire B is in 2 settings: B4ᵛ catchword: 'that' (F) or 'strayned' (O³, C⁵, quire B only). The latter has apparently been specially set to go w. the rest of the text in 22099; *see* note on O³, C⁵ copies there.

22102 — Vox populi Vox Dei. Vox regis. Digitus Dei. The Belgick pismire. The tongue-combat. Symmachia. The high-wayes of God and the king. The projector. 4°. [*Holland,* 1624.] L.O.C.D².E.+; F.HN.HD.MICH. NY.+
A reissue w. general tp, usually containing the sheets of 13264.8, 22069a, 22075, 22079, 22081, 22089, 22097a, 22101, 22105.5. The HN copy may represent an early issue as it has 22069 and 22105. The O and HD copies in 22064 have a mixture of 22100.4 and 22100.6 substituted for 22101. The L and F copies have 22080 bd. w. the collection.

22103 — The second part of Vox populi, or Gondomar appearing in the likenes of Matchiavell in a Spanish parliament. Faithfully transtated [*sic*] out of the Spanish coppie. [Init. T. S. of U.] 4°. *Goricom, A. Janss* [i.e. *London, N. Okes a. J. Dawson,*] 1624. O¹⁴.C.C⁵.D². SHEF.+; F(3).HD(2, see note).CU(see note).NY(lacks tp).
Engr. tp has blank spaces to left and right of Gondomar's head; D3ᵛ line 1 begins: 'thinke'. This typesetting of the text, with tp altered, is reissued in 22103.7.
Imprint, cropt in most copies, is present in 1 F, 1 HD. The other HD (in 22064) and CU copies have quire A of 22103.3.
The dedic. was pr. by Dawson.

22103.3 — [Anr. ed.] 4°. *Goricom, A. Janss* [i.e. *London, N. Okes,*] 1624. L.O.C.A(lacks tp).D(lacks dedic.).+; F.BO².COR. NY.NY⁵.+
Engr. tp has donkey-litter and motto: 'Simul Complectar omnia' to the left of Gondomar's head; D3ᵛ line 1 begins: 'vs thinke'. O and A copies in 22064; HD and CU have quire A only, w. the rest from 22103.

22103.7 — [Anr. issue of 22103, with engr. tp altered:] The second edition. *Goricom, A. Janss* [i.e. *London, N. Okes,*] 1624. L.L¹³.C.C³.ETON.; MIN.
Engr. tp has donkey-litter and motto with 'omnia' and 'The second edition'; D3ᵛ line 1 begins: 'thinke'.

22104 — [A forgery of 22103.7.] The second edition. 4°. *Goricom, A. Janss* [i.e. *London, W. Jones,*] 1624. L.O.C³. E(lacks tp).NOR².+; HN.HD.ILL.N.
Engr. tp has donkey-litter and motto with 'omina [*sic*]' and 'The second edition'; D3ᵛ line 1 begins: 'of *Buckinghams*'. In this ed. B1 is unsigned and B2–4 are signed B1–3; F4 is folded to precede F1.

22105 — Vox regis. [Init. T. S.] 4°. [*Utrecht, A. van Herwijck,* 1624.] L.C⁵.E.; F.HN(in 22102).HD(lacks engr.).N. NY¹¹.
I4ʳ catchword: 'the'. Engr. frontispiece is copied in 10021.4.

22105.5 — [Anr. issue, enlarged.] [*Utrecht, A. van Herwijck,* 1624.] L.O.C.DUL.NOR².+; F.HD.ILL(imp.).NY.U.+
I4ʳ catchword: 'iudgement'. O and HD are in 22064.

22105a — The wicked plots and practises of the Spaniards. [1642.] = Wing S 2087.

22106 — A briefe and true relation of the murther of T. Scott committed by J. Lambert the 18. of June. 1626. With his examination, confession, and execution. 4°. [*M. Flesher*] *f. N. Butter,* 1628. L.C⁵.E.

22107 **Scott, Thomas,** *Poet.* Foure paradoxes of arte, of lawe, of warre, of service. [In verse.] 8°. [*H. Ballard*] *f. T. Bushell,* 1602. L(lacks tp).; HN.
Dedic. to Marchioness of Northampton.

22107.5 — [Anr. ed.] 8°. *T. S[nodham] f. R. Redmer,* 1611. Ent. to Redmer by consent of T. Bushell 14 au. 1610. E². With new dedic. to Sir T. Gorges.

22108 **Scott, Thomas,** *Preacher at the Rolls Chapel.* A godlie sermon of repentaunce and amendment of life. 8°. *T. Purfoote,* 1585. Ent. 6 de. L.DEU(imp.). ⅍

22109 **Scott, William.** An essay of drapery: or, the compleate citizen. 12°. *Eli. All-de f. S. Pemell,* 1635. Ent. 28 fb. L.L⁸.L³⁰.O.E².+ ; F.HN.CU.HD.IND.+

Scottish Papists. A discouerie of the conspiracie of Scottisch papists. [1593, etc.] *See* 14937 sqq.

Scribonius, Gulielmus Adolphus. In physicam G. A. Scribonii, animaduersiones. 1584. *See* 3745.

22109.5 — Rerum physicarum juxta leges logicas methodica explicatio. Nunc denuó recognita. (Isagoge sphærica methodice proposita.) 8°. *H. Middletonus, imp. J. Harisoni,* 1581. PETWORTH(imp.).; Y.

22110 — [A revision.] Rerum naturalium doctrina methodica, post secundam editionem denuò copiosissimè adaucta. Vnà cum Isagoge sphærica. 8°. *H. Midletonus, imp. G. Bishop,* 1583. O.YK.; Y.

22110.5 — [A variant, w. imprint:] *H. Midletonus, imp. J. Harrisoni,* 1583. F(lacks L2).

22111 — [A trans.] Naturall philosophy: or a description of the world. [*Tr.* D. Widdowes; *ed.*] (J. Wydowes alias Woodhouse.) 4°. *J. D[awson] f. J. Bellamie,* 1621. Ent. 6 ja. L.L¹⁶.O.O¹³.; F.HN.PH².PN.Y.

22112 — Second edition, enlarged. [*Tr.*] By D. Widdowes. 4°. *T. Cotes f. J. Bellamie,* 1631. L.O.C.LONGLEAT.; HN. CHI.MICH.

22112.5 — [Anr. issue, w. imprint:] *T. Cotes, sold by B. Allen,* 1631. L¹⁶.; F.HN.ILL.NLM.Y.

22113 — = 22114.

22114 — Triumphus logicae Rameæ. Editio secunda. 8°. *T. Vautrollerius, imp. G. Bishop,* 1583. Ent. to J. Harrison a. G. Bishop 23 no. L.L².YK.

22114.5 — [A variant, w. imprint:] *T. Vautrollerius, imp. J. Harrison,* 1583. C¹⁰.

22115 **Scrougie, Alexander.** De imperfectione sanctorum in hac vita theses theologicæ. 1627. Now = 71.11.

Scudamore, James, *tr. See* 1543.

22115.5 **Scudder, Henry.** The christians daily walke in holy securitie and peace. [*Ed.*] (J. Davenport.) 12°. *J. D[awson] f. W. Sheffard,* 1627. Ent. 12 fb. F.U(imp.).

22116 — The second edition, inlarged. 12°. *J. D[awson] f. W. Sheffard,* 1628. F.DAR(imp.).

22117 — The fourth edition, corrected and amended. 12°. *J. B[eale] f. H. Overton,* 1631. Ass'd 13 my. 1630. L.; F.

22118 — The fift edition. 12°. *J. D[awson] f. H. Overton,* 1633. F.CHI.HD.

22119 — The sixt edition. 12°. *M. D[awson] f. H. Overton,* 1635. L.O.DUL(imp.).G².

22120 — The seventh edition. 12°. *J. D[awson] f. H. Overton,* 1637. O(2).O⁴¹.C.; Y.

22121 — A key of heaven: the Lords prayer opened. 12°. *R. Field f. T. Man,* 1620. Ent. to T. a. J. Man 8 mr. L.O.C.D.E.+ ; HN.U.

22122 — The second edition enlarged by the author. 12°. *T. Harper f. B. Fisher,* 1633. Ent. to T. Man 1 mr. 1624; to B. Fisher a. widow Man 12 au. 1635. O(imp.).; F.HN.HD.PN².

— *ed. See* 25317.

22123 **Scull, John.** Two sermons, upon that great embassie of Jesus Christ, recorded by his euangelist, saint Matthew, Chap. 10. v. 16. 4°. *T. Snodham,* 1624. Ent. 12 mr. L⁴.O.YK.; F.BO⁶.HD(tp def.).ILL.

22124 **Scultetus, Abraham.** A secular sermon concerning the doctrine of the Gospell. *Tr.* out of Latin. 4°. *W. Jones,* 1618. Ent. 6 fb. L.O.C.D².M.+ ; F.HD.U.

22125 — A sermon, preached before the two high borne princes, Fredericke the 5. And the princesse Elizabeth. *Tr.* out of High Dutch by J. Meddus. 8°. *J. Beale f. W. Welby,* 1613. Ent. 3 jy. L.L¹³.O.C².; F.HN.

22126 — A short information, but agreeable vnto scripture: of idol-images. *Tr.* according to the high Dutch copie. 4°. [*London?*] 1620. L.L⁴.O.O².M⁴.; F.HN.CAL.HART.

22126.3 **Scupoli, Lorenzo.** The spiritual conflict. Writen in Italian and lately *tr.* into English. [Anon. *Tr.* J. Gerard.] 12°. *Antwerp* [i.e. *English secret press,*] 1598. L.TMTH.
A&R 759.

Scupoli, Lorenzo—*cont.*

22126.7 — [Anr. ed.] 12°. [*Douai, C. Boscard,* 1603–10.] L². Rogers.
A&R 760.

22127 — = 22128.

22128 — [Anr. ed.] Newly reprinted, with the litanies of the B. virgine Mary, annexed. 12°. *Rouen, C. Hamillon,* 1613. O²⁵.C.DE.ST.W.+ ; F.
A&R 761.

22129 **Scute, Cornelius.** A pronostication. [1544.] Now = 508.5.

22130 **Sea Fight.** A true relation of a wonderfull sea fight betweene two great and well appointed Spanish ships. And a small English ship, at the iland of Dominico in her passage to Virginia. 4°. [*E. Allde*] *f. N. Butter,* 1621. L.O.; HN.

22131 — [An abridgement.] A notable and wonderfull sea-fight [etc.] 4°. *Amsterdam, G. Veseler,* 1621. L.; HN.
— A terrible sea-fight: related in a letter. 1640. *See* 21479.5.

Sea Fights. The true relation and description of 2. sea-fights. 1637. *See* 24335.5.

22132 — Two famous sea-fights. Lately made, betwixt the fleetes of the king of Spaine, and of the Hollanders. The one, in the West-Indyes: the other, the eight of this present moneth of February, betwixt Callis and Gravelin. 4°. [*B. Alsop a. T. Fawcet*] *f. N. Butter a. N. Bourne,* 1639. L.; F.HN.CB.NY.
The 1st pt. is trans. from Relacion verdadera, de la gran vitoria . . . en el Brasil, *Sevilla, N. Rodriguez,* 1638.

22133 **Seabrooke, Richard.** Seabrookes caveat: or his warning piece to all his country-men, to beware how they meddle with the eyes. 8°. *E. All-de,* 1620. L.L³⁹.

22134 **Seager, Francis.** Certayne psalmes drawn into Englyshe metre. 1553. = 2728.

22134.5 — [Headline:] THE SCOOLE/ OF VERTUE. [In verse.] 8°. [*London, c.* 1550.] DNPK(B2,4,5,7 only).
The text appears to be in an earlier form than the eds. that follow. The types and the method of signing leaf signatures, however, resemble those in 25439, *R. Jones,* [1567?]

22135 — [Anr. ed.] The schoole of vertue, and booke of good nourture for chyldren, and youth to learne theyr dutie by. Newely augmented by the fyrst auctour. With a briefe declaracion of the dutie of eche degree. 8°. *W. Seares,* 1557. L.
Seager's name in an acrostic. For a continuation, *see* 25265.

22136 — [Anr. ed.] Newlie perused, corrected, and augmented. Also certaine praiers and graces compiled by R. C(rowley.) 8°. *H. Denham, (the assigne of W. Seres,)* 1582. F.
Crowley's name also in an acrostic.

22137 — [Anr. ed.] 8°. [*J. Charlewood f.*] *R. Jones,* 1593. Ent. 28 no. 1586. HN.
Denham's rights yielded to the company 8 Jan. 1584; *see* Arber II.789.

22137.5 — [Anr. ed.] 8°. *E. All-de f. E. White,* 1620. Ent. 3 jy. 1601. L(tp only, Harl.5910, pt. IV,29).
See Court-Book C, pp. 112–13.

22137.7 — [Anr. ed.] 8°. *G. E[ld] f. T. P[avier] a. J. W[right,]* 1621. Ass'd to Pavier a. J. Wright 13 de. 1620. HD.
A8ʳ line 2: 'Bisket or Carrawayes,'.

22138 — [Anr. ed.] 8°. *M. Flesher f. R. Bird,* [1626?] Ass'd by widow Pavier to E. Brewster a. R. Bird 4 au. 1626. O(Mal.474(1)).
A8ʳ line 2: 'Bisket or Carrawaies,'.

22138.3 — [Anr. ed.] 8°. *M. Flesher f. R. Bird,* [c. 1630.] ILL.
A8ʳ line 2: 'Biskets or Carrawaies,'.

22138.5 — [Anr. ed.] 8°. *M. Flesher f. R. Bird,* [c. 1635.] Wright's share ass'd to Bird 29 ap. 1634. O(Wood 792(1)).
A8ʳ line 2: 'Biskets or Carrawayes,'.

22138.7 — [Anr. ed.] 8°. [*M. Flesher f. R. Bird?* c. 1640.] O (Douce A.385(4), lacks tp).
A8ʳ line 2: 'Biskets or Carrawaies' (no comma).
This is a different and earlier ed. from the ILL copy *M. Flesher f. J. Wright,* [1642?], Wing S 2171.

— *ed. See* 5058.

22139 **Seall, Robert.** A cõmendation of the aduēterus viage of the wurthy captain T. Stutely esquyer and others, towards the land called Terra florida. *Ballad.* s.sh. fol. *J. Alde,* [1563.] Ent. 1562–63. HN.

22140 **Seaman.** The sea-mans triumph. Declaring the honorable actions of such gentlemen as were at the takinge of the great carrick, lately brought to Dartmouth. 8°. *R. B[ourne] f. W. Barley,* 1592. L.O.; F.

Seaman, Lazarus, *ed. See* 24760.5.

22140.5 **Sea Piece.** A poeticall sea-peice [sic]: containing in a spacious table the lively description of a tempest at sea. Transcribed out of an elderly manuscript poem. [In verse.] fol. *T. Cotes,* 1633. Ent. to R. Cotes 1 oc. O.

22141 **Search.** [The search of confession.] 16° in 8's. (*R. Coplãd,* 1529 (20 se.)) A²(imp.).
E2ʳ has a heading: 'A lytell addycyon for more pfyte serche of confessyon.'

Searchfield, Rowland, *Bp. See* 25375a.5.

22142 **Searle, John.** An ephemeris for nine yeeres, inclusive, from 1609. to 1617. Whereunto is annexed three treatises, the first of the use of an ephemeris. The second of the fixed starres, and the third of astrologie. 4° in 8's. *J. Windet* [*a. E. Allde] f. W. Cotten* [sic] *a. J. Tapp,* 1609. Ent. 22 jy. 1608. L.O.O¹⁹.DUL. E⁵.+; F.Y.
Quires B–1st O pr. by Allde; the rest by Windet.

22142.3 **Searle, Robert.** To the honourable, the knights, citizens and burgesses of the commons house. Arguments, why the Posts should have free liberty to carry letters, &c. [Against the grant of T. Witherings.] By Robert Searle post, of Honyton, in Devon, who was the first that invented and set up a certaine weekly and speedy conveyance of letters within this kingdome. s.sh.4°. [*London,* 1640?] HD.
See also 9041, 25930.3, 25930.5.

22142.5 — To the honourable the knights, citizens, and burgesses of the house of commons. Arguments, why the Posts should be recompenced for the dammages sustained by T. Witherings. By Robert Searle post. s.sh.fol. [*London,* 1640?] HD.
Text refers to 'August last, [1640.]'

Sebastian, *King of Portugal.* The strangest adventure that ever happened. Containing a discourse of dom Sebastian. 1601. *See* 23864.
— The true historie of the adventures of don Sebastian. 1602. *See* 23865.

Seckford, Thomas. *See* 21805.1, 21805.7.

22142.7 **Second eighty-eight.** A second eighty eight or briefe relation of the late overthrowe of the Spainsh [sic] ships 10 of September 1631. 4°. *Delph,* [*A. Cloeting?*] 1631. O¹³.
Includes a reprint of 11128.5, initialled I. F.

Securis, John. Almanacks. 1562, etc. *See* 509 sqq.
22143 — A detection and querimonie of the daily enormities cõmitted in physick. 8°. (*in aed. T. Marshi,*) 1566. Ent. 1565–66. L.O.; HN.
22144 — No entry.
22145 — A newe prognosticatiõ. [1570.] Now = 511.5.
22146 — A prognostication. [1562.] Now = 510.3.
22147 — A prognostication. [1566.] Now = 510.5.
22148 — A prognostication. [1573.] Now = 511.9.

Seddon, John, *tr. See* 13030.

22149 **Sedgwick, John.** The bearing and burden of the spirit. In two sermons on Prov. 18. 14. 12°. *G. M[iller] f. R. Harford,* 1639. Ent. 20 au. 1638. L.O.C(lacks Q11).

22149.3 — [Anr. issue, w. cancel tp:] The bearing . . . spirit. Wherein . . . eight cases of conscience [are] cleared. *G. M[iller] f. R. Harford, sold by H. Blunden,* 1639. C¹⁰. M².; HN.HD.ILL.

22149.5 — The second edition corrected. 12°. *G. M[iller] f. R. Harford,* 1640. F.U.

22149.7 — The eye of faith open to God. Unfolded in a sermon preached at the funerall of Mʳˢ. Julian Blackwell. 12°. *G. Miller,* 1640. Ent. 18 au. HD.PN².

22150 — Fury fiered: or, crueltie scourged. [A sermon.] 12°. *J. L[egat] f. W. Sheffard,* 1624. Ent. 12 se. L(tp only, Ames II.688).LINC.

Sedgwick, John—*cont.*
22150a — [Anr. issue, w. cancel tp, w. imprint:] *J. L[egat] f. W. Sheffard,* 1625. O.
— *ed. See* 23829, 25023.5.

22151 **Sedgwick, Obadiah.** Christs counsell to his languishing church of Sardis. 8°. *T. B[adger] f. L. Fawne a. S. Gellibrand,* 1640. Ent. 22 oc. 1639. L.L².L³.O.C.+; F.HN.HD.N.U.+

22152 — Military discipline for the christian souldier. Drawne out in a sermon preached to the captaines in the Artillery Garden. 8°. *G. M[iller] f. T. Nicholes,* 1639. Ent. 19 de. 1638. L³.O.C³.BHP.M.; F.CHI.N.U.

22152.5 **Sedgwick, Richard.** A short summe of the principall things contained in the articles of our faith and ten commandements. [Init. R. S.] 8°. *J. Haviland f. F. Clifton,* 1624. Ent. as by Richard Sedgwick 20 se. L.O¹⁸.; F.

22153 **Seeing.** Here begynneth the seynge of uryns. 4°. [*J. Rastell f.*] (*R. Banckes,* 1525 (28 my.)) HN.
Leaf C4 has 2 paragraphs on pregnancy omitted in other eds. Most of the text is reprinted in 14834.
22153a — [Anr. ed.] 4°. [*J. Rastell f.*] (*R. Bankys,*) [1526?] C.
22153b — [Anr. ed.] 8° in 4's. (*R. wyer,*) [1540?] L.L¹⁶(imp.).G². M.; CHI.NLM.
There are at least 2 Wyer eds.: (1) with line 2 of title ending 'of all' and main text in 85 mm. bastard types (L); (2) with line 2 of title ending 'al the' and main text in 95 mm. textura (NLM).
22154 — [Anr. ed.] 8°. (*R. Redman,*) [1540?] L(1 imp., also tp only, Harl.5927/282; colophon only, Harl.5993/22). G².; CHI.
22155 — [Anr. ed.] 8°. (*Elysabeth late wyfe vnto R. Redman,*) [1541?] L.O.; CAL.Y.
22156 — [Anr. ed.] 8°. (*W. Myddylton,* 1544 (20 de.)) L.; Y.
22157 — [Anr. ed.] 8°. (*W. Powel,* 1548 (16 se.)) L¹⁶(2, 1 imp.). L¹⁷.BHP.M⁴(quires C–F, bd. w. 22161.5).
22158 — Now = 22161.5.
22159 — Now = 22160.5.
22160 — [Anr. ed.] Here begynneth the seynge of urynes. 8°. [*R. or W. Copland f.*] (*Johñ Waley,*) [1548?] L.L¹⁹.; HD(imp.).
22160.3 — [Anr. ed.] 8°. (*W. Copland f. R. Kele,* 1552 (12 au.)) O.; NLM.
22160.5 — [Anr. ed.] Here beginneth the seinge of urynes. 8°. [*f.*] (*Jhon Waley,*) [1557?] L.C.; HD.NY⁴. (Formerly 22159)
22161 — [Anr. ed.] 8°. (*W. Powel,* 1562 (14 ja.)) Ass'd by E. Marsh to T. Orwin ?23 jn. 1591. L¹⁶(imp.).P.; F.
22161.5 — [Anr. ed.] 8°. [*J. Awdley*] (*f. Ant. Kitson,*) [1575?] L. G².M⁴(quires A–B, bd. w. 22157, lacking tp).; ROCH. (Formerly 22158)

Segar, Francis. *See* 22134 sqq.

22162 **Segar,** *Sir William.* The blazon of papistes. obl.8°. *T. Purfoote,* [1587.] Ent. 22 mr. 1587. O.
22163 — The booke of honor and armes. [Anon.] 4°. [*T. Orwin f.*] *R. Jhones,* 1590. Ent. 13 de. 1589. L.O.C⁵.M. BRISTOL².+; F.HN.HD.N.NY.+
Most copies have 2 tpp; the 2nd is without imprint, and its title continues: 'Wherein is discoursed the causes of quarrell.' Segar is named, possibly by the publisher, on p. 102 (added quire Nn3ᵛ). Most of Bk. 5 and other portions are reprinted in 22164.
22164 — Honor military, and civill, contained in foure bookes. fol. *R. Barker,* 1602. L.O.C.E.M.+; F.HN.HD.N.NY.+
L has copies with both states of the engraved portraits: without (G.1183) and w. (137.e.6) Latin inscriptions in the lower right corners.

Seissel, Claude de. *See* Seyssel, C.

22165 **Selden, John.** A briefe discourse, concerning the power of the peeres and comons of Parliament, in point of judicature. [Anon.] 4°. [*T. Paine,*] *Printed in the yeere,* 1640. L.O.C.DUR⁵.M(deposit).+; F.HN.HD.ILL. NY.+
Pp. 9. Sometimes attrib. to Sir R. Cotton.
22166 — [Anr. ed.] 4°. [*London,*] *Printed in the yeere, that seacoale was exceeding deare,* 1640. L.O.C².D.E.+; F.HN. HD.N.Y.+
Pp. 6.

Selden, John—*cont.*

22167 — Joannis Seldeni I. C. de dis Syris syntagmata II. 8°. *G. Stansbeius, bibliopolarum corpori*, 1617. L.O.C.D. E².+; F.HN.CU.HD.N.+

Ent. to the ptnrs. in the Latin stock 27 se. 1616; *see* Arber III.681.

22168 — Joannis Seldeni de jure naturali & gentium, juxta disciplinam Ebræorum, libri septem. fol. *R. Bishopius*, 1640. Ent. 27 fb. 1639. L.O.C.D.E.+; F.HN.CHI.CU. HD.+

22169 — Joannis Seldeni J. C. de successionibus in bona defuncti, liber singularis. 4°. *typis G. Stanesbeij, prostant ap. E. Weaver & J. Smithick*, 1631. Ent. to Stansby 25 ap. L.O.C.D.DUR(Bamb.).+; F.HN. CHI.CU.HD.+

22170 — Editio altera, multùm auctior. Accedunt eiusdem de successione in pontificatum Ebræorum, libri duo. fol. *R. Bishop*, 1636. Ass'd 4 mr. 1639. L.O.C.D.E.+; F.HN.CU.HD.KAN.+

22171 — The duello or single combat. [Init. J. S.] 4°. *G. E[ld] f. J. Helme*, 1610. Ent. 22 de. 1609. L.O.C.LINC.SAL. +; F.HN.CU.HD.N.+

22172 — The historie of tithes. 4°. [*London*,] 1618. L¹³.O.C⁵.G². SHEF.+; F.CAL⁶.HD.ILL.NY¹¹.+

1st a2ʳ lines 3–4 of heading: 'Connington/Kight [*sic*]'; p. 249 misnumbered '149', line 1: 'litle'; 2nd a2ʳ line 5 begins: 'of a first borne,' (no hyphen).

Some copies (C, on Univ. Microfilms reel 1034; C⁹, ETON, 1 HD, SMU) have 1st a–e from 22172.3.

Answered by 18037, 18474, 21842, 22186, 24073.

22172.3 — [Anr. ed.] 4°. [*London*,] 1618. L³⁸.O.C.G².YK.+; HD(2). ILL.MICH.MIN.TORONTO².

1st a2ʳ lines 3–4 of heading: 'Connington./Knight' (w. stop), line 3 from bottom: 'be'; p. 249 misnumbered '149', line 1: 'little'; 2nd a–f from same setting as 22172.

Some copies (1 O, O⁸, O¹⁸, O²¹, O³¹, M², 1 HD) have 1st a–e from 22172.

22172.5 — [Anr. ed.] 4°. [*London*,] 1618. L.O.C².D.M.+; CHI.HD. MICH.NY.TEX.+

1st a2ʳ lines 3–4 of heading: 'Connington/Knight (no stop); p. 249 correctly numbered; 2nd a2ʳ line 5 begins: 'of a first-borne,' (w. hyphen), line 2 begins: 'in Works'.

A copy at F has some sheets from 22172.

22172.7 — [Anr. ed.] 4°. [*London*,] 1618. L.O.C.D.E.+; HN.CHI. CU.HD.LC.+

1st a2ʳ lines 3–4 of heading: 'Connington./Knight (with stop), line 3 from bottom: 'bee'; p. 249 misnumbered '146'; 2nd a2ʳ line 5 begins: 'of a first-borne,' (w. hyphen), line 2 begins: 'in Workes'.

A copy at N has some sheets from 22172.3.

22173 — [Anr. ed., w. title:] The history of tythes. 4°. [*London*,] 1618 [really 1680.] L.O.C⁷.D.E.+; HN.HD. ILL.U.WASH².+

The only ed. to have the tp printed all in black and to have medial 'v', e.g. 'give'.

22174 — Jani Anglorum facies altera. 12°. *typis T. S[nodham] procur. J. Helme, imp. auctor.*, 1610. Ent. to Helme 26 no. L.O.C.D².LINC.+; F.HN.CU.HD.ILL.

22175 — Joannis Seldeni mare clausum seu de dominio maris libri duo. fol. *W. Stanesbeius pro R. Meighen*, 1635. Ent. to Stansby 18 se. L.O.C.D.E.+; F.HN.CU.HD.N.+

22175.3 — [Anr. ed.] 12°. [*Leyden, B. a. A. Elzevir*,] *juxta exemplar Londinense, W. Stanesbeii pro R. Meighen*, 1636. L.O.C.DUR⁵.E.+; F.HN.COR.LC.PN.+

Importation of these foreign eds. forbidden in 9060. They qualify for STC because of passages in English in Bk. 2, ch. 14, 15, 22, 25, 30, 31.

22175.7 — [Anr. ed.] 4°. *Lugduni Batavorum, ap. J. & T. Maire*, 1636. L.O¹¹.O¹⁷.+; HD.NY.PN.

22176 — [Anr. ed., enlarged.] Accedunt M. Z. Boxhornii apologia pro navigationibus Hollandorum adversus Pontum Heuterum, et tractatus mutui commercii & navigationis inter Henricum VII. & Philippum archiducem Austriæ. 8°. *Londini* [i.e. *Amsterdam?*] *iuxta exemplar W. Stanesbeii pro R. Meighen*, 1636. L.O.C.D.E.+; F.HD.LC.NY.TEX.+

— Marmora Arundelliana. 1628, etc. *See* 823 sq.

22177 — Titles of honor by John Selden. 4°. *W. Stansby f. J. Helme*, 1614. Ent. 14 jy. L.O.C.D.E.+; F.HN.HD.N. NY.+

Selden, John—*cont.*

22178 — Second edition. fol. *W. Stansby f. R. Whitakers* [sic], 1631. Ent. to J. Bill 9 no. 1627; ass'd to Joyce Norton a. R. Whitaker 26 au. 1632. L.O.C.D.E.+; F.HN.CHI.CU.HD.+

— *ed. See* 7438, 11197.

— *See also* 24074.

22179 **Seldom.** Seldome comes the better: or, an admonition to husbands, wives, [etc.] *Ballad.* 2 pts. s.sh.fol. [*f. F. Grove*, 1629?] Ent. to F. Grove 20 jn. 1629. L.

Selim I, *Sultan.* The first part of the tragicall raigne of Selimus. 1594. *See* 12310a.

22180 **Selim II**, *Sultan.* A discourse of the bloody and cruell battaile, of late loste by sultan Selim. And also of the taking of Seruan. 1579. *Tr.* out of French. 8° in 4's. *T. Dawson*, [1579?] L.

22181 **Seller, John.** Five sermons preached upon severall occasions. 12°. [*B. Alsop a. T. Fawcet*] *f. J. Clark*, 1636. Ent. 1 ap. L.O²⁸(Bed.).C. Ickworth.; CHI.

22182 — A sermon against halting betweene two opinions. 4°. *T. Creede f. W. Welbie*, 1611. L.L².L³.C.NEP.+; HD.

22182a — [A variant, w. imprint:] *T. Creede f. R. Mabb*, 1611. L.O.C².; F(3).

— *See also* Bookplates.

22182a.5 **Selman, John.** The araignment of John Selman, who was executed neere Charing-Crosse. 4°. *W. H[all] f. T. Archer*, 1611 [1612.] Ent. 7 ja. 1612. F.

See also 22655.5.

22183 — [A variant, w. imprint:] *W. H[all] f. T. Archer*, 1612. L.E².; HN.HD.

22184 **Seminary Priest.** A seminary priest put to a non-plus. 1629. Now = 23507.5.

22185 **Seminary Priests.** To the seminarye priests lately come ouer, angelles of darkenes, who are not to be beleeued before they haue aunswered the author heerof. Which being printed more then X. yeeres past, and to this day not aunswered by R. Bristowe. 4°. *E. Allde*, 1592. C.C⁵.E.P.; F.HN

Tp verso has a type-facsimile of the orig. tp: 'The sixt new-yeres gift, and the fourth proclamacion of outlawrye &c. against . . . R. Bristowe. 1579.' Ent. to J. Allde 26 ja. 1579. Answers 3800.5.

22185.5 **Sempill**, *Sir James.* The pack-mans pater noster, or a dialogue betwixt a chapman and a priest. Newlie *tr.* out of Dutch, by S[ir] I. S[empill. In verse.] 4°. *Aberdene, E. Raban f. D. Melvill*, 1624. F.

(Formerly 19087)

22186 — Sacrilege sacredly handled. That is, according to Scripture onely. An appendix also added; answering some objections in J. Scaligers Diatribe, and J. Seldens Historie of tithes [22172]. 4°. *W. Jones f. E. Weaver*, 1619. Ent. to Weaver a. Jones 20 mr. L.O. C.D.E².+; F.HN.CU.HD.N.+

— *See also* 15110.

22187 **Sempill, Robert.** The admonitioun to the lordis. [Anon.] *Ballad.* s.sh.fol. *Edinburgh, R. Lekpreuik*, [15]70. L.

22187a — [Anr. ed.] s.sh.fol. [*Edinburgh, R. Lekpreuik*,] 1570. L⁵. This may be the earlier ed.

22187a.5 — The bird in the cage. [Signed 'Maddie Priores of the Caill mercat.'] *Ballad.* s.sh.fol. *Edinburgh, R. Lekpreuik*, 1570. L¹¹(S.P. Scot. Eliz., vol. 17, doc. 72).

(Formerly 3084)

22188 — The bischoppis lyfe and testament. *Ballad.* s.sh.fol. *Striuiling, R. Lekpreuik*, 1571. L⁵.

22189 — The complaint of Scotland. [Anon. On Regent Moray's death.] *Ballad.* s.sh.fol. [*Edinburgh, R. Lekpreuik*, 1570.] L.L¹¹(S.P. Scot. Eliz., vol. 13, doc. 48).

22190 — Ane complaint vpon fortoun. *Ballad.* s.sh.fol. *Edinburgh, R. Lekprewicke*, [1581.] L.

22191 — The cruikit liedis the blinde. [Anon.] *Ballad.* s.sh.fol. *Edinburgh, R. Lekpreuik*, 1570. L.L¹¹(S.P. Scot. Eliz., vol. 17, doc. 71).

22192 — ane deeclaratioun [*sic*] of the lordis iust quarrell. [Anon.] *Ballad.* s.sh.fol. *Edinburgh, R. Lekpreuik*, 1567. L(2).L¹¹(S.P. Scot. Eliz., vol. 14, doc. 73).

22192a — = 22192.

22192a.3 — The deploratioun of the cruell murther of James erle of Murray. [Anon.] *Ballad.* s.sh.fol. *Edinburgh, R. Lekpreuik*, 1570. Ent. to J. Sampson, i.e. Awdely 1569–70. L¹¹(S.P. Scot. Eliz., vol. 17, doc. 17).

(Formerly 23373)

Sempill, Robert—*cont.*

22192a.5 — [Anr. ed.] s.sh.fol. *Edinburgh, R. Lekpreuik, 1570.* L[5].
In title: 'cruel'.

22193 — The exhortatioun to all plesand thingis. [Anon.] *Ballad.* s.sh.fol. *Edinburgh, R. Lekpreuik, 1570.* L[5]. L[11](S.P. Scot. Eliz., vol. 17, doc. 18).

22194 — Ane exhortatioun derect to my lord regent. [Anon.] *Ballad.* s.sh.fol. [*Edinburgh, R. Lekpreuik, 1567.*] L[11](S.P. Scot. Eliz., vol. 14, doc. 72, imp.).

22194.5 — The exhortatioun to the lordis. [Anon. In praise of Regent Lennox.] *Ballad.* s.sh.fol. *Striuiling, R. Lekpreuik, 1571.* L[5].
(Formerly 22198) A different text from 22197.

22195 — The hailsome admonitioun &c. [Anon.] *Ballad.* s.sh. fol. *Edinburgh, R. Lekpreuik, 1570.* L[11](S.P. Scot. Eliz., vol. 17, doc. 73).

22196 — Heir followis ane ballat declaring the nobill and gude inclinatioun of our king. [Anon.] *Ballad.* s.sh.fol. *Edinburgh, R. Lekpreuik, 1567.* L[11](S.P. Scot. Eliz., vol. 13, doc. 47).

22197 — Heir followis ane exhortatioun to the lordis. [Anon. Against Queen Mary and Bothwell.] *Ballad.* s.sh.fol. *Edinburgh, R. Lekpreuik, 1567.* L[11](S.P. Scot. Eliz., vol. 13, doc. 62).

22198 — The exhortatioun to the lordis. 1571. Now = 22194.5.

22199 — Heir followis the testament and tragedie of vmquhile king Henrie Stewart. [Anon.] *Ballad.* s.sh.fol. *Edinburgh, R. Lekpreuik, 1567.* L(MS. Dept., Cotton MSS. Cal. C. I. fol. 17).
(Formerly also 23372)

22200 — The kingis complaint. [Anon.] *Ballad.* s.sh.fol. [*Edinburgh, R. Lekpreuik, 1567.*] L.

22200.5 — The lamentatiõ of the cõmounis of Scotland. [Anon.] *Ballad.* s.sh.fol. *Sanctandrois, R. Lekpreuik, 1572.* L[5].
(Formerly 22012)

22201 — Maddeis lamentatioun. [Anon.] *Ballad.* s.sh.fol. *Edinburgh, R. Lekpreuik, 1570.* L.

22201.5 — Maddeis proclamatioun. [Anon.] *Ballad.* s.sh.fol. [*Edinburgh, R. Lekpreuik, 1570.*] L.
(Formerly 17177)

22202 — My lord Methwenis tragedie. *Ballad.* s.sh.fol. *Sanctandrois, R. Lekpreuik, 1572.* L[5].

22203 — ane new ballet set out be ane fugitiue Scottisman that fled out of Paris. [On the St. Bartholomew massacre.] *Ballad.* s.sh.fol. *Sanctandrois, R. Lekpriuik, 1572.* L.

22204 — The poysonit schot. [Anon. On the murder of Regent Moray.] *Ballad.* s.sh.fol. *Edinburgh, R. Lekpreuik, 1570.* L.L[5].

22204.5 — ane premonitioun to the barnis of Leith. [Anon.] *Ballad.* s.sh.fol. *Sanctandrois, R. Lekpreuik, 1572.* L[5].
(Formerly 15436)

22205 — The regentis tragedie ending with ane exhortatoun [*sic*]. *Ballad.* s.sh.fol. *Edinburgh, R. Lekpreuik, 1570.* L.L[5].
For an Anglicized version *see* 22210.

22206 — [Anr. issue, partly reset.] *Edinburgh, R. Lekpreuik, 1570.* L[11](S.P. Scot. Eliz., vol. 17, doc. 16).
In title: 'Exhortatioun'.

22207 — The sege of the castel of Edinburgh. [In verse.] 4°. *Edinburgh, R. Lekpreuik, 1573.* L.

22208 — The spur to the lordis. [Anon.] *Ballad.* s.sh.fol. [*Edinburgh, R. Lekpreuik,*] 1570. L[5].

22209 — Ane tragedie in forme of ane diallog betuix honour gude fame, and the authour heirof in ane trance. [Anon. In verse.] 8°. *Edinburgh, R. Lekpreuik, 1570.* E.

22210 — The tragical end and death of the lord James regent of Scotland, lately set forth in Scottish, and printed at Edinburgh. 1570 [22205]. And now partly turned in to English. *Ballad.* s.sh.fol. *J. Awdely, 1570.* Ent. to J. Sampson, i.e. Awdely, 1569–70. HN.

22211 — The tressoun of Dunbartane. [Anon.] *Ballad.* s.sh.fol. *Edinburgh, R. Lekpreuik, 1570.* L[11](2, S.P. Scot. Eliz., vol. 18, docs. 23, 24).

22212 **Sendbrief.** Send-brief waer in de voorneempste stucken der pauwscher leere verhandelt, [etc.] 8°. *T. Vautrolier, 1581.* C(Sayle 1549).

22213 **Seneca, Lucius Annæus.** The workes of Lucius Annæus Seneca, both morrall and naturall. *Tr.* T. Lodge. (The life of Seneca by J. Lipsius.) fol. *W. Stansby,*

Seneca, Lucius Annæus—*cont.*

1614 (1613.) ?Ent. to E. Blount 15 ap. 1600. L.O.C.G[4].M.+; F.HN.HD.N.NY.+
In most copies b1–3 and b6 are missing; present in at least L, O[39], 1 F, HN, 1 HD.

22214 — [Anr. ed.] Newly inlarged by T. Lodge. fol. *W. Stansby,* (1620.) Ass'd by widow Stansby to R. Bishop 4 mr. 1639. L.O.C.D.E.+; F.HN.HD.N.NY.+

22215 — [*De beneficiis.*] The woorke of the excellent philosopher Lucius Annæus Seneca concerning benefyting. *Tr.* A. Golding. 4°. [*J. Kingston f.*] *J. Day, 1578.* Ent. 26 mr. 1579. L.O(2).; F.HN.BO.N(imp.).Y.
The tp is a cancel. For another trans. of Bks. 1–3, *see* 12939.

22215.5 — [*De brevitate vitæ.*] Lucius, Annæus, Seneca the philosopher: his booke of the shortnesse of life. *Tr.* into an English poem. ([Sir] R. F[reeman].) 4°. [*N. a. J. Okes*] *f. D. Frere, 1636.* C[5].DUL.WIN[2].; F.HD.

22215a — [*De consolatione.*] L. A. Seneca the philosopher, his booke of consolation to Marcia. *Tr.* into an English poem. (Philophrastes, *pseud.*) 4°. *E. P[urslowe] f. H. Seile, 1635.* Ent. as tr. by Sir R. Freeman 1 mr. 1634. L.O(2).C.DUL(imp.).STD.; F.HN.CHI.HD.Y.+
HN tp as above; the HD tp varies in having a comma after 'booke' but none after 'philosopher'. The HN copy has an extra leaf w. pr. dedic. to John Egerton, Earl of Bridgewater, signed in MS. by R. C., i.e. R. Codrington?

22216 — [*De remediis fortuitorum.*] Lucii Annei Senecæ ad Gallioneni de remediis fortuitorum. The remedyes agaynst all casuall chaunces. Dialogus inter sensum et rationem. A dialogue betwene sensualyte and reason. *Tr.* R. Whyttynton. *Lat. a. Eng.* 8°. (*W. Myddylton, 1547.*) L.O.; CU(B[8] C[4] only, bd. w. 1st quire of 17502).N.

22217 — [*Tragœdiæ.*] L. Annæi Senecæ Cordubensis tragoediæ. Maiore, quam antehac, cura recognitæ. 16° in 8's. *R. R[obinson,] imp. T. Man & T. Gubbin, 1589.* Ent. to T. Man a. W. Brome 6 se. 1585. L.L[13].O.C.; F.HN.MCG.
A paginary reprint of the *Lyons, A. Gryphius,* 1584 ed., w. an imitation (McK.262α) of its device.

22218 — L. & M. Annæi Senecae atque aliorum tragoediæ. Fideliter emendatæ atque illustratæ (T. Farnaby.) 8°. *F. Kingstonius, imp. G. Welby, 1613.* Ent. 20 no. 1612. L.O.C.A.M[4].+; F.HN.CU.HD.N.+

22219 — [Anr. ed.] Editæ denuò. 8°. *T. Snodham, 1624.* Ass'd 2 mr. 1618. L.O.C.E.M[4].+; F.HN.CU.HD.ILL.+

22220 — Editio tertia auctior. 8°. *F. Kyngston, imp. P. Stephani & C. Meredith, 1634.* Ass'd to W. Stansby 23 fb. 1626. L.O.C.CASHEL.LEEDS.+; HN.BO.HD.N.Y.+

22221 — [A trans.] Seneca his tenne tragedies, *tr.* into Englysh. [*Ed.*] (T. Newton.) 4° in 8's. *T. Marsh, 1581.* Ent. 4–9 jy. L.O.P.STU.WN.+; F.HN.HD.N.NY.+
Reprints the separate eds. 22222 sqq., w. a revised text of 22225; includes 1st ed. of *Thebais* tr. T. Newton, and *Hippolytus* and *Hercules Oetaeus* tr. J. Studley. The *Hippolytus* was ent. to H. Denham 1566–67 (Arber I.336) and ass'd to R. Jones a. J. Charlewood 31 au. 1579. A different? trans. of the *Hercules Oetaeus* was ent. to Denham 1566–67 (Arber I.327) and was apparently among the books printing rights to which Denham yielded to the company 8 Jan. 1584 (Arber II.789).

22222 — — [*Agamemnon.*] The eyght tragedie of Seneca. Entituled Agamemnon. *Tr.* J. Studley. 8°. *T. Colwell, 1566.* Ent. 1565–66. L.O.ETON(imp.).; HN. Greg 42.

22223 — — [*Hercules furens.*] Lucii Annei Senecæ tragedia prima quæ inscribitur Hercules furens nuper recognita. The first tragedie intituled Hercules furens, newly perused and *tr.* by Jasper Heywood. *Lat. a. Eng.* 8°. (*H. Sutton, 1561.*) L(2).O.C(imp.). ETON(imp.). HN(last leaf in facs.).ILL.LC(imp.).NY. PFOR. Greg 34.
See note to 22227a.

22224 — — [*Medea.*] The seuenth tragedie of Seneca, entituled Medea: tr. J. Studley. 8°. *T. Colwell, 1566.* Ent. 1565–66. L.; F.HN.PFOR. Greg 44.

22225 — — [*Oedipus.*] The lamentable tragedie of Oedipus. [*Tr.*] By A. Neuyle. 8°. *T. Colwell, 1563* (28 ap.) Ent. 1562–63. L.O.; HN. Greg 36.
Quartersheet F in 2 settings: w. (L, O) or without (HN) comma after 'London' in the colophon.

Seneca, Lucius Annæus—*cont.*

22226 — — [*Thyestes*.] The seconde tragedie of Seneca enti-
tuled Thyestes faithfully Englished by Jasper Hey-
wood. 8°. *in the hous late T. Berthelettes*, 1560 (26 mr.)
L(2).L¹³.O(imp.).C(frag.).ETON.+; F.HN.CH.HD.NY.+
Greg 29.
See note to 22227a.

22227 — — [*Troas*.] The sixt tragedie of . . . Lucius, Anneus,
Seneca, entituled Troas, with diuers addicions.
Newly set forth in Englyshe by Jasper Heywood. 8°.
(*R. Tottyll*,) 1559. Ent. 1558–59. L. Greg 28.

22227a — [Anr. ed.] 8°. (*R. Tottyll*,) 1559. L.ETON.
In title: 'Englishe'. Quires E and F and inner
forme of D partly from same setting as 22227.
Regarding the slovenly printing of this ed. Heywood writes on ❦1ʳ of 22226: 'And to the printer
thus I sayde:/ within these doores of thyne,/ I
make a vowe shall neuer more/come any worke of
myne.' *See* also 22223.

22228 — [Anr. ed.] 8°. *T. Powell f. G. Bucke*, [1562?] L.L¹³.C.;
F.HN(quire F in facs.).PFOR.
— *See* also 18136, 18155.

Suppositilious Works

— [*De moribus*.] A frutefull worke of L. A. Senecæ. Called
the myrrour or glasse of maners. 1547. *See* 17502.

— [*De quattuor virtutibus*.] Seneca moralissmus [*sic*]
philosophus de quattuor virtutibus. 1516, etc. *See*
17498 sqq.

— A frutefull worke of L. A. Seneca named the forme and
rule of honest lyuynge. 1546. *See* 17501.

22229 — [*Octavia*.] The ninth tragedie of Lucius Anneus
Seneca called Octavia. *Tr*. T. N[uce,] student in
Cambridge. 4°. *H. Denham*, [1566.] Ent. 1566–67.
L.O.; F.HN.HD.PFOR.TEX. Greg 45.

22230 **Senhouse, Richard**, *Bp*. Foure sermons preached at the
court. 4°. [*H. Lownes*] *f. R. Davlman*, 1627. Ent.
13 fb. L.O.C².D².DUR³.+; F.HN.HD.ILL.U.+
The D⁸ copy has the date altered in pen to 1637.

22231 **Sennertus, Daniel.** Danielis Sennerti Vratislaviensis
epitome naturalis scientiæ. Editio tertia. Auctior &
correctior. 8°. *Oxoniæ, J. Lichfield, imp. H. Cripps*,
1632. L.O.C³.D.STU.+; F.HN.LC.
Earlier eds. were pr. on the Continent.

22232 — The weapon-salves maladie: or, a declaration of its
insufficiencie. *Tr*. out of his 5ᵗʰ. booke, part. 4.
chap. 10. Practicæ medicinæ. 4°. [*B. Alsop a. T.
Fawcet*] *f. J. Clark*, 1637. Ent. 13 fb. L.O¹¹.SAL.STD.;
F.BO⁵.HD.NLM.

Sentence. March 7. 1623. Numb. 22. The sentence and
execution. 1623. *See* Newsbooks 101.

22233 **Seres**, really **Securis, John.** An almanacke and prognostication. [1574.] = 512.

22234 **Seres, William.** An aunswere to the proclamation of the
rebels in the north. [Init. W. S. In verse.] 8°. *W.
Seres*, 1569. Ent. 1569–70. L.L².O⁹.C.D².+; F.HN(1,
plus frag.).

Sergier, Richard, *tr*. *See* 22996.

Series. Series patefacti nuper parricidii. 1605. *See* 1401.

22235 **Serlio, Sebastiano.** The first (second—fift) booke of
architecture. *Tr*. out of Italian into Dutch, and out
of Dutch into English. (*R. Peake*.) 5 pts. fol. [*T.
Snodham? a.*] (*S. Stafford*) *f. R. Peake*, 1611. Ent. to
T. Snodham 14 de. L.O.C.D².E.+; F.HN.HD.N.NY.+
The woodcuts are from the same blocks used in
the Antwerp, 1553 and Basel, 1608 eds.; *see*
McK. & F. 253–5. Bk. 1 was app. pr. by Snodham.

Sermo. In die innocenciũ ꝑmo pro episcopo pueroꝝ.
[1499? etc.] *See* 282 sq.
— Sermo exhortatoriꝰ cancellarij Eboꝝ. [1510?] *See*
17806.

Sermon. A fruitfull sermon, [on Romans xii.3–8.] 1584,
etc. *See* 4926 sqq.
— A godly and fruitefull sermon [on Gen. xiv.20,21.]
[1584.] *See* 19103.

22236 — A godly and fruitfull sermon preached at Lieth [*sic*] in
Scotland. [By J. Murray, *Minister*.] 8°. [*W. Jones'
secret press*,] 1607. O.O⁵.C¹⁰.E.; F. Detroit PL.
Attrib. to J. Murray on *2ʳ of 14084.
— A godly and learned sermon, preached the 26. day of
Februarie, 1580. [1580?] *See* 11434 sq.

Sermon—*cont.*
— A godly sermon: preached at Detford. 1586. *See* 19105.

22237 — A godlye sermon: preached before the queens maiestie,
. . . shewing breefely that the authoritie which the
pope of Rome doth challenge to himselfe, is vnlaw-
fully vsurped. [On Matt. xvi.17–19.] 8°. *J. Windet f.
J. Perin*, 1585. L.O.P(2).; F(2).BO³.HD(lacks F8).
One P copy is bd. w. 19796.5, and both items may
be by the same author.
— A most excellent and heavenly sermon. [On Luke
xxiii.] 1595. *See* 20014 sq.
— A most godly and learned sermon, preached at Pauls
Crosse. [On Titus iii.1.] 1589. *See* 25432.
— A sermon, called Gods new-yeeres-guift. 1602. *See*
18547.
— A sermon concerning the eucharist. 1629. *See* 14441.

22238 — A sermon declaringe how vue [*sic*] ar iustified by faith.
(*Tr*. out of latin by E. T.) 8°. *W. hyl*, [1549?] O.; F.
— A sermon no lesse frutefull then famous. [On Luke
xvi.2. 1540? etc.] *See* 25823.3 sqq.
— A sermon, or homelie. [On Heb. xiii.16.] 1596. *See*
13680.9.
— A sermon preached at Plimmoth in New-England.
1622. *See* 6149.
— A sermon preached at S. Martins in the Fields. At the
funerall of the lady Blount. 1620. *See* 18226.
— A sermon preached at the Tower of London. [1570?
etc.] *See* 6694 sqq.

22239 — A sermon preached before the queenes maiestie, the
second of March An. 1575. [On Ps. cxxxi.] [1576?]
= 26110.

22240 — A verie fruitful sermon, . . . concerning predestination.
1583. Now = 19109.5.

Sermones. [Quatuor sermones.] 1483, etc. *See* 17957
sqq.

Sermonetta, *Cardinal*. Instructions for young gentlemen. 1633. *See* 11514.

Sermons. Certayne sermons or homilies. 1547, etc. *See*
13638.5 sqq.

22240.5 — Five especiall sermons, preached by severall men upon
severall occasions and subjects. 5 pts. 4°. *f. G.
Latham*, 1627. L¹³.; NY¹¹.PH.
A nonce collection of separate sermons w. orig.
tpp cancelled: 15301, 20767, 14693, 4588, 17470.
All these sermons were originally pub'd. by M.
Lownes, whose daughter Susan married Latham.
— Three sermons or homelies. 1596. *See* 13681 sq.

Serpent. This lytell treatyse declareth the damage caused
by the serpent of diuision. [c. 1535.] *See* 17027.5.

Serranus, John. A godlie and learned commentarie. *See*
22247.

Serre, Jean Puget de la. *See* 20487.5.

22241 **Serres, Jean de.** The fyrst parte of commentaries, concerning the state of religion, and the common wealthe
of Fraunce. [By P. de la Place.] *Tr*. T. Tymme. 4°.
H. Bynneman f. F. Coldocke, 1573. O(2).; HN.
A1ʳ line 1 of text ends: 'Commentaries,'. Although
prefatory verses attrib. authorship to P. Ramus,
this and the following are from *Commentariorum de statu religionis & reipublicæ in regno
Galliæ libri*, 1572–5, of which the 1st part is an
abridged trans. of la Place's *Commentaires de
l'estat de la religion*, 1565, and the rest by Serres.

22241.5 — [Anr. issue, w. a–b⁴ reprinted and pts. 2 and 3 by J. de
Serres added.] The three partes of commentaries,
containing the whole and perfect discourse of the
ciuill warres of Fraunce. With an addition of the
murther of the admirall Chastilion, 1572. *Tr*. out of
Latine by T. Timme. 3 pts. 4°. (*H. Middelton f.*) *F.
Coldocke*, 1574. L⁴³.O.O¹⁹.C.; F.CAL.ILL.N.NY.+ ﴾
A1ʳ line 1 of text ends: 'Commentaries,'. Bk. 9,
pp. 207–301, reprints pp. 59–218 of 11271. Bk. 10
reprints 13847.

22242 — [Anr. issue, w. pt. 1 reprinted.] 3 pts. 4°. (*H. Middelton
f.*) *F. Coldocke*, 1574. L.O.C⁵.A(imp.).BTU.+; F.
HN.HART².HD.
A1ʳ line 1 of text ends: 'commenta-'.

22243 — The fourth parte of cõmentaries . . . *tr*. T. Tymme.
[Anon.] 4°. *H. Binneman f. H. Toy*, 1576. L.O.C
(imp.).DUR³.G².+; F.HN.HD.N.NY.+

Serres, Jean de—*cont.*

22244 — A general inventorie of the history of France, unto 1598. Written by J. de Serres. And continued out off [*sic*] the best authors [P. Matthieu and others.] *Tr.* E. Grimeston. fol. *G. Eld,* 1607. Ent. to W. Ponsonby 7 no. 1597 a. 3 ja. 1600; to G. Eld 3 mr. 1606. L.O.C.INN.M⁴.+ ; F.HN.N.NY.Y.+

22245 — [Anr. ed., enlarged.] A generall historie of France. Much augmented. fol. *G. Eld,* 1611. L.O.C.A.D.+ ; F.HN.HD.ILL.NY.+

22246 — [Anr. ed.] Contynued by P. Mathew [i.e. *tr.* from P. Matthieu] to 1610. And unto 1622. By E. Grimston. fol. *G. Eld & M. Flesher,* 1624. L.O.C.A.M².+ ; F.HN.HD.N.NY¹¹.+

22246.5 — [Anr. issue of quires [b]–[gg] w. added tp:] A continuation of the generall history of France. *G. Eld a. M. Flesher,* 1624. N.NY(imp.).
The N copy also has an added dedic. to Lionel Cranfield, 1st Earl of Middlesex.

22247 — A godlie and learned commentarie vpon Ecclesiastes. Newly turned into English by J. Stockwood. 8°. *J. Windet f. J. Harrison the younger,* 1585. L.L².O.C.P. + ; F.HN.HD.PN².

— Gasparis Colinii Castilloni, magni quondam Franciae Amerallii, vita. 8°. [n.p.] 1575. L(2).; F.HD.
Sometimes attrib. to *London, J. Wolfe,* but more prob. pr. on the Continent, possibly at Geneva.

22248 — [A trans.] The lyfe of the most godly, valeant and noble capteine J. Colignie Shatilion. *Tr.* A. Golding. [Anon.] 8°. *T. Vautrollier,* 1576. L.O.O¹⁰.C(lacks H6).G².; F.HN.CU.HD.N.

22249 **Serres, Olivier de.** The perfect use of silk-wormes, and their benefit. Done out of the French by N. Geffe. With an annexed discourse of his owne. 4°. *F. Kyngston, sold by R. Sergier a. C. Purset w. the assignment of W. Stallenge,* 1607. Ent. to Purset a. Sergier 2 my. L(2).O.C.SH(imp.).Juel-Jensen(2).; F.HN.HD.NY.Y.+
Copies vary: with or without royal arms on tp verso; Juel-Jensen has both.

22249.3 — [A variant, w. imprint:] *F. Kyngston f. R. Sergier a. C. Purset, and are to be sold by them,* 1607. Oxford Univ., Hope Dept. of Entomology.

Servita, Paul. *See* 21765.

Servius Maurus Honoratus. *See* 695.

Servus. Fidelis serui, subdito infideli responsio. 1573. *See* 5407.

22249.5 **Seton, Alexander.** The declaraciō made at Poules Crosse in the cytye of London, the fourth sonday of Aduent by A. Seyton, and mayster W. Tolwyn, in M.D.XLI. Newly corrected & amēded. 8° in 4's. (*R. Lant,*) [1542?] L².R(frag.).
Tolwyn's confession reprinted and answered in 1309.

22250 **Seton, John.** [Dialectica. Bks. 1–3.] 8°. (*in off. T. Berthel[eti,]* 1545.) L(lacks tp).

22250.2 — [Anr. ed.] Dialectica breuem in contextum constricta. 8°. (*in off. nuper T. Berthel[eti,]* 1560.) YK. Stevens Cox.

22250.4 — [Anr. ed.] 8°. *in off. nuper T. Berthel[eti,]* 1563. L(tp only, Harl.5910, pt. I.259). DUL.LEIC.LK.

22250.5 — An earlier ed. of 22250.6.] 1563. *See* Addenda.

22250.6 — [Anr. ed., adding Bk. 4 and Carter's Annotations, w. title:] Petri Carteri Cantabrigiensis, in J. Setoni Dialecticam annotationes. 8°. *in æd. T. Marshi,* 1568. L(tp only, Harl.5993/53).D.DUL.K.

22250.8 — [Anr. ed., w. title:] Dialectica . . . annotationibus P. Carteri. Huic accessit G. Buclæi Arithmetica. 8°. *ap. T. Marshum,* 1570. O¹³.C⁷.HAT.LEIC.
Arithmetica reprinted from 4009.

22251 — [Anr. ed.] 8°. *ap. T. Marshum,* 1572. L(imp.).L¹⁶(Arith. only).C(imp.).

22252 — [Anr. ed.] 8°. *ap. T. Marsh,* 1574. L(lacks folding table).E².P.USHAW.; F.

22253 — [Anr. ed.] 8°. *ap. T. Marsh,* 1577. L.L².L⁴⁴.O.O³.+
There are 2 eds. w. this date: leaf signatures have roman numerals (L) or arabic numerals (O). In the O ed. the 3 of signature D3 is under the space after 'd' in 'sed'.

22253.3 — [Anr. ed.] 8°. [*T. Marsh,* 1580?] D(imp.).
Leaf signatures have arabic numerals. The 3 of signature D3 is beneath 'ed' in 'sed'.

Seton, John—*cont.*

22253.5 — [Anr. ed.] 8°. [*T. Marsh,* 1580?] O¹⁴(imp.).
Leaf signatures have arabic numerals. The 3 of signature D3 is beneath 's' in 'sed'.

22253.7 — [Anr. ed.] 8°. *ap. T. Marsh,* 1582. EX.

22254 — [Anr. ed.] 8°. *G. Dewes & H. Marsh, ex assign. T. Marsh,* 1584. L.C.C².D.P.+ ; HN.ILL.Y.

22254.3 — [Anr. ed.] Hac ultima editione, emendatissimè excusa. 8°. *ap. R. Dexter,* 1599. Ass'd by E. Marsh to T. Orwin ?23 jn. 1591. L¹³.GLOUC.YK(imp.).

22254.7 — [Anr. ed.] 8°. [*R. Bradock*] *ex typ. Soc. Stat.,* 1604. L(tp only, Ames II.79).COL.DUL.

22255 — [Anr. ed.] 8°. [*F. Kingston*] *ex typ. Soc. Stat.,* 1611. L.L³⁰.C.COL.; Y.

22256 — [Anr. ed.] 8°. [*F. Kingston*] *ex typ. Soc. Stat.,* 1617. Ent. to the English Stock 5 mr. 1620. L⁴.O⁶.C⁵.SAL.ST.+ ; F.ILL.U.

22257 — [Anr. ed.] 8°. *Cantabrigiæ, ex Acad. typog.,* 1631. L.O³.C.E⁸.YK.+ ; F.HD.

22257.5 — [Anr. ed.] 8°. *ex typ. T. Payne pro Soc. Stat.,* 1639. L(2).DUL.PARIS.; F.ILL.

22258 — Panegyrici in victoriam illustrissimæ D. Mariæ, reginæ. Item in coronationem eiusdem congratulatio. Ad hæc de sacrosancta eucharistia carmen. [In verse.] 4°. (*ex off. R. Wolfij,*) 1553. L(2).C.

22259 **Seton, John,** *of Aberdeen.* Theses philosophicae, . . . J. Setono præside. 1627. Now = 71.36.
22260 — — 1630. Now = 71.37.
22261 — — 1631. Now = 71.38.
22262 — — 1634. Now = 71.39.
22263 — — 1637. Now = 71.40.
22264 — — [1638.] Now = 71.41.

22265 **Settle, Dionyse.** A true reporte of the laste voyage into the west and northwest regions, &c. 1577. worthily achieued by capteine Frobisher. 8°. *H. Middleton,* 1577. L.O.; HN.CB.PH². Cincinnati U.
Collates A⁴ B–C⁸ D⁴.

22266 — [Anr. ed., enlarged.] 8°. *H. Middleton,* 1577. NY.
Collates A–C⁸; largely reimposed from standing type of 22265.

22267 **Settle, Thomas.** A catechisme briefly opening the misterie of our redemption. 8°. *W. How f. H. Car,* [1587.] Ent. to H. Carr a. H. Haslop 22 my. 1587. O.

Seven Wise Men. Sage and prudente saiynges of the seauen wyse men. 1545. *See* pt. 2 of 4853.5.
— *See* also 21254, 21297.

Seyfridt, George. An almanack. 1537. *See* 513.

22268 **Seymour, Edward,** *Duke of Somerset.* An epistle or exhortacion to vnitie & peace, sent to the inhabitauntes of Scotlande. 8°. (*in aed. R. Graftoni,* 1548.) L.C⁵.C⁷.E.M(2).; F.HN.
(Formerly also 9181) Tp varies: without (F) or with (L, HN) a comma after 'exhortacion'. Reprinted in 19137.5.

22269 — [A trans.] Epistola exhortatoria ad pacem, missa . . . ad Nobilitatem ac plebem, uniuersumq́; populum Regni Scotiæ. 4°. (*per R. Wolfium,*) 1548 (3 non. mr.) O.C. HAT. Budapest, Széchényi NL. Vatican Library (Palatine Collection).; HN.
(Formerly also 9180) C also has a frag. w. variants in A outer forme, w. tp: '. . . ad Nobiles, Generosos, Populumq́; Regni Scotiæ.'

22270 — The late expedicion in Scotlande, under the erle of Hertforde [i.e. Seymour. Not written by Seymour.] 8° in 4's. (*R. Wolfe,*) 1544. L.O.C⁹(frag.).E.G².+
— A spyrytuall and moost precyouse pearle. 1550. *See* 25255.

22270.5 **Seyssel, Claude de,** *Bp. of Marseilles.* Claudii de Seisello iurisconsulti christianissimi Ludouici duodecimi Francorum regis consiliarii et oratoris ad Henricū septimū: oratio in publico conuentu habita. 4° in 6. [*W. de Worde,* 1506?] F.
Device w. de Worde's name.
— *tr. See* 24056.

Sh., W. The first and second part of the troublesome raigne of John. 1611. *See* 14646.

22270.7 Shackley, William. To the right honorable assembly of the Commons. The humble petition of W. Shackley [against the] commission for buildings. s.sh.fol. [*London*, 1621?] L(2, Harl.MS.6803/111–12; Harl. MS.7608/146).
See Notestein VII.334.

22271 Shacklock, Richard. Impii cuiusdam epigrammatis . . . in mortem C. Scoti. 1565. = 7167.
— *tr. See* 13888, 18887.

22272 Shakelton, Francis. A blazyng starre or burnyng beacon, seene the 10. of October laste. 8°. *J. Kyngston f. H. Kirkham,* 1580. Ent. 17 oc. F.HN(C2 in facs.).
— *tr. See* 4042.7.

Shakerlaye, *Pore.* The knoledge of good and iuyle, other wyse calyd Ecclesiastes. [1551.] *See* 2761.5.

22272.5 Shakespeare, Katherine and **Elizabeth.** Katherine and Elizabeth Shakespeare, daughters of Thomas and Elizabeth Shakespeare, were baptized the seventh day of December, 1598. [Oblong slip measuring $3\frac{1}{4} \times 3\frac{3}{4}$ inches, w. letterpress text in border of type orns.] [*London?* 1598.] HD.

22273 Shakespeare, William. Mr. William Shakespeares comedies, histories, & tragedies. Published according to the true originall copies. fol. *Printed by Isaac Jaggard, and Ed. Blount.* 1623. [Colophon:] (*Printed at the charges of W. Jaggard, Ed. Blount, J. Smithweeke, and W. Aspley,* 1623.) Ent. to Blount a. I. Jaggard 8 no. L.O.C.D.E.+; F.HN.HD.N.NY.+
One o copy was delivered by the Stationers' Co. and sent for binding 7 Feb. 1624.

22274 — The second Impression. fol. *Printed by Tho. Cotes, for Robert Allot, and are to be fold* [sic] *at his shop at the signe of the Blacke Beare in Pauls Church-yard.* 1632. [Colophon:] (*Printed at London by Thomas Cotes, for John Smethwick, William Aspley, Richard Hawkins, Richard Meighen, and Robert Allot,* 1632.) Dorothy Jaggard's part ass'd to T. a. R. Cotes 19 jn. 1627; Blount's part to Allot 16 no. 1630, by a note of 26 June. L.O.BIRM².G².M.+; F.HN.MICH.NY.WEL.+
In imprint: 'Blacke'; *see* also 22274e.3 sq. For a discussion of the imprints and their order of printing *see* W. B. Todd, *Studies in Bibliography,* V (1952–3), pp. 81–108.

22274a — [A variant, w. imprint ending:] *and are to be fold* [sic] *at the signe of the Blacke Beare in Pauls Church-yard.* 1632. L.O¹⁰.C.E².ETON.+; F.HN.BO.ILL.NY.+
In imprint: 'Blacke'; omits 'at his shop'.

22274b — [A variant, w. imprint:] *Printed by Tho. Cotes, for William Aspley, and are to be sold at the signe of the Parrat in Pauls Church-yard.* 1632. PETWORTH.; F.HN.CAL.HD(impr. repaired).NY.+

22274c — [A variant, w. imprint:] *Printed by Tho. Cotes, for Richard Hawkins, and are to be sold at his shop in Chancery Lane, neere Serjeants Inne.* 1632. O(impr. def.).O⁷.O⁸.C⁴.LEEDS.+; F.HN.CAL.NY.PML.+
Imprint varies: with or without 'in' before 'Chancery'; both at F.

22274d — [A variant, w. imprint:] *Printed by Tho. Cotes, for Richard Meighen, and are to be sold at the middle Temple Gate in Fleetstreet.* 1632. L.O¹⁷.; F(2).HN. PML.

22274e — [A variant, w. imprint:] *Printed by Tho. Cotes, for John Smethwick, and are to be sold at his shop in Saint Dunstans Church-yard.* 1632. L. Ickworth.; F.HN. HD.ILL.NY.+

22274e.3 — [Anr. issue, w. A2,5 reprinted, w. imprint:] *Printed by Tho. Cotes, for Robert Allot, and are to be sold at his shop at the signe of the blacke Beare in Pauls Church-yard.* 1632. [after 1640.] Widow Allot's part ass'd to J. Legat a. A. Crooke 1 jy. 1637. L¹².O².C². D.; F(5).HN.NY.PH².
In imprint: 'blacke'. *See Court-Book C,* pp. 287, 294.

22274e.5 — [Anr. issue, w. A2,5 reprinted, w. imprint:] *Printed by Tho Cotes, for Robert Allot, and are to be sold at his shop at the signe of the blacke Beare in Pauls Church yard,* 1632. [after 1640.] O³(E).; F(3).CU.NY(tp only). Indianapolis PL, Indiana.
In imprint: 'blacke . . . Church yard,' (no hyphen).

22275 — [*Hamlet.*] The tragicall historie of Hamlet prince of Denmarke. 4°. [*V. Simmes*] *f. N. L[ing] a. J. Trundell,* 1603. Ent. to J. Roberts 26 jy. 1602. L(lacks tp).; HN(lacks I4). Greg 197.

Shakespeare, William—*cont.*

22276 — [Anr. version.] The tragicall historie of Hamlet, prince of Denmarke. Newly imprinted and enlarged to almost as much againe as it was, according to the true and perfect coppie. 4°. *J. R[oberts] f. N. L[ing,]* 1604. F.HN.Y².

22276a — [A variant, w. imprint:] *J. R[oberts] f. N. L[ing,]* 1605. L.C².VER. Wroclaw U, Poland.

22277 — [Anr. ed.] The tragedy of Hamlet prince of Denmarke. 4°. [*G. Eld*] *f. J. Smethwicke,* 1611. Ass'd by N. Ling 19 no. 1607. L.L⁶.O.C²(lacks tp).E²(lacks tp).+; F.HN. HD.PEN.Y².+

22278 — [Anr. ed.] 4°. *W. S[tansby] f. J. Smethwicke,* [c. 1625.] L(2).O.C².C¹⁰.PETWORTH.; F.HN.HD.NY.Y².+

22279 — [Anr. ed.] 4°. *R. Young f. J. Smethwicke,* 1637. L.O.C². E.ETON.+; F.HN.HD.ILL.NY.+

22279a — [*Henry IV,* pt. 1. Headline:] The Hystorie/of Henrie the fourth. 4°. [*P. Short f. A. Wise,* 1598.] Ent. 25 fb. 1598. F(quire C only). Greg 145.
Later eds. have in the headline 'Historie' or 'History'.

22280 — [Anr. ed.] The history of Henrie the fourth; with the battell at Shrewsburie. [Anon.] 4°. *P. S[hort] f. A. Wise,* 1598. L(imp.).C².; HN.

22281 — [Anr. ed.] Newly corrected by W. Shake-speare. 4°. *S. S[tafford] f. A. Wise,* 1599. L(2).O.C².G².; F(2).HN. HD(imp.).Y².

22282 — [Anr. ed.] 4°. *V. Simmes f. M. Law,* 1604. Ent. 25 jn. 1603. O(lacks C1).C²(imp.).E(imp.).; F(tp def.).

22283 — [Anr. ed.] 4°. [*J. Windet*] *f. M. Law,* 1608. L.O.E.; F(2). HN.HD.

22284 — [Anr. ed.] 4°. *W. W[hite] f. M. Law,* 1613. L(2, 1 lacks K4).O.C².VER.; F(2).HN(2).NY.Y²(2). Hickmott.

22285 — [Anr. ed.] 4°. *T. P[urfoot,] sold by M. Law,* 1622. L. L⁶.O.C².E.+; F(3, 1 w. date cropt).HN.BO.

22286 — [Anr. ed.] 4°. *J. Norton, sold by W. Sheares,* 1632. L. O⁶.C².E²(2). London, Sir John Soane's Museum.; F(4).BO.HD.

22287 — [Anr. ed.] 4°. *J. Norton, sold by H. Perry,* 1639. L.O. C².E.E².+; F.HN.HD.ILL.NY.+

22288 — [*Henry IV,* pt. 2.] The second part of Henrie the fourth. 4°. *V. S[immes] f. A. Wise a. W. Aspley,* 1600. Ent. 23 au. L².O.C².E.G².+; F.HN.N. Greg 167.
Quire E has 4 leaves.

22288a — [Anr. issue, w. E3,4 cancelled and replaced by E3–6.] *V. S[immes] f. A. Wise a. W. Aspley,* 1600. L(2). O.; F(2, 1 imp.).HN(3).HD(imp.)*.Y². Hickmott(imp.).

22289 — [*Henry V.*] The cronicle history of Henry the fift. [Anon.] 4°. *T. Creede f. T. Millington a. J. Busby,* 1600. Ent. to T. Pavier 14 au. L.O.C².; F(frag.).HN. Y². Greg 165.
Publication of this ed. 'staied' 4 Aug. 1600?; *see* Arber III.37.

22290 — [Anr. ed.] 4°. *T. Creede f. T. Pavier,* 1602. C².; F(impr. def.).HN.

22291 — [Anr. ed.] 4°. [*W. Jaggard*] *f. T. P[avier,]* 1608 [1619.] L.O(G1 def.).C².E.E².+; F.HN.HD.ILL.NY.+

— [*Henry VI,* pt. 2.] The first part of the contention betwixt the two famous houses of Yorke and Lancaster. [An abridged and mutilated version of the play afterwards known as *Henry VI,* pt. 2. Anon.] 1594, etc. *See* 26099 sq.

— [Anr. ed.] The whole contention. . . . Written by W. Shakespeare, Gent. 1619. *See* 26101.

— [*Henry VI,* pt. 3.] The true tragedie of Richard duke of Yorke. [An abridged and mutilated version of the play afterwards known as *Henry VI,* pt. 3.] 1595, etc. *See* 21006 sq.

22292 — [*King Lear.*] M. William Shak-speare: his true chronicle historie of the life and death of king Lear and his three daughters. 4°. [*N. Okes*] *f. N. Butter,* 1608. Ent. to Butter a. J. Busby 26 no. 1607. L(2, 1 lacks tp).O(2, 1 lacks tp; 1 lacks L4).C².VER.; F(2 imp.).HN. HD.NY.Y. Greg 265.

22293 — [Anr. ed.] M. William Shake-speare, his true chronicle history [etc.] 4°. [*W. Jaggard*] *f. N. Butter,* 1608 [1619.] L.O.C².E.E².+; F.HN.HD.ILL.NY.+

22294 — [*Love's labour's lost.*] A pleasant conceited comedie called, Loues labors lost. Newly corrected and augmented by W. Shakespere. 4°. *W. W[hite] f. C. Burby,* 1598. Ent. to N. Ling with consent of Burby 22 ja. 1607. L.O.C².E².; F.HN.HD.N.PN.+ Greg 150.

22295 — [Anr. ed.] Loues labours lost. A wittie and pleasant comedie. 4°. *W. S[tansby] f. J. Smethwicke,* 1631. Ass'd 19 no. 1607. L.O.C².E.E².+; F.HN.HD.ILL. NY.+

Shakespeare, William—*cont.*

22296 — [*Merchant of Venice.*] The most excellent historie of the Merchant of Venice. 4°. *J. R[oberts] f. T. Heyes,* 1600. Ent. to J. Roberts 22 jy. 1598; ass'd to T. Hayes 28 oc. 1600. L(3).L⁶.O.C².E(imp.).; F.HN.HD. NY.Y².+ Greg 172.

22297 — [Anr. ed.] The excellent history [etc.] 4°. *J. Roberts [W. Jaggard f. T. Pavier,]* 1600 [1619.] L.O.C².E² (imp.).ETON.+; F.HN.HD(imp.).ILL.NY.+

22298 — [Anr. ed.] The most excellent historie [etc.] 4°. *M. P[arsons] f. L. Hayes,* 1637. Ass'd 8 jy. 1619. L.O. C².E.E².+; F.HN.HD(lacks tp)*.ILL.NY.+
Reissued in 1652 w. cancel tp as Wing S 2938.

22299 — [*Merry Wives of Windsor.*] A most pleasaunt and excellent conceited comedie, of syr John Falstaffe, and the merrie wives of Windsor. 4°. *T. C[reede] f. A. Johnson,* 1602. Ent. to J. Busby a. ass'd to A. Johnson 18 ja. L.O.C².; F(lacks G3).HN. Greg 187.

22300 — [Anr. ed.] 4°. [*W. Jaggard*]*f. A. Johnson* [i.e. *T. Pavier,*] 1619. L.L⁶.O.C².E.+; F.HN.HD.ILL.NY.+

22301 — [Anr. ed.] The merry wives of Windsor. Newly corrected. 4°. *T. H[arper] f. R. Meighen,* 1630. Ass'd 29 ja. L.O.C².E(tp def.).E².+; F.HN.HD.NY.Y.+

22302 — [*Midsommer Night's Dream.*] A midsommer nights dreame. 4°. [*R. Bradock*] *f. T. Fisher,* 1600. Ent. 8 oc. L.O.C².; F.HN.BO.HD(imp.).Y². Greg 170.

22303 — [Anr. ed.] 4°. *J. Roberts* [*W. Jaggard f. T. Pavier,*] 1600 [1619.] L.O.C².E.ETON.+; F.HN.HD.ILL.NY.+

22304 — [*Much ado about Nothing.*] Much adoe about nothing. 4°. *V. S[immes] f. A. Wise a. W. Aspley,* 1600. Ent. 23 au. L(2).L⁶.O.C².E²(imp.).; F.HN.HD(imp.).N.Y².+ Greg 168.
Publication 'staied' 4 Aug. 1600?; *see* Arber III.37.

22305 — [*Othello.*] The tragœdy of Othello, the moore of Venice. 4°. *N. O[kes] f. T. Walkley,* 1622. Ent. 6 oc. 1621. L.L⁶.O.C².E²(imp.).+; F.HN.HD.NY.Y².+ Greg 379.

22306 — [Anr. ed.] 4°. *A. M[athewes] f. R. Hawkins,* 1630. Ass'd 1 mr. 1628. L.L⁶.O.C².E².+; F.HN.HD.ILL.NY.+

22307 — [*Richard II.*] The tragedie of king Richard the second. [Anon.] 4°. *V. Simmes f. A. Wise,* 1597. Ent. 29 au. L.C².PETWORTH(lacks tp).; HN. Greg 141.

22308 — [Anr. ed.] By W. Shake-speare. 4°. *V. Simmes f. A. Wise,* 1598. L.O.C².; F(2, 1 imp.).HN(2).BO.
In imprint: 'sold'.

22309 — [Anr. ed.] 4°. *V. Simmes f. A. Wise,* 1598. F.MCG(imp.).
In imprint: 'solde'.

22310 — [Anr. ed.] 4°. *W. W[hite] f. M. Law,* 1608. Ass'd 25 jn. 1603. L.; F.HN.HD(lacks tp)*.TCU.Y².+

22311 — [A variant, w. tp reset.] With new additions. *W. W[hite] f. M. Law,* 1608. O.E.

22312 — [Anr. ed.] 4°. [*T. Purfoot*] *f. M. Law,* 1615. L.O.C².E. E²(lacks F3).+; F.HN.BO.HD(imp.).NY.+

22313 — [Anr. ed.] The life and death of king Richard the second. 4°. *J. Norton,* 1634. L.O.C².E.E².+; F.HN.HD. ILL.NY.+

22314 — [*Richard III.*] The tragedy of king Richard the third. [Anon.] 4°. *V. Sims* [*a. P. Short*] *f. A. Wise,* 1597. Ent. 20 oc. L.O(imp.).; F.HN.Y²(frag.). Greg 142.
Quires A–G pr. by Simmes; the rest by Short.

22315 — [Anr. ed.] By William Shake-speare. 4°. *T. Creede f. A. Wise,* 1598. L(2 imp.).O.C².; HN(3, 1 imp.).

22316 — [Anr. ed.] Newly augmented. 4°. *T. Creede f. A. Wise,* 1602. L.C².VER.; HN.

22317 — [Anr. ed.] 4°. *T. Creede, sold by M. Lawe,* 1605. Ass'd 25 jn. 1603. L(2, 1 w. tp of 22318).O.E(imp.).; F(2). HN(imp.).

22318 — [Anr. ed.] 4°. *T. Creede, sold by M. Lawe,* 1612. L(tp only). O.C².E(impr. cropt).E².+; F(2, 1 imp.).HN.HD (impr. cropt).NY(2).PEN(imp.).
1st word of title is xylographic.

22319 — [Anr. ed.] 4°. *T. Purfoot, sold by M. Law,* 1622. L(3, 1 imp.).O.C².; F(imp.).HN.

22320 — [Anr. ed.] 4°. *J. Norton, sold by M. Law,* 1629. L.L⁶.O. C².E.+; F(5, 2 imp.).HN.HD(imp.).NY. Philadelphia, Shakspere Society.

22321 — [Anr. ed.] 4°. *J. Norton,* 1634. L.O.C²(lacks tp).E.E².+; F.HN.HD.ILL.NY.+

22322 — [*Romeo and Juliet.*] An excellent conceited tragedie of Romeo and Juliet. [Anon.] 4°. *J. Danter* [*a. E. Allde?*] 1597. L.O.C².; F(imp.).HN. Greg 143.
Danter pr. only quires A–D.

22323 — [Anr. version.] The most excellent and lamentable tragedie, of Romeo and Juliet. Newly corrected, augmented, and amended. 4°. *T. Creede f. C. Burby,* 1599. L.O.E².VER.; F(4, 2 imp.).HN.HD.LC(imp.).Y².

Shakespeare, William—*cont.*

22324 — [Anr. ed.] 4°. [*J. Windet*] *f. J. Smethwick,* 1609. Ass'd by Burby to N. Ling 22 ja. 1607; to Smethwick 19 no. 1607. L.O(lacks M2).C².Z.; F.HN(2).

22325 — [Anr. ed.] 4°. [*W. Stansby*] *f. J. Smethwicke,* [1622.] L.E²(imp.).; HN.

22325a — [A variant.] Written by W. Shake-speare. *f. J. Smethwicke,* [1622.] O.C²(tp def.).C⁴.PARIS.; F.HN. BO.HD.Y².

22326 — [Anr. ed.] 4°. *R. Young f. J. Smethwicke,* 1637. L.O. C².E.E².+; F.HN.HD.ILL.NY(tp def.).+

22327 — [*Taming of the Shrew.*] A wittie and pleasant comedie called The taming of the shrew. 4°. *W. S[tansby] f. J. Smethwicke,* 1631. Ent. to J. Smethwick 'books which did belong to N. Ling' 19 no. 1607. L.O.C².E.E².+; F.HN.HD.NY.Y².+ Greg 120e.
For the earlier text to which Ling had rights *see* 23667 sqq.

22328 — [*Titus Andronicus.*] The most lamentable Romaine tragedie of Titus Andronicus. [Anon.] 4°. *J. Danter, sold by E. White & T. Millington,* 1594. Ent. to Danter 6 fb. F. Greg 117.

22329 — [Anr. ed.] 4°. *J. R[oberts] f. E. White,* 1600. E².; HN.

22330 — [Anr. ed.] 4° w. perp. chainlines. [*E. Allde*] *f. E. White,* 1611. Ass'd by Millington to T. Pavier 19 ap. 1602. L(2 imp.).O.C².E.VER.; F.HN.HD.PFOR. Y².+

22331 — [*Troilus and Cressida.*] The historie of Troylus and Cresseida. As it was acted. 4°. *G. Eld f. R. Bonian a. H. Walley,* 1609. Ent. to J. Roberts 7 fb. 1603; to Bonian a. Walley 28 ja. 1609. L.BODMER.;HN.Y². Greg 279.

22332 — [Anr. issue, w. preface and cancel tp.] The famous historie of Troylus and Cresseid. *G. Eld f. R. Bonian a. H. Walley,* 1609. L.L⁶.O.C².E.+; F.HN.HD.PFOR. Y²(¶² only, bd. w. 22331).

Editions of plays excluded from the folio but previously ascribed to Shakespeare on their tpp.

22333 — The [xylographic] London prodigall. As it was plaide by the kings majesties servants. By W. Shakespeare. 4°. *T. C[reede] f. N. Butter,* 1605. L.O.C².ETON.; F.HN.HD.NY.Y².+ Greg 222.

— The first part of the true history, of the life of sir J. Old-castle. Written by W. Shakespeare. 1600 [1619.] *See* 18796.

22334 — The late, and much admired play, called Pericles, prince of Tyre. By William Shakespeare. 4°. [*W. White*] *f. H. Gosson,* 1609. Ent. to E. Blount 20 my. 1608. L.O.C².SH(imp.).; F.HN(imp.).BO.Y². Hickmott (lacks tp). Greg 284.
A2ʳ line 3: 'Enter Gower'.

22335 — [Anr. ed.] 4°. [*W. White*] *f. H. Gosson,* 1609. L.L³⁰ (lacks E4). Hamburg PL.; F(2).HN.
A2ʳ line 3: 'Eneer [*sic*] Gower'.

22336 — [Anr. ed.] 4°. *S. S[tafford,]* 1611. L(imp.).; F.ILL.Y².

— [Anr. ed.] *f. T. P[avier,]* 1619. *See* 3rd pt. of 26101.

22337 — [Anr. ed.] 4°. *J. N[orton] f. R. B[ird,]* 1630. Ass'd by R. Bird to R. Cotes 8 no. L.L⁶.E².; F.BO.NY. Y.
Imprint in 2 lines.

22338 — [A variant, w. imprint:] *J. N[orton] f. R. B[ird,]* 1630. L.O.C².E.E².; F.HN.BO.NY.PEN(imp.).
Imprint in 4 lines.

22339 — [Anr. ed.] 4° w. perp. chainlines. *T. Cotes,* 1635. L. O.C².E.E².+; F.HN.HD.ILL.NY.+

— The first and second part of the troublesome raigne of John. Written by W. Shakespeare. 1622. *See* 14647.

22340 — A Yorkshire tragedy. . . . Acted by his majesties players at the Globe. Written by W. Shakspere. 4°. *R. B[radock] f. T. Pavier,* 1608. Ent. 2 my. L.O. O⁵.; F.HN(2). Greg 272.
See also 18288.

22341 — [Anr. ed.] 4°. [*W. Jaggard*] *f. T. P[avier,]* 1619. L.O. C².E.E².+; F.HN.HD.ILL.NY.+
One L copy (C.12.g.26) has the last 2 figures in the date erased and '08' stamped in their place.

— The two noble kinsmen: . . . Written by Mʳ. John Fletcher and Mʳ. William Shakspere. 1634. *See* 11075.

Shakespeare, William—*cont.*

Poems

22341.5 — [The passionate pilgrim.] 8°. [*T. Judson? f. W. Jaggard? 1599?*] F(imp.).

F consists of 11 unsigned leaves in a different setting from the text pr. on A3–7, C5–D4 of 22342; 3 leaves are pr. on both sides. A few 1st line distinctions are: [3ʳ:] 'Dyd not'; [6ʳ:] 'On a day (alack'; [9ᵛ:] 'And to her wil'.

22342 — [Anr. ed.] The passionate pilgrime. Or certaine amorous sonnets. (Sonnets to sundry notes of musicke.) 8°. [*T. Judson*] *f. W. Jaggard, sold by W. Leake*, 1599. C².; F(quires B and D only).HN.

A1–D4 are pr. on the recto only. A5ʳ: 'Did not'; C5ʳ: 'On a day (alacke'; D3ʳ: 'And to her will'.

22343 — [Anr. ed.] Newly corrected and augmented. The third edition. Where-unto is newly added two loue-epistles, the first from Paris to Hellen, and Hellens answere [with others, reprinted from 13366.] 8°. *by W. Jaggard*, 1612. O.; F.

The O copy has 2 titles, 1 with (as in F copy) and 1 without Shakespeare's name, the latter prob. intended as a cancel. Quires A–C are pr. on the recto only.

— [The phœnix and the turtle. 1601.] *See* 5119.

22344 — Poems: written by Wil. Shake-speare. Gent. 8°. *T. Cotes, sold by J. Benson*, 1640. Ent. 4 no. 1639. L.O. C².G².M.+; F.HN.HD.ILL.NY.+

22345 — [*Rape of Lucrece.*] Lucrece. 4°. *R. Field f. J. Harrison*, 1594. Ent. 9 my. L(2, 1 lacks N1).L⁴.O(2).; F(2, plus a frag.).HN.Y². Kraus.

22346 — [Anr. ed.] 8°. *P. S[hort] f. J. Harrison*, 1598. C².

22347 — [Anr. ed.] 8°. *J. H[arrison 3] f. J. Harison [1,]* 1600. F. In imprint: 'London,' (w. comma); E3 correctly signed.

22348 — [Anr. ed.] 8°. *J. H[arrison 3] f. J. Harison [1,]* 1600. O(2, 1 imp.). In imprint: 'London.' (w. stop); E3 signed 'B3'.

22349 — [Anr. ed.] 8°. *N. O[kes] f. J. Harison [1,]* 1607. C².; HN.

22350 — [Anr. ed.] The rape of Lucrece. Newly revised. 8°. *T. S[nodham] f. R. Jackson*, 1616. Ass'd 1 mr. 1614. L.O.; F.HN.NY.

22351 — [Anr. ed.] 8°. *J. B[eale] f. R. Jackson*, 1624. L(2).; F(2).HN.PML.

22352 — [Anr. ed.] 8°. *R. B[adger] f. J. Harrison [4,]* 1632. Ass'd to F. Williams 16 ja. 1626; to J. Harrison 4 on 29 jn. 1630. O⁵.E²(imp.).; F.HN.

22353 — Shake-speares sonnets. Never before imprinted. (A lovers complaint.) 4°. *G. Eld f. T. T[horpe,] solde by W. Aspley*, 1609. Ent. to T. Thorpe 20 my. L.O.; F(imp.)*.HN.HD(imp.)*.

22353a — [A variant, w. imprint:] *G. Eld f. T. T[horpe,] solde by J. Wright*, 1609. L.O(date cropt).C²(imp.)*.BODMER. M.; F.HN.Y².

22354 — Venus and Adonis. 4°. *R. Field, sold [by J. Harrison 1,]* 1593. Ent. 18 ap. O.

22355 — [Anr. ed.] 4°. *R. Field, sold [by J. Harrison 1,]* 1594. Ass'd to J. Harrison 1 on 25 jn. L.O.SH(F1 only).; HN.Y². Hickmott(frags.).

22356 — [Anr. ed.] 8°. [*R. Field? f. J. Harrison 1, 1595?*] F(lacks A8).

22357 — [Anr. ed.] 8°. *R. F[ield] f. J. Harison [1,]* 1596. L.O.

22358 — [Anr. ed.] 8°. [*P. Short*] *f. W. Leake*, 1599. Ass'd 25 jn. 1596. HN. A2ʳ catchword: 'neuer'.

22358a — [Anr. ed.] 8°. [*R. Bradock*] *f. W. Leake*, 1599. F(lacks D1). A2ʳ catchword: '& neuer'.

22359 — [Anr. ed.] 8°. [*R. Bradock f. W. Leake*, 1602?] O (lacks tp). A2ʳ has no catchword. *See The Library*, III (1922–23), pp. 230–41 for facsimiles from the '1602' editions.

22360 — [Anr. ed.] 8°. [*R. Raworth*] *f. W. Leake*, 1602 [1607?] O. A2ʳ catchword: 'and'; on tp the top of 'l' in 'plena' is below left of tail of 'g' in 'vulgus'. Raworth was suppressed for printing this ed.; *see* Arber III.701, 703–4. *See also* 22363.

22360a — [Anr. ed.] 8°. [*H. Lownes*] *f. W. Leake*, 1602 [1608?] L. Earl of Macclesfield. A2ʳ catchword: 'ther'; on tp the top of 'l' in 'plena' is below centre of tail of 'g' in 'vulgus'. Copies vary: w. a comma (L) or colon (Macclesfield) after 'vulgus' in title.

22360b — [Anr. ed.] 8°. *f. W. Leake*, 1602 [1610?] L(tp only, Harl.5990/134). On tp the top of 'l' in 'plena' is below right of tail of 'g' in 'vulgus'.

22361 — [Anr. ed.] 8°. [*W. Stansby*] *f. W. B[arrett,]* 1617. Ass'd to W. Barrett 16 fb. O.

22362 — [Anr. ed.] 8°. [*F. Kingston*] *f. J. P[arker,]* 1620. Ass'd to J. Parker 8 mr. C².

22363 — [Anr. ed.] 8°. *Edinburgh, J. Wreittoun*, 1627. L.; HN. Uses 22360 as the copy text.

22364 — [Anr. ed.] 8°. *J. H[aviland,] sold by F. Coules*, 1630. Ass'd to J. Haviland a. J. Wright 7 my. 1626. O.

22365 — [Anr. ed.] 8°. [*J. Haviland, sold by F. Coules*, 1630–36?] O(lacks tp).

22366 — [Anr. ed.] 16° in 8's. *J. H[aviland,] sold by F. Coules*, 1636. Ent. to J. Haviland a. J. Wright 4 se. 1638. L.; F.

Shape. The shape and porportion [*sic*] of a perfit horse. 1607. *See* 17387.5.

— The shape of .ij. mōsters. [1562.] *See* 11485.

22367 — [The wonderful shape and natures of man. 1527?] Now = 13837.5.

22368 **Sharp, John.** Theses theologicæ de peccato. 1600. Now = 21555.6.

22369 **Sharp, Patrick.** Doctrinae christianae breuis explicatio: in tria priora Geneseos capita, symbolum Apostolorum, [etc.] 8°. *Edinburgi, R. Walde-graue.*, 1599. L.O¹⁹.C.D.E.+; F.NY¹¹.

Sharpe, E. Britaines busse. 1615. *See* 21486.

Sharpe, Edward, *B.D.*, *tr. See* 22372.

22370 **Sharpe, John.** The triall of the protestant private spirit. The second part, which is doctrinall. By J. S[harpe] of the society of Jesus. 4°. [*St. Omer, English College Press,*] 1630. L.O⁵.C³.A².D.+; F.HN.HD.N.U.+ A&R 762. Pt. 1 not pub'd.

22371 **Sharpe, Leonell.** Dialogus inter Angliam & Scotiam. [In verse.] 8°. *Cantabrigiæ, ex off. J. Legat*, 1603. C.; HD.

22372 — A looking-glasse for the pope. Together with the popes new creede, containing 12. articles refuted in two dialogues. Tr. E. Sharpe. 4°. *E. Griffin*, 1616. O.O². D.DUR(Bamb.).WI.+; F(imp.).PN². Athenaeum, Salem, Massachusetts(tp def.)*. This is a trans. of 22374.

22372.3 — [Anr. issue, w. cancel tp, w. imprint:] *E. Griffin, sold by John Barnes*, 1619. BTL.

22372.5 — [Anr. issue, w. cancel tp, w. imprint:] *sold by T. Bayly*, 1622. PETYT.

22373 — [Anr. issue, w. variant cancel tp, w. imprint:] *sold by T. Bayly*, 1623. L.C⁵.

22374 — Novum fidei symbolum, sive de novis multis articulis à Pio quarto . . . dialogus. Praefixum est Speculum papae. 4°. *R. Field*, 1612. L.O.C.D.E².+; HART. Translated in 22372.

22375 — Oratio funebris in honorem Henrici Walliæ principis. 4°. *G. Hall*, 1612. Ent. 17 de. L.O.C.E.P.+; F.HN. HD.N.Y.+

22376 — A sermon preached at Cambridge [on 1 Kings x.9.] 8°. *J. Legat, pr. to the Univ. of Camb., sold by S. Waterson*, [*London,*] 1603. L.O⁴.C(2).C¹⁰.P.

22377 **Sharpe, Lewis.** The noble stranger. As it was acted. 4°. *J. O[kes] f. J. Becket*, 1640. L.O.O⁶.E.ETON.+; F.HN. HD.N.NY.+ Greg 597.

22378 **Sharpe, Robert.** The confession and declaration of R. sharpe clerke, and other of that secte, tearmed the Familie of loue, the .xij. of June. 1575. s.sh.fol. *W. Seres*, [1575.] L⁵(Lemon 66).; HN. *See* 18548.5 sqq.

22379 **Sharpe, Roger.** More fooles yet. Written by R. S(harpe.) [In verse.] 4°. [*T. Purfoot*] *f. T. Castleton*, 1610. Ent. 1 jn. O.; F.

22379.5 **Sharpeigh,** *Sir* **Robert,** and **Haitley, Alexander.** Reasons most humbly offered to the house of Commons by . . . patentees for survey of sea-coales at Newcastle, &c. fol. [*London*, 1624.] HD. Patent discussed in Commons 13 Mar. and 26 May 1624; *see JHC* I.736, 795–6.

22380 **Sharpham, Edward.** Cupids whirligig. As it hath bene acted. [Init. E. S.] 4°. *E. Allde, solde by A. Johnson,* 1607. Ent. to J. Busby a. A. Johnson 29 jn. L.O.G².; F.HN(imp.).HD.MICH.NY.+ Greg 247.
　　One Y copy has an earlier variant of the tp, without the 3 lines of title following 'whirligig.'

22381 — [Anr. ed.] 4° w. perp. chainlines. *T. C[reede,] sold by A. Johnson,* 1611. L.L⁶.O.; F.HD.N.
　　Quire A has horizontal chainlines.

22382 — [Anr. ed.] 4°. *T. Creede a. B. Alsop, solde by A. Johnson,* 1616. L.L⁶(frag., bd. w. 22383).L⁸.O(3, 1 imp.).; F. HN(I2–K1 only, bd. w. 22380).BO.ILL.

22383 — [Anr. ed., omitting dedic. Anon.] 4°. *T. H[arper] f. R. Meighen,* 1630. Ass'd 29 ja. L.O.O⁶.E.ETON.+; F.HN. CHI.CU.HD.+

22384 — The fleire. As it hath beene often played. 4°. [*E. Allde,*] *printed a. solde by F. B[urton,]* 1607. Ent. to Trundle a. J. Busby 13 my. 1606; to Busby a. A. Johnson 21 no. 1606. L.M.; F.HN.HD.NY.Y. Greg 255.

22385 — [Anr. ed.] 4°. [*T. Purfoot*] *f. N. Butter,* 1610. L.L⁶. O(imp.).; F.HN.BO.CHI.

22386 — [Anr. ed.] 4°. [*T. Snodham*] *f. N. Butter,* 1615. L(2, 1 lacks B4).O.E.; F.HN.BO.LC.Y.

22387 — [Anr. ed.] 4°. *B. A[lsop] a. T. F[awcet] f. N. Butter,* 1631. L.L⁶.O.E.ETON.+; F.HN.HD.N.NY.+
— *See also* 21489.

22388 — No entry.

Sharrock, John, *tr. See* 18777.

22389 **Shaw, John,** *Divine.* Biblii summula: hoc est, argumenta singulorum capitum scripturæ canonicæ, utriusque Testamenti, alphabaticè [*sic*] distichis comprehensa. [In verse.] 8°. *R. Field, imp. R. Mylbourne,* 1621. Ent. 28 oc. 1620. L.O.C².C⁴.E.+; F.
　　Includes reprint of 22406. For an English version based on this *see* 25103.

22390 — [Anr. ed.] 8°. *R. Field, imp. R. Mylbourne,* 1623. L.O. O⁹.O²⁷.C.; HN.ILL.

22391 — The blessednes of Marie the mother of Jesus. [A sermon.] 8°. *R. Field,* 1618. Ent. 25 se. L.O(lacks dedic.).PLUME. Stevens Cox.

22391.3 **Shaw, John,** *Inventor.* Certaine easie and profitable points in husbandrie, for the improving and making of ground fertile. [Anon.] 4°. *B. Alsop, sold [by the author?] at the signe of the thr⟨e⟩e Flower-deluces, in Fleet-street, over against Saint Brides Lane end,* 1637. HN.
　　Collates A⁴. Known only in a nonce collection with gen. tp 22391.4.

22391.4 — [Gen. tp only:] Certaine helpes and remedies under God to prevent dearth and scarcitie. With divers other points of husbandrie never yet practised by any. [Anon.] 4°. *B. Alsop,* 1638. HN.
　　This is the general tp for a nonce collection which reissued sheets of 22391.6, 22391.3, 22391.5 in that order in the HN copy.
　　There is a single leaf at the end of the HN collection, w. Shaw's name in full, which offers a practical demonstration of methods at his house in Kent and which was prob. pr. at the same time as the gen. tp.

22391.5 — [Heading A1ʳ:] How to order any land, so as it may reteyne all the moysture that falleth thereon. [Anon.] 4°. [*B. Alsop,* 1637?] HN.
　　Collates A⁴. Known only in a nonce collection with gen. tp 22391.4.

22391.6 — Soli gloria Deo. Certaine rare and new inventions for the manuring and improving of all sorts of ground. [Init. I. S.] 4°. *B. A[lsop] a. T. Fawcet, sold by H. Seyle,* 1636. Ent. to Fawcet 24 ja. 1637. HN.
　　Collates A–D⁴ E². Known only in a nonce collection w. gen. tp 22391.4. On E2ʳ is a note offering further information at the address in the imprint of 22391.3.

Shawe, George. The doctrine of dying-well. [By G. Shawe?] 1628. *See* 6934.

Shaxton, Nicholas, *Bp.* Salisbury. Injunctions. *See* 10326.

Sheafe, Thomas. [Gift-plate.] *See* Bookplates.

22391.8 — Vindiciæ senectutis, or, a plea for old-age. 8°. *G. Miller,* 1639. Ent. 24 se. 1638. L(imp.).O.O⁶.YK.; CHI.
　　Sheafe is named on A5ʳ. The tp is a cancel.

Sheafe, Thomas—*cont.*

22392 — [Anr. issue, w. cancel tp, w. imprint:] *G. Miller, sold by J. Kirton a. T. Warren,* 1639. F.HN.

Sheen, *Carthusian Priory. See* Indulgences 15.

She-Jesuits. The suppressing of the assembly of the Shee-Jesuits. 1631. *See* 24524.

22393 **Sheldon, Richard.** Certain general reasons, proving the lawfulnesse of the oath of allegiance, written by R. S(heldon,) priest. Whereunto is added, the treatise of W. Barclay, concerning the temporall power of the pope [*ed. and tr.* J. Barclay.] And the sermon of T. Higgons, preached at Pauls Crosse the third of March. 3 pts. 4°. *F. Kyngston* [pt. 2:] (*A. Hatfield*) *f. W. Aspley,* 1611. Ent. 16 mr. L.O.C.D.E.+; F.HN. CHI.HD.U.+
　　(Pt. 2 formerly also 1409) Kingston also pr. 1st 2 quires of pt. 2. Pt. 3 reprints 13456.

22394 — Christ, on his throne; not in popish secrets. Laid open in a sermon preached and since much inlarged, and preached else-where. In the preface is a briefe inquirie into [17195–6]. 4°. *H. Lownes,* 1622. L.O. C³.D.YK.+; F(tp def.).HN.ILL.NY(lacks tp).

22395 — The first sermon of R. Sheldon priest, after his conversion. 4°. *J. B[eale] f. N. Butter,* 1612. L.O.C.D². YK.+; F.HD.U.

22396 — Mans last end, the glorious vision and fruition of God. 4°. *W. Jones,* 1634. Ent. 5 fb. L.O.LINC.P.YK.+; PN².

22396.5 — [Anr. issue, w. cancel tp, w. imprint:] *W. J[ones] f. A. Kembe in South-Worke* [*sic*], 1635. HN.

22397 — The motives of Richard Sheldon for his renouncing of communion with Rome. 4°. [*W. Hall a. W. Stansby*] *f. N. Butter,* 1612. Ent. 7 ja. L.O.C.D.E².+; F.HN.HD. MICH.U.+
　　Stansby pr. quires B–X; Hall the rest, including cancels for *2, E2, I3–4, Cc3.

22398 — A sermon preached at Paules Crosse. Upon the 14. of the Revelations, vers. 9.10.11. 4°. *W. Jones,* 1625. L.L⁴.L¹⁵.O.D.+; F.HN.NY.Y.

22399 — A survey of the miracles of the church of Rome, proving them to be Antichristian. Wherein are refuted the six reasons of J. Flood in defence of popish miracles [in 11114]. 4°. *E. Griffin f. N. Butter,* 1616. L.O.C.BIRM.D.+; F.HN.U.
　　Last chapter answers 11728.

22400 **Shelford, Robert.** Five pious and learned discourses. [2 sermons and 3 treatises.] 4°. [*T. Buck a. R. Daniel,*] *prs. to the Univ. of Camb.,* 1635. L.O.C.D.E. +; F.HN.CHI.HD.U.+
　　Answered in 20474.

22400.5 — Lectures or readings vpon the 6. verse of the 22. chapter of the Prouerbs, concerning the vertuous education of youth. [Anon.] 8°. *widdow Orwin f. T. Man,* 1596. Ent. 28 no. 1595. BUTE.

22401 — [Anr. ed., with author's name.] 8°. *F. Kingston f. T. Man,* 1602. O.

22402 — [Anr. ed.] 8°. *F. Kyngston f. T. Man,* 1606. L³.C.

22403 **Shelton, Thomas.** A centurie of [religious] similies. 8°. *J. Dawson,* 1640. Ent. 7 jy. L.O.C.; HN.

22404 — Short-writing the most exact methode. The second edition inlarged. 8°. *J. D[awson] f. S. C[artwright,] sould at the professors house in Cheapeside, over against Bowe Church,* 1630. Ent. to S. Cartwright 17 ap. 1626. L³⁰(imp.).L³².O.
　　See Court-Book C, p. 251 (2 entries).

22404.1 — Third edition. 8°. [*T. Cotes*] *f. S. Cartwright,* 1633. L(C.31.a.45, imp.).O.

22404.2 — [A revision.] Tachy graphy the most exact and compendious methode of short writing. 8°. *Prs. to the Univ. of Camb. f. I. H., sold at the professors house* [*etc.*], *London,* 1635. L³⁰.
　　End of text dated 1635.

22404.4 — [Anr. ed.] 8°. (*T. C[otes]*) *f. S. Cartwright,* 1639. Ent. 9 fb. 1638. G⁴. Munich, Bayerische Landesanstalt für Kurzschrift(imp.).

22404.5 — [Anr. ed.] 8°. (*R. C[otes]*) *f. S. Cartwright,* 1641 (1639.) M³.
— *ed. See* 15557.5.

Shelton, Thomas, *tr. See* 4915.

22404.7 **Shepard, Thomas.** The sincere convert, discovering the paucity of true believers. By T. Shepheard. 8°. *T. Paine f. M. Symmons,* 1640. Ent. to R. Dawlman 17 ap. L.; CB.

Shepard, Thomas—*cont.*

22404.8 — [A variant, w. imprint:] *T. P[aine] f. M. S[immons,] sold by H. Blunden,* 1640. PN².V.

22404.9 — [Anr. issue, w. imprint:] *T. Paine f. H. Blunden,* 1640. DUL.

22405 **Shepery, John.** Hyppolitus Ouidianæ Phaedræ respondens. [In verse. *Ed.* G. Edrychus, i.e. Etherege.] 8°. *J. Barnesius, typog. Oxoniensis,* [1586]. L.O(2).O⁸.; F.

— In nouum Testamentum carmen. [Pt. 2 of 'Gemma Fabri'.] 1598. *See* 22882.

22406 — Summa et synopsis Noui Testamenti distichis ducentis sexaginta, comprehensa: prior a J. Scheprevo conscripta: posterior ex Erasmi Roterodami editione [2800] decerpta: à L. Humfredo recognita. [In verse.] 8°. *Oxoniæ, ex off. J. Barnesii,* 1586. O.O⁵.YK.; F.
(Formerly also 13965) Shepery's part reprinted in 22389, 22882.

Shepheard, Thomas. *See* Shepard, T.

Shepherd. The affectionate shepheard. 1594. *See* 1480.
— The good shepheards sorrow. [1612.] *See* 13157.5.
— The passionate shepheard. 1604. *See* 3682.

22406.3 — The shepheard and the king, and of Gillian the shepheards wife. *Ballad.* 2 pts. s.sh.fol. [*London,* c. 1635.] Ent. to R. Jones 25 se. 1578; to ballad ptnrs. 14 de. 1624. c⁶.
Last line of 1st stanza: 'Jouiall'.

22406.4 — [Anr. ed.] 2 pts. s.sh.fol. [*London,* c. 1640.] G².
Last line of 1st stanza: 'Joviall'.
— The shepheards delight. To the tune of Frog Galliard. [1628–29.] *See* 3694.7.

22406.5 — The shepheards lamentation. To the tune of the plaine-dealing woman. *Ballad.* 2 pts. s.sh.fol. [*G. Eld] f. J. W[right,* c. 1617.] Ent. to T. Pavier 19 no. 1612; ?to E. White 20 fb. 1613. c⁶.

Shepherd, Luke. Antipus. [1548?] *See* 683.
— The comparison betwene the antipus and the antigraphe. [1548?] *See* 5605a.
— Doctour Doubble ale. [1548?] *See* 7071.
— A godlye and holesome preseruatyue against desperatiō. [1548?] *See* 20203.5.
— John Bon and Mast person. [1548?] *See* 3258.5.
— Pathose. [1548?] *See* 19463.
— Phylogamus. [1548?] *See* 19882.
— A pore helpe, The buklar and defence of mother holy kyrke. [1548?] *See* 13051.7.
— The vpcheringe of the messe. [1548?] *See* 17630.

22406.7 **Shepherdess.** The courteous shepherdesse. Who, though her love so often denies, the northern lad, at last, obtaines the prize. *Ballad.* 2 pts. s.sh.fol. [*M. Parsons] f. F. Grove,* [1639?] Ent. 6 se. 1639. M³.

22407 **Shepherds' Kalendar.** The kalendayr of the shyppars. [xylographic] [*Tr.* from 'Le Compost et Kalendrier des Bergiers' into Scottish.] fol. (*Paris,* [*A. Verard,*] 1503 (23 jn.)) L(2, 1 imp.).O(3 leaves).M(imp.).
See also 20480.

22408 — [Anr. ed., revised into English.] Here begynneth the Kalender of shepherdes. fol. (*R. Pynson,* 1506.) L(imp.).

22409 — [Anr. ed., revised by R. Copland.] The kalender of shepeherdes. 4° partly in 8's. (*W. de Worde,* 1508 (8 de.)) [really 1516.] O¹²(imp.).
The cuts and the device (McK. 19) are in a state c. 1516. C3ʳ catch title: 'Ka. of She.'

22409.3 — [Anr. ed. of 22408.] fol. (*R. Pynson,*) [c. 1510.] PARIS³ (imp.).

22409.5 — [Anr. ed. of 22409.] 4°. (*W. de Worde,* 1511.) O(imp.). Earl of Macclesfield.
C3ʳ catch title: 'Ka. of she.'
— [Anr. ed. 1516.] *See* 22409.

22409.7 — [Anr. ed. of 22408.] fol. [*R. Pynson,* 1517?] O(imp.).

22410 — [Anr. ed.] Here begynneth the kalender of shepardes. fol. [*J. Notary,* 1518?] L(imp.).C(A5 only, Syn. 2.50.1).M(imp.).; HN(imp., w. some leaves from 22412, 22415 and a faked last leaf w. colophon).

22411 — [Anr. ed.] The kalēder of shepeherdes. 4° ⁸·⁴. (*w. de worde,* 1528 (24 ja.)) O(lacks tp and col.).; HN(imp.).

22412 — [Anr. ed.] Here begynneth the kalender of shepardes. Newely augmented and corrected. fol. (*W. Powell,* 1556.) L².C(imp.).; HN(M5–7 only, w. 22410).

22413 — [Anr. ed.] fol. (*W. Powell f. J. Walley,* 1559.) Ent. bef. 4 my. 1560. C⁷.; HD. Arthur Vershbow, Newton Center, Mass.(imp.).

Shepherds' Kalendar—*cont.*

22414 — Now = 22416.5.

22415 — [Anr. ed.] The shepardes kalender. Here beginneth the kalender of shepardes newly augmented and corrected. fol. (*T. Este f. J. Wally,*) [1570?] L(imp.). O(Douce frag.d.6).HETH(imp.).OS(imp.).P(lacks tp).; F.HN(M6–N6 only, w. 22410).

22416 — [Anr. ed.] fol. [*J. Charlewood f.*](*Jhon Wally,*) [c. 1580.] L(imp.).
'K' of sig. K4 is under 'eg' of 'regulerly'.

22416.5 — [Anr. ed.] fol. [*J. Charlewood a. G. Robinson f.*] (*John Wally,*) [c. 1585.] O.C(N1 only, SSS.35.11²).NLW (lacks tp).
(Formerly 22414) K4 missigned 'K.iii.' The 'K' is under 1st 'g' of 'going'. Robinson app. pr. only A2–7, N1,8.

22417 — = 22418.

22418 — [Anr. ed.] fol. *V. S[immes,]* assigned by *T. Adams,* [1595?] Ass'd to R. Walley 7 mr. 1591; to T. Adams 12 oc. 1591. C(imp.).; Y.
(Formerly also 22417)

22419 — [Anr. ed.] fol. [*V. Simmes f. T. Adams?* 1600?] O (lacks tp).; Hollins College, Virginia(imp.).
Collates A–M⁸ N⁴ like 22418, but most leaf signatures have Arabic numerals like 22420 and later eds. which have different collations.

22420 — [Anr. ed.] Newly augmented and corrected. fol. *G. Elde f. T. Adams,* 1604. L.O(imp.).; HD(imp.).

22421 — [Anr. ed.] fol. *f. T. Adams,* 1611. L.INN.

22422 — [Anr. ed.] fol. *f. T. Adams,* 1618. L.O.C⁶.; HN.

22423 — [Anr. ed.] fol. [*Eliot's Court Press] f. J. Wright,* 1631. Ass'd to A. Hebb 6 my. 1625. L.O³.O¹⁷.; TOKYO. New York, Metropolitan Museum of Art (Print Dept.).

Sherborne School. Troposchematologiæ libri duo . . . in usum regiæ scholæ Shirburnensis. 1602, etc. *See* 11692.3 sq.

Sherburne, John, *tr. See* 18947.

Sheriffs. In this booke is contayned yᵉ offices of sheryffes. [1538? etc.] *See* 10984 sqq.

22424 **Sherley, *Sir* Anthony.** Sir Antony Sherley his relation of his travels into Persia. 4°. [*N. Okes] f. N. Butter a. J. Bagfet,* 1613. Ent. 17 ap. L.O.C¹⁷.G⁴.M².+; F.HN. BO.NY.Y.+
For related accounts *see* 4300, 4705, 6417, 17894, 18592, 19343.

22425 — A true report of sir Anthony Shierlies journey overland to Venice, . . . and soe to Casbine in Persia. 4°. *R. B[lower] f. J. J[aggard,]* 1600. L.L².O.; F.
Blower and Wm. Jaggard fined 23 oc. 1600; *see* Arber II.831, 833.

Sherley, *Sir* Robert. Sir Robert Sherley, sent ambassadour [etc.] 1609. *See* 17894 sq.

22425.5 **Sherley, *Sir* Thomas.** A true discourse, of the late voyage made by the right worshipfull sir Thomas Sherley the yonger, knight: on the coast of Spaine. Written by a gentleman that was in the voyage. 4°. [*E. Allde] f. T. Pavyer,* 1602. Ent. 20 au. L.

22426 **Sherly, Anthony,** *Poet.* Witts new dyall: or, a schollers prize. [In verse.] 4°. *W. W[hite] f. J. Browne,* 1604. Ent. to T. Man, jun., 29 oc. L.; HN.

Sherman, Abraham, *ed. See* 4937.

22427 **Sherrard, Robert.** The countryman with his houshold. Being a familiar conference, concerning faith and good workes. [Init. R. S., *preacher.*] 8°. *E. Griffin f. J. Man,* 1620. Ent. as by Sherrard to Man a. J. Bartlet 21 mr. O.; F(lacks C3).

22427a — [Anr. issue, w. imprint:] *E. Griffin f. J. Bartlet,* 1620. L.; Y.

22428 **Sherry, Richard.** A treatise of schemes & tropes. Wherunto is added a declamacion, that chyldren should be well and gently broughte vp in learnynge. Written fyrst in Latin by Erasmus [De civilitate morum puerilium.] 8°. (*J. Day,*) [1550.] L.O(2).C.P.; HN.Y. Dedic. dated 13 Dec. 1550.

22429 — A treatise of the figures of grammer and rhetorike, whereunto is ioygned the oration which Cicero made to Cesar, geuing thankes for pardonyng, Marcus Marcellus. Lat. a. Eng. 8°. [*R. Caly?*] *in æd. R. Totteli,* (1555 (4 my.)) L.L².C.M.P.; F.HN.
— *tr. See* 3603.

S'Hertogenbosch. A jornall of certaine principall passages in and before S'hertogenbosh. 1629. *See* 13248.4.
— A true relation of this present siege of Shertoken-Busse. 1629. *See* 13248.6.

Sherwood, Robert. Dictionaire, anglois et francois. 1632. *See* pt. 2 of 5831.
22429.5 — The French tutour: by way of grammar. Whereunto are also annexed three dialogues. [Init. R. S. L., i.e. R. Sherwood, *Londoner*.] 8°. [*H. Lownes*] *f. R. Young*, 1625. Ent. to H. Lownes 3 ja. O².; CHI(lacks B1).
22430 — [Anr. ed., enlarged.] Whereunto are also annexed . . . a touch of French compliments. The second edition, carefully corrected and enlarged. 8°. *R. Young*, 1634. L(2).O.O⁶.; F.
— *tr. See* 1782.

22431 **Sherwood, Thomas.** Murder upon murder, committed by T. Sherwood alias, Countrey Tom. And now he is hangd this 14 of Aprill, 1635. *Ballad.* 2 pts. s.sh.fol. *f. T. Langley, sold by T. Lambert*, [1635.] O.
For a pamphlet on this murder *see* 12010.

22432 **Sherwood, William.** A true report of the late horrible murder committed by W. Sherwood, vpon R. Hobson, gentleman, bothe prisoners in the Queenes Benche, for the profession of poperie, the 18. of Iune. 1581. 8°. *J. Charlwood a.* [i.e. *for*] *E. White*, 1581. Ent. to Charlewood 17 jy. L².

Shield. The shelde of saluacion. [1548?] *See* 20851.5.

Shilander, Cornelius. *See* 21817.

22433 **Shilling, Andrew.** The true relation of that worthy sea fight. 1622. Now = Newsbooks 57A.

22434 **Shillocke, Calebbe.** Calebbe Shillocke, his prophesie: or, the Jewes prediction. *Ballad.* 1/2 sh.fol. [*G. Eld*] *f. T. P[avier*, 1607.] C⁶.
Based on 4102.5; stanza 2 names 'this present yeere' as 1607.

Ship. The shyppe of fooles. 1509, etc. *See* 3547 sq.

Shirley, Sir Anthony. *See* Sherley.

22435 **Shirley, Henry.** The martyr'd souldier: as it was acted. 4°. *J. Okes, sold by F. Eglesfield*, 1638. Ent. to J. Okes 15 fb. L.O.E.ETON.M⁴.+; F.HN.HD.N.NY.+ Greg 533.
Copies vary; dedic. signed: 'I. K.' or 'Io. Kirke.'; both at HD.

22436 **Shirley, James.** The bird in a cage. A comedie. 4°. *B. Alsop a. T. Fawcet f. W. Cooke*, 1633. Ent. 19 mr. L.O.C.BRISTOL.E.+; F.HN.HD.N.Y.+ Greg 479.
22437 — Changes: or, love in a maze. A comedie. 4°. *G. P[urslowe] f. W. Cooke*, 1632. Ent. 9 fb. L.O.C.BRISTOL.E.+; F.HN.HD.N.Y.+ Greg 462.
22438 — The constant maid. A comedy. 4°. *J. Raworth f. R. Whitaker*, 1640. Ent. 28 ap. L.O.C.BRISTOL.E.+; F.HN.HD.N.Y.+ Greg 592.
Unsold sheets of this, w. impr. cropt, and of 22455, w. tp cancelled, reissued in 1657 as Wing S 3490 (Huth copy now at Williams College).
22439 — A contention for honour and riches. [A masque.] 4°. *E. A[llde] f. W. Cooke*, 1633. Ent. 9 no. 1632. L.O.C.BRISTOL.ETON.+; F.HN.HD.N.Y.+ Greg 473.
22440 — The coronation a comedy. . . . Written by J. Fletcher [or rather by J. Shirley.] 4°. *T. Cotes f. A. Crooke a. W. Cooke*, 1640. Ent. 25 ap. 1639. L.O.C.BRISTOL.E.+; F.HN.HD.N.Y.+ Greg 572.
Tp partly from same setting as 11072.
22441 — The dukes mistris, as it was presented. 4°. *J. Norton f. A. Crooke*, 1638. Ent. to Crooke a. W. Cooke 13 mr. L.O.C.BRISTOL.E.+; F.HN.HD.N.Y.+ Greg 536.
The probable order of printing of the variants is 22441b, 22441, 22441a.
22441a — [A variant, w. imprint:] *J. Norton f. W. Cooke*, 1638. L.O.E.LEEDS.NEK.+; F.HN.HD.ILL.Y.+
22441b — [A variant, w. imprint:] *J. Norton f. A. Crooke a. W. Cooke*, 1638. L.O(2).; F.HN.TEX.Y. McMaster U.+
22442 — The example. As it was presented. 4°. *J. Norton f. A. Crooke a. W. Cooke*, 1637. Ent. 18 oc. L.O.C.BRISTOL.E.+; F.HN.HD.N.Y.+ Greg 521.
22443 — The gamester. As it was presented. 4°. *J. Norton f. A. Crooke a. W. Cooke*, 1637. Ent. 15 no. L.O.C.BRISTOL.E.+; F.HN.HD.N.Y.+ Greg 523.

Shirley, James—*cont.*
22444 — The gratefull servant. A comedie. 4°. *B. A[lsop] a. T. F[awcet] f. J. Grove*, 1630. Ent. 26 fb. L.O.E.NEK(tp def.).WN.+; F.HN.HD.N.Y.+ Greg 429.
22445 — [Anr. ed.] 4°. *J. Okes f. W. Leake*, 1637. Ass'd 25 se. L.O.C.BRISTOL.E.+; F.HN.HD.N.Y.+
22446 — Hide Parke a comedie, as it was presented. 4°. *T. Cotes f. A. Crooke a. W. Cooke*, 1637. Ent. 13 ap. L.O.C.BRISTOL.E.+; F.HN.HD.N.Y.+ Greg 517.
22447 — The humorous courtier. A comedy. 4°. *T. C[otes] f. W. Cooke, sold by J. Becket*, 1640. Ent. to Cooke 29 jy. 1639. L.O.C.BRISTOL.E.+; F.HN.HD.N.Y.+ Greg 577.
22448 — The lady of pleasure. A comedie. 4°. *T. Cotes f. A. Crooke a. W. Cooke*, 1637. Ent. 13 ap. L.O.C.BRISTOL.E.+; F.HN.HD.N.Y.+ Greg 518.
22449 — Loves crueltie. A tragedy, as it was presented. 4°. *T. Cotes f. A. Crooke*, 1640. Ent. to Crooke a. W. Cooke 25 ap. 1639; entry to J. Williams a. F. Eglesfield 29 no. 1639 cancelled. L.O.C.BRISTOL.E(imp.).+; F.HN.HD.N.Y.+ Greg 573.
22450 — The maides revenge. A tragedy. 4°. *T. C[otes] f. W. Cooke*, 1639. Ent. 12 ap. L.O.C.BRISTOL.E.+; F.HN.HD.N.Y.+ Greg 562.
This setting of the imprint is prob. later than 22450a.
22450a — [A variant, w. imprint:] *f. W. Cooke*, 1639. L.; F(impr. def.).HD(impr.def.).N.TEX.
22451 — The opportunity a comedy, as it was presented. 4°. *T. Cotes f. A. Crooke a. W. Cooke*, 1640. Ent. 25 ap.1639. L.O.BRISTOL.E.NEK.+; F.HN.CHI.HD.Y.+ Greg 575.
22451a — [A variant, w. imprint:] *T. Cotes f. A. Crooke*, [1640.] L.O.C.ETON.LEEDS.+; F.HN.CH.N.TEX.+
22452 — [A variant, w. imprint:] *f. A. Crooke, sold [by T. Allot?] in Dublin*, 1640. HN.
22453 — A pastorall called the Arcadia. 4°. *J. D[awson] f. J. Williams a. F. Eglesfield*, 1640. Ent. 29 no. 1639. L.O.C.BRISTOL.E.+; F.HN.HD.N.Y.+ Greg 583.
22454 — The royall master; as it was acted in Dublin. 4°. *T. Cotes, sold by J. Crooke a. R. Serger*, 1638. Ent. to A. and J. Crooke a. R. Sergier 13 mr. L.O.C.BRISTOL.E.+; F.HN.HD.N.Y.+ Greg 538.
22454a — [A variant, w. imprint:] *T. Cotes, sold by T. Allot a. E. Crooke in Dublin*, 1638. L.; F.HN.CHI.HD.NY.+
22455 — S¹ Patrick for Ireland. The first part. 4°. *J. Raworth f. R. Whitaker*, 1640. Ent. 28 ap. L.O.C.BRISTOL.ETON.+; F.HN.HD.N.Y.+ Greg 593.
See note to 22438.
22456 — The schoole of complement. As it was acted. 4°. *E. A[llde] f. F. Constable*, 1631. Ent. 25 fb. L.L⁶.O.O⁶.E.+; F.HN.HD.N.Y.+ Greg 441.
22457 — [Anr. ed.] 4°. *J. H[aviland] f. F. Constable*, 1637. L(date cropt).O.C.BRISTOL.E.+; F.HN.HD.N.TEX.+
22458 — The traytor. A tragedie, written by J. Shirley. 4°. [*J. Norton] f. W. Cooke*, 1635. Ent. 3 no. 1634. L.O.C.BRISTOL.E.+; F.HN.HD.N.Y.+ Greg 498.
22458.5 — The triumph of peace. A masque. By J. Shirley, of Grayes Inne, Gent. 4°. *J. Norton f. W. Cooke*, 1633. Ent. 24 ja. 1634. L(2).L⁶.L⁸.O.C.; F(2, 1 imp.).HN(3). CAL.ILL.PFOR. Greg 488.
(Formerly 22459a) A1ᵛ line 19: 'bridle'; A2ʳ catchword: 'Next'; D1ᵛ line 1: 'Beneath . . . Wings,'. While this and 22459 have quires A–D largely from 2 settings, there are a number of variations in individual copies. For a study of the L copies *see* W. W. Greg's article in *The Library*, I (1946), pp. 113–26, where the 'bridle' setting w. its companion sheets (Greg's B, D, F copies) is considered earlier than the 'bride' setting (Greg's A, C, E copies).
The 1st quires in 22458.5–22459b are the same setting with the variant tpp produced by press alterations.
See also 19245.5.
22459 — [Anr. ed., w. title as 22458.5.] 4°. *J. Norton f. W. Cooke*, 1633. L(3).O.O⁶.; F.HN.HD.TEX.Y.+
A1ᵛ line 19: 'bride'; D1ᵛ line 1: 'Beneath . . . with [*sic*]'.
22459a — Now = 22458.5.
22459a.5 — [Anr. issue, partly reset.] By J. Shirley, Gent. *J. Norton f. W. Cooke*, 1633. L.O.O⁶.BRISTOL.E.; F(2). CHI.HD.N.Y.
(Formerly 22459c) A1ᵛ line 19: 'bride'; D1ᵛ line 1: '*beneath . . . wings*,'. In at least the L, F, and HD copies quires A–D are mainly from the same setting as 22459. One F copy has the extra Speech as in 22459b.

Shirley, James—*cont.*

22459b — [Anr. ed., partly reimposed.] By J. Shirley, of Grayes-Inne, Gent. The third impression. 4⁰. *J. Norton f. W. Cooke*, 1633. L.L⁶.O⁶.C.ETON.; F.BO(w. quire D of 22459a.5).

> A1ᵛ line 19: 'bridle'; A2ʳ catchword: 'fur-'; D1ᵛ line 1: '*Beneath . . . wings*' (no comma). In the L⁶ and F copies is an extra leaf: 'A Speech to the King and Queenes Maiesties,'.

22459c — Now = 22459a.5.

22460 — The wedding. As it was lately acted. 4⁰. [*J. Okes*] *f. J. Grove*, 1629. L.L⁶(2).O.BRISTOL.E.; F.HN.HD.CHI.Y.+ Greg 425.

22461 — [Anr. ed.] 4⁰. [*J. Beale*] *f. J. Grove*, 1633. Ass'd by Grove to W. Leake 25 se. 1637. L.O.C.E.ETON.+; F.HN.HD.N.Y.+

22462 — The wittie faire one. A comedie. 4⁰. B. *A*[*lsop*] *a. T. F*[*awcet*] *f. W. Cooke*, 1633. Ent. 15 ja. L.O.C. BRISTOL.E.+; F.HN.HD.N.Y.+ Greg 477.

22463 — The young admirall. As it was presented. 4⁰. *T. Cotes f. A. Crooke a. W. Cooke*, 1637. Ent. 13 ap. L.O.C. BRISTOL.E.+; F.HN.HD.N.Y.+ Greg 519.

— *See* also 4995, 4996.

Shirrye, Richard. *See* Sherry, R.

Shoemaker. The shomakers holiday. 1600, etc. *See* 6523 sqq.

22463.5 **Shore, Jane.** The wofull lamentation of mistris Jane Shore. *Ballad.* 2 pts. s.sh.fol. *G. P*[*urslowe*, c. 1620.] Ent. to W. White 11 jn. 1603; to ballad ptnrs. 14 de. 1624. M³(imp.).

Short, Richard. *See* 1571.5.

Shot. The poysonit shot. 1570. *See* 22204.

22463.7 **Shrewsbury, *Drapers of*.** To the right hon: the Lords spirituall and temporall, of Parliament. The humble petition of the drapers of the towne of Shrewsbury. [Against the bill passed in Commons for free trade of Welsh cloth.] s.sh.obl.fol. [*London*, 1621.] L⁸ (cropt, GL 5811).

> Commons passed the bill on 24 April 1621, and Lords passed an amended version 16 May 1621; *see* Notestein IV.252–3, 352.

22464 **Shute, John,** *Architect.* The first and chief groundes of architecture. *T. Marshe*, 1563. Ent. 1562–63. L²⁸.O.O⁴.C.D.; WASH².

22465 — [Anr. ed.] Of architecture; the first and chiefest grounds. fol. *T. Marsh*, 1584. J(untraced).

> PML does *not* have a copy of this.

22465.5 — [Anr. ed.] The first and chiefe groundes of architecture. fol. *H. Marshe*, 1587. O⁶.SAL.

Shute, John, *tr. See* 4470, 21507.5, 24777, 24778, 24782.

22466 **Shute, Nathaniel.** Corona charitatis, the crowne of charitie: a sermon preacht at the funerals of Mʳ. Richard Fishburne. 4⁰. *W. Stansby f. S. Man*, 1626. Ent. 17 my. L.O.C.CASHEL.G⁴.+; F.HN.HD.N.U.+

Shute, W., *tr. See* 7373.6, 11207, 17676.

22467 **Shutte, Christopher.** The testimonie of a true fayth: conteyned in a shorte catechisme. By C. S[hutte] preacher. 8⁰. *T. Dawson a. T. Gardyner*, 1577 (10 mr.) Ent. to Dawson 26 fb. O(imp.).

22468 — [Anr. ed., signed in full.] A compendious forme and summe of christian doctrine, called the testimonie of a true faith. Corrected, and newly augmented. 8⁰. *T. Dawson*, 1579. L.O(lacks tp).; U.

22469 — [Anr. ed.] 8⁰. *T. Dawson*, 1579. L.O

22469.3 — [Anr. ed.] 8⁰. *T. Dawson*, 1584. F.

22469.7 — [Anr. ed.] 8⁰. *M. D*[*awson*] *f. A. Boler*, 1637. E².; PH.

22470 — A verie godlie and necessary sermon, preached before the yong countesse of Comberland. 8⁰. [*H. Middleton? f.*] *C. Barker*, 1578. Ent. 26 ap. L.O(lacks tp). M. Woburn Abbey, Bedfordshire.

— *See* also 21482.

Shyrrey, Richard. *See* Sherry, R.

22471 **Sibbald, James.** Assertiones philosophicae. 1623. Now = 71.33.

22472 — Theses philosophicae. 1625. Now = 71.34.

22473 — Theses philosophicae. 1626. Now = 71.35.

22474 — Theses theologicæ. 1627. Now = 71.14.

22475 **Sibbes, Richard.** Beames of divine light, breaking forth in XXI. sermons. (The spirituall jubile.) 4⁰ in 8's. *G. M*[*iller a.*] (*E. P*[*urslowe*]) *f. N. Bourne a. R. Harford*, 1639 (1638.) Ent. 12 ja. 1638. L.O.C.D.E².+; F.HN.HD.N.U.+

22476 — Bowels opened, or, a discovery of the love, union and communion betwixt Christ and the church. Delivered in [20] sermons on the fourth fifth and sixt chapters of the Canticles. 4⁰ in 8's. *G. M*[*iller*] *f. G. Edwards*, 1639. Ent. 10 oc. 1632. L.O.C.G².OS.+; F.HN.CHI.HD.U.+

22477 — A breathing after God. Or a christians desire of Gods presence. 12⁰. *J. Dawson f. R. M*[*abb,*] *sold by T. Slater*, 1639. Ent. to R. Mabb 27 no. 1638. L.O.C. WN².; F.PN².

22478 — The brides longing for her bride-groomes second comming. A sermon preached at the funerall of sir Thomas Crew. 12⁰. *E. P*[*urslowe*] *f. G. Edwards*, 1638. Ent. to Edwards 13 fb.; half ass'd to R. Harford 12 mr. L.O.; HN.PN².Y.

22478a — [A variant, w. imprint:] *E. P*[*urslowe*] *f. R. Harford*, 1638. F.

22478b — [A variant, w. imprint:] *E. P*[*urslowe*] *f. E. Langham in Bambury*, 1638. C.; AAS.

22479 — The bruised reede, and smoaking flax. Some sermons contracted out of the 12. of Matth. 20. 12⁰. [*M. Flesher*] *f. R. Dawlman*, 1630. Ent. 13 jy. L.O.O¹⁷.; F.HD(lacks A10).ILL.LC.

22480 — Second edition, enlarged. 12⁰. [*M. Flesher*] *f. R. Dawlman*, 1631. L³.O.; F.PN².TORONTO².

22481 — Third edition, corrected. 12⁰. *M. F*[*lesher*] *f. R. Dawlman*, 1631. O.C³.DUR.; F.COR.PN².U.

22482 — Fourth edition. 12⁰. *M. F*[*lesher*] *f. R. Dawlman*, 1632. L².L⁴⁶.O⁶.SNU.WI.+; F.HN.HD.PEN.

22483 — Fifth edition. 12⁰. *M. F*[*lesher*] *f. R. Dawlman a. L. Faune*, 1635. L.C.LAMPORT.M.RGU.; F.HD.ILL.PN².Y.

22484 — Sixt edition. 12⁰. *M. F*[*lesher*] *f. R. Dawlman a. L. Faune*, 1638. L.L³⁰.O.C.C².+; F.HN.CHI.HD.NY¹¹.+

22485 — The christians end. Or, the sweet soveraignty of Christ, over his members. Being the substance of five sermons. 4⁰. *T. Harper* [*a. Eliot's Court Press*] *f. L. Chapman*, 1639. Ent. 18 oc. 1638. L.L².O.C². C⁵.+; F.HN.HD.ILL.U.+

> Eliot's Court Press pr. sermons 4 and 5.

22486 — The christians portion. Wherein is unfolded the unsearchable riches he hath by his interest in Christ. Published by T. G[oodwin] and P. N[ye.] 12⁰. *J. Norton f. J. Rothwell*, 1637. Ent. 10 no. L⁴.L³⁸.; F.HN.BO.PN².U.

22487 — [Anr. ed.] The christians portion, or, the charter of a christian. Corrected and enlarged. 12⁰. *J. O*[*kes*] *f. J. Rothwell*, 1638. Ent. 19 fb. L.L².O.O⁵.C.+; F(2). NY¹¹.PN².Y.

22488 — Christs exaltation purchast by humiliation. [3 sermons on Rom.xiv.9.] Published by T. G[oodwin] and P. N[ye.] 12⁰. *T. Cotes, sold by J. Bartlet*, 1639. L².L³. O.C.M⁴.+; F.HN.HD.ILL.PN².+

> Possibly these sermons were substituted for those on 1 John v.14 ent. to Bartlet 10 au. 1633, the same day he entered 22492.

22489 — The churches riches by Christs poverty. 1638. = pt. of 22498.

22490 — Divine meditations and holy contemplations. 12⁰. *T. Cotes f. J. Crooke a. R. Sergier*, 1638. Ent. 27 jy. L³. O.C.C⁵.BIRM.+; F.ILL.PN².U.Y.

22491 — Evangelicall sacrifices. In xix. sermons. The third tome. (The hidden life.) 4⁰ in 8's. *T. B*[*adger a.*] (*E. Purslow*) *f. N. Bourne a. R. Harford*, 1640 (1639.) Ent. 20 au. 1638. L.O.C³.BIRM.G².+; F.HN.HD.ILL (lacks gen. tp).U.+

> There are 11 sub tpp, all dated 1639, except that in some copies (F, 1 HD) Ll3–6 has been reprinted with sub tp on Ll5ʳ dated 1640.

22492 — The excellencie of the Gospell above the Law. Published by T. G[oodwin] and P. N[ye.] 12⁰. *T. Cotes, sold by J. Bartlet*, 1639. Ent. to Bartlet 10 au. 1633. L(destroyed).L².O.C.BRISTOL.D.+; F.HN.CHI.HD.U.+

22493 — An exposition of the third chapter of the Epistle to the Philippians: also Two sermons of christian watchfulnesse. An exposition of part of the second chapter of Philipp[ians]. A sermon upon Mal.4.2.3. 4⁰. *T. Cotes* [*a. J. Dawson*] *f. P. Cole*, 1639. Ent. 2 au. 1637. L(imp.).O.C.E².G².+; F.HN.HD.N.U.+

> Dawson pr. quires B–1st Ii. Unsold sheets reissued in 1647 as Wing S 3735.

— The fountaine opened. 1638. *See* 22498.

Sibbes, Richard—*cont.*

22494 — A fountain sealed: or, the duty of the sealed to the spirit. Being the substance of divers sermons [on Ephes.iv.30.] 12°. *T. Harper f. L. Chapman*, 1637. Ent. 27 au. 1633. L.O.C⁵.D.DUL.+; F. HN.ILL.PN².U.+ A3ʳ last line begins: 'Ladyship'.

22495 — [Anr. ed.] 12°. *T. Harper f. L. Chapman*, 1637. L.L². O.C.M.+; F.HN.HD.ILL.NY¹¹.+ Engr. tp has 'the 2ᵈ· edition.' A3ʳ last line begins: 'Ladyship'.

22496 — [Anr. ed.] 12°. *T. Harper f. L. Chapman*, 1638. L⁴⁶.O. C.E.M⁴.+; F.HN.HD.ILL.PN².+ Engr. tp has 'the 3ᵈ· edition.'

22496.5 — [Anr. ed.] 8°. *Amstelredam, [Richt Right Press,]* 1638. L.

22497 — A glance of heaven. Or, a pretious taste of a glorious feast. [4 sermons on 1 Cor.ii.9.] 12°. *E. G[riffin a. J. Okes] f. J. Rothwell*, 1638. Ent. 7 ap. C.; F(2).BO.ILL. Okes pr. quires L–N.

22497.5 — [Anr. issue, w. cancel tp, w. imprint:] *E. G[riffin] f. J. R[othwell], sold by H. Overton*, 1638. L.O.D.G².P.+; HN.CAL².HD.N. Tp set in duplicate; line 13 has 'preacher' (L) or 'Preacher' (HD).

— The hidden life. 1639. *See* 22491.

22498 — Light from heaven, discovering the fountaine opened. Angels acclamations. Churches riches. Rich povertie. In foure treatises. 4° in 8's. *E. Purslow [a.] (R. Badger) f. N. Bourne a. R. Harford*, 1638. Ent. 12 ja. L.O.C.CASHEL.M⁴.+; F.HN.HD.(imp.).PN².U.+ (22489 is part of this) Tp line 18 has 'Copies'; D2ʳ last line begins: 'it. God'.

22498a — [Anr. ed.] 4° in 8's. *E. Purslow [a.] (R. Badger) f. N. Bourne a. R. Harford*, 1638. L(lacks tp).O.C.BIRM. E⁸.+; F.HD.MIN.N.NY.+ Tp line 18 has 'Coppies'; D2ʳ last line begins: 'God'.

22499 — A miracle of miracles or Christ in our nature. [2 sermons on Isaiah vii.14.] 4°. *E. G[riffin a. J. Norton?] f. J. Rothwell*, 1638. Ent. 26 oc. L.L³.O.C².C⁵.+; F. HN.HD.ILL.U.+ Norton app. pr. quires F–I.

22500 — The returning backslider, or, a commentarie upon the whole XIIII. chapter of Hosea. (The saints priviledge.) [17 sermons.] 4° in 8's. *G. M[iller] f. G. Edwards*, 1639 (1638.) Ent. 10 oc. 1632. L.O.C.BIRM. M.+; F.HN.ILL.U.Y.+ Tp line 16 begins: 'Published by his owne Permission. . . .' Saints Privilege reprinted from 22505.

22500.5 — [Anr. issue, w. cancel tp.] *G. M[iller] f. G. Edwards*, 1639. HN(tp facs.)*.BO².HD.PN². Tp line 16 begins: 'Being allowed of in his life, . . .'

22501 — The riches of mercie. In two treatises; 1 Lydia's conversion. 2. A rescue from death. 12°. *J. D[awson] f. F. Eglesfield*, 1638. R. Mabb ent. Rescue 12 ap. and Lydia 11 my.; both ass'd to J. Dawson 2 au. L.L⁴. O(imp.).C. Rogers(imp.).; F.HD.PN².U.

22502 — The saints comforts. Being the substance of diverse sermons. 12°. *T. Cotes, sold by P. Cole*, 1638 (1637.) Ent. to R. Cotes 18 se. 1637. O.O²⁸(Bed.).; F. Copies vary: O, O²⁸ have on gen. tp: 'By a Reverent Divine now with God.' F has: 'By Richard Sibbes, D.D. now deceased.' O has sub tpp dated 1637, with Sibbes's name; O²⁸ has sub tpp, but with Sibbes's name cut out; F has sub tpp cancelled.

22503 — The saints cordials. As they were delivered in sundry sermons. [29 sermons by Sibbes and others, all anon.] fol. *(M. Flesher) f. R. Dawlman*, (1629.) Ent. 2 ap. 1629; ?'Judgments Reason' on 1 Cor.xi.30–1 ent. 20 ap. 1631. L.O.C³.M.NEK.+; F.HN.HD.ILL(imp.). U.+ (Formerly also 12110) Sermon 23 is the 1st printing of 13726.2.

22504 — The saints cordialls; delivered in [22] sundry sermons. Whereunto is now added, The saints safety. By R. Sibbs. fol. *M. F[lesher] f. H. Overton (a. R. Dawlman,)* 1637. L.O.C.E.LYU.+; F.HN.CHI.HD.U.+ Sub tpp on B1ʳ, H3ʳ, and N3ʳ have 'The second edition.' Reprints 11 sermons from 22503 and adds 11 others, 8 of which are reprinted from 22507.

22505 — The saints priviledge or a christians constant advocate. 12°. *G. M[iller] f. G. Edwards*, 1638. Ent. 2 ap. O. O²¹.; CAL².ILL.PN².U.Y. Reprinted in 22500.

Sibbes, Richard—*cont.*

22505.5 — [A variant, w. imprint:] *G. M[iller] f. E. Langham in Banbury*, 1638. AAS(imp.).

22506 — [Anr. ed.] 12°. *G. M[iller] f. G. Edwards*, 1639. SHEF.; F.

22507 — The saints safetie in evill times. Delivered at Sᵗ Maries in Cambridge. Whereunto is annexed a passion-sermon [on Matth. xxvii.46.] As also . . . the funerall of Mʳ Sherland. (The churches visitation.) 2 pts. 8°. *M. Flesher f. R. Dawlman*, 1633 (1634.) Ent. 16 au. 1633. L(lacks tp to pt. 2).L³(w. 2nd tp to pt. 1 cancelled).O(lacks 1st tp to pt. 1)*.O¹⁸(imp.)*.WI(w. 1st tp to pt. 1 bound as tp to pt. 2).; F(2, 1 w. 2nd tp to pt. 1 cancelled).HN(lacks tp to pt. 2).CHI(lacks 1st tp to pt. 1)*.PN²(w. 2nd tp to pt. 1 cancelled).U(w. 2nd tp to pt. 1 cancelled).+ The 1st tp to pt. 1, given above, is a cancel or added leaf. The 2nd tp, pr. as [a2]ʳ has: 'evill times. Shewing the nearenesse of God. *M. F. f. R. Dawlman*, 1634.' and does not mention the passion or funeral sermons. Reprinted in 22504.

22507.5 — [A variant, w. imprint on 1st tp to pt. 1, i.e. 'evill times. Delivered':] *M. Flesher f. R. Dawlman*, 1634. O(2nd tp to pt. 1 cancelled).STU.; HD(2nd tp to pt. 1 cancelled).

22508 — The soules conflict with it selfe. 8°. *M. Flesher f. R. Dawlman*, 1635. Ent. 16 my. 1632. L.O.C.A.M⁴.+; F.HN.HD.ILL.NY¹¹.+ Tp varies; lines 5–6: '/AND/VICTORIE/' or line 5: '/AND VICTORY/'; both at F. In the 2nd F copy G4,5 is a cancel bifolium w. G5ʳ last line having 'excellency' instead of 'excellencie'.

22508.5 — Second edition. 8°. *M. F[lesher] f. R. Dawlman*, 1635. O.C.D.

22509 — [A variant, w. imprint:] *M. F[lesher] f. R. Dawlman*, 1636. L.C.; AAS.PN².

22510 — Third edition. 8°. *M. F[lesher] f. R. Dawlman*, 1636. L.L².O.O².G².+; F.HN.ILL.PN².U.+

22511 — Fourth edition. 8°. *M. F[lesher] f. R. Dawlman*, 1638. L.O.C.BIRM.M⁴.+; F.HN.HD.ILL.NY¹¹.+ The Fourth edition, 1651, Wing S 3745, is completely reset.

22512 — The spiritual favorite at the throne of grace. 12°. *T. Paine f. R. Mabb*, 1640. Ent. 2 oc. 1639. C.; HD.LC. PN².U.

— The spirituall jubile. 1638. *See* 22475.

22512a — Now = 22513.5.

22513 — The spirituall-mans aime. Published by T. G[oodwin] and P. N[ye. A sermon.] 12°. *J. Norton f. J. Rothwell*, 1637. Ent. 12 jn. L.O²⁸.C⁵.; CU.

22513.5 — [Anr. ed., corrected.] 12°. *E. G[riffin] f. J. Rothwell*, 1637. L⁴.L³⁸.O.; F.HN.BO.ILL.U.+ (Formerly 22512a)

22514 — Third edition. 12°. *J. N[orton] f. J. Rothwell*, 1638. L³.O⁵.O²⁸(Bed.).C.WN².; F(2).CAL².HD.NY¹¹.PN².

22515 — Two sermons upon the first words of Christs last sermon. John XIIII.1. [Ed.] (T. Goodwin. P. Nye.) 4°. *T. Harper f. L. Chapman*, 1636. Ent. 14 ap. L.O.C². D.P.+; F.BO³.Y.

22516 — Second edition. 4°. *T. Harper f. L. Chapman*, 1636. L¹³.O.C¹⁰.E.PETYT.+; HN.HD.ILL.TORONTO².WASH².+ This has added: 'The Authors Prayer before his sermon.'

22517 — Third edition. 12°. *T. Harper f. L. Chapman*, 1637. L. L².O.C.M.+; F.HN.HD.N.U.+

22518 — Fourth edition. 12°. *T. Harper f. L. Chapman*, 1638. L⁴⁶.O.C.C³.E.+; F.HN.HD.ILL.PN².+

22519 — Two sermons: [on Canticles i.2; Coloss. iii.1.] 12°. *T. Cotes, sold by A. Kembe in Southwarke*, 1638. Ent. to Kemb 12 ap. O(imp.).OS.; F.HN(frag.).ILL.PN².

22520 — [Anr. ed.] 12°. *T. Cotes f. A. Kembe in Southwarke*, 1639. O.; HD.

22521 — Yea and amen: or, pretious promises, and priviledges. Spiritually unfolded. Perused by T. G[oodwin] and P. N[ye.] 12°. *R. Bishop f. R. Dawlman, sold by H. Mosley*, 1638. Ent. 11 ja. L.L³.O.C.NLW.+; F.HD. PN².U.WTL.

— ed. *See* 20208, 20241, 20251, 20262.

— *See* also 24048.

22522 **Sibthorp**, *Sir* **Christopher**. A friendly advertisement to the pretended catholickes of Ireland. In the end is added an epistle by J. Ussher that the religion anciently professed in Ireland is, the same with that, which at this day is established. 4° in 8's. *Dublin, Soc. of Statrs.*, 1622. L.O.C.D⁶.E².+; F.NY¹¹.PH².

Sibthorp, *Sir* **Christopher**—*cont.*
22523 — [A variant, w. imprint:] *Dublin, Soc. of Statrs.,* 1623.
L².O².C.D.D⁵.+; Y.
22524 — A reply to an answere [in manuscript] made by a
popish adversarie, to the two chapters in the first
part of [22523]. 4⁰. *Dublin, Soc. of Statrs.,* 1625.
L.O.C.D.D⁶.+
22525 — A surreplication to the rejoynder of a popish adversarie. 4⁰. *Dublin, Soc. of Statrs.,* 1627. C.
Text ends M3ʳ.
22525.3 — [Anr. issue, w. M3 cancelled and replaced by M3–5.]
Dublin, Soc. of Statrs., 1627. L²⁵.C.D(3).D⁶(imp.).
NEK.

Sibthorpe, Robert. Apostolike obedience. Shewing the
duty of subjects to pay tribute and taxes. A sermon.
4⁰. *M. Flesher f. R. M[ynne,]* 1627. Ent. to R. Mynne
10 my. O³.O¹⁹.C⁵.BURY.YK.+; F.CAL⁶.CU.HD.N.+
22525.7 — [A variant, w. imprint:] *M. Flesher, sold by J. Bowler,*
1627. L.O³.C².LINC.M.+; F.HN.CHI.HD.NY¹¹.+
22526 — [Anr. ed., partially reimposed.] 4⁰. *M. Flesher f. R.
M[ynne], sold by J. Bowler,* 1627. L.O.O¹⁸.C(2).D.;
N. Weissman.
22526a — [A variant, w. imprint:] *M. F[lesher] f. R. Mynne,*
1627. L.O²⁸.DUR³.DUR⁵.PLUME.+; F.HN.CU.HD.U.+
22527 — A counter-plea to an apostataes [*sic*] pardon. A sermon.
4⁰. *B. Alsop f. R. Fleming,* 1618. Ent. to Fleming a.
G. Fairbeard 13 ap. L⁸.O.C.C⁵.E.+; F.HN.CHI.U.
22527a — [A variant, w. imprint:] *B. Alsop f. G. Fairebeard,*
1618. L.L⁸.C.C³.E.+; CAL.CAL⁸.HD.

Sibyllarum Icones. XII Sibyllarum icones the pro-
22527a.5 phecies of the twelve sybills. [Engrs. w. verses.] 8⁰.
sold by R. Daniell, [c. 1625.] L(tp only, Print Dept.).
See Hind II.365.
22527a.7 — [Anr. state, w. imprint altered:] *sould by T. Johnson,*
[1630?] L(Print Dept.).

Sicelides. Sicelides a piscatory. 1631. *See* 11083.

22528 **Sicily.** A famous victorie, atchived in August last 1613.
by the christian gallies of Sicilia, against the Turkes.
4⁰. [*W. White?*] *f. T. Thorp,* 1613. L.; F.

22529 **Sictor, Joannes.** Carmina lugubria de infelici casu
17/7 Januarij 1629, principis Friderici Henrici . . .
Electoris Palatini primogeniti filii. [In verse.] 4⁰.
typis T. Cotes, [1629.] ?Ent. to R. Royston 26 ja.
1629. L.O¹⁷.C².M.; HN.TEX.
22529.5 — Epicedion apostrophicon honorabili et de patria
optimè merito viro, domino Ricardo Fenne equiti,
1639; die 19 Augusti mortuo. [In verse.] s.sh.fol.
[*T. Cotes?* 1639.] L.
22530 — Epicedion in honorabilem dominum Rodolphum
Freemannum, reipublicæ Londinensis prætorium
regium. [In verse.] s.sh.fol. [*R. Raworth,* 1634.]
?Ent. to R. Raworth 8 ap. 1634. L.
22531 — Lachrymæ reipublicæ Londinensis, sive epicedia
præcipuorum quatuor senatorum. [Latin verse in
honour of R. Freeman, M. Lumley, R. Ducy, and
H. Perry.] 4⁰. *typis T. Cotes,* 1635. L.O.O¹³.P.PETYT.;
F.HN.
22532 — Lacrymæ republicæ Londinensis, sive epicedia præcipuorum quinq; virorum, unius syndici. [Latin verse
in honour of R. Deane, R. Mason, H. Hammersley, R.
Parkhurst, J. Goare.] 4⁰. *typis T. Cotes,* 1637. O.C.; F.
22532.5 — Panegyricon Britannicum, quod pro auspicijs novi
anni, CIↃ IↃ CXXVII. In honorem serenissimi &
potentissimi principis Caroli Magnæ Britanniæ,
regis. [In verse.] 4⁰. [*B. Norton a. J. Bill,* 1626.]
O⁶.; F.
22533 — Panegyricon inaugurale . . . prætoris regii, sive majoris,
reipublicæ Londinensis, Richardi Fenn, sub finem
1637. (De celeberrima Trinobantiados Augustæ
civitate. [By] E. Benlowes.) [In verse.] 4⁰. *ex chalco-
graphia T. Harperi,* [1638.] C².
22533a — [Anr. ed., w. contents rearranged.] 4⁰. *Cantabrigiae, ex
off. R. Danielis,* [1638.] L⁸.O.C¹⁰.D.STD.+
Dedic. dated cal. Jan. 1638.

Sidney, Elizabeth. *See* 11729.

22533a.5 **Sidney,** *Sir* **Henry.** A very godly letter made, by the
right honourable sir Henry Sidney. Now XXV.
yeeres past vnto Phillip Sidney his sonne then at
schoole at Shrowesbury. (The epitaph of sir H.
Sidney. [By] W. Gruffith. [In verse.]) 8⁰. *T. Dawson,*
1591. Ent. 5 ja. SHR.

22534 **Sidney,** *Sir* **Philip.** An apologie for poetrie. 4⁰. [*J.
Roberts*] *f. H. Olney,* 1595. Ent. 12 ap.; entry can-
celled. L.O.C²(imp.).E².LINC(lacks A3).+; F.HN.HD.
NY.Y.+
A3, 4 have a preface by Olney and sonnets by H.
Constable not in either of the following. This
prob. was pr. after 22535.
22534.5 — [Anr. issue of quires B–L of 22534 w. tp to 22535 prefixed.] *f. W. Ponsonby,* 1595. O⁹.; HN. Mrs. Grant
H. Webb, Farms Road, Greenwich, Conn.
22535 — [Anr. ed.] The defence of poesie. 4⁰. [*T. Creede*] *f. W.
Ponsonby,* 1595. Ent. 29 no. 1594. L.O(lacks tp).
Juel-Jensen(frag.).; HD(tp facs.). Robert Taylor(tp
facs.).
The 1st authorized ed.
22536 — Syr P. S. his Astrophel and Stella. To the end of which
are added, sundry other rare sonnets of diuers
gentlemen [S. Daniel, etc. In verse.] 4⁰. [*J. Charle-
wood*] *f. T. Newman,* 1591. L.C²(imp.). Viscount De
L'Isle.
With an epistle by Newman and preface by T.
Nash. This ed. suppressed; *see* Arber I.555.
22537 — [Anr. ed., corrected.] Sir P. S. his Astrophel and
Stella. Wherein the excellence of sweete poesie is
concluded. 4⁰. [*J. Danter*] *f. T. Newman,* 1591. L(2).
CASHEL. Juel-Jensen(frag.).; HN.
Without the prefaces or the added sonnets.
22538 — [Anr. ed. of 22536.] Syr P. S. his Astrophel and Stella.
To the end of which [etc.] 4⁰. [*F. Kingston*] *f. M.
Lownes,* [1597?] Ent. to W. Ponsonby 23 oc. 1598.
O.; HN. Arthur Houghton.
Without the prefaces but w. the added sonnets.
22539 — The countesse of Pembrokes Arcadia. [*Ed.* M. Gwinne
and F. Greville?] 4⁰ in 8's. *J. Windet f. w. Ponsonbie,*
1590. Ent. 23 au. 1588. C².; HN.PFOR. Crocker.
See Greg, *Companion,* pp. 144–5.
22539a — [A variant, w. imprint:] *f. W. Ponsonbie,* 1590. L(2,
1 lacks A4).O³¹.BODMER. Juel-Jensen(imp.).; HN.CH.
IND.NY.TEX.+
22540 — [Anr. ed.] Now since the first edition augmented and
ended. [*Ed.*] (H. S[anford].) fol. [*J. Windet*] *f. W.
Ponsonbie,* 1593. L.C.BELVOIR. Juel-Jensen. Viscount
De L'Isle.+; F.HN.HD.NY.PML.+
22541 — [Anr. ed.] Now the third time published, with sundry
new additions of the author. fol. [*R. Field*] *f. W.
Ponsonbie,* 1598. L.O.C.BIRM.M.+; F.HN.HD.N.Y.+
22542 — [Anr. ed.] Now the third time published. fol. *Edinburgh,
R. walde-graue,* 1599. L.C²(tp def.).C¹³.E. Juel-
Jensen.+; F.CH.CHI.HD.NY.+
Printed for clandestine sale in England below
Ponsonby's price. *See* Greg, *Register B,* pp. 80,
82, 83, 87; and *The Library,* I (1900), pp. 195–
205.
22543 — [Anr. ed.] Now the fourth time published. fol. [*G. Eld
a. H. Lownes*] *f. S. Waterson,* 1605. Ass'd 3 se. 1604.
L.L.L³⁰.O.C⁴.LEEDS.+; F.CHI.ILL.WEL.Y.+
Eld pr. quires A–Aa; Lownes the rest.
22543a — [A variant, w. imprint:] *f. M. Lownes,* 1605. Ent. to S.
Waterson a. M. Lownes 5 no. 1604. L.C⁴. Juel-
Jensen.; F.HN.CH.HD. Indiana State U.
22544 — [Anr. ed.] Now the fourth time published. fol. *H.
L[ownes] f. S. Waterson,* 1613. L.L³⁸.C.G⁴.LEIC².+;
F.HN.HD.N.PN.+
Omits Sanford's preface and has 2 inserted leaves,
the 1st signed Ee5: 'Thus far the worthy Author'
and the second signed Ss11 with 'A dialogue
betweene two Shepherds.' John Buxton's copy and
one HD have 22544a.3 (*S.1*) inserted after Ee4.
22544a — [A variant, w. imprint:] *H. L[ownes] f. M. Lownes,*
1613. L³⁰.O.O³².SHR. Juel-Jensen.+; F.HN.CH.HD.Y.+
The SHR, Juel-Jensen, and CH copies have 22544a.5
(*S.2*) inserted after Ee4.
22544a.3 — — [Sir William Alexander's Supplement. *S.1.* ¶1ʳ
begins:] 'Thus the fire of rage. . . .' [Init. S. W. A.]
fol. [*W. Stansby f. W. Barrett?* 1617?] Ent. to W.
Barrett 31 au. 1616. L.O.E.LEEDS.LIV³.+; HN.DAR(w.
22546).HD(2, 1 w. 22544).ILL(2, 1 w. 22545.7).Y(2, w.
22545.5, 22545.7).+
10 leaves, the first 3 of which are foliated: '335',
'334', '335'. Copies listed above are bd. w. 22546a,
except as noted.
22544a.5 — — [Anr. ed. *S.2.* ¶1ʳ begins:] 'The fire of rage. . . .'
fol. [*W. Stansby f. W. Barrett?* 1617?] L(w. 22546).
O⁷(w. 22546).C³(w. 22546a).SHEF(w. 22545.7).+; F
(w. 22546a).CH(w. 22544a).TEX(w. 22545.7).
10 leaves without pagination or foliation.

Sidney, *Sir Philip*—*cont.*

22544a.7 —— [Anr. ed. *S.3.* 'Ee2ʳ' begins:] 'A supplement of the said defect by Sir W. A.' fol. [*Dublin*, 1621.] Ass'd to M. Lownes 22 mr. 1619. L.O.C.D.M.+; F.HN.HD. ILL.TEX.+

    10 leaves, paged 327–46. Found only w. 22545, except in rare cases, e.g. Juel-Jensen copy of 22545.5, the BRISTOL copy of 22545.7.

22545 — The countesse of Pembrokes Arcadia. Now the fift time published. Also a supplement. By sir W. Alexander. fol. *Dublin, Soc. of Statrs.*, 1621. L.O.C.D. M.+; F.HN.HD.ILL.TEX.+

    See Court-Book C, pp. 116, 141 (2 items), 170. Includes Sanford's preface. Copies w. the Dublin tp all have 22544a.7 (*S.3*) inserted after Ee1.

22545.5 — [Anr. issue, w. cancel tp:] Now the sixt time published. *H.* L[*ownes*] *f. S. Waterson a. M. Lownes*, 1622. Juel-Jensen(w. *S.3*).; BO²(imp., lacks Supplement). Y(w. *S.1*).

22545.7 — [Anr. issue, w. cancel tp:] Now the sixt time published. *H.* L[*ownes*] *f. S. Waterson*, 1622. O¹².BRISTOL.M⁴ (imp.).SHEF.; ILL.MCG.TEX.Y. Amherst C.

    TEX has *S.2*; O¹², BRISTOL have *S.3*; the rest have *S.1*, except SHEF, Amherst which were not checked.

22546 — [Anr. issue, w. variant cancel tp:] Now the sixt published. *H.* L[*ownes*] *f. M. Lownes*, 1622. L.O⁷ (lacks tp)*. Juel-Jensen.; F.DAR.N.

    F, DAR have *S.1*; the rest *S.2*.

22546a — [Anr. issue, w. cancel tp:] Now the sixt time published. *H.* L[*ownes*] *f. M. Lownes*, 1623. L.O.C³.E.LIV³.+; F. HN.HD.ILL.

    c³, 1 Juel-Jensen, John Buxton, F have *S.2*; the rest *S.1*.

22547 — [Anr. ed.] Now the sixt time published, with some new additions. Also a supplement by sir W. Alexander. (A sixth booke, by R. B[eling] of Lincolnes Inne Esquire.) fol. *W. S*[*tansby a.*] (*H.* L[*ownes*] *a. R. Y*[*oung,*]) *f. S. Waterson*, 1627 (1628.) M. Lownes' part ass'd to T. Lownes 10 ap.; to H. Lownes a. R. Young 30 my. 1627. L.L².O.C.DUR⁵.+; F.HN.CU.HD(imp.).N.+

    Beling's text reprinted from 1805. Stansby pr. prelims. and A–H; Lownes and Young the rest.

22548 — [Anr. issue, w. cancel tp:] Now the seventh time published, with some new additions. With the supplement by sir W. A. Whereunto is now added a sixth booke, by R. B. of Lincolnes Inne, Esq. *H.* L[*ownes*] *a. R. Y*[*oung,*] *sold by S. Waterson*, 1629. H. Lownes' part ass'd to G. Cole a. G. Latham 6 no. 1628; to R. Young 6 de. 1630. L.O.; HD(lacks Sidney's dedic.).

22548a — [A variant, w. imprint:] *H.* L[*ownes*] *a. R. Y*[*oung,*] *sold by R. Moore*, 1629. O.C.E.RGU. Juel-Jensen.+; HN.HD.N.PN.Y.+

22549 — [Anr. ed.] Now the eighth time published. fol. [*R. Young*] *f. S. Waterson a. R. Young* [*a.*] (*T. D*[*ownes,*]) 1633. L.O.ETON.M.NEK.+; F.HN.CHI.HD.NY.+

22550 — [Anr. ed.] Now the ninth time published, with a twofold supplement . . . the one by Sʳ W. A. knight; the other, by Mʳ Ja. Johnstoun Scoto-Brit. fol. [*R. Young a. T. Harper*] *f. S. Waterson a. R. Young* [*a.*] (*T. D*[*ownes,*]) 1638. S. Waterson's part ass'd to J. Waterson 19 au. 1635. L.O.C.INN.NMU.+; F.HN.HD. N.PML.+

    Harper pr. quires A–O; Young the rest. Juel-Jensen has a frag. w. variant tp; line 11: 'dedilcated [*sic*]' for 'dedicated' and 'Roung' for 'R. Young'. The prelims. are also in an earlier setting; recto catchword of dedic.: 'rest' instead of 'growne'; and recto catchword of preface: 'that' instead of 'To'.

— The defence of poesie. 1595. *See* 22535.

— *tr. See* 18149.

22551 — Exequiæ illustrissimi equitis, D. Philippi Sidnaei, gratissimae memoriae ac nomini impensæ. [In verse. Ed. W. Gager.] 4°. *Oxonii, ex off. J. Barnesii*, 1587. L.L².O.C.SHR.+; F.HN.CH. Lewis.

22552 — Peplus. Illustrissimi viri D. Philippi Sidnaei supremis honoribus dicatus. [In verse. Ed. J. Lloyd.] 4°. *Oxonii, J. Barnesius*, 1587. L.L².O.C².YK.+; F.HN. CH.HD(cropt).

— For laments on Sidney's death, *see* 3633, 4473, 5228, 6409, 15224, 19871, 23077, 25349.

Siecken troost. Der Siecken troost. 1566. *See* 5600.5.

Sierra, Pedro de la. *See* 18866.

Sighs. The sighes of Fraunce. 1610. *See* 13140.

Signs. The generall signes of Christs comming. [c. 1625.] *See* 14549.

— The signes that doe declare a person to be infected with the pestilence. [1625.] *See* 7021.3.

22553 **Silesio, Mariano.** The Arcadian princesse; or, the triumph of justice. Faithfully rendred to the originall Italian copy, by R. Brathwait. 8°. *T. Harper* [*a. Eliot's Court Press*] *f. R. Bostocke*, 1635. Ent. 19 oc. 1634. L.L³⁰.O.C(lacks *1).ETON.+; F.HN.HD.N.NY.+ Eliot's Court Press pr. quires Aa–Qq; Harper the rest.

Silva, Marcos da. The chronicle and institution of the order of S. Francis. 1618. *See* 11314.2.

— The life of the glorious virgin S. Clare. 1622. *See* 5350.

Silvayn, Alexander. *See* 4182.

22554 **Silver, George.** Paradoxes of defence, wherein is proued the true grounds of fight to be in the short auncient weapons. 4°. [*R. Field*] *f. E. Blount*, 1599. Ent. 30 ja. L.O.; F.HN.HD.Y.

Silvester, Joshua. *See* Sylvester, J.

22555 **Simeon,** *Metaphrastes.* Vitæ sanctorum euangelist. Johannis, & Lucæ, traductæ à R. Bretto. *Gr. a. Lat.* 8°. *Oxoniæ, ex off. J. Barnesii, veneunt Londini* [*by J. Broome,*] 1597. L.O.C.ETON.USHAW.+; F.HN.Y.

Simler, Josias. *See* 24668.

— *ed. See* 24671.

— *tr. See* 4078.

22555.5 **Simon.** A country new jigge betweene Simon and Susan. *Ballad.* 2 pts. s.sh.fol. *W. J*[*ones, c.* 1620.] c⁶.

22556 — [Anr. ed.] 2 pts. s.sh.fol. [*M. Flesher*] *f. H. Gosson,* [c. 1625.] c⁶.

22557 **Simon [Appleby],** *the Anker of London Wall.* The fruyte of redempcyon. 4° 8·4. (*W. de Worde,* 1514.) L.C. Sometimes attrib. to R. Whitford.

22558 — [Anr. ed.] 4° 8·4. (*W. Worde* [sic, no 'de'], 1417 [i.e. 1517.]) C.M.

22559 — [Anr. ed.] 4° 4·6. (*W. de Worde,* 1530 (21 my.)) L.; St. Mary's Seminary, Perryville, Missouri. (Formerly also 11407)

22559.5 — [Anr. ed.] 8°. (*R. Redman,* 1531.) M.

22560 — [Anr. ed.] 4°. (*W. de Worde,* 1532.) L.

Simon, *of Cologne.* The mirror of alchimy. 1597. *See* 1182.

22561 **Simotta, George.** A theater of the planetary houres for all dayes of the yeare. *Tr.* out of Greeke, into French, and now into English. 4°. *A. Matthewes, sold by G. Baker.* 1631. Ent. to G. Baker 23 jn. L(2).L¹⁰.O.C⁹.A.; HN.NLM.Y.

Simpell, Robert. *See* Sempill, R.

22562 **Simpson, Nathaniel.** N. S[impson] arithmeticæ compendium. Cui adjicitur arithmeticorum Aʼναμνήστης A. G[il, *the younger.*] 8°. [*T. Purfoot,*] 1623. L.

22563 **Simson, Andrew,** *Minister.* An exposition upon the second epistle generall of saint Peter. With two tables. 4° in 8's. *T. Cotes f. J. B*[*ellamy,*] *sold by B. Allen,* 1632. Ent. to Bellamy a. F. Clifton 24 ja. 1631; to Bellamy 29 no. 1631. L.L².O.E².G².+; F.HN.HD.U. Y.+

    See Court Book C, p. 250.

22564 **Simson, Andrew,** *Schoolmaster.* Rudimenta grammatices. Secunda tantùm: in gratiam iuventutis Scoto-Britannicæ conscripta. Aucta locis innumeris. [Init. M. A. S.] 4°. *Edinburgi, T. Finlason,* 1607. L.

    Collates A⁴; a different work from 15636 and 21438.

22565 **Simson, Archibald.** Christes testament unfolded: or, seaven sermons, on our Lords seaven last words. 8°. *Edinburgh, E. Raban,* 1620. L.C.E.; F.

22565.5 — A godly and fruitfull exposition on the twenty five psalme. 8°. *W. J*[*ones a. G. Eld*] *f. J. Bellamie,* 1622. F.

    An earlier issue w. special tp and dedic. to Mary Erskine, Countess of Mar, of the sheets of Ps. xxv (G4–L4) and Ps. li (Dd6–Mm3) of 22568. The tp is partly the same setting as the sub tp to Ps. xxv in 22568 dated 1623, which precedes a dedic. to William Douglas, Earl of Morton.

Simson, Archibald—*cont.*

22566 — Heptameron, the seven dayes: that is, meditations and prayers, upon the creation. 8°. *Sainct-Andrews, E. Raban*, 1621. L.DEU(lacks tp).E.; HD(imp.).

22567 — Hieroglyphica animalium terrestrium, . . . quæ in scripturis sacris inveniuntur. 4 pts. 4°. *Edinburgi, T. Finlason*, 1622 (1623, 1624.) L.O.C(1–3 only).E.G². + ; F.HN(1–3 only).HD(2–3 only).V.Y. +
    Pt. 1 dated 1622; pts. 2 (Volatilium) and 3 (Natatilium) dated 1623; pt. 4 (Reptilium) called 'Tomus secundus' dated 1624. There is a copy of pts. 1–3 in Salton Kirk Library, The Manse, East Saltoun, East Lothian, which has bd. at the end a proof tp to pt. 2 with 'Hieroglyphicorum [*sic*] volatilium.' O² also has this proof tp.

22567.5 — Nobilissimo et summo heroi, musarum Mecoenati, Alexandro Setono, . . . Eucharisticon de regis & reipublicae, salute. Novemb. V. 1605. [In verse.] s.sh.fol. *Andreapoli, E. Rabanus*, 1621. E.

22568 — A sacred septenarie, or, a godly and fruitful exposition on the seven psalmes of repentance. The second impression. 2 pts. 8°. *W. J[ones, G. Eld, a. J. Dawson] f. J. Bellamie*, 1623. Ent. 12 jn. 1622. L.O.E.G⁴.LINC. + ; F.NY¹¹.
    Eld pr. Ps.vi and xxv; Dawson Ps.xxxii; Jones the rest. Pts. of this issued earlier as 22565.5.

22569 — [Anr. ed.] 4°. *T. Paine f. J. Bellamie*, 1638. L.O.C.E. LYU. + ; F.HN.HD.U.Y. +

22570 — Samsons seaven lockes of haire: allegorically expounded. 8°. *Sainct-Andrewes, E. Raban*, 1621. L. DEU.E.; HD.
    — *ed. See* 23598, 23599.

22571 **Simson, Edward.** Edwardi Simsonî Mosaica: sive chronici historiam catholicam complectentis pars prima. Huic accessit Parasceve ad chronicon catholicum. 4°. *Cantabrigiæ, ex acad. typog.*, 1636. O.C. C³.D.SAL. +

22571.5 **Simson, Leonard.** The third step of the ladder to repentaunce: most needefull for this time present. 8°. [*J. Charlewood*] *f. T. Hacket*, 1585. YK.

Simson, Patrick. *See* Symson, P.

22572 **Sin.** Whether it be mortall sinne to transgresse ciuil lawes. [1570?] Now = 10391.5.

22573 **Singer, John.** Quips upon questions. 1600. Now = 775.5.

22574 **Singleton, Isaac.** The downefall of Shebna: together with an application to the bloudie Gowrie of Scotland. In two sermons. 4°. [*Eliot's Court Press*] *f. J. Bill*, 1615. Ent. 10 jn. L.O.C.D.G². + ; F.HN.HD.

22575 **Singleton, Robert.** A sermon preached at Poules Crosse . . . 1535. 4°. (*T. Godfraye,*) [1536]. LINC.
    — *tr. See* 909.5.

22576 **Sinner.** The sinners redemption. Wherein is described the blessed nativity of our Lord Jesus Christ. *Ballad.* 2 pts. s.sh.fol. [*f. J. Wright?* 1634?] Ent. to J. Wright, jun., 13 de. 1634. L.

22577 — [Running title:] The sinners sacrifice. [Collection of prayers.] 16° in 8's. (*Widdow Simson f. T. Pavier*, 1601.) Ent. 4 au. 1600. O(tp in pen facs.).
    B1ʳ has heading: 'The sinner to his sad soule'.

22578 — The sinners salvation: resolving . . . what course a poore soule should take that hee may be saved [on Acts xvi.31. By T. Hooker?] 12°. [*M. Flesher*] *f. R. Dawlman*, 1638. Ent. as by T. H. 13 no. 1637. L⁴.
    Collates A–C¹² D². *See* note to 23240.

22579 — The sinners supplication. Confessing his sins. *Ballad.* 2 pts. s.sh.fol. *f. H. Gosson*, [c. 1630.] L.

Sion. *See* Zion.

22579.5 **Sir.** Good sir, you wrong your britches, pleasantly discoursed by a witty youth, and a wily wench. *Ballad.* 2 pts. s.sh.fol. [*G. Purslowe*] *f. J. T[rundle, c. 1620.*] C⁶.

22580 **Sirectus, Antonius.** Formalitates Antonij sirecti summi ac preclari Parisien̄. theologi de mente Joannis duns Scoti . . . cum novis additionibus magistri Mauritii de portu hybernie . . . nouiter impresse. 4°. (*per me w. de worde*) *venūdantur in universitate Oxoniēn. ab H. Jacobi bibliopole Londoniēn.*, [1513?] L(imp.). O.O¹⁴(A1, 2 only).

22581 **Sisters.** The three divine sisters. 1616. *See* pt. 3 of 125.

22581 — The two loving sisters. *Ballad.* 2 pts. s.sh.fol. *f. E. B[lackmore*, 1631.] Ent. to E. Blackmore 4 no. 1631. L.

Sixesmith, Thomas, *ed. See* 3627, 3628.

22582 **Sixtus IV,** *Pope.* FRater Johannes kendale. [Indulgence, singular issue. 1480.] Now = Indulgences 107.

22582a — [Anr. ed.] [1480.] Now = Indulgences 108.

22583 — [Anr. ed.] [1480.] Now = Indulgences 109.

22584 — [Frater Johannes Kendale. Indulgence, plural issue. 1480.] Now = Indulgences 110.

22585 — [Anr. ed.] [1480.] Now = Indulgences 111.

— [J]Ohannes Abb⟨as⟩ Abendoñ [etc. 1476.] *See* Indulgences 106.

22586 — IOhannes de giglis [etc. Indulgence, singular issue. 1481.] Now = Indulgences 112.

22587 — IOhannis de giglis [etc. Indulgence, plural issue. 1481.] Now = Indulgences 113.

22588 — [c8ʳ:] Finiunt sex q̃elegantissime epistole, quarum tris a Sixto Quarto ad illustrissimum Venetiarum ducem Johannem Mocenigum totidemq̃ ab ipso conscripte sunt, . . . emendate per P. Cāmelianū [i.e. Carmelianum.] 4°. (*westmonasterio, per w. Caxton,*) [1483, after 14 fb.] L. Duff 371.
    — *See also* Indulgences 19.

22589 **Sixtus V,** *Pope.* The brutish thunderbolt. 1586. Now = 13843.5.

22590 — A declaration of the sentence and deposition of Elizabeth, the vsurper and pretensed quene of Englande. s.sh.fol. [*Antwerp, A. Conincx*, 1588.] L.O.
    A&R 770. Prob. drawn up by Cardinal Wm. Allen.

22591 — An oration of pope Sixtus the fifth. 1590. = 14002.
    — Antisixtus. 1590. *See* 14001 sqq.
    — Martine Mar-Sixtus. 1591. *See* 24913.
    — *See also* 25076.

22592 **Skay, John.** A friend to navigation plainely expressing to the capacity of the simpler sor⟨t⟩ the same art. 4°. *T. C[otes,]* 1628. L².C⁶.

Skeffington, *Sir* **William.** *See* Indulgences 55A.

22593 **Skelton, John.** A ballade of the scottysshe kynge. [Anon. In verse.] 4° in 2. [*R. Faques*, 1513.] L.
    A revised version is pr. in 22598.

22594 — Here after foloweth the boke of Phyllyp Sparowe. [In verse.] 8°. [*R. Copland f.*] (*R. Kele,*) [1545?] L. O(lacks tp).; HN.CH.PFOR.

22595 — [Anr. ed.] Here after foloweth a litle booke, of Phillyp Sparow. 8°. [*W. Copland f.*] (*J. wyght,*) [1554?] L.

22595.5 — [A variant, w. colophon:] [*W. Copland f.*] (*R. Toy,*) [1554?] O⁷.; PFOR.

22596 — [Anr. ed.] 8°. [*J. Day f.*] (*A. Kitson,*) [1558?] L.E.

22596a — [A variant, w. colophon:] [*J. Day f.*] (*A. Veale,*) [1558?] L.; HN.

22596b — [A variant, w. colophon:] [*J. Day f.*] (*J. Walley,*) [1558?] PFOR. Arthur Houghton.

22597 — Here begynneth a lytell treatyse named the bowge of courte. [Anon. In verse.] 4° in 6's. (*westmynster, W. the worde,*) [1499?] E. Duff 372.

22597.5 — [Anr. ed.] 4° ⁶·⁴. (*W. de worde,*) [c. 1510.] C.

22598 — Here after foloweth certayne bokes, cōpyled by mayster Skelton. Speke parrot The deth of kyng Edwarde the fourth. A treatyse of the Scottes. Ware the hawke The tunnyng of Elynour Rummynge. [In verse.] 8°. *R. Lant f. H. Tab,* [1545?] L.O⁷.; HN.N. PFOR(imp.).

22599 — [Anr. ed.] 8°. (*J. kynge a. T. Marche,*) [1554?] L.; HN. PFOR. Arthur Houghton.

22600 — [Anr. ed.] 8°. *J. Day,* [1563?] L.O(imp.).E(lacks D8).; N(imp.).PFOR.Y.
    (Formerly also 22606)

22600.5 — Here after foloweth a lytell boke called Collyn Clout. [In verse.] 8°. (*T. Godfray,*) [1531?] Woburn Abbey, Bedfordshire.

22601 — [Anr. ed.] 8°. [*R. Copland f.*] (*R. Kele,*) [1545?] L.O.; HN.NY.PFOR.

22602 — [Anr. ed.] 8°. [*W. Copland f.*] (*J. Wyghte,*) [1554?] L.; HN.

22602.5 — [A variant, w. colophon:] [*W. Copland f.*] (*T. Marshe,*) [1554?] O⁷.

22603 — [Anr. ed.] 8°. [*J. Day f.*] (*A. Kytson,*) [1558?] L.E (imp.).; F(imp.).HN.

22603a — [A variant, w. colophon:] [*J. Day f.*] (*A. Veale,*) [1558?] HN.

Skelton, John—*cont.*

22603b — [A variant, w. colophon:] [*J. Day f.*] (*J. Wallye,*) [1558?] L(lacks tp).; Arthur Houghton.

22604 — Here folowythe dyuers balettys and dyties solacyous. [In verse.] 4°. [*J. Rastell,* 1528?] HN.

— An elegy on the death of Henry the Seventh. 1509.] *See* 13075.

22605 — The epitaffe of Iasper late duke of Beddeforde. [Erroneously attrib. to Skelton.] [1496.] = 14477.

22606 — = 22600.

22607 — Magnyfycence, a goodly interlude and a mery. fol. [*Southwark, P. Treveris f. J. Rastell,* 1530?] L(lacks tp).O(G2, 3 only).C. Greg 11.

— [Old Christmas. An interlude.] 1533. *See* 18793.5.

22608 — Pithy pleasaunt and profitable workes of maister Skelton. Nowe collected and newly published (by J. S[tow]) 1568. [In verse.] 8°. *T. Marshe,* [1568.] Ent. 1566–67. L.O.C⁶.ETON(imp.).NOR².+; F(imp.).HN.N. NY.Y.+

22609 — Honorificatissimo, amplissimo, . . . A replycacion agaynst certayne yong scolers. [In verse.] 4° ⁶·⁴. (*R. Pynson,*) [1528.] C⁴(lacks tp).; HN. Queen's U.

22610 — A ryght delectable tratyse vpon a goodly garlande or chapelet of laurell. [In verse.] 4°. (*R. faukes,* 1523 (3 oc.)) L.

22611 — Skelton laureate agaynste a comely coystrowne. [In verse.] 4°. [*J. Rastell,* 1527?] HN.

22611.5 — [The tunning of Elinor Rumming. In verse.] 4°. [*W. de Worde,* 1521?] L.O(missing).C.; F.HN.HD. HD has 4 leaves of quire B; other locations have 2 leaves from the same quire.

22612 — [Anr. ed.] 1609. = pt. of 19936.

22613 — = 22614.

22614 — [Anr. ed.] Elynour Rummin, the famous ale-wife of England. 4°. [*B. Alsop*] *f. S. Rand,* 1624. O(2 imp.).; HN. (Formerly also 22613)

22615 — Here after foloweth a lytell boke, whiche hath to name, why come ye nat to courte. [In verse.] 8°. [*R. Copland f.*] (*R. kele,*) [1545?] L.; HN.CH.N.PFOR. Copies vary: with (HN,N,PFOR) or without (L,CH) woodcuts on A1ᵛ.

22616 — [Anr. ed.] 8°. [*W. Copland f.*] (*R. Toy,*) [1554?] L (imp.).O⁷(imp.).

22616.5 — [A variant, w. colophon:] [*W. Copland f.*] (*J. Wyght,*) [1554?] HN. (Formerly 22617b)

22617 — [Anr. ed.] 8°. [*J. Day f.*] (*A. Kytson,*) [1558?] L.E (imp.).*.; Robert Taylor.

22617a — [A variant, w. colophon:] [*J. Day f.*] (*A. Veale,*) [1558?] O.; PFOR.

22617a.5 — [A variant, w. colophon:] [*J. Day f.*] (*J. Wallye,*) [1558?] PFOR. Arthur Houghton.

22617b — Now = 22616.5.

22618 — Merie tales newly imprinted & made by master Skelton. 8°. *T. Colwell,* [1567.] Ent. 1566–67. HN.

22619 — A Skeltonicall salutation, or condigne gratulation, and just vexation of the Spanishe nation. (A question annexed, touching our sea-fishe.) [Poems in Eng. a. Lat. in Skelton's style about the Spanish Armada.] 4°. Oxford, *J. Barnes,* sold [*by T. Cooke in London,*] 1589. L².M.; F.HN.

22620 — [Anr. ed.] 4°. [*T. Orwin*] *f. T. Cooke,* 1589. L.O(3). LINC.; F(lacks tp).HN. Robert Taylor.

22621 **Skelton, John,** *of Peterhouse, Cambridge.* A mirror of modestie. (A monument of mortalitie.) 1621. Now = pts. 4 and 1 of 6427.5.

Skene, Gilbert. *See* Skeyne, G.

22622 **Skene, Sir John.** De verborum significatione. 1597. = pt. of 21877.

22623 — Second edition. 1599. = pt. of 21877.5.

22624 — Regiam majestatem Scotiæ veteres leges et constitutiones, recognitae, et notis illustratæ, operâ J. Skenaei. fol. *Edinburgi, T. Finlason,* 1609. L.O.C.D. E.+; F.HN.CH.CHI.CU.+ *See also* 11905.

22625 — [Anr. issue, w. cancel tp, w. imprint:] *ap. J. Billium,* 1613. L.O.C.DUR(Bamb.).E.+; F.HN.BO².CU.MICH.+

22626 — [A trans.] Regiam majestatem. The auld lawes and constitutions of Scotland. Tr. Be Sʳ. J. Skene. Quhereunto are adjoined twa treatises, the ane, anent the order of proces . . . the other of crimes, and

Skene, Sir John—*cont.* judges in criminall causes. fol. *Edinburgh, T. Finlason,* 1609. L.O.C.D.E.+; F.HN.HD.N.NY.+

— ed. *See* 21877, 21892.

22626.5 **Skeyne, Gilbert.** Ane breue descriptioun of the pest quhair in the causis, signis and sum speciall preseruatioun and cure thairof ar contenit. 8°. *Edinburgh, R. Lekpreuik,* 1568. E.

— Ane breif descriptioun of the qualiteis of the well. 1580. *See* 6767.

Skialetheia. Skialethia. 1598. *See* 12504.

22627 **Skinker, Tannakin.** A certaine relation of the hogfaced gentlewoman called mistris T. Skinker. 4°. *J. O[kes,]* sold *by F. Grove,* 1640. Ent. to Okes 5 de. 1639. L¹⁶. O.G².; HN.NLM.Y. B4ᵛ last line begins: 'the best,'.

22627.5 — [Anr. ed.] 4°. *J. O[kes,]* sold *by F. Grove,* 1640. HD. B4ᵛ last line begins: 'red, is'.

Skinner, Sir John. *See* 23705.

22628 **Skinner, Robert,** *Bp.* A sermon preached before the king at White-hall. 4°. *J. L[egat] f. A. Hebb,* 1634. Ent. 16 de. 1633. L.O.C.D.M.+; F(2).HN.NY.NY¹¹.U.

— *See also* 10145, 10145.3.

Skinner, Vincent, *tr. See* 11996.

Skipwith, Edward, *tr. See* 7312.

22629 **Skory, Edmund.** An extract out of the historie of the last French king Henry the fourth. To which is added his being murdered the 14. of May last 1610. Styl. Rom. With an apprecation [*sic*] for the safeguard of James the first. 4°. *R. Barker,* sold [*by J. Budge,*] 1610. L.O.C.E.G².+; F.HN.CHI.HD.NY.+

22630 **Slander.** A plaine description of the auncient petigree of dame Slaunder. 8°. [*H. Middleton f.*] *J. Harrison,* 1573. L.L².O.

22631 **Slater,** *Master.* The new-yeeres gift: presented at court, from the lady Parvula to little Jefferie [Hudson] . . . wherein is proved little things are better then great. [Microphilus, *pseud.* Attrib. to T. Heywood.] 12°. *N. a. J. Okes,* 1636. Ent. as by Master Slater to J. Okes 6 ap. L(lacks port.).c.Juel-Jensen.; F.HN.HD. PML.WTL. *See also* 13365.5.

22632 — [Anr. issue, w. cancel tp, w. imprint:] *J. O[kes] f. T. Andrewes,* 1638. L.

22633 **Slatyer, William.** Genethliacon. sive, stemma Jacobi . . . as an appendix, belonging to the first part of Palæ-Albion, the pedigree of king James, and king Charles. [In verse, w. engrs.] fol. *G. Miller,* 1630. Ent. 24 jn. L.L³⁰.O.C.E.+; HN.JH².

22634 — The history of Great Britanie to this present raigne. [In *Lat. a. Eng.* verse.] fol. *W. Stansby f. R. Meighen,* (1621.) L.O.C.D.E.+; F.HN.HD.N.NY.+ There is apparently only an engr. tp. Most copies lack the colophon, which is present in O,IC,IF,HD, and Juel-Jensen copies.

22634.5 — [Illustrations to the Book of Genesis. 40 plates engr. by J. van Langeren.] 4°. [*London,* c. 1635.] G²(proof copy).; HD(lacks plates 1, 2, 16). Plate 1: the tp, unfinished and without the title; 2: Latin verse dedics. to Charles I by Slatyer and van Langeren; 3–16: illustrations w. couplets in Latin, Hebrew, Greek, and English; 17–40: illustrations, w. text from the Bible in English.

22635 — Psalmes, or songs of Sion: turned into the language, and set to the tunes of a strange land. Intended for Christmas carols. 12°. *R. Young,* [1631.] C.LINC. Collates A–B¹² C⁶, w. table of tunes on C5,6. Anr. ed. at L,LINC collates A–B¹², has no table, and = Wing S 3985. Ordered burned 9 July 1631; *see Court-Book C,* p. 408. Slatyer reprimanded for 'scandalous table' citing ballad tunes in this, 20 Oct. 1631; *see Reports of Cases in the Court of Star Chamber,* ed. S. R. Gardiner, Camden Soc., 1886, p. 186.

22636 — Θρηνῳδία. Sive Pandionium melos, in perpetuam Annæ nuper Angliæ reginæ memoriam. Elegies and epitaphs. [In verse.] 4°. *J. Beale,* 1619. L.ETON.P.; HN. Slatyer's name in anagram.

Slatyer, William—*cont.*

22636.5 — A type of trew nobilitye or ye armes of a x̄ρtian emblazoned. Exornavit G. Slatyer. J[acob] v[an] L[angeren] fecit. [Engr. w. verses.] s.sh.4°. [*London*, c. 1635.] O.
    See Hind III.271–2.

Slave. The royall slave. 1639. *See* 4717.

Sleidanus, Joannes. *See* Philippson, J.

22637 **Sluys.** The true coppy of a certaine letter from Sluce. Concerning an exployt attempted by the enemie against the said towne. As it was printed at Flushing. [*Tr.*] 4°. *J. R[oberts] f. J. Flasket*, 1606. Ent. 11 jn. O.

Sm., Ra. Great thankes. [1566.] *See* 22644.

22638 **Smalle, Peter.** Mans May or a moneths minde: wherein the libertie of mans minde is compared to the moneth of May. [In verse.] 4°. *G. Purslowe f. S. Rand*, 1615. Ent. 3 se. L.O.

Smart, *Master of Henry VII's Hawks. See* 14477.

22639 **Smart, Peter.** [Heading B1ʳ:] Novemb. 3. 1640. To the honourable, . . . Commons House . . . the humble petition of Peter Smart, a poore prisoner in the Kings Bench [to be freed.] 4°. [*London*, 1640.] L. L³⁸.O.C².E.+; MIN.
    Petition presented 10 Nov. 1640; see *JHC* II.25. Smart had been fined and later imprisoned for 22640.

22640 — A sermon preached in the cathedrall church of Durham. 4°. [*London*,] 1628. L.O.C.DUR.E.+; F.HD.ILL. NY(imp.).U.
    Collates A–E⁴. Printing or circulation of this prohibited by the Scottish Secret Council 15 Sept. 1628; see Cr. 1509 (MS. only).

22640.3 — [Anr. issue, w. added prelims.] The vanitie & downefall of superstitious popish ceremonies: or, a sermon [etc.] Contayning [a] relation of popish ceremonies which J. Cosens hath lately brought into the said cathedrall church. *Edenborough, heyres of R. Charteris* [i.e. *London?*] 1628. L.O.C².BIRM²(K.N.). E⁸.+; F.HN.HD.
    (Formerly 22643) Collates *⁴ A–E⁴. In this and 22640.7, *⁴ is from the same typesetting. In both items *1 is a cancel. In some copies (O,E⁸,HN,HD) A1, the orig. tp, is present; in L,C⁵,F it is lacking (cancelled?).

22640.7 — [Anr. ed.] 4°. *Edenborough, heyres of R. Charteris* [i.e. *London?*] 1628. BUTE.DUL.E.NEK.; F.U(lacks *2–4).
    Collates *⁴ A–C⁴; text begins on A1ʳ.

22641 — [Anr. ed.] A sermon preached in the cathedrall church of Durham. 4°. [*B. Alsop a. T. Fawcet*,] 1640. L.O². C.D².DUR.+; F.HN.HD.N.Y.
    In title: 'CHVRCH'. This and the following collate A–E⁴ and are paginary reprints of 22640.

22641.5 — [Anr. ed.] 4°. [*B. Alsop a. T. Fawcet*,] 1640. O.C³.DUR³. LINC.M⁴.+; CAL.NY¹¹.
    In title: 'CHURCH'.

22642 — A short treatise of altars. 4°. [*London*, 1641.] C²(2). DUR.E.
    Not an STC book; prob. = Wing S 4014.

22643 — The vanitie. Now = 22640.3.

22644 **Smart, Ralph.** Great thankes to the welcome, in Churchyards behalfe. [Init. Ra. Sm.] *Ballad.* s.sh.fol. *A. Lacy f. F. Coldocke*, [1566.] Ent. 1565–66. HN.
    See also 5236.

Smeeton, Thomas. *See* Smeton, T.

22645 **Smell-knave, Simon,** *pseud.* The fearefull and lamentable effects of two comets, which shall appeare in 1591. 4°. *J. C[harlewood] f. J. Busbie*, [1590?] L(tp def.).O.
    The O copy has variant spelling 'Buzbie' in imprint.

Smerte, *Maister de ouzeaus. See* 14477.

22645.5 **Smethwike, Thomas.** A motion to the East India company by T. Smethwike (an adventurer with them) upon the reasons following. [Proposal to reduce the time ships are delayed in India waiting for a return cargo. 19 Feb. 1628(o.s.)] s.sh.fol. [*London*, 1629.] L⁵(Lemon 294).

22646 **Smetius, Heinrich.** Prosodia Henrici Smetii, medicinæ D. promptissima, quæ syllabarum positione & diphthongis carentium quantitates, exemplis demonstrat. 8°. [*R. Field*] *ex typ. Soc. Stat.*, 1615. Ent. to the English Stock 21 no. 1614. L.O.; HN.

22647 — [Anr. ed.] 8°. [*F. Kingston?*] *ex typ. Soc. Stat.*, 1622. Ent. to the English Stock 5 mr. 1620. C.; HN.

22648 — [Anr. ed.] 8°. [*W. Stansby*] *ex typ. Soc. Stat.*, 1628. L.L².L⁴.DUL. Warrington PL.; F.

— Editio decimatertia. *See* 22649.5.

22649 — [Anr. ed.] Ab auctore reformata, emendata, & quarta sui parte adaucta. Editio decimaquarta. Prioribus correctior. Cum appendice. 8°. [*F. Kingston*,] *imp. Soc. Stat.*, 1635. L.O.C⁵(imp.).D².G².+; CHI.HD.Y. Williams C.

22649.5 — Editio decimatertia [*sic*]. 8°. *G. M[iller] pro Soc. Stat.*, 1640. O⁶(lacks all after Ss2).
    Collates:)(⁸)⁚( )⁚(⁸)⁚( )⁚(⁴ A–Rr⁸ Ss⁴? Apparently reprinted from a Continental ed., prob. German.

22650 — Editio decimaquinta. 8°. [*F. Kingston*] *imp. Soc. Stat.*, 1640. L.O¹⁴.C.BTL.DUL.+; F.HN.BO².

22651 **Smeton, Thomas.** Ad virulentum Archibaldi Hamiltonii apostatæ dialogum, de confusione Caluinianæ sectæ apud Scotos, impiè conscriptum orthodoxa responsio. 4°. *Edinburgi, ap. J. Rosseum, pro H. Charteris*, 1579. L.O.C.D.E.+; F.HN.CH.HD.U.

22652 **Smiglecki, Marcin.** Logica Martini Smiglecii . . . selectis disputationibus illustrata, et in duos tomos distributa: in qua quicquid in Aristotelico Organo pertractatur. 4° in 8's. *Oxonii, J. L[ichfield,] imp. H. Crypps, E. Forrest, & H. Curteyne*, 1634. L.O.C.D².E².+; HN.BO².CHI.TORONTO².Y.+

22653 — [Anr. ed.] 4° in 8's. *Oxoniæ, G. Turner pro H. Crips, E. Forrest, H. Curteyne, & J. Wilmot*, 1638. L³.O.C².A. M⁴.+; F.HN.PH.Y. Redwood Library, Newport, R.I.

22653.3 **Smit, Hans.** [Advertisements, with directions for use, for 8 different medicines: laxatives, salves, worm powder, etc. Some begin: 'This master hath brought with him . . .', and each is signed: 'By me M. Hans Smit.'] s.sh.fol. [*London*, c. 1570.] Y(imp.).
    Prob. intended to be cut up to accompany each item sold.

22653.5 **Smith.** [The smith that forged him a new dame. In verse.] 4° in 6's. [*W. de Worde*, c. 1505.] O(leaves 2,5 only, imp.).
    Verso of leaf 2, line 28: 'He hente her vp than on hye'.

22653.7 — [Anr. ed.] 4°. [*R. Pynson*, c. 1510.] C⁹(frags. of leaves 3,4). Recto of leaf 3, line 5: 'He hent hyr vp than on hye'.

22653.9 — [Anr. ed.] Here begynneth a treatyse of the smyth whych that forged hym a new dame. 4°. (*W. Copland*,) [1565?] O(lacks A3).
    (Formerly 17036) A2ᵛ line 28: 'He hent her vp than on hye'.

22654 **Smith,** *Families of.* A congratulatory poem upon the noble feast made by the ancient and renouned families of the Smiths. *f. F. Smith*, [c. 1680.]
    Not an STC item.

Smith, —, *alias* **Norrice.** *See* 18661.

22654.5 **Smith, Edward.** The wofull lamentation of Edward Smith, a poore penitent prisoner in the jayle of Bedford, which he wrote a short time before his death. *Ballad.* 1/2 sh.fol. *f. C. W[right*, c. 1625.] Ent. to ballad ptnrs. 14 de. 1624. C⁶.

22655 — [Anr. ed.] 1/2 sh.fol. *assignes of T. Symcock*, [1628–29.] L.

22655.5 **Smith, Henry,** *Ballad Writer.* The captaine Cut-purse. A new ballad shewing the most notorious abuse of life of J. Selman, who for cutting a purse was executed. (The arraienment condemnation and execution of J. Selman, seventh of January 1612.) *Ballad.* 2 pts. s.sh.fol. [*G. Eld f. J. Wright*, 1612.] Ent. to J. Wright 9 ja. 1612. C⁶(I.130–1ᵛ).
    This has 11089 pr. on the verso. *See also* 22182a.5.

Smith, Henry, *Minister.*

Single Works

22656 — The affinitie of the faithfull: being a sermon, made vpon part of the eight chapter of Luke. 8°. *W. Hoskins, [J. Danter,] a. H. Chettle f. N. Ling a. J. Busbie*, 1591. Ent. to N. Ling 12 se. L.O.; HN.
    Reprinted in 22718–22 and 22735 sqq.

Smith, Henry, *Minister—Single Works—cont.*

22656.5 — [A variant, w. imprint:] *W. Hoskins a. J. Danter f. N. Ling a. J. Busbie,* 1591. L⁴³. Lord Kenyon.; F.PN².

22657 — [Anr. ed.] Nowe the second time imprinted. 8°. [*T. Scarlet*] *f. N. Ling a. J. Busbie,* 1591. L.
— The benefite of contentation. 1590, etc. *See* 22693 sqq.

22658 — The christians sacrifice. Seene, and allowed. 8°. *T. Orwin f. T. Man,* 1589. Ent. 3 oc. L.L⁴³.O. Lord Kenyon.; F(C1 in facs.).HD.
See Greg, *Register B,* p. 34. Reprinted in 22783.3 and 22718 sqq.

22659 — [Anr. ed.] 8°. [*J. Charlewood*] *f. T. Man,* 1591. L.O.C.; F.CAL.HD(imp.).PN².

22660 — The examination of vsury, in two sermons. Taken by characterie, and after examined. [Init. H. S.] 8°. *R. Field f. T. Man,* 1591. Ent. 4 fb. L.; F(lacks tp). 𝔄
Collates A–C⁸ D⁴; prob. pr. after 22661. Reprinted in 22685–7, 22783.3, and 22718 sqq.

22661 — [Anr. ed.] 8°. *T. Orwin f. T. Man,* 1591.
Collates A² B–E⁸ F⁴; = pt. 3 of 22685.
— [Anr. ed.] 8°. *T. Orwin f. T. Man,* 1591.
Collates H2–8 I–L⁸, with H3 missigned A3; *see* pt. 2 of 22687.

22662 — The fall of king Nabuchadnezzer. 8°. *T. Scarlet,* 1591. Ent. 19 jy. 1591; ass'd to T. Man 10 ap. 1592. L.; HD(quires B–C only).PN².
Running titles in all quires. Reprinted in 22783.7 and 22718 sqq.

22662.5 — [Anr. ed.] 8°. *T. Scarlet, (sold by W. Wright,)* 1591. O. Lord Kenyon.; HN.HD(quire A only).
No running titles.

22663 — The first sermon of Noahs drunkennes. 8°. [*E. Allde? f.*] *W. Kearney,* 1591. Ent. to C. Burby 28 ap. 1592. L.
On Gen. ix.20–1. Reprinted in 22718–19, 22747.3 sqq., and 22781 sqq.

22664 — A fruitfull sermon, [on 1 Thess. v.19–22.] Which sermon being taken by characterie, is now published. 8°. (*W. Hoskins, H. Chettle, a. J. Danter*) *f. N. Ling,* 1591. Ent. 18 au. L.L³⁰.L⁴³.O. Lord Kenyon.; F.PN².
Reprinted as 'The true trial' in 22718 sqq.

22665 — [Anr. ed.] 8°. [*W. Hoskins, H. Chettle, a. J. Danter*] *f. widdowe Broome,* 1591. L.

22666 — Gods arrowe against atheists. 4°. *J. Danter, sold by W. Barley,* 1593. Ent. to Danter 5 mr. L.O.C²(imp.).E⁴.; LC.
Extracts from chap. 5 are pr. in 18582.

22667 — [Anr. ed.] 4° in 8's. *F. K[ingston] f. T. Pavier,* 1604. Ent. 14 au. 1600. L.L³⁰.O.C.G².+ ; F.HN.HD.U.Y.
This and the following eds. usually bd. w. 22725 sqq.

22667.5 — [Anr. ed.] 4° in 8's. *R. B[radock] f. T. Pavier,* 1607. L.O²⁵. Stevens Cox.; F.ILL.NY¹¹.U.

22668 — [Anr. ed.] 4° in 8's. *F. K[ingston] f. T. Pavier,* 1609. L.O.C.BRISTOL².M.+ ; F.HD.ILL.MICH.U.+

22669 — [Anr. ed.] 4° in 8's. *F. K[ingston] f. T. Pavier,* 1611. L.O.C.C³.M⁴.+ ; HN.LC.N.STAN.

22670 — [Anr. ed.] 4° in 8's. *H. L[ownes] f. T. Pavier,* 1614. L.O.C.C³.; F.HN.CHI.HART.U.

22671 — [Anr. ed.] 4° in 8's. *F. K[ingston] f. T. Pavier,* 1617. L.O(3).BRISTOL.BTL.NLW.; F.HN.CHI.HD.TORONTO².+
G⁴ in 2 settings: p. 89, line 13 ends w. semicolon or w. comma; both at O.

22672 — [Anr. ed.] 4° in 8's. *F. K[ingston] f. T. Pavier,* 1622. L.O³⁹.C².BIRM.D.; F.HN.HD.MCG.NY.+

22673 — [Anr. ed.] 4° in 8's. *G. M[iller] f. E. Brewster a. R. Bird,* 1628. Ass'd 4 au. 1626. L.O.NLW.OS. Leicester PL.+ ; F(2).HN.ILL.Cincinnati U. Weissman.

22674 — [Anr. ed.] 4° in 8's. *G. M[iller] f. E. Brewster a. R. Bird,* 1631. L.C.; F.SMU.

22675 — [Anr. ed.] 4° in 8's. *J. H[aviland] f. E. Brewster a. R. Bird,* 1632. O.O¹⁰.C.; F.HD.ILL.NY.U.+

22676 — [Anr. ed.] 4° in 8's. *J. H[aviland] f. E. Brewster a. R. Bird,* 1637. O.BTL.LYD.STU.; F.COLG².DAR.

22677 — Jacobs ladder, or the high way to heauen. 4°. *widdow Orwin f. T. Man,* 1595. Ent. 3 mr. L.O⁹.C(tp only, bd. w. 22721).YK.
Reprinted in 22721 sqq.

22677.5 — Jonah, the messenger of Ninevehs repentance, set forth in his calling, rebellion, and punishment. [Init. H. S.] 12°. *G. M[iller] f. G. Edwards,* 1637. O.
(Formerly 21496) An abridgement of the Jonah sermons in 22775.7 to which Edwards now had the rights; cf. 22783.

22678 — Jurisprudentiæ medicinæ et theologiæ, dialogus dulcis. (Vita supplicium. [In verse.]) [*Ed.*] (B. Cavus.) 8°. *J. Danter, imp. T. Man,* 1592. L.O³(imp.).C.D.; F. Vita reprinted from 22712.5.

22679 — The lawiers question. The answere to the lawiers question. The censure of Christ vpon the answere. [Three sermons.] 4°. [*J. Danter*] *f. T. Gosson,* [1595.] Ass'd by T. Gosson to T. Man 5 ap. 1596. L.O⁹.
Reprinted in 22721 sqq.

22680 — The magistrates scripture, which treateth of their election, excellencie, qualities, dutie, and end: with two prayers. [A sermon.] 8°. [*R. Field f.*] *W. Kearney,* 1590. Ent. to T. Man 29 oc. 1591. O(imp.). Lord Kenyon.
Reprinted in 22717, 22783.5, and 22718 sqq.

22681 — [A variant, w. imprint:] [*R. Field f.*] *W. Kearney,* 1591. L(imp.).; F(imp.).*.ILL.

22682 — Maries choise. 1592. = pt. of 22697.

22683 — The poore mans teares, opened in a sermon. (The wedding garment.) 8°. *J. Wolfe, sold by W. Wright,* 1592. First serm. ent. to Wolfe 14 mr. L.O.; F(imp.).HN.
Collates A–H⁸ I². 1st serm. reprinted in 22719 sqq.; for the 2nd serm., *see* 22713.

22684 — The preachers proclamacion. Discoursing the vanity of all earthly things. 8°. [*E. Allde? f.*] *W. Kearney,* 1591. Ent. to T. Man 26 jy. L.
Reprinted as 'The trial of vanity' in 22717, 22783.5, and 22718 sqq.

22685 — A preparatiue to mariage. The summe whereof was spoken at a contract, and inlarged after. Whereunto is annexed a Treatise of the Lords supper, and another of Vsurie. 3 pts. 8°. *T. Orwin f. T. Man,* 1591. Ent. 4 fb. L.O.D(pt. 1 only, imp.).; F.
(Pt. 3 formerly also 22661) The collection collates A–H⁸; A–H⁸ I²; A² B–E⁸ F⁴ and is reprinted in 22718 sqq.

22685.5 — [Anr. ed.] 3 pts. 1591. *See* Addenda.

22686 — [Anr. ed., with Three prayers added.] Newly corrected, and augmented. 8°. *R. Field f. T. Man,* 1591. L(w. pt. 1 of 22685.5).L⁴³.O. Lord Kenyon.; F.
Collates A–R⁸ S⁴. Sub tpp G1ʳ Lords supper; N5ʳ Usury; R1ʳ Three prayers. For Three prayers *see* also 22703.

22687 — [Anr. ed.] 2 pts. 8°. *J. Charlewood* [*a.*] (*T. Orwin*) *f. T. Man,* 1591. L.O(pt. 2 only).C(pt. 2 only, imp.). c³(Usury and M⁴ only).; F(Usury only).CU(Lords supper only).HD.
Collates A–G⁸; A–L⁸ M⁴. 2nd A–L pr. by Orwin has Lords supper (A1–H1) and Usury (H2–L8). M⁴ pr. by Charlewood has Speech and Letter. L, O, and c³ copies have 22703.5, q.v., bd. before M⁴.

22688 — The pride of king Nabuchadnezzar. 8°. *T. Scarlet,* 1591. Ent. 19 jy. 1591; ass'd to T. Man 10 ap. 1592. L.O. Lord Kenyon.; HN.HD(A8 only).
Reprinted in 22783.7 and 22718 sqq.

22689 — [Anr. ed.] 8°. *T. Scarlet, sold by W. Wright,* 1591. L.; PN².

22690 — The restitution of king Nabuchadnezzer. 8°. *T. Scarlet, (sold by W. Wright,)* 1591. Ent. to Scarlet 19 jy. 1591; ass'd to T. Man 10 ap. 1592. L.
Unpaginated. Reprinted in 22783.7 and 22718 sqq.

22691 — [Anr. ed.] 8°. *T. Scarlet, (sold by W. Wright,)* 1591. L(2).O. Lord Kenyon.; HN.HD(imp.).PN².
41 pp.

22692 — Satans compassing the earth. (A sermon preached [on 1 Cor.x.12.]) 8°. *T. Scarlet,* 1592. C(2, 1 imp.).; F(2).NY¹¹(imp.).
See Greg, *Register B,* p. 40. 1st serm. reprinted in 22783.5 and 22718 sqq.; 2nd serm. reprinted as 'Caveat for Christians' in 22718 sqq.

22693 — A sermon of the benefite of contentation. Taken by characterie. 8°. *R. Ward f. J. Proctor,* 1590. L.
Collates A–C⁸ (A1, C7,8 blank?). Has a publisher's address to the reader not found in the following eds. Reprinted in 22783.3, 22718–22, and 22735 sqq.

22694 — [Anr. ed., anon.] The benefit of contentation. Taken by characterie, and examined after. 8°. *R. Ward f. J. Proctor,* 1590. L(4453.a.7).; HD.
Collates A⁴ B–C⁸ (C8 blank).

22694.5 — [Anr. ed., signed.] A sermon of the benefite. . . . 8°. *R. Ward f. H. Car,* 1590. L.
Collates A⁴ B–C⁸ (C8 blank).

22695 — [Anr. ed.] The benefite. . . . 8°. *A. Jeffes f. R. Ward,* 1590. L.BRISTOL².; F.
Collates A–B⁸ C⁴ (A1, C3,4 blank?).

Smith, Henry, *Minister—Single Works—cont.*

22695.5 — [Anr. ed.] 8°. *A. Jeffes,* 1590. C.; HD(A⁸ only).
Tp is A1.

22696 — [Anr. ed.] Newly examined and corrected by the author. 8°. *A. Jeffes,* 1591. L.L⁴³(imp.).O. Lord Kenyon(imp.).; PN².
Collates A–B⁸ C⁴, no blanks. With address to the reader by Smith.

22696.5 — [Anr. ed.] 8° in 4's. *A. Jeffes,* 1561 [i.e. 1591.] F.
Collates A–E⁴, no blanks.

22697 — The sinfull mans search: or seeking of God. Published according to a corrected copie, sent by the author. (Maries choise. With prayers.) 8°. (*T. Scarlet*) *f. C. Burby,* 1592. First serm. ent. to J. Charlewood 26 de. 1588. L(2).O(2).C.; Queen's U(lacks 1st tp).
(2nd serm. formerly also 22682) Both reprinted in 22779, 22747.5 sqq., and 22781 sqq.

22697.5 — [Anr. ed.] 8°. (*T. Scarlet*) *f. C. Burby,* (1593.) L(imp.).
O(2, 1 lacks 1st serm.).C².; F(2, 1 lacks 2nd serm.).
HN(lacks 2nd serm.).HD(frag.).
(Formerly 22700) In 1 F copy the 'S' in 'MANS' in tp line 2 has not pr.

22698 — [Anr. ed.] 8°. *T. S[carlet] f. C. Burby,* 1594. Ass'd to J. Roberts 31 my. L(2, 1 lacks 2nd serm.).P.; F(2).

22698.5 — [Anr. issue, w. imprint:] *T. Scarlet f. C. Burby,* 1594. YK.
Collates A–F⁸.

22699 — [Anr. ed.] 4°. *T. Scarlet f. C. Burby,* 1594. Both sermons ass'd by widow Scarlet to Burby 6 se. 1596. L.O.O⁹.SHEF(imp.).; F(imp.).
Collates A–H⁴.

22700 — Now = 22697.5.

22700.5 — The sinners confession. By Henrie Smith. 8°. [*J. Charlewood*] *f. W. Leake,* 1593. Ent. 18 mr. C²(lacks B8).; F.HD(2).
Reprinted in 22747.3, 22779, 22747.5–22748, 22765 sqq., and 22781 sqq.

22701 — [Anr. ed.] 8°. [*P. Short*] *f. W. Leake,* 1594. L.O.P.; F.HN.

22701.3 — [Anr. ed.] 8°. [*P. Short*] *f. w* [lower case]. *Leake,* 1594. P.

22701.5 — The sinners conuersion. By Henrie Smith. 8°. [*J. Charlewood*] *f. W. Leake,* 1593. Ent. 18 mr. C².; F.HD.
Reprinted in same collections as 22700.5.

22702 — [Anr. ed.] 8°. [*P. Short*] *f. W. Leake,* 1594. L.O.P.; F.HN.

22702.3 — [Anr. ed.] 8°. [*P. Short*] *f. w* [lower case]. *Leake,* 1594. P.

22703 — Three prayers, one for the morning, another for the euening: the third for a sick-man. Whereunto is annexed, a godly letter and a comfortable speech. [Anon.] 8°. [*J. Charlewood?*] *f. T. Man,* 1591. L.; F.HN.
24 pp. Reprinted in 22686–7, 22783.3, and 22719 sqq.

22703.5 — [Anr. ed.] 8°. [*T. Orwin*] *f. T. Man,* 1591. L.O.C³.
16 pp. Calls for Letter and Speech on the tp, but these appear only in M⁴ of 22687, w. which all copies are bd.

22704 — [Anr. ed.] 8°. [*R. Robinson*] *f. T. Man,* 1592. L.O.C.C².
YK.; F(3, 2 imp.).CAL². Queen's U.
Includes the Letter and Speech.

— A treatise of the Lords supper, in two sermons. [Anon.] 8°. *T. Orwin f. T. Man,* 1591.
Collates A–H⁸ I²; *see* pt. 2 of 22685. Pr. in 22685–7 and 22718 sqq.

— [Anr. ed.] 8°. *T. Orwin f. T. Man,* 1591.
Collates A–G⁸ H1; *see* pt. 2 of 22687.

22705 — [Anr. ed.] 8°. *R. Field f. T. Man,* 1591. L.C³.; F(lacks G4). ⅏
Collates A–F⁸ G⁴. A different setting of type from G1–N4 of 22686.

22706 — The trumpet of the soule, sounding to iudgement. 8°. [*E. Allde*] *f. J. Perrin,* 1591. L.L⁴³.O. Lord Kenyon (imp.).
Reprinted in 22719–21, 22747.3 sqq., and 22781 sqq.

22707 — [Anr. ed.] 8°. [*E. Allde*] *f. J. Perrin,* 1592. Ent. to Allde a. Perrin 19 my. F. Queen's U.

22708 — [Anr. ed.] 8° in 4's. *A. Jeffes,* 1592. F.HN.
Tp line 3 ends: 'sound-'.

22708.5 — [Anr. issue, w. first quire reprinted.] *A. Jeffes,* 1592. O.; F.
Tp line 3 ends: 'sounding'.

22709 — [Anr. ed.] 8°. [*J. Charlewood*] *f. the widdow Perrin,* 1593. L.C².; F.

— [Anr. ed., with 3 other sermons. 1595?] *See* 22747.3.

Smith, Henry, *Minister—Single Works—cont.*

22710 — [Anr. ed.] Whereunto is annexed a devout prayer. 8°. *E. All-de,* 1621. Ass'd by Allde to C. Burby 17 fb. 1595, with Allde retaining the right to print; ass'd by widow Burby to N. Bourne 16 oc. 1609. L.; HN (tp only).
See Court Book C, p. 133 and also 22759.

22711 — [Anr. ed.] 8°. *E. A[llde] f. G. Edwards, sold by J. Wright,* 1626. Ass'd by Bourne to G. Edwards, jun., 1 jn. 1624. O³.; F.

22711.5 — [Anr. ed.] 8°. *E[liz.] A[llde] f. G. Edwards,* 1630. HD.

22711.7 — [Anr. ed.] 8°. *E[liz.] A[llde] f. G. Edwards,* 1632. P (imp.).

22712 — [Anr. ed.] 8°. *E. G[riffin] f. G. Edwards,* 1640. L.

22712.5 — Vita supplicium: siue, de misera hominis conditione querela. [Init. H. S. In verse.] 8°. [*T. Orwin,*] *imp. T. Man,* 1590. ?Ent. 1 de. 1589. HN.
Reprinted in 22678; *tr.* in 23581.

22713 — The wedding garment. [Anon.] 8°. [*J. Wolfe?*] *f. W. Wright,* 1590. Ent. 18 my. L.C⁴. Lord Kenyon.; F.HN.
This and all the following eds. have a preface referring to previously pub'd false copies. Reprinted in 22783.3, 22683, 22783.7, and 22718 sqq.

22713.5 — [Anr. ed.] 8°. [*J. Wolfe?*] *f. T. Nelson,* 1590. HD.

22714 — [Anr. ed.] By H. Smith. 8°. [*E. Allde*] *f. W. Wright,* [1590?] L.

22714.5 — [Anr. ed.] 8°. *London,* [*A. Jeffes?*] 1591. F.
A3ᵛ line 2 begins: 'Christ'; A5ʳ last line ends: 'righteousnesse'.

22715 — [Anr. ed.] 8°. *London,* [*A. Jeffes?*] 1591. L.L⁴³.C.
A3ᵛ line 2 begins: 'Christ'; A5ʳ last line ends: 'Christ'.

22715.5 — [Anr. ed.] 8°. *London,* [*A. Jeffes?*] 1591. L.O.; PN².
A3ᵛ line 2 begins: 'christ' (lower case 'c'); A5ʳ last line ends: 'Christ'.

Collections of Sermons

With the exception of Man's first two collections (22716 and 22717), Waldegrave's piracy of the latter (22783.5), and Dexter's group (22775.3), the collections below are almost entirely made up of works previously published separately. As it was not until c. 1600 that the collections evolved to their final composition, it has seemed the most intelligible course to note *under the single works above* in what collections they appear and the bulk of information concerning copyrights. The interrelations of the Burby, Leake, and Dexter collections are so complicated that they are described in some detail below.

(a) Published by T. Man and his assigns

22716 — Seuen godly and learned sermons. Perused by the author before his death. 8°. *R. Field f. T. Man,* 1591. Ent. 26 jy. a. 4 oc. L.L⁴³.O. Lord Kenyon.; F.HD.

22717 — Thirteene sermons vpon seuerall textes of scripture. 8°. [*T. Scarlet a. J. Danter*] *f. T. Man,* 1592. 2 serm. ent. 26 jy. 1591, and 11 serm. ent. 29 oc. 1591. C(imp.).C²(missing). Kent U.; F(2, 1 imp.).NY¹¹.
Quire A pr. by Scarlet; the rest by Danter. Completely different sermons from 22716. Most of these sermons were pirated by Waldegrave in 22783.5.

22718 — The sermons of master Henrie Smith, gathered into one volume. Printed according to his corrected copies in his life time. 8°. *T. Orwin,* [*R. Robinson, a. T. Scarlet?*] *f. T. Man,* 1592. [Pp1ʳ:] (*J. Charlwood f. C. Burby,* 1592.) 4 serm. (22783.7) ass'd by T. Scarlet a. W. Wright to T. Man 10 ap. L.O(3, 1 lacks tp, 1 has tp def.).C(imp.).C²(imp.).M (imp.).+.; F(2 imp.).CAL. Queen's U(imp.).
Reprints 22716, 22717, 22783.7, w. 13 additional sermons, including 1 of Burby's: 22663. Orwin pr. A–Kk and Qqq–Ttt; R. Robinson pr. Rr–Ppp and prob. Oo. Charlewood pr. Ll–Nn, Qq, and 1 setting of Pp, w. his imprint on Pp1 and Pp2ʳ line 8 beginning: '*mids*'. T. Scarlet app. pr. the 2nd setting of Pp, with Pp1 cancelled and Pp2ʳ line 8 beginning: '*des*'; copies of both at O.

22719 — [Anr. ed., w. 4 more sermons.] 8°. *R. Field,* [*T. Orwin a. R. Robinson*] *f. T. Man,* 1593. 3 serm. ent. to J. Wolfe 14 mr. 1592. L.O(imp.).O²⁸(frag.).P(frag.).; HN(imp.).
Orwin pr. Aa–Zz and Nnn–Bbbb; Robinson pr. Aaa–Mmm; Field did the rest.

Smith, Henry, *Minister—Collections—cont.*

22720 — [Anr. ed.] 4° in 8's. *P. Short* [*a. J. Orwin*] *f. T. Man,* 1594. L.O.SHEF(lacks tp).; F.
Page 3 headline: 'mariage.' J. Orwin pr. Aa to end.

22720.5 — [Anr. ed.] 4° in 8's. *P. Short* [*a. J. Orwin*] *f. T. Man,* 1594. O⁹.O¹¹.; BO.
Page 3 headline: 'Mariage.' J. Orwin pr. Aa to end. O⁹ is bd. w. 22677, 22679, 22699, 22776.

22721 — [Anr. issue, w. added quires Ss⁸ Tt⁴ Vv–Xx⁸ Yy⁶, w. imprint on Vv1ʳ:] (*widdow Orwin f. T. Man,* 1595.) O(imp.).O⁹(imp.).C(imp.).
O, C copies lack before B1; O⁹ has A3,4 and the top of A2. All 3 copies are bd. w. 22779. The added sermons are Jacobs Ladder for which only the C copy has an inserted tp (*see* note at 22677); and Lawyers Question (cf. 22679) for which C copy has the tp only.

22722 — [Anr. ed.] large 8°. *F. Kingston* [*a. V. Sims*] *f. T. Man,* 1597. L³⁰.O(lacks Benefit and Affinity).; F(frag.).
Sims pr. Benefit and Affinity, on ¶–¶¶⁸ ¶¶¶².

22723 — [Anr. ed.] 4° in 8's. *F. Kingston f. T. Man,* 1599. L³⁰(imp.).O.M.; HN.CHI.HD.PN².

22724 — [Anr. ed.] 4° in 8's. *F. Kyngston f. T. Man,* 1601. L.O. C.C¹⁹.; F.

22725 — [Anr. ed.] Whereunto is added, Gods arrow against atheists. 4° in 8's. *F. Kyngston f. T. Man,* 1604. L(destroyed).LIV².Finedon.; F.U.
The table of contents of this and the following eds. calls for an ed. of 22737 as well as an ed. of 22667. Since different publishers held the copyrights and all 3 books were not always pr. simultaneously, it has seemed clearer to list eds. of the 3 separately.

22726 — [Anr. ed.] 4° in 8's. *F. Kyngston f. T. Man,* 1607. L.O²⁵.C².; F.ILL.NY¹¹.

22727 — [Anr. ed.] 4° in 8's. *F. Kyngston f. T. Man,* 1609. L.O.C⁴.BRISTOL². St. David's Cathedral, Wales.+; HN.HD.ILL(lacks gen. tp).IND(imp.).U(imp.).

22728 — [Anr. ed.] 4° in 8's. *F. Kyngston f. T. Man,* 1611. L(imp.).L⁴⁶.O.C.C³.+; F.LC. Bryn Mawr C.

22729 — [Anr. ed.] 4° in 8's. *H. Lownes f. T. Man,* 1614. O.C³.C¹⁰.G².; HN.U.

22730 — [Anr. ed.] 4° in 8's. *F. Kyngston f. T. Man,* 1618. L.O.O⁶.NOR².; F.HN.CHI.HD.IND.+

22731 — [Anr. ed.] 4° in 8's. *F. Kyngston f. T. Man,* 1622. L.L⁴⁸.C².E(imp.).NLW.; F.HD(imp.).ILL(imp.).NY.Y.+

22731.5 — [Anr. ed.] 4° in 8's. *F. Kyngston f. R. Meighen, by the assignment of P. a. Jonah Man,* 1628. Ass'd 3 my. 1624. O.NLW(2, 1 = St. Asaph).OS(tp def.).SHEF.; F(2).HD(imp.).TEX.

22732 — [Anr. ed.] 4° in 8's. [*J. Haviland f.*] *the assignes of T., P., a. Jonah Man,* 1631. Jonah Man's share ass'd to B. Fisher 6 jy. 1629. L.L².O.C.M.+; F.HN(lacks gen. tp).HD.ILL.U.+

22733 — No entry.

22734 — [Anr. ed.] 4° in 8's. *T. Harper, by the assignes of Joan Man a. B. Fisher,* 1637. Ass'd to B. Fisher a. widow Man 12 au. 1635. L.O.C¹⁵.LYD.STU.+; F.COLG².DAR.

(b) *Three Sermons published* (1599) *by N. Ling* (1609 *by J. Smethwick*)

22735 — Three sermons made by maister H. Smith. 1. The benefit of contentation. 2. The affinitie of the faithfull. 3. The lost sheepe is found. 4°. *J. Roberts f. N. Ling,* 1599. Third sermon ent. to J. Oxenbridge 9 fb. 1598. L.L³⁰.C.C²⁵.M.; F.HN(imp.).CHI.HD.

22736 — [Anr. ed.] 4°. *V. Simmes f. N. Ling,* 1601. L.O.; F.ILL.

22737 — [Anr. ed.] 4° in 8's. *F. K[ingston] f. N. Ling,* 1604. L.L³⁰.O.C.; F.HN.HD.U.
This and the following eds. usually bd. w. 22725 sqq.

22738 — [Anr. ed.] 4° in 8's. *F. K[ingston] f. N. Ling,* 1607. L.O²⁵.C. St. David's Cathedral, Wales.; F.HN.ILL. NY¹¹.U.+

22739 — [Anr. ed.] 4° in 8's. [*J. Windet f.*] *J. Smethwicke,* 1609. Three serm. ass'd 19 no. 1607. L.O.C³.BRISTOL². NLW.+; HN.HD.ILL.IND.

22740 — [Anr. ed.] 4° in 8's. [*W. Stansby?*] *f. J. Smethwicke,* 1611. L.O.C.; F.HN.LC.

22741 — [Anr. ed.] 4° in 8's. [*W. Stansby*] *f. J. Smethwick,* 1613. L.O.C.M.+; F.CAL.U. Bryn Mawr C.

22742 — [Anr. ed.] 4° in 8's. *H. L[ownes] f. J. Smethwicke,* 1616. O(2).O⁶.C.BRISTOL.; F.HN.HD.N.Y.+

22743 — [Anr. ed.] 4° in 8's. [*H. Lownes f.*] *J. Smethwicke,* 1619. L.O.C².BTL.NLW.+; F.HN.BO⁶.N.NY.+

22744 — [Anr. ed.] 4° in 8's. *W. S[tansby f.*] *J. Smethwicke,* 1624. L.L⁴⁸.D.EX.; F.HN.HD.Y. Cincinnati U.

Smith, Henry, *Monster—Collections—cont.*

22745 — [Anr. ed.] 4° in 8's. *W. S[tansby] f. J. Smethwicke,* 1628. L.O.O³⁹.BIRM.NLW.; F.HN.TEX. Weissman.

22746 — [Anr. ed.] 4° in 8's. *W. S[tansby] f. J. Smethwicke,* 1632. L.L².O.C.G².+; F.HN.HD.ILL.U.+

22747 — [Anr. ed.] 4° in 8's. [*J. Haviland f.*] *J. Smethwick,* 1637. L⁴⁶.O.LYD.STU.WI.; F(2).COLG².DAR.STAN.

(c) *Four, two, and six sermons published* [1595?] *by C. Burby* (1612 *by N. Bourne*; 1624 *by G. Edwards*)

22747.3 — [Four sermons, without tp. Heading A1ʳ:] The trumpet of the soule. By H. Smith. (The first sermon of Noahs drunkennesse.—The sinners conuersion.—The sinners confession.) 8°. [*P. Short f. C. Burby a. W. Leake,* 1595?] Trumpet ass'd by E. Allde to C. Burby 17 fb. 1595. L.; F.
Collates A–E⁸. Both copies orig. bd. w. 22698 and 22777.

22747.5 — [Anr. ed., w. 2 added sermons.] Foure sermons preached by master H. Smith: and published by a more perfect copie then heretofore. (Trumpet.—Sinfull mans search.—Maries choise.—Noahs drunkennesse.——Two sermons with three prayers.—Conuersion.—Confession.) 4°. *P. S[hort] f. C. Burby* [*a.*] (*W. Leake,*) 1598. L.L³⁰.; F(4 serm. only).HD.
The L³⁰ and HD copies are bd. as pt. 2 of 22780.

22748 — [Anr. ed.] 4°. *P. S[hort] f. C. Burby* [*a.*] (*W. Leake,*) 1599. L.L³⁰.O(2, 1 with 4 serm. only).M.; F.HN. BOWDOIN.CHI. Weissman.
See Greg, *Register B*, p. 73. Most copies bd. w. 22780.5. After this ed. Burby took over 2 of Dexter's sermons to replace Leake's (w. 22752 the result), and Leake added the 4 remaining Dexter items to his own 2 (with 22761 and 22765 the result).

22749 — = pt. of 22752.
22750 — = pt. of 22753.
22751 — = pt. of 22754.
22752 — Two sermons, of Jonahs punishment. (Four sermons.—Trumpet.—Sinfull.—Maries choise.—Noahs drunkennesse.) 4° in 8's. *S. S[tafford] f. C. Burby,* 1602. L(2).L³⁰.O.C.C¹⁹(2).; F(2 serm. only). HN.ILL.MICH(4 serm. only).U.
(22749 is pt. of this)

22753 — [Anr. ed.] 4° in 8's. *T. C[reede] f. C. Burby,* 1605. L(2 serm. only).O(2 serm. only).C. Finedon.; F.HN.CHI. HD.ILL.
(22750 is pt. of this)

22754 — [Anr. ed.] 4° in 8's. *T. D[awson] f. C. Burby,* 1607. L(4 serm. only).O²⁵.C(imp.).C².BRISTOL².+; F.HN.ILL. NY¹¹.U.
(22751 is pt. of this)

22755 — [Anr. ed.] 4° in 8's. *T. D[awson] f. E. Burby,* 1609. L.O(2 serm. only).C.C².NLW.+; F(4 serm. only, imp.). HN.HD(2, 1 imp.).ILL.IND.

22756 — [Anr. ed., w. title:] Six sermons. 4° in 8's. *T. D[awson] f. N. Bourne,* 1612. Ass'd by widow Burby to Bourne 16 oc. 1609. L.L⁴⁶.O(2).C. Kent U.; F(2 serm. only). HN.LC.N.U.+

22757 — [Anr. ed.] 4° in 8's. *T. D[awson] f. N. Bourne,* 1614. O.C.EX.; F(imp.).HN.U.

22758 — [Anr. ed.] 4° in 8's. *T. D[awson] f. N. Bourne,* 1617. L.O.C³.BRISTOL.NLW.+; F.HN.CHI.HD.Y.+

22759 — [Anr. ed.] 4° in 8's. *T. D[awson] f. N. Bourne,* 1620. L.O.; F.HN.BO.ILL.NY.+

22760 — [Anr. ed.] 4° in 8's. *J. D[awson] f. G. Edwards,* 1624. Ass'd 1 jn. L¹³.L⁴⁸.O.D.OS.; F(2).HN.CAL.HD(imp.).Y. (Formerly also 22774a) Reprinted in 22781 sqq.

(d) *Four, two, and six sermons published* (1602) *by W. Leake* (1615 *by W. Barret*; 1620 *by J. Parker*)

22761 — Foure sermons preached by maister H. Smith. And published by a more perfect coppie then heeretofore. (The sweete song of old father Simeon, in two sermons.—The calling of Jonah.—The rebellion of Jonah.) [*Ed.*] (W. S.) 4° in 8's. *J. R[oberts] f. W. Leake,* 1602. Ass'd by R. Dexter to Leake 3 se. 1599. L.L³⁰.O(2).C.; F.ILL.U.
See Greg, *Register B*, p. 73. Prob. issued w. 22765. See also 22748.

22762 — = pt. of 22767.
22763 — = pt. of 22768.
22764 — = pt. of 22769.
— [Two sermons. Conversion and confession. 1595? etc.] See 22747.3 sqq.

Smith, Henry, *Minister—Collections—cont.*

22765 — [Anr. ed.] Two sermons preached by maister H. Smith: with a prayer for the morning thereunto adjoyned. And published by a more perfect coppie then heere-to-fore. (The sinners conuersion.—The sinners confession.) 4⁰ in 8's. J. R[oberts] f. W. Leake, 1602. L.O.C.C⁴.C²⁵.+; F.HD. ILL.U.
    Prob. issued w. 22761. *See also* 22748.

22766 — [Anr. ed. of 22765 and 22761 on continuous signatures.] Two sermons [Conversion. Confession.] (Foure sermons [Simeon, etc.]) [Ed.] (W. S.) 4⁰ in 8's. [V. Simmes] f. W. Leake, 1605. L.C.; F.HN. CHI.Y.

22767 — [Anr. ed.] 4⁰ in 8's. [R. Raworth] f. W. Leake, 1608. L(imp.).O²⁵.C(2).C². Kent U(imp.).; F.HD.ILL. NY¹¹.U.
    (22762 is pt. of this)

22768 — [Anr. ed.] 4⁰ in 8's. [W. Hall] f. W. Leake, 1610. L.O.C.BRISTOL².NLW.+; F.HN.HD.ILL.IND.
    (22763 is pt. of this)

22769 — [Anr. ed.] 4⁰ in 8's. H. L[ownes] f. W. Leake, 1613 (1612.) L.L⁴⁶.O.C(1, plus 2 serm. only).M⁴.+; F.HN (4 serm. only).CAL.LC. Bryn Mawr C.
    (22764 is pt. of this)

22770 — = 22771.

22771 — [Anr. ed., w. title:] Six sermons. 4⁰ in 8's. W. Stansby f. W. Barret, 1615. Ass'd 16 fb. 1617. L.O.O⁶.C.C³.+; F.HN.CHI.N.U.+
    (Formerly also 22770)

22772 — [Anr. ed.] 4⁰ in 8's. W. Stansby f. W. Barret, 1618. L.O(imp.).BRISTOL.NLW.; F.HN.CHI.HD.IND.+

22773 — [A ghost.]

22774 — [Anr. ed.] 4⁰ in 8's. J. Beale f. J. Parker, 1621. Ass'd 8 mr. 1620. L.L⁴⁸.O.D.NLW.; F.HN.ILL.NY.

22774a — = 22760.

22775 — [Anr. ed.] 4⁰ in 8's. W. Stansby f. J. Parker, 1625. OS.; F.HN.HD.Y.
    Reprinted in 22781.

(e) Six, ten, and twelve sermons published by R. Dexter

22775.3 — Sixe sermons preached by maister H. Smith. With two prayers. (The sweete song of old father Simeon, in two sermons.—The calling of Jonah. The rebellion of Jonah, in two sermons.— The punishment of Jonah.) [Ed.] (W. S.) 8⁰. R. F[ield] f. R. Dexter, 1592. Ent. 23 se. O.; F.
    172 pp.

22775.7 — [Anr. ed., revised.] Published by a more perfect copie then heretofore. 8⁰. R. F[ield] f. R. Dexter, 1593. L³⁸.O.C².; F(2, 1 imp.).HN.CAL.
    201 pp. The Jonah sermons are entitled: The calling; The rebellion; The first (second) sermon of the punishment. This version is abridged in 22677.5.

22776 — [Anr. ed.] 4⁰. R. F[ield] f. R. Dexter, 1594. L.L³⁸.O. O⁹.C.; F.
    117 pp.

22777 — [Anr. ed.] 8⁰. R. F[ield] f. R. Dexter, 1594. L(2). SHEF.; F.
    182 pp.

22778 — [Anr. ed.] 1599. Now = 22780.5.

22779 — [Anr. ed., with 4 added sermons.] Ten sermons. With certaine prayers. 4⁰. R. Field [i.e. T. Scarlet?] f. R. Dexter, 1596. O.O⁹(imp.).O¹¹.C.; HN.
    The added sermons are Burby's Sinfull and Maries choise (cf. 22697 and 22747.5) and Leake's Confession and Conversion (cf. 22700.5, 22701.5, and 22747.3). The O, O⁹, and C copies are bd. w. 22721.
    The method of signing leaves is characteristic of Waldegrave but was also used by Scarlet in 7501 and 15028.

22780 — [Anr. ed., with 2 added sermons.] Twelve sermons. 2 pts. 4⁰ in 8's. R. Field f. R. Dexter, 1598. L³⁰.C(pt. 1 only).; HD.
    Pt. 1 has the same 6 sermons as 22775.7. Details of pt. 2, including its imprint, are listed separately at 22747.5.

22780.5 — [Anr. ed. of pt. 1.] Six sermons. 4⁰ in 8's. R. Field f. R. Dexter, 1599. L.L³⁰.O.M.; F.HN.BOWDOIN.CHI. Weissman.
    (Formerly 22778) *See* Greg, *Register B*, p. 73. Most copies bd. w. 22748, q.v.

Smith, Henry, *Minister—Collections—cont.*

(f) Twelve sermons published by G. Edwards

22781 — Twelve sermons, preached by Mr. H. Smith. With prayers, both for the morning and evening thereunto adjoyned. [Ed.] (W. S.) 2 pts. 4⁰ in 8's. J. Haviland f. G. Edwards, 1629. Pt. 1 ass'd by Parker to Haviland to Edwards 15 ja. L.O.BIRM.NLW.SHEF.+; F.HN(tp only).MICH.Y. Cincinnati U.
    Pt. 1 collates A–H⁸ I⁴ and reprints 22775; pt. 2 collates A–G⁸ H⁴ I² and reprints 22760.

22782 — [Anr. ed., w. continuous signatures.] 4⁰ in 8's. J. Haviland f. G. Edwards, 1632. L.L².O.C(lacks tp). M.+; F.HN.HD.N.U.+

22783 — [Anr. ed.] 4⁰ in 8's. J. Haviland f. G. Edwards, 1637. L⁴⁶.O.LYD(imp.).STU.; F.COLG²(imp.).DAR.ILL(frag.). MIN(imp.).
    See also 22677.5.

(g) Certain sermons pirated by R. Waldegrave

22783.3 — Certain sermons, preached by H. Smyth. Taken by characterie and examined after. 8⁰. Edinburgh, R. Walde-graue, [1591?] A(imp.).
    (Formerly 22873) Reprints 22693, 22713, 22660, 22658, 22703 in that order.

22783.5 — Certain sermons vpon seueral textes of scripture. 8⁰. Edinburgh, R. Walde-graue, 1592. INN.
    Contains 11 sermons all different from 22783.3; reprints the first 10 from 22717 and the first from 22692.

(h) Four sermons published by T. Scarlet, John Wolfe, and W. Wright

22783.7 — Foure sermons preached by M. Henrie Smith. The first, the pride of Nabuchadnezzer. The second, the fall. The third, the restitution. The fourth, the wedding garment. 8⁰. T. Scarlet, sold by W. Wrigstt [sic. Serm. 4:] (J. Wolfe f. W. Wright,) 1592. C⁴. A
    Reprints 22688, 22662, 22690, and 22713, and is reprinted in 22718.

Smith, John. An almanack. 1631. *See* 514.

22784 **Smith, John,** *Governor of Virginia.* An accidence or the path-way to experience. Necessary for all young sea-men. 4⁰. [N. Okes] f. Jonas Man a. B. Fisher, 1626. Ent. 23 oc. L.L³³(imp.).O³.LONGLEAT. London, Royal United Services Institute.; HN.CB.
    CB copy has a variant dedic. to Sir Robert Heath on A2ʳ. For an enlarged and rearranged version *see* 22794.

22785 — [A variant, w. imprint:] [N. Okes] f. Jonas Man a. B. Fisher, 1627. C¹²(imp.).; HN.NY.

22786 — [Anr. ed., anon., with altered prelims.] An accidence for the sea. 8⁰. T. H[arper] f. B. Fisher, 1636. L.; Y.
    Dedic. to Earl of Northumberland signed B. F., i.e. Fisher, the publisher.

22787 — Advertisements for the unexperienced planters of New-England, or any where. With the map, allowed by king Charles. 4⁰. J. Haviland, sold by R. Milbourne, 1631. L(2).O⁹.C(lacks map).; F.HN.HD. N.NY.+
    For the map of New England *see* Sabin 82815.

22788 — A description of New England: or the observations, and discoveries, of captain John Smith. 4⁰. H. Lownes f. R. Clerke, 1616 (18 jn.) Ent. 3 jn. L.L².O.E².WN.+; F.HN.HD.N.NY.+
    Some copies (L, HN, BO) have rare unsigned leaf w. Prince Charles's new names for New England places. The map of New England has imprint *Printed by G. Low,* in most states dated 1614; for a fuller discussion of states of the map *see* Sabin 82819, 82823.

22788.3 — [Anr. issue, w. cancel tp, beginning:] For the right honourable the lord Elesmore [sic]. . . . H. Lownes f. R. Clerke, 1616 (18 jn.) HN.

22788.5 — [Anr. issue, w. variant cancel tp, beginning:] For the right honourable, sir Edward Coke,. . . . H. Lownes f. R. Clerke, 1616 (18 jn.) Sotheby's 28 Feb. 1956, n. 474 (tp reproduced; bought by W. H. Robinson, untraced).

22789 — The generall history of Virginia, the Somer Iles, and New England. [A prospectus of the work first published in 1624.] fol. [J. Dawson, 1623.] L⁵(Lemon 209).

Smith, John, *Governor of Virginia—cont.*

22790 — The generall historie of Virginia, New-England, and the Summer Isles. Divided into six bookes. fol. *J. D[awson] a. J. H[aviland] f. M. Sparkes,* 1624. Ent. 12 jy. L.O.C.E.M.+; F.HN.HD.N.NY.+
Dawson pr.)(² A–N⁴. Haviland pr. P–Ii⁴. Some copies (F,NY) have errata slip pasted on Ii4ᵛ. This is largely a collected ed. of 22788, 22791, 22792, 22795, q.v. There are 4 maps: of New England; Virginia; Old Virginia; and the Summer Isles, the last 2 with *printed by James Reeve* in some states; *see Sabin 82823.*

22790a — [Anr. issue, w. letterpress tp, w. imprint:] *J. D[awson] a. J. H[aviland] f. M. Sparkes,* 1625. HN. Mellon. Henry Taylor.
With engr. tp as in 22790.

22790b — [Anr. issue, w. engr. tp only, w. date altered:] *J. D[awson] a. J. H[aviland] f. M. Sparkes,* 1626. L.O³.O⁸.C².; F.HN.HD(imp.).NY.Y.+

22790c — [A variant, w. date altered:] *J. D[awson] a. J. H[aviland] f. M. Sparkes,* 1627. L.O⁹.CHATS.M. Juel-Jensen(imp.).; HN.BO.LC.N.NY.+

22790c.5 — [A variant, w. date altered:] *J. D[awson] a. J. H[aviland] f. M. Sparkes,* 1631. F.CB.

22790d — [A variant, w. imprint altered:] *J. D[awson] a. J. H[aviland] f. E. Blackmore,* 1632. L³⁰.O³(E). D.DUL. ELY.+; HN.HD.LC.N.NY.+

22791 — A map of Virginia. With a description of the countrey, the commodities, people, government and religion. Written by captaine Smith. Whereunto is annexed the proceedings of those colonies. Taken out of the writings of ... R. Pots. [Ed.] By W. S[ymonds. The whole ed. by] (T. Abbay.) 2 pts. 4°. *Oxford, J. Barnes,* 1612. L.O.D(imp.).E².G²(imp.).+; HN.HD.LC.N.NY.+
NY,ROS have inserted dedic. to Earl of Hertford by Smith; PN has different dedic. to T. Watson and J. Bingley by Philip Fote: possibly a joke, as all copies have dedic. To the Hand by T. A[bbay.] For states of the map of Virginia *see Sabin 82832, 82823.*

22792 — New Englands trials. Declaring the successe of 26. ships employed thither. 4°. *W. Jones,* 1620. Ent. 11 de. L.O(1, plus duplicate tp and dedic.).; HN.N. There are 2 different dedic. texts: (1) beginning 'To the consideration of your favourable constructions . . .' headed To worthy adventers (both O) or To Fish-mongers (L); (2) a cancel, beginning: 'The great worke contained in this little Booke,' headed to Sir Edward Coke (N) or Earl of Bridgewater (HN).

22793 — [Anr. ed., enlarged.] With the present estate of that happie plantation. The second edition. 4°. *W. Jones,* 1622. L(2).L³.; HN.CB.N.NY.PH.+

22794 — A sea grammar, with the plaine exposition of Smiths accidence [22784] for young sea-men, enlarged. 4°. *J. Haviland,* 1627. Ent. to Mrs. Griffin a. J. Haviland 13 au. L³³.O.D.G².LINC.+; HN.CB.NY.PH².Y.+

22795 — A true relation of such occurrences as hath hapned in Virginia. [Ed.] (I. H.) 4°. *E. Allde] f. J. Tappe, solde by W. W[elby,]* 1608. Ent. to W. Welby a. J. Tappe 13 au. CHATS.; NY.NY².PH².
Line 10 of title: 'Written by a gentleman of the said collony, to a worshipfull/'. There are also copies at CB,HD,PN lacking tp.

22795.3 — [A variant, w. line 10 of title:] Written by Th. Watson Gent. one of the said collony, to a/. [*E. Allde] f. J. Tappe, solde by W. W[elby,]* 1608. L(2, 1 lacks preface).; HN.NY².

22795.5 — [A variant, w. line 10 of title:] Written by Captaine Smith Coronell of the said collony, to a/. [*E. Allde] f. J. Tappe, solde by W. W[elby,]* 1608. HN.BO. MICH.NY.V.+
In all copies 'Cor' and 'll' of 'Coronell' are inked out.

22795.7 — [A variant, w. line 10 of title:] Written by Captaine Smith one of the said collony, to a/. [*E. Allde] f. J. Tappe, solde by W. W[elby,]* 1608. HN(lacks preface).CB.NY(lacks preface). Henry Taylor.

22796 — The true travels, adventures, and observations of captaine J. Smith, from 1593. to 1629. Together with a continuation of his generall History of Virginia. fol. *J. H[aviland] f. T. Slater, sold [by M. Sparke,]* 1630. Ent. 29 au. 1629. L.O.C.D.E².+; F.HN.HD(lacks folding plate).N.NY.+
Smith's coat of arms engr. by Thomas Cecil usually found on verso of tp; sometimes on sep.

Smith, John, *Governor of Virginia—cont.*

leaf; both at HN, NY. Folding plate of Smith's adventures has imprint: *printed by James Reeve.*

22797 **Smith, John,** *Minister at Reading.* The doctrine of praier in generall for all men. 4°. *A. Islip,* 1595. L².O.C.LINC.YK.+; F.

22798 **Smith, John,** *of Clavering.* Essex dove, presenting the world with a few of her olive branches. Delivered in three severall treatises, viz. 1 His grounds of religion. 2 An exposition on the Lords prayer. 3 A treatise of repentance. [Ed.] (J. Hart.) 4° in 8's. *A. I[slip a.] (G. P[urslowe]) f. G. Edwardes,* 1629. Ent. 15 jn. L.O.C.COL.ETON.+; F.HN.BO.CHI.U.+
(2nd pt. formerly also 22804) Purslowe pr. the prelims, and the 2nd pt.; Islip did the rest.

22799 — The second edition, corrected and inlarged. 4° in 8's. *G. Miller f. G. Edwards,* 1633. L.O.C.; F.HN.BO⁵. ILL.NY¹¹.+

22800 — The third edition, corrected and amended. 4° in 8's. *G. Miller f. A. Crooke, J. Crooke a. R. Serger [a.] (f. G. Edwards,)* 1637. L.L³⁰.L⁴⁸.O.NOR.; F.HN.HD(date cropt).ROCH.Y.

22800.5 — [A variant, w. imprint:] *G. Miller (f. G. Edwards,) sould by A. Crooke, T. Allot in Dublin,* 1637. ILL (impr. on gen. tp shaved).

22801 — An exposition of the creed. Delivered in sermons. [Ed.] (A. Palmer.) fol. *F. Kyngston f. R. Allot,* 1632. Ent. to J. Legat a. A. Crooke 1 jy. 1637. L.O.C.A.NEP.+; F.HN(imp.).BO³.PN².U.+

22802 — A paterne of true prayer. 1605. Now = 22877.1.
22803 — [Anr. ed.] 1624. Now = 22877.2.
22804 — The substance and pith of prayer. 1629. = 2nd pt. of 22798.
— *tr. See* 14589, 14594.

Smith, John, *of Lincoln. See* 22874.

22805 **Smith, Jude.** A misticall deuise of the spirituall and godly loue betwene Christ and the church. [In verse.] And also a treatise of prodigalitie [by J. Carr.] 2 pts. 8°. [*f.*] *H. Kyrckham,* 1575. L(lacks pt. 2).C.
Pt. 2, which L has separately, is a reissue of 4685 and retains that tp.
— *See also* 21485.

Smith, M., *alias Norrice. See* 18661.

22806 **Smith, Miles,** *Bp.* Certaine plaine notes, vpon euery chapter of Genesis. 1596. = 1087.

22807 — A learned and godly sermon, preached at Worcester, at an assise. [Ed.] (R. Burhil.) 8°. *Oxford, Jos. Barnes, sold by John Barnes,* [London,] 1602. L.O⁴. C¹⁰.LINC.; HD.Y.

22808 — Sermons of the right reverend M. Smith, late lord bishop of Glocester. (A sermon at the funerall of Miles, bishop . . . preached 1624. by T. Prior.) fol. *Eliz. Allde f. R. Allot,* 1632. Ass'd by widow Allot to J. Legat a. A. Crooke 1 jy. 1637. L.O.C².BIRM² (K.N.).DEU.+; F.CHI.SMU.U.Y.+
— *ed. See* 1077.

Smith, Nicholas, *pseud. See* Wilson, Matthew.
— A brief inquisition into F. Nicholas Smith his discussion. 1630. *See* 22809a.5.

Smith, Peter, *ed. See* 25688, 25700a.

Smith, Reinold. Almanacks. 1620, etc. *See* 514.3 sqq.

22809 **Smith, Richard,** *Bp. of Chalcedon.* An answer to Thomas Bels late challeng named by him the downfal of popery [1818.] [Init. S. R.] 8°. *Doway, L. Kellam,* 1605. L.O.A².ST.W.+; F.HD.TEX.
A&R 771. Answered in 1824.

22809a — [A variant, w. imprint:] *Doway, L. Kellam,* 1606. L.O.ST.USHAW.W.+; F.HN.N.U.Y.+
A&R 772.

22809a.5 — A brief inquisition into F. Nicholas Smith his discussion [in 25779] of M. D. Kellison his treatise of the ecclesiasticall hierarchie. [Anon.] 12°. *Doway, widdowe of M. Wyon,* 1630. L²⁵.VAL.W.
A&R 773. Answered in 25779.3.

22810 — A conference of the catholike and protestante doctrine with the expresse words of holie scripture. Which is the second parte of the prudentiall balance of religion. Written first in Latin, but now augmented and tr. into English. [Anon.] 4°. *Doway, widdowe of M. Wyon,* 1631. L.O.A².D.W.+; F.HN.N.TEX.U.+
A&R 774.

Smith, Richard, *Bp. of Chalcedon—cont.*

22811 — The life of the most honourable and vertuous lady the La. Magdalen viscountesse Montague. Written in Latin. And now *tr.* into English, by C. F. [i.e. J. C. Fursdon.] 4°. [*St. Omer, English College Press,*] 1627. L.L³⁵.O.; N.
A&R 775.

22812 — Of the author and substance of the protestant church and religion, two bookes. Written first in Latin by R. S[mith] doctour of divinity, and now reviewed by the author, and *tr.* into English by W. Bas. 8°. [*St. Omer, English College Press,*] 1621. L.O.D.E.W.+; F.N.TEX.U. Notre Dame U.+
A&R 776.

22813 — The prudentiall ballance of religion, wherin the catholike and protestant religion are weighed together. The first part. [Anon.] 8°. [*St. Omer, F. Bellet,*] 1609. L.O.C.A².D.+; F.HN.HD(imp.).N.U.+
A&R 777. For pt. 2 *see* 22810.

22814 — The relection of a conference. 1635. Now = 15351.3.
— A treatise of the sacrament of confirmation. By W. R. 1629. *See* 20594.
— *See also* 8911, 8919, 10733, 10740, 15347.5, 18193.

22815 **Smith, Richard,** *Dean.* The assertion and defence of the sacramente of the aulter. 8°. (*J. Herforde, at the costes of R. Toye,*) 1546. L.L².O.C.P.+; F.HN.HD. N.U.+
At least L² copy has A1 uncancelled w. orig. tp: 'A treatyse concernyng the blessed sacramēt of the aulter. 1546.'

22816 — A bouclier of the catholike fayth . . . conteynyng diuers matters now of late called into controuersy, by the newe gospellers. 8°. (*R. Tottell,*) [1554.] L².O.P.; F.

22817 — The seconde parte of the booke called a boucklier of the catholyke fayeth. 8°. *in æd. R. Caly,* 1555 (ja.) L².M(imp.)*.; F.HN.

22817.5 — [Anr. issue, w. prelims. reset, w. title:] The seconde parte of . . . a bucklar. . . . *in æd. R. Caly,* 1555 (ja.) O.P(w. duplicate prelims.).; PML.

22818 — A brief treatyse settynge forth diuers truthes . . . left to yᵉ church by the apostles traditiõ. 8°. (*T. petit,*) 1547. L.L².O⁵.D².OS.+; F.U.

22819 — A confutation of à certen booke, called á defence of the doctrine of the sacramēt [6000], &c. sette fourth in the name of Thomas [Cranmer] archebysshoppe of Canterburye. 8°. [*Paris, R. Chaudière,* 1550?] L.O.C.C¹⁰.DUR⁵.+; F.HD.
Answered by 5990.5, 5991.

22820 — A defence of the blessed masse, and the sacrifice therof. 8°. (*J. Herforde,* 1546.) C(w. cancel tp and dedic. of 22820a bd. after A8).

22820a — [Anr. issue, w. cancel tp and dedic. to Henry VIII.] A defence of the sacrifice of the masse. (*J. Herforde,*) 1546. O.C.M.ST.WOR.+; F.HN.
The orig. tp on A1 is cancelled.

22821 — [Anr. ed.] 8°. (*W. Myddylton,*) 1546 (1547 (1 fb.)) L.L².O.G².M.+; F.CH.

22822 — A godly and faythfull retractation made by R. Smyth. Reuokyng certeyn errors in some of hys bookes. 8° in 4's. (*R. Wolfe,*) 1547. L²(2).O(2).C(2).C⁵.BUTE.
Standing type reimposed as pt. of 22824.

22823 — Of vnwryten verytyes. [Anon.] 8°. (*T. Raynalde,* 1548.) L².C.P.

22824 — A playne declaration made at Oxforde by R. Smyth, vpon hys Retractation. 8°. (*R. Wolfe,*) 1547. O.C.
Includes text of Retraction reimposed from 22822.

22824.3 **Smith, Richard,** *Murderer.* The reward of murther, in the execution of R. Smith, for murthering Mary Davis widdow, after he had gotten her with childe: . . . executed this present Saterday, being the 12. of Dccember [*sic*], 1640. *Ballad.* 2 pts. s.sh.fol. [*R. Oulton?* 1640.] M³(pt. 1 only).

Smith, Richard, *Preacher.* Munition against mans misery. 1610, etc. *See* 22877.8.

Smith, Richard, *Printer and Publisher, tr. See* 186.5.

Smith, Richard, *Protestant, tr. See* 24274.

22824.7 **Smith, Richard,** *Satirist.* The powder treason, propounded, by Sathan. Approved, by Antichrist. Enterprised, by Papists. [Engr. by Michael Droeshout.] s.sh.fol. [*London,* c. 1615.] L(Print Dept.).
Engraving of king in Parliament copied from 11922 or 17926. *See* Hind II.342.

22825 **Smith, Samuel,** *A.M.* Aditus ad logicam. In usum eorum qui primò academiam salutant. Autore S. S[mith] artium magistro. 8°. [*W. Stansby,*] 1613. O.

22826 — [Anr. ed.] Autore S. Smith. Editio secunda. 12°. *Oxoniæ, J. Barnesius,* 1615. L.

22827 — Editio tertia. 12°. *Oxoniæ, J. Barnesius,* 1617. L.O.O⁴.

22828 — Editio quarta à multis mendis repurgata. 12°. *Oxoniæ, J. Lichfield & J. Short, propter S. Jackson,* 1618. O.DUL.DUR⁵.G².YK.+

22829 — = 22831.

22830 — [Anr. ed., without edition number or mention of corrections.] 12°. *G. Stansby,* 1621. L(tp only, Harl. 5927/371).O(lacks tables).

22830.5 — [A variant, w. imprint:] [*London, W. Stansby f.*] *Genevæ, ap. J. Stoer,* 1621. L(part of tp only, w. device McK. 393 and imprint, Harl.5963/407).O⁴⁸.

22831 — Quarta editio, de nouo correcta, & emendata. 12°. *per G. Stansby,* 1627. L.O(lacks tp).CREDITON.D.E².+; HN.
(Formerly also 22829)

22831.3 — [Anr. ed., without edition number or mention of corrections.] 12°. *G. Stansby, veneunt ap. J. Grismond,* 1633. BRISTOL².DUL(2).

22831.7 — Editio quarta. 12°. *Oxoniæ, G. Turner, ipsius impensis,* 1634. O⁴⁸.LINC.; HD.ILL.

22832 — [A variant.] Editio quinta. *Oxoniæ, G. Turner, ipsius impensis,* 1634. O⁴.O³⁸.NLW.

22833 — [Anr. ed.] Editio quinta. 12°. *Oxoniæ, G. Turner, ipsius impensis,* 1639. L.O.O³⁸.A.P.+; F.HN.CHI.ILL.

22834 **Smith, Samuel,** *Minister in Essex.* The admirable convert: or, the miraculous conversion of the thiefe on the crosse. 8°. *T. Harper f. T. Alchorne,* 1632. Ent. 17 no. 1631. L(lacks folding table).L³.O.; F.CHI. HD.U.Y.+

22835 — The chiefe shepheard or, an exposition upon yᵉ xxiij, psalme. 8°. *N. Okes,* 1625. Ass'd by N. Okes to J. Okes 2 au. 1630. L.L³⁸.O.; F(2, 1 imp.).ILL.U.

22836 — A christian taske. A sermon, preached at the funerall of J. Lawson. 8°. *N. Okes,* 1620. Ent. 11 fb. L³(date defaced).M.; HN.
Reprinted in 22854.5.

22837 — Christs last supper or the doctrine of the sacrament set forth in five sermons. 8°. *T. D[awson] f. J. Bellamie,* 1620. Ent. to N. Bourne a. J. Bellamy 10 oc. O.; F.U.

22838 — Christs preparation to his owne death. Delivered in three sermons. 8°. *N. Okes,* 1620. Ass'd by N. Okes to J. Okes 2 au. 1630. L³(date defaced).O.
Reprinted in 22854.5.

22839 — Davids blessed man: or, a short exposition upon the first psalme. 8°. *N. Okes, sold by F. Faulkner,* 1614. Ent. to N. Okes 15 my. C.

22839.3 — Second edition profitably amplified. 8°. *N. Okes, sold by S. Waterson,* 1616. DUL(imp.).

22839.5 — [Anr. issue, w. imprint:] *N. Okes, sold by M. Law,* 1616. O.

22840 — Fourth edition. 8°. *N. Okes,* 1617. O.C⁴.COL.; F(imp.).

22840.5 — Sixt edition. 8°. *N. Okes a. J. Norton, sold by F. Falkner, Southwark,* 1628. F(imp.).U. Hope College, Holland, Mich.

22840.7 — Eighth edition. 8°. *N. Okes,* 1631. Ass'd to J. Okes 2 au. 1630. LK.

22841 — Ninth edition. 8°. *N. Okes,* 1635. L.; F.

22841.3 — Tenth edition. 8°. *J. Okes, sold by J. Becket,* 1638. HD.

22841.7 — Davids repentance: or, a plaine exposition of the 51. psalme. The second edition profitably amplified by the authour. 8°. *N. Okes,* 1614. Ent. 9 jy. 1613. O.; HD.

22842 — [A variant, w. imprint:] *N. Okes, sold by B. Lightfoot,* 1614. O⁵.LAMPORT.

22842.5 — Third edition. 8°. *N. Okes,* 1616. F.HN.

22843 — Fifth edition. 8°. *N. Okes,* 1620. O.

22844 — Sixth edition. 8°. *N. Okes,* 1623. E².; HN.

22845 — Seaventh edition, newly revised. 8°. *N. Okes,* 1625. C.

22845.3 — Ninth edition. 8°. *N. Okes, sold by T. Alchorn,* 1632. Ass'd to J. Okes 2 au. 1630. O⁴¹.; Y.

22845.7 — Twelfth edition. 8°. *J. Okes,* 1637. L(Davis).
The engr. tp has: 'tenth edition. *N. & J. Okes,* 1637,' w. the last digit altered from '5' to '7'.

22846 — Fourteenth edition. 8°. *J. Okes,* 1640. L.C¹⁹.; HN.U.
At least L, U copies have engr. tp: 'thirteenth edition. *N. & J. Okes,* 1642.'

22847 — The Ethiopian eunuchs conversion. Or, the summe of thirtie sermons. 8°. *T. Harper f. T. Alchorne,* 1632. Ent. 19 au. 1631. L².O.C.D.DUL.; HD.TORONTO².

Smith, Samuel, *Minister in Essex—cont.*

22847.3 — An exposition upon the sixt chapter of the prophesie of Hosea. 4° in 8's. *T. Purfoot f. R. Woodroffe,* 1616. Ent. 20 no. 1615. L.O(imp.).; F.HD.PN².
    (Formerly 22880)

22847.7 — The great assize, or, day of jubilee. The second impression, corrected. (A fold for Christs sheepe.) 8°. *N. Okes,* 1617. Ent. 28 ap. 1615. F.

22848 — Third impression. 8°. *N. Okes, sold by M. Law,* 1618 (1619.) L.; HN.Y.

22848.3 — [Anr. ed.] Third impression. 8°. *N. Okes,* 1622 (1623). E.

22848.7 — Fourth impression. 8°. *N. O[kes,] sold by F. Falkner, Southwarke,* 1624. U.

22849 — [Anr. ed.] Fourth impression. 8°. *N. Okes a. J. Norton, sold by W. Lee,* 1628. L.; F.

22849.1 — Fifth impression. 8°. *N. Okes, sold by T. Alchorn,* 1630. Assignment to F. Grove 16 fb. 1629 'crost out'; ass'd to J. Okes 2 au. 1630. F.

22849.3 — Sixt impression. 8°. *N. Okes, sold by T. Alchon* [sic], 1631. L.O.

22849.5 — Seventh impression. 8°. *N. Okes, sold by H. Taunton,* 1633. L(letterpress tp only, Ames II.1097).; U.

22849.7 — Ninth impression. 8°. *J. Okes, sold by H. Blunden,* 1637 (1638.) ILL(imp.).
    ILL copy has engr. tp: 'VIII Impression. *N. & J. Okes f. H. Blunden,* 1638.'

22849.9 — (Tenth impression.) 8°. (*J. Okes,* 1638.) F(imp.).
    Imprint from sub tp to 'A fold for Christs sheepe.'

22850 — Joseph and his mistresse. The faithfulnesse of the one, and the unfaithfulnesse of the other: laid downe in five sermons. 8°. *G. Purslowe f. J. Budge,* 1619. Ent. 12 jn. L⁴.O.LK.; F.HN.

22851 — Noahs dove, or, tydings of peace to the godly. A sermon preached at a funerall. 8°. *N. Okes, sold by T. Archer,* 1619. O.C⁵.; BO.

22852 — Second impression, corrected and amended by the author. 8°. *N. Okes,* 1620. L³(date defaced). LINC.

22853 — Third impression. 8°. *N. Okes, sold by F. Falkner, Southwarke,* 1624. O(lacks tp).C¹⁰.E.

22854 — Fourth impression. 1634. = pt. of 22854.5.

22854.5 — Three pious & religious treatises, viz. 1. Noah's dove (fourth impression.) 2. Christs preparation to his owne death (third impression.) 3. A christians taske. The third impression, corrected and amended. 8°. *N. O[kes,] sold by J. Rothwell,* 1634. Noah's dove ass'd by N. Okes to J. Okes 2 au. 1630. C(lacks gen. tp and next leaf).; F.PN².
    (1st part formerly 22854)

Smith, Thomas, *Artillerist.* The arte of gunnerie. (Certaine additions.) 2 pts. 4°. *[R. Field] f. W. Ponsonby,* 1600 (1601.) Ent. 13 de. 1599. PARIS.; HN.
    A2ʳ of pt. 1 has strapwork headpiece.

22855.5 — [Anr. ed.] The art of gunnery. 2 pts. 4°. *[H. Lownes] f. W. Ponsonby,* 1600 [1627? Pt. 2:] (*H. L[ownes,] sold by R. Dawlman,* 1627.) L³³(lacks pt. 2).C³.; HN.
    A2ʳ of pt. 1 has headpiece w. 'Cor unum' motto. Lownes apparently borrowed Field's device (McK. 192) and imitated the genuine 1600 tp. This tp is conjugate, and the device is quite worn.

22856 — [Anr. issue, w. added gen. tp:] The complete souldier. Containing the whole art of gunnery, with certaine additions. Second edition. *f. R. Dawlman,* 1628. L.

22856.5 **Smith, Sir Thomas,** *Doctor of Civil Laws.* De recta & emendata linguæ Anglicæ scriptione, dialogus. 4°. *Lutetiæ, ex off. R. Stephani,* 1568 (1567 (id. no.)) L.O.C.C².SHR.+; F.BO.ILL.N.Y.
    Contains numerous English words.

22857 — De republica Anglorum. The maner of gouernement of England. 4°. *H. Midleton f. G. Seton,* 1583. Ent. to J. Day 17 ja. 1581; to G. Seton 2 ja. 1584. L.O.C.M².P.+; F.HN.HD.N.NY.+

22858 — [Anr. ed.] 4°. *H. Midleton f. G. Seton,* 1584. L.O.C.D.E.+; F.HN.HD.ILL.NY⁸.+

22859 — [Anr. ed., enlarged. w. title:] The common-welth of England, and maner of gouernment thereof. With new additions of the cheefe courts in England, neuer before published. 4°. *J. Windet f. G. Seton,* 1589. L.O.C.M⁴.RGU.+; F.HN.COR.HD.Y.

22860 — [Anr. ed.] 4°. *V. Simmes f. G. Seton,* 1594. L.O.O⁶.O¹⁰.O¹¹.+; F.HN.HD.ILL.TEX.+

22861 — [Anr. ed.] Also a table of the principall matters. 4°. *J. Roberts f. G. Seton,* 1601. L.O².C.BTU.E.+; F.HN.HD.N.PN².+

Smith, *Sir* **Thomas,** *Doctor of Civil Laws—cont.*

22862 — [Anr. ed.] Newly corrected. 4°. *[J. Windet] f. J. Smethwicke,* 1609. Ass'd to N. Ling 22 ja. 1607; to J. Smethwick 19 no. 1607. L.O.C.E.P.+; F.HN.HD.N.Y.+

22863 — [Anr. ed.] 4°. *W. Stansby f. J. Smethwicke,* 1612. L.O.C.D².STU.+; F.HN.CU.HD.N.+

22864 — [Anr. ed.] 4°. *W. Stansby f. J. Smethwicke,* 1621. L.O.C.E.M.+; F.HN.HD.N.NY.+

22865 — [Anr. ed.] 12°. *W. Stansby f. J. Smethwicke,* 1633. L.O.C.D.E².+; F.HN.CHI.HD.N.+

22866 — [Anr. ed.] 12°. *W. Stansby f. J. Smethwicke,* 1635. L.O⁶.C.CASHEL.M².+; F.HN.CU.HD.N.+

22867 — [Anr. ed.] 12°. *R. Young f. J. Smethwicke,* 1640. L.O.C.M.NEP.+; F.HN.CU.HD(lacks engr. tp).ILL.+

22868 — [A trans.] De republica et administratione Anglorum libri tres: nunc primùm J. Buddeni, fide in Latinum conversi. 8°. *[Marburg, P. Egenolphus] pro off. Nortoniana Londini,* [1610.] L.O.C.D.G².+; F.HN.HD. ILL. Dickinson C.

22868.5 — The offer and order giuen forth by sir Thomas Smyth knight, and Thomas Smyth his sonne, vnto suche as be willing to accompanye the sayde sonne, in his voyage for the inhabiting some partes of the northe of Irelande. s.sh.fol. *[London,* 1572.] L⁵(Lemon 62). Cr. 73(Ireland).
    (Formerly 14140) Stipulates: 'The first payment to begin foure yeares hence, videlicet. 1576.' and mentions that the Letters Patent and Indentures may be examined at the sign of the Sun in Paul's Churchyard, i.e. the shop of Antony Kitson.

— *See also* 23133.

22869 **Smith,** *Sir* **Thomas,** *Merchant.* Sir Thomas Smithes voiage and entertainment in Rushia. 4°. *[J. Roberts a. W. Jaggard] f. N. Butter,* 1605. Ent. to J. Trundle 27 se. L.L⁴³.O.C⁶.E.+; F.HN.ILL.N.NY.+
    Relates the death of Boris Godonov; for a description of later events *see* 21461. Quires I–1st M pr. by Roberts; the rest by Jaggard.

22869.3 — [A variant, w. 'voyage' in title.] *[J. Roberts a. W. Jaggard] f. N. Butter,* 1605. C.; HD.

— *See also* 1415.7 and Virginia Company (24830.4, etc.)

22869.7 **Smith, Walter.** [Heading a1ʳ:] The wydow Edyth .xii. mery gestys of one callyd Edyth. [In verse.] fol. *[J. Rastell,]* (1525 (23 mr.)) L(frags., Harl. 5995/189, 191, 193). O(frags., Vet.A1.b.12). Earl Fitzwilliam (on deposit at C¹⁰).
    Has McK. 37 w. Rastell's name.

22870 — [Anr. ed., w. title:] XII. mery iests, of the wyddow Edyth. 4°. *[W. Williamson? f.]* (*R. Johnes,)* 1573. O.; HN.PFOR.

22871 **Smith, Wentworth.** The Hector of Germany. Or the palsgrave, prime elector. A new play. With new additions. 4°. *T. Creede f. Josias Harrison,* 1615. Ent. 24 ap. O(2).; F.HN.BO.HD.Y.+ Greg 329.

22871a — [Anr. issue, w. cancel tp:] The Hector of Germanie, or [etc.] *T. Creede f. Josias Harrison,* 1615. L(2). L⁶(both tpp).E(both tpp).; HN.HD(both tpp).N.PEN.

22871a.3 **Smith, William,** *Map-Maker.* [Set of 12 maps of English counties, engr. by J. Hondius? Anon.] fol (12). *H. Woutneel,* [1602?] L(6 sheets only, Map Room). London, Royal Geographical Society (7 sheets only).
    Skelton 3. Woutneel's imprint appears on the map of Essex.

22871a.5 **Smith, William,** *of Crissing-Temple, Essex.* An elegie upon the death of that worthy housekeeper, W. Smith. [In verse.] 4°. *G. P[urslowe,]* 1631. L.

22872 **Smith, William,** *Poet.* Chloris, or the complaint of the passionate despised shepheard. [In verse.] 4°. *E. Bollifant,* 1596. L.O.; Arthur Houghton.

22872.5 **Smith, William,** *Priest.* Qui non credit condemnabitur Marc. 16. or a discourse proving, that a man who beleeveth in the trinity, &c. & yet beleeveth not all other inferiour articles of christian fayth, cannot be saved. 4°. *S. Omers, [English College Press] f. J. Heigham,* 1625. L²⁵.C¹⁹.AMP.D.W.+
    A&R 779.

Smyth, Edward, *tr. See* 15516.

22873 **Smyth, Henry.** Certain sermons. [1591?] Now = 22783.3.

22874 **Smyth, John,** *Se-baptist.* The bright morning starre: or, the resolution and exposition of the 22. psalme, in foure sermons at Lincolne. 12°. *J. Legat, pr. to the Univ. of Camb., solde by S. Waterson,* [*London,*] 1603. C³.

22875 — The character of the beast: or the false constitution of the church. Discovered in certayne passages betwixt Mr. R. Clifton & John Smyth, concerning true christian baptisme. 4°. [*Middelburg, R. Schilders,*] 1609. L.L².O.LINC.STU.; F.U.
　　Answered by 5450.

22876 — The differences of the churches of the seperation [*sic*]: annexed: as a correction and supplement to Principles [22877.3]. 4°. [*Middelburg, R. Schilders,*] 1608. L.O.C⁵.C¹⁰.; F.HD.Y.
　　Answered by 235.

22877 — Paralleles, censures, observations. Aperteyning: to three several writings, 1. A lettre to Mr. R. Bernard, by J. Smyth. 2. The seperatists schisme [1927]. 3. An answer by H. Ainsworth [234]. 4°. [*Middelburg, R. Schilders,*] 1609. O.O²⁸.C.D. Blickling.; COLG.U.Y.
　　Answered by 1958.

22877.1 — A paterne of true prayer. A learned exposition upon the Lords prayer. 4°. *F. Kyngston f. T. Man,* 1605. Ent. to the T. Mans, sen. and jun., 22 mr. L.L³¹. O²⁸.E².YK.+; HN.COLG.PN².Y.
　　(Formerly 22802)

22877.2 — [Anr. ed.] 12°. *J. D[awson] f. T. Man, sold by W. Sheffard, J. Bellamie, a. B. Fisher,* 1624. Ass'd to P. a. J. Man 3 my. L.L³.O.D.P.+; F.COLG.U.
　　(Formerly 22803)

22877.3 — Principles and inferences concerning the visible church. 8°. [*Middelburg, R. Schilders,*] 1607. YK.; Y.
　　See also 22876.

22877.4 — [Heading A1ʳ:] Propositions and conclusions, concerning true christian religion, conteyning a confesion of faith [in 100 propositions] of certaine English people, livinge at Amsterdam. (The last booke of John Smith.—The life and death of John Smith.) [*Ed.*] (T. P[ygott.]) 8°. [*The Netherlands?* 1613?] YK(lacks gen. tp).
　　Answered by 21115.

Smyth, M. The reꝫne of. M. smythes enuoy. [1540.] *See* 12206a.7.

Smyth, Nicholas, *Pseud. See* Wilson, Matthew.

Smyth, Nicholas, *tr. See* 13221.

22877.6 **Smyth, R.,** *P.* An artificiall apologie, articulerlye [*sic*] answerynge to the obstreperous obgannynges of one W. G. [in 12206a.3]. Repercussed by R. Smyth P. with annotaciõs of master Mynterne. [In verse.] s.sh.fol. [*R. Grafton f.*] *R. Bankes, and be to sell* [*by J. Turke,* 1540.] L⁵(Lemon 11).
　　See 22880.2.

Smyth, Richard, *Doctor of Divinity. See* Smith.

22877.8 **Smyth, Richard,** *Preacher.* Munition against mans misery & mortality. A treatice containing the most effectuall remedies against the miserable state of man. 12°. *Oxford, J. Barnes,* 1610. PLUME.; F.

22878 — The second edition. 12°. *Oxford, J. Barnes,* 1612. L.O.O³.C.C³.

22879 — The third edition. (Heraclitus: first written in French by P. du Moulin and *tr.* by R. S[tafforde] gentleman.) 12°. *Oxford,* [*by a.*] *f. W. Turner,* 1634. Ent. to John Barnes a. ass'd to T. Langley 14 ap. 1619. L.O.O³⁸(imp.).C.SCL.; F.HD(lacks tp).PN².
　　Heraclitus reprinted from 7325.

Smyth, Rosier, *tr. See* 3170a, 4569, 4570.

22880 **Smyth, Samuel.** An exposition upon the sixt chapter of Hosea. 1616. Now = 22847.3.

22880.2 **Smyth, Thomas,** *Clerk of the Queen's Council.* An enuoye from Thomas Smyth vpon thaunswer of one W. G. [In verse.] s.sh.fol. [*R. Wyer?* 1540.] L⁵ (Lemon 9, printed on both sides).
　　The order of items in this controversy is: 1323.5, 22880.4, 22880.7, 22880.6, 12206a.3 (primarily answers 22880.4), 22880.2, 12206a.7, 22877.6, 4268.5.
　　Participants were called before the Privy Council in December 1540; see *Proceedings P.C.,* VII.105, 107. R. Bankes, prob. disingenuously,

Smyth, Thomas, *Clerk of the Queen's Council—cont.*
　　denied printing any of the items and blamed R. Grafton, who acknowledged his guilt, and R. Redman, deceased, who pr. none of them.

22880.4 — A lytell treatyse agaynst sedicyous persons. [In verse.] s.sh.fol. [*R. Lant,* 1540.] L⁵(Lemon 6, printed on both sides).
　　Reprinted and answered in 22880.7.

22880.6 — A treatyse declarynge the despyte of a secrete sedicyous person, that dareth not shewe hym selfe. [In verse.] s.sh.fol. *J. Redman,* [1540.] L⁵(Lemon 7).
— *ed. See* 20826.

———

22880.7 — [Heading A1ʳ:] A brefe apologye or answere to a certen craftye cloynar, or popyshe parasyte, called Thomas Smythe. [In verse.] 4°. [*Antwerp, M. Crom,* 1540.] L(imp.).
　　Reprints and answers 22880.4.
— The reꝫne of. M. smythes enuoy. [1540.] *See* 12206a.7.

Smyth, *Sir* **Thomas.** *See* Smith.

22880.9 **Smyth, William.** The black-smith. A sermon preached at White-Hall. By W. S[myth] Doct. in divinitie. 8°. *E. Allde f. M. Clerke,* 1606. Ent. 2 my. L²(lacks tp). O.C.E².LINC.
　　Pp. 62.

22881 — [Anr. ed.] 8°. *E. Allde f. M. Clarke,* 1606. L.O²⁴.C. G².P.+
　　Pp. 56.

22881.5 — [Anr. ed.] 8°. *E. Allde f. N. Ling,* 1606. L³.C⁴.STU.; SMITH.U.
　　Quire B and parts of quire A are reimposed from 22881. In the L³ copy the title appears to be a cancel.

22882 — Ad lectorem. Gemma Fabri: qua sacri Biblij margaritæ, fere omnes continentur. [Anon.] Adiecimus in novum Testamentum Schepreui carmen à doctore Humphredo olim æditum. [All in verse.] 8°. *ex typ. F. Kingstoni, imp. J. Porteri,* 1598. Ent. 21 au. L.L².O.C.P.+; F.HD.ILL.PN².Y.
　　Shepery's part reprinted from 22406.

22883 **Smythe,** *Sir* **John.** Certain discourses, written by sir J. Smythe, knight: concerning the formes and effects of diuers sorts of weapons, and other matters militarie. 4°. [*T. Orwin f.*] *R. Johnes,* 1590 (1 my.) Ent. 6 ap. L.O.C.D.E.+; F.HN.HD.ILL.Y.+
　　Suppressed by the Queen's command; see *Original Letters of Eminent Literary Men,* ed. Sir Henry Ellis, Camden Society, 1843, pp. 48–65, 88–97.

22884 — Certen instructions, obseruations, and orders militarie. 4°. [*P. Short f.*] *R. Johnes,* 1594. Ent. 12 ap. O⁸.; HN(tp def.).

22885 — [Anr. issue, w. prelims. expanded, w. title:] Instructions, obseruations, and orders mylitarie. [*J. Danter a. P. Short f.*] *R. Johnes,* 1595. L.O.CHATS.LINC.P.+; F.HN.LC.MICH.
　　Danter pr. only the prelims.

Smythe, Richard. *See* Smith.

Smythe, Robert. Straunge, hystories. *Tr.* by R. S[mythe.] 1577. *See* 1356.5.

Smythe, Thomas. A brefe apologye. [1540.] *See* 22880.7.

Snape, Nathaniel, *ed. See* 19089, 19092.

22886 **Snawsel, Robert.** A looking glasse for maried folkes. Set forth dialogue-wise. 8°. *N. O[kes] f. H. Bell,* 1610. Ent. 1 my. L.; F(imp.).

22886.5 — [Anr. ed.] 8°. *f. H. Bell,* 1619. TEX.

22887 — [Anr. ed.] 8°. *J. Haviland f. H. Bell,* 1631. L.O(2).; HN.U.

22888 **Snelling, Thomas.** Thibaldus sive vindictæ ingenium. Tragoedia. [Anon.] 8°. *Oxoniæ, L. Lichfield,* 1640. L⁴.O.O².C.C³.+; F.HN.BO.HD.N.+ Greg L 17.
　　Unsold sheets reissued in 1650 w. cancel tp as Wing P 1969.

Snuffe, Clunnyco de Curtanio, *Pseud. See* Armin, R.

Soave, Pietro. *See* 21760, 21761.

Society of Jesus, *A Father of, tr. See* 269, 4125.

Society of Saltmakers. *See* 21636.5.

22889 **Society of Twelve.** The booke of the holy societye commonly called of Twelve conteyning the lytanies, and prayers. *Tr.* out of the French by N. N. a catholicke gentleman. 24° in 6's. *Douay, L. Kellam,* 1626. C. A&R 130.

22890 **Sodom.** Of the horrible and wofull destruction of, Sodome and Gomorra. *Ballad.* s.sh.fol. *R. Johnes f. H. Kyrkham,* [1570]. Ent. to A. Lacy 1568–69; to H. Kirkham 1570–71. L.

22890.5 **Soezinger, Andreas.** Disputatio juridica de testamentis: quam, in Oxoniensium Anglorum academia, præside A. Reuter. discutiendam proponit, A. Sözinger Viennensis Austriacus. 4°. *Oxoniæ, J. Barnesius,* 1610. O⁵.C¹⁷.

Sofford, Arthur. Almanacks. 1618, etc. *See* 515 sqq.

22891 **Sohn, Georg.** A briefe and learned treatise, conteining a true description of the Antichrist. *Tr.* (N. G[rimald.]) 8°. *Cambridge, J. Legate,* 1592. L.O.C.C². 𝕬

So Ho. A pleasant new ditty called the new, So Ho. [c. 1615.] *See* 6924.5.

22891.5 **Solace.** A solace for this hard season: published by occasion of continuance of the scarsitie of corne. 8°. *London,* [*J. Orwin*] *f. J. Legate,* [*Cambridge,*] 1595. O²¹.; HD.
— The solace of the soule. 1548. *See* 1774.

22892 **Soldier.** A new ballad of the souldier and Peggy. [1640?] = 19554.

22892.5 — The souldiers delight in the north or, a new north-country jigge. *Ballad.* 2 pts. s.sh.fol. [*E. Griffin? f. A. Griffin,* 1640.] Ent. to Mrs. Griffin 24 ap. 1640. M³(imp.).

22893 — The souldiers farewel to his love. *f. F. Coles, T. Vere a. J. Wright,* [c. 1670.] = Wing S 4423.

Solemnity. May 3. Numb. 26. The solemnity of the marriage of the emperours sonne. 1631. *See* News-books 212.

22894 **Soliman.** The tragedye of Solyman and Perseda. [Attrib. to T. Kyd.] 4° w. perp. chainlines. *E. Allde f. E. White,* [1592?] Ent. 20 no. 1592. L. Greg 109.

22895 — [Anr. ed.] The tragedie of Soliman and Perseda. 4° w. perp. chainlines. *E. Allde f. E. White,* (1599.) L.L⁶. O.E. London, Bedford College.; F.HN.CH.HD.ILL.
With *N*[swash] in *FINIS* at the end; the Smeeton facsimile has *N*.

22895a — [Anr. issue, w. stamped addition to title:] Newly corrected and amended. *E. Allde f. E. White,* (1599.) L.; F.HN.BO.ILL.PFOR.
— *See also* 23424.5.

22895a.5 **Solinus, Caius Julius.** The worthie worke of Julius Solinus polyhistor. Contayning many noble actions of humaine creatures. *Tr.* out of Latine by A. Golding. 4°. *J. Charlewood f. T. Hacket,* 1587. HD. A2ʳ last line: 'wrighting'.

22896 — [Anr. issue, w. cancel tp:] The excellent and pleasant worke of J. Solinus. *J. Charlewoode f. T. Hacket,* 1587. L.O.C(2).G²(2).; F.CU.HD.MICH.N. A2ʳ last line: 'wrighting'. The O, 1 C, and HD copies are issued as pt. 2 of 17786.

22896.5 — [Anr. issue, w. quires A–C partly reset and reimposed.] The excellent and pleasant worke [etc.] *J. Charlewoode f. T. Hacket,* 1587. L.O.C².LEEDS.; F.HN.HD.Y. A2ʳ last line: 'wryting'. The L, F, HN copies are issued as pt. 2 of 17786.

22897 **Solme, Thomas.** Here begynnyth a traetys [*sic*] callyde the Lordis flayle handlyde by the bushops [*sic*] powre thresshere T. Solme. 8°. (*Basyl, T. Emlos,*) [i.e. *Antwerp, widow of C. Ruremund,* 1540?] L. LINC(imp.).
The printer's name is the author's name spelled backwards.

Soloma Hometh. *See* Sulaimán I, *the Magnificent.*

22898 **Solomon,** *King of Israel.* The judgement of Salomon: in discerning the true mother from the false. *Ballad.* 2 pts. s.sh.fol. *f. H. Gosson,* [c. 1630.] C⁶.

22899 — The sayinges or prouerbes of king Salomon, with the answers of Marcolphus, *tr.* out of frenche in to englysshe. [In verse.] 4°. (*R. Pynson, and be for to sell* [*by R. Wyer,*]) [1529?] HN.
For a different version *see* 22905.

Solomon, *King of Israel—cont.*

22900 — A most excellent new dittie, wherein is shewed the sage sayinges, and wise sentences of Salomon. *Ballad.* 1/2 sh. fol. *W. W*[*hite*] *f. T. P*[*avier, c.* 1615.] Ent. to E. White 1 au. 1586. HN.

22901 — [Anr. ed., w. title:] Solomons sentences. An excellent ditty. 1/2 sh.fol. [*f. H. Gosson, c.* 1635.] L(Rox. I.391ʳ).
Printed on the same sheet as 22904 and on the verso of 23012.

22902 — The reedifying of Salomons temple, and the laborers therof. *Ballad.* s.sh.fol. *f. W. Pickering,* [1564?] Ent. 4 se. 1564. HN.

22903 — Solomons charity. 1633. = pt. of 11199.

22904 — Solomons sacrifice. With his prayer in Gibeon. *Ballad.* 1/2 sh.fol. *f. H. Gosson,* [c. 1635.] L(Rox. I.390ᵛ). Pr. on the same sheet as 22901 and on the verso of 23012.

22905 — This is the dyalogus or cōmunyng betwxt [*sic*] the wyse king Salomon and Marcolphus. [*Tr.* from Latin.] 4°. (*andewerpe, G. leeu,*) [1492.] O. Duff 115. For a different version *see* 22899.

Solution. A solution of Doctor Resolutus. 1619. *See* 4364.

22906 **Some, Robert.** A godly and shorte treatise of the sacraments. 8°. (*T. Dawson*) *f. G. Bish.* [col.:] (*Byshoppe,*) 1582. Ent. to T. Dawson 24 my. L(lacks col.).L². C².P. 𝕬
Tp border has inits. T. D.

22906.5 — A godly and short treatise vpon the Lordes prayer, the xii. articles of the christian faith, and the ten commandements. 8°. *T. Dawson f. G. Bishop,* 1583. C²(imp.).P.

22907 — A godly sermon preached in Latin at Cambridge. 8°. *H. Middleton f. G. Bishop,* 1580. Ent. 17 my. L(3). L².O.C³.

22908 — A godly treatise containing and deciding certaine questions, touching the ministerie, sacraments, and church. 4°. *G. B*[*ishop,*] *deputie to C. Barker,* 1588. Ent. to G. Bishop 6 my. L.O.C².BRISTOL².E.+; F.HN.BO³.
Answers 19605.5; answered by 19604.

22909 — [Anr. ed., enlarged.] Whereunto one proposition more is added. After the ende you shall finde a defence . . . and a confutation of M. Penries last treatise. 4°. *G. B*[*ishop,*] *deputie to C. Barker,* 1588. L.O.C.E.P.+; F.HN.HD.N.U.+
2nd section reprints and answers 19604; answered by 12342.

22910 — A godlie treatise of the church. In the ende . . . a Treatise against oppression. 8°. (*T. Dawson,*) *imp. G. Bishop,* 1582 (1583.) Ent. 12 no. 1582. L².L³. O⁹(imp.).C¹⁵.P.+
(Formerly also 22911) Tp border has inits. T. D. Treatise of oppression reprinted in 19929 sq.

22911 — = 22910.

22912 — A godly treatise, wherein are examined and confuted many execrable fancies, giuen out by H. Barrow and J. Greenewood. 4°. *G. B*[*ishop,*] *deputie to C. Barker,* 1589. Ent. to G. Bishop 24 my. L.O.C.D².M.+; F.HN.HD.PN².U.+

22913 — Propositiones tres, piè, perspicuè, & breuitèr tractatæ. 1. Qui donantur à Deo. . . . 2. Verè fidelis, . . . 3. Christus mortuus est. . . . Addita est propositio consolationis. 8°. *Cantabrigiæ, ex off. J. Legat,* 1596. L⁴.C³.D.

22913a — [A trans.] Three questions, godly, plainly, and briefly handled. 8°. *J. Legat, pr. to the Univ. of Camb.,* 1596. O.C.

Some, Thomas, *ed. See* 15270.5.

22914 **Somer, Paulus van.** Figuræ variæ fictæ. [Post-1640.]

22915 **Somerset,** *County of.* 1607. A true report of certaine wonderfull overflowings of waters, in Summersetshire, Norfolke, and other places. 4°. *W. J*[*aggard*] *f. E. White,* [1607.] Ent. to E. White, jun., 6 fb. 1607. L.; HN. Penrose 357.
C3ʳ catchword: 'recouered'.

22915.5 — [Anr. ed.] 4°. *W. J*[*aggard*] *f. E. White,* [1607.] O.; F. C3ʳ catchword: 'downe'.

22916 — More strange newes: of wonderfull accidents hapning by the late overflowings of waters. 4°. *W. J*[*aggard*] *f. E. White,* [1607.] L.O.; HN. Includes reprint of 22915.

Somerset, Edward, *Duke of. See* Seymour, E.

Somerset, Thomas, *tr. See* 5010.5.

22917 **Sommers, William.** A briefe narration of the posses-sion, of W. Sommers. 1598. = 6281.

22917.5 **Sommers, William,** *Henry VIII's Jester.* A pleasant history of the life and death of Will Summers. And how hee came first to be knowne at the court, [etc.] 8⁰. *J. Okes, sold by F. Grove a. T. Lambart,* 1637. Ent. to J. Okes 25 ja. F.
    Film of F copy is on Univ. Microfilms reel 718 ('23434a').

22918 **Somner, William.** The antiquities of Canterbury. . . . With an appendix here annexed: wherein the manu-scripts, and records are exhibited. 4⁰. *J. L[egat] f. R. Thrale,* 1640. Ent. 4 no. 1639. L.O.C.D.E.+; F.HN. HD.N.Y.+
    1 copy each at F, HD has an extra leaf of errata after Vvv4. HN has added pr. dedic. to Charles II on his restoration.

22918.3 **Song.** A brave warlike song. Containing a briefe rehearsall of the deeds of chivalry, performed by the nine worthies [etc.] *Ballad.* 2 pts. s.sh.fol. *f. F. Coules,* [1626?] c⁶.
    Last stanza mentions Richard Peek, q.v.

22918.5 — A delicate new song, entituled, sweet-heart, I love thee. *Ballad.* 2 pts. s.sh.fol. *[E. Allde] f. H. G[osson,* c. 1625.] c⁶.

22918.7 — An excellent song wherein you shall finde great con-solation for a troubled minde. *Ballad.* 2 pts. s.sh.fol. *assignes of T. Symcocke,* [1628–29.] L.

22919 — A merry new song how a bruer meant to make a cooper cuckold. *Ballad.* s.sh.fol. [*H. Kirkham?* c. 1590.] L.

22919.1 — A merry new song of a rich widdowes wooing, that married a young man to her owne undooing. *Ballad.* 2 pts. s.sh.fol. *[M. Flesher] f. T. Langley,* [c. 1625.] c⁶.
— A merry new song. Wherein is shewed the cudgelling of the cobler of Colchester. [1589.] *See* 5530.5.

22919.2 — A most delicate, pleasant, amorous, new song, made by a gentleman that enjoyes his love, called, all lovers joy. *Ballad.* 2 pts. s.sh.fol. *[G. Purslowe] f. H. G[osson,* c. 1625.] c⁶.

22919.3 — A new little northren song called, under and over, over and under. *Ballad.* 2 pts. s.sh.fol. *[A. Mathewes] f. H. G[osson,* 1631?] Ent. to F. Coles and ballad ptnrs. 13 jn. 1631. c⁶.

22919.5 — A new song of a young mans opinion, of the difference betweene good and bad women. *Ballad.* 2 pts. s.sh.fol. *W. J[ones,* 1618?] Ent. to T. Lambert 7 fb. 1638. c⁶.
    (Formerly 25913) Begins: 'Shall I wrestling in dispaire,/ Dye because a womans faire,' and is a debased and augmented version of the Wither-Johnson poems in 6769.5. An abridgement of the ballad version is pr. in 14674.
— A new song to the great comfort of English harts. [1603.] *See* 14426.7.

22919.7 — A pleasant countrey Maying song. *Ballad.* 1/2 sh.fol. *f. T. L[angley?* c. 1625.] ?Ent. to F. Coles a. ballad ptnrs. 20 jn. 1629. c⁶.
— A pleasant new northerne song, called the two York-shire lovers. [c. 1630.] *See* 26103.5.

22919.9 — A pleasant new song, betwixt the saylor and his love. *Ballad.* 2 pts. s.sh.fol. *f. J. Grismond,* [c. 1625.] Ent. to ballad ptnrs. 14 de. 1624. c⁶.
    Has refrain: 'Kisse and bid me welcome home.'

22920 — [Anr. ed.] 2 pts. s.sh.fol. *f. F. C[oles,* c. 1640.] L.

22920.1 — A pleasant new song, if youle heare it, you may, of a north-country-lasse that had lost her way. *Ballad.* 2 pts. s.sh.fol. *[M. Flesher] f. H. Gosson,* [c. 1630.] Ent. to ballad ptnrs. 14 de. 1624. M³.
    First line begins: 'Within the North countrey, . . .'

22920.3 — A pleasant new songe of a joviall tinker [of 'Thurbie', i.e. Turvey.] *Ballad.* 2 pts. s.sh.fol. *[W. White] f. J. Trundle,* [1616?] Ent. 22 mr. 1616. c⁶.
    A considerably altered version of this is pr. in 4581, q.v.

22920.5 — ⟨   ⟩ Being a pleasant new song of the rites and ceremonies of mariage. *Ballad.* 2 pts. s.sh.fol. *[M. Flesher] f. F. Coules,* [c. 1630.] c⁶(I.428–9ᵛ, head-ing cropt).
    Printed on the verso of 7259.7.

Song—*cont.*

22920.7 — A pleasant song, made by a souldier, whose bringing up had bin dainty, [and who] tearmeth this his re-pentance, the fall of his folly. [By T. Stryde?] *Ballad.* 1/2 sh.fol. *f. J. Wright,* [c. 1630.] Ent. to R. Jones 24 ap. 1588; to ballad ptnrs. 14 de. 1624. c⁶.
    1st line: 'In Summer time when Phœbus rayes,'.

22920.9 — Here begins a pleasant song of a mayden faire, to purchase her desire, her coine she did not spare. *Ballad.* 2 pts. s.sh.fol. *f. H. Gosson,* [c. 1630.] c⁶.

22921 — A song made of nothing. *Ballad.* 2 pts. s.sh.fol. *f. J. Wright,* [c. 1635.] L.

22922 — A song or, story, for the lasting remembrance of divers famous works, which God hath done in our time. With an addition. [By J. Wilson, *of Boston.* In verse.] 4⁰. *R. Young f. J. Bartlet,* 1626. L(imp.).; HN.

22923 — A spiritual songe of thankesgiuing vnto God. Written by a close prisoner (with a coale) for his owne comforte. *Ballad.* s.sh.fol. [*London,*] 1592. HN.
— A very godly song, intituled, the earnest petition of a faithfull christian. [1624.] *See* 3194.5.

22924 **Songs.** In this boke ar cōteynyd .xx. sōges .ix. of .iiii. ptes, and .xi. of thre ptes. obl. 4⁰. (*Impryntyd in Londō at the signe of the black Morēs,*) 1530 (10 oc.) L(bassus, lacking colophon, and tp of triplex).L¹³ (frag. of tp and colophon only, of medius).
    The printer is unidentified and prob. dealt only in music; *see British Museum Quarterly,* XVI (1951), pp. 33–5. Chainlines in the tpp and colo-phon are perpendicular; in the text they are horizontal; a full leaf measures 5⅝ × 7¾ inches.

22925 **Sonnet.** An excellent sonnet: or, the swaines complaint. [By G. Wither.] *Ballad.* 2 pts. s.sh.fol. *f. J. Wright,* [1633?] Ent. to ballad ptnrs. 8 jy. 1633. L.G².
— A sweet and pleasant sonet. [1624.] *See* 7384.5.

22926 — A sweet sonnet, wherein the lover exclaimeth against fortune. *Ballad.* [post 1640.] L (sub 'Lover') has 3 eds. without imprint, c. 1650; cf. Wing S 6249.

22927 **Sonnibank, Charles.** The eunuche's conversion. A ser-mon. 8⁰. *H. L[ownes] f. R. Fleming,* 1617. Ent. 21 ja. L.O.C.C³.NLW.+; F.HD.

22928 **Soowthern, John.** Pandora, the musyque of the beautie, of his mistresse Diana. [In verse.] 4⁰. [*J. Charle-wood] f. T. Hackette,* 1584. L(lacks tp).; HN.

Sophister. The sophister. A comedy. 1639. *See* 26133.

22929 **Sophocles.** Sophoclis Antigone. Interprete T. Watsono. Huic adduntur pompæ quædam, ex singulis tra-gœdiæ actis deriuatæ. 4⁰. *J. Wolfius,* 1581. Ent. 31 jy. L.SHR.; F(imp.).HN.CHI. Greg L 1.

22930 **Sophronistes.** Sophronistes. A dialogue, perswading the people to reuerence God. 4⁰. *T. Orwin f. T. Man,* 1589. Ass'd by T. Man to R. Dexter 16 ja. 1598. L(2, 1 imp.).L²(2).O(3).C².; HD.SMITH.U.

Soppeth, Edward, *ed. See* 19816.

22931 **Soranzo, Lazzaro.** The Ottoman of Lazaro Soranzo. Wherein is delivered a report of the might and power of Mahamet the third. *Tr.* out of Italian by A. Hartwell. 4⁰. *J. Windet,* 1603. Ent. to J. Wolfe 8 de. 1599. L.L².O.YK. Athens, Gennadius Library.; HN. CHI.

Sorbonne. *See* Paris University.

22932 **Sorocold, Thomas.** Supplications of saints. A booke of prayers: divided into three parts. Wherein are three most excellent prayers made by queene Elizabeth. Third edition, enlarged. 12⁰. [*T. Snodham] f. N. Bourne,* 1612. Ent. to H. Rocket a. N. Bourne 24 se. 1608. L.

22933 — [Anr. ed., enlarged.] Supplications. . . . A booke of prayers and prayses. In foure parts. Sixth edition enlarged. 12⁰. *T. S[nodham] f. N. Bourne,* 1616. Rocket's pt. ass'd to Bourne 9 ap. C³.; F.

22933.3 — Eight edition. 12⁰. *T. S[nodham] f. N. Bourne,* 1619. LC.
    P. 242 line 2 of text: 'Winds and Sea'.

22933.5 — [Ninth? edition.] 12⁰. [*J. Beale f. N. Bourne,* 1619?] O(imp.).
    Dedic. dated 1 Feb. 1617; p. 131 prayers mention the Queen (Anne, d. 1619); p. 242 line 2 of text: 'windes and sea'. As Beale definitely pr. this, it most likely immediately precedes 22933.7.

Sorocold, Thomas—*cont.*

22933.7 — Tenth edition. 12°. *J. B[eale] f. N. Bourne,* 1622. O⁴.
P. 131 prayers omit the Queen.

22934 — Eleventh edition. 12°. *J. B[eale] f. N. Bourne,* 1623.
HN.

22934.2 — Sixteenth edition, corrected and enlarged. 12°. *J.
D[awson] f. H. Overton,* 1630. Ass'd to W. Sheffard
30 oc. 1627; to H. Overton 13 my. 1630. F.

22934.3 — Eighteenth edition. 12°. *J. D[awson] f. H. Overton,*
1631. L(imp.).

22934.5 — Twentie one edition. 12°. *J. D[awson] f. H. Overton,*
1634. MARL.

22934.7 — Twentietwo edition. 12°. *M. D[awson] f. H. Onerton*
[sic], 1635. O⁶.

22934.9 — Twentiefourth edition. 12°. *J. D[awson] f. H. Overton,*
1638. DUL.M².

22935 — Twentiefifth edition. 12°. *J. D[awson] f. H. Overton,*
1639. C(imp.).M².

22936 — Twentiesixth edition. 12°. *J. L[egat] f. H. Overton,*
1640. O.; PN².

Soter, Henrik, *ed. See* 23517.5.

22937 **Soto, Andreas de.** The ransome of time being captive.
Wherein is declared how precious a thing is time.
Tr. J. H(awkins.) 8°. *Doway, G. Pinsone,* 1634.
L.O.C.HP.; F.CU.
A&R 780. For anr. trans. *see* 20825.

22938 **Soto, Ferdinando de.** Virginia richly valued, by the
description of the maine land of Florida, out of the
foure yeeres continuall trauell of don Ferdinando de
Soto. Written by a Portugall gentleman of Elvas,
and *tr.* out of Portugese by R. Hakluyt. 4°. F.
Kyngston f. M. Lownes, 1609. L.O.C¹³.D.G².+; HN.
HD.LC.N.NY.+

22939 — [Anr. issue, w. cancel tp:] The worthye and famous
history, of the travailes, discovery, & conquest, of
Terra Florida. [*F. Kingston*] *f. M. Lownes,* 1611.
L.; NY.

22939a **Soul.** Desiderius. The soules desire, and the hope of
heaven. 1609. Now = 6777.4.
— The soules humiliation. 1637, etc. *See* 13728 sqq.
— The soules implantation. 1637, etc. *See* 13731 sq.
— The soules preparation. 1632, etc. *See* 13735 sqq.
— The soules request. 1618. *See* pt. 2 of 21097.

22940 — The soules solace. 1626. = 14494.
22941 — [Anr. ed.] 1631. = 14495.

22941.5 **Souterius, Daniel.** Bausme de Galaad, . . . en quatre
langues. (Dakrua basilika. That is, the princly [sic]
teares of Elisabetha, queene of Bohemia: over the
death, of her eldest sonne, Fridericus Henricus.—
Consolation chrestienne. — Christelicke vertroo-
stinge. — Trenodia & singultus.) [In verse.] *Eng.,
Fr., Dutch, a. Lat.* 4 pts. 12°. *Haarlem, (H. Cranepoel,*
1629.) L.O.; HN.

Southampton. The seuerall rates . . . set foorth for Southampton. [1563.] *See* 7957.5.

22942 **Southerne, Edmund.** A treatise concerning the right
vse and ordering of bees: newlie set forth. 4°. *T.
Orwin f. T. Woodcocke,* 1593. Ent. 30 jn. L.; HN.HD.

Southwark. The articles of lete and courte for the lyber-
ties of Southwarke. 4°. *J. Cawood,* 1561. O.
Prob. issued w. 22944.

22943 — The charge of the court baron [of Southwark.] 4°.
J. Cawood, 1561. O.
Prob. issued w. 22943.

22944

22945 — To the high court of parliament. [1642.] = pt. of
Wing T 1397.

Southwark, *Guild of St. George. See* Indulgences 70 sqq.

22945.5 **Southwark,** *St. Saviour's.* S⁺. Saivour [sic] of Southwarke. A rate of duties belonging to the corporation
of the churchwardens of the parish of S⁺. Saviour
of Southwarke, . . . 1613. s.sh.fol. [*J. Beale,* 1613.]
L⁵(Lemon 136).

Southwell, Robert. The dutifull advice of a loving sonne.
1632, etc. *See* 156 sqq.
— An epistle of a religious priest. [1597?] *See* 22968.5.

22946 — An epistle of comfort, to the reuerend priestes, & to
the laye sort restrayned in durance. [Anon.] 8°.
Paris, [i.e. *London, J. Charlewood? in Arundel
House,* 1587?] L.O.C.P.YK.+; F.HN.HD.N.Y.+
A&R 781.

Southwell, Robert—*cont.*

22947 — [Anr. ed.] 8°. [*English secret press,*] 1605. L.O.C².E.
W.+; F.HN.N.TEX.U.+
A&R 782.

22948 — [Anr. ed.] By R. S(outhwell) of the society of Jesus.
8°. [*St. Omer, English College Press,*] 1616. L.L⁹.C².
DE.OS.+; F.
A&R 783.

22949 — A foure-fould meditation, of the foure last things. By
R: S. The author of S. Peters complaint. [Actually
by Philip Howard, *Earl of Arundel.*] 1606. Now =
13868.7.

22949.5 — An humble supplication to her maiestie. [Against 8207.
Anon.] 8°. [*English secret press,*] 1595 [really 1600.]
L.L².CASHEL.DE.OS.+; F. 𝔄
(Formerly 7586) A&R 784.

22950 — Marie Magdalens funeral teares. [Init. S. W., i.e.
SouthWell.] 8°. *J. W[olfe] f. G. C[awood,]* 1591.
Ent. to G. Cawood 8 no. w(imp.).; HN.

22950.5 — [Anr. ed.] 8°. *J. W[olfe] f. G. C[awood,]* 1592. SN.; F.

22951 — [Anr. ed.] 8°. *A. I[slip] f.] G. C[awood,]* 1594. L².L⁹.O.

22951.5 — [Anr. ed.] [1596?] *See* Addenda.

22952 — [Anr. ed.] 8°. *J. R[oberts] f. W. L(eake,)* 1602. Ent. to
W. Leake 2 jy. L(imp.).C³.BUTE.; HN.

22953 — [Anr. ed.] 4°. [*T. Snodham*] *f. W. Leake,* 1609. L.C.
DUL.; F.CH.N.NY.

22954 — Now = 22955.5.

22955 — Mœoniæ. Or, certaine excellent poems and spirituall
hymnes: omitted in the last impression of Peters
Complaint. By R. S[outhwell.] 4°. *V. Sims f. J.
Busbie,* 1595. Ent. 17 oc. C.C².; HN(A2 only, in
22956).WEL(lacks A2; has A2 of 22956 inserted).
B3ʳ catchword: 'The'; B1ʳ line 1 ends: 'shroude,'.

22955.3 — [Anr. ed.] 4°. *V. Sims f. J. Busbie,* 1595. L(2).L⁶.O(2).
O¹⁸.C.; F.HN.CH.HD.Y.+
B3ʳ catchword: 'The'; B1ʳ line 1 ends: 'shrowde,'.
Really pr. [1599?] and later than 22955.5.

22955.5 — [Anr. ed.] 4°. *V. Sims f. J. Busbie,* 1595. SHEF.; F.
HN.HD.NY.
(Formerly 22954) B3ʳ catchword: 'His'.

22955.7 — Saint Peters complaint, with other poemes. [Anon.] 4°.
[*J. Windet f.*] *J. Wolfe,* 1595. O(imp.).; F(imp.).HN.
Pp. 56; no sidenotes.

22956 — [Anr. ed., corrected and enlarged.] 4°. *J. R[oberts] f.
G. C[awood,]* 1595. Ent. to G. Cawood 5 ap. C.;
F.HN(lacks A2; has A2 of 22955 inserted).WEL(A2
only, in 22955). 𝔄

22957 — [Anr. ed.] 4°. [*J. Windet f.*] *J. Wolfe,* 1595. C².BUTE.;
HN.
Pp. '65' (i.e. 70); with sidenotes pp. 1–30.

22958 — [Anr. ed.] 4°. *J. R[oberts] f. G. C[awood,]* 1597. E.
G²(imp.).SHEF.; HN.

22959 — [Anr. ed.] 4°. *J. R[oberts] f. G. C[awood,]* 1599. L.L⁶.;
F(2, 1 imp.).HN.

22960 — [Anr. ed.] 4°. *Edinburgh, R. Walde-graue,* [1600?] L.;
F(2). Hickmott.
A slightly altered version of the text is found only
in this ed.

22960a — [Anr. ed.] Newlie augmented with other poems. 4°.
J. R[oberts] f. G. C[awood,] 1602. O.; HD.

22961 — [Anr. ed.] 4°. *H. L[ownes] f. W. Leake,* [1609?] Ent.
2 jy. 1602. L.O¹⁸.C.DUL.; F.HN.CH.ILL.Y.+

22962 — [Anr. ed.] 4°. *W. Stansby f. W. Barret,* 1615. Ass'd 16 fb.
1617. L.O(imp.).C.; F(2, 1 imp.). Robert Taylor.
For Barret's next ed. *see* 22965; see also 22967.

22963 — S. Peters Complaint. And saint Mary Magdalens
funerall teares. With sundry other selected, and
devout poems. By R. S[outhwell] of the society of
Jesus. 8°. [*St. Omer, English College Press,*] 1616.
L.HP.ST.W.; F.HN.FORDHAM(imp.).PFOR.
A&R 785.

22964 — [Anr. ed.] By R. Southwell. 8°. [*St. Omer, English
College Press,*] 1620. L.C(tp only, inserted in 22966).
ROME(lacks tp).ST(2). Thomas Eyston, East Hendred,
Berks.; F(2).HD.WIS.
A&R 786.

22965 — [Anr. ed., enlarged, of 22962.] S⁺ Peters Complainte
Mary Magdal. teares wᵗʰ other workes. (Mœoniæ.—
The triumphs over death.—Short rules of good
life.) [Init. R. S.] 12°. [*R. Field*] *f. W. Barret,* 1620.
Short Rules ent. 13 jy. L.O.O¹⁸(lacks tp).OS(lacks
tp).USHAW(imp.).+; F.HN.TEX. Hickmott.

22966 — [Anr. ed.] 12°. *J. Haviland, sould by R. Allott,* 1630.
Ass'd to J. Parker 8 no. 1624. L.O.C(w. tp of 22964).
C³. Juel-Jensen(imp.).+; F.HN.HD(w. tp of 22968)
TEX.Y.+

Southwell, Robert—*cont.*

22967 — [Anr. ed., w. omissions, of 22962.] Saint Peters complaint. [Anon.] 4°. *Edinburgh, J. Wreittoun,* 1634. E.; F.

In addition to the Complaint this ed. has only 1 short poem: Content and rich.

22968 — [Anr. ed. of 22966, init. R. S.] 12°. *J. Haviland, sould by E. Benson,* 1636 (1634). Ass'd to J. Haviland a. J. Wright 4 se. 1638. L.O⁶.DUL.E.NOR².; F.HD(tp only, inserted in 22966).Y.

22968.5 — A short rule of good life. Newly set forth according to the authours direction before his death. [Anon.] (An epistle of a religious priest vnto his father. [Init. R. S.]) 2 pts. 12°. [*London? Fr. Garnet's second press,* 1597?] USHAW.; N(frag.).

A&R 787. Epistle on separate signatures; part of the Epistle is reprinted as 156 sqq.

22969 — [Anr. ed., on continuous signatures.] 12°. [*V. Simmes,* 1597?] Ent. to J. Wolfe 25 no. 1598. L²(2, 1 imp.).C³.

A&R 788. Collates A–I¹². tp line 2: 'Rule of good'.

22969.3 — [Anr. ed.] 12°. [*English secret press,* 1602–05.] O.

A&R 789. Collates A–I¹²; tp line 2: 'RVLE OF'.

22969.5 — [Anr. ed.] 12°. [*Douai, C. Boscard,* 1603–10.] AMP. COLWICH (lacks Epistle).W.YK².

A&R 790. Collates A–I¹² K⁶. AMP has quire A in a different setting from W.

22970 — [Anr. ed.] 24° in 8's. *S. Omers, [C. Boscard f.] J. Heigham,* 1622. L.

A&R 791.

22971 — The triumphs over death: or, a consolatorie epistle. [Init. R. S.] 4°. *V. S[immes] f. J. Busbie, sold at N. Lings shop,* 1595. Ent. 20 no. 1595. O⁵.C.; HN.

Reprinted in 22965.

22972 — [Anr. ed.] 4°. *V. Simmes f. J. Busbie, solde at N. Lings shop,* 1596. L(3).O.O¹⁸.C.; F.HN.CH.HD.

A3ᵛ line 2: 'Æsopes'. Really pr. [1600?] and later than 22973.

22973 — [Anr. ed.] 4°. *V. Simmes f. J. Busbie, solde at N. Lings shop,* 1596. L⁶.; F.HD.

A3ᵛ line 2: 'Esopes'.

Southworth, John. *See* 21505.

Sovereign of the Seas, *Ship. See* 19489.5.

22974 **Sowernam, Ester,** *pseud.* Ester hath hang'd Haman: or an answere to a lewd pamphlet, [23533]. 4°. [*T. Snodham] f. N. Bourne,* 1617. Ent. 4 ja. L(2, 1 imp.). O.; F(imp.).HN.

Sozinger, Andreas. Disputatio juridica. 1610. *See* 22890.5.

Sp., *Mr., of Queenes Colledge in Cambridge.* A sermon concerning confession of sinnes. 1637. *See* 23029.

Sp., Ed. *See* Spenser, Edmund.

22975 **Spa.** A briefe discourse of the hypostasis, or substance of the water of Spaw. *Tr.* out of French [partly from G. Philaretus] by G. T. This hypostasis is to be sold by doctor H. Seminus, Italian, in S. Paules Alley, in Red-crosse-street. 4°. [*W. Jaggard,* 1612?] L.; BO⁵.NLM(2).

22976 **Spackman, Norwich.** A sermon before his majestie at White-hall the first of May 1614. 8°. *J. Beale,* 1614. L⁴.

22977 **Spackman, Thomas.** A declaration of such greivous accidents as follow the biting of mad dogges, together with the cure thereof. 4°. [*Eliot's Court Press] f. J. Bill,* 1613. Ent. 3 jy. L.O.A.G²(lacks tp).SHEF.+; HN.HD.

22978 **Spagnuoli, Baptista.** [Colophon:] (Expliciunt bucolica fratris Baptistæ Mantuani). [In verse. *Ed.*] (J. Badius, *Ascensius.*) 4° 4·8. (*per W. de Worde,* 1523 (my.)) NOR(imp.).; HN(lacks A1).

22979 — [Anr. ed.] 4° 4·8. (*per W. de Worde,* 1526 (no.)) O(lacks A1).

22980 — [Anr. ed.] Baptistæ Mantuani Carmelitæ theologi adolescentia, seu bucolica, breuibus J. Badij commentarijs illustrata. His accesserunt J. Murmeillij argumenta. Accessit, & index, opera B. Laurentis. 8°. *J. Kyngstonus,* 1569. C.

22981 — [Anr. ed.] 8°. *J. Kyngstonus,* 1572. L³.; ILL.

22982 — [Anr. ed.] 8°. *ap. T. Marsh,* 1573. L.

Spagnuoli, Baptista—*cont.*

22982.3 — [Anr. ed.] 8°. *ap. T. Marsh,* 1576. F.

22982.5 — [Anr. ed.] 8°. *ap. T. Marsh,* 1577. F.Y.

22982.7 — [Anr. ed.] 8°. *ap. T. Marsh,* 1580. L(tp only, Harl. 5993/55). LK.; ILL.

22983 — [Anr. ed.] 16° in 8's. *ex off. typ. T. Marsh,* 1582. L.

22983.5 — [Anr. ed.] 8°. *G. Dewes & H. Marsh, ex ass. T. Marsh,* 1584. L(tp only, Ames I.429).; HD.

22984 — [Anr. ed.] 8°. *R. Robinsonus,* 1590. O.; HN.HD.ILL.

22984.1 — [Anr. ed.] 8°. *R. Robinsonus,* 1593. O.

22984.3 — [Anr. ed.] 8°. [*R. Robinson f.*] *R. Dexter,* 1598. L(tp only, Ames I.613).

A complete copy was offered in Colin Richardson, Catalogue 156 (1967), item 261, untraced.

22984.4 — [Anr. ed.] 8°. *ap. R. Dexter,* 1601. F.

22984.5 — [Anr. ed.] 8°. *pro Soc. Stat.,* 1606. O.

22984.6 — [Anr. ed.] 8°. [*F. Kingston*,] *ex typ. Soc. Stat.,* 1613. L.M⁴.P(imp.).; ILL.

22984.7 — [Anr. ed.] 8°. [*J. Beale?*] *ex typ. Soc. Stat.,* 1617. L(tp only, Ames II.467).

22984.9 — [Anr. ed.] 8°. *ex typ. Soc. Stat.,* 1622. Ent. to the English Stock 5 mr. 1620. O²⁸.; F.

22985 — [Anr. ed.] 8°. [*F. Kingston*,] *ex typ. Soc. Stat.,* 1627. L.O².

22986 — [Anr. ed.] 8°. *Cantabrigiæ, ex acad. typog.,* 1632. L¹³. O¹³.C.C¹⁹(imp.).; WEL.

22987 — [Anr. ed.] 8°. *Cantabrigiæ, ex acad. typog.,* 1634. C.C².

22988 — [Anr. ed.] 8°. *Cantabrigiæ, ex typog. acad.,* 1635. L.O. C.C¹⁰.; F.

22989 — [Anr. ed.] 8°. *ex typ. E. Purslow, imp. Soc. Stat.,* 1638. L.O.A.

22990 — [A trans.] The eglogs of the poet B. Mantuan Carmelitan, turned into English verse, by G. Turbervile gent. 1567. 8°. *H. Bynneman,* (1567.) Ent. 1566–67. L.O(imp.).O⁶.E.; F(imp.).HN.HD(imp.).NCU.

22991 — [Anr. ed.] 8°. *H. Bynneman,* 1572. HN.

22991.5 — [Anr. ed.] 8°. *J. Danter,* 1594. L(imp.).; F(imp.).

22992 — A lamentable complaynte of Baptista Mātuanus. Paraphrastically *tr.* into Englishe by J. Bale. 8°. [*S. Mierdman? f.*] (*J. Daye,*) [1551?] F.

22992.1 — Here begynnyth the lyfe of the gloryous martyr saynt George, *tr.* by a. barclay. [In verse.] 4° 8·4. [*R. Pynson,* 1515?] C²(imp.).

Has McK. 9 w. Pynson's name; end of text dated 3 non. Aug. 1515.

— *See also* Indulgences 25.

SPAIN

OFFICIAL DOCUMENTS (*Chronological*)

— A proclamation set out by the K. of Spaine. For the vse of merchandise. 1592. *See* 18464.5.

22992.3 — The edict and decree of Phillip, king of Spaine, touching the exchanging of monyes. First *tr.* out of Spanish, and now out of French into English by W. P[hilip?] 4°. [*f.*] *J. Wolfe,* 1597. Ent. 17 mr. L³⁰.O.

(Formerly 19833)

— The true copie of an edict, made by the king of Spaine, concerning Portugall. [1602.] *See* 20128.

— A proclamation or edict. Touching the traffique, of Spain. 1603. *See* 18472.

22992.5 — The severall proclamations lately published by the king of Spaine, and the French king: wherein are concluded certaine articles of amitie and commerce. 2 pts. 4°. *T. C[reede] f. C. Burbie,* 1604. O⁷.DUR.

(Formerly 19840) Pt. 2 also issued separately as 13122.

— A proclamation of the truce betweene Spayne, and the States generall. 1609. *See* 18472a.5.

22992.7 — Newes from Spaine. The king of Spaines edict, for the expulsion of Moores. *Tr.* out of Spanish by W. I. [12 Jan. 1610.] 4°. [*E. Allde*] *f. N. Butter,* 1611. Ent. 19 no. L.O.D²(imp.).; F.NCU.

(Formerly 22995)

22992.9 — A proclamation for reformation, published . . . by Philip the fourth. Wherein his majesty hath reformed many abuses in the common-wealth. *Tr.* out of Spanish. [10 Feb. 1623.] 4°. [*J. Dawson?*] *f. N. Butter, N. Bourne a. T. Archer,* [1623.] Ent. to N. Bourne 10 mr. 1623. L.L³⁰.O.C.DUR⁵.+; F.HN.HD.N.

(Formerly 19844) Tp varies; line 7 begins: 'Hie and Mighty' (HN) or 'High and Mighty' (HD).

— A proclamation made in the name of his majesty of Spaine. 1630. *See* 17916.6.

Spain—*cont.*

— A briefe declaration of the peace now intreating betweene the king of Spaine, [etc.] 1608. *See* 18455.3.

22993 — A discourse more at large of the late ouerthrowe giuen to the king of Spaines armie at Turnehaut, by Morris of Nassawe, wherunto is adioined praiers in Latine, found about diuerse of the Spaniards. *Tr.* out of French according to the copy printed in the Low Countries. 4°. [*P. Short,*] solde [*by J. Flasket a. P. Linley,*] 1597. L.
For a different account *see* 17678.

22994 — Newes from Spayne and Holland conteyning. An information of Inglish affayres in Spayne. Written by a gentleman trauelour borne in the Low Countryes, and brought vp in Ingland. [By R. Parsons. *Tr.* and augmented by H. Walpole.] 8°. [*Antwerp, A. Conincx,*] 1593. L.L².L⁴³.D².; F.
A&R 634.

22995 — Newes from Spaine. 1611. Now = 22992.7.
— Noua descriptio Hispaniae. [Map.] 1555. *See* 11718.7.

22996 — The present state of Spaine. *Tr.* out of French [by R. Sergier?] 4°. *P. S[hort] f. R. Serger,* 1594. Ent. 6 no. HAT(lacks all after E4)*.; F(lacks *1).HN.HD.N.
Collates A⁴(A1+*1) B–E⁴ Ee². As *1, the dedic. to R. Sonds, was pr. as H2 of 22997, it is clear that both 'issues' were pr. at the same time. Whether the copies listed above are imperfect or represent a distinct issue is uncertain.

22997 — [Anr. issue, w. extra quires F–G⁴ H² (H2 = *1), w. F1ʳ heading:] (A copy of speciall record, of the homage done by Philip archduke of Austria, to the king of France, Lewes the twelft in 1499.) *P. S[hort] f. R. Serger,* 1594. L.O(2).O⁸.YK. Chester PL.; F.PN. TEX.Y. Pirie.
One O copy (4° M36(9) Art.) has the tp date altered in ink to 1596.

22998 — A proclamation or edict. 1603. = 18472a.
— A true coppie of a discourse [etc.] 1589. *See* 6790.

22999 — A true discourse of the armie which the king of Spaine assembled in Lisbon. *Tr.* out of French by D. Archdeacon. Whereunto is added the verses that were printed in the first page of the Dutch copy printed at Colen. 8°. *J. Wolfe,* 1588. Ent. 30 au.; Distichon ent. 10 se. L(3).O(2).O⁵.C.; F.HN.HD(imp.).IND.NY.+
Copies vary: with or without the verses Distichon Coloniensium on E4; copies of both at L,O.
— Two famous sea fights. Betwixt the fleetes of Spaine, and the Hollanders. 1639. *See* 22132.
— Vox populi. Or newes from Spayne. 1620. *See* 22098 sqq.

Spalatro, *Archbishop of. See* Dominis, M. A. de.

Spalding, Augustine, *tr. See* 810.

23000 **Spangenberg, Johann.** [Heading A1ʳ:] De conficiendis epistolis liber. 8°. [*Edinburgh, J. Ross,* 1580?] Private owner.

23001 — Margarita theologica, continens praecipuos locos doctrinæ christianæ. 8°. [*Antwerp? f.*] *Londini, ap. G. Dewes,* 1566. L.C.

23002 — [Anr. ed.] 8°. *ap. H. Bynneman,* 1570. Ent. 1569–70. L.O.A.DUR³.ELY.+

23003 — [Anr. ed.] 8°. *ap. H. Bynneman,* 1573. L.BIRM²(K.N.). D(imp.).LK.WIN².; HD.

23004 — [A trans.] The sũ of diuinitie drawen out of the holy scripture. [Anon.] Drawen out of Latine into Englishe by R. Hutten. 8°. [*R. Grafton? f.*] (*J. Day a. W. Seres,*) 1548 (5 oc.) L.C.C⁴.; F.
A3ʳ line 4 ends: 'should'.

23004.5 — [Anr. ed.] 8°. [*R. Grafton? f.*] (*J. Day a. W. Seres,*) 1548 (5 oc.) L³.O(2, 1 lacks tp).BUTE.; F(imp.).
A3ʳ line 4 ends: 'shoulde'. Quire S is same setting as 23004.

23005 — [Anr. ed.] 8°. *J. Awdely,* 1560 (18 oc.) Ent. to J. Sampson, i.e. Awdeley, 20 se. F.
Colophon dated 24 Oct.

23006 — [Anr. ed.] 8°. *J. Awdely,* 1561 (8 au.) F.
23007 — [Anr. ed.] 8°. *J. Awdely,* 1567 (15 mr.) O.O⁹.C.C⁴.; ILL.

Spaniard. The Spaniards perpetuall designes. 1624. *See* 22086.

23008 **Spaniards.** A briefe discourse of the cruell dealings of the Spanyards, in Gulick and Cleue. A copie of [Prince Maurice's] letter to the states of the Westphalian

Spaniards—*cont.*
Creits. A copie of the letter of [Ernest,] archbishop of Colen, to the land-grave of Hessen. *Tr.* out of Dutch. 4°. [*J. Windet f.*] *J. Wolfe,* 1599. Ent. 19 fb. L.L².O².C.C⁹.
— A true reporte of the overthrowe given unto the Spaniards. 1605. *See* 1900.

Spanish Bawd. The Spanish bawd represented in Celestina. 1631. *See* 4911.

23009 **Spanish Fleet.** A true relation of that which lately hapned to the great Spanish fleet, and galeons of Terra Firma. *Tr.* out of the Spanish. 4°. [*G. Eld*] *f. N. Butter, N. Bourne, a. W. Sheffard,* 1623. Ent. 5 my. L.; F.HN.

23010 **Spanish Humours.** A pageant of Spanish humours. Wherin are naturally described, the kinds of a signior of Spaine. *Tr.* out of Dutche by H. w. 4°. [*J. Windet f.*] *J. Wolfe,* 1599. Ent. 23 ja. L.

23010.5 **Spanish Language.** [Heading A2ʳ:] The boke of Englysshe, and Spanysshe. 8°. (*R. wyer,*) [1554?] L(lacks tp).
Extracted and rearranged from the multilingual vocabularies, cf. 6832.7 sqq.

23010.7 — A very profitable boke to lerne the maner of redyng, writyng, & speakyng english & Spanish. 8°. (*J. Kyngston a. H. Sutton f. J. Wyght,*) 1554. L.
The Spanish is taken from the Barlement 4-language *Vocabulaer,* Louvain, 1551.

Spanish Lies. A libell of Spanish lies. 1596. *See* 6551.

23011 — A packe of Spanish lyes, sent abroad in the world: first printed in Spanish and *tr.* out of the originall. Now ripped vp, and condemned. 4°. *deputies of C. Barker,* 1588. L.L².O.C².D².+; F.HN.N.

Spanish Navy. Certaine aduertisements out of Ireland, concerning the losses to the Spanish nauie. 1588. *See* pt. 2 of 15412.

Spanish Pilgrim. The Spanish pilgrime. 1625. *See* 19838.5.

Spanish Practices. An experimentall discouerie of Spanish practises. 1623. *See* 22077.
— A second part of Spanish practises. 1624. *See* 22078.5.

Spanish Rodomontades. *See* 11691.5.

Spanish Ships. A second eighty eight or the overthrowe of the Spainsh [*sic*] ships. 1631. *See* 22142.7.
— A true relation of a wonderfull sea fight between Spanish ships. 1621. *See* 22130.

Spanish Tragedy. The Spanish tragedie. [1592, etc.] *See* 15086 sqq.

23012 — The Spanish tragedy, containing the lamentable murders of Horatio and Bellimperia. *Ballad.* 2 pts. s.sh.fol. *f. H. Gosson,* [1620?] L(2, Rox. I.364–5, Rox. I.390ʳ, 391ᵛ).
The 2nd L copy has 22901, 22904 pr. on the verso.

23013 **Spare.** Spare yo⟨ur good.⟩ [In verse.] 4°. [*W. de Worde,* c. 1515.] O(tp only, defective).
Tp verso line 2 from bottom: 'theym'.

23014 — [Anr. ed.] 4°. (*T. marshe,*) [1555?] F.
Tp verso line 2 from bottom: 'them'.

23014a — [A variant, w. colophon:] [*T. Marsh f.*] (*A. Kytson,*) [1555?] O.

Spark. A sparke of Christs beauty. 1622. *See* 14573.

23015 **Sparke, Edward.** The christians map of the world: drawne at the funerals of Mʳ. Henry Chitting esquire, Chester-Herauld at Armes. 8°. *J. N[orton] f. R. Thrale,* 1637. Ent. 5 mr. 1638. L.O.; F(impr. shaved).

23015.7 **Sparke, Michael.** Crumms of comfort, the valley of teares, and the hill of joy: with the thankefull remembrance, 1588. by water. The wonderful deliverance, 1605. by fire. And the miracle of mercy, 1625. by earth. The sixt edition. [Init. T. S.] 24° in 12's. [*I. Jaggard*] *f. M. Sparke,* 1627. Ent. 7 oc. 1623. ILL(imp.).
ILL also has engr. tp: 'The valley of teares. 6 edition. *f. M. Spark,* 1627.' This should apparently have 23018, q.v., cut up as folding plates. *See also* 21383.

Sparke, Michael—*cont.*

23016 — [Anr. ed.] The crums of comfort with godly prayers. Corrected and amended. 7. edition. (Thankfull remembrances of Gods wonderfull deliverances of this land.) [Init. M. S.] 2 pts. 24° in 12's. [*T. Cotes*] *f. M. Spark*, 1628. L.

23016.5 — 8. edition. 24° in 12's. [*T. Cotes*] *f. M. Spark*, 1628 (1629.) HD.
　　This and following eds. have Thankfull Remembrances on continuous signatures. P10ᵛ line 1: '65 A speciall Remedy for'.

23016.7 — 9. edition. 24° in 12's. [*T. Cotes*] *f. M. Spark*, 1629. Sotheby's 20 Oct. 1970, lot 60.
　　This was purchased by Hofmann & Freeman for Weissman but was lost in the mail.

23017 — 10. edition. 24° in 12's. [*T. Cotes*] *f. M. Spark*, 1629. (1630.) O(imp.).
　　P10ᵛ line 1 of this and 23017.3: '66 A good praier.' O also has O8–P12 (Douce frag.b.1(83)) in another setting with P10ᵛ line 1: '66 A good prayer.'

23017.3 — 12 edition. 24° in 12's. [*T. Cotes*] *f. M. Sparke*, 1631 (1630.) O.
　　Partly from same setting as 23017 (quires O–P at least).

23017.5 — 20. edition. 24° in 12's. (*Eliz. All-de*) *f. M. Sparke*, (1635.) L(imp.).

23017.7 — The poore orphans court, or orphans cry. [Init. M. S.] 4°. *A. G[riffin] f. M. S[parke,] jun.*, 1636. Ent. to Mrs. Griffin 7 no. L.O.C².G².LYD.; F.
　　(Formerly 21509)

23018 — To the glory of God in thankefull remembrance of our three great deliverances. [Anon. Engr. by J. Barra w. letterpress text above and below.] s.sh.fol. [*f. M. Sparke?* 1627.] ?Ent. to M. Flesher 30 no. 1624. L⁵(Lemon 266).
　　The engravings, w. text pr. on the verso, were also apparently issued as folding plates in 23016 sqq. *See* Hind III.101, 215. At the end of the text the reader is referred to 23015.7, which is described as '*printed by I. Jaggard, for M. Sparke,* . . . 1627.'

— Thankfull remembrances of Gods wonderfull deliverances of this land. 1628, etc. *See* pt. 2 of 23016 sqq.

— *See also* 21383.

23019 **Sparke, Thomas.** An answere to master John de Albines, notable discourse against heresies [274]. 4° in 8's. *Oxforde, J. Barnes*, 1591. L.O.C³.D.YK.+; F.HN.CHI.HD.U.

— A brief and short catechisme. [1580.] *See* 23025.

23019.5 — A brotherly perswasion to unitie, and uniformitie touching the received, and present ecclesiasticall government. 4°. *N. Okes f. Roger Jackson*, 1607. Ent. 29 ja. L.O³.C.BED.LIV².+; F.HN.HD.MICH.U.+
　　Answered in 13395.

23020 — [Anr. ed.] Newly corrected and enlarged. 4°. *N. Oakes [a. W. White] f. Roger Jackson*, 1607. L.O.C.CARLISLE.YK.+; BO³.HD.
　　Okes pr. only quires A–B.

— A catechisme, or short kind of instruction. Whereunto is prefixed a learned treatise. 1588. *See* 13030.

23021 — The high way to heauen by the cleare light of the gospell. 8°. *R. R[obinson] f. R. Dexter*, 1597. L.D.WI.; HD.U.

23021.5 — A sermon preached at Cheanies the 14. of September, 1585. at the buriall of the right honorable the earle of Bedford. 8°. *Oxford, J. Barnes*, [1585.] D.LINC.; F.

23022 — [Anr. ed.] 8°. *London,* [*J. Windet,*] 1585. L(imp.). O.C.D.COL.; HN.
　　For piracies by Windet of another book also pr. at Oxford see 19359, 19363.

23023 — [Anr. ed.] Newly corrected. 8°. *Oxford, J. Barnes*, 1594. L.O.C³.C⁵.LINC.+

23024 — A sermon preached at Whaddon in Buckinghamshyre the 22. of Nouember 1593. at the buriall of Arthur lorde Grey of Wilton. 8°. *Oxford, J. Barnes*, 1593. L(4).O(2).C.C.; F.

23025 — A short treatise, very comfortable for all troubled in theyr consciences. (A brief and short catechisme.) 8°. [*H. Bynneman f.*] *R. Newbery*, 1580. Ent. to H. Bynneman 26 oc. F.
　　C1ʳ catchword: 'nesse'; E2ʳ catchword: 'likelye'.

Sparke, Thomas—*cont.*

23025.5 — [Anr. ed.] 8°. [*H. Bynneman f.*] *R. Newbery*, 1580. L(2nd pt. only).L⁴(1st pt. only).C²(2nd pt. only).; HD.ILL.
　　C1ʳ catchword: 'is'; E2ʳ catchword: 'when'.

— *tr. See* 13030.

23026 **Sparke, William.** The mystery of godlinesse: a generall discourse of the reason that is in christian religion. (Booke I.—II.) 4°. *Oxford,* (*J. Lichfield*) *f. W. Webb*, 1628. O.O¹².C.C³.E.+; U.Y.

23027 — [A variant, w. imprint on gen. tp:] *Oxford, f. W. Webb*, 1629. L.O.C⁵.LINC.M.+; F.HD(lacks dedic. and Bk. II).
　　Has 1628 colophon as in 23026.

23028 — Vis naturæ et virtus vitæ explicatæ, comparatæ, ad universum doctrinæ ordinem constituendum. 8°. *R. Field*, 1612. Ent. 20 ja. L.L⁴³.O.C³.C¹⁰.

23029 **Sparrow, Anthony.** A sermon concerning confession of sinnes, and the power of absolution. Preached by Mʳ. Sp[arrow] of Queenes Colledge in Cambridge. 4°. *R. Bishop f. J. Clark dwelling . . . in Corne-hill*, 1637. Ent. 13 jy. L.O².C³.D.STU.+; HD.Y.

23029.5 — [Anr. issue, corrected and reimposed, w. imprint:] *R. Bishop f. J. Clark, and are to bee sold at his shop . . . in Corn-hill*, 1637. L.O.C.STD.YK.+; F.HD.U.

23029.7 — [Anr. ed.] 4°. *R. Bishop f. J. Clarke, and are to be sold at his shop . . . in Corne-hill,* [really *Dublin*,] 1637. SMU.

Sparry, Francis, *tr. See* 4864.

Speagle, Huldricke van, *pseud.* Drinke and welcome. 1637. *See* 23749.

Specimen. Specimen corruptelarum pontificiarum in Cypriano. 1626. *See* 14461.

23030 **Spectacle.** A spectacle for a blinde papist. 8°. *J. Charlewood a.* [i.e. *for*] *E. White,* [1582.] Ent. to E. White 2 my. 1582. L²(imp.).

— A spectacle for periurers. [1589.] *See* 11485.5.

23030.3 — A spectacle for usurers and succors of poore folkes bloud. Whereby they may see, Gods revenge, upon oppression. With a horrible murther. [*Tr.* from French.] 4°. [*G. Eld*] *f. J. Wright*, 1606. Ent. 21 no. HN.

Speculum. Speculum Xpristiani. [1486?] *See* 26012.

— Speculum iuuenum. 1547. *See* 19195.

23030.7 — Speculum spiritualiũ: in quo nõ solum de vita actiua et cõtemplatiua: verum etiã de viciis, ac virtutibus tractatur. [Sometimes attrib. to J. Wotton.] Additur opusculum Ricardi [Rolle] hampole de emẽdatione vite. 4° in 8's. (*in Parisioῳ academia p̃ W. hopyliũ, sumpt. G. brettoñ Londoñ.,*) *venale habeẽ Londonie ad signũ trinitatis* [*by H. Jacobi,*] (1510.) L.O.C. WOR.P.+; F(imp.).ILL.U.
　　IC copy, SAL have a variant imprint on the tp: 'Venale habetur in vico sancti Jacobi ad signum sancti Georgii', i.e. by W. Hopyl at Paris.

Speech. A speech, delivered at the visitation of Downe and Conner. 1639. *See* 15496.

— Speech of a Fife laird. [c. 1640.] *See* 10864.

— The speeche which the French king made to the lords of parliament. 1599. *See* 13119.5.

Speeches. Speeches deliuered to her maiestie this last progresse. 1592. *See* 7600.

23031 **Speed, John.** A clowd of witnesses: and they the holy genealogies of the sacred scriptures. (An alphabetical table.) 8°. *J. Beale f. D. Speed*, 1616. Ent. 6 my. L.O.C.D.G⁴.+; F.HN.HD.N.NY¹¹.+ ∄

23032 — Second addition [*sic*]. 8°. *J. Beale,* (1620). L.C⁴.C¹⁰ (Table only).CANT.; F.

23033 — [Anr. ed.] A cloud of witnesses, confirming the humanite of Christ Jesus. Newly corrected, and inlarged. 8°. *F. Kyngston, sold by E. Blackmore*, 1628. C.C³.C⁵.PLUME.; ILL.

23034 — [A description of England and Wales.] 1615. Now = 23041.2.

Speed, John—*cont.*

23034.5 — England, Wales, and Ireland. Their severall counties. Abridged from a farr larger, vollume: by J. Speed. [Engr. tp and maps, without text.] obl. 8°. *sold by G. Humble*, [c. 1620.] L(2, 1 imp., both in Map Room).

Most of the maps were engraved by P. van den Keere after Saxton's Atlas (21805.1); *see* Skelton 4, 12 and Hind I.206–7. Regarding this 1st Speed ed. of the maps *see* British Museum Society, *Bulletin*, no. 9 (Feb. 1972), p. 20, and Skelton p. 58, where the imperfect L copy is described as proofs.

23035 — [Anr. ed., w. added maps and text, and new engr. tp:] England Wales Scotland and Ireland described and abridged from a farr larger voulume done by J. Speed. obl. 8°. [*J. Dawson*,] *sould by G. Humble*, 1627. L(Maps C.7.a.27, lacks A8).O¹⁶.C(imp.).A.M³.+; DAR.ILL.

A2ᵛ line 14 of text ends: 'for our'. Skelton 17.

23036 — [Anr. ed.] obl. 8°. [*J. Dawson*,] *sould by G. Humble*, 1627 [1632?] L(Maps C.7.a.6, date cropt). O⁶.C. DUR⁵.LEEDS.+; HN.HD.BO⁵.LC.NY.

A2ᵛ line 14 of text ends: 'behoue-'. Skelton 19.

23036.5 — [Anr. ed.] obl.8°. [*M. Flesher*,] *sould by G. Humble*, 1627 [1646?] L(Maps C.7.a.3(1), imp.).O.C.G⁴. LEEDS.+; F.MICH.LC.NY.PN.+

A2ᵛ line 14 of text ends: 'behoue-'. Frequently bd. w. the 1646 Prospect, Wing S 4882.

23037 — A description of the civill warres of England. Collected by J. Speede citizen of London. Anno 1600. fol(4). [*T. East*, 1601?] C(Sayle 6830).

This is a different setting of the text headed 'A briefe description of the civill warres,' at the end of 23039g.7 sq. C's 4 sheets are pasted to margins of an earlier state of the engraving 'The invasions of England and Ireland' dedicated to Sir Oliver St. John, who was knighted 28 Feb. 1601. Speed's larger 'Map of Battles', engr. by R. Elstrack c. 1604, is at L(Map Room).

23038 — [Heading A1ʳ:] A direction to finde all those names expressed in that large table of Genealogies of scripture, lately gathered by J. S. [1595?] Now = 3859.5.

GENEALOGIES

What follows is a preliminary winnowing of the material, based almost exclusively on distinctions on A1ʳ–2ʳ. Though even these could have been refined further from my notes, such an effort seemed beyond the scope of STC. Enough is recorded to reveal a few interesting facts:

There were three printers of the Genealogies: J. Beale, 1611–23; T. Snodham, 1624–25; F. Kingston, 1626–40. On 20 August 1623 Beale had to surrender his Genealogies materials to Speed (*see Court-Book C*, p. 161). Snodham died in October of 1625, presumably from the plague, and as far as I yet have evidence, printed only 4° and 8° editions. Kingston then continued to 1640 and probably beyond. During his printing tenure, about 1630, additions were made in all formats but 12° to the Chelub genealogy (usually p. 21): two boxes, citing Numb. i. 27 and Numb. xxvi. 22, respectively. I have arbitrarily called all impressions in one format by the same printer 'issues' except for the unexpected Snodham 8° editions of 1624–25 (23039e.4 sq.).

Relationships between the various formats suggest some printing economies. In Beale's '1617–18' large fol. (23039.4) and small fol. (23039a.2) the typesetting of the tp recto and verso is identical, with adjustments made in imposing for the different areas of type page. It is quite likely that the same happened in earlier issues. In Kingston's work, what begins as the large fol. tp recto and verso (23039.6) ends as the small fol. (23039a.4) and vice versa.

In small fol., 4°, and 8° the same centre inset panel on A2ʳ (Adam and Eve), measuring approx. 90×74 mm., appears placed within outer compartments harmonizing with the respective formats. Marginal notes on the tp verso swim from 4° to 8° and back with great ease during Kingston's period, and appear to have invaded large fol. at least once during Beale's period (23039d.8, 23039.5). The 12° leads an isolated life of its own, and instead of having woodblocks, makes do with letterpress and rules.

Regarding Speed's various patents *see Cal. S.P.D., 1603–1610*, p. 639; *1611–1618*, p. 431; *1633–1634*, p. 576. For various transactions with the Stationers' Company *see Court-Book C*, pp. 78, 161, 215, 239, 241, 254, 256, 262 (*bis*), 295, 303, 316, 317 (*bis*), 328, 329, and Greg, *Companion*, pp. 301–4.

The copies cited below may be taken as standard copies for the purpose of A1ʳ–2ʳ. No attempt has been made to examine more

Speed, John—*Genealogies*—*cont.*

than a few locations, and I have not cited multiple copies at one location even when I knew they existed. Though I looked at most O copies myself, preliminary and further reports on O and O college copies were the drudgery of Paul Morgan, to whom I am deeply indebted. The shortcomings of the analysis are all my own. KFP.

Points of Distinction

The following distinctions are intended for identifying *only* those formats stipulated in the section headings, though they may appear in other formats. In sections I, II, and V the order is fairly chronological for the formats indicated. For large fol. begin with section I. For small fol., 4°, and 8° begin with section V. For 12° go directly to 23039f sqq. In the entries for each format the numbered distinctions are put in wide angle brackets at their first appearance or reappearance after intervening distinctions.

I have given each format its own STC designation so that if a copy lacks A1,2 it can have at least a partial identification; e.g. an imperfect 4° with additions to Chelub would be 23039d.12–.17.

Title-page

I. Border (fols. and 4°)
   a   no border
   b   double rules
   c   interlocking circles
   d   single rule
   e   type ornaments (sometimes within rules)
   f   thin woodcut strips (sometimes accompanied by type ornaments)

II. Ornaments (4° and 8°)
   a   woman's head with tiara, 28×103 mm.
   b   boys, scrolls, and animals, 22×100 mm.
   c   winged torso and blowing demons, 26×105 mm.
   d   woman's head with snakes and cornucopias, 12×73 mm.
   e   vase, scrolls, and birds, 18×74 mm.
   f   royal arms with 'I R'
   g   David playing harp, 18×45 mm.
   h   crowned rose, 16×44 mm.
   j   bearded face, 12×66 mm. or 12×36 mm.
   k   block of lace type ornaments
   m   small royal-emblem type ornaments (crowned rose, etc.)

Title-page verso

III. Last line of preface begins (fols. and 8°)
   a   *more, Amen.*
   b   *Amen.*
   c   *euermore, Amen.*
   d   *and Might . . .*
   e   *power and might . . .*
   f   *for euermore, Amen.*

IV. In lower marginal note (4° and 8°)
   a   1   *Rab Ha-/cadosh in/*
       2   ᶜ*Rab. Ha-/cadosh in his/*
       3   *Rab. Ha-/kadosh in/*
       4   ᵇ*Rab. Ha-/kadosh in/*
       5   *Rab. Ha-/kados in his/*
       6   ᶜ*Rab. Ha-/cadosh in/*
       7   *Rab. Haca-/dosh in his/*
   b   1   *the Iew/ in Suidas/*
       2   *the Jewe in/ Suidas on/*
       3   *the Jew/ in Suidsa/* [*sic*, in later issues the final 'a' disappears]
       4   *the Jew/ in Suidas/*
       5   *the Iew in/ suidas on/*
       6   *the Iew in/ Suidas on/*

Adam and Eve inset panel on A2ʳ (small fol., 4°, and 8°)

V. In the text
   a   Lines 1,2 'diso-/bedience . . . were/'; line 9 'raigne' [1611–17?]
   b   Lines 1,2 'dis-/obedienee [*sic*] . . . were/'; line 9 'reigne . . . righteousnes' [1618?]
   c   Lines 1,2 'dis-/obedience . . . were/'; line 9 'reigne . . righteousns [*sic*] [1619–24?]
   d   Lines 1,2 'dis-/obedience . . . were/'; line 9 'reign' [1624–25]
   e   Lines 1,2 'diso-/bedience . . . made/' [1626–40]

Speed, John—*Genealogies*—*cont.*

LARGE FOLIO

A–C⁶D²; the woodblocks measure approx. 340 × 228 mm. The references are to Francis Fry, *A description of the Great Bible*, 1865, pp. 31–5, 40–1, and plates 49–51, where much finer distinctions are made.

23039 — The genealogies recorded in the sacred scriptures. By J. S. [*J. Beale*, 1611.] O(Bib.Eng.1611 b.1, Fry 4). Fry 1–5.
    <Ia, IIIa.> Fry 4 has the tp blank.

23039.2 — [Anr. issue.] [*J. Beale*, 1612?] L(C.35.l.10, Fry 7). O(Bib.Eng.1611 b.6, Fry 7).O³⁸(Fry 10). Fry 7–8, 10–11, 20, 23.
    <Ib, IIIb.>

23039.2A—[Anr. issue, with Ib, <IIIf.>] *See* Addenda.

23039.3 — [Anr. issue.] [*J. Beale*, 1613?] L(L.9.c.4).O²⁰.O³⁸. Fry 9.
    Ib, <IIIc.>

23039.4 — [Anr. issue.] [*J. Beale*, 1617?] O²¹(Fry 13).O³⁸(imp., Fry 15).; HD(w. STC 2217, Fry 15). Fry 13–15.
    <Ic,> IIIc. In at least this issue the text on tp recto and verso is the same typesetting as 23039a.2, q.v. C,HN have Fry 14.

23039.5 — [Anr. issue.] [*J. Beale*, 1623?] O(Bib.Eng.1613 b.1). Fry 12.
    <Id,> IIIc. The marginal note on A1ᵛ is apparently the same typesetting as 23039d.8, i.e. has IVa5 and IVb5.

23039.6 — [Anr. ed.] [*F. Kingston*, 1627?] O(Bib.Eng.1617 b.2, imp.). Not in Fry.
    <Ie, IIId.> No additions to Chelub. This typesetting of the tp recto and verso is hereafter used for small fol. 23039a.4. The O copy has signature positions like Fry 22.

23039.7 — [Anr. issue.] [*F. Kingston*, 1630?] O(MS.Dugdale 33). Fry 17.
    <If, IIIe.> In title: 'Sauiour'. Beginning w. this issue there are additions to Chelub. This typesetting of the tp recto and verso was previously used in small fol. 23039a.3.

23039.8 — [Anr. issue.] [*F. Kingston*, 1634?] L(L.9.b.8, imp.). Fry 16.
    If, IIIe. In title: 'Saviour'.

SMALL FOLIO

A–C⁶ D²; the woodblocks measure approx. 260 × 175 mm.

23039a — The genealogies recorded in the sacred scriptures. By J. S. [*J. Beale*, 1612?] O⁹.O²⁸.O³⁵.
    <Ib, IIIb, Va.>

23039a.2 — [Anr. issue.] [*J. Beale*, 1618?] L(L.12.e.2).O(fol.St. Am.17).; HD(w. STC 16347).
    <Ic, IIIc, Vb.> The typesetting of the tp recto and verso is reimposed, w. smaller outer dimensions, from 23039a.4.

23039a.3 — [Anr. ed.] [*F. Kingston*, 1628?] L(3023.d.8).O(Bib. Eng.1629 c.2).; HD(*68–598F).
    <If, IIIe, Ve.> No additions to Chelub. This typesetting of the tp recto and verso is hereafter used in large fol. 23039.7.

23039a.4 — [Anr. issue.] [*F. Kingston*, 1632?] L(L.17.d.6).O(Bib. Eng.1632 c.1).
    <Ie, IIId,> Ve. With additions to Chelub. This typesetting of the tp recto and verso was previously used in large fol. 23039.6.

SMALL FOLIO WITH WOODBLOCKS FOR QUARTO

A–C⁶ D²; the woodblocks measure approx. 193 × 130 mm.

23039b — The genealogies recorded in the sacred scriptures. By J. S. [*F. Kingston*, 1630?] O(Bib.Eng.1629 c.1).
    <Ie, IIj, IVa6, IVb6, Ve.> With additions to Chelub. This differs from 23039d.12 only in being imposed on small fol. paper.

QUARTO WHOLLY ENGRAVED ON COPPER

23039c — The genealogies of the scriptures. Gathered and contrived by John Speed. [*London*, 1610?] L(689.e.9). O³.
    Both copies are bd. separately. This is the only form of the Genealogies w. Speed's name in full. Possibly the engraved form was too expensive for printing in such quantity and variety as eventually developed.

Speed, John—*Genealogies*—*cont.*

QUARTO WITH WOODBLOCKS

A–D⁴ E–F²; the woodblocks measure approx. 193 × 130 mm.

23039d — The genealogies recorded in the sacred scriptures. By J. S. [*J. Beale*, 1611–12.] L(3005.aaa.14).L¹⁴(201.C. 12.G²).O(Bib.Eng.1612 e.2, imp.).; F(imp., w. STC 2219, copy 1).
    <Ib, IIa, IIb, IVa1, IVb1, Va.>

23039d.2 — [Anr. issue.] [*J. Beale*, 1613–14.] L(3051.cc.9).L¹⁴ (D&M 256/1).O(Bib.Eng.1613 e.3, imp.).DUR(F.IV A.52(3)).M(R77137.2).; F(imp., w. STC 2220). HD (w. STC 16341).
    Ib, IIa, IIb, <IVa3, IVb3,> Va. An early state of this issue has IVb4 instead of IVb3; copies at M(R28656.2) and HD(*44–676); possibly earlier yet is O(Bib.Eng.1612 e.2), which has IVb1. The DUR copy is on large paper and bd. w. 3851 and 3867.9.

23039d.3 — [Anr. issue.] [*J. Beale*, 1615?] L(1008.c.6).L¹⁴(D&M 250).O(Bib.Eng.1615 e.1, imp.).M(R77136.2, imp.).; F(w. STC 2239).HD(imp., w. STC 2555).
    Ib, IIa, IIb, <IVa4,> IVb3, Va.

23039d.4 — [Anr. issue.] [*J. Beale*, 1616?] L(1411.e.2, imp.).L¹⁴ (D&M 251/1).O(Bib.Eng.1613 d.1, imp.).
    Ib, <IIc,> IIb, IVa4, IVb3, Va. In title: 'IN THE SA-/'.

23039d.5 — [Anr. issue.] [*J. Beale*, 1617?] L(3052.bb.19, imp.). L¹⁴(D&M 269).M(R77134.1).
    Ib, IIc, IIb, IVa4, IVb3, Va. In title: 'JN THE SA-/'. Another copy at L(1411.i.1) has distinctions like this except that it has IVb4 instead of IVb3.

23039d.6 — [Anr. issue.] [*J. Beale*, 1618?] L(C.47.g.4).L¹⁴(D&M 285/2).
    Ib, IIc, IIb, IVa4, <IVb4, Vb.> In title: 'JN THE SA-/'. C, HN have 'IN/' like 23039d.7.

23039d.7 — [Anr. issue.] [*J. Beale*, 1619–21?] L(3050.d.21).L¹⁴ (D&M 283).O(Bib.Eng.1620 e.1).M(21219.2).; F(w. STC 2258a, copy 1).
    Ib, IIc, IIb, IVa4, IVb4, <Vc.> In title: 'IN/'. Possibly later are copies at O³, O¹⁰ having Ia, IIa.

23039d.8 — [Anr. issue.] [*J. Beale*, 1622–23?] L(C.45.e.15).L¹⁴ (D&M 292/1).O(Bib.Eng.1619 e.1).M(12058.3).
    <Id, IIa,> IIb, <IVa5, IVb5,> Vc. The IV distinctions are the same as in 23039.5 and are apparently the same typesetting.

23039d.9 — [Anr. ed.] [*T. Snodham*, 1624–25.] L(1411.e.5). O(Bib.Eng.1625 d.1).; F(imp., w. STC 2270).HD (*58C–370).
    <Ie(with rules), IIg, IVa6, IVb1, Vd.> A copy at M(R28658.2) has distinctions like this except that it has Ve instead of Vd; O,HN have Vc.

23039d.10 — [Anr. ed.] [*F. Kingston*, 1626–27?] L(3037.e.13, imp.).L¹⁴(D&M 325).
    <Ie(no rules), IIj,> IVa6, IVb1, <Ve.>

23039d.11 — [Anr. issue.] [*F. Kingston*, 1628–29?] L(3037.e.12). L¹⁴(D&M 304/3).M(R77140.2, imp.).
    Ie, IIj, IVa6, <IVb6,> Ve. Page 34 is erroneously Manasseh.

23039d.12 — [Anr. issue.] [*F. Kingston*, 1630?] L(3053.dd.8).L¹⁴ (D&M 325).O(C.P.1630 e.2, imp.).; HD(*65–1956, imp.).
    Ie, IIj, IVa6, IVb6, Ve. Page 34 is correctly Salathiel. With additions to Chelub. This is the typesetting imposed for the small fol. 23039b.

23039d.13 — [Anr. issue.] [*F. Kingston*, 1631?] L(3049.e.4).
    Ie, IIj, <IVa7,> IVb6, Ve.

23039d.14 — [Anr. issue.] [*F. Kingston*, 1632–35?] L(C.128.f.1). L¹⁴(D&M 328/1).O(Bib.Eng.1634.e.1).M(R77141.2, imp.).; HD(*58C–374).
    Ie, <IIk,> IVa7, IVb6, Ve. Speed's inits. in the title are 'J S.'

23039d.15 — [Anr. issue.] [*F. Kingston*, 1636?] L(3049.d.12).L¹⁴ (D&M 390/1).; HN(62319).
    Ie, IIk, IVa7, IVb6, Ve. Speed's inits. in the title are 'I. S.'

23039d.16 — [Anr. issue.] [*F. Kingston*, 1637?] L(3408.f.28, imp.).
    Ie, <IIm,> IVa7, IVb6, Ve.

23039d.17 — [Anr. issue.] [*F. Kingston*,] 1638. L.L¹⁴.O.; HD.
    The distinctions are like 23039d.16, but this tp is dated.

Speed, John—*Genealogies*—*cont.*

OCTAVO

A–B⁸ C–D²; the woodblocks measure approx. 150 ×
95 mm.

23039e — The genealogies recorded in the sacred scriptures. By
J. S. [*J. Beale*, 1611?] O⁵.
<IId, IIe, IIIc, IVa6, IVb1, Va.>

23039e.2 — [Anr. issue.] [*J. Beale*, 1611?] L(C.108.c.21).
<IIf,> IIIc, IVa6, IVb1, Va. In title: 'ACORDING'.

23039e.3 — [Anr. issue.] [*J. Beale*, 1612?] L(C.15.a.7).
IIf, IIIc, <IVa2, IVb2,> Va. In title: 'ACORD-
ING'. 1 O²⁸ copy has IVb6, Vb.

23039e.4 — [Anr. ed.] [*T. Snodham*, 1624.] O¹⁹.; HD(*70–665).
<IIh, IIIb, IVa6, IVb1, Vc.>

23039e.5 — [Anr. ed.] [*T. Snodham*, 1625.] Broxbourne(O).; HD
(w. STC 2272).
IIh, IIIb, IVa6, IVb1, <Vd.> For this ed. the
set of woodblocks was entirely recut. The orig.
set had the names in the circles in letterpress.
This set has the names cut in wood.

23039e.6 — [Anr. ed.] [*F. Kingston*, 1626–27?] L(3049.bb.3).
<IIj,> IIIb, IVa6, IVb1, <Ve.>

23039e.7 — [Anr. issue.] [*F. Kingston*, 1628–29?] L(3050.a.43).;
HD(*58C–226).
IIj, IIIb, IVa6, <IVb6,> Ve. Broxbourne(O)
differs in distinction II in having no tp orn.

23039e.8 — [Anr. issue.] [*F. Kingston*, 1630–31?] L(1005.b.3).O
(Bib.Eng.1631 f.2).
IIj, IIIb, <IVa7,> IVb6, Ve. With additions
to Chelub.

23039e.9 — [Anr. issue.] [*F. Kingston*,] 1631. M.
<IIk,> IIIb, IVa7, IVb6, Ve. This and the other
dated issues have the same distinctions, except that
beginning in 1633 they have IIIa instead of IIIb.

23039e.10 — [Anr. issue.] [*F. Kingston*,] 1632. L.NLW.

23039e.11 — [Anr. issue.] [*F. Kingston*,] 1633. L.C.; PML.PTS.

23039e.12 — [Anr. issue.] [*F. Kingston*,] 1634. L.O.; HD.

23039e.13 — [Anr. issue.] [*F. Kingston*,] 1635. O³.; HD.

23039e.14 — [Anr. issue.] [*F. Kingston*,] 1636. L.L³⁰.O.; F.HD.
One L copy (3050.a.38) has no marginal notes on
the tp verso.

23039e.15 — [Anr. issue.] [*F. Kingston*,] 1637. L¹⁴.O¹³.E.

23039e.16 — [Anr. issue.] [*F. Kingston*,] 1638. L.O.C.A.E.+; HD.
PML.

23039e.17 — [Anr. issue.] [*F. Kingston*,] 1640. L.O¹⁶.C.LIV.

DUODECIMO

A¹² B⁶ C²; the outer rules measure approx. 128 × 65 mm.
So few 12°s have been examined that the dating below is
based largely on the Bibles most of them are bd. with.

23039f — The genealogies recorded in the sacred scriptures. By
J. S. [*J. Beale*, 1618?] L(C.25.d.17, imp.).
Tp compartment McK.&F. 34; signature position:
Kittam
A 2

23039f.2 — [Anr. issue.] [*J. Beale*, c. 1620.] O(Mar.358, bd. w. an
imp. Apocrypha).C(bd. w. 1620 Bible).
Tp compartment McK.&F. 34; signature position:
Kittim
A 2

23039f.4 — [Anr. ed.] [*F. Kingston*, 1626?] O(Bib.Eng.1625 f.1,
imp.).
Tp has panel strips; at bottom on right is a fleur-
de-lis with its top aimed left. Signature positions:
ifh K | nath
A 2 | A 3

23039f.5 — [Anr. issue.] [*F. Kingston*, 1632?] L(1481.ddd.60,
imp.).O(Bib.Eng.1632 f.1).O¹⁴(imp.).
Tp like 23039f.4; signature positions:
ifh K | Afen
A 2 | A 3

23039f.6 — [Anr. issue.] [*F. Kingston*, 1634?] L(3049.aa.22).;
HD(*68–625).
Tp like 23039f.4; signature position: fh K
A 2

23039f.7 — [Anr. issue.] [*F. Kingston*, 1638?] O(Bib.Eng.1638
f.3).
Tp has panel strips; at bottom on right is a dog,
upside down. Signature position: fh Kit
A 2

23039f.8 — [Anr. issue.] [*F. Kingston*,] 1638. Broxbourne(O).
This dated tp has panel strips; at bottom on right
is a fleur-de-lis with its top aimed right. Signature
position is identical to 23039f.6.

Speed, John—*Genealogies*—*cont.*

23039f.9 — [Anr. issue.] [*F. Kingston*,] 1639. L.
Like 23039f.8 except for the date.

———

23039g.3 — The most happy unions contracted betwixt the
princes of England & Scotland. [Genealogical tree
with text, engraved by R. Elstrack.] s.sh.fol. *J. Speed
excudebat*, [1603?] L(Print Dept.).C.
See Hind II.163, 209.

23039g.7 — A prospect of the most famous parts of the world.
Together with that large Theater of Great Brittaines
empire. fol. *J. Dawson f. G. Humble*, 1627. L.C.SAU.;
LC. Mellon.
Eds. of the Theatre are listed separately at
23041 sqq. *See also* 23037 and Hind II.91–5.

23040 — [Anr. ed.] fol. *J. Dawson f. G. Humble*, 1631. L.L³⁸.
O.C(impr. torn).G⁴.+; F.HN.CU.HD(imp.).MICH.+

23041 — The theatre of the empire of Great Britaine: presenting
an exact geography of England, Scotland, Ireland,
[etc.] fol. (*W. Hall*,) *solde by J. Sudbury & G.
Humble*, 1611 (1612.) L.O.C.D.E.+; HN.BO².ILL.
LC.NY.+
Humble was granted a privilege for 21 years to
print this on 29 April 1608; *see* Greg, *Companion*,
p. 154. *See also* Hind II.67–90. Skelton 7.
The engr. title is on a separate panel within an
engr. compartment. The compartment, which
includes imprint and date, was used for the
Theatre, the Theatrum (23044), and the History
(23045 sqq., large fol. eds.), the last 2 having
their own title panels.

23041.2 — [Anr. ed., without tp, imposed for cutting and mounting with maps.] fol. (*W. ⟨Hall⟩ [a.] T. Snodham f.
J. Sudburie a. G. Humble*, 1615.) L(796.a.1, de-
scriptive texts of 53 counties, without alphabetical
tables or maps). L⁵(frag. of text and table for
Surrey, Lemon 105).O(C.17.b.1, with 54 maps, 22
of them in the 1623? state).
(L copy formerly 23034) Text for each county
has an imprint. Hall's name appears on the description of England (O, defective); the rest pr. by
Snodham.
The L copy is cut up and bd. in 8° format. The
O copy has the text for each map cut into sections
and pasted at the sides of and below the map. The
text is described as proofs of 23041.4 in Skelton,
pp. 48, 53 and Hind II.89.

23041.4 — [Anr. issue, reimposed in regular folio format, w.
imprint on engr. tp:] *solde by J. Sudbury & G.
Humble*, 1614. [Sub tpp to Bks. 2,3,4:] (*T. Snodham
. . . 1616.*) L.O²⁶(imp.).C¹².C¹⁷.D.; F.ILL.
Map of Norfolk (ch. 18) has no engraver's name
in the right bottom corner. Skelton 10.

23041.6 — [Anr. issue, w. engr. tp and letterpress text as 23041.4,
but w. the maps altered.] [1623?] O¹¹.O¹⁶.LEEDS.
John Gardner, Monkswell, Coggeshall, Essex.
Map of Norfolk (ch.18) has: 'R. Elstrack sculpsit'
in the right bottom corner. Skelton 14.
All copies have the First Index from 23041,
signed w. asterisks, instead of the one signed
Ffff–Hhhh belonging with the 1614–16 text.

23041.8 — [Anr. ed.] fol. *sold by G. Humble*, 1623. [Bks. 2,3,4:]
(*J. Dawson*, 1627.) O⁷.

23042 — [A variant, w. imprint on engr. tp:] *sold by G. Humble*,
1627. [Bks. 2,3,4:] (*J. Dawson . . . 1627.*) L(C.7.e.
13(2)).C(imp.).C¹⁰.; HD(imp.).
Skelton 16.

23043 — [Anr. ed., w. engr. tp unaltered.] fol. *sold by G. Humble*,
1627. [Bks. 2,3,4:] (*J. Dawson . . . 1631.*) L.L³⁸.O.
C.D.+; F.HN.CU.HD.
Skelton 18. The 1627 engr. tp was used again for
a 1646 ed. of the Theatre, where the subtpp have
imprints: *J. Legatt f. W. Humble*, 1646. L,HD have
copies, both bd. w. 1646 folio Prospect with the
Legatt-Humble imprint.

23044 — [A trans.] Theatrum imperii Magnæ Britanniæ.
Opus, à P. Hollando, Latinitate donatum. fol. (*T.
Snodham*,) *solde by J. Sudbury & G. Humble*, 1616.
L.O(lacks A2).C⁹.A.LEEDS.+; F.LC.
John Gardner has a copy w. labels pasted over
the English imprint: '*Amstelodami, ex off. J.
Hondij*, 1621.' O has a copy w. a title label pasted
on a different tp: '*Theatrum* [etc.] *Amsterdami,
ap. J. Blaeu*, 1646.' Skelton 11.

Speed, John—*cont.*

23045 — The history of Great Britaine. large fol. (*W. Hall a. J. Beale,*) *solde by J. Sudbury & G. Humble,* 1611. L.O.C².D.E.+ ; F.HN.CU.HD.N.+
Numbered pages 151–894. The pagination and signatures are continuous w. 23041. The colophon precedes the 2nd index.

23046 — [A variant, w. impr. on engr. tp:] *solde by J. Sudbury & G. Humble,* 1614. L.O.C(Bury deposit).D.M.+ ; F.HN. CU.HD.MICH.+

23046.3 — [Anr. ed., w. letterpress tp:] The second edition revised, and enlarged. small fol. *J. Beale f. G. Humble,* 1623. L¹³.O(imp.).BIRM.G².P.+ ; F.HN.BO².CHI.Y.+
(Formerly 23047a) Numbered pages 11–1258. Separate pagination and signatures. *See Court-Book C,* p. 161, requiring Beale to print cancels for pp. 183, 188, 195, 219, 237, 281, 367, 883. Possibly cancel bifolia were pr., as the O²⁶ copy has Q2,5 (pp. 177–8, 183–4) on smaller paper than the rest of the quire.

23046.7 — [Anr. ed., w. engr. tp, without edition number in the title panel.] large fol. [*J. Beale,*] *sold by G. Humble,* 1623. L³⁰.O⁷.P.
Numbered pages 155–923. Pagination is continuous w. 23041, but signatures are separate. The 1650 'third' ed. Wing S4880 reprints this ed. but has the last numbered page 921.

23047 — [A variant, w. engr. title panel altered:] The second edition revised & enlarged. [*J. Beale,*] *sold by G. Humble,* 1623. L.L⁸.O²⁶.M².Bradford PL.+ ; Vassar C.

23047a — Now = 23046.3.

23048 — [A variant of 23047, w. imprint on engr. tp:] *sold by G. Humble,* 1627. L³⁰.O⁶.C.D.G⁴.+ ; HN.ILL.MIN.PN. Y.+

23048.5 — [Anr. ed., w. letterpress tp:] The third edition. Revised, enlarged, and newly corrected. small fol. *J. Dawson [a. T. Cotes] f. G. Humble,* 1631. ILL.
Numbered pages 1–1237. Separate pagination and signatures. T. Cotes pr. Aaaa to end.

23049 — [A variant, w. imprint:] *J. Dawson [a. T. Cotes] f. G. Humble,* 1632. L.O.C.D⁶.E².+ ; F.HN.BO.CU.N.+

23050 **Speed, Joshua.** Loves revenge. Wherein is briefly shewed from the historie of the holy scripture, the rising of the man of sinne. [In verse.] 8°. *Amsterdam, R. Raven,* 1631. O.

23050.5 **Speed, Robert.** The counter-scuffle. [Anon. In verse.] 4°. [*G. Purslowe*] *f. W. Butler,* 1621. PFOR.Y.

23051 — [Anr. ed. Init. R. S.] Whereunto is added, the Counter-ratt. 4°. *f. W. Butler,* 1623. HD(lacks Counter-ratt).

23051.5 — [Anr. ed.] 4°. *W. Stansby,* [1626?] Ass'd by Mary Butler to W. Stansby 4 jy. 1626. HD.
HD has MS. corrections (e.g. F1ʳ line 9 has 'ne'er' inserted) which are incorporated into the pr. text of 23052.

23052 — [Anr. ed.] 4°. *W. Stansby, sold by R. Meighen,* 1628. L.O(imp.).; F.HN.

23053 — [Anr. ed.] 4°. *W. Stansby,* 1635. L.O.C².; HN.

23054 — [Anr. ed.] 4°. *R. Bishop,* 1637. Ass'd 4 mr. 1639. L.; F.HD.Y. Pirie.

23055 **Speght, James.** A briefe demonstration, who have, . . . the spirit of Christ. 8°. *W. Hall f. T. Man,* 1613. Ent. to W. Hall a. J. Beale 11 de. 1612. L(2). STD.; F.

23056 — The day-spring of comfort. A sermon preached the 6. of January, 1610. 8°. *J. Beale,* 1615. Ent. 29 oc. LINC.; F.

23056.5 — [Anr. issue, w. cancel tp:] The christians comfort. *J. B[eale] f. S. Man,* 1616. LK.

23057 **Speght, Rachel.** Mortalities memorandum, with a dreame prefixed. [In verse.] 4°. *E. Griffin f. J. Bloome,* 1621. Ent. 18 ja. L.O¹¹(frag.).; F.HN.HD.N.Y.

23058 — A mouzell for Melastomus, the cynicall bayter of, . . . Evahs sex. Or an apologeticall answere to that pamphlet made by Jo. Sw[etnam]. The arraignement of women [23533]. (Certaine quaeres to the bayter of women.) 4°. *N. Okes f. T. Archer,* 1617. Ent. 14 no. 1616. L.O.; F.HN.HD(2, 1 lacks 1st pt.). N.Y.

Speght, Thomas, *ed. See* 5077, 5080.

23059 **Speidell, John.** An arithmeticall extraction or collection of divers questions with their answers. 8°. *Eliz. Allde,* 1628. L.L³⁰.O.

Speidell, John—*cont.*

23059.5 — A briefe treatise for the measuring of glasse, board, timber, or stone, square or round. By J. Speidell mathematitian, in Queenes-street, where you may have of these books at all times. 4°. *T. Harper,* 164[o?] L¹²(frag., bd. with 23060).L³⁸(6 leaves).; HN(8 leaves).

23060 — A breefe treatise of sphæricall triangles. Whereunto is annexed a geometricall extraction. 2 pts. 4°. *E. Allde,* 1627 (1617.) Ent. 24 my. 1627. L.L³⁰(pt. 1 only). O.E².ETON.+ ; F(pt. 1 only).HN(pt. 1 only).CHI.CU. MICH(pt. 1 only).+
Pt. 2 is a reissue of 23062.

23060.5 — Certaine verie necessarie and profitable tables: viz, a table of sines, tangents and secants. A table of the declination of the sunne: [etc.] 4°. [*E. Allde,*] *solde at the authors house in Coleman-Streete,* 1609. L³⁸.

23061 — A geometricall extraction, or a compendious collection of problemes, out of the best writers. Whereunto is added, about 30. problemes of the authors invention. 4°. *E. Allde, solde at the authors house in the fields . . .,* 1616. Ent. 15 ja. L.L³⁰.C.E.NEK.+ ; HN. BO.BR.MICH. Horblit(2).
Imprint varies: 'by' (L,C) or 'for' (HN) E. Allde.

23062 — [A variant, w. imprint:] *E. Allde, solde at the authors house . . .,* 1617. L³⁰.O.O³.C².C¹².+ ; F.HN.COR.NY.
Also issued as pt. 2 of 23060.

23062.5 — A most quicke and easie way, for the ready and speedy casting up of oyles at any rate whatsoever. 4° in 2. [*E. Allde?* c. 1625.] MICH(bd. w. 23060, 23064.3). Horblit (bd. w. 23060, 23061, 23064.5).
Refers to a 7-column table which is not w. the MICH or Horblit copies, nor does it seem to be 23060.5, though the L³⁸ copy of the latter has tables in 7 columns.

23063 — New logarithmes. The first invention whereof, was, by Lo: J. Nepair [i.e. Napier.] By J. Speidell, and are to bee solde at his dwelling house in the Fields. The first inpression [*sic*]. 1619. 4°. [*E. Allde? f. J. Speidell,* 1619.] L.C.
Quires B–M in this and the following are all from the same typesetting, whether pr. all at once or from standing type is not clear.
The tp and leaf following M4 are conjugate; the type of the title was kept standing and alterations in the impression number and date made as necessary.

23063.3 — The 2. inpression. 1620. 4°. [*E. Allde? f. J. Speidell,* 1620.] L³⁰.G².
This and the following have added quires N⁴ [O]⁴ P⁴ [Q]⁴, w. logarithms of whole numbers 1–1000. The G² copy is erroneously dated 1624 and lacks the additional quires.

23063.5 — The 4. inpression. 1622. [*E. Allde? f. J. Speidell,* 1622.] L.YK.

23063.7 — The 5. inpression. 1623. [*E. Allde? f. J. Speidell,* 1623.] L¹².L³⁰(imp.).A.E².

23064 — The 6. inpression. 1624. 4°. [*E. Allde? f. J. Speidell,* 1624.] L³⁰(2).; HN.BO.
One L³⁰ copy has the added quires as in 23063.3; the other has an abridged version of the logarithms of whole numbers, in 4 leaves.

23064.3 — The 7. inpression. 1625. [*E. Allde? f. J. Speidell,* 1625.] O.ETON.G².; MICH.
G², MICH have the long addition, ETON the short.

23064.5 — The 8. inpression. 1626. [*E. Allde? f. J. Speidell,* 1626.] CHI. Horblit.

23064.7 — The 9. inpression. 1627. [*E. Allde? f. J. Speidell,* 1627.] Sotheby's 7 May 1935, in lot 270 (bought by Maggs, untraced).

23064.9 — The 10. inpression. 1628. [*E. Allde? f. J. Speidell,* 1628.] L³⁸.

Spell, Thomas. [Bookplate.] *See* Bookplates.

23065 **Spelman,** *Sir* **Henry.** Henrici Spelmanni equit. Anglo-Brit. Archæologus. In modum glossarii ad rem antiquam posteriorem. fol. *ap. J. Beale,* 1626. L².O³.C².M.P.+ ; F.CU.LC.MICH.STAN.+
Tp line 13: 'Chartis & Formulis'. This consists of the 1st pt. only; rest not pub'd till 1664 in Wing S 4925. *See also* 23069.5.

23065.5 — [Anr. issue, w. tp and first leaf of main text reset.] *ap. J. Beale,* 1626. L.O.C.D.E.+ ; F.HN.HD.LC.N.+
Tp line 13: 'Chartis et Formulis'.

Spelman, *Sir Henry—cont.*

23066 — Concilia, decreta, leges, constitutiones, in re ecclesiarum orbis Britannici. Primus hic Tomus. [Ed. Jeremiah Stephens.] fol. *R. Badger, imp. P. Stephani & C. Meredith,* 1639. Ent. 10 au. 1637. L.O.C.D.E.+; F.HN.HD.N.NY.+

    Imprint varies: 'Excudebat Richardus Badger' (F, large paper) or 'Typis R. Badger' (F, regular paper). The rest not pub'd till 1664 in Wing S 4920.

23067 — De non temerandis ecclesiis. A tracte of the rights and respect due unto churches. 8°. *J. Beale,* 1613. Ent. 12 my. 1614. O²⁷.

    Text ends G6ᵛ: 'on earth.| Ω'; tp is a cancel and does not have the device, McK.374.

23067.2 — [Anr. issue, enlarged.] *J. Beale,* 1613. L(2, 1 imp.).; BO³.

    Quire G is reset, with G6ᵛ ending: 'on earth:| Therefore| MAR.12.17 [3-line quotation]| Ω'. Text continues G7–H8 w. 'A sermon of Sᵗ Augustines touching rendring of tithes.' Tp appears to be conjugate and does not have McK.374.

23067.4 — [Anr. issue, w. tp reset.] *J. Beale,* 1613. L.O.O⁵.C.C².+; F.HN.HD.U.

    In title: 'ecclesijs. A tract'; tp has McK.374. The L tp is on different paper from the rest of the book, but in other copies the tp appears to be conjugate.

    Some copies have cancels of B7, D1, F5, and G8. Orig. B7ʳ catchword: '4 Touching' (L,C², and the earlier issues above); cancel: '4 Tou-' (O,C²,F, HN).

23067.6 — [Anr. ed.] 8°. *Edinburgh, A. Hart,* 1616. L.O.E.G².STU.+

    (Formerly 23069) This ed. has an epistle to the Bishops of the Church of Scotland, signed I. S., which is not in other eds.

23067.8 — The second edition enlarged with an appendix. 8°. *J. Beale,* 1616. O.C.G².LINC.P.+; JH.

    (Formerly 23068a) Preface refers to Scottish ed., 23067.6.

23068 — [Anr. issue, w. cancel tp:] *J. Beale, sold by W. Welby,* 1616. L.C.C³.C⁵.BIRM.; F.U. Robert Taylor.

23068a — Now = 23067.8.

23069 — Now = 23067.6.

23069.5 — Series cancellariorum Angliæ; non dicam absoluta sed ut è Thinni, & MS. contexuimus. s.sh.fol. *ex off. J. Beale,* [1626?] L⁵(Lemon 189).

    Refers to Beale's ed. of 23065 and has the latter's text on pp. 132–5 reimposed, w. a cancel slip adding Bp. J. Williams, created Lord Keeper 10 July 1621.

Spelman, *Sir John, ed. See* 2369.

23070 **Spence, Robert.** Illustrissimi fortissimique domini, D. Georgii Villerii Buckinghamiæ ducis mortis διαγραφὴ ἐγκωκιαστικὴ [sic]. [In verse.] 4°. [*Edinburgh, J. Wreittoun,* 1628?] L.O¹⁷.C.E.; HD.Y.

Spencer, *John, ed. See* 12421, 13713.

23071 **Spencer, Robert,** *Baron.* The muses thankfulnesse, or a funerall elegie, consecrated to the memory of Robert, baron Spencer. 12°. [*I. Jaggard?* 1627.] L.

23072 **Spencer, Thomas.** The art of logick, delivered in the precepts of Aristotle and Ramus. 8°. *J. Dawson f. N. Bourne,* 1628. Ent. 23 fb. 1626. L.O.D.DUL.E².+; F.CU.HD.N.PN.+

23073 — Maschil unmasked. In a treatise. Against Mr. Cholmley [5144], and Mr. Butterfield [4205]. 4°. *W. Jones,* [1629.] L.O.C.D.E.+; F(2).HN.BO⁵.U.

    Jones called before the ecclesiastical commission for printing this; *see* Greg, *Companion,* pp. 243–7.

23074 **Spenser, Benjamin.** Vox civitatis, or Londons complaint against her children in the countrey. 4°. *J. D[awson] f. N. Bourne,* 1625. Ent. 2 de. L.L.L⁸.O.C. CARLISLE.; F.HN.HD.IND.

23075 — [Anr. ed.] 4°. *E. P[urslowe] f. W. Hope,* 1636. L.L¹⁶. L³⁰.O.; BO⁵.N.NY.U.Y.

    Answered by 18698.

Spenser, Edmund. [For collected poetical works, *see* 23083.3 sqq.]

Spenser, Edmund—*cont.*

23076 — Amoretti and Epithalamion. [In verse.] 8°. (*P. S[hort]*) f. *W. Ponsonby,* 1595. Ent. 19 no. 1594. L.O(imp.).C²(imp.).E².M.+; F(imp.).HN.JH²(imp.). PFOR.TEX(imp.).+

— Brittain's Ida. [Wrongly attrib. to E. Spenser.] 1628. *See* 11079.5.

23077 — Colin Clouts come home againe. (Astrophel.) [In verse.] 4°. (*T. C[reede]*) f. *W. Ponsonbie,* 1595. 'Mourning Muse of Thestylis' ent. to J. Wolfe 22 au. 1587. L.O.C².G².M.+; F.HN.HD.N.NY.+

    Includes laments on the death of Sidney by Raleigh and others.

23077.3 — [Anr. ed., including most of the minor poems.] fol. *H. L[ownes] f. M. Lownes,* (1611.) L.O.C.D.E.+; F.HN.HD.N.PML.+

    Usually issued w. 23083.3–23084.

23077.7 — [Anr. ed.] fol. *H. L[ownes] f. M. Lownes,* (1617). L.O.C.CASHEL(imp.).E².+; F.HN.HD.N.NY.+

    Usually issued w. 23085.

23078 — Complaints. Containing sundrie small poemes of the worlds vanitie. By Ed. Sp[enser.] (Teares of the muses.—Prosopopoia.—Muiopotmos.) 4°. [*T. Orwin*] f. *W. Ponsonbie,* 1591 (1590.) Ent. 29 de. 1590. L.O.C².E.M.+; F.HN.HD.N.NY.+

23079 — Daphnaïda. An elegie vpon the death of [Lady] Douglas Howard. By Ed. Sp[enser. In verse.] 4°. [*T. Orwin*] f. *W. Ponsonby,* 1591. L(lacks A2).; HN.BO.

23080 — The faerie queene. Disposed into twelue books, fashioning XII. morall vertues. [Bks. 1–3. In verse.] 4° in 8's. [*J. Wolfe*] f. *W. Ponsonbie,* 1590. Ent. 1 de. 1589. F.ILL.

    Verso of tp blank; 1st digit of tp date under 'r' in 'for'. Leaves Pp6,7 intended to be cancelled and replaced w. quire Qq⁴ in this, 23081, and 23081a. Most copies retain the cancellanda.

23081 — [A variant, w. dedic. on verso of tp and 1st digit of tp date under 'r' in 'for'.] [*J. Wolfe*] f. *W. Ponsonbie,* 1590. L.O.C.G².M.+; F.HN.HD.ILL.NY.+

23081a — [A variant, w. dedication on verso of tp and 1st digit of tp date under 'il' in 'William'.] [*J. Wolfe*] f. *W. Ponsonbie,* 1590. HN.BO⁵.JH².NY.TEX.+

    Copies of this and 23081 with the blank spaces on p. 332, lines 4,5 filled in are at L(C.12.h.7), C², HN(56741),BO⁵.JH².

23082 — [Anr. ed., enlarged.] (The second part of the faerie queene.) 2 pts. 4° in 8's. [*R. Field*] f. *W. Ponsonbie,* 1596. Pt. 2 ent. 20 ja. L.O.C².E².M.+; F.HN.HD.NY. TEX.+

    Sonnets at end of previous ed. are omitted. *See* also *Cal. S.P. Scot., 1509–1603,* II.723.

23083 — [Anr. ed., enlarged w. 'Two cantos of Mutabilitie.'] fol. *H. L[ownes] f. M. Lownes,* 1609. Ass'd to S. Waterson 3 se. 1604; to M. Lownes 5 no. 1604. L(C.57.f.6).O(Mal.7).C.D.E.+; F.HN.HD.N.NY.+

    Some copies w. the 1609 1st tp (L(78.g.13), O(Douce S 817), CAL, JH²) have bks. 4–7 in the 1612/13 setting; *see* 23083.7.

23083.3 — [Anr. issue, w. tp cancelled and replaced by tp and dedic.] The faerie queen: the shepheards calendar: together with the other works of England's archpoët, collected into one volume, and carefully corrected. 4 pts. *H. L[ownes] f. M. Lownes,* 1611. L³⁰.O³⁹(tp def.).C.M².NEK.; CAL.CHI.PML.PN.WEL.+

    Sub tp still dated 1609. B3ʳ stanza 1 begins: 'Yoũg knight,'; R3ʳ catchword: 'She'. 23083.3–23085 give locations *only for the gen. tp and FQ.*

    For a full analysis of the complicated issues of the Works *see* F. R. Johnson, *A Critical Bibliography,* 1933, pp. 33–48. In the interests of STC brevity the additional parts w. locations are listed separately though they are called for on the tp and are usually bd. w. the FQ. With this issue the pts. should ideally be: 23086.3, 23093.5, 23077.3.

23083.7 — [Anr. issue, w. bks. 4–7 reprinted, w. impr. on sub tp:] (*H. L[ownes] f. M. Lownes,* 1612 or 1613.) L³⁰ (1613).O(M 4.5 Art.).O⁵(1613).; F(1612).BO.JH².N. TEX.+

    Gen. tp still dated 1611. B3ʳ stanza 1 begins: 'Yoũg knight,'; R3ʳ catchword: 'And'. In some copies (JH², LC) the 1612/13 sub tp on R1 has been cancelled instead of the 1609 sub tp on Q5. The pts. bd. w. this should ideally be as in 23083.3, w. the addition of 23087. *See* note to 23083.

Spenser, Edmund—*cont.*

23084 — [Anr. issue, w. bks. 1–3 reprinted, but retaining the gen. tp:] *H. L[ownes] f. M. Lownes,* 1611 [1615?] L(79.h.23).O⁷(1612).C².BTU(1612).E(1613).+; F(both). HN.CU(1613).HD(both).TEX.+

　　　Sub tp still dated 1612/13. B3ʳ stanza 1 begins: 'Young Knight,'; R3ʳ catchword: 'And'. The pts. bd. w. this should ideally be as in 23083.7; but some copies have 1617 texts, e.g. O⁷(23077.7, 23086.7, 23094), TEX(23086.7).

23085 — [Anr. issue, w. tp and dedic. reprinted, w. imprint:] *H. L[ownes] f. M. Lownes,* 1617. Ass'd to T. Lownes 10 ap. 1627; to H. Lownes a. R. Young 30 my. 1627; by H. Lownes to G. Cole a. G. Latham 6 no. 1628; by Cole a. Latham to R. Young 6 de. 1630. L.O.C. DUR⁵.E².+; F(1613).HN.HD(both).N.NY.+

　　　Sub tp still dated 1612/13. B3ʳ stanza 1 begins: 'Young Knight,'; R3ʳ catchword: 'And'. The pts. bd. w. this should ideally be: 23086.7, 23094, 23077.7, 23087. Instead of the last, a few copies have 23087.5, q.v.

23086 — Fowre hymnes, made by Edm. Spenser. (Daphnaida.) [In verse.] 4°. [*R. Field*] f. *W. Ponsonby,* 1596. L.O.C⁴.DUL.M.+; F.HN.HD.NY.TEX.+

23086.3 — [Heading ¶1ʳ:] A letter of the authors. To sir Walter Raleigh. fol. [*H. Lownes f. M. Lownes,* 1611.] L.O.C.C².E.+; F.HN.HD.N.PML.+

　　　¶1ʳ line 1 of text ends: 'Alle-'. Usually issued w. 23083.3–23084.

23086.7 — [Anr. ed.] fol. [*H. Lownes f. M. Lownes,* 1617.] L.O.C. CASHEL.E².+; F.HN.HD.N.NY.+

　　　¶1ʳ line 1 of text ends: 'Allego-'. Usually issued w. 23085.

— Muiopotmos. 1590. *See* 23078.

— Prosopopoia. Or Mother Hubberds tale. 1591. *See* 23078.

23087 — [Anr. ed.] fol. *H. L[ownes] f. M. Lownes,* 1612 or 1613. L.O.C².D(1613).E(1612).+; F(both).HN.CHI.HD(1613). PML.+

　　　Usually issued w. 23083.7–23085.

23087.5 — [Anr. ed.] fol. *H. L[ownes,]* sold by *G. Lathum,* [1628?] O³⁸.C.C².G².; N.NY.PN(2).

　　　Issued w. some copies of 23085. App. included in the FQ rights ass'd by H. Lownes to Cole a. Latham 6 no. 1628; *see* 23085.

23088 — Prothalamion or a spousall verse. 4°. [*J. Orwin*] f. *W. Ponsonby,* 1596. L(2).L³⁰.O.; HN.HD.IND.JH².NY.+

23089 — The shepheardes calender conteyning twelue æglogues proportionable to the twelue monethes. [Immerito, *pseud.* In verse.] 4°. *H. Singleton,* 1579. Ent. 5 de. L.O.C².; HN(imp.).PFOR. Arthur Houghton.

23090 — [Anr. ed.] 4°. (*T. East*) f. *J. Harison the younger,* (1581.) Ass'd 29 oc. 1580. L(2).O.C².; HN.CH.N.TEX. Arthur Houghton.

23091 — [Anr. ed.] 4°. *J. Wolfe* [a.] (*T. East*) f. *J. Harrison the yonger,* 1586. L.O.C.DUL.M.+; F.HN.HD.ILL.JH².

　　　Colophon w. East's name possibly reprinted in error from 23090 as Wolfe apparently pr. all of this.

23092 — [Anr. ed.] 4°. *J. Windet* f. *J. Harrison the yonger,* 1591. L.L³⁰.O.C².G².+; F.HN.CH.N.TEX.+

23093 — [Anr. ed.] 4°. *T. Creede* f. *J. Harrison the yonger,* 1597. L(2).L⁸.O.O³⁰.C⁴.; F.HN.HD.PML.TCU.+

23093.5 — [Anr. ed.] fol. *H. L[ownes]* f. *M. Lownes,* 1611. L.O.C.D.E.+; F.HN.HD.N.PML.+

　　　Usually issued w. 23083.3–23084.

23094 — [Anr. ed.] fol. *B. Alsop* f. *J. Harrison the elder,* 1617. L.O.C.C².E².+; F.HN.HD.N.NY.+

　　　Usually issued w. 23085.

— Teares of the muses. 1591. *See* 23078.

23095 — Three proper, and wittie, familiar letters: lately passed betwene two vniuersitie men. (Two other, very commendable letters, of the same mens writing.) [Signed 'Immerito' and 'G. H.', i.e. G. Harvey.] 4°. *H. Bynneman,* 1580. Ent. 30 jn. L.O.O⁵.P.; F(imp.).HN(imp.).PFOR. Arthur Houghton (tp facs.).

— A view of the state of Ireland. 1633. *See* pt. 2 of 25067.

— *tr. See* 18602, 19974.6.

— *See also* 21488.

Spenser, Edw., *tr. See* 19974.6.

23096 **Spenser, John,** *D.D.* A learned and gracious sermon preached at Paules Crosse. Published by H. M(arshall.) 4°. *G. Purslowe* f. *S. Rande,* 1615. Ent. 13 ja. L¹⁵.O.O⁵.C².DUR³.+; F.HN.ILL.NY¹¹.Y.+

23097 — [A ghost.]

23098 **Spenser, John,** *Murderer.* John Spenser a Chesshire gallant, his life and repentance, who was lately executed at Burford a mile from Nantwich. (John Spenser his repentance.) *Ballad.* 2 pts. s.sh.fol. [*W. White*] f. *J. Trundle,* [c. 1617.] C⁶.

　　　T. Dickerson is named as author of pt. 1 and J. Spenser as author of pt. 2, but Dickerson prob. wrote both.

Sphinx. Sphinx theologica. [1636.] *See* 1880.

Sphyractes, Johannes, *Rector of Basle U. See* 14794.

23099 **Spicer, Alexander.** Davids petition. Inlarged by Alexander Spicer. 8°. *T. C[reede]* a. *B. A[lsop]* f. *R. Wilson,* 1616. Ent. to John [i.e. Robert?] Wilson 27 ja. O.

23100 — An elegie on the much lamented death of sir Arthur Chichester. 4°. *M. F[lesher]* f. *R. Bird,* 1625. Ent. 26 fb. L.; HN

　　　Reissued w. cancel tp in 1643 as Wing S 4972.

23100a — Nabuchadonosor at Rome or the pope at Babylon a sermon preached at Colaraine in the north of Ireland. 8°. *B. B[eale?]* f. *J. Harrison* [2,] 1617. Ent. to J. Harrison, jun., 26 ap. LINC(2).

　　　Isaiah xlviii.20 is quoted on the tp, but the sermon text is Daniel iii.6.

23101 **Spicer, John.** The sale of salt. Or the seasoning of soules. [Protestant propaganda in dialogue form.] 8°. *N. Okes,* sold [by *S. Waterson,*] 1611. Ent. to Okes 18 jy. L.D.P.WI.; F.HN.

23101.5 **Spicer, Richard.** Ad serenissimam Angliæ reginam Elizabetham oratio. (An oration made to the queenes maiestie, at Sandwiche, the first of September, 1573.) [Init. R. S.] 8°. [*J. Kingston*] ap. *J. Dayum,* [1573.] L.

Spigurnell, Andrew, *ed. See* 21740.

Spilbergen, Joris van. *See* 21507.

Spinola, Ambrogio. A certaine relation of the marquisse of Spinolas forces. 1625. *See* Newsbooks 353.

Spinola, Benedict. An epitaph vpon the death of B. Spinola. [1580.] *See* 1057.

Spira, Francis. A relation of the fearefull estate of F. Spira. 1638. *See* 1177.5.

Spirit. The spirit of detraction conjured. 1611. *See* 24622.

Spirito, Lorenzo. The booke of fortune. 1618. *See* 3306.

23102 **Splynter, Johan.** Here begynneth a mery gest and a true howe Johan splynter made his testament. [In verse.] 4°. (*J. Notary,*) [1520?] HN.

23103 **Spotiswood, John,** *Abp.* Refutatio libelli de regimine ecclesiae Scoticanae. 8°. *ex off. Nortoniana, ap. J. Billium,* 1620. L.O.C².E.M⁴.+; F.HN.HD.NY.U.+

23104 — A true relation, of the proceedings against John Ogilvie, a Jesuit, executed at Glasgow. [Anon.] 4°. *Edinburgh, A. Hart,* 1615. L.O.DUR⁵.E.M⁴.+; F(2).HN.SMU.

— *See also* 22034.

23105 **Spottiswood, James.** Concio Jacobi Spottiswodii, . . . quam habuit ad clerum Andreanopoli. 4°. *Edinburgi, A. Hart,* 1616. L.L³.C.E.STU.+

23106 — The execution of Neschech and the confyning of his kinsman Tarbith. Or a short discourse, shewing the difference betwixt damned usurie, and that which is lawfull. Whereunto is subjoyned an epistle of Mʳ. J. Calvin, *tr.* out of Latine. 4°. *Edinburgh, A. Hart* f. *C. Pounder, Norwich,* 1616. L.L³⁰.O.C.E.+; F.HN.HD(imp.).PN².Y.+

　　　The Calvin letter 'De usuris responsum' is in *Epistolae et responsa,* Geneva, 1575, pp. 355–7.

— *See also* 19474.

Sprint, *Doctor.* The christian sword. *See* 23108.2 sqq.

23107 **Sprint, John,** *Dean.* Ad illustrissimos comites Warwicensem et Leicestrensem oratio gratulatoria Bristolliæ habita. Anno 1587. 8°. *Oxonii, ex off. J. Barnesii,* [1587.] O.

Sprint, John, *Vicar.* The anatomy of the controversed ceremonies. [1618.] *See* folding leaf in 6469.

23108 — Cassander Anglicanus; shewing the necessity of conformitie to the prescribed ceremonies of our church, in case of deprivation. 4°. *J. Bill,* 1618. Ent. 4 mr. L.O.C.D.E.+; F.HN.HD.N.U.+

Sprint, John, *Vicar—cont.*

23108.2 — The christian sword and buckler. Or, a letter sent by D. Sprint, to a man seven yeares grievously afflicted in conscience. 8°. *B. Alsop f. S. Rand,* 1623. HD.

23108.3 — [Anr. ed.] 8°. *A. M[athewes] f. S. Rand,* 1625. E.

23108.4 — [Anr. ed.] 8°. *W. J[ones] f. S. Rand,* 1628. P.

23108.5 — [Anr. ed.] 8°. *A. M[athewes] f. S. Rand,* 1629. F.

23108.6 — [Anr. ed.] 8°. *A. M[athewes] f. S. Rand,* 1633. L(tp only, Ames II.1150).

23108.7 — [Anr. ed.] 8°. *f. S. Rand,* 1636. L(tp only, Harl. 5921/327).

23109 — Propositions, tending to proove the necessarie use of the christian sabbaoth. 4°. *H. L[ownes] f. T. Man,* 1607. Ent. 2 fb. L⁴.O.C³.E².M.+; F(date cropt).HD.

23110 — [Anr. ed.] 12°. [*A. Mathewes*] *f. J. Grismond,* 1635. L³.O²⁸.C.E.M.+; F.BALT.CHI.PN².U(imp.).+

23111 — The summe of the christian religion; contayning the chiefe points of the perswasion and practise of a christian. In question and answere. 8°. *W. Stansby f. W. Burre,* 1613. Ent. 15 my. O.; HN.BO.
A different text from 23432.3.

Spur. The spur to the lordis. 1570. *See* 22208.

23111.5 **Squire.** [The squire of low degree. A1ʳ:] Here begynneth vndo your dore. [In verse.] 4° 8.4? [*W. de Worde,* 1520?] HN(A1,2,7,8).

23112 — [Anr. ed. A1ʳ:] The squyr of lowe degre. 4°. (*W. Copland,*) [1560?] Ent. to J. King 10 jn. 1560. L.

Squire, D. *See* 21483.

Squire, Edward. A letter containing a report of a conspiracie. 1599. *See* 10017.

23113 **Squire, John,** *Minister.* A plaine exposition upon the first part of the second chapter of saint Paul his second epistle to the Thessalonians. Being lectures. 4° in 8's. [*M. Flesher*] *f. R. Allot,* 1630. Ent. 7 fb. L.D.WI.; F.HN.NY¹¹.

23114 — [A variant, w. imprint:] [*M. Flesher*] *f. P. Waterhouse,* 1630. L.O.C.G².P.+; F.HD.ILL.U.Y.+

23115 — A sermon on the second commandement. 4°. *W. S[tansby] f. N. Newbery,* 1624. Ent. 7 ja. L.O.C.D.M.+; F.HN.U.

23115.5 — A sermon preached at Hartford assises, March 14. 1616. 4°. *T. S[nodham] f. N. Bourne,* 1617. Ent. 27 mr. O.O².O³.P.

23116 — [Anr. ed.] 4°. *T. S[nodham] f. N. Bourne,* 1618. L³.C². E(2). Leeds PL.; F.HD.Y.

23117 — A sermon. Appointed for the New-church-yard, by London, on White-sunday, 1619. 4°. *N. Okes f. J. Piper,* 1621. Ent. 10 ja. 1620. L.L¹³.O.C.DUR³.+; F.HD.Y.

23118 — Tes irenes trophæa. 1620. Now = 23120.5.

23119 — A thankes-giving, for the decreasing, of the plague. Being a sermon. 4°. *B. A[lsop] a. T. F[awcet] f. J. Clark,* 1637. Ent. 11 ja. L.O⁶.C³.D.E.+; F.HN.BALT. HD.U.+

23119.5 — [Anr. ed.] The second edition revised. 4°. *B. A[lsop] a. T. F[awcet] f. J. Clark,* 1637. L².L³.O.C¹⁰.E.+; BO⁵ (imp.).BR.HD.PN.Y.
A2,3 and F outer forme are reimposed from 23119.

23120 — Three sermons: two of them appointed for the Spittle, preached in St. Pauls church, by J. Squier, and J. Lynch. 4°. *R. Young f. H. Blunden,* 1637. Ent. 4 jy. L.L².O.C¹⁹.G⁴.+; F.HN.HD.ILL.U.+
— *See also* 15569.

23120.5 **Squire, John,** *Triumph Writer.* Tes irenes trophæa. Or, the tryumphs of peace. [On the inauguration of Sir F. Jones as Lord Mayor.] 4°. *N. Okes,* 1620. L⁸. Greg 366.
(Formerly 23118)

Squire, William, *tr. See* 17229.

St., M. Newes out of Yorkshire. 1627. *See* 23228.

23121 **Stadius, Joannes.** Here after followeth a table of the sunnes declination. [1581.] = pt. of 18647.
— *ed. See* 11101.

23122 **Stafford, Anthony.** The day of salvation. Or, a homily upon the bloody sacrifice of Christ. 24° in 12's. *N. a. J. Okes f. D. Frere,* 1635. Ent. 15 ap. L(lacks engr. tp).; CH.

23123 — The femall glory: or, the life, and death of our blessed lady, the holy virgin Mary. 8°. *T. Harper f. J. Waterson,* 1635. Ent. 12 se. L.O.C.DUR⁵.OS.+; F. HN.HD.ILL.Y.+

Stafford, Anthony—*cont.*

— The golden meane. 1613, etc. *See* 17757 sqq.

23124 — The guide of honour, or the ballance wherin she may weigh her actions. 12°. *T. C[otes] f. T. Slater,* 1634. Ent. to S. Cartwright a. T. Slater 3 oc. 1633. L.O.; F.HN.HD.LC.N.

23124.5 — [A variant, w. imprint:] *T. C[otes] f. S. Cartwright,* 1634. C².DUL(2).P.PETYT(imp.).; ILL.Y.

23125 — Honour and vertue, triumphing over the grave. Exemplified in a life of Edward [or rather Henry] lord Stafford. Embelish'd by many elegies. 4°. *J. Okes* [*a. T. Cotes?*] *f. H. Seile,* 1640. Ent. 12 no. 1639. L.; HN.ILL.MIN.N.
N2–O4 missing in all copies; quires P–V may have been pr. by a different printer, possibly T. Cotes.

23126 — [A variant, w. 'Henry' on tp a. imprint:] *J. Okes, sold by R. Lownds,* 1640. L(2, 1 imp.).O(2).O¹².C².; F.HN. CH.Y.

23127 — Meditations, and resolutions, moral, divine, politicall. Century I. There is also annexed an oration of Justus Lipsius, against calumnie; tr. out of Latine. 12°. *H. L[ownes,] sold by T. Saunders,* 1612. Ent. 20 ap. L.O.O².C.DUL.+; F.HN.

23128 — Staffords heavenly dogge: or the life, and death of Diogenes. Taken out of the best authors. 12°. *G. Purslowe f. J. Budge,* 1615. Ent. 6 jn. L.O(2).C²¹. DUR.; F(2).HN.Y. Arthur Houghton.

23129 — Staffords Niobe: or his age of teares. A treatise. Wherein deaths visard is pulled off, and her face discovered not to be so fearefull. 12°. *H. Lownes,* 1611. Ent. 1 mr. L.L³.O(2).; F.BO.WTL.

23130 — [Anr. ed., enlarged.] The first part. The second edition; newlie corrected & amended. (Staffords Niobe, dissolv'd into a Nilus: serving as a second part.) 2 pts. 12°. *H. Lownes* (*f. M. Lownes,*) 1611. Pt. 2 ent. 10 oc. L(imp.).O(pt. 2 only).C³.LINC.P.+; F.HN.HD(pt. 1 only).ILL.N.+
Most copies have A3–6 in pt. 2 cancelled; these leaves, a dedic. to Anne Clifford Sackville, Countess of Dorset, are present in O,F.
— *tr. See* 7344, 24145.

Stafford, Henry, *First Baron Stafford, tr. See* 11220.

23131 **Stafford, Humphrey.** The [xylographic] arraignment, judgement, confession, and execution of H. Stafford. 4°. *E. A[llde] f. A. J[ohnson] a. F. B[urton,]* 1607. Ent. to F. Burton 18 jn. L.O⁵.

Stafford, Robert. *See* Stafforde, R.

23132 **Stafford, Thomas.** Pacata Hibernia. Ireland appeased and reduced. Or, an historie of the late warres. fol. *A. Mathewes f. R. Milbourne,* 1633. Ent. 3 au. 1632. L.O.C.D.E.+; F.HN.HD.ILL.NY.+
Most copies of this and the following have leaf w. engr. portrait of Eliz. and letterpress verses signed 'G. W[ither?]', with imprint: '*f. R. Milbourne,* 1633.'

23132a — [Anr. issue, w. cancel tp:] *A. M[athewes,] and part of the impression made over, to be vented for the benefit of the children of J. Mynshew, deceased,* 1633. L³⁸.O⁹.C.D.LIV³.+; F.HN.HD.N.Y.+

23132a.5 — [Anr. issue of 23132, w. imprint on cancel slip:] *f. R. M[ilborne,] and part of the impression made over, to be vented for the benefit of the children of J. Mynshew, deceased,* 1634. HD.

23133 **Stafford, William.** A compendious or briefe examination of certayne ordinary complaints. By [i.e. edited by?] William Stafford. 4°. *T. Marshe,* 1581. Ass'd by E. Marshe to T. Orwin ?23 jn. 1591. NEK.; F.
This was written in 1549; sometimes attrib. to J. Hales but more prob. by Sir T. Smith.

23133.5 — [A variant, w. tp altered:] By W. S. gentleman. *T. Marshe,* 1581. L³⁰.L³⁸.O.C.D².+; F(2).BO.
A1ʳ line 4 of heading: 'England.'; line 2 of text: 'sondry'. One F copy is sophisticated and has 'William Shakespeare' hand-stamped on the tp.

23133a — [Anr. ed.] 4°. *T. Marshe,* 1581. L.L³⁸.O.C.C⁶(lacks tp). +; F.HN.CU.HD.Y.+
A1ʳ line 4 of heading: 'Englande.'

23134 — [Anr. ed.] 4°. *T. Marshe,* 1581. L.L³⁰.L³⁸.O(5, 1 imp.). P(2).; F.HN.CHI.HD.TEX.+
A1ʳ line 4 of heading: 'England.'; line 2 of text: 'sundry'. Quires **, H–I, L largely reimposed from 23133a.

23135 **Stafforde, Robert.** A geographicall and anthologicall description of all the empires in this globe. 4°. *T. C[reede] f. S. Waterson,* 1607. Ent. 8 mr. 1608. L.L³⁰.O¹⁶.LONGLEAT.; HN.HD.KAN.LC.NY.+

23136 — [Anr. ed.] 4°. *N. Okes f. S. W[aterson,]* 1618. L.O(3).; HN.CB.N.NY.PN.

23136a — [Anr. issue, w. cancel tp, w. imprint:] *N. O[kes] f. J. Parker,* 1618. L.E. Blickling.; F.HN.CB.LC.NY.+

23137 — [Anr. ed.] 4°. *N. Okes f. S. Waterson,* 1634. L.O.O³. C.WOR.; F.HN.BO.CB.NY.+

— *tr. See* 7325, 22879.

Stalbrydge, Henry, *pseud. See* 1291.

23138 **Stallenge, William.** Instructions for the increasing of mulberie trees, and breeding of silke-wormes. [Init. W. S.] 4°. *E. A[llde] f. E. Edgar,* 1609. L.L³⁰.O¹⁸. C¹³.E².+; F.HN.CB.NY. Sexton.

Mostly a trans. of J. B. Le Tellier's 'Mémoires et instructions pour l'establissement des meuriers', Paris, 1603. For the licence granted on 5 Jan. 1607 to Stallenge to print this *see* Greg, *Companion,* p. 153.

23139 — [Anr. ed. Anon.] Newly printed. 4°. *[J. Windet,]* 1609. L(tp def.).L¹⁰. Phillipps 3183.

Stamford, Lincolnshire, *Benedictine Convent of Our Lady and St. Michael. See* Indulgences 74 sq.

STANBRIDGE, JOHN

Because of the difficulty of dealing with the complexity of texts, quantity of editions, and imperfections of copies, the title and colophon transcriptions are here given in more detail than elsewhere in STC. Line endings are indicated if they occur within the portion transcribed. Regarding types and letter forms cited *see* Frank Isaac, *English & Scottish Printing Types,* 2 vols.; regarding tp cuts *see* Edward Hodnett, *English Woodcuts.* Nearly every extant copy has been examined personally or by film or xerox, and readings have been selected to distinguish editions or issues. Should unrecorded copies come to light, however, it would be wise to have them checked against the much more extensive notes I have accumulated. KFP.

ACCIDENCE

There are three forms of Accidence listed below, all beginning: 'How many parts of reason be there?' Only 1 is positively connected with Stanbridge; 2 is sometimes attributed to Donatus.

1. The 'full' or 'regular' Accidence, having 16–18 leaves. In the section on nouns, usually in the first 10 lines of the text, is the sentence: 'And the name of every thing that may be felt, seen, heard or understood is in Latin a noun proper or appellative.'

2. The 'long' Accidence, having 12–14 leaves, with the sentence: 'For all manner thing that a man may see, feel, hear or understand that beareth the name of a thing is a noun. How many manner of nouns be there? Two. Which two? A noun substantive and a noun adjective.'

3. The 'short' Accidence, having 4 leaves, with the sentence: 'For all that you may see, feel, [etc. as in 2] is a noun. How many things belong to a noun? Six. Which six? Quality, comparison, [etc.]'

For an allied though distinct text with the same beginning sentence but having 20 leaves and the noun sentence: 'But noun of himself betokeneth a certain thing commonly or properly' *see* 14078 sq.

23139.5 — Here begynneth the accidens of maister Stan-/bridges awne makynge. 4° in 6's. *(Per Richardum Pynson,)* [1505?] O(4° A 18(2) Art.BS.).

23140 — [Anr. ed.] Here begynneth the Acci/dence of mayster Stanbrydges owue [*sic*] makynge. 4° in 6's. [*Rouen, P. Violet,* c. 1505.] O⁹(frags.).M(frags., R56258, R4519).

23140.5 — [Anr. ed.] The accydence of mayster [xylographic, white on black]/ Stanbrydges owne makynge. 4° in 6's. *(By wynkyn de worde,)* [1507?] C⁴(M.28.43/1). No catch titles.

23141 — Now = 23147.8.

23142 — [Anr. ed.] 4° in 6's. *(by wynkyn de worde,)* [1510?] L(G.16866, lacks A1,2). With catch titles; on A3, B3: 'Acci. stang. [*sic*]'

23143 — [Anr. ed.] Accidentia ex stanbrigiana editione. 4° in 6's. *(by Richarde Pynson, prynter vnto the/ Kynges noble grace,)* [1510?] L(C.54.bb.16).O(Mason H 44, lacks a1).

(Formerly also 23147 and 25509) Title is in 1 line.

Stanbridge, John—*Accidence*—*cont.*

23143.5 — [Anr. ed.] Accidentia ex stanbrigiana/ editione. 4° in 6's. [*R. Pynson,* c. 1510.] C(SSS.23.15/1, tp only).

Title is in 2 lines, over Hodnett 1508 in a state very similar to 23143.

23144 — Now = 23155.2.

23145 — Now = 23148.8.

23146 — Now = 23149.5.

23147 — = 23143.

23147.2 — [Anr. ed.] Accidētia ex stanbrigiana editio-/ne nuper recognita et castigata/ lima Roberti whitintoni Lichfeldien-/sis [etc.] 4°. [*Rouen, R. Auzoult,* c. 1515.] L(tp only, Harl.5974/16).

23147.4 — [Anr. ed.] 4° in 6's. *(by Wynkyn de Worde, in/ the Fletestrete,)* [1517?] MARL(lacks A1).SHR(B2,5,6 and C⁴ only).

23147.6 — [Anr. ed.] Roberti whittintoni stanbrigianis super/ Accidentibus vltima Recognitio. 4° in 6's. *(by wynkyn de worde,* 1519.) HN(59558).

Without de Worde's address in the colophon.

23147.8 — [Anr. ed.] 4° in 6's. *(by Rycharde Pynson, prynter/ vnto the Kynges most noble grace,)* [1520?] L(G.7560, lacks A1,6).

(Formerly 23141)

23148 — [Anr. ed.] Accidentia ex stābrigiana editione/ nup recognita & castigata lima Ro-/berti whitintoni Lichfeldiēsis [etc.] 4° in 6's. *(by Wykyn [sic] de worde in the/ Fletestrete,)* [1520?] ILL.

23148.2 — [Anr. ed.] Accidentia ex stanbrigiana editione/ nuper recognita & castigata [etc.] 4° in 6's. *(by me wynkyn de worde,* 1520.) WN(lacks B2–5).

23148.3 — [Anr. ed.] Accidentia ex stābrigiana editione nuper recognita/ et castigata [etc.] 4°. *(by Robert Coplāde,* 1522.) Mellon.

23148.4 — [Anr. ed.] Accidētia ex Stābrigiana editione nu-/per recognita et castigata [etc.] 4° ⁶·⁴. *(by Rycharde/ Pynson, printer to the kynges noble grace,)* [1523?] CREDITON. Lord Kenyon(imp.).

23148.5 — [Anr. ed.] 4° in 6's. *(by Wynkyn de Worde, in Fletestrete,* 1525.) LONGLEAT(lacks A1).

23148.7 — [Anr. ed.] Accidētia ex stanbrigiana editione/ nuper recognita et castigata [etc.] 4° in 6's. *(Rothomagi,) imp. iacobi Cousin,* (1526.) HN(88396).

Cf. 23159a.12.

23148.8 — [Anr. ed.] Accidentia ex stambrigiana/ editione. 4° in 6's. *(Impryntyd in chepe syde at the syne [sic] of the/ mearemayde [sic] next to pollys gate,) [by J. Rastell a. Southwark, P. Treveris,* 1527?] O(Tanner 239/1).

(Formerly 23145) Rastell's types with diamond 'T', in a fairly worn state, are in A⁶ and C⁴; Treveris's types with plain 'T' are in B⁶. There are approx. 2 lines of text missing between B4ᵛ and C1ʳ, so this item may represent a mixture of sheets from 2 eds. Catch titles on A2,3 and C2: 'Stam. accidence.'; on B1–3: 'Acci.stan.'

23148.10 — [Anr. ed.] Accidentia ex Stranbrigiana [*sic*] editione/ nuper recognita & castigata [etc.] 4° in 6's. *(by wynkyn de worde,/ in Fletestrete,)* [1528.] O(Mason H 36).

Letter on verso of tp dated 17 April [15]28. Catch title: 'Acci. stan.' on A3, B1,3, C1. Leaf signatures have stops.

23148.12 — [Anr. ed.] 4° in 6's. *(by me Wynkyn de Worde/ in Flete strete,)* [1529?] ILL(lacks A1).

Catch title: 'Acci. stan.' on A3, B1,3, C1. Leaf signatures have no stops. This has usual de Worde types: s³, w², w³; cf. 23174.3, 23150.3; cf. also 25577.

23148a — [Anr. ed.] Accidentia ex stanbrigiana editione nu-/per recognita & castigata [etc.] 4° in 6's. *(by me Wynkyn de Worde/ in Flete strete,)* [1529.] L(G.7563/1).

Letter on verso of tp dated 2 July [15]29. Has catch titles on A3, B1–3, C1–3; that on B1 is 'Acci. stā.' and on C3 is 'Acci.'

23149 — [Anr. ed.] Accidentia ex Stanbrigiana editione nu-/per recognita, et castigata, [etc.] 4° in 6's. *(at London in Poules chyrche/yarde, by Iohn̄ Skot,)* [1529?] C(Sel. 5.70).

23149.5 — [Anr. ed.] Accidētia [no 'ex'] stābrigia-/na editione nuper recognita et castigata [etc.] 4° ⁶·⁴. *(South-warke by me Peter Treuerys,)* [1529?] O(Mason H 22).

(Formerly 23146)

Stanbridge, John—*Accidence*—cont.

23150 — [Anr. ed.] 4° in 6's. (*by Wynkyn de Worde,/ in Flete-strete,*) [1530?] L(C.41.d.7, lacks A1).
   Catch title: 'Acci. stan.' on A3, B1,3, C1. Has 'TELOS./ TO THEO DOXA' before Additamenta on C4ᵛ.

23150.3 — [Anr. ed.] 4° in 6's. [*Wynkyn de Worde?*] (*for Iohn̄ Butler,*) [1530?] P(Sp.24/2, lacks A1).
   Catch title: 'Acci. stan.' on B1, C1. Has 'TELOS./ TO THEO DOXA' before Additamenta on C4ᵛ. The leaf signatures have no stops. This is in the same types as 23174.3, q.v.

23150.5 — [Anr. ed.] Accidentia ex Stanbrigiana editione nuper/ recognita, et castigata, [etc.]. 4°. (*by me Iohn̄ Skot/ dwellynge at the George alleygate,*) [1530?] O(Mason H 19).

23150.7 — [Anr. ed.] Accidētia ex stābrigiana editione/ nup recognita & castigata [etc.]. 4°. (*Southwarke by Peter/ Treueris,*) [1530?] M(9756).

23151 — [Anr. ed.] 4°. (*in yorke ... by Iohan WarWyke,* 1532.) L(C.70.bb.18, quires B–D4 only).

23151.3 — [Anr. ed.] Accidētia [no 'ex'] stābrigiana/ editione nuper recognita & castigata [etc.]. 4°. (*Southwarke/ by my* [sic] *Peter Treueris,*) [1532?] HN(30628).
   Though the letter on the verso of the tp is dated 16 kal. Oct., 1526, this is prob. the last Treveris ed.

23151.7 — [Anr. ed.] Accidentia ex Stan-/brigiana editione nuper recognita et/ castigata [etc.]. 4°. (*by me/ Wynkyn de Worde,* 1534 (20 fb.).) C5(A.2.11/12).

23152 — [Anr. issue, with C4 and D1ʳ, D4ᵛ reset, with colophon:] (*by me/ wynkyn de worde,* 1534 (16 my.).) L(C.33.b.18).

— [Anr. ed.] 1534. *See* 23153.2.

23152.3 — [Anr. ed.] Accidentia ex Stan-/brigiana editione nuper recognita et/ castigata [etc.]. 4°. (*by me Iohn̄ Byddell,*) [1538?] ILL.

23152.5 — [Anr. ed.] Accidentia ex Stan-/brigiana editione nuper recognita et castiga-/ta [etc.]. 4°. (*by Nycholas Bourman,* 1539.) M(R9761).

23152.7 — [A variant, with colophon:] (*by James Gauer,* 1539.) HD(frags., *63-1477F/65–66).

23153 — [Anr. ed.] 4°. (*at Cantorbury/ by Iohn̄ mychel,*) [1550?] C(Syn.7.51.25, C1,4 only; Syn. 7.55.20, D1,4 only).
   As the text continues from C4ᵛ to D1ʳ and the 2 frags. agree in types and in having catchwords, it is likely they belong to the same ed.

23153.2 — [An abridged version, with other extracts. B8ʳ:] (De Anomalum declinatione.—[D1ʳ:] Paruulo/rum Institutio). 8°. (*Antverpiae, Apud Martinum Cæsarem,/ ... Væneunt Londonij/ Apud Ioannem Toye ...* 1534 (my.).) C(Syn.8.53.74, lacks A1, D4).
   (Formerly 85) As the noun explanation is as in form 1 above, it seemed most logical to place this here, though the text is a considerable hodge-podge of selections.

Long Accidence

23153.4 — [Heading A1ʳ:] Accedence. [Anon.] 4° ⁸·⁶. (*West-mynstre, In Caxons* [sic] *hous by wynkyn de word',*) [1495.] O(Douce D 238). Duff 133.
   (Formerly 7009)

23153.5 — [Anr. ed.] Accedence. 4° ⁸·⁶. (*westmynstre, In Caxons hous/ by wynkyn de worde,*) [1499.] O(Arch.G e.4).c⁶. Duff 134.
   (Formerly 7010)

23153.6 — [Anr. ed.] Here begynneth the Accedence diligen/tly correcte and poyntyd. 4° in 6's. [*W. Faques,* 1504?] L²(frag. 14, leaves 1, 6).
   The title is over Hodnett 2019a.

23153.7 — [Anr. ed.] 4° ⁸·⁶? [*Antwerp,*] (*Hoc presens opusculū ꝑ me Iohānē/ de Doesborch est exaratum,*) [1509?] O⁵ (B1,2,5,6 only).
   Proctor 5; 30 lines a page; cf. 13606.5.

23153.9 — [Anr. ed.] Here beginnith the ac-/cedence. 4° ⁸·⁶. (*Antwerpe by me Godfroy Back,*) [c. 1510.] Philip Robinson, London.
   Cf. 23155.

23153.10 — [Anr. ed.] The longe Accydence. 4° ⁸·⁴. (*by Wynkyn de/ Worde,* 1513.) C5(A.2.9).

23154 — [Anr. ed.] The longe accydence/ newly correcte. 4° ⁸·⁴. (*By wynkyn de/ worde,*) [1518?] L(G.7561).

Stanbridge, John—*Long Accidence*—cont.

23154.3 — [Anr. ed.] 4°. (*by me Hary Pepwell,* 1519.) 2 leaves, untraced.
   Seen by E. G. Duff, when they were bd. at the end of Erasmus, *In evangelium Lucae,* Basle, Froben, 1548, belonging in 1908 to Mr. Barber, a bookseller of Manchester.

Short Accidence

23154.5 — [Begin A1ʳ:] How many partes of reson ben the/re. [Anon.] 4°. (*by Wynken* [sic] *de worde,*) [1500?] HN(152101, A1,4 only).

23154.7 — [Anr. ed.] 4°. [*W. Faques,* c. 1505.] C(Syn.5.50.2/2, 2nd and 3rd leaves only).
   In Faques's 97 textura with diamond 'T'.

23155 — [Anr. ed.] Here begynneth the shorte/ Accedence. 4°. (*Andwerp/ Be me Godfry Back,*) [c. 1510.] O(Antiq. e.N.1510.1).EX(1st and 4th leaves only).
   Cf. 23153.9.

23155.2 — [Anr. ed.] Accedence. 4°. [*Antwerp,*] (*by me Iohn̄ off Doesborch,*) [c. 1515.] O(4° A 18(1) Art.BS.).
   (Formerly 23144) Proctor 10; 29 lines a page, plus a headline; cf. 13606.5.

GRADUS COMPARATIONUM AND SUM, ES, FUI

This has 8 leaves, with text beginning: 'What nouns maketh comparison? All adjectives wellnear [etc.]' The section on irregular verbs begins: 'Sum, es, fui, esse, futurus.' For a different text on irregular verbs *see* 23163.4.

23155.4 — [Begin A1ʳ:] What nownys maketh comparison all ad-/ iectyues welnere [etc. Anon.] 4° in 8. (*by Rycharde Pynson,*) [c. 1505.] O(Arch.A.e.37/2).; HD(lacks A1,8).
   5-line init. on A1ʳ.

23155.6 — [Anr. ed.] 4° in 8. (*by Rycharde Pynson,*) [c. 1505.] HD(imp.).
   4-line init. on A1ʳ. Text begins like 23155.4.

23155.8 — [Anr. ed.] What nownys maketh comparison al/ adiectyues [etc.] 4° in 8. (*by Richarde Pynson / prynter vnto the kyngʒ noble grace,*) [1509?] CU.

23155.9 — [Anr. ed.] Gradus comparationū: cū verbis anomalis./ simul & eoꝛ cōpositis ex Stābrigiana editione. 4° in 8. [*Wynkyn de Worde,* 1509?] O(Mason H 38).
   (Formerly 23159) De Worde's device, McK. 19, is on A8ᵛ.

23156 — [Anr. ed.] Sum, es, fui, of Stanbrige. 4° in 8. (*by Rycharde pynson,/ prynter vnto yᵉ kynges noble grace,*) [1510?] L(C.33.i.3).

23156a — Now = 23159a.5.

23157 — [Anr. ed.] Gradus cōparationū cū verbis/ anormalis simul & eorū cōpositʒ. 4° in 8. (*by me wynkyn de worde,*) [1517?] L(C.40.e.7).c⁴(M.28.43/3).

23158 — Now = 23162.5.

23159 — Now = 23155.9.

23159.5 — [Anr. ed.] 4° in 8. (*by wynkn* [sic] *de worde,*) [1518?] O(Vet.A1.b.12, A7,8 only).
   With McK. 19 on A8ᵛ; the following de Worde eds. through 23159a.9 have McK. 20. As the wording and line endings of the full colophon resemble those in the de Worde group beginning 23159a.3, there is a bare chance the present frag. is the same ed. as 23159a.4 and the dates attrib. to both need slight adjustment.

23159a — [Anr. ed.] 4° in 8. (*at London ... by me wynkyn de Worde,*) [1519?] O(Mason H 37).
   Title like 23157 except: 'et eorū'.

23159a.1 — [Anr. ed.] 4° in 8. (*at Londō ... by me Wynkyn de Worde,*) [1520?] M(18936).; HN(59559).
   Title like 23159a.

23159a.2 — [Anr. ed.] 4° in 8. (*at Londō ... by/ me Wynkyn de worde,*) [1520?] WN.
   Title like 23159a.

23159a.3 — [Anr. ed.] Gradus comparationum cum/ verbis anomalis simul et/eorū compositis. 4° in 8. (*by Wynkyn de worde,*) [1521?] PML.
   5-line init. on A1ʳ.

23159a.4 — [Anr. ed.] 4° in 8. [*Wynkyn de Worde,* 1522?] MARL (lacks A7,8).
   Title like 23159a.3; 4-line init. on A1ʳ; A1 signed: 'A.i.'; cf. 23159a.7. Possibly earlier; *see* 23159.5.

Stanbridge, John—*Gradus Comparationum—cont.*

23159a.5 — [Anr. ed.] Sum es fui of Stambrige. 4⁰ in 8. (*by Richarde Pynson./ printer vnto the kyngʒ noble grace,*) [1523?] C(Sel.5.72.).CREDITON.
(Formerly 23156a)

23159a.7 — [Anr. ed.] Gradus [etc.] 4⁰ in 8. (*by wynkyn de worde,*) [1524?] C²(Grylls.3.392).
Title like 23159a.3; 4-line init. on A1ʳ; A1 signed: 'A.j.'; cf. 23159a.4.

23159a.8 — [Anr. ed.] 4⁰ in 8. (*by Wynkyn de Worde,*) [1525?] LONGLEAT.
Title like 23159a.3 except: '&/ eorū'.

23159a.9 — [Anr. ed.] Gradus comparationum stanbrigiane edi-/ tionis, cū verbis anomalis simul et eorū/ compositis. anno xxvj. supra sesqui-/millesimū, cultius solitoȼ ve-/rius excusi. 4⁰ in 8. (*by wynkyn de worde,*) [1526.] M(9759).

23159a.10— [Anr. ed.] Gradus comparatio-/num cum verbis anomalis simul/ et eorum compositis. 4⁰ in 8. (*apud V Vinandum de V Vorde,* 1526 (15 ka. au.)) M(9750).
The dated Latin colophon is on A8ᵛ; an undated English colophon is on A8ʳ in this and the following de Worde eds.

23159a.12— [Anr. ed.] Gradus comparationū cū verbis anomalis si-/mul et eorū cōpositis ex Stābrigiana editione. 4⁰ in 8. (*Rothomagi in sumptis ia/cobi Cousin,*) [1526?] O(Auct.2Q5.9/6).
Cf. 23148.7.

23159a.13 — [Anr. ed.] 4⁰ in 8. (*apud V Vinandum de V Vorde,* 1527 (17 ka. ap.)) C¹⁹(S.180/1, lacks A1,2).

23160 — [Anr. ed.] Gradus comparationum cum anoma-/lis simul et eorum compositis. 4⁰ in 8. (*apud V Vinandum de V Vorde,* 1527 (6 no.)) O(Arch.A.e.27).; CH.

23160.3 — [Anr. ed.] Gradus comparationum cū verbis anoma-/lis simul et eorum compositis. 4⁰ in 8. (*apud V Vinandum de V Vorde,* 1527 (6 no.)) CU.
A8ᵛ, including the colophon, is from the same typesetting as 23160, but the other pages are reset.

23160.7 — [Anr. ed.] Gradus comparationum cum/ verbis anomalis simul et/ eorum compositis. 4⁰. [*J. Skot f.*] (*by Iohn̄ Butler,*) [1529?] P(Sp.24/4).

23161 — [Anr. ed.] Gradus comparationū cū verbis anomalis/ simul cum eorum compositis. 4⁰ in 8. (*by me wynkyn/ de worde,* 1530.) F.
This has an English colophon only.

23162 — [Anr. ed.] Gradus cōparatiuū [*sic*] cum verbis ano-/malis simul cuu [*sic*] eorū compositis. 4⁰. [*J. Skot f.*] (*by me Iohn̄ Toye,* 1531 (30 my.)) L(C.59.e.21). O(Tanner 239/3).

23162.5 — [Anr. ed.] Gradus comparationum cum/ verbis anomalis simul et/ eorum compositis. 4⁰ in 8. *Southwarke by me Peter Treueris,*) [1531?] C⁵(A.2.11/15).; HN(29035).
(Formerly 23158)

23163 — [Anr. ed.] Sum es fui./ Gradus comparationū cum verbis ano-/malis simul cum eorum compositis. 4⁰. (*by Wynkyn de Worde,* 1532.) O(Douce frags.e.17, A⁴ only, misperfected). LIV³.MARL(frag. of quire A, misperfected).

23163.2 — [Anr. ed.] Sum es fui. 4⁰. (*by Thomas Godfray,*) [1534?] M(9763).

23163.4 — [A different text, having 4 leaves and beginning A1ʳ:] Sum es fui esse essendi do dū ens futur⁹/ Indicatiuo modo sum es est. Et pl'r su-/mus estis sunt. [Anon.] (*Explicit tractatulus verborų defectiuorų & anor/ malorų.*) 4⁰. (*Impressus per Winandū de worde,*) [1508?] C⁴(M.28.43/4).; CU.
Though this is *not* the Stanbridge text, in view of the heading it seems wise to put this here for purposes of comparison and distinction. The Stanbridge section begins on A2ᵛ of 23155.4: 'Sum es fui esse futurus Indicatiuo modo tem/pore presenti sum I am es est. In pl'ri sumus/ estis sūt.' Horman's Introductorium contains a similar though different section on F1ʳ of 13809: 'Sum. es. fui. esse. essendi. essendo. essendū./ ens. futurus./ Indicatiuo presenti Sum. es. est. sumus/ estis. sunt.'

23163.5 — [Anr. ed.] (*Explicit tractatul⁹ verborū defectiuo-rum. . . .*) 4⁰. (*Impressus per Wynandum de Worde,*) [c. 1525.] O(lacks A2).

Stanbridge, John—*cont.*

PARVULA AND PARVULORUM INSTITUTIO

There are three forms of Parvula listed below. 1 and 2 are not by Stanbridge but are the texts from which he derived 3.

1. Parvula, having 4–6 leaves, with the text beginning: 'What shalt thou do when thou hast an English to be made in Latin?'

2. Long Parvula, having 12 leaves, with text beginning as 1, except for the phrase 'English to make'.

3. Parvulorum Institutio, having 12 leaves, with text beginning: 'What is to be done when an English is given to be made in Latin?'

23163.6 — Peruula. [Anon.] 4⁰ in 6. [*Westminster, Wynkyn de Worde,* 1496?] O(Douce D 238). Duff 343.
(Formerly 19440) Hodnett 918 is on A6ᵛ.

23163.7 — [Anr. ed.] Here begynneth a treatyse called. Peruula. 4⁰ in 6. (*westmynstre In Caxtons/ hous by wynkyn de worde,*) [1497?] L(C.11.a.18). Duff 342.
(Formerly 19439)

23163.8 — [Anr. ed. d3ʳ begins:] noĩatif case supponēt to the verbe. as ego qui scribo se/deo. 4⁰ in 6's. [*R. Pynson,* 1497?] ETON(d2,3 only). Duff 240.
(Formerly 15295) As the text on d3ʳ is the same as on A2ᵛ of 23163.7, this fragment formed a later section of some unidentified grammar.

23163.9 — [Anr. ed. a1ʳ begins:] What shalt thou do whan thou haste an en-/glisshe [etc.] 4⁰. [*Paris,*] (*by me Nicole marcāt,*) [1500.] M(17321). Duff 345.
(Formerly 19442)

23163.11 — [Anr. ed.] Here begynneth a treatyse called Peruula. 4⁰ in 6. [*Wynkyn de Worde,* 1501?] C(Sel.5.152). Duff 344.
(Formerly 19441) With Hodnett 918 on the tp and the device McK.11 on A6ᵛ.

Long Parvula

23163.13 — [b2ʳ begins:] case As I muste goo to the mayster Oportet me ire/ ad preceptorem. 4⁰. [*Oxford, T. Rood,* 1482?] L(IA.55313, b2,5 only).; HD(Inc 9747, b2,5 only). Duff 239.
(Formerly 15294) The text on b2ʳ is the same as on b1ʳ of 23163.14.

23163.14 — [Anr. ed. a1ʳ begins:] What shalt thou doo whanne thou/ haste an englissh to make in laten/ 4⁰ in 6's. (*by Richard Pynson,*) [1496.] C⁶(1305/4). Duff 373.
(Formerly 23177)

23163.16 — [Anr. ed.] Here begynneth the boke of Englysshe rules or louge [*sic*] Peruula. 4⁰ in 6's. [*Westminster, Wynkyn de Worde,* 1499?] HN(152101, tp and 6th leaf only).
Tp has Hodnett 918.

23163.17 — [Anr. ed. a1ʳ begins:] What shalt thou whanne thou/ haste an englisshe [etc.] 4⁰ in 6's. [*Richard Pynson,* 1505?] L(C.122.h.2, a1,2,5,6 only).O¹²(7 copies of the same leaves).

23164 — [Anr. ed.] Longe paruula. 4⁰. (*by wynkyn de worde, prynter vnto my lady the/ kynges graundame,* 1509.) O(Arch.A.e.37/1).

23164.1 — [Anr. ed.] 4⁰. [*Antwerp, G. Bac,* c. 1510.] C(1 leaf, Syn. 7.51.23, Sayle 6074).
See Nijhoff and Kronenberg 3119. The text is the same as on B3ʳ and part of the verso of 23164.
— For a text with some resemblance to this, printed at Antwerp by Doesborch, 1507? *see* 13606.5.

Parvulorum Institutio

23164.2 — Paruuloȵ in/stitutio ex stābrigiana/ collectōe [*sic*]. 4⁰ ⁸·⁴. (*by Wynkyn de worde,*) [1507?] C⁴(M.28.43/2).

23164.4 — [Anr. ed.] Paruuloȵ institutio ex stan-/brigiana collectione. 4⁰ ⁸·⁴. (*by wynkyn de worde,*) [1508?] O(Mason H 14).
(Formerly 23171)

23164.6 — [Anr. ed.] Paruulorum institutio ex/ stanbrigiana collectione. 4⁰ ⁸·⁴. [*Wynkyn de Worde,* 1510?] L(G.16865, lacks B1,4).
(Formerly 23167) Tp has Hodnett 920; sidenotes are in 62 mm. textura.

23164.8 — [Anr. ed.] 4⁰ ⁸·⁴. (*by Wynkyn de worde,*) [1511?] CH.
Title like 23164.6; tp has Hodnett 920 with no break in right border; B4ᵛ has McK. 23b; sidenotes are in 53 mm. rotunda.

Stanbridge, John—*Parvula and Parvulorum Institutio*—*cont.*

23165 — Now = 23166.5.

23165.5 — [Anr. ed.] 4° 8·4. (*Enprynted . . . by wynkyn de worde,*) [1513?] PML(tp facs.).
Device McK.25 on B4ᵛ. This ed. has no catch titles.

23166 — [Anr. ed.] 4° 8·4. (*by Wynkyn de Worde,*) [1514?] Quaritch catalogue 436 (1930), item 1697 (tp reproduced, untraced).
Title like 23164.6; tp has Hodnett 920 in a state 1513–14, including an 11 mm. break in right border; B4ᵛ has McK. 23b.

23166.5 — [Anr. ed.] Paruulorum institutio ex/ Stambrigiana collectione. 4° in 6's. (*per me Richardum/ Pynson regium Impressorem,*) [1515?] L(G.7557).
(Formerly 23165)

— [Anr. ed.] 1515. *See* 23168.5.

23167 — Now = 23164.6.

23167.3 — [Anr. ed.] Paruulorū institutio ex/ stanbrigiana collectione. 4° 8·4. (*Inprynted . . . by wynkyn de worde,*) [1518?] HN(59560).
Tp has Hodnett 920; B4ᵛ has McK. 23c.

23167.5 — [Anr. ed.] Paruulorum institutio ex stā/brigiana collectione. 4° 8·4. (*by wynkyn de Worde,*) [1519?] WN.
Tp has Hodnett 921; B4ᵛ has McK. 30.

23167.7 — [Anr. ed.] 4° 8·4. (*by wynkyn de worde,* 1520 (mr.)) PML.
Title like 23167.5.

23168 — [Anr. ed.] 4° 8·4. (*by Wynkyn de Worde,* 1521.) L(G.7558).MARL(lacks tp).
Title like 23167.5.

23168.3 — [Anr. ed.] Paruulorum institutio ex/ Stambrigiana col-/lectione. 4° in 6's. (*by/ Richarde Pynson, printer to the/kynges noble grace,*) [1524?] CREDITON.

23168.5 — [Anr. ed.] 4° 8·4. (*by Wynkyn de Worde,* [1515] 'M.CCCEC.xv') [i.e. 1525?] LONGLEAT(lacks tp).
Device McK.23c on B4ᵛ; bd. with 23148.5 and 23182.

23168.7 — [Anr. ed.] Paruulorum institutio ex/ Stambrigiana collectione. 4° 8·4. (*by Wynkyn de worde,* 1526.) C(Sel.5.71).
Catch title on A3, B1: 'Par. stan.'

23169 — [Anr. ed.] 4° 8·4. (*by Wynkyn de worde,* 1526.) O(Mason H 39).
Title like 23168.7; catch title on A3: 'Paruu. stan.'; B1: 'Peruu. stan.'; A2ʳ last line has 'may'.

23169.5 — [Anr. ed.] 4° 8·4. [*Wynkyn de Worde, c.* 1526.] O(Arch. A.e.21, lacks A1, B2–4).
Catch title on A3: 'Paruu. stan.'; B1: 'Peruu. stan.'; A2ʳ last line has 'maye'.

23170 — Now = 23174.6.

23171 — Now = 23164.4.

23172 — [Anr. ed.] 4° 8·4. [*J. Skot f.*] (*by me Iohn̄ Butler,*) [1528?] O(Mason H 40, lacks tp).

23173 — [Anr. ed.] 4° 8·4. (*by Wynkyn de Worde,* 1528.) L(G.7563/2, lacks tp).

23174 — [Anr. ed.] Paruuloꝗ institutio ex/ Stanbrigiana collectiōe. 4° 8·4. (*by Wynkyn de Worde,* 1529.) L(tp only, Harl.5974/18).O(Auct.2Q5.9/5).

23174.3 — [Anr. ed.] Paruulorum institutio ex/ Stanbrigiana col-/lectione. 4° 6·4. [*Wynkyn de Worde?*] (*for Iohn̄ Butler,* 1529.) P(Sp.24/3).
This has w⁵ᵇ, not a usual de Worde letter, but it also has Hodnett 921, de Worde's cut. Leaf signatures have no stops; cf. 23150.3, 23148.12.

23174.5 — [Anr. ed.] 4° 8·4. (*by Wynkyn de Worde,* 1530.) C⁴ (Ref.39).
Title like 23174.

23174.6 — [Anr. ed.] Paruulorum institutio ex/ Stambrigiana collectione. 4° 8·4. (*Southwarke/ by my* [sic] *Peter Treueris,*) [1531?] C(Sel.5.153/2, lacks A1, B3,4). M(9755).
(Formerly 23170) A2ʳ begins: 'What is to be done whan an englys/she [etc.]'

23174.7 — [Anr. ed.] 4°. (*by Wynkyn de Worde,* 1534 (27 no.)) ILL(lacks tp).

23175 — [Anr. ed.] Paruulorum institutio ex Stan-/brigiana collectione. 4°. (*By me Roger Lathum,*) [1539?] O(Tanner 239/2).

23175.5 — [Anr. ed.] Paruulorum institutio ex Stanbrigiana col-/lectione. 4°. (*by Thomas Petyt,*) [c. 1545.] Thorp catalogue 255(1948), item 309(Bindley-Cunliffe copy, untraced).

Stanbridge, John—*cont.*

23176 — [Quatuor partes grammaticae. 1505.] Now = 696.3.

23177 — Now = 23163.14.

VOCABULA

This text has only vocabulary, the first three lines of mnemonic verse beginning respectively: 'Sinciput', 'Cincinnus', and 'Barba'. Editions through the year 1615 usually have 20 leaves.

23177.5 — [Begin:] Sinciput et vertex caput occiput et coma crinis. 4°. [*Wynkyn de Worde, c.* 1505.] L²(frag. 14a, one leaf).
This is the only ed. known w. the 1st page of text ending: 'hec bucca,e for a cheke'; other eds. with this last line omit 'for'. The verso of the leaf has app. the thirteenth page of text, ending: 'Discifer, et aphifer, [etc.]' from the De mensa section.

23178 — [Anr. ed.] Uocabula magistri stābrigi pri/mū iam edita sua saltē editione. 4° 6·4. (*by wynkyn de worde,* 1510.) L(G.7559).
The title is in a riband within a rectangular border, over Hodnett 920. On tp verso the heading has 'epystola.' and the last line begins: 'sum: vt'.

23178.3 — [Anr. ed.] 4° 6·4. (*by Wynkyn de worde,* 1510.) O(Auct. 2Q5.9/3).
Tp like 23178; on tp verso the heading has 'epistola.' and the last line begins: 'sum: vt'.

23178.7 — [Anr. ed.] 4° 6·4. [*Wynkyn de Worde,* 1511?] F(tp only, bd. before 18872).
Tp like 23178; on tp verso the heading has 'epistola.' and the last line begins: 'reat rudis'.

23179 — [Anr. ed.] Uocabula magistri stanbrigi primū/iam edita sua saltem editione. 4° in 6's. (*by Rychard pynson . . . prynter vnto the/ Kynges noble grace,* 1513.) O(Mason H 41).

23179.5 — [Anr. ed.] 4° in 6's. (*by Rychard pynson . . . prynter vnto the/ Kynges noble grace,* 1514.) C⁴(M.28.43/6).
Tp like 23179.

23180 — [Six leaves of two different texts, Sayle 314. Two leaves, including colophon: R. Pynson, 1516, now = 18874.5. Four leaves, D⁴, now = 23185.5.]

23180.3 — [Anr. ed.] (*by Wynkyn de worde,*) [1515?] *See* Addenda.

23180.5 — [Anr. ed.] Uocabula magistri stābrigi pri/mū iam edita sua saltē editione. 4° 6·4. (*by wynkyn de worde,*) [1517?] HN(59561).
(Formerly 23185) The title is in a riband without a border, over Hodnett 927; at the end is the device McK. 19.

23181 — [Anr. ed.] Uocabula magistri Stābrigi, primū/ iam edita sua saltem editione. [*Ed.*] (A. Barclay.) 4° 8·4·6·4. (*by Richarde Pynson,* 1519.) Earl of Macclesfield.
Barclay edited only this and the later Pynson eds., 23181.9 and 23182.3.

23181.2 — [Anr. ed.] 4° 6·4. (*by wynkyn de worde,*) [1520?] F(lacks A1,6).
(Formerly 23185) At the end is the device McK. 20; 'C' of the leaf signature on C3 is under 'ap' of 'capistror.'

23181.3 — [Anr. ed.] 4° 6·4. [*Wynkyn de Worde, c.* 1520.] O (Arch.A.e.22, lacks A1, D4).
(Formerly 23185) 'C' of the leaf signature on C3 is under 'or' of 'capistror.'

23181.4 — [Anr. ed.] Uocabula magistri Stābrigi/ sua saltem editione edita. 4° 6·4. [*Wynkyn de Worde, c.* 1520.] SHR(A1,6 only).
The title is in a riband without border, over Hodnett 921. This may be the same ed. as 23181.2, 23181.3, or 23181.5.

23181.5 — [Anr. ed.] 4° 6·4. (*by Wynkyn de Worde,* 1521.) MARL.
Tp like 23181.4. 'C' of the leaf signature on C3 is under 'ist' of 'capistror.'

23181.7 — [Anr. ed.] Uocabula mg̃ri Stābri/gi sui [sic] saltē editiōe edita. 4° 6·4. (*by Wynkyn de Worde,* 1523 (20 no.)) O¹².

23181.9 — [Anr. ed.] 4° 8·4·6·4. (*in edibus Pynsonianis rursus no-/uo recognita atꝗ impressa,* 1524 (id. ap.)) CREDITON.
Tp like 23181.

23182 — [Anr. ed.] Uocabula magistri/ Stābrigi: saltē editiōe. 4° 6·4. (*by wynkyn de Worde,* 1525 (16 fb.)) O(Mason H 42).LONGLEAT.

23182.2 — [Anr. ed.] Uocabula mg̃ri Stābri/gi sua saltē editione edita. 4° 6·4. [*Wynkyn de Worde,* 1526?] C¹⁹(S. 180/2, lacks D4).
The title is over Hodnett 921 in a state 1525–26; leaf A2 is missigned C2.

Stanbridge, John—*Vocabula*—*cont.*

23182.3 — [Anr. ed.] Uocabula magistri Stambrigi, pri-/mum iam edita sua saltem editione. 4° [8.4.4.4]. (*in edibus Pynsonianis rur-/sus nouo recognita atq; ipressa*, 1526 (21 fb.)) DUL.

23182.5 — [Anr. ed.] Uocabula mgr̄i Stābrigi/ sua saltem editione edita. 4° [6.4]. (*Southwarke/ by me Peter Treueris,*) [1527?] M(9758).

23182.6 — [Anr. ed.] Uocabula mgr̄i Stābri-/gi sua saltē editione edita. 4° [6.4]. (*by Wynkyn de worde*, 1529.) CU.

23182.8 — [Anr. ed.] Uocabula mgr̄i stābrigi/ sua saltē editione edita. 4° in 6's. [*J. Skot f.*] (*by me Iohn Butler,*) [1530?] P(Sp.24/5, lacks D6).

23182.9 — [Anr. ed.] Uocabula magistri stābrigi/ p̄mū iā edita sua saltē editiōe. 4° [6.4]. (*Southwarke/ by me Peter Treuerys,*) [1530?] O(Mason H 33).
(Formerly 23184.)

23183 — [Anr. ed.] Uocabula magistri/ Stābrigij sua saltē/ editione edita. 4°. (*by Wynkyn de Worde*, 1531 (17 no.)) O(Mason H 51).

23184 — Now = 23182.9.

23184.5 — [Anr. ed.] 4°. (*by Wynkyn de worde*, 1534 (6 ja.)) C⁵(A.2.11/13).
Tp like 23183.

23185 — Now = 23180.5, 23181.2, 23181.3.

23185.5 — [Anr. ed.] 4°. [*T. Godfray*, 1535?] C(Syn.7.51.28, D⁴ only).
(Formerly pt. of 23180) D4ᵛ catchword: 'Plata-'. This is the only ed. known with both catch titles and catchwords.

23186 — [Anr. ed.] Uocabula magistri/ Stābrigii sua saltē/editione edita. 4°. (*by me Ro/bert wyer,*) [c. 1538.] O(Tanner 239/4).

23187 — [Anr. ed.] Uocabula Ma-/gistri, Stābrigij,/ nuper emendata/ ac edita. [By] (*T. Paynellus.*) 4°. [*J. Day f.*] (*A. Vele,*) [1560?] L(G.7562).; ILL.

23188 — [Anr. ed.] Vocabula Magistri Stanbrigii, ab infinitis . . . mendis repurgata, obseruata interim . . . carminis ratione, studio et industria T. Newtoni Cestresbyrij. 4°. *J. Aldæus*, 1577. Ent. 30 se. C.

23189 — [Anr. ed.] 8°. *Edinburgi, R. Walde-graue*, 1596. E². This form of the text is reprinted in 23193, 23193.9.

23190 — [Anr. ed.] 4°. *E. A[llde], imp. & sumpt. C. Knight,* 1615. Ent. 26 jn. 1600. L.; HN.

23191 — [Anr. ed., revised.] Stanbrigii embryon relimatum, seu vocabularium metricum olim à J. Stanbrigio digestum, dein â T. Newtono . . . repurgatum, nunc verò locupletatum, . . . operâ & industriâ J. Brinslæi. 4°. [*T. Purfoot,*] *sumptibus C. Knight*, 1624. C.
With the Latin and English on facing pages.

23191.3 — [Anr. ed.] 4°. [*T. Purfoot,*] *sumpt. C. Knight*, 1627. C².

23191.7 — [Anr. ed.] 4°. [*T. Purfoot,*] *sumpt. C. Knight*, 1629. L(tp only, Harl.5927/391).

23192 — [Anr. ed.] 4°. [*T. Cotes,*] *sumpt. C. Knight*, 1630. L.C¹⁶.

23193 — [Anr. ed.] Vocabula Magistri Stanbrigii, [etc.] 8°. *Aberdoniæ, E. Rabanus, imp. D. Melvill*, 1631. L(tp only, Harl.5938/50).
Reprints 23189.

23193.2 — [Anr. ed.] Stanbrigii embryon relimatum, [etc.] 4°. *typis T. Cotes, imp. T. Knight: & venales prostant a T. Alchorne*, 1633. Ass'd to T. Knight 12 oc. 1629. BO⁵.

23193.4 — [Anr. ed.] 4°. *typis T. Cotes, & venales prostant a T. Alchorne*, 1636. Ass'd 8 mr. L.O³.O¹².STD.; F.

23193.6 — [Anr. ed.] 4°. *typis T. Cotes, & venales prostant a T. Alchorne*, 1638. L(tp only, Harl.5965/208).

23193.8 — [Anr. ed.] 4°. *typis R. Bishop, & venale prostat à T. Alchorne*, 1639. C(D2 only, Syn.7.61.158). WN.

23193.9 — [Anr. ed.] Vocabula Magistri Stanbrigii [etc.] 8°. *Edinburgi, R. Bryson*, 1639. CU.
Reprints 23189.

VULGARIA

This text has both vocabulary, with the first three lines of mnemonic verse beginning respectively: 'Sinciput', 'Cincinnus', and 'Os'; and phrases 'compilata juxta consuetudinem ludi literarii divi Pauli' beginning: 'Good morrow. Bonum tibi huius diei sit primordium.' Editions usually have 18 leaves.

23194 — Now = 18873.3.
23195 — Now = 18873.5.

23195.5 — Uulgaria stābrige [xylographic, white on black] 4° in 6's. (*by wynkyn/ de worde,*) [1509?] ILL.

23196 — [Anr. ed.] Uulgaria stanbryge. 4° in 6's. (*By wynkyn de/ Worde*, 1515.) M(R4520).

Stanbridge, John—*Vulgaria*—*cont.*

23196.2 — [Anr. ed.] Uulgaria stanbrige. 4° in 6's. (*by wynkyn/ de worde,*) [1517?] C⁴(M.28.43/5).

23196.4 — [Anr. ed.] 4° in 6's. [*Oxford, J. Scolar*, 1518?] O(Vet. A1.f.141, B⁶ only).
B2ʳ line 8 from bottom: 'God spede. Bona salus, salue, salue sis, optata sa/'.

23196.6 — [Anr. ed.] Uulgaria stābrigi. 4° in 6's. (*by wynkyn de/ worde,*) [1519?] WN.; F(lacks A1).

23196.8 — [Anr. ed.] Uulgaria stābrigiana. 4° in 6's. (*by wyn-/kyn de worde*, 1519.) HN(59562).

23196a — [Anr. ed.] Uulgaria stanbrigi. 4° in 6's. (*by wynkyn/ de worde,*) [1520?] L(C.33.b.37/1, A1–B1 only, 'completed' by A⁴ of 18875 with the leaf signatures altered). O(Auct.2Q5.9/4).MARL(lacks tp).; MEL.PML.
With Hodnett 926 on the tp in a later state than 23196.8; copies vary: C6ᵛ has McK. 19 very worn (O) or McK. 20(MEL, PML). B2ʳ line 8 from bottom: 'God spede. Bona salus, salue, saluus sis, optata sal⁹/'.

23196a.2 — [Anr. ed.] 4° in 6's. [*R. Pynson, c.* 1520.] C(Broadsides B 1520, 2 leaves = A3,4).
(Formerly 18873) A4ʳ last line: 'hec vrina'.

23196a.4 — [Anr. ed.] Uulgaria stābrige [xylographic, white on black] 4° in 6's. (*by Rycharde Pynson*, 1523.) CREDITON.
A4ʳ last line: 'hoc inguem for the share'.

23196a.5 — [Anr. ed.] Uulgaria stambrigi. 4° in 6's. (*by wynkyn/ de worde,*) [1524?] LONGLEAT.

23196a.6 — [Anr. ed.] Uulgaria stanbrigi. 4° in 6's. (*by wynkyn/ de worde,*) [1525?] O(Arch.A.e.23, A2–B6 only).C¹⁹ (S.180/3).
B2ʳ line 8 from bottom: 'God spede. Bona salus, salue, salu⁹ sis, optata sal⁹/'.

23196a.7 — [Anr. ed.] Uulgaria Stanbrigi. 4° in 6's. (*by me wyn-/kyn de worde,*) [1526?] O(Arch.A.e.23, C1–5 only). M(17327).
This and the following eds. have B2ʳ line 8 from bottom beginning: 'God spede you.'

23197 — [Anr. ed.] 4° in 6's. (*by me Wyn-/kyn de worde,*) [1527?] L(G.7563/3, lacks A1).

23198 — [Anr. ed.] Uulgaria Stanbrigi. 4° in 6's. (*by me Wynkyn de Worde/*) [1529?] O(Douce S 209).; LC.
— [Anr. ed.] (*J. Skot,*) [1529?] See 23199.

23198.3 — [Anr. ed.] Uulgaria Stambrigi. 4° in 6's. (*Southwarke by me/ Peter Treueris,*) [1530?] C⁵(A.2.11/14, C⁶ only).DUR⁵(S.R.4.A.2).

23198.7 — [Anr. ed.] Uulgaria/ Stanbrigij. 4°. [*Wynkyn de Worde*, 1534?] C⁵(A.2.11/14, A–C⁴ only).

23199 — [An extract.] 4°. (*by me/ Iohn̄ Skot,*) [1529?] C(Sel. 5.73, lacks A1,4).
This has only the phrases, which begin on A2ʳ, whereas in the full text they begin on B2ʳ.

Stanburne, Margaret. *See* Indulgences 75.

23199.7 **Standfast, Richard.** A little handfull of cordiall comforts. 12°. *R. B[adger] f. P. Stephens a. C. Meredith*, 1639. Ent. 26 oc. 1638. BRISTOL.

23200 Now = 23201.5.

23200.5 **Standish, Arthur.** The commons complaint. Wherein is contained two speciall grievances. The first is, the destruction of woods. The second is, the dearth of victuals. 4°. *W. Stansby*, 1611. Ent. 17 my. L(809. d.3).L³⁰.O(Tanner 820).O⁸.RD.+; NY.
(Formerly 23202) Pp. 33. The L copy has cancel slips and an extra leaf of pr. verses by H. Peacham, reprinted in the following. All eds. should have a folding cut of a fowl house.

23201 — [Anr. ed.] 4°. *W. Stansby*, 1611. L³⁸.O(Pamph.9). NLW.RD.WI.+; F.HD(lacks cut).Y.
Pp. 34. The O,WI and Y copies have inserted the Letters Patent for this book, 8470.5 sq., reprinted in the following and 23204.3. A has the dedic. only, bd. w. 23204.5.

23201.5 — [Anr. ed., enlarged.] 4°. *W. Stansby*, 1611. L(1028.i.1). O(4°.A.9.Art.BS., lacks cut).C.D.RD.+; HN.BOWDOIN. WIS.Y.
(Formerly 23200) Pp. '50' (i.e. 40.) Letters Patent reprinted on A2,3. At least L,HN have a leaf inserted after C4 beginning: 'If the aforesaid directions . . .'

23202 — Now = 23200.5.

Standish, Arthur—*cont.*

23203 — [Anr. ed.] Newly corrected and augmented. 4°. *W. Stansby*, 1612. L.O⁸.C¹⁵.LIV³.RD.+ ; F.HN.CU.
Pp. 46.

23204 — New directions of experience by the authour for the planting of timber and firewood. [Anon.] 4°. [*N. Okes*,] 1613. O(Ashm.1672).; HD.
Pp. 22; A–C⁴.

23204.3 — [Anr. ed., signed, w. title:] New directions of experience to the Commons complaint by the incouragement of the kings majesty. 4°. [*N. Okes*,] 1613. L¹⁶.L³⁰.LINDLEY.; HN.
Pp. 23; A–C⁴ D². Reprints the Letters Patent on A2.

23204.5 — [Anr. issue, w. additional pp. 25–34:] (A second direction, for the present increasing of fire-wood, agreeable to the nature of this age, 1613. February 1.) [*N. Okes*,] 1613. L(966.c.26).A(w. dedic. to King James inserted from 23201.); HD.Y.
Pp. 34; A–C⁴ D² E⁴ F² (F2 blank). 2nd direction begins: 'Hearing daily that this more then necessary business . . .'; *see also* 23206.4.

23204.7 — [Anr. issue, w. quires E–F reset, w. additions.] (A second direction, . . . encreasing. . . .) [*N. Okes*,] 1613. E.RD.; LC.WIS.
Pp. 36; A–C⁴ D² E⁴ F².

23205 — [Anr. ed., revised, w. title:] New directions of experience authorized by the kings majesty. 4°. [*N. Okes*,] 1614. E.; F(lacks cut).BO⁵(text of New directions only, with cut).CU(lacks 2nd A⁴ and cut; has Letters Patent app. inserted from 23204.3).
Pp. 28; a⁴(tp and dedic.) A⁴(To reader, beginning 'I thought') 2nd A⁴(To reader, beginning 'Thou hast') A–D⁴(A1, D4 blank, text of New directions). This has no 'Second direction' but contains much of the material formerly included in that section. This and the following eds. should have a folding cut of an orchard.

23206 — [Anr. ed., revised.] 4°. [*N. Okes*,] 1615. L(1146.d.32, lacks cut).O(Crynes 827).C(lacks cut).C².; HD(lacks cut). Penrose 359.
Pp. 28; A–F⁴. Omits To reader, beginning 'I thought'.

23206.2 — [Anr. ed.] 4°. [*N. Okes*,] 1616. C(lacks cut).
Pp. 28; A–F⁴.

23206.4 — [Heading A1ʳ:] A second direction, for the increasing of wood, and the destroying of vermine, this present yeare, 1613. Febr. 1. 4°. [*N. Okes*, 1613.] HD(bd. w. 23204).
A⁴; text begins: 'Acknowledging my selfe to bee animated by God, . . .'; *see also* 23204.5.

23206.6 — [Anr. ed., revised.] 4° in 2's. [*N. Okes*, 1613.] WIS(bd. w. 23204.7).
A–B².

23206.8 — [Heading A1ʳ:] A third edition [*sic*] by the authority of the king, June the nine and twentie day, 1614. [Anon.] 4°. [*N. Okes?* 1614.] HD(bd. w. 23204).
Text begins: 'For the better inducing of your Maiestie, . . .'

23207 **Standish, John.** A discourse wherin is debated whether the scripture should be in English. [Init. I. S.] 8°. *in æd. R. Caly*, 1554 (de.) L.C²(lacks tp).C⁴.BUTE. D².+ ; F.HN.HD.

23208 — [Anr. ed., signed in full.] In this second edition the authour hathe added sundrie thynges. 8°. (*R. Caly*, 1555 (8 fb.)) L.O(imp.).O⁴.WI.STD.; F.NY¹¹.PML.

23209 — A lytle treatise composyd by Johan Stãdysshe, agaĩst the ptestacion of R. Barnes at the tyme of his death. 8°. (*in æd. R. Redmani*, 1540 (3 non. oc.)) C.O³(lacks tp).O⁴(imp.).
Includes the text of Barnes's Protestation. Answered by 5888.

23210 — [Anr. ed.] Newly corrected with certayne addyciõs. 8°. (*ex æd. E. Pykerynge viduæ R. Redmani*, 1540 (13 cal. de.)) L.O.O⁶(imp.).LINC. Stevens Cox(lacks tp).+ ; F.

23211 — The triall of the supremacy wherein is set fourth yᵉ vnitie of christes church. 8°. (*T. Marshe*, 1556 (jy.)) O(1, plus a frag.).O⁴.C.
The O copy, Crynes 881, is on Univ. Microfilms reel 1188, erroneously identified as MICH.
— *ed. See* 2734.

23212 **Staney, William.** A treatise of penance, with an explication of the rule, of the third order of S. Frauncis. Whereunto is added, the epistle and annotations

Staney, William—*cont.*

upon this rule, of Fa. Peter Gonzales. By F. W. S(taney.) 8°. *Douay*, [*P. Auroi f.*] *J. Heigham*, 1617. L(lacks engr. tp).C.M.USHAW.W.+ ; F.TEX.
A&R 793.

Stanford, Robert, *tr. See* 4912, 7238, 7240.

23213 **Stanford, Sir William.** An exposicion of the kinges prerogatiue collected out of the great abridgement of justice Fitzherbert and other olde writers of the lawes of Englande. 1567. 4° in 8's. (*R. Tottel*, 1567.) L.O.C.C³.CASHEL.+ ; F.HN.CU.HD.MICH.+

23214 — [Anr. ed.] 1568. 4° in 8's. (*R. Tottel*, 1568.) L.O.O¹². C.YK.+ ; F.HN.HD.N.Y.+
A1–3 partly reimposed from 23213.

23215 — [Anr. ed.] 1573. 4° in 8's. *R. Tottle*, (1573.) L.O.C². D⁵.P.+ ; F.HN.CU.HD.MICH.+

23216 — [Anr. ed.] 1577. 4° in 8's. *R. Tottel*, (1577.) L.O.C.D. E².+ ; F.HN.HD.N.Y.+

23217 — [Anr. ed.] 4° in 8's. *R. Totthil*, 1590. Ent. 18 fb. 1583. L.O.O².E.E².+ ; F.HN.CU.HD.MICH.+

23218 — [Anr. ed.] 4° in 8's. [*A. Islip*] *f. the co. of Statrs.*, 1607. L.O.C².D.M².+ ; F.HN.CHI.CU.HD.+

23219 — Les plees del coron: diuisees in plusiours titles. 1557. 4° in 8's. *in æd. R. Tottelli*, (1557.) C.HOLK.YK.; CAL⁵.HD.LC.MICH.MIN.

23220 — [Anr. ed.] Dernieremt corrigee. 1560. 4° in 8's. *in æd. R. Tottelli*, (1560.) L.O.C³.LINC.NLW.+ ; F.HN.HD. MIN.Y.+

23221 — [Anr. ed.] 1567. 4° in 8's. *in æd. R. Tottelli*, (1567.) L.O.C⁷.A.NLW.+ ; F.HN.CHI.CU.HD.+

23222 — [Anr. ed.] Nouuelment reueu et corrigee. 1574. 4° in 8's. *in æd. R. Tottelli*, (1574.) L.O.C².D.E.+ ; F.HN. CU.HD.MICH.+

23223 — [Anr. ed.] 4° in 8's. *in æd. R. Tottellj*, 1583. Ent. 18 fb. L.O.C.D².E.+ ; F.HN.CU.HD.MICH.+

23224 — [Anr. ed.] 4° in 8's. [*A. Islip*,] *ex typ. Soc. Stat.*, 1607. L.O.C².D.M².+ ; F.HN.CHI.CU.HD.+
— *ed. See* 11905.

23224.5 **Stanhope, Sir Edward.** An epitaph upon the death of the right worthy and worsh: gent. S: Edward Stanhope knight deceased. [In verse.] s.sh.fol. [*R. Blower? f.*] *W. Barley*, 1607 [i.e. 1608.] L⁵(Lemon 118).

Stanhope, John, *1st Baron Stanhope of Harrington. See* 9198.7.

23225 **Stanhope, John,** *son of Philip, 1st Earl of Chesterfield.* Funerall elegies, upon the most untimely death of J. Stanhope. *Lat. a. Eng.* 4°. [*G. Purslowe*] *f. R. Mab*, 1624. LINC.M².P(imp.).; F.HN.HD. 𝔄

23226 **Stanhope, Michael.** Cures without care, or a summons to all to repaire to the northerne spaw. Wherein infirmities have received recovery, by vertue of minerall waters neare Knaresborow. 4°. *W. Jones*, 1632. Ent. 5 jy. L.L³.O.C⁴.G².+ ; F.HN.BO⁵.

23227
23228 — = 23228.
— Newes out of York-shire: or, an account of a journey, in the true discovery of medicinall water. [Init. M. St.] 4°. *J. H[aviland] f. G. Gibbes*, 1627. Ent. 14 de. 1626. L.O.C⁹.E.SHEF.+ ; F.
(Formerly also 23227) Most copies have the date cropt; it is present in one L(G.3115), and O.

23228.3 **Stanley, Henry.** Appendix ad libros omnes tam veteris quam novi testamenti. fol. *Oxoniæ*, 1630. L(Harl. 5932/45).
A specimen, consisting of tp and pp. 529–40, of a book of blank tables for listing biblical commentaries by their texts; *see* Madan I, p. 233.

23228.5 **Stanley, Thomas,** *Petitioner.* To the kings most excellent majesty, the Lords . . . in this present Parliament assembled. The humble petition of T. Stanley. [Appeal that the lands, money, and legacies given under Edward VI to Christ's Hospital, St. Thomas's Hospital, and Bridewell may be employed as intended.] s.sh.fol. [*London*, 1621?] L⁸(GL 5462).

Stanley, Thomas, *R. C. Bp. of Sodor and Man. See* 25858.7.

Stanley, William, *Earl of Derby. See* 19924.

23228.7 Stanley, *Sir* **William.** A short admonition or warning, vpon the detestable treason wherewith sir William Stanley and Rowland Yorke haue betraied and deliuered for monie vnto the Spaniards, the towne of Deuenter. [By G. Prouninck.] *Tr.* into English by C. C. 4°. *R. Jones,* (sold) [*by E. White,*] 1587. Ent. 9 ap. F.

23229 Stanyhurst, Richard. Harmonia seu catena dialectica, in Porphyrianas institutiones. Cum indice. fol. (*ap. R. Wolfium,*) 1570 (8 non. jn.) O⁷.O⁸.C.GLOUC.; F.
— *tr. See* 24806.
— *See also* 13568.

23230 Staphylus, Fridericus. The apologie of Fridericus Staphylus. Intreating of the true vnderstanding of holy scripture. *Tr.* out of Latin by Thomas Stapleton. Also a discourse of the translatour vppon the doctrine of the protestants. 4°. *Antwerp, J. Latius,* 1565. L.O.C.D²·E.+; F.HN.N.TEX.U.+
A&R 794. *See also* 17506.3 sq.

Stapleton, Richard, *tr. See* 19880.

Stapleton, *Sir* **Robert,** *tr. See* 24812.

23230.5 Stapleton, Theobald. Catechismus, seu doctrina christiana, Latino-Hibernica, per modum dialogi. *Lat. a. Irish.* 4°. *Bruxellis, typis H. A. Velpij,* 1639. L.O. O¹⁷.D.D⁸.+; N.
A&R 795.

23231 Stapleton, Thomas. A counterblast to M. Hornes vayne blaste [13818] against M. Fekenham. [In 4 books, based on material by N. Harpsfield.] 4°. *Louanii, ap. J. Foulerum,* 1567. L.O.C.USHAW.W.+; F.HN.CHI.HD.U.+
A&R 796. 1st bk. answered in 3737.

23232 — A fortresse of the faith first planted. Which protestants call, papistry. 4°. *Antwerpe, J. Laet,* 1565. L.O.C. DUR⁵(imp.).W.+; F.HN.HD.N.U.+
A&R 797. Based on material in 1778. Answered in 11456.

23233 — [Anr. ed.] 8°. *S. Omers, [C. Boscard] f. J. Heigham,* 1625. L.L⁹.O(imp.).USHAW.W.+; F.FORDHAM.N.PEN. TEX.+
A&R 798.

23234 — A returne of vntruthes vpon M. Jewelles replie [14606]. 4°. *Antwerpe, J. Latius,* 1566. L².O.C³.USHAW.W.+; NY¹¹.U.WASH³.
A&R 799.
— *tr. See* 1778, 13889, 23230.
— *See also* 25363.

Star. The bright star. 1603. *See* 6966.5.
— The new starre of the north. 1631, etc. *See* 11879.2 sqq.

Star-Chamber. *See* 7755 sqq.

23235 Staresmore, Sabine. The unlawfulnes of reading in prayer. Or, the answer of Mr. R. Maunsel vnto certain reasons. With a defence of the same reasons, by S. Staresmore. 8°. [*Amsterdam, G. Thorp,*] 1619. L. C.; Y(2).
— *ed. See* 227.
— *See also* 23605.

23235.5 Starkey, Ralph. The briefe contents of Ralph Starkye's bill, exhibited in Parliament, touching the practice for his dis-inherison of the lands of his ancestors. (A briefe of the proofes made by R. Starkie in Chancerie.) fol(2). [*London,* 1628?] L⁸(GL 465).
The matter was brought up in Parliament in 1624, 1626, and 1628. While both sheets may not refer to the same occasion, 1628 seems the likeliest possibility; see *JHL* III.710, 831.

23236 Starkey, Thomas. [Heading C4ʳ:] An exhortation to the people, instructynge theym to vnitie and obedience. 4°. (*in æd. T. Bertheleti,*) [1536.] L(lacks tp).
H. Dyson had a copy dated 1536 on the tp according to his MS. catalogue at O⁹.

23237 State. The true state of the business of glasse of all kinds. [1641.] = Wing T 3109.

23238 Statham, Nicholas. [Abridgement of cases to the end of Henry VI.] *Law Fr.* fol. [*Rouen, G. Le Talleur f.*] (*per me. R. pynson,*) [1490.] L.O.C.D(imp.).E.+; HN. HD.LC.N.PML.+ Duff 374.

23239 Statute. A statute for swearers and drunkards. *Ballad.* 2 pts. s.sh.fol. *f. J. T[rundle,* 1624.] C⁶.
The statutes referred to are in 9507, c.7, 20.

Staunford, *Sir* **William.** *See* Stanford, *Sir* W.

23239.5 Staveley, Leonard. A breef discour⟨se⟩ wherin is declared, of yᵉ trauailes an⟨d⟩ miseries of this painful life. Gathered out of ⟨di⟩uers writers. Wh⟨er⟩unto is annexed the authors muse of this life, in English vearse. 8° in 4's. *J. Allde,* [1575?] HN(tp def.).

23240 Stay. The stay of the faithfull [on Zeph.ii.3]: together with the properties of an honest heart [on Ps.li.16.] In two sermons. [By T. Hooker?] 2 pts. 12°. *M. F[lesher] f. R. Dawlman,* sold by *T. Nichols,* 1638. Ent. as by T. H. 13 no. 1637. L⁴(bd. w. 13739.7).
Collates [–]⁴ H–L¹²; A–B¹² C⁶. The 1st quire is on paper w. perp. chainlines and includes pp. 1–4 of the text. The rest has horizontal chainlines. Both parts use the same skeleton of rules beneath the headlines, and these also appear in 22578 and 23953, w. which the L⁴ copy is also bd.
All 4 sermons were ent. in the Stationers' Register at the same time, along w. 13734. In the entry is one sermon, on 1 Pet. v.5, which is unaccounted for; possibly it was intended to precede the 1st sermon of 23240.

Staynred, Philip. An almanack. 1635. *See* 515.25.

Stebbunhuth. *See* Stepney.

23241 Steenwyk. A true declaration of the streight siedge laide to Steenwich. Togither with the yeelding vp of the same. Printed first in Dutch, and *tr.* by I. T[horius?] 4°. *J. Wolfe,* 1592. Ent. 5 jy. L.O.C.; HD.

23242 Steingenius, Adolphus. Exemplar illius diplomatis regii. [*Printed abroad,*] 1620.
Not an STC book.

23242.5 Stella. Stella clericorum. 4° ⁸·⁶·⁶. [*R. Pynson,* 1497?] DUL.
Has device McK.6 w. Pynson's name.

23243 — [Anr. ed.] 4° in 6's. [*R. Pynson,* 1503?] L.; F.
Has device McK.9b w. Pynson's name.

23244 — [Anr. ed.] 8° in 4's. (*per me W. de Worde,* 1531 (20 oc.)) C(tp torn).; PML.

Stella, Diego de. *See* 10541 sqq.

23245 Stella, Joannes. A bewayling of the peace of Germany. Or, a discourse touching the peace of Prague. By Justus Asterius, otherwise Stella. *Tr.* out of the Latine copie. 4°. *J. L[egat a. Eliot's Court Press] f. J. H[unscott,]* sold [*by P. Stephens a. C. Meredith,*] 1637. Ent. to Stephens, Meredith a. Hunscott 13 ap. L.O.C².D.G⁴.+; F.HN.CU.HD(imp.).Y.+
Eliot's Court Press pr. a–f⁴. HD copy has orig. 2nd A1 with catchword 'their' and also cancel A1 with catchword 'at', the latter pr. as f4.

23246 Stella, Julius Caesar. Iulii Caesaris Stellae nob. Rom. Columbeidos, libri priores duo. [*Ed.*] (G. Castelvetri.) [In verse.] 4°. *ap. J. Wolfium,* 1585. L.L³.O. O⁸.M.; HN.
Dedic. to Raleigh on A2.

23246.5 — [Anr. issue, w. A2 blank, w. imprint:] *Lugduni,* [i.e. *London, J. Wolfe,*] 1585. L.; F.

Stephanides, Andreas. *See* 7487.22, 7487.26.

Stephanus, Henricus, *ed. See* Estienne, H.

Stephen, Henry. *See* Estienne, H.

23247 Stephens, Jeremiah. D. Caecilii Cypriani episcopi Carthaginiensis libellus. 1632. = 6154.
— *ed. See* 6153, 6154, 12348, 23066.

23248 Stephens, John. Cinthia's revenge: or Mænanders extasie. [Init. J. S.] 4°. *f. R. Barnes,* 1613. L(2).L⁶.O⁶ (imp.)*.P.; F.HN.BO.HD(tp def.)*.Y. Greg 314.
This variant prob. later than 23248a.

23248a — [A variant, w. author's name on tp.] L⁶.O(2, 1 imp.).; F(imp.).PFOR.

23249 — Satyrical essayes characters and others. [Partly in verse.] 8°. *N. Okes,* sold by *R. Barnes,* 1615. L.L³⁸.O. C².PETYT.; F.HN.HD.N.NY.+
321 pp.

23250 — [Anr. ed.] Essayes and characters, ironicall, and instructive. The second impression. With a new satyre in defence of common law and lawyers. Divers other things added; & every thing amended. 8°. *E. Allde f. P. Knight,* 1615. L.O.C².E.M².+; F.HN.HD.ILL.NY.+
434 pp.

Stephens, John—*cont.*

23250.5 — [Anr. issue, init. J. S., w. cancel tp:] The errors of men personated in sundry essaies. 8°. *f. W. Barrenger*, 1627. F.
(Formerly 10527 and 21502)

23251 — [Anr. issue, w. cancel tp:] New essayes and characters. With a new satyre in defence of the common law against [21445]. By J. Stephens. *f. L. Faune*, 1631. L.O.C.PETYT.SHEF.+; F.WTL.

Stephins, Thomas. An almanack. 1569. *See* 515.27.

23251.5 **Steple, Steven.** Steven Steple to mast Camell. [In verse.] s.sh.fol. *R. Lant*, [1552?] L⁵(Lemon 28).
Reprinted in 5225.

23252 **Stepney.** [Heading A1ʳ:] Hereafter ensueth the auncient severall customes, of the severall mannors of Stebbunhuth, and Hackney, 1587. 4°. [*T. Snodham*, c. 1610.] L(2).O.(imp.).O⁸.C².; F.HD.
Black letter.

23253 — [Anr. ed.] 4°. [*London*, c. 1615.] L.O.D⁵.; HN.
Roman.

23254 — [Anr. ed., revised and enlarged.] The free customes, benefits and priviledges of the copyhold tennants, of the mannors of Stepny and Hackny. Before which is prefixed an abstract of the assurance given by Thomas Lord Wentworth unto his tennants. Whereunto two tables are fitted. 4°. *W. Jones* [3,] 1617 (4 de.) Ent. 14 ap. L.L³⁰.L³⁸. Bradford PL.; F.
Colophon on I4ʳ has: 'Imprinted . . . with consent of Thomas Lord Wentworth.'

23254.5 — [Anr. issue, w. additions:] (Anno. 21. Jacobi regis. Memorandum, . . . An acte for confirmation of the copyhold estates and customes . . . of Stepny and Hackney.) [Additions: *London*, 1624.] L(2).L⁸.O.D².
Bill enacted 4 May 1624; *see JHL* III.339.

23255 — The liberty of the mannor of Stepney. [post-1640.]
Not an STC item.

23256 **Stepney, William.** The Spanish schoole-master. Containing seven dialogues. Whereunto, are annexed the Lords prayer, [etc.] *Span. a. Eng.* 16° in 8's. *R. Field f. J. Harison* [1,] 1591. Ent. to J. Harrison the elder 13 ja. L.E. Madrid NL.; HN.ILL.
Largely based on 1431.6 sqq.; *see Revue Hispanique*, LXXXI¹ (1933), pp. 283–318.

23257 — [Anr. ed.] Now newly corrected by a new author (J. Grange.) 12°. *N. Okes f. J. Harison* [4,] 1619. Ass'd to J. Harrison 2 on 11 ap. 1614. L(tp only, Harl. 5993/112).C.

23258 — [A variant, w. imprint:] *N. Okes f. J. Harison*, [4,] 1620. L(imp.). Lisbon NL.

Sternhold, Thomas. *See* 2419, 16561, 16578.5.

23259 **Sterrie, D.** A briefe sonet declaring the lamentation of Beckles, a market towne in Suffolke. 1586. *Ballad.* 1/2 sh.fol. *R. Robinson f. N. Colman of Norwich*, [1586.] Ent. to N. Colman 13 de. 1586. L.C(imp.). R.WOR.; HN.N.
R copy on undivided sheet w. 6564.
— *See also* 21485.

Stevens, Charles. *See* 10547 sqq.

23260 **Stevens, John.** The godly end, and wofull lamentation of one J. Stevens, a youth, that was hang'd, the seventh day of March last, 1632. *Ballad.* 2 pts. s.sh.fol. *f. H. Gosson*, [1633.] Ent. to ballad ptnrs. 8 jy. 1633. L.

23261 **Stevenson, Andrew.** Theses philosophicæ. 1625. Now = 7487.22.

23262 — — 1629. Now = 7487.26.

23263 **Stevenson, William.** A ryght pithy, pleasaunt and merie comedie: intytuled Gammer gurtons nedle. [Init. Mr. S., *Mr. of Art*.] 4°. *T. Colwell*, (1575.) Ent. as 'Dyccon of Bedlam' 1562–63. L(2).L⁶.O.; F.HN.IND. NY.Y.+ Greg 67.
(Formerly also 23268) Some copies (HN, PFOR) have 'anp' for 'and' on title, and other misprints. Stevenson's authorship is disputed.

23264 **Stevin, Simon.** Disme: the art of tenths, or, decimall arithmetike. Published in English with some additions by R. Norton. 4°. *S. S[tafford] f. H. Astley*, 1608. Ent. 23 jn. L.C.C³.PLUME(frag.).; HD.Y.

Stevin, Simon—*cont.*

23265 — The hauen-finding art, or, the way to find any hauen or place at sea, by the latitude and variation. *Tr.* (E. Wright.) 4°. *G. B[ishop,] R. N[ewberry,] a. R. B[arker,]* 1599. L.L³³.O(2). Rotterdam, Prins Hendrik Maritime Museum.; F.HN.LC.NY³(lacks tp).

Stewart, Theophilus, *ed. See* 24623.7.

Stewart, William, *tr. See* 11684.

23266 **Stile, Christopher.** Psalmes of inuocation vpon God, to preserue her maiestie. Collected by C. Stile. 4°. *J. Wolfe*, 1588. Ent. 21 au. COL.; F.

23267 **Stile, Elizabeth.** A rehearsall both straung and true, of hainous actes committed by Elizabeth Stile, alias Rockingham, mother Dutten, mother Deuell, mother Margaret, fower notorious witches. 1579. 8°. [*J. Kingston*] *f. E. White*, [1579.] Ent. 24 mr. 1579. L.E(imp.).
See also 11537.5.

23268 **Still, John,** *Bp.* A ryght pithy, comedie: intytuled Gammer gurtons nedle. 1575. = 23263.
— *See also* 10137.2 sq.

Stinnet, William. An hundred heavenly thoughts. 1616. *See* 21527.

23269 **Stint, Thomas.** An exposition upon the cxii. psalme. [Init. T. S.] 8°. *B. Alsop*, 1621. Ent. 19 oc. O.C² (imp.).; F.

23270 — An exposition on the cxxiiii.cxxv.cxxvi. psalmes, called the psalmes of degrees: or, the churches deliverance. 8°. *B. A[lsop] f. W. Lee*, 1621. Ent. to B. Alsop 7 no., ass'd to W. Lee 15 de. 1620. O.P.; F.

23271 **Stinton, George.** A sermon preached in the cathedrall of Worcester. 8°. *Oxford, L. Lichfield f. H. C.* [i.e. *Cripps?* or *Curteyn?*] *printer to the univ.*, 1637. O.C¹⁰.

23272 **Stirk, George.** Musæ Somerenses: id est, sacræ historiæ series, à mundi creatione, ad lingarum confusionem poeticè deducta. Ad usum scholæ. 8°. *E. P[urslowe,]* 1635. Ent. to N. Bourne 1 au. L.O.; Y.

23273 **Stock, Richard.** The churches lamentation for the losse of the godly: delivered in a sermon, at the funerals of John lord Harington, baron of Exton. 8°. *J. Beale*, 1614. Ent. 12 my. L.O.C².C⁵.NLW.+; F(2). HN.ILL.
B1ʳ catchword: 'Church,'.

23273.5 — [Anr. issue, w. impr. on cancel tp:] *f. E. Weaver a. W. Welby*, 1614. L(tp only, Ames II.356).BUTE.LINC.; HD(lacks H7).

23274 — [Anr. ed.] 8°. *J. Beale*, 1614. L(impr. def.).O(date cropt).C.C³(date cropt).EX.
B1ʳ catchword: 'stitute,'.

23274.5 — The doctrine and use of repentance. Preached in sundrie sermons. 8°. *F. Kyngston f. E. Weaver a. W. Welby*, 1608. Ent. 7 de. 1607. L(tp only, Harl.5919/114).; PN².

23275 — [Anr. ed.] 8°. *F. Kyngston f. E. Weaver a. W. Welby*, 1610. L.O.G².; F.PN².TEX.
— A learned and very usefull commentary upon Malachy. Whereunto is added an exercitation upon the same. By S. Torshell. 1641 (1640.) *See* Wing S 5692.

23276 — A sermon preached at Paules Crosse, the second of November. 1606. 8°. *T. C[reede] f. E. Weaver a. W. Welby*, 1609. Ent. 7 de. 1608. L.O.C.; F.HN.PN².U.
— *tr. See* 25360.

— Upon the pious life of R. Stocke. 1626. *See* 7021.7.

Stock, Simon. *See* 7072.5 sqq.

Stockbery. A most true and lamentable report, of haile which fell vpon Stockbery. 1590. *See* 20889.7.

Stocker, Thomas, *tr. See* 2029, 2779.5, 4409, 4437, 4440, 4460, 4870, 6893, 7373.4, 17450.3, 24775, 24786.5.

23277 **Stockwood, John.** A Bartholmew [*sic*] fairing for parentes, shewing that children are not to marie, without the consent of their parentes. 8°. *J. Wolfe f. J. Harrison the yonger*, 1589. Ent. 9 au. L.O.C².

Stockwood, John—*cont.*

23277.5 — Disputatiuncularum grammaticalium libellus, ad puerorum in scholis excogitatus: iam vero denuo reuisus. 8°. *T. Judson pro J. Harrison iuniore,* 1589 [i.e. 1598.] Ent. to J. Harrison 14 au. 1598; cancelled a. ent. to T. Dawson, E. White, W. Leake a. C. Burby 12 de. 1598. SHR.; CU.
Dedic. dated 1598.

23278 — [A variant, w. tp date corrected.] *T. Judson pro J. Harrison iuniore,* 1598. L(tp only, Harl.5927/166). O.O⁵.P.; ILL.

23278.7 — [Anr. ed.] Editio tertia: duabus prioribus castigatior. 8°. *typis J. Norton,* 1607. O.CHEL².SCL(lacks tp).; Y.

23279 — [Anr. ed.] Editio quarta. 8°. [*T. Dawson,*] *typis J. Battersbie,* 1619. L.O.O⁶.C².C¹⁶.

23279.5 — [Anr. ed.] Editio quinta. 12°. [*R. Young?*] *per assign. B. Norton,* 1634. O.BIRM²(K.N.).MARL.; F.HN. Auckland PL.

23280 — A plaine and easie laying open of . . . construction in the English Accidence [cf. 15622.3.] 4°. [*Eliot's Court Press? f.*] *assignes of F. Flower,* 1590. Ent. to R. Watkins 24 oc. L.O(2).C.P.

23281 — Progymnasma scholasticum. Hoc est, epigrammatum Græcorum, ex anthologia selectorum ab H. Stephano. Opera J. Stockwoodi. *Greek a. Lat.* [In verse.] 8°. *ex typ. A. Islip,* 1597. L.O.C.BIRM²(K.N.).G⁴.+; F.HN.ILL.N.PN.

23282 — [A ghost.]

23283 — Quæstiones, & responsiones grammaticales, ad faciliorem illarum regularum explanationem, quæ in Grammatica Liliana [cf. 15622.7] habentur, accommodatæ. 8°. *T. Dawson pro J. Harrisone,* 1592. Ent. to J. Harrison, jun., 27 jn. 1586. L.

23284 — A sermon preached at Paules Crosse on Barthelmew day, being the 24. of August. 1578. 8°. *H. Bynneman f. G. Byshop,* [1578.] Ent. 11 se. 1578. L.L².O.C.P.+; F.PN².Y.

— A short catechisme for housholders. Gathered by J. Stockwood. 1580, etc. *See* 6710.5 sqq.

23284.5 — The treatise of the figures at the end of the rules of construction in the Latine grammar [cf. pt. 2 of 15626] construed. 8°. [*Eliot's Court Press f.*] *J. Norton,* 1609. MARL.

23285 — A very fruiteful sermon prached at Paules Crosse the tenth of May last. 8°. (*T. Dawson*) *f. G. Bishop,* 1579. Ent. 12 oc. L.L².O.C⁵.WOR.; HN.PN².

23286 — A very fruitfull and necessarye sermon of the destruction of Ierusalem. 8°. *T. Dawson,* 1584. L(2).L².O.

23287 — A verie godlie and profitable sermon of the necessitie, properties and office of a good magistrate. 8°. *J. C[harlewood] f. T. Butter,* 1584. L.L².O.

— ed. *See* 6710.5 sqq.

— tr. *See* 2046, 2049, 3602, 4055, 6227, 10607, 22247, 24528.

Stoics. The moral philosophie of the Stoicks. 1598. *See* 7374.

Stokesley, John, *Bp. See* 24321.

Stone, Thomas. An answer to the arguments written by Mr. Stone. 1608. *See* 25852.7.

23288 **Stone, William.** A curse become a blessing: or, a sermon preached at the funerall of Paul Cleybrooke esquire. 4°. *J. Haviland f. W. Sheffard,* 1623. Ent. 17 de. 1622. L.O¹⁰.C(tp def.).BRISTOL.P.+; HD.Y.

23289 **Stoneham, Matthew.** A treatise on the first psalme. 4°. *G. Eld f. W. Burre,* 1610. L.O.C³.G².LINC.+; F.HN. AAS.PN².

23290 — Two sermons of direction for judges and magistrates. 8°. *R. Field,* 1608. Ent. 6 jn. L.L⁴.O³.C¹⁰.NEP.; F. BO⁵.

23291 **Stoole, George.** A lamentable new ditty, made upon the death of G. Stoole. *Ballad.* 2 pts. s.sh.fol. *f. H. Gosson,* [1630?] Ass'd by M. Trundle to ballad ptnrs. 1 jn. 1629. L.
In refrain: 'Heighho, . . . Georgie.' = Wing L 274.

23292 **Stopes, Leonard.** An Aue Maria in commendation of our most vertuous queene. [In verse.] s.sh.fol. *R. Lant,* [1553?] L⁵(Lemon 35).
— *See also* 17559.

23293 **Storehouse.** A storehouse of physicall and philosophicall secrets. 1633. Now = 19182.5.

23294 **Storer, Thomas.** The life and death of Thomas Wolsey cardinall. [In verse.] 4°. [*V. Simmes f.*] *T. Dawson,* 1599. Ent. 7 se. L.O.C.C².ETON.+; F.HN.HD.N.NY.+

23295 **Storre, William.** The manner of the cruell outragious murther of W. Storre mast. of art, at Market Raisin committed by F. Cartwright. 4°. *Oxford, J. Barnes,* 1603. L².O.E(imp.).; HN.
Reprinted in 18287. *See also* 4704.

23296 **Story, John,** *D.C.L.* A copie of a letter lately sent by a gentleman, student in the lawes of the realme, to a frende of his concernyng. D. Story. 8° in 4's. [*J. Day?* 1571.] L.O.C⁵.D².G².+; F.HN.
End of text dated 4 June 1571. One L copy (C.27.a. 16) has a fake tp adding John Prestall's name.

23297 — A declaration of the lyfe and death of J. Story. 1571. 8° in 4's. *T. Colwell,* [1571.] Ent. 1570–71. L².O (lacks last leaf).C⁵.D².G².+

23298 — An historicall discource of yᵉ life and death of doctor Story. [1571?] Now = 15033.7.

Story, John, *Gent., tr. See* 23517.5.

23299 **Stoughton, John.** The arraignement of covetousnesse, in three sermons [on Luke xii.15.] 4°. [*R. Badger*] *f. J. Bellamie, H. Overton, J. Rothwell, R. Serger a. R. Smith,* 1640. Ent. to Rothwell, Overton a. Smith 13 se. 1639. O.D.; F.
Also issued as pt. 4 of 23311.

23300 — Baruch's sore gently opened: God's salve skilfully applied: in two sermons [on Jer.xlv.5.] 4°. *R. B[adger] f. J. Bellamie, H. Overton, J. Rothwell a. R. Smith,* 1640. Ent. to Overton, Rothwell, jun., a. Smith 3 se. 1639. O.D.; F.
Also issued as pt. 3 of 23311.

23301 — The burning light. A sermon preached in Christs Church, London. 1640. = pt. of 23302.

23302 — Choice sermons preached upon selected occasions. Viz. The happinesse of peace [on Ps. cxliv.15.] The love-sick spouse [Cantic.v.8.] The burning light [John v.35.] The magistrates commission [Ps.ii.10–12.] (Published by A. B[urgess.]) 4°. *R. Hodgkinson [a.] (T. Cotes) f. D. Frere,* 1640. Serm.1, 2 ent. 23 au. 1639; serm. 3, 4 ent. 2 se. 1639. ?Serm. 4 also ent. to J. Rothwell, jun., 17 se. 1639. L³.O³.C².G². NLW.+; F(imp.).CAL².HD(serm. 2 only).PN².TORONTO².
(23301 is pt. of this) Also issued as pt. 1 of 23306.

23303 — The christians prayer for the churches peace. Or, a sermon [on Ps. cxxii.6.] (A sermon upon 1 Sam. 2.30.) 4°. *J. Dawson f. J. Bellamie a. R. Smith,* 1640. Ent. 10 se. 1639. L⁴.O.; F(2, 1 imp.).
Also issued as pt. 1 of 23311.

23304 — XI. choice sermons, . . . viz. I. The preachers dignity, and duty: in five sermons [on 2 Cor. v. 20.] II. Christ crucified, in six sermons [on 1 Cor. ii. 2.] (Published by A. B[urgess.]) 2 pts. 4°. *R. B[adger] f. J. Bellamie, H. Overton, J. Rothwell a. R. Smith,* 1640. 5 serm. ent. to Smith 3 se. 1639, to Bellamy a. Smith 18 oc. and 29 no. 1639; 6 serm. ent. to Rothwell, Overton, a. Smith 18 se. 1639. O⁶(D).DUR(Bamb.).; F.NY¹¹ TORONTO².
Also issued as pts. 2, 3 of 23306. Six Sermons possibly issued separately as 23312.

23305 — Felicitas ultimi sæculi: epistola in qua, calamitosus ævi præsentis status seriò deploratur. [*Ed.*] S. H(artlibus.) 8°. *typis R. Hodgkinson, imp. D. Frere,* 1640. Ent. 23 au. 1639. L.O.C².D.G².+; F.HN.HD.N. U.+

23306 — XV. choice sermons, preached upon selected occasions. 3 pts. 4°. *f. J. Bellamie, H. Overton, J. Rothwell, R. Royston, D. Frere a. R. Smith,* 1640. L.O.C.A.D.+; F.HN.HD.N.U.+
A reissue, w. added gen. tp, of 23302, 23304.
— Five sermons. 1640. *See* pt. 1 of 23304.

23307 — A forme of wholsome words; or, an introduction to the body of divinity: in three sermons on 2 Timothy,1. 13. [*Ed.*] (A. B[urgess.]) 4°. *J. R[aworth] f. J. Bellamy, H. Overton, A. Crook, J. Rothwell, R. Sergeir, D. Frere a. R. Smith,* 1640. Ent. 17 se. 1639 to bksellers in imprint, omitting Bellamy and Frere, and including J. Crook. O⁸.D².LINC.; F.
Also issued as pt. 1 of 23313.

23307.5 — [A variant, w. 'J. Crook' added to the imprint, following 'R. Sergeir'.] 1640. L².O⁵.C.BIRM²(K.N.).D.+; BO². CHI.MICH.PEN.Y.

Stoughton, John—*cont.*

23308 — The heavenly conversation. And the naturall mans condition. In two treatises [on Phil. iii. 20. *Ed.*] (A. B[urgess.]) 12°. *T. C[otes] f. J. Bellamie a. R. Smith*, 1640. Ent. 18 oc. 1639. L.L³.O³(date cropt).C.C³(date cropt).+; F.CHI.Y.

23308.5 — [A variant, w. impr. on gen. tp:] *T. Cotes f. D. Frere*, 1640. Ent. to Bellamy, Smith a. Frere 29 oc. 1639. O.C¹⁰.; U.

23309 — A learned treatise: in three parts, 1 The definition 2 The distribution of divinity. 3 The happinesse of man. [*Ed.*] (A. B[urgess.]) 4°. *R. Hodgkinson f. J. Bellamy, D. Frere a. R. Smith*, 1640. Ent. 29 no. 1639. L².O⁵.C.D.DUR.+; F.HN.BO.CHI.U.+
Also issued as pt. 3 of 23313.

— The magistrates commission. 1640. *See* 23302.

23310 — The righteous mans plea to true happinesse. In ten sermons on Psal.4.ver.6. 4°. *T. Cotes, [R. Badger, a. assigns of T. Purfoot] f. J. Bellamie, H. Overton, A. Crooke, J. Rothwell, J. Crooke, R. Sergier, D. Freere a. R. Smith*, 1640. Ent. to A. and J. Crook a. R. Sergier 4 se. 1639; also to Overton, Rothwell, a. Smith 17 se. 1639. L².O⁵.C.D.DUR.+; F.HN.BO².MICH. U.+ 𝔄
Also issued as pt. 2 of 23313. Collates tp+(*)⁴ **⁴ Aaa–Rrr⁴ Aaaa–Mmmm⁴ Nnnn² Oooo–Tttt⁴. Cotes pr. through Rrr; Badger Aaaa–Nnnn; and Purfoot's assigns Oooo–Tttt.

23311 — Seaven sermons, preached upon severall occasions. 3 pts. 4°. *J. D[awson] f. J. Bellamie a. R. Smith*, 1640. L³⁰.O.C².A.D.+; F.HN.HD.N.U.+
A reissue, w. added gen. tp, of 23303, 23300, 23299.

23311.5 — [Anr. issue, w. gen. tp reset, w. imprint:] *f. H. Overton a. J. Rothwell*, 1640. L.C.C³.

23312 — Sixe sermons, on I Cor.II.II. 4°. *R. B[adger] f. J. Bellamie, H. Overton, J. Rothwell a. R. Smith*, 1640. M.
Usually issued as pt. 2 of 23304, pt. 3 of 23306.

23313 — XIII. sermons, preached in the church of Aldermanbury. To which is added, An exact and learned discourse. 3 pts. 4°. *J. Raworth f. J. Bellamy, H. Overton, A. Crook, J. Rothwell, R. Sergeir, J. Crook, D. Frere a. R. Smith*, 1640. L.O.C.E.NLW.+; F.HN. HD.N.U.+
A reissue, w. added gen. tp, of 23307, 23310, 23309.

23314 **Stoughton, Thomas.** The christians sacrifice: . . . Or, a logicall and theologicall exposition of [Rom. xii.1,2.] 4°. *W. Jones*, 1622. Ent. 2 se. L.O.C.BED.BIRM² (K.N.).; F.ILL.U.Y.

23315 — The dignitie of Gods children. Or an exposition of 1.John 3.1.2.3. 4° in 8's. *T. Haveland f. T. Man the yonger*, 1610. Ent. to T. Man, sen. and jun., a. J. Man 16 oc. 1609. L(destroyed).
Notes by F. S. Ferguson confirm the L copy had this imprint.

23315.5 — [A variant, w. imprint:] *T. Haveland f. T. Man*, 1610. L³.L⁴.BIRM²(K.N.).DUL.; F.HN.PN².Y.

23316 — A generall treatise against poperie. 8°. *J. Legat, pr. to the Univ. of Camb.*, 1598. L.O.C.BIRM²(K.N.).E.+; U.

23317 — Two profitable treatises: I. Of Davids love to the word: II. Of Davids meditation on the word of God. 4° in 8's. *E. Griffin f. A. Johnson*, 1616. Ent. 20 jy. L.O.C. BIRM²(K.N.).D.+; LC.PN².TEX.

23318 **Stoughton, William.** An assertion for true and christian church-policie. [Anon.] 8°. [*Middelburg, R. Schilders*,] 1604. L.O.C.D.E.+; F.HN.HD.N.U.+
Some copies (L, 1 O, 1 O⁵, F) have 2 halfsheets inserted after the tp: 'To the apprentices and students of the Innes of Court' w. Stoughton's name pr. at the end but defaced or deleted in at least the Oxford copies. Most copies have line 6 of tp: 'Pastours'; the other O⁵ copy, without the dedic., has: 'Pastors' and quires A–L in a different typesetting.

— *See also* 10394.

23318.3 **Stourton, Charles,** *Baron Stourton.* The copye of the self same wordes, that mi lorde Sturton spake at his death, beyng [executed for murder] the .vi. day of March, 1557. s.sh.fol. [*f.*] *W. Pickeringe*, [1557.] L⁵(Lemon 41).

23318.7 — [Anr. version.] A prayer sayd by the lorde Sturton and also his confession. s.sh.fol. *T. Marshe*, [1557.] L⁵ (Lemon 42).

Stow, John. The abridgement or summarie of the English chronicle. 1607, etc. *See* 23330 sqq.
— The annales of England. 1592, etc. *See* 23334 sqq.
— The chronicles of England. [1580.] *See* 23333.

The Chronicles come in 2 ever-expanding forms: the *Summary*, which grows from 8° (23319) to 4° (23333) to fol. ending as the *Annals*; and the *Abridgement*, which grows from 16° (23325.4) to 8°. Each ed. differs to some extent from all others, but in general each abridgement is adapted from the most recent large version.

THE SUMMARY—8°

23319 — A summarie of Englyshe chronicles. Collected by J. Stow 1565. 8°. *in æd. T. Marshi*, (1565.) Ent. 1564–65. L.L⁸.O.C².DUR³.+; F.HN.CH.HD.Y.+
Copies differ: orig. Gg4ʳ has 'The Constable of Fraunce'; the cancel, set in duplicate, has 'The duke of Montmorency [or 'Montmorency,' (with comma) in binding frag. w. both settings at USHAW] Constable of France'. Orig. quire Hh has Hh8 cancelled and replaced by a bifolium w. the Ages of the World on the recto of the 2nd leaf; the cancel quire has this list on Hh8ᵛ. Examples of all but the USHAW cancel are at L.

23319.5 — [Anr. ed.] Collected 1566. 8°. *T. Marshe*, [1566.] L⁸ (imp.).O.A(imp.).D(imp.).NEK.+; KAN(imp.).LC.

23320 — Now = 23325.4.
23321 — Now = 23325.5.
23322 — [Anr. ed.] A summarye of the chronicles of England, . . . vnto 1570. Nowe newly corrected and enlarged. 8°. *T. Marshe*, [1570.] L⁸.O(lacks tp).LIV³.; F(imp.).HN.

23323 — Now = 23325.6.
23323.5 — [Anr. issue, w. 1st quire and Fff8 reset, and additions.] Vnto 1573. 8°. *T. Marshe*, [1573.] E(lacks tp).; F.

23324 — [Anr. issue, w. 1st quire and Iii8 reset, and additions.] Vnto 1574. 8°. *H. Binneman*, [1574.] L⁸.O.; F.
Marsh exchanged Stow for Binneman's Terence 31 Mar. 1573; *see* Arber I.272, 418.

23325 — [Anr. ed.] Vnto 1575. 8°. *R. Tottle a. H. Binneman*, [1575.] L(last leaf facs.).L⁴³.O(2 imp.).NLW.ST.; N (missing).

23325.2 — [Anr. ed.] Vnto 1590. 8°. *R. Newbery*, 1590. Ent. to Newbery a. H. Denham 30 de. 1584. L.L⁸.O. Stevens Cox.; F(imp.).HD.WIS.Y. W. Stirling Maxwell, Chicago.
(Formerly 23327)

ABRIDGEMENT—16° and 8°

23325.4 — The summarie of Englyshe chronicles. (Lately collected and published) nowe abridged and continued tyl March, 1566. By J. S(tow.) 16° in 8's. *T. Marshe*, [1566.] L(imp.).L⁸(imp.).; F(2 imp.).
(Formerly 23320) L⁸ has a quartersheet w. Stow's dedic. to Sir Richard Champion, Lord Mayor, which is in none of the other copies.

23325.5 — [Anr. ed.] Continued til Nouember. 1567. 16° in 8's. *T. Marshe*, [1567.] L.L⁸.O.LAMPORT.; CAL(imp.).HD. TEX.
(Formerly 23321)

23325.6 — [Anr. ed.] The summarye of the chronicles of Englande . . . abridged and continued, vnto 1573. 16° in 8's. *T. Marshe*, [1573.] L(2).L⁸(imp.).O(lacks tp). Broxbourne(E).; Y.
(Formerly 23323)

23325.7 — [Anr. ed.] Vnto 1579. 16° in 8's. *R. Tottle a. H. Binneman*, [1579.] L⁸.O.C². Rogers(imp.).; F.HN.HD (imp.).NCU(imp.).

23325.8 — [Anr. issue, w. prelims. reset, and additions.] Vnto 1584. 16° in 8's. *R. Newbery a. H. Denham*, 1584. Ent. 30 de. L⁸.O³(imp.).; PN.
Title omits the word 'abridged'. Newbery and Denham yielded the 16° rights to the company 8 Jan. 1584; *see* Arber II.788.

23326 — [Anr. ed.] Vnto 1587. 16° in 8's. *R. Newberie a. H. Denham*, [1587.] L.L⁸.O.C(lacks tp). E.+

23327 — Now = 23325.2.
23328 — [Anr. ed.] Vnto 1598. 16° in 8's. *R. Bradocke*, 1598. L.O.C.D(lacks tp).E.+; F.HN.CU.PN(2).TEX.
Page 4 catchword: 'Betwene'. O³⁷ has a copy, imp. at beginning and end, with ¶1–Ff5 in this typesetting. Ff6 to the end is cancelled and replaced by *–***⁸, bringing the text to 1604 and pr. by T. Dawson.

Stow, John—*cont.*

23328.5 —[Anr. ed.] Vnto 1598. 16° in 8's. *R. Bradocke*, 1598. E.
Page 4 catchword: 'Betweene'. c³ has a copy lack-
ing tp and Syracuse U has a copy, imp. at the
beginning, in this typesetting. Ff6–8 are cancelled
and replaced by *–***⁸ as in the O³⁷ copy above.
The Syracuse U copy also has a cancel dedic. to
Sir T. Bennet, the proper dedicatee for 23329, with
dedic. ending: 'pardon, if I do / offend.' while
23329 has: 'par- / don if I do offend.'

23329 — [Anr. ed.] Unto 1604. 16° in 8's. *J. Harison* [3,] 1604.
Ent. to J. Harrison 3 to print for the company 12 jy.
1602. L.O.C(imp.).D.E.+ ; F.HN.HD.N(imp.).Y.+
See Greg, *Register B*, p. 90. *See also* 23328.

23330 — [Anr. ed.] The abridgement or summarie of the English chronicle, continued unto 1607. By E. H(owes.)
8°. [*J. Windet*] *f. the Co. of Statrs.*, [1607.] L.O.C
(imp.).M².P.+ ; F.HN.CHI.HD.NY¹¹.+

23331 — [Anr. ed.] Continued unto 1610. By E. H(owes.) 8°.
[*N. Okes, W. Hall a. T. Haveland*,] *f. the Co. of
Statrs.*, 1611. L.O.C⁵.M.NEK.+ ; F.HN.HD.N.Y.+
Okes pr. through quire P; Hall and Haveland the
rest.

23332 — [Anr. ed.] Continued unto 1618. By E. H(owes.) 8°.
[*E. Allde a. N. Okes*] *f. the Co. of Statrs.*, 1618. Ent.
to the English Stock 5 mr. 1620. L.O.C.E⁴.SHEF.+ ;
F.HN.CU.HD.ILL.+
(Formerly also 23339) Allde pr. through quire U;
Okes the rest.

CHRONICLES AND ANNALS—4° and fol.

23333 — The chronicles of England, from Brute vnto this
present yeare 1580. 4° in 8's. [*H. Bynneman f.*] *R.
Newberie, at the assign. of H. Bynneman*, [1580.]
L.L⁸.O(imp.).C(imp.).G²(imp.).+ ; F.HN.COR.LC.PN.

23334 — [Anr. ed.] The annales of England, . . . vntill 1592. 4°
in 8's. *R. Newbery* [*a. Eliot's Court Press*, 1592.] Ent.
to Newbery a. Denham 30 de. 1584. L.O.C.E.M².+ ;
F.HN.HD.N.NY.+
Newbery pr. A–Ll; Eliot's Court Press the rest.

23335 — [Anr. ed.] Untill 1600. 4° in 8's. [*Eliot's Court Press a.
F. Kingston f.*] *R. Newbery*, [1600.] Ass'd by R. to
John Newbery 30 se. 1594. L.L⁸.O¹¹(imp.).OS.; CAL².
CHI.PEN. Mount Holyoke C(imp.).
Eliot's Court Press pr. prelims., A–Y, and also
prob. Aaa–Yyy, Oooo–Rrrr; Kingston pr. Aa–Yy;
a 3rd printer or compositor did Aaaa–Nnnn.

23336 — [A variant, w. title:] Untill 1601. [*Eliot's Court Press a.
F. Kingston f.*] *R. Newbery*, [1601.] L⁸.O.C.G².LEEDS.
+ ; F.HN.HD(2, 1 imp.).WTL.

23337 — [Anr. issue, w. cancel tp and additions.] Untill 1605.
[Additions pr. by *G. Eld*] *f. G. Bishop a. T. Adams*,
[1605.] Ass'd by R. Newbery to John Newbery a. T.
Adams 18 ja. 1602. L.O.C.C².STU.+ ; F.HN.ILL.LC
(imp.).STAN.+

23338 — [Anr. ed.] Continued unto 1614. by E. Howes. (An
appendix of three universities. The thirde was collected by syr G. Buck.) fol. (*T. Dawson*,) *imp. T.
Adams*, 1615. Ass'd by widow Bishop 14 mr. 1611;
ent. 29 jy. 1613. L.O.C.D.E.+ ; F.HN.HD.N.NY.+
The FBL copy omits the colophon on Qqqq6ᵛ.

23339 — = 23332.
23340 — [Anr. ed.] Continued unto 1631. By E. Howes. fol. [*J.
Beale, B. Alsop a. T. Fawcet, a.*] (*A. Matthewes*,)
imp. R. Meighen, 1631 (1632.) Ass'd to A. Hebb
6 my. 1625 a. 28 jy. 1631. L.O.C.D.E².+ ; F.HN.HD.N.
NY.+
Beale pr. the prelims., A–G, Aa–Ccc; Alsop and
Fawcet did H–Z; Mathewes did Ddd–Ssss.

23341 — A suruay of London. Contayning the originall, antiquity, increase, moderne estate, and description of
that citie. With an appendix, containing in Latine,
Libellum de situ Londini: written by W. Fitz-
stephen, in the raigne of Henry the second. 4° in 8's.
[*J. Windet f.*] *J. Wolfe*, 1598. Ent. 7 jy. L.O.C².D.G².
+ ; F.HN.HD.NY.Y.+
The outer sheet of quire Hh is in 2 settings: without errata on Hh10ᵛ and Hh1ʳ line 2 ending:
'whome'; or w. errata on Hh10ᵛ and Hh1ʳ line 2
ending: 'whom'; both at L, F.

23342 — [A variant, w. imprint:] [*J. Windet f.*] *J. Wolfe*, 1599.
L.O.C².CARLISLE.P.+ ; F(lacks Hh10).HN.HD.ILL.WIS.+

Stow, John—*cont.*

23343 — [Anr. ed.] 4° in 8's. *J. Windet*, 1603. L.O.C.E².M.+ ; F.
HN.HD.N.Y.+
See Greg, *Register B*, p. 90.

23344 — [Anr. ed.] Continued, and enlarged. [By A. M., i.e. A.
Munday.] 4° in 8's. *G. Purslowe*, 1618. Ass'd to J.
Pindley 27 ap. 1612; to Purslowe 2 no. 1613. L.O.
C².D.E.+ ; F.HN.HD.N.PML.+
End of title varies: 'this present yeere 1617.' or
'. . . 1618.'; both at HN.
Pp. 624–47 reprint most of 13583; *see Court-
Book C*, p. 114.

23345 — [Anr. ed.] Completely finished by the study of A.
M[unday,] H. D[yson] and others. [*Ed.*] (C. I.) fol.
E. Purslow, sold by N. Bourne, 1633. L.O.C.D.E.+ ;
F.HN.HD.N.NY.+

23345.5 — [Anr. issue, w. cancel tp, w. imprint:] *f. N. Bourn*,
1633 [post-1640.] HD.
— *ed. See* 5075, 17028, 21499, 22608.
— *See also* 13569, 16738.5.

— [Brief for collections for J. Stow. 8 Mar. 1603, o.s.] *See*
8345.
— [Brief for collections for J. Stow. 26 Oct. 1604.] *See*
8362.

23346 — A recital of Stow's collection concerning the rise of the
court of Requests. s.sh.fol. [*London*, 1640?] L.O.;
LC.

23347 **Strachan, Andrew.** Panegyricus inauguralis, quo autores,
vindices & euergetæ illustris universitatis Aberdonensis justis elogiis ornabantur. [In verse.] 4°. *Aberdoniis*,
E. Rabanus, 1631. L(imp.).C¹⁰.A.E².G².

— Propositiones, & problemata philosophica. Præs. A.
Strachano. 1629. *See* 71.16.

23348 — Schediasmata philosophica. Præside A. Strachano.
1631. Now = 71.17.

23349 — Vindiciæ cultus divini. 1634. Now = 71.19A.

23350 **Strachey, William.** For the colony in Virginea Britannia.
Lawes divine, morall and martiall. [*Ed.*] (W.
Strachey.) 4°. [*W. Stansby*] *f. W. Burre*, 1612. Ent.
13 de. 1611. L(2).O(frag.).D(imp.).HOLK.; F.HN.BO⁵.
PH.PN.+
Some copies have added pr. dedic. leaf: to Sir A.
Auger (L, G.7126), to Sir E. Sandys (HOLK), to Sir
W. Wade (PN). Some copies have added pr. verses
to Lord de la Warre and Sir T. Smith (L, C.33.c.
30; HOLK, HN, CB, PN).

23351 **Strada, Famianus.** Famiani Stradae Romani e Societate
Jesu. Prolusiones academicæ. 8°. *Oxoniæ, G. Turner*,
1631. L.O.C⁵.A.YK.+ ; F.HN.ILL.PN².WIS.+

23352 **Stradling,** *Sir* **John.** Beati pacifici: a divine poem.
Written to the kings most excellent majestie. 4°. [*F.
Kingston*] *f. the Co. of Statrs.*, 1623. Ent. to E.
Weaver for the English Stock 4 jn. L.NLW.USHAW.;
F.HN.

23353 — Divine poemes. In seven severall classes. 4° in 8's. *W.
Stansby*, 1625. Ent. 29 mr. L.O¹⁸.C.WN.; F.HN.HD.
PML.

23354 — Joannis Stradlingi epigrammatum libri quatuor. 8°.
[*Eliot's Court Press*,] imp. *G. Bishop & J. Norton*,
1607. L.O.O⁴.C².NLW.+ ; F.HN.CU.HD.N.+
— *tr. See* 15694.7, 15696.

Strafford, *Earl of. See* Wentworth, T.

Strang, John. Theses ex uberrimis logicæ. Sub præs. J.
Strangii. 1611. *See* 21555.17.

Strangling. The strangling and death of the great Turke.
1622. *See* Newsbooks 62.

Stranguage, William, *pseud. See* 24509.

Strassburg, *Preachers of.* [A treatise declaring that images
are not to be suffered. 1535.] *See* 24238.

Strata Marcella, Montgomeryshire, *Monastery of
B. Mary de. See* Indulgences 76.

Stratford, Edmond. *See* Lechmere, E.

23355 **Stratford Langton.** [A petition to the lord mayor. 1648.]
= Wing T 1656.

Stratford-on-Avon. [Brief for relief.] 1616. *See* 8541.

23356 **Straw, Jack.** The life and death of Jacke Straw, a notable rebell. [A play.] 4°. *J. Danter, solde by W. Barley,* 1593 (1594.) Ent. to Danter 23 oc. 1593. L.E(lacks tp).; HN(tp only). Greg 114.

23357 — [Anr. ed.] 4°. [*W. Jaggard*] *f. T. Pavyer,* 1604. Ent. 14 au. 1600. O.E(lacks tp).; HN.HD(lacks tp).

23358 **Strigelius, Victorinus.** Part of the harmony of king Dauids harp. Conteining the first XXI. psalmes. Newly *tr.* by R. Robinson. 4°. *J. Wolfe,* 1582. L.O. C.SCL(lacks tp).; F.HN.BO.NY.

23359 — A proceeding in the harmonie of king Dauids harpe. [Psalms 22–34.] *Tr.* out of Latin by R. Robinson. 1591. 4°. *J. Wolfe* [a. *J. Charlewood,* 1591.] Ent. 8 mr. 1591. L.O(2, 1 imp.).C.; F.HD.
Wolfe pr. quire A; Charlewood B to end.

23360 — A second proceeding. [Psalms 35–44.] *Tr.* R. Robinson. 1592. 4°. *J. C[harlewood*] *f. A. Kitson,* 1593. Ent. to Charlewood 22 de. 1592. L.O.C.P.

23361 — A third proceeding. [Psalms 45–61.] *Tr.* R. Robinson. 4°. *V. Sims,* 1595. L.O.C.; F.HN.
This and 23362 pr. 'at the charges of R. Banckworth' according to Robinson's Eupolemia; *see The Library,* XI (1930), p. 177.

23362 — A fourth proceeding. [Psalms 62–7.] *Tr.* R. Robinson. 4°. *V. Simmes,* 1596. L.O.O³.P.
See note to 23361.

23363 — A fift proceeding. [Psalms 68–72.] *Tr.* R. Robinson. 1594. 4°. *P. S[hort*] *f. M. Lownes,* 1598. L(tp only, Ames I.610).L⁴.P(imp.).; F(imp.).LC.

Stripping. Stripping, whipping, and pumping. 1638. *See* 23795.3.

23364 **Strode, George.** The anatomie of mortalitie: devided into these eight heads. [etc.] 4° in 8's. *W. Jones, sold by E. Weaver,* 1618. Ent. to Jones 28 jn. L.L².O.C³.BIRM² (K.N.).+; F.CAL.

23365 — The second edition somewhat enlarged. 4° in 8's. *W. Jones, sold by T. Weaver,* 1632. L.O.C¹⁷.BTU.WI.+; F.ILL.PN².V.Y.+

Strof, Walter. Almanacks. 1626, etc. *See* 516 sq.

23366 **Strumsdorf.** The forme of the agreement made at Strumsdorff. Of the truce betwixt the kings majesty of Poland. And the queenes majestie, of Sweden. *Lat. a. Eng.* 4°. *T. Harper f. N. Butter a. N. Bourne,* 1635. O.C.; F.HN.Y.
In at least the F copy 'tter' of Butter's name in the English imprint has not pr.

23367 **Struther, William.** Christian observations and resolutions. I. Centurie. With a Resolution for death, &c. Newlie published. 2 pts. 8°. *Edinburgh, heires of A. Hart,* 1628. Ent. to R. Allot 1 no. L.O.C².E.G².+; F.HN.NY.U.
For II. Centurie *see* 23368.5.

23367.5 — [Anr. ed.] 12°. *J. Dawson f. R. Mabb,* 1629. L.C¹⁰. CHATS(imp.).E.E⁴.; BO.

23368 — [Anr. issue, w. imprint on cancel gen. tp:] *f. R. M., sould by R. Swayne,* 1629. L⁴(lacks tp)*.C.YK.; HD. TORONTO².

23368.5 — Christian observations and resolutions. II. Centurie. Newlie published. 8°. *Edinburgh, heires of A. Hart,* 1629. L.O.E.ELY.G².+; HN.HD.PN².U. Rutgers U.
Found bd. w. both Scottish and English eds. of I. Centurie.

23369 — A looking glasse for princes and people. Delivered in a sermon. And since augmented. Together with a vindication of princes, &c. 2 pts. 4°. *Edinburgh, heires of A. Hart,* 1632. L.O.BTU.E.YK.+; F.HN.U.

23370 — Scotlands warning, or a treatise of fasting. 8°. *Edinburgh, heires of A. Hart,* 1628. O.O⁵.E.E².G².; Y.

23371 — True happines, or, king Davids choice. Begunne in sermons, and now digested into a treatise. 4°. *Edinburgh, R. Young f. J. Wood,* 1633. L.C.E.G².P.+; F.HD.

Stryde, Thomas. *See* 22920.7.

Stuart, Henry, *King Consort of Mary Q. of Scots.* Heir followis ane ballat declaring the inclinatioun of our king. 1567. *See* 22196.
— A dolefull ditty, of the lord Darly [*sic*], sometime king of Scots. [c. 1585.] *See* 4270.5.
— The kingis complaint. [1567.] *See* 22200.

23372 — Heir followis the testament of king Henrie. 1567. = 22199.

23373 **Stuart, James,** *Earl of Moray.* The deploratioun of the cruell murther of James erle of Murray. 1570. Now = 22192a.3.
— Ane exhortatioun derect to my lord regent. [1567.] *See* 22194.
— *See* also 22189, 22204, 22205.

Stuart Family. A trewe description of the nobill race of the Stewards. [1602?] *See* 14787.2.
— Vera descriptio Stewartorum familiae. [1602?] *See* 14787.6.

23374 **Stubbe, Edmund.** Fraus honesta comœdia Cantabrigiæ olim acta. 12°. *typis A. Math[ewes,*] *imp. R. Thrale,* 1632. Ent. 28 se. 1631. L.O.C.D.E².+; F.HN.HD(tp def.).N.Y.+ Greg L 10.

23375 **Stubbe Peter.** A true discourse. Declaring the damnable life and death of one Stubbe Peeter, a sorcerer. *Tr.* out of the high Duch. according to the copie brought into England the xj. daye of this present moneth of Iune 1590. 8°. [*R. Ward?*] *f. E. Venge,* [1590.] Ent. 22 jn. 1590. L.L².

23376 **Stubbes, Philip.** The anatomie of abuses: contayning a discouerie, of vices in a verie famous ilande called Ailgna. Made dialogue-wise. 8°. [*J. Kingston f.*] *R. Jones,* 1583 (1 my.) Ent. 1 mr. O(4, 1 imp.).NLW.; F(lacks colophon).HN.ROS.
Contains a preface to the reader omitted in 23377 sqq.

23376.5 — [A variant, w. imprint:] *R. Jones,* 1583 (29 my.) P.

23377 — [Anr. ed.] 8°. [*J. Kingston f.*] *R. Jones,* 1583 (16 au.) L(2).O(2 imp.).HETH(imp.).; F.HN(imp.).N(imp.).

23377.5 — [Anr. ed.] Now augmented the third time. 8°. *R. Jones,* 1584 (12 oc.) HD.ILL(imp.).

23378 — [A variant, w. imprint:] *R. Jones,* 1585. L.C(imp.).SH.; F.Y.
The date in the colophon is also altered in press to 1585.

23379 — [Anr. ed., w. prelims. revised.] Now, the fourth time, newly corrected and inlarged. 4°. [*J. Danter f.*] *R. Johnes,* 1595. L.O.O⁸.C³.BIRM²(K.N.).+; F.HN.HD.
'Ailgna' in this ed. is openly called England.

23380 — The second part of the Anatomie of abuses, conteining the display of corruptions. 8°. *R. W(ard) f. W. Wright,* (1583.) Ent. 7 no. L.L².O(2).SCL.; F.N.

23380.5 — [Anr. issue, w. prelims. cancelled, and cancel tp.] *R. W(ard) f. W. Wright,* (1583.) L.
In title: 'containing'.

23381 — A christal glasse for christian women. Contayning an excellent discourse, of the life and death of Katherine Stubbes. [Init. P. S., *Gent.*] 4°. *R. Jhones,* 1591. Ent. 15 jn. L.

23382 — [Anr. ed.] By P. Stubbes. 4°. [*T. Orwin f.*] *R. Jhones,* 1592. O⁸.; F(2).
The imperfect L copy (1417.h.6) is post-1640.

23382.3 — [Anr. ed.] 4°. [*J. Roberts*] *f. E. White,* 1600. Ent. 3 jy. 1601. F.

23382.7 — [Anr. ed.] 4°. [*E. Allde*] *f. E. White,* 1603. HD.

23383 — [Anr. ed.] 4°. [*E. Allde*] *f. E. White,* 1606. L.

23383.5 — [Anr. ed.] 4°. [*J. Windet*] *f. E. White,* 1608. F.

23384 — [Anr. ed.] 4°. [*E. Allde*] *f. E. White,* 1610. F.

23385 — [Anr. ed.] 4°. [*E. Allde*] *f. E. White,* 1612. C.

23386 — [Anr. ed.] 4°. [*G. Purslowe*] *f. E. White,* 1618. O.

23387 — [Anr. ed.] 4°. *E. Allde f. T. Pavier a. J. Wright,* 1620. Ass'd 13 de. S.
See Court-Book C, pp. 112–13.

23388 — [Anr. ed.] 4°. *W. J[ones] f. T. Pavier a. J. Wright,* 1621. Y.

23389 — [Anr. ed.] 4°. *W. J[ones] f. T. Pavier a. J. Wright,* 1623. M(deposit).; HD.
Tp line 5 ends: 'discourse, of/'.

23389.3 — [Anr. ed.] 4°. *W. J[ones] f. T. Pavier a. J. Wright,* 1623. O.
Tp line 5 ends: 'discourse/'.

23389.7 — [Anr. ed.] 4°. *W. Jones f. T. Pavier a. J. Wright,* 1624. C¹³.

23390 — [Anr. ed.] 4°. [*J. Haviland*] *f. J. Wright,* 1626. Pavier's pt. ass'd to E. Brewster a. R. Bird 4 au. O.YK.

23390.5 — [Anr. ed.] 4°. [*J. Haviland*] *f. J. Wright,* 1627. SHEF.

23391 — [Anr. ed.] 4°. [*J. Haviland*] *f. J. Wright,* 1629. L.

23391.5 — [Anr. ed.] 4°. [*J. Haviland*] *f. J. Wright,* 1630. N.

23392 — [Anr. ed.] 4°. *f. J. Wright,* 1631. S.

23392.5 — [Anr. ed.] 4°. [*J. Haviland*] *f. J. Wright,* 1632. HD.

23393 — [Anr. ed.] 4°. *f. J. Wright,* 1633. L.L³.

23394 — [Anr. ed.] 4°. *f. J. Wright,* 1634. Bird's pt. ass'd to Wright 29 ap. S.; HN.

Stubbes, Philip—*cont.*

23394.5 — [Anr. ed.] 4°. *f. J. Wright*, 1635. E²(2, both with date shaved).

23395 — [Anr. ed.] 4°. *f. J. Wright*, 1637. E.S.

23395a — [Anr. ed.] *W. Thackery*, [after 1665.]
   Not an STC book.

23396 — The intended treason, of doctor Parrie. With a letter from the pope. 4°. *f. H. Car*, [1585.] L.L².O³.O¹⁷.E.; HN.

23397 — A motiue to good workes. 8°. *f. T. Man*, 1593. Ent. 14 oc. L.C³.; F.

23398 — A perfect pathway to felicitie, conteining godly meditations, and praiers. 16° in 8's. *R. Yardly f. H. Lownes*, 1592. Ent. 22 mr. L(2, 1 imp.).

23399 — [Anr. ed., enlarged.] 16° in 8's. *H. Lownes*, 1610. O(imp.).; HN.

23399.3 — The theater of the popes monarchie: wherein is described as well the vncleane liues of that wicked generation. 8°. *T. Dawson*, 1585. HD(imp.).

23399.7 — Two wunderfull and rare examples of the vndeferred iudgement of God: the one vpon a blasphemer. The other vpon a woman, to whome the deuill appeared. In June last. 1581. [In verse.] 4°. *f. W. Wright*, [1581.] L².

23400 **Stubbs, John.** The discouerie of a gaping gulf whereinto England is like to be swallowed by an other French mariage. [Anon.] 8°. [*H. Singleton f. W. Page*,] 1579 (au.) L.O.C.E.M.+; F.HN.HD.N.NY.+
   Suppressed by proclamation; see 8114.
   — *tr.* See 2004, 2017, 19292a.
   — *See also* 21504, 21506.

Stubbs, Justinian, *ed. See* 1636.

23401 **Stuckley, Sir Lewis.** [Heading A2ʳ:] To the kings most excellent majestie. The humble petition of sir L. Stucley, touching the bringing up of sir W. Raleigh. 4°. (*B. Norton a. J. Bill*, 1618.) L.O.C².D.E².+; F.HN. HD.N.NY.+
   Colophon from same setting as 20652.5.

23401.5 **Student.** A students lamentation that hath sometime been in London an apprentice, for the rebellious tumults lately in the citie hapning: for which fiue suffred death on Thursday the 24. of July last. 4°. [*E. Allde*] *f. W. Blackwall*, [1595.] Ent. 1 au. 1595. F(impr. cropt).

Studia. Studiorum puerilium clauis. 1597. *See* 7353.

23402 **Studley, Christopher.** Treason pretended against the king of Scots. 1585. Now = 21949.5.

Studley, John, *tr. See* 1304, 22221, 22222, 22224.

23403 **Studley, Peter.** The looking-glasse of schisme: wherein by a narration of the murders, done by Enoch ap Evan, a downe-right Separatist, on his mother and brother, the disobedience of that sect, is set forth. 12°. *R. B[adger] f. T. Alchorne*, 1634. Ent. 10 jn. L.O.C.D².WI.+; HN.BO³.ILL.PN².U.+
   See also 10581.5 sq.

23404 — The second edition enlarged and corrected: together with an answer to certaine criminations against this historie. 2 pts. 12°. *R. B[adger] f. T. Alchorne*, 1635. L.O.DUR⁵.P.; F(2).HN.HD.NY¹¹.Y.

23405 **Stukeley, Thomas.** The famous historye of the life and death of captaine T. Stukeley. As it hath beene acted. 4°. [*W. Jaggard*] *f. T. Pavyer*, 1605. Ent. 11 au. 1600. L(2).L⁶.O.E.; F.HN.HD.KAN.Y.+ Greg 220.

23406 — Newe newes contayning a shorte rehersall of the late enterprise of certaine fugytiue rebelles: fyrst pretended by captaine Stukeley, and sithence continued, by Mac Morice vpon Ireland. [etc.] *Tr.* out of Dutch the sixth of October, 1579. 8°. *J. C[harlewood*, 1579.] L.O.D.

Sture, Phillip. *See* 12967.5.

23407 **Sturmius, Joannes.** The epistle that Johan Sturmius, . . . sent to the cardynalles and prelates, . . . *tr.* into englysshe by R. Morysine. 8°. (*in aed. T. Bertheleti*, 1538.) L.C(lacks tp).C³.; F.

23408 — A ritch storehouse or treasurie . . . called Nobilitas literata, *tr.* by T. B(rowne, from Lyncolnes Inne.) 8°. *H. Denham*, 1570. Ent. 1569–70. L.L¹³.; F(lacks tp).HN.CAL.
   — *ed. See* 167.
   — *See also* 829, 5301.6.

23408.2 **Sturtevant, Simon.** Anglo-Latinus nomenclator Græcorum primitiuorum. E J. Scapula Lexico desumptorum. Or, the English-Latin nomenclator of Greeke primitiue words. Compiled by S. Sturteuant. 8°. *ex off. V. Sems* [sic], *imp. T. Gellebrand*, 1597. Ent. to T. Man 26 se. L(tp only, Harl.5936/345).

23408.4 — [Anr. issue? w. cancel tp, w. imprint:] *ex off. S. Macham*, 1610. O.D.; Y(lacks tp).

23408.6 — The Latin nomenclator conteining simple, primitiue, and meere latine words. 8°. *V. Sims, sold by T. Salisbury*, 1597. NMU.

23408.8 — [Anr. ed.] Anglolatinus or the Latine nomenclator. The second edition corrected and augmented. 8°. *E. Griffin, sold by T. Salisbury*, 1614. D.; Y(lacks F8).

23409 — דברי אדם [xylographic] Dibre Adam, or Adams Hebrew dictionarie. 8°. [*F. Kingston*,] 1602. O (preface only). Tobias Rodgers, London(sheet A, with only outer forme printed).

23410 — The etymologist of Æsops fables, containing the construing of his Latine fables into English: also . . . of Phædrus fables. 8°. *R. Field f. R. Dexter*, 1602. C.; F(tp def.).
   — The Latin nomenclator. 1597. *See* 23408.6.

23411 — Metallica. Or the treatise of metallica. Briefly comprehending how to neale, melt, and worke all kinde of mettle-oares. 4°. *G. Eld*, 1612 (22 my.) L.O.C².E². G².+; HN. Horblit.
   See also 21355.
   — *See also* 6455.5.

Sturton, Lord. *See* 23318.3.

Style, William, *tr. See* 6879, 12145.

23412 **Styles, Christopher.** The gaines of seeking God. In two sermons. 4°. *W. Stansby*, 1620. L.; F.

23412.5 — A receite for grace. In a sermon. 4°. *F. Kyngston*, 1620. HN.

Styles, Matthias. *See* 19044.

23413 **Styward, Thomas.** The pathwaie to martiall discipline, deuided into two bookes. 4°. *T. E[ast] f. M. Jenyngs*, 1581. Ent. 14 fb. L.C(impr. def.).DUL(imp.).*.G² (lacks tp)*.LONGLEAT.; F.HD.N.

23413.5 — [A variant, w. imprint:] *T. East f. M. Jenyngs*, 1581. L(date def.).O.; HN.LC.
   (Formerly 23415)

23414 — [Anr. ed.] 1582. Januarij decimus. The pathwaie to martiall discipline. Now newly imprinted, and deuided into three bookes. 2 pts. 4°. *T. E[ast*,) [*J. Kingston, W. How, a. J. Charlewood*,] *imp. M. Jenyngs*, [1582.] L(tp only, Harl.5965/43).L³⁸.O¹⁷. C⁸.; F.HN(lacks pt. 2).
   Pt. 2 = Bk. 3, also issued sep. as 12538. East pr. the tp to pt. 1 and all of pt 2. In pt. 1 Kingston pr. B–D, K–N, Q–T, and possibly Y; How pr. E–P; Charlewood pr. V–X.

23415 — Now = 23413.5.

Suavis, Petrus. *See* 21764.

23416 **Subject.** The subiects thankfulnesse: or, God-a-mercie good Scot. Ballad. 2 pts. s.sh.fol. [*London*,] 1640. L.

23417 **Subpoena.** A subpoena from the high imperiall court of heaven. 1617. Now = 595.6.

23418 — [Anr. ed.] 1618. Now = 595.7.

23419 — [Anr. ed.] 1620. Now = 595.8.
   — [Anr. ed.] 1623. *See* 595.9.

Suchtelensis, Aegidius. *See* 7566.

23419.5 **Suckling, Edmund.** [Headline:] A Sermon / of Obedience. [On Luke xx.25.] 8°. [*f. T. Chard a. W. Lownes*, 1590.] Ent. to W. Lownes 6 ap. 1590. LINC(lacks tp).
   See Maunsell, 17669, pt. 1, p. 105, and Arber V.157.

23420 **Suckling, Sir John.** Aglaura. [Anon.] fol. *J. Haviland f. T. Walkley*, 1638. Ent. as by Suckling 18 ap. L.O(2). O³(2, 1 imp.), 1 Evelyn).; HN.HD(lacks tp, has sub tp substituted). Greg 541.
   — [Gift-plate.] *See* Bookplates.

Sucquet, Antoine, *S.J. See* 17542.7.

Sudbury, Suffolk, *Hospital of St. Sepulchre. See* Indulgences 151 sq.

23421 Sudlow, Edward. The arraignment and executi⟨on⟩ of E. Sudlow. H. Stockley. [etc.] Who were executed at West-Chester, the three and twenty of September last. 4°. [*W. Jaggard*, 1609.] Ent. to J. Hunt 5 de. 1609. L(destroyed).; HD(photostat only).

23422 Suetonius Tranquillus, Caius. The historie of twelve cæsars. [*Tr.* P. Holland.] fol. [*H. Lownes a. G. Snowdon*] *f. M. Lownes*, 1606. Ent. 9 mr. 1605. L⁸.O¹⁸.C.HER.LIV.; CAL.ILL.LC(w. added engr. tp).PN. SMITH.+
    Letterpress tp only, omitting Holland's name. Snowdon pr. the prelims., indexes, and annotations; H. Lownes the rest.

23423 — [A variant, w. Holland's name on the letterpress tp.] *f. M. Lownes*, 1606. L.L³⁰.O.C².M.+; F.HN.HD.N.Y.+

23424 — [Anr. issue, w. letterpress tp cancelled and replaced by engr. tp, also w. Holland's name.] *f. M. Lownes*, 1606. L³.O.C.E².M³.+; F.CH.CHI.IND.NY.+
    Tp from same copperplate as 7489.

23424.3 Suffolk, *County of*. Suff.ss. Memorandum that the [   ] day [etc. Blank licence for ale-house keepers.] s.sh. fol. [*London*, c. 1625.] HN.

Suffolk, *Duchess of*. The life of the dutches of Suffolke. 1631. *See* 7242.
— The most rare history of the dutchess of Suffolke's calamity. [c. 1625.] *See* 6557.8.

Suffrage. The collegiat suffrage of the divines of Great Britaine. 1629. *See* 7070.

Suffragium. Suffragium collegiale theologorum Magnæ Britanniæ. 1626, etc. *See* 7067 sqq.

23424.5 Sulaimán I, *the Magnificent*. A true and fearfull pronouncing of warre against the Roman imperiall majesty, and withall against the king of Poland, by the late emperour of Turkey, Soloma Hometh. Confirmed by diverse letters. 4°. [*T. Harper*] *f. N. Butter*, 1640. HD.
    The vaunting letter is evidently based on one written by Sulaimán at the siege of Vienna in 1529, as the letter is dated: 'after our Nativity 39 yeares, after our mighty Reigne the tenth yeare.' It appears to have been used by Turkish or European propagandists as a form letter since slightly different versions are ascribed to Murad III in 1593 (STC 15052, p. 1024) and to Muhammad IV in 1663 (Wing S 3622A, pp. 25–6).
    The 'diverse letters', mainly from Venice, are dated 23 March–10 April 1640 and report the death of Murad IV and Turkish war news. *See* also Newsbooks 333.

23424.7 — [A ballad version.] The great Turks terrible challenge, this yeare 1640. Pronounced by Soloma Hometh. *Ballad.* 2 pts. s.sh.fol. *f. R. Harper*, [1640.] M³ (imp.).
— *See* also 22894.

Sulpitius, Joannes. Carmen iuuenile. 1572. *See* 23431.

23425 — [a1ʳ:] Pagina prima. Sulpitii Verulani oratoris prestãtissimi opus insigne grammaticum feliciter incipit. 4° mostly in 6's. (*per R. Pynson*, 1494 (4 id. ja.)) M.; PML. Duff 388.

23426 — [Anr. ed.] 4° mostly in 6's. (*p R. Pynson*, 1498.) L.C⁶. Duff 389.

23427 — [Anr. ed.] 4° in 6's. (*apud westmonasterium, per w. de worde*, 1499 (4 de.)) L.O.C. Duff 390.

23427.3 — [Anr. ed., enlarged.] Posterior editio Sulpitiana in partes tris divisa que complectuntur. Prima. De octo partibus. . . . Cũ textu ascensiano. Carmen iuuenile. Secunda. De constructione. . . . Tertia. . . . Donatũ et mancinellum de figuris. 4° mostly in 6's. (*Impressum a A. boccardo in parrhisiorũ gymnasio: ubi venũdaĩ ab J. paruo. Et a J. balduino* [i.e. *Boeidens*] *londonie & handwerpie*, 1502 (ad id. mr.)) Lyons PL.

23427.7 — [Anr. ed.] 4° ⁸·⁴. (*per W. de Worde*, 1504 (19 de.)) C(f⁴ only).SHR(lacks tp).

23427a — [Anr. ed.] Grammatice Sulpitiana cũ textu Ascẽsiano recognito & aucto. 4° in 6's. (*per R. Pynson*, 1505 (11 au.)) L.; ILL.

23427a.3 — Quĩta recognitio atꝗ additio. 4° mostly in 8's. *venundantur Lõdonijs a W. de worde* [&6ᵛ: *Paris*,] (*J. barbier, sũptibus w. de worde, Lõdon*, 1511 (4 non. ap.))

Sulpitius, Joannes—*cont.*
    [Ss8: *Paris*,] (*ex aed. J. barbier*, 1511 [i.e. 1512] (*ad non. mr.*)) L(imp.).O(imp.).GLOUC.
    Copies vary: L has Petit's device on the tp while O has de Worde's, McK. 24; L has 1st colophon as above while O has '*sũptibus J. parui*, [*Paris*].

23427a.7 — [Anr. ed.] Quinta recognitio. 4° ⁸·⁴. (*per W. de Worde*,) [1514?] ETON.G²(imp.). Ghent U.; WES.
    Preface dated 1510 ad idus Aprilis, but the device, McK. 19, is in a 1514? state.

23428 — [A1ʳ:] Stãs puer ad mensã. [A1ᵛ:] Joannis Sulpitii Verulani de moribus pueroꝛ carmen iuuenile ab Ascensio explanatum. [Verse w. prose commentary.] 4° in 6. (*per W. de Worde*, 1515.) L.MARL(imp.). 𝔄

23428a — [Anr. ed.] 4° in 6. (*per w. de worde*, 1516.) M.

23428a.5 — [Anr. ed.] 4° in 6. (*per R. Pynson*, 1516.) M.

23429 — [Anr. ed.] 4° in 6. (*per w. de worde*, 1518.) L.C⁴.

23429.5 — [Anr. ed.] 4° in 6. (*in ed. w. de worde*, 1520.) C⁷.

23429a — [Anr. ed.] Pristine rursus valetudini per W. de Worde restitutum. 4° in 6. (*in ed. W. de Worde*, 1524 (prid. kal. no.)) L.

23429a.5 — [Anr. ed.] 4° in 6. [*Southwark, P. Treveris f.*] (*per me J. boteler*,) [1530?] P.

23430 — Now = 17030.5.

23431 — [Anr. ed., enlarged.] Sulpitii Verulani carmen iuuenile. (Dialogi pueriles.) 8°. *J. Kyngstonus*, 1572. Ent. to J. King 1557–58; to W. Norton 1562–63. HN.

23431.3 — [Anr. ed., without commentary or dialogues.] Ioan. Sulpitii Verulani, de moribus & civilitate puerorum carmen. 8° in 4. *Edinburgi, A. Hart*, 1619. E².

23431.7 — [Anr. ed.] 8° in 4. *Edinburgi, R. Bryson*, 1639. CU.
— ed. *See* 16882.

Sum. A compendyouse somme of the very christen relygyon. 1535. *See* 14821.

23432 — A short summe of the trueth which is according to godlines. s.sh.fol. [*London*,] 1592. L.

23432.3 — The summe of christian religion, comprehended in six principall questions, serving for instruction of the simpler sort. 8°. *T. Creed f. T. Man*, 1607. E². A different text from 23111.

23432.5 — [Anr. ed.] 8°. *F. Kyngston f. T. Man*, 1617. O.
— The summe of christianitie, reduced vnto eight propositions. [1578, etc.] *See* 21183.

23432.7 — [Heading A1ʳ:] The summe of christianitie, set downe in familiar questions and answers. 8°. [*London*, c. 1600.] F.
    Collates A⁸; text in 8 sections, beginning: 'There haue bene alwayes, are, & will be . . . such as denie the Lord.' Film of F copy on Univ. Microfilms reel 561 ('21183a').
— The sũ of diuinitie. 1548, etc. *See* 23004 sqq.
— The summe of true catholike doctrine: plainly laid downe. 1613. *See* 24282.5.
— The summe of what I have written concerning mathematickes. [1638?] *See* 19564.5.

23433 — A sum or a brief collection of holy signes, sacrifices and sacraments. *Tr.* out of French by N. Lynge. 8°. *R. Hall*, 1563. Ent. 1562–63. L(tp only, Harl.5919/74). O¹⁰.C.C³.P.+; F.U(lacks tp).

23433.5 — [Anr. ed., omitting translator's name, w. 5 more tracts.] Six godlie treatises necessarie for christian instruction. 8°. *N. Okes f. L. Becket*, 1608. Ent. to Okes to print for the Company 6 jy. 1607. L.L⁴.C. (Formerly 5161)

23434 — [Anr. issue, w. new prelims., including dedic. to Sir Wm. Cavendish.] A summe or a briefe collection of holy signes. [*S. Stafford*] *f. W. C[otton,]* 1609. L. O(imp.).

23434.5 — [Anr. issue, omitting prelims., w. cancel tp:] A most godly and worthy treatis of holy signes. [*S. Stafford*] *f. G. H[umble?]* 1609. E.
— The totall summe. 1639. *See* 11117.

Sum, Es, Fui. *See* 23155.4, 23163.4.

Summer Islands. Orders and constitutions. 1622. *See* 1905.

Summers, William. A pleasant history. 1637. *See* 22917.5.

Supper. The souper of the Lorde. 1533. *See* 24468 sqq.

Supplicatio. Supplicatio ad imperatorem. 1513 [i.e. 1613.] *See* 1703.

Supplication. An humble supplicacion vnto God. 1554. *See* 1730.

Supplication—*cont.*
— A most humble supplication. 1620. *See* 563.5.
— A supplicacyon for the beggers. [1529?] *See* 10883.
— The supplication of certaine masse-priests. 1604. *See* 14430.
— The supplication of Great Brittaines friends. 1628. *See* 10021.4.
— A supplication of the Family of Love. 1606. *See* 10683.

23435 — The supplicacion. O most dere [etc.] 1554. = 1730.
23435.5 — A supp⟨lication⟩ of the p⟨oor⟩ cōmons. 8°. [*London?* 1546.] C.
While spelling is 'normal' for London printing, the fact that the 62 mm. textura fount has no upper-case W nor 'sh' ligature may indicate continental (Dutch?) printing. Authorship has been attrib. to R. Crowley and to H. Brinkelow; reprinted in 10884.
— The supplicacion: that the nobles made vnto Ferdinandus. [1543?] *See* 10808.
— A supplycacion to Henry the eyght. 1544. *See* 24165.
— A supplication to the kings most excellent majestie. 1604. *See* 14432.

Surat. Two memorable relations. The former, of conflicts at Surat. 1631. *See* 20865.

23435a **Surdit.** [A prose romance, of Surdit, king of Ireland. c. 1510.] Now = 20107.5.

Sureau, Hugues. *See* 7368 sq.

Surphlet, Richard, *tr. See* 7304, 10547.

Surprisal. The surprisall of two imperial townes. 1622. *See* Newsbooks 65.

Surrey, Earl of. *See* 13860.

Survey. A surveigh and critique censure. 1615. *See* 4792.
— A suruay of the pretended holy discipline. 1593. *See* 1352.

Surveying. Surueyenge. [1533? etc.] *See* 11006.5 sqq.

23435a.5 **Susanna.** The ballad of constant Susanna. *Ballad.* 1/2 sh.fol. [*G. Purslowe*] *f. H. Gosson,* [c. 1625.] Ent. to T. Colwell 1562–63; to J. Wolfe 8 se. 1592; to ballad ptnrs. 14 de. 1624. C⁶.
23435a.7 — [Anr. ed.] 1/2 sh.fol. *assignes of T. Symcocke,* [1628–29.] M³(imp.).
23436 — [Anr. ed., w. title:] An excellent ballad intituled, The constancy of Susanna. 2 pts. s.sh.fol. *f. J. Wright,* [c. 1640.] L.
— Susanna: or, the arraignment of the elders. 1622. *See* 1003.

23437 **Susenbrotus, Joannes.** Σὺν δὲ θεοὶ μάκαρες. Epitome troporum ac schematum et grammaticorum & rhetorum. 8°. *ap. G. Dewes,* 1562. C.
23438 — [Anr. ed.] 8°. *in æd. H. Wykes,* 1570. L.; Union College, Schenectady, N.Y.
B1ʳ last line: 'latēs'.
23438.3 — [Anr. ed.] 8°. *in æd. H. Wykes,* 1572. LK.
The last digit in the date is badly inked and might be a 'I'. B1ʳ last line: 'latens'.
23438.7 — [Anr. ed.] 8°. *in æd. H. Middelton,* 1574. L(tp only, Harl.5927/348).
23439 — [Anr. ed.] 8°. *J. Kyngstonus,* 1576. O.D².
23439.5 — [Anr. ed.] 8°. *G. Robisonus* [sic], 1586. Ass'd from Kingston and Robinson to T. Orwin 7 my. 1593. L(tp only, Harl. 5919/60).
O³ has a copy lacking tp which collates A–G⁸ like 23437–9 but has the main text in roman type like 23440 sqq. and might be this ed.
23440 — [Anr. ed.] 8°. [*G. Eld,*] *ex typ. Soc. Stat.,* 1608. L.O.
23440.3 — [Anr. ed.] 8°. [*F. Kingston,*] *ex typ. Soc. Stat.,* 1612. O³.C¹⁰.
23440.7 — [Anr. ed.] 8°. [*F. Kingston,*] *ex typ. Soc. Stat.,* 1616. L(tp only, Harl.5937/220).SAL.
23441 — [Anr. ed.] 8°. [*F. Kingston,*] *ex typ. Soc. Stat.,* 1621. Ent. to the English Stock 5 mr. 1620. L.; HN.ILL.
23442 — [Anr. ed.] 8°. [*F. Kingston,*] *ex typ. Soc. Stat.,* 1627. O².O¹⁷(imp.).
23443 — [Anr. ed.] 8°. [*F. Kingston,*] *ex typ. Soc. Stat.,* 1635. O.; ILL.

23443.5 **Suso, Henry.** Certayne sweete prayers of the glorious name of Iesus, commonly called, Iesus mattens. [*Tr.* from Latin.] 16° in 8's. [*W. Carter,* 1575–78.] L.
A&R 801. Other versions, in Latin and in English, are found in some Sarum primers, e.g. 15899 and 15992.

23444 **Sussex.** Articles of enquirie to be ministred concerning the admiraltie in the county of Sussex. 4°. B. *A[lsop] f. R. Meighen,* 1638. L.
23445 — [Anr. ed.] 4°. *R. Hearne,* 1640. HN.
23445.5 — The constant wife of Sussex. *Ballad.* 2 pts. s.sh.fol. *f. F. Coles,* [1632?] Ent. to ballad ptnrs. 24 my. 1632. C⁶.

23446 **Sustain.** Susteine, absteine, kepe well in your mind. [An exhortation to abstain from controversy. In verse.] s.sh.fol. [*J. Cawood,* c. 1555.] L⁵(Lemon 14).

23447 **Sutcliffe, Alice.** Meditations of man's mortalitie. Or, a way to true blessednesse. The second edition, enlarged. [Partly in verse.] 12°. B. *A[lsop] a. T. F[awcet] f. H. Seyle,* 1634. Ent. 30 ja. 1633. L.P.; F.HN.

23448 **Sutcliffe, Matthew.** An abridgement or survey of poperie, opposed unto [14913]. 4°. *M. Bradwood f. C. Burbie,* 1606. L.O.C.BIRM²(K.N.).D.+; F.HN.BO³. NY¹¹.U.
23449 — Matthæi Sutliuii Aduersus Roberti Bellarmini de purgatorio disputationem, liber unus. 4°. *G. Bishop, R. Newberie & R. Barker,* 1599. Ent. 9 fb. 1600. L.O⁴. C.D.DUR⁵.+; U.
23450 — An answere to a certaine libel supplicatorie [1521]. 4°. *deputies of C. Barker,* 1592. L.O.C².DUR⁵.G².+; F.HN. BO³.U.Y.+
Answered by 24055.
23451 — An answere vnto a certaine calumnious letter published by M. J. Throkmorton [24055]. 4°. *deputies of C. Barker,* 1595. Ent. to G. Bishop, R. Newbery a. R. Barker 16 jn. L.O.C.D.DUR⁵.+; F.HN.U.Y.
Includes reprint of the letter.
— Apologia pro Christiano Batavo. 1610. *See* 1708.
— The blessings on mount Gerizzim. [1625?] *See* 23466.
23452 — A briefe examination, of a certaine peremptorie menacing and disleal petition [4835] presented, by certaine laye papistes. 4°. [*R. Bradock*] *f. W. Cotton,* 1606. Ent. to C. Burbie 26 de. 1604. L.L².YK(2).; HN.
Includes reprint of the petition.
23452a — [Anr. issue, w. cancel tp:] The petition apologeticall of lay papists, . . . contradicted, examined, glozzed, and refuted. [*R. Bradock*] *f. W. Cotton a. W. Welby,* 1606. L.O.O³.C.E.+; F.
23452a.5 — [Anr. issue, w. cancel tp reset:] The petition, of lay papistes. [*R. Bradock*] *f. W. Cotton a. W. Welby,* 1606. F.
23453 — A briefe replie to a certaine odious libel [19415], lately published by a Jesuite N. D. Hereunto is added a new Challenge to N. D. Together with a briefe refutation of [1st ed. of 19413]. [Init. O. E.] 4° in 8's. *A. Hatfield,* 1600. Ent. to E. Bollifant a. Hatfield 8 de. L.O.C.D.DUR⁵.+; F.HN. HD.N.U.+
Answered by 18754, 19418, 19413, 24994.5.
23454 — A challenge concerning the romish church [1st pub'd in 23453], now againe reuiewed, enlarged, and fortified. Thereunto also is annexed an answere unto [18754]. 2 pts. 4° in 8's. *A. Hatfield,* [*J. Windet, a. J. Harrison 3,*] 1602. L.O.C.D.DUR⁵.+; F.HN.BO³.U.Y.+
Hatfield pr. pt. 1; in pt. 2 Windet app. pr. A–D and E outer sheet; Harrison pr. E inner sheet and the rest. Answered by 19413.
23455 — Matthæi Sutliuii De catholica, orthodoxa, et vera Christi ecclesia, libri duo. 4°. *Reg. typog.* [*deputies of C. Barker,*] 1592. L².O.C.D.E.+; F.
— Matthæi Sutlivii De concilijs. 1600. *See* 23462.
23456 — Matthæi Sutliuii De missa papistica, . . . aduersus R. Bellarminum, libri quinque. 2 pts. 4° in 8's. *per A. Islip,* 1603. Ent. 6 de. 1602. L.O.D.E.P.+; F(pt. 1 only).HN.U(pt. 1 only).
See Greg, *Register B,* p. 92.
— Matthæi Sutlivii De monachis. 1600. *See* 23462.
23457 — Matthæi Sutliuii De pontifice romano, aduersùs R. Bellarminum, libri quinque. 4°. *G. Bishop, R. Newberie & R. Barker,* 1599. Ent. 9 fb. 1600. L.O.C.D.DUR⁵.+; F.

Sutcliffe, Matthew—*cont.*

23458 — De presbyterio, eiusque noua in ecclesia christiana politeia. 4°. *G. Bishop & R. Newbery,* 1591. Ent. 3 jy. L.O.C.D.E².+; HD.ILL.

23459 — Matthæi Sutlivii De recta studij theologici ratione, liber unus. Adjunctus est breuis de concionum ad populum formulis, libellus. (Religionis christianæ prima institutio.) 2 pts. 8°. *ap. M. Bradwood,* 1602. L².O.C(lacks pt. 2).A.DUR⁵.+; F.

23460 — De turcopapismo, hoc est, de Turcarum & papistarum aduersùs Christi ecclesiam & fidem coniuratione, liber unus. Adiuncti sunt, aduersus Gulielmi Giffordi Caluinoturcismum libri quatuor. [Anon.] 4°. *G. Bishop, R. Newberie & R. Barker,* 1599. Ent. 9 fb. 1600. L.O.C.D.DUR⁵.+; F.U.

23461 — [Anr. ed., init. T. M. S.] 8°. *Londini, G. Bishop, R. Newberie & R. Barker* [actually *Hanau,*] 1604. L.O.C.G².LYD.+; HN.HD.PN.

23462 — Matthæi Sutlivii De vera Christi ecclesia adversus R. Bellarminum, liber unus. (De concilijs.—De monachis.) 4° in 8's. *E. Bollifantus,* 1600. Ent. to Bollifant a. A. Hatfield 8 de. L.O.C².D.E².+; F.HN.CHI(3rd pt. only).U.Y.

23463 — The examination of M. Thomas Cartwrights late apologie [4706]. 4°. *deputies of C. Barker,* 1596. L.O.C².D.YK.+; F.BO³.NY.Y.

23464 — The examination and confutation of a certaine scurrilous treatise [14913] published by M. Kellison. 4°. *E. Allde f. R. Serger a. E. Weaver,* 1606. Ent. 4 mr. L.O.C.D(imp.).E².+; F.HN.HD.U.Y.+

23465 — A ful and round answer to N. D. alias R. Parsons his Warne-word [19418]. 4° in 8's. [*R. Field*] *f. G. Bishop,* 1604. Ent. 27 jn. L.O.C(lacks tp).D.E.+; F. HN.BO³.CHI.HD.+

23466 — [Anr. issue, w. cancel tp:] The blessings on mount Gerizzim. Or, the happie estate of protestants. By M. S. doctor of divinitie. *f. A. Hebb,* [1625?] L(2). O.C⁵.; HD.NY.Y.
   One L and HD copies also have the dedic., A2–4, cancelled.

23467 — [Anr. issue, w. A1–7 cancelled, w. tp:] A true relation of Englands happinesse; under the raigne of queene Elizabeth. And the miserable estate of papists, under the popes tyrany. By M. S. [*London,*] 1629. L.C.; F.
   — The petition apologeticall examined. 1606. *See* 23452a.
   — The petition, of lay papistes. 1606. *See* 23452a.5.

23468 — The practice, proceedings, and lawes of armes. 4°. *deputies of C. Barker,* 1593. L.O.C.D.E².+; F.HN.HD. ILL.Y.+
   Possibly by a different Sutcliffe as in the dedic. (B4ᵛ) he refers to his book as 'all which I have wonne not onely by long observation, but also by dangerous experience both in France, Italy, Flanders, and Portugall.'
   — Religionis christianæ prima institutio. 1602. *See* pt. 2 of 23459.

23469 — The subversion of Robert Parsons his confused and worthlesse worke [19416]. 4° in 8's. [*R. Field*] *f. J. Norton,* 1606. L.O.C.D².E.+; F.HN.HD.MICH.U.+

23470 — A threefold answer unto the third part of a certaine triobolar treatise [19416]. 4° in 8's. [*R. Field*] *f. J. Norton,* 1606. L.O.C.D.E.+; F.ILL.PN.U.

23471 — A treatise of ecclesiasticall discipline. 4°. *G. Bishop a. R. Newberie,* 1590 (1591.) Ent. 3 jy. 1591. L.L².O.E⁴. YK.+; F.HN.HD.U(imp.).

23472 — [Anr. ed.] Newly corrected and amended. 4°. [*Eliot's Court Press f.*] *G. Bishop,* 1591. L.O.C.D.STU.+; F. HN.HD.ILL.Y.+

23473 — The unmasking of a masse-monger. In the counterfeit habit of S. Augustine. 4°. *B. A[lsop] a. T. Fawcet f. N. Bourne,* 1626. Ent. 21 ap. and 12 jn. L.O.C².E². LEIC.+; BO.HD.U.
   Attacks 910.
   — *See also* 14429.5.

Sutton, *Doctor. See* Sutton, T.

Sutton, *Mother. See* 25872.

23474 **Sutton, Christopher.** Disce mori. Learne to die. A religious discourse. 12°. [*J. Windet f.*] *J. Wolfe,* 1600. Ent. 21 au. L.C.NOR².; CAL².

23475 — [Anr. ed.] 12°. [*J. Windet f.*] *J. Wolfe, sold by C. Burby,* 1601. Ent. to Wolfe a. Burby 19 ja. BIRM(imp.).DUL.; F.HN.

23475.5 — [Anr. ed.] 12°. *J. Windet f. C. Burby,* 1602. O³.; CHI.
23476 — [Anr. ed.] 12°. *J. Windet f. C. Burby,* 1604. L.; F.HD.

Sutton, Christopher—*cont.*

23477 — [Anr. ed.] Newly enlarged. 12°. *J. Windet f. C. Burby,* 1607. O.; F.ILL.Y.

23478 — [Anr. ed.] 12°. *J. Windet f. widdew Burby,* 1609. Ass'd by E. Burby to W. Welby 16 oc. L.BIRM. Stevens Cox.; F.HN.

23479 — [Anr. ed.] 12°. *f. A. Garbrand,* 1613. Ass'd by Welby to Garbrand 15 jn. 1610. Wolfe's pt. ass'd to J. Pindley 27 ap. 1612. C.C².; NY¹¹. Arthur Freeman, Cambridge, Mass.
   See Court-Book C, p. 56.

23480 — [Anr. ed.] 12°. *G. Purslowe f. N. Bourne,* 1616. Pindley's pt. ass'd to Purslowe 2 no. 1613; Garbrand's pt. ass'd to Bourne 22 mr. 1616. L.O.C⁵.; F.HN.LC.

23481 — [Anr. ed.] 12°. *G. Purslowe f. N. Bourne,* 1618. L(lacks H1).O(tp only).; F.ILL.

23482 — [Anr. ed.] 1626. Now = pt. 2 of 23488.
23483 — Disce vivere. Learne to live. 12°. *J. Windet f. C. Burby,* 1602. Ent. 7 no. 1601. L(date cropt).O.C(lacks tp). G².NLW.; F.HN.
   (Formerly also 23485)

23484 — [Anr. ed.] Perused and corrected. 12°. *E. Short f. C. Burby,* [1604?] L.C. Broxbourne(O).; F(imp.).HD.NY.

23485 — = 23483.
23485.5 — [Anr. ed.] 12°. *f. E. Burby,* 1608. E.; Y.
23486 — [Anr. ed.] 12°. *T. S[nodham] f. N. Bourne,* 1611. Ass'd 16 oc. 1609. L.L³⁰.O.DUL.NOR².; F.HN.

23487 — Fourth edition. 12°. *W. J[ones] f. N. Bourne,* 1617. L.O³.A.

23488 — [Anr. ed., w. pt. 2 added and gen. tp:] Disce vivere: learne to live. Disce mori: learne to dye. Two briefe treatises joyned together. 2 pts. 12°. *J. D[awson;* pt. 2:] (*R. Badger a. G. Miller) f. N. Bourne,* 1626. Ass'd to J. Beale 27 my. 1623; entry cancelled 20 ap. 1625 with rights returning to Bourne. O(lacks gen. tp).WI.; F.

23489 — [Anr. ed.] 2 pts. 12°. *J. B(eal) a. T. B(rudenell) f. N. Bourne,* 1629. O.C³.; F.U.

23490 — [Anr. ed.] 2 pts. 12°. *R. Badger f. the partners of the Irish Stock,* 1634. L.O.C¹⁹.; F.HN.ILL(pt. 1 only).N.

23491 — Godly meditations upon the most holy sacrament of the Lordes supper. In the end. De eucharistiæ controversia, admonitio brevis. 12°. *J. W[indet,] sold by C. Burby,* 1601. Ent. to J. Wolfe 13 ja. and to Wolfe a. Burby 19 ja. L.O⁴.O¹⁰.C. Stevens Cox.; F.HN.TEX.

23492 — [Anr. ed., enlarged, w. the Admonitio *tr.* into English.] 12°. *T. S[nodham] f. N. Bourne,* 1613. Burby's pt. ass'd to Bourne 16 oc. 1609; Wolfe's pt. ass'd to Pindley 27 ap. 1612, to Bourne 25 jn. 1612. The assignment of Pindley's pt. to G. Purslowe 2 no. 1613 is crossed out. L.O².C².; F(imp.).

23493 — [Anr. ed.] 12°. *W. Jaggard f. N. Bourne,* 1616. L.O. DUL.; F.U.

23493.5 — [Anr. ed.] 12°. *J. Dawson f. N. Bourne,* 1622. O³¹.; F. HD(tp def.).

23493.7 — [Anr. ed.] 12°. *G. M[iller] a. R. B[adger] f. N. Bourne, sold by H. Perrie,* 1626. C.

23494 — [Anr. ed.] 12°. *R. Badger f. N. Bourne,* 1630. L.C.C³. BTU.; F.MCG.U.

23495 — [Anr. ed.] 12°. *R. Badger f. N. Bourne,* 1635. L. O(imp.).; F.HD.

23495.5 **Sutton, Edward.** Anthropophagus: or, a caution for the credulous. A morall discourse upon [Prov. xxvi.25. Init. E. S., *B. of D.*] 4°. [*G. Eld*] *f. J. Marriot,* 1623. Ent. as by Sutton 19 jn. 1623. O⁶.O¹⁰.; HD.Y.

23496 — [Anr. ed.] Anthropophagus: the man-eater. Or a caution [etc.] 4°. *G. E[ld] f. J. Marriot,* 1624. L.O.C². STU.YK.+; F(3).HN.HD.Y. Sydney U.

23497 — [Anr. issue, w. dedic. cancelled and cancel tp:] The serpent anatomized. A morall discourse. By E. Sutton. 4°. [*M. Flesher*] *f. J. Marriot,* 1626. L.O.C. C³.D.; CAL(imp.).

23498 **Sutton, J.** A newe reuenge for an olde grudge. Lately sette foorth by J. S[utton. Anti-Catholic pamphlet.] 8°. *H. Wykes f. F. Coldocke,* [1567.] Ent. as by Sutton 1566–67. L².

23499 **Sutton, Thomas.** The christians jewell, to adorne the heart of every protestant taken out of Sᵗ Mary Overis church in the lecturship of doctor Sutton 1624. [Engr. w. text, including verses by W. Grant.] s.sh.fol. *sold by T. Jener,* [1624.] L⁵ (Lemon 231).

23500 — Englands summons. A sermon preached at Pauls Crosse the third of January, 1612. 8°. *W. Hall f. M. Law,* 1613. L(2).L¹⁵.O(imp.).C.; F.HN.NY.NY¹¹.U.

Sutton, Thomas—*cont.*

23501 — Englands second summons. A sermon. 8º. *E. Griffin f. M. Lawe*, 1615. O.

23502 — Englands first and second summons. The second impression, perused and corrected. 8º. *N. Okes f. M. Law*, 1616. L(tp def.).O².P.; F(tp def.).

23503 — Third impression. 12º. *J. Norton*, 1633. L.O.C.M².YK. +; F.HN.

23504 — The good fight of faith. A sermon preached unto the gentlemen of the Artillery Garden. 4º. *H. Lownes f. R. Milbourne*, 1624. Ent. 11 fb. L.O.C.D.YK.+; HN. NY¹¹.

23505 — Jethroes counsell to Moses: or, a direction for magistrates. A sermon preached March 5. 1621. 4º. *W. Jones*, 1631. Ent. 3 jy. 1630. L.O.C².G².YK.+; F.HN. HD.N.Y.+

23506 — King James his hospitall. 1618. Now = 5056.5.

23507 — Lectures upon the eleventh chapter to the Romans. [*Ed.* J. Downame.] 4º in 8's. *J. H[aviland] f. N. Bourne*, 1632. Ent. 12 jy. 1631. L.O.C.D.G⁴.+; F.HN. HD.U.Y.+

23507.5 **Sutton, William,** *Senior.* A seminary priest put to a nonplus. Or, a christian and modest answere, to certaine Motives sent by a popish priest to a worthy gentleman. [Anon.] 4º. [*B. Alsop a. T. Fawcet*] *f. W. Sheeres*, 1629. L.O.DUL.E.M².+; F.HN.U.
(Formerly 22184) Includes text of the Motives, app. pr. from MS.

23508 — [Anr. ed., corrected, w. title:] The falshood of the cheife grounds of the romish religion. Descried in a briefe answere to certaine Motives. By W. S. [*Ed.*] (W. Sutton, *jun.*) 12º. [*Oxford, L. Lichfield*] *f. the author*, 1635. O.; U.
As Sutton, sen., died in 1632, the 'author' referred to in the imprint is prob. the son.

Sutton, William, *Junior, ed. See 23508.*

23509 **Swadling, Thomas.** Sermons, meditations, and prayers, upon the plague. 1636. [Init. T. S.] 8º. *N. a. J. Okes f. J. Benson*, 1637. Ent. as by Swadling 28 fb. L.L¹⁶. M.M⁴.PLUME.; HD.

23510 **Swadon, William.** In obitum serenissimæ principis, Annæ, carmen funebre. s.sh.fol. [*B. Norton a. J. Bill*, 1619.] L⁵(Lemon 163–4).

23511 — [Anr. ed., w. heading in English:] Upon the death of queene Anne, wife of king James. Funerall verses. *Lat.* s.sh.fol. [*N. Okes*, 1623.] = pt. of 4523.
Even when found separately (e.g. at L, F, HD) the sheet shows signs of folding and usually retains the instructions at the bottom for binding in after p. 344.

Swain. An excellent sonnet: or, the swaines complaint. [1633?] *See 22925.*

23511.5 **Swaine, Richard.** A table concerning Christ our advocate, and whether remission of sinnes once obtained, can againe be made frustrate. s.sh.fol. [*N. Okes*] *f. H. Bell*, 1615. L⁵(Lemon 148).

23512 **Swale, Christopher.** Jacobs vow. A sermon preached before his majestie, at Hampton Court. 4º. *J. Bill*, 1621. L.YK.; F.HD.

Swallow, Thomas. Almanacks. 1628, etc. *See 517 sqq.*

Swan, John, *of Christ's College, Camb., tr. See 6229.*

23513 **Swan, John,** *of Trinity College, Camb., Senior.* Profanomastix. Or, a briefe and necessarie direction concerning the respects wee owe to God, and his house. 4º. *J. D[awson,] sold by D. Pakeman*, 1639. Ent. to J. Dawson 17 oc. 1638. L.O¹⁰.C².D.E.+; F.NY.U.

23514 — Redde debitum. Or, a discourse in defence of three chiefe fatherhoods, first intended for the pulpit, extended since to a larger tract. 4º partly in 8's. *J. D[awson] f. J. Williams*, 1640. Ent. 29 no. 1639. L.O.C⁵.D².G².+; F.HN.ILL(imp.).NY¹¹.U.

23515 — A sermon, pointing out the chiefe causes, and cures, of such unruly stirres, as are not seldome found in the church of God. 4º. *J. D[awson,] sold by D. Pakeman*, 1639. O.O¹⁰.C².D.P.+; F.HART.HD.PH.

23516 **Swan, John,** *of Trinity College, Camb., Junior.* Speculum mundi. Or a glasse representing the face of the world. Whereunto is joyned an Hexameron, or discourse of creation. 4º. *prs. to the Univ. of Camb.*, 1635. L.O. C.D.E⁵.+; F.HN.HD(lacks engr. tp).N.U.+
The engr. tp has imprint: '*T. Buck a. R. Daniel*'.

23517 **Swan, John,** *Student in Divinity.* A true and briefe report, of Mary Glovers vexation, and of her deliverance by fastinge and prayer. 8º in 4's. [*London?*] 1603. L.L²².G²(lacks tp).

Swayne, W., *Publisher. See 6220, 6221.*

Sweden. The king of Swethens progresse into Germanie. 1632. *See 12534.4.*

23517.5 — A short survey of the kingdome of Sweden. [An abridged *tr.* by J. Story, *Gent.* of Suecia, sive de Suecorum regis dominiis, 1631, *ed.* H. Soter.] 4º. [*J. Beale*] *f. M. Sparke*, 1632. Ent. 31 ja. L.O¹³.C.D². DUR⁵.+; F.HD.ILL.

23518 — [Anr. issue, w. pt. 2 added and cancel tp:] A short survey or history of the kingdome of Sweden. With a Genealogy and pedegree of the kings of Sweden. 2 pts. [*J. Beale*] *f. M. Sparke, sold by J. Boler*, 1632. O(3, 2 imp.).C⁵.BIRM.D.; HN.IND.Y.
Pt. 2 also issued separately as 13458.

23518.5 — [Anr. issue, w. quire A cancelled, and cancel tp:] The history of Gustavus Adolphus, now king of Sweden. *J. B[eale] f. J. Boler*, 1633. E.; F.
Film of F copy on Univ. Microfilms reel 714 ('12534a'). F is separate; E has 13458 bd. w. it.

23519 **Swedish Devotion.** The Swedish devotion. Expressed by certaine prayers. 8º. *T. Cotes f. J. Bartlet*, 1632. Ent. 18 my. and crossed out. O.C⁵.
An unauthorized ed.; *see 23519.5.*

23519.5 **Swedish Discipline.** The devotions and formes of prayer, daily used in the king of Swedens army: being the first part of our intended booke concerning the Swedish discipline. The reason for our publishing this by it selfe, looke for in the epistle. [*Tr.* Sir T. Roe? or W. Watts?] 4º. [*J. Dawson*] *f. N. Butter a. N. Bourne*, 1632. L.O.C¹³.
The Stationer's Epistle deplores the trans. in 23519 and suggests buying the present item and keeping it 'till next weeke that the other two Parts come out also: at which time they may be bound together, as was at first intended. The second part of the Intelligencer [23524] is likewise now in hand.'

23520 — [Anr. issue, w. the complete text, and new prelims.] The Swedish discipline, religious, civile, and military. The first . . . second . . . third part. Last of all, is the famous battell of Leipsich, in two fayre figures also set forth: and now this second time more fully and particularly described. *J. Dawson*, [*B. Alsop a. T. Fawcet*] *f. N. Butter a. N. Bourne*, 1632. Ent. 28 my. L.O.C.DUR⁵.E.+; F.HN.CU.HD.N.+
Also issued as pt. 5 of 23525.2; advertised in Newsbooks 255, 258. Alsop and Fawcet pr. 2nd F–M. The 2 engraved plates titled respectively: 'The figure of the Battell of Leipsich fought the 7ᵗʰ of September 1631 as it was first ranged' and 'The figure of the battell as it was in fighting when Tilley was overthrowing' are frequently missing; present in O,C,MICH copies.

Swedish Intelligence. September 1. Numb. 42. The continuation of our Swedish intelligence. 1632. *See Newsbooks 266.*

23521 **Swedish Intelligencer.** The Swedish Intelligencer. The first part. [By W. Watts.] 4º. [*J. Dawson*] *f. N. Butter a. N. Bourne*, 1632. Ent. 9 ja. L.C².DUL.E. YK.+; HN.BO².MICH.NY.Y.+

23522 — [Anr. ed.] Newly revised, and corrected. 4º. [*J. Dawson*] *f. N. Butter a. N. Bourne*, 1632. L.O.C.C⁴. E⁴.+; F.HN.Y. Indiana State U.

23523 — [Anr. ed.] Now the third time, revised, corrected, and augmented. 4º. [*J. Dawson*] *f. N. Butter a. N. Bourne*, 1632. L.O.C.D⁸.E.+; F.HN.HD.N.TEX.+
First 2 quires reimposed from 23522.

23523.5 — [Anr. ed.] Now the fourth time, revised. 4º. [*J. Legat*] *f. N. Butter a. N. Bourne*, 1634. O⁶.O¹⁰.D.G².; CU. ILL.
Also issued as pt. 1 of 23525.2.

Swedish Intelligencer—*cont.*

23524 —— The second part. [By W. Watts.] 4°. [*J. Legat a. J. Dawson*] *f. N. Butter a. N. Bourne*, 1632. Ent. 19 jy.
2 sections are found in 2 settings. Quires A–F are distinguished by A1ʳ having:
(1) a 10-line initial, pr. by Dawson.
(2) an 8-line initial, pr. by Legat.
Quires L, N–O, Q–V, Z, Aa, Cc–Dd are in both settings app. pr. by Legat and are distinguished by Z1ʳ line 2 having:
(3) 'townes'
(4) 'Townes'
Copies w. the above imprint are found w. the following combination of quires:
i. has 1, 3. L(C.133.c.1).E.; F.

23524a —— [A variant, w. imprint:] *J. L[egat a. J. Dawson*] *f. N. Butter a. N. Bourne*, 1632.
Copies with the above imprint are found with the following combinations of quires:
i. has 1, 3. L².O⁹.C².C⁵.YK.+; F.
ii. has 1, 4. L.O⁶.C.DUR⁵.NEP.+; HN.HD.ILL.MICH.Y.+
iii. has 2, 3. L(1054.i.19).O.C.C².DUL.+; MCG.N.
iv. has 2, 4. L³.O.C.D.E.+; HN.CU.TEX.WASH².

23525 —— The third part. Unto which is added the fourth part. [Both by W. Watts.] 2 pts. 4°. *J. L[egat a. M. Flesher*] *f. N. Butter a. N. Bourne*, 1633. Ent. 13 fb. L.O.C.E.M.+; F.HN.CU.HD(imp.).MICH.+
Flesher pr. the Fourth Part. A1ʳ line 1 of text: 'euen'; Aa2ʳ line 2 of text: 'cõming' (most copies) or 'comming' (MICH, an early, badly spaced state of this line).

23525.1 —— [Anr. ed.] 2 pts. 4°. *J. L[egat a. M. Flesher*] *f. N. Butter a. N. Bourne*, 1633. L(in 23525.2).O⁶.D.DUR⁵.G².+; CAL². ILL.Y (Third part only).
Flesher pr. the Fourth Part. A1ʳ line 1 of text: 'even'; Aa2ʳ line 2 of text: 'com-' (most copies) or 'con-' (CAL²).

23525.2 — [A reissue of 23523.5, 23524a(ii), 23525.1, 23520, w. gen. tp:] The Swedish Intelligencer, compleat: all 4 parts; with the Discipline. 5 pts. 4°. *f. N. Butter a. N. Bourne*, 1634. L Stockholm RL. Lord Kenyon (w. 23523 as pt. 1). Mrs. Folke Dahl, Lund, Sweden.
The Stockholm copy has an inserted dedic. to Queen Christina by W. Watts.

23525.3 —— The continuation of the German history. The fifth part [of the Swedish Intelligencer.] 4°. [*T. Harper*] *f. N. Butter a. N. Bourne*, 1633. Ent. 23 oc. O.O¹⁷.
Tp lines 8–9: 'downe to/ this present time.'

23525.4 — [Anr. issue, w. cancel tp.] [*T. Harper*] *f. N. Butter a. N. Bourne*, 1633. L.O.C.DUR⁵.E.+; HN.CU(tp def.)*. MICH(tp def.)*.
(Formerly 11783) Tp lines 8–9: 'downe,/ To the late Treaty in Silesia, . . .'

23525.5 — The history of the present warres of Germany. A sixt part [of the Swedish Intelligencer.] 4°. *T. Harper f. N. Butter a. N. Bourne*, 1634. Ent. 2 jn. L.O.O⁶.C². PETYT.+; F.CU.HD.MICH.Y.
(Formerly 11790)

23525.6 — A supplement to the sixth part of the Germane history [i.e. of the Swedish Intelligencer.] 4°. *T. H[arper, M. Flesher, a. Eliz. Allde?*] *f. N. Butter a. N. Bourne*, 1634. Ent. 25 jn. O.O⁶.O¹⁴.O¹⁷.; CU.HD.
Harper pr. A–E and I3–6 (pp. 57–64); Flesher pr. G–I (pp. 37–56); Eliz. Allde app. pr. I, L (pp. 61–75).

23525.7 — The German history continued. The seventh part [of the Swedish Intelligencer. By N. C.] 4°. [*T. Harper, M. Flesher, Eliz. Allde? a. J. Dawson*] *f. N. Butter a. N. Bourne*, 1634. Ent. 15 no. L.O⁶.C².DUR⁵.SHEF.+; HN.
(Formerly 11784) Harper pr. A, A¶–E¶, aaa–ccc; Flesher pr. B–K; Eliz. Allde app. pr. aa*–ee*; Dawson pr. aa–dd.

23525.8 — [A variant, w. imprint:] *f. N. Butter a. N. Bourne*, 1635. O.O¹⁴.; CU.HD.

23525.9 — The modern history of the world. Or, an historicall relation since the beginning of 1635. Divided into three sections. The eighth part [of the Swedish Intelligencer. By N. C.] 4°. [*T. Harper a. M. Flesher*] *f. N. Butter a. N. Bourn*, 1635. Ent. 14 no. L.L³.O(imp.).O³.C².+; HN.CU.HD.
(Formerly 13528) The relation of events is continued in 4293 sqq. Harper pr. the 1st section and app. Ggg–Iii; Flesher the rest.

23526 **Sweeper, Walter.** A briefe treatise declaring the true noble-man, and the base worldling. [A sermon.] 4°. *W. Jones*, 1622. Ent. 10 jy. L⁴.C.P. Gloucester PL.

23527 — Israels redemption by Christ. Wherein is confuted the Arminian universall redemption. [A sermon.] 4°. *W. Jones*, 1622. Ent. 27 no. L.O.DUR⁵.E.LIV².; F.HN. CHI. McMaster U. Weissman.

23528 **Sweet, John.** A defence of the Appendix [18658.5]. Or a reply to certaine authorities alleaged in answere to An appendix to the Antidote. Wherein also [10732] is censured. By L. D. [i.e. J. Sweet?] To syr H. Lynde. 4°. [*St. Omer, English College Press,*] 1624. O.A.OS.P.USHAW.+; F.HN.U.
A&R 802. App. answers a MS. of Lynde's, cf. the book ent. to R. Milbourne and Eliz. Jaggard 12 ja. 1625. Answered by 10738.5.

23529 — Monsig. fate voi. Or a discovery of the Dalmatian apostata, M. A. de Dominis, and his bookes. By C. A. [i.e. J. Sweet.] 4°. [*St. Omer, English College Press,*] 1617. L.O.C.DUR⁵.YK.+
A&R 803.

23530 — True relations of sundry conferences. By A. C. 1626. Now = 10916.5.

23531 **Sweetnam, John.** The paradise of delights. Or the B. virgins garden of Loreto. By J. S. of the society of Jesus. 8°. [*St. Omer, English College Press,*] 1620. L. O.OS.USHAW.W.+; F.HN.
A&R 804.

23532 — S. Mary Magdalens pilgrimage to paradise. By J. S. of the society of Jesus. 8°. [*St. Omer, English College Press,*] 1617. L.O.OS.; F(2).NY.
A&R 805.

— *tr. See* 18000.

23533 **Swetnam, Joseph.** The araignment of lewde, idle, froward, and unconstant women. [Tho. Tel-troth, *pseud.*] 4°. *E. Allde f. T. Archer*, 1615. Ent. 8 fb. O.; F.
Answered by 18257, 18508, 22974, 23058, 24393. *See also* 23544.

23534 — [Anr. ed., signed in full.] 4°. *G. Purslowe f. T. Archer*, 1615. L.SAL.; N.

23535 — [Anr. ed.] 4°. [*T. Snodham*] *f. T. Archer*, 1616. HN.

23536 — [Anr. ed.] 4°. [*T. Snodham*] *f. T. Archer*, 1617. L.; HN.HD(impr. cropt).

23537 — [Anr. ed.] 4°. [*T. Snodham*] *f. T. Archer*, 1619. L.; F(lacks tp).HD.

23538 — [Anr. ed.] 4°. *B. Alsop f. T. Archer*, 1622. F.

23539 — [Anr. ed.] 4°. *A. M[athewes*] *f. T. Archer*, 1628. Ass'd to F. Grove 10 se. L.O(2).

23540 — [Anr. ed. Tom Tel-Trouth, *pseud.*] 8°. *Edinburgh, J. Wreittoun*, 1629. L.

23541 — [Anr. ed., signed in full.] 4°. *T. C[otes*], sold by *F. Grove*, 1634. Ass'd to R. Cotes 9 no. 1633. L.O.

23542 — [Anr. ed.] 4°. *T. C[otes*] *f. F. Gro[ve,*] 1637. L⁶.O.

23543 — The schoole of the noble and worthy science of defence. 4°. *N. Okes*, 1617. O.

23544 — Swetnam, the woman-hater, arraigned by woman. A new comedie. 4°. [*W. Stansby*] *f. R. Meighen*, 1620. Ent. 17 oc. 1619. L.L⁶.O.E.ETON.+; F.HN.HD.N.PML.+ Greg 362.

23545 **Swift, John.** The divine eccho, or, resounding voice from heaven. The first part. [Short meditations.] 12°. [*W. Stansby*] *f. R. Bonion*, 1612. L.

23546 **Swift, William.** A sermon preached at the funerall of M. Thomas Wilson, in Canterbury. 4°. *J. D[awson*] *f. F. Clifton*, 1622. Ent. 15 mr. L.L³.O.O¹⁰.A.; F.HD.U.

23547 **Swinburne, Henry.** A briefe treatise of testaments and last willes. 4° in 8's. *J. Windet*, 1590 (1591.) Ent. 10 se. 1590. L.O.C.A.D.+; F.HN.CU.HD.N.+
Copies vary: with or without extra leaf with 35 errata; both at F, HD. A copy w. the tp dated 1591 was offered in Ravenstree Catalogue 17 (Nov. 1971), item 174.

23548 — [Anr. ed.] Newly corrected and augmented. 4° in 8's. [*W. Stansby? a. T. Snodham*] *f. the Co. of Statrs.*, 1611. Ent. to E. Weaver 6 my. 1605; 'this belongs to the company' i.e. English stock, 2 mr. 1607. L. O¹⁴.C³.D².E⁸.+; F.HN.CU.HD.LC.+
See Court-Book C, p. 43. App. Stansby pr. through quire Ff; Snodham did Gg to the end.

Swinburne, Henry—*cont.*

23549 — = 23550.
23550 — [Anr. ed.] 4° in 8's. *W. S[tansby a. T. Harper] f. the Co. of Statrs.*, 1635. Ent. to the English Stock 5 mr. 1620. L.O.C.DUR.NLW.+; F.HN.HD.ILL.PML.+
 (Formerly also 23549) Stansby pr. A–Z, aa; Harper pr. Aa–Qq.
23551 — [Anr. ed.] 4° in 8's. *J. L[egat, F. Kingston, R. Bishop, a. J. Dawson] f. the Co. of Statrs.*, 1640. L.O.C.M².SAL.+; F.HN.CU.HD.ILL.+
 Legat pr. A–L; Kingston M–X; Bishop Y–Z, aa, Aa–Ff; Dawson Gg–Qq.

23551.5 **Swinnerton, Thomas.** A litel treatise ageynste the mutterynge of some papistis in corners. [Anon.] 8°. *in aed. T. Bertheleti*, 1534. L.O.C².; HN.
 (Formerly 19177)
23552 — A mustre of scismatyke bysshoppes of Rome. (First a prologue. After that a hystory of pope Gregory the seuenth. Last of al the lyfe of yᵉ fourth Henry, emperour. [Both *tr.* from the Latin of Cardinal Benno by J. Roberts, *pseud.*]) 2 pts. 8°. (*w. de worde f.*) *J. Byddell*, (1534 (21 mr.)) L(1, plus pt. 2 only).O.

23553 **Switzerland,** *Reformed Church of.* The confescion of the fayth of the Sweserlãdes. (*Tr.* out of laten by G. Ussher [i.e. Wishart], who was burned in Scotland M.v.Cxl.vi.) 8°. [*H. Singleton*, 1548?] F.
23554 — A confession of fayth, made by common consent of diuers reformed churches beyonde the seas [the Helvetian Confession of 1566 by H. Bullinger, and the French Confession of 1561]: with an exhortation to the reformation of the churche. [By] (T. Beza.) [All *tr.* by] (J. O[lde].) 8°. *H. Wykes f. L. Harrison*, [1568?] Ent. 1566–67. L.O.C.E(imp.).M.+; F(imp.). HN.
23555 — [Anr. ed.] 8°. *H. Bynneman f. L. Harison*, (1571.) L. O(lacks col.).C³.E²(lacks col.).M.; F(imp.).NY¹¹.
 (Formerly also 23556)
23556 — = 23555.
23557 — [Anr. trans.] Belijdenisse ende eenuoudige wtlegghinge des gheloofs, van de dienaers der kercken in Switzerlant. 8°. *Nordwitz, A. de Solemne*, 1568. L.C.M. NOR².; HD.
 Without Beza's exhortation.

Sword. A sword against swearers. 1609, etc. *See* 3050.3 sqq.
— The sworde of maintenance. 1600. *See* pt. 2 of 25282.

23558 **Swynnerton, John.** A christian love-letter: sent particularly to K. T. but intended to all of the romish religion. 4°. *W. Jaggard*, 1606. Ent. to M. Lownes a. Jaggard 17 my. L.O².C.C⁹.CASHEL.+; F.HN.HD.

23559 **Sydenham, Humphrey.** The arraignment of the Arrian. A sermon. 4°. [*Eliot's Court Press*] *f. J. Parker*, 1626. L⁸.O.C².BIRM.BRISTOL.+; BO³.N.Y.
 Also issued as pt. 3 of 23563.
23560 — [Anr. ed.] 1636. = pt. of 23565.
23561 — The Athenian babler. A sermon. 4°. *B. A[lsop] a. T. Fawcet f. J. Parker*, 1627. O.C.C³.BRISTOL.; HN.HD.Y.
 Also issued as pt. 1 of 23563.
23562 — The christian duell. 1637. = pt. of 23573.
23563 — Five sermons, upon severall occasions. 5 pts. 4°. [*Eliot's Court Press*] *f. J. Parker*, 1626 (1627.) Ent. 19 my. 1627. L.O.C⁵.D.E.+; F.ILL.MCG.Y.
 A reissue, w. gen. tp and prelims., of 23561, 23567, 23559, 23568, 23569.
23564 — [Anr. ed.] 4°. *J. Haviland f. N. Fussell a. H. Mosley [a.]* (*f. J. Parker*) 1627. L⁴³.O.C³.BRISTOL.D².+; F (Serm. 1 only)*.ILL.PN².U(Serm. 1–4 only)*.
 Continuous signatures.
23564.5 — [Anr. issue, w. gen. tp, w. imprint:] *J. Haviland f. N. Fussell*, 1627. L³.O⁶.O⁷(imp.).CHEL².; CHI.
23565 — [Anr. ed.] 4°. *J. Haviland*, 1636. L¹⁵.; HN.ILL.
 (23560, 23567a, 23568a, and 23569b are pt. of this) The gen. tp in this and the following is a separate leaf, or possibly part of a bifolium with the other leaf blank.
23566 — [Anr. issue, w. gen. tp reset, w. imprint:] *J. Haviland, sold by N. Fussell*, 1637. Ass'd to Haviland a. J. Wright 4 se. 1638. L(2, 1 imp.).; F.HN.
23566.5 — [A variant.] The third edition. *J. Haviland, sold by N. Fussell*, 1637. L³.O⁴.O¹²; F.CU.HD.U.Y.

Sydenham, Humphrey—*cont.*

23567 — Jacob and Esau: election. Reprobation. [A sermon.] 4°. [*Eliot's Court Press*] *f. J. Parker*, 1626. L⁸.O.C. BIRM.BRISTOL.+; N.Y.
 Also issued as pt. 2 of 23563.
23567a — [Anr. ed.] 1636. = pt. of 23565.
23568 — Moses and Aaron or the affinitie of civill and ecclesiasticke power. A sermon. 4°. [*Eliot's Court Press*] *f. J. Parker*, 1626. O.C².C³.BIRM.BRISTOL.; BO³.N. Sydney U.
 Also issued as pt. 4 of 23563.
23568a — [Anr. ed.] 1636. = pt. of 23565.
23569 — Natures overthrow, and deaths triumph. A sermon. 4°. [*Eliot's Court Press*] *f. J. Parker*, 1626. L.L³.O.C. BIRM.+; BO³.HD.N.
 Also issued as pt. 5 of 23563.
23569a — [A ghost.]
23569b — [Anr. ed.] 1636. = pt. of 23565.
23570 — The rich mans warning-peece. A sermon. 4°. *F. Kyngston [a. W. Stansby] f. N. Butter*, 1630. Ent. 12 my. L⁴³.O.C³.E.NLW.+; F.HN.HD.N.NY¹¹.
 Also issued as pt. 2 of 23572. Stansby pr. C–F, including F4: gen. tp for 23572.
23571 — The royall passing-bell: or, Davids summons to the grave. A sermon. 4°. *W. Stansby f. N. Butter*, 1630. Ent. 12 my. L.O.C³.BRISTOL.E.+; F.HN.HD(w. ¶² of 23572).N. Weissman.
 Also issued as pt. 1 of 23572.
23572 — Sermons by Humph. Sydenham. 3 pts. 4°. *W. Stansby f. N. Butter*, 1630. L.O³.C².D.LINC.+; F.HN.PN².U (prelims. and Serm. 3).Y.+
 A reissue, w. gen. tp (pr. as F4 of 23570) and dedic. (¶², pr. by Stansby), of 23571, 23570, 23574.
23573 — Sermons upon solemne occasions: preached in severall auditories. 4°. *J. Beale f. H. Robinson*, 1637. Ent. 12 de. L.O.C.BRISTOL.NLW.+; F.HN.HD.N.Y.+
 (23562 is pt. of this)
23574 — Waters of Marah, and Meribah: by way of advice, against the pseudo-zelots of our age. 4°. *Eliz. Allde f. N. Butter*, 1630. Ent. 12 my. L¹⁵.O.C³.E.NLW.+; F.CHI.HD.N.NY¹¹.+
 Also issued as pt. 3 of 23572.

Sylvester, Bernard. Here begynneth the cure of a household. [c. 1535.] *See* 1967.5.

Sylvester, Joshua. [The complete works.] 1620, etc. *See* 21653 sq.
23575 — The sacred workes of that famous poet J. Silvester. Gathered into one volume. 2 pts. 8°. *London*, 1620. HN.
 A reissue, w. gen. tp, of 23581, 23582, q.v. The HN copy has 23582a appended but has neither pair of extra leaves in 23582.
23575.5 — [A variant, w. gen. tp:] All the small workes [etc.] *London*, 1620. F.
 The F copy does not have 23582a but has 1 pair of extra leaves, Dd3*, in 23582.
23576 — Lachrimæ lachrimarum. or the distillation of teares shede for the death of prince Panaretus [xylographic.] 4°. (*H. Lownes*, 1612.) Ent. to H. Lownes, jun., 27 no. L.O.C.E².M.+; F.HN.HD.ILL.Y.+
 The colophon and device McK. 211 within a frame of woodcuts are on D4ʳ. O(85.d.5), HN, HD have A3ʳ line 4: 'Cedars'; B3ʳ line 10: 'He'.
 Other copies w. the colophon, e.g. O(4° P 35(19) Th.) and O⁵, have A3 and B3 readings like 23577 and may represent mixed sheets or reimpositions of the text.
23577 — [Anr. ed.] 4°. [*H. Lownes*, 1612.] O¹⁷.; HN.PN.
 Omits colophon and device on D4ʳ but retains the frame of woodcuts. O¹⁷ and HN have A3ʳ line 4: 'Cædars'; B3ʳ line 10: 'Hee'.
23577.5 — Third edition, with addition of his owne. and other elegies [xylographic.] 4°. (*H. Lownes*, 1613.) L³⁸.M. M²(imp.).; F(imp.).HD(imp., w. quire C of 23578).Y. B3ʳ last line: 'oftentymes.'; C1ʳ catchword: 'Weepe'. HD, Y have an early state of G outer forme, with G1, 3 missigned F1, 3 and G3ʳ last line beginning: 'In whom all Grace' instead of 'In whom thou mightst'.
23578 — [Anr. issue, w. quires B–C reset.] (*H. Lownes*, 1613.) L.L³⁰.D.LIV³.WI.+; F.HN(imp.).HD(imp.).N.PML.+ B3ʳ last line: 'oftentimes.'; C1ʳ catchword: 'Weep'.
23579 — Monodia. (An elegie in commemoration of dame Hellen Branch.—The triumph of W. Salustius.) 4°. *P. short*, [1594.] L.; HN(Elegie only).

Sylvester, Joshua—*cont.*
— The mysterie of mysteries. [1621.] *See* 21653.
23580 — Panthea: or, divine wishes and meditations. Revised by J. M(artin.) Whereunto is added an Appendix, containing an excellent elegy, by [F. Bacon] viscount St Albans. [All in verse.] 4°. [*G. Purslowe*] *f. F. Coules*, 1630. Ent. 14 no. 1629. L(2).; HN.CH.HD.
23581 — The parliament of vertues royal: of prince Panaretus. [By J. Bertaut.] (Bethulians rescue. [By Saluste du Bartas.]—Little Bartas.— [By Saluste du Bartas.]— Micro-cosmo-graphia; from H. Smith [in 22712.5.] —Lachrymæ lachrymarum [from 23576.]—Elegiac-Epistle [from 23578.]) 8°. [*H. Lownes*,] (1614.) Ent. to H. Lownes, sen., pts. 1–3, 13 ja. 1614, and pt. 4, 22 de. 1612; to Lownes, jun., pt. 5, 27 no. 1612. L. L².O.C.C⁴.+; F.HN.HD.N.NY.+
The dated sub tp is on G1^r. Reissued as pt. 1 of 23575 sq.
23582 — The second session of the parliament of vertues reall: transcribed by J. Sylvester. (Job triumphant.— Memorials of mortalitie: by P. Mathieu.—Henrie the great, his tropheis and tragedie. By P. Mathieu. [Pt. 2:] S^t. Lewis.—A hymn of alms.—The batail of Yvry: by du Bartas.—Honor's farwel.) 2 pts. 8°. [*H. Lownes*,] (1615.) Job ent. to H. Lownes, sen., 23 de. 1615; pt. 2 ent. 29 de. 1614. L(3).L².O(2, 1 imp.).C⁴.; F.HN.HD.ILL.NY.+
Pt. 2 (formerly 16829) has the dated sub tp on Aa1^r. In some copies, e.g. L(C.34.a.11(4)), 1 O, 1 F, 1 HD(bd. sep.), NY, this pt. has 2 pairs of extra dedic. leaves: Aa3¶ (to Prince Charles) and Dd3* (to Abp. G. Abbot).
Both pts. are reissued together as pt. 2 of 23575 sq.
Some copies, e.g. L(C.34.a.11), HD, NY, have 23582a appended as a 3rd part.
23582a — Tobacco battered; & the pipes shattered. (Simile non est idem.—A glimpse of heavenly joyes.—Auto-machia [by G. Goodwin.]) 8°. [*H. Lownes*, 1616–17.] Ent. to H. Lownes 13 de. 1616. L(1038.a.43(2)). O.C.; HN.HD(imp.).LC(imp.).NY(imp.).
Collates F–I⁸ K⁴ L⁸, with F2,3 (tp and dedic. to Villiers as Earl of Buckingham [created 5 Jan. 1617]) being a cancel bifolium, and the 'Simile' tp and dedic. pr. as H4,5. C has the orig. 1st quire, lacking the 1st leaf and with the 4th signed A4 instead of F4; its dedic. is to Villiers as Viscount [created 27 Aug. 1616]. This item is sometimes also issued w. 23582, 23575.
23583 — The wood-mans bear. A poeme. 8°. [*B. Alsop*?] *f. T. Jones a. L. Chapman*, 1620. Ent. to Jones 12 ja. HN. *See Court Book C*, p. 119.
23583.5 — [Six-line poem, signed Jos. Syl., underneath engraved portrait by R. Elstrack of M. A. de Dominis, aged 57.] s.sh.fol. *M. Sparke*, [1617.] DALK.; Washington, D.C., National Gallery of Art.
For this and later states *see* Hind II.173–4.
— *tr. See* 7353.5, 11253, 12028, 15216, 17661, 21649, 21661, 21665, 21669, 21672. Some of these are reprinted in the Sylvester items listed above, and they are all reprinted in 21653.

Sylvius, Aeneas. *See* Pius II, *Pope*.

Symcocke, Thomas. *See* 3217.5, 8615, 8716.5.

23584 **Syme, John.** Lifes preservative against self-killing. 4°. *M. Flesher f. R. Dawlman a. L. Fawne*, 1637. Ent. 18 no. 1636. L.O.C.D².DUR⁵.+; F.HN.CHI.HD.U.+
23585 — The sweet milke of christian doctrine: in question and answere. 8°. *G. Purslowe f. J. Hodges*, 1617. O.; F.

Symmachia. Symmachia: or, a true-loves knot. [1623?] *See* 22089.

23586 **Symmer, Archibald.** Αναπαυσις Rest for the restlesse soule. 4°. *J. Haviland f. W. Sheres*, 1637. F.NYS.
23587 — Rest for the weary, or a briefe treatise. 4°. *J. N[orton] f. W. Sheres*, 1630. L.L³.
23588 — A spirituall posie for Zion. Or two decades of observations. 4°. [*M. Flesher*] *f. W. Sheares*, 1629. L.L³. LINC.P.; HN.U.

23588.5 **Symmes, Thomas.** [An invective against such runnin-gate papists that greedily go about to disturb the concord of the church.] *Ballad.* s.sh.fol. *R. Johnes*, 1584 (22 oc.) Ent. 19 oc. EX(binding frag.).
Title from Stationers' Register; 3rd? from last

Symmes, Thomas—*cont.*
stanza begins: 'As men possest with wicked sprits,/ to mischiefe wholy bent:/ They study and apply theyr wits,/ to cause vs to dissent.'

23589 **Symon, John.** A pleasant posie, or sweete nosegay of fragrant smellyng flowers: gathered [from] the Bible. *Ballad.* s.sh.fol. *R. Johnes*, 1572. ?Ent. to J. Charlewood 15 ja. 1582. L.

23590 **Symonds, Joseph.** The case and cure of a deserted soule. 8°. *M. Flesher f. L. Fawne*, 1639. Ent. 13 no. 1638. L.D.G².; F.HN.LC.MICH.Y.+
23590.5 — [A variant, w. imprint:] *M. Flesher f. L. Fawne a. S. Gellibrand*, 1639. L⁴⁶.O.C².E.ETON.; BO.HD.ILL.N.U.+

23591 **Symonds, William.** A heavenly voyce. A sermon . . . preached at Paules Crosse the 12 of Januarie. 4°. *J. R[oberts] f. E. Weaver*, 1606. Ent. 18 ja. L.O.C⁴. DUL.M.+; HN.U.
23592 — Pisgah evangelica. By the method of the Revelation. In a briefe ecclesiasticall historie, containing the mutations which have befallen the church, unto 1603. as they have been shewed unto S. John and recorded by historiographers. 4°. *F. Kyngston f. E. Weaver*, 1605. Ent. 24 au. O.D.DUL.G².WOR.; HN (imp.).HART.U.
23593 — [A variant, w. imprint:] *F. Kyngston f. E. Weaver*, 1606. L.O¹².C.CASHEL.G⁴.+; F.CAL(imp.).NY¹¹.
— The proceedings of the English colonie in Virginia. 1612. *See* pt. 2 of 22791.
23594 — Virginia. A sermon preached at White-Chappel, in the presence of the adventurers and planters for Virginia. 25. April. 1609. 4°. *J. Windet f. E. Edgar a. W. Welby*, 1609. Ent. to Edgar 8 my. L.O.C.BIRM²(K.N.). DUR³.+; F.HN.BO.N.NY.+

23594.5 **Symondson, Philip.** A new description of Kent . . . 1596. [Map w. text engr. by C. Whitwell.] fol(2). [*London*, 1596?] L. London, Royal Geographical Society (eastern sheet only).
For later states w. P. Stent's imprint *see* Hind I.223–4 and *Archaeologia Cantiana*, XLIV (1937), pp. 272–7.

23595 **Sympson, William.** A full and profitable interpretation of all the proper names within the genealogie of Jesus Christ. 4°. *C. Legge, pr. to the Univ. of Camb.*, 1619. L.C.C².E.USHAW.+; F.HN.

23596 **Syms, Christopher.** An apology for Christopher Syms gent. and his way and method of teaching. 4°. [*Dublin, Soc. of Statrs.*,] 1633. C.
23597 — An introduction to, or, the art of teaching, the Latine speach. 4°. *Dublin, Soc. of Statrs.*, 1634. L.O(lacks tp).D.E.; F.

Symson, Andrew. *See* Simson.

Symson, Archibald. *See* Simson.

23598 **Symson, Patrick.** The historie of the church. Devided into foure bookes. [Ed.] (A. Symson.) 4° in 8's. *J. D[awson] f. J. Bellamie a. W. Sheffard*, 1624. Ent. to Dawson a. Bellamy 29 jn. 1622. L.O.C.D².E.+; F. HN.N.U.Y.+
Centuries 1–9 are rearranged extracts of pt. of the text of 23601; Centuries 10–16 are new material.
23598.5 — Third edition corrected and inlarged. fol. *J. Dawson [a. W. Jones] f. J. Bellamie*, 1634. Dawson's pt. ass'd to Bellamie 30 ja. 1633. L.O.C.D.E.+; F.HN.HD(lacks Nnn3).N.NY¹¹.+
(Formerly 23600) Jones pr. Aaa-Hhh; Dawson the rest.
23599 — The historie of the church. The second part. Containing a discoverie of the noveltie of popish religion. Digested into 34. treatises. [Ed.] (A. Symson.) 4° in 8's. *R. Field f. N. Newberie*, 1625. Ent. 1 ap. 1624. O.C⁵.G².LINC.YK.+; F.HN.ILL.NY.
Centuries 1–9 are rearranged extracts of the rest of the text of 23601; Centuries 10–12 are new material. This text is not reprinted in 23598.5.
23600 — Now = 23598.5.

Symson, Patrick—*cont.*

23601 — A short compend of the historie of the first ten persecutions divided into III. centuries. 4° in 8's. *Edinburgh, A. Hart,* 1613. [Vol. II, Centuries 4–6:] (A short compend, of the Arrian and Eutychian persecutions. 4°. *Edinburgh, A. Hart,* 1615.) [Vol. III, Centuries 7–9:] (A short compend, of the grouth of the romane antichrist. 4°. *Edinburgh, A. Hart,* 1616.) L.O.C.CASHEL.E.+; F.HN.ILL(imp.).U.Y.+

 Sections on the Emperors, Popes, etc. reprinted in 23598, while the various treatises are reprinted in 23599.

Symson, Rafe. *See* Indulgences 84.

23602 **Symson, William.** De accentibus Hebraicis breves & perspicuæ regulæ. 8°. *typis G. Stansby, venduntur in æd. J. Woodcocke,* [1617.] L³.O.C¹⁵.E².WOR.+; PN².

 The dedic. is dated 1617.

Synagogue. The synagogue, or, the shadow of the Temple. 1640. *See* 12898.

23603 **Synesius,** *Bp.* A paradoxe, prouing by reason and example, that baldnesse is much better than bushie haire. Englished by A. Fleming. Hereunto is annexed the tale of Hemetes the heremite. Newly recognised both in Latine and Englishe, by the said A. F. 8°. *H. Denham,* 1579. Ent. 22 se. L.O.; F.

 The anon. Tale also appears in 7596; the Latin trans. is by G. Gascoigne.

23604 **Synge, George.** A rejoynder to the reply [17213] published by the jesuites. The first part. 4° in 8's. *Dublin, Soc. of Statrs.,* 1632. L.O.C.D.STU.+; F.HN.HD.

 In at least O, 2 C, HD copies this is bound w. the prelims. of 20520 and vice versa.

— *See also* 14265.7.

Syon, *Brigittine Convent of.* See Indulgences 18.

Szegedinus, Stephanus. *See* Kis, S.

T

23605   **T., A.** A christian reprofe against contention. Against such slanders which S. Staresmore hath layd upon us. An answer to a letter by Mr. Robinson. [By A. Thatcher?] 4°. [*Amsterdam, successors of G. Thorpe,*] 1631. L.

         Answers 227 and a book by Staresmore, *A loving tender,* 1623, no copy of which is known.

23606   **T., A.,** *Practitioner in Physic.* A rich store-house or treasury for the diseased. Now set foorth for the benefit of the poorer sort. By A. T. 4°. [*T. Purfoot*] *f. T. Purfoot a. R. Blower,* 1596. Ent. to Blower 9 au. L(imp.).L¹⁶.E⁵.G².; F.HN.NY⁴.

23606.5   — [Anr. ed.] First set foorth by A. T. And now newly corrected, augmented and inlarged by G. W. practi-cioner in phisicke and chirurgerie. 4°. *R. Blower, solde by W. Barley,* 1601. L(imp.).G².; F.

23607   — [Anr. ed.] First set foorth by A. T. Now fourthly augmented, by G. W. 4°. *R. Blower,* 1607. L.L¹⁶.; F.HD.

23608   — [Anr. ed.] First set foorth by G. W. And now fifthly augmented by A. T. practitioner in phisicke. 4°. *R. Blower,* 1612. L.L¹⁶.L³⁹.O³(imp.).; HD.NY⁴.Y.

23609   — Now sixtly augmented. 4°. *R. Blower,* 1616. L³⁰.; HN.NLM.WIS.

23610   — Now seventhly augmented. 4° in 8's. *R. Badger f. P. Stephens a. C. Meredith,* 1630. Blower's pt. ass'd to W. Jones 4 on 22 jn. 1626. S. Stafford's pt. ass'd to Stephens a. Meredith 13 ja. 1630. L¹⁶.O.C.G².P.+; COR.HD(lacks tp).NLM.

         Copies vary: colophon dated 1630 (HD) or 1631 (G²).

23611   — [A variant, w. tp imprint:] *R. Badger f. P. Stephens a. C. Meredith,* 1631. L.L¹⁶.O.G².SH(lacks colophon).+; F.HN.HD(imp.).NLM. Philadelphia, College of Physicians.

23612   **T., C.** An advice how to plant tobacco in England. 4°. *N. Okes, sold by W. Burre,* 1615. Ent. to Burre 29 no. 1614. L.O.; F.HN.CU.NY.

         Jaggard's catalogue (14341), B2ʳ last line, lists this as written by W. R.

   — Laugh and lie down. 1605. *See* 24148.7.

   — A short inuentory of certayne idle inuentions. 1581. *See* 23952.3.

   — *tr.* A notable historye of Nastagio. 1569. *See* 3184.

T., D. Asylum Veneris. 1616. *See* 24393.

   — Christian purposes and resolutions. 1611. *See* 24393.3.

   — The dove and the serpent. 1614. *See* 24394.

   — Essayes. 1609. *See* 24395.

   — Vade mecum. 1629. *See* 24397.

T., D., *Gent.* Essaies. 1608. *See* 24396.

T., E. The christian souldier. 1639. *See* 24331.

   — Here beginneth a song of the Lordes supper. [1550?] *See* 24078.

23613   — That neither temporallities nor tythes is due to the bishops. 4°. [n.p. 1630?] J(untraced).

   — *tr. See* 22238.

T., F. An adjoynder to the supplement. 1613. *See* 11022.

23614   — The case is altered. How? Aske Dalio, and Millo. [Sometimes attrib. to N. Breton.] 4°. *T. C[reede] f. J. Smethicke,* 1604. Ent. 16 fb. L.O.; PFOR.

23615   — [Anr. ed.] 4°. [*W. Jaggard*] *f. T. Pavyer,* 1605. O.; HN.

23616   — [Anr. ed.] 4°. *J. Norton f. R. Bird,* 1630. T. Pavier's rights ass'd to E. Brewster a. Bird 4 au. 1626. O.; HN.

23617   — [Anr. ed.] 4°. *J. N[orton] f. R. Bird,* 1635. L.

   — The debate betweene pride and lowlines. [1577?] *See* 24061.

   — A defence of the catholyke cause. 1602. *See* 11016.

T., F.—*cont.*

   — The obmutesce of F. T. 1621. *See* 11020.

   — A supplement to the discussion. 1613. *See* 11021.

23617.5   **T., G.** [Heading *1ʳ:*] A table gathered owt of a booke named a treatise of treasons [7601]. 8°. [*Antwerp, J. Fowler,* 1573.] L².

         A&R 806.

   — *tr.* An epistle of the persecution of catholickes. [1582.] *See* 19406.

   — *See also* 22975.

23618   **T., H.** Certaine articles or forcible reasons. 1600. Now = 26038.6.

   — A relation of the travells. 1631. *See* 24086.

   — *ed. See* 1383, 5846.4.

   — *tr. See* 11759.

23619   **T., I.** or **J.** An apologie or defence agaynst the calumna-cion of certayne men, which haue abandoned theyr liuinges and vocacion, abydinge as exyles. 8°. [*Wesel? H. Singleton?*] 1555 (21 jy.). L.

         Pr. in the same types as 9981.

23619.5   — Funerall elegie. 1615. *See* Addenda.

23620   — The hauen of pleasure: containing a direction how to liue well. 4°. *P. S[hort] f. P. Linley a. J. Flasket,* 1596. F.

23621   — [A variant, w. imprint:] *P. S[hort] f. P. Linley a. J. Flasket,* 1597. O.P.; Lewis.

   — A horrible creuel murther. 1614. *See* 12630.

   — The just down⟨fall of⟩ ambition. [1616?] *See* 18920.

   — A most plaine and easie way for finding the azimuth. [c. 1630.] *See* 1590.5.

23621.5   — The ready path to the pleasant pasture of delitesome, and eternall paradyse. 8° in 4's. *H. Denham f. J. Judson,* [1570?] Ent. 1569-70. F(lacks tp).HD(imp.).

23622   — [Anr. ed., w. title:] The pathway to the pleasant pasture of paradise. 8°. *H. Bynneman,* [1577.] Ass'd 1 jy. 1577. L.

   — A warning for swearers and blasphemers. 1626. *See* 23812.7.

   — *ed. See* 3225, 12630.

   — *tr. See* 3161.5, 3202, 4066, 23241.

T., John. Keepe within compasse. [1619, etc.] *See* 14898.5 sqq.

23623   **T., J.,** *Gent.* The A, B, C, of armes, or, an introduction directorie; whereby the order of militarie exercises may bee understood. 8°. *W. Stansby f. J. Helmes,* 1616. Ent. 12 my. L.O.

23624   — An ould facioned loue. 1594. = 25118.

T., I., *Minister.* A sermon preached at Paules Crosse. 1596. *See* 23670.

23624.3   **T., I.,** *Sacræ Theologiæ Doctor.* Problema theologicum propositum primò & disceptatum, de natura, usu, subscriptionis doctrinæ fidei, & ceremonijs, in qua-que ecclesia constitutis. 8°. *ex off. H. L[ownes,] imp. C. Knight,* 1607. Ent. 28 fb. D.; F.

         The F tp has the author's first init. altered in ink from 'I.' to 'L'.

23624.7   **T., I.,** *Westminster.* The hunting of the pox: a pleasant discourse betweene the authour, and Pild-Garlicke. Wherein is declared the nature of the disease. [In verse.] 4°. *J. W[hite] f. J. T[rundle,] sold by P. Birch,* 1619. Ent. to J. Trundle 19 fb. HN.

T., L. An answere to certein assertions of M. Fecknam. [1570.] *See* 24113.

   — Prosopopeia. 1596. *See* 16662b.

   — *tr. See* 983.

T., M., *tr. See* 7233.

T., M. P. Descriptio erysipelatis. [1621?] *See* 24368.5.

T., N. A true relation of the . . . murther. 1616. *See* 14054.5.
— *tr. See* 21676.

T., R. A brief treatise of the use of the globe. 1616. *See* 23672.

23625 — De templis, a treatise of temples: wherein is discovered the ancient manner of building churches. 12°. *R. Bishop f. T. Alchorn,* 1638. Ent. 2 oc. L.O.C.A. DUR⁵.+; F(2).CHI.ILL.Y. Sexton.
— A discourse. Wherein is plainly proued that Peter was neuer at Rome. 1572. *See* 4655.

23625.5 — Epicedium Ludoici [*sic*] regis Galliae, de caede patris Henrici magni. [In verse.] 8° in 4's. [*N. Okes,*] 1611. C².
— A learned and very profitable exposition made vppon the hundred & eleuenth psalme. 1583. *See* 24180.3.
— A prettie newe ballad, intytuled: the crowe sits vpon the wall. [1592.] *See* 23683.

T., R., *Bachelor of Divinity.* Five godlie sermons. 1602. *See* 24475 sq.

T., R., *Gent.* Alba. The months minde. 1598. *See* 24096.
— Laura. The toyes of a traueller. 1597. *See* 24097.
— *tr. See* 749, 3216, 23690, 24593.

23626 **T., T.** A booke, containing the true portraiture of the kings of England, together with a briefe report of some of the principall acts of the same kings. 4°. [*R. Field f.*] *J. de Beauchesne,* 1597. L(2, 1 in MS. Dept., Lansdowne 218).; HN.CH.NY.
(Formerly also 24415) Has been attrib. to T. Twyne and T. Tymme.
— A discourse against painting of women. 1616. *See* 24316a.

23626.5 — A handfull of goates-haire: that is, certaine principles of christian religion, easie for beginners to understand, and to remember. [By T. Thompson?] 8°. *T. S[nodham] f. J. Hodgets,* 1616. E².
23627 — Now = 23628.5.
23628 — A myrror for Martinists, and all other schismatiques. 4°. *J. Wolfe,* 1590. Ent. 22 de. 1589. L².O⁶.C.E.M.+; F.HN.PFOR.Y.
— New essayes: meditations, and vowes. 1614. *See* 24312.3.
— The schoolemaster. 1576. *See* 24411.
— A shorte and pithie discourse. 1580. *See* 24413.
— A silver watch-bell. 1606. *See* 24422.

23628.5 — ⟨Some f⟩yne gloues deuised for newyeare gyftes to teche yonge peop⟨le to⟩ knowe good from euyll. [Woodcut diagrams. Partly in verse.] s.sh.fol. *W. Powell,* [after 1559.] HN.
(Formerly 23627)
23629 — A view of certain wonderful effects, of the comete. [By T. Twyne.] 4°. [*J. Charlewood f.*] ⟨*R. Jhones,* 1578 (1 de.)⟩ Ent. 24 mr. 1579. L.O⁵.
— *ed. See* 18951.

T., T., *Fellow of Christ's College.* Davids learning. 1617. *See* 23827.

23630 **T., T.,** *Sacristan.* The whetstone of reproofe. Or a reproving censure of the misintitled Safe way [17097]. (An appendix.) 2 pts. 8°. *Catuapoli* [*Douai,*] *ap. viduam M. Wyonis,* 1632. L.O.C.A².USHAW.+ A&R 807.

23631 **T., T. W.** A mery balade, how a wife entreated her husband to haue her owne wyll. *Ballad.* s.sh.fol. *A. Lacy,* [1568.] Ent. 1567–68. L.

23632 **T., W.** A casting up of accounts of certain errors, being answered in items, to the Summa totalis. (An opinion touching the pestilence.) 8°. *T. Creede f. J. Hippon,* 1603. L.O.PETYT.SAL. Attacks 1338.
— A discourse of eternitie. 1633. *See* 24473.
— An exposicion vppon the. v. vi. vii. chapters of Mathew. [1533?] *See* 24440.
— The exposition of the fyrste epistle of seynt Jhon. 1531. *See* 24443.
23633 — A godlie & comfortable letter written by W. T. to a godly friende of his, beeing troubled in minde with sinne. 12°. [*London,* c. 1590.] C(frags.).
Text begins: 'Because it is/ the duetie of/'; a different text from 25624, 25624.5.

T., W.—cont.
23633.5 — [Anr. ed.] 12°. [*J. Windet?* c. 1590.] F(lacks tp). Text begins: 'Because it/ is yᵉ duety/'.
23633a — A godly and profitable treatise, intituled Absolom his fall. 8°. *T. Orwin f. N. L[ing] a. J. Busbie,* [1590.] O.
— The practyse of prelates. 1530. *See* 24465.
— ⟨A return of⟩ thankfullnesse. 1640. *See* 24473.7.
— The shepheards delight. [1624.] *See* 3694.3.
— Vindiciæ ecclesiæ Anglicanæ. 1630. *See* 24188.
— *ed. See* 20036.5.
— *tr. See* 18348.

Table. The holy table. 1637. *See* 25724.
23633a.5 — In this second table is contained the law of God being the second principall part of his heavenly honour. fol(3). *R. Field,* [c. 1590.] YK(pasted together and inserted in XV.C.22, a copy of 21226).
— A logarithmeticall table. 1635. *See* 25851.
— A most exact alphabeticall table. 1640. *See* 12503.5.
23633a.7 — A necessarie table of losse or gaine after tenne in the hundred, both by the moneth, and the yeare, as shall be required. s.sh.fol. *V. Simmes,* [1598.] Ent. 11 de. 1598. HD.
— A plaine and perfect two-fold table: shewing interest. [1624.] *See* 19600.2.
23634 — A plaine table and most perfit description of the yeare politicall. Also here is added the Gregorian calendar, and a perpetuall concordance of the diuers Romane calendars. s.sh.fol. *London,* [1592.] L(impr. cropt).
Refers to this present year 1592 and the 'Triple Almanacke for 1591', prob. 433.5.
23634.3 — [Heading A1ʳ:] A short and plaine table orderly disposing the principles of religion. 8°. [*T. Dawson?* c. 1580.] C².
23634.5 — A table declaring what planet dooth raigne euery day and houre enduring for euer. s.sh.fol. *G. Simson f. W. Kirkham,* 1598. HD.
— Une table logarithmetique. 1635. *See* 25851.5.
23634.7 — Table-observations. Picke no quarrels [etc. Rules for conduct.] s.sh.fol. [*R. Barker,* c. 1615.] L⁵(Lemon 244).
— [A table of compound interest at £8 per centum. 1625?] *See* 19600.6.
23635 — A table of good nurture. (The second table.) *Ballads.* s.sh.fol. *f. H. G[osson,* 1625?] Ent. to ballad ptnrs. 14 de. 1624. L.
— A table of the cheiffest citties. [c. 1600.] *See* 10021.7.
— A table or short view off all ecclesiasticall discipline. [1574.] *See* 24184.
23636 — A table plainly teaching yᵉ making and use of a wetherglas. [Engr. w. text.] s.sh.fol. [*London,* 1631.] L.
Also advertises sale of the glasses 'at the Princes armes in Leaden Hall street.'
— ⟨A table⟩ shewing the most profitable order and m⟨ethod for r⟩eading of history. [c. 1620.] *See* 13528.5.
23636.5 — A table shewing the true value of the hundred, and the halfe quartern of haperdepois [*sic*] weight: at any price whatsoever. s.sh.fol. *W. J[ones,] sold by N. Bourne,* 1625. L⁵(Lemon 269).
23637 — A verie plaine and perfecte table, called of some mariners the flye. 1569. = pt. of 484.

23638 **Tables.** Tables of leasses and interest, with their grounds expressed in foure tables of fractions. [By A. Acroyd?] 8°. *W. Jones,* 1628. L².O.C.C³.LINC.+
23639 — [A variant, w. imprint:] *W. Jones,* [1628?] HN.

23640 **Tablet.** [A tablet for gentlewomen.] (Here foloweth the Letanie.) 32° in 8's. (*W. Seres,* 1574.) Ass'd by W. Seres to J. Judson 26 mr. 1577. L(lacks all before D2).
23641 — A tablet of deuout prayers and godly meditations. 24° in 8's. *T. East & H. Middelton f. N. Blond,* 1571. Ent. 1569–70. L(frags. of outer forme of 1st quire, Harl.5936/355; and of both formes of B and C, Harl.5936/106). O³(frag. of outer formes of 1st 3 quires).
The text is pr. within circular borders having a diameter of 33 mm. each.

23641.5 **Tabula.** Tabula, Graecas declinationes et coniugationes omnes, partem grammaticæ potissimam & maximè necessariam, breuissima methodo comprehendens. s.sh.fol. *R. Robinsonus,* [c. 1590.] ILL.

23642 **Tacitus, Publius Cornelius.** The ende of Nero and beginning of Galba. Fower bookes of the Histories of Cornelius Tacitus. The life of Agricola. [*Tr.* and *ed.* by *Sir*] (H. Savile.) fol. (*Oxforde, J. Barnes* [really *London, R. Robinson*] *f. R. Wright,*) 1591. L.O.C.D.DUR⁵.+; F.HN.CAL.NY.Y.+
    Wright granted a patent to print this 25 May 1591; *see* Arber II.16.

23643 — Second edition. fol. (*E. Bollifant f. B. a. J. Norton,*) 1598. L.O.C.G².M.+; F.HN.HD.N.NY.+
    Issued w. 23644.

23644 — The annales of Cornelius Tacitus. The description of Germanie. [*Tr.*] (R. Grenewey.) fol. (*A. Hatfield f. B. a. J. Norton,*) 1598. L.O.C.G².M.+; F.HN.HD.N.NY.+
    Issued w. 23643.

23645 — [Anr. ed. of 23644, 23643.] The annales. The description. (The end of Nero. Foure bookes. The life of Agricola. The third edition.) 2 pts. fol. (*A. Hatfield f. J. Norton,*) 1604 (1605.) L.O.C.D.E.+; F.HN.CU. HD.N.+

23646 — (Fourth edition.) 2 pts. fol. (*A. Hatfield f. J. Norton,*) 1612. L.O.C.DEU.M.+; F.HN.CU.HD.N.+

23647 — (Fifth edition.) 2 pts. fol. (*J. Bill,*) 1622. L.O.C.D.E².+; F.HN.HD.N.NY.+

23648 — (Sixth edition.) 2 pts. fol. *J. L*[*egat*] *f. R. Whitaker,* 1640. Ass'd by J. Bill to Joyce Norton a. R. Whitaker 26 au. 1632. L.O.C.BIRM²(K.N.).E.+; F.HN.CHI.CU.HD(imp.).+

23649 — La vita di Giulio Agricola. Messa in volgare da G. M. Manelli. 4°. *nella stamperia di G. Wolfio,* 1585. L.O.C.; F.

Taets, Elizabeth Goossens. Two most remarkable histories. 1620. *See* 13525.

23650 **Taffin, Jean.** The amendment of life, comprised in fower bookes: *tr.* according to the French coppie. 4° in 8's. [*J. Windet,*] *imp. G. Bishop,* 1595. Ent. to J. Wolfe 20 se. 1594. L.O.C.BIRM²(K.N.).M.+; F(2).HN.IND.N.
    (23651 is pt. of this)

23651 — = pt. of 23650.

23652 — Of the markes of the children of God, and of their comforts in afflictions. Ouerseene againe and augmented by the author, and *tr.* out of French by A. Prowse. 8°. *T. Orwin f. T. Man,* 1590. Ent. to E. Aggas 30 oc. 1587; to T. Man 26 mr. 1590. L.; F.HN.PN².

23652.3 — [Anr. ed.] 8°. *R. Field f. T. Man,* 1591. C⁴.

23652.5 — [Anr. ed.] 8°. *R. Robinson f. T. Man,* 1597. F.

23652.7 — [Anr. ed.] 8°. *F. Kingston f. T. Man,* 1599. L(tp only, Ames I.632).DUL.

23653 — [Anr. ed.] 8°. *T. E*[*ast*] *f. T. Man,* 1608. L.O²⁸.; MCG.

23654 — [Anr. ed.] 8°. *T. C*[*reede*] *f. T. Man,* 1609. O.; F.

23655 — [Anr. ed.] 8°. *T. Snodham f. T. Man,* 1615. O.C.

23656 — Third edition. 12°. *assignes of T., P., a. J. Man, sold by J. Grismond,* 1634. Ass'd to P. a. J. Man 3 my. 1624; to B. Fisher 6 jy. 1629; to Fisher a. widow Man 12 au. 1635. L.

23656.5 — The practice of charity. Pressed upon the conscience by sundry effectuall and forcible arguments. [*Tr.*] (C. Cotton.) 8°. *f. N. Newberry,* 1625. ELY.

23657 **Tailboys, Samuel.** A new lachrymentall and funerall elegy: or, a distillation of teares, shed for the death of Lodowicke, duke of Richmond and Lenox. [In verse.] 4°. *B. Alsop,* 162[4]. L.

23658 **Tailor, Robert.** The hogge hath lost his pearle. A comedy. 4°. [*J. Beale*] *f. R. Redmer,* 1614. Ent. 23 my. L.O.C⁶.E.ETON.+; F.HN.CHI.HD.NY.+ Greg 321.

Tailour, Robert, *Composer.* Sacred hymns. Set to be sung. 1615. *See* 21723.

23659 **Taisnier, Joannes.** A very necessarie and profitable booke concerning nauigation. *Tr.* R. Eden. 4°. *R. Jugge,* [1575?] L.C³.C⁶.M.STU.+; F.CB.MICH.
    Advertised for sale in 5799.5 sqq.

23659.3 **Talæus, Audomarus.** Audomari Talaei rhetorica, e P. Rami praelectionibus observata. Nunc primúm hac manuali forma edita. 24° in 12's. *Cantabrigiæ, ex off. J. Legat,* 1592. Ent. to W. Norton a. J. Harrison 1 on 11 no. 1577; to J. Harrison 1 on 6 de. 1588. ILL.
    Issued w. 15244.3.

23659.5 — [Anr. ed.] 8°. *F. Kingston,* 1599. LK(imp.).

Talæus, Audomarus—*cont.*

23659.7 — [Anr. ed.] Cui præfixa est epistola [by A. Wechelus.] 8°. [*T. Snodham,*] *ex tipographica* [sic] *Soc. Stat.,* 1614. L(date defective, 1473.aa.39).

23659.9 — [Anr. ed.] 8°. [*T. Snodham*] *pro Soc. Stat.,* [c. 1620.] HN(date, if any, cropt).
    Tp device McK.305, w. motto: 'Sed adhuc . . .'

23660 — [Anr. ed., omitting the Epistola.] 8°. *Edinburgi, A. Hart,* 1621. F.

23660.5 — [Anr. ed., w. the Epistola.] 8°. [*J. Dawson*] *pro Soc. Stat.,* 1627. Ent. to the English Stock 20 mr. 1620. L(tp only, Ames II.773).
    Lace orn. on the tp.

23661 — [Anr. ed.] 8°. *Cantabrigiæ, ex acad. typog.,* 1631. C.E.PLUME.

23661.5 — [Anr. ed.] 12°. *Cantabrigiæ, ex acad. typog.,* 1635. C.C².; F.

23662 — [Anr. ed.] 8°. [*E. Purslowe,*] *imp. Soc. Stat.,* 1636. L⁴⁴.C.
    — *See also* 4196.5, 10765.5, 11338, 21106.

23662.5 **Talbot, Thomas,** *Antiquary.* Vnio rosarum. . . . The vnion of the roses of the famelies of Lancaster and Yorke wᵗʰ the armes of knights of the garter from that tyme vnto 1589. *Lat. a. Eng.* [Engr. by J. Hondius.] s.sh.fol. *solde in Black-friers,* [1589?] L(Print Dept.).
    See Hind I.177.

Talbot, Thomas, *Roman Catholic, tr. See* 4125.

Talent. [The talent of devotion. 1609?] *See* 13507.5.

23663 **Tales.** A, C, mery talys. fol. [*J. Rastell,* 1526?] L(imp.). SH(8 leaves).; F(2 leaves). Nash (2 leaves).
    Has Rastell's name in the device, McK.37.

23664 — [Anr. ed., w. omissions and additions.] fol. [*J. Rastell a. Southwark, P. Treveris,*] (1526 (22 no.)) Göttingen U.
    Has Rastell's name in the device, McK.37. This may be the earlier ed.

23664.5 — [Anr. ed.] 8°. [*R. Copland?* 1548?] P(4 leaves, in the binding of E.4.28).
    Includes Tales 97 and 99 of 23663, which do not appear in 23664.

23665 — Tales, and quicke answeres, very mery, and pleasant to rede. 4°. (*in the house of T. Berthelet,*) [1532?] HN.

23665.5 — [Anr. ed., enlarged.] Mery tales, wittie questions, and quicke answeres. 8°. *H. Wykes,* 1567. Ent. to H. Bynneman 3 no. 1576. HD(imp.).
    — The thrie tailes of the thrie priests of Peblis. 1603. *See* 19528.

Talley, David, *ed. See* 15610.6.

Tallis, Thomas. *See* 2729.

23666 **Tallis, Thomas,** and **Byrd, William.** Discantus (Tenor.—Contra tenor.—Bassus.—Superius.—Sexta Pars.) Cantiones, quae ab argumento sacrae vocantur, quinque et sex partium. 6 ptbks. obl.4°. *T. Vautrollerius,* 1575. L.L⁷.O³.D.YK(imp.).+; F(1, plus superius only).HN(superius only).LC.N(discantus only).
    H4 of all but sexta pars has Extract of Letters Patent to Byrd and Tallis to print music and music paper for 21 years, dated 22 Jan. 1575.

Talpin, Jean. A forme of christian pollicie. 1574. *See* 10793a.

Tamburlaine. Tamburlaine the great. 1590, etc. *See* 17425 sqq.

23667 **Taming.** A pleasant conceited historie, called The taming of a shrew. 4°. *P. Short, sold by C. Burbie,* 1594. Ent. to Short 2 my. HN. Greg 120.
    For the authorized Shakespeare text *see* 22327.

23668 — [Anr. ed.] 4°. *P. S*[*hort,*] *sold by C. Burbie,* 1596. L.; HN.

23669 — [Anr. ed.] 4°. *V. S*[*immes*] *f. N. Ling,* 1607. Ass'd by Burby to Ling 22 ja.; by Ling to J. Smethwick 19 no. O.; F.HN.HD.

23670 **Tanner, John.** A sermon preached at Paules Crosse the first day of June. 1596. by I. T[anner,] minister of Gods word. 8°. *Widow Orwin f. R. Ockold, sold* [*by J. Broome.*] Ent. as by Tanner 29 no. L.; F.

23670.5 — [A variant, w. imprint:] *Widow Orwin f. R. Ockold,* 1597. P. Stevens Cox.; F.

Tanner, Robert. [An almanack. 1584.] *See* 517.9.

23671 — Anno domini. 1592. A briefe treatise for the ready vse of the sphere. 16° in 8's. (*J. Charlwood,*) 1592. O.

23672 — A brief treatise of the use of the globe celestiall and terrestriall. [Init. R. T.] 8°. *F. Kyngston f. T. Man,* 1616. L.O.G⁴.USHAW.

23673 — [Anr. ed.] 8°. *R. Field f. T. Man,* 1620. L.INN.; F.

23674 — A mirror for mathematiques: a golden gem for geometricians: a sure safety for saylers. 4°. *J. C[harlewood,] solde by Richarde Watkins,* 1587. Ent. to Charlewood 6 ap. L.L³⁰.; N.

23674.5 — [A variant, w. imprint:] *J. C[harlewood,] sold by Richard Watkins,* 1587. O.C².E.G².M.+; F. Horblit. Henry Taylor.

23675 — = 23676.

23676 — A prognosticall iudgement of the great coniunction of the two superiour planets, Saturne and Iupiter, which shall happen the 28. day of Aprill. 1583. 8°. (*T. Dawson, at the assignement of R. W[atkins?]*) 1583. Ent. to Dawson 11 mr. O(2, 1 lacks tp).O⁵.; HN(lacks tp).
    (Formerly also 23675) A different text from 517.9.

Taphæa, Malumpertus, *tr. See* 12000.

23677 **Tapp, John.** The path-way to knowledge; containing the whole art of arithmeticke. By way of dialogue. Wherewith is a briefe order for the keeping of accompts, by way of debitor and creditor. 8°. *T. Purfoot f. T. Pavier,* 1613. Ent. 14 au. 1600. L.L³⁰.O.C.STU.+
    Partly based on G. Gosselin's French ed. of N. Tartalia; and partly *tr.* from V. Mennher.

23678 — [Anr. ed.] 8°. *T. Purfoot f. T. Pavier,* 1621. L⁴ (missing).L³⁸.; HN.CU.

23679 — The seamans kalender, or an ephemerides of the sun, moone and certaine starres. By J. T(app.) 4°. *E. Allde f. J. Tapp,* 1602. Ent. 1 de. 1601. L.C¹⁵.; Y. Penrose 243.

23679.5 — Third edition: newly corrected. 4° in 8's. *E. Allde f. J. Tappe,* 1608. L.O³(lacks tp).

23680 — Fifth edition newly corrected and enlarged. 4° in 8's. *E. Allde f. J. Tappe,* 1615. L.

23680.3 — Sixth edition. 4° in 8's. *E. All-de f. J. Tappe,* 1617. E².

23680.5 — Seventh edition. 4° in 8's. *E. All-de f. J. Tap,* 1620. PARIS.

23680.7 — Eighth edition. 4° in 8's. *E. All-de f. J. Tap,* 1622. Horblit.

23681 — Ninth edition. 4° in 8's. *E. All-de f. J. Tap,* 1625. HN.

23682 — Twelfth impression. 4° in 8's. *B. Alsop a. T. Fawcet f. J. Tap,* 1631. O.(tp only, Harl.5921/33). O.

23682.5 — Thirteenth impression. 4° in 8's. *B. A[lsop] a. T. F[awcet] f. J. Hurlocke,* 1632. Ass'd 1 au. 1631. A. London, Trinity House (imp.).

23682.7 — [Fourteenth? impression.] 4° in 8's. [*B. Alsop a. T. Fawcet f. J. Hurlock,* 1634?] Horblit (lacks tp).
    In the calendar on C8ʳ the date of Easter in 1636 is correctly given as 17 Apr. while previous eds. have 16 Apr.

— *ed. See* 5803.

— *See also* 1590.5.

23683 **Tarlton, Richard.** A prettie newe ballad, intytuled: the crowe sits vpon the wall. [Init. R. T.] Ballad. s.sh.fol. *f. H. Kyrkham,* [1592.] Ent. 18 ja. 1592. L.

23683.3 — Tarltons jests. Drawne into these three parts. 4°. [*T. Snodham*] *f. J. Budge,* 1613. Pt. 2 ent. to T. Pavier 4 au. 1600; the whole ass'd by J. Budge to C. Knight 21 fb. 1609. F(imp.).
    C2ʳ line 5 from bottom: 'Globe on the Banckeside/'.

23683.5 — [Anr. ed.] 4°. [*London,* c. 1620.] F(frag. of C2,3).
    C2ʳ lines 4, 5 from bottom: 'Globe on/ the Bankes side'.

23683.7 — [Anr. ed.] 4°. [*G. Purslowe,* c. 1630.] L(lacks tp).
    C2ʳ lines 4, 5 from bottom: 'Globe on the/Bankes side'.

23684 — [Anr. ed.] 4°. *J. H[aviland] f. A. Crook,* 1638. Ass'd by M. Allot to J. Legat a. A. Crooke 1 jy. 1637. O.; HN(lacks tp).
    C2ʳ lines 4, 5 from bottom: 'Globe on the/Banks side'.

23685 — Tarltons newes out of purgatorie. Onely such a jest as his iigge. Published by Robin Goodfellow. 4°. [*R. Robinson*] *f. T. G[ubbin] a. T. N[ewman,]* 1590. Ent. to Gubbin a. Newman 26 jn. L.
    Attacked in 4579. Possibly by R. Armin.

Tarlton, Richard—*cont.*

23685a — [Anr. ed.] 4°. [*E. Allde*] *f. E. White,* [c. 1600.] O.; HN.

23686 — [Anr. ed.] 4°. *G. Purslowe, sold by F. Grove,* 1630. L.O(3, 2 imp.).C².; F(imp.).HD(imp.).

23687 — [Tarltons toyes of an idle head. c. 1585.] Now = 3655.5.

23687.5 — Tarltons tragical treatises, contayning sundrie discourses and prety conceytes, both in prose and verse. 8°. *H. Bynneman,* 1578. Ent. 5 fb. F(*⁸ only).

23688 — A very lamentable and woful discours of the fierce fluds, in Bedford shire, in Lincoln shire, and other places, the v. of October. 1570. [In verse.] s.sh.fol. *J. Allde,* 1570. Ent. 1570–71. HN.

— The cobler of Caunterburie, or an inuectiue against Tarltons newes out of purgatorie. 1590. *See* 4579.

23689 **Tartaglia, Niccolò.** Three bookes of colloquies concerning the arte of shooting artillerie, written in Italian. *Tr.* by C. Lucar. Also . . . annexed a treatise named Lucar appendix. fol. (*T. Dawson*) *f. J. Harrison (the elder),* 1588. Ent. 30 oc. 1587. L(tp def.).L¹⁰.L³⁰.A. London, Royal Artillery Institution.+; F(2, 1 imp.). HD.N.TEX(imp.).Y.
    Orig. sub tp on G5 w. device McK.236 is sometimes replaced by cancel bifolium w. sub tp w. cut of mortar shooting and errata on verso of 2nd leaf; both varieties in HD copy. HD also has cancel G3,4 w. G3ʳ line 5 from bottom ending: 'saide' instead of 'sayde' (L).

— *See also* 3420, 23677.

23690 **Tasso, Ercole** and **Torquato.** Of mariage and wiuing. An excellent, pleasant, and philosophicall controuersie, betweene the two Tassi. Done into English, by R. T[ofte?] gentleman. 4°. *T. Creede, sold by J. Smythicke,* 1599. Ent. to Creede 6 mr. L.O.C⁵.; F.HN.HD.
    Ordered burned by Abp. Whitgift 1 June 1599; *see* Arber III.677–8.

Tasso, Torquato. Aminta favola boschereccia. 1591. *See* 12414.

23691 — Amyntas Thomæ Watsoni. 1585. Now = 25118.2.

23692 — [A trans.] The lamentations of Amyntas. 1587. Now = 25118.4.

23693 — [Anr. ed.] 1588. Now = 25118.5.

23694 — [Anr. ed.] 1589. Now = 25118.6.

23695 — [Anr. ed.] 1596. Now = 25118.8.

23696 — Torquato Tasso's Aminta Englisht [by H. Reynolds.] To this is added Ariadne's complaint in imitation of Anguillara; written by the translater of Tasso's Aminta. 4°. *A. Mathewes f. W. Lee,* 1628. Ent. as tr. by H. Reynolds 7 no. 1627. L.O.O⁶.O⁸.DUL.+; F. HN.HD.N.PML.+ Greg 417.
    For an adaptation of Aminta see 11340.

23697 — Godfrey of Bulloigne, or the recouerie of Hierusalem. *Tr.* by R. C[arew] esquire: and now the first part containing fiue cantos, imprinted in both languages. [In verse.] Eng. a. Ital. 4°. *J. Windet f. C. Hunt of Exceter,* 1594. Ent. 26 ja. L.O.C.C².BTU.+; F.HD. N.NY.Y.+

23697a — [A variant, w. imprint:] *J. Windet f. T. Man,* [1594.] L(1st four leaves only, Harl. 5995/281-4).L³⁸.O. LINC.; HN.ILL.Y.

23698 — Godfrey of Bulloigne, . . . [Anon.] Done in English heroicall verse, by E. Fairefax. fol. *A. Hatfield f. J. Jaggard a. M. Lownes,* 1600. Ent. 22 no. 1599. L.O.C.E.M.+; F.HN.HD.N.NY.+
    Orig. B1 has 1st stanza beginning: 'I Sing the sacred armies' (HN 69619). Cancel B1 begins: 'The sacred armies' (most copies), over which is, or was, pasted a cancel 1st stanza beginning: 'I Sing the warre' (1 L, 2 F).

23699 — Now the second time imprinted. fol. [*Eliot's Court Press f.*] *J. Bill,* 1624. L.O.C.D.E.+; F.HN.CHI. HD.PML.+
    With extra preliminaries, including the publisher's dedic. naming Tasso as author. Some copies have an engr. portrait of Godfrey and/or an extra leaf of verses: 'The Genius of Godfrey to Prince Charles'; both at L.

23700 — Torquati Tassi Solymeidos, liber primus latinis numeris expressus a S. Gentili. [In verse.] fol. *J. Wolfius,* 1584. L.O⁸.ETON.YK.; HN.

Tasso, Torquato—*cont.*

23701 — Scipii Gentilis Solymeidos libri duo priores de T. Tassi Italicis expressi. [In verse.] 4°. *ap. J. Wolfium,* 1584. L.C.E.M.; F.

    Copies vary: with (L) or without (C) the inits. 'S.G.' following the verses 'De Tasso'.

23702 — Plutonis concilium. Ex initio quarti libri Solymeidos. [*Tr.*] (S. Gentilis.) [In verse.] 4°. *ap. J. Wolfium,* 1584. C.

23702.5 — The housholders philosophie. Wherein is perfectly described, the true oeconomia of housekeeping. *Tr.* T. K[yd.] 4°. *J. C[harlewood] f. T. Hacket,* 1588. Ent. 6 fb. O.

23703 — [Anr. issue, w. pt. 2 added, and cancel gen. tp:] Whereunto is anexed a dairie booke for all good huswiues. [By] (B. Dowe.) 2 pts. 4°. *J. C[harlewood] f. T. Hacket,* 1588. Pt. 2 ent. 9 jy. L(lacks pt. 2). O.SH(lacks tp)*.; HN.BO[5].

    — *See also* 11728.8.

23704 **Tatham, John.** The fancies theater. (Love crownes the end. A pastorall.) [In verse.] 8°. *J. Norton f. R. Best,* 1640. Ent. 15 oc. L.L[6].O.C[3].D[9].+; F.HN.N.NY.Y.

23705 **Tatius, Titus.** Rapta Tatio. The mirrour of his majesties present government, tending to the union. 4°. *W. W[hite] f. S. Waterson,* 1604. L.O.C.D[2].E[2].+; F.HN. HD.NY.

    One L copy (600.d.29/6) has MS. attrib. to Sir John Skinner or N. Douglas; the motto on tp verso: 'Ignibus vnionis ardenS.' would seem to support the former.

    B4 is a cancel in app. all copies. The cancel was set in duplicate: B4[r] line 8 ends: 'friendes,' or 'frindes [*sic*],' both at L.

23706 **Tattlewell, Mary.** The womens sharpe revenge: or an answer to sir Seldome Sober [in 23747, 23766]. 12°. *J. O[kes,] sold by J. Becket,* 1640. Ent. to J. Okes 24 ap. 1639. O(imp.).

    This answer may have been written by John Taylor as well as the 2 works it attacks.

23707 **Tavern.** Here ensueth a lytell treatyse named the tauerne of goostly helthe. 16° in 8. (R. Coplande, 1522.) A[2](lacks 6th leaf).

23708 **Taverner, John.** Certaine experiments concerning fish and fruite. 4°. [R. Field] f. W. Ponsonby, 1600. Ent. 10 ja. L.O.C[2].; F.HN.CH.HD.Y.+

23709 **Taverner, Richard.** A catechisme or institution of the christen religion. Newely setforthe. 8°. [R. Bankes,] 1539. L(imp.).

23710 — An epitome of the psalmes. 1539. = 2748.

23711 — [A ghost.]

23711a — The garden of wysdom wherin ye maye gather moste pleasaunt flowres, wytty sayenges of princes, [etc. Based on Erasmus' Apophthegmata.] 8°. [R. Bankes] (in æd. R. Tauerneri,) solde by J. Haruye, 1539. L(tp facs.).LEEDS.; F(frag.).HN.

23712 — [Anr. ed.] Newly recognised and augmented. 8°. E. Whytchurche, (sold by W. Telotson,) [1543?] L.O(imp.).C.; CH.ILL(imp.).

23712.5 — The second booke of the Garden of wysdome. (The thyrde boke.) 8°. (R. Bankes,) 1539. HETH(imp.).; F(imp.).

    Bk. 2 is based on Erasmus' Apophthegmata. The text of bk. 3, derived from Erasmus' Adagia, is not included in the following eds. but is reprinted separately as 10437.

23713 — [Anr. ed.] The secōd booke . . . wysedome. 8°. [E. Whitchurch f.] (R. Bankes,) 1539 [1542?] L(2).O.C. LEEDS.; HN.CH.ILL.

23714 — [Anr. ed. of bks. 1 and 2.] 2 pts. 8°. W. Myddylton, [1547?] O.C[4].; CHI(bk. 2 only).LC.

    This and the following generally bd. w., issued? with, 10446 sqq.

23715 — [Anr. ed.] 2 pts. W. Copland f. R. Kele, [1550?] L.; HN.WIS.

23715.5 — [A variant, w. imprint:] W. Copland, [1550?] F(3, 2 imp.).

23716 — [Anr. ed.] 2 pts. 8°. [J. King, 1556?] O(lacks tp). C(imp.).DUL(imp.).

    — The summe or pith of the 150. psalmes. 1539. See 2747.5.

    — *ed. See* 2967.2, 2967.6, 4843, 4845, 10437.

    — *tr. See* 908, 2067, 2747.5, 2844, 10445, 10492, 21752.5.

23716.5 **Tavernier, Melchior.** A true and most exact map of the siedge of Rochell, presented to the [French] kings majestie the first day of May, 1628. by M. Tavernor graver & printer. [Engr. map w. letterpress text.] s.sh.fol. *Paris, M. Tavernor, sold by T. Walkely,* [London,] 1628. L[5](Lemon 284).P(G.10.14).; HN. *See also* 21590.5.

23717 **Tayler, Francis,** *B. D.* Selfe-satisfaction occasionally taught the citizens in the lecture at St. Magnes neere London-bridge. 4°. *J. Norton f. R. Bird,* 1633. Ent. 17 se. L[3].D.P.; F.U.

23718 — Vocatio divina, seu meditationes succintæ. 8°. *B. A[lsop] a. T. Fawcet, imp. N. Butter,* 1627. L[2].L[3]. O.D.E.+

23719 **Tayler, Francis,** *Preacher.* A godly, zealous and learned sermon, vpon the 18. 19. 20. 21. verses of the 10. chap. to the Romaines. 8°. *T. D[awson] f. T. Woodcocke* 1583. L(2).L[2].O.O[19](frag.). DEU.; F.TORONTO[2].

23720 **Taylor, Augustine.** [Engr. gen. tp:] Divine epistles dedicated to right hon.[ble] & worthy guests invited to ye nuptialls of the great kings sonne. [In verse.] 8°. (*N. Okes,* 1623.) L(sub tp on L4[r]: 'A watch', Harl.5993/67). LONGLEAT(imp.).; HN.

    There are numerous letterpress sub tpp, all beginning w. 'Epistle . . .' except L4[r]: 'A watch' and M4[r]: 'The defence of divine poesie.'

23721 — Encomiasticke elogies. Written by Augustine Taylor. [In verse.] 8°. *N. Okes,* 1614. O.; HN.

23722 — Epithalamium upon the all-desired nuptials of Frederike the fift. And Elizabeth. [In verse.] 4°. [*N. Okes*] f. S. Rand, sold by E. Marchant, 1613. O.CHATS.

23722.5 — [Anr. issue, w. imprint:] [*N. Okes*] f. S. Rand, 1613. O[13].

23723 — Newes from Jerusalem: containing, 1. The beauty of the citie of the great king. 2. The vanitie of the isles of the sonns of men. 3. The comming of the kings sonne. [Partly in verse.] 8°. *A. Matthewes,* 1623. Ent. 30 ap. L(tp only, Harl.5910, pt.IV/20).; HN.

23724 **Taylor, Jeremy,** *Bp.* A sermon preached in saint Maries church in Oxford. Upon the anniversary of the Gunpowder-treason. 4°. *Oxford, L. Lichfield,* 1638. L.O.C.D.G[2].+; F.HN.HD(pt. of Wing T 403).N.NY.+

    Unsold sheets retaining orig. tp reissued in 1648 as pt. of Wing T 403.

23725 **Taylor, John.** All the workes of John Taylor the Water-Poet. Beeing sixty and three in number. With sundry new additions, corrected, revised and newly imprinted. fol. *J. B[eale, Eliz. Allde, a. B. Alsop a. T. Fawcet] f. J. Boler,* 1630. L.O.C.D.E.+; F.HN. HD.N.NY.+

    Beale pr. A, Aa–Ss, and 1st Aaa–Kkk; Allde pr. B–O; Alsop and Fawcet pr. 2nd Aaa–Mmm. For possible nonce collections of Taylor's works, *see The Library,* XVIII (1963), pp. 51–7.

23726 — An armado, or navye, of 103. ships & other vessels; who have the art to sayle by land, as well as by sea. 8°. *E. A[llde] f. H. Gosson,* 1627. Ent. 25 ja. L.; HN.NY.

23726a — [Anr. issue, w. title:] An armado, or navy, [etc.] *E. A[llde] f. H. Gosson,* 1627. O.; HD.

    Sheet B is reset; sheet A and inner forme of C are largely reimposed w. new headings; the rest is from same setting as 23726.

23727 — [Anr. ed.] 8°. [*A. Mathewes*] f. H. Gosson, 1635. O.; HN.Y.

23728 — An arrant thiefe, whom every man may trust. With a comparison betweene a thiefe and a booke. [In verse.] 8°. *E. All-de f. H. Gosson,* 1622. L(2).L[8]. Gloucester PL.; F.HN.HD.ILL.NY.+

23729 — [Anr. ed.] 8°. [*M. Flesher*] f. H. Gosson, sold [by E. Wright?] 1625. L(3).O.

23730 — [Anr. ed.] 8°. [*A. Mathewes*] f. H. Gosson, 1635. O.; HN.HD.

23731 — A bawd. A vertuous bawd, a modest bawd. 8°. [*A. Mathewes?*] f. H. Gosson, 1635. O.; HN.

23731.3 — The booke of martyrs. [In verse.] 2 pts. 64° in 16's. [*J. Beale?*] f. J. Hamman, 1616. Ent. 27 fb. O.

23731.5 — [Anr. ed.] 2 pts. 64° in 16's. [*J. Beale?*] f. J. Hamman, 1617. O(imp.).

23731.7 — [Anr. ed.] 2 pts. 64° in 16's. *J. H[aviland] f. J. Hammond,* 1627. Arthur Houghton (imp.).

Taylor, John—*cont.*

23732 — [Anr. ed.] 2 pts. 64° in 16's. *J. Beale*, 1631. Ass'd 16 de. 1630. No copy traced.

> W. A. Jackson noted an unlocated frag. of quire B from pt. 2, unfolded, w. the above imprint, but attempts to trace it have failed.

23732.3 — [Anr. ed.] 2 pts. 64° in 16's. *J. Beale*, 1633. O(frag. of quire C from pt. 1).; Miss Julia P. Wightman, New York City (pt. 1 only).

23732.7 — [Anr. ed. Anon.] 8°. *J. B[eale,]* sold by *J. Wright [jun.]*, 1635. O[6].; PN[2].

23733 — [Anr. ed.] 8°. *J. B[eale,]* 1639. L.; HN.

23734 — A brave and valiant sea-fight, upon the coast of Cornewall. 1640. Now = 23809.5.

23735 — A brave memorable and dangerous sea-fight, foughten neere the road of Tittawan in Barbary. [In verse.] 4°. [*N. Okes?*] *f. H. Gosson*, 1636. O(lacks tp).; HN.

23736 — A briefe remembrance of all the English monarchs, from the Normans conquest. [Engraved portraits w. verses.] 8°. *G. Eld f. H. Gosson*, 1618. Ent. 24 jy. L.

> C2[r] last line: 'waite'; half-length portraits in this and next 2 eds. *See* H. C. Levis, *Notes on the Early British Engraved Royal Portraits*, pp. 101 ff.

23737 — [Anr. ed.] 8°. *G. Eld f. H. Gosson*, 1618. HN.

> C2[r] last line: 'wait'.

23737.5 — [Anr. ed.] 8°. [*G. Eld?*] *f. C. Holland*, 1621. HD.LC (2 imp.).

23738 — [Anr. ed.] 8°. *G. Eld*, 1622. L.L[30].

> Full-length portraits.

23738.5 — [An advertisement.] A briefe remembrance [etc.] 1/2 sh.fol. *G. Eld*, 1622. L(Harl.5952/37).

> The sheet is divided into 4 quarters, the bottom 2 containing the title and verses on Prince Charles reimposed from 23738. The upper left has an engraving of the royal arms, while the upper right is cut away. It may have contained a full-length portrait of Prince Charles.

23739 — Bull, beare, and horse, cut, curtaile, and longtaile. With tales, and tales of buls, clenches, and flashes. [In verse.] 8°. *M. Parsons f. H. Gosson*, 1638. Ent. 25 oc. 1637. O.

23740 — The carriers cosmographie. or a briefe relation, of the innes, . . . in, and neere London. 4°. *A. G[riffin,]* 1637. Ent. to Mrs. Griffin 16 my. L.L[8].O(2).LINC.; HN.HD.ILL.Y.

> An abridged version w. heading on A1[r]: 'A brief director . . .' was pub'd anonymously c. 1642 (HD).

23741 — A cast over the water. Given gratis to William Fennor, the rimer, from London to the Kings Bench. [In verse.] 8°. [*G. Eld*] *f. W. Butler [1,]* sold by *E. Marchant*, 1615. L.

> Answers 10783.

23741.5 — Christian admonitions, against the two fearefull sinnes of cursing and swearing, most fit to be set up in every house. s.sh.fol. *Eliz. Allde f. H. Gosson*, [c. 1630.] ?Ent. 5 de. 1626. L[5](Lemon 233).

> Reprinted from 23754.

— The coaches overthrow. [1636.] *See* 5451.

23742 — A common whore with all these graces grac'd. [In verse.] 8°. [*E. Allde*] *f. H. Gosson*, 1622. Ent. 31 ja. L(quire B, Ashley 2028).; HN.HD.ILL.NY(2).

> In imprint: 'Pannier-Alley'; B1[r] last line: 'sensuality'.

23742.5 — [Anr. ed.] 8°. [*E. Allde*] *f. H. Gosson*, 1622. L(C.30.b. 26, and quire A in Ashley 2028).L[8].

> In imprint: 'Panier-Alley'; B1[r] last line: 'sensuality'.

23743 — [Anr. ed.] 8°. [*M. Flesher*] *f. H. Gosson*, solde [by *E. Wright?*] 1625. L.

23744 — [Anr. ed.] 8°. [*A. Mathewes*] *f. H. Gosson*, 1635. O.; HN.

23745 — The complaint of Christmas. And the teares of twelfe-tyde. 4°. [*J. Beale*] *f. J. B[oler]* a. *H. G[osson,]* sold [by *J. Boler*,] 1631. Ent. to Boler a. Gosson 4 de. 1630. C.; HN.

23745.5 — [A variant, w. imprint:] *f. J. Boler*, 1631. HN.HD.

23746 — Differing worships, or, the oddes, betweene some knights service and God's. Or Tom Nash his ghost. [In verse.] 4°. [*R. Bishop?*] *f. W. Ley*, 1640. Ent. 17 jn. L(3).L[8].O.M.; F.HN.N.Y.+

23747 — Divers crabtree lectures. Expressing the severall languages that shrews read to their husbands. [Mary Make-peace, *pseud.*] 12°. *J. Okes f. J. Sweeting*, 1639. Ent. to Okes 24 ap. with 23706. O.

> *See* also 23706 and 23766.

Taylor, John—*cont.*

23748 — A dog of war, or, the travels of Drunkard, the famous curre of the Round-Woolstaple in Westminster. [In verse.] 8°. *Printed by I Perse I, for O perse O, and & perse &, solde at the signe of the Æ dipthong* [i.e. London, 1628?] O.; HN.

> Preceding the tp is a half-title reading: 'A dogg of warre.' On C5[r]: 'This storie's writ the day and yeare, That Seacoles were exceeding deere.'

23748.5 — The Dolphins danger: and deliverance. Being a ship of 220. tunne. Set forth by the appoyntment of M. Edward Nichols. 4°. [*E. Allde?*] *f. H. Gosson*, 1617. L.

> A refutation of 6993.

23749 — Drinke and welcome: or the famous historie of the most part of drinks, in use now in Great Brittaine and Ireland. Compiled in the high Dutch tongue, by H. van Speagle, and now *tr.* By J. Taylor. 4°. *A. Griffin*, 1637. Ent. to Mrs. Griffin 16 my. L.L[6].L[8]. O.M.; HN.HD. Lehigh U.

> An orig. work by Taylor rather than a trans.

23750 — The eighth wonder of the world, or Coriats escape from his supposed drowning. With his entertainment at Constantinople. [In verse.] 8°. *Printed at Pancridge* [i.e. London, *N. Okes,*] 1613. Ent. to T. Thorpe 2 au. L.; HN.

23751 — An English-mans love to Bohemia. [In verse.] 4°. *Dort* [i.e. London, *G. Eld,*] 1620. L.O.; HN.HD(lacks tp).

23752 — Faire and fowle weather: or a sea and land storme. [In verse.] 4°. [*R. Blower*] *f. W: B[utler?]* solde by *E. Wright*, 1615. O.

23753 — A famous fight at sea. Where foure English ships fought in the Gulfe of Persia. 4°. *J. Haviland f. H. Gosson*, 1627. Ent. 28 mr. L.C[2].; F.HN(date cropt).CH.HD(date cropt).TEX.

> Tp varies: w. (HN) or without (HD) 2 lines at end of title beginning: 'With a farewell . . .'

23754 — The fearefull summer: or Londons calamity, the countries courtesy, and both their misery. [In verse.] 8°. *Oxford, J. Lichfield a. W. Turner*, 1625. L.O.

> Includes earlier printing of 23741.5 and 23812.7.

23755 — [Anr. ed., revised.] The fearefull sommer: . . . 8°. *Oxford, J. L[ichfield]* a. *W. T[urner*, really London, *E. Allde,*] 1625. L.

> Omits text of 23741.5.

23756 — [Anr. ed.] Now reprinted with some editions [*sic*]. 4°. *E. P[urslowe]* *f. H. Gosson*, 1636. L(impr. cropt).; HN.

> Omits both 23741.5 and 23812.7.

23757 — Fill gut, & pinch belly. [Anon. In verse.] s.sh.fol. *E. All-de f. H. Gosson*, 1620. L[5](Lemon 175).

> Prob. not by Taylor.

23757.5 — The first (second) part of the discourse held betweene the felt-hat, the beaver, French hood, and black-bagge. [Anon.] 2 pts. 8°. *J. O[kes]* *f. A. Kembe in Southwarke*, 1639. Ent. as by Taylor to Okes 17 oc. 1638. Brent Gration-Maxfield, London.

23758 — For the sacred memoriall of . . . Charles Howard earle of Nottingham. 4°. [*M. Flesher?*] *f. H. G[osson,]* 1625. L[8].; HD.

23759 — A funerall elegie, in memory of the rare, famous, and admired poet, M[r]. Benjamin Jonson deceased. Who dyed the sixteenth day of August last. 4°. *E. P[urslowe]* *f. H. Gosson*, 1637. Ent. 9 oc. O[5].E.; Y.

23760 — Great Britaine, all in blacke. For the incomparable losse of Henry, our late worthy prince. [In verse.] 4°. *E. A[llde]* *f. J. Wright*, 1612. Ent. to H. Gosson 7 no. HN.NY.

23760.5 — [Anr. issue, w. poems by W. Rowley added.] *E. A[llde]* *f. J. Wright*, 1612. L.; HD.

23761 — The great eater, of Kent, or part of the exploits of Nicholas Wood. 4°. *Eliz. Allde f. H. Gosson*, 1630. Ent. 20 de. 1629. L.O[8].; HN.

23762 — The great O Toole. [In verse.] 8°. [*E. Allde*] *f. H. Gosson*, 1622. L.C.; HN.HD.NY.Y.

> Reissued as pt. 2 of 23812.3.

23763 — Heavens blessing, and earths joy. Or a true relation, of the al-beloved mariage, of Fredericke & Elizabeth. With triumphall encomiasticke verses. 4°. [*E. Allde*] *f. J. Hunt [a.]* (*H. Gosson,*) solde by *J. Wright*, 1613. Ent. to H. Gosson 30 ja. L(impr. cropt).L[8].

23764 — The honorable, and memorable foundations, . . . within ten shires. Also, a relation of the wine tavernes. 8°. *A. M[athewes,]* 1636. O(2).; F.HN.

Taylor, John—_cont._

23764a — [Anr. issue, w. imprint:] _f. H. Gosson,_ 1636. L.

23765 — Jack a Lent. His beginning and entertainment. 4⁰. [_G. Eld f. J. Trundle?_ 1617?] O(impr. cropt).

23765.5 — [Anr. ed.] With new additions. 4⁰. [_G. Purslowe_] _f. J. T[rundle?_] 1620. L.L⁸.

23766 — A juniper lecture. With the description of all sorts of women. The second impression. 12⁰. _J. O[kes] f. W. Ley,_ 1639. Ent. to Okes 4 au. 1638. HN.
Answered by 23706.

23767 — A kicksey winsey: or a lerry come-twang: wherein John Taylor hath satyrically suited 800. of his bad debters. 8⁰. _N. Okes f. M. Walbanck,_ 1619. Ent. 8 no. L.O.

23768 — [Anr. ed., w. title:] The scourge of basenesse. Or the old lerry with a new kicksey. 8⁰. _N. O[kes] f. M. Walbancke,_ 1624. L(date cropt). Sheffield PL (imp.).; HN.

23769 — [Heading B1ʳ:] Laugh, and be fat, or a commentary upon the Odcombyan banket. [In verse.] 8⁰. [_W. Hall?_] 1612.] Ent. to H. Gosson 9 my. 1612. L(lacks prelims.).

23770 — The life and death of . . . the virgin Mary. [In verse.] 8⁰. _G. E[ld], sold [by E. Wright?]_ 1620. L(lacks tp).O.

23771 — [Anr. ed.] 8⁰. _G. E[ld] f. J. T[rundle,]_ 1622. Ass'd from widow Trundle to J. Wright a. others 1 jn. 1629. L.L⁸.; F.HD(lacks tp).NY.

23772 — A living sadnes, in duty consecrated to the immortall memory of our late soveraigne James. [In verse.] 4⁰. [_E. Allde f. H. Gosson,_ 1625.] L.; HN.

23772a — [A variant, w. imprint:] _E. All-de f. H. Gosson,_ [1625.] L.

23772a.5 — A meditation on the passion. [In verse.] s.sh.fol. _T. Harper,_ 1630. Private owner.
The meditation is anon., followed by 3 poems by Taylor.

23773 — A memorial of all the English monarchs, from Brute to king James. In heroyicall verse. 8⁰. [_N. Okes,_] 1622. L.O.; F.HN.HD(2).NY.TEX.

23774 — [Anr. ed.] . . . to king Charles. 8⁰. _J. Beale f. J. Bowler,_ 1630. L(2, 1 imp.).L⁸.O.; F.HN.NY.
Some copies (L(1077.b.73), O) have added portrait of Charles I, w. imprint: '_sould by J. Stafford,_ 1631.'

23774.5 — [Heading A4ʳ:] A most horrible, terrible, tollerable, termagant satyre. [In verse.] 8⁰. [_T. Cotes,_ 1639.] Ent. to J. Okes 23 fb. 1639. HN(lacks tp).

23775 — The muses mourning: or, funerall sonnets on the death of John Moray esquire [xylographic.] 8⁰. [_London,_ 1615.] L.

23775.5 — The needles excellency a new booke wherin are divers admirable workes wrought with the needle. [In verse.] obl. 4⁰. [_T. Harper_] _f. J. Boler,_ 1631. Ent. 24 no. 1629. C⁶(engr. tp and plates only).; HD.

23776 — [Anr. ed.] The 10th edition inlarged. obl. 4⁰. _f. J. Boler,_ 1634. HN.

23776.5 — [Anr. ed.] The 10th edition inlarged. obl. 4⁰. _f. J. Boler,_ 1636. Sotheby's, 7 May 1929, lots 288 (bought by Thorp, untraced) and 289 (bought in?, untraced).

23777 — [Anr. ed.] The 12th edition inlarged. obl. 4⁰. [_J. Dawson?_] _f. J. Boler,_ 1640. L.O.C.M.; HD.PN.

23778 — A new discovery by sea, with a wherry from London to Salisbury. [Partly in verse.] 8⁰. _E. Allde f. the author,_ 1623. O.STD(lacks tp).

23778.5 — Newes and strange newes from St. Christophers of a hurry-cano. In August last, about the 5. day. 1638. Whereunto is added [in verse] the accident at Withicombe in Devonshire the 21. of October. [Anon.] 8⁰. _J. O[kes] f. F. Coules,_ 1638. Ent. as by Taylor to J. Okes 4 de. O⁶.; HN.
(Formerly 21558) See also 25607.

23779 — The nipping or snipping of abuses. [In verse.] 4⁰. _E. Griffin f. N. Butter,_ 1614. Ent. 7 de. 1613. L.O.; F(2, 1 lacks tp, 1 imp.).HN.NY(date cropt).Y.

23780 — Odcombs complaint: or Coriats funerall epicedium. [In verse.] 8⁰. _Printed for merrie recreation, sold at the salutation in Utopia_ [i.e. London, _G. Eld f. W. Burre?_] 1613. Ent. to W. Burre 15 my. L.M.

23781 — The olde, old, very olde man: or the age and long life of Thomas Par. [In verse.] 4⁰. [_A. Mathewes_] _f. H. Gosson,_ 1635. Ent. 7 de. L.L⁶.L³⁰.ETON.M.+; BO.HD.NY.PML.Y.
The SR entry prob. refers to 23782.5.

23782 — [Anr. ed.] The old, old, very old man. Whereunto is added a postscript [in prose]. 4⁰. [_A. Mathewes_] _f. H. Gosson,_ 1635. L(2).O(2).O⁹.NEK.Blickling*.; F.HN.HD.PML.

Taylor, John—_cont._

23782.5 — [Anr. issue, w. tp reset, adding:] Hee . . . departed this life the 15 of Novem. 1635, and is buried at Westminster. [_A. Mathewes_] _f. H. Gosson,_ 1635. O.C².; HN.HD.NCU.NY.PN.

23783 — Part of this summers travels, or news from Hell, Hull, and Hallifax. . . . 8⁰. _J. O[kes,_ 1639.] L.O.; HN.

23784 — The pennyles pilgrimage, or the money-lesse perambulation, of J. Taylor. From London to Edenborough. [Partly in verse.] 4⁰. _E. All-de, at the charges of the author,_ 1618. Ent. to H. Gosson 2 no. L.L⁸.O(2).; HN.HD.NY.Y.

23785 — The praise and vertue of a jayle, and jaylers. [In verse.] 8⁰. _J. H[aviland] f. R. B[adger,]_ 1623. Ent. to Badger 25 ja. L(2).L⁸.O.; HN(tp def.).

23786 — The praise, antiquity, and commodity, of beggery, beggers, and begging. [In verse.] 4⁰. _E. A[llde] f. H. Gosson, sold by E. Wright,_ 1621. Ent. 16 ja. L.O.; HN.HD.NY.

23787 — The praise, of cleane linnen. With the commendable use of the laundresse. [In verse.] 8⁰. _E. All-de f. H. Gosson,_ 1624. Ent. 22 oc. Gloucester PL.; HN.

23787.5 — [Anr. ed.] 8⁰. _E. Allde_] _f. H. Gosson,_ 1624. Y.
Quire B is from the same typesetting as 23787.

23788 — The praise of hemp-seed. With the voyage of Mʳ. Roger Bird and the writer hereof, in a boat of brown-paper, to Quinborough in Kent. [In verse.] 4⁰. [_E. Allde_] _f. H. Gosson, sold [by E. Wright?]_ 1620. Ent. 22 my. L.; F.HN.NY.

23789 — [Anr. ed.] 4⁰. [_E. Allde_] _f. H. Gosson, sold [by E. Wright?_ 1623.] HD(imp.).*.NY.

23789.3 — [A variant, dated:] 1623. O.

23789.7 — Prince Charles his welcome from Spaine. [Anon.] 4⁰. _G. E[ld] f. J. Wright,_ 1623. Ent. to J. Trundle a. H. Gosson 7 oc. as by Taylor. YK.; HD.

23790 — A sad and deplorable loving elegy to the memory of M. Richard Wyan deceased. The 16. of August last. 1638. s.sh.fol. [_J. Okes,_ 1638.] O.
— The scourge of basenesse. 1624. See 23768.

23791 — The sculler, rowing from Tiber to Thames. [In verse.] 4⁰. _E. A[llde] solde [by N. Butter,]_ 1612. Ent. to H. Gosson 4 oc. 1611. O(impr. cropt).; HN.HD.

23792 — [Anr. ed., with title:] Taylors water-worke: or the scullers travels, from Tiber to Thames. 4⁰. [_T. Snodham?_] _f. N. Butter,_ 1614. L(lacks tp).O.

23793 — A shilling, or, the travailes of twelve-pence. [In verse.] 8⁰. [_E. Allde f. H. Gosson,_ 1621.] Ent. to H. Gosson 3 no. 1621. L.L⁸.O.; F(lacks tp).HN.HD.ILL.NY.+

23794 — [Anr. ed., with title:] The travels of twelve-pence. 8⁰. [_A. Mathewes_] _f. H. Gosson,_ 1635. O(imprint shaved).; HD(imprint cropt).

23795 — Sir Gregory Nonsence his newes from no place. [In verse.] 8⁰. (_N. O[kes,]_) sold betweene Charing-Crosse, and Algate, 1700 [sic] (1622.) L.L⁸.; F(2, both w. tp date cropt).NY(2).TEX. Arthur Houghton.

23795.3 — Stripping, whipping, and pumping. Or, the five mad shavers of Drury-Lane. [Anon.] 8⁰. _J. O[kes] f. T. Lambert,_ 1638. Ent. as by Taylor to Okes 17 oc. HN.

23795.7 — The subjects joy, for the Parliament. [In verse.] s.sh.fol. _E. All-de f. H. G[osson,] solde by E. Wright,_ [1621.] L⁵(Lemon 177).

23796 — Superbiæ flagellum, or, the whip of pride. [In verse.] 8⁰. _G. Eld,_ 1621. Ent. to Eld a. M. Flesher 31 my. L(2).L⁸.O.; F.HN.HD.N.NY.+
Some copies dedic. to Sir Thomas Richardson, others to Wm. Seymour, Earl of Hertford; both at L. Engr. frontispiece w. letterpress verses should precede tp.

23797 — Taylors farewell, to the Tower-bottles. [In verse.] 8⁰. _Dort_ [i.e. London, A. Mathewes] 1622. L.L⁸.O.; F.HN.HD.NY.SMITH.

23798 — Taylors feast: contayning twenty-seaven dishes of meate. 8⁰. _J. Okes,_ 1638. Ent. 10 no. 1637. HN.

23799 — Taylors goos⟨e,⟩ describing the wilde goose. [In verse.] 4⁰. _E. A[llde] f. H. Gosson, sold ⟨by⟩ E. Wright,_ 1621. L⁸.O(lacks tp).

23800 — Taylor's motto. Et habeo, et careo, et curo. [In verse.] 8⁰. [_E. Allde_] _f. J. T[rundle] & H. G[osson,]_ 1621. Ent. to Gosson 18 jn. L.O.LINC. Gloucester PL (imp.).; F(2, 1 lacks tp).HN.HD.NY.
B4ʳ line 1: 'Libles'. See also 25925.

23800.5 — [Anr. ed.] 8⁰. [_E. Allde_] _f. J. T[rundle] & H. G[osson,]_ 1621. L(lacks tp).L⁸.O(lacks tp).C².
B4ʳ line 1: 'Libels'. Quire D reimposed from 23800; quire E from same setting, not reimposed.

Taylor, John—*cont.*

23801 — Taylors pastorall: being both historicall and satyricall: or the noble antiquitie of shepheards. [In verse.] 4°. *G. P[urslowe] f. H. Gosson, sold at E. Wrights shop,* 1624. L.O.; HN.HD(imp.).

23802 — Taylor his travels: from the citty of London to Prague. [Partly in verse.] 4°. *N. Okes f. H. Gosson, sold by E. Wright,* 1620. L.; F.HN.HD.

23802.5 — The second edition, corrected, and much enlarged. 4°. *N. Okes f. H. Gosson, sold by E. Wright,* 1621. F.HD. With omissions as well as additions.

23803 — Taylor on Thame Isis: or the description of the Thame and Isis. [In verse.] 8°. *J. Haviland,* 1632. Ent. to H. Gosson 5 my. L(impr. cropt). O.; HN.

23804 — Taylors revenge or the rymer William Fennor firkt. [In verse.] 8°. *Rotterdam, at the signe of the blew bitch in Dog-Lane, and are to be sold, almost anywhere. And transported over sea in a cods belly, and cast up at Cuckolds Haven the last spring-tide* [i.e. *London, E. Allde,*] 1615. L⁸. Answered by 10783.

23805 — Taylors travels and circular perambulation, of London and Westminster. With an alphabeticall description, of all the taverne signes. [Partly in verse.] 8°. *A. M[athewes,]* 1636. Ent. to H. Gosson 12 fb. O.; HN.

23806 — Taylors Urania, or his heavenly muse. With a briefe narration of the thirteene sieges, of Jerusalem. In heroicall verse. 8°. *E. Griffin f. N. Butter,* 1615 (1616.) L.L⁸.O.; F(last leaf in facs.).HN.
— Taylors water-worke. 1614. *See* 23792.

23807 — Three weekes, three daies, and three houres observations and travel, from London to Hamburgh. 4°. *E. Griffin, sold by G. Gybbs,* 1617. Ent. to Griffin 15 mr. L.O.LONGLEAT.; F.HN.HD(imp.).
— The travels of twelve-pence. 1635. *See* 23794.

23808 — The triumphs of fame and honour: or the noble solemnity, at the inauguration of R. Parkhurst, into the office of lord maior. 8°. *London,* 1634. M.Greg 495.

23808.5 — True loving sorow, attired in a robe of unfeigned griefe, presented upon occasion of the funerall of prince Lewis Steward duke of Richmond and Linox. [In verse.] s.sh.fol. *f. H. Gosson,* 1624. L⁵(Lemon 218).

23808a — The unnaturall father: or, the cruell murther committed by ⟨one⟩ John Rowse. [Anon.] 4°. *[G. Purslowe] f. J. T[rundle] a. H. G[osson,]* 1621. Ent. 10 jy. L.

23809 — A valorous and perillous sea-fight. Fought with three Turkish ships, on the coast of Cornewall. 4°. *E. P[urslowe] f. E. Wright,* 1640. Ent. to N. Butter a. N. Bourne 13 jy. L.DUR⁵(frag.)*.

23809.5 — [Anr. issue, w. cancel tp and quire D added:] A brave and valiant sea-fight, upon the coast of Cornewall. [Additions by: *B. Alsop a. T. Fawcet] f. N. Butter,* 1640 (14 jy.) O.; HN. (Formerly 23734)

23810 — Verbum sempiternæ [*sic*]. (Salvator mundi.) [A thumb-Bible. In verse.] 2 pts. 64° in 16's. *J. Beale f. J. Hamman,* 1614. Ent. 4 mr. A(imp.).; Miss Frances Dunn, Saginaw, Michigan.

23811 — [Anr. ed., corrected.] Verbum sempiternum. 2 pts. 64° in 16's. *J. Beale f. J. Hamman,* 1616. L.; HN.

23811.3 — [Anr. ed.] 2 pts. 64° in 16's. *J. H[aviland] f. J. Hamman,* 1627. L.

23811.7 — [Anr. ed.] 2 pts. 64° in 16's. *J. B(eale,)* 1631. Ass'd to Beale 16 de. 1630. F.

23812 — A verry merry wherry-ferry voyage: or Yorke for my money. [In verse.] 8°. *E. All-de,* 1622. Ent. to H. Gosson 11 se. L.; HN.

23812.3 — [Anr. ed.] Whereunto is annexed a very pleasant discription of O Toole the great. 2 pts. 8°. *E. All-de f. H. Gosson,* 1623 (1622.) HD. Pt. 2 also issued separately as 23762.

23812.7 — A warning for swearers and blasphemers. Shewing Gods fearfull judgements. [Init. I. T. In verse.] s.sh.fol. *f. F. Couls,* 1626. Ass'd to Coules by H. Gosson 5 jn. Private owner. Reprinted from 23754.

23813 — The water-cormorant his complaint. [In verse.] 4°. *G. Eld,* 1622. Ent. to Eld a. M. Flesher 26 oc. 1621. L(A1 in facs.).L⁸(impr. cropt).O.; F.HD.NY.

23813.3 — [Heading A2ʳ:] The watermens suit, concerning players. [Anon.] 4°. *[G. Eld,* 1614?] F(A2 only). HD(A2, 3 only). The text mentions 'Ianuary last 1613', i.e. 1614, but the HD frag. was bd. w. items dated 1620, 1621; cf. 16787.

Taylor, John—*cont.*

23813.5 — Wit and mirth. Chargeably collected out of tavernes, ordinaries, innes. 8°. *[M. Flesher] f. H. Gosson, sold [by E. Wright,]* 1626. NY.

23813.7 — [Anr. ed.] 8°. *[A. Mathewes] f. H. Gosson, sold [by E. Wright,]* 1628. HD.

23814 — [Anr. ed.] 8°. *T. C[otes] f. J. Boler,* 1629. HN.HD.

23815 — [Anr. ed.] 8°. *[T. Cotes] f. J. Boler,* 1635. HN.
— The womens sharpe revenge. 1640. *See* 23706.

23816 — The world runnes on wheeles. 8°. *E. A[llde] f. H. Gosson,* 1623. Ent. 21 jn. L.; NY(impr. cropt).

23817 — [Anr. ed.] 8°. *[A. Mathewes] f. H. Gosson,* 1635. O.
— *ed. See* 5809.

Taylor, John, *Bp.* Lincoln. Visitation articles. *See* 10228.

Taylor, Joseph, *ed.* A court of guard for the heart. 1626. *See* 5876.5.

Taylor, Nathaniel. *See* 23857.5.

23818 **Taylor, Stephen.** A whippe for worldlings or the centre of content. [In verse.] 4°. *[Printed abroad,* 1637?] L(imp.).O(2 imp., both lacking tp).LINC(tp cropt).; HN(imp.).

23819 **Taylor, Theophilus.** The mappe of Moses: or, a guide for governours. Two sermons preached before the judges and magistrates of Reding. 4°. *T. Harper,* 1629. L.O.C.NOR².RGU.+; F.HD.LC.

23819.5 **Taylor, Thomas.** An answer to that question, how farre it is lawfull to flee in the time of the plague; extracted out of a sermon preached in Alderman-bury. s.sh.fol. *T. P[urfoot] f. J. Bartlet,* [1636?] HD. Although the sermon was prob. preached during the 1625 plague, this extract was more likely pr. during the 1636 plague as it has medial 'v'; e.g. 'have'.

23820 — The beawties of Beth-el. . . . Preached in Cambridge. 8°. *G. Eld f. T. Man,* 1609. Ent. to T. Man, sen., a. J. Man 7 ap. L.C.; F.

23821 — Christ revealed: or the Old Testament explained. A treatise of the types and shadowes of our saviour. [*Ed.*] (W. Jemmat.) 4° in 8's. *M. F[lesher] f. R. Dawlman a. L. Fawne,* 1635. Ent. to Dawlman 25 jy. 1632. L.O.C.E².M.+; F.HN.CHI.HD.NY¹¹.+

23822 — Christs combate and conquest: or, the lyon of Judah. [A treatise.] 4° in 8's. *C. Legge, pr. to the Univ. of Camb.,* 1618. Ent. to T. Man, L. Greene a. C. Legge 20 no. O⁶(D).O²⁸(Bed.).C.C².A.; F.

23822a — [A variant, w. imprint:] *[Cambridge,] C. Legge f. T. Man, [London,]* 1618. O.G⁴.M². Lord Kenyon.; F.HN.HD.ILL.U.+

23822a.5 — [A variant, w. imprint:] *[Cambridge,] C. Legge f. L. Greene,* 1618. L.C⁵.LINC.

23823 — Christs victorie over the dragon. In a plaine exposition of the twelfth chapter of S. Johns Revelation. [*Ed.*] (W. Jemmat.) 4° in 8's. *M. F[lesher] f. R. Dawlman,* 1633. Ent. 10 au. 1632. L.O.C.D.G².+; F.HN.HD. N.U.+

23823.5 — Circumspect walking: describing the severall rules, as so many steps in the way of wisedome. 12°. *C. Legge, pr. to the Univ. of Camb.,* 1619. Ent. to Legge a. L. Greene 28 no. 1622. C.

23824 — [Anr. ed.] 12°. *[J. Beale?] f. J. Boler,* 1631. Ass'd by widow Legge 1 jn. 1629. L.O.C.YK.; CAL⁶(imp.).

23825 — Ἀρχὴν ἁπάντων. . . . A commentarie upon the Epistle to Titus. Preached in Cambridge. 4° in 8's. *[Cambridge, C. Legge] f. L. Greene,* 1612. L.O.C.C⁴.M.+; HN.BO.HART.HD.Y.+

23825a — [A variant, w. imprint:] *C. Legge, pr. to the Univ. of Camb.,* 1612. O.C³.G⁴.M.YK.+; F.BO².NY¹¹.U.Y.+

23826 — [Anr. ed.] Reviewed and enlarged with some notes. 4° in 8's. *C. Legge, pr. to the Univ. of Camb.,* 1619. Ent. to T. Man, L. Greene a. C. Legge 20 no. 1618. L.O.C.E².LYU.+; F.HN.CHI.HD(imp.).U.+

23827 — Davids learning, or the way to true happiness: in a commentarie upon the 32. psalme. Preached and now published by T. T[aylor] late fellow of Christs Colledge in Cambridge. 4° in 8's. *W. Stansby f. H. Fetherstone,* 1617. L.O.LYD.M.STU.; F.HN. BOWDOIN.HD(imp.).ILL.

23828 — [Anr. ed.] The second time corrected. 4° in 8's. *W. Stansby f. H. Fetherstone,* 1618. C.C¹⁰.; F.N.PN².U.Y.+

23829 — A good husband and a good wife: layd open in a sermon. Published by J. Sedgwicke. 4°. *[G. Miller] f. W. Sheffard,* 1625. L.O.; F.HD.Y.

Taylor, Thomas—*cont.*

23830 — Japhets first publique perswasion into Sems tents: or Peters sermon, preached before Cornelius. 4°. *C. Legge, pr. to the Univ. of Camb.*, 1612. Ent. to Legge, L. Greene a. R. Mab 28 no. 1622. L.O.C.C³.E².+; Y.

23830.3 — [A variant, w. imprint:] *f. L. Greene, [Cambridge,]* 1612. O.C⁴.BURY.M.; ILL(imp.).

23830.5 — [A variant, w. imprint:] *C. Legge, pr. to the Univ. of Camb., sold by R. Mab, [London,]* 1612. L(tp only, Ames II.281).O².; F.HN.HD.U.

23830.7 — The kings bath. Affording many sweet observations from the baptisme of Christ. 8°. *F. Kyngston f. J. Bartlet, sold [by T. Man,]* 1620. Ent. 7 ja. HN.

23831 — [Anr. issue, w. imprint:] *F. Kyngston f. T. Man a. J. Bartlet,* 1620. L(imp.).O.C¹⁰.D.DUL.+; F.PN².Y.

23832 — A man in Christ, or a new creature. To which is added a treatise, containing Meditations from the creatures. 2 pts. 12°. *[H. Lownes] f. J. Bartlet,* 1628. Ent. 2 ap. 1629. O.C.
This and the following eds. usually bd. w. 23845 sqq.

23833 — Second edition. Corrected. 2 pts. 12°. *[H. Lownes] f. J. Bartlet,* 1629. L(pt. 1 only).O²⁸.; F.HD.Y.

23834 — Third edition. 2 pts. 12°. *[R. Young] f. J. Bartlet,* 1632. L².C.DUL.; F.
(Pt. 2 formerly also 23839)

23835 — Fourth edition. 1635. = pt. of 23848.

23836 — The manifold wisedome of God. 1640. Now = 24959.5.

23837 — A mappe of Rome: lively exhibiting her mercilesse meeknesse, preached in five sermons, on occasion of the Gunpowder treason, and now published by W. J(emmat.) 4°. *F. Kyngston f. J. Bartlet, sould [by T. Man,]* 1619. Ent. 27 oc. O¹⁰.O(J, tp only).YK.; F.HN.NY.U.Y.

23838 — [A variant, w. imprint:] *F. Kyngston f. J. Bartlet, sould [by T. Man,]* 1620. L.O.C.A.D.+; F(2).HN.CHI. Reprinted in 23842.

23839 — Meditations from the creatures. 1632. = pt. of 23834.

23840 — The parable of the sower and of the seed. [On Luke viii. 4–8.] 4° in 8's. *F. Kyngston f. J. Bartlet,* 1621. Ent. 8 au. 1620. L.O.C.G².M².+; F.HN.HD.PEN.U.+

23841 — [Anr. ed.] 4° in 8's. *J. Dawson f. J. Bartlet,* 1623. L.O(2, 1 lacks engr. tp).WOR.; F(lacks engr. tp).HN.CHI.HD(lacks engr. tp).Y.+
Engr. tp has: 'Second edition. *f. J. Bartlet,* 1623.'

23842 — [Anr. ed.] To which is added, A mappe of Rome. The third edition. 2 pts. 4° in 8's. *T. Purfoot [a. J. Beale] f. J. Bartlet,* 1634. L.L³.O.C.NLW.+; F.HN.BO.N.NY¹¹(imp.).+
Beale printed pt. 2.

23843 — The pilgrims profession. Or a sermon preached at the funerall of Mris Mary Gunter. 12°. *J. D[awson] f. J. Bartlet,* 1622. Ent. 14 jn. L.

23844 — [Anr. ed.] 1625. = pt. 2 of 23854.

23845 — The practise of repentance, laid downe in sundry directions. As it was preached. 12°. *[H. Lownes] f. J. Bartlet,* 1628. Ent. 2 ap. 1629. O.C.; BO.
This and the following eds. usually bd. w. 23832 sqq.

23846 — Second edition. Reviewed and corrected. 12°. *[H. Lownes] f. J. Bartlet,* 1629. L.O²⁸.; F.HD.U.Y.

23847 — Third edition. 12°. *[R. Badger] f. J. Bartlet,* 1632. L².C.; F.

23847.5 — [A variant, w. imprint:] *f. J. Bartlet,* 1633. DUL.

23848 — Fourth edition. (A man in Christ.—Meditations.) 12°. *[T. Cotes] f. J. Bartlet,* 1635. L.O.C.; F.HN.HD(imp.).NY¹¹.U.
(23835 is pt. of this)

23849 — The principles of christian practice. [Ed.] (W. Jemmat.) 12°. *R. Y[oung a. J. Beale] f. J. Bartlet,* 1635. Ent. 2 oc. 1634. L.O.C.PLUME.; F.HN.
Beale pr. quires 2nd R–Dd.

23850 — The progresse of saints to full holinesse. [A treatise.] 4° in 8's. *W. J[ones] f. J. Bartlet,* 1630. Ent. 19 no. L.L³.O.LEEDS.M.+; HN.NY¹¹.Y.

23850a — [Anr. issue, w. cancel tp, w. imprint:] *W. J[ones] f. J. Bartlet,* 1631. L.O.C¹⁰.G².; F.HD.TORONTO².U.

23851 — Regula vitæ, the rule of the law under the gospel. Containing a discovery of the pestiferous sect of Libertines, Antinomians, [etc.] 12°. *W. J[ones] f. R. Dawlman,* 1631. Ent. 15 se. L².O.C³.G².M.+; F.HN.PN.U(2).

23852 — [Anr. ed.] 12°. *M. F[lesher] f. R. Dawlman,* 1635. L.O²⁸.C.C¹⁰.M⁴.+; F.PN².

Taylor, Thomas—*cont.*

— Three treatises. 1633. *See* 23856.

23853 — Two sermons: the one a heavenly voice, calling all Gods people out of Romish Babylon. The other an everlasting record of the utter ruine of Romish Amalek. 4°. *J. H[aviland] f. J. Bartlet,* 1624. Ent. 24 my. L.O.C.BRISTOL.E.+; F.HN.PN.U.V.

23854 — Two treatises: the pearle of the gospell, and the pilgrims profession: to which is added a glasse for gentlewomen. 3 pts. 12°. *J. H[aviland] f. J. Bartlet,* 1624 (1625.) Ent. 1 de. 1621, 14 jn. 1622, and 13 de. 1624. O.
(Pt. 2 formerly also 23844) All tpp dated 1624 except pt. 2.

23855 — [A variant, w. imprint on gen. tp:] *J. H[aviland] f. J. Bartlet,* 1625. L(2 imp.).BIRM²(K.N.).; F.
All tpp dated 1625 except pt. 3, which is dated 1624.

23856 — [Anr. ed.] Three treatises: . . . To which is added A short introduction to the Lords supper. 12°. *J. B[eale] f. J. Bartlet,* 1633. L.L³(2nd pt. only).O.C.; F.TORONTO².U.

23857 — The value of true valour, or, the probation of a military man. In a sermon. 4°. *A. Mathewes f. T. Jones,* 1629. Ent. 13 de. L.O.C.D.RGU.+; F.

— *ed. See* 19724.
— *See* also 24048.

23857.5 **Taylour, Nathaniel.** Meditations for the passion weeke. 12°. *[T. a. J. Buck,] prs. to the Univ. of Camb.,* 1627. P.; AAS.ILL(imp.).

Tears. Three precious teares of blood. 1611. *See* 13142.

23857.7 **Tedder, Richard.** A sermon preached at Wimondham, at the primary visitation of the bishop of Norwich. 4°. *T. Harper, sold by G. Emerson,* 1637. Ent. to Emerson 8 fb. M⁴.; F.

23858 — [Anr. issue, w. cancel tp, w. imprint:] *T. Harper f. G. Emerson,* 1637. L.O.O¹⁰.C.STD.; ILL.

23858.5 **Tedder, William.** A coppie of a recantation made at Paules Crosse, by W. Tedder. Whereunto is added: A. Tyrell. 4°. *J. Charlewoode a. W. Broome,* 1588. Ent. to Brome 12 de. HD.
This is the tp on A2. Two O, G² copies of 23859 also have this title.

23858.7 — [Anr. issue, w. tp on A2 reset.] The recantation . . . by W. Tedder. Wherunto is adioyned: A. Tyrell. *J. Charlewoode a. W. Brome,* 1588. O⁹.DUR³.DUR⁵(imp.).; ILL.
Most copies of 23859 sq. have this title.

23859 — [Anr. issue, w. added prelims., w. title on *1:] The recantations as they were seuerallie pronounced by W. Tedder and A. Tyrrell. With an epistle dedicatorie vnto her maiestie. *J. Charlewood a. W. Brome, sold by T. Gubbin,* 1588. L².O.C.D².G².+; F.HN.BO³.

23859.3 — [A variant.] The recantations [etc.] *J. Charlewood a. W. Brome,* 1588. L.; U.Y.

23860 **Teelinck, Willem.** The ballance of the sanctuarie, shewing how we must behave our selves when wee see people under the tyranny of their enemies. [*Tr.* from Dutch. *Ed.* by] (T. Gataker.) 4°. *J. D[awson] f. W. Sheffard,* 1621. Ent. 13 jn. L.L³⁰.O.O⁸.O²⁸.+; F.HN.PN².

23861 — Pauls complaint against his naturall corruption. Set forth in two sermons. [*Tr.* from Dutch by] (C. Harmar.) 4°. *J. Dawson f. J. Bellamie,* 1621. Ent. 12 ap. L.O.C.D.E.+; AAS.LC.PN².U.

23862 — The resting place of the minde. That is, a propounding of the providence of God. [A sermon. *Tr.* from Dutch. *Ed.* by] (T. Gataker.) 4°. *J. Haviland f. E. Brewster,* 1622. Ent. 22 ja. L(2).O.C².E².; F.BO⁵.ILL.PN².

23863 **Teixeira, José.** The Spanish pilgrime. [Anon.] 1625. Now = 19838.5.

23864 — The strangest adventure that ever happened. Containing a discourse of the king of Portugall dom Sebastian, from 1578. unto 1601. First done in Spanish, then in French, and now into English. [By] (A. M[unday].) 4°. *R. Field f. F. Henson,* 1601. Ent. 30 mr. L.L².O.C.YK.+; F(imp.).HN.BO⁵.HD.N.
The texts of this and the next 2 items are all different from one another.

Teixeira, José—*cont.*

23865 — The true historie of the late and lamentable adventures of don Sebastian, after his imprisonment in Naples, vntill this present day, being now in Spaine. [Anon.] 4°. *S. Stafford a.* [i.e. *for*] *J. Shaw,* 1602. Ent. to Stafford a. Shaw 27 se. L.

23866 — A continuation of the lamentable and admirable adventures of dom Sebastian. Since 1578. untill this present yeare 1603. [*Tr.* from French.] 4°. [*R. Field*] *f. J. Shaw,* 1603. Ent. 27 se. 1602. L.C(imp.).C²(2). London, Foreign Office (lacks tp).; F.

23867 **Telin, Guillaume.** Archaioplutos. Or the riches of elder ages. Proouing that the auncient emperors were more rich then such as liue in these daies. *Tr.* (A. Munday.) 4°. *J. C[harlewood] f. R. Smith,* 1592. Ent. to Charlewood 16 ap. L.O(2).P.

Tellisford, Worcester Diocese. *See* Indulgences 122.

23867.5 **Tell-Troth.** Tell-trothes new-yeares gift beeing Robin Good-fellowes newes. With his owne inuectiue against ielosy. 4°. *R. Bourne* [*f. J. Oxenbridge,*] 1593. Ent. to J. Oxenbridge 16 de. 1592. F(2, 1 imp.). Y(2 leaves).
(Formerly 313) Tp has Oxenbridge's device McK.289. Text continued in STC 1.

Tel-Trouth, Thomas. The araignment of lewde, women. 1615, 1629. *See* 23533, 23540.

23868 — Tom Tell Troath or a free discourse touching the manners of the tyme. [Anti-Catholic propaganda.] 4°. [*Holland?* 1630?] C.C².C⁶.A.SHEF.; F.HN.PN. Anr. F ed., '23868a' on Univ. Microfilms reel 718, has 'Troth' in the title and = Wing T 1786.

Temperance. [An enterlude of temperance. c. 1528.] *See* 14109.5.

Temple. The temple of glas. [1477, etc.] *See* 17032 sqq.

23869 **Temple, Robert.** A sermon teaching discretion in matters of religion. Preached at Paules Crosse. 8°. *R. B[ourne] f. E. Aggas,* 1592. L.L¹⁵.O.YK.

23870 **Temple,** *Sir* **William.** A logicall analysis of twentie select psalmes. 4°. *F. Kyngston f. T. Man,* 1605. Ent. to T. Man, sen., 27 jy. L.L².C.D.E.+; F.HN.CHI.U (imp.).Tufts U.

23871 — Analysis logica triginta psalmorum, a primo scilicet ad tricesimum primum. 8°. *R. Field,* 1611. Ent. 14 oc. L².O.C³.D.D².

23872 — Francisci Mildapetti Navarreni [*pseud.*] ad Everardum Digbeium Anglum admonitio de vnica P. Rami methodo reiectis cæteris retinenda. 8°. *H. Middletonus, imp. T. Man,* 1580. L.O.C.C³.E².+
Answers 6841; answered by 6838.

23873 — Gulielmi Tempelli philosophi Cantabrigiensis epistola de dialectica P. Rami, ad J. Piscatorem Argentinens. vná cum J. Piscatoris responsione. 8°. *H. Middletonus pro J. Harrisono & G. Bishop,* 1582. Ent. 27 no. L.O.O³.D².R.; F.ILL. ¶

23873.5 — [A variant, w. tp dated:] 1583. HN.

23874 — Pro Mildapetti de vnica methodo defensione contra Diplodophilum, commentatio G. Tempelli. Huc accessit nonnullarum e physicis & ethicis quæstionum explicatio, vná cum epistola de Rami dialectica ad J. Piscatorem. 8°. [*H. Middleton*] *pro T. Man,* 1581. Ent. 18 my. L.O.C.C³.E².+; F.HD. This was app. all pr. in Middleton's shop, but by 2 different compositors: (1) ¶ and 2nd A–F, with medial 'v'; (2) 1st A–H, with medial 'u'. Answers 6838.

— *ed. See* 15243.

23875 **Tempus.** Temporis filia veritas. A mery deuise called the troublsome trauell of tyme. [A plea for religious tolerance.] 4°. [*Printed abroad,*] 1589. C.

23876 **Ten Commandments.** Ihesus. The floure of the commaundementes of god. [*Tr.* from French by A. Chertsey.] fol. (*W. de Worde,* 1510 (14 se.)) L.O.C. C⁴.M.+; HN(imp.).Y. St. John's Seminary, Camarillo, California.
See also 10613.

23877 — [Anr. ed.] fol. (*w. de worde,* 1521 (8 oc.)) L.O.C.E¹². M.+; F.HN.CH.JH.PML.+

— A plaine and familiar exposition of the Ten Commandements. 1604, etc. *See* 6968 sqq.

Ten Commandments—*cont.*

23877.3 — Here foloweth the .X. cōmaundeme⟨nts⟩ in englyshe, the crede with the pater noster, *tr.* by the auctorite of the bysshops [in] cōuocation, & the kynges grace iniunc⟨t⟩ions. s.sh.fol. [*W. Powell f.*] *J. Waley,* [1548?] Seven Gables (2 imp.).

— A treatise or exposition upon the ten commandments. 1603. *See* 6967.

Tenure. The tenure and forme of indentures. 1583. *See* 23884a.2.

23877.7 **Tenures.** [The old tenures. a2ʳ:] Tenir per seruice de chiualer: est a tenir per ho-/mage foialte [etc.] *Law Fr.* fol. (*by me R. Pynson at the instance of my maistres of the cōpany of stronde Inne with oute tempyll Barre,*) [1494?] HN.PML.
Linked in the colophon w. 18385. Reprinted in 18394 sq., 18397, 20703.5 sqq.

23878 — [Anr. ed. a2ʳ:] Tenir per seruice de chiualer: est a tenir per homage foi/alte [etc.] fol. (*per R. Pynson,*) [1496.] L.O.D.; HD. Duff 335.

23878.5 — [Anr. ed. A1ʳ:] Tenir per seruice de chiualer: est a tenir p homage foi-/alte [etc.] fol. [*J. Rastell,* 1511?] L².O.

23879 — [Anr. ed. A1ʳ:] Tenir per seruice de chiualer: est a tenir p homage/foialte [etc.] fol. [*R. Pynson,* c. 1515.] L.L²².; HN.

23879.5 — [Anr. ed. A1ʳ:] Tenir p seruyce de chiualer: est a tenir per homage/foialte, [etc.] fol. [*R. Pynson,* c. 1520.] HD.

23879.7 — [Anr. ed.] The tenuris. *Law Fr. a. Eng.* fol. [*J. Rastell,* c. 1523.] C.C⁴.
A1ʳ line 6 of English ends: 'of the'. Rastell's name in the device, McK. 37. Both copies bd. w. 20701.

23880 — [Anr. ed.] Olde teners newly corrected. *Law Fr.* 16° in 8's. (*in ẹd. R. Pynsoni,* 1525 (4 id. oc.)) L.L²².O. Lord Kenyon.; HD(2).LC.

23880.3 — [Anr. ed.] The tennris [*sic*]. *Law Fr. a. Eng.* fol. [*J. Rastell,* c. 1525.] HD.
A1ʳ line 6 of English ends: 'of yᵉ'. Rastell's name in the device, McK. 37. HD bd. w. 20702.

23880.5 — [Anr. ed.] Olde teners newly corrected. *Law Fr.* 16° in 8's. (*in ed. R. Redmā,* 1528 (20 ja.)) HD.

23881 — [Anr. ed.] The olde tenures. 8°. (*T. Bertheletus,* 1530.) C.; HD.

23882 — [Anr. ed.] 8°. (*by me R. Redman,* 1532.) L.O.O¹⁰(imp.). C.M.; HD.LC. Cincinnati U.

23883 — [Anr. ed.] 8°. *in aed. T. Bert[heleti,*] 1538. L.P.; HD.LC.

23884 — [Anr. ed.] 8°. (*W. Myddylton,*) [c. 1542.] HD.LC.Y(2).

23884.5 — The tenours and fourme of indentures, obligations, quittaunces, [etc.] 8°. (*f. A. Vele,*) [c. 1560.] P.

23884a — [Anr. ed.] 8°. (*J. Tysdale,*) [1560?] (29 de.) O.

23884a.2 — [Anr. ed.] The tenure and forme [etc.] 8°. *T. Marsh,* 1583. Ass'd from E. Marsh to T. Orwin ?23 jn. 1591. AAS.

23884a.4 **Teramano, Pietro.** Dechreuad a rhyfedhus esmudiad eglwys yr arglwdhes Fair o Loreto. [Anon. Adapted and *tr.* from Teramano's Latin by R. Corbington.] s.sh.fol. *Loreto, F. Serafini,* 1635. L(Add.MS. 22912/395ᵇ).
A&R 808.

23884a.6 — [Anr. trans.] The miraculous origin and translation of the church of our B. lady of Loreto. [Anon. *Tr.* R. Corbington.] s.sh.fol. *Loreto, F. Serafini,* 1635. O.
(Formerly 16826) A&R 809.

23884a.8 — [Anr. trans.] The wondrus flitting of the kirk of our B. lady of Loreto. [Anon. *Tr.* R. Corbington.] s.sh.fol. *Loreto, F. Serafini,* 1635. L(Add.MS. 22912/393ᵇ).
A&R 810.

Terceira, *Island of.* Relation of the expongnable attempt. [1583?] *See* 1104.

— A true and strange relation of fire. 1639. *See* 20863.

23885 **Terentius, Publius,** *Afer.* [Comœdiæ sex: Andria, Eunuchus, Heauton timorumenos, Adelphoe, Phormio, Hecyra.] 6 pts. 4° in 8's and 6's. [Andria:] (*R. Pynson,* 1497.) [Hecyra:] (*p R. Pynson,* 1495 (20 ja.)) L(imp.).O(Phormio only.)CHATS(Eunuchus only.).; MEL(Hecyra colophon). Duff 391.
MEL also has a frag. of the 1st leaf of the Andria in a different setting from L: line 2 of recto ends: 'Philome-/' (MEL) or 'Philomena:altera/' (L). The MEL frag. has Pynson types 2, 3, 5 and may be [1494?]
The other plays have no colophons and are pr. in differing types, prob. all 1495-7.

Terentius, Publius, *Afer—cont.*

23885.3 — [Anr. ed.] P. Terentij aphri comicorū elegantissimi comedie a G. Iuuenale explanate: & ab J. Badio Ascensio annotate. fol. (*Impresse Parrhisijs,*) *venū-dātur londonie in edib⁹ winādi de worda. Michael' Morini & Johānis Brachij* [i.e. Bray?] *Et in edibus ipsius Ascensij Parrhisijs,* (1504 (15 jy.)) L.C.PARIS. Dijon PL.; N.

23885.5 — [Anr. ed.] 4°. [*W. de Worde,* c. 1510.] ETON(2 leaves from Adelphoe).

23885.7 — [Anr. ed.] Publii Terentii Aphri comoediæ sex. P. Nannij in hunc auctorem obseruationibus. 8°. *ex off. T. Marshi,* 1575. O.

23886 — [Anr. ed.] Pub. Terentii Afri comoediæ sex, ex M. Antonii Mureti exemplari emendatæ. Additis ex P. Bembi codice lectionibus. Item libellus de comœdia & tragœdia Donato, Afro, Cornuto adscriptus. 8°. *ex off. T. Marsh,* 1583. L.

23886.5 — [Anr. ed.] Terentius a M. Antonio Mureto, . . . emendatus. Aucta a F. F. Marcodurano. Variæ lectiones è exemplarib. T. Pulmanni. 16° in 8's. *ex off. T. Marshi,* [1585?] ETON.

23887 — [Anr. ed., without notes.] Pub. Terentii Afri comoediæ sex. 12°. *Cantabrigiae, ex off. J. Legatt,* 1589. L.O (imp.).C.CHATS. Bradford PL.; HN.

23888 — [Anr. ed., without notes.] 24° in 12's. *ex off. R. Robinsoni* [f.] (*R. Dexter,*) 1597. L(lacks A5).M⁴.

23888.5 — [Anr. ed.] Terentius a M. Antonio Mureto emendatus. Denuò emendatissime excusus. 8°. [*F. Kingston*] *ex typ. Soc. Stat.,* 1611. L.

23889 — [Anr. ed., without notes.] Pub. Terentii comoediæ sex. 8°. *Edinburgi, A. Hart,* 1619. L.E⁵.; F(frags.).

23889.2 — [Anr. ed.] Terentius a M. Antonio Mureto emendatus. Denuò emendatissimè excusus. 8°. [*F. Kingston*] *ex typ. Soc. Stat.,* 1624. Ent. to the English Stock 5 mr. 1620. F.
  Film of F copy is on Univ. Microfilms reel 718 ('23885a').

23889.3 — [Anr. ed.] 8°. [*F. Kingston*] *ex typ. Soc. Stat.,* 1627. ILL.

23889.4 — [Anr. ed.] 8°. [*F. Kingston*] *ex typ. Soc. Stat.,* 1629. L³⁸.

23889.5 — [Anr. ed.] 8°. [*F. Kingston*] *ex typ. Soc. Stat.,* 1633. L(tp only, Ames II.1094).

23889.6 — [Anr. ed., without notes.] Pub. Terentii comoediæ sex à R. Wintertono recognitæ. 24° in 12's. *Cantabrigiæ, ap. T. Buck & R. Daniell,* 1633. F.

23889.7 — [Anr. ed.] Terentius a M. Antonio Mureto emendatus. 8°. [*F. Kingston*] *ex typ. Soc. Stat.,* 1635. L(tp only, Ames II.1275).PLUME.

23889.8 — [Anr. ed.] 8°. [*J. Beale*] *ex typ. Soc. Stat.,* 1636. ILL.

23889.9 — [Anr. ed.] Pub. Terentius a M. Antonio Mureto emendatus. 8°. *Cantabrigiæ, ex acad. typog.,* 1636. Y.

23890 — Terence in English. Fabulae comici facetissimi omnes Anglicæ factae opera R. B(ernard.) *Lat. a. Eng.* 4° in 8's. *Cantabrigiæ, ex off. J. Legat,* 1598. L.O.C.C².P.+; F.HN.HD.N.NY.+

23891 — Secunda editio multò emendatior. 4° in 8's. *Cantabrigiae, ex off. J. Legat,* 1607. L.O.C.D.E.+; F.HN.ILL.N.TEX.+

23892 — Quarta editio. 4° in 8's. *Londini, ex off. J. Legatt,* 1614. L.O.C.D⁹.DUR⁵.+; F.HN.HD.N.Y.+

23893 — Quinta editio. 4° in 8's. *J. Legatt, sold by J. Boler,* 1629. Ass'd from Legat sen. to jun. 2 ja. 1621. L.O.C. E⁴.M⁴.+; F.HN.HD.N.Y.+

23894 — Terens in englysh. [A3ʳ:] (The translacyon of the furst comedy callyd Andria.) *Lat. a. Eng.* 4° in 6's. [*Paris, P. le Noir?* c. 1520.] L. Greg 12.

23895 — Andria the first comoedie of Terence, in English. *Tr.* M. Kyffin. 4°. *T. E[ast] f. T. Woodcocke,* 1588. All Woodcock's rights ass'd by his widow to P. Linley 9 fb. 1596; to J. Flasket 26 jn. 1600. L.O.O⁵.LINC.; F.HN.Y². Greg 91.

23896 — The first comedy of Pub. Terentius, called Andria, claused after the method of Dᵣ. [Joseph] Webbe. Priviledged by patent from his majestie. *Eng. a. Lat.* 4°. *F. Kyngston f. P. Waterhouse,* 1629. L(lacks errata).O.C.DUR(Bamb.).E.+; F.HN.HD.N.Y.+
  See also 23898, 25170.5.

23897 — The two first comedies of Terence called Andria, and the Eunuch newly Englished by T. Newman. 8°. *G. M[iller] sold at the house of M. Fenricus,* 1627. Ent. to Miller 26 ap. L(imp.).O.; F.

23898 — The second comedie of Pub. Terentius, called Eunuchus, claused after the method of Dr.

Terentius, Publius, *Afer—cont.*

[Joseph] Webbe. Priviledged by patent from his majestie. *Eng. a. Lat.* 4°. *A. I[slip,] sold by N. Bourne,* 1629. L.I.².O.C⁵.E.+; HN.N.Y.
  The tp w. imprint as above is on ¶1ʳ. All the copies cited above also have the tp 23898a. See also 23896, 25170.5.

23898a — [A variant, w. tp on ¶2ʳ, w. imprint:] *A. I[slip] f. P. Waterhouse,* 1629. C.; F.HD.
  In the F copy ¶1 is blank and genuine.

23899 — Floures for Latine spekynge selected and gathered oute of Terence, and *tr.* by N. Udall. *Lat. a. Eng.* 8°. (*in aed. T. Bertheleti,* 1533) [1534.] L.O.M.; F(2, 1 imp.).HN.
  Preface dated prid. cal. Mar. 1534.

23900 — [Anr. ed.] Newly corrected and imprinted. 8°. (*in aed. T. Bertheleti,* 1538.) ETON(imp.).; HD.ILL.PFOR.

23900.5 — [Anr. ed.] 8°. (*in æd. T. Bertheleti,*) 1544. L.; F.CU.ILL. N(lacks tp).Y.

23901 — [Anr. ed.] 8°. [*T. Powell*] (*in the house late T. Berthelettes,*) 1560. L.O.C.P.; HN.BO².CAL². Toronto PL.

23901.3 — [Anr. ed.] 8°. *T. Marshe,* 1568. Ent. 1567–68. ETON.; F.ILL.

23901.7 — [Anr. ed.] 8°. *T. Marshe,* 1572. Sheffield PL.; LC.

23902 — [Anr. ed., enlarged.] Flowers or eloquent phrases of the Latine speach, gathered out of all the sixe comedies of Terence: those of the first three by N. Udall. And those of the latter three, nowe annexed by J. Higgins. *Lat. a. Eng.* 8°. *T. Marshe,* 1575. L.; F(2).ILL.

23903 — [Anr. ed.] 8°. *T. Marshe,* 1581. L.L⁴⁴.; F(2, 1 imp.). HN.LC.PEN.Y.

23904 — [Heading n1ʳ:] Vulgaria quedam abs Terencio in Anglicā linguam traducta. *Lat. a. Eng.* 4° in 8's. [*Oxford, T. Rood a. T. Hunte,* 1483.] L.O.C.M(imp.). Duff 392.
  Collates n–q⁸ and was prob. intended to follow an ed. of Anwykyll's Compendium; see 696.

23905 — [Anr. ed. Heading a2ʳ:] Vulgaria quedam . . . anglicam. 4° in 8's. [*W. de Machlinia,* 1483?] L.C(imp.). Duff 393.
  Collates a–d⁸.

23906 — [Anr. ed.] Vulgaria q̄dā . . . Anglicam. 4° in 8's. [*W. de Machlinia,* 1486?] L(lacks 3 leaves).C(4 leaves).C⁹ (lacks 12 leaves).; PML(2 leaves). Duff 394.
  Collates [a–d⁸], i.e. no leaf signatures.

23907 — [Anr. ed.] Vulgaria Therentii in anglicanam linguam traducta. *p* partly in 6's. (*Antwerpie, p̄ me G. leeu,* 1486 (11 kal. ja.)) C. Duff 395.

23907.3 — [Anr. ed.] 8°. (*per me G. faques,*) [c. 1505.] C⁷(imp.).

23907.7 — [Anr. ed.] 8°. [*W. de Worde,* c. 1510.] C(Sayle 245, frag.).
  Latin and English both in B.L.

23908 — [Anr. ed.] Vulgaria quedam . . . collecta, et in Ang⟨li⟩cam lin⟩guam traducta. 8°. (*W. de Worde,* 1529 (3 au.)) C(A1 def.).
  Latin in italic, English in B.L.

Teresa, *of Jesus, Saint. See* 23948.5.

23909 **Terilo, William,** *Pseud.* A piece of friar Bacons brazenheads prophesie. [A poem on the decline of manners from the Golden Age. Probably by N. Breton.] 4°. *T. C[reede] f. A. Johnson,* 1604. Ent. 4 jn. O.

23910 **Term.** The colde tearme: or the frozen age: or the metamorphosis of the river of Thames. 1621. [By J. Taylor, *the Water Poet?* In verse.] s.sh.fol. [*London,* 1621.] L(C.20.f.2(3)).

Termini. [Begins:] [Q]Voniā ex t'mis. [1483.] *See* 16693.

Terms. Les termes de la ley. 1624, etc. *See* 20716 sqq.

23911 **Terry, John.** The defence of protestancie. 1635. Now = 23915.5.

23912 — The reasonablenesse of wise and holy truth. [A sermon.] 4°. *Oxford, J. Lichfield a. W. Wrench,* 1617. O.C.; HN.

23913 — The triall of truth: containing a plaine and short discovery of the doctrine of the great Antichrist. 4°. *Oxford, Jos. Barnes, sold* [*by J. Broome, London,*] 1600. L.O.O¹⁰.D.M.+; F(2).BO³.HD.

23913.5 — The second part of the Trial of truth: wherein is set downe the fountaine of good works. 4°. *Oxford, Jos. Barnes, solde by John Barnes,* [*London,*] 1602. L.O.O¹⁰.D.M.+; F(2).HD.
  On the last page are errata for both pts.

Terry, John—*cont.*

23914 — Theologicall logicke: or the third part of the Tryall of truth: wherein is declared the excellency and æquity of the christian faith, fortified by right reason. 4°. *Oxford, J. Lichfield a. W. Turner,* 1625. L.O(2).; CHI.U(imp.).*

At least the L copy has a final quire: G[g]⁴ with Questions handled in the 3rd pt. and errata.

23915 — [Anr. issue, w. cancel tp, w. imprint:] *Oxford, J. Lichfield a. W. Turner f. W. T[urner] a. H. Curtaine,* 1626. L¹³.C(a copy lacking tp, plus a separate tp only).BTL(lacks tp)*. Finedon.

23915.5 — [Anr. issue, w. cancel tp:] The defence of protestancie. Second edition. *f. W. Millard, bookeseller in Shrewsbury,* 1635. O².C¹⁷.; U.
(Formerly 23911)

23916 **Tertullian, Quintus.** The seconde booke of Tertullian vnto his wyf, *tr.* [by J. Hoper, i.e. Hooper] wherī is cōteined coūsel how those vnmaryed, may chese godly companyons. 8°. [*N. Hill f.*] (*R. Jugge,* 1550.) O.
Tp comp. McK. & F. 33 has inits. 'N. H.' in the sill.

23916.5 **Tesauro, Emmanuele.** Reverendi patris Emanuelis Thesauri . . . Cæsares; quibus accesserunt pontificium elogia, & varia opera poëtica. Editio secunda emendatior, cum auctariolo. 12°. *Oxonii, L. Lichfield, imp. G. Webb,* 1637. O.O².C.C³.E.+; F.HN.HD.ILL.N.
Collates ¶² C–H¹² I⁴.

23917 — [Anr. issue, completely reimposed for 8°.] Reverendi patris Emanuelis [etc.] 8°. *Oxonii, L. Lichfield, imp. G. Webb,* 1637. O¹¹.O³⁸.C.BIRM²(K.N.).; HN.FBL.
Collates ¶⁴ C–L⁸ M⁴.

23917.5 — [A variant, w. title beginning:] R. P. Emanuelis [etc.] 8°. *Oxonii, L. Lichfield, imp. G. Webb,* 1637. L.O⁶. C².M².SCL.+; Y.

23918 **Tessier, Charles.** Superius (Contratenor—Bassus—[etc.]) Le premier liure de chansons & airs de court tant Enfrançois qu'en Italien & Gascon a 4. & 5. parties. 5 ptbks? 4°. *par T. Este, se treuvent ches E. Blount,* 1597. L²(contratenor tp only, MS 661).; HN(superius, bassus only).

Testament. The testament of Gad. [1542?] *See* 19465.3.

Testaments. The testaments of the twelue patriarches. 1574, etc. *See* 19465.7 sqq.

Testimony. A testimonie of antiquitie. [1566.] *See* 159 sq.

Teverton. *See* Tiverton.

23918.5 **Tewkesbury.** Reasons, why the county of Glocester, ought to joyne with the towne of Tewkesbury, in repayring of a decayed bridge. [Arguments presented to Parliament.] s.sh.fol. [*W. Jaggard,* 1621.] L⁸(GL 4944).
See Notestein III.171–2.

23919 **Texeda, Fernando de.** The exhortation. 1624. = 23922.
23920 — Hispanus conversus. Potens est Deus [etc.] 4°. *T. S[nodham] pro R. Mylbourne,* 1623. L.O.C.DUR⁵. YK.+; F.HN.BO².HART.HD(2).
Translated in 23923.

23921 — Miracles unmasked. A treatise proving that miracles are not infallible signes of faith. [*Tr.* by Texeda from a Spanish work of his.] 4°. *T. S[nodham] f. E. Blackamore,* 1625. L.O.C.DUR(Bamb.).LINC.+; F.HN. ILL.LC.

23922 — Scrutamini scripturas: the exhortation of a Spanish converted monke: collected out of the Spanish authours themselves, to read the holy scriptures. 4°. [*J. Bill f.*] *T. Harper,* 1624. Ent. 8 ap. L.O.C. DUR⁵.SAL.+; F(cropt).HART.HD.
(Formerly also 23919)

23923 — Texeda retextus: or the Spanish monke his bill of divorce against Rome. [A trans. of 23920.] 4°. *T. S[nodham] f. R. Mylbourne,* 1623. Ent. 14 ja. L.O.C. DUR⁵.YK.+; F.HN.HD.N.Y.
Copies vary: To Reader signed 'D.F.' or 'Daniel Featly.'; both at HN.
— *tr. See* 16434.

Texere, Joseph. *See* Teixeira, J.

23924 **Text.** Keepe your text. Or a short discourse, wherein is sett downe a method to instruct, how a catholike may defend his fayth . . . in keeping to the text of the scripture. Composed by a catholike priest. 4°. [*Lancs., Birchley Hall Press?*] 1619. L.O¹⁰.C⁵.HP.; F. A&R 421. Freely based on 24675.5.

Textoris, Johannes Ravisius. *See* Ravisius, J.

Th., R. In obitum Jo. Barclaii elegia. [1621.] *See* 24034.

23925 **Thachame, T.** [An exhortation to despise the gifts], whych we receaue by faylynge fortune. *Ballad.* s.sh.fol. [*T. Raynald,* 1552?] O(imp.).
(Formerly also 10618)

23926 **Thacker, R.** A godlie dittie to be song for the preseruation of the queenes maiesties raigne. *Ballad* w. music. s.sh.fol. *A. Jeffes,* 1586. L⁵(Lemon 86).

Thamara, Francisco. *See* 11255.

23927 **Thame School.** Preces matutinæ, in schola ante alia exercitia dicendæ. [Prayers, followed by 10 school rules in Latin verse.] fol(5). (*T. Vautrollerius,*) [1578.] L.O¹⁴.
Heading of the 4th leaf is dated cal. Feb. 1578. Prayers reprinted from 23928.

23928 — 1575. Schola Thamensis ex fundatione Johannis Williams. [Covenants, statutes, etc.] fol. [*H. Bynneman,* 1575.] L.O.O¹⁴.WN. Thame School, Thame, Oxfordshire.+; CH.HD.
All copies are imperfect except one L(128.e.23) and HD which have 55 printed leaves. Most copies still in orig. binding w. a title label reimposed from the tp; *see* Bookplates.

Thames. The colde tearme: or the metamorphosis of the river of Thames. [1621.] *See* 23910.

Thatcher, Anthony. *See* 23605.

23929 **Thayre, Thomas.** A treatise of the pestilence. 4°. *E. Short,* 1603. Ent. to F. Kingston 12 jy. L.L¹⁶.O(imp.). NEP. Blackburn PL.; F. Philadelphia, College of Physicians.
Dedic. to Sir Robert Lee, Lord Mayor.

23930 — [Anr. ed.] An excellent and best approved treatise of the plague. 4°. [*N. Okes*] *f. T. Archer,* 1625. L.L¹⁶. O.C⁹. Preston PL.; F.HD.NLM.
Dedic. to John Gore, Lord Mayor.

23931 **Theatre.** The theatre of the earth. Containing very short descriptions of all countries, gathered out of the cheefest cosmographers. [By J. Thorius.] 4°. *A. Islip,* 1599. Ent. to J. Wolfe 15 fb. 1593. L(imp.). PLUME.

23932 — [Anr. issue, w. cancel tp, w. imprint:] *f. W. Jones* [2,] 1601. O.O⁵.DUL.; F.HN.

23932.5 — [Anr. issue, w. cancel tp and added dedic.] Orbe inferiore, or, theatre of the earth. *A. Islip,* 1602. L.
Dedic. to Lady Mary Neville is signed Giovanni Thorisi.

23933 — Wits theater of the little world. 1599. = 382.

Thebes. Prologus/ Here begynneth the prologue of the storye of Thebes. [1497?] *See* 17031.

23934 **Theloall, Simon.** Le digest des briefes originals. 8°. *in æd. R. Tottelli,* 1579 (14 oc.) Ent. 18 fb. 1583. L.O².C.D.E.+; F.HN.CU.HD.MICH.+

Thelsford, Warks., *Trinitarians of. See* Indulgences 122.

Thémines, *Marquis de. See* 15317.

23934.2 **Themylthorp, Nicholas.** The posie of godly prayers, fit for every christian to use. Now newly altered and enlarged and the third time imprinted. 12°. *T. S[nodham] f. G. Vincent,* 1611. Ent. to T. Dawson 18 ja. 1608; to G. Vincent 18 ap. 1609. CHATS.

23934.5 — The ninth time imprinted. 12°. *T. Dawson f. K. V[incent,]* sould by *J. Parker,* 1618. C⁴(imp.).; HD.

23934.6 — The tenth time imprinted. 12°. *T. Dawson, sold by J. Parker,* 1619. Broxbourne(O).

23934.8 — The thirteenth time imprinted. 12°. *J. Dawson, sold by J. Parker,* 1623. E².

23934.9 — The foureteenth time imprinted. 12°. *J. Dawson, sold by J. Parker,* 1624 (1623.) C².

23935 — [Anr. ed., without edition number.] 12° in 6's. *Aberdene, E. Raban,* 1636. O.; F.

Themylthorp, Nicholas—*cont.*

23936 — The twentie and ninth time imprinted. 12°. *J. L[egat a.] (J. Dawson) f. R. Thrale,* 1638. Ass'd by widow of G. Vincent, jun., 28 ap. 1637. L.
Dawson pr. quires G to end.

Theocritus. A paraphrase upon the third of the canticles. 1591. *See* 3508.

23937 — Sixe idillia that is, sixe, small, or petty poems, or æglogues, *tr.* into English verse. 8°. *Oxford, J. Barnes,* 1588. O.

23938 **Theodoret,** *Bp.* The ecclesiasticall history of Theodoret. Now *tr.* into our English tongue [by R. Cadwallader. *Ed.*] (G. E.) 4°. [*St. Omer, English College Press,*] 1612. L.O.C.DE.USHAW.+; F.GRO.NY[11].
A&R 813.

23939 — The mirror of divine providence. Taken out of his workes De providentia. [*Ed.*] (J. C.) [*Tr.* by 'a divine, now deceased'.] 8°. *T. C[reede] f. J. Smithick,* 1602. Ent. 5 de. 1601. L.O.

23939.5 **Theodulus.** [Liber Theoduli cum commento. *Ed.* Odo Picardus.] 4°. [*R. Pynson,* 1497?] L(a2 and another leaf).
Text begins a2[r].

23940 — [Anr. ed.] Liber theodoli cum cōmento incipit feliciter. 4° in 6's. [*R. Pynson,* 1503?] L(2, 1 imp.).C[5].; HN. (Formerly also 23942) Collates A–G[6] H[8]. Text begins A2[r].

23940.3 — [Anr. ed.] Theodolus cum commento. 4° in 6's. (*per J. Notary,* 1505 (1 jn.)) D(lacks tp).; F.
Collates a–f[6] g[8]; text begins a1[v].

23940.7 — [Anr. ed.] Liber theodoli cum commento.... 4° in 6's. [*R. Pynson,* 1508?] D.
Collates a–d[6] e–f[4] g–h[6]; text begins a1[v].

23940a — [Anr. ed.] Nouiter impressus. 4° in 6's. [*Antwerp, T. Martens,*] *venundatur Londini ap. bibliopolas in cimiterio sancti Pauli* (imp. *J. pelgrim & H. Jacobi,* 1508.) L.O(lacks tp).C.C[2].; HN.

23941 — [Anr. ed.] 4° 8.4. *per w. de worde,* (imp. *w. de worde,* 1509 (28 ap.)) L.; ILL.

23942 — = 23940.

23943 — [Anr. ed.] 4° 8.4. (imp. *w. de worde,* 1515 (10 mr.)) L.O(lacks tp).C(imp.).E[5](imp.).; BALT(imp.).

23944 **Theognis.** Theognidis Megarensis sententiæ: cum versione Latina, addita earundem explicatione. A P. Melancthone. *Gr. a. Lat.* 8°. *typis E. G[riffin,] sumpt. G. Emerson,* 1639. Ent. 1 jn. 1638. L(tp only, Harl.5921/235).O.

Theologia. Theologia Germanica. *See* 11786.

23945 **Theophile,** *D. L.* A tragicall historie. [1583.] Now = 17450.3.

23946 — [A ghost.]

Theophilus. Divine and politike observations. 1638. *See* 15309.

Theophilus, *tr. See* 17450.

Theophilus, Joannes, *pseud., tr. See* 11786.

23947 **Theophrastus.** Θεοφραστου ηθικοι χαρακτῆρες. Theophrasti notationes morum. *Gr.* 4°. *Oxoniae, J. Barnesius,* 1604. O.; CU.
For an Eng. trans. *see* 10426.

23947.5 — [Anr. ed.] 4° in 2's. *Oxoniæ, J. Lichfield propter H. Cripps,* 1628. PARIS[3].; ILL.

23948 **Theophylact,** *Abp. of Achrida.* Θεοφυλακτου...εξηγησις. Theophylacti...in D. Pauli epistolas commentarii: studio A. Lindselli. Cum Latina P. Montani versione. [Pub'd by T. Bailius, i.e. Bayly, *Sub-Dean of Wells.*] *Gr. a. Lat.* fol. *e typog. regio* [*R. Barker a. assigns of J. Bill,*] 1636. L.O.C.D.E.+; F.HN.HD. CHI.NY[11].+

23948.5 **Theresa,** *de Jesus, Saint.* The lyf of the mother Teresa of Jesus. Written by her self, and now *tr.* into English, out of Spanish. By W. M. of the Society of Jesus. [i.e. M. Walpole?] 4°. *Antwerp, H. Jaye,* 1611. L.O.D[2].SN.W.+; F.HD.N.TEX.V.
(Formerly 20971) A&R 811.

23949 **Thersytes.** A new enterlude called Thersytes. [Adapted from J. Ravisius by N. Udall?] 4°. (*J. Tysdale,*) [1562?] HN.JH.PFOR. Greg 37.

Thesaurus, Emanuel. *See* 23916.5.

Thetford, Norfolk, *Hospital of St. Sepulchre. See* Indulgences 151 sq.

Theutobocus. A true relation of a mighty giant, named Theutobocus. 1615. *See* 24091.5.

23950 **Thevet, André.** The new found worlde, or Antarctike, wherin is contained beastes, fishes, [etc.] written in French. And now newly *tr.* 4° in 8's. *H. Bynneman f. T. Hacket,* (1568.) Ent. 1567–68. L.L[16].O.O[4].G[2].+; F.HN.HD.N.NY.+

Thibaldus. Thibaldus sive vindictæ ingenium. Tragoedia. 1640. *See* 22888.

23951 **Thibault, John.** Pronosticacyon. [1530.] Now = 517.10.
23952 — Pronostycacyon. [1533.] Now = 517.12.

Thief. Save a thiefe from the gallowes. [c. 1618, etc.] *See* 21776.3 sq.

Thierry. The tragedy of Thierry king of France. 1621. *See* 11074.

23952.3 **Thimelthorpe, C.** A short inuentory of certayne idle inuentions the fruites of a close and secret garden of great ease, and litle pleasure. By C. T. [Partly in verse.] 8°. *T. Marsh,* 1581. Ass'd by E. Marsh to T. Orwin ?23 jn. 1591. HN.
On L1[v] the compositor calls the author 'Thimelthorpe'.

23952.7 **Things.** Things lost the 24. of December. 1614. A ring with a table diamond in an open claw [and 15 other rings, with their values] all in a leather boxe. s.sh.4°. [*London,* 1614?] L(Harl.5919/75, imp.?).
No owner's name or address is given. *See* also 17120.5.

23953 **Thirst.** Spirituall thirst: a sermon preached upon John 7.37. [By T. Hooker?] 12°. [*M. Flesher*] *f. R. Davlman,* 1638. Ent. as by T. H. 13 no. 1637. L[4].
Collates A[6] B–C[12] D[10]. *See* note to 23240.

23954 **Thomas,** *à Becket, Saint.* [Heading A1[r]:] Here begynneth the lyfe of the blessed martyr saynte Thomas. [In prose. Extracted from 24873.] 4° in 8. (*R. Pynson,*) [c. 1520.] L.

23954.3 — [Verse life of St. Thomas.] 4°. (*Imprented in chepe syde next to Paulis gate,*) [i.e. *J. Rastell,* c. 1520.] Nash (frag.).

Thomas [Haemmerlein], *à Kempis.*

DE IMITATIONE CHRISTI

[A supposititious work. Thomas is not named in any of the following translations except those of Rogers (23973), B. F. (23987), and Page (23993).]

Atkinson's translation

23954.7 — A ful deuout and gostely treatyse of the Imytacyon and folowynge the blessed lyfe of our sauyour cryste: cōpiled in Laten by J. Gerson: and *tr.* into Englysshe M.ð.ii. By w. Atkynson. (Here begīnethe the forthe boke. Inprynted at the cōmaūdement of Margarete [Countess of Richmond and Derby]: aud [*sic*] by the same prynces *tr.* oute of frenche M & D.iiii.) 2 pts. 4° in 6's. [col. to Bk. 3:] (*Emprynted in London by R. Pynson,* 1503 (27 jn.)) [Bk. 4:] (*Inprinted at lōdon by R. Pynson,*) [1504.] C[5].

23955 — [Anr. issue, w. outer sheet of 1st quire reprinted.] A full...Imytacion...oure sauyoure criste: compiled ...Englysshe: M.D.ii. (*R. Pynson,* 1503 (27 jn.)) [1504?] L(imp.).

23956 — [Anr. ed.] 2 pts. 4° in 6's. [col. to Bk. 3:] (*Emprynted in Lōdon by w. de worde,*) [1518?] [Bk. 4:] (*Inprynted at london...by w. de worde,*) [1519?] L(G.12041). c(Sel.5.28, Sel.5.26).M.; F(pt. 1 only, imp.).

23957 — [Anr. ed.] 2 pts. 4° in 6's. [Col. to Bk. 3:] (*Emprynted in London by R. Pynson,* 1517 (7 oc.)) [Bk. 4:] (*Inprinted at lōdō...by R. Pynson,*) [1517.] C.

23958 — [A variant, w. end of Bk. 3 undated.] (*R. Pynson,*) [1517.] O.C(imp.).

23959 — = 23960.
23960 — [Anr. ed. of Bks. 1–3.] 4° in 6's. [col. to Bk. 3:] (*Imprynted in Lōdon by w. de worde,*) [1528?] L(C.25. k.1, imp.).C(2, 1 imp., Sel.5.64, Sel.5.3).; St. John's Seminary, Camarillo, California.

23960a — = 23968.

Thomas, *à Kempis—cont.*

Whitford's translation

23961 — A boke newely translated out of Laten in to Englysshe, called the folowynge of Cryste. (Here after folowyth the fourthe boke of the folowynge of Cryste.) [*Tr.* R. Whitford.] 2 pts. 8°. (*R. wyer*,) [1531?] C³(imp.). YK(imp.).; HN.
　　In the preface the authorship is attrib. to Gerson. For extracts *see* 23968.5. P. Treveris app. pr. Bk. 4.

23962 — [Anr. ed. of Bk. 4.] Here after foloweth the fourth boke, of the folowyng of Chryste. 8° in 4's. (*R. wyer*,) [1531?] F.

23963 — [Anr. ed. of all 4 bks.] The folowyng of Christ. Lately translated in to Englisshe, and newly examyned. 8°. (*T. Godfray*,) [1531?] L(2).C(imp.).
　　Prob. issued w. 1915. Tp varies: with (L, IX.Eng. 128) or without (L, G.19949) woodcut panel to the right of the large cut on the tp.

23964 — [Anr. ed., w. additions.] A boke ne⟨we⟩ly translated . . . with the Golden epistel of saynt Barnard [and four revelations of St. Bridget.] 8°. [*R. Redman*, 1531?] C(imp.).
　　C1ʳ line 4 ends: 'invayne'. The last 2 items are reprinted from 1915.

23964.3 — [Anr. ed.] 8°. [*R. Redman*, 1531?] HD(A3–H5 only).
　　C1ʳ line 4 ends: 'i vayne'.

23964.7 — [Anr. ed.] 8°. [*R. Redman*, 1535?] L(imp.).ST(imp.).
　　C1ʳ line 4 ends: 'in vaine'.

23965 — [Anr. ed.] 8°. (*W. Myddylton*,) [1545?] L(imp.). O(imp.).
　　C1ʳ line 4 ends: 'vayne oft erreth'.

23966 — [Anr. ed.] The folowinge of Chryste, newly corrected and amended. Whereunto is added the golden epystell. [*Ed.* W. Peto.] 8°. (*J. Cawood*,) 1556 (18 se.) L².C(imp.). Rogers(imp.).; F(frag.).HN.HD.
　　Collates A–T⁸ V⁴; A–E⁸. The Golden Epistle is a dif. trans., reprinted from 1912, w. Whitford's name at the end.

23967 — [Anr. ed.] The folowing of Christ. 8°. (*J. Cawood*,) 1556 (18 se.) [i.e. *W. Carter, c.* 1575.] L.L².CHATS.P.; F(2).TEX.
　　Collates A–Y⁸.

23967.5 — [Anr. ed.] 8°. (*J. Cawood*,) 1566 (2 de.) F.
　　Collates A–T⁸ V⁴; A–E⁸.

23968 — [Anr. ed.] And now lastelie [added] the rules of a christian lyfe, made by John Picus the elder earle of mirãdula. 12°. [*Rouen, G. L'Oyselet*,] 1585. L.O.C⁵(imp.).E.W.+; F.HD(lacks tp).N.Y.
　　(Formerly also 23960a) A&R 814. The Pico Rules are in Sir T. Elyot's trans., reprinted from 6157. The Golden Epistle and the Rules are reprinted in 23988.

23968.5 — [Extracts from Whitford's trans.] Here ben cõteyned fyue notable chapytres: moche profytable for euery man, dylygently to recorde. And after do folowe thyrtene degrees of mortyfycacyon. [Anon.] 8°. (*R. wyer*,) [1533?] O(tp and col. only, Douce Add. 142/614–5).
　　The chapters listed on the tp verso appear to correspond w. those in Wyer's ed. (23961): Bk. 1, chap. 25; 3.61; 1.24; 3.52; 4.9.

Hake's translation

23969 — The imitation or following of Christ, amended by S. Castalio, & Englished by E. H(ake.) 8°. *H. Denham*, 1567. Ent. 1566–67. F.HN.
　　Collates A⁸ A–S⁸.

23969.5c — [Anr. ed., omitting reference to Castalio from the title and adding:] Whereunto, we haue adioyned another pretie treatise, The perpetuall reioyce of the godlye. 2 pts. 8°. *H. Denham*, 1568. Pt. 2 ent. 1568–69. O.C⁵.; ILL(pt. 1 only).
　　Pt. 2 also issued sep. as 24230. Collates A–T⁸; A–C⁸ D⁴. 1st C3ʳ last line ends: 'wholie'; sub tp line 8: 'the order appointed'.

23970 — [Anr. ed.] 2 pts. 8°. *H. Denham*, 1568. L(lacks 1st B4). C(pt. 1 only).SHEF(with A1, 7 of 23969.5).; F.HD.
　　Collates A–T⁸; A–C⁸ D⁴. 1st C3ʳ last line ends: 'wholye'; sub tp line 8: 'order appointed'.

23971 — [Anr. ed.] 8°. *H. Denham*, (1568) [1571?] L.C(2nd pt. only).M².; F.HN.HD(1st pt. only, lacking tp).
　　(2nd pt. formerly also 24231) Collates A–U⁸ X⁴; 1st tp undated; sub tp on S3ʳ dated 1568. Sub tp line 8: 'order appoynted'.

Thomas, *à Kempis—cont.*

23972 — No entry.

Rogers's translation

23973 — Of the imitation of Christ, three, both for wisedome, and godlines, most excellent bookes; made by Thomas of Kempis, now newlie corrected, translated, and illustrated by T. Rogers. 12°. *H. Denham*, (*the assigne of W. Seres*, 1580.) L.C⁵.; F.HN.HD.

23974 — [Anr. ed.] 12°. *H. Denham*, (1582.) L.

23975 — [Anr. ed.] 12°. *H. Denham*, 1584. L.Rogers.; HN.LC.

23976 — [Anr. ed.] 12°. *in the now dwelling house of H. Denham*, 1585. L.C⁵.

23977 — [Anr. ed.] 12°. *H. Midleton*, 1587. L.; F.

23978 — [Anr. ed.] 12°. *H. Denham*, 1589. NY.

23979 — [Anr. ed.] 12°. *R. Yardly a. P. Short f. the assignes of W. Seres*, 1592. L(imp.).; F.HD(2, 1 imp.).
　　This and following eds. frequently have 23995 sqq. bd. w. them as a fourth book.

23980 — [Anr. ed.] 12°. *P. Short*, 1596. L.O.YK.; HD.PML. WEL.

23980.5 — [Anr. ed.] 12°. *P. Short*, 1600. HD(very imp.). Pirie.

23981 — [Anr. ed.] 12°. *P. Short*, 1602. L.O.; HD(imp.).

23982 — [Anr. ed.] 12°. [*H. Lownes*] *f. the Co. of Stacioners*, 1605. L.

23982.3 — [Anr. ed.] 12°. [*W. Jaggard a. N. Okes*] *f. the Co. of Stacioners*, 1607. HD.
　　Jaggard pr. quires A–G; Okes the rest.

23982.5 — [Anr. ed.] 12°. [*H. Lownes*] *f. the Co. of Statrs.*, 1609. L(imp.).; HD(lacks O12).

23983 — [Anr. ed.] 12°. (*H. L[ownes]*) *f. the Co. of Statrs.*, 1617. L.O.C.C⁵.; F.HN.HD.

23984 — [Anr. ed.] 12°. [*H. Lownes a. R. Young*] *f. the Co. of Statrs.*, 1629. Ent. to the English Stock 5 mr. 1620. L.O(imp.).M.; F.CH.HD.N.

23985 — [Anr. ed.] 12°. [*M. Dawson*] *f. the Co. of Statrs.*, 1636. L.C⁴.G².M².; F.ILL.

23986 — [Anr. ed.] 12°. *E. P[urslowe] f. the Co. of Statrs.*, 1640. L⁴.NLW.; HD.

B. F.'s (or F. B.'s) translation

23987 — The following of Christ. Devided into foure bookes. Written in Latin by Thomas a Kempis and *tr.* by B. F. [i.e. A. Hoskins.] 8°. [*St. Omer, English College Press*,] 1613. O.C⁵.AMP.PARIS.W.+ A&R 815.

23988 — [Anr. ed.] Whereunto also is added the golden epistle of S. Bernard [*tr.* R. Whitford.] And also certaine rules of a christian life, by J. Picus, earle of Mirandula [*tr.* Sir T. Elyot.] 12°. [*English secret press*,] 1615. L.ST.; HN.
　　A&R 816. The St. Bernard and Pico sections are revised and reprinted from 23968 and appear only in this ed.

23988.5 — [Anr. ed.] 18°. *Mackline, H. Jaye*, 1616. DE(imp.).
　　A&R 817.

23989 — [Anr. ed.] *Tr.* by F. B. 12°. [*St. Omer, English College Press*,] 1620. L.C.
　　A&R 818.

23989.5 — The third edition. 12°. [*St. Omer, English College Press*,] 1624. C⁵.W.
　　A&R 819.

23990 — [Anr. ed.] 24° in 8's. [*St. Omer, C. Boscard f.*] *J. Heigham*, 1624. O³.; F.
　　A&R 820.

23991 — Fourth edition. 16° in 8's. [*Rouen*,] *J. Cousturier*, 1633. L.C¹⁸(imp.).PARIS.; HD.
　　A&R 821.

23992 — [Anr. ed.] Reviewed and corrected by M. C[ar, i.e. M. Pinkney,] confessor to the English nuns at Paris. Who also added the authours life in this last edition. 16° in 8's. *Paris, Mistris Blageart*, 1636. L.O.SN.W.; HD.Y.
　　A&R 822.

Page's translation

23993 — The imitation of Christ, divided into four books. Written in Latin by Thomas à Kempis, and the translations of it corrected & amended by W. P(age.) 12°. *Oxford, L. Lichfield f. E. Forrest*, 1639. L.O(2).; F.
　　Largely based on 23987.

Thomas, *à Kempis—cont.*

SOLILOQUIUM ANIMAE

[A genuine work by Thomas.]

23994 — = 23995.
23995 — Soliloquium animæ. The sole-talke of the soule. Now
entituled the fourth booke of the Imitation of Christ.
Tr. by T. Rogers. Neuer before published. 12°. (*R.*
Yardley a. P. Short,) *solde at the shop of A. Maunsell,*
1592. Ent. to Denham 3 jy. 1587; to Yardley a. Short
17 fb. 1592. O(imp.).; F.HD(2 imp.). NY.WEL.
This and the following eds. are frequently bd. w.
23979 sqq.
23996 — [Anr. ed.] Corrected. 12°. *P. S[hort,] sold by W.*
Leake, 1598. L(imp., with A⁸ of 23998).O.; HD(imp.).
Pirie.
23996.5 — [Anr. ed.] 12°. *H. L[ownes,] sold by W. Leake,* 1608.
HD.
23997 — [Anr. ed.] 12°. *H. Lownes,* 1616. L.O.C.C⁵.; F.HD(2).
23998 — [Anr. ed.] 12°. *H. Lownes a. R. Young,* 1628. L(A⁸
only, w. 23996).C⁴.; F(2).HD.
A3ʳ line 1: 'BEeing'.
23999 — [Anr. ed.] 12°. *H. Lownes a. R. Young,* 1628 (1629.)
L.O(imp.).; F.CH.HD(imp.).N.
A3ʳ line 1: 'BEing'.
24000 — [Anr. ed.] 12°. *R. Young,* 1640. L.; HN.HD.

Thomas, *of Erfurt.* See 268, 270 sqq.

24000.5 **Thomas,** *Sir* **Anthony.** The propositions of sir Anthony
Thomas knight, and John Worsop esquire, for
making the bargaine with the country, and H. Briggs
professor of the mathematicks in the universitie of
Oxford [for draining the fens in Norfolk, Suffolk,
Cambridge, etc. 11 Jan. 1629.] s.sh.fol. [*London?*
1629.] C²⁶(3: CUR 3.3(128–9), CUR 11.13(5)).

24000.7 **Thomas,** **Joan.** To the honourable assembly of the
Commons. The humble petition of J. Thomas, a
poore distressed widdow. [For relief from a decree
in Chancery.] s.sh.fol. [*London,* 1624.] L(Harl.MS.
7614/94).Lᴵᴵ(S.P.D. Jas.1, vol. 164, doc. 26).
The Lᴵᴵ copy is docketed for 5 May 1624.

24001 **Thomas,** **John.** [Almanack. 1612.] Now = 517.14.

24002 **Thomas,** **Lewis.** Demegoriai. Certaine lectures upon
sundry portions of scripture. 8°. *J. R[oberts] f. E.*
White, 1600. Ent. 21 oc. L.O⁴.C³.NLW.SCL.+; F.PN².
24003 — Seauen sermons, or, the exercises of seuen Sabbaoths.
Together with a short treatise vpon the commaunde-
ments. 8°. *V. Sims,* 1599. Ent. 5 mr. L.NLW.; F(imp.).
HN.
24004 — Editio quarta. 8°. *V. Simmes,* 1602. L(destroyed).O.
24005 — Editio septima. 8°. *T. Purfoot f. V. Sims,* 1610. L.;
Haverford C.
24005.5 — The ninth time imprinted. 8°. *G. E[ld] f. J. Wright,*
1615. DUL.M.; F.
24006 — The tenth time imprinted. 8°. *N. O[kes] f. T. Langley,*
1619. Ass'd by Sims to E. Griffin 20 de. L.
24006.5 — The eleventh time imprinted. 8°. *J. Haviland,* 1638.
Ent. to A. Griffin a. J. Haviland 7 jn. 1621;
Haviland's half shared w. J. Wright, sen., 4 se.
1638. L.O⁴.

24007 **Thomas,** **Oliver.** Car-wr y Cymru, yn anfon ychydig
gymmorth i bôb Tâd. [Anon. A catechism.] 8°.
N. Okes dros P. Stephens a C. Meredyth, 1630.
L.NLW.
24007a — Car-wr y Cymru, yn annog ei genedl anwyl. [Anon. A
religious treatise. With a note on pronunciation by
E. Kyffin.] 8°. *F. Kyngston* (*dros yr awdur*) *drwy*
awdurdod, 1631. Ent. 13 jn. L.NLW(2).
One NLW copy is misdated '1361'.

24008 **Thomas,** **Thomas.** Dictionarium linguæ Latinae et
Anglicanæ. 8°. *Cantebrigiæ, ex off. T. Thomasii,*
extant Londini ap. R. Boyle, [1587.] C.BRISTOL.HAT.
Based on 18101, q.v.; see also 21032. See Greg,
Companion, p. 44.
24008.5 — [Anr. ed.] Nunc denuo recognitum. 8°. *Cantabrigiæ,*
ex off. J. Legatt, extant Londini ap. A. Kitson, 1589.
C.C⁴.; ILL.TEX.
24009 — [Anr. ed.] Thomae Thomasii dictionarium tertiò iam
emendatum, longè auctius. Huic accessit de ponde-
rum, mensurarum, & monetarum tractatus. 4° in
8's. *Cantabrigiæ, ex off. J. Legate, extant Londini ap.*
A. Kitson, 1592. L.O.C.A.CARLISLE.

Thomas, **Thomas**—*cont.*
24009.5 — Quarta editio superioribus multò auctior. 8°. *Canta-*
brigiæ, ex off. J. Legatt, extant Londini ap. A. Kitson,
1593. C(imp.).
24010 — [A variant, w. imprint:] *Cantabrigiæ, ex off. J. Legatt,*
extant Londini ap. A. Kitson, 1594. O³.C.C².WI.
Göttingen U.+; F.TEX.Y. Indiana State U.
24011 — Quinta editio cum Græcarum dictionum, adiectione
auctior. 4° in 8's. *Cantabrigiæ, ex off. J. Legati, extant*
Londini [*at R. Bankworth's shop,*] 1596. L.C.NLW.;
F.HN.HD.ILL.TEX.
24012 — Sexta editio. 8°. *Cantabrigiæ, ex off. J. Legat,* 1600.
L.O⁹.C.BIRM.NLW.+
Without the Greek supplement. Copies vary: tp
date in arabic numerals (L) or roman numerals (C).
24013 — Septima editio. 4° in 8's. *Cantabrigiæ, ex off. J. Legati,*
extant Londini [*at S. Waterson's shop,*] 1606.
L.L¹⁵.C.C².YK.; F.CAL.ILL.MICH.TEX.
With the Greek supplement. See *Court-Book C,*
p. 18.
24014 — Octava editio. 8°. *Cantabrigiæ, ex off. J. Legati, extant*
Londini [*at S. Waterson's shop,*] 1610. L.C(2).
CANT.; F.CAL(imp.).
Without the Greek supplement.
24015 — Decima editio. Cui demum adiectum est Supplementum, authore P. Hollando unà cum novo Anglo-
latino dictionario. 4° in 8's. *Londini, ex off. J. Legati,*
1615. L¹³.O.O³.LIV³.NEK.+
With the Greek supplement.
24016 — Undecima editio. 8°. *ex off. J. Legati,* 1619. L.L³⁰.O.C.
E².+; F.HN.ILL.JH. Indiana State U.
Without the Greek, Holland's or Eng.–Lat. sup-
plements.
24017 — Duodecima editio. 4° in 8's. *ex off. J. Legati,* 1620.
L⁴.C(2). Rouen PL.; CHI(imp.).ILL(3).Y.
With all supplements. See Greg, *Companion,* pp.
60, 178.
24017.5 — Decima tertia editio. 4° in 8's. *ex off. J. Legati, ap.*
P. Stephens & C. Meredith venale, 1631. O⁵.C⁵.E.;
ILL.
With all supplements.
— ed. See 18951.

Thomas, **William.** An argument, wherin the apparaile
of women is both reproued and defended. 1551. See
16612a.7.
24018 — The historie of Italie, . . . [which] intreateth of the
astate of many and diuers common weales. 4°. (*in*
the house of T. Berthelet,) 1549. L.O.C.D.E².+;
F.HN.CH.CHI.NY.+
24019 — [Anr. ed.] 4°. *T. Marshe,* (1561.) Ent. 24 jn. L.O.C.D.
G².+; F.HN.CU.HD.N.+
Quire 2nd A in 2 settings; A1ᵛ catchword:
'enough' or 'enoughe'; both at C², F.
24020 — Principal rules of the Italian grammer, with a dictionarie. 2 pts. 4°. (*in the house of T. Berthelet,*) 1550.
L(imp.).O.C.NLW.P.+; F(2).HN.HD.ILL. Indiana State
U.
24021 — [Anr. ed.] Newly corrected and imprinted. 2 pts. 4°.
(*T. Powell,*) 1562. L.O.C¹⁹.P.SHR.+; F(imp.).HN.CHI.
HD.ILL.+
24022 — [Anr. ed.] 2 pts. 4°. *in æd. H. Wykes,* 1567. L.O.C.
E.M.+; F.HN.CU.HD.N.+
24023 — The vanitee of this world. 8°. (*in the house of T.*
Berthelet,) 1549. C.; F.

24024 **Thompson,** **Henry,** *Esquire.* The soules alarum-bell.
Wherein the sicke soule hath recourse to God by
meditation and prayer. 12°. *J. Beale,* 1618. Ent. 14
my. L.L⁴.DUL.
Thompson is called 'esq.' in the SR entry.

Thompson, **Henry,** *Parson of Edenham.* [Brief granted
by James I. 1613.] See 9236.5.

24025 **Thompson,** **Thomas.** Antichrist arraigned: in a sermon
at Pauls Crosse. With the tryall of guides. 4° in 8's.
W. Stansby f. R. Meighen, 1618. Ent. 30 mr. L⁴.L¹⁵.
O.C⁹.NEP.+; F.HN.CAL.
(24029 is pt. of this)
24026 — Claviger ecclesiæ, seu concio ad clerum de clavibus
regni cœlorum. Cui adiectæ sunt theses duæ de
votis monasticis. 8°. *R. Field, imp. N. Butter,* 1612.
Ent. 22 jn. O.C⁵.A.D.DUR(Bamb.).+; F.BO⁵.
24027 — A diet for a drunkard. Delivered in two sermons in
Bristol, 1608. 4°. [*W. Stansby*] *f. R. Bankworth,*
1612. Ent. 9 de. 1611. L.O.BRISTOL.DUR³.STU.; F.HN.
NY.Y.

Thompson, Thomas—*cont.*

24028 — A friendly farewell from a faithfull flocke: taken in a sermon, preached in Bristoll, 1612. 4°. *T. Snodham f. J. Hodgets*, 1616. Ent. 3 jn. L.O.C(lacks tp). BRISTOL.DEU(lacks tp).+; F(tp def.).HN.AAS.PN².

24029 — The trial of guides. 1618. = pt. of 24025.
— *See also* 23626.5.

24030 **Thomson, George.** Ἀνακεφαλαίωσις sive de reductione regnorum Britanniæ ad unum principem, poema. (De pompa in ejus introitu in Londinum sylva.) [In verse.] 8°. *M. Bradwood, imp. S. Waterson*, 1604. L.O(Pompa only).C.D.E.+; HD(imp.).

24031 — Vindex veritatis. Adversus Iustum Lipsium libri duo. 8°. [*Eliot's Court Press*,] *ex off. Nortoniana*, 1606. Ent. to J. Bill 7 ja. L.O.C.D.E.+; F.HN.HD.ILL.U. Attacks portions of the Politicorum libri (cf. 15700.7) and the Diva Sichemiensis (pr. abroad).

24032 **Thomson, Richard.** Elenchus refutationis Torturae Torti. . . . Adversus M. Becanum. 8°. *R. Barkerus*, 1611. L.O.C.D.DUR³.+ Defends 626 against the Latin original of 1699; *see also* 1702.

Thorisi, Giovanni. *See* 23932.5.

Thorius, John. A spiritual wedding. *Tr.* J. Thorius. 1597. *See* 25195.
— The theatre of the earth. 1599, etc. *See* 23931 sqq.
— *tr. See* 5790, 10753, 23241, 24570.

24033 **Thorius, Raphael.** Hymnus tabaci, autore Raphaele Thorio. [In verse.] 12° ⁸·⁴. [*J. Haviland,*] *imp. J. Waterson*, 1626. Ent. 25 no. L.O.C.ETON.G².+; F.HN.HD.NY.PH.+

24034 — In obitum Jo. Barclaii elegia. (Venator [A defense of Abp. G. Abbot.]) [Init. R. Th. In verse.] 4°. *Londini* [*W. Stansby*, 1621.] L(date cropt).

24035 **Thornborough, John,** *Bp.* A discourse plainely proving the evident utilitie and urgent necessitie of the union of England and Scotland: by way of answer to certaine objections. [Signed J. Bristol.] 4°. *R. Field f. T. Chard*, 1604. L.L³⁰.O.C³.E.+; F.HN(imp.).HD. N.NY.+ Copies vary: A3ᵛ last line 'sensure' or 'censure'; A4ʳ and F2ʳ have 'Ioh.' or 'Io.'; both at F. The House of Commons took offence at the book and attempted to suppress it; see *JHC* I.226–32, 234, 236, 238, 244, and *JHL* II.314.

24036 — The joiefull and blessed reuniting the two kingdomes, England & Scotland. By J. Bristoll. 4°. *Oxford, J. Barnes, sold by S. Waterson,* [*London*, 1605?] L.O.C⁵.E.YK.+; F.HN.HD.ILL(imp.).NY¹¹.+

24037 — The last will and testament of Jesus Christ, touching the blessed sacrament. 4°. *Oxford, W. Turner*, 1630. L.O.C².D.E².+; F(date cropt).CAL.U.Y.

24038 — Λιθοθεωρικος, sive, nihil, aliquid, omnia, antiquorum sapientum depicta, in gratiam eorum qui artem auriferam physico-chymicè & piè profitentur. 4°. *Oxoniæ, J. Lichfield & J. Short*, 1621. L.O.C.E.M².+; F.HN.HD.MICH.NY.

24039 — A sermon preached before his majestie. 1618. = 4005.
— *See also* 10143, 10368, 10369, 10371.

Thornburgh, W. [Indulgence. 1505, etc.] *See* Indulgences 62 sq.

24040 **Thorndike, Herbert.** Epitome lexici Hebraici. 1635. Now = 21817.5.

24040.5 **Thorne, Henry.** [Heading A6ʳ:] The confutation of follie. [A dialogue between Falsiloquuus and Veriloquus.] 8°. (*H. Denham*,) [1584.] Ent. 22 se. 1584. L⁴(lacks tp).
— Phisicke for the soule. *Tr.* H. Thorne. [1567?] *See* 19893a.7.

24041 **Thorne, William.** Ἔσοπτρον βασιλικόν. Or a kenning-glasse for a christian king. 8°. *R. R[ead] f. J. Harrison* [2,] 1603. Ent. to J. Harrison, jun., 15 jn. L.O.E(lacks tp).G².

24042 — Ducente Deo. Willelmi Thorni Tullius, seu ῥήτωρ in tria stromata diuisus. 8°. *Oxoniae, J. Barnesius, væneunt cum Oxoniæ, tum ad caput tigridis Londinensium* [*by T. Cooke,*] 1592. O.O².O⁸.C².LK.; F.BOWDOIN.HD.

24043 **Thornes, Edward.** Encomium Salopiæ, or the description of Shrowesbury. [In verse.] 8°. [*W. Stansby*] *f. R. Meighen*, 1615. L.

24043.5 **Thornton,** *Captain.* [Heading A1ʳ:] Hereafter followeth the uttermost and [*sic*] course round about all Ireland. 4°. [*London*, 1606.] C⁶. End of text dated 1606.

24044 **Thornton, Richard.** The Ægyptian courtier. Delivered in two sermons. 4°. *E. P[urslowe] f. H. Seile*, 1635. Ent. 10 ap. L.O.C.RGU.WOR.+; F.NY¹¹.

24044a — = 24044.

24044a.5 **Thorold, Edmond.** To the most honourable assembly of the Commons. The humble petition of E. Thorold, marshall of [the] court of exchequer. [Against infringements of his right to apprehend sheriffs, etc. for accounts not rendered.] s.sh.fol. [*London*, 1621.] L(Harl.MS.7608/215).

Thorpe, John, *tr. See* 3161.5.

24045 **Thorpe, William.** The examinacion of master William Thorpe preste accused of heresye. The examinacion of syr J. Oldcastell. [*Ed.* W. Tyndale? or G. Constantine?] 8°. [*Antwerp, J. van Hoochstraten*, 1530.] L.O⁴.G².Blickling.

24046 **Thou, Jacques Auguste de.** Monumenta litteraria sive, obitus et elogia doctorum virorum. Ex historiis J. A. Thuani. Opera C. B[arksdale.] 4°. *J. Norton, sumpt. J. Kirton & T. Warren*, 1640. Ent. 4 no. 1639. L.O.C.D.E.+; F.HN.HD.N.NY.

24047 **Thrace.** A pleasant history of a gentleman in Thracia, which have foure sonnes. *Ballad.* s.sh.fol. *f. H. G[osson*, 1633.] Ent. to ballad ptnrs. 8 jy. 1633. L.

24048 **Threnoikos.** Θρηνοικος. The house of mourning. Delivered in XLVII. sermons, preached at funeralls. By D. Featly M. Day R. Sibbs T. Taylor. And other reverend divines. [*Ed.*] (H. W.) fol. *J. Dawson f. R. M[abb,*) sold by P. Nevill, 1640 (1639.) Ent. to Mabb 18 oc. 1638; Featley's pt. ent. to N. Bourne 28 jn. 1639. L.O.C⁵.D.YK.+; F.HN(imp.).HD.N.U.+ The only sermons w. the author identified are Featley's Hexalexium, which has imprint: *J. Dawson f. N. Bourne*, 1639.

24049 — [Anr. issue, w. imprint on gen. tp:] *J. Dawson f. R. M[abb,*] sold by J. Bellamie a. R. Smith, 1640. C.NLW.; TORONTO².

Thrissels-Banner. *See* 6120.

Throckmerton, Michael, *tr. See* 15693.

24050 **Throckmorton, Francis.** A discouerie of the treasons practised by F. Throckmorton. [With a letter by Q. Z., of Lion's Inn.] 4°. [*C. Barker*,] 1584. L.L³⁰. O.C².E.+; F(2).HD.NY.PML. [-]2ʳ line 4 of text ends: 'Throckmorton &' (no comma).

24050.5 — [Anr. issue, partially reset and reimposed.] [*C. Barker*,] 1584. L³⁰.O.C.E.M²(imp.).+; HN.BO⁵.PN.Y. [-]2ʳ line 4 of text ends: 'Throckmorton, &'.

24051 — [Anr. ed.] 4°. [*C. Barker*,] 1584. L⁸.O.C².D.DUR⁵.+ F.HD.N.TEX. [-]2ʳ line 4 of text ends: 'Throckemorton,'.

24051.5 — [A trans.] Indicium proditionum, quas Franciscus Throckmortonus . . . concepit. 8°. [*C. Barker.* 1584.] L.

24052 **Throgmorton, George.** A treatise of faith, and of some principal fruits thereof. Delivered in two sermons. With some additions and enlargements. 12°. *J. L[egat] f. W. Sheffard*, 1624. Ent. 12 se. L³.O.SCL.

24053 **Throgmorton, Robert.** The lives, apprehension, araignment & execution, of R. Throgmorton. W. Porter. J. Bishop. 4°. [*E. Allde*] *f. H. Gosson*, 1608. L.; F(frag. of tp only)*. A3ʳ lines 7, 17: 'George Throgmorton'.

24053.5 — [Anr. issue, w. quire A reset.] [*E. Allde*] *f. H. Gosson*, 1608. O. A3ʳ lines 6, 16: 'Robert Throgmorton'.

24054 — = 24053.

24055 **Throkmorton, Job.** The defence of Job Throkmorton, against the slaunders of maister Sutcliffe [in 23450]. 4°. [*London*,] 1594. L.O.G². In all recto headlines: 'SCLAN.' Reprinted and answered in 23451.

Throkmorton, Job—*cont.*

24055.5 — [Anr. ed.] 4°. [*London*,] 1594. C⁵.; F.
    In all recto headlines: 'SLAN.'
— *ed. See* 4706.
— *See also* 12342.

24056 **Thucydides.** The hystory writtone by Thucidides . . . *tr.*
    oute of Frenche [from C. de Seyssel's trans.] by T.
    Nicolls. fol. [*W. Tylle*,] 1550 (25 jy.) L.O.C.D.E.+;
    F.HN.CU.HD.N.+

24057 — History. *Tr.* into Englishe. fol. [*W. Jaggard*,] 1607.
    Ent. to W. Jaggard 2 jy. J(untraced, presumably
    a ghost).

24058 — Eight bookes of the Peloponnesian warre. Interpreted
    immediately out of the Greeke by T. Hobbes. fol.
    [*Eliot's Court Press*] *f.* H. Seile, 1629. Ent. 18 mr.
    1628. L.O.C³.DUR⁵.G².+; F.HN.HD.N.NY.+

24059 — [Anr. issue, w. engr. tp altered:] *f.* R. Mynne, 1634.
    L.O.C.BTU.E.+; F.HN.CU.HD.ILL.+
    Unsold sheets reissued in 1648 as Wing T 1133A.

24059.5 **Thunder.** Thunder haile, & lightni⟨ng⟩ from heaven.
    Sent against certaine covetous persons, inhabitants
    of Humerstone ⟨Lin⟩colneshire, 5. miles from
    Grimsby: the 3. of July last, 1616. 4°. [*G. Eld*, 1616.]
    L(cropt).

Thunderbolt. The brutish thunderbolt. 1586. *See*
13843.5.

Thybault, John. [Prognostication. 1530, etc.] *See*
517.10 sq.

24060 **Thylesius, Antonius.** Cassius of Parma his Orpheus:
    with N. Chitræus his commentarie. *Tr.* and abridged
    by R. Rawlyns. (Nestor his Antilochus [*tr.* from the
    Iliad xxiii.304–25.]—Certaine generall conclusions
    concerning our common lawes.) [Partly in verse.] 4°.
    [*T. Orwin*,] 1587. L.; HN.
        The Orpheus is a spurious work usually attrib. to
        Thylesius though his name does not appear in
        this ed.

Thynne, *Sir* Egremont. The lawes resolutions. 1632.
    See 7437.

24061 **Thynne, Francis.** The debate betweene pride and lowli-
    nes, pleaded to an issue in assise. [Init. F. T. In
    verse.] 8°. *J.* Charlwood *f.* R. Newbery, [1577?] HN.
        The attrib. to Thynne is erroneous.

24062 — Newes from the north. Otherwise called the con-
    ference betweene Simon Certain, and Pierce Plow-
    man, faithfully collected by T. F. student. 4°. *J.*
    Allde, 1579. Ent. 19 oc. O(3, 2 imp.).; F.HN.
        The attrib. to Thynne is erroneous.

24062a — [Anr. ed.] 4°. E. Allde, 1585. L.C.; HN.CH.
    — *See also* 13569.

Thynne, William, *ed. See* 5068.

24063 **Tiberius,** *Emperor of Rome.* The tragedie of Claudius
    Tiberius Nero, Romes greatest tyrant. 4°. [*E. Allde*]
    f. F. Burton, 1607. Ent. 10 ap. L(3).L⁶.O.O⁶(imp.)*.
    ETON.; F.HN.CHI.HD.Y².+ Greg 240.

24063a — [A variant, w. title:] The statelie tragedie of Claudius
    Tiberius Nero. [*E. Allde*] *f.* F. Burton, 1607. O.E.;
    F(imp.).

Tichborne, Chidiock. *See* 7605.

24064 **Tichborne, John.** A triple antidote, against certaine very
    common scandals. 4°. N. Okes *f.* C. Knight, 1609.
    L.L³.O³.C².E.+; F.HN.BO.

24065 **Tidings.** Glad tydings from heaven: or Christs glorious
    invitation to sinners. *Ballad.* 2 pts. s.sh.fol. *f.*
    C. W[right, c. 1630.] L.

24066 — O maruelous tydynges both wonders old and new the
    deuyll is endited yf many mens wordes be tru. [In
    verse.] s.sh.fol. C. Woltrop, [c. 1570.] L.

24067 **Tilenus, Daniel.** De disciplina ecclesiastica brevis &
    modesta dissertatio, ad ecclesiam Scoticam. Autore
    Gallo quodam theologo. [Anon.] 8°. *Abredoniæ*,
    E. Rabanus, imp. D. Melvill, 1622. L.O.C.D².E.+;
    HN.U.

24068 — A defence of the sufficiency of the holy scripture. 1606.
    = pt. 2 of 24071.
    — Novum et solenne decretum. Sub correctione D.
    Tileni. 1604. *See* 11548.5.

Tilenus, Daniel—*cont.*

24069 — Parænesis ad Scotos, Genevensis disciplinæ zelotas.
    8°. *Andreapoli*, E. Rabanus, 1620. L.D.E.E².G².+;
    Dickinson C.

24070 — [Anr. ed.] 8°. *typis* G. Stansby, *pro* N. Buttero, 1620.
    Ent. 24 jy. L.O.C.D².E.+; F.HN.BO.U.

24071 — Positions lately held by the L. du Perron, against
    the sufficiency of the scriptures. Verie learnedly
    answered. With a defence of the sufficiency of the
    scriptures. Faithfully *tr.* 2 pts. 4°. L. S[nowden] *f.*
    N. Butter, 1606. Ent. 5 my. L(1, plus pt. 2 only).
    E².P.YK.; ILL(pt. 2 only).
        (Pt. 2 formerly also 24068) Includes trans. from
        an unpublished version of J. Davy du Perron's
        Discours sur l'autorité.

24072 — The true copy of two letters, with their answeres, con-
    tayning the apostasie of the earle of Lavall [G. P.
    de Coligny, *Comte de Laval.*] By D. Tilenus. *Tr.* by
    D. D. S. 4°. S. Stafford *f.* N. Butter, 1605. L.C.A.D.
    YK.+; F.HN.ILL.MCG.WASH².

24073 **Tillesley, Richard.** Animadversions upon M. Seldens
    History of tithes [22172]. 4°. *J.* Bill, 1619. L.O.C.
    D.DUR³.+; F.HN.HD.N.NY.+

24074 — Second edition newly corrected and much augmented,
    together with an Answer to an unprinted pamphlet
    [by Selden] divulged against the former [24073].
    4° in 8's. N. Okes [a.] (R. Field) *f.* A. Johnson, 1621.
    Ent. 12 fb. L.O.C.D.E².+; F.HN.CU.HD.U.+
        Prints text of Selden's pamphlet. Field pr. quires
        Aa–Hh; Okes the rest.

24075 **Tillinghast, John.** Saint Paul's ship-wrack in his voyage
    to Rome. Delivered in a sermon. 12°. R. B[adger] *f.*
    A. Kembe, in South-warke, 1637. Ent. 24 ja. O.

24076 **Tilney, Edmund.** [A brief and pleasant discourse of
    duties in mariage.] 8°. (H. Denham, 1568.) Ent.
    1567–68. L(lacks tp).; Y(imp.).
        D2ʳ line 3 from bottom ends: 'drew neere,'.

24076.3 — [Anr. ed.] A brief and pleasant discourse of duties in
    mariage, called the Flower of friendshippe. 8°.
    H. Denham, 1568. HN.
        D2ʳ line 3 from bottom ends: 'drewe neere,'.

24076.7 — [Anr. ed.] A briefe and pleasant [etc.] 8°. H. Denham,
    1568. O(lacks colophon).
        D2ʳ line 3 from bottom ends: 'drewe nere,'.

24077 — [Anr. ed.] 8°. H. Denham, 1571. O(3).
24077.5 — [Anr. ed.] 8°. H. Denham, 1573. C⁵.
24077a — [Anr. ed.] 8°. H. Denham, 1577. O.; PML.Y.
24077a.5 — [Anr. ed.] 8°. A. Jeffs, 1587. F.

24078 **Tilney, Emery.** [Heading A1ʳ:] Here beginneth a song
    of the Lordes supper. [Init. E. T. In verse.] 4°.
    (W. Copland, solde by R. Stoughton,) [1550?] F.

24079 **Timberlake, Henry.** A true and strange discourse of the
    travailes of two English pilgrimes: to Jerusalem,
    [etc.] [Anon.] 4°. [R. Bradock] *f.* T. Archer, 1603.
    Ent. to R. Jones 21 oc. 1601; to T. Archer 4 fb. 1603.
    L.C⁵(imp.).; F.

24080 — [Anr. ed.] 4°. [E. Allde] *f.* T. Archer, 1608. L(2).L¹³.;
    F.HN.

24081 — [Anr. ed.] Written by H. Timberlake. 4°. *f.* T. Archer,
    1609. L.; CU.ILL. Penrose 253.

24082 — [Anr. ed.] 4° w. perp. chainlines. [N. Okes] *f.* T. Archer,
    1611. L.O⁵.CHATS. School of Oriental and African
    Studies, London Univ.; HN(imp.).HD.N.

24083 — [Anr. ed.] 4°. [E. Allde] *f.* T. Archer, 1612. DUR
    (Bamb.).; HN.

24084 — [Anr. ed.] 4°. N. Okes *f.* T. Archer, 1616. L(3, 1 lacks
    tp).; NY.

24085 — [Anr. ed.] 4°. N. Okes *f.* T. Archer, 1620. L.O.; F.Y.

24086 — [Anr. ed., w. title:] A relation of the travells. [Init.
    H. T.] 4°. *J.* N[orton] *f.* H. Perry, 1631. Ass'd 10 fb.
    L.O.CASHEL.; F.HN. Penrose 254.

24087 **Time.** Take time, while time is. *Ballad.* 2 pts. s.sh.fol.
    M. P[arsons] *f.* H. Gosson, [1638?] L.
    — Time vindicated. [1623.] *See* 14782.5.

24088 — The times abuses: or, muld-sacke his grievances
    briefly exprest. *Ballad.* 2 pts. s.sh.fol. *f.* *J.* Wright,
    [*sen.*, c. 1635.] L.
    — Times alteration. [c. 1630.] *See* 19271.5.
    — The troublsome trauell of tyme. 1589. *See* 23875.

Times. The times, places, and persons of the holie
    scripture. 1607. *See* 12981.

Timme, Thomas. *See* Tymme, T.

Tindall. *See* Tyndale.

Tinker. [The tinker of Turvey.] *See* 4581, 22920.3.

Tipping, William. *See* Typing, W.

Tiptoft, John, *Earl of Worcester, tr. See* 4337, 5275, 5293.

Tirwhit, William, *tr. See* 12452.

24089 **Tis.** Tis not otherwise: or: the praise of a married life. *Ballad.* 2 pts. s.sh.fol. G. E[ld, c. 1617.] c⁶.

24090 **Tisdale, Roger.** The lawyers philosophy: or, law brought to light. Poetized in a divine rhapsodie. [In verse.] 8°. [*G. Purslowe*] *f. J. T[rundle] a. H. G[osson,] sold at the widdow* [*A.*] *Gossons,* 1622. L.GK.; F(impr. cropt).HD.

24091 — Pax vobis, or, wits changes: tuned in a Latine hexameter of peace. Whereof, the numerall letters present the yeare of our Lord: and the verse it selfe (consisting only of nine words) admitteth 1623 transpositions. With a congratulatorie poem and other chronograms. [English verse.] 4°. *G. Eld a. M. Flesher,* 1623. Ent. 30 my. L.O.; HN.CH.

24091.5 **Tissot, Jacques.** A true relation of a mighty giant, named Theutobocus, overthrowne by consul Marius, 1700 yeares agone. Whose bones were found 1613. [Anon.] (A true relation of the bones of giants, to be seene at this day. By, I. B., *G.*) 4°. *E. Allde,* 1615. Ent. 8 fb. E².; HD.

24092 **Tithes.** Tithes and oblations. 1595. Now = 4323.2.

Titus Andronicus. The most lamentable Romaine tragedie of Titus Andronicus. 1594, etc. *See* 22328 sqq.

24092.3 — Titus Andronicus complaint. To the tune of Fortune. *Ballad.* 1/2 sh.fol. *f. E. Wright,* [c. 1625.] ?Ent. to ballad ptnrs. as 'Titus and Audconmus' 14 de. 1624. c⁶.

24092.7 — [Anr. ed.] 1/2 sh.fol. ⟨*f. the assigns*⟩ *of T. Symcocke,* [1628–29.] o(imp.).

24093 **Tiverton.** The true lamentable discourse of the burning of Teuerton the third day of Aprill 1598. 4°. *T. Purfoot f. T. Millington,* [1598.] Ent. to Purfoot, sen. and jun., 14 ap. 1598. o(2).
— Wofull newes. Being the burning of Teverton. 1612. *See* 10025.
— *See also* 8480.5.

To Have. To have, or not to have. 1627. *See* 5362.

Tobacco. A counter-blaste to tobacco. 1604. *See* 14363.

24094 **Tobias.** A pleasant new ballad of Tobias. *Ballad.* 2 pts. s.sh.fol. *f. F. Coules,* [c. 1640.] Ent. to ballad ptnrs. 14 de. 1624. L.

24095 **Tobias,** *Fellow Elder with H. Niclas.* Mirabilia opera Dei: certaine wonderfull works of God which hapned to H. N[iclas.] *Tr.* out of Base Almain. 4°. [*London,* c. 1650?] L(3).O.C.; HD.U(imp.).Y.
Not an STC book; *see also* 18548.5 sqq.

Tocsin. The tocsin. 1611. *See* 1845.

24096 **Tofte, Robert.** Alba. The months minde of a melancholy louer, diuided into three parts: by R. T. gentleman. [In verse.] Hereunto is added a letter, sent by [J. L. de Nogaret de la Valette,] duke D'Epernoun, vnto the late French king, Henry the 3. *Tr.* into English by the foresaid author. (Certaine diuine poems.) 8°. *F. Kingston f. M. Lownes,* 1598. F(imp.).HN.
— Honours academie. Or the famous pastorall, of Julietta. 1610. *See* 18053.

24097 — Laura. The toyes of a traueller. Or the feast of fancie. Diuided into three parts. By R. T. gentleman. [In verse.] 8°. *V. Sims,* 1597. L.; HN.
While 'A frends iust excuse' on E7ʳ asserts over 30 poems are not Tofte's, the statement is prob. false.
— *tr. See* 744, 745, 749, 3216, 6476, 23690, 24593.

24098 **Tokens.** Faire fall all good tokens. Or, a pleasant new song. *Ballad.* 2 pts. s.sh.fol. *f. H. Gosson,* [c. 1630.] L.

Tolwyn, William. *See* 22249.5.

Tombes, John, *ed. See* 19576a.

24099 **Tomkins, Thomas.** Songs of 3. 4. 5. and 6. parts. 6 ptbks. 4°. [*T. Snodham*] *f. M. Lownes, John Browne* [*1,*] *a. T. Snodham,* 1622. L(lacks quintus). O.O³.E².M³(cantus, quintus only).+; HN(tenor, bassus, sextus only).
Tpp vary: dated 1622 (o, 4 ptbks only) or w. the date replaced by 'Cum Privilegio' (o, 6 ptbks). Sets may be mixed, e.g. o³, which has the bassus dated, the others not.

24100 **Tomkis, Thomas.** Albumazar. A comedy presented before the kings majestie at Cambridge. [Anon.] 4°. *N. Okes f. W. Burre,* 1615. Ent. to Okes 28 ap. L.O.C(cropt).C²(imp.).G².+; F.HN.HD.NY.Y. Greg 330.
Collates A² B–L⁴. Adapted from G. B. della Porta's L'astrologo.

24101 — [Anr. ed.] 4°. *N. Okes f. W. Burre,* 1615. L.L⁶.C.; F.BO.CAL.NY. Cleveland PL.+
Collates A–I⁴; part of quires A and I reimposed from 24100.

24102 — [Anr. ed.] Newly reuised and corrected. 4°. *N. Okes,* 1634. Ass'd to J. Okes 2 au. 1630. L.L³⁸.O.C².ETON.; F.HN.HD.ILL.NY⁸.+
D1ʳ catchword: 'O'.

24103 — [Anr. ed.] Newly revised [etc.] 4°. *N. Okes,* 1634 [c. 1640.] L.O.C.C².DUR(Bamb.).+; F.HN.HD.N.NY.+
D1ʳ catchword: 'drops'. Unused sheets reissued w. cancel tp in 1668 as Wing T 1841.

24104 — Lingua: or the combat of the tongue, and the five senses. A comœdie. [Anon.] 4°. *G. Eld f. S. Waterson,* 1607. Ent. 23 fb. L.O.C⁴.CANT.; F.HN.LC. Greg 239.

24105 — [Anr. ed.] 4°. *N. Okes f. S. Waterson,* [c. 1615.] L.O⁶.E.G²(imp.).; HN.

24106 — [Anr. ed.] 4°. *N. Okes f. S. Waterson,* 1617. L.L⁶.C². ETON.E.+; F.HN.HD.CHI.NY.+

24107 — [Anr. ed.] 4°. *N. Okes f. S. Waterson,* 1622. L.O.C. D.E.+; F(lacks tp).HN.BO.HD.Y.+

24108 — [Anr. ed.] 4°. *A. Mathewes f. S. Waterson,* 1632. L.L⁶.O.C².E.+; F.HN.HD.N.NY.+

24109 **Tomkys, John.** A briefe exposition of the Lordes prayer, contained in questions and answeres: collected . . . 1585. 8°. *R. Walde-grave f. W. Ponsonbye,* [1585.] Ent. 8 jn. 1585. O.; F.

24110 — A sermon preached the 26. day of May. 1584. in Shrewesbury. 8°. *R. Walde-graue f. W. Ponsonby,* 1586. L.L².O.C².C¹⁰.; F.HN.
— *tr. See* 4066, 4067, 4077.

24111 **Tomlinson, Francis.** The holy salutation of the blessed apostle saint Jude. Preached at Pauls Crosse. 4°. *F. Kyngston f. G. Norton,* 1612. O.O³.C².; F(2).PN².

24112 **Tommai, Petrus.** The art of memory, that otherwyse is called the phenix. [Anon.] (*Tr.* out of french in to englyshe by R. Coplande.) 8°. (*W. Myddylton,*) [c. 1545.] c.

24113 **Tomson, Laurence.** An answere to certein assertions of M. Fecknam [Feckenham], sometime abbot of Westminster, against a godly sermon of J. Goughes, preached the .xv. of Ianuarie. 1570. [Init. L. T.] 8°. *H. Bynneman f. L. Harison & G. Bishop,* [1570.] Ent. to L. Harrison 1569–70. L.L².O.C.P.+; ILL.
Includes Feckenham's assertions and objections. *See also* 12131.
— *tr. See* 2146, 2878, 4441, 15231.

24114 **Tomson, William.** In canticum canticorum quod scripsit Schelomo explanatio. 8°. *ex off. R. Walde-graue,* 1583. L.L².C.E².P.+

Tom Tel-trouth. *See* Tel-trouth, T.

Tom Thumb. The history of Tom Thumbe. 1621. *See* 14056.

24115 — Tom Thumbe, his life and death. [In verse.] 8°. [*A. Mathewes?*] *f. J. Wright,* 1630. Ent. to H. Gosson as a ballad 18 jy. 1623. O.

24115.5 **Tongues.** Of euyll tonges. [In verse.] 4°. (*J. Notary,*) [c. 1510.] M. 𝕬

Tonstall, Cuthbert, *Bp. See* Tunstall, C.

24116 **Tooke, George.** The legend of Brita-mart: otherwise Britaines Mars; or, a paraphrase upon our provisionall martiall discipline. Presented dialoguewise. 8°. *J. B[eale] f. N. Fussell,* 1635. L.C.

24117 = 24118.

24118 **Tooker, William.** Charisma siue donum sanationis. Seu explicatio . . . de solenni & sacra curatione strumæ [i.e. of the King's Evil.] 4°. *J. Windet,* 1597. L.O. C.D.E².+; F.HN.HD.NY⁴.Y.+

24119 — Duellum sive singulare certamen cum M. Becano jesuita, futuliter refutante Apologiam et monitoriam præfationem. 8°. *G. Eld, imp. N. Butter & R. Mab,* 1611. Ent. to Butter 7 fb. L.O.C.D.E.+; F.HN.N. Defends 14405; *see also* 1702.

24120 — Of the fabrique of the church and church-mens livings. 8°. *M. Bradwood f. J. Norton,* 1604. Ent. 2 ap. L.O.C.D.E.+; F.HN.NW.NY.U.

Top, Alexander. The book of prayses, called the psalmes of David. 1629. *See* 2415.

24121 — The olive leafe: or, universall abce. Wherein is set foorth the creation of letters. [With] two tables, characericall and syllabicall. 4°. *W. White f. G. Vincent,* 1603. L.O.CHATS.

24122 — Saint Peters rocke, vnder which title is deciphered the faith of Peter. 4°. [*Deputies of C. Barker,*] 1597. L.C.M.

24123 **Topsell, Edward.** The [xylographic] historie of foure-footed beastes. Collected out of all the volumes of C. Gesner, and all other writers to this present day. fol. *W. Jaggard,* 1607. L.O.C³.M.SHEF.+; F.HN.CU. HD.N.+
　　Tp varies: w. cut of hyena (used for sea wolf on p. 749) or of gorgon (most copies; not illustrated in the text pp. 262–3); examples of both at L. B1,2,5,6 in 2 settings; B2ʳ catchword: 'they'; B6ʳ line 1: 'crowne' (HN) or 'gers' and 'Crowne' (HD). In some copies (2 L) there is an extra leaf after F4 w. heading: 'The Picture of the vulger Bugill Folio 57.'

24124 — The [xylographic] historie of serpents. Or, the second booke of living creatures. Collected out of divine scriptures, [etc.] fol. *W. Jaggard,* 1608. L.L³⁰.O.E. SHEF.+; F.HN.HD.N.PEN.+
　　Ee3, 4 in 2 settings; Ee3ᵛ line 18: 'waters, as in a Boate.' or 'in a boate.'; both at F.

24125 — The house-holder: or, perfect man. Preached in three sermons. 8°. [*W. Jaggard*] *f. H. Rockyt,* 1609. Ent. to W. Jaggard 22 se. PN².U.

24126 — [A variant, w. imprint:] [*W. Jaggard*] *f. H. Rockyt,* 1610. L.O.C¹⁰.; F.

24127 — The reward of religion. Deliuered in sundrie lectures vpon the booke of Ruth. 8°. *J. Windet,* 1596. Ent. 5 ap. L.O.O⁴.; F(2, 1 imp.).

24128 — [Anr. ed.] 8°. *J. Windet,* 1597. L.L².C².P.; F.HN.BO.BO⁶.

24129 — [Anr. ed.] 8°. *J. Windet,* 1601. L.O.; F.HN.CAL⁶.U.

24130 — [Anr. ed.] Newly corrected and augmented. 8°. *W. Stansby, sold by J. Budge,* 1613. Ass'd to Stansby 11 se. 1611. L.O.C³.P.STU.+; HD.PN².Y.

24131 — Times lamentation: or an exposition on the prophet Joel, in sundry sermons or meditations. 4° in 8's. *E. Bollifant f. G. Potter,* 1599. Ent. 11 ap. L.O.C.P.WI. +; F.HN.HD(imp.).N.U.+

24132 — [Anr. ed.] Newly corrected and augmented. 4° in 8's. *W. Stansby f. N. Butter,* 1613. Ass'd 13 no. 1609. L⁴.O.A.BIRM.PLUME.; F.HD.ILL.N.V.

24133 **Torent,** *of Portyngale.* [Torent of Portyngale. In verse.] 4°. [*R. Pynson,* 1505?] O(2 leaves).
　　30 lines a page, in 95 mm. textura w. s¹ and occasional use of w⁶.

24133.5 — [Anr. ed.] 4°. [*W. de Worde,* 1510?] O(4 pp. only, on the verso of 13075).
　　32 lines a page, in 95 mm. textura w. s², w² and rare use of an early form of w².

Tormes, Lazarillo de. *See* Lazarillo.

24134 **Torporley, Nathanael.** Diclides coelometricæ seu valuæ astronomicæ universales. 4°. *F. Kingston,* 1602. L.O.C.D.E⁵.+; MICH.NY.

24135 **Torquemada, Antonio de.** The Spanish Mandevile of miracles. Or the garden of curious flowers. Wherin are handled sundry points of humanity, philosophy, [etc.] *Tr.* (L. Lewkenor.) [*Ed.*] (F. Walker.) 4°. *J. R[oberts] f. E. Matts,* 1600. Ent. 4 mr. L.O.C.C³. CASHEL.+; F.HN.HD.N.NY.+

24136 — [Anr. ed.] 4° mostly in 8's. *B. Alsop, by the assigne of R. Hawkins, solde at his* [*Alsop's*] *house by Saint Annes church neere Aldersgate,* 1618. Ass'd to R. Barnes 17 fb. 1612; to R. Hawkins 11 oc. 1613. L.O.C².C⁵.G².; F.HN.CHI.HD.U.+

24137 **Torriano, Giovanni.** The Italian tutor or a new and most compleat Italian grammer. To which is annexed a display of the monasillable particles. 2 pts. 4°. *T. Paine, sold by H. Robinson,* 1640. Ent. to Robinson 21 no. 1639. L.O.C³.C⁵.C¹⁰.+; HN.HD. MICH. Syracuse U.

24137.5 — [A variant, w. imprint:] *T. Payne, sold by H. Robinson . . . for the author,* 1640. O.O⁷.C.YK.; F.Y.
　　At least the C, Y copies have a cancel dedic. on A2 to Sir H. Garraway, Lord Mayor, instead of the usual one in Italian to Elizabeth Grey, Countess of Kent.

24138 — New and easie directions for attaining the Thuscan Italian tongue. With a nomenclator, or little dictionarie. 8°. *R. O[ulton] f. R. Mab, sold by the professour at his lodging in Abchurch lane, adjoyning to Lumbard-street,* 1639. Ent. 27 no. 1638. C³.

24139 — [Anr. ed.] 4°. *Cambridge, R. Daniel,* [1645?] = Wing T 1926.

24140 **Torsellino, Orazio.** The admirable life of S. Francis Xavier. Written in Latin and *tr.* by T. F[itz-Herbert.] 4°. *Paris* [i.e. *St. Omer, English College Press,*] 1632. L.O³.C. M.USHAW.+; F.HN.HD(Iiii4 in facs.).TEX.WASH³.
　　A&R 824.

24140.5 — The history of our B. lady of Loreto. Translated out of Latin [from Lauretanæ historiæ libri quinque] into English. (T. P[rice].) 8°. [*St. Omer, English College Press,*] 1608. SN.
　　A&R 825. Letterpress tp on *1ʳ.

24141 — [Anr. issue, w. cancel engr. tp.] The history . . . Loreto. Trãslated out of Latyn, into English. [*St. Omer, English College Press,*] 1608. L.O.C.D.E.+; F.HN.HD(lacks **8).N.Y.+
　　A&R 826. In this issue **8ᵛ has an engr. illustration instead of being blank.

Torshell, Samuel. An exercitation upon the prophecie of Malachy. 1640. = pt. of Wing S 5692.

24142 — The saints humiliation. Being the substance of nine sermons. 4°. *J. Dawson* [*a. R. Young*] *f. H. Overton,* 1633. Ent. 24 no. 1632. L.L³.C.C².LINC.+; F.HN. SMU.U.Y.
　　Young pr. Aa–Ii.

24143 — The three questions of free justification. Christian liberty. The use of the law. In a comment on Galatians, [ii.16–iii.26.] 12°. *J. B[eale] f. H. Overton,* 1632. Ent. 6 se. 1631. L.O.C².D.LEIC.+; F.ILL.U.Y.

24144 **Tossanus, Daniel.** The exercise of the faithfull soule: that is to say, prayers & meditations. Englished out of the French, by F. Filding. 8°. *H. Middleton f. H. Denham,* 1583. Ent. 15 de. 1579. L.O³.C.P(2).; F.HD.v(lacks tp)*.
　　Tp line 6: 'maner'.

24144.5 — [Anr. issue, w. first quire reset.] *H. Middleton f. H. Denham,* 1583. L(tp only, Ames I.417).O.
　　Tp line 6: 'manner'.

— The lamentations . . . of Jeremiah. [1587.] *See* 2779.5.

24145 — A synopsis or compendium of the Fathers, as also of the Schoolmen. Englished by A. S[tafford] gent. 8°. [*J. Beale*] *f. D. Frere,* 1635. Ent. as tr. by Stafford 15 ap. L.O.C(date cropt).D.E.+; F.HN.HD.ILL.LC.+

24145.3 — [Anr. ed.] 8°. [*R. Hodgkinson*] *f. D. Frere,* 1637. O⁵.O¹³.C¹³.; F.HD.Y.

Totenham, St. Anne of. *See* Indulgences 23.

Tottel, Richard, *Publisher.* [Tottel's Miscellany.] 1557, etc. *See* 13860 sqq.

Touchet, *Lady* **Eleanor.** *See* Audeley, E.

Touchstone. The touch-stone of the reformed ghospell. 1634. *See* 13033.8.

24145.7 — The touchstone of true religion, decyphering the right use & finall ende there-of. [Anon.] 8°. *R. Blower f. W. Holmes, dwelling at yᵉ signe of the spread Eagle . . . ,* [c. 1600.] L⁴(date cropt).
　　Maunsell in 17669, pt. 1, p. 115, lists a 1590 ed. as written by D. A., of which this may be a re-issue w. preliminaries cancelled, as it collates tp+B–N⁸ O⁴.

Toulon. *See* 10611.

Tourneur, Cyril. The atheist's tragedie: or the honest man's revenge. 4º. [*T. Snodham*] *f. J. Stepneth a. R. Redmer,* 1611. Ent. to Stepneth 14 se. L(3, 1 lacks tp*).O.O⁶.C⁴.ETON(imp.).; F.HN.HD.N.Y².+ Greg 293.

    In some copies (1 L, O, 1 HN) the imprint has misprints 'Stepney' and 'Redmere'.

24147 — [A variant, w. imprint:] *f. J. Stepneth a. R. Redmer,* 1612. L.L.L⁶(2, 1 imp.).E.; HN.HD.NY.

24148 — A funerall poeme. Upon the death of sir Francis Vere. 4º. [*J. Windet*] *f. E. Edgar,* 1609. Ent. 16 oc. L.; HN.

24148.3 — A griefe on the death of prince Henrie. [In verse.] 4º. [*F. Kingston*] *f. W. Welbie,* 1613. O.YK.Juel-Jensen.; F.WES.Y.

    A reissue, w. gen. tp cancelled, of pt. 1 of 24151.

24148.7 — Laugh and lie downe: or, the worldes folly. [Init. C. T.] 4º. [*W. Jaggard*] *f. J. Chorlton,* 1605. F.HN.

    Film of F copy on Univ. Microfilms reel 738 ('15316a').

24149 — The revengers tragædie. As it hath beene acted. [Anon.] 4º. *G. Eld,* 1607. Ent. 7 oc. L.L.L⁶.O(imp.). DUL.E.+; F.HN.HD.TCU.Y.+ Greg 253.

24150 — [A variant, w. imprint:] *G. Eld,* 1608. L.L.L⁶.O.O⁶.C⁴.+; F.HN.PN.Y.

24151 — Three elegies on the most lamented death of prince Henrie, by C. Tourneur. J. Webster. and T. Heywood. [xylographic] 3 pts. 4º. [*F. Kingston a.*] (*N. O[kes]*) *f. W. Welbie,* 1613. Ent. 25 de. 1612. L.ETON.; F(imp.).HN.HD.

    The parts were also issued separately as 24148.3, 25174, 13323.

24152 — The transformed metamorphosis. By Cyril Turner. [In verse.] 8º. *V. Sims,* 1600. L.

  — *See also* 22086.5.

Toussain, Daniel. *See* Tossanus, D.

Toutevile, Daniel. Christian purposes and resolutions. 1622. *See* 24393.7.

24153 — St. Pauls threefold cord. 1635. Now = 24396.5.

24154 **Tower.** [A fragment concerning the Toure melodyous. 1509.] = pt. of 12948.

Towers, John, *Bp.* Peterborough. Visitation Articles. *See* 10320.

24155 **Townshend, Aurelian.** Albions triumph. Personated in a maske at court. 4º. *A. Mathewes f. R. Allet,* 1631 [1632.] L.L.L⁶.O⁶.E.WN.; F.HN.Y. Robert Taylor. Greg 453.

    Townshend's name is on C4ᵛ; this is prob. the later variant.

24155a — [A variant, anon.] *A. Mathewes f. R. Allet,* 1631 [1632.] L.O.; HN.HD.ILL.

24156 — Tempe restord. A masque. 4º. *A. M[athewes] f. R. Allet a. G. Bakek* [sic], 1631 [1632.] L.L.L⁶.O.; F.HN.BO.LC.Y.+ Greg 454.

    Only the songs are by Townshend; the rest is by Inigo Jones w. portions derived from Beaujoyeulx's *Balet comique de la royne,* Paris, 1582.

Townson, Robert, *Bp.* Salisbury. Visitation Articles. *See* 10329.7.

Toxites, Michael. Onomastica. 1574. *See* headnote preceding 6832.1.

24157 **Toy, John.** Worcester's elegie, and eulogie. [In verse.] 4º. *T. Cotes f. H. Blunden,* 1638. Ent. 28 ap. L.O(2).; F.HN.HD.Y.

24158 **Tozer, Henry.** A christian amendment delivered in a sermon. 8º. *Oxford, J. Lichfield,* 1633. L.O(2).O³.C².

24159 — Christian wisdome, or the excellency of true wisdome. As it was delivered in a sermon. 8º. *Oxford, L. Lichfield,* 1639. L.L.L³.O.LIV³.; F(2).

24160 — Christus: sive dicta & facta Christi. [A treatise in outline form.] 8º. *Oxoniæ, G. Turner,* 1634. L.L³.O. C².D.+; HN.HD.NY¹¹.

24161 — Directions for a godly life: especially for communicating at the Lord's table. 12º. *Oxford, W. Turner,* 1628. O.

24161.3 — Third edition. 12º. *Oxford, W. Turner,* 1634. HN.

24161.5 — Fifth edition. 12º. *Oxford, f. L. Lichfield,* 1640. O⁶.

Tract. Here begynneth a newe tracte. [1523? etc.] *See* 10994 sqq.

  — A tract against usurie. 1621, etc. *See* 6108 sqq.

Tractatulus. Tractatulus verboꝝ defectiuoꝝ & anormaloꝝ. [1508?] *See* 23163.4.

Tractatus. Doctissimi viri tractatus contra missæ sacrificium. 1578. *See* pt. 2 of 1492.

  — Tractatus de legibus. [1554? etc.] *See* 11905 sq.

  — Tractatus secundarum intentionum. 1527. *See* 15574.

24162 **Tracy, Richard.** A bryef & short declaracyon made, wherbye euerye chrysten man maye knowe, what is a sacrament. 8º. *R. Stoughton,* (1548 (10 no.)) L.O. C.D.E.+; F.HN.BO⁶.CAL.PML.

24163 — A most godly enstruction and very necessarie lesson [concerning] yᵉ communion of the bodie & bloud of Christe. 8º. (*J. Day a. W. Seres,*) 1548 (5 au.) O(frag.).BUTE.D.DUR⁵.P.; F. 𝔄

  — Of the preparation to the crosse. Tr. R. Tracy. 1540. *See* 11393.

24164 — The profe and declaration of thys proposition: fayth only iustifieth. 8º. [*E. Whitchurch,* 1543?] L.O³. O¹⁷.C.

24165 — A supplycacion to our moste soueraigne lorde kynge Henry the eyght. [Anon.] 8º. [*Antwerp, widow of C. Ruremond,*] (1544 (de.)) L.O.O².C.M.+; F. C5ᵛ, C6ʳ misimposed; C3ʳ catchword: 'les'. Some copies (1 O, 2 C, F) have title misprint 'te' instead of 'to'.

24165.5 — [Anr. issue, w. C3–6 reprinted.] [*London?*] (1544 (de.)) [1545?] L.; F. C3ʳ catchword: 'ted'.

24166 — [Anr. ed.] A supplication. . . . Nowe newly imprinted. 8º. (1544 (de.)) [i.e. *T. Dawson? c.* 1585.] L.O.C.C⁵. BUTE.+; F.HN.BO.N. Detroit PL.+

24167 **Tracy, William.** The testament of master Wylliam Tracie esquier, expounded both by W. Tindall and J. Frith. 8º ⁸·⁴. [*Antwerp, H. Peetersen van Middelburch?*] 1535. L.C.M.; F.HD(lacks tp).

    Tyndale section reprinted in 25590 sq.; the whole in 25591 sq. The printing was formerly attrib. to J. Hoochstraten.

24167.3 **Tradescant, John.** Plantarum in horto Johannem [*sic*] Tradescanti nascentium catalogus. 8º. [*London?*] 1634. O¹².

Tragedies. Tragedies and comedies. 1633. *See* 17472.

Tragedy. A divine tragedie lately acted. 1636. *See* 4140.7.

24167.5 — A most rare and wonderfull tragedy . . . of the life and death of a miserable ⟨u⟩surer of Fraunce [named Lanton], which hanged himselfe in Hell streete. Printed at Paris, for M. Breuille, 1583. 8º. [*J. Charlewood*] *f. T. Hacket,* 1584. Ent. 1 au. 1583. HN. Film of HN copy on Univ. Microfilms reel 538 ('24558+').

  — The Spanish tragedie. [1592, etc.] *See* 15086 sqq.

  — Ane tragedie in forme of ane diallog. 1570. *See* 22209.

24167.7 **Traheron, Bartholomew.** An aunswere made by Bar. Traheron to a priuie papiste, which crepte in to the english congregation. 8º. [*Wesel? P. A. de Zuttere?*] 1558. L².

24168 — An exposition of a parte of S. Johannes gospel made in [six] sondrie readings in the English congregation at Wesel. 8º. [*Wesel? P. A. de Zuttere?*] 1557. L.O. O¹⁷.BUTE.P.

24168.5 — [Anr. issue, w. cancel tp omitting 'at Wesel' from title.] [*Wesel? P. A. de Zuttere?*] 1557. O(lacks tp)*.C(3). D.DUL*.LINC.; F(lacks tp)*. Queen's U(lacks tp)*. Tp varies: 'AN EX-/POSITION [sic]' or corrected to 'AN EX-/POSITION'; both at C.

24169 — [Anr. ed.] Ouerseen againe, corrected, and augmēted in many places by the autor, with addition of [four] sondrie other lectures. 8º. [*Wesel? P. A. de Zuttere?*] 1558. L.O.C.C².YK.+; F.COLG.ILL.Y.

24170 — An expositiō of the .4. chap. of S. Joans Reuelation. With an aunswer made to the obiections of a gentle aduersarie. (An exposition of . . . Leade vs not in to tentation.) 8º. [*Wesel? P. A. de Zuttere?*] 1557 (1558.) L(destroyed).L²(2).O³⁸(imp.).DUL.; F.U.

24171 — [Anr. ed.] 8º. *H. Bynneman f. H. Toy,* 1573. L.O.C.; F.NY².

24172 — [Anr. ed.] 8º. *T. Dawson a. T. Gardiner f. E. Aggas* (*a. T. Charde,* 1577.) L.O.LINC.; F.

24173 — [Anr. ed.] 8º. (*T. Dawson*) *f. T. Chard,* 1583. L.C(2). C⁵.; HN.

Traheron, Bartholomew—*cont.*

24174 — A warning to England to repente, by the terrible exemple of Calece, giuen the 7. of March. Anno. D. 1558. By Benthalmai Outis [i.e. B. Traheron.] 8º. [*Wesel? P. A. de Zuttere?*] 1558. L.L².

— *tr. See* 24720.

Traheron, W., *tr. See* 17851, 18348.

24175 **Trapp, John.** Gods love-tokens, and the afflicted mans lessons: in two discourses upon Revel. 3.19. 12º. *R. Badger*, 1637. Ent. 25 se. L(imp.).L³.O.O²⁸(Bed.). C.; F.HN.WTL.

24175.3 **Traske, John.** Christs kingdome discovered. Or, that the true church of God is in England. [Anon.] 8º. *T. Creede f. Josias Harrison*, 1615. Ent. 22 jn. O.; F.HN.U.
(Formerly 14542)

24175.7 — [Anr. ed.] By J. Traske. Second edition. 8º. *T. Creede a. B. Alsop f. Josias Harrison*, 1616. HD(imp.).

24176 — A pearle for a prince, . . . Delivered in two sermons. 8º. *W. Stansby f. M. Lownes*, 1615. Ent. 29 mr. O.C¹⁰.

24177 — The power of preaching. Or, the powerfull effects of the word . . . delivered in one or moe sermons. 8º. *T. S[nodham] f. N. Butter*, 1623. Ent. 1 fb. O(2).

24178 — A treatise of libertie from Judaisme, or an acknowledgement of true christian libertie. 4º. *W. Stansby f. N. Butter*, 1620. Ent. 1 my. L.O.C².D.PETYT.+; HN.

24178.5 — The true gospel vindicated, from the reproach of a new gospel. 8º. [*London?*] *Printed in the yeere* 1636. C². Answered by 18645.

Tratado. Tratado para confirmar los pobres catiuos de Beruería. 1594. *See* 24582.

Traveller. The travellers breviat. 1601. *See* 3398.

24179 **Travels.** The travels of time: loaden with popish trumperies. [In verse, w. engr.] s.sh.fol. [*London*, 1624.] L⁵(Lemon 229).
Contains a reference to 8726.

24180 **Travers, Robert.** A learned and a very profitable exposition made vpon the CXI. psalme. [Anon.] 16º in 8's. *T. Vautroullier*, 1579. O(2).LINC.

24180.3 — [Anr. ed.] By R. T. 16º in 8's. *T. Vautrollier*, 1583. L(tp only, Ames I.411).D.

24180.7 **Travers, Walter.** An answere to a supplicatorie epistle, of G. T. for the pretended catholiques: to the priuy Councell. 8º. [*J. Wolfe, R. Waldegrave, and others?*] *f. T. Smith*, [1583.] Ent. 18 ja. 1583. L.L².O.C.P.+; F.HN.HD.U.Y.+
(Formerly 24182) Answers first section of 19406. Wolfe pr. quires A–G; K, R, T, U, Aa are signed in Waldegrave's manner. Other prs. or compositors are responsible for the tp, H, I; M–O; L, P, Q, S, X–Z, Bb, Cc.

24181 — [Anr. ed.] 8º. *T. Vautroullier f. T. Smith*, 1583. L.O.C³. D.E⁴.+; F(imp.).CAL.NY¹¹.PML.

24182 — Now = 24180.7.

24183 — A defence of the ecclesiastical discipline ordayned of God to be vsed in his church. Against a replie of maister Bridges [3734]. [Anon.] 4º. [*Middelburg, R. Schilders,*] 1588. L.O.C².D.E.+; F.HD.NY.U.Y.+
Defends 10395.

24184 — A full and plaine declaration of ecclesiasticall discipline. [Anon. *Tr.* from Latin by T. Cartwright.] 4º. [*Heidelberg, M. Schirat,*] 1574. L.O.C.D.E.+; F.HN. HD.N.U.+
With a folding sheet: 'A table or short view off [*sic*] all ecclesiasticall discipline.'

24185 — [Anr. ed.] 8º. *Geneva*, 1580. L.O.C.E⁴.M.+; LC. TORONTO².U(imp.).Y.

24186 — [Anr. ed.] 4º. [*Leyden, W. Brewster,*] 1617. L.L².O.C². C¹³.+; F(imp.).HN.HD.Y. Pilgrim Hall, Plymouth, Mass.

24187 — A supplication made to the privy counsel. 4º. *Oxford, Jos. Barnes, sold by John Barnes,* [*London,*] 1612. L.O.C.D.E.+; F.HN.BO⁶.U.Y.+
Answered by 13706 and reprinted w. it in 13716 sqq. The orig. controversy took place in 1586.

24188 — Vindiciæ ecclesiæ Anglicanæ: or a justification of the religion now professed in England. By W. T[ravers. Ed.] (A. B.) 4º. *T. C[otes] & R. C[otes] f. M. Sparke,* 1630. Ent. as by Travers 20 de. 1629. L.O.C.D.E.+; F.HN.HD.NY¹¹.U.+
Possibly by Walter Travers the nephew, chaplain to Charles I.

24188.5 **Traversanus, Laurentius Gulielmus.** [Begin:] Fratris laurencij guilelmi de saona . . . p̄hemiũ ī nouā r̄tho̅rīcā. [End:] (Explicit . . . opus . . . appellandū fore Margaritam eloquentie castigate.) fol. [*Westminster, W. Caxton,* 1479.] Savona U. Uppsala U. 1st quire has 10 leaves, the 1st 2 being blank. End of text dated 6 July 1478. The MS. used as printer's copy (in the Vatican Library) is dated 26 July 1478; *see Bulletin of the John Rylands Library,* XXXVI (1953), p. 193.

24189 — [Anr. issue, reimposed to eliminate the blanks, with 1st quire having 6 leaves and the 2nd quire 2 leaves.] [*Westminster, W. Caxton,* 1479.] C⁷. Turin U. Duff 368.

24190 — [Anr. ed.] 4º in 8's. (*ap. villā sancti Albani,* 1480.) L.O.O⁸.C.M.+ Duff 369.

24190.3 — [An epitome. Begin:] [Q] Vom homines maxime appetant vt sermones sui acceptabiles sint. [End:] (Explicit epitonia siue isagogicū magarite castigate eloquencie.) fol. [*Westminster, W. Caxton,* 1480?] LEEDS(Ripon copy). Not in Duff.
End of text dated 21 Jan. 1480; *see The Library,* VIII (1953), pp. 37–42.

24190.7 **Treasure.** Thys booke is called the Treasure of gladnesse and semeth by the copy (beeing a verye litle manuel, and written in velam) to be made aboue CC. yeres past at the least. . . . The coppy hereof is for the antiquity of it, preserued and to be seene in the Printers Hall. Now first imprinted. 16º in 8's. [*H. Denham f.*] (*J. Charlewood,*) 1563. Ent. 1562–63. F.

24191 — [Anr. ed.] This booke. . . . Now fyrst imprinted. 16º in 8's. [*H. Denham f.*] (*J. Charlwood,*) 1563. O.

24191a — [Anr. ed.] Now fyrst imprinted. 16º in 8's. (*H. Denham f. J. Charlewood,*) 1563 (1564 (6 se.)) O.

24192 — [Anr. ed.] Newly imprinted. 16º in 8's. [*J. Charlewood?*] 1568. HN(lacks last leaf).

24193 — [Anr. ed.] And first imprinted, 1563. 8º. (*W. Williamson f. J. Charlewood,* 1572 (28 jy.)) L(2, 1 imp.). O(frag.).

24193.5 — [Anr. ed.] 16º in 8's. [*J. Charlewood,*] 1574. F(lacks last leaf).

24194 — [Anr. ed.] 16º in 8's. (*J. charlewood,*) 1575. HN.

24195 — [Anr. ed.] 16º in 8's. (*J. Charlewood,*) 1577. L.

24196 — [Anr. ed.] 16º in 8's. [*J. Charlewood,*] 1579. L(imp.).

24197 — [Anr. ed.] 16º in 8's. *J. Charlewood,* 1581. O.
This has additional Litany and Graces apparently unique to this ed.

24197.3 — [Anr. ed.] 16º in 8's. [*J. Charlewood,*] 1590. O(imp.).

24197.5 — [Anr. ed.] 16º in 8's. (*J. Roberts,*) 1601. L¹⁵(imp.).; HD.

24198 — The treasure of knowledge. 1626. = pt. 4 of 11395.

24199 — [Treasure of poor men.] Here begynneth a newe boke in medecynes intytulyd or callyd the treasure of poor men. 4º. [*J. Rastell f.*] (*R. Bankes,*) [1526?] C.; HN.

24200 — [Anr. ed.] Here beginneth a good boke of medecines [etc.] 8º. (*R. Redman,* 1539 (24 ja.)) L(imp.).G². ; CAL.CHI.

24201 — [Anr. ed.] 8º. (*T. Petyt,* 1539.) L. Traylen.

24202 — [Anr. ed.] 8º. (*T. Petyt,* 1540.) O.

24202.5 — [Anr. ed.] 8º. (*R. Redman,* 1540 (31 my.)) L.; NLM.Y.

24203 — [Anr. ed.] 8º. (*W. Myddylton,* 1544 (13 de.)) L.O.M. Stevens Cox(imp.).

24203.3 — [Anr. ed.] 8º. [*N. Hill*](*f. T. Petyt,*) [1546?] L¹⁹.; NY⁴. Hill's inits. are in the slot in the sill of tp border McK. & F. 33.

24203.5 — [Anr. ed.] 8º. (*R. Lant,* 1547 (8 mr.)) L(prelims. only, w. 24206a). Phillipps 3220.; WIS.

24203.7 — [Anr. ed.] 8º. [*R. Copland f.*] (*H. Tab* [a.] *J. waley,*) [1548?] O.M⁴.
(Formerly 24205a) Tab's name appears on 1st A4ᵛ and Walley's at the end.

24204 — [Anr. ed.] 8º. (*w. powell,* 1551 (25 jy.)) L.E.; WIS.

24204.5 — [Anr. ed.] 8º. [*J. Wayland,* 1555?] G².
Tp border McK. & F. 64; in title: 'medecins'. This ed. never had a colophon.

24205 — [Anr. ed.] 8º. (*J. Waylande,*) 1556. L.O.G².; HD.
Tp border McK. & F. 64; in title: 'medecynes'.

24205a — Now = 24203.7.

24206 — [A ghost.]

24206a — [Anr. ed.] 8º. (*T. Colwell: dwellyng in the house of R. Wyer,*) [1560?] L(2, 1 imp.).L¹⁶.O⁸.; F(lacks colophon).NY⁴(imp.).Y(imp.).
The imp. L copy is C.31.a.27, w. prelims. of 24203.5.

Treasure—*cont.*

24206a.5 — [Anr. ed.] 8°. (*T. Colwell*, 1565.) NLM.

24207 — [Anr. ed.] 8°. (*T. Colwell*, 1575.) Ent. to W. Aspley 13 no. 1600. C.C²(imp.).

24208 — The treasure of the soule. Newly *tr.* by A. P(oyntz) [from Spill de la vida religiosa by M. de Comalada.] 12°. [*J. Windet f.*] *J. Wolfe*, 1596. Ent. 5 mr. 1593; again ent. to Wolfe 9 fb. 1599 'as it was printed by R. Waldegraue 1598.' L(Davis).O(imp.).O²(imp.). C.; F.HN.HD(imp.).U(imp.). St. Mary's Seminary, Perryville, Missouri.
For another trans. *see* 6777.

24209 — The treasure of tranquillitie. Or a manuall of morall discourses, tending to the tranquillity of minde. *Tr.* out of French by J. M(axwell,) master of arts. 12°. *N. Okes f. S. Rand*, 1611. Ent. 23 my. C.

24209.5 **Treasurer.** [The treasurer's almanac.] The money monger. Or, the usurers almanacke. With necessary tables of interest, the usurers gaine, and borrowers losse, of 8, 7, and 6, in the hundred. 8°. *W. Jones f. J. Boler a. M. Sparke*, 1626. Ent. to Sparke 25 ja. O.O⁵.
(Formerly 18010) Preface init. M. S., i.e. M. Sparke.

24210 — [Anr. ed., revised, w. title:] The treasurers almanacke, or the money-master: with necessary tables of interest, the lenders gaine, and borrowers losse, of 10. 8. 7. 6. in the 100. Second edition. 8°. *f. M. Sparke*, 1627. O.

24211 — [Anr. issue, w. date altered and most of quire B reset.] Second edition. *f. M. Sparke*, 1628. L.

24212 — Third edition. 8°. *f. M. Sparke*, 1629. O⁵.

24213 — Fourth edition. 8°. *f. M. Sparke*, 1630. L.

24214 — [Anr. ed.] This last edition corrected and amended. 8°. *f. M. Sparke*, 1631. O.

24214.5 — [Anr. ed.] 8°. *f. M. Sparke*, 1636. O.

Treasury. The treasurie of auncient and moderne times. 1613. *See* 17936.
— The treasurie of hidden secrets. 1596, etc. *See* 19429.5 sqq.

Treatise. A brief treatise conteinyng many proper tables. [1573? etc.] *See* 12155 sqq.

24215 — A briefe treatise. Discouering in substance the offences . . . of the late 14. traitors [William Deane and others.] Who were all executed. 8°. *J. Wolfe f. H. Carre*, 1588. Ent. 28 au. L².O²⁴.C⁵.
Copies differ; title continues: 'With the maner of the execution of eight of them, . . .' (L²) or 'Who were all executed. . . . Hereunto is adioyned the death of Margaret Ward, . . .' (O²⁴). *See also* 25089.5.
— A briefe treatise in which, is made playne, that catholikes may be saued. 1623. *See* 26044.
— A briefe treatise of oathes. [1590?] *See* 18106.

24216 — A breefe treatise of the vertue of the crosse. *Tr.* out of French [by A. Munday.] 8°. [*E. Allde*] *f. E. White*, 1599. L.C³.D.; F(2).Y.
Copies vary: dedic. signed by Munday (D) or unsigned (F).
— A briefe treatise touching the preseruation of the eie sight. 1586, etc. *See* 1193, 1195.
— A compendious olde treatyse, shewynge, howe that we ought to haue yᵉ scripture in Englysshe. 1530. *See* 3021.

24216a — A compendyous treatyse of sclaūdre, declarynge what sclaundre is. 8° in 4's. (*R. Lant*,) [1545?] L².; F.
— A deuout treatyse called the tree & xii. frutes of the holy goost. 1534. *See* 13608.

24217 — A frutefull treatis of baptyme and the Lordis souper. [By G. Joye.] 8°. (*at Grunning* [i.e. *Antwerp, widow of C. Ruremond*,] 1541 (27 ap.)) P.; F.

24217.5 — [Anr. ed., w. additions.] (Most comfortable lessons, touching our saluation handled by T. Beza, in his 45. epistle.) 8°. *R. Walde-graue*, [1584?] C².D.

24218 — Now = 24219.5.

24218.5 — A godly and comfortable treatise, very necessary for all such as are ouer-laden with the burden of their sinnes. 8°. *R. Walde-graue*, 1585. D.P.

24219 — A godlye and learned treatise, wherin is proued the true iustificacion of a christian manne. Wherunto is

Treatise—*cont.*

ioyned a cōference betwene the law and the gospel. [*Tr.* by M. Coverdale from O. Werdmueller's Vom höchsten Artikel.] 16° in 8's. [*Wesel? H. Singleton?* 1555?] L.
Pr. in the same types as 9981.
— A godly and short treatise vpon the Lordes prayer. 1580. *See* 16814.5.
— A godlie treatice concerning the lawfull vse of ritches. 1578. *See* 4342.
— A godlie treatisse declaryng the benefites of prayer. [1560.] *See* 10888.

24219.5 — A goodly treatise of faith, hope, and charite . . . *tr.* into englyshe [by M. Coverdale from Een profitelic eñ troostelic boexken, Nijhoff and Kronenberg 440.] 8°. *Southwarke, for* [i.e. *by*] *J. Nicolson*, 1537. C.
(Formerly 24218)
— [Begin:] In this tretyse that is cleped Gouernayle of helthe. [1489.] *See* 12138.
— Here begynneth a lytell necessarye treatyse the whiche speketh of the estate of the comonalte, and of good manners. [1531–4.] *See* 15399.5.
— Here begynneth a lytyll new treatyse intytuled the .ix. drunkardes. 1523. *See* 7260.
— Here after foloweth a lytyll treatyse agaynst Mahumet. [c. 1530.] *See* 17994.5.
— A litel treatise ageynste the mutterynge of some papistis. 1534. *See* 23551.5.
— Here begynneth a lytel treatyse called the dysputacyon or cōplaynt of the herte. [c. 1515.] *See* 6915.
— Here begynneth a lytell treatyse called the gouernall of helthe. [1510?] *See* 12139.
— A lyttle treatyse called the Image of idlenesse. [1558?] *See* 25196.
— Here after foloweth a lytell treatyse called the newe addicions. 1531. *See* 21563.
— Here begynneth a lytell treatyse for to lerne Englysshe and Frensshe. [1497.] *See* 24866.
— Here begynneth a lytell treatyse named the bowge of courte. [1499, etc.] *See* 22597 sq.
— Here ensueth a lytell treatyse named the tauerne of goostly helthe. 1522. *See* 23707.

24220 — Here foloweth a lytell treatyse of the Beaute of women. [c. 1525.] = 1696.

24221 — [Anr. ed. c. 1540.] = 1697.
— Here begynneth a lytell treatyse of the dyenge creature. 1506, etc. *See* 6033.5 sqq.

24222 — Here begynneth a lytel treatyse . . . of the xv. tokens. [1505?] Now = 793.3.

24223 — Here begynneth a litell treatise of the knight of Curtesy and the lady of Faguell. [In verse.] 4°. (*W. Copland*,) [1556?] O.

24223.3 — A lytle treatous or dialoge very necessary for all christen men to learne and to knowe. [*Tr.* from W. Capito's De pueris instituendis by] (*W. Roye.*) 8°. [*Strassburg, J. Schott*, 1527.] LONGLEAT. Vienna NL.
Preface dated 31 Aug. 1527.

24223.5 — [Anr. issue, w. cancel dedic. signed by Lynne and title:] The true beliefe in Christ and his sacramentes, set forth in a Dialoge betwene a christen father and his sonne. [*S. Mierdman*] *f. G. Lynne*, 1550. L.O.C. D.M.+; F.HN.
(Formerly 14576)

24224 — Here begynneth a lytel treatyse that sheweth how every man & woman ought to faste on yᵉ wednesday. [In verse.] 4°. [*W. de Worde*, 1500.] C⁶. Duff 413.

24225 — [Anr. ed.] Wednesdayes faste. 4°. (*W. de Worde*, 1532.) O¹¹.M.
— A moste briefe and pleasant treatise of the interpretation of dreames. 1601, etc. *See* 13499 sq.
— A most frutefull, piththye and learned treatise. [1555?] *See* 25251.
— A most godly and worthy treatis of holy signes. 1609. *See* 23434.5.

24226 — A moche profitable treatise against the pestilence, *tr.* by T. Paynel chanon of Martin abbey. 8°. (*in aed. T. Bertheleti*,) [1534?] L(2).
Tp comp. McK. & F. 30 dated 1534.

24227 — = 24226.

24227.5 — A neawe treatys: as cōcernynge the excellency of the nedle worcke spānisshe stitche and weavynge in the frame. [*Tr.* from French.] 4°. *Andwarp, these boekes be to sell at W. Vorstermans*, [c. 1530?] Rijksprentenkabinet, Rijksmuseum, Amsterdam (tp only, '27: 310).

Treatise—*cont.*

24228 — Here begyñeth a newe treatyse deuyded in thre parties. The fyrst parte is to know, the wretchednes, of all mankynde. The seconde . . . of the vnstedfastnes, of this world. The thyrde . . . of bytter death. [In verse. A version of the first three sections of the Prick of Conscience.] 4°. (by me R. wyer,) [1542?] L. 𝔄

— A new treatyse in maner of a dialogue. [1550?] *See* 13560.

24229 — A notable treatyse wherin is shewed, that we may eat at al times such meates as god hath created. 8°. *R. Stoughton,* [1550?] O.D.

24229.5 — A pithie and short treatise by way of dialogue, whereby a godly christian is directed how to make his last will. 16° in 8's. [*R. Field*] *f. W. Jones* [3,] 1612. Ent. to W. Jones, printer, 23 jy. L.
(Formerly 14746)

— A plaine and godlye treatise, concernynge the masse. [1555?] *See* 17629.

— Here after ensueth a propre treatyse of good workes. [1535?] *See* 16988.

24230 — A short and pretie treatise touching the perpetuall reioyce of the godly. 8°. *H. Denham,* 1568. Ent. 1568–69. L.; F.
Tp line 8: 'the order appointed.' Also issued as pt. 2 of 23969.5.

— [Anr. ed.] 1568. *See* pt. 2 of 23970.
Tp line 8: 'order appointed.'

24231 — [Anr. ed.] 1568. = 2nd pt. of 23971.
Tp line 8: 'order appoynted.'

24232 — A shorte treatise against stage-playes. 1625. Now = 15431.5.

— A short treatise: containing all the grounds of christian religion. 1617, etc. *See* 1314.3 sqq.

— A shorte treatise, of the crosse in baptisme. 1604. *See* 3526.

24233 — A theological and philosophical treatise of the nature and goodnesse of salt. 4°. *F. Kyngston f. R. Boyle,* 1612. Ent. 26 fb. L.O.C.G².LINC.+; F.HN.HD. Penrose 353.

— [End:] Here endeth thys lytle treatyse of the instruction of chyldren. 1543. *See* 14106.2.

24234 — [Begin:] This tretyse is of loue . . . whiche tretyse was *tr.* out of frenshe into englyshe, the yere of our lord M cccc lxxxxiij. fol. [*Westminster, W. de Worde,* 1493.] C.C⁶(imp.).G².LINC.M.+; HN.IND.PML.SMU (2 leaves). Duff 399.
Based on a French adaptation of Ancren Riwle. Has sections on the Passion, seven deadly sins, signs of spiritual love, virtues of the apple tree, love of Jesus, and avoiding evil thoughts. Possibly issued w. 5065.

— [Begin:] These ben the chapitres of thys tretyse of yᵉ seuen poyntes of trewe loue. [1491.] *See* 3305.

24235 — Here begynneth a treatyse agaynst pestelẽce. [c. 1510.] = 4592.

— A treatise against the proclamation published by the king of Spayne. [1581.] *See* 15208.

24236 — A treatise cõcernynge diuers of the constitucyons pro-uynciall and legantines. [By C. Saint German?] 8°. *T. Godfray,* [1535?] L.O².C(2, 1 imp.).C².BTL.; F.HN.HD.
(Formerly also 10084)

24237 — A treatise concernynge generall councilles, the by-shoppes of Rome, and the clergy. [By A. Alesius?] 8°. (*in aed. T. Bertheleti,* 1538.) L².C⁷.DUR⁵(imp.).

— A treatise concernynge the diuision betwene the spirytualtie and temporaltie. [1530?] *See* 21586.

— A treatyse concernĩge the power of the clergye. [1535?] *See* 21588.

— A treatice cõteining certain meditatiõs. [1564.] *See* 16988.5.

— A treatise containing the aequity of an humble supplication. 1587. *See* 19611.

24237.5 — A treatyse: contaynynge the orygynall causes, and occasions of the diseases, growynge on horses. And the remedyes. Collected by a cũnynge horse mayster. 4°. (*J. Kynge,*) 1560. Ent. 1560–61. Clark Art Institute, Williamstown, Mass.

24238 — [A treatise declaring and showing that images are not to be suffered in churches. *Tr.* by W. Marshall from the Latin trans. by J. Bedrote of M. Bucer's Das einigerlei Bild.] 8°. (*T. Godfray*) (*f. W. Marshall,*) [1535.] L(lacks tp).
Collates A–F⁸.

Treatise—*cont.*

24239 — [Anr. ed., w. added appendix.] A treatise declaryng & shewĩg dyuers causes that pyctures & other ymages ar ĩ no wise to be suffred in churches. The authours ar the opẽ preachers of Argtẽyne [*sic,* i.e. Argentina or Strassburg.] 8°. [*T. Godfray*] (*f. W. Marshall,*) [1535?] L(G4 def.).O.C(imp.).; F.IND.
Collates A–F⁸ G⁴. In the appendix (G3ʳ) the trans. says he has been 'compelled agayne to printe this lytell treatyse.'

— Here begynneth a treatyse how yᵉ hye fader of heuen sendeth dethe. [1528, etc.] *See* 10606 sq.

24240 — [Heading a1ʳ:] Here begynneth a treatyse of a galaũt. [Doubtfully attrib. to J. Lydgate. In verse.] 4°. (*w. de worde,*) [1510?] L(a1,4 only).; F(a1,4 only). HN(imp.).

24241 — [Anr. ed. Heading A1ʳ:] Here begȳneth a treatise of a galaũt. 4°. (*W. de worde,*) [1520?] L.

24242 — [Anr. ed., w. additions, w. tp:] Here begynneth a treatyse of this galaunt with the maryage of the bosse of Byllyngesgate vnto London stone. 4° in 6. [*J. Skot f. W. de Worde,* 1521?] L. 𝔄
In Skot's types, w. de Worde's device (McK. 20) at the end.

24242.3 — [An extract? without heading.] s.sh.4°. [*W. de Worde,* 1521?] MEL.
The first 4 stanzas are on the recto and the last 4 on the verso. The state of the text, particularly the last stanza is closest to 24242.

— A treatise of auricular confession. 1622. *See* 13036.

— A treatise of blazing starres. 1618. *See* 18413.3.

— A treatise of charitie. 1533. *See* 16939.

24242.5 — A treatise of daunses, wherin it is shewed, that they are accessories to whoredome: where also is proued, that playes are ioyned with them. 8°. [*H. Middleton?*] 1581. L.L².

— A treatise of divine worship. 1604. *See* 3528.

— A treatise of ecclesiasticall and politike power. 1612. *See* 21024.

24243 — Here begynneth a treatyse of fysshynge with an angle. [1533?] Now = 3313.5.

24244 — [Anr. ed.] [n.d.] Now = 3313.7.

— [Treatise of hunting. 1530?] *See* 3313.3.

24245 — A treatie [*sic*] of iustification. 1569. = 20088.

24246 — A treatise of the cohabitacyon of the faithfull. 1555. Now = 24673.5.

24247 — A treatise of the groundes of the old and newe religion. 1608. Now = 17197.5.

— A treatise of the Lords supper. 1591. *See* 22705.

— A treatise of the nature and use of things indifferent. 1605. *See* 3530.

— A treatise of the nature of God. 1599. *See* 18198.

— A treatise of the perpetuall visibilitie of the church. 1624. *See* 39.

— A treatise of the principles of Christ. [1588?] *See* 14573.5.

— A treatise of use and custome. 1638. *See* 4753.

— A treatise or exposition upon the ten commandments. 1603. *See* 6967.

— A treatise parænetical. 1598. *See* 19838.

24248 — A treatise prouynge by the kynges lawes, that the byshops of Rome, had neuer ryght to any supremitie within this realme. 8°. *in æd. T. Berthelet,* (1538.) L.D.; F(1, plus a frag.).HN.

24249 — A treatise, shewing the possibilitie, of the reall presence in the blessed sacrament. 1596. Now = 26043.5.

— here after foloweth a treatyse takẽ out of a boke. [1511?] *See* 14806.

24250 — A treatyse to teche a mã to dye, and not to feare dethe. 8°. (by me R. Redman,) [1537?] F.
Also printed in 11390.

— A treatise wherin Christe and his techinges, are compared. 1534. *See* 14575.

24251 — A two-fold treatise, the one decyphering the worth of speculation, and of a retired life. The other containing a discouerie of youth and old age. 12°. *Oxford, J. Barnes,* 1612. L.C³.

24251.3 — A very godly and learned treatise, of the exercise of fastyng. (A generall confession of sins.—A confession of sinnes, with fayth and repentaunce.) [By T. Cartwright? *Ed.*] (*W. Wilkinson.*) 8° in 4's. *J. Daye,* 1580. C.; F.HN.
(Formerly 25666) Reprinted in 4314.

Treatise—*cont.*

24251.5 — [Anr. ed., omitting Wilkinson's dedic. and adding 'A prayer for the Queene', w. title:] The holie exercise of a true fast. 16° in 8's. [*H. Middleton?*] *f. J. Harison* [2,] *a. T. Man*, 1580. Ass'd from Day to Harrison, jun., a. Man 17 my. L.O.C³.; F.HN.
  (Formerly 25667) Man was fined 6 May 1580 for publishing this; *see* Arber II.851. This has a monogram which can be read as including the letters of Cartwright's name. All copies bd. w. 22044.

24251.7 — A verie plaine and well grownded treatise concerninge baptisme. [Anabaptist propaganda.] 4°. [*The Netherlands?*] 1618. F(third digit in date defective).
  Film of F copy on Univ. Microfilms reel 719 ('24662a'). F also has a later ed. [1648?] w. spellings 'very plain . . . grounded' which is on Univ. Microfilms reel 672 ('24662b').

24252 — A very proper treatise, wherein is briefly sett forthe the arte of limming. 4°. *R. Tottill*, 1573. L(2).O.G².; F.HN.HD.N.Y.+

24253 — [Anr. ed.] 4°. *R. Tottill*, 1581. L.D.M².; HN.

24254 — [Anr. ed.] 4°. *T. Purfoote, the assigne of R. Tottill*, 1583. Ent. to Tottell 18 fb. L.O.LIV³.
  This and the following eds. sometimes bd. w. corresponding eds. of 17590 sqq.

24255 — [Anr. ed.] 4°. *T. Purfoote, the assigne of R. Tottill*, 1588. L¹⁸.O.; F.PN. New York, Metropolitan Museum of Art.

24256 — [Anr. ed.] 4°. *T. Purfoot*, 1596. L.; HN.BO.LC.

24257 — [Anr. ed.] 1605. = 2nd pt. of 17593.

Treatises. Six godlie treatises. 1608. *See* 23433.5.

24258 — Three severall treatises concerning the truce at this present propounded. The first, considerations and reasons, why a truce ought not to bee contracted: propounded unto the States Generall of the United Provinces: by the [Dutch] company of West India. The second, whether it bee lawfull to make truce with the king of Spaine. Lastly, a remonstrance, to the States in the behalfe of the king of Bohemia. *Tr.* out of the Low Dutch copie. 4°. [*B. Alsop a. T. Fawcet*] *f. N. Butter a. N. Bourne*, 1630. Ent. 26 fb. L.L³⁰.L.³⁸.O².C.+; F.HN.BO².CB.TEX.

24259 — Three small and plaine treatises. 1. Of prayer, or active divinitie. 2. Of principles. 3. Resolutions. *Tr.* and collected out of the auncient writers for the private use of a most noble ladie. By an old praebendary of the church of Lincolne [Abp. J. Williams.] 8° in 4's. [*J. Bill*, 1620.] L.L³. Finedon.

— Two treatises concerning regeneration. 1597, etc. *See* 18200.5 sq.

24260 — Two treaties [*sic*] the first concerning the holy scriptures in generall; the second concerning the psalmes in particular. 12°. *Hamburgk* [sic], 1640. O(imp.).

Treaty. The treaty of thassociation made by the prince of Condee. 1562. *See* 16852.

Treboun, Salohcin, *Pseud. See* 3678.

Tregony. Somewhat: written by occasion of three sunnes seene at Tregnie. 1622. *See* 10599.

24261 **Trelcatius, Lucas.** A briefe institution of the common places of sacred divinitie. Wherein, the sophismes of Bellarmine are reproved. Written in Latine, and Englished by J. Gawen. 8°. *T. P[urfoot] f. F. Burton*, 1610. Ent. to Burton a. M. Baker 21 jy.; ass'd to Burton 31 au. L.O.C.D.OS.+; F.
  A trans. of 24262.

24262 — Scholastica et methodica locorum communium S. theologiæ institutio, in epitome explicata. 8°. *J. Bill*, 1604. Ent. 28 no. O³.C.A.YK.
  Translated in 24261.

24263 — [Anr. ed.] 8°. *Oxoniæ, J. Barnesius*, 1606. L.O.C.A.D.+; F.HN.
  Issued w. 24881.

24263.3 — [Anr. ed., w. additions, w. title:] Locorum communium . . . per epitomen. Indice errorum ecclesiæ Rom. adiecto unà cum antidoto: per C. Vorstium. (Enchiridion . . . editio altera; auctior.) 12°. [*R. Field*,] *ex off. Nortoniana, ap. J. Billium*, 1608. L¹³.O.O¹¹.A.ETON.+; F.
  Includes reprint of 24881.

Tremellius, Joannes Immanuel, *ed. See* 2779.
— *tr. See* 2056, 2359.

24263.7 **Trendle, John.** Tren: Arke, against the dragons flood. Buy and try, no cost lost. [A religious treatise, against temptation.] 8°. *T. C[reede] f. W. Welbie*, 1608. L(tp only, Harl.5990/136).STU.; PN²(lacks tp).

Trent, *Council of.* Consilium delectorum cardinalium. 1609. *See* 4610.

24264 — The declaration of the fathers of the councell of Trent. [1593.] Now = pt. 2 of 11617.8.

24265 — A godly and necessarye admonition of the decrees and canons of the counsel of Trent. *Tr.* out of Latine [by Abp. M. Parker?] 4°. *J. Day*, 1564 (19 fb.) L(lacks 1st B1).O.C.D.DUR⁵.+; F.HN.HD(tp def.). ILL.U.+ 𝔄
  C1ʳ catchword: 'regard'.

24265.5 — [Anr. ed.] 4°. *J. Day*, 1564 (19 fb.) O.C³.D.LINC.STD.+; F(2).N. Notre Dame U.
  C1ʳ catchword: 'that'; prelims. are from same setting as 24265.

24266 — Newes concernynge the general coūcell, holden at Trydent by the emperoure and the Germaynes . . . *tr.* oute of Germayne by J. Holibush. Anno. 1548. 8° in 10. (*T. Raynalde*,) [1549?] F.
  End of text dated from Augsburg 6 Dec. 1548.

24267 **Trental.** [End:] This trental is wryten in . . . latyn frenche and englysshe. [1500?] Now = 12351.5.

Tresame, *Sir* **Thomas.** [Bookplate.] *See* Bookplates.

24267.5 **Treswell, Ralph.** A publication of surveying and measuring of mannors, lands and lordships: and arts mathematicall, geometrie, astrologie, geomancie, and the art of dialling. By R. Treswell the younger, in the Strand at the signe of the sunne diall; and are there to be sold. 4°. *W. White*, 1616. O⁴³.

Treswell, Robert. [Bookplate.] *See* Bookplates.

24268 — A relation of such things as were observed in the journey of Charles earle of Nottingham, to Spaine: for the maintenance of peace betweene Great Brittaine and Spaine. 4°. *M. Bradwood f. G. Seaton*, 1605. Ent. 27 jy. L.O.C.DUR⁵.M².+; F.HN.HD.WIS.Y.+
  Corrects the account in 13857.

— *See also* 16768.32.

24268.3 **Treves Endt.** Treves endt. The funerall of the Netherlands peace. Anno 1621. [Dutch engr. w. English letterpress verses.] s.sh.fol. [*The Netherlands*, 1621.] L⁵(Lemon 192).

Trevisa, John, *tr. See* 1536, 12511, 13438.

24268.7 **Trevor**, *Sir* **Sackville.** A true and most exact relation of the taking of the goodly ship called the Saint Esprit, the 28. day of September, by sir Sackevill Trever. Likewise, the proceedings of the duke of Buckingham in the isle of Ree. 4°. *A. M[athewes] f. T. Walkley*, 1627. Ent. 4 oc. L.; HD.
  The Buckingham section has events following those in 24744.

Triades. The triades or trinites of Rome. [c. 1535.] *See* 14027.5.

24269 **Trial.** The fierie tryall of Gods saints; as a counter-poyze to I. W. priest his English martyrologe [25771]. (A Post-script.) 4°. *T. P[urfoot a. T. Creede] f. A. Johnson*, 1611. Ent. 12 oc. L.DALK.
  1st quire has 4 leaves. Creede pr. the Postscript. There appear 2 versions of the author's monogram, w. letters A B C F I N O R S T, later used by F. Burton as publisher's devices; cf. McK. 364 and especially *The Library*, XV (1934), pp. 365–7.

24270 — [Anr. issue, omitting dedic. to Lord Salisbury (died 24 May 1612) and w. 1st quire reimposed to fill 2 leaves.] *T. P[urfoot] f. A. Johnson*, 1612. L.O.C.E². YK.+; F.HN.HD.U.

24271 — A new and mery enterlude, called the Triall of treasure, neuer before imprinted. 4°. *T. Purfoote*, 1567. L(imp.).O(imp.).; HN(imp.).PFOR.ROS. Greg 49.

24272 — No entry.

24273 — A triall of subscription, by way of a preface vnto certaine subscribers; and, reasons for lesse rigour against non-subscribers. [By W. Bradshaw.] 8°. [*Middelburg, R. Schilders*,] 1599. L².L³.O.C⁵.E.+; F(imp.).BALT.COR.U.

Trial—*cont.*

24274 — The trial of trueth or a treatise wherein is declared who should be iudge betwene the reformed churches, and the romish. Published in Latine by a certaine Hungarian, and *tr.* by Richard Smith. 4°. (*J. Windet*) *f. R. Dexter*, 1591. Ent. 5 jn. L.O.YK. Budapest, Széchényi NL.; F(lacks col.).N.Y(lacks col.).

At least L and F copies have B4 and C1 cancelled and replaced by a bifolium w. the leaves signed * and C1. *Tr.* from Oratio de constituendo iudice controversiarum religionis, Basel, 1591; *see* K. Szabó, *Régi Magyar Könyvtár*, III, no. 810.

— The true tryall and examination of a mans owne selfe. 1586. *See* 11761.3.

Trick. A trick to catch the old-one. 1608. *See* 17896.

Tridentino, Accontio. *See* 3161.

24275 **Trigge, Francis.** Analysis capitis vicesimi quarti euangelii secundum Matthæum, in qua prophetiæ omnes, clarè explicantur. 4°. *Oxoniæ, ex off. J. Barnesii*, 1591. L.O.O3.C17.D.

24276 — An apologie, or defence of our dayes. [In praise of the Reformation.] 4°. *J. Wolfe*, 1589. Ent. 7 no. L.L2.O.

24277 — A godly and fruitfull sermon preached at Grantham. 8°. *Oxford, J. Barnes*, 1594. L.O(imp.).

24277.5 — [Anr. ed.] Newly corrected and enlarged. 8°. *Oxford, J. Barnes*, 1595. L.

24278 — [A ghost.]

24279 — Noctes sacrae, seu lucubrationes in primam partem Apocalypseos: in quibus docetur, quænam sit vera ecclesia. 4°. *Oxoniæ, ex off. J. Barnesii*, 1590. L2.C.D(2).SCL.; PN.

24280 — To the kings most excellent majestie. The humble petition of two sisters; the church and Commonwealth. [Against enclosures.] 8°. [*F. Kingston,*] *imp. G. Bishop*, 1604. Ent. 22 mr. L(date cropt).O.

24280.5 — [Anr. ed.] 8°. [*F. Kingston,*] *imp. G. Bishop*, 1604. L30.C2.; F.N.

In title: 'Common wealth' (no hyphen).

24281 — A touchstone, whereby may easilie be discerned, which is the true catholike faith. Taken out of the epistle of S. Jude. 4°. *P. Short*, 1599. Ent. 5 oc. L.O.; HD.

24281a — [A variant, w. imprint:] *P. Short*, 1600. L.C.P.YK.; F.HN.

24282 — The true catholique, formed according to the truth of the scriptures. 4°. *P. Short*, 1602. Ent. 23 oc. 1601. L2.O.C5(2).NOR2.; NY11.

24282.5 — [Anr. issue, anon., w. prelims. cancelled and cancel tp:] The summe of true catholike doctrine. H. L[ownes] *f. J. Royston*, 1613. YK.

Trinitarian Order. *See* Indulgences 115A, 121B, 122.

Trinity College, Dublin. *See* 7265.

24283 **Trinity House.** The answer of the masters of the Trinitie-house, to the speciall objections of the patentee, for the keeping of Winterton lights. [Arguments addressed to Parliament.] s.sh.fol. [*W. Jones*, 1621.] L5(Lemon 183).L8(GL 1435).

Answered by 25856.5.

24284 **Triplet, Robert.** Writing tables. 1604. Now = 26050.6.
24285 — [Anr. ed.] 1611. Now = 26050.10.
— *See also* 16050.4.

Triplici Nodo. Triplici nodo, triplex cuneus. 1607. *See* 14400, 14403 sqq.

Tripp, Henry, *tr. See* 4769, 11759.
— *See also* 6075.

24285.5 **Tritheim, Johann von.** A three-fold mirrour of man's vanitie and miserie. The first by J. Trithemius. The two others by catholicke authors unknown: faithfully Englished by A. Batt. [Third part is in verse.] 8° in 4's. *Doway, L. Kellam*, 1633. O(lacks tp).AMP (imp.).; F(imp.).

A&R 830.

Triumph. A triumph for true subiects. 1581. *See* 7564.

24286 **Triumphs.** The rare triumphs of loue and fortune. Plaide before the queenes maiestie. 4°. *E. A[llde] f. E. White*, 1589. HN. Greg 92.

Troes. Fuimus Troes. 1633. *See* 10886.

24287 **Trogus Pompeius.** Iustini ex Trogi Pompeij historia, libri .xliiij. Supra plurimorum æditiones doctorum hominum opera castigatissimi. Cum eruditissimis scholiolis. Adiecimus monarchiarum omnium tabulam. 8°. *ap. H. Bynneman*, 1572. L.D.

24287.3 — [Anr. ed.] 8°. *H. Bynneman*, 1577. L(tpp only, Ames I.319; Harl.5993/94).

24287.7 — [Anr. ed.] Justini ex Trogi Pompeii historiis externis libri XLIIII. His accessit, ex Sexto Aurelio Victore De vita & moribus Romanorum imperatorum epitome. 8°. *G. Robinsonus*, 1586. O.

24288 — [Anr. ed.] 8°. *T. Orwinus*, 1593. L.C.C2.LINC.

See Greg, *Register B*, p. 45.

24288.5 — [Anr. ed.] 8°. *T. Haveland*, 1609. L(date faultily printed; plus tp only, Harl.5927/196, date is distinct). LK(2).

24289 — [Anr. ed.] 8°. *F. Kyngstonius, ex imp. J. Grismundi*, 1633. L.O.C19.D.; F.

24289.5 — [Anr. ed.] 8°. *F. Kyngstonius, ex imp. P. Nevilli*, 1640. L.O6.C5.DUL.; F.BOWDOIN.

24290 — [A trans.] Thabridgment of the histories of Trogus Pompeius, collected by Justine, and *tr.* by A. Goldyng. 4° in 8's. *T. Marshe*, 1564 (my.) Ent. 1562–63. L.O3.C.; F.HN.CU.HD(lacks tp).N.+

Quires A and B in 2 settings; A3r last line: 'yt,'; B5r catchword: 'that' (HN) or 'it,' and 'vse' (HD).

24291 — [Anr. ed.] Newlie conferred with the Latin copye. 4° in 8's. *T. Marshe*, 1570. L.O.LEEDS.NLW.P.+; F.HN.HD. TEX.WEL.

24292 — [Anr. ed.] 4° in 8's. *T. Marsh*, 1578. L.L43.O.C12. BIRM.+; F.HN.ILL.Y.

24293 — [Anr. trans.] The historie of Justine. . . . Whereunto is newly added a briefe collection of the lives of the emperours (taken out of Sext. Aurelius Victor.) Newly *tr.* by G. W[ilkins?] fol. *W. Jaggard*, 1606. L.L30.O.C2.LIV3.+; F.HN.HD.N.NY.+

24293.3 **Trollop, Thomas.** [Heading:] Certaine necessary considerations and orders to encorage the lord maior, and aldermen of London . . . accordinge to the letter of requeste made to certaine of them by the queenes maiesties priuy counsell. [Proposals for increasing and controlling the manufacture of cloth.] 4°. [*W. Powell*, c. 1563.] HD.

Trotman, Edward, *tr. See* 5527.

Trouhertighe Vermaninghe. Trouhertighe vermaninghe aen alle swangere vroutgens. 1618. *See* 13684.5.

Troy. The faythfull and true storye of the destruction of Troye. 1553. *See* 6274.5.
— The hystorye, sege and dystruccyon of Troye. 1513. *See* 5579.
— Here foloweth the .C. hystoryes of Troye. [1540?] *See* 7272.
— A most pithi and plesant history of Troye. [By F. Edderemane?] *See* 7481.7.

24293.5 — A proper new ballad, intituled, the wandring prince of Troy. *Ballad.* 2 pts. s.sh.fol. *f. John Wright*, [c. 1630.] Ent. to E. Allde 8 jn. 1603; to ballad ptnrs. 14 de. 1624. C6.

24293.7 — [Anr. ed.] 2 pts. s.sh.fol. [*A. Mathewes*] *f. J. Wright*, [c. 1635.] O.
— hEre begynneth . . . the recuyell of the historyes of Troye. [1475, etc.] *See* 15375 sqq.

Trubach, Volradus a, *Pseud. See* 11406.

True, Patrick. An almanack. 1636. *See* 517.16.

24294 **Truman, Richard.** A christian memorandum, or advertisement wherein is handled the doctrine of reproofe. 8°. *Oxford, J. Lichfield, sold by H. Seale*, [*London,*] 1629. O(2).PLUME.WOR.

24295 **Trumpet.** A trumpet to call souldiers on to noble actions. By the rare and new examples of two kings. Viz. Gustanus [*sic*] of Sweden, against Sigismond of Poland. *Tr.* out of the Latine copie. 4°. [*M. Flesher*] *f. N. Bourne a. T. Archer*, 1627. O.

Trundle, John. *See* 14898.5.

24296 **Trussell, John.** Raptus I. Helenae. The first rape of faire Hellen. Done into a poeme. [*Tr.* from the Latin version of T. Coluthus in 5586.] 4°. *R. Johnes*, 1595. Ent. 16 ap. CASHEL(imp.).; ROS.

Trussell, John—*cont.*

24297 — A continuation of the collection of the history of England, beginning where S. Daniell ended. fol. *M. D[awson] f. E. Dawson*, 1636. Ent. to D. Pakeman 29 jy. 1635. L.O.C.D.E².+; F.HN.HD.N.NY.+

— *tr. See* 25118.

24298 **Trussell, Thomas.** The souldier pleading his owne cause. With an epitome of the qualities required in the severall officers of a private company. Second edition, much enlarged. 8°. *N. Okes, sold by T. Walkley*, 1619. L.

24299 — [Anr. ed., enlarged.] Third impression. 8°. *N. Okes, sold by T. Walkley*, 1626. L.O.

24299.5 **Trusswell, William.** ⟨T⟩he true hearted l⟨over⟩ or a young man sent a letter to his love. *Ballad.* 2 pts. s.sh.fol. *R. Oulton f. John ⟨Wrigh⟩t t⟨he⟩ younger*, [c. 1640.] HD(imp.).

24300 **Truth.** The truth of three things. 1633. Now = 21347.7.

24301 — Truths integrity: or, a curious northerne ditty, called, love will finde out the way. *Ballad.* 2 pts. s.sh.fol. [*E. Purslowe?*] *f. F. Coules*, [c. 1635.] L.

24301.5 **Tryamour.** [Sir Tryamour. In verse.] 4° in 6's. [*R. Pynson*, 1503?] HN(leaves 8, 9 of the text, plus a duplicate of leaf 9).MEL(leaf 8).
30 lines a complete page.

24302 — [Anr. ed.] 4°. [*W. de Worde*, c. 1530.] C(B1, 4).
32 lines a complete page.

24303 — [Anr. ed.] Syr Tryamoure. 4°. (*w. Copland, in Temes strete vp̄o the thre Crane wharfe,*) [1561?] L.
34 lines a page.

24303.3 — [Anr. ed.] 4°. (*W. Copland,*) [1565.] O.
34 lines a page; no address in colophon.

24303.7 **Tuke, Thomas.** Christian and heavenly directions to the holy land: or a treatise, shewing the right way to heavenly happinesse. 8°. *T. Snodham f. J. Budge*, 1610. Ent. 12 oc. 1609. HAT.

24304 — The christians looking-glasse: wherein hee may cleerely see, his love to God. 8°. *N. Okes, sold by R. Bolton*, 1615. Ent. to Okes 30 jn. 1614. O.

24305 — Concerning the holy eucharist, and the popish breaden-god. [In verse.] 4°. [*Amsterdam, successors of G. Thorp,*] 1625. L⁴.O.E.; F(date shaved).

24306 — [Anr. ed.] 4°. [*Amsterdam?*] 1636. L.C⁴(lacks tp). LYD.; F.HN.HD.
The postscript on p. 26 refers to 'the second impression'.

24307 — A discourse of death, bodily, ghostly, and eternall. 4°. *W. Stansbie f. G. Norton*, 1613. L.L³.O.O³(imp.). C.+; HD.

24308 — A fit guest for the Lords table. 8°. *E. Allde, sold by H. Rockit*, 1609. C.; F(imp.).CAL.
(Formerly also 12424)

24308a — [Anr. issue, w. cancel tp, w. imprint:] *E. Allde, sold by H. Rockit*, 1610. LINC.

24309 — The high-way to heaven: or, the doctrine of election, effectuall vocation, [etc.] 8°. *N. Okes*, 1609. Ent. 20 fb. L(lacks K8).CHATS(2).M.; BO.

24310 — [Anr. ed.] 12°. [*T. Cotes f.*] *N. Okes*, 1635. L(imp.). L³.D.; F.HN.U.

24310.5 — Improbus foeneratorum spiritus variis tormentis exercitatus. Sive tractatus de usurariorum statu calamitoso. Auctore T. Tuko, Anglo. 4°. *Francofurti, apud* [i.e. *for?*] *J. Bill,* [*London*,] 1618. O²⁴.C.

24311 — Index fidei, et religionis, sive dilucidatio primi, & secundi capitis epistolę catholicæ divi Jacobi. 4°. *Londoni, ex off. Nortoniana, ap. J. Bill,* [really printed at Frankfurt?* 1617.] L(destroyed).O²⁴.C.C¹² (lacks tp).DUR³.YK.
The tp has a device formerly used at Lyons by T. Payen (Silvestre 657; Baudrier IV.210, no. 4), but the prelims. are signed in a manner characteristic of Frankfurt: '(:)'; *see The Library*, XXI (1966), pp. 9–10.

24312 — New essayes: meditations, and vowes: including in them the chiefe duties of a christian. By T. Tuke. 12°. *N. O[kes] f. W. Bladon*, 1614. Ent. to Okes 1 jy. O.
Tp, dedic., and To the reader are all signed in full. The O copy does not have the contents bifolium, but this may be an imperfection.

Tuke, Thomas—*cont.*

24312.3 — [Anr. issue, init. T. T., with added? bifolium with contents.] *N. O[kes] f. W. Bladon*, 1614. L.O.
Tp is anon.; dedic. and To the reader are init. T. T.

24312.7 — The picture of a picture: or, the character of a painted woman. [Anon.] s.sh.fol. [*T. Creede*, 1615?] O.
Reprinted in 24316 sq.

24313 — The picture of a true protestant: or, Gods house and husbandry. 8°. *N. Okes, sold by T. Archer*, 1609. Ent. to Okes 10 no. L.PLUME(lacks tp)*.

24313.3 — [A variant, w. imprint:] *N. Okes*, 1609. C⁵.

24313.5 — [A variant, w. imprint:] *N. Okes, sold by S. Rande*, 1609. F.

24314 — The practise of the faithfull: containing many godly praiers. 12°. *J. Beale f. S. Man*, 1613. Ent. 27 ja. O.
In the dedic. Tuke says he is only the editor.

24314.3 — The ninth edition corrected. 12°. *W. Jones f. S. Man*, 1636. PLUME.

24314.7 — A sermon of the last and great judgement. 8°. *R. Badger*, 1632. Ent. 29 oc. 1631. L(tp only, Ames II.1027).

24315 — A theological discourse of the gracious and blessed conjunction of Christ and a sincere christian. 8°. *E. Griffin*, 1617. Ent. 30 my. L(tp only, Harl. 5963/353).O.; HD(imp.).

24315.5 — The treasure of true love. Or a lively description of the love of Christ. 8°. *T. Creede, solde by T. Archer*, 1608. F.

24315.7 — [A variant, w. imprint:] *T. Creede, solde by J. Budge*, 1608. EX.; HN.

24316 — A treatise against paintng [*sic*] and tincturing of men and women: against murther and poysoning: [etc.] Whereunto is added the picture of a picture, or, the character of a painted woman. By T. Tuke. 4°. *T. Creed a. B. Allsope f. E. Merchant*, 1616. L.O(2). C³.; F.HD.N. Hickmott.
In both O and F copies the tp is clearly a cancel. Includes reprint of 24312.7.

24316a — [Anr. issue, w. anon. cancel tp and end of text still init. T. T.] A discourse against painting and tincturing of women. [etc.] *f. E. Marchant*, 1616. O.C(impr. cropt). C³.LIV³.PLUME(lacks tp)*.; HN(both tpp).HD.ILL.
The O tp is clearly a cancel.

24317 — The true trial and turning of a sinner. Or, three sermons. 8°. *T. Creede*, 1607. Ent. 13 mr. L.C³.P.; F.

— *tr. See* 19683, 19735.4, 24753.

24318 **Tunstall, Cuthbert**, *Bp.* Certaine godly and deuout prayers. Made in latin and *tr.* by T. Paynell. *Lat. a. Eng.* 8°. (*J. Cawoode*, 1558.) Ent. to R. Harvey 1557–58. L.L¹⁵.O.DE.; F.HN.

24319 — De arte supputandi libri quattuor. 4°. (*in aed. R. Pynsoni*, 1522 (prid. id. oc.)) L.O.C.E.M.+; F.HN.CU. HD.PML.+ 𝔄

24320 — Cutheberti Tonstalli in laudem matrimonii oratio. 4° in 8's. (*per R. Pynson*, 1518 (id. no.)) L.O(2).BUTE.; HN.PML.

24321 — A letter written by Cutbert Tunstall and J. Stokesley somtime byshop of London, sente vnto R. Pole, cardinall. 8°. (*R. Woulfe*, 1560.) Ent. 18 my. L.L².C. C⁵.ST.+; F.HN.
Reprinted in 11629.

24322 — A sermon of Cuthbert bysshop of Duresme, made vpon Palme sondaye before kynge Henry the .viii. 8°. (*in æd. T. Bertheleti*, 1539.) L.O.C³.DUR³.P.+

24322a — [Anr. ed.] A sermon . . . before kyng Henry. 8°. (*in æd. T. Bertheleti*, 1539.) L(2).CHATS.; F.HN.

24323 — [Anr. ed., w. title:] A sermon preached on Palme-Sunday, before king Henry the VIII. 4°. *T. Harper*, 1633. Ent. 18 my. 1631. L.O.C.DUR⁵.YK.+; HN.HD.U.

24323.5 — Vniuersis Christifidelibus, ad quos præsentes literę siue hoc pręsens publicum [etc. An inspeximus, dated 15 Mar. 1528/9, of the bull of Clement VII, dated 13 May 1528, granting privileges to Wolsey's Cardinall College (later Christ Church), Oxford.] s.sh.fol. [*R. Pynson*, 1529.] O.
With woodcut notary's mark, etc., of William Claiburgh at the foot.

— *See also* 24633.5.

24324 **Turberville, George.** The booke of faulconrie or hauking, . . . collected out of the best aucthors. 4° in 8's. [*H. Bynneman*] *f. C. Barker*, 1575. L.L¹⁸.O.A.E.+; F.HN.HD(tp def.).PN.TEX.+
This and the following usually bd. w. 24328 sq.

Turberville, George—*cont.*

24325 — [Anr. ed.] Newly reuiued, with many new additions proper to these present times. 4° in 8's. *T. Purfoot,* 1611. L.O.O⁶.C.M.+; F.HN.HD.N.Y.+
Aⁱʳ catchword: 'of'.

24325.5 — [Anr. issue, with quires A–K reset.] *T. Purfoot,* 1611. Lord Kenyon.; BO.HD.ILL.PN.
Aⁱʳ catchword: 'com-'.

24326 — Epitaphes, epigrams, songs and sonets. Newly corrected with additions. 8°. *H. Denham,* 1567. Ent. 1566–67. O(imp.).C(frag.).; HN.

24327 — [Anr. ed.] 8°. *H. Denham,* (1570.) L(imp.).O(2, 1 imp.). C²(imp.).; F.HN.HD(imp.).

24328 — The noble arte of venerie or hunting. *Tr.* and collected out of the best authors. [Anon. Not by Turberville; actually adapted by G. Gascoigne from J. de Fouilloux's La Venerie, 1573.] 4° in 8's. (*H. Bynneman f. C. Barker,*) [1575.] L.O.A.E.M.+; F. HN.PN.TEX. Pearson.+
This and the following usually bd. w. 24324 sqq.

24329 — [Anr. ed.] 4° in 8's. *T. Purfoot,* 1611. L.O.C.LIV².M.+; F.HN.HD.N.Y.+

24330 — Tragical tales, *tr.* by Turbervile out of sundrie Italians. (Epitathes [*sic*] and sonnettes.) [All in verse.] 8°. *A. Jeffs,* 1587. L(imp.).O(2, 1 imp.).C(1, plus a frag.).E²(missing).; HN(tp and portions of other leaves in facs.).BO.
Tales 2, 5, 8 are from M. Roseo da Fabriano's Ital. trans. and enlargement of P. Mexia's Silva (cf. 17849); the rest are from Boccaccio.
— *tr. See* 17244, 18939.5, 22990.

Turcopapismus. De Turcopapismo. 1599. *See* 23460.

24331 **Turges, Edward.** The christian souldier, his combat, conquest, and crowne. [Init. E. T.] 12°. *R. Hodgkinsonne f. J. Spencer,* 1639. Ent. as by Turges 6 de. 1638. L⁴.NLW.; N.

24331.5 — [Anr. issue, w. cancel tp, w. imprint:] *R. H[odgkinson] f. J. S[pencer,] sold by B. Langford,* 1639. F.PN² (tp def.).

Turk, *the Great.* The greate Turkes defiance. 1613. *See* 206.
— The great Turks terrible challenge. [1640.] *See* 23424.7.
— Letters from the great Turke. 1606. *See* 207.
— The strangling and death of the great Turke. 1622. *See* Newsbooks 62.
— The Turkes secretorie. 1607. *See* 17996.
— True copies of the insolent letter by the great Turke. 1621. *See* 208.

Turkey. History of the imperiall estate of the grand seigneurs. 1635. *See* 1593.

24332 — Newes from Turkie and Poland. 1622. Now = Newsbooks 36.

24333 — Newes from Turkie. Or a true and perfect relation sent from Constantinople. Touching the death of Achmet. 4°. *W. Jones f. S. Nealand a. N. Browne,* 1618. L⁴³.C³. London, Foreign Office.

24334 — The order of the great Turckes courte. *Tr.* oute of Frenche [from A. Geuffroy's Estat de la court du grant Turc] 1524 [*sic*]. 8°. *R. Grafton,* (1542.) L.O⁵(imp.).
The sub tp on aⁱʳ is dated 1542.

24335 — The policy of the Turkish empire. The first booke. [On religion.] 4°. *J. Windet f. W. S(tansby,)* 1597. Ent. 28 ap. L.O.C.C²(imp.).P.+; F.HN.HD.Y.
The P copy has an early MS. attrib. to G. Fletcher, the Elder. No more published.
— True newes of a notable victorie obtayned against the Turkes. [1598.] *See* 20595.5.

24335.5 — The true relation and description of 2. most strange and true remarkable sea-fights against the Turkes. 4°. *E. P[urslowe] f. H. Gosson,* 1637. L.

24336 **Turler, Hieronymus.** The traueiler of Jerome Turler, deuided into two bookes. The first of the maner, of traueiling ouersea. The second of the realme of Naples. *Tr.* from the Latin. 8°. *W. How f. A. Veale,* 1575. L(2).O.C(tp def.).; F.HN.ROS.

24337 **Turnbull, Charles.** A perfect and easie treatise of the vse of the cœlestiall globe. 8°. [*G. Robinson*] *f. S. Waterson,* [1585.] Ent. 8 mr. 1585. L.; HN.

24338 — [Anr. ed.] 8°. *f. S. Waterson,* 1597. L.O.

24339 **Turnbull, Richard.** An exposition vpon the canonicall epistle of saint James. (Saint Jude.—The xv. psalme.) 3 pts. 8°. *J. Windet,* 1591. Pt. 1 ent. 12 ja. L(pts. 2, 3).L²(pts. 1, 2).O(pt. 2).C²(pt. 2).LEEDS(pt. 3).+; F (pt. 1).HN(pt. 1).NY(pts. 1, 2).
The parts were evidently issued separately throughout the year.

24339.5 — [Anr. ed.] Newly corrected. 3 pts. 8°. *J. Windet,* 1592. L.O.; F.CAL⁶.PN².TEX.Y.+
Jude has on the title: 'Lately reuised and augmented' and Psalm xv: 'Lately perused, and augmented.'

24340 — [Anr. issue, w. gen. tp:] An exposition vpon the canonical epistle of S. James . . . sainte Jude . . . the fiftenth psalme. All lately corrected, enlarged. *J. Windet,* 1592. C.P.; HART.
C has the pt. tpp cancelled; P retains them.

24341 — [Anr. ed.] 4° in 8's. *J. Windet, solde by R. Bankworth,* 1606. L(destroyed).O.C.C²().C³.YK.; F.HN.ILL(imp.). U.Y.+

Turner, *Dr., one of his majesty's chaplains. See* 24349.

24341.5 **Turner, Anne.** Mistris Turners farewell to all women. [Woodcut w. letterpress verses against the sin of pride.] s.sh.fol. *f. J. Trundle,* [1615.] L⁵(Lemon 143).
— *See also* 3720, 18919.3.

24342 **Turner, John.** An essay on ecclesiastical authority. [Concerning nonjurors.] 8° in 4's. *f. J. Wyat,* 1617 [really 1717?] L⁴(lacks F3).

24343 **Turner, Peter,** *the Elder.* The opinion of Peter Turner doct: in physicke, concerning amulets or plague cakes. 4°. [*R. Read*] *f. E. Blount,* 1603. L.
— *See also* 19916.3, 24367.

Turner, Peter, *the Younger. See* 19009.

24344 **Turner, Richard.** Constant Lusina. The amorous passions of Paurinio. 4°. [*J. Roberts*] *f. W. Kirkham,* 1599. O(frag.).; HN.

24345 — The garland of a greene witte. Discouering the constancie of Calipolis. A precious spectacle for wanton wiues. 4°. [*J. Roberts*] *f. W. Kirkham,* [1595?] Ent. 28 ap. 1595. HN.

24346 — Nosce te, (Humors.) By Richard Turner. [In verse.] 4°. *J. W[indet] f. J. Chorlton,* 1607. Ent. 30 oc. 1606. L.L¹³(imp.).O.O⁶(frag.).; F.HN.

24347 — Youth know thy selfe. [Anon. In verse.] 4°. *A. Mathewes a. J. Norton, sold [by R. Milbourne,]* 1624. Ent. to R. Milbourne 17 au. L.; F(tp def.).HN.

24348 **Turner, Roger.** The usurers plea answered. In a sermon preached at Southampton. 4°. *E. P[urslowe] f. R. Bostocke,* 1634. Ent. 11 ja. L.O.EX.SNU.WOR.; HN. HD.Y.

24349 **Turner, Thomas,** *Chaplain to Charles I.* A sermon preached before the king at White-hall, the tenth of March. By doctor Turner, one of his majesties chaplaines. 4°. *R. Badger,* 1635. Ent. 26 mr. L.O.C. D.G².+; F.CAL.HD.MCG.Y.

Turner, Thomas, *Mathematician.* Almanacke. 1633, etc. *See* 518 sq.

24350 **Turner, W.** Turners dish of lentten stuffe, or a galymaufery. 2 pts. Ballad. s.sh.fol. [*S. Stafford?*] *f. J. W[right? 1612?]* C⁶.
Cf. the Turner ballads ent. to T. Pavier 19 no. 1612.

24350.5 **Turner, William.** Avium praecipuarum, quarum apud Plinium et Aristotelem mentio est, historia. Adiectis nominibus Græcis, Germanicis & Britannicis. 8°. *Coloniæ, J. Gymnicus,* 1544. L(2).O.C.PARIS.; HD.

24351 — A booke of the natures and properties, of the bathes in Englande. 1562. = pt. 2 of 24366.

24352 — [Anr. issue.] 1568. = pt. 4 of 24367.

24353 — The huntyng & fyndyng out of the romishe fox. [W. Wraghton, *pseud.*] 8°. (*Basyl* [i.e. *Bonn, L. Mylius,*]) 1543 (14 se.) L.C².C¹⁵.; F.HD(imp.).
Collates A–E⁸ F⁴.

24354 — [Anr. ed.] The huntyng and fyndyng out of the romyshe foxe. 8°. (*Basyll,* 1543 (xiiij se.)) [i.e. *Antwerp, S. Mierdman,* 1544?] L.O.C.C¹⁵.E².+; BO.NY¹¹.
Collates A–F⁸.

Turner, William—*cont.*

24355 — The rescuynge of the romishe fox other wyse called the examination of the hunter deuised by steuen gardiner. The seconde course of the hunter at the romishe fox. [W. Wraghton, *pseud.*] 8°. (*winchester, by me Hanse hit prik* [i.e. Bonn, L. Mylius,] 1545 (4 non. mr.)) L.O.C.E.M.+; F.HN.BO.CU.Y.

    Prints and answers Gardiner's Examination, which app. circulated only in MS.

24356 — The huntyng of the romyshe vuolfe. 8°. [*Emden, E. van der Erve, 1555?*] L.O.C.D².BRISTOL.+; F(2).HN.BO (imp.).HD.WIS.

    Collates A–E⁸ F⁴. F, HN have the last halfsheet printed in Erve's 73 mm. Schwabacher like the rest of the book (F1ʳ catchword 'lowe'). The HD copy has the halfsheet printed in 78 mm. lettersnijder (F1ʳ catchword 'pre-') and possibly represents a reissue, with the halfsheet printed [*London? J. Day? 1558?*]

24357 — [Anr. ed., anon., w. new prelims. and title:] The hunting of the fox and the wolfe. 8°. [*London, c. 1565.*] L.O(imp.).C.C³.; Y.

    Collates A–D⁸ E⁴. The new preface is sometimes attrib. to J. Knox.

24358 — Libellus de re herbaria nouus, in quo herbarum aliquot nomina greca, latina, & Anglica habes. 4°. (*ap. J. Byddellum, 1538.*) L.O⁴³.; Lownes.

24359 — The names of herbes in Greke, Latin, Englishe Duche & Frenche. 8°. [*S. Mierdman f.*] (*J. Day a. W. Seres,*) [1548.] L.O³(E).C.D.E².+; HD.

    Dedic. dated 15 Mar. 1548.

24360 — A new boke of the natures of all wines commonlye vsed in England. Wherunto is annexed the booke of the natures of triacles, newly corrected. 8°. *W. Seres,* 1568. Ent. 1567–68. L.L⁴⁰.O.P.; HD.LC.WIS.Y.

24361 — A new booke of spirituall physik for dyuerse diseases of the nobilite and gentlemen of Englande. 8°. (*Imprented at Rome by the vaticane churche, by Marcus Antonius Constantius. Otherwyse called, thraso miles gloriosus* [i.e. Emden, E. van der Erve,]) 1555 (10 cal. mr.) L.O.C⁹.C¹⁵.ETON(imp.).; F.HN.WIS.

24361.5 — A new dialogue where in is conteyned the examinatiõ of the masse. 8°. [*E. Whitchurch f.*] (*J. Day a. W. Seres,*) [1548?] L.O(8° K 96 Art. BS.).C³. BHP(imp.).; BO³.HD.

    (Formerly 24364)

24362 — [Anr. ed.] A newe dialogue wherin is conteyned the examinatiõ of the messe. 8°. [*E. Whitchurch f.*] *J. Day a. W. Seres,* [1548?] L.O(Tanner 47(6)).C⁵.E². NLW.; F.

    Parts of quire E and all of F and G are from the same typesetting, reimposed, as 24361.5. E8ʳ line 5 ends 'Messe' while 24361.5 has erroneous 'Masse or'. At the bottom of A1ᵛ are 5 lines of type from D7ᵛ intended as bearers but pr. by mistake.

24363 — [Anr. ed.] A new dialogue wherein is conteyned the examination of the messe. 8°. [*W. Hill,* 1548.] O.C(2).

24364 — Now = 24361.5.

24364a — [Anr. ed.] A new dialogue wherin is contayned the examinacion of the messe. 8°. (*Richarde wyer,*) [1549?] L.C⁵.

24365 — A new herball, wherin are conteyned the names of herbes. fol. *S. Mierdman, solde (by J. Gybken,)* 1551. L.L¹⁶.O.C.E⁵.+; F.HD.ILL.LC.NY.+

24366 — The seconde parte of William Turners herball. Here vnto is ioyned also a booke of the bath of Baeth in Englande. 2 pts. fol. *Collen, A. Birckman,* 1562. L.L¹⁶.O.C.E.+; F.HD.ILL.LC.NY.+

    (Pt. 2 formerly 24351) All copies should have errata on Gg². Some copies (LC) have an extra slip with 'Errours in Figures' bd. after or pasted on Gg2. 13433 is frequently bd. w. this and the following. See also 24707.

24367 — The first and seconde partes of the herbal lately ouersene, corrected and enlarged with the thirde parte, lately gathered. Also a booke of the bath of Baeth. 4 pts. fol. *Collen, [heirs of] A. Birckman,* 1568. L.O.C(lacks tp).E.M.+; F.HN.HD.ILL.PML.+

    (Pt. 4 formerly 24352) Pt. 1 is a reprint of 24365; pt. 2 is a reissue w. new prelims. of 24366 (pt. 1); pt. 3 is completely new; pt. 4 is a reissue w. new prelims. of 24366 (pt. 2).

    Errata for pt. 2 should be retained from 24366. Further errata were prepared, though they are very rare. BO has 2 leaves signed ¶: 'Errata.

Turner, William—*cont.*

Faultes escaped in the printing' with errata for the preface and pts. 1, 3. HN has a later form on 3 leaves: A²: 'Peter Turner to the Reader' w. errata for the prelims. and pt. 1; and *1: 'Faultes to be amended in the thirde part.'

— The olde learnyng and the newe. 1548. See 20842.

24368 — A preseruatiue, or triacle, agaynst the poyson of Pelagius, lately renued, by the furious secte of the annabaptistes. 8°. [*S. Mierdman*] (*f. A. Hester,* 1551 (30 ja.)) L(lacks col.).L².O(2, 1 imp.).C.C⁵.

— The rescuynge of the romishe fox. 1545. *See* 24355.

— *tr. See* 13028, 20840, 25127.

24368.5 **Turnet, Patrick.** Descriptio erysipelatis, ab experientia. [Init. M. P. T. In verse.] s.sh.fol. [*St. Andrews, E. Raban,* 1621?] E.

    Bd. in a copy of 22567.

Turnhaut. A discourse of the ouerthrowe. 1597. *See* 22993.

— A true discourse of the ouerthrowe. 1597. *See* 17678.

24369 **Turtledove.** The turtle dove. Or, the wooing in the wood. *Ballad.* 2 pts. s.sh.fol. *assignes of T. Symcocke,* [1628–9.] L.

Turtledoves. A paire of turtle doves. 1606. *See* 11094.

24370 **Turtles.** The paire of northerne turtles. [c. 1640.] = 18672.

Turquet. *See* Mayern Turquet.

Turvallius, I. L. Summus dux. [1623?] *See* 16695.5.

24371 **Turvell, Thomas.** The poore mans path-way to heaven. [A dialogue between a professor, an atheist, and a civilian.] 8°. *W. Stansby, sold by T. Pavier,* 1616. L².YK.

Turvey, *Tinker of. See* 4581, 22920.3.

24372 **Tusser, Thomas.** A hundreth good pointes of husbandrie. [In verse.] 4°. (*R. Tottel,* 1557 (3 fb.)) Ent. to J. Day 1557–58. L.

24372.5 — [Anr. ed., enlarged.] Lately maried vnto a hundreth good poyntes of huswifry, newly corrected, and amplified. 1562. 4°. *in æd. R. Tottelli,* [1562.] Ent. 1561–62. NOR²(imp.).

    O. Rogers was fined for printing an ed. 1561–62; *see* Arber I.184.

24373 — [Anr. ed.] 4°. [*H. Denham?*] *in æd. R. Tottylli,* 1570. O³(imp.).; HN.

    Tp border of this, 24374, and 24375 (McK. & F. 139) has the inits. 'H D' at the bottom.

24374 — [Anr. ed.] 4°. [*H. Denham?*] *in aed. R. Tottelli,* 1571. L.

24375 — [Anr. ed., enlarged.] Fiue hundreth points of good husbandry vnited to as many of good huswiferie, nowe lately augmented. 4°. [*H. Denham f.?*] *R. Tottill,* 1573. L(imp.).P.RD.; F(imp.).

    Collates A–Aa⁴.

24376 — [Anr. ed., w. additions.] 4°. *R. Tottell,* 1573. L(lacks Bb4).

    Collates A–Bb⁴; A2ʳ line 1: 'husbandry'.

24377 — [Anr. ed.] 4°. *R. Tottell,* 1573. L.; F(imp.).HN.WEL.

    Collates A–Bb⁴; A2ʳ line 1: 'husbãdry'.

24378 — [Anr. ed.] 4°. *R. Tottell,* 1574. L.L³⁰(imp.).RD.

24378.5 — [Anr. ed.] 4°. *R. Tottell,* 1576. L(tp only, Harl.1919/181). L³⁰(imp.).DALK.LINC.

24379 — [Anr. ed.] 4°. *R. Tottell,* 1577. L.O.; F.CU.

24380 — [Anr. ed.] Corrected, and newly augmented to a fourth part more. Newly set foorth. 4°. *H. Denham (the assigne of W. Seres,)* 1580. L.O(imp.).C.C²(frag.). RD.+; F.HN(imp.).HD.IND.WIS.+

24381 — [Anr. ed.] 1585. 4° in 8's. *in the now dwelling house of H. Denham,* [1585.] L.HETH(imp.).M.RD.; HN(imp., completed by 24385.5).

24382 — [Anr. ed.] 1586. 4° in 8's. *in the now dwelling house of H. Denham,* [1586.] C.C²².; F.HD.WIS.

24383 — [Anr. ed.] 1590. 4° in 8's. [*R. Yardley a. P. Short*] *f. the assignes of W. Seres,* [1590.] L.O.D⁶.E.P.+; WIS. Penrose 363.

24384 — [Anr. ed.] 1593. 4° in 8's. *R. Yardley a. P. Short,* [1593.] L.O.ETON(imp.).LEEDS.; HN.DAR.HD.WIS.

24385 — [Anr. ed.] 1597. 4° in 8's. *P. Short,* (1597.) O.HETH (imp.).M.STU.; Rutgers U.

24385.5 — [Anr. ed.] 1599. 4° in 8's. *P. Short,* (1599.) L.C²(imp.). RD.; F.HN(frag., including tp, completing 24381).BO.

Tusser, Thomas—*cont.*

24386 — [Anr. ed.] 4° in 8's. *Edinburgh, R. Walde-graue,* 1599. L.L[38].
Not signed in Waldegrave's manner.

24387 — [Anr. issue, w. cancel tp.] 1604. *f. the Co. of Statrs.,* [1604.] L.C.P.; HN.ILL.WIS. Hobart and William Smith Colleges, Geneva, N.Y.

24388 — [Anr. ed.] 1610. 4° in 8's. [*N. Okes*] *f. the Co. of Statrs.,* [1610.] L[30].D.NOR[2].RD.YK.+; F(2).HN.WIS.

24389 — [Anr. ed.] 4° in 8's. [*T. Purfoot*] *f. the Co. of Statrs.,* 1614. L.RD. London, Royal Agricultural Society.; F.PEN.

24390 — [Anr. ed.] 4° in 8's. [*T. Purfoot*] *f. the Co. of Statrs.,* 1620. Ent. to the English Stock 5 mr. L.L[16].O[7]. RD.SH.; F.HN.

24391 — [Anr. ed.] 4° in 8's. [*T. Purfoot*] *f. the Co. of Statrs.,* 1630. L.O.HETH(imp.).RD.; F(imp.).HD.LC.WIS.

24392 — [Anr. ed.] 4° in 8's. *J. O*[*kes*] *f. the Co. of Statrs.,* 1638. L.O.C[14].BHP.RD.+; F.HN.HD.NY.WIS.+

24393 **Tuvil** or **Toutevile, Daniel.** Asylum Veneris, or a sanctuary for ladies. Justly protecting them, from the foule aspersions of traducing spirits [cf. 23533]. [Init. D. T.] 8°. *E. Griffin f. L. L'isle,* 1616. Ent. 7 my. L[4].O.C[2].; F.HN.

24393.3 — Christian purposes and resolutions. [Init. D. T.] 12°. *f. S. Macham,* 1611. G[2].

24393.7 — [Anr. ed., w. dedic. signed in full.] 12°. [*W. Jaggard*] *f. T. Dewe,* 1622. HN.

24394 — The dove and the serpent. In which is conteined a description of such points as tend either to conversation, or negotiation. [Init. D. T.] 4°. *T. C*[*reede*] *f. L. L'isle,* 1614. Ent. 14 oc. 1613. L.C.C[2].LIV[3]. YK.+; F.HN.HD.ILL.N.+

24394a — [Anr. issue, w. cancel tp.] The dove, and the serpent. *T. C*[*reede*] *f. L. L'isle,* 1614. L.O.C[4].; F. Cincinnati U.
With a comma after 'dove'.

24395 — Essayes, morall and theologicall. [Init. D. T.] 12°. *J. W*[*indet*] *f. E. Edgar,* 1609. Ent. to Edgar, a. W. Burre 17 oc. 1608. L.L[30].ETON.; F.HN.N.PML.Y.+
Reprinted in 24397.

24396 — Essaies politicke, and morall. By D. T. gent. 8°. *H. L*[*ownes*] *f. M. Lownes,* 1608. Ent. 19 ap. L.L[30].O. C.E.+; F.HN.HD.N.Y.+
Sometimes attrib. to Dr. John Tovey, chaplain to John, Lord Harington, to whose wife this is dedicated.

24396.5 — S[t]. Pauls threefold cord: wherewith are combined, oeconomicall duties, betwixt husband. Wife. [etc.] 12°. *A. Griffin f. H. Seile,* 1635. Ent. 10 oc. L[4].O. C[5].D.; F.HD.
(Formerly 24153)

24397 — Vade mecum: a manuall of essayes morrall, theologicall. [Init. D. T.] 12°. [*N. Okes*] *f. J. S*[*pencer,*] *sold by J. Day,* 1629. Edgar's pt. ass'd as 'master Tuvalles essayes' to J. Hodgets 19 ap. 1613. L.O.C. C[3].PETYT.; F.HN.CHI.GRO.HD.
Reprints 24395. On A4[r] 'Anonym. Musophil.' mentions this was 'first composed by Mr. D. T.'

24398 — [Anr. ed., omitting preface and w. letterpress tp init. D. T.] 12°. [*G. Purslowe*] *f. J. S*[*pencer,*] *sold by J. Day a. D. Pakeman,* 1631. L.O.O[27].BUTE.DUL.; F.HN.HD.NY[7].
The engr. tp calls this 'A new edition wth some additions. *f. J. S*[*pencer,*] 1631.'

24399 — Third edition. 12°. *E. P*[*urslowe*] *f. J. S*[*pencer,*] *sold by B. Langford,* 1638. L.L[43].O.C.; F.HN.HD.ILL.N.+

Tweed, *River.* Tweeds tears of joy, to Charles great Brittains king. [1639.] *See* 15313.5.

Twells, William. Almanacks. 1637, etc. *See* 518.4 sqq.

Twine. *See* Twyne.

24400 **Twisse, William.** A briefe catecheticall exposition of christian doctrine. Divided into foure catechismes. [Anon.] 8°. *G. M*[*iller*] *f. R. Bird,* 1632. Ent. as by William Twisse 23 jn. 1631. L.; HN.

24401 — [Anr. ed.] 8°. *J. N*[*orton*] *f. R. Bird,* 1633. O.

24401.3 — [Anr. ed.] 8°. *G. M*[*iller*] *f. R. Bird,* 1636. L.
(Formerly 4138)

24401.7 — [Anr. ed.] 8°. *G. M*[*iller*] *f. R. Bird,* 1637. Y.

Twisse, William—*cont.*

24402 — A discovery of D. Jacksons vanitie. 4°. [*Amsterdam, successors of G. Thorp a. London, W. Jones,*] 1631. L.O.C.D.E[2].+; F.HN.ILL.U.Y.+
Jones pr. only the errata. An attack on Thomas Jackson, Dean of Peterborough.

24403 — The doctrine of the synod of Dort and Arles, reduced to the practise. [Anon.] 4°. [*Amsterdam, successors of G. Thorp,* 1631?] L.O.C[2].D.YK(imp.).+; F.HD. TORONTO[2].U.
Wing T 3420 is this ed.

24404 **Twittee, Thomas.** Ad clerum pro forma concio habita Martij 13. 1634. 4°. *Oxoniæ, L. Lichfield,* 1640. L.O.O[2].CARLISLE.; U.

24405 **Twyne, Brian.** Antiquitatis academiæ Oxoniensis apologia. In tres libros divisa. 4°. *Oxoniæ, J. Barnesius,* 1608. L.O.C.D.E.+; F.HN.HD.N.NY.+

24406 — [Anr. issue, w. cancel tp.] Ultima editio. *Oxoniæ, J. L*[*ichfield*] & *J. S*[*hort,*] 1620. L.O.O[15].O[17].M.; Y.
— *ed. See* 19005.

24407 **Twyne, John.** Joannis Twini Bolingdunensis, Angli, de rebus Albionicis, Britannicis atque Anglicis, commentariorum libri duo. [*Ed.*] Ad T. Twinum. 8°. *E. Bollifantus pro R. Watkins,* 1590. Ent. 15 jy. L.O.C.D.E.+; F.HN.HD.N.NY.+
Copies vary: M2 blank or w. errata on the recto; both at L. Possibly based in part on a MS. by Sir T. Elyot; *see Transactions of the Cambridge Bib. Soc.,* II (1957), pp. 352–8.
— *ed. See* 3186.

Twyne, Laurence, *tr. See* 709.

Twyne, Thomas. Almanacks. 1579, etc. *See* 518.8 sqq.

24408 — The garlande of godly flowers, bewtifully adorned. Yeeldyng foorth a sauour to the afflicted soule. Carefully collected, 1574. 8° in 4's. *W. How,* [1574.] L.L[30].O.; F.HN.

24409 — [Anr. ed.] The garlande of godlie flowers, (commonly called Twynes praiers,) carefully collected. Newly corrected, and augmented. 16° in 8's. (*H. Denham,*) *the assigne of W. Seres,* (1580.) L.

24409.5 — [Anr. ed.] 16° in 8's. (*P. S*[*hort,*] *by the assignes of W. Seres,* 1596.) L[30](lacks tp).

24410 — [Anr. ed.] 16° in 8's. *P. S*[*hort,*] *the assigne of W. Seres,* 1602. Ent. to the English Stock 5 mr. 1620. L.

24411 — The schoolemaster, or teacher of table philosophie. [Init. T. T. on U2[v].] 4°. *R. Jones,* 1576. O.E(lacks tp).ETON(imp.).; F(lacks tp).HN.HD(imp.).CHI[2].
Loosely based on the Mensa Philosophica attrib. to T. Anguilbertus and to Sir M. Scott; *see* also 22061.5.

24412 — [Anr. ed. Anon.] 4°. *R. Johnes,* 1583. Ent. to H. Gosson 22 de. 1632. L.O.G[2](lacks tp).; F.BO.ILL.Y.

24413 — A shorte and pithie discourse, concerning earthquakes. By T. T[wyne]. 4°. [*J. Charlewood f.*] *R. Johnes,* 1580. Ent. 11 ap. L.L[30].O.C[3].; F(2).HN.HD.
— A view of certain effects, of the comete. 1578. *See* 23629.
— *ed. See* 24407.
— *tr. See* 710, 4078, 6231, 6901, 7241, 16636, 19809, 24801.
— *See* also 23626.

Tychborne, Chidiock. Tychbornes lamentation. 1586. *See* 7605.

Tye, Christopher. The actes of the apostles, translated into Englyshe metre by C. Tye. [1553?] *See* 2983.8 sqq.

24414 **Tye, William.** A matter of moment: or, a case of waight. To be pleaded in the heart of every christian before the Lords supper. Set forth dialogue wise. 8°. *R. Raworth f. H. Bell,* 1608. Ent. 1 fb. L[2].C.

24414.5 — [Anr. issue, w. cancel tp, w. imprint:] [*N. Okes*] *f. H. Bell,* 1608. P(imp.).

Tyler, Margaret. The mirrour of princely deedes. [1578, etc.] *See* 18859 sqq.

24415 **Tymme, Thomas.** A booke, containing the kings of England. 1597. = 23626.

24415a — The chariot of devotion. [A treatise.] 8°. *G. Eld f. T. Baylie,* 1618. Ent. 9 jn. L.O.; F.

Tymme, Thomas—*cont.*

24416 — A dialogue philosophicall. Wherein natures secret closet is opened, and the cause of all motion shewed. 4°. *T. S[nodham] f. C. Knight*, 1612. Ent. 16 ja. L.O.C⁹.D².G².+; F.LC.PEN.WIS. Horblit.+
　Copies vary: in title 'philosophicall' is in lower case italics, or in italic caps.; both at L.

24417 — The figure of Antichriste, with the tokens of the end of the world, most plainly disciphered by a catholike exposition of the seconde epistle to the Thessalonians. 8°. [*T. Dawson*] *f. F. Coldocke*, 1586. Ent. 31 ja. L.L².DUL.

24418 — A plaine discouerie of ten English lepers, verie noisome [*sic*] to the church and common wealth. [i.e. schismatics, church robbers, etc.] 4°. *P. Short*, 1592. Ent. to J. Wolfe 13 ja.; to Short 5 my. L.O.C.C³.P.+; F(3, 1 imp.).HN. CHI.STAN.U(lacks tp.).

24419 — The poore mans pater noster, with a preparatiue to praier: wherto are annexed diuers psalmes and meditations. Newly imprinted the second time. 16° in 8's. *P. Short*, 1598. Ent. to Short a. R. Yardley 5 jy. 1591. L.

24420 — A preparation against the prognosticated dangers of this yeare, 1588. 8°. *J. Wolfe*, 1588. Ent. 14 de. 1587. F.
— The schoole of wisedome. 1601. *See* 2759.5.

24421 — A silver watch-bell. The sound wherof is able to win the worldling, to become a true christian. Whereunto is annexed, a treatise of the Lords supper. [Anon.] 8°. *T. C[reede] f. W. Cotton*, 1605. Ent. 11 oc. 1604. F.BR.

24422 — [Anr. ed. Init. T. T.] Third time imprinted and enlarged. 8°. [*W. Jaggard, T. Creede? a. G. Eld*] *f. W. Cotton*, 1606. O⁹.C.G².YK.; F.Y.
　Jaggard pr. 1st A, B–D, F–G, O–S; Eld pr. H–N; anr. pr. or compositor, poss. T. Creede, pr. 2nd A and E.

24422.5 — Fourth time imprinted. 8°. *H. L[ownes] f. W. Cotton*, 1607. BTL.

24423 — Fift time imprinted: and now newly perused and amended. 8°. [*W. Jaggard*] *f. W. Cotton*, 1608. O.DUL.; HN.AAS.HD(tp only).ILL.

24424 — [Anr. ed.] By T. Timme. Seauenth time imprinted. 8°. *T. Snodham f. C. Knight*, 1610. Ass'd 27 no. 1609. L³⁸(2).; F.

24424.7 — Ninth impression. 8°. *H. Lownes f. C. Knight*, 1613. F.

24425 — Tenth impression. 8°. [*H. Lownes*] *f. C. Knight*, 1614. L.C.; F.HD(w. tp to 24432).LC.U.

24426 — Eleventh impression. 8°. [*T. Purfoot*] *f. C. Knight*, 1616. C(2, 1 imp.).WOR.; F.LC.

24427 — Twelfth impression. 8°. [*T. Purfoot*] *f. C. Knight*, 1617. L.

24428 — Thirteenth impression. 8°. [*T. Purfoot*] *f. C. Knight*, 1619. E⁴.; F.

24429 — Fourteenth impression. 8°. [*T. Purfoot*] *f. C. Knight*, 1621. L(tp only, w. sheets of 24432).L³⁸.E⁴.LEIC².; F.

24429.5 — Fifteenth impression. 8°. [*T. Purfoot*] *f. C. Knight*, 1625. C(imp.).E².; F.NYS.

24430 — Sixteenth impression. 8°. *Aberdene, E. Raban*, 1627. Private owner.

24431 — [Anr. ed.] Sixteenth impression. 8°. [*T. Purfoot*] *f. T. Knight*, 1630. Ass'd 12 oc. 1629. L.O.C.C².STU.+; F.

24431a — Seauenteenth impression. 8°. *Aberdene, E. Raban*, 1630. A.; F(imp.).

24432 — [Anr. ed.] Seventeenth impression. 8°. *T. Harper f. T. Knight*, 1634. L(2, 1 w. tp of 24429). O.LAMPORT. M⁴.; F.HN.HD(imp.).N.Y.+

24433 — Eighteenth impression. 8°. *J. Haviland f. T. Alchorn*, 1638. Ass'd 8 mr. 1636. L(imp.).O.C.C¹²(imp.).; F.ILL.NY¹¹.U.

24434 — [Anr. ed., w. additions.] Eighteenth impression. (Certaine godly rules concerning christian practise.) 8°. *E. P[urslowe] f. T. Knight*, 1640. Ass'd 23 mr. 1639. L.M².; F.HN.U.Y.
— *ed. See* 12448.
— *tr. See* 152, 2759.5, 3601, 4393, 4400, 7276, 17404, 17405, 17406, 22241, 22241.5, 22243.

24435 **Tyndal,** *Sir* **John.** A true relation of a most desperate murder, committed upon sir J. Tindall . . . by J. Barterham gent: which Barterham afterwards hanged himselfe. 4°. *E. All-de f. L. L[isle,]* 1617. Ent. to Lisle 26 no. 1616. L.L⁸.O.HAT.; F.HD(impr. def.).
　(Formerly also 14055) For anr. account of the murder, *see* 14054.

24435.5 **Tyndale, Nathaniel.** The penitent sonnes teares, for his murdered mother. By N. Tyndale, a prisoner now in New-gate.—The much-afflicted mothers teares, for her drowned daughter. [By] A. Musket, the wofull mother. [In verse.] s.sh.fol. *f. J. Trundle*, [1624.] Ent. to R. Hodgkinson 2 jy. 1624. L⁵(Lemon 243).

24436 **Tyndale, William.** The whole workes of W. Tyndall, John Frith, and Doct. Barnes. [*Ed.*] (J. Foxe.) fol. *J. Daye*, 1573 (1572.) L.O.C.D.E.+; F.HN.HD.N.NY.+
　Several copies (L⁸, C⁴, 2 F, 1 HN, HD) have the gen. tp dated 1572 and altered in ink to 1573.

24437 — An answere vnto sir Thomas Mores dialoge [18084]. 8°. [*Antwerp, S. Cock*, 1531.] L.C.D.; F.
　Answered by 18079, 18080.
— A briefe declaration of the sacraments. [1548?] *See* 24445.

24438 — A compendious introduccion, prologe or preface vn to the pistle off Paul to the Romayns. [Anon.] 8°. [*Worms, P. Schoeffer*, 1526.] O.

24438.5 — [Anr. ed.] 16° in 8's. *J. Charlewood*, 1564. Ent. 1563–64. L².

24439 — = 24440.

24440 — An exposicion vppon the. v. vi. vij. chapters of Mathew. [Init. W. T.] 8°. [*Antwerp, J. Grapheus?* 1533?] L(tp facs., imp.).C.M.; F.NY.
　Collates a–p⁸.

24441 — [Anr. ed.] ⟨A⟩n exposi⟨tion v⟩pon th⟨e⟩ v. vi. vij. chapt⟨er⟩s of Mathew⟨ ⟩ 8°. [*R. Redman*, 1536?] L(F3–6 only).; F(tp def.).
　Collates A–N⁸ O⁶ P⁴; leaf signatures have roman numerals.

24441.3 — [Anr. ed.] An exposycyon vpon the. v. vi. vij. chapters of Mathewe. 8°. [*R. Redman*, 1536?] L(F1–3 only). L².O.C(F2, G3 only).
　Collates A–N⁸ O⁶ P⁴; leaf signatures have arabic numerals.

24441.7 — [Anr. ed.] An exposycyon vpō the. v. vi. & vij. chapters of Mathewe. 8°. [*R. Redman*, 1537?] D(imp.).M.; F.CAL⁶.
　Collates A–O⁸.

24441a — [Anr. ed., signed in full.] An exposiciō vpon [etc.] Newly set furth according to his first copy. 1548. 8°. *J. Day a. W. Seres*, [1548.] O²¹.C(2).G².LINC.M.

24442 — [Anr. ed.] An exposicion vpon [etc.] Newly set forth and corrected. 8°. (*W. Hill,*) [1549?] L.O(col. def.). C.C³.M.+; HN.HD.N.PML.

24443 — The exposition of the fyrste epistle of seynt Jhon with a prologge before it: by W. T[yndale.] 8°. [*Antwerp, M. de Keyser,*] (1531 (se.)) L.M.; F.

24443.5 — [Anr. ed., anon., with added expositions on II and III John by L. Ridley, also anon.] 8°. [*Southwark, J. Nicholson*, 1537?] O(imp.).
　B3ʳ last line begins: 'haue handled of . . .'

24444 — [Anr. ed.] The exposition of the fyrste, seconde, and thyrde epistles of S. Jhon. 8°. *Southwarke, J. Nicolson*, [1538.] L¹⁵(imp.).O.O³.D.P.
　Dated 1538 in the tp compartment. B3ʳ last line begins: 'sawe wyth oure . . .'.
— A fruitefull and godly treatise expressing the right institution and vsage of the sacramentes. [1533?] No copy survives.

24445 — [Anr. ed.] A briefe declaration of the sacraments. 8°. *R. Stoughton*, [1548?] L.O.C.D.M.+; F.HN.HD.N.U.+

24446 — The obediē/ce of a Christen man and how Chr/istē rulers ought to governe,/ [etc.] 8°. (*Marlborow in the lāde of Hesse, H. luft* [i.e. *Antwerp, J. Hoochstraten,*] 1528 (2 oc.)) L.O.C².E(lacks tp).M.+; F.CH(lacks tp). Y(lacks tp).
　See also 5189.7.

24447 — [Anr. ed.] The Obe-/dience of a Christen man,/ and how Christen rulers ought to go-/uerne, [etc.] Newly printed and diligently corrected M.D.XXXV. 8°. (*Marlborow in the lande of Hesse, H. luft* [i.e. *Antwerp, H. Peetersen van Middelburch?*] 1535 (29 oc.)) L.C.C²(imp.).E(imp.).M.+; F.HN.HD(lacks tp). NY.U.
　The printing of this and the following ed. was formerly attrib. to J. Hoochstraten.

24447.3 — [Anr. ed.] The Obe/dience of a christen mā/ and howe Christen rulers ought to/ gouerne, [etc.] Newly printed and diligently corrected MDXXXvi. 8°. (*Marlborow in the lande of Hesse, H. luft,* [i.e. *Antwerp, H. Peetersen van Middelburch?*] 1537 (11 de.)) O³(imp.).M(2).; BO(imp.).

Tyndale, William—*cont.*

24447.7 — [Anr. ed.] The obedyence of a/ Chrysten man: and/ howe Chrysten rulers ought to go-/uerne, [etc.] 4° in 8's. [*London*, 1537?] L(C.37.e.24, imp.).O.C.D.; F.CAL²(imp.).CAL⁶(lacks tp).HD(lacks tp).Y.
(Formerly 24452) A2ʳ last line: 'with'. When filmed (Univ. Microfilms reel 156, '24452') the L copy had inserted the tp to 24448, which has now been removed. The F copy (reel 670 '24448ᵃ') has had a triangle drawn in ink around the title. Possibly issued w. 24455.5.

24448 — [Anr. ed.] THE/ Obedyence of/ A Christian man: And how christen/ Rulers ought to gouerne: [etc.] 4° in 8's. [*W. Hill*, 1548.] L(C.25.d.11).O.C⁶.DUR⁵.M.+; F.HN.BO⁶.CAL²(lacks tp).Y.
Title varies; as above, or: 'THE O/BedyEnce of/'; both now in the L copy. A2ʳ last line: 'wyth'.

24449 — = 24450.

24450 — [Anr. ed.] The Obe-/dience of [*sic*, no 'a'] Christen/ man, & how christē/ rulers ought to gouerne,/ [etc.] 8°. (*T. Ranalde a. W. Hyll, solde by R. Jugge*,) [1548?] L(imp.).O(imp.).C(2, lacking tp).E⁴.NEK.+; F(imp.).NY¹¹.
B3 is a cancel in some copies; orig. B3ʳ line 2 from bottom: 'mercy'; the cancel: 'mercye'; both at C.

24451 — [Anr. ed.] The O/bediēce of a Chri-/sten man, and how/ christen rulers ought to/ gouerne, [etc.] 8°. (*W. Coplande, in Fletstrete*,) [1548?] L.O(imp.).C². D.M.+; F.HN.HD(tp only, inserted in 24447.7).N.Y.

24452 — Now = 24447.7.

24453 — [Anr. ed.] The O/bedyence of a Chry-/sten man, and howe/ christen rulers ought to/ gouerne, [etc.] 8°. (*W. Coplande*, 1561.) L.O.C.E(imp.).M.+; F.HN.BO⁵. ILL.U(imp.).+

24454 — [The parable of the wicked mammon. Begin A1ʳ:] That fayth the mother of all good workes iustifieth vs, [etc.] 8°. (*Malborowe in the londe off hesse, H. luft* [i.e. *Antwerp, J. Hoochstraten,*] 1528 (8 my.)) L.; F.NY.PML.

— [Anr. ed.] 1528. See 24455.5.

24455 — [Anr. ed.] A treatyse of the iustificacyon by faith only, otherwise called the parable of the wyked mammon. 8°. (*Southwarke, f.* [i.e. by] *J. Nycolson*, 1536.) L.

24455.5 — [Anr. ed.] The parable of the wycked mammō . . . lately corrected. 4° in 8's. (*Malborowe in the lande of Hesse, H. Luft*, 1528 (8 my.)) [i.e. *London*, 1537?] L(imp.).O.C.E⁴.M.+; HN.CAL⁶(lacks col.).SMU.Y. Scheide.
(Formerly 24460) From the state of the tp comp. (McK. & F. 16) this was pr. between 1535 and Oct. 1537. Possibly issued w. 24447.7.

24456 — [A ghost.]

24457 — [Anr. ed.] The parable of the wycked mammon. 8°. *J. daye*, 1547. L(2).O.C.BUTE.NEK.; F.NY¹¹.

24458 — [Anr. ed.] Lately corrected. 4° in 8's. (*W. hill*,) [1548] (15 se.) L.O.DUR⁵.M.P.+; F.HN.BO.ILL.U.

24459 — [Anr. ed.] 8°. *W. Copland*, 1549. L.O.O⁸.D.M.+; F.HD.N.NY.Y.

— [Anr. ed.] The parable of the wycked mammō. 1528 [1537?] Now = 24455.5.

24460 — [Anr. ed.] 8°. (*w. Coplande in the Vyntre vpon the thre krayned warfe*,) [1561?] L.O⁹.C¹⁰.M.P.+; F.BO⁶. CAL⁶.CH.

24461 — A path way īto the holy scripture. [Anon.] 8°. (*Thomas Godfray*,) [1536?] C³.
A2ʳ last line: 'oure'. This may be the later ed. Reprinted from the prologue of 2823.

24462 — [Anr. ed.] 8°. (*Tho. Godfray*,) [1536?] F.
A2ʳ last line: 'our'. This may be the earlier ed.

24464 — [Anr. ed.] 16° in 8's. *J. Charlwood*, 1564. Ent. 1563–64. L².

24465 — The practyse of prelates. [Init. W. T.] 8°. *marborch* [i.e. *Antwerp, J. Hoochstraten*,] 1530. L.O.C.G².M.+; F.HN.HD(lacks K10).N.NY.+
An ed. after 1553 'wᵗ the augmentacions of J. Bale, & a plentuouse table in yᵉ ende therof' is announced on H4ʳ of 11587.

24466 — [Anr. ed.] Compyled by W. Tyndale. 8°. *A. Scoloker a. W. Seres*, 1548. L.O¹⁷.D.G².

24467 — [Anr. issue, w. quire a reprinted, w. imprint:] *A. Scoloker a. W. Seres*, [1549?] L.O.C¹⁰.M.NEK.+; F.N.Y.

24468 — The souper of the Lorde. . . . wheryn incidently M. Moris letter agenst J. Frythe [18090] is confuted. [Anon.] 8°. (*Nornburg, N. twonson*, [i.e. *Antwerp?*]

Tyndale, William—*cont.*

1533 (5 ap.)) [or *London, N. Hill?* 1546?] O.C. BUTE.M.; F.
Answered by 18077. While this ed. answers More's description in the preface and beginning of 18077 of a 'new come ouer boke' of 32 leaves, the initial 'W' is used by N. Hill on A3ʳ of 2083 and Cc3ʳ of 5071, so that 24468 may be a reprint of the original ed., including the imprint; cf. 24455.5.

24468a — = 24469–24471.

24469 — [Anr. ed.] The supper of the Lorde after the true meanyng of the sixte of Johñ and the. xi. of the fyrst epistle to the Corhinthiās, wher vnto is added an epystle to the reader. 8°. [n.p.] 1533 (5 ap.) [i.e. *London*, 1547?] L.O(2).C(2).M(2). Stevens Cox.; F(2). HN.NY.Y. Vermont U.
Text ends E6ʳ. Added epistle signed by R. Crowley.

24470 — [Anr. ed.] The supper of the Lorde.[with stop] . . . epystle to the Corhinthis [see note]. 8°. [n.p.] 1533 (5 ap.) [i.e. *J. Day?* 1547?] L².O.D(imp.).M.; F.HN.BO.
Ends E4ᵛ. With Crowley's preface, but without his name. Tp varies; originally line 5 began: 'rhinthiās' (D); the 'ā' was pulled out accidentally, producing 'rhinthis' (O, M, F, BO); it was then corrected to 'rynthians' (L²).

24471 — [Anr. ed.] The supper of the Lorde.[with stop] . . . epistle to the Corhinthiās. 8°. [n.p.] 1533 (5 ap.) [i.e. *J. Day?* 1547?] L.; F.
Ends E4ᵛ. With Crowley's preface, and signed by him.

— *ed.* See 20036, 24045.
— *tr.* See 2066, 2350, 2788, 2823, 10479.
— See also 24167.

24472 **Tynley, Robert.** Two learned sermons. . . . Preached, the one at Paules Crosse. The other at the Spittle. 4°. *W. Hall f. T. Adams*, 1609. L.L¹³.O.O¹².BURY.; HN.CAL.CAL².MIN.U.
Attacks 19408, 18746.

24473 **Typing, William.** A discourse of eternitie. Collected and composed for the common good, by W. T[yping.] 4°. *Oxford, J. Lichfield f. W. Webbe*, 1633. O.O²⁸ (Bed.).C³.C⁵.A.+; F(imp.).CHI.HD.N.PN².+
Tp has device McK. 408 with lady at bottom.

24473.3 — [Anr. issue, w. ¶⁴ cancelled and cancel tp.] *Oxford, J. Lichfield f. W. Webbe*, 1633 [i.e. *Oxford, W. Turner, c.* 1640?] L.ETON.
Tp has device McK. 407 w. rose and thistle at bottom.

24473.7 — ⟨A return of⟩ thankfullnesse, or a thankfull remembrance of Gods mercy. By Mʳ W. T[yping.] 8°. *Oxford, L. Lichfield, sold by T. Wilkins*, [*London*,] 1640. O(frag.).

24474 **Tyrell, Anthony.** A fruitfull sermon preached in Christschurch the 13. of Julie. 1589. Conteining an admonition vnto vertue, and a dehortation from vice. Taken by characterye. 8°. *J. Windet, sold by Abraham Kitson*, [1589.] Ent. to Windet 30 se. 1589. L.C.BUTE.E.; HN.
— The recantation. 1588. See 23858.5.

24475 **Tyrer, Ralph.** Five godlie and learned sermons, preached at Kendall by R. T. bachiler of divinitie. 8°. *J. H[arrison 3,] f. J. Harison* [1,] 1602. Ent. as by 'Raffe Tiroll' to J. Harrison 3 on 6 my. C(tp only).
This is presumably the orig. tp, cancelled in the following.

24475.5 — [Anr. issue, w. tp cancelled and new prelims.] Five godlie sermons, preached by R. T. bachiler of divinitie. *J. H[arrison 3,] f. J. Harison* [1,] 1602. L.L¹⁵.C¹⁰.E².; F.
All copies have A1 cancelled.

24476 **Tyrie, James.** The refutation of ane ansuer made be schir Johne Knox. 8°. *Parisiis, ap. T. brumenium*, 1573. L.O.O⁶.E.E².+; F.PML.
A&R 832. Includes Tyrie's orig. letter, Knox's answer reprinted from 15062, and Tyrie's refutation.

Tyrius, Maximus. See 20612.7.

24477 **Tyro, T.** Tyros roring megge. Planted against the walles of melancholy. (The meane in spending.) *Eng. a. Lat.* [Partly in verse.] 4°. *V. Simmes,* 1598. L(imp.). O(1, plus Meane only).; HN.
(17760 is pt. of this)

Tyrone, *Earl of. See* 18813, 18814.

24477.5 **Tyrwhit,** *Lady* **Elizabeth.** Morning and euening prayers, with diuers psalmes himnes and meditations. 32° in

Tyrwhit, *Lady* **Elizabeth**—*cont.*
8's. *H. Middelton f. C. Barker,* (1574.) Ent. 1569–70. L(Dept. of Medieval Antiquities).
Reprinted w. alterations in Lamp 2 of 1892.

Tyrwhit, William, *tr. See* 18003.

24478 **Tyson, John.** The Lancashire wonder, to warn all sinners to repentance. Being a true account of Mr. Jeremiah Carter. [c. 1700.]
Not an STC book.

U

24479   **Ubaldini, Petruccio.** Parte prima delle breui dimostra-
tioni, et precetti ne i quale si trattano diuersi pro-
positi morali, politici, & iconomici. 4°. [*R. Field*,]
1592. Ent. to R. Field 6 de. 1591. L.C³.HAT.;
F.HD.

24480   — Descrittione del regno di Scotia. fol. *Anuersa* [i.e.
London, J. Wolfe,] 1588 (1 ja.) Ent. to J. Wolfe
27 no. 1587. L.O.C².E.G².+; F.HN.HD.MIN.NY.+
    Freely *tr.* from 3203.

24481   — A discourse concerninge the Spanishe fleete inuadinge
Englande 1588 . . . written in Italian and *tr.* for A.
Ryther: vnto the wch discourse are annexed certaine
tables. 4°. (*A. Hatfield*,) *solde at the shoppe of A.
Ryther*, (1590.) Ent. to J. Wolfe 13 oc. L.L².O(lacks
tp).C⁵.C⁶.+; F(lacks E2).BO.HD. Penrose 261.
    The 'tables', i.e. engravings, were issued sepa-
rately as 24481a.

24481a   — Expeditionis Hispanorum in Angliam vera descriptio
Anno Do: MDLXXXVIII. [Engr. by A. Ryther
after designs by R. Adams.] fol. [*London*, 1590.]
Ent. to J. Wolfe 13 oc. 1590. L(2, one: Maps
C.7.c.1, the other: Print Dept.).L³³.C⁵.C⁶. London,
Royal Geographical Society (2 imp.).; HN.
    See Hind I.142–9; the L Maps copy and one
R.G.S. are bd. w. 21805.5.

24482   — Militia del gran duca di Thoscana. 4°. [*R. Field*,] 1597.
L.C.HAT.

24483   — Rime di Petruccio Vbaldino. 4°. [*R. Field*,] 1596.
L.LINC.; PFOR.

24484   — Scelta di alcune attioni, . . . occorsi tra alcune nationi
differenti del mondo. 4°. [*R. Field*,] 1595. L.C.
HAT(2).; HD.Y.

24485   — Lo stato delle tre corti. Della corte Romana, di
Napoli, & del gran duca di Thoscana. 4°. [*R. Field*,
1594.] L.O.O⁵.C².HAT.+
    Preface dated 1 Jan. 1594.

24486   — La vita di Carlo Magno imperadore. 4°. *G. Wolfio*,
1581. Ent. 17 ja. L.O.C.D.E.+; F.HN.HD.ILL.Y.

24487   — [Anr. ed.] Di nueuo corretta. 4°. [*R. Field*,] 1599.
L.O.E².LINC(lacks tp).M.; F.HD.Y.

24487.5   — Le vite delle donne illustri. del regno d'Inghilterra, &
del regno di Scotia. 4°. [*J. Wolfe*,] 1591. Ent. to
J. Wolfe 23 jy. 1590. O.C¹⁷.; Y.

24488   — [Anr. issue, w. added dedic. to Queen Elizabeth, w.
imprint:] *G. Volfio*, 1591. L.O.C.E.LINC(lacks tp).+;
F.HN.HD.TEX.Y.+
    Most copies have the orig. tp (A1) cancelled; still
present in one L(137.b.1) and E. The other L(G.
1364) and 1 copy each at O, HD lack A⁴.

24489   **Udall, John.** Amendment of life: three sermons, vpon
Actes 2. verses 37.38. 8°. [*J. Windet?*] *f. T. Man,
W. B[rome] a. N. L[ing,]* 1584. L. Stevens Cox.

24490   — [Anr. ed.] 8°. *R. Walde-graue f. T. Man a. T. Gubbins*,
1588. L.O.DUL.E.YK.; F.CU.HD.ILL. Goucher College,
Baltimore, Maryland (imp.).*

24491   — Certaine sermons, taken out of seuerall places of
scripture. 8°. *A. Islip f. T. Man*, 1596. L.O.C.D.YK.
+; CHI.HD.PH.U.Y.+
    Reprints 24503, 24489, 24507, 24492, 24501.

24492   — The combate betwixt Christ and the deuill. Foure
sermons. 8°. *R. Walde-graue f. T. Man a. W. Brome*,
[1588?] L.O. London, Sir John Soane's Museum.;
F.LC.PN².

24493   — [Anr. ed.] 8°. *T. Orwin f. T. Man a. T. Gubbin*, 1589.
O⁹.DUL(imp.).E.; F.HD.U.

24494   — A commentarie vpon the Lamentations of Jeremy.
[Anon.] 4°. *Widdow Orwin f. T. Man*, 1593. L⁴.O.
C.M⁴.YK(tp def.).+; F.HN.CHI.HD(imp.).Y.+
    In this and the following eds. sheet B is a set of 3
folding leaves w. an analysis of the contents. In
the present ed. the 1st leaf is signed 'B' and
the 3rd '¶'.

Udall, John—*cont.*

24495   — [Anr. ed.] 4°. *P. Short f. T. Man*, 1595. L.O.SCL.STU.
Lord Kenyon.; F.BO³.HD.U.

24496   — [Anr. ed.] 4°. *F. Kingston f. T. Man*, 1599. L(imp.).C.
HETH.; F.TORONTO².

24497   — [Anr. ed.] 4°. *T. C[reede] f. T. Man*, 1608. L.L².L³.D.
PLUME.; F(imp.).HD(imp.).NY.U.Y.

24498   — [Anr. ed.] 4°. [*T. Harper f.*] *assignes of Joane Man a.
B. Fisher*, 1637. L.C.

24498.5   — [A variant.] By J. Udall. [*T. Harper f.*] *assignes of
Joane Man a. B. Fisher f. P. Stephens a. C. Meredith*,
1637. L³.L¹³.O.O².E.+; F(imp.).CAL².HD.U.

24499   — A demonstration of the trueth of that discipline which
Christe hath prescribed for the gouernement of
his church. [Anon.] 8° in 4's. [*East Molesey, R.
Waldegrave*, 1588.] L.O.C.D.E.+; F.HART².HD(imp.).
U.Y.+
    Answered by 20881. Udall tried and imprisoned
for writing this; *see* references in *DNB*.

24500   — [Anr. ed. In title 'Christ'. 1593?] = pt. 2 of 10400.
  — . . . the key of the holy tongue: [etc.] All Englished by
J. Udall. 1593. *See* 17523.

24501   — Obedience to the gospell. Two sermons, conteining
fruteful matter, both of doctrine, and exhortation.
[On Luke ii.15–20.] 8°. [*J. Windet?*] *f. T. Man,
W. B[rome] a. N. L[ing,]* 1584. L. Stevens Cox.

24502   — [Anr. ed.] 8°. *T. Orwin f. T. Man*, 1588. O.O⁹.DUL.
E.YK.; F.HD.

24503   — Peters fall. Two sermons vpon the historie of Peters
denying Christ. [On Matt. xxvi.34–5, 72–4 and
Luke xxii.54–8, 60–2.] 8°. *J. Windet a. T. Judson f.
N. Lyng*, 1584. L.L².; F(2).

24503.3   — [Anr. issue, w. cancel tp:] Peters fall. A godlie sermon:
vpon the historie [etc.] *f. J. Perin*, 158(5?) P(imp.).

24503.7   — [Anr. ed.] Peters fall. Two sermons. 8°. *R. Walde-graue
f. T. Man*, [c. 1585.] L.PLUME.; TORONTO².

24504   — [Anr. ed.] 8°. [*R. Waldegrave*] *f. T. Man*, [1587?]
L.O.E.YK.; F.HN(imp.).HD.

24504.5   — [Anr. ed.] 8°. *T. Dawsonne f. T. Man*, 1589. O⁹.

24505   — The state of the church of Englande, laide open in a
conference betweene Diotrephes a Byshop, Tertullus
a Papist, [etc. Anon.] 8° in 4's. [*R. Waldegrave*,
1588.] L.L²(3).O(imp.).E.; Y(missing)*.
    (Formerly also 19609) *See* Greg, *Register B*,
pp. 27–8.

24506   — [Anr. ed.] 8° in 4's. [*R. Waldegrave*, 1588.] L³.O⁸.C.; Y.
    In title: 'Bishop'.

24506a   — [Anr. ed.] 8° in 8's. [*R. Waldegrave*, 1588.] L².O.STU.
    In title: 'Byshopp' and 'Papiste'.

24507   — The true remedie against famine and warres. Fiue
sermons vpon the firste chapter of Joel, . . . preached
1586. 8°. *R. Walde-graue f. T. Man a. T. Gubbins*,
[1588.] Ent. 6 mr. 1588. L.O.C.E.G².+; F.HD.

———

  —A remonstrance: or plaine detection of faults in A
demonstration of discipline. 1590. *See* 20881.

Udall, Nicholas. A new enterlude called Thersytes.
[1562?] *See* 23949.

24508   — [Ralph Roister Doister.] 4°. [*H. Denham f. T. Hacket?*
1566?] Ent. to T. Hacket 1566–67. ETON(lacks tp).
Greg 46.
  — *ed. See* 2854, 2866.
  — *tr. See* 10443, 11715.5, 23899, 24665.

24508.3   **Udall, Thomas.** A briefe replie of Thomas Udall, gent.
to a short memorandum, or shew of answere against
his booke intituled: A briefe view . . . by B. C.
student in divinitie. 8°. *W. S[tansby] f. S. Macham*,
109 [i.e. 1609.] Ent. 21 au. 1609. F.
    Answers 25972.2.

Udall, Thomas—*cont.*

24508.5 — A briefe viewe of the weake grounds of popery; as it was propounded to D. Norrice, priest, by T. V. gent. 8°. *H. Lownes f. S. Macham a. M. Cooke*, 1606. Ent. 11 oc. L⁴.O.C.P.; U.
(Formerly 24567) Answered by 25972.2.

24508.7 **Udall, William.** The historie of the life and death of Mary Stuart. fol. *J. Haviland f. R. Whitaker*, 1624. Ent. to W. Barret a. Whitaker 29 ja. D.D⁶.PARIS.; F.PML.
(Formerly 24509b) The dedic. is signed by Udall. This is largely a *tr.* of the relevant passages in 4496.

24509 — [Anr. issue, w. cancel dedic. signed W. Stranguage, *pseud.*] *J. Haviland f. W. Barret*, 1624. O.O¹³.C⁵. BUTE.WOR.; PML.
In the O¹³ copy the orig. dedic. has been used as an endpaper.

24509a — [A variant, w. same cancel dedic. and imprint:] *J. Haviland f. R. Whitaker*, 1624. L.O.C.D².E.+; F.HN. HD.N.PML.+

24509b — Now = 24508.7.

24510 — [Anr. ed., w. dedic. signed by Udall.] 12°. *J. Haviland, sold by W. Sheares*, 1636. Ass'd to J. Parker 3 ap. L.O.C.D.E.+; F.HN.HD.NY.Y.+
Some copies (O, HD) have letterpress tp only; most (L, G², 3 F, NY¹¹) have engr. tp also.

24511 — [Anr. issue, w. letterpress tp cancelled and w. only the engr. tp.] *f. W. Sheares*, [1636.] O.

24512 **Udny, Alexander.** A golden bell, and a pomgranate. A sermon. 4°. *A. M[athewes] a. J. N[orton] f. A. Uphill*, 1625. Ent. 17 fb. L.O.C².D.NLW.+; F.HN.HD.PN².Y.

24513 — The voyce of the cryer. Delivered in two sermons. 4°. *T. C[otes] f. S. Cartwright*, 1628. Ent. 23 oc. 1627. O.A.BTL.; F.Y.

24513a — [A variant, w. imprint:] *T. C[otes] f. J. Bowler*, 1628. L.L³.NOR².P.; F.HN.HD(imp.).

24514 **Ulric, Saint, Bp.** An epistel of moche learnīg, sent by saint Huldericus, vnto Nicolas bysshoppe of Rome, agaynst the vnmaried chastitie of pryests. 8°. [*London?* 1547?] L.O.O⁵(frag.).C.; F.
In the same 95 mm. textura types as 17627 and 20795, with s³, wˢᵇ, W¹², Y⁵, and a distinctive ſh ligature. 17627 has three woodcut initials used by A. Scoloker, though he is not recorded by Isaac as using the types. Possibly printed by Scoloker or an unidentified predecessor of his. See also 17517.

24515 **Ulster.** A collection of such orders and conditions, as are to be observed by the undertakers, upon the distribution of the eschaeted lands in Ulster. 4°. *R. Barker*, 1608. L.L³⁸.O.C².D.+; F.HN.HD.
C1 partly reset; C1ʳ line 16: 'yeeres' or 'yeres'; both at L.

24515.5 — [Anr. ed.] 4°. *Edinburgh, T. Finlason*, 1609. E.

24516 — Conditions to be observed by the Brittish undertakers of the escheated lands in Ulster. 4°. *R. Barker*, 1610. L.L³⁰.O.C.D⁶.+; F.HN.MCG.Y.
With some parallels to 24515, but essentially a different text.

Ulysses. Ulysses upon Aiax. 1596. See 12782.

Uncasing. The uncasing of heresie. 1624. See 13.

24517 **Underdowne, Thomas.** The excellent historye of Theseus and Ariadne. [In verse.] 8°. *R. Johnes*, 1566 (28 ja.) Ent. 1565–66. M.
— *tr. See* 13041, 18949.

24518 **Underhill, John.** Newes from America; or, a new discoverie of New England; containing, a true relation of their war-like proceeding these two yeares last past, with a figure [map] of the Indian fort. 4°. *J. D[awson] f. P. Cole*, 1638. Ent. 26 ap. L.C².C³. C⁶.G².; HN.HD.LC.N.NY.+
HN has map in facsimile; HD has defective map, and LC lacks it.

24519 **Underwood, Robert.** A new anatomie. Wherein the body of man is compared: 1 To a household. 2 To a cittie. With divers approved medicines, wittie, and pleasant to be read. [In verse.] 4°. [*W. White*] *f. W. Jones* [2,] 1605. F(imp.).LC.

24519.5 — [Anr. issue, w. prelims. cancelled and new title:] The little world. Or, a lively description of all the partes of man. By Ro. Vn. bachelor of divinitie. [*W. White*] *f. W. Jones* [2,] 1612. HN.
This has been erroneously attrib. to R. Vaughan.

Undo. Here begynneth vndo your dore. [1520?] *See* 23111.5.

United Provinces. *See* Netherlands (18437, 18450, 18454, etc.)

Unreasonableness. The unreasonablenesse of the separation. 1614. *See* 3532.

24520 **Unton, Sir Henry.** Funebria nobilissimi ac præstantissimi equitis, D. H. Untoni, à musis Oxoniensibus apparata. [In verse. *Ed. R. Wright.*] 4°. *Oxoniæ, J. Barnesius*, 1596. O.; Lewis.
'Liber ad Lectorem' on ¶2ʳ.

24520.5 — [Anr. issue, w. added preface, and 'Liber ad Lectorem' on ¶1ᵛ.] *Oxoniæ, J. Barnesius*, 1596. L(2).O.C².C⁷.; F.HN.NY⁹.Y.

Upchering. The vpcheringe of the messe. [1548?] *See* 17630.

Upcote, Augustine. Almanacks. 1614, etc. *See* 519 sqq.

24521 **Urban VI, Pope.** UNiuersis scē matris ecclesie filiis [etc. c. 1515.] Now = Indulgences 82.

24522 **Urban VIII, Pope.** A breeve of our holy father the pope to the king [28 Nov. 1628.] 1629. = pt. of 12641.

24522.5 — [Heading:] A copie of the briefe of our holy father pope Urban. VIII. for appeasing the late controversies in the clergy and laytie of England. [*Tr.* from the Brief, *Britannia.*] 4°. [*Douai, widow of M. Wyon?* 1631.] DAI.DE. Brussels, Archives du Royaume (4). A&R 833.

24523 — The popes conclave: or, a speech made by his holinesse, upon the covenant of Scotland. [A satire, w. verses by J. Durie, D. Primrose, etc.] 4°. [*Edinburgh, R. Bryson*,] 1640. L.L³⁰.O.E.G⁴.+; F.HN.N.
This is continued in Wing U 130.

24524 — The suppressing of the assembly of the pretended shee-jesuites. By the edict of Urbanus [13 Jan. 1630.] *Tr.* out of the Low-dutch coppie, printed at Bruxells. 4°. [*J. Dawson?*] *f. N. Butter a. N. Bourne*, 1631. L.C.C³.
— *See also* 4137.

Urdemann, Heinrich. De libertate ecclesiastica tractatꝰ. [1483?] *See* 13922.

24525 **Urfé, Honoré d'.** The history of Astrea. The first part. In twelve bookes: newly *tr.* out of French. [Anon.] 4°. *N. Okes* [*a. T. Creede*] *f. J. Pyper*, 1620. Ent. as by 'Durfe' to M. Lownes 17 oc. 1611; to J. Pyper 6 mr. 1620. L.O.O⁸.C.
Creede pr. Aaa–Hhh; Okes the rest.

24526 **Ursinus, Joachimus, pseud.** The Romane conclave. Wherein, by way of history, exemplified upon the lives of the Romane emperours, the usurpations of the jesuited statists, are truely reported. [By I. Gentillet.] 4°. [*J. Windet*] *f. J. Jagger*, 1609. L.O.C. D²(imp.).G².+; F.HN.CHI.HD.Y.+

24527 **Ursinus, Zacharias.** A collection of certaine learned discourses. For explication of divers difficult points, in his catechisme. Lately put in print in Latin by Dauid Parry: and now newlie *tr.* by I. H. [A funerall oration of F. Junius.] 8°. *Oxford, J. Barnes, solde* [*by J. Broome, London*,] 1600. O.O³⁸.; F.HD(imp.).N.

24527.5 — [Anr. issue, w. cancel tp:] Certaine learned and excellent discourses. *H. L[ownes,] sould by J. Royston*, 1613. F.
Omits the translator's inits. Possibly Lownes acquired the unused sheets of this along w. the rights to 24537, q.v.

24528 — A verie profitable and necessarie discourse concerning the keeping of the sabboth. *Tr.* J. Stockwood. 8°. [*T. East?*] *f. J. Harrison the yonger*, 1584. O.D. E.E².; PN²(imp.).

24529 — Doctrinæ christianæ compendium: seu, commentarii catechetici, diuerso tempore ab ipsius discipulis excepti. Auctiores facti, & nunc denuo locupletati. 8°. *ex off. T. Thomasii, acad. Cantabrigiensis typog.* 1585. O.C.DUR(Bamb.).LYD.M.+; BO.U.
Reprinted from the *Geneva*, 1584, ed. w. preface by S. G. S., i.e. S. Goulart de Senlis.

24530 — [A pirated ed.] Cum indice preçipuorum capitum. 8°. *H. Midletonus, imp. T. Chardi*, 1586. L.D².DUL. E⁴.G².+; F.HN.ILL.
See also 25364b.

Ursinus, Zacharias—*cont.*

24531 — [Anr. ed. of 24529, w. title:] Explicationum catecheti-carum, quae tractationem locorum theologicorum κατ' ἐπιτομὴν complectuntur. Editio altera. 8°. *Cantebrigiae, ex off. T. Thomasii,* 1587. L.C.C².A.; F.HN.

The tp calls 24530 'vitiosissima'.

24532 — [A trans.] The summe of christian religion: delivered by Z. Ursinus in his lectures vpon the [Heidelberg] catechism. *Tr.* by H. Parrie, out of the last & best Latin editions, together with some supplie of wāts out of his Discourses of diuinitie. 8°. *Oxford, J. Barnes, sold [by T. Cooke, London,]* 1587. L(imp.). O.C.DUR³.M.+; F.HN.ILL.N.Y.+

24533 — [Anr. ed.] 8°. *Oxford, J. Barnes, solde [by T. Cooke, London,]* 1589. L.L⁴³.O.; F.ILL.SMU.

24534 — [Anr. ed.] 8°. *Oxford, J. Barnes, solde [by T. Cooke, London,]* 1591. O.O³¹.O³⁸.LINC.LYU.; F.HN.BO.U.

24535 — [Anr. ed.] 8°. *Oxford, J. Barnes, solde [by T. Cooke, London,]* 1595. L.O.DUL.M⁴.P.+; CAL.HD.

24536 — [Anr. ed., w. additions.] Lately conferred with the Latine edition of David Pareus. [*Ed.*] (R. Crosse.) 4° in 8's. *Oxford, J. Barnes, sold [by J. Broome, London,]* 1601. L.L².O(imp.).O⁶.P.+; DAR.ILL.NY¹¹. Schwenkfelder Library, Pennsburg, Pennsylvania.

24537 — [Anr. ed.] 4° in 8's. *H. L[ownes,] sold by A. Johnson,* 1611. Ent. to P. Short a. T. Hayes 31 ja. 1602; Hayes' pt. to H. Lownes 6 fb. 1604. L.O.C.D.SHEF.+; F.HN.HD.ILL.U.+

24538 — [Anr. ed.] 4° in 8's. *H. L[ownes,] sold by A. Johnson,* 1617. L.O.O¹³.C.STU.+; F.HN.HD.ILL.U.+

24539 — [Anr. ed.] Whereunto is added a large table of matters. fol. *R. Young, sold by J. Rothwell,* 1633. Ent. to H. Lownes a. R. Young 30 my. 1627; Lownes' pt. ass'd to G. Cole a. G. Latham 6 no. 1628; to R. Young 6 de. 1630. L.O.BTL.G⁴.NLW.; HN.BO⁵.CHI.Y.

24539.3 — [A variant, w. imprint:] *R. Young, sold by R. More,* 1633. DUR⁵.STD.; F.GRO.PTS.

24539.5 — [A variant, w. imprint:] *R. Young, sold by G. Lathum,* 1633. O⁶(D).G².; LC.U.Y.

24539.7 — [A variant, w. imprint:] *R. Young, sold by T. Alcorne,* 1633. E.M.; HD.ILL.

— A verie profitable and necessarie discourse. 1584. *See* 24528.

— *See also* Heidelberg Catechism (13023 sqq.)

Urstitius, Christian. The elements of arithmeticke most methodically deliuered. *Tr.* T. Hood. 8°. *R. Field,* 1596. Ent. 5 mr. L.L³⁰.L⁴⁴.; HN.

24540

24541 **Ursula,** *Saint.* The confraternyte of seynt Ursula. [c. 1520.] Now = Indulgences 59.

24541.3 — Here begyñeth yᵉ lyf of saynt Vrsula after yᵉ cronycles of englōde. (*Tr.* e sermone latino [by] E. hatfeild.) [In verse.] 4° ⁸·⁴. (*per me W. de Worde,*) [1509?] L.

Use. The use of the law. 1629. *See* pt. 2 of 6983.

Usselincx, Willem. More excellent observations. 1622. *See* 13573.

24541.7 **Ussher, Ambrose.** A briefe cathechisme, very well serving for the instruction of youth. 8°. *Dublin, the Co. of Stationers,* [c. 1620.] D(imp.).

Ussher, George, *tr. See* 23553.

Ussher, James, *Abp.* The workes. 1631. *See* 24544.5.

24542 — An answer to a challenge made by a jesuite [W. Malone] in Ireland. 4°. *Dublin, Soc. of Statrs.* [*a. London, Eliot's Court Press,*] 1624. Ent. to the Irish Stock 29 jy. 1629. L.O.C.A.D².+; F.HN.HD.ILL.U.+

Answered by 17213. Quires B–Ooo pr. in Dublin; the rest in London.

24543 — [Anr. ed.] Whereunto is added a sermon preached at Wansted. 2 pts. 4° in 8's. [*H. Lownes*] *f. the Soc. of Statrs.,* 1625. L.O.C.D.E.+; F.HN.ILL.U.Y.+

Usually 24546 is found as pt. 2, but at least one F copy has 24547. Tp as above is on A1; there is a sub tp on A2 w. the same imprint which does not mention 24546.

24544 — [Anr. ed.] Whereunto certain other treatises are ad-joyned. 5 pts. 4°. *R. Y(oung) f. the partners of the Irish Stocke,* 1631. L.O.C.D.E.+; F.HN.HD.ILL.NY.+

The gen. tp is conjugate w. a leaf of contents. Pt. 1

Ussher, James, *Abp.*—*cont.*

has a sub tp on a2: 'An answer. The third edition, corrected and enlarged. *R. Young f. the partners of the Irish stocke,* 1631.'

Ideally the other 4 pts. should be 24554a, 24548, 24549, 24555; but as contents of vols. differ, copies of the pts. are listed separately. Among the various forms in which copies survive are the following: pt. 1 by itself (1 D); gen. tp and contents leaf present, pt. 1 sub tp cancelled, pt. 3 lacking (1 G²); all 5 pts. present but gen. tp and contents leaf lacking (1 G²,CHI).

24544.5 — [Anr. issue, w. gen. tp and contents leaf cancelled, and cancel gen. tp:] The workes of the most reverend father in God, J. Ussher. Containing, I. An answer. [etc.] All newly revised. [*R. Young*] *for the Co. of Statrs., adventurers in the factorie for Ireland, and are to be sold at the shops of N. Butter a. P. Stephens,* 1631. O.O¹³.DUR⁵.LK.; F(imp.).

24545 — A briefe declaration of the universalitie of the church of Christ, delivered in a sermon before his majestie the 20ᵗʰ of June, 1624. at Wansted. 4°. *R. Young f. T. Downes a. E. Dawson,* [1624.] Ent. 27 jy. 1624. L.O.C.D⁸.E.+; F.HN.HD.U.Y.+

Answered by 12808.3.

24546 — Second impression. 4°. *R. Young f. T. Downes a. E. Dawson,* 1625. L.O.C.D².E.+; F.HN.ILL.U.Y.+

Usually found as pt. 2 of 24543.

24547 — Third impression. 4°. *J. Dawson f. E. Dawson,* 1629. L.O.C.D⁶.E.+; F.HN.PH.U.

24548 — [Anr. ed.] Third impression, corrected. 4°. *T. C[otes] f. T. Downes,* 1631. L.O.C.D.G².+; F.HN.CHI.HD.NY.+

Usually found as pt. 3 of 24544 sq.

24548a — Britannicarum ecclesiarum antiquitates. Quibus inserta est pestiferae adversùs Dei gratiam à Pelagio Britanno in ecclesiam inductæ hæreseos historia. 4°. *Dublinii, ex off. typog. Soc. Bibliopolarum,* 1639. L.O.C.D.E.+; F.HN.HD.N.U.+

Tp varies: most copies pr. in black, a few in red and black; both at L, O, C. Two quires are in 2 settings; Bbb1ʳ catchword is 'sa' or 'evagari'; Mmm1ʳ line 1 begins 'ranarum' or 'ranarū'; both at L¹⁵.

24549 — A discourse of the religion anciently professed by the Irish and Brittish. 4° in 8's. *R. Y[oung] f. the partners of the Irish stocke,* 1631. L.O.C.D.E.+; F.HN.HD. N.NY.+

Usually found as pt. 4 of 24544 sq.

24550 — Gotteschalci, et prædestinatianæ controversiæ ab eo motæ, historia: unà cum duplice eiusdem [i.e. of Gotteschalcus] confessione, nunc primùm in lucem editâ. 4°. *Dublinii, ex typog. Soc. Bibliopolarum,* 1631. L.O.C.D.E.+; F.HN.CHI.HD.U.+

24551 — Gravissimae quæstionis, de christianarum ecclesiarum, continuâ successione historica explicatio. 4°. [*Eliot's Court Press f.*] *B. Norton,* 1613. Ent. to B. Norton a. J. Bill 4 au. L.O.C.D.E.+; F.HN.BO³.CHI.U.+

24552 — Immanuel, or, the mystery of the incarnation. 4°. *Dublin, Soc. of Statrs.,* 1638. Ent. to J. Parker a. W. Bladen for ptnrs. in the Irish stock 14 fb. L.O¹⁰.C. D.DUR³.+; F.HN.HD.Y.

C, HN have an inserted leaf, signed A3, w. dedic. to Thomas, Viscount Wentworth.

24553 — [Anr. ed.] 4°. *J. H[aviland] f. J. Parker, &c.* [i.e. the partners in the Irish stock,] 1638. L.O.C.E.M.+; F.HN.HD.ILL.U.+

24553.5 — The substance of that which was delivered in a sermon before the Commons House the 18. of February, 1620. 4°. *F. Kyngston f. J. Bartlet,* 1621. Ent. 30 mr. L.O.C.D.M.+; F.HN.HD.N.U.+

(Formerly 24556)

24554 — [Anr. issue, w. cancel tp:] A sermon preached before the Commos [*sic*]-House. *J. D[awson] f. J. Bartlett,* 1624. L³.O.; PH².

24554a — Second edition corrected. 4°. *J. L[egat] f. J. Bartlet,* 1631. L.O.C.D.G².+; F.HN.CHI.HD.NY.+

Usually found as pt. 2 of 24544 sq. Omits Ussher's preface addressed to Parliament.

24555 — A speech delivered in the castle-chamber at Dublin, the XXII. of November, 1622. [Concerning] the oath of supremacie. 4°. *R. Y[oung] f. the partners of the Irish Stocke,* 1631. L.O.C.D.G².+; F.HN.CHI. HD.NY.+

Usually found as pt. 5 of 24544 sq.

24556 — The substance of that which was delivered in a sermon. Now = 24553.5.

Ussher, James, *Abp.—cont.*

24557 — Veterum epistolarum hibernicarum sylloge; quæ partim ab Hibernis, . . . sunt conscriptæ. 4°. *Dublinii, ex off. typog. Soc. Bibliopolarum,* 1632. L.O.C.D.E.+; F.HN. HD.N.Y.+

Copies differ in the last quire: 1: text ends Xx3ʳ (p. 165) w. the verso blank (4 L, 1 O, 7 C, F, 2 HD); 2: Xx3ᵛ numbered p. 166 with 7 lines of additional errata (1 O, 2 C); 3: like 2, but w. an extra leaf paged 167–8 w. corrected text of letters XXXV and XXXVI (1 O, 1 C, 1 HD).

One HD copy has the orig. Bb1 with letter IIII pr. as prose, corrected in the cancel to verse.

— *See* also 6030, 14265.5, 22522.

Usurer. A most rare tragedy of a ⟨u⟩surer of Fraunce. 1584. *See* 24167.5.

24557.5 **Usury.** The ruinate fall of the pope Vsury, deriued from the pope Idolatrie, reueled by a Saxon of antiquitie. [A dialogue between flesh and spirit.] 8°. (*J. Allde a.* [i.e. *for*] *J. Hunter,*) [c. 1580.] HN.

24558 — Usurie araigned and condemned. Or a discouerie of the infinite injuries this kingdome endureth by the unlawfull trade of usurie. 4°. *W. S[tansby] f. J.*

Usury—*cont.*

Smethwicke, 1625. Ent. 25 oc. 1624. L.O.C³.D.E.+; CU.HART².HD.ILL.

Utenhove, Jan, *tr. See* 2738.7, 2739, 15260.

24559 **Uthalmus, Lerimos,** *Pseud.* Fasciculus florum: or, a nosegay of flowers, *tr.* out of the gardens of severall poets. [In verse.] *Lat. a. Eng.* 12°. *A. M[athewes,]* 1636. Ent. to Mathewes 10 oc. 1635. L.O.C.DUL (imp.).E.+; F.HN.HD.N.Y.+

The pseudonym is sometimes interpreted as an anagram for Thomas Willmers.

24559a — [Anr. issue, w. cancel tp, w. imprint:] *M. P[arsons,] sold by R. Wilson,* 1638. L.E.E².; F.CU.

24560 **Utie, Emanuel.** Mathew the publican. A funerall sermon. By E. V. sometimes fellow of Sᵗ. Johns colledge in Cambridge. 4°. *E. Griffin f. N. Butter,* 1616. L.O. C.C⁵.DUL(imp.).+; F.HN.HD.

24561 **Utrecht.** A proclamation by the states of Utrecht. 1623. Now = Newsbooks 100.

Uxbridge, Middlesex, *Confraternity of Chapel of St. Margaret. See* Indulgences 79.

V

V., *Double. See* 17463.

V., A. Ephemerides of the celestiall motions. 1635. *See* 24864.

24562 V., B. The [xylographic] run-awyaes [*sic*] answer, to a booke called, A rodde for runne-awayes [6520]. [Init. B. V.; S. O.; etc.] 4°. [*A. Mathewes,*] 1625. L.O.; HD.

V., C. D. Dos tratados. 1588. *See* 24579.

24563 V., D. An enlargement of a former catechisme. That shewed what wee ought to beleeve, this upon what ground we ought so to beleeve. Gathered at the first, and since enlarged by D. V. 8°. *M. Dawson f. Jone Newbery,* 1637. M.
— *tr. See* 24675.5.

V., E., *sometime fellow of St. John's College in Cambridge. See* 24560.

24564 V., G. D. Holy meditations upon seaven penitentiall psalmes. 1612. Now = 7373.6.

V., I. A nomenclator. 1637. *See* 24674.
— *tr. See* 18143.

24565 V., I. D. The translation of a letter [signed I. D. V.] written by a Frenche gentilwoman vpon the death of Elenor of Roye, princes of Conde. Doone by H. Myddelmore at the request of the ladye Anne Throkmorton. 8°. *J. Daye f. H. Toye,* 1564. L.O.; ILL.

V., I. P., *Ox. See* 20343.7.

V., R. Englands joy. 1601. *See* 24636.3.
— Odes. 1606. *See* 21359.

24566 — The olde fayth of greate Brittaygne, and the newe learnynge of Inglande. Wherunto is added a symple instruction, concernynge the kinges maiesties procedinges in the cõmunyon. 8°. *A. Scoloker,* [1549?] L.O.C.M.M².+; F.HN.
— The true testimonie. [1605.] *See* 24639.
— *ed. See* 16094.
— *tr. See* 4401, 4403, 5116, 11762, 14609.5, 19815, 24627a.8.

V., R., *Preacher.* Jonah's contestation about his gourd. 1625. *See* 24594.

V., T., *B. of D. See* 24700.

24567 V., T., *Gent.* A briefe viewe of the weake grounds of popery. 1606. Now = 24508.5.

V., W. The honourable prentice. 1615. *See* 24588.

Vachan, Simon, *tr. See* 17495.

Vænius, Otto. Amorum emblemata. 1608. *See* 24627a.8.

Vaghane, Robert. A dyalogue. [1542.] *See* 24601.

Val. Den val der roomscher kercken. 1553. *See* 21307.3.

24568 Valdes, Alfonso de. Dialogo en que particularmente se tratan las cosas acaecidas en Roma, el año de M.D.XXVII. [Anon. *Ed.* A. del Corro.] 8°. *Paris* [i.e. *Oxford, J. Barnes,*] 1586. L(2).O(2).O⁵.C². Regarding minor press variants in the imprint *see The Library,* XX (1965), p. 191. The Address of the corrector is in the same typesetting as in 5789 sq.

24569 — [A trans.] The sacke of Roome, exsequuted by the emperour Charles armie. Notablie described in a Spanish dialogue. *Tr.* latelie into the English tounge. [Anon.] 4°. *A. Jeffes f. R. Ward,* 1590. Ent. to Jeffes 2 no. L.L²O⁷(lacks tp)*.; F.

24569.5 — [A variant, w. imprint:] *A. Jeffes,* 1590. DUR⁵.; HN.

24570 Valdes, Francisco de. The sergeant maior. A dialogue of the office of a sergeant maior. *Tr.* into Englishe, by J. Thorius. 4°. *J. Wolfe,* 1590. Ent. 5 de. 1589. L.L²SAL.; HN.

24571 Valdes, Juan de. The hundred and ten considerations of signior J. Valdesso: treating of our christian profession. Written in Spanish, and first set forth in Italian at Basil by C. S. Curio, 1550. Now *tr.* into English [by N. Ferrar], with notes [by] (G. Herbert.) 4°. *Oxford, L. Lichfield,* 1638. L.O.C.D.YK.+; F.HN.HD.ILL.Y.+

Valence, Peter. *See* 14125.5.

Valentia, Jacobus Perez de, *Bp. See* 19627.

24571.3 Valentine. [The history of Valentine and Orson. *Tr.* H. Watson.] 4° in 8's? [*W. de Worde,* c. 1510.] L(B₃–6 only). Text of chap. 4 begins on B5ʳ: 'Whan the Archebysshop . . .'

24571.7 — [Anr. ed.] The hystory of the two valyaunte brethren Valentyne and Orson. [*Tr.*] (H. Watson.) 4° partly in 8's. (*Imprinted in Fletestrete at the sygne of the Rose Garland by me W. Copland f. J. walley,*) [c. 1555.] HN(imp.). (Formerly 24572a) Text of chap. 4 begins on D1ʳ: 'When the Archebisshop . . .'

24572 — [Anr. ed.] 4° in 8's. (*Imprinted over agaynst S. Margaretes Churche in Lothbery be W. Coplande,*) [c. 1565.] L(imp.).; Y. Text of chap. 4 begins on C1ʳ: 'When the Archebysshop . . .'

24572a — Now = 24571.7.
24573 — [An abbreviated version.] Valentine and Orson. The two sonnes of the emperour of Greece. Newly corrected. 4° in 8's. *T. Pnrfoot* [sic], 1637. Ent. 8 au. 1586 and 6 no. 1615. L.E(imp.).

24574 Valentine, Henry. Foure sea-sermons, preached at the annuall meeting of the Trinitie Companie, in Deptford. [With prayers used at sea.] 4°. *M. Flesher f. J. Marriot,* 1635. Ent. 30 se. 1634. L.O¹¹.C.D.E.+; F.HN.HD.ILL.Y.

24575 — God save the king. A sermon preached in Sᵗ. Pauls church the 27ᵗʰ. of March. 1639. 4°. *M. F[lesher] f. J. Marriott,* 1639. Ent. 29 mr. L.O.C.D.PETYT.+; F.CU.HD.ILL.Y.

24576 — Noahs dove: or a prayer for the peace of Jerusalem. Delivered in a sermon at Pauls Crosse. 4°. *J. H[aviland] f. J. Marriot,* 1627. Ent. 25 ja. L.O.C.P.STU.+; F.CAL.CU.U(imp.).

24576.3 — Private devotions digested into six letanies. I. Of confession. II. Of deprecation. [etc.] The seventh edition enlarged. 24° in 12's. (*M. F[lesher]) f. J. Marriot,* 1635. Ent. erroneously as by S. Page on 28 ap. 1631. F(imp.). Correctly assigned as by Valentine to R. Marriot 3 May 1651.

24576.5 — The eighth edition. 24° in 12's. (*M. F[lesher]) f. J. Marriot,* 1636. L(letterpress and engr. tpp only, Ames II.1303).O.

24576.7 — The eleventh edition. 24° in 12's. [*M. Flesher*] f. J. Marriot,* 1640. L.O.

24577 Valentinus, Petrus Pomarius. Enchiridion medicum: containing, an epitome of the whole course of physicke: with the Examination of a chirurgion. (By S. H[obbs].) With a Definition of diseases . . . and an Antidotary. 8°. *H. Ballard f. G. Potter,* 1609. Ent. 3 oc. 1608. L¹³.C(date shaved).C¹⁰.DUL.SH.; HD(lacks errata). Nebraska U(date shaved). Sydney, Royal Australasian College of Physicians.

Valentinus, Petrus Pomarius—*cont.*

24578 — Second impression, enlarged with a second part, containing a particular practise of physicke, with the Flowers of Celsus, [etc.] 4°. *N. O[kes a. T. Snodham] f. J. Royston a. W. Bladon*, 1612. Ass'd 24 oc. 1611, and 2nd pt. ent. 7 de. 1611. L.O.C.BRISTOL².E⁵.+; F.HN.HD.NLM.Y.

Snodham pr. Aa–Yy; Okes the rest. Tp varies: with or without Valentinus' name; both at L.

24578.3 **Valera, Cipriano de.** Aviso a los de la iglesia Romana, sobre la indiccion del jubiléo, por la bulla del papa Clemente octavo. [Anon.] 8°. *en casa de R. del Campo [i.e. R. Field,]* 1600. L. Paris, Société de l'Histoire du Protestantisme Français.

24578.5 — [A trans.] An answere or admonition to those of the church of Rome, touching the jubile, proclaimed . . . by Clement the eyght, for 1600. *Tr. out of French.* [Anon.] 4°. *E. Allde f. J. Wolfe*, [1600.] L(lacks A4). O.O⁶.A.PETYT.+; F.HN.NY¹¹.Y.

(Formerly 21304) *See also* 21291.

24579 — Dos tratados. El primero es del papa. El segundo es de la missa. [Init. C. D. V.] 8°. *en casa de A. Hatfildo*, 1588. Ent. to E. Bollifant, Hatfield, a. J. Jackson 24 ap. L(2, 1(4061.bbb.33) with A2–7 of 24580 and type facs. tp).O.E⁸.M.; HN.HD(lacks I18).Y.

24580 — [Anr. ed., enlarged.] Iten, un enxambre de los falsos milagros. Segunda edicion, augmentada por el mismo autor. 8°. *en casa de R. del Campo [i.e. R. Field,]* 1599. L.O.O³.P.STU.+; F.HN.HD.NY⁵.

24581 — [A trans.] Two treatises: the first, of the lives of the popes. The second, of the masse. Also, a swarme of false miracles. The second edition in Spanish augmented by the author himselfe, M. Cyprian Valera, and *tr.* by J. Golburne. 4° in 8's. *J. Harison [3,] sold [by J. Harrison 1,]* 1600. Ent. to J. Harrison 3 on 14 jy. L.O.C.D.E.+; F.HN.HD.ILL.NY⁵.+

24582 — Tratado para confirmar los pobres catiuos de Berueria [i.e. Barbary] en la catolica fe. Al fin hallareys un enxambre de los falsos milagros. [Anon.] 8°. *en casa de P. Shorto*, 1594. L(851.a.8).O.M.P.

— *ed. See* 2959, 4391.5.
— *tr. See* 4426.

Valerian, Johan. *See* 19902.

24583 **Valerius, Cornelius.** The casket of iewels: contaynynge a playne description of morall philosophie. Lately turned out of Latin by J. C(harlton [i.e. Chardon.]) 8°. *W. How f. R. Johnes*, 1571. Ent. 1570–71. L. LEEDS.

On Univ. Microfilms reel 1042 is reproduced a HN photostat of the L copy, w. duplicates of quires D, H made directly from L.

24584 — Cornelii Valerii Vltraiectini in vniuersam benedicendi rationem tabula, summam artis rhetoricae complectens. Recognita, & emendatius excusa. 8°. *H. Middletonus, imp. G. B[ishop]*, 1580. C.

— *See also* 21106.

24585 **Valesco,** *Signior, pseud.* Newes from Rome. [1606.] Now = 4102.5.

24586 — [Anr. ed.] A Jewes prophesy. [1607.] Now = 4102.9.

Valesius, Joannes, *Bellomayus, ed. See* 25469.

24587 **Valesius [i.e. Wallace], Michael.** In serenissimi regis Jacobi, . . . ab immanissima papanæ factionis hominum conjuratione, liberationem carmen ἐπιχάρτικον. [In verse.] 4°. *R. Field*, 1606. L.

Valesius [i.e. Wallace], Thomas. Theses theologicæ. 1631. *See* 7487.29.

Valla, Laurentius. A treatyse of the donation. [1534.] *See* 5641.
— *tr. See* 170.3.
— *See also* 695.

24588 **Vallans, William.** The honourable prentice: or, this taylor is a man. Shewed in the life and death of sir John Hawkewood, [with other short historical narratives. Init. W. V.] 4°. [*J. Beale*] *f. H. Gosson*, 1615. O.O⁵.

24589 — [A variant, w. imprint:] [*J. Beale*] *f. H. Gosson*, 1616. O(2, 1 imp.).

Vallans, William—*cont.*

24590 — A tale of two swannes. Wherein is comprehended the original and increase of the riuer Lee. [In verse, with commentary.] 4°. *R. Ward f. J. Sheldrake*, 1590. HN.

Valtellina. A discourse upon the reasons [etc.] 1628. *See* 21757a.

24591 **Valuation.** The valuacyō of golde and syluer made i yᵉ yere. M.C.CCC.lxxxxix. [*Tr.* L. Andrewe.] 8°. [*Antwerp, J. van Doesborch?* c. 1520?] L.

24592 **Vandermer, Tarquatus.** Tarquatus Vandermers seauen yeares studie. 1569. = pt. of 5324.5.

Vandernote, John. *See* Noot, J. van der.

Vanderstegen, Michael, *tr. See* 3541.

Varamundus, Ernestus, *pseud. See* Hotman, F.

24593 **Varchi, Benedetto.** The blazon of jealousie. . . . First written in Italian, and *tr.* into English, with speciall notes by R. T[ofte] gentleman. (The fruits of jealousie. [In verse.]) 4°. *T. S[nodham] f. J. Busbie*, 1615. Ent. as by Robert 'Toffe' 14 oc. 1614. L.O. O³.O⁸.NEK.; F.HN.HD.N.Y.+

See also 744 sqq.

Varennius, Johannes. *See* 20130.

24594 **Vase, Robert.** Jonah's contestation about his gourd. In a sermon. By R. V[ase] preacher. 4°. *J. L[egat] f. R. Bird*, 1625. Ent. as by Vase 30 no. 1624. L.L¹⁵.C².; HN.NY¹¹.U.

24595 **Vasseus, Joannes.** Here beginnith a litel treatise conteyninge the iugemēt of vrynes . . . englished by H. Lloyd. 8°. *R. Tottyl*, 1553. L.O.NLW.

Vassy. The destruction . . . of Vassy. [1562.] *See* 11312.

24596 **Vaughan, Edward.** A divine discoverie of death, directing all people to triumphant resurrection. 8°. [*R. Field*] *f. W. Jones [3] a. R. Boyle*, 1612. Ent. to Jones 23 jn. L⁴.O.D(imp.).

24596.5 — [Anr. ed.] 8°. *W. J[ones 3,] sold by John Barnes*, 1619. TEX.

24597 — A method, or briefe instruction; verie profitable and speedy, for the reading and vnderstanding of the old and new Testament. 8°. *T. Orwin f. W. Holme*, 1590. Ent. to W. Holme, jun., 6 jy. L.C.; F(imp.).

24597–24599.5 are all different texts.

24598 — Nine obseruations howe to read the Bible. 8°. [*J. Charlewood*] *f. T. Gosson*, 1591. Ent. 8 no. C³.

24599 — Ten introductions: how to read, . . . all the bookes, . . . in the holie Bible. 8°. *A. Islip*, 1594. L.O²¹.C⁵. NLW.P(2).; HN.NY.

24599.5 — A plaine and perfect method, for understanding the Bible; containing seven observations, dialoguewise, betweene the parishioner, and the pastor. 12°. *f. W. Holme*, 1603. L(tp only, Harl.5993/61).; CHI.

24600 — [Anr. ed.] 12°. *T. S[nodham] f. the widow [A.] Helme*, 1617. Ass'd by W. Holme to J. Helme 20 ap. 1612. O. Leeds PL.; PN².TEX.

— *tr. See* 19153.

Vaughan, Edward, *Bp. See* Indulgences 117B.

Vaughan, Lewes. Almanacks. 1559, etc. *See* 520 sqq.

Vaughan, Millicent. *See* 20795.5.

24600.5 **Vaughan, Richard,** *Bp.* The baites, and methode of right fishing, delivered in two sermons, at Christchurch in Oxforde. 8°. [*Oxford, J. Barnes*,] 1599. L.

— *See also* 10175, 10256.

Vaughan, Richard, *of Bodeiliog in Denbighshire, tr. See* 1838.

24601 **Vaughan, Robert.** A dyalogue defensyue for women, agaynst malycyous detractoures. [Really by R. Burdet? In verse.] 4°. (*R. wyer f. R. Banckes,*) [1542.] HN.PFOR.

End of text dated 1542. Answers 12104.5.

Vaughan, Robert, *B.D.* The little world. By Ro. Vn. 1612. *See* 24519.5.

24602 **Vaughan, Robert,** *Engraver.* The pourtraitures at large of nine moderne worthies with a short relation of theire lives and deaths. fol. *sould* [*by* C. *Holland,*] 1622. Ent. to H. Holland 30 mr. HN.
　　　　Some of the plates were issued separately; *see* Hind III.89–91.
　　— *See also* 6271.5, 12561.4.

Vaughan, Rowland, *of Jesus College, Oxford, tr. See* 1623.5.

24603 **Vaughan, Rowland,** *of New Court, Herefordshire.* Most approved, and long experienced water-workes. Containing, the manner of winter and summer-drowning of medow and pasture. [With verse by J. Davies of Hereford, etc.] 4°. *G. Eld,* 1610. Ent. 14 no. 1609. L.O.C³.NLW.RD.+; F.HN.CU.HD.Y.+
　　　　Copies vary: S4ᵛ blank or w. a promissory note dated 29 Nov. 1609; both at L,F.

24604 **Vaughan, William.** Cambrensium Caroleia. Quibus nuptiᵉ regales celebrantur. [In verse.] 8°. *G. Stansbeius,* 1625. L(2).O(imp.).WN.; F.HN.NY(imp.).
24605 — [Anr. issue, w. cancel tp:] Cambrensium Caroleia. Quibus prᵉcepta necessaria ad rempublicam interxuntur [*sic*]. [*N. Okes,*] *imp. F. Constable,* 1630. HN.
24606 — The church militant, historically continued from the yeare of our saviours incarnation 33. untill this present, 1640. [In verse.] 8°. *T. Paine f. H. Blunden,* 1640. Ent. 16 ja. L.O.C.D².E.+; F.HN.HD.N.NY.+
　　　　At least 1 HD copy has errata on Aa4ʳ.
24607 — *Ερωτοπαιγνιον* pium: continens Canticum canticorum Salomonis: et psalmos aliquot selectiores una cum quibusdam aliis poëmatis. [In verse.] 8°. *ap. R. Johnesum,* 1597 (26 oc.) L(date cropt).L².O.; F.
　　　　Although the tp verso has R. Field's device, McK. 192, the whole seems to have been pr. by Jones.
24608 — Erotopainion pium. Pars secunda. = pt. of 24620.
24609 — The golden fleece divided into three parts, under which are discovered the errours of religion, the vices and decayes of the kingdome, and lastly the wayes to get wealth, and to restore trading. [Orpheus Junior, *pseud.*] 4°. [*W. Stansby, M. Flesher and another*] *f. F. Williams,* 1626. L.O.C.E.NLW.+; F.HN.HD.N.NY.+
　　　　Stansby pr. the prelims. and A–V; Flesher pr. Aaa–Mmm. The rest was done by an unidentified printer.
24610 — The golden-grove, moralized in three books: necessary for all such, as would know how to governe themselves, their houses, or their countrey. 8°. *S. Stafford,* 1600. L².O.; F.HN.PN. Robert Taylor.
　　　　Tp varies: 'books:' (F) or 'Bookes:' (HN).
24611 — Second edition, now lately reviewed and enlarged. 8°. *S. Stafford, sold by R. Serger and J. Browne,* 1608. L.O.C.BRISTOL².M².+; F.CAL(imp.).CHI.HD.Y.+
24612 — Naturall and artificiall directions for health. 8°. *R. Bradocke,* 1600. Ent. 17 mr. L.; NY.
24613 — [Anr. ed.] 8°. *R. Bradocke,* 1602. L.
24613.5 — [Anr. issue, w. imprint:] *R. Bradocke, soulde by John Newbery,* 1602. O(quire A only).
24614 — Third edition, newly corrected, revised and enlarged. 8°. [*R. Bradock*] *f. Roger Jackson,* 1607. Ass'd 14 se. L.; HD(imp.).
24614.5 — [Anr. ed.] Approved directions for health, both naturall and artificiall. Newly corrected and augmented. The fourth edition. 8°. *T. S[nodham]* f. *Roger Jackson,* 1611. NY.
24615 — [A variant, w. imprint:] *T. S[nodham]* f. *Roger Jackson,* 1612. L¹⁶.; F.
24616 — [Anr. ed.] Directions for health, . . . Newly enriched with large additions. The fift edition. 8°. *T. S[nodham]* f. *Roger Jackson,* 1617. L.O.DUL.M⁴.; HN.FBL.NY(2).NY⁴.
24617 — The sixth edition reviewed. Whereunto is annexed Two treatises of the eyes. The first by doctor Baily, the other collected out of Fernelius and Riolanus. 4°. *J. Beale f. F. Williams,* 1626. Ass'd 16 ja. L.O.C.G².NLW.+; CH.HD.NLM.NY.Y.+
　　　　(2nd pt. formerly also 1197)
24618 — The seventh edition. 4°. *T. Harper f. J. Harison* [4,] 1633. Ass'd 29 jn. 1630. L.O.C.DUL.M².+; F.HN.HD.NLM.NY.+
　　　　(2nd pt. formerly also 1198) Imprint on gen. tp varies: w. Harison's address at the Unicorn, or with no address; both at F.

Vaughan, William—*cont.*
24619 — The Newlanders cure. Aswell of those violent sicknesses as also to preserve the body free from diseases. [Partly in verse.] 8°. *N. O[kes]* f. *F. Constable,* 1630. L.; F(imp.).HN.CB.HD.NY.+
24620 — Poematum libellus continens 1. Encomium . . . Roberti comitis Essexii. 2. De sphærarum ordine tractatiunculam. 3. Palæmonis amores philosophicos. (Erotopainion pium continens 1. Natiuitatem & quædam Christi acta. 2. Speculum pudicitiæ. 3. Psalmos aliquot selectiores. Pars secunda.—Speculum humanᵉ condicionis.) 8°. *ap. G. Shaw,* 1598. L.O.M².; F. (24608, 24621 are pt. of this) The Erotopainion sub tp is on 1st E3ʳ; the Speculum sub tp is on 2nd C8ʳ.
24621 — Speculum humanᵉ condicionis. 1598. = pt. of 24620.
24622 — The spirit of detraction, conjured and convicted in seven circles. A worke both divine and morall. [Anon.] 4°. *W. Stansby* [*a. T. Snodham*] f. *G. Norton,* 1611. Ent. 17 my. L.O.
　　　　On A4ᵛ is mentioned 'the death of Elizabeth, the wife of William Vaughan.' Snodham pr. Oo–Bbb.
24622.5 — [Anr. issue, w. title reset, w. imprint:] *W. S[tansby a. T. Snodham]* f. *G. Norton,* 1611. L².C.C².D.P.+; F.BO.HD.NY.
24623 — [Anr. issue, w. tp and Epistolarie Preface cancelled, and cancel tp:] The arraignment of slander. Published by sir W. Vaughan. f. *F. Constable,* 1630. L.
　　— *tr. See* 3185.

24623.3 **Vaus, John.** [Rudimenta puerorum in artem grammaticam. Begin recto:] in latī onythīg at in terminatiōis of pticipil [etc.] *Scots a. Lat.* 4°. [*Edinburgh, A. Myllar,* 1507.] A(1 leaf only).
24623.5 — [Anr. ed.] Rudimenta puerorum in artem grammaticam per J. Vaus Scotum: ex variis collecta. 4° in 8's. [*Paris,*] (*prelo J. Badii Ascensii,* 1531 (8 cal. no.)) A.
24623.7 — [A selection.] Rudimenta artis grammaticæ per Jo. Vaus Scotum selecta, & in duo diuisa. *Scots a. Lat.* [*Ed.* T. Stewart.] 4° partly in 8's. *Parisiis, ex off. R. Massellin,* 1553. A.
24623a — [Anr. ed.] 4°. *Edinburgi, R. Lekpreuik,* 1566. HN.

24624 **Vautor, Thomas.** Cantus. (Altus.—Tenor.—Bassus.—Quintus.—Sextus.) The first set: beeing songs of divers ayres of five and sixe parts: apt for vyols and voyces. 6 ptbks. 4°. *T. Snodham f. M. Lownes a. J. Browne,* 1619. L.; F(sextus only).N(cantus only).

Vaux, John. Almanacks. 1621, etc. *See* 522 sqq.

24625 **Vaux, Laurence.** A brief fourme of confession. 1576. = 11181.
24625.5 — [Heading A2ʳ:] A catechisme, or a christian doctrine necessarie for chyldren and the ignorant people. (The vse and meaning of ceremonies.) 16° in 8's. [*Louvain, J. Fowler,* 1568.] L(imp.).
　　　　(Formerly 4801) A&R 834. Approbation on S7ᵛ dated 20 Apr. 1568.
24626 — [Anr. ed.] A catechisme, or a christian doctrine. With an instruction newly added of the laudable ceremonies vsed in the catholike church. (Godly contemplations.) 16° in 8's. *Antuerpiæ, ap. J. Foulerum,* 1574. O.
　　　　A&R 835. The Godly contemplations called for on P7 of this and the next ed. may refer to a series of woodcuts; *see* pt. 2 of 14563.3.
24626.3 — [Anr. ed.] 16° in 8's. *Rothomagi,* [*G. L'Oyselet,*] *ap. H. Mareschalum,* 1580. L(C.110.a.16, imp.).; TEX(bd. w. 14564).
　　　　(Formerly 5645) A&R 836.
24626.7 — [Anr. ed., w. title:] A catechisme or christian doctrine . . . with an addition of the ceremonies. Whereunto are adioyned certayne briefe notes of dyuers godly matters. 16° in 8's. [*Rouen, Fr. Parson's press?*] 1583. BUTE.SAL.
　　　　A&R 837.
24627 — [Anr. ed.] Whereunto is adioyned a brief forme of confession. 16° in 8's. [*Rouen, G. L'Oyselet,*] 1583. L.A(lacks tp).LK(imp.).W.YK.; CU(lacks Confession). HD.TEX.
　　　　A&R 838. The Confession is reprinted from 11181.
24627a — [Anr. ed.] 16° in 8's. [*Rouen, G. L'Oyselet,*] 1590. L².LINC.USHAW.; Toronto PL.
　　　　A&R 839.

Vaux, Laurence—*cont.*

24627a.2 — [Anr. ed.] 12°. [*English secret press,*] 1599. O⁵.P. Rogers.
    A&R 840.

24627a.3 — [Anr. ed.] 12°. *Roan* [really *English secret press,*] 1605 (1599.) BUTE.HP.OS.
    A&R 841. The Confession sub tp repeats the date 1599 from 24627a.2.

24627a.4 — [Anr. ed.] Reuewed and amplified in this edition by J. Heigham. 24° in 8's. *S. Omers,* [*C. Boscard,*] 1620. F.
    A&R 842. A reprint of this ed. [c. 1670?] but w. tp repeating the 1620 date is found in 12° at the Capuchin Friary, Pantasaph, near Holywell, Flints.

Vaux, Robert, *tr. See* 4401, 4403, 5116, 11762, 14609.5.

24627a.6 **Vecellio, Cesare.** The true perfection of cutworks. Wherein is set forth all manner of faire patternes of new cutworks, for falling bandes, ruffes, cuffes, handkerchers. First printed in Venice, next at Basill, and now in England. [Anon. *Tr.?* by] (R. B.) obl.4°. [*R. Field*] *f. W. Jaggard,* 1598. Ent. 23 ja. LAMPORT(6 leaves only).

24627a.8 **Veen, Otto van.** Amorum emblemata, figuris æneis incisa studio Othonis Væni. Emblemes of love. with verses in Latin, English, and Italian. [Eng. *tr.* by R. V., i.e. R. Verstegan or Rowlands.] obl.4°. *Antuerpiæ,* (*typis H. Swingenij,*) *venalia ap. auctorem,* 1608. L.L³⁰.O.C.G².+; F.HN.CH.HD.ILL.+
    1 imp. F copy (on Univ. Microfilms reel 602 '24567c') has an additional quire and slips w. a Spanish trans.

24627a.9 — [A variant, w. imprint:] *Antuerpiæ,* (*typis H. Swingenij,*) *venalia ap. auctorem,* [1608.] F.
    F copy on Univ. Microfilms reel 602 '24567b'.

24627a.10 — [Anr. issue, w. imprint:] *Antuerpiæ,* (*typis H. Swingenij,*) *ap. H. Verdussen,* 1608. BRISTOL (missing). ㋐

24628 **Veer, Gerrit de.** The true and perfect description of three voyages, . . . by the ships of Holland and Zeland, on the north sides of Norway, Muscovia, and Tartaria. [Anon. *Tr.*] (W. Phillip.) 4°. [*W. White*] *f. T. Pavier,* 1609. Ent. as by Veer to J. Wolfe 13 jn. 1598; to T. Pavier 15 my. 1609. L(2). G².M. Rotterdam, Prins Hendrik Maritime Museum.; CB.CH.LC(imp.).MICH.NY.+

Vega, Luis Gutierres de la. *See* 12538.

24629 **Vega Carpio, Lope Felix de.** The pilgrime of Casteele. Written in Spanish. *Tr.* into English. [Anon.] 4°. [*E. Allde f.*] *J. Norton,* 1621. Ent. 18 se. L(lacks A2). DUL(imp.).
    In the O⁶ copy of 24630.5 the trans. is ascribed in contemporary MS. to William Dutton.

24630 — [Anr. issue, w. cancel prelims.] *E. All-de f. J. N*[*orton,*] *solde by T. Dewe,* 1623. L.C¹³.; HD.Y.

24630.5 — [A variant, w. imprint:] *London,* [*E. Allde,*] 1623. O⁵.O⁶.; F.

24631 **Vegetius Renatus, Flavius.** The foure bookes of Flauius Vegetius Renatus, briefelye contayninge a plaine forme, of martiall policye. *Tr.* out of [*sic*] lattine, by J. Sadler. 1572. 4° in 8's. *T. Marshe,* [1572.] L.O.C.NOR².P.+; F.HN.HD.N.Y.+
    — *See also* 7269, 18842.

Veghelman, S., *tr. See* 5188, 15514.5.

Vegius, Maphaeus. *See* 24789, 24797, 24802.

24632 **Velcurio, Joannes.** Joannis Velcurionis commentariorum libri iiii. In vniuersam Aristotelis Physicen: nunc recèns castigati. Plenissimus index præfixus. 16° in 8's. [*Deputies of C. Barker,*] *imp. G. Bishop,* 1588. Ent. 24 se. 1582. L.L¹⁶.C.C³.; HN.Y.

24633 **Velleius Paterculus, Caius.** Velleius Paterculus his Romane historie: in two bookes. *Tr.* out of the Latine edition supervised by J. Gruterus. By Sʳ R. Le Grys. 12°. *M. F*(*lesher*) *f. R. Swaine,* 1632. Ent. 9 my. L.O.C.M.YK.+; F.HN.HD.N.NY.+
    Imprimatur on verso of tp in 2 settings: line 2 has '*EVELLEIVS*' or the corrected '[*V*]*ELLEIVS*'; both at O.

Velthoven, Adrian. The pnostication. [1520.] *See* 406.7.

Vemius, Jacobus. Theses philosophicae. 1616. *See* 21555.27.

24633.5 **Venæus, Joannes.** A notable oration, made by J. Venæus a Parisien in the defence of the sacrament of the aultare, pronounced before the vniuersitie of Parise 1.5.3.7. Whereunto is added a preface, taken out of De veritate corporis . . . in eucharistia, by C. Tunstall. *Tr.* oute of Latin by J. Bullingham. 8°. (*J. Cawood,* 1554 (2 oc.)) L.

Vendôme, *Duke of.* The French kings declaration against the dukes of Vendosme [etc.] 1617. *See* 16834.

Venice. A declaration of the variance. 1606. *See* 19482.

24634 — Letters sent from Venice. Anno. 1571. Containing the certaine newes of the victorie of the christians ouer the great Turke [in the battle of Lepanto.] *Tr.* oute of the Frenche copie printed at Paris by G. de Niuerd. 8° in 4's. *H. Bynneman, sold by Ant. Kitson,* [1571?] L.

24634.5 — News from Venice. An extract of certaine poyntes of religion, maintained in Venice, against the doctrine of the church of Rome. s.sh.fol. *f. F. Burton,* 1607. Ent. 22 ap. Venice, Biblioteca dell'Archivio di Stato.
    Suppressed at the request of the Venetian ambassador; *see Cal.S.P.Ven., 1603–1607,* pp. 495–6.

24635 — A true copie of the sentence of the high Councell of tenne . . . against Ridolfo Poma, Michael Viti priest, [etc.] who attempted murder upon Paolo Servite [i.e. Sarpi], theologue. *Tr.* out of Italian. 4°. *H. Lownes f. S. Macham,* 1608. Ent. 12 fb. L.O.O⁵.D.; F.HN(lacks tp).N.

24636 **Vennard, Richard.** An apology: written, by R. Vennar of Lincolnes Inne, abusively called Englands Joy. 8°. *N. Okes,* 1614. L.C.

24636.3 — Englands joy. [Verses on the defeat by Lord Mountjoy of the Irish rebels under Tyrone. Init. R. V.] 4°. [*P. Short,* 1601?] L.
    (Formerly 21358)

24636.7 — [An advertisement.] The plot of the play, called Englands joy. To be playd at the Swan this 6. of November. 1602. [Anon.] s.sh.fol. [*J. Windet,* 1602.] L⁵ (Lemon 98).
    Regarding Vennard's fraud in issuing this playbill w. no intention of producing a play, *see* Sir Edm. K. Chambers, *Elizabethan Stage,* III.500–3.

24637 — The right way to heaven: and the true testimonie of a loyall subject. Compiled by R. Vennard. [Partly in verse.] 4°. *T. Este,* 1601. Ent. 19 no. L(imp.).; F(imp.).

24638 — [Anr. issue, w. omissions and additions, w. title:] The right way to heaven, and a good presedent for lawyers and all other good christians. *T. Este, sould under Lincolnes gate* [by *T. Este?*] 1602. HN.
    Quires B–F are the same typesetting as 24637.

24639 — [An extract, w. new verse.] The true testimonie of a faithfull subject: containing severall exhortations. Also a thanksgiving [for the frustration of the Gunpowder plot. Init. R. V.] 8°. [*R. Field,* 1605.] L.; HN.
    Reprints most of the prose portion 'Reward of a faithfull subject' from 24637.

24640 — = 24639.

24641 **Venner, Tobias.** The baths of Bathe. 4°. *F. Kyngston f. R. Moore,* 1628. L(2).O¹⁷(imp.).C¹⁰.G².; NLM.PH².
    Also issued as pt. 2 of 24645.

24642 — A briefe and accurate treatise, concerning, the taking of the fume of tobacco. 4°. *W. J*[*ones*] *f. R. Moore,* 1621. Ent. 23 se. 1620. L.BRISTOL.STD. London, The Athenaeum.; F.HN.HD.NLM.NY.+
    Reprinted in 24646.

24643 — Via recta ad vitam longam, or a plaine philosophical discourse of such things, as make for health. Also, by way of introduction, the true use of our famous bathes of Bathe. 4°. *E. Griffin f. R. Moore,* 1620. Ent. 5 my. L.O.C.BRISTOL.M.+; F.HD.NLM.NY⁴. NWM.

24643.5 — The second edition, corrected, and enlarged. Whereunto is also annexed a Treatise of tobacco, . . . 4°. *T. S*[*nodham*] *f. R. Moore,* 1622. O.C.; HD.NY.Y.
    HD is the only copy having 24642 bd. w. it. The C copy has a blank slip of paper pasted over the portion of the title calling for the treatise.

Venner, Tobias—*cont.*

24644 — [A variant, w. ornament replacing 'Whereunto . . . tobacco, ...'] *T. S[nodham] f. R. Moore*, 1622. L.O².C.BRISTOL.STD.; CAL.NLM.PH.

24645 — [Anr. ed., enlarged.] Whereunto is annexed a Treatise of the baths of Bathe, lately published. 2 pts. 4°. *F. Kyngston f. R. Moore*, 1628. L(pt. 1 only).O.C. BRISTOL.E².+; F.HN.HD.N.Y.+
    Pt. 2 also issued sep. as 24641. Pt. 1 includes reprint of 24648.

24646 — [Anr. ed., enlarged.] As also an accurate treatise concerning tobacco. 4°. *R. Bishop f. H. Hood*, 1637. Ass'd 12 my. 1641. L.O.C⁴.BRISTOL.P.+; F.HN.CHI. ILL.NY.+

24647 — [A variant, w. imprint on gen. tp:] *R. Bishop f. H. Hood*, 1638. L.O².C.BRISTOL.NEK.+; F.HN.HD.NLM. NY.+
    Sub tpp retain 1637 date.

24648 — Viæ rectæ ad vitam longam, pars secunda. Wherein the true use of sleepe, exercise, [etc.] is, discussed. 4°. *G. Eld f. G. Winder*, 1623. Ent. 9 my. 1623; ass'd to M. Flesher 21 my. 1628. L.L².O.C².BRIS-TOL.+; F.HN.HD.NY.Y.+
    Reprinted in 24645.

24649 **Venner, William.** The beame of brightnesse. Or the three faire sisters of Christendome. Viz. Venice, Paris and London. [In verse.] 4°. [*G. Eld*] *f. J. Wright*, 1611. O.

24650 **Venus.** [The court of Venus. With the Pilgrim's Tale. In verse.] 8°. [*T. Gybson*, 1538?] O(frags. of quires E and F).
    E1 verso/recto headline: 'The court of / Venus'. The pseudo-Chaucerian Pilgrim's Tale was presumably omitted from later eds.

24650.5 — [Anr. ed.] The courte of Venus. Newly and diligently corrected with many proper ballades newly amended, and also added therunto which haue not before bene imprinted. 8°. [*T. Marshe*, 1563?] Ent. to H. Sutton 1557–58. F(quire A only, w. comp. McK. & F. 107). A4ᵛ/5ʳ headline: 'The Court / of Venus'. For a fragment with some of the same poems, attrib. to Sir T. Wyatt, with the headline: 'A Boke / of Balettes.' *see* 26053.5.

Verdere, *Monsieur*. *See* 21775.

24651 **Vere**, *Sir Francis.* Extremities urging the lord generall sir Fra: Veare to the anti-parle with the archduke Albertus. Written by an English gentleman from Ostend. 4°. [*T. Purfoot*] *f. T. Pavyer*, 1602. Ent. 10 ja. O².O⁵.O⁹.; HN.HD.ILL.Y.
    Ends C3ᵛ.

24651a — [Anr. issue.] Extremities urging the lord general sir Fra: Veare to offer the late anti-parle. . . . [*W. White a. T. Purfoot*] *f. T. Pavier*, 1602. L.O.O⁵.HAGUE.; F.HN. Lewis.
    Ends C3ᵛ. O, F have quires B–C in the same setting as 24651: C3ᵛ line 1 'winde'; O⁵, HN are partly reset and have 'wind'. In this and the following White pr. quire A; Purfoot B–C.

24651b — [Anr. issue, w. quire C reimposed, w. additions.] With an addition of some farther particulars. [*W. White a. T. Purfoot*] *f. T. Pavier*, 1602. O⁵.; HN.
    Ends C4ʳ.

24652 — True newes from one of sir Fraunces Veres companie. Concerning Delftes-Isle, and other townes. With the bloody persecution in Spaine. *Tr.* out of Dutch. 4°. [*E. Allde*] *f. T. Nelson*, 1591. L.O.O⁸.LINC.YK.+; HN.ILL.LC.TEX.

24653 **Verepæus, Simon.** Simonis Verepaei de epistolis Latine conscribendis libri V. Denuo illustrati, & accessione aucti. 8°. *R. Field, imp. J. Harisoni* [*1,*] 1592. Ent. to J. Harrison, sen., 16 mr. L(2).O.DUR³.ETON.

Verger, Susan du, *tr.* *See* 4549.

Vergerio, Pietro Paolo. *See* 3218, 10532.

24654 **Vergilius, Polydorus.** An abridgemēt of the notable worke of Polidore Vergile conteygnyng the deuisers and first finders out aswell of artes, . . . ciuill ordinaunces, as of rites, & ceremonies, in the churche. Compēdiousely gathered by T. Langley. 8°. *R. Grafton*, 1546 (25 ja.) L.O⁶.C.G².NLW.+; F (lacks col.).CAL(imp.).PN(lacks col.).TEX.
    a2ʳ catchword: 'hym'.

Vergilius, Polydorus—*cont.*

24655 — [Anr. ed.] An abridgemēt . . . worke of Polidore Virgile. 8°. *R. Grafton*, 1546 (25 ja.) [col.:] ((16 ap.)) L.O.; HN.CHI(imp.).ILL.LC.WIS.
    a2ʳ catchword: 'life'.

24656 — [Anr. issue, with quire A largely reimposed and quire a reprinted:] An abridgement . . . woorke of Polidore Vergile. 8°. *R. Grafton*, 1546 (16 ap.) L.O.G². M.P.+; HD.N.Y. Horblit. Barnet Kottler, Purdue Univ., Lafayette, Indiana.
    a2ʳ catchword: 'lyfe'.

24657 — [Anr. ed.] 8°. (*R. Grafton*,) 1551 (jy.) L.L⁴³.O.C.G².+; F.HN.HD.ILL(imp.).

24658 — [Anr. ed.] Newlye perused. 8°. (*J. Tisdale*,) [c. 1560.] L.O.C.G².NLW.+; F.HN.CHI.HD.NY.+

— *ed.* *See* 11892.

24659 [A ghost.]

24660 **Verheiden, Jacobus.** The history of the moderne protestant divines. With a register of all their writings that are extant. [Anon.] *Tr.* out of Latine by D. L(upton.) 8°. *N. a. J. Okes*, 1637. Ent. to J. Okes 5 se. 1636; ass'd to J. Stafford 18 no. 1637. L.O.C. G⁴.M.+; F.HN.HD.NY.+
    The engr. tp has imprint: *J. Okes*, 1637, or *J. Okes, sold by A. Crooke*, 1637; both at HD.

Verheiden, Willem. *See* 18837.

Verheile, P., *tr.* *See* 18451.

24661 **Veridicus, Paulus.** A briefe confutation. 1627. Now = 12808.3.

24662 — The second edition. 1639. Now = 12808.7.

Verino, Michael. *See* 18991.

Verities. Of vnwryten verytyes. 1548. *See* 22823.

24662.5 **Vermigli, Caterina.** De Katherinæ nuper vxoris doctissimi viri D. Petri Martyris vermilij . . . regnante Maria, effossæ exhumatione, ac eiusdem ad honestam sepulturam sub Elisabetha regina restitutione, studiosorum quorundam tam Oxoniensium quàm aliorum carmina, cum præfatione. [Latin verse by J. Calfhill and others.] 4°. *in off. J. Day*, 1561. O³. O⁸.; HN.
    Film of HN copy on Univ. Microfilms reel 341 ('24663+').

24663 **Vermigli, Pietro Martire.** A briefe and most excellent exposition, of the .xij. articles of our fayth, commonly called the apostles creede. Written in Italian, and *tr.* by T. E. 8°. *H. Jackson*, (1578). Ent. 15 no. L(tp only, Harl.5993/45). O.O⁹.E².LEEDS(imp.).

24664 — A briefe treatise, concerning the vse and abuse of dauncing. Collected oute of P. Martyr, by R. Massonius: and *tr.* into English by I. K. 8°. [*J. Charlewood f.*] *John Jugge*, [1580?] L.O(frag.).

24665 — A discourse or traictise of Petur Martyr Vermill a Florētine, wherin he declared his iudgemente concernynge the sacrament of the Lordes supper. (*Tr.* N. Udall.) 4°. (*R. Stoughton* [really *E. Whitchurch*] *f. N. Udall*,) [1550.] L.O.C⁴.D.E.+; F.HN.HD.ILL.Y.+
    A trans. of 24673. Copies differ in quire z: with 4 leaves, in which some text is omitted; or w. 6 leaves, the second of which has the verso blank and is intended to be pasted down over orig. z1ʳ; both at F.

24666 — An epistle vnto the right honorable . . . the duke of Somerset written in Latin, and *tr.* by T. Norton. Anno M.D.L. 8°. [*N. Hill*] (*f. G. Lynne*, 1550.) L.L².O.M.P.+; F.HD.

24667 — Petri Martyris Vermilii, . . . loci communes. In vnum volumen collecti. [*Ed.*] (R. Massonius.) fol. *ex typ. J. Kyngstoni*, 1576. L.O.C.E.LYD.+; HN.BO.CHI.HD.U.+

24668 — [Anr. ed., enlarged.] Loci communes D. Petri Martyris Vermilii. Quam multa accesserint. (Oratio de vita et obitu à J. Simlero.) [*Ed.*] (R. Massonius.) fol. *T. Vautrollerius*, 1583. L.O³.C.D².G².+; F.HN.HD. TORONTO².Y.

24669 — [A trans.] The common places of . . . Peter Martyr, with a large addition of manie discourses, some neuer extant before. *Tr.* and partlie gathered by A. Marten. fol. [*H. Denham a. H. Middleton*] (*at the costs of H. Denham, T. Chard, W. Broome a. A. Maunsell*, 1583.) Ent. 3 my. 1582. L.O.C.E². LYD.+; F.HN.HD.N(imp.).U.+
    Middleton pr. 2nd Aa–Yy (roman letter signatures); Denham the rest.

Vermigli, Pietro Martire—*cont.*

24670 — Most fruitfull & learned cŏmentaries [upon the Book of Judges. *Tr.*] fol. *J. Day*, (1564 (28 se.)) L.O.C⁵. CASHEL.P.+; F.HN(lacks col.).CHI.HD(lacks col.).U.+
　　Yielded by Day to the Company 8 Jan. 1584; see Arber II.787.

24671 — Most godly prayers compiled out of Dauids psalmes. *Tr.* out of Latin [from the ed. of J. Simler] by C. Glemhan. 8°. *W. Seres*, 1569. Ent. 1566–67. L.L⁴⁴.O.C.; F.CAL².HD.

24672 — Most learned and fruitfull commentaries . . . vpon the epistle to the Romanes. *Tr.* out of Latine by H. B[illingsley.] (Perused by D. Whitehead.) fol. *J. Daye*, (1568 (31 au.)) L.O.C.BIRM.E⁴.+; F.HN.HD. N.Y.+
　　Yielded by Day to the Company 8 Jan. 1584; see Arber II.787.

24673 — Tractatio de sacramento eucharistiæ, habita in uniuersitate Oxoniensi [on 1 Cor.xi.] Ad hec. Disputatio habita M.D.XLIX. 2 pts. 4°. [*R. Wolfe*,] *ad ænum serpentem*, [1549]. L.O.C.DUR⁵.E².+; F.BO².NY¹¹.U.
　　For a trans. *see* 24665; *see also* 25388.

24673.5 — A treatise of the cohabitacyon of the faithfull with the vnfaithfull. [Anon.] Wherunto is added. A sermon made [by H. B., i.e. H. Bullinger] of the confessing of Christe and his gospell. Anno M.D.LV. [*Tr.* T. Becon?] 8°. [*Strassburg, W. Rihel*, 1555.] L.O.O³.C.M.+; F.HN.PH.
　　(Formerly 24246)
　　— *See also* 10387, 10391.5.

24674 **Verneuil, Jean.** A nomenclator of such tracts and sermons as have beene printed or translated into English upon any place of holy scripture. Operâ, studio & impensis J. V[erneuil.] 12°. *Oxford, W. Turner*, 1637. L.O.; F.HD.
　　— *ed. See* 14448.
　　— *tr. See* 4532, 7338, 18143.

24675 **Vernon, John.** The young horse-man. 4°. [*London*, 1644.] HN(impr. cropt).
　　= Wing V 253.

24675.5 **Veron, François.** M. le Hucher minister of Amyens in France compelled to fly from the pure word of holy write. Vppon the subject of the B. sacrament of the altar. By F. Veron encountring him with the Bible of Geneva only. [*Tr.* D. V., i.e. E. Catcher *alias* Burton.] 12°. [*Douai, widow of L. Kellam*, 1616.] L⁴.; F.
　　(Formerly 15400) A&R 843. *See also* 23924.

24676 **Veron, Jean.** Certayne litel treaties setforth by J. Veron for the erudition and learnyng, of the symple & ingnorant [*sic*] peopell. 8°. (*H. Powell*, 1548.) L(imp.).O.BUTE.D.; CHI.

24677 — A dictionary in Latine and English, corrected by R. W(addingtonus.) 4° in 8's. *H. Middelton f. J. Harison* [1,] 1575.; HN.ILL.Y.
　　A revised and enlarged ed., omitting French, of 10555.

24678 — [Anr. ed., corrected by A. Fleming.] 4° in 8's. *R. Newberie a. H. Denham*, [1584.] Ent. 30 de. 1584. O.C.P.; F.CU.HD(imp.).
　　Tp comp. dated 1584 in the sill.

24679 — The .V. abhominable blasphemies cŏteined in the masse, with a short ãswere to them, that saie, we ronne before the kyng and his counsayle. 8°. (*H. Powell*, 1548.) L²(imp.).; F.PN².

24680 — A fruteful treatise of predestination, . . . as far forth as the holy scriptures shal lead vs, and an answer to the obiections [of] epicures and anabaptistes. Set forth dialoge wise. 8°. (*J. Tisdale*,) [1561.] Ent. 11 my. 1561. L³⁸.O.O⁵.C.P.+; F(lacks A8).HN.CHI.HD (lacks tp).PML.+
　　Unfoliated. Some copies (1 O, F) have ✻⁴ with To the readers and Argument, more often found with 24681. Another O and O³ have ✻2–4.

24681 — [Anr. ed., with additions.] With an apology of the same, against the swynyshe gruntinge of the epicures and atheystes of oure time. Whereunto are added, a boke againste the free wyll men, and another of the true iustification of faith, made dialoge wyse. 2 pts. 8°. *J. Tisdale*, [1561.] L(lacks pt. 2).O(pt. 2 bd. separately).O³.D.P.+; F.HN(tp facs.).CHI(lacks ✻⁴). HD(tp, ✻⁴, Q⁸, and pt. 2 only, bd. w. text of 24680). U(lacks tp).+
　　Both pts. are foliated, and pt. 1 should include Q⁸

Veron, Jean—*cont.*

(Table). Copies listed above have pt. 2 (Apology) bd. w. them unless otherwise indicated. Free will and Justification are rarely bd. in, and all copies are listed separately at 24684, 24685. The HD copy has all 4 pts. but is evidently sophisticated.

24682 — The godly saiyngs of the old auncient faithful fathers, vp on the sacrament of the bodye and bloude of Chryste. Newlye compyled and *tr.* oute of Latin. By J. Veron. 8°. (*worceter, J. Oswen, also to sell at Shrewesburye*, 1550 (11 oc.)) L.O.C.BIRM(imp.).G².+; F(imp.).

24683 — The huntynge of purgatorye to death, made dialoge-wyse. Newly setfoorth. 8°. (*J. Tysdale*, 1561.) Ent. betw. 24 jn. and 8 jy. L.O.C.D.G².+; F.HN.CHI.HD (imp.).U.+
　　Colophon varies: 'ne vnto grace' or 'nere vnto grace'; both at F.
　　— A most necessary & frutefull dialogue. *Tr.* J. Veron. 1551. *See* 4068.

24684 — A moste necessary treatise of free wil, not onlye against the papistes, but also against the anabaptistes. Made dialoge wyse. 8°. (*J. Tisdale*,) [1561.] Ent. 11 my. 1561. L.O.C⁴.NEK.P.+; F.CHI.HD.ILL.U.+
　　Intended to be issued w. 24681.

24685 — The ouer throw of the iustification of workes sette foorth dialoge wise. Newlye set foorthe 1561. 8°. (*J. Tysdale*, 1561.) Ent. 1561–62. L.O.O².C⁴.P.+; F. HD.U.
　　Intended to be issued w. 24681.

24686 — A stronge battery against the idolatrous inuocation of the dead saintes, made dialoguewise. 8°. (*H. Sutton f. T. Hacket*, 1562 (10 mr.)) Ent. 1561–62. L.O.O³. C⁴(lacks tp).DUL.+; F.CHI.U.

24687 — A stronge defence of the maryage of pryestes, agaynste the pope Eustachians, made dialogue wise. 8°. *T. Marshe*, [1562?] Ass'd by E. Marshe to T. Orwin ?23 jn. 1591. L.O⁵.O¹⁷.D.; F.
　　— *tr. See* 4059, 4068, 4069, 10555, 26141, 26142.

24688 **Verro, Sebastian.** Sebast. Verronis . . . physicorum libri X. Nunc primùm in lucem editi. 8°. *ex off. H. Bynneman*, 1581. L.O.C.C¹².C¹³.+; F.HN.

24689 — [Anr. ed.] 8°. [*Eliot's Court Press*,] imp. *J. Harison*, 1590. L(tp only, Harl.5993/89).O.; HD.

24689.5 — [A variant, w. imprint:] imp. *G. Bishop*, 1590. L(tpp only, Ames I.499; Harl.5936/259, date cropt).L¹⁶.

24690 **Verslyn, Francis.** The state of the suite in chancerie, betweene F. Verslyn pl': agaynst P. Manning, M. Palmer . . . defendants [etc. Appeal to the House of Commons to dismiss a bill offered by the defendants, 17257.5.] s.sh.fol. [*London*, 1621.] L.L⁸.
　　Chancery had decreed in Verslyn's favour in a dispute over inheritance.

Verstegan, Richard. *See* Rowlands, R.

24691 **Vertue, Henry.** A plea for peace: or a sermon preached in S^t. Pauls. 4°. *M. F[lesher] f. J. Clark*, 1637. Ent. 11 oc. L.L³.L¹⁵.O.C.; F.HD.U.

24692 = 24693.

24693 **Verus Pater.** Verus Pater, or, a bundell of truths. Containing a prognostication. And dedicated to the memory of old Erra-Pater [439.3]. [By G. Markham.] 8°. [*N. Okes*] f. *T. L[angley]*, 1622. Ent. as by Markham to T. Langley 4 my. 1620. L(2).O.; HN.

Verzelline, Francis. *See* 17257.5, 24690.

Vesalius, Andreas. *See* 11714, 20779.

24693.5 **Vesey, Henry.** The scope of the scripture. . . . By short questions and answeres. 8°. *N. O[kes] f. S. Man*, 1614. Ent. 18 jy. LK.
24694 — [Anr. ed.] 8°. *W. J[ones] f. S. Man*, 1621. L.
24694.3 — [Anr. ed.] 8°. *W. J[ones] f. S. Man*, 1623. L.
24694.5 — [Anr. ed.] 8°. *W. J[ones] f. S. Man*, 1626. COL.
24695 — [Anr. ed.] 8°. *J. B[eale] f. S. Man*, 1633. L.O(3).; F.
24695a — [Anr. ed.] 8°. *W. J[ones] f. S. Man*, 1637. M.

Vespasian. The dystruccyon of Iherusalem by Vaspazyan and Tytus. [1513, etc.] *See* 14517 sqq.

24695a.5 **Via.** Nova et expedita via comparandae linguae Latinæ. 8°. *ex off. J. Legatt, acad. Cantab. typog.*, [c. 1590.] O.O¹³.

Vic., Tho. *See* 24700.

24696 **Vicars, John,** *Linguist.* Decapla in psalmos: sive commentarius ex decem linguis mss. et impressis. A J. Viccars. fol. *ap. R. Young,* 1639. Ent. 9 my. 1638. L².O.C.D.E.+; CAL.CHI.HART.HD(lacks engr. tp). ILL.+

In most copies the dedic. is a cancel, w. paragraph 2 line 1 ending: 'lin-'. In one C copy the orig. dedic., also to Laud, is found as endpapers and has: 'linguas'; this leaf is also present in O², O³, O⁸, O²⁷.

24697 **Vicars, John,** *Poet.* Englands hallelu-jah. . . . For Gods gratious benediction. In our deliverances [from Catholic plots], since the halcyon-dayes of queene Elizabeth. Together, with divers of Davids psalmes. [In verse.] 8°. *T. Purfoot f. H. Seile,* 1631. Ent. 8 no. 1630. O.; HN(lacks tp).

24697.3 — In honor. Caro. Princ: Mag: Bri: . . . Nat. 29 Maii, 1630. [Engr. by W. Marshall, w. verses.] s.sh.fol. *sould by T. Jenner,* [1630.] BUTE.DALK.

For this and the later states, *see* Hind III.109–10.

24697.5 — [Anr. state, w. right column of verses and Vicars' name erased and replaced by:] The effigies of the Lady Anna . . . baptized . . . 1637. *sould by T. Jenner,* [1637.] O³⁴(Sutherland C.III.43).WIN.

24697.7 — [States with further alterations:] The most hopefull . . . Henry Duke of Lancaster [or 'Glocester'] borne . . . 1640. *sould by T. Jenner,* [1640.] O³⁴(Sutherland C.III.43, both states).

24698 — A prospective glasse to looke into heaven, or the cœlestiall Canaan described. [In verse.] 8°. *W. Stansby f. J. Smethwicke,* 1618. Ent. 17 se. L.O.; HN.

— *tr. See* 3569, 12030, 13247, 18993, 24809.

Vicars, Thomas. [Gift-plate.] *See* Bookplates.

24699 — Edom and Babylon against Jerusalem, or meditations on psal. 137.7. Being the summe of divers sermons. [On the anniversary of the Gunpowder Plot.] 8°. *E. P[urslowe] f. H. Seyle,* 1633. O.C⁴(lacks tp).; NY.

24700 — The grounds of that doctrine which is according to godlinesse. Or a briefe and easie catechisme, (gathered out of many other). By T(ho.) V(ic.) B. of D. Second edition. 8°. *T. C[otes] a. R. C[otes] f. M. Sparke,* 1630. Ent. 1 oc. 1628. DUR(Bamb.).

24701 — [Anr. ed., enlarged.] Third edition. 8°. *T. Cotes f. M. Sparke,* 1631. O.

With Vicars' name in an acrostic on tp verso.

24702 — Χειραγωγια manuductio ad artem rhetoricam. 8°. *typis A. Matthæi,* 1621. Ent. to W. Bladen 20 no. 1620. L.O.

24702.5 — [Anr. ed.] Editio nova. 12°. *G. E[ld] & M. F[lesher,]* 1624. L(tp only, Ames II.694).O.

24703 — Editio tertia altera parte auctior. 12°. *typis J. Haviland, imp. R. Milbourne,* 1628. L.O²⁷.C⁵.A.; F.Y.

24704 — Pusillus grex. Ελεγχος. Refutatio cuiusdam libelli De amplitudine regni coelestis sub ementito C. S. Curionis nomine emissi. 4°. *Oxoniæ, G. Turner,* 1627. L³.O.O³.O¹⁰.O¹⁸.

24705 — Ρομφαιοφορος the sword-bearer. . . . In a sermon. 4°. *B. A[lsop] a. T. Fawcet f. R. Milburne,* 1627. O.NEP.PETYT.STD.; F.HN.HD.

— *ed. See* 4630, 17245.

— *tr. See* 14896.

24706 [A ghost.]

24707 **Vicary, Thomas.** The Englishemans treasure, or treasor for Englishmen: with the true anatomye of mans body. Also the rare treasor of the English bathes, written by W. Turner. Gathered by W. Bremer. 4°. *J. Windet f. J. Perin,* 1586. L.L¹⁶.L³⁹.O⁵(imp.). BRISTOL.; HN(imp.).NLM. Duke U.

A reprint of 24713 w. several additions including extracts from pt. 2 of 24366.

24708 — [Anr. ed.] 4°. *G. Robinson f. J. Perin,* 1587. L.L¹⁶. O³.BHP.BRISTOL.+; F.Y.

24709 — [Anr. ed.] 4°. *T. Creede,* 1596. Ent. 28 ja. L¹⁰.O.G². Warrington PL.; F.NLM.NY⁴.

24709.5 — [Anr. ed.] 4°. *T. Creede,* 1599. HD(imp.).NLM.WIS.

24710 — [Anr. ed.] Now sixtly augmented and enlarged, by G. E. 4°. *T. Creede,* 1613. L.O.BHP.E⁵.G².+; F(2 imp.).HN.NLM(2).NY⁴(imp.).WIS.

Vicary, Thomas—*cont.*

24711 — [Anr. ed.] Now seventhly augmented. 4°. *B. Alsop a. T. Fawcet,* 1626. L.O⁴³(imp.).C.G²(2, 1 imp.).; F (imp.).ILL.

The imp. G² copy has date altered in ink to 1696.

24712 — [Anr. ed.] Now eighthly augmented: by W. B(oraston.) 4°. *B. Alsop a. T. Fawcet,* 1633. L.O.C.BIRM.G².+; HN.HD.NLM.NWM.NY⁴.+

24713 — A profitable treatise of the anatomie of mans body. Newly reuyued, corrected, and published by the chirurgions of [St. Bartholomew's] hospital. 1577. 8° in 4's. *H. Bamforde,* [1577.] Ent. 13 ja. L.C.

Reprinted in 24707. Regarding the earlier ed. *see* 11715.5.

Viccars, John. Decapla. 1639. *See* 24696.

24714 **Victor,** *Bp. of Vita.* The memorable, and tragical history, of the persecution in Africke: under Gensericke and Hunricke, Arrian kinges of the Vandals. With the life and acts of bishop Fulgentius. [*Tr.* R.Y.S.M. L.A.D., i.e. R. Buckland.] 8°. [*English secret press,*] 1605. L.L².O.PARIS.; F.HN.STL.Y.

A&R 847. The author is erroneously called Victor of Utica on the tp.

Victor Amadeus, *Duke of Savoy. See* 5045.3.

24715 **Victorinus, Georgius.** Siren coelestis centum harmoniarum, duarum, trium, & quatuor vocum. Eandem, methodo docendi, et discendi musicam . . . W. Bray-thwaitus . . . communicavit. Editio altera correctior. Suprema. 4°. *ex typ. J. Norton [a. J. Dawson,]* 1638 (1639.) L(lacks Methodus).O³(lacks Methodus).c.c⁶.c¹⁷(Methodus only).+

Dawson pr. first A⁴. The music is in a unique notation devised by Braithwait. Apparently only the 2-pt. songs in the Suprema voice were pub'd, together w. Braithwait's Methodus, which gives another musical setting of the same texts.

Victory. The great victory which God hath given. 1613. *See* 13572.

— The tryumphant vyctory. 1532. *See* 5018.

24716 **Vienna.** Newes from Vienna the .5. day of August .1566. of Jula in Hungary, assaulted by the great Turke. *Tr.* out of hye Almaine. 4°. *J. Awdeley,* 1566 (21 se.) Ent. to J. Sampson, i.e. Awdeley, 1566–67. L.

24716.5 — True and most certaine newes, sent from Vienna in Austria, the 17. of June last, 1595. Howe Ferdinand earle of Hardeck, generall ouer Raab in Hungaria, trecherously yeelded to the Turke. 4°. [*P. Short*] *f. W. Leake,* 1595. Ent. 12 au. O.

24717 **Vienna.** Vienna. Noe art can cure this hart. [1632?] = 17202.

24718 **Vieta, Franciscus.** Francisci Vietæi opera mathematica, in quibus tractatur canon mathematicus, seu ad triangula. Item Canonion triangulorum . . . unà cum Vniuersalium inspectionum . . . libro singulari. Quæ quidem omnia illustrantur Tabula. fol. 4 pts. *Londini, ap. F. Bouuier,* 1589. L.O.; F(Cashel copy).

A reissue w. added gen. tp of the ed. pr. at Paris by J. Mettayer, 1579, and w. the latter's imprints uncancelled.

Vignay, Jean de. *See* 24873.

24719 **Vignier, Nicolas.** Concerning the excommunication of the Venetians a discourse against C. Baronius. Written in Latine and *tr.* after the copie printed at Samur 1606. Whereunto is added the bull of pope Paulus the fift, against Venice. As also an Apologie of frier Paul of Servi [P. Sarpi.] 4°. *M. B[radwood] f. C. B[urby,]* 1607. Ent. to Burby 10 de. 1606. L.O.C. D.M(deposit).+; F.HN.BO.ILL.U.+

24720 **Vigo, Joannes de.** The most excellent workes of chirurgerye, made by J. Vigon, *tr.* (B. Traheron.) fol. *E. Whytchurch,* 1543. L.L¹⁶.O.G².E.+; HD.NLM. WASH³.WIS. Duke U.+

24721 — [Anr. ed.] fol. *E. Whytchurch,* 1550. L.O.C(imp.). A.M.+; F.HN.HD(lacks tp).PML.WIS.+

24722 — [Anr. ed.] M.D.LXXI. The most [etc.] fol. *T. East a. H. Middelton,* 1571 (17 jy.) L.L¹⁶.O.G².P.+; CAL. NLM.NY⁴.WIS(lacks tp).Y.+

Vigo, Joannes de—*cont.*

24723 — [Anr. ed., enlarged.] The whole worke of . . . J. Vigo: newly corrected. Whereunto are annexed certain works, compiled and published by T. Gale. 3 pts. 4° in 8's. *T. East*, 1586. Ent. 12 mr. 1582; *see also* 6 se. 1585. L.O(lacks pt. 3).C.G².M⁴.+; F. HD.LC. NLM.Y(pt. 1 only).+

Locations listed above have all 3 pts., except as noted, though it has not been ascertained if they are in each case bd. together. Copies of pts. 2 and 3 listed at 11529a and 11531, respectively, are locations where no copy of 24723 was reported.

24724 — Now = 24725.5.

24725 — This lytell practyce of Johānes de Vigo in medycyne, is *tr.* out of Laten for the health of the body of man. 8°. (*Robert wyer*,) [1550?] L.O.; NLM. In colophon: 'at/ charynge'.

24725.3 — [Anr. ed.] 8°. (*Robart Wyer*,) [1552?] G².; HN. In colophon: 'at cha-/rynge'.

24725.5 — [Anr. ed.] 8° in 4's. (*Robert Wyer*,) [1555?] L(2). (Formerly 24724) In colophon: 'besyde Cha-/rynge'.

24725.7 — [Anr. ed.] 8°. (*T. Colwell*,) 1562 (1 ap.) O⁸.

24726 — [Anr. ed.] 8°. [*J. Awdley*](*f. A. Kitson*,) 1564 (1 ap.) L.

24726.5 **Vigor, Simon,** *Abp.* Actes of conference in religion, holden at Paris, betweene two papist doctours of Sorbone [S. Vigor and C. de Sainctes] and two godlie ministers of the church [J. de L'Espine and H. du Rosier.] Drawen out of French by G. Fenton. 4°. *H. Bynneman f. W. Norton a. H. Toye*, [1571.] L.O³.C⁹.DUR³.E².+; U. (Formerly 10790) Dedic. dated 4 July 1571.

24727 — [Anr. trans.] Acts of the dispute and conference holden at Paris, 1566. Tr. J. Golburne. 4° in 8's. *T. Creede*, 1602. L.O.C.D.DUR⁵.+; F(imp.).HN.

Villacastin, Tomás de. A manuall of devout meditations. 1618. *See* 16877.

Villainies. Villainies discovered by lanthorne and candle-light. 1616, etc. *See* 6488 sq.

24728 **Villa Sancta, Alphonsus de.** De libero arbitrio aduersus Melanchtonem. 4°. (*in æd. Pinsonianis*, 1523 (14 kal. no.)) L.C³.

24729 — Problema indulgentiarum, quo Lutheri errata dissoluuntur. 4°. (*in æd. Pynsonianis*,) [1523.] L.L².O. C³.C⁷.+

Villegagnon, *Sir* **Nicholas.** *See* 24894.

24730 **Villegas, Alfonso de.** Flos sanctorum. The liues of saints. Written in Spanish. *Tr.* out of Italian into English, and compared with the Spanish by W. & E. K[insman] B[rothers.] The first tome. 4°. [*Douai, P. Auroi*, 1609.] L.O.O¹³(imp.).C.YK.+; F.HD. A&R 851. Although 6 months are called for, only Jan.–April were published.

24731 — [Anr. ed.?] 8°. [n.p.] 1610. No copy located; possibly a confusion with 24734. A&R 852.

24731.5 — The lives of saints. 8°. *Douai, widow of L. Kellam*, 1614. L.DE.; TEX. • All copies contain Sept.–Dec. only.

24731a — [Anr. ed. w. all 12 months.] The lives of saints. The first part contayning the six first monethes. (The second part contayning the six last monethes.) 2 vols. 8°. *Doway, widow of L. Kellam*, 1615. L(vol. 2). L¹⁵.O.M²(imp.).W(imp.).+; N. A&R 853.

24731b — [Anr. ed.] Wherunto are added the lives of sundrie other saints. Extracted out of F. Ribadeniera [*sic*], and other authors. The second edition, set forth by J. Heigham, more correct, and more exact then the former. 4°. [*St. Omer, C. Boscard*,] 1621. O.W. A&R 854.

24732 — [Anr. issue of 24731a, w. added Appendix in vol. 1, and cancel prelims.] The lives of saints gathered out of father P. Ribadeneyra . . . A. Villegas, [etc.] The first (last) six monethes. With an appendix prefixed of the saintes lately canonized, and beatified by Paulus V. & Gregory XV. By E. Kinesman. 2 vols. 8°. [*St. Omer, English College Press*,] 1623. L(vol. 1). O¹³.C(vol. 1).ST(imp.).KILLINEY.+; F(vol. 2). A&R 855. Appendix reprinted in 24738.

Villegas, Alfonso de—*cont.*

24733 — [Anr. ed., enlarged.] This last edition. Newly perused, corrected amplefied & adorned with many faire brasen images. And in the end the lives of S. Patricke, [etc.] 4°. [*Rouen, J. Cousturier*,] f. W. H., 1628 (1627.) L².O.C.D⁶.DUR³.+; GRO.Y(imp.). A&R 856. The additional Lives are reprinted from 14626 and next appear in 24736.

24734 — [Anr. ed.] The third edition, set forth by J. Heigham. 4°. [Main text: *St. Omer, widow of C. Boscard*; Appendix: *St. Omer, G. Seutin?*] 1630. L.O.O⁵. DUR⁵(imp.).W.+; HN.HD.NY. A&R 857. *2ʳ catchword: 'more'.

24735 — [Anr. issue, w. cancel prelims. and engr. tp:] The fourth, & last edition. *Paris* [really *St. Omer, English College Press*,] 1634. O. A&R 858. *2ʳ catchword: 'stianity,'. The engr. tp was earlier used in 17181, w. a different engr. title-panel in the centre.

24736 — [Anr. ed.] With the lives of S. Patrick [etc.] All newly corrected and adorned with many brasen picteurs in this last edition. 4°. [*Rouen*,] J. Cousturier, 1636. L.L⁹(imp.).O³.SBK(imp.).W.+; F.HN.N.NLA. A&R 859.

24737 — [Anr. issue of 24734, w. engr. tp of 24735, w. date altered.] The fourth, & last edition. *Paris* [really *St. Omer?*] 1638. C(lacks Appendix). A&R 860. *2ʳ catchword: 'more'.

24738 — An appendix of the saints lately canonized, and beatifyed. [Anon. Not by Villegas. Tr.] (E. Kinsman.) 12°. *Doway, H. Taylor*, 1624. L.L²⁶.DAI.; HN. A&R 33. Reprinted from 24732.

24739 **Villiers, George,** *Duke of Buckingham.* [Heading A1ʳ:] April 4. The proceeding of the Parliament, being this day related to the King. [Heading A2ʳ:] The Duke of Buckingham his Speach . . . the 4ᵗʰ. of Aprill, 1628. 4°. [*London*, 1628.] L(2, 1 lacks A1). O⁸.C².M(lacks A1).; HD.Y.

24739.5 — A journall of all the proceedings of the duke of Buckingham his grace, in the isle of Ree. Set forth by a gentleman of speciall note. 4°. [*A. Mathewes*] f. T. Walkley, 1627. Ent. 1 au. O³.O⁸.; F.BO. Portions of the title and imprint in 24739.5–24743 are from standing type.

24740 — [A variant, with additions to the title:] Whereunto is added the names of the French nobilitie that were slaine. 4°. [*A. Mathewes*] f. T. Walkley, 1627. L.

24741 — A continued journall. August 17. (The relation of Mr. Garetson [master of a Dutch ship.]) 4°. [*A. Mathewes*] f. T. Walkley, 1627. L.O.O⁶.LAMPORT.; F.HN.

24742 — — August 30. As also the portaiture [*sic*] of the knife with which his excellence should have been murdered. 4°. [*A. Mathewes*] f. T. Walkley, 1627. Ent. 25 au. L(2).M⁴.; HN.DAR.HD. The cut of the knife is on a folding leaf; on B2ʳ is an advt. for a map of Ré and Oléron, which is a different item from 21590.5.

24743 — — September 18. 4°. A. M[athewes] f. T. Walkley, 1627. Ent. 15 se. L.L³⁸.G².; F.HN.

24744 — — October 2. 4°. A. M[athewes] f. T. Walkley, 1627. Ent. 4 oc. L.O⁵.; F.HN. *See also* 24268.7.

24745 — — November 2. 4°. A. M[athewes] f. T. Walkley, 1627. O⁸.; HN.Y.

— For other accounts of these events *see* Newsbooks 186 sqq. and 20779.5.

24746 — A manifestation or remonstrance. Of the duke of Buckingham; containing a declaration of his majesties intention for this present arming. Tr. out of the originall French copie. *Eng. a. Fr.* 4°. [*J. Bill*] f. T. Walkley, 1627. Ent. 25 au. L.O.C.M⁴.SHEF.+; HN.CAL.HD.ILL.Y.+ Tp varies; most copies have: 'Tr. . . . copie.' as above. At least 1 copy each at C, C², HN has instead: 'Printed according to the originall, given aboard the shippe Admirall, on Wednesday the 21. of July, and signed Buckingham.'

24746.3 — The right high, and right mightie prince George Villiers, duke, [etc.] A catalogue of all the kings ships, as also of all other ships, . . . with their squadrons, captaines, . . . in his majesties service, the 27. of June, 1207 [*sic*]. s.sh.fol. f. H. Gosson, [1627.] O⁵.

24746.5 — [A variant, with corrections.] . . . the 27. of June, 1627. f. J. Wright, [1627.] L⁵(Lemon 276).

24747 **Vincent,** *of Lerins, Saint.* A boke writtē by one Vincētius Leriniensis, . . . against certain heretikes, in the time of Theodosius . . . *tr.* out of Latin. 8º. (*R. Tottel,*) 1554 (12 jn.) O.; F.
This and the following are all eds., in English or Latin, of the same text: Pro catholicae fidei antiquitate libellus.

24748 — The golden treatise of . . . Vincentius Lirinensis. For the antiquitie, and vniuersalitie, of the catholicke religion: against all heresies: newly *tr.* by A. P. 8º. [*London?* *Fr. Garnet's second press,* 1596?] L.O.W. Brailes Presbytery, Warwickshire.; HN. A&R 861.

24748.5 — [Anr. ed.] 8º. *S. Omers,* [*widow of C. Boscard*] *f. J. Heigham,* 1631. L.A²ST(2). A&R 862.

24749 — Peregrini, id est, ut vulgo perhibetur, Vincentii Lirinensis, adversus prophanas hæreses, commonitoria duo. Editio repurgata. Huic adijcitur Augustini liber de hæresibus. 12º. *Oxoniæ, G. T*[*urner,*] *imp. G. Webb,* 1631. L.O.C.D.E.+; F.HN.HD.N.Y.+

24750 — Vincentii Lirinensis Galli pro catholicæ fidei antiquitate libellus verè aureus: nunc primum per capita distinctus. 12º. [*R. Robinson,*] 1591. L.O.O³.C. LEEDS.+; F.HD.TORONTO².U.Y. Issued w. 14584.

24751 — No entry.

24752 — Vincentius Lirinensis . . . for the antiquitie and veritie of the catholik fayth, aganis ye prophane nouationis of al hæreseis, neulie *tr.* in Scottis be N. Winzet. 8º. *Antuerpiae, ex off. Æ. Diest,* 1563 (1 de.) L(lacks tp).E.; F. A&R 863. The errata include some for 25859.

24753 — A very christian, learned, and briefe discourse, concerning the true, ancient, and catholicke faith. *Tr.* and illustrated with marginall notes. By T. Tuke. 12º. (*N. Okes*) *f. L. Becket,* 1611. Ent. 23 ap. L.OS.

24754 — The waie home to Christ and truth. Englished [by J. Proctor], and by the quenes highnes authorised to be sette furthe. 8º. (*R. Caly,* 1554 (22 oc.)) O.P. ST.; F(2, 1 lacks col.).

24755 — [Anr. ed.] 8º. (*R. Caly,* 1556 (20 ja.)) L.C.DUR⁵ (imp.).; F.

24756 **Vincent, Augustine.** A discoverie of errours in the first edition of the Catalogue of nobility, published by R. Brooke, 1619 [3832]. And printed heerewith word for word, according to that edition. With a continuance untill 1622. At the end whereof, is annexed a review of a later edition, by him stolne into the world. 1621. fol. *W. Jaggard,* 1622. Ent. 29 oc. 1621. L.O.C.D.M.+; F.HN.HD.N.NY.+
Concerning added leaves and cancels, see *The Library,* XIII (1958), pp. 124–7.
— See also 16768.32.

24757 **Vincent, Margret.** A pittilesse mother. That most unnaturally murthered two of her owne children. Beeing a gentlewonan [*sic*] named M. Vincent. Whereunto is added Andersons repentance [in verse], who was executed the 18. of May 1616. 4º. [*G. Eld*] *f. J. T*[*rundle,*] *sold by J. Wright,* [1616.] L(impr. cropt).O.; HD(tp cropt).

24758 **Vincent, Philip.** A true relation of the late battell fought in New England, between the English, and the salvages. 4º w. perp. chainlines. *M. P*[*arsons*] *f. N. Butter a. J. Bellamie,* 1637. Ent. to Butter 13 no. L.O⁹.C⁴(lacks tp)*.; HN.BO⁵.CB.MICH(imp.).NY.+

24759 — [A variant, w. title:] A true relation . . . and the Pequet salvages: in which was slaine and taken prisoners about 700 of the salvages. *M. P*[*arsons*] *f. N. Butter a. J. Bellamie,* 1638. O¹³.G².; F.HN.BO.N.NY.+

24760 — [Anr. ed.] 4º w. perp. chainlines. *T. Harper f. N. Butter a. J. Bellamie,* 1638. L.HAT.; F.HN.CB.HD(C4 def.). NY.+

24760.5 — The lamentations of Germany. Wherein, as in a glasse, we may behold her miserable condition. [*Ed.* L. Seaman.] 8º. *E. G*[*riffin*] *f. J. Rothwell,* 1638. Ent. 19 de. 1637. L¹⁶. Waddesdon Manor, Aylesbury, Bucks. (*see note*).
Collates A–F⁸. Chap. 1 begins on B2ʳ, p. 1. Copies differ; line 2 of imprint ends: 'to be' (L¹⁶) or 'are to' (Waddesdon). The Waddesdon copy is signed in MS. 'Laz. Seaman' at the end of the preface; it also has B3–6 cancelled and replaced by the enlarged chap. 2 of 24761 and has the latter's a⁸.

Vincent, Philip—*cont.*

24760.7 — [Anr. ed., with additions.] Hereunto are added three letters, [etc.] 8º. *E. G*[*riffin*] *f. J. Rothwell,* 1638. C².; Y.
Collates A⁸ a⁸ B–E⁸. Chap. 1 begins on B1ʳ, p. 1; a2ᵛ catchword: 'nay,'. C² has orig. E8 w. line 1 of the recto beginning: 'soules' and imprimatur on the verso; Y has the first cancel mentioned in 24761.

24761 — [Anr. ed., with the text of chap. 2 enlarged.] 8º. *E. G*[*riffin*] *f. J. Rothwell,* 1638. L(2).O.C(2).SHEF.; F(imp.).HN.CU.HD.N.+
Collates A⁸ a⁸ B⁸ b⁸ C–E⁸. Chap. 1 begins on B1ʳ, unpaged; a2ᵛ catchword: 'at'. E8 is known in 3 settings: the original has line 1 of the recto beginning: 'that' and imprimatur on the verso (L(G.6312), C(Acton)); both cancels have the verso blank, and line 18 on the recto beginning 'loke' (O, C(also in Acton), HN, and Y copy of 24760.7) or 'looke' (C(Syn), CU, HD, N).

24762 **Vincentius,** *Bellovacensis.* [a6ʳ:] Hier begynneth the book callid the myrrour of the worlde. [Anon. Not by Vincentius. *Tr.* by W. Caxton from Image du monde.] fol. [*Westminster, W. Caxton,* 1481.] L.O. C(imp.).M.WIN².+; HN.LC.MIN.PML.Mellon.+ Duff 401.

24763 — [Anr. ed. a4ᵛ:] Hier begynneth the booke callyd the, Myrrour of the worlde. fol. [*Westminster,*] (*Caxton me fieri fecit,*) [1490.] L.O¹⁰.C.G².M.+; HN.ILL.LC.NY. PML.+ Duff 402.

24764 — [Anr. ed., revised.] The myrrour: [xylographic] & dyscrypcyon of the worlde. fol. (*L. Andrewe,*) [1527?] L(imp.).L³⁰.C.C⁶.M.+; F(2, 1 imp.).HN.BO.

24765 **Vinciolo, Federico di.** Les singuliers et nouueaux pourtraicts, pour touttes sortes d'ouurages de lingerie. 4º. *Paris, J. le Clerc le jeune,* 1587. Not an STC book.

24765.3 — [A trans.] New and singular patternes & workes of linnen. Seruing for paternes to make all sortes of lace. (New . . . patterns. . . . Wherein are represented the seauen planets, [etc.]) [Anon. *Tr.*] (A. Poyntz.) 4º. *J. Wolfe a.* [i.e. *for*] *E. White,* 1591. Ent. to Wolfe 11 se. 1587. L(frags., incl. sub tp, Harl.5927/40–46; 5963/178).; HD(lacks quire H).
(Formerly 20180) All leaves have signatures. The sub tp has imprint: '*J. Wolfe,* 1591.'

24765.7 — [An imitation?] 4º. [*London?* c. 1605.] O(imp., Douce L 204*).
(Formerly 15116) O has only patterns and leaf signatures; only leaves 1 and 3 in each quire are signed.
A few of the patterns are identical to those in continental eds. of Vinciolo though from different blocks, and a number of the other patterns are generally similar in style. None of the patterns is identical w. those in 24765.3.

Vindication. The vindication of the cobler. 1640. *See* 13855.4.

24766 **Vineis, Raimundus de.** [Heading a1ʳ:] Here begynneth the lyf of saint katherin of senis. (Here begynnen the reuelaciōs of Saynt Elysabeth of hungarye. [By J. Montanus.]) [*Tr.* from Latin.] fol. [*Westminster, W. de Worde,* 1492?] L(2).C.M.WN. Copenhagen RL.; F(imp.). Mellon. Duff 403.
Text ends: 'Here enden the reuelacions . . . hungarye,'.

24766.3 — [Anr. issue, with h2,5; n1,6; and q1,4 reset.] (*westemynster, W. de worde,*) [1500?] HN(lacks l 2–5). Duff 403a.
Text ends: 'Here endeth the reuelacyons . . . hūgarye,'.
— See also 4815, 4830.

24766.7 **Vineyard.** The viniard of deuotion. Comprehending sundry godly praiers, psalmes and meditations. Newly corrected and augmen⟨ted.⟩ 16º in 8's. [*R. Bradock?*] (*f. E. White,* 1599.) Ent. 3 my. 1591. L(imp.).

24767 **Viques,** *Captain.* The rodomantades of captayne Viques, . . . a traytour to his king, slayne in fight vnder the banner of the Leaguers. Wherein is expressed, the desire of a bloudy minde, and the reward of a false traitour. 4º. *J. Wolfe,* 1591. Ent. 4 no. 1590. P.
(Pt. 2 now = 5400.3) Entered in the SR together with 5400.3 but apparently a separate publication.

24767.5 **Virel, Matthieu.** A learned and excellent treatise containing all the principall grounds of christian religion. Turned into English [by] (S. Egerton.) 8°. *R. Field f. R. Dexter*, 1594. Ent. 5 ja. o.

24768 — Second impression, corrected and amended. 8°. *R. Field f. R. Dexter*, 1594. L.C.C².C¹⁰.P.; F.HD.

24768.5 — Third impression. 8°. *R. Robinson [a. R. Field] f. R. Dexter*, 1595. L(tp only, Ames I.567).P.; F.
Field app. pr. quires M–S.

24769 — Fourth and last impression. 8°. *R. Robinson f. R. Dexter*, 1597. L.O.C.; U.

24769.5 — Fifth impression. 8°. *R. Field f. R. Dexter*, 1600. C(imp.).; PML.

24769a — Sixt impression. 8°. *R. Bradock f. R. Dexter*, 1603. O(2).E⁴.

24770 — Seventh impression: now newly revised, with a table annexed. 8°. [*Eliot's Court Press*] *f. E. Bishop*, 1607. Ent. to the Stat. Co. 28 no. 1603; to Bishop 14 mr. 1605. O⁶.C.C³.BRISTOL.LK.; F.U.

24770.5 — Eighth impression. 8°. *M. Bradwood f. E. Bishop*, 1609. L.C¹².; Y.

24771 — Ninth impression. 8°. *M. Bradwood f. E. Bishop*, 1612. L.YK.; HN.

24771.3 — Tenth impression. 8°. *J. Legatt f. E. Bishop*, 1615. O¹².C⁵.

24771.7 — Eleventh impression. 8°. *T. Dawson f. Eliz. Bishop*, 1620. Stevens Cox.; HD.

24772 — Twelfth [*sic*] impression. 8°. *H. L[ownes] f. G. Lathum*, 1626. Ass'd 31 ja. 1620. L³.C¹³.; HD.NY⁸.

24772.5 — Thirteenth edition. 12°. *R. Y[oung] f. G. Lathum*, 1633. L(engr. tp only, Harl.5927/109).O.DUL.E.G⁴.+; CHI.HART.
The engr. tp reads: 'The grounds of christian religion. *f. G. Latham*, 1633.'

24773 — Fourteenth edition. 12°. *R. Y[oung] f. G. Lathum*, 1635. L.L⁴.O.M.SCL.; F.DAR(imp.).FBL.HD(lacks engr. tp).U.
The engr. tp is like 24772.5, w. date altered to 1636.

24774 **Viret, Pierre.** De cautelen (dat is te segghen, de waerschouwinghe ofte onderwijsinghe) met het canon ende ceremonien vander Misse. Eerst ghemaeckt int Frācois . . . nu nieuwelyck ouergesedt. *Lat. a. Dutch.* 8°. *Londen,* [*H. Bynneman,*] 1568. L.O.O³¹.C(2).; F.HN.HD.
With Bynneman's device (McK. 149) at the end. O³¹ has the date unaltered; HD has the date altered in ink to 1578. Copies bd. w. and prob. issued w. 6581.

24775 — [*Anr. trans.*] The cauteles, canon, and ceremonies, of the popish masse. Fully set downe, both in Latine and Englishe. With annotations by P. Viret, and *tr.* out of French by T. Sto(cker) gent. *Lat. a. Eng.* 8°. *T. Vautrollier f. A. Maunsell*, 1584. Ent. 7 ja. L.O.C.A.D.+; F.HN.BO.ILL.

24776 — The christian disputations, by master P. Viret. Deuided into three partes, dialogue wise. *Tr.* out of French by J. Brooke of Ashe. 4° in 8's. *T. East*, 1579. L.O.C³. D.P.+; F.HN(imp.).

24777 — The firste parte of the christian instruction, wherein the principall pointes of the religion are handled by dialogues. *Tr.* by J. Shute . . . 1565. 4°. *J. Day,* [1565.] L.L².DUL(imp.).P.; F.

24778 — A christian instruction, conteyning the law and the gospell. Done in certayne dialogues in french. *Tr.* by J. S[hute.] 8°. [*H. Bynneman? f.*] *A. Veale,* 1573. L(2).C(imp.).P.; F.HN(imp.).
A different text from 24777.

24779 — An epistle to the faithfull, necessary for all the children of God: especially in these dangerous dayes. Written in French, and englished by F. H. esquier. 8°. [*T. Dawson*] *f. T. Smith*, 1582. L.L².C³.P.; F.
The inits. 'T.D.' are in the tp border.

24780 — A faithfull and familiar exposition vpon the prayer of our Lorde . . . written in French, dialogue wise, and *tr.* by J. Brooke. 4°. *H. Middleton f. R. Sergier*, 1582. L.O.C.D.E⁴.+; F.PN².

24781 — A notable collection of diuers and sōdry places of the sacred scriptures, which make to the declaratyon of the Lordes prayer. *Tr.* oute of Frenche by A. Scoloker. 8°. *A. Scoloker a. W. Seres,* [1548.] L.O.C.LINC(imp.).; HN.CH.
A2ʳ has sub tp: 'The Places of Holye Scripture', n.d.

24782 — The principal points which are at this daye in controuersie, concerning the holy supper and of the masse. *Tr.* J. S(houte.) 8°. *C. Barker*, 1579. Ent. 17 au. L².O⁹.D.E⁴.P.; F(imp.).

Viret, Pierre—*cont.*

24783 — The schoole of beastes, intituled, the good housholder, or the oeconomickes. Made dialogue-wise, and *tr.* out of French by I. B. 8°. *R. Walde-graue*, 1585. L.E⁴.; Y.

24784 — A verie familiare & fruiteful exposition of the .xii. articles in the Apostles crede, made in dialoges. *Tr.* in to englishe. 8°. [*S. Mierdman f.*] (*J. Day a. W. Seres,*) [1548?] L.O.C⁵(lacks col.).E⁴.P.; F.HN(lacks col.).HD(lacks tp and col.).U.

24785 — The worlde possessed with deuils, conteyning three dialogues. 1. Of the deuill let loose. 2. Of blacke deuils. 3. Of white deuils. [Anon. *Tr.* W. Chauncie.] 8°. [*H. Bynneman?*] *f. J. Perin*, 1583. Ent. 17 ja. L.C³.G².; Syracuse U (imp.).
Collates A–G⁸ H² a–d⁸ e⁴.

24786 — [Anr. ed.] 8°. [*J. Kingston*] *f. J. Perin*, 1583. L.O¹⁴.C¹⁹. P.; F.HN.COR.LC.PEN.
Collates A–L⁸. For pt. 2 *see* 24786.5.

24786.5 — The second part of the demoniacke worlde, conteining three dialogues. 1. Of familiar diuels. 2. Of lunaticke diuels. 3. Of the coniuring of diuels. *Tr.* out of French by T. S(tocker) 8°. (*T. Dawson*) *f. J. Perin*, 1583. L(2).L².O¹⁴.P.; F.HN.COR.PEN.

— See also 21507.5.

Virgidemiarum. Virgidemiarum. 1597, etc. *See* 12716 sqq.

24787 **Virgilius Maro, Publius.** Vergiliana poesis que latinitatis norma est et propulsatis & elimatis [*sic*] omnibus mendis felici gaudet exordio. 8°. *Venalis extat Londoñ* [*by R. Pynson, c.* 1515.] O¹⁰(imp.).M.
Tp has Pynson's name in device McK. 9; the last 3 quires are in long 12's. Both copies lack colophon, if any.

24788 — Pub. Virgilii Maronis opera. Annotationibus P. Manutij illustrata. 8°. *ap. H. Bynneman*, 1570. Ent. 1569–70. L.O.; F.

24788a — [Anr. ed.] 8°. *ap. H. Bynneman*, 1572. O⁶.C.

24788a.5 — [Anr. ed.] Opera P. Virgilii Maronis. P. Manutii annotationes. G. Fabricii obseruationes. 8°. *ex typ. J. Kyngstoni*, 1576. L(tp only, Harl.5927/89).

24789 — [Anr. ed.] 16° in 8's. *H. Middletonus, imp. J. H[arrison 1,]* 1580. L.
With an addition to the Aeneid by M. Vegius.

24790 — [Anr. ed.] 16° in 8's. *H. Midletonus, imp. J. H[arrison 1,]* 1583. L.O. Warrington PL.

24790.3 — [A variant, w. imprint:] *H. Midletonus, imp. J. H[arrison 1,]* 1584. ETON.; PN.

24790.7 — [Anr. ed.] Publii Virgilii Maronis poemata. Novis scholiis illustrata, quæ H. Steph[anus] partim domi nata, partim è virorum doctissimorum libris excerpta dedit. Secunda editio. 8°. *Vidua T. Orwini*, 1593. L.

24791 — [Anr. ed.] Pub. Virgilii Maronis opera. P. Manutij annotationes. G. Fabricij annotationes. 8°. *F. Kingston*, 1597. L.O.M⁴.; HN.

24791.3 — [Anr. ed.] 16° in 8's. *ap. R. Dexter*, 1602. C¹².

24791.7 — [Anr. ed.] 8°. [*R. Field,*] *ex typ. Soc. Stat.*, 1613. L(tp only, Ames II.306).O.LK.

24792 — [Anr. ed.] 16° in 8's. [*London, R. Field and unidentified Continental press,*] *ex typ. Soc. Stat.*, 1616. L.
Field pr. only the tp.

24792.5 — [Anr. ed.] 8°. *ex typ. Soc. Stat.*, 1622. Ent. to the English Stock 5 mr. 1620. MARL.

24793 — [Anr. ed.] 8°. *Cantabrigiæ, ex acad. typog.*, 1632. L.O.; ILL.

24794 — [Anr. ed.] Notis à T. Farnabio. 8°. *F. Kyngston, imp. R. Allot*, 1634. L.O.; ILL.

24794.5 — Pub. Virgilii Maronis poemata, cum optimis, exemplaribus collata. Quibus annotationes in margine adscriptæ sunt. 8°. *Edinburgi, A. Hart*, 1612 (24 jy.) E(imp.).

24795 — [Anr. ed.] 8°. *Aberdoniae, E. Rabanus, imp. D. Melvil*, 1629. E.G⁴.

24796 — [*Aeneid.*] [L7ʳ:] (Here fynyssheth the boke yf Eneydos, compyled by Vyrgyle, . . . *tr.* oute of latyne in to frensshe, and oute of frensshe reduced in to Englysshe by me w. Caxton.) fol. [*Westminster, W. Caxton,* 1490.] L.O(imp.).C.G²(imp.).M.+; HN.PFOR(imp.). PML. Mellon. Syracuse U.+ Duff 404.
From G. le Roy's French version of an Italian paraphrase of parts of the Aeneid and Boccaccio's Fall of Princes (cf. 3175).

Virgilius Maro, Publius—*cont.*

24797 — The .xiii. bukes of Eneados . . . *tr.* into Scottish metir, bi G. Douglas. [The 13th bk. by M. Vegius.] 4° in 8's. [*W. Copland*,] 1553. L.O.C.E.M.+; F.HN.HD (imp.).N.NY.+

24798 — Certain bokes [2 and 4] of Virgiles Aenæis turned into English meter by Henry [Howard] earle of Surrey. small 4°. *ap. R. Tottel*, 1557 (21 jn.) L.O(2).DUL.; PN.

Book 4 reprinted from 24810a.5.

24799 — The seuen first bookes of the Eneidos conuerted in Englishe meter by T. Phaer. 4°. (*J. Kyngston f. R. Jugge*,) 1558 (28 my.) L.O(3, 2 imp.).M.; HN.HD. MICH.PN.

24800 — [Anr. ed., enlarged.] The nyne fyrst bookes . . . conuerted into Englishe vearse by T. Phaer. [*Ed.*] (W. Wightman.) 4°. *R. Hall f. N. Englande*, 1562. Ent. 1562–63. L.O.G².NLW.P.+; F.HN.HD(imp.). PN.Y.+

24801 — [Anr. ed., enlarged.] The whole .xii. bookes of the Æneidos. The residue supplied, and the whole newly set forth, by T. Twyne. 4°. *W. How f. A. Veale*, 1573. L.O⁵.C².LIV³.M.+; F.HN.CU.HD.ILL.+

24802 — [Anr. ed., enlarged.] The .xiii. bookes of Æneidos. The thirteenth [*sic*] the supplement of Maphæus Vegius. Now the second time setforth. 4° in 8's. *W. How f. A. Veale*, 1584. L.O.C.BIRM.LIV³.+; F.HN.HD.N. NY.+

24803 — [Anr. ed.] Now newly set forth. 4° in 8's. *T. Creede*, 1596. Ent. 23 fb. L.O.C(imp.).C⁴.G².+; F.HN.CHI. HD(imp.).NY.+

24804 — [Anr. ed.] 4° in 8's. *T. Creede*, 1600. Ent. to C. Knight 26 jn. L.L²⁴.O.BIRM.ST.+; F.

24805 — [Anr. ed.] 4° in 8's. *T. Creede*, 1607. L.O.C.BRISTOL. NEK.+; F.HN.CU.HD.N.+

24805a — [Anr. ed.] 4° in 8's. *B. Alsop, by the assignement of C. Knight*, 1620. L.O.C⁵.E.LYD.+; F(tp def.).HN.ILL. PN.Y.+

(Formerly also 24808)

24806 — Thee first foure bookes of Virgil his Aeneis *tr.* intoo English heroical verse by R. Stanyhurst, wyth oother poëtical diuises thereto annexed. 4°. *Leiden, J. Pates*. 1582. L(lacks last leaf).O.; HN(imp.).

A&R 865.

24807 — [Anr. ed.] 8°. *H. Bynneman*, 1583. Ent. 24 ja. L(2). O(3, 1 imp.).C(2).C².E².; F.HN.HD.ILL.Y.+

24808 — = 24805a.

24809 — The XII Aeneids of Virgil, *tr.* into English deca-syllables, by J. Vicars. 8°. [*Cambridge, T. Buck*,] *sold by N. Alsop*, [*London*,] 1632. L.L³⁰.O.C.E.+; F.HN.HD.N.NY.+

Some copies (1 F, 1 HN) have errata at the end.

24809a — [A ghost.]

— [Single books. Book 1. *Tr.* G. Sandys. 1632.] *See* 18966.

24810 — The destruction of Troy, or the acts of Aeneas. *Tr.* out of the second booke of the Æneads. As also a Centurie of epigrams. By Sʳ T. Wrothe. *Lat. a. Eng.* 4°. *T. D[awson], sold by N. Bourne*, 1620. Ent. to J. Dawson 4 ap. L.O.; F(tp def.).HN.

(26052 is pt. of this)

24810a — Publij Vergilij Maronis Aeneidos liber secundus: Græcis uersibus redditus per G. Ethrigeum. *Lat. a. Gr.* 8°. (*ap. R. Wolfium*,) 1553 (8 id. jn.) L.O²¹(imp.). M.

24810a.5 — The fourth boke of Virgill, intreating of the loue betwene Aeneas & Dido, *tr.* into English, and drawne into a straūge metre by Henrye [Howard] late earle of Surrey. 4°. *J. Day f. W. Awen*, [1554.] PFOR.

Reprinted in 24798.

24811 — Didos death. *Tr.* out of the best of Latine poets, into the best of vulgar languages. By one that hath no name [Sir D. Digges.] *Lat. a. Eng.* 12°. *N. O[kes] f. W. Burre*, 1622. Ent. 11 de. 1621. O.

Regarding the translator *see The Letters of John Chamberlain*, ed. N. E. McClure, II.429–30.

24812 — Dido and Aeneas the fourth booke of Virgils Aeneis now Englished by R. Stapylton. 8°. *f. W. Cooke*, [1634?] Ent. 11 no. 1634. L(lacks tp).O.; HN.

24813 — [*Bucolics.*] Bucolica Virgilii cum commento familiari. 4° 8·4. (*per w. de worde*, 1512 (8 ap.)) L(imp.).M².

24814 — [Anr. ed.] 4° 8·4. (*per w. de worde*, 1514 (21 no.)) O. DNPK.M.

24814.5 — [Anr. ed.] 4° 6·4. (*in æd. W. de Worde*, 1522 (22 au.)) O(2 imp.).; PN.

Virgilius Maro, Publius—*cont.*

24815 — [Anr. ed.] 4° 6·4. (*in æd. W. de Worde*, 1529 (12 mr.)) PN(imp.).

24816 — The Bucolikes of Publius Virgilius Maro, with alphabeticall annotations. Drawne into Englishe by A. Fleming. 4°. *J. Charlewood f. T. Woodcocke*, 1575. O.E.G².M.

In rhymed verse.

24817 — The Bucoliks. . . . Together with his Georgiks. All newly *tr.* by A. F[leming.] 2 pts. 4°. *T. O[rwin] f. T. Woodcocke*, 1589. Ass'd from Woodcock to P. Linley 9 fb. 1596; to J. Flasket 26 jn. 1600. L.O.C.C⁴.E².+; F.HN.HD.N.Y².+

A different trans., in unrhymed verse.

— [Eclogues 1 and 2. *Tr.* W. Webbe.] 1586. *See* 25172.

24818 — Virgils eclogues, with his booke De apibus, *tr.* grammatically [by] (J. Brinsley.) To be used according to the directions in . . . Ludus Literarius, Chap. 8. [cf. 3768.] 4°. *R. Field f. T. Man*, 1620. Ent. to T. and Jonas Man 3 se. 1619. L.L³⁰.O.DUL.E².+; F.HN. ILL.N.PN.

24819 — [Anr. ed.] 4°. [*Eliot's Court Press f.*] assignes of T. Man, P. Man, a. Jonah Man, 1633. Ass'd to P. a. Jonas Man 3 my. 1624; to B. Fisher 6 jy. 1629. L.L³⁰.O. O⁵.C.+; F.HN.HD.N.PN.+

24820 — Virgils eclogues *tr.* into English [verse]: by W. L[atham,] gent. [With the commentary of J. L. Vives.] 8°. *W. Jones*, 1628. Ent. as tr. by Master Latham 17 jy. L.O.O⁷.C⁴.C⁵.+; F.HN(lacks M8). HD.PN.Y.+

24821 — Virgil's bucolicks Englished [*sic*]. Whereunto is added the two first satyrs of Juvenal. By J. Bidle. [In verse.] 8°. *J. L[egat,]* 1634. Ent. 11 jn. L(tp only, Harl. 5986/83).O.; HN.

24821.5 — [Single Eclogues. Heading A1ʳ:] Ecloga Virgilii prima Sapphico carmine, reddita ab A. Richardsono. [A Latin paraphrase in Sapphic meter.] 4°. [*London?* c. 1600.] F.

— [Eclogue 2. *Tr.* A. Fraunce.] 1591. *See* 11340.

24822 — [*Georgics.*] Nicolai Grimoaldi . . . in quatuor libros Georgicorum paraphrasis. [Virgil's text with Latin prose paraphrase.] 8°. *G. Bishop & R. Newbery*, [1591.] L.L².O.A.C.+; F.N.STAN.

Tp comp. dated 1591 in the sill.

24823 — Virgil's Georgicks Englished by T. May. [In verse.] 16° in 8's. [*H. Lownes] f. T. Walkley*, 1628. Ent. 24 my. L(2).O(2).HETH(imp.). London, Birkbeck College.; F.HN.HD.N(imp.).Y.+

Ends K2.

24824 — [Anr. ed.] 16° in 8's. [*A. Mathewes*] f. T. Walkley, 1628. L⁶.O(3).O⁷.O¹⁸.; HN.FBL.HD. Haverford C. Phillips Academy, Andover, Mass.

Ends L2.

— *See also* 24817, 24818.

24825 — The epigrams of P. Virgilius Maro, and others. Englished by J. P(enkethman.) 8°. *G. P[urslowe,]* 1624. L.C.; HN.PN.

HN lacks the inserted leaf after B5, which has epigrams 10, 11; present in L.

—————

24826 — Virgilius evangelisans. Sive historia domini & salvatoris nostri Jesu Christi, Virgilianis verbis & versibus descripta. Operâ A. Rossæi. 8°. *per J. Legatum, pro R. Thralo*, 1634. Ent. 27 jn. 1633. L.O.C.A.NEK.+; F.HN.CHI.HD.PN.+

E4ʳ last line: 'læthi'.

24826.5 — [Anr. ed.] 8°. *per J. Legatum, pro R. Thralo*, 1634. L.O(imp.).C³.E.STD.+; F.Y.

E4ʳ last line: 'lethi'.

24827 — [Anr. ed., extensively revised and enlarged.] Virgilii evangelisantis Christiados libri XIII. 8°. *typis J. Legate, sumpt. R. Thrale*, 1638. L.O.C.D.E.+; F.HN. HD.N.U.+

The engr. tp has imprint: 'pro R. Thralo, 1638.' X4 varies: text ends, incomplete, on the recto; or is completed on the verso; both at L, O, C. At least F has an extra leaf of errata.

24827.5 — Les faictz merueilleux de virgille. [c. 1520.] *See* Addenda.

24828 — Virgilius. [xylographic] This boke treath [*sic*] of the lyfe of Virgilius and of his deth and many maruayles that he dyd by whychcraft. [*Tr.* from Dutch?] 4° 6·4. (*Anwarpe, J. Doesborcke*,) [1518?] O(lacks A1).C(D3,4 only).; PML.

Virgilius Maro, Publius—*cont.*

24829 — [Anr. ed.] Virgilius. This boke treateth of the lyfe of Virgil. 4°. [*W. Copland*, 1562?] Ent. to Copland 1561–62. L(imp.).

24829.5 **Virgin.** The loving virgins complaint. Or, her destre [*sic*, for 'desire'] to obtaine the love of a young man. *Ballad.* 2 pts. s.sh.fol. *f. F. Coules*, [c. 1630.] C⁶.

24830 — The virgins A. B. C. Or, an alphabet of vertuous admonitions. *Ballad.* 2 pts. s.sh.fol. *M. P[arsons] f. F. Coules*, [1638?] L.

24830.2 **Virginia.** Good newes from Virginia, sent from James his Towne March, 1623. *Ballad.* 2 pts. s.sh.fol. *f. J. Trundle*, [1623.] v. Thomas Gilcrease Institute, Tulsa, Oklahoma.

— To the minister and church-wardens of [   ] [Brief for collections to convert the Indians of Virginia. 1616.] *See* 4587.7.

Virginia Company.

For further details of most of the following *see* Sabin 99854–99888.

24830.4 — [Bills of adventure.] Whereas [   ] hath paid in readie monie to sir Thomas Smith knight, treasurer of Virginia, the somme of [   ] for his adventures towards the said voyage . . . Anno domini. 1608. s.sh.fol. [*London*, 1608.] HN(dated in MS. 22 Mar.). *See also Court-Book C*, pp. 342–4.

24830.5 — [Anr. ed.] Whereas [   ] hath paid in ready mony [etc.] 1610. s.sh.fol. [*London*, 1610.] HN(dated in MS. 4 Apr.).

24830.6 — [Anr. ed., without printed date.] s.sh.fol. [*f. W. Welby*, 1611?] Bills of adventure ent. to Welby 11 ap. 1611. HAT(dated in MS. 14 Nov. 1611).; HN(dated in MS. 2 Dec. 1613).
Line 6 ends: 'shall haue ra-'.

24830.7 — [Anr. ed., without printed date.] s.sh.fol. [*f. W. Welby*, 1613?] HAT(dated in MS. 10 Nov. 1613).
Line 6 ends: 'shall haue'.

***

Arranged chronologically

24830.9 — Considering there is no publicke action, [etc. Offer of stock in the Company at £12 10s. a share.] s.sh.fol. [*London*, 1609?] CB.NY.ROS.
The text indicates a blank bill of adventure and some books on Virginia were to accompany this. CB is bd. in 22791; NY in 14699.

24831 — For the plantation in Virginia. Or Nova Britannia. Whereas . . . for the better setling of the colony [etc. Terms on which labourers will be accepted as colonists.] s.sh.fol. *J. Windet*, 1609. L.

24831.3 — By the counsell of Virginea. Whereas the good shippe, called the Hercules, is now preparing, [etc. Appeal to labourers to join the expedition.] s.sh.obl. 4°. [*T. Haveland*, 1610.] L⁵(Lemon 128).

24831.7 — A publication by the counsell of Virginea, touching the plantation there. [A further appeal for labourers to join the settlement.] s.sh.fol. *T. Haveland f. W. Welby*, 1610. L⁵(Lemon 122).

24832 — A true and sincere declaration of the purpose and ends of the plantation begun in Virginia. Sett forth by the authority of the governors and councellors established for that plantation. 4°. [*G. Eld*] *f. J. Stepneth*, 1610. Ent. 14 de. 1609. L.; LC.PN(2).ROS.
This is the later variant as 'Stepneth' is the correct spelling.

24832a — [A variant, w. imprint:] *f. J. Stepney*, 1610. DUR³.; HN.CB.HD.PH².
This is the earlier variant.

24833 — A true declaration of the estate of the colonie in Virginia, with a confutation of scandalous reports. Published by advise and direction of the councell of Virginia. 4°. [*Eliot's Court Press a. W. Stansby*] *f. W. Barret*, 1610. Ent. 8 no. L.O.D².G².M.+; F.HN. HD.N.NY.+
Eliot's Court Press pr. A–1st F; Stansby the rest.

24833.2 — By the counsell of Virginea. Seeing it hath pleased God, [etc. A further appeal for labourers.] 1/2 sh.fol. [*T. Haveland*] *f. W. Welby*, 1611. L⁵(Lemon 127).

24833.4 — By his majesties counsell of Virginea. Forasmuch as notwithstanding the late publication [etc. Regarding deferring of the lottery.] s.sh.fol. *F. Kyngston f. W. Welby*, 1612. Ent. 16 my. CB.
For various transactions of the Stationers' Co.

Virginia Company—*cont.*

regarding the lottery *see Court-Book C*, pp. 53, 65, 345–7. The item mentioned on p. 346, A true declaration, of which no copy survives, was entered to F. Kingston 9 Mar. 1614. *See also* 16756.5.

24833.6 — By his majesties councell for Virginia. Whereas sundrie the adventurers to Virginia [etc. Announcement that the lottery is to be drawn beginning 10 May.] s.sh.fol. *F. Kyngston f. W. Welby*, 1613. L⁵(Lemon 135).

24833.8 — A declaration for the certaine time of drawing the great standing lottery. . . . The 26. of June next. [With a list of the prizes.] s.sh.fol. *F. Kyngston f. W. Welby*, 1615 (22 fb.). L⁵(Lemon 151).
For a proclamation suppressing the lotteries *see* 8660.

24834 — [Heading A1ʳ:] By his majesties counseil for Virginia. A briefe declaration of the present state of things and of a division to be now made, of lands as well to all such as have adventured their monyes, as also to planters there. 4°. [*T. Snodham*, 1616.] L.; HN.CB.

24835 — Now = 24841.4.
24836 — Now = 24841.6.
24837 — Now = 24844.3.
24838 — ⟨The Vi⟩rginia trade stated. [Includes reference to Navigation Acts. after 1647.]
Not an STC item.

24839 — By his majesties councell for Virginia. Whereas upon the returne of sir Thomas Dale knight, (marshall of Virginia) [etc. An appeal for emigrants; Samuel Argall made governor.] s.sh.fol. [*T. Snodham*, 1617?] HN.

24840 — Orders and constitutions. 1620. = pt. of 24841.3 sq.

24841 — By the treasuror, councell and company for Virginia. [A proclamation for the erection of a guest house and the appointment of a godly minister in every borough. 17 May 1620.] s.sh.fol. [*F. Kingston*, 1620.] C¹⁰.; NY.

24841.2 — A declaration of the state of the colonie and affaires in Virginia: with the names of the adventurors, and summes adventured in that action. By his majesties counseil for Virginia. 22 Junij. 1620. 4°. *T. S[nodham a. F. Kingston,]* 1620. Ent. to Kingston a. Snodham 11 jy. CB. Detroit PL.
Collates A–B⁴ ⅃€⁴ C–F⁴ A². Kingston pr. C–2nd A; Snodham the rest. ⅃€⁴ is a Note of the shipping, and reprints 24842.

24841.3 — [Anr. issue, w. added A–E⁴:] (Orders and constitutions.) *T. S[nodham a. F. Kingston,]* 1620. O².O¹⁷. STD.; BO⁵.CB.CH.N.
The addition (formerly 24840) was pr. by Snodham; either this or STC 1905 may have been the text of which W. Jones pr. an illegal ed.; *see Court-Book C*, pp. 467, 471.

24841.4 — [Anr. issue, w. added C⁴:] (A declaration of the supplies.) *T. S[nodham a. F. Kingston,]* 1620. L.O.O². CHATS(imp. at beginning and made up w. A–C⁴ of 24841.6).; F.HN.CB.HD.NY.+
(Formerly 24835) The addition was pr. by Snodham.

24841.6 — [Anr. ed.] 4°. *T. Snodham [a. F. Kingston,]* 1620. L.O.C(lacks M4).C³.E.+; CB.LC.NY.PN.Y.+
(Formerly 24836) Collates A–M⁴. Kingston pr. D–G, which is partly reimposed from his section of 24841.4.

24841.8 — [Anr. issue, w. added N⁴:] (By his majesties councell for Virginia. [etc. Proposals and inducements for settlers. 15 Nov. 1620.]) *T. Snodham [a. F. Kingston,]* 1620. F.HN.MICH.MIN.NY.+
The addition was pr. by Kingston; *see The Library*, XV (1960), p. 130.

— Observations to be followed, to keepe silke-wormes. 1620. *See* 18761.

24842 — A note of the shipping, men and provisions, sent to Virginia, in the yeere 1619. fol. [*F. Kingston*, 1620.] NY.
With information to April 1620; reprinted with some revision in 24841.2.

24842a — A note of the shipping, men, and provisions, sent and provided for Virginia, . . . this yeare, 1620. fol. [*T. Snodham*, 1621 (30 ap.)] L.L⁵(Lemon 180).; NY. Mellon.
With information to Feb. 1621. Regarding the date of printing *see The Library*, XV (1960), p. 129.

Virginia Company—*cont.*

24843 — A note of the shipping, men, and provisions, sent and provided for Virginia, . . . in the yeere 1621. &c. fol. [*F. Kingston*, 1622.] L(Harl.MS.7617/18–9).L[5] (Lemon 194).; HN.NY.ROS.

With information to May 1622. Copies vary on A1[r]: top of page has orn. w. goat's head (L[5]) or woodcut seals of James I and of the Virginia Company (L).

24844 — The inconveniencies that have happened to some persons which transported themselves from England to Virginia, [etc. With a list of items necessary to be taken along.] s.sh.fol. *F. Kyngston*, 1622. L[5](Lemon 195).; HN.NY.PN.

Also issued w. 25104.

— Orders and constitutions, . . . for the Summer-Ilands. 1622. *See* 1905.

— To . . . Commons. The information of J. Bargrave shewing the severall abuses of the government of the plantation in Virginia. [1624.] *See* 1415.7.

24844.3 — By his majesties commissioners for Virginia. [A notice of their weekly sittings.] s.sh.fol. *F. Kingston*, 1624. L(Add.MS.12496.f.458).

(Formerly 24837) The King's commissioners were appointed by the Privy Council in July 1624, after the Virginia Company was dissolved.

24844.7 **Virtue.** The admirable vertue, property, and operation of the quintessence of rosemary flowers, for the sicknesses and diseases herein mentioned. s.sh.fol. [*R. Barker?* 1615?] O(MS.Ashmole 457(f.3), imp.).

24844a — [Virtue and his lieutenant Reason. Two leaves of a poem. c. 1505.] Now = 17007.5.

— [The virtue of the mass. c. 1500, etc.] *See* 17037.5 sq.

24844a.3 — Vertues reward wherein the living are incouraged unto good workes. (Sions suite, or a treatise to helpe forward the work of a publique reconciliation amongst protestants.) 4°. [*Amsterdam, Richt Right Press*,] 1639. C.C[2].STD.

Virtues. The enterlude of the .iiii. cardynal vertues. [c. 1545.] *See* 14109.7.

— [Verses on the seven virtues. Doubtfully attrib. to Lydgate. 1500?] *See* 17037.

24845 **Vis.** Minima vis potest mouere maximum pondus. [Cambridge Act verses. 1585.] Now = 4474.72.

Vitell, Christopher, *tr. See* 7573, 10843, 18551, 18554, 18556, 18560, 18561, 18562.

— *See also* 21180.

24846 **Vives, Joannes Ludovicus.** Joannis Lodovici Vivis Valentini, ad sapientiam introductio. 12°. *Aberdoniæ, E. Rabanus, imp. D. Melvil*, 1623. L.O.E.G[2].M[4].+; TEX.

24846.5 — [A trans.] [An introduction to wisdom. *Tr.* R. Morison.] 8°. (*in æd. T. Bertheleti*, 1539.) O(lacks tp).

24847 — [Anr. ed.] An introduction to wysedome, . . . *tr.* R. Morysine. 8°. (*in æd. T. Bertheleti*, 1540.) L(imp.).C.; F.CH.

24848 — [Anr. ed., w. additions:] (For the fyllyng of void pages we haue inserted certain floures [selections from 10478.7 and 10445.]) 8°. (*in æd. T. Bertheleti*, 1544.) L.O(lacks tp).; HN.

This form of the text is reprinted in 24850 sq.

24848.5 — [Anr. ed., w. more additions:] Introduction to wisedome. Banket of sapience. Preceptes of Agapetus. 16° in 8's. (*T. Berthelet*, 1546 (13 se.)) HD(imp.).

Reprints 7630, tr. by Sir T. Elyot, and 193, tr. by T. Paynell.

24849 — [Anr. ed.] 16° in 8's. (*in the hous of T. Berthelet*, 1550.) F(imp.).ILL. Iowa U.

24850 — [Anr. ed. of 24848.] 8°. *J. Daye*, [1558?] L(imp.). O(frag.).

24850.3 — [A variant, w. imprint:] *J. Daye f. A. Vele*, [1558?] L(tp only, Harl.5936/321).

24850.7 — [Anr. ed. of 24848.5.] 16° in 8's. (*T. Powell*, 1563.) F.HN.

24851 — [A ghost.]

24851.5 — [Anr. ed.] 16° in 8's. *T. East f. A. Veale*, [c. 1575.] L.; F.

24852 — Joannis Ludovici Vivis. . . . Libri. XII. De disciplinis. 8°. [*W. Stansby*,] 1612. Ent. to J. Crosley 10 fb. L.O.O[5].C[2].D.+; F.

Contents on verso of tp.

Vives, Joannes Ludovicus—*cont.*

24852.3 — [Anr. issue, w. cancel tp:] Joannis. . . . Libri. XII. Quorum septem priores sunt de corruptis artibus quinqʒ posteriores de trahendis disciplinis. [*W. Stansby*,] 1612. L[44].O.O[11].

Verso of tp blank.

24852.7 — Linguæ Latinæ exercitatio, Joanne Lodovico Vive auctore. 8°. *N. Okes, imp. J. Harisoni* [1, 1612?] Ent. to T. Gubbin 25 jn. 1590. L(tp only, Harl. 5919/69).

Partly reprinted, w. trans., in 6735.

24853 — [Anr. ed.] 8°. *Edinburgi, A. Hart*, 1620. L.

24853.3 — [Anr. ed.] 8°. [*G. Purslowe*] *pro Soc. Stat.*, 1624. Ent. to the English Stock 5 mr. 1620. C[5].D.

24853.7 — [Anr. ed.] 8°. [*G. Purslowe*] *pro Soc. Stat.*, 1628. ILL.Y.

24854 — [Anr. ed.] 8°. *Cantabrigiæ, ex acad. typog.*, 1633. C.DUL.DUR[3].; F.

24854.5 — [Anr. ed.] 12°. *Cantabrigiæ, ex acad. typog.*, 1635. L(tp only, Harl.5967/228).O[7].ETON.; HD.

24855 — The office and duetie of an husband, *tr.* into Englyshe by T. Paynell. 8°. *J. Cawood*, [1555?] L.O.C.P.; F.N.

24856 — A very frutefull and pleasant boke called the instructiõ of a christen womã, turned out of Laten into Englysshe by R. Hyrd. 4°. (*in the house of T. Berthelet*,) [1529?] L.O[9](lacks tp).

B2[r] catchword: 'to'; C2[r] line 1: 'cõmaund'.

24856.5 — [Anr. ed.] 4°. (*in the house of T. Berthelet*,) [1529?] F.

B2[r] catchword: 'to'; C2[r] line 1: 'cõmaunde'.

24857 — [Anr. ed.] 4°. (*in the house of T. Berthelet*,) [1531?] L(lacks quire A).C[17].; ILL.

B2[r] catchword: 'to withall'.

24858 — [Anr. ed.] 4°. (*in ȩd. T. Berth[eleti,*] 1541.) L.O.O[3].C. BRISTOL[2].+; F.HN.

This and following eds. omit Hyrd's dedic.

24859 — [Anr. ed.] 4°. (*in ȩd. T. Berth[eleti,*]) 1547 (1541.) L(imp.).; HN.PH.

The tp date is correct.

24860 — [Anr. ed.] 4°. (*T. Powell*,) 1557. O(2, 1 imp.). NLW.; F.HN.

24861 — [Anr. ed.] 4°. (*H. Wykes*,) 1557 [i.e. 1567?] L.O.C.G[2]. PETYT.+; F.HD.N.NY.Y.+

24862 — [Anr. ed.] 8°. *R. Walde-graue*, 1585. L[4](lacks tp).C[12].; F.HD.

24863 — [Anr. ed.] 8°. *J. Danter*, 1592. L.O.C.LIV[3].YK.; F.BR. CU.ILL.

See Greg, *Register B*, p. 42.

— *ed. See* 916, 24820.

— *See also* 6735, 11181.

24864 **Vlacq, Adrian.** Ephemerides of the celestiall motions, for 1633. 1634. 1635. 1636. Calculated out of the tables of P. Lansberg by A. V[lacq] and out of the Rudolphine tables by J. Kepler. [*Tr.* from Latin.] 4°. *W. Jones*, 1635. O.O[18].C.

(Formerly also 10422)

— *See also* 25234.

Vliederhoven, Gerardus de. [Cordiale. 1479, etc.] *See* 5758 sq.

Vn., Ro., *B.D.* The little world. 1612. *See* 24519.5.

24865 **Vocabulary.** [Headline:] Frensshe Englissh. [Ends:] (Here endeth this doctrine in the whiche one euerich may shortly lerne Frenssh and englissh. *Fr. a. Eng.* fol. (*westmestre*,) [*W. Caxton*, 1480.] O(2 leaves, Douce frag.d.2.). C.DUR(Bamb.).M.; HN(last 5 leaves in facs.). Duff 405.

24866 — Here begynneth a lytell treatyse for to lerne Englysshe and Frensshe. . . . Soo that I maye doo my marchaundyse. (Here foloweth the booke of curtesye. [In verse.]) *Eng. a. Fr.* 4° in 6's. (*Westmynster, by my W. de worde*,) [1497.] L. Duff 407.

The 1st line of verse is: Little children here may ye learn. *See also* 3303, 17030, 20953.

24867 — [Anr. ed.] Here is a good boke to lerne to speke french. 4°. (*per me R. Pinson*,) [1500?] L. Duff 406.

24868 — [Anr. ed.] 4°. [*R. Wyer?* c. 1533.] L(B2–4 only, C.40.m.9(21)).

Portions of the Book of Courtesy only.

24868.3 — [An edition in three languages, *Fr., Ger., a. Eng.*, with title:] Sensuyt vng petit liure pour apprendre a parler Francoys, Alemant, et Ancloys. Pour apprẽdre a cõter, a vẽdre & acheter [etc.] 4°. (*Lyon, P. Mareschal*,) [c. 1525.] Y(Lxh.519s).

Vocabulary—*cont.*

24868.7 — [An edition in three languages, Eng., Fr., a. Dutch.] 4°. [*Antwerp, C. van Ruremond,* c. 1530.] HN(frags. of 2 leaves).MEL(1 leaf).

Portions of the Book of Courtesy only, w. head-line: 'Englysshe. Frenche. Dutche.' Nijhoff and Kronenberg 3916.

24869 — Den grooten vocabulaer, Engels ende Duyts. The great vocabuler, . . . also lettres and obligations to write. With a dictionarie and the conjugation. Desen lesten druck, op nieus oversien. 8°. *Rotterdam, P. van Waes-berge,* 1639. C.CANT.DUR³.LINC. Leiden U.+

Derived from Barlement.

24869.5 — [Anr. ed.] Den grooten vocabulaer, Enghels ende Duyts. Den vierden druck. The fourth impression. 8°. *Rotterdam, de weduwe van M. Bastiaensz, boeck-verkooper,* 1639. L(tp only, Harl.5949/189).O(date cropped).

24870 **Voice.** The voyce of the Lord in the temple. Or, a relation of Gods power, in sending sounds, fires, and a fiery ball into the church of Anthony in Cornwall neere Plimmouth. The truth whereof will be maintained by persons; having been examined by Richard Carew of Anthony, esquire; and Arthur Bache, vicar of Anthony. 4°. *T. Paine f. F. Eglesfield,* 1640. L(date cropt).O.C².C³.CASHEL.+; F.

24870.5 — [A variant, w. imprint:] *T. P[aine] f. F. Eglesfield, sold by W. Russell, in Plimmouth,* 1640. HD.

24871 **Voilleret, François.** Le preau des fleurs mesle'es. Cueilly & extraict de bons autheurs, tant anciens que modernes. [Essays.] 4°. *chez W. S[tansby,* 1621.] Ent. to G. Fairbeard 3 fb. 1621. L.L².O.; F.HN.HD.

Voisin, Lancelot. *See* 11276.

Volusenus, Florentius, *ed. See* 5317.5.

Volusenus, Thomas, *ed. See* 146, 148.

24872 **Volusianus,** *Bp.* Epistolæ duæ D. Volusiani . . . de cęlibatu cleri. Inquisitio discipuli et solutio magistri reperta inter libros Anselmi olim Cantuariensis archiepiscopi. [etc.] 8°. *in æd. H. Bynneman,* 1569 (au.) Ent. 1569–70. L.O.C.D.YK.+

Vopell, Jasper. An almanack. 1549. *See* 522.20.

24873 **Voragine, Jacobus de.** [kk5ʳ:] (Thus endeth the legende named in latyn legenda aurea.) [Anon. *Tr.* by W. Caxton? from the French of J. de Vignay.] fol. (*westmestre, wyllyam Caxton,*) [1483, after 20 no.] L(imp.).O(imp.).C.LINC(imp.).M.+; BO.LC.NY(imp.). PH. St. John's Seminary, Camarillo, California.+ Duff 408.

Headlines are in Duff's de Worde type 3 (135 mm.). Includes feasts of the church, stories from the Bible, and legends of the saints. In copies of this and the following eds. the life of St. Thomas à Becket is sometimes cut out or defaced. For a separate printing of the Becket portion *see* 23954.

24874 — [Anr. ed.] fol. (*westmestre, wylyam Caxton,*) [1487?] L(portions completing imp. copy of 24873).O(imp.). C(imp.).A(imp.).G².+; HN(imp.).LC(imp.).PML. Duff 409.

Quires a–t and A–E are the same typesetting as 24873. In the rest, headlines are in Duff's de Worde type 5 (113 mm.). Most copies of this and the preceding have same mixed sheets.

24875 — [Anr. ed.] fol. (*westmestre, wyllyam Caxton* [really *W. de Worde,*] 1493 (20 my.)) L(imp.).O(imp.).O¹⁶. LINC(imp.).M.+; F(imp.).HN(lacks 1st leaf).CB.HD (imp.).PML.+ Duff 410.

This is the only ed. to omit the stories from the Bible.

24876 — [Anr. ed.] fol. (*westmynster, w. de worde,* 1498 (8 ja.)) L(imp.).O(imp.).C(imp.).M.NLW.+; F(1 leaf).CAL² (frag.).N(frag.).PML(imp.).WTL.+ Duff 411.

— [Anr. ed.] 4°. [1500?] *See* 24880.5.

24877 — [Anr. ed.] fol. (*J. Notary,* 1503 [1504] (16 fb.)) L.O. C(imp.).G².M.+; F.IND.NCU.PML. Mellon.+

24878 — Now = 24880.5.

24878.3 — [Anr. ed.] fol. (*w. de worde,* 1507 (4 se.)) C²(frags.)*. E(imp.)*. Lord Kenyon.; HD(imp.)*.

24878.5 — [A variant, w. imprint:] [*W. de Worde f.*] (*R. Pynson,* 1507 (4 se.)) L².

Voragine, Jacobus de—*cont.*

24879 — [Anr. ed.] fol. (*w. de worde,* 1512 (15 fb.)) L.O.C(imp.). M.P.+; BO⁶(lacks tp).CAL².TEX.

24879.5 — [Anr. ed.] fol. (*W. de Worde,* 1521 (30 [*sic*] fb.)) L.C (Sayle 194). DUR(Bamb.).DUR³.M.+; F.HN.PML.

All copies are imperfect; HN is the only one with a colophon.

24880 — [Anr. ed.] fol. (*w. de worde,* 1527 (27 au.)) L.L⁴.O. C².M.+; F.HN.BO(imp.).N.NY.+

24880.5 — [An extract, comprised of the stories of the Bible: Adam-Judith.] 4° 8·4. [*W. de Worde,* 1500?] L(imp.). (Formerly 24878) 31 lines a column.

Vorstius, Conrad. Declaration du roy. 1612. *See* 9229.

24881 — Enchiridion controuersiarum: seu index errorum ecclesiæ Romanæ, vnà cum antidoto. 8°. *Oxoniæ, J. Barnesius,* 1606. L.O.O³⁸.C.D.+; F.HN.Y.

Issued w. 24263; reprinted in 24263.3.

24881.5 **Vossius, Gerardus.** Ger. Jo. Vossii elementa rhetorica, oratoriis ejusdem Partitionibus accommodata: inque usum scholarum Hollandiæ & west-Frisiæ edita. 8°. *Aberdoniæ, E. Rabanus, imp. D. Melvil,* 1631. A(imp.).; F.

Collates A–C⁸ and does not appear to be an extract or abridgment of 24882.

24882 — Gerardi Joannis Vossi rhetorices contractæ, sive partitionum oratoriarum. Libri V. Ex decreto Hollandiæ, & west-Frisiæ in usum scholarum excusi. Editio altera castigatior. 12°. *Oxoniæ, pro G. Turner & T. Huggins,* 1631. L.O.C.D.DUL.+; F.HD(tp def.).MICH.

24882.3 — [Anr. ed.] 12°. *Oxoniæ, G. Turner, imp. J. Godwin,* 1640. L¹³.O.C.BIRM²(K.N.).YK.+; HD.

24882.7 — Gerardi Joh. Vossii V. CL. theses theologicæ et historicæ, de varijs doctrinæ christianæ capitibus. 4° in 8's. *Bellositi Dobunorum,* [i.e. Oxford,] *W. T[urner,] imp. W. W[ebb,]* 1628. O.C².DUR³.E⁴.YK.+; BO²(imp.). HD.TORONTO².Y.

The-place name in the imprint is whimsical as the Dobuni tribe once inhabited the district near Oxford.

24883 — [A variant, w. imprint:] *Bellositi Dobunorum, G. Turner, imp. G. Webb,* 1628. L.O⁶.C.D².E².+; F.HART.U.Y. 𝔄

24884 — [Anr. issue, w. *4 reprinted.] *Oxonii,* [*J. Lichfield,*] *imp. G. Webb,* 1631. L³⁸.O⁶.C³.C⁴.E⁴.+; ILL.HD.

The C⁴ copy contains extra errata for 19096.

— *See also* 12401.

24885 **Vowell, John,** *alias* **Hooker.** A catalog of the bishops of Excester. 4° in 2's. *H. Denham,* 1584. Ent. 20 de. 1583. L(2).O.O³.C.; F.

Prob. issued w. 24889.

24886 — The discription of the cittie of Excester. 4°. [*J. Allde,* 1575?] L(imp.).C.

Also issued as pt. 2 of 24887.

24886.3 — Isca Damnoniorum britañice Kaier penhuelgorte . . . at nunc vulgo Exeter. 1587. [Bird's eye view, engr. by R. Hogenberg.] s.sh.fol. *imp. J. Hokeri* [i.e. *Vowell,* 1587.] L(Maps, C.5.a.3). Exeter PL.

See Hind I.77–8.

24886.7 — The order and vsage of keeping of the parlements in England. 4°. [*J. Charlewood?* 1572?] O.; Y.

Dedic. to Sir W. Fitzwilliam, Lord Deputy of Ireland, dated 3 Oct. 1572.

24887 — [Anr. issue, w. new dedic. to mayor and senators of Exeter, and pt. 2 added.] The order and vsage of the keeping of a parlement in England, and the description of Fxcester [*sic*]. 2 pts. 4°. [*J. Allde a. J. Charlewood?* 1575?] L.O.; HN.HD(pt. 1 only).

Quires 2nd C–I in pt. 1 are app. pr. by Charlewood, and E–I are in the same typesetting as 24886.7. Pt. 2 also issued sep. as 24886.

24888 — Orders enacted for orphans and for their portions within the citie of Excester. 4°. *J. Allde,* [1575?] L(imp.).C.

24889 — A pamphlet of the offices, and duties of euerie particular sworne officer, of the citie of Excester. 4° in 2's. *H. Denham,* 1584. Ent. 20 de. 1583. L.O.C.; F.HN.

Prob. issued w. 24885.

— *ed. See* 13569.

Vox. Vox cœli. 1624. *See* 20946.4.

— Vox Dei. [1623?] *See* 22097a.

— Vox militis. 1625. *See* 20980.

— Vox piscis. 1627. *See* 11395.

— Vox populi. 1620. *See* 22098.

— Vox regis. [1623.] *See* 22105.

24890 **Voyon, Simon de.** A discourse vpon the catalogue of doctors of Gods church, together with the continuall succession of the true church vntill 1565. *Tr.* by J. Golburne. 8°. *R. Bradocke f. J. Browne,* 1598. Ent. 24 oc. L.O.C.D.DUR⁵.+; F.HN.U.

24891 — [Anr. trans.] A testimonie of the true church of God. *Tr.* out of French by W. Phiston. 4°. *H. M[iddleton] f. T. Charde,* [1585?] Ent. to J. Harrison 3 oc. 1580. L.C.A.G².P.+; F.HN.HD.N.U.+

Quires B–C in 2 settings; C1ʳ last line begins 'led with' (HN) or 'a diuelish' (HD).

24892 — [Anr. issue, w. cancel tp:] A testimonie of the true church, from the false. ... And may fitly be annexed to the abridgement [of Foxe's *Martyrs*] lately published [1762₂]. *f. L. Becket,* 1618. L³.D.; HD.

Phiston's dedic. is also missing or cancelled in the HD copy.

24893 **Vrillac,** *Monsieur de.* An epistle sent by monsieur de Vrillac upon his conversion. *Tr.* according to the French copie; by C. C. 4°. *J. D[awson] f. W. Sheffard,* 1621. Ent. 5 se. L⁴.O⁶.E².G².

24893.3 **Vulcanius, Bonaventura.** De literis & lingua Getarum, siue Gothorum. Quibus accesserunt specimina variarum linguarum. Editore Bon. Vulcanio. 8°. *Lugduni Batavorum, ex off. Plantiniana, ap. F. Raphelengium,* 1597. L.O.O⁵.C.E².+; HD.

Pp. 73–80 are in Anglo-Saxon and English.

24893.5 — [Anr. issue, w. prelims. cancelled, as the third section of:] Gothicarum et Langobardicarum rerum scriptores aliquot veteres. *Lugduni Batavorum, ap. J. Maire,* 1617. O².O¹².O¹⁸.DUR³.E.+

24893.7 — [A variant, w. imprint:] *Lugduni Batavorum, ap. J. Maire,* 1618. O(2).O².

24894 **Vyllagon** or **Villegagnon,** *Sir* **Nicholas.** A lamentable and piteous treatise, ... wherin is contayned, not onely the enterprise of Charles V. to Angier in Affrique. But also the myserable chaunces of wynde and wether. *Tr.* out of Latyn into Frenche, and out of French into English. 1542. 8°. *R. Grafton,* [1542.] L²(not found).

The description above is taken from Hazlitt, *Handbook,* p. 635.

W

W. Double V. *See* 17463.

24895 **W., A.** A booke of cookry. . . . Now newly enlarged with the seruing in of meats to the table. And the proper sauces to eche of them moste conuenient. 8°. *J. Allde,* 1584. L(tp only, Harl.5910, pt.IV/2).LEEDS(imp.).
24896 — [Anr. ed., enlarged.] 8°. *E. Allde,* 1587. LEEDS.; NY (imp.).
24897 — [Anr. ed.] 8°. *E. Allde,* 1591. O.
24898 — [Anr. ed.] 8°. *E. Allde,* 1594. L(destroyed).
24899 — A fruitfull and godly sermon, preached at Paules crosse. [By A. Willet.] 8°. *R. B[ourne] f. T. Man,* 1592. Ent. 19 jy. C.LINC.LK(imp.).; F(date cropt).
 The attribution to Willet is from Maunsell (17669), pt. 1, p. 107.

W., A., *tr. See* 18135.

W., B., *Esquire. See* 25349.

24900 **W., C.** The crying murther: contayning the cruell butcher⟨y⟩ of Mr. Trat, curate of olde Cleave. For this fact Peter Smethwicke, [and 3 others] were executed the 24. of July, at Stone Gallowes, neere Taunton. 4°. *E. Allde f. N. Butter,* 1624. L(tp cropt).; HD(tp cropt).

W., C., *B.* A summarie of controversies. 1616. *See* 26047.

W., D. The loves of the Lord. 1637. *See* 2776.5.

24901 **W., D.,** *Archd.* Certaine godly instructions, verie necessarie to be learned of the younger sorte. Also certaine articles. [By Dr. [George] Wither, *Archdeacon*?] 8°. [*J. Kingston*] *f. H. Kirkham,* 1580. Ent. 22 fb. 1578. L(2).
 For an earlier ed. *see* 20974.
24902 — [Anr. ed. Heading A1ʳ:] Certaine necessarie instructions, meet to be taught the yonger sort. 8° in 4. (*J. C[harlewood] f. H. Kirkham,*) [1586?] L.
 Possibly the ed. dated 1586 in Maunsell (17669), pt. 1, p. '32' (C3ᵛ).

W., D. I. P. B. R. A shorte treatise of politike power. 1556, etc. *See* 20178 sq.

W., E. E. W. his Thameseidos. 1600. *See* 25642.
— Good newes from New-England. 1624. *See* 25855.

W., E., *ed. See* 21549.

W., E., *tr. See* 19459, 21023.

W., E., *Doctor, and Professor of Divinity.* A triple cure. 1616. *See* 25290.7.

24903 **W., Ez.** The answere of a mother unto hir seduced sonnes letter. 8°. [*Amsterdam, J. F. Stam,*] 1627. C.; F.
 (Formerly also 657) The inits. 'Ez.', 'W.' are at the sides of a block of type orns. on the tp. The son's letter is signed 'I. MADD.' Of this ed. 500 copies were pr. according to the pref. of 24903.5.
24903.5 — [Anr. ed., enlarged. Anon.] A mothers teares over hir seduced sonne: or a dissuasive from idolatry. 8°. [*London,*] 1627. O.Cˢ.
 (Formerly 18212)

W., G. A briefe exposition of christian religion. 1612. *See* 25158.
— Cantica sacra. [1623?] *See* 25899.5.
— The censure of a loyall subiect. 1587. *See* 25334.
— The cures of the diseased. 1598. *See* 25106.
— The hymnes and songs of the church. 1623. *See* 25908.
24904 — Newes out of Cheshire of the new found well. [With examples of the cures its waters effected.] 4°. *F. Kingston f. T. Man,* 1600. Ent. 18 se. L.O.YK.; F.TEX.
— A rich store-house. 1612. *See* 23608.

W., G., *tr. See* 24293.

W., G., *Gent.* Aurelia. 1593. *See* 25338.

W., G., *of Lincoln's Inn.* Fidelia. 1617. *See* 25906.

W., G., *Practitioner in physic, ed. See* 23606.5.

24904.5 **W., H.** Clasmata H. W. [Religious poems in English.] 4°. [*London,* c. 1640.] HN.
 At the bottom of the 19th leaf is: 'H. W. Ætatis suæ 76, 1636.' The versos of all leaves are blank.
24905 — [Heading A1ʳ:] A meditation upon the XXIIᵗʰ [*sic*] chapter of Genesis. By H. W[otton.] 4°. (*A. M[athewes] f. G. Baker,* 1631.) L.O.O¹¹.LINC.OS.; F.HN.
 Mathewes and Baker fined for printing Wotton's book without entrance 9 Feb. 1631; *see Court-Book C,* p. 224. Text reprinted in 20645.
24905.3 — A paterne of a passionate minde. Conteining a briefe description of the sundry straunge affects of the minde of man. 8°. *T. East,* 1580. HD.
 An abridgement of 21239, to which there is a reference on C7ʳ.

W., H., *ed. See* 24048.

W., H., *tr. See* 13119.5, 17323.5, 18465, 18467, 18468, 23010.

W., I. or **J.** A booke declaring the vexasion, of A. Nyndge. [1573?] *See* 18752.
— A breefe of scripture. 1624. *See* 24953.3.
24905.7 — A briefe treatise of the plague wherein is shewed, the naturall cause. Preservations. Way to cure. Newly corrected with new additions. 4°. *V. Sims,* 1603. HN.
24906 — [Heading A1ʳ:] The copie of a letter sent by a learned physician to his friend, wherein are detected the errors of the apothecaries, in preparing their compositions. 8°. [*J. Wolfe,* 1586?] L.; HN.NLM.
 End of text dated 21 Mar. 1586.
— De neutralibus & mediis. 1626. *See* 25614.
24907 — A table briefly pointing out such places of scripture. 1625. Now = 24953.5.

W., I., *tr.* Miles gloriosus, the Spanish braggadocio. 1630. *See* 11691.5.
— *See also* 4932.5, 12457, 18897, 21148.

W., I., *Esquire.* Sciographia, or the art of shadowes. 1635. *See* 25234.

24908 **W., I.,** *Gent.* The merchants hand-maide: or, a booke containing tables, for the speedie casting up, and true valuing of any commoditie. By J. W(arre) Gent. 4°. *W. Jones,* 1622. L.L³⁰.O. Edinburgh, Institute of Chartered Accountants.
24909 — A speedie poste, with certaine new letters. Published for the helpe of such as are desirous to learne to write letters. 4°. *M. F[lesher] f. W. Sheares,* 1625. Ent. 15 ja. L(date cropt).; PN².
24909.5 — [Anr. ed.] 4°. *Eliz. All-de f. F. Coules,* 1629. HN.
24910 — The valiant Scot. By I. W. Gent. 4°. *T. Harper f. J. Waterson,* 1637. Ent. 26 ap. L.O.C².M².E.+; F.HN. CU.HD.N.+ Greg 520.

W., I., *Priest.* The English martyrologe. 1608. *See* 25771.
— The fierie tryall of Gods saints. 1611. *See* 24269.

W., I., *Printer.* The treasurie of hidden secrets. 1608. *See* 19430.5.

W., Is. The copy of a letter. [1567?] *See* 25439.
— A sweet nosgay. [1573.] *See* 25440.

W., I. H., *tr. See* 12091.

W., L., *C.* A verie perfect discourse. 1601, etc. *See* 4286 sqq.

W., M. Academiarum catalogus. 1590. *See* 25841.
— Europaei orbis, academiae. 1592. *See* 25841a.5.

W., M., *Master in Arts.* The redemption of time. 1606. *See* 25318.

W., N. The moste pleasante historie. 1639. *See* 25437.
— Nature and grace in conflict. 1638. *See* 25023.5.

W., N., *Master in Arts.* Le hore di recreatione. 1637. *See* 25436.

W., P. A checke or reproofe. 1581. *See* 25586.

W., P., *tr. See* 12349.

W., P., *Minister.* A godlye and fruitefull sermon. 1581. *See* 25402.

24911   W., R. A castle for the soule, conteining many godly prayers, and diuine meditations. 8°. (*T. Dawson*) *f. R. Walgraue* [sic], 1578. Ent. 17 jn. F.
    The inits. are those of the publisher, Waldegrave.
— The honest wooer. [1632?] *See* 25972.8.
— Iter boreale. 1605 [i.e. 1665.] *See* Wing W 2135.

24912   — A looking-glasse for papists: to see their owne deformities. With a briefe history of the popes lives. [By] (R. W. a poore minister in Norffolke.) 4°. *T. S[nodham] f. N. Newbery*, 1621. Ent. 13 ja. L.O. O⁶(2).E.; F.HN.U.
    The Printer to the Reader mentions 5364 and adds, 'I could not keepe backe this second [treatise], committed vnto my dispose by the same learned man, a little before his trauailes into forraine countries.' i.e. by John Burges. By R. Wrathall?

24912.5   — [Anr. issue, w. new prelims. Anon.] The popes wound is deadly. [*T. Snodham,*] 1624. O⁶(prelims. only). C¹⁷.DUR⁵.
    The prelims. w. the contents there listed indicate a reissue of 5364 was prob. contemplated; C¹⁷ and DUR⁵ both have as text the sheets of 24912.
— Lots wife. 1607. *See* 25656.

24913   — Martine Mar-Sixtus. A second replie against the defensory and apology of Sixtus the fift. Wherein the saide apology is faithfully translated, directly answered, and fully satisfied. [By R. Wilson?] 4°. [*T. Orwin*] *f. T. Woodcock*, 1591. Ent. 8 no. L(2). O.C.E.; HN.PFOR.Y.
    For the 1st reply *see* 14002, which has a different trans. of the Sixtus work.

24913a   — [A variant, w. imprint:] [*T. Orwin*] *f. T. Woodcock*, 1592. O(imp.).O⁶.C².C¹³.BIRM.+; F.HN.HD.PFOR. Pirie.
— The order of matrimonie. 1580. *See* 18841.3.
— The pleasant and stately morall, of the three lordes. 1590. *See* 25783.

24913a.5   — A recantation of famous Pasquin of Rome. [In verse.] 8° in 4's. *J. Daye*, 1570. Ent. 1569–70. L.
— A receyt to stay the plague. 1625. *See* 26037.
— A right excellent comœdy called the three ladies. 1584. *See* 25784.

24914   — [Heading A2ʳ:] To my ingenuous friend, R. W. [1646.] = an imperfect copy of Wing V 124.

W., R., *tr. See* 5827, 18412.

W., R., *Esquire.* Mount Tabor. 1639. *See* 25752.

W., R., *a Poor Minister. See* 24912.

24915   W., S. The appollogie of the illustrious prince Ernestus, earle of Mansfield, &c. Tr. out of the French coppie. 4°. *Heidelbergh* [i.e. *London, E. Allde,*] 1622. L.O.C. C².D.+; F.HN.HD.
— Marie Magdalens funeral teares. 1591. *See* 22950.

24916   W., T. The araignement and execution of the late traytors [in the Gunpowder Plot], with a relation of other traytors, executed at Worcester, the 27. of January. 4° w. perp. chainlines. [*J. Windet*] *f. J. Chorlton*, 1606. Ent. 4 fb. L.L³.L⁴.O.O².+; F.NY.Y.
    (Formerly also 784)

24916.3   — [Anr. issue, w. title reset:] A true report of the imprisonment, the arraignement, and execution of the late traytors. [*J. Windet*] *f. J. Chorlton*, 1606. OS.; F.
— An attestation [concerning H. Airay's suit for the rectory of Charleton.] 1621. *See* 244.
— A catalogue of the dukes, [etc.] 1632, etc. *See* 24975 sqq.
— A catalogue of the nobility. 1630. *See* 24974.

W., T.—*cont.*

24916.7   — Certaine wholesome observations and rules fo [sic] inne-keepers, and their guests, meet to be fixed vpon the wall of every chamber, but meant more specially for Mʳ. Henry Hunter of Smithfield. s.sh.fol. [*J. Beale?* c. 1615?] L⁵(Lemon 249).

24917   — A concordance or table made after the order of the alphabet, conteyning the principall both wordes & matters, in the newe Testament. [By T. Wilcox.] 8°. *C. Barker*, 1579. L³.; F.
— Exercitatio scholastica. 1623. *See* 25867.5.
— An exposition vppon the booke of the Canticles. 1585. *See* 25622.
— A forme of preparation to the Lordes supper. [1587.] *See* 25622.5.
— A glasse for gamesters. 1581. *See* 25623.
— A ninuectyue [sic] agaynst treason. [1553.] *See* 25105.

24918   — The lamentation of Melpomene, for the death of Belphæbe our late queene. [Init. T. W., *Gent.* In verse.] 4°. *W. W[hite] f. C. K[night,]* 1603. HN.
— A mirror of mans lyfe made by a virgine. 1570. *See* 5104.
— A profitable, and comfortable letter. [1584?] *See* 25624.5.
— A relation of sixtene martyrs. 1601. *See* 26000.9.
— A right godly and learned exposition. 1586. *See* 25625.
— A sermon preached at Pawles Crosse. 1578. *See* 25405, 25406.
— A short, yet sound commentarie; on the Prouerbes. [1589.] *See* 25627.
— A succinct philosophicall declaration. 1604. *See* 26043.3.
— The summe of a sermon, preached at Sowthell. 1597. *See* 25630.

24919   — Summarie and short meditations, touching sundry poyntes of christian religion. [By T. Wilcox.] 8°. [*T. Dawson*] *f. G. Byshop*, 1580. Ent. 30 jn. 1579. L(2).L⁴.; Y.
    Text in B.L. A 1579 ed. is attrib. to Wilcox in Maunsell (17669), pt. 1, p. 121.

24919.5   — [Anr. ed., revised.] 8°. [*F. Kingston,* 1610?] C(imp.).
    Text in roman.
— The tears of fancie. 1593. *See* 25122.
— A true report of the imprisonment. 1606. *See* 24916.3.
— The vnfoldyng of sundry vntruths. 1581. *See* 25631.
— A very godly and learned exposition. 1591. *See* 25626.

W., T., *ed. See* 20751, 21434.

W., T., *tr. See* 540, 937, 2014, 2051, 4464, 5307, 15450, 15489, 16812, 25710, 26124.5.

W., T., *Gent. See* 24918.

W., T., *Master of Arts.* The optick glasse of humors. 1607. *See* 24967.

W., T., *Minister of the Word.* An exposition of the two first verses. 1609. *See* 24966.

W., T., *P.* Whyte dyed black. 1615. *See* 26001.

W., T., *Preacher.* Theologicall rules. 1615. *See* 25798.

W., T., *Sem. Pr.* The second part of an anker. 1620. *See* 26000.3.

W., Th. An anker of christian doctrine. 1618, etc. *See* 26000 sqq.
— A christian and learned exposition vpon certaine verses of that eight chapter of Romanes. 1587. *See* 25620.5.
— The passions of the minde. 1601. *See* 26039.

24920   W., W. The anchor of faith. 1628. Now = 25763.5.
— A bride-bush. 1617. *See* 25296.
— A dialogue betwixt a secular priest, and a lay gentleman. 1601. *See* 25124.
— Important considerations. 1601. *See* 25125.
— Menaecmi. 1595. *See* 20002.

24920.5   — A merie and p⟨leasant⟩ prognostica⟨tion⟩ Deuised after the finest fashion, Made and written for this presen⟨t year⟩ By fower wittie doctors as shall ap⟨pear⟩ Spendall, Whoball, & doctor Deusac⟨e⟩ With them Will Somer takes his place. [In verse.] 8°. [*J. Kingston*] *f. J. Rowbothom*, [1577.] Ent. as by J. Dernyll to W. Pickering 1566–67; to E. Allde 8 au. 1586; this was Rowbotham's copy, *see* cancelled ent. to T. Purfoot 5 se. 1586. O⁵(imp.).
    The Prognostication is init. W. W. The pref. is init. I. D. (altered in ink to I. B.) and is dated 1577 on A3ʳ. This incorporates most of the text of 394.5.

W., W.—*cont.*

24921 — [Anr. ed., w. title:] A new, and merrie prognostication. 4°. w. perp. chainlines. *E. All-de, sold by J. Tapp,* 1623. L.O.; F(cropt).HN.

    The pref. is init. W. W.; the prognostication has no inits.

— Physicke to cure the most dangerous disease. 1607. *See* 25763.

— A sparing discoverie. 1601. *See* 25126.

24922 — A true and iust recorde, of the information, examination and confession of all the witches, at S. Oses in Essex. 8°. *T. Dawson,* 1582. Ent. 6 mr. (ap.?) L.O⁵. C².

    At least L has a folding table headed: 'The names of xiii. Witches, . . .'

W., W., *tr. See* 4102.5, 5636.2, 14527, 16985, 20002.

24923 **W., W.,** *Doctor in Divinity.* Englands unthankfulnes for Gods mercie. 1621. Now = 25970.5.

W., W., *Gent., tr. See* 1707.

Wackerzeele, Jean de. *See* 1375.5.

24924 **Wadding, Luke.** The history of the angelicall virgin glorious S. Clare. Extracted by F. Hendricq and now donne into English. By sister Magdalen Augustine, of the Poore Clarcs [*sic*] in Aire [i.e. C. Bentley? or E. Evelinge?] 8° in 4's. *Douay, M. Bocart,* 1635. L.O. C.OS.W(imp.).+; F.TEX.

    A&R 869.

Waddington, John, *tr. See* Weddington, J.

Waddington, Ralph, *ed. See* 24677.

24924.5 **Wadsworth, James,** *the elder.* The contrition of a protestant preacher, converted to be a catholique scholler. Conteyning certayne meditations upon the fourth penitentiall psalme, Miserere. 4°. *S. Omers, C. Boscard,* 1615. C².HP(imp.). Preshome Presbytery, Port Gordon, Banffshire.; HD.

    A&R 870.

24925 — The copies of certaine letters which have passed betweene Spaine and England in matter of religion. Betweene J. Wadesworth, and W. Bedell. [*Ed.* W. Bedel.] 4°. *W. Stansby f. W. Barret a. R. Milbourne,* 1624. Ent. to Milbourne 7 ap. L.O.C.D².M.+; F.HN. N.U.Y.+

24925a — [A variant, w. the spelling 'Milburne' in the imprint.] L².O.D(imp.).DUR⁵.P.+; HD.PH².

— *See also* 15562.

24926 **Wadsworth, James,** *the younger.* The English Spanish pilgrime. Or, a new discoverie of Spanish popery, and jesuiticall stratagems. 4°. *T. C[otes] f. M. Sparke,* 1629. Ent. 31 au. L.O.C.CASHEL.M(deposit).+; F.HN. CHI.ILL.Y.+

    Dedic. to the Earl of Pembroke.

24926a — [A variant, w. imprint:] *T. C[otes] f. M. Sparke,* 1630. L.O⁸.C(date mutilated).E.M².+; F.HN.HD.N.NY.+

    The dedic. is also altered, to the Earl of Holland.

24927 — Second edition, corrected and amended. 4°. *T. Cotes a. R. C[otes] f. M. Sparke,* 1630. L.O.C.LINC.M.+; F. HN.HD.N.NY.+

24928 — Further observations of the English Spanish pilgrime, concerning Spaine. 4°. *F. Kyngston f. N. Butter,* 1630. Ent. to Butter a. R. Allot 1 fb. L.O¹⁷.C.CASHEL. M.+; HN.IND.

24928a — [A variant, w. imprint:] *F. Kyngston f. R. Allot,* 1630. L.O.O¹³.DUR⁵.M².+; F.HN.HD.IND.NY.+

24929 — The present estate of Spayne, . . . touching the court, and government with a catalogue of all the nobility, with their revenues. 4°. *A. M[athewes] f. R. Thrale a. A. Ritherdon,* 1630. Ent. 24 ap. L.O.C.DUR⁵.SHEF. +; F(2).HN.HD.IND.N.

24929a — [A variant, w. imprint:] *A. M[athewes] f. A. Ritherdon,* 1630. L⁴.L³⁸.O.O³.C.+; HN.IND.LC.NY⁵.Y.+

— *tr. See* 5570, 11691.5.

Waerdenburgh, Dirk van. *See* 25219.

24930 **Waferer, Myrth.** An apologie for Daniel Featley, against the calumnies of S. E. [in 15347.5.] 4°. *J. D[awson] f. N. Bourne,* 1634. Ent. 6 ap. L.O.C².SHEF.YK.+; HN.HART.

    Answered by 15351.3.

24931 **Wagenaer, Lucas Janssen.** The mariners mirrour. . . . Now [*tr.* and] fitted with necessarie additions by A. Ashley. fol. [*J. Charlewood,* 1588?] Ent. to H. Haslop 3 ap. 1587. L.O.C³.D.E(imp.).+; F.HN.CB.LC.Y.+

    Dedic. dated 20 Oct. 1588.

24931.5 — [Anr. ed.] fol. [*Amsterdam,*] *J. Hondius,* 1605. Lund U.; Y(imp.).

    Engr. title and chart titles in English; letterpress text in Dutch; omits Ashley's dedic.

24932 **Wager, Lewis.** A new enterlude, neuer before this tyme imprinted, of the life and repentaunce of Marie Magdalene. 4°. *J. Charlewood,* 1566. Ent. 1566–67. HN. Greg 47.

24932a — [A variant, w. imprint:] *J. Charlewood,* 1567. L(2, 1 imp.).

24933 **Wager, W.** A comedy or enterlude intituled, Inough is as good as a feast. 4°. *J. Allde,* [1570?] HN. Greg 57.

24934 — [Headline C3ʳ:] The cruell Debtter. 4°. [*T. Colwell,* 1566.] Ent. as by 'Wager' to Colwell 1565–66. L(frags.). Greg 43.

24935 — A very mery and pythie commedie, called The longer thou liuest, the more foole thou art. 4°. *W. How f. R. Johnes,* [1569.] Ent. 1568–69. L. Greg 53.

24935a — The history of the tryall of chevalry. [Erroneously attrib. to Wager.] 1605. = 13527.

24935b — [Anr. issue.] This gallant cavaliero. 1605. Now = 13527.5.

24935b.5 **Waggoners.** To the honorable assembly of Commons. The humble petition of the waggoners or carriers of the cities of Oxford, Cambridge, Norwich, . . . and other townes. [For relief from the effects of 8689.] s.sh.fol. [*W. Jones,* 1624.] L⁵(Lemon 215).

24936 **Wake,** *Sir* **Isaac.** Oratio funebris habita in templo beatæ Mariæ Oxon. [on J. Rainolds.] 12°. *Oxoniæ, J. Barnesius,* 1608. O.O²⁸.; F.

    For earlier and later eds. *see* 24939.5 sqq., 20613 sq.

24937 — [Anr. ed.] 1614. = pt. of 20613.

24938 — [Anr. ed.] 1627. = pt. of 24941.

24939 — Rex Platonicus: sive, de . . . Jacobi regis, ad academiam Oxoniensem, adventu, narratio. 4°. *Oxoniæ, J. Barnesius,* 1607. L.O.C.D.LINC.+; F.HN.HD.NY.TEX.+

24939.5 — [Anr. ed., w. additions.] Multis in locis auctior & emendatior. Editio secunda. (Oratio funebris [on J. Rainolds.]) 12°. *Oxoniæ, J. Barnesius,* 1607. L.O.C². E².P.+; F(2, 1 imp.).HN.TORONTO².

24940 — Editio tertia. 12°. *Oxoniae, J. Barnesius,* 1615. L.O.C³. E.P.+; HN.CH.CHI.U.Y.+

24941 — Editio quarta. 12°. *Oxoniæ, J. Lichfield,* 1627. L.O.C.D. NEP.+; F.HN.HD.ILL.U.+

    (24938 is pt. of this)

24942 — Editio quinta. 12°. *Oxoniæ, L. Lichfield,* 1635. L.O.C². D².M⁴.+; F(3).CAL.ILL.Y. St. Mark's Church Rectory, Niagara-on-the-lake, Ontario.

24942.5 — [A variant, w. imprint:] *Oxoniæ, L. Lichfield,* 1636. HD.

Wakefield. The pinder of Wakefield. 1632. *See* 12213.

24943 **Wakefield, Robert.** Kotser codicis R. Wakfeldi, quo probatur coniugium cum fratria carnaliter cognitum, illicitum omnino. (The copie of a lettre by mayster R. Payce.) 4°. (*T. Berthelet,*) [1533?] L.O.C. D.DUR³.+

24944 — Roberti Wakfeldi . . . oratio de laudibus triũ linguaꝛ Arabicę Chaldaicæ & Hebraicę. 4°. *ap. W. de Vorde* [sic], [1528?] L.O.C.DUR⁵.M.+; HD(imp.).ILL. Hebrew Union C.

24945 — Roberti wakfeldi . . . paraphrasis in librũ Koheleth (quem vulgo Ecclesiasten vocāt). 4°. [*T. Gybson,* 1536?] O.

24946 — Roberti Wakfeldi . . . syntagma de hebreorum codicũ incorruptione. Item eiusdem oratio Oxonij habita. 4°. [*W. de Worde,* 1530?] L.L².O.C.D.+; F.ILL.

24947 **Wakeman, Robert.** The christian practise. A sermon. 8°. *Oxford, J. Barnes, sold by S. Waterson,* [*London,*] 1605. O.C¹⁰.P.; F(2).

24947.3 — Second impression. 8°. *Oxford, Jos. Barnes, sold by John Barnes,* [*London,*] 1612. O⁶.O¹¹.; PN².

24947.7 — Jonahs sermon and Ninevehs repentence. A sermon. 8°. *Oxford, J. Barnes, sold by S. Waterson,* [*London,*] 1603. L⁴⁴.O¹⁷.P.

24948 — Second impression. 8°. *Oxford, J. Barnes, sold by S. Waterson,* [*London,*] 1606. L¹⁵.O.P.; F.

Wakeman, Robert—*cont.*

24949 — Third impression. 8°. *Oxford, Jos. Barnes, sold by John Barnes, [London,]* 1612. L¹⁵.L³⁰.L⁴¹.; F.BO⁵. PN².

24950 — The judges charge. As it was given at Exceter. In a sermon. 8°. [*W. Stansby*] *f. G. Norton,* 1610. Ent. 4 jy. O(lacks tp).LINC.; BO⁵.PN².

24951 — The poore-mans preacher. A sermon. 8°. *A. Hatfield f. J. Bill,* 1607. Ent. 10 jn. L.O.C.LINC.P.+; F.HART. PN².U(lacks tp).

24952 — Salomons exaltation. A sermon preached before the kings majestie. 8°. *Oxford, J. Barnes, sold by S. Waterson, [London,]* 1605. L.O.O³.P.; F.BO⁵.PN².

24953 — The true professor. Opposed against the formall hypocrites. A sermon. 8°. *F. Kyngston f. J. Bartlet,* 1620. Ent. 9 se. O.LINC.; PN²(imp.).

24953.3 **Waker, I.** A breefe of scripture, disproving the principall points of popery. [Init. I. W.] s.sh.fol. [*Dublin, Society of Stationers,*] 1624. L⁵.

24953.5 — [Anr. ed., w. title:] A table briefly pointing out such places of scripture, as condemne popery. s.sh.fol. [*London,*] 1625. L.; HN. (Formerly 24907)

24953.7 — [Anr. ed., revised.] A table . . . gathered by I. Waker. s.sh.fol. [*London,*] 1628. L⁵(Lemon 292).; HD.

Wakering, Essex, *Confraternity of St. John. See* Indulgences 80.

24954 **Walbancke, Matthew.** Annalia Dubrensia. Upon the yeerely celebration of Mᵣ· Robert Dovers Olimpick games upon Cotswold-Hills. Written by M. Drayton. [and others. In verse.] 4°. *R. Raworth f. M. Walbancke,* 1636. Ent. 11 ja. L.L¹³.O.BIRM.BRISTOL². +; F.HN.HD.N.Y.+

Copies are known w. added dedic. leaves: to Sir T. Trevor (L); to Sir P. Kiligree (Y); and to S. Rolston (Chew copy, untraced).

There is an 18th-century reprint (at L, LIV³, CH, ILL) which has on A2ᵛ: 'Dr. Dover thought it his Duty to perpetuate the Memory of that Good Man his Grandfather.'

24955 — No entry.

24956 **Waldstein, Albrecht von.** The relation of the death of that great generalissimo . . . the duke of Meckleburg, [etc., commonly known as Wallenstein.] 4°. *T. Harper [a. J. Beale] f. N. Butter a. N. Bourne,* 1634. Ent. 22 mr. L.O.O³.C.C². +; F.HN.ILL.WEL.Y.
Harper pr. A–C; Beale quire E; and possibly a 3rd printer or compositor quire D.

Wales. Ban wedy i dynny. . . . A certaine case of the auncient law of Hoel da, kyng of Wales. 1550. *See* 21612.

24956.3 — South-Wales . . . North-Wales [Names of the 13 counties enclosed within woodcut border strips, 188× 270 mm.] obl. 1/2 sh.fol. [*London,* c. 1595.] L⁵ (Lemon 104).
Possibly intended to accompany a private collection of maps as it does not appear to be connected w. Saxton, Camden, or Speed.

24956.5 **Wales, Samuel.** Totum hominis: or the whole dutie of a christian. Abridged in certaine sermons expounding [2 Thess. i.11–12.] 8°. *J. Haviland f. W. Sheffard,* 1627. C².

Walker, Ferdinando, *ed. See* 24135.

24957 **Walker, George.** The doctrine of the sabbath. Delivered in divers sermons. 4°. *Amsterdam, [Richt Right Press,]* 1638. L.O²⁸.C.E².YK.+; CHI.

24958 — [Anr. issue, w. quires A–D reset.] *Amsterdam, [Richt Right Press,]* 1639. Ent. to J. Bartlet 7 de. 1640. L.L³.D⁸.EX.PETYT.; F.HN.

24959 — Fishers folly unfolded: or the vaunting jesuites vanity discovered. 4°. [*Eliot's Court Press,*] 1624. L.O.DUR (Bamb.).SNU. Rogers.+; F.HN.HD.U.

24959.5 — The manifold wisedome of God: in the divers dispensation of grace by Jesus Christ. In the Old [and] New Testament. Their agreement and difference. [Anon.] 12°. *R. H[odgkinson] f. J. Bartlet,* 1640. Ent. as by T. Taylor 24 au. L(4410.aaa.27).L³.C. CREDITON(tp only).; HD.TORONTO².U.
(Formerly 23836) Reissued in 1641, w. A1–4 cancelled and new prelims. naming Walker, as Wing W 361.

Walker, George—*cont.*

24960 — The summe of a disputation, betweene Mr. Walker and a popish priest, . . . Norrice. 4°. [*London,*] 1624. L.O.O³.C.PETYT.+; F.HN.HD.Y.
A4ᵣ line 3 ends: 'Church'. Answered by 18661.

24960.5 — [Anr. ed.] 4°. [*London,*] 1624. O.O⁶.C².C⁴.DUL.+; F. TEX.U.
A4ᵣ line 3 ends: 'no'.

24961 **Walker, Gilbert.** A manifest detection of the moste vyle and detestable vse of diceplay. [Anon. Dubiously attrib. to Walker.] 8°. [*f.*] (*A. Vele,*) [c. 1555.] O. C.; HN.
Reprinted with some alterations in 17916.

Walker, John, *Demonologist. See* 6439, 6440.

24962 **Walker, John,** *of Leeds.* The English pharise, or religious ape. [A dialogue between Protestant and Puritan.] 12°. [*London?*] 1616. L.C.

24962.5 — A glasse for papists and puritans. Or, a true description of the chiefest hypocrites and pharisies [*sic*] of these last dayes. 8°. *A. Mathewes,* 1623. Ent. as by J. Walker, Gent., to W. Lee, jun., 2 jy. O.
A different text from 24962, but prob. by the same author.

24963 **Walker, Ralph.** A learned and profitable treatise of Gods providence. 8°. *F. Kyngston f. T. Man,* 1608. Ent. to T. Man, sen., a. Jonas Man 18 ja. O.C.A.; F.HN.

24964 **Walker, William.** A sermon preached at the funerals of William, lord Russell. 4°. [*T. Snodham*] *f. J. Hodgets,* 1614. Ent. 6 no. 1613. L³.O.C.BIRM.E.+; F.HN.HD. N.U.+

24965 — A sermon preached in Sᵗ. Pauls-Church Novemb. 28. 1628. And since enlarged. 4°. *B. Alsop a. T. Fawcet f. R. Allot,* 1629. Ent. 22 ja. L.O.C.C².LEIC.+; F.CHI. HD.Y.

Walker, William, *tr. from German and Dutch. See* 539, 18417.

24966 **Walkington, Thomas.** An exposition of the two first verses of the sixt chapter to the Hebrewes, in forme of a [catechism.] (Two sermons: the practise . . . the perseverance of the saints.—Two learned treatises of the Lords supper.) [Init. T. W., *Minister of the Word.*] 4°. *T. Snodham f. T. Man,* 1609. Ent. to T. Man, sen., a. Jonas Man 18 my. L(imp.).L¹⁵.D⁸.G². G⁴(imp.).+; F(2).HD.NY¹¹.
(24972 is pt. of this) The 2 sub tpp have: *T. S. f. T. Man,* 1609.

24966a — [Anr. issue, w. cancel tpp, w. imprint:] *f. J. Bulkley,* 1609. O¹⁰(frag.).; HN.
Of the tpp, HN has only the 1st; the sub tpp are cancelled and not replaced, and gg⁴ is lacking. O¹⁰ has only the Two sermons tp, w. the Bulkley imprint, and the text of the 1st sermon.

24967 — The optick glasse of humors. Wherein the foure complections are succinctly painted forth. [Init. T. W., *Master of Arts.*] 8°. *J. Windet f. M. Clerke,* 1607. L.O.CANT.; HN.
CANT tp varies in having 'Walkington' in full.

24968 — [Anr. ed.] 8°. *Oxford, W. T[urner,] sold by M. S[parke, London,* 1631?] L.L¹⁶.O.C.BRISTOL². +; F.HN.HD.NY. WIS.+
See Greg, *Companion,* pp. 268–73.

24969 — [Anr. ed.] 8°. *for [and by] J. D[awson,] sould by L. B[laiklock,]* 1639. Ass'd from Sparke to Dawson 2 au. 1638. L.L¹⁶.O.C.LIV³.+; F.HN.HD.N.Y.+

24970 — Rabboni; Mary Magdalens teares, of sorrow, solace. Preached at S. Pauls Crosse, and newly revised and enlarged. 8°. *E. Griffin f. R. Whittakers,* 1620. Ent. 25 ja. L.O.C³.E.P.+; F.HN.HD.LC.Y.

24971 — Salomons sweete harpe: . . . Preached of late at Thetford. 8°. *C. Legge, pr. to the Univ. of Camb.,* 1608. O.C.C².C⁵.; HN.

— Theologicall rules. 1615. *See* 25798.

24972 — Two learned treatises. 1609. := pt. of 24966.

24973 **Walkley, Thomas.** A most exact catalogue of the Lords. And Commons, . . . for this Parliament. Fourth edition. 1628. Now = 7746.3.

Walkley, Thomas—*cont.*

24973.5 — A most exact catalogue of the nobilitie of England, Scotland, and Ireland. Whereunto is added the baronets and knights of the Bath of England. [Anon.] 8°. [*E. Allde*? *f. T. Walkley*,] *Printed* 1628. Quaritch (Penrose 85).; TEX.

Issued w. 7746.4 and represents an enlarged version of the Lords portion of the Parliamentary catalogues, cf. 7746.3.

24974 — [Anr. ed., enlarged.] A catalogue of the nobility of England, Scotland, and Ireland. With an addition of the baronets of England, the dates of their patents, [etc.] Collected by T. W[alkley.] 4°. [*Eliz. Allde*] *f. T. Walkley*, 1630. L.L[16].O(2).E.LINC.; F.ILL. NY.Y.

24975 — [Anr. ed., enlarged.] A catalogue of the dukes, marquesses, . . . barons, with their names, surnames, and titles of honour. Whereunto is added a catalogue of the knights of the Garter, [etc.] 4°. *f. T. Walkley*, 1632. L(2).O[8].D.; F.HN.CAL.

24976 — [Anr. ed., enlarged.] Whereunto is added a perfect list of the lords, and others of his majesties Privy Counsell; . . . the names of the judges. 8°. *f. T. Walkley*, 1634. C[3].LINC.M.SHEF.

24977 — [Anr. ed.] 8°. *f. T. Walkley*, 1635. L.O(2).M.; F(tp def.). CU.LC.

24978 — [Anr. ed., enlarged.] With an addition of the knights, from the first of king Charles to this present. 8°. *T. Harper f. T. Walkley*, 1639. C.C[10].D.DUR[3].; LC.

24979 — [Anr. ed.] 8°. *J. D[awson] f. T. Walkely*, 1640. L.O[11].C[2].M[2].; CU.HD.PN.

A2–7 reimposed in 7746.6.

24980 — A catalogue of the dukes, . . . in Parliament. [Anon.] 1640. Now = 7746.9.

24981 — [Anr. ed.] 1640. Now = 7746.10.

24981a — A catalogue of the Lords spirituall and temporall. 1640. Now = 7746.6.

24982 — A catalogue of the names of the knights, . . . 13. of Aprill, 1640. Now = 7746.7.

24983 — A catalogue of the names of the knights, . . . 3. of November, 1640. Now = 7746.13.

— *tr. See* 16927.

24984 **Wall, George.** A sermon at the lord arch-bishop of Canterbury his visitation metropoliticall, in Worcester. 4°. *T. Cotes f. R. Allot*, 1635. O.C.DUR[5].E. LINC.+

24985 **Wall, John.** Alæ seraphicæ the seraphins wings to raise us unto heaven. Delivered in six sermons. 4°. *G. M[iller] f. R. Allot*, 1627. L.O.C[2].DUL.LINC.+; F(2). HN.HD.TEX(imp.).U.

Copies vary: w. or without errata on T4[r]; both at F.

24986 — Christ in progresse. Delivered in a sermon. 8°. *Oxford, J. Lichfield a. W. Turner*, 1627. O.; HN.

24987 — Evangelicall spices, or, the incense of the Gospell. Delivered in a sermon. 8°. *M. F[lesher] f. J. Clarke*, 1627. Ent. 21 mr. L.C[10].; F.

24987.5 — [A variant, w. imprint:] *M. Flesher f. J. Clarke*, 1627. O[3].C[3].

24988 — Jacobs ladder, or christian advancement. Delivered in a sermon. 8°. *Oxford, J. Lichfield a. W. Turner f. W. Turner, T. Huggins a. E. Forrest*, 1626. L.O.BURY. LINC.; HN.

24989 — The lion in the lambe. Delivered in a sermon. 8°. *Oxford, J. Lichfield, sold by T. Butler*, 1628. L[15].O.; F.HN.

24990 — A sermon preached at Shelford, in Nottinghamshire; on the death of M. John Stanhope. 12°. *H. L[ownes] f. M. Lownes*, 1623. Ent. 15 se. L.O.

24991 — The watering of Apollos. Delivered in a sermon. 8°. *Oxford, J. Lichfield a. W. Turner f. E. Forrest*, 1625. L.O.O[5].C[3].LINC.+; F.HD(frag.).Y.

Wallace, John. *See* 21555.7.

Wallace, Michael. *See* 24587.

Wallace, Thomas. *See* 7487.29.

Wallace, *Sir* **William.** [The acts and deeds. 1508? etc.] *See* 13148 sqq.

Wallenstein, Albrecht von. *See* 24956.

24991.5 **Wallis, Thomas.** The path-way to please god. Which way whomsoever [*sic*] walketh, . . . shalbe defended against all temptations. [Anon.] 32° in 8's. *W. Jaggard, (solde by J. Hammon*, 1617.) Ass'd from J. Roberts to Jaggard 29 oc. 1615. F.

For an ed. of 1583 naming Wallis as the author, *see* Maunsell (17669), pt. 1, p. 87.

Walpole, Edward, *tr. See* 21023.

Walpole, Henry, *tr. See* 22994.
— *See also* 4537.

24992 **Walpole, Michael.** A briefe admonition to all English catholikes, concerning a late proclamation [8447]. Togeather with the confutation of a pamphlet [19204]. And an epistle to doctor King. By M. C[hristopherson] P[riest, i.e. M. Walpole.] 4°. [*St. Omer, English College Press*,] 1610. L.O.C[2].C[3].D.+; F.U. A&R 871.

24993 — A treatise of Antichrist. Conteyning the defence of cardinall Bellarmines arguments, that the pope is not Antichrist. Against [7120]. By M. Christopherson priest. The first part. 4°. [*St. Omer, English College Press*,] 1613. L[30].O.C[3].W.YK.+; N(lacks tp).TEX. A&R 872.

24994 — A treatise concerning Antichrist. Conteyning an answere to [7120]. By M. Christoferson priest. The second part. 4°. [*St. Omer, English College Press*,] 1614. L[4].C.D.USHAW.W.+; F.TEX. A&R 873.

— *tr. See* 3202, 20967, 23948.5.

24994.5 **Walpole, Richard.** A brief, and cleere confutation, of a chalenge, made by O. E. [in 23453.] By W. R. 8°. [*Antwerp, A. Conincx*,] 1603. L.O.C.D.YK.+; F.HN. TEX.U.

(Formerly 19391) A&R 874.

— A letter . . . containing a report of a conspiracie. 1599. *See* 10017.

Walraven, Jacob. *See* 25340.

24995 **Walsall, John.** A sermon preached at Pauls Crosse . . . 5. October. 1578. 8°. (*H. Middleton*) *f. G. Byshop*, [1578.] Ent. 23 mr. 1579. L.L[2](2).L[15].O.WOR.

24996 **Walsall, Samuel.** The life and death of Jesus Christ. In a sermon. 4°. [*G. Eld*] *f. T. Thorppe*, 1607. Ent. to L. Green 14 no. 1606. L.L[4].O[16].C[2].PETYT.+; F.HD.ILL.

The ILL copy has the date misprinted '1600' w. the last digit altered in ink to '7'.

24996.5 — [Anr. issue, w. imprint:] [*G. Eld*] *f. J. Porter a. L. Greene of Cambridge*, 1607. O[17].C.

In imprint: 'Cambridge'; B3[r] last line begins: 'gainst'. Quires C, E, F are reset.

24996a — [Anr. ed.] 4°. [*G. Eld*] *f. J. Porter a. L. Greene of Cambridge*, 1607. L[3].C.C[10].O.O[17].; F(imp.).

In imprint: 'CAMBRIDGE'; B3[r] last line begins: 'against'.

24997 — [Anr. ed.] 8°. *f. T. Thorp*, 1615. O.C.

24998 — [Anr. ed.] 8°. *f. J. Wright*, 1622. L.C.LINC.

24999 **Walsh, John.** The examination of John Walsh, vpon certayne interrogatories touchyng wytchcrafte and sorcerye. 8°. *J. Awdely*, 1566 (23 de.) L.

25000 **Walshe, Edward.** The office and duety in fightyng for our countrey. 8°. (*J. Herford, at the costes of R. Toye*,) 1545. L.

25001 **Walsingham.** [Begins:] Of this chapell se here the fundacyon [etc. In verse.] 4°. [*R. Pynson*, 1496?] c[6]. Duff 412.

With device McK. 9, with Pynson's name.

25002 **Walsingham, Francis,** *Jesuit.* A search made into matters of religion, by F. Walsingham deacon of the protestants church, before his change to the catholicke. 4°. [*St. Omer, English College Press*,] 1609. L.O.C[5].D.E.+; F.HN.HD.N.U.+ A&R 875.

25003 — Second edition. 4°. [*St. Omer, English College Press*,] 1615. L.O.C.A[2].YK.+; F(2, 1 imp.).HN.N.TEX.U. A&R 876.

Walsingham, *Sir* **Francis.** *See* 9188, 13869, and Bookplates.

25004 **Walsingham, Thomas.** Historia breuis Thomæ Walsingham, ab Edwardo primo, ad Henricum quintum. [*Ed.* Abp. M. Parker.] fol. *ap.* H. Binneman, 1574. L.O.C.D.E.+; F.HN.HD.N.NY.+
Issued w. 863, 25005.

25005 — Ypodigma Neustriæ vel Normanniæ: ... ab irruptione Normannorum vsq; ad annum. 6. regni Henrici quinti. [*Ed.* Abp. M. Parker.] fol. *in æd. J. Daij*, 1574. L.O.C.D.E.+; F.HN.HD.N.NY.+
Issued w. 863, 25004.

25006 — [A ghost.]

Walsoken, Norfolk, *Hospital of Holy Trinity. See* Indulgences 81 sq.

25007 **Walter,** *of Henley.* Boke of husbandry [xylographic, white on black.] [Anon. *Tr.* from French by R. Groshede, i.e. Grosseteste.] 4° [8.4]. [*W. de Worde,* 1508?] C.A
The attribution of the trans. to Grosseteste is dubious.

25007.3 — [Anr. trans., w. additions.] The booke of thrift, containing a perfite order, to profite lands, and other things belonging to husbandry. Newly Englished, by J. B(ellot.) 8°. *J. Wolfe,* 1589. G²RD.
(Formerly 1850) Includes a trans. of the anon. text 'Hosebondrie'.

Walter, M. and **Ry, Henry.** An almanack. 1544. *See* 523.

Walter, William. Guystarde and Sygysmonde. Here foloweth the amerous hystory. *Tr.* W. Walter. 1532. *See* 3183.5.
— Here begynneth yᵉ hystory of Tytus & Gesyppus, *tr.* W. Walter. [c. 1525.] *See* 3184.5.

25008 — The spectacle of louers. Here after foloweth a lytell contrauers dyalogue bytwene loue and councell. [In verse.] 4°. (*W. de worde,*) [1533?] L.; HN.

25009 **Walther, Rudolph.** Antichrist, that is to saye: a true reporte, that Antichriste is come, *tr.* out of Latine. By J. O[lde.] 8°. *Sothwarke, Christophor Trutheall* [i.e. *Emden, E. van der Erve,*] 1556. L.O.O⁴.C.DUR⁵. +; F.HN.BO.Y.

25010 — Certaine godlie homelies or sermons vpon the prophets Abdias and Jonas. *Tr.* R. Norton, minister of the worde in Suffolke. 8°. *H. Bynneman f. R. Newberie,* 1573. L.O.C⁴.CASHEL.DUR⁵.+; F(imp.).NY.NY⁸.

25011 — De syllabarum et carminum ratione, libri duo. 8°. *G. Williamsonus,* 1573. L(2).C³.; F.

25012 — The homilies or familiar sermons ... vpon the prophet Joel. *Tr.* from Latine by J. Ludham. 8°. (*T. Dawson*) *f. W. Ponsonnby,* 1582. Ent. 1 ja. L.O.DUL.HER.P.; F.
In the colophon is the spelling 'Ponnsonby'.

25013 — An hundred, threescore and fiftene homelyes or sermons, vppon the Actes of the apostles, *tr.* out of Latine. [By] (J. Bridges, *Vicar of Herne.*) fol. (*H. Denham,*) 1572. Ent. 1570–71. L.O.C.E².M.+; F.HN. N.NY.U.+

25014 — The sermons of master Ralfe Gualter vpon the prophet Zephaniah written in Latine. *Tr.* M. Wilton. 8°. *T. Dawson f. T. Cooke,* 1580. Ent. 15 jn. L.O.; F.Y.

Walton, John, *tr. See* 3200.

25015 **Wandering Jew.** The wandring Jew; or, the shoomaker of Jerusam [sic]. Ballad. *f. E. Wright in Gilt-spur-street,* [post-1640.]
Not an STC item.
— The wandering-Jew, telling fortunes. 1640. *See* 11512.

25016 **Wanton.** A preaty interlude called, Nice wanton. 4°. (*J. Kyng,*) 1560. Ent. 10 jn. L. Greg 31.

25017 — [Anr. ed.] A pretie enterlude [etc.] 4°. *J. Allde,* [1565?] L.; HN.

25018 **Wapull, George.** The tyde taryeth no man. A moste pleasant and merry commody. 4°. *H. Jackson,* 1576. Ent. 22 oc. L.C(frag.).; F.HN.PFOR.Y². Greg 70.
— *See also* 1849.

25018.5 **Warboys.** The most strange and admirable discouerie of the three witches of Warboys. [J. Samuel and others.] 4°. *f. J. Windet, J. Danter, R. Field, a. others] f. T. Man a. J. Winnington,* 1593. Ent. to Winnington a. T. Newman 30 jn. O(2).E.G².; HD(imp.).
Collates ¶² B–P⁴. Windet pr. at least halfsheet ¶; Danter B–D; Field H–O; the rest unidentified.

25019 — [Anr. ed.] 4°. *Widdowe Orwin f. T. Man a. J. Winnington,* 1593. L.O(imp.).C¹⁴(imp.).; F.
Collates A–O⁴.

25020 **Warburton, George.** King Melchizedech. A sermon preached at the court, at East-Hamsted. 4°. B. *Norton a. J. Bill,* 1623. L.O.E.PETYT.YK.+; HN. PML.U. Sydney U.

25021 **Warcop, Ralph.** Encomion Rodolphi Warcoppi. 1605. Now = 19049.5.

25022 **Ward, John,** *Captain.* Newes from sea, of two notorious pyrats Ward the Englishman and Danseker the Dutchman. With a true relation of all or the most piraces [sic] by them committed. 4°. [*E. Allde*] *f. N. Butter,* 1609. Ent. to J. Busby, sen., 2 jn. L(date crop).; HN(date shaved). Joseph M. Roebling, Harbourton, N.J.
With a dedic. to William Cockin, i.e. Cokayne.

25022.5 — [Anr. ed., omitting dedic.] Ward and Danseker, two notorious pyrates, [etc.] 4°. [*E. Allde*] *f. N. Butter,* 1609. O.; F(tp crop).

25023 **Ward, John.** The first set of English madrigals to 3. 4. 5. and 6. parts: apt both for viols and voyces. 6 ptbks. 4°. *T. Snodham,* 1613. L.L³⁰.O.C.E².+; F.HN.HD(sextus only).ILL(tenor, bassus, quintus only).
App. in all copies the quintus tp is undated; tenor tp varies: dated (F) or undated (O³, HN, ILL).

25023.5 **Ward, Nathaniel.** Nature and grace in conflict. Or, the opposition of the flesh to the spirit. [A treatise on Gal. v. 17. Init. N. W. Ed.] (J. Sedgwick.) 12°. *G. M[iller] f. R. Harford, sold by H. Overton,* 1638. Ent. as by Ward 9 ap. ELY.
— *ed. See* 25046.

25024 **Ward, Richard.** Theologicall questions, dogmaticall observations, and evangelicall essays, upon the gospel according to St. Matthew. fol. [*M. Parsons a. others*] *f. P. Cole,* 1640. Ent. 28 ja. 1639. L(destroyed).L⁴³.O¹³.C.D.E².+; HN.HD.ILL.LC.U.+
Parsons pr. Pp–Yyy; others, possibly including T. Cotes and J. Legat, did the rest.

25025 **Ward, Robert.** Anima'dversions of warre; or, a militarie magazine of the truest rules. fol. *J. Dawson,* [*T. Cotes a. R. Bishop,*] *sold by F. Eglesfield,* 1639. Ent. to Dawson 15 de. 1638. L.O³.C.A.SHEF.+; F.HN.HD. N(lacks engr. tp).Y.+
Cotes pr. quires bb–ee; Bishop Aa–Ii; Dawson the rest. The letterpress tp is a cancel.

25025a — [Anr. issue, w. letterpress tp, w. imprint:] *J. Dawson,* 1639. O.E⁸.G⁴.; HN. Penrose 364.
This is the earlier issue, w. letterpress tp clearly conjugate in HN copy.

25026 **Ward, Samuel,** *of Cambridge.* Gratia discriminans. Concio ad clerum. 4°. *M. Flesher, imp. R. Mylbourne,* 1626. Ent. 12 jn. L.O.C².D.E.+; F.HN.HD.Y.

25027 — [Anr. ed.] Emendatior et auctior. 4°. *M. Flesher, imp. R. Mylbourne,* 1627. L³.O.O⁵.C.DUL.; HN.
Also issued as pt. 2 of 7068.

25027.5 — Magnetis reductorium theologicum tropologicum. 8°. *imp. A. M[athewes,]* 1637. Ent. to Mathewes 12 jn. O⁶.O¹⁷.; F.NY³.
Dedic. to King Charles begins ✦2ʳ.

25028 — [Anr. issue, w. prelims. reprinted and added index.] *imp. A. M[athewes,]* 1637. L.O.C.LINC.NEP.+; HN.BO. CHI.TORONTO².
Dedic. to King Charles begins *1ʳ.

25029 — [Anr. ed.] 12°. *typis J. L[egat,] imp. P. Stephani & C. Meredith,* 1639. Ass'd 25 ja. 1638. L.O.C.C⁵.C¹⁰.; F. HN.HD. David P. Wheatland, Topsfield, Mass.

25030 — [A trans.] The wonders of the load-stone or, the loadstone reduc't into a divine and morall use. [*Tr.*] (H. Grimeston.) 12°. *E. P[urslowe] f. P. Cole,* 1640. Ent. 29 ap. L.L¹⁶.L³⁸.O.O¹³.; F.HN.HD.NY.Y.+
Ward is erroneously identified as 'of Ipswich' on the tp.
— *ed. See* 19734.

25030.5 **Ward, Samuel,** *of Ipswich.* The sermons and treatises which have beene heretofore severally published: and are now newly revised, corrected and augmented. 8 pts. 8°. *A. Mathewes f. J. Marriott a. J. Grismand,* 1623. F.
A reissue, w. added gen. tp and contents leaf, of 25033a, 25050, 25052, 25042, 25037, 25048, 25044.5, 25055.

Ward, Samuel, *of Ipswich—cont.*

25031 — [Anr. ed.] A collection of such sermons and treatises
as have beene written by S. Ward. 9 pts. 8°. *M.
F[lesher] f. J. Grismand*, 1627 (1628.) Marriot's share
in 6 sermons ass'd to Grismand 22 jn. 1626. L.O.C³.
C¹⁰.BTL.; F.HN.HD.N.NY.+
     Includes gen. tp and contents leaf w. 25033a.5,
25051.5, 25053.5, 25042.5, 25038(HD, NY, U) or
25038.5(L, O, F, BO, ILL), 25048.5, 25054.5,
25056.5, 25045.5. Some copies (C¹⁰, I F, HN)
have 25037 and 25054 instead. Single sermons
or collections lacking gen. tp are listed separately.

25032 — [Anr. ed., w. continuous signatures.] 8°. [*A. Mathewes*]
f. J. Grismond, 1636 (1635.) L.O.C.G².NOR².+; F.HN.
HD.N.U.+
     The Balme of Gilead has imprint: *f. E. Brewster*,
1635.

25033 — [A ghost.]

25033a — All in all. [A sermon.] 8°. (*A. Mathewes f. J. Marriott
a. J. Grismand*, 1622.) Ent. 28 my. L.O.C.C¹⁵.M.+;
F.HN.CHI.HD.NY.+
     Also issued as pt. 1 of 25030.5.

25033a.5 — [Anr. ed.] 8°. (*M. Flesher f. J. Grismand*, 1627.)
L(imp.).L³.C⁵.E.G².; CB.
     Also issued as pt. 1 of 25031.

25034 — = 25035.

25035 — Balme from Gilead to recover conscience. In a sermon.
[Ed.] (T. Gatacre.) 8°. *T. S[nodham] f. Roger Jackson
a. W. Bladen*, 1617. Ent. 14 no. 1616. L.L³(lacks tp).
L¹⁵.O.D.+; F.HN(date shaved).HD(lacks G4).ILL.

25036 — [Anr. ed.] 8°. *T. S[nodham] f. Roger Jackson a. W.
Bladen*, 1618. L.L¹⁵.C(date cropt).C².; F.HN.HART².
HD.ILL.+

25037 — [Anr. ed.] 8°. *J. H[aviland] f. Roger Jackson a.
W. Bladen*, 1622. L.O.C.M.YK.+; F.HN.CHI.NY.
Weissman.
     Also issued as pt. 5 of 25030.5 and some copies of
25031.

25038 — [Anr. ed.] 8°. *G. M[iller] f. E. Brewster*, 1628. Ass'd
4 au. 1626. L.C⁵.; F.CB.
     This and the following also issued as pt. 5 of
25031.

25038.5 — [A variant, w. imprint:] *G. M[iller] f. W. Sheffard*,
1628. L³.O.E.G².; F.HD.Y.

25039 — A coal from the altar. In a sermon. [Ed.] (A. Wood.)
8°. *H. L[ownes] f. S. Macham*, 1615. Ent. 21 no.
1614. L.O.C.D.G².+; Y. Amherst C.

25040 — Second edition, corrected & much amended. 8°. *H.
L[ownes] f. Joyce Macham, widow*, 1616. L³.O.C.C³.
CREDITON.; F.HN.HD.ILL.

25041 — Third edition. 8°. *E. G[riffin] f. Joyce Macham, widow*,
1618. L.C.D.; BO⁵.HD. Jacobson.

25042 — Fourth edition. 8°. *A. M[athewes] f. J. Marriott a. J.
Grismand*, 1622. L.O.C.C².YK.+; F.HN.CHI.HD.NY.+
     Also issued as pt. 4 of 25030.5.

25042.5 — Fift edition. 8°. *M. Flesher f. J. Grismand*, 1627. L.
L³.C⁵.E.G².; CB.HD(2).Y.
     Also issued as pt. 4 of 25031.

25043 — 1588. Deo trin-vniBritanniæ bis ultori in memoriam . . .
to God, in memorye of his double deliveraunce from
yᵉ invincible navie and yᵉ unmatcheable powder
treason. 1605. [Engr. with verses.] s.sh.fol. *Amsterdam*, 1621. L(Dept. of P&D).O³⁴(Sutherland 118–
113).
     See Hind II.393–4. Copies advertised for sale
by J. Marriot and J. Grismand at the end of
25049a.

25044 — The happinesse of practice. [A sermon.] 8°. [*G.
Purslowe*] *f. J. Marriot a. J. Grismond*, 1621. Ent.
19 fb. L.L².O.C.C³.; F.HN(lacks A3).CHI. Jacobson.
A4ʳ catchword: 'Pepuza'.

25044.5 — [Anr. ed.] 8°. [*A. Mathewes*] *f. J. Marriot a. J.
Grismond*, 1621. C.C².; HD.NY.
A4ʳ catchword: 'Spirit'. Also issued as pt. 7 of
25030.5.

25045 — [A variant, w. imprint:] [*A. Mathewes*] *f. J. Marriot
a. J. Grismond*, 1622. L.L⁴⁶.O.CARLISLE.YK.+; F.HN.
CHI.HD.ILL.+

25045.5 — [Anr. ed.] 8°. *M. Flesher f. J. Grismand*, 1627. L(2,
I imp.).L³.C⁵.E.G².; CB.U.Y.
     Also issued as pt. 9 of 25031.

25046 — Jethro's justice of peace. A sermon. [Ed.] (N. Ward.) 8°.
E. Griffin f. J. Marriot, 1618. Ent. 22 ap. L.O.C.C³.
D.+; F.BO⁵.ILL.

25047 — [Anr. ed.] 8°. *A. Mathewes f. J. Marriot a. J. Grismand*,
1621. L.C.C².C¹⁷.; HN.HD.MICH. Jacobson.

Ward, Samuel, *of Ipswich—cont.*

25048 — [Anr. ed.] 8°. *A. Math[ewes] f. J. Marriott a. J.
Grismand*, 1623. L.O(2).O²¹.M.YK.+; F.HN.CHI.HD.
NY.+
     Also issued as pt. 6 of 25030.5.

25048.5 — [Anr. ed.] 8°. *M. Flesher f. J. Grismand*, 1627. L.L³.
C⁵.E.G².+; CB.HD.MICH.Y.
     Also issued as pt. 6 of 25031.

25049 — The life of faith. [A treatise.] 8°. *A. Math[ewes] f. J.
Marriot a. J. Grismand*, 1621. Ent. 9 oc. 1620. O.C.;
HN(imp.).ILL.

25049a — Second edition, corrected and amended. 8°. *A.
Mathewes f. J. Marriot a. J. Grismand*, 1621. L.O.
O¹⁸.C.C².+; HD. Jacobson.
     With a bookseller's notice at the end for 25043.

25050 — Third edition. 8°. *A. Mathewes f. J. Marriot a. J.
Grismand*, 1622. L.O.O²¹.M.YK.+; F.HN.CHI.HD.NY.+
     Also issued as pt. 2 of 25030.5.

25051 — [Anr. ed.] 8°. [*M. Flesher*] *f. J. Marriot a. J. Grismand*,
1625. L.L⁴⁶.C.

25051.5 — [Anr. ed.] 8°. *M. Flesher f. J. Grismand*, 1627. L.L³.C.
E.G².+; CB(imp.).MICH.Y.
     Also issued as pt. 2 of 25031.

25052 — The life of faith in death. Exemplified in the living
speeches of dying christians. [With two sermons.]
8°. *A. Mathewes f. J. Marriot a. J. Grismand*, 1622.
Ent. 29 oc. 1621. L.O.C.M.YK.+; F.HN.CHI.HD.NY.+
     Page 4 catchword: 'onely'. Also issued as pt. 3 of
25030.5.

25053 — [Anr. ed.] 8°. *A. Mathewes f. J. Marriot a. J. Grismand*,
1622. L.O.C².; F.CHI.ILL.Y. Jacobson.
     Page 4 catchword: 'only'.

25053.5 — [Anr. ed.] 8°. *M. Flesher f. J. Grismand*, 1627. L.L³.
C(imp.).C⁵.E.+; CB.Y.
     Also issued as pt. 3 of 25031.

25054 — A peace-offring to God. In a sermon. 8°. *A. Math[ewes]
f. J. Marriott a. J. Grismand*, 1624. Ent. 7 de. 1623.
L.L⁴⁶.O.C.C³.+; F.HN.BO⁵.ILL.Y.+
     A1, cancelled in most copies, is present in O²¹ and
is a tp, w. line 5 ending: 'enjoy'; most copies have
only the tp on a3, w. line 5 ending 'vnder'. Occasionally issued as pt. 7 of 25031.

25054.5 — [Anr. ed.] 8°. [*M. Flesher*] *f. J. Grismond*, [1627.] L.
L³.C⁵.E.G².
     Also issued as pt. 7 of 25031.

25055 — Woe to drunkards. A sermon. 8°. *A. Math[ewes] f. J.
Marriott a. J. Grismand*, 1622. Ent. 28 my. O³.C.M.
YK.; F.HN.NY.U. Weissman.
     A3ʳ catchword: 'nities'. Also issued as pt. 8 of
25030.5.

25055.5 — [Anr. issue, partly reset and reimposed.] *A. Math[ewes]
f. J. Marriott a. J. Grismand*, 1622. L.C².; F.HN.CHI.HD.
     A3ʳ catchword: 'of'.

25056 — [Anr. ed.] 8°. *A. Math[ewes] f. J. Marriott a. J.
Grismand*, 1624. L.L⁴⁶.O²¹.C.; HD. Weissman.

25056.5 — [Anr. ed.] 8°. [*M. Flesher*] *f. J. Grismand*, 1627. L
(frag.).L³.C⁵.E.G².; CB.MICH.NY.WIS.Y.
     Also issued as pt. 8 of 25031.

— The wonders of the load-stone. 1640. *See* 25030.

— *See* also 18030.

25057 **Ward, William,** *Minister.* Gods arrowes, or, two sermons, concerning the pestilence. 8°. *H. Ballard*,
1607. L.O.C.NLW.; HN.

25058 — Short grounds of catechisme: delivered by way of
question and answer. 8°. *Cambridge, prs. to the Univ.*,
[T. a. J. Buck,] 1627. O.O³.C³.DUR(Bamb.).E⁴.+

25059 — Short questions upon the eight parts of speech, with
the concords, in English. 8°. *J. Beale*, [1628.] Ent.
7 jy. 1628. L(C.27.d.11/8).

25060 — [Anr. ed.] 4°. *J. Beale, sold by W. Lee*, 1629. L(tp only,
Harl. 5974/111).; HN.HD.

25061 — A sinners inditement. [A sermon.] 8°. *T. Purfoot f. T.
Pavier*, 1613. Ent. 20 no. 1612. O.O³.

25062 — [Anr. ed.] 8°. *W. White f. T. Pavier*, 1615. C.

Warde, William, *Physician.* The arte of angling. 1577.
See 793.7.

— *tr. See* 293, 300, 305, 312, 724, 4458.

25062.5 **Wardlaw, Henry.** Catalogus librorum, qui summa quin-
gentarum minarum, D. Henrico Wardlaw, à Pitravia
milite, testamento legatâ, comparati sunt, Anno
Dom. 1638. [List of 22 works in 48 vols.] s.sh.4°.
[*Edinburgh*, 1638.] E².

Ware. Another bloody murther committed neere Ware.
[1633.] *See* 3945.7.

Ware—*cont.*

25063 — The post of Ware: with a packet full of strange newes. [Largely satiric; includes a reference to Spinola, Spanish general in the Netherlands.] *Ballad.* 2 pts. s.sh.fol. [*G. Purslowe*] *f. J. Trundle*, [1622?] c⁶.

25064 **Ware**, *Sir James.* Archiepiscoporum Casseliensium & Tuamensium vitæ. 4°. *Dublini, ex off. Soc. Bibliopolarum*, 1626. L.O.C.D.G².+; F(2).HN.CAL².HD.

25065 — De præsulibus Lageniae, sive provinciæ Dubliniensis. Liber unus. 4°. *Dublini, ex off. Soc. Bibliopolarum*, 1628. L.O.C.D.SHR.+; F(2).HN.HD.N.

25066 — De scriptoribus Hiberniæ. Libri duo. 4°. *Dublinii, ex typog. Soc. Bibliopolarum*, 1639. L.O.C.D.E.+; F. HN. CHI.HD.NY.+
   Tp varies: pr. all in black, or in red and black; both at c.

25067 — Two histories of Ireland. The one written by E. Campion, the other by M. Hanmer. (A view of the state of Ireland. By E. Spenser. Published by sir J. Ware.) fol. 2 pts. *Dublin, Soc. of Stationers,* [*a. London, T. Harper,*] 1633. View ent. to M. Lownes 14 ap. 1598. L.O.C.D.M.+; F(View only, imp.).HN.JH. CHI.Y.+
   Harper pr. the Hanmer section. Some copies (c, M, PFOR) have an early state of the View tp, w. an orn.; others (c, F) have the orn. replaced by: 'Whereunto is added the history of Ireland, by E. Campion'; others (L, O, C, HN) have, in addition, annotations (k⁴) in the View. For a more detailed analysis of issues and copies *see* F. R. Johnson, *A Critical Bibliography of Spenser,* pp. 48–53.

25067a — [Anr. issue, w. cancel gen. tp:] The historie of Ireland, collected by M. Hanmer . . . E. Campion . . . and E. Spenser. *Dublin, Soc. of Stationers,* 1633. L.O.C.D. E.+; F.HN.HD.N.NY.+
   A few copies (c, HD, LC) have Hanmer's chronicle bd. 1st, w. a cancel dedic. by M. Manwaring, Hanmer's son-in-law; most copies (L, O, C, F, HN, HD) retain Ware's dedic.

Warfare. The warfare of Christians. 1576. *See* 5201.

25068 **Warford, William.** A briefe instruction. By way of dialogue, concerning the principall poyntes of christian religiõ. [*G. Doulye, pseud.*] 8°. *Lovaine, L. Kellam* [really *Seville, F. Perez?*] 1604. L.C⁵.D.E². YK.+; F.
   A&R 877. *See Cal.S.P.D., 1603–1610,* p. 261.

25069 — [Anr. ed.] 8°. [*St. Omer, English College Press,*] 1616. L.O.AMP(imp.).OS.USHAW.+; HN.
   A&R 878.

25070 — Fourth edition. 12°. [*St. Omer, English College Press,*] 1637. L.
   A&R 879.

25070.5 — A briefe treatise of pennance. With necessary instructions for the preparation to that sacramẽt. 12°. [*St. Omer, English College Press,*] 1624. C¹⁵.
   A&R 880.

25071 — [Anr. ed.] 12°. [*St. Omer, widow of C. Boscard,*] 1633. L.W.
   A&R 881.

25071.5 **Warham, William,** *Abp.* Uniuersis [xylographic] Sancte matris ecclesie filijs . . . Willms . . . Cant. Archiepus. . . . [Inspeximus by Warham, dated 5 Apr. 1508, of bull of Julius II, dated 18 Mar. 1508, granting indulgences to contributors to the rebuilding of St. Peter's.] s.sh.fol. [*R. Pynson,* 1508.] c⁷(MS.106. 378).
   For the indulgences themselves *see* Indulgences 103B sqq.

25072 — Willmus . . . vobis auctoritate apostolica [etc. 1508.] Now = Indulgences 105C.
   — *See also* Indulgences 43, 103B sqq., 117B, 124, 126.

25073 — O quantum in rebus inane. Intronizatio Wilhelmi Warham. A. D. 1504. *Eng. a. Lat.* fol(10). [*J. Cawood,* 1570?] L²('Provisiones' sheet only).O.
   The O copy, which has 18482.5 pr. on the verso of sheets 4–8, is mounted in a roll with 3419.5, 6832.22, 19286. 3835 was formerly bd. in also.

25074 **Waring, Robert.** Amoris effigies. [1657.] = Wing W 860.

25075 **Warming Stone.** The warming stone. 1640. Now = 4615.5.

25076 **Warmington, William.** A moderate defence of the oath of allegiance: wherein the author proueth the said oath to be most lawful, notwithstanding the popes breves. Together with the oration of Sixtus 5. upon the murther of Henrie 3. 4°. [*R. Field,*] 1612. L.O. C.D.M.+; F.HN.HD(imp.).TEX.U.+
   A&R 882. The trans. of the Sixtus oration is reprinted from 14002.

25076.5 **Warmstrey, Gervase.** Virescit vulnere virtus. Englands wound and cure. [An appeal to patriotism following the Isle of Ré disaster. In verse.] 4°. [*W. Jones?*] 1628. O.

25077 **Warmstrey, Thomas.** Suspiria ecclesiæ. The sighs of the church. 1648. = Wing W 891. In most copies the lower loop of the 8 has not printed.

25078 **Warner, John.** Christ in the clouds, or Gods comming to judgement. A short treatise. [*Anon.*] 8°. *f. F. Coles,* 1635. Ent. as by John Warner 25 mr. 1630. L.O⁶.; F.

Warner, John, *Bp.* Rochester. Visitation Articles. *See* 10321.5.

Warner, Walter, *ed. See* 12784.

25079 **Warner, William.** Albions England. Or historicall map of the same island. [4 bks. In verse.] 4°. *G. Robinson* [*a. R. Ward*] *f. T. Cadman,* (1586.) Ent. 7 no. HN. HD.JH.PFOR.WIS.
   Ward illegally pr. A–F; *see* Greg, *Register B,* p. 20. Copies differ; quire A in 2 settings, both by Ward; A1ʳ last line: 'euerie' (HN) or 'euery' (HD). HD has both formes of quire F pr. by Ward; F2ʳ last line: 'Wench said'; HN has the outer forme by Ward, the inner by Robinson; F2ʳ last line: 'wench sayd'.

25080 — [Anr. ed., enlarged to 6 bks.] The first and second parts of Albions England. The former reuised and corrected. 4°. *T. Orwin f. T. Cadman,* 1589. L.O(2, 1 imp.).; F.HN.HD(imp.).ILL.LC(imp.).+

25081 — [Anr. ed., enlarged to 9 bks.] Albions England: the third time corrected and augmented. 4°. *T. Orwin f. J. B[roome,*] 1592. L.O.C.BTU.NOR².+; F.HN.CHI. PN.TEX.+

25082 — [Anr. ed., enlarged to 12 bks.] Now reuised, and newly inlarged. 4° in 8's. *Widow Orwin f. J. B[roome,*] 1596. Ent. to Mrs. Broome 6 de. L.L⁶.L³⁰.; HN.ILL.

25082a — [A variant, w. imprint:] *Widow Orwin f. J. B[roome,*] 1597. L.O.BTU.E².; F.HN.HD.ILL.Y.+

25083 — [Anr. ed., enlarged to 13 bks. and Epitome.] Whereunto is also newly added an Epitome of the whole historie of England. 4° in 8's. *E. Bollifant f. G. Potter,* 1602. Ass'd 23 au. 1601. L.O.C.D².E.+; F.HN. HD.ILL.NY.+

25084 — [Anr. ed.] 4° in 8's. [*W. Stansby*] *f. G. P[otter,*] *sold by R. Moore,* 1612. L.O.C¹⁹.D.E.+; F.HN.HD.N.Y.+

25085 — A continuance of Albions England. [Bks. 14–16. In verse.] 4°. *F. Kyngston f. G. Potter,* 1606. L⁶.L⁴³.O. M².P.+; F.HN.HD.N.NY.+
   R. Bradock may have pr. quire B.
   — Menaecmi. Written in English, by W. W[arner.] 1595. *See* 20002.

25086 — Pan his syrinx, or pipe, . . . including seuen tragical and comicall arguments. 4°. *T. Purfoote,* [1584.] Ent. 22 se. 1584. L.L¹⁶.O⁶.; HD(imp.).

25087 — [Anr. ed.] Syrinx, or a seauenfold historie. Newly perused. 4°. *T. Purfoot, sould* [*by J. Broome,*] 1597. L.L⁶.; F(imp.).HN.PFOR.

25088 **Warning.** A warning for all murderers. [On the murder, probably fictitious, of David Williams.] *Ballad.* 2 pts. s.sh.fol. *f. H. Gosson,* [c. 1620.] ?Ent. to F. Grove 8 se. 1638. L.
   — A warnyng for Englande. 1555. *See* 10024.

25089 — A warning for faire women. Containing, the most tragicall murther of master G. Sanders. 4°. *V. Sims f. W. Aspley,* 1599. Ent. 17 no. L.L⁶.O(imp.).; F.HN. CH.HD.Y.+ Greg 155.
   — [Warning of a second deluge and other disasters, predicted for Feb. 1524.] *See* 389.7.

25089.5 — A warning to all false traitors by example of 14. Wherof vi. were executed in diuers places neere about London, and 2. neere Braintford the 28. day of August, 1588. Also at Tyborne . . . vi. *Ballad.* s.sh. fol. *E. Allde,* [1588.] Private owner.
   See also 24215.

Warning—*cont.*
— A warning to the dragon. 1625. *See* 904.

Warre, James. The merchants hand-maide. 1622. *See* 24908.

25090 — The touch-stone of truth. Wherein veritie, by scripture is plainely confirmed. [Tables of scriptural citations on various topics, w. an anti-Catholic bias.] 8°. *A. Mathewes*, 1621. Ent. 2 no. 1620. L.O.C.; F. Duke U.

25090a — Second impression inlarged and corrected. 8°. *A. Mathewes a. J. Norton, sold by T. Jones*, 1624. O.D. YK.; HD.

25091 — Third impression inlarged and corrected. 8°. *A. Mathewes, sold by T. Jones*, 1630. L.O.C.C⁶.STU.+; F.HN.

25092 — Fourth impression. 8°. *A. Mathewes, sold by T. Jones*, 1634. L.L⁴.D.LK.YK.; F.CHI.

25093 **Warren, Arthur.** The poore mans passions. And poverties patience. Written . . . 1605. [In verse.] 4°. *J. R[oberts] f. R. B[ankworth*, 1605.] Ent. to Bankworth 14 ja. 1605. L.O.; F.HN.HD.ILL.Y.

25094 **Warren, John.** Domus ordinata. A funerall sermon, preached in Bristoll, at the buriall of mistresse Needes. 4°. *N. Okes, solde by J. Harison* [4,] 1618. L.L⁴⁶.O.O¹⁰.; F.HN.HD.PN.Y.
Copies vary: 1st halfsheet has no leaf signature (o) or is signed ¶ (o¹⁰).

25095 **Warren, William.** A pleasant new fancie of a fondlings deuice: intitled and cald the Nurcerie of names. [In verse.] 4°. [*J. Charlewood f.*] *R. Jhones*, 1581. Ent. 15 ap. F.HN.

Warrin, John, *Priest, tr. See* 18571.

Warwick. A briefe discours of bathes in Warwicke. 1587. *See* 1192.

25096 **Warwick, Arthur.** Spare-minutes; or, resolved meditations. Second edition corrected and enlarged. 12°. *R. B[adger a.]* (*G. M[iller]) f. W. Hammond, sold by M. Sparke*, 1634. Ent. to Hammond 24 mr. 1632. O. Badger app. pr. quires A–B. Engr. tp by T. Clark has imprint 'f. W. Hammond.'

25097 — [A variant, w. imprint on 1st tp:] *G. M[iller] f. W. Hammond, sold by M. Sparke*, 1634. F(2, both lacking engr. tp and verses).

25097.5 — [Anr. ed.] Third edition. 12°. *G. M[iller] f. W. Hammond, sold by M. Sparke*, 1635. L.O.E(imp.).; F.
Quires G–I are largely reimposed from 25097. With a different 1st engr. tp by T. Clark, w. imprint 'f. W. H.', and the engr. tp of 25096 used as a sub tp.

25098 — Fourth edition. 12°. *G. M[iller] f. W. Hammond, sold by M. Sparke*, 1635. L⁴.

25099 — Fift edition. 12°. *G. M[iller] f. W. Hammond, sold by M. Sparke*, 1636. L(lacks 1st engr. tp and verses).; F.

25100 — Sixt edition. 12°. *G. M[iller] f. W. Hammond, sold by M. Sparke*, 1637. L(2).E.; F.HN.HD.Y.

25100.5 — Seventh edition. 12°. *G. M[iller] f. W. Hammond, sold by M. Sparke*, 1639. C⁵.; HD.
Both engr. tpp dated 1640.

25101 — [A variant, w. letterpress tp:] Seventh edition. *G. M[iller] f. W. Hammond, sold by F. Eglesfield*, 1640. L.NOR².; HN.V.
All copies but L have the misprint 'sod by' in the letterpress imprint. Sheets reissued w. cancel letterpress tp: 'Seventh edition. 1641.' as Wing W 989.

Washington, Thomas, *tr. See* 18574.

25102 **Wastell, Simon.** Microbiblion or the Bibles epitome: in verse. (A true christians daily delight: being the summe of every chapter of the new Testament, in verse.) 12°. [*M. Flesher] f. R. Mylbourne*, 1629. L. O.E.G².PETYT.+; F.HN.HD.N.NY.+
The N.T. text is the same as in 25103, but the O.T. is different and longer. In some copies (ILL, U) the date is blurred and can be misread as 1620.

25103 — A true christians daily delight: being the summe of every chapter of the Old and New Testaments. [In verse.] 12°. *G. Eld a. M. Flesher f. R. Mylbourne*, 1623. Ent. 6 au. 1621. L.O.O².; F.HN.NY.Y.
In the Preface Wastell mentions 22389 as the inspiration for this work.

Watchbell. A silver watch-bell. 1605. *See* 24421.

25104 **Waterhouse, Edward.** A declaration of the state of the colony in Virginia. With a relation of the barbarous massacre. And a treatise annexed, by H. Briggs, of the Northwest passage. And a note of necessary provisions. 4°. *G. Eld f. R. Mylbourne*, 1622. Ent. 21 au. L.L².CHATS.G².M.+; F(lacks Note).HN.HD (lacks Note).N.NY.+
The broadside Note of provisions also issued sep. as 24844.

Waterman, William, *tr. See* 3197.

Watermen. The watermens suit. [1614?] *See* 23813.3.

Waters, Fr. An almanack. 1624. *See* 524.

25105 **Watertoune, Thomas.** A ninuectyue [*sic*] agaynst treason. [Init. T. W. In verse.] s.sh.fol. *R. Madeley*, [1553.] L.; MEL.

25106 **Wateson, George.** The cures of the diseased, in remote regions [especially in hot climates like Spain.] [Init. G. W.] 4°. *F. K(ingston) f. H. L(ownes,)* 1598. Ent. 6 my. L.C.

25106a — [A variant, w. dedic. signed in full.] *F. K(ingston) f. H. L(ownes,)* 1598. L.L¹⁷.

25107 **Watkins, *Mother*.** A ditty delightfull of mother watkins ale. *Ballad.* s.sh.fol. [*London,* c. 1590.] L.

Watkinson, William, *tr. See* 15256, 21064.5.

25108 **Watling Street.** The first part of the faire widow of Watling street. *Ballad.* 2 pts. s.sh.fol. *f. T. P[avier*, 1625?] Ent. to R. Jones 15 au. 1597; to T. Pavier and ballad ptnrs. 14 de. 1624. L.

25108.5 — [Anr. ed.] 2 pts. s.sh.fol. *f. F. Cowles*, [c. 1635.] L.C⁶.

Wats, Gilbert, *tr. See* 1167.

25109 **Wats, James.** The controversie debated about the reverend gesture of kneeling, in the act of receiving the holy communion. 4°. *W. J[aggard] f. W. Burre*, 1621. L.O.C⁵.BTL(imp.).PLUME.+; F.U.

Wats, William. *See* Watts, W.

Watson, Anthony, *Bp.* Chichester. Visitation Articles. *See* 10180.

25109.5 **Watson, Christopher.** Briefe [etc.] 1578. *See* Addenda.
25110 — [Anr. ed. Heading A1ʳ:] Briefe principles of religion, for the exercise of youth. 8° in 4. (*H. Singleton,* 1581.) L.O.; F.HN.
— *tr. See* 20097.

Watson, Henry, *tr. See* 1966, 3547, 12091, 18808, 20107, 24571.3.

25111 **Watson, Robert.** Aetiologia . . . de transubstantiatione. [*Emden,*] 1556.
Not an STC book.

Watson, Robert. Almanacks. 1595, etc. *See* 525 sqq.

25112 **Watson, Thomas,** *Bp.* Holsome and catholyke doctryne concerninge the seuen sacramentes . . . set forth in maner of shorte sermons. 4° in 8's. *in æd. R. Caly,* 1558 (fb.) [in col.:] (10 fb.) O¹⁷.C.C⁴.DE.ST.; N.Y.
A1ʳ catchword: 'working', last line: 'onely'.

25112.5 — [Anr. ed.] 4° in 8's. *in æd. R. Caly,* 1558 (fb.) [in col.:] (10 fb.) L.O.C.P.ST.+; F.HN.HD.TEX.U.+
A1ʳ catchword: 'working', last line: 'onelye'.

25113 — [Anr. ed.] 4° in 8's. *in æd. R. Caly* [really *J. Kingston,*] 1558 (fb.) L.O.C⁴.D.P.+; F.ILL.LC.N.PML.
A1ʳ catchword: 'It'. The woodcut inits. are those of Kingston, but regarding T. Marsh's possible help in printing this *see Acts P.C., 1556–1558,* p. 346. Caly refers to this pirated ed. in 25114.

25114 — [Anr. ed.] 4° in 8's. *in æd. R. Caly,* 1558 (7 jn.) L.O.C. DE.YK.+
This has an added 2-leaf printer's pref.

25115 — Twoo notable sermons, made . . . before the quenes highnes, concernynge the reall presence. 8°. (*J. Cawood,* 1554 (10 my.)) D.LONGLEAT.; F.ILL(lacks tp).
In colophon: 'churcheyarde, at/'; H5ʳ last line: 'drynke'. Reprinted and answered in 6093.

25115.3 — [Anr. ed.] 8°. (*J. Cawood,* 1554 (10 my.)) L².O.C⁵(lacks col.).DE(w. at least quire A of 25115.5).USHAW(imp.). +; F.HN.
In title: 'concernynge'; in col.: 'churche yarde,/'; H5ʳ last line: 'drynk'.

Watson, Thomas, *Bp.*—*cont.*

25115.5 — [Anr. ed.] 8°. (*J. Cawood*, 1554 (10 my.)) L.O(lacks
col.).O⁵.C.P.+; CH.HD.U.Y.
In title: 'concerninge'; in col.: 'churchyarde,/';
H5ʳ last line: 'drink'.

Watson, Thomas, *Gent.* A true relation of occurrences
in Virginia. 1608. *See* 22795.3.

25116 Now = 25118.10.

25117 **Watson, Thomas,** *Poet.* Amintæ gaudia authore Thoma
Watsono. [In verse.] 4°. [*P. Short,*] *imp. G.
Ponsonbei,* 1592. Ent. 10 no. L.O.C.C².LINC.+; F(3).
HN.HD.

25118 — [An extract, translated.] An ould facioned loue. . . .
[*Anon. Tr.* in verse.] By I. T[russel?] gent. (The
answer of Phillis . . . by the translator.) 4°. *P. S[hort]
f. W. Mattes,* 1594. L⁴.O⁵.C².
(Formerly also 23624)

25118.2 — Amyntas Thomæ Watsoni Londinensis. I. V. studiosi.
[In verse.] 8°. *H. Marsh, ex assig. T. Marsh,* 1585.
Ass'd by E. Marsh to T. Orwin ?23 jn. 1591. L.
(Formerly 23691)

25118.4 — [A trans.] The lamentations of Amyntas for the death
of Phillis, paraphrastically *tr.* into English hexa-
meters by A. Fraunce. [*Anon.*] 4°. *J. Wolfe f. T.
Newman a. T. Gubbin,* 1587. O.; HN.
(Formerly 23692) Reprinted w. alterations in
11340.

25118.5 — [Anr. ed.] Newelie corrected. 4°. *J. Charle-wood f. T.
Newman a. T. Gubbin,* 1588. O⁵.; HN.
(Formerly 23693)

25118.6 — [Anr. ed.] 4°. *R. Robinson f. T. Newman a. T. Gubbin,*
1589. O.DUL.; HN.
(Formerly 23694)

25118.8 — [Anr. ed.] 4°. *R. Robinson f. T. Gubbin,* 1596. Ent. to
John Newbery 12 jn. 1600. L.D².; F.ILL.
(Formerly 23695)
— Coluthi Thebani . . . Helenae raptus. 1586. *See* 5586.

25118.10 — Compendium memoriæ localis. Autore Thoma
Watsono. 8° in 4's. [*T. Vautrollier,* 1585?] C.;
HN(imp.).
(Formerly 25116)

25118a — The EʹKATOMΠAΘIʹA [*sic*] or passionate centurie of
loue, diuided into two parts. [In verse.] 4°. *J. Wolfe
f. G. Cawood,* [1582.] Ent. 31 mr. 1582. L.L⁶.O(3,
1 imp.).; F(2).HN.HD(imp.).PML. Arthur Houghton.

25119 — Superius. (Medius.—Contratenor.—Tenor.—Bassus.
—Sextus.) The first sett, of Italian madrigalls Englished, not to the sense of the originall dittie, but
after the affection of the noate. Also two madrigalls
of W. Byrds. 6 ptbks. 4°. *T. Este, the assigné of W.
Byrd, sold at the house of T. Este,* 1590. Ent. 6 de.
1596. L.O.C.G².M³.+; F(1, plus medius, contratenor,
and sextus).HN.HD(1, of which tenor is imp.).LC
(bassus only).N.
The medius imprint omits 'sold . . . T. Este' and
further varies in having 'assigné' (1 O, HN) or
'assigne' (no accent, 1 O, F, HD).
— A gratification vnto master John Case. 1589. *See*
4246.

25120 — Meliboeus Thomæ Watsoni siuè, ecloga in obitum F.
Walsinghami. [In verse.] 4°. *R. Robinsonus,* 1590.
L.O¹⁷.; F(2).HN.PML.Y.

25121 — [A trans.] An eglogue vpon the death of sir F.
Walsingham. Now *tr.* [by T. Watson.] 4°. *R.
Robinson,* 1590. L.

25122 — The tears of fancie. Or, loue disdained. [Init. T. W.
Not by Watson. In verse.] 4°. [*J. Danter*] *f. W.
Barley,* 1593. Ent. to Danter 11 au. HN(imp.).
— *tr. See* 22929.

25123 **Watson, William.** A decacordon of ten quodlibeticall
questions concerning religion and state. Newly
imprinted. 4° in 8's. [*R. Field,*] 1602. L.O.C.D.E.+;
F.HN.HD.N.Y.+
A&R 883. Answered by 10765, 20562. Watson's
name as author appears on p. 361.

25124 — A dialogue betwixt a secular priest, and a lay gentleman. Being an abstract of matters in controversie
betwixt the priests and the Spanish or jesuiticall
faction. [Init. W. W. Preface by Watson; main text
by J. Mush.] 4°. *Rhemes,* [i.e. *London, A. Islip,*] 1601.
L.O⁴.C.DUR⁵.W.+; F.U.
A&R 553.

Watson, William—*cont.*

25124.5 — [Anr. issue, w. cancel tp:] A dialogue . . . gentleman.
Concerning some points objected by the jesuiticall
faction against such secular priests, as have shewed
their dislike. *Rhemes,* [i.e. *London, A. Islip,*] 1601.
O.O¹⁸.C.D(imp.)*.E.+; HN.TEX(lacks tp)*.
A&R 554.

25125 — Important considerations, which ought to move all
true catholikes, to acknowledge that the proceedings
of her majesty, have bene mild. [Init. W. W. Preface
by Watson; main text by T. Bluet.] 4°. [*R. Field,*]
1601. L.O.C.DUR³.YK.+; F.HN.HD.NY.TEX.
A&R 122.

25126 — A sparing discoverie of our English jesuits, and of Fa.
Parsons. [Init. W. W. Preface by Watson; main
text by C. Bagshaw?] 4°. [*F. Kingston,*] 1601. L.
O¹⁷.C.D.E.+; F.HN.HD.U.Y.+
A&R 64.
— *tr. See* 780, 19449.

25127 **Watt, Joachim von.** A worke entytled of yᵉ olde god &
the newe. [*Anon. Tr.* by W. Turner from H.
Dulichius' Latin trans. of Watt's Vom alten und
neuen Gott.] 8°. (*J. Byddell* [*f. W. Marshall,*] 1534
(15 jn.)) L.O.C.C⁴.LINC.+; F(2).HN.HD(imp.).ILL.
WIS.
Regarding Marshall's connection w. this *see* L. &
P. Henry VIII, VII.178.

Watton, John. *See* Wotton, J.

25128 **Watts, Thomas.** The entrie to christianitie, or, an admonition to housholders, for instruction of their
families. 8°. *T. O[rwin] f. T. Woodcocke,* 1589. Ent.
15 ja. F.

25129 **Watts, William.** Mortification apostolicall. Delivered in
a sermon. 4°. *J. L[egat] f. J. Cowper,* 1637. Ent.
5 jn. L.O.C.D.LEEDS.+; F(lacks tp).HN.HD.N.U.+
— The Swedish Intelligencer. [Pts. 1–4 by W. Watts.]
1632, etc. *See* 23521, 23524, 23525.
— *ed. See* 19210.
— *tr. See* 912, 23519.5 sq.

Way. The richt vay to the kingdome of heuine. 1533. *See*
19525.
— The true way to vertue. 1623. *See* 7373.2.

25130 — The way how a religious correspondencie may be procured amongst the churches. [*London,* c. 1655?]
Not an STC book; a copy at D⁸ is bd. w. STC
7367.5 and Wing T 863.

25131 — The waye to commende our selues to God in the
morning. [1580–81.] Now = pt. 3 of 17278.4.
— The way to the holy lande. 1515, etc. *See* 14082 sq.

25132 — The way to true happines leading to the gate of knowledge. By questions and answers. 8°. [*W. Jaggard*] *f.
T. Pavier,* 1610. Ent. 20 au. 1602. C.BRISTOL.; F.PN.
For other eds. entitled 'The doctrine of the Bible'
see 3022.7 sqq.

25133 — Now = 25135.5.

25134 — [Anr. ed.] 8°. *T. S[nodham] f. T. Pavier,* 1613. L.O.C.;
ILL.

25135 — [Anr. ed.] 8°. *T. Snodham f. T. Pavier,* 1615. L.O.C.;
F.CAL.PML.U.

25135.5 — [Anr. ed.] 8°. [*T. Snodham*] *f. T. Pavier,* [1620?] L.
L¹⁴(2).BRISTOL.; F.
(Formerly 25133)

25136 — [Anr. ed.] 8°. [*G. Miller*] *f. E. Brewster a. R. Bird,*
[1630?] Ass'd 4 au. 1626. L(2).L¹⁴(2).BRISTOL. Brox-
bourne(O).; F.HN.NY.NY⁶.PML.+

25137 — [Anr. ed.] Now newly corrected, and augmented. 8°.
R. Young, 1633. Ass'd 5 ap. 1634. L¹⁴.O⁶.C.BRISTOL.
E.+; CAL.HD(lacks tp).ILL.PH⁵.+
A2ʳ has a headpiece of 15 type orns. in a row.

25138 — [Anr. ed.] 8°. *R. Young,* [1637?] L.O.C.BRISTOL.; F.HD.
NY(imp.).
(Formerly also 25140) A2ʳ has a headpiece of
24 type orns. in a row; A2ʳ, col. 2, last line: 'Hee
cursed'.

25139 — [Anr. ed.] 8°. *R. Young,* [1640?] L(2).C.BRISTOL.P.;
F.HN.ILL.LC.Y(lacks tp).+
(Formerly also 25141) A2ʳ has a headpiece of
24 type orns. in a row; A2ʳ, col. 2, last line: 'He
cursed'.

25140 — = 25138.
25141 — = 25139.

25142 **Waymouth, John.** Low-Countrie trayning: or, certaine demonstrations, how a company should march. According to the methode now perfected, by prince Maurice of Nassau. obl.4°. *T. S[nodham] f. W. Welby a. E. Brewster,* 1617. Ent. to Brewster 26 se. 1616. L.O.C.C¹⁴.WI.; HN.

25143 — A plaine and easie table, whereby to read the whole Bible in a yeere. 8°. *F. Kyngston f. W. Welbie,* 1613. Ent. 25 de. 1612. L.
The tables are pr. only on rectos.

Waynman, Humfrey, *ed. See* 17649.

25144 **Weakest.** The weakest goeth to the wall. [A tragi-comedy.] 4°. *T. Creede f. R. Olive,* 1600. Ent. 23 oc. L.O.; F.HN.HD.PFOR.Y. Greg 171.

25145 — [Anr. ed.] 4°. *G. P[urslowe] f. R. Hawkins,* 1618. Ass'd to P. Knight 6 no. 1615; to Hawkins 18 oc. 1617. L.L⁶(2).O.DUL.E.; F.HN.HD.N.Y.+

Wealsh, Luke, *ed. See* 13143.

25146 **Weapons.** Seven weapons to conquer the devill. With some excellent motives to stirre us up to this conquest. 8°. *[G. Purslowe] f. F. Coules,* [1628?] F (impr. shaved).

25147 Now = 25149.5.

25148 **Weaver, R.** An enterlude called lusty Iuuentus. 4°. *[John Wyer f.]* (*A. Vele,*) [1550?] O. Greg 41.
This is the only ed. w. a prayer for the king at the end; the next 2 substitute queen.

25149 — [Anr. ed.] 4°. (*J. Awdely,*) [c. 1565.] Ent. to J. King 14 au. 1560. L.; HN(last leaf facs.).

25149.5 — [Anr. ed.] 4°. (*W. Copland, in Lothbury,*) [c. 1565.] L.; HN.PFOR.
(Formerly 25147)

25150 **Web, Richard.** Christs kingdome. Described in seven fruitfull sermons upon the second psalme. 4°. *N. Okes f. H. Rockit,* 1610. Ent. to Okes 30 jn. C.G².PLUME.

25150a — [A variant, w. imprint:] *N. Okes f. H. Rockit,* 1611. L. L⁴.C.BIRM²(K.N.).E.; F.HN.HD.Y.

25150a.5 — A key of knowledge for catechizing children in Christ. 8°. *G. P[urslowe] f. Roger Jackson,* 1622. Ass'd by widow Jackson to F. Williams 16 ja. 1626. E⁴.; PN².

25151 — The lot or portion of the righteous. A comfortable sermon. 4°. *T. Creede f. Roger Jackson,* 1616. Ent. 9 oc. 1615. O.D.; F.
— *See also* 5381.

25151.5 **Webbe, Edward.** The rare and most wonderfull things which E. Webbe hath seene in the landes of Jewrie, Egypt, Grecia, Russia, and Prester John. 4°. *[J. Wolfe] f. W. Wright,* 1590. Ent. 19 my. PML.
B1ʳ catchword: 'Noble'.

25151.7 — [Anr. ed.] Newly enlarged. [B1ʳ catchword: 'Noble'.] *See* Addenda.

25152 — [Anr. ed.] Newly enlarged. 4°. *[J. Wolfe] f. W. Wright,* 1590. L.D².
B1ʳ catchword: 'their'.

25153 — [Anr. ed. of 25151.5.] 4°. *A. J[effes] f. W. Barley,* [1592?] L.; F.
B1ʳ catchword: 'the'. Some of the cuts (e.g. wild man) are from the same blocks as 25151.5 sqq. and are more worn.

25154 — [Anr. ed.] 4°. *R. Blower f. T. Pavier,* [1600.] Ent. 14 au. 1600. L(imp.).; F.HN.NY.

25155 **Webbe, George,** *Bp.* Agurs prayer. Or, the christians choyce. Describing the miserie of povertie, the vanitie of wealth, the excellencie of a middle estate. 12°. *[Eliot's Court Press] f. J. Budge,* 1621. Ent. 15 de. 1620. O.; F.HN.

25156 — The araignement of an unruly tongue. 12°. *G. P[urslowe] f. J. Budge,* 1619. Ent. 24 no. 1618. L.O.

25157 — The bride royall, or the spirituall marriage. Delivered by way of congratulation upon the marriage betweene the palsegrave, and the ladie Elizabeth. In a sermon. 8°. *W. Stansby f. R. Mabbe,* 1613. Ass'd from Mab to W. Arundell 13 ap. 1614. L.O.C.; HN.

25158 — A briefe exposition of the principles of christian religion. [Init. G. W. A catechism.] 8°. *T. S[nodham] f. R. Mabb,* 1612. Ent. 20 mr. L⁴.O.O³.C.; F.
Imprint varies: 'Mab'(O) or 'Mabb'(F).

Webbe, George, *Bp.—cont.*

25159 — [Anr. ed., signed in full.] Reviewed by the authour. 8°. *B. Alsop f. W. Arundell,* 1617. Ass'd 13 ap. 1614. L.O.

25160 — [A ghost.]

25160.7 — Catalogus protestantium: or, the protestants kalender. Containing a surview of the protestants religion long before Luthers daies. [Anon.] 4°. *[M. Flesher] f. N. Butter,* 1624. Ent. 28 jn. O.O⁴(imp.).C.D.P.; F.BO.HD.
Tp pr. in black. The epistle by John Gee, ¶², was pr. as N2,3 and is still found there in some copies (P, F).

25161 — [Anr. issue, w. added gen. tp in red and black.] By G. Web. *[M. Flesher] f. N. Butter,* 1624. L.O.O¹⁰. BRISTOL(tp def.).D².; F.HN.NY¹¹.U.Y.+
In at least O, O¹⁰ copies the black tp is cancelled.

25161.5 — [Anr. issue, w. variant red and black gen. tp, w. imprint:] *f. T. Walkcliffe [i.e. Walkley?]* 1624. L. O¹⁴.C¹⁰.BIRM²(K.N.).ETON(lacks Gee's epistle).+; F.ILL.

25162 — Gods controversie with England. [A sermon.] 8°. *F. K[ingston] f. W. Leake,* 1609. Ent. 8 jy. L.O³.C.P.; LC.

25163 — The path-way to honor. [A sermon.] 8°. *W. S[tansby] f. R. Mabbe,* 1612. Ent. 23 jn. L.O.O³.C.LINC.; HD.U.

25164 — A posie of spirituall flowers, taken out of the scriptures. 8°. *[F. Kingston] f. W. Leake,* 1610. Ent. 27 mr. L.L⁴.O.C(2).

25165 — The practice of quietnes. . . . In six sermons. 8°. *E. Griffin f. R. Mab,* 1615. O.C.E(imp.).YK.

25166 — Second edition profitably amplified by the author. 12°. *[E. Griffin] f. G. Edwards,* 1617. Ass'd by Mab 19 de. 1616. L.

25166.3 — Third edition. 12°. *[E. Griffin] f. G. Edwards,* 1618. F.Y.

25166.5 — Fourth edition. 12°. *f. G. Hodges,* 1623. Ass'd 4 jn. 1621. L.O.

25166.7 — Fifth edition. 12°. *M. F[lesher,] sold by P. Waterhouse,* 1631. L(tp only, Ames II.992).; F.

25167 — Sixt edition. 12°. *M. F[lesher,] sold by G. Edwards,* 1633. L.; HN.

25168 — The 7ᵗʰ edition. 12°. *M. F[lesher,] sold by G. Edwards,* 1638. L.L²(lacks tp).O(2, 1 imp.).C.SCL.; F(tp def.). HD.NY¹¹.PN².
— *See also* 21204.5.

25169 **Webbe, Joseph.** An appeale to truth, in the controversie betweene art, & use; about the best and most expedient course in languages. 4°. *H. L[ownes] f. G. Latham,* 1622. Ent. 11 ja. L.O.C³.D².E².+; F.HN.BO². PN.TEX.+

25170 — A petition to the high court of parliament, in the behalfe of auncient and authentiqne [*sic*] authors. [Requesting grant of a patent for 21 years for his method of teaching languages.] 4°. *[London,]* 1623 [o.s.]. L.L⁴³. O(imp.).C³.LINC.; HN.HD.LC.

25170.5 — Pueriles confabulatiunculæ, or childrens talke: claused and drawne into lessons, after the method of Dʳ. Webbe. Lately priviledged by patent from his maiestie for 31. yeeres. And are to be sold by every master licensed to teach by that way, as we have further intimated in [5306.5]. [Adapted from Evaldus Gallus.] *Lat. a. Eng.* 4°. *F. K[ingston,]* 1627. L(tp only, Ames II.780).L⁴⁴.; HN.
For another adaptation from Gallus *see* 3773. For other examples of Webbe's method *see* 5306.5, 23896, 23898. Concerning Webbe's patent *see* Arber V.lviii and *Court-Book C,* p. 188.

25171 — Usus et authoritas, id est, liber loquens, sub titulo entheati materialis primi hexametra & pentametra primo introitu abundè largientis. [A metrical dictionary.] 12°. *F. Kyngstonus,* 1626. L.L².O.SAL.; F. CHI.HD.
— *tr. See* 5305.

25172 **Webbe, William.** A discourse of English poetrie. [With a trans. of Virgil's 1st 2 Eclogues, etc.] 4°. *J. Charlewood f. R. Walley,* 1586. Ent. to Walley and Charlewood 4 se. O(1, plus frags.).O⁵.; HN.

25173 **Webster, John.** The devils law-case. Or, when women goe to law, the devill is full of businesse. 4°. *A. M[athewes] f. J. Grismand,* 1623. L.O.C.E.ETON.+; F.HN.HD.N.NY.+ Greg 388.

25174 — A monumental columne, erected to the memory of Henry, late prince of Wales. [In verse.] 4°. *N. O[kes] f. W. Welby,* 1613. L.YK.; F.HD.ILL.NY.TEX.+
Also issued as pt. 2 of 24151.

Webster, John—*cont.*

25175 — Monuments of honor. Derived from remarkable antiquity, and celebrated in London. At the confirmation of John Gore [as Lord Mayor.] 4°. *N. Okes,* 1624. HN. Greg 409.

25176 — The tragedy of the dutchesse of Malfy. 4°. *N. Okes f. J. Waterson,* 1623. L.O.C¹⁰.E.ETON.+; HN.HD.LC.N. NY.+ Greg 389.

25177 — [Anr. ed.] The dutchesse of Malfy. 4°. *J. Raworth f. J. Benson,* 1640. L.L⁶.O.C.E.+; F.HN.HD.PEN.TEX.+
Unsold sheets reissued c. 1664 w. cancel tp as Wing W 1222.

25177a — [A variant, w. imprint:] *J. Raworth f. J. Waterson a. J. Benson,* 1640. HN.HD.

25178 — The white divel, . . . with the life and death of Vittoria Corombona. 4°. *N. O[kes] f. T. Archer,* 1612. L.L⁶. O.E.ETON.+; F.HN.HD.ILL.Y.+ Greg 306.

25179 — [Anr. ed.] 4°. *J. N[orton] f. H. Perry,* 1631. Ass'd from Archer 10 fb. L.L⁶.O.C.E.+; F.HN.HD.N.Y.+

25179.5 — [Twenty-six lines of verse underneath engraved portrait by G. Mountin of James I and his progeny, including the infant James II.] s.sh.fol. *sould by W. Riddiard,* [1634?] L(Dept. of P&D).
See Hind II.311–12.
— *See also* 6537, 6539, 6540, 12863, 17481, 18908.

Webster, William, *Poet.* The [xylographic] most pleasant and delightful historie of Curan, and Argentile. [In verse.] 4°. *B. Alsop f. R. Higgenbotham,* 1617. L(date cropt).BTU.; HN.

25181 **Webster, William,** *Treatise Writer.* The plaine mans pilgrimage. Or journey towards heaven. 8°. *G. Eld,* 1613. Ent. 9 no. 1612. O.

25182 **Webster, William,** *of the Salters' Company.* The principles of arithmetick: . . . teaching the performance of multiplication and division, onely by addition and subtraction. 8°. *M. Flesher,* 1634. Ent. 26 jy. L⁴⁴. Stevens Cox.; HN.
On tp verso: 'This Booke is sold by the Author, who dwelleth in Bearebinder lane in London.'

25182.5 — A plaine and most necessarie booke of tables. For simple interest (direct) at 8 pound and 7 pound per centum. Simple interest (to rebate) [etc.] 8°. *M. Flesher f. G. Hodges,* 1625. Ent. 15 jn. Y.

25183 — [Anr. ed., enlarged.] Websters tables: for simple interest direct, at 10, 8, 7, and 6 l'. per centum. . . . Together with a necessary table for summing up of the price of commodities. The second edition, with very large additions. 8°. *M. Flesher f. N. Bourne,* 1629. Ass'd 4 au. 1626. L.L³⁰.O(2).

25183.5 — [Anr. ed., revised.] Third edition. 8°. *M. Flesher f. N. Bourne,* 1634. D.; HD.

25184 — Fourth edition. 8°. *M. Flesher f. N. Bourne,* 1639. L (tp only, Harl.5967/206).O.DUL. Warrington PL.; F.

Wechelus, Andreas. *See* 23659.7.

25185 **Wecker, Hanss Jacob.** A compendious chyrurgerie: gathered, & *tr.* (especially) out of Wecker, but encreased with certaine annotations, by J. Banester. 12°. *J. Windet f. J. Harrison the elder,* 1585. Ent. to Harrison a. T. Man 6 se. L¹⁹.L³⁹*.C.; NLM.WIS.
Reprinted in pt. 1 of 1357.

25185a — [A variant, w. imprint:] *J. Windet f. T. Man a. W. Brome,* 1585. L.L¹⁶.L¹⁷.G².; HD.NLM.

25185a.5 **Weckherlin, Georg Rudolf.** A panegyricke to the most honourable the lord Hays vicount of Doncaster, ambassadour in Germanie. [In verse.] 4°. (*Stutgart, J.-W. Rösslin,* 1619.) HN.

25186 — Triumphall shews set forth lately at Stutgart. Written first in German, and now in English by G. R. Weckherlin. 8°. *Stutgart, J.-W. Resslin,* 1616. L.

25187 **Wedderburn, David.** Abredonia atrata, sub obitum serenissimi & potentissimi monarchæ, Jacobi VI. [In verse.] 4°. *Abredoniæ, E. Rabanus,* 1625. L.C.A. E²(imp.).; HN.

25188 — In obitu summæ spei principis Henrici lessus. [In verse.] 4°. *Edinburgi, A. Hart,* 1613. L.E.E².

25189 — Institutiones grammaticae, in tres partes distributae: quarum 1. De etymologia, 2. De syntaxi, 3. De orthographia. 8°. *Abredoniæ, E. Rabanus,* 1634. O. A.E.
Collates a–i⁸ A⁴, w. A⁴ being Tabulæ Rhethoricæ.

Wedderburn, David—*cont.*

25190 — Editio secunda. 8°. *Abredoniæ, E. Rabanus,* 1633 [for 1635?] L(lacks K4).A.E.G².
Collates A⁴ B–I⁸ K⁴, w. no Tabulæ Rhethoricæ.

25191 — Invictissimo . . . Jacobi VI, . . . Scotiam suam revisenti συνευφραντήριον. 4° in 6. *Edinburgi, A. Hart,* 1617. L¹³.E.YK.

25192 — A short introduction to grammar. [*Anon.*] *Eng. a. Lat.* 8°. *Aberdene, E. Raban,* 1632. O.A(lacks tp).G².

25193 — [Anr. ed.] 8°. *Aberdene, E. Raban,* 1637. A.

25194 — Vivat rex, seu προσευκτικόν pro incolumitate Caroli. [In verse.] 4°. *Abredoniæ, E. Rabanus,* 1633. L.A. G².

Wedderburn, John. Theses philosophicae. 1629. *See* 21555.38.

Wedderburn, John, James, and **Robert.** *See* 2996.5.

Wedderburn, William. Theses aliquot logicae. 1608. *See* 21555.12.

25195 **Wedding.** A spiritual wedding. Wherein we are taught, how the faithfull soule, is prepared [for] the heauenly wedding. Writen first in the high Dutch tongue, now newly *tr.* (J. Thorius.) 12°. [*R. Robinson f.*] *J. Wolfe,* 1597. Ent. as Die gheestelyck Bruyloft 26 mr. 1590. O(imp.).P.; F.HN.Y.

Wedding Garment. The wedding garment. 1590. *See* 22713.

25195.5 **Weddington, John.** A breffe instruction and manner, howe to kepe, marchantes bokes of accomptes after the order of debitor and creditor. fol. *Andwarpe, P. van Keerberghen,* 1567. A².
— *tr. See* 11105.5.

Wedhouse, John. Almanacks. 1610, etc. *See* 531 sqq.

25196 **Wedlocke, Walter.** A lyttle treatyse called the Image of idlenesse . . . betwene W. Wedlocke and Bawdin Bacheler. *Tr.* out of the Troyane or Cornyshe tounge by Olyuer Oldwanton. 8°. [*W. Powell f.*] (*W. Seres,*) [1555?] L.

25196.5 — [Anr. ed.] A lyttle . . . yᵉ Image [etc.] 8°. [*W. Copland f.*] (*W. Seres,*) [1558?] Ent. 1558–59. LINC.; HN.

25197 — [Anr. ed.] Newly corrected and augmented. 8°. *W. Seres,* 1574. L.

25197.5 — [Anr. ed.] 8°. [*H. Denham,*] *the assigne of W. Seres,* 1581. C².

Wednesday's Fast. Here beginneth a lytel treatyse . . to faste on yᵉ wednesday. [1500.] *See* 24224.

Wedyral, William. *See* Indulgences 101A.

25198 **Weekly Avisoes.** The continuation of our weekely avisoes. [Nos. 32, 35.] 1632. Now = Newsbooks 257, 259.
— *See also* the other listings in the Newsbooks section.

25199 **Weekly News.** The weekely newes. [No. 7.] 1624. Now = Newsbooks 352.

25200 — A continuation of the former newes. [No. 23.] [1624.] Now = Newsbooks 346.

25201 — The continuation of our weekly newes. [No. 42.] 1624. Now = Newsbooks 157.

25201a — The continuation of our weekly newes. [No. 20.] 1625. Now = Newsbooks 169.

25201b — The continuation of our weekly newes. [Nos. 23, 31.] 1631. Now = Newsbooks 209, 218.

25201c — The continuation of our weekly newes. [No. 26.] 1632. Now = Newsbooks 254.
— *See also* the other listings in the Newsbooks section.

25202 **Weelkes, Thomas.** Cantus (Tenor—Bassus) Ayeres or phantasticke spirites for three voices. 3 ptbks. 4°. [*J. Windet f.*] *W. Barley,* 1608. L(2).L⁷.O(1, plus bassus only).C. St. Michael's College, Tenbury (imp.).; F.HN.LC.NY(bassus only, imp.).

25203 — Cantus (Altus—Tenor—Bassus—Quintus) Balletts and madrigals to fiue voyces, with one to 6. voyces: newly published. 5 ptbks. 4°. *T. Este,* 1598. Ent. 7 au. L(altus, bassus only).L⁷.O.; F(cantus only).HN (altus, bassus only).
At least O, HN have the sextus leaf (E1) bd. w. the bassus ptbk.

Weelkes, Thomas—*cont.*

25204 — [Anr. ed.] 5 ptbks. 4°. *T. Este, the assigne of W. Barley,* 1608. L(imp.).L[7](imp.).C.E².; F(1, plus altus, quintus). HD(cantus, tenor, bassus only).LC.N(cantus only).
>
> At least F, LC have the sextus leaf (E1) bd. w. the quintus ptbk.

25205 — Cantus prim⁹. (Cantus secund⁹.—Altus.—Bassus.—Quintus.—Sextus.) Madrigals to 3. 4. 5. & 6. voyces. 6 ptbks. 4°. *T. Este,* 1597. Ent. 15 oc. 1603 (Arber III.246.). L.L[7](imp.).O(lacks cantus primus, sextus). G²(imp.).PARIS.; F(1, plus altus, quintus, sextus).HD (sextus only).LC(1, with bassus imp.).

25206 — Canto. (Alto.—Tenore.—Basso.—Quinto.—Sesto.) Madrigals of 5. and 6. parts, apt for the viols and voices. 6 ptbks. 4°. *T. Este, the assigne of T. Morley,* 1600. L.L[7](imp.).O(1, plus quinto, sesto).O³.; F(1, plus alto, tenore, sesto).HN.HD(lacks quinto; canto and basso are imp.).LC.

Weemes, John

The attempt at a systematic listing of Weemes's works has been foiled by the insuperable complications surviving copies present. In a preliminary report on O and O college copies Paul Morgan noted 13 different combinations for 19 sets of volumes. As a result, I have broken down the entries not only into volumes but into sections of volumes and added explanatory notes. Copies are generally listed under the most complete form of their contents, but volumes lacking a general tp (except 25207.5) are listed under their sections. KFP.

25207 — [Works. Vol. 1.] The workes of Mr. John Weemse [*sic*]. In three volumnes. 2 pts. 4° in 8's. *T. Cotes f. J. Bellamie,* 1633. L.O.C.E.SCL.+; HD.MICH.NY.PN². TORONTO².
>
> A reissue, w. added gen. tp, of 25217.3 and 25216; 1 O, C, E copies also have 25211.3.

25207.3 — — [Vol. 2.] An exposition of the lawes of Moses. Viz. morall, ceremoniall, judiciall. In two volumes. 2 pts. 4°. *T. C(otes) f. J. Bellamie,* 1632. L.O.C.E.SCL.+; F.HN.HD.
>
> A reissue, w. added gen. tp, of 25215. The imprint on the gen. tp is in the same typesetting as 25217.3. This and 25207.5 were apparently issued as a pair (O, HD) before being issued as vols. 2, 3 w. 25207. O⁸, O¹², F are single volumes and possibly were issued in that form in spite of the 2-vol. gen. tp.

25207.5 — — [Vol. 3.] An exposition of the lawes of Moses. Viz. Morall. Ceremoniall. Judiciall. The second [*sic*] volume. 2 pts. 4°. *J. Dawson [a.] (T. Cotes) f. J. Bellamie,* 1632. L.O¹².C.E.SCL.+; F.HN.HD.ILL.Y.+
>
> A reissue, w. gen. tp, of 25213a and 25214. The gen. tp, which at least HD has at the beginning of the vol., was pr. as *4 of 25214 where it is sometimes found (F). In view of this obscure position of the gen. tp, copies of 25213a and 25214 bd. together are listed here. Most copies (not HD) have 25212 bd. w. this.

25208 — [Anr. ed. Vol. 1.] The workes . . . in three volumes. Containing these eight bookes. Viz. 1. The christian synagogue. 2. The portraiture. 3. Observations. [etc.] 4° in 8's. *T. Cotes [a.] (M. Dawson) f. J. Bellamie,* 1636. L.O⁵.C².E.LYU.+; F.HN.HD.ILL.Y.+
>
> Dawson pr. quires Mm to end. Most copies have 25211.3; L, O⁸, and 1 HD have 25211.5.

25208.3 — — The second volumne. Containing an exposition of the morall law. 4° in 8's. *T. Cotes f. J. Bellamie,* 1636. L.O.C².D.E.+; F.HN.HD.ILL.U.+
>
> Issued w. 25208 and 25209. Sometimes 25212.5 (HN, 1 HD) is bd. w. this.

25208.5 — — The third volumne. Containing an exposition of the lawes of Moses, viz. ceremoniall and judiciall. With Exercitations divine. Proving the sence of the scriptures. 4° in 8's. *M. Dawson f. J. Bellamie,* 1636. L. O.C².D.E.+; F.HN.HD.ILL.U.+
>
> Issued w. 25208 and 25209. The Exercitations ideally included is 25212.5; O⁷, 1 F, Y lack Exercitations; 1 HD set has 25212, but it is bd. in vol. 2.

25209 — [Anr. issue of vol. 1, w. cancel gen. tp:] The workes . . . in foure volumnes. *T. Cotes f. J. Bellamie,* 1637. O.O³.C⁹.D.E².+; F.HD.PN.U.Y.+
>
> For vol. 4 *see* 25218. O, O⁶ have 25211.3; O³, O¹⁰, O²², O²⁸, F have 25211.5.

Weemes, John—*cont.*

25210 — The christian synagogue. Wherein is contayned the diverse reading, poynting, translation, and collation of scripture with scripture. 4°. *J. D[awson a. G. Eld] f. J. Bellamie,* 1623. Ent. 6 se. 1622. L.O¹².C.E.M⁴.+; HN.HD(imp.).Y.
>
> Collates)(⁴ A–Ff⁴ A–L⁴; Eld pr. 2nd A–L⁴.

25210a — [A ghost.]

25210a.5 — Second edition, corrected, and amended. 4°. *J. D[awson] f. J. Bellamie,* 1623. L.O.C¹⁷.DUR³.E.+; F. ILL.SMITH.U.Y.+
>
> The copy on Univ. Microfilms reel 1160 is L(473.a.40), wrongly identified as DUR³.

25211 — Third edition. 4°. *T. a. R. Cotes f. J. Bellamy,* 1630. L. O.C¹⁰.CASHEL.STU.+; F.CU.HD.ILL.ROCH.+

25211.3 — Fourth edition. 4° in 8's. *T. Cotes f. J. Bellamy,* 1633. L.O⁵.C.E.+; F.HN.HD.ILL.U.+
>
> Usually bd. w. 25207, 25208, or 25209. 1 O, O²⁸ (imp.) are bd. separately.

25211.5 — Fifth edition. 4° in 8's. *T. Cotes, sold by J. Bellamie,* 1636. L.O².O³.O⁸.M.+; HN.COR.HD.
>
> The copies above are pt. of 25208 or 25209.

— Exercitations divine. Containing an explanation of diverse positions, for the right understanding of the first table of the morall law. *T. C[otes] f. J. Bellamy,* 1632.
>
> This is the 2nd tp in 25215.

25212 — Exercitations divine. Containing diverse questions and solutions for the right understanding of the scriptures. 4°. *T. Cotes f. J. Bellamie,* 1632. Ent. 29 no. 1631. L².O.C².E.M.+; F.HN.HD.ILL.Y.+
>
> Most of the copies above are bd. w. 25207.5; 1 F is sep. bd. in contemporary vellum.

25212.5 — [Anr. ed.] 4° in 8's. *T. Cotes f. J. Bellamie,* 1634. L.O. O³.C.PETYT.+; F.HN.HD.ILL.U.+
>
> Most of the copies above are pt. of 25208.5, though sometimes (HN, 1 HD) bd. w. 25208.3; at least C and 1 HD are in a vol. lacking a gen. tp. While the imprint date of 1634 is prob. correct, it is interesting to note that the collation is Aaaaaaa–Ooooooo⁸, which places it at the end of vol. 3 of the 1636 Works.

25213 — [A ghost.]

25213a — An explanation of the ceremoniall lawes of Moses. 4°. *T. Cotes f. J. Bellamie,* 1632. Ent. 29 fb. L(3155.l. 10).
>
> Other copies that may be sep. bd. are at E⁸, NEK, STU. Reissued in 25207.5, q.v.

25213a.5 — [Anr. ed.] 4° in 8's. *M. Dawson f. J. Bellamie,* 1636. C.
>
> This is usually pt. of 25208.5; the C copy lacks that gen. tp.

25214 — An explication of the judiciall lawes of Moses. 4°. *J. Dawson f. J. Bellamie,* 1632. Ent. 16 mr. L(493.f.28). C(Sayle 3888).
>
> Other copies that may be sep. bd. are at E², G². At the end of the preliminaries (*4) is the gen. tp for 25207.5.

25214.5 — [Anr. ed.] 4° in 8's. *M. Dawson f. J. Bellamie,* 1636. C.; HN.HD.
>
> This is usually pt. of 25208.5; the copies above lack that gen. tp.

— An exposition of the lawes of Moses. 1632. *See* 25207.3, 25207.5.

25215 — An exposition of the morall law, or ten commandements . . . set downe by way of exercitations. (Exercitations divine. Containing an explanation. —An exposition of the second table of the morall law.) 2 pts. 4°. *T. Cotes f. J. Bellamie,* 1632. Ent. 29 no. 1631 and 16 mr. 1632. NOR².; LC.
>
> Usually found, w. added gen. tp, as 25207.3. Other copies without that gen. tp may be at L², C², BIRM, NEK.

— [Anr. ed.] *T. Cotes f. J. Bellamie,* 1636.
>
> This is 25208.3. As the only other tp besides the vol. tp is that for the Second table, copies lacking the vol. tp should be considered imperfect.

25216 — Observations, naturall and morall. With a short treatise of the numbers, weights, and measures, used by the Hebrews. 4° in 8's. *T. Cotes f. J. Bellamie, sold by B. Allen,* 1633. Ent. 13 mr. 1632. O.O⁸.; F.COR.
>
> Reissued in 25207; other copies without that gen. tp may be at STU, YK. The O copy is sep. bd.

25216.5 — [Anr. ed.] 4° in 8's. *M. Dawson f. J. Bellamie,* 1636. Hebrew Union C.
>
> This is usually pt. of 25208, 25209; Hebrew Union is separate in a modern binding.

Weemes, John—*cont.*

25217 — The pourtraiture of the image of God in man. 4°. [*M. Flesher a. G. Wood*] *f. J. Bellamie*, 1627. Ent. 5 se. 1626. L.O.C.E.M².+; F.CAL.CHI.U.Y.+

25217.3 — Second edition, corrected and enlarged. 4° in 8's. *T. C[otes] f. J. Bellamie*, 1632. O⁸.; F.COR.ILL.
    Reissued in 25207; another copy without that gen. tp may be at YK.

25217.5 — Third edition. 4° in 8's. *T. C[otes] f. J. Bellamie*, 1636. O².
    This is usually pt. of 25208, 25209; O² lacks a gen. tp.

25218 — A treatise of the foure degenerate sonnes, viz. the atheist the magician the idolater and the Jew. Being the fourth volume, of the Workes. 4°. *T. Cotes, sold by J. Bellamie*, 1636. Ent. 18 jn. L.O.C.D.E.+; F.HN.HD.ILL.U.+
    This is sometimes bd. separately (1 O, C, 1 HD); bd. uniformly as a 4th vol. with 25208 (M) or 25209 (F); bd. in 25208.5 (1 HD), or bd. in a mixed vol. (1 HD).

25219 **Weerdenburck** or **Waerdenburgh, Dirk van.** Two memorable relations. The one a letter out of West-India touching the surprisall of the towne of Olinda in [Pernambuco.] *Tr.* out of Dutch. The other, the relation of the taking of Pignerolle. *Tr.* out of the French coppy. 4°. *f. N. Bourne*, 1630. HN. 𝔄

25219.5 **Weersburch.** A most straunge and wounderfull accident, happened at Weersburch [Würzburg?] by Franckford, by a most fearefull earthquake. *Tr.* out of Duch by *T. C.* 4°. [*H. Ballard f.*] *W. Barley*, 1600. HD.

25220 **Weever, John.** An agnus Dei. [Life of Christ. In verse.] 128°? in 8's. *V. Sims f. N. Lyng*, 1601. Arthur Houghton. Miss Julia P. Wightman, New York City.

25221 — [Anr. ed.] 128°? in 8's. *V. Sims f. N. Lyng*, 1603. L¹⁸.

25222 — [Anr. ed.] 128°? in 8's. *V. S[ims] f. N. Lyng*, 1606. L⁸.; Arthur Houghton.

25222.5 — [Anr. ed.] 128°? in 8's. *N. O[kes] f. J. Smethwicke*, 1610. Ass'd by Sims 18 fb. 1611. HN. Julian I. Edison, St. Louis, Missouri(imp.).

25223 — Ancient funerall monuments within the united monarchie of Great Britaine, Ireland, and the islands adjacent. fol. *T. Harper, sold by L. Sadler*, 1631. Ent. to Harper 21 se. 1630. L.O.C.D.E.+; F.HN.HD(lacks letterpress tp).N.NY.+
    Some copies (3 F, HD) lack the index (a–b⁴). Some (6 O, HN) have the genuine index, w. a1ʳ, column 3, line 9 from bottom: 'Ball . . . wicked/' while others (1 O, 1 F) have a reprint c. 1800 w.: 'Ball . . . wick/'.

25224 — Epigrammes in the oldest cut, and newest fashion. [In verse.] 8°. *V. S[ims] f. T. Bushell*, 1599. O.; HD (imp.).

25225 — Faunus and Melliflora or, the original of our English satyres. [In verse, w. translations of the first satires of Horace, Persius, and Juvenal.] 4°. *V. Simmes*, 1600. HN.

25226 — The mirror of martyrs, or the life and death of sir John Old-castle. [In verse.] 8°. *V. S[ims] f. W. Wood*, 1601. L(tp facs.).O.C⁶.; F(imp.).HN. Pirie.
    Quires B, D, F have horizontal chainlines.

— *See also* 14071.

25226.5 **Welby, Henry.** The phœnix of these late times. Or the life of H. Welby. [By T. Heywood.] With epitaphs and elegies. 4°. *N. Okes, sold by R. Clotterbuck*, 1637. Ent. to J. Okes 25 ja. L.L⁶.O.C(imp.).C².+; F.HN.HD.ILL.NY.+ 𝔄
    (Formerly 25228) Ends F3.

25227 — [Anr. ed.] With some new epitaphs. 4°. *N. Okes, sold by R. Clotterbuck*, 1637. L.O.O¹¹.C¹⁷.; N.NLM.PH.PML.PN.+
    Ends F4.

25228 — Now = 25226.5.

Welde, William, *tr. See* 14466.

25228.5 **Weldon,** *Sir* **Anthony.** A discription of Scotland, by observation of doctor Corbett in his majesties progresse into that country. The fourth edition. [Anon. An attack on Scotland.] 4°. [*The Netherlands?*] 1626. F.

25229 **Weldon, John.** A true report of the inditement, and execution of J. Weldon, W. Hartley and R. Sutton: who suffred for high treason, the fifth of October. 1588. 4°. [*R. Waldegrave f.*] *R. Jones*, 1588. Ent. 18 oc. L².
    End of text undated.

25229.3 — [Anr. issue, with C⁴ reprinted.] *R. Jones*, 1588. L.O³. C⁵.OS.P.; F.HN.
    End of text dated 24 Oct. 1588. C⁴ not signed in Waldegrave's manner. Part of B1ʳ in 2 settings; line 3 ends: 'open-' (F) or 'openly' (L, O³, HN).

Well-wisher. A quench-coale. . . . By a well-wisher. 1637. *See* 20474.

25229.5 — A wel-wisher. Wherein is briefly shewed, a ready way and meanes to procure the publike good. 4°. [*Amsterdam, Richt Right Press,*] 1639. F.

25229.7 **Well-wishing.** A well-wishing to a place of pleasure. (An inconstant female.) *Ballads.* s.sh.fol. [*M. Flesher*] *f. F. Coules*, [c. 1627.] C⁶(I.335, 370).
    Though to the same tune, these are 2 separate ballads.

25230 — [Anr. ed.] s.sh.fol. *assignes of T. Symcocke*, [1628–29.] L.

25231 **Welles, John.** The soules progresse to the celestiall Canaan. By way of godly meditation. Collected out of the scriptures, [etc.] 4° in 8's. *E. G[riffin,] sold by H. Shephard*, 1639. Ent. to A. Griffin 27 se. 1638. L.O.C.BRISTOL.E².+; F.HN.CHI.HD.U.+

25232 **Wellington, Alice.** The late commotion of certaine papists in Herefordshire. Occasioned by the death of A. Wellington, a recusant. [By T. Hamond and E. R.] 4°. *S. S[tafford] f. J. Chorlton a. F. Burton*, 1605. Ent. 16 jy. L.O(3).O⁵.O¹⁷.C.

25232.5 — [Anr. issue, w. 4-leaf quire added after C3:] (An induction into the sequent discourse.) *S. S[tafford] f. J. Chorlton a. F. Burton*, 1605. O.; HD.

25233 **Wells,** *Dr.* A true and ample relation of occurrences in the Palatinate since the first of June. 4°. *J. D[awson] f. J. Bartlet*, 1622. L(Burney 2/27).C.
    Title varies: line 12 gives the day of printing as '13' (L) or '14' (C) of June. This belongs in the Newsbooks section following 51A.

Wells, John. The compleat art of dyalling. 1637. *See* 25234.5.

25234 — Sciographia, or the art of shadowes. Plainly demonstrating, out of the sphere, how to project both great and small circles, [etc.] By I. W. esquire. 8°. *T. Harper, sold [by A. Hebb,]* 1635. Ent. 30 jn. 1634. L.O.C.D.E.+; F.HN.HD.N.NY.+
    A few copies (1 L, O, 1 C, F) have bd. w. them unsold sheets of H. Briggs's and A. Vlacq's logarithmic tables pub'd at Gouda by P. Rammaseyn, 1626. The above copies have the Gouda title cancelled, but the O³(E) copy retains it, though slashed for cancellation, w. title in French: 'Table des logarithmes . . .'

25234.5 — [Anr. issue, w. cancel tp:] The compleat art of dyalling. *T. Harper f. N. Fussell*, 1637. L³⁰.O³.YK.
    At least O³ also has the Briggs–Vlacq tables, lacking tp.

Wellspring. The welspring of wittie conceites. 1584. *See* 5615.

25235 **Welsch, John.** A reply against M. Gilbert Browne priest. Wherein is handled many pointes of controversie betweene us and the papists. 4°. *Edinburgh, R. Walde-grave*, 1602. L.D.E.G².YK.+; F.HN.BOWDOIN.
    Also prints for the 1st time Welsch's orig. letter and Browne's answer. Only [–]2 and 1st B3 are signed in Waldegrave's manner.

Welsh. Car-wr y Cymru. 1630. *See* 24007.

Welsh Grammar. Dosparth byrr ar y rhann gyntaf. 1567. *See* 21076.

Welshmen. A cōmendacion/Of welshmen. 1546. *See* 14919.

25236 **Welsthed, Robert.** The cure of a hard-heart. First preached in divers sermons. Since digested into questions and answers. [*Ed.*] (J. Hart.) 12º. *W. Stansby f. S. Man*, 1630. Ent. 10 se. 1624. O³.C³. C¹⁰(2).; PN².

25237 **Welwood, William.** An abridgement of all sea-lawes; . . . found among any people or nation. 4º. *H. Lownes f. T. Man*, 1613. Ent. to T. Man, sen., and Jonas Man 20 de. 1612. L.L³⁰.O.C.E.+; F.HN.CU. HD.KAN.+
An expanded and revised version of 25242.

25238 — [*Anr. ed.*] 8º. [*T. Harper f.*] *assignes of Joane Man a. B. Fisher*, 1636. Ass'd 12 au. 1635. L.O.C.E.G⁴.+; F.HN. HD.MICH.NY.+

25238.5 — Aurei D. de verb. oblig. tituli, aliorumq; obiter titulorum numero 24. illi rei affinium inst. C. et D. temere sparsorum epitome methodica. 4º. *S. Stafford*, 1605. L¹³.

25239 — Guilielmi Velvod de aqua in altum per fistulas plumbeas facile exprimenda apologia demonstrativa. 4º. *Edimburgh, ap. A. Arbuthnetum*, 1582. E.E².

25240 — De dominio maris, juribusque ad dominum praecipue spectantibus assertio brevis et methodica. 4º. *Cosmopoli, G. Fonti-silvius* [i.e. *London, T. Creede f. W. Welwood*,] 1615 (16 cal. ja.) L.O.C.E.E².+; F.HN.HD. MCG.

25241 — Dubiorum quæ tam in foro poli quam in foro fori occurrrere [*sic*] solent, brevis expeditio. 8º. *R. Field*, 1622. O.C⁵.CANT.D.

25242 — The sea-law of Scotland shortly gathered for the vse of all seafairingmen. 8º. *Edinburgh, R. Waldegraue*, 1590. O.C.; NY².

Wemyss, George. Theses aliquot logicae. Præside G. Wemio. 1635. *See* 21555.46.
— Theses aliquot philosophicæ. Præside G. Wemio. [1631.] *See* 21555.41.

Wemyss, James. Theses philosophicae. Sub præsidio J. Wemii. 1612. *See* 21555.19.
—— 1616. *See* 21555.27.

25243 **Wemyss,** *Sir* **John.** Βασιλέως ὑπεροχη. Sive de regis primatu libellus. 4º. *Edinburgi, T. Finlason*, 1623. L.O.DUR⁵.E.M⁴.+; F.HN.HART.ILL.

25244 **Wentworth, Paul.** The miscellanie, or, a registrie, and methodicall directorie of orizons. 4º. [*W. White a. T. Creede*] *f. J. Harison, dwelling at . . . the golden Anchor*, 1615. Ent. to J. Harrison 4 on 22 jn. 1614. L.L².O.C⁵.YK.+; F.HN.HART.HD.ILL.+
Creede pr. Y to end. The shop is that of John Harrison 2.

25245 **Wentworth, Peter,** *Parliamentarian.* A pithie exhortation to her majestie for establishing her successor. 8º. [*Edinburgh, R. Waldegrave*,] 1598. L.O.C.E.YK.+; F.HN.HD.N.U.+
Signed in Waldegrave's manner. In part, an answer to 19398. *See Acts P.C., 1600–1601*, p. 216, regarding inquiries started 11 Mar. 1601 concerning an ed. reportedly pr. at Middelburg.

25246 **Wentworth, Peter,** *Preacher.* A sermon faithfullie and trulie published: according as it was preached at the courte, at Greenewiche. 8º. *J. Windet f. T. Gubbin a. J. Winnington*, 1587. O.

Wentworth, Thomas, *Earl of Strafford*
Copies of the following editions and issues, also listed as Wing E 2572, frequently have mixed sheets and formes, particularly between 25247.5, 25248, and 25248.3. Distinctions below offer a coarse sifting but cannot guarantee that a particular copy is not mixed in one of the other sheets or formes. For that reason shelfmarks are listed for a few copies at O, C, F, HD which have been checked in all formes and judged to represent the most rational standard for each entry. Other copies listed among the locations have all the specified distinctions. Following the distinctions are still other copies with mixed sheets.

25247 — Depositions and articles against Thomas earle of Strafford. 4º. *Printed in the yeare* 1640 [o.s.] L.O(Antiq.e.E 72).C(R.9.62¹).C⁵.D⁸.; CAL.CAL⁶.HD (Gay 640.321.144). NY.
A3ʳ line 3 ends: '*England*, and those'

Wentworth, Thomas, *Earl of Strafford—cont.*
B2ʳ line 4 begins: 'Court of *Chancery*,' (with plain italic C)
D1ʳ line 3 ends: 'Officers of'
E1ʳ line 1 ends: 'appoin-'.

25247.5 — [*Anr. ed.*] 4º. *Printed in the yeare* 1640 [o.s.] L¹³.O (Pamph. C.39(15)).C².LIV³.M.+; F(Wing E 2572).HN. HD(2).IND.
At least sheet B was pr. by B. Alsop.
A3ʳ line 3 ends: 'England, and those'
B2ʳ line 4 begins: 'Court of *Chancery*,' (with swash C)
D1ʳ line 3 ends: 'State,' (with comma), line 4 has: 'Iustices'
E1ʳ line 1 ends: 'appointed'.
Mixed copies: O, with B, D of 25248.3; F, with B, D of 25247.
A few copies with the D1ʳ readings as above have D1ᵛ reset with line 2 beginning: 'and thirtieth of Ianuary': C(R.10.19²⁶), F(Wing E 2572.2), instead of 'aud [*sic*] thirtieth of *Ianuary*' like most copies. These 2 copies are also mixed: C, with B of 25248; F, with A, B of 25248.

25248 — [*Anr. issue, with sheets A and B, C inner forme and D outer forme reset.*] *Printed in the yeare,* 1640 [o.s.] L²².L³⁰.O⁵(LH.2.51).; F.HN.HD(Gay 640.321. 145).ILL.U.+
At least sheets A and B were pr. by E. Purslowe.
A3ʳ line 3 ends: 'England, and' (tp has: 'yeare, 1640.')
B2ʳ line 4 begins: 'of Chancery,' line 5 has 'precincts'
D1ʳ line 3 ends: 'State,' (with comma), line 4 has: 'Justices'
E1ʳ line 1 ends: 'appointed'.
Mixed copies: L, L⁴, L³⁸, G⁴, LIV³, NY, Y, with D of 25247.5; HN, LC, NY-Arents, with B of 25248.3; O, with D of 25248.3; O³, with E of 25248.5.

25248.3 — [*Anr. issue, with A1ʳ, B inner forme, sheet C, and D outer forme reset.*] *Printed in the yeare* 1640 [o.s.] O(4º L 79(5)Art.).C(2 copies, Hib.7.64.2 and Syn. 7.64.28).BTU.LIV³.M.+; F(Wing E 2572.3).HN.CHI.HD (Law School).TORONTO².
At least sheets A and B were pr. by E. Purslowe.
A3ʳ line 3 ends: 'England, and' (tp has: 'yeare 1640.')
B2ʳ line 4 begins: 'of Chancery,' line 5 has: 'Precincts'
D1ʳ line 3 ends: '& made . . . State' (no comma)
E1ʳ line 1 ends: 'appointed'.
Mixed copies: LIV³, with A of 25248; O, Y, with B of 25248.

25248.5 — [*Anr. ed.*] 4º. *Printed in the yeare* 1640 [o.s.] L⁴⁸.O² (Z.b.21(5)).D⁸.E.M(deposit).+; HN.CU.N.PN.Y.+
At least sheets A and B were pr. by T. Harper.
A3ʳ line 3 ends: 'England, and those of'
B2ʳ line 4 begins: 'Chancery,'
D1ʳ line 3 ends: 'and made . . . State' (no comma)
E1ʳ line 1 ends: 'appointed a'.
Copies differ in the tp ornament: O³(Wc.6.23), I MCG: a woodcut orn. with winged heads; O⁶ (AA.a.6(1)), HN: a rectangle of type orns. measuring 29×91 mm.; O², YK(XXVIII.K.8(8)): a square of type orns. measuring 18×18 mm.

25248.7 — [*Anr. ed.*] 4º. *Printed Anno Dom.* 1640 [o.s.] O⁶(BB. w.4(12)).C(Hib.7.64.1).BHP. Dr. J. McL. Emmerson, New College, Oxford.; CAL.NY.
At least sheet A was pr. by T. Harper. This ed. collates A–D⁴ while the previous items collate A–F⁴.
— *See also* 21781.5.

Werdmueller, Otto. A godlye and learned treatise wherin is the iustificacion of a christian manne. [1555?] *See* 24219.

25249 — The hope of the faythfull, declaryng the resurreccion of our lorde Jesus Chryst. [Anon. *Tr.* M. Coverdale.] 16º in 8's. [*Wesel? H. Singleton?* 1555?] L.O.C.; HD.
Pr. in the types of 9981.

25250 — [*Anr. ed.*] Newly imprinted and corrected. 16º in 8's. (*H. Singleton*,) 1574. HN.

25250.5 — [*Anr. ed.*] 16º in 8's. (*H. Singleton*, 1579.) O(last leaf only).O³.D.

Werdmueller, Otto—*cont.*

25251 — A moste frutefull, piththye and learned treatise, how a christen mā ought to behaue himself in the daūger of death. [Anon. *Tr.* M. Coverdale.] (An exhortacion by the lady Jane [Dudley], the night before she suffred.) 16⁰ in 8's. [*Wesel? H. Singleton?* 1555?] L.O.G².M. Broxbourne(E, imp.)*.+; F(imp.)*.
  Pr. in the types of 9981. There is a sub tp on A1ʳ: 'A most . . . piththie . . . treatyse . . . ought . . . him selfe.'

25252 — [Anr. issue, w. first 8 leaves reprinted.] A most . . . piththye . . . treatyse . . . oughte . . . hymselfe. [*Wesel? H. Singleton?* 1555?] O.C⁵.

25253 — [Anr. ed.] 16⁰ in 8's. (*H. Singleton,*) [1574?] Ent. 1561–62. HN.
  See Greg, Register B, p. 8.

25254 — [Anr. ed.] 12⁰. [*E. Allde*] *f. W. Blackwall,* [1595?] L. O.; F.
  With the author's preface omitted, and a dedic. by Blackwall added, attributing authorship of the whole to Lady Jane Dudley.

25255 — A spyrytuall and moost precyouse pearle. Teachyng all men howe, consolacyon in afflyccyons is to be soughte. Sett forth by the duke of Somerset. [Anon. *Tr.* M. Coverdale.] 8⁰. [*S. Mierdman*] (*f. G. Lynne,* 1550.) L.O¹⁷.C.M.P.+; F.HD.
  Copies vary in the colophon: 'Londen' or 'London'; both at L. This has at the end some prayers by T. Becon not reprinted in later eds.

25256 — [Anr. ed.] A spiritual and most precious perle. 16⁰ in 8's. [*Wesel? H. Singleton?* 1555?] L.O.; F.HN(2).
  In the types of 9981; *see* note to 25258.3. Copies vary in the marginal notes; e.g. p. 120 has 1 note of 2 lines, or 2 notes totalling 7 lines; both at HN.

25257 — [Anr. ed.] 1560. Now = 25259.5.

25258 — [Anr. ed.] 16⁰ in 8's. *J. Allde f. H. Singleton,* [1561?] Ent. to A. Smith 1558–59; to Singleton 1561–62. L.D.DUR⁵.

25258.3 — [Anr. ed.] By O. Wermullerus [*sic*]. *Tr.* by M. Coverdale. 16⁰ in 8's. (*H. Singleton,*) [1574?] F.
  B2ʳ line 1: 'this'. In the printer's pref. of this and the next ed. Singleton calls 25258 a corrupt ed. brought out by 'sinister dealing'. He also indicates he had pr. the text before (25256?) and had received the trans. of this and Werdmueller's other 3 books (cf. 24219, 25249, 25251) direct from Coverdale's hands.

25258.5 — [Anr. ed.] 16⁰ in 8's. (*H. Singleton,*) [1579.] O³(tp def.); HD(imp.).
  B2ʳ line 1: 'thys'.

25259 — [Anr. ed.] 16⁰ in 8's. *R. Robinson,* 1593. Ent. 25 jn. L.CHATS.SHR.; F.HN.

25259.5 — [Anr. ed.] 16⁰ in 8's. [*R. Bradock*] *f. W. Leake,* 1560 [1605.] Ass'd 19 ap. 1602. L.O.
  (Formerly 25257)

25259.7 — [Anr. issue, w. imprint:] [*R. Bradock*] *f. W. Leake,* 1605. F.

25260 — [A trans.] Perl mewn adfyd neu, Perl ysprydawl. [*Tr.*] H. L(ewys.) 12⁰. Rhydychen [*Oxford,*] *J. Barnes,* 1595. L.NLW.

25261 **Wescombe, Martin.** Fabulæ pontificiæ evangelicæ veritatis radiis dissipatæ. 8⁰. *Oxoniæ, L. Lichfield,* 1639. L.O.C.D.DUR⁵.+; F.HN.

West India Company. *See* 18459.5, 18460.

25261.5 **West, John.** The severall notorious and lewd cousnages of John West, and Alice West. Practised in this citie, and many places neere adjoyning, . . . who were arraigned and convicted the 14. of Januarie. 4⁰. [*W. Stansby*] *f. E. Marchant,* 1613. Ent. to J. Trundle 30 ja. O(2).; HN(date cropt).

25262 **West, Richard,** *of Magdalen Coll., Oxford.* Wits A. B. C. Or a centurie of epigrams. [Anon. In verse.] 4⁰. [*G. Eld*] *f. T. Thorp, sould* [by *L. Lisle,* 1608.] Ent. as by 'R. W. bachelor of Artes in Oxon' 21 ap. 1608. O.; HN.

25263 **West, Richard.** The court of conscience or Dick Whippers sessions. [In verse.] 4⁰. *G. Eld f. J. Wright,* 1607. Ent. 6 au. L.; F.

25264 — [Heading A2ʳ:] Newes from Bartholmew fayre. [Anon. In verse.] 4⁰. [*f. J. Wright,* 1606.] Ent. as by Richard West to J. Wright 16 jy. 1606. O(lacks tp).

West, Richard—*cont.*

25265 — The schoole of vertue, the second part: or, the young schollers paradice. Contayning verie good precepts. Fit for all children. [In verse.] 8⁰. *E. Griffin f. N. Butter,* 1619. L.
  West's name is in an acrostic on tp verso. A continuation of 22135.

25266 **West, Thomas,** *Baron De La Warre.* The relation of the most honourable the lord De-la-Warre, lord governour of the colonie, planted in Virginea. 4⁰. *W. Hall f. W. Welbie,* 1611. Ent. 6 jy. L.O.O⁵.O⁹.DUR³.; HN. HD.LC.N.NY.+
  See Court-Book C, p. 447.

25267 **West, William.** [Pt. 1.] Συμβολαιογραφία. Symbolæographia. Which may be termed the art, description, or image of instruments. 4⁰ in 8's. *R. Tothill,* 1590. L.O.O¹⁷(imp.).CREDITON. Sheffield PL(imp.).; F.HD (imp.).MIN.Y.

25267.5 — [Anr. ed., revised.] Symbolæography, . . . The first part and second booke, newly corrected. 4⁰ in 8's. *R. Tottle,* 1592. HD.
  This has no Bk. 1; colophon on Oo8ᵛ.

25267.7 — [Anr. issue, w. tp cancelled and Bk. 1 added.] The first part, newly corrected, and augmented. *R. Tottle,* 1592. NOR²(imp., w. tp of 25267.5 uncancelled).; F.CAL.
  Bk. 1 and the new tp are in preliminary quires A–B⁸ C²; colophon on Oo8ᵛ.

25267a — [Anr. ed.] 4⁰ in 8's. *R. Tottle,* 1592. L(imp.).L¹³.L³⁸. O(imp.).O³.+; CAL.
  Colophon on Nn8ᵛ.

25268 — The third time corrected. 4⁰ in 8's. *C. Yetsweirt, Esq.,* 1594. O.O⁵.CLEEDS.P.+; HN(tp only, DeVinne II.735).CAL.CAL⁵.Y.
  Pt. 2 now = 25276.7.

25268.5 — The fourth time corrected. 4⁰ in 8's. *Jane Yetsweirt, widowe of C. Yetsweirt Esquire,* 1597. L(tp only, Ames I.592).YK.; F.HD.MIN.PH.

25269 — [Anr. ed.] The first part of Symboleography. Lately amended. 4⁰ in 8's. *T. Wight a. B. Norton,* 1598. L.O¹¹.D.G².P.+; CAL⁵.LC.NY⁸.PH.

25270 — [Anr. ed.] Now newly augmented with diuers presidents touching marchants affaires. 4⁰ in 8's. [*A. Islip f.*] *T. Wight,* 1603. O.E.LEEDS.NLW.; F.HN.HD (lacks tp).Y.

25271 — [Anr. ed.] 4⁰ in 8's. [*A. Islip*] *f. the Co. of Statrs.,* 1605. O(2).C⁵.DUL.DUR³.LEEDS.; F.HN.COR.HD.ILL.+
  See Court-Book C, p. 16.

25272 — [Anr. ed.] 4⁰ in 8's. [*A. Islip*] *f. the Co. of Statrs.,* 1610. L.O.C².E.LEEDS.; F.HN.CU.HD.ILL.+
  Pt. 2 now = 25279.3.

25273 — [Anr. ed.] 4⁰ in 8's. [*A. Islip*] *f. the Co. of Statrs.,* 1615. L.L³⁰.O.NLW.RGU.+; F.CAL.CU.HD.MICH.+

25274 — [Anr. ed.] 1618. Now = 25279.5.

25275 — [Anr. ed.] 4⁰ in 8's. [*A. Islip*] *f. the Co. of Statrs.,* 1622. L.O.BRISTOL².G⁴.LEEDS.+; F.CAL.HD.MICH.Y.+
  Pt. 2 now = 25279.7.

25276 — [Anr. ed.] 4⁰ in 8's. [*M. Flesher f.*] *assignes of J. More, Esq.* 1632. L.O.C.D.NLW.+; F.HN.CU.HD.MICH.+

25276.3 — [Pt. 2. Heading B1ʳ:] A treatise concerning the forms of fines, concords, recoueries, arbitrementes and indictments &c. being a parcell of Symbolæography judiciall. 4⁰ in 8's. [*R. Tottell,* 1593.] L¹³.; HN.
  Collates B⁴ C–G⁸, ending w. Recoueries. The text is like 25276.5, w. the latter having extra sections. Possibly printing was interrupted by Tottell's death.

25276.5 — [Anr. ed., enlarged.] Foure treatises, of the second part of Symbolæographie. 4⁰ in 8's. *C. Yetsweirt Esq.,* 1594. HD.
  Dedic. to Sir J. Puckering, dated 1 May 1594, is conjugate w. the above tp (*²). The tp and Coke dedic. of 25276.7 are also in the HD copy, preceding the Chancery section. The 1st quire of Chancery is A⁸, w. sections 1–29, largely in Latin.

25276.7 — [Anr. issue, w. cancel? prelims.] Three treatises, of the second part of Symbolæographie. Wherunto is annexed another of . . . Chauncerie. *C. Yetsweirt, Esq.,* 1594. L.O.O⁵.C.LEEDS.+; F.CAL⁵.HD. Amherst C. (Formerly pt. 2 of 25268) Dedic. to Sir E. Coke, dated 2 May 1594, is conjugate w. the above tp (A²). The Puckering dedic. and tp of 25276.5 is lacking in F, HD (all?) copies. The 1st quire of Chancery is A⁴, w. sections 20–9, largely in English.

West, William—*cont.*

25277 — [Anr. ed.] Of Symboleography the second part. Newly corrected, and much enlarged. 4° in 8's. *T. Wight a. B. Norton*, 1597. L¹³.L³⁸.O.BRISTOL².P.+ ; PH.
This is the only ed. besides 25276.5 to have the Puckering dedic., on a1ᵛ of the Chancery section.

25278 — [Anr. ed.] The second part of Symboleography, newly corrected and very much enlarged. Hereunto is also added a table. 4° in 8's. *T. Wight*, 1601. L.O.D.G². LEEDS.+ ; F.HN.HD.LC.

25279 — [Anr. ed.] 4° in 8's. [*A. Islip*] *f. the Co. of Statrs.*, 1606. L.O.C².C⁵. Leeds PL.; F.HN.COR.HD.ILL.+

25279.3 — [Anr. ed.] 4° in 8's. [*A. Islip*] *f. the Co. of Statrs.*, 1611. L.O.E.HAT.; F.HN.CU.HD.ILL.+
(Formerly pt. 2 of 25272)

25279.5 — [Anr. ed.] With an addition of some exemplars to be used in Exchequer, [etc.] 4° in 8's. [*A. Islip*] *f. the Co. of Statrs.*, 1618. L.O.D².G⁴.LEEDS.+ ; HN.HD(2). LC.MICH.Y.
(Formerly 25274)

25279.7 — [Anr. ed.] 4° in 8's. [*A. Islip*] *f. the Co. of Statrs.*, 1627. L.O.C.D.LEEDS.+ ; F.CU.HD.MICH.PN.+
(Formerly pt. 2 of 25275)
— *ed. See* 15745.

25280 **Westerman, William.** The faithfull subject: or Mephiboseth. And Salomons porch: or a caveat for them that enter Gods house: in two sermons. 8°. [*W. Jaggard*] *f. G. Seaton a. S. Waterson*, 1608. Ent. to Seton 11 oc. L.O.C.CASHEL.LINC.+ ; F.HN.BO⁵.

25281 — Jacobs well: or, a sermon. 8°. *J. Beale f. M. Lawe*, 1613. L(2).O.C.D².LINC.; F.BO⁵.

25282 — Two sermons of assise: the one intituled; a prohibition of revenge: the other, a sword of maintenance. 2 pts. 8°. *R. B[radock] f. G. Seaton*, 1600. Ent. 3 mr. L.L³.O.C.LINC.+ ; F.NY¹¹.
Pt. 2 is anon.

25283 **Western Knight.** The westerne knight, and the young maid of Bristoll. *Ballad*. 2 pts. s.sh.fol. *f. F. Coules*, [1629.] Ass'd by widow Trundle to ballad ptnrs. 1 jn. 1629. C⁶.

25284 **Westerne, Thomas.** The flaming bush. Or, an embleme of the true church. [*A treatise*.] 8°. *N. Okes*, 1624. Ent. 7 oc. L.C².LINC.PLUME(lacks tp).; F.HN.

25285 **Westfaling, Herbert,** *Bp.* A treatise of reformation in religion, diuided into seuen sermons preached in Oxford. Hereunto are added two sermons touching the supper of the Lorde. 4°. (*T. Dawson*) *imp. G. Byshop*, 1582. Ent. 7 no. 1581. L.O.C.D.YK.+ ; F. BO³.ILL.U.
With inits. T. D. in the tp border.
— *See also* 10215, 10215.5.

Westhawe, Robert. Almanacks. 1594, etc. *See* 526 sq.

25286 **Westminster.** The declaracyon of the procedynge of a conference, begon at Westminster the laste of Marche. 1559. 8°. *R. Jugge a. J. Cawood*, [1560?] L. L².O.C⁵.; F.

25287 — A generall or great bill for burials, in Westminster, [etc.] 1625. Now = 16741.7.
— The hole īdulgēce of pdō grāuted to blessed s. Cornelis. [c. 1520.] *See* Indulgences 23A.

25288 — The pardon grauntyd to the fraternyte of Seynt Cornelys at Westmynster. [c. 1518.] Now = Indulgences 83.

Westminster, *Dean of.* A prayer made by the deane. [1555.] *See* 25291.5.

25289 **Weston, Edward.** The repaire of honour, falsely impeached by Featley [in 10738]. Wherein the apostles disciple S. Ignatius bishop & martyr, his religion, against protestantisme, is layd open. 8° in 4's. *Bruges*, [i.e. *St. Omer, English College Press,*] 1624. Lᴼ.O.ST. A&R 884.

25290 — The triall of christian truth by the rules of faith, hope, charitie, and religion. The first parte, entreating of faith. 4°. *Douay*, [*widow of L. Kellam,*] 1614. L.L² (lacks tp).O(2).O².W.
A&R 885.

25290.3 — The triall of christian truht [*sic*]. . . . The second parte, entreating of hope. 4°. *Doway, widdow of L. Kellam*, 1615. L².O²(imp.).DE(imp.).USHAW.
A&R 886.

Weston, Edward—*cont.*

25290.7 — A triple cure of a triple malady. That is, of vanity in apparell. Excesse in drinking. Impiety in swearing. By E. W. doctor, and professor of divinity. 8°. [*St. Omer, English College Press,*] 1616. AMP.USHAW. Dr. R. A. Hunter, London (lacks tp).; F.HD.
A&R 887.

25291 **Weston, Hugh.** Oratio coram clero. 1553. = pt. of 12794.

25291.5 — A prayer made by the deane of Westminster, and delyuered to the chyldren of yᵉ queenes maiesties gramer scole there. s.sh.fol. *in æd. J. Cawodi*, [1555.] P.
— *See also* 19836.

Weston, *Sir* **Richard.** A discours of husbandrie used in Brabant. 1605 [1650.] *See* Wing W 1482.

25292 **Westward.** Westward for smelts. Or, the water-mans fare of mad-merry western wenches. By kinde Kit of Kingstone. 4°. [*G. Purslowe*] *f. J. Trundle*, 1620. Ent. 15 ja. C².; F.HD.

Wetham, John. *See* Indulgences 82.

25292.3 **Wetherel, Thomas.** Five sermons, preached upon several texts. [*Ed.*] (*F. Quarles.*) 12°. *J. B[eale] f. S. Man*, 1635. Ent. 23 mr. L(tp only, Ames II.1294). O.PLUME.; F.

Wetherall, William. *See* Indulgences 101A.

Wever, R. *See* Weaver, R.

25293 **Wh., Ih.** English paradise. Discovered in the Latine prospect of Jacobs blessing. [Two sermons.] 4°. *W. Hall f. R. Redmer*, 1612. Ent. to Hall 17 jn. L(imp.). O.C¹⁰.; F.HN.AAS.ILL.
Usually attrib. to John White, D.D., but not included in 25389.

25294 **Whalley, John.** Gods plentie, feeding true pietie. In a sermon preached at Pauls crosse. 4°. *W. Stansby, sold by R. Mabbe*, 1616. Ent. to Stansby 20 ja. L.L¹⁵. O.C.C².; F.U. Weissman.

25294.5 — [Anr. issue, w. cancel tp, w. imprint:] *W. Stansby*, [1616?] HD.

Wharton, *Lady* **Dorothy.** *See* 25759.5.

25295 **Wharton, John.** Whartons dreame. Conteyninge an inuectiue agaynst vsurers, [etc. In verse.] 4°. *J. J. Charlewod f. P. Conyngton*, 1578. Ent. 13 de. 1577. L.

25296 **Whately, William.** A bride-bush, or a wedding sermon. [*Init.* W. W.] 4°. *W. Jaggard f. N. Bourne*, 1617. Ent. 15 mr. 1616. O.C⁵.; F.U.Y.

25297 — [Anr. ed., enlarged into a treatise.] A bride-bush: or, a direction for married persons. By W. Whately. 4°. *F. Kyngston f. T. Man*, 1619. L.O.C⁵.M.SH.+ ; F.HN. HD.N.NY¹¹.+
For Whately's revocation of his opinion that adultery and desertion are grounds for divorce *see* Cal. S.P.D., *1619–1623*, p. 253 (4 May 1621). The text in 25298 is unaltered, but Whately adds an advertisement (Ff3) that his argument was erroneous.

25298 — [Anr. ed.] 4°. *B. Alsop f. B. Fisher*, 1623. Ent. to T. Man 1 mr. 1624. L.O.C.DUR⁵.SHEF.+ ; F.CAL.HD.N. U(lacks Ff3).+
Imprint varies; sold at 'Taulbut' or 'Talbot'; both at C.

25299 — A care-cloth: or a treatise of the troubles of marriage. (Mortification.—Charitable teares. [Both sermons.]) 4° in 8's. *F. Kyngston f. T. Man*, 1624 (1623.) Ent. 1 mr. 1624. L.O.O¹⁷.LIV².NEK.+ ; F.HN.HD.N.Y.+
(25307, 25303 are pt. of this)

25300 — A caveat for the covetous, in a sermon preached at Paules Crosse. 8°. *T. C[reede] f. T. Man a. M. Lawe*, 1609. Ent. to Man, sen., and Law 30 ja. L.YK.; NY².

25300.5 — [Anr. ed., w. added preface.] 8°. *T. S[nodham] f. T. Man a. M. Lawe*, 1609. L³(lacks tp).C¹⁰.; F.

25301 — [Anr. ed.] 8°. *F. Kyngston f. T. Man a. M. Lawe*, 1610. O.

25302 — [Anr. ed.] 8°. *H. Lownes f. T. Man & M. Law*, 1616. O.G².; F(imp.).

25303 — Charitable teares. 1623. = pt. of 25299.

Whately, William—*cont.*

25304 — A godlie treatise, intituled the view of pride. 8°. *T. Creede f. J. Deane a. J. Baily*, 1602. Ent. to Creede 28 de. 1601. C[3].

25305 — Gods husbandry: the first part. Tending to shew the difference betwixt the hypocrite and the true-hearted christian. As it was delivered in certaine sermons. 4°. *F. Kyngston f. T. Man*, 1619. Ent. to T. a. J. Man a. H. Sharp 13 fb. L.O.C[5].D.PETYT.+; F.NY[11].

25305a — [A variant, w. imprint:] *F. Kingston f. H. Sharpe, in Banburie*, 1619. C(imp.).; HN.

25306 — [Anr. ed., enlarged.] The first (second) part. 2 pts. 4° in 8's. *B. Alsop [a.] (F. Kyngston) f. T. Man*, 1622. Pt. 2 ent. to T. and Jonah Man 16 no. 1621. L.O.C.D. YK.+; F.HN.HD.IND.U.+

25307 — Mortification. 1623. = pt. of 25299.

25308 — The new birth: or, a treatise of regeneration, delivered in certaine sermons. 4° in 8's. *F. Kingston f. T. Man*, 1618. L(imp.).O.O[10].C.YK.+; HD.

25309 — [Anr. ed.] 4°. *F. Kyngston f. T. Man*, 1619. L.C[5].PLUME. STD.

25309.3 — [A variant, w. imprint:] *F. Kyngston f. H. Sharpe, in Banbury*, 1619. Kent U.

25309.7 — [Anr. ed.] 4° partly in 8's. *B. Alsop f. T. Man*, 1622. BURY.; HN.

25310 — [A variant, w. imprint:] *B. Alsop f. Jonas a. P. Man*, 1622. Ass'd from T. Man 3 my. 1624. L(destroyed). O.; CAL.CAL[6].

25311 — [Anr. ed.] 4°. *F. Kyngston f. R. Moore*, 1628. L.L[4].; F (2).ILL.IND.

25312 — [Anr. ed.] 4°. *[J. Haviland f.] assignes of T. Man, &c., sold by F. Clifton*, 1630. Ass'd to B. Fisher 6 jy. 1629. O.O[3].O[19].DUR[5].; F.HN(tp only, DeVinne I.340). PN[2].

25313 — [Anr. ed.] 4°. *[T. Harper f.] assignes of Joane Man a. B. Fisher*, 1635. Ass'd 12 au. L.O.C[10].D.NLW.+; F.HN NY[11].U.Y.+

25314 — The oyle of gladnesse. . . . Certaine sermons. 12°. *G. M[iller] f. G. Edwards*, 1637. Ent. 2 my. O.E(frags.).; U.

25315 — A pithie, short, and methodicall opening of the ten commandments. 12°. *J. Haviland f. T. Pavier a. L. Greene, [Cambridge,]* 1622. Ent. 29 mr. L.O.C[10].D.; HN.

25316 — The poore mans advocate, or, a treatise of liberality to the needy. Delivered in sermons. 12°. *G. M[iller] f. G. Edwards*, 1637. Ent. 22 ap. O.C.; F.

25317 — Prototypes, or, the primarie precedent presidents out of Genesis. Published by those who were appointed by the authour. (E. Leigh; H. Scudder.) fol. *G. M[iller, R. Hearne, a. Eliot's Court Press] f. G. Edwards*, 1640. Ent. 19 fb. L[2].O[2].C.E[2].M[2].+; HN.CAL. MICH.N.U.+
Hearne pr. Aa–Ll; Eliot's Court Press Aaa–Ccc; Miller the rest.

25317.3 — [Anr. issue, w. cancel tp:] Together with M[r]. Whatelyes life and death. Published by E. Leigh and H. Scudder. *G. M[iller] f. G. Edwards*, 1640. L.O.O[12]. O[26].D.; F.

25317.5 — [Anr. issue, w. variant cancel tp, w. imprint:] *G. M[iller] f. E. Langham, in Banbury*, 1640. O.O[28]. EX.; ILL.TORONTO[2].

25318 — The redemption of time, or a sermon. By M. W[hately] master in arts. 8°. *T. E[ast] f. T. Man*, 1606. Ent. to T. Man, sen. and jun., 14 ap. L.; HD.

25319 — [Anr. ed.] 8°. *T. Este f. T. Man*, 1607. L.LINC.

25319.3 — [Anr. ed.] 8°. *T. Este f. T. Man*, 1608. HN.

25319.5 — [Anr. ed.] 8°. *T. Snodham f. T. Man*, 1609. C[10].YK.; HD.

25320 — [Anr. ed.] By W. Whately. 4°. *F. Kyngston f. T. Man*, 1619. L.L[4].O.C[2].WI.+; F.HN.CAL[6].HD(lacks G4).U.

25321 — [Anr. ed.] 4°. *f. B. Fisher*, 1634. Ass'd 6 jy. 1629. L[3]. O.A.EX.M.

25322 — Sinne no more, or a sermon preached in the parish church of Banbury . . . upon occasion of a fire. Now published. 4°. *[Eliot's Court Press] f. G. Edwards*, 1628. Ent. 6 jn. L.L[2].O[3](imp.).O[5].C.+; F.HN.HD.
B[1r] catchword: 'beene'. *See also* 9248.5.

25322.3 — [Anr. issue, w. cancel tp.] Now published. *[Eliot's Court Press] f. E. Langham, in Banbury*, 1628. Ass'd 24 jn. HN.

25322.7 — [Anr. ed.] The second time published and enlarged. 4°. *[Eliot's Court Press] f. G. Edwards*, 1628. O(w. A[4] of 25322).O[3].A(lacks tp)*.E.; F.
B[1r] catchword: 'ten'.

Whately, William—*cont.*

25322a — [A variant, w. imprint:] *[Eliot's Court Press] f. E. Langham in Banbury*, 1628. O(2).O[26].; F.
The F copy has 1342.5 bd. in it.

25323 — [Anr. ed.] The third time published. 4°. *[Eliot's Court Press] f. G. Edwards, sold by E. Langham of Banbury*, 1630. L.

25324 — [A variant, w. imprint:] *[Eliot's Court Press] f. G. Edwards*, 1630. L.O.D.P.STU.+; F.HN.ILL.Y.

25325 **Whear, Diggory.** De ratione et methodo legendi historias dissertatio. 8° in 4's. *J. H[aviland,]* 1623. O(2). WOR.; ILL.

25326 — [Anr. ed., revised, w. additions.] Huic praemittitur oratio auspicalis. 8° in 4's. *Oxoniæ, J. Lichfield & G. Turner*, 1625. L[3].L[44].O.C.INN.+; F.HN.NY.
For a further revision, omitting the Oratio *see* 25328.

25326.5 — Degorei Wheari prael. hist. Camdeniani. Pietas erga benefactore. 8°. *Oxon., G. Turner*, 1628. O.C.C[2].; CAL[4].PN[2].
Collates *[4] A–C[8].

25327 — [Anr. ed., w. additions.] Necnon epistolarum eucharisticarum fasciculum. *Oxon., G. Turner*, 1628. L.O.O[6].C[5]. Sparrow.; F.HN.HD.Y.
Collates *[4] A–C[8] a–h[8] i[4]. The last halfsheet is in 2 settings: signed i (L, O, Sparrow, HD) or I (O[6], O[38], C[5], F, HN); the latter setting has an added inscription to N. Brent on p. 129.

25328 — Relectiones hyemales, de ratione & methodo legendi utrasq; historias, civiles et ecclesiasticas. 8°. *Oxoniæ, L. Lichfield, imp. H. Curteyne*, 1637. L.O[38].C[2].D.E.+; F.HN.COLG.
A revision of 25326.

25328.3 — [A variant, w. imprint:] *Oxoniæ, L. Lichfield, imp. E. Forrest & H. Curteyne*, 1637. L.O.C.D.M[4].+

25328.5 — [A variant, w. imprint:] *Oxoniæ, L. Lichfield, imp. E. Forrest*, 1637. O.O[2].O[4].O[6](2).; CHI.N.Y.
— *See also* 19028.

25329 **Wheathill, Anne.** A handfull of holesome (though homelie) hearbs, gathered out of the goodlie garden of Gods most holie word. [Prayers.] 12°. *H. Denham*, 1584. Ent. 22 ja. Broxbourne(E).; F.

Wheatlie, William. *See* Whately, W.

25330 **Wheeler, John.** A treatise of commerce, wherin are shewed the commodies [*sic*] arising by a wel ordered, and ruled trade, such as that of the societie of Merchantes Adventurers. 4°. *Middelburgh, R. Schilders*, 1601. L.L[2].C[5].G[2].RGU.+; F.HN.HD.MIN.NY.+
Answered by 17932.

25331 — [Anr. ed.] 4°. *J. Harison*, 1601. Ent. to J. Harrison 3 on 14 au. L.L[30].O.C.DUR(Bamb.).+; HN.HD(imp.).ILL. LC.NY.+

Whete, Thomas, *Prior. See* Indulgences 51.

25332 **Whetenhall, Thomas.** A discourse of the abuses now in question in the churches of Christ. 4°. *[W. Jones's secret press,]* 1606. L.O.C.E[2].YK.+; F.HN.HD.N.NY.+

25333 — [Anr. ed.] Now distinguished into chapters, and enlarged in the index. 8°. *[Leyden, W. Brewster,] Reprinted*, 1617. L.L[2](2).O[5].A.E.; F.HN.

Whetham, Johannes. *See* Indulgences 82.

25333.5 **Whetstone.** A whetstone for lyers. A song of strange wonders. *Ballad.* 2 pts. s.sh.fol. *f. F. Grove, [c. 1630.]* C[6].
Pr. on the verso of 19252.5.

Whetstone, George. Aurelia. 1593. *See* 25338.

25334 — The censure of a loyall subiect: vpon those traitors, at the place of their executions, the xx. and xxi. of September. [Init. G. W.] 4°. *R. Jones*, 1587. Ent. 4 ja. L.L[30].O.C.E.+; F.HN.ILL.Y.
G2[r] catchword: 'turne'.

25334a — [Anr. issue, w. cancel tp and G2.] As also, of the Scottish queen, cut off by justice. On Wednesday the 8. of Februarie. *R. Jones, [1587.]* L.O.O[3].C[5].E.+; F.HD.
G2[r] catchword: 'same'.

25335 — The enemie to vnthryftinesse. 1586. Now = 25341.5.

25336 — The English myrror. A regard wherein al estates may behold the conquests of enuy: containing ruine of common weales, [etc.] 4° in 8's. *J. Windet f. G. Seton*, 1586. Ent. 29 ap. L.L[30].L[38].O.C.+; F.HN.HD (tp def.).N.NY.+

450

Whetstone, George—*cont.*

25337 — An heptameron of ciuill discourses. Containing: the Christmasse exercise of sundrie well courted gentlemen and gentlewomen. 4°. *R. Jones*, 1582 (3 fb.) Ent. 11 ja. L(2).O.C(frag.).; F(3).HN.ILL.PML.ROS.

25338 — [Anr. ed., w. title:] Aurelia. The paragon of pleasure and princely delights. By G. W. Gent. 4°. [*T. Orwin f.*] *R. Johnes*, 1593. L.O.; HN.

25339 — The honorable reputation of a souldier. Drawen out of the liues, of Romaine, Grecian, and other martialistes. 4°. *R. Jones*, 1585. L.O(imp.).; HN(tp facs.). HD.

25340 — [Anr. ed., w. additions.] Verduytscht ende by een ghevoecht, door J. Walraven. (English pronounciation: or a shorte introduction to the English speache. [By] J. Walraven.) *Eng. a. Dutch.* 4°. *Leyden, J. P. Jacobszoon ende J. Bouwenszoon, [sold] by T. Basson,* 1586. L.O(frag.).C.P.; F.HN.

25341 — A mirour for magestrates of cyties. Representing the ordinaunces, of the emperour, Alexander Severus, to suppresse vices. Hereunto, is added, a touchstone for the time: containyng: mischiefes, bred in London. 4°. *R. Jones*, 1584. Ent. 15 ap. L.L[8].O.O[5]. NEP.+; F.HN.CH.HD.ILL.+

25341.5 — [Anr. issue, w. A1–¶1 cancelled, and new tp and dedic.] The enemie to vnthryftinesse. *R. Jones*, 1586. L(2, 1 imp.).
(Formerly 25335)

25342 — A mirror of treue honnour and christian nobilitie, exposing: the life, death, and vertues of Frauncis earle of Bedford. [In verse.] 4°. *R. Jones*, 1585. O(2). Woburn Abbey, Bedfordshire.; F.HN.

25343 — A remembraunce, of the woorthie life, of sir Nicholas Bacon who deceased, the 20 daye of Februarie 1578 [o.s.] [In verse.] 4°. [*J. Kingston*] *f. M. Jennyngs,* [1579.] Ent. 6 ap. 1579. HN.

25344 — A remembraunce of the life, death, and vertues, of Thomas late erle of Sussex. [In verse.] 4°. *J. Wolfe a. R. Jones*, 1583. Ent. to Wolfe 17 jy. L.; HN.
Wolfe pr. the whole.

25345 — A remembraunce of the precious vertues of the right honourable iudge, sir James Dier, who disseased the 24. of Marche, 1582. [In verse.] 4°. *J. Charlewood,* [1582.] HN.

25346 — A remembraunce of the wel imployed life, of George Gaskoigne esquire, who deceased the 7. of October. 1577. [In verse.] 4°. *f. E. Aggas,* [1577.] Ent. 15 no. O.

25347 — The right excellent and famous historye, of Promos and Cassandra. [A drama in 2 parts.] 4°. [*J. Charlewood f.*] (*R. Jhones*, 1578 (20 au.)) Ent. 31 jy. L.O(imp.). C[2].; F(2, 1 imp.).HN. Greg 73.

25348 — The rocke of regard, diuided into foure parts. [Mostly in verse.] 4° in 8's. [*H. Middleton*] (*f. R. Waley,* 1576.) L.O.C(1 leaf).C[2].; HN.HD(frag.).

25349 — Sir Phillip Sidney, his honorable life, his valiant death, and his true vertues. Whereunto is adioyned, one other commemoration. By B. W. esquire. [In verse.] 4°. [*T. Orwin*] *f. T. Cadman,* [1587.] Ent. 15 jn. 1587. HN.PML.

25350 **Whight, Nicholas.** A commendation of musicke, and a confutation of them which disprayse it. [In verse.] s.sh.fol. *A. Lacy,* [1563?] Ent. 1562–63. HN.

25351 **Whipper.** The whipper of the satyre. 1601. = 12504.5.

25351.5 **Whippet You Priests.** [Ballad with repeated lines: 'Whippet you prestes, and tourne you . . . Leaue that you prestes I warne you'.] *Ballad.* s.sh.fol. [*London,* 1549?] HN(frag.).

Whipping. No whippinge, nor trippinge. 1601. *See* 3672.
25352 — The whipping of the satyre. 1601. = 14071.
25353 — Whipping cheare. Or the wofull lamentations of the three sisters in the Spittle. *Ballad.* 2 pts. s.sh.fol. *f. H. G[osson, c.* 1625.] c[6].

Whit, James, *tr. See* 192.

25354 **Whitaker, Alexander.** Good newes from Virginia. Sent to the counsell and company of Virginia. And a preface prefixed [by] (W. Crashawe.) 4°. *F. Kyngston f. W. Welby,* 1613. L.; HN.CB.LC.NN.NY.+

25355 **Whitaker, Tobias.** Περι υδροποσιας: or, a discourse of waters. 12°. [*A. Mathewes*] *f. J. Grismond,* 1634. Ent. 13 my. L.O[19].C.M[2].NLW.+; F.CHI.

Whitaker, Tobias—*cont.*

25356 — The tree of humane life, or, the bloud of the grape. Proving the possibilitie of maintaining humane life by the use of wine. 8°. *J. D[awson] f. H. O[verton,]* 1638. Ent. to Overton 19 se. 1637. L.L[16].O.C.NEK.+; LC.NLM.NY[4].

25357 **Whitaker, William.** Ad Nicolai Sanderi demonstrationes quadraginta, in octavo libro visibilis Monarchiæ positas, responsio. Accesit eiusdem thesis de Antichristo. 8°. *T. Vautrollerius, imp. T. Chardi,* 1583. L.O.C.D[2].E[2].+; F.HN.HD.NCU.Y.+
Prints and answers Sanders; remarks in the Pref. against 2884 are answered in 20632. *See also* 25365.3.

25358 — Ad rationes decem Edmundi Campiani jesuitæ [4536.5], responsio. 8°. *T. Vautrollerius, imp. T. Chardi,* 1581. L.O.C.CASHEL.E[4].+; F.HN.HD.ILL. NY[11].+

25359 — Editio secunda. 8°. *T. Vautrollerius, imp. T. Chardi,* 1581. O.C[4].C[5].OS.STD.+; HN.

25360 — [A trans.] An answere to the ten reasons of E. Campian. Whereunto is added the summe of the defence of those reasons by John Duræus the Scot, a jesuit, with a reply unto it. *Tr.* R. Stocke. 4°. *F. Kyngston f. C. Burby a. E. Weaver,* 1606. Ent. 18 fb. L.O.C.D.STU.+; F.HN.BO.CHI.NY.+
Includes excerpts tr. from 25362.

25361 — [A ghost.]

25362 — Responsionis ad decem illas rationes, quibus fretus E. Campianus, defensio contra confutationem J. Duræi Scoti. 8°. *H. Midletonus, imp. T. Chardi,* 1583. Ent. 10 jn. L.O.C.CASHEL.E.+; F.HN.HD(imp.).U.Y.+
Prints and answers Durie; partly tr. in 25360.

25363 — Adversus Thomæ Stapletoni Anglopapistae . . . Defensionem ecclesiasticæ authoritatis, duplicatio, pro authoritate S. scripturæ. fol. *Cantabrigiæ, J. Legatus,* 1594 (20 ap.) L.O.C.D.E[2].+; F.HN.CHI.HD.U.+
Prints and answers Stapleton.

25364 — An aunswere to a certaine booke, written by M. W. Rainoldes [20632]. 8°. *T. Thomas, pr. to the Univ. of Cambridge, sold at the white Horse in Canon-Lane, ouer-against the North Doore of Paules,* 1585. C.D. E[2].M[4].YK.+; F(2).ILL.U.Y. 𝔄
The address may be that of R. Waldegrave; *see* Herbert II.1139. A book w. Waldegrave's name and this address still has not been noted.

25364a — [Anr. issue, w. cancel tp, w. imprint:] *Printed at London,* [*Eliot's Court Press?*] *f. T. Chard,* 1585. L.L[43].O[2].C[5].R.; F(lacks dedic.).HD.Y.

25364b — [A pirated ed.] 8°. *Printed at London,* [*Eliot's Court Press,*] 1585. L[4].O(imp.).C.C[2].E.+; F.HN.HD.N.NY[11].
For other piracies of Cambridge eds. *see* 15252, 24530.

25365 — [Anr. issue of 25364, w. cancel tp, w. imprint:] *Cambridge, J. Legate,* 1590. O.O[13].C[5].; U.

25365.3 — Antichristi. Nolumus hunc regnare in nos. Luc. 19.14. Theses quædam publicè . . . propositæ iamq; in tabulam digestæ. s.sh.fol. [*Cambridge, J. Legat,* 1589?] O(2).
The theses are different from that in 25357.

25365.5 — [A trans.] Antichrist. We will not haue this man to rule ouer vs. Luc. 19.14. Certaine articles publicklie propounded . . . now enlarged in a table. s.sh.fol. [*Cambridge, J. Legat,* 1589?] L[2].
L[2] is bd. w. 20834.3.

25366 — Disputatio de sacra scriptura, contra R. Bellarminum & T. Stapletonum. 4° in 8's. *Cantabrigiæ, ex off. T. Thomasii,* 1588 (2 my.) L(imp.).O.C.D.E[4].+; F.HN. BO.CHI.U.+ 𝔄

25367 — Prælectiones doctissimi viri Guilielmi Whitakeri . . . In quibus tractatur controuersia de concilijs. Editæ opera J. Allenson. 8°. *Cantabrigiæ, J. Legat,* 1600. L.O.C.D.E[2].+; F.BO[2].TEX.

25368 — Praelectiones doctissimi viri Guilielmi Whitakeri, . . . In quibus tractatur controuersia de ecclesia. Opera J. Allenson. His accessit Doct. Whitakeri ultima concio ad clerum, unà cum descriptione vitæ & mortis, authore A. Assheton. 4°. *ex off. J. Legat, acad. Cantab. typog.,* 1599. L.O.C.CASHEL.E.+; F. BO[2].CHI.U.Y.+

25369 — A short summe of christianity. Delivered by way of catechisme. [*Ed.*] (J. Martinus.) 8°. [*G. Purslowe*] *f. J. Emery,* 1630. Ent. 6 no. 1629. O.C[3].; Y.

— Theses quædam . . . propositæ. [1589?] *See* 25365.3.

Whitaker, William—*cont.*

25370 — Tractatus doctissimi viri Guilielmi Whitakeri, . . . De peccato originali. Opera J. Allenson. 8º. *ex off. J. Legat, acad. Cantab. typog.*, 1600. L.O.C.CASHEL.E⁴.+; BO².CU.HD. Cleveland PL.
— *tr. See* 14607.5, 16429.5, 18707, 18711a, 18726.

25371 **Whitbie, Oliver.** Londons returne, after the decrease of the sicknes: in a sermon. 4º. *N. a. J. Okes, sold by R. Whitaker*, 1637. L.L¹⁵.O.P.; F.HN.U.

25372 **Whitbourne, Richard.** A discourse and discovery of New-found-land, with many reasons how a plantation may there be made, after a far better manner. With certaine abuses [in] trade. 4º. *F. Kyngston f. W. Barret*, 1620. L.O².C⁶.DUR⁵.STD.+; F.HN.HD.N.NY.+
For indications of a special reissue in 1622 *see* 25375a.2, 25375a.4.

25373 — [Anr. ed., w. additions.] As also, an Invitation: and likewise certaine letters. 4º. *F. Kingston*, 1622. L.L². O.C.D(lacks tp).+; F.HN.HD.IND.NY.+
Includes a reimposition of 25375a.2 and a revised version of 25375a.

25374 — [Anr. ed.] 4º. *F. Kingston*, 1623. L.O(3).O³.O⁵.BED.; F. HN(imp.).BO.N.NY.+
Some copies (F, HN, N) have the misprint 'DIS-COERVS' in the title. The Invitation is further revised.

25375 — A discourse containing a loving invitation to adventurers, in the New-found-land. 4º. *F. Kyngston*, 1622. D.G².; F.HN.HD.N.NY.+
Ends G3ᵛ.

25375a — [Anr. issue, w. added A–B⁴ C²:] (A letter from captaine E. Wynne, vnto sir G. Calvert July 1622. [And others.]) *F. Kyngston*, 1622. L(2).O²².C⁶.STD.; F.HN. HD.N.NY.+
Revised in 25373. The Winne letters are different from 25854.

25375a.2 — [Heading ¶1ʳ:] At Theobalds, the 12. of Aprill 1622. The copy of a reference [from King James and others concerning collections of money; also granting Whitbourne a 21-year privilege to print his books.] 4º in 2. [*F. Kingston*, 1622.] L.O²².; F.HN.HD.N.NY(2).
Usually found when 25372 and 25375a are bd. together; the typesetting is reimposed as A2, 3 in 25373.

25375a.4 — [Bishops' letters instructing parishes to collect money for Whitbourne.] [By G. Montaigne, Bp. of London. 16 Sept. 1622.] 1/2 sh.fol. [*F. Kingston*, 1622.] L. O²²(frag.)*.; F.HN.N.NY.
Text in 2 paragraphs; *see also* 25375a.7. Usually found when 25372 and 25375a are bd. together. This and the following are all pr. from standing type w. various amounts of alteration. For further details *see Essays Honoring L. C. Wroth*, pp. 223–33.

25375a.5 — [Anr. issue, by R. Searchfield, Bp. of Bristol. 5 Oct. 1622.] CB(in 25373).NY(in 25372).

25375a.6 — [Anr. issue, by S. Harsnet, Bp. of Norwich. 2 Dec. 1622.] L(in 25373).; BO⁵(in 25373).

25375a.7 — [Anr. issue, by G. Montaigne, Bp. of London. 16 Sept. 1622 (actually after 2 Dec. 1622.)] HN(in 25373).
Text in 3 paragraphs.

25375a.8 — [Anr. issue, by N. Felton, Bp. of Ely. 2 June 1623.] NY(in 25374).

25375a.10 **White, Andrew, S.J.** [Heading A1ʳ:] A declaration of the lord Baltemore's plantation in Mary-land, manifesting the nature, quality, condition, and rich utilities it contayneth. [Anon.] 4º. [*B. Alsop a. T. Fawcet*, 1633.] W.
A4ʳ dated 10 Feb. 1633.

25376 **White, Anthony.** Truth and error discovered in two sermons. 4º. *Oxford, J. Lichfield f. H. Curteyne*, 1628. L.O.C(lacks D4).D(lacks tp).E.+; F.HN.HD.U (imp.).Y.+

White, Charles, *ed. See* 5410.

25377 **White, Christopher.** Of oathes: their object, forme, and bond: perjurie, and papall dispensations. Delivered in three sermons. 4º. [*G. Purslowe*] *f. R. Mab*, 1627. L.O.C.A.M⁴.+; F.HN.CHI.HD.U.+

White, Christopher—*cont.*

25378 — A sermon preached in Christ-Church in Oxford. 4º. *B. Norton a. J. Bill*, 1622. L.O.C.DUR³.E.+; F.HN. CAL.CHI.Y.+

25379 **White, Francis,** *Bp.* An examination and confutation of a lawlesse pamphlet, [4137.7]. 4º. *R. B[adger,] sold in S. Dunstans Churchyard . . . at the little shop turning up to Cliffords-Inne*, 1637. Ent. to Badger 13 fb. O.C.DUR.; F(lacks Y1).ILL.U.WASH³.

25379.5 — [A variant, w. imprint:] *R. Badger, sold in S. Pauls Church-yard*, 1637. O³(imp.).C¹⁰.

25379a — [A variant, w. imprint:] *R. B[adger] f. A. Crooke*, 1637. L.O.C.D.E.+; F.HN.CHI.HD.Y.+
B⁴ and Y² in 2 settings: B2ʳ line 1 ends: 'pub-', Y1ʳ line 11 ends: 'confor-' (O, D², HD; also C copy of 25379); or 'publi-' and 'con-' (D, imp., F.ll.53, no. 2). At least 1 P has them mixed.

25380 — The orthodox faith and way to the church . . . in answer to a popish treatise [26001]. 4º in 8's. *R. Field f. W. Barret*, 1617. Ent. 7 ja. L.O.C.D.E².+; F.HN.BO.U. Y.+
Tp varies; line 5 of title: 'IVSVIFIED [*sic*]' (C) or 'IVSTIFIED' (O, ELY, HN); line 2 of imprint ends 'BAR-' (C, ELY) or 'BARRET,' (O, HN).

25381 — Second edition, enlarged. fol. *J. Haviland f. W. Barret*, 1624. = pt. 4 of 25389 sqq.

25382 — A replie to jesuit Fishers answere to certain questions propoūded by king James. Hereunto is annexed, a conference of the B: of Sᵗ Davids [W. Laud] wᵗʰ the same jesuit [written by R. B., chaplain to Laud, i.e. R. Baillie.] 2 pts. fol. *A. Islip*, 1624. L.O.C.D.E.+; F.HN.HD.CHI.U.+
Pt. 2 (formerly also 1204) is reprinted in an enlarged version in 15298. Answered in 10910.7, 10916.5.

25383 — A treatise of the sabbath-day. . . . Against sabbatarian-novelty. 4º. *R. Badger*, 1635. Ent. 13 jy. L.O.C. CASHEL.E.+; F.HN.HD.ILL.U.+
Answers 3473; answered by 4137.7.

25384 — Second edition. 4º. *R. Badger*, 1635. L.O.C.D.G⁴.+; F.HN.HD.N.NY¹¹.+

25384.5 — Third edition. 4º. *R. Badger*, 1635. G².

25385 — [A variant, w. imprint:] *R. B[adger,] sold at St. Dunstans Church-yard in Fleetstreet*, 1636. L.O.C. D.E².+; F.CHI.NY¹¹.U.
— *See also* 10172.5, 10295.

— A reply to D. White and D. Featly. 1625. *See* pt. 3 of 10916.5.

25386 **White, Francis,** *M. A.* Londons warning, by Jerusalem. A sermon preached at Pauls Crosse. 4º. *G. Purslowe f. R. Flemming*, 1619. Ent. 29 jy. L(lacks A4).O.C. BIRM²(K.N.).E.+; F(2).HN.HD.Y(tp def.). Sydney U.

25387 **White, Harim.** The ready way to true repentance: in divers sermons. 8º. *G. E[ld] f. T. B[ushell,]* 1618. Ent. to Bushell 13 de. 1617. L.C.LINC.

White, James, *tr. See* 192.

25388 **White, John,** *Bp.* Diacosiomartyrion. id est ducentorum virorum testimonium, de veritate corporis, et sanguinis Christi, in eucharistia, aduersus Petrum Martyrem. [In verse.] 4º in 8's. *in aed. R. Cali*, 1553 (de.) L.O.C.D.DUR⁵.+; F(2).CH.HD.
1 F, CH have an inserted leaf w. approbation of Queen Mary dated 15 Mar. 1554. *See also* 24673.

25389 **White, John,** *D. D.* The workes of that learned . . . divine, John White. Together with a Defence of the way. By F. White. 4 pts. fol. *R. F. for J. Bill a. W. Barret*, 1624. O¹⁸(lacks pt. 3).C(2).DUR³.E².; CAL.
(Pts. 1–4 formerly also 25398, 25391, 25393, 25381, q.v. for imprints)

25389.5 — [A variant, w. imprint on gen. tp:] *f. W. Barret*, 1624. L.O.C.D.G².+; F.HN.HD.ILL.U.+

25389a — [Anr. issue, w. added bifolium with engr. portrait and gen. tp w. imprint:] *f. W. Barret, sold by M. Lownes a. R. Moore*, 1624. L.O².C⁵.BIRM.DUR.+; BO⁵.CHI. MICH.PML.
Copies usually have the 2nd tp as in 25389.5; O¹³ has the 2nd tp as in 25389; C⁵ has the 2nd tp cancelled.

White, John, *D. D.—cont.*

25390 — A defence of the Way to the true church against A. D. [10914]. 4° in 8's. [*R. Field*] *f. W. Barret*, 1614. Ent. 15 my. L.O.C.D.E².+; F.HN.HD(imp.).U.Y.+
Answered by 26045.

25391 — [Anr. ed.] fol. *F. Kyngston f. W. Barret*, 1624. = pt. 2 of 25389 sqq.

25392 — Two sermons; the former delivered at Pauls Crosse. The latter at the Spittle. 4°. *R. Field f. W. Barret*, 1615. Ent. 20 ap. L⁴.O.C.DUR⁵.G².+; F.HN.HART². NY¹¹.Y.+

25393 — [Anr. ed.] fol. *J. Haviland f. W. Barret*, 1624. = pt. 3 of 25389 sqq.

25394 — The way to the true church: contrived into an answer to a popish discourse, concerning the rule of faith. 4° in 8's. [*R. Field*]*f. J. Bill a. W. Barret*, 1608. Ent. to Barret 27 jn. L.O⁵.C.D.STU.+; F.HD.ILL.U.Y.+
Answers an earlier MS. version of 10915.5 (*see* d5ᵛ of 25395); answered by 10914, 26001, 26049.

25395 — Second impression corrected and augmented. 4° in 8's. [*R. Field*] *f. J. Bill a. W. Barret*, 1610. L.O.C.E².M. +; F(imp.).HD.ILL.U(lacks Gg1).Y.+

25396 — Third impression. 4° in 8's. [*R. Field*] *f. J. Bill a. W. Barret*, 1612. L.O.C.BIRM.D.+; F.HN.HD.U. Iowa U.+

25397 — Fourth impression, to which is annexed the authors protestation made upon his deathbed. 4° in 8's. *R. Field f. J. Bill a. W. Barret*, 1616. L.O.C.BIRM² (K.N.).E.+; F(2).HN.NY⁷.U.

25398 — Fift impression. fol. *R. Field f. J. Bill a. W. Barret*, 1624. = pt. 1 of 25389 sqq.
— *See also* 25293.

White, John, *Mathematician.* Almanacks. 1613, etc. *See* 527 sqq.

25399 **White, John,** *of Dorchester.* The planters plea. Or the grounds of plantations examined. [Anon.] 4°. *W. Jones,* [*M. Flesher, a. J. Dawson*] 1630. Ent. 8 jy. L.O.C.C³.SAL.+; F.HN.HD.N.NY.+
Jones pr. quire A and possibly H–I; Flesher B–G; Dawson K–M.

White, John, *Painter. See* 12786.

25399.5 **White, Josias.** A plaine and familiar exposition upon the creed, ten commandements, . . . by question and answer. 8°. *G. Miller f. E. Brewster*, 1632. Ent. to W. Bladen 26 mr. 1623; ass'd to R. Bird and Brewster 4 au. 1626. E⁴.

25400 — [Anr. ed.] 8°. *W. J[ones] f. E. Brewster*, 1637. O.
— A short catechisme. 1632. *See* 4803.2.

White, Matthew, *pseud.* Newes from Ipswich. [1636?] *See* 20469.

25401 **White, Peter.** An answeare vnto certaine crabbed questions: by some secret papist. (A discouerie of the iesuitical opinion of iustification vttered by Sherwine at his execution.) 2 pts. 8°. *J. Wolfe a. H. Kirkham,* (1582.) L.L².O(pt. 2 only).C.D.+

25402 — A godlye and fruitefull sermon against idolatrie. [Init. P. W., *Minister.*] 8°. *f. F. Coldocke*, 1581. Ent. 4 jy. L.L².O(tp only, Douce Add.142/121).LINC.P.; F.HD.
Imprint varies: 'by' (F) or 'for' (HD) F. Coldocke.

25403 **White, Richard.** Richardi Whiti Angli, orationes duę: vna, de omnium artium ac philosophiæ circulo: altera de laudibus Ciceronis & eloquentiæ. 8°. (*ap. R. Wolfium,*) 1565 (1566.) Ent. 1565–66. c(lacks tp).D.
With an epistle by C. Jonson.

25403.5 **White, Thomas,** *Catholic.* A catechisme of christian doctrine. [Anon.] 24° in 8's. *Paris,* [*widow Blagaert,*] 1637. O.BUTE.OS.W(lacks tp).WOR².; Pirie. A&R 888.

White, Thomas, *Founder of St. John's College, Oxford.* Rerum gestarum ab Th: White ἀπομνημόνευμα. [1608?] *See* 15266.5.

25404 **White, Thomas,** *Founder of Sion College.* A godlie sermon preached . . . at the buriall of sir H. Sidney. 8°. *H. Midleton,* 1586. Ent. 7 no. L.C³.; F.

25405 — A sermon preached at Pawles Crosse on Sunday the ninth of December 1576. by T. W[hite]. 8°. [*H. Bynneman f.*] *F. Coldock,* 1578. L.L².L⁴.O⁹.LINC.+; F.HN.N.U(imp.).

White, Thomas, *Founder of Sion College—cont.*

25406 — A sermõ preached at Pawles Crosse on Sunday the thirde of Nouember 1577. in the time of the plague, by T. W[hite.] 8°. [*H. Bynneman f.*] *F. Coldock,* 1578 (10 fb.) L(2, 1 lacks tp).L².L⁴.O⁹.; F.HN.N.

25407 — A sermon preached at Paules Crosse the 17. of Nouember 1589. 8° in 4's. *R. Robinson a. T. Newman,* 1589. Ent. to Robinson 22 no. L.

— Schola moralis philosophiae Oxon. In funere Whiti pullata. 1624. *See* 19029.

25408 **White, Thomas,** *Writer against the Brownists.* A discoverie of Brownisme: or, a briefe declaration of errors among the English at Amsterdam. 4°. *E. A[llde] f. N. Fosbroke,* 1605. Ent. 26 oc. L.O.C.D². M.+; F.BO³.TORONTO².U.Y.+

25409 **White, Tristram.** The martyrdome of saint George of Cappadocia. [In verse.] 4°. [*T. Snodham*] *f. W. Barley,* 1614. Ent. to J. Beale by consent of widow M. Barley 12 no. L.L⁸.O(2).; F(impr. shaved).HN.

Whitehead, David, *ed. See* 24672.

Whitehorne, Peter. Certain waies of the orderyng of souldiers. 1562, etc. *See* 17164 sqq.
— *tr. See* 17164, 18815.

25409.5 **Whitfeld, Henry.** Some helpes to stir up to christian duties. 12°. [*T. Cotes?*]*f. J. Bartlet,* 1634. Ent. 12 au. 1633. L(tp only, Ames II.1210).; F.PN².

25410 — Second edition, corrected and amended. 12°. *f. J. Bartlet,* 1634. L.O.D.INN.; F.CHI.PN.U.Y.
Tp varies; last word of title 'amended' (F) or 'enlarged' (O).

25411 — Third edition. 12°. *f. J. Bartlet,* 1636. L.NLW.; F.

25412 **Whitford, Richard.** The contêtes of this boke. A werke of preparacion, vnto cõmunion, or howselyng. The werke for housholders with the golden pistle and alphabete or a crosrowe called an .A.B.C. all duely corrected and newly prynted. 2 pts. 8°. (*R. Redman,*) [1531?] c(imp.).; F.
For pt. 2 *see* 25422.5. Pt. 1 includes reprints from 1915 (the Godfray version of St. Bernard w. St. Bridget's revelations) as well as Whitford's trans., 1912, and his St. Bonauentura ABC, 3273.3. On L8ᵛ is the statement: 'We haue prynted this golden pystle agayn, bycause yᵉ other before is nat of the trãslation nor ediciõ of this auctor.'

25413 — [Anr. ed., w. omissions and additions.] With A dayly exercyce all duely corrected and newly prynted. 3 pts. 8°. (*R. Redman,*) [1537?] C¹⁰.; F.
For pts. 2, 3 *see* 25415, 25425. The Godfray texts are omitted from pt. 1.

25413.5 — [Anr. ed., w. additional prefaces, with title:] A dialoge or cõmunicacion. . . . For preparacion vnto howselynge. The werke for housholders wᵗ the golden pystle and alphabete or a crosrowe. (A dayly exercyse.) 3 pts. 8°. (*J. Waylande,* 1537.) L.
(Formerly 25416) For pts. 2, 3 *see* 25414, 25425.5. In the pref. to pt. 3 Whitford refers to a 'moche vicyous and faultye' ed. in which 'is one of my workes left out, whiche werke is nombred amonge the contentes. . . . And in stede of my werke, is an other heretyke or heretycall werke set in place.' In the pref. to 25420 the omitted work is identified as A daily exercise, cf. 25415, but the heretical work is nameless.

25413.7 — A dayly exercice . . . dethe. *See* Addenda.

25414 — A dayly exercyse and experyence of dethe. 8°. (*J. Waylande,* 1537.) L.
This is pt. 2 of 25413.5.

25415 — [Anr. ed.] A dayly exercice [etc.] 8°. (*R. Redman,*) [1538?] C¹⁰.; F.
Intended (retrospectively?) to be pt. 2 of 25413. As almost all the leaf signatures have arabic numerals, this could very well have been pr. after 25413, 25425. In title: 'deathe'.

25416 — A dialoge. 1537. Now = 25413.5.

25417 — The rule of saynt Augustyne. 1525. Now = 922.3.

25418 — No entry.

25419 — [Anr. ed.] 1527. Now = 922.4.
— The fruyte of redempcyon. [Sometimes attrib. to Whitford.] 1514, etc. *See* 22557 sqq.

Whitford, Richard—*cont.*

25420 — Here foloweth dyuers holy instrucyons and teachynges very necessarye for the helth of mannes soule. 4°. (*W. Myddylton*, 1541.) L.C.; F(imp.).
Includes a trans. of St. Isidore's Instruction to avoid vices (cf. 14270) and John Chrysostom's Of detraction, from the 3rd homily to the people of Antioch.

— The Jesus Psalter. [Sometimes attrib. to Whitford.] 1529, etc. *See* 14563 sqq.

25421 — Here begynneth the boke called the Pype, or tonne, of the lyfe of perfection. 4° 8.4. (*R. Redman*, 1532 (23 mr.)) L.L².O.C.M.+; F.CH.PML.Y³(imp.).
Includes a trans. of St. Bernard's Of commandment and dispensation.

25421.2 — The pomander of prayer. [*Ed.*] (by a broder of Syon [i.e. Whitford.]) 4°. (*R. Coplande*, 1528 (24 de.)) Lord Kenyon.
In the pref. the author is described as 'one of the deuout fathers of yᵉ Charterhous of Shene.'

25421.3 — [Anr. ed.] 4°. (*R. Coplande*, 1530 (31 oc.)) O⁵.BUTE.; F.

25421.5 — [Anr. ed.] 8°. (*R. Redman*, 1531.) M.

25421.6 — [Anr. ed.] 4°. (*W. de Worde*, 1532.) M(imp.).

25421.8 — A werke for housholders, or for them that haue the gydynge or gouernaunce of ony cōpany. 4° 4.6. (*R. Redman*,) [1530?] C.
(Formerly 25426)

25422 — [Anr. ed.] Newly corrected & prynted agayne wᵗ an addicion of policy (out of Bernarde syluestre.) 4°. (*W. de Worde*, 1530 (20 de.)) O.
The Bernardus portion is reprinted w. minor alterations from 1967.5.

25422.3 — [Anr. ed.] 4°. [*Southwark*,] (*P. Treueris*) [1531?] O. O⁵.
(Formerly 25424)

25422.5 — [Anr. ed.] 8°. (*R. Redman*, 1531 (19 au.)) c(imp.).; F. This is pt. 2 of 25412.

25423 — [Anr. ed.] 4°. (*W. de worde*, 1533 (2 my.)) L.; F.
25424 — Now = 25422.3.
25425 — [Anr. ed.] 8°. (*R. Redman*, 1537 (8 no.)) L.C¹⁰. Intended to be pt. 3 of 25413.

25425.5 — [Anr. ed.] 8°. (*J. waylande*, 1537.) L.USHAW(frag. of proof sheet of H4,7 in XVIII.E.5.6).
This is pt. 3 of 25413.5, q.v.

25426 — Now = 25421.8.

— *tr. See* 922.3, 1912, 1967.5, 3273.3, 17532, 23961, 23966, 23988.

25427 **Whitgift, John**, *Abp.* An answere to a certen libel intituled, An admonition [10847]. 4°. *H. Bynneman f. H. Toy*, 1572. L.O.C².D.M.+; F.HN.BO³.N.NY.+
C1ʳ last line begins: 'cōtempt'. Answered by 4711.

25428 — [Anr. ed.] 4°. *H. Bynneman f. H. Toy*, 1572 (1573.) O⁴. C⁹.CASHEL.D².P.+; F(imp.).HD.
C1ʳ last line begins: 'contempt'.

25429 — [Anr. ed.] Newly augmented. 4°. *H. Bynneman f. H. Toy*, 1573. L.O.C.D.M².+; F.HN.BO³.SMU.U.+
C1ʳ last line begins: 'order'.

25430 — The defense of the aunswere to the Admonition, against the Replie [4711]. fol. *H. Binneman f. H. Toye*, 1574. L.O².C.D(imp.).E².+; F.HN.CAL².ILL.PN.+
A1ʳ catchword: 'fence'; errata on b8ʳ. Answered by 4714, 4715, 25433.

25430.5 — [Anr. ed.] fol. *H. Binneman f. H. Toye*, 1574. L.O.C. D².E.+; F.HD.N.SMU.U.+
A1ʳ catchword: 'fense'; errata corrected; orn. on b8ʳ.

25431 — A godlie sermon preched before the queenes maiestie. 8°. *H. Bynneman f. H. Toy*, 1574. L.L².O⁹.C.DUR⁵.+

25432 — A most godly and learned sermon, preached at Pauls Crosse. [Anon.] 8°. *T. Orwin f. T. Chard*, 1589. L. L²(2).O.O⁹.

25433 — An examination of M. doctor Whytgiftes censures, contained in two tables, [in 25430]. [By W. Fulke?] 8° in 4's. [*English secret Puritan press?*] 1575. L. L².C.
Pr. in very small roman and italic types (about 46 mm.), w. normal 'w' and 'ſh' ligature.

25433.3 **Whitgre, Thomas.** A necessary instruction to cast account by, serving for all such as are unskilfull in the art of arithmaticke, comprehended in two tables. fol(2). *W. Stansby, sold by J. Budge*, 1615. Ent. to L. Greene 28 ap. L⁵(Lemon 147).

Whithalkus, Nicolaus. Christianæ fidei ac veræ religionis compendium. 1575. *See* 5159.

25433.7 **Whiting, Giles.** Short questions and answeres to be learned of such as be ignorant, before they be admitted to the Lords supper. 8°. *T. Orwin f. R. Dexter*, 1593. F.

25434 — [Anr. ed.] 8°. *London*, [*W. Stansby?*] *f. C. L[egge, Cambridge*,] 1613. F.

25435 — [Anr. ed.] 8°. *T. C[otes] f. R. Birde*, 1629. Ass'd from T. Pavier to E. Brewster a. R. Bird 4 au. 1626. DUR (Bamb.).

25436 **Whiting, Nathaniel.** Le hore di recreatione: or, the pleasant historie of Albino and Bellama, by N. W[hiting] master in arts. [In verse.] 12°. *J. D[awson] f. C. G[reene,] sold [by H. Moseley*,] 1637. Ent. as by Whiting to Greene 1 se. L(2, 1 lacks engr. tp).O(lacks engr. tp).; HN.
The engr. tp varies: dated 1637 (HN) or 1638(L).

25436a — [Anr. issue, w. cancel letterpress tp, w. imprint:] *J. D[awson] f. C. G[reene,] sold [by H. Moseley*,] 1638. L.O⁶.; F(lacks engr. tp).DAR(lacks tpp)*.HD.N.WTL.

25437 — [Anr. issue, w. letterpress tp cancelled, and engr. tp altered:] The most pleasante historie of Albino and Bellama. [Init. N. W.] *sould by N. Fussell*, 1639. L.; HN.

25438 **Whitney, Geffrey.** A choice of emblemes and other deuises. [In verse.] 2 pts. 4°. *Leyden, in the house of C. Plantyn, by F. Raphelengius*, 1586. L.O.C.G².M.+; F.HN.HD.N.NY.+
Copies differ: **3ʳ line 18 ends: 'and' or 'behalfe.', the latter (most copies) partly reset and reimposed; both at HD. Quires O–P in 2 impositions, each w. an emblem not in the other: p. 109 has 'Fato non Fortuna', or p. 119 has 'Ex damno alterius' (most copies); both at F.

25439 **Whitney, Isabella.** The copy of a letter, lately written in meeter, by a yonge gentilwoman: to her vnconstant louer. By Is. W[hitney.] 8°. *R. Jhones*, [1567?] Ent. 1566–67. O.
Includes 2 more poems: 'A loueletter' by W. G., i.e. G. Whitney? and one 'Against the inconstancie of his deare foe E. T.' (formerly 25873) signed R. Witc.

25440 — [Heading B2ʳ:] A sweet nosgay, or pleasant posye: contayning a hundred and ten phylosophicall flowers. [Init. Is. W. In verse.] 8°. [*R. Jones*, 1573.] L(lacks tp).
Dedic. dated 20 Oct. 1573.

25441 **Whittell, Robert.** The way to the celestiall paradise. Declaring how a sinner may be saved. In three bookes. 4° in 8's. *E. Griffin f. R. Rounthwaite*, 1620. Ent. 3 se. 1619 (Arber III.652). L.L³⁰.O.C.C⁹.+; ILL.PN².U.

25442 **Whittingham, William.** A brieff discours off the troubles begonne at Franckford Anno Domini 1554. Abowte the Booke off off [*sic*] common prayer. [Anon.] 4°. [*Heidelberg, M. Schirat*,] 1574. O.

25443 — [A variant, w. imprint:] [*Heidelberg, M. Schirat*,] 1575. L.O.C.D.E.+; F.HN.HD.ILL.NY.+

— To my faythfull brethren now afflycted. [1566.] *See* 10389.

— *tr. See* 2001, 2871.

Whittinton, Robert

Because a number of the editions are undated and other difficulties occur, Whittinton has been treated nearly as elaborately as Stanbridge. Transcriptions of title and colophon include line endings when they occur within the portion transcribed. Dating the Treveris editions has been particularly troublesome as their relationship with the later de Worde editions is not clear, especially which printer first published a revised form of each text. On three occasions, however, it seems fairly certain de Worde had the last word; *see* 25477, 25493.3, 25507.5. Should unrecorded copies of undated editions come to light, they should be checked against my own more copious notes. KFP.

Whittinton, Robert—*cont.*

Antilycon

25443.2 — Antilycon, in defensione Ro-/berti VVhitintoni ī florētissima oxo-/niensi Achademia Laureati, con/tra quendam Zoilum suæ/grammaticæ oblatrā/tem sub lyci pro/sopope-/ia. [In verse.] 4° in 6. (*in ædibus VVinandi VVordensis*, 1521 (nonis ja.)) L(C.132.i.37).
    See also 13807, 15606.

Declinationes Nominum

25443.4 — Whytthyntoni Editio./ Declinationes nominū tam latinorum φ̄ grecorum. 4° 8·6. (*nouiter impressa Londoñ per wynandum de worde,*) [1511?] L(G.7550/1).
    B1ʳ 7th line of 95 mm. textura: '& icis'.
25443.6 — [Anr. ed.] 4° 8·6. (*nouiter impressa Londoñ per wynandum de worde,*) [1512?] HN(59572).
    (Formerly 25447) Title is like 25443.4. B1ʳ 7th line of 95 mm. textura: 'et icis'.
25443.8 — [Anr. ed.] whyttyntoni Editio./ Declinationes nominum tam latinorū φ̄ grecorum. 4° in 6's. (*nouiter impressa Londoñ per Rychardū/Pynson,*) [1513?] C⁵(A.2.10/4, with B3,4 misbound after C2).
25444 — [Anr. ed., w. title:] Editio roberti whittinoni lich-feldien-/sis grāmatices magistri & prothouatis An/glie in florentissima Oxoniensi achademia/ laureati./ Declinationes noīm tā latinorū φ̄ grecorū. 4° 8·6. (*Impressa Londoñ. per wynandū de worde,*) [1516?] O¹²(Arch.C.I.1.21).; F.HN(59564).
25444.5 — [Anr. ed.] 4° 8·6. (*Impressa Londoñ. per wynandū de worde,*) [1517?] C²(VIᵈ.8.15/3).; HN(12956, lacks A4).
    In title: 'pthouatis An-/glie ī florētissima Oxoniēsi academia'.
25445 — [Anr. ed.] 4° 8·6. (*per wynandū de worde,* 1517.) L(C. 40. e. 13). O(Mason H 45/2). C⁴(No. 41).; F.HN(79720).
25446 — [Anr. ed.] 4° 8·6. (*per wynandū de worde,* 1519.) L(C.40.e.15).O(Mason H 1/5).; ILL.LC.
25446.5 — [Anr. ed.] whyttyntoni Editio./ Declinationes nominū [etc.] 4° in 6's. (*nouiter impressa Londoñ per Richardū/Pynson,*) [c. 1520.] M(9746).
25447 — Now = 25443.6.
25448 — [Anr. ed.] Editio Roberti whitinoni [etc.] 4° 8·6. (*per wynādum de worde,* 1521.) L(C.40.e.1/6).E(H.32.b.40).MARL. Seville, Biblioteca Colombina.; HN(30006). ILL. Mellon.
25449 — [Anr. ed., w. title:] GRAMMATICAE VVhitin-/tonianæ Liber secundus de no-/minum declinatione. 4° 4·6. (*in ædibus VVinandi de VVorde,* 1523.) L(G.7551/2).C(B1,5 only, Syn.7.52.29).; ILL.
25450 — [Anr. ed.] GRAMMATICAE VVHITIN-/tonianæ liber Secundus [etc.] 4° 4·6. (*in ædibus Richardi Pyn-/sonis,* 1523 (16 my.)) O(Arch.A e.41).CREDI-TON.; HN(61688).
25450.3 — [Anr. ed.] 4° 4·6. (*in ædibus VVinandi de VVorde,* 1523 (de.)) C(Sel.5.75, colophon def.).; CH. Mellon.
    (C copy formerly 25455) Title is like 25449.
25450.7 — [Anr. ed.] Grammaticæ VVhitintonianæ Liber/secūdus [etc.] 4° 4·6. (*in ædibus VVinandi de VVorde,* 1524.) HN(61714).
25451 — [Anr. ed.] 4° 4·6. (*in ædibus Richardi Pyn-/sonis,* 1525 (30 jy.)) L(C.40.e.2/4).DUL. Copenhagen RL. Lord Kenyon.
    Title is like 25450, except: 'VVHITIM-/[*sic*]'.
25452 — [Anr. ed.] Grāmaticę VVhitintonianæ Liber/ secundus [etc.] 4° 4·6. (*in ędibus VVinandi de VVorde,* 1525.) L(G.7555/1).O(Mason H 8a).
    This appears to have A outer forme corrected; e.g. A2ᵛ 1st marginal note has: 'ablatiuo.'
25453 — [A variant, with A outer forme reimposed.] Grammaticę VVhitintonianæ Li/ber secūdus [etc.] (*in ędibus VVinandi de VVorde,* 1525.) L(C.40.e.39/7).O Mason H 8*).P(Sp.26/2).
    This appears to be the earlier variant; e.g. A2ᵛ 1st marginal note has the misprint: 'ablotiuo.'
25453a — [A ghost.]
25454 — [Anr. ed.] 4° 4·6. (*in ędibus VVinandi de VVorde,* 1527.) O(Mason H 27).C¹⁹(lacks C4).; HN(61704).
25455 — Now = 25450.3.
25455.5 — [Anr. ed.] Editio Roberti VVhitintoni/ Lichefeldiensis grammatices . . . nupe-/rime recognita. 4°. [*Southwark,*] (*per me Petrum Treueris,*) [1527–28?] O⁵.C⁵(A.2.11/4).NEK.; ILL.

Whittinton, Robert—*Declinationes Nominum*—*cont.*

25456 — [Anr. ed.] Grāmaticę VVhitintonianæ Liber/ secundus [etc.] 4° 4·6. (*in ędibus VVinandi de VVorde,* 1529.) O(Mason H 12/1, with A2,3 of 25456.7).; ILL.
25456.3 — [Anr. ed.] EDITIO RO-/BERTI VVHITINTONI/ Lichefeldiensis . . . nupe-/rime recognita. 4°. [*Southwark,*] (*per me Petrum Treueris,*) [1529–30?] L⁴.O(Arch.A e.35).
25456.7 — [Anr. ed.] Nominum de-/clinatio,/ Grammaticę VVhitintonianæ Liber/ secundus. 4° 4·6. (*in ędibus VVinandi de VVorde,* 1531.) O(A2,3 only, in Mason H 12/1).; ILL.PN(imp.).
25457 — [Anr. ed.] EDITIO RO/BERTI VVHITINTONI/ Lichefeldiensis . . . nupe-/rime recognita. 4°. [*Southwark,*] (*Impressum diligenterφ̄ correctum per/ me Petrum Treueris,*) [1531?] L(C.40.e.29, plus tp only, Harl.5974/36).O(Douce WW 74/4).; ILL.
25458 — [Anr. ed.] EDITIO ROBERTI WHI-/tintoni Liche-feldiensis . . . nuperime/ recognita. 4°. (*sub prælo diserti viri VVinandi de VVorde,* 1533.) M(9747).
25459 — = 25548.

De Concinnitate

— whittyntoni Editio secūda de Concin-/nitate. 1512, etc. *See* 25541 sqq.

De Heteroclitis Nominibus

25459.2 — De heteroclitis nominibus./ Editio Roberti whittintoni lichfeldien/sis Grammatice magistri: et prothouatis/ anglie in florentissima Oxoniensi achade-/mia Laureati, de heteroclitis nominibus/ et gradibus comparationis. 4° 6·4. (*Londini impres-/sa per wynandum de worde,*) [1513?] HN(59573).
    With the device McK. 23b below the title.
25459.3 — [Anr. ed.] De heteroclitis nominibus. 4° 6·4. (*Londini impressa/ per wynandum de worde,*) [1513?] COR.
    Title continues like 25459.2, but the tp has no device.
25459.4 — [Anr. ed.] De heteroclitis noībus. 4° 6·4. (*Londini impressa/ per wynandū de worde,*) [1514?] C²(VIᵈ.8.15/2).
    Title continues like 25459.2, but line 5 ends: 'nominibus et/'.
25459.5 — [Anr. ed.] De heteroclitis noībus. 4° 6·4. (*Londini impres-/sa p wynādū de worde,*) [1515?] Mellon.
    Title continues like 25459.4.
25459.6 — [Anr. ed.] De heteroclitis nominibus./ EDitio Roberti whittītoni lichfeldiensis Gram/matice magistri: . . . de hete-/roclitis nominibus et gradibus cōparationis. 4° 6·4. (*Impresse Londonii pe* [*sic*] *me Iulianū Notariū,* 1516.) C⁵(A.2.11/2).
25459.8 — [Anr. ed.] De heteroclitis noībus./ Editio Roberti whittintoni lichfeldien-/sis Grāmatice magistri, et prothouatis An/glie . . . de heteroclitis nominibus & gradi/bus comparationis. 4° 6·4. (*Londini impressa/ per wynādum de worde,*) [1516?] C(Syn.7.52.24).
25459.9 — [Anr. ed.] De heteroclitis nominibus. 4° 6·4. (*Lōdini impressa/ per wynādū de worde,*) [1517?] O(Mason H 45/3).C(Syn.7.52.16).M(R4529).; HN(59566).
    (Formerly 25463 and 25477a) Title has line endings like 25459.8, but line 3 has: '& protouatis'.
25459.11 — [Anr. ed.] De heteroclytis nominibus. 4° 6·4. (*Londini impres-/sa p Wynandum de worde,*) [1518?] O(Mason H 29).
    (Formerly 25477b)
25460 — [Anr. ed.] De heteroclitis nominibus. 4° 6·4. (*Oxonie impressa p/ Ioannē Scolar,* 1518 (27 jn.)) O(2 imp., Arch.A f.39 and Auct.4 Q 1.21/20, plus frags.). C(Syn.7.51.20, plus frags.).M(19619).; ILL.
25461 — [Anr. ed.] De heteroclytis nominibus. 4° 6·4. (*Impres-/sa Londini per wynādū de worde,* 1519 (7 id. jy.)) O (Mason H 1/3).MARL.P(Sp.25/1, imp.).; PML.
25461.5 — [Anr. ed.] De heteroclitis nominibus. 4° 6·4. (*Impresse Londo-/nii per me Richardum Pynson,* 1519.) C⁵(A.2.10/5).
25462 — [Anr. ed.] De heteroclytis nominibus. 4° 6·4. (*Londini apud wynādū de worde,* 1520.) L(C.40.e.1/4).O(Arch.A e.24).
25463 — Now = 25459.9.
25464 — [Anr. ed.] 4° 6·4. (*Londini apud winandū de worde,* 1521.) L(tp only, Harl.5974/20).O(Mason H 4).C⁴(M.25.3). DNPK. Seville, Biblioteca Colombina.; HN(30005). ILL.

Whittinton, Robert—*De Heteroclitis Nominibus*—*cont.*

25464.5 — [Anr. ed., w. title:] De heteroclitis nominibus./ Grāmaticæ VVhitintonianæ Liber/tertius de nominum hete-/roclisi. 4°. (*in ędibus VVinandi de Vorde*, 1522 (id. mr.)) YK(lacks B1,2).
  HD has a single leaf, B2, bd. in 25560.7 and differing from all known eds., which may belong to this.

25465 — [Anr. ed.] 4° 6.4. (*per me Richardum/Pynson*, 1523.) O(Arch.A e.42).CREDITON(lacks B4).

25466 — [Anr. ed.] 4°. (*in ędibus VVinandi de VVorde*, 1523 (id. fb.)) O(Mason H 5).M(21531).; HN(61691).

25466.5 — [Anr. ed.] 4°. (*in ædibus VVinandi de VVorde*, 1524 (cał. fb.)) CH.

25467 — [Anr. ed.] 4°. (*in ędibus VVinandi de VVorde*, 1524 (19 de.)) L(G.7551/3).O(Mason H 28).; ILL.

25468 — [Anr. ed.] 4°. (*in ædibus VVinandi de VVorde*, 1525 (pridie cał. au.)) C(Sel.5.77).; HN(61715).

25468.5 — [Anr. ed.] 4° 6.4. (*per me Richardum/Pynson*, 1525.) DUL.

25469 — [Anr. ed.] 4°. (*apud prœlum VVinquin* [sic] *de/VVorde, nuper ad purum restituit Idem Valesi⁹*, 1526 (ad id. jy.)) L(C.40.e.39/6).P(lacks A1,4).; PML.

25470 — [Anr. ed.] 4°. (*apud prœlum VVinandi de VVorde*, 1527 (ad id. my.)) L(G.7555/2).O(Arch.A e.34, lacks tp).c¹⁹.

05471 — [Anr. ed.] 4° 6.4. (*per me Richardum/ Pynson*, 1527.) L(C.40.e.2/5). Copenhagen RL. Lord Kenyon.

25471.5 — [Anr. ed.] DE HETEROCLITIS NO-/minibus/ Grammaticæ VVhitintonianæ/ Liber tertius de nomi-/num heteroclisi. 4°. [*Southwark*,] (*per me Petrum Treueris*) [1527?] L(C.40.e.25, plus tp only, Harl.5974/24).O⁵.M(9757).NEK.SHR.; ILL.
  (Formerly 25473) Collates A–B⁴.

25472 — [Anr. ed.] De heteroclitis Nominibus./ [etc.] 4°. (*apud prœlum VVynandi de/VVorde*, 1529 (20 my.)) M (9760, quire B only).M².; HN(61708).

25473 — Now = 25471.5.

25474 — [Anr. ed., revised and enlarged.] 4°. [*Southwark*,] (*per me Petrum Treueris*,) [1529–30?] L(C.40.e.26).L⁴. c⁵(A.2.11/6).
  Title is like 25471.5. Collates [–]⁴ B–E⁴; recto of 2nd leaf, last line: 'hebreū'.

25474.3 — [Anr. ed.] DE HETEROCLITIS NOMINIBUS/ ET DE VLTIMA CORRE-/CTIONE./ . . . M.D.XXXI. 4°. (*per me VVynãdum de VVorde*, 1531 (mr.)) M (9760, quire A only).; ILL.
  (Formerly 25476) Collates A–C⁴ D⁶.

25474.7 — [Anr. ed. of orig. text, A–B⁴.] De heteroclitis/ nomini-bus,/ Grammaticæ [etc.] 4°. (*in ędibus VVinandi de Vorde*, 1531 (10 no.)) ILL.

25475 — [Anr. ed. of the revised text.] 4°. [*Southwark*,] (*per me Petrum Treueris*,) [1531?] L(C.40.e.27).O(Douce WW 74/2).; F.BALT.ILL.
  Title is like 25471.5, except '/minibus./' and 'tertius qe [sic]'. Collates A–E⁴; A2ʳ last line: 'hebreum'.

25476 — Now = 25474.3.

25477 — [Anr. ed. of the revised text, w. more marginal notes.] DE HETEROCLITIS NO-/minibus VVhitintoni æditio re-/centior, et limatior, . . . M.D.XXXIII. 4°. (*per me VVinandum de VVorde*, 1533.) L(C.40.e.30).M(9764).; F.
  Collates A–E⁴; A1ᵛ has verses against Treveris.

25477a — Now = 25459.9.
25477b — Now = 25459.11.

De Magistratibus

— De magistratibus veterum Romanorū. 1515, etc. *See* 25525.3 sqq.

De Metris

25478 — whittyntoni Editio cum interpretamento/ Frācisci Nigri diomedes de accētu [etc.] 1515. Now = pt. 2 of 25509.7.
— For other eds. *see* 25509.3 sqq.

De Nominum Generibus

25479 — [Early version, usually collating A⁸ B–C⁴.] Opusculum affabre recognitum/ et ad vnguem elimatum./ De nominum generibus./ De verborum preteritis et supinis. [Anon.] 4° 8.4. (*Here endeth Opusculum affabre Enprynted at/ London . . . by wynkyn de worde*,) [1511?] L(G.7550/2).

Whittinton, Robert—*De Nominum Generibus*—*cont.*

25479.2 — [Anr. ed.] 4° in 6's. (*Here endeth Opusculum affabre Enprynted at/ London by (Richarde Pynson*,)) [1512?] O(Arch.A e.38).
  (Formerly 25495) Though this collates A–C⁶, it is the same text as 25479.

25479.3 — [Anr. ed.] 4° 8.4. (*Here endeth Opusculum affabre enprynted at Lon-/don by Richarde Pynson*,) [1515?] c⁵(A.2.10/3).

25479.5 — [Anr. ed., w. title:] Whittintoni editio secunda./ Opusculum affabre recognitum et ad vnguem eli-/matum./ De noīm generibus. [etc.] 4° 8.4. (*Here endeth Opusculū affabre Enprynted at Lon/don . . . by wynkyn de worde*,) [1516?] HN(17289, lacks B1).

25479.6 — [Anr. issue, w. quire C reset.] (*Finit Opusculū Affabre. Impressum Londoñ./ þ wynandū de worde*,) [1517?] O(Mason H 18).; HN(59563).BR(Annmary Brown Memorial Library). Mellon(w. quire C of 25479.8).
  (Formerly 25496)

25479.8 — [Anr. ed.] whittintoni editio secundo [sic]./ Opusculum affabre recognitum et ad vnguē eli-/matum. 4° 8.4. (*Finis* [sic] *opusculū affabre. Impressum Lōdoñ. þ/ wynandū de worde*,) [1517?] M(R4534).; Mellon (quire C only, with 25479.6).

25479.9 — [Anr. ed.] Whittyntoni editio secundo [sic]./ Opusculum affabre recognitū & ad vnguem eli-/matum. 4° 8.4. (*Finit opusculū affabre. Impressum Londoñ. þ/ Wynandū de worde*,) [1518?] O(Mason H 45/4).

25479.11 — [Anr. ed.] Whittyntoni editio secunda./ Opusculum affabre recognitum et ad vnguem/ elimatum. 4° 8.4. (*Finis* [sic] *opusculū affabre. Impressum Londoñ, þ/ Wynandū de worde*,) [1518?] c²(VIᵈ.8.15/4).

25479.14 — [Anr. ed.] Opusculū Roberti whitintoni Lichfel/diēsis Oxonie laureati affabre recognitū./ De nominum generibus./ De verborum preteritis et supinis. 4° 8.4. (*per wynãdū de worde*, 1520.) HD.

25479.15 — [Anr. ed.] whittintoni editio secunda./ Opusculum [etc.] 4° 8.4. (*ex officina Richardi/Pynsonis*,) 1520 (nonis se.)) M(9753).

25479.17 — [Anr. ed.] Opusculum Roberti whitintoni Lichfeldiensis/ [etc.] 4° 8.4. (*in edibus winandi de worde*, 1522.) M(9749).

25480 — [A ghost.]

25480.3 — [Later version, usually collating A⁴ B⁶ C⁴.] GRAMMATICES Primæ partis/ Liber primus Roberti VV. L. L./ nuperrime recogni-/tus./ De nominum generibus. 4° 4.6. (*ex typis VVinandi VVordensis*, 1521 (cal. fb.)) O(Arch.A e.25, lacks C4).; PML.

25480.7 — [Anr. ed.] 4° 4.6. (*ex typis VVinandi VVordensis*, 1521 (pridie nonas fb.)) L(T.1340/2, lacks C4).MARL. SHR(lacks C4). Seville, Biblioteca Colombina(lacks C4).
  (Formerly 25483)

25481 — [Anr. ed.] 4° 4.6. (*ex typis VVinãdi VVordēsis*, 1521 (id. jn.)) M(21530).; ILL. Mellon.

25482 — [Anr. ed.] 4° 4.6. (*ex typis VVinandi VVordensis*, 1521 (pridie id. oc.)) L(C.40.e.1/2, lacks C4).

25483 — Now = 25480.7.

25483.5 — [Anr. ed.] 4° 4.6. (*ex typis VVinandi de VVorden*, 1522 (pridie cał. au.)) P(Sp.25/1a, lacks quire A).

25484 — [Anr. ed.] 4° 4.6. (*ex typis VVinandi de VVorden*, 1522 (pridie cał. se.)) ILL.

25484.5 — [Anr. ed.] 4° 4.6. (*ex typis VVinandi VVordensis*, 1522 (pridie nonas se.)) CH.

25485 — [Anr. ed.] 4° 4.6. (*in ædibus Richardi Pynsoñ*, 1523 (mr.)) O(Arch.A e.44).

25486 — [Anr. ed.] 4° 4.6. (*ex typis VVinandi de VVorden*, 1524 (13 kał. mr.)) L(G.7551/1).
  In title: 'VVhitītoni. L.'

25486.3 — [Anr. ed.] 4° 4.6. (*ex typis VVinandi de VVorden*, 1524 (13 kał. mr.)) HN(61689).
  In title: 'Vhitintoni. L. L.'

25486.7 — [Anr. ed.] 4° 4.6. (*in ædibus Richardi Pynsoñ*, 1525 (ap.)) CREDITON(lacks B3,4).DUL. Lord Kenyon.
  In title: 'VV. L. L.'

25487 — [Anr. ed.] 4° 4.6. (*ex typis VVinandi de VVorde*, 1525 (8 kał. my.)) O(Mason H 1/6).; HN(61712).
  In title: 'VV. L. L.'

25488 — [Anr. ed.] 4° 4.6. (*ex typis VVinandi de VVorde*, 1526 (3 kalendas se.)) O(Douce WW 73/1).G².
  In title: 'VVitintoni. L.'

25488.5 — [Anr. ed.] 4° 4.6. (*ex typis VVinandi de VVorde*, 1526 (3 kalen. se.)) C(Sel.5.78, with B3,4 misbound after A2).c¹⁹.
  In title: 'VVhitītoni. L.'

Whittinton, Robert—*De Nominum Generibus*—*cont.*

25489 — [Anr. ed.] 4° 4·6. (*ex typis VVinandi VVordensis*, 1527 (pridie nonas mr.)) O(Arch.A e.29, lacks C4).P (Sp.26/1).
  In title: 'VV. L. L.'

25489.3 — [Anr. ed.] 4° 4·6. (*in edibus Richardi Pynsoñ*, 1527 (my.)) Copenhagen RL.
  In title: 'VV. L. L.'

25489.7 — [Anr. ed.] 4° 4·6. [*Southwark*,] (*per me Petrum Treueris*,) [1527.] L(C.40.e.23).O(Tanner 239/5).O⁵.C⁵(A.2. 11/5).NEK.+; CU.ILL.
  (Formerly 25493) In title: 'VV L. L.' Pref. on tp verso is dated id. Aug. 1527.

25490 — [Anr. ed.] 4° 4·6. (*ex typis VVinandi VVordēsis*, 1528 (pridie kal. jy.)) O(Mason H 46).
  In title: 'VVhitintoni. Li. L.'

25491 — [Anr. ed.] 4° 4·6. (*ex typis VVinandi VVordensis*, 1529 (pridie kal. jn.)) L(C.40.e.39/2).O(Mason H 12/2).; HN(61707).
  In title: 'VVhitintoni. Li. L.' Pref. dated 1 June 1529.

25491.3 — [Anr. issue, w. quire A reset.] (*ex typis VVinandi VVordensis*, 1529 (pridie kal. jn.)) O(Mason H 17, lacks C4).
  In title: 'VVhitintoni. L. L'. Pref. incorrectly dated id. Mar. 1521, like 25486 sq., 25488, and 25490; possibly the earlier issue.

25491.7 — [Anr. ed.] 4°. (*Expliciunt genera nominum reuisa re-/ cognitaɟ . . . per Petrum/ Treueris/ in suburbio . . . (Sowthwarke*)) [1530?] L(frags., Harl.5974/21–3).L⁴.
  In title: 'florentissimū'.

25492 — [Anr. ed.] 4°. (*Expliciunt genera nominū reuisa re-/ cognitaɟ . . . per me Petrum/ Treueris/ in suburbio . . . (Southwarke*)) [1531?] L(C.40.e.24).O(Douce WW 74/5).; F.ILL(2).
  In title: 'florētissimū'.

25493 — Now = 25489.7.

25493.3 — [Anr. ed., w. title:] ROBERTI VVhitintoni Lichfeldi-/ ensis, poætæ laureati æditio recentior,/ primæ partis grammatices/ liber secundus,/ de nominum generi-bus. 4°. (*ex typis VVinandi Vordensis*, 1533.) ILL (lacks D4).
  Whittinton's pref. attacks Treueris.

25493.7 — [Anr. ed.] 4°. (*ex typis VVinandi VVordensis*, 1533 (6 au.)) HN(81976, lacks D4).

25494 — [Anr. ed.] 4°. (*ex typis VVinandi VVordensis*, 1534 (16 oc.)) L(C.40.e.2/2, lacks A1,2).

25495 — Now = 25479.2.

25496 — Now = 25479.6.

De Octo Partibus

25496.3 — Roberti whittintoni lichfeldiensis grā/matices magistri et prothouatis Anglie/ in florentissima Oxoniensi achademia lau/reati de octo partibus orationis. 4° 4·6. (*per/ me Wynandum de Worde*,) [1514?] O¹² (lacks C4).; HN(59574).

25496.5 — [Anr. ed.] 4° 4·8. (*per me Ri-/chardū Pynson*,) [1515?] C⁵(A.2.10/2).
  In title: '& prothouatis Anglie in/ florētissima . . . laurea/ti'.

25496.7 — [Anr. ed.] 4° 4·6. (*p/ me wynanduȝ de worde*,) [1516?] O(Mason H 45/1).C²(VIᵈ.8.15/1, lacks A1).; Scheide.
  Title like 25496.3, except 'Anglie in/ . . . laurea-/ti'.

25497 — Now = 25498.7.

25498 — [Anr. ed.] Roberti whittinoti [*sic*, etc.] 4° 4·6. (*per me Iulianū/ notary*, 1516 (27 au.)) C(Sel.5.74).

25498.3 — [Anr. ed.] Roberti whittintoni Lichfeldiēsis [etc.] 4° 4·6. (*p me Wynādum de worde*,) [1517?] C(Sel.5.156/1, lacks C4).; HN(59562).

25498.7 — [Anr. ed.] Robert [*sic*] wihittintoni [*sic*, etc.] 4° 4·6. (*p me wynādū de worde*,) [1518?] L(68.b.25/2).M (R4530).
  (Formerly 25497 and 25504a)

25499 — [Anr. ed.] Roberti whittintoni alma in vniuersi-/tate Oxoniensi laureati de octo partib⁹ ora/tionis opus-culū: de nouo recognitum. 4° 4·6. (*per Wynādum de worde*, 1519 (8 id. ap.)) L(C.40.e.16).O(Mason H 1/2).C(Adv.b.70.15 (p. 80), C4 only).; F.

25500 — [Anr. ed.] 4° 4·6. (*in edibus winandi de worde*, 1521 (id. jy.)) L(C.40.e.1/1).MARL. Seville, Biblioteca Colombina.; F.ILL.
  In title: 'orationis opusculū:/ iterum recognitū.'

25501 — [Anr. ed.] 4° 4·6. (*in ędibus VVinandi de VVorde*, 1522 (id. ap.)) ILL.
  In title: 'orationis/ ęditio.'

Whittinton, Robert—*De Octo Partibus*—*cont.*

25502 — [Anr. ed.] 4° 4·6. (*in ædibus Richardi Pynsoñ.*, 1522.) O(Mason H 23).CREDITON.DUL.M(R4531).
  In title: 'orationis opuscu-/lum: iterum recogni-tum.'

25502.5 — [Anr. ed.] 4°. (*in edibus Henricum* [*sic*] *Pepwell*, 1523 (id. fb.)) L(colophon only, Harl.5974/40).

25503 — [Anr. ed.] 4° 4·6. (*in ædibus VVinandi de VVorde*, 1523 (de.)) L(G.7546).O(A 4.11 Linc.).LONGLEAT. Broxbourne(E).; HN(2 copies 61687 and 61711). CU.
  In title: 'orationis/ æditio.'

25504 — [Anr. ed.] 4° 4·6. (*in edibus VVinandi de Vorde*, 1525 (ja.)) O(Mason H 7).

25504a — Now = 25498.7.

25505 — [Anr. ed.] 4° 4·6. (*in ędibus VVinandi de VVorde*, 1527 (19 fb.)) O(Mason H 24).C¹⁹(lacks C4).; HN(61702).

25505.5 — [Anr. ed.] 4° 4·6. (*in ædibus Richardi Pynsoñ.*, 1527.) L(Lord Kenyon's copy).
  In title: 'orationis opuscu-/lum: iterum recogni-tum.'

25506 — [Anr. ed.] 4° 4·6. (*in ędibus VVinandi de Vorde*, 1529 (29 my.)) L(C.40.e.39/1).M(21533).
  In title: 'Robertti [*sic*] . . . orationis/ æditio.'

25506.3 — [Anr. ed.] 4° 4·6. [*Southwark*,] (*per me Petrum Treueris*,) [1530?] L⁴.O⁵.MARL(lacks C4).NEK.
  In title: 'Roberti . . . orationis/ æditio.'

25506.7 — [Anr. ed.] De octo partibus/ whitintoni,/ Authoris distichon./ 4° 4·6. (*in ędibus VVinandi de VVorde*, 1531 (oc.)) BALT³.

25507 — [Anr. ed.] ROBRTI [*sic*], VVHITINTONI/ alma . . . orationis./ æditio. 4° 4·6. [*Southwark*,] (*Impressum diligenterɟ enucleatum per me/ Petrum Treueris*,) [1531?] L(C.40.e.2/1).O(Douce WW 74/1)C⁵(A.2.11/3).

25507.5 — [Anr. ed.] De octo partibus/ whitintoni,/ æditio nouis-sima. 4° 4·6. (*in ędibus VVinandi de VVorde*, 1533.) ILL.
  On the verso of the tp are 6 lines of verse against Treueris.

25508 — [Anr. ed.] 4° 4·6. (*in ædibus VVinandi de VVorde*, 1533 (3 se.)) L(C.40.e.76).

25509 — = 23143.

De Syllabarum Quantitate

Note: The colophons below are found at the end of pt. 2, except for 25517.

25509.3 — whyttyntoni lych-/feldiensis Editio/ Secunda pars grammatices./ De sillaba et eius quantitate./ (whittyn-toni Editio cum interpretamēto/ Francisci Nigri diomedes de accentu [etc.]) 2 pts. 4° 8·4. (*per wynan-dum de worde*,) [1512?] O(Mason H 26).
  (Formerly 25525)

25509.5 — [Anr. ed.] Roberti whyttyntoni/ lychfeldiensis Editio./ Secunda pars [etc.] 2 pts. 4° 8·4. (*per wynandū de worde*, 1513 (12 au.)) HN(59570).CU.
  Tp has the device McK. 19.

25509.7 — [Anr. ed.] Roberti whittintoni lychfeldiēsis editio./ 2 pts. 4° 8·4. (*per me Richardum pynson*, 1515.) L (C.40.e.12, pt. 2 only).O¹¹(frags. of pt. 1).C⁵(A.2. 10/8). Lord Kenyon(pt. 2 only).; PML.
  (Pt. 2 formerly 25478)

25510 — [Anr. ed.] Roberti whittintoni/ lichfeldiensis Editio./ 2 pts. 4° 8·4. (*per wynandū de worde*, 1516.) O(Mason H 45/7).; BO(pt. 1 only, imp.).

25511 — [Anr. ed.] Roberti whyttyntoni/ lychfeldiensis Editio./ 2 pts. 4° 8·4. (*per Iulianum Notari*, 1516 (23 jy.)) C (pt. 1: Sel.5.82; pt. 2: Sel.5.76).
  Tp has the woodcut Hodnett 2168.

25511.5 — [Anr. ed.] Roberti whittintoni Lichfeldiensis de/ sylla-barum quantitate Editio./ Secunda pars grammas-tices./ (whittintoni editio cum interpretamēto . . . de accentu.) 2 pts. 4° 8·4. (*nup impres-/sa Londoñ. per wynandum de worde*, 1517 (10 au.)) C²(VIᵈ.8.15/7, lacks colophon).; ILL.

25512 — [Anr. ed.] whittintoni primā in Anglia Lauri coro-/ nam gestantis de sillabarū quātitate conge-/ries. (whittintoni editio cum interpretamento . . . de accētu.) 2 pts. 4° 8·4. (*nuperrime recognita: . . . im-/pressa Londini per wynandū de worde*, 1519 (7 Id⁹ mr.)) L(C.122.bb.1/1).; HN(59569).CAL(pt. 2 only).

25513 — = 25514.

Whittinton, Robert—*De Syllabarum Quantitate*—*cont.*

25514 — [Anr. ed.] Roberti whitintoni Lauricomi Lichfel/diensis de syllabarū quantitatibus Opus-/culū recognitū Anno dñi XIX. supra sesqui-/millesimum. (whitintoni editio cū interpretamēto Frā/cisci nigri Diomedes de Accentu.) 2 pts. 4° 8·4. (*nuperrime re-/cognita:* . . . *impressa Lōdini per winādū de worde,* 1519 (kał. no.)) L(C.40.e.17).O(Mason H 1/8).

25515 — [Anr. ed.] Roberti VVhitintoni L. Secunda gram-/maticę pars de syllabarū quantitate./ . . . nuprime recēsita, [etc.] (VVHITINTONI ęditio cum inter-/pretamēto Fran-/cisci nigri. Diomedes de accentu.) 2 pts. 4° 4·6. (*in ædibus VVinādi de VVorden,* 1521.) O(Mason H 3, lacks 2nd B2,5).MARL. Seville, Biblioteca Colombina.; CH(quire A of pt. 1 only).ILL.
In 1st title: 'Calco-/gra-/phorum'; in 2nd title: 'obseruanda.'

25515a — [Anr. ed.] 2 pts. 4° 4·6. (*in ædibus VVinādi de VVorden,* 1521.) L(C.40.e.1/7,8).O8(pt. 1 only).G4.P(Sp.25/3). SHR.; CH(B–M of pt. 1 only).HD(pt. 2 only). Mellon.
In 1st title: 'Calco-/gra-/phorū'; in 2nd title: 'obseruāda.'

25516 — = pt. 2 of 25517.

25517 — [Anr. ed.] 2 pts. 4° 4·6. [Pt. 1:] (*in ædibus Richardi Pynsoñ.,* 1522 (24 jy.)) [Pt. 2:] (*in ædibus Richardi Pynsonis,* 1523 (10 jy.)) O(Mason H 25 and Arch.A e.40, both pt. 1 only; pt. 2: Arch.A e.46).CREDITON. DUL. Lord Kenyon(pt. 1 only).; HN(61694–5). Vermont U(pt. 1 only).
(Pt. 2 formerly 25516)

25518 — [Anr. ed.] 2 pts. 4° 4·6. (*in ædibus VVinandi de VVorden,* 1524.) L(G.7548).O(A 13.16a Linc.).; HN(2, 61718 and 17288).KAN.
In 1st title 'gram-/maticæ . . . syllabarū quantitate,/ accētu.'

25519 — = 25520.

25520 — [Anr. ed.] 2 pts. 4° 4·6. (*in ædibus VVinādi de VVorde,* 1526.) O(pt. 1: Arch.A e.30; pt. 2: Arch.A e.26). C(frags. in Syn.7.52.27).C19(lacks 2nd C6).G2.P (Sp.26/4).; ILL(1 imp., plus pt. 1 only, imp.).
(Formerly also 25519 and 25524) In 1st title: 'gram-/maticę . . . syllabarum quantitate./ accētu.'

25521 — [Anr. ed.] 2 pts. 4° 4·6. (*in ædibus VVinādi de VVorde,* 1528.) L(C.40.e.39/8, imp.).O(Douce WW 73/3, pt. 1 only).M(17698).; HN(61709).ILL(pt. 1 only). MEL(pt. 1 only).
(Pt. 1 formerly also 25523) In 1st title: 'gram-/maticæ . . . syllabarū quantitate,/ accentu.'; 2nd A1r line 6 from bottom: 'quē'.

25521.5 — [Anr. issue, with quires A, D, G–H of pt. 1 and A of pt. 2 reset.] 2 pts. (*in ædibus VVinādi de VVorde,* 1528.) O(Mason H 10).
In 1st title: 'gram-/maticę . . . syllabarū quantitate./ accētu.'; 2nd A1r line 6 from bottom: 'quem'.

25522 — [Anr. ed.] 2 pts. 4° partly 4·6. [*Southwark,*] (*in officina Petri/ Treueris,*) [1529?] L(C.40.e.2/9).L4.O(Mason H 34, imp., plus pt. 2 only: Douce WW 73/3).C5 (A.2.11/8).NEK.+; ILL(imp.).
In 1st title: 'ROBERTI,/'.

25523 — = pt. 1 of 25521.
25524 — = pt. 1 of 25520.
25525 — Now = 25509.3.

De Synonymis (*Lucubrationes*) and *De Magistratibus*

25525.3 — [Pt. 2; AA4.] De magistratibus veterum Romanorū. 4°. [*W. de Worde,*] (1515 (octauo kal. mr.)) c2 (VId.8.15/8).
c2 bd. w. 25526.5.

25525.5 — [Anr. ed.] 4°. [*R. Pynson,*] (1515 (actauo [*sic*] kal. mr.)) c5(A.2.10/7).
c5 bd. w. 25527.8.

25525.7 — [Anr. ed.] 4°. [*W. de Worde,*] (1517 (9 kal. au.)) L (C.40.e.14).; HN(59565).
L bd. w. 25527; HN w. 25527.2. Reprinted as E4 of 25528 sqq.

25526 — Now = 25527.6.

25526.5 — [Pt. 1.] Roberti whittintoni lichfeldiensis grā-/matices magistri et prothouatis Anglie in/ florentissima Oxoniensi academia laurea-/ti lucubrationes. De noīm appellatiuorū, deorū, . . . locorumꝗ synonimis. . . . De veterū romanorū magistratibus. 4° 8·4. (*p wynandū de wor-/de,* 1517.) C2(VId.8.15/6).
c2 bd. w. 25525.3. This is the only example of a dated colophon to pt. 1 except for Pynson's 25529.

Whittinton, Robert—*De Synonymis*—*cont.*

25527 — [Anr. issue, with D outer sheet reset.] (*per wynandū de wor/de,*) [1517?] L(C.40.e.14).O(4° E 6 Art.Seld.). (Formerly also 25540) L bd. w. 25525.7.

25527.2 — [Anr. ed.] 4° 8·4. (*per wynandum/ de worde,*) [1517?] HN(59567).
HN bd. w. 25525.7. In title: 'whittintoni . . . oxoniensi . . . deoꝛ, . . . synonimis.'

25527.3 — [Anr. ed.] 4° 8·4. (*per wynandum/ de worde,* [1517?] O (Mason H 45/6).
(Formerly 25539) In title: 'wittintoni [*sic*] . . . gram/matices . . . in flo/rentissima Oxoniensi achademia . . . deorū, . . . sinonymis.'

25527.5 — [Anr. ed.] 4° 8·4. (*per wynandum/ de worde,*) [1518?] O(Arch.A e.32).
(Formerly 25538) In title: 'whittintoni . . . grā-/matices . . . in/ florētissima . . . achademia . . . deorū, . . . synonymis.'

25527.6 — [Anr. issue, with quires A–B reset.] (*per wynandum/ de worde,*) [1518?] C4(N.23.1). Broxbourne (E).
(Formerly 25526) In title: 'whitintoni lichfeldiensis, grāma-/tices . . . lucu-/brationes. De synoni-/mis'.

25527.8 — [Anr. ed.] 4° 8·6. (*per Richardū/ pynchon* [*sic*],) [1518?] O12(lacks B6).C5(A.2.10/7).
c5 is bd. w. 25525.5. In title: 'whitintoni lichfel-/diensis, grāmati-/ces . . . lucubrationes./ De synoni-/mis.'

25528 — [Anr. ed. of pts. 1 and 2.] Roberti whittintoni . . . lucubraitones [*sic*]./ De synonimis/ 4° 8·4. (*p me wynandū de worde,* 1519 (9 kał. fb.)) O(Mason H 1/7).SHR.; PML.

25529 — [Anr. ed.] 4° 8·6. (*per Richardum/ Pynsonem,* 1520.) c(Adv.b.70.15 (p. 112), last leaf only).DUL. Lord Kenyon.
This is the only later ed. not to include De Magistratibus.

25530 — [Anr. ed.] 4° 8·4. (*in edibus Winādi de Worde,* 1521.) L (2 copies, G.7552 and C.40.e.1/9).MARL. Seville, Biblioteca Colombina.

25531 — [Anr. ed.] Roberti VVhitintoni Lichfeldiensis lucu-/brationes. De synonimis. 4° 8·4. (*in ędibus VVinādi de VVorde,* 1522.) DNPK.P(Sp.25/4). Saffron Walden Museum(lacks E4).; ILL.

25532 — [Anr. ed.] 4°. (*in ædibus Richardi Pynsonis,* 1523 (16 jn.)) L(C.40.e.2/8).O(Mason H 16).CREDITON. LIV3.; HN(61693, imp.).

25533 — [Anr. ed.] 4° 8·4. (*in ędibus VVinandi de VVorde,* 1523 (au.)) L(C.40.e.20).C(Sel.5.80).C19.; CH.

25534 — [Anr. ed.] 4° 8·4. (*in ędibus VVinandi de VVorde,* 1525 (fb.)) L(2 copies, G.7553 and 68.b.25/3).C5(A.2.11/9).; HN(61719, lacks A3–6).CH.

25535 — [Anr. ed.] 4° 8·4. (*in ędibus VVinādi de VVorde,* 1527 (fb.)) L(C.40.e.39/4).O(Arch.A e.31).P(Sp.26/5).; F (lacks C4).

25536 — [Anr. ed.] 4° 8·4. (*in ędibus VVinnndi* [*sic*] *de VVorde,* 1529 (mr.)) O(Mason H 11).C(SSS.17.25).G2.; HN (quires D–E only, in 61706).CH.

25536.5 — [Anr. ed.] 4° 8·4. [*Southwark, P. Treveris,* 1531?] L4. O5.MARL(lacks E4).NEK.SHR(E4 only).; F(C8 only, in 25535).HD(C2,4,5,7 only).
In title: 'lucus [*sic*]/brationes./ De synonimis/'.

25537 — [Anr. ed.] 4°. (*in ædibus VVinandi de VVorde,* 1533.) O(Douce WW 74/3, quires F–G only).; ILL.

25538 — Now = 25527.5.
25539 — Now = 25527.3.
25540 — = 25527.

Libellus Epigrammaton

25540.5 — Opusculū Roberti whittintoni in florē/tissima Oxoniensi achademia Laureati./ . . . Libellus epygrammaton. [In verse.] 4° 4·6·8. (*per me wynandū de worde,* 1519 (10 kal. my.)) L(C.132.i.36).C4(M.29.7).C5(A.2.13/1, lacks tp).ETON.; HN(59198).

Syntaxis (*De Concinnitate*)

25541 — whittyntoni Editio secūda de Concin-/nitate grāmatices et Cōstructione. 4° 8·4. *Noui-/ter impressa Londoniis, Per wynandum/ de worde,* (1512 (3 se.)) O(Mason H 47).; HN(59571).

25541.5 — [Anr. ed.] Roberti whittintoni lichfeldiensis gram-/matices magistri et prothouatis anglie in flo-/rētissima Oxoniēsi achademia laureati. Edi/tio de cōcinnitate grammatices et cōstructiōe. 4° 8·4. (*per wi/nandū de Worde,* 1516.) M(R4532).

Whittinton, Robert—*Syntaxis*—cont.

25542 — [Anr. ed.] whittyntoni Editio de consinitate grāmatices et Con/structione. 4° [8.4]. *nouiter impressa Eboꝝ Per me Ursyñ Mylner,* (1516 (20 de.)) L(68.b.21).

25543 — [Anr. ed.] Roberti whittintoni. . . . Editio de concinnitate grammatices/ et constructione./ 4° [8.4]. (*per/ winandū de worde,* 1517.) L(G.7545).O(Mason H 45/5).C⁵(A.2.11/1).

25544 — Now = 25545.5.

25545 — [Anr. ed.] 4° [8.4]. (*per/ winandū de worde,* 1518.) O (Mason H. 20).C²(VIᵈ.8.15/5, lacks A1).

25545.3 — [Anr. ed.] 4° [8.4]. (*per wynandū de worde,* 1518.) HN (59568).

25545.5 — [Anr. ed.] 4° in 8's. (*per/ me Richardum Pynson,* 1518 (id. de.)) O(Mason H 21, lacks D6).O¹²(imp.).C⁵ (A.2.10/6).
(Formerly 25544)

25546 — [Anr. ed.] Re-/cognitū anno dñi xix. supra sesquimil-lesi/mum. 4° [8.4]. (*per winandū de worde,* 1519 (id. jn.)) O(Mason H 1/4, lacks D6).O³(frags.).C(Sel.5.156/2, lacks A1).; CU.

25547 — [Anr. ed.] Syntaxis./ Roberti VVhitintoni . . . de Syn-taxi,/ siue constructione recen-/sitū [1521] Idi./ Februa./ 4° [4.6]. (*in ędibus VVinādi VVordensis,* 1520 (Ibib⁹ [*sic*] mr.)) L(C.40.e.1/5).SHR(D–G only, with 25547.5).; ILL(quire A only, with 25548). Mellon.

25547.3 — [Anr. ed.] Syntaxis./ Roberti VVhitintoni Lich/feldien-sis, . . . de Synta/xi, siue constructione,/ recensitū [1521] /Idi. Iuñ./ 4°. [*R. Pynson,* 1521.] Oberlin C(imp., w. C2–4 of 25554).
With tp border McK.&F. 7. This is the only ed. mentioning the month of June in the title.

25547.5 — [Anr. ed.] 4° [4.6]. (*in ędibus VVinādi VVordensis,* 1521 (Idib⁹ oc.)) MARL.SHR(A–C only, with 25547).
In title: '/anno. Idibus Februa./'

25548 — [Anr. ed.] Syntaxis./ Roberti VV. L. in florentissima Oxo-/niensi academia laureati Opuscu-/lum de Syn-taxi, siue cōstru-/ctione recensitū [1521] Idi. Februa./ 4° [4.6]. (*in ædibus VVinandi VVordensis,* 1521 (no.)) O(Mason H 48). Seville, Biblioteca Colombina.; ILL (quires B–G only, with A of 25547). Mellon.
(Formerly also 25459)

25549 — [Anr. ed.] Syntaxis./ Roberti VV. L. in florentissima Oxoni-/ensi . . . recensitum [1521] Idi. Februa./ 4°. (*in ædibus Richardi Pynsonis,* 1523 (12 my.)) O (Arch.A e.43).

25550 — [Anr. ed.] SINTAXIS./ Roberti VVhitintoni . . . de Syntaxi,/ siue constructione recen-/sitū [1522] Idi./ Februa./ 4° [4.6]. (*in ædibus VVinandi VVordensis,* 1524 (Idibus ja.)) HN(61692).ILL.

25551 — [Anr. ed.] 4°⸴[4.6]. (*in ædibus VVinandi VVordensis,* 1524 (Idibus no.)) L(G.7549).O(Mason H 6).c(Sel.5.81).; HN(61701).CU.

25552 — [Anr. ed.] SYNTAXIS. 4° [4.6]. (*in ędibus VVinandi de VVorde,* 1525 (Idibus ap.)) L(68.b.25/1).; HN (61716).
In title 'Vuhitintoni'.

25552.5 — [Anr. ed.] Syntaxis./ Roberti VV. L. in . . . recensitum [1521] Id'. Februa./ 4°. (*in ædibus Richardi Pynsonis,* 1525 (16 my.)) CREDITON.DUL.P(Sp.24/6). Copenhagen RL. Lord Kenyon.

25553 — = 25564.

25553.5 — [Anr. ed.] SYTAXIS [*sic*]./ Roberti VVhitintoni . . . recen-/sitū [1522] Idi./ Februa./ 4° [4.6]. (*in ędibus VVinādi VVordensis,* 1527 (pridie no. mr.)) O(2 copies, Mason H 9 and Arch.A e.33, imp.).c¹⁹.

25554 — [Anr. ed.] SYNTAXIS. 4° [4.6]. (*in ædibus VVinandi VVordensis,* 1527 (pridie Caɫ. no.)) L(66.a.23, lacks G4).; Oberlin C(C2–4 only, in 25547.3).

25555 — [Anr. ed.] SYNTAXIS./ Roberti VVhitintoni . . . recen-/sitū [1522] Idi./ Februa./ 4°. [*Southwark,*] (*per me Petrum Treueris,*) [1529?] L(C.40.e.2/6, plus tp only, Harl.5974/26).L⁴.O⁵.C(SSS.23.18).NEK.+

25556 — [Anr. ed.] Syntaxis./ 4° [4.6]. (*in ædibus VVinandi VVordensis,* 1529 (Id. no.)) L(C.40.e.39/5).O(Mason H 15).G².

25556.5 — [Anr. ed.] Sintaxis.'/ Roberti VV.L. . . . recensitum [1521] Id⁹/ Februa./ 4°. [*Southwark,*] (*per me petrum Treueris,*) [1531?] L(G.7556).O(Douce WW 74/6). C²(VIᵈ.7.21).; Auckland PL.
Though the 'recensitum' year would indicate this is an earlier ed., the state of wear of the tp orns. suggests this is the later Treveris ed. Possibly Treveris was using a Pynson ed. as copy; cf. 25552.5.

Whittinton, Robert—*Syntaxis*—cont.

25557 — [Anr. ed.] Syntaxis./ Roberti VVhitintoni . . . recen-situm/ [1532]. 4°. (*in ædibus VVinandi VVordensis,* 1533.) L(C.40.e.77).O(2 copies, Tanner 239/7 and A 3.6 Linc.).M(9754).; ILL(3).

Verborum Praeterita

25558 — Verborū præterita & supina./ GRAMMATICAE PRIMA PARS/ Roberti VVhitintoni. L. L. nup-/rime recēsita. Liber/ quintus/ De verborum præteritis et supinis. (LIBER SEXTUS DE VERBORUM FORMIS.) 4° [4.6]. (*in edib⁹ VVinādi de VVorde,* 1521.) L(C.40.e.1/3, lacks B3,4).MARL.SHR.; Mellon (quire D only, with 25558.5).

25558.5 — [Anr. ed.] Præterita verboꝝ./ Grāmaticę prima pars [etc.] 4° [4.6]. (*i ędibus VVinādi de VVorde,* 1521.) O (Mason H 49).; Mellon(A–C only, with 25558).

25559 — [Anr. ed.] GRAMMATICAE PRIMA PARS/ Roberti VVhitintoni. L. nuper-/rime recensita./ Liber quint⁹ / De verborum Præteritis et supi-/nis. 4° [4.6]. (*in ędibus VVinādi de VVorde,* 1521.) L(C.40. e.18). Seville, Biblioteca Colombina.; ILL.

25560 — [Anr. ed.] Præterita verborum. 4° [4.6]. (*in ædibus VVinandi de VVorde,* 1522.) CH.ILL.
In title: 'VVhitin-/toni'.

25560.3 — [Anr. ed.] Præterita verborum. 4° [4.6]. (*in ędib⁹ VVinādi de VVorde,* 1522.) P(Sp.25/2).
In title: 'vvhi-/tintoni'.

25560.7 — [Anr. ed.] Verborū præterita & supina. 4° [4.6]. (*in ędib⁹ VVinādi de VVorde,* 1522.) HD(lacks B1).

25561 — [Anr. ed.] Verborū preterita & supina. 4° [4.6]. (*in ędibus pynsonianis,* 1522.) O(Mason H 13).M(9752, lacks B3,4).

25561.5 — [Anr. ed.] Verborum præterita et supina. 4°. [*R. Pynson,* 1523?] O(Arch.A e.45).CREDITON.
(Formerly 25569)

25562 — [Anr. ed.] Verborū præterita & supina. 4° [4.6]. (*in ędib⁹ VVinādi de VVorde,* 1524.) L(G.7547).O(A 13.16b Linc.).M(21532).

25562.3 — [Anr. ed.] Prēterita verborum. 4° [4.6]. (*in ędibus VVinādi de VVorde,* 1524.) HN(61690). Mellon.

25562.7 — [Anr. ed.] Verborum preterita et supina. 4°. [*R. Pynson,* 1524?] DUL. Copenhagen RL*. Lord Kenyon.
Collates A⁴ B⁶ C–E⁴; in title: 'pars/ Roberti VVhitintoni.'; cf. 25561.5, 25566.3.

25563 — [Anr. ed.] Verborū præterita & supina. 4° [4.6]. (*in ędib⁹ VVinādi de VVorde,* 1525.) O(Mason H 1/1).; HN (61713).

25564 — [Anr. ed.] Verborū præterita & supina. 4° [4.6]. (*in ędib⁹ VVinādi de VVorde,* 1526 (ad id. se.)) L(C.40.e.21, plus tp only, Harl.5974/29).O(Arch.A e.28, lacks A1). c(Sel.5.79).c¹⁹.
(Formerly also 25553)

25564.2 — [Anr. ed.] Verborū præterita & supina. 4° [4.6]. (*in ędib⁹ VVinādi de VVorde,* 1527 (ad id⁹ my.)) P(Sp.26/3, lacks A1).; MEL.

25564.6 — [Anr. ed.] Verborū præterita & supina. 4° [4.6]. (*in ędib⁹ VVinādi de VVorde,* 1528 (4 my.)) HN(61705).

25564.8 — [Anr. ed.] Verborum præterita & supina. 4° [4.6]. [*Southwark, P. Treveris,* 1528?] L(C.40.e.28).O⁵. c⁵(A.2.11/7).NEK(lacks A1).SHR.; HN(88440).
(Formerly 25566)

25565 — [Anr. ed.] Verborū præterita & supina. 4° [4.6]. (*in ędib⁹ VVinādi de VVorde,* 1529 (ad Caɫ. se.)) L(2 copies, C.40.e.22 and C.40.e.39/3).O(Tanner 239/6).G².

25565.5 — [Anr. ed.] Verborum præterita & supina. 4° [4.6]. (*in ędib⁹ VVinādi de VVorde,* 1530.) ILL(lacks B3,4).

25566 — Now = 25564.8.

25566.3 — [Anr. ed.] Verborum preterita et supina. 4°. [*Southwark, P. Treveris,* 1530?] L(tp only, Harl.5974/25). L⁴.
In title: 'pars/ Roberti VVitintoni [*sic*]'; cf. 25562.7.

25566.7 — [Anr. ed.] GRAMMATICE/ PRIMA PARS, ROBERTI, VVi/tintōi. L. L. nouiter diligēterꝗ/ recensita, Liber quintus./ Verborum pręterita et supina./ 4°. [*Southwark, P. Treveris,* 1531?] L (C.122.d.15, lacks G6).O(Douce WW 73/2).C(Sel. 5. 153/1, lacks G3–6).; HN(61700).ILL.
(Formerly 25568) This is a revised text, found only in this ed.

25567 — [Anr. ed.] [Verborum præterita & supina.] 4°. (*in ædib⁹ VVinādi de VVorde,* 1533.) L(C.40.e.2/3, lacks A1).
Catch title on B3, C3, D3, E3: 'Prætęr [*sic*]. & supi. verborū.'

Whittinton, Robert—*Verborum Praeterita*—*cont.*

25567.5 — [Anr. ed.] Verborum præterita & supina. 4°. (*in ædib⁹ VVinādi de VVorde*, 1533.) ILL.
All catch titles: 'Præte. & supi. verborū.'

25568 — Now = 25566.7.

25569 — Now = 25561.5.

Vulgaria

25569.3 — Uulgaria Roberti whitintoni Lichfel-/diensis, et de institutione grāma-/ticulorū Opusculum: libello/ suo de concinnitate Grā-/matices accōmodatū:/ et ī quattuor par-/tes dige-/stum. 4° ⁴·⁸. (*apud wynandū/ de worde*, 1520 (Nonis mr.)) c⁵(A.2.10/1).

25569.5 — [Anr. ed.] 4° ⁴·⁸. (*apud/ wynādum de worde*, 1520.) M (R4535).

25569.7 — [Anr. ed.] 4° ⁴·⁸. (*in edibus winandi de worde/*, 1520.) HN(79721).
(Formerly 25571)

25570 — [Anr. ed.] VVLGARIA [etc.] 4°. (*ex calcographia Richardi Pyn-/sonis*,) 1520 (id. oc.) O(Arch.A e.39). c(SSS.17.24, lacks M3,4).CREDITON.
With an extra epistle to the reader by 'typographus Thomas Bercula', i.e. Berthelet, stating 'typis nostris uulgaria sua [Whittinton's] . . . cudimus.'
See also 25577.5, 5639.

25571 — Now = 25569.7.

25572 — [Anr. ed.] Uulgaria [etc.] 4° ⁴·⁸. (*i edibus winandi de worde/*, 1521.) L(C.40.e.19).O(Mason H 2).MARL. SHR. Seville, Biblioteca Colombina.

25572.5 — [Anr. ed.] Vulgaria Roberti VVhitintoni [etc.] 4° ⁴·⁸. (*in edibus Winandi de worde/*, 1522.) ILL.

25573 — [Anr. ed.] 4° ⁴·⁸. (*in edibus Winandi de Worde/*, 1523.) HN(61696).ILL.

25574 — [Anr. ed.] 4° ⁴·⁸. (*in edibus Winandi de Wqrde/*, 1524.) O(Mason H 30).G².; ILL.

25575 — Now = 25577.5.

25576 — [Anr. ed.] 4° ⁴·⁸. (*in edibus Winandi de Worde/*, 1525.) L(G.7554).O(Mason H 31).C¹⁹(quires B, F, H, with 25577.).; HN(61720).CH.

25577 — [Anr. ed.] 4° ⁴·⁸. (*in edibus Winandi de Worde*, 1526.) O(Arch.A e.36, lacks H8).c(Sel.5.83).C¹⁹(quires A, D outer sheet, E, G, with 25576).
(Formerly also 25580)Leaf signatures have no stops; cf. 23148.12. C¹⁹ has quire C and D inner sheet in a different setting, possibly the same as 25572.5.

25577.5 — [Anr. ed.] VVLGARIA [etc.] M.D.xxv. 4°. (*ex calcographia Richardi Pyn-/sonis*, 1526.) L(2 copies, C.122.bb.33 and C.40.e.2/7, lacks M3,4). Lord Kenyon(imp.).
(Formerly 25575) Reprints 25570, including the epistle by Berthelet.

25578 — [Anr. ed.] Vulgaria [etc.] 4° ⁴·⁸. (*in edibus winandi de worde*, 1527.) L(C.40.e.39/9).; HN(61703).WIS.

25578.5 — [Anr. ed.] Vulgaria Roberti VVhitintoni/ Lichfeldien-sis [etc.] 4° ⁴·⁸. [*Southwark, P. Treveris*, 1528–29?] L⁴.O(2 copies, Mason H 32 and Mason H 52). O⁵. c⁵(2 copies, A.2.11/10 and A.2.11/11).NEK(imp.).; WIS. Oberlin C(imp.).
(Formerly 25581)

25579 — [Anr. ed.] 4°. (*in edibus Winandi de Worde*, 1533.) O (Douce WW 73/4).O²⁴(frags.).; F.ROS.

25580 — = 25577.

25581 — Now = 25578.5.

— ed. *See* 23147.2.

— tr. *See* 5278, 5292, 5313, 10467, 17501, 17502, 22216.

Whitwell, Charles. *See* 18638.5, 23594.5.

Whobals, Harry. *See* 1656.

25582 **Whore.** The costlie whore. A comicall historie. 4°. *A. Mathewes f. W. Sheares a. H. Perrie*, 1633. Ent. to Sheares 2 no. 1632. L(2).L⁶(2).O.O⁶.ETON.; BO.ILL. PEN. Greg 472.

25582a — [A variant, w. imprint:] *A. Mathewes f. W. Sheares*, 1633. L.O.O⁹.E.; F.HN.HD.N.NY.+

Whyte, John. Almanacks. 1613, etc. *See* 527 sqq.

Whytford, Richard. *See* Whitford, R.

25583 **Whythorne, Thomas.** Cantus. (Bassus.) Of duos, or songs for two voices. 2 ptbks. 4°. *T. Este, the assigné of W. Byrd*, 1590. L.O(bassus only).CASHEL.

25584 — Triplex (Medius—Bassus—Contratenor—Tenor), of songes, for three, fower, and fiue voyces. 5 ptbks. obl.4°. *J. Daye*, 1571. L(lacks tenor and all tpp).O (tenor only, lacking tp).O³(lacks contratenor).; HN (lacks all tpp, imp.).NY(contratenor only).

25585 **Whytstons, James.** De iusticia & scitate belli per Juliū pontificē secūdū in scismaticos. 4° ⁸·⁴. (*opa & ipensis R. Pynson*, 1512.) O.C⁷.D. Orihuela PL, Spain.

25586 **Wiburn, Perceval.** A checke or reproofe of M. Howlets vntimely shreeching [*sic*] with an answeare to [19394]. [Init. P. W.] 4°. *T. Dawson f. T. Smyth*, 1581. Ent. 25 au. L.O.C³.D.DUR⁵.+; F.HN.BO³.HD.U.+
The inits. P. W. appear on Zz2ᵛ in the Appendix.

Wicelius, Georgius. *See* 25935.

Wiche, Sir Peter. *See* 26057.3.

Wickham, William, *Bp.* Lincoln. Visitation Articles. *See* 10231 sqq.
— *See also* Bookplates.

25587 **Wickins, Nathaniel.** Woodstreet-compters-plea, for its prisoner. Or the sixteen reasons, which induce mee N. Wickins, late servant to W. Prynne. To refuse to take the oath ex officio. 4°. [*Amsterdam, Richt Right press*,] *Printed in the second yeare of remembrance*, 1638. L.O¹⁰.C².D.E².+; HN.HD.U.WEL.Y. Copies vary: tp verso blank (HN) or with addi-tional errata (HD).

25587.5 **Wiclif, John.** The dore of holy scripture. Matthew.vij. Omnis enim [etc. The general prologue of the Wycliffite Bible.] [Anon. Attrib. to J. Purvey.] 8°. [*J. Mayler f.*] *J. Gowgh*, (1540 (12 mr.)) L.O.LINC(imp.).
(Formerly 3033)

25588 — [Anr. ed., from a different MS.] The true copye of a prolog wrytten about two C. yeres paste by J. Wycklife . . . the originall whereof is founde written in an olde English Bible bitwixt the olde Testament and the newe. Whych Bible remaynith now in yᵉ kyng hys maiesties chamber. 8°. [*R. Grafton f.*] *R. Crowley*, 1550. L.O.C.LEIC².M.+; F.HN.HD.NY.Y.+
Quires K and L are in 2 settings; K1ʳ last line: 'Egypt:' or 'Egipt:'; L1ʳ last line: 'al' or 'all'; both at O, F.

25589 — Two short treatises, against the orders of the begging friars. Faithfully printed according to two ancient manuscript copies, extant, the one in Benet Colledge in Cambridge, the other remaining in the publike librarie at Oxford. [Ed.] (T. James.) 4°. *Oxford, J. Barnes*, 1608. L.O.C.D.G².+; F.HN.HD.N.NY.+
Issued with 14445.

25590 — wycklyffes wycket: whyche he made in kyng Rycards days the second in the yere of our lorde God M.CCC.XCV. (The testament of w. Tracie ex-pounded by W. Tyndall.) 8°. (*Norenburch*, [*i.e. London, J. Day?*] 1546.) L.O.; F.NY.
The Tracy portion is reprinted from 24167.

25590.5 — [Anr. ed.] 8°. (*Norenburch*, [*i.e. London, J. Day?*] 1546.) O(2).C.BUTE.M.; NY¹¹.
In title: 'whych . . . Rychards'.

25591 — [Anr. ed.] Uvicklieffes wicket. Faythfully ouerseene and corrected. Hereunto is added an epistle to the reader. With the protestacion of J. Lassels late burned in Smythfelde: and the Testament of W. Tracie expounded by W. Tyndall, and J. Frythe. (Ouerseene by M. C[overdale].) 8°. [*J. Day?* 1548?] L.C.C³.D.DUR⁵.; F.HN.NY. Vermont U.
a1ᵛ line 1: 'studious'.

25591a — [Anr. ed.] 8°. [*J. Day?* 1548?] L.L².O.O³.M.+; F. a1ᵛ line 1: 'studiouse'.

25592 — [Anr. ed. of the Wiclif portion only.] Wickliffes wicket, or a learned treatise of the sacrament. Set forth according to an ancient printed copie. [Ed.] (H. Jackson.) 4°. *Oxford, Jos. Barnes, sold by John Barnes*, [*London*,] 1612. Ent. to H. Denham 1567–68. L.O.C.D.E.+; F.HN.HD.N.U.+

Widdowes, Daniel. Naturall philosophy. 1621, etc. *See* 22111 sq.

25593 **Widdowes, Giles.** The lawlesse kneelesse schismaticall puritan. Or a confutation of the author of an Appen-dix [in 20458]. 4°. *Oxford, [J. Lichfield] f. the author*, 1631 [1630?] L.O.C.D.E.+; F.HN.HD.N.U.+
Supported by 19096; answered by 20465.

25594 — The schysmatical puritan. A sermon concerning the lawfulnesse of church-authority. 4°. *Oxford, [J. Lichfield] f. the author*, 1630. L.O.C.A.LYU.+; F.HN. HD.U.Y.+
Most copies (L, O³, 2 C, F, HN, HD) have an 'I hand-stamped over the 'Y' in 'schysmatical'; 3 O, O¹⁰, O³⁸ copies apparently are altered in MS.

Widdowes, Giles—*cont.*

25595 — The second edition, augmented. 4°. *Oxford*, [*J. Lichfield*] *f. the author*, 1631. L.O(3).O³(imp.).O⁸.A.; F.BO.U.

25596 **Widdrington, Roger**, *pseud*. [i.e. Thomas Preston.] Apologia cardinalis Bellarmini pro iure principum. Adversùs suas ipsius rationes. 8°. *Cosmopoli, ap. Theophilum Pratum* [i.e. *London, R. Field*,] 1611. L.O.C.D.E.+; F(2).HN(imp.).COR.U.
    A&R 661. 'Pratum' is Latin for 'Field'. Lines 3–4 of title: 'IV–/RE'.

25596.5 — [Anr. ed.] 8°. *Cosmopoli, ap. Theophilum Pratum* [i.e. *Paris, D. Binet?*] 1611. O.C.DE.DUR⁵.W.+; WASH³. Dickinson C.
    A&R 662. Line 3 of title ends: 'IVRE/'.

25597 — Rogeri Widdringtoni catholici Angli responsio apologetica. ad libellum cuiusdam doctoris theologi, qui eius apologiam criminatur. 8°. *Cosmopoli, ap. Pratum* [i.e. *London, R. Field*,] 1612. L.O.C.D.E.+; F.HN.TEX.U.
    A&R 674. With a pref., which is reprinted in 25602.

25598 — A cleare, sincere, and modest confutation of the Reply of T. Fitzherbert [11023]. Wherein also are confuted the objections which Card. Bellarmine, hath made against Widdrintons [*sic*] Apologie. (An adjoinder.) 4°. [*Eliot's Court Press a. G. Eld*,] 1616. L.O.C.D.E.+; F.HN.HART.HD(imp.).
    A&R 664. Eld pr. quires Pp–2nd N.

25599 — Roger Widdringtons last rejoynder to Mʳ. Fitz-herberts Reply concerning the oath of allegiance [11023]. 4° in 8's. [*J. Bill*,] 1619. L.O.C.D.E.+; F.HART.TEX.
    A&R 671. The tp is a cancel.

25600 — [Anr. issue, w. cancel tp dated:] 1633. L.O¹⁸.C.M².OS.+
    A&R 672.

25601 — Discussio discussionis decreti magni concilii Lateranensis, adversus L. Lessium nomine Guilhelmi Singletoni personatum. 8°. *Augustæ, ap. Joan. Libium,* [i.e. *London, J. Bill*,] 1618. L.O.C.D.E.+; TEX.
    A&R 666. 'Libium' is an anagram for 'Bill'.

25602 — Disputatio theologica de juramento fidelitatis sanctissimo patri Paulo papæ quinto dedicata. (R. Widdringtoni Apologeticæ responsionis præfatio ad lectorem.) 8°. *Albionopoli, ex off. Theophili Fabri* [i.e. *London, E. Allde*,] 1613. L.O.C.D.E².+; F.HN(lacks T8).TEX.
    A&R 667. See 25597.

25602.5 — [Anr. ed.] 8°. *Albionopoli, ex off. Theophili Fabri* [i.e. *Frankfurt?*] 1614. L.PARIS.W.
    A&R 668.

25603 — [A trans.] A theologicall disputation concerning the oath of allegiance. *Tr.* out of Latin by the author himselfe, whereunto hee hath also added an appendix. 4°. [*F. Kingston*,] 1613. L.O¹⁸.C².E.USHAW.+
    A&R 676.

25604 — Appendix ad Disputationem theologicam de juramento fidelitatis. 8°. *Albionopoli, ap. Ruardum Phigrum* [i.e. *London, E. Griffin*,] 1616. L.O.C.D.E.+; F.HN.N (imp.).TEX.U(imp.).
    A&R 663. 'Phigrum' is an anagram for 'Griffin', one of the members of Eliot's Court Press.

25605 — Rogeri Widdringtoni, catholici Angli ad Paulum quintun [*sic*], humillima supplicatio. Cui adjungitur appendix, in quo plurimæ calumniæ deteguntur. 2 pts. 8°. *Albionopoli, ap. Rufum Lipsium* [i.e. *London, A. Islip a. Eliot's Court Press*,] 1616. L.O.C.D.E.+; F.HN.N(imp.).STL.U.
    A&R 673. 'Lipsium' is an anagram for 'Islip', who pr. only pt. 1.

25605.5 — Exemplar decreti: in quo duo libri R. Widdringtoni condemnantur, & authori ut se purget præceptum imponitur. 8°. *Albionopoli, ap. Theophilum Fabrum,* [i.e. *London, J. Beale*,] 1614. Ent. to W. and T. Harper 1 au. O(imp.).C⁵.
    A&R 669.

25606 — [A trans.] A copy of the decree: wherein two bookes of R. Widdrington are condemned, and a copy of the purgation sent to Paul the fift. *Tr.* out of Latine by the author, whereunto he hath also adjoined an admonition concerning the Reply of T. F. [11023]. 8°. [*London*,] 1614. Ent. to John Barnes 31 jy. L.L².
    L²⁵.O¹⁷.C.+; NY.
    A&R 665.
    — See also 13871, 14049, 14050, 14050.5, 14969.5, 20286.3, 20286.7.

25607 **Widecombe.** A true relation of those sad and lamentable accidents, which happened in the parish church of Withycombe on Sunday the 21. of October last, 1638. [Struck by lightning.] 4°. *G. M[iller] f. R. Harford*, 1638. Ent. 17 no. L.O.O⁹.C².; F.HN.HD.
    Pp. 14. See also 23778.5.

25608 — [Anr. issue, largely reimposed, with additions.] *G. M[iller] f. R. Harford*, 1638. Ent. 19 no. L.O(2).C.E.; F.Y.
    Pp. 15.

25609 — [Anr. ed., enlarged.] A second and most exact relation of those sad accidents. 4°. *G. M[iller] f. R. Harford*, 1638. Ent. 27 no. L.O(3).ETON.; F.HN.HD.Y.
    Includes the 1st account, which is largely reimposed from 25608.

25610 **Widley, George.** The doctrine of the sabbath, handled in foure treatises. 4°. *F. Kyngston f. T. Man*, 1604. Ent. to Man, sen. and jun., 27 jn. L.O³.C.C³.E².+; F.HN.CHI.U.Y.+

Widow. A merry new song of a rich widdowes wooing. [c. 1625.] See 22919.1.
    — The widowes treasure. 1585, etc. See 19433.3 sqq.

Wied, Herman von. See Herman V, *Abp. of Cologne*.

25610.5 **Wife.** A constant wife, a kinde wife, a loving wife, and a fine wife. *Ballad.* 2 pts. s.sh.fol. *f. F. C[oules*, 1631?] Ent. 5 se. 1631. C⁶(imp.).
    — The constant wife of Sussex. [1632?] See 23445.5.

25611 — A good wife, or none. *Ballad.* 2 pts. s.sh.fol. *f. F. Coules*, [c. 1640.] Ent. to ballad ptnrs. 14 de. 1624; ? to F. Coules 18 jn. 1639. L.
    Begins: 'The blazing Torch is soone burnt out.'
    — The good wife. 1618. See 3568.5.
    — A wife, now a widowe. 1614. See 18903.5.

25612 **Wigand, Johann.** De neutralibus et mediis. Grosly Inglyshed, Jacke of both sydes. A godly admonition, touching those that be neutres, holding vpon no certayne religion. [Anon. *Tr.* from Latin.] 8°. *R. Harrison*, 1562. Ent. 1561–62. O.P.R*.; F.
    Errata on N7ᵛ; B1ʳ line 1: 'compte'.

25612.5 — [Anr. ed., corrected.] 8°. *R. Harrison*, 1562. L.D.M.; HD.
    N7ᵛ blank; B1ʳ line 1: 'compt'. At least HD has quires M–N from the same setting as the F copy of 25612, except HD omits the errata.

25613 — [Anr. ed.] 8°. *T. Dawson f. E. White*, 1591. Ent. to J. Sheldrake 12 ap. L.C.

25614 — [Anr. ed., init. J. W.] 4°. *G. M[iller] f. E. Blackmore*, 1626. L.O.O⁶.; U.

Wightman, Gilbert. [Bookplate.] *See* Bookplates.

Wightman, William, *ed. See* 24800.

25615 **Wigmore, Michael.** The good adventure: importing, 1 that there is a God, 2 that there is a trinity. A sermon. 4°. *G. P[urslowe] f. J. Budge*, 1620. L².L¹⁵.O.; Y.

25616 — The holy citie. 1 Discovered. 2 Besieged. 3 Delivered. A sermon. 4°. *A. M[athewes] f. R. Redmer*, 1619. Ent. 13 ap. L.O.C.P.; F.HD.N.PN². Lewis.

25617 — The meteors. A sermon preached at a visitation. 4°. *T. Harper f. N. Butter*, 1633. L.C.C³.D.YK.; F.HN.HD.

25618 — The way of all flesh. A sermon. 4°. *G. Purslow f. J. Budge*, 1619. L(imp.).O.C².M².; Y.

25619 **Wilbye, John.** Cantus. (Altus.—Tenor.—Bassus.—Quintus.—Sextus.) The first set of English madrigals to 3. 4. 5. and 6. voices. 6 ptbks. 4°. *T. Este*, 1598. Ent. 7 au. L(altus: 55.b.20, and quintus: Hirsch III.1150).; F(1, plus altus, sextus).ILL(tenor).PN(sextus).
    In all ptbks. song 23 has: 'Subdue her hart, who makes mee glad'. In the F copy only tenor and sextus have the dedic. to Sir C. Cavendish, w. Table on the verso.

25619.3 — [Anr. ed.] 6 ptbks. 4°. *T. Este*, 1598. L(K.3.k.17, complete, plus cantus, tenor, bassus: Hirsch III.1150). L³⁰.O.E².G².+; HD.ILL(cantus, altus, sextus).LC.N.PN (w. sextus of 25619).+
    In all ptbks. song 23 has: 'Subdue her hart, who makes me glad'. In 1 L(K.3.k.17) all but altus and quintus have the leaf w. dedic. and table; in LC all but bassus and quintus have it; in G², N, PN only cantus has it.

Wilbye, John—*cont.*

25619.5 — [Anr. ed.] 6 ptbks. 4°. *T. Este*, 1598. L(altus, sextus: Hirsch III.1150).L[7](tenor).; F.

In all ptbks. song 23 has: 'Subdue hir hart,'. In the F copy all ptbks. have the leaf w. dedic. and table, though leaf signatures have been tampered with; in L, only sextus has it.

25619a — Cantus. (Altus.—Tenor.—Bassus.—Quintus.—Sextus.) The second set of madrigales to 3. 4. 5. and 6. parts, apt for voyals and voyces. 6 ptbks. 4°. *T. Este alias Snodham f. J. Browne* [1,] 1609. L.O.C.E[2].G[2].+; F.HN(lacks tenor tp).HD.LC.N.+

Wilcocks, Elijahu, *tr. See* 20083.7.

25620 **Wilcox, Thomas.** The works of that late divine, Mr. T. Wilcocks, containing an exposition upon the Psalmes, Proverbs, Canticles, and part of the 8. chapter of Romans. 3 pts. fol. *J. Haviland*, 1624. L.O.C.LYU.M. +; F.HN.HD.ILL.U.+

— An admonition to the Parliament. [1572.] *See* 10847.

25620.5 — A christian and learned exposition, vpon certaine verses of that eight chapter of Romanes. Written long agoe, and now lately published. [Init. Th. W.] 8°. *R. Walde-graue f. T. Man*, 1587. Ent. as by Wilcox 11 jn. L(tpp only, Ames I.470 and Harl. 5995/21).O.; F.U.

— A concordance . . . in the newe Testament. 1579. *See* 24917.

25621 — A discourse touching the doctrine of doubting. In which the arguments, that our popish aduersaries vse, are aunswered. Written long since and now published. 8°. *J. Legat, pr. to the Univ. of Camb.*, 1598. L.C(lacks tp).LK.P(2).

25622 — An exposition vppon the booke of the Canticles. [Init. T. W.] 8°. [*R. Waldegraue*] *f. T. Man*, 1585. Ent. as by Wilcox to Man a. W. Broome 28 jn. L.L[2].O.O[4]. P.+; F.HN.CHI.ILL.

25622.5 — A forme of preparation to the Lordes supper. [A catechism. Init. T. W.] 8°. *R. Waldegraue f. T. Man*, [1587.] Ent. as 'Master Wilcoxe Catechisme' 11 jn. 1587. HD.

25622.7 — [A variant, w. imprint:] *R. Waldegraue f. W. Brome*, [1587.] L[2].

25623 — A glasse for gamesters: and namelie for suche as delight in cards & dise. [Init. T. W.] 8°. *J. Kyngston f. T. Man*, 1581. Ent. 20 de. 1580. O.; F.Y.

25624 — Large letters. Three in number, for the instruction of such, as are distressed in conscience. 8°. *R. warde f. T. Man*, 1589. O.C.

25624.5 — A profitable, and comfortable letter for afflicted consciences: written and sent . . . 1582. [Anon.] 12°. *R. Walde-graue f. T. Man*, [1584?] F(imp., date cropt).

Maunsell (17669), pt. 1, p. 67, cites a 1584 ed. by T. W., i.e. Wilcox.

25625 — A right godly and learned exposition, vpon the whole booke of Psalmes. [Init. T. W.] 4° in 8's. [*T. Dawson*] *f. T. Man a. W. Brome*, 1586. Ent. as by Wilcox 7 fb. L(imp.).O.C(imp.).BTL.NEP.+; F(2, 1 imp.).HN.CAL[6].HART.NY(imp.).

25626 — [Anr. ed., enlarged.] A very godly and learned exposition, [etc.] Diligētly reuiued by the author. 4° in 8's. *T. Orwin f. T. Man*, 1591. L.O.C[19].D.E[2].+; F.HN.CHI. HD.NY[11].+

25627 — A short, yet sound commentarie; written on the Prouerbes of Salomon. [Init. T. W.] 4°. *T. Orwin f. T. Man*, [1589.] L.O.C[4].BIRM.G[4].+; F(2).HN.ILL.NY.

Dated 1589 in the slot in the sill of tp border McK. & F. 117.

25628 — [A ghost.]

25629 — A short yet a true and faithfull narration of the fire in Wooburne. 8°. *the Widdow Orwin f. T. Man*, 1595. Ent. 28 no. L(lacks tp).O.D.

— The substance of the Lordes supper. 1610. *See* 4314.

25630 — The summe of a sermon, preached at Sowthell. [Init. T. W.] 8°. *the Widow Orwin f. T. Man*, 1597. L.O. LINC.; F.

— Summarie and short meditations. 1580. *See* 24919.

— A treatise of the Lords supper. 1588. *See* 2051.

25631 — The vnfouldyng of sundry vntruths and absurde propositions, latelye propounded by one I. B. a fauourer of the heresie of the Libertines. [Init. T. W.] 8°. (*T. Dawson*) *f. T. Man*, 1581. Ent. 9 my. L[3].O(2).D.

The SR entry identifies the opponent as 'one Bannester'.

— *ed. See* 18151, 20084, 20751.

Wilcox, Thomas—*cont.*

— *tr. See* 2014, 2051, 4464, 15450, 15489, 16812, 18146, 26124.5.

— *See also* 10850.

25632 **Wild, Robert.** Alas poore scholler, whither wilt thou goe. [Anon.] *Ballad.* 2 pts. s.sh.fol. [*London*, 1641.] L. Written in early 1641 and very possibly pr. before the end of the legal year 1640 on 24 March.

25633 **Wilkes, William.** Obedience or ecclesiasticall union. 4°. *G. Elde f. Roger Jackson*, 1605. L.O.C.C[2].LINC.+; F.HN.HD.U.

Copies vary: errata on L3[v](L, O, HD) or L4[r](F, HN).

25634 — [Anr. issue, w. cancel tp:] A second memento for magistrates. *f. Roger Jackson*, 1608. C.

25634a — [Anr. issue, w. variant cancel tp:] *f. Roger Jackson*, 1609. L[4].C[2].C[5].

Wilkie, Daniel. Theses philosophicæ quædam, sub presidio D. Willikij. 1603. *See* 21555.11.

Wilkins, George. Jests to make you merie. 1607. *See* 6541.

25635 — The miseries of inforst mariage. As it is now playd. 4°. [*W. Jaggard*] *f. G. Vincent*, 1607. Ent. 31 jy. L.O. E(lacks tp).; F.HN.HD.TCU.Y.+ Greg 249.

In some copies (O, F, 1 HN) the device on the tp, McK. 136, is upside down. *See also* 18288.

25636 — [Anr. ed.] 4°. [*W. White*] *f. G. Vincent*, 1611. L(2).L[6]. O.; F.HN.HD.ILL.NY.+

In this and the following, the 1st word of the title is xylographic.

25637 — [Anr. ed.] 4°. *A. Mathewes f. R. Thrale*, [col.:] (*A. Mathewes f. G. Vincent* [2,] sold by *R. Thrale*,) 1629. L.L[6].; F.HN.HD.N.Y.+

25638 — [Anr. ed.] 4°. *J. N[orton] f. R. Thrale*, 1637. Ass'd by widow of G. Vincent, jun., 28 ap. L.O.C.G[2].SHEF.+; F.HN.CHI.HD.NY.+

25638.5 — The painfull adventures of Pericles prince of Tyre. Being the true history of the play of Pericles, as presented by J. Gower. 4°. *T. P[urfoot] f. N. Butter*, 1608. Ent. to E. Blount 20 my. L(lacks dedic.).Z. (Formerly 19628)

25639 — Three miseries of Barbary: Plague. Famine. Civill warre. With a relation of the death of Mahamet the late emperour. 4°. *W. J[aggard] f. H. Gosson*, [1607.] L.L[13].O.C[5].LONGLEAT.; F(2).HD.Y. Robert H. Chapman, Cambridge, Mass.

— The travailes of the three English brothers. 1607. *See* 6417.

— *tr. See* 24293.

25640 **Wilkins, John,** *Bp.* The discovery of a world in the moone. [Anon.] 8°. *E. G[riffin] f. M. Sparke a. E. Forrest*, [*Oxford*,] 1638. Ent. 30 mr. O.O[18].C[5].BHP. G[2].+; HN.HD.ILL.NY.PH.+

B1[r] line 3 from bottom ends: 'at'.

25640.5 — [Anr. ed.] 8°. *E. G[riffin] f. M. Sparke a. E. Forrest*, [*Oxford*,] 1638. L.O.C.G[2].M.+; F.CAL.HD.N.U.+

B1[r] line 3 from bottom ends: 'first'. Quires K–M and part of A and P are reimposed from 25640.

25641 — [Anr. ed., w. additions.] The first book. The discovery of a new world. The third impression. Corrected and enlarged. (A discourse concerning a new planet. The second booke, now first published.) [Anon.] 2 pts. *J. Norton* [a.] (*R. H[earne]*) *f. J. Maynard*, 1640. Ent. 15 fb. L.O.C.G[2].M[4].+; F.HN.HD.N.NY.+

With engr. gen. tp: 'A discourse concerning a new world & another planet in 2 bookes. *f. J. Maynard*, 1640.'

25642 **Wilkinson, Edward.** E. W[ilkinson] his Thameseidos. Devided into three bookes, or cantos. [In verse.] 4° w. perp. chainlines. *W. W[hite] f. S. Waterson*, 1600. Ent. 28 au. L.L[2].O.O[14](frag.).LONGLEAT.; F.HN.HD.

25643 — Isahacs [*sic*] inheritance; dew to our prince, James the sixt of Scotland, of England, France and Ireland the first. [In verse.] 4°. [*R. Read*] *f. J. Harrison* [4,] 1603. Ent. 16 jn. HN.

25644 **Wilkinson, Henry.** A catechisme, contayning a short exposition of the points in the ordinary catechisme. For the use of the congregation of Wadsdon. Second edition. 8°. *T. S[nodham] f. R. Pott*, 1624. Ent. 7 fb. 1623. O.

25645 — Third edition. 8°. *T. C[otes] f. R. Birde*, 1629. L.C[3].; F.U.

25645.5 — Fourth edition. 8°. *R. Bishop f. R. Bird*, 1637. PH.

Wilkinson, Henry—*cont.*

25646 — The debt book: or, a treatise upon Romans 13. ver. 8. 8⁰. *R. B[adger] a. G. M[iller] f. R. Bird,* 1625. Ent. 19 my. L.O.O¹¹.D.LINC(lacks tp).+; F.

25647 **Wilkinson, John,** *Dissenter.* An exposition of the 13. chapter of the Revelation. 4⁰. [*Amsterdam, G. Thorp,*] 1619. O.C².C⁵(lacks tp).

25648 **Wilkinson, John,** *of Barnard's Inn.* A treatise collected out of the statutes concerning the office of coroners and sherifes. 8⁰. [*A. Islip*] *f. the Co. of Statrs.,* 1618. Ent. to the English Stock 29 au. L.O.C³.C¹⁵.DUL.; F.HN.CU.HD.N.
See Court-Book C, pp. 101–2.

25649 — [Anr. ed.] 8⁰. [*A. Islip*] *f. the Co. of Statrs.,* 1620. L.O.O¹³.C³.D.DUL.+; CAL⁵.HD.PEN.

25650 — [Anr. ed.] 8⁰. [*A. Islip*] *f. the Co. of Statrs.,* 1628. L.O¹⁹.C.M⁴.RGU.+; F.CU.HD.ILL.LC.+

25650.5 — [Anr. ed.?] 8⁰. *Dublin, f. the Co. of Statrs.,* 1634. L(tp only, Ames II.1166).

25651 — [Anr. ed.] 8⁰. [*M. Flesher,*] *by the assignes of J. More,* 1638. L.O.C².E.WI.; F.HN.HD.IND.Y.+

Wilkinson, John, *Servant to the Earl of Derby, tr.* See 754, 987.

Wilkinson, Richard, *ed.* See 1092.

25652 **Wilkinson, Robert.** Barwick bridge: or England and Scotland coupled. In a sermon. Preached before the king at Saint Andrewes. 4⁰. *E. Griffin f. W. Aspley,* 1617. L.C.YK.; HD.
Also issued w. tp cancelled as pt. 1 of 25664.

25652.5 — A sermon of hearing, or, jewell for the eare. 8⁰. [*T. Orwin*] *f. T. Woodcocke,* 1593. Ent. 30 jn. YK.
With dedic. to Lancelet Batherst and others.

25652.7 — [Anr. ed., w. title:] A jewell for the eare. 8⁰. [*f. T. Pavier?* c. 1602.] F(device and impr. cut out of tp).
The dedic. is replaced by a pref. to the reader, which in this ed. has, on A2ʳ: '. . . al Scripture is profitable, but set this apart and we shall [be] like him . . .' while at least 25653 and 25654.5 have: '. . . profitable, But set this Art of hearing aside, and all will be vnprofitable.' and further revisions in text.

25653 — [Anr. ed.] 8⁰. *f. T. Pavyer,* 1905 [i.e. 1605.] L.O.C.C³.

25653.5 — [Anr. ed.] 8⁰. [*T. East*] *f. T. Pavyer,* 1608. D.WI.

25654 — [Anr. ed.] 8⁰. [*R. Blower*] *f. T. Pavyer,* 1610. L(tp only, Harl. 5993/106).C³.

25654.5 — [Anr. ed.] 8⁰. [*W. Jones f. T. Pavier,* c. 1625.] E(imp.).
Main text has 28 lines a page like 25655, while earlier eds. have 26 lines. 'B' of sig. B1 is below 'ne' of 'onely'.

25655 — [Anr. ed.] 8⁰. [*W. Jones*] *f. T. Pavier,* 1625. Ass'd by widow Pavier to E. Brewster a. R. Bird 4 au. 1626. L.
'B' of sig. B1 is below the space preceding 'onely'.

25656 — Lots wife. A sermon preached at Paules Crosse. [Init. R. W.] *F. Kyngston f. J. Flasket,* 1607. Ent. 12 se. L.L³.O.C⁸.M.+; F.CHI.HD.U.

25657 — The merchant royall. A sermon preached at the nuptials of lord Hay. 4⁰. *F. Kyngston f. J. Flasket,* 1607. L.O.C.COL.YK.+; F.HN.HD.N. Weissman.+
Page 2, line 1: 'dignity'. Quire A in this and the next 2 eds. is from the same typesetting.

25658 — [Anr. ed.] 4⁰. *F. Kyngston f. J. Flasket,* 1607. O¹⁴.; HN.HD. Weissman.
Page 2, line 1: 'dignitie'; line 2: 'holy'. This is prob. the earliest ed.; quire F and E outer forme are from the same typesetting as 25657.

25658.5 — [Anr. ed.] 4⁰. *F. Kyngston f. J. Flasket,* 1607. L.L³.O.C⁵.M⁴.+; F.HN.CHI.DAR.TEX.+
Page 2, line 1: 'dignitie'; line 2: 'holie'.

25659 — [Anr. ed.] 4⁰. *Edinburgh, T. Finlason,* 1607. L.E(lacks dedic.).; HART.

25659.5 — [Anr. ed.] 4⁰. *W. Stansby f. E. Blunt a. W. Barret,* 1613. L.CHELM².P.; F.LC.

25660 — [Anr. ed.] 4⁰. *G. Eld f. E. Blount,* 1615. L(2).O.; F.CAL.HART.TEX.Y.+

25661 — A paire of sermons. The former as an ante-funerall to the late prince Henry. The latter to the now living prince Charles. 4⁰. *F. Kyngston f. W. Aspley,* 1614. Ent. 18 mr. L.L³.O.C².YK.+; F.HN.HD.N.
Also issued as pt. 2 of 25664.
— A sermon of hearing. 1593. *See* 25652.5.

Wilkinson, Robert—*cont.*

25662 — A sermon preached at North-Hampton upon occasion of the late rebellion and riots. 4⁰. [*G. Eld*] *f. J. Flasket,* 1607. Ent. 7 jy. L.O.C.COL.YK.+; F.HN.HD (tp def.).N.Y.+
C4 a cancel in some copies; orig. C4ʳ line 3 ends: 'men' (HN); the cancel: 'were' (HD).

25663 — The stripping of Joseph, or the crueltie of brethren. In a sermon. With a consolatorie epistle, to the English-East-India companie, for wrongs sustayned in Amboyna. Published by T. Myriell. 4⁰. *W. S[tansby] f. H. Holland a. G. Gibbs,* 1625. Ent. 3 fb. L.L³⁰.O.C.G².+; F.HN.HD.MIN.

25664 — Three sermons. 2 pts. 4⁰. *E. Griffin f. W. Aspley,* 1617. CARLISLE.DUR³.
A reissue, w. added gen. tp, of 25652 and 25661.

25665 **Wilkinson, William.** A confutation of certaine articles deliuered [by H. Niclas] vnto the Familye of Loue. 4⁰. *J. Daye,* 1579. L.O.C.DUR⁵.YK.+; F.HN.HD.U.Y.
Reprints and answers portions of various Niclas texts; *see* 18548.5 sqq. 𝕬

25666 — A very godly and learned treatise, of fastyng. 1580. Now = 24251.3.

25667 — [Anr. ed.] The holie exercise of a true fast. 1580. Now = 24251.5.
— *tr.* See 16985.

Will. A mad kinde of wooing, . . . betweene Will the simple, and Nan the subtill. [c. 1630.] *See* 14960.5.

25668 — Slippery Will, or the old bachelors complaint. *Ballad.* 2 pts. s.sh.fol. *f. E. B[lackmore,* c. 1630.] L.G².

25668.5 — westerne Wyll, vpon the debate betwyxte Churchyarde and Camell. [By W. Baldwin? In verse.] 4⁰. (*W. Powell,*) [1552?] L⁵(Lemon 24).
Includes reprint of 5225.5; reprinted in 5225.

Will. The wyll of the deuyll. [1548? etc.] *See* 6793.6 sqq.

25669 **Willan, Robert.** Conspiracie against kings, heavens scorne. A sermon. 4⁰. *J. Bill,* 1622. L.O.C.D.G⁴.+; F.HN.CAL.N.U.+

25670 — Eliah's wish: a prayer for death. A sermon preached at the funerall of viscount Sudbury, lord Bayning. 4⁰. [*T. Cotes*] *f. J. S[pencer,] Hypo-Bibliothecary of Syon Colledge, sold by R. Royston,* 1630. L.O.C.G².P.+; F.HN.HD.Y.

25671 **Willes, Richard.** Ricardi Willeii poematum liber. (In suorum poemat. librum scholia.) 2 pts. 8⁰. *ex bibliotheca Tottellina,* 1573. L.O.C.A.D(lacks tp).+; F.HN.CHI.HD.Y.+
Pt. 2 includes reprint of 14656.7.
— *ed.* See 649.

Willet, Andrew. The larger workes. 1610. *See* 25698.7.

25672 — An antilogie or counterplea to an Apologicall epistle [3893]. 4⁰. [*R. Field a. F. Kingston*] *f. T. Man,* 1603. L.O.C.D.E.+; HN.HD.PN².Y.
Kingston pr. B–Ii; Field the rest.

25673 — A catholicon, that is, a generall preservative or remedie against the pseudocatholike religion, gathered out of the epistle of S. Jude. 8⁰. *J. Legat, pr. to the Univ. of Camb., sold by S. Waterson,* [*London,*] 1602. L.O.C.A.D.+; F.HD.ILL.PN².U.+
Reprinted in 25677.

25674 — De animæ natura et viribus quæstiones quædam, partim ex Aristotelicis scriptis decerptæ: partim ex vera philosophia. 8⁰. *ex off. T. Thomasii, Acad. Cantab. typog.* 1585. L.O.C.D.E².+; F.

25675 — De vniuersali et nouissima Judæorum vocatione, liber vnus. Vbi demonstratur, quem in modum illius gentis conversio expectanda sit. 4⁰. *ex off. J. Legati, Cantab. typog.,* 1590. L.O(tp def.).C.D.LINC.+; F.NY¹¹.U.Y.

25676 — Ecclesia triumphans: that is, the joy of the English church, for the coronation of the prince, James. With a briefe exposition of the 122. psalme. 8⁰. *J. Legat, pr. to the Univ. of Camb., sold by S. Waterson,* [*London,*] 1603. L.L².O.C³.CARLISLE.

25677 — [Anr. ed., w. additions.] Ecclesia triumphans. Second edition. (Thesaurus ecclesiæ.—A catholicon.) fol. [*London,*] *J. Legat,* 1614. L.O³.C.CASHEL.G².+; F.HN.ILL.NY¹¹.Y.+
— A fruitfull and godly sermon. 1592. *See* 24899.

Willet, Andrew—*cont.*

25678 — An harmonie upon the first booke of Samuel. 4° in 8's. [*Cambridge, C. Legge*] *f. L. Greene of Cambridge, sold by R. Bankeworth,* [*London,*] 1607. Ent. to Greene and Legge 26 no. L.O.C.D.M⁴.+; F.HD.ILL.Y.
  A outer sheet is in 2 settings: A1ʳ line 4 from bottom has *Elkanah* with plain italic *E* (F) or swash *E* (O, HD).

25678a — [A variant, w. imprint:] *C. Legge, pr. to the Univ. of Camb., sold by R. Bankeworth,* [*London,*] 1607. C. C².E.G⁴.SHR.; F.

25679 — [Anr. ed.] fol. [*Cambridge,*] *C. Legge f. L. Greene,* 1614. Ent. to Legge a. Greene 28 no. 1622. L.O.C.G².M.+; F.HN.ILL.PN².U.+

25679.5 — [A variant, w. imprint:] *C. Legge, pr. to to* [sic] *the Univ. of Camb.,* 1614. L.O².C.CASHEL.G².+; DAR.PTS.Y.

25680 — An harmonie upon the second booke of Samuel. fol. *C. Legge, pr. to to* [sic] *the Univ. of Camb.,* 1614. Ent. to Legge a. L. Greene 28 no. 1622. L.O.C.CASHEL. G².+; F.HN.ILL.U.Y.+
  In the 4-leaf 'preliminaries' the 1st leaf is R1 of 25679 sq.; the 2nd is signed ¶2 and is the tp for the present text.

25681 — [A ghost.]

25682 — Hexapla in Genesin: that is, a sixfold commentarie upon Genesis. Divided into two tomes. fol. *J. Legat, pr. to the Univ. of Camb.,* 1605. Ent. to T. Man, sen., a. J. Norton 9 my. L.O.C.E.NEP.+; F.HN.BO³. TEX.U.+

25683 — Second time revised, corrected, and with divers additions enlarged. fol. *T. Creede f. T. Man,* 1608. L. O⁴.O²⁸(Bed.).C.NLW.+; F.HN.LC.V.

25683a — [Anr. issue, w. imprint on gen. tp:] *T. Creede f. J. Norton,* 1608. O.C.DUR.LIV².WN.+; HN.HD.ILL.

25684 — The third time revised. fol. [*J. Haviland f.*] *the assignes of T. Man, P. Man, a. Jonah Man,* 1632 (1633.) Ass'd to P. a. J. Man 3 my. 1624. L.O.C.D.E.+; F.HN. CHI.HD.Y.+
  The sub tp on Dd2ʳ is dated 1633. Usually bd. w. 25687.

25685 — [Anr. issue.] Hexapla in Genesin & Exodum. Now the fourth time imprinted. *J. Haviland, sold by J. Boler,* 1633. C.
  A reissue of 25684 and 25687 w. added gen. tp.

25685a — [A variant, w. imprint on gen. tp:] *J. Haviland, sold by J. Grismond,* 1633. HN.ILL.

25685a.3 — [A variant, w. imprint on gen. tp:] *J. Haviland, sold by W. Lee,* 1633. O¹⁸.

25685a.5 — [A variant, w. imprint on gen. tp:] *J. Haviland, sold by J. Parker,* 1633. U.

25686 — Hexapla in Exodum:. . . . Divided into two parts. fol. *F. Kyngston f. T. Man a. J. Norton,* 1608. L.O.C.G². YK.+; F.HN.BO³.ILL.PN².

25687 — [Anr. ed.] fol. [*J. Haviland f.*] *the assignes of T. Man, P. Man, a. Jonah Man,* 1633. Ass'd by T. Man to P. and J. Man 3 my. 1624. L.O.C.D.E.+; F.HN.CHI. HD.Y.+
  Usually bd. w. 25684; reissued in 25685 sqq.

25688 — Hexapla in Leviticum. . . . Perused and finished by P. S(mith.) fol. *A. Matthewes f. R. Milbourne,* 1631. Ent. 27 au. 1629. L.O.C.D.E².+; F.HN.HD.ILL.U.+

25689 — Hexapla in Danielem. fol. *C. Legge, pr. to the Univ. of Camb.,* 1610. Ent. to T. Man, Legge, a. L. Greene 28 no. 1622. L.O.C.E².M.+; F.HN.HD.U.Y.+

25689.3 — [A variant, w. imprint on 1st tp:] *f. L. Greene,* 1610. L².O⁵.C⁵.CASHEL.E.+; BO³.CHI.N.PTS.

25689.7 — Hexapla: that is, a six-fold commentarie upon the epistle to the Romanes. fol. *C. Legge, pr. to the Univ. of Camb.,* 1611. Ent. to Legge a. Greene 28 no. 1622. L.O¹².C⁵.D.E.+; F.HD.ILL.NY.U.+

25690 — [A variant, w. imprint on 1st tp:] *f. L. Greene,* 1611. L.O.C.NEK.SCL.+; F.HN.CHI.PN².Y.+

25691 — [Anr. ed.] fol. *C. Legge, pr. to the Univ. of Camb.,* 1620. O³.O¹¹.C.G².SCL.+; HN.HD.CHI.FORDHAM.PEN.+

25691.5 — [A variant, w. imprint on 1st tp:] *f. L. Greene,* 1620. L.O.O⁶.C³.M².+; F.HD(lacks ¶4).SMU.U.

25692 — Limbo-mastix: that is, a canvise of Limbus patrum, shewing that Christ descended not in soule to hell. Containing also a briefe replie to [19296]. [Anon.] 4°. [*F. Kingston*] *f. T. Man,* 1604. Ent. to T. Man, sen., 14 my. L.O.C.LEIC.LIV³.+; HN.DAR.N.U.
  Answered by 19295.

25693 — Loidoromastix: that is, a scourge for a rayler; containing a full answer unto [19295]. 4°. *C. Legge, pr. to the Univ. of Camb., sold by R. Bankeworth,* [*London,*] 1607. L.O.C.D(imp.).G².+; HN.DAR.U.Y.

Willet, Andrew—*cont.*

25694 — A retection, or discoverie of a false detection: containing a true defence of [25696, 25701]. 8°. *F. Kyngston f. T. Man,* 1603. L.C.C³.D.D².+; ILL.
  Answers 18754.

25695 — Sacrorum emblematum centuria vna, ... [In verse.] *Lat. a. Eng.* 4°. *ex off. J. Legate, acad. Cantab. typog.,* [1592?] L.L⁴⁶.C.A.; HN.HD(imp.).

25696 — Synopsis papismi, that is, a generall viewe of papistry: deuided into three hundreds of popish errors. 4° in 8's. *T. Orwin f. T. Man,* 1592. Ent. 8 my. L.O.O³. C.CHEL².+; F.HN.BO⁵.CHI.

25697 — Now this second time published and augmented with a fourth hundred of errors. 4° in 8's. *widdow Orwin f. T. Man,* 1594. L.O⁶.C⁹.DUL.EX.+; F.HN(imp.). BOWDOIN.HD.U.+
  At least L, O⁶, HN, HD lack *2, the dedic. to Sir W. Russell, present in F. Answered by 18754.

25698 — Now this third time published and augmented with a fift hundred of errors. fol. *F. Kyngston f. T. Man,* 1600. L.C.CASHEL.DUR⁵.E.+; F.HN.HD.ILL.U.+
  The prelims. collate A⁴ B⁶, w. A3–B1 the dedic. to Queen Elizabeth; B2–3 the Latin dedic. to Abp. Whitgift and Bp. Bancroft; B4–6 the pref. to the reader.

25698.3 — [Anr. issue, w. dedic. to Queen Elizabeth cancelled.] *F. Kyngston f. T. Man,* 1600 [1603.] L.O.
  The L copy has the Latin dedic. also cancelled and a new dedic. to King James added.

25698.5 — [Anr. issue, w. cancel dedic. to King James, and imprint:] *F. Kyngston f. T. Man,* 1603. O.LYU (dedic. to Q. Eliz. uncancelled).

25698.7 — [Anr. issue of 25698, w. added prelims., w. title:] The larger workes of Andrew Willet which containe his [Synopsis], and his commentaries upon certaine bookes of the scriptures. [*Cambridge, C. Legge,*] 1610. LEEDS.
  LEEDS has the prelims. of 25698 intact. The added tp is followed by a dedic. to Prince Henry, whose arms are on the binding.

25699 — [Anr. ed., w. additions.] Now this fourth time published. (Tetrastylon papismi.) fol. *F. Kyngston f. T. Man, sold by H. Fetherston,* 1613. L.C.CHES.NEP. STU.+; AAS.

25699a — [A variant, w. imprint:] *F. Kyngston f. T. Man, sold by H. Fetherston,* 1614. L⁴³.O⁵.C.D.E².+; F.HN.NY¹¹. PTS.
  All sub tpp still dated 1613.

25700 — [A ghost.]

25700a — Now the fifth time published by the authoritie of his majesties royall letters patens [sic], with addition of a preface. By P. Smith. fol. *J. Haviland, sold by R. Allot,* 1634. Ass'd to P. and J. Man 3 my. 1624. L. O.C².D.G².+; CAL²(lacks tp)*.IND.MIN.
  In this and the following the sub tp to bk. 2 has the imprint: *J. Haviland, sold by R. Allot, J. Grismond, R. Milbourne,* 1634; the sub tp to bk. 4 has the imprint: *by the assignes of T. Man, P. Man, a. Jonah Man,* 1634; The other sub tpp have imprints like the respective gen. tpp.
  A section around Nnnnn seems to have been pr. by J. Legat and another around Vvvvv by T. Cotes.
  Willet's son Paul had the patent to publish this; *see* Arber V.lviii.

25700a.3 — [A variant, w. imprint on gen. tp:] *J. Haviland,* 1634. C³.; F.HD.MICH.

25700a.5 — [A variant, w. imprint on gen. tp:] *J. Haviland, sold by J. Grismond,* 1634. O⁸.C⁵.BED.E.SCL.+; F.HN.HD. ILL.

25700a.7 — [A variant, w. imprint on gen. tp:] *J. Haviland, sold by R. Milbourne,* 1634. O¹⁰.O¹³.C.M².STU.+; HD.ILL. N.U. Iowa U.+

25701 — Tetrastylon papisticum, that is, the foure principal pillers of papistrie. 4° in 8's. *R. Robinson f. T. Man,* 1593. L.C⁹.D.DUL.YK.+; F.HN.BOWDOIN. CHI.HD.U.

25702 — [Anr. ed.] 4° in 8's. *widdow Orwin f. T. Man,* 1596. L.; HD.U.Y.
  Answered by 18754.

25703 — [Anr. ed., w. title:] Tetrastylon papismi. . . . Reuiewed againe and inlarged throughout, and the third time published. 4° in 8's. *F. Kingston f. T. Man,* 1599. L.O.C.D.E².+; F.HN.N.NY¹¹.Y.+ 𝔄
  Reprinted in 25699.

Willet, Andrew—*cont.*

25704 — Thesaurus ecclesiæ: that is, the treasure of the church set forth in the 17. chapter of the gospel by S. John. 8°. *J. Legat, pr. to the Univ. of Camb.* [*a. R. Field,*] *sold by S. Waterson,* [*London,*] 1604. L.O.A.; F.U.
Legat app. pr. only the 1st 2 quires. Reprinted in 25677.

25705 — A treatise of Salomons mariage, or, a congratulation for the happie mariage betweene Frederike the V. And the princesse, the ladie Elizabeth. 4°. *F. K[ingston] f. T. Man the elder a. W. Welby,* 1612 [o.s.] L(impr. cropt).O.C.E.M.+; F(tp def.).HN.BO³.N.U.+

25706 — [Anr. issue, w. cancel tp, w. imprint:] *R. B[adger] f. R. Allot, sold by J. Stafford,* 1634. L⁴.

25707 — [A trans.?] Tractatus de Salomonis nuptiis. 4°. *typis F. Kingston, imp. T. Man,* 1612 [o.s.] L.O.C².C³.M.+; F.HD.Y.
This may be the orig. and 25705 the trans.
— *See also* 13721.

Willet, Roland, *tr. See* 21510.

William, *Bp. of Ruremunde. See* 15653.

William, *of Malmesbury. See* 21783.

William, *of Occam. See* 12510.

25707.5 **William,** *of Palermo.* [William of Palermo, a prose romance.] 4°. [*W. de Worde,* c. 1515.] O(collotype only, of 2 leaves: P3, 4).
P3ʳ has the catch title: 'kyng Wyl.'

25708 **William I,** *Prince of Orange.* A declaration and publication of the prince of Orange, contaynyng the cause of his necessary defence against the duke of Alba. *Tr.* out of French. 8°. *J. Day,* [1568?] L.L².; F.
End of text dated 20 July 1568.

25709 — Now = 25710.5.
25710 — A supplication to the kinges maiestie of Spayne. By which is declared the troubles in the low Countrie. *Tr.* out of Duytsch by T. W. 8° in 4's. *H. Middleton,* 1573. L.L².; F(date shaved).HN.
— A treatise of the peace made between the states and the prince of Orenge, published the viij day of Nouember. 1576. [1577.] *See* 18448.

25710.5 — The aduise and answer of yᵉ prince of Orenge, made by the estates generall vpon the articles between don John of Austrich, and the said estates. *Tr.* out of Dutch. 8°. *John Jugge a. J. Allde,* [1577.] L².; F.
(Formerly 25709) End of text dated 19 Feb. 1577.

25711 — Antwerpes vnitye. An accord or peace in religion, and gouernment, concluded by his highnes, the 12. of June 1579. Englished by the printer hereof [i.e. R. Day.] 8°. *R. Daye,* 1579. L.L².; HN.

— The apologie or defence, of prince William. 1581. *See* 15207.5.

25712 — A iustification or cleering of the prince of Orendge agaynst the false sclaunders. 8°. *J. Day,* (1575(24 fb.)) L.L².O.C².P.+; F.HN.HD.ILL.Y.+
Tp varies; a few copies (C², C³, 1 HN) have: 'Translated out of French by Arthur Goldyng', omitted in most copies.

25713 — A true discourse of the assault committed vpon the prince of Orange, by J. Jauregui. *Tr.* out of the frenche copie printed at Antwerp by C. Plantin. Anno. 1582. [With depositions, etc. in *Span. a. Eng.*] 8° in 4's. [*H. Bynneman*] *f. T. Charde a. W. Broome,* (1582.) Ent. 12 ap. L.O(2, 1 imp.).HAGUE.; F.
This is the later ed.

25714 — [Anr. ed.] A briefe discourse of the assault. 4°. *T. Dawson f. T. C[hard] a. W. B[roome,]* 1582. L.O.; HD.
This is the earlier ed. 2nd A1–E3 is prob. by anr. printer.

25715 **Williams, Caleb.** Autodidactus a round-hand coppybook. *sold by I. Pask,* [c. 1690.] = Wing W 2643, with the erroneous date '1593' handstamped on another tp, which begins: 'Nuncius oris'.

Williams, Griffith, *Bp.* The best religion. 1636. *See* 25718.

25716 — The delights of the saints. A most comfortable treatise, of grace and peace. 8°. [*Eliot's Court Press*] *f. N. Butter.* 1622. Ent. 14 de. 1621. L².O.G².NLW.PLUME.; F.

Williams, Griffith, *Bp.*—*cont.*

25717 — The resolution of Pilate. A sermon. 8°. *E. Gryffin,* [1614.] Ent. 22 jy. 1614. L².

25718 — The right way to the best religion, wherein is largely explained the summe and principall heads of the gospell. In certaine sermons. fol. *G. Miller f. P. Stephens a. C. Meredith,* 1636 (1635.) Ent. 9 fb. 1635. L.O.C.D.E².+; F.HN.ILL.PN².U.
The above tp is conjugate w. A3, the dedic., in the F copy, which also has the tp: 'The best religion; wherein is largely explaned [etc.]' conjugate with To the reader and Contents and bd. as A1,4. It is not clear whether this is intended as an additional or a cancel tp; O has the 'best' tp on a stub, followed by the 'right' tp; C has the 'best' tp mounted, and the 'right' tp is lacking.

25719 — Seven goulden candlestickes houlding the seauen greatest lights of christian religion: 1624. 4° in 8's. [*T. Snodham*] *f. N. Butter,* [1624.] Ent. 8 fb. 1624. L.O.BTL.E.P.+; F.HD.U.WASH².
The above tp is engraved.

25720 — [Anr. issue, w. cancel letterpress tp, w. imprint:] *f. N. Butter,* 1627. L.O.C³.G².NLW.+; F.U.

25720.5 — [Anr. issue, w. cancel engr. tp, a copy of that in 25719.] Seven golden candlesticks . . . 1627. *f. N. Butter,* [1627.] L.

25721 — The true church: shewed to all men. In six bookes. fol. *J. Haviland f. N. Butter,* 1629. L.O.C.D.E².+; HN.ILL.LC.U.Y.+

25722 **Williams, John,** *of Oxford University.* De Christi iustitia, et in regno spirituali ecclesiæ pastorum officio. Concio. 4°. *Oxoniæ, ex off. J. Barnesij,* 1597. L².
— *See also* 1181.

25723 **Williams, John,** *Abp.* Great Britains Salomon. A sermon preached at the funerall, of the king, James. 4°. [*Eliot's Court Press f.*] *J. Bill,* 1625. L.O.C.NLW.P.+; F.HN.HD.N.U.+
A3ʳ line 1 begins: 'on,'.

25723a — [Anr. ed.] 4°. [*Eliot's Court Press f.*] *J. Bill,* 1625. L.O.C.DUR⁵.E.+; F.HN.HD.NY¹¹.Y.+
A3ʳ line 1 begins: 'mole'. Part of quire G and all of H–K have the text in the same typesetting as 25723.

25724 — The holy table, name & thing, more anciently, properly, and literally used under the New Testament, then that of an altar: written by a minister in Lincolnshire, in answer to D. Coal [13270]. [Anon.] 4°. [*Eliot's Court Press,*] *Printed for the Diocese of Lincoln,* 1637. L.O.C³.D.E.+; BO³.HD.NY¹¹.PH².U.
Page 234, last line begins: 'votions'. At least 1 copy each at O³(F.116) and D(P.mm.33/2) has some sheets from 25725 mixed in. Answered by 13267.
It is reasonably certain that no one compositor and prob. no one printing house produced the whole of this or any of the following eds. The printers supplied in the imprints have been identified from the orns. in the prelims. and A1ʳ, and how much they contributed to the rest of the respective eds. is undetermined.
Arber IV.528 has a list of printers, 3 of whom (Alsop, Mathewes, A. Griffin of Eliot's Court Press) are stated to have reprinted eds., and a 4th, N. Okes, who 'printed yᵉ booke yᵃᵗ was lately Burnt' (i.e. 25726?).

25725 — [Anr. ed.] 4°. [*Eliot's Court Press,*] *Printed for the Diocese of Lincoln,* 1637. L.O.C.BIRM.D.+; F.ILL.NY¹¹.Y.
Page 234, last line begins: 'saying'; page 1, sidenote (a), line 2: 'in the Cause of' (with swash C).

25725.2 — [Anr. ed.] 4°. [*Eliot's Court Press,*] *Printed for the Diocese of Lincoln,* 1637. L¹³.O⁸.C.CASHEL.M(deposit). +; F(2).HN.CHI.HD.N.
Page 234, last line begins: 'saying'; page 1, sidenote (a), line 2: 'in the Cause of' (with plain C); page 1, third line of text from the bottom has 'Judgement' (with roman J).
In the F (and other?) copies of this and 25725, part of quire X and all of Y and Gg1 are the same typesetting, reimposed.

25725.4 — [Anr. ed.] 4°. *Printed for the Diocese of Lincoln,* 1637. L³.O²⁷.C.CASHEL.NLW.+; CAL.ILL.
Page 234, last line begins: 'saying'; page 1, sidenote (a), line 2: 'cha. in the Cause'.

Williams, John, *Abp.—cont.*

25725.6 — [Anr. ed.] 4°. [*J. Dawson?*] *Printed for the Diocese of Lincoln,* 1637. O.C⁴.D.DUR⁵.NLW.+
Page 234, last line begins: 'saying'; page 1, sidenote (a), line 2: '*cham. in the*'. In the O (and other?) copies of this and 25725.8, quires R–Aa are in the same typesetting.

25725.8 — [Anr. ed.] 4°. *Printed for the Diocesse* [sic] *of Lincoln,* 1637. L⁴⁶.O.C.D.E.+; CU.HD.
Page 234, last line begins: 'saying'; page 1, sidenote (a), line 2: '*in the cause of*' (with lowercase c).

25726 — [Anr. ed.] 4°. [*N. Okes,*] *Printed for the Diocese of Lincoln,* 1637. L.O.O². C⁵. York U.+; F.HN.CAL⁶.HD (lacks tp).WASH².
Page 234, last line begins: 'thereunto'. In the O, HD (and other?) copies of this and 25725.8, quires V–Y, Aa are in the same typesetting.

25727 — *Perseverantia sanctorum. A sermon of persevering in patience, repentance, and humiliation. Preached before the lords of the parliament the 18. day of February* 1628. 4°. [*T. Harper f.*] *J. Bill,* 1628. L.O. C.DUR⁵.M.+; F.HN.HD.N.U.+

25728 — *A sermon of apparell, preached the 22. of February.* 4°. *J. Bill,* 1620. L.O.C.DUR⁵.YK.+; F.HN.NY¹¹.Y.

25728.5 — [A variant, w. imprint:] *R. Barker a. J. Bill,* 1620. L³.; HD.U.

25729 — *A sermon preached . . . the sixth of April.* 1628. *Before the lords.* 4°. *J. Bill,* 1628. L.O.C.A.BTL.+; HN.BO. Sydney U.
— *Three small and plaine treatises.* [1620.] *See* 24259.
— *See also* 10240 sqq., 13270.

25730 **Williams, John,** *Abp., pseud.* Punition de Dieu arrive a Londres. *S. Omer,* 1626.
Not an STC book.

25731 **Williams, Sir Roger.** The actions of the Lowe Countries. [*Ed.*] (J. Haywarde.) 4°. *H. Lownes f. M. Lownes,* 1618. Ent. 1 de. 1617. L.O.C.E.YK.+; F.HN.HD.N. NY.+
Date at end of dedic. varies: 1617 or 1618; both at F.

25732 — *A briefe discourse of warre.* 4°. *T. Orwin,* 1590. L.L². L¹³.; F(lacks I4).HD.LC.PN.
B2ʳ line 1: 'All those'. L, HD have 3 lines of errata on I4ʳ.

25732.5 — [Anr. ed.] 4°. *T. Orwin,* 1590. O.C².; F(2).HN.
B2ʳ line 1: 'Al those'. Quire A is from the same typesetting as 25732.

25733 — [Anr. ed.] Newly perused. 4°. *T. Orwin,* 1590. O(lacks H4).C².D².ETON.NLW.+; HN.HD.MICH.

25733.5 — *In obitum illustrisismi* [sic] *nobilissimique viri . . . R. Dudlæi, . . . Leicestriæ comitis, . . . carmina funebria.* [In verse.] s.sh.fol. *T. Orwinus, imp. J. Daldern,* 1588. C⁵.

25734 — *Newes from sir Roger Williams. With a discourse printed at Rheines* [sic] *containing the most happie victorie, lately obtained by the prince de Conty.* 4°. *J. Woolfe, sold by A. White,* 1591. L².O.P.
— *A particuler, of the yeelding of Zutphen. With the enterprise of sir R. Williams.* 1591. *See* 26134.

Williams, Stephen, *tr. See* 18012.

25735 **Williams, Thomas.** The strange and cruell martyrdome of an English man [T. Williams] in Dunkerke. 4°. [*W. Kearney?*] *f. W. Wright,* 1591. Ent. 21 ja. O.; F.

25736 **Williams, Wat.** Wat Williams will. Well-wishing Williams will and testament. *Ballad.* 2 pts. s.sh.fol. *f. H. Gosson,* [c. 1635.] L.

25736.3 **Williamson, Robert.** Elementa linguæ Latinæ, præuia Despauterianæ grammaticæ. Editio altera, priore auctior & limatior. 8°. *Edinburgi, ex off. J. Wreittoun,* 1624. E.

25736.5 — [Anr. issue.] Elementa linguæ Latinæ, e grammaticorum imprimis Donati, Despauterij, &c. cornucopiæ grammaticali excerpta. Editio tertia. 8°. *Edinburgi, J. Wreittoun,* 1625. D.
The text on A1–B2 has been revised and reset. The rest is the same setting as 25736.3.

25737 — Grammatica Latina, ad artium methodum, discentium statum, et unius anni studium, è grãmaticorum cornucopiæ, præcipue J. Despauterij & Linacri commode concinnata. Iam tertiò limata. 8°. *Edinburgi, J. Wreittoun,* 1632. L(tp only, Harl.5938/25). E²(2). STD.

Williamson, Robert—*cont.*

25737.5 — Paedagogia moralis tertiâ R. Williamsoni Cuprensis curâ aucta et limata. 8°. *Edinopoli, J. Wreittoun,* 1635. E.
Collates [–]⁸ B–D⁸.

25737.7 — [Anr. ed.] 8°. [*Edinburgh, J. Wreittoun?* c. 1635.] C³ (imp.).
Collates A–C⁸ D⁴.

25738 **Williamson, Thomas.** A comfortable meditation of humane frailtie, and divine mercie: in two sermons. 4°. *J. Haviland f. J. Boler,* 1630. L.O.C.E².NOR².+; F.HD(lacks tp).LC.

25739 — = 25740.

25740 — The sword of the spirit to smite in pieces that antichristian Goliah, who daily defieth the Lords people. 8°. *E. Griffin,* 1613. Ent. to T. Purfoot, jun., 29 jn. 1606; to E. Griffin 2 no. 1613. L(2, 1 lacks tp).O.OS.; F.HN.U.
— *tr. See* 12136.

Williatt, Andrew. *See* Willet, A.

25741 **Willis, Edmond.** An abreviation of writing by character. 8°. (*G. Purslow,* 1618.) Ent. 28 jn. L.O.O².LINC(lacks tp).; LC.
Copies vary: the dedic. to Nicholas [Felton] erroneously terms him Bishop of Coventry and Lichfield (L) or is corrected to Bishop of Bristol (O, O², LC).

25742 — Second edition, much enlarged. 8°. *G. Purslowe, sold by N. Bourne a. P. Stephens,* 1627. L.O.C⁶.M². Warrington PL.+; HD.Y.

25743 **Willis, Edward.** The blinde mans staffe, or the poore mans comfort: dialogue-wise. 8°. *G. Purslowe f. H. Bell,* 1615. Ent. 1 au. 1614. L.M.

25743.5 **Willis, John,** *Petitioner.* [Petition to King James for the repair of causeways near Bristol, with letters of the Earl of Pembroke addressed to Sir John Herbert.] 4°. [*R. Barker,* 1611.] O(lacks tp).
The last letter is dated 27 Apr. 1611.

25744 — = 25744a.

25744a **Willis, John,** *Stenographer.* The art of stenographie, teaching by plaine and certaine rules, the way of compendious writing. Whereunto is annexed a direction for steganógraphie, or, secret writing. [*Anon.*] 8°. [*W. White*] *f. C. Burbie,* 1602. Ent. 19 ap. L.L³⁰.L⁴⁴.O.O⁵.+; F.

25744a.5 — [Anr. ed.] The art of stenographie: or, short writing. Invented by J. Willis and now newly inlarged. The fift edition. 8°. *W. White,* 1617. Ass'd to W. Welby 16 oc. 1609. M².

25744a.6 — [Anr. ed.] Now fully perfected. The sixt edition. 8°. *f. Robert Willis, sould by W. Jones* [3,] 1618. Ass'd by Welby to R. Willis 10 oc. 1617. C⁶.
See Court-Book C, pp. 94, 460.

25744a.8 — The eighth edition. 8°. *f. H. Seile,* 1623. Ass'd 2 de. 1622. L³⁰.; NY.
See Court-Book C, p. 152.

25745 — The ninth edition. Whereunto is now adjoyned the Schoolemaster. 8°. [*G. Purslowe*] *f. H. Seyle,* 1628. L.O(2).PARIS.
Although the letterpress tp of this and the following eds. calls for 25751, the latter is rarely found, and all copies are listed at 25751.

25746 — The tenth edition. 8°. [*G. Purslowe*] *f. H. Seyle,* 1632. L(imp.).PLUME.; LC.Y.
PLUME and LC have an engr. tp: '10ᵗʰ edition' dated 1628, also found separately at L(Harl.5927/486).

25746.5 — The twelfth edition. 8°. *f. H. Seile,* 1638. E.
E and one L copy of the 1647 ed. (Wing W 2810) have bd. w. them 4 engr. pages headed 'Certaine exemplary sentences in stenographicall characters' and dated 20 Aug. 1634 at the end.

25746.7 — [A variant, w. imprint:] *f. H. Seile,* 1639. C⁶.M³.
Both copies have an engr. tp: '10ᵗʰ edition' dated 1628.

25747 — [A trans.] Stenographia, sive ars compendiosè scribendi. Item, Mnemonica. 12°. *per H. Lownes, sumpt. R. Willis & N. Browne,* 1618. Ent. to R. Willis 15 de. 1617. O.; Y.
Neither copy has 25748 bd. w. it.

Willis, John, *Stenographer—cont.*

25748 — Mnemonica, sive reminiscendi ars: . . . in tres libros digesta. 12°. *per H. Lownes, sumpt. N. Browne,* 1618. Ent. to R. Willis 16 oc. 1617. L.L³⁰.O.C³.D.+; F.HD. ILL.NY.

25749 — [A trans. of the 3rd bk., w. revisions.] The art of memory, so far forth as it dependeth upon places and idea's. Now published in English by the said author. 12°. *W. Jones, sold by H. Seely,* 1621. Ent. to R. Willis 16 oc. 1617. L.L¹⁶.L³⁰.O.O⁵.; Y.

25750 — The school-maister to the art of stenographie. Explayning the rules, and teaching the practise thereof. 12°. *W. Jones f. R. Willis, sould by H. Seile,* 1622. Ent. to R. Willis 13 no. 1621. C.

25751 — Second edition. 8°. [*G. Purslowe*] *f. H. Seyle,* 1628. L. L⁸.O.C⁶. London, Science Museum Library.; HN.Y. O is bd. w. 25745; L and Y w. 25746.

25752 **Willis, R.** Mount Tabor. Or private exercises of a penitent sinner. By R. W[illis] esquire. 12°. *R. B[adger] f. P. Stephens a. C. Meredith,* 1639. Ent. 19 no. L(2). O.SH.; F.HN.HD.NY¹¹.Y.+
(Formerly also 20595)

25753 **Willis, Timothy.** Propositiones tentationum: sive propaedeumata de vitis et faecunditate compositorum naturalium: quæ sunt elementa chymica. 8°. *per J. Legatt,* 1615. L.O.C.D.ETON.; WIS.Y.

25754 — The search of causes. Containing a theophysicall investigation of the possibilitie of transmutatorie alchemie. 8°. *J. Legatt,* 1616. L.L¹⁶.O.C.E².

Willmers, Thomas. *See* 24559.

25755 **Willoby, Henry.** Willobie his Auisa. Or the true picture of a modest maid. In hexamiter verse. 4°. *J. Windet,* 1594. Ent. 3 se. L. Wallington, Cambo, near Morpeth, Northumberland.; F(2, 1 imp.).PFOR.

25756 — [Anr. ed.] Whereunto is added an Apologie, [etc.] never before published. The fourth time corrected and augmented. 4°. *J. Windet,* 1605. F.HD(*2, 3 in facs.). The Apologie is dated 30 June 1596. An ed. was called in by the Stat. Co. 4 June 1599; *see* Arber III.678.

25757 — [Anr. ed.] The fourth time corrected. 4°. *J. Windet,* 1609. F.HN. Robert Taylor.

25758 — The fifth time corrected. 8°. *W. Stansby,* 1635. Ass'd 11 se. 1611. L(imp.).; F.HN.N(imp.).ROS.Y.+

25759 **Willoughbie, John.** Mnemosynon Kyrio-euchariston: a treatise on the supper of the Lord. 8°. *Oxford, J. Barnes, sold by S. Waterson,* [*London,*] 1603. L(tp def.).O³.YK.
— *tr. See* 14641.

Willoughby, Giles, *tr. See* 19794.

25759.5 **Willughby, Edward.** To the right honorable the lords in Parliament assembled. The humble petition of E. Willughby . . . William Pargiter . . . Montague Wood [to dismiss two bills in Chancery and make Lady Dorothy Wharton deliver up a deed of lease to the petitioners.] s.sh.fol. [*London,* 1621.] L⁸(cropt, GL 6410).
For a petition to Commons in the same dispute, accusing Lord Chancellor Bacon of accepting a bribe, *see* Notestein II.246, etc.

25760 **Willymat, William.** A loyal subjects looking-glasse, or a direction, to the duties of an honest and obedient subject to his king. 4°. *G. Elde f. R. Boulton,* 1604. Ent. 27 jn. L.L³⁰.C(2).D(lacks tp)*.EX(lacks tp)*.; Elmira College, Elmira, N.Y.

25761 — [A variant, w. imprint:] *G. Elde f. R. Boulton,* [1604.] O.O².C.C².C⁹(2).; F.HD.

25761.5 — Physicke, to cure the most dangerous disease of desperation. 8°. [*W. White*] *f. R. Boulton,* 1604. Ent. 29 au. D(imp.).

25762 — [A variant, w. imprint:] [*W. White*] *f. R. Boulton,* 1605. L.C.NLW.

25763 — [Anr. ed., omitting dedic., init. W. W.] 8°. *f. R. Boulton,* 1607. L.LK.; PN².

25763.5 — [Anr. ed., init. W. W., w. title:] The anchor of faith. . . . Especially in that gulfe of desperation. 8°. [*M. Flesher*] *f. R. Wilson,* 1628. O³(imp.).C.
(Formerly 24920)
— *tr. See* 14357.

25764 **Wilmot, Robert.** The tragedie of Tancred and Gismund. Compiled by the gentlemen of the Inner Temple. Newly reuiued and polished according to the decorum of these daies. 4°. *T. Scarlet, solde by R. Robinson,* 1591. HN. Greg 104.

25764a — [A variant, w. imprint:] *T. Scarlet, solde by R. Robinson,* 1592. L(3, 2 imp.*).L⁶.O.C⁶.ETON(lacks tp)*.; F.HN.HD.

25765 — Syrophænissa or, the Cananitish womans conflicts: in twelue seuerall tractats discouered, sectio prima. At Horndon on the hil, in the countie of Essex. 1598. 8°. *V. Simmes,* 1601. C.
The c copy has only Tractates 1–6.

25765.5 — [Anr. ed.?] 8°. *V. Sims,* 1610. L(tp only, Ames II.218). The title has no mention of 'sectio prima'.

25766 **Wilson, Christopher,** *Poet.* Almightie God I pray, his holy spirite to send. [In verse.] s.sh.fol. *A. Lacy,* 1566 (16 au.) Ent. 1566–67. L.

25767 **Wilson, Christopher,** *Preacher.* Selfe deniall: or, a christians hardest taske. 4°. *N. Okes f. R. Whitakers,* 1625. L.O.C.C².INN.+; F.HN.HD.PN².Y.

25767a — [A ghost.]

Wilson, Florence. Florentii Voluzeni scholia in Scipionis somnium. [1535?] *See* 5317.5.

Wilson, Galfridus. An almanack. 1634. *See* 529.8.

25768 **Wilson, George.** The commendation of cockes, and cockfighting. 4°. [*T. Purfoot*] *f. H. Tomes,* 1607. Ent. to R. Ockold 24 no. 1606. L.CHATS.; F.HN.BO⁵.Y.

Wilson, Jeffrey. Almanacks. 1625, etc. *See* 529 sqq.

Wilson, John, *of Boston. See* 22922.

25769 **Wilson, John,** *Preacher.* Some helpes to faith. Shewing the necessitie, grounds, kinds, degrees, signes of it. 12°. *J. L[egat] f. R. Mylbourne,* 1625. Ent. 14 oc. 1624. L.O.

25769.3 — Second edition, explaining and inlarging something in the former. 12°. *f. R. Milbourne,* 1629. C¹⁰.D.DUL.; PN².

25769.5 — [Anr. ed., enlarged.] Third edition. 12°. [*A. Mathewes*] *f. R. Milbourne,* 1630. D.M.; F.HD(2).PN².

25770 — Zacheus converted: or, the rich publicans repentance. Restitution. 12°. *T. Cotes f. F. Clifton,* 1631. Ent. to J. Bellamy a. Clifton 27 ja. L.L².O.; F.U.

25770.5 — [A variant, w. imprint:] *T. Cotes f. J. Bellamy,* 1631. O²⁸.C.; PN².TORONTO².Y.

25771 **Wilson, John,** *Priest.* The English martyrologe conteyning a summary of the lives of the saintes of England, Scotland, and Ireland. Collected and distributed into monethes. [Init. I. W. Priest.] 8°. [*St. Omer, English College Press,*] 1608. L.O.C.E.M.+; F.HN. HD.N(imp.).Y.+
A&R 889. Answered by 24269. On Aa⁸ is 'A catalogue of those who have suffered death in England, 1535. unto 1608.', which is a different text from 26000.8.

25772 — [Anr. ed.] Reviewed, & much augmented in this second edition. [Init. I. W. P.] 8°. [*St. Omer, English College Press,*] 1640. L.L⁹.L³⁵.A²(imp.).ST.+; F.HN.BR.ILL.TEX.+
A&R 890.
— The fierie tryall . . . as a counter-poyze to I. W. priest. 1611. *See* 24269.
— The Roman martyrologe. 1627. *See* 17533.

25773 — The treasury of devotion. Contayning divers pious prayers. Togeather with the seaven little offices in Latin and English. Collected by I. W. P. 12°. [*St. Omer, English College Press,*] 1622. L.O.
A&R 891.
— *ed. See* 14945.5.
— *tr. See* 1699, 1702, 3103, 4932.5, 12144.5, 15117.3, 15524.
— *See also* 6777.7, 6798.3, 16877, 17533, 21148.

25774 **Wilson, Matthew.** Charity mistaken, with the want whereof, catholickes are unjustly charged. [E. Knott, *pseud.*] 8°. [*St. Omer, widow of C. Boscard,*] 1630. L(imp.).C.C².USHAW(imp.).W.+
A&R 892. Sometimes attrib. to Sir T. Matthew. Answered by 20135.

Wilson, Matthew—*cont.*

25775 — Christianity maintained. Or a discovery of sundry doctrines tending to the overthrowe of christian religion: contayned in [5138]. [Init. I. H.] 4°. [*St. Omer, English College Press,*] 1638. L.O.C.D.DUR⁵.+; F.U.Y. (Formerly also 5149) A&R 893.

25776 — The church conquerant. 1638. = 11110.
— A defence of Nicholas Smith. 1631. *See* 1017.

25777 — A direction to be observed by N. N. [i.e. W. Chillingworth] if hee meane to proceede in answering the booke intituled Mercy and truth. [E. Knott, *pseud.*] 8°. [*English secret press,*] 1636. O.C.E.
A&R 895. An attempt to discredit in advance the arguments in 5138.

25778 — Mercy & truth. Or charity maintayned by catholiques. By way of reply upon [20135]. [Init. I. H.] 4°. [*St. Omer, English College Press,*] 1634. L.O.C¹⁰.E.M.+; F.HN.BO³.N.U.+
A&R 897. Answered by 5138.

25779 — A modest briefe discussion of some points taught by doctour Kellison in [14914]. By N. Smyth [i.e. M. Wilson.] 8°. *Rouan* [i.e. *English secret press,*] 1630. C.BRISTOL.HP.ST.W.; N.
A&R 898. Answered by 6929, 22809a.5. Extracts are reprinted in 11109.5.

25779.3 — The second edition. 8°. *Rouen,* [*J. Boulanger,*] 1630. AMP.VAL.W(imp.).
A&R 899. Includes 'A charitable qualification [of 22809a.5]' by [M. Wilson] and an 'Admonition to the reader' by the editor, [J. Floyd.] The latter is in 2 typesettings: 1 pr. [*St. Omer, G. Seutin*] and the other [*Rouen, N. Courant.*]

25779.5 — [Anr. issue, w. cancel tp and additional prelims.] The second edition. Whereunto is annexed a charitable qualificatiō of [22809a.5]. *Rouen, J. Boulenger,* 1630. C³.HP.
A&R 900. The additions were pr. [*St. Omer, G. Seutin.*]

25780 — Motives maintained. Or a reply unto M. Chillingworthes answere to his owne motives [in 5138]. [Anon.] 4°. [*St. Omer, English College Press,*] 1638. L.O.C.LINC.P.+; F.U.Y.
A&R 901.
— *tr. See* 15523.

25781 **Wilson, Robert.** The coblers prophesie. Written by R. Wilson. 4°. *J. Danter f. C. Burbie,* 1594. Ent. 8 jn. L(imp.).L⁶.O(2).C⁶.E.; F(imp.).HN.HD.ILL.PFOR.+ Greg 124.

25782 — The pedlers prophecie. [Anon.] 4°. *T. Creede, sold by W. Barley,* 1595. Ent. to Creede 13 my. 1594. L. L⁶(lacks tp).O(lacks tp).C⁶(lacks tp).; F.HN.HD.PFOR. Hickmott. Greg 134.

25783 — The pleasant and stately morall, of the three lordes and three ladies of London. [Init. R. W.] 4°. *R. Jhones,* 1590. Ent. 31 jy. L.L⁶(imp.).O(tp def.).; F(2 imp.). HN.PFOR. Greg 93.

25784 — A right excellent and famous comœdy called the three ladies of London. [Init. R. W.] 4°. *R. Warde,* 1584. L.O.C⁶.; HN(tp facs.). Greg 85.

25785 — [Anr. ed.] 4°. *J. Danter,* 1592. L(imp.).; F(2).HN.HD. PFOR. Mrs. Donald Hyde, Somerville, N.J.
— *See also* 7675, 24913.

25786 **Wilson, Thomas,** *Divine.* A christian dictionarie, opening the signification of the chiefe wordes of the Old and New Testament. 4° in 8's. *W. Jaggard,* 1612. Ent. 27 jn. 1611. L.O(imp.).BRISTOL².D.G².+; F.CHI. HD.ILL.Y.+

25787 — Second edition, augmented. 4° in 8's. *W. Jaggard,* 1616. L.O.C.G².SH.+; F.HN.CHI.GRO.PH.+

25788 — Third edition, augmented. 4° in 8's. *W. Jaggard,* 1622. L.O.C.E.LYU.+; F.HN.HD.ILL.N.+
Some copies have the misprint 'Jaggad' in the imprint; both variants at C.

25789 — Fourth edition; augmented. Whereunto is added a large edition [*sic*], of words and phrases by J. Bagwell. 4° in 8's. *T. Cotes, sold by F. Clifton,* [c. 1635.] Ass'd from I. Jaggard to T. a. R. Cotes 19 jn. 1627. L.O.BIRM.D.G⁴.+; F.HN.NY¹¹(imp.). Tufts U.

25790 — Christs farewell to Jerusalem, and last prophesie. A sermon at the funerall of doctor Colfe. 8°. [*T. Snodham*] *f. F. Burton,* 1614. Ent. 3 no. 1613. L³.O.C.LINC.; U.Y.
(Formerly also 25797a)

Wilson, Thomas, *Divine*—*cont.*

25791 — A commentarie vpon the most divine epistle of S. Paul to the Romanes. In forme of a dialogue. 4° in 8's. *W. Jaggard,* 1614. Ent. 13 ap. 1613. L.O.D.G⁴.HER.+; F.HN.HD.ILL.U.+

25792 — [Anr. ed.] fol. *W. Jaggard,* 1620. J(untraced).

25793 — Second edition. fol. *I. Jaggard,* 1627. L.O.C².BTU.E².+; F.HN.HD.N.U.+

25794 — A dialogue about justification. 1610. = pt. of 25795.

25795 — Jacobs ladder, or a short treatise laying forth Gods eternall purpose. (Dialogue about justification.—Receite against heresie.—Sermon of sanctification.—Sermon of the spirituall combat.) 8°. *W. Hall f. N. Butter,* 1611. Ent. 19 oc. 1610. L.O.LIV³.P.; F.U(2). (25794 is pt. of this) The date on the Dialogue sub tp varies: 1610 (O) or 1611 (L, F).

25796 — Saints by calling: or called to be saints. A godly treatise. 4°. *W. Jaggard,* 1620. Ent. 19 my. L.O.C.BIRM.; F. HD(lacks Gg4).ILL.NY¹¹.U.

25797 — A sermon preached . . . in Canterbury to the corporation of black-smiths. Whereunto are annexed a short catechisme, with two short tables. 8°. [*N. Okes*] *f. S. Waterson,* 1610. Ent. 25 oc. LINC.; F.

25797a — A sermon . . . at the funerall of doctor Colfe. 1614. = 25790.

25798 — Theologicall rules, to guide us in the holy scriptures: two centuries. Also Ænigmata sacra, holy riddles; with their resolutions. Foure centuries. By T. W[ilson] Preacher. 8°. *E. Griffin f. F. Burton,* 1615. Ent. 8 de. 1614. L.L³.O.C.G².+; F.HN.HD.U.Y.+
Sometimes erroneously attrib. to T. Walkington.

25799 **Wilson, Thomas,** *Secretary of State.* The arte of rhetorique, for the vse of all suche as are studious of eloquence. 4°. (*R. Graftonus,*) 1553 (ja.) L.O.C.G⁴. Warrington PL.; F.HN.CU.HD(lacks col.).N.+
Includes a trans. of Erasmus on marriage; cf. 10492.

25800 — [Anr. ed.] Newlie sette forthe again, with a prologue to the reader. 4° in 8's. *J. Kingston,* 1560 (10 de.) L.O.C(imp.).E.P.+; HN.BR(imp.).ILL.TORONTO².

25801 — [Anr. ed.] 4° in 8's. *J. Kingston,* 1562. L.O(2, 1 imp.). C⁴.G².P.; F.HN.BO.ILL.PH²(imp.).+

25802 — [Anr. ed.] 4° in 8's. *J. Kingston,* 1563. L³.O.BIRM² (K.N.).HETH.; F.CH. Pirie.
At least L³, HETH, CH are bd. w. 20925a.5 and apparently have the 1563 sheets. O, F are bd. separately and have a few sheets from 25801 and 25803 mixed in, the latter having 36 lines a page.

25803 — [Anr. ed.] 4° in 8's. *J. Kingston,* 1567. L.O⁴⁸(imp.).C. G².P.+; F.CHI.ILL.PEN.STAN.+

25804 — [Anr. ed.] 4° in 8's. *J. Kyngston,* 1580. L.L³⁰.O.C⁴.LYD. +; CAL.CU.HD.N.WIS.

25805 — [Anr. ed.] 4° in 8's. *J. Kingston,* 1584. L.O(imp.).O²⁶ (frags.).E².G².; HN.CU.ILL.PEN.TEX.

25806 — [Anr. ed.] 4° in 8's. *G. Robinson,* 1585. L.O.C.BRISTOL². E².+; F.HN.ILL.NY¹¹.WIS.+

25807 — A discourse vppon vsurye, by waye of dialogue. 8°. (*in æd. R. Tottelli,*) 1572. Ent. 18 fb. 1583. L.O.C².E.P. +; F.HN.HD.ILL.PEN.+

25808 — [Anr. ed.] 8°. *R. Warde,* 1584. L.L³⁰.O.C(imp.).P.+; F. CU.HD.MIN.PEN.+
Tottell's rights yielded to the company 8 Jan. 1584; see Arber II.787.

25809 — The rule of reason, conteinyng the arte of logique. 8°. (*R. Grafton,*) 1551. L.O.CARLISLE.P.; ILL(imp.). N.

25810 — [Anr. ed.] Newely corrected. Wherunto is added a table. 8°. (*R. Grafton,* 1552.) L.O.C.D.E².+; F.HN.CU. HD. Auckland PL.

25811 — [Anr. ed.] 4°. (*R. Grafton,*) 1553 (ja.) L.C.E.M.P(imp.). +; HD.ILL.Y.

25812 — [Anr. ed.] 4°. *J. Kingston,* 1563 (ap.) L.O.C⁴.P.LEEDS.+; F.HN.CHI.COR.PH.+

25813 — [Anr. ed.] 4°. *J. Kingston,* 1567 (fb.) L.O.BIRM²(K.N.). G².P.+; F.CH.CHI.ILL.NY.
Ff. 89. A copy at O⁴⁸ has a1ᵛ and a3ᵛ misimposed, with the last numbered leaf 90; otherwise it is identical in setting w. the O copies.

25814 — [Anr. ed.] 4°. *J. Kingston,* 1567 (fb.) [1584?] L.O³(E). C.C⁴.E².+; HN.CU.N.ROS.TEX.+
Ff. 88. This is the only ed. to have the dedic. in roman type.

25815 — [Anr. ed.] 4°. *J. Kyngston,* 1580. Ent. to T. Orwin 7 my. 1593. L.L³⁰.O.; F.CU.WIS.Y.

Wilson, Thomas, *Secretary of State—cont.*

25816 — Vita et obitus duorum fratrum Suffolciensium, Henrici et Caroli Brandoni duabus epistolis explicata. Adduntur epitaphia. Affiguntur praeterea epigrammata. 4°. (*in aed. R. Graftoni,*) 1551. L.C⁵(imp.).M.
The 1st letter is by W. Haddon.

25817 — [A variant, omitting the date from the tp.] (*in aed. R. Graftoni,*) [1551.] L.O.C.C².HOLK.+; F.PML.
(Formerly also 12594a)
— *tr. See* 3981, 6578.
— *See also* 3978.

Wilton, Moses, *tr. See* 25014.

25818 **Wily.** A pleasant comedie, called Wily beguilde. 4°. H. L[*ownes*] f. C. Knight, 1606. Ent. 12 no. L⁶.O(imp.).; F(imp.).HN. Greg 234.

25819 — [Anr. ed., omitting the Epilogue.] 4°. W. W[*hite*] f. C. Knight, 1614. L(impr. def.).; F(lacks tp).HN.

25820 — [Anr. ed.] 4°. T. Purfoot f. C. Knight, 1623. L.L⁶(impr. cropt).O(2).; F(imp.).ILL.

25821 — [Anr. ed.] 4°. Eliz. Allde f. T. Knight, 1630. Ass'd 12 oc. 1629. L.; F.HD. Paul S. Newman, Stamford, Connecticut.

25822 — [Anr. ed.] 4°. [*J. Haviland?*] f. T. Knight, sold by E. Blackmore a. F. Coules, 1635. L.L⁶.O.O⁶.ETON.+; F.HN.HD.N.WIS.

25823 — [Anr. ed.] 4°. J. B[*eale*] f. T. Alchorn, 1638. Ass'd 8 mr. 1636. L(2).L⁶.O.E(imp.).; F.HN.HD.ILL. Hickmott.
Copies differ: tp verso blank or w. imprimatur, possibly hand stamped; both at L.

25823.3 **Wimbledon, Richard.** A sermon [on Luke xvi.2] no lesse fruteful then famous made in the yeare M.CCC.lxxxvij. in these oure latter dayes moost necessary to be knowen. Nether addyng to, neyther demynyshynge fro. Saue tholde and rude Englysh ther of mended here and there. [Anon.] 8°. [*J. Mayler?* 1540?] C³(imp.).; F.
(Formerly 25825) The author's 1st name may actually be 'Thomas'.

25823.7 — [Anr. ed.] 8°. E. Whytchurche, [c. 1548.] Canterbury PL.

25824 — [Anr. ed.] Made . . . m.CCC.lxxxviij. 16° in 8's. [*R. Grafton f.*] (*R. Kele,*) [c. 1550.] C³.E.
The C³ copy has the last quartersheet (F⁴) in duplicate, folded and bd. as a halfsheet; i.e. one set is on leaves 1, 4, 5, 8, the other on leaves 2, 3, 6, 7. This suggests some form of halfsheet imposition.

25825 — Now = 25823.3.
25825.3 — [Anr. ed.] 8°. (*J. Kynge,*) [1561?] YK.
25825.7 — [Anr. ed.] Made M.CCC.lxxxviij. and founde out hyd in a wall. 8° in 4's. J. Awdely, 1572. Ent. to W. Lobley 1562–63. L¹⁵.

25826 — [Anr. ed.] 8°. J. Awdely, 1573 (1574.) L.O(imp.).; F.Y.
25827 — [Anr. ed.] 8°. J. Awdely, 1575. L.L¹⁵.O.O⁵(imp.).C⁴.; F(imp.).
In title: 'no lesse fruitful then'.

25827.5 — [Anr. ed.] 16° in 8's. J. Awdeley, 1575. HN.
In title: 'no les fruitfull thē'.

25828 — [Anr. ed.] 8°. J. Charlewood, 1578 (1579.) L.; ILL.
25829 — [Anr. issue, w. quire A reprinted, w. imprint:] J. Charlewood, 1579. L.L⁴³(imp.).O.
25830 — [Anr. ed.] Preached at Paules Crosse, by R. Wimbeldon. 8°. J. Charlewood, 1582. L(2).L¹⁵.O²(imp.).C⁵.; F.HN.
Copies have portions in 2 settings: C3ʳ last line has: 'geuen' (HN) or 'gyuen' (O², C⁵, F).

25831 — [Anr. ed.] 8°. J. Charlewood, 1584. L.L².L¹⁵.C³.SCL.+; F(2, 1 imp.).Y.
25832 — [Anr. ed.] J. Charlewoode, 1588. L.; F.
25833 — [Anr. ed.] 8°. J. Charlewood, 1593. O.C¹⁰.
25834 — [Anr. ed.] 4°. J. Roberts, 1593 (1599.) Ass'd from Charlewood 31 my. 1594. L.; F.LC.
The tail of the 2nd 9 in the colophon of the F copy has been erased.

25834.5 — [Anr. ed.] 8°. J. Roberts, 1603. L¹⁵.
25835 — Eleventh edition. 8°. W. Jaggard, 1617. L(2).L¹⁵.C.E. LINC.; F.Y.
25836 — Twelfth edition. 8°. W. Jaggard, solde by D. Speed, 1617. O(imp.).C(2).; HD.
25837 — Thirteenth edition. 8°. T. Cotes a. R. Cotes, 1629. Ass'd 19 jn. 1627. L.L¹⁵.
25838 — Fourteenth edition. 8°. T. Cotes, 1634. L.L¹⁵.; HN.
25839 — Fifteenth edition. 8°. T. Cotes, 1635. L.; F.

Winchester, *Bishop of. See* Gardiner, S.

Winchester, *Diocese of.* An order of praier and thanksgiuing. [1585.] *See* 16516.

25840 **Winds.** The last terrible tempestious windes and weather. Truely relating many ship-wracks, [etc.] 4°. [*E. Allde a. J. Beale*] f. Jos. Hunt, sold by J. Wright, 1613. Ent. to Hunt a. Gosson 7 ja. L.O.; HN(impr. shaved).
Beale pr. only quire B. All copies have D², w. heading: 'These things heereafter following were related to me by certaine saylers and countrey people, since the first were printed.' *See also* 19792.

25841 **Windsor, Miles.** Academiarum quæ aliquando fuere et hodie sunt in Europa, catalogus. [Init. M. W.] 4°. G. Bishop & R. Newberie, 1590. Ent. 25 jn. L(impr. torn).O.C².D.DUR⁵.+; F.HN.NY.
The tp, which has the royal arms on the recto, is a cancel, so this is the later issue. The text is a revised and enlarged version of 10568.

25841a — [Anr. issue, w. large orns. on the recto of the tp and 3 stars below the title.] G. Bishop & R. Newberie, 1590. L.L¹³.O⁵.C.D.

25841a.5 — [Anr. ed., revised and abridged.] Europaei orbis, ac⟨ademiae⟩ celebriores et aliqua⟨ndo⟩ flore⟨nte⟩s. [Init. M. W.] fol(2). Oxoniæ, J. Barnesius, 1592. O⁵ (imp.).

Wine. Wine, beere, and ale, together by the eares. 1629. *See* 11541.

25842 **Wing, John.** Abels offering. Or the earely, and most accepted sacrifice of a christian. A sermon preached at Hamburg 1617. 4°. Flushing, M. A. vander Nolck, 1621. L³.L¹³.O.C(2).; HN.BALT.Y.

25843 — The best merchandise or, a cleare discovery of the difference, betweene our traffike with God, and with men. Preached at Middleburgh. 4°. Flushing, M. A. vander Nolck, 1622. L.O.; F(imp.).HN(2).PH.PN².

25844 — The crowne conjugall or, the spouse royall. [Two sermons.] 4°. Middelburgh, J. Hellenius, 1620. L.O.C.D. E².+; F.HN.HD(date deft.).ILL.Y.+

25845 — [Anr. ed.] 12°. J. Beale f. R. Mylbourne, 1632. Ent. 8 ja. 1621. L.O(date cropt).O⁶.PETYT.; F(date cropt). N. Mrs. Donald G. Wing, Woodbridge, Connecticut.

25846 — Jacobs staffe. To beare up, the faithfull. Formerly preached at Hamburg. 4°. Flushing, M. A. vander Nolck, 1621. Ent. to R. Milbourne 13 oc. L.L².O.C. G².; F.HN. ꝛ

25847 — The saints advantage or the welfare of the faithfull. A sermon. 4°. Flishing [sic], M. A. vander Nolck, 1623. L.O.D.P(imp.).; HN.DAR.

25848 — [Anr. ed.] 4°. J. Dawson f. J. Bellamie, 1624. Ent. 7 ap. L.O.P.; F.HD.LC.U.NY¹¹.+

25848.5 — [Anr. ed.] 12°. T. Paine f. A. Kembe in South-warke, 1637. F.

25849 **Wingate, Edmund.** Arithmetique made easie, in two bookes. The former, of naturall arithmetique. The other of artificiall arithmetique [logarithms.] 8°. [*M. Flesher*] f. P. Stephens a. C. Meredith, 1630. Ent. 12 ja. L.O.C.A.NEP.+; F.HN.CU.MICH.PH.

25850 — The construction, and use of the line of proportion. 8°. J. Dawson, 1628. Ent. 30 jn. L.O¹⁷.

25850.5 — Λογαριθμοτεχνία, or the construction, and use of the logarithmeticall tables. First published in the French tongue by E. Wingate and now *tr.* by the author himselfe. (The first chiliad of logarithmes, called in the discourse aforegoing the table of numbers. By H. Brigs.—Canon triangulorum, or a logarithmeticall table. By E. Gunter.) 2 pts. 24° in 12's. W. Stansby, 1626. Ent. 1 mr.; 'crossed out' by Stansby's consent; possibly intended to be ass'd to Flesher 23 ap. 1635. O(pt. 2 only). Keele U. London, Royal Institution of Chartered Surveyors.; F.Y.
Pt. 2 (formerly 3742) is 24° 8.4.

25851 — The second edition, much enlarged. (A logarithmeticall table.) 2 pts. 12°. M. Flesher, 1635. L.O.C².DUL.E¹³ (pt. 2 only).+; HN.Y.
The Table is anon.

25851.5 — [Anr. issue of pt. 2, w. tp reset:] Une table logarithmetique. Londres, [*M. Flesher,*] 1635. L.L⁴⁴.O.ETON. O, ETON are bd. with Wing W 3018A.
— *ed. See* 3804.
— *See also* 21151.

Wingfield, Anthony. A true coppie of a discourse. 1589. *See* 6790.

25852 **Wingfield, Henry.** A compendious or shorte treatise, conteynynge preceptes necessary to the preseruacion of healthe. 8°. (*R. Stoughten,*) [1551?] L(2, 1 lacks tp).c(2, 1 imp.).; HD.NLM. Dedic. dated 1 Jan. 1551.

25852.3 **Wingfield, John.** Atheisme close and open, anatomized. And a refuge in affliction. Being prayers fitted for severall occasions. 12°. *T. Harper, sold by T. Ellis,* 1634. F.TORONTO².

25852.7 **Wingrave, Francis,** *ed.* An answer to the arguments written by Mr. Stone, intituled Reasons to prove the parish assemblies in England to be the true visible churches of Christ. 8°. [*London,*] 1608. D.
    Prints (from MS.?) the Reasons of Thomas Stone, minister of 'Warton', i.e. Warkton, Northants., together w. answers by an unnamed friend of Wingrave, who is a nonconformist.

25853 **Winifred,** *Saint.* Here begynneth the lyf of saynt Wenefryde. [By Robertus, *Prior of Shrewsbury.*] (Reduced in to Englysshe by me W. Caxton.) fol. [*Westminster, W. Caxton,* 1485.] L.L².O(1 leaf).; PML. Duff 414.
    For anr. trans. *see* 21102.

25854 **Winne, Edward.** A letetr [*sic*] written by captaine E. Winne, to sir G. Calvert, from Feryland in New-foundland, the 26. of August. 1621. 8°. [*B. Alsop,*] 1621. L.; COR.
    For other letters of Winne *see* 25375a.

25855 **Winslow, Edward.** Good newes from New-England. Written by E. W[inslow.] 4°. *J. D[awson a. Eliot's Court Press] f. W. Bladen a. J. Bellamie,* 1624. Ent. to Bladen 14 no. 1623. L.LINC.; HN.BO.N.NY.PH.+ K2ʳ has an advertisement for 18483, 20074. Eliot's Court Press pr. quires B–E. A copy at Y has)(2 from 25856 bd. in at the end.

25856 — [Anr. issue, w. tp cancelled and replaced by a bifolium, the 2nd leaf of which is signed)(2 and sometimes bd. after K1.] Whereunto is added a briefe relation of Virginia. *J. D[awson] f. W. Bladen,* 1624. L.CHATS. G². Blickling.; HN.BO⁵.CB.MICH. Henry Taylor.

Winter, Frig. Almanacks. 1633, etc. *See* 530 sqq.

Winter, Simon, *of Syon Abbey. See* 14508.

Winter, Thomas, *tr. See* 21659, 21660.

25856.5 **Winterton.** Reasons why the contribution of one pennie per tunne of every ship that goeth on the north coast of England, towards lighthouses at Winterton should not be any grievance; with an answere unto [24283]. [Arguments addressed to Parliament by the patentees.] fol(3). [*London,* 1621.] L(2, 1 = Harl.MS. 7611/2–6).L⁵(Lemon 184).L⁸(GL 4943).
    (Formerly 10020) For the patent *see* 8559; *see also* Notestein VII.400–2.

25857 — A true medium of the monies payable from 1613. to 1618. by the masters and owners of divers ships for the lights at Winterton. [Financial details submitted to Parliament by the patentees.] s.sh.fol. [*London,* 1621.] L(2, 1 = Harl.MS.7611/8).L⁸(GL 5917).; Y.

Winterton, Ralph. Poetæ minores Græci. 1635. *See* 12211.
— *ed. See* 23889.6.
— *tr. See* 7235, 11769, 11772, 11780, 13518.

25858 **Winthrop, John.** The humble request. 1630. = 18485.

25858.3 **Wintter, Georgius.** Disputatio juridica de injuriis. Quam D.A.N. in Oxoniensi academia, sub præsidio A. Reuter. Exhibet G. Wintter, Neotreptoviensis Pomeranus. 4°. *Oxoniæ, J. Barnesius,* 1610. C¹⁷(2). PLUME.; F.

25858.7 **Winwick,** *Lancashire.* To the right honorable the knights . . . of Parliament. The humble petition of the parishioners of Winwick. [Appeal to set aside the lease, granted in 1537 to Bp. Thomas Stanley and now held by the recusant John Fortescue, of the

Winwick, *Lancashire—cont.*
parsonage house and tithes of Winwick and allow them to be bestowed on the present curate, Josiah Horne.] fol(6). [*London,* 1621?] L⁵(sheets 2–5 only, Lemon 250).L⁸(GL 6427).
    The petition is on the 1st sheet; the others are documents in support: (2) headed 'Josiah Horne plaintiffe'; (3–5) connected by catchwords, w. (3) beginning: 'Tho. Stanly his Dispensation of Perinde valere.'; (6) headed 'A threefold dilemma from the premises.'

25859 **Winzet, Ninian.** The buke of fourscoir-thre questions, tueching doctrine, ordour, and maneris proponit to ye precheouris of ye protestants in Scotland. 8°. *Antuerpiæ, ex off. Æ. Diest,* 1563 (13 oc.) E².; F.HN. A&R 902. Errata for this are in 24752. There is a letter to John Knox on H4ʳ, dated 27 Oct. 1563.

25860 — Certane tractatis for reformatioun of doctryne and maneris. 4°. *Edinburgi,* [*J. Scot,*] 1562 (21 my.) A². E².LAMPORT.; F.
    A&R 903. The pref. to the 3rd tractate is dated 24 May 1562 (D2ᵛ). E4 possibly was used to print the tp and beginning of pref. of 25861.

25861 — The last blast of the trompet of Godis worde aganis the vsurpit auctoritie of J. Knox. 4°. *Edinburgi,* [*J. Scot,*] 1562 (31 jy.) E²(imp.).; F(imp.).
    A&R 904. This is the work Scot was printing when he was arrested.
— *tr. See* 1884.5, 24752.

25862 **Wirsung, Christoph.** Praxis medicinæ vniuersalis; or a generall practise of physicke. Compiled in Germane and now *tr.* and augmented, by J. Mosan. fol. *E. Bollifant,* 1598. Ent. to G. Bishop and master Ascanias 6 jn. 1597. L¹⁶.O.C.G².M.+; JH.NLM.NWM. PEN.WIS.

25863 — [Anr. issue, w. imprint:] *imp. G. Bishop,* 1598. L.O³. LIV³.; F.

25864 — [Anr. ed.] The general practise of physicke. fol. [*R. Field,*] *imp. G. Bishop,* 1605. L.L¹⁶.O¹².C².STU.+; F. HN.HD.NWM.WIS.+

25865 — [Anr. ed.] fol. [*J. Legat*] *f. T. Adams,* 1617. Ass'd 14 mr. 1611. L.O(imp.).C.E².M⁴.+; F.HD.NLM.NY⁴. Y.+

Wisbech. A true relation of the faction. 1601. *See* 1188.
— A true reporte of a conference. 1581. *See* 11457.

25866 **Wischart, William.** An exposition of the Lords prayer. Delivered in two and twenty lectures. 12°. *M. Flesher f. N. Bourne,* 1633. Ent. 21 se. 1632. L.O. C.D.E.+; F.HN(imp.).ILL.NY¹¹.ROS.+

Wisdom. The manifold wisedome of God. 1640. *See* 24959.5.
— Wisdome crying out to sinners. 1639. *See* 17919.
— The wisdome of doctor Dodypoll. 1600. *See* 6991.

25867 **Wise, Thomas,** *M.A.* Animadversions upon Lillies grammar [15610.5 sqq.], or Lilly scanned. Set downe by way of question, and answere. [Anon.] 8°. *W. Stansby f. R. Hawkins,* 1625. Ent. as by Wise 22 se. 1624. L(2).O.C².M.; F(imp.).CU.HD.LC.
    At least O, HD have an extra leaf w. an address to the reader and errata.

25867.5 — Exercitatio scholastica, ad linguam Latinam viam muniens: sive, fasciculus argutiorum sententiarum. Collectore, T. W[ise.] 8°. [*G. Purslowe,*] *imp. R. Hawkins,* 1623. Ent. 16 jn. HD.
    Ass'd as by Wise 29 May 1638 (Arber IV.420).

Wiseman, *Sir William, pseud. See* 10926.

Wishart, George, *tr. See* 23553.

25868 **Wit.** A pleasant comoedie, wherein is merily shewen: The wit of a woman. 4° with perp. chainlines. [*E. Allde*] *f. E. White,* 1604. L.O.E.; F.HN(2). Arthur Houghton. Greg 206.
— Wits A. B. C. Or a centurie of epigrams. [1608.] *See* 25262.
— Wits Bedlam. 1617. *See* 6343.
— Wits fittes and fancies. 1614. *See* 5740.

25869 — Wit's never good till 'tis bought. [By M. Parker?] *Ballad.* 2 pts. s.sh.fol. [*M. Flesher*] *f. T. Lambert,* [1634?] Ent. 9 my. 1634. L.

Wit—*cont.*

25870 — Wits recreations. Selected from the finest fancies of moderne muses. (Outlandish proverbs, selected by G. H[erbert].) [In verse.] 2 pts. 8°. *R. H[odgkinson*; pt. 2:] (*T. P[aine]*) *f. H. Blunden*, 1640. Ent. 15 oc. 1639. L(2 imp.).O.BTU(imp.).; F.HN.HD.ILL(lacks letterpress tp). NY.+

> The engr. tp has: 'Witts recreations . . . with outlandish proverbs. *f. H. Blunden*, 1640.' At least 1 L, 2 F, HN also have a dedic. by Blunden to Francis Newport.
> Pt. 2 also issued sep. as 13182.

25871 — [Heading A3ʳ:] Witts tearme. [A satire on London characters.] 8°. [*T. Cotes*, 1634?] Ent. to T. Lambert 22 au. 1634. L(imp.).

— Wits theater of the little world. 1599. *See* 381.

Witchcrafts. Witchcrafts, strange and wonderfull. 1635. *See* 11107.7.

25872 **Witches.** Witches apprehended, examined and executed. [Mother Sutton and her daughter.] With a strange triall how to know a witch. 4°. [*W. Stansby*] *f. E. Marchant*, 1613. Ent. to J. Trundell 23 ja. O.; HN.

25873 **Witc., R.** R W against his deare foe E. T. [1567?] = pt. of 25439.

25874 **Withals, John.** A shorte dictionarie for yonge begynners. Gathered of good authours. *Eng. a. Lat.* 4°. (*in the house of T. Berthelet*,) 1553. CU(imp.). Arthur Houghton.

25875 — [Anr. ed.] 4°. (*J. Kingstun* [sic] *f. J. Waley a. A. Vele*,) 1556. L.; HN.

25876 — [Anr. ed.] 4°. [*T. Powell*] (*in the late house of T. Barthelet*,) 1562. Ent. to R. Jugge 1557–58. O.; ILL(imp.).

25877 — [Anr. ed.] 4°. (*H. Wykes*,) 1566. Ent. to T. Purfoot 1564–65. L(tp and col. only, Harl.5919/240, 237). O(lacks A3).

> Wykes fined in 1565–66 for printing this without licence; *see* Arber I.316.

25878 — [Anr. ed.] 4°. (*H. Wykes*,) 1568. L.O³⁰.; HN.LC.

25878.5 — [Anr. ed.] A short dictionarie most profitable. Nowe newelie corrected, and augmented, with diuerse phrasys, & other thinges necessarie thereunto added. By L. Euans. 4° in 8's. (*T. Purfoote*,) 1568. F.

25879 — The seconde tyme corrected. 4° in 8's. (*T. Purfoote*,) 1574. L.O.

25879.5 — [Anr. ed.] The second time corrected. 4° in 8's. (*T. Purfoot*,) 1579. L(tp only, Harl.5974/100).; F.

25880 — The thirde time corrected. 4° in 8's. (*T. Purfoote*,) 1581. L.

25880.5 — [Anr. ed.] A shorte dictionarie in Latine and English. And nowe lastlie augmented with more than six hundred rythmical verses, newlie done by A. Fleming. 4° in 8's. *T. Purfoote*, 1584. O(2 leaves, imp.).; F(imp.).ILL(imp.).

25881 — [Anr. ed.] 4° in 8's. *T. Purfoote*, 1586. L.C.C⁵.G².NEK. +; F.

> For details of a stock of 750 copies acquired by the Stationers' Co. and sold 1587–93, *see* Arber I.520, 521, 530, etc.

25882 — [Anr. ed.] 4° in 8's. *T. Purfoot*, 1594. O(frag.).; HN.

25883 — [Anr. ed.] 4° in 8's. *T. Purfoot*, 1599. L.O.; F(2).

25884 — [Anr. ed.] A dictionarie in English and Latine for children. Now augmented. By W. Clerk. 8°. *T. Purfoot*, 1602. L.O.DUL.LEEDS. Stevens Cox(lacks tp).; F (imp.).HD.ILL.Y.

25885 — [Anr. ed.] 8°. *T. Purfoot*, 1608. O(imp.).*.; F(imp.).ILL.

25885.5 — [Anr. issue, w. imprint:] *T. Purfoot, sold by N. Butter*, 1608. L.G².; F.

25886 — [Anr. ed.] Now at this last impression enlarged. 8°. *T. Purfoot*, 1616. Ass'd 6 no. 1615. L.L³⁰.O.O⁶.NLW.+; F.HD(imp.).ILL.N.PEN.

25887 — [Anr. ed.] Corrected and amended in divers places. 8°. *T. Purfoot*, 1634. L.O.C.NLW.PETYT.+; F.HN.CU.N. SMITH.+

25888 **Wither, Fabian,** *tr. See* 6275.

— *See also* Withers, F., who may be the same person.

Wither, George, *Archdeacon.* An A. B. C. for laye-men, otherwise called, the lay-mans letters. 8°. *R. Waldegraue f. T. Man a. W. Brome*, 1585. Ent. 18 ja. O(2, 1 imp.).C.; F(2).

Wither, George, *Archdeacon*—*cont.*

25889 — A view of the marginal notes of the popish Testament [2884]. 4°. *E. Bollifant f. T. Woodcocke*, [1588.] L. O.C.D.E.+; F.HN.HD.ILL.NY.+

> Dedic. dated 12 Apr. 1588.

— *See also* 24901.

25890 **Wither, George,** *Poet.* The workes of master George Wither. Containing satyrs. Epigrams. Eclogues. Sonnets. and poems. Whereunto is annexed a paraphrase on the creed and the Lords prayer. 8°. *J. Beale f. T. Walkley*, 1620. L.O.C⁴.E.LEEDS.+; F.HN. CHI.HD.Y.

> A pirated collection; *see The Library*, VI(1925), pp. 271–7. Includes a reprint of the Shepheards Pipe (formerly also 3918) from which Wither's eclogues have been cancelled as the text also appears as nos. 4, 5 in Shepheards Hunting. L8, cancelled in most copies, has the beginning of no. 5 on the verso (HN, CH, HD).

25891 — Abuses stript, and whipt. Or satirical essayes. [In verse.] 8°. *G. Eld f. F. Burton*, 1613. Ent. 16 ja. L. L⁴.C².LEEDS.; F.HN.CAL.HD.

> Collates A⁸ a⁴ B–V⁸; A4ʳ line 4: 'quareld'. This and 25891.5 may have been pr. after 25894. Wither was imprisoned for this; cf. 25920.

25891.5 — [Anr. ed.] 8°. *G. Eld f. F. Burton*, 1613. L(imp.). BIRM²(imp.).; NY.Y.

> Collates A⁸ a⁴ B–V⁸; A4ʳ line 4: 'quareled'.

25892 — [Anr. ed.] 8°. *G. Eld f. F. Burton*, 1613. L.O.C⁴(2). E².; F.HN.HD.N.PFOR.+

> Collates A–X⁸; A4ʳ line 1 of text: 'whome'.

25893 — [Anr. ed.] 8°. *G. Eld f. F. Burton* [really *T. Creede*,] 1613. L(2, 1 imp.).L⁶.C⁴(lacks tp).C¹⁷.; F.HN.HD.Y.

> Collates A–X⁸; A4ʳ line 1 of text: 'whom', line 2 from bottom ends 'will'. A forged ed.; *see The Library*, XV (1934), pp. 365–7. *See also Court-Book C*, p. 73.

25894 — [Anr. ed.] 8°. *G. Eld f. F. Burton*, 1613. L.L³⁰.O.C⁴.G². +; F(3).HD.PML.WEL.

> Collates A–X⁸; A4ʳ line 1 of text: 'whom', line 2 from bottom ends 'wil'. This is the only ed. to mention in the title: 'Also the Scourge. Epigrams.' though the poems are included in all eds.

25895 — [Anr. ed.] 8°. *T. S[nodham] f. F. Burton*, 1614. L.O.C. E².M.+; F.HN.HD.Y.

25896 — [Anr. ed.] 8°. *H. Lownes f. F. Burton*, 1615. L.O.C². BHP.BIRM(imp.).+; F.HN.HD.MICH.Y.+

> WEL has an imp. copy of this ed. with faked tp w. imprint: 'T. Snodham f. G. Norton, 1615.'

25897 — [Anr. ed.] Reviewed and enlarged. (Prince Henries obsequies.) 8°. *H. Lownes f. F. Burton*, 1617. L.O.C. BIRM.E.+; F.HN.CHI.HD.Y.+

25898 — [Anr. ed.] 1622. = pt. of 25911.

25899 — Britain's remembrancer containing a narration of the plague lately past; a declaration of the mischiefs present; and a prediction of judgments to come. [In verse.] 12°. *Imprinted for Great Britaine, sold by J. Grismond*, 1628. L.O.C.BTL.E.+; F.HN.HD.N.NY.+

> One HD copy has the last 2 leaves, *², w. the text in roman type rather than italic, and possibly pr. c. 1645.

25899.5 — Cantica sacra. Or the hymns and songs of the church. Faithfully, and briefely *tr.*, into lyricke verse. By G. W[ither.] 12°. [*A. Mathewes*, 1623?] Ent. to A. Mathewes 7 de. 1622. L¹⁵.

> Contains 41 songs without music, all but 1 of which (Song of the vineyard) appear in the 1st pt. of 25908.

25900 — A collection of emblemes, ancient and moderne. The first (second—third—fourth) booke. [In verse.] fol. *A. M(athewes) f. R. Allot*, 1635 (1634.) Ent. to Allot, Grismond, Milbourne, Royston, a. Taunton 10 mr. 1634. L.BIRM.G². Leeds PL.; F.FBL.HD.LC. MIN.+

> The emblems are pr. from plates brought over from Holland and originally engraved by C. van de Passe, the Elder, for G. Rollenhagen's Nucleus Emblematorum, 1611–13.

25900a — [A variant, w. imprint on gen. tp:] *A. M. f. J. Grismond*, 1635. L.L⁴.; HN.CAL.CU.HD.ILL.+

25900b — [A variant, w. imprint on gen. tp:] *A. M. f. R. Milbourne*, 1635. L.O³⁸.C.BHP.G².+; F.HN.HD.KAN. NY.+

25900c — [A variant, w. imprint on gen. tp:] *A. M. f. R. Royston*, 1635. L.O¹².C.D⁶.E.+; F.HN.BO.HD.WIS.+

Wither, George, *Poet—cont.*

25900d — [A variant, w. imprint on gen. tp:] *A. M. f. H. Taunton,* 1635. L.L²⁶.O.C⁴.M.; FBL.HD.N.PML.PN².+

25901 — Epithalamia: or nuptiall poems upon the mariage betweene prince Frederick the fifth, and the princesse, Elizabeth. 4°. [*F. Kingston*] *f. E. Marchant,* 1612 [o.s.] Ent. to W. Welby 10 fb. 1613. L.C.; F.HD.ILL.PML.Y.+

25902 — Exercises upon the first psalme. Both in prose and verse. 8°. *E. Griffin f. J. Harrison,* 1620. Ent. 30 mr. L.L⁶.O.STU.YK.+; F.HN.HD.WIS.Y.+
    With an advertisement on M7ᵛ for 25914.

25903 — Faire-Virtue, the mistresse of Phil'Arete. Written by him-selfe. [Anon. In verse.] 8°. [*A. Mathewes*] *f. J. Grismand,* 1622. Ent. to J. Marriot a. Grismand 31 ja. L.O.BRISTOL².G².M.+; F(imp.).HN.HD.N.Y.+

25903a — [A variant.] Written by Geo: Wither. *f. J. Grismand,* 1622. L(2).; HN.HD.ILL.PN.Y.+
    HN and HD both have the title in the same setting as 25903. In the right-hand tp border HD has the ends of the 2 rules even, like 25903, and appears to be conjugate; HN has the inner rule 2 mm. lower than the outer rule and is a cancel.

25903b — [Anr. issue, w. cancel tp:] Written by George Wither. *f. J. Grismand,* 1622. C⁴.; F(lacks tp)*.HN.HD.

25904 — [Anr. ed.] 1633. = pt. of 25929.

25905 — Fidelia. [Anon. In verse.] 12°. *N. Okes,* 1615. O.

25906 — [Anr. ed.] Written by G. W[ither] of Lincolnes Inne, gentleman. 12°. *N. Okes (f. G. Norton,)* 1617. O(imp.).; CH(imp.).PML.
    Author's pref. of previous ed. is replaced by a new stationer's pref.

25907 — [Anr. ed.] Newly corrected and augmented, by G. Withers. (Sonnets.) 8°. *E. G[riffin] f. T. Walkley,* 1619. L.O(imp.).+; F.HN.Y.
    An unauthorized ed.

25907.5 — [The 4 continents. A set of 4 anon. engravings w. female allegorical figures representing Europa, Asia, Africa, and America. Each engr. has 6 lines of verse, those on Europa signed G: Wither.] fol. *sold by J. Stafforde,* [c. 1635.] L(Dept. of P&D, 166.c.1).

25908 — The hymnes and songs of the church. Divided into two parts. *Tr.* and composed by G. W[ither. With music by O. Gibbons.] 16° in 8's. [*J. Bill*] *f. G. W[ither,]* 1623. L.O.C¹⁰.E.NLW.+; F.HN.HD.ILL.NY.+
    Contains 90 hymns; enlarged and developed from 25899.5 and 25923, q.v.
    At least O, F, I HD are bd. w. 2735. Regarding Wither's patent and objections to it *see* 8704.5, 16768.10, 25919. *See also Court-Book C,* pp. 156, 162, 192, 247, Greg, *Companion,* pp. 212–18, and *Studies in Bibliography,* XIX (1966), pp. 210–15.

25909 — = 25910a.

25909.5 — [Anr. ed., w. dedic. to King James signed by Wither.] fol. [*J. Legat?*] *by the assignes of G. Wither,* 1623. L⁴.C⁴.; F(imp.).
    Collates A–H⁴ I².

25910 — [Anr. ed.] 4°. [*J. Bill*] *by the assignes of G. Wither,* 1623. WIS.
    Collates A–P⁴.

25910.5 — [Anr. ed.] 4°. [*J. Bill*] *by the assignes of G. Wither,* 1623. O¹⁰(imp.).; HD.NY.
    Collates A–H⁴ I²; B1ʳ in roman type.

25910.7 — [Anr. ed.] 4°. [*J. Bill*] *by the assignes of G. Wither,* 1623. F.BO.CAL.
    Collates A–H⁴ I²; B1ʳ in B.L. type.

25910a — [Anr. ed.] 8°. [*J. Bill*] *by the assignes of G. Wither,* [1623.] L.O.C³.E.M².+; F.HN.HD.TEX.Y.+
    (Formerly also 25909) Collates A–O⁸ P⁴, w. errata on P4ᵛ; this is the only undated ed.

25910a.3 — [Anr. ed.] 8°. [*J. Bill*] *by the assignes of G. Wither,* 1623. G².P.; F.HD.TEX.Y.
    Collates A–O⁸.

25910a.5 — [Anr. ed.] 8°. [*J. Bill?*] *by the assignes of G. Wither,* 1623. L.O(imp.).C(2).; F.BO(imp.).N.PML.PN².+
    Collates A–D⁸ E⁴.

25910a.7 — [Anr. ed.] 12°. *by the assignes of G. Wither,* 1623. O⁸.; HN.BO⁵.
    Collates A⁶ B–C¹²; without music.

25911 — Juvenilia. A collection of those poemes heretofore imprinted, and written by G. Wither. 8°. (*T. S[nodham]*) *f. J. Budge,* 1622. L.O⁶(imp.).C(imp.).BRISTOL².STU.+; F.HN.HD.N.NY.+
    (25898 is pt. of this)

Wither, George, *Poet—cont.*

25911a — [Anr. issue, w. imprint on engr. tp altered:] *f. R. Allott,* 1626. 'Abuses' ass'd from Budge to Allot 4 se. L.O.; F(imp.).HN.PFOR.

25912 — [Anr. ed.] 12°. (*R. Badger*) *f. R. Allott,* 1633 (1632.) L.L⁶.O.C.NEK(imp.).+; F.HN.HD(imp.).N(imp.).Y.+

25912.5 — [Anr. issue, w. added? letterpress bifolium:] The poems of Geo: Wither: heretofore imprinted, and now comprised in two volumes. . . . The second volume containes only, [25899]. *f. J. Grismond,* 1633. F.HD.
    Neither F nor HD has 25899 bd. uniformly. Vol. 1 is a reissue of 25912 and 25929, the engr. tpp of which are lacking in F but present in HD.

25913 — A new song of a young mans opinion. [1618?] Now = 22919.5.
    — The poems. 1633. *See* 25912.5.

25914 — A preparation to the psalter. fol. (*N. Okes,* 1619.) Ent. 13 au. L.O.C³.CASHEL.DEU.+; F.HN.HD.ILL.NY.+
    Most copies (L, O, F, HD) have the engr. tp only; in addition HN has a letterpress tp, in border McK.&F. 147 and w. imprint: *N. Okes,* 1619, prob. pr. before the engr. one was ready. *See Court-Book C,* pp. 111, 463. 25902 has an advertisement for this.

25915 — Prince Henries obsequies or mournefull elegies upon his death. [In verse.] 4°. *E. Allde f. A. Johnson,* 1612. Ent. to F. Burton 18 de. L.L³.L⁴.L³⁰.O.; F(date shaved).HN(date cropt).HD.PFOR(date cropt).Y.
    — The psalmes of David *tr.* into lyrick-verse. 1632. *See* 2735.

25916 — A satyre: dedicated to his most excellent majestie. [In verse.] 8°. [*T. Snodham*] *f. G. Norton,* 1614. Ent. 8 au. L.O.O⁵.; F.HN.HD.NY. Iowa U.+

25917 — [Anr. ed.] 8°. *T. Snodham f. G. Norton,* 1615. L(2).L³⁰.O(2).SH.; F.HN(2, 1 w. mixed sheets).ILL.Y.
    A4ʳ line 7: 'slight'; B3ʳ line 2: 'ne're'.

25917.5 — [Anr. ed.] 8°. *T. Snodham f. G. Norton,* 1615. L(imp.). O.C³.BIRM.E.+; F.HN.HD.N.PML.+
    A4ʳ line 7: 'sleight'; B3ʳ line 2: 'nere'.

25918 — [Anr. ed.] 8°. *T. Snodham f. G. Norton,* 1616. L.L³⁰.C⁴. DUL.; F.HN.CH.TEX. Pirie.

25919 — The schollers purgatory, discovered in the stationers common-wealth. [A defence of Wither's patent for 25908.] 8°. [*G. Wood*] *f. the Honest Stationers,* [1624.] L.L⁶.O.C.E².+; HN.HD.Y.
    Regarding G. Wood's printing of part of this *see Court-Book C,* pp. 169–70; *see also* Greg, *Companion,* pp. 230–3. Quires A–D are app. from 1 type font and E–I from anr., w. (∴)⁴ possibly pr. at the 2nd press.

25920 — The shepherds hunting: being, certaine eglogs written during the authors imprisonment in the Marshalsey. [In verse.] 8°. *T. Snodham f. G. Norton,* 1615. Ent. 8 oc. 1614. L(lacks H1).L³⁰.O.O¹².; F.HD.
    Pref. signed: 'Geo. Wyther'.

25921 — [Anr. ed.] 8°. *T. Snodham f. G. Norton,* 1615. L.L⁶.O. Juel-Jensen (imp.).; HN.CHI.PFOR.
    Pref. signed: 'Geo. Wither'.

25922 — [Anr. ed.] 8°. *W. White f. G. Norton,* 1615. L.O.C³. BIRM(imp.).E.+; F.HN.HD.N.PML.+

25923 — The songs of the Old Testament, *tr.* into English measures. To every song is added a new tune. [In verse.] 12°. *T. S[nodham,]* 1621. Ent. to Snodham 8 de. 1620. L.
    Contains 14 songs which, w. revised texts and different music, appear in the 1st pt. of 25908.

25924 — Now = 25926.5.

25925 — Wither's motto. Nec habeo, nec careo, nec curo. [In verse.] 8°. [*A. Mathewes,*] 1621. Provisionally ent. to E. Weaver 14 my.; to J. Marriot a. J. Grismand 16 jn. L.
    Ends F2ᵛ w. 'FINIS.'; F2ᵛ line 2 of heading: 'own'. This issue has only a letterpress tp.
    Regarding various actions taken against the printers and publishers of this, and also Wither's imprisonment in the Marshalsea, *see Court-Book C,* p. 135; *Cal. S.P.D., 1619–1623,* pp. 268, 274–5; *Acts P.C., 1619–1621,* pp. 406, 408, *1621–1623,* pp. 12, 161. *See also* 11509, 23800.

25925.5 — [Anr. issue, w. letterpress tp cancelled and replaced by a bifolium with engr. tp, *without imprint or date,* and explanatory verses.] L.C(bifolium only).

Wither, George, *Poet—cont.*

25926 — [Anr. ed.] 8°. [*N. Okes*] *f. J. Marriott*, 1621. L(2, 1 imp.: 238.b.20, with F3,4 added from a copy of 25927).C⁴.E².LEEDS.; F.Y.
 Ends F2ᵛ w. '*FINIS.*'; F2ᵛ line 2 of heading: '*owne*', line 1 of heading: '*An*' (w. plain *A*).

25926.5 — [Anr. ed.] 8°. [*A. Mathewes*] *f. J. Marriott*, 1621. L⁶.; HN.
 (Formerly 25924) Ends F2ᵛ w. '*FINIS.*'; F2ᵛ line 2 of heading: '*owne*', line 1 of heading: '*An*' (w. swash *A*).

25927 — [Anr. ed.] 8°. [*N. Okes*] *f. J. Marriott*, 1621. L(2).O. O⁶.DUR⁵(imp.).LIV³.; F.HN.HD.ILL.Y.+
 F2ᵛ has catchword: '*A Post-*'.

25928 — [Anr. ed.] 8°. [*A. Mathewes*] *f. J. Marriott*, 1621. L⁶. O.O¹⁰.BRISTOL²*.; CHI.
 Copies of this and the following eds. at L, O, F, HD, LC have been checked in all formes. The number of typesettings found varies from two for sheet B to four for A and C outer formes. The order and distinctions below reveal the gross differences, but a thorough analysis has not been attempted.
 Postscript begins on F2ᵛ
 A7ʳ line 3: 'For it is' and line 7: 'No; . . . chaines,'
 C8ᵛ line 7 from bottom: '*Rosie-Crosse,*' (w. swash *C*) and line 9 from bottom: '*Chymists*' (with swash *C*)
 D8ʳ line 8: 'mad;'
 F3ʳ line 3 from bottom: 'bark, and'.
 At least L⁶, O, O¹⁰ (all copies?) have sheet D in the same setting as 25926.5.

25928.3 — [Anr. issue.] [*A. Mathewes*] *f. J. Marriott*, 1621. C⁴(2).; LC.PFOR.Y. Pirie.
 Postscript begins on F2ᵛ
 A7ʳ line 3: 'For it is' and line 7: 'No; . . . chaines:'
 C8ᵛ line 7 from bottom: '*Rosie-Crosse,*' (w. plain *C*)
 D8ʳ line 8: 'madd;'
 F3ʳ line 3 from bottom: 'bark, and'.
 At least LC, Pirie (all copies?) have sheets B, E, F in the same setting as 25928; sheet D in the same setting as 25928.5; A inner forme in the same setting as 25928.7; and A and C outer formes in a unique setting.

25928.5 — [Anr. ed.] 8°. [*A. Mathewes*] *f. J. Marriott*, 1621. L. LEEDS(with A of 25928.7).; F.BO⁵.CH.CU(with D of 25928.7).
 Postscript begins on F2ᵛ
 A7ʳ line 3: 'For, it is'
 C8ᵛ line 7 from bottom: '*Rosy-Crosse,*' (with swash *R*)
 D8ʳ line 8: 'madd;'
 F3ʳ line 3 from bottom: 'barke, and'.
 At least L, F (all copies?) have sheet D in the same setting as 25928.3.

25928.7 — [Anr. ed.] 8°. [*A. Mathewes*] *f. J. Marriott*, 1621. G² (mixed).STU(imp.).; F(mixed).HN(2 mixed).HD(2, 1 mixed).ILL(2).PFOR.PML.+
 Postscript begins F2ᵛ
 A7ʳ line 3: 'For it is' and line 7: 'No:'
 C8ᵛ line 7 from bottom: '*Rosie-Crosse,*' (w. swash *C*) and line 9 from bottom: '*Chymists*' (with plain *C*)
 D8ʳ line 8: 'mad,'
 F3ʳ line 3 from bottom: 'barke, &'.
 At least F, HN, HD (all copies?) have sheet B in the same setting as 25928.5. The G², CAL, IHN, HD, N, WIS mixed copies have sheet A of 25928.5; F, PN have C, F of 25928.5; the other HN copy has C of 25928.5.

25929 — [Anr. ed., w. additions.] (Faire-Virtue.) 12°. (*T. Harper*) *f. J. Grismond*, 1633. L.L³⁰.O.C.NEK(imp.).; F.HN.HD.ILL.Y.+
 (25904 is pt. of this) Usually bd. w. 25912; reissued as pt. of 25912.5.

25929.5 — [Eight-line poem, signed Ge. Wi., underneath engr. portrait by S. van de Passe of Lancelot Andrewes, dated 1618.] s.sh.4°. [*London*, 1618.] L(Dept. of P&D).O³⁴.WIN.; HN. Washington, D.C., National Gallery of Art.
 The orig. engr. identifies Andrewes as Bp. of Ely; there is a copy in reverse, also at O³⁴, where he is identified as Bp. of Winchester. See Hind II.247–8.

— *tr. See* 18427.

— *See also* 3917, 22919.5, 22925, 23132.

25930 **Witherings, John.** The orders lawes and ancient customes of swanns. Caused to be printed by J. Witherings. 4°. *A. Mathewes*, 1632. L.; HD.
 See also 9342.2 *sqq*.

25930.3 **Witherings, Thomas.** To all people to whom this present declaration may concerne [etc. List of rates for the post and where payment is to be made.] s.sh.fol. *E. P[urslowe] at the instance of the said Tho. Withrings, his Majesties Postmaster for forraigne parts: sold at the shop of N. Bourne*, 1635. L(Harl.5954/1).
 See also 9041, 22142.3, 22142.5, 25930.5.

25930.5 — To the honourable the house of Commons. The humble remonstrance of the grievances of all his majesties posts miserably sustained by the unlawfull projects of T. Witherings. s.sh.fol. [*London*, 1640.] L(C.112.h.4(75)).
 (Formerly 7753)

Withers, Fabian, *tr. See* 14075, 20087.
— *See also* Wither, F., who may be the same person.

Withers, Stephen, *tr. See* 4467, 19849.

Withycombe. *See* 25607.

Witness of Jesus Christ. *See* 4154.

25931 **Witt, Richard.** Arithmeticall questions, touching the buying or exchange of annuities; [etc.] 4°. *H. L[ownes] f. R. Redmer*, 1613. Ent. 22 ja. L.L³⁰.O. C.LINC.+; F.HN.HD.Y.

25932 — [Anr. ed.] To which are added sundry sorts of breviats. By T. Fisher. (Briefe solutions of questions of intrest.—A table of right proportionall intrest.) 3 pts. 8°. *T. Harper, sold by J. Parker*, 1634. Pts. 2, 3 ent. to Harper 25 my. 1633. L.O.O³.
 (Pts. 2, 3 formerly also 10918)

25932.5 — [A variant, w. 1st tp:] The second edition. *T. Harper*, 1634. O³.; MICH.

25933 **Wittenberg University.** The consideration and judgement, of the divines of the electorall principality of Saxony, in the universitie of Wittenberge: whether a state of the empire ought to ayde the Roman emperour in these warres of Bohemia? *Tr.* out of the high Dutch tongue. 4°. [*London*,] 1620. L.O².C.C⁴. PETWORTH.; F.HN.

25934 **Wittenhorst, Walraven van.** Propositions made by monsieur vander Hurst at the assembly of the generall states of the United Provinces. With the answer of the sayd generall states. 4°. [*M. Bradwood*] *f. P. Harison*, 1609. Ent. to J. Hardy 13 fb. L.L¹³.C⁵. HAGUE.PETWORTH.; F.HN.Y.

25934.5 **Wittewronghelus, Jacobus.** De vera christiani hominis fide, dialogus. Huc accessit oratio pia quae petitionibus complectitur: per A. Fleming. 8°. *ex off. T. Purfutij*, 1581. Ent. 4 ja. HAT.
 Trans. in 4301.

Wittie, Robert, *tr. See* 20383.

25935 **Witzell, Georg.** Georgii Wicelii methodus concordiæ ecclesiasticæ, cum exhortatione ad concilium; juxta exemplar excusum apud N. Wolrab. 1533. [*Ed.*] T. J(ames). 8°. *per J. Billium*, 1625. L.O³.C.C⁵.D.+

25936 **Wives.** The good wives fore-cast. [1685–88.] = Wing G 1084.

25937 — Halfe a dozen of good wives. All for a penny. *Ballad.* 2 pts. s.sh.fol. [*E. Purslowe*] *f. F. C[oules, c.* 1640.] Ent. to the ballad ptnrs. 16 jy. 1634. L.

25938 — The proude wyues pater noster that wolde go gaye, and vndyd her husbonde. [In verse.] 4°. (*J. Kynge*), 1560. Ent. 10 jn. L.O.; HN.
 Tp has a border (McK.&F. 37, w. different sil' piece).

25938.5 — [Anr. ed.] 4°. [*W. Copland*, 1561?] Ent. to J. Sampson, i.e. Awdley, 14 au. 1560. O(lacks col.).
 Tp has 2 factotum figures.

25939 **Wodroephe, John.** The spared houres of a souldier in his travels. Or the true marrowe of the French tongue. *Fr. a. Eng.* fol. *Dort, N. Vincentz pour G. Waters*, 1623. L.L³⁸.O.C.C²(2).; F.HN.CAL(imp.).HD.
 Pp. 427–47 reprint the 1st hour of STC 338. Quires † and Z–Vv have horizontal chainlines.

Wodroephe, John—*cont.*

25940 — [Anr. ed.] The marrow of the French tongue. The second edition: reviewed and purged of much grosse English. fol. [*M. Flesher*] *f. R. Meighen*, 1625. Ent. 22 ja. L.C⁴.DUR³.E².G².+; F.HN.JH.N.Y.+

— *tr. See* 18897.

25941 **Wolcomb, Robert.** A glasse for the godly. Contayning many comfortable treatises. The first (second) part. 8°. *T. P[urfoot a. T. Creede] f. A. Johnson*, 1612. Ent. 12 mr. L.O.; F(imp.).HD(imp.).ILL.PN²(imp.). Purfoot apparently pr. only quire A.

25941.5 — The sinners salue or medicine of the soule. Heerunto is annexed the Armour of the soule. 12°. *R. R[obinson] f. J. Winnington*, 1595. Ass'd from widow Winnington to J. Busby 30 oc. HD(imp.).

25942 — The state of the godly both in this life, and in the life to come: delivered in a sermon at the funeralls of ladie Elizabeth Courtney. 8°. [*R. Bradock*] *f. Roger Jackson*, 1606. L.L³.O.P.; F.

— *tr. See* 14630.5.

Wolfe, William, *S.J. See* 15117.

Wolfius, Hieronymus. Admonitio de vero astrologiæ vsu. 1558. *See* 15483.

— *tr. See* 14275.

25943 **Wollay, Edward.** A new yeres gyft, intituled, A playne pathway to perfect rest. [Partly in verse.] s.sh.fol. *W. How f. R. Johnes*, 1571. Ent. 1570–71. HN.

25944 **Wolsey, Thomas,** *Cardinal.* Rudimenta grammatices. 1529. Now = pt. of 5542.3.

25945 — [Anr. ed.] 153[5.] = pt. of 5543a.

25946 — [Anr. ed.] 1536. = pt. of 5543b.

25947 — [Anr. ed.] 1539. Now = pt. 1 of 5543b.7.

25947.3 — Thomas [Wolsey] Miseratione diuina Tituli Sanctę Cecilię sacrosāctę Romanę ecclesię presbiter Cardinalis Eboracen̄. [etc. Notification of Wolsey's visitation as papal legate.] s.sh.fol. [*R. Pynson*, 1525?] L¹³(Muniment No. 12,788, filled out in MS. for the Monastery of Westminster, 30 May 1525).

25947.7 — Vniuersis [xylographic] sancte matris ecclesie filijs. . . . [An inspeximus by Wolsey as Dean of Lincoln, dated 22 Sept. 1512, of the bull of Julius II absolving the subjects of Louis XII of France from their allegiance.] s.sh.fol. [*R. Pynson*, 1512.] L(2 copies, C.18.e.2(70) and Harl.5919/187, imp.). (Formerly 14839)

— UNiuersis sancte matris ecclesie filiis. [Letter of confraternity for the Chapel of St. Margaret in Uxbridge. 1527.] *See* Indulgences 79.

— *See also* Indulgences 42, 43, 68, 76, 83, 146.

Wolton, John, *Bp. See* Woolton, J.

Woman. English-men for my money: or, a comedy, called, A woman will have her will. 1616, etc. *See* 12931 sqq.

25948 — Everie woman in her humor. 4°. *E. A[llde] f. T. Archer*, 1609. L(3).L⁶.O.; F.HN.CHI.HD.NY.+ Greg 283.

— The woman hater. 1607. *See* 1692.

Wonder. A wonder beyond mans expectation. [1632.] *See* 12326.

— The wonder of this age. 1635. *See* 13372.5.

— A wonder woorth the reading. 1617. *See* 14935.

Wonders. Looke up and see wonders. 1628. *See* 1904.

— The three wonders of this age. 1636. *See* 13365.5.

25949 — The wonders of this windie winter. 4°. *G. Eld f. J. Wright*, 1613. Ent. to T. Bushell a. Wright 7 ja. L.; F. *See also* 19792.

25950 — [A variant, w. imprint:] *f. J. Hunt, sold by J. Wright*, 1613. O.; HN.

25951 **Wood, Family of.** Jacobus Dei gratia Magnæ Britanniæ, . . . rex, [etc. Recognition of services of Thomas Wood and family, dated 6 Apr. 1624.] s.sh.fol. [*London*, c. 1687.] O. Pr. after the Restoration from an MS. document in Rymer's *Foedera*, cf. 2nd ed., XVI (1727), p. 720 (under the date 1612).

Wood, Ambrose, *ed. See* 25039.

Wood, George. An abstract of his majesties Letters Patents. [25 Oct. 1619.] *See* 8614.

Wood, George—*cont.*

25951.5 — The particular grievances of those his majesties subjects throughout England and Wales, which lye under the oppression of G. Woods patent for the sole printing upon linnen cloth. [Petition to Parliament.] s.sh.fol. [*W. Stansby*, 1621.] L⁵(Lemon 222).

25952 **Wood, John,** *D.D.* The true honor of navigation and navigators: or, holy meditations for sea-men. 4°. *F. Kyngston*, 1618. Ent. 31 de. 1617. L.; F.CB.DAR. PN².Y.

25953 **Wood, John,** *M.D.* Practicæ medicinæ liber, vocatus Amalgama, quo, causæ, . . . præcipuorum capitis morborum. exponuntur. 4°. [*J. Windet,*] imp. H. Hooper, 1596. Ent. 1 mr. L.L².O.O².C⁹.

25954 — [Anr. issue, w. prelims. cancelled and new tp.] Authore D. Johnson. *imp. J. Bayly*, 1602. L(2). L¹⁶.O.O¹⁴.

25954.5 **Wood, John,** *Petitioner.* To the most honourable assembly of Commons. An abstract of the greevances of J. Wood, against the earle of Derby. [Concerning a dispute over land leases.] s.sh.fol. [*London*, 1621?] L(Harl.MS.7608/144).L⁸(GL 6448).

Wood, Montague. *See* 25759.5.

25955 **Wood, Owen.** An alphabetical book of physicall secrets, for diseases in the body of man. 8°. *J. Norton f. W. Edmonds*, 1639. Ent. 4 my. L.L¹⁶.O.; NLM.NY.

Wood, Robert, *tr. See* 795.

Wood, Roger. *See* 3217.5, 8615, 8716.5.

Wood, Thomas, *tr. See* 18837, 19459.

Wood, William, *Milit. See* 10003.

25956 **Wood, William,** *of Middleton Cheney.* A fourme of cathechising in true religion. 8°. *T. Dawson f. G. Bishop*, 1581. Ent. 4 se. L⁴.O⁹.C².LINC.

25957 **Wood, William,** *Settler in New England.* New Englands prospect. A true, lively, and experimentall description of that part of America. 4°. *T. Cotes f. J. Bellamie*, 1634. Ent. 7 jy. L.O.C.E².M.+; HN.HD.LC. MICH.NY.+

25958 — [Anr. ed.] 4°. *T. Cotes f. J. Bellamie*, 1635. L.O.CHATS. G²(2).M.; F.HN.HD.N.NY.+

25959 — [Anr. ed.] 4°. *J. Dawson, sold by J. Bellamy*, 1639. Ass'd to Dawson 2 au. 1638. L.C².C⁹.D².; HN.BO².N. NY.PH.+

25960 **Woodall, John.** The cure of the plague by an antidote called aurum vitæ. 4°. *E. P[urslowe] f. N. Bourne*, 1640. L. B4ᵛ line 1 begins: 'Yet considering'.

25961 — [Anr. issue, w. cancel B4.] *E. P[urslowe] f. N. Bourne*, 1640. L.L¹⁶. B4ᵛ line 1 begins: 'dreadfull disease,'.

25962 — The surgions mate, or a treatise discovering the contents of the surgions chest. Chiefly for the benefit of young sea-surgions, imployed in the East-India companies affaires. 4°. *E. Griffin f. L. Lisle*, 1617. Ent. 18 fb. L.L¹⁶.L¹⁹.C.LEEDS.; HN.HD.LC.MICH.Y.+

25963 — [Anr. ed., enlarged.] The surgeons mate or military & domestique surgery. With a treatise of yᵉ cure of yᵉ plague. (Viaticum. Revised and inlarged.) fol. *R. Young, [J. Legat? a.] (E. P[urslowe]) f. N. Bourne*, 1639. Ass'd 23 au. 1624. L.O.C.G².M⁴.+; F.HD.NWM. NY⁴.TEX.+ Young pr. the 1st set of signatures; app. Legat the 2nd; Purslowe the 3rd.

25964 — Woodalls viaticum: the path-way to the surgions chest. For the yonger surgions now imployed for the intended reliefe of Rochell. 4°. [*J. Dawson,*] 1628. Ent. to N. Bourne 7 au. L.

25965 **Woodcoke, Richard.** A godly and learned answer, to a lewd and unlearned pamphlet: intituled, A few, plaine and forcible reasons for the catholike faith, against the religion of the protestants. 4°. *N. O[kes] f. J. Bache a. N. Bourne*, 1608. O.C.C².D.YK.+; TEX.U. Includes the text of the pamphlet, which was in MS. and is a different text from 26038.4 sqq.

25966 **Woodes, Nathaniel.** An excellent new commedie, intituled: the conflict of conscience. Contayninge, the most lamentable hystorie, of the desperation of F. Spera. 4°. *R. Bradocke*, 1581. O.; PFOR. Greg 78.

25966.5 — [Anr. issue, with cancel A1,2 and I4.] An excellent . . . conscience. Contayninge, . . . the dolefull desperation of . . . Philologus. *R. Bradocke*, 1581. L(2 imp.). O(imp.).; F.HN.CH.HD(imp., with tp, partly in pen facs., of 25966).Y².

Woodhouse, John. Almanacks. 1610, etc. *See* 531 sqq.
— Naturall philosophy. 1621. *See* 22111.

25967 **Woodhouse, Peter.** The flea: sic parva componere magnis. [A beast fable. In verse.] 4°. [*E. Allde*] *f. J. Smethwick*, 1605. Ent. 22 mr. M.; HN.

25968 **Woodhouse, W.** The .xv. fearfull tokens preceding I say, the generall iudgement called domesday. [In verse.] 8°. *W. How f. W. Pickeryng*, [1566.] Ent. 1565–66. L².
For anr. trans. of the same original *see* 793.3.

Woodhouse, William. Almanacks. 1602, etc. *See* 532 sqq.

Woods, Richard, *tr. See* 18480.

25968.5 **Woodstreet Counter.** The humble petition of the poore prisoners in the loathsome hole of Woodstreet Compter, being above 70. in number. [Appeal for alms for Easter, to be put into 'this bearers Box. 1614.'] s.sh.*obl*.4°. [*R. Blower?* 1614.] L⁸.
The title is taken from the pr. endorsement on the verso.

25969 — To the worshipful our good benefactor. . . . Wee the poore distressed prisoners, in the hole of Wood-streete Counter, in nomber fiftie [etc. An appeal for alms for Easter.] s.sh.*obl*.8°. [*V. Simmes*, c. 1595.] L.

Woodville, Anthony, *Earl Rivers. See* Wydeville, A.

25970 **Woodwall, William.** A sermon upon the xii. xiij. and xiiij. verses of the xiiij. chapter of Ezechiel. Wherein are shewed the causes of dearth and famine. Preached at Strowd. 4°. *E. A[llde] f. E. White*, 1609. O.STU.; F(K1 in facs.).

25970.5 — [Anr. issue, w. cancel tp, init. W. W., *Doctor in Divinity*.] Englands unthankfulnes for Gods mercie. A sermon preached at a funerall at Strowd the 16. of August. 1621. [*A. Mathewes?*] *f. J. Marriott*, 1621. L.O¹⁰.D(lacks tp)*.; F(imp.).ILL.
(Formerly 24923)

25971 **Woodward, Ezekias.** A childes patrimony laid out upon the good tilling over his whole man. The first part. (A child's portion. The second part.) 2 pts. 4°. *J. Legatt*, 1640. Ent. to P. Stephens a. C. Meredith 13 se. 1639. L⁴.C².; F.HN.ILL.
Because of the inscrutability of Woodward's prose and the apparent vacillation of his purpose, copies of this and the following show disheartening variety. The most intelligible collation for 25971 is, pt. 1: *-*** (Patrimony tp and dedic. to Sir R. Pye); 2nd **² (To Reader by W. Gouge); b–g⁴ (pref.); h⁴ (contents); A–Z⁴ (text); pt. 2: 1–4⁴ (Portion tp; iii, dedic. to J. Croker; 2iii, pref.; 4ii, contents); Aa–Ccc⁴ Ddd² (text). For the leaf signed 11 i *see* 25972.
At least F is bd. sep. and in this order, and the same order is followed, but w. both tpp and the Pye dedic. cancelled, in the 1649 reissue at HD (*62–719, Wing W 3500). The HN copy has b–g⁴ at the end of the volume, following 25972, which is bd. after pt. 2.

25971a — [Anr. issue, w. 25972 added, and added? gen. tp:] A childes patrimony. In two parts. [With an] Appendix. 3 pts. *J. L[egat,] sold by H. Overton*, 1640. C. C³.LEIC.; HD(*67–872).
c³ has the added gen. tp at the beginning but otherwise follows the order in the HN copy of 25971/25972 (i.e. with b–g⁴ at the end of the vol.). The HD copy has the gen. tp immediately followed by 25972 and b–g⁴, then the 1st tp of 25971 and the rest of that item. However, the HD copy has ***1 cancelled (1st leaf of 'Epistle' of 25972; stub

Woodward, Ezekias—*cont.*
visible) and replaced by a bifolium of which the 1st leaf is still another tp in a different setting: 'A childes patrimony. The first part., *J. L.*, 1640' and the 2nd leaf is signed ***1 and is the same setting as the leaf it replaces.
The 1643 reissue at O⁶ (Wing W 3506) begins w. the gen. tp 25971a, followed by [–]² (An appendix. . . . To the reader); then b–g⁴; 25972 lacking [-]⁴; then the rest of 25971 with the 1st tp cancelled and replaced by the 1643 tp and an unsigned leaf (A premonition to the parent). These 2 last-mentioned leaves are at the beginning of the 1643 reissue at ILL, followed by the 1st tp to 25971.

25972 — Vestibulum or, a manuduction towards a faire edifice. 4°. *J. L[egat,]* 1640. C².; F.HN.ILL.
The orig. collation of this is [-]⁴ (Vestibulum tp and anon. To Reader); *⁴ (*1–3, dedic. to H. Garraway; *4 (signed '11'), dedic. to Lady M. Garraway); ***-12*⁴ (text = Epistle to Ministers).
The dedic. to Lady Garraway was intended to be removed and placed after the tp of pt. 2 of 25971, where HN, the C³ copy of 25971a, and the O⁶ copy of Wing W 3506 have it; the F copy, bd. sep., lacks this leaf; the HD copy of 25971a retains it at *4.

25972.2 **Woodward, Philip.** Bels trial examined that is a refutation of [1832]. By B. C. student in divinitie. 8°. *Roane*, [i.e. *Douai, P. Auroi,*] 1608. L².L²⁵.L²⁶. CHATS.E².+; F.
A&R 905. Also attacks 21228, 24508.5. Answered by 1815, 24508.3.
— A detection, of divers notable untruthes. 1602. *See* 18754.

25972.4 — The dolefull knell, of Thomas Bell. That is a full answer, to [1825]. By B. C. student in divinitye. 8°. *Roane*, [i.e. *Douai, P. Auroi a. L. Kellam,*] 1607. L.O.C.D.E.+; F.HN.U.Y.
(Formerly 19403) A&R 907. Auroi pr. the prelims.; Kellam the rest.

25972.5 — The fore-runner of Bels downefall, wherin, is breifely answered [1818]. [Init. B. C.] 8°. [*Douai, C. Boscard,*] 1605. L².L⁹.O(2).YK.; HN.
(Formerly 19407) A&R 908. Answered by 1825.

25972.6 — The second time set forth, & corrected. 8°. [*English secret press*, 1605?] C.; F.
(Formerly 19407a) A&R 909.
— *tr. See* 12349.

25972.8 **Wooer.** The honest woer, his minde expressing. [Init. R. W.] *Ballad*. 2 pts. s.sh.fol. [*E. Purslowe?*] *f. H. G[osson*, 1632?] Ent. to Gosson a. F. Coules 24 my. 1632. C⁶.

25973 — [Anr. ed. Anon.] The honest wooer. 2 pts. s.sh.fol. [*E. Purslowe?*] *f. F. Coules*, [c. 1635.] Ent. to ballad ptnrs. 16 jy. 1634. L.

Wooing. A mad kinde of wooing. [c. 1630.] *See* 14960.5.

25974 **Woolton, John,** *Bp.* An armoure of proufe: very profitable, as well for princes, as all other in authoritie. 8°. [*H. Bynneman f.*] *J. Shepperde*, 1576. L(tp only, Harl.5927/250).O⁴.C(lacks tp).; F.

25975 — The castell of christians and fortresse of the faithfull, beseeged, and defended. 8°. (*J. C[harlewood] f. T. Sturrup*, 1577.) Ent. 30 mr. L.O.O⁴.P.; F.

25976 — The christian manuell, or of the life and maners of true christians. 8°. *J. C[harlewood] f. T. Sturruppe*, 1576. Ent. 29 oc. L.O.O⁴.C⁴.D.; F.U.

25977 — A newe anatomie of whole man, aswell of his body, as of his soule. 8°. *T. Purfoote*, 1576. L.O⁴.; F.HN.

25978 — Of the conscience, a discourse. . . . Anno. 1576. 8° in 4's. *H. Jackson f. H. Toye*, [1576.] O⁴.; F.

25979 — A treatise of the immortalitie of the soule. 8°. (*T. Purfoote f.*) *J. Shepperd*, 1576. L.O.O⁴.C(2, 1 imp.). C².; F(3).CHI.
— *See also* 10203.

25980 **Worcestershire.** A briefe discourse of two most cruell and bloudie murthers, committed in Worcestershire. 8°. *R. Warde*, 1583. L.

Work. More worke for a masse-priest. 1621. *See* 5663.
— A notable and very excellente woorke, how to kepe a boke of accōptes. [1547.] *See* 26093.5.

Work—*cont.*

    — A worke entytled of yᵉ olde god & the newe. 1534. *See* 25127.

    — Worke for a masse-priest. 1617. *See* 5662.

    — Work for chimny-sweepers. 1602. *See* 12571.

25981 — Worke for cutlers. Or, a merry dialogue betweene sword, rapier, and dagger. Acted in the universitie of Cambridge. 4°. *T. Creede f. R. Meighen a. T. Jones*, 1615. Ent. to Meighen 4 jy. L.O⁶.; HN.PFOR. Greg 331.

25982 **World.** Here begynneth a propre newe interlude of the worlde and the chylde, otherwyse called [Mundus & Infans]. 4° ⁶·⁴. (*W. de worde*, 1522 (17 jy.)) D. Greg 5.

    — Of the ende of this world. 1577. *See* 11804.

    — The worlde, or an historicall description. 1601. *See* 3399.

    — The worlde possessed with deuils. 1583. *See* 24785.

25983 — [Heading A3ʳ:] The worlds anotomy [*sic*]. [c. 1660.] Not an STC book.

    — The worlds great restauration. 1621. *See* 10874.5.

25984 — The worlds sweet-heart: whereby it is shewed that mistris Money, is the worlds sweet-heart and hony. *Ballad.* 2 pts. s.sh.fol. *f. T. Lambert*, [1634.] Ent. 19 au. 1634. L.

    Worming. The worming of a mad dogge. 1617. *See* 18257.

25985 **Worship, William.** The christians jewell. Or, the treasure of a good conscience. 12°. *W. Stansby f. J. Parker*, 1617. Ass'd by H. Fetherstone to Parker 3 ap. 1626. L.O.; F.FBL.U.

25986 — [Anr. ed.] Revised, and inlarged. 12°. *W. Stansby f. J. Parker*, 1618. C⁵.; F.HN.

25987 — The christians mourning garment. The third edition. [A treatise.] 8°. *f. T. Pavier*, 1603. Ent. 7 au. 1602. L.

    See also 25992.

25988 — [Anr. ed.] 8°. [*R. Bradock*] *f. T. Pavier*, 1608. L(imp.).; LC.

25989 — [Anr. ed.] 8°. [*R. Blower?*] *f. T. P[avier,]* 1610. C.

25989.5 — [Anr. ed.] 8°. *W. J[ones] f. T. Pavier*, 1618. HD.

25990 — [Anr. ed.] 8°. *J. Norton f. R. Bird*, 1630. Ass'd to E. Brewster a. Bird 4 au. 1626. C(frag.).D.

25991 — [Anr. ed.] 8°. *J. B[eale] f. R. Bird*, 1636. L.

25992 — The christians mourning garment. Aarons bells. The fisher. Three sermons. 8°. *G. Eld f. T. Pavier a. F. Burton*, 1612. Ent. 23 se. L.O.C³.C¹⁰(2).; F(lacks A8). The 1st sermon is the orig. form of the text, which was altered and pub'd as a treatise in 25987.

25993 — [Anr. ed., w. additions.] The christians mourning garment. Foure sermons. 8°. *L. S[nowdon] f. T. Pavier*, 1615. L.O(imp.).E(lacks tp).LINC.NEP.+; F.BO.U.Y. The 4th sermon reprints 25994.

25994 — Earth raining upon heaven. A sermon. 4°. [*T. Snodham*] *f. T. Pavier*, 1614. Ent. 16 se. L.O.C.D.YK.+; F.HN.

25995 — The patterne of an invincible faith. A sermon. 4°. *N. Okes f. M. Law*, 1616. Ent. 21 jn. L.O.E.G².P.+; F(imp.).FBL.

25996 — Three sermons, preached at three severall visitations, at Boston, in the county of Lincolne. 4°. *F. Kyngston f. J. Parker*, 1625. Ent. 31 my. L.DUL.PLUME.; F. HN.U.

25997 **Worsop, Edward.** A discouerie of sundrie errours committed by landemeaters, ignorant of arithmetike and geometrie, written dialoguewise. 4°. *H. Middleton f. G. Seton*, 1582. Ent. 6 mr. [ap.?] L.O.C.; HN.

    Worsop, John. *See* 24000.5.

25998 **Worst.** The worst is past. Or, a merry new song that lately was pend. *Ballad.* 2 pts. s.sh.fol. *f. R. Harper*, [c. 1640.] Ent. to F. Coules and ballad ptnrs. 20 jn. 1629. L.G².

    Worthington, Lawrence, *tr. See* 5827.

25999 **Worthington, Robert.** The ground of a christians life. Delivered in a sermon. 8°. *R. Field f. R. Mylbourne*, 1620. Ent. 17 fb. L.LINC.P.

26000 **Worthington, Thomas.** An anker of christian doctrine. Whearein the most principal pointes of catholique religion are proved by the only written word of God. [Init. Th. W.] 4°. *Doway, T. Kellam* [really *Lancs., Birchley Hall Press?*] 1618. L.O.C.M(imp.).W.+; F. HN.HD.N.
    A&R 910. For pts. 2–4 *see* 26000.3 sqq.

26000.2 — [Anr. issue, w. cancel tp.] Auctore T.W.S.T.D.P.A. *Doway, L. Kellam*, 1622. L²⁶.A².D.HP(imp.).W.; N.U.
    A&R 911. In title: 'points of Catholike'; the title is in a border of rules; cf. 26000.4, 26000.6.

26000.3 — The second part of an anker of christian doctrine. Auctore T.W.S.T.D.P.A. 4°. *Mackline, H. Jaey*, 1620. O⁴.D².DAI.DE.HP.+; BO.
    A&R 912. Pref. init. 'T. W. Sem[inary]. Pr[iest].'

26000.4 — [Pts. 3 and 4 on continuous signatures.] An anker of christian doctrine. Auctore T.W.S.T.D.P.A. 4°. *Doway, L. Kellam*, 1622. O.C(imp.).A².D².W.+
    A&R 913. In title: 'pointes of Catholique'. The preface has Worthington's name in full.

26000.5 — [Anr. issue of pts. 2–4.] *Doway, L. Kellam*, 1622. L.O⁴(imp.).C.D.M.+; TEX. William and Mary C, Williamsburg, Virginia(imp.).
    A&R 914. This consists of 26000.3, w. prelims. cancelled, inserted between the prelims. and the text of 26000.4. At least L, C, D have a cancel slip w. 'The second part of an' pasted over 'An' on the tp.

26000.6 — [Anr. issue of all 4 pts.] *Doway, L. Kellam*, 1622. A².
    A&R 915. This consists of 26000.2 w. variant tp without border of rules, and 26000.5 w. tp cancelled.

26000.8 — [Heading:] A catalogue of martyrs in England: since 1535 vnto 1608. [Anon.] 8°. [*Douai, L. Kellam?* 1608.] OS.
    A&R 916. Collates A⁸ B⁶ and is a different text from that at the end of 25771.

26000.9 — A relation of sixtene martyrs: glorified in England in twelve monethes. With a declaration. That the seminarie priests agree with the jesuites. [Init. T. W.] 8°. *Doway, widow of J. Boscard*, 1601. L⁹(2, 1 imp.).C(imp.).OS(imp.).; HD(imp.).
    A&R 917.

    — The rosarie of our ladie. 1600. *See* 17546.

26001 — Whyte dyed black. Or a discovery of many deceiptes, which D. Whyte haith practysed in his book [25394]. [Init. T. W. P.] 4° partly in 2's. [*Lancs., Birchley Hall Press?*] 1615. L.O.C.D.E².+; F.HN.BO³.
    A&R 919. Answered by 25380.

26002 **Wotton, Anthony.** An answere to a popish pamphlet, of late the second time printed, entituled: Certaine articles [26038.6]. 4°. *G. Eld f. W. Timme*, 1605. Ent. 8 my. L.O.C.D.E.+; F.HN.ILL.U.Y.
    Answered by 10914.

26003 — A dangerous plot discovered. By a discourse, wherein is proved, that, R. Mountague, in his two bookes; [18038 and 18030] laboureth to bring in the faith of Rome, and Arminius. [Anon.] 4°. [*J. Dawson*] *f. N. Bourne*, 1626. L.O.C.D.E.+; F.HN.HD.N.U.+

26004 — A defence of M. Perkins booke, [19735.8] against the cavils in [3096]. 4° in 8's. *F. Kyngston f. C. Burby*, 1606. Ent. 16 ja. L.O.C.D.E².+; F.HN.CHI.HD.U.+
    Includes reprints of both books.

26005 — Runne from Rome. Or, a treatise shewing the necessitie of separating from the church of Rome. 4°. *W. J[ones] f. N. Bourne*, 1624. Ent. 2 jn. L.O.C.D.G².+; F.HN.ILL.U.Y.+

26006 — [Anr. ed.] 12°. *T. Cotes f. W. Hope*, 1636. L.L³.C.D.E⁸. +; F.ILL.TORONTO².

26007 — Runne from Rome. [A different text.] 1640. Now = 21307a.3.

26008 — Sermons upon a part of the first chap. of the gospell of S. John. 4° in 8's. *H. L[ownes] f. S. Macham*, 1609. Ent. 21 ap. L.O.C.CHATS.STU.; F.HN(imp.).TORONTO². U.Y.

26009 — A trial of the romish clergies title to the church. By way of answer to [10915.5]. 4°. [*R. Field*] *f. E. Burby widow*, 1608. Ent. to E. Burby a. W. Timme 17 oc. and 3 no. 1607. L.O.C².D.E.+; F.HN.HD. WASH².U.

    — *ed. See* 15248.

    Wotton, Edward. *See* 17993.

Wotton, Henry. A courtlie controuersie of Cupids cautels. *Tr.* by H. W(otton.) 1578. *See* 5647.

26009.5 **Wotton, *Sir* Henry.** Ad illustrissimum virum Marcum Velserum duumvirum Augustæ Vindeliciæ H. Wottonij epistola. 4°. [*London*, 1612.] LINC.M.
　　End of text dated 5 Dec. 1612.

26010 — Ad regem è Scotia reducem Henrici Wottonij plausus et vota. fol. *typis A. Mathusij,* 1633. Ent. to H. Robinson 21 no. L.O.C.A.YK.+; F.HN.HD.Y.
　　Most copies are on paper w. no watermark, in some examples (L, 1 O, 1 ETON) cropt to 4° size, and have the device McK. 249β on the tp. Large paper copies have a pot or shield watermark; 1 ETON has the device; 1 O, O⁵, O⁶, F have no device.

26010.5 — [Anr. issue, w. imprint:] *typis A. Mathusij, sumpt. H. Robinson,* 1633. ETON(lacks dedic.).
　　The tp has no device; the paper is without watermarks except for N1.

26011 — The elements of architecture, collected from the best authors and examples. 4°. *J. Bill,* 1624. Ent. to T. Harper 24 ja. L.O.C.D.G².+; F.HN.HD.N.NY.+
　　B4 is a cancel in some copies; the orig. has no leaf signature; the cancel is signed 'B4'; both at L.
— A meditation upon Genesis. 1631. *See* 24905.

26012 **Wotton, John.** Incipit liber qui vocatur Speculum Xpristiani [*sic*]. [Anon.] 4° in 8's. (*p me w. de Machlinia ad expensas H. Vrankenbergh mercatoris,*) [1486?] L.O.C.LEEDS.M.+; F.HN.N.PML.NY.+ Duff 415.
— Speculum spiritualiũ. [Sometimes attrib. to J. Wotton.] 1510. *See* 23030.7.

Wotton, Samuel, *tr. See* 15248.

26013 **Wouwerus, Joannes à.** Joannis Wouweri dies æstiva, sive de umbra pægnion. Unà cum Jani Dousæ F. in eandem declamatione. Editio postrema castigatior. 12°. *Oxonii, G. Turner, imp. G. Webb,* 1636. L.O.C².D.E.+; F.HN.HD.ILL.NY.+

Wr., Tho. The passions of the minde. 1604. *See* 26040.

Wraghton, William, *pseud. See* Turner, W.

Wrathall, Richard. *See* 24912.

26013.5 **Wray, Thomas.** Sundry lawes against swearing, cursing and blaspheming the most holy name of God. s.sh. fol. *f. S. Stafford, sold by R. Milbourne,* 1624. Ent. 24 jn. M(deposit).

26014 **Wrednot, William.** Palladis palatium: wisedoms pallace. Or the fourth part of Wits commonwealth. [Anon.] 8°. *G. Elde f. F. Burton,* 1604. Ent. as by W. Wrednot 4 jn. HN.
　　The other parts in the 'Wits Series' are 381, 15685, 17834.

Wren, Christopher, *Dean of Windsor.* Stafford. Archdeaconry. Visitation Articles. *See* 10336.

26015 **Wren, Matthew,** *Bp.* A sermon preached before the kings majestie. 4°. *Cambridge, T. a. J. Buck,* 1627. L.O.C.E.YK.+; F.HN.HD.U(imp.).Y.+
— *See also* 10197, 10217, 10298.

26016 — The wrens nest defil'd, or, bishop Wren anatomiz'd. With a true relation of his persecuting ministers. 4°. *f. J. Thomas,* 1640. C.; HD.Y.

Wrenham, John. The true state of foure severall suites. [1621?] *See* 10885.5.

26017 **Wright, Abraham.** Delitiæ delitiarum sive epigrammatum ex optimis poetis in illâ bibliothecâ Bodleiana, ἀνθολογία, operâ A. Wright. 12°. *Oxoniæ, L. Lichfield, imp. G. Webb,* 1637. O.C.PLUME.; F.HD.

26017a — [A variant, w. errata on p. 247, and imprint:] *Oxoniæ, L. Lichfield, imp. Gulielmi Webb,* 1637. L.O.C.D.G².+; F.HN.HD.N.Y.+

26018 **Wright, Benjamin,** *Engraver.* The armes of all the cheife corporatons [*sic*] of England wᵗ the Companees of London. [Completely engraved.] fol(2). *sould at the hartshorne in pater-noster-rowe,* 1596. Ent. to H. Denham 1 de. 1589. L(1 imp. in Dept. of MSS.; frags. in Dept. of P&D).; F.HN(imp.).
　　See Hind I.214–15. The sheets may have been pasted together before printing.

Wright, Edward. The arte of dialing. 1614. *See* 26022.5.

26019 — Certaine errors in nauigation, . . . detected and corrected. (Voyage of George earle of Cumberl. to the Azores.) 2 pts. 4°. *V. Sims [a. W. White,]* 1599. L(2).O.C⁹.; F(pt. 2 only).CB.NY.NY³.Y.+ White pr. pt. 2.

26019a — [Anr. issue, w. cancel tp:] Errors in nauigation. . . . Whereto is adioyned, the voyage to the Azores. *f. E. Agas,* 1599. C⁶.; HN.

26020 — [Anr. ed.] With many additions. (The whole art of navigation. [*Tr.* from R. Zamorano's Compendio.]) 4°. *F. Kingstō,* 1610. L.O.C⁶.D.G².+; LC.NY.NY³(imp.). Y.

26021 — The description and use of the sphære. 4°. [*E. Allde*] *f. J. Tap,* 1613. L.L³⁰.O.E².PETYT.+; F.LC.NY³.PH².Y.

26022 — [Anr. ed.] 4°. *B. A[lsop] a. T. Fawcet f. J. Tap,* 1627. Ass'd by widow Tap to J. Hurlock 1 au. 1631. L(tp def.).L³⁰.L³⁸.C.C¹⁵.+; HN(lacks N4).

26022.5 — The arte of dialing: shewing, how to make any kind of diall vpon a plaine superficies howsoever placed. 4°. *J. Beale f. W. Welby,* 1614. Ent. 15 my. L⁴⁴.O³.O¹⁶. D²(imp.).M².+
　　With 3 unnumbered figures on a folding sheet signed H.

26023 — [Anr. issue, with 3 figures, numbered 16–18, on a bifolium signed G, G2; and new prelims., w. title:] A short treatise of dialling. *J. Beale f. W. Welby,* 1614. L.L³⁸.O.C.D.+; F.BOWDOIN.HD. Horblit.
— *ed. See* 21549.
— *tr. See* 18351, 23265.

26024 **Wright, Henry.** The first part of the disquisition of truth, concerning political affaires. 4°. *N. Okes,* 1616. L.L³⁸.L⁴³.C.C².+; F.HN.HD.N.Y.+ 𝔄

Wright, John. Two notorious murders. 1595. *See* 18289.

26025 **Wright, Leonard.** A display of dutie, dect [*sic*] with sage sayings, pythie sentences, and proper similies. 4°. *J. Wolfe,* 1589. Ent. 13 oc. L.O⁸.M.; F(2).Y.

26026 — [Anr. ed.] 4°. *V. S[ims] f. N. Lyng,* 1602. Ent. to E. Aggas 7 de. 1601. L.; TEX.

26027 — [Anr. ed.] 4°. *E. Griffin f. G. Purslowe,* 1614. Ass'd by widow Wolfe to J. Pindley 27 ap. 1612; to Purslowe 2 no. 1613. L.O.M.; F.

26028 — [Anr. ed.] 4°. *G. Purslowe,* 1616. L³.C.SH.; F.HN.

26029 — [Anr. ed.] 8°. *G. Purslowe,* 1621. O.; F.

26030 — A friendly admonition to Martine Marprelate, and his mates. 4°. *J. Wolfe,* 1590. Ent. 19 ja. L.L².O(date shaved).D.M.; F.PFOR.

26031 — The hunting of Antichrist. With a caueat to the contentious. 4°. *J. Wolfe,* 1589. Ent. 7 jn. L.L².O.C.M.+; F.HN.CHI.HD.U.

26032 — The pilgrimage to paradise. Compiled for the direction, of Gods children. 4°. *J. Wolfe,* 1591. Ent. 23 ja. L.L²(2).SAL.; Pirie.

26033 — [Anr. ed.] Newly augmented. 8°. *H. L[ownes] f. W. Leake,* 1608. Ass'd 5 oc. 1601. L.

26033.5 — A summons for sleepers. Wherein offenders are cited to repentance. Hereunto is annexed, A patterne for pastors. 4°. [*J. Wolfe, sold by E. Aggas,*] 1589. Ent. to J. Wolfe 4 mr. L²(2).; BO³.CHI.
　　Collates [-]² B–H⁴. The tp of this and the following has McK. 199, the device of Aggas.

26034 — [Anr. ed.] Newly reprinted, corrected and amended. 4°. [*J. Wolfe, sold by E. Aggas,*] 1589. O⁸(tp def., lacks sheet C).; U.
　　This and the following collate [-]² A–G⁴ and have [-]² in the same typesetting. In the present ed. sheets A–G are in a different setting from all others.
　　B1ʳ last line begins: 'they be', line 1 has: 'vsurie:'
　　C3ʳ line 7 from bottom begins: 'ceiue'
　　E1ʳ lines 5,6: 'praising . . . bruite'
　　F2ʳ subheading: 'A Prayer.'

26034.3 — [Anr. ed.] 4°. [*J. Wolfe, sold by E. Aggas,*] 1589. L.O (Douce WW 106).M.P(H.6.2).; F.HN(imp.). Pirie.
　　In this and the next there are at least 5 settings of B outer forme and only 1 of sheets A and G, though the type for the latter 2 is in 2 impositions. Copies display a relationship rather than a simple mixture. The standard copies for this are a different setting or imposition in all sheets from the standard copies of 26034.7. The other copies are related to their respective standards, though

Wright, Leonard—*cont.*

they have some formes in common w. the other
standard as well as some unique formes.
For this M, P, HN, Pirie are the standard,
represented below by P; L, O, F all show identical
variations, represented below by O.
B1[r] last line begins: 'they be', line 1 has 'vsury:'
(P) or B1[r] last line begins: 'they he [*sic*]' (O)
C3[r] line 7 from bottom begins: 'wise men' (all
copies).
E1[v] lines 4,5: 'praising . . . brute' (P) or 'praysing
. . . bruit' (O)
F2[r] subheading: 'A prayer.' (all copies).

26034.7 — [Anr. ed.] 4°. [*J. Wolfe, sold by E. Aggas,*] 1589. O
(Tanner 270).O[16].C[2].C[5](lacks tp).P(H.3.151).STD.STU.;
F(2, 1 imp.).
For this O[16], C[2], C[5], P, F(imp.) are the standard,
represented below by P; O, STD, STU all show identical variations, represented below by O, except
in the imposition of sheet G; the 2nd F copy is
more distantly related, and no other copy w. its
unique readings is now known.
B1[r] last line begins: 'shal they be . . . from' (P) or
'shal they be . . . frõ' (O) or 'they bee' (2nd F)
C3[r] line 7 from bottom begins: 'ceyue' (P, O) or
'fooles.' (2nd F)
E1[v] lines 4,5: 'praising . . . bruit' (all copies)
F2[r] subheading: 'A Praier.' (all copies but 2nd F,
which has the 26034.3 setting).

26035 — [Anr. ed.] 4°. *A. Islip, sold by E. white,* 1596. L.O.P.
YK.; F(2).U.

26036 — [Anr. ed.] Newly corrected and augmented. 4°. *G.
Purslowe,* 1615. Ass'd by widow Wolfe to J. Pindley
22 jn. 1612; to Purslowe 2 no. 1613. L.L[2].C.; F.HD.
U.Y.

26036.5 — [Anr. ed.] 4°. *E. Purslow,* 1637. O.DUL.EX.

26037 **Wright, Robert,** *Bp.* A receyt to stay the plague. Delivered [in a sermon] by R. W[right.] 4°. *A. M[athewes]
a. J. N[orton] f. M. Law,* 1625. Ent. to J. Norton
25 jn. L(imp.).O.C[8].BRISTOL.; Y.

26037a — [Anr. ed., with new preface by T. R., *Minister.*] 4°. *J.
N[orton,] sold by R. Bird,* 1630. O(2).
One O copy has the tp in an early state, without
the quotation from Numb. xvi.46 and w. the misprint 'Rird' in the imprint.

26038 — [Anr. issue, w. cancel tp, w. imprint:] *J. Norton,* 1636.
HN.
— ed. *See* 24520.
— *See also* 10144, 10227.5 sqq.

Wright, Samuel. Divers godly and learned sermons.
1612. *See* 21203.

26038.2 **Wright, Thomas,** *Bookseller.* Memento mori. s.sh.4°?
sould by T. Wright, [1636?] O(not traced).
Reproduced in F. P. Wilson, *Plague in Shakespeare's London,* p. 128. Title and imprint are
xylographic in a woodcut compartment enclosing
3 lines of letterpress; *see also* 17816.5.

26038.4 **Wright, Thomas,** *Priest.* Certaine articles or forcible
reasons. Discovering the absurdities, and errors of
the protestants religion. [Init. H. T.] 8°. *Anwerpe*
[really *English secret press,*] 1600. OS.; F(imp.).
A&R 920. Collates A–B[8] C[4] D[2]. Reprinted and
answered in 1449, 4025; *see also* 25965.

26038.5 — [Anr. ed.] 8°. *Anwerp* [really *English secret press,*]
1600. L[2].OS.VAL.WOR.
A&R 921. Collates A–B[8] C[6].

26038.6 — [Anr. ed., enlarged.] 8°. *Antwerpe,* 1600 [really *English
secret press,* 1604?] L.C.; HN.
(Formerly 23618) A&R 922. Collates A–C[8]. Reprinted and answered in 26002.

26038.8 — The disposition or garnishmente of the soule to
receiue worthily the blessed sacrament, deuyded into
three discourses. [Init. T. N.] 8°. *Antwerpe, J.
Trognesius* [really *English secret press,*] 1596. L.O.C[3].
W.YK.+; F.N.STL.TEX.
(Formerly 18335) Copies differ: without (F; A&R
923) or with (L, O, N, TEX; A&R 924) y[8] containing
'A conclusion'.

26039 — The passions of the minde. [Init. Th. W.] 8°. *V.
S[ims] f. W. B[urre,]* 1601. Ent. to V. Sims 12 jn.
L.O.C[2].E[2].LIV[2].+; F.HN.MICH.

Wright, Thomas, *Priest*—*cont.*

26040 — [Anr. ed.] Corrected, enlarged, and augmented. With
a treatise occasioned by the death of queene Elizabeth. 2 pts. 4° in 8's. *V. Simmes* [*a. A. Islip*] *f. W.
Burre* [Pt. 2:] (*f. T. Thorpe, sold by W. Burre,*) 1604.
L.O.C.E[2].YK.+; F.HN.HD(lacks folding table).PEN.Y.+
Pt. 2 is a reissue of 26043.3; it is not reprinted in
26041 sqq. Quire A of pt. 1 is in 2 settings: uncorrected, w. tp line 7 beginning: 'Newly enlarged,' and A2[v] line 10 having: 'continuall' (P);
or corrected, w.: 'With a treatise' and 'conna-
turall' (O, C, both HD). The tp, which is largely
from standing type in both settings, varies further:
O, P, C, and 1 HD have 'By Thomas Wright.'; the
other HD has 'By Tho. Wr.'. Islip pr. quires G–O
in pt. 1.

26041 — [Anr. ed.] In six bookes. Corrected, . . . by T. Wright.
4° in 8's. *A. M[athewes] f. A. Helme,* 1620. L[38].O.C[5].
A.G[4].+; F(2).ILL.KAN.
Most copies have the dedic. signed by the editor's
inits. 'T. D.'; the HN copy of 26042 has 'Thomas
Dewe.'

26042 — [A variant, w. imprint:] *A. M[athewes] f. A. Helme,*
1621. L.O[11].C.E.G[4](tp def.).+; F.HN.LC.NY[4].PN.+

26043 — [Anr. ed.] 4° in 8's. *M. Flesher, sold by R. Dawlman,*
1630. Ass'd by A. Helme to W. Washington 3 de.
1627; to Flesher 21 my. 1628. L.O.C.BIRM.D.+; F.
HN.HD.N.Y.+

26043.3 — A succinct philosophicall declaration of the nature of
clymactericall yeeres, occasioned by the death of
queene Elizabeth. [Init. T. W.] 4°. [*V. Sims*] *f. T.
Thorpe, sold by W. Burre,* 1604. L(2).LONGLEAT.;
F.HN.ILL.NLM. Vassar C.
Also issued as pt. 2 of 26040.

26043.5 — A treatise, shewing the possibilitie, and conueniencie
of the reall presence of our sauiour in the blessed
sacrament. [Anon.] 8°. *Antwerp, J. Trognesius*
[really *London, V. Sims,*] 1596. L.O.C[2].A[2].W.+; F.
HD.ILL.U.Y.+
(Formerly 14574 and 24249) A&R 925.
— *See also* 21152.

26044 **Wright, William.** A briefe treatise in which, is made
playne, that catholikes living and dying in their profession, may be saved. Against a minister [N. E.]
who in his Epistle exhorteth an honourable person,
to forsake his ancient catholike roman religion.
[Anon.] 4°. [*St. Omer, English College Press,*] 1623.
L.; HD.
A&R 926. Apparently against the same book or
MS. as 26046.5.

26045 — A discovery of certaine notorious shifts, evasions, and
untruthes uttered in [25390]. By W. G. professour
in divinity, in manner of a dialogue. 4°. [*St. Omer,
English College Press,*] 1614. L[25].O.C[2].USHAW.YK.
A&R 927.

26046 — [Anr. ed., enlarged.] Second edition. 4°. [*St. Omer,
English College Press,*] 1619. L.O.C.OS.USHAW.+; F.
A&R 928.

26046.5 — An epistle dedicated to an honourable person. In the
which, are discovered a dozen bad spirits, who have
haunted the protestant congregation. [Anon.] 4°.
[*St. Omer, English College Press,*] 1622. L[9](lacks
tp).; HD.
A&R 929. Attacks an Epistle written by N. E.;
see also 26044.

26047 — A summarie of controversies: wherein the chiefest
points of the catholike faith, are proved. [Init. C. W.,
B. Erroneously attrib. to W. Wright.] 8°. [*English
secret press,*] 1616. L.O.A[2].DE.W.+; HN.N(lacks tp).
TEX.
A&R 866. A different text from 13998.

26048 — The II. edition. 8°. *S. Omers,* [*English College Press*] *f.
J. Heigham,* 1623. L.L[2].O. USHAW.W.+; F.HD.N.TEX.
U.
A&R 867.

26049 — A treatise of the church. In which is proved J. White
his Way [25394] to be no way at all. By W. G. professour in divinity: in manner of dialogue. 4°. [*St.
Omer, English College Press,*] 1616. L.E.P.
A&R 930.
— *tr. See* 1700, 1707, 13996, 13996a, 13997, 13997a,
13997b, 13998, 14527, 15517.

26049.2 **Writing Tables** or **Tablets.** Wryting tables, with a
necessarie calender for xxv. (yea)res, with all the
principall fayres in Englande, the festiuall holydayes,

Writing Tables—*cont.*

the hie wayes from one towne to another [etc.] Made by Franke Adams. 16° in 8's. [*H. Singleton f. F. Adams*, 1577?] o(quires A–B only).

With Singleton's device, McK. 127, on B7ʳ. This is the only ed. w. the text in roman types. In the imprint Adams's address is 'dwelling in the Greene Arbour without Newgate', which is crossed out and his later address added in ink: 'black raven nere London brydge'.

26049.4 — [Anr. ed.] 16° in 8's. (*made by F. Adams*,) [1579?] o (B2–D8 only).

In this ed. through 26049.14 the last date in the text is 9 Aug. 1577. In these eds. differing portions are pr. from standing type.

26049.6 — [Anr. ed.] Writing tables with a kalender for xxij yeares. 16° in 8's. [*R. Watkins a. J. Roberts f.*] *F. Adams, sold [by him] or else by T. Chayre*, 1580. Y.

The colophon also has Chayre's name.

26049.8 — [Anr. ed.] Writing tables with a kalender for xxiiij. yeres. 16° in 8's, gathered at the top. [*R. Watkins a. J. Roberts f.*] *F. Adams, sold [by him] or else by T. Chayre* [col.:] (*F. Adams, solde [by him] or els by T. Frethren*,) 1581. HD.

26049.10 — [A variant, w. imprint on tp:] *F. Adams, sold [by him] or else by T. Frethren*, 1581. L(lacks last leaf). Bos. cxciii.

(Formerly 101)

26049.14 — [Anr. ed., revised.] 16° in 8's, gathered at the top. [*R. Watkins a. J. Roberts f.*] *F. Adams*, 1584. F.

With added quire E⁸, w. Godly exercises of prayer. A copy w. a similar quire but dated 1583 was offered for sale by Frank B. Benger, Leatherhead, Surrey, Catalogue 8 (Nov. 1950), item 1 (tp reproduced, not traced).

26049.16 — [Anr. ed., revised.] 16° in 8's, gathered at the top. [*R. Watkins a. J. Roberts f.*] *F. Adams*, 1594. C.

(Formerly 102) In this ed. through 26050.8 the text ends w. events of 1587. In this ed. through 26050.4 differing portions are pr. from standing type.

26050 — [Anr. ed.] 16° in 8's. *J. Roberts f. E. White*, 1598. ILL. Pirie. Bos. cxcix.

(Formerly also 103) In this and 26050.2 there is no mention of any maker of the tablets.

26050.2 — [Anr. ed.] 16° in 8's. *J. Roberts f. E. White*, 1601. ILL (imp.).

26050.4 — [Anr. ed.] (Made by R. Triplet.) 16° in 8's, gathered at the top. [*J. Roberts f. E. White*, 1602?] o(B2–D8 only, Douce Add.330).

This is the only Triplet ed. mentioning his name on D8ᵛ. Quires B–C are in the same setting as 26050, w. C8ᵛ line 3 ending 'prisoners'; 26050.2 has 'prysoners'.

26050.6 — [Anr. ed.] Writing tables with a kalendar for xxiiij. yeeres. The tables made by Robert Triplet. 16° in 8's. *f. the Co. of Stationers*, 1604. L.O(tp def.).; F.

(Formerly 24284) See Court-Book C, p. 4. This and the following eds. appear to be largely from different typesettings.

26050.8 — [Anr. ed.] 16° in 8's, gathered at the top. *f. the Co. of Stationers*, 1609. PML.

In the date the tail of the '9' has not pr. This is the last ed. w. text ending w. events of 1587.

26050.10 — [Anr. ed., revised.] 16° in 8's. *f. the Co. of Stationers*, 1611. L.; HD.

(Formerly 24285) Last date in text is 4 June 1610.

26050.12 — [Anr. ed.] 16° in 8's, gathered at the top. *f. the Co. of Stationers*, 1615. HN(imp.).

Last date in text is 14 Feb. 1613. This is the last ed. to name Triplet as maker of the tablets.

26050.14 — [Anr. ed.] Writing tables with a kalender for xxiiij. yeeres. The tables made by J. Hammond. 16° in 8's. [*W. Jaggard?*] *f. the Co. of Stationers*, 1618. Mrs. W. A. Potter, Lambley House, Woodborough, Notts.

26050.16 — [Anr. ed.] 16° in 8's, gathered at the top. [*f. the Co. of Stationers*, after 1625.] Ent. to the English Stock 5 mr. 1620. F(imp. at beginning and end).

Events end in 1625, w. Charles I's marriage to Henrietta Maria. After this are listed the foundations of the colleges at Cambridge and Oxford.

26050.18 — [Anr. ed.?] ⟨ ⟩ Whereunto are added writing-tables made by Oliver Ridge. 16° in 8's. *f. the Co. of Stationers*, 1628. F(frag. of two leaves, missing).

26051 **Wroth**, *Lady* **Mary**. The countesse of Mountgomeries Urania. (Pamphilia, to Amphilanthus. [In verse.]) fol. [*A. Mathewes?*] *f. J. Marriott a. J. Grismand*, [1621.] Ent. 13 jy. 1621. L.L⁴.O.C⁴.M²(imp.).+; F. HN.HD.N.Y.+

While the orn. on Oo1ʳ belonged to F. Kingston, the woodcut init. letters are not his and prob. belonged to A. Mathewes at this time.

26052 **Wroth**, *Sir* **Thomas**. The abortive of an idle houre. 1620. = pt. of 24810.

26053 — Sir Thomas Wrothe his sad encomion, upon his dearest consort. [In verse.] 4°. [*E. Purslowe*] *f. H. Seile*, 1635. HN.

— *tr. See* 24810.

Wuerzburg. *See* 25219.5.

Wurstisen, Christian. *See* 24540.

26053.5 **Wyatt**, *Sir* **Thomas**. [Verso/recto headline:] A Boke / of Balettes. [Anon. In verse.] 8°. [*W. Copland?* 1549?] TEX(2 leaves).

See also 24650.5.

26054 — [Heading A1ʳ:] An excellent epitaffe of syr Thomas wyat, with two other dytties, [upon] the state of mannes lyfe. [In verse.] 4°. (*J. Herforde f. R. Toye*,) [1545?] HN.

The 1st poem is by H. Howard, Earl of Surrey; the 3rd is anr. printing of 6920.

— *tr. See* 2726, 20058.5.

26055 **Wybarne**, **Joseph**. The new age of old names. [Miscellaneous essays.] 4°. [*J. Windet*] *f. W. Barret a. H. Fetherstone*, 1609. Ent. 25 au. L.L³⁸.O.C.STD.+; F. HN.HD.N.Y.+

Wyberd, **John**. Almanacks. 1635, etc. *See* 532.9 sqq.

26056 — Horologiographia nocturna. Or lunar horologiographie. Together with an addition for the mensuration of circles and spheres, and also cylinders. 4°. *T. Cotes*, 1639. L.L³⁰.O.C³.G².+; F.HN.

26057 — Synopsis anni 1637. Now = 532.11.

26057.3 **Wyche**, *Sir* **Peter**. Illustrissimus dominus, Petrus Wiche. Eques auratus, [etc. Declaration of the style and titles of Sir P. Wyche, ambassador to the Sultan Hanmorat, i.e. Amureth, or Murad IV, 1627.] s.sh.fol. [*London*, 1627.] L⁵(Lemon 280).

Wyclif, John. *See* Wiclif, J.

Wydeville, Anthony, *Earl Rivers*, *tr.* Cordiale. [1479.] *See* 5758.

— The dictes or sayengis of the philosophhres. 1477. *See* 6826.

— The morale prouerbes of Cristyne. [1478.] *See* 7273.

Wydowes, John. Almanacks. 1610, etc. *See* 531 sqq.

— Naturall philosophy. 1621. *See* 22111.

26057.5 **Wye**, *River*. The river of Wye (in true examination) very difficult and chargeable to be reduced portable beneath Hereford, but upward more difficult. [Against proposals in Parliament to make the river navigable.] fol(2). [*London*, 1624.] L⁸(GL 5012).; HN.

A bill for prostrating the weirs on the Wye was first read 25 Mar. 1624 and sent to committee 3 Apr. 1624; see *JHC* I.749, 753.

26057.7 **Wye**, **T.**, *Captain*. A briefe discourse, dedicated to the right honorable, the lord Charles Howarde, in maner of a dialogue, betwene Baldwyne & a sayler. [In verse.] 8°. *R. Waldegraue*, 1580. Ent. 2 no. C⁶.

Wyer, Robert, *tr. See* 7272.

Wykeham, William of. *See* 17516.

26058 **Wylshman**, **Walter**. The sincere preacher: proving that in whom is adulation, avarice, or ambition, he cannot be sincere. Delivered in three sermons. 8°. *F. Kyngston f. Jonas Man*, 1616. Ent. to T. a. J. Man 20 de. 1615. L.O.O²⁷.C(missing).LINC.

26059 **Wymesley**, **John**. Oratio. 1553. = pt. of 12794.

Wynne, William. [Bookplate.] *See* Bookplates.

Wynne, William—*cont.*

26060 — Morall observations. By W. W(ynne) Gent. 8°. [*by and*] *f. E. Allde*, 1616. L(tp only, Harl.5910, pt. IV/24).O.

26061 — Selected sentences out of sacred antiquitie, conducing to the establishment of faith and good manners. 12°. *E. A*[*llde*] *f. N. Butter*, 1624. L.NLW.; F.

26062 **Wyrley, William.** The true vse of armorie, shewed by historie, and plainly proued by example. (The life of sir J. Chandos.—The life of sir J. de Gralhy

Wyrley, William—*cont.*

Capitall de Buz. [Two poems.]) 4°. *J. Jackson f. G. Cawood*, 1592. Ent. 22 de. 1591. L.O.BTU.E.M².+; F.HN.HD.N.PML.+

26063 **Wyse, Nicholas.** A consolacyon for chrysten people . . . for yᵉ expellyng of ydolatry, & to instruct thē, of loue and obedience. 8°. (*J. Waylande*, 1538 (16 oc.)) O.C.

Wythers, Stephen. *See* Withers, S.

X

26064 **Xenophon.** [*Anabasis.*] The historie of Xenophon: containing the ascent of Cyrus. Whereunto is added a comparison of the Roman manner of warres out of Justus Lipsius. *Tr.* J. Bingham. fol. *J. Haviland f. R. Mabb*, 1623. Ent. 22 mr. L.O.C.E². M.+; F.HN.HD. N.Y.+

26065 — [*Cyropaedia.*] Ξενοφῶντος Κύρου παιδείας βιβλία η. Xenophontis de Cyri institutione libri octo. [*Ed.* Sir H. Savile.] *Gr.* 4º. *Etonae, in Collegio Regali* [*M. Bradwood*,] 1613. L.O.C.DUR³. M.+; F.HN.HD.N.Y.+

26066 — [A trans.] The [vi] bookes of Xenophon contayning the discipline, schole, and education of Cyrus. *Tr.* out of Greeke by W. Barkar. 8º. *R. Wolfe*, [1552?] L.G². R.; F.HN.ILL.

26067 — [Anr. issue, w. new prelims. and additions.] The VIII. bookes . . . also his expedition into Babylon, Syria and Aegypt, and his exhortation before his death, to his children. *Tr.* out of Greeke by W. Bercker [*sic*]. 8º. (*R. Wolfe*,) 1567. L.O.C.C². STU.+; HN.HD. ILL.N.Y.

　　At least L, HN retain the orig. dedic. to Pembroke from 26066, not present in HD. Final bifolium F set in duplicate; F1ʳ line 4 begins: 'spende.' or 'spend.'; both at O.

26068 — [Anr. trans.] Cyrupædia. The institution and life of Cyrus. *Tr.* out of Greeke by P. Holland. (Naumachia. Or, a poeticall description of the battaile of Lepanto.

Xenophon—*cont.*

　　By A. Holland.) fol. *J. L*[*egat*] *f. R. Allot* [*a.*] (*H. Holland*,) 1632. Ass'd by widow Allot to Legat a. A. Crooke 1 jy. 1637. L.O.C.E². LIV³.+; F.HN.HD.ILL.Y.+

　　Naumachia, which is a reprint of 13580 w. different prelims., is not found in many copies. Copies w. it (1 each at L, C, F, HD) also have added to Cyrupædia a dedic. by H. Holland to Henry Rich, Earl of Holland, to whom Naumachia is also dedicated. Unused sheets reissued in 1654, w. letterpress tp cancelled and engr. tp altered, as Wing X 17.

26069 — [*Economicus.*] Xenophons treatise of house holde. (*Tr.* out of the greke tonge by G. Heruet.) 8º. (*T. Berthelet*, 1532.) O.O⁶(imp.).RD.; F(imp.).

26070 — No entry.

26071 — [Anr. ed.] 8º. (*T. Berthelet*, 1537.) L.O.C.G². RD.+; F. HN.CU.N.Y.+

26072 — [Anr. ed.] 8º. (*in æd. T. Bertheleti*, 1544.) L.O.DUL. HAT(imp.).RD.+; F.HN.CU.WIS.Y.+

26073 — [Anr. ed.] 8º. (*in the house of T. Berthelet*,) [1550?] L. L¹³.C⁵.M.; F.HN.HD.Y².

　　Tp border McK.&F. 30 dated 1534.

26074 — [Anr. ed.] 8º. [*W. Copland f.*] (*A. Vele*,) 1557. L(2). O(2, 1 imp.).O¹⁰.C².LONGLEAT.; HN. Frank Altschul, Stamford, Conn.

26075 — [Anr. ed.] 8º. (*J. Allde*,) 1573. L.O(2).RD.; HN.

Y

Y., J., *tr. See* 11316.5.

Y., R. The state of a christian. 1636. *See* 26112.7.
— The victory of patience. 1636. *See* 26113.

Yakesley, John, *tr. See* 11316.5.

26076 Yarington, Robert. Two lamentable tragedies. The one, of the murther of maister Beech. The other of a young childe murthered in a wood. 4°. [*R. Read*] f. *M. Lawe*, 1601. L(2).L⁶.O.; HN. Greg 182.

26076.5 Yarmouth. For the selling of herrings in and neere the towne of Yarmouth during the faire. [Brief of a bill in Parliament for freer trade.] s.sh.fol. [*W. Jones*, 1624?] L(Harl.MS.7608/381).

26077 Yarrow, Robert. Soveraigne comforts for a troubled conscience. [*Ed.*] (J. Maunsell.) 8°. [*G. Purslowe*] f. *R. Rounthwaite*, 1619. O.DUL.E².WI. Dr. R. A. Hunter, London.

26078 — [Anr. ed.] 12°. *G. M[iller]* f. *P. Stephens a. C. Meredith*, 1634. L.L⁴.O.C(imp.).; F.HN.HD.LC.PN².+

26078.5 Yate, George, *Engraver*. The miraculous week of our blessed saviours pilgrimage. [Engravings, with verse.] fol. [*London*, c. 1620.] C.
See Hind II.244.

26079 Yates, James. The castell of courtesie, whereunto is adioyned the holde of humilitie: with the chariot of chastitie. Also a dialogue betweene age and youth. 1582. [In verse.] 2 pts. 4°. *J. Wolfe*, (1582.) Ent. 7 jn.; the Dialogue ?ent. to H. Carre 13 ja. 1581. L(imp.).; HN.
Tp to pt. 2, line 5: 'seruingman'.

26080 — [Anr. issue of pt. 2, w. variant title.] The hould of humilitie. *J. Wolfe*, (1582.) L.
Tp line 5: 'Seruingman'.

26081 Yates, John. Gods arraignment of hypocrites: . . . [With] a defence of Mʳ. Calvine against Bellarmine; and of M. Perkins against Arminius. 4°. *C. Legge, pr. to the Univ. of Camb.*, 1615. L.O²⁴.C.D.E⁴.+; F.HN.HD.ILL.U.+
HD has dedicatee's name in 2 states: 'Alofe' or 'Aylofe'.

26082 — [Anr. issue, w. cancel tp, w. imprint:] *C. Legge, pr. to the Univ. of Camb., sold by A. Johnson*, [*London*,] 1616. C.C³.LYU*.; PH².
Orn. above imprint measures 12×36 mm. The tp was pr. in London by F. Kingston, and was prob. set in duplicate w. the following.

26082.5 — [Anr. issue, w. cancel tp, w. imprint:] *C. Legge, pr. to the Univ. of Camb., sould by A. Johnson*, [*London*,] 1616. HD.
Orn. above imprint measures 12×67 mm.

26083 — Ibis ad Cæsarem. Or a submissive appearance before Cæsar; in answer to Mʳ Mountagues Appeale [1803o]. 4°. [*M. Flesher a. Eliot's Court Press?*] f. *R. Mylbourne*, 1626. L.O.C.A.DUR⁵.+; F.HN.HD.N.U.+
The middle section was app. pr. by Eliot's Court Press.

26084 — Imago mundi, et regnum Christi. The foure monarchies, and Christs twofold kingdome. The gentiles converted, [etc.] 4°. *M. Flesher* [*a. T. Cotes*] f. *R. Milbourne*, 1640. Ent. 28 no. 1639. L.L⁴.O.PETYT. PLUME.; F.HN.HD.
Cotes pr. quires B–1st Dd.

26085 — A modell of divinitie, catechistically composed. [*Ed.* T. Goad.] 4°. *J. Dawson* f. *F. Clifton*, 1622. Ent. 10 oc. 1621. L.O.C.G².M⁴.+: F.HD(tp def.).LC.PN². U.+
In the Advt. to the Reader Yates indicates the outline of the treatise came from Alexander Richardson, who is erroneously cited as the author in the SR entry. *See also* 26088.

Yates, John—*cont.*
26086 — Second edition corrected and inlarged. 4° in 8's. *J. Legatt* f. *F. Clifton*, 1623. L.E².NOR².PLUME.STU.; F.PN².

26087 — The saints sufferings, and sinners sorrowes. Or, the evident tokens of salvation and perdition. 12°. *T. Cotes* f. *N. Bourne*, 1631. Ent. 27 ap. L³.L⁴.

26088 — A short and briefe summe of saving knowledge. [A catechism.] 8°. *J. D[awson]* f. *F. Clifton*, 1621. L.C³.
Reprinted in chapter 1 of 26085.

26089 — A treatise of the honor of Gods house: or, the true paterne of the church. With a discovery of the true cause and cure of our present contentions. 4°. *T. C[otes]* f. *W. Cooke*, 1637. Ent. 15 jn. L.O.C.D.E.+; F.HN.HD(lacks tp).NY¹¹.U.+

26090 Yaxlee, Henry. Morbus et antidotus the disease with the antidote. Or a declaration of H. Yaxlee how he was a papist, and is now converted. 4°. *W. Jones* f. *N. Bourne*, 1630. Ent. 24 jn. L.O.C.DUR⁵.YK.+; F. HN.HD.

26091 Year. The cold yeare. 1614. A deepe snow: in which men and cattell have perished. Written dialogue-wise, betweene a London shop-keeper, and a north-country-man. 4°. *W. W[hite]* f. *T. Langley*, 1615. ?Ent. to J. Trundle 12 mr. L(imp.).O(2, 1 w. date cropt).; HN(impr. shaved).HD.
Has a few passages derived from 11403; attrib. to T. Dekker.

26092 — The windie yeare. Shewing many strange accidents. With a particular relation of that which happened at Great Chart in Kent. 4°. *G. Eld* f. *A. Johnson*, 1613. Ent. 12 ja. L(2, 1 lacks tp, 1 has date altered in ink to 1612).O(2).; F.
See also 19792.

— The wonderfull yeare. 1603. *See* 6535.

26093 Yelverton, *Sir* Henry. A treatise conteining divers benefits and priviledges, of charter warren. 4°. [*R. Barker*,] 1617. C.M(deposit).; CU.
— ed. *See* 19853.

Yes. O yes. If any man or woman [etc. c. 1630.] *See* 17234.

26093.5 Ympyn Christoffels, Jan. A notable and very excellente woorke, how to kepe a boke of accōptes. *Tr.* out of the Italian toung into Dutche, and out of Dutche, into French, and now out of Frenche into English. 1547. [*Anon.*] fol. [*R. Grafton*, 1547.] Moscow, Lenin Library (lacks pt. 2).

Yong, John. *See* Young, J.

26094 Yonge, Nicholas. Musica transalpina. Cantus. (Altus.—Tenor.—Bassus.—Quintus.—Sextus.) Madrigales translated [from Italian] of foure, fiue and six partes. 6 ptbks. 4°. *T. East, the assigné of W. Byrd*, 1588. Ent. 6 de. 1596. L⁷(cantus, quintus).O.C³ (lacks bassus).D²(lacks quintus, sextus).G²(tenor).+; F.HN(cantus, altus, quintus).HD(altus, tenor, quintus, sextus).LC(altus, tenor, bassus).PFOR(quintus).+
In all ptbks. line 1 of the Table heading has 'conteyned'. L¹⁸ has a copy of the tenor only, in a binding w. the arms of the dedicatee, Gilbert Talbot, Earl of Shrewsbury.

26094.5 — [Anr. ed.] 6 ptbks. 4°. *T. East, the assigné of W. Byrd*, 1588. L.O.C(with sextus of 26094).E².M³.+; HN (tenor, bassus, sextus).HD(cantus, bassus).ILL(altus, bassus, quintus).LC(cantus, quintus, sextus).N.+
In all ptbks. the title has 'parts.'; line 1 of the Table heading has 'contayned'.

Yonge, Nicholas—*cont.*

26095 — Musica Transalpina. Cantus. (Altus.—Tenor.—Bassus.—Quintus.—Sextus.) The second booke of madrigalles, to 5. & 6. voices: *tr.* out of sundrie Italian authors. 6 ptbks. 4°. *T. Este*, 1597. L.O³.D². E².G².+; F.HN.HD.ILL.PFOR(lacks sextus).+

26096 **Yonger, William.** The nurses bosome. A sermon. Hereunto is added, Judahs penance. 4°. *J. Beale*, 1617. Ent. 14 au. L.L¹³.O.G⁴.M⁴.+; F.HN.ILL.

26096a — [A variant, w. imprint:] *f. E. Causon*, [*Norwich*,] 1617. L.; HD.

26097 —A sermon preached at great Yarmouth, upon the 12. of September. 1599. 8°. *S. Stafford*, 1600. O.C.; F.

26097.5 — [A variant, w. imprint:] *S. Stafford, sold by T. Man*, 1600. O.; BO⁵.

26098 — The unrighteous judge: or, judex Cretensis. A sermon. 4°. *G. Eld f. H. Fetherstone*, 1621. Ent. 20 jy. HN.HD.

26098.3 — [A variant, w. imprint:] *G. Eld f. H. Fetherstone, solde by C. Puntar of Norwich*, 1621. L.O.; HD.

York, *City of.* A speciall grace, appointed to haue been said at Yorke. [1558.] *See* 7599.

26098.5 — Yule in Yorke. [Two carols. c. 1570.] *See* Addenda.
— *Confraternity of St. Mary of Mt. Carmel. See* Indulgences 84.
— *Guild of SS. Christopher and George. See* Indulgences 84A.

York, *Diocese of.* Certaine necessarie articles to be obserued in the diocese of Yorke. [1584.] *See* 8145.5.

26098.7 — Instructions for the curates. First that he examine euery his parishoner [about reconciliation to the Roman Catholic faith.] A declaration to be made in euery church within the diocese of Yorke, by the curate [concerning the terms of Pope Julius III for absolution.] s.sh.fol. [*R. Lant?*] *ap. Robertum Holder*, [1554?] YK.
See also Indulgences 147.

26099 **York,** *House of.* The first part of the contention betwixt the two famous houses of Yorke and Lancaster. 4°. *T. Creede f. T. Millington*, 1594. Ent. 12 mr. O. CANT(Elham deposit).; F. Greg 119.
An abridged and corrupt version of Shakespeare's Henry VI, pt. 2.

26100 — [Anr. ed.] 4°. *V. Simmes f. T. Millington*, 1600. O(2, 1 lacks tp).C²(imp.).; HN(2).

26101 — [Anr. ed., w. additions.] The whole contention betweene the two famous houses, Lancaster and Yorke. Newly corrected and enlarged. Written by W. Shakespeare, Gent. 4°. [*W. Jaggard*] *f. T. P[avier]*, (1619.) Ass'd to Pavier 19 ap. 1602. L.O (imp.).C².BIRM².E.+; F.HN.HD.N.PML.+
This also reprints the True Tragedie (21006 sq.) and Pericles (22334 sqq.).

26102 **York,** *Province of.* A grant of the benevolence or contribution to his majestie, by the clergie of the province of Yorke. 4°. *R. Barker a. assignes of J. Bill*, 1640. C².; HN.
Anr. issue of 4586, largely from standing type, with substitution of names, etc., pertaining to York.
— Orders set downe . . . for the reforming of abuses. [By Abp. S. Harsnett.] 1629. *See* 12884.

26102.5 **Yorke, James.** The union of honour. Containing the armes, matches and issues of the kings, dukes, . . . from the Conquest, untill 1640. fol. *E. Griffin*, 1640. Ent. to Griffin a. W. Leake 31 ja. L⁴³.O.C.LINC.RGU. +; F.BO.CHI.HD.Y.
The above imprint is on the letterpress tp; at least C, F have no engr. tp (lacking?); O has engr. tp without imprint; O¹⁹, O²⁴, RGU, BO, HD have engr. tp w. imprint: *E. Griffin*, 1641.

26103 — [A variant, w. imprint on letterpress tp:] *E. Griffin f. W. Leake*, 1640. L.O.C.BTL.E.+; F.HN.N.NY.PN.+
Most copies have engr. tp w. imprint: *E. Griffin*, 1641; 1 O² and 1 CAL² have engr. tp without imprint; O¹³ and 1 CAL² have no engr. tp.

Yorkshire, *East Riding.* Eastriding in the countie of Yorke. A certificate of the rate of wages. 1593. *See* 8231.

26103.5 **Yorkshire Lovers.** A pleasant new northerne song, called the two York-shire lovers. *Ballad.* 2 pts. s.sh.fol. [*G. Purslowe*] *f. J. W[right*, c. 1630.] C⁶.

26104 — [Anr. ed.] 2 pts. s.sh.fol. [*E. Purslowe*] *f. J. Wright*, [c. 1635.] L.

26105 **Youll, Henry.** Canzonets to three voyces newly composed. 3 ptbks. 4°. *T. Este, the assigne of W. Barley*, 1608. Ent. to East 25 se. 1607. L.O(bassus only). C.; F(cantus only).ILL(altus only).

26106 **Young, Andrew.** Theses . . . philosophiæ . . . præs. A. Junio. 1607. Now = 7487.7.
26107 — — 1613. Now = 7487.10.
26108 — — 1617. Now = 7487.14.
26109 — — 1621. Now = 7487.18.

Young, Bartholomew, *tr. See* 3179, 12423, 18044.

Young, Francis, *tr. See* 1840.

Young, John, *Bp. of Callipolis. See* Indulgences 5, 56, 60A, 70.

26110 **Young, John,** *Bp. of Rochester.* A sermon preached before the queenes maiestie, the second of March. An. 1575. [On Ps. cxxxi. Anon.] 8°. *R. Watkins*, [1576?] L². O(tp only, Douce Add. 142/652).C.
(Formerly also 22239) Quire C is in different B.L. types, w. 29 lines a page, while quires A–B have 27 or 28 lines a page.

26110.3 — [A variant.] By J. Yong. *R. Watkins*, [1576?] O.C¹⁵. B1ʳ line 2: 'briers'.

26110.5 — [Anr. ed.] By J. Yong. 8°. *R. Watkins*, [1576?] L³.O (imp.).P. B1ʳ line 2: 'bryers'.

Young, Patrick, *ed. See* 5398.
— *tr. See* 14346, 18527.

26111 **Young, Richard.** The drunkard's character, or, a true drunkard. Together with Compleat armour against evill society. By R. Junius. 8°. *R. Badger, f. G. Latham*, 1638. Ent. to J. Crump 10 jy. L.L¹⁶.O.C (imp.).E².+; F.HN.CHI.N.Y.+

26112 — [Anr. issue, with added? tp:] Sinne stigmatized: or, the art to know savingly. Whereunto is annexed, Compleat armor. *f. G. Latham*, 1639. C.C³.BIRM² (K.N.).PETYT.; HD.ILL.Y.
Some copies (C, PETYT, HD) retain 'Drunkard's' tp; in others (C³, ILL, Y) it is cancelled.

26112.3 — [Anr. issue, w. a bifolium signed A2,3, containing a recommendation by T. Gataker and others, and a Pref. collating A–C⁸ D⁴.] Sinne stigmatized: [etc.] *f. G. Latham*, 1639. L('Drunkard's' tp cancelled). O³ (Preface only).
Gataker's letter cautions not to buy the book without the additional 3½ sheets.

26112.7 — The state of a christian, lively set forth by an allegorie of a shippe under sayle. [Init. R. Y.] s.sh.fol. *T. Cotes f. the author, sold by Sarah Fairbeard*, 1636. L(2, 1 bd. w. 26113; 1 in Thomason Tracts, 669.f. 10/70, w. date altered in ink to 1646 = Wing Y 5).

26113 — The victory of patience, and benefit of affliction. Extracted out of the choisest authors. [Init. R. Y.] 12°. *R. B[adger,]* sold [by M. Allot,] 1636. Ent. to Badger 23 oc. 1637. L.; F.HART².

26114 — [A variant, w. imprint:] *R. Badger, sold [by M. Allot,]* 1637. O.

Young, Thomas, *Abp.* York. Injunctions. *See* 10374.

26115 **Young, Thomas,** *Vicar of Stowmarket.* Dies Dominica, sive succincta narratio ex S. scripturarum, testimoniis concinnata. [Theophilus, Philokuriaces, *pseud.*] [*Printed abroad,*] 1639.
Not an STC book.

26116 **Young, Thomas,** *Student of Staple Inn.* Englands bane: or, the description of drunkennesse. 4°. *W. Jones, sold by T. Baylee*, 1617. Ent. 10 no. L.O.DUR⁵.; HN. HD.NY.
Spelling in imprint varies: 'Baylee' (L, HN, HD) or 'Bayle' (O).

26117 — [Anr. ed.] 8°. *W. J[ones] f. T. Bayly*, 1634. L.; F(date cropt).

Young Man. A new song of a young mans opinion. [1618?] *See* 22919.5.

26118 — A yong-mans most earnest affection to his sweetheart. *Ballad.* 2 pts. s.sh.fol. [*A. Mathewes*, c. 1630.] L.

Youth. Youth know thyself. 1624. *See* 24347.

26119 **Ypres.** The forme and maner of subuētion or helpyng for pore people, practysed ī Hypres. (*Tr.* from Laten [by W. Marshall.]) 8°. (*T. Godfray*, 1535 (jn.)) L. c(imp.).

Yver, Jacques. *See* 5647.

Z

Z., Q., *of Lion's Inn. See* 24050.

Z., R., *P. R. Oxoniæ. See* Zouch, R.

Zamorano, Rodrigo. *See* 26020.

26119.5 **Zanchius, Hieronymus.** An excellent and learned treatise, of the spirituall mariage betweene Christ and the church, and euery faithfull man. Written in Latine and *tr.* 8°. *J. Legate, pr. to the Univ. of Camb.,* 1592. Ent. 9 au. LK.P.; HD.U.

26120 — H. Zanchius his confession of christian religion. Englished in sense agreeable, to his owne latine copie. 8°. *J. Legat, pr. to the Univ. of Camb.,* 1599. Ent. to S. Waterson 26 jn. 1598. L.O.C.C².P.+; F.HN.HD.SMU. U.+

A trans. of 26121.

26121 — Hieron. Zanchii, de religione christiana, fides: quam nunc demùm, annum agens LXX. in lucem edendam curavit. 8°. *Londini, J. Rimeus,* 1605. C.

Collates A⁸ (w. A1 being a cancel tp) B–Ff⁸. The sheets are from a continental ed., but not the one at L, *Neostadii Palatinorum,* [1586?] which collates a–c⁸ A–S⁸ T⁴ a–l⁸.

For Rime's licence of 26 June 1605 to publish the Latin works of Zanchius *see* Greg, *Companion,* p. 153.

26121.3 — Hieronymi Zanchii theologi clarissimi in D. Pauli apostoli epistolas ad [Eph., Phil., Col., Thess.] et [1 John i–ii.] Comentarii. Editio altera recognita et aucta. 4°. *Londini, J. Rimeus,* 1605. L(tpp only, Harl.5963/361 and Harl.5927/165, date cropt).

Possibly intended as a cancel gen. tp for the ed. *Neustadii Palatinorum,* 1600.

26121.7 — Hieron. Zanchii in Hoseam primum et difficilimum inter eos quos minores vocant prophetam commentarius. 4°. *Londini, J. Rimeus,* 1605. O⁴.

A reissue, w. cancel tp, of the ed. *Neustadii,* 1600.

26121a — Hieronymi Zanchii Miscellaneorum libri tres. 4°. *Londini, J. Rimeus,* 1605, (*Neustadii in Palatinatu, typis N. Schrammij, sumt. haeredum W. Harnisij,* 1603.) DUR(Bamb.).; F.

The gen. tp is a cancel.

26121a.3 — Hieronymi Zanchii theologi celeberrimi Miscellaneorum tomus alter in quo SS. theologiae loci & quæstiones plurimæ, pertractantur. Nunc primùm in lucem editus. 4°. *Neostadii, typis N. Schrammii, sumpt. J. Bill Nortonian. Londinens. bibliopol.,* 1608. O.O².O⁴.O⁵.C.

26121a.7 — Speculum christianum or, a christian survey for the conscience. Containing three tractates of H. Zanchius. Englished. By H. N(elson). 8°. *G. Eld,* 1614. Ent. 17 ja. O.BURY.E².P(lacks tp).; F.HD.

(Formerly 18422)

— *See* also 555, 19665.

26122 **Zarain.** A relation of the late seidge and taking of Babylon by the Turke. *Tr.* out of Turkish, into Italian. And Englished by W. H(olloway.) 4°. *J. Raworth f. N. Butter a. N. Bourne,* 1639. Ent. 30 my. L.O(imp.). O¹¹.C.M.+; F.HN.HD(imp.).ILL.NY.+

Collates A–E⁴. Copies vary: C1ʳ last line has 'our most Potent' or 'our Omni Potent'; both at L. L⁴³, M have A1 blank; Y has A1 with half-title and woodcut on the recto.

26122.5 — [Anr. ed.] 4°. *J. Raworth f. N. Butter a. N. Bourne,* 1639. O.O⁶.; CB.HD(D2 def.).

Collates A–C⁴ D². O has A1 blank; O⁶, HD have A1 w. half-title and woodcut on the recto.

26123 **Zarate, Augustin de.** [A1ʳ:] The discouerie and conquest of the prouinces of Peru. And also of the riche mines of Potosi. [A2ʳ:] (The strange and delectable history of Peru. By A. Sarate. *Tr.* out of

---

Zarate, Augustin de—*cont.*

Spanish by T. Nicholas.) 4°. [*J. Charlewood, W. How, a. J. Kingston f.*] *R. Jhones,* 1581 (6 fb.) Ent. 13 ja. L.O.C(imp.).A.G².+; F.HN.HD.N.NY.+

Charlewood app. pr. quires A, T–X; How ¶, B–N, R–S, Aa; Kingston O–Q, Y–Z.

26124 **Zepheria.** Zepheria. [A sonnet sequence.] 4°. *Widdowe Orwin f. N. L[ing] a. J. Busbie,* 1594. L.O.E².; F (imp.).HN.

26124.5 **Zepper, Wilhelm.** The art or skil, well and fruitfullie to heare the holy sermons of the church. Written first in Latin, and now *tr.* by T. W[ilcox?] 8°. *F. Kingston,* 1599. Ent. 4 de. C⁴.

Zimara, Marco Antonio. *See* 761.

26125 **Zion.** A guide unto Sion. Or certaine positions, concerning a true visible church. [By H. Ainsworth?] 8°. *Amstelredam,* [*Richt Right Press,*] 1638. L.

26126 — [Anr. ed.] 8°. [*Leyden, W. Christiaens*] *f. T. Crafford,* [*Amsterdam?*] 1639. L.L³.O.; HD.

26126.5 — [Anr. ed.] The second edition, corrected & much enlarged. 8°. *Amstelredam,* [*Richt Right Press,*] 1639. O(tp def.).; Y.

26127 — Third edition. 8°. *Amstelredam,* [*Richt Right Press,*] 1640. L.C².C¹⁰.; F.

Zion, *Convent of. See* Indulgences 18.

Zouch, Edward 1a, *Lord Warden of the Cinque Ports.* After my verie heartie commendations, [etc. 1619.] *See* 5323a.2.

26128 **Zouch, Richard.** Descriptio juris et judicii feudalis, secundum consuetudines Mediolani & Normanniæ. [Init. R. Z., *I.C.P.R. Oxoniæ.*] 8°. *Oxoniæ, J. Lichfield,* 1634. O.O³.C.D.E.+; F.HN.HD(missing).WASH³.

Reprinted in 26132.

26129 — Descriptio juris & judicii militaris. . . . Nec non juris & judicii maritimi. [Init. R. Z., *P.R. Oxoniæ.*] 2 pts. 4°. *Oxoniæ, L. Lichfield,* 1640. O.O².O⁸.C.C³.+; COR. CU.HD.PEN.NY.+

26130 — The dove: or passages of cosmography. [In verse.] 8°. [*T. Snodham*] *f. G. Norton,* 1613. Ent. 15 no. L.O. CHATS.M.; F.HN.PML.

26131 — = 26131a.

26131a — Elementa jurisprudentiæ, definitionibus, regulis, et sententijs selectioribus juris civilis illustrata. [Init. R. Z., *P.R. Oxon.*] 8°. *Oxoniæ, J. Lichfield,* 1629. L.O.C.D.NEP.+; HN.HD(2).ILL.PH.

26132 — [Anr. ed., w. additions.] Quibus accessit descriptio juris & judicii temporalis secundum consuetudines feudales. Nec non descriptio juris & judicii ecclesiastici. 4°. *Oxoniæ, L. Lichfield,* 1636. L.O.C.D.E⁸.+; F.HN.CU.HD.N.+

The dedic. is signed Ric. Zouchæus.

26133 — The sophister. A comedy. [Anon.] 4°. *J. O[kes] f. H. Mosley,* 1639. Ent. 7 no. 1638. L.O.C⁴.E.M⁴.+; F. HN.CU.HD.N.+ Greg 556.

— ed. *See* 19005.

26134 **Zutphen.** A particuler, of the yeelding vppe of Zutphen, and the beleagering of Deuenter. With the honourable enterprise of sir R. Williams, at Cinque Saunce. 4°. *J. Charlwood, solde by W. Wright,* 1591. Ent. 2 jn. L.O.LINC.

26134.5 — [Anr. issue, w. quire A reprinted, w. title:] The politique takinge of Zutphen Skonce. 4°. *J. Charlwood, solde by W. Wright,* 1591. YK.; F.

Zwinger, Jacob. *See* 21805.9.

Zwinger, Theodor. *See* 19156.

Zwingli, Ulrich. The accompt . . . of the faith. 1555. *See* 26140.

Zwingli, Ulrich—*cont.*

26135 — A briefe rehersal of the death resurrectiō, & ascension of Christ, written first in Latin, and now *tr.* 8°. (*J. Daye*,) [1561?] C.C[4].C[5].ETON.; F.

26136 — Certeyne preceptes, . . . declaring howe the ingenious youth ought to be instructed and brought vnto Christ. *Tr.* oute of latin by R. Argentyne. 8°. *Ippeswich, A. Scoloker,* 1548. L.O(2).C.M.; F.

26137 — The ymage of bothe pastoures. = 26143.

26138 — The rekening and declaraciō of the faith of H. Zwingly. *Tr.* [G. Joye.] 8°. *Zijryk* [really *Antwerp, widow of C. Ruremond,*] 1543 (mr.) L.L[43].O.O[14].C.+; F.HD (imp.).U.Y.

26138.5 — [Anr. ed.] The rekenynge and declaracion of the fayth of H. zwyngly. 8°. *ziiryk* [really *London,*] (*by me Rycharde wyer,*) 1543 (mr.) [1548?] D.

26139 — [A variant, w. date on tp altered in press.] *ziiryk* [really *London,*] (*by me Rycharde wyer,*) 1548 (mr.) L.L[15].O.; HD.

Zwingli, Ulrich—*cont.*

26140 — [Anr. trans.] The accompt rekenynge and confession of the faith of H. Zwinglius. *Tr.* out of latyn by T. Cotsforde. 8°. *Geneva* [really *Emden, E. van der Erve,*] 1555 (ap.) L.O.C.D.P.+; F(2).HN.
  With 2 epistles by Cottesford at the end, which are both reprinted in 5841.5, and the 2nd epistle also in 14631.

26141 — A short pathwaye to the ryghte and true vnderstanding of the holye scriptures: *tr.* out of Laten, by J. Veron. 8°. (*worceter, J. Oswen,* 1550 (24 my.)) L(lacks tp). L[2].O.C.M.+; F.HN. Mellon.

26142 — The ymage of bothe pastoures, *tr.* out of Latin by J. Veron. (Of the metynge of J. Hooper & doctoure [H.] Cole.) 8°. (*T. Raynald,*) 1550. C.

26143 — [A variant, w. colophon:] [*T. Raynald f.*] (*W. Seris & R. Kele,*) 1550. O.O[17].; F.U.
  (Formerly also 26137)

  — *See* also 19137.5.

ADDENDA AND CORRIGENDA

Where possible, the addenda and corrigenda have been indicated in the main text by 𝔄 following the locations in an entry or by a numbered reference. None of the new headings and cross-references cited below by page and column has been indicated in the main text.

The following, however, have no indicator in the main text ('new' signifies new entries to be added):

14068.5	18617.6 (new)	22697
14425.3	19546	22868.5
16633.3 (new)	19855	23439.5
16353	19861.3	23059.3
16739.5	20397	23845
16743.4	20612.5	23918
16743.9	21134.5	23918.3 (new)
16790	21215	24667
17576	21500	25899

14068.5   *Add after date*: Ent. to A. Jeffes 30 jy. *Freeman copy now* = F.

14104   *Add note*: This is by Humfrey Braham. Copies vary: with (P) or without (L, O) his name at end of dedic.

     Add new entry:
14109.2   — [Enterlude of detraction, light judgement, verity, and justice.] 4°. [*London*, c. 1550.] HN(frags., consisting of most of E1 and E3).
     Unique in having a fairly consistent rhyme scheme of abbacc.

14117   *Add note*: One C copy has cancel slips on tp and in colophon, w. imprint: *W. Middiltoñ* and colophon dated 1 May 1546.

     Add new entry:
14323.3   — [Anr. ed.] Thystorye of Jacob and his twelue sones. 4° 6·8. (*W. de Worde*,) [1510?] C.

14371   *Continue note*: P may have the orig. tp as endpapers in D.5.15, w. misprint: '*indepencie*'.

14425.3   *In SR entry delete*: or 6.

     Add new entry:
14467.7   — [Anr. ed. of 14466.] Janua linguarum, sive modus maxime accommodatus. [Editio tertia?] *Lat. a. Eng.* 4°. [*H. Lownes f. M. Lownes*, 1619?] C(tp def.).
     Unique in having the Prooemium begin on ¶1ʳ.

14628   *Continue note*: The title identifies the translator as 'Philip [Howard] late Earl of Arundell'.

14634   *Add note*: At least 1 C copy has paper w. horizontal chainlines.

14651   *Add note*: At least P has the misprint: 'Mylborne' instead of 'Mylbourne' in the imprint.

14691   *Continue note*: One O copy is an intermediate state, w. tp correctly dated 1612 but w. only the author's inits. on A3ʳ and A4ᵛ.

p. 40²   *Add new heading*:
Kirkby, John. *See* Bookplates.

p. 46²   *Add new heading*:
Lake, Anne. *See* Bookplates.

15192   *Continue note*: Some copies (O, 2 P) have a slip pasted on the cut on the tp verso or inserted after the tp w. 8 lines of verse beginning: 'In effigiem . . .' Quaritch catalogue 829 (1962), back cover, describes a copy w. tp verso blank and other indications of early issue.

15203   *Add note*: There are 2 eds.; B2ᵛ line 2 has: 'beganne' (2 C) or 'began' (L, O, HD).

15217   *Add note*: The colophon date is correct. C has the tp date corrected in MS. to 'M.D.XLIX.'

15259   *Add note*: The dedic. is reprinted and tr. in 555.

15309   *Add note*: The heading on A1ʳ varies: '. . . *Observations upon a speech . . .*' (F, HD) or corrected to 'OB/SERVA-TIONS *Upon the Arch-Bishops Epistle Dedicatory* | . . .' (O).

     Add new entry:
15326.7   — [Anr. ed.] 4°. *R. Badger*, 1637. C.C².
     Tp line 5: 'MAIESTIE'. This ed. is the same setting as 15327, the latter having a variant tp w. 'Second edition' and different imprint. The present item is a different setting throughout from 15326 sq., which have 'MAIESTY' in line 5 of the tp.

15334   *Continue note*: C has the date unaltered and variant tp w. commas after 'Sermon' and 'Funerall'.

p. 54¹   *Add new heading*:
Lee, Robert. *See* Bookplates.

p. 55¹   *Add new heading*:
Leigh, Edmund. *See* Bookplates.

15485   *Add note*: The engr. tp exists in different states, including a variation in the portion transcribed: 'discription' (P, HD) or 'description' (2 O, C).

p. 62¹   *Add new heading*:
Lightfoot, Edward. *See* Bookplates.

     Add new entry:
15622.8   — [Anr. ed.] 8°. *assignes of F. Flowar*, 1593. L¹³(frags. of 8 leaves, in bdg. of P.2.36).

p. 67¹   *Add new heading*:
Little, Clement. *See* Bookplates.

p. 67¹   *Add new heading*:
Littleton, *Sir* Edward. *See* Bookplates.

15826   *Add note*: The Psalter collates a–q⁸, 40 lines to a column. C has substituted the Psalter from a different ed., collating a–q⁸, 38 lines to a column, like 15810, 15811.5, and 15815. It is a different setting from those three and is unique in having g8ᵛ, col. 1, last line beginning: 'Adesto . . .'

15836   *Add note*: Only the P.H. tp is dated 1554; both colophons and the P.E. tp are dated 1555.

16002a   *Add note*: The Inglis copy was sold at Sotheby's, 11 June 1900, lot 601, bought by Ellis, untraced. The tp was lacking and prob. supplied from a facs. of 16001 sq. The text sheets prob. belonged to 15971.

16259.7   *Continue note*: C has an imp. 20-line ed. (Rit.e.451.2) similar to HD, but C has lower-case signatures so that the 1st Canticle is on s7. It was also prob. pr. by de Worde and is possibly later than HD.

p. 90   *Extend Series 16/7 to include*: 1596   16321a.5 (Addenda)

     Extend Series 24/3 to include: 1608   16333.3 (Addenda)

16291   *Continue note*: The C copy mentioned above also has, inserted after πA11, quires ππA² πB⁸ as in 16292a (copy 4), w. Almanack beginning 1561 on πB1ᵛ.

     Add new entry:
16321a.5   — [Anr. ed.] 16° in 8's. (*Deputies of C. Barker*, 1596.) O³(imp.).
     1 col., B.L., ending Ss8; series 16/7. The Catechism begins Y8ʳ and has as line 3 of the heading: 'of euerie childe, before hee'; in the C² copy of 16315, the only other extant copy of this series yet known, Y8ʳ line 3 of heading is: 'euery childe, before hee he [*sic*, for 'be']'.

     Add new entry:
16333.3   — [Anr. ed.] 24° in 12's. *R. Barker*, 1608. T. C Nicholas, Trinity College, Cambridge.
     1 col., rom., ending P12; series 24/3.

16353   *Continue note*: The psalter sub tp varies: imprint names *R. Barker and J. Bill* or *R. Barker* alone; both at HN.

16524   *Add note*: Tp varies: with (HN) or without (C) 'and commended . . . &c.' in the title.

p. 109²   *Add new heading*:
Lodington, William. *See* Bookplates.

16699   *Add note*: This is an anon. report of Loncq's expedition. It also includes a letter by D. van Waerdenburgh, of which a different trans. is pr. in 25219.

16739.5   *Add after 'Ent.'*: to J. Wolfe 14 jy. 1593; to Windet

16743.4   *Add after 'Ent.'*: to J. Wolfe 14 jy. 1593;

16743.9   *Add after 'Ent.'*: to J. Wolfe 14 jy. 1593; to Windet

16753   *Add following title*: [Ed. H. Holland.]

    Add new entry:
16763.3   — [Anr. ed.] The othe of euerie free man, of the cittie of London. s.sh.4°. [*J. Windet? f.*] *J. Wolfe*, [c. 1595.] HN.

p. 115²   *Add new heading*:
London, *Doctors' Commons*. *See* Bookplates.

16790   *Continue note*: While both sections of 16790 have Pynson's colophon and leaf sigs. w. arabic numerals, the prelims. (A⁴) have leaf sigs. w. roman numerals and tp border McK. & F. 19 and may have been pr. by [*R. Redman?* 1532?]

    Add new entry:
16857.9   — Index postillanum [*sic*]. A briefe and plaine direction for the use of postils. 12°. *f. J. Boler*, 1632. Ent. to A. Hebb 14 no. 1631. C⁵.

p. 129¹   **M., A.** *Add cross-reference*:
— Chruso-thriambos. 1611. *See* 18267.

17154   *Continue note*: Ordered burned 1 June 1599; *see* Arber III.677–8.

p. 130²   *Add new heading*:
M., Thomas. *See* Bookplates.

p. 132²   *Add new heading*:
Malet, John. *See* Bookplates.

p. 134¹   *Add new heading*:
Manfield, Thomas. *See* Bookplates.

    Add new entry:
17311.5   **Marckant, John.** [A notable instruction for all men to beware the abuses] of dice, wyne and women. [In verse.] s.sh.fol. *W. Griffith*, 1571. Ent. 1565–66. O⁸(title torn).
      Beginning of title supplied from Griffith's 1st entry in SR; *see* Arber I.293, 296.

17445.5   *Add note*: The cancel tp is in 2 settings; in imprint: 'soulde' (P) or 'solde' (C).

17492   *Add note*: Tp varies: with 'epigrammatωn' as transcribed (O, HD) or 'epigrammaton' (C).

17576   *Add after date*: 'The seconde Edicon' ent. to H. Bynneman 3 no. 1580.

17627   *Add note*: This has the same types as 24514 and is prob. earlier than 17628.

17653a   *Insert before last sentence of note*: Some copies omit the beginning of the errata on ✱✱3ᵛ; both at C.

17687   *Substitute for 1st sentence of note*: The title as transcribed is a cancel. HN now has 2 copies w. the cancel, 1 of which also has the orig. tp omitting 'Together with the Agony of Christ', i.e. not calling for the reissue of 17691 as pt. 2.

17764   *Add note*: The end of the Mecare news is dated 26 Jan. 1597, and the compiler's name is given as James Drucateen.

17770.7   *Add note*: Prob. pr. on 1 sheet together w. 10626.5.

17810   *Add note*: This is more prob. pr. in the Netherlands, in which case it does not belong in STC. The Palinodia is tr. from 149.

17823   *Continue note*: In both HD copies of this and most copies of 17823.5 G3 is cancelled. It is present in the C copy of 17823.5 and contains T. Norton's 'reporte unto the Reader' w. an MS. note: 'An approbation . . . unapproved'.

    Add new entry:
17857.7   **Michell,** *Sir* **John.** [Heading 1ᵛ:] Sir Anthonie Strelley. had issue [etc. In support of claims by Michell to the manors of Bilborough and Strelley.] 4° in 2. [*A. Mathewes*, c. 1629?] L¹¹(S.P. 14/203:29). Docketed: 'Sʳ John Michells case to bee communicated with My lord Keeper.' On 28 Jan. 1629 Michell petitioned the House of Commons, expressing a grievance against Bp. J. Williams, Lord Keeper from July 1621 to Oct. 1625; *see* JHC I.923. Though the present item may derive from that earlier period, it more likely accompanied or followed Michell's approach to Parliament.

p. 154²   *Add new heading*:
Middleton, *Sir* **Thomas.** *See* Bookplates.

p. 155²   *Add new heading*:
Miller, James. *See* Bookplates.

p. 157²   *Add new heading*:
Mitton, Thomas. *See* Bookplates.

18044   *Add note*: This also includes the Second part tr. from Alonso Perez and Enamoured Diana tr. from G. Gil Polo. *See also* 153.3.

18180   *Continue note*: C has another state of this halfsheet, signed Ss.

p. 165²   *Add new heading*:
Moseley, *Sir* **Edward.** *See* Bookplates.

    Add new entry:
18214a.5   — [Anr. ed.] 8° in 4's. [*R. Wyer*, bef. 1536.] L(imp.). 121 chapters in the Table. On d4ᵛ 'by egall porcyon.' is the 2nd line while in 18214a.3 it is the 1st line.

18225.6   *Continue note*: a⁴ is in 2 settings; tp line 2 has: 'Helthe,' (WIS) or 'helth.' (G²), the latter prob. pr. [1549?] In 18225.8 tp line 2 has: 'Helthe:'.

18249   *Add after date*: Ent. to T. Stirrop 6 no. 1599. *Continue note*: The St. Paul's School copy, which lacks A1,2, is a different ed. from O and was pr. by [F. Kingston]. It has a 3-line ornamental init. on A6ʳ while O has a 2-line type init. Both eds. have the dedic. dated 17 Nov. 1599, and the St. Paul's School copy may represent an ed. of that year.

18267   *Add after title*: [Init. A. M.]

18421   *Continue note*: This is a trans. of 7006.

p. 176²   *Add new heading*:
Nevill, Charles. *See* Bookplates.

18597   *Correct format*: 4° w. perp. chainlines.

18617.5   *Amend beginning of note*: D3ʳ last line ends: 'diuers waies indaun-/';

    Add new entry:
18617.6   — [Anr. ed.] 12°. *R. Robinson*, 1595. LAMPORT. D3ʳ last line ends: 'to thy diuine care and/'.

18641.2   *Add note*: See Hind I.229–30.

18658   *Continue note*: Pt. 2 is in 2 settings, ending p. '207' [i.e. 307] (OS, HD, U) or p. 247 (O, F).

18724   *Add note*: There are 2 eds.; A5ʳ is signed: 'NOVVELLUS' (O⁴, O¹⁷, I C) or 'NOWELLUS' (I C).

p. 193¹   *Add new heading*:
Nowell, Robert. *See* Bookplates.

18816   *Add note*: The author is actually Eusebius Pagit; Maunsell (17669), pt. 1, C4ʳ, lists a 1591 ed. of 'Paget his Catechisme' and a 1582 ed. of the enlarged version, 18830.2A sqq., as Openshaw's 'setting downe the testimonies . . . quoted in Pagets Catechisme.' 19101 is a trans. of the orig. Pagit text.

18845a   *Substitute this note*: Although the text of the dedic. is the same setting in all copies, the dedicatees vary: Earl of Craven (L), Sir T. Middleton, kt. and bt. (F), Sir H. Berkeley, kt. and bt. (AAS), S. Marow (HD).

18920   *Add note*: This adds reprints of 11332.5 and 23619.5 (Addenda).

18990   *Add note*: Imprint varies: 'sumptibus' (O¹⁴, C, F) or 'sumtibus' (O).

18991   *Add note*: Imprint varies: 'sumptibus' or 'sumtibus'; both at C.

19016.3   *Add location*: Daniel H. Woodward, Pasadena, Calif. (left half). *Add note*: See *The Book Collector*, XVI (1967), pp. 81–2.

19048   *Add note*: C2ʳ line 3 has 'quærat' (all Oxford copies, P, HN, HD). C has a frag. of leaves C2,3 only, in a different setting w. 'quẹrat'.

p. 207¹   P., E. *Add cross-reference*: — *ed. See* 240.

19078.6   *Correct title, etc.*: . . . to a friend of his at Rome: [on] the late treaty betweene the queene mother . . . Nauarre. *Tr. out of French.* 8⁰ in 4's. *Add note*: Tp has Aggas's device, McK. 199.

19096a   *Add note*: The cancel tp has a press variant in the portion transcribed: 'Command' (HD) or 'Commande' (C).

19101   *Add note*: The orig. English, erroneously attrib. to R. Openshaw, is listed at 18816.

19110.5   *Add new entry*:
— — [A publisher's prospectus for 19110, w. heading:] A description of the multitude of Christians in the world. s.sh.fol. *W. J[ones,] sold by T. Alchorne*, 1635. HD(in bdg. of 19111).
     Imposed in 1 long and 4 short columns and prob. intended to accompany a map like 19111.5.

p. 210¹   *Add new heading*:
Paine, Hugh. *See* Bookplates.

p. 210²   *Add new heading*:
Palladius Rutilius Taurus Aemilianus. *See* 25007 (Addenda).

p. 211¹   *Add new heading*:
Palmer, Thomas, *Book owner. See* Bookplates.

19209a   *Add note*: F is a further variant, w. the colophon leaf (Yyyyy8) blank.

19223   *Add note*: Also entered as Wing B 4811.

19226   *Add note*: Also erroneously entered as Wing D 1143.

p. 215²   *Add new heading*:
Parkhurst, *Sir* Robert. *See* Bookplates.

19409   *Continue note*: One P copy has errata for the preface on (q)2ᵛ.

19433.2   *Add new entry*:
— The widowes treasure, plentifully furnished with secretes in phisicke: & chirurgery. Hereunto adioyned, sundrie prety practises of cookerie. [Anon.] 8⁰. *[J. Kingston] f. H. Disle*, 1582. Devon Record Office, Exeter(2309B/Z 8/1).
     It was Disle's copy that Rider entered; *see* 19433.3.

p. 222¹   *Add new heading*:
Paynton, Dorothy. *See* Bookplates.

19546   *Add note*: For a record that Jones paid the fee for this but the transaction was not entered in SR *see* Arber II.36.

19596   *Add note*: This is tr. from St. Francis of Assisi.

p. 225¹   *Add new heading*:
Penketh, Thomas, *ed. See* 581.

19596.5   *Add note*: For an earlier ed. *see* 3059.6.

p. 226¹   *Add new heading*:
Percivall, Geoffrey. *See* Bookplates.

p. 226¹   *Add new heading*:
Perez, Alonso. *See* 18044 (Addenda).

19689.5   *Add new entry*:
— [Anr. ed.] 12⁰. *J. Legate, pr. to the Univ. of Camb.*, 1600. NLW.

19736   *Add note*: There are 2 eds.; A1ʳ line 2 of text ends: 'descrip-' (P, HN) or 'discrip-' (2 C).

19742   *Add note*: There are 2 eds.; in title: 'man, . . . manner' (HN) or 'man: . . . maner' (C).

19743.3   *Add new entry*:
— [Anr. ed. of 19742.5.] 12⁰. *J. Legate, pr. to the Univ. of Camb.*, 1600. NLW.

19760   *Add note*: 19760–19761.1 are called 'second edition'; 19761.3 sqq. have no ed. number except for 19761.5.

p. 230²   *Add new heading*:
Perne, Andrew. *See* Bookplates.

p. 230²   *Add new heading*:
Perot, William. *See* Bookplates.

19776   *Continue note*: This is a trans. deriving ultimately from the MS. relation in Spanish by M. Garayzabal, in religion Prosper a Spiritu Sancto.

p. 233¹   *Add new heading*:
Phesaunt, Peter. *See* Bookplates.

19830   *Continue note*: ¶ outer forme is in 2 settings; ¶4ᵛ line 21: 'Arch' or 'Arche'; both at P.

19838.5   *Continue note*: The dedic. mentioned is init. 'M. V.' and altered in ink to 'M. W.' in both the copies cited. O¹⁰ also has the dedic.

19855   *Add after date*: Ent. to J. Parnell 25 fb.

19861.3   *Phillipps copy now* = L.

19930   *Add note*: The report is not by Pilkington, but it includes an account of his sermon of 8 June.

p. 239¹   *Add new heading*:
Plat, John. *See* Bookplates.

20083.3   *Add location*: F. *Substitute for beginning of note*: '279' [i.e. 261] pp. On re-examination this ed. appears to be later: [*London, R. Young, after* 1635.] O has another ed. w. '350' [i.e. 250] pp., which may be English printed, prob. after 1640.

p. 244¹   *Add new heading*:
Popham, John. *See* Bookplates.

20135.7   *Add note*: The HN tp is conjugate; the L tp may be a cancel.

20141   *Continue note*: Although much of the type of this and the next two appears in only 1 setting and at most 2, there appear to be 3 distinct issues. In the present issue C4ᵛ line 12 ends: '& abrode.'; D3ʳ line 5 has: 'Consequence' (L, 1 C, 1 E, and prob. all the copies listed at this number).

20141.3   *Add note*: C4ᵛ line 12 ends: 'and abrode.'; D3ʳ line 5 has: 'Consequence' (1 O, 2 C, HD, and some of the other copies listed at this number).

20141.5   *Add new entry*:
— [Anr. issue.] *F. Kyngston f. E. Weaver*, 1603. O.E.P. C4ᵛ line 12 ends: 'and abrode.'; D3ʳ line 5 has: 'consequence' (1 O, 1 E, P, and some of the other copies listed at 20141.3).

20163   *Continue note*: At least L, O, F copies also have extra leaves w. dedics. to Sir James Ley, Sir Henry Hobart, and Sir Thomas Coventry, which are not reprinted in the following eds.

20221.5   *Continue note*: Tp varies; init. 'J. P.' (L) or 'John Preston' (HN).

20397   *Add after date*: Ent. 20 ja. 1579.

20399   *Continue note*: There are 2 eds.; 1st line of title: 'The Descripcion of the' (NLM, [1550?]) or 'The Descripci-' (L, L², C, [c. 1553]).

20458   *Continue note*: ¶2 is a cancel in some copies; orig. ¶2ʳ line 1 of text ends: 'the'; the cancel has: 'pro-'; both at C.

20474   *Add note*: One C copy has 2 leaves of errata inserted after Yy3.

20506   *Add note*: The tp and at least 4 other leaves are in 2 settings. In title: 'Second edition, much enlarged.' or 'Second edition, of the first part (of fower intended). Much enlarged.'; both at F.

20565   *Add after title*: Lat., Eng., Fr., a. Ital.

p. 262²   *Add new heading*:
Radcliffe, Samuel. *See* Bookplates.

20612.5   *Continue note*: The Oratio in laudem artis poeticae is a different version of the text of 6787.4.

p. 263²   *Add new heading*:
Raith, James. *See* Bookplates.

20757   *Add note*: Copies vary: with (L, LC) or without (O) inits. 'T. R.' on A3ᵛ.

p. 268² | *Add new headings:*
Reade, John, *of Brasenose. See* Bookplates.
Reade, John, *of St. John's, Oxford. See* Bookplates.

20825 | *Add note:* This is tr. from A. de Soto; for anr. trans. *see* 22937.

p. 271² | *Add new heading:*
Remey, James. *See* Bookplates.

20917.5 | *Add note: See* Hind I.254–5.

21053.7 | *Add note:* The order is issued by Ridley as Vicar General to the Abp. of Canterbury.

p. 278² | *Add new heading:*
Ritch, Peter. *See* Bookplates.

21079 | *Add note:* Tp varies in the portion transcribed: '*Christian the fourth, famous*' (HD) or '*Christian, the fourth famous*' (C).

p. 280¹ | *Add new heading:*
Robinson, Bernard. *See* Bookplates.

p. 280¹ | *Add new heading:*
Robinson, Henry. *See* Bookplates.

21134.5 | *Add note:* Tp varies: as transcribed (HD) or omitting the 1st line: 'A . . . gift.' (L).

p. 281² | *Add new heading:*
Rodeknight, John. *See* Bookplates.

21215 | *Add note: See also* 5694.

21256 | *Add note:* For further details of this and the following eds. *see The Bibliotheck,* V (1967), pp. 67–72.

Add new entry:
21286.2 | — [Gesta Romanorum.] *Eng.* 4° in 8's and 6's. (*w. de worde,*) [1502?] BTU(lacks tp).
G1ʳ line 2: 'emperour named Andromyke'. The 16th story begins D4ᵛ 25 lines from the bottom: 'Somtyme there dwelled . . . Pompey'. This ed. has no woodcuts.

Add new entry:
21299.3 | — [Anr. ed.] The history of the seuen wise maisters of Rome, now newly corrected with a pleasant stile, & purged from all old and rude wordes and phrases. [*Ed.*] (T. Greene.) 8°. T. Purfoote, 1576. L.
Collates A–Q⁸ R⁴; B1ᵛ last line is: 'or not.' Purfoot's SR entry for 1565–66 should be transferred from 21299.5 to the present entry.

21324 | *Continue note:* Pt. 1 reprints 21325.

21360 | *Add note:* C, HN lack *–**⁴, w. the 1st tp, Almanack, and Kalendar of saints' days, and may be a separate issue or at least a purchaser's option rather than imperfect.

21386 | *Add note:* This is largely composed of selections from 21385.5 and 21395.

p. 291² | *Add new heading:*
Rumsey, Walter. *See* Bookplates.

21500 | *Add after date:* Ent. 16 my.

21555.10 | *Add note:* O⁶, which is imp., has the imprint corrected to: 'Walde-graue'.

21714 | *Add note:* The tp is a cancel in O, C, P, HD (all?) copies.

21746 | *Continue note:* There are 2 eds.; A3ʳ line 1 of text ends: 'e-' (O³, O⁵, O⁶, P) or 'E-' (O, O⁶, O⁷, O⁸, C, HD).

Add new entry:
21806.5 | **Scarbrough, Gervase.** The summe of all godly and profitable catechismes, reduced into one. 12°. G. Eld, 1623. Ent. to Eld a. M. Flesher 30 my. L.

21844 | *Add note:* Tp varies; the author's and editor's names are spelt 'Slater' (HD) or corrected to 'Sclater' (C, F).

21869 | *Add note:* This Scot may also be the author of 22064 sqq.

Add new entry:
21949.7 | — [Heading 1ʳ:] Ane act and proclamatioun for cunzie. [Reforming the coinage of Scotland. 13 Jan. 1591 (o.s.)] 8° in 4. (*Edinburgh, R. Walde-graue,*) [1592.] E. Cr.726(MS. only).
Printed, like STC 1562, in 81 mm. Lettersnijder, which Waldegrave had previously used in Marprelate tracts, e.g. 17453.

22058 | *Continue note:* The 'deliberations' setting varies: with or without 'VII.' in the margin of B3ᵛ. Quire A also has press variants; tp line 11 is misdated '1628' or corrected to '1638'; A4ʳ line 19 ends: 'Law-' and is with or without 'III' in the margin or ends: 'law-'; copies of all varieties at M.

22060 | *Add note:* At least quire D is in 2 settings; D1ʳ catchword: 'Com-' (HN) or 'Commissi-' (HD).

22064 | *Continue note:* This Scott may also be the author of 21869 sqq. He is the son of the author of 22108.

22074 | *Continue note:* This is by the elder Scott, the author of 22108.

22076 | *Add note:* Reprinted in 10009.

22083 | *Add note:* This is not by Scott; it is a trans. from the Dutch 'Den Compaignon van den verresienden Waerschouwer' pr. by Meuris.

22108 | *Add note:* This Scott, who is also the author of 22074, actually preached only once at the Rolls Chapel. He was rector of Northwold and of Oxburgh in Norfolk and the father of the author of 22064 sqq.

p. 319¹ | *Add new heading:*
Scott, William, *of Queen's College, Oxford. See* Bookplates.

p. 320² | *Add new heading:*
Segar, Thomas. *See* Bookplates.

22241.5 | *Continue note:* The prelims. (a–b⁴) are in the same setting in this and 22242. The gen. tp varies: with (O, F) or without (C) 'With an addition of the murther . . .', which refers to Bk. 10; that portion is present in all 3 copies.

Add new entry:
22250.5 | — [Anr. ed., w. the same contents as 22250.6.] Petri Carteri Cantabrigiensis in J. Setoni Dialecticam annatationes [*sic*]. 8°. *in æd. T. Marshi,* 1563. Ent. 1562–63. L(tp only, Ames I.225).PLUME.

p. 329¹ | *Add new heading:*
Shepheard, Richard. *See* Bookplates.

p. 329² | *Add new heading:*
Sherard, Roland. *See* Bookplates.

p. 335¹ | *Add new heading:*
Singleton, Thomas. *See* Bookplates.

22660 | *Continue note:* Also issued as pt. 3 of 22685.5 (Addenda).

Add new entry:
22685.5 | — [Anr. ed.] 3 pts. R. Field f. T. Man, 1591. L(pt. 1 only, completed by 22686).; HD(imp.).
Collates A⁴ B–F⁸ G⁴ (Preparative); A–F⁸ G⁴ (Lords supper, also issued sep. as 22705); A–C⁸ D⁴ (Usury, also issued sep. as 22660).

22697 | *Delete:* First serm. . . . 1588.

22705 | *Continue note:* Also issued as pt. 2 of 22685.5 (Addenda).

22783.7 | *Add after title:* 3 pts. *Add location:* L. *Continue note:* C⁴ collates: A⁴ (b)⁸ B⁸ (Pride); A–E⁸ F⁴ (Fall and Restitution, w. sub tp on C6ʳ); A–C⁸ (Wedding garment); w. all tpp dated 1592. In the L copy the Wedding garment is a reissue of 22714.

22868.5 | *Continue note:* Reprinted in 1048.

22891 | *Correct end of title to: Tr.* (N. G.).

22906 | *Continue note:* Tp imprint varies: 'Bish.' (L, C²) or 'Bishop.' (P).

22949.5 | *Continue note:* Although written by the end of 1591, the text as pr. is dated 14 Dec. 1595 at the end. It was not pr. until shortly before 17 Dec. 1600; *see Cal. S.P.D., 1598–1600,* p. 499.

Add new entry:
22951.5 | — [Anr. ed.] 8°. [*J. Roberts f. G. Cawood,* 1596?] USHAW(lacks tp).
Collates A–L⁸; it is the only ed. to have a woodcut orn. w. 'IHS' on A8ʳ.

22956 | *Add note:* Pr. later than 22957.

23031 | *Add note:* C has an early state of some sheets, including blank tp verso; P, HD have errata on tp verso.

23039.2A — Add new entry:
— [Anr. issue.] [*J. Beale*, 1613?] L(L.9.c.3, Fry 6).O¹⁶ (Fry 6).; HN(Fry 6 and Fry 22). Fry 6, 22. Ib, <IIIf.>

23180.3 — Add new entry:
— [Anr. ed.] Uocabula magistri stābrigi pri/mū iam edita sua saltem editiōe. 4° ⁶·⁴. (*by Wynkyn de worde*,) [1515?] HN(69538).
The title is in a riband without a border, over Hodnett 920; at the end is the device McK. 19. Quires B–C are the same setting as 23180.5.

23225 — Add note: The extra leaf among the prelims.: 'Ad Lectorem.' is in 2 settings; line 5 of verse has: '*Causa*' (P) or '*causa*' (HN, HD).

p. 367¹ — Add new heading:
Stone, Richard. *See* Bookplates.

23310 — Continue note: The tp, a separate leaf, was set in duplicate; 1st line of imprint ends: 'H.' or 'Bellamie,'; both at C.

p. 370¹ — Add new heading:
Stuart, Frances, *Duchess of Lennox and Richmond. See* Bookplates.

23428 — Add note: For other items called 'Stans puer ad mensam' but w. texts in English *see* 17030 and 20953.

23439.5 — Add after date: Ent. to J. Kingston 3 se. 1579.

23619.5 — Add new entry:
— Funerall elegie upon the untimely death of the honourable knight sir T. Overberie. [In verse.] s.sh.fol. *f. H. Gosson*, 1615. LAMPORT.
Reprinted in 18920.

23659.3 — Add before '6 de. 1588.': 5 de. 1582 and

23845 — Continue note: Tp in 2 settings; line 2 has: 'PRACTISE' (O) or 'PRACTICE' (C).

p. 390¹ — Add new heading:
Temple, Alexander. *See* Bookplates.

23873 — Add note: This and the next are usually bd. w. 19962.

23918 — After title correct to: 4 ptbks. Add note: The ptbks. have dedic. to Lady Penelope Rich on the recto of the 2nd leaf and 2 commendatory poems on the verso.

23918.3 — Add new entry:
— [Anr. issue, w. imprint:] *par T. Este*, 1597. PARIS.
The dedic. to Lady Rich is omitted in all ptbks. and the 1st commendatory poem 'Alla louange' is moved from the verso of the 2nd leaf to the recto. The ptbks. collate: superius, contratenor, bassus: π² B–E⁴ F²; tenor: A–E⁴ F², w. the 2 quintus songs pr. on A4ᵛ and B1ᵛ.

p. 398² — Add new heading:
Tomlinson, Robert. *See* Bookplates.

24115.5 — Add note: For a later ed. *see* 10608.

24163 — Add note: Intended as a preface to 3816.

24228 — Add note: For the 4th pt. of the Prick of Conscience *see* 3360.

24242 — Continue note: P has frags. of a later ed. w. tp, but pr. in de Worde's types.

p. 404¹ — Add new heading:
Tredway, Robert and **Edmund.** *See* Bookplates.

24265 — Continue note: This is a trans. of Pia et necessaria admonitio, Frankfurt, 1563, attrib. to M. Flacius.

24319 — Add note: Tp verso is blank or has errata. Quires C and Z are in 3 settings; C1ʳ has no catchword, or catchword: 'Quęstio' or 'Verum,' (the last at O, HN, HD); Z1ʳ line 12 has: 'communis' and line 21 has: 'additę' or 'cōmunis / additę' or 'communis / additæ'. Copies of all are at C except as noted.

p. 414¹ — Add new heading:
Underhill, William. *See* Bookplates.

p. 419² — Add new heading:
Vaughn, Walter. *See* Bookplates.

24627a.10 — Add note: There are copies at O, HN, HD w. tp imprint: *Antuerpiæ, venalia ap. auctorem, prostant ap. H. Verdussen*, 1608, but they have French verses substituted for the English and so do not qualify for STC. The imprint and text of the BRISTOL copy could not be checked.

24667 — Add note: Tp varies; line 5 ends: 'col-' (P) or 'volumen' (C).

p. 422¹ — Add new heading:
Vernon, Henry. *See* Bookplates.

24827.5 — Add new entry:
— Les faictz merueilleux de virgille. 8° in 4's. (*Paris, pour J. sainct Denis*) [*a. for W. de Worde*, London, c. 1520.] O.
With de Worde's device, McK. 24, on D4ᵛ; Brunet II.1167 describes a copy w. McK. 11.

24883 — Add note: The C and P copies have (*)2 'Typographus lectori S.' removed; it is present in the C copy of 24882.7.

p. 437² — Add new heading:
Walrond, John. *See* Bookplates.

25007 — Continue note: Includes a few precepts on planting trees and vines derived partly from Palladius and partly from a text similar to 5952.5.

p. 441¹ — Add new heading:
Warren, Richard. *See* Bookplates.

p. 441¹ — Add new heading:
Washington, *Sir* **Laurence.** *See* Bookplates.

25109.5 — Add new entry:
Watson, Christopher. Briefe principles of religion, collected for the exercise of youth. [Init. Chr. Wats. De., i.e. deacon.] 1/2 sh.fol. *H. Singleton*, 1578. C⁴.
The 1581 ed., 25110, has Watson's name in full.

p. 442² — Add new heading:
Waune, George. *See* Bookplates.

25151.7 — Add new entry:
— [Anr. ed.] Newly enlarged. 4°. [*J. Wolfe*] *f. W. Wright*, 1590. O⁶.
B1ʳ catchword: 'Noble'; C2ʳ catchword: 'I haue'; 25151.5 has C2ʳ catchword: 'When'. The present item is largely reimposed, w. additions, from the standing type of 25151.5. These additions but no new ones appear in 25152, which in turn is partly reimposed from the present item. 25153 sq. are completely reset and reprint the unaugmented text of 25151.5.

25219 — Add note: For a different trans. of the 1st pt. *see* 16699.

25226.5 — Add note: Tp varies; in line 7: 'any. Aged' or 'any, aged'; both at HN.

p. 451¹ — Add new heading:
Whistler, John. *See* Bookplates.

25364 — Substitute this note: The address is prob. that of R. Waldegrave as 571 is pr. by him and sold there in [1586]. By 1589 the shop belonged to J. Daldern (7538, 19898a.3).
The 'Answer to Master Rainolds Preface' on 1st B–D⁸ is not present in one of 3 C copies, and its absence prob. indicates an early issue. In the piracy, 25364b, the 'Answer' is on additional quires A⁸ (1st 3 leaves signed A11, A13, A15) a⁴, intended to be inserted after orig. A5. The additional quires are present in the C and HD copies of 25364b but not in the P copy.

25366 — Add note: C has copies w. quires A, B, Mm, and Nn reimposed w. some correction and resetting; e.g. tp line 11 has 'magistro' or 'Magistro'; Nn2ʳ has grotesque mask or block of type orns.

25413.7 — Add new entry:
— A dayly exercice and experience of dethe, gadred, [etc.] 8°. [*R. Redman*, 1534?] LINC(imp.).
This is a different ed. from 25415, which has in the title: 'deathe, gathered, . . .'

25665 — Continue note: Copies vary; Y4ᵛ is blank or has errata; both at P.

25703 — Continue note: A4ᵛ varies; dedic. dated 'this present December. 1598.' (C) or 'this first of Ianuarie. 1599.' (P).

p. 466¹ — Add new heading:
Williams, Richard. *See* Bookplates.

p. 467¹ — Add new heading:
Willmer, William. *See* Bookplates.

p. 467¹ — Add new heading:
Willoughby, William. *See* Bookplates.

493

25846   *Add note*: At least O, C, F (all?) copies have the misprint: 'preachcd' in the portion of the title transcribed.

25899   *In the note for 'and . . . 1645' substitute*: inserted from a later (c. 1675?), unidentified ed.

26024   *Add note*: Tp varies in the portion transcribed: with (HD) or without (C) a comma after 'TRVTH'.

p. 479²   *Add new heading*:
Wyndham, George. *See* Bookplates.

Add new entry:

26098.5   — Yule in Yorke. [Two carols in verse, w. explanatory notes.] s.sh.fol. [*London*, c. 1570.] O.
       Apparently pr. in defence of the ceremony of 'Yule riding' celebrated on 21 Dec.; the ceremony was suppressed in 1572.